Italian
Dictionary
Plus Italian in Action

HarperResource
An Imprint of HarperCollins*Publishers*

Dizionario Inglese

italiano › inglese inglese › italiano

MONDADORI

first edition/prima edizione 2000

© HarperCollins Publishers 2000

latest reprint 2002

HarperCollins Publishers
Westerhill Road, Bishopbriggs, Glasgow G64 2QT
Great Britain

www.collinsdictionaries.com

Collins® and Bank of English® are registered trademarks of
HarperCollins Publishers Limited

Collins is an imprint of HarperCollins Publishers

ISBN 0-00-470786-9

Pubblicato in Italia dalla
Arnoldo Mondadori Editore, Milano
ISBN 88-04-47612-5

http://www.mondadori.com/libri

HarperCollins Publishers, Inc.
10 East 53rd Street, New York, NY 10022

ISBN 0-06-095677-1

Library of Congress Catalog Card Number: 99-76598*
*Published in the U.S. as *HarperCollins Italian Concise Dictionary*

www.harpercollins.com

First HarperCollins edition published 2000

HarperCollins books may be purchased for educational, business, or sales
promotional use. For information, please write to: Special Markets Department,
HarperCollins Publishers Inc., 10 East 53rd Street, New York, NY 10022

Typeset by Morton Word Processing Ltd, Scarborough

Printed by Legoprint S.P.A.

INDICE

CONTENTS

Catherine E. Love ● Michela Clari

with/hanno collaborato
Gabriella Bacchelli ● Donatella Boi
Angela Jack ● Daphne Day

editorial staff/segreteria di redazione
Megan Thomson ● Isobel Gordon
Elspeth Anderson ● Anne Convery ● Anne Marie Banks

series editor/collana a cura di
Lorna Sinclair Knight
editorial management/coordinamento redazionale
Vivian Marr

INTRODUZIONE

Se desiderate imparare l'inglese o approfondire le conoscenze già acquisite, se volete leggere o redigere dei testi in inglese, oppure conversare con interlocutori di madrelingua inglese, se siete studenti, turisti, uomini o donne d'affari avete scelto il compagno di viaggio ideale per esprimervi e comunicare in inglese sia a voce che per iscritto. Strumento pratico e moderno, il vostro dizionario dà largo spazio al linguaggio quotidiano in campi quali l'attualità, gli affari, la gestione d'ufficio, l'informatica e il turismo. Come in tutti i nostri dizionari, grande importanza è stata data alla lingua contemporanea e alle espressioni idiomatiche.

COME USARE IL DIZIONARIO

Troverete qui di seguito alcune spiegazioni sul modo in cui le informazioni sono state presentate nel testo. L'obiettivo del dizionario è quello di darvi il maggior numero possibile di informazioni senza tuttavia sacrificare la chiarezza all'interno delle voci.

Le voci

Qui di seguito verranno descritti i vari elementi di cui si compone una voce tipo del vostro dizionario.

La trascrizione fonetica

Come regola generale è stata data la pronuncia di tutte le parole inglesi e quella delle parole italiane che potevano presentare qualche difficoltà per il parlante inglese. Nella parte inglese-italiano, tuttavia, per la pronuncia di nomi composti formati da due parole non unite dal trattino si dovrà cercare la trascrizione di ciascuna di queste parole alla rispettiva posizione alfabetica. La pronuncia si trova tra parentesi quadra, subito dopo il lemma. Come nella maggior parte dei dizionari moderni è stato adottato il sistema noto come "alfabeto fonetico internazionale". Troverete qui di seguito, a pagina xiii e xiv, un elenco completo dei caratteri utilizzati in questo sistema.

La categorie grammaticali

Tutte le parole appartengono ad una categoria grammaticale, cioè possono essere sostantivi, verbi, aggettivi, avverbi, pronomi, articoli, congiunzioni o abbreviazioni. I sostantivi possono essere singolari o plurali, sia in italiano che in inglese, e maschili o femminili in italiano. I verbi possono essere transitivi o intransitivi in entrambe le lingue, ma anche riflessivi o impersonali in italiano. La categoria grammaticale è stata introdotta in *corsivo* subito dopo la pronuncia ed eventuali informazioni di tipo morfologico (plurali irregolari ecc.).

Numerose voci sono state suddivise in varie categorie grammaticali. Per esempio la parola italiana **bene** può essere sia un avverbio che un aggettivo o un sostantivo, e la parola inglese **sneeze** può essere sia un sostantivo (starnuto) che un verbo intransitivo (starnutire). Analogamente il verbo italiano **correre** può essere usato sia come verbo intransitivo ("correre alla stazione") che come transitivo ("correre un rischio"). Per presentare la voce con maggior chiarezza e permettervi di trovare rapidamente la traduzione che cercate, è stato introdotto il simbolo ♦ per contrassegnare il passaggio da una categoria grammaticale ad un'altra.

Suddivisioni semantiche

La maggior parte delle parole ha più di un significato. Per esempio, la parola **fiocco** può essere sia un'annodatura di un nastro che una falda di neve. Molte parole si traducono in modo diverso a seconda del contesto in cui sono usate: per esempio **scala** si tradurrà in inglese con "staircase" o "stairs" se si tratta di una scala con gradini, con "ladder" se è una scala a pioli. Per permettervi di scegliere la traduzione giusta per ciascuno dei contesti in cui la parola si può trovare, le voci sono state suddivise in categorie di significato. Ciascuna suddivisione è introdotta da un "indicatore d'uso" tra parentesi in *corsivo*. Le voci **fiocco** e **scala** compariranno

vii

quindi nel testo nel modo seguente:

fiocco, chi *sm (di nastro)* bow; *(di stoffa, lana)* flock; *(di neve)* flake
scala *sf (a gradini etc)* staircase, stairs *pl*; *(a pioli, di corda)* ladder

Per segnalare la traduzione appropriata sono stati introdotti anche degli indicatori d'ambito d'uso in CORSIVO MAIUSCOLO tra parentesi, spesso in forma abbreviata, come per esempio nel caso della voce **tromba**:

tromba *sf (MUS)* trumpet; *(AUT)* horn

Troverete un elenco completo delle abbreviazioni adottate all'interno del dizionario alle pp x, xi, xii.

Le traduzioni

Per la maggior parte delle parole inglesi ed italiane ci sono traduzioni precise a seconda del significato o del contesto, come risulta dagli esempi riportati fin qui. A volte, tuttavia, le parole non hanno un preciso equivalente nella lingua d'arrivo: in questi casi è stato fornito un equivalente approssimativo, preceduto dal segno ≈, come ad esempio per l'abbreviazione **RAC**, per cui è stato dato l'equivalente italiano "A.C.I.", dato che le due associazioni svolgono nei due paesi funzioni analoghe:

RAC *n abbr (BRIT.* = *Royal Automobile Club)* ≈ *A.C.I. m (= Automobile Club d' Italia)*

A volte è persino impossibile trovare un equivalente approssimativo. Questo è il caso, per esempio, di piatti tipici di un certo paese, come ad esempio **pandoro**:

pandoro *sm type of sponge cake eaten at Christmas*

In questi casi, al posto della traduzione, che non esiste, comparirà una spiegazione: per maggiore chiarezza questa spiegazione o glossa è stata messa in *corsivo*.

Molto spesso la traduzione di una parola può non funzionare all'interno di una data locuzione. Ad esempio alla voce **dare**, verbo spesso tradotto con "to give" in inglese, troviamo varie locuzioni per alcune delle quali la traduzione fornita all'inizio della voce non si può utilizzare: **quanti anni mi dai?** "how old do you think I am?" **danno ancora quel film?** "is that film still showing?", **dare per certo qc** "to consider sth certain", e così via. Ed è proprio in questi casi che potrete verificare l'utilità e la completezza del dizionario, che contiene una ricca gamma di composti, locuzioni e frasi idiomatiche.

Il registro linguistico

In italiano sapete istintivamente scegliere l'espressione corretta da usare a seconda del contesto in cui vi esprimete. Per esempio saprete quando dire **Non me ne importa!** e quando invece potete dire **Chi se ne frega?** Più difficile sarà farlo in inglese, dove avete minore consapevolezza delle sfumature di registro linguistico. Per questo motivo nella parte inglese-italiano le parole ed espressioni inglesi di uso più familiare sono segnalate dall'abbreviazione *(col)*, mentre *(col!)* segnala le parole ed espressioni volgari. Nella parte italiano-inglese *(!)* dopo una traduzione segnala che si tratta di una parola od espressione volgare.

Parole chiave

Come vedrete, ad alcune voci è stato riservato un trattamento particolare sia dal punto di vista grafico che da quello linguistico. Si tratta di voci come **essere** o **fare**, o dei loro equivalenti inglesi **be** e **do**, che per la loro importanza e complessità meritano una strutturazione più articolata ed un maggior numero di locuzioni illustrative. Queste voci sono strutturate in diverse categorie di significato contrassegnate da numeri, e le costruzioni sintattiche e locuzioni che illustrano quel particolare significato sono riportate all'interno della relativa categoria.

Informazioni culturali

Le voci che compaiono nel testo delimitate da due linee approfondiscono aspetti della cultura italiana o di quella dei paesi di lingua inglese in argomenti quali la politica, la scuola, i mass media e le festività nazionali.

INTRODUCTION

You may be starting to learn Italian, or you may wish to extend your knowledge of the language. Perhaps you want to read and study Italian books, newspapers and magazines, or perhaps simply have a conversation with Italian speakers. Whatever the reason, whether you're a student, a tourist or want to use Italian for business, this is the ideal book to help you understand and communicate. This modern, user-friendly dictionary gives priority to everyday vocabulary and the language of current affairs, business and tourism. As in all Collins dictionaries, the emphasis is firmly placed on contemporary language and expressions.

HOW TO USE THE DICTIONARY

Below you will find an outline of how information is presented in your dictionary. Our aim is to give you the maximum amount of detail in the clearest and most helpful way.

Entries

A typical entry in your dictionary will be made up of the following elements:

Phonetic transcription

Phonetics appear in square brackets immediately after the headword. They are shown using the International Phonetic Alphabet (IPA), and a complete list of the symbols used in this system can be found on pages xiii and xiv.

Grammatical information

All words belong to one of the following parts of speech: noun, verb, adjective, adverb, pronoun, article, conjunction, preposition, abbreviation. Nouns can be singular or plural and, in Italian, masculine or feminine. Verbs can be transitive, intransitive, reflexive or impersonal. Parts of speech appear in *italics* immediately after the phonetic spelling of the headword.

Often a word can have more than one part of speech. Just as the English word **chemical** can be an adjective or a noun, the Italian word **fondo** can be an adjective ("deep") or a masculine noun ("bottom"). In the same way the verb **to walk** is sometimes transitive, ie it takes an object ("to walk the dog") and sometimes intransitive, ie it doesn't take an object ("to walk to school"). To help you find the meaning you are looking for quickly and for clarity of presentation, the different part of speech categories are separated by a black lozenge ♦.

Meaning divisions

Most words have more than one meaning. Take, for example, **punch** which can be, amongst other things, a blow with the fist or an object used for making holes. Other words are translated differently depending on the context in which they are used. The transitive verb **to roll up**, for example, can be translated by "arrotolare" or "rimboccare" depending on *what* it is you are rolling up. To help you select the most appropriate translation in every context, entries are divided according to meaning. Each different meaning is introduced by an "indicator" in *italics* and in brackets. Thus, the examples given above will be shown as follows:

> **punch** n (*blow*) pugno; (*tool*) punzone m
> **roll up** vt (*carpet, cloth, map*) arrotolare; (*sleeves*) rimboccare

Likewise, some words can have a different meaning when used to talk about a specific subject area or field. For example, **bishop**, which is generally used to mean a high-ranking clergyman, is also the name of a chess piece. To show English speakers which translation to use, we have added "subject field labels" in capitals and in brackets, in this case (*CHESS*):

bishop *n* vescovo; (*CHESS*) alfiere *m*

Field labels are often shortened to save space. You will find a complete list of abbreviations used in the dictionary on pages x, xi, xii.

Translations

Most English words have a direct translation in Italian and vice versa, as shown in the examples given above. Sometimes, however, no exact equivalent exists in the target language. In such cases we have given an approximate equivalent, indicated by the sign ≈. Such is the case of **National Insurance**, the Italian equivalent of which is "Previdenza Sociale". This is not an exact translation since the systems of the two countries in question are quite different:

National Insurance *n* (*BRIT*) ≈ Previdenza Sociale

On occasion it is impossible to find even an approximate equivalent. This may be the case, for example, with the names of types of food:

cottage pie *n piatto a base di carne macinata in sugo e purè di patate*

Here the translation (which doesn't exist) is replaced by an explanation. For increased clarity the explanation, or "gloss", is shown in *italics*.

It is often the case that a word, or a particular meaning of a word, cannot be translated in isolation. The translation of **Dutch**, for example, is "olandese". However, the phrase **to go Dutch** is rendered by "fare alla romana". Even an expression as simple as **washing powder** needs a separate translation since it translates as "detersivo (in polvere)", not "polvere per lavare". This is where your dictionary will prove to be particularly informative and useful since it contains an abundance of compounds, phrases and idiomatic expressions.

Levels of formality and familiarity

In English you instinctively know when to say **I'm broke** *or* **I'm a bit short of cash** and when to say **I don't have any money**. When you are trying to understand someone who is speaking Italian, however, or when you yourself try to speak Italian, it is important to know what is polite and what is less so, and what you can say in a relaxed situation but not in a formal context. To help you with this, on the Italian-English side we have added the label (*fam*) to show that an Italian word or expression is colloquial, while those word or expressions which are vulgar are given an exclamation mark (*fam!*), warning you they can cause serious offence. Note also that on the English-Italian side, translations which are vulgar are followed by an exclamation mark in brackets.

Keywords

Words labelled in the text as *KEYWORDS*, such as **be** and **do** or their Italian equivalents **essere** and **fare**, have been given special treatment because they form the basic elements of the language. This extra help will ensure that you know how to use these complex words with confidence.

Cultural information

Entries which appear separated from the main text by a line above and below them explain aspects of culture in Italy and English-speaking countries. Subject areas covered include politics, education, media and national festivals.

ABBREVIAZIONI

ABBREVIATIONS

abbreviazione	**abbr**	abbreviation
aggettivo	**adj**	adjective
amministrazione	**ADMIN**	administration
avverbio	**adv**	adverb
aeronautica, viaggi aerei	**AER**	flying, air travel
aggettivo	**ag**	adjective
agricoltura	**AGR**	agriculture
amministrazione	**AMM**	administration
anatomia	**ANAT**	anatomy
architettura	**ARCHIT**	architecture
astronomia, astrologia	**ASTR**	astronomy, astrology
l'automobile	**AUT**	the motor car and motoring
verbo ausiliare	**aux vb**	auxiliary verb
avverbio	**av**	adverb
aeronautica, viaggi aerei	**AVIAT**	flying, air travel
biologia	**BIOL**	biology
botanica	**BOT**	botany
inglese della Gran Bretagna	**BRIT**	British English
consonante	**C**	consonant
chimica	**CHIM, CHEM**	chemistry
familiare (! da evitare)	**col(!)**	colloquial usage (! particularly offensive)
commercio, finanza, banca	**COMM**	commerce, finance, banking
informatica	**COMPUT**	computing
congiunzione	**cong**	conjunction
congiunzione	**conj**	conjunction
edilizia	**CONSTR**	building
sostantivo usato come aggettivo, non può essere usato né come attributo, né dopo il sostantivo qualificato	**cpd**	compound element: noun used as adjective and which cannot follow the noun it qualifies
cucina	**CUC, CULIN**	cookery
davanti a	**dav**	before
determinante: articolo, aggettivo dimostrativo o indefinito etc	**det**	determiner: article, demonstrative etc
diritto	**DIR**	law
economia	**ECON**	economics
edilizia	**EDIL**	building
elettricità, elettronica	**ELETTR, ELEC**	electricity, electronics
esclamazione, interiezione	**escl, excl**	exclamation, interjection
specialmente	**esp**	especially
femminile	**f**	feminine
familiare (! da evitare)	**fam(!)**	colloquial usage (! particularly offensive)
ferrovia	**FERR**	railways
figurato	**fig**	figurative use
fisiologia	**FISIOL**	physiology
fotografia	**FOT**	photography
(verbo inglese) la cui particella è inseparabile dal verbo	**fus**	(phrasal verb) where the particle cannot be separated from main verb
nella maggior parte dei sensi; generalmente	**gen**	in most or all senses; generally
geografia, geologia	**GEO**	geography, geology
geometria	**GEOM**	geometry
impersonale	**impers**	impersonal

informatica	*INFORM*	computing
insegnamento, sistema scolastico e universitario	*INS*	schooling, schools and universities
invariabile	*inv*	invariable
irregolare	*irreg*	irregular
grammatica, linguistica	*LING*	grammar, linguistics
maschile	*m*	masculine
matematica	*MAT(H)*	mathematics
termine medico, medicina	*MED*	medical term, medicine
il tempo, meteorologia	*METEOR*	the weather, meteorology
maschile o femminile	*m/f*	either masculine or feminine depending on sex
esercito, linguaggio militare	*MIL*	military matters
musica	*MUS*	music
sostantivo	*n*	noun
nautica	*NAUT*	sailing, navigation
sostantivo che non si usa al plurale	*no pl*	uncountable noun: not used in the plural
numerale (aggettivo, sostantivo)	*num*	numeral adjective or noun
	o.s.	oneself
peggiorativo	*peg, pej*	derogatory, pejorative
fotografia	*PHOT*	photography
fisiologia	*PHYSIOL*	physiology
plurale	*pl*	plural
politica	*POL*	politics
participio passato	*pp*	past participle
preposizione	*prep*	preposition
pronome	*pron*	pronoun
psicologia, psichiatria	*PSIC, PSYCH*	psychology, psychiatry
tempo passato	*pt*	past tense
qualcosa	*qc*	
qualcuno	*qn*	
religione, liturgia	*REL*	religions, church service
sostantivo	*s*	noun
	sb	somebody
insegnamento, sistema scolastico e universitario	*SCOL*	schooling, schools and universities
singolare	*sg*	singular
soggetto (grammaticale)	*sog*	(grammatical) subject
	sth	something
congiuntivo	*sub*	subjunctive
soggetto (grammaticale)	*subj*	(grammatical) subject
termine tecnico, tecnologia	*TECN, TECH*	technical term, technology
telecomunicazioni	*TEL*	telecommunications
tipografia	*TIP*	typography, printing
televisione	*TV*	television
tipografia	*TYP*	typography, printing
inglese degli Stati Uniti	*US*	American English
vocale	*V*	vowel
verbo (ausiliare)	*vb (aus)*	(auxiliary) verb
verbo o gruppo verbale con funzione intransitiva	*vi*	verb or phrasal verb used intransitively
verbo riflessivo	*vr*	reflexive verb
verbo o gruppo verbale con funzione transitiva	*vt*	verb or phrasal verb used transitively
zoologia	*ZOOL*	zoology
marchio registrato	®	registered trademark
introduce un'equivalenza culturale	≈	introduces a cultural equivalent

TRASCRIZIONE FONETICA

Consonanti

Consonants

NB. **p, b, t, d, k, g** sono seguite da un'aspirazione in inglese.

NB. **p, b, t, d, k, g** are not aspirated in Italian.

_p_adre	p	_pupp_y
_b_am_b_ino	b	_b_a_b_y
_tutt_o	t	_t_en_t_
_dad_o	d	_dadd_y
_c_ane _ch_e	k	_c_ork _k_iss _ch_ord
gola _gh_iro	g	_gag gu_ess
_s_ano	s	_s_o ri_ce_ ki_ss_
_s_vago e_s_ame	z	cou_s_in bu_zz_
_sc_ena	ʃ	_sh_eep _s_ugar
	ʒ	plea_s_ure bei_ge_
pe_ce_ lan_ci_are	tʃ	_ch_ur_ch_
giro _gi_oco	dʒ	_j_ud_ge_ _g_eneral
a_ta t_aro	t	_t_arm ra_tt_le
_v_ero bra_v_o	v	_v_ery re_v_
	θ	_th_in ma_th_s
	ð	_th_at o_th_er
_l_etto a_l_a	l	_l_itt_le_ ba_ll_
_gl_i	ʎ	
_r_ete ar_c_o	r	_r_at b_r_at
ra_m_o _m_adre	m	_m_u_mm_y co_mb_
_n_o fuma_nt_e	n	_n_o ra_n_
_gn_omo	ɲ	
	ŋ	si_ng_ing ba_n_k
	h	_h_at re_h_eat
bu_i_o p_i_acere	j	_y_et
_u_omo g_u_aio	w	_w_all be_w_ail
	x	lo_ch_

Varie

Miscellaneous

per l'inglese: la "r" finale viene pronunciata se seguita da una vocale	*

precede la sillaba accentata	'	precedes the stressed syllable

Come regola generale, in tutte le voci la trascrizione fonetica in parentesi quadra segue il termine cui si riferisce. Tuttavia, dalla parte inglese-italiano del dizionario, per la pronuncia di composti che sono formati da più parole non unite da trattino che appaiono comunque nel dizionario, si veda la trascrizione fonetica di ciascuna di queste parole alla rispettiva posizione alfabetica.

PHONETIC TRANSCRIPTION

Vocali

NB. La messa in equivalenza di certi suoni indica solo una rassomiglianza approssimativa.

Vowels

NB. The pairing of some vowel sounds only indicates approximate equivalence.

Vocali		Vowels
vino idea	i iː	heel bead
	ɪ	hit pity
stella edera	e	
epoca eccetto	ɛ	set tent
mamma amore	a æ	apple bat
	ɑː	after car calm
	ʌ	fun cousin
	ə	over above
	əː	urn fern work
rosa occhio	ɔ	wash pot
	ɔː	born cork
ponte ognuno	o	
utile zucca	u	full soot
	uː	boon lewd

Dittonghi

Diphthongs

	ɪə	beer tier
	ɛə	tear fair there
	eɪ	date plaice day
	aɪ	life buy cry
	au	owl foul now
	əu	low no
	ɔɪ	boil boy oily
	uə	poor tour

In general, we give the pronunciation of each entry in square brackets after the word in question. However, on the English-Italian side, where the entry is composed of two or more unhyphenated words, each of which is given elsewhere in this dictionary, you will find the pronunciation of each word in its alphabetical position.

ITALIAN PRONUNCIATION

Vowels

Where the vowel **e** or the vowel **o** appears in a stressed syllable it can be either open [ɛ], [ɔ] or closed [e], [o]. As the open or closed pronunciation of these vowels is subject to regional variation, the distinction is of little importance to the user of this dictionary. Phonetic transcription for headwords containing these vowels will therefore only appear where other pronunciation difficulties are present.

Consonants

c before "e" or "i" is pronounced *tch*.

ch is pronounced like the "k" in "kit".

g before "e" or "i" is pronounced like the "j" in "jet".

gh is pronounced like the "g" in "get".

gl before "e" or "i" is normally pronounced like the "lli" in "million", and in a few cases only like the "gl" in "glove".

gn is pronounced like the "ny" in "canyon".

sc before "e" or "i" is pronounced *sh*.

z is pronounced like the "ts" in "stetson", or like the "d's" in "bird's-eye".

Headwords containing the above consonants and consonantal groups have been given full phonetic transcription in this dictionary.

NB. All double written consonants in Italian are fully sounded: e.g. the *tt* in "tutto" is pronounced as in "hat *trick*".

ITALIAN VERBS

1 Gerundio **2** Participio passato **3** Presente **4** Imperfetto **5** Passato remoto **6** Futuro
7 Condizionale **8** Congiuntivo presente **9** Congiuntivo passato **10** Imperativo

accadere *like* **cadere**
accedere *like* **concedere**
accendere 2 acceso **5** accesi, accendesti
accludere *like* **alludere**
accogliere *like* **cogliere**
accondiscendere *like* **scendere**
accorgersi *like* **scorgere**
accorrere *like* **correre**
accrescere *like* **crescere**
addirsi *like* **dire**
addurre *like* **ridurre**
affiggere 2 affisso **5** affissi, affiggesti
affliggere 2 afflitto **5** afflissi, affliggesti
aggiungere *like* **giungere**
alludere 2 alluso **5** allusi, alludesti
ammettere *like* **mettere**
andare 3 vado, vai, va, andiamo, andate, vanno **6** andrò *etc* **8** vada **10** va'!, vada!, andate!, vadano!
annettere 2 annesso **5** annessi *o* annettei, annettesti
apparire 2 apparso **3** appaio, appari *o* apparisci, appare *o* apparisce, appaiono *o* appariscono **5** apparvi *o* apparsi, apparisti, apparve *o* apparì *o* apparse, apparvero *o* apparirono *o* apparsero **8** appaia *o* apparisca
appartenere *like* **tenere**
appendere 2 appeso **5** appesi, appendesti
apporre *like* **porre**
apprendere *like* **prendere**
aprire 2 aperto **3** apro **5** aprii *o* apersi, apristi **8** apra
ardere 2 arso **5** arsi, ardesti
ascendere *like* **scendere**
aspergere 2 asperso **5** aspersi, aspergesti
assalire *like* **salire**
assistere 2 assistito
assolvere 2 assolto **5** assolsi *o* assolvei *o* assolvetti, assolvesti
assumere 2 assunto **5** assunsi, assumesti
astenersi *like* **tenere**
attendere *like* **tendere**
attingere *like* **tingere**
AVERE 3 ho, hai, ha, abbiamo, avete, hanno **5** ebbi, avesti, ebbe, avemmo, aveste, ebbero **6** avrò *etc* **8** abbia *etc* **10** abbi!, abbia!, abbiate!, abbiano!
avvedersi *like* **vedere**
avvenire *like* **venire**
avvincere *like* **vincere**
avvolgere *like* **volgere**
benedire *like* **dire**
bere 1 bevendo **2** bevuto **3** bevo *etc* **4** bevevo *etc* **5** bevvi *o* bevetti, bevesti **6** berrò

etc **8** beva *etc* **9** bevessi *etc*
cadere 5 caddi, cadesti **6** cadrò *etc*
chiedere 2 chiesto **5** chiesi, chiedesti
chiudere 2 chiuso **5** chiusi, chiudesti
cingere 2 cinto **5** cinsi, cingesti
cogliere 2 colto **3** colgo, colgono **5** colsi, cogliesti **8** colga
coincidere 2 coinciso **5** coincisi, coincidesti
coinvolgere *like* **volgere**
commettere *like* **mettere**
commuovere *like* **muovere**
comparire *like* **apparire**
compiacere *like* **piacere**
compiangere *like* **piangere**
comporre *like* **porre**
comprendere *like* **prendere**
comprimere 2 compresso **5** compressi, comprimesti
compromettere *like* **mettere**
concedere 2 concesso *o* conceduto **5** concessi *o* concedei *o* concedetti, concedesti
concludere *like* **alludere**
concorrere *like* **correre**
condurre *like* **ridurre**
confondere *like* **fondere**
congiungere *like* **giungere**
connettere *like* **annettere**
conoscere 2 conosciuto **5** conobbi, conoscesti
consistere *like* **assistere**
contendere *like* **tendere**
contenere *like* **tenere**
contorcere *like* **torcere**
contraddire *like* **dire**
contraffare *like* **fare**
contrarre *like* **trarre**
convenire *like* **venire**
convincere *like* **vincere**
coprire *like* **aprire**
correggere *like* **reggere**
correre 2 corso **5** corsi, corresti
corrispondere *like* **rispondere**
corrompere *like* **rompere**
costringere *like* **stringere**
costruire 5 costrussi, costruisti
crescere 2 cresciuto **5** crebbi, crescesti
cuocere 2 cotto **3** cuocio, cociamo, cuociono **5** cossi, cocesti
dare 3 do, dai, dà, diamo, date, danno **5** diedi *o* detti, desti **6** darò *etc* **8** dia *etc* **9** dessi *etc* **10** da'!, dai!, date!, diano!
decidere 2 deciso **5** decisi, decidesti
decrescere *like* **crescere**
dedurre *like* **ridurre**

deludere *like* **alludere**
deporre *like* **porre**
deprimere *like* **comprimere**
deridere *like* **ridere**
descrivere *like* **scrivere**
desumere *like* **assumere**
detergere *like* **tergere**
devolvere *2* devoluto
difendere *2* difeso *5* difesi, difendesti
diffondere *like* **fondere**
dipendere *like* **appendere**
dipingere *like* **tingere**
dire *1* dicendo *2* detto *3* dico, dici, dice, diciamo, dite, dicono *4* dicevo *etc 5* dissi, dicesti *6* dirò *etc 8* dica, diciamo, diciate, dicano *9* dicessi *etc 10* di'!, dica!, dite!, dicano!
dirigere *2* diretto *5* diressi, dirigesti
discendere *like* **scendere**
dischiudere *like* **chiudere**
disciogliere *like* **sciogliere**
discorrere *like* **correre**
discutere *2* discusso *5* discussi, discutesti
disfare *like* **fare**
disilludere *like* **alludere**
disperdere *like* **perdere**
dispiacere *like* **piacere**
disporre *like* **porre**
dissolvere *2* dissolto *o* dissoluto *5* dissolsi *o* dissolvetti *o* dissolvei, dissolvesti
dissuadere *like* **persuadere**
distendere *like* **tendere**
distinguere *2* distinto *5* distinsi, distinguesti
distogliere *like* **togliere**
distrarre *like* **trarre**
distruggere *like* **struggere**
divenire *like* **venire**
dividere *2* diviso *5* divisi, dividesti
dolere *3* dolgo, duoli, duole, dolgono *5* dolsi, dolesti *6* dorrò *etc 8* dolga
DORMIRE *1* GERUNDIO dormendo
2 PARTICIPIO PASSATO dormito
3 PRESENTE dormo, dormi, dorme, dormiamo, dormite, dormono
4 IMPERFETTO dormivo, dormivi, dormiva, dormivamo, dormivate, dormivano
5 PASSATO REMOTO dormii, dormisti, dormì, dormimmo, dormiste, dormirono
6 FUTURO dormirò, dormirai, dormirà, dormiremo, dormirete, dormiranno
7 CONDIZIONALE dormirei, dormiresti, dormirebbe, dormiremmo, dormireste, dormirebbero
8 CONGIUNTIVO PRESENTE dorma, dorma, dorma, dormiamo, dormiate, dormano
9 CONGIUNTIVO PASSATO dormissi, dormissi, dormisse, dormissimo, dormiste, dormissero
10 IMPERATIVO dormi!, dorma!, dormite!, dormano!
dovere *3* devo *o* debbo, devi, deve, dobbiamo, dovete, devono *o* debbono *6* dovrò *etc*

8 debba, dobbiamo, dobbiate, devano *o* debbano
eccellere *2* eccelso *5* eccelsi, eccellesti
eludere *like* **alludere**
emergere *2* emerso *5* emersi, emergesti
emettere *like* **mettere**
erigere *like* **dirigere**
escludere *like* **alludere**
esigere *2* esatto
esistere *2* esistito
espellere *2* espulso *5* espulsi, espellesti
esplodere *2* esploso *5* esplosi, esplodesti
esporre *like* **porre**
esprimere *like* **comprimere**
ESSERE *2* stato *3* sono, sei, è, siamo, siete, sono *4* ero, eri, era, eravamo, eravate, erano *5* fui, fosti, fu, fummo, foste, furono *6* sarò *etc 8* sia *etc 9* fossi, fossi, fosse, fossimo, foste, fossero *10* sii!, sia!, siate!, siano!
estendere *like* **tendere**
estinguere *like* **distinguere**
estrarre *like* **trarre**
evadere *2* evaso *5* evasi, evadesti
evolvere *2* evoluto
fare *1* facendo *2* fatto *3* faccio, fai, fa, facciamo, fate, fanno *4* facevo *etc 5* feci, facesti *6* farò *etc 8* faccia *etc 9* facessi *etc 10* fa'!, faccia!, fate!, facciano!
fingere *like* **cingere**
FINIRE *1* GERUNDIO finendo
2 PARTICIPIO PASSATO finito
3 PRESENTE finisco, finisci, finisce, finiamo, finite, finiscono
4 IMPERFETTO finivo, finivi, finiva, finivamo, finivate, finivano
5 PASSATO REMOTO finii, finisti, finì, finimmo, finiste, finirono
6 FUTURO finirò, finirai, finirà, finiremo, finirete, finiranno
7 CONDIZIONALE finirei, finiresti, finirebbe, finiremmo, finireste, finirebbero
8 CONGIUNTIVO PRESENTE finisca, finisca, finisca, finiamo, finiate, finiscano
9 CONGIUNTIVO PASSATO finissi, finissi, finisse, finissimo, finiste, finissero
10 IMPERATIVO finisci!, finisca!, finite!, finiscano!
flettere *2* flesso
fondere *2* fuso *5* fusi, fondesti
friggere *2* fritto *5* frissi, friggesti
fungere *2* funto *5* funsi, fungesti
giacere *3* giaccio, giaci, giace, giac(c)iamo, giaciate, giacciono *5* giacqui, giacesti *8* giaccia *etc 10* giaci!, giaccia!, giac(c)iamo!, giacete!, giacciano!
giungere *2* giunto *5* giunsi, giungesti
godere *6* godrò *etc*
illudere *like* **alludere**
immergere *like* **emergere**
immettere *like* **mettere**
imporre *like* **porre**
imprimere *like* **comprimere**

incidere *like* decidere
includere *like* alludere
incorrere *like* correre
incutere *like* discutere
indulgere *2* indulto *5* indulsi, indulgesti
indurre *like* ridurre
inferire[1] *2* inferto *5* infersi, inferisti
inferire[2] *2* inferito *5* inferii, inferisti
infliggere *like* affliggere
infrangere *2* infranto *5* infransi, infrangesti
infondere *like* fondere
insistere *like* assistere
intendere *like* tendere
interdire *like* dire
interporre *like* porre
interrompere *like* rompere
intervenire *like* venire
intraprendere *like* prendere
introdurre *like* ridurre
invadere *like* evadere
irrompere *like* rompere
iscrivere *like* scrivere
istruire *like* costruire
ledere *2* leso *5* lesi, ledesti
leggere *2* letto *5* lessi, leggesti
maledire *like* dire
mantenere *like* tenere
mettere *2* messo *5* misi, mettesti
mordere *2* morso *5* morsi, mordesti
morire *2* morto *3* muoio, muori, muore, moriamo, morite, muoiono *6* morirò *o* morrò *etc* *8* muoia
mungere *2* munto *5* munsi, mungesti
muovere *2* mosso *5* mossi, movesti
nascere *2* nato *5* nacqui, nascesti
nascondere *2* nascosto *5* nascosi, nascondesti
nuocere *2* nuociuto *3* nuoccio, nuoci, nuoce, nociamo *o* nuociamo, nuocete, nuocciono *4* nuocevo *etc* *5* nocqui, nuocesti *6* nuocerò *etc* *7* nuoccia
occorrere *like* correre
offendere *like* difendere
offrire *2* offerto *3* offro *5* offersi *o* offrii, offristi *8* offra
omettere *like* mettere
opporre *like* porre
opprimere *like* comprimere
ottenere *like* tenere
parere *2* parso *3* paio, paiamo, paiono *5* parvi *o* parsi, paresti *6* parrò *etc* *8* paia, paiamo, paiate, paiano
PARLARE *1* GERUNDIO parlando
2 PARTICIPIO PASSATO parlato
3 PRESENTE parlo, parli, parla, parliamo, parlate, parlano
4 IMPERFETTO parlavo, parlavi, parlava, parlavamo, parlavate, parlavano
5 PASSATO REMOTO parlai, parlasti, parlò, parlammo, parlaste, parlarono
6 FUTURO parlerò, parlerai, parlerà, parleremo, parlerete, parleranno

7 CONDIZIONALE parlerei, parleresti, parlerebbe, parleremmo, parlereste, parlerebbero
8 CONGIUNTIVO PRESENTE parli, parli, parli, parliamo, parliate, parlino
9 CONGIUNTIVO PASSATO parlassi, parlassi, parlasse, parlassimo, parlaste, parlassero
10 IMPERATIVO parla!, parli!, parlate!, parlino!
percorrere *like* correre
percuotere *2* percosso *5* percossi, percotesti
perdere *2* perso *o* perduto *5* persi *o* perdei *o* perdetti, perdesti
permettere *like* mettere
persuadere *2* persuaso *5* persuasi, persuadesti
pervenire *like* venire
piacere *2* piaciuto *3* piaccio, piacciamo, piacciono *5* piacqui, piacesti *8* piaccia *etc*
piangere *2* pianto *5* piansi, piangesti
piovere *5* piovve
porgere *2* porto *5* porsi, porgesti
porre *1* ponendo *2* posto *3* pongo, poni, pone, poniamo, ponete, pongono *4* ponevo *etc* *5* posi, ponesti *6* porrò *etc* *8* ponga, poniamo, poniate, pongano *9* ponessi *etc*
posporre *like* porre
possedere *like* sedere
potere *3* posso, puoi, può, possiamo, potete, possono *6* potrò *etc* *8* possa, possiamo, possiate, possano
prediligere *2* prediletto *5* predilessi, prediligesti
predire *like* dire
prefiggersi *like* affiggere
preludere *like* alludere
prendere *2* preso *5* presi, prendesti
preporre *like* porre
prescrivere *like* scrivere
presiedere *like* sedere
presumere *like* assumere
pretendere *like* tendere
prevalere *like* valere
prevedere *like* vedere
prevenire *like* venire
produrre *like* ridurre
proferire *like* inferire[2]
profondere *like* fondere
promettere *like* mettere
promuovere *like* muovere
proporre *like* porre
prorompere *like* rompere
proscrivere *like* scrivere
proteggere *2* protetto *5* protessi, proteggesti
provenire *like* venire
provvedere *like* vedere
pungere *2* punto *5* punsi, pungesti
racchiudere *like* chiudere
raccogliere *like* cogliere
radere *2* raso *5* rasi, radesti

raggiungere *like* giungere
rapprendere *like* prendere
ravvedersi *like* vedere
recidere *like* decidere
redigere 2 redatto
redimere 2 redento 5 redensi, redimesti
reggere 2 retto 5 ressi, reggesti
rendere 2 reso 5 resi, rendesti
reprimere *like* comprimere
rescindere *like* scindere
respingere *like* spingere
restringere *like* stringere
ricadere *like* cadere
richiedere *like* chiedere
riconoscere *like* conoscere
ricoprire *like* coprire
ricorrere *like* correre
ridere 2 riso 5 risi, ridesti
ridire *like* dire
ridurre 1 riducendo 2 ridotto 3 riduco *etc* 4 riducevo *etc* 5 ridussi, riducesti 6 ridurrò *etc* 8 riduca *etc* 9 riducessi *etc*
riempire 1 riempiendo 3 riempio, riempi, riempie, riempiono
rifare *like* fare
riflettere 2 riflettuto *o* riflesso
rifrangere *like* infrangere
rimanere 2 rimasto 3 rimango, rimangono 5 rimasi, rimanesti 6 rimarrò *etc* 8 rimanga
rimettere *like* mettere
rimpiangere *like* piangere
rinchiudere *like* chiudere
rincrescere *like* crescere
rinvenire *like* venire
ripercuotere *like* percuotere
riporre *like* porre
riprendere *like* prendere
riprodurre *like* ridurre
riscuotere *like* scuotere
risolvere *like* assolvere
risorgere *like* sorgere
rispondere 2 risposto 5 risposi, rispondesti
ritenere *like* tenere
ritrarre *like* trarre
riuscire *like* uscire
rivedere *like* vedere
rivivere *like* vivere
rivolgere *like* volgere
rodere 2 roso 5 rosi, rodesti
rompere 2 rotto 5 ruppi, rompesti
salire 3 salgo, sali, salgono 8 salga
sapere 3 so, sai, sa, sappiamo, sapete, sanno 5 seppi, sapesti 6 saprò *etc* 8 sappia *etc* 10 sappi!, sappia!, sappiate!, sappiano!
scadere *like* cadere
scegliere 2 scelto 3 scelgo, scegli, sceglie, scegliamo, scegliete, scelgono 5 scelsi, scegliesti 8 scelga, scegliamo, scegliate, scelgano 10 scegli!, scelga!, scegliamo!, scegliete!, scelgano!
scendere 2 sceso 5 scesi, scendesti

schiudere *like* chiudere
scindere 2 scisso 5 scissi, scindesti
sciogliere 2 sciolto 3 sciolgo, sciolgi, sciolglie, sciogliamo, sciogliete, sciolgono 5 sciolsi, sciogliesti 8 sciolga, sciogliamo, sciogliate, sciolgano 10 sciogli!, sciolga!, sciogliamo!, sciogliete!, sciolgano!
scommettere *like* mettere
scomparire *like* apparire
scomporre *like* porre
sconfiggere 2 sconfitto 5 sconfissi, sconfiggesti
sconvolgere *like* volgere
scoprire *like* aprire
scorgere 2 scorto 5 scorsi, scorgesti
scorrere *like* correre
scrivere 2 scritto 5 scrissi, scrivesti
scuotere 2 scosso 3 scuoto, scuoti, scuote, scotiamo, scotete, scuotono 5 scossi, scotesti 6 scoterò *etc* 8 scuota, scotiamo, scotiate, scuotano 10 scuoti!, scuota!, scotiamo!, scotete!, scuotano!
sedere 3 siedo, siedi, siede, siedono 8 sieda
seppellire 2 sepolto
smettere *like* mettere
smuovere *like* muovere
socchiudere *like* chiudere
soccorrere *like* correre
soddisfare *like* fare
soffriggere *like* friggere
soffrire 2 sofferto 5 soffersi *o* soffrii, soffristi
soggiungere *like* giungere
solere 2 solito 3 soglio, suoli, suole, sogliamo, solete, sogliono 8 soglia, sogliamo, sogliate, sogliano
sommergere *like* emergere
sopprimere *like* comprimere
sorgere 2 sorto 3 sorsi, sorgesti
sorprendere *like* prendere
sorreggere *like* reggere
sorridere *like* ridere
sospendere *like* appendere
sospingere *like* spingere
sostenere *like* tenere
sottintendere *like* tendere
spandere 2 spanto
spargere 2 sparso 5 sparsi, spargesti
sparire 5 sparii *o* sparvi, sparisti
spegnere 2 spento 3 spengo, spengono 5 spensi, spegnesti 8 spenga
spendere 2 speso 5 spesi, spendesti
spingere 2 spinto 5 spinsi, spingesti
sporgere *like* porgere
stare 2 stato 3 sto, stai, sta, stiamo, state, stanno 5 stetti, stesti 6 starò *etc* 8 stia *etc* 9 stessi *etc* 10 sta'!, stia!, state!, stiano!
stendere *like* tendere
storcere *like* torcere
stringere 2 stretto 5 strinsi, stringesti
struggere 2 strutto 5 strussi, struggesti
succedere *like* concedere

supporre *like* **porre**
svenire *like* **venire**
svolgere *like* **volgere**
tacere *2* taciuto *3* taccio, tacciono *5* tacqui, tacesti *8* taccia
tendere *2* teso *5* tesi, tendesti *etc*
tenere *3* tengo, tieni, tiene, tengono *5* tenni, tenesti *6* terrò *etc* *8* tenga
tingere *2* tinto *5* tinsi, tingesti
togliere *2* tolto *3* tolgo, togli, toglie, togliamo, togliete, tolgono *5* tolsi, togliesti *8* tolga, togliamo, togliate, tolgano *10* togli!, tolga!, togliamo!, togliete!, tolgano!
torcere *2* torto *5* torsi, torcesti
tradurre *like* **ridurre**
trafiggere *like* **sconfiggere**
transigere *like* **esigere**
trarre *1* traendo *2* tratto *3* traggo, trai, trae, traiamo, traete, traggono *4* traevo *etc* *5* trassi, traesti *6* trarrò *etc* *8* tragga *9* traessi *etc*
trascorrere *like* **correre**
trascrivere *like* **scrivere**
trasmettere *like* **mettere**
trasparire *like* **apparire**
trattenere *like* **tenere**
uccidere *2* ucciso *5* uccisi, uccidesti
udire *3* odo, odi, ode, odono *8* oda
ungere *2* unto *5* unsi, ungesti
uscire *3* esco, esci, esce, escono *8* esca
valere *2* valso *3* valgo, valgono *5* valsi, valesti *6* varrò *etc* *8* valga

vedere *2* visto *o* veduto *5* vidi, vedesti *6* vedrò *etc*
VENDERE *1* GERUNDIO vendendo
2 PARTICIPIO PASSATO venduto
3 PRESENTE vendo, vendi, vende, vendiamo, vendete, vendono
4 IMPERFETTO vendevo, vendevi, vendeva, vendevamo, vendevate, vendevano
5 PASSATO REMOTO vendei *o* vendetti, vendesti, vendé *o* vendette, vendemmo, vendeste, venderono *o* vendettero
6 FUTURO venderò, venderai, venderà, venderemo, venderete, venderanno
7 CONDIZIONALE venderei, venderesti, venderebbe, venderemmo, vendereste, venderebbero
8 CONGIUNTIVO PRESENTE venda, venda, venda, vendiamo, vendiate, vendano
9 CONGIUNTIVO PASSATO vendessi, vendessi, vendesse, vendessimo, vendeste, vendessero
10 IMPERATIVO vendi!, venda!, vendete!, vendano!
venire *2* venuto *3* vengo, vieni, viene, vengono *5* venni, venisti *6* verrò *etc* *8* venga
vincere *2* vinto *5* vinsi, vincesti
vivere *2* vissuto *5* vissi, vivesti
volere *3* voglio, vuoi, vuole, vogliamo, volete, vogliono *5* volli, volesti *6* vorrò *etc* *8* voglia *etc* *10* vogli!, voglia!, vogliate!, vogliano!
volgere *2* volto *5* volsi, volgesti

VERBI INGLESI

present	pt	pp	present	pt	pp
arise	arose	arisen	drive	drove	driven
awake	awoke	awoken	dwell	dwelt	dwelt
be (am, is,	was, were	been	eat	ate	eaten
are;			fall	fell	fallen
being)			feed	fed	fed
bear	bore	born(e)	feel	felt	felt
beat	beat	beaten	fight	fought	fought
become	became	become	find	found	found
befall	befell	befallen	flee	fled	fled
begin	began	begun	fling	flung	flung
behold	beheld	beheld	fly	flew	flown
bend	bent	bent	forbid	forbad(e)	forbidden
beset	beset	beset	forecast	forecast	forecast
bet	bet, betted	bet, betted	forget	forgot	forgotten
bid (at	bid	bid	forgive	forgave	forgiven
auction,			forsake	forsook	forsaken
cards)			freeze	froze	frozen
bid (say)	bade	bidden	get	got	got, (US)
bind	bound	bound			gotten
bite	bit	bitten			
bleed	bled	bled	give	gave	given
blow	blew	blown	go (goes)	went	gone
break	broke	broken	grind	ground	ground
breed	bred	bred	grow	grew	grown
bring	brought	brought	hang	hung	hung
build	built	built	hang	hanged	hanged
burn	burnt,	burnt,	(execute)		
	burned	burned	have	had	had
burst	burst	burst	hear	heard	heard
buy	bought	bought	hide	hid	hidden
can	could	(been able)	hit	hit	hit
cast	cast	cast	hold	held	held
catch	caught	caught	hurt	hurt	hurt
choose	chose	chosen	keep	kept	kept
cling	clung	clung	kneel	knelt,	knelt,
come	came	come		kneeled	kneeled
cost	cost	cost	know	knew	known
cost (work	costed	costed	lay	laid	laid
out price			lead	led	led
of)			lean	leant,	leant,
creep	crept	crept		leaned	leaned
cut	cut	cut	leap	leapt,	leapt,
deal	dealt	dealt		leaped	leaped
dig	dug	dug	learn	learnt,	learnt,
do (3rd	did	done		learned	learned
person:			leave	left	left
he/she/it			lend	lent	lent
does)			let	let	let
			lie (lying)	lay	lain
draw	drew	drawn	light	lit, lighted	lit, lighted
dream	dreamed,	dreamed,	lose	lost	lost
	dreamt	dreamt	make	made	made
drink	drank	drunk	may	might	—

present	pt	pp	present	pt	pp
mean	meant	meant	speed	sped,	sped,
meet	met	met		speeded	speeded
mistake	mistook	mistaken	spell	spelt,	spelt,
mow	mowed	mown,		spelled	spelled
		mowed	spend	spent	spent
must	(had to)	(had to)	spill	spilt,	spilt,
pay	paid	paid		spilled	spilled
put	put	put	spin	spun	spun
quit	quit,	quit,	spit	spat	spat
	quitted	quitted	spoil	spoiled,	spoiled,
read	read	read		spoilt	spoilt
rid	rid	rid	spread	spread	spread
ride	rode	ridden	spring	sprang	sprung
ring	rang	rung	stand	stood	stood
rise	rose	risen	steal	stole	stolen
run	ran	run	stick	stuck	stuck
saw	sawed	sawed,	sting	stung	stung
		sawn	stink	stank	stunk
say	said	said	stride	strode	stridden
see	saw	seen	strike	struck	struck
seek	sought	sought	strive	strove	striven
sell	sold	sold	swear	swore	sworn
send	sent	sent	sweep	swept	swept
set	set	set	swell	swelled	swollen,
sew	sewed	sewn			swelled
shake	shook	shaken	swim	swam	swum
shear	sheared	shorn,	swing	swung	swung
		sheared	take	took	taken
shed	shed	shed	teach	taught	taught
shine	shone	shone	tear	tore	torn
shoot	shot	shot	tell	told	told
show	showed	shown	think	thought	thought
shrink	shrank	shrunk	throw	threw	thrown
shut	shut	shut	thrust	thrust	thrust
sing	sang	sung	tread	trod	trodden
sink	sank	sunk	wake	woke,	woken,
sit	sat	sat		waked	waked
slay	slew	slain	wear	wore	worn
sleep	slept	slept	weave	wove	woven
slide	slid	slid	weave	weaved	weaved
sling	slung	slung	(wind)		
slit	slit	slit	wed	wedded,	wedded,
smell	smelt,	smelt,		wed	wed
	smelled	smelled	weep	wept	wept
sow	sowed	sown,	win	won	won
		sowed	wind	wound	wound
speak	spoke	spoken	wring	wrung	wrung
			write	wrote	written

I NUMERI   NUMBERS

uno(a)	1	one
due	2	two
tre	3	three
quattro	4	four
cinque	5	five
sei	6	six
sette	7	seven
otto	8	eight
nove	9	nine
dieci	10	ten
undici	11	eleven
dodici	12	twelve
tredici	13	thirteen
quattordici	14	fourteen
quindici	15	fifteen
sedici	16	sixteen
diciassette	17	seventeen
diciotto	18	eighteen
diciannove	19	nineteen
venti	20	twenty
ventuno	21	twenty-one
ventidue	22	twenty-two
ventitré	23	twenty-three
ventotto	28	twenty-eight
trenta	30	thirty
quaranta	40	forty
cinquanta	50	fifty
sessanta	60	sixty
settanta	70	seventy
ottanta	80	eighty
novanta	90	ninety
cento	100	a hundred, one hundred
centouno	101	a hundred and one
duecento	200	two hundred
mille	1 000	a thousand, one thousand
milleduecentodue	1 202	one thousand two hundred and two
cinquemila	5 000	five thousand
un milione	1 000 000	a million, one million

I NUMERI

NUMBERS

primo(a), 1°	first, 1st
secondo(a), 2°	second, 2nd
terzo(a), 3°	third, 3rd
quarto(a)	fourth, 4th
quinto(a)	fifth, 5th
sesto(a)	sixth, 6th
settimo(a)	seventh
ottavo(a)	eighth
nono(a)	ninth
decimo(a)	tenth
undicesimo(a)	eleventh
dodicesimo(a)	twelfth
tredicesimo(a)	thirteenth
quattordicesimo(a)	fourteenth
quindicesimo(a)	fifteenth
sedicesimo(a)	sixteenth
diciassettesimo(a)	seventeenth
diciottesimo(a)	eighteenth
diciannovesimo(a)	nineteenth
ventesimo(a)	twentieth
ventunesimo(a)	twenty-first
ventiduesimo(a)	twenty-second
ventitreesimo(a)	twenty-third
ventottesimo(a)	twenty-eighth
trentesimo(a)	thirtieth
centesimo(a)	hundredth
centunesimo(a)	hundred-and-first
millesimo(a)	thousandth
milionesimo(a)	millionth

L'ORA

THE TIME

che ora è?, che ore sono?
what time is it?

è ..., sono ...
it's ...

mezzanotte	midnight
l'una (del mattino)	one o'clock (in the morning) , one (am)
l'una e cinque	five past one
l'una e dieci	ten past one
l'una e un quarto, l'una e quindici	a quarter past one, one fifteen
l'una e venticinque	twenty-five past one, one twenty-five
l'una e mezzo o mezza, l'una e trenta	half past one, one thirty
l'una e trentacinque	twenty-five to two, one thirty-five
le due meno venti, l'una e quaranta	twenty to two, one forty
le due meno un quarto, l'una e quarantacinque	a quarter to two, one forty-five
le due meno dieci, l'una e cinquanta	ten to two, one fifty
mezzogiorno	twelve o'clock, midday, noon
le tre, le quindici	three o'clock (in the afternoon), three (pm)
le sette (di sera), le diciannove	seven o'clock (in the evening), seven (pm)

a che ora?
at what time?

a mezzanotte	at midnight
alle sette	at seven o'clock
fra venti minuti	in twenty minutes
venti minuti fa	twenty minutes ago

LA DATA

THE DATE

oggi	today
domani	tomorrow
dopodomani	the day after tomorrow
ieri	yesterday
l'altro ieri	the day before yesterday
il giorno prima	the day before, the previous day
il giorno dopo	the next or following day

la mattina	morning
la sera	evening
stamattina	this morning
stasera	this evening
questo pomeriggio	this afternoon
ieri mattina	yesterday morning
ieri sera	yesterday evening
domani mattina	tomorrow morning
domani sera	tomorrow evening
nella notte tra sabato e domenica	during Saturday night, during the night of Saturday to Sunday
viene sabato	he's coming on Saturday
il sabato	on Saturdays
tutti i sabati	every Saturday
sabato scorso, lo scorso sabato	last Saturday
il prossimo sabato	next Saturday
fra due sabati	a week on Saturday
fra tre sabati	a fortnight or two weeks on Saturday
da lunedì a sabato	from Monday to Saturday
tutti i giorni	every day
una volta alla settimana	once a week
una volta al mese	once a month
due volte alla settimana	twice a week
una settimana fa	a week ago
quindici giorni fa	a fortnight or two weeks ago
l'anno scorso or passato	last year
fra due giorni	in two days
fra una settimana	in a week
fra quindici giorni	in a fortnight or two weeks
il mese prossimo	next month
l'anno prossimo	next year

che giorno è oggi?	*what day is it?*
il primo/24 ottobre 1996	the 1st/24th of October 1996, October 1st/24th 1996
nel 1996	in 1996
il millenovecentonovantacinque	nineteen ninety-five
44 a.C.	44 BC
14 d.C.	14 AD
nel diciannovesimo secolo, nel XIX secolo, nell'Ottocento	in the nineteenth century
negli anni trenta	in the thirties
c'era una volta ...	once upon a time ...

Italiano-Inglese
Italian-English

Aa

A, a [a] *sf o m inv* (*lettera*) A, a; **A come Ancona** ≈ A for Andrew (*BRIT*), A for Able (*US*), **dalla a alla z** from a to z. **A** *abbr* (= *altezza*) h; (– *area*) A; (= *autostrada*) ≈ M (*BRIT*).

═════════════════ PAROLA CHIAVE

à (*a* + *il* = **al**, *a* + *lo* = **allo**, *a* + *l'* = **all'**, *a* + *la* = **alla**, *a* + *i* = **ai**, *a* + *gli* = **agli**, *a* + *le* = **alle**) *prep* **1** (*stato in luogo*) at; (: *in*) in; **essere alla stazione** to be at the station; **essere ~ casa/~ scuola/~ Roma** to be at home/at school/in Rome; **è ~ 10 km da qui** it's 10 km from here, it's 10 km away; **restare ~ cena** to stay for dinner
2 (*moto a luogo*) to; **andare ~ casa/~ scuola/alla stazione** to go home/to school/to the station; **andare ~ Roma/al mare** to go to Rome/to the seaside
3 (*tempo*) at; (*epoca, stagione*) in; **alle cinque** at five (o'clock); **~ mezzanotte/Natale** at midnight/Christmas; **al mattino** in the morning; **~ maggio/primavera** in May/spring; **~ cinquant'anni** at fifty (years of age); **~ domani!** see you tomorrow!; **~ lunedì!** see you on Monday!; **~ giorni** within (a few) days
4 (*complemento di termine*) to; **dare qc ~ qn** to give sb sth, give sth to sb; **l'ho chiesto ~ lui** I asked him
5 (*mezzo, modo*) with, by; **~ piedi/cavallo** on foot/horseback; **viaggiare ~ 100 km all'ora** to travel at 100 km an *o* per hour; **alla televisione/radio** on television/the radio; **fatto ~ mano** made by hand, handmade; **una barca ~ motore** a motorboat; **una stufa ~ gas** a gas heater;

~ uno ~ uno one by one; **~ fatica** with difficulty; **all'italiana** the Italian way, in the Italian fashion
6 (*rapporto*) a, per; (: *con prezzi*) at; **due volte al giorno/mese** twice a day/month; **prendo 500.000 lire al mese** I get 500,000 lire a *o* per month; **pagato ~ ore** paid by the hour; **vendere qc ~ 500 lire il chilo** to sell sth at 500 lire a *o* per kilo; **cinque ~ zero** (*punteggio*) five nil.

AA *sigla* = Alto Adige.
AAS *sigla f* = Azienda Autonoma di Soggiorno.
AA.VV. *abbr* = autori vari.
ab. *abbr* = abitante.
a'bate *sm* abbot.
abbacchi'ato, a [abbak'kjato] *ag* downhearted, in low spirits.
abbacin'are [abbatʃi'nare] *vt* to dazzle.
abbagli'ante [abbaʎ'ʎante] *ag* dazzling; **~i** *smpl* (*AUT*): **accendere gli ~i** to put one's headlights on full (*BRIT*) *o* high (*US*) beam.
abbagli'are [abbaʎ'ʎare] *vt* to dazzle; (*illudere*) to delude.
ab'baglio [ab'baʎʎo] *sm* blunder; **prendere un ~** to blunder, make a blunder.
abbai'are *vi* to bark.
abba'ino *sm* dormer window; (*soffitta*) attic room.
abbando'nare *vt* to leave, abandon, desert; (*trascurare*) to neglect; (*rinunciare a*) to abandon, give up; **~rsi** *vr* to let o.s. go; **~ il campo** (*MIL*) to retreat; **~ la presa** to let go; **~rsi a** (*ricordi, vizio*) to give o.s. up to.
abbando'nato, a *ag* (*casa*) deserted;

(*miniera*) disused; (*trascurato*: *terreno*, *podere*) neglected; (*bambino*) abandoned.

abban'dono *sm* abandoning; neglecting; (*stato*) abandonment; neglect; (*SPORT*) withdrawal; (*fig*) abandon; **in** ~ (*edificio*, *giardino*) neglected.

abbarbi'carsi *vr*: ~ (**a**) (*anche fig*) to cling (to).

abbassa'mento *sm* lowering; (*di pressione*, *livello dell'acqua*) fall; (*di prezzi*) reduction; ~ **di temperatura** drop in temperature.

abbas'sare *vt* to lower; (*radio*) to turn down; ~**rsi** *vr* (*chinarsi*) to stoop; (*livello*, *sole*) to go down; (*fig*: *umiliarsi*) to demean o.s.; ~ **i fari** (*AUT*) to dip (*BRIT*) o dim (*US*) one's lights; ~ **le armi** (*MIL*) to lay down one's arms.

ab'basso *escl*: ~ **il re!** down with the king!

abbas'tanza [abbas'tantsa] *av* (*a sufficienza*) enough; (*alquanto*) quite, rather, fairly; **non è** ~ **furbo** he's not shrewd enough; **un vino** ~ **dolce** quite a sweet wine, a fairly sweet wine; **averne** ~ **di qn/qc** to have had enough of sb/sth.

ab'battere *vt* (*muro*, *casa*, *ostacolo*) to knock down; (*albero*) to fell; (: *sog*: *vento*) to bring down; (*bestie da macello*) to slaughter; (*cane*, *cavallo*) to destroy, put down; (*selvaggina*, *aereo*) to shoot down; (*fig*: *sog*: *malattia*, *disgrazia*) to lay low; ~**rsi** *vr* (*avvilirsi*) to lose heart; ~**rsi a terra** o **al suolo** to fall to the ground; ~**rsi su** (*sog*: *maltempo*) to beat down on; (: *disgrazia*) to hit, strike.

abbatti'mento *sm* knocking down; felling; (*di casa*) demolition; (*prostrazione*: *fisica*) exhaustion; (: *morale*) despondency.

abbat'tuto, a *ag* despondent, depressed.

abba'zia [abbat'tsia] *sf* abbey.

abbece'dario [abbetʃe'darjo] *sm* primer.

abbelli'mento *sm* embellishment.

abbel'lire *vt* to make beautiful; (*ornare*) to embellish.

abbeve'rare *vt* to water; ~**rsi** *vr* to drink.

abbevera'toio *sm* drinking trough.

'abbi, 'abbia, abbi'amo, 'abbiano, abbi'ate *vb vedi* **avere.**

abbiccì [abbit'tʃi] *sm inv* alphabet; (*sillabario*) primer; (*fig*) rudiments *pl*.

abbi'ente *ag* well-to-do, well-off.

abbi'etto, a *ag* = **abietto.**

abbiezi'one [abbjet'tsjone] *sf* = **abiezione.**

abbiglia'mento [abbiʎʎa'mento] *sm* dress *no pl*; (*indumenti*) clothes *pl*; (*industria*) clothing industry.

abbigli'are [abbiʎ'ʎare] *vt* to dress up.

abbina'mento *sm* combination; linking; matching.

abbi'nare *vt*: ~ (**con** o **a**) (*gen*) to combine (with); (*nomi*) to link (with); ~ **qc a qc** (*colori etc*) to match sth with sth.

abbindo'lare *vt* (*fig*) to cheat, trick.

abbocca'mento *sm* (*colloquio*) talks *pl*, meeting; (*TECN*: *di tubi*) connection.

abboc'care *vt* (*tubi*, *canali*) to connect, join up ♦ *vi* (*pesce*) to bite; (*tubi*) to join; ~ (**all'amo**) (*fig*) to swallow the bait.

abboc'cato, a *ag* (*vino*) sweetish.

abbona'mento *sm* subscription; (*alle ferrovie etc*) season ticket; **in** ~ **for** subscribers only; for season ticket holders only; **fare l'**~ (**a**) to take out a subscription (to); to buy a season ticket (for).

abbo'nare *vt* (*cifra*) to deduct; (*fig*: *perdonare*) to forgive; ~**rsi** *vr*: ~**rsi a un giornale** to take out a subscription to a newspaper; ~**rsi al teatro/alle ferrovie** to take out a season ticket for the theatre/ the train.

abbo'nato, a *sm/f* subscriber; season-ticket holder; **elenco degli** ~**i** telephone directory.

abbon'dante *ag* abundant, plentiful; (*giacca*) roomy.

abbon'danza [abbon'dantsa] *sf* abundance; plenty.

abbon'dare *vi* to abound, be plentiful; ~ **in** o **di** to be full of, abound in.

abbor'dabile *ag* (*persona*) approachable; (*prezzo*) reasonable.

abbor'dare *vt* (*nave*) to board; (*persona*) to approach; (*argomento*) to tackle; ~ **una curva** to take a bend.

abbotto'nare *vt* to button up, do up; ~**rsi** *vr* to button (up).

abbotto'nato, a *ag* (*camicia etc*) buttoned (up); (*fig*) reserved.

abbottona'tura *sf* buttons *pl*; **questo cappotto ha l'**~ **da uomo/da donna** this coat buttons on the man's/woman's side.

abboz'zare [abbot'tsare] *vt* to sketch, outline; (*SCULTURA*) to rough-hew; ~ **un sorriso** to give a hint of a smile.

ab'bozzo [ab'bɔttso] *sm* sketch, outline; (*DIR*) draft.

abbracci'are [abbrat'tʃare] *vt* to embrace; (*persona*) to hug, embrace; (*professione*) to take up; (*contenere*) to include; ~**rsi** *vr* to hug o embrace (one another).

ab'braccio [ab'brattʃo] *sm* hug, embrace.

abbrevi'are *vt* to shorten; (*parola*) to abbreviate, shorten.

abbreviazi'one [abbrevjat'tsjone] *sf* abbreviation.

abbron'zante [abbron'dzante] *ag* tanning,

sun cpd.

abbron'zare [abbron'dzare] vt (pelle) to tan; (metalli) to bronze; ~rsi vr to tan, get a tan.

abbron'zato, a [abbron'dzato] ag (sun)tanned.

abbronza'tura [abbrondza'tura] sf tan, suntan.

abbrusto'lire vt (pane) to toast; (caffè) to roast.

abbruti'mento sm exhaustion; degradation.

abbru'tire vt (snervare, stancare) to exhaust; (degradare) to degrade; **essere abbrutito dall'alcool** to be ruined by drink.

abbuf'farsi vr (fam): ~ (di qc) to stuff o.s. (with sth).

abbuf'fata sf (fam) nosh-up; (fig) binge; **farsi un'**~ to stuff o.s.

abbuo'nare vt = abbonare.

abbu'ono sm (COMM) allowance, discount; (SPORT) handicap.

abdi'care vi to abdicate; ~ a to give up, renounce.

abdicazi'one [abdikat'tsjone] sf abdication.

aberrazi'one [aberrat'tsjone] af aberration.

abe'taia sf fir wood.

a'bete sm fir (tree); ~ **bianco** silver fir; ~ **rosso** spruce.

abi'etto, a ag despicable, abject.

abiezi'one [abjet'tsjone] sf abjection.

'abile ag (idoneo): ~ **(a qc/a fare qc)** fit (for sth/to do sth); (capace) able; (astuto) clever; (accorto) skilful; ~ **al servizio militare** fit for military service.

abilità sf inv ability; cleverness; skill.

abili'tante ag qualifying; **corsi** ~**i** (INS) ≈ teacher training sg.

abili'tare vt: ~ **qn a qc/a fare qc** to qualify sb for sth/to do sth; **è stato abilitato all'insegnamento** he has qualified as a teacher.

abili'tato, a ag qualified; (TEL) which has an outside line.

abilitazi'one [abilitat'tsjone] sf qualification.

abis'sale ag abysmal; (fig: senza limiti) profound.

abis'sino, a ag, sm/f Abyssinian.

a'bisso sm abyss, gulf.

abitabilità sf: **licenza di** ~ document stating that a property is fit for habitation.

abi'tacolo sm (AER) cockpit; (AUT) inside; (di camion) (driver's) cab.

abi'tante sm/f inhabitant.

abi'tare vt to live in, dwell in ♦ vi: ~ **in**

campagna/a Roma to live in the country/ in Rome.

abi'tato, a ag inhabited; lived in ♦ sm (anche: **centro** ~) built-up area.

abitazi'one [abitat'tsjone] sf residence; house.

'abito sm dress no pl; (da uomo) suit; (da donna) dress; (abitudine, disposizione, REL) habit; ~**i** smpl (vestiti) clothes; **in** ~ **da cerimonia** in formal dress; **in** ~ **da sera** in evening dress; **'è gradito l'**~ **scuro"** "dress formal"; ~ **mentale** way of thinking.

abitu'ale ag usual, habitual; (cliente) regular.

abitual'mente av usually, normally.

abitu'are vt: ~ **qn a** to get sb used to, accustom to; ~**rsi a** to get used to, accustom o.s. to.

abitudi'nario, a ag of fixed habits ♦ sm/f creature of habit.

abi'tudine sf habit; **aver l'**~ **di fare qc** to be in the habit of doing sth; **d'**~ usually; **per** ~ from o out of habit.

abiu'rare vt to renounce.

abla'tivo sm ablative.

abnegazi'one [abnegat'tsjone] sf (self-) abnegation, self-denial.

ab'norme ag (enorme) extraordinary; (anormale) abnormal.

abo'lire vt to abolish; (DIR) to repeal.

abolizi'one [abolit'tsjone] sf abolition; repeal.

abomi'nevole ag abominable.

abo'rigeno [abo'rid3eno] sm aborigine.

abor'rire vt to abhor, detest.

abor'tire vi (MED: accidentalmente) to miscarry, have a miscarriage; (: deliberatamente) to have an abortion; (fig) to miscarry, fail.

abor'tista, i, e ag pro-choice, pro-abortion ♦ sm/f pro-choicer.

a'borto sm miscarriage; abortion; (fig) freak; ~ **clandestino** backstreet abortion.

abrasi'one sf abrasion.

abra'sivo, a ag, sm abrasive.

abro'gare vt to repeal, abrogate.

abrogazi'one [abrogat'tsjone] sf repeal.

abruz'zese [abrut'tsese] ag of (o from) the Abruzzi.

A'bruzzo [a'bruttso] sm: **l'**~, **gli** ~**i** the Abruzzi.

'abside sf apse.

'Abu 'Dhabi sf Abu Dhabi.

a'bulico, a, ci, che ag lacking in willpower.

abu'sare vi: ~ **di** to abuse, misuse; (approfittare, violare) to take advantage of;

~ **dell'alcool/dei cibi** to drink/eat to excess.

abusi'vismo *sm* (*anche:* ~ **edilizio**) unlawful building, building without planning permission (*BRIT*).

abu'sivo, a *ag* unauthorized, unlawful; (**occupante**) ~ (*di una casa*) squatter.

a'buso *sm* abuse, misuse; excessive use; **fare** ~ **di** (*stupefacenti, medicine*) to abuse.

a.C. *abbr av* (= *avanti Cristo*) BC.

a'cacia, cie [a'katʃa] *sf* acacia.

'acca *sf* letter H; **non capire un'**~ not to understand a thing.

ac'cadde *vb vedi* **accadere.**

acca'demia *sf* (*società*) learned society; (*scuola: d'arte, militare*) academy; ~ **di Belle Arti** art school.

acca'demico, a, ci, che *ag* academic ♦ *sm* academician.

acca'dere *vi* to happen, occur.

acca'duto *sm* event; **raccontare l'**~ to describe what has happened.

accalappia'cani *sm inv* dog-catcher.

accalappi'are *vt* to catch; (*fig*) to trick, dupe.

accal'care *vt*, ~**rsi** *vr* to crowd, throng.

accal'darsi *vr* to grow hot.

accalo'rarsi *vr* (*fig*) to get excited.

accampa'mento *sm* camp.

accam'pare *vt* to encamp; (*fig*) to put forward, advance; ~**rsi** *vr* to camp; ~ **scuse** to make excuses.

accani'mento *sm* fury; (*tenacia*) tenacity, perseverance.

acca'nirsi *vr* (*infierire*) to rage; (*ostinarsi*) to persist.

accanita'mente *av* fiercely; assiduously.

acca'nito, a *ag* (*odio, gelosia*) fierce, bitter; (*lavoratore*) assiduous; (*giocatore*) inveterate; (*tifoso, sostenitore*) keen; **fumatore** ~ chain smoker.

ac'canto *av* near, nearby; ~ **a** *prep* near, beside, close to; **la casa** ~ the house next door.

accanto'nare *vt* (*problema*) to shelve; (*somma*) to set aside.

accaparra'mento *sm* (*COMM*) cornering, buying up.

accapar'rare *vt* (*COMM*) to corner, buy up; (*versare una caparra*) to pay a deposit on; ~**rsi** *vr*: ~**rsi qc** (*fig: simpatia, voti*) to secure sth (for o.s.).

accapigli'arsi [akkapiʎ'ʎarsi] *vr* to come to blows; (*fig*) to quarrel.

accappa'toio *sm* bathrobe.

accappo'nare *vi*: **far** ~ **la pelle a qn** (*fig*) to bring sb out in goosepimples.

accarez'zare [akkaret'tsare] *vt* to caress, stroke, fondle; (*fig*) to toy with.

accartocci'are [akkartot'tʃare] *vt* (*carta*) to roll up, screw up; ~**rsi** *vr* (*foglie*) to curl up.

acca'sarsi *vr* to set up house; to get married.

accasci'arsi [akkaʃ'ʃarsi] *vr* to collapse; (*fig*) to lose heart.

accatas'tare *vt* to stack, pile.

accatto'naggio [akkatto'naddʒo] *sm* begging.

accat'tone, a *sm/f* beggar.

accaval'lare *vt* (*gambe*) to cross; ~**rsi** *vr* (*sovrapporsi*) to overlap; (*addensarsi*) to gather.

acce'care [attʃe'kare] *vt* to blind ♦ *vi* to go blind.

ac'cedere [at'tʃɛdere] *vi*: ~ **a** to enter; (*richiesta*) to grant, accede to; (*fonte*) to gain access to.

accele'rare [attʃele'rare] *vt* to speed up ♦ *vi* (*AUT*) to accelerate; ~ **il passo** to quicken one's pace.

accele'rato, a [attʃele'rato] *ag* quick, rapid ♦ *sm* (*FERR*) local train, stopping train.

accelera'tore [attʃelera'tore] *sm* (*AUT*) accelerator.

accelerazi'one [attʃelerat'tsjone] *sf* acceleration.

ac'cendere [at'tʃɛndere] *vt* (*fuoco, sigaretta*) to light; (*luce, televisione*) to put *o* switch *o* turn on; (*AUT: motore*) to switch on; (*COMM: conto*) to open; (: *debito*) to contract; (: *ipoteca*) to raise; (*fig: suscitare*) to inflame, stir up; ~**rsi** *vr* (*luce*) to come *o* go on; (*legna*) to catch fire, ignite; (*fig: lotta, conflitto*) to break out.

accen'dino [attʃen'dino], **accendi'sigaro** [attʃendi'sigaro] *sm* (*cigarette*) lighter.

accen'nare [attʃen'nare] *vt* to indicate, point out; (*MUS*) to pick out the notes of; to hum ♦ *vi*: ~ **a** (*fig: alludere a*) to hint at; (: *far atto di*) to make as if; ~ **un saluto** (*con la mano*) to make as if to wave; (*col capo*) to half nod; ~ **un sorriso** to half smile; **accenna a piovere** it looks as if it's going to rain.

ac'cenno [at'tʃenno] *sm* (*cenno*) sign; nod; (*allusione*) hint.

accensi'one [attʃen'sjone] *sf* (*vedi accendere*) lighting; switching on; opening; (*AUT*) ignition.

accen'tare [attʃen'tare] *vt* (*parlando*) to stress; (*scrivendo*) to accent.

accentazi'one [attʃentat'tsjone] *sf* accentuation; stressing.

ac'cento [at'tʃɛnto] *sm* accent; (*FONETICA,*

fig) stress; (*inflessione*) tone (of voice).

accentra'mento [attʃentra'mento] *sm* centralization.

accen'trare [attʃen'trare] *vt* to centralize.

accentra'tore, 'trice [attʃentra'tore] *ag* (*persona*) unwilling to delegate; **politica** ~**trice** policy of centralization.

accentu'are [attʃentu'are] *vt* to stress, emphasize; ~**rsi** *vr* to become more noticeable.

accerchi'are [attʃer'kjare] *vt* to surround, encircle.

accerta'mento [attʃerta'mento] *sm* check; assessment.

accer'tare [attʃer'tare] *vt* to ascertain; (*verificare*) to check; (*reddito*) to assess; ~**rsi** *vr*: ~**rsi (di qc/che)** to make sure (of sth/that).

ac'ceso, a [at'tʃeso] *pp di* **accendere** ♦ *ag* lit; on; open; (*colore*) bright; ~ **di** (*ira, entusiasmo etc*) burning with.

acces'sibile [attʃes'sibile] *ag* (*luogo*) accessible; (*persona*) approachable, (*prezzo*) reasonable; (*idea*): ~ **a qn** within the reach of sb.

ac'cesso [at'tʃɛsso] *sm* (*anche INFORM*) access; (*MED*) attack, fit; (*impulso violento*) fit, outburst, **programmi dell'**~ (*TV*) educational programmes; **tempo di** ~ (*INFORM*) access time; ~ **casuale/seriale/ sequenziale** (*INFORM*) random/serial/ sequential access.

accessori'ato, a [attʃesso'rjato] *ag* with accessories.

acces'sorio, a [attʃes'sɔrjo] *ag* secondary, of secondary importance; ~**i** *smpl* accessories.

ac'cetta [at'tʃetta] *sf* hatchet.

accet'tabile [attʃet'tabile] *ag* acceptable.

accet'tare [attʃet'tare] *vt* to accept; ~ **di fare qc** to agree to do sth.

accettazi'one [attʃettat'tsjone] *sf* acceptance; (*locale di servizio pubblico*) reception; ~ **bagagli** (*AER*) check-in (desk); ~ **con riserva** qualified acceptance.

ac'cetto, a [at'tʃetto] *ag* (*persona*) welcome; (**ben**) ~ **a tutti** well-liked by everybody.

accezi'one [attʃet'tsjone] *sf* meaning.

acchiap'pare [akkjap'pare] *vt* to catch; (*afferrare*) to seize.

ac'chito [ak'kito] *sm*: **a primo** ~ at first sight.

acciac'cato, a [attʃak'kato] *ag* (*persona*) full of aches and pains; (*abito*) crushed.

acci'acco, chi [at'tʃakko] *sm* ailment; ~**chi** *smpl* aches and pains.

acciaie'ria [attʃaje'ria] *sf* steelworks *sg*.

acci'aio [at'tʃajo] *sm* steel; ~ **inossidabile** stainless steel.

acciden'tale [attʃiden'tale] *ag* accidental.

accidental'mente [attʃidental'mente] *av* (*per caso*) by chance; (*non deliberatamente*) accidentally, by accident.

acciden'tato, a [attʃiden'tato] *ag* (*terreno etc*) uneven.

acci'dente [attʃi'dɛnte] *sm* (*caso imprevisto*) accident; (*disgrazia*) mishap; ~**i!** (*fam: per rabbia*) damn (it)!; (: *per meraviglia*) good heavens!; ~**i a lui!** damn him!; **non vale un** ~ it's not worth a damn; **non capisco un** ~ it's as clear as mud to me; **mandare un** ~ **a qn** to curse sb.

ac'cidia [at'tʃidja] *sf* (*REL*) sloth.

accigli'ato, a [attʃiʎ'ʎato] *ag* frowning.

ac'cingersi [at'tʃindʒersi] *vr*: ~ **a fare** to be about to do.

acciotto'lato [attʃotto'lato] *sm* cobbles *pl*.

acciuf'fare [attʃuf'fare] *vt* to seize, catch.

acci'uga, ghe [at'tʃuga] *sf* anchovy; **magro come un'**~ as thin as a rake.

accla'mare *vt* (*applaudire*) to applaud; (*ologgere*) to acclaim.

acclamazi'one [akklamat'tsjone] *sf* applause; acclamation.

acclima'tare *vt* to acclimatize; ~**rsi** *vr* to become acclimatized.

acclimatazl'one [akklimatat'tsjone] *sf* acclimatization.

ac'cludere *vt* to enclose.

ac'cluso, a *pp di* **accludere** ♦ *ag* enclosed.

accocco'larsi *vr* to crouch.

acco'darsi *vr* to follow, tag on (behind).

accogli'ente [akkoʎ'ʎɛnte] *ag* welcoming, friendly.

accogli'enza [akkoʎ'ʎɛntsa] *sf* reception; welcome; **fare una buona** ~ **a qn** to welcome sb.

ac'cogliere [ak'kɔʎʎere] *vt* (*ricevere*) to receive; (*dare il benvenuto*) to welcome; (*approvare*) to agree to, accept; (*contenere*) to hold, accommodate.

ac'colgo *etc vb vedi* **accogliere**.

accol'lare *vt* (*fig*): ~ **qc a qn** to force sth on sb; ~**rsi** *vr*: ~**rsi qc** to take sth upon o.s., shoulder sth.

accol'lato, a *ag* (*vestito*) high-necked.

ac'colsi *etc vb vedi* **accogliere**.

accol'tellare *vt* to knife, stab.

ac'colto, a *pp di* **accogliere**.

accoman'dita *sf* (*DIR*) limited partnership.

accomia'tare *vt* to dismiss; ~**rsi** *vr*: ~**rsi (da)** to take one's leave (of).

accomoda'mento *sm* agreement,

settlement.
accomo'dante *ag* accommodating.
accomo'dare *vt* (*aggiustare*) to repair, mend; (*riordinare*) to tidy; (*sistemare*: *questione, lite*) to settle; ~**rsi** *vr* (*sedersi*) to sit down; (*fig*: *risolversi*: *situazione*) to work out; **si accomodi!** (*venga avanti*) come in!; (*si sieda*) take a seat!
accompagna'mento [akkompaɲɲa'mento] *sm* (*MUS*) accompaniment; (*COMM*): **lettera di** ~ accompanying letter.
accompa'gnare [akkompaɲ'ɲare] *vt* to accompany, come *o* go with; (*MUS*) to accompany; (*unire*) to couple; ~**rsi** *vr* (*armonizzarsi*) to go well together; ~ **qn a casa** to see sb home; ~ **qn alla porta** to show sb out; ~ **un regalo con un biglietto** to put in *o* send a card with a present; ~ **qn con lo sguardo** to follow sb with one's eyes; ~ **la porta** to close the door gently; ~**rsi a** (*frequentare*) to frequent; (*colori*) to go with, match; (*cibi*) to go with.
accompagna'tore, 'trice [akkompaɲɲa'tore] *sm/f* companion, escort; (*MUS*) accompanist; (*SPORT*) team manager; ~ **turistico** courier; tour guide.
accomu'nare *vt* to pool, share; (*avvicinare*) to unite.
acconcia'tura [akkontʃa'tura] *sf* hairstyle.
accondiscen'dente [akkondiʃʃen'dɛnte] *ag* affable.
accondi'scendere [akkondiʃ'ʃendere] *vi*: ~ **a** to agree *o* consent to.
accondi'sceso, a [akkondiʃ'ʃeso] *pp di* **accondiscendere**.
acconsen'tire *vi*: ~ **(a)** to agree *o* consent (to); **chi tace acconsente** silence means consent.
acconten'tare *vt* to satisfy; ~**rsi** *vr*: ~**rsi di** to be satisfied with, content o.s. with; **chi si accontenta gode** there's no point in complaining.
ac'conto *sm* part payment; **pagare una somma in** ~ to pay a sum of money as a deposit; ~ **di dividendo** interim dividend.
accoppia'mento *sm* pairing off; mating; (*ELETTR, INFORM*) coupling.
accoppi'are *vt* to couple, pair off; (*BIOL*) to mate; ~**rsi** *vr* to pair off; to mate.
accoppia'tore *sm* (*TECN*) coupler; ~ **acustico** (*INFORM*) acoustic coupler.
acco'rato, a *ag* heartfelt.
accorci'are [akkor'tʃare] *vt* to shorten; ~**rsi** *vr* to become shorter; (*vestiti*: *nel lavaggio*) to shrink.
accor'dare *vt* to reconcile; (*colori*) to match; (*MUS*) to tune; (*LING*): ~ **qc con qc** to make sth agree with sth; (*DIR*) to grant;

~**rsi** *vr* to agree, come to an agreement; (*colori*) to match.
ac'cordo *sm* agreement; (*armonia*) harmony; (*MUS*) chord; **essere d'**~ to agree; **andare d'**~ to get on well together; **d'**~! all right!, agreed!; **mettersi d'**~ **(con qn)** to agree *o* come to an agreement with sb; **prendere** ~**i con** to reach an agreement with; ~ **commerciale** trade agreement; **A**~ **generale sulle tariffe ed il commercio** General Agreement on Tariffs and Trade, GATT.
ac'corgersi [ak'kɔrdʒersi] *vr*: ~ **di** to notice; (*fig*) to realize.
accorgi'mento [akkordʒi'mento] *sm* shrewdness *no pl*; (*espediente*) trick, device.
ac'correre *vi* to run up.
ac'corsi *vb vedi* **accorgersi; accorrere.**
ac'corso, a *pp di* **accorrere.**
accor'tezza [akkor'tettsa] *sf* (*avvedutezza*) good sense; (*astuzia*) shrewdness.
ac'corto, a *pp di* **accorgersi** ♦ *ag* shrewd; **stare** ~ to be on one's guard.
accosta'mento *sm* (*di colori etc*) combination.
accos'tare *vt* (*avvicinarsi a*) to approach; (*socchiudere*: *imposte*) to half-close; (*: porta*) to leave ajar ♦ *vi*: ~ **(a)** (*NAUT*) to come alongside; (*AUT*) to draw up (at); ~**rsi** *vr*: ~**rsi a** to draw near, approach; (*somigliare*) to be like, resemble; (*fede, religione*) to turn to; (*idee politiche*) to come to agree with; ~ **qc a** (*avvicinare*) to bring sth near to, put sth near to; (*colori, stili*) to match sth with; (*appoggiare*: *scala etc*) to lean sth against.
accovacci'arsi [akkovat'tʃarsi] *vr* to crouch.
accoz'zaglia [akkot'tsaʎʎa] *sf* (*peg*: *di idee, oggetti*) jumble, hotchpotch; (*: di persone*) odd assortment.
ac'crebbi *etc vb vedi* **accrescere.**
accredi'tare *vt* (*notizia*) to confirm the truth of; (*COMM*) to credit; (*diplomatico*) to accredit; ~**rsi** *vr* (*fig*) to gain credit.
ac'credito *sm* (*COMM*: *atto*) crediting; (*: effetto*) credit.
ac'crescere [ak'kreʃʃere] *vt* to increase; ~**rsi** *vr* to increase, grow.
accresci'mento [akkreʃʃi'mento] *sm* increase, growth.
accresci'tivo, a [akkreʃʃi'tivo] *ag, sm* (*LING*) augmentative.
accresci'uto, a [akkreʃ'ʃuto] *pp di* **accrescere.**
accucci'arsi [akkut'tʃarsi] *vr* (*cane*) to lie down; (*persona*) to crouch down.
accu'dire *vi*: ~ **a** *vt* to attend to; to look

after.

acculturazi'one [akkulturat'tsjone] *sf* (*SOCIOLOGIA*) integration.

accumu'lare *vt* to accumulate; **~rsi** *vr* to accumulate; (*FINANZA*) to accrue.

accumula'tore *sm* (*ELETTR*) accumulator.

accumulazi'one [akkumulat'tsjone] *sf* accumulation.

ac'cumulo *sm* accumulation.

accurata'mente *av* carefully.

accura'tezza [akkura'tettsa] *sf* care; accuracy.

accu'rato, a *ag* (*diligente*) careful; (*preciso*) accurate.

ac'cusa *sf* accusation; (*DIR*) charge; **l'~, la pubblica ~** (*DIR*) the prosecution; **mettere qn sotto ~** to indict sb; **in stato di ~** committed for trial.

accu'sare *vt* (*sentire*: *dolore*) to feel; **~ qn di qc** to accuse sb of sth, (*DIR*) to charge sb with sth; **~ ricevuta di** (*COMM*) to acknowledge receipt of; **~ la fatica** to show signs of exhaustion; **ha accusato il colpo** (*anche fig*) you could see that he had felt the blow.

accusa'tivo *sm* accusative.

accu'sato, a *sm/f* accused.

accusa'tore, 'trice *ag* accusing ♦ *sm/f* accuser ♦ *sm* (*DIR*) prosecutor.

a'cerbo, a [a'tʃerbo] *ag* bitter; (*frutta*) sour, unripe; (*persona*) immature.

'acero ['atʃero] *sm* maple.

a'cerrimo, a [a'tʃerrimo] *ag* very fierce.

ace'tato [atʃe'tato] *sm* acetate.

a'ceto [a'tʃeto] *sm* vinegar; **mettere sotto ~** to pickle.

ace'tone [atʃe'tone] *sm* nail varnish remover.

'A.C.I. ['atʃi] *sigla m* (= *Automobile Club d'Italia*) ≈ AA (*BRIT*), AAA (*US*).

acidità [atʃidi'ta] *sf* acidity; sourness; **~ (di stomaco)** heartburn.

'acido, a ['atʃido] *ag* (*sapore*) acid, sour; (*CHIM, colore*) acid ♦ *sm* (*CHIM*) acid.

a'cidulo, a [a'tʃidulo] *ag* slightly sour, slightly acid.

'acino ['atʃino] *sm* berry; **~ d'uva** grape.

'ACLI *sigla fpl* (= *Associazioni Cristiane dei Lavoratori Italiani*) Christian Trade Union Association.

'acme *sf* (*fig*) acme, peak; (*MED*) crisis.

'acne *sf* acne.

ACNUR *sigla m* (= *Alto Commissariato delle Nazioni Unite per i Rifugiati*) UNHCR.

'acqua *sf* water; (*pioggia*) rain; **~e** *sfpl* waters; **fare ~** (*NAUT*) to leak, take in water; **essere con o avere l'~ alla gola** to be in great difficulty; **tirare ~ al proprio**

mulino to feather one's own nest; **navigare in cattive ~e** (*fig*) to be in deep water; **~ in bocca!** mum's the word!; **~ corrente** running water; **~ dolce** fresh water; **~ di mare** sea water; **~ minerale** mineral water; **~ ossigenata** hydrogen peroxide; **~ piovana** rain water; **~ potabile** drinking water; **~ salata** *o* **salmastra** salt water; **~ tonica** tonic water.

acqua'forte, *pl* **acque'forti** *sf* etching.

a'cquaio *sm* sink.

acqua'ragia [akkwa'radʒa] *sf* turpentine.

a'cquario *sm* aquarium; (*dello zodiaco*): **A~** Aquarius; **essere dell'A~** to be Aquarius.

acquartie'rare *vt* (*MIL*) to quarter.

acqua'santa *sf* holy water.

a'cquatico, a, ci, che *ag* aquatic; (*sport, sci*) water *cpd*.

acquat'tarsi *vr* to crouch (down).

acqua'vite *sf* brandy.

acquaz'zone [akkwat'tsone] *sm* cloudburst, heavy shower.

acque'dotto *sm* aqueduct; waterworks *pl*, water system.

'acqueo, a *ag*. **vapore ~** water vapour (*BRIT*) *o* vapor (*US*); **umore ~** aqueous humour (*BRIT*) *o* humor (*US*).

acque'rello *sm* watercolour (*BRIT*), watercolor (*US*).

acque'rugiola [akkwe'rudʒola] *sf* drizzle.

acquie'tare *vt* to appease; (*dolore*) to ease; **~rsi** *vr* to calm down.

acqui'rente *sm/f* purchaser, buyer.

acqui'sire *vt* to acquire.

acquisizi'one [akkwizit'tsjone] *sf* acquisition.

acquis'tare *vt* to purchase, buy; (*fig*) to gain ♦ *vi* to improve; **~ in bellezza** to become more beautiful; **ha acquistato in salute** his health has improved.

a'cquisto *sm* purchase; **fare ~i** to go shopping; **ufficio ~i** (*COMM*) purchasing department; **~ rateale** instalment purchase, hire purchase (*BRIT*).

acqui'trino *sm* bog, marsh.

acquo'lina *sf*: **far venire l'~ in bocca a qn** to make sb's mouth water.

a'cquoso, a *ag* watery.

'acre *ag* acrid, pungent; (*fig*) harsh, biting.

a'credine *sf* (*fig*) bitterness.

a'crilico, a, ci, che *ag, sm* acrylic.

a'critico, a, ci, che *ag* uncritical.

a'crobata, i, e *sm/f* acrobat.

acro'batico, a, ci, che *ag* (*ginnastica*) acrobatic; (*AER*) aerobatic ♦ *sf* acrobatics *sg*.

acroba'zia [akrobat'tsia] *sf* acrobatic feat;

~e aeree aerobatics.

a'cronimo *sm* acronym.

a'cropoli *sf inv*: **l'A~** the Acropolis.

acu'ire *vt* to sharpen; **~rsi** *vr* (*gen*) to increase; (*crisi*) to worsen.

a'culeo *sm* (*ZOOL*) sting; (*BOT*) prickle.

a'cume *sm* acumen, perspicacity.

acumi'nato, a *ag* sharp.

a'custico, a, ci, che *ag* acoustic ♦ *sf* (*scienza*) acoustics *sg*; (*di una sala*) acoustics *pl*; **apparecchio** ~ hearing aid; **cornetto** ~ ear trumpet.

acu'tezza [aku'tettsa] *sf* sharpness; shrillness; acuteness; high pitch; intensity; keenness.

acutiz'zare [akutid'dzare] *vt* (*fig*) to intensify; **~rsi** *vr* (*fig*: *crisi, malattia*) to become worse, worsen.

a'cuto, a *ag* (*appuntito*) sharp, pointed; (*suono, voce*) shrill, piercing; (*MAT, LING, MED*) acute; (*MUS*) high-pitched; (*fig: dolore, desiderio*) intense; (: *perspicace*) acute, keen ♦ *sm* (*MUS*) high note.

A.D. *sigla f* (*POL*) = **Alleanza Democratica.**

ad *prep* (*dav V*) = **a.**

adagi'are [ada'dʒare] *vt* to lay *o* set down carefully; **~rsi** *vr* to lie down, stretch out.

a'dagio [a'dadʒo] *av* slowly ♦ *sm* (*MUS*) adagio; (*proverbio*) adage, saying.

ada'mitico, a, ci, che *ag*: **in costume** ~ in one's birthday suit.

adat'tabile *ag* adaptable.

adattabilità *sf* adaptability.

adatta'mento *sm* adaptation; **avere spirito di** ~ to be adaptable.

adat'tare *vt* to adapt; (*sistemare*) to fit; **~rsi** *vr*: **~rsi (a)** (*ambiente, tempi*) to adapt (to); (*essere adatto*) to be suitable (for); (*accontentarsi*): **~rsi a qc/a fare qc** to make the best of sth/of doing sth.

adatta'tore *sm* (*ELETTR*) adapter, adaptor.

a'datto, a *ag*: ~ **(a)** suitable (for), right (for).

addebi'tare *vt*: ~ **qc a qn** to debit sb with sth; (*fig: incolpare*) to blame sb for sth.

ad'debito *sm* (*COMM*) debit.

addensa'mento *sm* thickening; gathering.

adden'sare *vt* to thicken; **~rsi** *vr* to thicken; (*nuvole*) to gather.

adden'tare *vt* to bite into.

adden'trarsi *vr*: ~ **in** to penetrate, go into.

ad'dentro *av* (*fig*): **essere molto** ~ **in qc** to be well-versed in sth.

addestra'mento *sm* training; ~ **aziendale** company training.

addes'trare *vt*, **~rsi** *vr* to train; **~rsi in qc** to practise (*BRIT*) *o* practice (*US*) sth.

ad'detto, a *ag*: ~ **a** (*persona*) assigned to; (*oggetto*) intended for ♦ *sm* employee; (*funzionario*) attaché; ~ **commerciale/stampa** commercial/press attaché; ~ **al telex** telex operator; **gli ~i ai lavori** authorized personnel; (*fig*) those in the know; "**vietato l'ingresso ai non ~i ai lavori**" "authorized personnel only".

addì *av* (*AMM*): ~ **3 luglio 1989** on the 3rd of July 1989 (*BRIT*), on July 3rd 1989 (*US*).

addi'accio [ad'djattʃo] *sm* (*MIL*) bivouac; **dormire all'**~ to sleep in the open.

addi'etro *av* (*indietro*) behind; (*nel passato, prima*) before, ago.

ad'dio *sm*, *escl* goodbye, farewell.

addirit'tura *av* (*veramente*) really, absolutely; (*perfino*) even; (*direttamente*) directly, right away.

ad'dirsi *vr*: ~ **a** to suit, be suitable for.

'Addis A'beba *sf* Addis Ababa.

addi'tare *vt* to point out; (*fig*) to expose.

addi'tivo *sm* additive.

addizio'nale [addittsjo'nale] *ag* additional ♦ *sf* (*anche*: **imposta** ~) surtax.

addizio'nare [addittsjo'nare] *vt* (*MAT*) to add (up).

addizi'one [addit'tsjone] *sf* addition.

addob'bare *vt* to decorate.

ad'dobbo *sm* decoration.

addol'cire [addol'tʃire] *vt* (*caffè etc*) to sweeten; (*acqua, fig: carattere*) to soften; **~rsi** *vr* (*fig*) to mellow, soften; ~ **la pillola** (*fig*) to sugar the pill.

addolo'rare *vt* to pain, grieve; **~rsi** *vr*: **~rsi (per)** to be distressed (by).

addolo'rato, a *ag* distressed, upset; **l'A~a** (*REL*) Our Lady of Sorrows.

ad'dome *sm* abdomen.

addomesti'care *vt* to tame.

addomi'nale *ag* abdominal; (**muscoli** *mpl*) **~i** stomach muscles.

addormen'tare *vt* to put to sleep; **~rsi** *vr* to fall asleep, go to sleep.

addormen'tato, a *ag* sleeping, asleep; (*fig: tardo*) stupid, dopey.

addos'sare *vt* (*appoggiare*): ~ **qc a qc** to lean sth against sth; (*fig*): ~ **la colpa a qn** to lay the blame on sb; **~rsi** *vr*: **~rsi qc** (*responsabilità etc*) to shoulder sth.

ad'dosso *av* (*sulla persona*) on; ~ **a** *prep* (*sopra*) on; (*molto vicino*) right next to; **mettersi** ~ **il cappotto** to put one's coat on; **andare** (*o* **venire**) ~ **a** (*AUT*: *altra macchina*) to run into; (: *pedone*) to run over; **non ho soldi** ~ I don't have any money on me; **stare** ~ **a qn** (*fig*) to breathe down sb's neck; **dare** ~ **a qn** (*fig*) to attack sb; **mettere gli occhi** ~ **a qn/qc** to take quite a fancy to sb/sth; **mettere le**

mani ~ **a qn** (*picchiare*) to hit sb; (*catturare*) to seize sb; (*molestare*: *donna*) to touch sb up.

ad'dotto, a *pp di* **addurre.**

ad'duco *etc vb vedi* **addurre.**

ad'durre *vt* (*DIR*) to produce; (*citare*) to cite.

ad'dussi *etc vb vedi* **addurre.**

adegu'are *vt*: ~ **qc a** to adjust sth to; ~**rsi** *vr* to adapt.

adegua'tezza [adegwa'tettsa] *sf* adequacy; suitability; fairness.

adegu'ato, a *ag* adequate; (*conveniente*) suitable; (*equo*) fair.

a'dempiere *vt* to fulfil (*BRIT*), fulfill (*US*), carry out; (*comando*) to carry out.

adempi'mento *sm* fulfilment (*BRIT*), fulfillment (*US*); carrying out; **nell'**~ **del proprio dovere** in the performance of one's duty.

adem'pire *vt* = **adempiere.**

'Aden: il golfo di ~ *sm* the Gulf of Aden.

ade'noidi *sfpl* adenoids.

a'depto *sm* disciple, follower

ade'rente *ag* adhesive; (*vestito*) close-fitting ♦ *sm/f* follower.

ade'renza [ade'rɛntsa] *sf* adhesion; ~**e** *sfpl* (*fig*) connections, contacts.

ade'rire *vi* (*stare attaccato*) to adhere, stick; ~ **a** to adhere to, stick to; (*fig*: *società, partito*) to join; (: *opinione*) to support; (*richiesta*) to agree to.

ades'care *vt* (*attirare*) to lure, entice; (*TECN*: *pompa*) to prime.

adesi'one *sf* adhesion; (*fig*: *assenso*) agreement, acceptance; (*appoggio*) support.

ade'sivo, a *ag*, *sm* adhesive.

a'desso *av* (*ora*) now; (*or ora, poco fa*) just now; (*tra poco*) any moment now; **da** ~ **in poi** from now on; **per** ~ for the moment, for now.

adia'cente [adja't ʃɛnte] *ag* adjacent.

adi'bire *vt* (*usare*): ~ **qc a** to turn sth into.

'Adige ['adidʒe] *sm*: **l'**~ the Adige.

'adipe *sm* fat.

adi'poso, a *ag* (*tessuto, zona*) adipose.

adi'rarsi *vr*: ~ (**con** *o* **contro qn per qc**) to get angry (with sb over sth).

adi'rato, a *ag* angry.

a'dire *vt* (*DIR*): ~ **le vie legali** to take legal proceedings; ~ **un'eredità** to take legal possession of an inheritance.

'adito *sm*: **dare** ~ **a** (*sospetti*) to give rise to.

ADN *sigla m* (= *acido deossiribonucleico*) DNA.

adocchi'are [adok'kjare] *vt* (*scorgere*) to catch sight of; (*occhieggiare*) to eye.

adole'scente [adoleʃ'ʃɛnte] *ag*, *sm/f*

adolescent.

adole'scenza [adoleʃ'ʃɛntsa] *sf* adolescence.

adolescenzi'ale [adoleʃʃen'tsjale] *ag* adolescent.

adom'brarsi *vr* (*cavallo*) to shy; (*persona*) to grow suspicious; (: *aversene a male*) to be offended.

adope'rare *vt* to use; ~**rsi** *vr* to strive; ~**rsi per qn/qc** to do one's best for sb/sth.

ado'rabile *ag* adorable.

ado'rare *vt* to adore; (*REL*) to adore, worship.

adorazi'one [adorat'tsjone] *sf* adoration; worship.

ador'nare *vt* to adorn.

a'dorno, a *ag*: ~ (**di**) adorned (with).

adot'tare *vt* to adopt; (*decisione, provvedimenti*) to pass.

adot'tivo, a *ag* (*genitori*) adoptive; (*figlio, patria*) adopted.

adozi'one [adot'tsjone] *sf* adoption.

adrena'linico, a, ci, che *ag* (*fig*: *vivace, eccitato*) charged-up.

adri'atico, a, ci, che *ag* Adriatic ♦ *sm*: **l'A-, il mare A**~ the Adriatic, the Adriatic Sea.

adu'lare *vt* to flatter.

adula'tore, 'trice *sm/f* flatterer.

adula'torio, a *ag* flattering.

adulazi'one [adulat'tsjone] *sf* flattery.

adulte'rare *vt* to adulterate.

adul'terio *sm* adultery.

a'dultero, a *ag* adulterous ♦ *sm/f* adulterer/adulteress.

a'dulto, a *ag* adult; (*fig*) mature ♦ *sm* adult, grown-up.

adu'nanza [adu'nantsa] *sf* assembly, meeting.

adu'nare *vt*, ~**rsi** *vr* to assemble, gather.

adu'nata *sf* (*MIL*) parade, muster.

a'dunco, a, chi, che *ag* hooked.

AEDA *sigla mpl* (= *Autori Editori Associati*) association of authors and publishers.

aerazi'one [aerat'tsjone] *sf* ventilation; (*TECN*) aeration.

a'ereo, a *ag* air *cpd*; (*radice*) aerial ♦ *sm* aerial; (*aeroplano*) plane; ~ **da caccia** fighter (plane); ~ **di linea** airliner; ~ **a reazione** jet (plane).

ae'robica *sf* aerobics *sg*.

aerodi'namico, a, ci, che *ag* aerodynamic; (*affusolato*) streamlined ♦ *sf* aerodynamics *sg*.

aeromo'dello *sm* model aircraft.

aero'nautica *sf* (*scienza*) aeronautics *sg*; ~ **militare** air force.

aerona'vale *ag* (*forze, manovre*) air and sea

cpd.
aero'plano sm (aero)plane (BRIT),
(air)plane (US).
aero'porto sm airport.
aeroportu'ale ag airport cpd.
aeros'calo sm airstrip.
aero'sol sm inv aerosol.
aerospazi'ale [aerospat'tsjale] ag
aerospace.
aeros'tatico, a, ci, che ag aerostatic;
pallone ~ air balloon.
ae'rostato sm aerostat.
A.F. abbr (= alta frequenza) HF; (AMM)
= assegni familiari.
'afa sf sultriness.
af'fabile ag affable.
affabilità sf affability.
affaccen'darsi [affattʃen'darsi] vr: ~
intorno a qc to busy o.s. with sth.
affaccen'dato, a [affattʃen'dato] ag busy.
affacci'arsi [affat'tʃarsi] vr: ~ **(a)** to appear
(at); ~ **alla vita** to come into the world.
affa'mato, a ag starving; (fig): ~ **(di)** eager
(for).
affan'nare vt to leave breathless; (fig) to
worry; ~**rsi** vr: ~**rsi per qn/qc** to worry
about sb/sth.
af'fanno sm breathlessness; (fig) anxiety,
worry.
affannosa'mente av with difficulty;
anxiously.
affan'noso, a ag (respiro) difficult; (fig)
troubled, anxious.
af'fare sm (faccenda) matter, affair; (COMM)
piece of business, (business) deal;
(occasione) bargain; (DIR) case; (fam: cosa)
thing; ~**i** smpl (COMM) business sg; ~
fatto! done!, it's a deal!; **sono** ~**i miei**
that's my business; **bada agli** ~**i tuoi!**
mind your own business!; **uomo d'**~**i**
businessman; **ministro degli A**~**i Esteri**
Foreign Secretary (BRIT), Secretary of
State (US).
affa'rista, i sm profiteer, unscrupulous
businessman.
affasci'nante [affaʃʃi'nante] ag fascinating.
affasci'nare [affaʃʃi'nare] vt to bewitch;
(fig) to charm, fascinate.
affatica'mento sm tiredness.
affati'care vt to tire; ~**rsi** vr (durar fatica) to
tire o.s. out.
af'fatto av completely; **non ...** ~ not .,. at
all; **niente** ~ not at all.
affer'mare vi (dire di sì) to say yes ♦ vt
(dichiarare) to maintain, affirm; ~**rsi** vr to
assert o.s., make one's name known.
affermativa'mente av in the affirmative,
affirmatively.

afferma'tivo, a ag affirmative.
affer'mato, a ag established, well-known.
affermazi'one [affermat'tsjone] sf
affirmation, assertion; (successo)
achievement.
affer'rare vt to seize, grasp; (fig: idea) to
grasp; ~**rsi** vr: ~**rsi a** to cling to.
Aff. Est. abbr = Affari Esteri.
affet'tare vt (tagliare a fette) to slice;
(ostentare) to affect.
affet'tato, a ag sliced; affected ♦ sm sliced
cold meat.
affetta'trice [affetta'tritʃe] sf meat slicer.
affettazi'one [affettat'tsjone] sf
affectation.
affet'tivo, a ag emotional, affective.
af'fetto, a ag: **essere** ~ **da** to suffer from
♦ sm affection; **gli** ~**i familiari** one's
nearest and dearest.
affettuosa'mente av affectionately; (nelle
lettere): **(ti saluto)** ~, **Maria** love, Maria.
affettuosità sf inv affection; ~ sfpl
(manifestazioni) demonstrations of
affection.
affettu'oso, a ag affectionate.
affezio'narsi [affettsjo'narsi] vr: ~ **a** to
grow fond of.
affezio'nato, a [affettsjo'nato] ag: ~ **a qn/**
qc fond of sb/sth; (attaccato) attached to
sb/sth.
affezi'one [affet'tsjone] sf (affetto)
affection; (MED) ailment, disorder.
affian'care vt to place side by side; (MIL) to
flank; (fig) to support; ~ **qc a qc** to place
sth next to o beside sth; ~**rsi** vr: ~**rsi a qn**
to stand beside sb.
affiata'mento sm understanding.
affia'tato, a ag: **essere** ~**i** to work well
together o get on; **formano una squadra**
~**a** they make a good team.
affibbi'are vt to buckle, do up; (fig: dare) to
give.
affi'dabile ag reliable.
affidabilità sf reliability.
affida'mento sm (DIR: di bambino) custody;
(fiducia): **fare** ~ **su qn** to rely on sb; **non**
dà nessun ~ he's not to be trusted.
affi'dare vt: ~ **qc o qn a qn** to entrust sth o
sb to sb; ~**rsi** vr: ~**rsi a** to place one's
trust in.
affievo'lirsi vr to grow weak.
af'figgere [af'fiddʒere] vt to stick up, post
up.
affi'lare vt to sharpen.
affi'lato, a ag (gen) sharp; (volto, naso)
thin.
affili'are vt to affiliate; ~**rsi** vr: ~**rsi a** to
become affiliated to.

affi'nare vt to sharpen.

affinché [affin'ke] cong in order that, so that.

af'fine ag similar.

affinità sf inv affinity.

affio'rare vi to emerge.

af'fissi etc vb vedi **affiggere**.

affissi'one sf billposting.

af'fisso, a pp di **affiggere** ♦ sm bill, poster; (LING) affix.

affitta'camere sm/f inv landlord/landlady.

affit'tare vt (dare in affitto) to let, rent (out); (prendere in affitto) to rent.

af'fitto sm rent; (contratto) lease; **dare in** ~ to rent (out), let; **prendere in** ~ to rent.

affittu'ario sm lessee.

af'fliggere [af'fliddʒere] vt to torment; ~**rsi** vr to grieve.

af'flissi etc vb vedi **affliggere**.

af'flitto, a pp di **affliggere**.

afflizi'one [afflit'tsjone] sf distress, torment.

afflosci'arsi [afflos'ʃarsi] vr to go limp; (frutta) to go soft.

afflu'ente sm tributary.

afflu'enza [afflu'entsa] sf flow; (di persone) crowd.

afflu'ire vi to flow; (fig: merci, persone) to pour in.

af'flusso sm influx.

affo'gare vt, vi to drown; ~**rsi** vr to drown; (deliberatamente) to drown o.s.

affo'gato, a ag drowned; (CUC: uova) poached.

affolla'mento sm crowding; (folla) crowd.

affol'lare vt, ~**rsi** vr to crowd.

affol'lato, a ag crowded.

affonda'mento sm (di nave) sinking.

affon'dare vt to sink.

affran'care vt to free, liberate; (AMM) to redeem; (lettera) to stamp; (: meccanicamente) to frank (BRIT), meter (US); ~**rsi** vr to free o.s.

affranca'trice [affranka'tritʃe] sf franking machine (BRIT), postage meter (US).

affranca'tura sf (di francobollo) stamping; franking (BRIT), metering (US); (tassa di spedizione) postage; ~ **a carico del destinatario** postage paid.

af'franto, a ag (esausto) worn out; (abbattuto) overcome.

af'fresco, schi sm fresco.

affret'tare vt to quicken, speed up; ~**rsi** vr to hurry; ~**rsi a fare qc** to hurry o hasten to do sth.

affret'tato, a ag (veloce: passo, ritmo) quick, fast; (frettoloso: decisione) hurried, hasty; (: lavoro) rushed.

affron'tare vt (pericolo etc) to face; (assalire: nemico) to confront; ~**rsi** vr (reciproco) to confront each other.

af'fronto sm affront, insult; **fare un** ~ **a qn** to insult sb.

affumi'care vt to fill with smoke; to blacken with smoke; (alimenti) to smoke.

affuso'lato, a ag tapering.

af'gano, a ag, sm/f Afghan.

Af'ghanistan [af'ganistan] sm: l'~ Afghanistan.

af'ghano, a ag, sm/f = **afgano**.

afo'risma, i sm aphorism.

a'foso, a ag sultry, close.

'Africa sf: l'~ Africa.

afri'cano, a ag, sm/f African.

afroasi'atico, a, ci, che ag Afro-Asian.

afrodi'siaco, a, ci, che ag, sm aphrodisiac.

AG sigla = Agrigento.

a'genda [a'dʒɛnda] sf diary; **tavolo** ~ pocket/desk diary.

a'gente [a'dʒɛnte] sm agent; ~ **di cambio** stockbroker; ~ **di custodia** prison officer; ~ **marittimo** shipping agent; ~ **di polizia** police officer; ~ **provocatore** agent provocateur; ~ **delle tasse** tax inspector; ~ **di vendita** sales agent; **resistente agli** ~**i atmosferici** weather-resistant.

agen'zia [adʒen'tsia] sf agency; (succursale) branch; ~ **di collocamento** employment agency; ~ **immobiliare** estate agent's (office) (BRIT), real estate office (US); **A**~ **Internazionale per l'Energia Atomica (AIEA)** International Atomic Energy Agency (IAEA); ~ **matrimoniale** marriage bureau; ~ **pubblicitaria** advertising agency; ~ **di stampa** press agency; ~ **viaggi** travel agency.

agevo'lare [adʒevo'lare] vt to facilitate, make easy.

agevolazi'one [adʒevolat'tsjone] sf (facilitazione economica) facility; ~ **di pagamento** payment on easy terms; ~**i creditizie** credit facilities; ~**i fiscali** tax concessions.

a'gevole [a'dʒevole] ag easy; (strada) smooth.

aggan'ciare [aggan'tʃare] vt to hook up; (FERR) to couple; ~**rsi** vr: ~**rsi a** to hook up to; (fig: pretesto) to seize on.

ag'gancio [ag'gantʃo] sm (TECN) coupling; (fig: conoscenza) contact.

ag'geggio [ad'dʒeddʒo] sm gadget, contraption.

agget'tivo [add3et'tivo] sm adjective.

agghiacci'ante [aggjat'tʃante] ag (fig) chilling.

agghiacci'are [aggjat'tʃare] vt to freeze;

(*fig*) to make one's blood run cold; ~**rsi** *vr* to freeze.

agghin'darsi [aggin'darsi] *vr* to deck o.s. out.

aggiorna'mento [addʒorna'mento] *sm* updating; revision; postponement; **corso di** ~ refresher course.

aggior'nare [addʒor'nare] *vt* (*opera, manuale*) to bring up-to-date; (: *rivedere*) to revise; (*listino*) to maintain, up-date; (*seduta etc*) to postpone; ~**rsi** *vr* to bring (*o* keep) o.s. up-to-date.

aggior'nato, a [addʒor'nato] *ag* up-to-date.

aggio'taggio [addʒo'taddʒo] *sm* (*ECON*) rigging the market.

aggi'rare [addʒi'rare] *vt* to go round; (*fig: ingannare*) to trick; ~**rsi** *vr* to wander about; **il prezzo s'aggira sul milione** the price is around the million mark.

aggiudi'care [addʒudi'kare] *vt* to award; (*all'asta*) to knock down; ~**rsi qc** to win sth.

aggi'ungere [ad'dʒundʒere] *vt* to add.

aggi'unsi [ad'dʒunsi] *etc vb vedi* **aggiungere**.

aggi'unto, a [ad'dʒunto] *pp di* **aggiungere** ♦ *ag* assistant *cpd* ♦ *sm* assistant ♦ *sf* addition; **sindaco** ~ deputy mayor; **in** ~**a** ... what's more ....

aggius'tare [addʒus'tare] *vt* (*accomodare*) to mend, repair; (*riassettare*) to adjust; (*fig: lite*) to settle; ~**rsi** *vr* (*arrangiarsi*) to make do; (*con senso reciproco*) to come to an agreement; **ti aggiusto io!** I'll fix you!

agglome'rato *sm* (*di rocce*) conglomerate; (*di legno*) chipboard; ~ **urbano** built-up area.

aggrap'parsi *vr*: ~ **a** to cling to.

aggrava'mento *sm* worsening.

aggra'vante *ag* (*DIR*) aggravating ♦ *sf* aggravation.

aggra'vare *vt* (*aumentare*) to increase; (*appesantire: anche fig*) to weigh down, make heavy; (*fig: pena*) to make worse; ~**rsi** *vr* (*fig*) to worsen, become worse.

ag'gravio *sm*: ~ **di costi** increase in costs.

aggrazi'ato, a [aggrat'tsjato] *ag* graceful.

aggre'dire *vt* to attack, assault.

aggre'gare *vt*: ~ **qn a qc** to admit sb to sth; ~**rsi** *vr* to join; ~**rsi a** to join, become a member of.

aggre'gato, a *ag* associated ♦ *sm* aggregate; ~ **urbano** built-up area.

aggressi'one *sf* aggression; (*atto*) attack; ~ **a mano armata** armed assault.

aggressività *sf* aggressiveness.

aggres'sivo, a *ag* aggressive.

aggres'sore *sm* aggressor, attacker.

aggrot'tare *vt*: ~ **le sopracciglia** to frown.

aggrovigli'are [aggroviʎ'ʎare] *vt* to tangle; ~**rsi** *vr* (*fig*) to become complicated.

agguan'tare *vt* to catch, seize.

aggu'ato *sm* trap; (*imboscata*) ambush; **tendere un** ~ **a qn** to set a trap for sb.

agguer'rito, a *ag* (*sostenitore, nemico*) fierce.

agia'tezza [adʒa'tettsa] *sf* prosperity.

agi'ato, a [a'dʒato] *ag* (*vita*) easy; (*persona*) well-off, well-to-do.

'agile ['adʒile] *ag* agile, nimble.

agilità [adʒili'ta] *sf* agility, nimbleness.

'agio ['adʒo] *sm* ease, comfort; ~**i** *smpl* comforts; **mettersi a proprio** ~ to make o.s. at home *o* comfortable; **dare** ~ **a qn di fare qc** to give sb the chance of doing sth.

a'gire [a'dʒire] *vi* to act; (*esercitare un'azione*) to take effect; (*TECN*) to work, function; ~ **contro qn** (*DIR*) to take action against sb.

agi'tare [adʒi'tare] *vt* (*bottiglia*) to shake; (*mano, fazzoletto*) to wave; (*fig: turbare*) to disturb; (: *incitare*) to stir (up); ~**rsi** *vr* (*mare*) to be rough; (*malato, dormitore*) to toss and turn; (*bambino*) to fidget; (*emozionarsi*) to get upset; (*POL*) to agitate.

agi'tato, a [adʒi'tato] *ag* rough; restless; fidgety; upset, perturbed.

agita'tore, 'trice [adʒita'tore] *sm/f* (*POL*) agitator.

agitazi'one [adʒitat'tsjone] *sf* agitation; (*POL*) unrest, agitation; **mettere in** ~ **qn** to upset *o* distress sb.

'agli ['aʎʎi] *prep* + *det vedi* **a**.

'aglio ['aʎʎo] *sm* garlic.

a'gnello [aɲ'ɲɛllo] *sm* lamb.

a'gnostico, a, ci, che [aɲ'ɲɔstiko] *ag, sm/f* agnostic.

'ago, *pl* **'aghi** *sm* needle; ~ **da calza** knitting needle.

ago. *abbr* (= *agosto*) Aug.

ago'nia *sf* agony.

ago'nistico, a, ci, che *ag* athletic; (*fig*) competitive.

agoniz'zante [agonid'dzante] *ag* dying.

agoniz'zare [agonid'dzare] *vi* to be dying.

agopun'tura *sf* acupuncture.

agorafo'bia *sf* agoraphobia.

a'gosto *sm* August; *per fraseologia vedi* **luglio**.

a'grario, a *ag* agrarian, agricultural; (*riforma*) land *cpd* ♦ *sm* landowner ♦ *sf* agriculture.

a'gricolo, a *ag* agricultural, farm *cpd*.

agricol'tore *sm* farmer.

agricol'tura *sf* agriculture, farming.

agri'foglio [agri'fɔʎʎo] *sm* holly.

agrimen'sore *sm* land surveyor.

agritu'rismo *sm* farm holidays *pl*.

agritu'ristico, a, ci, che *ag* farm holiday *cpd*.

'agro, a *ag* sour, sharp.

agro'dolce [agro'doltʃe] *ag* bittersweet; (*salsa*) sweet and sour.

agrono'mia *sf* agronomy.

a'gronomo *sm* agronomist.

a'grume *sm* (*spesso al pl: pianta*) citrus; (: *frutto*) citrus fruit.

agru'meto *sm* citrus grove.

aguz'zare [agut'tsare] *vt* to sharpen; ~ **gli orecchi** to prick up one's ears; ~ **l'ingegno** to use one's wits.

aguz'zino, a [agud'dzino] *sm/f* jailer; (*fig*) tyrant.

a'guzzo, a [a'guttso] *ag* sharp.

'ahi *escl* (*dolore*) ouch!

ahimè *escl* alas!

'ai *prep* + *det vedi* **a**.

'Aia *sf*: **L'**~ The Hague.

'aiuola *sf* flowerbed.

AIDDA *sigla f* (= *Associazione Imprenditrici Donne Dirigenti d'Azienda*) *association of women entrepreneurs and managers*.

AIDS ['aids] *abbr m o f* AIDS.

AIE *sigla f* (= *Associazione Italiana degli Editori*) *publishers' association*.

AIEA *sigla f vedi* **Agenzia Internazionale per l'Energia Atomica**.

AIED *sigla f* (= *Associazione Italiana Educazione Demografica*) ≈ FPA (= *Family Planning Association*).

AIG *sigla f* (= *Associazione Italiana Alberghi per la Gioventù*) ≈ YHA (*BRIT*).

ai'ola *sf* = **aiuola**.

AIPI *sigla f* = *Associazione Italiana Protezione Infanzia*.

airbag *sm inv* air bag.

AIRC *abbr f* = *associazione italiana per la ricerca sul cancro*.

ai'rone *sm* heron.

ai'tante *ag* robust.

aiu'ola *sf* flower bed.

aiu'tante *sm/f* assistant ♦ *sm* (*MIL*) adjutant; (*NAUT*) master-at-arms; ~ **di campo** aide-de-camp.

aiu'tare *vt* to help; ~ **qn (a fare)** to help sb (to do).

ai'uto *sm* help, assistance, aid; (*aiutante*) assistant; **venire in** ~ **di qn** to come to sb's aid; ~ **chirurgo** assistant surgeon.

aiz'zare [ait'tsare] *vt* to incite; ~ **i cani contro qn** to set the dogs on sb.

al *prep* + *det vedi* **a**.

a.l. *abbr* = **anno luce**.

'ala, *pl* **'ali** *sf* wing; **fare** ~ to fall back,

make way; ~ **destra/sinistra** (*SPORT*) right/left wing.

ala'bastro *sm* alabaster.

'alacre *ag* quick, brisk.

alacrità *sf* promptness, speed.

alam'bicco, chi *sm* still (*CHIM*).

a'lano *sm* Great Dane.

a'lare *ag* wing *cpd*; ~**i** *smpl* firedogs.

A'laska *sf*: **l'**~ Alaska.

a'lato, a *ag* winged.

'alba *sf* dawn; **all'**~ at dawn.

alba'nese *ag, sm/f, sm* Albanian.

Alba'nia *sf*: **l'**~ Albania.

'albatro *sm* albatross.

albeggi'are [albed'dʒare] *vi, vb impers* to dawn.

albe'rato, a *ag* (*viale, piazza*) lined with trees, tree-lined.

albera'tura *sf* (*NAUT*) masts *pl*.

alber'gare *vt* (*dare albergo*) to accommodate ♦ *vi* (*poetico*) to dwell.

alberga'tore, 'trice *sm/f* hotelier, hotel owner.

alberghi'ero, a [alber'gjero] *ag* hotel *cpd*.

al'bergo, ghi *sm* hotel; ~ **diurno** *public toilets with washing and shaving facilities etc*; ~ **della gioventù** youth hostel.

'albero *sm* tree; (*NAUT*) mast; (*TECN*) shaft; ~ **a camme** camshaft; ~ **genealogico** family tree; ~ **a gomiti** crankshaft; ~ **maestro** mainmast; ~ **di Natale** Christmas tree; ~ **di trasmissione** transmission shaft.

albi'cocca, che *sf* apricot.

albi'cocco, chi *sm* apricot tree.

al'bino, a *ag, sm/f* albino.

'albo *sm* (*registro*) register, roll; (*AMM*) notice board.

'album *sm* album; ~ **da disegno** sketch book.

al'bume *sm* albumen; (*bianco d'uovo*) egg white.

albu'mina *sf* albumin.

'alce ['altʃe] *sm* elk.

al'chimia [al'kimja] *sf* alchemy.

alchi'mista, i [alki'mista] *sm* alchemist.

'alcol *sm inv* = **alcool**.

alcolità [alkolit'ʃi'ta] *sf* alcohol(ic) content.

al'colico, a, ci, che *ag* alcoholic ♦ *sm* alcoholic drink.

alco'lismo *sm* alcoholism.

alco'lista, i, e *sm/f* alcoholic.

alcoliz'zato, a [alkolid'dzato] *sm/f* alcoholic.

'alcool *sm inv* alcohol; ~ **denaturato** methylated spirits *pl* (*BRIT*), wood alcohol (*US*); ~ **etilico** ethyl alcohol; ~ **metilico**

methyl alcohol.

alco'olico *etc vedi* **alcolico** *etc*.

alco'test *sm inv* Breathalyser ® (*BRIT*), Breathalyzer ® (*US*).

al'cova *sf* alcove.

al'cuno, a *det* (*dav sm*: **alcun** + *C, V*, **alcuno** + *s impura, gn, pn, ps, x, z; dav sf*: **alcuna** + *C*, **alcun'** +*V*) (*nessuno*): **non ...** ~ no, not any; ~**i(e)** *det pl, pron pl* some, a few; **non c'è** ~**a fretta** there's no hurry, there isn't any hurry; **senza alcun riguardo** without any consideration.

aldilà *sm inv*: **l'**~ the next life, the after-life.

alea'torio, a *ag* (*incerto*) uncertain.

aleggi'are [aled'dʒare] *vi* (*fig*: *profumo, sospetto*) to be in the air.

Ales'sandria *sf* (*anche*: ~ **d'Egitto**) Alexandria.

a'letta *sf* (*TECN*) fin; tab.

alet'tone *sm* (*AER*) aileron.

Aleu'tine *sfpl*: **le isole** ~ the Aleutian Islands.

alfa'betico, a, ci, che *ag* alphabetical.

alfa'beto *sm* alphabet.

alfanu'merico, a, ci, che *ag* alphanumeric.

alfi'ere *sm* standard-bearer; (*SCACCHI*) bishop.

al'fine *av* finally, in the end.

'alga, ghe *sf* seaweed *no pl*, alga.

'algebra ['aldʒebra] *sf* algebra.

Al'geri [al'dʒeri] *sf* Algiers.

Alge'ria [aldʒe'ria] *sf*: **l'**~ Algeria.

alge'rino, a [aldʒe'rino] *ag, sm/f* Algerian.

algo'ritmo *sm* algorithm.

ALI *sigla f* (= *Associazione Librai Italiani*) *booksellers' association*.

ali'ante *sm* (*AER*) glider.

'alibi *sm inv* alibi.

a'lice [a'litʃe] *sf* anchovy.

alie'nare *vt* (*DIR*) to transfer; (*rendere ostile*) to alienate; ~**rsi qn** to alienate sb.

alie'nato, a *ag* alienated; transferred; (*fuor di senno*) insane ♦ *sm* lunatic, insane person.

alienazi'one [aljenat'tsjone] *sf* alienation; transfer; insanity.

ali'eno, a *ag* (*avverso*): ~ (**da**) opposed (to), averse (to) ♦ *sm/f* alien.

alimen'tare *vt* to feed; (*TECN*) to feed, supply; (*fig*) to sustain ♦ *ag* food *cpd*; ~**i** *smpl* foodstuffs; (*anche*: **negozio di** ~**i**) grocer's shop; **regime** ~ diet.

alimenta'tore *sm* (*ELETTR*) feeder.

alimentazi'one [alimentat'tsjone] *sf* feeding; (*cibi*) diet; ~ **di fogli** (*INFORM*) sheet feed.

ali'mento *sm* food; ~**i** *smpl* food *sg*; (*DIR*) alimony.

a'liquota *sf* share; ~ **d'imposta** tax rate; ~ **minima** (*FISCO*) basic rate.

alis'cafo *sm* hydrofoil.

'alito *sm* breath.

all. *abbr* (= *allegato*) enc., encl.

'alla *prep* + *det vedi* **a**.

allaccia'mento [allattʃa'mento] *sm* (*TECN*) connection.

allacci'are [allat'tʃare] *vt* (*scarpe*) to tie, lace (up); (*cintura*) to do up, fasten; (*due località*) to link; (*luce, gas*) to connect; (*amicizia*) to form; ~**rsi** *vr* (*vestito*) to fasten; ~ *o* ~**rsi la cintura** to fasten one's belt.

allaccia'tura [allattʃa'tura] *sf* fastening.

allaga'mento *sm* flooding *no pl*; flood.

alla'gare *vt*, ~**rsi** *vr* to flood.

allampa'nato, a *ag* lanky.

allar'gare *vt* to widen; (*vestito*) to let out; (*aprire*) to open; (*fig*: *dilatare*) to extend; ~**rsi** *vr* (*gen*) to widen; (*scarpe, pantaloni*) to stretch; (*fig*: *problema, fenomeno*) to spread.

allar'mare *vt* to alarm; ~**rsi** *vr* to become alarmed.

al'larme *sm* alarm; **mettere qn in** ~ to alarm sb; ~ **aereo** air-raid warning.

allar'mismo *sm* scaremongering.

allar'mista, i, e *sm/f* scaremonger, alarmist.

allat'tare *vt* (*sog*: *donna*) to (breast-)feed; (: *animale*) to suckle; ~ **artificialmente** to bottle-feed.

'alle *prep* + *det vedi* **a**.

alle'anza [alle'antsa] *sf* alliance; **A**~ **Democratica** (*POL*) *moderate centre-left party*; **A**~ **Nazionale** (*POL*) *party on the far right*.

alle'arsi *vr* to form an alliance.

alle'ato, a *ag* allied ♦ *sm/f* ally.

alleg. *abbr* = **all**.

alle'gare *vt* (*accludere*) to enclose; (*DIR*: *citare*) to cite, adduce; (*denti*) to set on edge.

alle'gato, a *ag* enclosed ♦ *sm* enclosure; **in** ~ enclosed; **in** ~ **Vi inviamo ...** please find enclosed ....

allegge'rire [alleddʒe'rire] *vt* to lighten, make lighter; (*fig*: *sofferenza*) to alleviate, lessen; (: *lavoro, tasse*) to reduce.

allego'ria *sf* allegory.

alle'gorico, a, ci, che *ag* allegorical.

alle'gria *sf* gaiety, cheerfulness.

al'legro, a *ag* cheerful, merry; (*un po' brillo*) merry, tipsy; (*vivace*: *colore*) bright ♦ *sm* (*MUS*) allegro.

allena'mento *sm* training.

alle'nare *vt*, ~**rsi** *vr* to train.

allena'tore *sm* (*SPORT*) trainer, coach.

allen'tare *vt* to slacken; (*disciplina*) to relax; ~**rsi** *vr* to become slack; (*ingranaggio*) to work loose.

aller'gia, **'gie** [aller'dʒia] *sf* allergy.

al'lergico, **a**, **ci**, **che** [al'lɛrdʒiko] *ag* allergic.

allesti'mento *sm* preparation, setting up; **in** ~ in preparation.

alles'tire *vt* (*cena*) to prepare; (*esercito, nave*) to equip, fit out; (*spettacolo*) to stage.

allet'tante *ag* attractive, alluring.

allet'tare *vt* to lure, entice.

alleva'mento *sm* breeding, rearing; (*luogo*) stock farm; **pollo d'**~ battery hen.

alle'vare *vt* (*animale*) to breed, rear; (*bambino*) to bring up.

alleva'tore *sm* breeder.

allevi'are *vt* to alleviate.

alli'bire *vi* to turn pale; (*essere turbato*) to be disconcerted.

alli'bito, **a** *ag* pale; disconcerted.

allibra'tore *sm* bookmaker.

allie'tare *vt* to cheer up, gladden.

alli'evo *sm* pupil; (*apprendista*) apprentice; ~ **ufficiale** cadet.

alliga'tore *sm* alligator.

allinea'mento *sm* alignment.

alline'are *vt* (*persone, cose*) to line up; (*TIP*) to align; (*fig: economia, salari*) to adjust, align; ~**rsi** *vr* to line up; (*fig: a idee*): ~**rsi a** to come into line with.

alline'ato, **a** *ag* aligned, in line; **paesi non** ~**i** (*POL*) non-aligned countries.

'allo *prep* + *det vedi* **a**.

allo'care *vt* to allocate.

al'locco, **a**, **chi**, **che** *sm* tawny owl ♦ *sm/f* oaf.

allocuzi'one [allokut'tsjone] *sf* address, solemn speech.

al'lodola *sf* (sky)lark.

alloggi'are [allod'dʒare] *vt* to accommodate ♦ *vi* to live.

al'loggio [al'lɔddʒo] *sm* lodging, accommodation (*BRIT*), accommodations (*US*); (*appartamento*) flat (*BRIT*), apartment (*US*).

allontana'mento *sm* removal; dismissal; estrangement.

allonta'nare *vt* to send away, send off; (*impiegato*) to dismiss; (*pericolo*) to avert, remove; (*estraniare*) to alienate; ~**rsi** *vr*: ~**rsi (da)** to go away (from); (*estraniarsi*) to become estranged (from).

al'lora *av* (*in quel momento*) then ♦ *cong* (*in questo caso*) well then; (*dunque*) well then, so; **la gente d'**~ people then *o* in those days; **da** ~ **in poi** from then on; **e** ~**?** (*che fare?*) what now?; (*e con ciò?*) so what?

allor'ché [allor'ke] *cong* (*formale*) when, as soon as.

al'loro *sm* laurel; **riposare** *o* **dormire sugli** ~**i** to rest on one's laurels.

'alluce ['allutʃe] *sm* big toe.

alluci'nante [allutʃi'nante] *ag* (*scena, spettacolo*) awful, terrifying; (*fam: incredibile*) amazing.

alluci'nato, **a** [allutʃi'nato] *ag* terrified; (*fuori di sé*) bewildered, confused.

allucinazi'one [allutʃinat'tsjone] *sf* hallucination.

al'ludere *vi*: ~ **a** to allude to, hint at.

allu'minio *sm* aluminium (*BRIT*), aluminum (*US*).

allu'naggio [allu'naddʒo] *sm* moon landing.

allu'nare *vi* to land on the moon.

allun'gare *vt* to lengthen; (*distendere*) to prolong, extend; (*diluire*) to water down; ~**rsi** *vr* to lengthen; (*ragazzo*) to stretch, grow taller; (*sdraiarsi*) to lie down, stretch out; ~ **le mani** (*rubare*) to pick pockets; **gli allungò uno schiaffo** he took a swipe at him.

al'lusi *etc vb vedi* **alludere**.

allusi'one *sf* hint, allusion.

al'luso, **a** *pp di* **alludere**.

alluvi'one *sf* flood.

alma'nacco, **chi** *sm* almanac.

al'meno *av* at least ♦ *cong*: (**se**) ~ **if** only; (**se**) ~ **piovesse!** if only it would rain!

a'logeno, **a** [a'lɔdʒeno] *ag*: **lampada** ~**a** halogen lamp.

a'lone *sm* halo.

al'pestre *ag* (*delle alpi*) alpine; (*montuoso*) mountainous.

'Alpi *sfpl*: **le** ~ the Alps.

alpi'nismo *sm* mountaineering, climbing.

alpi'nista, **i**, **e** *sm/f* mountaineer, climber.

al'pino, **a** *ag* Alpine; mountain *cpd*; ~**i** *smpl* (*MIL*) Italian Alpine troops.

al'quanto *av* rather, a little; ~, **a** *det* **a** certain amount of, some ♦ *pron* a certain amount, some; ~**i(e)** *det pl*, *pron pl* several, quite a few.

Al'sazia [al'sattsja] *sf* Alsace.

alt *escl* halt!, stop! ♦ *sm*: **dare l'**~ to call a halt.

alta'lena *sf* (*a funi*) swing; (*in bilico, anche fig*) seesaw.

alta'mente *av* extremely, highly.

al'tare *sm* altar.

alte'rare *vt* to alter, change; (*cibo*) to adulterate; (*registro*) to falsify; (*persona*) to irritate; ~**rsi** *vr* to alter; (*cibo*) to go bad; (*persona*) to lose one's temper.

alterazi'one [alterat'tsjone] *sf* alteration, change; adulteration; falsification; annoyance.

al'terco, chi *sm* altercation, wrangle.

alter'nanza [alter'nantsa] *sf* alternation; (*AGR*) rotation.

alter'nare *vt*, ~**rsi** *vr* to alternate.

alterna'tivo, a *ag* alternative ♦ *sf* alternative; **non abbiamo** ~**e** we have no alternative.

alter'nato, a *ag* alternate; (*ELETTR*) alternating.

alterna'tore *sm* alternator.

al'terno, a *ag* alternate; **a giorni** ~**i** on alternate days, every other day; **circolazione a targhe** ~**e** (*AUT*) *system of restricting vehicle use to odd/even registrations on alternate days.*

al'tero, a *ag* proud.

al'tezza [al'tettsa] *sf* (*di edificio, persona*) height; (*di tessuto*) width, breadth; (*di acqua, pozzo*) depth; (*di suono*) pitch; (*GEO*) latitude; (*titolo*) highness; (*fig: nobiltà*) greatness; **essere all'**~ **di** to be on a level with; (*fig*) to be up to *o* equal to; **all'**~ **della farmacia** near the chemist's.

altez'zoso, a [altet'tsoso] *ag* haughty.

al'ticcio, a, ci, ce [al'tittʃo] *ag* tipsy.

altipi'ano *sm* = altopiano.

altiso'nante *ag* (*fig*) high-sounding, pompous.

alti'tudine *sf* altitude.

'alto, a *ag* high; (*persona*) tall; (*tessuto*) wide, broad; (*sonno, acque*) deep; (*suono*) high(-pitched); (*GEO*) upper; (: *settentrionale*) northern ♦ *sm* top (part) ♦ *av* high; (*parlare*) aloud, loudly; **il palazzo è** ~ **20 metri** the building is 20 metres high; **il tessuto è** ~ **70 cm** the material is 70 cm wide; **ad** ~**a voce** aloud; **a notte** ~**a** in the dead of night; **in** ~ up, upwards; at the top; **mani in** ~! hands up!; **dall'**~ **in** *o* **al basso** up and down; **degli** ~**i e bassi** (*fig*) ups and downs; **andare a testa** ~**a** (*fig*) to carry one's head high; **essere in** ~ **mare** (*fig*) to be far from a solution; ~**a fedeltà** high fidelity, hi-fi; ~**a moda** haute couture; **l'A**~ **Medioevo** the Early Middle Ages; **l'**~ **Po** the upper reaches of the Po.

altoate'sino, a *ag* of (*o* from) the Alto Adige.

alto'forno *sm* blast furnace.

altolo'cato, a *ag* of high rank, highly placed.

altopar'lante *sm* loudspeaker.

altopi'ano, *pl* **alti'piani** *sm* upland plain, plateau.

'Alto 'Volta *sm*: **l'**~ Upper Volta.

altret'tanto, a *ag, pron* as much; (*pl*) as many ♦ *av* equally; **tanti auguri!** — **grazie,** ~ all the best! — thank you, the same to you.

'altri *pron inv* (*qualcuno*) somebody; (: *in espressioni negative*) anybody; (*un'altra persona*) another (person).

altri'menti *av* otherwise.

══════════════ *PAROLA CHIAVE*

'altro, a *det* **1** (*diverso*) other, different; **questa è un'**~**a cosa** that's another *o* a different thing; **passami l'**~**a penna** give me the other pen

2 (*supplementare*) other; **prendi un** ~ **cioccolatino** have another chocolate; **hai avuto** ~**e notizie?** have you had any more *o* any other news?; **hai** ~ **pane?** have you got any more bread?

3 (*nel tempo*): **l'**~ **giorno** the other day; **l'altr'anno** last year; **l'**~ **ieri** the day before yesterday; **domani l'**~ the day after tomorrow; **quest'**~ **mese** next month

4: **d'**~**a parte** on the other hand

♦ *pron* **1** (*persona, cosa diversa o supplementare*): **un** ~, **un'**~**a** another (one); **lo farà un** ~ someone else will do it; ~**i, e** others; **gli** ~**i** (*la gente*) others, other people; **l'uno e l'**~ both (of them); **aiutarsi l'un l'**~ to help one another; **prendine un** ~ have another (one); **da un giorno all'**~ from day to day; (*nel giro di 24 ore*) from one day to the next; (*da un momento all'altro*) any day now

2 (*sostantivato*: *solo maschile*) something else; (: *in espressioni interrogative*) anything else; **non ho** ~ **da dire** I have nothing else *o* I don't have anything else to say; **desidera** ~? do you want anything else?; **più che** ~ above all; **se non** ~ if nothing else, at least; **tra l'**~ among other things; **ci mancherebbe** ~! that's all we need!; **non faccio** ~ **che lavorare** I do nothing but work; **contento?** — ~ **che!** are you pleased? — I certainly am!; *vedi anche* **senza; noialtri; voialtri; tutto.**

altroché [altro'ke] *escl* certainly!, and how!

al'tronde *av*: **d'**~ on the other hand.

al'trove *av* elsewhere, somewhere else.

al'trui *ag inv* other people's ♦ *sm*: **l'**~ other people's belongings *pl.*

altru'ismo *sm* altruism.

altru'ista, i, e *ag* altruistic ♦ *sm/f* altruist.

al'tura *sf* (*rialto*) height, high ground; (*alto mare*) open sea; **pesca d'**~ deep-sea fishing.

a'lunno, a *smlf* pupil.

alve'are *sm* hive.

'alveo *sm* riverbed.

alzabandi'era [altsaban'djera] *sm inv* (*MIL*): **l'**~ the raising of the flag.

al'zare [al'tsare] *vt* to raise, lift; (*issare*) to hoist; (*costruire*) to build, erect; ~**rsi** *vr* to rise; (*dal letto*) to get up; (*crescere*) to grow tall (*o taller*); ~ **le spalle** to shrug one's shoulders; ~ **le carte** to cut the cards; ~ **il gomito** to drink too much; ~ **le mani su qn** to raise one's hand to sb; ~ **i tacchi** to take to one's heels; ~**rsi in piedi** to stand up, get to one's feet; ~**rsi col piede sbagliato** to get out of bed on the wrong side.

al'zata [al'tsata] *sf* lifting, raising; **un'**~ **di spalle** a shrug.

A.M. *abbr* = **aeronautica militare**.

a'mabile *ag* lovable; (*vino*) sweet.

'AMAC *sigla f* = Aeronautica Militare-Aviazione Civile.

a'maca, che *sf* hammock.

amalga'mare *vt*, ~**rsi** *vr* to amalgamate.

a'mante *ag*: ~ **di** (*musica etc*) fond of ♦ *smlf* lover/mistress.

amara'mente *av* bitterly.

ama'ranto *sm* (*BOT*) love-lies-bleeding ♦ *ag inv*: **color** ~ reddish purple.

a'mare *vt* to love; (*amico, musica, sport*) to like.

amareggi'are [amared'dʒare] *vt* to sadden, upset; ~**rsi** *vr* to get upset; ~**rsi la vita** to make one's life a misery.

amareggi'ato, a [amared'dʒato] *ag* upset, saddened.

ama'rena *sf* sour black cherry.

ama'retto *sm* (*dolce*) macaroon; (*liquore*) bitter liqueur made with almonds.

ama'rezza [ama'rettsa] *sf* bitterness.

a'maro, a *ag* bitter ♦ *sm* bitterness; (*liquore*) bitters *pl*.

ama'rognolo, a [ama'roɲɲolo] *ag* slightly bitter.

a'mato, a *ag* beloved, loved, dear ♦ *smlf* loved one.

ama'tore, 'trice *smlf* (*amante*) lover; (*intenditore: di vini etc*) connoisseur; (*dilettante*) amateur.

a'mazzone [a'maddzone] *sf* (*MITOLOGIA*) Amazon; (*cavallerizza*) horsewoman; (*abito*) riding habit; **cavalcare all'**~ to ride sidesaddle; **il Rio delle A**~**i** the (river) Amazon.

Amaz'zonia [amad'dzonja] *sf* Amazonia.

amaz'zonico, a, ci, che [amad'dzɔniko] *ag* Amazonian; Amazon *cpd*.

ambasce'ria [ambaʃʃe'ria] *sf* embassy.

ambasci'ata [ambaʃ'ʃata] *sf* embassy; (*messaggio*) message.

ambascia'tore, 'trice [ambaʃʃa'tore] *smlf* ambassador/ambassadress.

ambe'due *ag inv*: ~ **i ragazzi** both boys ♦ *pron inv* both.

ambi'destro, a *ag* ambidextrous.

ambien'tale *ag* (*temperatura*) ambient *cpd*; (*problemi, tutela*) environmental.

ambienta'lismo *sm* environmentalism.

ambienta'lista, i, e *ag* environmental ♦ *smlf* environmentalist.

ambien'tare *vt* to acclimatize; (*romanzo, film*) to set; ~**rsi** *vr* to get used to one's surroundings.

ambientazi'one [ambjentat'tsjone] *sf* setting.

ambi'ente *sm* environment; (*fig: insieme di persone*) milieu (*mezza*) room.

ambigu'ità *sf inv* ambiguity.

am'biguo, a *ag* ambiguous; (*persona*) shady.

am'bire *vt* (*anche: vi:* ~ **a**) to aspire to; **un premio molto ambito** a much sought-after prize.

'ambito *sm* sphere, field.

ambiva'lente *ag* ambivalent; **questo apparecchio e** ~ this is a dual-purpose device.

ambizi'one [ambit'tsjone] *sf* ambition.

ambizi'oso, a [ambit'tsjoso] *ag* ambitious.

'ambo *ag inv* both.

'ambra *sf* amber; ~ **grigia** ambergris.

ambu'lante *ag* travelling, itinerant.

ambu'lanza [ambu'lantsa] *sf* ambulance.

ambulatori'ale *ag* (*MED*) outpatients *cpd*; **operazione** ~ operation as an outpatient; **visita** ~ visit to the doctor's surgery (*BRIT*) *o* office (*US*).

ambula'torio *sm* (*studio medico*) surgery (*BRIT*), doctor's office (*US*).

'AMDI *sigla f* = Associazione Medici Dentisti Italiani.

'AME *sigla m* = Accordo Monetario Europeo.

a'meba *sf* amoeba (*BRIT*), ameba (*US*).

amenità *sf inv* pleasantness *no pl*; (*facezia*) pleasantry.

a'meno, a *ag* pleasant; (*strano*) funny, strange; (*spiritoso*) amusing.

A'merica *sf*: **l'**~ America; **l'**~ **latina** Latin America; **l'**~ **del sud** South America.

america'nata *sf* (*peg*): **le Olimpiadi sono state una vera** ~ the Olympics were a typically vulgar American extravaganza.

america'nismo *sm* Americanism;

(*ammirazione*) love of America.
ameri'cano, a *ag, sm/f* American.
ame'tista *sf* amethyst.
ami'anto *sm* asbestos.
a'mica *sf vedi* **amico**.
ami'chevole [ami'kevole] *ag* friendly.
ami'cizia [ami'tʃittsja] *sf* friendship; ~**e** *sfpl* (*amici*) friends; **fare** ~ **con qn** to make friends with sb.
a'mico, a, ci, che *sm/f* friend; (*amante*) boyfriend/girlfriend; ~ **del cuore** o **intimo** bosom friend; ~ **d'infanzia** childhood friend.
'amido *sm* starch.
ammac'care *vt* (*pentola*) to dent; (*persona*) to bruise; ~**rsi** *vr* to bruise.
ammacca'tura *sf* dent; bruise.
ammaes'trare *vt* (*animale*) to train; (*persona*) to teach.
ammai'nare *vt* to lower, haul down.
amma'larsi *vr* to fall ill.
amma'lato, a *ag* ill, sick ♦ *sm/f* sick person; (*paziente*) patient.
ammali'are *vt* (*fig*) to enchant, charm.
ammalia'tore, 'trice *sm/f* enchanter/enchantress.
am'manco, chi *sm* (*ECON*) deficit.
ammanet'tare *vt* to handcuff.
ammani'cato, a, ammanigli'ato, a [ammaniʎ'ʎato] *ag* (*fig*) with friends in high places.
amman'sire *vt* (*animale*) to tame; (*fig*: *persona*) to calm down, placate.
amman'tarsi *vr*: ~ **di** (*persona*) to wrap o.s. in; (*fig*: *prato etc*) to be covered in.
amma'raggio [amma'raddʒo] *sm* (sea) landing; splashdown.
amma'rare *vi* (*AER*) to make a sea landing; (*astronave*) to splash down.
ammas'sare *vt* (*ammucchiare*) to amass; (*raccogliere*) to gather together; ~**rsi** *vr* to pile up; to gather.
am'masso *sm* mass; (*mucchio*) pile, heap; (*ECON*) stockpile.
ammat'tire *vi* to go mad.
ammaz'zare [ammat'tsare] *vt* to kill; ~**rsi** *vr* (*uccidersi*) to kill o.s.; (*rimanere ucciso*) to be killed; ~**rsi di lavoro** to work o.s. to death.
am'menda *sf* amends *pl*; (*DIR, SPORT*) fine; **fare** ~ **di qc** to make amends for sth.
am'messo, a *pp di* **ammettere** ♦ *cong*: ~ **che** supposing that.
am'mettere *vt* to admit; (*riconoscere: fatto*) to acknowledge, admit; (*permettere*) to allow, accept; (*supporre*) to suppose; **ammettiamo che ...** let us suppose that ....

ammez'zato [ammed'dzato] *sm* (*anche*: **piano** ~) entresol, mezzanine.
ammic'care *vi*: ~ (**a**) to wink (at).
amminis'trare *vt* to run, manage; (*REL, DIR*) to administer.
amministra'tivo, a *ag* administrative.
amministra'tore *sm* administrator; (*COMM*) director; ~ **aggiunto** associate director; ~ **delegato** managing director; ~ **fiduciario** trustee; ~ **unico** sole director.
amministrazi'one [amministrat'tsjone] *sf* management; administration; **consiglio d'**~ board of directors; **l'**~ **comunale** local government; ~ **fiduciaria** trust.
ammi'raglia [ammi'raʎʎa] *sf* flagship.
ammiragli'ato [ammiraʎ'ʎato] *sm* admiralty.
ammi'raglio [ammi'raʎʎo] *sm* admiral.
ammi'rare *vt* to admire.
ammira'tore, 'trice *sm/f* admirer.
ammirazi'one [ammirat'tsjone] *sf* admiration.
am'misi *etc vb vedi* **ammettere**.
ammis'sibile *ag* admissible, acceptable.
ammissi'one *sf* admission; (*approvazione*) acknowledgement.
Amm.ne *abbr* = **amministrazione**.
ammobili'are *vt* to furnish.
ammobili'ato, a *ag* (*camera, appartamento*) furnished.
ammoder'nare *vt* to modernize.
am'modo, a 'modo *av* properly ♦ *ag inv* respectable, nice.
ammogli'are [ammoʎ'ʎare] *vt* to find a wife for; ~**rsi** *vr* to marry, take a wife.
am'mollo *sm*: **lasciare in** ~ to leave to soak.
ammo'niaca *sf* ammonia.
ammoni'mento *sm* warning; admonishment.
ammo'nire *vt* (*avvertire*) to warn; (*rimproverare*) to admonish; (*DIR*) to caution.
ammonizi'one [ammonit'tsjone] *sf* (*monito*: *anche SPORT*) warning; (*rimprovero*) reprimand; (*DIR*) caution.
ammon'tare *vi*: ~ **a** to amount to ♦ *sm* (total) amount.
ammonticchi'are [ammontik'kjare] *vt* to pile up, heap up.
ammor'bare *vt* (*diffondere malattia*) to infect; (*sog: odore*) to taint, foul.
ammorbi'dente *sm* fabric softener.
ammorbi'dire *vt* to soften.
ammorta'mento *sm* redemption; amortization; ~ **fiscale** capital allowance.
ammor'tare *vt* (*FINANZA: debito*) to pay off,

redeem; (: *spese d'impianto*) to write off.

ammortiz'zare [ammortid'dzare] *vt* (*FINANZA*) to pay off, redeem; (: *spese d'impianto*) to write off; (*AUT, TECN*) to absorb, deaden.

ammortizza'tore [ammortiddza'tore] *sm* (*AUT, TECN*) shock absorber.

Amm.re *abbr* = **amministratore**.

ammucchi'are [ammuk'kjare] *vt*, ~**rsi** *vr* to pile up, accumulate.

ammuf'fire *vi* to go mouldy (*BRIT*) *o* moldy (*US*).

ammutina'mento *sm* mutiny.

ammuti'narsi *vr* to mutiny.

ammuti'nato, a *ag* mutinous ♦ *sm* mutineer.

ammuto'lire *vi* to be struck dumb.

amne'sia *sf* amnesia.

amnis'tia *sf* amnesty.

'amo *sm* (*PESCA*) hook; (*fig*) bait.

amo'rale *ag* amoral.

a'more *sm* love; ~**i** *smpl* love affairs; **il tuo bambino è un** ~ your baby's a darling; **fare l'**~ *o* **all'**~ to make love; **andare d'**~ **e d'accordo con qn** to get on like a house on fire with sb; **per** ~ **o per forza** by hook or by crook; **amor proprio** self-esteem, pride.

amoreggi'are [amored'dʒare] *vi* to flirt.

amo'revole *ag* loving, affectionate.

a'morfo, a *ag* amorphous; (*fig: persona*) lifeless.

amo'rino *sm* cupid.

amo'roso, a *ag* (*affettuoso*) loving, affectionate; (*d'amore: sguardo*) amorous; (: *poesia, relazione*) love *cpd*.

am'pere [ã'pɛr] *sm inv* amp(ère).

ampi'ezza [am'pjettsa] *sf* width, breadth; spaciousness; (*fig: importanza*) scale, size; ~ **di vedute** broad-mindedness.

'ampio, a *ag* wide, broad; (*spazioso*) spacious; (*abbondante: vestito*) loose; (: *gonna*) full; (: *spiegazione*) ample, full.

am'plesso *sm* (*sessuale*) intercourse.

amplia'mento *sm* (*di strada*) widening; (*di aeroporto*) expansion; (*fig*) broadening.

ampli'are *vt* (*allargare*) to widen; (*fig: discorso*) to enlarge on; ~**rsi** *vr* to grow, increase; ~ **la propria cultura** to broaden one's mind.

amplifi'care *vt* to amplify; (*magnificare*) to extol.

amplifica'tore *sm* (*TECN, MUS*) amplifier.

amplificazi'one [amplifikat'tsjone] *sf* amplification.

am'polla *sf* (*vasetto*) cruet.

ampol'loso, a *ag* bombastic, pompous.

ampu'tare *vt* (*MED*) to amputate.

amputazi'one [amputat'tsjone] *sf* amputation.

'Amsterdam *sf* Amsterdam.

amu'leto *sm* lucky charm.

AN *sigla* = *Ancona*.

A.N. *sigla f* (*POL*) = **Alleanza Nazionale**.

'ANA *sigla f* (*MIL*) = *Associazione Nazionale Alpini*.

ANAAO *sigla f* (= *Associazione Nazionale Aiuti e Assistenti Ospedalieri*) *trade union for hospital workers*.

anabbagli'ante [anabbaʎ'ʎante] *ag* (*AUT*) dipped (*BRIT*), dimmed (*US*); ~**i** *smpl* dipped *o* dimmed headlights.

anacro'nismo *sm* anachronism.

a'nagrafe *sf* (*registro*) register of births, marriages and deaths; (*ufficio*) registry office (*BRIT*), office of vital statistics (*US*).

ana'grafico, a, ci, che *ag* (*AMM*): **dati** ~**ci** personal data; **comune di residenza** ~**a** district where resident.

ana'gramma, i *sm* anagram.

anal'colico, a, ci, che *ag* non-alcoholic ♦ *sm* soft drink; **bevanda** ~**a** soft drink.

a'nale *ag* anal.

analfa'beta, i, e *ag, smlf* illiterate.

analfabe'tismo *sm* illiteracy.

anal'gesico, a, ci, che [anal'dʒɛziko] *ag, sm* analgesic.

a'nalisi *sf inv* analysis; (*MED: esame*) test; **in ultima** ~ in conclusion, in the final analysis; ~ **grammaticale** parsing; ~ **del sangue** blood test; ~ **dei sistemi/costi** systems/cost analysis.

ana'lista, i, e *smlf* analyst; (*PSIC*) (psycho)analyst; ~ **finanziario** financial analyst; ~ **di sistemi** systems analyst.

ana'litico, a, ci, che *ag* analytic(al).

analiz'zare [analid'dzare] *vt* to analyse (*BRIT*), analyze (*US*); (*MED*) to test.

analo'gia, 'gie [analo'dʒia] *sf* analogy.

ana'logico, a, ci, che [ana'lɔdʒiko] *ag* analogical; (*calcolatore, orologio*) analog(ue).

a'nalogo, a, ghi, ghe *ag* analogous.

'ananas *sm inv* pineapple.

anar'chia [anar'kia] *sf* anarchy.

a'narchico, a, ci, che [a'narkiko] *ag* anarchic(al) ♦ *smlf* anarchist.

'A.N.A.S. *sigla f* (= *Azienda Nazionale Autonoma delle Strade*) *national roads department*.

ana'tema, i *sm* anathema.

anato'mia *sf* anatomy.

ana'tomico, a, ci, che *ag* anatomical; (*sedile*) contoured.

'anatra *sf* duck; ~ **selvatica** mallard.

ana'troccolo *sm* duckling.

'**ANCA** sigla f = Associazione Nazionale Cooperative Agricole.

'**anca, che** sf (ANAT) hip; (ZOOL) haunch.

'**ANCAB** sigla f (= Associazione Nazionale delle Cooperative di Abitazione) national association of housing cooperatives.

ANCC sigla f = Associazione Nazionale Carabinieri.

'**ANCE** ['antʃe] sigla f (= Associazione Nazionale Costruttori Edili) national association of builders.

'**anche** ['anke] cong also; (perfino) even; **vengo anch'io!** I'm coming too!; ~ **se** even if; ~ **volendo, non finiremmo in tempo** even if we wanted to, we wouldn't finish in time.

ancheggi'are [anked'dʒare] vi to wiggle (one's hips).

anchilo'sato, a [ankilo'zato] ag stiff.

'**ANCI** ['antʃi] sigla f (= Associazione Nazionale dei Comuni Italiani) national confederation of local authorities.

ancone'tano, a ag of (o from) Ancona.

an'cora av still; (di nuovo) again; (di più) some more; (persino): ~ **più forte** even stronger; **non** ~ not yet; ~ **una volta** once more, once again; ~ **un po'** a little more; (di tempo) a little longer.

'**ancora** sf anchor; **gettare/levare l'**~ to cast/weigh anchor; ~ **di salvezza** (fig) last hope.

anco'raggio [anko'raddʒo] sm anchorage.

anco'rare vt, ~**rsi** vr to anchor.

ANCR sigla f (= Associazione Nazionale Combattenti e Reduci) servicemen's and ex-servicemen's association.

Andalu'sia sf: l'~ Andalusia.

anda'luso, a ag,'sm/f Andalusian.

anda'mento sm (di strada, malattia) course; (del mercato) state.

an'dante ag (corrente) current; (di poco pregio) cheap, second-rate ♦ sm (MUS) andante.

an'dare sm: **a lungo** ~ in the long run; **con l'andar del tempo** with the passing of time; **racconta storie a tutto** ~ she's forever talking rubbish ♦ vi (gen) to go; (essere adatto): ~ **a** to suit; (piacere): **il suo comportamento non mi va** I don't like the way he behaves; **ti va di** ~ **al cinema?** do you feel like going to the cinema?; ~ **a cavallo** to ride; ~ **in macchina/aereo** to go by car/plane; ~ **a fare qc** to go and do sth; ~ **a pescare/sciare** to go fishing/skiing; **andarsene** to go away; **vado e vengo** I'll be back in a minute; ~ **per i 50** (età) to be getting on for 50; ~ **a male** to go bad; ~ **fiero di qc/qn** to be proud of sth/sb; ~

perduto to be lost; **come va?** (lavoro, progetto) how are things?; **come va?** — **bene, grazie!** how are you? — **fine, thanks!**; **va fatto entro oggi** it's got to be done today; **ne va della nostra vita** our lives are at stake; **se non vado errato** if I'm not mistaken; **le mele vanno molto** apples are selling well; **va da sé** (è naturale) it goes without saying; **per questa volta vada** let's say no more about it this time.

an'data sf (viaggio) outward journey; **biglietto di sola** ~ single (BRIT) o one-way ticket; **biglietto di** ~ **e ritorno** return (BRIT) o round-trip (US) ticket.

anda'tura sf (modo di andare) walk, gait; (SPORT) pace; (NAUT) tack.

an'dazzo [an'dattso] sm (peg): **prendere un brutto** ~ to take a turn for the worse.

'**Ande** sfpl: **le** ~ the Andes.

an'dino, a ag Andean.

andiri'vieni sm inv coming and going.

'**andito** sm corridor, passage.

An'dorra sf Andorra.

andrò etc vb vedi **andare**.

an'drone sm entrance hall.

ANDS sigla f (= Associazione Nazionale Docenti Subalterni) teachers' union.

'**ANDU** sigla f (= Associazione Nazionale Docenti Universitari) association of university teachers.

a'neddoto sm anecdote.

ane'lare vi: ~ **a** (fig) to long for, yearn for.

a'nelito sm (fig): ~ **di** longing o yearning for.

a'nello sm ring; (di catena) link.

ane'mia sf anaemia (BRIT), anemia (US).

a'nemico, a, ci, che ag anaemic (BRIT), anemic (US).

a'nemone sm anemone.

aneste'sia sf anaesthesia (BRIT), anesthesia (US).

aneste'sista, i, e sm/f anaesthetist (BRIT), anesthetist (US).

anes'tetico, a, ci, che ag, sm anaesthetic (BRIT), anesthetic (US).

anestetiz'zare [anestetid'dzare] vt to anaesthetize (BRIT), anesthetize (US).

anfeta'mina sf amphetamine.

anfeta'minico, a, ci, che ag (fig) hyper.

an'fibio, a ag amphibious ♦ sm amphibian; (AUT) amphibious vehicle.

anfite'atro sm amphitheatre (BRIT), amphitheater (US).

anfitri'one sm host.

'**anfora** sf amphora.

an'fratto sm ravine.

an'gelico, a, ci, che [an'dʒɛliko] ag

angelic(al).

'**angelo** ['andʒelo] *sm* angel; ~ **custode** guardian angel; **l'~ del focolare** (*fig*) the perfect housewife.

anghe'ria [ange'ria] *sf* vexation.

an'gina [an'dʒina] *sf* tonsillitis; ~ **pectoris** angina.

angli'cano, a *ag* Anglican.

angli'cismo [angli'tʃizmo] *sm* anglicism.

an'glofilo, a *ag* anglophilic ♦ *sm/f* anglophile.

anglo'sassone *ag* Anglo-Saxon.

An'gola *sf*: **l'~** Angola.

ango'lano, a *ag, sm/f* Angolan.

ango'lare *ag* angular.

angola'tura *sf* angle.

angolazi'one [angolat'tsjone] *sf* (*di angolo*) angulation; (*FOT, CINE, TV, fig*) angle.

'**angolo** *sm* corner; (*MAT*) angle; ~ **cottura** (*di appartamento etc*) cooking area; **fare** ~ **con** (*strada*) to run into; **dietro l'~** (*anche fig*) round the corner.

ango'loso, a *ag* (*oggetto*) angular; (*volto, corpo*) angular, bony.

'**angora** *sf*: **lana d'~** angora.

an'goscia, sce [an'gɔʃʃa] *sf* deep anxiety, anguish *no pl*.

angosci'are [angoʃ'ʃare] *vt* to cause anguish to; ~**rsi** *vr*: ~**rsi (per)** (*preoccuparsi*) to become anxious (about); (*provare angoscia*) to get upset (about *o* over).

angosci'oso, a [angoʃ'ʃoso] *ag* (*d'angoscia*) anguished; (*che dà angoscia*) distressing, painful.

angu'illa *sf* eel.

an'guria *sf* watermelon.

an'gustia *sf* (*ansia*) anguish, distress; (*povertà*) poverty, want.

angusti'are *vt* to distress; ~**rsi** *vr*: ~**rsi (per)** to worry (about).

an'gusto, a *ag* (*stretto*) narrow; (*fig*) mean, petty.

'**anice** ['anitʃe] *sm* (*CUC*) aniseed; (*BOT*) anise; (*liquore*) anisette.

ani'dride *sf* (*CHIM*): ~ **carbonica/solforosa** carbon/sulphur dioxide.

'**anima** *sf* soul; (*abitante*) inhabitant; ~ **gemella** soul mate; **un'~ in pena** (*anche fig*) a tormented soul; **non c'era** ~ **viva** there wasn't a living soul; **volere un bene dell'~ a qn** to be extremely fond of sb; **rompere l'~ a qn** to drive sb mad; **il nonno buon'~** ... Grandfather, God rest his soul ....

ani'male *sm, ag* animal.

anima'lesco, a, schi, sche *ag* (*gesto, atteggiamento*) animal-like.

anima'lista, i, e *ag* animal rights *cpd* ♦ *sm/f* animal rights activist.

ani'mare *vt* to give life to, liven up; (*incoraggiare*) to encourage; ~**rsi** *vr* to become animated, come to life.

ani'mato, a *ag* animate; (*vivace*) lively, animated; (*: strada*) busy.

anima'tore, 'trice *sm/f* guiding spirit, (*CINE*) animator; (*di festa*) life and soul.

animazi'one [animat'tsjone] *sf* liveliness; (*di strada*) bustle; (*CINE*) animation; ~ **teatrale** amateur dramatics.

'**animo** *sm* (*mente*) mind; (*cuore*) heart; (*coraggio*) courage; (*disposizione*) character, disposition; **avere in** ~ **di fare qc** to intend *o* have a mind to do sth; **farsi** ~ to pluck up courage; **fare qc di buon/ mal** ~ to do sth willingly/unwillingly; **perdersi d'**~ to lose heart.

animosità *sf* animosity.

A'NITA *sigla f* = Associazione Nazionale dell'Industria dei Trasporti Automobilistici, Associazione Naturista Italiana.

'**anitra** *sf* = anatra.

'**Ankara** *sf* Ankara.

ANM *sigla f* (= Associazione Nazionale dei Magistrati) national association of magistrates.

ANMI *sigla f* (= Associazione Nazionale Marinai d'Italia) national association of seamen.

ANMIG *sigla f* (= Associazione Nazionale fra Mutilati e Invalidi di Guerra) national association for disabled ex-servicemen.

anna'cquare *vt* to water down, dilute.

annaffi'are *vt* to water.

annaffia'toio *sm* watering can.

an'nali *smpl* annals.

annas'pare *vi* (*nell'acqua*) to flounder; (*fig*: *nel buio, nell'incertezza*) to grope.

an'nata *sf* year; (*importo annuo*) annual amount; **vino di** ~ vintage wine.

annebbi'are *vt* (*fig*) to cloud; ~**rsi** *vr* to become foggy; (*vista*) to become dim.

annega'mento *sm* drowning.

anne'gare *vt, vi* to drown; ~**rsi** *vr* (*accidentalmente*) to drown; (*deliberatamente*) to drown o.s.

anne'rire *vt* to blacken ♦ *vi* to become black.

annessi'one *sf* (*POL*) annexation.

an'nesso, a *pp di* annettere ♦ *ag* attached; (*POL*) annexed; **... e tutti gli** ~**i e connessi** ... and so on and so forth.

an'nettere *vt* (*POL*) to annex; (*accludere*) to attach.

annichi'lire [anniki'lire] *vt* to annihilate.

anni'darsi *vr* to nest.

annienta'mento *sm* annihilation, destruction.

annien'tare *vt* to annihilate, destroy.

anniver'sario *sm* anniversary.

'anno *sm* year; **quanti ~i hai? — ho 40 ~i** how old are you? **— I'm 40** (years old); **gli ~i 20** the 20s; **porta bene gli ~i** she doesn't look her age; **porta male gli ~i** she looks older than she is; **~ commerciale** business year; **~ giudiziario** legal year; **~ luce** light year; **gli ~i di piombo** the Seventies in Italy, characterized by terrorist attacks and killings.

anno'dare *vt* to knot, tie; (*fig: rapporto*) to form.

annoi'are *vt* to bore; (*seccare*) to annoy; **~rsi** *vr* to be bored; to be annoyed.

an'noso, a *ag* (*albero*) old; (*fig: problema etc*) age-old.

anno'tare *vt* (*registrare*) to note, note down (*BRIT*); (*commentare*) to annotate.

annotazi'one [annotat'tsjone] *sf* note; annotation.

annove'rare *vt* to number.

annu'ale *ag* annual.

annual'mente *av* annually, yearly.

annu'ario *sm* yearbook.

annu'ire *vi* to nod; (*acconsentire*) to agree.

annulla'mento *sm* annihilation, destruction; cancellation; annulment; quashing.

annul'lare *vt* to annihilate, destroy; (*contratto, francobollo*) to cancel; (*matrimonio*) to annul; (*sentenza*) to quash; (*risultati*) to declare void.

an'nullo *sm* (*AMM*) cancelling.

annunci'are [annun'tʃare] *vt* to announce; (*dar segni rivelatori*) to herald.

annuncia'tore, 'trice [annuntʃa'tore] *sm/f* (*RADIO, TV*) announcer.

Annunciazi'one [annuntʃat'tsjone] *sf* (*REL*): **l'~** the Annunciation.

an'nuncio [an'nuntʃo] *sm* announcement; (*fig*) sign; **~ pubblicitario** advertisement; **~i economici** classified advertisements, small ads; **piccoli ~i** small ads, classified ads; **~i mortuari** (*colonna*) obituary column.

'annuo, a *ag* annual, yearly.

annu'sare *vt* to sniff, smell; **~ tabacco** to take snuff.

annuvola'mento *sm* clouding (over).

annuvo'lare *vt* to cloud; **~rsi** *vr* to become cloudy, cloud over.

'ano *sm* anus.

'anodo *sm* anode.

anoma'lia *sf* anomaly.

a'nomalo, a *ag* anomalous.

anoni'mato *sm* anonymity; **conservare l'~** to remain anonymous.

a'nonimo, a *ag* anonymous ♦ *sm* (*autore*) anonymous writer (*o* painter *etc*); **un tipo ~** (*peg*) a colourless (*BRIT*) *o* colorless (*US*) character.

anores'sia *sf* anorexia; **~ nervosa** anorexia nervosa.

ano'ressico, a, ci, che *ag* anorexic.

anor'male *ag* abnormal ♦ *sm/f* subnormal person; (*eufemismo*) homosexual.

anormalità *sf inv* abnormality.

'ANSA *sigla f* (= *Agenzia Nazionale Stampa Associata*) national press agency.

'ansa *sf* (*manico*) handle; (*di fiume*) bend, loop.

an'sante *ag* out of breath, panting.

'ANSEA *sigla f* (= *Associazione delle Nazioni del Sud-Est asiatico*) ASEAN.

'ansia *sf* anxiety; **stare in ~ (per qn/qc)** to be anxious (about sb/sth).

ansietà *sf* anxiety.

ansi'mare *vi* to pant.

ansi'oso, a *ag* anxious.

'anta *sf* (*di finestra*) shutter; (*di armadio*) door.

antago'nismo *sm* antagonism.

antago'nista, i, e *sm/f* antagonist.

an'tartico, a, ci, che *ag* Antarctic ♦ *sm*: **l'A~** the Antarctic.

An'tartide *sf*: **l'~** Antarctica.

ante'bellico, a, ci, che *ag* prewar *cpd*.

antece'dente [antetʃe'dɛnte] *ag* preceding, previous.

ante'fatto *sm* previous events *pl*; previous history.

antegu'erra *sm* pre-war period.

ante'nato *sm* ancestor, forefather.

an'tenna *sf* (*RADIO, TV*) aerial; (*ZOOL*) antenna, feeler; **rizzare le ~e** (*fig*) to prick up one's ears; **~ parabolica** (*TV*) satellite dish.

ante'porre *vt*: **~ qc a qc** to place *o* put sth before sth.

ante'posto, a *pp di* **anteporre**.

ante'prima *sf* preview.

anteri'ore *ag* (*ruota, zampa*) front *cpd*; (*fatti*) previous, preceding.

antesi'gnano [antesiɲ'ɲano] *sm* (*STORIA*) standard-bearer; (*fig*) forerunner.

antia'ereo, a *ag* anti-aircraft *cpd*.

antial'lergico, a [antial'lɛrdʒiko] *ag, sm* hypoallergenic.

antia'tomico, a, ci, che *ag* anti-nuclear; **rifugio ~** fallout shelter.

antibi'otico, a, ci, che *ag, sm* antibiotic.

anti'caglia [anti'kaʎʎa] *sf* junk *no pl*.

anti'camera *sf* anteroom; **fare** ~ to be kept waiting; **non mi passerebbe neanche per l'**~ **del cervello** it wouldn't even cross my mind.

anti'carie *ag inv* which fights tooth decay.

antichità [antiki'ta] *sf inv* antiquity; (*oggetto*) antique.

antici'clone [antitʃi'klone] *sm* anticyclone.

antici'pare [antitʃi'pare] *vt* (*consegna, visita*) to bring forward, anticipate; (*somma di denaro*) to pay in advance; (*notizia*) to disclose ♦ *vi* to be ahead of time.

antici'pato, a [antitʃi'pato] *ag* (*prima del previsto*) early; **pagamento** ~ payment in advance.

anticipazi'one [antiʃipat'tsjone] *sf* anticipation; (*di notizia*) advance information; (*somma di denaro*) advance.

an'ticipo [an'titʃipo] *sm* anticipation; (*di denaro*) advance; **in** ~ early, in advance; **con un sensibile** ~ well in advance.

antic'lan *ag inv* (*magistrato, processo*) anti-Mafia.

an'tico, a, chi, che *ag* (*quadro, mobili*) antique; (*dell'antichità*) ancient; **all'**~**a** old-fashioned.

anticoncezio'nale [antikontʃettsjo'nale] *sm* contraceptive.

anticonfor'mista, i, e *ag, sm/f* nonconformist.

anticonge'lante [antikondʒe'lante] *ag, sm* antifreeze.

anticongiuntu'rale [antikondʒuntu'rale] *ag* (*ECON*): **misure** ~**i** measures to remedy the economic situation.

anti'corpo *sm* antibody.

anticostituzio'nale [antikostituttsjo'nale] *ag* unconstitutional.

antidiluvi'ano, a *ag* (*fig: antiquato*) ancient.

anti'doping *sm inv* (*SPORT*) dope test.

an'tidoto *sm* antidote.

anti'droga *ag inv* anti-drugs *cpd*.

antie'stetico, a, ci, che *ag* unsightly.

an'tifona *sf* (*MUS, REL*) antiphon; **capire l'**~ (*fig*) to take the hint.

anti'furto *sm* anti-theft device.

anti'gelo [anti'dʒɛlo] *ag inv* antifreeze *cpd* ♦ *sm* (*per motore*) antifreeze; (*per cristalli*) de-icer.

an'tigene [an'tidʒene] *sm* antigen.

antigi'enico, a, ci, che [anti'dʒɛniko] *ag* unhygienic.

An'tille *sfpl*: **le** ~ the West Indies.

an'tilope *sf* antelope.

anti'mafia *ag inv* anti-mafia *cpd*.

antin'cendio [antin'tʃɛndjo] *ag inv* fire *cpd*; **bombola** ~ fire extinguisher.

anti'nebbia *sm inv* (*anche*: **faro** ~: *AUT*) fog

lamp.

antine'vralgico, a, ci, che [antine'vraldʒiko] *ag* painkilling ♦ *sm* painkiller.

antio'rario *ag*: **in senso** ~ in an anticlockwise (*BRIT*) *o* counterclockwise (*US*) direction, anticlockwise, counterclockwise.

anti'pasto *sm* hors d'œuvre.

antipa'tia *sf* antipathy, dislike.

anti'patico, a, ci, che *ag* unpleasant, disagreeable.

an'tipodi *smpl*: **essere agli** ~ (*fig: di idee opposte*) to be poles apart.

antiquari'ato *sm* antique trade; **un pezzo d'**~ an antique.

anti'quario *sm* antique dealer.

anti'quato, a *ag* antiquated, old-fashioned.

antirici'claggio [antiritʃi'kladdʒo] *ag* (*attività, operazioni*) anti-laundering.

antiri'flesso *ag inv* (*schermo*) non-glare *cpd*.

antirug'gine [anti'ruddʒine] *ag* anti-rust *cpd* ♦ *sm inv* rust-preventer.

antise'mita, i, e *ag* anti-semitic.

antisemi'tismo *sm* anti-semitism.

anti'settico, a, ci, che *ag, sm* antiseptic.

antista'minico, a, ci, che *ag, sm* antihistamine.

anti'stante *ag* opposite.

antiterro'rismo *sm* anti-terrorist measures *pl*.

an'titesi *sf* antithesis.

antolo'gia, 'gie [antolo'dʒia] *sf* anthology.

antono'masia *sf* antonomasia; **per** ~ par excellence.

antra'cite [antra'tʃite] *sf* anthracite.

'antro *sm* cavern.

antro'pofago, gi *sm* cannibal.

antropolo'gia [antropolo'dʒia] *sf* anthropology.

antropo'logico, a, ci, che [antropo'lɔdʒiko] *ag* anthropological.

antro'pologo, a, gi, ghe *sm/f* anthropologist.

anu'lare *ag* ring *cpd* ♦ *sm* ring finger.

An'versa *sf* Antwerp.

'anzi ['antsi] *av* (*invece*) on the contrary; (*o meglio*) or rather, or better still.

anzianità [antsjani'ta] *sf* old age; (*AMM*) seniority.

anzi'ano, a [an'tsjano] *ag* old; (*AMM*) senior ♦ *sm/f* old person; senior member.

anziché [antsi'ke] *cong* rather than.

anzi'tempo [antsi'tɛmpo] *av* (*in anticipo*) early.

anzi'tutto [antsi'tutto] *av* first of all.

AO *sigla* = *Aosta*.

a'orta *sf* aorta.

aos'tano, a *ag* of (*o* from) Aosta.
AP *sigla* = Ascoli Piceno.
a'partheid [a'partheit] *sm* apartheid.
apar'titico, a, ci, che *ag* (*POL*) non-party
cpd.
apa'tia *sf* apathy, indifference.
a'patico, a, ci, che *ag* apathetic,
indifferent.
a.p.c. *abbr* = **a pronta cassa.**
'ape *sf* bee.
aperi'tivo *sm* apéritif.
aperta'mente *av* openly.
a'perto, a *pp di* **aprire** ♦ *ag* open ♦ *sm*: **all'~**
in the open (air); **rimanere a bocca ~a**
(*fig*) to be taken aback.
aper'tura *sf* opening; (*ampiezza*) width,
spread; (*POL*) approach; (*FOT*) aperture; **~**
alare wing span; **~ mentale** open-
mindedness; **~ di credito** (*COMM*)
granting of credit.
API *sigla f* = Associazione Piccole e Medie
Industrie.
'apice ['apit∫e] *sm* apex; (*fig*) height.
apicol'tore *sm* beekeeper.
apicol'tura *sf* beekeeping.
ap'nea *sf*: **immergersi in ~** to dive without
breathing apparatus.
apoca'lisse *sf* apocalypse.
apo'geo [apo'dʒɛo] *sm* (*ASTR*) apogee; (*fig*:
culmine) zenith.
a'polide *ag* stateless.
apo'litico, a, ci, che *ag* (*neutrale*)
nonpolitical; (*indifferente*) apolitical.
apolo'gia, gie [apolo'dʒia] *sf* (*difesa*)
apologia; (*esaltazione*) praise; **~ di reato**
attempt to defend criminal acts.
apoples'sia *sf* (*MED*) apoplexy.
apop'lettico, a, ci, che *ag* apoplectic;
colpo ~ apoplectic fit.
a'postolo *sm* apostle.
apostro'fare *vt* (*parola*) to write with an
apostrophe; (*persona*) to address.
a'postrofo *sm* apostrophe.
app. *abbr* (= appendice) app.
appaga'mento *sm* satisfaction; fulfilment.
appa'gare *vt* to satisfy; (*desiderio*) to fulfil;
~rsi *vr*: **~rsi di** to be satisfied with.
appa'gato, a *ag* satisfied.
appai'are *vt* to couple, pair.
ap'paio *etc vb vedi* **apparire.**
Appa'lachi [appa'laki] *smpl*: **i Monti ~ the**
Appalachian Mountains.
appalottol'are *vt* (*carta, foglio*) to screw
into a ball; **~rsi** *vr* (*gatto*) to roll up into a
ball.
appalta'tore *sm* contractor.
ap'palto *sm* (*COMM*) contract; **dare/**
prendere in ~ un lavoro to let out/

undertake a job on contract.
appan'naggio [appan'naddʒo] *sm*
(*compenso*) annuity; (*fig*) privilege,
prerogative.
appan'nare *vt* (*vetro*) to mist; (*metallo*) to
tarnish; (*vista*) to dim; **~rsi** *vr* to mist
over; to tarnish; to grow dim.
appa'rato *sm* equipment, machinery;
(*ANAT*) apparatus; **~ scenico** (*TEAT*) props
pl.
apparecchi'are [apparek'kjare] *vt* to
prepare; (*tavola*) to set ♦ *vi* to set the
table.
apparecchia'tura [apparekkja'tura] *sf*
equipment; (*macchina*) machine, device.
appa'recchio [appa'rekkjo] *sm* piece of
apparatus, device; (*aeroplano*) aircraft
inv; **~i sanitari** bathroom *o* sanitary
appliances; **~ televisivo/telefonico**
television set/telephone.
appa'rente *ag* apparent.
apparente'mente *av* apparently.
appa'renza [appa'rɛntsa] *sf* appearance; **in**
o **all'~** apparently, to all appearances.
appa'rire *vi* to appear; (*sembrare*) to seem,
appear.
appari'scente [appariʃ'ʃɛnte] *ag* (*colore*)
garish, gaudy; (*bellezza*) striking.
apparizi'one [apparit'tsjone] *sf* apparition.
ap'parso, a *pp di* **apparire.**
apparta'mento *sm* flat (*BRIT*), apartment
(*US*).
appar'tarsi *vr* to withdraw.
appar'tato, a *ag* (*luogo*) secluded.
apparte'nenza [apparte'nɛntsa] *sf*: **~ (a)**
(*gen*) belonging (to); (*a un partito, club*)
membership (of).
apparte'nere *vi*: **~ a** to belong to.
ap'parvi *etc vb vedi* **apparire.**
appassio'nante *ag* thrilling, exciting.
appassio'nare *vt* to thrill; (*commuovere*) to
move; **~rsi** *vr*: **~rsi a qc** to take a great
interest in sth; to be deeply moved by
sth.
appassio'nato, a *ag* passionate;
(*entusiasta*): **~ (di)** keen (on).
appas'sire *vi* to wither.
appel'larsi *vr* (*ricorrere*): **~ a** to appeal to;
(*DIR*): **~ contro** to appeal against.
ap'pello *sm* roll-call; (*implorazione, DIR*)
appeal; (*sessione d'esame*) exam session;
fare ~ a to appeal to; **fare l'~** (*INS*) to call
the register *o* roll; (*MIL*) to call the roll.
ap'pena *av* (*a stento*) hardly, scarcely;
(*solamente, da poco*) just ♦ *cong* as soon as;
(non) ~ furono arrivati ... as soon as they
had arrived ...; **~ ... che** *o* **quando** no
sooner ... than.

ap'pendere vt to hang (up).
appendi'abiti sm inv hook, peg; (mobile) hall stand (BRIT), hall tree (US).
appen'dice [appen'ditʃe] sf appendix; **romanzo d'~** popular serial.
appendi'cite [appendi'tʃite] sf appendicitis.
appen'dino sm (coat) hook.
Appen'nini smpl: **gli ~** the Apennines.
appesan'tire vt to make heavy; **~rsi** vr to grow stout.
ap'peso, a pp di **appendere**.
appe'tito sm appetite.
appeti'toso, a ag appetising; (fig) attractive, desirable.
appezza'mento [appettsa'mento] sm (anche: ~ **di terreno**) plot, piece of ground.
appia'nare vt to level; (fig) to smooth away, iron out; **~rsi** vr (divergenze) to be ironed out.
appiat'tire vt to flatten; **~rsi** vr to become flatter; (farsi piatto) to flatten o s; **~rsi al suolo** to lie flat on the ground.
appic'care vt: **~ il fuoco a** to set fire to, set on fire.
appicci'care [appittʃi'kare] vt to stick; (fig): **~ qc a qn** to palm sth off on sb; **~rsi** vr to stick; (fig: persona) to cling.
appiccica'ticcio, a, ci, ce [appittʃika'tittʃo] ag, **appicci'coso, a** [appittʃi'koso] ag sticky; (fig: persona): **essere ~** to cling like a leech.
appie'dato, a ag: **rimanere ~** to be left without means of transport.
appi'eno av fully.
appigli'arsi [appiʎ'ʎarsi] vr: **~ a** (afferrarsi) to take hold of; (fig) to cling to.
ap'piglio [ap'piʎʎo] sm hold; (fig) pretext.
appiop'pare vt: **~ qc a qn** (nomignolo) to pin sth on sb; (compito difficile) to saddle sb with sth; **gli ha appioppato un pugno sul muso** he punched him in the face.
appiso'larsi vr to doze off.
applau'dire vt, vi to applaud.
ap'plauso sm applause no pl.
appli'cabile ag: **~ (a)** applicable (to).
appli'care vt to apply; (regolamento) to enforce; **~rsi** vr to apply o.s.
appli'cato, a ag (arte, scienze) applied ♦ sm (AMM) clerk.
applica'tore sm applicator.
applicazi'one [applikat'tsjone] sf application; enforcement; **~i tecniche** (INS) practical subjects.
appoggi'are [appod'dʒare] vt (mettere contro): **~ qc a qc** to lean o rest sth against sth; (fig: sostenere) to support; **~rsi** vr: **~rsi a** to lean against; (fig) to rely upon.

ap'poggio [ap'pɔddʒo] sm support.
appollai'arsi vr (anche fig) to perch.
ap'pongo, ap'poni etc vb vedi **apporre**.
ap'porre vt to affix.
appor'tare vt to bring.
ap'porto sm (gen, FINANZA) contribution.
ap'posi etc vb vedi **apporre**.
apposita'mente av (apposta) on purpose; (specialmente) specially.
ap'posito, a ag appropriate.
ap'posta av on purpose, deliberately; **neanche a farlo ~, ...** by sheer coincidence, ...
appos'tarsi vr to lie in wait.
ap'posto, a pp di **apporre**.
ap'prendere vt (imparare) to learn; (comprendere) to grasp.
apprendi'mento sm learning.
appren'dista, i, e sm/f apprentice.
apprendi'stato sm apprenticeship.
appren'sione sf apprehension.
appren'sivo, a ag apprehensive.
ap'preso, a pp di **apprendere**.
ap'presso av (accanto, vicino) close by, near; (dietro) behind; (dopo, più tardi) after, later ♦ ag inv (dopo): **il giorno ~** the next day; **~ a** prep (vicino a) near, close to.
appres'tare vt to prepare, get ready; **~rsi** vr: **~rsi a fare qc** to prepare o get ready to do sth.
ap'pretto sm starch.
apprez'zabile [appret'tsabile] ag (notevole) noteworthy, significant; (percepibile) appreciable.
apprezza'mento [apprettsa'mento] sm appreciation; (giudizio) opinion; (commento) comment.
apprez'zare [appret'tsare] vt to appreciate.
ap'proccio [ap'prɔttʃo] sm approach.
appro'dare vi (NAUT) to land; (fig): **non ~ a nulla** to come to nothing.
ap'prodo sm landing; (luogo) landing place.
approfit'tare vi: **~ di** (persona, situazione) to take advantage of; (occasione, opportunità) to make the most of, profit by.
approfon'dire vt to deepen; (fig) to study in depth; **~rsi** vr (gen, fig) to deepen; (peggiorare) to get worse.
appron'tare vt to prepare, get ready.
appropri'arsi vr: **~ di qc** to appropriate sth, take possession of sth; **~ indebitamente di** to embezzle.
appropri'ato, a ag appropriate.
appropriazi'one [approprjat'tsjone] sf appropriation; **~ indebita** (DIR)

embezzlement.

approssi'mare *vt* (*cifra*): ~ **per eccesso/per difetto** to round up/down; ~**rsi** *vr*: ~**rsi a** to approach, draw near.

approssima'tivo, a *ag* approximate, rough; (*impreciso*) inexact, imprecise.

approssimazi'one [approssimat'tsjone] *sf* approximation; **per** ~ approximately, roughly.

appro'vare *vt* (*condotta, azione*) to approve of; (*candidato*) to pass; (*progetto di legge*) to approve.

approvazi'one [approvat'tsjone] *sf* approval.

approvvigiona'mento [approvvidʒona 'mento] *sm* supplying; stocking up; ~**i** *smpl* (*MIL*) supplies.

approvvigio'nare [approvvidʒo'nare] *vt* to supply; ~**rsi** *vr* to lay in provisions, stock up; ~ **qn di qc** to supply sb with sth.

appunta'mento *sm* appointment; (*amoroso*) date; **darsi** ~ to arrange to meet (one another).

appun'tare *vt* (*rendere aguzzo*) to sharpen; (*fissare*) to pin, fix; (*annotare*) to note down.

appun'tato *sm* (*CARABINIERI*) corporal.

appun'tino *av* perfectly.

appun'tire *vt* to sharpen.

ap'punto *sm* note; (*rimprovero*) reproach ♦ *av* (*proprio*) exactly, just; **per l'**~**!**, ~**!** exactly!

appu'rare *vt* to check, verify.

apr. *abbr* (= *aprile*) Apr.

apribot'tiglie [apribot'tiʎʎe] *sm inv* bottleopener.

a'prile *sm* April; **pesce d'**~**!** April Fool!; *per fraseologia vedi* **luglio**.

a'prire *vt* to open; (*via, cadavere*) to open up; (*gas, luce, acqua*) to turn on ♦ *vi* to open; ~**rsi** *vr* to open; ~ **le ostilità** (*MIL*) to start up *o* begin hostilities; ~ **una sessione** (*INFORM*) to log on; ~**rsi a qn** to confide in sb, open one's heart to sb; **mi si è aperto lo stomaco** I feel rather peckish; **apriti cielo!** heaven forbid!

apris'catole *sm inv* tin (*BRIT*) *o* can opener.

APT *sigla f* (= *Azienda di Promozione Turistica*) ≈ tourist board.

AQ *sigla* = *L'Aquila*.

a'quario *sm* = **acquario**.

'aquila *sf* (*ZOOL*) eagle; (*fig*) genius.

aqui'lino, a *ag* aquiline.

aqui'lone *sm* (*giocattolo*) kite; (*vento*) North wind.

AR *sigla* = *Arezzo*.

ara'besco *sm* (*decorazione*) arabesque.

A'rabia Sau'dita *sf*: **l'**~ Saudi Arabia.

a'rabico, a, ci, che *ag*: **il Deserto** ~ **the** Arabian Desert.

a'rabile *ag* arable.

'arabo, a *ag*, *sm/f* Arab ♦ *sm* (*LING*) Arabic; **parlare** ~ (*fig*) to speak double Dutch (*BRIT*).

a'rachide [a'rakide] *sf* peanut.

ara'gosta *sf* spiny lobster.

a'raldica *sf* heraldry.

a'raldo *sm* herald.

aran'ceto [aran'tʃeto] *sm* orange grove.

a'rancia, ce [a'rantʃa] *sf* orange.

aranci'ata [aran'tʃata] *sf* orangeade.

a'rancio [a'rantʃo] *sm* (*BOT*) orange tree; (*colore*) orange ♦ *ag inv* (*colore*) orange; **fiori di** ~ orange blossom *sg*.

aranci'one [aran'tʃone] *ag inv*: **(color)** ~ bright orange.

a'rare *vt* to plough (*BRIT*), plow (*US*).

ara'tore *sm* ploughman (*BRIT*), plowman (*US*).

a'ratro *sm* plough (*BRIT*), plow (*US*).

ara'tura *sf* ploughing (*BRIT*), plowing (*US*).

a'razzo [a'rattso] *sm* tapestry.

arbi'traggio [arbi'traddʒo] *sm* (*SPORT*) refereeing; umpiring; (*DIR*) arbitration; (*COMM*) arbitrage.

arbi'trare *vt* (*SPORT*) to referee; to umpire; (*DIR*) to arbitrate.

arbi'trario, a *ag* arbitrary.

arbi'trato *sm* arbitration.

ar'bitrio *sm* will; (*abuso, sopruso*) arbitrary act.

'arbitro *sm* arbiter, judge; (*DIR*) arbitrator; (*SPORT*) referee; (: *TENNIS, CRICKET*) umpire.

arbo'scello [arboʃ'ʃello] *sm* sapling.

ar'busto *sm* shrub.

'arca, che *sf* (*sarcofago*) sarcophagus; **l'**~ **di Noè** Noah's ark.

ar'caico, a, ci, che *ag* archaic.

arca'ismo *sm* (*LING*) archaism.

ar'cangelo [ar'kandʒelo] *sm* archangel.

ar'cano, a *ag* arcane, mysterious ♦ *sm* mystery.

ar'cata *sf* (*ARCHIT, ANAT*) arch; (*ordine di archi*) arcade.

archeolo'gia [arkeolo'dʒia] *sf* arch(a)eology.

archeo'logico, a, ci, che [arkeo'lɔdʒiko] *ag* arch(a)eological.

arche'ologo, a, gi, ghe [arke'ɔlogo] *sm/f* arch(a)eologist.

ar'chetipo [ar'kɛtipo] *sm* archetype.

ar'chetto [ar'ketto] *sm* (*MUS*) bow.

architet'tare [arkitet'tare] *vt* (*fig: ideare*) to devise; (: *macchinare*) to plan, concoct.

archi'tetto [arki'tetto] *sm* architect.

architet'tonico, a, ci, che [arkitet'tɔniko] *ag* architectural.
architet'tura [arkitet'tura] *sf* architecture.
archivi'are [arki'vjare] *vt* (*documenti*) to file; (*DIR*) to dismiss.
archiviazi'one [arkivjat'tsjone] *sf* filing; dismissal.
ar'chivio [ar'kivjo] *sm* archives *pl*; (*INFORM*) file; ~ **principale** (*INFORM*) master file.
archi'vista, i, e [arki'vista] *sm/f* (*AMM*) archivist; (*in ufficio*) filing clerk.
'ARCI ['artʃi] *sigla f* (= *Associazione Ricreativa Culturale Italiana*) *cultural society*.
arci'duca, chi [artʃi'duka] *sm* archduke.
arci'ere [ar'tʃεre] *sm* archer.
ar'cigno, a [ar'tʃiɲɲo] *ag* grim, severe.
arci'one [ar'tʃone] *sm* saddlebow.
arci'pelago, ghi [artʃi'pεlago] *sm* archipelago.
arci'vescovo [artʃi'veskovo] *sm* archbishop.
'arco, chi *sm* (*arma, MUS*) bow, (*ARCHIT*) arch; (*MAT*) arc; **nell'**~ **di 3 settimane** within the space of 3 weeks; ~ **costituzionale** *political parties involved in formulating Italy's post-war constitution*.
arcoba'leno *sm* rainbow.
arcu'ato, a *ag* curved, bent; **dalle gambe** ~**e** bow-legged.
ar'dente *ag* burning; (*fig*) burning, ardent.
'ardere *vt, vi* to burn; **legna da** ~ firewood.
ar'desia *sf* slate.
ardi'mento *sm* daring.
ar'dire *vi* to dare ♦ *sm* daring.
ar'dito, a *ag* brave, daring, bold; (*sfacciato*) bold.
ar'dore *sm* blazing heat; (*fig*) ardour, fervour.
'arduo, a *ag* arduous, difficult.
'area *sf* area; (*EDIL*) land, ground; **nell'**~ **dei partiti di sinistra** among the parties of the left; ~ **fabbricabile** building land; ~ **di rigore** (*SPORT*) penalty area; ~ **di servizio** (*AUT*) service area.
a'rena *sf* arena; (*per corride*) bullring; (*sabbia*) sand.
are'naria *sf* sandstone.
are'narsi *vr* to run aground; (*fig: trattative*) to come to a standstill.
areo'plano *sm* = **aeroplano**.
are'tino, a *ag* of (*o* from) Arezzo.
'argano *sm* winch.
argen'tato, a [ardʒen'tato] *ag* silver-plated; (*colore*) silver, silvery; (*capelli*) silver(-grey).
ar'genteo, a [ar'dʒεnteo] *ag* silver, silvery.
argente'ria [ardʒente'ria] *sf* silverware,

silver.
Argen'tina [ardʒen'tina] *sf*: **l'**~ Argentina.
argen'tino, a [ardʒen'tino] *ag, sm/f* (*dell'Argentina*) Argentinian ♦ *sf* crewneck sweater.
ar'gento [ar'dʒεnto] *sm* silver; ~ **vivo** quicksilver; **avere l'**~ (**vivo**) **addosso** (*fig*) to be fidgety.
ar'gilla [ar'dʒilla] *sf* clay.
argil'loso, a [ardʒil'loso] *ag* (*contenente argilla*) clayey; (*simile ad argilla*) clay-like.
argi'nare [ardʒi'nare] *vt* (*fiume, acque*) to embank; (: *con diga*) to dyke up; (*fig: inflazione, corruzione*) to check; (: *spese*) to limit.
'argine ['ardʒine] *sm* embankment, bank; (*diga*) dyke, dike; **far** ~ **a, porre un** ~ **a** (*fig*) to check, hold back.
argomen'tare *vi* to argue.
argo'mento *sm* argument; (*materia, tema*) subject; **tornare sull'**~ to bring the matter up again.
argu'ire *vt* to deduce.
ar'guto, a *ag* sharp, quick-witted; (*spiritoso*) witty.
ar'guzia [ar'quttsja] *sf* wit; (*battuta*) witty remark.
'aria *sf* air; (*espressione, aspetto*) air, look; (*MUS: melodia*) tune; (: *di opera*) aria; **all'**~ **aperta** in the open (air); **manca l'**~ it's stuffy; **andare all'**~ (*piano, progetto*) to come to nothing; **mandare all'**~ **qc** to ruin *o* upset sth; **darsi delle** ~**e** to put on airs and graces; **ha la testa per** ~ his head is in the clouds; **che** ~ **tira?** (*fig: atmosfera*) what's the atmosphere like?
aridità *sf* aridity, dryness; (*fig*) lack of feeling.
'arido, a *ag* arid.
arieggi'are [arjed'dʒare] *vt* (*cambiare aria*) to air; (*imitare*) to imitate.
ari'ete *sm* ram; (*MIL*) battering ram; (*dello zodiaco*): **A**~ Aries; **essere dell'A**~ to be Aries.
a'ringa, ghe *sf* herring *inv*; ~ **affumicata** smoked herring, kipper; ~ **marinata** pickled herring.
ari'oso, a *ag* (*ambiente, stanza*) airy; (*MUS*) ariose.
'arista *sf* (*CUC*) chine of pork.
aristo'cratico, a, ci, che *ag* aristocratic.
aristocra'zia [aristokrat'tsia] *sf* aristocracy.
arit'metica *sf* arithmetic.
arit'metico, a, ci, che *ag* arithmetical.
arlec'chino [arlek'kino] *sm* harlequin.
'arma, i *sf* weapon, arm; (*parte dell'esercito*) arm; **alle** ~**i!** to arms!; **chiamare alle** ~**i** to call up (*BRIT*), draft (*US*); **sotto le** ~**i** in

the army (*o* forces); **combattere ad ~i
pari** (*anche fig*) to fight on equal terms;
essere alle prime ~i (*fig*) to be a novice;
passare qn per le ~i to execute sb;
battersi all'~ bianca to fight with blades;
~ a doppio taglio (*anche fig*) double-
edged weapon; **~ da fuoco** firearm.
ar'madio *sm* cupboard; (*per abiti*)
wardrobe; **~ a muro** built-in cupboard.
armamen'tario *sm* equipment,
instruments *pl.*
arma'mento *sm* (*MIL*) armament;
(: *materiale*) arms *pl*, weapons *pl*; (*NAUT*)
fitting out; manning; **la corsa agli ~i** the
arms race.
ar'mare *vt* to arm; (*arma da fuoco*) to cock;
(*NAUT: nave*) to rig, fit out; to man; (*EDIL:
volta, galleria*) to prop up, shore up; **~rsi** *vr*
to arm o.s.; (*MIL*) to take up arms.
ar'mato, a *ag*: **~ (di)** (*anche fig*) armed
(with) ♦ *sf* (*MIL*) army; (*NAUT*) fleet; **rapina
a mano ~a** armed robbery.
arma'tore *sm* shipowner.
arma'tura *sf* (*struttura di sostegno*)
framework; (*impalcatura*) scaffolding;
(*STORIA*) armour *no pl* (*BRIT*), armor *no pl*
(*US*), suit of armo(u)r.
armeggi'are [armed'dʒare] *vi*
(*affaccendarsi*): **~ (intorno a qc)** to mess
about (with sth).
Ar'menia *sf*: **l'~** Armenia.
ar'meno, a *ag*, *sm/f*, *sm* Armenian.
arme'ria *sf* (*deposito*) armoury (*BRIT*),
armory (*US*); (*collezione*) collection of
arms.
armis'tizio [armis'tittsjo] *sm* armistice.
armo'nia *sf* harmony.
ar'monico, a, ci, che *ag* harmonic; (*fig*)
harmonious ♦ *sf* (*MUS*) harmonica; **~a a
bocca** mouth organ.
armoni'oso, a *ag* harmonious.
armoniz'zare [armonid'dzare] *vt* to
harmonize; (*colori, abiti*) to match ♦ *vi* to
be in harmony; to match.
ar'nese *sm* tool, implement; (*oggetto
indeterminato*) thing, contraption; **male in
~** (*malvestito*) badly dressed; (*di salute
malferma*) in poor health; (*di condizioni
economiche*) down-at-heel.
'arnia *sf* hive.
a'roma, i *sm* aroma; fragrance; **~i** *smpl*
herbs and spices; **~i naturali/artificiali**
natural/artificial flavouring *sg* (*BRIT*) *o*
flavoring *sg* (*US*).
aromatera'pia *sf* aromatherapy.
aro'matico, a, ci, che *ag* aromatic; (*cibo*)
spicy.
aromatiz'zare [aromatid'dzare] *vt* to

season, flavour (*BRIT*), flavor (*US*).
'arpa *sf* (*MUS*) harp.
ar'peggio [ar'peddʒo] *sm* (*MUS*) arpeggio.
ar'pia *sf* (*anche fig*) harpy.
arpi'one *sm* (*gancio*) hook; (*cardine*) hinge;
(*PESCA*) harpoon.
arrabat'tarsi *vr* to do all one can, strive.
arrabbi'are *vi* (*cane*) to be affected with
rabies; **~rsi** *vr* (*essere preso dall'ira*) to get
angry, fly into a rage.
arrabbi'ato, a *ag* (*cane*) rabid, with rabies;
(*persona*) furious, angry.
arrabbia'tura *sf*: **prendersi un'~ (per qc)** to
become furious (over sth).
arraf'fare *vt* to snatch, seize; (*sottrarre*) to
pinch.
arrampi'carsi *vr* to climb (up); **~ sui vetri**
o **sugli specchi** (*fig*) to clutch at straws.
arrampi'cata *sf* climb.
arrampica'tore, 'trice *sm/f* (*gen, SPORT*)
climber; **~ sociale** (*fig*) social climber.
arran'care *vi* to limp, hobble; (*fig*) to
struggle along.
arrangia'mento [arrandʒa'mento] *sm* (*MUS*)
arrangement.
arran'giare [arran'dʒare] *vt* to arrange; **~rsi**
vr to manage, do the best one can.
arre'care *vt* to bring; (*causare*) to cause.
arreda'mento *sm* (*studio*) interior design;
(*mobili etc*) furnishings *pl.*
arre'dare *vt* to furnish.
arreda'tore, 'trice *sm/f* interior designer.
ar'redo *sm* fittings *pl*, furnishings *pl*; **~ per
uffici** office furnishings.
arrem'baggio [arrem'baddʒo] *sm* (*NAUT*)
boarding.
ar'rendersi *vr* to surrender; **~ all'evidenza
(dei fatti)** to face (the) facts.
arren'devole *ag* (*persona*) yielding,
compliant.
arrendevo'lezza [arrendevo'lettsa] *sf*
compliancy.
ar'reso, a *pp di* **arrendersi**.
arres'tare *vt* (*fermare*) to stop, halt;
(*catturare*) to arrest; **~rsi** *vr* (*fermarsi*) to
stop.
arres'tato, a *sm/f* person under arrest.
ar'resto *sm* (*cessazione*) stopping; (*fermata*)
stop; (*cattura, MED*) arrest; (*COMM: in
produzione*) stoppage; **subire un ~** to
come to a stop *o* standstill; **mettere agli
~i** to place under arrest; **~i domiciliari**
(*DIR*) house arrest.
arre'trare *vt*, *vi* to withdraw.
arre'trato, a *ag* (*lavoro*) behind schedule;
(*paese, bambino*) backward; (*numero di
giornale*) back *cpd*; **~i** *smpl* arrears; **gli ~i
dello stipendio** back pay *sg.*

arricchi'mento [arrikki'mento] *sm* enrichment.

arric'chire [arrik'kire] *vt* to enrich; **~rsi** *vr* to become rich.

arric'chito, a [arrik'kito] *sm/f* nouveau riche.

arricci'are [arrit't∫are] *vt* to curl; **~ il naso** to turn up one's nose.

ar'ridere *vi*: **~ a qn** (*fortuna, successo*) to smile on sb.

ar'ringa, ghe *sf* harangue; (*DIR*) address by counsel.

arrischi'are [arris'kjare] *vt* to risk; **~rsi** *vr* to venture, dare.

arrischi'ato, a [arris'kjato] *ag* risky; (*temerario*) reckless, rash.

ar'riso, a *pp di* **arridere**.

arri'vare *vi* to arrive; (*avvicinarsi*) to come; (*accadere*) to happen, occur; **~ a** (*livello, grado etc*) to reach; **lui arriva a Roma alle 7** he gets to *o* arrives at Rome at 7; **~ a fare qc** to manage to do sth, succeed in doing sth; **non ci arrivo** I can't reach it; (*fig: non capisco*) I can't understand it.

arri'vato, a *ag* (*persona: di successo*) successful ♦ *sm/f*: **essere un ~** to have made it; **nuovo ~** newcomer; **ben ~!** welcome!; **non sono l'ultimo ~!** (*fig*) I'm no fool!

arrive'derci [arrive'dert∫i] *escl* goodbye!

arrive'derla *escl* (*forma di cortesia*) goodbye!

arri'vismo *sm* (*ambizione*) ambitiousness; (*sociale*) social climbing.

arri'vista, i, e *sm/f* go-getter.

ar'rivo *sm* arrival; (*SPORT*) finish, finishing line.

arro'gante *ag* arrogant.

arro'ganza [arro'gantsa] *sf* arrogance.

arro'gare *vt*: **~rsi il diritto di fare qc** to assume the right to do sth; **~rsi il merito di qc** to claim credit for sth.

arro'lare *vb* = **arruolare**.

arrossa'mento *sm* reddening.

arros'sare *vt* (*occhi, pelle*) to redden, make red; **~rsi** *vr* to go *o* become red.

arros'sire *vi* (*per vergogna, timidezza*) to blush; (*per gioia*) to flush, blush.

arros'tire *vt* to roast; (*pane*) to toast; (*ai ferri*) to grill.

ar'rosto *sm, ag inv* roast; **~ di manzo** roast beef.

arro'tare *vt* to sharpen; (*investire con un veicolo*) to run over.

arro'tino *sm* knife-grinder.

arroto'lare *vt* to roll up.

arroton'dare *vt* (*forma, oggetto*) to round; (*stipendio*) to add to; (*somma*) to round off.

arrovel'larsi *vr* (*anche*: **~ il cervello**) to rack one's brains.

arroven'tato, a *ag* red-hot.

arruf'fare *vt* to ruffle; (*fili*) to tangle; (*fig: questione*) to confuse.

arruggi'nire [arrudʒi'nire] *vt* to rust; **~rsi** *vr* to rust; (*fig*) to become rusty.

arruola'mento *sm* (*MIL*) enlistment.

arruo'lare *vt* (*MIL*) to enlist; **~rsi** *vr* to enlist, join up.

arse'nale *sm* (*MIL*) arsenal; (*cantiere navale*) dockyard.

ar'senico *sm* arsenic.

'arsi *vb vedi* **ardere**.

'arso, a *pp di* **ardere** ♦ *ag* (*bruciato*) burnt; (*arido*) dry.

ar'sura *sf* (*calore opprimente*) burning heat; (*siccità*) drought.

art. *abbr* (= *articolo*) art.

'arte *sf* art; (*abilità*) skill; **a regola d'~** (*fig*) perfectly, senz' **né parte** penniless and out of a job; **~i figurative** visual arts.

arte'fatto, a *ag* (*stile, modi*) affected; (*cibo*) adulterated.

ar'tefice [ar'tefit∫e] *sm/f* craftsman/woman; (*autore*) author.

ar'teria *sf* artery.

arterioscle'rosi *sf* arteriosclerosis, hardening of the arteries.

arteri'oso, a *ag* arterial.

'artico, a, ci, che *ag* Arctic ♦ *sm*: **l'A~** the Arctic; **il Circolo polare ~** the Arctic Circle; **l'Oceano ~** the Arctic Ocean.

artico'lare *ag* (*ANAT*) of the joints, articular ♦ *vt* to articulate; (*suddividere*) to divide, split up; **~rsi** *vr*: **~rsi in** (*discorso, progetto*) to be divided into.

artico'lato, a *ag* (*linguaggio*) articulate; (*AUT*) articulated.

articolazi'one [artikolat'sjone] *sf* (*ANAT, TECN*) joint; (*di voce, concetto*) articulation.

ar'ticolo *sm* article; **~ di fondo** (*STAMPA*) leader, leading article; **~i di marca** branded goods; **un bell'~** (*fig*) a real character.

'Artide *sm*: **l'~** the Arctic.

artifici'ale [artifi't∫ale] *ag* artificial.

artifici'ere [artifi't∫ere] *sm* (*MIL*) artificer; (: *per disinnescare bombe*) bomb-disposal expert.

arti'ficio [arti'fit∫o] *sm* (*espediente*) trick, artifice; (*ricerca di effetto*) artificiality.

artifici'oso, a [artifi't∫oso] *ag* cunning; (*non spontaneo*) affected.

artigia'nale [artidʒa'nale] *ag* craft *cpd*.

artigia'nato [artidʒa'nato] *sm*

craftsmanship; craftsmen *pl.*

artigi'ano, a [arti'dʒano] *sm/f* craftsman/ woman.

artigli'ere [artiʎ'ʎɛre] *sm* artilleryman.

artiglie'ria [artiʎʎe'ria] *sf* artillery.

ar'tiglio [ar'tiʎʎo] *sm* claw; (*di rapaci*) talon; **sfoderare gli ~i** (*fig*) to show one's claws.

ar'tista, i, e *sm/f* artist; **un lavoro da ~** (*fig*) a professional piece of work.

ar'tistico, a, ci, che *ag* artistic.

'arto *sm* (*ANAT*) limb.

ar'trite *sf* (*MED*) arthritis.

ar'trosi *sf* osteoarthritis.

arzigogo'lato, a [ardzigogo'lato] *ag* tortuous.

arzi'gogolo [ardzi'gɔgolo] *sm* tortuous expression.

ar'zillo, a [ar'dzillo] *ag* lively, sprightly.

a'scella [aʃ'ʃɛlla] *sf* (*ANAT*) armpit.

ascen'dente [aʃʃen'dɛnte] *sm* ancestor; (*fig*) ascendancy; (*ASTR*) ascendant.

a'scendere [aʃ'ʃendere] *vi:* ~ **al trono** to ascend the throne.

ascensi'one [aʃʃen'sjone] *sf* (*ALPINISMO*) ascent; (*REL*): **l'A~** the Ascension; **isola dell'A~** Ascension Island.

ascen'sore [aʃʃen'sore] *sm* lift.

a'scesa [aʃ'ʃesa] *sf* ascent; (*al trono*) accession; (*al potere*) rise.

a'scesi [aʃ'ʃɛzi] *sf* asceticism.

a'sceso, a [aʃ'ʃeso] *pp di* **ascendere**.

a'scesso [aʃ'ʃɛsso] *sm* (*MED*) abscess.

a'sceta, i [aʃ'ʃɛta] *sm* ascetic.

'ascia, *pl* **'asce** ['aʃʃa] *sf* axe.

asciugaca'pelli [aʃʃugaka'pelli] *sm* hair dryer.

asciuga'mano [aʃʃuga'mano] *sm* towel.

asciu'gare [aʃʃu'gare] *vt* to dry; **~rsi** *vr* to dry o.s.; (*diventare asciutto*) to dry.

asciuga'trice [aʃʃuga'tritʃe] *sf* spin-dryer.

asciut'tezza [aʃʃut'tettsa] *sf* dryness; leanness; curtness.

asci'utto, a [aʃ'ʃutto] *ag* dry; (*fig: magro*) lean; (: *burbero*) curt ♦ *sm:* **restare all'~** (*fig*) to be left penniless; **restare a bocca ~a** (*fig*) to be disappointed.

asco'lano, a *ag* of (*o from*) Ascoli.

ascol'tare *vt* to listen to; ~ **il consiglio di qn** to listen to *o* heed sb's advice.

ascolta'tore, 'trice *sm/f* listener.

as'colto *sm:* **essere** *o* **stare in** ~ to be listening; **dare** *o* **prestare** ~ **(a)** to pay attention (to); **indice di** ~ (*TV, RADIO*) audience rating.

AS. COM. *sigla f* = *Associazione Commercianti*.

as'critto, a *pp di* **ascrivere**.

as'crivere *vt* (*attribuire*): ~ **qc a qn** to attribute sth to sb; ~ **qc a merito di qn** to give sb credit for sth.

a'settico, a, ci, che *ag* aseptic.

asfal'tare *vt* to asphalt.

as'falto *sm* asphalt.

asfis'sia *sf* asphyxia, asphyxiation.

asfissi'ante *ag* (*gas*) asphyxiating; (*fig: calore, ambiente*) stifling, suffocating; (: *persona*) tiresome.

asfissi'are *vt* to asphyxiate, suffocate; (*fig: opprimere*) to stifle; (: *infastidire*) to get on sb's nerves ♦ *vi* to suffocate, asphyxiate.

'Asia *sf:* **l'~** Asia.

asi'atico, a, ci, che *ag, sm/f* Asiatic, Asian.

a'silo *sm* refuge, sanctuary; ~ **(d'infanzia)** nursery(-school); ~ **nido** day nursery, crèche (*for children aged 0 to 3*); ~ **politico** political asylum.

asim'metrico, a, ci, che *ag* asymmetric(al).

'asino *sm* donkey, ass; **la bellezza dell'~** (*fig: di ragazza*) the beauty of youth; **qui casca l'~!** there's the rub!

'asma *sf* asthma.

as'matico, a, ci, che *ag, sm/f* asthmatic.

asoci'ale [aso'tʃale] *ag* antisocial.

'asola *sf* buttonhole.

as'parago, gi *sm* asparagus *no pl.*

as'pergere [as'pɛrdʒere] *vt:* ~ **(di o con)** to sprinkle (with).

asperità *sf inv* roughness *no pl*; (*fig*) harshness *no pl.*

as'persi *etc vb vedi* **aspergere**.

as'perso, a *pp di* **aspergere**.

aspet'tare *vt* to wait for; (*anche COMM*) to await; (*aspettarsi*) to expect; (*essere in serbo: notizia, evento etc*) to be in store for, lie ahead of ♦ *vi* to wait; **~rsi qc** to expect sth; ~ **un bambino** to be expecting (a baby); **questo non me l'aspettavo** I wasn't expecting this; **me l'aspettavo!** I thought as much!

aspetta'tiva *sf* expectation; **inferiore all'~** worse than expected; **essere/mettersi in** ~ (*AMM*) to be on/take leave of absence.

as'petto *sm* (*apparenza*) aspect, appearance, look; (*punto di vista*) point of view; **di bell'~** good-looking.

aspi'rante *ag* (*attore etc*) aspiring ♦ *sm/f* candidate, applicant.

aspira'polvere *sm inv* vacuum cleaner.

aspi'rare *vt* (*respirare*) to breathe in, inhale; (*sog: apparecchi*) to suck (up) ♦ *vi:* ~ **a** to aspire to.

aspira'tore *sm* extractor fan.

aspirazi'one [aspirat'tsjone] *sf* (*TECN*) suction; (*anelito*) aspiration.

aspi'rina *sf* aspirin.

aspor'tare vt (anche MED) to remove, take away.

as'prezza [as'prettsa] sf sourness, tartness; pungency; harshness; roughness; rugged nature.

'aspro, a ag (sapore) sour, tart; (odore) acrid, pungent; (voce, clima, fig) harsh; (superficie) rough; (paesaggio) rugged.

Ass. abbr = assicurazione; assicurata; assegno.

assaggi'are [assad'dʒare] vt to taste.

assag'gini [assad'dʒini] smpl (CUC) selection of first courses.

as'saggio [as'saddʒo] sm tasting; (piccola quantità) taste; (campione) sample.

as'sai av (molto) a lot, much; (: con ag) very; (a sufficienza) enough ♦ ag inv (quantità) a lot of, much; (numero) a lot of, many; ~ **contento** very pleased.

as'salgo etc vb vedi **assalire**.

assa'lire vt to attack, assail.

assali'tore, 'trice sm/f attacker, assailant.

assal'tare vt (MIL) to storm; (banca) to raid; (treno, diligenza) to hold up.

as'salto sm attack, assault; **prendere d'**~ (fig: negozio, treno) to storm; (: personalità) to besiege; **d'**~ (editoria, giornalista etc) aggressive.

assapo'rare vt to savour (BRIT), savor (US).

assassi'nare vt to murder; (POL) to assassinate; (fig) to ruin.

assas'sinio sm murder; assassination.

assas'sino, a ag murderous ♦ sm/f murderer; assassin.

'asse sm (TECN) axle; (MAT) axis ♦ sf board; ~ **da stiro** ironing board.

assecon'dare vt: ~ **qn (in qc)** to go along with sb (in sth); ~ **i desideri di qn** to go along with sb's wishes; ~ **i capricci di qn** to give in to sb's whims.

assedi'are vt to besiege.

as'sedio sm siege.

asse'gnare [assen'ɲare] vt to assign, allot; (premio) to award.

assegna'tario [assenɲa'tarjo] sm (DIR) assignee; (COMM) recipient; **l'**~ **del premio** the person awarded the prize.

assegnazi'one [assenɲat'tsjone] sf (di casa, somma) allocation; (di carica) assignment; (di premio, borsa di studio) awarding.

as'segno [as'seɲɲo] sm allowance; (anche: ~ **bancario**) cheque (BRIT), check (US); **contro** ~ cash on delivery; ~ **circolare** bank draft; ~ **di invalidità** o **di malattia** injury o sickness benefit; ~ **post-datato** post-dated cheque; ~ **sbarrato** crossed cheque; ~ **non sbarrato** uncrossed cheque; ~ **di studio** study grant; "~ **non**

trasferibile" "account payee only"; ~ **di viaggio** travel(l)er's cheque; ~ **a vuoto** dud cheque; ~**i alimentari** alimony sg; ~**i familiari** ≈ child benefit sg.

assem'blaggio [assem'bladdʒo] sm (INDUSTRIA) assembly.

assem'blare vt to assemble.

assem'blea sf assembly; (raduno, adunanza) meeting.

assembra'mento sm public gathering; **divieto di** ~ ban on public meetings.

assen'nato, a ag sensible.

as'senso sm assent, consent.

assen'tarsi vr to go out.

as'sente ag absent; (fig) faraway, vacant ♦ sm/f absentee.

assente'ismo sm absenteeism.

assente'ista, i, e sm/f (dal lavoro) absentee.

assen'tire vi: ~ **(a)** to agree (to), assent (to).

as'senza [as'sɛntsa] sf absence.

asse'rire vt to maintain, assert.

asserragli'arsi [asserraʎ'ʎarsi] vr: ~ **(in)** to barricade o.s. (in).

asser'vire vt to enslave; (fig: animo, passioni) to subdue; ~**rsi** vr: ~**rsi (a)** to submit (to).

asserzi'one [asser'tsjone] sf assertion.

assesso'rato sm councillorship.

asses'sore sm councillor.

assesta'mento sm (sistemazione) arrangement; (EDIL, GEO) settlement.

asses'tare vt (mettere in ordine) to put in order, arrange; ~**rsi** vr to settle in; (GEO) to settle; ~ **un colpo a qn** to deal sb a blow.

asse'tato, a ag thirsty, parched.

as'setto sm order, arrangement; (NAUT, AER) trim; **in** ~ **di guerra** on a war footing; ~ **territoriale** country planning.

assicu'rare vt (accertare) to ensure; (infondere certezza) to assure; (fermare, legare) to make fast, secure; (fare un contratto di assicurazione) to insure; ~**rsi** vr (accertarsi): ~**rsi (di)** to make sure (of); (contro il furto etc): ~**rsi (contro)** to insure o.s. (against).

assicu'rato, a ag insured ♦ sf (anche: **lettera** ~**a**) registered letter.

assicura'tore, 'trice ag insurance cpd ♦ sm/f insurance agent; **società** ~**trice** insurance company.

assicurazi'one [assikurat'tsjone] sf assurance; insurance; ~ **multi-rischio** comprehensive insurance.

assidera'mento sm exposure.

asside'rare vt to freeze; ~**rsi** vr to freeze; **morire assiderato** to die of exposure.

as'siduo, a *ag* (*costante*) assiduous;
(*regolare*) regular.

assi'eme *av* (*insieme*) together ♦ *prep*: ~ a
(together) with.

assil'lante *ag* (*dubbio, pensiero*) nagging;
(*creditore*) pestering.

assil'lare *vt* to pester, torment.

as'sillo *sm* (*fig*) worrying thought.

assimi'lare *vt* to assimilate.

assimilazi'one [assimilat'tsjone] *sf*
assimilation.

assi'oma, i *sm* axiom.

assio'matico, a, ci, che *ag* axiomatic.

as'sise *sfpl* (*DIR*) assizes (*BRIT*); corte *f* d'~
court of assizes, ≈ crown court (*BRIT*);
vedi anche Corte d'Assise.

assis'tente *sm/f* assistant; ~ sociale social
worker; ~ universitario (assistant)
lecturer; ~ di volo (*AER*) steward/
stewardess.

assis'tenza [assis'tɛntsa] *sf* assistance; ~
legale legal aid; ~ ospedaliera free
hospital treatment; ~ sanitaria health
service; ~ sociale welfare services *pl*.

assistenzi'ale [assisten'tsjale] *ag* (*ente,
organizzazione*) welfare *cpd*; (*opera*)
charitable.

assistenzia'lismo [assistentsja'lizmo] *sm*
(*peg*) excessive state aid.

as'sistere *vt* (*aiutare*) to assist, help; (*curare*) to treat ♦ *vi*: ~ (a qc) (*essere presente*)
to be present (at sth), attend (sth).

assis'tito, a *pp di* assistere.

'asso *sm* ace; piantare qn in ~ to leave sb
in the lurch.

associ'are [asso'tʃare] *vt* to associate;
(*rendere partecipe*): ~ qn a (*affari*) to take
sb into partnership in; (*partito*) to make
sb a member of; ~rsi *vr* to enter into
partnership; ~rsi a to become a member
of, join; (*dolori, gioie*) to share in; ~ qn
alle carceri to take sb to prison.

associazi'one [assotʃat'tsjone] *sf*
association; ~ di categoria trade
association; ~ a o per delinquere (*DIR*)
criminal association; A~ Europea di
Libero Scambio European Free Trade
Association, EFTA; ~ in partecipazione
(*COMM*) joint venture.

asso'dare *vt* (*muro, posizione*) to
strengthen; (*fatti, verità*) to ascertain.

asso'dato, a *ag* well-founded.

assogget'tare [assoddʒet'tare] *vt* to
subject, subjugate; ~rsi *vr*: ~rsi a to
submit to.

asso'lato, a *ag* sunny.

assol'dare *vt* to recruit.

as'solsi *etc vb vedi* assolvere.

as'solto, a *pp di* assolvere.

assoluta'mente *av* absolutely.

asso'luto, a *ag* absolute.

assoluzi'one [assolut'tsjone] *sf* (*DIR*)
acquittal; (*REL*) absolution.

as'solvere *vt* (*DIR*) to acquit; (*REL*) to
absolve; (*adempiere*) to carry out,
perform.

assomigli'are [assomiʎ'ʎare] *vi*: ~ a to
resemble, look like.

asson'nato, a *ag* sleepy.

asso'pirsi *vr* to doze off.

assor'bente *ag* absorbent ♦ *sm*: ~ igienico
sanitary towel; ~ interno tampon.

assor'bire *vt* to absorb; (*fig: far proprio*) to
assimilate.

assor'dante *ag* (*rumore, musica*) deafening.

assor'dare *vt* to deafen.

assorti'mento *sm* assortment.

assor'tire *vt* (*disporre*) to arrange.

assor'tito, a *ag* assorted; (*colori*) matched,
matching.

as'sorto, a *ag* absorbed, engrossed.

assottigli'are [assottiʎ'ʎare] *vt* to make
thin, thin; (*aguzzare*) to sharpen; (*ridurre*)
to reduce; ~rsi *vr* to grow thin; (*fig:
ridursi*) to be reduced.

A.S.S.T. *sigla f* (= *Azienda di Stato per i
Servizi Telefonici*) *state-run
telecommunications company*.

assue'fare *vt* to accustom; ~rsi *vr*: ~rsi a to
get used to, accustom o.s. to.

assue'fatto, a *pp di* assuefare.

assuefazi'one [assuefat'tsjone] *sf* (*MED*)
addiction.

as'sumere *vt* (*impiegato*) to take on,
engage; (*responsabilità*) to assume, take
upon o.s.; (*contegno, espressione*) to
assume, put on; (*droga*) to consume.

as'sunsi *etc vb vedi* assumere.

as'sunto, a *pp di* assumere ♦ *sm* (*tesi*)
proposition.

assunzi'one [assun'tsjone] *sf* (*di impiegati*)
employment, engagement; (*REL*): l'A~ the
Assumption.

assurdità *sf inv* absurdity; dire delle ~ to
talk nonsense.

as'surdo, a *ag* absurd.

'asta *sf* pole; (*modo di vendita*) auction.

as'tante *sm* bystander.

astante'ria *sf* casualty department.

as'temio, a *ag* teetotal ♦ *sm/f* teetotaller.

aste'nersi *vr*: ~ (da) to abstain (from),
refrain (from); (*POL*) to abstain (from).

astensi'one *sf* abstention.

astensio'nista, i, e *sm/f* (*POL*)
abstentionist.

aste'risco, schi *sm* asterisk.

aste'roide *sm* asteroid.
'astice ['astitʃe] *sm* lobster.
astigi'ano, a [asti'dʒano] *ag* of (*o* from) Asti.
astig'matico, a, ci, che *ag* astigmatic.
asti'nenza [asti'nɛntsa] *sf* abstinence; **essere in crisi di ~** to suffer from withdrawal symptoms.
'astio *sm* rancour, resentment.
asti'oso, a *ag* resentful.
astrat'tismo *sm* (*ARTE*) abstract art.
as'tratto, a *ag* abstract.
astrin'gente [astrin'dʒɛnte] *ag, sm* astringent.
'astro *sm* star.
astrolo'gia [astrolo'dʒia] *sf* astrology.
astro'logico, a, ci, che [astro'lɔdʒiko] *ag* astrological.
as'trologo, a, ghi, ghe *sm/f* astrologer.
astro'nauta, i, e *sm/f* astronaut.
astro'nautica *sf* astronautics *sg*.
astro'nave *sf* spaceship.
astrono'mia *sf* astronomy.
astro'nomico, a, ci, che *ag* astronomic(al).
as'tronomo *sm* astronomer.
as'truso, a *ag* (*discorso, ragionamento*) abstruse.
as'tuccio [as'tuttʃo] *sm* case, box, holder.
as'tuto, a *ag* astute, cunning, shrewd.
as'tuzia [as'tuttsja] *sf* astuteness, shrewdness, (*azione*) trick.
AT *sigla* = Asti.
A.T. *abbr* (= alta tensione) HT.
ATA *sigla f* = Associazione Turistica Albergatori.
a'tavico, a, ci, che *ag* atavistic.
ate'ismo *sm* atheism.
atelier [atə'lje] *sm inv* (*laboratorio*) workshop; (*studio*) studio; (*sartoria*) fashion house.
A'tene *sf* Athens.
ate'neo *sm* university.
ateni'ese *ag, sm/f* Athenian.
'ateo, a *ag, sm/f* atheist.
a'tipico, a, ci, che *ag* atypical.
at'lante *sm* atlas; **i Monti dell'A~** the Atlas Mountains.
at'lantico, a, ci, che *ag* Atlantic ♦ *sm*: **l'A~**, **l'Oceano A~** the Atlantic, the Atlantic Ocean.
at'leta, i, e *sm/f* athlete.
at'letica *sf* athletics *sg*; **~ leggera** track and field events *pl*; **~ pesante** weightlifting and wrestling.
ATM *sigla f* = Azienda Tranviaria Municipale.
atmos'fera *sf* atmosphere.
atmos'ferico, a, ci, che *ag* atmospheric.

a'tollo *sm* atoll.
a'tomico, a, ci, che *ag* atomic; (*nucleare*) atomic, atom *cpd*, nuclear.
atomizza'tore [atomiddza'tore] *sm* (*di acqua, lacca*) spray; (*di profumo*) atomizer.
'atomo *sm* atom.
'atono, a *ag* (*FONETICA*) unstressed.
'atrio *sm* entrance hall, lobby.
a'troce [a'trotʃe] *ag* (*che provoca orrore*) dreadful; (*terribile*) atrocious.
atrocità [atrotʃi'ta] *sf inv* atrocity.
atro'fia *sf* atrophy.
attacca'brighe [attakka'brige] *sm/f inv* quarrelsome person.
attacca'mento *sm* (*fig*) attachment, affection.
attacca'panni *sm* hook, peg; (*mobile*) hall stand.
attac'care *vt* (*unire*) to attach; (*cucendo*) to sew on; (*far aderire*) to stick (on); (*appendere*) to hang (up); (*assalire: anche fig*) **to attack**; (*iniziare*) to begin, start, (*fig. contagiare*) to pass on ♦ *vi* to stick, adhere; **~rsi** *vr* to stick, adhere; (*trasmettersi per contagio*) to be contagious, (*afferrarsi*): **~rsi (a)** to cling (to); (*fig: affezionarsi*): **~rsi (a)** to become attached (to); **~ discorso** to start a conversation; **con me non attaccal** that won't work with me!
attacca'ticcio, a, ci, ce [attakka'tittʃo] *ag* sticky.
attacca'tura *sf* (*di manica*) join; **~ (dei capelli)** hairline.
at'tacco, chi *sm* (*azione offensiva: anche fig*) attack; (*MED*) attack, fit; (*SCI*) binding; (*ELETTR*) socket.
attanagli'are [attanaʎ'ʎare] *vt* (*anche fig*) to grip.
attar'darsi *vr*: **~ a fare qc** (*fermarsi*) to stop to do sth; (*stare più a lungo*) to stay behind to do sth.
attec'chire [attek'kire] *vi* (*pianta*) to take root; (*fig*) to catch on.
atteggia'mento [atteddʒa'mento] *sm* attitude.
atteggi'arsi [atted'dʒarsi] *vr*: **~ a** to pose as.
attem'pato, a *ag* elderly.
atten'dente *sm* (*MIL*) orderly, batman.
at'tendere *vt* to wait for, await ♦ *vi*: **~ a** to attend to.
atten'dibile *ag* (*scusa, storia*) credible; (*fonte, testimone, notizia*) reliable; (*persona*) trustworthy.
atte'nersi *vr*: **~ a** to keep o stick to.
atten'tare *vi*: **~ a** to make an attempt on.
atten'tato *sm* attack; **~ alla vita di qn** attempt on sb's life.
at'tento, a *ag* attentive; (*accurato*) careful,

thorough ♦ *escl* be careful!; **stare ~ a qc** to pay attention to sth; **~i!** (*MIL*) attention!; **~i al cane** beware of the dog.

attenu'ante *sf* (*DIR*) extenuating circumstance.

attenu'are *vt* to alleviate, ease; (*diminuire*) to reduce; **~rsi** *vr* to ease, abate.

attenuazi'one [attenuat'tsjone] *sf* alleviation; easing; reduction.

attenzi'one [atten'tsjone] *sf* attention ♦ *escl* watch out!, be careful!; **coprire qn di ~i** to lavish attention on sb.

atter'raggio [atter'raddʒo] *sm* landing; **~ di fortuna** emergency landing.

atter'rare *vt* to bring down ♦ *vi* to land.

atter'rire *vt* to terrify.

at'tesa *sf vedi* **atteso**.

at'tesi *etc vb vedi* **attendere**.

at'teso, a *pp di* **attendere** ♦ *sf* waiting; (*tempo trascorso aspettando*) wait; **essere in ~a di qc** to be waiting for sth; **in ~a di una vostra risposta** (*COMM*) awaiting your reply; **restiamo in ~a di Vostre ulteriori notizie** (*COMM*) we look forward to hearing (further) from you.

attes'tare *vt*: **~ qc/che** to testify to sth/(to the fact) that.

attes'tato *sm* certificate.

attestazi'one [attestat'tsjone] *sf* (*certificato*) certificate; (*dichiarazione*) statement.

'attico, ci *sm* attic.

at'tiguo, a *ag* adjacent, adjoining.

attil'lato, a *ag* (*vestito*) close-fitting, tight; (*persona*) dressed up.

'attimo *sm* moment; **in un ~** in a moment.

atti'nente *ag*: **~ a** relating to, concerning.

atti'nenza [atti'nɛntsa] *sf* connection.

at'tingere [at'tindʒere] *vt*: **~ a o da** (*acqua*) to draw from; (*denaro, notizie*) to obtain from.

at'tinto, a *pp di* **attingere**.

atti'rare *vt* to attract; **~rsi delle critiche** to incur criticism.

atti'tudine *sf* (*disposizione*) aptitude; (*atteggiamento*) attitude.

atti'vare *vt* to activate; (*far funzionare*) to set going, start.

atti'vista, i, e *sm/f* activist.

attività *sf inv* activity; (*COMM*) assets *pl*; **~ liquide** (*COMM*) liquid assets.

at'tivo, a *ag* active; (*COMM*) profit-making ♦ *sm* (*COMM*) assets *pl*; **in ~** in credit; **chiudere in ~** to show a profit; **avere qc al proprio ~** (*fig*) to have sth to one's credit.

attiz'zare [attit'tsare] *vt* (*fuoco*) to poke; (*fig*) to stir up.

attizza'toio [attittsa'tojo] *sm* poker.

'atto, a *ag*: **~ a** a fit for, capable of ♦ *sm* act;

(*azione, gesto*) action, act, deed; (*DIR: documento*) deed, document; **~i** *smpl* (*di congressi etc*) proceedings; **essere in ~** to be under way; **mettere in ~** to put into action; **fare ~ di fare qc** to make as if to do sth; **all'~** **pratico** in practice; **dare ~ a qn di qc** to give sb credit for sth; **~ di nascita/morte** birth/death certificate; **~ di proprietà** title deed; **~ pubblico** official document; **~ di vendita** bill of sale; **~i osceni (in luogo pubblico)** (*DIR*) indecent exposure; **~i verbali** transactions.

at'tonito, a *ag* dumbfounded, astonished.

attorcigli'are [attortʃiʎ'ʎare] *vt*, **~rsi** *vr* to twist.

at'tore, 'trice *sm/f* actor/actress.

attorni'are *vt* (*circondare*) to surround; **~rsi** *vr*: **~rsi di** to surround o.s. with.

at'torno *av*, **~ a** *prep* round, around, about.

attrac'care *vt, vi* (*NAUT*) to dock, berth.

at'tracco, chi *sm* (*NAUT: manovra*) docking, berthing; (*luogo*) berth.

at'trae *etc vb vedi* **attrarre**.

attra'ente *ag* attractive.

at'traggo *etc vb vedi* **attrarre**.

at'trarre *vt* to attract.

at'trassi *etc vb vedi* **attrarre**.

attrat'tiva *sf* attraction, charm.

at'tratto, a *pp di* **attrarre**.

attraversa'mento *sm* crossing; **~ pedonale** pedestrian crossing.

attraver'sare *vt* to cross; (*città, bosco, fig: periodo*) to go through; (*sog: fiume*) to run through.

attra'verso *prep* through; (*da una parte all'altra*) across.

attrazi'one [attrat'tsjone] *sf* attraction.

attrez'zare [attret'tsare] *vt* to equip; (*NAUT*) to rig.

attrezza'tura [attrettsa'tura] *sf* equipment *no pl*; rigging; **~e per uffici** office equipment.

at'trezzo [at'trettso] *sm* tool, instrument; (*SPORT*) piece of equipment.

attribu'ire *vt*: **~ qc a qn** (*assegnare*) to give o award sth to sb; (*quadro etc*) to attribute sth to sb.

attri'buto *sm* attribute.

at'trice [at'tritʃe] *sf vedi* **attore**.

at'trito *sm* (*anche fig*) friction.

attu'abile *ag* feasible.

attuabilità *sf* feasibility.

attu'ale *ag* (*presente*) present; (*di attualità*) topical; (*che è in atto*) actual.

attualità *sf inv* topicality; (*avvenimento*) current event; **notizie d'~** (*TV*) the news *sg*.

attualiz'zare [attualid'dzare] *vt* to update,

bring up to date.
attual'mente *av* at the moment, at present.
attu'are *vt* to carry out; ~**rsi** *vr* to be realized.
attuazi'one [attuat'tsjone] *sf* carrying out.
attu'tire *vt* to deaden, reduce; ~**rsi** *vr* to die down.
A.U. *abbr* = **allievo ufficiale.**
au'dace [au'datʃe] *ag* audacious, daring, bold; (*provocante*) provocative; (*sfacciato*) impudent, bold.
au'dacia [au'datʃa] *sf* audacity, daring; boldness; provocativeness; impudence.
'audio *sm* (*TV, RADIO, CINE*) sound.
audiocas'setta *sf* (audio) cassette.
audio'leso, a *sm/f* person who is hard of hearing.
audiovi'sivo, a *ag* audiovisual.
audi'torio *sm*, **audi'torium** *sm inv* auditorium.
audizi'one [audit'tsjone] *sf* hearing, (*MUS*) audition.
'auge ['audʒe] *sf* (*della gloria, carriera*) height, peak; **essere in** ~ to be at the top.
augu'rale *ag*: **messaggio** ~ greeting; **biglietto** ~ greetings card.
augu'rare *vt* to wish; ~**rsi qc** to hope for sth.
au'gurio *sm* (*presagio*) omen; (*voto di benessere etc*) (good) wish; **essere di buon/cattivo** ~ to be of good omen/be ominous; **fare gli ~i a qn** to give sb one's best wishes; **tanti ~i!** all the best!
'aula *sf* (*scolastica*) classroom; (*universitaria*) lecture theatre; (*di edificio pubblico*) hall; ~ **magna** main hall; ~ **del tribunale** courtroom.
aumen'tare *vt*, *vi* to increase; ~ **di peso** (*persona*) to put on weight; **la produzione è aumentata del 50%** production has increased by 50%.
au'mento *sm* increase.
'aureo, a *ag* (*di oro*) gold *cpd*; (*fig: colore, periodo*) golden.
au'reola *sf* halo.
au'rora *sf* dawn.
ausili'are *ag*, *sm*, *sm/f* auxiliary.
au'silio *sm* aid.
auspi'cabile *ag* desirable.
auspi'care *vt* to call for, express a desire for.
aus'picio [aus'pitʃo] *sm* omen; (*protezione*) patronage; **sotto gli ~i di** under the auspices of; **è di buon** ~ it augurs well.
austerità *sf inv* austerity.
aus'tero, a *ag* austere.
aus'trale *ag* southern.

Aus'tralia *sf*: **l'**~ Australia.
australi'ano, a *ag*, *sm/f* Australian.
'Austria *sf*: **l'**~ Austria.
aus'triaco, a, ci, che *ag*, *sm/f* Austrian.
au'tarchico, a, ci, che [au'tarkiko] *ag* (*sistema*) self-sufficient, autarkic; (*prodotto*) home *cpd*, home-produced.
'aut 'aut *sm inv* ultimatum.
autenti'care *vt* to authenticate.
autenticità [autentitʃi'ta] *sf* authenticity.
au'tentico, a, ci, che *ag* (*quadro, firma*) authentic, genuine; (*fatto*) true, genuine.
au'tista, i *sm* driver; (*personale*) chauffeur.
'auto *sf inv* car; ~ **blu** official car.
autoade'sivo, a *ag* self-adhesive ♦ *sm* sticker.
autoarticolato *sm* articulated lorry (*BRIT*), semi (trailer) (*US*).
autobiogra'fia *sf* autobiography.
autobio'grafico, a, ci, che *ag* autobiographic(al).
auto'blinda *sf* armoured (*BRIT*) o armored (*US*) car.
auto'bomba *sf inv* car carrying a bomb; **l'**~ **si trovava a pochi metri** the car bomb was a few metres away.
auto'botte *sf* tanker.
'autobus *sm inv* bus.
auto'carro *sm* lorry (*BRIT*), truck.
autocertificazi'one [autotʃertifikat'tsjone] *sf* self-declaration.
autocis'terna [autotʃis'tɛrna] *sf* tanker.
autoco'lonna *sf* convoy.
autocon'trollo *sm* self-control.
autocopia'tivo, a *ag*: **carta** ~**a** carbonless paper.
autocorri'era *sf* coach, bus.
auto'cratico, a, ci, che *ag* autocratic.
auto'critica, che *sf* self-criticism.
au'toctono, a *ag*, *sm/f* native.
autodemolizi'one [autodemolit'tsjone] *sf* breaker's yard (*BRIT*).
autodi'datta, i, e *sm/f* autodidact, self-taught person.
autodi'fesa *sf* self-defence.
autoferrotranvi'ario, a *ag* public transport *cpd*.
autogesti'one [autodʒes'tjone] *sf* worker management.
autoges'tito, a [autodʒes'tito] *ag* under worker management.
au'tografo, a *ag*, *sm* autograph.
auto'grill *sm inv* motorway café (*BRIT*), roadside restaurant (*US*).
autoim'mune *ag* autoimmune.
autolesio'nismo *sm* (*fig*) self-destruction.
auto'linea *sf* bus route.
au'toma, i *sm* automaton.

auto'matico, a, ci, che *ag* automatic ♦ *sm* (*bottone*) snap fastener; (*fucile*) automatic; **selezione** ~**a** (*TEL*) direct dialling.

automazi'one [automat'tsjone] *sf*: ~ **delle procedure d'ufficio** office automation.

automedicazi'one [automedikat'tsjone] *sf* (*medicine, farmaci*): **medicinale di** ~ self-medication.

auto'mezzo [auto'mɛddzo] *sm* motor vehicle.

auto'mobile *sf* (motor) car; ~ **da corsa** racing car (*BRIT*), race car (*US*).

automobi'lismo *sm* (*gen*) motoring; (*SPORT*) motor racing.

automobi'lista, i, e *sm/f* motorist.

automobi'listico, a, ci, che *ag* car *cpd* (*BRIT*), automobile *cpd* (*US*); (*sport*) motor *cpd*.

autono'leggio [autono'leddʒo] *sm* car hire (*BRIT*), car rental.

autono'mia *sf* autonomy; (*di volo*) range.

au'tonomo, a *ag* autonomous; (*sindacato, pensiero*) independent.

auto'parco, chi *sm* (*parcheggio*) car park (*BRIT*), parking lot (*US*); (*insieme di automezzi*) transport fleet.

auto'pompa *sf* fire engine.

autop'sia *sf* post-mortem (examination), autopsy.

auto'radio *sf inv* (*apparecchio*) car radio; (*autoveicolo*) radio car.

au'tore, 'trice *sm/f* author; **l'**~ **del furto** the person who committed the robbery; **diritti d'**~ copyright *sg*; (*compenso*) royalties.

autoregolamentazi'one [autoregolamentat'tsjone] *sf* self-regulation.

auto'revole *ag* authoritative; (*persona*) influential.

autori'messa *sf* garage.

autorità *sf inv* authority.

autori'tratto *sm* self-portrait.

autoriz'zare [autorid'dzare] *vt* to authorize, give permission for.

autorizzazi'one [autoriddzat'tsjone] *sf* authorization; ~ **a procedere** (*DIR*) authorization to proceed.

autos'catto *sm* (*FOT*) timer.

autos'contro *sm* dodgem car (*BRIT*), bumper car (*US*).

autoscu'ola *sf* driving school.

autosno'dato *sm* articulated vehicle.

autos'top *sm* hitchhiking.

autostop'pista, i, e *sm/f* hitchhiker.

autos'trada *sf* motorway (*BRIT*), highway (*US*); ~ **informatica** information superhighway.

autosuffici'ente [autosuffi'tʃɛnte] *ag* self-sufficient.

autosuffici'enza [autosuffi'tʃɛntsa] *sf* self-sufficiency.

autotassazi'one [autotassat'tsjone] *sf* system of taxation where individual himself assesses and pays tax due.

auto'treno *sm* articulated lorry (*BRIT*), semi (trailer) (*US*).

autove'icolo *sm* motor vehicle.

auto'velox® *sm inv* (police) speed camera.

autovet'tura *sf* (motor) car.

autun'nale *ag* (*di autunno*) autumn *cpd*; (*da autunno*) autumnal.

au'tunno *sm* autumn.

AV *sigla* = *Avellino*.

a/v *abbr* = **a vista**.

aval'lare *vt* (*FINANZA*) to guarantee; (*fig: sostenere*) to back; (: *confermare*) to confirm.

a'vallo *sm* (*FINANZA*) guarantee.

avam'braccio, *pl*(*f*) **-cia** [avam'brattʃo] *sm* forearm.

avam'posto *sm* (*MIL*) outpost.

A'vana *sf*: **l'**~ Havana.

a'vana *sm inv* (*sigaro*) Havana (cigar); (*colore*) Havana brown.

avangu'ardia *sf* vanguard; (*ARTE*) avant-garde.

avansco'perta *sf* (*MIL*) reconnaissance; **andare in** ~ to reconnoitre.

a'vanti *av* (*stato in luogo*) in front; (*moto: andare, venire*) forward; (*tempo: prima*) before ♦ *prep* (*luogo*): ~ **a** before, in front of; (*tempo*): ~ **Cristo** before Christ ♦ *escl* (*entrate*) come (*o* go) in!; (*MIL*) forward!; (*coraggio*) come on! ♦ *sm inv* (*SPORT*) forward; **il giorno** ~ the day before; ~ **e indietro** backwards and forwards; **andare** ~ to go forward; (*continuare*) to go on; (*precedere*) to go (*on*) ahead; (*orologio*) to be fast; **essere** ~ **negli studi** to be well advanced with one's studies; **mandare** ~ **la famiglia** to provide for one's family; **mandare** ~ **un'azienda** to run a business; ~ **il prossimo!** next please!

avan'treno *sm* (*AUT*) front chassis.

avanza'mento [avantsa'mento] *sm* (*gen*) advance; (*fig*) progress; promotion.

avan'zare [avan'tsare] *vt* (*spostare in avanti*) to move forward, advance; (*domanda*) to put forward; (*promuovere*) to promote; (*essere creditore*): ~ **qc da qn** to be owed sth by sb ♦ *vi* (*andare avanti*) to move forward, advance; (*fig: progredire*) to make progress; (*essere d'avanzo*) to be left, remain; **basta e avanza** that's more than enough.

avan'zato, a [avan'tsato] *ag* (*teoria, tecnica*)

advanced ♦ *sf* (*MIL*) advance; **in età ~a** advanced in years, up in years.

a'**vanzo** [a'vantso] *sm* (*residuo*) remains *pl*, left-overs *pl*; (*MAT*) remainder; (*COMM*) surplus; (*eccedenza di bilancio*) profit carried forward; **averne d'~ di qc** to have more than enough of sth; **~ di cassa** cash in hand; **~ di galera** (*fig*) jailbird.

ava'**ria** *sf* (*guasto*) damage; (*: meccanico*) breakdown.

avari'**ato, a** *ag* (*merce*) damaged; (*cibo*) off.

ava'**rizia** [ava'rittsja] *sf* avarice; **crepi l'~!** to hang with the expense!

a'**varo, a** *ag* avaricious, miserly ♦ *sm* miser.

a'**vena** *sf* oats *pl*.

========================= PAROLA CHIAVE

a'**vere** *sm* (*COMM*) credit; **gli ~i** (*ricchezze*) wealth *sg*, possessions
♦ *vt* **1** (*possedere*) to have; **ha due bambini/una bella casa** she has (got) two children/a lovely house; **ha i capelli lunghi** he has (got) long hair; **non ho da mangiare/bere** I've (got) nothing to eat/drink, I don't have anything to eat/drink
2 (*indossare*) to wear, have on; **aveva una maglietta rossa** he was wearing *o* he had on a red T-shirt; **ha gli occhiali** he wears *o* has glasses
3 (*ricevere*) to get; **hai avuto l'assegno?** did you get *o* have you had the cheque?
4 (*età, dimensione*) to be; **ha 9 anni** he is 9 (years old); **la stanza ha 3 metri di lunghezza** the room is 3 metres in length; *vedi* **fame; paura; sonno** *etc*
5 (*tempo*): **quanti ne abbiamo oggi?** what's the date today?; **ne hai per molto?** will you be long?
6 (*fraseologia*): **avercela con qn** to be angry with sb; **cos'hai?** what's wrong *o* what's the matter (with you)?; **non ha niente a che vedere** *o* **fare con me** it's got nothing to do with me
♦ *vb aus* **1** to have; **aver bevuto/mangiato** to have drunk/eaten; **l'ho già visto** I have seen it already; **l'ho visto ieri** I saw it yesterday; **ci ha creduto?** did he believe it?
2 (+ *da* + *infinito*): **~ da fare qc** to have to do sth; **non ho niente da dire** I have nothing to say; **non hai che da chiederlo** you only have to ask him.

avia'**tore, 'trice** *sm/f* aviator, pilot.

aviazi'**one** [avjat'tsjone] *sf* aviation; (*MIL*) air force; **~ civile** civil aviation.

avicol'**tura** *sf* bird breeding; (*di pollame*) poultry farming.

avidi'**tà** *sf* eagerness; greed.

'**avido, a** *ag* eager; (*peg*) greedy.

avi'**ere** *sm* (*MIL*) airman.

avitami'**nosi** *sf* vitamin deficiency.

'**avo** *sm* (*antenato*) ancestor; **i nostri ~i** our ancestors.

avo'**cado** *sm* avocado.

a'**vorio** *sm* ivory.

a'**vulso, a** *ag*: **parole ~e dal contesto** words out of context; **~ dalla società** (*fig*) cut off from society.

Avv. *abbr* = **avvocato**.

avva'**lersi** *vr*: **~ di** to avail o.s. of.

avvalla'**mento** *sm* sinking *no pl*; (*effetto*) depression.

avvalo'**rare** *vt* to confirm.

avvantaggi'**are** [avvantad'dʒare] *vt* to favour (*BRIT*), favor (*US*); **~rsi di** (*trarre vantaggio*): **~rsi di** to take advantage of; (*prevalere*): **~rsi negli affari/sui concorrenti** to get ahead in business/of one's competitors.

avve'**dersi** *vr*: **~ di qn/qc** to notice sb/sth.

avve'**duto, a** *ag* (*accorto*) prudent; (*scaltro*) astute.

avvelena'**mento** *sm* poisoning.

avvele'**nare** *vt* to poison.

avve'**nente** *ag* attractive, charming.

avve'**nenza** [avve'nentsa] *sf* good looks *pl*.

av'**vengo** *etc vb vedi* **avvenire**.

avveni'**mento** *sm* event.

avve'**nire** *vi, vb impers* to happen, occur ♦ *sm* future.

av'**venni** *etc vb vedi* **avvenire**.

avven'**tarsi** *vr*: **~ su** *o* **contro qn/qc** to hurl o.s. *o* rush at sb/sth.

avven'**tato, a** *ag* rash, reckless.

avven'**tizio, a** [avven'tittsjo] *ag* (*impiegato*) temporary; (*guadagno*) casual.

av'**vento** *sm* advent, coming; (*REL*): **l'A~** Advent.

avven'**tore** *sm* customer.

avven'**tura** *sf* adventure; (*amorosa*) affair; **avere spirito d'~** to be adventurous.

avventu'**rarsi** *vr* to venture.

avventuri'**ero, a** *sm/f* adventurer/adventuress.

avventu'**roso, a** *ag* adventurous.

avve'**nuto, a** *pp di* **avvenire**.

avve'**rarsi** *vr* to come true.

av'**verbio** *sm* adverb.

avver'**rò** *etc vb vedi* **avvenire**.

avver'**sare** *vt* to oppose.

avver'**sario, a** *ag* opposing ♦ *sm* opponent, adversary.

avversi'**one** *sf* aversion.

avversi'**tà** *sf inv* adversity, misfortune.

av'verso, a *ag* (*contrario*) contrary; (*sfavorevole*) unfavourable (*BRIT*), unfavorable (*US*).

avver'tenza [avver'tɛntsa] *sf* (*ammonimento*) warning; (*cautela*) care; (*premessa*) foreword; ~**e** *sfpl* (*istruzioni per l'uso*) instructions.

avverti'mento *sm* warning.

avver'tire *vt* (*avvisare*) to warn; (*rendere consapevole*) to inform, notify; (*percepire*) to feel.

av'vezzo, a [av'vettso] *ag*: ~ **a** used to.

avvia'mento *sm* (*atto*) starting; (*effetto*) start; (*AUT*) starting; (: *dispositivo*) starter; (*COMM*) goodwill.

avvi'are *vt* (*mettere sul cammino*) to direct; (*impresa, trattative*) to begin, start; (*motore*) to start; ~**rsi** *vr* to set off, set out.

avvicenda'mento [avvitʃenda'mento] *sm* alternation; (*AGR*) rotation; **c'è molto** ~ **di personale** there is a high turnover of staff.

avvicen'dare [avvitʃen'dare] *vt*, ~**rsi** *vr* to alternate.

avvicina'mento [avvitʃina'mento] *sm* approach.

avvici'nare [avvitʃi'nare] *vt* to bring near; (*trattare con: persona*) to approach; ~**rsi** *vr*: ~**rsi (a qn/qc)** to approach (sb/sth), draw near (to sb/sth); (*somigliare*) to be similar (to sb/sth), be close (to sb/sth).

avvi'lente *ag* (*umiliante*) humiliating; (*scoraggiante*) discouraging, disheartening.

avvili'mento *sm* humiliation; disgrace; discouragement.

avvi'lire *vt* (*umiliare*) to humiliate; (*degradare*) to disgrace; (*scoraggiare*) to dishearten, discourage; ~**rsi** *vr* (*abbattersi*) to lose heart.

avvilup'pare *vt* (*avvolgere*) to wrap up; (*ingarbugliare*) to entangle.

avvinaz'zato, a [avvinat'tsato] *ag* drunk.

avvin'cente [avvin'tʃɛnte] *ag* (*film, racconto*) enthralling.

av'vincere [av'vintʃere] *vt* to charm, enthral.

avvinghi'are [avvin'gjare] *vt* to clasp; ~**rsi** *vr*: ~**rsi a** to cling to.

av'vinsi *etc vb vedi* **avvincere**.

av'vinto, a *pp di* **avvincere**.

av'vio *sm* start, beginning; **dare l'**~ **a qc** to start sth off; **prendere l'**~ to get going, get under way.

avvi'saglia [avvi'zaʎʎa] *sf* (*sintomo: di temporale etc*) sign; (*di malattia*) manifestation, sign, symptom; (*scaramuccia*) skirmish.

avvi'sare *vt* (*far sapere*) to inform; (*mettere in guardia*) to warn.

avvisa'tore *sm* (*apparecchio d'allarme*) alarm; ~ **acustico** horn; ~ **d'incendio** fire alarm.

av'viso *sm* warning; (*annuncio*) announcement; (*affisso*) notice; (*inserzione pubblicitaria*) advertisement; **a mio** ~ in my opinion; **mettere qn sull'**~ to put sb on their guard; **fino a nuovo** ~ until further notice; ~ **di consegna/spedizione** (*COMM*) delivery/consignment note; ~ **di garanzia** (*DIR*) notification (*of impending investigation and of the right to name a defence laywer*); ~ **di pagamento** (*COMM*) payment advice.

avvista'mento *sm* sighting.

avvis'tare *vt* to sight.

avvi'tare *vt* to screw down (*o* in).

avviz'zire [avvit'tsire] *vi* to wither.

avvo'cato, 'essa *sm/f* (*DIR*) barrister (*BRIT*), lawyer; (*fig*) defender, advocate; ~ **del diavolo: fare l'**~ **del diavolo** to play devil's advocate; ~ **difensore** counsel for the defence; ~ **di parte civile** counsel for the plaintiff.

av'volgere [av'vɔldʒere] *vt* to roll up; (*bobina*) to wind up; (*avviluppare*) to wrap up; ~**rsi** *vr* (*avvilupparsi*) to wrap o.s. up.

avvol'gibile [avvol'dʒibile] *sm* roller blind (*BRIT*), blind.

avvolgi'mento [avvoldʒi'mento] *sm* winding.

av'volsi *etc vb vedi* **avvolgere**.

av'volto, a *pp di* **avvolgere**.

avvol'toio *sm* vulture.

aza'lea [addza'lɛa] *sf* azalea.

Azerbaigi'an [addzɛrbai'dʒan] *sm* Azerbaijan.

azerbaig'iano, a [addzɛrbai'dʒano] *ag* Azerbaijani ♦ *sm/f* (*abitante*) Azerbaijani ♦ *sm* (*LING*) Azerbaijani.

a'zero, a [ad'dzɛro] *sm/f* Azeri.

azi'enda [ad'dzjɛnda] *sf* business, firm, concern; ~ **agricola** farm; ~ (**autonoma**) **di soggiorno** tourist board; ~ **a partecipazione statale** *business in which the State has a financial interest*; ~**e pubbliche** public corporations.

azien'dale [addzjen'dale] *ag* company *cpd*; **organizzazione** ~ business administration.

azio'nare [attsjo'nare] *vt* to activate.

azio'nario, a [attsjo'narjo] *ag* share *cpd*; **capitale** ~ share capital; **mercato** ~ stock market.

azi'one [at'tsjone] *sf* action; (*COMM*) share;

~ **sindacale** industrial action; **~i preferenziali** preference shares (*BRIT*), preferred stock *sg* (*US*).
azio'nista, i, e [attsjo'nista] *sm/f* (*COMM*) shareholder.
a'zoto [ad'dzɔto] *sm* nitrogen.
az'teco, a, ci, che [as'tɛko] *ag*, *sm/f* Aztec.
azzan'nare [attsan'nare] *vt* to sink one's teeth into.
azzar'dare [addzar'dare] *vt* (*soldi, vita*) to risk, hazard; (*domanda, ipotesi*) to hazard, venture; **~rsi** *vr*: **~rsi a fare** to dare (to) do.
azzar'dato, a [addzar'dato] *ag* (*impresa*) risky; (*risposta*) rash.
az'zardo [ad'dzardo] *sm* risk; **gioco d'~** game of chance.
azzec'care [attsek'kare] *vt* (*bersaglio*) to hit, strike; (*risposta, pronostico*) to get right; (*fig: indovinare*) to guess.
azzera'mento [addzera'mento] *sm* (*INFORM*) reset.
azze'rare [addze'rare] *vt* (*MAT, FISICA*) to make equal to zero, reduce to zero; (*TECN: strumento*) to (re)set to zero.
'azzimo, a ['addzimo] *ag* unleavened ♦ *sm* unleavened bread.
azzop'pare [attsop'pare] *vt* to lame, make lame.
Az'zorre [ad'dzorre] *sfpl*: **le ~** the Azores.
azzuf'farsi [attsuf'farsi] *vr* to come to blows.
az'zurro, a [ad'dzurro] *ag* blue ♦ *sm* (*colore*) blue; **gli ~i** (*SPORT*) the Italian national team.
azzur'rognolo, a [addzur'roɲɲolo] *ag* bluish.

B b

B, b [bi] *sf o m inv* (*lettera*) B, b; **~ come Bologna** ≈ B for Benjamin (*BRIT*), B for Baker (*US*).
BA *sigla* = *Bari*.
ba'bau *sm inv* ogre, bogey man.
bab'beo *sm* simpleton.
'babbo *sm* (*fam*) dad, daddy; **B~ Natale** Father Christmas.
bab'buccia, ce [bab'buttʃa] *sf* slipper; (*per neonati*) bootee.
babbu'ino *sm* baboon.

babilo'nese *ag*, *sm/f* Babylonian.
Babi'lonia *sf* Babylonia.
ba'bordo *sm* (*NAUT*) port side.
baby'sitter ['beɪbɪsitə*] *sm/f inv* baby-sitter.
ba'cato, a *ag* worm-eaten, rotten; (*fig: mente*) diseased; (: *persona*) corrupt.
'bacca, che *sf* berry.
baccalà *sm* dried salted cod; (*fig: peg*) dummy.
bac'cano *sm* din, clamour (*BRIT*), clamor (*US*).
bac'cello [bat'tʃɛllo] *sm* pod.
bac'chetta [bak'ketta] *sf* (*verga*) stick, rod; (*di direttore d'orchestra*) baton; (*di tamburo*) drumstick; **comandare a ~** to rule with a rod of iron; **~ magica** magic wand.
ba'checa, che [ba'kɛka] *sf* (*mobile*) showcase, display case; (*UNIVERSITÀ, in ufficio*) notice board (*BRIT*), bulletin board (*US*).
bacia'mano [batʃa'mano] *sm*: **fare il ~ a qn** to kiss sb's hand.
baci'are [ba'tʃare] *vt* to kiss; **~rsi** *vr* to kiss (one another).
ba'cillo [ba'tʃillo] *sm* bacillus, germ.
baci'nella [batʃi'nɛlla] *sf* basin.
ba'cino [ba'tʃino] *sm* basin; (*MINERALOGIA*) field, bed; (*ANAT*) pelvis; (*NAUT*) dock; **~ carbonifero** coalfield; **~ di carenaggio** dry dock; **~ petrolifero** oilfield.
'bacio ['batʃo] *sm* kiss.
'baco, chi *sm* worm; **~ da seta** silkworm.
'bada *sf*: **tenere qn a ~** (*tener d'occhio*) to keep an eye on sb; (*tenere a distanza*) to hold sb at bay.
ba'dare *vi* (*fare attenzione*) to take care, be careful; **~ a** (*occuparsi di*) to look after, take care of; (*dar ascolto*) to pay attention to; **è un tipo che non bada a spese** money is no object to him; **bada ai fatti tuoi!** mind your own business!
ba'dia *sf* abbey.
ba'dile *sm* shovel.
'baffi *smpl* moustache *sg*, mustache *sg* (*US*); (*di animale*) whiskers; **leccarsi i ~** to lick one's lips; **ridere sotto i ~** to laugh up one's sleeve.
bagagli'aio [bagaʎ'ʎajo] *sm* luggage van (*BRIT*) *o* car (*US*); (*AUT*) boot (*BRIT*), trunk (*US*).
ba'gaglio [ba'gaʎʎo] *sm* luggage *no pl*, baggage *no pl*; **fare/disfare i ~i** to pack/ unpack; **~ a mano** hand luggage.
bagat'tella *sf* trifle, trifling matter.
Bag'dad *sf* Baghdad.
baggia'nata [baddʒa'nata] *sf* foolish action; **dire ~e** to talk nonsense.
bagli'ore [baʎ'ʎore] *sm* flash, dazzling light;

un ~ di speranza a sudden ray of hope.

ba'gnante [baɲ'ɲante] *sm/f* bather.

ba'gnare [baɲ'ɲare] *vt* to wet; (*inzuppare*) to soak; (*innaffiare*) to water; (*sog: fiume*) to flow through; (*: mare*) to wash, bathe; (*brindare*) to drink to, toast; **~rsi** *vr* (*al mare*) to go swimming *o* bathing; (*in vasca*) to have a bath.

ba'gnato, a [baɲ'ɲato] *ag* wet; **era come un pulcino ~** he looked like a drowned rat.

ba'gnino [baɲ'ɲino] *sm* lifeguard.

'bagno ['baɲɲo] *sm* bath; (*locale*) bathroom; **~i** *smpl* (*stabilimento*) baths; **fare il ~** to have a bath; (*nel mare*) to go swimming *o* bathing; **fare il ~ a qn** to give sb a bath; **mettere a ~** to soak.

bagnoma'ria [baɲɲoma'ria] *sm*: **cuocere a ~** to cook in a double saucepan (*BRIT*) *o* double boiler (*US*).

bagnoschi'uma [baɲɲoskj'uma] *sm inv* bubble bath.

Ba'hama [ba'ama] *sfpl*: **le ~** the Bahamas.

Bah'rein [ba'rein] *sm*: **il ~** Bahrain *o* Bahrein.

'baia *sf* bay.

baio'netta *sf* bayonet.

'baita *sf* mountain hut.

balaus'trata *sf* balustrade.

balbet'tare *vi* to stutter, stammer; (*bimbo*) to babble ♦ *vt* to stammer out.

bal'buzie [bal'buttsje] *sf* stammer.

balbuzi'ente [balbut'tsjɛnte] *ag* stuttering, stammering.

Bal'cani *smpl*: **i ~** the Balkans.

bal'canico, a, ci, che *ag* Balkan.

bal'cone *sm* balcony.

baldac'chino [baldak'kino] *sm* canopy; **letto a ~** four-poster (bed).

bal'danza [bal'dantsa] *sf* self-confidence; boldness.

'baldo, a *ag* bold, daring.

bal'doria *sf*: **fare ~** to have a riotous time.

Bale'ari *sfpl*: **le isole ~** the Balearic Islands.

ba'lena *sf* whale.

bale'nare *vb impers*: **balena** there's lightning ♦ *vi* to flash; **mi balenò un'idea** an idea flashed through my mind.

baleni'era *sf* (*per la caccia*) whaler, whaling ship.

ba'leno *sm* flash of lightning; **in un ~** in a flash.

ba'lera *sf* (*locale*) dance hall; (*pista*) dance floor.

ba'lestra *sf* crossbow.

'balia *sf* wet-nurse; **~ asciutta** nanny.

ba'lìa *sf*: **in ~ di** at the mercy of; **essere lasciato in ~ di se stesso** to be left to one's own devices.

ba'lilla *sm inv* (*STORIA*) *member of Fascist youth group.*

ba'listico, a, ci, che *ag* ballistic ♦ *sf* ballistics *sg*; **perito ~** ballistics expert.

'balla *sf* (*di merci*) bale; (*fandonia*) (tall) story.

bal'labile *sm* dance number, dance tune.

bal'lare *vt, vi* to dance.

bal'lata *sf* ballad.

balla'toio *sm* (*terrazzina*) gallery.

balle'rina *sf* dancer; ballet dancer; (*scarpa*) pump; **~ di rivista** chorus girl.

balle'rino *sm* dancer; ballet dancer.

bal'letto *sm* ballet.

'ballo *sm* dance; (*azione*) dancing *no pl*; **~ in maschera** *o* **mascherato** fancy-dress ball; **essere in ~** (*fig: persona*) to be involved; (*: cosa*) to be at stake; **tirare in ~ qc** to bring sth up, raise sth.

ballot'taggio [ballot'taddʒo] *sm* (*POL*) second ballot.

balne'are *ag* seaside *cpd*; (*stagione*) bathing.

ba'locco, chi *sm* toy.

ba'lordo, a *ag* stupid, senseless.

bal'samico, a, ci, che *ag* (*aria, brezza*) balmy; **pomata ~a** balsam.

'balsamo *sm* (*aroma*) balsam; (*lenimento, fig*) balm; (*per capelli*) (hair) conditioner.

'baltico, a, ci, che *ag* Baltic; **il (mar) B~** the Baltic (Sea).

balu'ardo *sm* bulwark.

'balza ['baltsa] *sf* (*dirupo*) crag; (*di stoffa*) frill.

bal'zano, a [bal'tsano] *ag* (*persona, idea*) queer, odd.

bal'zare [bal'tsare] *vi* to bounce; (*lanciarsi*) to jump, leap; **la verità balza agli occhi** the truth of the matter is obvious.

'balzo ['baltso] *sm* bounce; jump, leap; (*del terreno*) crag; **prendere la palla al ~** (*fig*) to seize one's opportunity.

bam'bagia [bam'badʒa] *sf* (*ovatta*) cotton wool (*BRIT*), absorbent cotton (*US*); (*cascame*) cotton waste; **tenere qn nella ~** (*fig*) to mollycoddle sb.

bam'bina *sf vedi* **bambino**.

bambi'naia *sf* nanny, nurse(maid).

bam'bino, a *sm/f* child; **fare il ~** to behave childishly.

bam'boccio [bam'bɔttʃo] *sm* plump child; (*pupazzo*) rag doll.

'bambola *sf* doll.

bambo'lotto *sm* male doll.

bambù *sm* bamboo.

ba'nale *ag* banal, commonplace.

banalità *sf inv* banality.

ba'nana *sf* banana.
ba'nano *sm* banana tree.
'banca, che *sf* bank; ~ d'affari merchant bank; ~ (di) dati data bank.
banca'rella *sf* stall.
ban'cario, a *ag* banking, bank *cpd* ♦ *sm* bank clerk.
banca'rotta *sf* bankruptcy; fare ~ to go bankrupt.
bancarotti'ere *sm* bankrupt.
ban'chetto [ban'ketto] *sm* banquet.
banchi'ere [ban'kjɛre] *sm* banker.
ban'china [ban'kina] *sf (di porto)* quay; *(per pedoni, ciclisti)* path; *(di stazione)* platform; ~ cedevole *(AUT)* soft verge *(BRIT)* o shoulder *(US)*; ~ spartitraffico *(AUT)* central reservation *(BRIT)*, median (strip) *(US)*.
ban'chisa [ban'kiza] *sf* pack ice.
'banco, chi *sm* bench; *(di negozio)* counter; *(di mercato)* stall; *(di officina)* (work)bench; *(GEO, banca)* bank; sotto ~ *(fig) under the counter*; tenère il ~ *(nei giochi)* to be (the) banker; tener ~ *(fig)* to monopolize the conversation; medicinali da ~ over-the-counter medicines; ~ di chiesa pew; ~ di corallo coral reef; ~ degli imputati dock; ~ del Lotto lottery-ticket office; ~ di prova *(fig)* testing ground; ~ dei testimoni witness box *(BRIT)* o stand *(US)*.
banco'giro [banko'dʒiro] *sm* credit transfer.
'Bancomat ® *sm inv* automated banking; *(tessera)* cash card.
banco'nota *sf* banknote.
'banda *sf* band; *(di stoffa)* band, stripe; *(lato, parte)* side; *(di calcolatore)* tape; ~ perforata punch tape.
banderu'ola *sf (METEOR)* weathercock, weathervane; essere una ~ *(fig)* to be fickle.
bandi'era *sf* flag, banner; battere ~ italiana *(nave etc)* to fly the Italian flag; cambiare ~ *(fig)* to change sides; ~ di comodo flag of convenience.
ban'dire *vt* to proclaim; *(esiliare)* to exile; *(fig)* to dispense with.
ban'dito *sm* outlaw, bandit.
bandi'tore *sm (di aste)* auctioneer.
'bando *sm* proclamation; *(esilio)* exile, banishment; mettere al ~ qn to exile sb; *(fig)* to freeze sb out; ~ alle ciance! that's enough talk!
'bandolo *sm (di matassa)* end; trovare il ~ della matassa *(fig)* to find the key to the problem.
Bang'kok [ban'kɔk] *sf* Bangkok.

Bangla'desh [bangla'dɛʃ] *sm*: il ~ Bangladesh.
bar *sm inv* bar.
'bara *sf* coffin.
ba'racca, che *sf* shed, hut; *(peg)* hovel; mandare avanti la ~ to keep things going; piantare ~ e burattini to throw everything up.
barac'cato, a *sm/f person living in temporary camp*.
barac'chino [barak'kino] *sm (chiosco)* stall; *(apparecchio)* CB radio.
barac'cone *sm* booth, stall; ~i *smpl (luna park)* funfair *sg (BRIT)*, amusement park; fenomeno da ~ circus freak.
barac'copoli *sf inv* shanty town.
bara'onda *sf* hubbub, bustle.
ba'rare *vi* to cheat.
'baratro *sm* abyss.
barat'tare *vt*: ~ qc con to barter sth for, swap sth for.
ba'ratto *sm* barter.
ba'rattolo *sm (di latta)* tin; *(di vetro)* jar; *(di coccio)* pot.
'barba *sf* beard, farsi la ~ to shave; farla in ~ a qn *(fig)* to fool sb; servire qn di ~ e capelli *(fig)* to teach sb a lesson; che ~! what a bore!
barbabi'etola *sf* beetroot *(BRIT)*, beet *(US)*; ~ da zucchero sugar beet.
Bar'bados *sfsg* Barbados.
bar'barico, a, ci, che *ag (invasione)* barbarian; *(usanze, metodi)* barbaric.
bar'barie *sf* barbarity.
'barbaro, a *ag* barbarous ♦ *sm* barbarian; i B~ the Barbarians.
'barbecue ['baːbikjuː] *sm inv* barbecue.
barbi'ere *sm* barber.
barbi'turico, a, ci, che *ag* barbituric ♦ *sm* barbiturate.
bar'bone *sm (cane)* poodle; *(vagabondo)* tramp.
bar'buto, a *ag* bearded.
'barca, che *sf* boat; una ~ di *(fig)* heaps of, tons of; mandare avanti la ~ *(fig)* to keep things going; ~ a remi rowing boat *(BRIT)*, rowboat *(US)*; ~ a vela sailing boat *(BRIT)*, sailboat *(US)*.
barcai'olo *sm* boatman.
barcame'narsi *vr (nel lavoro)* to get by; *(a parole)* to beat about the bush.
Barcel'lona [bartʃel'lona] *sf* Barcelona.
barcol'lare *vi* to stagger.
bar'cone *sm (per ponti di barche)* pontoon.
ba'rella *sf (lettiga)* stretcher.
'Barents: il mar di ~ *sm* the Barents Sea.
ba'rese *ag* of *(o* from) Bari.
bari'centro [bari'tʃentro] *sm* centre *(BRIT)* o

center (*US*) of gravity.
ba'rile *sm* barrel, cask.
ba'rista, i, e *sm/f* barman/barmaid; bar owner.
ba'ritono *sm* baritone.
bar'lume *sm* glimmer, gleam.
'baro *sm* (*CARTE*) cardsharp.
ba'rocco, a, chi, che *ag, sm* baroque.
ba'rometro *sm* barometer.
ba'rone *sm* baron; **i ~i della medicina** (*fig peg*) the top brass in the medical faculty.
baro'nessa *sf* baroness.
'barra *sf* bar; (*NAUT*) helm; (*segno grafico*) stroke.
bar'rare *vt* to bar.
barri'care *vt* to barricade.
barri'cata *sf* barricade; **essere dall'altra parte della ~** (*fig*) to be on the other side of the fence.
barri'era *sf* barrier; (*GEO*) reef; **la Grande B~ Corallina** the Great Barrier Reef.
bar'roccio [bar'rɔttʃo] *sm* cart.
ba'ruffa *sf* scuffle; **fare ~** to squabble.
barzel'letta [bardzel'letta] *sf* joke, funny story.
basa'mento *sm* (*parte inferiore, piedestallo*) base; (*TECN*) bed, base plate.
ba'sare *vt* to base, found; **~rsi** *vr:* **~rsi su** (*sog: fatti, prove*) to be based *o* founded on; (*: persona*) to base one's arguments on.
'basco, a, schi, sche *ag* Basque ♦ *sm/f* Basque ♦ *sm* (*lingua*) Basque; (*copricapo*) beret.
bas'culla *sf* weighing machine, weighbridge.
'base *sf* base; (*fig: fondamento*) basis; (*POL*) rank and file; **di ~** basic; **in ~ a** on the basis of, according to; **in ~ a ciò ...** on that basis ...; **a ~ di caffè** coffee-based; **essere alla ~ di qc** to be at the root of sth; **gettare le ~i per qc** to lay the basis *o* foundations for sth; **avere buone ~i** (*INS*) to have a sound educational background.
'baseball ['beisbɔːl] *sm* baseball.
ba'setta *sf* sideburn.
basi'lare *ag* basic, fundamental.
Basi'lea *sf* Basle.
ba'silica, che *sf* basilica.
ba'silico *sm* basil.
bas'sezza [bas'settsa] *sf* (*d'animo, di sentimenti*) baseness; (*azione*) base action.
'basso, a *ag* low; (*di statura*) short; (*meridionale*) southern ♦ *sm* bottom, lower part; (*MUS*) bass; **a occhi ~i** with eyes lowered; **a ~ prezzo** cheap; **scendere da ~** to go downstairs; **cadere in ~** (*fig*) to come down in the world; **la ~a Italia**

southern Italy; **il ~ Medioevo** the late Middle Ages.
basso'fondo, *pl* **bassi'fondi** *sm* (*GEO*) shallows *pl*; **i bassifondi (della città)** the seediest parts of the town.
bassorili'evo *sm* bas-relief.
bas'sotto, a *ag* squat ♦ *sm* (*cane*) dachshund.
bas'tardo, a *ag* (*animale, pianta*) hybrid, crossbreed; (*persona*) illegitimate, bastard (*peg*) ♦ *sm/f* illegitimate child, bastard (*peg*); (*cane*) mongrel.
bas'tare *vi, vb impers* to be enough, be sufficient; **~ a qn** to be enough for sb; **~ a se stesso** to be self-sufficient; **basta chiedere *o* che chieda a un vigile** you have only to *o* need only ask a policeman; **basti dire che ...** suffice it to say that ...; **basta!** that's enough!, that will do!; **basta così?** (*al bar etc*) will that be all?; **punto e basta!** and that's that!
basti'an *sm:* **~ contrario** awkward customer.
basti'mento *sm* ship, vessel.
basti'one *sm* bastion.
basto'nare *vt* to beat, thrash; **avere l'aria di un cane bastonato** to look crestfallen.
basto'nata *sf* blow (with a stick); **prendere qn a ~e** to give sb a good beating.
baston'cino [baston'tʃino] *sm* (*piccolo bastone*) small stick; (*TECN*) rod; (*SCI*) ski pole; **~i di pesce** (*CUC*) fish fingers (*BRIT*), fish sticks (*US*).
bas'tone *sm* stick; **~i** *smpl* (*CARTE*) *suit in Neapolitan pack of cards*; **~ da passeggio** walking stick; **mettere i ~i fra le ruote a qn** to put a spoke in sb's wheel.
bat'tage [ba'taʒ] *sm inv:* **~ promozionale** *o* **pubblicitario** publicity campaign.
bat'taglia [bat'taʎʎa] *sf* battle.
bat'taglio [bat'taʎʎo] *sm* (*di campana*) clapper; (*di porta*) knocker.
battagli'one [battaʎ'ʎone] *sm* battalion.
bat'tello *sm* boat.
bat'tente *sm* (*imposta: di porta*) wing, flap; (*: di finestra*) shutter; (*per bussare*) knocker; (*di orologio*) hammer; **chiudere i ~i** (*fig*) to shut up shop.
'battere *vt* to beat; (*grano*) to thresh; (*percorrere*) to scour; (*rintoccare: le ore*) to strike ♦ *vi* (*bussare*) to knock; (*urtare*): **~ contro** to hit *o* strike against; (*pioggia, sole*) to beat down; (*cuore*) to beat; (*TENNIS*) to serve; **~rsi** *vr* to fight; **~ le mani** to clap; **~ i piedi** to stamp one's feet; **~ su un argomento** to hammer home an argument; **~ a macchina** to type; **~ il marciapiede** (*peg*) to walk the

streets, be on the game; ~ **un rigore**
(*CALCIO*) to take a penalty; ~ **in testa**
(*AUT*) to knock; **in un batter d'occhio** in
the twinkling of an eye; **senza** ~ **ciglio**
without batting an eyelid; **battersela** to
run off.
batte'ria *sf* battery; (*MUS*) drums *pl*; ~ **da
cucina** pots and pans *pl*.
bat'terio *sm* bacterium; ~**i** *smpl* bacteria.
batteriolo'gia [batterjolo'dʒia] *sf*
bacteriology.
bat'tesimo *sm* (*sacramento*) baptism; (*rito*)
baptism, christening; **tenere qn a** ~ to be
godfather (*o* godmother) to sb.
battez'zare [batted'dzare] *vt* to baptize; to
christen.
battiba'leno *sm*: **in un** ~ in a flash.
batti'becco, chi *sm* squabble.
batticu'ore *sm* palpitations *pl*; **avere il** ~ to
be frightened to death.
bat'tigia [bat'tidʒa] *sf* water's edge.
batti'mano *sm* applause.
batti'panni *sm inv* carpet-beater.
battis'tero *sm* baptistry.
battis'trada *sm inv* (*di pneumatico*) tread;
(*di gara*) pacemaker.
battitap'peto *sm inv* upright vacuum
cleaner.
'battito *sm* beat, throb; ~ **cardiaco**
heartbeat; ~ **della pioggia/dell'orologio**
beating of the rain/ticking of the clock.
batti'tore *sm* (*CRICKET*) batsman;
(*BASEBALL*) batter; (*CACCIA*) beater.
batti'tura *sf* (*anche*: ~ **a macchina**) typing;
(*del grano*) threshing.
bat'tuta *sf* blow; (*di macchina da scrivere*)
stroke; (*MUS*) bar; beat; (*TEAT*) cue; (*di
caccia*) beating; (*POLIZIA*) combing,
scouring; (*TENNIS*) service; **fare una** ~ to
crack a joke, make a witty remark; **aver
la** ~ **pronta** (*fig*) to have a ready answer;
è ancora alle prime ~**e** it's just started.
ba'tuffolo *sm* wad.
ba'ule *sm* trunk; (*AUT*) boot (*BRIT*), trunk
(*US*).
bau'xite [bauk'site] *sf* bauxite.
'bava *sf* (*di animale*) slaver, slobber; (*di
lumaca*) slime; (*di vento*) breath.
bava'glino [bavaʎ'ʎino] *sm* bib.
ba'vaglio [ba'vaʎʎo] *sm* gag.
bava'rese *ag, smf* Bavarian.
'bavero *sm* collar.
Bavi'era *sf* Bavaria.
ba'zar [bad'dzar] *sm inv* bazaar.
baz'zecola [bad'dzekola] *sf* trifle.
bazzi'care [battsi'kare] *vt* (*persona*) to hang
about with; (*posto*) to hang about ♦ *vi*: ~
in/con to hang about/hang about with.

BCE *sigla f* (= *Banca centrale europea*) ECB.
be'arsi *vr*: ~ **di qc/a fare qc** to delight in
sth/in doing sth; ~ **alla vista di** to enjoy
looking at.
beati'tudine *sf* bliss.
be'ato, a *ag* blessed; (*fig*) happy; ~ **te!**
lucky you!
bebè *sm inv* baby.
bec'care *vt* to peck; (*fig: raffreddore*) to pick
up, catch; ~**rsi** *vr* (*fig*) to squabble.
bec'cata *sf* peck.
beccheggi'are [bekked'dʒare] *vi* to
pitch.
beccherò *etc* [bekke'rɔ] *vb vedi* **beccare**.
bec'chime [bek'kime] *sm* birdseed.
bec'chino [bek'kino] *sm* gravedigger.
'becco, chi *sm* beak, bill; (*di caffettiera etc*)
spout; lip; **mettere** ~ (*fam*) to butt in;
chiudi il ~! (*fam*) shut your mouth!; **non
ho il** ~ **di un quattrino** (*fam*) I'm broke.
Be'fana *sf old woman who, according to
legend, brings children their presents at
the Epiphany*; (*Epifania*) Epiphany; (*donna
brutta*): **b**~ hag, witch; *vedi nota nel riquadro*.

BEFANA

*Marking the end of the traditional 12 days of
Christmas on 6 January, the* **Befana**, *or the
feast of the Epiphany, is a national holiday in
Italy. It is named after the old woman who,
legend has it, comes down the chimney the
night before, bringing gifts to children who
have been good during the year and leaving
lumps of coal for those who have not.*

'beffa *sf* practical joke; **farsi** ~ *o* ~**e di qn**
to make a fool of sb.
bef'fardo, a *ag* scornful, mocking.
bef'fare *vt* (*anche*: ~**rsi di**) to make a fool
of, mock.
'bega, ghe *sf* quarrel.
'begli ['beʎʎi], **'bei** *ag vedi* **bello**.
beige [bɛʒ] *ag inv* beige.
Bei'rut *sf* Beirut.
bel *ag vedi* **bello**.
be'lare *vi* to bleat.
'belga, gi, ghe *ag, smf* Belgian.
'Belgio ['bɛldʒo] *sm*: **il** ~ Belgium.
Bel'grado *sf* Belgrade.
'bella *sf vedi* **bello**.
bel'lezza [bel'lettsa] *sf* beauty; **chiudere** *o*
finire qc in ~ to finish sth with a flourish;
che ~! fantastic!; **ho pagato la** ~ **di**
60.000 lire I paid 60,000 lire, no less.
belli'coso, a *ag* warlike.
bellige'rante [bellidʒe'rante] *ag* belligerent.
bellim'busto *sm* dandy.

======================= PAROLA CHIAVE

'bello, a (ag: dav sm bel + C, bell' + V,
bello + s impura, gn, pn, ps, x, z, pl bei +
C, begli + s impura etc o V) ag 1 (oggetto,
donna, paesaggio) beautiful; (uomo)
handsome; (tempo) beautiful, fine, lovely;
farsi ~ di qc to show off about sth; fare la
~a vita to have an easy life; le ~e arti
fine arts
2 (quantità): una ~a cifra a considerable
sum of money; un bel niente absolutely
nothing
3 (rafforzativo): è una truffa ~a e buona!
it's a real fraud!; oh ~a!, anche questa è
~a! (ironico) that's nice!; è bell'e finito it's
already finished
♦ sm/f (innamorato) sweetheart
♦ sm 1 (bellezza) beauty; (tempo) fine
weather
2: adesso viene il ~ now comes the best bit;
sul più ~ at the crucial point; cosa fai di ~?
are you doing anything interesting?
♦ sf (anche: ~a copia) fair copy; (SPORT,
CARTE) decider
♦ av: fa ~ the weather is fine, it's fine; alla
bell'e meglio somehow or other.

bellu'nese ag of (o from) Belluno.
'belva sf wild animal.
belve'dere sm inv panoramic viewpoint.
benché [ben'ke] cong although.
'benda sf bandage; (per gli occhi) blindfold.
ben'dare vt to bandage; to blindfold.
bendis'posto, a ag: ~ a qn/qc well
disposed towards sb/sth.
'bene av well; (completamente, affatto): è
ben difficile it's very difficult ♦ ag inv:
gente ~ well-to-do people ♦ sm good;
(COMM) asset; ~i smpl (averi) property sg,
estate sg; io sto ~/poco ~ I'm well/not
very well; va ~ all right; ben più lungo/
caro much longer/more expensive; lo
spero ~ I certainly hope so; volere un ~
dell'anima a qn to love sb very much; un
uomo per ~ a respectable man; fare ~ to
do the right thing; fare ~ a (salute) to be
good for; fare del ~ a qn to do sb a good
turn; di ~ in meglio better and better; ~i
ambientali environmental assets; ~i di
consumo consumer goods; ~i di consumo
durevole consumer durables; ~i culturali
cultural heritage; ~i immateriali
immaterial o intangible assets; ~i
patrimoniali fixed assets; ~i privati
private property sg; ~i pubblici public
property sg; ~i reali tangible assets.
bene'detto, a pp di benedire ♦ ag blessed,

holy.
bene'dire vt to bless; to consecrate; l'ho
mandato a farsi ~ (fig) I told him to go to
hell.
benedizi'one [benedit'tsjone] sf blessing.
benedu'cato, a ag well-mannered.
benefat'tore, 'trice sm/f benefactor/
benefactress.
benefi'cenza [benefi'tʃentsa] sf charity.
benefici'are [benefi'tʃare] vi: ~ di to benefit
by, benefit from.
benefici'ario, a [benefi'tʃarjo] ag, sm/f
beneficiary.
bene'ficio [bene'fitʃo] sm benefit; con ~
d'inventario (fig) with reservations.
be'nefico, a, ci, che ag beneficial;
charitable.
'Benelux sm: il ~ Benelux, the Benelux
countries.
beneme'renza [beneme'rentsa] sf merit.
bene'merito, a ag meritorious.
bene'placito [bene'platʃito] sm
(approvazione) approval; (permesso)
permission.
be'nessere sm well-being.
benes'tante ag well-to-do.
benes'tare sm consent, approval.
benevo'lenza [benevo'lentsa] sf
benevolence.
be'nevolo, a ag benevolent.
ben'godi sm land of plenty.
benia'mino, a sm/f favourite (BRIT),
favorite (US).
be'nigno, a [be'niɲɲo] ag kind, kindly;
(critica etc) favourable (BRIT), favorable
(US); (MED) benign.
benintenzio'nato, a [benintentsjo'nato] ag
well-meaning.
benin'teso av of course; ~ che cong
provided that.
benpen'sante sm/f conformist.
benser'vito sm: dare il ~ a qn (sul lavoro)
to give sb the sack, fire sb; (fig) to send
sb packing.
bensì cong but (rather).
benve'nuto, a ag, sm welcome; dare il ~ a
qn to welcome sb.
ben'visto, a ag: essere ~ (da) to be well
thought of (by).
benvo'lere vt: farsi ~ da tutti to win
everybody's affection; prendere a ~ qn/
qc to take a liking to sb/sth.
ben'zina [ben'dzina] sf petrol (BRIT), gas
(US); fare ~ to get petrol o gas; rimanere
senza ~ to run out of petrol o gas; ~
verde unleaded petrol, lead-free petrol.
benzi'naio [bendzi'najo] sm petrol (BRIT) o
gas (US) pump attendant.

be'one *sm* heavy drinker.
'bere *vt* to drink; (*assorbire*) to soak up; **questa volta non me la dai a ~!** I won't be taken in this time!
berga'masco, a, schi, sche *ag* of (*o* from) Bergamo.
'Bering ['beriŋ]: **il mar di ~** *sm* the Bering Sea.
ber'lina *sf* (*AUT*) saloon (car) (*BRIT*), sedan (*US*); **mettere alla ~** (*lig*) to hold up to ridicule.
Ber'lino *sf* Berlin; **~ est/ovest** East/West Berlin.
Ber'muda *sfpl:* **le ~** Bermuda *sg*.
ber'muda *smpl* (*calzoncini*) Bermuda shorts.
'Berna *sf* Bern.
ber'noccolo *sm* bump; (*inclinazione*) flair.
ber'retto *sm* cap.
berrò *etc vb vedi* **bere**.
bersagli'are [bersaʎ'ʎare] *vt* to shoot at; (*colpire ripetutamente, fig*) to bombard; **bersagliato dalla sfortuna** dogged by ill fortune.
bersagli'ere [bersaʎ'ʎɛre] *sm member of rifle regiment in Italian army*.
ber'saglio [ber'saʎʎo] *sm* target.
bes'temmia *sf* curse; (*REL*) blasphemy.
bestemmi'are *vi* to curse, swear; to blaspheme ♦ *vt* to curse, swear at; to blaspheme; **~ come un turco** to swear like a trooper.
'bestia *sf* animal; **lavorare come una ~** to work like a dog; **andare in ~** (*fig*) to fly into a rage; **una ~ rara** (*fig: persona*) an oddball; **~ da soma** beast of burden.
besti'ale *ag* bestial, brutish; (*fam*): **fa un caldo ~** it's terribly hot; **fa un freddo ~** it's bitterly cold.
besti'ame *sm* livestock; (*bovino*) cattle *pl*.
Bet'lemme *sf* Bethlehem.
betoni'era *sf* cement mixer.
'bettola *sf* (*peg*) dive.
be'tulla *sf* birch.
be'vanda *sf* drink, beverage.
bevi'tore, 'trice *sm/f* drinker.
'bevo *etc vb vedi* **bere**.
be'vuto, a *pp di* **bere** ♦ *sf* drink.
'bevvi *etc vb vedi* **bere**.
BG *sigla* = Bergamo.
BI *sigla f* = Banca d'Italia ♦ *sigla* = Biella.
bi'ada *sf* fodder.
bianche'ria [bjanke'ria] *sf* linen; **~ intima** underwear; **~ da donna** ladies' underwear, lingerie.
bi'anco, a, chi, che *ag* white; (*non scritto*) blank ♦ *sm* white; (*intonaco*) whitewash ♦ *sm/f* white, white man/woman; **in ~**
(*foglio, assegno*) blank; **in ~ e nero** (*TV, FOT*) black and white; **mangiare in ~** to follow a bland diet; **pesce in ~** boiled fish; **andare in ~** (*non riuscire*) to fail; (*in amore*) to be rejected; **notte ~a** o **in ~** sleepless night; **voce ~a** (*MUS*) treble (voice); **~ dell'uovo** egg-white.
bianco'segno [bjanko'seɲɲo] *sm* signature to a blank document.
biancos'pino *sm* hawthorn.
biasci'care [bjaʃʃi'kare] *vt* to mumble.
biasi'mare *vt* to disapprove of, censure.
'bibbia *sf* bible.
bibe'ron *sm inv* feeding bottle.
'bibita *sf* (soft) drink.
bibliogra'fia *sf* bibliography.
biblio'teca, che *sf* library; (*mobile*) bookcase.
bibliote'cario, a *sm/f* librarian.
bicame'rale *ag* (*POL*) two-chamber *cpd*.
bicarbo'nato *sm*: **~ (di sodio)** bicarbonate (of soda).
bicchi'ere [bik'kjɛre] *sm* glass; **è (facile) come bere un bicchier d'acqua** it's as easy as pie.
bici'cletta [bitʃi'kletta] *sf* bicycle; **andare in ~** to cycle.
bi'cipite [bi'tʃipite] *sm* bicep.
bidè *sm inv* bidet.
bi'dello, a *sm/f* (*INS*) janitor.
bi'det *sm inv* = **bidè**.
bido'nare *vt* (*fam: piantare in asso*) to let down; (: *imbrogliare*) to cheat, swindle.
bido'nata *sf* (*fam*) swindle.
bi'done *sm* drum, can; (*anche: ~ dell'immondizia*) (dust)bin; (*fam: truffa*) swindle; **fare un ~ a qn** (*fam*) to let sb down; to cheat sb.
bidon'ville [bidɔ'vil] *sf inv* shanty town.
bi'eco, a, chi, che *ag* sinister.
Bielo'russia *sf* Belarus.
bielo'russo, a *ag, sm/f* Belarussian.
bien'nale *ag* biennial ♦ *sf:* **la B~ di Venezia** the Venice Arts Festival; *vedi nota nel riquadro*.

BIENNALE DI VENEZIA

Dating back to 1895, the **Biennale di Venezia** *is an international festival of the contemporary arts. It takes place every two years in the "Giardini Pubblici". The various countries taking part each put on exhibitions in their own pavilions. There is a section dedicated to the work of young artists, as well as a special exhibition organized around a specific theme for that year.*

bi'ennio *sm* period of two years.
bi'erre *sm/f* member *of the Red Brigades.*
bi'etola *sf* beet.
bifo'cale *ag* bifocal.
bi'folco, a, chi, che *sm/f* (*peg*) bumpkin, yokel.
'bifora *sf* (*ARCHIT*) mullioned window.
bifor'carsi *vr* to fork.
biforcazi'one [biforkat'tsjone] *sf* fork.
bifor'cuto, a *ag* (*anche fig*) forked.
biga'mia *sf* bigamy.
'bigamo, a *ag* bigamous ♦ *sm/f* bigamist.
bighello'nare [bigello'nare] *vi* to loaf (about).
bighel'lone, a [bigel'lone] *sm/f* loafer.
bigiotte'ria [bidʒotte'ria] *sf* costume jewellery (*BRIT*) *o* jewelry (*US*); (*negozio*) jeweller's (shop) (*BRIT*) *o* jewelry store (*US*) (*selling only costume jewellery*).
bigli'ardo [biʎ'ʎardo] *sm* = **biliardo.**
bigliet'taio, a [biʎʎet'tajo] *sm/f* (*nei treni*) ticket inspector; (*in autobus etc*) conductor/conductress; (*CINE, TEAT*) box-office attendant.
bigliette'ria [biʎʎette'ria] *sf* (*di stazione*) ticket office; booking office; (*di teatro*) box office.
bigli'etto [biʎ'ʎetto] *sm* (*per viaggi, spettacoli etc*) ticket; (*cartoncino*) card; (*anche:* ~ **di banca**) (bank)note; ~ **d'auguri/da visita** greetings/visiting card; ~ **d'andata e ritorno** return (*BRIT*) *o* round-trip (*US*) ticket; ~ **omaggio** complimentary ticket.
bignè [biɲ'ɲɛ] *sm inv* cream puff.
bigo'dino *sm* roller, curler.
bi'gotto, a *ag* over-pious ♦ *sm/f* church fiend.
bi'kini *sm inv* bikini.
bi'lancia, ce [bi'lantʃa] *sf* (*pesa*) scales *pl*; (*: di precisione*) balance; (*dello zodiaco*): **B~** Libra; **essere della B~** to be Libra; ~ **commerciale/dei pagamenti** balance of trade/payments.
bilanci'are [bilan'tʃare] *vt* (*pesare*) to weigh; (*: fig*) to weigh up; ~ **le uscite e le entrate** (*COMM*) to balance expenditure and revenue.
bi'lancio [bi'lantʃo] *sm* (*COMM*) balance (sheet); (*statale*) budget; **far quadrare il** ~ to balance the books; **chiudere il** ~ **in attivo/passivo** to make a profit/loss; **fare il** ~ **di** (*fig*) to assess; ~ **consolidato** consolidated balance; ~ **consuntivo** (final) balance; ~ **preventivo** budget; ~ **pubblico** national budget; ~ **di verifica** trial balance.
bilate'rale *ag* bilateral.
'bile *sf* bile; (*fig*) rage, anger.
bili'ardo *sm* billiards *sg*; (*tavolo*) billiard table.
'bilico, chi *sm*: **essere in** ~ to be balanced; (*fig*) to be undecided; **tenere qn in** ~ to keep sb in suspense.
bi'lingue *ag* bilingual.
bili'one *sm* (*mille milioni*) thousand million, billion (*US*); (*milione di milioni*) billion (*BRIT*), trillion (*US*).
'bimbo, a *sm/f* little boy/girl.
bimen'sile *ag* fortnightly.
bimes'trale *ag* two-monthly, bimonthly.
bi'mestre *sm* two-month period; **ogni** ~ every two months.
bi'nario, a *ag* binary ♦ *sm* (*railway*) track *o* line; (*piattaforma*) platform; ~ **morto** dead-end track.
bi'nocolo *sm* binoculars *pl.*
bio... *prefisso* bio....
bio'chimica [bio'kimika] *sf* biochemistry.
biodegra'dabile *ag* biodegradable.
biodiversità *sf* biodiversity.
bio'etica *sf* bioethics *sg.*
bio'etico, a, ci, che *ag* bioethical.
bio'fabbrica *sf factory producing biological control agents.*
bio'fisica *sf* biophysics *sg.*
biogra'fia *sf* biography.
bio'grafico, a, ci, che *ag* biographical.
bi'ografo, a *sm/f* biographer.
biolo'gia [biolo'dʒia] *sf* biology.
bio'logico, a, ci, che [bio'lɔdʒiko] *ag* biological.
bi'ologo, a, ghi, ghe *sm/f* biologist.
bi'ondo, a *ag* blond, fair.
bi'onico, a, ci, che *ag* bionic.
biop'sia *sf* biopsy.
bio'ritmo *sm* biorhythm.
bios'fera *sf* biosphere.
bipar'tito, a *ag* (*POL*) two-party *cpd* ♦ *sm* (*POL*) two-party alliance.
'birba *sf* rascal, rogue.
bir'bante *sm* rascal, rogue.
birbo'nata *sf* naughty trick.
bir'bone, a *ag* (*bambino*) naughty ♦ *sm/f* little rascal.
biri'chino, a [biri'kino] *ag* mischievous ♦ *sm/f* scamp, little rascal.
bi'rillo *sm* skittle (*BRIT*), pin (*US*); ~**i** *smpl* (*gioco*) skittles *sg* (*BRIT*), bowling *no pl* (*US*).
Bir'mania *sf:* **la** ~ Burma.
bir'mano, a *ag, sm/f* Burmese (*inv*).

'**biro** ® *sf inv* biro ®.
'**birra** *sf* beer; ~ **scura** stout; **a tutta** ~ (*fig*) at top speed.
birre'ria *sf* (*locale*) ≈ bierkeller; (*fabbrica*) brewery.
bis *escl*, *sm inv* encore ♦ *ag inv* (*treno, autobus*) relief *cpd* (*BRIT*), additional; (*numero*): **12** ~ **12a**.
bi'saccia, ce [bi'zattʃa] *sf* knapsack.
Bi'sanzio [bi'zantsjo] *sf* Byzantium.
bis'betico, a, ci, che *ag* ill-tempered, crabby.
bisbigli'are [bizbiʎ'ʎare] *vt, vi* to whisper.
bis'biglio [biz'biʎʎo] *sm* whisper; (*notizia*) rumour (*BRIT*), rumor (*US*).
bisbi'glio [bizbiʎ'ʎio] *sm* whispering.
bis'boccia, ce [biz'bottʃa] *sf* binge, spree; **fare** ~ to have a binge.
'**bisca, sche** *sf* gambling house.
Bis'caglia [bis'kaʎʎa] *sf*: **il golfo di** ~ the Bay of Biscay.
'**bischero** ['biskero] *sm* (*MUS*) peg; (*fam: toscano*) fool, idiot.
'**biscia, sce** ['biʃʃa] *sf* snake; ~ **d'acqua** water snake.
biscot'tato, a *ag* crisp; **fette** ~**e** rusks.
bis'cotto *sm* biscuit.
bisessu'ale *ag*, *smf* bisexual.
bi'sestile *ag*: **anno** ~ leap year.
bisec'zione [bisɛt'tsjone] *sf* dichotomy.
bis'lacco, a, chi, che *ag* odd, weird.
bis'lungo, a, ghi, ghe *ag* oblong.
biso'gnare [bizoɲ'ɲare] *vb impers*: **bisogna che tu parta/lo faccia** you'll have to go/do it; **bisogna parlargli** we'll (*o* I'll) have to talk to him ♦ *vi* (*esser utile*) to be necessary.
bi'sogno [bi'zoɲɲo] *sm* need; ~**i** *smpl* (*necessità corporali*): **fare i propri** ~**i** to relieve o.s.; **avere** ~ **di qc/di fare qc** to need sth/to do sth; **al** ~, **in caso di** ~ if need be.
biso'gnoso, a [bizoɲ'ɲoso] *ag* needy, poor; ~ **di** in need of, needing.
bi'sonte *sm* (*ZOOL*) bison.
bis'tecca, che *sf* steak, beefsteak; ~ **al sangue/ai ferri** rare/grilled steak.
bisticci'are [bistit'tʃare] *vi*, ~**rsi** *vr* to quarrel, bicker.
bis'ticcio [bis'tittʃo] *sm* quarrel, squabble; (*gioco di parole*) pun.
bistrat'tare *vt* to maltreat.
'**bisturi** *sm inv* scalpel.
bi'sunto, a *ag* very greasy.
bi'torzolo [bi'tortsolo] *sm* (*sulla testa*) bump; (*sul corpo*) lump.
'**bitter** *sm inv* bitters *pl*.
bi'tume *sm* bitumen.

bivac'care *vi* (*MIL*) to bivouac; (*fig*) to bed down.
bi'vacco, chi *sm* bivouac.
'**bivio** *sm* fork; (*fig*) dilemma.
bizan'tino, a [biddzan'tino] *ag* Byzantine.
'**bizza** ['biddza] *sf* tantrum; **fare le** ~**e** to throw a tantrum.
biz'zarro, a [bid'dzarro] *ag* bizarre, strange.
biz'zeffe [bid'dzɛffe]: **a** ~ *av* in plenty, galore.
BL *sigla* = *Belluno*.
blan'dire *vt* to soothe; to flatter.
'**blando, a** *ag* mild, gentle.
blas'femo, a *ag* blasphemous ♦ *sm/f* blasphemer.
bla'sone *sm* coat of arms.
blate'rare *vi* to chatter.
'**blatta** *sf* cockroach.
blin'dare *vt* to armour (*BRIT*), armor (*US*).
blin'data *sf* (*macchina*) armoured car *o* limousine.
blin'dato, a *ag* armoured (*BRIT*), armored (*US*); **camera** ~**a** strongroom; **mezzo** ~ armoured vehicle; **porta** ~**a** reinforced door; **vita** ~**a** life amid maximum security; **vetro** ~ bulletproof glass.
bloc'care *vt* to block; (*isolare*) to isolate, cut off; (*porto*) to blockade; (*prezzi, beni*) to freeze; (*meccanismo*) to jam; ~**rsi** *vr* (*motore*) to stall, (*freni, porta*) to jam, stick; (*ascensore*) to get stuck, stop; **ha bloccato la macchina** (*AUT*) he jammed on the brakes.
bloccas'terzo [blokkas'tertso] *sm* (*AUT*) steering lock.
bloccherò *etc* [blokke'rɔ] *vb vedi* **bloccare**.
bloc'chetto [blok'ketto] *sm* notebook.
'**blocco, chi** *sm* block; (*MIL*) blockade; (*dei fitti*) restriction; (*quadernetto*) pad; (*fig: unione*) coalition; (*il bloccare*) blocking; isolating, cutting-off; blockading; freezing; jamming; **in** ~ (*nell'insieme*) as a whole; (*COMM*) in bulk; ~ **cardiaco** cardiac arrest.
bloc-'notes [blɔk'nɔt] *sm inv* notebook, notepad.
blu *ag inv*, *sm inv* dark blue.
bluff [blœf] *sm inv* bluff.
bluf'fare *vi* (*anche fig*) to bluff.
'**blusa** *sf* (*camiciotto*) smock; (*camicetta*) blouse.
BMT *sigla m* = *bollettino meteorologico*.
BN *sigla* = *Benevento*.
BO *sigla* = *Bologna*.
'**boa** *sm inv* (*ZOOL*) boa constrictor; (*sciarpa*) feather boa ♦ *sf* buoy.
bo'ato *sm* rumble, roar.

bob [bɔb] *sm inv* bobsleigh.
bo'bina *sf* reel, spool; (*di pellicola*) spool; (*di film*) reel; (*ELETTR*) coil.
'bocca, che *sf* mouth; **essere di buona** ~ **to** be a hearty eater; (*fig*) to be easily satisfied; **essere sulla** ~ **di tutti** (*persona, notizia*) to be the talk of the town; **rimanere a** ~ **asciutta** to have nothing to eat; (*fig*) to be disappointed; **in** ~ **al lupo!** good luck!; ~ **di leone** (*BOT*) snapdragon.
boc'caccia, ce [bok'kattʃa] *sf* (*malalingua*) gossip; (*smorfia*): **fare le** ~**ce** to pull faces.
boc'caglio [bok'kaʎʎo] *sm* (*TECN*) nozzle; (*di respiratore*) mouthpiece.
boc'cale *sm* jug; ~ **da birra** tankard.
bocca'scena [bokkaʃ'ʃɛna] *sm inv* proscenium.
boc'cata *sf* mouthful; (*di fumo*) puff; **prendere una** ~ **d'aria** to go out for a breath of (fresh) air.
boc'cetta [bot'tʃetta] *sf* small bottle.
boccheggi'are [bokked'dʒare] *vi* to gasp.
boc'chino [bok'kino] *sm* (*di sigaretta, sigaro: cannella*) cigarette-holder; cigar-holder; (*di pipa, strumenti musicali*) mouthpiece.
'boccia, ce ['bottʃa] *sf* bottle; (*da vino*) decanter, carafe; (*palla di legno, metallo*) bowl; **gioco delle** ~**ce** bowls *sg*.
bocci'are [bot'tʃare] *vt* (*proposta, progetto*) to reject; (*INS*) to fail; (*BOCCE*) to hit.
boccia'tura [bottʃa'tura] *sf* failure.
bocci'olo [bot'tʃɔlo] *sm* bud.
'boccolo *sm* curl.
boccon'cino [bokkon'tʃino] *sm* (*pietanza deliziosa*) delicacy.
boc'cone *sm* mouthful, morsel; **mangiare un** ~ to have a bite to eat.
boc'coni *av* face downwards.
Bo'emia *sf* Bohemia.
bo'emo, a *ag, sm/f* Bohemian.
bofonchi'are [bofon'kjare] *vi* to grumble.
Bogotá *sf* Bogotá.
'boia *sm inv* executioner; hangman; **fa un freddo** ~ (*fam*) it's cold as hell; **mondo** ~**!**, ~ **d'un mondo ladro!** (*fam*) damn!, blast!
boi'ata *sf* botch.
boicot'taggio [boikot'taddʒo] *sm* boycott.
boicot'tare *vt* to boycott.
'bolgia, ge ['bɔldʒa] *sf* (*fig*): **c'era una tale** ~ **al cinema** the cinema was absolutely mobbed.
'bolide *sm* (*ASTR*) meteor; (*macchina: da corsa*) racing car (*BRIT*), race car (*US*); (: *elaborata*) performance car; **come un** ~ like a flash, at top speed; **entrare/uscire come un** ~ to charge in/out.
Bo'livia *sf*: **la** ~ Bolivia.

bolivi'ano, a *ag, sm/f* Bolivian.
'bolla *sf* bubble; (*MED*) blister; (*COMM*) bill, receipt; **finire in una** ~ **di sapone** (*fig*) to come to nothing; ~ **di accompagnamento** waybill; ~ **di consegna** delivery note; ~ **papale** papal bull.
bol'lare *vt* to stamp; (*fig*) to brand.
bol'lente *ag* boiling; boiling hot; **calmare i** ~**i spiriti** to sober up, calm down.
bol'letta *sf* bill; (*ricevuta*) receipt; **essere in** ~ to be hard up; ~ **di consegna** delivery note; ~ **doganale** clearance certificate; ~ **di trasporto aereo** air waybill.
bollet'tino *sm* bulletin; (*COMM*) note; ~ **meteorologico** weather forecast; ~ **di ordinazione** order form; ~ **di spedizione** consignment note.
bol'lire *vt, vi* to boil; **qualcosa bolle in pentola** (*fig*) there's something brewing.
bol'lito *sm* (*CUC*) boiled meat.
bolli'tore *sm* (*TECN*) boiler; (*CUC: per acqua*) kettle; (: *per latte*) milk pan.
bolli'tura *sf* boiling.
'bollo *sm* stamp; **imposta di** ~ stamp duty; ~ **auto** road tax; ~ **per patente** driving licence tax; ~ **postale** postmark.
bol'lore *sm*: **dare un** ~ **a qc** to bring sth to the boil (*BRIT*) *o* a boil (*US*); **i** ~**i della gioventù** youthful enthusiasm *sg*.
Bo'logna [bo'lɔɲɲa] *sf* Bologna.
bolo'gnese [boloɲ'ɲese] *ag* Bolognese; **spaghetti alla** ~ spaghetti bolognese.
'bomba *sf* bomb; **tornare a** ~ (*fig*) to get back to the point; **sei stato una** ~**!** you were tremendous!; ~ **atomica** atom bomb; ~ **a mano** hand grenade; ~ **ad orologeria** time bomb.
bombarda'mento *sm* bombardment; bombing.
bombar'dare *vt* to bombard; (*da aereo*) to bomb.
bombardi'ere *sm* bomber.
bom'betta *sf* bowler (hat) (*BRIT*), derby (*US*).
'bombola *sf* cylinder; ~ **del gas** gas cylinder.
bomboni'era *sf* box of sweets (*as souvenir at weddings, first communions etc*).
bo'naccia, ce [bo'nattʃa] *sf* dead calm.
bonacci'one, a [bonat'tʃone] *ag* good-natured, easy-going ♦ *sm/f* good-natured sort.
bo'nario, a *ag* good-natured, kind.
bo'nifica, che *sf* reclamation; reclaimed land.
bo'nifico, ci *sm* (*riduzione, abbuono*) discount; (*versamento a terzi*) credit transfer.

Bonn *sf* Bonn.

bontà *sf* goodness; (*cortesia*) kindness; **aver la ~ di fare qc** to be good *o* kind enough to do sth.

'bonus-'malus *sm inv* ≈ no-claims bonus.

bor'bonico, a, ci, che *ag* Bourbon; (*fig*) backward, out of date.

borbot'tare *vi* to mumble; (*stomaco*) to rumble.

borbot'tio, ii *sm* mumbling; rumbling.

'borchia ['borkja] *sf* stud.

borda'tura *sf* (*SARTORIA*) border, trim.

bor'deaux [bor'dɔ] *sm* (*colore*) burgundy, maroon; (*vino*) Bordeaux.

bor'dello *sm* brothel.

'bordo *sm* (*NAUT*) ship's side; (*orlo*) edge; (*striscia di guarnizione*) border, trim; **a ~ di** (*nave, aereo*) aboard, on board; (*macchina*) in; **sul ~ della strada** at the roadside; **persona d'alto ~** (*fig*) VIP.

bor'dura *sf* border.

bor'gata *sf* hamlet; (*a Roma*) working-class suburb.

bor'ghese [bor'geze] *ag* (*spesso peg*) middle-class; bourgeois; **abito ~** civilian dress; **poliziotto in ~** plainclothes policeman

borghe'sia [borge'zia] *sf* middle classes *pl*; bourgeoisie.

'borgo, ghi *sm* (*paesino*) village; (*quartiere*) district; (*sobborgo*) suburb.

'boria *sf* self-conceit, arrogance.

bori'oso, a *ag* arrogant.

bor'lotto *sm* kidney bean.

'Borneo *sm*: **il ~** Borneo.

boro'talco *sm* talcum powder.

bor'raccia, ce [bor'rattʃa] *sf* canteen, water-bottle.

'borsa *sf* bag; (*anche: ~ da signora*) handbag; (*ECON*): **la B~ (valori)** the Stock Exchange; **~ dell'acqua calda** hot-water bottle; **B~ merci** commodity exchange; **~ nera** black market; **~ della spesa** shopping bag; **~ di studio** grant.

borsai'olo *sm* pickpocket.

bor'seggio [bor'seddʒo] *sm* pickpocketing.

borsel'lino *sm* purse.

bor'sello *sm* gent's handbag.

bor'setta *sf* handbag.

bor'sista, i, e *sm/f* (*ECON*) speculator; (*INS*) grant-holder.

bos'caglia [bos'kaʎʎa] *sf* woodlands *pl*.

boscai'olo, boscaiu'olo *sm* woodcutter; forester.

bos'chetto [bos'ketto] *sm* copse, grove.

'bosco, schi *sm* wood.

bos'coso, a *ag* wooded.

bos'niaco, a, ci, che *ag, sm/f* Bosnian.

'Bosnia-Erze'govina ['bɔsnja erdze'govina] *sf*: **la ~** Bosnia-Herzegovina.

'bossolo *sm* cartridge case.

Bot, bot *sigla m inv vedi* **buono ordinario del Tesoro.**

bo'tanico, a, ci, che *ag* botanical ♦ *sm* botanist ♦ *sf* botany.

'botola *sf* trap door.

Bots'wana [bots'vana] *sm*: **il ~** Botswana.

'botta *sf* blow; (*rumore*) bang; **dare (un sacco di) ~e a qn** to give sb a good thrashing; **~ e risposta** (*fig*) cut and thrust.

'botte *sf* barrel, cask; **essere in una ~ di ferro** (*fig*) to be as safe as houses; **volere la ~ piena e la moglie ubriaca** to want to have one's cake and eat it.

bot'tega, ghe *sf* shop; (*officina*) workshop; **stare a ~ (da qn)** to serve one's apprenticeship (with sb); **le B~ghe Oscure** *headquarters of the P.D.S.*

botte'gaio, a *sm/f* shopkeeper.

botte'ghino [botte'gino] *sm* ticket office; (*del lotto*) public lottery office.

bot'tiglia [bot'tiʎʎa] *sf* bottle.

bottiglie'ria [bottiʎʎe'ria] *sf* wine shop.

bot'tino *sm* (*di guerra*) booty; (*di rapina, furto*) loot; **fare ~ di qc** (*anche fig*) to make off with sth.

'botto *sm* bang; crash; **di ~** suddenly; **d'un ~** (*fam*) in a flash.

bot'tone *sm* button; (*BOT*) bud; **stanza dei ~i** control room; (*fig*) nerve centre; **attaccare (un) ~ a *o* con qn** to buttonhole sb; **bottton d'oro** buttercup.

bo'vino, a *ag* bovine; **~i** *smpl* cattle.

box [bɔks] *sm inv* (*per cavalli*) horsebox; (*per macchina*) lock-up; (*per macchina da corsa*) pit; (*per bambini*) playpen.

boxe [bɔks] *sf* boxing.

'boxer ['bɔkser] *sm inv* (*cane*) boxer ♦ *smpl* (*mutande*): **un paio di ~** a pair of boxer shorts.

'bozza ['bɔttsa] *sf* draft; (*TIP*) proof; **~ di stampa/impaginata** galley/page proof.

boz'zetto [bot'tsetto] *sm* sketch.

'bozzolo ['bɔttsolo] *sm* cocoon.

BR *sigla fpl* = **Brigate Rosse** ♦ *sigla* = *Brindisi*.

'braca, che *sf* (*gamba di pantalone*) trouser leg; **~che** *sfpl* (*fam*) trousers, pants (*US*); (*mutandoni*) drawers; **calare le ~che** (*fig fam*) to chicken out.

brac'care *vt* to hunt.

brac'cetto [brat'tʃetto] *sm*: **a ~** arm in arm.

braccherò *etc* [brakke'rɔ] *vb vedi* **braccare.**

bracci'ale [brat'tʃale] *sm* bracelet; (*distintivo*) armband.

braccia'letto [brattʃa'letto] *sm* bracelet,

bangle.

bracci'ante [brat't∫ante] *sm* (*AGR*) day labourer.

bracci'ata [brat't∫ata] *sf* armful; (*nel nuoto*) stroke.

'braccio ['bratt∫o] *sm* (*pl*(*f*) **braccia**: *ANAT*) arm; (*pl*(*m*) **bracci**: *di gru, fiume*) arm; (*: di edificio*) wing; **camminare sotto** ~ **to** walk arm in arm; **è il suo** ~ **destro** he's his right-hand man; ~ **di ferro** (*anche fig*) trial of strength; ~ **di mare** sound.

bracci'olo [brat't∫olo] *sm* (*appoggio*) arm.

'bracco, chi *sm* hound.

bracconi'ere *sm* poacher.

'brace ['brat∫e] *sf* embers *pl*.

braci'ere [bra't∫ere] *sm* brazier.

braci'ola [bra't∫ola] *sf* (*CUC*) chop.

'bradipo *sm* (*ZOOL*) sloth.

'brado, a *ag*: **allo stato** ~ in the wild *o* natural state.

'brama *sf*: ~ (**di/di fare**) longing (for/to do), yearning (for/to do).

bra'mare *vt*: ~ (**qc/di fare qc**) to long (for sth/to do sth), yearn (for sth/to do sth).

bramo'sia *sf*: ~ (**di**) longing (for), yearning (for).

'branca, che *sf* branch.

'branchia ['brankja] *sf* (*ZOOL*) gill.

'branco, chi *sm* (*di cani, lupi*) pack; (*di uccelli, pecore*) flock; (*peg: di persone*) gang, pack.

branco'lare *vi* to grope, feel one's way.

'branda *sf* camp bed.

bran'dello *sm* scrap, shred; **a** ~**i** in tatters, in rags; **fare a** ~**i** to tear to shreds.

bran'dina *sf* camp bed (*BRIT*), cot (*US*).

bran'dire *vt* to brandish.

'brano *sm* piece; (*di libro*) passage.

bra'sare *vt* to braise.

bra'sato *sm* braised beef.

Bra'sile *sm*: **il** ~ Brazil.

Bra'silia *sf* Brasilia.

brasili'ano, a *ag, sm/f* Brazilian.

bra'vata *sf* (*azione spavalda*) act of bravado.

'bravo, a *ag* (*abile*) clever, capable, skilful; (*buono*) good, honest; (*: bambino*) good; (*coraggioso*) brave; ~! well done!; (*al teatro*) bravo!; **su da** ~! (*fam*) there's a good boy!; **mi sono fatto le mie** ~**e 8 ore di lavoro** I put in a full 8 hours' work.

bra'vura *sf* cleverness, skill.

'breccia, ce ['brett∫a] *sf* breach; **essere sulla** ~ (*fig*) to be going strong; **fare** ~ **nell'animo** *o* **nel cuore di qn** to find the way to sb's heart.

'Brema *sf* Bremen.

bre'saola *sf* kind of dried salted beef.

bresci'ano, a [bre∫'∫ano] *ag* of (*o* from) Brescia.

Bre'tagna [bre'taɲɲa] *sf*: **la** ~ Brittany.

bre'tella *sf* (*AUT*) link; ~**e** *sfpl* braces.

'bret(t)one *ag, sm/f* Breton.

'breve *ag* brief, short; **in** ~ in short; **per farla** ~ to cut a long story short; **a** ~ (*COMM*) short-term.

brevet'tare *vt* to patent.

bre'vetto *sm* patent; ~ **di pilotaggio** pilot's licence (*BRIT*) *o* license (*US*).

brevità *sf* brevity.

'brezza ['breddza] *sf* breeze.

'bricco, chi *sm* jug; ~ **del caffè** coffeepot.

bricco'nata *sf* mischievous trick.

bric'cone, a *sm/f* rogue, rascal.

'briciola ['brit∫ola] *sf* crumb.

'briciolo ['brit∫olo] *sm* (*specie fig*) bit.

bridge [brid3] *sm* bridge.

'briga, ghe *sf* (*fastidio*) trouble, bother; **attaccar** ~ to start a quarrel; **pigliarsi la** ~ **di fare qc** to take the trouble to do sth.

brigadi'ere *sm* (*dei carabinieri etc*) ≈ sergeant.

bri'gante *sm* bandit.

bri'gata *sf* (*MIL*) brigade; (*gruppo*) group, party; **le B**~**e Rosse** (*POL*) the Red Brigades.

briga'tismo *sm* phenomenon of the Red Brigades.

briga'tista, i, e *sm/f* (*POL*) member of the Red Brigades.

'briglia ['briʎʎa] *sf* rein; **a** ~ **sciolta** at full gallop; (*fig*) at full speed.

bril'lante *ag* bright; (*anche fig*) brilliant; (*che luccica*) shining ♦ *sm* diamond.

brillan'tina *sf* brilliantine.

bril'lare *vi* to shine; (*mina*) to blow up ♦ *vt* (*mina*) to set off.

'brillo, a *ag* merry, tipsy.

'brina *sf* hoarfrost.

brin'dare *vi*: ~ **a qn/qc** to drink to *o* toast sb/sth.

'brindisi *sm inv* toast.

'brio *sm* liveliness, go.

bri'oche [bri'ɔ∫] *sf inv* brioche (bun).

bri'oso, a *ag* lively.

'briscola *sf* type of card game; (*seme vincente*) trump(s); (*carta*) trump card.

bri'tannico, a, ci, che *ag* British ♦ *sm/f* Briton; **i B**~**ci** the British *pl*.

'brivido *sm* shiver; (*di ribrezzo*) shudder; (*fig*) thrill; **racconti del** ~ suspense stories.

brizzo'lato, a [brittso'lato] *ag* (*persona*) going grey; (*barba, capelli*) greying.

'brocca, che *sf* jug.

broc'cato *sm* brocade.

'broccolo *sm* broccoli *no pl.*

bro'daglia [bro'daʎʎa] *sf* (*peg*) dishwater.

'brodo *sm* broth; (*per cucinare*) stock; ~ ristretto consommé; **lasciare** (**cuocere**) **qn nel suo** ~ to let sb stew (in his own juice); **tutto fa** ~ every little bit helps.

'broglio ['brɔʎʎo] *sm*: ~ **elettorale** gerrymandering; ~**i** *smpl* (*DIR*) malpractices.

'bromo *sm* (*CHIM*) bromine.

bron'chite [bron'kitɛ] *sf* (*MED*) bronchitis.

'broncio ['brontʃo] *sm* sulky expression; **tenere il** ~ to sulk.

'bronco, chi *sm* bronchial tube.

bronto'lare *vi* to grumble; (*tuono, stomaco*) to rumble.

bronto'lio *sm* grumbling, mumbling.

bronto'lone, a *ag* grumbling ♦ *sm/f* grumbler.

bron'zina [bron'dzina] *sf* (*TECN*) bush.

'bronzo ['brondzo] *sm* bronze; **che faccia di** ~**!** what a brass neck!

bross *abbr* = in brossura.

bros'sura *sf*: **in** ~ (*libro*) limpback.

'browser ['brauzɛ] *sm inv* (*INFORM*) browser.

bru'care *vt* to browse on, nibble at.

brucherà *etc* [bruke'ra] *vb vedi* **brucare**.

bruciacchi'are [brutʃak'kjare] *vt* to singe, scorch; ~**rsi** *vr* to become singed o scorched.

brucia'pelo [brutʃa'pelo]: **a** ~ *av* point-blank.

bruci'are [bru'tʃare] *vt* to burn; (*scottare*) to scald ♦ *vi* to burn; ~ **gli avversari** (*SPORT, fig*) to leave the rest of the field behind; ~ **le tappe o i tempi** (*SPORT, fig*) to shoot ahead; ~**rsi la carriera** to put an end to one's career.

brucia'tore [brutʃa'tore] *sm* burner.

brucia'tura [brutʃa'tura] *sf* (*atto*) burning *no pl*; (*segno*) burn; (*scottatura*) scald.

bruci'ore [bru'tʃore] *sm* burning o smarting sensation.

'bruco, chi *sm* grub; (*di farfalla*) caterpillar.

'brufolo *sm* pimple, spot.

brughi'era [bru'gjɛra] *sf* heath, moor.

bruli'care *vi* to swarm.

bruli'chio, ii [bruli'kio] *sm* swarming.

'brullo, a *ag* bare, bleak.

'bruma *sf* mist.

'bruno, a *ag* brown, dark; (*persona*) dark(-haired).

brusca'mente *av* (*frenare, fermarsi*) suddenly; (*rispondere, reagire*) sharply.

'brusco, a, schi, sche *ag* (*sapore*) sharp; (*modi, persona*) brusque, abrupt; (*movimento*) abrupt, sudden.

bru'sio *sm* buzz, buzzing.

bru'tale *ag* brutal.

brutalità *sf inv* brutality.

'bruto, a *ag* (*forza*) brute *cpd* ♦ *sm* brute.

'brutta *sf vedi* **brutto**.

brut'tezza [brut'tettsa] *sf* ugliness.

'brutto, a *ag* ugly; (*cattivo*) bad; (*malattia, strada, affare*) nasty, bad ♦ *sm*: **guardare qn di** ~ to give sb a nasty look ♦ *sf* rough copy, first draft; ~ **tempo** bad weather; **passare un** ~ **quarto d'ora** to have a nasty time of it; **vedersela** ~**a** (*per un attimo*) to have a nasty moment; (*per un periodo*) to have a bad time of it.

brut'tura *sf* (*cosa brutta*) ugly thing; (*sudiciume*) filth; (*azione meschina*) mean action.

Bru'xelles [bry'sɛl] *sf* Brussels.

BS *sigla* = Brescia.

B.T. *abbr* (= *bassa tensione*) LT ♦ *sigla m inv* = **buono del Tesoro**.

btg *abbr* = **battaglione**.

Btp *sigla m* (= *buono del Tesoro pluriennale, vedi* **buono**.

bub'bone *sm* swelling.

'buca, che *sf* hole; (*avvallamento*) hollow; ~ **delle lettere** letterbox.

buca'neve *sm inv* snowdrop.

bu'care *vt* (*forare*) to make a hole (o holes) in; (*pungere*) to pierce; (*biglietto*) to punch; ~**rsi** *vr* (*con eroina*) to mainline; ~ **una gomma** to have a puncture; **avere le mani bucate** (*fig*) to be a spendthrift.

'Bucarest *sf* Bucharest.

bu'cato *sm* (*operazione*) washing; (*panni*) wash, washing.

'buccia, ce ['buttʃa] *sf* skin, peel; (*corteccia*) bark.

bucherel'lare [bukerel'lare] *vt* to riddle with holes.

bucherò *etc* [buke'rɔ] *vb vedi* **bucare**.

'buco, chi *sm* hole; **fare un** ~ **nell'acqua** to fail, draw a blank; **farsi un** ~ (*fam*: *drogarsi*) to have a fix; ~ **nero** (*anche fig*) black hole.

'Budapest *sf* Budapest.

'Budda *sm inv* Buddha.

bud'dismo *sm* Buddhism.

bu'dello *sm* intestine; (*fig*: *tubo*) tube; (*vicolo*) alley; ~**a** *sfpl* bowels, guts.

bu'dino *sm* pudding.

'bue, *pl* **bu'oi** *sm* ox; (*anche*: **carne di** ~) beef; **uovo all'occhio di** ~ fried egg.

Bu'enos 'Aires *sf* Buenos Aires.

'bufalo *sm* buffalo.

bu'fera *sf* storm.

buf'fetto *sm* flick.

'buffo, a *ag* funny; (*TEAT*) comic.

buffo'nata *sf* (*azione*) prank, jest; (*parola*) jest.

buf'fone *sm* buffoon.

bugge'rare [buddʒe'rare] *vt* to swindle, cheat.

bu'gia, 'gie [bu'dʒia] *sf* lie; (*candeliere*) candleholder.

bugi'ardo, a [bu'dʒardo] *ag* lying, deceitful ♦ *sm/f* liar.

bugi'gattolo [budʒi'gattolo] *sm* poky little room.

'buio, a *ag* dark ♦ *sm* dark, darkness; **fa** ~ **pesto** it's pitch-dark.

'bulbo *sm* (*BOT*) bulb; ~ **oculare** eyeball.

Bulga'ria *sf*: **la** ~ Bulgaria.

'bulgaro, a *ag*, *sm/f*, *sm* Bulgarian.

buli'mia *sf* bulimia.

'bullo *sm* (*persona*) tough.

bul'lone *sm* bolt.

bu'oi *smpl di* **bue**.

buona'fede *sf* good faith.

buon'anima *sf* = **buon'anima**; *vedi* **anima**.

buona'notte *escl* good night! ♦ *sf*: **dare la** ~ **a** to say good night to.

buona'sera *escl* good evening!

buoncos'tume *sm* public morality; **la (squadra del)** ~ (*POLIZIA*) the vice squad.

buondì *escl* hello!

buongi'orno [bwon'dʒorno] *escl* good morning (*o* afternoon)!

buon'grado *av*: **di** ~ willingly.

buongus'taio, a *sm/f* gourmet.

buon'gusto *sm* good taste.

=============== *PAROLA CHIAVE* ===============

bu'ono, a (*ag*: *dav sm* **buon** + *C o V*, **buono** + *s impura, gn, pn, ps, x, z*; *dav sf* **buon'** + *V*) *ag* **1** (*gen*) good; **un buon pranzo/ ristorante** a good lunch/restaurant; (**stai**) ~**!** behave!; **che** ~**!** (*cibo*) this is nice!

2 (*benevolo*): ~ (**con**) good (to), kind (to)

3 (*giusto, valido*) right; **al momento** ~ at the right moment

4 (*adatto*): ~ **a/da** fit for/to; **essere** ~ **a nulla** to be no good *o* use at anything

5 (*auguri*): **buon compleanno!** happy birthday!; **buon divertimento!** have a nice time!; ~**a fortuna!** good luck!; **buon riposo!** sleep well!; **buon viaggio!** have a good trip!

6: **ad ogni buon conto** in any case; **tante** ~**e cose!** all the best!; **di buon cuore** (*persona*) goodhearted; **di buon grado** willingly; **le** ~**e maniere** good manners; **di buon mattino** early in the morning; **a buon mercato** cheap; **di buon'ora** early; **mettere una** ~**a parola** to put in a good word; **di buon passo** at a good pace; **buon pro ti faccia!** much good may it do you!; **buon senso** common sense; **la** ~**a società** the upper classes; **una** ~**a volta** once and for all; **alla** ~**a** *ag* simple ♦ *av* in a simple way, without any fuss; **un tipo alla** ~**a** an easy-going sort ♦ *sm/f*: **essere un** ~**/una** ~**a** to be a good person; ~ **a nulla** good for nothing; **i** ~**i e i cattivi** (*in storia, film*) the goodies and the baddies; **accetterà con le** ~**e o con le cattive** one way or another he's going to agree to it ♦ *sm* **1** (*bontà*) goodness, good

2 (*COMM*) voucher, coupon; ~ **d'acquisto** credit note; ~ **di cassa** cash voucher; ~ **di consegna** delivery note; ~ **fruttifero** interest-bearing bond; ~ **ordinario del Tesoro** short-term Treasury bond; ~ **postale fruttifero** interest-bearing bond (*issued by Italian Post Office*); ~ **del Tesoro** Treasury bill.

buon'senso *sm* = **buon senso**.

buontem'pone, a *sm/f* jovial person.

buonu'scita [bwonuʃ'ʃita] *sf* (*INDUSTRIA*) golden handshake; (*di affitti*) sum paid for the relinquishing of tenancy rights.

buratti'naio *sm* puppeteer, puppet master.

burat'tino *sm* puppet.

'burbero, a *ag* surly, gruff.

'burla *sf* prank, trick.

bur'lare *vt*: ~ **qc/qn**, ~**rsi di qc/qn** to make fun of sth/sb.

bu'rocrate *sm* bureaucrat.

buro'cratico, a, ci, che *ag* bureaucratic.

burocra'zia [burokrat'tsia] *sf* bureaucracy.

bur'rasca, sche *sf* storm.

burras'coso, a *ag* stormy.

'burro *sm* butter.

bur'rone *sm* ravine.

bus'care *vt* (*anche*: ~**rsi**: *raffreddore*) to get, catch; **buscarle** (*fam*) to get a hiding.

buscherò *etc* [buske'rɔ] *vb vedi* **buscare**.

bus'sare *vi* to knock; ~ **a quattrini** (*fig*) to ask for money.

'bussola *sf* compass; **perdere la** ~ (*fig*) to lose one's bearings.

'busta *sf* (*da lettera*) envelope; (*astuccio*) case; **in** ~ **aperta/chiusa** in an unsealed/ sealed envelope; ~ **paga** pay packet.

busta'rella *sf* bribe, backhander.

bus'tina *sf* (*piccola busta*) envelope; (*di cibi, farmaci*) sachet; (*MIL*) forage cap; ~ **di tè** tea bag.

'busto *sm* bust; (*indumento*) corset, girdle; **a mezzo** ~ (*fotografia, ritratto*) half-length.

bu'tano *sm* butane.

but'tare *vt* to throw; (*anche*: ~ **via**) to throw away; ~**rsi** *vr* (*saltare*) to jump; ~ **giù** (*scritto*) to scribble down, dash off;

(*cibo*) to gulp down; (*edificio*) to pull down, demolish; (*pasta, verdura*) to put into boiling water; **ho buttato là una frase** I mentioned it in passing; **buttiamoci!** (*saltiamo*) let's jump!; (*rischiamo*) let's have a go!; **~rsi dalla finestra** to jump out of the window.

'**buzzo** ['buddzo] *sm* (*fam: pancia*) belly, paunch; **di ~ buono** (*con impegno*) with a will.

Cc

C, c [tʃi] *sf o m inv* (*lettera*) C, c ♦ *abbr* (*GEO*) = **capo**; (= *Celsius, centigrado*) C; (= *conto*) a/c; **~ come Como** ≈ C for Charlie.

CA *sigla* = *Cagliari*.

c.a. *abbr* (*ELETTR*) *vedi* **corrente alternata**; (*COMM*) = *corrente anno*.

cab. *abbr* = *cablogramma*.

caba'ret [kaba'rɛ] *sm inv* cabaret.

ca'bina *sf* (*di nave*) cabin; (*da spiaggia*) beach hut; (*di autocarro, treno*) cab; (*di aereo*) cockpit; (*di ascensore*) cage; **~ di proiezione** (*CINE*) projection booth; **~ di registrazione** recording booth; **~ telefonica** callbox, (tele)phone box *o* booth.

cabi'nato *sm* cabin cruiser.

ca'blaggio [ka'bladdʒo] *sm* wiring.

cablo'gramma *sm* cable(gram).

ca'cao *sm* cocoa.

'**cacca** *sf* (*fam: anche fig*) shit (*!*).

'**caccia** ['kattʃa] *sf* hunting; (*con fucile*) shooting; (*inseguimento*) chase; (*cacciagione*) game ♦ *sm inv* (*aereo*) fighter; (*nave*) destroyer; **andare a ~** to go hunting; **andare a ~ di guai** to be asking for trouble; **~ grossa** big-game hunting; **~ all'uomo** manhunt.

cacciabombardi'ere [kattʃabombar'djɛre] *sm* fighter-bomber.

cacciagi'one [kattʃa'dʒone] *sf* game.

cacci'are [kat'tʃare] *vt* to hunt; (*mandar via*) to chase away; (*ficcare*) to shove, stick ♦ *vi* to hunt; **~rsi** *vr* (*fam: mettersi*): **~rsi tra la folla** to plunge into the crowd; **dove s'è cacciata la mia borsa?** where has my bag got to?; **~rsi nei guai** to get into trouble; **~ fuori qc** to whip *o* pull sth out; **~ un**

urlo to let out a yell.

caccia'tora [kattʃa'tora] *sf* (*giacca*) hunting jacket; (*CUC*): **pollo** *etc* **alla ~** chicken *etc* chasseur.

caccia'tore [kattʃa'tore] *sm* hunter; **~ di frodo** poacher; **~ di dote** fortune-hunter.

cacciatorpedini'ere [kattʃatorpedi'njɛre] *sm* destroyer.

caccia'vite [kattʃa'vite] *sm inv* screwdriver.

cache'mire [kaʃ'mir] *sm inv* cashmere.

ca'chet [ka'ʃɛ] *sm* (*MED*) capsule; (*: compressa*) tablet; (*compenso*) fee; (*colorante per capelli*) rinse.

'**cachi** ['kaki] *sm inv* (*albero, frutto*) persimmon; (*colore*) khaki ♦ *ag inv* khaki.

'**cacio** ['katʃo] *sm* cheese; **essere come il ~ sui maccheroni** (*fig*) to turn up at the right moment.

'**cactus** *sm inv* cactus.

ca'davere *sm* (dead) body, corpse.

cada'verico, a, ci, che *ag* (*fig*) deathly pale.

'**caddi** *etc vb vedi* **cadere**.

ca'dente *ag* falling; (*casa*) tumbledown; (*persona*) decrepit.

ca'denza [ka'dɛntsa] *sf* cadence; (*andamento ritmico*) rhythm; (*MUS*) cadenza.

ca'dere *vi* to fall; (*denti, capelli*) to fall out; (*tetto*) to fall in; **questa gonna cade bene** this skirt hangs well; **lasciar ~** (*anche fig*) to drop; **~ dal sonno** to be falling asleep on one's feet; **~ ammalato** to fall ill; **~ dalle nuvole** (*fig*) to be taken aback.

ca'detto *sm* cadet.

cadrò *etc vb vedi* **cadere**.

ca'duto, a *ag* (*morto*) dead ♦ *sm* dead soldier ♦ *sf* fall; **monumento ai ~i** war memorial; **~a di temperatura** drop in temperature; **la ~a dei capelli** hair loss; **~a del sistema** (*INFORM*) system failure.

caffè *sm inv* coffee; (*locale*) café; **~ corretto** coffee with liqueur; **~ in grani** coffee beans; **~ macchiato** coffee with a dash of milk; **~ macinato** ground coffee.

caffe'ina *sf* caffeine.

caffel'latte *sm inv* white coffee.

caffette'ria *sf* coffee shop.

caffetti'era *sf* coffeepot.

ca'fone *sm* (*contadino*) peasant; (*peg*) boor.

cagio'nare [kadʒo'nare] *vt* to cause, be the cause of.

cagio'nevole [kadʒo'nevole] *ag* delicate, weak.

cagli'are [kaʎ'ʎare] *vi* to curdle.

cagliari'tano, a [kaʎʎari'tano] *ag* of (*o* from) Cagliari.

'**cagna** ['kaɲɲa] *sf* (*ZOOL, peg*) bitch.

ca'gnara [kaɲ'ɲara] *sf* (*fig*) uproar.

ca'gnesco, a, schi, sche [kaɲ'ɲesko] *ag* (*fig*): **guardare qn in** ~ to scowl at sb.
CAI *sigla m* = *Club Alpino Italiano*.
'Cairo *sm*: **il** ~ Cairo.
cala'brese *ag, sm/f* Calabrian.
cala'brone *sm* hornet.
Cala'hari [kala'ari]: **il Deserto di** ~ *sm* the Kalahari Desert.
cala'maio *sm* inkpot; inkwell.
cala'maro *sm* squid.
cala'mita *sf* magnet.
calamità *sf inv* calamity, disaster; ~ **naturale** natural disaster.
ca'lare *vt* (*far discendere*) to lower; (*MAGLIA*) to decrease ♦ *vi* (*discendere*) to go (*o* come) down; (*tramontare*) to set, go down; ~ **di peso** to lose weight.
ca'lata *sf* (*invasione*) invasion.
'calca *sf* throng, press.
cal'cagno [kal'kaɲɲo] *sm* heel.
cal'care *sm* limestone ♦ *vt* (*premere coi piedi*) to tread, press down; (*premere con forza*) to press down; (*mettere in rilievo*) to stress; ~ **la mano** to overdo it, exaggerate; ~ **le scene** (*fig*) to be on the stage; ~ **le orme di qn** (*fig*) to follow in sb's footsteps.
'calce ['kaltʃe] *sm*: **in** ~ at the foot of the page ♦ *sf* lime; ~ **viva** quicklime.
calces'truzzo [kaltʃes'truttso] *sm* concrete.
calcherò [kalke'rɔ] *vb vedi* **calcare**.
calci'are [kal'tʃare] *vt, vi* to kick.
calcia'tore [kaltʃa'tore] *sm* footballer (*BRIT*), (football) player.
cal'cina [kal'tʃina] *sf* (lime) mortar.
calci'naccio [kaltʃi'nattʃo] *sm* flake of plaster.
'calcio ['kaltʃo] *sm* (*pedata*) kick; (*sport*) football, soccer; (*di pistola, fucile*) butt; (*CHIM*) calcium; ~ **d'angolo** (*SPORT*) corner (kick); ~ **di punizione** (*SPORT*) free kick.
'calco, chi *sm* (*ARTE*) casting, moulding (*BRIT*), molding (*US*); cast, mo(u)ld.
calco'lare *vt* to calculate, work out, reckon; (*ponderare*) to weigh (up).
calcola'tore, 'trice *ag* calculating ♦ *sm* calculator; (*fig*) calculating person ♦ *sf* (*anche*: **macchina calcolatrice**) calculator; ~ **digitale** digital computer; ~ **elettronico** computer; ~ **da tavolo** desktop computer.
'calcolo *sm* (*anche MAT*) calculation; (*infinitesimale etc*) calculus; (*MED*) stone; **fare il** ~ **di qc** to work sth out; **fare i propri** ~**i** (*fig*) to weigh the pros and cons; **per** ~ out of self-interest.
cal'daia *sf* boiler.

caldar'rosta *sf* roast chestnut.
caldeggi'are [kalded'dʒare] *vt* to support.
'caldo, a *ag* warm; (*molto* ~) hot; (*fig: appassionato*) keen ♦ *sm* heat; **ho** ~ I'm warm; I'm hot; **fa** ~ it's warm; it's hot; **non mi fa né** ~ **né freddo** I couldn't care less; **a** ~ (*fig*) in the heat of the moment.
caleidos'copio *sm* kaleidoscope.
calen'dario *sm* calendar.
ca'lende *sfpl* calends; **rimandare qc alle** ~ **greche** to put sth off indefinitely.
ca'lesse *sm* gig.
'calibro *sm* (*di arma*) calibre, bore; (*TECN*) callipers *pl*; (*fig*) calibre; **di grosso** ~ (*fig*) prominent.
'calice ['kalitʃe] *sm* goblet; (*REL*) chalice.
Cali'fornia *sf* California.
californi'ano, a *ag* Californian.
ca'ligine [ka'lidʒine] *sf* fog; (*mista con fumo*) smog.
calligra'fia *sf* (*scrittura*) handwriting; (*arte*) calligraphy.
'callo *sm* callus; (*ai piedi*) corn; **fare il** ~ **a qc** to get used to sth.
'calma *sf* calm; **faccia con** ~ take your time.
cal'mante *sm* sedative, tranquillizer.
cal'mare *vt* to calm; (*lenire*) to soothe; ~**rsi** *vr* to grow calm, calm down; (*vento*) to abate; (*dolori*) to ease.
calmi'ere *sm* controlled price.
'calmo, a *ag* calm, quiet.
'calo *sm* (*COMM: di prezzi*) fall; (: *di volume*) shrinkage; (: *di peso*) loss.
ca'lore *sm* warmth; (*intenso, FISICA*) heat; **essere in** ~ (*ZOOL*) to be on heat.
calo'ria *sf* calorie.
calo'rifero *sm* radiator.
calo'roso, a *ag* warm; **essere** ~ not to feel the cold.
calpes'tare *vt* to tread on, trample on; "**è vietato** ~ **l'erba**" "keep off the grass".
ca'lunnia *sf* slander; (*scritta*) libel.
calunni'are *vt* to slander.
cal'vario *sm* (*fig*) affliction, cross.
cal'vizie [kal'vittsje] *sf* baldness.
'calvo, a *ag* bald.
'calza ['kaltsa] *sf* (*da donna*) stocking; (*da uomo*) sock; **fare la** ~ to knit; ~**e di nailon** nylons, (nylon) stockings.
calza'maglia [kaltsa'maʎʎa] *sf* tights *pl*; (*per danza, ginnastica*) leotard.
cal'zare [kal'tsare] *vt* (*scarpe, guanti: mettersi*) to put on; (: *portare*) to wear ♦ *vi* to fit; ~ **a pennello** to fit like a glove.
calza'tura [kaltsa'tura] *sf* footwear.
calzaturi'ficio [kaltsaturi'fitʃo] *sm* shoe *o* footwear factory.

cal'zetta [kal'tsetta] *sf* ankle sock; **una mezza ~** (*fig*) a nobody.

calzet'tone [kaltset'tone] *sm* heavy knee-length sock.

cal'zino [kal'tsino] *sm* sock.

calzo'laio [kaltso'lajo] *sm* shoemaker; (*che ripara scarpe*) cobbler.

calzole'ria [kaltsole'ria] *sf* (*negozio*) shoe shop; (*arte*) shoemaking.

calzon'cini [kaltson'tʃini] *smpl* shorts; **~ da bagno** (swimming) trunks.

cal'zone [kal'tsone] *sm* trouser leg; (*CUC*) savoury turnover made with pizza dough; **~i** *smpl* trousers (*BRIT*), pants (*US*).

camale'onte *sm* chameleon.

cambi'ale *sf* bill (of exchange); (*pagherò cambiario*) promissory note; **~ di comodo** *o* **di favore** accommodation bill.

cambia'mento *sm* change.

cambi'are *vt* to change; (*modificare*) to alter, change; (*barattare*): **~ (qc con qn/ qc)** to exchange (sth with sb/for sth) ♦ *vi* to change, alter; **~rsi** *vr* (*variare abito*) to change; **~ casa** to move (house); **~ idea** to change one's mind; **~ treno** to change trains; **~ le carte in tavola** (*fig*) to change one's tune; **~ (l')aria in una stanza** to air a room; **è ora di ~ aria** (*andarsene*) it's time to move on.

cambiava'lute *sm inv* exchange office.

'cambio *sm* change; (*modifica*) alteration, change; (*scambio*, *COMM*) exchange; (*corso dei cambi*) rate (of exchange); (*TECN*, *AUT*) gears *pl*; **in ~ di** in exchange for; **dare il ~ a qn** to take over from sb; **fare il *o* un ~** to change (over); **~ a termine** (*COMM*) forward exchange.

'Cambital *sigla m = Ufficio Italiano dei Cambi.*

Cam'bogia [kam'bɔdʒa] *sf*: **la ~** Cambodia.

cambogi'ano, a [kambo'dʒano] *ag*, *sm/f* Cambodian.

cam'busa *sf* storeroom.

'camera *sf* room; (*anche*: **~ da letto**) bedroom; (*POL*) chamber, house; **~ ardente** mortuary chapel; **~ d'aria** inner tube; (*di pallone*) bladder; **~ blindata** strongroom; **C~ di Commercio** Chamber of Commerce; **C~ dei Deputati** Chamber of Deputies, ≈ House of Commons (*BRIT*), ≈ House of Representatives (*US*); *vedi nota nel riquadro*; **~ a gas** gas chamber; **~ del lavoro** trades union centre (*BRIT*), labor union center (*US*); **~ a un letto/a due letti/matrimoniale** single/twin-bedded/double room; **~ oscura** (*FOT*) dark room; **~ da pranzo** dining room.

CAMERA DEI DEPUTATI

The **Camera dei deputati** is the lower house of the Italian Parliament and is presided over by the "Presidente della Camera", who is chosen by the "deputati". Elections to the Chamber are normally held every five years. Since the electoral reform of 1993 members have been voted in via a system which combines a first-past-the-post element with proportional representation. See also **Parlamento**.

---

came'rata, i, e *sm/f* companion, mate ♦ *sf* dormitory.

camera'tismo *sm* comradeship.

cameri'era *sf* (*domestica*) maid; (*che serve a tavola*) waitress; (*che fa le camere*) chambermaid.

cameri'ere *sm* (man)servant; (*di ristorante*) waiter.

came'rino *sm* (*TEAT*) dressing room.

'Camerun *sm*: **il ~** Cameroon.

'camice ['kamitʃe] *sm* (*REL*) alb; (*per medici etc*) white coat.

cami'cetta [kami'tʃetta] *sf* blouse.

ca'micia, cie [ka'mitʃa] *sf* (*da uomo*) shirt; (*da donna*) blouse; **nascere con la ~** (*fig*) to be born lucky; **sudare sette ~cie** (*fig*) to have a hell of a time; **~ di forza** straitjacket; **~ da notte** (*da donna*) nightdress; (*da uomo*) nightshirt; **C~ nera** (*fascista*) Blackshirt.

camici'ola [kami'tʃɔla] *sf* vest.

camici'otto [kami'tʃɔtto] *sm* casual shirt; (*per operai*) smock.

cami'netto *sm* hearth, fireplace.

ca'mino *sm* chimney; (*focolare*) fireplace, hearth.

'camion *sm inv* lorry (*BRIT*), truck (*US*).

camion'cino [kamjon'tʃino] *sm* van.

camio'netta *sf* jeep.

camio'nista, i *sm* lorry driver (*BRIT*), truck driver (*US*).

'camma *sf* cam; **albero a ~e** camshaft.

cam'mello *sm* (*ZOOL*) camel; (*tessuto*) camel hair.

cam'meo *sm* cameo.

cammi'nare *vi* to walk; (*funzionare*) to work, go; **~ a carponi** *o* **a quattro zampe** to go on all fours.

cammi'nata *sf* walk; **fare una ~** to go for a walk.

cam'mino *sm* walk; (*sentiero*) path; (*itinerario, direzione, tragitto*) way; **mettersi in ~** to set *o* start off; **cammin facendo** on the way; **riprendere il** ~ to continue on one's way.

camo'milla *sf* camomile; (*infuso*) camomile tea.

ca'morra *sf* Camorra; (*fig*) racket.

camor'rista, i, e *sm/f* member of the Camorra; (*fig*) racketeer.

ca'moscio [ka'moʃʃo] *sm* chamois.

cam'pagna [kam'paɲɲa] *sf* country, countryside; (*POL, COMM, MIL*) campaign; **in** ~ in the country; **andare in** ~ to go to the country; **fare una** ~ to campaign; ~ **promozionale vendite** sales campaign.

campa'gnolo, a [kampaɲ'ɲɔlo] *ag* country *cpd* ♦ *sf* (*AUT*) cross-country vehicle.

cam'pale *ag* field *cpd*; (*fig*): **una giornata** ~ a hard day.

cam'pana *sf* bell; (*anche:* ~ **di vetro**) bell jar; **sordo come una** ~ as deaf as a doorpost; **sentire l'altra** ~ (*fig*) to hear the other side of the story.

campa'nella *sf* small bell; (*di tenda*) curtain ring.

campa'nello *sm* (*all'uscio, da tavola*) bell.

campa'nile *sm* bell tower, belfry.

campani'lismo *sm* parochialism.

cam'pano, a *ag* of (*o* from) Campania.

cam'pare *vi* to live; (*tirare avanti*) to get by, manage; ~ **alla giornata** to live from day to day.

cam'pato, a *ag*: ~ **in aria** unsound, unfounded.

campeggi'are [kamped'dʒare] *vi* to camp; (*risaltare*) to stand out.

campeggia'tore, 'trice [kampedjʒa'tore] *sm/f* camper.

cam'peggio [kam'peddʒo] *sm* camping; (*terreno*) camp site; **fare (del)** ~ to go camping.

cam'pestre *ag* country *cpd*, rural; **corsa** ~ cross-country race.

Campi'doglio [kampi'dɔʎʎo] *sm*: **il** ~ the Capitol; *vedi nota nel riquadro*.

CAMPIDOGLIO

The **Campidoglio**, *one of the Seven Hills of Rome, is the home of the "Comune di Roma".*

'camping ['kæmpiŋ] *sm inv* camp site.

campiona'mento *sm* sampling.

campio'nario, a *ag*: **fiera** ~a a trade fair ♦ *sm* collection of samples.

campio'nato *sm* championship.

campiona'tura *sf* (*COMM*) production of samples; (*STATISTICA*) sampling.

campi'one, 'essa *sm/f* (*SPORT*) champion ♦ *sm* (*COMM*) sample; ~ **gratuito** free

sample; **prelievi di** ~ product samples.

'campo *sm* (*gen*) field; (*MIL*) field; (: *accampamento*) camp; (*spazio delimitato: sportivo etc*) ground; field; (*di quadro*) background; **i** ~**i** (*campagna*) the countryside; **padrone del** ~ (*fig*) victor; ~ **da aviazione** airfield; ~ **di concentramento** concentration camp; ~ **di golf** golf course; ~ **lungo** (*CINE, TV, FOT*) long shot; ~ **da tennis** tennis court; ~ **visivo** field of vision.

campobas'sano, a *ag* of (*o* from) Campobasso.

campo'santo, pl campi'santi *sm* cemetery.

camuf'fare *vt* to disguise; ~**rsi** *vr*: ~**rsi (da)** to disguise o.s. (as); (*per ballo in maschera*) to dress up (as).

CAN *abbr* (= *Costo, Assicurazione e Nolo*) CIF.

Can. *abbr* (*GEO*) = **canale**.

'Canada *sm*: **il** ~ Canada.

cana'dese *ag, sm/f* Canadian ♦ *sf* (*anche:* **tenda** ~) ridge tent.

ca'naglia [ka'naʎʎa] *sf* rabble, mob; (*persona*) scoundrel, rogue.

ca'nale *sm* (*anche fig*) channel; (*artificiale*) canal.

'canapa *sf* hemp; ~ **indiana** cannabis.

Ca'narie *sfpl*: **le (isole)** ~ the Canary Islands, the Canaries.

cana'rino *sm* canary.

Can'berra *sf* Canberra.

cancel'lare [kantʃel'lare] *vt* (*con la gomma*) to rub out, erase; (*con la penna*) to strike out; (*annullare, disdire*) to cancel.

cancel'lata [kantʃel'lata] *sf* railing(s) (*pl*).

cancelle'ria [kantʃelle'ria] *sf* chancery; (*quanto necessario per scrivere*) stationery.

cancelli'ere [kantʃel'ljɛre] *sm* chancellor; (*di tribunale*) clerk of the court.

can'cello [kan'tʃello] *sm* gate.

cance'rogeno, a [kantʃe'rɔdʒeno] *ag* carcinogenic ♦ *sm* carcinogen.

cance'rologo, a, gi, ghe [kantʃe'rɔlogo] *sm/f* cancer specialist.

cance'roso, a [kantʃe'roso] *ag* cancerous ♦ *sm/f* cancer patient.

can'crena *sf* gangrene.

'cancro *sm* (*MED*) cancer; (*dello zodiaco*): **C**~ Cancer; **essere del C**~ to be Cancer.

candeggi'are [kanded'dʒare] *vt* to bleach.

candeg'gina [kanded'dʒina] *sf* bleach.

can'dela *sf* candle; ~ **(di accensione)** (*AUT*) spark(ing) plug; **una lampadina da 100** ~**e** (*ELETTR*) a 100 watt bulb; **a lume di** ~ by candlelight; **tenere la** ~ (*fig*) to play gooseberry (*BRIT*), act as chaperone.

cande'labro *sm* candelabra.
candeli'ere *sm* candlestick.
cande'lotto *sm* candle; ~ **di dinamite** stick of dynamite; ~ **lacrimogeno** tear gas grenade.
candi'dare *vt* to present as candidate; ~**rsi** *vr* to present o.s. as candidate.
candi'dato, a *sm/f* candidate; (*aspirante a una carica*) applicant.
candida'tura *sf* candidature; application.
'candido, a *ag* white as snow; (*puro*) pure; (*sincero*) sincere, candid.
can'dito, a *ag* candied.
can'dore *sm* brilliant white; purity; sincerity, candour (*BRIT*), candor (*US*).
'cane *sm* dog; (*di pistola, fucile*) cock; **fa un freddo** ~ it's bitterly cold; **non c'era un** ~ there wasn't a soul; **quell'attore è un** ~ he's a rotten actor; ~ **da caccia** hunting dog; ~ **da guardia** guard dog; ~ **lupo** alsatian; ~ **da salotto** lap dog; ~ **da slitta** husky.
ca'nestro *sm* basket; **fare un** ~ (*SPORT*) to shoot a basket.
'canfora *sf* camphor.
cangi'ante [kan'dʒante] *ag* iridescent; **seta** ~ shot silk.
can'guro *sm* kangaroo.
ca'nicola *sf* scorching heat.
ca'nile *sm* kennel; (*di allevamento*) kennels *pl*; ~ **municipale** dog pound.
ca'nino, a *ag, sm* canine.
'canna *sf* (*pianta*) reed; (: *indica, da zucchero*) cane; (*bastone*) stick, cane; (*di fucile*) barrel; (*di organo*) pipe; (*DROGA: gergo*) joint; ~ **fumaria** chimney flue; ~ **da pesca** (fishing) rod; ~ **da zucchero** sugar cane.
can'nella *sf* (*CUC*) cinnamon; (*di conduttura, botte*) tap.
cannel'loni *smpl* pasta tubes stuffed with sauce and baked.
can'neto *sm* bed of reeds.
can'nibale *sm* cannibal.
cannocchi'ale [kannok'kjale] *sm* telescope.
canno'nata *sf*: **è una vera** ~! (*fig*) it's (*o* he's *etc*) fantastic!
can'none *sm* (*MIL*) gun; (: *STORIA*) cannon; (*tubo*) pipe, tube; (*piega*) box pleat; (*fig*) ace; **donna** ~ fat woman.
cannoni'ere *sm* (*NAUT*) gunner; (*CALCIO*) goal scorer.
can'nuccia, ce [kan'nuttʃa] *sf* (drinking) straw.
'canone *sm* canon, criterion; (*mensile, annuo*) rent; fee; **legge dell'equo** ~ fair rent act.
ca'nonica, che *sf* presbytery.

ca'nonico, ci *sm* (*REL*) canon.
canoniz'zare [kanonid'dzare] *vt* to canonize.
ca'noro, a *ag* (*uccello*) singing, song *cpd*.
ca'notta *sf* vest.
canot'taggio [kanot'taddʒo] *sm* rowing.
canotti'era *sf* vest (*BRIT*), undershirt (*US*).
ca'notto *sm* small boat, dinghy; canoe.
cano'vaccio [kano'vattʃo] *sm* (*tela*) canvas; (*strofinaccio*) duster; (*trama*) plot.
can'tante *sm/f* singer.
can'tare *vt, vi* to sing; ~ **vittoria** to crow; **fare** ~ **qn** (*fig*) to make sb talk.
cantas'torie *sm/f inv* storyteller.
cantau'tore, 'trice *sm/f* singer-composer.
canterel'lare *vt, vi* to hum, sing to o.s.
canticchi'are [kantik'kjare] *vt, vi* to hum, sing to o.s.
canti'ere *sm* (*EDIL*) (building) site; (*anche:* ~ **navale**) shipyard.
canti'lena *sf* (*filastrocca*) lullaby; (*fig*) singsong voice.
can'tina *sf* (*locale*) cellar; (*bottega*) wine shop.
'canto *sm* song; (*arte*) singing; (*REL*) chant; chanting; (*POESIA*) poem, lyric; (*parte di una poesia*) canto; (*parte, lato*): **da un** ~ on the one hand; **d'altro** ~ on the other hand.
canto'nata *sf* (*di edificio*) corner; **prendere una** ~ (*fig*) to blunder.
can'tone *sm* (*in Svizzera*) canton.
cantoni'era *ag*: (**casa**) ~ road inspector's house.
can'tuccio [kan'tuttʃo] *sm* corner, nook.
ca'nuto, a *ag* white, whitehaired.
canzo'nare [kantso'nare] *vt* to tease.
canzona'tura [kantsona'tura] *sf* teasing; (*beffa*) joke.
can'zone [kan'tsone] *sf* song; (*POESIA*) canzone.
canzoni'ere [kantso'njere] *sm* (*MUS*) songbook; (*LETTERATURA*) collection of poems.
'caos *sm inv* chaos.
ca'otico, a, ci, che *ag* chaotic.
CAP *sigla m vedi* **codice di avviamento postale**.
cap. *abbr* (= *capitolo*) ch.
ca'pace [ka'patʃe] *ag* able, capable; (*ampio, vasto*) large, capacious; **sei** ~ **di farlo?** can you *o* are you able to do it?; ~ **d'intendere e di volere** (*DIR*) in full possession of one's faculties.
capacità [kapatʃi'ta] *sf inv* ability; (*DIR, di recipiente*) capacity; ~ **produttiva** production capacity.
capaci'tarsi [kapatʃi'tarsi] *vr*: ~ **di** to make out, understand.

ca'panna *sf* hut.

capan'nello *sm* knot (of people).

ca'panno *sm* (*di cacciatori*) hide; (*da spiaggia*) bathing hut.

capan'none *sm* (*AGR*) barn; (*fabbricato industriale*) (factory) shed.

caparbietà *sf* stubbornness.

ca'parbio, a *ag* stubborn.

ca'parra *sf* deposit, down payment.

capa'tina *sf*: **fare una ~ da qn/in centro** to pop in on sb/into town.

capeggi'are [kaped'dʒare] *vt* (*rivolta etc*) to head, lead.

ca'pello *sm* hair; **~i** *smpl* (*capigliatura*) hair *sg*; **averne fin sopra i ~i di qc/qn** to be fed up to the (back) teeth with sth/sb; **mi ci hanno tirato per i ~i** (*fig*) they dragged me into it; **tirato per i ~i** (*spiegazione*) far-fetched.

capel'lone, a *sm/f* hippie.

capel'luto, a *ag*: **cuoio ~** scalp.

capez'zale [kapet'tsale] *sm* bolster; (*fig*) bedside.

ca'pezzolo [ka'pettsolo] *sm* nipple.

capi'ente *ag* capacious.

capi'enza [ka'pjɛntsa] *sf* capacity.

capiglia'tura [kapiʎʎa'tura] *sf* hair.

capil'lare *ag* (*fig*) detailed ♦ *sm* (*ANAT*: *anche*: **vaso ~**) capillary.

ca'pire *vt* to understand; **~ al volo** to catch on straight away; **si capisce!** (*certamente!*) of course!, certainly!

capi'tale *ag* (*mortale*) capital; (*fondamentale*) main *cpd*, chief *cpd* ♦ *sf* (*città*) capital ♦ *sm* (*ECON*) capital; **~ azionario** equity capital, share capital; **~ d'esercizio** working capital; **~ fisso** capital assets, fixed capital; **~ immobile** real estate; **~ liquido** cash assets *pl*; **~ mobile** movables *pl*; **~ di rischio** risk capital; **~ sociale** (*di società*) authorized capital; (*di club*) funds *pl*; **~ di ventura** venture capital, risk capital.

capita'lismo *sm* capitalism.

capita'lista, i, e *ag*, *sm/f* capitalist.

capitaliz'zare [kapitalid'dzare] *vt* to capitalize.

capitalizzazi'one [kapitaliddzat'tsjone] *sf* capitalization.

capita'nare *vt* to lead; (*CALCIO*) to captain.

capitane'ria *sf*: **~ (di porto)** port authorities *pl*.

capi'tano *sm* captain; **~ di lungo corso** master mariner; **~ di ventura** (*STORIA*) mercenary leader.

capi'tare *vi* (*giungere casualmente*) to happen to go, find o.s.; (*accadere*) to happen; (*presentarsi: cosa*) to turn up,

present itself ♦ *vb impers* to happen; **~ a proposito/bene/male** to turn up at the right moment/at a good time/at a bad time; **mi è capitato un guaio** I've had a spot of trouble.

capi'tello *sm* (*ARCHIT*) capital.

capito'lare *vi* to capitulate.

capitolazi'one [kapitolat'tsjone] *sf* capitulation.

ca'pitolo *sm* chapter; **~i** *smpl* (*COMM*) items; **non ho voce in ~** (*fig*) I have no say in the matter.

capi'tombolo *sm* headlong fall, tumble.

'capo *sm* (*ANAT*) head; (*persona*) head, leader; (: *in ufficio*) head, boss; (: *in tribù*) chief; (*estremità*: *di tavolo, scale*) head, top; (: *di filo*) end; (*GEO*) cape; **andare a ~** to start a new paragraph; **"punto a ~"** "full stop – new paragraph"; **da ~** over again; **in ~ a** (*tempo*) within; **da un ~ all'altro** from one end to the other; **fra ~ e collo** (*all'improvviso*) out of the blue; **un discorso senza né ~ né coda** a senseless o meaningless speech; **~ d'accusa** (*DIR*) charge; **~ di bestiame** head *inv* of cattle; **C~ di Buona Speranza** Cape of Good Hope; **~ di vestiario** item of clothing.

capo'banda, *pl* **capi'banda** *sm* (*MUS*) bandmaster; (*di malviventi, fig*) gang leader.

ca'poccia [ka'pɔttʃa] *sm inv* (*di lavoranti*) overseer; (*peg*: *capobanda*) boss.

capo'classe, *pl(m)* **capi'classe,** *pl(f)* *inv sm/f* (*INS*) ≈ form captain (*BRIT*), class president (*US*).

capocu'oco, chi *sm* head cook.

Capo'danno *sm* New Year.

capofa'miglia, *pl(m)* **capifa'miglia,** *pl(f) inv* [kapofa'miʎʎa] *sm/f* head of the family.

capo'fitto: a ~ *av* headfirst, headlong.

capo'giro [kapo'dʒiro] *sm* dizziness *no pl*; **da ~** (*fig*) astonishing, staggering.

capo'gruppo, *pl(m)* **capi'gruppo,** *pl(f) inv sm/f* group leader.

capola'voro, i *sm* masterpiece.

capo'linea, *pl* **capi'linea** *sm* terminus; (*fig*) end of the line.

capo'lino *sm*: **far ~** to peep out (*o in etc*).

capo'lista, *pl(m)* **capi'lista,** *pl(f) inv sm/f* (*POL*) top candidate on electoral list.

capolu'ogo, *pl* **ghi** *o* **capilu'oghi** *sm* chief town, administrative centre (*BRIT*) *o* center (*US*).

capo'mastro, *pl* **i** *o* **capi'mastri** *sm* master builder.

capo'rale *sm* (*MIL*) lance corporal (*BRIT*), private first class (*US*).

capore'parto, *pl(m)* **capire'parto,** *pl(f) inv*

sm/f (*di operai*) foreman; (*di ufficio, negozio*) head of department.

capo'sala *sf inv* (*MED*) ward sister.

capo'saldo, *pl* **capi'saldi** *sm* stronghold; (*fig: fondamento*) basis, cornerstone.

capo'squadra, *pl* **capi'squadra** *sm* (*di operai*) foreman, ganger; (*MIL*) squad leader; (*SPORT*) team captain.

capostazi'one, *pl* **capistazi'one** [kapostat'tsjone] *sm* station master.

capos'tipite *sm* progenitor; (*fig*) earliest example.

capo'tavola, *pl*(*m*) **capi'tavola,** *pl*(*f*) *inv sm/f* (*persona*) head of the table; **sedere a** ~ to sit at the head of the table.

ca'pote [ka'pɔt] *sf inv* (*AUT*) hood (*BRIT*), soft top.

capo'treno, *pl* **capi'treno** *o* **capo'treni** *sm* guard.

capouf'ficio, *pl*(*m*) **capiuf'ficio,** *pl*(*f*) *inv* [kapouf'fitʃo] *sm/f* head clerk.

capo'verso *sm* (*di verso, periodo*) first line; (*TIP*) indent; (*paragrafo*) paragraph; (*DIR: comma*) section.

capo'volgere [kapo'vɔldʒerc] *vt* to overturn; (*fig*) to reverse; ~**rsi** *vr* to overturn; (*barca*) to capsize; (*fig*) to be reversed.

capovolgi'mento [kapovoldʒi'mento] *sm* (*fig*) reversal, complete change.

capo'volto, a *pp di* **capovolgere ♦** *ag* upside down; (*barca*) capsized.

'cappa *sf* (*mantello*) cape, cloak; (*del camino*) hood.

cap'pella *sf* (*REL*) chapel.

cappel'lano *sm* chaplain.

cap'pello *sm* hat; **ti faccio tanto di** ~**!** (*fig*) I take my hat off to you!; ~ **a bombetta** bowler (hat), derby (*US*); ~ **a cilindro** top hat.

'cappero *sm* caper.

cap'pone *sm* capon.

cappot'tare *vi* (*AUT*) to overturn.

cap'potto *sm* (over)coat.

cappuc'cino [kapput'tʃino] *sm* (*frate*) Capuchin monk; (*bevanda*) cappuccino.

cap'puccio [kap'puttʃo] *sm* (*copricapo*) hood; (*della biro*) cap.

'capra *sf* (she-)goat.

ca'prese *ag* from (*o* of) Capri.

ca'pretto *sm* kid.

ca'priccio [ka'prittʃo] *sm* caprice, whim; (*bizza*) tantrum; **fare i** ~**i** to be very naughty; ~ **della sorte** quirk of fate.

capricci'oso, a [kaprit'tʃoso] *ag* capricious, whimsical; naughty.

Capri'corno *sm* Capricorn; **essere del** ~ (*dello zodiaco*) to be Capricorn.

capri'foglio [kapri'fɔʎʎo] *sm* honeysuckle.

capri'ola *sf* somersault.

capri'olo *sm* roe deer.

'capro *sm* billy-goat; ~ **espiatorio** (*fig*) scapegoat.

ca'prone *sm* billy-goat.

'capsula *sf* capsule; (*di arma, per bottiglie*) cap.

cap'tare *vt* (*RADIO, TV*) to pick up; (*cattivarsi*) to gain, win.

CAR *sigla m* = *Centro Addestramento Reclute.*

cara'bina *sf* rifle.

carabini'ere *sm* member of Italian military police force; *vedi nota nel riquadro.*

CARABINIERI

Originally part of the armed forces, the **Carabinieri** *are police who now have civil as well as military duties, such as maintaining public order. They include various units and mounted divisions and report to either the Minister of the Interior or the Minister of Defence, depending on the function they are performing.*

Ca'racas *sf* Caracas.

ca'raffa *sf* carafe.

Ca'raibi *smpl*: **il mar dei** ~ the Caribbean (Sea).

cara'ibico, a, ci, che *ag* Caribbean.

cara'mella *sf* sweet.

cara'mello *sm* caramel.

ca'rato *sm* (*di oro, diamante etc*) carat.

ca'rattere *sm* character; (*caratteristica*) characteristic, trait; **avere un buon** ~ to be good-natured; **informazione di** ~ **tecnico/confidenziale** information of a technical/confidential nature; **essere in** ~ **con qc** (*intonarsi*) to be in harmony with sth.

caratte'rino *sm* difficult nature *o* character.

caratte'ristico, a, ci, che *ag* characteristic **♦** *sf* characteristic, feature; **segni** ~**ci** (*su passaporto etc*) distinguishing marks.

caratteriz'zare [karatterid'dzare] *vt* to characterize, distinguish.

carboi'drato *sm* carbohydrate.

carbo'naio *sm* (*chi fa carbone*) charcoal-burner; (*commerciante*) coalman, coal merchant.

car'bone *sm* coal; ~ **fossile** (pit) coal; **essere** *o* **stare sui** ~**i ardenti** to be like a cat on hot bricks.

car'bonio *sm* (*CHIM*) carbon.

carboniz'zare [karbonid'dzare] *vt* (*legna*) to carbonize; (: *parzialmente*) to char; **morire carbonizzato** to be burned to death.
carbu'rante *sm* (motor) fuel.
carbura'tore *sm* carburettor.
car'cassa *sf* carcass; (*fig: peg: macchina etc*) (old) wreck.
carce'rato, a [kartʃe'rato] *sm/f* prisoner.
'carcere ['kartʃere] *sm* prison; (*pena*) imprisonment; ~ **di massima sicurezza** top-security prison.
carceri'ere, a [kartʃe'rjɛre] *sm/f* (*anche fig*) jailer.
carci'ofo [kar'tʃɔfo] *sm* artichoke.
cardel'lino *sm* goldfinch.
car'diaco, a, ci, che *ag* cardiac, heart *cpd.*
cardi'nale *ag, sm* cardinal.
'cardine *sm* hinge.
cardiolo'gia [kardjolo'dʒia] *sf* cardiology.
cardi'ologo, gi *sm* heart specialist, cardiologist.
'cardo *sm* thistle.
ca'rente *ag*: ~ **di** lacking in.
ca'renza [ka'rɛntsa] *sf* lack, scarcity; (*vitaminica*) deficiency.
cares'tia *sf* famine; (*penuria*) scarcity, dearth.
ca'rezza [ka'rettsa] *sf* caress; **dare** *o* **fare una** ~ **a** (*persona*) to caress; (*animale*) to stroke, pat.
carez'zare [karet'tsare] *vt* to caress, stroke, fondle.
carez'zevole [karet'tsevole] *ag* sweet, endearing.
cari'are *vt*, ~**rsi** *vr* (*denti*) to decay.
'carica *sf vedi* **carico.**
caricabatte'rie *sm inv* (*ELETTR*) battery charger.
cari'care *vt* to load; (*aggravare: anche fig*) to weigh down; (*orologio*) to wind up; (*batteria, MIL*) to charge; (*INFORM*) to load; ~**rsi** *vr*: ~**rsi di** to burden *o* load o.s. with; (*fig: di responsabilità, impegni*) to burden o.s. with.
carica'tura *sf* caricature.
'carico, a, chi, che *ag* (*che porta un peso*): ~ **di** loaded *o* laden with; (*fucile*) loaded; (*orologio*) wound up; (*batteria*) charged; (*colore*) deep; (*caffè, tè*) strong ♦ *sm* (*il caricare*) loading; (*ciò che si carica*) load; (*COMM*) shipment; (*fig: peso*) burden, weight ♦ *sf* (*mansione ufficiale*) office, position; (*MIL, TECN, ELETTR*) charge; ~ **di debiti** up to one's ears in debt; **persona a** ~ dependent; **essere a** ~ **di qn** (*spese etc*) to be charged to sb; (*accusa, prova*) to be against sb; **testimone a** ~ witness for the prosecution; **farsi** ~ **di** (*problema,*

responsabilità) to take on; **a** ~ **del cliente** at the customer's expense; ~ **di lavoro** (*di ditta, reparto*) workload; ~ **utile** payload; **capacità di** ~ cargo capacity; **entrare/ essere in** ~**a** to come into/be in office; **ricoprire** *o* **rivestire una** ~**a** to hold a position; **uscire di** ~**a** to leave office; **dare la** ~**a a** (*orologio*) to wind up; (*fig: persona*) to back up; **tornare alla** ~**a** (*fig*) to insist, persist; **ha una forte** ~**a di simpatia** he's very likeable.
'carie *sf* (*dentaria*) decay.
ca'rino, a *ag* lovely, pretty, nice; (*simpatico*) nice.
ca'risma [ka'rizma] *sm* charisma.
caris'matico, a, ci, che *ag* charismatic.
carità *sf* charity; **per** ~! (*escl di rifiuto*) good heavens, no!
carita'tevole *ag* charitable.
carnagi'one [karna'dʒone] *sf* complexion.
car'nale *ag* (*amore*) carnal; (*fratello*) blood *cpd.*
'carne *sf* flesh; (*bovina, ovina etc*) meat; **in** ~ **e ossa** in the flesh, in person; **essere (bene) in** ~ to be well padded, be plump; **non essere né** ~ **né pesce** (*fig*) to be neither fish nor fowl; ~ **di manzo/ maiale/pecora** beef/pork/mutton; ~ **in scatola** tinned *o* canned meat; ~ **tritata** mince (*BRIT*), hamburger meat (*US*), minced (*BRIT*) *o* ground (*US*) meat.
car'nefice [kar'nefitʃe] *sm* executioner; hangman.
carnefi'cina [karnefi'tʃina] *sf* carnage; (*fig*) disaster.
carne'vale *sm* carnival; **C**~ *vedi nota nel riquadro.*

CARNEVALE

Carnevale *is the name given to the period between Epiphany (6 January) and the beginning of Lent, when people throw parties, put on processions with spectacular floats, build bonfires in the "piazze" and dress up in fabulous costumes and masks. Building to a peak just before Lent,* Carnevale *culminates in the festivities of "Martedì grasso" (Shrove Tuesday).*

---

car'nivoro, a *ag* carnivorous.
car'noso, a *ag* fleshy; (*pianta, frutto, radice*) pulpy; (*labbra*) full.
'caro, a *ag* (*amato*) dear; (*costoso*) dear, expensive.
ca'rogna [ka'roɲɲa] *sf* carrion; (*fig fam*) swine.
caro'sello *sm* merry-go-round.

ca'rota *sf* carrot.
caro'vana *sf* caravan.
caro'vita *sm* high cost of living.
'carpa *sf* carp.
Car'pazi [kar'patsi] *smpl*: **i** ~ the Carpathian Mountains.
carpente'ria *sf* carpentry.
carpenti'ere *sm* carpenter.
car'pire *vt*: ~ **qc a qn** (*segreto etc*) to get sth out of sb.
car'poni *av* on all fours.
car'rabile *ag* suitable for vehicles; **"passo ~"** "keep clear".
car'raio, a *ag*: **passo** ~ vehicle entrance.
carré *sm* (*acconciatura*) bob.
carreggi'ata [karred'dʒata] *sf* carriageway (*BRIT*), roadway; **rimettersi in** ~ (*fig: recuperare*) to catch up; **tenersi in** ~ (*fig*) to keep to the right path.
carrel'lata *sf* (*CINE, TV: tecnica*) tracking; (*; scena*) running shot; ~ **di successi** medley of hit tunes.
car'rello *sm* trolley; (*AER*) undercarriage; (*CINE*) dolly; (*di macchina da scrivere*) carriage.
car'retta *sf*: **tirare la** ~ (*fig*) to plod along.
car'retto *sm* handcart.
carri'era *sf* career; **fare** ~ to get on; **ufficiale di** ~ (*MIL*) regular officer; **a gran** ~ at full speed.
carri'ola *sf* wheelbarrow.
'carro *sm* cart, wagon; **il Gran/Piccolo C**~ (*ASTR*) the Great/Little Bear; **mettere il** ~ **avanti ai buoi** (*fig*) to put the cart before the horse; ~ **armato** tank; ~ **attrezzi** (*AUT*) breakdown van (*BRIT*), tow truck (*US*); ~ **funebre** hearse; ~ **merci/bestiame** (*FERR*) goods/animal wagon.
car'roccio [kar'rɔtʃo] *sm* (*POL*): **il C**~ symbol of Lega Nord.
car'rozza [kar'rɔttsa] *sf* carriage, coach; ~ **letto** (*FERR*) sleeper; ~ **ristorante** (*FERR*) dining car.
carroz'zella [karrot'tsɛlla] *sf* (*per bambini*) pram (*BRIT*), baby carriage (*US*); (*per invalidi*) wheelchair.
carrozze'ria [karrottse'ria] *sf* body, coachwork (*BRIT*); (*officina*) coachbuilder's workshop (*BRIT*), body shop.
carrozzi'ere [karrot'tsjɛre] *sm* (*AUT: progettista*) car designer; (*: meccanico*) coachbuilder.
carroz'zina [karrot'tsina] *sf* pram (*BRIT*), baby carriage (*US*).
carroz'zone [karrot'tsone] *sm* (*da circo, di zingari*) caravan.
car'rucola *sf* pulley.

'carta *sf* paper; (*al ristorante*) menu; (*GEO*) map; plan; (*documento, da gioco*) card; (*costituzione*) charter; ~**e** *sfpl* (*documenti*) papers, documents; **alla** ~ (*al ristorante*) à la carte; **cambiare le** ~**e in tavola** (*fig*) to shift one's ground; **fare** ~**e false** (*fig*) to go to great lengths; ~ **assegni** bank card; ~ **assorbente** blotting paper; ~ **bollata** *o* **da bollo** (*AMM*) official stamped paper; ~ **di credito** credit card; ~ **di debito** cash card; ~ (**geografica**) map; ~ **d'identità** identity card; ~ **igienica** toilet paper; ~ **d'imbarco** (*AER, NAUT*) boarding card, boarding pass; ~ **da lettere** writing paper; ~ **libera** (*AMM*) unstamped paper; ~ **millimetrata** graph paper; ~ **oleata** waxed paper; ~ **da pacchi**, ~ **da imballo** wrapping paper, brown paper; ~ **da parati** wallpaper; ~ **verde** (*AUT*) green card; ~ **vetrata** sandpaper; ~ **da visita** visiting card.
cartacar'bone *pl* **cartecar'bone** *sf* carbon paper.
car'taccia, ce [kar'tattʃa] *sf* waste paper.
cartamo'dello *sm* (*CUCITO*) paper pattern.
cartamo'neta *sf* paper money.
carta'pecora *sf* parchment.
carta'pesta *sf* papier-mâché.
cartas'traccia [kartas'trattʃa] *sf* waste paper.
car'teggio [kar'teddʒo] *sm* correspondence.
car'tella *sf* (*scheda*) card; (*custodia: di cartone*) folder; (*: di uomo d'affari etc*) briefcase; (*: di scolaro*) schoolbag, satchel; ~ **clinica** (*MED*) case sheet.
cartel'lino *sm* (*etichetta*) label; (*su porta*) notice; (*scheda*) card; **timbrare il** ~ (*all'entrata*) to clock in; (*all'uscita*) to clock out; ~ **di presenza** clock card, timecard.
car'tello *sm* sign; (*pubblicitario*) poster; (*stradale*) sign, signpost; (*in dimostrazioni*) placard; (*ECON*) cartel.
cartel'lone *sm* (*pubblicitario*) advertising poster; (*della tombola*) scoring frame; (*TEAT*) playbill; **tenere il** ~ (*spettacolo*) to have a long run.
carti'era *sf* paper mill.
carti'lagine [karti'ladʒine] *sf* cartilage.
car'tina *sf* (*AUT, GEO*) map.
car'toccio [kar'tɔttʃo] *sm* paper bag; **cuocere al** ~ (*CUC*) to bake in tinfoil.
cartogra'fia *sf* cartography.
carto'laio, a *sm/f* stationer.
cartole'ria *sf* stationer's (shop) (*BRIT*).
carto'lina *sf* postcard; ~ **di auguri** greetings card; ~ **precetto** *o* **rosa** (*MIL*) call-up card.
carto'mante *sm/f* fortune-teller (*using*

cards).

carton'cino [karton'tʃino] *sm* (*materiale*) thin cardboard; (*biglietto*) card; ~ **della società** compliments slip.

car'tone *sm* cardboard; (*del latte, dell'aranciata*) carton; (*ARTE*) cartoon; ~**i animati** (*CINE*) cartoons.

car'tuccia, ce [kar'tuttʃa] *sf* cartridge; ~ **a salve** blank cartridge; **mezza** ~ (*fig: persona*) good-for-nothing.

'casa *sf* house; (*specialmente la propria* ~) home; (*COMM*) firm, house; **essere a** ~ **to** be at home; **vado a** ~ **mia/tua** I'm going home/to your house; ~ **di correzione** ≈ community home (*BRIT*), reformatory (*US*); ~ **di cura** nursing home; ~ **editrice** publishing house; ~ **dello studente** student hostel; ~ **di tolleranza,** ~ **d'appuntamenti** brothel; ~**e popolari** ≈ council houses (*o* flats) (*BRIT*), ≈ public housing units (*US*).

Casa'blanca *sf* Casablanca.

ca'sacca, che *sf* military coat; (*di fantino*) blouse.

ca'sale *sm* (*gruppo di case*) hamlet; (*casa di campagna*) farmhouse.

casa'lingo, a, ghi, ghe *ag* household, domestic; (*fatto a casa*) home-made; (*semplice*) homely; (*amante della casa*) home-loving ♦ *sf* housewife; ~**ghi** *smpl* (*oggetti*) household articles; **cucina** ~**a** plain home cooking.

ca'sata *sf* family lineage.

ca'sato *sm* family name.

Casc. *abbr* (*GEO*) = cascata.

casca'morto *sm* woman-chaser; **fare il** ~ **to** chase women.

cas'care *vi* to fall; ~ **bene/male** (*fig*) to land lucky/unlucky; ~ **dalle nuvole** (*fig*) to be taken aback; ~ **dal sonno** to be falling asleep on one's feet; **caschi il mondo** no matter what; **non cascherà il mondo se ...** it won't be the end of the world if ....

cas'cata *sf* fall; (*d'acqua*) cascade, waterfall.

cascherò *etc* [kaske'rɔ] *vb vedi* cascare.

ca'scina [kaʃ'ʃina] *sf* farmstead.

casci'nale [kaʃʃi'nale] *sm* (*casolare*) farmhouse; (*cascina*) farmstead.

'casco, schi *sm* helmet; (*del parrucchiere*) hair-dryer; (*di banane*) bunch; ~ **blu** (*MIL*) blue helmet (*UN soldier*).

caseggi'ato [kased'dʒato] *sm* (*edificio*) large block of flats (*BRIT*) *o* apartment building (*US*); (*gruppo di case*) group of houses.

casei'ficio [kazei'fitʃo] *sm* creamery.

ca'sella *sf* pigeonhole; ~ **postale** (**C.P.**) post

office box (P.O. box).

casel'lario *sm* (*mobile*) filing cabinet; (*raccolta di pratiche*) files *pl*; ~ **giudiziale** court records *pl*; ~ **penale** police files *pl*.

ca'sello *sm* (*di autostrada*) tollgate.

case'reccio, a, ci, ce [kase'rettʃo] *ag* home-made.

ca'serma *sf* barracks *pl*.

caser'tano, a *ag* of (*o* from) Caserta.

ca'sino *sm* (*confusione*) row, racket; (*casa di prostituzione*) brothel.

casinò *sm inv* casino.

ca'sistica (*MED*) record of cases; **secondo la** ~ **degli incidenti stradali** according to road accident data.

'caso *sm* chance; (*fatto, vicenda*) event, incident; (*possibilità*) possibility; (*MED, LING*) case; **a** ~ at random; **per** ~ by chance, by accident; **in ogni** ~, **in tutti i** ~**i** in any case, at any rate; **in** ~ **contrario** otherwise; **al** ~ should the opportunity arise; **nel** ~ **che** in case; ~ **mai** if by chance; **far** ~ **a qc/qn** to pay attention to sth/sb; **fare** *o* **porre** *o* **mettere il** ~ **che** to suppose that; **fa proprio al** ~ **nostro** it's just what we need; **guarda** ~ **...** strangely enough **...; è il** ~ **che ce ne andiamo** we'd better go; ~ **limite** borderline case.

caso'lare *sm* cottage.

'Caspio *sm*: **il mar** ~ the Caspian Sea.

'caspita *escl* (*di sorpresa*) good heavens!; (*di impazienza*) for goodness' sake!

'cassa *sf* case, crate, box; (*bara*) coffin; (*mobile*) chest; (*involucro: di orologio etc*) case; (*macchina*) cash register; (*luogo di pagamento*) cash desk, checkout (*counter*); (*fondo*) fund; (*istituto bancario*) bank; **battere** ~ (*fig*) to come looking for money; ~ **automatica prelievi** automatic telling machine, cash dispenser; ~ **continua** night safe; **mettere in** ~ **integrazione** ≈ to lay off; **C**~ **del Mezzogiorno** *development fund for the South of Italy*; ~ **mutua** *o* **malattia** health insurance scheme; ~ **di risonanza** (*MUS*) soundbox; (*fig*) platform; ~ **di risparmio** savings bank; ~ **rurale e artigiana** credit institution (*serving farmers and craftsmen*); ~ **toracica** (*ANAT*) chest.

cassa'forte, pl casse'forti *sf* safe.

cassa'panca, pl cassa'panche *o* **casse'panche** *sf* settle.

casseru'ola, casse'rola *sf* saucepan.

cas'setta *sf* box; (*per registratore*) cassette; (*CINE, TEAT*) box-office takings *pl*; **pane a** *o* **in** ~ toasting loaf; **film di** ~ (*commerciale*) box-office draw; **far** ~ to be a box-office success; ~ **delle lettere** letterbox; ~ **di**

sicurezza strongbox.
cas'setto *sm* drawer.
casset'tone *sm* chest of drawers.
cassi'ere, a *sm/f* cashier; (*di banca*) teller.
cassinte'grato, a *sm/f person who has been laid off.*
cas'sone *sm* (*cassa*) large case, large chest.
'casta *sf* caste.
cas'tagna [kas'taɲɲa] *sf* chestnut; **prendere qn in ~** (*fig*) to catch sb in the act.
cas'tagno [kas'taɲɲo] *sm* chestnut (tree).
cas'tano, a *ag* chestnut (brown).
cas'tello *sm* castle; (*TECN*) scaffolding.
casti'gare *vt* to punish.
casti'gato, a *ag* (*casto, modesto*) pure, chaste; (*emendato: prosa, versione*) expurgated, amended.
cas'tigo, ghi *sm* punishment.
castità *sf* chastity.
'casto, a *ag* chaste, pure.
cas'toro *sm* beaver.
cas'trante *ag* frustrating.
cas'trare *vt* to castrate; to geld; to doctor (*BRIT*), fix (*US*); (*fig: iniziativa*) to frustrate.
castrone'ria *sf* (*fam*): **dire ~e** to talk rubbish.
casu'ale *ag* chance *cpd.*
ca'supola *sf* simple little cottage.
catac'lisma, i *sm* (*fig*) catastrophe.
cata'comba *sf* catacomb.
cata'fascio [kata'faʃʃo] *sm*: **andare a ~** to collapse; **mandare a ~** to wreck.
cata'litico, a, ci, che *ag*: **marmitta ~a** (*AUT*) catalytic converter.
cataliz'zare [katalid'dzare] *vt* (*fig*) to act as a catalyst (up)on.
cataliz'zato, a [katalid'dzato] *ag* (*AUT*) with catalytic converter.
catalizza'tore [kataliddza'tore] *sm* (*anche fig*) catalyst; (*AUT*) catalytic converter.
Cata'logna [kata'loɲɲa] *sf*: **la ~** Catalonia.
ca'talogo, ghi *sm* catalogue; **~ dei prezzi** price list.
cata'nese *ag* of (*o* from) Catania.
catanza'rese [katandza'rese] *ag* of (*o* from) Catanzaro.
cata'pecchia [kata'pekkja] *sf* hovel.
cata'pulta *sf* catapult.
catarifran'gente [katarifran'dʒɛnte] *sm* (*AUT*) reflector.
ca'tarro *sm* catarrh.
ca'tarsi *sf inv* catharsis.
ca'tasta *sf* stack, pile.
ca'tasto *sm* land register; land registry office.
ca'tastrofe *sf* catastrophe, disaster.
catas'trofico, a, ci, che *ag* (*evento*) catastrophic; (*persona, previsione*) pessimistic.
cate'chismo [kate'kizmo] *sm* catechism.
catego'ria *sf* category; (*di albergo*) class.
cate'gorico, a, ci, che *ag* categorical.
ca'tena *sf* chain; **reazione a ~** chain reaction; **susseguirsi a ~** to happen in quick succession; **~ alimentare** food chain; **~ di montaggio** assembly line; **~ montuosa** mountain range; **~e da neve** (*AUT*) snow chains.
cate'naccio [kate'nattʃo] *sm* bolt.
cate'nella *sf* (*ornamento*) chain; (*di orologio*) watch chain; (*di porta*) door chain.
cate'ratta *sf* cataract; (*chiusa*) sluice gate.
ca'terva *sf* (*di cose*) loads *pl*, heaps *pl*; (*di persone*) horde.
cate'tere *sm* (*MED*) catheter.
cati'nella *sf*: **piovere a ~e** to pour, rain cats and dogs.
ca'tino *sm* basin.
ca'todico, a, ci, che *ag*: **tubo a raggi ~ci** cathode-ray tube.
ca'torcio [ka'tɔrtʃo] *sm* (*peg*) old wreck.
ca'trame *sm* tar.
'cattedra *sf* teacher's desk; (*di università*) chair; **salire** *o* **montare in ~** (*fig*) to pontificate.
catte'drale *sf* cathedral.
catte'dratico, a, ci, che *ag* (*insegnamento*) university *cpd*; (*ironico*) pedantic ♦ *sm/f* professor.
catti'veria *sf* (*qualità*) wickedness; (*di bambino*) naughtiness; (*azione*) wicked action; **fare una ~** to do something wicked; to be naughty.
cattività *sf* captivity.
cat'tivo, a *ag* bad; (*malvagio*) bad, wicked; (*turbolento: bambino*) bad, naughty; (*: mare*) rough; (*odore, sapore*) nasty, bad ♦ *sm/f* bad *o* wicked person; **farsi ~ sangue** to worry, get in a state; **farsi un ~ nome** to earn o.s. a bad reputation; **i ~i** (*nei film*) the baddies (*BRIT*), the bad guys (*US*).
cattocomu'nista, i, e *ag* combining Catholic and communist ideas.
cattoli'cesimo [kattoli'tʃezimo] *sm* Catholicism.
cat'tolico, a, ci, che *ag*, *sm/f* (Roman) Catholic.
cat'tura *sf* capture.
cattu'rare *vt* to capture.
cau'casico, a, ci, che *ag*, *sm/f* Caucasian.
'Caucaso *sm*: **il ~** the Caucasus.
cauc'ciù [kaut'tʃu] *sm* rubber.
'causa *sf* cause; (*DIR*) lawsuit, case, action;

a ~ di because of; per ~ sua because of him; fare o muovere ~ a qn to take legal action against sb; parte in ~ litigant.
cau'sale ag (LING) causal ♦ sf cause, reason.
cau'sare vt to cause.
'caustico, a, ci, che ag caustic.
cau'tela sf caution, prudence.
caute'lare vt to protect; ~rsi vr: ~rsi (da o contro) to take precautions (against).
'cauto, a ag cautious, prudent.
cauzio'nare [kauttsjo'nare] vt to guarantee.
cauzi'one [kaut'tsjone] sf security; (DIR) bail; rilasciare dietro ~ to release on bail.
cav. abbr = cavaliere.
'cava sf quarry.
caval'care vt (cavallo) to ride; (muro) to sit astride; (sog: ponte) to span.
caval'cata sf ride; (gruppo di persone) riding party.
cavalca'via sm inv flyover.
cavalci'oni [kaval't ʃoni]: a ~ di prep astride.
cavali'ere sm rider; (feudale, titolo) knight; (soldato) cavalryman; (al ballo) partner.
cavalleg'gero [kavalled'dʒɛro] sm (MIL) light cavalryman.
cavalle'resco, a, schi, sche ag chivalrous.
cavalle'ria sf chivalry; (milizia a cavallo) cavalry.
cavalle'rizzo, a [kavalle'rittso] sm/f riding instructor; circus rider.
caval'letta sf grasshopper; (dannosa) locust.
caval'letto sm (FOT) tripod; (da pittore) easel.
caval'lina sf (GINNASTICA) horse; (gioco) leap-frog; correre la ~ (fig) to sow one's wild oats.
ca'vallo sm horse; (SCACCHI) knight; (AUT: anche: ~ vapore) horsepower; (dei pantaloni) crotch; a ~ on horseback; a ~ di astride, straddling; siamo a ~ (fig) we've made it; da ~ (fig: dose) drastic; (: febbre) raging; vivere a ~ tra due periodi to straddle two periods; ~ di battaglia (TEAT) tour de force; (fig) hobbyhorse; ~ da corsa racehorse; ~ a dondolo rocking horse; ~ da sella saddle horse; ~ da soma packhorse.
ca'vare vt (togliere) to draw out, extract, take out; (: giacca, scarpe) to take off; (: fame, sete, voglia) to satisfy; ~rsi vr: ~rsi da (guai, problemi) to get out of; cavarsela to get away with it; to manage, get on all right; non ci caverà un bel nulla you'll get nothing out of it (o him etc).
cava'tappi sm inv corkscrew.
ca'verna sf cave.

caver'noso, a ag (luogo) cavernous; (fig: voce) deep; (: tosse) raucous.
ca'vezza [ka'vettsa] sf halter.
'cavia sf guinea pig.
cavi'ale sm caviar.
ca'viglia [ka'viʎʎa] sf ankle.
cavil'lare vi to quibble.
ca'villo sm quibble.
cavil'loso, a ag quibbling, hair-splitting.
cavità sf inv cavity.
'cavo, a ag hollow ♦ sm (ANAT) cavity; (grossa corda) rope, cable; (ELETTR, TEL) cable.
cavo'lata sf (fam) stupid thing, foolish thing.
cavolfi'ore sm cauliflower.
'cavolo sm cabbage; non m'importa un ~ (fam) I don't give a hoot; che ~ vuoi? (fam) what the heck do you want?; ~ di Bruxelles Brussels sprout.
caz'zata [kat'tsata] sf (fam!: stupidaggine) stupid thing, something stupid.
'cazzo ['kattso] sm (fam!: pene) prick (!); non gliene importa un ~ (fig fam!) he doesn't give a damn about it; fatti i ~i tuoi (fig fam!) mind your own damn business.
caz'zotto [kat'tsɔtto] sm punch; fare a ~i to have a punch-up.
cazzu'ola [kat'tswɔla] sf trowel.
CB sigla = Campobasso.
CC abbr = Carabinieri.
cc abbr (= centimetro cubico) cc.
C.C. abbr = codice civile.
c.c. abbr (= conto corrente) c/a, a/c; (ELETTR) vedi corrente continua.
c/c abbr (= conto corrente) c/a, a/c.
C.C.D. sigla m (POL = Centro Cristiano Democratico) party originating from Democrazia Cristiana.
CCI sigla f (= Camera di Commercio Internazionale) ICC (= International Chamber of Commerce).
CCIAA abbr = Camera di Commercio Industria, Agricoltura e Artigianato.
CCT sigla m vedi certificato di credito del Tesoro.
C.D. abbr (= Corpo Diplomatico) CD ♦ sm inv (= compact disc) CD.
c.d. abbr = cosiddetto.
c.d.d. abbr (= come dovevasi dimostrare) QED (= quod erat demonstrandum).
C.d.M. abbr = Cassa del Mezzogiorno.
CD-Rom [tʃidi'rɔm] sigla m inv (= Compact Disc Read Only Memory) CD-Rom.
CE sigla = Caserta.
ce [tʃe] pron, av vedi ci.
C.E. sigla = Consiglio d'Europa.

CECA *sigla f* (= *Comunità Europea del Carbone e dell'Acciaio*) ECSC (= *European Coal and Steel Community*).

cec'chino [tʃek'kino] *sm* sniper; (*POL*) *member of parliament who votes against his own party*.

'cece ['tʃetʃe] *sm* chickpea, garbanzo (*US*).

cecità [tʃetʃi'ta] *sf* blindness.

'ceco, a, chi, che ['tʃɛko] *ag, sm/f, sm* Czech; **la Repubblica C~a** the Czech Republic.

Cecoslo'vacchia [tʃɛkozlo'vakkja] *sf*: **la ~** Czechoslovakia.

cecoslo'vacco, a, chi, che [tʃɛkozlo'vakko] *ag, sm/f* Czechoslovakian.

CED [tʃɛd] *sigla m* = **centro elaborazione dati**.

'cedere ['tʃɛdere] *vt* (*concedere: posto*) to give up; (*DIR*) to transfer, make over ♦ *vi* (*cadere*) to give way, subside; **~ (a)** to surrender (to), yield (to), give in (to); **~ il passo (a qn)** to let (sb) pass in front; **~ il passo a qc** (*fig*) to give way to sth; **~ la parola (a qn)** to hand over (to sb).

ce'devole [tʃe'devole] *ag* (*materiale*) soft; (*fig*) yielding.

'cedola ['tʃɛdola] *sf* (*COMM*) coupon; voucher.

ce'drata [tʃe'drata] *sf* citron juice.

'cedro ['tʃɛdro] *sm* cedar; (*albero da frutto, frutto*) citron.

'CEE ['tʃɛe] *sigla f vedi* **Comunità Economica Europea**.

'ceffo ['tʃɛffo] *sm* (*peg*) ugly mug.

cef'fone [tʃef'fone] *sm* slap, smack.

'ceko, a ['tʃɛko] *ag, sm/f, sm* = **ceco**.

ce'lare [tʃe'lare] *vt* to conceal; **~rsi** *vr* to hide.

cele'brare [tʃele'brare] *vt* to celebrate; (*cerimonia*) to hold; **~ le lodi di qc/qn** to sing the praises of sth/sb.

celebrazi'one [tʃelebrat'tsjone] *sf* celebration.

'celebre ['tʃɛlebre] *ag* famous, celebrated.

celebrità [tʃelebri'ta] *sf inv* fame; (*persona*) celebrity.

'celere ['tʃɛlere] *ag* fast, swift; (*corso*) crash *cpd* ♦ *sf* (*POLIZIA*) riot police.

ce'leste [tʃe'lɛste] *ag* celestial; heavenly; (*colore*) sky-blue.

'celia [tʃɛlja] *sf* joke; **per ~** for a joke.

celi'bato [tʃeli'bato] *sm* celibacy.

'celibe ['tʃɛlibe] *ag* single, unmarried ♦ *sm* bachelor.

'cella ['tʃɛlla] *sf* cell; **~ di rigore** punishment cell.

cello'phane ® [sɛlo'fan] *sm* cellophane ®.

'cellula ['tʃɛllula] *sf* (*BIOL, ELETTR, POL*) cell.

cellu'lare [tʃellu'lare] *ag* cellular ♦ *sm*

(*furgone*) police van; (*telefono*) cellphone; **segregazione ~** (*DIR*) solitary confinement.

cellu'lite [tʃellu'lite] *sf* cellulitis.

'celta ['tʃɛlta] *sm/f* Celt.

'celtico, a, ci, che ['tʃɛltiko] *ag, sm* Celtic.

'cembalo ['tʃembalo] *sm* (*MUS*) harpsichord.

cemen'tare [tʃemen'tare] *vt* (*anche fig*) to cement.

ce'mento [tʃe'mento] *sm* cement; **~ armato** reinforced concrete.

'cena ['tʃena] *sf* dinner; (*leggera*) supper.

ce'nacolo [tʃe'nakolo] *sm* (*circolo*) coterie, circle; (*REL, dipinto*) Last Supper.

ce'nare [tʃe'nare] *vi* to dine, have dinner.

'cencio ['tʃentʃo] *sm* piece of cloth, rag; (*per spolverare*) duster; **essere bianco come un ~** to be as white as a sheet.

'cenere ['tʃenere] *sf* ash.

Cene'rentola [tʃene'rɛntola] *sf* (*anche fig*) Cinderella.

'cenno ['tʃenno] *sm* (*segno*) sign, signal; (*gesto*) gesture; (*col capo*) nod; (*con la mano*) wave; (*allusione*) hint, mention; (*breve esposizione*) short account; **far ~ di si/no** to nod (one's head)/shake one's head; **~ d'intesa** sign of agreement; **~i di storia dell'arte** an outline of the history of art.

censi'mento [tʃensi'mento] *sm* census.

cen'sire [tʃen'sire] *vt* to take a census of.

'CENSIS ['tʃensis] *sigla m* (= *Centro Studi Investimenti Sociali*) *independent institute carrying out research on Italy's social and cultural welfare*.

cen'sore [tʃen'sore] *sm* censor.

cen'sura [tʃen'sura] *sf* censorship; censor's office; (*fig*) censure.

censu'rare [tʃensu'rare] *vt* to censor; to censure.

cent. *abbr* = **centesimo**.

centelli'nare [tʃentelli'nare] *vt* to sip; (*fig*) to savour (*BRIT*), savor (*US*).

cente'nario, a [tʃente'narjo] *ag* (*che ha cento anni*) hundred-year-old; (*che ricorre ogni cento anni*) centennial, centenary *cpd* ♦ *sm/f* centenarian ♦ *sm* centenary.

cen'tesimo, a [tʃen'tɛzimo] *ag, sm* hundredth; **essere senza un ~** to be penniless.

cen'tigrado, a [tʃen'tigrado] *ag* centigrade; **20 gradi ~i** 20 degrees centigrade.

cen'tilitro [tʃen'tilitro] *sm* centilitre.

cen'timetro [tʃen'timetro] *sm* centimetre (*BRIT*), centimeter (*US*); (*nastro*) measuring tape (*in centimetres*).

centi'naio, a *pl(f)* **-aia** [tʃenti'najo] *sm*: **un ~**

(di) a hundred; about a hundred.

'cento ['tʃɛnto] *num* a hundred, one hundred; **per** ~ per cent; **al** ~ **per** ~ a hundred per cent; ~ **di questi giorni!** many happy returns (of the day)!

centodi'eci [tʃɛnto'djɛtʃi] *num* one hundred and ten; ~ **e lode** (*UNIVERSITÀ*) ≈ first-class honours.

cento'mila [tʃɛnto'mila] *num* a *o* one hundred thousand; **te l'ho detto** ~ **volte** (*fig*) I've told you a thousand times.

Cen'trafrica [tʃɛn'trafrika] *sm*: **il** ~ the Central African Republic.

cen'trale [tʃɛn'trale] *ag* central ♦ *sf*: ~ **elettrica** electric power station; ~ **del latte** dairy; ~ **di polizia** police headquarters *pl*; ~ **telefonica** (telephone) exchange; **sede** ~ head office.

centrali'nista [tʃɛntrali'nista] *sm/f* operator.

centra'lino [tʃɛntra'lino] *sm* (telephone) exchange; (*di albergo etc*) switchboard.

centraliz'zare [tʃɛntralid'dzare] *vt* to centralize.

cen'trare [tʃɛn'trare] *vt* to hit the centre (*BRIT*) *o* center (*US*) of; (*TECN*) to centre; ~ **una risposta** to get the right answer; **ha centrato il problema** you've hit the nail on the head.

centra'vanti [tʃɛntra'vanti] *sm inv* centre forward.

cen'trifuga [tʃɛn'trifuga] *sf* spin-dryer.

centrifu'gare [tʃɛntrifu'gare] *vt* (*TECN*) to centrifuge; (*biancheria*) to spin-dry.

'centro ['tʃɛntro] *sm* centre (*BRIT*), center (*US*); **fare** ~ to hit the bull's eye; (*CALCIO*) to score; (*fig*) to hit the nail on the head; ~ **balneare** seaside resort; ~ **commerciale** shopping centre; (*città*) commercial centre; ~ **di costo** cost centre; ~ **elaborazione dati** data-processing unit; ~ **ospedaliero** hospital complex; ~ **sociale** community centre; ~**i vitali** (*anche fig*) vital organs.

centromedi'ano [tʃɛntrome'djano] *sm* (*CALCIO*) centre half.

'ceppo ['tʃeppo] *sm* (*di albero*) stump; (*pezzo di legno*) log.

'cera ['tʃera] *sf* wax; (*aspetto*) appearance, look; ~ **per pavimenti** floor polish.

cera'lacca [tʃera'lakka] *sf* sealing wax.

ce'ramica, che [tʃe'ramika] *sf* ceramic; (*ARTE*) ceramics *sg*.

cerbi'atto [tʃer'bjatto] *sm* fawn.

'cerca ['tʃerka] *sf*: **in** *o* **alla** ~ **di** in search of.

cercaper'sone [tʃerkaper'sone] *sm inv* bleeper.

cer'care [tʃer'kare] *vt* to look for, search for ♦ *vi*: ~ **di fare qc** to try to do sth.

cercherò *etc* [tʃerke'rɔ] *vb vedi* **cercare**.

'cerchia ['tʃerkja] *sf* circle.

cerchi'ato, a [tʃer'kjato] *ag*: **occhiali** ~**i d'osso** horn-rimmed spectacles; **avere gli occhi** ~**i** to have dark rings under one's eyes.

'cerchio ['tʃerkjo] *sm* circle; (*giocattolo, di botte*) hoop; **dare un colpo al** ~ **e uno alla botte** (*fig*) to keep two things going at the same time.

cerchi'one [tʃer'kjone] *sm* (wheel)rim.

cere'ale [tʃere'ale] *sm* cereal.

cere'brale [tʃere'brale] *ag* cerebral.

ceri'monia [tʃeri'mɔnja] *sf* ceremony; **senza tante** ~**e** (*senza formalità*) informally; (*bruscamente*) unceremoniously, without so much as a by-your-leave.

cerimoni'ale [tʃerimo'njale] *sm* etiquette; ceremonial.

cerimoni'ere [tʃerimo'njɛre] *sm* master of ceremonies.

cerimoni'oso, a [tʃerimo'njoso] *ag* formal, ceremonious.

ce'rino [tʃe'rino] *sm* wax match.

CERN [tʃɛrn] *sigla m* (= *Comitato Europeo di Ricerche Nucleari*) CERN.

'cernia ['tʃɛrnja] *sf* (*ZOOL*) stone bass.

cerni'era [tʃer'njɛra] *sf* hinge; ~ **lampo** zip (fastener) (*BRIT*), zipper (*US*).

'cernita ['tʃɛrnita] *sf* selection; **fare una** ~ **di** to select.

'cero ['tʃero] *sm* (church) candle.

ce'rone [tʃe'rone] *sm* (*trucco*) greasepaint.

ce'rotto [tʃe'rɔtto] *sm* sticking plaster.

certa'mente [tʃerta'mente] *av* certainly, surely.

cer'tezza [tʃer'tettsa] *sf* certainty.

certifi'care [tʃertifi'kare] *vt* to certify.

certifi'cato [tʃertifi'kato] *sm* certificate; ~ **medico/di nascita** medical/birth certificate; ~ **di credito del Tesoro (CCT)** treasury bill.

certificazi'one [tʃertifikat'tsjone] *sf* certification; ~ **di bilancio** (*COMM*) external audit.

═══════════════════════ *PAROLA CHIAVE*

'certo, a ['tʃɛrto] *ag* (*sicuro*): ~ **(di/che)** certain *o* sure (of/that)

♦ *det* **1** (*tale*) certain; **un** ~ **signor Smith** a (certain) Mr Smith

2 (*qualche; con valore intensivo*) some; **dopo un** ~ **tempo** after some time; **un fatto di una** ~**a importanza** a matter of some importance; **di una** ~**a età** past one's prime, not so young

♦ *pron*: ~**i, e** *pl* some

◆ av (*certamente*) certainly; (*senz'altro*) of course; **di** ~ certainly; **no (di)** ~!, ~ **che no!** certainly not!; **sì** ~ yes indeed, certainly.

certo'sino [tʃerto'zino] sm Carthusian monk; (*liquore*) chartreuse; **è un lavoro da** ~ it's a pernickety job.

cer'tuni [tʃer'tuni] pron pl some (people).

ce'rume [tʃe'rume] sm (ear) wax.

'cerva ['tʃɛrva] sf (female) deer, doe.

cer'vello, pl **i** (*anche:* pl(f) **a** o **e**) [tʃer'vɛllo] sm brain; ~ **elettronico** computer; **avere il** o **essere un** ~ **fino** to be sharp-witted; **è uscito di** ~, **gli è dato di volta il** ~ he's gone off his head.

cervi'cale [tʃervi'kale] ag cervical.

'cervo, a ['tʃɛrvo] sm/f stag/hind ◆ sm deer; ~ **volante** stag beetle.

cesel'lare [tʃezel'lare] vt to chisel; (*incidere*) to engrave.

ce'sello [tʃe'zɛllo] sm chisel.

'CESIS ['tʃɛsis] sigla m (= Comitato Esecutivo per i Servizi di Informazione e di Sicurezza) committee on intelligence and security matters, reporting to the Prime Minister.

ce'soie [tʃe'zoje] sfpl shears.

ces'puglio [tʃes'puʎʎo] sm bush.

ces'sare [tʃes'sare] vi, vt to stop, cease; ~ **di fare qc** to stop doing sth; **"cessato allarme"** "all clear".

ces'sate il fu'oco [tʃes'sate-] sm ceasefire.

cessazi'one [tʃessat'tsjone] sf cessation; (*interruzione*) suspension.

cessi'one [tʃes'sjone] sf transfer.

'cesso ['tʃesso] sm (*fam: gabinetto*) bog.

'cesta ['tʃesta] sf (large) basket.

ces'tello [tʃes'tɛllo] sm (*per bottiglie*) crate; (*di lavatrice*) drum.

cesti'nare [tʃesti'nare] vt to throw away; (*fig: proposta*) to turn down; (*: romanzo*) to reject.

ces'tino [tʃes'tino] sm basket; (*per la carta straccia*) wastepaper basket; ~ **da viaggio** (FERR) packed lunch (o dinner).

'cesto ['tʃesto] sm basket.

ce'sura [tʃe'zura] sf caesura.

ce'taceo [tʃe'tatʃeo] sm sea mammal.

'ceto ['tʃeto] sm (*social*) class.

'cetra ['tʃetra] sf zither; (*fig: di poeta*) lyre.

cetrio'lino [tʃetrio'lino] sm gherkin.

cetri'olo [tʃetri'ɔlo] sm cucumber.

Cf., Cfr. abbr (= confronta) cf.

CFC [tʃiɛffe'tʃi] abbr mpl (= clorofluorocarburi) CFC.

CFS sigla m (= Corpo Forestale dello Stato) body responsible for the planting and management of forests.

cg abbr (= centigrammo) cg.

C.G.I.L. [tʃidʒi'ɛlle] sigla f (= Confederazione Generale Italiana del Lavoro) trades union organization.

CH sigla = Chieti.

cha'let [ʃa'lɛ] sm inv chalet.

cham'pagne [ʃã'paɲ] sm inv champagne.

chance [ʃãs] sf inv chance.

charme [ʃarm] sm charm.

'charter ['tʃaːtər] ag inv (*volo*) charter cpd; (*aereo*) chartered ◆ sm inv chartered plane.

=========== **PAROLA CHIAVE**

che [ke] pron **1** (*relativo: persona: soggetto*) who; (: *oggetto*) whom, that; (: *cosa, animale*) which, that; **il ragazzo** ~ **è venuto** the boy who came; **l'uomo** ~ **io vedo** the man (whom) I see; **il libro** ~ **è sul tavolo** the book which o that is on the table; **il libro** ~ **vedi** the book (which o that) you see; **la sera** ~ **ti ho visto** the evening I saw you

2 (*interrogativo, esclamativo*) what; ~ **(cosa) fai?** what are you doing?; **a** ~ **(cosa) pensi?** what are you thinking about?; **non sa** ~ **(cosa) fare** he doesn't know what to do; **non sa** ~ **(cosa) succede?** what's happening?; **ma** ~ **dici!** what are you saying!

3 (*indefinito*): **quell'uomo ha un** ~ **di losco** there's something suspicious about that man; **un certo non so** ~ an indefinable something; **non è un gran** ~ it's nothing much

◆ det **1** (*interrogativo: tra tanti*) what; (: *tra pochi*) which; ~ **tipo di film preferisci?** what sort of film do you prefer?; ~ **vestito ti vuoi mettere?** what (o which) dress do you want to put on?

2 (*esclamativo: seguito da aggettivo*) how; (: *seguito da sostantivo*) what; ~ **buono!** how delicious!; ~ **bel vestito!** what a lovely dress!; ~ **macchina!** what a car!

◆ cong **1** (*con proposizioni subordinate*) that; **credo** ~ **verrà** I think he'll come; **voglio** ~ **tu studi** I want you to study; **so** ~ **tu c'eri** I know (that) you were there; **non** ~ **sia sbagliato, ma**... not that it's wrong, but...

2 (*finale*) so that; **vieni qua,** ~ **ti veda** come here, so (that) I can see you; **stai attento** ~ **non cada** mind it doesn't fall

3 (*temporale*): **arrivai** ~ **eri già partito** you had already left when I arrived; **sono anni** ~ **non lo vedo** I haven't seen him for years

4 (*in frasi imperative, concessive*): ~ **venga**

pure! let him come by all means!; ~ **tu sia benedetto!** may God bless you!; ~ **tu venga o no partiamo lo stesso** we're going whether you come or not
5 (*comparativo: con più, meno*) than; **è più lungo** ~ **largo** it's longer than it's wide; **più bella** ~ **mai** more beautiful than ever; *vedi anche* **più; meno; così** *etc.*

'checca, che ['kekka] *sf* (*fam: omosessuale*) fairy.
chef [ʃef] *sm inv* chef.
chemiotera'pia [kemjotera'pia] *sf* chemotherapy.
chero'sene [kero'zɛne] *sm* kerosene.
cheru'bino [keru'bino] *sm* cherub.
che'tare [ke'tare] *vt* to hush, silence; ~**rsi** *vr* to quieten down, fall silent.
cheti'chella [keti'kɛlla]: **alla** ~ *av* stealthily, unobtrusively; **andarsene alla** ~ to slip away.
'cheto, a ['keto] *ag* quiet, silent.

═══════════ *PAROLA CHIAVE*

chi [ki] *pron* **1** (*interrogativo: soggetto*) who; (: *oggetto*) who, whom; ~ **è?** who is it?; **di** ~ **è questo libro?** whose book is this?, whose is this book?; **con** ~ **parli?** who are you talking to?; **a** ~ **pensi?** who are you thinking about?; ~ **di voi?** which of you?; **non so a** ~ **rivolgermi** I don't know who to ask
2 (*relativo*) whoever, anyone who; **dillo a** ~ **vuoi** tell whoever you like; **portate** ~ **volete** bring anyone you like; **so io di** ~ **parlo** I know who I'm talking about; **lo riferirò a** ~ **di dovere** I'll pass it on to the relevant person
3 (*indefinito*): ~ ... ~ ... some ... others ...; ~ **dice una cosa,** ~ **dice un'altra** some say one thing, others say another.

chiacchie'rare [kjakkje'rare] *vi* to chat; (*discorrere futilmente*) to chatter; (*far pettegolezzi*) to gossip.
chiacchie'rata [kjakkje'rata] *sf* chat; **farsi una** ~ to have a chat.
chi'acchiere ['kjakkjere] *sfpl* chatter *no pl*; gossip *no pl*; **fare due** *o* **quattro** ~ to have a chat; **perdersi in** ~ to waste time talking.
chiacchie'rone, a [kjakkje'rone] *ag* talkative, chatty; gossipy ♦ *sm/f* chatterbox; gossip.
chia'mare [kja'mare] *vt* to call; (*rivolgersi a qn*) to call (in), send for; ~**rsi** *vr* (*aver nome*) to be called; **mi chiamo Paolo** my name is Paolo, I'm called Paolo; **mandare**

a ~ **qn** to send for sb, call sb in; ~ **alle armi** to call up; ~ **in giudizio** to summon; ~ **qn da parte** to take sb aside.
chia'mata [kja'mata] *sf* (*TEL*) call; (*MIL*) call-up; ~ **interurbana** long-distance call; ~ **con preavviso** person-to-person call; ~ **alle urne** (*POL*) election.
chi'appa ['kjappa] *sf* (*fam: natica*) cheek; ~**e** *sfpl* bottom *sg*.
chi'ara ['kjara] *sf* egg white.
chia'rezza [kja'rettsa] *sf* clearness; clarity.
chiarifi'care [kjarifi'kare] *vt* (*anche fig*) to clarify.
chiarificazi'one [kjarifikat'tsjone] *sf* clarification.
chiari'mento [kjari'mento] *sm* clarification *no pl*, explanation.
chia'rire [kja'rire] *vt* to make clear; (*fig: spiegare*) to clear up, explain; ~**rsi** *vr* to become clear; **si sono chiariti** they've sorted things out.
chi'aro, a ['kjaro] *ag* clear; (*luminoso*) clear, bright; (*colore*) pale, light ♦ *av* (*parlare, vedere*) clearly; **si sta facendo** ~ the day is dawning; **sia** ~**a una cosa** let's get one thing straight; **mettere in** ~ **qc** (*fig*) to clear sth up; **parliamoci** ~ let's be frank; **trasmissione in** ~ (*TV*) uncoded broadcast.
chia'rore [kja'rore] *sm* (*diffuse*) light.
chiaroveg'gente [kjaroved'dʒɛnte] *sm/f* clairvoyant.
chi'asso ['kjasso] *sm* uproar, row; **far** ~ to make a din; (*fig*) to make a fuss; (: *scalpore*) to cause a stir.
chias'soso, a [kjas'soso] *ag* noisy, rowdy; (*vistoso*) showy, gaudy.
'chiatta ['kjatta] *sf* barge.
chi'ave ['kjave] *sf* key ♦ *ag inv* key *cpd*; **chiudere a** ~ to lock; ~ **d'accensione** (*AUT*) ignition key; ~ **a forcella** fork spanner; ~ **inglese** monkey wrench; **in** ~ **politica** in political terms; ~ **di volta** (*anche fig*) keystone; ~**i in mano** (*contratto*) turn-key *cpd*; **prezzo** ~**i in mano** (*di macchina*) on-the-road price.
chiavis'tello [kjavis'tɛllo] *sm* bolt.
chi'azza ['kjattsa] *sf* stain, splash.
chiaz'zare [kjat'tsare] *vt* to stain, splash.
chic [ʃik] *ag inv* chic, elegant.
chicches'sia [kikkes'sia] *pron* anyone, anybody.
'chicco, chi ['kikko] *sm* (*di cereale, riso*) grain; (*di caffè*) bean; ~ **di grandine** hailstone; ~ **d'uva** grape.
chi'edere ['kjɛdere] *vt* (*per sapere*) to ask; (*per avere*) to ask for ♦ *vi*: ~ **di qn** to ask after sb; (*al telefono*) to ask for *o* want sb;

~**rsi** *vr*: ~**rsi (se)** to wonder (whether); ~ **qc a qn** to ask sb sth; to ask sb for sth; ~ **scusa a qn** to apologize to sb; ~ **l'elemosina** to beg; **non chiedo altro** that's all I want.

chieri'chetto [kjeri'ketto] *sm* altar boy.

chi'erico, ci ['kjɛriko] *sm* cleric; altar boy.

chi'esa ['kjɛza] *sf* church.

chi'esi *etc* ['kjɛzi] *vb vedi* **chiedere**.

chi'esto, a ['kjɛsto] *pp di* **chiedere**.

'**Chigi** ['kidʒi]: **palazzo** ~ *sm* (POL) *offices of the Italian Prime Minister.*

'**chiglia** ['kiʎʎa] *sf* keel.

'**chilo** ['kilo] *sm* kilo.

chilo'grammo [kilo'grammo] *sm* kilogram(me).

chilome'traggio [kilome'traddʒo] *sm* (AUT) ≈ mileage.

chilo'metrico, a, ci, che [kilo'mɛtriko] *ag* kilometric; (*fig*) endless.

chi'lometro [ki'lɔmetro] *sm* kilometre (BRIT), kilometer (US).

'**chimico, a, ci, che** ['kimiko] *ag* chemical ♦ *sm/f* chemist ♦ *sf* chemistry.

chi'mono [ki'mɔnɔ] *sm inv* kimono.

'**china** ['kina] *sf* (*pendio*) slope, descent; (BOT) cinchona; (**inchiostro di**) ~ Indian ink; **risalire la** ~ (*fig*) to be on the road to recovery.

chi'nare [ki'nare] *vt* to lower, bend; ~**rsi** *vr* to stoop, bend.

chincaglie'ria [kinkaʎʎe'ria] *sf* fancy-goods shop; ~**e** *sfpl* fancy goods, knick-knacks.

chi'nino [ki'nino] *sm* quinine.

'**chino, a** ['kino] *ag*: **a capo** ~, **a testa** ~**a** head bent *o* bowed.

chi'occia, ce ['kjɔttʃa] *sf* brooding hen.

chi'occio, a, ci, ce ['kjɔttʃo] *ag* (*voce*) clucking.

chi'occiola ['kjɔttʃola] *sf* snail; **scala a** ~ spiral staircase.

chi'odo ['kjɔdo] *sm* nail; (*fig*) obsession; ~ **scaccia** ~ (*proverbio*) one problem drives away another; **roba da** ~**i!** it's unbelievable!; ~ **di garofano** (CUC) clove.

chi'oma ['kjɔma] *sf* (*capelli*) head of hair; (*di albero*) foliage.

chi'osco, schi ['kjɔsko] *sm* kiosk, stall.

chi'ostro ['kjɔstro] *sm* cloister.

chiro'mante [kiro'mante] *sm/f* palmist; (*indovino*) fortune-teller.

chirur'gia [kirur'dʒia] *sf* surgery.

chi'rurgico, a, ci, che [ki'rurdʒiko] *ag* (*anche fig*) surgical.

chi'rurgo, ghi *o* **gi** [ki'rurgo] *sm* surgeon.

chissà [kis'sa] *av* who knows, I wonder.

chi'tarra [ki'tarra] *sf* guitar.

chitar'rista, i, e [kitar'rista] *sm/f* guitarist, guitar player.

chi'udere ['kjudere] *vt* to close, shut; (*luce, acqua*) to put off, turn off; (*definitivamente: fabbrica*) to close down, shut down; (*strada*) to close; (*recingere*) to enclose; (*porre termine*) to end ♦ *vi* to close, shut; to close down, shut down; to end; ~**rsi** *vr* to shut, close; (*ritirarsi: anche fig*) to shut o.s. away; (*ferita*) to close up; ~ **un occhio su** (*fig*) to turn a blind eye to; **chiudi la bocca!** *o* **il becco!** (*fam*) shut up!

chi'unque [ki'unkwe] *pron* (*relativo*) whoever; (*indefinito*) anyone, anybody; ~ **sia** whoever it is.

'**chiusi** *etc* ['kjusi] *vb vedi* **chiudere**.

chi'uso, a ['kjuso] *pp di* **chiudere** ♦ *ag* (*porta*) shut, closed; (: *a chiave*) locked; (*senza uscita: strada etc*) blocked off, (*rubinetto*) off; (*persona*) uncommunicative; (*ambiente, club*) exclusive ♦ *sm*: **stare al** ~ (*fig*) to be shut up ♦ *sf* (*di corso d'acqua*) sluice, lock; (*recinto*) enclosure; (*di discorso etc*) conclusion, ending; "~" (*negozio etc*) "closed"; "~ **al pubblico**" "no admittance to the public".

chiu'sura [kju'sura] *sf* closing; shutting; closing *o* shutting down; enclosing; putting *o* turning off; ending; (*dispositivo*) catch; fastening; fastener; **orario di** ~ closing time; ~ **lampo** ® zip (fastener) (BRIT), zipper (US).

════════════════ *PAROLA CHIAVE*

ci [tʃi] (*dav lo, la, li, le, ne diventa* **ce**) *pron* **1** (*personale: complemento oggetto*) us; (: *a noi: complemento di termine*) (to) us; (: *riflessivo*) ourselves; (: *reciproco*) each other, one another; (*impersonale*): ~ **si veste** we get dressed; ~ **ha visti** he's seen us; **non** ~ **ha dato niente** he gave us nothing; ~ **vestiamo** we get dressed; ~ **amiamo** we love one another *o* each other; ~ **siamo divertiti** we had a good time

2 (*dimostrativo: di ciò, su ciò, in ciò etc*) about (*o* on *o* of) it; **non** ~ **capisco nulla** I can't make head nor tail of it; **non so cosa far**~ I don't know what to do about it; **che** ~ **posso fare?** what can I do about it?; **che c'entro io?** what have I got to do with it?; ~ **puoi giurare** you can bet on it; ~ **puoi contare** you can depend on it; ~ **sei?** (*sei pronto?*) are you ready?; (*hai capito?*) are you with me?

♦ *av* (*qui*) here; (*lì*) there; (*moto attraverso*

luogo): ~ **passa sopra un ponte** a bridge passes over it; **non ~ passa più nessuno** nobody comes this way any more; **qui ~ abito da un anno** I've been living here for a year; **esser~** *vedi* **essere**.

CIA ['tʃia] *sigla f* (= *Central Intelligence Agency*) CIA.

C.ia *abbr* (= *compagnia*) Co.

cia'batta [tʃa'batta] *sf* mule, slipper.

ciabat'tino [tʃabat'tino] *sm* cobbler.

ciac [tʃak] *sm* (*CINE*) clapper board; ~, **si gira!** action!

Ci'ad [tʃad] *sm*: **il** ~ Chad.

ci'alda ['tʃalda] *sf* (*CUC*) wafer.

cial'trone [tʃal'trone] *sm* good-for-nothing.

ciam'bella [tʃam'bɛlla] *sf* (*CUC*) ring-shaped cake; (*salvagente*) rubber ring.

ci'ancia, ce ['tʃantʃa] *sf* gossip *no pl*, tittle-tattle *no pl*.

cianfru'saglie [tʃanfru'zaʎʎe] *sfpl* bits and pieces.

cia'nuro [tʃa'nuro] *sm* cyanide.

ci'ao ['tʃao] *escl* (*all'arrivo*) hello!; (*alla partenza*) cheerio! (*BRIT*), bye!

ciar'lare [tʃar'lare] *vi* to chatter; (*peg*) to gossip.

ciarla'tano [tʃarla'tano] *sm* charlatan.

cias'cuno, a [tʃas'kuno] (*dav sm*: **ciascun** +C, V, **ciascuno** +s *impura, gn, pn, ps, x, z*; *dav sf*: **ciascuna** +C, **ciascun'** +V) *det, pron* each.

ci'bare [tʃi'bare] *vt* to feed; ~**rsi** *vr*: ~**rsi di** to eat.

ci'barie [tʃi'barje] *sfpl* foodstuffs.

ciber'netica [tʃiber'netika] *sf* cybernetics *sg*.

'cibo ['tʃibo] *sm* food.

ci'cala [tʃi'kala] *sf* cicada.

cica'trice [tʃika'tritʃe] *sf* scar.

cicatriz'zarsi [tʃikatrid'dzarsi] *vr* to form a scar, heal (up).

'cicca, che ['tʃikka] *sf* cigarette end; (*fam*: *sigaretta*) fag; **non vale una** ~ (*fig*) it's worthless.

'ciccia ['tʃittʃa] *sf* (*fam*: *carne*) meat; (: *grasso umano*) fat, flesh.

cicci'one, a [tʃit'tʃone] *sm/f* (*fam*) fatty.

cice'rone [tʃitʃe'rone] *sm* guide.

cicla'mino [tʃikla'mino] *sm* cyclamen.

ci'clismo [tʃi'klizmo] *sm* cycling.

ci'clista, i, e [tʃi'klista] *sm/f* cyclist.

'ciclo ['tʃiklo] *sm* cycle; (*di malattia*) course.

ciclomo'tore [tʃiklomo'tore] *sm* moped.

ci'clone [tʃi'klone] *sm* cyclone.

ciclos'tile [tʃiklos'tile] *sm* cyclostyle (*BRIT*).

ci'cogna [tʃi'koɲɲa] *sf* stork.

ci'coria [tʃi'kɔrja] *sf* chicory.

'CIDA ['tʃida] *sigla f* = *Confederazione Italiana Dirigenti d'Azienda*.

ci'eco, a, chi, che ['tʃɛko] *ag* blind ♦ *sm/f* blind man/woman; **alla** ~**a** (*anche fig*) blindly.

ciel'lino, a [tʃiel'lino] *sm/f* (*POL*) member of CL movement.

ci'elo ['tʃɛlo] *sm* sky; (*REL*) heaven; **toccare il** ~ **con un dito** (*fig*) to walk on air; **per amor del** ~! for heavens' sake!

'cifra ['tʃifra] *sf* (*numero*) figure, numeral; (*somma di denaro*) sum, figure; (*monogramma*) monogram, initials *pl*; (*codice*) code, cipher.

ci'frare [tʃi'frare] *vt* (*messaggio*) to code; (*lenzuola etc*) to embroider with a monogram.

'ciglio ['tʃiʎʎo] *sm* (*margine*) edge, verge; (*pl(f)* **ciglia**: *delle palpebre*) (eye)lash; (*sopracciglio*) eyebrow; **non ha battuto** ~ (*fig*) he didn't bat an eyelid.

'cigno ['tʃiɲɲo] *sm* swan.

cigo'lante [tʃigo'lante] *ag* squeaking, creaking.

cigo'lare [tʃigo'lare] *vi* to squeak, creak.

CIIS *sigla m* (= *Comitato Interparlamentare per l'Informazione e la Sicurezza*) all-party committee on intelligence and security.

'Cile ['tʃile] *sm*: **il** ~ Chile.

ci'lecca [tʃi'lekka] *sf*: **far** ~ to fail.

ci'leno, a [tʃi'lɛno] *ag, sm/f* Chilean.

cili'egia, gie *o* **ge** [tʃi'ljedʒa] *sf* cherry.

cilie'gina [tʃilje'dʒina] *sf* glacé cherry; **la** ~ **sulla torta** (*fig*) the icing *o* cherry on the cake.

cili'egio [tʃi'ljedʒo] *sm* cherry tree.

cilin'drata [tʃilin'drata] *sf* (*AUT*) (cubic) capacity; **una macchina di grossa** ~ a big-engined car.

ci'lindro [tʃi'lindro] *sm* cylinder; (*cappello*) top hat.

CIM [tʃim] *sigla m* = *centro d'igiene mentale*.

'cima ['tʃima] *sf* (*sommità*) top; (*di monte*) top, summit; (*estremità*) end; (*fig*: *persona*) genius; **in** ~ **a** at the top of; **da** ~ **a fondo** from top to bottom; (*fig*) from beginning to end.

ci'melio [tʃi'mɛljo] *sm* relic.

cimen'tarsi [tʃimen'tarsi] *vr*: ~**rsi in** (*atleta, concorrente*) to try one's hand at.

'cimice ['tʃimitʃe] *sf* (*ZOOL*) bug; (*puntina*) drawing pin (*BRIT*), thumbtack (*US*).

cimini'era [tʃimi'njera] *sf* chimney; (*di nave*) funnel.

cimi'tero [tʃimi'tɛro] *sm* cemetery.

ci'murro [tʃi'murro] *sm* (*di cani*) distemper.

'Cina ['tʃina] *sf*: **la** ~ China.

cin'cin, cin cin [tʃin'tʃin] *escl* cheers!

cincischi'are [tʃintʃis'kjare] *vi* to mess about, fiddle about.

'cine ['tʃine] *sm inv* (*fam*) cinema.

cine'asta, i, e [tʃine'asta] *sm/f* person in the film industry; film-maker.

cinegior'nale [tʃinedʒor'nale] *sm* newsreel.

'cinema ['tʃinema] *sm inv* cinema; ~ **muto** silent films; ~ **d'essai** (*locale*) avant-garde cinema, experimental cinema.

cinemato'grafico, a, ci, che [tʃinemato'grafiko] *ag* (*attore, critica*) movie *cpd*, film *cpd*; (*festival*) film *cpd*; **sala** ~**a** cinema; **successo** ~ box-office success.

cinema'tografo [tʃinema'tografo] *sm* cinema.

cine'presa [tʃine'presa] *sf* cine-camera.

ci'nese [tʃi'nese] *ag, sm/f, sm* Chinese *inv*.

cine'teca, che [tʃine'tɛka] *sf* (*collezione*) film collection, film library; (*locale*) film library.

ci'netico, a, ci, che [tʃi'nɛtiko] *ag* kinetic.

'cingere ['tʃindʒere] *vt* (*attorniare*) to surround, encircle; ~ **la vita con una cintura** to put a belt round one's waist; ~ **d'assedio** to besiege, lay siege to.

'cinghia ['tʃingja] *sf* strap; (*cintura, TECN*) belt; **tirare la** ~ (*fig*) to tighten one's belt.

cinghi'ale [tʃin'gjale] *sm* wild boar.

cinguet'tare [tʃingwet'tare] *vi* to twitter.

'cinico, a, ci, che ['tʃiniko] *ag* cynical ♦ *sm/f* cynic.

ci'nismo [tʃi'nizmo] *sm* cynicism.

cin'quanta [tʃin'kwanta] *num* fifty.

cinquante'nario [tʃinkwante'narjo] *sm* fiftieth anniversary.

cinquan'tenne [tʃinkwan'tɛnne] *sm/f* fifty-year-old man/woman.

cinquan'tesimo, a [tʃinkwan'tɛzimo] *num* fiftieth.

cinquan'tina [tʃinkwan'tina] *sf* (*serie*): **una** ~ (**di**) about fifty; (*età*): **essere sulla** ~ to be about fifty.

'cinque ['tʃinkwe] *num* five; **avere** ~ **anni** to be five (years old); **il** ~ **dicembre 1988** the fifth of December 1988; **alle** ~ (*ora*) at five (o'clock); **siamo in** ~ there are five of us.

cinquecen'tesco, a, schi, sche [tʃinkwetʃen'tesko] *ag* sixteenth-century.

cinque'cento [tʃinkwe'tʃɛnto] *num* five hundred ♦ *sm*: **il C**~ the sixteenth century.

cinque'mila [tʃinkwe'mila] *num* five thousand.

'cinsi *etc* ['tʃinsi] *vb vedi* **cingere**.

'cinta ['tʃinta] *sf* (*anche*: ~ **muraria**) city walls *pl*; **muro di** ~ (*di giardino etc*)

surrounding wall.

cin'tare [tʃin'tare] *vt* to enclose.

'cinto, a ['tʃinto] *pp di* **cingere**.

'cintola ['tʃintola] *sf* (*cintura*) belt; (*vita*) waist.

cin'tura [tʃin'tura] *sf* belt; ~ **di salvataggio** lifebelt (*BRIT*), life preserver (*US*); ~ **di sicurezza** (*AUT, AER*) safety o seat belt.

cintu'rino [tʃintu'rino] *sm* strap; ~ **dell'orologio** watch strap.

CIO *sigla m* (= *Comitato Internazionale Olimpico*) IOC (= *International Olympic Committee*).

ciò [tʃɔ] *pron* this; that; ~ **che** what; ~ **nonostante** o **nondimeno** nevertheless, in spite of that; **con tutto** ~ for all that, in spite of everything.

ci'occa, che ['tʃɔkka] *sf* (*di capelli*) lock.

ciocco'lata [tʃokko'lata] *sf* chocolate; (*bevanda*) (hot) chocolate; ~ **al latte/ fondente** milk/plain chocolate.

cioccola'tino [tʃokkola'tino] *sm* chocolate.

ciocco'lato [tʃokko'lato] *sm* chocolate.

cio'è [tʃo'ɛ] *av* that is (to say).

ciondo'lare [tʃondo'lare] *vt* (*far dondolare*) to dangle, swing ♦ *vi* to dangle; (*fig*) to loaf (about).

ci'ondolo [tʃondolo] *sm* pendant; ~ **portafortuna** charm.

ciondo'loni [tʃondo'loni] *av*: **con le braccia/ gambe** ~ with arms/legs dangling.

cionono'stante [tʃononos'tante] *av* nonetheless, nevertheless.

ci'otola ['tʃɔtola] *sf* bowl.

ci'ottolo ['tʃɔttolo] *sm* pebble; (*di strada*) cobble(stone).

C.I.P. [tʃip] *sigla m* (= *comitato interministeriale prezzi*) *vedi* **comitato**.

Cipe ['tʃipe] *sigla m* (= *comitato interministeriale per la programmazione economica*) *vedi* **comitato**.

'**Cipi** ['tʃipi] *sigla m* (= *comitato interministeriale per lo sviluppo industriale*) *vedi* **comitato**.

ci'piglio [tʃi'piʎʎo] *sm* frown.

ci'polla [tʃi'polla] *sf* onion; (*di tulipano etc*) bulb.

ci'presso [tʃi'prɛsso] *sm* cypress (tree).

'cipria ['tʃiprja] *sf* (*face*) powder.

cipri'ota, i, e [tʃipri'ɔta] *ag, sm/f* Cypriot.

'Cipro ['tʃipro] *sm* Cyprus.

'circa ['tʃirka] *av* about, roughly ♦ *prep* about, concerning; **a mezzogiorno** ~ about midday.

'circo, chi ['tʃirko] *sm* circus.

circo'lare [tʃirko'lare] *vi* to circulate; (*AUT*) to drive (along), move (along) ♦ *ag* circular ♦ *sf* (*AMM*) circular; (*di autobus*) circle (line); **circola voce che** ... there is a rumour going about that ...; **assegno** ~ banker's draft.

circolazi'one [tʃirkolat'tsjone] *sf* circulation; (*AUT*): **la** ~ (**the**) traffic; **libretto di** ~ log book, registration book; **tassa di** ~ road tax; ~ **a targhe alterne** *vedi nota nel riquadro.*

CIRCOLAZIONE A TARGHE ALTERNE

Circolazione a targhe alterne *was introduced by some town councils to combat the increase in traffic and pollution in town centres. It stipulates that on days with an even date, only cars whose number plate ends in an even number or a zero may be on the road; on days with an odd date, only cars with odd registration numbers may be used. Public holidays are generally, but not always, exempt.*

'circolo ['tʃirkolo] *sm* circle; **entrare in** ~ (*ANAT*) to enter the bloodstream.
circoncisi'one [tʃirkontʃi'zjone] *sf* circumcision.
circon'dare [tʃirkon'dare] *vt* to surround.
circondari'ale [tʃirkonda'rjale] *ag*: **casa di pena** ~ district prison.
circon'dario [tʃirkon'darjo] *sm* (*DIR*) administrative district; (*zona circostante*) neighbourhood (*BRIT*), neighborhood (*US*).
circonfe'renza [tʃirkonfe'rɛntsa] *sf* circumference.
circonvallazi'one [tʃirkonvallat'tsjone] *sf* ring road (*BRIT*), beltway (*US*); (*per evitare una città*) by-pass.
circos'critto, a [tʃirkos'kritto] *pp di* circoscrivere.
circos'crivere [tʃirkos'krivere] *vt* to circumscribe; (*fig*) to limit, restrict.
circoscrizi'one [tʃirkoskrit'tsjone] *sf* (*AMM*) district, area; ~ **elettorale** constituency.
circos'petto, a [tʃirkos'pɛtto] *ag* circumspect, cautious.
circos'tante [tʃirkos'tante] *ag* surrounding, neighbouring (*BRIT*), neighboring (*US*).
circos'tanza [tʃirkos'tantsa] *sf* circumstance; (*occasione*) occasion; **parole di** ~ words suited to the occasion.
circu'ire [tʃirku'ire] *vt* (*fig*) to fool, take in.
cir'cuito [tʃir'kuito] *sm* circuit; **andare in** *o* **fare corto** ~ to short-circuit; ~ **integrato** integrated circuit.
ci'rillico, a, ci, che [tʃi'rilliko] *ag* Cyrillic.
cir'rosi [tʃir'rɔzi] *sf*: ~ **epatica** cirrhosis (of the liver).
'C.I.S.A.L. ['tʃizal] *sigla f* (= *Confederazione Italiana Sindacati Autonomi dei Lavoratori*) trades union organization.

C.I.S.L. [tʃizl] *sigla f* (= *Confederazione Italiana Sindacati Lavoratori*) trades union organization.
'C.I.S.N.A.L. ['tʃiznal] *sigla f* (= *Confederazione Italiana Sindacati Nazionali dei Lavoratori*) trades union organization.
'ciste ['tʃiste] *sf* = **cisti**.
cis'terna [tʃis'tɛrna] *sf* tank, cistern.
'cisti ['tʃisti] *sf inv* cyst.
cis'tite [tʃis'tite] *sf* cystitis.
C.I.T. [tʃit] *sigla f* = *Compagnia Italiana Turismo.*
cit. *abbr* (= *citato, citata*) cit.
ci'tare [tʃi'tare] *vt* (*DIR*) to summon; (*autore*) to quote; (*a esempio, modello*) to cite; ~ **qn per danni** to sue sb.
citazi'one [tʃitat'tsjone] *sf* summons *sg*; quotation; (*di persona*) mention.
ci'tofono [tʃi'tɔfono] *sm* entry phone; (*in uffici*) intercom.
cito'logico, a, ci, che [tʃito'lɔdʒiko] *ag*: **esame** ~ *test for detection of cancerous cells.*
'citrico, a, ci, che ['tʃitriko] *ag* citric.
città [tʃit'ta] *sf inv* town; (*importante*) city; ~ **giardino** garden city; ~ **mercato** shopping centre, mall; ~ **universitaria** university campus; **C**~ **del Capo** Cape Town.
citta'della [tʃitta'dɛlla] *sf* citadel, stronghold.
cittadi'nanza [tʃittadi'nantsa] *sf* citizens *pl*, inhabitants *pl* of a town (*o* city); (*DIR*) citizenship.
citta'dino, a [tʃitta'dino] *ag* town *cpd*; city *cpd* ♦ *smlf* (*di uno Stato*) citizen; (*abitante di città*) town dweller, city dweller.
ci'uccio ['tʃuttʃo] *sm* (*fam*) comforter, dummy (*BRIT*), pacifier (*US*).
ci'uco, a, chi, che ['tʃuko] *smlf* ass.
ci'uffo ['tʃuffo] *sm* tuft.
ci'urma ['tʃurma] *sf* (*di nave*) crew.
ci'vetta [tʃi'vetta] *sf* (*ZOOL*) owl; (*fig: donna*) coquette, flirt ♦ *ag inv*: **auto/nave** ~ decoy car/ship; **fare la** ~ **con qn** to flirt with sb.
civet'tare [tʃivet'tare] *vt* to flirt.
civette'ria [tʃivette'ria] *sf* coquetry, coquettishness.
civettu'olo, a [tʃivet'twɔlo] *ag* flirtatious.
'civico, a, ci, che ['tʃiviko] *ag* civic; (*museo*) municipal, town *cpd*; **guardia** ~**a** town policeman; **senso** ~ public spirit.
ci'vile [tʃi'vile] *ag* civil; (*non militare*) civilian; (*nazione*) civilized ♦ *sm* civilian; **stato** ~ marital status; **abiti** ~**i** civvies.
civi'lista, i, e [tʃivi'lista] *smlf* (*avvocato*) civil lawyer; (*studioso*) expert in civil law.

civiliz'zare [tʃivilid'dzare] *vt* to civilize.
civilizzazi'one [tʃiviliddzat'tsjone] *sf* civilization.
civiltà [tʃivil'ta] *sf* civilization; (*cortesia*) civility.
ci'vismo [tʃi'vizmo] *sm* public spirit.
CL [tʃi'ɛlle] *sigla f* (*POL*: = *Comunione e Liberazione*) *Catholic youth movement* ♦ *sigla* = *Caltanissetta*.
cl *abbr* (= *centilitro*) cl.
'clacson *sm inv* (*AUT*) horn.
cla'more *sm* (*frastuono*) din, uproar, clamour (*BRIT*), clamor (*US*); (*fig*) outcry.
clamo'roso, a *ag* noisy; (*fig*) sensational.
clan *sm inv* clan.
clandestinità *sf* (*di attività*) secret nature; **vivere nella** ~ to live in hiding; (*ricercato politico*) to live underground.
clandes'tino, a *ag* clandestine; (*POL*) underground, clandestine ♦ *sm/f* stowaway.
clari'netto *sm* clarinet.
'classe *sf* class; **di** ~ (*fig*) with class; of excellent quality; ~ **turistica** (*AER*) economy class.
classi'cismo [klassi'tʃizmo] *sm* classicism.
'classico, a, ci, che *ag* classical; (*tradizionale: moda*) classic(al) ♦ *sm* classic; classical author; (*anche: liceo* ~) *secondary school with emphasis on the humanities*.
clas'sifica, che *sf* classification; (*SPORT*) placings *pl*; (*di dischi*) charts *pl*.
classifi'care *vt* to classify; (*candidato, compito*) to grade; ~**rsi** *vr* to be placed.
classifica'tore *sm* filing cabinet.
classificazi'one [klassifikat'tsjone] *sf* classification; grading.
clas'sista, i, e *ag* class-conscious ♦ *sm/f* class-conscious person.
claudi'cante *ag* (*zoppo*) lame; (*fig: prosa*) halting.
'clausola *sf* (*DIR*) clause.
claustro'fobico, a, ci, che *ag* claustrophobic.
clau'sura *sf* (*REL*): **monaca di** ~ nun belonging to an enclosed order; **fare una vita di** ~ (*fig*) to lead a cloistered life.
'clava *sf* club.
clavi'cembalo [klavi'tʃembalo] *sm* harpsichord.
cla'vicola *sf* (*ANAT*) collarbone.
cle'mente *ag* merciful; (*clima*) mild.
cle'menza [kle'mɛntsa] *sf* mercy, clemency; mildness.
clep'tomane *sm/f* kleptomaniac.
cleri'cale *ag* clerical.
'clero *sm* clergy.

cles'sidra *sf* (*a sabbia*) hourglass; (*ad acqua*) water clock.
clic'care *vi* (*INFORM*): ~ **su** to click on.
cliché [kli'ʃe] *sm inv* (*TIP*) plate; (*fig*) cliché.
cli'ente *sm/f* customer, client.
clien'tela *sf* customers *pl*, clientèle.
cliente'lismo *sm*: ~ **politico** political nepotism.
'clima, i *sm* climate.
cli'matico, a, ci, che *ag* climatic; **stazione** ~**a** health resort.
climatizzazi'one [klimatiddzat'tsjone] *sf* air conditioning.
'clinico, a, ci, che *ag* clinical ♦ *sm* (*medico*) clinician ♦ *sf* (*scienza*) clinical medicine; (*casa di cura*) clinic, nursing home; (*settore d'ospedale*) clinic; **quadro** ~ anamnesis; **avere l'occhio** ~ (*fig*) to have an expert eye.
clis'tere *sm* (*MED*) enema; (: *apparecchio*) *device used to give an enema*.
clo'aca, che *sf* sewer.
cloche [klɔʃ] *sf inv* (*AER*) control stick, joystick; **cambio a** ~ (*AUT*) floor-mounted gear lever.
'cloro *sm* chlorine.
cloro'filla *sf* chlorophyll.
cloro'formio *sm* chloroform.
club *sm inv* club.
cm *abbr* (= *centimetro*) cm.
c.m. *abbr* (= *corrente mese*) inst.
CN *sigla* = *Cuneo*.
c/n *abbr* = *conto nuovo*.
CNEN *sigla m* (= *Comitato Nazionale per l'Energia Nucleare*) ≈ AEA (*BRIT*), AEC (*US*).
CNIOP *sigla m* = *Centro Nazionale per l'Istruzione e l'Orientamento Professionale*.
CNR *sigla m* (= *Consiglio Nazionale delle Ricerche*) science research council.
CNRN *sigla m* = *Comitato Nazionale Ricerche Nucleari*.
CO *sigla* = *Como*.
Co. *abbr* (= *compagnia*) Co.
c/o *abbr* (= *care of*) c/o.
coabi'tare *vi* to live together.
coagu'lare *vt* to coagulate ♦ *vi*, ~**rsi** *vr* to coagulate; (*latte*) to curdle.
coalizi'one [koalit'tsjone] *sf* coalition.
co'atto, a *ag* (*DIR*) compulsory, forced; **condannare al domicilio** ~ to place under house arrest.
'COBAS *sigla mpl* (= *Comitati di base*) *independent trades unions*.
'cobra *sm inv* cobra.
'coca 'cola ® *sf* coca cola ®.
coca'ina *sf* cocaine.
coc'carda *sf* cockade.

cocchi'ere [kok'kjɛre] *sm* coachman.
'cocchio ['kɔkkjo] *sm* (*carrozza*) coach; (*biga*) chariot.
cocci'nella [kottʃi'nɛlla] *sf* ladybird (*BRIT*), ladybug (*US*).
'coccio ['kɔttʃo] *sm* earthenware; (*vaso*) earthenware pot; ~i *smpl* fragments (of pottery).
cocciu'taggine [kottʃu'taddʒine] *sf* stubbornness, pig-headedness.
cocci'uto, a [kot'tʃuto] *ag* stubborn, pigheaded.
'cocco, chi *sm* (*pianta*) coconut palm; (*frutto*): **noce di** ~ coconut ♦ *sm/f* (*fam*) darling; **è il** ~ **della mamma** he's mummy's darling.
cocco'drillo *sm* crocodile.
cocco'lare *vt* to cuddle, fondle.
co'cente [ko'tʃɛnte] *ag* (*anche fig*) burning.
cocerò *etc* [kotʃe'rɔ] *vb vedi* **cuocere**.
co'comero *sm* watermelon.
co'cuzzolo [ko'kuttsolo] *sm* top; (*di capo, cappello*) crown.
cod. *abbr* = **codice**.
'coda *sf* tail; (*fila di persone, auto*) queue (*BRIT*), line (*US*); (*di abiti*) train; **con la** ~ **dell'occhio** out of the corner of one's eye; **mettersi in** ~ to queue (up) (*BRIT*), line up (*US*); to join the queue *o* line; ~ **di cavallo** (*acconciatura*) ponytail; **avere la** ~ **di paglia** (*fig*) to have a guilty conscience; ~ **di rospo** (*CUC*) frogfish tail.
codar'dia *sf* cowardice.
co'dardo, a *ag* cowardly ♦ *sm/f* coward.
co'desto, a *ag, pron* (*poetico*) this; that.
'codice ['kɔditʃe] *sm* code; (*manoscritto antico*) codex; ~ **di avviamento postale** (*CAP*) postcode (*BRIT*), zip code (*US*); ~ **a barre** bar code; ~ **civile** civil code; ~ **fiscale** tax code; ~ **penale** penal code; ~ **segreto** (*di tessera magnetica*) PIN (number); ~ **della strada** highway code.
co'difica *sf* codification; (*INFORM*: *di programma*) coding.
codifi'care *vt* (*DIR*) to codify; (*cifrare*) to code.
codificazi'one [kodifikat'tsjone] *sf* coding.
coercizi'one [koertʃit'tsjone] *sf* coercion.
coe'rente *ag* coherent.
coe'renza [koe'rɛntsa] *sf* coherence.
coesi'one *sf* cohesion.
coe'sistere *vi* to coexist.
coe'taneo, a *ag, sm/f* contemporary; **essere** ~ **di qn** to be the same age as sb.
cofa'netto *sm* casket; ~ **dei gioielli** jewel case.
'cofano *sm* (*AUT*) bonnet (*BRIT*), hood (*US*); (*forziere*) chest.

'coffa *sf* (*NAUT*) top.
'cogli ['koʎʎi] *prep* + *det vedi* **con**.
'cogliere ['kɔʎʎere] *vt* (*fiore, frutto*) to pick, gather; (*sorprendere*) to catch, surprise; (*bersaglio*) to hit; (*fig: momento opportuno etc*) to grasp, seize, take; (: *capire*) to grasp; ~ **l'occasione (per fare)** to take the opportunity (to do); ~ **sul fatto** *o* **in flagrante/alla sprovvista** to catch red-handed/unprepared; ~ **nel segno** (*fig*) to hit the nail on the head.
cogli'one [koʎ'ʎone] *sm* (*fam!: testicolo*): ~i balls (*!*); (: *fig: persona sciocca*) jerk; **rompere i** ~**i a qn** to get on sb's tits (*!*).
co'gnac [kɔ'ɲak] *sm inv* cognac.
co'gnato, a [koɲ'ɲato] *sm/f* brother-/sister-in-law.
cognizi'one [koɲɲit'tsjone] *sf* knowledge; **con** ~ **di causa** with full knowledge of the facts.
co'gnome [koɲ'ɲome] *sm* surname.
'coi *prep* + *det vedi* **con**.
coi'bente *ag* insulating.
coinci'denza [kointʃi'dɛntsa] *sf* coincidence; (*FERR, AER, di autobus*) connection.
coin'cidere [koin'tʃidere] *vi* to coincide.
coin'ciso, a [koin'tʃizo] *pp di* **coincidere**.
coinqui'lino *sm* fellow tenant.
cointeres'senza [kointeres'sɛntsa] *sf* (*COMM*): **avere** ~ **in qc** to own shares in sth; ~ **dei lavoratori** profit-sharing.
coin'volgere [koin'vɔldʒere] *vt*: ~ **in** to involve in.
coinvolgi'mento [koinvoldʒi'mento] *sm* involvement.
coin'volto, a *pp di* **coinvolgere**.
col *prep* + *det vedi* **con**.
Col. *abbr* (= *colonnello*) Col.
colà *av* there.
cola'brodo *sm inv* strainer.
cola'pasta *sm inv* colander.
co'lare *vt* (*liquido*) to strain; (*pasta*) to drain; (*oro fuso*) to pour ♦ *vi* (*sudore*) to drip; (*botte*) to leak; (*cera*) to melt; ~ **a picco** *vt, vi* (*nave*) to sink.
co'lata *sf* (*di lava*) flow; (*FONDERIA*) casting.
colazi'one [kolat'tsjone] *sf* (*anche*: **prima** ~) breakfast; (*anche*: **seconda** ~) lunch; **fare** ~ to have breakfast (*o* lunch); ~ **di lavoro** working lunch.
Coldi'retti *abbr f* (= *Confederazione nazionale coltivatori diretti*) *federation of Italian farmers*.
co'lei *pron vedi* **colui**.
co'lera *sm* (*MED*) cholera.
coleste'rolo *sm* cholesterol.
colf *abbr f* = **collaboratrice familiare**.

'**colgo** *etc vb vedi* **cogliere**.
colibrì *sm* hummingbird.
'**colica** *sf* (*MED*) colic.
co'lino *sm* strainer.
'**colla** *prep* + *det vedi* **con** ♦ *sf* glue; (*di farina*)
paste.
collabo'rare *vi* to collaborate; (*con la
polizia*) to co-operate; ~ **a** to collaborate
on; (*giornale*) to contribute to.
collabora'tore, 'trice *sm/f* collaborator; (*di
giornale, rivista*) contributor; ~ **esterno**
freelance; ~**trice familiare** home help; ~
di giustizia = **pentito, a**.
collaborazi'one [kollaborat'tsjone] *sf*
collaboration; contribution.
col'lana *sf* necklace; (*collezione*) collection,
series.
col'lant [kɔ'lã] *sm inv* tights *pl*.
col'lare *sm* collar.
col'lasso *sm* (*MED*) collapse.
collate'rale *ag* collateral; **effetti** ~**i** side
effects.
col'laudo *sm* testing *no pl*; test.
'**colle** *prep* + *det vedi* **con** ♦ *sm* hill.
col'lega, ghi, ghe *sm/f* colleague.
collega'mento *sm* connection; (*MIL*)
liaison; (*RADIO*) link(-up); **ufficiale di** ~
liaison officer.
colle'gare *vt* to connect, join, link; ~**rsi** *vr*
(*RADIO, TV*) to link up; ~**rsi con** (*TEL*) to get
through to.
collegi'ale [kolle'dʒale] *ag* (*riunione,
decisione*) collective; (*INS*) boarding
school *cpd* ♦ *sm/f* boarder; (*fig: persona
timida e inesperta*) schoolboy/girl.
col'legio [kol'lɛdʒo] *sm* college; (*convitto*)
boarding school; ~ **elettorale** (*POL*)
constituency.
'**collera** *sf* anger; **andare in** ~ to get angry.
col'lerico, a, ci, che *ag* quick-tempered,
irascible.
col'letta *sf* collection.
collettività *sf* community.
collet'tivo, a *ag* collective; (*interesse*)
general, everybody's; (*biglietto, visita etc*)
group *cpd* ♦ *sm* (*POL*) (political) group;
società in nome ~ (*COMM*) partnership.
col'letto *sm* collar; ~**i bianchi** (*fig*) white-
collar workers.
collezio'nare [kollettsjo'nare] *vt* to collect.
collezi'one [kollet'tsjone] *sf* collection.
collezio'nista [kollettsjo'nista] *sm/f*
collector.
colli'mare *vi* to correspond, coincide.
col'lina *sf* hill.
colli'nare *ag* hill *cpd*.
col'lirio *sm* eyewash.
collisi'one *sf* collision.

'**collo** *prep* + *det vedi* **con** ♦ *sm* neck; (*di abito*)
neck, collar; (*pacco*) parcel; ~ **del piede**
instep.
colloca'mento *sm* (*impiego*) employment;
(*disposizione*) placing, arrangement;
ufficio di ~ ≈ Jobcentre (*BRIT*), state (*o
federal*) employment agency (*US*); ~ **a
riposo** retirement.
collo'care *vt* (*libri, mobili*) to place;
(*persona: trovare un lavoro per*) to find a job
for, place; (*COMM: merce*) to find a market
for; ~ **qn a riposo** to retire sb.
collocazi'one [kollokat'tsjone] *sf* placing;
(*di libro*) classification.
colloqui'ale *ag* (*termine etc*) colloquial;
(*tono*) informal.
col'loquio *sm* conversation, talk; (*ufficiale,
per un lavoro*) interview; (*INS*)
preliminary oral exam; **avviare un** ~ **con
qn** (*POL etc*) to start talks with sb.
col'loso, a *ag* sticky.
col'lottola *sf* nape o scruff of the neck;
afferrare qn per la ~ to grab sb by the
scruff of the neck.
collusi'one *sf* (*DIR*) collusion.
colluttazi'one [kolluttat'tsjone] *sf* scuffle.
col'mare *vt*: ~ **di** (*anche fig*) to load o
(*dare in abbondanza*) to load o overwhelm
with; ~ **un divario** (*fig*) to bridge a gap.
'**colmo, a** *ag*: ~ (**di**) full (of) ♦ *sm* summit,
top; (*fig*) height; **al** ~ **della disperazione** in
the depths of despair, **è il** ~! it's the last
straw!; **e per** ~ **di sfortuna** ... and to cap
it all ....
co'lomba *sf vedi* **colombo**.
Co'lombia *sf*: **la** ~ Colombia.
colombi'ano, a *ag, sm/f* Colombian.
co'lombo, a *sm/f* dove; pigeon; ~**i** (*fig fam*)
lovebirds.
Co'lonia *sf* Cologne.
co'lonia *sf* colony; (*per bambini*) holiday
camp; (**acqua di**) ~ (eau de) cologne.
coloni'ale *ag* colonial ♦ *sm/f* colonist,
settler.
co'lonico, a, ci, che *ag*: **casa** ~**a**
farmhouse.
coloniz'zare [kolonid'dzare] *vt* to colonize.
co'lonna *sf* column; ~ **sonora** (*CINE*) sound
track; ~ **vertebrale** spine, spinal column.
colon'nello *sm* colonel.
co'lono *sm* (*coltivatore*) tenant farmer.
colo'rante *sm* colouring (*BRIT*), coloring
(*US*).
colo'rare *vt* to colour (*BRIT*), color (*US*);
(*disegno*) to colo(u)r in.
co'lore *sm* colour (*BRIT*), color (*US*); (*CARTE*)
suit; **a** ~**i** in colo(u)r, colo(u)r *cpd*; **la
gente di** ~ colo(u)red people; **diventare di**

tutti i ~**i** to turn scarlet; **farne di tutti i** ~**i** to get up to all sorts of mischief; **passarne di tutti i** ~**i** to go through all sorts of problems.

colo'rito, a *ag* coloured (*BRIT*), colored (*US*); (*viso*) rosy, pink; (*linguaggio*) colourful (*BRIT*), colorful (*US*) ♦ *sm* (*tinta*) colour (*BRIT*), color (*US*); (*carnagione*) complexion.

co'loro *pron pl vedi* **colui.**

colos'sale *ag* colossal, enormous.

co'losso *sm* colossus.

'colpa *sf* fault; (*biasimo*) blame; (*colpevolezza*) guilt; (*azione colpevole*) offence; (*peccato*) sin; **di chi è la** ~**?** whose fault is it?; **è** ~ **sua** it's his fault; **per** ~ **di** through, owing to; **senso di** ~ sense of guilt; **dare la** ~ **a qn di qc** to blame sb for sth.

col'pevole *ag* guilty.

colpevoliz'zare [kolpevolid'dzare] *vt*: ~ **qn** to make sb feel guilty.

col'pire *vt* to hit, strike; (*fig*) to strike; **rimanere colpito da qc** to be amazed *o* struck by sth; **è stato colpito da ordine di cattura** there is a warrant out for his arrest; ~ **nel segno** (*fig*) to hit the nail on the head, be spot on (*BRIT*).

'colpo *sm* (*urto*) knock; (*fig: affettivo*) blow, shock; (*: aggressivo*) blow; (*di pistola*) shot; (*MED*) stroke; (*furto*) raid; **di** ~, **tutto d'un** ~ suddenly; **fare** ~ to make a strong impression; **il motore perde** ~**i** (*AUT*) the engine is misfiring; **è morto sul** ~ he died instantly; **mi hai fatto venire un** ~**!** what a fright you gave me!; **ti venisse un** ~**!** (*fam*) drop dead!; ~ **d'aria** chill; ~ **in banca** bank job *o* raid; ~ **basso** (*PUGILATO, fig*) punch below the belt; ~ **di fulmine** love at first sight; ~ **di grazia** coup de grâce; (*fig*) finishing blow; **a** ~ **d'occhio** at a glance; ~ **di scena** (*TEAT*) coup de théâtre; (*fig*) dramatic turn of events; ~ **di sole** sunstroke; ~**i di sole** (*nei capelli*) highlights; ~ **di Stato** coup d'état; ~ **di telefono** phone call; ~ **di testa** (sudden) impulse *o* whim; ~ **di vento** gust (of wind).

col'poso, a *ag*: **omicidio** ~ manslaughter.

'colsi *etc vb vedi* **cogliere.**

coltel'lata *sf* stab.

col'tello *sm* knife; **avere il** ~ **dalla parte del manico** (*fig*) to have the whip hand; ~ **a serramanico** clasp knife.

colti'vare *vt* to cultivate; (*verdura*) to grow, cultivate.

coltiva'tore *sm* farmer; ~ **diretto** small independent farmer.

coltivazi'one [koltivat'tsjone] *sf* cultivation; growing; ~ **intensiva** intensive farming.

'colto, a *pp di* **cogliere** ♦ *ag* (*istruito*) cultured, educated.

'coltre *sf* blanket.

col'tura *sf* cultivation; ~ **alternata** crop rotation.

co'lui, co'lei, *pl* **co'loro** *pron* the one; ~ **che parla** the one *o* the man *o* the person who is speaking; **colei che amo** the one *o* the woman *o* the person (whom) I love.

com. *abbr* = **comunale; commissione.**

'coma *sm inv* coma.

comanda'mento *sm* (*REL*) commandment.

coman'dante *sm* (*MIL*) commander, commandant; (*di reggimento*) commanding officer; (*NAUT, AER*) captain.

coman'dare *vi* to be in command ♦ *vt* to command; (*imporre*) to order, command; ~ **a qn di fare** to order sb to do.

co'mando *sm* (*ingiunzione*) order, command; (*autorità*) command; (*TECN*) control; ~ **generale** general headquarters *pl*; ~ **a distanza** remote control.

co'mare *sf* (*madrina*) godmother; (*donna pettegola*) gossip.

co'masco, a, schi, sche *ag* of (*o* from) Como.

combaci'are [komba't ʃare] *vi* to meet; (*fig: coincidere*) to coincide, correspond.

combat'tente *ag* fighting ♦ *sm* combatant; **ex-**~ ex-serviceman.

com'battere *vt* to fight; (*fig*) to combat, fight against ♦ *vi* to fight.

combatti'mento *sm* fight; fighting *no pl*; (*di pugilato*) match; **mettere fuori** ~ to knock out.

combat'tivo, a *ag* pugnacious.

combat'tuto, a *ag* (*incerto: persona*) uncertain, undecided; (*gara, partita*) hard fought.

combi'nare *vt* to combine; (*organizzare*) to arrange; (*fam: fare*) to make, cause ♦ *vi* (*corrispondere*): ~ (**con**) to correspond (with).

combinazi'one [kombinat'tsjone] *sf* combination; (*caso fortuito*) coincidence; **per** ~ by chance.

com'briccola *sf* (*gruppo*) party; (*banda*) gang.

combus'tibile *ag* combustible ♦ *sm* fuel.

combusti'one *sf* combustion.

com'butta *sf* (*peg*) gang; **in** ~ in league.

================================ PAROLA CHIAVE

'come *av* **1** (*alla maniera di*) like; **ti comporti** ~ **lui** you behave like him *o* like he does; **bianco** ~ **la neve** (as) white as snow; ~ **se** as if, as though; **com'è vero Dio!** as God is my witness!
2 (*in qualità di*) as a; **lavora** ~ **autista** he works as a driver
3 (*interrogativo*) how; ~ **ti chiami?** what's your name?; ~ **sta?** how are you?; **com'è il tuo amico?** what is your friend like?; ~**?** (*prego?*) pardon?, sorry?; ~ **mai?** how come?; ~ **mai non ci hai avvertiti?** how come you didn't warn us?
4 (*esclamativo*): ~ **sei bravo!** how clever you are!; ~ **mi dispiace!** I'm terribly sorry!
♦ *cong* **1** (*in che modo*) how; **mi ha spiegato** ~ **l'ha conosciuto** he told me how he met him; **non so** ~ **sia successo** I don't know how it happened; **attento a** ~ **parli!** watch your mouth!
2 (*correlativo*) as; (*con comparativi di maggioranza*) than; **non è bravo** ~ **pensavo** he isn't as clever as I thought; **è meglio di** ~ **pensassi** it's better than I thought
3 (*quasi se*) as; **è** ~ **se fosse ancora qui** it's as if he was still here; ~ **se niente fosse** as if nothing had happened; ~ **non detto!** let's forget it!
4 (*appena che, quando*) as soon as; ~ **arrivò, iniziò a lavorare** as soon as he arrived, he set to work; *vedi anche* **così**; **oggi**; **ora**.

'COMECON *abbr m* (= *Consiglio di Mutua Assistenza Economica*) COMECON.
come'done *sm* blackhead.
co'meta *sf* comet.
'comico, a, ci, che *ag* (*TEAT*) comic; (*buffo*) comical ♦ *sm* (*attore*) comedian, comic actor; (*comicità*) comic spirit, comedy.
co'mignolo [ko'miɲɲolo] *sm* chimney top.
cominci'are [komin'tʃare] *vt, vi* to begin, start; ~ **a fare/col fare** to begin to do/by doing; **cominciamo bene!** (*ironico*) we're off to a fine start!
comi'tato *sm* committee; ~ **direttivo** steering committee; ~ **di gestione** works council; ~ **interministeriale prezzi** interdepartmental committee on prices; ~ **interministeriale per la programmazione economica** interdepartmental committee for economic planning; ~ **interministeriale per lo sviluppo industriale** interdepartmental committee for industrial development.
comi'tiva *sf* party, group.
co'mizio [ko'mittsjo] *sm* (*POL*) meeting, assembly; ~ **elettorale** election rally.
'comma, i *sm* (*DIR*) subsection.
com'mando *sm inv* commando (squad).
com'media *sf* comedy; (*opera teatrale*) play; (: *che fa ridere*) comedy; (*fig*) playacting *no pl*.
commedi'ante *sm/f* (*peg*) third-rate actor/actress; (: *fig*) sham.
commedi'ografo, a *sm/f* (*autore*) comedy writer.
commemo'rare *vt* to commemorate.
commemorazi'one [kommemorat'tsjone] *sf* commemoration.
commenda'tore *sm* official title awarded for services to one's country.
commen'sale *sm/f* table companion.
commen'tare *vt* to comment on; (*testo*) to annotate; (*RADIO, TV*) to give a commentary on.
commenta'tore, 'trice *sm/f* commentator.
com'mento *sm* comment; (*a un testo, RADIO, TV*) commentary; ~ **musicale** (*CINE*) background music.
commerci'ale [kommer'tʃale] *ag* commercial, trading; (*peg*) commercial.
commercia'lista, i, e [kommertʃa'lista] *sm/f* (*laureato*) graduate in economics and commerce; (*consulente*) business consultant.
commercializ'zare [kommertʃalid'dzare] *vt* to market.
commercializzazi'one [kommertʃaliddzat'tsjone] *sf* marketing.
commerci'ante [kommer'tʃante] *sm/f* trader, dealer; (*negoziante*) shopkeeper; ~ **all'ingrosso** wholesaler; ~ **in proprio** sole trader.
commerci'are [kommer'tʃare] *vi:* ~ **in** *vt* to deal *o* trade in.
com'mercio [kom'mertʃo] *sm* trade, commerce; **essere in** ~ (*prodotto*) to be on the market *o* on sale; **essere nel** ~ (*persona*) to be in business; ~ **all'ingrosso/al minuto** wholesale/retail trade.
com'messo, a *pp di* **commettere** ♦ *sm/f* shop assistant (*BRIT*), sales clerk (*US*) ♦ *sm* (*impiegato*) clerk ♦ *sf* (*COMM*) order; ~ **viaggiatore** commercial traveller.
commes'tibile *ag* edible; ~**i** *smpl* foodstuffs.
com'mettere *vt* to commit; (*ordinare*) to commission, order.
commi'ato *sm* leave-taking; **prendere** ~ **da**

qn to take one's leave of sb.
commi'nare *vt* (*DIR*) to make provision for.
commise'rare *vt* to sympathize with, commiserate with.
commiserazi'one [kommizerat'tsjone] *sf* commiseration.
com'misi *etc vb vedi* **commettere**.
commissaria'mento *sm* temporary receivership.
commissari'are *vt* to put under temporary receivership.
commissari'ato *sm* (*AMM*) commissionership; (: *sede*) commissioner's office; (: *di polizia*) police station.
commis'sario *sm* commissioner; (*di pubblica sicurezza*) ≈ (police) superintendent (*BRIT*), (police) captain (*US*); (*SPORT*) steward; (*membro di commissione*) member of a committee *o* board; **alto** ~ high commissioner; ~ **di bordo** (*NAUT*) purser; ~ **d'esame** member of an examining board; ~ **di gara** race official; ~ **tecnico** (*SPORT*) national coach.
commissio'nare *vt* to order, place an order for.
commissio'nario *sm* (*COMM*) agent, broker.
commissi'one *sf* (*incarico*) errand; (*comitato, percentuale*) commission; (*COMM: ordinazione*) order; ~**i** *sfpl* (*acquisti*) shopping *sg*; ~ **d'esame** examining board; ~ **d'inchiesta** committee of enquiry; ~ **permanente** standing committee; ~**i bancarie** bank charges.
commit'tente *sm/f* (*COMM*) purchaser, customer.
com'mosso, a *pp di* **commuovere**.
commo'vente *ag* moving.
commozi'one [kommot'tsjone] *sf* emotion, deep feeling; ~ **cerebrale** (*MED*) concussion.
commu'overe *vt* to move, affect; ~**rsi** *vr* to be moved.
commu'tare *vt* (*pena*) to commute; (*ELETTR*) to change *o* switch over.
commutazi'one [kommutat'tsjone] *sf* (*DIR, ELETTR*) commutation.
comò *sm inv* chest of drawers.
como'dino *sm* bedside table.
comodità *sf inv* comfort; convenience.
'comodo, a *ag* comfortable; (*facile*) easy; (*conveniente*) convenient; (*utile*) useful, handy ♦ *sm* comfort; convenience; **con** ~ at one's convenience *o* leisure; **fare il proprio** ~ to do as one pleases; **far** ~ to be useful *o* handy; **stia** ~! don't bother to

get up!
'compact disc *sm inv* compact disc.
compae'sano, a *sm/f* fellow-countryman/woman; person from the same town.
com'pagine [kom'padʒine] *sf* (*squadra*) team.
compa'gnia [kompaɲ'ɲia] *sf* company; (*gruppo*) gathering; **fare** ~ **a qn** to keep sb company; **essere di** ~ to be sociable.
com'pagno, a [kom'paɲɲo] *sm/f* (*di classe, gioco*) companion; (*POL*) comrade; ~ **di lavoro** workmate; ~ **di scuola** schoolfriend; ~ **di viaggio** fellow traveller.
com'paio *etc vb vedi* **comparire**.
compa'rare *vt* to compare.
compara'tivo, a *ag*, *sm* comparative.
comparazi'one [komparat'tsjone] *sf* comparison.
com'pare *sm* (*padrino*) godfather; (*complice*) accomplice; (*fam: amico*) old pal, old mate.
compa'rire *vi* to appear; ~ **in giudizio** (*DIR*) to appear before the court.
comparizi'one [komparit'tsjone] *sf* (*DIR*) appearance; **mandato di** ~ summons *sg*.
com'parso, a *pp di* **comparire** ♦ *sf* appearance; (*TEAT*) walk-on; (*CINE*) extra.
comparteci'pare [kompartetʃi'pare] *vi* (*COMM*): ~ **a** to have a share in.
compartecipazi'one [kompartetʃipat'tsjone] *sf* sharing; (*quota*) share; ~ **agli utili** profit-sharing; **in** ~ jointly.
comparti'mento *sm* compartment; (*AMM*) district.
com'parvi *etc vb vedi* **comparire**.
compas'sato, a *ag* (*persona*) composed; **freddo e** ~ cool and collected.
compassi'one *sf* compassion, pity; **avere** ~ **di qn** to feel sorry for sb, pity sb; **fare** ~ to arouse pity.
compassio'nevole *ag* compassionate.
com'passo *sm* (pair of) compasses *pl*; callipers *pl*.
compa'tibile *ag* (*scusabile*) excusable; (*conciliabile, INFORM*) compatible.
compati'mento *sm* compassion; indulgence; **con aria di** ~ with a condescending air.
compa'tire *vt* (*aver compassione di*) to sympathize with, feel sorry for; (*scusare*) to make allowances for.
compatri'ota, i, e *sm/f* compatriot.
compat'tezza [kompat'tettsa] *sf* (*solidità*) compactness; (*fig: unità*) solidarity.
com'patto, a *ag* compact; (*roccia*) solid; (*folla*) dense; (*fig: gruppo, partito*) united, close-knit.

com'pendio *sm* summary; (*libro*) compendium.

compen'sare *vt* (*equilibrare*) to compensate for, make up for; ~**rsi** *vr* (*reciproco*) to balance each other out; ~ **qn di** (*rimunerare*) to pay *o* remunerate sb for; (*risarcire*) to pay compensation to sb for; (*fig: fatiche, dolori*) to reward sb for.

compen'sato *sm* (*anche*: **legno** ~) plywood.

com'penso *sm* compensation; payment, remuneration; reward; **in** ~ (*d'altra parte*) on the other hand.

'compera *sf* purchase; **fare le** ~**e** to do the shopping.

compe'rare *vt* = **comprare**.

compe'tente *ag* competent; (*mancia*) apt, suitable; (*capace*) qualified; **rivolgersi all'ufficio** ~ to apply to the office concerned.

compe'tenza [kompe'tɛntsa] *sf* competence; (*DIR: autorità*) jurisdiction, (*TECN, COMM*) expertise; ~**e** *sfpl* (*onorari*) fees; **definire le** ~**e** to establish responsibilities.

com'petere *vi* to compete, vie; (*DIR: spettare*): ~ **a** to lie within the competence of.

competitività *sf inv* competitiveness.

competi'tivo, a *ag* competitive.

competi'tore, 'trice *sm/f* competitor.

competizi'one [kompetit'tsjone] *sf* competition; **spirito di** ~ competitive spirit.

compia'cente [kompja'tʃɛnte] *ag* courteous, obliging.

compia'cenza [kompja'tʃɛntsa] *sf* courtesy.

compia'cere [kompja'tʃere] *vi*: ~ **a** to gratify, please ♦ *vt* to please; ~**rsi** *vr* (*provare soddisfazione*): ~**rsi di** *o* **per qc** to be delighted at sth; (*rallegrarsi*): ~**rsi con qn** to congratulate sb; (*degnarsi*): ~**rsi di fare** to be so good as to do.

compiaci'mento [kompjatʃi'mento] *sm* satisfaction.

compiaci'uto, a [kompja'tʃuto] *pp di* **compiacere**.

compi'angere [kom'pjandʒere] *vt* to sympathize with, feel sorry for.

compi'anto, a *pp di* **compiangere** ♦ *ag*: **il** ~ **presidente** the late lamented president ♦ *sm* mourning, grief.

'compiere *vt* (*concludere*) to finish, complete; (*adempiere*) to carry out, fulfil; ~**rsi** *vr* (*avverarsi*) to be fulfilled, come true; ~ **gli anni** to have one's birthday.

compi'lare *vt* to compile; (*modulo*) to

complete, fill in (*BRIT*), fill out (*US*).

compila'tore, 'trice *sm/f* compiler.

compilazi'one [kompilat'tsjone] *sf* compilation; completion.

compi'mento *sm* (*termine, conclusione*) completion, fulfilment; **portare a** ~ **qc** to conclude sth, bring sth to a conclusion.

com'pire *vb* = **compiere**.

'compito *sm* (*incarico*) task, duty; (*dovere*) duty; (*INS*) exercise; (*: a casa*) piece of homework; **fare i** ~**i** to do one's homework.

com'pito, a *ag* well-mannered, polite.

compiu'tezza [kompju'tettsa] *sf* (*completezza*) completeness; (*perfezione*) perfection.

compi'uto, a *pp di* **compiere** ♦ *ag*: **a 20 anni** ~**i** at 20 years of age, at age 20; **un fatto** ~ a fait accompli.

comple'anno *sm* birthday.

complemen'tare *ag* complementary; (*INS: materia*) subsidiary.

comple'mento *sm* complement; (*MIL*) reserve (troops); ~ **oggetto** (*LING*) direct object.

comples'sato, a *ag, sm/f*: **essere (un)** ~ to be full of complexes *o* hang-ups (*fam*).

complessità *sf* complexity.

complessiva'mente *av* (*nell'insieme*) on the whole; (*in tutto*) altogether.

comples'sivo, a *ag* (*globale*) comprehensive, overall; (*totale: cifra*) total; **visione** ~**a** overview.

com'plesso, a *ag* complex ♦ *sm* (*PSIC, EDIL*) complex; (*MUS: corale*) ensemble; (*: orchestrina*) band; (*: di musica pop*) group; **in** *o* **nel** ~ on the whole.

completa'mento *sm* completion.

comple'tare *vt* to complete.

com'pleto, a *ag* complete; (*teatro, autobus*) full ♦ *sm* suit; **al** ~ full; (*tutti presenti*) all present; **essere al** ~ (*teatro*) to be sold out; ~ **da sci** ski suit.

compli'care *vt* to complicate; ~**rsi** *vr* to become complicated.

complicazi'one [komplikat'tsjone] *sf* complication; **salvo** ~**i** unless any difficulties arise.

'complice ['kɔmplitʃe] *sm/f* accomplice.

complicità [komplitʃi'ta] *sf inv* complicity; **un sorriso/uno sguardo di** ~ a knowing smile/look.

complimen'tarsi *vr*: ~ **con** to congratulate.

compli'mento *sm* compliment; ~**i** *smpl* (*cortesia eccessiva*) ceremony *sg*; ~**i!** congratulations!; **senza** ~**i!** don't stand on ceremony!; make yourself at home!;

help yourself!
complot'tare *vi* to plot, conspire.
com'plotto *sm* plot, conspiracy.
com'pone *etc vb vedi* **comporre**.
compo'nente *sm/f* member ◆ *sm* component.
com'pongo *etc vb vedi* **comporre**.
compo'nibile *ag* (*mobili, cucina*) fitted.
componi'mento *sm* (*DIR*) settlement; (*INS*) composition; (*poetico, teatrale*) work.
com'porre *vt* (*musica, testo*) to compose; (*mettere in ordine*) to arrange; (*DIR: lite*) to settle; (*TIP*) to set; (*TEL*) to dial; **comporsi** *vr*: **comporsi di** to consist of, be composed of.
comportamen'tale *ag* behavioural (*BRIT*), behavioral (*US*).
comporta'mento *sm* behaviour (*BRIT*), behavior (*US*); (*di prodotto*) performance.
compor'tare *vt* (*implicare*) to involve, entail; (*consentire*) to permit, allow (of); **~rsi** *vr* (*condursi*) to behave.
com'posi *etc vb vedi* **comporre**.
composi'tore, 'trice *sm/f* composer; (*TIP*) compositor, typesetter.
composizi'one [kompozit'tsjone] *sf* composition; (*DIR*) settlement.
com'posta *sf vedi* **composto**.
compos'tezza [kompos'tettsa] *sf* composure; decorum.
com'posto, a *pp di* **comporre** ◆ *ag* (*persona*) composed, self-possessed; (*: decoroso*) dignified; (*formato da più elementi*) compound *cpd* ◆ *sm* compound; (*CUC etc*) mixture ◆ *sf* (*CUC*) stewed fruit *no pl*; (*AGR*) compost.
com'prare *vt* to buy; (*corrompere*) to bribe.
compra'tore, 'trice *sm/f* buyer, purchaser.
compra'vendita *sf* (*COMM*) (contract of) sale; **un atto di ~** a deed of sale.
com'prendere *vt* (*contenere*) to comprise, consist of; (*capire*) to understand.
compren'donio *sm*: **essere duro di ~** to be slow on the uptake.
compren'sibile *ag* understandable.
comprensi'one *sf* understanding.
compren'sivo, a *ag* (*prezzo*): **~ di** inclusive of; (*indulgente*) understanding.
compren'sorio *sm* area, territory; (*AMM*) district.
com'preso, a *pp di* **comprendere** ◆ *ag* (*incluso*) included; **tutto ~** all included, all-in (*BRIT*).
com'pressa *sf vedi* **compresso**.
compressi'one *sf* compression.
com'presso, a *pp di* **comprimere** ◆ *ag* (*vedi* comprimere) pressed; compressed; repressed ◆ *sf* (*MED*: garza) compress;

(*: pastiglia*) tablet.
compres'sore *sm* compressor; (*anche*: **rullo ~**) steamroller.
compri'mario, a *sm/f* (*TEAT*) supporting actor/actress.
com'primere *vt* (*premere*) to press; (*FISICA*) to compress; (*fig*) to repress.
compro'messo, a *pp di* **compromettere** ◆ *sm* compromise.
compro'mettere *vt* to compromise; **~rsi** *vr* to compromise o.s.
comproprietà *sf* (*DIR*) joint ownership.
compro'vare *vt* to confirm.
com'punto, a *ag* contrite; **con fare ~** with a solemn air.
compunzi'one [kompun'tsjone] *sf* contrition; solemnity.
compu'tare *vt* to calculate; (*addebitare*): **~ qc a qn** to debit sb with sth.
com'puter [kəm'pjuːtər] *sm inv* computer.
computeriz'zato, a [komputerid'dzato] *ag* computerized.
computerizzazi'one [komputeriddzat 'tsjone] *sf* computerization.
computiste'ria *sf* accounting, book-keeping.
'computo *sm* calculation; **fare il ~ di** to count.
comu'nale *ag* municipal, town *cpd*; **consiglio/palazzo ~** town council/hall; **è un impiegato ~** he works for the local council.
Co'mune *sm* (*AMM*) town council; (*sede*) town hall; *vedi nota nel riquadro*.

COMUNE

The **Comune** is the smallest autonomous political and administrative unit. It keeps records of births, marriages and deaths and has the power to levy taxes and vet proposals for public works and town planning. It is run by a "Giunta comunale", which is elected by the "Consiglio comunale". Both of these are headed by the "Sindaco" (mayor).

---

co'mune *ag* common; (*consueto*) common, everyday; (*di livello medio*) average; (*ordinario*) ordinary ◆ *sf* (*di persone*) commune; **fuori del ~** out of the ordinary; **avere in ~** to have in common, share; **mettere in ~** to share; **un nostro ~ amico** a mutual friend of ours; **fare cassa ~** to pool one's money.
comuni'care *vt* (*notizia*) to pass on, convey; (*malattia*) to pass on; (*ansia etc*) to communicate; (*trasmettere: calore etc*) to transmit, communicate; (*REL*) to

administer communion to ♦ *vi* to communicate; ~**rsi** *vr* (*propagarsi*): ~**rsi a** to spread to; (*REL*) to receive communion.

comunica'tivo, a *ag* (*sentimento*) infectious; (*persona*) communicative ♦ *sf* communicativeness.

comuni'cato *sm* communiqué; ~ **stampa** press release.

comunicazi'one [komunikat'tsjone] *sf* communication; (*annuncio*) announcement; (*TEL*): ~ **(telefonica)** (telephone) call; **dare la** ~ **a qn** to put sb through; **ottenere la** ~ to get through; **salvo** ~**i contrarie da parte Vostra** unless we hear from you to the contrary.

comuni'one *sf* communion; ~ **dei beni** (*DIR*: *tra coniugi*) joint ownership of property.

comu'nismo *sm* communism.

comu'nista, i, e *ag*, *sm/f* communist.

comunità *sf inv* community; **C~ Economica Europea (CEE)** European Economic Community (EEC): ~ **terapeutica** rehabilitation centre run by voluntary organizations for people with drug, alcohol etc dependency.

comuni'tario, a *ag* community *cpd*.

co'munque *cong* however, no matter how ♦ *av* (*in ogni modo*) in any case; (*tuttavia*) however, nevertheless.

con *prep* (*nei seguenti casi* **con** *può fondersi con l'articolo definito*: **con** + *il* = **col**, **con** + *la* = **colla**, **con** + *gli* = **cogli**, **con** + *i* = **coi**, **con** + *le* = **colle**) with; **partire col treno** to leave by train; ~ **mio grande stupore** to my great astonishment; ~ **la forza** by force; ~ **questo freddo** in this cold weather; ~ **il 1° di ottobre** as of October 1st; ~ **tutto ciò** in spite of that, for all that; ~ **tutto che era arrabbiato** even though he was angry, in spite of the fact that he was angry; **e** ~ **questo?** so what?

co'nato *sm*: ~ **di vomito** retching.

'conca, che *sf* (*GEO*) valley.

concate'nare *vt* to link up, connect; ~**rsi** *vr* to be connected.

'concavo, a *ag* concave.

con'cedere [kon'tʃedere] *vt* (*accordare*) to grant; (*ammettere*) to admit, concede; ~**rsi qc** to treat o.s. to sth, allow o.s. sth.

concentra'mento [kontʃentra'mento] *sm* concentration.

concen'trare [kontʃen'trare] *vt*, ~**rsi** *vr* to concentrate.

concen'trato [kontʃen'trato] *sm* concentrate; ~ **di pomodoro** tomato purée.

concentrazi'one [kontʃentrat'tsjone] *sf* concentration; ~ **orizzontale/verticale** (*ECON*) horizontal/vertical integration.

con'centrico, a, ci, che [kon'tʃɛntriko] *ag* concentric.

conce'pibile [kontʃe'pibile] *ag* conceivable.

concepi'mento [kontʃepi'mento] *sm* conception.

conce'pire [kontʃe'pire] *vt* (*bambino*) to conceive; (*progetto, idea*) to conceive (of); (*metodo, piano*) to devise; (*situazione*) to imagine, understand.

con'cernere [kon'tʃɛrnere] *vt* to concern; **per quanto mi concerne** as far as I'm concerned.

concer'tare [kontʃer'tare] *vt* (*MUS*) to harmonize; (*ordire*) to devise, plan; ~**rsi** *vr* to agree.

concer'tista, i, e [kontʃer'tista] *sm/f* (*MUS*) concert performer.

con'certo [kon'tʃɛrto] *sm* (*MUS*) concert; (: *componimento*) concerto.

con'cessi *etc* [kon'tʃɛssi] *vb vedi* **concedere**.

concessio'nario [kontʃessjo'narjo] *sm* (*COMM*) agent, dealer; ~ **esclusivo (di)** sole agent (for).

concessi'one [kontʃes'sjone] *sf* concession.

con'cesso, a [kon'tʃɛsso] *pp di* **concedere**.

con'cetto [kon'tʃetto] *sm* (*pensiero, idea*) concept; (*opinione*) opinion; **è un impiegato di** ~ ≈ he's a white-collar worker.

concezi'one [kontʃet'tsjone] *sf* conception; (*idea*) view, idea.

con'chiglia [kon'kiʎʎa] *sf* shell.

'concia ['kontʃa] *sf* (*di pelli*) tanning; (*di tabacco*) curing; (*sostanza*) tannin.

conci'are [kon'tʃare] *vt* (*pelli*) to tan; (*tabacco*) to cure; (*fig: ridurre in cattivo stato*) to beat up; ~**rsi** *vr* (*sporcarsi*) to get in a mess; (*vestirsi male*) to dress badly; **ti hanno conciato male o per le feste!** they've really beaten you up!

concili'abile [kontʃi'ljabile] *ag* compatible.

concili'abolo [kontʃi'ljabolo] *sm* secret meeting.

concili'ante [kontʃi'ljante] *ag* conciliatory.

concili'are [kontʃi'ljare] *vt* to reconcile; (*contravvenzione*) to pay on the spot; (*favorire: sonno*) to be conducive to, induce; (*procurare: simpatia*) to gain; ~**rsi qc** to gain o win sth (for o.s.); ~**rsi qn** to win sb over; ~**rsi con** to be reconciled with.

conciliazi'one [kontʃiljat'tsjone] *sf* reconciliation; (*DIR*) settlement; **la C~** (*STORIA*) the Lateran Pact.

con'cilio [kon'tʃiljo] *sm* (*REL*) council.

conci'mare [kontʃi'mare] *vt* to fertilize; (*con letame*) to manure.
con'cime [kon'tʃime] *sm* manure; (*chimico*) fertilizer.
concisi'one [kontʃi'zjone] *sf* concision, conciseness.
con'ciso, a [kon'tʃizo] *ag* concise, succinct.
conci'tato, a [kontʃi'tato] *ag* excited, emotional.
concitta'dino, a [kontʃitta'dino] *sm/f* fellow citizen.
con'clave *sm* conclave.
con'cludere *vt* to conclude; (*portare a compimento*) to conclude, finish, bring to an end; (*operare positivamente*) to achieve ♦ *vi* (*essere convincente*) to be conclusive; ~**rsi** *vr* to come to an end, close.
conclusi'one *sf* conclusion; (*risultato*) result.
conclu'sivo, a *ag* conclusive; (*finale*) final.
con'cluso, a *pp di* **concludere**.
concomi'tanza [konkomi'tantsa] *sf* (*di circostanze, fatti*) combination.
concor'danza [konkor'dantsa] *sf* (*anche* LING) agreement.
concor'dare *vt* (*prezzo*) to agree on; (LING) to make agree ♦ *vi* to agree; ~ **una tregua** to agree to a truce.
concor'dato *sm* agreement; (REL) concordat.
con'corde *ag* (*d'accordo*) in agreement; (*simultaneo*) simultaneous.
con'cordia *sf* harmony, concord.
concor'rente *ag* competing; (MAT) concurrent ♦ *sm/f* (SPORT, COMM) competitor; (*a un concorso di bellezza*) contestant.
concor'renza [konkor'rentsa] *sf* competition; ~ **sleale** unfair competition; **a prezzi di** ~ at competitive prices.
concorrenzi'ale [konkorren'tsjale] *ag* competitive.
con'correre *vi*: ~ (**in**) (MAT) to converge *o* meet (in); ~ (**a**) (*competere*) to compete (for); (: INS: *a una cattedra*) to apply (for); (*partecipare: a un'impresa*) to take part (in), contribute (to).
con'corso, a *pp di* **concorrere** ♦ *sm* competition; (*esame*) competitive examination; ~ **di bellezza** beauty contest; ~ **di circostanze** combination of circumstances; ~ **di colpa** (DIR) contributory negligence; **un** ~ **ippico** a showjumping event; ~ **in reato** (DIR) complicity in a crime; ~ **per titoli** competitive examination for qualified candidates.
con'creto, a *ag* concrete ♦ *sm*: **in** ~ in reality.
concu'bina *sf* concubine ♦ *sm*: **sono** ~**i** they are living together.
concussi'one *sf* (DIR) extortion.
con'danna *sf* condemnation; sentence; conviction; ~ **a morte** death sentence.
condan'nare *vt* (*disapprovare*) to condemn; (DIR): ~ **a** to sentence to; ~ **per** to convict of.
condan'nato, a *sm/f* convict.
con'densa *sf* condensation.
conden'sare *vt*, ~**rsi** *vr* to condense.
condensa'tore *sm* capacitor.
condensazi'one [kondensat'tsjone] *sf* condensation.
condi'mento *sm* seasoning; dressing.
con'dire *vt* to season; (*insalata*) to dress.
condiscen'dente [kondiʃʃen'dɛnte] *ag* obliging; compliant.
condiscen'denza [kondiʃʃen'dɛntsa] *sf* (*disponibilità*) obligingness; (*arrendevolezza*) compliance.
condi'scendere [kondiʃ'ʃendere] *vi*: ~ **a** to agree to.
condi'sceso, a [kondiʃ'ʃeso] *pp di* **condiscendere**.
condi'videre *vt* to share.
condi'viso, a *pp di* **condividere**.
condizio'nale [kondittsjo'nale] *ag* conditional ♦ *sm* (LING) conditional ♦ *sf* (DIR) suspended sentence.
condiziona'mento [kondittsjona'mento] *sm* conditioning; ~ **d'aria** air conditioning.
condizio'nare [kondittsjo'nare] *vt* to condition; **ad aria condizionata** air-conditioned.
condiziona'tore [kondittsjona'tore] *sm* air conditioner.
condizi'one [kondit'tsjone] *sf* condition; ~**i** *sfpl* (*di pagamento etc*) terms, conditions; **a** ~ **che** on condition that, provided that; **a nessuna** ~ on no account; ~**i a convenirsi** terms to be arranged; ~**i di lavoro** working conditions; ~**i di vendita** sales terms.
condogli'anze [kondoʎ'ʎantse] *sfpl* condolences.
condomini'ale *ag*: **riunione** ~ residents' meeting; **spese** ~**i** common charges.
condo'minio *sm* joint ownership; (*edificio*) jointly-owned building.
con'domino *sm* joint owner.
condo'nare *vt* (DIR) to remit.
con'dono *sm* remission; ~ **fiscale** *conditional amnesty for people evading tax*.
con'dotta *sf vedi* **condotto**.
con'dotto, a *pp di* **condurre** ♦ *ag*: **medico** ~

local authority doctor (*in country district*)
♦ *sm* (*canale, tubo*) pipe, conduit; (*ANAT*)
duct ♦ *sf* (*modo di comportarsi*) conduct,
behaviour (*BRIT*), behavior (*US*); (*di un
affare etc*) handling; (*di acqua*) piping;
(*incarico sanitario*) country medical
practice controlled by a local authority.

condu'cente [kondu'tʃɛnte] *sm* driver.

con'duco *etc vb vedi* **condurre**.

con'durre *vt* to conduct; (*azienda*) to
manage; (*accompagnare: bambino*) to take;
(*automobile*) to drive; (*trasportare: acqua,
gas*) to convey, conduct; (*fig*) to lead ♦ *vi*
to lead; **condursi** *vr* to behave, conduct
o.s.; ~ **a termine** to conclude.

con'dussi *etc vb vedi* **condurre**.

condut'tore, 'trice *ag*: **filo** ~ (*fig*) thread;
motivo ~ leitmotiv ♦ *sm* (*di mezzi pubblici*)
driver; (*FISICA*) conductor.

condut'tura *sf* (*gen*) pipe; (*di acqua, gas*)
main.

conduzi'one [kondut'tsjone] *sf* (*di affari,
ditta*) management; (*DIR: locazione*) lease;
(*FISICA*) conduction.

confabu'lare *vi* to confab.

confa'cente [konfa'tʃɛnte] *ag*: ~ **a qn/qc**
suitable for sb/sth; **clima** ~ **alla salute**
healthy climate.

CONFAGRICOL'TURA *abbr f*
(= *Confederazione generale dell'Agricoltura
Italiana*) confederation of Italian farmers.

CON'FAPI *sigla f* = *Confederazione Nazionale
della Piccola Industria*.

con'farsi *vr*: ~ **a** to suit, agree with.

CONFARTIGIA'NATO [konfartidʒa'nato]
abbr f = *Confederazione Generale
dell'Artigianato Italiano*.

con'fatto, a *pp di* **confarsi**.

CONFCOM'MERCIO [konfkom'mɛrtʃo]
abbr f = *Confederazione Generale del
Commercio*.

confederazi'one [konfederat'tsjone] *sf*
confederation; ~ **imprenditoriale**
employers' association.

confe'renza [konfe'rɛntsa] *sf* (*discorso*)
lecture; (*riunione*) conference; ~ **stampa**
press conference.

conferenzi'ere, a [konferen'tsjɛre] *sm/f*
lecturer.

conferi'mento *sm* conferring, awarding.

confe'rire *vt*: ~ **qc a qn** to give sth to sb,
confer sth on sb ♦ *vi* to confer.

con'ferma *sf* confirmation.

confer'mare *vt* to confirm.

confes'sare *vt*, ~**rsi** *vr* to confess; **andare a**
~**rsi** (*REL*) to go to confession.

confessio'nale *ag, sm* confessional.

confessi'one *sf* confession; (*setta religiosa*)

denomination.

con'fesso, a *ag*: **essere reo** ~ to have
pleaded guilty.

confes'sore *sm* confessor.

con'fetto *sm* sugared almond; (*MED*) pill.

confet'tura *sf* (*gen*) jam; (*di arance*)
marmalade.

confezio'nare [konfettsjo'nare] *vt* (*vestito*)
to make (up); (*merci, pacchi*) to package.

confezi'one [konfet'tsjone] *sf* (*di abiti: da
uomo*) tailoring; (: *da donna*)
dressmaking; (*imballaggio*) packaging; ~
regalo gift pack; ~ **risparmio** economy
size; ~ **da viaggio** travel pack; ~**i per
signora** ladies' wear *no pl*; ~**i da uomo**
menswear *no pl*.

confic'care *vt*: ~ **qc in** to hammer o drive
sth into; ~**rsi** *vr* to stick.

confi'dare *vi*: ~ **in** to confide in, rely on
♦ *vt* to confide; ~**rsi con qn** to confide in
sb.

confi'dente *sm/f* (*persona amica*) confidant/
confidante; (*informatore*) informer.

confi'denza [konfi'dɛntsa] *sf* (*familiarità*)
intimacy, familiarity; (*fiducia*) trust,
confidence; (*rivelazione*) confidence;
prendersi (troppe) ~**e** to take liberties;
fare una ~ **a qn** to confide something to
sb.

confidenzi'ale [konfiden'tsjale] *ag* familiar,
friendly; (*segreto*) confidential; **in via** ~
confidentially.

configu'rare *vt* (*INFORM*) to set; ~**rsi** *vr*: ~ **a**
to assume the shape o form of.

configurazi'one [konfigurat'tsjone] *sf*
configuration; (*INFORM*) setting.

confi'nante *ag* neighbouring (*BRIT*),
neighboring (*US*).

confi'nare *vi*: ~ **con** to border on ♦ *vt* (*POL*)
to intern; (*fig*) to confine; ~**rsi** *vr* (*isolarsi*):
~**rsi in** to shut o.s. up in.

confi'nato, a *ag* interned ♦ *sm/f* internee.

CONFIN'DUSTRIA *sigla f* (= *Confederazione
Generale dell'Industria Italiana*) employers'
association, ≈ CBI (*BRIT*).

con'fine *sm* boundary; (*di paese*) border,
frontier; **territorio di** ~ border zone.

con'fino *sm* internment.

con'fisca *sf* confiscation.

confis'care *vt* to confiscate.

conflagrazi'one [konflagrat'tsjone] *sf*
conflagration.

con'flitto *sm* conflict; **essere in** ~ **con qc** to
clash with sth; **essere in** ~ **con qn** to be at
loggerheads with sb.

conflittu'ale *ag*: **rapporto** ~ relationship
based on conflict.

conflittualità *sf* conflicts *pl*.

conflu'enza [konflu'εntsa] *sf* (*di fiumi*) confluence; (*di strade*) junction.

conflu'ire *vi* (*fiumi*) to flow into each other, meet; (*strade*) to meet.

con'fondere *vt* to mix up, confuse; (*imbarazzare*) to embarrass; ~**rsi** *vr* (*mescolarsi*) to mingle; (*turbarsi*) to be confused; (*sbagliare*) to get mixed up; ~ **le idee a qn** to mix sb up, confuse sb.

confor'mare *vt* (*adeguare*): ~ **a** to adapt *o* conform to; ~**rsi** *vr*: ~**rsi** (**a**) to conform (to).

con'forme *ag*: ~ **a** (*simile*) similar to; (*corrispondente*) in keeping with.

conforme'mente *av* accordingly; ~ **a** in accordance with.

confor'mismo *sm* conformity.

confor'mista, i, e *sm/f* conformist.

conformità *sf* conformity; **in** ~ **a** in conformity with.

confor'tare *vt* to comfort, console.

confor'tevole *ag* (*consolante*) comforting; (*comodo*) comfortable.

con'forto *sm* (*consolazione, sollievo*) comfort, consolation; (*conferma*) support; **a** ~ **di qc** in support of sth; **i** ~**i** (*religiosi*) the last sacraments.

confra'ternita *sf* brotherhood.

confron'tare *vt* to compare; ~**rsi** *vr* (*scontrarsi*) to have a confrontation.

con'fronto *sm* comparison; (*DIR, MIL, POL*) confrontation; **in** *o* **a** ~ **di** in comparison with, compared to; **nei miei** (*o* **tuoi** *etc*) ~**i** towards me (*o* you *etc*).

con'fusi *etc vb vedi* **confondere**.

confusi'one *sf* confusion; (*imbarazzo*) embarrassment; **far** ~ (*disordine*) to make a mess; (*chiasso*) to make a racket; (*confondere*) to confuse things.

con'fuso, a *pp di* **confondere** ♦ *ag* (*vedi* confondere) confused; embarrassed.

confu'tare *vt* to refute.

conge'dare [kondʒe'dare] *vt* to dismiss; (*MIL*) to demobilize; ~**rsi** *vr* to take one's leave.

con'gedo [kon'dʒedo] *sm* (*anche MIL*) leave; **prendere** ~ **da qn** to take one's leave of sb; ~ **assoluto** (*MIL*) discharge.

conge'gnare [kondʒeɲ'ɲare] *vt* to construct, put together.

con'gegno [kon'dʒeɲɲo] *sm* device, mechanism.

congela'mento [kondʒela'mento] *sm* (*gen*) freezing; (*MED*) frostbite; ~ **salariale** wage freeze.

conge'lare [kondʒe'lare] *vt*, ~**rsi** *vr* to freeze.

congela'tore [kondʒela'tore] *sm* freezer.

con'genito, a [kon'dʒεnito] *ag* congenital.

con'gerie [kon'dʒεrje] *sf inv* (*di oggetti*) heap; (*di idee*) muddle, jumble.

congestio'nare [kondʒestjo'nare] *vt* to congest; **essere congestionato** (*persona, viso*) to be flushed; (*zona: per traffico*) to be congested.

congesti'one [kondʒes'tjone] *sf* congestion.

conget'tura [kondʒet'tura] *sf* conjecture, supposition.

con'giungere [kon'dʒundʒere] *vt*, ~**rsi** *vr* to join (together).

congiunti'vite [kondʒunti'vite] *sf* conjunctivitis.

congiun'tivo [kondʒun'tivo] *sm* (*LING*) subjunctive.

congi'unto, a [kon'dʒunto] *pp di* **congiungere** ♦ *ag* (*unito*) joined ♦ *sm/f* (*parente*) relative.

congiun'tura [kondʒun'tura] *sf* (*giuntura*) junction, join; (*ANAT*) joint; (*circostanza*) juncture; (*ECON*) economic situation.

congiuntu'rale [kondʒuntu'rale] *ag* of the economic situation; **crisi** ~ economic crisis.

congiunzi'one [kondʒun'tsjone] *sf* (*LING*) conjunction.

congi'ura [kon'dʒura] *sf* conspiracy.

congiu'rare [kondʒu'rare] *vi* to conspire.

conglome'rato *sm* (*GEO*) conglomerate; (*fig*) conglomeration; (*EDIL*) concrete.

'Congo *sm*: **il** ~ the Congo.

congo'lese *ag, sm/f* Congolese *inv*.

congratu'larsi *vr*: ~ **con qn per qc** to congratulate sb on sth.

congratulazi'oni [kongratulat'tsjoni] *sfpl* congratulations.

con'grega, ghe *sf* band, bunch.

congregazi'one [kongregat'tsjone] *sf* congregation.

congres'sista, i, e *sm/f* participant at a congress.

con'gresso *sm* congress.

'congruo, a *ag* (*prezzo, compenso*) adequate, fair; (*ragionamento*) coherent, consistent.

conguagli'are [kongwaʎ'ʎare] *vt* to balance; (*stipendio*) to adjust.

congu'aglio [kon'gwaʎʎo] *sm* balancing; adjusting; (*somma di denaro*) balance; **fare il** ~ **di** to balance; to adjust.

coni'are *vt* to mint, coin; (*fig*) to coin.

coniazi'one [konjat'tsjone] *sf* mintage.

'conico, a, ci, che *ag* conical.

co'nifere *sfpl* conifers.

conigli'era [koniʎ'ʎera] *sf* (*gabbia*) rabbit hutch; (*più grande*) rabbit run.

conigli'etta [koniʎ'ʎetta] *sf* bunny girl.
conigli'etto [koniʎ'ʎetto] *sm* bunny.
co'niglio [ko'niʎʎo] *sm* rabbit; **sei un** ~! (*fig*) you're chicken!
coniu'gale *ag* (*amore, diritti*) conjugal; (*vita*) married, conjugal.
coniu'gare *vt* to combine; (*LING*) to conjugate; ~**rsi** *vr* to get married.
coniu'gato, a *ag* (*AMM*) married.
coniugazi'one [konjugat'tsjone] *sf* (*LING*) conjugation.
'coniuge ['kɔnjudʒe] *sm/f* spouse.
connatu'rato, a *ag* inborn.
connazio'nale [konnattsjo'nale] *sm/f* fellow-countryman/woman.
connessi'one *sf* connection.
con'nesso, a *pp di* **connettere**.
con'nettere *vt* to connect, join ♦ *vi* (*fig*) to think straight.
connet'tore *sm* (*ELETTR*) connector.
conni'vente *ag* conniving.
conno'tati *smpl* distinguishing marks; **rispondere ai** ~**i** to fit the description; **cambiare i ~i a qn** (*fam*) to beat sb up.
con'nubio *sm* (*matrimonio*) marriage; (*fig*) union.
'cono *sm* cone; ~ **gelato** ice-cream cone.
co'nobbi *etc vb vedi* **conoscere**.
cono'scente [konoʃ'ʃente] *sm/f* acquaintance.
cono'scenza [konoʃ'ʃentsa] *sf* (*il sapere*) knowledge *no pl*; (*persona*) acquaintance; (*facoltà sensoriale*) consciousness *no pl*; **essere a** ~ **di qc** to know sth; **portare qn a** ~ **di qc** to inform sb of sth; **per vostra** ~ for your information; **fare la** ~ **di qn** to make sb's acquaintance; **perdere** ~ to lose consciousness; ~ **tecnica** know-how.
co'noscere [ko'noʃʃere] *vt* to know; **ci siamo conosciuti a Firenze** we (first) met in Florence; ~ **qn di vista** to know sb by sight; **farsi** ~ (*fig*) to make a name for o.s.
conosci'tore, 'trice [konoʃʃi'tore] *sm/f* connoisseur.
conosci'uto, a [konoʃ'ʃuto] *pp di* **conoscere** ♦ *ag* well-known.
con'quista *sf* conquest.
conquis'tare *vt* to conquer; (*fig*) to gain, win.
conquista'tore, 'trice *sm/f* (*in guerra*) conqueror ♦ *sm* (*seduttore*) lady-killer.
cons. *abbr* = **consiglio**.
consa'crare *vt* (*REL*) to consecrate; (: *sacerdote*) to ordain; (*dedicare*) to dedicate; (*fig: uso etc*) to sanction; ~**rsi a** to dedicate o.s. to.
consangu'ineo, a *sm/f* blood relation.
consa'pevole *ag*: ~ **di** aware *o* conscious

of.
consapevo'lezza [konsapevo'lettsa] *sf* awareness, consciousness.
conscia'mente [konʃa'mente] *av* consciously.
'conscio, a, sci, sce ['kɔnʃo] *ag*: ~ **di** aware *o* conscious of.
consecu'tivo, a *ag* consecutive; (*successivo: giorno*) following, next.
con'segna [kon'seɲɲa] *sf* delivery; (*merce consegnata*) consignment; (*custodia*) care, custody; (*MIL: ordine*) orders *pl*; (: *punizione*) confinement to barracks; **alla** ~ on delivery; **dare qc in** ~ **a qn** to entrust sth to sb; **passare le** ~**e a qn** to hand over to sb; ~ **a domicilio** home delivery; ~ **in contrassegno, pagamento alla** ~ cash on delivery; ~ **sollecita** prompt delivery.
conse'gnare [konseɲ'ɲare] *vt* to deliver; (*affidare*) to entrust, hand over; (*MIL*) to confine to barracks.
consegna'tario [konseɲɲa'tarjo] *sm* consignee.
consegu'ente *ag* consequent.
conseguente'mente *av* consequently.
consegu'enza [konse'gwentsa] *sf* consequence; **per** *o* **di** ~ consequently.
consegui'mento *sm* (*di scopo, risultato etc*) achievement, attainment; **al** ~ **della laurea** on graduation.
consegu'ire *vt* to achieve ♦ *vi* to follow, result; ~ **la laurea** to graduate, obtain one's degree.
con'senso *sm* approval, consent.
consensu'ale *ag* (*DIR*) by mutual consent.
consen'tire *vi*: ~ **a** to consent *o* agree to ♦ *vt* to allow, permit; **mi si consenta di ringraziare** ... I would like to thank ....
consenzi'ente [konsen'tsjɛnte] *ag* (*gen, DIR*) consenting.
con'serto, a *ag*: **a braccia** ~**e** with one's arms folded.
con'serva *sf* (*CUC*) preserve; ~ **di frutta** jam; ~ **di pomodoro** tomato purée; ~**e alimentari** tinned (*o* canned *o* bottled) foods.
conser'vare *vt* (*CUC*) to preserve; (*custodire*) to keep; (: *dalla distruzione etc*) to preserve, conserve; ~**rsi** *vr* to keep.
conserva'tore, 'trice *ag, sm/f* (*POL*) conservative.
conserva'torio *sm* (*di musica*) conservatory.
conservato'rismo *sm* (*POL*) conservatism.
conservazi'one [konservat'tsjone] *sf* preservation; conservation; **istinto di** ~ instinct for self-preservation; **a lunga** ~

(*latte, panna*) long-life *cpd.*
con'sesso *sm* (*assemblea*) assembly;
(*riunione*) meeting.
conside'rabile *ag* worthy of consideration.
conside'rare *vt* to consider; (*reputare*) to
consider, regard; ~ **molto qn** to think
highly of sb.
conside'rato, a *ag* (*prudente*) cautious,
careful; (*stimato*) highly thought of,
esteemed.
considerazi'one [konsiderat'tsjone] *sf*
(*esame, riflessione*) consideration; (*stima*)
regard, esteem; (*pensiero, osservazione*)
observation; **prendere in** ~ to take into
consideration.
conside'revole *ag* considerable.
consigli'abile [konsiʎ'ʎabile] *ag* advisable.
consigli'are [konsiʎ'ʎare] *vt* (*persona*) to
advise; (*metodo, azione*) to recommend,
advise, suggest; **~rsi** *vr*: **~rsi con qn** to
ask sb for advice.
consigli'ere, a [konsiʎ'ʎere] *sm/f* adviser
♦ *sm*: ~ **d'amministrazione** board
member; ~ **comunale** town councillor; ~
delegato (*COMM*) managing director.
con'siglio [kon'siʎʎo] *sm* (*suggerimento*)
advice *no pl*, piece of advice; (*assemblea*)
council; ~ **d'amministrazione** board; **C~**
d'Europa Council of Europe; ~ **di fabbrica**
works council; **il C~ dei Ministri** (*POL*) ≈
the Cabinet; **C~ di stato** *advisory body to*
the Italian government on administrative
matters and their legal implications; **C~**
superiore della magistratura *state body*
responsible for judicial appointments
and regulations; *vedi nota nel riquadro.*

CONSIGLI

The **Consiglio dei Ministri**, *the Italian*
Cabinet, is headed by the "Presidente del
Consiglio", the Prime Minister, who is the
leader of the Government.
The **Consiglio superiore della**
Magistratura, *the magistrates' governing*
body, ensures their autonomy and independ-
ence as enshrined in the Constitution. Chaired
by the "Presidente della Repubblica", it
mainly deals with appointments and transfers,
and can take disciplinary action as required.
Of the 30 magistrates elected to the **Consiglio**
for a period of four years, 20 are chosen by
their fellow magistrates and 10 by Parliament.
The "Presidente della Repubblica" and
the "Vicepresidente" are ex officio
members.

---

con'simile *ag* similar.
consis'tente *ag* solid; (*fig*) sound,
valid.
consis'tenza [konsis'tɛntsa] *sf* (*di impasto*)
consistency; (*di stoffa*) texture; **senza** ~
(*sospetti, voci*) ill-founded, groundless; ~
di cassa/di magazzino cash/stock in hand;
~ **patrimoniale** financial solidity.
con'sistere *vi*: ~ **in** to consist of.
consis'tito, a *pp di* **consistere.**
'CONSOB *sigla f* (= *Commissione nazionale*
per le società e la borsa) *regulatory body*
for the Italian Stock Exchange.
consoci'arsi [konso'tʃarsi] *vr* to go into
partnership.
consociati'vismo [konsotʃati'vizmo] *sm*
(*POL*) pact-building.
consocia'tivo, a [konsotʃa'tivo] *ag* (*POL:*
democrazia) based on pacts.
consoci'ato, a [konso'tʃato] *ag* associated
♦ *sm/f* associate.
conso'lante *ag* consoling, comforting.
conso'lare *ag* consular ♦ *vt* (*confortare*)
to console, comfort; (*rallegrare*) to cheer
up; **~rsi** *vr* to be comforted; to cheer
up.
conso'lato *sm* consulate.
consolazi'one [konsolat'tsjone] *sf*
consolation, comfort.
'console *sm* consul ♦ *sf* [kɔ̃'sɔl] (*quadro di*
comando) console.
consolida'mento *sm* strengthening;
consolidation.
consoli'dare *vt* to strengthen, reinforce;
(*MIL, terreno*) to consolidate; **~rsi** *vr* to
consolidate.
consolidazi'one [konsolidat'tsjone] *sf*
strengthening; consolidation.
consommé [kɔ̃sɔ'me] *sm inv* consommé.
conso'nante *sf* consonant.
conso'nanza [konso'nantsa] *sf* consonance.
'consono, a *ag*: ~ **a** consistent with,
consonant with.
con'sorte *sm/f* consort.
con'sorzio [kon'sɔrtsjo] *sm* consortium;
~ **agrario** farmers' cooperative;
~ **di garanzia** (*COMM*) underwriting
syndicate.
con'stare *vi*: ~ **di** to consist of ♦ *vb impers*:
mi consta che it has come to my
knowledge that, it appears that; **a quanto**
mi consta as far as I know.
consta'tare *vt* to establish, verify; (*notare*)
to notice, observe.
constatazi'one [konstatat'tsjone] *sf*
observation; ~ **amichevole** (*in incidenti*)
jointly-agreed statement for insurance
purposes.

consu'eto, a *ag* habitual, usual ♦ *sm*: come di ~ as usual.

consuetudi'nario, a *ag*: diritto ~ (*DIR*) common law.

consue'tudine *sf* habit; (*usanza*) custom.

consu'lente *sm/f* consultant; ~ aziendale/ tecnico management/technical consultant.

consu'lenza [konsu'lɛntsa] *sf* consultancy; ~ medica/legale medical/legal advice; ufficio di ~ fiscale tax consultancy office; ~ tecnica technical consultancy *o* advice.

consul'tare *vt* to consult; ~rsi *vr*: ~rsi con qn to seek the advice of sb.

consultazi'one [konsultat'tsjone] *sf* consultation; ~i *sfpl* (*POL*) talks, consultations; libro di ~ reference book.

consul'tivo, a *ag* consultative.

consul'torio *sm*: ~ familiare o matrimoniale marriage guidance centre; ~ pediatrico children's clinic.

consu'mare *vt* (*logorare: abiti, scarpe*) to wear out; (*usare*) to consume, use up; (*mangiare, bere*) to consume; (*DIR*) to consummate; ~rsi *vr* to wear out; to be used up; (*anche fig*) to be consumed; (*combustibile*) to burn out.

consu'mato, a *ag* (*vestiti, scarpe, tappeto*) worn; (*persona: esperto*) accomplished.

consuma'tore *sm* consumer.

consumazi'one [konsumat'tsjone] *sf* (*bibita*) drink; (*spuntino*) snack; (*DIR*) consummation.

consu'mismo *sm* consumerism.

con'sumo *sm* consumption; wear; use; generi *o* beni di ~ consumer goods; beni di largo ~ basic commodities; imposta sui ~i tax on consumer goods.

consun'tivo *sm* (*ECON*) final balance.

con'sunto, a *ag* worn-out; (*viso*) wasted.

'conta *sf* (*nei giochi*): fare la ~ to see who is going to be "it".

con'tabile *ag* accounts *cpd*, accounting ♦ *sm/f* accountant.

contabilità *sf* (*attività, tecnica*) accounting, accountancy; (*insieme dei libri etc*) books *pl*, accounts *pl*; (*ufficio*) ~ accounts department; ~ finanziaria financial accounting; ~ di gestione management accounting.

contachi'lometri [kontaki'lɔmetri] *sm inv* ≈ mileometer.

conta'dino, a *sm/f* countryman/woman; farm worker; (*peg*) peasant.

contagi'are [konta'dʒare] *vt* to infect.

con'tagio [kon'tadʒo] *sm* infection; (*per contatto diretto*) contagion; (*epidemia*) epidemic.

contagi'oso, a [konta'dʒoso] *ag* infectious; contagious.

conta'giri [konta'dʒiri] *sm inv* (*AUT*) rev counter.

conta'gocce [konta'gottʃe] *sm inv* dropper.

contami'nare *vt* to contaminate.

contaminazi'one [kontaminat'tsjone] *sf* contamination.

con'tante *sm* cash; pagare in ~i to pay cash.

con'tare *vt* to count; (*considerare*) to consider ♦ *vi* to count, be of importance; ~ su qn to count *o* rely on sb; ~ di fare qc to intend to do sth; ha i giorni contati, ha le ore contate his days are numbered; la gente che conta people who matter.

contas'catti *sm inv* telephone meter.

conta'tore *sm* meter.

contat'tare *vt* to contact.

con'tatto *sm* contact; essere in ~ con qn to be in touch with sb; fare ~ (*ELETTR: fili*) to touch.

'conte *sm* count.

con'tea *sf* (*STORIA*) earldom; (*AMM*) county.

conteggi'are [konted'dʒare] *vt* to charge, put on the bill.

con'teggio [kon'tedd30] *sm* calculation.

con'tegno [kon'teɲɲo] *sm* (*comportamento*) behaviour (*BRIT*), behavior (*US*); (*atteggiamento*) attitude; darsi un ~ (*ostentare disinvoltura*) to act nonchalant; (*ricomporsi*) to pull o.s. together.

conte'gnoso, a [konteɲ'ɲoso] *ag* reserved, dignified.

contem'plare *vt* to contemplate, gaze at; (*DIR*) to make provision for.

contempla'tivo, a *ag* contemplative.

contemplazi'one [kontemplat'tsjone] *sf* contemplation.

con'tempo *sm*: nel ~ meanwhile, in the meantime.

contemporanea'mente *av* simultaneously; at the same time.

contempo'raneo, a *ag*, *sm/f* contemporary.

conten'dente *sm/f* opponent, adversary.

con'tendere *vi* (*competere*) to compete; (*litigare*) to quarrel ♦ *vt*: ~ qc a qn to contend with *o* be in competition with sb for sth.

conte'nere *vt* to contain; ~rsi *vr* to contain o.s.

conteni'tore *sm* container.

conten'tabile *ag*: difficilmente ~ difficult to please.

conten'tare *vt* to please, satisfy; ~rsi *vr*: ~rsi di to be satisfied with, content o.s. with; si contenta di poco he is easily

satisfied.
conten'tezza [konten'tettsa] *sf* contentment.
conten'tino *sm* sop.
con'tento, a *ag* pleased, glad; ~ **di** pleased with.
conte'nuto *ag* (*ira, entusiasmo*) restrained, suppressed; (*forza*) contained ♦ *sm* contents *pl*; (*argomento*) content.
contenzi'oso, a [konten'tsjɔso] *ag* (*DIR*) contentious ♦ *sm* (*AMM*: *ufficio*) legal department.
con'teso, a *pp di* **contendere** ♦ *sf* dispute, argument.
con'tessa *sf* countess.
contes'tare *vt* (*DIR*) to notify; (*fig*) to dispute; ~ **il sistema** to protest against the system.
contesta'tore, 'trice *ag* anti-establishment ♦ *sm/f* protester.
contestazi'one [kontestat'tsjone] *sf* (*DIR*: *disputa*) dispute; (: *notifica*) notification; (*POL*) anti-establishment activity; **in caso di** ~ if there are any objections.
con'testo *sm* context.
con'tiguo, a *ag*: ~ (**a**) adjacent (to).
continen'tale *ag* continental.
conti'nente *ag* continent ♦ *sm* (*GEO*) continent; (: *terra ferma*) mainland.
conti'nenza [konti'nɛntsa] *sf* continence.
contin'gente [kontin'dʒɛnte] *ag* contingent ♦ *sm* (*COMM*) quota; (*MIL*) contingent.
contin'genza [kontin'dʒɛntsa] *sf* circumstance; (**indennità di**) ~ cost-of-living allowance.
continua'mente *av* (*senza interruzione*) continuously, nonstop; (*ripetutamente*) continually.
continu'are *vt* to continue (with), go on with ♦ *vi* to continue, go on; ~ **a fare qc** to go on *o* continue doing sth; **continua a nevicare/a fare freddo** it's still snowing/cold.
continua'tivo, a *ag* (*occupazione*) permanent; (*periodo*) consecutive.
continuazi'one [kontinuat'tsjone] *sf* continuation.
continuità *sf* continuity.
con'tinuo, a *ag* (*numerazione*) continuous; (*pioggia*) continual, constant; (*ELETTR*: *corrente*) direct; **di** ~ continually.
'conto *sm* (*calcolo*) calculation; (*COMM, ECON*) account; (*di ristorante, albergo*) bill; (*fig*: *stima*) consideration, esteem; **avere un** ~ **in sospeso (con qn)** to have an outstanding account (with sb); (*fig*) to have a score to settle (with sb); **fare i** ~**i con qn** to settle one's account with sb;

fare ~ **su qn** to count *o* rely on sb; **fare** ~ **che** (*supporre*) to suppose that; **rendere** ~ **a qn di qc** to be accountable to sb for sth; **rendersi** ~ **di qc/che** to realize sth/that; **tener** ~ **di qn/qc** to take sb/sth into account; **tenere qc da** ~ to take great care of sth; **ad ogni buon** ~ in any case; **di poco/nessun** ~ of little/no importance; **per** ~ **di** on behalf of; **per** ~ **mio** as far as I'm concerned; (*da solo*) on my own; **a** ~**i fatti, in fin dei** ~**i** all things considered; **mi hanno detto strane cose sul suo** ~ I've heard some strange things about him; ~ **capitale** capital account; ~ **cifrato** numbered account; ~ **corrente** current account (*BRIT*), checking account (*US*); ~ **corrente postale** Post Office account; ~ **economico** profit and loss account; ~ **in partecipazione** joint account; ~ **passivo** account payable; ~ **profitti e perdite** profit and loss account; ~ **alla rovescia** countdown; ~ **valutario** foreign currency account.
con'torcere [kon'tɔrtʃere] *vt* to twist; (*panni*) to wring (out); ~**rsi** *vr* to twist, writhe.
contor'nare *vt* to surround; ~**rsi** *vr*: ~**rsi di** to surround o.s. with.
con'torno *sm* (*linea*) outline, contour; (*ornamento*) border; (*CUC*) vegetables *pl*; **fare da** ~ **a** to surround.
contorsi'one *sf* contortion.
con'torto, a *pp di* **contorcere**.
contrabban'dare *vt* to smuggle.
contrabbandi'ere, a *sm/f* smuggler.
contrab'bando *sm* smuggling, contraband; **merce di** ~ contraband, smuggled goods *pl*.
contrab'basso *sm* (*MUS*) (double) bass.
contraccambi'are *vt* (*favore etc*) to return; **vorrei** ~ I'd like to show my appreciation.
contraccet'tivo, a [kontratt∫et'tivo] *ag, sm* contraceptive.
contrac'colpo *sm* rebound; (*di arma da fuoco*) recoil; (*fig*) repercussion.
con'trada *sf* street; district; *vedi anche* **Palio**.
contrad'detto, a *pp di* **contraddire**.
contrad'dire *vt* to contradict; ~**rsi** *vr* to contradict o.s.; (*uso reciproco*: *persone*) to contradict each other *o* one another; (: *testimonianze etc*) to be contradictory.
contraddis'tinguere *vt* (*merce*) to mark; (*fig*: *atteggiamento, persona*) to distinguish.
contraddis'tinto, a *pp di* **contraddistinguere**.
contraddit'torio, a *ag* contradictory; (*sentimenti*) conflicting ♦ *sm* (*DIR*) cross-

examination.
contraddizi'one [kontraddit'tsjone] *sf*
contradiction; **cadere in** ~ to contradict
o.s.; **essere in** ~ (*tesi, affermazioni*) to
contradict one another; **spirito di** ~
argumentativeness.
con'trae *etc vb vedi* **contrarre**.
contra'ente *sm* contractor.
contra'erea *sf* (*MIL*) anti-aircraft artillery.
contra'ereo, a *ag* anti-aircraft.
contraf'fare *vt* (*persona*) to mimic; (*voce*)
to disguise; (*firma*) to forge, counterfeit.
contraf'fatto, a *pp di* **contraffare** ♦ *ag*
counterfeit.
contraffazi'one [kontraffat'tsjone] *sf*
mimicking *no pl*; disguising *no pl*; forging
no pl; (*cosa contraffatta*) forgery.
contraf'forte *sm* (*ARCHIT*) buttress; (*GEO*)
spur.
con'traggo *etc vb vedi* **contrarre**.
con'tralto *sm* (*MUS*) contralto.
contrap'pello *sm* (*MIL*) second roll call.
contrappe'sare *vt* to counterbalance; (*fig:
decisione*) to weigh up.
contrap'peso *sm* counterbalance,
counterweight.
contrap'porre *vt*: ~ **qc a qc** to counter sth
with sth; (*paragonare*) to compare sth
with sth; **contrapporsi** *vr*: **contrapporsi a**
qc to contrast with sth, be opposed to
sth.
contrap'posto, a *pp di* **contrapporre**.
contraria'mente *av*: ~ **a** contrary to.
contrari'are *vt* (*contrastare*) to thwart,
oppose; (*irritare*) to annoy, bother; ~**rsi** *vr*
to get annoyed.
contrari'ato, a *ag* annoyed.
contrarietà *sf* adversity; (*fig*) aversion.
con'trario, a *ag* opposite; (*sfavorevole*)
unfavourable (*BRIT*), unfavorable (*US*)
♦ *sm* opposite; **essere** ~ **a qc** (*persona*) to
be against sth; **al** ~ on the contrary; **in**
caso ~ otherwise; **avere qualcosa in** ~ to
have some objection; **non ho niente in** ~ I
have no objection.
con'trarre *vt* (*malattia, debito*) to contract;
(*muscoli*) to tense; (*abitudine, vizio*) to pick
up; (*accordo, patto*) to enter into; **contrarsi**
vr to contract; ~ **matrimonio** to marry.
contrasse'gnare [kontrassen'ɲare] *vt* to
mark.
contras'segno [kontras'seɲɲo] *sm*
(*distintivo*) distinguishing mark; **spedire**
in ~ (*COMM*) to send COD.
con'trassi *etc vb vedi* **contrarre**.
contras'tante *ag* contrasting.
contras'tare *vt* (*avversare*) to oppose;
(*impedire*) to bar; (*negare: diritto*) to

contest, dispute ♦ *vi*: ~ **(con)** (*essere in
disaccordo*) to contrast (with); (*lottare*) to
struggle (with).
con'trasto *sm* contrast; (*conflitto*) conflict;
(*litigio*) dispute.
contrat'tacco *sm* counterattack; **passare al**
~ (*fig*) to fight back.
contrat'tare *vt, vi* to negotiate.
contrat'tempo *sm* hitch.
con'tratto, a *pp di* **contrarre** ♦ *sm* contract;
~ **di acquisto** purchase agreement; ~ **di**
affitto, ~ **di locazione** lease; ~ **collettivo**
di lavoro collective agreement; ~ **di**
lavoro contract of employment; ~ **a**
termine forward contract.
contrattu'ale *ag* contractual; **forza** ~ (*dl
sindacato*) bargaining power.
contravve'nire *vi*: ~ **a** (*legge*) to
contravene; (*obbligo*) to fail to meet.
contravven'tore, 'trice *sm/f* offender.
contravve'nuto, a *pp di* **contravvenire**.
contravvenzi'one [kontravven'tsjone] *sf*
contravvention; (*ammenda*) fine.
contrazi'one [kontrat'tsjone] *sf*
contraction; (*di prezzi etc*) reduction.
contribu'ente *sm/f* taxpayer; ratepayer
(*BRIT*), property tax payer (*US*).
contribu'ire *vi* to contribute.
contribu'tivo, a *ag* contributory.
contri'buto *sm* contribution; (*sovvenzione*)
subsidy, contribution; (*tassa*) tax; ~**i**
previdenziali ≈ national insurance (*BRIT*)
o welfare (*US*) contributions; ~**i sindacali**
trade union dues.
con'trito, a *ag* contrite, penitent.
'contro *prep* against; ~ **di me/lui** against
me/him; **pastiglie** ~ **la tosse** throat
lozenges; ~ **pagamento** (*COMM*) on
payment; ~ **ogni mia aspettativa**
contrary to my expectations; **per** ~ on
the other hand.
contro'battere *vt* (*fig: a parole*) to answer
back; (*: confutare*) to refute.
controbilanci'are [kontrobilan'tʃare] *vt* to
counterbalance.
controcor'rente *av*: **andare** ~ (*anche fig*) to
swim against the tide.
controcul'tura *sf* counterculture.
contro'esodo *sm* return from holiday.
contro'fax *sm inv* reply to a fax.
controffen'siva *sf* counteroffensive.
controfi'gura *sf* (*CINE*) double.
controfir'mare *vt* to countersign.
control'lare *vt* (*accertare*) to check;
(*sorvegliare*) to watch, control; (*tenere nel
proprio potere, fig: dominare*) to control;
~**rsi** *vr* to control o.s.
control'lato, a *ag* (*persona*) self-possessed;

(*reazioni*) controlled ♦ *sf* (*COMM*: *società*) associated company.

con'trollo *sm* check; watch; control; **base di** ~ (*AER*) ground control; **telefono sotto** ~ tapped telephone; **visita di** ~ (*MED*) checkup; ~ **doganale** customs inspection; ~ **di gestione** management control; ~ **delle nascite** birth control; ~ **di qualità** quality control.

control'lore *sm* (*FERR, AUTOBUS*) (ticket) inspector; ~ **di volo** *o* **del traffico aereo** air traffic controller.

contro'luce [kontro'lutʃe] *sf inv* (*FOT*) backlit shot ♦ *av*: **(in)** ~ against the light; (*fotografare*) into the light.

contro'mano *av*: **guidare** ~ to drive on the wrong side of the road; (*in un senso unico*) to drive the wrong way up a one-way street.

contropar'tita *sf* (*fig*: *compenso*): **come** ~ in return.

contropi'ede *sm* (*SPORT*): **azione di** ~ sudden counter-attack; **prendere qn in** ~ (*fig*) to catch sb off his (*o* her) guard.

controprodu'cente [kontroprodu'tʃɛnte] *ag* counterproductive.

con'trordine *sm* counter-order; **salvo** ~ unless I (*o* you *etc*) hear to the contrary.

contro'senso *sm* (*contraddizione*) contradiction in terms; (*assurdità*) nonsense.

controspio'naggio [kontrospio'naddʒo] *sm* counterespionage.

controva'lore *sm* equivalent (value).

contro'vento *av* against the wind; **navigare** ~ (*NAUT*) to sail to windward.

contro'versia *sf* controversy; (*DIR*) dispute; ~ **sindacale** industrial dispute.

contro'verso, a *ag* controversial.

contro'voglia [kontro'vɔʎʎa] *av* unwillingly.

contu'mace [kontu'matʃe] *ag* (*DIR*): **rendersi** ~ to default, fail to appear in court ♦ *sm/f* (*DIR*) defaulter.

contu'macia [kontu'matʃa] *sf* (*DIR*) default.

contun'dente *ag*: **corpo** ~ blunt instrument.

contur'bante *ag* (*sguardo, bellezza*) disturbing.

contur'bare *vt* to disturb, upset.

contusi'one *sf* (*MED*) bruise.

convale'scente [konvaleʃ'ʃɛnte] *ag*, *sm/f* convalescent.

convale'scenza [konvaleʃ'ʃɛntsa] *sf* convalescence.

con'valida *sf* (*DIR*) confirmation; (*di biglietto*) stamping.

convali'dare *vt* (*AMM*) to validate; (*fig*:

sospetto, dubbio) to confirm.

con'vegno [kon'veɲɲo] *sm* (*incontro*) meeting; (*congresso*) convention, congress; (*luogo*) meeting place.

conve'nevoli *smpl* civilities.

conveni'ente *ag* suitable; (*vantaggioso*) profitable; (: *prezzo*) cheap.

conveni'enza [konve'njɛntsa] *sf* suitability; advantage; cheapness; ~**e** *sfpl* social conventions.

conve'nire *vi* to agree upon ♦ *vi* (*riunirsi*) to gather, assemble; (*concordare*) to agree; (*tornare utile*) to be worthwhile ♦ *vb impers*: **conviene fare questo** it is advisable to do this; **conviene andarsene** we should go; **ne convengo** I agree; **come convenuto** as agreed; **in data da** ~ on a date to be agreed; **come (si) conviene ad una signorina** as befits a young lady.

conven'ticola *sf* (*cricca*) clique; (*riunione*) secret meeting.

con'vento *sm* (*di frati*) monastery; (*di suore*) convent.

conve'nuto, a *pp di* **convenire** ♦ *sm* (*cosa pattuita*) agreement ♦ *sm/f* (*DIR*) defendant; **i** ~**i** (*i presenti*) those present.

convenzio'nale [konventsjo'nale] *ag* conventional.

convenzio'nato, a [konventsjo'nato] *ag* (*ospedale, clinica*) providing free health care, ≈ National Health Service *cpd* (*BRIT*).

convenzi'one [konven'tsjone] *sf* (*DIR*) agreement; (*nella società*) convention; **le** ~**i (sociali)** social conventions.

conver'gente [konver'dʒɛnte] *ag* convergent.

conver'genza [konver'dʒɛntsa] *sf* convergence.

con'vergere [kon'vɛrdʒere] *vi* to converge.

con'versa *sf* (*REL*) lay sister.

conver'sare *vi* to have a conversation, converse.

conversazi'one [konversat'tsjone] *sf* conversation; **fare** ~ (*chiacchierare*) to chat, have a chat.

conversi'one *sf* conversion; ~ **ad U** (*AUT*) U-turn.

con'verso, a *pp di* **convergere; per** ~ *av* conversely.

conver'tire *vt* (*trasformare*) to change; (*INFORM, POL, REL*) to convert; ~**rsi** *vr*: ~**rsi (a)** to be converted (to).

conver'tito, a *sm/f* convert.

converti'tore *sm* (*ELETTR*) converter.

con'vesso, a *ag* convex.

convin'cente [konvin'tʃɛnte] *ag* convincing.

con'vincere [kon'vint∫ere] *vt* to convince; ~ **qn di qc** to convince sb of sth; (*DIR*) to prove sb guilty of sth; ~ **qn a fare qc** to persuade sb to do sth.

con'vinto, a *pp di* **convincere** ♦ *ag*: **reo** ~ (*DIR*) convicted criminal.

convinzi'one [konvin'tsjone] *sf* conviction, firm belief.

convis'suto, a *pp di* **convivere**.

convi'tato, a *sm/f* guest.

con'vitto *sm* (*INS*) boarding school.

convi'venza [konvi'ventsa] *sf* living together; (*DIR*) cohabitation.

con'vivere *vi* to live together.

convivi'ale *ag* convivial.

convo'care *vt* to call, convene; (*DIR*) to summon.

convocazi'one [konvokat'tsjone] *sf* meeting; summons *sg*; **lettera di** ~ (letter of) notification to appear *o* attend.

convogli'are [konvoʎ'ʎare] *vt* to convey; (*dirigere*) to direct, send.

con'voglio [kon'vɔʎʎo] *sm* (*di veicoli*) convoy; (*FERR*) train; ~ **funebre** funeral procession.

convo'lare *vi*: ~ **a (giuste) nozze** (*scherzoso*) to tie the knot.

convulsi'one *sf* convulsion.

con'vulso, a *ag* (*pianto*) violent, convulsive; (*attività*) feverish.

COOP *abbr f* = **cooperativa**.

coope'rare *vi*: ~ **(a)** to cooperate (in).

coopera'tiva *sf* cooperative.

cooperazi'one [kooperat'tsjone] *sf* cooperation.

coordina'mento *sm* coordination.

coordi'nare *vt* to coordinate.

coordi'nato, a *ag* (*movimenti*) coordinated ♦ *sf* (*LING, GEO, MAT*) coordinate ♦ *smpl*: ~**i** (*MODA*) coordinates.

coordinazi'one [koordinat'tsjone] *sf* coordination.

co'perchio [ko'perkjo] *sm* cover; (*di pentola*) lid.

co'perta *sf* cover; (*di lana*) blanket; (*da viaggio*) rug; (*NAUT*) deck.

coper'tina *sf* (*STAMPA*) cover, jacket.

co'perto, a *pp di* **coprire** ♦ *ag* covered; (*cielo*) overcast ♦ *sm* place setting; (*posto a tavola*) place; (*al ristorante*) cover charge; ~ **di** covered in *o* with.

coper'tone *sm* (*telo impermeabile*) tarpaulin; (*AUT*) rubber tyre.

coper'tura *sf* (*anche ECON, MIL*) cover; (*di edificio*) roofing; **fare un gioco di** ~ (*SPORT*) to play a defensive game; ~ **assicurativa** insurance cover.

'copia *sf* copy; (*FOT*) print; **brutta/bella** ~

rough/final copy; ~ **conforme** (*DIR*) certified copy; ~ **omaggio** presentation copy.

copi'are *vt* to copy.

copia'trice [kopja'trit∫e] *sf* copier, copying machine.

copi'one *sm* (*CINE, TEAT*) script.

'coppa *sf* (*bicchiere*) goblet, (*per frutta, gelato*) dish; (*trofeo*) cup, trophy; ~**e** *sfpl* (*CARTE*) suit in Neapolitan pack of cards; ~ **dell'olio** oil sump (*BRIT*) *o* pan (*US*).

'coppia *sf* (*di persone*) couple; (*di animali, SPORT*) pair.

cop'rente *ag* (*colore, cosmetico*) covering; (*calze*) opaque.

copri'capo *sm* headgear; (*cappello*) hat.

coprifu'oco, chi *sm* curfew.

copri'letto *sm* bedspread.

co'prire *vt* to cover; (*occupare: carica, posto*) to hold; ~**rsi** *vr* (*cielo*) to cloud over; (*vestirsi*) to wrap up, cover up; (*ECON*) to cover *o* s; ~**rsi di** (*macchie, muffa*) to become covered in; ~ **qn di baci** to smother sb with kisses; ~ **le spese** to break even; ~**rsi le spalle** (*fig*) to cover o.s.

coque [kɔk] *sf*: **uovo alla** ~ boiled egg.

co'raggio [ko'raddʒo] *sm* courage, bravery; ~**!** (*forza!*) come on!; (*animo!*) cheer up!; **farsi** ~ to pluck up courage; **hai un bel** ~**!** (*sfacciataggine*) you've got a nerve *o* a cheek!

coraggi'oso, a [korad'dʒoso] *ag* courageous, brave.

co'rale *ag* choral; (*approvazione*) unanimous.

co'rallo *sm* coral; **il mar dei C~i** the Coral Sea.

co'rano *sm* (*REL*) Koran.

co'razza [ko'rattsa] *sf* armour (*BRIT*), armor (*US*); (*di animali*) carapace, shell; (*MIL*) armo(u)r(-plating).

coraz'zato, a [korat'tsato] *ag* (*MIL*) armoured (*BRIT*), armored (*US*) ♦ *sf* battleship.

corazzi'ere [korat'tsjɛre] *sm* (*STORIA*) cuirassier; (*guardia presidenziale*) *carabiniere of the President's guard.*

corbelle'ria *sf* stupid remark; ~**e** *sfpl* (*sciocchezze*) nonsense *no pl*.

'corda *sf* cord; (*fune*) rope; (*spago, MUS*) string; **dare** ~ **a qn** (*fig*) to let sb have his (*o* her) way; **tenere sulla** ~ **qn** (*fig*) to keep sb on tenterhooks; **tagliare la** ~ (*fig*) to slip away, sneak off; **essere giù di** ~ to feel down; ~**e vocali** vocal cords.

cor'data *sf* (*ALPINISMO*) roped party; (*fig*) *alliance system in financial and business*

world.
cordi'ale *ag* cordial, warm ♦ *sm* (*bevanda*) cordial.
cordialità *sf inv* warmth, cordiality; ~ *sfpl* (*saluti*) best wishes.
cor'doglio [kor'dɔʎʎo] *sm* grief; (*lutto*) mourning.
cor'done *sm* cord, string; (*linea: di polizia*) cordon; ~ **ombelicale** umbilical cord; ~ **sanitario** quarantine line.
Co'rea *sf*: **la** ~ Korea; **la** ~ **del Nord/Sud** North/South Korea.
core'ano, a *ag*, *sm/f* Korean.
coreogra'fia *sf* choreography.
core'ografo, a *sm/f* choreographer.
cori'aceo, a [ko'rjatʃeo] *ag* (*BOT*, *ZOOL*) coriaceous; (*fig*) tough.
cori'andolo *sm* (*BOT*) coriander; ~**i** *smpl* (*per carnevale etc*) confetti *no pl.*
cori'care *vt* to put to bed; ~**rsi** *vr* to go to bed.
coricherò *etc* [korike'rɔ] *vb vedi* **coricare**.
Co'rinto *sf* Corinth.
co'rista, i, e *sm/f* (*REL*) choir member, chorister; (*TEAT*) member of the chorus.
'corna *sfpl vedi* **corno**.
cor'nacchia [kor'nakkja] *sf* crow.
corna'musa *sf* bagpipes *pl.*
'cornea *sf* (*ANAT*) cornea.
'corner *sm inv* (*CALCIO*) corner (kick); **salvarsi in** ~ (*fig: in gara, esame etc*) to get through by the skin of one's teeth.
cor'netta *sf* (*MUS*) cornet; (*TEL*) receiver.
cor'netto *sm* (*CUC*) croissant; ~ **acustico** ear trumpet.
cor'nice [kor'nitʃe] *sf* frame; (*fig*) background, setting.
cornici'one [korni'tʃone] *sm* (*di edificio*) ledge; (*ARCHIT*) cornice.
'corno *sm* (*ZOOL*: *pl(f)* ~**a**, *MUS*) horn; (*fam*): **fare le** ~**a a qn** to be unfaithful to sb; **dire peste e** ~**a di qn** to call sb every name under the sun; **un** ~! not on your life!
Corno'vaglia [korno'vaʎʎa] *sf*: **la** ~ Cornwall.
cor'nuto, a *ag* (*con corna*) horned; (*fam!*: *marito*) cuckolded ♦ *sm* (*fam!*) cuckold; (: *insulto*) bastard (*!*).
'coro *sm* chorus; (*REL*) choir.
corol'lario *sm* corollary.
co'rona *sf* crown; (*di fiori*) wreath.
corona'mento *sm* (*di impresa*) completion; (*di carriera*) crowning achievement; **il** ~ **dei propri sogni** the fulfilment of one's dreams.
coro'nare *vt* to crown.
coro'naria *sf* coronary artery.
'corpo *sm* body; (*cadavere*) (dead) body;

(*militare, diplomatico*) corps *inv*; (*di opere*) corpus; **prendere** ~ to take shape; **darsi anima e** ~ **a** to give o.s. heart and soul to; **a** ~ **a** ~ hand-to-hand; ~ **d'armata** army corps; ~ **di ballo** corps de ballet; ~ **dei carabinieri** ≈ police force; ~ **celeste** heavenly body; ~ **di guardia** (*soldati*) guard; (*locale*) guardroom; ~ **insegnante** teaching staff; ~ **del reato** material evidence.
corpo'rale *ag* bodily; (*punizione*) corporal.
corpora'tura *sf* build, physique.
corporazi'one [korporat'tsjone] *sf* corporation.
cor'poreo, a *ag* bodily, physical.
cor'poso, a *ag* (*vino*) full-bodied.
corpu'lento, a *ag* stout, corpulent.
corpu'lenza [korpu'lɛntsa] *sf* stoutness, corpulence.
cor'puscolo *sm* corpuscle.
corre'dare *vt*: ~ **di** to provide o furnish with; **domanda corredata dai seguenti documenti** application accompanied by the following documents.
cor'redo *sm* equipment; (*di sposa*) trousseau.
cor'reggere [kor'rɛddʒere] *vt* to correct; (*compiti*) to correct, mark.
cor'rente *ag* (*fiume*) flowing; (*acqua del rubinetto*) running; (*moneta, prezzo*) current; (*comune*) everyday ♦ *sm*: **essere al** ~ **(di)** to be well-informed (about) ♦ *sf* (*movimento di liquido*) current, stream; (*spiffero*) draught; (*ELETTR, METEOR*) current; (*fig*) trend, tendency; **mettere al** ~ **(di)** to inform (of); **la vostra lettera del 5** ~ **mese** (*in lettere commerciali*) in your letter of the 5th inst.; **articoli di qualità** ~ average-quality products; ~ **alternata (c.a.)** alternating current (AC); ~ **continua (c.c.)** direct current (DC).
corrente'mente *av* (*comunemente*) commonly; **parlare una lingua** ~ to speak a language fluently.
corren'tista, i, e *sm/f* (current (*BRIT*) o checking (*US*)) account holder.
cor'reo, a *sm/f* (*DIR*) accomplice.
'correre *vi* to run; (*precipitarsi*) to rush; (*partecipare a una gara*) to race, run; (*fig: diffondersi*) to go round ♦ *vt* (*SPORT: gara*) to compete in; (*rischio*) to run; (*pericolo*) to face; ~ **dietro a qn** to run after sb; **corre voce che ...** it is rumoured that ....
corresponsabilità *sf* joint responsibility; (*DIR*) joint liability.
corresponsi'one *sf* payment.
cor'ressi *etc vb vedi* **correggere**.
corret'tezza [korret'tettsa] *sf* (*di*

comportamento) correctness; (*SPORT*) fair play.

cor'retto, , a *pp di* **correggere** ♦ *ag* (*comportamento*) correct, proper; **caffè** ~ **al cognac** coffee laced with brandy.

corret'tore, 'trice *sm/f*: ~ **di bozze** proofreader ♦ *sm*: (**liquido**) ~ correction fluid.

correzi'one [korret'tsjone] *sf* correction; marking; ~ **di bozze** proofreading.

cor'rida *sf* bullfight.

corri'doio *sm* corridor; **manovre di** ~ (*POL*) lobbying *sg*.

corri'dore *sm* (*SPORT*) runner; (: *su veicolo*) racer.

corri'era *sf* coach (*BRIT*), bus.

corri'ere *sm* (*diplomatico, di guerra*) courier; (*posta*) mail, post; (*spedizioniere*) carrier.

corri'mano *sm* handrail.

corrispet'tivo *sm* amount due; **versare a qn il** ~ **di una prestazione** to pay sb the amount due for his (o her) services.

corrispon'dente *ag* corresponding ♦ *sm/f* correspondent.

corrispon'denza [korrispon'dentsa] *sf* correspondence; ~ **in arrivo/partenza** incoming/outgoing mail.

corris'pondere *vi* (*equivalere*): ~ **(a)** to correspond (to); (*per lettera*): ~ **con** to correspond with ♦ *vt* (*stipendio*) to pay; (*fig: amore*) to return.

corris'posto, a *pp di* **corrispondere**.

corrobo'rare *vt* to strengthen, fortify; (*fig*) to corroborate, bear out.

cor'rodere *vt*, **~rsi** *vr* to corrode.

cor'rompere *vt* to corrupt; (*comprare*) to bribe.

corrosi'one *sf* corrosion.

corro'sivo, a *ag* corrosive.

cor'roso, a *pp di* **corrodere**.

corrotta'mente *av* corruptly.

cor'rotto, a *pp di* **corrompere** ♦ *ag* corrupt.

corrucci'arsi [korrut'tʃarsi] *vr* to grow angry *o* vexed.

corru'gare *vt* to wrinkle; ~ **la fronte** to knit one's brows.

cor'ruppi *etc vb vedi* **corrompere**.

corrut'tela *sf* corruption, depravity.

corruzi'one [korrut'tsjone] *sf* corruption; bribery; ~ **di minorenne** (*DIR*) corruption of a minor.

'corsa *sf* running *no pl*; (*gara*) race; (*di autobus, taxi*) journey, trip; **fare una** ~ to run, dash; (*SPORT*) to run a race; **andare** *o* **essere di** ~ to be in a hurry; ~

automobilistica/ciclistica motor/cycle racing; ~ **campestre** cross-country racing; ~ **ad ostacoli** (*IPPICA*) steeplechase; (*ATLETICA*) hurdles race.

cor'saro, a *ag*: **nave** ~ a privateer ♦ *sm* privateer.

'corsi *etc vb vedi* **correre**.

cor'sia *sf* (*AUT, SPORT*) lane; (*di ospedale*) ward; ~ **di emergenza** (*AUT*) hard shoulder; ~ **preferenziale** ≈ bus lane; (*fig*) fast track; ~ **di sorpasso** (*AUT*) overtaking lane.

'Corsica *sf*: **la** ~ Corsica.

cor'sivo *sm* cursive (writing); (*TIP*) italics *pl*.

'corso, a *pp di* **correre** ♦ *ag*, *sm/f* Corsican ♦ *sm* course; (*strada cittadina*) main street; (*di unità monetaria*) circulation; (*di titoli, valori*) rate, price; **dar libero** ~ a to give free expression to; **in** ~ in progress, under way; (*annata*) current; ~ **d'acqua** river, stream; (*artificiale*) waterway; ~ **serale** evening class; **aver** ~ **legale** to be legal tender.

'corte *sf* (court)yard; (*DIR, regale*) court; **fare la** ~ **a qn** to court sb; ~ **d'appello** court of appeal; ~ **di cassazione** final court of appeal; **C**~ **dei Conti** *State audit court*; **C**~ **Costituzionale** *special court dealing with constitutional and ministerial matters*; ~ **marziale** court-martial; *vedi nota nel riquadro.*

CORTI

The **Corte d'Appello** *hears appeals against sentences passed by courts in both civil and criminal cases and can modify sentences where necessary. The* **Corte d'Assise** *tries serious crimes such as manslaughter and murder; its judges include both legal professionals and members of the public. Similar in structure, the* **Corte d'Assise d'Appello** *hears appeals imposed by these two courts. The* **Corte di Cassazione** *is the highest judicial authority and ensures that the law is correctly applied by the other courts; it may call for a retrial if required. The politically independent* **Corte Costituzionale** *decides whether laws comply with the principles of the Constitution, and has the power to impeach the "Presidente della Repubblica". The* **Corte dei Conti** *ensures the Government's compliance with the law and the Constitution. Reporting directly to Parliament, it oversees the financial aspects of the state budget and of the nationalized industries.*

cor'teccia, , ce [kor'tettʃa] *sf* bark.
corteggia'mento [korteddʒa'mento] *sm* courtship.
corteggi'are [korted'dʒare] *vt* to court.
corteggia'tore [korteddʒa'tore] *sm* suitor.
cor'teo *sm* procession; ~ **funebre** funeral cortège.
cor'tese *ag* courteous.
corte'sia *sf* courtesy; **fare una** ~ **a qn** to do sb a favour; **per** ~, **dov'è** ...? excuse me, please, where is ...?
cortigi'ano, a [korti'dʒano] *sm/f* courtier ♦ *sf* courtesan.
cor'tile *sm* (court)yard.
cor'tina *sf* curtain; (*anche fig*) screen.
corti'sone *sm* cortisone.
'corto, a *ag* short ♦ *av*: **tagliare** ~ to come straight to the point; **essere a** ~ **di qc** to be short of sth; **essere a** ~ **di parole** to be at a loss for words; **la settimana** ~**a** the 5-day week; ~ **circuito** short-circuit.
cortocir'cuito [kortotʃir'kuito] *sm* = **corto circuito**.
cortome'traggio [kortome'traddʒo] *sm* short (feature film).
cor'vino, a *ag* (*capelli*) jet-black.
'corvo *sm* raven.
'cosa *sf* thing; (*faccenda*) affair, matter, business *no pl*; **(che)** ~? what?; **(che) cos'è?** what is it?; **a** ~ **pensi?** what are you thinking about?; **tante belle** ~**e!** all the best!; **ormai è** ~ **fatta!** (*positivo*) it's in the bag!; (*negativo*) it's done now!; **a** ~**e fatte** when it's all over.
'Cosa 'Nostra *sf* Cosa Nostra.
'cosca, sche *sf* (*di mafiosi*) clan.
'coscia, sce ['kɔʃʃa] *sf* thigh; ~ **di pollo** (*CUC*) chicken leg.
cosci'ente [koʃ'ʃɛnte] *ag* conscious; ~ **di** conscious *o* aware of.
cosci'enza [koʃ'ʃɛntsa] *sf* conscience; (*consapevolezza*) consciousness; ~ **politica** political awareness.
coscienzi'oso, a [koʃʃen'tsjoso] *ag* conscientious.
cosci'otto [koʃ'ʃɔtto] *sm* (*CUC*) leg.
cos'critto *sm* (*MIL*) conscript.
coscrizi'one [koskrit'tsjone] *sf* conscription.

================= PAROLA CHIAVE

così *av* **1** (*in questo modo*) like this, (in) this way; (*in tal modo*) so; **le cose stanno** ~ this is the way things stand; **non ho detto** ~! I didn't say that!; **come stai?** — **(e)** ~ how are you? — so-so; **e** ~ **via** and so on; **per** ~ **dire** so to speak; ~ **sia** amen **2** (*tanto*) so; ~ **lontano** so far away; **un**

ragazzo ~ **intelligente** such an intelligent boy
♦ *ag inv* (*tale*): **non ho mai visto un film** ~ I've never seen such a film
♦ *cong* **1** (*perciò*) so, therefore; **e** ~ **ho deciso di lasciarlo** so I decided to leave him
2: ~ ... **come** as ... as; **non è** ~ **bravo come te** he's not as good as you; ~ ... **che** so ... that.

cosicché [kosik'ke] *cong* so (that).
cosid'detto, a *ag* so-called.
cos'mesi *sf* (*scienza*) cosmetics *sg*; (*prodotti*) cosmetics *pl*; (*trattamento*) beauty treatment.
cos'metico, a, ci, che *ag*, *sm* cosmetic.
'cosmico, a, ci, che *ag* cosmic.
'cosmo *sm* cosmos.
cosmo'nauta, i, e *sm/f* cosmonaut.
cosmopo'lita, i, e *ag* cosmopolitan.
'coso *sm* (*fam*: *oggetto*) thing, thingumajig; (: *aggeggio*) contraption; (: *persona*) what's his name, thingumajig.
cos'pargere [kos'pardʒere] *vt*: ~ **di** to sprinkle with.
cos'parso, a *pp di* **cospargere**.
cos'petto *sm*: **al** ~ **di** in front of; in the presence of.
cospicuità *sf* vast quantity.
cos'picuo, a *ag* considerable, large.
cospi'rare *vi* to conspire.
cospira'tore, 'trice *sm/f* conspirator.
cospirazi'one [kospirat'tsjone] *sf* conspiracy.
'cossi *etc vb vedi* **cuocere**.
Cost. *abbr* = **costituzione**.
'costa *sf* (*tra terra e mare*) coast(line); (*litorale*) shore; (*pendio*) slope; (*ANAT*) rib; **navigare sotto** ~ to hug the coast; **la C**~ **Azzurra** the French Riviera; **la C**~ **d'Avorio** the Ivory Coast; **velluto a** ~**e** corduroy.
costà *av* there.
cos'tante *ag* constant; (*persona*) steadfast ♦ *sf* constant.
cos'tanza [kos'tantsa] *sf* (*gen*) constancy; (*fermezza*) constancy, steadfastness; **il Lago di C**~ Lake Constance.
cos'tare *vi*, *vt* to cost; ~ **caro** to be expensive, cost a lot; ~ **un occhio della testa** to cost a fortune; **costi quel che costi** no matter what.
'Costa 'Rica *sf*: **la** ~ Costa Rica.
cos'tata *sf* (*CUC*: *di manzo*) large chop.
cos'tato *sm* (*ANAT*) ribs *pl*.
costeggi'are [kosted'dʒare] *vt* to be close to; to run alongside.

cos'tei *pron vedi* **costui.**

costellazi'one [kostellat'tsjone] *sf* constellation.

coster'nare *vt* to dismay.

coster'nato, a *ag* dismayed.

costernazi'one [kosternat'tsjone] *sf* dismay, consternation.

costi'ero, a *ag* coastal, coast *cpd* ♦ *sf* stretch of coast.

costi'pato, a *ag* (*stitico*) constipated.

costitu'ire *vt* (*comitato, gruppo*) to set up, form; (*collezione*) to put together, build up; (*sog: elementi, parti: comporre*) to make up, constitute; (*rappresentare*) to constitute; (*DIR*) to appoint; ~**rsi** *vr*: ~**rsi** (**alla polizia**) to give o.s. up (to the police); ~**rsi parte civile** (*DIR*) *to associate in an action with the public prosecutor for damages*; **il fatto non costituisce reato** this is not a crime.

costitu'tivo, a *ag* constituent, component; **atto** ~ (*DIR*: *di società*) memorandum of association.

costituzio'nale [kostituttsjo'nale] *ag* constitutional.

costituzi'one [kostitut'tsjone] *sf* setting up; building up; constitution.

'costo *sm* cost; **sotto** ~ **for less than cost price**; **a ogni** *o* **qualunque** ~, **a tutti i** ~**i** at all costs; ~**i di esercizio** running costs; ~**i fissi** fixed costs; ~**i di gestione** operating costs; ~**i di produzione** production costs.

'costola *sf* (*ANAT*) rib; **ha la polizia alle** ~**e** the police are hard on his heels.

costo'letta *sf* (*CUC*) cutlet.

cos'toro *pron pl vedi* **costui.**

cos'toso, a *ag* expensive, costly.

cos'tretto, a *pp di* **costringere.**

cos'tringere [kos'trindʒere] *vt*: ~ **qn a fare qc** to force sb to do sth.

costrit'tivo, a *ag* coercive.

costrizi'one [kostrit'tsjone] *sf* coercion.

costru'ire *vt* to construct, build.

costrut'tivo, a *ag* (*EDIL*) building *cpd*; (*fig*) constructive.

costruzi'one [kostrut'tsjone] *sf* construction, building; **di** ~ **inglese** British-made.

cos'tui, cos'tei, *pl* **cos'toro** *pron* (*soggetto*) he/she; *pl* they; (*complemento*) him/her; *pl* them; **si può sapere chi è** ~? (*peg*) just who is that fellow?

cos'tume *sm* (*uso*) custom; (*foggia di vestire, indumento*) costume; **il buon** ~ public morality; **donna di facili** ~**i** woman of easy morals; ~ **da bagno** bathing *o* swimming costume (*BRIT*), swimsuit; (*da uomo*) bathing *o* swimming trunks *pl*.

costu'mista, i, e *sm/f* costume maker, costume designer.

co'tenna *sf* bacon rind.

co'togna [ko'toɲɲa] *sf* quince.

coto'letta *sf* (*di maiale, montone*) chop; (*di vitello, agnello*) cutlet.

coto'nare *vt* (*capelli*) to backcomb.

co'tone *sm* cotton; ~ **idrofilo** cotton wool (*BRIT*), absorbent cotton (*US*).

cotoni'ficio [kotoni'fitʃo] *sm* cotton mill.

'cotta *sf* (*REL*) surplice; (*fam: innamoramento*) crush.

'cottimo *sm*: **lavorare a** ~ to do piecework.

'cotto, a *pp di* **cuocere** ♦ *ag* cooked; (*fam: innamorato*) head-over-heels in love ♦ *sm* brickwork; ~ **a puntino** cooked to perfection; **dirne di** ~ **e e di crude a qn** to call sb every name under the sun; **farne di** ~ **e di crude** to get up to all kinds of mischief; **mattone di** ~ fired brick; **pavimento in** ~ tile floor.

cot'tura *sf* cooking, (*in forno*) baking; (*in umido*) stewing; ~ **a fuoco lento** simmering; **angolo** (**di**) ~ cooking area.

co'vare *vt* to hatch; (*fig: malattia*) to be sickening for; (*: odio, rancore*) to nurse ♦ *vi* (*fuoco, fig*) to smoulder (*BRIT*), smolder (*US*).

co'vata *sf* (*anche fig*) brood.

'covo *sm* den; ~ **di terroristi** terrorist base.

co'vone *sm* sheaf.

'cozza ['kɔttsa] *sf* mussel.

coz'zare [kot'tsare] *vi*: ~ **contro** to bang into, collide with.

'cozzo ['kɔttso] *sm* collision.

C.P. *abbr* (= *cartolina postale*) pc; (*POSTA*) *vedi* **casella postale**; (*NAUT*) = **capitaneria (di porto)**; (*DIR*) = **codice penale.**

crack *sm inv* (*droga*) crack.

Cra'covia *sf* Cracow.

'crampo *sm* cramp.

'cranio *sm* skull.

cra'tere *sm* crater.

cra'vatta *sf* tie; ~ **a farfalla** bow tie.

cravat'tino *sm* bow tie.

cre'anza [kre'antsa] *sf* manners *pl*; **per buona** ~ out of politeness.

cre'are *vt* to create.

creatività *sf* creativity.

cre'ato *sm* creation.

crea'tore, 'trice *ag* creative ♦ *sm/f* creator; **un** ~ **di alta moda** fashion designer; **andare al C**~ to go to meet one's maker.

crea'tura *sf* creature; (*bimbo*) baby, infant.

creazi'one [kreat'tsjone] *sf* creation; (*fondazione*) foundation, establishment.

'crebbi *etc vb vedi* **crescere.**

cre'dente *sm/f* (*REL*) believer.

cre'denza [kre'dɛntsa] *sf* belief; (*armadio*) sideboard.
credenzi'ali [kreden'tsjali] *sfpl* credentials.
'credere *vt* to believe ♦ *vi*: ~ **in**, ~ **a** to believe in; ~ **qn onesto** to believe sb (to be) honest; ~ **che** to believe *o* think that; ~**rsi furbo** to think one is clever; **lo credo bene!** I can well believe it!; **fai quello che credi** *o* **come credi** do as you please.
cre'dibile *ag* credible, believable.
credibilità *sf* credibility.
credi'tizio, a [kredi'tittsjo] *ag* credit.
'credito *sm* (*anche COMM*) credit; (*reputazione*) esteem, repute; **comprare a** ~ to buy on credit; ~ **agevolato** easy credit terms; ~ **d'imposta** tax credit.
credi'tore, 'trice *sm/f* creditor.
'credo *sm inv* creed.
'credulo, a *ag* credulous.
credu'lone, a *sm/f* simpleton, sucker (*fam*).
'crema *sf* cream; (*con uova, zucchero etc*) custard; ~ **idratante** moisturizing cream; ~ **pasticciera** confectioner's custard; ~ **solare** sun cream.
cre'mare *vt* to cremate.
crema'torio *sm* crematorium.
cremazi'one [kremat'tsjone] *sf* cremation.
'cremisi *ag inv*, *sm inv* crimson.
Crem'lino *sm*: **il** ~ the Kremlin.
cremo'nese *ag* of (*o* from) Cremona.
cre'moso, a *ag* creamy.
'crepa *sf* crack.
cre'paccio [kre'pattʃo] *sm* large crack, fissure; (*di ghiacciaio*) crevasse.
crepacu'ore *sm* broken heart.
crepa'pelle *av*: **ridere a** ~ to split one's sides laughing.
cre'pare *vi* (*fam: morire*) to snuff it (*BRIT*), kick the bucket; ~ **dalle risa** to split one's sides laughing; ~ **dall'invidia** to be green with envy.
crepi'tare *vi* (*fuoco*) to crackle; (*pioggia*) to patter.
crepi'tio, ii *sm* crackling; pattering.
cre'puscolo *sm* twilight, dusk.
cre'scendo [kreʃ'ʃɛndo] *sm* (*MUS*) crescendo.
cre'scente [kreʃ'ʃɛnte] *ag* (*gen*) growing, increasing; (*luna*) waxing.
'crescere ['kreʃʃere] *vi* to grow ♦ *vt* (*figli*) to raise.
cre'scione [kreʃ'ʃone] *sm* watercress.
'crescita ['kreʃʃita] *sf* growth.
cresci'uto, a [kreʃ'ʃuto] *pp di* **crescere**.
'cresima *sf* (*REL*) confirmation.
cresi'mare *vt* to confirm.
'crespo, a *ag* (*capelli*) frizzy; (*tessuto*) puckered ♦ *sm* crêpe.

'cresta *sf* crest; (*di polli, uccelli*) crest, comb; **alzare la** ~ (*fig*) to become cocky; **abbassare la** ~ (*fig*) to climb down; **essere sulla** ~ **dell'onda** (*fig*) to be riding high.
'Creta *sf* Crete.
'creta *sf* (*gesso*) chalk; (*argilla*) clay.
cre'tese *ag*, *sm/f* Cretan.
creti'nata *sf* (*fam*): **dire/fare una** ~ to say/do a stupid thing.
cre'tino, a *ag* stupid ♦ *sm/f* idiot, fool.
CRI *sigla f* = *Croce Rossa Italiana.*
cric *sm inv* (*TECN*) jack.
'cricca, che *sf* clique.
'cricco, chi *sm* = **cric**.
cri'ceto [kri'tʃeto] *sm* hamster.
crimi'nale *ag*, *sm/f* criminal.
criminalità *sf* crime; ~ **organizzata** organized crime.
'Criminalpol *abbr* = **polizia criminale**.
'crimine *sm* (*DIR*) crime.
criminolo'gia [kriminolo'dʒia] *sf* criminology.
crimi'noso, a *ag* criminal.
cri'nale *sm* ridge.
'crine *sm* horsehair.
crini'era *sf* mane.
'cripta *sf* crypt.
crip'tare *vt* (*TV: programma*) to encrypt.
crip'tato, a *ag* (*programma, messaggio*) encrypted.
crisan'temo *sm* chrysanthemum; *vedi anche* **Giorno dei Morti**.
'crisi *sf inv* crisis; (*MED*) attack, fit; **essere in** ~ (*partito, impresa etc*) to be in a state of crisis; ~ **energetica** energy crisis; ~ **di nervi** attack *o* fit of nerves.
cristalle'ria *sf* (*fabbrica*) crystal glassworks *sg*; (*oggetti*) crystalware.
cristal'lino, a *ag* (*MINERALOGIA*) crystalline; (*fig: suono, acque*) crystal clear ♦ *sm* (*ANAT*) crystalline lens.
cristalliz'zare [kristallid'dzare] *vi*, ~**rsi** *vr* to crystallize; (*fig*) to become fossilized.
cris'tallo *sm* crystal.
cristia'nesimo *sm* Christianity.
cristianità *sf* Christianity; (*i cristiani*) Christendom.
cristi'ano, a *ag*, *sm/f* Christian; **un povero** ~ (*fig*) a poor soul *o* beggar; **comportarsi da** ~ (*fig*) to behave in a civilized manner.
'cristo *sm*: **C**~ Christ; **(un) povero** ~ (a) poor beggar.
cri'terio *sm* criterion; (*buon senso*) (common) sense.
'critica, che *sf vedi* **critico**.
criti'care *vt* to criticize.
'critico, a, ci, che *ag* critical ♦ *sm* critic ♦ *sf*

criticism; la ~a (*attività*) criticism;
(*persone*) the critics *pl.*

criti'cone, a *sm/f* faultfinder.

crivel'lare *vt*: ~ **(di)** to riddle (with).

cri'vello *sm* riddle.

cro'ato, a *ag, sm/f* Croatian, Croat.

Cro'azia [kro'attsja] *sf*: **la** ~ Croatia.

croc'cante *ag* crisp, crunchy ♦ *sm* (*CUC*)
almond crunch.

'crocchia ['krɔkkja] *sf* chignon, bun.

'crocchio ['krɔkkjo] *sm* (*di persone*) small
group, cluster.

'croce ['krotʃe] *sf* cross; **in** ~ (*di traverso*)
crosswise; (*fig*) on tenterhooks; **mettere
in** ~ (*anche fig*: *criticare*) to crucify;
(: *tormentare*) to nag to death; **la C~ Rossa**
the Red Cross; ~ **uncinata** swastika.

croce'figgere *etc* [krotʃe'fidd3ere]
= **crocifiggere** *etc.*

croceros'sina [krotʃeros'sina] *sf* Red Cross
nurse.

croce'via [krotʃe'via] *sm inv* crossroads *sg.*

cruci'ato, a [kro'tʃato] *ag* cross-shaped
♦ *sm* (*anche fig*) crusader ♦ *sf* crusade.

cro'cicchio [kro'tʃikkjo] *sm* crossroads *sg.*

croci'era [kro'tʃɛra] *sf* (*viaggio*) cruise;
(*ARCHIT*) transept; **altezza di** ~ (*AER*)
cruising height; **velocità di** ~ (*AER, NAUT*)
cruising speed.

croci'figgere [krotʃi'fidd3ere] *vt* to crucify.

crocifissi'one [krotʃifis'sjone] *af*
crucifixion.

croci'fisso, a [krotʃi'fisso] *pp di* **crocifiggere**
♦ *sm* crucifix.

crogio'larsi [krod3o'larsi] *vr*: ~ **al sole** to
bask in the sun.

crogi'olo [kro'd3ɔlo], **crogiu'olo**
[kro'd3wɔlo] *sm* crucible; (*fig*) melting pot.

crol'lare *vi* to collapse.

'crollo *sm* collapse; (*di prezzi*) slump,
sudden fall.

'croma *sf* (*MUS*) quaver (*BRIT*), eighth note
(*US*).

cro'mato, a *ag* chromium-plated.

'cromo *sm* chrome, chromium.

cromo'soma, i *sm* chromosome.

'cronaca, che *sf* chronicle; (*STAMPA*) news
sg; (: *rubrica*) column; (*TV, RADIO*)
commentary; **fatto** o **episodio di** ~ news
item; ~ **nera** crime news *sg*; crime
column.

'cronico, a, ci, che *ag* chronic.

cro'nista, i *sm* (*STAMPA*) reporter,
columnist.

cronis'toria *sf* chronicle; (*fig*: *ironico*)
blow-by-blow account.

cro'nografo *sm* (*strumento*) chronograph.

cronolo'gia [kronolo'd3ia] *sf* chronology.

crono'metrare *vt* to time.

cro'nometro *sm* chronometer; (*a scatto*)
stopwatch.

'crosta *sf* crust; (*MED*) scab; (*ZOOL*) shell;
(*di ghiaccio*) layer; (*fig peg*: *quadro*) daub.

cros'tacei [kros'tatʃei] *smpl* shellfish.

cros'tata *sf* (*CUC*) tart.

cros'tino *sm* (*CUC*) croûton; (: *da antipasto*)
canapé.

crucci'are [krut'tʃare] *vt* to torment, worry;
~**rsi** *vr*: ~**rsi per** to torment o.s. over.

'cruccio ['kruttʃo] *sm* worry, torment.

cruci'ale [kru'tʃale] *ag* crucial.

cruci'verba [krutʃi'verba] *sm inv* crossword
(puzzle).

cru'dele *ag* cruel.

crudeltà *sf* cruelty.

'crudo, a *ag* (*non cotto*) raw; (*aspro*) harsh,
severe.

cru'ento, a *ag* bloody.

cru'miro *sm* (*peg*) blackleg (*BRIT*), scab.

'cruna *sf* eye (of a needle).

'crusca *sf* bran.

crus'cotto *sm* (*AUT*) dashboard.

CS *sigla* – Cosenza.

C.S. *sigla* (*MIL*) = comando supremo; (*AUT*)
= codice della strada.

c.s. *abbr* = come sopra.

Csce [tʃi'esse'tʃie] *sigla f* (= Conferenza sulla
sicurezza e la cooperazione in Europa) CSCE.

CSI [tʃi'esse'i] *sigla f* (= Comunità di Stati
Indipendenti) CIS.

CSM [tʃiesse'emme] *sigla m* (= consiglio
superiore della magistratura) Magistrates'
Board of Supervisors.

CT *sigla* = Catania.

c.t. *abbr* = commissario tecnico.

'Cuba *sf* Cuba.

cu'bano, a *ag, sm/f* Cuban.

cu'betto *sm* (small) cube; ~ **di ghiaccio** ice
cube.

'cubico, a, ci, che *ag* cubic.

'cubo, a *ag* cubic ♦ *sm* cube; **elevare al** ~
(*MAT*) to cube.

cuc'cagna [kuk'kaɲɲa] *sf*: **paese della** ~
land of plenty; **albero della** ~ greasy pole
(*fig*).

cuc'cetta [kut'tʃetta] *sf* (*FERR*) couchette;
(*NAUT*) berth.

cucchiai'ata [kukkja'jata] *sf* spoonful;
tablespoonful.

cucchia'ino [kukkja'ino] *sm* teaspoon;
coffee spoon.

cucchi'aio [kuk'kjajo] *sm* spoon; (*da tavola*)
tablespoon; (*cucchiaiata*) spoonful;
tablespoonful.

'cuccia, ce ['kuttʃa] *sf* dog's bed; **a** ~!
down!

cuccio'lata [kuttʃo'lata] sf litter.

'cucciolo ['kuttʃolo] sm cub; (di cane) puppy.

cu'cina [ku'tʃina] sf (locale) kitchen; (arte culinaria) cooking, cookery; (le vivande) food, cooking; (apparecchio) cooker; di ~ (libro, lezione) cookery cpd; ~ **componibile** fitted kitchen; ~ **economica** kitchen range.

cuci'nare [kutʃi'nare] vt to cook.

cuci'nino [kutʃi'nino] sm kitchenette.

cu'cire [ku'tʃire] vt to sew, stitch; ~ **la bocca a qn** (fig) to shut sb up.

cu'cito, a [ku'tʃito] sm sewing; (INS) sewing, needlework.

cuci'trice [kutʃi'tritʃe] sf (TIP: per libri) stitching machine; (per fogli) stapler.

cuci'tura [kutʃi'tura] sf sewing, stitching; (costura) seam.

cucù sm inv, **cu'culo** sm cuckoo.

'cuffia sf bonnet, cap; (da infermiera) cap; (da bagno) (bathing) cap; (per ascoltare) headphones pl, headset.

cu'gino, a [ku'dʒino] sm/f cousin.

══════════ PAROLA CHIAVE

'cui pron 1 (nei complementi indiretti: persona) whom; (: oggetto, animale) which; **la persona/le persone a** ~ **accennavi** the person/people you were referring to o to whom you were referring; **la penna con** ~ **scrivo** the pen I'm writing with; **il paese da** ~ **viene** the country he comes from; **i libri di** ~ **parlavo** the books I was talking about o about which I was talking; **parla varie lingue, fra** ~ **l'inglese** he speaks several languages, including English; **il quartiere in** ~ **abito** the district where I live; **visto il modo in** ~ **ti ha trattato** ... considering how he treated you ...; **la ragione per** ~ the reason why; **per** ~ **non so più che fare** that's why I don't know what to do
2 (inserito tra articolo e sostantivo) whose; **la donna i** ~ **figli sono scomparsi** the woman whose children have disappeared; **il signore, dal** ~ **figlio ho avuto il libro** the man from whose son I got the book.

culi'naria sf cookery.

culi'nario, a ag culinary.

'culla sf cradle.

cul'lare vt to rock; (fig: idea, speranza) to cherish; ~**rsi** vr (gen) to sway; ~**rsi in vane speranze** (fig) to cherish fond hopes; ~**rsi nel dolce far niente** (fig) to sit back and relax.

culmi'nante ag: **posizione** ~ (ASTR) highest point; **punto** o **momento** ~ (fig) climax.

culmi'nare vi: ~ **in** o **con** to culminate in.

'culmine sm top, summit.

'culo sm (fam!) arse (BRIT!), ass (US!); (: fig: fortuna): **aver** ~ to have the luck of the devil; **prendere qn per il** ~ to take the piss out of sb (!).

'culto sm (religione) religion; (adorazione) worship, adoration; (venerazione: anche fig) cult.

cul'tura sf (gen) culture; (conoscenza) education, learning; **di** ~ (persona) cultured; (istituto) cultural, of culture; ~ **generale** general knowledge; ~ **di massa** mass culture.

cultu'rale ag cultural.

cultu'rismo sm body-building.

cumu'lare vt to accumulate, amass.

cumula'tivo, a ag cumulative; (prezzo) inclusive; (biglietto) group cpd.

'cumulo sm (mucchio) pile, heap; (METEOR) cumulus; ~ **dei redditi** (FISCO) combined incomes; ~ **delle pene** (DIR) consecutive sentences.

'cuneo sm wedge.

cu'netta sf (di strada etc) bump; (scolo: nelle strade di città) gutter; (: di campagna) ditch.

cu'nicolo sm (galleria) tunnel; (di miniera) pit, shaft; (di talpa) hole.

cu'oca sf vedi **cuoco.**

cu'ocere ['kwɔtʃere] vt (alimenti) to cook; (mattoni etc) to fire ♦ vi to cook; ~ **in umido/a vapore/in padella** to stew/ steam/fry; ~ **al forno** (pane) to bake; (arrosto) to roast.

cu'oco, a, chi, che sm/f cook; (di ristorante) chef.

cuoi'ame sm leather goods pl.

cu'oio sm leather; ~ **capelluto** scalp; **tirare le** ~**a** (fam) to kick the bucket.

cu'ore sm heart; ~**i** smpl (CARTE) hearts; **avere buon** ~ to be kind-hearted; **stare a** ~ **a qn** to be important to sb; **un grazie di** ~ heartfelt thanks; **ringraziare di** ~ to thank sincerely; **nel profondo del** ~ in one's heart of hearts; **avere la morte nel** ~ to be sick at heart; **club dei** ~**i solitari** lonely hearts club.

cupi'digia [kupi'didʒa] sf greed, covetousness.

'cupo, a ag dark; (suono) dull; (fig) gloomy, dismal.

'cupola sf dome; (più piccola) cupola; (fig) Mafia high command.

'cura sf care; (MED: trattamento) (course of)

treatment; **aver ~ di** (*occuparsi di*) to look after; **a ~ di** (*libro*) edited by; **fare una ~** to follow a course of treatment; **~ dimagrante** diet.

cu'rabile *ag* curable.

cu'rante *ag*: **medico ~** doctor (in charge of a patient).

cu'rare *vt* (*malato, malattia*) to treat; (*: guarire*) to cure; (*aver cura di*) to take care of; (*testo*) to edit; **~rsi** *vr* to take care of o.s.; (*MED*) to follow a course of treatment; **~rsi di** to pay attention to; (*occuparsi di*) to look after.

cu'rato *sm* parish priest; (*protestante*) vicar, minister.

cura'tore, 'trice *sm/f* (*DIR*) trustee; (*di antologia etc*) editor; **~ fallimentare** (official) receiver.

'curdo, a *ag* Kurdish ♦ *sm/f* Kurd.

'curia *sf* (*REL*): **la ~ romana** the Roman curia; **~ notarile** notaries' association *o* guild.

curio'saggine [kurjo'saddʒine] *sf* nosiness.

curio'sare *vi* to look round, wander round; (*tra libri*) to browse; **~ nei negozi** to look *o* wander round the shops; **~ nelle faccende altrui** to poke one's nose into other people's affairs.

curiosità *sf inv* curiosity; (*cosa rara*) curio, curiosity.

curi'oso, a *ag* (*che vuol sapere*) curious, inquiring; (*ficcanaso*) curious, inquisitive; (*bizzarro*) strange, curious ♦ *sm/f* busybody, nosy parker; **essere ~ di** to be curious about; **una folla di ~i** a crowd of onlookers.

cur'riculum *sm inv*: **~ (vitae)** curriculum vitae.

cur'sore *sm* (*INFORM*) cursor.

'curva *sf* curve; (*stradale*) bend, curve.

cur'vare *vt* to bend ♦ *vi* (*veicolo*) to take a bend; (*strada*) to bend, curve; **~rsi** *vr* to bend; (*legno*) to warp.

'curvo, a *ag* curved; (*piegato*) bent.

CUS *sigla m* = Centro Universitario Sportivo.

cusci'netto [kuʃʃi'netto] *sm* pad; (*TECN*) bearing ♦ *ag inv*: **stato ~** buffer state; **~ a sfere** ball bearing.

cu'scino [kuʃ'ʃino] *sm* cushion; (*guanciale*) pillow.

'cuspide *sf* (*ARCHIT*) spire.

cus'tode *sm/f* (*di museo*) keeper, custodian; (*di parco*) warden; (*di casa*) concierge; (*di fabbrica, carcere*) guard.

cus'todia *sf* care; (*DIR*) custody; (*astuccio*) case, holder; **avere qc in ~** to look after sth; **dare qc in ~ a qn** to entrust sth to sb's care; **agente di ~** prison warder; **~**

delle carceri prison security; **~ cautelare** (*DIR*) remand.

custo'dire *vt* (*conservare*) to keep; (*assistere*) to look after, take care of; (*fare la guardia*) to guard.

'cute *sf* (*ANAT*) skin.

cu'ticola *sf* cuticle.

C.V. *abbr* = **cavallo vapore**.

c.v.d. *abbr* (= *come volevasi dimostrare*) QED (= *quod erat demonstrandum*).

c.vo *abbr* = **corsivo**.

cy'clette ® [si'klɛt] *sf inv* exercise bike.

CZ *sigla* = Catanzaro.

D d

D, d [di] *sf o m inv* (*lettera*) D, d; **D come Domodossola ~** D for David (*BRIT*), D for Dog (*US*).

D *abbr* (= *destra*) R; (*FERR*) = **diretto**.

═══════════════ PAROLA CHIAVE

da (*da + il* = **dal**, *da + lo* = **dallo**, *da + l'* = **dall'**, *da + la* = **dalla**, *da + i* = **dai**, *da + gli* = **dagli**, *da + le* = **dalle**) *prep* **1** (*agente*) by; **dipinto ~ un grande artista** painted by a great artist

2 (*causa*) with; **tremare dalla paura** to tremble with fear

3 (*stato in luogo*) at; **abito ~ lui** I'm living at his house *o* with him; **sono dal giornalaio** I'm at the newsagent's; **era ~ Francesco** she was at Francesco's (house)

4 (*moto a luogo*) to; (*moto per luogo*) through; **vado ~ Pietro/dal giornalaio** I'm going to Pietro's (house)/to the newsagent's; **sono passati dalla finestra** they came in through the window

5 (*provenienza, allontanamento*) from; **~ ... a** from ... to; **arrivare/partire ~ Milano** to arrive/depart from Milan; **scendere dal treno/dalla macchina** to get off the train/ out of the car; **viene ~ una famiglia povera** he comes from a poor background; **viene dalla Scozia** he comes from Scotland; **ti chiamo ~ una cabina** I'm phoning from a call box; **si trova a 5 km ~ qui** it's 5 km from here

6 (*tempo: durata*) for; (*: a partire da: nel passato*) since; (*: nel futuro*) from; **vivo qui ~ un anno** I've been living here for a year; **è dalle 3 che ti aspetto** I've been waiting for you since 3 (o'clock); ~ **mattina a sera** from morning till night; ~ **oggi in poi** from today onwards; ~ **bambino** as a child, when I (*o he etc*) was a child

7 (*modo, maniera*) like; **comportarsi ~ uomo** to behave like a man; **l'ho fatto ~ me** I did it (by) myself; **non è ~ lui** it's not like him

8 (*descrittivo*): **una macchina ~ corsa** a racing car; **è una cosa ~ poco** it's nothing special; **una ragazza dai capelli biondi** a girl with blonde hair; **sordo ~ un orecchio** deaf in one ear; **abbigliamento ~ uomo** menswear; **un vestito ~ 100.000 lire** a 100,000 lire dress; **qualcosa ~ bere/mangiare** something to drink/eat.

dà *vb vedi* **dare**.

dab'bene *ag inv* honest, decent.

'Dacca *sf* Dacca.

dac'capo, da 'capo *av* (*di nuovo*) (once) again; (*dal principio*) all over again, from the beginning.

dacché [dak'ke] *cong* since.

'dado *sm* (*da gioco*) dice *o* die (*pl* dice); (*CUC*) stock cube (*BRIT*), bouillon cube (*US*); (*TECN*) (screw) nut; ~**i** *smpl* (game of) dice.

daf'fare, da 'fare *sm* work, toil; **avere un gran ~** to be very busy.

'dagli ['daʎʎi], **'dai** *prep + det vedi* **da**.

'daino *sm* (fallow) deer *inv*; (*pelle*) buckskin.

Da'kar *sf* Dakar.

dal *prep + det vedi* **da**.

dal. *abbr* (= *decalitro*) dal.

dall', 'dalla, 'dalle, 'dallo *prep + det vedi* **da**.

dal'tonico, a, ci, che *ag* colour-blind (*BRIT*), colorblind (*US*).

dam. *abbr* (= *decametro*) dam.

'dama *sf* lady; (*nei balli*) partner; (*gioco*) draughts *sg* (*BRIT*), checkers *sg* (*US*); **far ~** (*nel gioco*) to make a crown; **~ di compagnia** lady's companion; **~ di corte** lady-in-waiting.

Da'masco *sf* Damascus.

dami'gella [dami'dʒɛlla] *sf* (*STORIA*) damsel; (: *titolo*) mistress; **~ d'onore** (*di sposa*) bridesmaid.

damigi'ana [dami'dʒana] *sf* demijohn.

dam'meno *ag inv*: **per non essere ~ di qn** so as not to be outdone by sb.

DAMS *sigla m* (= *Disciplina delle Arti, della Musica, dello Spettacolo*) *study of the performing arts.*

da'naro *sm* = **denaro**.

dana'roso, a *ag* wealthy.

da'nese *ag* Danish ♦ *smf* Dane ♦ *sm* (*LING*) Danish.

Dani'marca *sf*: **la ~** Denmark.

dan'nare *vt* (*REL*) to damn; **~rsi** *vr*: **~rsi** (**per**) (*fig: tormentarsi*) to be worried to death (by); **far ~ qn** to drive sb mad; **~rsi l'anima per qc** (*affannarsi*) to work o.s. to death for sth; (*tormentarsi*) to worry o.s. to death over sth.

dan'nato, a *ag* damned.

dannazi'one [dannat'tsjone] *sf* damnation.

danneggi'are [danned'dʒare] *vt* to damage; (*rovinare*) to spoil; (*nuocere*) to harm; **la parte danneggiata** (*DIR*) the injured party.

'danno *vb vedi* **dare** ♦ *sm* damage; (*a persona*) harm, injury; ~**i** *smpl* (*DIR*) damages; **a ~ di qn** to sb's detriment; **chiedere/risarcire i ~i** to sue for/pay damages.

dan'noso, a *ag*: **~ (a o per)** harmful (to), bad (for).

dan'tesco, a schi, sche *ag* Dantesque; **l'opera ~a** Dante's work.

Da'nubio *sm*: **il ~** the Danube.

'danza ['dantsa] *sf*: **la ~** dancing; **una ~** a dance.

dan'zante [dan'tsante] *ag* dancing; **serata ~** dance.

dan'zare [dan'tsare] *vt, vi* to dance.

danza'tore, 'trice [dantsa'tore] *smf* dancer.

dapper'tutto *av* everywhere.

dap'poco *ag inv* inept; worthless.

dap'prima *av* at first.

Darda'nelli *smpl*: **i ~** the Dardanelles.

'dardo *sm* dart.

'dare *sm* (*COMM*) debit ♦ *vt* to give; (*produrre: frutti, suono*) to produce ♦ *vi* (*guardare*): **~ su** to look (out) onto; **~rsi** *vr*: **~rsi a** to dedicate o.s. to; **quanti anni mi dai?** how old do you think I am?; **danno ancora quel film?** is that film still showing?; **~ da mangiare a qn** to give sb something to eat; **~ per certo qc** to consider sth certain; **~ ad intendere a qn che** … to lead sb to believe that …; **~ per morto qn** to give sb up for dead; **~ qc per scontato** to take sth for granted; **~rsi ammalato** to report sick; **~rsi alla bella vita** to have a good time; **~rsi al bere** to take to drink; **~rsi al commercio** to go into business; **~rsi da fare per fare qc** to go to a lot of bother to do sth; **~rsi per vinto** to give in; **può ~rsi** maybe, perhaps; **si dà il caso che** … it so happens that …; **darsela a gambe** to take to one's heels; **il ~ e l'avere** (*ECON*) debits and credits *pl.*

Dar-es-Sa'laam *sf* Dar-es-Salaam.

'darsena *sf* dock.

'data *sf* date; **in ~ da destinarsi** on a date still to be announced; **in ~ odierna** as of today; **amicizia di lunga** *o* **vecchia ~** long-standing friendship; **~ di emissione** date of issue; **~ di nascita** date of birth; **~ di scadenza** expiry date; **~ limite d'utilizzo** *o* **di consumo** (*COMM*) best-before date.

da'tare *vt* to date ♦ *vi:* **~ da** to date from.

da'tato, a *ag* dated.

da'tivo *sm* dative.

'dato, a *ag* (*stabilito*) given ♦ *sm* datum; **~i** *smpl* data *pl;* **~ che** given that; **in ~i casi** in certain cases; **è un ~ di fatto** it's a fact.

da'tore, 'trice *sm/f:* **~ di lavoro** employer.

'dattero *sm* date (*BOT*).

dattilogra'fare *vt* to type.

dattilogra'fia *sf* typing.

datti'lografo, a *sm/f* typist.

dattilos'critto *sm* typescript.

da'vanti *av* in front; (*dirimpetto*) opposite ♦ *ag inv* front ♦ *sm* front; **~ a** *prep* in front of; (*dirimpetto a*) facing, opposite; (*in presenza di*) before, in front of.

davan'zale [davan'tsale] *sm* windowsill.

da'vanzo, d'a'vanzo [da'vantso] *av* more than enough.

dav'vero *av* really, indeed; **dico ~** I mean it.

dazi'ario, a [dat'tsjarjo] *ag* excise *cpd.*

'dazio ['dattsjo] *sm* (*somma*) duty; (*luogo*) customs *pl;* **~ d'importazione** import duty.

db *abbr* (= *decibel*) dB.

DC *sigla f* = **Democrazia Cristiana** (*former political party*).

d.C. *av abbr* (= *dopo Cristo*) A.D.

D.D.T. *abbr m* (= *dicloro-difenil-tricloroetano*) D.D.T.

'dea *sf* goddess.

'debbo *etc vb vedi* **dovere.**

debel'lare *vt* to overcome, conquer.

debili'tare *vt* to debilitate.

debita'mente *av* duly, properly.

'debito, a *ag* due, proper ♦ *sm* debt; (*COMM: dare*) debit; **a tempo ~** at the right time; **portare a ~ di qn** to debit sb with; **~ consolidato** consolidated debt; **~ d'imposta** tax liability; **~ pubblico** national debt.

debi'tore, 'trice *sm/f* debtor.

'debole *ag* weak, feeble; (*suono*) faint; (*luce*) dim ♦ *sm* weakness.

debo'lezza [debo'lettsa] *sf* weakness.

debut'tante *sm/f* (*gen*) beginner, novice;

(*TEAT*) actor/actress at the beginning of his (*o* her) career.

debut'tare *vi* to make one's début.

de'butto *sm* début.

'decade *sf* period of ten days.

deca'dente *ag* decadent.

deca'denza [deka'dɛntsa] *sf* decline; (*DIR*) loss, forfeiture.

deca'dere *vi* to decline.

deca'duto, a *ag* (*persona*) impoverished; (*norma*) lapsed.

decaffei'nato, a *ag* decaffeinated.

de'calogo *sm* (*fig*) rulebook.

de'cano *sm* (*REL*) dean.

decan'tare *vt* (*virtù, bravura etc*) to praise; (*persona*) to sing the praises of.

decapi'tare *vt* to decapitate, behead.

decappot'tabile *ag, sf* convertible.

dece'duto, a [detʃe'duto] *ag* deceased.

decele'rare [detʃele'rare] *vt, vi* to decelerate, slow down.

decen'nale [detʃen'nale] *ag* (*che dura 10 anni*) ten-year *cpd;* (*che ricorre ogni 10 anni*) ten-yearly, every ten years ♦ *sm* (*ricorrenza*) tenth anniversary.

de'cenne [de'tʃɛnne] *ag:* **un bambino ~** a ten-year-old child, a child of ten.

de'cennio [de'tʃɛnnjo] *sm* decade.

de'cente [de'tʃɛnte] *ag* decent, respectable, proper; (*accettabile*) satisfactory, decent.

decentraliz'zare [detʃentralid'dzare] *vt* (*AMM*) to decentralize.

decentra'mento [detʃentra'mento] *sm* decentralization.

decen'trare [detʃen'trare] *vt* to decentralize, move out of the centre.

de'cenza [de'tʃɛntsa] *sf* decency, propriety.

de'cesso [de'tʃɛsso] *sm* death; **atto di ~** death certificate.

de'cidere [de'tʃidere] *vi* to decide, make up one's mind ♦ *vt:* **~ qc** to decide on sth; (*questione, lite*) to settle sth; **~rsi** *vr:* **~rsi (a fare)** to decide (to do), make up one's mind (to do); **~ di fare/che** to decide to do/that; **~ di qc** (*sog: cosa*) to determine sth.

deci'frare [detʃi'frare] *vt* to decode; (*fig*) to decipher, make out.

de'cilitro [de'tʃilitro] *sm* decilitre (*BRIT*), deciliter (*US*).

deci'male [detʃi'male] *ag* decimal.

deci'mare [detʃi'mare] *vt* to decimate.

de'cimetro [de'tʃimetro] *sm* decimetre.

'decimo, a ['dɛtʃimo] *num* tenth.

de'cina [de'tʃina] *sf* ten; (*circa dieci*): **una ~ (di)** about ten.

de'cisi [de'tʃizi] *etc vb vedi* **decidere.**

decisio'nale [detʃizjo'nale] *ag* decision-making *cpd*.

decisi'one [detʃi'zjone] *sf* decision; **prendere una** ~ to make a decision; **con** ~ decisively, resolutely.

deci'sivo, a [detʃi'zivo] *ag* (*gen*) decisive; (*fattore*) deciding.

de'ciso, a [de'tʃizo] *pp di* **decidere** ♦ *ag* (*persona, carattere*) determined; (*tono*) firm, resolute.

declas'sare *vt* to downgrade; to lower in status; **1ª declassata** (*FERR*) *first-class carriage which may be used by second-class passengers*.

decli'nare *vi* (*pendio*) to slope down; (*fig: diminuire*) to decline; (*tramontare*) to set, go down ♦ *vt* to decline; ~ **le proprie generalità** (*fig*) to give one's particulars; ~ **ogni responsabilità** to disclaim all responsibility.

declinazi'one [deklinat'tsjone] *sf* (*LING*) declension.

de'clino *sm* decline.

de'clivio *sm* (downward) slope.

decodifi'care *vt* to decode.

decodifica'tore *sm* decoder.

decol'lare *vi* (*AER*) to take off.

décolleté [dekol'te] *ag inv* (*abito*) low-necked, low-cut ♦ *sm* (*di abito*) low neckline; (*di donna*) cleavage.

de'collo *sm* take-off.

decolo'rare *vt* to bleach.

decom'porre *vt*, **decomporsi** *vr* to decompose.

decomposizi'one [dekompozit'tsjone] *sf* decomposition.

decom'posto, a *pp di* **decomporre**.

decompressi'one *sf* decompression.

deconge'lare [dekondʒe'lare] *vt* to defrost.

decongestio'nare [dekondʒestjo'nare] *vt* (*MED, traffico*) to relieve congestion in.

deco'rare *vt* to decorate.

decora'tivo, a *ag* decorative.

decora'tore, 'trice *sm/f* (interior) decorator.

decorazi'one [dekorat'tsjone] *sf* decoration.

de'coro *sm* decorum.

deco'roso, a *ag* decorous, dignified.

decor'renza [dekor'rɛntsa] *sf*: **con** ~ **da** (as) from.

de'correre *vi* to pass, elapse; (*avere effetto*) to run, have effect.

de'corso, a *pp di* **decorrere** ♦ *sm* (*evoluzione: anche MED*) course.

de'crebbi *etc vb vedi* **decrescere**.

de'crepito, a *ag* decrepit.

de'crescere [de'kreʃʃere] *vi* (*diminuire*) to

decrease, diminish; (*acque*) to subside, go down; (*prezzi*) to go down.

decresci'uto, a [dekreʃ'ʃuto] *pp di* **decrescere**.

decre'tare *vt* (*norma*) to decree; (*mobilitazione*) to order; ~ **lo stato d'emergenza** to declare a state of emergency; ~ **la nomina di qn** to decide on the appointment of sb.

de'creto *sm decree with the force of law*; ~ **di sfratto** eviction order.

decur'tare *vt* (*debito, somma*) to reduce.

decurtazi'one [dekurtat'tsjone] *sf* reduction.

'dedalo *sm* maze, labyrinth.

'dedica, che *sf* dedication.

dedi'care *vt* to dedicate; ~**rsi** *vr*: ~**rsi a** (*votarsi*) to devote o.s. to.

dedicherò *etc* [dedike'rɔ] *vb vedi* **dedicare**.

'dedito, a *ag*: ~ **a** (*studio etc*) dedicated *o* devoted to; (*vizio*) addicted to.

de'dotto, a *pp di* **dedurre**.

de'duco *etc vb vedi* **dedurre**.

de'durre *vt* (*concludere*) to deduce; (*defalcare*) to deduct.

de'dussi *etc vb vedi* **dedurre**.

deduzi'one [dedut'tsjone] *sf* deduction.

defal'care *vt* to deduct.

defenes'trare *vt* to throw out of the window; (*fig*) to remove from office.

defe'rente *ag* respectful, deferential.

defe'rire *vt* (*DIR*): ~ **a** to refer to.

defezi'one [defet'tsjone] *sf* defection, desertion.

defici'ente [defi'tʃɛnte] *ag* (*mancante*): ~ **di** deficient in; (*insufficiente*) insufficient ♦ *sm/f* mental defective; (*peg: cretino*) idiot.

defici'enza [defi'tʃɛntsa] *sf* deficiency; (*carenza*) shortage; (*fig: lacuna*) weakness.

'deficit ['dɛfitʃit] *sm inv* (*ECON*) deficit.

defi'nire *vt* to define; (*risolvere*) to settle; (*questione*) to finalize.

defini'tivo, a *ag* definitive, final ♦ *sf*: **in** ~**a** (*dopotutto*) when all is said and done; (*dunque*) well then.

defi'nito, a *ag* definite; **ben** ~ clear, clear cut.

definizi'one [definit'tsjone] *sf* (*gen*) definition; (*di disputa, vertenza*) settlement; (*di tempi, obiettivi*) establishment.

deflagrazi'one [deflagrat'tsjone] *sf* explosion.

deflazi'one [deflat'tsjone] *sf* (*ECON*) deflation.

deflet'tore *sm* (*AUT*) quarterlight (*BRIT*),

deflector (US).

deflu'ire vi: ~ **da** (liquido) to flow away from; (fig: capitali) to flow out of.

de'flusso sm (della marea) ebb.

defor'mare vt (alterare) to put out of shape; (corpo) to deform; (pensiero, fatto) to distort; ~**rsi** vr to lose its shape.

deformazi'one [deformat'tsjone] sf (MED) deformation; **questa è** ~ **professionale!** that's force of habit because of your (o his etc) job!

de'forme ag deformed; disfigured.

deformità sf inv deformity.

defrau'dare vt: ~ **qn di qc** to defraud sb of sth, cheat sb out of sth.

de'funto, a ag late cpd ♦ sm/f deceased.

degene'rare [dedʒene'rare] vi to degenerate.

degenerazi'one [dedʒenerat'tsjone] sf degeneration.

de'genere [de'dʒenere] ag degenerato.

de'gente [de'dʒɛnte] sm/f bedridden person; (ricoverato in ospedale) in-patient.

de'genza [de'dʒɛntsa] sf confinement to bed; ~ **ospedaliera** period in hospital.

'degli ['deʎʎi] prep + det vedi **di**.

deglu'tire vt to swallow.

de'gnare [deɲ'ɲare] vt: ~ **qn della propria presenza** to honour sb with one's presence; ~**rsi** vr: ~**rsi di fare qc** to deign o condescend to do sth; **non mi ha degnato di uno sguardo** he wouldn't even look at me.

'degno, a ['deɲɲo] ag dignified; ~ **di** worthy of; ~ **di lode** praiseworthy.

degra'dare vt (MIL) to demote; (privare della dignità) to degrade; ~**rsi** vr to demean o.s.

de'grado sm: ~ **urbano** urban decline.

degus'tare vt to sample, taste.

degustazi'one [degustat'tsjone] sf sampling, tasting; ~ **di vini** (locale) specialist wine bar; ~ **di caffè** (locale) specialist coffee shop.

'dei smpl di **dio** ♦ prep + det vedi **di**.

del prep + det vedi **di**.

dela'tore, 'trice sm/f police informer.

delazi'one [delat'tsjone] sf informing.

'delega, ghe sf (procura) proxy; **per** ~ **notarile** ≈ through a solicitor (BRIT) o lawyer.

dele'gare vt to delegate.

dele'gato sm delegate.

delegazi'one [delegat'tsjone] sf delegation.

delegherò etc [delege'rɔ] vb vedi **delegare**.

dele'terio, a ag deleterious, noxious.

del'fino sm (ZOOL) dolphin; (STORIA) dauphin; (fig) probable successor.

'Delhi ['dɛli] sf Delhi.

de'libera sf decision.

delibe'rare vt to come to a decision on ♦ vi (DIR): ~ **(su qc)** to rule (on sth).

delica'tezza [delika'tettsa] sf delicacy; frailty; thoughtfulness; tactfulness.

deli'cato, a ag delicate; (salute) delicate, frail; (fig: gentile) thoughtful, considerate; (: che dimostra tatto) tactful.

delimi'tare vt (anche fig) to delimit.

deline'are vt to outline; ~**rsi** vr to be outlined; (fig) to emerge.

delin'quente sm/f criminal, delinquent.

delin'quenza [delin'kwentsa] sf criminality, delinquency; ~ **minorile** juvenile delinquency.

de'liquio sm (MED) swoon; **cadere in** ~ to swoon.

deli'rante ag (MED) delirious; (fig: folla) frenzied; (: discorso, mente) insane.

deli'rare vi to be delirious, rave; (fig) to rave.

de'lirio sm delirium; (ragionamento insensato) raving; (fig): **andare/mandare in** ~ to go/send into a frenzy.

de'litto sm crime; ~ **d'onore** crime committed to avenge one's honour.

delittu'oso, a ag criminal.

de'lizia [de'littsja] sf delight.

delizi'are [delit'tsjare] vt to delight; ~**rsi** vr: ~**rsi di qc/a fare qc** to take delight in sth/in doing sth.

delizi'oso, a [delit'tsjoso] ag delightful; (cibi) delicious.

dell', 'della, 'delle, 'dello prep + det vedi **di**.

'delta sm inv delta.

delta'plano sm hang-glider; **volo col** ~ hang-gliding.

delucidazi'one [delutʃidat'tsjone] sf clarification no pl.

delu'dente ag disappointing.

de'ludere vt to disappoint.

delusi'one sf disappointment.

de'luso, a pp di **deludere** ♦ ag disappointed.

dema'gogico, a, ci, che [dema'gɔdʒiko] ag popularity-seeking, demagogic.

dema'gogo, ghi sm demagogue.

de'manio sm state property.

de'mente ag (MED) demented, mentally deranged; (fig) crazy, mad.

de'menza [de'mɛntsa] sf dementia; madness; ~ **senile** senile dementia.

demenzi'ale [demen'tsjale] ag (fig) off-the-wall.

'demmo vb vedi **dare**.

demo'cratico, a, ci, che ag democratic.

democra'zia [demokrat'tsia] sf democracy; **la D**~ **Cristiana** the Christian Democrat Party.

democristi'ano, a *ag, sm/f* Christian Democrat.

demogra'fia *sf* demography.

demo'grafico, a, ci, che *ag* demographic; **incremento** ~ increase in population.

demo'lire *vt* to demolish.

demolizi'one [demolit'tsjone] *sf* demolition.

'demone *sm* demon.

de'monio *sm* demon, devil; **il D**~ the Devil.

demoniz'zare [demonid'dzare] *vt* to make a monster of.

demonizzazi'one [demoniddzat'tsjone] *sf* demonizing, demonization.

demoraliz'zare [demoralid'dzare] *vt* to demoralize; ~**rsi** *vr* to become demoralized.

de'mordere *vi*: **non** ~ **(da)** to refuse to give up.

demoti'vare *vt*: ~ **qn** to take away sb's motivation.

demoti'vato, a *ag* unmotivated, lacking motivation.

de'naro *sm* money; ~**i** *smpl* (*CARTE*) *suit in Neapolitan pack of cards*.

denatu'rato, a *ag vedi* **alcool**.

deni'grare *vt* to denigrate, run down.

denomi'nare *vt* to name; ~**rsi** *vr* to be named *o* called.

denomina'tore *sm* (*MAT*) denominator.

denominazi'one [denominat'tsjone] *sf* name; denomination; ~ **di origine controllata** (**D.O.C.**) *label guaranteeing the quality and origin of a wine.*

deno'tare *vt* to denote, indicate.

densità *sf inv* density; (*di nebbia*) thickness, denseness; **ad alta/bassa** ~ **di popolazione** densely/sparsely populated.

'denso, a *ag* thick, dense.

den'tale *ag* dental.

den'tario, a *ag* dental.

denta'tura *sf* set of teeth, teeth *pl*; (*TECN: di ruota*) serration.

'dente *sm* tooth; (*di forchetta*) prong; (*GEO: cima*) jagged peak; **al** ~ (*CUC: pasta*) *cooked so as to be firm when eaten*; **mettere i** ~**i** to teethe; **mettere qc sotto i** ~**i** to have a bite to eat; **avere il** ~ **avvelenato contro** *o* **con qn** to bear sb a grudge; ~ **di leone** (*BOT*) dandelion; ~**i del giudizio** wisdom teeth.

'dentice ['dentitʃe] *sm* (*ZOOL*) sea bream.

denti'era *sf* (set of) false teeth *pl*.

denti'fricio [denti'fritʃo] *sm* toothpaste.

den'tista, i, e *sm/f* dentist.

'dentro *av* inside; (*in casa*) indoors; (*fig: nell'intimo*) inwardly ♦ *prep*: ~ **(a)** in;

piegato in ~ folded over; **qui/là** ~ in here/there; ~ **di sé** (*pensare, brontolare*) to oneself; **tenere tutto** ~ to keep everything bottled up (inside o.s.); **darci** ~ (*fig fam*) to slog away, work hard.

denucleariz'zato, a [denuklearid'dzato] *ag* denuclearized, nuclear-free.

denu'dare *vt* (*persona*) to strip; (*parte del corpo*) to bare; ~**rsi** *vr* to strip.

de'nuncia, ce *o* **cie** [de'nuntʃa], **de'nunzia** [de'nuntsja] *sf* denunciation; declaration; **fare una** ~ *o* **sporgere** ~ **contro qn** (*DIR*) to report sb to the police; ~ **del reddito** (income) tax return.

denunci'are [denun'tʃare], **denunzi'are** [denun'tsjare] *vt* to denounce; (*dichiarare*) to declare; ~ **qn/qc (alla polizia)** to report sb/sth to the police.

denu'trito, a *ag* undernourished.

denutrizi'one [denutrit'tsjone] *sf* malnutrition.

deodo'rante *sm* deodorant.

deontolo'gia [deontolo'dʒia] *sf* (*professionale*) professional code of conduct.

depenalizzazi'one [depenaliddzat'tsjone] *sf* decriminalization.

dépen'dance [depā'dās] *sf inv* outbuilding.

depe'ribile *ag* perishable; **merce** ~ perishables *pl*, perishable goods *pl*.

deperi'mento *sm* (*di persona*) wasting away; (*di merci*) deterioration.

depe'rire *vi* to waste away.

depi'lare *vt* to depilate.

depila'torio, a *ag* hair-removing, depilatory ♦ *sm* hair remover, depilatory.

depilazi'one [depilat'tsjone] *sf* hair removal, depilation.

depis'taggio [depis'taddʒo] *sm* diversion.

depis'tare *vt* to set on the wrong track.

dépli'ant [depli'ā] *sm inv* leaflet; (*opuscolo*) brochure.

deplo'rare *vt* to deplore; to lament.

deplo'revole *ag* deplorable.

de'pone, de'pongo *etc vb vedi* **deporre**.

de'porre *vt* (*depositare*) to put down; (*rimuovere: da una carica*) to remove; (*: re*) to depose; (*DIR*) to testify; ~ **le armi** (*MIL*) to lay down arms; ~ **le uova** to lay eggs.

depor'tare *vt* to deport.

depor'tato, a *sm/f* deportee.

deportazi'one [deportat'tsjone] *sf* deportation.

de'posi *etc vb vedi* **deporre**.

deposi'tante *sm* (*COMM*) depositor.

deposi'tare *vt* (*gen, GEO, ECON*) to deposit; (*lasciare*) to leave; (*merci*) to store; ~**rsi** *vr* (*sabbia, polvere*) to settle.

deposi'tario *sm* (*COMM*) depository.

de'posito *sm* deposit; (*luogo*) warehouse; depot; (: *MIL*) depot; ~ **bagagli** left-luggage office; ~ **di munizioni** ammunition dump.

deposizi'one [depozit'tsjone] *sf* deposition; (*da una carica*) removal; **rendere una falsa** ~ to perjure o.s.

de'posto, a *pp di* **deporre**.

depra'vare *vt* to corrupt, pervert.

depra'vato, a *ag* depraved ♦ *sm/f* degenerate.

depre'care *vt* to deprecate, deplore.

depre'dare *vt* to rob, plunder.

depressi'one *sf* depression; **area** *o* **zona di** ~ (*METEOR*) area of low pressure; (*ECON*) depressed area.

de'presso, a *pp di* **deprimere** ♦ *ag* depressed.

deprezza'mento [deprettsa'mento] *sm* depreciation.

deprez'zare [depret'tsare] *vt* (*ECON*) to deprezíate

depri'mente *ag* depressing.

de'primere *vt* to depress.

depu'rare *vt* to purify.

depura'tore *sm*: ~ **d'acqua** water purifier; ~ **di gas** scrubber.

depu'tato, a *sm/f* (*POL*) deputy, ≈ Member of Parliament (*BRIT*), ≈ Congressman/woman (*US*); *vedi anche* **Camera dei Deputati**.

deputazi'one [deputat'tsjone] *sf* deputation; (*POL*) position of deputy, ≈ parliamentary seat (*BRIT*), ≈ seat in Congress (*US*).

deraglia'mento [deraʎʎa'mento] *sm* derailment.

deragli'are [deraʎ'ʎare] *vi* to be derailed; **far** ~ to derail.

dera'pare *vi* (*veicolo*) to skid; (*SCI*) to sideslip.

derattizzazi'one [derattiddzat'tsjone] *sf* rodent control.

deregolamen'tare *vt* to deregulate.

deregolamentazi'one [deregolamentat'tsjone] *sf* deregulation.

dere'litto, a *ag* derelict.

dere'tano *sm* (*fam*) bottom, buttocks *pl*.

de'ridere *vt* to mock, deride.

de'risi *etc vb vedi* **deridere**.

derisi'one *sf* derision, mockery.

de'riso, a *pp di* **deridere**.

deri'sorio, a *ag* (*gesto, tono*) mocking.

de'riva *sf* (*NAUT, AER*) drift; (*dispositivo*: *AER*) fin; (: *NAUT*) centre-board (*BRIT*), centerboard (*US*); **andare alla** ~ (*anche fig*) to drift.

deri'vare *vi*: ~ **da** to derive from ♦ *vt* to derive; (*corso d'acqua*) to divert.

deri'vato, a *ag* derived ♦ *sm* (*CHIM, LING*) derivative; (*prodotto*) by-product.

derivazi'one [derivat'tsjone] *sf* derivation; diversion.

derma'tite *sf* dermatitis.

dermatolo'gia [dermatolo'dʒia] *sf* dermatology.

derma'tologo, a, gi, ghe *sm/f* dermatologist.

dermoprotet'tivo, a *ag* (*crema, azione*) protecting the skin.

'deroga, ghe *sf* (special) dispensation; **in** ~ **a** as a (special) dispensation to.

dero'gare *vi*: ~ **a** (*DIR*) to repeal in part.

der'rate *sfpl* commodities; ~ **alimentari** foodstuffs.

deru'bare *vt* to rob.

des'critto, a *pp di* **descrivere**.

des'crivere *vt* to describe.

descrizi'one [deskrit'tsjone] *sf* description.

de'serto, a *ag* deserted ♦ *sm* (*GEO*) desert; **isola** ~**a** desert island.

deside'rabile *ag* desirable.

deside'rare *vt* to want, wish for; (*sessualmente*) to desire; ~ **fare/che qn faccia** to want o wish to do/sb to do; **desidera fare una passegglata?** would you like to go for a walk?; **farsi** ~ (*fare il prezioso*) to play hard to get; (*farsi aspettare*) to take one's time; **lascia molto a** ~ it leaves a lot to be desired.

desi'derio *sm* wish; (*più intenso, carnale*) desire.

deside'roso, a *ag*: ~ **di** longing o eager for.

desi'gnare [desiɲ'ɲare] *vt* to designate, appoint; (*data*) to fix; **la vittima designata** the intended victim.

designazi'one [desiɲɲat'tsjone] *sf* designation, appointment.

desi'nare *vi* to dine, have dinner ♦ *sm* dinner.

desi'nenza [dezi'nɛntsa] *sf* (*LING*) ending, inflexion.

de'sistere *vi*: ~ **da** to give up, desist from.

desis'tito, a *pp di* **desistere**.

deso'lante *ag* distressing.

deso'lato, a *ag* (*paesaggio*) desolate; (*persona: spiacente*) sorry.

desolazi'one [dezolat'tsjone] *sf* desolation.

'despota, i *sm* despot.

'dessi *etc vb vedi* **dare**.

destabiliz'zare [destabilid'dzare] *vt* to destabilize.

des'tare *vt* to wake (up); (*fig*) to awaken, arouse; ~**rsi** *vr* to wake (up).

'deste *etc vb vedi* **dare.**
desti'nare *vt* to destine; (*assegnare*) to appoint, assign; (*indirizzare*) to address; ~ qc a qn to intend to give sth to sb, intend sb to have sth.
destina'tario, a *sm/f* (*di lettera*) addressee; (*di merce*) consignee; (*di mandato*) payee.
destinazi'one [destinat'tsjone] *sf* destination; (*uso*) purpose.
des'tino *sm* destiny, fate.
destitu'ire *vt* to dismiss, remove.
destituzi'one [destitut'tsjone] *sf* dismissal, removal.
'desto, a *ag* (wide) awake.
'destra *sf vedi* **destro.**
destreggi'arsi [destred'dʒarsi] *vr* to manoeuvre (*BRIT*), maneuver (*US*).
des'trezza [des'trettsa] *sf* skill, dexterity.
'destro, a *ag* right, right-hand; (*abile*) skilful (*BRIT*), skillful (*US*), adroit ♦ *sf* (*mano*) right hand; (*parte*) right (side); (*POL*): **la ~a** the right ♦ *sm* (*BOXE*) right; **a ~a** (*essere*) on the right; (*andare*) to the right; **tenere la ~a** to keep to the right.
de'sumere *vt* (*dedurre*) to infer, deduce; (*trarre: informazioni*) to obtain.
de'sunto, a *pp di* **desumere.**
detas'sare *vt* to remove the duty (*o* tax) from.
dete'nere *vt* (*incarico, primato*) to hold; (*proprietà*) to have, possess; (*in prigione*) to detain, hold.
de'tengo, de'tenni *etc vb vedi* **detenere.**
deten'tivo, a *ag*: **mandato ~** imprisonment order; **pena ~a** prison sentence.
deten'tore, 'trice *sm/f* (*di titolo, primato etc*) holder.
dete'nuto, a *sm/f* prisoner.
detenzi'one [deten'tsjone] *sf* holding; possession; detention.
deter'gente [deter'dʒɛnte] *ag* detergent; (*crema, latte*) cleansing ♦ *sm* detergent.
de'tergere [de'tɛrdʒere] *vt* (*gen*) to clean; (*pelle, viso*) to cleanse; (*sudore*) to wipe (away).
deteriora'mento *sm*: **~ (di)** deterioration (in).
deterio'rare *vt* to damage; **~rsi** *vr* to deteriorate.
deteri'ore *ag* (*merce*) second-rate; (*significato*) pejorative; (*tradizione letteraria*) lesser, minor.
determi'nante *ag* decisive, determining.
determi'nare *vt* to determine.
determina'tivo, a *ag* determining; **articolo ~** (*LING*) definite article.
determi'nato, a *ag* (*gen*) certain;

(*particolare*) specific; (*risoluto*) determined, resolute.
determinazi'one [determinat'tsjone] *sf* determination; (*decisione*) decision.
deter'rente *ag, sm* deterrent.
deterrò *etc vb vedi* **detenere.**
deter'sivo *sm* detergent; (*per bucato: in polvere*) washing powder (*BRIT*), soap powder.
de'terso, a *pp di* **detergere.**
detes'tare *vt* to detest, hate.
deti'ene *etc vb vedi* **detenere.**
deto'nare *vi* to detonate.
detona'tore *sm* detonator.
detonazi'one [detonat'tsjone] *sf* (*di esplosivo*) detonation, explosion; (*di arma*) bang; (*di motore*) pinking (*BRIT*), knocking.
de'trae, de'traggo *etc vb vedi* **detrarre.**
de'trarre *vt*: **~ (da)** to deduct (from), take away (from).
de'trassi *etc vb vedi* **detrarre.**
de'tratto, a *pp di* **detrarre.**
detrazi'one [detrat'tsjone] *sf* deduction; **~ d'imposta** tax allowance.
detri'mento *sm* detriment, harm; **a ~ di** to the detriment of.
de'trito *sm* (*GEO*) detritus.
detroniz'zare [detronid'dzare] *vt* to dethrone.
'detta *sf*: **a ~ di** according to.
dettagli'ante [dettaʎ'ʎante] *sm/f* (*COMM*) retailer.
dettagli'are [dettaʎ'ʎare] *vt* to detail, give full details of.
dettagliata'mente [dettaʎʎata'mente] *av* in detail.
det'taglio [det'taʎʎo] *sm* detail; (*COMM*): **il ~** retail; **al ~** (*COMM*) retail; separately.
det'tame *sm* dictate, precept.
det'tare *vt* to dictate; **~ legge** (*fig*) to lay down the law.
det'tato *sm* dictation.
detta'tura *sf* dictation.
'detto, a *pp di* **dire** ♦ *ag* (*soprannominato*) called, known as; (*già nominato*) above-mentioned ♦ *sm* saying; **~ fatto** no sooner said than done; **presto ~!** it's easier said than done!
detur'pare *vt* to disfigure; (*moralmente*) to sully.
devas'tante *ag* (*anche fig*) devastating.
devas'tare *vt* to devastate; (*fig*) to ravage.
devastazi'one [devastat'tsjone] *sf* devastation, destruction.
devi'are *vi*: **~ (da)** to turn off (from) ♦ *vt* to divert.
devi'ato, a *ag* (*fig: persona, organizzazione*)

corrupt, bent (col).

deviazi'one [devjat'tsjone] sf (anche AUT)
diversion; **fare una** ~ to make a detour.

'devo etc vb vedi **dovere.**

devo'luto, a pp di **devolvere.**

devoluzi'one [devolut'tsjone] sf (DIR)
devolution, transfer.

de'volvere vt (DIR) to transfer, devolve; ~
qc in beneficenza to give sth to charity.

de'voto, a ag (REL) devout, pious;
(affezionato) devoted.

devozi'one [devot'tsjone] sf devoutness;
(anche REL) devotion.

dg abbr (= decigrammo) dg.

═══════════════ PAROLA CHIAVE

di (di + il = **del**, di + lo = **dello**, di + l'
= **dell'**, di + la = **della**, di + i = **dei**, di + gli
= **degli**, di + le = **delle**) prep **1** (possesso,
specificazione) of; (composto da, scritto da)
by; **la macchina** ~ **Paolo/**~ **mio fratello**
Paolo's/my brother's car; **un amico** ~ **mio
fratello** a friend of my brother's, one of
my brother's friends; **la grandezza della
casa** the size of the house; **le foto delle
vacanze** the holiday photos; **la città** ~
Firenze the city of Florence; **il nome** ~
Maria the name Mary; **un quadro** ~
Botticelli a painting by Botticelli

2 (caratterizzazione, misura) of; **una casa** ~
mattoni a brick house; **un orologio d'oro** a gold watch; **un
bimbo** ~ **3 anni** a child of 3, a 3-year-old
child; **una trota** ~ **un chilo** a trout
weighing a kilo; **una strada** ~ **10km** a
road 10km long; **un quadro** ~ **valore** a
valuable picture

3 (causa, mezzo, modo) with; **tremare** ~
paura to tremble with fear; **morire** ~
cancro to die of cancer; **spalmare** ~ **burro**
to spread with butter

4 (argomento) about, of; **discutere** ~
sport to talk about sport; **parlare** ~
politica/lavoro to talk about politics/work

5 (luogo: provenienza) from; out of; **essere**
~ **Roma** to be from Rome; **uscire** ~ **casa**
to come out of o leave the house

6 (tempo) in; **d'estate/d'inverno** in (the)
summer/winter; ~ **notte** by night, at
night; ~ **mattina/sera** in the morning/
evening; ~ **lunedì** on Mondays; ~ **ora in
ora** by the hour

7 (partitivo) of; **alcuni** ~ **voi/noi** some of
you/us; **il più bravo** ~ **tutti** the best of all;
il migliore del mondo the best in the
world; **non c'è niente** ~ **peggio** there's
nothing worse

8 (paragone) than; **più veloce** ~ **me** faster

than me; **guadagna meno** ~ **me** he earns
less than me

♦ det (una certa quantità di) some;
(: negativo) any; (: interrogativo) any, some;
del pane (some) bread; **delle caramelle**
(some) sweets; **degli amici miei** some
friends of mine; **vuoi del vino?** do you
want some o any wine?

dì sm day; **buon** ~! hallo!; **a** ~ = **addì.**

DIA sigla f = Direzione investigativa antimafia.

dia'bete sm diabetes sg.

dia'betico, a, ci, che ag, sm/f diabetic.

dia'bolico, a, ci, che ag diabolical.

di'acono sm (REL) deacon.

dia'dema, i sm diadem; (di donna) tiara.

di'afano, a ag (trasparente) diaphanous;
(pelle) transparent.

dia'framma, i sm (divisione) screen; (ANAT,
FOT, contraccettivo) diaphragm.

di'agnosi [di'aɲɲozi] sf diagnosis sg.

diagnosti'care [diaɲɲosti'kare] vt to
diagnose.

dia'gnostico, a, ci, che [diaɲ'ɲostiko] ag
diagnostic; **aiuti** ~ **ci** (INFORM) debugging
aids.

diago'nale ag, sf diagonal.

dia'gramma, i sm diagram; ~ **a barre** bar
chart; ~ **di flusso** flow chart.

dialet'tale ag dialectal; **poesia** ~ poetry in
dialect.

dia'letto sm dialect.

di'alisi sf dialysis.

dialo'gante ag: **unità** ~ (INFORM)
interactive terminal.

dialo'gare vi: ~ (con) to have a dialogue
(with); (conversare) to converse (with)
♦ vt (scena) to write the dialogue for.

di'alogo, ghi sm dialogue.

dia'mante sm diamond.

di'ametro sm diameter.

di'amine escl: **che** ~ ...? what on
earth ...?

diaposi'tiva sf transparency, slide.

di'aria sf daily (expense) allowance.

di'ario sm diary; ~ **di bordo** (NAUT)
log(book); ~ **di classe** (INS) class register;
~ **degli esami** (INS) exam timetable.

diar'rea sf diarrhoea.

dia'triba sf diatribe.

diavole'ria sf (azione) act of mischief;
(aggeggio) weird contraption.

di'avolo sm devil; **è un buon** ~ he's a good
sort; **avere un** ~ **per capello** to be in a
foul temper; **avere una fame/un freddo
del** ~ to be ravenously hungry/frozen
stiff; **mandare qn al** ~ (fam) to tell sb to
go to hell; **fare il** ~ **a quattro** to kick up a

fuss.

di'battere *vt* to debate, discuss; **~rsi** *vr* to struggle.

dibatti'mento *sm* (*dibattito*) debate, discussion; (*DIR*) hearing.

di'battito *sm* debate, discussion.

dic. *abbr* (= *dicembre*) Dec.

dicas'tero *sm* ministry.

'dice ['ditʃe] *vb vedi* **dire.**

di'cembre [di'tʃɛmbre] *sm* December; *per fraseologia vedi* **luglio.**

dice'ria [ditʃe'ria] *sf* rumour (*BRIT*), rumor (*US*), piece of gossip.

dichia'rare [dikja'rare] *vt* to declare; **~rsi** *vr* to declare o.s.; (*innamorato*) to declare one's love; **si dichiara che ...** it is hereby declared that ...; **~rsi vinto** to acknowledge defeat.

dichia'rato, a [dikja'rato] *ag* (*nemico, ateo*) avowed.

dichiarazi'one [dikjarat'tsjone] *sf* declaration; **~ dei redditi** statement of income; (*modulo*) tax return.

dician'nove [ditʃan'nɔve] *num* nineteen.

dicianno'venne [ditʃanno'vɛnne] *ag, sm/f* nineteen-year-old.

dicias'sette [ditʃas'sɛtte] *num* seventeen.

diciasset'tenne [ditʃasset'tɛnne] *ag, sm/f* seventeen-year-old.

diciot'tenne [ditʃot'tɛnne] *ag, sm/f* eighteen-year-old.

dici'otto [di'tʃɔtto] *num* eighteen ♦ *sm inv* (*INS*) *minimum satisfactory mark awarded in Italian universities.*

dici'tura [ditʃi'tura] *sf* words *pl*, wording.

'dico *etc vb vedi* **dire.**

didasca'lia *sf* (*di illustrazione*) caption; (*CINE*) subtitle; (*TEAT*) stage directions *pl*.

di'dattico, a, ci, che *ag* didactic; (*metodo, programma*) teaching; (*libro*) educational ♦ *sf* didactics *sg*; teaching methodology.

di'dentro *av* inside, indoors.

didi'etro *av* behind ♦ *ag inv* (*ruota, giardino*) back, rear *cpd* ♦ *sm* (*di casa*) rear; (*fam*: *sedere*) backside.

di'eci ['djɛtʃi] *num* ten.

dieci'mila [djɛtʃi'mila] *num* ten thousand.

die'cina [dje'tʃina] *sf* = **decina.**

di'edi *etc vb vedi* **dare.**

di'eresi *sf* dieresis *sg*.

'diesel ['di:zəl] *sm inv* diesel engine.

di'eta *sf* diet; **essere a ~** to be on a diet.

die'tetica *sf* dietetics *sg*.

die'tologo, a, gi, ghe *sm/f* dietician.

di'etro *av* behind; (*in fondo*) at the back ♦ *prep* behind; (*tempo: dopo*) after ♦ *sm* (*di foglio, giacca*) back; (*di casa*) back, rear ♦ *ag inv* back *cpd*; **le zampe di ~** the hind legs; **~ ricevuta** against receipt; **~ richiesta** on demand; (*scritta*) on application; **andare ~ a** (*anche fig*) to follow; **stare ~ a qn** (*sorvegliare*) to keep an eye on sb; (*corteggiare*) to hang around sb; **portarsi ~ qn/qc** to bring sb/sth with one, bring sb/sth along; **gli hanno riso/parlato ~** they laughed at/talked about him behind his back.

di'etro 'front *escl* about turn! (*BRIT*), about face! (*US*) ♦ *sm* (*MIL*) about-turn, about-face; (*fig*) volte-face, about-turn, about-face; **fare ~** (*MIL, fig*) to about-turn, about-face; (*tornare indietro*) to turn round.

di'fatti *cong* in fact, as a matter of fact.

di'fendere *vt* to defend; **~rsi** *vr* (*cavarsela*) to get by; **~rsi da/contro** to defend o.s. from/against; **~rsi dal freddo** to protect o.s. from the cold; **sapersi ~** to know how to look after o.s.

difen'sivo, a *ag* defensive ♦ *sf*: **stare sulla ~a** (*anche fig*) to be on the defensive.

difen'sore, a *sm/f* defender; **avvocato ~** counsel for the defence (*BRIT*) o defense (*US*).

di'fesa *sf vedi* **difeso.**

di'fesi *etc vb vedi* **difendere.**

di'feso, a *pp di* **difendere** ♦ *sf* defence (*BRIT*), defense (*US*); **prendere le ~e di qn** to defend sb, take sb's part.

difet'tare *vi* to be defective; **~ di** to be lacking in, lack.

difet'tivo, a *ag* defective.

di'fetto *sm* (*mancanza*): **~ di** lack of; (*di fabbricazione*) fault, flaw, defect; (*morale*) fault, failing, defect; (*fisico*) defect; **far ~** to be lacking; **in ~** at fault; in the wrong.

difet'toso, a *ag* defective, faulty.

diffa'mare *vt* (*a parole*) to slander; (*per iscritto*) to libel.

diffama'torio, a *ag* slanderous; libellous.

diffamazi'one [diffamat'tsjone] *sf* slander; libel.

diffe'rente *ag* different.

diffe'renza [diffe'rɛntsa] *sf* difference; **a ~ di** unlike; **non fare ~ (tra)** to make no distinction (between).

differenzi'ale [differen'tsjale] *ag, sm* differential; **classi ~i** (*INS*) special classes (*for backward children*).

differenzi'are [differen'tsjare] *vt* to differentiate; **~rsi da** to differentiate o.s. from; to differ from.

diffe'rire *vt* to postpone, defer ♦ *vi* to be different.

diffe'rita *sf*: **in ~** (*trasmettere*) prerecorded.

dif'ficile [dif'fitʃile] *ag* difficult; (*persona*)

hard to please, difficult (to please); (poco probabile): è ~ che sia libero it is unlikely that he'll be free ♦ sm/f: fare il(la) ~ to be difficult, be awkward ♦ sm difficult part; difficulty; essere ~ nel mangiare to be fussy about one's food.

difficil'mente [diffitʃil'mente] av (con difficoltà) with difficulty; ~ verrà he's unlikely to come.

difficoltà sf inv difficulty.

difficol'toso, a ag (compito) difficult, hard; (persona) difficult, hard to please; digestione ~a poor digestion.

dif'fida sf (DIR) warning, notice.

diffi'dare vi: ~ di to be suspicious o distrustful of ♦ vt (DIR) to warn; ~ qn dal fare qc to warn sb not to do sth, caution sb against doing sth.

diffi'dente ag suspicious, distrustful.

diffi'denza [diffi'dentsa] sf suspicion, distrust.

dif'fondere vt (luce, calore) to diffuse; (notizie) to spread, circulate; ~rsi vr to spread.

dif'fusi etc vb vedi **diffondere**.

diffusi'one sf diffusion; spread, (anche di giornale) circulation; (FISICA) scattering.

dif'fuso, a pp di **diffondere** ♦ ag (FISICA) diffuse; (notizia, malattia etc) widespread; è opinione ~a che ... it's widely held that ....

difi'lato av (direttamente) straight, directly; (subito) straight away.

difte'rite sf diphtheria.

'diga, ghe sf dam; (portuale) breakwater.

dige'rente [didʒe'rɛnte] ag (apparato) digestive.

dige'rire [didʒe'rire] vt to digest.

digesti'one [didʒes'tjone] sf digestion.

diges'tivo, a [didʒes'tivo] ag digestive ♦ sm (after-dinner) liqueur.

Digi'one [di'dʒone] sf Dijon.

digi'tale [didʒi'tale] ag digital; (delle dita) finger cpd, digital ♦ sf (BOT) foxglove.

digi'tare [didʒi'tare] vt (dati) to key (in); (tasto) to press.

digiu'nare [didʒu'nare] vi to starve o.s.; (REL) to fast.

digi'uno, a [di'dʒuno] ag: essere ~ not to have eaten ♦ sm fast; a ~ on an empty stomach.

dignità [diɲɲi'ta] sf inv dignity.

digni'tario [diɲɲi'tarjo] sm dignitary.

digni'toso, a [diɲɲi'toso] ag dignified.

'DIGOS sigla f (= Divisione Investigazioni Generali e Operazioni Speciali) police department dealing with political security.

digressi'one sf digression.

digri'gnare [digriɲ'ɲare] vt: ~ i denti to grind one's teeth.

dila'gare vi to flood; (fig) to spread.

dilani'are vt to tear to pieces.

dilapi'dare vt to squander, waste.

dila'tare vt to dilate; (gas) to cause to expand; (passaggio, cavità) to open (up); ~rsi vr to dilate; (FISICA) to expand.

dilatazi'one [dilatat'tsjone] sf (ANAT) dilation; (di gas, metallo) expansion.

dilazio'nare [dilattsjo'nare] vt to delay, defer.

dilazi'one [dilat'tsjone] sf deferment.

dileggi'are [diled'dʒare] vt to mock, deride.

dilegu'are vi, ~rsi vr to vanish, disappear.

di'lemma, i sm dilemma.

dilet'tante sm/f dilettante; (anche SPORT) amateur.

dilet'tare vt to give pleasure to, delight; ~rsi vr: ~rsi di to take pleasure in, enjoy.

dilet'tevole ag delightful.

di'letto, a ag dear, beloved ♦ sm pleasure, delight.

dili'gente [dili'dʒɛnte] ag (scrupoloso) diligent; (accurato) careful, accurate.

dili'genza [dili'dʒɛntsa] sf diligence; care; (carrozza) stagecoach.

dilu'ire vt to dilute.

dilun'garsi vr (fig): ~ su to talk at length on o about.

diluvi'are vb impers to pour (down).

di'luvio sm downpour; (inondazione, fig) flood; il ~ universale the Flood.

dima'grante ag slimming cpd.

dima'grire vi to get thinner, lose weight.

dime'nare vt to wave, shake; ~rsi vr to toss and turn; (fig) to struggle; ~ la coda (sog: cane) to wag its tail.

dimensi'one sf dimension; (grandezza) size; considerare un discorso nella sua ~ politica to look at a speech in terms of its political significance.

dimenti'canza [dimenti'kantsa] sf forgetfulness; (errore) oversight, slip; per ~ inadvertently.

dimenti'care vt to forget; ~rsi vr: ~rsi di qc to forget sth.

dimentica'toio sm (scherzoso): cadere/mettere nel ~ to sink into/consign to oblivion.

di'mentico, a, chi, che ag: ~ di (che non ricorda) forgetful of; (incurante) oblivious of, unmindful of.

di'messo, a pp di **dimettere** ♦ ag (voce) subdued; (uomo, abito) modest, humble.

dimesti'chezza [dimesti'kettsa] sf familiarity.

di'mettere *vt*: ~ **qn da** to dismiss sb from; (*dall'ospedale*) to discharge sb from; ~**rsi** *vr*: ~**rsi (da)** to resign (from).

dimez'zare [dimed'dzare] *vt* to halve.

diminu'ire *vt* to reduce, diminish; (*prezzi*) to bring down, reduce ♦ *vi* to decrease, diminish; (*rumore*) to die down, die away; (*prezzi*) to fall, go down.

diminu'tivo, a *ag, sm* diminutive.

diminuzi'one [diminut'tsjone] *sf* decreasing, diminishing; **in** ~ on the decrease; ~ **della produttività** fall in productivity.

di'misi *etc vb vedi* **dimettere**.

dimissio'nario, a *ag* outgoing, resigning.

dimissi'oni *sfpl* resignation *sg*; **dare** *o* **presentare le** ~ to resign, hand in one's resignation.

di'mora *sf* residence; **senza fissa** ~ of no fixed address *o* abode.

dimo'rare *vi* to reside.

dimos'trante *sm/f* (*POL*) demonstrator.

dimos'trare *vt* to demonstrate, show; (*provare*) to prove, demonstrate; ~**rsi** *vr*: ~**rsi molto abile** to show o.s. *o* prove to be very clever; **non dimostra la sua età** he doesn't look his age; **dimostra 30 anni** he looks about 30 (years old).

dimostra'tivo, a *ag* (*anche LING*) demonstrative.

dimostrazi'one [dimostrat'tsjone] *sf* demonstration; proof.

di'namico, a, ci, che *ag* dynamic ♦ *sf* dynamics *sg*.

dina'mismo *sm* dynamism.

dinami'tardo, a *ag*: **attentato** ~ dynamite attack ♦ *sm/f* dynamiter.

dina'mite *sf* dynamite.

'dinamo *sf inv* dynamo.

di'nanzi [di'nantsi]: ~ **a** *prep* in front of.

dinas'tia *sf* dynasty.

dini'ego, ghi *sm* (*rifiuto*) refusal; (*negazione*) denial.

dinocco'lato, a *ag* lanky; **camminare** ~ to walk with a slouch.

dino'sauro *sm* dinosaur.

din'torno *av* round, (round) about; ~**i** *smpl* outskirts; **nei** ~**i di** in the vicinity *o* neighbourhood of.

'dio, *pl* **'dei** *sm* god; **D**~ God; **gli dei** the gods; **si crede un** ~ he thinks he's wonderful; **D**~ **mio!** my God!; **D**~ **ce la mandi buona** let's hope for the best; **D**~ **ce ne scampi e liberi!** God forbid!

di'ocesi [di'ɔtʃezi] *sf inv* diocese.

dios'sina *sf* dioxin.

dipa'nare *vt* (*lana*) to wind into a ball; (*fig*) to disentangle, sort out.

diparti'mento *sm* department.

dipen'dente *ag* dependent ♦ *sm/f* employee.

dipen'denza [dipen'dɛntsa] *sf* dependence; **essere alle** ~**e di qn** to be employed by sb *o* in sb's employ.

di'pendere *vi*: ~ **da** to depend on; (*finanziariamente*) to be dependent on; (*derivare*) to come from, be due to.

di'pesi *etc vb vedi* **dipendere**.

di'peso, a *pp di* **dipendere**.

di'pingere [di'pindʒere] *vt* to paint.

di'pinsi *etc vb vedi* **dipingere**.

di'pinto, a *pp di* **dipingere** ♦ *sm* painting.

di'ploma, i *sm* diploma.

diplo'mare *vt* to award a diploma to, graduate (*US*) ♦ *vi* to obtain a diploma, graduate (*US*).

diplo'matico, a, ci, che *ag* diplomatic ♦ *sm* diplomat.

diplo'mato, a *ag* qualified ♦ *sm/f* qualified person, holder of a diploma.

diploma'zia [diplomat'tsia] *sf* diplomacy.

di'porto *sm*: **imbarcazione** *f* **da** ~ pleasure craft.

dira'dare *vt* to thin (out); (*visite*) to reduce, make less frequent; ~**rsi** *vr* to disperse; (*nebbia*) to clear (up).

dira'mare *vt* to issue ♦ *vi*, ~**rsi** *vr* (*strade*) to branch.

'dire *vt* to say; (*segreto, fatto*) to tell; ~ **qc a qn** to tell sb sth; ~ **a qn di fare qc** to tell sb to do sth; ~ **di si/no** to say yes/no; **si dice che ...** they say that ...; **mi si dice che ...** I am told that ...; **si direbbe che ...** it looks (*o* sounds) as though ...; **dica, signora?** (*in un negozio*) yes, Madam, can I help you?; **sa quello che dice** he knows what he's talking about; **lascialo** ~ (*esprimersi*) let him have his say; (*ignoralo*) just ignore him; **come sarebbe a** ~? what do you mean?; **che ne diresti di andarcene?** how about leaving?; **chi l'avrebbe mai detto!** who would have thought it!; **si dicono esperti** they say they are experts; **per così** ~ so to speak; **a dir poco** to say the least; **non c'è che** ~ there's no doubt about it; **non dico di no** I can't deny it; **il che è tutto** ~ need I say more?

di'ressi *etc vb vedi* **dirigere**.

di'retta *sf vedi* **diretto**.

diretta'mente *av* (*immediatamente*) directly, straight; (*personalmente*) directly; (*senza intermediari*) direct, straight.

diret'tissima *sf* (*tragitto*) most direct route; (*DIR*): **processo per** ~ summary

trial.
diret'tissimo *sm* (*FERR*) fast (through) train.
diret'tivo, a *ag* (*POL, AMM*) executive; (*COMM*) managerial, executive ♦ *sm* leadership, leaders *pl* ♦ *sf* directive, instruction.
di'retto, a *pp di* **dirigere** ♦ *ag* direct ♦ *sm* (*FERR*) through train ♦ *sf*: **in (linea)** ~**a** (*RADIO, TV*) live; **il mio** ~ **superiore** my immediate superior.
diret'tore, 'trice *sm/f* (*di azienda*) director; manager/ess; (*di scuola elementare*) head (teacher) (*BRIT*), principal (*US*); ~ **amministrativo** company secretary (*BRIT*), corporate executive secretary (*US*); ~ **del carcere** prison governor (*BRIT*) *o* warden (*US*); ~ **di filiale** branch manager; ~ **d'orchestra** conductor; ~ **di produzione** (*CINE*) producer; ~ **sportivo** team manager; ~ **tecnico** (*SPORT*) trainer, coach.
direzi'one [diret'tsjone] *sf* (*senso: anche fig*) direction; (*conduzione: gen*) running; (: *di partito*) leadership; (: *di società*) management; (: *di giornale*) editorship; (*direttori*) management; **in** ~ **di** in the direction of, towards.
diri'gente [diri'dʒɛnte] *ag* managerial ♦ *sm/f* executive; (*POL*) leader; **classe** ~ ruling class.
diri'genza [diri'dʒɛntsa] *sf* management; (*POL*) leadership.
dirigenzi'ale [diridʒɛn'tsjale] *ag* managerial.
di'rigere [di'ridʒere] *vt* to direct; (*impresa*) to run, manage; (*MUS*) to conduct; ~**rsi** *vr*: ~**rsi verso** *o* **a** to make *o* head for; ~ **i propri passi verso** to make one's way towards; **il treno era diretto a Pavia** the train was heading for Pavia.
diri'gibile [diri'dʒibile] *sm* airship.
dirim'petto *av* opposite; ~ **a** *prep* opposite, facing.
di'ritto, a *ag* straight; (*onesto*) straight, upright ♦ *av* straight, directly ♦ *sm* right side; (*TENNIS*) forehand; (*MAGLIA*) plain stitch, knit stitch; (*prerogativa*) right; (*leggi, scienza*): **il** ~ law; **stare** ~ to stand up straight; **aver** ~ **a qc** to be entitled to sth; **punto** ~ plain (stitch); **andare** ~ to go straight on; **a buon** ~ quite rightly; ~**i** (*d'autore*) royalties; ~ **di successione** right of succession.
dirit'tura *sf* (*SPORT*) straight; (*fig*) rectitude.
diroc'cato, a *ag* tumbledown, in ruins.
dirom'pente *ag* (*anche fig*) explosive.

dirotta'mento *sm*: ~ (**aereo**) hijack.
dirot'tare *vt* (*nave, aereo*) to change the course of; (*aereo: sotto minaccia*) to hijack; (*traffico*) to divert ♦ *vi* (*nave, aereo*) to change course.
dirotta'tore, 'trice *sm/f* hijacker.
di'rotto, a *ag* (*pioggia*) torrential; (*pianto*) unrestrained; **piovere a** ~ to pour, rain cats and dogs; **piangere a** ~ to cry one's heart out.
di'rupo *sm* crag, precipice.
disabi'tato, a *ag* uninhabited.
disabitu'arsi *vr*: ~ **a** to get out of the habit of.
disac'cordo *sm* disagreement.
disadat'tato, a *ag* (*PSIC*) maladjusted.
disa'dorno, a *ag* plain, unadorned.
disaffezi'one [dizaffet'tsjone] *sf* disaffection.
disa'gevole [disa'dʒevole] *ag* (*scomodo*) uncomfortable; (*difficile*) difficult.
disagi'ato, a [diza'dʒato] *ag* poor, needy; (*vita*) hard.
di'sagio [di'zadʒo] *sm* discomfort; (*disturbo*) inconvenience; (*fig: imbarazzo*) embarrassment; ~**i** *smpl* hardship *sg*, poverty *sg*; **essere a** ~ to be ill at ease.
dl'samina *sf* close examination.
disappro'vare *vt* to disapprove of.
disapprovazi'one [dizapprovat'tsjone] *sf* disapproval.
disap'punto *sm* disappointment.
disarcio'nare [dizartʃo'nare] *vt* to unhorse.
disar'mante *ag* (*fig*) disarming.
disar'mare *vt, vi* to disarm.
di'sarmo *sm* (*MIL*) disarmament.
di'sastro *sm* disaster.
disas'troso, a *ag* disastrous.
disat'tento, a *ag* inattentive.
disattenzi'one [dizatten'tsjone] *sf* carelessness, lack of attention.
disatti'vare *vt* (*bomba*) to de-activate, defuse.
disa'vanzo [diza'vantso] *sm* (*ECON*) deficit.
disavven'tura *sf* misadventure, mishap.
dis'brigo, ghi *sm* (prompt) clearing up *o* settlement.
dis'capito *sm*: **a** ~ **di** to the detriment of.
dis'carica, che *sf* (*di rifiuti*) rubbish tip *o* dump.
discen'dente [diʃʃen'dɛnte] *ag* descending ♦ *sm/f* descendant.
di'scendere [diʃ'ʃendere] *vt* to go (*o* come) down ♦ *vi* to go (*o* come) down; (*smontare*) to get off; ~ **da** (*famiglia*) to be descended from; ~ **dalla macchina/dal treno** to get out of the car/out of *o* off the train; ~ **da cavallo** to dismount, get off one's horse.

di'scepolo, a [diʃ'ʃepolo] *sm/f* disciple.
di'scernere [diʃ'ʃɛrnere] *vt* to discern.
discerni'mento [diʃʃerni'mento] *sm*
discernment.
disce'sista [diʃʃe'sista] *sm/f* downhill skier.
di'sceso, a [diʃ'ʃeso] *pp di* **discendere** ♦ *sf*
descent; (*pendio*) slope; **in** ~**a** (*strada*)
downhill *cpd*, sloping; ~**a libera** (*SCI*)
downhill race.
dischi'udere [dis'kjudere] *vt* (*aprire*) to
open; (*fig*: *rivelare*) to disclose, reveal.
dischi'usi *etc* [dis'kjusi] *vb vedi* **dischiudere**.
dischi'uso, a [dis'kjuso] *pp di* **dischiudere**.
di'scinto, a [diʃ'ʃinto] *ag* (*anche*: **in abiti** ~**i**)
half-undressed.
disci'ogliere [diʃ'ʃɔʎʎere] *vt*, ~**rsi** *vr* to
dissolve; (*fondere*) to melt.
disci'plina [diʃʃi'plina] *sf* discipline.
discipli'nare [diʃʃipli'nare] *ag* disciplinary
♦ *vt* to discipline.
'disco, schi *sm* disc, disk; (*SPORT*) discus;
(*fonografico*) record; (*INFORM*) disk; ~
magnetico (*INFORM*) magnetic disk; ~
orario (*AUT*) parking disc; ~ **rigido**
(*INFORM*) hard disk; ~ **volante** flying
saucer.
discogra'fia *sf* (*tecnica*) recording, record-
making; (*industria*) record industry.
disco'grafico, a, ci, che *ag* record *cpd*,
recording *cpd* ♦ *sm* record producer; **casa**
~**a** record(ing) company.
'discolo, a *ag* (*bambino*) undisciplined,
unruly ♦ *sm/f* rascal.
discol'pare *vt* to clear of blame; ~**rsi** *vr* to
clear o.s., prove one's innocence;
(*giustificarsi*) to excuse o.s.
disco'noscere [disko'noʃʃere] *vt* (*figlio*) to
disown; (*meriti*) to ignore, disregard.
disconosci'uto, a [diskonoʃ'ʃuto] *pp di*
disconoscere.
discon'tinuo, a *ag* (*linea*) broken;
(*rendimento, stile*) irregular; (*interesse*)
sporadic.
dis'corde *ag* conflicting, clashing.
dis'cordia *sf* discord; (*dissidio*)
disagreement, clash.
dis'correre *vi*: ~ (**di**) to talk (about).
dis'corso, a *pp di* **discorrere** ♦ *sm* speech;
(*conversazione*) conversation, talk.
dis'costo, a *ag* faraway, distant ♦ *av* far
away; ~ **da** *prep* far from.
disco'teca, che *sf* (*raccolta*) record library;
(*luogo di ballo*) disco(theque).
discre'panza [diskre'pantsa] *sf*
discrepancy.
dis'creto, a *ag* discreet; (*abbastanza buono*)
reasonable, fair.
discrezi'one [diskret'tsjone] *sf* discretion;

(*giudizio*) judgment, discernment; **a** ~ **di**
at the discretion of.
discrimi'nante *ag* (*fattore, elemento*)
decisive ♦ *sf* (*DIR*) extenuating
circumstance.
discrimi'nare *vt* to discrimate.
discriminazi'one [diskriminat'tsjone] *sf*
discrimination.
dis'cussi *etc vb vedi* **discutere**.
discussi'one *sf* discussion; (*litigio*)
argument; **mettere in** ~ to bring into
question; **fuori** ~ out of the question.
dis'cusso, a *pp di* **discutere**.
dis'cutere *vt* to discuss, debate;
(*contestare*) to question, dispute ♦ *vi*
(*conversare*): ~ (**di**) to discuss; (*litigare*) to
argue.
discu'tibile *ag* questionable.
disde'gnare [dizdeɲ'ɲare] *vt* to scorn.
dis'degno [diz'deɲɲo] *sm* scorn, disdain.
disde'gnoso, a [dizdeɲ'ɲoso] *ag*
disdainful, scornful.
dis'detto, a *pp di* **disdire** ♦ *sf* cancellation;
(*sfortuna*) bad luck.
disdi'cevole [dizdi'tʃevole] *ag* improper,
unseemly.
dis'dire *vt* (*prenotazione*) to cancel; ~ **un**
contratto d'affitto (*DIR*) to give notice (to
quit).
dise'gnare [diseɲ'ɲare] *vt* to draw;
(*progettare*) to design; (*fig*) to outline.
disegna'tore, 'trice [diseɲɲa'tore] *sm/f*
designer.
di'segno [di'zeɲɲo] *sm* drawing; (*su stoffa*
etc) design; (*fig*: *schema*) outline; ~
industriale industrial design; ~ **di legge**
(*DIR*) bill.
diser'bante *sm* weedkiller.
disere'dare *vt* to disinherit.
diser'tare *vt*, *vi* to desert.
diser'tore *sm* (*MIL*) deserter.
diserzi'one [dizer'tsjone] *sf* (*MIL*) desertion.
disfaci'mento [disfatʃi'mento] *sm* (*di*
cadavere) decay; (*fig*: *di istituzione, impero,*
società) decline, decay; **in** ~ in decay.
dis'fare *vt* to undo; (*valigie*) to unpack;
(*meccanismo*) to take to pieces; (*lavoro,*
paese) to destroy; (*neve*) to melt; ~**rsi** *vr* to
come undone; (*neve*) to melt; ~ **il letto** to
strip the bed; ~**rsi di qn** (*liberarsi*) to get
rid of sb.
dis'fatta *sf vedi* **disfatto**.
disfat'tista, i, e *sm/f* defeatist.
dis'fatto, a *pp di* **disfare** ♦ *ag* (*gen*) undone,
untied; (*letto*) unmade; (*persona: sfinito*)
exhausted, worn-out; (: *addolorato*) grief-
stricken ♦ *sf* (*sconfitta*) rout.
disfunzi'one [disfun'tsjone] *sf* (*MED*)

dysfunction; ~ **cardiaca** heart trouble.
disge'lare [dizdʒe'lare] *vt, vi,* ~**rsi** *vr* to thaw.
dis'gelo [diz'dʒɛlo] *sm* thaw.
dis'grazia [diz'grattsja] *sf (sventura)* misfortune; *(incidente)* accident, mishap.
disgrazi'ato, a [dizgrat'tsjato] *ag* unfortunate ♦ *sm/f* wretch.
disgre'gare *vt,* ~**rsi** *vr* to break up.
disgu'ido *sm* hitch; ~ **postale** error in postal delivery.
disgus'tare *vt* to disgust; ~**rsi** *vr:* ~**rsi di** to be disgusted by.
dis'gusto *sm* disgust.
disgus'toso, a *ag* disgusting.
disidra'tare *vt* to dehydrate.
disidra'tato, a *ag* dehydrated.
disil'ludere *vt* to disillusion, disenchant.
disillusi'one *sf* disillusion, disenchantment.
disimpa'rare *vt* to forget.
disimpe'gnare [dizimpeɲ'ɲare] *vt (persona: da obblighi):* ~ **da** to release from; *(oggetto dato in pegno)* to redeem, get out of pawn; ~**rsi** *vr:* ~**rsi da** *(obblighi)* to release o.s. from, free o.s. from.
disincagli'are [dizinkaʎ'ʎare] *vt (barca)* to refloat; ~**rsi** *vr* to get afloat again.
disincan'tato, a *ag* disenchanted, disillusioned.
disincenti'vare [dizintʃenti'vare] *vt* to discourage.
disinfes'tare *vt* to disinfest.
disinfestazi'one [dizinfestat'tsjone] *sf* disinfestation.
disinfet'tante *ag, sm* disinfectant.
disinfet'tare *vt* to disinfect.
disinfezi'one [dizinfet'tsjone] *sf* disinfection.
disingan'nare *vt* to disillusion.
disin'ganno *sm* disillusion.
disini'bito, a *ag* uninhibited.
disinnes'care *vt* to defuse.
disinnes'tare *vt (marcia)* to disengage.
disinqui'nare *vt* to free from pollution.
disinte'grare *vt, vi* to disintegrate.
disinteres'sarsi *vr:* ~ **di** to take no interest in.
disinte'resse *sm* indifference; *(generosità)* unselfishness.
disintossi'care *vt (alcolizzato, drogato)* to treat for alcoholism (*o* drug addiction); ~**rsi** *vr* to clear out one's system; *(alcolizzato, drogato)* to be treated for alcoholism (*o* drug addiction).
disintossicazi'one [dizintossikat'tsjone] *sf* treatment for alcoholism (*o* drug addiction).

disin'volto, a *ag* casual, free and easy.
disinvol'tura *sf* casualness, ease.
disles'sia *sf* dyslexia.
disli'vello *sm* difference in height; *(fig)* gap.
dislo'care *vt* to station, position.
dismi'sura *sf* excess; **a** ~ to excess, excessively.
disobbe'dire *etc* = **disubbidire** *etc.*
disoccu'pato, a *ag* unemployed ♦ *sm/f* unemployed person.
disoccupazi'one [dizokkupat'tsjone] *sf* unemployment.
disonestà *sf* dishonesty.
diso'nesto, a *ag* dishonest.
disono'rare *vt* to dishonour (*BRIT*), dishonor (*US*), bring disgrace upon.
diso'nore *sm* dishonour (*BRIT*), dishonor (*US*), disgrace.
di'sopra *av (con contatto)* on top; *(senza contatto)* above; *(al piano superiore)* upstairs ♦ *ag inv (superiore)* upper ♦ *sm inv* top, upper part; **la gente** ~ the people upstairs; **il piano** ~ the floor above.
disordi'nare *vt* to mess up, disarrange; *(MIL)* to throw into disorder.
disordi'nato, a *ag* untidy; *(privo di misura)* irregular, wild.
di'sordine *sm (confusione)* disorder, confusion; *(sregolatezza)* debauchery; ~**i** *smpl (POL etc)* disorder *sg;* *(tumulti)* riots.
disor'ganico, a, ci, che *ag* incoherent, disorganized.
disorganiz'zato, a [dizorganid'dzato] *ag* disorganized.
disorienta'mento *sm (fig)* confusion, bewilderment.
disorien'tare *vt* to disorientate; ~**rsi** *vr (fig)* to get confused, lose one's bearings.
disorien'tato, a *ag* disorientated.
disos'sare *vt (CUC)* to bone.
di'sotto *av* below, underneath; *(in fondo)* at the bottom; *(al piano inferiore)* downstairs ♦ *ag inv (inferiore)* lower; bottom *cpd* ♦ *sm inv (parte inferiore)* lower part; bottom; **la gente** ~ the people downstairs; **il piano** ~ the floor below.
dis'paccio [dis'pattʃo] *sm* dispatch.
dispa'rato, a *ag* disparate.
'dispari *ag inv* odd, uneven.
disparità *sf inv* disparity.
dis'parte : **in** ~ *av (da lato)* aside, apart; **tenersi** *o* **starsene in** ~ to keep to o.s., hold aloof.
dis'pendio *sm (di denaro, energie)* expenditure; *(: spreco)* waste.
dispendi'oso, a *ag* expensive.
dis'pensa *sf* pantry, larder; *(mobile)*

sideboard; (*DIR*) exemption; (*REL*) dispensation; (*fascicolo*) number, issue.

dispen'sare *vt* (*elemosine, favori*) to distribute; (*esonerare*) to exempt.

dispe'rare *vi*: ~ **(di)** to despair (of); **~rsi** *vr* to despair.

dispe'rato, a *ag* (*persona*) in despair; (*caso, tentativo*) desperate.

disperazi'one [disperat'tsjone] *sf* despair.

dis'perdere *vt* (*disseminare*) to disperse; (*MIL*) to scatter, rout; (*fig: consumare*) to waste, squander; **~rsi** *vr* to disperse; to scatter.

dispersi'one *sf* dispersion, dispersal; (*FISICA, CHIM*) dispersion.

disper'sivo, a *ag* (*lavoro etc*) disorganized.

dis'perso, a *pp di* **disperdere** ♦ *sm/f* missing person; (*MIL*) missing soldier.

dis'petto *sm* spite *no pl*, spitefulness *no pl*; **fare un** ~ **a qn** to play a (nasty) trick on sb; **a** ~ **di** in spite of; **con suo grande** ~ much to his annoyance.

dispet'toso, a *ag* spiteful.

dispia'cere [dispja't∫ere] *sm* (*rammarico*) regret, sorrow; (*dolore*) grief ♦ *vi*: ~ **a** to displease ♦ *vb impers*: **mi dispiace (che)** I am sorry (that); **~i** *smpl* (*preoccupazioni*) troubles, worries; **se non le dispiace, me ne vado adesso** if you don't mind, I'll go now.

dispiaci'uto, a [dispja't∫uto] *pp di* **dispiacere** ♦ *ag* sorry.

dis'pone, dis'pongo *etc vb vedi* **disporre**.

dispo'nibile *ag* available; (*persona: solerte, gentile*) helpful.

disponibilità *sf inv* availability; (*solerzia, gentilezza*) helpfulness; **disponibilità** *sfpl* (*economiche*) resources.

dis'porre *vt* (*sistemare*) to arrange; (*preparare*) to prepare; (*DIR*) to order; (*persuadere*): ~ **qn a** to incline *o* dispose sb towards ♦ *vi* (*decidere*) to decide; (*usufruire*): ~ **di** to use, have at one's disposal; (*essere dotato*): ~ **di** to have; **disporsi** *vr* (*ordinarsi*) to place o.s., arrange o.s.; **disporsi a fare** to get ready to do; **disporsi all'attacco** to prepare for an attack; **disporsi in cerchio** to form a circle.

dis'posi *etc vb vedi* **disporre**.

disposi'tivo *sm* (*meccanismo*) device; (*DIR*) pronouncement; ~ **di controllo** *o* **di comando** control device; ~ **di sicurezza** (*gen*) safety device; (*di arma da fuoco*) safety catch.

disposizi'one [dispozit'tsjone] *sf* arrangement, layout; (*stato d'animo*) mood; (*tendenza*) bent, inclination;

(*comando*) order; (*DIR*) provision, regulation; **a** ~ **di qn** at sb's disposal; **per** ~ **di legge** by law; ~ **testamentaria** provisions of a will.

dis'posto, a *pp di* **disporre** ♦ *ag* (*incline*): ~ **a fare** disposed *o* prepared to do.

dis'potico, a, ci, che *ag* despotic.

dispo'tismo *sm* despotism.

disprez'zare [dispret'tsare] *vt* tó despise.

dis'prezzo [dis'prɛttso] *sm* contempt; **con** ~ **del pericolo** with a total disregard for the danger involved.

'disputa *sf* dispute, quarrel.

dispu'tare *vt* (*contendere*) to dispute, contest; (*SPORT: partita*) to play; (*: gara*) to take part in ♦ *vi* to quarrel; ~ **di** to discuss; **~rsi qc** to fight for sth.

disqui'sire *vi* to discourse on.

disquisizi'one [diskwizit'tsjone] *sf* detailed analysis.

dissa'crare *vt* to desecrate.

dissangua'mento *sm* loss of blood.

dissangu'are *vt* (*fig: persona*) to bleed white; (*: patrimonio*) to suck dry; **~rsi** *vr* (*MED*) to lose blood; (*fig*) to ruin o.s.; **morire dissanguato** to bleed to death.

dissa'pore *sm* slight disagreement.

'disse *vb vedi* **dire**.

disse'care *vt* to dissect.

dissec'care *vt*, **~rsi** *vr* to dry up.

dissemi'nare *vt* to scatter; (*fig: notizie*) to spread.

dissenna'tezza [dissenna'tettsa] *sf* foolishness.

dis'senso *sm* dissent; (*disapprovazione*) disapproval.

dissente'ria *sf* dysentery.

dissen'tire *vi*: ~ **(da)** to disagree (with).

disseppel'lire *vt* (*esumare: cadavere*) to disinter, exhume; (*dissotterrare: anche fig*) to dig up, unearth; (*: rancori*) to resurrect.

dissertazi'one [dissertat'tsjone] *sf* dissertation.

disser'vizio [disser'vittsjo] *sm* inefficiency.

disses'tare *vt* (*ECON*) to ruin.

disses'tato, a *ag* (*fondo stradale*) uneven; (*economia, finanze*) shaky; **"strada ~a"** (*per lavori in corso*) "road up" (*BRIT*), "road out" (*US*).

dis'sesto *sm* (financial) ruin.

disse'tante *ag* refreshing.

disse'tare *vt* to quench the thirst of; **~rsi** *vr* to quench one's thirst.

dissezi'one [disset'tsjone] *sf* dissection.

'dissi *vb vedi* **dire**.

dissi'dente *ag, sm/f* dissident.

dis'sidio *sm* disagreement.

dis'simile *ag* different, dissimilar.

dissimu'lare vt (fingere) to dissemble; (nascondere) to conceal.

dissimula'tore, 'trice sm/f dissembler.

dissimulazi'one [dissimulat'tsjone] sf dissembling; concealment.

dissi'pare vt to dissipate; (scialacquare) to squander, waste.

dissipa'tezza [dissipa'tettsa] sf dissipation.

dissi'pato, a ag dissolute, dissipated.

dissipazi'one [dissipat'tsjone] sf squandering.

dissoci'are [disso't∫are] vt to dissociate.

dis'solto, a pp di **dissolvere**.

disso'lubile ag soluble.

dissolu'tezza [dissolu'tettsa] sf dissoluteness.

dissolu'tivo, a ag (forza) divisive; **processo** ~ (anche fig) process of dissolution.

disso'luto, a pp di **dissolvere** ♦ ag dissolute, licentious.

dissol'venza [dissol'ventsa] sf (CINE) fading.

dis'solvere vt to dissolve; (nube) to melt; (fumo) to disperse; ~**rsi** vr to dissolve; to melt; to disperse.

disso'nante ag discordant.

disso'nanza [disso'nantsa] sf (fig: di opinioni) clash.

dissotter'rare vt (cadavere) to disinter, exhume; (tesori, rovine) to dig up, unearth; (fig: sentimenti, odio) to bring up again, resurrect.

dissu'adere vt: ~ qn da to dissuade sb from.

dissuasi'one sf dissuasion.

dissu'aso, a pp di **dissuadere**.

distacca'mento sm (MIL) detachment.

distac'care vt to detach, separate; (SPORT) to leave behind; ~**rsi** vr to be detached; (fig) to stand out; ~**rsi da** (fig: allontanarsi) to grow away from.

dis'tacco, chi sm (separazione) separation; (fig: indifferenza) detachment; (SPORT): **vincere con un** ~ **di** ... to win by a distance of ....

dis'tante av far away ♦ ag distant, far away; **essere** ~ (da) to be a long way (from); **è** ~ **da qui?** is it far from here?; **essere** ~ **nel tempo** to be in the distant past.

dis'tanza [dis'tantsa] sf distance; **comando a** ~ remote control; **a** ~ **di 2 giorni** 2 days later; **tener qn a** ~ to keep sb at arm's length; **prendere le** ~**e da qc/qn** to dissociate o.s. from sth/sb; **tenere** o **mantenere le** ~**e** to keep one's distance; ~ **focale** focal length; ~ **di sicurezza** safe distance; (AUT) braking distance; ~ **di**

tiro range; ~ **di visibilità** visibility.

distanzi'are [distan'tsjare] vt to space out, place at intervals; (SPORT) to outdistance; (fig: superare) to outstrip, surpass.

dis'tare vi: **distiamo pochi chilometri da Roma** we are only a few kilometres (away) from Rome; **dista molto da qui?** is it far (away) from here?; **non dista molto** it's not far (away).

dis'tendere vt (coperta) to spread out; (gambe) to stretch (out); (mettere a giacere) to lay; (rilassare: muscoli, nervi) to relax; ~**rsi** vr (rilassarsi) to relax; (sdraiarsi) to lie down.

distensi'one sf stretching; relaxation; (POL) détente.

disten'sivo, a ag (gen) relaxing, restful; (farmaco) tranquillizing; (POL) conciliatory.

dis'teso, a pp di **distendere** ♦ ag (allungato: persona, gamba) stretched out; (rilassato: persona, atmosfera) relaxed ♦ sf expanse, stretch; **avere un volto** ~ to look relaxed.

distil'lare vt to distil.

distil'lato sm distillate.

distillazi'one [distillat'tsjone] sf distillation.

distille'ria sf distillery.

dis'tinguere vt to distinguish; ~**rsi** vr (essere riconoscibile) to be distinguished; (emergere) to stand out, be conspicuous, distinguish o.s.; **un vino che si distingue per il suo aroma** a wine with a distinctive bouquet.

dis'tinguo sm inv distinction.

dis'tinta sf (nota) note; (elenco) list; ~ **di pagamento** receipt; ~ **di versamento** pay-in slip.

distin'tivo, a ag distinctive; distinguishing ♦ sm badge.

dis'tinto, a pp di **distinguere** ♦ ag (dignitoso ed elegante) distinguished; ~**i saluti** (in lettera) yours faithfully.

distinzi'one [distin'tsjone] sf distinction; **non faccio** ~**i** (tra persone) I don't discriminate; (tra cose) it's all one to me; **senza** ~ **di razza/religione** ... no matter what one's race/creed ....

dis'togliere [dis'tɔʎʎere] vt: ~ **da** to take away from; (fig) to dissuade from.

dis'tolto, a pp di **distogliere**.

dis'torcere [dis'tɔrt∫ere] vt to twist; (fig) to twist, distort; ~**rsi** vr (contorcersi) to twist.

distorsi'one sf (MED) sprain; (FISICA, OTTICA) distortion.

dis'torto, a pp di **distorcere**.

dis'trarre vt to distract; (divertire) to entertain, amuse; **distrarsi** vr (non fare *attenzione*) to be distracted, let one's mind wander; (*svagarsi*) to amuse o enjoy o.s.; ~ **lo sguardo** to look away; **non distrarti!** pay attention!

distratta'mente *av* absent-mindedly, without thinking.

dis'tratto, a *pp di* **distrarre** ♦ *ag* absent-minded; (*disattento*) inattentive.

distrazi'one [distrat'tsjone] *sf* absent-mindedness; inattention; (*svago*) distraction, entertainment; **errori di ~** careless mistakes.

dis'tretto *sm* district.

distribu'ire *vt* to distribute; (*CARTE*) to deal (out); (*consegnare: posta*) to deliver; (*lavoro*) to allocate, assign; (*ripartire*) to share out.

distribu'tore *sm* (*di benzina*) petrol (*BRIT*) o gas (*US*) pump; (*AUT, ELETTR*) distributor; (*automatico*) vending machine.

distribuzi'one [distribut'tsjone] *sf* distribution; delivery; allocation, assignment; sharing out.

distri'care *vt* to disentangle, unravel; **~rsi** *vr* (*tirarsi fuori*): **~rsi da** to get out of, disentangle o.s. from; (*fig: cavarsela*) to manage, get by.

dis'truggere [dis'truddʒere] *vt* to destroy.

distrut'tivo, a *ag* destructive.

dis'trutto, a *pp di* **distruggere**.

distruzi'one [distrut'tsjone] *sf* destruction.

distur'bare *vt* to disturb, trouble; (*sonno, lezioni*) to disturb, interrupt; **~rsi** *vr* to put o.s. out; **non si disturbi** please don't bother.

dis'turbo *sm* trouble, bother, inconvenience; (*indisposizione*) (slight) disorder, ailment; **~i** *smpl* (*RADIO, TV*) static *sg*; **~ della quiete pubblica** (*DIR*) disturbance of the peace; **~i di stomaco** stomach trouble *sg*.

disubbidi'ente *ag* disobedient.

disubbidi'enza [dizubbi'djɛntsa] *sf* disobedience; **~ civile** civil disobedience.

disubbi'dire *vi*: **~ (a qn)** to disobey (sb).

disuguagli'anza [dizugwaʎ'ʎantsa] *sf* inequality.

disugu'ale *ag* unequal; (*diverso*) different; (*irregolare*) uneven.

disumanità *sf* inhumanity.

disu'mano, a *ag* inhuman; **un grido ~** a terrible cry.

disuni'one *sf* disunity.

disu'nire *vt* to divide, disunite.

di'suso *sm*: **andare** o **cadere in ~** to fall into disuse.

'dita *sfpl di* **dito**.

di'tale *sm* thimble.

di'tata *sf* (*colpo*) jab (with one's finger); (*segno*) fingermark.

'dito, *pl(f)* **'dita** *sm* finger; (*misura*) finger, finger's breadth; **~ (del piede)** toe; **mettersi le ~a nel naso** to pick one's nose; **mettere il ~ sulla piaga** (*fig*) to touch a sore spot; **non ha mosso un ~ (per aiutarmi)** he didn't lift a finger (to help me); **ormai è segnato a ~** everyone knows about him now.

'ditta *sf* firm, business; **macchina della ~** company car.

dit'tafono *sm* Dictaphone ®.

ditta'tore *sm* dictator.

ditta'tura *sf* dictatorship.

dit'tongo, ghi *sm* diphthong.

di'urno, a *ag* day *cpd*, daytime *cpd*; **ore ~e** daytime *sg*; **spettacolo ~** matinee; **turno ~** day shift; *vedi anche* **albergo**.

'diva *sf vedi* **divo**.

diva'gare *vi* to digress.

divagazi'one [divagat'tsjone] *sf* digression; **~i sul tema** variations on a theme.

divam'pare *vi* to flare up, blaze up.

di'vano *sm* sofa; (*senza schienale*) divan; **~ letto** bed settee, sofa bed.

divari'care *vt* to open wide.

di'vario *sm* difference.

di'vengo *etc vb vedi* **divenire**.

dive'nire *vi* = **diventare**.

di'venni *etc vb vedi* **divenire**.

diven'tare *vi* to become; **~ famoso/ professore** to become famous/a teacher; **~ vecchio** to grow old; **c'è da ~ matti** it's enough to drive you mad.

dive'nuto, a *pp di* **divenire**.

di'verbio *sm* altercation.

diver'gente [diver'dʒɛnte] *ag* divergent.

diver'genza [diver'dʒɛntsa] *sf* divergence; **~ d'opinioni** difference of opinion.

di'vergere [di'vɛrdʒere] *vi* to diverge.

diverrò *etc vb vedi* **divenire**.

diversa'mente *av* (*in modo differente*) differently; (*altrimenti*) otherwise; **~ da quanto stabilito** contrary to what had been decided.

diversifi'care *vt* to diversify, vary; **~rsi** *vr*: **~rsi (per)** to differ (in).

diversificazi'one [diversifikat'tsjone] *sf* diversification; difference.

diversi'one *sf* diversion.

diversità *sf inv* difference, diversity; (*varietà*) variety.

diver'sivo, a *ag* diversionary ♦ *sm* diversion, distraction; **fare un'azione ~a** to create a diversion.

di'verso, a *ag* (*differente*): **~ (da)** different (from) ♦ *sm* (*omosessuale*) homosexual;

~**i, e** *det pl* several, various; (*COMM*) sundry ♦ *pron pl* several (people), many (people).

diver'tente *ag* amusing.

diverti'mento *sm* amusement, pleasure; (*passatempo*) pastime, recreation; **buon** ~**!** enjoy yourself!, have a nice time!

diver'tire *vt* to amuse, entertain; ~**rsi** *vr* to amuse *o* enjoy o.s.; **divertiti!** enjoy yourself, have a good time!; ~**rsi alle spalle di qn** to have a laugh at sb's expense.

diver'tito, a *ag* amused.

divez'zare [divet'tsare] *vt* (*anche fig*): ~ **(da)** to wean (from).

divi'dendo *sm* dividend.

di'videre *vt* (*anche MAT*) to divide; (*distribuire, ripartire*) to divide (up), split (up); ~**rsi** *vr* (*persone*) to separate, part; (*coppia*) to separate; ~**rsi (in)** (*scindersi*) to divide (into), split up (into); (*ramificarsi*) to fork; **è diviso dalla moglie** he's separated from his wife; **si divide tra casa e lavoro** he divides his time between home and work.

divi'eto *sm* prohibition; *"*~ **di accesso"** "no entry"; *"*~ **di caccia"** "no hunting"; *"*~ **di parcheggio"** "no parking"; *"*~ **di sosta"** (*AUT*) "no waiting".

divinco'larsi *vr* to wriggle, writhe.

divinità *sf inv* divinity.

di'vino, a *ag* divine.

di'visa *sf* (*MIL etc*) uniform; (*COMM*) foreign currency.

di'visi *etc vb vedi* **dividere**.

divisi'one *sf* division; ~ **in sillabe** syllable division; (*a fine riga*) hyphenation.

di'vismo *sm* (*esibizionismo*) playing to the crowd.

di'viso, a *pp di* **dividere**.

divi'sorio, a *ag* (*siepe, muro esterno*) dividing; (*muro interno*) dividing, partition *cpd* ♦ *sm* (*in una stanza*) partition.

'divo, a *sm/f* star; **come una** ~**a** like a prima donna.

divo'rare *vt* to devour; ~ **qc con gli occhi** to eye sth greedily.

divorzi'are [divor'tsjare] *vi*: ~ **(da qn)** to divorce (sb).

divorzi'ato, a [divor'tsjato] *ag* divorced ♦ *sm/f* divorcee.

di'vorzio [di'vɔrtsjo] *sm* divorce.

divul'gare *vt* to divulge, disclose; (*rendere comprensibile*) to popularize; ~**rsi** *vr* to spread.

divulgazi'one [divulgat'tsjone] *sf* (*vedi vb*) disclosure; popularization; spread.

dizio'nario [dittsjo'narjo] *sm* dictionary.

dizi'one [dit'tsjone] *sf* diction; pronunciation.

Dja'karta [dʒa'karta] *sf* Djakarta.

dl *abbr* (= *decilitro*) dl.

dm *abbr* (= *decimetro*) dm.

DNA [di'ennɛa] *sigla m* (*BIOL*: = *acido deossiribonucleico*) DNA ♦ *sigla f* = *direzione nazionale antimafia*.

do *sm* (*MUS*) C; (: *solfeggiando la scala*) do(h).

dobbi'amo *vb vedi* **dovere**.

D.O.C. [dɔk] *sigla vedi* **denominazione di origine controllata**.

doc. *abbr* = **documento**.

'doccia, ce ['dottʃa] *sf* (*bagno*) shower; (*condotto*) pipe; **fare la** ~ to have a shower; ~ **fredda** (*fig*) slap in the face.

do'cente [do'tʃɛnte] *ag* teaching ♦ *sm/f* teacher; (*di università*) lecturer; **personale non** ~ non-teaching staff.

do'cenza [do'tʃɛntsa] *sf* university teaching *o* lecturing; **ottenere la libera** ~ to become a lecturer.

D.O.C.G. *sigla* (= *denominazione di origine controllata e garantita*) *label guaranteeing the quality and origin of a wine*.

'docile ['dɔtʃile] *ag* docile.

docilità [dotʃili'ta] *sf* docility.

documen'tare *vt* to document; ~**rsi** *vr*: ~**rsi (su)** to gather information *o* material (about).

documen'tario, a *ag*, *sm* documentary.

documentazi'one [dokumentat'tsjone] *sf* documentation.

docu'mento *sm* document; ~**i** *smpl* (*d'identità etc*) papers.

Dodecan'neso *sm*: **le Isole del** ~ the Dodecanese Islands.

dodi'cenne [dodi'tʃɛnne] *ag*, *sm/f* twelve-year-old.

dodi'cesimo, a [dodi'tʃɛzimo] *num* twelfth.

'dodici ['doditʃi] *num* twelve.

do'gana *sf* (*ufficio*) customs *pl*; (*tassa*) (customs) duty; **passare la** ~ to go through customs.

doga'nale *ag* customs *cpd*.

dogani'ere *sm* customs officer.

'doglie ['dɔʎʎe] *sfpl* (*MED*) labour *sg* (*BRIT*), labor *sg* (*US*), labo(u)r pains.

'dogma, i *sm* dogma.

dog'matico, a, ci, che *ag* dogmatic.

'dolce ['doltʃe] *ag* sweet; (*colore*) soft; (*carattere, persona*) gentle, mild; (*fig: mite: clima*) mild; (*non ripido: pendio*) gentle ♦ *sm* (*sapore* ~) sweetness, sweet taste; (*CUC: portata*) sweet, dessert; (: *torta*) cake; **il** ~ **far niente** sweet idleness.

dol'cezza [dol'tʃettsa] *sf* sweetness;

softness; mildness; gentleness.

dolci'ario, a [dol'tʃarjo] *ag* confectionery *cpd*.

dolci'astro, a [dol'tʃastro] *ag* (*sapore*) sweetish.

dolcifi'cante [doltʃifi'kante] *ag* sweetening ♦ *sm* sweetener.

dolci'umi [dol'tʃumi] *smpl* sweets.

do'lente *ag* sorrowful, sad.

do'lere *vi* to be sore, hurt, ache; ~**rsi** *vr* to complain; (*essere spiacente*): ~**rsi di** to be sorry for; **mi duole la testa** my head aches, I've got a headache.

'dolgo *etc vb vedi* **dolere**.

'dollaro *sm* dollar.

'dolo *sm* (*DIR*) malice; (*frode*) fraud, deceit.

Dolo'miti *sfpl*: **le** ~ the Dolomites.

dolo'rante *ag* aching, sore.

do'lore *sm* (*fisico*) pain; (*morale*) sorrow, grief; **se lo scoprono sono** ~**i!** if they find out there'll be trouble!

dolo'roso, a *ag* painful; sorrowful, sad.

do'loso, a *ag* (*DIR*) malicious; **incendio** ~ arson.

'dolsi *etc vb vedi* **dolere**.

dom. *abbr* (= *domenica*) Sun.

do'manda *sf* (*interrogazione*) question; (*richiesta*) demand; (: *cortese*) request; (*DIR: richiesta scritta*) application; (*ECON*): **la** ~ demand; **fare una** ~ **a qn** to ask sb a question; **fare** ~ **(per un lavoro)** to apply (for a job); **far regolare** ~ **(di qc)** to apply through the proper channels (for sth); **fare** ~ **all'autorità giudiziaria** to apply to the courts; ~ **di divorzio** divorce petition; ~ **di matrimonio** proposal.

doman'dare *vt* (*per avere*) to ask for; (*per sapere*) to ask; (*esigere*) to demand; ~**rsi** *vr* to wonder, ask o.s.; ~ **qc a qn** to ask sb for sth; to ask sb sth.

do'mani *av* tomorrow ♦ *sm* (*l'indomani*) next day, following day; **il** ~ (*il futuro*) the future; (*il giorno successivo*) the next day; **un** ~ some day; ~ **l'altro** the day after tomorrow; ~ **(a) otto** tomorrow week, a week tomorrow; **a** ~**!** see you tomorrow!

do'mare *vt* to tame.

doma'tore, 'trice *sm/f* (*gen*) tamer; ~ **di cavalli** horsebreaker; ~ **di leoni** lion tamer.

domat'tina *av* tomorrow morning.

do'menica, che *sf* Sunday; *per fraseologia vedi* **martedì**.

domeni'cale *ag* Sunday *cpd*.

domeni'cano, a *ag*, *sm/f* Dominican.

do'mestica, che *sf vedi* **domestico**.

do'mestico, a, ci, che *ag* domestic ♦ *sm/f* servant, domestic; **le pareti** ~**che** one's

own four walls; **animale** *m* ~ pet; **una** ~**a a ore** a daily (woman).

domicili'are [domitʃi'ljare] *ag vedi* **arresto**.

domicili'arsi [domitʃi'ljarsi] *vr* to take up residence.

domi'cilio [domi'tʃiljo] *sm* (*DIR*) domicile, place of residence; **visita a** ~ (*MED*) house call; "**recapito a** ~" "deliveries"; **violazione di** ~ (*DIR*) breaking and entering.

domi'nante *ag* (*colore, nota*) dominant; (*opinione*) prevailing; (*idea*) main *cpd*, chief *cpd*; (*posizione*) dominating *cpd*; (*classe, partito*) ruling *cpd*.

domi'nare *vt* to dominate; (*fig: sentimenti*) to control, master ♦ *vi* to be in the dominant position; ~**rsi** *vr* (*controllarsi*) to control o.s.; ~ **su** (*fig*) to surpass, outclass.

domina'tore, 'trice *ag* ruling *cpd* ♦ *sm/f* ruler.

dominazi'one [dominat'tsjone] *sf* domination.

domini'cano, a *ag*: **la Repubblica D**~**a** the Dominican Republic.

do'minio *sm* dominion; (*fig: campo*) field, domain; ~**i coloniali** colonies; **essere di** ~ **pubblico** (*notizia etc*) to be common knowledge.

don *sm* (*REL*) Father.

do'nare *vt* to give, present; (*per beneficenza etc*) to donate ♦ *vi* (*fig*): ~ **a** to suit, become; ~ **sangue** to give blood.

dona'tore, 'trice *sm/f* donor; ~ **di sangue/di organi** blood/organ donor.

donazi'one [donat'tsjone] *sf* donation; **atto di** ~ (*DIR*) deed of gift.

'donde *av* (*poetico*) whence.

dondo'lare *vt* (*cullare*) to rock; ~**rsi** *vr* to swing, sway.

'dondolo *sm*: **sedia/cavallo a** ~ rocking chair/horse.

dongio'vanni [dondʒo'vanni] *sm* Don Juan, ladies' man.

'donna *sf* woman; (*titolo*) Donna; (*CARTE*) queen; **figlio di buona** ~**!** (*fam*) son of a bitch!; ~ **di casa** housewife; ~ **a ore** daily (help *o* woman); ~ **delle pulizie** cleaning lady, cleaner; ~ **di servizio** maid; ~ **di vita** *o* **di strada** prostitute, streetwalker.

donnai'olo *sm* ladykiller.

'donnola *sf* weasel.

'dono *sm* gift.

'dopo *av* (*tempo*) afterwards; (: *più tardi*) later; (*luogo*) after, next ♦ *prep* after ♦ *cong* (*temporale*): ~ **aver studiato** after having studied ♦ *ag inv*: **il giorno** ~ the following day; ~ **mangiato va a dormire**

after having eaten *o* after a meal he goes for a sleep; **un anno** ~ a year later; ~ **di me/lui** after me/him; ~ **che** = **dopoché.**

dopo'barba *sm inv* after-shave.

dopoché [dopo'ke] *cong* after, when.

dopodiché [dopodi'ke] *av* after which.

dopodo'mani *av* the day after tomorrow.

dopogu'erra *sm* postwar years *pl.*

dopola'voro *sm* recreational club.

dopo'pranzo [dopo'prandzo] *av* after lunch (*o* dinner).

doposcì [dopoʃ'ʃi] *sm inv* après-ski outfit.

doposcu'ola *sm inv* school club *offering extra tuition and recreational facilities.*

dopo'sole *sm inv, ag inv*: **(lozione/crema)** ~ aftersun (lotion/cream).

dopo'tutto *av* after all.

doppi'aggio [dop'pjaddʒo] *sm* (*CINE*) dubbing.

doppi'are *vt* (*NAUT*) to round; (*SPORT*) to lap; (*CINE*) to dub.

doppia'tore, 'trice *sm/f* dubber.

doppi'etta *cf* (*fucile*) double-barrelled (*BRIT*) *o* double-barreled (*US*) shotgun; (*sparo*) shot from both barrels; (*CALCIO*) double; (*PUGILATO*) one-two; (*AUT*) double-declutch (*BRIT*), double-clutch (*US*).

doppi'ezza [dop'pjettsa] *sf* (*fig: di persona*) duplicity, double-dealing.

'doppio, a *ag* double; (*fig: falso*) double-dealing, deceitful ♦ *sm* (*quantità*): **il** ~ **(di)** twice as much (*o* many), double the amount (*o* number) of; (*SPORT*) doubles *pl* ♦ *av* double; **battere una lettera in** ~**a copia** to type a letter with a carbon copy; **fare il** ~ **gioco** (*fig*) to play a double game; **chiudere a** ~**a mandata** to double-lock; ~ **senso** double entendre; **frase a** ~ **senso** sentence with a double meaning; **un utensile a** ~ **uso** a dual-purpose utensil.

doppio'fondo *sm* (*di valigia*) false bottom; (*NAUT*) double hull.

doppi'one *sm* duplicate (copy).

doppio'petto *sm* double-breasted jacket.

dop'pista *sm/f* (*TENNIS*) doubles player.

do'rare *vt* to gild; (*CUC*) to brown; ~ **la pillola** (*fig*) to sugar the pill.

do'rato, a *ag* golden; (*ricoperto d'oro*) gilt, gilded.

dora'tura *sf* gilding.

dormicchi'are [dormik'kjare] *vi* to doze.

dormi'ente *ag* sleeping ♦ *sm/f* sleeper.

dormigli'one, a [dormiʎ'ʎone] *sm/f* sleepyhead.

dor'mire *vi* to sleep; (*essere addormentato*) to be asleep, be sleeping; **il caffè non mi fa** ~ coffee keeps me awake; ~ **come un**

ghiro to sleep like a log; ~ **della grossa** to sleep soundly; ~ **in piedi** (*essere stanco*) to be asleep on one's feet.

dor'mita *sf*: **farsi una** ~ to have a good sleep.

dormi'torio *sm* dormitory; ~ **pubblico** doss house (*BRIT*) *o* flophouse (*US*) (*run by local authority*).

dormi'veglia [dormi'veʎʎa] *sm* drowsiness.

dorrò *etc vb vedi* **dolere.**

dor'sale *ag*: **spina** ~ backbone, spine.

'dorso *sm* back; (*di montagna*) ridge, crest; (*di libro*) spine; (*NUOTO*) backstroke; **a** ~ **di cavallo** on horseback.

do'saggio [do'zaddʒo] *sm* (*atto*) measuring out; **sbagliare il** ~ to get the proportions wrong.

do'sare *vt* to measure out; (*MED*) to dose.

'dose *sf* quantity, amount; (*MED*) dose.

dossi'er [do'sje] *sm inv* dossier, file.

'dosso *sm* (*rilievo*) rise; (: *di strada*) bump; (*dorso*): **levarsi di** ~ **i vestiti to take one's** clothes off; **levarsi un peso di** ~ (*fig*) to take a weight off one's mind.

do'tare *vt*: ~ **di** to provide *o* supply with; (*fig*) to endow with.

do'tato, a *ag*: ~ **di** (*attrezzature*) equipped with; (*bellezza, intelligenza*) endowed with; **un uomo** ~ a gifted man.

dotazi'one [dotat'tsjone] *sf* (*insieme di beni*) endowment; (*di macchine etc*) equipment; **dare qc in** ~ **a qn** to issue sb with sth; **i macchinari in** ~ **alla fabbrica** the machinery in use in the factory.

'dote *sf* (*di sposa*) dowry; (*assegnata a un ente*) endowment; (*fig*) gift, talent.

Dott. *abbr* (= *dottore*) Dr.

'dotto, a *ag* (*colto*) learned ♦ *sm* (*sapiente*) scholar; (*ANAT*) duct.

dotto'rato *sm* degree; ~ **di ricerca** doctorate, doctor's degree.

dot'tore, 'essa *sm/f* doctor.

dot'trina *sf* doctrine.

Dott.ssa *abbr* (= *dottoressa*) Dr.

double-'face [dubl'fas] *ag inv* reversible.

'dove *av* where; (*in cui*) where, in which; (*dovunque*) wherever ♦ *sm*: **per ogni** ~ everywhere; **di dov'è?** where are you from?; **da** ~ **abito vedo tutta la città** I can see the whole city from where I live; **per** ~ **si passa?** which way should we go?; **le dò una mano fin** ~ **posso** I'll help you as much as I can.

do'vere *sm* (*obbligo*) duty ♦ *vt* (*essere debitore*): ~ **qc (a qn)** to owe (sb) sth ♦ *vi* (*seguito dall'infinito: obbligo*) to have to; **lui deve farlo** he has to do it, he must do it; **è dovuto partire** he had to leave; **ha dovuto**

pagare he had to pay; (: *intenzione*): **devo partire domani** I'm (due) to leave tomorrow; (: *probabilità*) **dev'essere tardi** it must be late; **doveva accadere** it was bound to happen; **avere il senso del** ~ to have a sense of duty; **rivolgersi a chi di** ~ to apply to the appropriate authority *o* person; **a** ~ (*bene*) properly; (*debitamente*) as he (*o* she *etc*) deserves; **come si deve** (*bene*) properly; (*meritatamente*) properly, as he (*o* she *etc*) deserves; **una persona come si deve** a respectable person.

dove'roso, a *ag* (right and) proper.

do'vizia [do'vittsja] *sf* abundance.

dovrò *etc vb vedi* **dovere.**

do'vunque *av* (*in qualunque luogo*) wherever; (*dappertutto*) everywhere; ~ **io vada** wherever I go.

dovuta'mente *av* (*debitamente: redigere, compilare*) correctly; (: *rimproverare*) as he (*o* she *etc*) deserves.

do'vuto, a *ag* (*causato*): ~ **a** due to ♦ *sm* due; **nel modo** ~ in the proper way; **ho lavorato più del** ~ I worked more than was necessary.

doz'zina [dod'dzina] *sf* dozen; **una** ~ **di uova** a dozen eggs; **di** *o* **da** ~ (*scrittore, spettacolo*) second-rate.

dozzi'nale [doddzi'nale] *ag* cheap, second-rate.

DP *sigla f* (= *Democrazia Proletaria*) *political party.*

'draga, ghe *sf* dredger.

dra'gare *vt* to dredge.

dragherò *etc* [drage'rɔ] *vb vedi* **dragare.**

'drago, ghi *sm* dragon; (*fig fam*) genius.

'dramma, i *sm* drama; **fare un** ~ **di qc** to make a drama out of sth.

dram'matico, a, ci, che *ag* dramatic.

drammatiz'zare [drammatid'dzare] *vt* to dramatize.

dramma'turgo, ghi *sm* playwright, dramatist.

drappeggi'are [drapped'dʒare] *vt* to drape.

drap'peggio [drap'peddʒo] *sm* (*tessuto*) drapery; (*di abito*) folds.

drap'pello *sm* (*MIL*) squad; (*gruppo*) band, group.

'drappo *sm* cloth.

'drastico, a, ci, che *ag* drastic.

dre'naggio [dre'naddʒo] *sm* drainage.

dre'nare *vt* to drain.

'Dresda *sf* Dresden.

drib'blare *vi* (*CALCIO*) to dribble ♦ *vt* (*avversario*) to dodge, avoid.

'dritto, a *ag, av* = **diritto** ♦ *sm/f* (*fam: furbo*): **è un** ~ he's a crafty *o* sly one ♦ *sf* (*destra*)

right, right hand; (*NAUT*) starboard; **a** ~**a e a manca** (*fig*) on all sides, right, left and centre.

driz'zare [drit'tsare] *vt* (*far tornare diritto*) to straighten; (*volgere: sguardo, occhi*) to turn, direct; (*innalzare: antenna, muro*) to erect; ~**rsi** *vr* to stand up; ~ **le orecchie** to prick up one's ears; ~**rsi in piedi** to rise to one's feet; ~**rsi a sedere** to sit up.

'droga, ghe *sf* (*sostanza aromatica*) spice; (*stupefacente*) drug; ~**ghe pesanti/leggere** hard/soft drugs.

dro'gare *vt* to season, spice; to drug, dope; ~**rsi** *vr* to take drugs.

dro'gato, a *sm/f* drug addict.

droghe'ria [droge'ria] *sf* grocer's (shop) (*BRIT*), grocery (store) (*US*).

drogherò *etc* [droge'rɔ] *vb vedi* **drogare.**

droghi'ere, a [dro'gjɛre] *sm/f* grocer.

drome'dario *sm* dromedary.

D.T. *abbr* = **direttore tecnico.**

'dubbio, a *ag* (*incerto*) doubtful, dubious; (*ambiguo*) dubious ♦ *sm* (*incertezza*) doubt; **avere il** ~ **che** to be afraid that, suspect that; **essere in** ~ **fra** to hesitate between; **mettere in** ~ **qc** to question sth; **nutrire seri** ~**i su qc** to have grave doubts about sth; **senza** ~ doubtless, no doubt.

dubbi'oso, a *ag* doubtful, dubious.

dubi'tare *vi*: ~ **di** (*onestà*) to doubt; (*risultato*) to be doubtful of; ~ **di qn** to mistrust sb; ~ **di sé** to be unsure of o.s.

Du'blino *sf* Dublin.

'duca, chi *sm* duke.

'duce ['dutʃe] *sm* (*STORIA*) captain; (: *del fascismo*) duce.

du'chessa [du'kessa] *sf* duchess.

'due *num* two; **a** ~ **a** ~ two at a time, two by two; **dire** ~ **parole** to say a few words; **ci metto** ~ **minuti** I'll have it done in a tick (*BRIT*) *o* jiffy.

duecen'tesco, a, schi, sche [duetʃen'tesko] *ag* thirteenth-century.

due'cento [due'tʃɛnto] *num* two hundred ♦ *sm*: **il D**~ the thirteenth century.

duel'lare *vi* to fight a duel.

du'ello *sm* duel.

due'mila *num* two thousand ♦ *sm inv*: **il** ~ the year two thousand.

due'pezzi [due'pɛttsi] *sm* (*costume da bagno*) two-piece swimsuit; (*abito femminile*) two-piece suit.

du'etto *sm* duet.

'dulcis in 'fundo ['dultʃisin'fundo] *av* to cap it all.

'duna *sf* dune.

'dunque *cong* (*perciò*) so, therefore; (*riprendendo il discorso*) well (then) ♦ *sm*

inv: **venire al** ~ to come to the point.
'duo *sm inv* (*MUS*) duet; (*TEAT, CINE, fig*) duo.
du'ole *etc vb vedi* **dolere**.
du'omo *sm* cathedral.
'duplex *sm inv* (*TEL*) party line.
dupli'cato *sm* duplicate.
'duplice ['duplitʃe] *ag* double, twofold; **in** ~
  copia in duplicate.
duplicità [duplitʃi'ta] *sf* (*fig*) duplicity.
du'rante *prep* during; **vita natural** ~ for
  life.
du'rare *vi* to last; **non può** ~! this can't go
  on any longer!; ~ **fatica a** to have
  difficulty in; ~ **in carica** to remain in
  office.
du'rata *sf* length (of time); duration; **per**
  tutta la ~ **di** throughout; ~ **media della**
  vita life expectancy.
dura'turo, a *ag*, **du'revole** *ag* (*ricordo*)
  lasting; (*materiale*) durable.
du'rezza [du'rettsa] *sf* hardness;
  stubbornness; harshness; toughness.
'duro, a *ag* (*pietra, lavoro, materasso,*
  problema) hard; (*persona: ostinato*)
  stubborn, obstinate; (: *severo*) harsh,
  hard; (*voce*) harsh; (*carne*) tough ♦ *sm/f*
  (*persona*) tough one ♦ *av*: **tener** ~ (*resistere*)
  to stand firm, hold out; **avere la pelle** ~**a**
  (*fig: persona*) to be tough; **fare il** ~ to act
  tough; ~ **di comprendonio** slow-witted; ~
  d'orecchi hard of hearing.
du'rone *sm* hard skin.
'duttile *ag* (*sostanza*) malleable; (*fig:*
  carattere) docile, biddable; (: *stile*)
  adaptable.

E e

E, e [e] *sf o m inv* (*lettera*) E, e; **E come Empoli**
  ≈ E for Edward (*BRIT*), E for Easy (*US*).
E *abbr* (= *est*) E; (*AUT*) = *itinerario europeo*.
e, *dav V spesso* **ed** *cong* and; (*avversativo*) but;
  (*eppure*) and yet; ~ **lui?** what about him?;
  ~ **compralo!** well buy it then!
è *vb vedi* **essere**.
E.A. *abbr* = *ente autonomo*.
E.A.D. *sigla f vedi* **elaborazione automatica**
  dei dati.
ebaniste'ria *sf* cabinet-making; (*negozio*)
  cabinet-maker's shop.
'ebano *sm* ebony.

eb'bene *cong* well (then).
'ebbi *etc vb vedi* **avere**.
eb'brezza [eb'brettsa] *sf* intoxication.
'ebbro, a *ag* drunk; ~ **di** (*gioia etc*) beside
  o.s. ~ wild with.
'ebete *ag* stupid, idiotic.
ebe'tismo *sm* stupidity.
ebollizi'one [ebollit'tsjone] *sf* boiling;
  punto di ~ boiling point.
e'braico, a, ci, che *ag* Hebrew, Hebraic
  ♦ *sm* (*LING*) Hebrew.
e'breo, a *ag* Jewish ♦ *sm/f* Jew/Jewess.
'Ebridi *sfpl*: **le (isole)** ~ the Hebrides.
e'burneo, a *ag* ivory *cpd*.
E/C *abbr* = *estratto conto*.
eca'tombe *sf* (*strage*) slaughter, massacre.
ecc. *abbr av* (= *eccetera*) etc.
ecce'dente [ettʃe'dɛnte] *sm* surplus.
ecce'denza [ettʃe'dɛntsa] *sf* excess,
  surplus; (*INFORM*) overflow.
ec'cedere [et'tʃedere] *vt* to exceed ♦ *vi* to go
  too far; ~ **nel bere/mangiare** to indulge in
  drink/food to excess.
eccel'lente [ettʃel'lɛnte] *ag* excellent;
  (*cadavere, arresto*) of a prominent person.
eccel'lenza [ettʃel'lɛntsa] *sf* excellence;
  (*titolo*): **Sua E**~ His Excellency.
ec'cellere [et'tʃellere] *vi*: ~ (**in**) to excel
  (at); ~ **su tutti** to surpass everyone.
ec'celso, a [et'tʃelso] *pp di* **eccellere** ♦ *ag*
  (*cima, montagna*) high; (*fig: ingegno*) great,
  exceptional.
ec'centrico, a, ci, che [et'tʃɛntriko] *ag*
  eccentric.
ecces'sivo, a [ettʃes'sivo] *ag* excessive.
ec'cesso [et'tʃɛsso] *sm* excess; **all'**~
  (*gentile, generoso*) to excess, excessively;
  dare in ~**i** to fly into a rage; ~ **di velocità**
  (*AUT*) speeding; ~ **di zelo**
  overzealousness.
ec'cetera [et'tʃetera] *av* et cetera, and so
  on.
ec'cetto [et'tʃetto] *prep* except, with the
  exception of; ~ **che** *cong* except, other
  than; ~ **che (non)** unless.
eccettu'are [ettʃettu'are] *vt* to except;
  eccettuati i presenti present company
  excepted.
eccezio'nale [ettʃettsjo'nale] *ag*
  exceptional; **in via del tutto** ~ in this
  instance, exceptionally.
eccezi'one [ettʃet'tsjone] *sf* exception;
  (*DIR*) objection; **a** ~ **di** with the exception
  of, except for; **d'**~ exceptional; **fare un'**~
  alla regola to make an exception to the
  rule.
ec'chimosi [ek'kimozi] *sf inv* bruise.
ec'cidio [et'tʃidjo] *sm* massacre.

ecci'tante [ettʃi'tante] ag (gen) exciting; (sostanza) stimulating ♦ sm stimulant.

ecci'tare [ettʃi'tare] vt (curiosità, interesse) to excite, arouse; (folla) to incite; ~rsi vr to get excited; (sessualmente) to become aroused.

eccitazi'one [ettʃitat'tsjone] sf excitement.

ecclesi'astico, a, ci, che ag ecclesiastical, church cpd; clerical ♦ sm ecclesiastic.

'ecco av (per dimostrare): ~ il treno! here's o here comes the train!; (dav pronome): ~mi! here I am!; ~ne uno! here's one (of them)!; (dav pp): ~ fatto! there, that's it done!

ec'come av rather; ti piace? — ~! do you like it? — I'll say! o and how! o rather! (BRIT).

ECG sigla m = elettrocardiogramma.

echeggi'are [eked'dʒare] vi to echo.

e'clettico, a, ci, che ag, sm/f eclectic.

eclet'tismo sm eclecticism.

eclis'sare vt to eclipse; (fig) to eclipse, overshadow; ~rsi vr (persona: scherzoso) to slip away.

e'clissi sf eclipse.

'eco, pl(m) 'echi sm o f echo; suscitò o ebbe una profonda ~ it caused quite a stir.

ecogra'fia sf (MED) ultrasound.

ecolo'gia [ekolo'dʒia] sf ecology.

eco'logico, a, ci, che [eko'lɔdʒiko] ag ecological.

ecolo'gista, i, e [ekolo'dʒista] ag ecological ♦ sm/f ecologist, environmentalist.

e'cologo, a, gi, ghe sm/f ecologist.

econo'mato sm (INS) bursar's office.

econo'mia sf economy; (scienza) economics sg; (risparmio: azione) saving; fare ~ to economize, make economies; l'~ sommersa the black (BRIT) o underground (US) economy; ~ di mercato market economy; ~ pianificata planned economy.

eco'nomico, a, ci, che ag economic; (poco costoso) economical; edizione ~a economy edition.

econo'mista, i sm economist.

economiz'zare [ekonomid'dzare] vt, vi to save.

e'conomo, a ag thrifty ♦ sm/f (INS) bursar.

ecosis'tema, i sm ecosystem.

'ECU, 'ecu abbr m inv (= European Currency Unit) ECU, ecu.

'Ecuador sm: l'~ Ecuador.

ecu'menico, a, ci, che ag ecumenical.

ec'zema [ek'dzɛma] sm eczema.

ed cong vedi e.

Ed. abbr = editore.

ed. abbr = edizione.

'edera sf ivy.

e'dicola sf newspaper kiosk o stand (US).

edico'lante sm/f news vendor (in kiosk).

edifi'cante ag edifying.

edifi'care vt to build; (fig: teoria, azienda) to establish; (indurre al bene) to edify.

edi'ficio [edi'fitʃo] sm building; (fig) structure.

e'dile ag building cpd.

edi'lizio, a [edi'littsjo] ag building cpd ♦ sf building, building trade.

Edim'burgo sf Edinburgh.

'edito, a ag published.

edi'tore, 'trice ag publishing cpd ♦ sm/f publisher; (curatore) editor.

edito'ria sf publishing.

editori'ale ag publishing cpd ♦ sm (articolo di fondo) editorial, leader.

e'ditto sm edict.

edizi'one [edit'tsjone] sf edition; (tiratura) printing; ~ a tiratura limitata limited edition.

edo'nismo sm hedonism.

e'dotto, a ag informed; rendere qn ~ su qc to inform sb about sth.

edu'canda sf boarder.

edu'care vt to educate; (gusto, mente) to train; ~ qn a fare to train sb to do.

educa'tivo, a ag educational.

edu'cato, a ag polite, well-mannered.

educazi'one [edukat'tsjone] sf education; (familiare) upbringing; (comportamento) (good) manners pl; per ~ out of politeness; questa è pura mancanza d'~! this is sheer bad manners!; ~ fisica (INS) physical training o education.

educherò etc [eduke'rɔ] vb vedi educare.

E.E.D. sigla f vedi elaborazione elettronica dei dati.

EEG sigla m = elettroencefalogramma.

e'felide sf freckle.

effemi'nato, a ag effeminate.

effe'rato, a ag brutal, savage.

efferve'scente [efferveʃ'ʃɛnte] ag effervescent.

effettiva'mente av (in effetti) in fact; (a dire il vero) really, actually.

effet'tivo, a ag (reale) real, actual; (impiegato, professore) permanent; (MIL) regular ♦ sm (MIL) strength; (di patrimonio etc) sum total.

ef'fetto sm effect; (COMM: cambiale) bill; (fig: impressione) impression; far ~ (medicina) to take effect, (start to) work; cercare l'~ to seek attention; in ~i in fact; ~i attivi (COMM) bills receivable; ~i passivi (COMM) bills payable; ~i personali personal effects, personal belongings; ~

serra greenhouse effect; ~**i speciali** (*CINE*) special effects.
effettu'are *vt* to effect, carry out.
effi'cace [effi'katʃe] *ag* effective.
effi'cacia [effi'katʃa] *sf* effectiveness.
effici'ente [effi'tʃɛnte] *ag* efficient.
efficien'tismo [effitʃen'tizmo] *sm* maximum efficiency.
effici'enza [effi'tʃɛntsa] *sf* efficiency.
effigi'are [effi'dʒare] *vt* to represent, portray.
ef'figie [ef'fidʒe] *sf inv* effigy.
ef'fimero, a *ag* ephemeral.
ef'fluvio *sm* (*anche peg, ironico*) scent, perfume.
effusi'one *sf* effusion.
e.g. *abbr* (= *exempli gratia*) e.g.
egemo'nia [edʒemo'nia] *sf* hegemony.
E'geo [e'dʒɛo] *sm*: **l'~, il mare ~** the Aegean (Sea).
'egida ['ɛdʒida] *sf*: **sotto l'~ di** under the aegis of.
E'gitto [e'dʒitto] *sm*: **l'~** Egypt.
egizi'ano, a [edʒit'tsjano] *ag, sm/f* Egyptian.
e'gizio, a [e'dʒittsjo] *ag, sm/f* (ancient) Egyptian.
'egli ['eʎʎi] *pron* he; **~ stesso** he himself.
'ego *sm inv* (*PSIC*) ego.
ego'centrico, a, ci, che [ego'tʃɛntriko] *ag* egocentric(al) ♦ *sm/f* self-centred (*BRIT*) o self-centered (*US*) person.
egocen'trismo [egotʃen'trizmo] *sm* egocentricity.
ego'ismo *sm* selfishness, egoism.
ego'ista, i, e *ag* selfish, egoistic ♦ *sm/f* egoist.
ego'istico, a, ci, che *ag* egoistic, selfish.
ego'tismo *sm* egotism.
ego'tista, i, e *ag* egotistic ♦ *sm/f* egotist.
Egr. *abbr* = **Egregio.**
e'gregio, a, gi, gie [e'grɛdʒo] *ag* distinguished; (*nelle lettere*): **E~ Signore** Dear Sir.
eguagli'anza *etc* [egwaʎ'ʎantsa] *vedi* **uguaglianza** *etc*.
eguali'tario, a *ag, sm/f* egalitarian.
E.I. *abbr* = *Esercito Italiano*.
eiaculazi'one [ejakulat'tsjone] *sf* ejaculation; **~ precoce** premature ejaculation.
elabo'rare *vt* (*progetto*) to work out, elaborate; (*dati*) to process; (*digerire*) to digest.
elabora'tore *sm* (*INFORM*): **~ elettronico** computer.
elaborazi'one [elaborat'tsjone] *sf* elaboration; processing; digestion; **~ automatica dei dati (E.A.D.)** (*INFORM*)

automatic data processing (A.D.P.); **~ elettronica dei dati (E.E.D.)** (*INFORM*) electronic data processing (E.D.P.); **~ testi** (*INFORM*) text processing.
elar'gire [elar'dʒire] *vt* to hand out.
elargizi'one [elardʒit'tsjone] *sf* donation.
elasticiz'zato, a [elastitʃid'dzato] *ag* (*tessuto*) stretch *cpd*.
e'lastico, a, ci, che *ag* elastic; (*fig: andatura*) springy; (: *decisione, vedute*) flexible ♦ *sm* (*gommino*) rubber band; (*per il cucito*) elastic *no pl*.
ele'fante *sm* elephant.
ele'gante *ag* elegant.
ele'ganza [ele'gantsa] *sf* elegance.
e'leggere [e'lɛddʒere] *vt* to elect.
elemen'tare *ag* elementary; **le (scuole) ~i** *vedi* **scuola elementare; prima ~** first year of primary school, ≈ infants' class (*BRIT*), ≈ 1st grade (*US*).
ele'mento *sm* element; (*parte componente*) element, component, part; **~i** *smpl* (*della scienza etc*) elements, rudiments.
ele'mosina *sf* charity, alms *pl*; **chiedere l'~** to beg.
elemosi'nare *vt* to beg for, ask for ♦ *vi* to beg.
elen'care *vt* to list.
elencherò *etc* [elenke'rɔ] *vb vedi* **elencare.**
e'lenco, chi *sm* list; **~ nominativo** list of names; **~ telefonico** telephone directory.
e'lessi *etc vb vedi* **eleggere.**
elet'tivo, a *ag* (*carica etc*) elected.
e'letto, a *pp di* **eleggere** ♦ *sm/f* (*nominato*) elected member.
eletto'rale *ag* electoral, election *cpd*.
eletto'rato *sm* electorate.
elet'tore, 'trice *sm/f* voter, elector.
elet'trauto *sm inv* workshop for car electrical repairs; (*tecnico*) car electrician.
elettri'cista, i [elettri'tʃista] *sm* electrician.
elettricità [elettritʃi'ta] *sf* electricity.
e'lettrico, a, ci, che *ag* electric(al).
elettrifi'care *vt* to electrify.
elettriz'zante [elettrid'dzante] *ag* (*fig*) electrifying, thrilling.
elettriz'zare [elettrid'dzare] *vt* to electrify; **~rsi** *vr* to become charged with electricity; (*fig: persona*) to be thrilled.
e'lettro... *prefisso* electro....
elettrocardio'gramma, i *sm* electrocardiogram.
e'lettrodo *sm* electrode.
elettrodo'mestico, a, ci, che *ag*: **apparecchi ~ci** domestic (electrical) appliances.
elettroencefalo'gramma, i

[elettroentʃefalo'gramma] *sm* electroencephalogram.

elet'trogeno, a [elet'trɔdʒeno] *ag*: **gruppo ~ generator.**

elet'trolisi *sf* electrolysis.

elettroma'gnetico, a, ci, che [elettromaɲ'ɲetiko] *ag* electromagnetic.

elettromo'trice [elettromo'tritʃe] *sf* electric train.

elet'trone *sm* electron.

elet'tronico, a, ci, che *ag* electronic ♦ *sf* electronics *sg*.

elettro'shock [elettroʃ'ʃɔk] *sm inv* (electro)shock treatment.

elettro'tecnico, a, ci, che *ag* electrotechnical ♦ *sm* electrical engineer.

ele'vare *vt* to raise; (*edificio*) to erect; (*multa*) to impose; **~ un numero al quadrato** to square a number.

eleva'tezza [eleva'tettsa] *sf* (*altezza*) elevation; (*di animo, pensiero*) loftiness.

ele'vato, a *ag* (*gen*) high; (*cime*) high, lofty; (*fig: stile, sentimenti*) lofty.

elevazi'one [elevat'tsjone] *sf* elevation; (*l'elevare*) raising.

elezi'one [elet'tsjone] *sf* election; **~i** *sfpl* (*POL*) election(s); **patria d'~** chosen country.

'elica, che *sf* propeller.

eli'cottero *sm* helicopter.

e'lidere *vt* (*FONETICA*) to elide; **~rsi** *vr* (*forze*) to cancel each other out.

elimi'nare *vt* to eliminate.

elimina'toria *sf* eliminating round.

eliminazi'one [eliminat'tsjone] *sf* elimination.

'elio *sm* helium.

eli'porto *sm* heliport.

elisabetti'ano, a *ag* Elizabethan.

eli'sir *sm inv* elixir.

e'liso, a *pp di* **elidere.**

elisoc'corso *sm* helicopter ambulance.

eli'tario, a *ag* elitist.

é'lite [e'lit] *sf inv* élite.

'ella *pron* she; (*forma di cortesia*) you; **~ stessa** she herself; you yourself.

el'lisse *sf* ellipse.

el'littico, a, ci, che *ag* elliptic(al).

el'metto *sm* helmet.

'elmo *sm* helmet.

elogi'are [elo'dʒare] *vt* to praise.

elogia'tivo, a [elodʒa'tivo] *ag* laudatory.

e'logio [e'lɔdʒo] *sm* (*discorso, scritto*) eulogy; (*lode*) praise; **~ funebre** funeral oration.

elo'quente *ag* eloquent; **questi dati sono ~i** these facts speak for themselves.

elo'quenza [elo'kwɛntsa] *sf* eloquence.

e'loquio *sm* speech, language.

elucu'brare *vt* (*piano*) to ponder about, ponder over.

elucubrazi'oni [elukubrat'tsjoni] *sfpl* (*anche ironico*) cogitations, ponderings.

e'ludere *vt* to evade.

e'lusi *etc vb vedi* **eludere.**

elusi'one *sf*: **~ d'imposta** tax evasion.

elu'sivo, a *ag* evasive.

e'luso, a *pp di* **eludere.**

el'vetico, a, ci, che *ag* Swiss.

emaci'ato, a [ema't ʃato] *ag* emaciated.

ema'nare *vt* to send out, give off; (*fig: leggi*) to promulgate; (: *decreti*) to issue ♦ *vi*: **~ da** to come from.

emanazi'one [emanat'tsjone] *sf* (*di raggi, calore*) emanation; (*di odori*) exhalation; (*di legge*) promulgation; (*di ordine, circolare*) issuing.

emanci'pare [emantʃi'pare] *vt* to emancipate; **~rsi** *vr* (*fig*) to become liberated *o* emancipated.

emancipazi'one [emantʃipat'tsjone] *sf* emancipation.

emargi'nare [emardʒi'nare] *vt* (*fig: socialmente*) to cast out.

emargi'nato, a [emardʒi'nato] *sm/f* outcast.

ematolo'gia [ematolo'dʒia] *sf* haematology (*BRIT*), hematology (*US*).

ema'toma, i *sm* haematoma (*BRIT*), hematoma (*US*).

em'blema, i *sm* emblem.

emble'matico, a, ci, che *ag* emblematic; (*fig: atteggiamento, parole*) symbolic.

embo'lia *sf* embolism.

embrio'nale, i, e *ag* embryonic, embryo *cpd*; **allo stadio ~** at the embryo stage.

embri'one *sm* embryo.

emenda'mento *sm* amendment.

emen'dare *vt* to amend.

emer'gente [emer'dʒɛnte] *ag* emerging.

emer'genza [emer'dʒɛntsa] *sf* emergency; **in caso di ~** in an emergency.

e'mergere [e'mɛrdʒere] *vi* to emerge; (*sommergibile*) to surface; (*fig: distinguersi*) to stand out.

e'merito, a *ag* (*insigne*) distinguished; **è un ~ cretino!** he's a complete idiot!

e'mersi *etc vb vedi* **emergere.**

e'merso, a *pp di* **emergere** ♦ *ag* (*GEO*): **terre ~e** lands above sea level.

e'messo, a *pp di* **emettere.**

e'mettere *vt* (*suono, luce*) to give out, emit; (*onde radio*) to send out; (*assegno, francobollo, ordine*) to issue; (*fig: giudizio*) to express, voice; **~ la sentenza** (*DIR*) to pass sentence.

emi'crania *sf* migraine.

emi'grante *ag, sm/f* emigrant.
emi'grare *vi* to emigrate.
emi'grato, a *ag* emigrant ◊ *sm/f* emigrant; (*STORIA*) émigré.
emigrazi'one [emigrat'tsjone] *sf* emigration.
emili'ano, a *ag* of (*o* from) Emilia.
emi'nente *ag* eminent, distinguished.
emi'nenza [emi'nɛntsa] *sf* eminence; ~ grigia (*fig*) éminence grise.
emi'rato *sm* emirate; gli E~i Arabi Uniti the United Arab Emirates.
e'miro *sm* emir.
emis'fero *sm* hemisphere; ~ boreale/australe northern/southern hemisphere.
e'misi *etc vb vedi* emettere.
emis'sario *sm* (*GEO*) outlet, effluent; (*inviato*) emissary.
emissi'one *sf* (*vedi emettere*) emission; sending out; issue; (*RADIO*) broadcast.
emit'tente *ag* (*banca*) issuing; (*RADIO*) broadcasting, transmitting ◊ *sf* (*RADIO*) transmitter.
emofi'lia *sf* haemophilia (*BRIT*), hemophilia (*US*).
emofi'liaco, a, ci, che *ag, sm/f* haemophiliac (*BRIT*), hemophiliac (*US*).
emoglo'bina *sf* haemoglobin (*BRIT*), hemoglobin (*US*).
emolli'ente *ag* soothing.
emorra'gia, 'gie [emorra'dʒia] *sf* haemorrhage (*BRIT*), hemorrhage (*US*).
emor'roidi *sfpl* haemorrhoids (*BRIT*), hemorrhoids (*US*).
emos'tatico, a, ci, che *ag* haemostatic (*BRIT*), hemostatic (*US*); laccio ~ tourniquet; matita ~a styptic pencil.
emotività *sf* emotionalism.
emo'tivo, a *ag* emotional.
emozio'nante [emottsjo'nante] *ag* exciting, thrilling.
emozio'nare [emottsjo'nare] *vt* (*appassionare*) to thrill, excite; (*commuovere*) to move; (*innervosire*) to upset; ~rsi *vr* to be excited; to be moved; to be upset.
emozi'one [emot'tsjone] *sf* emotion; (*agitazione*) excitement.
'empio, a *ag* (*sacrilego*) impious; (*spietato*) cruel, pitiless; (*malvagio*) wicked, evil.
em'pirico, a, ci, che *ag* empirical.
em'porio *sm* general store.
emu'lare *vt* to emulate.
'emulo, a *sm/f* imitator.
emulsi'one *sf* emulsion.
EN *sigla* = Enna.
en'ciclica, che [en'tʃiklika] *sf* (*REL*) encyclical.
enciclope'dia [entʃiklope'dia] *sf* encyclop(a)edia.
encomi'abile *ag* commendable, praiseworthy.
encomi'are *vt* to commend, praise.
en'comio *sm* commendation; ~ solenne (*MIL*) mention in dispatches.
endove'noso, a *ag* (*MED*) intravenous ◊ *sf* intravenous injection.
E'NEA *sigla f* = Comitato nazionale per la ricerca e lo sviluppo dell'Energia Nucleare e delle Energie Alternative.
'E.N.E.L. *sigla m* (= *Ente Nazionale per l'Energia Elettrica*) national electricity company.
ener'getico, a, ci, che [ener'dʒɛtiko] *ag* (*risorse, crisi*) energy *cpd*; (*sostanza, alimento*) energy-giving.
ener'gia, 'gie [ener'dʒia] *sf* (*FISICA*) energy; (*fig*) energy, strength, vigour (*BRIT*), vigor (*US*).
e'nergico, a, ci, che [e'nɛrdʒiko] *ag* energetic, vigorous.
'enfasi *sf* emphasis, (*peg*) bombast, pomposity.
en'fatico, a, ci, che *ag* emphatic; pompous.
enfatiz'zare [enfatid'dzare] *vt* to emphasize, stress.
enfi'sema *sm* emphysema.
'ENI *sigla m* = Ente Nazionale Idrocarburi.
e'nigma, i *sm* enigma.
enig'matico, a, ci, che *ag* enigmatic.
'ENIT *sigla m* (= *Ente Nazionale Italiano per il Turismo*) Italian tourist authority.
en'nesimo, a *ag* (*MAT, fig*) nth; per l'~a volta for the umpteenth time.
enolo'gia [enolo'dʒia] *sf* oenology (*BRIT*), enology (*US*).
e'nologo, gi *sm* wine expert.
e'norme *ag* enormous, huge.
enormità *sf inv* enormity, huge size; (*assurdità*) absurdity; non dire ~! don't talk nonsense!
eno'teca, che *sf* (*negozio*) wine bar.
'E.N.P.A. *sigla m* (= *Ente Nazionale Protezione Animali*) ≈ RSPCA (*BRIT*), ≈ SPCA (*US*).
'E.N.P.A.S. *sigla m* (= *Ente Nazionale di Previdenza e Assistenza per i Dipendenti Statali*) welfare organization for State employees.
'ente *sm* (*istituzione*) body, board, corporation; (*FILOSOFIA*) being; ~ locale local authority (*BRIT*), local government (*US*); ~ pubblico public body; ~ di ricerca research organization.
ente'rite *sf* enteritis.

entità *sf* (*FILOSOFIA*) entity; (*di perdita, danni, investimenti*) extent; (*di popolazione*) size; **di molta/poca** ~ (*avvenimento, incidente*) of great/little importance.

en'trambi, e *pron pl* both (of them) ♦ *ag pl*: ~ **i ragazzi** both boys, both of the boys.

en'trante *ag* (*prossimo: mese, anno*) next, coming.

en'trare *vi* to enter, go (*o* come) in; ~ **in** (*luogo*) to enter, go (*o* come) into; (*trovar posto, poter stare*) to fit into; (*essere ammesso a: club etc*) to join, become a member of; ~ **in automobile** to get into the car; **far** ~ **qn** (*visitatore etc*) to show sb in; ~ **in società/in commercio con qn** to go into partnership/business with sb; **questo non c'entra** (*fig*) that's got nothing to do with it.

en'trata *sf* entrance, entry; ~**e** *sfpl* (*COMM*) receipts, takings; (*ECON*) income *sg*; "~ **libera**" "admission free"; **con l'**~ **in vigore dei nuovi provvedimenti** ... once the new measures come into effect ...; ~**e tributarie** tax revenue *sg*.

'entro *prep* (*temporale*) within; ~ **domani** by tomorrow; ~ **e non oltre il 25 aprile** no later than 25th April.

entro'terra *sm inv* hinterland.

entusias'mante *ag* exciting.

entusias'mare *vt* to excite, fill with enthusiasm; ~**rsi** *vr*: ~**rsi (per qc/qn)** to become enthusiastic (about sth/sb).

entusi'asmo *sm* enthusiasm.

entusi'asta, i, e *ag* enthusiastic ♦ *sm/f* enthusiast.

entusi'astico, a, ci, che *ag* enthusiastic.

enucle'are *vt* (*formale: chiarire*) to explain.

enume'rare *vt* to enumerate, list.

enunci'are [enun'tʃare] *vt* (*teoria*) to enunciate, set out.

en'zima, i *sm* enzyme.

e'patico, a, ci, che *ag* hepatic; **cirrosi** ~**a** cirrhosis of the liver.

epa'tite *sf* hepatitis.

'epico, a, ci, che *ag* epic.

epide'mia *sf* epidemic.

epi'dermico, a, ci, che *ag* (*ANAT*) skin *cpd*; (*fig: interesse, impressioni*) superficial.

epi'dermide *sf* skin, epidermis.

Epifa'nia *sf* Epiphany.

e'pigono *sm* imitator.

e'pigrafe *sf* epigraph; (*su libro*) dedication.

epiles'sia *sf* epilepsy.

epi'lettico, a, ci, che *ag, sm/f* epileptic.

e'pilogo, ghi *sm* conclusion.

epi'sodico, a, ci, che *ag* (*romanzo, narrazione*) episodic; (*fig: occasionale*) occasional.

epi'sodio *sm* episode; **sceneggiato a** ~**i** serial.

e'pistola *sf* epistle.

episto'lare *ag* epistolary; **essere in rapporto** *o* **relazione** ~ **con qn** to correspond *o* be in correspondence with sb.

e'piteto *sm* epithet.

'epoca, che *sf* (*periodo storico*) age, era; (*tempo*) time; (*GEO*) age; **mobili d'**~ period furniture; **fare** ~ (*scandalo*) to cause a stir; (*cantante, moda*) to mark a new era.

epo'pea *sf* (*anche fig*) epic.

ep'pure *cong* and yet, nevertheless.

EPT *sigla m* (= *Ente Provinciale per il Turismo*) district tourist bureau.

epu'rare *vt* (*POL*) to purge.

equ'anime *ag* (*imparziale*) fair, impartial.

equa'tore *sm* equator.

equazi'one [ekwat'tsjone] *sf* (*MAT*) equation.

e'questre *ag* equestrian.

equi'latero, a *ag* equilateral.

equili'brare *vt* to balance.

equili'brato, a *ag* (*carico, fig: giudizio*) balanced; (*vita*) well-regulated; (*persona*) stable, well-balanced.

equi'librio *sm* balance, equilibrium; **perdere l'**~ to lose one's balance; **stare in** ~ **su** (*persona*) to balance on; (*oggetto*) to be balanced on.

equili'brismo *sm* tightrope walking; (*fig*) juggling.

e'quino, a *ag* horse *cpd*, equine.

equi'nozio [ekwi'nɔttsjo] *sm* equinox.

equipaggia'mento [ekwipaddʒa'mento] *sm* (*operazione: di nave*) equipping, fitting out; (: *di spedizione, esercito*) equipping, kitting out; (*attrezzatura*) equipment.

equipaggi'are [ekwipad'dʒare] *vt* to equip; ~**rsi** *vr* to equip o.s.

equi'paggio [ekwi'paddʒo] *sm* crew.

equipa'rare *vt* to make equal.

é'quipe [e'kip] *sf* (*SPORT, gen*) team.

equità *sf* equity, fairness.

equitazi'one [ekwitat'tsjone] *sf* (horse-) riding.

equiva'lente *ag, sm* equivalent.

equiva'lenza [ekwiva'lɛntsa] *sf* equivalence.

equiva'lere *vi*: ~ **a** to be equivalent to; ~**rsi** *vr* (*forze etc*) to counterbalance each other; (*soluzioni*) to amount to the same thing; **equivale a dire che** ... that is the same as saying that ....

equi'valso, a *pp di* equivalere.

equivo'care *vi* to misunderstand.

e'quivoco, a, ci, che *ag* equivocal, ambiguous; (*sospetto*) dubious ♦ *sm* misunderstanding; a scanso di ~ci to avoid any misunderstanding; giocare sull'~ to equivocate.

'equo, a *ag* fair, just.

'era *sf* era.

'era *etc vb vedi* essere.

erari'ale *ag*: ufficio ~ ≈ tax office; imposte ~i revenue taxes; spese ~i public expenditure *sg*.

e'rario *sm*: l'~ ≈ the Treasury.

'erba *sf* grass; (*aromatica, medicinale*) herb; in ~ (*fig*) budding; fare di ogni ~ un fascio (*fig*) to lump everything (*o* everybody) together.

er'baccia, ce [cr'battʃa] *sf* weed.

er'bivoro, a *ag* herbivorous ♦ *sm/f* herbivore.

erbo'rista, i, e *sm/f* herbalist.

erborìste'ria *sf* (*scienza*) study of medicinal herbs; (*negozio*) herbalist's (shop).

er'boso, a *ag* grassy.

e'rede *sm/f* heir; ~ legittimo heir-at-law.

eredità *sf* (*DIR*) inheritance; (*BIOL*) heredity; lasciare qc in ~ a qn to leave *o* bequeath sth to sb.

eredi'tare *vt* to inherit.

eredi'tario, a *ag* hereditary.

erediti'era *sf* heiress.

ere'mita, i *sm* hermit.

eremi'taggio [eremi'taddʒo] *sm* hermitage.

'eremo *sm* hermitage; (*fig*) retreat.

ere'sia *sf* heresy.

e'ressi *etc vb vedi* erigere.

e'retico, a, ci, che *ag* heretical ♦ *sm/f* heretic.

e'retto, a *pp di* erigere ♦ *ag* erect, upright.

erezi'one [eret'tsjone] *sf* (*FISIOL*) erection.

ergasto'lano, a *sm/f* prisoner serving a life sentence, lifer (*fam*).

er'gastolo *sm* (*DIR*: *pena*) life imprisonment; (: *luogo di pena*) prison (*for those serving life sentences*).

ergono'mia *sf* ergonomics *sg*.

ergo'nomico, a, ci, che *ag* ergonomic(al).

'erica *sf* heather.

e'rigere [e'ridʒere] *vt* to erect, raise; (*fig*: *fondare*) to found.

eri'tema *sm* (*MED*) inflammation, erythema; ~ solare sunburn.

Eri'trea *sf* Eritrea.

ermel'lino *sm* ermine.

er'metico, a, ci, che *ag* hermetic.

'ernia *sf* (*MED*) hernia; ~ del disco slipped disc.

'ero *vb vedi* essere.

e'rodere *vt* to erode.

e'roe *sm* hero.

ero'gare *vt* (*somme*) to distribute; (*gas, servizi*) to supply.

erogazi'one [erogat'tsjone] *sf* distribution; supply.

e'roico, a, ci, che *ag* heroic.

ero'ina *sf* heroine; (*droga*) heroin.

ero'ismo *sm* heroism.

'eros *sm* Eros.

erosi'one *sf* erosion.

e'roso, a *pp di* erodere.

e'rotico, a, ci, che *ag* erotic.

ero'tismo *sm* eroticism.

'erpete *sm* herpes *sg*.

'erpice ['erpitʃe] *sm* (*AGR*) harrow.

er'rare *vi* (*vagare*) to wander, roam; (*sbagliare*) to be mistaken.

er'roneo, a *ag* erroneous, wrong.

er'rore *sm* error, mistake; (*morale*) error; per ~ by mistake; ~ giudiziario miscarriage of justice.

'erto, a *ag* (very) steep ♦ *sf* steep slope; stare all'~a to be on the alert.

eru'dire *vt* to teach, educate.

eru'dito, a *ag* learned, erudite.

erut'tare *vt* (*sog: vulcano*) to throw out, belch.

eruzi'one [erut'tsjone] *sf* eruption; (*MED*) rash.

es. *abbr* (= *esempio*) e.g.

E.S. *sigla m* (= *elettroshock*) ECT.

E.S.A. ['eza] *sigla m* (= *European Space Agency*) ESA.

esacer'bare [ezatʃer'bare] *vt* to exacerbate.

esage'rare [ezadʒe'rare] *vt* to exaggerate ♦ *vi* to exaggerate; (*eccedere*) to go too far; senza ~ without exaggeration.

esage'rato, a [ezadʒe'rato] *ag* (*notizia, proporzioni*) exaggerated; (*curiosità, pignoleria*) excessive; (*prezzo*) exorbitant ♦ *sm/f*: sei il solito ~ you are exaggerating as usual.

esagerazi'one [esadʒerat'tsjone] *sf* exaggeration.

esago'nale *ag* hexagonal.

e'sagono *sm* hexagon.

esa'lare *vt* (*odori*) to give off ♦ *vi*: ~ (da) to emanate (from); ~ l'ultimo respiro (*fig*) to breathe one's last.

esalazi'one [ezalat'tsjone] *sf* (*emissione*) exhalation; (*odore*) fumes *pl*.

esal'tante *ag* exciting.

esal'tare *vt* to exalt; (*entusiasmare*) to excite, stir; ~rsi *vr*: ~rsi (per qc) to grow excited (about sth).

esal'tato, a *sm/f* fanatic.

esaltazi'one [ezaltat'tsjone] *sf* (*elogio*)

extolling, exalting; (*nervosa*) intense excitement; (*mistica*) exaltation.

e'same *sm* examination; (*INS*) exam, examination; **fare** *o* **dare un** ~ to sit *o* take an exam; **fare un** ~ **di coscienza** to search one's conscience; ~ **di guida** driving test; ~ **del sangue** blood test.

esami'nare *vt* to examine.

e'sangue *ag* bloodless; (*fig*: *pallido*) pale, wan; (: *privo di vigore*) lifeless.

e'sanime *ag* lifeless.

esaspe'rare *vt* to exasperate; (*situazione*) to exacerbate; ~**rsi** *vr* to become annoyed *o* exasperated.

esasperazi'one [ezasperat'tsjone] *sf* exasperation.

esatta'mente *av* exactly; accurately, precisely.

esat'tezza [ezat'tettsa] *sf* exactitude, accuracy, precision; **per l'**~ to be precise.

e'satto, a *pp di* **esigere** ♦ *ag* (*calcolo, ora*) correct, right, exact; (*preciso*) accurate, precise; (*puntuale*) punctual.

esat'tore *sm* (*di imposte etc*) collector.

esatto'ria *sf*: ~ **comunale** district rates office (*BRIT*) *o* assessor's office (*US*).

esau'dire *vt* to grant, fulfil (*BRIT*), fulfill (*US*).

esauri'ente *ag* exhaustive.

esauri'mento *sm* exhaustion; ~ **nervoso** nervous breakdown; **svendita (fino) ad** ~ **della merce** clearance sale.

esau'rire *vt* (*stancare*) to exhaust, wear out; (*provviste, miniera*) to exhaust; ~**rsi** *vr* to exhaust o.s., wear o.s. out; (*provviste*) to run out.

esau'rito, a *ag* exhausted; (*merci*) sold out; (*libri*) out of print; **essere** ~ (*persona*) to be run down; **registrare il tutto** ~ (*TEAT*) to have a full house.

e'sausto, a *ag* exhausted.

esauto'rare *vt* (*dirigente, funzionario*) to deprive of authority.

esazi'one [ezat'tsjone] *sf* collection (of taxes).

'esca, *pl* **'esche** *sf* bait.

escamo'tage [ɛskamɔ'taʒ] *sm* subterfuge.

escande'scenza [eskandeʃ'ʃɛntsa] *sf*: **dare in** ~**e** to lose one's temper, fly into a rage.

'esce ['ɛʃʃe] *vb vedi* **uscire**.

eschi'mese [eski'mese] *ag, sm/f, sm* Eskimo.

'esci ['ɛʃʃi] *vb vedi* **uscire**.

escl. *abbr* (= *escluso*) excl.

escla'mare *vi* to exclaim, cry out.

esclama'tivo, a *ag*: **punto** ~ exclamation mark.

esclamazi'one [esklamat'tsjone] *sf* exclamation.

es'cludere *vt* to exclude.

es'clusi *etc vb vedi* **escludere**.

esclusi'one *sf* exclusion; **a** ~ **di, fatta** ~ **per** except (for), apart from; **senza** ~ **(alcuna)** without exception; **procedere per** ~ to follow a process of elimination; **senza** ~ **di colpi** (*fig*) with no holds barred.

esclu'siva *sf vedi* **esclusivo**.

esclusiva'mente *av* exclusively, solely.

esclu'sivo, a *ag* exclusive ♦ *sf* (*DIR, COMM*) exclusive *o* sole rights *pl*.

es'cluso, a *pp di* **escludere** ♦ *ag*: **nessuno** ~ without exception; **IVA** ~**a** excluding VAT, exclusive of VAT.

'esco *vb vedi* **uscire**.

escogi'tare [eskodʒi'tare] *vt* to devise, think up.

'escono *vb vedi* **uscire**.

escoriazi'one [eskorjat'tsjone] *sf* abrasion, graze.

escre'menti *smpl* excrement *sg*, faeces.

es'cudo *sm* (*pl* ~**s**) escudo.

escursi'one *sf* (*gita*) excursion, trip; (: *a piedi*) hike, walk; (*METEOR*): ~ **termica** temperature range.

escursio'nista, i, e *sm/f* (*gitante*) (day) tripper; (: *a piedi*) hiker, walker.

ese'crare *vt* to loathe, abhor.

esecu'tivo, a *ag, sm* executive.

esecu'tore, 'trice *sm/f* (*MUS*) performer; (*DIR*) executor.

esecuzi'one [ezekut'tsjone] *sf* execution, carrying out; (*MUS*) performance; ~ **capitale** execution.

ese'geta, i [eze'dʒɛta] *sm* commentator.

esegu'ire *vt* to carry out, execute; (*MUS*) to perform, execute.

e'sempio *sm* example; **per** ~ for example, for instance; **fare un** ~ to give an example.

esem'plare *ag* exemplary ♦ *sm* example; (*copia*) copy; (*BOT, ZOOL, GEO*) specimen.

esemplifi'care *vt* to exemplify.

esen'tare *vt*: ~ **qn/qc da** to exempt sb/sth from.

esen'tasse *ag inv* tax-free.

e'sente *ag*: ~ **da** (*dispensato da*) exempt from; (*privo di*) free from.

esenzi'one [ezen'tsjone] *sf* exemption.

e'sequie *sfpl* funeral rites; funeral service *sg*.

eser'cente [ezer'tʃɛnte] *sm/f* trader, dealer; shopkeeper.

eserci'tare [ezertʃi'tare] *vt* (*professione*) to practise (*BRIT*), practice (*US*); (*allenare:*

corpo, mente) to exercise, train; (*diritto*) to exercise; (*influenza, pressione*) to exert; ~**rsi** *vr* to practise; ~**rsi nella guida** to practise one's driving.

esercitazi'one [ezertʃitat'tsjone] *sf* (*scolastica, militare*) exercise; ~**i di tiro** target practice *sg.*

e'sercito [e'zɛrtʃito] *sm* army.

eser'cizio [ezer'tʃittsjo] *sm* practice; (*compito, movimento*) exercise; (*azienda*) business, concern; (*ECON*): ~ **finanziario** financial year; **in** ~ (*medico etc*) practising (*BRIT*), practicing (*US*); **nell'**~ **delle proprie funzioni** in the execution of one's duties.

esfoli'ante *sm* exfoliator.

esi'bire *vt* to exhibit, display; (*documenti*) to produce, present; ~**rsi** *vr* (*attore*) to perform; (*fig*) to show off.

esibizi'one [ezibit'tsjone] *sf* exhibition; (*di documento*) presentation; (*spettacolo*) show, performance.

esibizio'nista, i, e [ezibittsjo'nista] *sm/f* exhibitionist.

esi'gente [ezi'dʒɛnte] *ag* demanding.

esi'genza [ezi'dʒɛntsa] *sf* demand, requirement.

e'sigere [e'zidʒere] *vt* (*pretendere*) to demand; (*richiedere*) to demand, require; (*imposte*) to collect.

esi'gibile [ezi'dʒibile] *ag* payable.

e'siguo, a *ag* small, slight.

esila'rante *ag* hilarious; **gas** ~ laughing gas.

'esile *ag* (*persona*) slender, slim; (*stelo*) thin; (*voce*) faint.

esili'are *vt* to exile.

esili'ato, a *ag* exiled ♦ *sm/f* exile.

e'silio *sm* exile.

e'simere *vt*: ~ **qn/qc da** to exempt sb/sth from; ~**rsi** *vr*: ~**rsi da** to get out of.

esis'tente *ag* existing; (*attuale*) present, current.

esis'tenza [ezis'tɛntsa] *sf* existence.

esistenzia'lismo [ezistentsja'lizmo] *sm* existentialism.

e'sistere *vi* to exist; **esiste più di una versione dell'opera** there is more than one version of the work; **non esiste!** (*fam*) no way!

esis'tito, a *pp di* **esistere**.

esi'tante *ag* hesitant; (*voce*) faltering.

esi'tare *vi* to hesitate.

esitazi'one [ezitat'tsjone] *sf* hesitation.

'esito *sm* result, outcome.

'eskimo *sm* (*giaccone*) parka.

'esodo *sm* exodus.

e'sofago, gi *sm* oesophagus (*BRIT*),

esophagus (*US*).

esone'rare *vt*: ~ **qn da** to exempt sb from.

esorbi'tante *ag* exorbitant, excessive.

esor'cismo [ezor'tʃizmo] *sm* exorcism.

esor'cista, i [ezor'tʃista] *sm* exorcist.

esorciz'zare [ezortʃid'dzare] *vt* to exorcize.

esordi'ente *sm/f* beginner.

e'sordio *sm* debut.

esor'dire *vi* (*nel teatro*) to make one's debut; (*fig*) to start out, begin (one's career); **esordì dicendo che ...** he began by saying (that) ....

esor'tare *vt*: ~ **qn a fare** to urge sb to do.

esortazi'one [ezortat'tsjone] *sf* exhortation.

e'soso, a *ag* (*prezzo*) exorbitant; (*persona: avido*) grasping.

eso'terico, a, ci, che *ag* esoteric.

e'sotico, a, ci, che *ag* exotic.

es'pandere *vt* to expand; (*confini*) to extend; (*influenza*) to extend, spread; ~**rsi** *vr* **to** expand.

espansi'one *sf* expansion.

espansività *sf* expansiveness.

espan'sivo, a *ag* expansive, communicative.

es'panso, a *pp di* **espandere**.

espatri'are *vi* to leave one's country.

es'patrio *sm* expatriation; **permesso di** ~ authorization to leave the country.

espedi'ente *sm* expedient; **vivere di** ~**i** to live by one's wits.

es'pellere *vt* to expel.

esperi'enza [espe'rjɛntsa] *sf* experience; (*SCIENZA: prova*) experiment; **parlare per** ~ to speak from experience.

esperi'mento *sm* experiment; **fare un** ~ to carry out *o* do an experiment.

es'perto, a *ag, sm/f* expert.

espi'anto *sm* (*MED*) removal.

espi'are *vt* to atone for.

espiazi'one [espiat'tsjone] *sf*: ~ (**di**) expiation (of), atonement (for).

espi'rare *vt, vi* to breathe out.

espleta'mento *sm* (*AMM*) carrying out.

esple'tare *vt* (*AMM*) to carry out.

espli'care *vt* (*attività*) to carry out, perform.

esplica'tivo, a *ag* explanatory.

es'plicito, a [es'plitʃito] *ag* explicit.

es'plodere *vi* (*anche fig*) to explode ♦ *vt* to fire.

esplo'rare *vt* to explore.

esplora'tore, 'trice *sm/f* explorer; (*anche: giovane* ~) (boy) scout/(girl) guide (*BRIT*) *o* scout (*US*) ♦ *sm* (*NAUT*) scout (ship).

esplorazi'one [esplorat'tsjone] *sf* exploration; **mandare qn in** ~ (*MIL*) to send sb to scout ahead.

esplosi'one *sf* (*anche fig*) explosion.

esplo'sivo, a *ag, sm* explosive.

es'ploso, a *pp di* **esplodere.**

es'pone *etc vb vedi* **esporre.**

espo'nente *sm/f* (*rappresentante*) representative.

esponenzi'ale [esponen'tsjale] *ag* (*MAT*) exponential.

es'pongo, es'poni *etc vb vedi* **esporre.**

es'porre *vt* (*merci*) to display; (*quadro*) to exhibit, show; (*fatti, idee*) to explain, set out; (*porre in pericolo, FOT*) to expose; **esporsi** *vr*: **esporsi a** (*sole, pericolo*) to expose o.s. to; (*critiche*) to lay o.s. open to.

espor'tare *vt* to export.

esporta'tore, 'trice *ag* exporting ♦ *sm* exporter.

esportazi'one [esportat'tsjone] *sf* (*azione*) exportation, export; (*insieme di prodotti*) exports *pl.*

es'pose *etc vb vedi* **esporre.**

espo'simetro *sm* exposure meter.

esposizi'one [espozit'tsjone] *sf* displaying; exhibiting; setting out; (*anche FOT*) exposure; (*mostra*) exhibition; (*narrazione*) explanation, exposition.

es'posto, a *pp di* **esporre** ♦ *ag*: ~ **a nord** facing north, north-facing ♦ *sm* (*AMM*) statement, account; (: *petizione*) petition.

espressi'one *sf* expression.

espres'sivo, a *ag* expressive.

es'presso, a *pp di* **esprimere** ♦ *ag* express ♦ *sm* (*lettera*) express letter; (*anche*: **treno** ~) express train; (*anche*: **caffè** ~) espresso.

es'primere *vt* to express; ~**rsi** *vr* to express o.s.

espropri'are *vt* (*terreni, edifici*) to place a compulsory purchase order on; (*persona*) to dispossess.

espropriazi'one [esproprjat'tsjone] *sf*, **es'proprio** *sm* expropriation; ~ **per pubblica utilità** compulsory purchase.

espu'gnare [espuɲ'ɲare] *vt* to take by force, storm.

es'pulsi *etc vb vedi* **espellere.**

espulsi'one *sf* expulsion.

es'pulso, a *pp di* **espellere.**

'essa *pron f*, **'esse** *pron fpl vedi* **esso.**

es'senza [es'sɛntsa] *sf* essence.

essenzi'ale [essen'tsjale] *ag* essential; (*stile, linea*) simple ♦ *sm*: **l'**~ the main o most important thing.

═══════════════ **PAROLA CHIAVE**

'essere *sm* being; ~ **umano** human being

♦ *vb copulativo* **1** (*con attributo, sostantivo*) to be; **sei giovane/simpatico** you are *o* you're young/nice; **è medico** he is *o* he's a doctor

2 (+ *di: appartenere*) to be; **di chi è la penna?** whose pen is it?; **è di Carla** it is *o* it's Carla's, it belongs to Carla

3 (+ *di: provenire*) to be; **è di Venezia** he is *o* he's from Venice

4 (*data, ora*): **è il 15 agosto** it is *o* it's the 15th of August; **è lunedì** it is *o* it's Monday; **che ora è?, che ore sono?** what time is it?; **è l'una** it is *o* it's one o'clock; **sono le due** it is *o* it's two o'clock

5 (*costare*): **quant'è?** how much is it?; **sono 20.000 lire** it's 20,000 lire

♦ *vb aus* **1** (*attivo*): ~ **arrivato/venuto** to have arrived/come; **è già partita** she has already left

2 (*passivo*) to be; ~ **fatto da** to be made by; **è stata uccisa** she has been killed

3 (*riflessivo*): **si sono lavati** they washed, they got washed

4 (+ *da* + *infinito*): **è da farsi subito** it must be done *o* is to be done immediately

♦ *vi* **1** (*esistere, trovarsi*) to be; **sono a casa** I'm at home; ~ **in piedi/seduto** to be standing/sitting

2 (*succedere*): **sarà quel che sarà** what will be will be; **sia quel che sia, io me ne vado** come what may, I'm going now

3: **esserci**: **c'è** there is; **ci sono** there are; **che c'è?** what's the matter?, what is it?; **non c'è niente da fare** there's nothing we can do; **è da sperare che ...** one can only hope that ...; **ci sono!** (*sono pronto*) I'm ready; (*ho capito*) I get it!; *vedi anche* **ci**

♦ *vb impers*: **è tardi/Pasqua** it's late/Easter; **è mezzanotte** it's midnight; **è bello/caldo/freddo** it's nice/hot/cold; **è possibile che venga** he may come; **è così** that's the way it is.

'essi *pron mpl vedi* **esso.**

essic'care *vt* (*gen*) to dry; (*legname*) to season; (*cibi*) to desiccate; (*bacino, palude*) to drain; ~**rsi** *vr* (*fiume, pozzo*) to dry up; (*vernice*) to dry (out).

'esso, a *pron* it; (*riferito a persona: soggetto*) he/she; (: *complemento*) him/her; ~**i, e** *pron pl* they; (*complemento*) them.

est *sm* east; **i paesi dell'E**~ the Eastern bloc *sg.*

'estasi *sf* ecstasy.

estasi'are *vt* to send into raptures; ~**rsi** *vr*: ~**rsi (davanti a)** to go into ecstasies (over), go into raptures (over).

es'tate *sf* summer.

es'tatico, a, ci, che *ag* ecstatic.

estempo'raneo, a *ag* (*discorso*) extempore, impromptu; (*brano musicale*) impromptu.

es'tendere *vt* to extend; ~**rsi** *vr* (*diffondersi*) to spread; (*territorio, confini*) to extend.

estensi'one *sf* extension; (*di superficie*) expanse; (*di voce*) range.

estenu'ante *ag* wearing, tiring.

estenu'are *vt* (*stancare*) to wear out, tire out.

esteri'ore *ag* outward, external.

esteriorità *sf inv* outward appearance.

esterioriz'zare [esterjorid'dzare] *vt* (*gioia etc*) to show.

ester'nare *vt* to express; ~ **un sospetto to** voice a suspicion.

es'terno, a *ag* (*porta, muro*) outer, outside; (*scala*) outside; (*alunno, impressione*) external ♦ *sm* outside, exterior ♦ *sm/f* (*allievo*) day pupil; "**per uso ~**" "for external use only"; **gli ~i sono stati giratl a Glasgow** (*CINE*) the location shots were taken in Glasgow.

'**estero, a** *ag* foreign ♦ *sm*: **all'~** abroad; **Ministero degli E~i, gli E~i** Ministry for Foreign Affairs, ≈ Foreign Office (*BRIT*), ≈ State Department (*US*).

esterofi'lia *sf* excessive love of foreign things.

esterre'fatto, a *ag* (*costernato*) horrified; (*sbalordito*) astounded.

es'tesi *etc vb vedi* **estendere**.

es'teso, a *pp di* **estendere** ♦ *ag* extensive, large; **scrivere per** ~ to write in full.

estetica'mente *av* aesthetically.

es'tetico, a, ci, che *ag* aesthetic ♦ *sf* (*disciplina*) aesthetics *sg*; (*bellezza*) attractiveness; **chirurgia** ~**a** cosmetic surgery; **cura** ~**a** beauty treatment.

este'tista, i, e *sm/f* beautician.

'**estimo** *sm* valuation; (*disciplina*) surveying.

es'tinguere *vt* to extinguish, put out; (*debito*) to pay off; (*conto*) to close; ~**rsi** *vr* to go out; (*specie*) to become extinct.

es'tinsi *etc vb vedi* **estinguere**.

es'tinto, a *pp di* **estinguere**.

estin'tore *sm* (*fire*) extinguisher.

estinzi'one [estin'tsjone] *sf* putting out; (*di specie*) extinction; (*di debito*) payment; (*di conto*) closing.

estir'pare *vt* (*pianta*) to uproot, pull up; (*dente*) to extract; (*tumore*) to remove;

(*fig: vizio*) to eradicate.

es'tivo, a *ag* summer *cpd*.

'**estone** *ag, sm/f, sm* Estonian.

Es'tonia *sf*: l'~ Estonia.

es'torcere [es'tortʃere] *vt*: ~ **qc (a qn)** to extort sth (from sb).

estorsi'one *sf* extortion.

es'torto, a *pp di* **estorcere**.

estra'dare *vt* to extradite.

estradizi'one [estradit'tsjone] *sf* extradition.

es'trae, es'traggo *etc vb vedi* **estrarre**.

es'traneo, a *ag* foreign; (*discorso*) extraneous, unrelated ♦ *sm/f* stranger; **rimanere** ~ **a qc** to take no part in sth; **sentirsi** ~ **a** (*famiglia, società*) to feel alienated from; "**ingresso vietato agli ~i**" "no admittance to unauthorized personnel".

estrani'arsi *vr*: ~ (**da**) to cut o.s. off (from).

es'trarre *vt* to extract; (*minerali*) to mine; (*sorteggiare*) to draw; ~ **a sorte** to draw lots.

es'trassi *etc vb vedi* **estrarre**.

es'tratto, a *pp di* **estrarre** ♦ *sm* extract; (*di documento*) abstract; ~ **conto** (*bank*) statement; ~ **di nascita** birth certificate.

estrazi'one [estrat'tsjone] *sf* extraction; mining; drawing *no pl*; draw.

estrema'mente *av* extremely.

estre'mismo *sm* extremism.

estre'mista, i, e *sm/f* extremist.

estremità *sf inv* extremity, end ♦ *sfpl* (*ANAT*) extremities.

es'tremo, a *ag* extreme; (*ultimo: ora, tentativo*) final, last ♦ *sm* extreme; (*di pazienza, forza*) limit, end; ~**i** *smpl* (*DIR*) essential elements; (*AMM: dati essenziali*) details, particulars; **l'E~ Oriente** the Far East.

estrinse'care *vt* to express, show.

'**estro** *sm* (*capriccio*) whim, fancy; (*ispirazione creativa*) inspiration.

estro'messo, a *pp di* **estromettere**.

estro'mettere *vt*: ~ (**da**) (*partito, club etc*) to expel (from); (*discussione*) to exclude (from).

estromissi'one *sf* expulsion.

es'troso, a *ag* whimsical, capricious; inspired.

estro'verso, a *ag, sm* extrovert.

estu'ario *sm* estuary.

esube'rante *ag* exuberant; (*COMM*) redundant (*BRIT*).

esube'ranza [ezube'rantsa] *sf* (*di persona*) exuberance; ~ **di personale** (*COMM*) overmanning (*BRIT*), over-staffing (*US*).

e'subero *sm*: ~ **di personale** surplus staff; **in** ~ redundant, due to be laid off.

esu'lare *vi*: ~ **da** (*competenza*) to be beyond; (*compiti*) not to be part of.

'esule *smlf* exile.

esul'tanza [ezul'tantsa] *sf* exultation.

esul'tare *vi* to exult.

esu'mare *vt* (*salma*) to exhume, disinter; (*fig*) to unearth.

età *sf inv* age; **all'**~ **di 8 anni** at the age of 8, at 8 years of age; **ha la mia** ~ he (*o* she) is the same age as me *o* as I am; **di mezza** ~ middle-aged; **raggiungere la maggiore** ~ to come of age; **essere in** ~ **minore** to be under age.

eta'nolo *sm* ethanol.

etc. *abbr* etc.

'etere *sm* ether; **via** ~ on the airwaves.

e'tereo, a *ag* ethereal.

eternità *sf* eternity.

e'terno, a *ag* eternal; (*interminabile*: *lamenti, attesa*) never-ending; **in** ~ for ever.

etero'geneo, a [etero'dʒɛneo] *ag* heterogeneous.

eterosessu'ale *ag*, *smlf* heterosexual.

'etica *sf vedi* **etico.**

eti'chetta [eti'ketta] *sf* label; (*cerimoniale*): **l'**~ etiquette.

'etico, a, ci, che *ag* ethical ♦ *sf* ethics *sg*.

eti'lometro *sm* Breathalyzer ®.

etimolo'gia, 'gie [etimolo'dʒia] *sf* etymology.

etimo'logico, a, ci, che [etimo'lɔdʒiko] *ag* etymological.

e'tiope *ag*, *smlf* Ethiopian.

Eti'opia *sf*: **l'**~ Ethiopia.

eti'opico, a, ci, che *ag*, *sm* (*LING*) Ethiopian.

'Etna *sm*: **l'**~ Etna.

'etnico, a, ci, che *ag* ethnic.

e'trusco, a, schi, sche *ag*, *smlf* Etruscan.

'ettaro *sm* hectare (= *10,000 m²*).

'etto *sm abbr* = **ettogrammo.**

etto'grammo *sm* hectogram(me) (= *100 grams*).

et'tolitro *sm* hectolitre (*BRIT*), hectoliter (*US*).

et'tometro *sm* hectometre.

EU *abbr* = **Europa.**

euca'lipto *sm* eucalyptus.

Eucaris'tia *sf*: **l'**~ the Eucharist.

eufe'mismo *sm* euphemism.

eufe'mistico, a, ci, che *ag* euphemistic.

eufo'ria *sf* euphoria.

eu'forico, a, ci, che *ag* euphoric.

Eu'rasia *sf* Eurasia.

eurasi'atico, a, ci, che *ag*, *smlf* Eurasian.

Eura'tom *sigla f* (= *Comunità Europea dell'Energia Atomica*) Euratom.

'euro *sm inv* (*divisa*) euro.

euro'corpo *sm* European force.

eurodepu'tato *sm* Euro MP.

eurodi'visa *sf* Eurocurrency.

euro'dollaro *sm* Eurodollar.

Euro'landia *sf* Euroland.

euromer'cato *sm* Euromarket.

euro'missile *sm* Euro-missile.

Eu'ropa *sf*: **l'**~ Europe.

euro'peo, a *ag*, *smlf* European.

euro'scettico, a, ci, che [euroʃ'ʃettiko] *smlf* Euro-sceptic.

eutana'sia *sf* euthanasia.

E.V. *abbr* = *Eccellenza Vostra.*

evacu'are *vt* to evacuate.

evacuazi'one [evakuat'tsjone] *sf* evacuation.

e'vadere *vi* (*fuggire*): ~ **da** to escape from ♦ *vt* (*sbrigare*) to deal with, dispatch; (*tasse*) to evade.

evan'gelico, a, ci, che [evan'dʒɛliko] *ag* evangelical.

evange'lista, i [evandʒe'lista] *sm* evangelist.

evapo'rare *vi* to evaporate.

evaporazi'one [evaporat'tsjone] *sf* evaporation.

e'vasi *etc vb vedi* **evadere.**

evasi'one *sf* (*vedi* evadere) escape; dispatch; **dare** ~ **ad un ordine** to carry out *o* execute an order; **letteratura d'**~ escapist literature; ~ **fiscale** tax evasion.

eva'sivo, a *ag* evasive.

e'vaso, a *pp di* **evadere** ♦ *sm* escapee.

eva'sore *sm*: ~ (**fiscale**) tax evader.

eveni'enza [eve'njɛntsa] *sf*: **nell'**~ **che ciò succeda** should that happen; **essere pronto ad ogni** ~ to be ready for anything *o* any eventuality.

e'vento *sm* event.

eventu'ale *ag* possible.

eventualità *sf inv* eventuality, possibility; **nell'**~ **di** in the event of.

eventual'mente *av* if need be, if necessary.

'Everest *sm*: **l'**~, **il Monte** ~ (Mount) Everest.

eversi'one *sf* subversion.

ever'sivo, a *ag* subversive.

evi'dente *ag* evident, obvious.

evidente'mente *av* evidently; (*palesemente*) obviously, evidently.

evi'denza [evi'dɛntsa] *sf* obviousness; **mettere in** ~ to point out, highlight; **tenere in** ~ **qc** to bear sth in mind.

evidenzi'are [eviden'tsjare] *vt* (*sottolineare*) to emphasize, highlight; (*con*

evidenziatore) to highlight.
evidenzia'tore [evidentsja'tore] *sm* (*penna*) highlighter.
evi'rare *vt* to castrate.
evi'tabile *ag* avoidable.
evi'tare *vt* to avoid; ~ **di fare** to avoid doing; ~ **qc a qn** to spare sb sth.
'evo *sm* age, epoch.
evo'care *vt* to evoke.
evoca'tivo, a *ag* evocative.
evocherò *etc* [evoke'rɔ] *vb vedi* **evocare.**
evolu'tivo, a *ag* (*gen, BIOL*) evolutionary; (*MED*) progressive.
evo'luto, a *pp di* **evolversi** ♦ *ag* (*popolo, civiltà*) (highly) developed, advanced; (*persona: emancipato*) independent; (: *senza pregiudizi*) broad-minded.
evoluzi'one [evolut'tsjone] *sf* evolution.
e'volversi *vr* to evolve; **con l'~ della situazione as the** situation develops.
ev'viva *escl* hurrah!; ~ **il re!** long live the king!, hurrah for the king!
ex *prefisso* ex-, former ♦ *sm/f inv* ex-boyfriend/girlfriend.
ex 'aequo [cq'zɛkwo] *av*: **classificarsi primo** ~ to come joint first, come equal first.
'extra *ag inv, sm inv* extra.
extracomuni'tario, a *ag* non-EEC ♦ *sm/f* non-EEC national (*often referring to non-European immigrant*).
extraconiu'gale *ag* extramarital.
extraparlamen'tare *ag* extraparliamentary.
extrasensori'ale *ag*: **percezione** *f* ~ extrasensory perception.
extrater'restre *ag*, *sm/f* extraterrestrial.
extraur'bano, a *ag* suburban.

Ff

F, f ['effe] *sf o m inv* (*lettera*) F, f; **F come Firenze** ≈ F for Frederick (*BRIT*), F for Fox (*US*).
F *abbr* (= *Fahrenheit*) F.
F. *abbr* (= *fiume*) R.
fa *vb vedi* **fare** ♦ *sm inv* (*MUS*) F; (: *solfeggiando la scala*) fa ♦ *av*: **10 anni** ~ 10 years ago.
fabbi'sogno [fabbi'zoɲɲo] *sm* needs *pl*, requirements *pl*; **il** ~ **nazionale di petrolio** the country's oil requirements; ~ **del**

settore pubblico public sector borrowing requirement (*BRIT*), government debt borrowing (*US*).
'fabbrica *sf* factory.
fabbri'cante *sm* manufacturer, maker.
fabbri'care *vt* to build; (*produrre*) to manufacture, make; (*fig*) to fabricate, invent.
fabbri'cato *sm* building.
fabbricazi'one [fabbrikat'tsjone] *sf* building, fabrication; making, manufacture, manufacturing.
'fabbro *sm* (black)smith.
fac'cenda [fat't∫ɛnda] *sf* matter, affair; (*cosa da fare*) task, chore; **le** ~**e domestiche** the housework *sg*.
faccendi'ere [fatt∫en'djɛre] *sm* wheeler-dealer, (shady) operator.
fac'cetta [fat't∫etta] *sf* (*di pietra preziosa*) facet.
fac'chino [fak'kino] *sm* porter.
'faccia, ce [fat'tʃa] *sf* face; (*di moneta, medaglia*) side; ~ **a** ~ face to face; **di** ~ **a** opposite, facing; **avere la** ~ **(tosta) di dire/fare qc** to have the cheek o nerve to say/do sth; **fare qc alla** ~ **di qn** to do sth to spite sb; **leggere qc in** ~ **a qn** to see sth written all over sb's face.
facci'ata [fat't∫ata] *sf* façade; (*di pagina*) side.
'faccio *etc* ['fatt∫o] *vb vedi* **fare.**
fa'cente [fa't∫ente]: ~ **funzione** *sm* (*AMM*) deputy.
fa'cessi *etc* [fa't∫essi] *vb vedi* **fare.**
fa'ceto, a [fa't∫eto] *ag* witty, humorous.
fa'cevo *etc* [fa't∫evo] *vb vedi* **fare.**
fa'cezia [fa't∫ɛttsja] *sf* witticism, witty remark.
fa'chiro [fa'kiro] *sm* fakir.
'facile ['fat∫ile] *ag* easy; (*affabile*) easy-going; (*disposto*): ~ **a** inclined to, prone to; (*probabile*): **è** ~ **che piova** it's likely to rain; **donna di** ~**i costumi** woman of easy virtue, loose woman.
facilità [fat∫ili'ta] *sf* easiness; (*disposizione, dono*) aptitude.
facili'tare [fat∫ili'tare] *vt* to make easier.
facilitazi'one [fat∫ilitat'tsjone] *sf* (*gen*) facilities *pl*; ~**i di pagamento** easy terms, credit facilities.
facil'mente [fat∫il'mente] *av* (*gen*) easily; (*probabilmente*) probably.
faci'lone, a [fat∫i'lone] *sm/f* (*peg*) happy-go-lucky person.
facino'roso, a [fat∫ino'roso] *ag* violent.
facoltà *sf inv* faculty; (*CHIM*) property; (*autorità*) power.
facolta'tivo, a *ag* optional; (*fermata*

d'autobus) request *cpd*.

facol'toso, a *ag* wealthy, rich.

fac'simile *sm* facsimile.

'faggio ['faddʒo] *sm* beech.

fagi'ano [fa'dʒano] *sm* pheasant.

fagio'lino [fadʒo'lino] *sm* French (*BRIT*) o string bean.

fagi'olo [fa'dʒɔlo] *sm* bean; **capitare a** ~ **to** come at the right time.

fagoci'tare [fagotʃi'tare] *vt* (*fig*: *industria etc*) to absorb, swallow up; (*scherzoso*: *cibo*) to devour.

fa'gotto *sm* bundle; (*MUS*) bassoon; **far** ~ (*fig*) to pack up and go.

'fai *vb vedi* **fare**.

'faida *sf* feud.

'fai-da-'te *sm inv* DIY, do-it-yourself.

fa'ina *sf* (*ZOOL*) stone marten.

'Fahrenheit ['faːrənheit] *sm* Fahrenheit.

fa'lange [fa'landʒe] *sf* (*ANAT, MIL*) phalanx.

fal'cata *sf* stride.

'falce ['faltʃe] *sf* scythe; ~ **e martello** (*POL*) hammer and sickle.

fal'cetto [fal'tʃetto] *sm* sickle.

falci'are [fal'tʃare] *vt* to cut; (*fig*) to mow down.

falcia'trice [faltʃa'tritʃe] *sf* (*per fieno*) reaping machine; (*per erba*) mowing machine.

'falco, chi *sm* (*anche fig*) hawk.

fal'cone *sm* falcon.

'falda *sf* (*GEO*) layer, stratum; (*di cappello*) brim; (*di cappotto*) tails *pl*; (*di monte*) lower slope; (*di tetto*) pitch; (*di neve*) flake; **abito a** ~**e** tails *pl*.

fale'gname [falen'ɲame] *sm* joiner.

fa'lena *sf* (*ZOOL*) moth.

'Falkland ['fɔːlklənd] *sfpl*: **le isole** ~ **the** Falkland Islands.

fal'lace [fal'latʃe] *ag* misleading, deceptive.

'fallico, a, ci, che *ag* phallic.

fallimen'tare *ag* (*COMM*) bankruptcy *cpd*; **bilancio** ~ negative balance, deficit; **diritto** ~ bankruptcy law.

falli'mento *sm* failure; bankruptcy.

fal'lire *vi* (*non riuscire*): ~ (**in**) to fail (in); (*DIR*) to go bankrupt ♦ *vt* (*colpo, bersaglio*) to miss.

fal'lito, a *ag* unsuccessful; bankrupt ♦ *sm/f* bankrupt.

'fallo *sm* error, mistake; (*imperfezione*) defect, flaw; (*SPORT*) foul; fault; (*ANAT*) phallus; **senza** ~ without fail; **cogliere qn in** ~ to catch sb out; **mettere il piede in** ~ to slip.

fal'locrate *sm* male chauvinist.

falò *sm inv* bonfire.

fal'sare *vt* to distort, misrepresent.

falsa'riga, ghe *sf* lined page, ruled page; **sulla** ~ **di** ... (*fig*) along the lines of ....

fal'sario *sm* forger; counterfeiter.

falsifi'care *vt* to forge; (*monete*) to forge, counterfeit.

falsità *sf inv* (*di persona, notizia*) falseness; (*bugia*) falsehood, lie.

'falso, a *ag* false; (*errato*) wrong; (*falsificato*) forged; fake; (: *oro, gioielli*) imitation *cpd* ♦ *sm* forgery; **essere un** ~ **magro** to be heavier than one looks; **giurare il** ~ to commit perjury; ~ **in atto pubblico** forgery (of a legal document).

'fama *sf* fame; (*reputazione*) reputation, name.

'fame *sf* hunger; **aver** ~ to be hungry; **fare la** ~ (*fig*) to starve, exist at subsistence level.

fa'melico, a, ci, che *ag* ravenous.

famige'rato, a [famidʒe'rato] *ag* notorious, ill-famed.

fa'miglia [fa'miʎʎa] *sf* family.

famili'are *ag* (*della famiglia*) family *cpd*; (*ben noto*) familiar; (*rapporti, atmosfera*) friendly; (*LING*) informal, colloquial ♦ *sm/f* relative, relation; **una vettura** ~ a family car.

familiarità *sf* familiarity; friendliness; informality.

familiariz'zare [familjarid'dzare] *vi*: ~ **con** **qn** to get to know sb; **abbiamo familiarizzato subito** we got on well together from the start.

fa'moso, a *ag* famous, well-known.

fa'nale *sm* (*AUT*) light, lamp (*BRIT*); (*luce stradale, NAUT*) light; (*di faro*) beacon.

fa'natico, a, ci, che *ag* fanatical; (*del teatro, calcio etc*): ~ **di** o **per** mad o crazy about ♦ *sm/f* fanatic; (*tifoso*) fan.

fana'tismo *sm* fanaticism.

fanciul'lezza [fantʃul'lettsa] *sf* childhood.

fanci'ullo, a [fan'tʃullo] *sm/f* child.

fan'donia *sf* tall story; ~**e** *sfpl* nonsense *sg*.

fan'fara *sf* brass band; (*musica*) fanfare.

fanfa'rone *sm* braggart.

fan'ghiglia [fan'giʎʎa] *sf* mire, mud.

'fango, ghi *sm* mud; **fare i** ~**ghi** (*MED*) to take a course of mud baths.

fan'goso, a *ag* muddy.

'fanno *vb vedi* **fare**.

fannul'lone, a *sm/f* idler, loafer.

fantasci'enza [fantaʃ'ʃɛntsa] *sf* science fiction.

fanta'sia *sf* fantasy, imagination; (*capriccio*) whim, caprice ♦ *ag inv*: **vestito** ~ patterned dress.

fantasi'oso, a *ag* (*dotato di fantasia*) imaginative; (*bizzarro*) fanciful, strange.

fan'tasma, i *sm* ghost, phantom.
fantasti'care *vi* to daydream.
fantastiche'ria [fantastike'ria] *sf* daydream.
fan'tastico, a, ci, che *ag* fantastic; (*potenza, ingegno*) imaginative.
'fante *sm* infantryman; (*CARTE*) jack, knave (*BRIT*).
fante'ria *sf* infantry.
fan'tino *sm* jockey.
fan'toccio [fan'tɔttʃo] *sm* puppet.
fanto'matico, a, ci, che *ag* (*nave, esercito*) phantom *cpd*; (*personaggio*) mysterious.
FAO *sigla f* FAO (= *Food and Agriculture Organization*).
fara'butto *sm* crook.
fara'ona *sf* guinea fowl.
fara'one *sm* (*STORIA*) Pharaoh.
fara'onico, a, ci, che *ag* of the Pharaohs; (*fig*) enormous, huge.
far'cire [far'tʃire] *vt* (*carni, peperoni etc*) to stuff; (*torta*) to fill.
fard [far] *sm inv* blusher.
far'dello *sm* bundle; (*fig*) burden.

════════ *PAROLA CHIAVE*

'fare *sm* **1** (*modo di fare*): **con ~ distratto** absent-mindedly; **ha un ~ simpatico** he has a pleasant manner
2: **sul far del giorno/della notte** at daybreak/nightfall
♦ *vt* **1** (*fabbricare, creare*) to make; (: *casa*) to build; (: *assegno*) to make out; **~ una promessa/un film** to make a promise/a film; **~ rumore** to make a noise
2 (*effettuare: lavoro, attività, studi*) to do; (: *sport*) to play; **cosa fa?** (*adesso*) what are you doing?; (*di professione*) what do you do?; **~ psicologia/italiano** to do psychology/Italian; **~ tennis** to play tennis; **~ un viaggio** to go on a trip *o* journey; **~ una passeggiata** to go for a walk; **~ la spesa** to do the shopping
3 (*funzione*) to be; (*TEAT*) to play; **~ il medico** to be a doctor; **~ il malato** (*fingere*) to act the invalid
4 (*suscitare: sentimenti*): **~ paura a qn** to frighten sb; **mi fa rabbia** it makes me angry; **(non) fa niente** (*non importa*) it doesn't matter
5 (*ammontare*): **3 più 3 fa 6** 3 and 3 are *o* make 6; **fanno 6.000 lire** that's 6,000 lire; **Roma fa oltre 2.000.000 di abitanti** Rome has over 2,000,000 inhabitants; **che ora fai?** what time do you make it?
6 (+ *infinito*): **far ~ qc a qn** (*obbligare*) to make sb do sth; (*permettere*) to let sb do sth; **~ piangere/ridere qn** to make sb

cry/laugh; **~ venire qn** to send for sb; **fammi vedere** let me see; **far partire il motore** to start (up) the engine; **far riparare la macchina/costruire una casa** to get *o* have the car repaired/a house built
7: **~rsi**: **~rsi una gonna** to make o.s. a skirt; **~rsi un nome** to make a name for o.s.; **~rsi la permanente** to get a perm; **~rsi notare** to get o.s. noticed; **~rsi tagliare i capelli** to get one's hair cut; **~rsi operare** to have an operation
8 (*fraseologia*): **farcela** to succeed, manage; **non ce la faccio più** I can't go on; **ce la faremo** we'll make it; **me l'hanno fatta!** I've been done!; **lo facevo più giovane** I thought he was younger; **fare si/no con la testa** to nod/shake one's head
♦ *vi* **1** (*agire*) to act, do; **fate come volete** do as you like; **~ per** to be quick; **~ da** to act as; **non c'è niente da ~** it's no use; **saperci ~ con qn/qc** to know how to deal with sb/sth; **ci sa ~** she's very good at it; **faccia pure!** go ahead!
2 (*dire*) to say; **"davvero?" fece** "really?" he said
3: **~ per** (*essere adatto*) to be suitable for; **~ per ~ qc** to be about to do sth; **fece per andarsene** he made as if to leave
4: **~rsi**: **si fa così** you do it like this, this is the way it's done; **non si fa così!** (*rimprovero*) that's no way to behave!; **la festa non si fa** the party is off
5: **~ a gara con qn** to compete with sb; **~ a pugni** to come to blows; **~ in tempo a ~** to be in time to do
♦ *vb impers*: **fa bel tempo** the weather is fine; **fa caldo/freddo** it's hot/cold; **fa notte** it's getting dark
♦ *vr*: **~rsi 1** (*diventare*) to become; **~rsi prete** to become a priest; **~rsi grande/vecchio** to grow tall/old
2 (*spostarsi*): **~rsi avanti/indietro** to move forward/back; **fatti più in là** move along a bit
3 (*fam: drogarsi*) to be a junkie.

fa'retra *sf* quiver.
far'falla *sf* butterfly.
farfugli'are [farfuʎ'ʎare] *vt, vi* to mumble, mutter.
fa'rina *sf* flour; **~ gialla** maize (*BRIT*) *o* corn (*US*) flour; **~ integrale** wholemeal (*BRIT*) *o* whole-wheat (*US*) flour; **questa non è ~ del tuo sacco** (*fig*) this isn't your own idea (*o* work).
fari'nacei [fari'natʃei] *smpl* starches.
fa'ringe [fa'rindʒe] *sf* (*ANAT*) pharynx.
farin'gite [farin'dʒite] *sf* pharyngitis.

fari'noso, a *ag* (*patate*) floury; (*neve, mela*) powdery.

farma'ceutico, a, ci, che [farma't∫eutiko] *ag* pharmaceutical.

farma'cia, 'cie [farma't∫ia] *sf* pharmacy; (*negozio*) chemist's (shop) (*BRIT*), pharmacy.

farma'cista, i, e [farma't∫ista] *sm/f* chemist (*BRIT*), pharmacist.

'farmaco, ci *o* **chi** *sm* drug, medicine.

farneti'care *vi* to rave, be delirious.

'faro *sm* (*NAUT*) lighthouse; (*AER*) beacon; (*AUT*) headlight, headlamp (*BRIT*).

farragi'noso, a [farradʒi'noso] *ag* (*stile*) muddled, confused.

'farsa *sf* farce.

far'sesco, a, schi, sche *ag* farcical.

fasc. *abbr* = **fascicolo**.

'fascia, sce ['fa∫∫a] *sf* band, strip; (*MED*) bandage; (*di sindaco, ufficiale*) sash; (*parte di territorio*) strip, belt; (*di contribuenti etc*) group, band; **essere in** ~**sce** (*anche fig*) to be in one's infancy; ~ **oraria** time band.

fasci'are [fa∫'∫are] *vt* to bind; (*MED*) to bandage; (*bambino*) to put a nappy (*BRIT*) *o* diaper (*US*) on.

fascia'tura [fa∫∫a'tura] *sf* (*azione*) bandaging; (*fascia*) bandage.

fa'scicolo [fa∫'∫ikolo] *sm* (*di documenti*) file, dossier; (*di rivista*) issue, number; (*opuscolo*) booklet, pamphlet.

'fascino ['fa∫∫ino] *sm* charm, fascination.

'fascio ['fa∫∫o] *sm* bundle, sheaf; (*di fiori*) bunch; (*di luce*) beam; (*POL*): **il F**~ the Fascist Party.

fa'scismo [fa∫'∫izmo] *sm* fascism.

fa'scista, i, e [fa∫'∫ista] *ag, sm/f* fascist.

'fase *sf* phase; (*TECN*) stroke; **in** ~ **di espansione** in a period of expansion; **essere fuori** ~ (*motore*) to be rough (*BRIT*), run roughly; (*fig*) to feel rough (*BRIT*) *o* rotten.

fas'tidio *sm* bother, trouble; **dare** ~ **a qn** to bother *o* annoy sb; **sento** ~ **allo stomaco** my stomach's upset; **avere** ~**i con la polizia** to have trouble *o* bother with the police.

fastidi'oso, a *ag* annoying, tiresome; (*schifiltoso*) fastidious.

'fasto *sm* pomp, splendour (*BRIT*), splendor (*US*).

fas'toso, a *ag* sumptuous, lavish.

fa'sullo, a *ag* (*gen*) fake; (*dichiarazione, persona*) false; (*pretesto*) bogus.

'fata *sf* fairy.

fa'tale *ag* fatal; (*inevitabile*) inevitable; (*fig*) irresistible.

fata'lismo *sm* fatalism.

fatalità *sf inv* inevitability; (*avversità*) misfortune; (*fato*) fate, destiny.

fa'tato, a *ag* (*spada, chiave*) magic; (*castello*) enchanted.

fa'tica, che *sf* hard work, toil; (*sforzo*) effort; (*di metalli*) fatigue; **a** ~ with difficulty; **respirare a** ~ to have difficulty (in) breathing; **fare** ~ **a fare qc** to find it difficult to do sth; **animale da** ~ beast of burden.

fati'caccia, ce [fati'katt∫a] *sf*: **fu una** ~ it was hard work, it was a hell of a job (*fam*).

fati'care *vi* to toil; ~ **a fare qc** to have difficulty doing sth.

fati'cata *sf* hard work.

fa'tichi *etc* [fa'tiki] *vb vedi* **faticare**.

fati'coso, a *ag* (*viaggio, camminata*) tiring, exhausting; (*lavoro*) laborious.

fa'tidico, a, ci, che *ag* fateful.

'fato *sm* fate, destiny.

Fatt. *abbr* (= **fattura**) inv.

fat'taccio [fat'tatt∫o] *sm* foul deed.

fat'tezze [fat'tettse] *sfpl* features.

fat'tibile *ag* feasible, possible.

fattis'pecie [fattis'pɛt∫e] *sf*: **nella** *o* **in** ~ in this case *o* instance.

'fatto, a *pp di* **fare ♦** *ag*: **un uomo** ~ **a** grown man **♦** *sm* fact; (*azione*) deed; (*avvenimento*) event, occurrence; (*di romanzo, film*) action, story; ~ **a mano/in casa** hand-/home-made; **è ben** ~**a** she has a nice figure; **cogliere qn sul** ~ to catch sb red-handed; **il** ~ **sta** *o* **è che** the fact remains *o* is that; **in** ~ **di** as for, as far as ... is concerned; **fare i** ~**i propri** to mind one's own business; **è uno che sa il** ~ **suo** he knows what he's about; **gli ho detto il** ~ **suo** I told him what I thought of him; **porre qn di fronte al** ~ **compiuto** to present sb with a fait accompli.

fat'tore *sm* (*AGR*) farm manager; (*MAT*: *elemento costitutivo*) factor.

fatto'ria *sf* farm; (*casa*) farmhouse.

fatto'rino *sm* errand boy; (*di ufficio*) office boy; (*d'albergo*) porter.

fattucchi'era [fattuk'kjɛra] *sf* witch.

fat'tura *sf* (*COMM*) invoice; (*di abito*) tailoring; (*malia*) spell; **pagamento contro presentazione** ~ payment on invoice.

fattu'rare *vt* (*COMM*) to invoice; (*prodotto*) to produce; (*vino*) to adulterate.

fattu'rato *sm* (*COMM*) turnover.

fatturazi'one [fatturat'tsjone] *sf* billing, invoicing.

'fatuo, a *ag* vain, fatuous; **fuoco** ~ (*anche fig*) will-o'-the-wisp.

'fauci ['faut∫i] *sfpl* (*di leone etc*) jaws; (*di vulcano*) mouth *sg*.

'**fauna** sf fauna.

'**fausto, a** ag (formale) happy; **un ~ presagio** a good omen.

fau'**tore, 'trice** sm/f advocate, supporter.

'**fava** sf broad bean.

fa'**vella** sf speech.

fa'**villa** sf spark.

'**favo** sm (di api) honeycomb.

'**favola** sf (fiaba) fairy tale; (d'intento morale) fable; (fandonia) yarn; **essere la ~ del paese** (oggetto di critica) to be the talk of the town; (zimbello) to be a laughing stock.

favo'**loso, a** ag fabulous; (incredibile) incredible.

fa'**vore** sm favour (BRIT), favor (US); **per ~** please; **prezzo/trattamento di ~** preferential price/treatment; **condizioni dl ~** (COMM) favo(u)rable terms; **fare un ~ a qn** to do sb a favo(u)r; **col ~ delle tenebre** under cover of darkness.

favoreggia'**mento** [favoreddʒa'mento] sm (DIR) aiding and abetting.

favo'**revole** ag favourable (BRIT), favorable (US).

favo'**rire** vt to favour (BRIT), favor (US); (il commercio, l'industria, le arti) to promote, encourage; **vuole ~?** won't you help yourself?; **favorisca in salotto** please come into the sitting room; **mi favorisca i documenti** please may I see your papers?

favori'**tismo** sm favouritism (BRIT), favoritism (US).

favo'**rito, a** ag, sm/f favourite (BRIT), favorite (US).

fax sm inv fax; **mandare qc via ~** to fax sth.

fa'**xare** vt to fax.

fazi'**one** [fat'tsjone] sf faction.

fazio'**sità** [fattsjosi'ta] sf sectarianism.

fazzo'**letto** [fattso'letto] sm handkerchief; (per la testa) (head)scarf.

F.B.I. sigla f (= Federal Bureau of Investigation) FBI.

F.C. abbr = **fuoricorso**.

f.co abbr = **franco**.

FE sigla = Ferrara.

febb. abbr (= febbraio) Feb.

feb'**braio** sm February; per fraseologia vedi **luglio**.

'**febbre** sf fever; **aver la ~** to have a high temperature; **~ da fieno** hay fever.

feb'**brile** ag (anche fig) feverish.

'**feccia, ce** ['fettʃa] sf dregs pl.

'**feci** ['fɛtʃi] sfpl faeces, excrement sg.

'**feci** ['fɛtʃi] vb vedi **fare**.

'**fecola** sf potato flour.

fecon'**dare** vt to fertilize.

fecondazi'**one** [fekondat'tsjone] sf fertilization; **~ artificiale** artificial insemination.

fecon'**dità** sf fertility.

fe'**condo, a** ag fertile.

'**Fedcom** sigla m = Fondo Europeo di Cooperazione Monetaria.

'**fede** sf (credenza) belief, faith; (REL) faith; (fiducia) faith, trust; (fedeltà) loyalty; (anello) wedding ring; (attestato) certificate; **aver ~ in qn** to have faith in sb; **tener ~ a** (ideale) to remain loyal to; (giuramento, promessa) to keep; **in buona/ cattiva ~** in good/bad faith; "**in ~ ~**" (DIR) "in witness whereof".

fe'**dele** ag (leale): **~ (a)** faithful (to); (veritiero) true, accurate ♦ sm/f follower; **i ~i** (REL) the faithful.

fedel'**tà** sf faithfulness; (coniugale) fidelity; (esattezza: di copia, traduzione) accuracy; **alta ~** (RADIO) high fidelity.

'**federa** sf pillowslip, pillowcase.

fede'**rale** ag federal.

federa'**lismo** sm (POL) federalism.

federa'**lista, i, e** ag, sm/f (POL) federalist.

federazi'**one** [federat'tsjone] sf federation.

Feder'**caccia** [feder'kattʃa] abbr f (= Federazione Italiana della Caccia) hunting federation.

Feder'**calcio** [feder'kaltʃo] abbr m (= Federazione Italiana Gioco Calcio) Italian football association.

Federcon'**sorzi** [federkon'sɔrtsi] abbr f (= Federazione Italiana dei Consorzi Agrari) federation of farmers' cooperatives.

fe'**difrago, a, ghi, ghe** ag faithless, perfidious.

fe'**dina** sf (DIR): **~ (penale)** record; **avere la ~ penale sporca** to have a police record.

'**fegato** sm liver; (fig) guts pl, nerve; **mangiarsi o rodersi il ~** to be consumed with rage.

'**felce** ['feltʃe] sf fern.

fe'**lice** [fe'litʃe] ag happy; (fortunato) lucky.

felici'**tà** [felitʃi'ta] sf happiness.

felici'**tarsi** [felitʃi'tarsi] vr (congratularsi): **~ con qn per qc** to congratulate sb on sth.

felicitazi'**oni** [felitʃitat'tsjoni] sfpl congratulations.

fe'**lino, a** ag, sm feline.

'**felpa** sf sweatshirt.

fel'**pato, a** ag (tessuto) brushed; (passo) stealthy; **con passo ~** stealthily.

'**feltro** sm felt.

'**femmina** sf (ZOOL, TECN) female; (figlia) girl, daughter; (spesso peg) woman.

femmi'**nile** ag feminine; (sesso) female; (lavoro, giornale) woman's, women's;

(*moda*) women's ♦ *sm* (*LING*) feminine.
femmini'nismo *sf* femininity.
femmi'nismo *sm* feminism.
femmi'nista, i, e *ag, sm/f* feminist.
'femore *sm* thighbone, femur.
'fendere *vt* to cut through.
fendi'nebbia *sm* (*AUT*) fog lamp.
fendi'tura *sf* (*gen*) crack; (*di roccia*) cleft, crack.
fenome'nale *ag* phenomenal.
fe'nomeno *sm* phenomenon.
'feretro *sm* coffin.
feri'ale *ag*: **giorno** ~ weekday, working day.
'ferie *sfpl* holidays (*BRIT*), vacation *sg* (*US*); **andare in** ~ to go on holiday *o* vacation; **25 giorni di** ~ **pagate** 25 days' holiday *o* vacation with pay.
feri'mento *sm* wounding.
fe'rire *vt* to injure; (*deliberatamente*: *MIL etc*) to wound; (*colpire*) to hurt; ~**rsi** *vr* to hurt o.s., injure o.s.
fe'rito, a *sm/f* wounded *o* injured man/woman ♦ *sf* injury; wound.
feri'toia *sf* slit.
'ferma *sf* (*MIL*) (period of) service; (*CACCIA*): **cane da** ~ pointer.
ferma'carte *sm inv* paperweight.
fermacra'vatta *sm inv* tiepin (*BRIT*), tie tack (*US*).
fer'maglio [fer'maʎʎo] *sm* clasp; (*gioiello*) brooch; (*per documenti*) clip.
ferma'mente *av* firmly.
fer'mare *vt* to stop, halt; (*POLIZIA*) to detain, hold; (*bottone etc*) to fasten, fix ♦ *vi* to stop; ~**rsi** *vr* to stop, halt; ~**rsi a fare qc** to stop to do sth.
fer'mata *sf* stop; ~ **dell'autobus** bus stop.
fermen'tare *vi* to ferment; (*fig*) to be in a ferment.
fermentazi'one [fermentat'tsjone] *sf* fermentation.
fer'mento *sm* (*anche fig*) ferment; (*lievito*) yeast.
fer'mezza [fer'mettsa] *sf* (*fig*) firmness, steadfastness.
'fermo, a *ag* still, motionless; (*veicolo*) stationary; (*orologio*) not working; (*saldo*: *anche fig*) firm; (*voce, mano*) steady ♦ *escl* stop!; keep still! ♦ *sm* (*chiusura*) catch, lock; (*DIR*): ~ **di polizia** police detention; ~ **restando che** ... it being understood that ....
'fermo 'posta *av, sm inv* poste restante (*BRIT*), general delivery (*US*).
fe'roce [fe'rotʃe] *ag* (*animale*) wild, fierce, ferocious; (*persona*) cruel, fierce; (*fame, dolore*) raging.

fe'rocia, cie [fe'rotʃa] *sf* ferocity.
Ferr. *abbr* = **ferrovia**.
fer'raglia [fer'raʎʎa] *sf* scrap iron.
ferra'gosto *sm* (*festa*) feast of the Assumption; (*periodo*) August holidays *pl* (*BRIT*) *o* vacation (*US*); *vedi nota nel riquadro*.

FERRAGOSTO

Ferragosto, 15 August, is a national holiday. Marking the feast of the Assumption, its origins are religious but in recent years it has simply become the most important public holiday of the summer season. Most people take some extra time off work and head out of town to the holiday resorts. Consequently, most of industry and commerce grind to a standstill.

---

ferra'menta *sfpl* ironmongery *sg* (*BRIT*), hardware *sg*; **negozio di** ~ ironmonger's (*BRIT*), hardware shop *o* store (*US*).
fer'rare *vt* (*cavallo*) to shoe.
fer'rato, a *ag* (*FERR*): **strada** ~**a** railway line (*BRIT*), railroad line (*US*); (*fig*): **essere** ~ **in** (*materia*) to be well up in.
ferra'vecchio [ferra'vɛkkjo] *sm* scrap merchant.
'ferreo, a *ag* iron *cpd*.
ferri'era *sf* ironworks *sg o pl*.
'ferro *sm* iron; **una bistecca ai** ~**i** a grilled steak; **mettere a** ~ **e fuoco** to put to the sword; **essere ai** ~**i corti** (*fig*) to be at daggers drawn; **tocca** ~! touch wood!; ~ **battuto** wrought iron; ~ **di cavallo** horseshoe; ~ **da stiro** iron; ~**i da calza** knitting needles; **i** ~**i del mestiere** the tools of the trade.
ferrotranvi'ario, a *ag* public transport *cpd*.
Ferrotranvi'eri *abbr f* (= *Federazione Nazionale Lavoratori Autoferrotranvieri e Internavigatori*) *transport workers' union*.
ferro'vecchio [ferro'vɛkkjo] *sm* = **ferravecchio**.
ferro'via *sf* railway (*BRIT*), railroad (*US*).
ferrovi'ario, a *ag* railway *cpd* (*BRIT*), railroad *cpd* (*US*).
ferrovi'ere *sm* railwayman (*BRIT*), railroad man (*US*).
'fertile *ag* fertile.
fertilità *sf* fertility.
fertiliz'zante [fertilid'dzante] *sm* fertilizer.
fertiliz'zare [fertilid'dzare] *vt* to fertilize.
fer'vente *ag* fervent, ardent.
'fervere *vi*: **fervono i preparativi per** ... they are making feverish preparations for ....
'fervido, a *ag* fervent, ardent.
fer'vore *sm* fervour (*BRIT*), fervor (*US*),

ardour (BRIT), ardor (US); (punto
culminante) height.
'**fesa** sf (CUC) rump of veal.
fesse'ria sf stupidity; **dire** ~**e** to talk
nonsense.
'**fesso, a** pp di **fendere** ♦ ag (fam: sciocco)
crazy, cracked.
fes'sura sf crack, split; (per gettone,
moneta) slot.
'**festa** sf (religiosa) feast; (pubblica) holiday;
(compleanno) birthday; (onomastico)
name day; (ricevimento) celebration,
party; **far** ~ to have a holiday; (far
baldoria) to live it up; **far** ~ **a qn** to give sb
a warm welcome; **essere vestito a** ~ to be
dressed up to the nines; ~ **comandata**
(REL) holiday of obligation; **la** ~ **della
mamma/del papà** Mother's/Father's Day;
la F~ **della Repubblica** vedi nota nel riquadro.

FESTA DELLA REPUBBLICA

The **Festa della Repubblica**, 2 June,
celebrates the founding of the Italian Republic
after the fall of the monarchy and the
subsequent referendum in 1946. It is marked by
military parades and political speeches.

---

festeggia'menti [festeddʒa'menti] smpl
celebrations.
festeggi'are [fested'dʒare] vt to celebrate;
(persona) to have a celebration for.
fes'tino sm party; (con balli) ball.
fes'tivo, a ag (atmosfera) festive; **giorno** ~
holiday.
fes'toso, a ag merry, joyful.
fe'tente ag (puzzolente) fetid;
(comportamento) disgusting.
fe'ticcio [fe'tittʃo] sm fetish.
'**feto** sm foetus (BRIT), fetus (US).
fe'tore sm stench, stink.
'**fetta** sf slice.
fet'tuccia, ce [fet'tuttʃa] sf tape, ribbon.
fettuc'cine [fettut'tʃine] sfpl (CUC) ribbon-
shaped pasta.
feu'dale ag feudal.
'**feudo** sm (STORIA) fief; (fig) stronghold.
ff abbr (AMM) = **facente funzione**; (= fogli)
pp.
FF.AA abbr = **forze armate**.
FF.SS. abbr (= Ferrovie dello Stato) Italian
railways.
FG sigla = Foggia.
FI sigla = Firenze.
fi'aba sf fairy tale.
fia'besco, a, schi, sche ag fairy-tale cpd.
fi'acca sf weariness; (svogliatezza)
listlessness; **battere la** ~ to shirk.

fiac'care vt to weaken.
fiaccherò etc [fjakke'rɔ] vb vedi **fiaccare**.
fi'acco, a, chi, che ag (stanco) tired,
weary; (svogliato) listless; (debole) weak;
(mercato) slack.
fi'accola sf torch.
fiacco'lata sf torchlight procession.
fi'ala sf phial.
fi'amma sf flame; (NAUT) pennant.
fiam'mante ag (colore) flaming; **nuovo** ~
brand new.
fiam'mata sf blaze.
fiammeggi'are [fjammed'dʒare] vi to blaze.
fiam'mifero sm match.
fiam'mingo, a, ghi, ghe ag Flemish ♦ sm/f
Fleming ♦ sm (LING) Flemish; (ZOOL)
flamingo; **i F**~**ghi** the Flemish.
fian'cata sf (di nave etc) side; (NAUT)
broadside.
fiancheggi'are [fjanked'dʒare] vt to border;
(fig) to support, back (up); (MIL) to flank.
fi'anco, chi sm side; (di persona) hip; (MIL)
flank; **di** ~ sideways, from the side; **a** ~ **a**
~ side by side; **prestare il proprio** ~ **alle
critiche** to leave o.s. open to criticism; ~
destr/sinistr! (MIL) right/left turn!
Fi'andre sfpl: **le** ~ Flanders sg.
fiaschette'ria [fjaskette'ria] sf wine shop.
fi'asco, schi sm flask; (fig) fiasco; **fare** ~ to
be a fiasco.
fia'tare vi (fig: parlare): **senza** ~ without
saying a word.
fi'ato sm breath; (resistenza) stamina; ~**i**
smpl (MUS) wind instruments; **avere il** ~
grosso to be out of breath; **prendere** ~ to
catch one's breath; **bere qc tutto d'un** ~
to drink sth in one go o gulp.
'**fibbia** sf buckle.
'**fibra** sf fibre, fiber (US); (fig) constitution;
~ **ottica** optical fibre; ~ **di vetro**
fibreglass (BRIT), fiberglass (US).
ficca'naso, pl(m) ~**i,** pl(f) inv sm/f busybody,
nos(e)y parker.
fic'care vt to push, thrust, drive; ~**rsi** vr
(andare a finire) to get to; ~ **il naso negli
affari altrui** (fig) to poke o stick one's nose
into other people's business; ~**rsi nei
pasticci** o **nei guai** to get into a fix.
ficcherò etc [fikke'rɔ] vb vedi **ficcare**.
fiche [fiʃ] sf inv (nei giochi d'azzardo) chip.
'**fico, chi** sm (pianta) fig tree; (frutto) fig; ~
d'India prickly pear; ~ **secco** dried fig.
fidanza'mento [fidantsa'mento] sm
engagement.
fidan'zarsi [fidan'tsarsi] vr to get engaged.
fidan'zato, a [fidan'tsato] sm/f fiancé/
fiancée.
fi'darsi vr: ~ **di** to trust; ~**rsi è bene non**

~rsi è meglio (*proverbio*) better safe than sorry.

fi'dato, a *ag* reliable, trustworthy.

fide'ismo *sm* unquestioning belief.

fide'istico, a, ci, che *ag* (*atteggiamento, posizione*) totally uncritical.

fideius'sore *sm* (*DIR*) guarantor.

'fido, a *ag* faithful, loyal ♦ *sm* (*COMM*) credit.

fi'ducia [fi'dutʃa] *sf* confidence, trust; **incarico di** ~ position of trust, responsible position; **persona di** ~ reliable person; **è il mio uomo di** ~ he is my right-hand man; **porre la questione di** ~ (*POL*) to ask for a vote of confidence.

fiduci'oso, a [fidu'tʃoso] *ag* trusting.

fi'ele *sm* (*MED*) bile; (*fig*) bitterness.

fie'nile *sm* hayloft.

fi'eno *sm* hay.

fi'era *sf* fair; (*animale*) wild beast; ~ **di beneficenza** charity bazaar; ~ **campionaria** trade fair.

fie'rezza [fje'rettsa] *sf* pride.

fi'ero, a *ag* proud; (*crudele*) fierce, cruel; (*audace*) bold.

fi'evole *ag* (*luce*) dim; (*suono*) weak.

F.I.F.A. *sigla f* (= *Fédération Internationale de Football Association*) FIFA.

'fifa *sf* (*fam*): **aver** ~ to have the jitters.

fi'fone, a *sm/f* (*fam, scherzoso*) coward.

fig. *abbr* (= *figura*) fig.

FIGC *sigla f* (= *Federazione Italiana Gioco Calcio*) *Italian football association.*

'Figi ['fidʒi] *sfpl*: **le isole** ~ Fiji, the Fiji Islands.

'figlia ['fiʎʎa] *sf* daughter; (*COMM*) counterfoil (*BRIT*), stub.

figli'are [fiʎ'ʎare] *vi* to give birth.

figli'astro, a [fiʎ'ʎastro] *sm/f* stepson/daughter.

'figlio ['fiʎʎo] *sm* son; (*senza distinzione di sesso*) child; ~ **d'arte: essere** ~ **d'arte** to come from a theatrical (*o* musical *etc*) family; ~ **di puttana** (*fam!*) son of a bitch (*!*); ~ **unico** only child.

figli'occio, a, ci, ce [fiʎ'ʎottʃo] *sm/f* godchild, godson/daughter.

figli'ola [fiʎ'ʎola] *sf* daughter; (*fig: ragazza*) girl.

figli'olo [fiʎ'ʎolo] *sm* (*anche fig: ragazzo*) son.

fi'gura *sf* figure; (*forma, aspetto esterno*) form, shape; (*illustrazione*) picture, illustration; **far** ~ to look smart; **fare una brutta** ~ to make a bad impression; **che** ~! how embarrassing!

figu'raccia, ce [figu'rattʃa] *sf*: **fare una** ~ to create a bad impression.

figu'rare *vi* to appear ♦ *vt*: ~**rsi qc** to

imagine sth; ~**rsi** *vr*: **figurati!** imagine that!; **ti do noia?** — **ma figurati!** am I disturbing you? — not at all!

figura'tivo, a *ag* figurative.

figu'rina *sf* (*statuetta*) figurine; (*cartoncino*) picture card.

figuri'nista, i, e *sm/f* dress designer.

figu'rino *sm* fashion sketch.

fi'guro *sm*: **un losco** ~ a suspicious character.

figu'rone *sm*: **fare un** ~ (*persona, oggetto*) to look terrific; (*persona: con un discorso etc*) to make an excellent impression.

'fila *sf* row, line; (*coda*) queue; (*serie*) series, string; **di** ~ in succession; **fare la** ~ to queue; **in** ~ **indiana** in single file.

fila'mento *sm* filament.

fi'lanca ® *sf stretch material.*

fi'landa *sf* spinning mill.

fi'lante *ag*: **stella** ~ (*stella cadente*) shooting star; (*striscia di carta*) streamer.

filantro'pia *sf* philanthropy.

filan'tropico, a, ci, che *ag* philanthropic(al).

fi'lantropo *sm* philanthropist.

fi'lare *vt* to spin; (*NAUT*) to pay out ♦ *vi* (*baco, ragno*) to spin; (*formaggio fuso*) to go stringy; (*liquido*) to trickle; (*discorso*) to hang together; (*fam: amoreggiare*) to go steady; (*muoversi a forte velocità*) to go at full speed; (*andarsene lestamente*) to make o.s. scarce ♦ *sm* (*di alberi etc*) row, line; ~ **diritto** (*fig*) to toe the line.

filar'monico, a, ci, che *ag* philharmonic.

filas'trocca, che *sf* nursery rhyme.

filate'lia *sf* philately, stamp collecting.

fi'lato, a *ag* spun ♦ *sm* yarn ♦ *av*: **vai dritto** ~ **a casa** go straight home; **3 giorni** ~**i** 3 days running *o* on end.

fila'tura *sf* spinning; (*luogo*) spinning mill.

fi'letto *sm* (*ornamento*) braid, trimming; (*di vite*) thread; (*di carne*) fillet.

fili'ale *ag* filial ♦ *sf* (*di impresa*) branch.

filibusti'ere *sm* pirate; (*fig*) adventurer.

fili'grana *sf* (*in oreficeria*) filigree; (*su carta*) watermark.

fi'lippica *sf* invective.

Filip'pine *sfpl*: **le** ~ the Philippines.

filip'pino, a *ag, sm/f* Filipino.

film *sm inv* film.

fil'mare *vt* to film.

fil'mato *sm* short film.

fil'mina *sf* film strip.

'filo *sm* (*anche fig*) thread; (*filato*) yarn; (*metallico*) wire; (*di lama, rasoio*) edge; **con un** ~ **di voce** in a whisper; **un** ~ **d'aria** (*fig*) a breath of air; **dare del** ~ **da torcere a qn** to create difficulties for sb, make

life difficult for sb; **fare il ~ a qn**
(*corteggiare*) to be after sb, chase sb; **per
~ e per segno** in detail; **~ d'erba** blade of
grass; **~ interdentale** dental floss; **~ di
perle** string of pearls; **~ di Scozia** fine
cotton yarn; **~ spinato** barbed wire.

filoameri'cano, a *ag* pro-American.

'filobus *sm inv* trolley bus.

filodiffusi'one *sf* rediffusion.

filodram'matico, a, ci, che *ag*:
(compagnia) ~a amateur dramatic
society ♦ *sm/f* amateur actor/actress.

filon'cino [filon't∫ino] *sm* ≈ French stick.

fi'lone *sm* (*di minerali*) seam, vein; (*pane*) ≈
Vienna loaf; (*fig*) trend.

filoso'fia *sf* philosophy.

filo'sofico, a, ci, che *ag* philosophical.

fi'losofo, a *sm/f* philosopher.

filosovi'etico, a, ci, che *ag* pro-Soviet.

filo'via *sf* (*linea*) trolley line; (*bus*) trolley
bus.

fil'trare *vt, vi* to filter.

'filtro *sm* filter; (*pozione*) potion; **~ dell'olio**
(*AUT*) oil filter.

'filza ['filtsa] *sf* (*anche fig*) string.

FIN *sigla f = Federazione Italiana Nuoto.*

fin *av, prep* = **fino**.

fi'nale *ag* final ♦ *sm* (*di libro, film*) end,
ending; (*MUS*) finale ♦ *sf* (*SPORT*) final.

fina'lista, i, e *sm/f* finalist.

finalità *sf* (*scopo*) aim, purpose.

finaliz'zare [finalid'dzare] *vt*: **~ a** to direct
towards.

final'mente *av* finally, at last.

fi'nanza [fi'nantsa] *sf* finance; **~e** *sfpl* (*di
individuo, Stato*) finances; **(Guardia di) ~**
(*di frontiera*) ≈ Customs and Excise (*BRIT*),
≈ Customs Service (*US*); **(Intendenza di)
~** ≈ Inland Revenue (*BRIT*), ≈ Internal
Revenue Service (*US*); **Ministro delle ~e**
Minister of Finance, ≈ Chancellor of the
Exchequer (*BRIT*), ≈ Secretary of the
Treasury (*US*).

finanzia'mento [finantsja'mento] *sm*
(*azione*) financing; (*denaro fornito*) funds
pl.

finanzi'are [finan'tsjare] *vt* to finance, fund.

finanzi'ario, a [finan'tsjarjo] *ag* financial
♦ *sf* (*anche*: **società ~a**) investment
company; (*anche*: **legge ~a**) finance act,
≈ budget (*BRIT*).

finanzia'tore, 'trice *ag*: **ente ~, società
~trice** backer ♦ *sm/f* backer.

finanzi'ere [finan'tsjere] *sm* financier;
(*guardia di finanza: doganale*) customs
officer; (: *tributaria*) Inland Revenue
official (*BRIT*), Internal Revenue official
(*US*).

finché [fin'ke] *cong* (*per tutto il tempo che*) as
long as; (*fino al momento in cui*) until; **~
vorrai** as long as you like; **aspetta ~ non
esca** wait until he goes (*o* comes) out.

'fine *ag* (*lamina, carta*) thin; (*capelli, polvere*)
fine; (*vista, udito*) keen, sharp; (*persona*:
raffinata) refined, distinguished;
(*osservazione*) subtle ♦ *sf* end ♦ *sm* aim,
purpose; (*esito*) result, outcome; **in o alla
~** in the end, finally; **alla fin ~** at the end
of the day, in the end; **che ~ ha fatto?**
what became of him?; **buona ~ e buon
principio!** (*augurio*) happy New Year!; **a
fin di bene** with the best of intentions; **al
~ di fare qc** (in order) to do sth; **condurre
qc a buon ~** to bring sth to a successful
conclusion; **secondo ~** ulterior motive.

'fine setti'mana *sm o f inv* weekend.

fi'nestra *sf* window.

fines'trino *sm* (*di treno, auto*) window.

fi'nezza [fi'nettsa] *sf* thinness; fineness;
keenness, sharpness; refinement;
subtlety.

'fingere ['find3ere] *vt* to feign; (*supporre*) to
imagine, suppose; **~rsi** *vr*: **~rsi ubriaco/
pazzo** to pretend to be drunk/crazy; **~ di
fare** to pretend to do.

fini'menti *smpl* (*di cavallo etc*) harness *sg*.

fini'mondo *sm* pandemonium.

fi'nire *vt* to finish ♦ *vi* to finish, end ♦ *sm*: **sul
~ della festa** towards the end of the
party; **~ di fare** (*compiere*) to finish doing;
(*smettere*) to stop doing; **~ in galera** to
end up *o* finish up in prison; **farla finita**
(*con la vita*) to put an end to one's life;
farla finita con qc to have done with sth;
com'è andata a ~? what happened in the
end?; **finiscila!** stop it!

fini'tura *sf* finish.

finlan'dese *ag* Finnish ♦ *sm/f* Finn ♦ *sm*
(*LING*) Finnish.

Fin'landia *sf*: **la ~** Finland.

'fino, a *ag* (*capelli, seta*) fine; (*oro*) pure; (*fig*:
acuto) shrewd ♦ *av* (*spesso troncato in* **fin**:
pure, anche) even ♦ *prep* (*spesso troncato in*
fin: *tempo*): **fin quando?** till when?;
(: *luogo*): **fin qui** as far as here; **~ a**
(*tempo*) until, till; (*luogo*) as far as, (up)
to; **fin da domani** from tomorrow
onwards; **fin da ieri** since yesterday; **fin
dalla nascita** from *o* since birth.

fi'nocchio [fi'nɔkkjo] *sm* fennel; (*fam peg*:
pederasta) queer.

fi'nora *av* up till now.

'finsi *etc vb vedi* **fingere**.

'finto, a *pp di* **fingere** ♦ *ag* (*capelli, dente*)
false; (*fiori*) artificial; (*cuoio, pelle*)
imitation *cpd*; (*fig: simulato: pazzia etc*)

feigned, sham ♦ *sf* pretence (*BRIT*), pretense (*US*), sham; (*SPORT*) feint; **far ~a (di fare)** to pretend (to do); **l'ho detto per ~a** I was only pretending; (*per scherzo*) I was only kidding.

finzi'one [fin'tsjone] *sf* pretence (*BRIT*), pretense (*US*), sham.

fioc'care *vi* (*neve*) to fall; (*fig: insulti etc*) to fall thick and fast.

fi'occo, chi *sm* (*di nastro*) bow; (*di stoffa, lana*) flock; (*di neve*) flake; (*NAUT*) jib; **coi ~chi** (*fig*) first-rate; **~chi di granoturco** cornflakes.

fi'ocina ['fjɔtʃina] *sf* harpoon.

fi'oco, a, chi, che *ag* faint, dim.

fi'onda *sf* catapult.

fio'raio, a *sm/f* florist.

fiorda'liso *sm* (*BOT*) cornflower.

fi'ordo *sm* fjord.

fi'ore *sm* flower; **~i** *smpl* (*CARTE*) clubs; **nel ~ degli anni** in one's prime; **a fior d'acqua** on the surface of the water; **a fior di labbra** in a whisper; **aver i nervi a fior di pelle** to be on edge; **fior di latte** cream; **è costato fior di soldi** it cost a pretty penny; **il fior ~ della società** the cream of society; **~ all'occhiello** feather in the cap; **~i di campo** wild flowers.

fio'rente *ag* (*industria, paese*) flourishing; (*salute*) blooming; (*petto*) ample.

fioren'tino, a *ag, sm/f* Florentine ♦ *sf* (*CUC*) T-bone steak.

fio'retto *sm* (*SCHERMA*) foil.

fio'rino *sm* florin.

fio'rire *vi* (*rosa*) to flower; (*albero*) to blossom; (*fig*) to flourish.

fio'rista, i, e *sm/f* florist.

fiori'tura *sf* (*di pianta*) flowering, blooming; (*di albero*) blossoming; (*fig: di commercio, arte*) flourishing; (*insieme dei fiori*) flowers *pl*; (*MUS*) fioritura.

fi'otto *sm* (*di lacrime*) flow, flood; (*di sangue*) gush, spurt.

'FIPE *sigla f* = *Federazione Italiana Pubblici Esercizi*.

Fi'renze [fi'rɛntse] *sf* Florence.

'firma *sf* signature; (*reputazione*) name.

firma'mento *sm* firmament.

fir'mare *vt* to sign.

firma'tario, a *sm/f* signatory.

fisar'monica, che *sf* accordion.

fis'cale *ag* fiscal, tax *cpd*; (*meticoloso*) punctilious; **medico ~** *doctor employed by Social Security to verify cases of sick leave*.

fisca'lista, i, e *sm/f* tax consultant.

fiscaliz'zare [fiskalid'dzare] *vt* to exempt from taxes.

fischi'are [fis'kjare] *vi* to whistle ♦ *vt* to whistle; (*attore*) to boo, hiss; **mi fischian le orecchie** my ears are singing; (*fig*) my ears are burning.

fischiet'tare [fiskjet'tare] *vi, vt* to whistle.

fischi'etto [fis'kjetto] *sm* (*strumento*) whistle.

'fischio ['fiskjo] *sm* whistle; **prendere ~i per fiaschi** to get hold of the wrong end of the stick.

'fisco *sm* tax authorities *pl*, ≈ Inland Revenue (*BRIT*), ≈ Internal Revenue Service (*US*).

'fisica *sf vedi* **fisico**.

fisica'mente *av* physically.

'fisico, a, ci, che *ag* physical ♦ *sm/f* physicist ♦ *sm* physique ♦ *sf* physics *sg*.

'fisima *sf* fixation.

fisiolo'gia [fizjolo'dʒia] *sf* physiology.

fisiono'mia *sf* face, physiognomy.

fisiotera'pia *sf* physiotherapy.

fisiotera'pista *sm/f* physiotherapist.

fis'saggio [fis'saddʒo] *sm* (*FOT*) fixing.

fis'sante *ag* (*spray, lozione*) holding.

fis'sare *vt* to fix, fasten; (*guardare intensamente*) to stare at; (*data, condizioni*) to fix, establish, set; (*prenotare*) to book; **~rsi** *vr*: **~rsi su** (*sog: sguardo, attenzione*) to focus on; (*fig: idea*) to become obsessed with.

fissazi'one [fissat'tsjone] *sf* (*PSIC*) fixation.

fissi'one *sf* fission.

'fisso, a *ag* fixed; (*stipendio, impiego*) regular ♦ *av*: **guardar ~ qn/qc** to stare at sb/sth; **avere un ragazzo ~** to have a steady boyfriend; **senza ~a dimora** of no fixed abode.

fitoterma'lismo *sm* herbal hydrotherapy.

'fitta *sf vedi* **fitto**.

fit'tavolo *sm* tenant.

fit'tizio, a [fit'tittsjo] *ag* fictitious, imaginary.

'fitto, a *ag* thick, dense; (*pioggia*) heavy ♦ *sm* (*affitto, pigione*) rent ♦ *sf* sharp pain; **una ~a al cuore** (*fig*) a pang of grief; **nel ~ del bosco** in the heart *o* depths of the wood.

fiu'mana *sf* torrent; (*fig*) stream, flood.

fi'ume *sm* river ♦ *ag inv*: **processo ~** long-running trial; **scorrere a ~i** (*acqua, sangue*) to flow in torrents.

fiu'tare *vt* to smell, sniff; (*sog: animale*) to scent; (*fig: inganno*) to get wind of, smell; **~ tabacco** to take snuff; **~ cocaina** to snort cocaine.

fi'uto *sm* (*sense of*) smell; (*fig*) nose.

'flaccido, a ['flattʃido] *ag* flabby.

fla'cone *sm* bottle.

flagel'lare [fladʒel'lare] *vt* to flog, scourge; (*sog: onde*) to beat against.

fla'gello [fla'dʒɛllo] *sm* scourge.

fla'grante *ag* flagrant; **cogliere qn in** ~ to catch sb red-handed.

fla'nella *sf* flannel.

flash [flaʃ] *sm inv* (*FOT*) flash; (*giornalistico*) newsflash.

flau'tista, i *sm/f* flautist.

'flauto *sm* flute.

'flebile *ag* faint, feeble.

fle'bite *sf* phlebitis.

'flemma *sf* (*calma*) coolness, phlegm; (*MED*) phlegm.

flem'matico, a, ci, che *ag* phlegmatic, cool.

fles'sibile *ag* pliable; (*fig: che si adatta*) flexible.

flessi'one *sf* (*gen*) bending; (*GINNASTICA; a terra*) sit-up; (*: in piedi*) forward bend; (*: sulle gambe*) knee-bend; (*diminuzione*) slight drop, slight fall; (*LING*) inflection; **fare una** ~ to bend; **una** ~ **economica** a downward trend in the economy.

'flesso, a *pp di* **flettere.**

flessu'oso, a *ag* supple, lithe, (*andatura*) flowing, graceful.

'flettere *vt* to bend.

'flipper ['flipper] *sm inv* pinball machine.

flirt [fləːt] *sm inv* brief romance, flirtation.

flir'tare *vi* to flirt.

F.lli *abbr* (= *fratelli*) Bros.

'flora *sf* flora.

'florido, a *ag* flourishing; (*fig*) glowing with health.

'floscio, a, sci, sce ['flɔʃʃo] *ag* (*cappello*) floppy, soft; (*muscoli*) flabby.

'flotta *sf* fleet.

flot'tante *sm* (*ECON*): **titoli a largo** ~ blue chips, stocks on the market.

'fluido, a *ag, sm* fluid.

flu'ire *vi* to flow.

fluore'scente [fluoreʃ'ʃɛnte] *ag* fluorescent.

flu'oro *sm* fluorine.

fluo'ruro *sm* fluoride.

'flusso *sm* flow; (*FISICA, MED*) flux; ~ **e riflusso** ebb and flow; ~ **di cassa** (*COMM*) cash flow.

'flutti *smpl* waves.

fluttu'are *vi* to rise and fall; (*ECON*) to fluctuate.

fluvi'ale *ag* river *cpd*, fluvial.

FM *abbr vedi* **modulazione di frequenza.**

FMI *sigla m vedi* **Fondo Monetario Internazionale.**

FO *sigla* = Forlì.

fo'bia *sf* phobia.

'foca, che *sf* (*ZOOL*) seal.

fo'caccia, ce [fo'kattʃa] *sf* kind of pizza; (*dolce*) bun; **rendere pan per** ~ to get one's own back, give tit for tat.

fo'cale *ag* focal.

focaliz'zare [fokalid'dzare] *vt* (*FOT*: *immagine*) to get into focus; (*fig*: *situazione*) to get into perspective; ~ **l'attenzione su** to focus one's attention on.

'foce ['fotʃe] *sf* (*GEO*) mouth.

fo'chista, i [fo'kista] *sm* (*FERR*) stoker, fireman.

foco'laio *sm* (*MED*) centre (*BRIT*) o center (*US*) of infection; (*fig*) hotbed.

foco'lare *sm* hearth, fireside; (*TECN*) furnace.

fo'coso, a *ag* fiery; (*cavallo*) mettlesome, fiery.

'fodera *sf* (*di vestito*) lining; (*di libro, poltrona*) cover.

fode'rare *vt* to line; to cover.

'fodero *sm* (*di spada*) scabbard; (*di pugnale*) sheath; (*di pistola*) holster.

'foga *sf* enthusiasm, ardour (*BRIT*), ardor (*US*).

'foggia, ge ['fɔddʒa] *sf* (*maniera*) style, (*aspetto*) form, shape; (*moda*) fashion, style.

foggi'are [fod'dʒare] *vt* to shape; to style.

'foglia ['fɔʎʎa] *sf* leaf; **ha mangiato la** ~ (*fig*) he's caught on; ~ **d'argento/d'oro** silver/gold leaf.

fogli'ame [foʎ'ʎame] *sm* foliage, leaves *pl*.

fogli'etto [foʎ'ʎetto] *sm* (*piccolo foglio*) slip of paper, piece of paper; (*manifestino*) leaflet, handout.

'foglio ['fɔʎʎo] *sm* (*di carta*) sheet (of paper); (*di metallo*) sheet; (*documento*) document; (*banconota*) (bank)note; ~ **rosa** (*AUT*) provisional licence; ~ **di via** (*DIR*) expulsion order; ~ **volante** pamphlet.

'fogna ['foɲɲa] *sf* drain, sewer.

fogna'tura [foɲɲa'tura] *sf* drainage, sewerage.

föhn [føːn] *sm inv* hair-dryer.

fo'lata *sf* gust.

fol'clore *sm* folklore.

folclo'ristico, a, ci, che *ag* folk *cpd*.

folgo'rare *vt* (*sog: fulmine*) to strike down; (*: alta tensione*) to electrocute.

folgorazi'one [folgorat'tsjone] *sf* electrocution; **ebbe una** ~ (*fig*: *idea*) he had a brainwave.

'folgore *sf* thunderbolt.

'folla *sf* crowd, throng.

'folle *ag* mad, insane; (*TECN*) idle; **in** ~ (*AUT*) in neutral.

folleggi'are [folled'dʒare] *vi* (*divertirsi*) to

paint the town red.
fol'letto *sm* elf.
fol'lia *sf* folly, foolishness; foolish act;
(*pazzia*) madness, lunacy; **amare qn alla ~**
to love sb to distraction; **costare una ~** to
cost the earth.
'folto, a *ag* thick.
fomen'tare *vt* to stir up, foment.
fon *sm inv* = **föhn**.
fon'dale *sm* (*del mare*) bottom; (*TEAT*)
backdrop; **il ~ marino** the sea bed.
fondamen'tale *ag* fundamental, basic.
fondamenta'lista, i, e *ag, sm/f* (*REL*)
fundamentalist.
fonda'mento *sm* foundation; **~a** *sfpl* (*EDIL*)
foundations.
fon'dare *vt* to found; (*fig: dar base*): **~ qc su**
to base sth on; **~rsi** *vr* (*teorie*): **~rsi (su)** to
be based (on).
fonda'tezza [fonda'tettsa] *sf* (*di ragioni*)
soundness; (*di dubbio, sospetto*) basis in
fact.
fon'dato, a *ag* (*ragioni*) sound; (*dubbio,
sospetto*) well-founded.
fondazi'one [fondat'tsjone] *sf* foundation.
'fondere *vt* (*neve*) to melt; (*metallo*) to fuse,
melt; (*fig: colori*) to blend;
(: *imprese, gruppi*) to merge ♦ *vi* to melt;
~rsi *vr* to melt; (*fig: partiti, correnti*) to
unite, merge.
fonde'ria *sf* foundry.
fondi'ario, a *ag* land *cpd*.
fon'dina *sf* (*piatto fondo*) soup plate;
(*portapistola*) holster.
'fondo, a *ag* deep ♦ *sm* (*di recipiente, pozzo*)
bottom; (*di stanza*) back; (*quantità di
liquido che resta, deposito*) dregs *pl*;
(*sfondo*) background; (*unità immobiliare*)
property, estate; (*somma di denaro*) fund;
(*SPORT*) long-distance race; **~i** *smpl*
(*denaro*) funds; **a notte ~a** at dead of
night; **in ~ a** at the bottom of; at the back
of; (*strada*) at the end of; **laggiù in ~**
(*lontano*) over there; (*in profondità*) down
there; **in ~** (*fig*) after all, all things
considered; **andare fino in ~ a** (*fig*) to
examine thoroughly; **andare a ~** (*nave*) to
sink; **conoscere a ~** to know inside out;
dar ~ a (*fig: provvisti, soldi*) to use up;
toccare il ~ (*fig*) to plumb the depths; **a ~
perduto** (*COMM*) without security; **~
comune di investimento** investment
trust; **F~ Monetario Internazionale (FMI)**
International Monetary Fund (IMF); **~ di
previdenza** social insurance fund; **~ di
riserva** reserve fund; **~ urbano** town
property; **~i di caffè** coffee grounds; **~i
d'esercizio** working capital *sg*; **~i liquidi**

ready money *sg*, liquid assets; **~i di
magazzino** old *o* unsold stock *sg*; **~i neri**
slush fund *sg*.
fondo'tinta *sm inv* (*cosmetico*) foundation.
fo'nema *sm* phoneme.
fo'netica *sf* phonetics *sg*.
fo'netico, a, ci, che *ag* phonetic.
fon'tana *sf* fountain.
fonta'nella *sf* drinking fountain.
'fonte *sf* spring, source; (*fig*) source ♦ *sm*: **~
battesimale** (*REL*) font.
fon'tina *sm full fat hard, sweet cheese
from Valle d'Aosta.*
'footing ['futiŋ] *sm* jogging.
forag'giare [forad'dʒare] *vt* (*cavalli*) to
fodder; (*fig: partito etc*) to bankroll.
fo'raggio [fo'raddʒo] *sm* fodder, forage.
fo'rare *vt* to pierce, make a hole in;
(*pallone*) to burst; (*pneumatico*) to
puncture; (*biglietto*) to punch; **~rsi** *vr* (*gen*)
to develop a hole; (*AUT, pallone, timpano*)
to burst; **~ una gomma** to burst a tyre
(*BRIT*) *o* tire (*US*).
fora'tura *sf* piercing; bursting; puncturing;
punching.
'forbici ['fɔrbitʃi] *sfpl* scissors.
forbi'cina [forbi'tʃina] *sf* earwig.
for'bito, a *ag* (*stile, modi*) polished.
'forca, che *sf* (*AGR*) fork, pitchfork;
(*patibolo*) gallows *sg*.
for'cella [for'tʃɛlla] *sf* (*TECN*) fork; (*di
monte*) pass.
for'chetta [for'ketta] *sf* fork; **essere una
buona ~** to enjoy one's food.
for'cina [for'tʃina] *sf* hairpin.
'forcipe ['fɔrtʃipe] *sm* forceps *pl*.
for'cone *sm* pitchfork.
fo'rense *ag* (*linguaggio*) legal; **avvocato ~**
barrister (*BRIT*), lawyer.
fo'resta *sf* forest; **la F~ Nera** the Black
Forest.
fores'tale *ag* forest *cpd*; **guardia ~** forester.
foreste'ria *sf* (*di convento, palazzo etc*) guest
rooms *pl*, guest quarters *pl*.
foresti'ero, a *ag* foreign ♦ *sm/f* foreigner.
for'fait [fɔr'fɛ] *sm inv*: (**prezzo a**) **~** fixed
price, set price; **dichiarare ~** (*SPORT*) to
withdraw; (*fig*) to give up.
forfe'tario, a *ag*: **prezzo ~** (*da pagare*) fixed
o set price; (*da ricevere*) lump sum.
'forfora *sf* dandruff.
'forgia, ge ['fɔrdʒa] *sf* forge.
forgi'are [for'dʒare] *vt* to forge.
'forma *sf* form; (*aspetto esteriore*) form,
shape; (*DIR: procedura*) procedure; (*per
calzature*) last; (*stampo da cucina*) mould
(*BRIT*), mold (*US*); **~e** *sfpl* (*del corpo*) figure,
shape; **le ~e** (*convenzioni*)

appearances; **errori di** ~ stylistic errors; **essere in** ~ to be in good shape; **tenersi in** ~ to keep fit; **in** ~ **ufficiale/privata** officially/privately; **una** ~ **di formaggio** a (whole) cheese.

formag'gino [formad'dʒino] *sm* processed cheese.

for'maggio [for'maddʒo] *sm* cheese.

for'male *ag* formal.

formalità *sf inv* formality.

formaliz'zare [formalid'dzare] *vt* to formalize.

for'mare *vt* to form, shape, make; (*numero di telefono*) to dial; (*fig: carattere*) to form, mould (*BRIT*), mold (*US*); ~**rsi** *vr* to form, take shape; **il treno si forma a Milano** the train starts from Milan.

for'mato *sm* format, size.

format'tare *vt* (*INFORM*) to format.

formattazi'one [formattat'tsjone] *sf* (*INFORM*) formatting.

formazi'one [format'tsjone] *sf* formation; (*fig: educazione*) training; ~ **professionale** vocational training.

for'mica, che *sf* ant.

formi'caio *sm* anthill.

formico'lare *vi* (*gamba, braccio*) to tingle; (*brulicare: anche fig*): ~ **di** to be swarming with; **mi formicola la gamba** I've got pins and needles in my leg, my leg's tingling.

formico'lio *sm* pins and needles *pl*; swarming.

formi'dabile *ag* powerful, formidable; (*straordinario*) remarkable.

for'moso, a *ag* shapely.

'formula *sf* formula; ~ **di cortesia** (*nelle lettere*) letter ending.

formu'lare *vt* to formulate.

for'nace [for'natʃe] *sf* (*per laterizi etc*) kiln; (*per metalli*) furnace.

for'naio *sm* baker.

for'nello *sm* (*elettrico, a gas*) ring; (*di pipa*) bowl.

for'nire *vt*: ~ **qn di qc**, ~ **qc a qn** to provide *o* supply sb with sth, supply sth to sb; ~**rsi** *vr*: ~**rsi di** (*procurarsi*) to provide o.s. with.

for'nito, a *ag*: **ben** ~ (*negozio*) well-stocked.

forni'tore, 'trice *ag*: **ditta** ~**trice di** ... company supplying ... ♦ *sm/f* supplier.

forni'tura *sf* supply.

'forno *sm* (*di cucina*) oven; (*panetteria*) bakery; (*TECN: per calce etc*) kiln; (: *per metalli*) furnace; **fare i** ~**i** (*MED*) to undergo heat treatment.

'foro *sm* (*buco*) hole; (*STORIA*) forum; (*tribunale*) (law) court.

'forse *av* perhaps, maybe; (*circa*) about; **essere in** ~ to be in doubt.

forsen'nato, a *ag* mad, crazy, insane.

'forte *ag* strong; (*suono*) loud; (*spesa*) considerable, great ♦ *av* strongly; (*velocemente*) fast; (*a voce alta*) loud(ly); (*violentemente*) hard ♦ *sm* (*edificio*) fort; (*specialità*) forte, strong point; **piatto** ~ (*CUC*) main dish; **avere un** ~ **mal di testa/ raffreddore** to have a bad headache/cold; **essere** ~ **in qc** to be good at sth; **farsi** ~ **di qc** to make use of *o* avail o.s. of sth; **dare man** ~ **a qn** to back sb up, support sb; **usare le maniere** ~**i** to use strong-arm tactics.

for'tezza [for'tettsa] *sf* (*morale*) strength; (*luogo fortificato*) fortress.

fortifi'care *vt* to fortify, strengthen.

for'tuito, a *ag* fortuitous, chance *cpd*.

for'tuna *sf* (*destino*) fortune, luck; (*buona sorte*) success, fortune; (*eredità, averi*) fortune; **per** ~ luckily, fortunately; **di** ~ makeshift, improvised; **atterraggio di** ~ emergency landing.

fortu'nale *sm* storm.

fortunata'mente *av* luckily, fortunately.

fortu'nato, a *ag* lucky, fortunate; (*coronato da successo*) successful.

fortu'noso, a *ag* (*vita*) eventful; (*avvenimento*) unlucky.

fo'runcolo *sm* (*MED*) boil.

forvi'are *vt, vi* = **fuorviare**.

'forza ['fortsa] *sf* strength; (*potere*) power; (*FISICA*) force ♦ *escl* come on!; ~ **e** *sfpl* (*fisiche*) strength *sg*; (*MIL*) forces; **per** ~ against one's will; (*naturalmente*) of course; **per** ~ **di cose** by force of circumstances; **a viva** ~ by force; **a** ~ **di** by dint of; **farsi** ~ (*coraggio*) to pluck up one's courage; **bella** ~! (*ironico*) how clever of you (*o* him *etc*)!; ~ **lavoro** work force, manpower; **per causa di** ~ **maggiore** (*DIR*) by reason of an act of God; (*per estensione*) due to circumstances beyond one's control; **la** ~ **pubblica** the police *pl*; ~ **di vendita** (*COMM*) sales force; ~ **di volontà** willpower; **le** ~**e armate** the armed forces; **F**~ **Italia** (*POL*) *moderate right-wing party*.

for'zare [for'tsare] *vt* to force; (*cassaforte, porta*) to force (open); (*voce*) to strain; ~ **qn a fare** to force sb to do.

for'zato, a [for'tsato] *ag* forced ♦ *sm* (*DIR*) prisoner sentenced to hard labour (*BRIT*) *o* labor (*US*).

forzi'ere [for'tsjere] *sm* strongbox; (*di pirati*) treasure chest.

for'zista, i, e [for'tsista] *ag* of Forza Italia ♦ *sm/f* member (*o* supporter) of Forza Italia.

for'zuto, a [for'tsuto] *ag* big and strong.

fos'chia [fos'kia] *sf* mist, haze.

'fosco, a, schi, sche *ag* dark, gloomy; **dipingere qc a tinte** ~**sche** (*fig*) to paint a gloomy picture of sth.

fos'fato *sm* phosphate.

fosfore'scente [fosforeʃ'ʃɛnte] *ag* phosphorescent; (*lancetta dell'orologio etc*) luminous.

'fosforo *sm* phosphorous.

'fossa *sf* pit; (*di cimitero*) grave; ~ **biologica** septic tank; ~ **comune** mass grave.

fos'sato *sm* ditch; (*di fortezza*) moat.

fos'setta *sf* dimple.

'fossi *etc vb vedi* **essere**.

'fossile *ag*, *sm* fossil (*cpd*).

'fosso *sm* ditch; (*MIL*) trench.

'foste *etc vb vedi* **essere**.

'foto *sf inv* photo; ~ **ricordo** souvenir photo; ~ **tessera** passport(-type) photo.

foto... *prefisso* photo....

fotocomposi'tore *sm* filmsetter.

fotocomposizi'one [fotokompozit'tsjone] *sf* film setting.

foto'copia *sf* photocopy.

fotocopi'are *vt* to photocopy.

foto'genico, a, ci, che [foto'dʒɛniko] *ag* photogenic.

fotogra'fare *vt* to photograph.

fotogra'fia *sf* (*procedimento*) photography; (*immagine*) photograph; **fare una** ~ to take a photograph; **una** ~ **a colori/in bianco e nero** a colour/black and white photograph.

foto'grafico, a, ci, che *ag* photographic; **macchina** ~**a** camera.

fo'tografo, a *sm/f* photographer.

foto'gramma, i *sm* (*CINE*) frame.

fotomo'dello, a *sm/f* fashion model.

fotomon'taggio [fotomon'taddʒo] *sm* photomontage.

fotore'porter *sm/f inv* newspaper (*o* magazine) photographer.

fotoro'manzo [fotoro'mandzo] *sm* romantic picture story.

foto'sintesi *sf* photosynthesis.

'fottere *vt* (*fam!: avere rapporti sessuali*) to fuck (*!*), screw (*!*); (: *rubare*) to pinch, swipe; (: *fregare*): **mi hanno fottuto** they played a dirty trick on me; **vai a farti** ~! fuck off! (*!*).

fot'tuto, a *ag* (*fam!*) bloody, fucking (*!*).

fou'lard [fu'lar] *sm inv* scarf.

FR *sigla* = Frosinone.

fr. *abbr* (*COMM*) = **franco**.

fra *prep* = **tra**.

fracas'sare *vt* to shatter, smash; ~**rsi** *vr* to shatter, smash; (*veicolo*) to crash.

fra'casso *sm* smash; crash; (*baccano*) din, racket.

'fradicio, a, ci, ce ['fraditʃo] *ag* (*guasto*) rotten; (*molto bagnato*) soaking (wet); **ubriaco** ~ blind drunk.

'fragile ['fradʒile] *ag* fragile; (*salute*) delicate; (*nervi, vetro*) brittle.

fragilità [fradʒili'ta] *sf* (*vedi ag*) fragility; delicacy; brittleness.

'fragola *sf* strawberry.

fra'gore *sm* (*di cascate, carro armato*) roar; (*di tuono*) rumble.

frago'roso, a *ag* deafening; **ridere in modo** ~ to roar with laughter.

fra'grante *ag* fragrant.

fraintendi'mento *sm* misunderstanding.

frain'tendere *vt* to misunderstand.

frain'teso, a *pp di* **fraintendere**.

fram'mento *sm* fragment.

fram'misto, a *ag*: ~ **a** interspersed with, mixed with.

'frana *sf* landslide; (*fig: persona*): **essere una** ~ to be useless, be a walking disaster area.

fra'nare *vi* to slip, slide down.

franca'mente *av* frankly.

fran'cese [fran'tʃeze] *ag* French ♦ *sm/f* Frenchman/woman ♦ *sm* (*LING*) French; **i F**~**i** the French.

fran'chezza [fran'kettsa] *sf* frankness, openness.

fran'chigia, gie [fran'kidʒa] *sf* (*AMM*) exemption; (*DIR*) franchise; (*NAUT*) shore leave; ~ **doganale** exemption from customs duty.

'Francia ['frantʃa] *sf*: **la** ~ France.

'franco, a, chi, che *ag* (*COMM*) free; (*sincero*) frank, open, sincere ♦ *sm* (*moneta*) franc; **farla** ~**a** (*fig*) to get off scot-free; ~ **a bordo** free on board; ~ **di dogana** duty-free; ~ **a domicilio** delivered free of charge; ~ **fabbrica** ex factory, ex works; **prezzo** ~ **fabbrica** ex-works price; ~ **magazzino** ex warehouse; ~ **di porto** carriage free; ~ **vagone** free on rail; ~ **tiratore** *sm* sniper; (*POL*) *member of parliament who votes against his own party*.

franco'bollo *sm* (*postage*) stamp.

franco-cana'dese *ag*, *sm/f* French Canadian.

Franco'forte *sf* Frankfurt.

fran'gente [fran'dʒɛnte] *sm* (*onda*) breaker; (*scoglio emergente*) reef; (*circostanza*) situation, circumstance.

'**frangia, ge** ['frandʒa] *sf* fringe.
frangi'flutti [frandʒi'flutti] *sm inv*
breakwater.
frangi'vento [frandʒi'vɛnto] *sm* windbreak.
fran'toio *sm* (*AGR*) olive press; (*TECN*)
crusher.
frantu'mare *vt*, **~rsi** *vr* to break into
pieces, shatter.
fran'tumi *smpl* pieces, bits; (*schegge*)
splinters; **andare in ~**, **mandare in ~** to
shatter, smash to pieces *o* smithereens.
frappé *sm* (*CUC*) milk shake.
fra'sario *sm* (*gergo*) vocabulary, language.
'**frasca, sche** *sf* (leafy) branch; **saltare di
palo in ~** to jump from one subject to
another.
'**frase** *sf* (*LING*) sentence; (*locuzione,
espressione*, *MUS*) phrase; **~ fatta** set
phrase.
fraseolo'gia [frazeolo'dʒia] *sf* phraseology.
'**frassino** *sm* ash (tree).
frastagli'ato, a [frastaʎ'ʎato] *ag* (*costa*)
indented, jagged.
frastor'nare *vt* (*intontire*) to daze;
(*confondere*) to bewilder, befuddle.
frastor'nato, a *ag* dazed; bewildered.
frastu'ono *sm* hubbub, din.
'**frate** *sm* friar, monk.
fratel'lanza [fratel'lantsa] *sf* brotherhood;
(*associazione*) fraternity.
fratel'lastro *sm* stepbrother.
fra'tello *sm* brother; **~i** *smpl* brothers; (*nel
senso di fratelli e sorelle*) brothers and
sisters.
fra'terno, a *ag* fraternal, brotherly.
fratri'cida, i, e [fratri'tʃida] *ag* fratricidal
♦ *sm/f* fratricide; **guerra ~** civil war.
frat'taglie [frat'taʎʎe] *sfpl* (*CUC: gen*) offal
sg; (: *di pollo*) giblets.
frat'tanto *av* in the meantime, meanwhile.
frat'tempo *sm*: **nel ~** in the meantime,
meanwhile.
frat'tura *sf* fracture; (*fig*) split, break.
frattu'rare *vt* to fracture.
fraudo'lento, a *ag* fraudulent.
fraziona'mento [frattsjona'mento] *sm*
division, splitting up.
frazio'nare [frattsjo'nare] *vt* to divide, split
up.
frazi'one [frat'tsjone] *sf* fraction; (*borgata*):
~ di comune hamlet.
'**freccia, ce** ['frettʃa] *sf* arrow; **~ di
direzione** (*AUT*) indicator.
frec'ciata [fret'tʃata] *sf*: **lanciare una ~** to
make a cutting remark.
fred'dare *vt* to shoot dead.
fred'dezza [fred'dettsa] *sf* coldness.
'**freddo, a** *ag*, *sm* cold; **fa ~** it's cold; **aver ~**

to be cold; **soffrire il ~** to feel the cold; **a
~** (*fig*) deliberately.
freddo'loso, a *ag* sensitive to the cold.
fred'dura *sf* pun.
'**freezer** ['frizer] *sm inv* fridge-freezer.
fre'gare *vt* to rub; (*fam: truffare*) to take in,
cheat; (: *rubare*) to swipe, pinch;
fregarsene (*fam!*): **chi se ne frega?** who
gives a damn (about it)?
fre'gata *sf* rub; (*fam*) swindle; (*NAUT*)
frigate.
frega'tura *sf* (*fam: imbroglio*) rip-off;
(: *delusione*) let-down.
fregherò *etc* [frege'rɔ] *vb vedi* **fregare**.
'**fregio** ['fredʒo] *sm* (*ARCHIT*) frieze;
(*ornamento*) decoration.
'**fremere** *vi*: **~ di** to tremble *o* quiver with;
~ d'impazienza to be champing at the bit.
'**fremito** *sm* tremor, quiver.
fre'nare *vt* (*veicolo*) to slow down; (*cavallo*)
to rein in; (*lacrime*) to restrain, hold back
♦ *vi* to brake; **~rsi** *vr* (*fig*) to restrain o.s.,
control o.s.
fre'nata *sf*: **fare una ~** to brake.
frene'sia *sf* frenzy.
fre'netico, a, ci, che *ag* frenetic.
'**freno** *sm* brake; (*morso*) bit; **tenere a ~**
(*passioni etc*) to restrain; **tenere a ~ la
lingua** to hold one's tongue; **~ a disco**
disc brake; **~ a mano** handbrake.
'**freon** ® *sm inv* (*CHIM*) Freon ®.
frequen'tare *vt* (*scuola, corso*) to attend;
(*locale, bar*) to go to, frequent; (*persone*) to
see (often).
frequen'tato, a *ag* (*locale*) busy.
fre'quente *ag* frequent; **di ~** frequently.
fre'quenza [fre'kwɛntsa] *sf* frequency; (*INS*)
attendance.
fre'sare *vt* (*TECN*) to mill.
fres'chezza [fres'kettsa] *sf* freshness.
'**fresco, a, schi, sche** *ag* fresh;
(*temperatura*) cool; (*notizia*) recent, fresh
♦ *sm*: **godere il ~** to enjoy the cool air;
~ di bucato straight from the wash,
newly washed; **stare ~** (*fig*) to be in for it;
mettere al ~ to put in a cool place; (*fig: in
prigione*) to put inside *o* in the cooler.
fres'cura *sf* cool.
'**fresia** *sf* freesia.
'**fretta** *sf* hurry, haste; **in ~** in a hurry; **in ~
e furia** in a mad rush; **aver ~** to be in a
hurry; **far ~ a qn** to hurry sb.
frettolosa'mente *av* hurriedly, in a rush.
fretto'loso, a *ag* (*persona*) in a hurry;
(*lavoro etc*) hurried, rushed.
fri'abile *ag* (*terreno*) friable; (*pasta*)
crumbly.
'**friggere** ['friddʒere] *vt* to fry ♦ *vi* (*olio etc*)

to sizzle; **vai a farti** ~! (*fam*) get lost!

frigidità [fridʒidi'ta] *sf* frigidity.

'frigido, a ['fridʒido] *ag* (*MED*) frigid.

fri'gnare [friɲ'ɲare] *vi* to whine, snivel.

fri'gnone, a [friɲ'ɲone] *sm/f* whiner, sniveller.

'frigo, ghi *sm* fridge.

frigo'rifero, a *ag* refrigerating ♦ *sm* refrigerator; **cella** ~**a** a cold store.

fringu'ello *sm* chaffinch.

'frissi *etc vb vedi* **friggere**.

frit'tata *sf* omelet(te); **fare una** ~ (*fig*) to make a mess of things.

frit'tella *sf* (*CUC*) pancake; (: *ripiena*) fritter.

'fritto, a *pp di* **friggere** ♦ *ag* fried ♦ *sm* fried food; **ormai siamo** ~**i!** (*fig fam*) now we've had it!; **è un argomento** ~ **e rifritto** that's old hat; ~ **misto** mixed fry.

frit'tura *sf* (*cibo*) fried food; ~ **di pesce** mixed fried fish.

friu'lano, a *ag* of (*o* from) Friuli.

frivo'lezza [frivo'lettsa] *sf* frivolity.

'frivolo, a *ag* frivolous.

frizi'one [frit'tsjone] *sf* friction; (*di pelle*) rub, rub-down; (*AUT*) clutch.

friz'zante [frid'dzante] *ag* (*anche fig*) sparkling.

'frizzo ['friddzo] *sm* witticism.

fro'dare *vt* to defraud, cheat.

'frode *sf* fraud; ~ **fiscale** tax evasion.

'frodo *sm*: **di** ~ illegal, contraband; **pescatore di** ~, **cacciatore di** ~ poacher.

'frogia, gie ['frɔdʒa] *sf* (*di cavallo etc*) nostril.

'frollo, a *ag* (*carne*) tender; (: *di selvaggina*) high; (*fig: persona*) soft; **pasta** ~**a** short(crust) pastry.

'fronda *sf* (leafy) branch; (*di partito politico*) internal opposition; ~**e** *sfpl* (*di albero*) foliage *sg*.

fron'tale *ag* frontal; (*scontro*) head-on.

'fronte *sf* (*ANAT*) forehead; (*di edificio*) front, façade ♦ *sm* (*MIL, POL, METEOR*) front; **a** ~, **di** ~ facing, opposite; **di** ~ **a** (*posizione*) opposite, facing, in front of; (*a paragone di*) compared with; **far** ~ **a** (*nemico, problema*) to confront; (*responsabilità*) to face up to; (*spese*) to cope with.

fronteggi'are [fronted'dʒare] *vt* (*avversari, difficoltà*) to face, stand up to; (*spese*) to cope with.

frontes'pizio [frontes'pittsjo] *sm* (*ARCHIT*) frontispiece; (*di libro*) title page.

fronti'era *sf* border, frontier.

fron'tone *sm* pediment.

'fronzolo ['frondzolo] *sm* frill.

'frotta *sf* crowd; **in** ~, **a** ~**e** in their

hundreds, in droves.

'frottola *sf* fib; **raccontare un sacco di** ~**e** to tell a pack of lies.

fru'gale *ag* frugal.

fru'gare *vi* to rummage ♦ *vt* to search.

frugherò *etc* [fruge'rɔ] *vb vedi* **frugare**.

frui'tore *sm* user.

fruizi'one [fruit'tsjone] *sf* use.

frul'lare *vt* (*CUC*) to whisk ♦ *vi* (*uccelli*) to flutter; **cosa ti frulla in mente?** what is going on in that mind of yours?

frul'lato *sm* (*CUC*) milk shake; (: *con solo frutta*) fruit drink.

frulla'tore *sm* electric mixer.

frul'lino *sm* whisk.

fru'mento *sm* wheat.

frusci'are [fruʃ'ʃare] *vi* to rustle.

fru'scio [fruʃ'ʃio] *sm* rustle; rustling.

'frusta *sf* whip; (*CUC*) whisk.

frus'tare *vt* to whip.

frus'tata *sf* lash.

frus'tino *sm* riding crop.

frus'trare *vt* to frustrate.

frus'trato, a *ag* frustrated.

frustrazi'one [frustrat'tsjone] *sf* frustration.

'frutta *sf* fruit; (*portata*) dessert; ~ **candita/secca** candied/dried fruit.

frut'tare *vi* (*investimenti, deposito*) to bear dividends, give a return; **il mio deposito in banca (mi) frutta il 10%** my bank deposits bring (me) in 10%; **quella gara gli fruttò la medaglia d'oro** he won the gold medal in that competition.

frut'teto *sm* orchard.

frutticol'tura *sf* fruit growing.

frut'tifero, a *ag* (*albero etc*) fruit-bearing; (*fig: che frutta*) fruitful, profitable; **deposito** ~ interest-bearing deposit.

frutti'vendolo, a *sm/f* greengrocer (*BRIT*), produce dealer (*US*).

'frutto *sm* fruit; (*fig: risultato*) result(s); (*ECON: interesse*) interest; (: *reddito*) income; **è** ~ **della tua immaginazione** it's a figment of your imagination; ~**i di mare** seafood *sg*.

fruttu'oso, a *ag* fruitful, profitable.

FS *abbr* (= *Ferrovie dello Stato*) Italian railways.

f.t. *abbr* = **fuori testo**.

f.to. *abbr* (= *firmato*) signed.

fu *vb vedi* **essere** ♦ *ag inv*: **il** ~ **Paolo Bianchi** the late Paolo Bianchi.

fuci'lare [futʃi'lare] *vt* to shoot.

fuci'lata [futʃi'lata] *sf* rifle shot.

fucilazi'one [futʃilat'tsjone] *sf* execution (by firing squad).

fu'cile [fu'tʃile] *sm* rifle, gun; (*da caccia*)

shotgun, gun; ~ **a canne mozze** sawn-off shotgun.

fu'cina [fu't∫ina] *sf* forge.

'fuco, chi *sm* drone.

'fucsia *sf* fuchsia.

'fuga, ghe *sf* escape, flight; (*di gas, liquidi*) leak; (*MUS*) fugue; **mettere qn in** ~ to put sb to flight; ~ **di cervelli** brain drain.

fu'gace [fu'gat∫e] *ag* fleeting, transient.

fu'gare *vt* (*dubbi, incertezze*) to dispel, drive out.

fug'gevole [fud'dʒevole] *ag* fleeting.

fuggi'asco, a, schi, sche [fud'dʒasko] *ag, sm/f* fugitive.

fuggi'fuggi [fuddʒi'fuddʒi] *sm* scramble, stampede.

fug'gire [fud'dʒire] *vi* to flee, run away; (*fig: passar veloce*) to fly ♦ *vt* to avoid.

fuggi'tivo, a [fuddʒi'tivo] *sm/f* fugitive, runaway.

'fui *vb vedi* **essere**.

'fulcro *sm* (*FISICA*) fulcrum; (*fig: di teoria, questione*) central *o* key point.

ful'gore *sm* brilliance, splendour (*BRIT*), splendor (*US*).

fu'liggine [fu'liddʒine] *sf* soot.

fulmi'nare *vt* (*sog: elettricità*) to electrocute; (*con arma da fuoco*) to shoot dead; ~**rsi** *vr* (*lampadina*) to go, blow; (*fig: con lo sguardo*): **mi fulminò** (**con uno sguardo**) he looked daggers at me.

'fulmine *sm* bolt of lightning; ~**i** *smpl* lightning *sg*; ~ **a ciel sereno** bolt from the blue.

ful'mineo, a *ag* (*fig: scatto*) rapid; (: *minaccioso*) threatening.

'fulvo, a *ag* tawny.

fumai'olo *sm* (*di nave*) funnel; (*di fabbrica*) chimney.

fu'mante *ag* (*piatto etc*) steaming.

fu'mare *vi* to smoke; (*emettere vapore*) to steam ♦ *vt* to smoke.

fu'mario, a *ag*: **casa** ~**a** flue.

fu'mata *sf* (*segnale*) smoke signal; **farsi una** ~ to have a smoke; ~ **bianca/nera** (*in Vaticano*) signal that a new pope has/has not been elected.

fuma'tore, 'trice *sm/f* smoker.

fu'metto *sm* comic strip; **giornale** *m* **a** ~**i** comic.

'fummo *vb vedi* **essere**.

'fumo *sm* smoke; (*vapore*) steam; (*il fumare tabacco*) smoking; ~**i** *smpl* (*industriali etc*) fumes; **vendere** ~ to deceive, cheat; **è tutto** ~ **e niente arrosto** it has no substance to it; **i** ~**i dell'alcool** (*fig*) the after-effects of drink; ~ **passivo** passive smoking.

fu'mogeno, a [fu'mɔdʒeno] *ag* (*candelotto*) smoke *cpd* ♦ *sm* smoke bomb; **cortina** ~**a** smoke screen.

fu'moso, a *ag* smoky; (*fig*) muddled.

fu'nambolo, a *sm/f* tightrope walker.

'fune *sf* rope, cord; (*più grossa*) cable.

'funebre *ag* (*rito*) funeral; (*aspetto*) gloomy, funereal.

fune'rale *sm* funeral.

fu'nesto, a *ag* (*incidente*) fatal; (*errore, decisione*) fatal, disastrous; (*atmosfera*) gloomy, dismal.

'fungere ['fundʒere] *vi*: ~ **da** to act as.

'fungo, ghi *sm* fungus; (*commestibile*) mushroom; ~ **velenoso** toadstool; **crescere come i** ~**ghi** (*fig*) to spring up overnight.

funico'lare *sf* funicular railway.

funi'via *sf* cable railway.

'funsi *etc vb vedi* **fungere**.

'funto, a *pp di* **fungere**.

funzio'nare [funtsjo'nare] *vi* to work, function; (*fungere*): ~ **da** to act as.

funzio'nario [funtsjo'narjo] *sm* official; ~ **statale** civil servant.

funzi'one [fun'tsjone] *sf* function; (*carica*) post, position; (*REL*) service; **in** ~ (*meccanismo*) in operation; **in** ~ **di** (*come*) as; **vive in** ~ **dei figli** he lives for his children; **far** ~ **di** to act as; **fare la** ~ **di qn** (*farne le veci*) to take sb's place.

fu'oco, chi *sm* fire; (*fornello*) ring; (*FOT, FISICA*) focus; **dare** ~ **a qc** to set fire to sth; **far** ~ (*sparare*) to fire; **prendere** ~ to catch fire; ~ **d'artificio** firework; ~ **di paglia** flash in the pan; ~ **sacro** *o* **di Sant'Antonio** (*MED fam*) shingles *sg*.

fuorché [fwor'ke] *cong, prep* except.

FU'ORI *sigla m* (= *Fronte Unitario Omosessuale Rivoluzionario Italiano*) *gay liberation movement*.

fu'ori *av* outside; (*all'aperto*) outdoors, outside; (~ *di casa, SPORT*) out; (*esclamativo*) get out! ♦ *prep*: ~ (**di**) out of, outside ♦ *sm* outside; **essere in** ~ (*sporgere*) to stick out; **lasciar** ~ **qc/qn** to leave sth/sb out; **far** ~ (*fam: soldi*) to spend; (: *cioccolatini*) to eat up; (: *rubare*) to nick; **far** ~ **qn** (*fam*) to kill sb, do sb in; **essere tagliato** ~ (*da un gruppo, ambiente*) to be excluded; **essere** ~ **di sé** to be beside oneself; ~ **luogo** (*inopportuno*) out of place, uncalled for; ~ **mano** out of the way, remote; ~ **pasto** between meals; ~ **pericolo** out of danger; ~ **dai piedi!** get out of the way!; ~ **servizio** out of order; ~ **stagione** out of season; **illustrazione** ~ **testo** (*STAMPA*) plate; ~ **uso** out of use.

fuori'bordo *sm inv* speedboat (with outboard motor); outboard motor.
fuori'busta *sm inv* unofficial payment.
fuori'classe *sm/f inv* (undisputed) champion.
fuori'corso *ag inv* (*moneta*) no longer in circulation; (*INS*): **(studente)** ~ undergraduate who has not completed a course in due time.
fuorigi'oco [fwori'dʒɔko] *sm* offside.
fuori'legge [fwori'leddʒe] *sm/f inv* outlaw.
fuoriprog'ramma *sm inv* (*TV, RADIO*) unscheduled programme; (*fig*) change of plan *o* programme.
fuori'serie *ag inv* (*auto etc*) custom-built ♦ *sf* custom-built car.
fuoris'trada *sm* (*AUT*) cross-country vehicle.
fuoru'scito, a, fuoriu'scito, a [fwor(i)uʃ'ʃito] *sm/f* exile ♦ *sf* (*di gas*) leakage, escape; (*di sangue, linfa*) seepage.
fuorvi'are *vt* to mislead; (*fig*) to lead astray ♦ *vi* to go astray.
furbacchi'one, a [furbak'kjone] *sm/f* cunning old devil.
fur'bizia [fur'bittsja] *sf* (*vedi ag*) cleverness; cunning; **una** ~ a cunning trick.
'furbo, a *ag* clever, smart; (*peg*) cunning ♦ *sm/f*: **fare il** ~ to (try to) be clever *o* smart; **fatti** ~! show a bit of sense!
fu'rente *ag*: ~ **(contro)** furious (with).
fure'ria *sf* (*MIL*) orderly room.
fu'retto *sm* ferret.
fur'fante *sm* rascal, scoundrel.
furgon'cino [furgon'tʃino] *sm* small van.
fur'gone *sm* van.
'furia *sf* (*ira*) fury, rage; (*fig: impeto*) fury, violence; (*fretta*) rush; **a** ~ **di** by dint of; **andare su tutte le** ~**e** to fly into a rage.
furi'bondo, a *ag* furious.
furi'ere *sm* quartermaster.
furi'oso, a *ag* furious; (*mare, vento*) raging.
'furono *vb vedi* **essere**.
fu'rore *sm* fury; (*esaltazione*) frenzy; **far** ~ to be all the rage.
furtiva'mente *av* furtively.
fur'tivo, a *ag* furtive.
'furto *sm* theft; ~ **con scasso** burglary.
'fusa *sfpl*: **fare le** ~ to purr.
fu'scello [fuʃ'ʃɛllo] *sm* twig.
fu'seaux *smpl inv* leggings.
'fusi *etc vb vedi* **fondere**.
fu'sibile *sm* (*ELETTR*) fuse.
fusi'one *sf* (*di metalli*) fusion, melting; (*colata*) casting; (*COMM*) merger; (*fig*) merging.
'fuso, a *pp di* **fondere** ♦ *sm* (*FILATURA*)

spindle; **diritto come un** ~ as stiff as a ramrod; ~ **orario** time zone.
fusoli'era *sf* (*AER*) fusillage.
fus'tagno [fus'taɲɲo] *sm* corduroy.
fus'tella *sf* (*su scatola di medicinali*) tear-off tab.
fusti'gare *vt* (*frustare*) to flog; (*fig: costumi*) to censure, denounce.
fus'tino *sm* (*di detersivo*) tub.
'fusto *sm* stem; (*ANAT, di albero*) trunk; (*recipiente*) drum, can; (*fam*) he-man.
'futile *ag* vain, futile.
futilità *sf inv* futility.
futu'rismo *sm* futurism.

G g

G, g [dʒi] *sf o m inv* (*lettera*) G, g; **G come Genova** ≈ G for George.
g. *abbr* (= *grammo*) g.
G7 [dʒi'sɛtte] *smpl* G7 (*Group of Seven*).
gabar'dine [gabar'din] *sm* (*tessuto*) gabardine; (*soprabito*) gabardine raincoat.
gab'bare *vt* to take in, dupe; ~**rsi** *vr*: ~**rsi di qn** to make fun of sb.
'gabbia *sf* cage; (*DIR*) dock; (*da imballaggio*) crate; **la** ~ **degli accusati** (*DIR*) the dock; ~ **dell'ascensore** lift (*BRIT*) *o* elevator (*US*) shaft; ~ **toracica** (*ANAT*) rib cage.
gabbi'ano *sm* (sea)gull.
gabi'netto *sm* (*MED etc*) consulting room; (*POL*) ministry; (*di decenza*) toilet, lavatory; (*INS: di fisica etc*) laboratory.
Ga'bon *sm*: **il** ~ Gabon.
ga'elico, a, ci, che *ag, sm* Gaelic.
gaffe [gaf] *sf inv* blunder, boob (*fam*).
gagli'ardo, a [gaʎ'ʎardo] *ag* strong, vigorous.
gai'ezza [ga'jettsa] *sf* gaiety, cheerfulness.
'gaio, a *ag* cheerful.
'gala *sf* (*sfarzo*) pomp; (*festa*) gala.
ga'lante *ag* gallant, courteous; (*avventura, poesia*) amorous.
galante'ria *sf* gallantry.
galantu'omo, *pl* galantu'omini *sm* gentleman.
Ga'lapagos *sfpl*: **le (isole)** ~ the Galapagos Islands.
ga'lassia *sf* galaxy.
gala'teo *sm* (good) manners *pl*, etiquette.

gale'otto *sm* (*rematore*) galley slave; (*carcerato*) convict.

ga'lera *sf* (*NAUT*) galley; (*prigione*) prison.

'galla *sf*: a ~ afloat; venire a ~ to surface, come to the surface; (*fig: verità*) to come out.

galleggia'mento [galleddʒa'mento] *sm* floating; linea di ~ (*di nave*) waterline.

galleggi'ante [galled'dʒante] *ag* floating ♦ *sm* (*natante*) barge; (*di pescatore, lenza, TECN*) float.

galleggi'are [galled'dʒare] *vi* to float.

galle'ria *sf* (*traforo*) tunnel; (*ARCHIT, d'arte*) gallery; (*TEAT*) circle; (*strada coperta con negozi*) arcade; ~ del vento o aerodinamica (*AER*) wind tunnel.

'Galles *sm*: il ~ Wales.

gal'lese *ag* Welsh ♦ *smf* Welshman/woman ♦ *sm* (*LING*) Welsh; i G~i the Welsh.

gal'letta *sf* cracker; (*NAUT*) ship's biscuit.

gal'letto *sm* young cock, cockerel; (*fig*) cocky young man; fare il ~ to play the gallant.

'Gallia *sf*: la ~ Gaul.

gal'lina *sf* hen; andare a letto con le ~e to go to bed early.

gal'lismo *sm* machismo.

'gallo *sm* cock; al canto del ~ at daybreak, at cockcrow; fare il ~ to play the gallant.

gal'lone *sm* piece of braid; (*MIL*) stripe; (*unità di misura*) gallon.

galop'pare *vi* to gallop.

galop'pino *sm* errand boy; (*POL*) canvasser.

ga'loppo *sm* gallop; al o di ~ at a gallop.

galvaniz'zare [galvanid'dzare] *vt* to galvanize.

'gamba *sf* leg; (*asta: di lettera*) stem; in ~ (*in buona salute*) well; (*bravo, sveglio*) bright, smart; prendere qc sotto ~ (*fig*) to treat sth too lightly; scappare a ~e levate to take to one's heels; ~e! scatter!

gam'bale *sm* legging.

gambe'retto *sm* shrimp.

'gambero *sm* (*di acqua dolce*) crayfish; (*di mare*) prawn.

'Gambia *sf*: la ~ the Gambia.

gambiz'zare [gambid'dzare] *vt* to kneecap.

'gambo *sm* stem; (*di frutta*) stalk.

ga'mella *sf* mess tin.

'gamma *sf* (*MUS*) scale; (*di colori, fig*) range; ~ di prodotti product range.

ga'nascia, sce [ga'naʃʃa] *sf* jaw; ~sce del freno (*AUT*) brake shoes.

'gancio ['gantʃo] *sm* hook.

'Gange ['gandʒe] *sm*: il ~ the Ganges.

'gangheri ['gangeri] *smpl*: uscire dai ~ (*fig*) to fly into a temper.

gan'grena *sf* = cancrena.

'gara *sf* competition; (*SPORT*) competition; contest; match; (: *corsa*) race; fare a ~ to compete, vie; ~ d'appalto (*COMM*) tender.

ga'rage [ga'raʒ] *sm inv* garage.

ga'rante *smf* guarantor.

garan'tire *vt* to guarantee; (*debito*) to stand surety for; (*dare per certo*) to assure.

garan'tismo *sm* protection of civil liberties.

garan'tista, i, e *ag* concerned with civil liberties.

garan'zia [garan'tsia] *sf* guarantee; (*pegno*) security; in ~ under guarantee.

gar'bare *vi*: non mi garba I don't like it (o him *etc*).

garba'tezza [garba'tettsa] *sf* courtesy, politeness.

gar'bato, a *ag* courteous, polite.

'garbo *sm* (*buone maniere*) politeness, courtesy; (*di vestito etc*) grace, style.

gar'buglio [gar'buʎʎo] *sm* tangle; (*fig*) muddle, mess.

gareggi'are [gared'dʒare] *vi* to compete.

garga'nella *sf*: a ~ from the bottle.

garga'rismo *sm* gargle; fare i ~i to gargle.

ga'ritta *sf* (*di caserma*) sentry box.

ga'rofano *sm* carnation; chiodo di ~ clove.

gar'retto *sm* hock.

gar'rire *vi* to chirp.

'garrulo, a *ag* (*uccello*) chirping; (*persona: loquace*) garrulous, talkative.

'garza ['gardza] *sf* (*per bende*) gauze.

gar'zone [gar'dzone] *sm* (*di negozio*) boy.

gas *sm inv* gas; a tutto ~ at full speed; dare ~ (*AUT*) to accelerate; ~ lacrimogeno tear gas; ~ naturale natural gas.

ga'sare *etc* = gassare *etc*.

ga'sato, a *smf* (*fam: persona*) freak.

gas'dotto *sm* gas pipeline.

ga'solio *sm* diesel (oil).

ga's(s)are *vt* to aerate, carbonate; (*asfissiare*) to gas; ~rsi *vr* (*fam*) to get excited.

ga's(s)ato, a *ag* (*bibita*) aerated, fizzy.

gas'soso, a *ag* gaseous; gassy ♦ *sf* fizzy drink.

'gastrico, a, ci, che *ag* gastric.

gast'rite *sf* gastritis.

gastroente'rite *sf* gastroenteritis.

gastrono'mia *sf* gastronomy.

gas'tronomo, a *smf* gourmet, gastronome.

G.A.T.T. *sigla m* (= *General Agreement on Tariffs and Trade*) GATT.

'gatta *sf* cat, she-cat; una ~ da pelare (*fam*) a thankless task; qui ~ ci cova! I smell a rat!, there's something fishy going on

here!
gatta'buia *sf (fam scherzoso: prigione)* clink.
gat'tino *sm* kitten.
'gatto *sm* cat, tomcat; ~ **delle nevi** (*AUT, SCI*) snowcat; ~ **a nove code** cat-o'-nine-tails; ~ **selvatico** wildcat.
gatto'pardo *sm*: ~ **africano** serval; ~ **americano** ocelot.
gat'tuccio [gat'tuttʃo] *sm* dogfish.
gau'dente *sm/f* pleasure-seeker.
'gaudio *sm* joy, happiness.
ga'vetta *sf (MIL)* mess tin; **venire dalla** ~ (*MIL, fig*) to rise from the ranks.
'gazza ['gaddza] *sf* magpie.
gaz'zarra [gad'dzarra] *sf* racket, din.
gaz'zella [gad'dzɛlla] *sf* gazelle; (*dei carabinieri*) (high-speed) police car.
gaz'zetta [gad'dzetta] *sf* news sheet; **G~ Ufficiale** *official publication containing details of new laws*.
gaz'zoso, a [gad'dzoso] *ag* = **gassoso**.
Gazz. Uff. *abbr* = **Gazzetta Ufficiale**.
GB *sigla* (= *Gran Bretagna*) GB.
G.C. *abbr* = **genio civile**.
G.d.F. *abbr* = **guardia di finanza**.
GE *sigla* = *Genova*.
gel [dʒɛl] *sm inv* gel.
ge'lare [dʒe'lare] *vt, vi, vb impers* to freeze; **mi ha gelato il sangue** (*fig*) it made my blood run cold.
ge'lata [dʒe'lata] *sf* frost.
gela'taio, a [dʒela'tajo] *sm/f* ice-cream vendor.
gelate'ria [dʒelate'ria] *sf* ice-cream shop.
gela'tina [dʒela'tina] *sf* gelatine; ~ **esplosiva** gelignite; ~ **di frutta** fruit jelly.
gelati'noso, a [dʒelati'noso] *ag* gelatinous, jelly-like.
ge'lato, a [dʒe'lato] *ag* frozen ♦ *sm* ice cream.
'gelido, a ['dʒɛlido] *ag* icy, ice-cold.
'gelo ['dʒɛlo] *sm (temperatura)* intense cold; (*brina*) frost; (*fig*) chill.
ge'lone [dʒe'lone] *sm* chilblain.
gelo'sia [dʒelo'sia] *sf* jealousy.
ge'loso, a [dʒe'loso] *ag* jealous.
'gelso ['dʒɛlso] *sm* mulberry (tree).
gelso'mino [dʒelso'mino] *sm* jasmine.
gemel'laggio [dʒemel'laddʒo] *sm* twinning.
gemel'lare [dʒemel'lare] *ag* twin *cpd* ♦ *vt* (*città*) to twin.
ge'mello, a [dʒe'mɛllo] *ag, sm/f* twin; ~**i** *smpl* (*di camicia*) cufflinks; (*dello zodiaco*): **G~i** Gemini *sg*; **essere dei G~i** to be Gemini.
'gemere ['dʒɛmere] *vi* to moan, groan; (*cigolare*) to creak; (*gocciolare*) to drip, ooze.

'gemito ['dʒɛmito] *sm* moan, groan.
'gemma ['dʒɛmma] *sf (BOT)* bud; (*pietra preziosa*) gem.
Gen. *abbr (MIL: = generale)* Gen.
gen. *abbr* (= *generale, generalmente*) gen.
gen'darme [dʒen'darme] *sm* policeman; (*fig*) martinet.
'gene ['dʒɛne] *sm* gene.
genealo'gia, 'gie [dʒenealo'dʒia] *sf* genealogy.
genea'logico, a, ci, che [dʒenea'lɔdʒiko] *ag* genealogical; **albero** ~ family tree.
gene'rale [dʒene'rale] *ag, sm* general; **in** ~ (*per sommi capi*) in general terms; (*di solito*) usually, in general; **a** ~ **richiesta** by popular request.
generalità [dʒenerali'ta] *sfpl* (*dati d'identità*) particulars.
generaliz'zare [dʒeneralid'dzare] *vt, vi* to generalize.
generalizzazi'one [dʒeneraliddzat'tsjone] *sf* generalization.
general'mente [dʒeneral'mente] *av* generally.
gene'rare [dʒene'rare] *vt* (*dar vita*) to give birth to; (*produrre*) to produce; (*causare*) to arouse; (*TECN*) to produce, generate.
genera'tore [dʒenera'tore] *sm* (*TECN*) generator.
generazi'one [dʒenerat'tsjone] *sf* generation.
'genere ['dʒɛnere] *sm* kind, type, sort; (*BIOL*) genus; (*merce*) article, product; (*LING*) gender; (*ARTE, LETTERATURA*) genre; **in** ~ generally, as a rule; **cose del o di questo** ~ such things; **il** ~ **umano** mankind; ~**i alimentari** foodstuffs; ~**i di consumo** consumer goods; ~**i di prima necessità** basic essentials.
ge'nerico, a, ci, che [dʒe'nɛriko] *ag* generic; (*vago*) vague, imprecise; **medico** ~ general practitioner.
'genero ['dʒɛnero] *sm* son-in-law.
generosità [dʒenerosi'ta] *sf* generosity.
gene'roso, a [dʒene'roso] *ag* generous.
'genesi ['dʒɛnezi] *sf* genesis.
ge'netico, a, ci, che [dʒe'nɛtiko] *ag* genetic ♦ *sf* genetics *sg*.
gen'giva [dʒen'dʒiva] *sf (ANAT)* gum.
ge'nia [dʒe'nia] *sf (peg)* mob, gang.
geni'ale [dʒe'njale] *ag* (*persona*) of genius; (*idea*) ingenious, brilliant.
'genio ['dʒɛnjo] *sm* genius; (*attitudine, talento*) talent, flair, genius; **andare a** ~ **a qn** to be to sb's liking, appeal to sb; ~ **civile** civil engineers *pl*; **il** ~ (**militare**) the Engineers.
geni'tale [dʒeni'tale] *ag* genital; ~**i** *smpl*

genitals.
geni'tore [dʒeni'tore] *sm* parent, father *o* mother; ~**i** *smpl* parents.
genn. *abbr* (= *gennaio*) Jan.
gen'naio [dʒen'najo] *sm* January; *per fraseologia vedi* **luglio.**
geno'cidio [dʒeno'tʃidjo] *sm* genocide.
'Genova ['dʒɛnova] *sf* Genoa.
geno'vese [dʒeno'vese] *ag*, *sm/f* Genoese (*pl inv*).
gen'taglia [dʒen'taʎʎa] *sf* (*peg*) rabble.
'gente ['dʒɛnte] *sf* people *pl.*
gentil'donna [dʒentil'dɔnna] *sf* lady.
gen'tile [dʒen'tile] *ag* (*persona, atto*) kind; (: *garbato*) courteous, polite; (*nelle lettere*): **G**~ **Signore** Dear Sir; (: *sulla busta*): **G**~ **Signor Fernando Villa** Mr Fernando Villa.
genti'lezza [dʒenti'lettsa] *sf* kindness; courtesy, politeness; **per** ~ (*per favore*) please.
gentilu'omo, *pl* **gentilu'omini** [dʒenti'lwɔmo] *sm* gentleman.
genuflessi'one [dʒenufles'sjone] *sf* genuflection
genu'ino, a [dʒenu'ino] *ag* (*prodotto*) natural; (*persona, sentimento*) genuine, sincere.
geogra'fia [dʒeogra'fia] *sf* geography.
geo'grafico, a, ci, che [dʒeo'grafiko] *ag* geographical.
ge'ografo, a [dʒe'ografo] *sm/f* geographer.
geolo'gia [dʒeolo'dʒia] *sf* geology.
geo'logico, a, ci, che [dʒeo'lɔdʒiko] *ag* geological.
ge'ometra, i, e [dʒe'ɔmetra] *sm/f* (*professionista*) surveyor.
geome'tria [dʒeome'tria] *sf* geometry.
geo'metrico, a, ci, che [dʒeo'mɛtriko] *ag* geometric(al).
geopo'litico, a, ci, che [dʒeopo'litiko] *ag* geopolitical.
Ge'orgia [dʒe'ɔrdʒa] *sf* Georgia.
geor'giano, a [dʒeor'dʒano] *ag*, *sm/f* Georgian.
ge'ranio [dʒe'ranjo] *sm* geranium.
ge'rarca, chi [dʒe'rarka] *sm* (*STORIA: nel fascismo*) party official.
gerar'chia [dʒerar'kia] *sf* hierarchy.
ge'rarchico, a, ci, che [dʒe'rarkiko] *ag* hierarchical.
ge'rente [dʒe'rɛnte] *sm/f* manager/manageress.
ge'renza [dʒe'rɛntsa] *sf* management.
ger'gale [dʒer'gale] *ag* slang *cpd.*
'gergo, ghi ['dʒɛrgo] *sm* jargon; slang.
geria'tria [dʒerja'tria] *sf* geriatrics *sg.*
geri'atrico, a, ci, che [dʒe'rjatriko] *ag* geriatric.

'gerla ['dʒɛrla] *sf* conical wicker basket.
Ger'mania [dʒer'manja] *sf:* **la** ~ Germany; **la** ~ **occidentale/orientale** West/East Germany.
'germe ['dʒɛrme] *sm* germ; (*fig*) seed.
germinazi'one [dʒerminat'tsjone] *sf* germination.
germogli'are [dʒermoʎ'ʎare] *vi* (*emettere germogli*) to sprout; (*germinare*) to germinate.
ger'moglio [dʒer'moʎʎo] *sm* shoot; (*gemma*) bud.
gero'glifico, ci [dʒero'glifiko] *sm* hieroglyphic.
geron'tologo, a, gi, ghe [dʒeron'tɔlogo] *sm/f* specialist in geriatrics.
ge'rundio [dʒe'rundjo] *sm* gerund.
Gerusa'lemme [dʒeruza'lɛmme] *sf* Jerusalem.
'gesso ['dʒɛsso] *sm* chalk; (*SCULTURA, MED, EDIL*) plaster; (*statua*) plaster figure; (*minerale*) gypsum.
'gesta ['dʒɛsta] *sfpl* (*letterario*) deeds, feats.
ges'tante [dʒes'tante] *sf* expectant mother.
gestazi'one [dʒestat'tsjone] *sf* gestation.
gestico'lare [dʒestiko'lare] *vi* to gesticulate.
gestio'nale [dʒestjo'nale] *ag* administrative, management *cpd.*
gesti'one [dʒes'tjone] *sf* management; ~ **di magazzino** stock control; ~ **patrimoniale** investment management.
ges'tire [dʒes'tire] *vt* to run, manage.
'gesto ['dʒɛsto] *sm* gesture.
ges'tore [dʒes'tore] *sm* manager.
Gesù [dʒe'zu] *sm* Jesus; ~ **bambino** Christ Child.
gesu'ita, i [dʒezu'ita] *sm* Jesuit.
get'tare [dʒet'tare] *vt* to throw; (*anche*: ~ **via**) to throw away *o* out; (*SCULTURA*) to cast; (*EDIL*) to lay; (*acqua*) to spout; (*grido*) to utter; ~**rsi** *vr*: ~**rsi in** (*impresa*) to throw o.s. into; (*mischia*) to hurl o.s. into; (*sog: fiume*) to flow into; ~ **uno sguardo su** to take a quick look at.
get'tata [dʒet'tata] *sf* (*di cemento, gesso, metalli*) cast; (*diga*) jetty.
'gettito ['dʒettito] *sm* revenue.
'getto ['dʒetto] *sm* (*di gas, liquido, AER*) jet; (*BOT*) shoot; **a** ~ **continuo** uninterruptedly; **di** ~ (*fig*) straight off, in one go.
get'tone [dʒet'tone] *sm* token; (*per giochi*) counter; (: *roulette etc*) chip; ~ **di presenza** attendance fee; ~ **telefonico** telephone token.
gettoni'era [dʒetto'njɛra] *sf* telephone-token dispenser.

'geyser ['gaizə] *sm inv* geyser.

'Ghana ['gana] *sm*: **il** ~ Ghana.

'ghenga, ghe ['gɛnga] *sf (fam)* gang, crowd.

ghe'pardo [ge'pardo] *sm* cheetah.

gher'mire [ger'mire] *vt* to grasp, clasp, clutch.

'ghetta ['getta] *sf (gambale)* gaiter.

ghettiz'zare [gettid'dzare] *vt* to segregate.

'ghetto ['getto] *sm* ghetto.

ghiacci'aia [gjat'tʃaja] *sf (anche fig)* icebox.

ghiacci'aio [gjat'tʃajo] *sm* glacier.

ghiacci'are [gjat'tʃare] *vt* to freeze; *(fig)*: ~ qn to make sb's blood run cold ♦ *vi* to freeze, ice over.

ghiacci'ato, a [gjat'tʃato] *ag* frozen; *(bevanda)* ice-cold.

ghi'accio ['gjattʃo] *sm* ice.

ghiacci'olo [gjat'tʃɔlo] *sm* icicle; *(tipo di gelato)* ice lolly *(BRIT)*, popsicle *(US)*.

ghi'aia ['gjaja] *sf* gravel.

ghi'anda ['gjanda] *sf (BOT)* acorn.

ghi'andola ['gjandola] *sf* gland.

ghiando'lare [gjando'lare] *ag* glandular.

ghigliot'tina [giʎʎot'tina] *sf* guillotine.

ghi'gnare [giɲ'ɲare] *vi* to sneer.

'ghigno ['giɲɲo] *sm (espressione)* sneer; *(risata)* mocking laugh.

'ghingheri ['gingeri] *smpl*: **in** ~ all dolled up; **mettersi in** ~ to put on one's Sunday best.

ghi'otto, a ['gjotto] *ag* greedy; *(cibo)* delicious, appetizing.

ghiot'tone, a [gjot'tone] *sm/f* glutton.

ghiottone'ria [gjottone'ria] *sf* greed, gluttony; *(cibo)* delicacy, titbit *(BRIT)*, tidbit *(US)*.

ghiri'goro [giri'gɔro] *sm* scribble, squiggle.

ghir'landa [gir'landa] *sf* garland, wreath.

'ghiro ['giro] *sm* dormouse.

'ghisa ['giza] *sf* cast iron.

G.I. *abbr* = **giudice istruttore**.

già [dʒa] *av* already; *(ex, in precedenza)* formerly ♦ *escl* of course!, yes indeed!; ~ **che ci sei ...** while you are at it ....

gi'acca, che ['dʒakka] *sf* jacket; ~ **a vento** windcheater *(BRIT)*, windbreaker *(US)*.

giacché [dʒak'ke] *cong* since, as.

giac'chetta [dʒak'ketta] *sf* (light) jacket.

'giaccio *etc* ['dʒattʃo] *vb vedi* **giacere**.

giac'cone [dʒak'kone] *sm* heavy jacket.

gia'cenza [dʒa'tʃɛntsa] *sf*: **merce in** ~ goods in stock; **capitale in** ~ uninvested capital; **~e di magazzino** unsold stock.

gia'cere [dʒa'tʃere] *vi* to lie.

giaci'mento [dʒatʃi'mento] *sm* deposit.

gia'cinto [dʒa'tʃinto] *sm* hyacinth.

giaci'uto, a [dʒa'tʃuto] *pp di* **giacere**.

gi'acqui *etc* ['dʒakkwi] *vb vedi* **giacere**.

gi'ada ['dʒada] *sf* jade.

giaggi'olo [dʒad'dʒɔlo] *sm* iris.

giagu'aro [dʒa'gwaro] *sm* jaguar.

gial'lastro, a [dʒal'lastro] *ag* yellowish; *(carnagione)* sallow.

gi'allo ['dʒallo] *ag* yellow; *(carnagione)* sallow ♦ *sm* yellow; *(anche: romanzo* ~*)* detective novel; *(anche:* **film** ~*)* detective film; ~ **dell'uovo** yolk; **il mar G**~ the Yellow Sea.

gial'lognolo, a [dʒal'loɲɲolo] *ag* yellowish, dirty yellow.

Gia'maica [dʒa'maika] *sf*: **la** ~ Jamaica.

giamai'cano, a [dʒamai'kano] *ag, sm/f* Jamaican.

giam'mai [dʒam'mai] *av* never.

Giap'pone [dʒap'pone] *sm*: **il** ~ Japan.

giappo'nese [dʒappo'nese] *ag, sm/f, sm* Japanese *inv*.

gi'ara ['dʒara] *sf* jar.

giardi'naggio [dʒardi'nadddʒo] *sm* gardening.

giardi'netta [dʒardi'netta] *sf* estate car *(BRIT)*, station wagon *(US)*.

giardini'ere, a [dʒardi'njɛre] *sm/f* gardener ♦ *sf (misto di sottaceti)* mixed pickles *pl*; *(automobile)* = **giardinetta**.

giar'dino [dʒar'dino] *sm* garden; ~ **d'infanzia** nursery school; ~ **pubblico** public gardens *pl*, (public) park; ~ **zoologico** zoo.

giarretti'era [dʒarret'tjɛra] *sf* garter.

Gi'ava ['dʒava] *sf* Java.

giavel'lotto [dʒavel'lɔtto] *sm* javelin.

gib'boso, a [dʒib'boso] *ag (superficie)* bumpy; *(naso)* crooked.

Gibil'terra [dʒibil'tɛrra] *sf* Gibraltar.

gi'gante, 'essa [dʒi'gante] *sm/f* giant ♦ *ag* giant, gigantic; *(COMM)* giant-size.

gigan'tesco, a, schi, sche [dʒigan'tesko] *ag* gigantic.

gigantogra'fia [dʒigantogra'fia] *sf (FOT)* blow-up.

'giglio ['dʒiʎʎo] *sm* lily.

gilè [dʒi'le] *sm inv* waistcoat.

gin [dʒin] *sm inv* gin.

gin'cana [dʒin'kana] *sf* gymkhana.

ginecolo'gia [dʒinekolo'dʒia] *sf* gynaecology *(BRIT)*, gynecology *(US)*.

gine'cologo, a, gi, ghe [dʒine'kɔlogo] *sm/f* gynaecologist *(BRIT)*, gynecologist *(US)*.

gi'nepro [dʒi'nepro] *sm* juniper.

gi'nestra [dʒi'nɛstra] *sf (BOT)* broom.

Gi'nevra [dʒi'nevra] *sf* Geneva; **il Lago di** ~ Lake Geneva.

gingil'larsi [dʒindʒil'larsi] *vr* to fritter away one's time; *(giocare)*: ~ **con** to fiddle with.

gin'gillo [dʒin'dʒillo] *sm* plaything.
gin'nasio [dʒin'nazjo] *sm the 4th and 5th year of secondary school in Italy.*
gin'nasta, i, e [dʒin'nasta] *sm/f* gymnast.
gin'nastica [dʒin'nastika] *sf* gymnastics *sg*; (*esercizio fisico*) keep-fit exercises *pl*; (*INS*) physical education.
'ginnico, a, ci, che ['dʒinniko] *ag* gymnastic.
gi'nocchio [dʒi'nɔkkjo], *pl(m)* **gi'nocchi** o *pl(f)* **gi'nocchia** *sm* knee; **stare in** ~ to kneel, be on one's knees; **mettersi in** ~ to kneel (down).
ginocchi'oni [dʒinok'kjoni] *av* on one's knees.
gio'care [dʒo'kare] *vt* to play; (*scommettere*) to stake, wager, bet; (*ingannare*) to take in ♦ *vi* to play; (*a roulette etc*) to gamble; (*fig*) to play a part, be important; (*TECN: meccanismo*) to be loose; ~ **a** (*gioco, sport*) to play; (*cavalli*) to bet on; ~ **d'astuzia** to be crafty; ~**rsi la carriera** to put one's career at risk; ~**rsi tutto** to risk everything; **a che gioco giochiamo?** what are you playing at?
gioca'tore, 'trice [dʒoka'tore] *sm/f* player; gambler.
gio'cattolo [dʒo'kattolo] *sm* toy.
giocherel'lare [dʒokerel'lare] *vi*: ~ **con** to play with.
giocherò *etc* [dʒoke'rɔ] *vb vedi* **giocare**.
gio'chetto [dʒo'ketto] *sm* (*gioco*) game; (*tranello*) trick; (*fig*): **è un** ~ it's child's play.
gi'oco, chi ['dʒɔko] *sm* game; (*divertimento, TECN*) play; (*al casinò*) gambling; (*CARTE*) hand; (*insieme di pezzi etc necessari per un gioco*) set; **per** ~ for fun; **fare il doppio** ~ **con qn** to double-cross sb; **prendersi** ~ **di qn** to pull sb's leg; **stare al** ~ **di qn** to play along with sb; **è in** ~ **la mia reputazione** my reputation is at stake; ~ **d'azzardo** game of chance; ~ **della palla** ball game; ~ **degli scacchi** chess set; **i G~chi Olimpici** the Olympic Games.
gioco'forza [dʒoko'fɔrtsa] *sm*: **essere** ~ to be inevitable.
giocoli'ere [dʒoko'ljere] *sm* juggler.
gio'coso, a [dʒo'koso] *ag* playful, jesting.
gio'gaia [dʒo'gaja] *sf* (*GEO*) range of mountains.
gi'ogo, ghi ['dʒogo] *sm* yoke.
gi'oia ['dʒɔja] *sf* joy, delight; (*pietra preziosa*) jewel, precious stone.
gioielle'ria [dʒojelle'ria] *sf* jeweller's (*BRIT*) o jeweler's (*US*) craft; (*negozio*) jewel(l)er's (shop).
gioielli'ere, a [dʒojel'ljere] *sm/f* jeweller

(*BRIT*), jeweler (*US*).
gioi'ello [dʒo'jello] *sm* jewel, piece of jewellery (*BRIT*) o jewelry (*US*); ~**i** *smpl* (*gioie*) jewel(l)ery *sg*.
gioi'oso, a [dʒo'joso] *ag* joyful.
Gior'dania [dʒor'danja] *sf*: **la** ~ Jordan.
Gior'dano [dʒor'dano] *sm*: **il** ~ the Jordan.
glor'dano, a [dʒor'dano] *ag, sm/f* Jordanian.
giorna'laio, a [dʒorna'lajo] *sm/f* newsagent (*BRIT*), newsdealer (*US*).
gior'nale [dʒor'nale] *sm* (news)paper; (*diario*) journal, diary; (*COMM*) journal; ~ **di bordo** (*NAUT*) ship's log; ~ **radio** radio news *sg*.
giorna'letto [dʒorna'letto] *sm* (children's) comic.
giornali'ero, a [dʒorna'ljero] *ag* daily.
giorna'lino [dʒorna'lino] *sm* children's comic.
giorna'lismo [dʒorna'lizmo] *sm* journalism.
giorna'lista, i, e [dʒorna'lista] *sm/f* journalist.
giorna'listico, a, ci, che [dʒorna'listiko] *ag* journalistic; **stile** ~ journalese.
giornal'mente [dʒornal'mente] *av* daily.
gior'nata [dʒor'nata] *sf* day; (*paga*) day's wages, day's pay; **durante la** ~ **di ieri** yesterday; **fresco di** ~ (*uovo*) freshly laid; **vivere alla** ~ to live from day to day; ~ **lavorativa** working day.
gi'orno ['dʒorno] *sm* day; (*opposto alla notte*) day, daytime; (*luce del* ~) daylight; **al** ~ per day; **di** ~ by day; ~ **per** ~ day by day; **al** ~ **d'oggi** nowadays; **tutto il santo** ~ all day long; **il G~ dei Morti** *vedi nota nel riquadro.*

IL GIORNO DEI MORTI

Il Giorno dei Morti, *All Souls' Day, falls on 2 November. At this time of year people visit cemeteries to lay flowers on the graves of their loved ones.*

---

gi'ostra ['dʒɔstra] *sf* (*per bimbi*) merry-go-round; (*torneo storico*) joust.
gios'trare [dʒos'trare] *vi* (*STORIA*) to joust, tilt; ~**rsi** *vr* to manage.
giov. *abbr* (= *giovedì*) Thur(s).
giova'mento [dʒova'mento] *sm* benefit, help.
gi'ovane ['dʒovane] *ag* young; (*aspetto*) youthful ♦ *sm/f* youth/girl, young man/woman; **i** ~**i** young people; **è** ~ **del mestiere** he's new to the job.
giova'netto, a [dʒova'netto] *sm/f* young man/woman.
giova'nile [dʒova'nile] *ag* youthful; (*scritti*)

early; (*errore*) of youth.

giova'notto [dʒova'nɔtto] *sm* young man.

gio'vare [dʒo'vare] *vi*: ~ **a** (*essere utile*) to be useful to; (*far bene*) to be good for ♦ *vb impers* (*essere bene, utile*) to be useful; **~rsi** *vr*: **~rsi di qc** to make use of sth; **a che giova prendersela?** what's the point of getting upset?

Gi'ove ['dʒɔve] *sm* (*MITOLOGIA*) Jove; (*ASTR*) Jupiter.

giovedì [dʒove'di] *sm inv* Thursday; *per fraseologia vedi* **martedì**.

gio'venca, che [dʒo'vɛnka] *sf* heifer.

gioventù [dʒoven'tu] *sf* (*periodo*) youth; (*i giovani*) young people *pl*, youth.

giovi'ale [dʒo'vjale] *ag* jovial, jolly.

giovi'nastro [dʒovi'nastro] *sm* young thug.

giovin'cello [dʒovin'tʃɛllo] *sm* young lad.

giovi'nezza [dʒovi'nettsa] *sf* youth.

gip [dʒip] *sigla m inv* (= *giudice per le indagini preliminari*) judge for preliminary enquiries.

gira'dischi [dʒira'diski] *sm inv* record player.

gi'raffa [dʒi'raffa] *sf* giraffe; (*TV, CINE, RADIO*) boom.

gira'mento [dʒira'mento] *sm*: ~ **di testa** fit of dizziness.

gira'mondo [dʒira'mondo] *sm/f inv* globetrotter.

gi'randola [dʒi'randola] *sf* (*fuoco d'artificio*) Catherine wheel; (*giocattolo*) toy windmill; (*banderuola*) weather vane, weathercock.

gi'rante [dʒi'rante] *sm/f* (*di assegno*) endorser.

gi'rare [dʒi'rare] *vt* (*far ruotare*) to turn; (*percorrere, visitare*) to go round; (*CINE*) to shoot; (: *film: come regista*) to make; (*COMM*) to endorse ♦ *vi* to turn; (*più veloce*) to spin; (*andare in giro*) to wander, go around; **~rsi** *vr* to turn; ~ **attorno a** to go round; to revolve round; **si girava e rigirava nel letto** he tossed and turned in bed; **far** ~ **la testa a qn** to make sb dizzy; (*fig*) to turn sb's head; **gira al largo** keep your distance; **girala come ti pare** (*fig*) look at it whichever way you like; **gira e rigira ...** after a lot of driving (*o* walking) about ...; (*fig*) whichever way you look at it; **cosa ti gira?** (*fam*) what's got into you?; **mi ha fatto** ~ **le scatole** (*fam*) he drove me crazy.

girar'rosto [dʒirar'rɔsto] *sm* (*CUC*) spit.

gira'sole [dʒira'sole] *sm* sunflower.

gi'rata [dʒi'rata] *sf* (*passeggiata*) stroll; (*con veicolo*) drive; (*COMM*) endorsement.

gira'tario, a [dʒira'tarjo] *sm/f* endorsee.

gira'volta [dʒira'vɔlta] *sf* twirl, turn; (*curva*) sharp bend; (*fig*) about-turn.

gi'rello [dʒi'rɛllo] *sm* (*di bambino*) Babywalker ® (*BRIT*), go-cart (*US*); (*taglio di carne*) topside (*BRIT*), top round (*US*).

gi'retto [dʒi'retto] *sm* (*passeggiata*) walk, stroll; (: *in macchina*) drive, spin; (: *in bicicletta*) ride.

gi'revole [dʒi'revole] *ag* revolving, turning.

gi'rino [dʒi'rino] *sm* tadpole.

'giro ['dʒiro] *sm* (*circuito, cerchio*) circle; (*di chiave, manovella*) turn; (*viaggio*) tour, excursion; (*passeggiata*) stroll, walk; (*in macchina*) drive; (*in bicicletta*) ride; (*SPORT: della pista*) lap; (*di denaro*) circulation; (*CARTE*) hand; (*TECN*) revolution; **fare un** ~ to go for a walk (*o* a drive *o* a ride); **fare il** ~ **di** (*parco, città*) to go round; **andare in** ~ (*a piedi*) to go about, walk around; **guardarsi in** ~ to look around; **prendere in** ~ **qn** (*fig*) to take sb for a ride; **nel** ~ **di un mese** in a month's time; **essere nel** ~ (*fig*) to belong to a circle (of friends); ~ **d'affari** (*viaggio*) business tour; (*COMM*) turnover; ~ **di parole** circumlocution; ~ **di prova** (*AUT*) test drive; ~ **turistico** sightseeing tour; ~ **vita** waist measurement.

giro'collo [dʒiro'kɔllo] *sm*: **a** ~ crewneck *cpd*.

giro'conto [dʒiro'konto] *sm* (*ECON*) credit transfer.

gi'rone [dʒi'rone] *sm* (*SPORT*) series of games; ~ **di andata/ritorno** (*CALCIO*) first/second half of the season.

gironzo'lare [dʒirondzo'lare] *vi* to stroll about.

giro'tondo [dʒiro'tondo] *sm* ring-a-ring-o'roses (*BRIT*), ring-around-the-rosey (*US*); **in** ~ in a circle.

girova'gare [dʒirova'gare] *vi* to wander about.

gi'rovago, a, ghi, ghe [dʒi'rɔvago] *sm/f* (*vagabondo*) tramp; (*venditore*) peddler; **una compagnia di** ~**ghi** (*attori*) a company of strolling actors.

'gita ['dʒita] *sf* excursion, trip; **fare una** ~ to go for a trip, go on an outing.

gi'tano, a [dʒi'tano] *sm/f* gipsy.

gi'tante [dʒi'tante] *sm/f* member of a tour.

giù [dʒu] *av* down; (*dabbasso*) downstairs; **in** ~ downwards, down; **la mia casa è un po'** più in ~ my house is a bit further on; ~ **di lì** (*pressappoco*) thereabouts; **bambini dai 6 anni in** ~ children aged 6 and under; **cadere** ~ **per le scale** to fall down the stairs; ~ **le mani!** hands off!; **essere** ~

(*fig: di salute*) to be run down;
(: *di spirito*) to be depressed; **quel tipo non
mi va** ~ I can't stand that guy.
gi'ubba ['dʒubba] *sf* jacket.
giub'botto [dʒub'bɔtto] *sm* jerkin; ~
antiproiettile bulletproof vest.
giubi'lare [dʒubi'lare] *vi* to rejoice.
gi'ubilo ['dʒubilo] *sm* rejoicing.
giudi'care [dʒudi'kare] *vt* to judge;
(*accusato*) to try; (*lite*) to arbitrate in; ~
qn/qc bello to consider sb/sth (to be)
beautiful.
giudi'cato [dʒudi'kato] *sm* (*DIR*): **passare in**
~ to pass final judgment.
gi'udice ['dʒuditʃe] *sm* judge; ~ **collegiale**
member of the court; ~ **conciliatore**
justice of the peace; ~ **istruttore**
examining (*BRIT*) o committing (*US*)
magistrate; ~ **popolare** member of a
jury.
giudizi'ale [dʒudit'tsjale] *ag* judicial.
giudizi'ario, a [dʒudit'tsjarjo] *ag* legal,
judicial.
giu'dizio [dʒu'dittsjo] *sm* judgment;
(*opinione*) opinion; (*DIR*) judgment,
sentence; (: *processo*) trial; (: *verdetto*)
verdict; **aver** ~ to be wise o prudent;
essere in attesa di ~ to be awaiting trial;
citare in ~ to summons; **l'imputato è
stato rinviato a** ~ the accused has been
committed for trial.
giudizi'oso, a [dʒudit'tsjoso] *ag* prudent,
judicious.
gi'uggiola ['dʒuddʒola] *sf*: **andare in brodo
di** ~**e** (*fam*) to be over the moon.
gi'ugno ['dʒuɲɲo] *sm* June; *per fraseologia vedi*
luglio.
giu'livo, a [dʒu'livo] *ag* merry.
giul'lare [dʒul'lare] *sm* jester.
giu'menta [dʒu'menta] *sf* mare.
gi'unco, chi ['dʒunko] *sm* (*BOT*) rush.
gi'ungere ['dʒundʒere] *vi* to arrive ♦ *vt*
(*mani etc*) to join; ~ **a** to arrive at, reach;
~ **nuovo a qn** to come as news to sb; ~ **in
porto** to reach harbour; (*fig*) to be
brought to a successful outcome.
gi'ungla ['dʒungla] *sf* jungle.
gi'unsi *etc* ['dʒunsi] *vb vedi* **giungere**.
gi'unto, a ['dʒunto] *pp di* **giungere** ♦ *sm*
(*TECN*) coupling, joint ♦ *sf* addition;
(*organo esecutivo, amministrativo*) council,
board; **per** ~**a** into the bargain, in
addition; ~**a militare** military junta; *vedi
anche* **Comune; Provincia; Regione**.
giun'tura [dʒun'tura] *sf* joint.
giuo'care [dʒwo'kare] *vt, vi* = **giocare**.
giu'oco ['dʒwɔko] *sm* = **gioco**.
giura'mento [dʒura'mento] *sm* oath; ~ **falso**

perjury.
giu'rare [dʒu'rare] *vt* to swear ♦ *vi* to swear,
take an oath; **gliel'ho giurata** I swore I
would get even with him.
giu'rato, a [dʒu'rato] *ag*: **nemico** ~ sworn
enemy ♦ *sm/f* juror, juryman/woman.
giu'ria [dʒu'ria] *sf* jury.
giu'ridico, a, ci, che [dʒu'ridiko] *ag* legal.
giurisdizi'one [dʒurizdit'tsjone] *sf*
jurisdiction.
giurispru'denza [dʒurispru'dentsa] *sf*
jurisprudence.
giu'rista, i, e [dʒu'rista] *sm/f* jurist.
giustap'porre [dʒustap'porre] *vt* to
juxtapose.
giustapposizi'one [dʒustappozit'tsjone] *sf*
juxtaposition.
giustap'posto, a [dʒustap'posto] *pp di*
giustapporre.
giustifi'care [dʒustifi'kare] *vt* to justify;
~**rsi** *vr*: ~**rsi di** o **per qc** to justify o excuse
o.s. for sth.
giustifica'tivo, a [dʒustifika'tivo] *ag* (*AMM*):
nota o **pezza** ~**a** receipt.
giustificazi'one [dʒustifikat'tsjone] *sf*
justification; (*INS*) (note of) excuse.
gius'tizia [dʒus'tittsja] *sf* justice; **farsi** ~ **(da
sé)** (*vendicarsi*) to take the law into one's
own hands.
giustizi'are [dʒustit'tsjare] *vt* to execute,
put to death.
giustizi'ere [dʒustit'tsjɛre] *sm* executioner.
gi'usto, a ['dʒusto] *ag* (*equo*) fair, just;
(*vero*) true, correct; (*adatto*) right,
suitable; (*preciso*) exact, correct ♦ *av*
(*esattamente*) exactly, precisely; (*per
l'appunto, appena*) just; **arrivare** ~ to
arrive just in time; **ho** ~ **bisogno di te**
you're just the person I need.
'glabro, a *ag* hairless.
glaci'ale [gla'tʃale] *ag* glacial.
gla'diolo *sm* gladiolus.
'glandola *sf* = **ghiandola**.
'glassa *sf* (*CUC*) icing.
glau'coma *sm* glaucoma.
gli [ʎi] *det mpl* (*dav V, s impura, gn, pn, ps, x, z*)
the ♦ *pron* (*a lui*) to him; (*a esso*) to it; (*in
coppia con lo, la, li, le, ne: a lui, a lei, a loro
etc*): **gliele do** I'm giving them to him (o
her o them); **gliene ho parlato** I spoke to
him (o her o them) about it; *vedi anche* **il**.
glice'mia [glitʃe'mia] *sf* glycaemia.
glice'rina [glitʃe'rina] *sf* glycerine.
'glicine ['glitʃine] *sm* wistaria.
gli'ela *etc* ['ʎela] *vedi* **gli**.
glo'bale *ag* overall; (*vista*) global.
'globo *sm* globe.
'globulo *sm* (*ANAT*): ~ **rosso/bianco** red/

white corpuscle.

'gloria *sf* glory; farsi ~ di qc to pride o.s. on sth, take pride in sth.

glori'arsi *vr*: ~ di qc to pride o.s. on sth, glory *o* take pride in sth.

glorifi'care *vt* to glorify.

glori'oso, a *ag* glorious.

glos'sario *sm* glossary.

glu'cosio *sm* glucose.

'gluteo *sm* gluteus; ~i *smpl* buttocks.

GM *abbr* = genio militare.

G.N. *abbr* = gas naturale.

'gnocchi ['ɲɔkki] *smpl* (CUC) small dumplings made of semolina pasta or potato.

'gnomo ['ɲɔmo] *sm* gnome.

'gnorri ['ɲɔrri] *sm/f inv*: non fare lo ~! stop acting as if you didn't know anything about it!

GO *sigla* = Gorizia.

'goal ['goul] *sm inv* (SPORT) goal.

'gobba *sf* (ANAT) hump; (protuberanza) bump.

'gobbo, a *ag* hunchbacked; (ricurvo) round-shouldered ♦ *sm/f* hunchback.

'Gobi *smpl*: il Deserto dei ~ the Gobi Desert.

'goccia, ce ['gottʃa] *sf* drop; ~ di rugiada dewdrop; somigliarsi come due ~ce d'acqua to be as like as two peas in a pod; è la ~ che fa traboccare il vaso! it's the last straw!

'goccio ['gottʃo] *sm* drop, spot.

goccio'lare [gottʃo'lare] *vi, vt* to drip.

goccio'lio [gottʃo'lio] *sm* dripping.

go'dere *vi* (compiacersi): ~ (di) to be delighted (at), rejoice (at); (trarre vantaggio): ~ di to enjoy, benefit from ♦ *vt* to enjoy; ~rsi la vita to enjoy life; godersela to have a good time, enjoy o.s.

godi'mento *sm* enjoyment.

godrò *etc vb vedi* godere.

gof'faggine [gof'faddʒine] *sf* clumsiness.

'goffo, a *ag* clumsy, awkward.

'gogna ['goɲɲa] *sf* pillory.

gol *sm inv* = goal.

'gola *sf* (ANAT) throat; (golosità) gluttony, greed; (di camino) flue; (di monte) gorge; fare ~ (anche fig) to tempt; ricacciare il pianto *o* le lacrime in ~ to swallow one's tears.

go'letta *sf* (NAUT) schooner.

golf *sm inv* (SPORT) golf; (maglia) cardigan.

'golfo *sm* gulf.

goli'ardico, a, ci, che *ag* (canto, vita) student *cpd*.

go'loso, a *ag* greedy.

'golpe *sm inv* (POL) coup.

gomi'tata *sf*: dare una ~ a qn to elbow sb; farsi avanti a (forza *o* furia di) ~e to elbow one's way through; fare a ~e per qc to fight to get sth.

'gomito *sm* elbow; (di strada etc) sharp bend.

go'mitolo *sm* ball.

'gomma *sf* rubber; (colla) gum; (per cancellare) rubber, eraser; (di veicolo) tyre (BRIT), tire (US); ~ da masticare chewing gum; ~ a terra flat tyre.

gommapi'uma ® *sf* foam rubber.

gom'mino *sm* rubber tip; (rondella) rubber washer.

gom'mista, i, e *sm/f* tyre (BRIT) *o* tire (US) specialist; (rivenditore) tyre *o* tire merchant.

gom'mone *sm* rubber dinghy.

gom'moso, a *ag* rubbery.

'gondola *sf* gondola.

gondoli'ere *sm* gondolier.

gonfa'lone *sm* banner.

gonfi'are *vt* (pallone) to blow up, inflate; (dilatare, ingrossare) to swell; (fig: notizia) to exaggerate; ~rsi *vr* to swell; (fiume) to rise.

'gonfio, a *ag* swollen; (stomaco) bloated; (palloncino, gomme) inflated, blown up; (con pompa) pumped up; (vela) full; occhi ~i di pianto eyes swollen with tears; ~ di orgoglio (persona) puffed up (with pride); avere il portafoglio ~ to have a bulging wallet.

gonfi'ore *sm* swelling.

gongo'lare *vi* to look pleased with o.s.; ~ di gioia to be overjoyed.

'gonna *sf* skirt; ~ pantalone culottes *pl*.

'gonzo ['gondzo] *sm* simpleton, fool.

gorgheggi'are [gorged'dʒare] *vi* to warble; to trill.

gor'gheggio [gor'geddʒo] *sm* (MUS, di uccello) trill.

'gorgo, ghi *sm* whirlpool.

gorgogli'are [gorgoʎ'ʎare] *vi* to gurgle.

gorgo'glio [gorgoʎ'ʎio] *sm* gurgling.

go'rilla *sm inv* gorilla; (guardia del corpo) bodyguard.

'Gotha *sm inv* (del cinema, letteratura, industria) leading lights *pl*.

'gotico, a, ci, che *ag, sm* Gothic.

'gotta *sf* gout.

gover'nante *sm/f* ruler ♦ *sf* (di bambini) governess; (donna di servizio) housekeeper.

gover'nare *vt* (stato) to govern, rule; (pilotare, guidare) to steer; (bestiame) to tend, look after.

governa'tivo, a *ag* (politica, decreto)

government *cpd*, governmental; (*stampa*) pro-government.

governa'tore *sm* governor.

go'verno *sm* government; ~ **ombra** shadow cabinet.

'gozzo ['gottso] *sm* (*ZOOL*) crop; (*MED*) goitre; (*fig fam*) throat.

gozzovigli'are [gottsoviʎˈʎare] *vi* to make merry, carouse.

gpm *abbr* (= *giri per minuto*) rpm.

GR [dziˈerre] *sigla* = *Grosseto* ♦ *sigla m* (= **giornale radio**) radio news.

gracchi'are [grakˈkjare] *vi* to caw.

graci'dare [gratʃiˈdare] *vi* to croak.

graci'dio, ii [gratʃiˈdio] *sm* croaking.

'gracile ['gratʃile] *ag* frail, delicate.

gra'dasso *sm* boaster.

gradata'mente *av* gradually, by degrees.

gradazi'one [gradatˈtsjone] *sf* (*sfumatura*) gradation; ~ **alcolica** alcoholic content, strength.

gra'devole *ag* pleasant, agreeable.

gradi'mento *sm* pleasure, satisfaction; **essere di mio** (*o* **tuo** *etc*) ~ to be to my (*o* your *etc*) liking.

gradi'nata *sf* flight of steps; (*in teatro, stadio*) tiers *pl*.

gra'dino *sm* step; (*ALPINISMO*) foothold.

gra'dire *vt* (*accettare con piacere*) to accept; (*desiderare*) to wish, like; **gradisce una tazza di tè?** would you like a cup of tea?

gra'dito, a *ag* welcome.

'grado *sm* (*MAT, FISICA etc*) degree; (*stadio*) degree, level; (*MIL, sociale*) rank; **essere in ~ di fare** to be in a position to do; **di buon** ~ willingly; **per ~i** by degrees; **un cugino di primo/secondo** ~ a first/second cousin; **subire il terzo** ~ (*anche fig*) to be given the third degree.

gradu'ale *ag* gradual.

gradu'are *vt* to grade.

gradu'ato, a *ag* (*esercizi*) graded; (*scala, termometro*) graduated ♦ *sm* (*MIL*) non-commissioned officer.

gradua'toria *sf* (*di concorso*) list; (*per la promozione*) order of seniority.

'graffa *sf* (*gancio*) clip; (*segno grafico*) brace.

graf'fetta *sf* paper clip.

graffi'are *vt* to scratch.

graffia'tura *sf* scratch.

'graffio *sm* scratch.

graf'fiti *smpl* graffiti.

gra'fia *sf* spelling; (*scrittura*) handwriting.

'grafico, a, ci, che *ag* graphic ♦ *sm* graph; (*persona*) graphic designer ♦ *sf* graphic arts *pl*; ~ **a torta** pie chart.

gra'migna [graˈmiɲɲa] *sf* weed; couch grass.

gram'matica, che *sf* grammar.

grammati'cale *ag* grammatical.

'grammo *sm* gram(me).

gram'mofono *sm* gramophone.

'gramo, a *ag* (*vita*) wretched.

gran *ag vedi* **grande**.

'grana *sf* (*granello, di minerali, corpi spezzati*) grain; (*fam: seccatura*) trouble; (: *soldi*) cash ♦ *sm inv* cheese similar to Parmesan.

gra'naglie [graˈnaʎʎe] *sfpl* corn *sg*, seed *sg*.

gra'naio *sm* granary, barn.

gra'nata *sf* (*frutto*) pomegranate; (*pietra preziosa*) garnet; (*proiettile*) grenade.

granati'ere *sm* (*MIL*) grenadier; (*fig*) fine figure of a man.

Gran Bre'tagna [granbreˈtaɲɲa] *sf*: **la** ~ Great Britain.

gran'cassa *sf* (*MUS*) bass drum.

'granchio ['grankjo] *sm* crab; (*fig*) blunder; **prendere un** ~ (*fig*) to blunder.

grandango'lare *sm* wide-angle lens *sg*.

gran'dangolo *sm* (*FOT*) wide-angle lens *sg*.

'grande *ag* (*qualche volta* **gran** +*C*, **grand'** +*V*) (*grosso, largo, vasto*) big, large; (*alto*) tall; (*lungo*) long; (*in sensi astratti*) great ♦ *sm/f* (*persona adulta*) adult, grown-up; (*chi ha ingegno e potenza*) great man/woman; **mio fratello più** ~ my big *o* older brother; **il gran pubblico** the general public; **di gran classe** (*prodotto*) high-class; **cosa farai da te?** what will you be *o* do when you grow up?; **fare le cose in** ~ to do things in style; **fare il** ~ (*strafare*) to act big; **una gran bella donna** a very beautiful woman; **non è una gran cosa** *o* **un gran che** it's nothing special; **non ne so gran che** I don't know very much about it.

grandeggi'are [grandedˈdʒare] *vi* (*emergere per grandezza*): ~ **su** to tower over; (*darsi arie*) to put on airs.

gran'dezza [granˈdettsa] *sf* (*dimensione*) size; (*fig*) greatness; **in** ~ **naturale** lifesize; **manie di** ~ delusions of grandeur.

grandi'nare *vb impers* to hail.

'grandine *sf* hail.

grandi'oso, a *ag* grand, grandiose.

gran'duca, chi *sm* grand duke.

grandu'cato *sm* grand duchy.

grandu'chessa [granduˈkessa] *sf* grand duchess.

gra'nello *sm* (*di cereali, uva*) seed; (*di frutta*) pip; (*di sabbia, sale etc*) grain.

gra'nita *sf* kind of water ice.

gra'nito *sm* granite.

'grano *sm* (*in quasi tutti i sensi*) grain;

(*frumento*) wheat; (*di rosario, collana*) bead; ~ **di pepe** peppercorn.

gran'turco *sm* maize.

'granulo *sm* granule; (*MED*) pellet.

'grappa *sf* rough, strong brandy.

'grappolo *sm* bunch, cluster.

'graspo *sm* bunch (of grapes).

gras'setto *sm* (*TIP*) bold (type) (*BRIT*), bold face.

'grasso, a *ag* fat; (*cibo*) fatty; (*pelle*) greasy; (*terreno*) rich; (*fig: guadagno, annata*) plentiful; (: *volgare*) coarse, lewd ♦ *sm* (*di persona, animale*) fat; (*sostanza che unge*) grease.

gras'soccio, a, ci, ce [gras'sɔttʃo] *ag* plump.

gras'sone, a *sm/f* (*fam: persona*) dumpling.

'grata *sf* grating.

gra'ticcio [gra'tittʃo] *sm* trellis; (*stuoia*) mat.

gra'ticola *sf* grill.

gra'tifica, che *sf* bonus; ~ **natalizia** Christmas bonus.

gratificazi'one [gratifikat'tsjone] *sf* (*soddisfazione*) satisfaction, reward.

grati'nare *vt* (*CUC*) to cook au gratin.

'gratis *av* free, for nothing.

grati'tudine *sf* gratitude.

'grato, a *ag* grateful.

gratta'capo *sm* worry, headache.

grattaci'elo [gratta'tʃɛlo] *sm* skyscraper.

grat'tare *vt* (*pelle*) to scratch; (*raschiare*) to scrape; (*pane, formaggio, carote*) to grate; (*fam: rubare*) to pinch ♦ *vi* (*stridere*) to grate; (*AUT*) to grind; ~**rsi** *vr* to scratch o.s.; ~**rsi la pancia** (*fig*) to twiddle one's thumbs.

grat'tata *sf* scratch; **fare una** ~ (*AUT: fam*) to grind the gears.

grat'tugia, gie [grat'tudʒa] *sf* grater.

grattugi'are [grattu'dʒare] *vt* to grate; **pane** *m* **grattugiato** breadcrumbs *pl*.

gratuità *sf* (*fig*) gratuitousness.

gra'tuito, a *ag* free; (*fig*) gratuitous.

gra'vame *sm* tax; (*fig*) burden, weight.

gra'vare *vt* to burden ♦ *vi*: ~ **su** to weigh on.

'grave *ag* (*danno, pericolo, peccato etc*) grave, serious; (*responsabilità*) heavy, grave; (*contegno*) grave, solemn; (*voce, suono*) deep, low-pitched; (*LING*): **accento** ~ grave accent ♦ *sm* (*FISICA*) (heavy) body; **un malato** ~ a person who is seriously ill.

grave'mente *av* (*ammalato, ferito*) seriously.

gravi'danza [gravi'dantsa] *sf* pregnancy.

'gravido, a *ag* pregnant.

gravità *sf* seriousness; (*anche FISICA*) gravity.

gravi'tare *vi* (*FISICA*): ~ **intorno a** to gravitate round.

gra'voso, a *ag* heavy, onerous.

'grazia ['grattsja] *sf* grace; (*favore*) favour (*BRIT*), favor (*US*); (*DIR*) pardon; **di** ~ (*ironico*) if you please; **troppa** ~! (*ironico*) you're too generous!; **quanta** ~ **di Dio!** what abundance!; **entrare nelle** ~**e di qn** to win sb's favour; **Ministero di G**~ **e Giustizia** Ministry of Justice, ≈ Lord Chancellor's Office (*BRIT*), ≈ Department of Justice (*US*).

grazi'are [grat'tsjare] *vt* (*DIR*) to pardon.

'grazie ['grattsje] *escl* thank you!; ~ **mille!** *o* **tante!** *o* **infinite!** thank you very much!; ~ **a** thanks to.

grazi'oso, a [grat'tsjoso] *ag* charming, delightful; (*gentile*) gracious.

'Grecia ['grɛtʃa] *sf*: **la** ~ Greece.

'greco, a, ci, che *ag, sm/f, sm* Greek.

gre'gario *sm* (*CICLISMO*) supporting rider.

'gregge, pl(f) i ['greddʒe] *sm* flock.

'greggio, a, gi, ge ['greddʒo] *ag* raw, unrefined; (*diamante*) rough, uncut; (*tessuto*) unbleached ♦ *sm* (*anche*: **petrolio** ~) crude (oil).

grembi'ule *sm* apron; (*sopravveste*) overall.

'grembo *sm* lap; (*ventre della madre*) womb.

gre'mito, a *ag*: ~ **(di)** packed *o* crowded (with).

'greto *sm* (exposed) gravel bed of a river.

'gretto, a *ag* mean, stingy; (*fig*) narrow-minded.

'greve *ag* heavy.

'grezzo, a ['greddzo] *ag* = **greggio**.

gri'dare *vi* (*per chiamare*) to shout, cry (out); (*strillare*) to scream, yell ♦ *vt* to shout (out), yell (out); ~ **aiuto** to cry *o* shout for help.

'grido, pl(m) i *o* **pl(f) a** *sm* shout, cry; scream, yell; (*di animale*) cry; **di** ~ famous; **all'ultimo** ~ in the latest style.

'grigio, a, gi, gie ['gridʒo] *ag, sm* grey (*BRIT*), gray (*US*).

'griglia ['griʎʎa] *sf* (*per arrostire*) grill; (*ELETTR*) grid; (*inferriata*) grating; **alla** ~ (*CUC*) grilled.

grigli'ata [griʎ'ʎata] *sf* (*CUC*) grill.

gril'letto *sm* trigger.

'grillo *sm* (*ZOOL*) cricket; (*fig*) whim; **ha dei** ~**i per la testa** his head is full of nonsense.

grimal'dello *sm* picklock.

'grinfia *sf*: **cadere nelle** ~**e di qn** (*fig*) to fall into sb's clutches.

'grinta *sf* grim expression; (*SPORT*) fighting

spirit; **avere molta** ~ to be very
determined.
grintoso, a *ag* forceful.
'**grinza** ['grintsa] *sf* crease, wrinkle; (*ruga*)
wrinkle; **il tuo ragionamento non fa una**
~ your argument is faultless.
grin'zoso, a [grin'tsoso] *ag* wrinkled;
creased.
grip'pare *vi* (*TECN*) to seize.
gris'sino *sm* bread-stick.
groenlan'dese *ag* Greenland *cpd* ♦ *sm/f*
Greenlander.
Groen'landia *sf*: **la** ~ Greenland.
'**gronda** *sf* eaves *pl*.
gron'daia *sf* gutter.
gron'dante *ag* dripping.
gron'dare *vi* to pour; (*essere bagnato*): ~ **di**
to be dripping with ♦ *vt* to drip with.
'**groppa** *sf* (*di animale*) back, rump; (*fam*:
dell'uomo) back, shoulders *pl*.
'**groppo** *sm* tangle; **avere un** ~ **alla gola**
(*fig*) to have a lump in one's throat.
'**grossa** *sf* (*unità di misura*) gross.
gros'sezza [gros'settsa] *sf* size; thickness.
gros'sista, i, e *sm/f* (*COMM*) wholesaler.
'**grosso, a** *ag* big, large; (*di spessore*) thick;
(*grossolano: anche fig*) coarse; (*grave*,
insopportabile) serious, great; (*tempo*,
mare) rough ♦ *sm*: **il** ~ **di** the bulk of; **un**
pezzo ~ (*fig*) a VIP, a bigwig; **farla** ~**a** to
do something very stupid; **dirle** ~**e** to tell
tall stories (*BRIT*) *o* tales (*US*); **questa è**
~**a!** that's a good one!; **sbagliarsi di** ~ to
be completely wrong; **dormire della** ~**a** to
sleep like a log.
grossolanità *sf* coarseness.
grosso'lano, a *ag* rough, coarse; (*fig*)
coarse, crude; (: *errore*) stupid.
grosso'modo *av* roughly.
'**grotta** *sf* cave; grotto.
grot'tesco, a, schi, sche *ag* grotesque.
grovi'era *sm o f* gruyère (cheese).
gro'viglio [gro'viλλo] *sm* tangle; (*fig*)
muddle.
gru *sf inv* crane.
'**gruccia, ce** ['gruttʃa] *sf* (*per camminare*)
crutch; (*per abiti*) coat-hanger.
gru'gnire [gruɲ'ɲire] *vi* to grunt.
gru'gnito [gruɲ'ɲito] *sm* grunt.
'**grugno** ['gruɲɲo] *sm* snout; (*fam*: *faccia*)
mug.
'**grullo, a** *ag* silly, stupid.
'**grumo** *sm* (*di sangue*) clot; (*di farina etc*)
lump.
gru'moso, a *ag* lumpy.
'**gruppo** *sm* group; ~ **sanguigno** blood
group.
gruvi'era *sm o f* = **groviera**.

'**gruzzolo** ['gruttsolo] *sm* (*di denaro*) hoard.
GT *abbr* (*AUT*: = *gran turismo*) GT.
G.U. *abbr* = **Gazzetta Ufficiale**.
guada'gnare [gwadaɲ'ɲare] *vt* (*ottenere*) to
gain; (*soldi*, *stipendio*) to earn; (*vincere*) to
win; (*raggiungere*) to reach; **tanto di**
guadagnato! so much the better!
gua'dagno [gwa'daɲɲo] *sm* earnings *pl*;
(*COMM*) profit; (*vantaggio*, *utile*)
advantage, gain; ~ **di capitale** capital
gains *pl*; ~ **lordo/netto** gross/net earnings
pl.
gu'ado *sm* ford; **passare a** ~ to ford.
gu'ai *escl*: ~ **a te** (*o lui etc*)! woe betide you
(*o him etc*)!
gua'ina *sf* (*fodero*) sheath; (*indumento per*
donna) girdle.
gu'aio *sm* trouble, mishap; (*inconveniente*)
trouble, snag.
gua'ire *vi* to whine, yelp.
gua'ito *sm* (*di cane*) yelp, whine; (*il guaire*)
yelping, whining.
gu'ancia, ce ['gwantʃa] *sf* cheek.
guanci'ale [gwan'tʃale] *sm* pillow; **dormire**
fra due ~**i** (*fig*) to sleep easy, have no
worries.
gu'anto *sm* glove; **trattare qn con i** ~**i** (*fig*)
to handle sb with kid gloves; **gettare/**
raccogliere il ~ (*fig*) to throw down/take
up the gauntlet.
guan'tone *sm* boxing glove.
guarda'boschi [gwarda'bɔski] *sm inv*
forester.
guarda'caccia [gwarda'kattʃa] *sm inv*
gamekeeper.
guarda'coste *sm inv* coastguard; (*nave*)
coastguard patrol vessel.
guarda'linee *sm inv* (*SPORT*) linesman.
guarda'macchine [gwarda'makkine] *sm/f inv*
car-park (*BRIT*) *o* parking lot (*US*)
attendant.
guar'dare *vt* (*con lo sguardo: osservare*) to
look at; (*film*, *televisione*) to watch;
(*custodire*) to look after, take care of ♦ *vi*
to look; (*badare*): ~ **a** to pay attention to;
(*luoghi: esser orientato*): ~ **a** to face; ~**rsi** *vr*
to look at o.s; ~ **di** to try to; ~**rsi da**
(*astenersi*) to refrain from; (*stare in*
guardia) to beware of; ~**rsi dal fare** to take
care not to do; **ma guarda un po'!** good
heavens!; **e guarda caso** ... as if by
coincidence ...; ~ **qn dall'alto in basso** to
look down on sb; **non** ~ **in faccia a**
nessuno (*fig*) to have no regard for
anybody; ~ **di traverso** to scowl *o* frown
at; ~ **a vista qn** to keep a close watch on
sb.
guarda'roba *sm inv* wardrobe; (*locale*)

cloakroom.
guardarobi'ere, a *sm/f* cloakroom
attendant.
guardasi'gilli [gwardasi'dʒilli] *sm inv* ≈ Lord
Chancellor (*BRIT*), ≈ Attorney General
(*US*).
gu'ardia *sf* (*individuo, corpo*) guard;
(*sorveglianza*) watch; **fare la ~ a qc/qn** to
guard sth/sb; **stare in ~** (*fig*) to be on
one's guard; **il medico di ~** the doctor on
call; **il fiume ha raggiunto il livello di ~**
the river has reached the high-water
mark; **~ carceraria** (prison) warder (*BRIT*)
o guard (*US*); **~ del corpo** bodyguard; **~**
di finanza (*corpo*) customs *pl*; (*persona*)
customs officer; **~ forestale** forest
ranger; **~ giurata** security guard; **~**
medica emergency doctor service; **~**
municipale town policeman; **~ notturna**
night security guard; **~ di pubblica**
sicurezza policeman; *vedi nota nel riquadro.*

GUARDIA DI FINANZA

The **Guardia di Finanza** *is a military body*
which deals with infringements of the laws
governing income tax and monopolies. It
reports to the Ministers of Finance, Justice or
Agriculture, depending on the function it is
performing.

---

guardia'caccia [gwardja'kattʃa] *sm inv*
= **guardacaccia**.
guardi'ano, a *sm/f* (*di carcere*) warder
(*BRIT*), guard (*US*); (*di villa etc*) caretaker;
(*di museo*) custodian; (*di zoo*) keeper; **~**
notturno night watchman.
guar'dina *sf* cell.
guar'dingo, a, ghi, ghe *ag* wary,
cautious.
guardi'ola *sf* porter's lodge; (*MIL*) look-out
tower.
guarigi'one [gwari'dʒone] *sf* recovery.
gua'rire *vt* (*persona, malattia*) to cure;
(*ferita*) to heal ♦ *vi* to recover, be cured;
to heal (up).
guarnigi'one [gwarni'dʒone] *sf* garrison.
guar'nire *vt* (*ornare: abiti*) to trim; (*CUC*) to
garnish.
guarnizi'one [gwarnit'tsjone] *sf* trimming;
garnish; (*TECN*) gasket.
guasta'feste *sm/f inv* spoilsport.
guas'tare *vt* to spoil, ruin; (*meccanismo*) to
break; **~rsi** *vr* (*cibo*) to go bad;
(*meccanismo*) to break down; (*tempo*) to
change for the worse; (*amici*) to quarrel.
gu'asto, a *ag* (*non funzionante*) broken;
(: *telefono etc*) out of order; (*andato a*

male) bad, rotten; (: *dente*) decayed, bad;
(*fig: corrotto*) depraved ♦ *sm* breakdown;
(*avaria*) failure; **~ al motore** engine
failure.
Guate'mala *sm*: **il ~** Guatemala.
guatemal'teco, a, ci, che *ag, sm/f*
Guatemalan.
guazza'buglio [gwattsa'buʎʎo] *sm* muddle.
gu'ercio, a, ci, ce ['gwertʃo] *ag* cross-eyed.
gu'erra *sf* war; (*tecnica: atomica, chimica etc*)
warfare; **fare la ~ (a)** to wage war
(against); **la ~ fredda** the Cold War; **~**
mondiale world war; **la prima/seconda ~**
mondiale the First/Second World War.
guerrafon'daio *sm* warmonger.
guerreggi'are [gwerred'dʒare] *vi* to wage
war.
guerri'ero, a *ag* warlike ♦ *sm* warrior.
guer'riglia [gwer'riʎʎa] *sf* guerrilla
warfare.
guerrigli'ero [gwerriʎ'ʎεro] *sm* guerrilla.
'gufo *sm* owl.
'guglia ['guʎʎa] *sf* (*ARCHIT*) spire; (*di roccia*)
needle.
Gui'ana *sf*: **la ~ francese** French Guiana.
gu'ida *sf* (*persona*) guide; (*libro*) guide(book);
(*comando, direzione*) guidance, direction;
(*AUT*) driving; (: *sterzo*) steering;
(*tappeto, di tenda, cassetto*) runner; **~ a**
destra/sinistra (*AUT*) right-/left-hand
drive; **essere alla ~ di** (*governo*) to head;
(*spedizione, paese*) to lead; **far da ~ a qn**
(*mostrare la strada*) to show sb the way;
(*in una città*) to show sb (a)round; **~**
telefonica telephone directory.
gui'dare *vt* to guide; (*condurre a capo*) to
lead; (*auto*) to drive; (*aereo, nave*) to pilot;
sa ~? can you drive?
guida'tore, 'trice *sm/f* (*conducente*) driver.
Gui'nea *sf*: **la Repubblica di ~** the Republic
of Guinea; **la ~ Equatoriale** Equatorial
Guinea.
guin'zaglio [gwin'tsaʎʎo] *sm* leash, lead.
gu'isa *sf*: **a ~ di** like, in the manner of.
guiz'zare [gwit'tsare] *vi* to dart; to flicker;
to leap; **~ via** (*fuggire*) to slip away.
gu'izzo ['gwittso] *sm* (*di animali*) dart; (*di*
fulmine) flash.
'guru *sm inv* (*REL, anche fig*) guru.
'guscio ['guʃʃo] *sm* shell.
gus'tare *vt* (*cibi*) to taste; (: *assaporare con*
piacere) to enjoy, savour (*BRIT*), savor
(*US*); (*fig*) to enjoy, appreciate ♦ *vi*: **~ a** to
please; **non mi gusta affatto** I don't like it
at all.
gusta'tivo, a *ag*: **papille** *fpl* **~e** taste buds.
'gusto *sm* (*senso*) taste; (*sapore*) taste,
flavour (*BRIT*), flavor (*US*); (*godimento*)

enjoyment; **al ~ di fragola** strawberry-
flavo(u)red; **di ~ barocco** in the baroque
style; **mangiare di ~** to eat heartily;
prenderci ~: ci ha preso ~ he's acquired a
taste for it, he's got to like it.
gus'toso, a *ag* tasty; (*fig*) agreeable.
guttu'rale *ag* guttural.
Gu'yana [gu'jana] *sf*: **la ~** Guyana.

H h

H, h ['akka] *sf o m inv* (*lettera*) H, h ♦ *abbr*
(= *ora*) hr; (= *etto, altezza*) h; **H come hotel**
≈ H for Harry (*BRIT*), H for How (*US*).
ha¹, 'hai [a, ai] *vb vedi* **avere**.
ha² *abbr* (= *ettaro*) ha.
Ha'iti [a'iti] *sf* Haiti.
haiti'ano, a [ai'tjano] *ag, sm/f* Haitian.
hall [hɔːl] *sf inv* hall, foyer.
'handicap ['handikap] *sm inv* handicap.
handicap'pato, a [andikap'pato] *ag*
handicapped ♦ *sm/f* handicapped person,
disabled person.
'hanno ['anno] *vb vedi* **avere**.
ha'scisc [aʃ'ʃiʃ] *sm* hashish.
hawai'ano, a [ava'jano] *ag, sm/f* Hawaiian.
Ha'waii [a'vai] *sfpl*: **le ~** Hawaii *sg*.
'Helsinki ['ɛlsinki] *sf* Helsinki.
'herpes ['ɛrpes] *sm* (*MED*) herpes *sg*; **~
zoster** shingles *sg*.
hg *abbr* (= *ettogrammo*) hg.
'hi-fi ['haifai] *sm inv, ag inv* hi-fi.
Hima'laia [ima'laja] *sm*: **l'~** the Himalayas
pl.
hl *abbr* (= *ettolitro*) hl.
ho [ɔ] *vb vedi* **avere**.
'hobby ['hɔbi] *sm inv* hobby.
'hockey ['hɔki] *sm* hockey; **~ su ghiaccio**
ice hockey.
'holding ['houldiŋ] *sf inv* holding company.
Hon'duras [on'duras] *sm inv* Honduras.
'Hong Kong ['ɔŋkɔŋg] *sf* Hong Kong.
Hono'lulu [ono'lulu] *sf* Honolulu.
'hostess ['houstis] *sf inv* air hostess (*BRIT*) *o*
stewardess.
ho'tel [o'tɛl] *sm inv* hotel.
Hz *abbr* (= *hertz*) Hz.

I i

I, i [i] *sf o m inv* (*lettera*) I, i; **I come Imola** ≈ I
for Isaac (*BRIT*), I for Item (*US*).
i *det mpl* the; *vedi anche* **il**.
IACP *sigla m* (= *Istituto Autonomo per le Case
Popolari*) public housing association.
i'ato *sm* hiatus.
i'berico, a, ci, che *ag* Iberian; **la Penisola
I~a** the Iberian Peninsula.
iber'nare *vi* to hibernate ♦ *vt* (*MED*) to
induce hypothermia in.
ibernazi'one [ibernat'tsjone] *sf*
hibernation.
ibid. *abbr* (– *ibidem*) ib(id).
'ibrido, a *ag, sm* hybrid.
'ICE ['itʃe] *sigla m* (= *Istituto nazionale per il
Commercio Estero*) overseas trade board.
i'cona *sf* icon.
id *abbr* (– *idem*) do.
Id'dio *sm* God.
i'dea *sf* idea; (*opinione*) opinion, view;
(*ideale*) ideal; **avere lc ~e chiare** to know
one's mind; **cambiare ~** to change one's
mind; **dare l'~ di** to seem, look like;
neanche *o* **neppure per ~!** certainly not!,
no way!; **~ fissa** obsession.
ide'ale *ag, sm* ideal.
idea'lismo *sm* idealism.
idea'lista, i, e *sm/f* idealist.
idea'listico, a, ci, che *ag* idealistic.
idealiz'zare [idealid'dzare] *vt* to idealize.
ide'are *vt* (*immaginare*) to think up,
conceive; (*progettare*) to plan.
idea'tore, 'trice *sm/f* author.
i'dentico, a, ci, che *ag* identical.
identifi'care *vt* to identify.
identificazi'one [identifikat'tsjone] *sf*
identification.
identità *sf inv* identity.
ideolo'gia, 'gie [ideolo'dʒia] *sf* ideology.
ideo'logico, a, ci, che [ideo'lɔdʒiko] *ag*
ideological.
idil'liaco, a, ci, che *ag* = **idillico**.
i'dillico, a, ci, che *ag* idyllic.
i'dillio *sm* idyll; **tra di loro è nato un ~** they
have fallen in love.
idi'oma, i *sm* idiom, language.
idio'matico, a, ci, che *ag* idiomatic; **frase** *f*
~a idiom.

idiosincra'sia *sf* idiosyncrasy.
idi'ota, i, e *ag* idiotic ♦ *sm/f* idiot.
idio'zia [idjot'tsia] *sf* idiocy; (*atto, discorso*) idiotic thing to do (*o* say).
ido'latra, i, e *ag* idolatrous ♦ *sm/f* idolater.
idola'trare *vt* to worship; (*fig*) to idolize.
idola'tria *sf* idolatry.
'idolo *sm* idol.
idoneità *sf* suitability; **esame** *m* **di** ~ qualifying examination.
i'doneo, a *ag:* ~ **a** suitable for, fit for; (*MIL*) fit for; (*qualificato*) qualified for.
i'drante *sm* hydrant.
idra'tante *ag* (*crema*) moisturizing ♦ *sm* moisturizer.
idra'tare *vt* (*pelle*) to moisturize.
idratazi'one [idratat'tsjone] *sf* moisturizing.
i'draulico, a, ci, che *ag* hydraulic ♦ *sm* plumber ♦ *sf* hydraulics *sg*.
'idrico, a, ci, che *ag* water *cpd*.
idrocar'buro *sm* hydrocarbon.
idroe'lettrico, a, ci, che *ag* hydroelectric.
i'drofilo, a *ag:* **cotone** *m* ~ cotton wool (*BRIT*), absorbent cotton (*US*).
idrofo'bia *sf* rabies *sg*.
i'drofobo, a *ag* rabid; (*fig*) furious.
i'drogeno [i'drɔdʒeno] *sm* hydrogen.
idroli'pidico, a, ci, che *ag* hydrolipid.
idro'porto *sm* (*AER*) seaplane base.
idrorepel'lente *ag* water-repellent.
idros'calo *sm* = idroporto.
idrovo'lante *sm* seaplane.
i'ella *sf* bad luck.
iel'lato, a *ag* plagued by bad luck.
i'ena *sf* hyena.
ie'ratico, a, ci, che *ag* (*REL: scrittura*) hieratic; (*fig: atteggiamento*) solemn.
i'eri *av, sm* yesterday; **il giornale di** ~ yesterday's paper; ~ **l'altro** the day before yesterday; ~ **sera** yesterday evening.
ietta'tore, 'trice *sm/f* jinx.
igi'ene [i'dʒɛne] *sf* hygiene; **norme d'**~ sanitary regulations; **ufficio d'**~ public health office; ~ **mentale** mental health; ~ **pubblica** public health.
igi'enico, a, ci, che [i'dʒɛniko] *ag* hygienic; (*salubre*) healthy.
IGM *sigla m* (= *Ispettorato Generale della Motorizzazione*) road traffic inspectorate.
i'gnaro, a [iɲ'ɲaro] *ag:* ~ **di** unaware of, ignorant of.
i'gnifugo, a, ghi, ghe [iɲ'ɲifugo] *ag* flame-resistant, fireproof.
i'gnobile [iɲ'ɲɔbile] *ag* despicable, vile.
igno'minia [iɲɲo'minja] *sf* ignominy.
igno'rante [iɲɲo'rante] *ag* ignorant.

igno'ranza [iɲɲo'rantsa] *sf* ignorance.
igno'rare [iɲɲo'rare] *vt* (*non sapere, conoscere*) to be ignorant *o* unaware of, not to know; (*fingere di non vedere, sentire*) to ignore.
i'gnoto, a [iɲ'ɲɔto] *ag* unknown ♦ *sm/f:* **figlio di** ~**i** child of unknown parentage; **il Milite I**~ the Unknown Soldier.

━━━━━━━━━━ *PAROLA CHIAVE*

il (*pl* (*m*) **i**; *diventa* **lo** (*pl* **gli**) *davanti a s impura, gn, pn, ps, x, z; f* **la** (*pl* **le**)) *det m* **1** the; ~ **libro/lo studente/l'acqua** the book/ the student/the water; **gli scolari** the pupils
2 (*astrazione*): ~ **coraggio/l'amore/la giovinezza** courage/love/youth
3 (*tempo*): ~ **mattino/la sera** in the morning/evening; ~ **venerdì** (*abitualmente*) on Fridays; (*quel giorno*) on (the) Friday; **la settimana prossima** next week
4 (*distributivo*) a, an; **2.500 lire** ~ **chilo/ paio** 2,500 lire a *o* per kilo/pair
5 (*partitivo*) some, any; **hai messo lo zucchero?** have you added sugar?; **hai comprato** ~ **latte?** did you buy (some *o* any) milk?
6 (*possesso*): **aprire gli occhi** to open one's eyes; **rompersi la gamba** to break one's leg; **avere i capelli neri/**~ **naso rosso** to have dark hair/a red nose; **mettiti le scarpe** put your shoes on
7 (*con nomi propri*): ~ **Petrarca** Petrarch; ~ **Presidente Clinton** President Clinton; **dov'è la Francesca?** where's Francesca?
8 (*con nomi geografici*): ~ **Tevere** the Tiber; **l'Italia** Italy; ~ **Regno Unito** the United Kingdom; **l'Everest** Everest.

'ilare *ag* cheerful.
ilarità *sf* hilarity, mirth.
ill. *abbr* (= *illustrazione; illustrato*) ill.
illangui'dire *vi* to grow weak *o* feeble.
illazi'one [illat'tsjone] *sf* inference, deduction.
il'lecito, a [il'letʃito] *ag* illicit.
ille'gale *ag* illegal.
illegalità *sf* illegality.
illeg'gibile [illed'dʒibile] *ag* illegible.
illegittimità [illedʒittimi'ta] *sf* illegitimacy.
ille'gittimo, a [ille'dʒittimo] *ag* illegitimate.
il'leso, a *ag* unhurt, unharmed.
illette'rato, a *ag* illiterate.
illiba'tezza [illiba'tettsa] *sf* (*di donna*) virginity.
illi'bato, a *ag:* **donna** ~**a** virgin.
illimi'tato, a *ag* boundless; unlimited.

illivi'dire *vi* (*volto, mani*) to turn livid; (*cielo*) to grow leaden.

ill.mo *abbr* = **illustrissimo.**

il'logico, a, ci, che [il'lɔdʒiko] *ag* illogical.

il'ludere *vt* to deceive, delude; **~rsi** *vr* to deceive o.s., delude o.s.

illumi'nare *vt* to light up, illuminate; (*fig*) to enlighten; **~rsi** *vr* to light up; **~ a giorno** (*con riflettori*) to floodlight.

illumi'nato, a *ag* (*fig: sovrano, spirito*) enlightened.

illuminazi'one [illuminat'tsjone] *sf* lighting; illumination; floodlighting; (*fig*) flash of inspiration.

illumi'nismo *sm* (*STORIA*): **l'I~** the Enlightenment.

il'lusi *etc vb vedi* **illudere.**

illusi'one *sf* illusion; **farsi delle ~i** to delude o.s.

illusio'nismo *sm* conjuring.

illusio'nista, i, e *sm/f* conjurer.

il'luso, a *pp di* **illudere.**

illu'sorio, a *ag* illusory

illu'strare *vt* to illustrate.

illustra'tivo, a *ag* illustrative.

illustrazi'one [illustrat'tsjone] *sf* illustration.

il'lustre *ag* eminent, renowned.

illus'trissimo, a *ag* (*negli indirizzi*) very revered.

'ILOR *sigla f vedi* **imposta locale sui redditi.**

IM *sigla* = *Imperia.*

imbacuc'care *vt,* **~rsi** *vr* to wrap up.

imbaldan'zire [imbaldan'tsire] *vt* to give confidence to; **~rsi** *vr* to grow bold.

imbal'laggio [imbal'laddʒo] *sm* packing *no pl.*

imbal'lare *vt* to pack; (*AUT*) to race; **~rsi** *vr* (*AUT*) to race.

imbalsa'mare *vt* to embalm.

imbalsa'mato, a *ag* embalmed.

imbambo'lato, a *ag* (*sguardo, espressione*) vacant, blank.

imban'dire *vt*: **~ un banchetto** to prepare a lavish feast.

imban'dito, a *ag*: **tavola ~a** lavishly *o* sumptuously decked table.

imbaraz'zante [imbarat'tsante] *ag* embarrassing, awkward.

imbaraz'zare [imbarat'tsare] *vt* (*mettere a disagio*) to embarrass; (*ostacolare: movimenti*) to hamper; (: *stomaco*) to lie heavily on; **~rsi** *vr* to become embarrassed.

imbaraz'zato, a [imbarat'tsato] *ag* embarrassed; **avere lo stomaco ~** to have an upset stomach.

imba'razzo [imba'rattso] *sm* (*disagio*)

embarrassment; (*perplessità*) puzzlement, bewilderment; **essere** *o* **trovarsi in ~** to be in an awkward situation *o* predicament; **mettere in ~** to embarrass; **~ di stomaco** indigestion.

imbarbari'mento *sm* (*di civiltà, costumi*) barbarization.

imbarca'dero *sm* landing stage.

imbar'care *vt* (*passeggeri*) to embark; (*merci*) to load; **~rsi** *vr*: **~rsi su** to board; **~rsi per l'America** to sail for America; **~rsi in** (*fig: affare*) to embark on.

imbarcazi'one [imbarkat'tsjone] *sf* (small) boat, (small) craft *inv*; **~ di salvataggio** lifeboat.

im'barco, chi *sm* embarkation; loading; boarding; (*banchina*) landing stage; **carta d'~** boarding pass (*BRIT*), boarding card.

imbastar'dire *vt* to bastardize, debase; **~rsi** *vr* to degenerate, become debased.

imbas'tire *vt* (*cucire*) to tack; (*fig: abbozzare*) to sketch, outline.

im'battersi *vr*: **~ in** (*incontrare*) to bump *o* run into.

imbat'tibile *ag* unbeatable, invincible.

imbavagli'are [imbavaʎ'ʎare] *vt* to gag.

imbec'care *vt* (*uccelli*) to feed; (*fig*) to prompt, put words into sb's mouth.

imbec'cata *sf* (*TEAT*) prompt; **dare l'~ a qn** to prompt sb; (*fig*) to give sb their cue.

imbe'cille [imbe't'fille] *ag* idiotic ♦ *sm/f* idiot; (*MED*) imbecile.

imbecillità [imbetʃilli'ta] *sf inv* (*MED, fig*) imbecility, idiocy; **dire ~** to talk nonsense.

imbellet'tare *vt* (*viso*) to make up, put make-up on; **~rsi** *vr* to make o.s. up, put on one's make-up.

imbel'lire *vt* to adorn, embellish ♦ *vi* to grow more beautiful.

im'berbe *ag* beardless; **un giovanotto ~** a callow youth.

imbestia'lire *vt* to infuriate; **~rsi** *vr* to become infuriated, fly into a rage.

im'bevere *vt* to soak; **~rsi** *vr*: **~rsi di** to soak up, absorb.

imbe'vuto, a *ag*: **~ (di)** soaked (in).

imbian'care *vt* to whiten; (*muro*) to whitewash ♦ *vi* to become *o* turn white.

imbianca'tura *sf* (*di muro: con bianco di calce*) whitewashing; (: *con altre pitture*) painting.

imbian'chino [imbjan'kino] *sm* (house) painter, painter and decorator.

imbion'dire *vt* (*capelli*) to lighten; (*CUC: cipolla*) to brown; **~rsi** *vr* (*capelli*) to lighten, go blonde, go fair; (*messi*) to turn golden, ripen.

imbizzar'rirsi [imbiddzar'rirsi] vr (cavallo) to become frisky.

imboc'care vt (bambino) to feed; (entrare: strada) to enter, turn into ♦ vi: ~ in (sog: strada) to lead into; (: fiume) to flow into.

imbocca'tura sf mouth; (di strada, porto) entrance; (MUS, del morso) mouthpiece.

im'bocco, chi sm entrance.

imboni'tore sm (di spettacolo, circo) barker.

imborghe'sire [imborge'zire] vi, ~rsi vr to become bourgeois.

imbos'care vt to hide; ~rsi vr (MIL) to evade military service.

imbos'cata sf ambush.

imbos'cato sm draft dodger (US).

imboschi'mento [imboski'mento] sm afforestation.

imbottigli'are [imbottiʎ'ʎare] vt to bottle; (NAUT) to blockade; (MIL) to hem in; ~rsi vr to be stuck in a traffic jam.

imbot'tire vt to stuff; (giacca) to pad; ~rsi vr: ~rsi di (rimpinzarsi) to stuff o.s. with.

imbot'tito, a ag (sedia) upholstered; (giacca) padded ♦ sf quilt.

imbotti'tura sf stuffing; padding.

imbracci'are [imbrat'tʃare] vt (fucile) to shoulder; (scudo) to grasp.

imbra'nato, a ag clumsy, awkward ♦ sm/f clumsy person.

imbratta'carte sm/f (peg) scribbler.

imbrat'tare vt to dirty, smear, daub; ~rsi vr: ~rsi (di) to dirty o.s. (with).

imbratta'tele sm/f (peg) dauber.

imbrigli'are [imbriʎ'ʎare] vt to bridle.

imbroc'care vt (fig) to guess correctly.

imbrogli'are [imbroʎ'ʎare] vt to mix up; (fig: raggirare) to deceive, cheat; (: confondere) to confuse, mix up; ~rsi vr to get tangled; (fig) to become confused.

im'broglio [im'brɔʎʎo] sm (groviglio) tangle; (situazione confusa) mess; (truffa) swindle, trick.

imbrogli'one, a [imbroʎ'ʎone] sm/f cheat, swindler.

imbronci'ato, a [imbron'tʃato] ag (persona) sulky; (cielo) cloudy, threatening.

imbru'nire vi, vb impers to grow dark; all'~ at dusk.

imbrut'tire vt to make ugly ♦ vi to become ugly.

imbu'care vt to post.

imbur'rare vt to butter.

imbuti'forme ag funnel-shaped.

im'buto sm funnel.

I.M.C.T.C. sigla (= Ispettorato Generale della Motorizzazione Civile e dei Trasporti in Concessione) ≈ DVLA.

i'mene sm hymen.

imi'tare vt to imitate; (riprodurre) to copy; (assomigliare) to look like.

imita'tore, 'trice sm/f (gen) imitator; (TEAT) impersonator, impressionist.

imitazi'one [imitat'tsjone] sf imitation.

immaco'lato, a ag spotless; immaculate.

immagazzi'nare [immagaddzi'nare] vt to store.

immagi'nabile [immadʒi'nabile] ag imaginable.

immagi'nare [immadʒi'nare] vt to imagine; (supporre) to suppose; (inventare) to invent; s'immagini! don't mention it!, not at all!

immagi'nario, a [immadʒi'narjo] ag imaginary.

immagina'tiva [immadʒina'tiva] sf imagination.

immaginazi'one [immadʒinat'tsjone] sf imagination; (cosa immaginata) fancy.

im'magine [im'madʒine] sf image; (rappresentazione grafica, mentale) picture.

immagi'noso, a [immadʒi'noso] ag (linguaggio, stile) fantastic.

immalinco'nire vt to sadden, depress; ~rsi vr to become depressed, become melancholy.

imman'cabile ag unfailing.

immancabil'mente av without fail, unfailingly.

im'mane ag (smisurato) huge; (spaventoso, inumano) terrible.

imma'nente ag (FILOSOFIA) inherent, immanent.

immangi'abile [imman'dʒabile] ag inedible.

immatrico'lare vt to register; ~rsi vr (INS) to matriculate, enrol.

immatricolazi'one [immatrikolat'tsjone] sf registration; matriculation, enrolment.

immaturità sf immaturity.

imma'turo, a ag (frutto) unripe; (persona) immature; (prematuro) premature.

immedesi'marsi vr: ~ in to identify with.

immediata'mente av immediately, at once.

immedia'tezza [immedja'tettsa] sf immediacy.

immedi'ato, a ag immediate.

immemo'rabile ag immemorial; da tempo ~ from time immemorial.

im'memore ag: ~ di forgetful of.

immensità sf immensity.

im'menso, a ag immense.

im'mergere [im'mɛrdʒere] vt to immerse, plunge; ~rsi vr to plunge; (sommergibile) to dive, submerge; (dedicarsi a): ~rsi in to immerse o.s. in.

immeri'tato, a ag undeserved.

immeri'tevole *ag* undeserving, unworthy.
immersi'one *sf* immersion; (*di sommergibile*) submersion, dive; (*di palombaro*) dive; **linea di** ~ (*NAUT*) water line.
im'merso, a *pp di* **immergere.**
im'messo, a *pp di* **immettere.**
im'mettere *vt*: ~ (**in**) to introduce (into); ~ **dati in un computer** to enter data on a computer.
immi'grante *ag, sm/f* immigrant.
immi'grare *vi* to immigrate.
immi'grato, a *sm/f* immigrant.
immigrazi'one [immigrat'tsjone] *sf* immigration.
immi'nente *ag* imminent.
immi'nenza [immi'nɛntsa] *sf* imminence.
immischi'are [immis'kjare] *vt*: ~ **qn in** to involve sb in; ~**rsi** *vr*: ~**rsi in** to interfere *o* meddle in.
immiseri'mento *sm* impoverishment.
immise'rire *vt* to impoverish.
immis'sario *sm* (*GEO*) affluent, tributary.
immissi'one *sf* (*gas*) introduction; (*di aria, gas*) intake; ~ **di dati** (*INFORM*) data entry.
im'mobile *ag* motionless, still; (**beni**) ~**i** *smpl* real estate *sg*.
immobili'are *ag* (*DIR*) property *cpd*; **patrimonio** ~ real estate; **società** ~ property company.
immobi'lismo *sm* inertia.
immobilità *sf* immobility.
immobiliz'zare [immobilid'dzare] *vt* to immobilize; (*ECON*) to lock up.
immo'bilizzo [immobi'liddzo] *sm*: **spese d'**~ capital expenditure.
immo'destia *sf* immodesty.
immo'desto, a *ag* immodest.
immo'lare *vt* to sacrifice.
immondez'zaio [immondet'tsajo] *sm* rubbish dump.
immon'dizia [immon'dittsja] *sf* dirt, filth; (*spesso al pl: spazzatura, rifiuti*) rubbish *no pl*, refuse *no pl*.
immo'rale *ag* immoral.
immoralità *sf* immorality.
immorta'lare *vt* to immortalize.
immor'tale *ag* immortal.
immortalità *sf* immortality.
im'mune *ag* (*esente*) exempt; (*MED, DIR*) immune.
immunità *sf* immunity; ~ **diplomatica** diplomatic immunity; ~ **parlamentare** parliamentary privilege.
immuniz'zare [immunid'dzare] *vt* (*MED*) to immunize.
immunizzazi'one [immuniddzat'tsjone] *sf* immunization.

immunodefi'cienza [immunodefi'tʃentsa] *sf*: ~ **acquisita** acquired immunodeficiency.
immuno'logico, a, ci, che [immuno'lɔdʒiko] *ag* immunological.
immu'tabile *ag* immutable; unchanging.
impac'care *vt* to pack.
impacchet'tare [impakket'tare] *vt* to pack up.
impacci'are [impat'tʃare] *vt* to hinder, hamper.
impacci'ato, a [impat'tʃato] *ag* awkward, clumsy; (*imbarazzato*) embarrassed.
im'paccio [im'pattʃo] *sm* obstacle; (*imbarazzo*) embarrassment; (*situazione imbarazzante*) awkward situation.
im'pacco, chi *sm* (*MED*) compress.
impadro'nirsi *vr*: ~ **di** to seize, take possession of; (*fig: apprendere a fondo*) to master.
impa'gabile *ag* priceless.
impagi'nare [impadʒi'nare] *vt* (*TIP*) to paginate, page (up).
impaginazi'one [impadʒinat'tsjone] *sf* pagination.
impagli'are [impaʎ'ʎare] *vt* to stuff (with straw).
impa'lato, a *ag* (*fig*) stiff as a board.
impalca'tura *sf* scaffolding; (*anche fig*) framework.
impalli'dire *vi* to turn pale; (*fig*) to fade.
impalli'nare *vt* to riddle with shot.
impal'pabile *ag* impalpable.
impa'nare *vt* (*CUC*) to dip (*o* roll) in breadcrumbs, bread (*US*).
impanta'narsi *vr* to sink (in the mud); (*fig*) to get bogged down.
impape'rarsi *vr* to stumble over a word.
impappi'narsi *vr* to stammer, falter.
impa'rare *vt* to learn; **così impari!** that'll teach you!
impara'ticcio [impara'tittʃo] *sm* half-baked notions *pl*.
impareggi'abile [impared'dʒabile] *ag* incomparable.
imparen'tarsi *vr*: ~ **con** (*famiglia*) to marry into.
'impari *ag inv* (*disuguale*) unequal; (*dispari*) odd.
impar'tire *vt* to bestow, give.
imparzi'ale [impar'tsjale] *ag* impartial, unbiased.
imparzialità [impartsjali'ta] *sf* impartiality.
impas'sibile *ag* impassive.
impas'tare *vt* (*pasta*) to knead; (*colori*) to mix.
impastic'carsi *vr* to pop pills.
im'pasto *sm* (*l'impastare: di pane*) kneading;

(: *di cemento*) mixing; (*pasta*) dough; (*anche fig*) mixture.

im'patto *sm* impact; ~ **ambientale** impact on the environment.

impau'rire *vt* to scare, frighten ♦ *vi* (*anche:* ~**rsi**) to become scared *o* frightened.

im'pavido, a *ag* intrepid, fearless.

impazi'ente [impat'tsjɛnte] *ag* impatient.

impazi'enza [impat'tsjɛntsa] *sf* impatience.

impaz'zata [impat'tsata] *sf*: **all'**~ (*precipitosamente*) at breakneck speed; (*colpire*) wildly.

impaz'zire [impat'tsire] *vi* to go mad; ~ **per qn/qc** to be crazy about sb/sth.

impec'cabile *ag* impeccable.

impedi'mento *sm* obstacle, hindrance.

impe'dire *vt* (*vietare*): ~ **a qn di fare** to prevent sb from doing; (*ostruire*) to obstruct; (*impacciare*) to hamper, hinder.

impe'gnare [impeɲ'ɲare] *vt* (*dare in pegno*) to pawn; (*onore etc*) to pledge; (*prenotare*) to book, reserve; (*obbligare*) to oblige; (*occupare*) to keep busy; (*MIL: nemico*) to engage; ~**rsi** *vr* (*vincolarsi*): ~**rsi a fare** to undertake to do; (*mettersi risolutamente*): ~**rsi in qc** to devote o.s. to sth; ~**rsi con qn** (*accordarsi*) to come to an agreement with sb.

impegna'tivo, a [impeɲɲa'tivo] *ag* binding; (*lavoro*) demanding, exacting.

impe'gnato, a [impeɲ'ɲato] *ag* (*occupato*) busy; (*fig: romanzo, autore*) committed, engagé.

im'pegno [im'peɲɲo] *sm* (*obbligo*) obligation; (*promessa*) promise, pledge; (*zelo*) diligence, zeal; (*compito, d'autore*) commitment; ~**i di lavoro** business commitments.

impego'larsi *vr* (*fig*): ~ **in** to get heavily involved in.

impela'garsi *vr* = **impegolarsi**.

impel'lente *ag* pressing, urgent.

impene'trabile *ag* impenetrable.

impen'narsi *vr* (*cavallo*) to rear up; (*AER*) to go into a climb; (*fig*) to bridle.

impen'nata *sf* (*di cavallo*) rearing up; (*di aereo*) climb, nose-up; (*fig: scatto d'ira*) burst of anger; (*: di prezzi etc*) sudden increase.

impen'sabile *ag* (*inaccettabile*) unthinkable; (*difficile da concepire*) inconceivable.

impen'sato, a *ag* unforeseen, unexpected.

impensie'rire *vt*, ~**rsi** *vr* to worry.

impe'rante *ag* prevailing.

impe'rare *vi* (*anche fig*) to reign, rule.

impera'tivo, a *ag*, *sm* imperative.

impera'tore, 'trice *sm/f* emperor/empress.

impercet'tibile [impertʃet'tibile] *ag* imperceptible.

imperdo'nabile *ag* unforgivable, unpardonable.

imper'fetto *ag* imperfect ♦ *sm* (*LING*) imperfect (tense).

imperfezi'one [imperfet'tsjone] *sf* imperfection.

imperi'ale *ag* imperial.

imperia'lismo *sm* imperialism.

imperia'lista, i, e *ag* imperialist.

imperi'oso, a *ag* (*persona*) imperious; (*motivo, esigenza*) urgent, pressing.

imperi'turo, a *ag* everlasting.

impe'rizia [impe'rittsja] *sf* lack of experience.

imperma'lirsi *vr* to take offence.

imperme'abile *ag* waterproof ♦ *sm* raincoat.

imperni'are *vt*: ~ **qc su** to hinge sth on; (*fig: discorso, relazione etc*) to base sth on; ~**rsi** *vr* (*fig*): ~**rsi su** to be based on.

im'pero *sm* empire; (*forza, autorità*) rule, control.

imperscru'tabile *ag* inscrutable.

imperso'nale *ag* impersonal.

imperso'nare *vt* to personify; (*TEAT*) to play, act (the part of); ~**rsi** *vr*: ~**rsi in un ruolo** to get into a part, live a part.

imper'territo, a *ag* unperturbed.

imperti'nente *ag* impertinent.

imperti'nenza [imperti'nɛntsa] *sf* impertinence.

impertur'babile *ag* imperturbable.

imperver'sare *vi* to rage.

im'pervio, a *ag* (*luogo*) inaccessible; (*strada*) impassable.

'impeto *sm* (*moto, forza*) force, impetus; (*assalto*) onslaught; (*fig: impulso*) impulse; (*: slancio*) transport; **con** ~ (*parlare*) forcefully, energetically.

impet'tito, a *ag* stiff, erect; **camminare** ~ to strut.

impetu'oso, a *ag* (*vento*) strong, raging; (*persona*) impetuous.

impian'tare *vt* (*motore*) to install; (*azienda, discussione*) to establish, start.

impian'tistica *sf* plant design and installation.

impi'anto *sm* (*installazione*) installation; (*apparecchiature*) plant; (*sistema*) system; ~ **elettrico** wiring; ~ **sportivo** sports complex; ~**i di risalita** (*SCI*) ski lifts.

impias'trare, impiastricci'are [impjastrit'tʃare] *vt* to smear, dirty.

impi'astro *sm* poultice; (*fig fam: persona*) nuisance.

impiccagi'one [impikka'dʒone] *sf* hanging.

impic'care *vt* to hang; ~**rsi** *vr* to hang o.s.

impicci'are [impit'tʃare] *vt* to hinder, hamper; ~**rsi** *vr* to meddle, interfere; **impicciati degli affari tuoi!** mind your own business!

im'piccio [im'pittʃo] *sm* (*ostacolo*) hindrance; (*seccatura*) trouble, bother; (*affare imbrogliato*) mess; **essere d'~** to be in the way; **cavare** *o* **togliere qn dagli** ~**i** to get sb out of trouble.

impicci'one, a [impit'tʃone] *sm/f* busybody.

impie'gare *vt* (*usare*) to use, employ; (*assumere*) to employ, take on; (*spendere*: *denaro, tempo*) to spend; (*investire*) to invest; ~**rsi** *vr* to get a job, obtain employment; **impiego un quarto d'ora per andare a casa** it takes me *o* I take a quarter of an hour to get home.

impiega'tizio, a [impjega'tittsjo] *ag* clerical, white-collar *cpd*; **lavoro/ceto** ~ clerical *o* white-collar work/workers *pl*.

impie'gato, a *sm/f* employee; ~ **statale** state employee.

impi'ego, ghi *sm* (*uso*) use; (*occupazione*) employment; (*posto di lavoro*) (regular) job, post; (*ECON*) investment; ~ **pubblico** job in the public sector.

impieto'sire *vt* to move to pity; ~**rsi** *vr* to be moved to pity.

impie'toso, a *ag* pitiless, cruel.

impie'trire *vt* (*anche fig*) to petrify.

impigli'are [impiʎ'ʎare] *vt* to catch, entangle; ~**rsi** *vr* to get caught up *o* entangled.

impi'grire *vt* to make lazy ♦ *vi* (*anche*: ~**rsi**) to grow lazy.

impingu'are *vt* (*maiale etc*) to fatten; (*fig*: *tasche, casse dello Stato*) to stuff with money.

impiom'bare *vt* (*pacco*) to seal (with lead); (*dente*) to fill.

impla'cabile *ag* implacable.

implemen'tare *vt* to implement.

impli'care *vt* to imply; (*coinvolgere*) to involve; ~**rsi** *vr*: ~**rsi (in)** to become involved (in).

implicazi'one [implikat'tsjone] *sf* implication.

im'plicito, a [im'plitʃito] *ag* implicit.

implo'rare *vt* to implore.

implorazi'one [implorat'tsjone] *sf* plea, entreaty.

impolli'nare *vt* to pollinate.

impollinazi'one [impollinat'tsjone] *sf* pollination.

impolve'rare *vt* to cover with dust; ~**rsi** *vr* to get dusty.

impoma'tare *vt* (*pelle*) to put ointment on;

(*capelli*) to pomade; (*baffi*) to wax; ~**rsi** *vr* (*fam*) to get spruced up.

imponde'rabile *ag* imponderable.

im'pone *etc vb vedi* **imporre.**

impo'nente *ag* imposing, impressive.

im'pongo *etc vb vedi* **imporre.**

impo'nibile *ag* taxable ♦ *sm* taxable income.

impopo'lare *ag* unpopular.

impopolarità *sf* unpopularity.

im'porre *vt* to impose; (*costringere*) to force, make; (*far valere*) to impose, enforce; **imporsi** *vr* (*persona*) to assert o.s.; (*cosa*: *rendersi necessario*) to become necessary; (*aver successo*: *moda, attore*) to become popular; ~ **a qn di fare** to force sb to do, make sb do.

impor'tante *ag* important.

impor'tanza [impor'tantsa] *sf* importance; **dare** ~ **a qc** to attach importance to sth; **darsi** ~ to give o.s. airs.

impor'tare *vt* (*introdurre dall'estero*) to import ♦ *vi* to matter, be important ♦ *vb impers* (*essere necessario*) to be necessary; (*interessare*) to matter; **non importa!** it doesn't matter!; **non me ne importa!** I don't care!

importa'tore, 'trice *ag* importing ♦ *sm/f* importer.

importazi'one [importat'tsjone] *sf* importation; (*merci importate*) imports *pl*.

im'porto *sm* (total) amount.

importu'nare *vt* to bother.

impor'tuno, a *ag* irksome, annoying.

im'posi *etc vb vedi* **imporre.**

imposizi'one [impozit'tsjone] *sf* imposition; (*ordine*) order, command; (*onere, imposta*) tax.

imposses'sarsi *vr*: ~ **di** to seize, take possession of.

impos'sibile *ag* impossible; **fare l'**~ to do one's utmost, do all one can.

impossibilità *sf* impossibility; **essere nell'**~ **di fare qc** to be unable to do sth.

impossibili'tato, a *ag*: **essere** ~ **a fare qc** to be unable to do sth.

im'posta *sf* (*di finestra*) shutter; (*tassa*) tax; ~ **indiretta sui consumi** excise duty *o* tax; ~ **locale sui redditi (ILOR)** tax on unearned income; ~ **patrimoniale** property tax; ~ **sul reddito** income tax; ~ **sul reddito delle persone fisiche (IRPEF)** personal income tax; ~ **di successione** capital transfer tax (*BRIT*), inheritance tax (*US*); ~ **sugli utili** tax on profits; ~ **sul valore aggiunto (I.V.A.)** value added tax (VAT) (*BRIT*), sales tax (*US*).

impos'tare *vt* (*imbucare*) to post; (*servizio*,

organizzazione) to set up; (lavoro) to organize, plan; (resoconto, rapporto) to plan; (problema) to set out, formulate; (TIP: pagina) to lay out; ~ **la voce** (MUS) to pitch one's voice.

impostazi'one [impostat'tsjone] sf (di lettera) posting (BRIT), mailing (US); (di problema, questione) formulation, statement; (di lavoro) organization, planning; (di attività) setting up; (MUS: di voce) pitch.

im'posto, a pp di **imporre.**

impos'tore, a sm/f impostor.

impo'tente ag weak, powerless; (anche MED) impotent.

impo'tenza [impo'tentsa] sf weakness, powerlessness; impotence.

impove'rire vt to impoverish ♦ vi (anche: ~rsi) to become poor.

imprati'cabile ag (strada) impassable; (campo da gioco) unplayable.

imprati'chire [imprati'kire] vt to train; ~rsi vr: ~rsi in qc to practise (BRIT) o practice (US) sth.

impre'care vi to curse, swear; ~ **contro** to hurl abuse at.

imprecazi'one [imprekat'tsjone] sf abuse, curse.

impreci'sato, a [impretʃi'zato] ag (non preciso: quantità, numero) indeterminate.

imprecisi'one [impretʃi'zjone] sf imprecision; inaccuracy.

impre'ciso, a [impre'tʃizo] ag imprecise, vague; (calcolo) inaccurate.

impre'gnare [impreɲ'ɲare] vt: ~ (di) (imbevere) to soak o impregnate (with); (riempire: anche fig) to fill (with).

imprendi'tore sm (industriale) entrepreneur; (appaltatore) contractor; **piccolo** ~ small businessman.

imprendito'ria sf enterprise; (imprenditori) entrepreneurs pl.

imprenditori'ale ag (ceto, classe) entrepreneurial.

imprepa'rato, a ag: ~ (a) (gen) unprepared (for); (lavoratore) untrained (for); **cogliere qn** ~ to catch sb unawares.

impreparazi'one [impreparat'tsjone] sf lack of preparation.

im'presa sf (iniziativa) enterprise; (azione) exploit; (azienda) firm, concern; ~ **familiare** family firm; ~ **pubblica** state-owned enterprise.

impre'sario sm (TEAT) manager, impresario; ~ **di pompe funebri** funeral director.

imprescin'dibile [impreʃʃin'dibile] ag not to be ignored.

im'pressi etc vb vedi **imprimere.**

impressio'nante ag impressive; upsetting.

impressio'nare vt to impress; (turbare) to upset; (FOT) to expose; ~rsi vr to be easily upset.

impressi'one sf impression; (fig: sensazione) sensation, feeling; (stampa) printing; **fare** ~ (colpire) to impress; (turbare) to frighten, upset; **fare buona/ cattiva** ~ **a** to make a good/bad impression on.

im'presso, a pp di **imprimere.**

impres'tare vt: ~ **qc a qn** to lend sth to sb.

impreve'dibile ag unforeseeable; (persona) unpredictable.

imprevi'dente ag lacking in foresight.

imprevi'denza [imprevi'dentsa] sf lack of foresight.

impre'visto, a ag unexpected, unforeseen ♦ sm unforeseen event; **salvo** ~i unless anything unexpected happens.

imprezio'sire [imprettsjo'sire] vt: ~ **di** to embellish with.

imprigiona'mento [impridʒona'mento] sm imprisonment.

imprigio'nare [impridʒo'nare] vt to imprison.

im'primere vt (anche fig) to impress, stamp; (comunicare: movimento) to transmit, give.

impro'babile ag improbable, unlikely.

'improbo, a ag (fatica, lavoro) hard, laborious.

improdut'tivo, a ag (investimento) unprofitable; (terreno) unfruitful; (fig: sforzo) fruitless.

im'pronta sf imprint, impression, sign; (di piede, mano) print; (fig) mark, stamp; ~ **digitale** fingerprint; **rilevamento delle** ~**e genetiche** genetic fingerprinting.

impro'perio sm insult.

impropo'nibile ag which cannot be proposed o suggested.

im'proprio, a ag improper; **arma** ~**a** offensive weapon.

improro'gabile ag (termine) that cannot be extended.

improvvisa'mente av suddenly; unexpectedly.

improvvi'sare vt to improvise; ~rsi vr: ~rsi **cuoco** to (decide to) act as cook.

improvvi'sata sf (pleasant) surprise.

improvvisazi'one [improvvizat'tsjone] sf improvisation; **spirito d'**~ spirit of invention.

improv'viso, a ag (imprevisto) unexpected;

(*subitaneo*) sudden; **all'~** unexpectedly; suddenly.

impru'dente *ag* foolish, imprudent; (*osservazione*) unwise.

impru'denza [impru'dɛntsa] *sf* foolishness, imprudence; **è stata un'~** that was a foolish *o* an imprudent thing to do.

impu'dente *ag* impudent.

impu'denza [impu'dɛntsa] *sf* impudence.

impudi'cizia [impudi'tʃittsja] *sf* immodesty.

impu'dico, a, chi, che *ag* immodest.

impu'gnare [impuɲ'ɲare] *vt* to grasp, grip; (*DIR*) to contest.

impugna'tura [impuɲɲa'tura] *sf* grip, grasp; (*manico*) handle; (: *di spada*) hilt.

impulsività *sf* impulsiveness.

impul'sivo, a *ag* impulsive.

im'pulso *sm* impulse; **dare un ~ alle vendite** to boost sales.

impune'mente *av* with impunity.

impunità *sf* impunity.

impun'tarsi *vr* to stop dead, refuse to budge; (*fig*) to be obstinate.

impun'tura *sf* stitching.

impurità *sf inv* impurity.

im'puro, a *ag* impure.

impu'tare *vt* (*ascrivere*): **~ qc a** to attribute sth to; (*DIR*: *accusare*): **~ qn di** to charge sb with, accuse sb of.

impu'tato, a *sm/f* (*DIR*) accused, defendant.

imputazi'one [imputat'tsjone] *sf* (*DIR*) charge; (*di spese*) allocation.

imputri'dire *vi* to rot.

—————————— *PAROLA CHIAVE*

in (*in* + *il* = **nel**, *in* + *lo* = **nello**, *in* + *l'* = **nell'**, *in* + *la* = **nella**, *in* + *i* = **nei**, *in* + *gli* = **negli**, *in* + *le* = **nelle**) *prep* **1** (*stato in luogo*) in; **vivere ~ Italia/città** to live in Italy/town; **essere ~ casa/ufficio** to be at home/the office; **è nel cassetto/~ salotto** it's in the drawer/in the sitting room; **se fossi ~ te** if I were you

2 (*moto a luogo*) to; (: *dentro*) into; **andare ~ Germania/città** to go to Germany/town; **andare ~ ufficio** to go to the office; **entrare ~ macchina/casa** to get into the car/go into the house

3 (*tempo*) in; **nel 1989** in 1989; **~ giugno/ estate** in June/summer; **l'ha fatto ~ sei mesi** he did it in six months; **~ gioventù, io ...** when I was young, I ...

4 (*modo, maniera*) in; **~ silenzio** in silence; **parlare ~ tedesco** to speak (in) German; **~ abito da sera** in evening dress; **~ guerra** at war; **~ vacanza** on holiday; **Maria Bianchi ~ Rossi** Maria

Rossi née Bianchi

5 (*mezzo*) by; **viaggiare ~ autobus/treno** to travel by bus/train

6 (*materia*) made of; **~ marmo** made of marble, marble *cpd*; **una collana ~ oro** a gold necklace

7 (*misura*) in; **siamo ~ quattro** there are four of us; **~ tutto** in all

8 (*fine*): **dare ~ dono** to give as a gift; **spende tutto ~ alcool** he spends all his money on drink; **~ onore di** in honour of.

i'nabile *ag*: **~ a** incapable of; (*fisicamente, MIL*) unfit for.

inabilità *sf*: **~ (a)** unfitness (for).

inabis'sare *vt* (*nave*) to sink; **~rsi** *vr* to go down.

inabi'tabile *ag* uninhabitable.

inabi'tato, a *ag* uninhabited.

inacces'sibile [inattʃes'sibile] *ag* (*luogo*) inaccessible; (*persona*) unapproachable; (*mistero*) unfathomable.

inaccet'tabile [inattʃet'tabile] *ag* unacceptable.

inacer'bire [inatʃer'bire] *vt* to exacerbate; **~rsi** *vr* (*persona*) to become embittered.

inaci'dire [inatʃi'dire] *vt* (*persona, carattere*) to embitter; **~rsi** *vr* (*latte*) to go sour; (*fig*: *persona, carattere*) to become sour, become embittered.

ina'datto, a *ag*: **~ (a)** unsuitable *o* unfit (for).

inadegu'ato, a *ag* inadequate.

inadempi'ente *ag* defaulting ♦ *sm/f* defaulter.

inadempi'enza [inadem'pjɛntsa] *sf*: **~ a un contratto** non-fulfilment of a contract; **dovuto alle ~e dei funzionari** due to negligence on the part of the officials.

inadempi'mento *sm* non-fulfilment.

inaffer'rabile *ag* elusive; (*concetto, senso*) difficult to grasp.

'INAIL *sigla m* (= *Istituto Nazionale per l'Assicurazione contro gli Infortuni sul Lavoro*) state body providing sickness benefit in the event of accidents at work.

ina'lare *vt* to inhale.

inala'tore *sm* inhaler.

inalazi'one [inalat'tsjone] *sf* inhalation.

inalbe'rare *vt* (*NAUT*) to hoist, raise; **~rsi** *vr* (*fig*) to flare up, fly off the handle.

inalte'rabile *ag* unchangeable; (*colore*) fast, permanent; (*affetto*) constant.

inalte'rato, a *ag* unchanged.

inami'dare *vt* to starch.

inami'dato, a *ag* starched.

inammis'sibile *ag* inadmissible.

inani'mato, a *ag* inanimate; (*senza vita*:

corpo) lifeless.
inappa'gabile *ag* insatiable.
inappel'labile *ag* (*decisione*) final, irrevocable; (*DIR*) final, not open to appeal.
inappe'tenza [inappe'tɛntsa] *sf* (*MED*) lack of appetite.
inappun'tabile *ag* irreproachable, flawless.
inar'care *vt* (*schiena*) to arch; (*sopracciglia*) to raise; ~**rsi** *vr* to arch.
inaridi'mento *sm* (*anche fig*) drying up.
inari'dire *vt* to make arid, dry up ♦ *vi* (*anche*: ~**rsi**) to dry up, become arid.
inarres'tabile *ag* (*processo*) irreversible; (*emorragia*) that cannot be stemmed; (*corsa del tempo*) relentless.
inascol'tato, a *ag* unheeded, unheard.
inaspettata'mente *av* unexpectedly.
inaspet'tato, a *ag* unexpected.
inas'prire *vt* (*disciplina*) to tighten up, make harsher; (*carattere*) to embitter; (*rapporti*) to make worse; ~**rsi** *vr* to become harsher; to become bitter; to become worse.
inattac'cabile *ag* (*anche fig*) unassailable; (*alibi*) cast-iron.
inatten'dibile *ag* unreliable.
inat'teso, a *ag* unexpected.
inat'tivo, a *ag* inactive, idle; (*CHIM*) inactive.
inattu'abile *ag* impracticable.
inau'dito, a *ag* unheard of.
inaugu'rale *ag* inaugural.
inaugu'rare *vt* to inaugurate, open; (*monumento*) to unveil.
inaugurazi'one [inaugurat'tsjone] *sf* inauguration; unveiling.
inavve'duto, a *ag* careless, inadvertent.
inavver'tenza [inavver'tɛntsa] *sf* carelessness, inadvertence.
inavvertita'mente *av* inadvertently, unintentionally.
inavvici'nabile [inavvitʃi'nabile] *ag* unapproachable.
'Inca *ag inv*, *sm/f inv* Inca.
incagli'are [inkaʎ'ʎare] *vi* (*NAUT: anche:* ~**rsi**) to run aground.
incalco'labile *ag* incalculable.
incal'lito, a *ag* calloused; (*fig*) hardened, inveterate; (: *insensibile*) hard.
incal'zante [inkal'tsante] *ag* urgent, insistent; (*crisi*) imminent.
incal'zare [inkal'tsare] *vt* to follow *o* pursue closely; (*fig*) to press ♦ *vi* (*urgere*) to be pressing; (*essere imminente*) to be imminent.
iname'rare *vt* (*DIR*) to expropriate.

incammi'nare *vt* (*fig: avviare*) to start up; ~**rsi** *vr* to set off.
incana'lare *vt* (*anche fig*) to channel; ~**rsi** *vr* (*folla*): ~**rsi verso** to converge on.
incancre'nire *vi*, **incancre'nirsi** *vi* to become gangrenous.
incande'scente [inkandeʃ'ʃɛnte] *ag* incandescent, white-hot.
incan'tare *vt* to enchant, bewitch; ~**rsi** *vr* (*rimanere intontito*) to be spellbound; to be in a daze; (*meccanismo: bloccarsi*) to jam.
incanta'tore, 'trice *ag* enchanting, bewitching ♦ *sm/f* enchanter/enchantress.
incan'tesimo *sm* spell, charm.
incan'tevole *ag* charming, enchanting.
in'canto *sm* spell, charm, enchantment; (*asta*) auction; **come per** ~ as if by magic; **ti sta d'**~**!** (*vestito etc*) it really suits you!; **mettere all'**~ to put up for auction.
incanu'tire *vi* to go white.
inca'pace [inka'patʃe] *ag* incapable.
incapacità [inkapatʃi'ta] *sf* inability; (*DIR*) incapacity; ~ **d'intendere e di volere** diminished responsibility.
incapo'nirsi *vr* to be stubborn, be determined.
incap'pare *vi*: ~ **in qc/qn** (*anche fig*) to run into sth/sb.
incappucci'are [inkapput'tʃare] *vt* to put a hood on; ~**rsi** *vr* (*persona*) to put on a hood.
incapricci'arsi [inkaprit'tʃarsi] *vr*: ~ **di** to take a fancy to *o* for.
incapsu'lare *vt* (*dente*) to crown.
incarce'rare [inkartʃe'rare] *vt* to imprison.
incari'care *vt*: ~ **qn di fare** to give sb the responsibility of doing; ~**rsi** *vr*: ~**rsi di** to take care *o* charge of.
incari'cato, a *ag*: ~ (**di**) in charge (of), responsible (for) ♦ *sm/f* delegate, representative; **docente** ~ (*di università*) lecturer without tenure; ~ **d'affari** (*POL*) chargé d'affaires.
in'carico, chi *sm* task, job; (*INS*) temporary post.
incar'nare *vt* to embody; ~**rsi** *vr* to be embodied; (*REL*) to become incarnate.
incarnazi'one [inkarnat'tsjone] *sf* incarnation; (*fig*) embodiment.
incarta'mento *sm* dossier, file.
incartapeco'rito, a *ag* (*pelle*) wizened, shrivelled (*BRIT*), shriveled (*US*).
incar'tare *vt* to wrap (in paper).
incasel'lare *vt* (*posta*) to sort; (*fig: nozioni*) to pigeonhole.
incas'sare *vt* (*merce*) to pack (in cases); (*gemma: incastonare*) to set; (*ECON: riscuotere*) to collect; (*PUGILATO: colpi*) to

take, stand up to.
in'casso *sm* cashing, encashment; (*introito*) takings *pl*.
incasto'nare *vt* to set.
incastona'tura *sf* setting.
incas'trare *vt* to fit in, insert; (*fig*: *intrappolare*) to catch; ~**rsi** *vr* (*combaciare*) to fit together; (*restare bloccato*) to become stuck.
in'castro *sm* slot, groove; (*punto di unione*) joint; **gioco a** ~ interlocking puzzle.
incate'nare *vt* to chain up.
incatra'mare *vt* to tar.
incatti'vire *vt* to make wicked; ~**rsi** *vr* to turn nasty.
in'cauto, a *ag* imprudent, rash.
inca'vare *vt* to hollow out.
inca'vato, a *ag* hollow; (*occhi*) sunken.
in'cavo *sm* hollow; (*solco*) groove.
incavo'larsi *vr* (*fam*) to lose one's temper, get annoyed.
incaz'zarsi [inkat'tsarsi] *vr* (*fam!*) to get steamed up.
in'cedere [in'tʃɛdere] *vi* (*poetico*) to advance solemnly ♦ *sm* solemn gait.
incendi'are [intʃen'djare] *vt* to set fire to; ~**rsi** *vr* to catch fire, burst into flames.
incendi'ario, a [intʃen'djarjo] *ag* incendiary ♦ *sm/f* arsonist.
in'cendio [in'tʃɛndjo] *sm* fire.
incene'rire [intʃene'rire] *vt* to burn to ashes, incinerate; (*cadavere*) to cremate; ~**rsi** *vr* to be burnt to ashes.
inceneri'tore [intʃeneri'tore] *sm* incinerator.
in'censo [in'tʃɛnso] *sm* incense.
incensu'rato, a [intʃensu'rato] *ag* (*DIR*): **essere** ~ to have a clean record.
incenti'vare [intʃenti'vare] *vt* (*produzione, vendite*) to boost; (*persona*) to motivate.
incen'tivo [intʃen'tivo] *sm* incentive.
incen'trarsi [intʃen'trarsi] *vr*: ~ **su** (*fig*) to centre (*BRIT*) *o* center (*US*) on.
incep'pare [intʃep'pare] *vt* to obstruct, hamper; ~**rsi** *vr* to jam.
ince'rata [intʃe'rata] *sf* (*tela*) tarpaulin; (*impermeabile*) oilskins *pl*.
incer'tezza [intʃer'tettsa] *sf* uncertainty.
in'certo, a [in'tʃɛrto] *ag* uncertain; (*irresoluto*) undecided, hesitating ♦ *sm* uncertainty; **gli** ~**i del mestiere** the risks of the job.
incespi'care [intʃespi'kare] *vi*: ~ **(in qc)** to trip (over sth).
inces'sante [intʃes'sante] *ag* incessant.
in'cesto [in'tʃɛsto] *sm* incest.
incestu'oso, a [intʃestu'oso] *ag* incestuous.
in'cetta [in'tʃetta] *sf* buying up; **fare** ~ **di qc**

to buy up sth.
inchi'esta [in'kjɛsta] *sf* investigation, inquiry.
inchi'nare [inki'nare] *vt* to bow; ~**rsi** *vr* to bend down; (*per riverenza*) to bow; (*: donna*) to curtsy.
in'chino [in'kino] *sm* bow; curtsy.
inchio'dare [inkjo'dare] *vt* to nail (down); ~ **la macchina** (*AUT*) to jam on the brakes.
inchi'ostro [in'kjɔstro] *sm* ink; ~ **simpatico** invisible ink.
inciam'pare [intʃam'pare] *vi* to trip, stumble.
inci'ampo [in'tʃampo] *sm* obstacle; **essere d'**~ **a qn** (*fig*) to be in sb's way.
inciden'tale [intʃiden'tale] *ag* incidental.
incidental'mente [intʃidental'mente] *av* (*per caso*) by chance; (*per inciso*) incidentally, by the way.
inci'dente [intʃi'dente] *sm* accident; (*episodio*) incident; **e con questo l'**~ **è chiuso** and that is the end of the matter; ~ **d'auto** car accident; ~ **diplomatico** diplomatic incident.
inci'denza [intʃi'dentsa] *sf* incidence; **avere una forte** ~ **su qc** to affect sth greatly.
in'cidere [in'tʃidere] *vi*: ~ **su** to bear upon, affect ♦ *vt* (*tagliare incavando*) to cut into; (*ARTE*) to engrave; to etch; (*canzone*) to record.
in'cinta [in'tʃinta] *ag f* pregnant.
incipi'ente [intʃi'pjɛnte] *ag* incipient.
incipri'are [intʃi'prjare] *vt* to powder.
in'circa [in'tʃirka] *av*: **all'**~ more or less, very nearly.
in'cisi *etc* [in'tʃizi] *vb vedi* **incidere**.
incisi'one [intʃi'zjone] *sf* cut; (*disegno*) engraving; etching; (*registrazione*) recording; (*MED*) incision.
inci'sivo, a [intʃi'zivo] *ag* incisive; (*ANAT*): **(dente)** ~ incisor.
in'ciso, a [in'tʃizo] *pp di* **incidere** ♦ *sm*: **per** ~ incidentally, by the way.
inci'sore [intʃi'zore] *sm* (*ARTE*) engraver.
incita'mento [intʃita'mento] *sm* incitement.
inci'tare [intʃi'tare] *vt* to incite.
inci'vile [intʃi'vile] *ag* uncivilized; (*villano*) impolite.
incivi'lire [intʃivi'lire] *vt* to civilize.
inciviltà [intʃivil'ta] *sf* (*di popolazione*) barbarism; (*fig*: *di trattamento*) barbarity; (*: maleducazione*) incivility, rudeness.
incl. *abbr* (= *incluso*) encl.
incle'mente *ag* (*giudice, sentenza*) severe, harsh; (*fig*: *clima*) harsh; (*: tempo*) inclement.
incle'menza [inkle'mentsa] *sf* severity; harshness; inclemency.

incli'nabile *ag* (*schienale*) reclinable.

incli'nare *vt* to tilt ♦ *vi* (*fig*): ~ **a qc/a fare** to incline towards sth/doing; to tend towards sth/to do; ~**rsi** *vr* (*barca*) to list; (*aereo*) to bank.

incli'nato, a *ag* sloping.

inclinazi'one [inklinat'tsjone] *sf* slope; (*fig*) inclination, tendency.

in'cline *ag*: ~ **a** inclined to.

in'cludere *vt* to include; (*accludere*) to enclose.

inclusi'one *sf* inclusion.

inclu'sivo, a *ag*: ~ **di** inclusive of.

in'cluso, a *pp di* **includere** ♦ *ag* included; enclosed.

incoe'rente *ag* incoherent; (*contraddittorio*) inconsistent.

incoe'renza [inkoe'rɛntsa] *sf* incoherence; inconsistency.

in'cognito, a [in'kɔɲɲito] *ag* unknown ♦ *sm*: **in** ~ incognito ♦ *sf* (*MAT, fig*) unknown quantity.

incol'lare *vt* to glue, gum; (*unire con colla*) to stick together; ~ **gli occhi addosso a qn** (*fig*) to fix one's eyes on sb.

incolla'tura *sf* (*IPPICA*): **vincere/perdere di un'**~ to win/lose by a head.

incolon'nare *vt* to draw up in columns.

inco'lore *ag* colourless (*BRIT*), colorless (*US*).

incol'pare *vt*: ~ **qn di** to charge sb with.

in'colto, a *ag* (*terreno*) uncultivated; (*trascurato: capelli*) neglected; (*persona*) uneducated.

in'colume *ag* safe and sound, unhurt.

incolumità *sf* safety.

incom'bente *ag* (*pericolo*) imminent, impending.

incom'benza [inkom'bɛntsa] *sf* duty, task.

in'combere *vi* (*sovrastare minacciando*): ~ **su** to threaten, hang over.

incominci'are [inkomin'tʃare] *vi, vt* to begin, start.

incomo'dare *vt* to trouble, inconvenience; ~**rsi** *vr* to put o.s. out.

in'comodo, a *ag* uncomfortable; (*inopportuno*) inconvenient ♦ *sm* inconvenience, bother.

incompa'rabile *ag* incomparable.

incompa'tibile *ag* incompatible.

incompatibilità *sf* incompatibility; ~ **di carattere** (mutual) incompatibility.

incompe'tente *ag* incompetent.

incompe'tenza [inkompe'tɛntsa] *sf* incompetence.

incompi'uto, a *ag* unfinished, incomplete.

incom'pleto, a *ag* incomplete.

incompren'sibile *ag* incomprehensible.

incomprensi'one *sf* incomprehension.

incom'preso, a *ag* not understood; misunderstood.

inconce'pibile [inkontʃe'pibile] *ag* inconceivable.

inconcili'abile [inkontʃi'ljabile] *ag* irreconcilable.

inconclu'dente *ag* inconclusive; (*persona*) ineffectual.

incondizio'nato, a [inkondittsjo'nato] *ag* unconditional.

inconfes'sabile *ag* (*pensiero, peccato*) unmentionable.

inconfon'dibile *ag* unmistakable.

inconfu'tabile *ag* irrefutable.

incongru'ente *ag* inconsistent.

incongru'enza [inkongru'ɛntsa] *sf* inconsistency.

in'congruo, a *ag* incongruous.

inconsa'pevole *ag*: ~ **di** unaware of, ignorant of.

inconsapevo'lezza [inkonsapevo'lettsa] *sf* ignorance, lack of awareness.

in'conscio, a, sci, sce [in'kɔnʃo] *ag* unconscious ♦ *sm* (*PSIC*): **l'**~ the unconscious.

inconsis'tente *ag* (*patrimonio*) insubstantial; (*dubbio*) unfounded; (*ragionamento, prove*) tenuous, flimsy.

inconsis'tenza [inkonsis'tɛntsa] *sf* insubstantial nature; lack of foundation; flimsiness.

inconso'labile *ag* inconsolable.

inconsu'eto, a *ag* unusual.

incon'sulto, a *ag* rash.

inconte'nibile *ag* (*rabbia*) uncontrollable; (*entusiasmo*) irrepressible.

inconten'tabile *ag* (*desiderio, avidità*) insatiable; (*persona: capriccioso*) hard to please, very demanding.

incontes'tabile *ag* incontrovertible, indisputable.

incontes'tato, a *ag* undisputed.

inconti'nenza [inkonti'nɛntsa] *sf* incontinence.

incon'trare *vt* to meet; (*difficoltà*) to meet with; ~**rsi** *vr* to meet.

incon'trario *av*: **all'**~ (*sottosopra*) upside down; (*alla rovescia*) back to front; (*all'indietro*) backwards; (*nel senso contrario*) the other way round.

incontras'tabile *ag* incontrovertible, indisputable.

incontras'tato, a *ag* (*successo, vittoria, verità*) uncontested, undisputed.

in'contro *av*: ~ **a** (*verso*) towards ♦ *sm* meeting; (*SPORT*) match; meeting; (*fortuito*) encounter; **venire** ~ **a** (*richieste,* *esigenze)* to comply with; ~ **di calcio** football match (*BRIT*), soccer game (*US*).

incontrol'labile *ag* uncontrollable.

inconveni'ente *sm* drawback, snag.

incoraggia'mento [inkoraddʒa'mento] *sm* encouragement; **premio d'~** consolation prize.

incoraggi'are [inkorad'dʒare] *vt* to encourage.

incor'nare *vt* to gore.

incornici'are [inkorni'tʃare] *vt* to frame.

incoro'nare *vt* to crown.

incoronazi'one [inkoronat'tsjone] *sf* coronation.

incorpo'rare *vt* to incorporate; (*fig: annettere*) to annex.

incorreg'gibile [inkorred'dʒibile] *ag* incorrigible.

in'correre *vi:* ~ **in** to meet with, run into.

incorrut'tibile *ag* incorruptible.

in'corso, a *pp di* **incorrere**.

incosci'ente [inkoʃ'ʃɛnte] *ag* (*inconscio*) unconscious; (*irresponsabile*) reckless, thoughtless.

incosci'enza [inkoʃ'ʃɛntsa] *sf* unconsciousness; recklessness, thoughtlessness.

incos'tante *ag* (*studente, impiegato*) inconsistent; (*carattere*) fickle, inconstant; (*rendimento*) sporadic.

incos'tanza [inkos'tantsa] *sf* inconstancy, fickleness.

incostituzio'nale [inkostituttsjo'nale] *ag* unconstitutional.

incre'dibile *ag* incredible, unbelievable.

incredulità *sf* incredulity.

in'credulo, a *ag* incredulous, disbelieving.

incremen'tare *vt* to increase; (*dar sviluppo a*) to promote.

incre'mento *sm* (*sviluppo*) development; (*aumento numerico*) increase, growth.

incresci'oso, a [inkreʃ'ʃoso] *ag* (*spiacevole*) unpleasant; regrettable.

incres'pare *vt* (*capelli*) to curl; (*acque*) to ripple; ~**rsi** *vr* (*vedi vt*) to curl; to ripple.

incrimi'nare *vt* (*DIR*) to charge.

incriminazi'one [inkriminat'tsjone] *sf* (*atto d'accusa*) indictment, charge.

incri'nare *vt* to crack; (*fig: rapporti, amicizia*) to cause to deteriorate; ~**rsi** *vr* to crack; to deteriorate.

incrina'tura *sf* crack; (*fig*) rift.

incroci'are [inkro'tʃare] *vt* to cross; (*incontrare*) to meet ♦ *vi* (*NAUT, AER*) to cruise; ~**rsi** *vr* (*strade*) to cross, intersect; (*persone, veicoli*) to pass each other; ~ **le braccia/le gambe** to fold one's arms/cross one's legs.

incrocia'tore [inkrotʃa'tore] *sm* cruiser.

in'crocio [in'krotʃo] *sm* (*anche FERR*) crossing; (*di strade*) crossroads.

incrol'labile *ag* (*fede*) unshakeable, firm.

incros'tare *vt* to encrust; ~**rsi** *vr:* ~**rsi di** to become encrusted with.

incrostazi'one [inkrostat'tsjone] *sf* encrustation; (*di calcare*) scale; (*nelle tubature*) fur (*BRIT*), scale.

incru'ento, a *ag* (*battaglia*) without bloodshed, bloodless.

incuba'trice [inkuba'tritʃe] *sf* incubator.

incubazi'one [inkubat'tsjone] *sf* incubation.

'incubo *sm* nightmare.

in'cudine *sf* anvil; **trovarsi** *o* **essere tra l'~ e il martello** (*fig*) to be between the devil and the deep blue sea.

incul'care *vt:* ~ **qc in** to inculcate sth into, instill sth into.

incune'are *vt* to wedge.

incu'pire *vt* (*rendere scuro*) to darken; (*fig: intristire*) to fill with gloom ♦ *vi* (*vedi vt*) to darken; to become gloomy.

incu'rabile *ag* incurable.

incu'rante *ag:* ~ (**di**) heedless (of), careless (of).

in'curia *sf* negligence.

incurio'sire *vt* to make curious; ~**rsi** *vr* to become curious.

incursi'one *sf* raid.

incur'vare *vt*, ~**rsi** *vr* to bend, curve.

in'cusso, a *pp di* **incutere**.

incusto'dito, a *ag* unguarded, unattended; **passaggio a livello** ~ unmanned level crossing.

in'cutere *vt* to arouse; ~ **timore/rispetto a qn** to strike fear into sb/command sb's respect.

'indaco *sm* indigo.

indaffa'rato, a *ag* busy.

inda'gare *vt* to investigate.

indaga'tore, 'trice *ag* (*sguardo, domanda*) searching; (*mente*) inquiring.

in'dagine [in'dadʒine] *sf* investigation, inquiry; (*ricerca*) research, study; ~ **di mercato** market survey.

indebita'mente *av* (*immeritatamente*) undeservedly; (*erroneamente*) wrongfully.

indebi'tare *vt:* ~ **qn** to get sb into debt; ~**rsi** *vr* to run *o* get into debt.

in'debito, a *ag* undeserved; wrongful.

indeboli'mento *sm* weakening; (*debolezza*) weakness.

indebo'lire *vt*, *vi* (*anche:* ~**rsi**) to weaken.

inde'cente [inde'tʃɛnte] *ag* indecent.

inde'cenza [inde'tʃɛntsa] *sf* indecency; **è un'~!** (*vergogna*) it's scandalous!, it's a disgrace!

indeci'frabile [indetʃi'frabile] *ag* indecipherable.

indecisi'one [indetʃi'zjone] *sf* indecisiveness; indecision.

inde'ciso, a [inde'tʃizo] *ag* indecisive; (*irresoluto*) undecided.

indeco'roso, a *ag* (*comportamento*) indecorous, unseemly.

inde'fesso, a *ag* untiring, indefatigable.

indefi'nibile *ag* indefinable.

indefi'nito, a *ag* (*anche LING*) indefinite; (*impreciso, non determinato*) undefined.

indefor'mabile *ag* crushproof.

in'degno, a [in'deɲɲo] *ag* (*atto*) shameful; (*persona*) unworthy.

inde'lebile *ag* indelible.

indelica'tezza [indelika'tettsa] *sf* tactlessness.

indeli'cato, a *ag* (*domanda*) indiscreet, tactless.

indemoni'ato, a *ag* possessed (by the devil).

in'denne *ag* unhurt, uninjured.

indennità *sf inv* (*rimborso: di spese*) allowance; (: *di perdita*) compensation, indemnity; ~ **di contingenza** cost-of-living allowance; ~ **di fine rapporto** severance payment (*on retirement, redundancy or when taking up other employment*); ~ **di trasferta** travel expenses *pl*.

indenniz'zare [indennid'dzare] *vt* to compensate.

inden'nizzo [inden'niddzo] *sm* (*somma*) compensation, indemnity.

indero'gabile *ag* binding.

indescri'vibile *ag* indescribable.

indeside'rabile *ag* undesirable.

indeside'rato, a *ag* unwanted.

indetermina'tezza [indetermina'tettsa] *sf* vagueness.

indetermina'tivo, a *ag* (*LING*) indefinite.

indetermi'nato, a *ag* indefinite, indeterminate.

in'detto, a *pp di* indire.

'India *sf*: l'~ India; le ~e occidentali the West Indies.

indi'ano, a *ag* Indian ♦ *sm/f* (*d'India*) Indian; (*d'America*) Red Indian; l'Oceano I~ the Indian Ocean.

indiavo'lato, a *ag* possessed (by the devil); (*vivace, violento*) wild.

indi'care *vt* (*mostrare*) to show, indicate; (: *col dito*) to point to, point out; (*consigliare*) to suggest, recommend.

indica'tivo, a *ag* indicative ♦ *sm* (*LING*) indicative (mood).

indi'cato, a *ag* (*consigliato*) advisable; (*adatto*): ~ **per** suitable for, appropriate for.

indica'tore, 'trice *ag* indicating ♦ *sm* (*elenco*) guide; directory; (*TECN*) gauge; indicator; **cartello** ~ sign; ~ **della benzina** petrol (*BRIT*) *o* gas (*US*) gauge, fuel gauge; ~ **di velocità** (*AUT*) speedometer; (*AER*) airspeed indicator.

indicazi'one [indikat'tsjone] *sf* indication; (*informazione*) piece of information; ~i **per l'uso** instructions for use.

'indice ['inditʃe] *sm* (*ANAT: dito*) index finger, forefinger; (*lancetta*) needle, pointer; (*fig: indizio*) sign; (*TECN, MAT, nei libri*) index; ~ **azionario** share index; ~ **di gradimento** (*RADIO, TV*) popularity rating; ~ **dei prezzi al consumo** ≈ retail price index.

indicherò *etc* [indike'rɔ] *vb vedi* indicare.

indi'cibile [indi'tʃibile] *ag* inexpressible.

indiciz'zare [inditʃid'dzare] *vt*: ~ **al costo della vita** to index-link (*BRIT*), index (*US*).

indiciz'zato, a [inditʃid'dzato] *ag* (*polizza, salario etc*) index-linked (*BRIT*), indexed (*US*).

indicizzazi'one [inditʃiddzat'tsjone] *sf* indexing.

indietreggi'are [indjetred'dʒare] *vi* to draw back, retreat.

indi'etro *av* back; (*guardare*) behind, back; (*andare, cadere: anche*: all'~) backwards; **rimanere** ~ to be left behind; **essere** ~ (*col lavoro*) to be behind; (*orologio*) to be slow; **rimandare qc** ~ to send sth back; **non vado né avanti né** ~ (*fig*) I'm not getting anywhere, I'm getting nowhere.

indi'feso, a *ag* (*città, confine*) undefended; (*persona*) defenceless (*BRIT*), defenseless (*US*), helpless.

indiffe'rente *ag* indifferent ♦ *sm*: **fare l'**~ to pretend to be indifferent, be *o* act casual; (*fingere di non vedere o sentire*) to pretend not to notice.

indiffe'renza [indiffe'rɛntsa] *sf* indifference.

in'digeno, a [in'didʒeno] *ag* indigenous, native ♦ *sm/f* native.

indi'gente [indi'dʒɛnte] *ag* poverty-stricken, destitute.

indi'genza [indi'dʒɛntsa] *sf* extreme poverty.

indigesti'one [indidʒes'tjone] *sf* indigestion.

indi'gesto, a [indi'dʒɛsto] *ag* indigestible.

indi'gnare [indiɲ'ɲare] *vt* to fill with indignation; ~**rsi** *vr* to be (*o* get) indignant.

indignazi'one [indiɲɲat'tsjone] *sf* indignation.
indimenti'cabile *ag* unforgettable.
'**indio, a** *ag, sm/f* (South American) Indian.
indipen'dente *ag* independent.
indipendente'mente *av* independently; ~ **dal fatto che gli piaccia o meno, verrà!** he's coming, whether he likes it or not!
indipen'denza [indipen'dɛntsa] *sf* independence.
in'dire *vt* (*concorso*) to announce; (*elezioni*) to call.
indi'retto, a *ag* indirect.
indiriz'zare [indirit'tsare] *vt* (*dirigere*) to direct; (*mandare*) to send; (*lettera*) to address; ~ **la parola a qn** to address sb.
indiriz'zario [indirit'tsarjo] *sm* mailing list.
indi'rizzo [indi'rittso] *sm* address; (*direzione*) direction; (*avvio*) trend, course; ~ **assoluto** (*INFORM*) absolute address.
indisci'plina [indiʃʃi'plina] *sf* indiscipline
indi'scipli'nato, a [indiʃʃipli'nato] *ag* undisciplined, unruly.
indis'creto, a *ag* indiscreet.
indiscrezi'one [indiskret'tsjone] *sf* indiscretion.
indiscrimi'nato, a *ag* indiscriminate.
indis'cusso, a *ag* unquestioned.
indiscu'tibile *ag* indisputable, unquestionable.
indispen'sabile *ag* indispensable, essential.
indispet'tire *vt* to irritate, annoy ♦ *vi* (*anche*: ~**rsi**) to get irritated *o* annoyed.
indispo'nente *ag* irritating, annoying.
indis'porre *vt* to antagonize.
indisposizi'one [indispozit'tsjone] *sf* (slight) indisposition.
indis'posto, a *pp di* **indisporre** ♦ *ag* indisposed, unwell.
indisso'lubile *ag* indissoluble.
indissolubil'mente *av* indissolubly.
indistinta'mente *av* (*senza distinzioni*) indiscriminately, without exception; (*in modo indefinito*: *vedere, sentire*) vaguely, faintly.
indis'tinto, a *ag* indistinct.
indistrut'tibile *ag* indestructible.
in'divia *sf* endive.
individu'ale *ag* individual.
individua'lismo *sm* individualism.
individua'lista, i, e *sm/f* individualist.
individualità *sf* individuality.
individual'mente *av* individually.
individu'are *vt* (*dar forma distinta a*) to characterize; (*determinare*) to locate; (*riconoscere*) to single out.

indi'viduo *sm* individual.
indivi'sibile *ag* indivisible; **quei due sono** ~**i** (*fig*) those two are inseparable.
indizi'are [indit'tsjare] *vt*: ~ **qn di qc** to cast suspicion on sb for sth.
indizi'ato, a [indit'tsjato] *ag* suspected ♦ *sm/f* suspect.
in'dizio [in'dittsjo] *sm* (*segno*) sign, indication; (*POLIZIA*) clue; (*DIR*) piece of evidence.
Indo'cina [indo'tʃina] *sf*: **l'**~ Indochina.
'**indole** *sf* nature, character.
indo'lente *ag* indolent.
indo'lenza [indo'lɛntsa] *sf* indolence.
indolen'zire [indolen'tsire] *vt* (*gambe, braccia etc*) to make stiff, cause to ache; (: *intorpidire*) to numb; ~**rsi** *vr* to become stiff; to go numb.
indolen'zito, a [indolen'tsito] *ag* stiff, aching; (*intorpidito*) numb.
indo'lore *ag* (*anche fig*) painless.
indo'mani *sm*: **l'**~ the next day, the following day.
Indo'nesia *sf*: **l'**~ Indonesia.
indonesi'ano, a *ag, sm/f, sm* Indonesian.
indo'rare *vt* (*rivestire in oro*) to gild; (*CUC*) to dip in egg yolk; ~ **la pillola** (*fig*) to sugar the pill.
indos'sare *vt* (*mettere indosso*) to put on; (*avere indosso*) to have on.
indossa'tore, 'trice *sm/f* model
in'dotto, a *pp di* **indurre**.
indottri'nare *vt* to indoctrinate.
indovi'nare *vt* (*scoprire*) to guess; (*immaginare*) to imagine, guess; (*il futuro*) to foretell; **tirare a** ~ to make a shot in the dark.
indovi'nato, a *ag* successful; (*scelta*) inspired.
indovi'nello *sm* riddle.
indo'vino, a *sm/f* fortuneteller.
indù *ag, sm/f* Hindu.
indubbia'mente *av* undoubtedly.
in'dubbio, a *ag* certain, undoubted.
in'duco *etc vb vedi* **indurre**.
indugi'are [indu'dʒare] *vi* to take one's time, delay.
in'dugio [in'dudʒo] *sm* (*ritardo*) delay; **senza** ~ without delay.
indul'gente [indul'dʒɛnte] *ag* indulgent; (*giudice*) lenient.
indul'genza [indul'dʒɛntsa] *sf* indulgence; leniency.
in'dulgere [in'duldʒere] *vi*: ~ **a** (*accondiscendere*) to comply with; (*abbandonarsi*) to indulge in.
in'dulto, a *pp di* **indulgere** ♦ *sm* (*DIR*) pardon.

indu'mento *sm* article of clothing, garment; ~**i** *smpl* (*vestiti*) clothes; ~**i intimi** underwear *sg*.
induri'mento *sm* hardening.
indu'rire *vt* to harden ♦ *vi* (*anche:* ~**rsi**) to harden, become hard.
in'durre *vt*: ~ **qn a fare qc** to induce *o* persuade sb to do sth; ~ **qn in errore** to mislead sb; ~ **in tentazione** to lead into temptation.
in'dussi *etc vb vedi* **indurre**.
in'dustria *sf* industry; **la piccola/grande** ~ small/big business.
industri'ale *ag* industrial ♦ *sm* industrialist.
industrializ'zare [industrjalid'dzare] *vt* to industrialize.
industrializzazi'one [industrjaliddzat'tsjone] *sf* industrialization.
industri'arsi *vr* to do one's best, try hard.
industri'oso, a *ag* industrious, hardworking.
induzi'one [indut'tsjone] *sf* induction.
inebe'tito, a *ag* dazed, stunned.
inebri'are *vt* (*anche fig*) to intoxicate; ~**rsi** *vr* to become intoxicated.
inecce'pibile [inettʃe'pibile] *ag* unexceptionable.
i'nedia *sf* starvation.
i'nedito, a *ag* unpublished.
inef'fabile *ag* ineffable.
ineffi'cace [ineffi'katʃe] *ag* ineffective.
ineffi'cacia [ineffi'katʃa] *sf* inefficacy, ineffectiveness.
ineffici'ente [ineffi'tʃɛnte] *ag* inefficient.
ineffici'enza [ineffi'tʃɛntsa] *sf* inefficiency.
ineguagli'abile [inegwaʎ'ʎabile] *ag* incomparable, matchless.
ineguagli'anza [inegwaʎ'ʎantsa] *sf* (*sociale*) inequality; (*di superficie, livello*) unevenness.
inegu'ale *ag* unequal; (*irregolare*) uneven.
inelut'tabile *ag* inescapable.
ineluttabilità *sf* inescapability.
inenar'rabile *ag* unutterable.
inequivo'cabile *ag* unequivocal.
ine'rente *ag*: ~ **a** concerning, regarding.
i'nerme *ag* unarmed, defenceless (*BRIT*), defenseless (*US*).
inerpi'carsi *vr*: ~ (**su**) to clamber (up).
i'nerte *ag* inert; (*inattivo*) indolent, sluggish.
i'nerzia [i'nɛrtsja] *sf* inertia; indolence, sluggishness.
inesat'tezza [inezat'tettsa] *sf* inaccuracy.
ine'satto, a *ag* (*impreciso*) inaccurate, inexact; (*erroneo*) incorrect; (*AMM: non*

riscosso) uncollected.
inesau'ribile *ag* inexhaustible.
inesis'tente *ag* non-existent.
ineso'rabile *ag* inexorable, relentless.
inesorabil'mente *av* inexorably.
inesperi'enza [inespe'rjɛntsa] *sf* inexperience.
ines'perto, a *ag* inexperienced.
inespli'cabile *ag* inexplicable.
inesplo'rato, a *ag* unexplored.
ines'ploso, a *ag* unexploded.
inespres'sivo, a *ag* (*viso*) expressionless, inexpressive.
ines'presso, a *ag* unexpressed.
inespri'mibile *ag* inexpressible.
inespu'gnabile [inespuɲ'ɲabile] *ag* (*fortezza, torre etc*) impregnable.
ineste'tismo *sm* beauty problem.
inesti'mabile *ag* inestimable; (*valore*) incalculable.
inestir'pabile *ag* ineradicable.
inestri'cabile *ag* (*anche fig*) impenetrable.
inetti'tudine *sf* ineptitude.
i'netto, a *ag* (*incapace*) inept; (*che non ha attitudine*): ~ (**a**) unsuited (to).
ine'vaso, a *ag* (*ordine, corrispondenza*) outstanding.
inevi'tabile *ag* inevitable.
inevitabil'mente *av* inevitably.
i'nezia [i'nɛttsja] *sf* trifle, thing of no importance.
infagot'tare *vt* to bundle up, wrap up; ~**rsi** *vr* to wrap up.
infal'libile *ag* infallible.
infallibilità *sf* infallibility.
infa'mante *ag* (*accusa*) defamatory, slanderous.
infa'mare *vt* to defame.
in'fame *ag* infamous; (*fig: cosa, compito*) awful, dreadful.
in'famia *sf* infamy.
infan'gare *vt* (*sporcare*) to cover with mud; (*nome, reputazione*) to sully; ~**rsi** *vr* to get covered in mud; to be sullied.
infan'tile *ag* child *cpd*; childlike; (*adulto, azione*) childish; **letteratura** ~ children's books *pl*.
in'fanzia [in'fantsja] *sf* childhood; (*bambini*) children *pl*; **prima** ~ babyhood, infancy.
infari'nare *vt* to cover with (*o* sprinkle with *o* dip in) flour; ~ **di zucchero** to sprinkle with sugar.
infarina'tura *sf* (*fig*) smattering.
in'farto *sm* (*MED*): ~ (**cardiaco**) coronary.
infasti'dire *vt* to annoy, irritate; ~**rsi** *vr* to get annoyed *o* irritated.
infati'cabile *ag* tireless, untiring.
in'fatti *cong* as a matter of fact, in fact,

actually.
infatu'arsi *vr*: ~ **di** *o* **per** to become
infatuated with, fall for.
infatuazi'one [infatuat'tsjone] *sf*
infatuation.
in'fausto, a *ag* unpropitious, unfavourable
(*BRIT*), unfavorable (*US*).
infecondità *sf* infertility.
infe'condo, a *ag* infertile.
infe'dele *ag* unfaithful.
infedeltà *sf* infidelity.
infe'lice [infe'litʃe] *ag* unhappy; (*sfortunato*)
unlucky, unfortunate; (*inopportuno*)
inopportune, ill-timed; (*mal riuscito:
lavoro*) bad, poor.
infelicità [infelitʃi'ta] *sf* unhappiness.
infel'trire *vi*, ~**rsi** *vr* (*lana*) to become
matted.
infe'renza [infe'rɛntsa] *sf* inference.
inferi'ore *ag* lower; (*per intelligenza, qualità*)
inferior ♦ *sm/f* inferior; ~ **a** (*numero,
quantità*) less *o* smaller than; (*meno
buono*) inferior to; ~ **alla media** below
average.
inferiorità *sf* inferiority.
infe'rire *vt* (*dedurre*) to infer, deduce.
inferme'ria *sf* infirmary; (*di scuola, nave*)
sick bay.
infermi'ere, a *sm/f* nurse.
infermità *sf inv* illness; infirmity; ~ **di
mente** mental illness.
in'fermo, a *ag* (*ammalato*) ill; (*debole*)
infirm; ~ **di mente** mentally ill.
infer'nale *ag* infernal; (*proposito,
complotto*) diabolical; **un tempo** ~ (*fam*)
hellish weather.
in'ferno *sm* hell; **soffrire le pene dell'**~ (*fig*)
to go through hell.
infero'cire [infero'tʃire] *vt* to make fierce
♦ *vi*, ~**rsi** *vr* to become fierce.
inferri'ata *sf* grating.
infervo'rare *vt* to arouse enthusiasm in;
~**rsi** *vr* to get excited, get carried away.
infes'tare *vt* to infest.
infet'tare *vt* to infect; ~**rsi** *vr* to become
infected.
infet'tivo, a *ag* infectious.
in'fetto, a *ag* infected; (*acque*) polluted,
contaminated.
infezi'one [infet'tsjone] *sf* infection.
infiac'chire [infjak'kire] *vt* to weaken ♦ *vi*
(*anche*: ~**rsi**) to grow weak.
infiam'mabile *ag* inflammable.
infiam'mare *vt* to set alight; (*fig, MED*) to
inflame; ~**rsi** *vr* to catch fire; (*MED*) to
become inflamed; (*fig*): ~**rsi di** to be fired
with.
infiammazi'one [infjammat'tsjone] *sf*

(*MED*) inflammation.
infias'care *vt* to bottle.
infici'are [infi'tʃare] *vt* (*DIR*: *atto,
dichiarazione*) to challenge.
in'fido, a *ag* unreliable, treacherous.
infie'rire *vi*: ~ **su** (*fisicamente*) to attack
furiously; (*verbalmente*) to rage at;
(*epidemia*) to rage over.
in'figgere [in'fiddʒere] *vt*: ~ **qc in** to thrust
o drive sth into.
infi'lare *vt* (*ago*) to thread; (*mettere: chiave*)
to insert; (: *vestito*) to slip *o* put on;
(*strada*) to turn into, take; ~**rsi** *vr*: ~**rsi in**
to slip into; (*indossare*) to slip on; ~ **un
anello al dito** to slip a ring on one's
finger; ~ **l'uscio** to slip in; to slip out; ~**rsi
la giacca** to put on one's jacket.
infil'trarsi *vr* to penetrate, seep through;
(*MIL*) to infiltrate.
infil'trato, a *sm/f* infiltrator.
infiltrazi'one [infiltrat'tsjone] *sf* infiltration.
infil'zare [infil'tsare] *vt* (*infilare*) to string
together; (*trafiggere*) to pierce.
'infimo, a *ag* lowest; **un albergo di** ~ **ordine**
a third-rate hotel.
in'fine *av* finally; (*insomma*) in short.
infin'gardo, a *ag* lazy ♦ *sm/f* slacker.
infinità *sf* infinity; (*in quantità*): **un'**~ **di** an
infinite number of.
infinitesi'male *ag* infinitesimal.
infi'nito, a *ag* infinite; (*LING*) infinitive ♦ *sm*
infinity; (*LING*) infinitive; **all'**~ (*senza fine*)
endlessly; (*LING*) in the infinitive.
infinocchi'are [infinok'kjare] *vt* (*fam*) to
hoodwink.
infiore'scenza [infjoreʃ'ʃɛntsa] *sf*
inflorescence.
infir'mare *vt* (*DIR*) to invalidate.
infischi'arsi [infis'kjarsi] *vr*: ~ **di** not to care
about.
in'fisso, a *pp di* **infiggere** ♦ *sm* fixture; (*di
porta, finestra*) frame.
infit'tire *vt*, *vi* (*anche*: ~**rsi**) to thicken.
inflazio'nare [inflattsjo'nare] *vt* to inflate.
inflazi'one [inflat'tsjone] *sf* inflation.
inflazio'nistico, a, ci, che
[inflattsjo'nistiko] *ag* inflationary.
infles'sibile *ag* inflexible; (*ferreo*)
unyielding.
inflessi'one *sf* inflexion.
in'fliggere [in'fliddʒere] *vt* to inflict.
in'flissi *etc vb vedi* **infliggere**.
in'flitto, a *pp di* **infliggere**.
influ'ente *ag* influential.
influ'enza [influ'ɛntsa] *sf* influence; (*MED*)
influenza, flu.
influen'zare [influen'tsare] *vt* to influence,
have an influence on.

influ'ire *vi*: ~ **su** to influence.
in'flusso *sm* influence.
INFN *sigla m* = *Istituto Nazionale di Fisica Nucleare.*
info'cato, a *ag* = **infuocato.**
info'gnarsi [infoɲ'ɲarsi] *vr (fam)* to get into a mess; ~ **in un mare di debiti** to be up to one's *o* the eyes in debt.
infol'tire *vt, vi* to thicken.
infon'dato, a *ag* unfounded, groundless.
in'fondere *vt*: ~ **qc in qn** to instill sth in sb; ~ **fiducia in qn** to inspire sb with confidence.
infor'care *vt* to fork (up); *(bicicletta, cavallo)* to get on; *(occhiali)* to put on.
infor'male *ag* informal.
infor'mare *vt* to inform, tell; ~**rsi** *vr*: ~**rsi (di** *o* **su)** to inquire (about); **tenere informato qn** to keep sb informed.
infor'matico, a, ci, che *ag (settore)* computer *cpd* ♦ *sf* computer science.
informa'tivo, a *ag* informative; **a titolo** ~ for information only.
informatiz'zare [informatid'dzare] *vt* to computerize.
infor'mato, a *ag* informed; **tenersi** ~ **to keep** o.s. (well-)informed.
informa'tore *sm* informer.
informazi'one [informat'tsjone] *sf* piece of information; ~**i** *sfpl* information *sg*; **chiedere un'**~ to ask for (some) information; ~ **di garanzia** *(DIR)* = **avviso di garanzia.**
in'forme *ag* shapeless.
informico'larsi *vr*, **informico'lirsi** *vr*: **mi si è informicolata una gamba** I've got pins and needles in my leg.
infor'nare *vt* to put in the oven.
infor'nata *sf (anche fig)* batch.
infortu'narsi *vr* to injure o.s., have an accident.
infortu'nato, a *ag* injured, hurt ♦ *sm/f* injured person.
infor'tunio *sm* accident; ~ **sul lavoro** industrial accident, accident at work.
infortu'nistica *sf* study of (industrial) accidents.
infos'sarsi *vr (terreno)* to sink; *(guance)* to become hollow.
infos'sato, a *ag* hollow; *(occhi)* deep-set; (*: per malattia*) sunken.
infradici'are [infradi'tʃare] *vt (inzuppare)* to soak, drench; *(marcire)* to rot; ~**rsi** *vr* to get soaked, get drenched; to rot.
in'frangere [in'frandʒere] *vt* to smash; *(fig: legge, patti)* to break; ~**rsi** *vr* to smash, break.
infran'gibile [infran'dʒibile] *ag*

unbreakable.
in'franto, a *pp di* **infrangere** ♦ *ag* broken.
infra'rosso, a *ag, sm* infrared.
infrasettima'nale *ag* midweek *cpd.*
infrastrut'tura *sf* infrastructure.
infrazi'one [infrat'tsjone] *sf*: ~ **a breaking of, violation of.**
infredda'tura *sf* slight cold.
infreddo'lito, a *ag* cold, chilled.
infre'quente *ag* infrequent, rare.
infrol'lire *vi*, ~**rsi** *vr (selvaggina)* to become high.
infruttu'oso, a *ag* fruitless.
infuo'cato, a *ag (metallo)* red-hot; *(sabbia)* burning; *(fig: discorso)* heated, passionate.
infu'ori *av* out; **all'**~ outwards; **all'**~ **di** *(eccetto)* except, with the exception of.
infuri'are *vi* to rage; ~**rsi** *vr* to fly into a rage.
infusi'one *sf* infusion.
in'fuso, a *pp di* **infondere** ♦ *ag*: **scienza** ~**a** *(anche ironico)* innate knowledge ♦ *sm* infusion; ~ **di camomilla** camomile tea.
Ing. *abbr* = **ingegnere.**
ingabbi'are *vt* to (put in a) cage.
ingaggi'are [ingad'dʒare] *vt (assumere con compenso)* to take on, hire; *(SPORT)* to sign on; *(MIL)* to engage.
in'gaggio [in'gaddʒo] *sm* hiring; signing on.
ingagliar'dire [ingaʎʎar'dire] *vt* to strengthen, invigorate ♦ *vi (anche:* ~**rsi)** to grow stronger.
ingan'nare *vt* to deceive; *(coniuge)* to be unfaithful to; *(fisco)* to cheat; *(eludere)* to dodge, elude; *(fig: tempo)* to while away ♦ *vi (apparenza)* to be deceptive; ~**rsi** *vr* to be mistaken, be wrong.
inganna'tore, 'trice *ag* deceptive; *(persona)* deceitful.
ingan'nevole *ag* deceptive.
in'ganno *sm* deceit, deception; *(azione)* trick; *(menzogna, frode)* cheat, swindle; *(illusione)* illusion.
ingarbugli'are [ingarbuʎ'ʎare] *vt* to tangle; *(fig)* to confuse, muddle; ~**rsi** *vr* to become confused *o* muddled.
ingarbugli'ato, a [ingarbuʎ'ʎato] *ag* tangled; confused, muddled.
inge'gnarsi [indʒeɲ'ɲarsi] *vr* to do one's best, try hard; ~ **per vivere** to live by one's wits; **basta** ~ **un po'** you just need a bit of ingenuity.
inge'gnere [indʒeɲ'ɲere] *sm* engineer; ~ **civile/navale** civil/naval engineer.
ingegne'ria [indʒeɲɲe'ria] *sf* engineering.
in'gegno [in'dʒeɲɲo] *sm (intelligenza)* intelligence, brains *pl*; *(capacità creativa)*

ingenuity; (*disposizione*) talent.

ingegnosità [indʒeɲɲosi'ta] *sf* ingenuity.

inge'gnoso, a [indʒeɲ'ɲoso] *ag* ingenious, clever.

ingelo'sire [indʒelo'sire] *vt* to make jealous ♦ *vi* (*anche:* ~**rsi**) to become jealous.

in'gente [in'dʒɛnte] *ag* huge, enormous.

ingenti'lire [indʒenti'lire] *vt* to refine, civilize; ~**rsi** *vr* to become more refined, become more civilized.

ingenuità [indʒenui'ta] *sf* ingenuousness.

in'genuo, a [in'dʒɛnuo] *ag* ingenuous, naïve.

inge'renza [indʒe'rɛntsa] *sf* interference.

inge'rire [indʒe'rire] *vt* to ingest.

inges'sare [indʒes'sare] *vt* (*MED*) to put in plaster.

ingessa'tura [indʒessa'tura] *sf* plaster.

Inghil'terra [ingil'tɛrra] *sf:* l'~ England.

inghiot'tire [ingjot'tire] *vt* to swallow.

in'ghippo [in'gippo] *sm* trick.

ingial'lire [indʒal'lire] *vi* **ta** gʊ jɛllow.

ingigan'tire [indʒigan'tire] *vt* to enlarge, magnify ♦ *vi* to become gigantic *o* enormous.

inginocchi'arsi [indʒinok'kjarsi] *vr* to kneel (down).

inginocchia'toio [indʒinokkja'tojo] *sm* prie-dieu.

ingioiel'lare [indʒojel'lare] *vt* to bejewel, adorn with jewels.

ingiù [in'dʒu] *av* down, downwards.

ingi'ungere [in'dʒundʒere] *vt:* ~ **a qn di fare qc** to enjoin *o* order sb to do sth.

ingi'unto, a [in'dʒunto] *pp di* **ingiungere**.

ingiunzi'one [indʒun'tsjone] *sf* injunction, command; ~ **di pagamento** final demand.

ingi'uria [in'dʒurja] *sf* insult; (*fig: danno*) damage.

ingiuri'are [indʒu'rjare] *vt* to insult, abuse.

ingiuri'oso, a [indʒu'rjoso] *ag* insulting, abusive.

ingiusta'mente [indʒusta'mente] *av* unjustly.

ingiustifi'cabile [indʒustifi'kabile] *ag* unjustifiable.

ingiustifi'cato, a [indʒustifi'kato] *ag* unjustified.

ingius'tizia [indʒus'tittsja] *sf* injustice.

ingi'usto, a [in'dʒusto] *ag* unjust, unfair.

in'glese *ag* English ♦ *sm/f* Englishman/woman ♦ *sm* (*LING*) English; **gli l~i** the English; **andarsene** *o* **filare all'**~ to take French leave.

inglori'oso, a *ag* inglorious.

ingob'bire *vi*, ~**rsi** *vr* to become stooped.

ingoi'are *vt* to gulp (down); (*fig*) to swallow (up); **ha dovuto** ~ **il rospo** (*fig*) he had to

accept the situation.

ingol'fare *vt*, ~**rsi** *vr* (*motore*) to flood.

ingolo'sire *vt:* ~ **qn** to make sb's mouth water; (*fig*) to attract sb ♦ *vi* (*anche:* ~**rsi**): ~ (**di**) (*anche fig*) to become greedy (for).

ingom'brante *ag* cumbersome.

ingom'brare *vt* (*strada*) to block; (*stanza*) to clutter up.

in'gombro, a *ag:* ~ **di** (*strada*) blocked by; (*stanza*) cluttered up with ♦ *sm* obstacle; **essere d'**~ to be in the way; **per ragioni di** ~ for reasons of space.

ingor'digia [ingor'didʒa] *sf:* ~ (**di**) greed (for); avidity (for).

in'gordo, a *ag:* ~ **di** greedy for; (*fig*) greedy *o* avid for ♦ *sm/f* glutton.

ingor'gare *vt* to block; ~**rsi** *vr* to be blocked up, be choked up.

in'gorgo, ghi *sm* blockage, obstruction; (*anche:* ~ **stradale**) traffic jam.

ingoz'zare [ingot'tsare] *vt* (*animali*) to fatten; (*fig: persona*) to stuff; ~**rsi** *vr:* ~**rsi** (**di**) to stuff o.s. (with).

ingra'naggio [ingra'naddʒo] *sm* (*TECN*) gear; (*di orologio*) mechanism; **gli ~i della burocrazia** the bureaucratic machinery.

ingra'nare *vi* to mesh, engage ♦ *vt* to engage; ~ **la marcia** to get into gear.

ingrandi'mento *sm* enlargement; extension; magnification; growth; expansion.

ingran'dire *vt* (*anche FOT*) to enlarge; (*estendere*) to extend; (*OTTICA, fig*) to magnify ♦ *vi* (*anche:* ~**rsi**) to become larger *o* bigger; (*aumentare*) to grow, increase; (*espandersi*) to expand.

ingrandi'tore *sm* (*FOT*) enlarger.

ingras'saggio [ingras'saddʒo] *sm* greasing.

ingras'sare *vt* to make fat; (*animali*) to fatten; (*AGR: terreno*) to manure; (*lubrificare*) to grease ♦ *vi* (*anche:* ~**rsi**) to get fat, put on weight.

ingrati'tudine *sf* ingratitude.

in'grato, a *ag* ungrateful; (*lavoro*) thankless, unrewarding.

ingrazi'are [ingrat'tsjare] *vt:* ~**rsi qn** to ingratiate o.s. with sb.

ingredi'ente *sm* ingredient.

in'gresso *sm* (*porta*) entrance; (*atrio*) hall; (*l'entrare*) entrance, entry; (*facoltà di entrare*) admission; "~ **libero**" "admission free"; ~ **principale** main entrance; ~ **di servizio** tradesmen's entrance.

ingros'sare *vt* to increase; (*folla, livello*) to swell ♦ *vi* (*anche:* ~**rsi**) to increase; to swell.

in'grosso *av:* **all'**~ (*COMM*) wholesale; (*all'incirca*) roughly, about.

ingru'gnato, a [ingruɲ'ɲato] *ag* grumpy.
inguai'arsi *vr* to get into trouble.
inguai'nare *vt* to sheathe.
ingual'cibile [ingwal'tʃibile] *ag* crease-resistant.
ingua'ribile *ag* incurable.
'inguine *sm* (*ANAT*) groin.
ingurgi'tare [ingurdʒi'tare] *vt* to gulp down.
ini'bire *vt* to forbid, prohibit; (*PSIC*) to inhibit.
ini'bito, a *ag* inhibited ♦ *sm/f* inhibited person.
inibi'torio, a *ag* (*PSIC*) inhibitory, inhibitive; (*provvedimento, misure*) restrictive.
inibizi'one [inibit'tsjone] *sf* prohibition; inhibition.
iniet'tare *vt* to inject; ~**rsi** *vr*: ~**rsi di sangue** (*occhi*) to become bloodshot.
iniet'tore *sm* injector.
iniezi'one [injet'tsjone] *sf* injection.
inimi'care *vt* to alienate, make hostile; ~**rsi** *vr*: ~**rsi con qn** to fall out with sb; **si è inimicato gli amici di un tempo** he has alienated his old friends.
inimi'cizia [inimi'tʃittsja] *sf* animosity.
inimi'tabile *ag* inimitable.
inimmagi'nabile [inimmadʒi'nabile] *ag* unimaginable.
ininfiam'mabile *ag* non-flammable.
inintelli'gibile [inintelli'dʒibile] *ag* unintelligible.
ininterrotta'mente *av* non-stop, continuously.
ininter'rotto, a *ag* (*fila*) unbroken; (*rumore*) uninterrupted.
iniquità *sf inv* iniquity; (*atto*) wicked action.
i'niquo, a *ag* iniquitous.
inizi'ale [init'tsjale] *ag, sf* initial.
inizializ'zare [inittsjalid'dzare] *vt* (*INFORM*) to boot.
inizial'mente [inittsjal'mente] *av* initially, at first.
inizi'are [init'tsjare] *vi, vt* to begin, start; ~ **qn a** to initiate sb into; (*pittura etc*) to introduce sb to; ~ **a fare qc** to start doing sth.
inizia'tiva [inittsja'tiva] *sf* initiative; ~ **privata** private enterprise.
inizia'tore, 'trice [inittsja'tore] *sm/f* initiator.
i'nizio [i'nittsjo] *sm* beginning; **all'**~ at the beginning, at the start; **dare** ~ **a qc** to start sth, get sth going; **essere agli** ~**i** (*progetto, lavoro etc*) to be in the initial stages.
innaffi'are *etc* = **annaffiare** *etc*.
innal'zare [innal'tsare] *vt* (*sollevare, alzare*)

to raise; (*rizzare*) to erect; ~**rsi** *vr* to rise.
innamora'mento *sm* falling in love.
innamo'rare *vt* to enchant, charm; ~**rsi** *vr*: ~**rsi (di qn)** to fall in love (with sb).
innamo'rato, a *ag* (*che nutre amore*): ~ **(di)** in love (with); (*appassionato*): ~ **di** very fond of ♦ *sm/f* lover; (*anche scherzoso*) sweetheart.
in'nanzi [in'nantsi] *av* (*stato in luogo*) in front, ahead; (*moto a luogo*) forward, on; (*tempo: prima*) before ♦ *prep* (*prima*) before; ~ **a** in front of; **d'ora** ~ from now on; **farsi** ~ to step forward; ~ **tempo** ahead of time.
innanzi'tutto [innantsi'tutto] *av* above all; (*per prima cosa*) first of all.
in'nato, a *ag* innate.
innatu'rale *ag* unnatural.
inne'gabile *ag* undeniable.
inneggi'are [inned'dʒare] *vi*: ~ **a** to sing hymns to; (*fig*) to sing the praises of.
innervo'sire *vt*: ~ **qn** to get on sb's nerves; ~**rsi** *vr* to get irritated *o* upset.
innes'care *vt* to prime.
in'nesco, schi *sm* primer.
innes'tare *vt* (*BOT, MED*) to graft; (*TECN*) to engage; (*inserire: presa*) to insert.
in'nesto *sm* graft; grafting *no pl*; (*TECN*) clutch; (*ELETTR*) connection.
'inno *sm* hymn; ~ **nazionale** national anthem.
inno'cente [inno'tʃɛnte] *ag* innocent.
inno'cenza [inno'tʃɛntsa] *sf* innocence.
in'nocuo, a *ag* innocuous, harmless.
innomi'nato, a *ag* unnamed.
inno'vare *vt* to change, make innovations in.
innova'tivo, a *ag* innovative.
innovazi'one [innovat'tsjone] *sf* innovation.
innume'revole *ag* innumerable.
inocu'lare *vt* (*MED*) to inoculate.
ino'doro, a *ag* odourless (*BRIT*), odorless (*US*).
inoffen'sivo, a *ag* harmless.
inol'trare *vt* (*AMM*) to pass on, forward; ~**rsi** *vr* (*addentrarsi*) to advance, go forward.
inol'trato, a *ag*: **a notte** ~**a** late at night; **a primavera** ~**a** late in the spring.
i'noltre *av* besides, moreover.
i'noltro *sm* (*AMM*) forwarding.
inon'dare *vt* to flood.
inondazi'one [inondat'tsjone] *sf* flooding *no pl*; flood.
inope'roso, a *ag* inactive, idle.
inopi'nato, a *ag* unexpected.
inoppor'tuno, a *ag* untimely, ill-timed; (*poco adatto*) inappropriate; (*momento*)

inopportune.

inoppu'gnabile [inoppuɲ'ɲabile] *ag* incontrovertible.

inor'ganico, a, ci, che *ag* inorganic.

inorgo'glire [inorgoʎ'ʎire] *vt* to make proud ♦ *vi* (*anche:* ~rsi) to become proud; ~rsi di qc to pride o.s. on sth.

inorri'dire *vt* to horrify ♦ *vi* to be horrified.

inospi'tale *ag* inhospitable.

inosser'vante *ag:* **essere** ~ **di** to fail to comply with.

inosser'vato, a *ag* (*non notato*) unobserved; (*non rispettato*) not observed, not kept; **passare** ~ to go unobserved, escape notice.

inossi'dabile *ag* stainless.

INPS *sigla m* (= *Istituto Nazionale Previdenza Sociale*) social security service.

inqua'drare *vt* (*foto, immagine*) to frame; (*fig*) to situate, set.

inquadra'tura *sf* (*CINE, FOT: atto*) framing; (*: immagine*) shot; (*: inquadrata*) sequence.

inqualifi'cabile *ag* unspeakable.

inquie'tante *ag* disturbing, worrying.

inquie'tare *vt* (*turbare*) to disturb, worry; ~rsi *vr* to worry, become anxious; (*impazientirsi*) to get upset.

inqui'eto, a *ag* restless; (*preoccupato*) worried, anxious.

inquie'tudine *sf* anxiety, worry.

inqui'lino, a *sm/f* tenant.

inquina'mento *sm* pollution.

inqui'nare *vt* to pollute.

inqui'rente *ag* (*DIR*): **magistrato** ~ examining (*BRIT*) *o* committing (*US*) magistrate; **commissione** ~ commission of inquiry.

inqui'sire *vt, vi* to investigate.

inqui'sito, a *ag* (*persona*) under investigation.

inquisi'tore, 'trice *ag* (*sguardo*) inquiring.

inquisizi'one [inkwizit'tsjone] *sf* inquisition.

insabbia'mento *sm* (*fig*) shelving.

insabbi'are *vt* (*fig: pratica*) to shelve; ~rsi *vr* (*barca*) to run aground; (*fig: pratica*) to be shelved.

insac'care *vt* (*grano, farina etc*) to bag, put into sacks; (*carne*) to put into sausage skins.

insac'cati *smpl* (*CUC*) sausages.

insa'lata *sf* salad; (*pianta*) lettuce; ~ **mista** mixed salad.

insalati'era *sf* salad bowl.

insa'lubre *ag* unhealthy.

insa'nabile *ag* (*piaga*) which cannot be healed; (*situazione*) irremediable; (*odio*) implacable.

insangui'nare *vt* to stain with blood.

in'sania *sf* insanity.

in'sano, a *ag* (*pazzo, folle*) insane.

insapo'nare *vt* to soap; ~rsi **le mani** to soap one's hands.

insapo'nata *sf:* **dare un'**~ **a qc** to give sth a (quick) soaping.

insapo'rire *vt* to flavour (*BRIT*), flavor (*US*); (*con spezie*) to season; ~rsi *vr* to acquire flavo(u)r.

insa'poro, a *ag* tasteless, insipid.

insa'puta *sf:* **all'**~ **di qn** without sb knowing.

insazi'abile [insat'tsjabile] *ag* insatiable.

inscato'lare *vt* (*frutta, carne*) to can.

insce'nare [inʃe'nare] *vt* (*TEAT*) to stage, put on; (*fig*) to stage.

inscin'dibile [inʃin'dibile] *ag* (*fattori*) inseparable; (*legame*) indissoluble.

insec'chire [insek'kire] *vt* (*seccare*) to dry up; (*: piante*) to wither ♦ *vi* to dry up, become dry; to wither.

insedia'mento *sm* (*AMM: in carica, ufficio*) installation; (*villaggio, colonia*) settlement.

insedi'are *vt* (*AMM*) to install; ~rsi *vr* (*AMM*) to take up office; (*colonia, profughi eto*) to settle; (*MIL*) to take up positions.

in'segna [in'seɲɲa] *sf* sign; (*emblema*) sign, emblem; (*bandiera*) flag, banner; ~**e** *sfpl* (*decorazioni*) insignia *pl*.

insegna'mento [inseɲɲa'mento] *sm* teaching; **trarre** ~ **da un'esperienza** to learn from an experience, draw a lesson from an experience; **che ti serva da** ~ let this be a lesson to you.

inse'gnante [inseɲ'ɲante] *ag* teaching ♦ *sm/f* teacher.

inse'gnare [inseɲ'ɲare] *vt, vi* to teach; ~ **a qn qc** to teach sb sth; ~ **a qn a fare qc** to teach sb (how) to do sth; **come lei ben m'insegna** ... (*ironico*) as you will doubtless be aware ....

insegui'mento *sm* pursuit, chase; **darsi all'**~ **di qn** to give chase to sb.

insegu'ire *vt* to pursue, chase.

insegui'tore, 'trice *sm/f* pursuer.

insel'lare *vt* to saddle.

inselvati'chire [inselvati'kire] *vt* (*persona*) to make unsociable ♦ *vi* (*anche:* ~rsi) to grow wild; (*persona*) to become unsociable.

inseminazi'one [inseminat'tsjone] *sf* insemination.

insena'tura *sf* inlet, creek.

insen'sato, a *ag* senseless, stupid.

insen'sibile *ag* (*anche fig*) insensitive.

insensibilità *sf* insensitivity, insensibility.

insepa'rabile *ag* inseparable.

inse'polto, a *ag* unburied.
inseri'mento *sm* (*gen*) insertion; **problemi di** ~ (*di persona*) adjustment problems.
inse'rire *vt* to insert; (*ELETTR*) to connect; (*allegare*) to enclose; ~**rsi** *vr* (*fig*): ~**rsi in** to become part of; ~ **un annuncio sul giornale** to put *o* place an advertisement in the newspaper.
in'serto *sm* (*pubblicazione*) insert; ~ **filmato** (film) clip.
inser'vibile *ag* useless.
inservi'ente *sm/f* attendant.
inserzi'one [inser'tsjone] *sf* insertion; (*avviso*) advertisement; **fare un'**~ **sul giornale** to put an advertisement in the newspaper.
inserzio'nista, i, e [insertsjo'nista] *sm/f* advertiser.
insetti'cida, i [insetti'tʃida] *sm* insecticide.
in'setto *sm* insect.
insicu'rezza [insiku'rettsa] *sf* insecurity.
insi'curo, a *ag* insecure.
in'sidia *sf* snare, trap; (*pericolo*) hidden danger; **tendere un'**~ **a qn** to lay *o* set a trap for sb.
insidi'are *vt* (*MIL*) to harass; ~ **la vita di qn** to make an attempt on sb's life.
insidi'oso, a *ag* insidious.
insi'eme *av* together; (*contemporaneamente*) at the same time ♦ *prep*: ~ **a** *o* **con** together with ♦ *sm* whole; (*MAT, servizio, assortimento*) set; (*MODA*) ensemble, outfit; **tutti** ~ all together; **tutto** ~ all together; (*in una volta*) at one go; **nell'**~ on the whole; **d'**~ (*veduta etc*) overall.
in'signe [in'siɲɲe] *ag* (*persona*) famous, distinguished, eminent; (*città, monumento*) notable.
insignifi'cante [insiɲɲifi'kante] *ag* insignificant.
insi'gnire [insiɲ'ɲire] *vt*: ~ **qn di** to honour (*BRIT*) *o* honor (*US*) sb with, decorate sb with.
insin'cero, a [insin'tʃero] *ag* insincere.
insinda'cabile *ag* unquestionable.
insinu'ante *ag* (*osservazione, sguardo*) insinuating; (*maniere*) ingratiating.
insinu'are *vt* (*introdurre*): ~ **qc in** to slip *o* slide sth into; (*fig*) to insinuate, imply; ~**rsi** *vr*: ~**rsi in** to seep into; (*fig*) to creep into; to worm one's way into.
insinuazi'one [insinuat'tsjone] *sf* (*fig*) insinuation.
in'sipido, a *ag* insipid.
insis'tente *ag* insistent; (*pioggia, dolore*) persistent.
insistente'mente *av* repeatedly.

insis'tenza [insis'tɛntsa] *sf* insistence; persistence.
in'sistere *vi*: ~ **su qc** to insist on sth; ~ **in qc/a fare** (*perseverare*) to persist in sth/in doing.
insis'tito, a *pp di* **insistere.**
'insito, a *ag*: ~ **(in)** inherent (in).
insoddis'fatto, a *ag* dissatisfied.
insoddisfazi'one [insoddisfat'tsjone] *sf* dissatisfaction.
insoffe'rente *ag* intolerant.
insoffe'renza [insoffe'rɛntsa] *sf* impatience.
insolazi'one [insolat'tsjone] *sf* (*MED*) sunstroke.
inso'lente *ag* insolent.
insolen'tire *vi* to grow insolent ♦ *vt* to insult, be rude to.
inso'lenza [inso'lɛntsa] *sf* insolence.
in'solito, a *ag* unusual, out of the ordinary.
inso'lubile *ag* insoluble.
inso'luto, a *ag* (*non risolto*) unsolved; (*non pagato*) unpaid, outstanding.
insol'vente *ag* (*DIR*) insolvent.
insol'venza [insol'vɛntsa] *sf* (*DIR*) insolvency.
insol'vibile *ag* insolvent.
in'somma *av* (*in breve, in conclusione*) in short; (*dunque*) well ♦ *escl* for heaven's sake!
inson'dabile *ag* unfathomable.
in'sonne *ag* sleepless.
in'sonnia *sf* insomnia, sleeplessness.
insonno'lito, a *ag* sleepy, drowsy.
insonorizzazi'one [insonoriddzat'tsjone] *sf* soundproofing.
insoppor'tabile *ag* unbearable.
insoppri'mibile *ag* insuppressible.
insor'genza [insor'dʒɛntsa] *sf* (*di malattia*) onset.
in'sorgere [in'sordʒere] *vi* (*ribellarsi*) to rise up, rebel; (*apparire*) to come up, arise.
insormon'tabile *ag* (*ostacolo*) insurmountable, insuperable.
in'sorsi *etc vb vedi* **insorgere.**
in'sorto, a *pp di* **insorgere** ♦ *sm/f* rebel, insurgent.
insospet'tabile *ag* (*al di sopra di ogni sospetto*) above suspicion; (*inatteso*) unsuspected.
insospet'tire *vt* to make suspicious ♦ *vi* (*anche*: ~**rsi**) to become suspicious.
insoste'nibile *ag* (*posizione, teoria*) untenable; (*dolore, situazione*) intolerable, unbearable; **le spese di manutenzione sono** ~**i** the maintenance costs are excessive.
insostitu'ibile *ag* (*persona*) irreplaceable; (*aiuto, presenza*) invaluable.

insoz'zare [insot'tsare] *vt* (*pavimento*) to make dirty; (*fig*: *reputazione, memoria*) to tarnish, sully; ~**rsi** *vr* to get dirty.

inspe'rabile *ag*: **la guarigione/salvezza era** ~ there was no hope of a cure/of rescue; **abbiamo ottenuto risultati** ~**i** the results we achieved were far better than we had hoped.

inspe'rato, a *ag* unhoped-for.

inspie'gabile *ag* inexplicable.

inspi'rare *vt* to breathe in, inhale.

in'stabile *ag* (*carico, indole*) unstable; (*tempo*) unsettled; (*equilibrio*) unsteady.

instabilità *sf* instability; (*di tempo*) changeability.

instal'lare *vt* to install; ~**rsi** *vr* (*sistemarsi*): ~**rsi in** to settle in.

installazi'one [installat'tsjone] *sf* installation.

instan'cabile *ag* untiring, indefatigable.

instau'rare *vt* to establish.

instaurazi'one [instaurat'tsjone] *sf* establishment.

instil'lare *vt* to instil.

instra'dare *vt* = **istradare**.

insù *av* up, upwards; **guardare all'**~ to look up *o* upwards; **naso all'**~ turned-up nose.

insubordinazi'one [insubordinat'tsjone] *sf* insubordination.

insuc'cesso [insut'tʃɛsso] *sm* failure, flop.

insudici'are [insudi'tʃare] *vt* to dirty; ~**rsi** *vr* to get dirty.

insuffici'ente [insuffi'tʃɛnte] *ag* insufficient; (*compito, allievo*) inadequate.

insuffici'enza [insuffi'tʃɛntsa] *sf* insufficiency; inadequacy; (*INS*) fail; ~ **di prove** (*DIR*) lack of evidence.

insu'lare *ag* insular.

insu'lina *sf* insulin.

in'sulso, a *ag* (*sciocco*) inane, silly; (*persona*) dull, insipid.

insul'tare *vt* to insult, affront.

in'sulto *sm* insult, affront.

insupe'rabile *ag* (*ostacolo, difficoltà*) insuperable, insurmountable; (*eccellente*: *qualità, prodotto*) unbeatable; (: *persona, interpretazione*) unequalled.

insuper'bire *vt* to make proud, make arrogant; ~**rsi** *vr* to become arrogant.

insurrezi'one [insurret'tsjone] *sf* revolt, insurrection.

insussis'tente *ag* non-existent.

intac'care *vt* (*fare tacche*) to cut into; (*corrodere*) to corrode; (*fig*: *cominciare ad usare: risparmi*) to break into; (: *ledere*) to damage.

intagli'are [intaʎ'ʎare] *vt* to carve.

intaglia'tore, 'trice [intaʎʎa'tore] *sm/f*

engraver.

in'taglio [in'taʎʎo] *sm* carving.

intan'gibile [intan'dʒibile] *ag* (*bene, patrimonio*) untouchable; (*fig*: *diritto*) inviolable.

in'tanto *av* (*nel frattempo*) meanwhile, in the meantime; (*per cominciare*) just to begin with; ~ **che** *cong* while.

intarsi'are *vt* to inlay.

in'tarsio *sm* inlaying *no pl*, marquetry *no pl*; inlay.

intasa'mento *sm* (*ostruzione*) blockage, obstruction; (*AUT*: *ingorgo*) traffic jam.

inta'sare *vt* to choke (up), block (up); (*AUT*) to obstruct, block; ~**rsi** *vr* to become choked *o* blocked.

intas'care *vt* to pocket.

in'tatto, a *ag* intact; (*puro*) unsullied.

intavo'lare *vt* to start, enter into.

inte'gerrimo, a [inte'dʒɛrrimo] *ag* honest, upright.

inte'grale *ag* complete; (*pane, farina*) wholemeal (*BRIT*), wholewheat (*US*); **film in versione** ~ uncut version of a film; **calcolo** ~ (*MAT*) integral calculus; **edizione** ~ unabridged edition.

inte'grante *ag*: **parte** *f* ~ integral part.

inte'grare *vt* to complete; (*MAT*) to integrate; ~**rsi** *vr* (*persona*) to become integrated.

integra'tivo, a *ag* (*assegno*) supplementary; (*INS*): **esame** ~ assessment test sat when changing schools.

integra'tore *sm*: ~**i alimentari** nutritional supplements.

integrazi'one [integrat'tsjone] *sf* integration.

integrità *sf* integrity.

'integro, a *ag* (*intatto, intero*) complete, whole; (*retto*) upright.

intelaia'tura *sf* frame; (*fig*) structure, framework.

intel'letto *sm* intellect.

intellettu'ale *ag, sm/f* intellectual.

intellettua'loide (*peg*) *ag* pseudo-intellectual ♦ *sm/f* pseudo-intellectual, would-be intellectual.

intelli'gente [intelli'dʒɛnte] *ag* intelligent.

intelli'genza [intelli'dʒɛntsa] *sf* intelligence.

intelli'ghenzia [intelli'gɛntsja] *sf* intelligentsia.

intelli'gibile [intelli'dʒibile] *ag* intelligible.

inteme'rato, a *ag* (*persona, vita*) blameless, irreproachable; (*coscienza*) clear; (*fama*) unblemished.

intempe'rante *ag* intemperate,

immoderate.

intempe'ranza [intempe'rantsa] *sf*
intemperance; ~**e** *sfpl* (*eccessi*) excesses.

intem'perie *sfpl* bad weather *sg*.

intempes'tivo, a *ag* untimely.

inten'dente *sm*: ~ **di Finanza** inland (*BRIT*)
o internal (*US*) revenue officer.

inten'denza [inten'dɛntsa] *sf*: ~ **di Finanza**
inland (*BRIT*) *o* internal (*US*) revenue
office.

in'tendere *vt* (*avere intenzione*): ~ **fare qc** to
intend *o* mean to do sth; (*comprendere*) to
understand; (*udire*) to hear; (*significare*) to
mean; ~**rsi** *vr* (*conoscere*): ~**rsi di** to know
a lot about, be a connoisseur of;
(*accordarsi*) to get on (well); ~**rsi con qn**
su qc to come to an agreement with sb
about sth; **intendersela con qn** (*avere una
relazione amorosa*) to have an affair with
sb; **mi ha dato a** ~ **che** ... he led me to
believe that ...; **non vuole** ~ **ragione** he
won't listen to reason; **s'intende!**
naturally!, of course!; **intendiamoci** let's
get it quite clear; **ci siamo intesi?** is that
clear?, is that understood?

intendi'mento *sm* (*intelligenza*)
understanding; (*proposito*) intention.

intendi'tore, 'trice *sm/f* connoisseur,
expert; **a buon intenditor poche parole**
(*proverbio*) a word is enough to the wise.

intene'rire *vt* (*fig*) to move (to pity); ~**rsi** *vr*
(*fig*) to be moved.

intensifi'care *vt*, ~**rsi** *vr* to intensify.

intensità *sf* intensity; (*del vento*) force,
strength.

inten'sivo, a *ag* intensive.

in'tenso, a *ag* (*luce, profumo*) strong;
(*colore*) intense, deep.

inten'tare *vt* (*DIR*): ~ **causa contro qn** to
start *o* institute proceedings against sb.

inten'tato, a *ag*: **non lasciare nulla d'**~ to
leave no stone unturned, try everything.

in'tento, a *ag* (*teso, assorto*): ~ **(a)** intent
(on), absorbed (in) ♦ *sm* aim, purpose;
fare qc con l'~ **di** to do sth with the
intention of; **riuscire nell'**~ to achieve
one's aim.

intenzio'nale [intentsjo'nale] *ag*
intentional; (*DIR*: *omicidio*) premeditated;
fallo ~ (*SPORT*) deliberate foul.

intenzio'nato, a [intentsjo'nato] *ag*: **essere**
~ **a fare qc** to intend to do sth, have the
intention of doing sth; **ben** ~ well-
meaning, well-intentioned; **mal** ~ ill-
intentioned.

intenzi'one [inten'tsjone] *sf* intention; (*DIR*)
intent; **avere** ~ **di fare qc** to intend to do
sth, have the intention of doing sth.

intera'gire [intera'dʒire] *vi* to interact.

intera'mente *av* entirely, completely.

interat'tivo, a *ag* interactive.

interazi'one [interat'tsjone] *sf* interaction.

interca'lare *sm* pet phrase, stock phrase
♦ *vt* to insert.

interca'pedine *sf* gap, cavity.

inter'cedere [inter'tʃedere] *vi* to intercede.

intercessi'one [intertʃes'sjone] *sf*
intercession.

intercetta'mento [intertʃetta'mento] *sm*
= **intercettazione**.

intercet'tare [intertʃet'tare] *vt* to intercept.

intercettazi'one [intertʃettat'tsjone] *sf*: ~
telefonica telephone tapping.

intercity [inter'siti] *sm inv* (*FERR*) ≈ intercity
(train).

intercon'nettere *vt* to interconnect.

inter'correre *vi* (*esserci*) to exist; (*passare:
tempo*) to elapse.

inter'corso, a *pp di* **intercorrere**.

inter'detto, a *pp di* **interdire** ♦ *ag* forbidden,
prohibited; (*sconcertato*) dumbfounded
♦ *sm* (*REL*) interdict; **rimanere** ~ to be
taken aback.

inter'dire *vt* to forbid, prohibit, ban; (*REL*)
to interdict; (*DIR*) to deprive of civil
rights.

interdizi'one [interdit'tsjone] *sf*
prohibition, ban.

interessa'mento *sm* interest; (*intervento*)
intervention, good offices *pl*.

interes'sante *ag* interesting; **essere in
stato** ~ to be expecting (a baby).

interes'sare *vt* to interest; (*concernere*) to
concern, be of interest to; (*far intervenire*):
~ **qn a** to draw sb's attention to ♦ *vi*: ~ **a**
to interest, matter to; ~**rsi** *vr* (*mostrare
interesse*): ~**rsi a** to take an interest in, be
interested in; (*occuparsi*): ~**rsi di** to take
care of; **precipitazioni che interessano le
regioni settentrionali** rainfall affecting
the north; **si è interessato di farmi avere
quei biglietti** he took the trouble to get
me those tickets.

interes'sato, a *ag* (*coinvolto*) interested,
involved; (*peg*): **essere** ~ to act out of
pure self-interest ♦ *sm/f* (*coinvolto*) person
concerned; **a tutti gli** ~**i** to all those
concerned, to all interested parties.

inte'resse *sm* (*anche COMM*) interest;
(*tornaconto*): **fare qc per** ~ to do sth out of
self-interest; ~ **maturato** (*ECON*) accrued
interest; ~ **privato in atti di ufficio** (*AMM*)
abuse of public office.

interes'senza [interes'sɛntsa] *sf* (*ECON*)
profit-sharing.

inter'faccia, ce [inter'fattʃa] *sf* (*INFORM*)

interface; ~ **utente** user interface.
interfacci'are [interfat't∫are] *vt* (*INFORM*) to interface.
interfe'renza [interfe'rɛntsa] *sf* interference.
interfe'rire *vi* to interfere.
inter'fono *sm* intercom; (*apparecchio*) internal phone.
interiezi'one [interjet'tsjone] *sf* exclamation, interjection.
'**interim** *sm inv* (*periodo*) interim, interval; **ministro ad** ~ acting *o* interim minister; (*incarico*) temporary appointment.
interi'ora *sfpl* entrails.
interi'ore *ag* inner *cpd*; **parte** *f* ~ inside.
interiorità *sf* inner being.
interioriz'zare [interjorid'dzare] *vt* to internalize.
inter'linea *sf* (*DATTILOGRAFIA*) spacing; (*TIP*) leading; **doppia** ~ double spacing.
interlocu'tore, 'trice *sm/f* speaker.
interlocu'torio, a *ag* interlocutory.
inter'ludio *sm* (*MUS*) interlude.
intermedi'ario, a *ag, sm/f* intermediary.
intermediazi'one [intermedjat'tsjone] *sf* mediation.
inter'medio, a *ag* intermediate.
inter'mezzo [inter'mɛddzo] *sm* (*intervallo*) interval; (*breve spettacolo*) intermezzo.
intermi'nabile *ag* interminable, endless.
intermit'tente *ag* intermittent.
intermit'tenza [intermit'tɛntsa] *sf*: **ad** ~ intermittent.
interna'mento *sm* internment; confinement (to a mental hospital).
inter'nare *vt* (*arrestare*) to intern; (*MED*) to confine to a mental hospital.
inter'nato, a *ag* interned; confined (to a mental hospital) ♦ *sm/f* internee; inmate (of a mental hospital) ♦ *sm* (*collegio*) boarding school; (*MED*) period as a houseman (*BRIT*) *o* an intern (*US*).
internazio'nale [internattsjo'nale] *ag* international.
'**Internet** ['internet] *sf* Internet; **in** ~ on the Internet.
inter'nista, i, e *sm/f* specialist in internal medicine.
in'terno, a *ag* (*di dentro*) internal, interior, inner; (: *mare*) inland; (*nazionale*) domestic; (*allievo*) boarding ♦ *sm* inside, interior; (*di paese*) interior; (*fodera*) lining; (*di appartamento*) flat (*BRIT*) *o* apartment (*US*) (number); (*TEL*) extension ♦ *sm/f* (*INS*) boarder; ~**i** *smpl* (*CINE*) interior shots; **commissione** ~**a** (*INS*) internal examination board; "**per uso** ~" (*MED*) "to be taken internally"; **all'**~ inside;

Ministero degli I~**i** Ministry of the Interior, ≈ Home Office (*BRIT*), ≈ Department of the Interior (*US*); **notizie dall'**~ (*STAMPA*) home news.
in'tero, a *ag* (*integro, intatto*) whole, entire; (*completo, totale*) complete; (*numero*) whole; (*non ridotto: biglietto*) full.
interpel'lanza [interpel'lantsa] *sf*: **presentare un'**~ (*POL*) to ask a (parliamentary) question; ~ **parlamentare** interpellation.
interpel'lare *vt* to consult; (*POL*) to question.
INTER'POL *sigla f* (= *International Criminal Police Organization*) INTERPOL.
inter'porre *vt* (*ostacolo*): ~ **qc a qc** to put sth in the way of sth; (*influenza*) to use; **interporsi** *vr* to intervene; ~ **appello** (*DIR*) to appeal; **interporsi fra** (*mettersi in mezzo*) to come between.
inter'posto, a *pp di* **interporre**.
interpre'tare *vt* (*spiegare, tradurre*) to interpret; (*MUS, TEAT*) to perform; (*personaggio, sonata*) to play; (*canzone*) to sing.
interpretari'ato *sm* interpreting.
interpretazi'one [interpretat'tsjone] *sf* interpretation.
in'terprete *sm/f* interpreter; (*TEAT*) actor/ actress, performer; (*MUS*) performer; **farsi** ~ **di** to act as a spokesman for.
interpunzi'one [interpun'tsjone] *sf* punctuation; **segni di** ~ punctuation marks.
inter'rare *vt* (*seme, pianta*) to plant; (*tubature etc*) to lay underground; (*MIL: pezzo d'artiglieria*) to dig in; (*riempire di terra: canale*) to fill in.
interro'gare *vt* to question; (*INS*) to test.
interroga'tivo, a *ag* (*occhi, sguardo*) questioning, inquiring; (*LING*) interrogative ♦ *sm* question; (*fig*) mystery.
interroga'torio, a *ag* interrogatory, questioning ♦ *sm* (*DIR*) questioning *no pl*.
interrogazi'one [interrogat'tsjone] *sf* questioning *no pl*; (*INS*) oral test; (*POL*): ~ **(parlamentare)** question.
inter'rompere *vt* to interrupt; (*studi, trattative*) to break off, interrupt; ~**rsi** *vr* to break off, stop.
inter'rotto, a *pp di* **interrompere**.
interrut'tore *sm* switch.
interruzi'one [interrut'tsjone] *sf* (*vedi interrompere*) interruption; break; ~ **di gravidanza** termination of pregnancy.
interse'care *vt*, ~**rsi** *vr* to intersect.
inter'stizio [inter'stittsjo] *sm* interstice, crack.
interur'bano, a *ag* inter-city; (*TEL*:

chiamata) trunk *cpd* (*BRIT*), long-distance; (: *telefono*) long-distance ♦ *sf* trunk call (*BRIT*), long-distance call.

inter'vallo *sm* interval; (*spazio*) space, gap; ~ **pubblicitario** (*TV*) commercial break.

interve'nire *vi* (*partecipare*): ~ **a** to take part in; (*intromettersi: anche POL*) to intervene; (*MED: operare*) to operate.

interven'tista, i, e *ag*, *sm/f* interventionist.

inter'vento *sm* participation; (*intromissione*) intervention; (*MED*) operation; (*breve discorso*) speech; **fare un ~ nel corso di** (*dibattito, programma*) to take part in.

interve'nuto, a *pp di* **intervenire** ♦ *sm*: **gli ~i** those present.

inter'vista *sf* interview.

intervis'tare *vt* to interview.

intervista'tore, 'trice *sm/f* interviewer.

in'teso, a *pp di* **intendere** ♦ *ag* agreed ♦ *sf* understanding; (*accordo*) agreement, understanding; **resta ~ che ...** it is understood that ...; **non darsi per ~ di qc** to take no notice of sth; **uno sguardo d'~a** a knowing look.

in'tessere *vt* to weave together; (*fig: trama, storia*) to weave.

intes'tare *vt* (*lettera*) to address; (*proprietà*): ~ **a** to register in the name of; ~ **un assegno a qn** to make out a cheque to sb.

intesta'tario, a *sm/f* holder.

intes'tato, a *ag* (*proprietà, casa, conto*) in the name of; (*assegno*) made out to; **carta ~a** headed paper.

intestazi'one [intestat'tsjone] *sf* heading; (*su carta da lettere*) letterhead; (*registrazione*) registration.

intesti'nale *ag* intestinal.

intes'tino, a *ag* (*lotte*) internal, civil ♦ *sm* (*ANAT*) intestine.

intiepi'dire *vt* (*riscaldare*) to warm (up); (*raffreddare*) to cool (down); (*fig: amicizia etc*) to cool; ~**rsi** *vr* to warm (up); to cool (down); to cool.

Inti'fada *sf* Intifada.

intima'mente *av* intimately; **sono ~ convinto che ...** I'm firmly *o* deeply convinced that ...; **i due fatti sono ~ connessi** the two events are closely connected.

inti'mare *vt* to order, command; ~ **la resa a qn** (*MIL*) to call upon sb to surrender.

intimazi'one [intimat'tsjone] *sf* order, command.

intimida'torio, a *ag* threatening.

intimidazi'one [intimidat'tsjone] *sf* intimidation.

intimi'dire *vt* to intimidate ♦ *vi* (*anche:* ~**rsi**) to grow shy.

intimità *sf* intimacy; privacy; (*familiarità*) familiarity.

'intimo, a *ag* intimate; (*affetti, vita*) private; (*fig: profondo*) inmost ♦ *sm* (*persona*) intimate *o* close friend; (*dell'animo*) bottom, depths *pl*; **parti ~e** (*ANAT*) private parts; **rapporti ~i** (*sessuali*) intimate relations.

intimo'rire *vt* to frighten; ~**rsi** *vr* to become frightened.

in'tingere [in'tindʒere] *vt* to dip.

in'tingolo *sm* sauce; (*pietanza*) stew.

in'tinto, a *pp di* **intingere**.

intiriz'zire [intirid'dzire] *vt* to numb ♦ *vi* (*anche:* ~**rsi**) to go numb.

intiriz'zito, a [intirid'dzito] *ag* numb (with cold).

intito'lare *vt* to give a title to; (*dedicare*) to dedicate; ~**rsi** *vr* (*libro, film*) to be called.

intolle'rabile *ag* intolerable.

intolle'rante *ag* intolerant.

intolle'ranza [intolle'rantsa] *sf* intolerance.

intona'care *vt* to plaster.

in'tonaco, ci *o* **chi** *sm* plaster.

into'nare *vt* (*canto*) to start to sing; (*armonizzare*) to match; ~**rsi** *vr* (*colori*) to go together; ~**rsi a** (*carnagione*) to suit; (*abito*) to go with, match.

intonazi'one [intonat'tsjone] *sf* intonation.

inton'tire *vt* to stun, daze ♦ *vi*, ~**rsi** *vr* to be stunned *o* dazed.

inton'tito, a *ag* stunned, dazed; ~ **dal sonno** stupid with sleep.

in'toppo *sm* stumbling block, obstacle.

intorbi'dire *vt* (*liquido*) to make turbid; (*mente*) to cloud; ~ **le acque** (*fig*) to muddy the waters.

in'torno *av* around; ~ **a** *prep* (*attorno a*) around; (*riguardo, circa*) about.

intorpi'dire *vt* to numb; (*fig*) to make sluggish ♦ *vi* (*anche:* ~**rsi**) to grow numb; (*fig*) to become sluggish.

intossi'care *vt* to poison.

intossicazi'one [intossikat'tsjone] *sf* poisoning.

intradu'cibile [intradu'tʃibile] *ag* untranslatable.

intralci'are [intral'tʃare] *vt* to hamper, hold up.

in'tralcio [in'traltʃo] *sm* hitch.

intrallaz'zare [intrallat'tsare] *vi* to intrigue, scheme.

intral'lazzo [intral'lattso] *sm* (*POL*) intrigue, manoeuvre (*BRIT*), maneuver (*US*); (*traffico losco*) racket.

intramon'tabile *ag* timeless.

intramusco'lare *ag* intramuscular.

'Intranet ['intranet] *sf* intranet.

intransi'gente [intransi'dʒɛnte] *ag* intransigent, uncompromising.
intransi'genza [intransi'dʒɛntsa] *sf* intransigence.
intransi'tivo, a *ag, sm* intransitive.
intrappo'lare *vt* to trap; **rimanere intrappolato** to be trapped; **farsi** ~ to get caught.
intrapren'dente *ag* enterprising, go-ahead; (*con le donne*) forward, bold.
intrapren'denza [intrapren'dɛntsa] *sf* audacity, initiative; (*con le donne*) boldness.
intra'prendere *vt* to undertake; (*carriera*) to embark (up)on.
intra'preso, a *pp di* **intraprendere**.
intrat'tabile *ag* intractable.
intratte'nere *vt* (*divertire*) to entertain; (*chiacchierando*) to engage in conversation; (*rapporti*) to have, maintain; ~**rsi** *vr* to linger; ~**rsi su qc** to dwell on sth.
intratteni'mento *sm* entertainment
intrave'dere *vt* to catch a glimpse of; (*fig*) to foresee.
intrecci'are [intret't∫are] *vt* (*capelli*) to plait, braid; (*intessere*: *anche fig*) to weave, interweave, intertwine; ~**rsi** *vr* to intertwine, become interwoven; ~ **le mani** to clasp one's hands; ~ **una relazione amorosa** (*fig*) to begin an affair.
in'treccio [in'trett∫o] *sm* (*fig*: *trama*) plot, story.
in'trepido, a *ag* fearless, intrepid.
intri'care *vt* (*fili*) to tangle; (*fig*: *faccenda*) to complicate; ~**rsi** *vr* to become tangled; to become complicated.
in'trico, chi *sm* (*anche fig*) tangle.
intri'gante *ag* scheming ♦ *sm/f* schemer, intriguer.
intri'gare *vi* to manoeuvre (*BRIT*), maneuver (*US*), scheme.
in'trigo, ghi *sm* plot, intrigue.
in'trinseco, a, ci, che *ag* intrinsic.
in'triso, a *ag*: ~ (**di**) soaked (in).
intris'tire *vi* (*persona*: *diventare triste*) to grow sad; (*pianta*) to wilt.
intro'dotto, a *pp di* **introdurre**.
intro'durre *vt* to introduce; (*chiave etc*): ~ **qc in** to insert sth into; (*persona*: *far entrare*) to show in; **introdursi** *vr* (*moda, tecniche*) to be introduced; **introdursi in** (*persona*: *penetrare*) to enter; (: *entrare furtivamente*) to steal *o* slip into.
in'troito *sm* income, revenue.
intro'messo, a *pp di* **intromettersi**.
intro'mettersi *vr* to interfere, meddle; (*interporsi*) to intervene.

intromissi'one *sf* interference, meddling; intervention.
introspezi'one [introspet'tsjone] *sf* introspection.
intro'vabile *ag* (*persona, oggetto*) who (*o* which) cannot be found; (*libro etc*) unobtainable.
intro'verso, a *ag* introverted ♦ *sm/f* introvert.
intrufo'larsi *vr*: ~ (**in**) (*stanza*) to sneak in(to), slip in(to); (*conversazione*) to butt in (on).
in'truglio [in'truʎʎo] *sm* concoction.
intrusi'one *sf* intrusion; interference.
in'truso, a *sm/f* intruder.
intu'ire *vt* to perceive by intuition; (*rendersi conto*) to realize.
in'tuito *sm* intuition; (*perspicacia*) perspicacity.
intuizi'one [intuit'tsjone] *sf* intuition.
inturgi'dire [inturdʒi'dire] *vi,* ~**rsi** *vr* to swell.
inumanità *sf inv* inhumanity.
inu'mano, a *ag* inhuman.
inu'mare *vt* (*seppellire*) to bury, inter.
inumazi'one [inumat'tsjone] *sf* burial, interment.
inumi'dire *vt* to dampen, moisten; ~**rsi** *vr* to become damp *o* wet.
inurba'mento *sm* urbanization.
inusi'tato, a *ag* unusual.
i'nutile *ag* useless; (*superfluo*) pointless, unnecessary; **è stato tutto** ~! it was all in vain!
inutilità *sf* uselessness; pointlessness.
inutliz'zabile [inutilid'dzabile] *ag* unusable.
inutil'mente *av* (*senza risultato*) fruitlessly; (*senza utilità, scopo*) unnecessarily, needlessly; **l'ho cercato** ~ I looked for him in vain; **ti preoccupi** ~ there's nothing for you to worry about, there's no need for you to worry.
inva'dente *ag* (*fig*) intrusive.
inva'denza [inva'dɛntsa] *sf* intrusiveness.
in'vadere *vt* to invade; (*affollare*) to swarm into, overrun; (*sog: acque*) to flood.
invadi'trice [invadi'trit∫e] *ag f vedi* **invasore**.
inva'ghirsi [inva'girsi] *vr*: ~ **di** to take a fancy to.
invali'cabile *ag* (*montagna*) impassable.
invali'dare *vt* to invalidate.
invalidità *sf* infirmity; disability; (*DIR*) invalidity.
in'valido, a *ag* (*infermo*) infirm; (*al lavoro*) disabled; (*DIR*: *nullo*) invalid ♦ *sm/f* invalid; disabled person; ~ **di guerra** disabled ex-serviceman; ~ **del lavoro** industrially disabled person.

in'valso, a *ag (diffuso)* established.
in'vano *av* in vain.
invari'abile *ag* invariable.
invari'ato, a *ag* unchanged.
inva'sare *vt (pianta)* to pot.
inva'sato, a *ag* possessed (by the devil)
♦ *sm/f* person possessed by the devil;
urlare come un ~ to shout like a
madman.
invasi'one *sf* invasion.
in'vaso, a *pp di* **invadere.**
inva'sore, invadi'trice [invadi'tritʃe] *ag*
invading ♦ *sm* invader.
invecchia'mento [invekkja'mento] *sm*
growing old; ageing; **questo whisky ha un**
~ **di 12 anni** this whisky has been
matured for 12 years.
invecchi'are [invek'kjare] *vi (persona)* to
grow old; *(vino, popolazione)* to age;
(moda) to become dated ♦ *vt* to age; *(far
apparire più vecchio)* to make look older; **lo
trovo invecchiato** I find he has aged.
in'vece [in'vetʃe] *av* instead; *(al contrario)*
on the contrary; ~ **di** *prep* instead of.
inve'ire *vi:* ~ **contro** to rail against.
invele'nire *vt* to embitter; ~**rsi** *vr* to
become bitter.
inven'duto, a *ag* unsold.
inven'tare *vt* to invent; *(pericoli,
pettegolezzi)* to make up, invent.
inventari'are *vt* to make an inventory of,
inventory.
inven'tario *sm* inventory; *(COMM)*
stocktaking *no pl.*
inven'tivo, a *ag* inventive ♦ *sf*
inventiveness.
inven'tore, 'trice *sm/f* inventor.
invenzi'one [inven'tsjone] *sf* invention;
(bugia) lie, story.
invere'condia *sf* shamelessness,
immodesty.
inver'nale *ag* winter *cpd*; *(simile all'inverno)*
wintry.
in'verno *sm* winter; **d'**~ in (the) winter.
invero'simile *ag* unlikely ♦ *sm:* **ha dell'**~
it's hard to believe, it's incredible.
inversi'one *sf* inversion; **"divieto d'**~**"**
(AUT) "no U-turns".
in'verso, a *ag* opposite; *(MAT)* inverse ♦ *sm*
contrary, opposite; **in senso** ~ in the
opposite direction; **in ordine** ~ in reverse
order.
inverte'brato, a *ag, sm* invertebrate.
inver'tire *vt* to invert; *(disposizione, posti)*
to change; *(ruoli)* to exchange; ~ **la
marcia** *(AUT)* to do a U-turn; ~ **la rotta**
(NAUT) to go about; *(fig)* to do a U-turn.
inver'tito, a *sm/f* homosexual.

investi'gare *vt, vi* to investigate.
investiga'tivo, a *ag:* **squadra** ~**a** detective
squad.
investiga'tore, 'trice *sm/f* investigator,
detective.
investigazi'one [investigat'tsjone] *sf*
investigation, inquiry.
investi'mento *sm (ECON)* investment; *(di
veicolo)* crash, collision; *(di pedone)*
knocking down.
inves'tire *vt (denaro)* to invest; *(sog:
veicolo: pedone)* to knock down; *(: altro
veicolo)* to crash into; *(apostrofare)* to
assail; *(incaricare):* ~ **qn di** to invest sb
with; ~**rsi** *vr (fig):* ~**rsi di una parte** to
enter thoroughly into a role.
investi'tore, 'trice *sm/f* driver responsible
for an accident.
investi'tura *sf* investiture.
invete'rato, a *ag* inveterate.
invet'tiva *sf* invective.
invi'are *vt* to send.
invi'ato, a *sm/f* envoy; *(STAMPA)*
correspondent.
in'vidia *sf* envy; **fare** ~ **a qn** to make sb
envious.
invidi'abile *ag* enviable.
invidi'are *vt:* ~ **qn (per qc)** to envy sb (for
sth); ~ **qc a qn** to envy sb sth; **non aver
nulla da** ~ **a nessuno** to be as good as the
next one.
invidi'oso, a *ag* envious.
invin'cibile [invin'tʃibile] *ag* invincible.
in'vio, 'vii *sm* sending; *(insieme di merci)*
consignment.
invio'labile *ag* inviolable.
invio'lato, a *ag (diritto, segreto)* inviolate;
(foresta) virgin *cpd*; *(montagna, vetta)*
unscaled.
invipe'rire *vi,* ~**rsi** *vr* to become furious,
fly into a temper.
invipe'rito, a *ag* furious.
invis'chiare [invis'kjare] *vt (fig):* ~ **qn in qc**
to involve sb in sth, mix sb up in sth; ~**rsi**
vr: ~**rsi (con qn/in qc)** to get mixed up *o*
involved (with sb/in sth).
invi'sibile *ag* invisible.
in'viso, a *ag:* ~ **a** unpopular with.
invi'tante *ag (proposta, odorino)* inviting;
(sorriso) appealing, attractive.
invi'tare *vt* to invite; ~ **qn a fare** to invite
sb to do.
invi'tato, a *sm/f* guest.
in'vito *sm* invitation; **dietro** ~ **del sig. Rossi**
at Mr Rossi's invitation.
invo'care *vt (chiedere: aiuto, pace)* to cry
out for; *(appellarsi: la legge, Dio)* to appeal
to, invoke.

invogli'are [invoʎ'ʎare] *vt*: ~ qn a fare to tempt sb to do, induce sb to do.

involon'tario, a *ag* (*errore*) unintentional; (*gesto*) involuntary.

invol'tino *sm* (*CUC*) roulade.

in'volto *sm* (*pacco*) parcel; (*fagotto*) bundle.

in'volucro *sm* cover, wrapping.

involu'tivo, a *ag*: subire un processo ~ to regress.

invo'luto, a *ag* involved, intricate.

involuzi'one [involut'tsjone] *sf* (*di stile*) convolutedness; (*regresso*): subire un'~ to regress.

invulne'rabile *ag* invulnerable.

inzacche'rare [intsakke'rare] *vt* to spatter with mud; ~rsi *vr* to get muddy.

inzup'pare [intsup'pare] *vt* to soak; ~rsi *vr* to get soaked; inzuppò i biscotti nel latte he dipped the biscuits in the milk.

'io *pron* I ♦ *sm inv*: l'~ the ego, the self; ~ stesso(a) I myself; sono ~ it's me.

i'odio *sm* iodine.

l'ogurt *sm inv* = yoghurt.

i'one *sm* ion.

l'onio *sm*: lo ~, il mar ~ the Ionian (Sea).

ionizza'tore [joniddza'tore] *sm* ioniser.

'iosa: a ~ *av* in abundance.

'IPAB *sigla fpl* (= *Istituzioni pubbliche di Assistenza e Beneficenza*) *charitable institutions.*

i'perbole *sf* (*LETTERATURA*) hyperbole; (*MAT*) hyperbola.

iper'bolico, a, ci, che *ag* (*LETTERATURA, MAT*) hyperbolic(al); (*fig: esagerato*) exaggerated.

ipermer'cato *sm* hypermarket.

ipersen'sibile *ag* (*persona*) hypersensitive; (*FOT: lastra, pellicola*) hypersensitized.

ipertecno'logico, a, ci, che [ipertekno'lɔdʒiko] *ag* hi-tech.

ipertensi'one *sf* high blood pressure, hypertension.

iper'testo *sm* hypertext.

ip'nosi *sf* hypnosis.

ip'notico, a, ci, che *ag* hypnotic.

ipno'tismo *sm* hypnotism.

ipnotiz'zare [ipnotid'dzare] *vt* to hypnotize.

ipoaller'genico, a, ci, che [ipoaller'dʒeniko] *ag* hypoallergenic.

ipocon'dria *sf* hypochondria.

ipocon'driaco, a, ci, che *ag, sm/f* hypochondriac.

ipocri'sia *sf* hypocrisy.

i'pocrita, i, e *ag* hypocritical ♦ *sm/f* hypocrite.

ipo'sodico, a, ci, che *ag* low sodium *cpd*.

ipo'teca, che *sf* mortgage.

ipote'care *vt* to mortgage.

ipote'nusa *sf* hypotenuse.

i'potesi *sf inv* hypothesis; facciamo l'~ che ..., ammettiamo per ~ che ... let's suppose *o* assume that ...; nella peggiore/migliore delle ~ at worst/best; nell'~ che venga should he come, if he comes; se per ~ io partissi ... just supposing I were to leave....

ipo'tetico, a, ci, che *ag* hypothetical.

ipotiz'zare [ipotid'dzare] *vt*: ~ che to form the hypothesis that.

'ippico, a, ci, che *ag* horse *cpd* ♦ *sf* horse-racing.

ippocas'tano *sm* horse chestnut.

ip'podromo *sm* racecourse.

ippo'potamo *sm* hippopotamus.

'ipsilon *sf o m inv* (*lettera*) Y, y; (: *dell'alfabeto greco*) epsilon.

IP'SOA *sigla m* (= *Istituto Post-Universitario per lo Studio dell'Organizzazione Aziendale*) *postgraduate institute of business administration.*

IRA *sigla f* (= *Irish Republican Army*) IRA.

'ira *sf* anger, wrath.

ira'cheno, a [ira'keno] *ag, sm/f* Iraqi.

l'ran *sm*: l'~ Iran.

irani'ano, a *ag, sm/f* Iranian.

l'raq *sm*: l'~ Iraq.

iras'cibile [iraʃ'ʃibile] *ag* irascible, quick-tempered.

'IRCE ['irtʃe] *sigla m* = *Istituto per le relazioni culturali con l'Estero.*

'IRI *sigla m* (= *Istituto per la Ricostruzione Industriale*) *state-controlled industrial investment office.*

'iride *sf* (*arcobaleno*) rainbow; (*ANAT, BOT*) iris.

Ir'landa *sf*: l'~ Ireland; l'~ del Nord Northern Ireland, Ulster; la Repubblica d'~ Eire, the Republic of Ireland; il mar d'~ the Irish Sea.

irlan'dese *ag* Irish ♦ *sm/f* Irishman/woman; gli I~i the Irish.

iro'nia *sf* irony.

i'ronico, a, ci, che *ag* ironic(al).

ironiz'zare [ironid'dzare] *vt, vi*: ~ su to be ironical about.

i'roso, a *ag* (*sguardo, tono*) angry, wrathful; (*persona*) irascible.

'IRPEF *sigla f vedi* imposta sul reddito delle persone fisiche.

ir'pino, a *ag* of (*o* from) Irpinia.

irradi'are *vt* to radiate; (*sog: raggi di luce: illuminare*) to shine on ♦ *vi* (*diffondersi: anche*: ~rsi) to radiate.

irradiazi'one [irradjat'tsjone] *sf* radiation.

irraggiun'gibile [irraddʒun'dʒibile] *ag* unreachable; (*fig: meta*) unattainable.

irragio'nevole [irradʒo'nevole] *ag* (*privo di ragione*) irrational; (*fig*: *persona, pretese, prezzo*) unreasonable.

irrazio'nale [irrattsjo'nale] *ag* irrational.

irre'ale *ag* unreal.

irrealiz'zabile [irrealid'dzabile] *ag* (*sogno, desiderio*) unattainable, unrealizable; (*progetto*) unworkable, impracticable.

irrealtà *sf* unreality.

irrecupe'rabile *ag* (*gen*) irretrievable; (*fig*: *persona*) irredeemable.

irrecu'sabile *ag* (*offerta*) not to be refused; (*prova*) irrefutable.

irreden'tista, i, e *ag, smf* (*STORIA*) Irredentist.

irrefre'nabile *ag* uncontrollable.

irrefu'tabile *ag* irrefutable.

irrego'lare *ag* irregular; (*terreno*) uneven.

irregolarità *sf inv* irregularity; unevenness *no pl.*

irremo'vibile *ag* (*fig*) unshakeable, unyielding.

irrepa'rabile *ag* irreparable; (*fig*) inevitable.

irrepe'ribile *ag* nowhere to be found.

irrepren'sibile *ag* irreproachable.

irrequi'eto, a *ag* restless.

irresis'tibile *ag* irresistible.

irreso'luto, a *ag* irresolute.

irrespi'rabile *ag* (*aria*) unbreathable; (*fig*: *opprimente*) stifling, oppressive; (: *malsano*) unhealthy.

irrespon'sabile *ag* irresponsible.

irrestrin'gibile [irrestrin'dʒibile] *ag* unshrinkable, non-shrink (*BRIT*).

irre'tire *vt* to seduce.

irrever'sibile *ag* irreversible.

irrevo'cabile *ag* irrevocable.

irricono'scibile [irrikonoʃ'ʃibile] *ag* unrecognizable.

irridu'cibile [irridu'tʃibile] *ag* irreducible; (*fig*) unshakeable.

irrifles'sivo, a *ag* thoughtless.

irri'gare *vt* (*annaffiare*) to irrigate; (*sog: fiume etc*) to flow through.

irrigazi'one [irrigat'tsjone] *sf* irrigation.

irrigidi'mento [irridʒidi'mento] *sm* stiffening; hardening; tightening.

irrigi'dire [irridʒi'dire] *vt* to stiffen; (*disciplina*) to tighten; ~rsi *vr* to stiffen; (*posizione, atteggiamento*) to harden.

irriguar'doso, a *ag* disrespectful.

irrile'vante *ag* (*trascurabile*) insignificant.

irrimedi'abile *ag*: **un errore** ~ a mistake which cannot be rectified; **non è** ~! we can do something about it!

irrinunci'abile [irrinun'tʃabile] *ag* vital; which cannot be abandoned.

irripe'tibile *ag* unrepeatable.

irri'solto, a *ag* (*problema*) unresolved.

irri'sorio, a *ag* derisory.

irrispet'toso, a *ag* disrespectful.

irri'tabile *ag* irritable.

irri'tante *ag* (*atteggiamento*) irritating, annoying; (*MED*) irritant.

irri'tare *vt* (*mettere di malumore*) to irritate, annoy; (*MED*) to irritate; ~rsi *vr* (*stizzirsi*) to become irritated *o* annoyed; (*MED*) to become irritated.

irritazi'one [irritat'tsjone] *sf* irritation; annoyance.

irrive'rente *ag* irreverent.

irrobus'tire *vt* (*persona*) to make stronger, make more robust; (*muscoli*) to strengthen; ~rsi *vr* to become stronger.

ir'rompere *vi*: ~ **in** to burst into.

irro'rare *vt* to sprinkle; (*AGR*) to spray.

ir'rotto, a *pp di* **irrompere**.

irru'ente *ag* (*fig*) impetuous, violent.

irru'enza [irru'entsa] *sf* impetuousness; **con** ~ impetuously.

ir'ruppi *etc vb vedi* **irrompere**.

irruvi'dire *vt* to roughen ♦ *vi* (*anche*: ~rsi) to become rough.

irruzi'one [irrut'tsjone] *sf*: **fare** ~ **in** to burst into; (*sog: polizia*) to raid.

ir'suto, a *ag* (*petto*) hairy; (*barba*) bristly.

'irto, a *ag* bristly; ~ **di** bristling with.

Is. *abbr* (= *isola*) I.

ISBN *abbr* (= *International Standard Book Number*) ISBN.

is'crissi *etc vb vedi* **iscrivere**.

is'critto, a *pp di* **iscrivere** ♦ *smf* member; **gli** ~**i alla gara** the competitors; **per** *o* **in** ~ in writing.

is'crivere *vt* to register, enter; (*persona*): ~ (**a**) to register (in), enrol (in); ~rsi *vr*: ~rsi (**a**) (*club, partito*) to join; (*università*) to register *o* enrol (at); (*esame, concorso*) to register *o* enter (for).

iscrizi'one [iskrit'tsjone] *sf* (*epigrafe etc*) inscription; (*a scuola, società etc*) enrolment; registration.

'ISEF *sigla m* = *Istituto Superiore di Educazione Fisica*.

Is'lam *sm*: **l'** ~ Islam.

is'lamico, a, ci, che *ag* Islamic.

Is'landa *sf*: **l'** ~ Iceland.

islan'dese *ag* Icelandic ♦ *smf* Icelander ♦ *sm* (*LING*) Icelandic.

'isola *sf* island; ~ **pedonale** (*AUT*) pedestrian precinct.

isola'mento *sm* isolation; (*TECN*) insulation; **essere in cella di** ~ to be in solitary confinement; ~ **acustico** soundproofing; ~ **termico** thermal

insulation.
iso'lano, a *ag* island *cpd* ♦ *sm/f* islander.
iso'lante *ag* insulating ♦ *sm* insulator.
iso'lare *vt* to isolate; (*TECN*) to insulate; (*: acusticamente*) to soundproof.
iso'lato, a *ag* isolated; insulated ♦ *sm* (*edificio*) block.
isolazio'nismo [isolattsjo'nismo] *sm* isolationism.
i'sotopo *sm* isotope.
ispessi'mento *sm* thickening.
ispes'sire *vt* to thicken; ~**rsi** *vr* to get thicker, thicken.
ispetto'rato *sm* inspectorate.
ispet'tore, 'trice *sm/f* inspector; (*COMM*) supervisor; ~ **di zona** (*COMM*) area supervisor *o* manager; ~ **di reparto** shop walker (*BRIT*), floor walker (*US*).
ispezio'nare [ispettsjo'nare] *vt* to inspect.
ispezi'one [ispet'tsjone] *sf* inspection.
'ispido, a *ag* bristly, shaggy.
ispi'rare *vt* to inspire; ~**rsi** *vi*. ~**rsi a** to draw one's inspiration from; (*conformarsi*) to be based on, l'**luea** m'**ispirò** the luea appeals to me.
Ispira'tore, 'trice *ag* inspiring ♦ *sm/f* inspirer; (*di ribellione*) instigator.
ispirazi'one [ispiral'tsjone] *sf* inspiration, **secondo l'**~ **del momento** according to the mood of the moment.
israeli'ano, a *ag, sm/f* Israeli.
israe'lita, i, e *sm/f* Jew/Jewess; (*STORIA*) Israelite.
israe'litico, a, ci, che *ag* Jewish.
is'sare *vt* to hoist; ~ **l'ancora** to weigh anchor.
'Istanbul *sf* Istanbul.
istan'taneo, a *ag* instantaneous ♦ *sf* (*FOT*) snapshot.
is'tante *sm* instant, moment; **all'**~, **sull'**~ instantly, immediately.
is'tanza [is'tantsa] *sf* petition, request; **giudice di prima** ~ (*DIR*) judge of the court of first instance; **giudizio di seconda** ~ (*fig*) judgment on appeal; **in ultima** ~ (*fig*) finally; ~ **di divorzio** petition for divorce.
'ISTAT *sigla m* = *Istituto Centrale di Statistica.*
'ISTEL *sigla f* = *Indagine sull'ascolto delle televisioni in Italia.*
is'terico, a, ci, che *ag* hysterical.
isteri'lire *vt* (*terreno*) to render infertile; (*fig: fantasia*) to dry up; ~**rsi** *vr* to become infertile; to dry up.
iste'rismo *sm* hysteria.
isti'gare *vt* to incite.
istigazi'one [istigat'tsjone] *sf* instigation; ~ **a delinquere** (*DIR*) incitement to crime.

istin'tivo, a *ag* instinctive.
is'tinto *sm* instinct.
istitu'ire *vt* (*fondare*) to institute, found; (*porre: confronto*) to establish; (*intraprendere: inchiesta*) to set up.
isti'tuto *sm* institute; (*di università*) department; (*ente, DIR*) institution; ~ **di bellezza** beauty salon; ~ **di credito** bank, banking institution; ~ **tecnico commerciale** ≈ commercial college; ~ **tecnico industriale statale** ≈ technical college.
istitu'tore, 'trice *sm/f* (*fondatore*) founder; (*precettore*) tutor/governess.
istituzi'one [istitut'tsjone] *sf* institution; ~**i** *sfpl* (*DIR*) institutes; **lotta alle** ~**i** struggle against the Establishment.
'istmo *sm* (*GEO*) isthmus.
isto'gramma, i *sm* histogram
istra'dare *vt* (*fig: persona*): ~ (**a/verso**) to direct (to/towards).
istri'ano, a *ag* *sm/f* Istrian.
'istrice l'istritʃe] *sm* porcupine.
istri'one *sm* (*peg*) ham (actor).
istru'ire *vt* (*insegnare*) to teach; (*ammaestrare*) to train; (*informare*) to instruct, inform; (*DIR*) to prepare.
istru'ito, a *ag* educated.
istrut'tivo, a *ag* instructive.
istrut'tore, 'trice *sm/f* instructor ♦ *ag*: **giudice** ~ examining (*BRIT*) *o* committing (*US*) magistrate.
istrut'toria *sf* (*DIR*) (preliminary) investigation and hearing; **formalizzare un'**~ to proceed to a formal hearing.
istruzi'one [istrut'tsjone] *sf* (*gen*) training; (*INS, cultura*) education; (*direttiva*) instruction; (*DIR*) = **istruttoria; Ministero della Pubblica I**~ Ministry of Education; ~**i di spedizione** forwarding instructions; ~**i per l'uso** instructions (for use).
istupi'dire *vt* (*sog: colpo*) to stun, daze; (*: droga, stanchezza*) to stupefy; ~**rsi** *vr* to become stupid.
'ISVE *sigla m* (= *Istituto di Studi per lo Sviluppo Economico*) institute for research into economic development.
l'talia *sf*: **l'**~ Italy.
itali'ano, a *ag* Italian ♦ *sm/f* Italian ♦ *sm* (*LING*) Italian; **gli I**~**i** the Italians.
ITC *sigla m* = *istituto tecnico commerciale.*
'iter *sm* passage, course; **l'**~ **burocratico** the bureaucratic process.
itine'rante *ag* wandering, itinerant; **mostra** ~ touring exhibition; **spettacolo** ~ travelling (*BRIT*) *o* traveling (*US*) show, touring show.
itine'rario *sm* itinerary.

'ITIS *sigla m* = **istituto tecnico industriale statale.**

itte'rizia [itte'rittsja] *sf* (*MED*) jaundice.

'ittico, a, ci, che *ag* fish *cpd*; fishing *cpd.*

IUD *sigla m inv* (= *intra-uterine device*) IUD.

Iugos'lavia *sf* = **Jugoslavia.**

iugos'lavo, a *ag, sm/f* = **jugoslavo, a.**

i'uta *sf* jute.

'I.V.A. *sigla f vedi* **imposta sul valore aggiunto.**

'ivi *av* (*formale, poetico*) therein; (*nelle citazioni*) ibid.

—————————— *J j*

J, j [i'lunga] *sm o f inv* (*lettera*) J, j; ~ **come Jersey** ≈ J for Jack (*BRIT*), J for Jig (*US*).

jazz [dʒaz] *sm* jazz.

jaz'zista, i [dʒad'dzista] *sm* jazz player.

jeans [dʒinz] *smpl* jeans.

jeep [dʒip] *sm inv* jeep.

'jersey ['dʒɛrzi] *sm inv* jersey (cloth).

'jockey ['dʒɔki] *sm inv* (*CARTE*) jack; (*fantino*) jockey.

'jogging ['dʒɔgiŋ] *sm* jogging; **fare** ~ to go jogging.

'jolly ['dʒɔli] *sm inv* joker.

jr. *abbr* (= *junior*) Jr., jr.

ju'do [dʒu'dɔ] *sm* judo.

Jugos'lavia [jugoz'lavja] *sf*: **la** ~ Yugoslavia.

jugos'lavo, a *ag, sm/f* Yugoslav(ian).

'juke 'box ['dʒuk'bɔks] *sm inv* jukebox.

—————————— *K k*

K, k ['kappa] *sf o m inv* (*lettera*) K, k ♦ *abbr* (= *kilo-, chilo-*) k; (*INFORM*) K; **K come Kursaal** ≈ K for King.

Kam'pala *sf* Kampala.

kara'kiri *sm* harakiri.

karatè [kara'tɛ] *sm* karate.

'Kashmir ['kaʃmir] *sm*: **il** ~ Kashmir.

ka'yak [ka'jak] *sm inv* kayak.

'Kenia ['kenja] *sm*: **il** ~ Kenya.

keni'ano, a, keni'ota, i, e *ag, sm/f* Kenyan.

'Kenya ['kenja] *sm*: **il** ~ Kenya.

kero'sene [kero'zɛne] *sm* = **cherosene.**

kg *abbr* (= *chilogrammo*) kg.

kib'butz [kib'buts] *sm inv* kibbutz.

Kilimangi'aro [kiliman'dʒaro] *sm*: **il** ~ Kilimanjaro.

'killer ['killer] *sm inv* gunman, hired gun.

'kilo *etc* = **chilo** *etc.*

kilt [kilt] *sm inv* kilt.

ki'mono [ki'mɔno] *sm* = **chimono.**

kitsch [kitʃ] *sm* kitsch.

'kiwi ['kiwi] *sm inv* kiwi (fruit).

km *abbr* (= *chilometro*) km.

kmq *abbr* (= *chilometro quadrato*) km².

ko'ala [ko'ala] *sm inv* koala (bear).

KR *sigla* = Crotone.

'krapfen ['krapfən] *sm inv* doughnut.

Ku'ala Lum'par *sf* Kuala Lumpur.

Ku'wait [ku'vait] *sm*: **il** ~ Kuwait.

kW *abbr* (= *kilowatt, chilowatt*) kW.

kWh *abbr* (= *kilowattora*) kW/h.

—————————— *L l*

L, l ['ɛlle] *sf o m inv* (*lettera*) L, l ♦ *abbr* (= *lira*) L; **L come Livorno** ≈ L for Lucy (*BRIT*), L for Love (*US*).

l *abbr* (= *litro*) l.

l' *det vedi* **la, lo.**

la *det f* (*dav V l'*) the ♦ *pron* (*dav V l'*) (*oggetto: persona*) her; (*: cosa*) it; (*: forma di cortesia*) you ♦ *sm inv* (*MUS*) A; (*: solfeggiando la scala*) la; *vedi anche* **il.**

là *av* there; **di** ~ (*da quel luogo*) from there; (*in quel luogo*) in there; (*dall'altra parte*) over there; **di** ~ **di** beyond; **per di** ~ that way; **più in** ~ further on; (*tempo*) later on; ~ **dentro/sopra/sotto** in/up (*o* on)/under there; ~ **per** ~ (*sul momento*) there and then; **essere in** ~ **con gli anni** to be getting on (in years); **essere più di** ~ **che di qua** to be more dead than alive; **va'** ~! come off it!; **stavolta è andato troppo in** ~ this time he's gone too far; *vedi anche* **quello.**

'labbro *sm* (*pl(f)*: **labbra**: *solo nel senso ANAT*) lip.

'labile *ag* fleeting, ephemeral.

labi'rinto *sm* labyrinth, maze.

labora'torio sm (di ricerca) laboratory; (di arti, mestieri) workshop; ~ **linguistico** language laboratory.

labori'oso, a ag (faticoso) laborious; (attivo) hard-working.

labu'rista, i, e ag Labour cpd (BRIT) ♦ sm/f Labour Party member (BRIT).

'lacca, che sf lacquer; (per unghie) nail varnish (BRIT), nail polish.

lac'care vt (mobili) to varnish, lacquer.

'laccio ['lattʃo] sm noose; (legaccio, tirante) lasso; (di scarpa) lace; ~ **emostatico** (MED) tourniquet.

lace'rante [latʃe'rante] ag (suono) piercing, shrill.

lace'rare [latʃe'rare] vt to tear to shreds, lacerate; ~**rsi** vr to tear.

lacerazi'one [latʃerat'tsjone] sf (anche MED) tear.

'lacero, a ['latʃero] ag (logoro) torn, tattered; (MED) lacerated; **ferita ~-contusa** injury with lacerations and bruising.

la'conico, a, ci, che ag laconic, brief.

'lacrima sf tear; (goccia) drop; in ~**e** in tears.

lacri'mare vi to water.

lacri'mevole ag heartrending, pitiful.

lacri'mogeno, a [lakri'mɔdʒeno] ag: **gas ~** tear gas.

lacri'moso, a ag tearful.

la'cuna sf (fig) gap.

la'custre ag lake cpd.

lad'dove cong whereas.

'ladro sm thief; **al ~!** stop thief!

ladro'cinio [ladro'tʃinjo] sm theft, robbery.

la'druncolo, a sm/f petty thief.

laggiù [lad'dʒu] av down there; (di là) over there.

'lagna ['laɲɲa] sf (fam: persona, cosa) drag, bore; **fare la ~** to whine, moan.

la'gnanza [laɲ'ɲantsa] sf complaint.

la'gnarsi [laɲ'ɲarsi] vr: ~ **(di)** to complain (about).

'lago, ghi sm lake.

'Lagos ['lagos] sf Lagos.

'lagrima etc = **lacrima** etc.

la'guna sf lagoon.

lagu'nare ag lagoon cpd.

'laico, a, ci, che ag (apostolato) lay; (vita) secular; (scuola) non-denominational ♦ sm/f layman/woman ♦ sm lay brother.

'laido, a ag filthy, foul; (fig: osceno) obscene, filthy.

'lama sf blade ♦ sm inv (ZOOL) llama; (REL) lama.

lambic'care vt to distil; ~**rsi il cervello** to rack one's brains.

lam'bire vt (fig: sog: fiamme) to lick; (: acqua) to lap.

lam'bretta ® sf scooter.

la'mella sf (di metallo etc) thin sheet, thin strip; (di fungo) gill.

lamen'tare vt to lament; ~**rsi** vr (emettere lamenti) to moan, groan; (rammaricarsi): ~**rsi (di)** to complain (about).

lamen'tela sf complaining no pl.

lamen'tevole ag (voce) complaining, plaintive; (stato) lamentable, pitiful.

la'mento sm moan, groan; (per la morte di qn) lament.

lamen'toso, a ag plaintive.

la'metta sf razor blade.

lami'era sf sheet metal.

'lamina sf (lastra sottile) thin sheet (o layer o plate); ~ **d'oro** gold leaf; gold foil.

lami'nare vt to laminate.

lami'nato, a ag laminated; (tessuto) lamé ♦ sm laminate.

'lampada sf lamp; ~ **a petrolio/a gas** oil/gas lamp; ~ **a spirito** blowlamp (BRIT), blowtorch; ~ **a stelo** standard lamp (BRIT), floor lamp; ~ **da tavolo** table lamp.

lampa'dario sm chandelier.

lampa'dina sf light bulb; ~ **tascabile** pocket torch (BRIT), flashlight (US).

lam'pante ag (fig: evidente) crystal clear, evident.

lam'para sf fishing lamp; (barca) boat for fishing by lamplight (in Mediterranean).

lampeggi'are [lamped'dʒare] vi (luce, fari) to flash ♦ vb impers: **lampeggia** there's lightning.

lampeggia'tore [lampeddʒa'tore] sm (AUT) indicator.

lampi'one sm street light o lamp (BRIT).

'lampo sm (METEOR) flash of lightning; (di luce, fig) flash ♦ ag inv: **cerniera ~** zip (fastener) (BRIT), zipper (US); **guerra ~** blitzkrieg; ~**i** smpl (METEOR) lightning no pl; **passare come un ~** to flash past o by.

lam'pone sm raspberry.

'lana sf wool; ~ **d'acciaio** steel wool; **pura ~ vergine** pure new wool; ~ **di vetro** glass wool.

lan'cetta [lan'tʃetta] sf (indice) pointer, needle; (di orologio) hand.

'lancia, ce ['lantʃa] sf (arma) lance; (: picca) spear; (di pompa antincendio) nozzle; (imbarcazione) launch; **partire ~ in resta** (fig) to set off ready for battle; **spezzare una ~ in favore di qn** (fig) to come to sb's defence; ~ **di salvataggio** lifeboat.

lancia'bombe [lantʃa'bombe] sm inv (MIL) mortar.

lanciafi'amme [lantʃa'fjamme] sm inv

flamethrower.
lancia'missili [lantʃa'missili] _ag inv_ missile-launching ♦ _sm inv_ missile launcher.
lancia'razzi [lantʃa'raddzi] _ag inv_ rocket-launching ♦ _sm inv_ rocket launcher.
lanci'are [lan'tʃare] _vt_ to throw, hurl, fling; (_SPORT_) to throw; (_far partire: automobile_) to get up to full speed; (_bombe_) to drop; (_razzo, prodotto, moda_) to launch; (_emettere: grido_) to give out; ~**rsi** _vr_: ~**rsi contro/su** to throw _o_ hurl _o_ fling o.s. against/on; ~**rsi in** (_fig_) to embark on; ~ **un cavallo** to give a horse his head; ~ **il disco** (_SPORT_) to throw the discus; ~ **il peso** (_SPORT_) to put the shot; ~**rsi all'inseguimento di qn** to set off in pursuit of sb; ~**rsi col paracadute** to parachute.
lanciasi'luri [lantʃasi'luri] _sm inv_ torpedo tube.
lanci'ato, a [lan'tʃato] _ag_ (_affermato: attore, prodotto_) well-known, famous; (_veicolo_) speeding along, racing along.
lanci'nante [lantʃi'nante] _ag_ (_dolore_) shooting, throbbing; (_grido_) piercing.
'lancio ['lantʃo] _sm_ throwing _no pl_; throw; dropping _no pl_; drop; launching _no pl_; launch; ~ **del disco** (_SPORT_) throwing the discus; ~ **del peso** (_SPORT_) putting the shot.
'landa _sf_ (_GEO_) moor.
'languido, a _ag_ (_fiacco_) languid, weak; (_tenero, malinconico_) languishing.
langu'ire _vi_ to languish; (_conversazione_) to flag.
langu'ore _sm_ weakness, languor.
lani'ero, a _ag_ wool _cpd_, woollen (_BRIT_), woolen (_US_).
lani'ficio [lani'fitʃo] _sm_ woollen (_BRIT_) _o_ woolen (_US_) mill.
lano'lina _sf_ lanolin(e).
la'noso, a _ag_ woolly.
lan'terna _sf_ lantern; (_faro_) lighthouse.
lanter'nino _sm_: **cercarsele col** ~ to be asking for trouble.
la'nugine [la'nudʒine] _sf_ down.
'Laos _sm_ Laos.
lapalissi'ano, a _ag_ self-evident.
La 'Paz [la'pas] _sf_ La Paz.
lapi'dare _vt_ to stone.
lapi'dario, a _ag_ (_fig_) terse.
'lapide _sf_ (_di sepolcro_) tombstone; (_commemorativa_) plaque.
la'pin [la'pɛ̃] _sm inv_ coney.
'lapis _sm inv_ pencil.
'lappone _ag, sm/f, sm_ Lapp.
Lap'ponia _sf_: **la** ~ Lapland.
'lapsus _sm inv_ slip.

laptop ['læp tɔp] _sm inv_ laptop (computer).
'lardo _sm_ bacon fat, lard.
lar'ghezza [lar'gettsa] _sf_ width; breadth; looseness; generosity; ~ **di vedute** broad-mindedness.
lar'gire [lar'dʒire] _vt_ to give generously.
'largo, a, ghi, ghe _ag_ wide, broad; (_maniche_) wide; (_abito: troppo ampio_) loose; (_fig_) generous ♦ _sm_ width; breadth; (_mare aperto_): **il** ~ the open sea ♦ _sf_: **stare o tenersi alla** ~**a** (**da qn/qc**) to keep one's distance (from sb/sth), keep away (from sb/sth); ~ **due metri** two metres wide; ~ **di spalle** broad-shouldered; **di** ~**ghe vedute** broad-minded; **in** ~**a misura** to a great _o_ large extent; **su** ~**a scala** on a large scale; **di manica** ~**a** generous, open-handed; **al** ~ **di Genova** off (the coast of) Genoa; **farsi** ~ **tra la folla** to push one's way through the crowd.
'larice ['laritʃe] _sm_ (_BOT_) larch.
la'ringe [la'rindʒe] _sf_ larynx.
larin'gite [larin'dʒite] _sf_ laryngitis.
laringoi'atra, i, e _sm/f_ (_medico_) throat specialist.
'larva _sf_ larva; (_fig_) shadow.
la'sagne [la'zaɲɲe] _sfpl_ lasagna _sg_.
lasciapas'sare [laʃʃapas'sare] _sm inv_ pass, permit.
lasci'are [laʃ'ʃare] _vt_ to leave; (_abbandonare_) to leave, abandon, give up; (_cessare di tenere_) to let go of ♦ _vb aux_: ~ **qc to** let sb do sth ♦ _vi_: ~ **di fare** (_smettere_) to stop doing; ~**rsi andare/truffare** to let o.s. go/be cheated; ~ **andare** _o_ **correre** _o_ **perdere** to let things go their own way; ~ **stare qc/qn** to leave sth/sb alone; ~ **qn erede** to make sb one's heir; ~ **la presa** to lose one's grip; ~ **il segno (su qc)** to leave a mark (on sth); (_fig_) to leave one's mark (on sth); ~ **(molto) a desiderare** to leave much to be desired; **ci ha lasciato la vita** it cost him his life.
'lascito ['laʃʃito] _sm_ (_DIR_) legacy.
la'scivia [laʃ'ʃivja] _sf_ lust, lasciviousness.
la'scivo, a [laʃ'ʃivo] _ag_ lascivious.
'laser ['lazer] _ag, sm inv_: (_raggio_) ~ laser (beam).
lassa'tivo, a _ag, sm_ laxative.
las'sismo _sm_ laxity.
'lasso _sm_: ~ **di tempo** interval, lapse of time.
lassù _av_ up there.
'lastra _sf_ (_di pietra_) slab; (_di metallo, FOT_) plate; (_di ghiaccio, vetro_) sheet; (_radiografica_) X-ray (plate).
lastri'care _vt_ to pave.
lastri'cato _sm_ paving.

'lastrico, ci *o* chi *sm* paving; essere sul ~ (*fig*) to be penniless; gettare qn sul ~ (*fig*) to leave sb destitute.

las'trone *sm* (*ALPINISMO*) sheer rock face.

la'tente *ag* latent.

late'rale *ag* lateral, side *cpd*; (*uscita, ingresso etc*) side *cpd* ♦ *sm* (*CALCIO*) half-back.

lateral'mente *av* sideways.

late'rizio [late'rittsjo] *sm* (perforated) brick.

latifon'dista, i, e *sm/f* large agricultural landowner.

lati'fondo *sm* large estate.

la'tino, a *ag, sm* Latin.

la'tinoameri'cano, a *ag, sm/f* Latin-American.

lati'tante *ag*: essere ~ to be on the run ♦ *sm/f* fugitive (from justice).

lati'tanza [lati'tantsa] *sf*: darsi alla ~ to go into hiding.

lati'tudine *sf* latitude.

'lato, a *ag*: in senso ~ broadly speaking ♦ *sm* side; (*fig*) aspect, point of view; d'altro ~ (*d'altra parte*) on the other hand.

la'trare *vi* to bark.

lat'rato *sm* howling.

la'trina *sf* public lavatory.

latro'cinio [latro'tʃinjo] *sm* = ladrocinio.

'latta *sf* tin (plate); (*recipiente*) tin, can.

lat'taio, a *sm/f* (*distributore*) milkman/woman; (*commerciante*) dairyman/woman.

lat'tante *ag* unweaned ♦ *sm/f* breast-fed baby.

'latte *sm* milk; fratello di ~ foster brother; avere ancora il ~ alla bocca (*fig*) to be still wet behind the ears; tutto ~ e miele (*fig*) all smiles; ~ detergente cleansing milk *o* lotion; ~ intero full-cream milk; ~ magro *o* scremato skimmed milk; ~ secco *o* in polvere dried *o* powdered milk.

'latteo, a *ag* milky; (*dieta, prodotto*) milk *cpd*.

latte'ria *sf* dairy.

latti'cini [latti'tʃini] *smpl* dairy *o* milk products.

lat'tina *sf* (*di birra etc*) can.

lat'tuga, ghe *sf* lettuce.

'laurea *sf* ≈ degree; ~ breve *university degree awarded at the end of a three-year course*; avere una ~ in chimica to have a degree in chemistry *o* a chemistry degree; *vedi nota nel riquadro*.

LAUREA

The **Laurea** *is awarded to students who successfully complete their degree courses. Traditionally, this takes between four and six years; a major element of the final examinations is the presentation and discussion of a dissertation. A shorter, more vocational course of study, taking from two to three years, is also available; at the end of this time students receive a diploma called the* **Laurea breve**.

laure'ando, a *sm/f* final-year student.

laure'are *vt* to confer a degree on; ~rsi *vr* to graduate.

laure'ato, a *ag, sm/f* graduate.

'lauro *sm* laurel.

'lauto, a *ag* (*pranzo, mancia*) lavish.

'lava *sf* lava.

la'vabo *sm* washbasin.

la'vaggio [la'vaddʒo] *sm* washing *no pl*; ~ del cervello brainwashing *no pl*.

la'vagna [la'vaɲɲa] *sf* (*GEO*) slate; (*di scuola*) blackboard; ~ luminosa overhead projector.

la'vanda *sf* (*anche MED*) wash; (*BOT*) lavender; fare una ~ gastrica a qn to pump sb's stomach.

lavande'ria *sf* (*di ospedale, caserma etc*) laundry; ~ automatica launderette; ~ a secco dry-cleaner's.

lavan'dino *sm* sink; (*del bagno*) washbasin.

lavapi'atti *sm/f* dishwasher.

la'vare *vt* to wash; ~rsi *vr* to wash, have a wash; ~ a secco to dry-clean; ~rsi le mani/i denti to wash one's hands/clean one's teeth.

lava'secco *sm o f inv* dry-cleaner's.

lavasto'viglie [lavasto'viʎʎe] *sm o f inv* (*macchina*) dishwasher.

la'vata *sf* wash; (*fig*): dare una ~ di capo a qn to give sb a good telling-off.

lava'tivo *sm* (*clistere*) enema; (*buono a nulla*) good-for-nothing, idler.

lava'trice [lava'tritʃe] *sf* washing machine.

lava'tura *sf* washing *no pl*; ~ di piatti dishwater.

la'vello *sm* (kitchen) sink.

la'vina *sf* snowslide.

lavo'rare *vi* to work; (*fig: bar, studio etc*) to do good business ♦ *vt* to work; ~ a to work on; ~ a maglia to knit; ~ di fantasia (*suggestionarsi*) to imagine things; (*fantasticare*) to let one's imagination run free; ~rsi qn (*convincere*) to work on sb.

lavora'tivo, a *ag* working.

lavora'tore, 'trice *sm/f* worker ♦ *ag* working.

lavorazi'one [lavorat'tsjone] *sf* (*gen*) working; (*di legno, pietra*) carving; (*di film*) making; (*di prodotto*) manufacture; (*modo di esecuzione*) workmanship.

lavo'rio *sm* intense activity.

la'voro *sm* work; (*occupazione*) job, work *no pl*; (*opera*) piece of work, job; (*ECON*) labour (*BRIT*), labor (*US*); **Ministero del L**~ Department of Employment (*BRIT*), Department of Labor (*US*); (**fare**) **i** ~**i di casa** (to do) the housework *sg*; ~**i forzati** hard labour *sg*; **i** ~**i del parlamento** the parliamentary session *sg*; ~**i pubblici** public works.

lazi'ale [lat'tsjale] *ag* of (*o* from) Lazio.

lazza'retto [laddza'retto] *sm* leper hospital.

lazza'rone [laddza'rone] *sm* scoundrel.

'lazzo ['laddzo] *sm* jest.

LC *sigla* = Lecco.

LE *sigla* = Lecce.

le *det fpl* the ♦ *pron* (*oggetto*) them; (: *a lei, a essa*) (to) her; (: *forma di cortesia*) (to) you; *vedi anche* **il.**

le'ale *ag* loyal; (*sincero*) sincere; (*onesto*) fair.

lea'lista, i, e *sm/f* loyalist.

lealtà *sf* loyalty; sincerity; fairness.

'leasing ['li:ziŋ] *sm* leasing; lease.

'lebbra *sf* leprosy.

'lecca 'lecca *sm inv* lollipop.

leccapi'edi *sm/f inv* (*peg*) toady, bootlicker.

lec'care *vt* to lick; (*sog: gatto: latte etc*) to lick *o* lap up; (*fig*) to flatter; ~**rsi** *vr* (*fig*) to preen o.s.; ~**rsi i baffi** to lick one's lips.

lec'cato, a *ag* affected ♦ *sf* lick.

leccherò *etc* [lekke'rɔ] *vb vedi* **leccare.**

'leccio ['lettʃo] *sm* holm oak, ilex.

leccor'nia *sf* titbit, delicacy.

'lecito, a ['letʃito] *ag* permitted, allowed; **se mi è** ~ if I may; **mi sia** ~ **far presente che** ... may I point out that ....

'ledere *vt* to damage, injure; ~ **gli interessi di qn** to be prejudicial to sb's interests.

'lega, ghe *sf* (*anche POL*) league; (*di metalli*) alloy; **metallo di bassa** ~ base metal; **gente di bassa** ~ common *o* vulgar people; **L**~ **Nord** (*POL*) *federalist party.*

le'gaccio [le'gattʃo] *sm* string, lace.

le'gale *ag* legal ♦ *sm* lawyer; **corso** ~ **delle monete** official exchange rate; **medicina** ~ forensic medicine; **studio** ~ lawyer's office.

legalità *sf* legality, lawfulness.

legaliz'zare [legalid'dzare] *vt* to legalize; (*documento*) to authenticate.

legalizzazi'one [legaliddzat'tsjone] *sf* (*vedi*

vt) legalization; authentication.

le'game *sm* (*corda, fig: affettivo*) tie, bond; (*nesso logico*) link, connection; ~ **di sangue** *o* **di parentela** family tie.

lega'mento *sm* (*ANAT*) ligament.

le'gare *vt* (*prigioniero, capelli, cane*) to tie (up); (*libro*) to bind; (*CHIM*) to alloy; (*fig: collegare*) to bind, join ♦ *vi* (*far lega*) to unite; (*fig*) to get on well; **è pazzo da** ~ (*fam*) he should be locked up.

lega'tario, a *sm/f* (*DIR*) legatee.

le'gato *sm* (*REL*) legate; (*DIR*) legacy, bequest.

legato'ria *sf* (*attività*) bookbinding; (*negozio*) bookbinder's.

lega'tura *sf* (*di libro*) binding; (*MUS*) ligature.

legazi'one [legat'tsjone] *sf* legation.

le'genda [le'dʒɛnda] *sf* (*di carta geografica etc*) = **leggenda.**

'legge ['leddʒe] *sf* law; ~ **procedurale** procedural law.

leg'genda [led'dʒɛnda] *sf* (*narrazione*) legend; (*di carta geografica etc*) key, legend.

leggen'dario, a [leddʒen'darjo] *ag* legendary.

'leggere ['lɛddʒere] *vt, vi* to read; ~ **il pensiero di qn** to read sb's mind *o* thoughts.

legge'rezza [leddʒe'rettsa] *sf* lightness; thoughtlessness; fickleness.

leg'gero, a [led'dʒero] *ag* light; (*agile, snello*) nimble, agile, light; (*tè, caffè*) weak; (*fig: non grave, piccolo*) slight; (: *spensierato*) thoughtless; (: *incostante*) fickle; free and easy; **una ragazza** ~**a** (*fig*) a flighty girl; **alla** ~**a** thoughtlessly.

leggi'adro, a [led'dʒadro] *ag* pretty, lovely; (*movimenti*) graceful.

leg'gibile [led'dʒibile] *ag* legible; (*libro*) readable, worth reading.

leg'gio, 'gii [led'dʒio] *sm* lectern; (*MUS*) music stand.

legherò *etc* [lege'rɔ] *vb vedi* **legare.**

le'ghismo [le'gismo] *sm political movement with federalist tendencies.*

le'ghista, i, e [le'gista] (*POL*) *ag* of a "lega" (*especially Lega Nord*) ♦ *sm/f* member (*o* supporter) of a "lega" (*especially Lega Nord*).

legife'rare [ledʒife'rare] *vi* to legislate.

legio'nario [ledʒo'narjo] *sm* (*romano*) legionary; (*volontario*) legionnaire.

legi'one [le'dʒone] *sf* legion; ~ **straniera** foreign legion.

legisla'tivo, a [ledʒizla'tivo] *ag* legislative.

legisla'tore [ledʒizla'tore] *sm* legislator.

legisla'tura [ledʒizla'tura] *sf* legislature.
legislazi'one [ledʒizlat'tsjone] *sf*
legislation.
legitti'mare [ledʒitti'mare] *vt* (*figlio*) to
legitimize; (*comportamento etc*) to justify.
legittimità [ledʒittimi'ta] *sf* legitimacy.
le'gittimo, a [le'dʒittimo] *ag* legitimate;
(*fig: giustificato, lecito*) justified,
legitimate; ~ **a difesa** (*DIR*) self-defence
(*BRIT*), self-defense (*US*).
'legna ['leɲɲa] *sf* firewood.
le'gnaia [leɲ'naja] *sf* woodshed.
legnai'olo [leɲɲa'jɔlo] *sm* woodcutter.
le'gname [leɲ'ɲame] *sm* wood, timber.
le'gnata [leɲ'ɲata] *sf* blow with a stick;
dare a qn un sacco di ~e to give sb a
good hiding.
'legno ['leɲɲo] *sm* wood; (*pezzo di ~*) piece
of wood; **di ~** wooden; ~ **compensato**
plywood.
lo'gnoso, a [leɲ'ɲoso] *ag* (*di legno*) wooden;
(*come il legno*) woody; (*carne*) tough.
lo'gume *sm* (*BOT*) pulse; ~**i** *smpl* (*fagioli,
piselli etc*) pulses.
'lei *pron* (*soggetto*) she; (*oggetto: per dare
rilievo, con preposizione*) her; (*forma di
cortesia: anche: L~*) you ♦ *sf inv.* **la mia ~**
my beloved ♦ *sm*: **dare del ~ a qn** to
address sb as "lei"; ~ **stessa** she herself;
you yourself; **è ~** it's her.
'lembo *sm* (*di abito, strada*) edge; (*striscia
sottile: di terra*) strip.
lemma, i *sm* headword.
'lemme 'lemme *av* (very) very slowly.
'lena *sf* (*fig*) energy, stamina; **di buona ~**
(*lavorare, camminare*) at a good pace.
Lenin'grado *sf* Leningrad.
le'nire *vt* to soothe.
lenta'mente *avv* slowly.
'lente *sf* (*OTTICA*) lens *sg*; ~
d'ingrandimento magnifying glass; ~**i a
contatto**, ~**i corneali** contact lenses; ~**i (a
contatto) morbide** soft lenses; ~**i (a
contatto) rigide** hard lenses.
len'tezza [len'tettsa] *sf* slowness.
len'ticchia [len'tikkja] *sf* (*BOT*) lentil.
len'tiggine [len'tiddʒine] *sf* freckle.
'lento, a *ag* slow; (*molle: fune*) slack; (*non
stretto: vite, abito*) loose ♦ *sm* (*ballo*) slow
dance.
'lenza ['lɛntsa] *sf* fishing line.
lenzu'olo [len'tswɔlo] *sm* sheet; ~**a** *sfpl* pair
of sheets; ~ **funebre** shroud.
leon'cino [leon'tʃino] *sm* lion cub.
le'one *sm* lion; (*dello zodiaco*): **L~** Leo;
essere del L~ to be Leo.
leo'pardo *sm* leopard.
lepo'rino, a *ag*: **labbro ~** harelip.

'lepre *sf* hare.
'lercio, a, ci, ce ['lɛrtʃo] *ag* filthy.
lerci'ume [ler'tʃume] *sm* filth.
'lesbico, a, ci, che *ag, sf* lesbian.
'lesi *etc vb vedi* **ledere.**
lesi'nare *vt* to be stingy with ♦ *vi*: ~ **(su)** to
skimp (on), be stingy (with).
lesi'one *sf* (*MED*) lesion; (*DIR*) injury,
damage; (*EDIL*) crack.
le'sivo, a *ag*: ~ **(di)** damaging (to),
detrimental (to).
'leso, a *pp di* **ledere** ♦ *ag* (*offeso*) injured;
parte ~a (*DIR*) injured party; ~**a maestà**
lese-majesty.
les'sare *vt* (*CUC*) to boil.
'lessi *etc vb vedi* **leggere.**
lessi'cale *ag* lexical.
'lessico, ci *sm* vocabulary; (*dizionario*)
lexicon.
lessicogra'fia *sf* lexicography.
lessi'cografo, a *sm/f* lexicographer.
'lesso, a *ag* boiled ♦ *sm* boiled meat.
'lesto, a *ag* quick; (*agile*) nimble; ~ **di
mano** (*per rubare*) light-fingered; (*per
picchiare*) free with one's fists.
lesto'fante *sm* swindler, con man.
le'tale *ag* lethal, deadly.
leta'maio *sm* dunghill.
le'tame *sm* manure, dung.
le'targo, ghi *sm* lethargy; (*ZOOL*)
hibernation.
le'tizia [le'tittsja] *sf* joy, happiness.
'letta *sf*: **dare una ~ a qc** to glance o look
through sth.
'lettera *sf* letter; ~**e** *sfpl* (*letteratura*)
literature *sg*; (*studi umanistici*) arts
(subjects); **alla ~** literally; **in ~e** in
words, in full; **diventar ~ morta** (*legge*) to
become a dead letter; **restar ~ morta**
(*consiglio, invito*) to go unheeded; ~ **di
accompagnamento** accompanying letter;
~ **assicurata** registered letter; ~ **di
cambio** (*COMM*) bill of exchange; ~ **di
credito** (*COMM*) letter of credit; ~ **di
intenti** letter of intent; ~ **di presentazione**
o **raccomandazione** letter of introduction;
~ **raccomandata** recorded delivery (*BRIT*)
o certified (*US*) letter; ~ **di trasporto
aereo** (*COMM*) air waybill.
lette'rale *ag* literal.
letteral'mente *av* literally.
lette'rario, a *ag* literary.
lette'rato, a *ag* well-read, scholarly.
lettera'tura *sf* literature.
let'tiga, ghe *sf* (*portantina*) litter; (*barella*)
stretcher.
let'tino *sm* cot (*BRIT*), crib (*US*).
'letto, a *pp di* **leggere** ♦ *sm* bed; **andare a ~**

to go to bed; ~ **a castello** bunk beds *pl;* ~ **a una piazza/a due piazze** *o* **matrimoniale** single/double bed.
'lettone *ag, sm/f* Latvian ♦ *sm (LING)* Latvian, Lettish.
Let'tonia *sf:* **la** ~ Latvia.
lettorato *sm (INS)* lectorship, assistantship; *(REL)* lectorate.
let'tore, 'trice *sm/f* reader; *(INS)* (foreign language) assistant *(BRIT)*, (foreign) teaching assistant *(US)* ♦ *sm:* ~ **ottico (di caratteri)** optical character reader; ~ **CD** CD player.
let'tura *sf* reading.
leuce'mia [leutʃe'mia] *sf* leukaemia.
'leva *sf* lever; *(MIL)* conscription; **far** ~ **su qn** to work on sb; **essere di** ~ to be due for call-up; ~ **del cambio** *(AUT)* gear lever.
le'vante *sm* east; *(vento)* East wind; **il L**~ the Levant.
le'vare *vt (occhi, braccio)* to raise; *(sollevare, togliere: tassa, divieto)* to lift; *(: indumenti)* to take off, remove; *(rimuovere)* to take away; *(: dal di sopra)* to take off; *(: dal di dentro)* to take out; ~**rsi** *vr* to get up; *(sole)* to rise; ~ **le tende** *(fig)* to pack up and leave; ~**rsi il pensiero** to put one's mind at rest; **levati di mezzo** *o* **di lì** *o* **di torno!** get out of my way!
le'vata *sf (di posta)* collection.
leva'taccia, ce [leva'tattʃa] *sf* early rise.
leva'toio, a *ag:* **ponte** ~ drawbridge.
leva'trice [leva'tritʃe] *sf* midwife.
leva'tura *sf* intelligence, mental capacity.
levi'gare *vt* to smooth; *(con carta vetrata)* to sand.
levi'gato, a *ag (superficie)* smooth; *(fig: stile)* polished; *(: viso)* flawless.
levità *sf* lightness.
levri'ere *sm* greyhound.
lezi'one [let'tsjone] *sf* lesson; *(all'università, sgridata)* lecture; **fare** ~ to teach; to lecture.
lezi'oso, a [let'tsjoso] *ag* affected; simpering.
'lezzo ['leddzo] *sm* stench, stink.
lg *abbr (= lira sterlina)* £.
LI *sigla = Livorno.*
li *pron pl (oggetto)* them.
lì *av* there; **di** *o* **da** ~ from there; **per di** ~ that way; **di** ~ **a pochi giorni** a few days later; ~ **per** ~ there and then; at first; **essere** ~ **(~) per fare** to be on the point of doing, be about to do; ~ **dentro** in there; ~ **sotto** under there; ~ **sopra** on there; up there; **tutto** ~ that's all; *vedi anche* **quello**.
libagi'one [liba'dʒone] *sf* libation.

liba'nese *ag, sm/f* Lebanese *inv.*
Li'bano *sm:* **il** ~ the Lebanon.
'libbra *sf (peso)* pound.
li'beccio [li'bettʃo] *sm* south-west wind.
li'bello *sm* libel.
li'bellula *sf* dragonfly.
libe'rale *ag, sm/f* liberal.
liberaliz'zare [liberalid'dzare] *vt* to liberalize.
libe'rare *vt (rendere libero: prigioniero)* to release; *(: popolo)* to free, liberate; *(sgombrare: passaggio)* to clear; *(: stanza)* to vacate; *(produrre: energia)* to release; ~**rsi** *vr:* ~**rsi di qc/qn** to get rid of sth/sb.
libera'tore, 'trice *ag* liberating ♦ *sm/f* liberator.
liberazi'one [liberat'tsjone] *sf (di prigioniero)* release; *(di popolo)* liberation; **che** ~! what a relief!; **la L**~ *vedi nota nel riquadro.*

LIBERAZIONE

The **Liberazione** *is a national holiday which falls on 25 April. It commemorates the liberation of Italy in 1945 from German forces and Mussolini's government and marks the end of the war on Italian soil.*

Li'beria *sf:* **la** ~ Liberia.
liberi'ano, a *ag, sm/f* Liberian.
libe'rismo *sm (ECON)* laissez-faire.
'libero, a *ag* free; *(strada)* clear; *(non occupato: posto etc)* vacant, free; *(TEL)* not engaged; ~ **di fare qc** free to do sth; ~ **da** free from; **una donna dai** ~**i costumi** a woman of loose morals; **avere via** ~**a** to have a free hand; **dare via** ~**a a qn** to give sb the go-ahead; **via** ~**a!** all clear!; ~ **arbitrio** free will; ~ **professionista** self-employed professional person; ~ **scambio** free trade; ~**a uscita** *(MIL)* leave.
liberoscam'bismo *sm (ECON)* free trade.
libertà *sf inv* freedom; *(tempo disponibile)* free time ♦ *sfpl (licenza)* liberties; **essere in** ~ **provvisoria/vigilata** to be released without bail/be on probation; ~ **di riunione** right to hold meetings.
'liberty ['liberti] *ag inv, sm* art nouveau.
'Libia *sf:* **la** ~ Libya.
'libico, a, ci, che *ag, sm/f* Libyan.
li'bidine *sf* lust.
libidi'noso, a *ag* lustful, libidinous.
li'bido *sf* libido.
li'braio *sm* bookseller.
li'brario, a *ag* book *cpd.*
li'brarsi *vr* to hover.
libre'ria *sf (bottega)* bookshop; *(stanza)*

library; (*mobile*) bookcase.

li'bretto *sm* booklet; (*taccuino*) notebook; (*MUS*) libretto; ~ **degli assegni** chequebook (*BRIT*), checkbook (*US*); ~ **di circolazione** (*AUT*) logbook; ~ **di deposito** (bank) deposit book; ~ **di risparmio** (savings) bankbook, passbook; ~ **universitario** student's report book.

'libro *sm* book; ~ **bianco** (*POL*) white paper; ~ **di cassa** cash book; ~ **di consultazione** reference book; ~ **mastro** ledger; ~ **paga** payroll; ~ **tascabile** paperback; ~ **di testo** textbook; ~**i contabili** (account) books; ~**i sociali** company records.

li'cantropo *sm* werewolf.

lice'ale [litʃe'ale] *ag* secondary school *cpd* (*BRIT*), high school *cpd* (*US*) ♦ *sm/f* secondary school *o* high school pupil.

li'cenza [li'tʃɛntsa] *sf* (*permesso*) permission, leave; (*di pesca, caccia, circolazione*) permit, licence (*BRIT*), license (*US*); (*MIL*) leave; (*INS*) school-leaving certificate; (*libertà*) liberty; (*sfrenatezza*) licentiousness; **andare in** ~ (*MIL*) to go on leave; **su** ~ **di ...** (*COMM*) under licence from ...; ~ **di esportazione** export licence; ~ **di fabbricazione** manufacturer's licence; ~ **poetica** poetic licence.

licenzia'mento [litʃentsja'mento] *sm* dismissal.

licenzi'are [litʃen'tsjare] *vt* (*impiegato*) to dismiss; (*INS*) to award a certificate to; ~**rsi** *vr* (*impiegato*) to resign, hand in one's notice; (*INS*) to obtain one's school-leaving certificate.

licenziosità [litʃentsjosi'ta] *sf* licentiousness.

licenzi'oso, a [litʃen'tsjoso] *ag* licentious.

li'ceo [li'tʃɛo] *sm* (*INS*) secondary (*BRIT*) *o* high (*US*) school (*for 14 to 19-year-olds*); ~ **classico/scientifico** secondary or high school specializing in classics/scientific subjects.

li'chene [li'kɛne] *sm* (*BOT*) lichen.

'lido *sm* beach, shore.

'Liechtenstein ['liktənstain] *sm*: **il** ~ Liechtenstein.

li'eto, a *ag* happy, glad; **"molto** ~**"** (*nelle presentazioni*) "pleased to meet you"; **a** ~ **fine** with a happy ending.

li'eve *ag* light; (*di poco conto*) slight; (*sommesso: voce*) faint, soft.

lievi'tare *vi* (*anche fig*) to rise ♦ *vt* to leaven.

li'evito *sm* yeast; ~ **di birra** brewer's yeast.

'ligio, a, gi, gie ['lidʒo] *ag* faithful, loyal.

li'gnaggio [liɲ'naddʒo] *sm* descent, lineage.

'ligure *ag* Ligurian; **la Riviera L~** the Italian Riviera.

Li'kud [li'kud] *sm* Likud.

'lilla, lillà *sm inv* lilac.

'Lima *sf* Lima.

'lima *sf* file; ~ **da unghie** nail file.

limacci'oso, a [limat'tʃoso] *ag* muddy.

li'mare *vt* to file (down); (*fig*) to polish.

'limbo *sm* (*REL*) limbo.

li'metta *sf* nail file.

limi'tare *vt* to limit, restrict; (*circoscrivere*) to bound, surround.

limitata'mente *av* to a limited extent; ~ **alle mie possibilità** in so far as I am able.

limi'tato, a *ag* limited, restricted.

limitazi'one [limitat'tsjone] *sf* limitation, restriction.

'limite *sm* limit; (*confine*) border, boundary ♦ *ag inv*: **caso** ~ extreme case; **al** ~ if the worst comes to the worst (*BRIT*), if worst comes to worst (*US*); ~ **di velocità** speed limit.

li'mitrofo, a *ag* neighbouring (*BRIT*), neighboring (*US*).

'limo *sm* mud, slime; (*GEO*) silt.

limo'nata *sf* lemonade (*BRIT*), (lemon) soda (*US*); (*spremuta*) lemon squash (*BRIT*), lemonade (*US*).

li'mone *sm* (*pianta*) lemon tree; (*frutto*) lemon.

limpi'dezza [limpi'dettsa] *sf* clearness; (*di discorso*) clarity.

'limpido, a *ag* (*acqua*) limpid, clear; (*cielo*) clear; (*fig: discorso*) clear, lucid.

'lince ['lintʃe] *sf* lynx.

linci'aggio [lin'tʃaddʒo] *sm* lynching.

linci'are [lin'tʃare] *vt* to lynch.

'lindo, a *ag* tidy, spick and span; (*biancheria*) clean.

'linea *sf* (*gen*) line; (*di mezzi pubblici di trasporto: itinerario*) route; (: *servizio*) service; (*di prodotto: collezione*) collection; (: *stile*) style; **a grandi** ~**e** in outline; **mantenere la** ~ to look after one's figure; **è caduta la** ~ (*TEL*) I (*o you etc*) have been cut off; **di** ~: **aereo di** ~ airliner; **nave di** ~ liner; **volo di** ~ scheduled flight; **in** ~ **diretta da** (*TV, RADIO*) coming to you direct from; ~ **aerea** airline; ~ **continua** solid line; ~ **di partenza/d'arrivo** (*SPORT*) starting/finishing line; ~ **punteggiata** dotted line; ~ **di tiro** line of fire.

linea'menti *smpl* features; (*fig*) outlines.

line'are *ag* linear; (*fig*) coherent, logical.

line'etta *sf* (*trattino*) dash; (*d'unione*) hyphen.

'linfa *sf* (*BOT*) sap; (*ANAT*) lymph; ~ **vitale**

(*fig*) lifeblood.

lin'gotto *sm* ingot, bar.

'lingua *sf* (*ANAT, CUC*) tongue; (*idioma*) language; **mostrare la** ~ to stick out one's tongue; **di** ~ **italiana** Italian-speaking; ~ **madre** mother tongue; **una** ~ **di terra** a spit of land.

lingu'accia [lin'gwattʃa] *sf* (*fig*) spiteful gossip.

linguacci'uto, a [lingwat'tʃuto] *ag* gossipy.

lingu'aggio [lin'gwaddʒo] *sm* language; ~ **giuridico** legal language; ~ **macchina** (*INFORM*) machine language; ~ **di programmazione** (*INFORM*) programming language.

lingu'etta *sf* (*di strumento*) reed; (*di scarpa, TECN*) tongue; (*di busta*) flap.

lingu'ista, i, e *sm/f* linguist.

lingu'istico, a, ci, che *ag* linguistic ♦ *sf* linguistics *sg*.

lini'mento *sm* liniment.

'lino *sm* (*pianta*) flax; (*tessuto*) linen.

li'noleum *sm inv* linoleum, lino.

liofiliz'zare [liofilid'dzare] *vt* to freeze-dry.

liofiliz'zati [liofilid'dzati] *smpl* freeze-dried foods.

Li'one *sf* Lyons.

liposuzi'one [liposut'tsjone] *sf* liposuction.

'LIPU *sigla f* (= *Lega Italiana Protezione Uccelli*) *society for the protection of birds.*

liqu'ame *sm* liquid sewage.

lique'fare *vt* (*render liquido*) to liquefy; (*fondere*) to melt; ~**rsi** *vr* to liquefy; to melt.

lique'fatto, a *pp di* **liquefare**.

liqui'dare *vt* (*società, beni, persona*: *uccidere*) to liquidate; (*persona*: *sbarazzarsene*) to get rid of; (*conto, problema*) to settle; (*COMM: merce*) to sell off, clear.

liquidazi'one [likwidat'tsjone] *sf* (*di società, persona*) liquidation; (*di conto*) settlement; (*di problema*) settling; (*COMM: di merce*) clearance sale; (*AMM*) severance pay (*on retirement, redundancy, or when taking up other employment*).

liquidità *sf* liquidity.

'liquido, a *ag, sm* liquid; **denaro** ~ cash, ready money; ~ **per freni** brake fluid.

liqui'gas ® *sm inv* Calor gas ® (*BRIT*), butane.

liqui'rizia [likwi'rittsja] *sf* liquorice.

li'quore *sm* liqueur.

liquo'roso, a *ag*: **vino** ~ dessert wine.

'lira *sf* (*unità monetaria*) lira; (*MUS*) lyre; ~ **sterlina** pound sterling.

'lirico, a, ci, che *ag* lyric(al); (*MUS*) lyric ♦ *sf* (*poesia*) lyric poetry; (*componimento*

poetico) lyric; (*MUS*) opera; **cantante/teatro** ~ opera singer/house.

li'rismo *sm* lyricism.

Lis'bona *sf* Lisbon.

'lisca, sche *sf* (*di pesce*) fishbone.

lisci'are [liʃ'ʃare] *vt* to smooth; (*fig*) to flatter; ~**rsi i capelli** to straighten one's hair.

'liscio, a, sci, sce ['liʃʃo] *ag* smooth; (*capelli*) straight; (*mobile*) plain; (*bevanda alcolica*) neat; (*fig*) straightforward, simple ♦ *av*: **andare** ~ to go smoothly; **passarla** ~**a** to get away with it.

'liso, a *ag* worn out, threadbare.

'lista *sf* (*striscia*) strip; (*elenco*) list; ~ **elettorale** electoral roll; ~ **delle vivande** menu.

lis'tare *vt*: ~ (**di**) to edge (with), border (with).

lis'tato *sm* (*INFORM*) list, listing.

lis'tino *sm* list; ~ **di borsa** the Stock Exchange list; ~ **dei cambi** (foreign) exchange rate; ~ **dei prezzi** price list.

lita'nia *sf* litany.

'lite *sf* quarrel, argument; (*DIR*) lawsuit.

liti'gare *vi* to quarrel; (*DIR*) to litigate.

li'tigio [li'tidʒo] *sm* quarrel.

litigi'oso, a [liti'dʒoso] *ag* quarrelsome; (*DIR*) litigious.

litogra'fia *sf* (*sistema*) lithography; (*stampa*) lithograph.

lito'grafico, a, ci, che *ag* lithographic.

lito'rale *ag* coastal, coast *cpd* ♦ *sm* coast.

lito'raneo, a *ag* coastal.

'litro *sm* litre (*BRIT*), liter (*US*).

lit'torio, a *ag* (*STORIA*) lictorial; **fascio** ~ fasces *pl*.

Litu'ania *sf*: **la** ~ Lithuania.

litu'ano, a *ag, sm/f, sm* Lithuanian.

litur'gia, 'gie [litur'dʒia] *sf* liturgy.

li'uto *sm* lute.

li'vella *sf* level; ~ **a bolla d'aria** spirit level.

livel'lare *vt* to level, make level; ~**rsi** *vr* to become level; (*fig*) to level out, balance out.

livella'trice [livella'tritʃe] *sf* steamroller.

li'vello *sm* level; (*fig*) level, standard; **ad alto** ~ (*fig*) high-level; **a** ~ **mondiale** world-wide; **a** ~ **di confidenza** confidentially; ~ **di magazzino** stock level; ~ **del mare** sea level; **sul** ~ **del mare** above sea level; ~ **occupazionale** level of employment; ~ **retributivo** salary level.

'livido, a *ag* livid; (*per percosse*) bruised, black and blue; (*cielo*) leaden ♦ *sm* bruise.

li'vore *sm* malice, spite.

Li'vorno *sf* Livorno, Leghorn.

li'vrea *sf* livery.

'lizza *sf* lists *pl*; **essere in** ~ **per** (*fig*) to compete for; **scendere in** ~ (*anche fig*) to enter the lists.

LO *sigla* = *Lodi.*

lo *det m* (*dav s impura, gn, pn, ps, x, z; dav V l'*) the ♦ *pron* (*dav V l'*) (*oggetto: persona*) him; (: *cosa*) it; ~ **sapevo** I knew it; ~ **so** I know; **sii buono, anche se lui non** ~ **è** be good, even if he isn't; *vedi anche* **il**.

lob'bista, i, e *sm/f* lobbyist.

'lobby *sf inv* lobby.

'lobo *sm* lobe; ~ **dell'orecchio** ear lobe.

lo'cale *ag* local ♦ *sm* room; (*luogo pubblico*) premises *pl*; ~ **notturno** nightclub.

località *sf inv* locality.

localiz'zare [lokalid'dzare] *vt* (*circoscrivere*) to confine, localize; (*accertare*) to locate, place.

lo'canda *sf* inn.

locandi'ere, a *sm/f* innkeeper.

locan'dina *sf* (*TEAT*) poster.

lo'care *vt* (*casa*) to rent out, let; (*macchina*) to hire out (*BRIT*), rent (out).

loca'tario, a *sm/f* tenant.

loca'tivo, a *ag* (*DIR*) rentable.

loca'tore, 'trice *sm/f* landlord/lady.

locazi'one [lokat'tsjone] *sf* (*da parte del locatario*) renting *no pl*; (*da parte del locatore*) renting out *no pl*, letting *no pl*; (**contratto di**) ~ lease; (**canone di**) ~ rent; **dare in** ~ to rent out, let.

locomo'tiva *sf* locomotive.

locomo'tore *sm* electric locomotive.

locomot'rice [lokomo'tritʃe] *sf* = **locomotore**.

locomozi'one [lokomot'tsjone] *sf* locomotion; **mezzi di** ~ vehicles, means of transport.

'loculo *sm* burial recess.

lo'custa *sf* locust.

locuzi'one [lokut'tsjone] *sf* phrase, expression.

lo'dare *vt* to praise.

'lode *sf* praise; (*INS*): **laurearsi con 110 e** ~ ≈ to graduate with first-class honours (*BRIT*), ≈ to graduate summa cum laude (*US*).

'loden *sm inv* (*stoffa*) loden; (*cappotto*) loden overcoat.

lo'devole *ag* praiseworthy.

loga'ritmo *sm* logarithm.

'loggia, ge ['lɔddʒa] *sf* (*ARCHIT*) loggia; (*circolo massonico*) lodge.

loggi'one [lod'dʒone] *sm* (*di teatro*): **il** ~ the Gods *sg*.

logica'mente [lodʒika'mente] *av* naturally, obviously.

logicità [lodʒitʃi'ta] *sf* logicality.

'logico, a, ci, che ['lɔdʒiko] *ag* logical ♦ *sf* logic.

lo'gistica [lo'dʒistika] *sf* logistics *sg*.

'logo *sm inv* logo.

logora'mento *sm* (*di vestiti etc*) wear.

logo'rante *ag* exhausting.

logo'rare *vt* to wear out; (*sciupare*) to waste; ~**rsi** *vr* to wear out; (*fig*) to wear o.s. out.

logo'rio *sm* wear and tear; (*fig*) strain.

'logoro, a *ag* (*stoffa*) worn out, threadbare; (*persona*) worn out.

'Loira *sf*: **la** ~ the Loire.

lom'baggine [lom'baddʒine] *sf* lumbago.

Lombar'dia *sf*: **la** ~ Lombardy.

lom'bardo, a *ag, sm/f* Lombard.

lom'bare *ag* (*ANAT, MED*) lumbar.

lom'bata *sf* (*taglio di carne*) loin.

'lombo *sm* (*ANAT*) loin.

lom'brico, chi *sm* earthworm.

'londinese *ag* London *cpd* ♦ *sm/f* Londoner.

'Londra *sf* London.

lon'ganime *ag* forbearing.

longevità [londʒevi'ta] *sf* longevity.

lon'gevo, a [lon'dʒevo] *ag* long-lived.

longi'lineo, a [londʒi'lineo] *ag* long-limbed.

longi'tudine [londʒi'tudine] *sf* longitude.

lontana'mente *av* remotely; **non ci pensavo neppure** ~ it didn't even occur to me.

lonta'nanza [lonta'nantsa] *sf* distance; absence.

lon'tano, a *ag* (*distante*) distant, faraway; (*assente*) absent; (*vago: sospetto*) slight, remote; (*tempo: remoto*) far-off, distant; (*parente*) distant, remote ♦ *av* far; **è** ~**a la casa**? is it far to the house?, is the house far from here?; **è** ~ **un chilometro** it's a kilometre away *o* a kilometre from here; **più** ~ farther; **da** *o* **di** ~ from a distance; ~ **da** a long way from; **alla** ~**a** slightly, vaguely.

'lontra *sf* otter.

lo'quace [lo'kwatʃe] *ag* talkative, loquacious; (*fig: gesto etc*) eloquent.

loquacità [lokwatʃi'ta] *sf* talkativeness, loquacity.

'lordo, a *ag* dirty, filthy; (*peso, stipendio*) gross; ~ **d'imposta** pre-tax.

Lo'rena *sf* (*GEO*) Lorraine.

'loro *pron pl* (*oggetto, con preposizione*) them; (*complemento di termine*) to them; (*soggetto*) they; (*forma di cortesia: anche*: **L**~) you; to you; **il(la)** ~, **i(le)** ~ *det* their; (*forma di cortesia: anche*: **L**~) your ♦ *pron* theirs; (*forma di cortesia: anche*: **L**~) yours ♦ *sm inv*: **il** ~ their (*o* your) money ♦ *sf inv*:

la ~ (*opinione*) their (*o* your) view; **i** ~ (*famiglia*) their (*o* your) family; (*amici etc*) their (*o* your) own people; **un** ~ **amico** a friend of theirs; **è dalla** ~ he's on their (*o* your) side; **ne hanno fatto un'altra delle** ~ they've (*o* you've) done it again; ~ **stessi(e)** they themselves; you yourselves.

lo'sanga, ghe *sf* diamond, lozenge.

Lo'sanna *sf* Lausanne.

'losco, a, schi, sche *ag* (*fig*) shady, suspicious.

'lotta *sf* struggle, fight; (*SPORT*) wrestling; **essere in** ~ **(con)** to be in conflict (with); **fare la** ~ **(con)** to wrestle (with); ~ **armata** armed struggle; ~ **di classe** (*POL*) class struggle; ~ **libera** (*SPORT*) all-in wrestling (*BRIT*), freestyle.

lot'tare *vi* to fight, struggle; to wrestle.

lotta'tore, 'trice *sm/f* wrestler.

lotte'ria *sf* lottery; (*di gara ippica*) sweepstake.

lottiz'zare [lottid'dzare] *vt* to divide into plots; (*fig*) to share out.

lottizzazi'one [lottiddzat'tsjone] *sf* division into plots; (*fig*) share-out.

'lotto *sm* (*gioco*) (state) lottery; (*parte*) lot; (*EDIL*) site; **vincere un terno al** ~ (*anche fig*) to hit the jackpot.

lozi'one [lot'tsjone] *sf* lotion.

L.st. *abbr* (= *lire sterline*) £.

LT *sigla* = *Latina*.

LU *sigla* = *Lucca*.

lubrifi'cante *sm* lubricant.

lubrifi'care *vt* to lubricate.

lu'cano, a *ag* of (*o* from) Lucania.

luc'chetto [luk'ketto] *sm* padlock.

lucci'care [luttʃi'kare] *vi* to sparkle; (*oro*) to glitter; (*stella*) to twinkle; (*occhi*) to glisten.

lucci'chio [luttʃi'kio] *sm* sparkling; glittering; twinkling; glistening.

lucci'cone [luttʃi'kone] *sm*: **avere i** ~**i agli occhi** to have tears in one's eyes.

'luccio ['luttʃo] *sm* (*ZOOL*) pike.

'lucciola ['luttʃola] *sf* (*ZOOL*) firefly; glowworm; (*fam, fig: prostituta*) girl (*o* woman) on the game.

'luce ['lutʃe] *sf* light; (*finestra*) window; **alla** ~ **di** by the light of; **fare qc alla** ~ **del sole** (*fig*) to do sth in the open; **dare alla** ~ (*bambino*) to give birth to; **fare** ~ **su qc** (*fig*) to shed *o* throw light on sth; ~ **del sole/della luna** sun/moonlight.

lu'cente [lu'tʃɛnte] *ag* shining.

lucen'tezza [lutʃen'tettsa] *sf* shine.

lu'cerna [lu'tʃɛrna] *sf* oil lamp.

lucer'nario [lutʃer'narjo] *sm* skylight.

lu'certola [lu'tʃɛrtola] *sf* lizard.

luci'dare [lutʃi'dare] *vt* to polish; (*ricalcare*) to trace.

lucida'trice [lutʃida'tritʃe] *sf* floor polisher.

lucidità [lutʃidi'ta] *sf* lucidity.

'lucido, a ['lutʃido] *ag* shining, bright; (*lucidato*) polished; (*fig*) lucid ♦ *sm* shine, lustre (*BRIT*), luster (*US*); (*per scarpe etc*) polish; (*disegno*) tracing.

lu'cignolo [lu'tʃiɲɲolo] *sm* wick.

luc'rare *vt* to make money out of.

lucra'tivo, a *ag* lucrative; **a scopo** ~ for gain.

'lucro *sm* profit, gain; **a scopo di** ~ for gain; **organizzazione senza scopo di** ~ nonprofit-making (*BRIT*) *o* non-profit (*US*) organization.

lu'croso, a *ag* lucrative, profitable.

luculli'ano, a *ag* (*pasto*) sumptuous.

lu'dibrio *sm* mockery *no pl*; (*oggetto di scherno*) laughing stock.

'lue *sf* syphilis.

'luglio ['luʎʎo] *sm* July; **nel mese di** ~ in July, in the month of July; **il primo** ~ the first of July; **arrivare il 2** ~ to arrive on the 2nd of July; **all'inizio/alla fine di** ~ at the beginning/at the end of July; **durante il mese di** ~ during July; **a** ~ **del prossimo anno** in July of next year; **ogni anno a** ~ every July; **che fai a** ~**?** what are you doing in July?; **ha piovuto molto a** ~ **quest'anno** July was very wet this year.

'lugubre *ag* gloomy.

'lui *pron* (*soggetto*) he; (*oggetto: per dare rilievo, con preposizione*) him ♦ *sm inv*: **il mio** ~ my beloved; ~ **stesso** he himself; **è** ~ it's him.

lu'maca, che *sf* slug; (*chiocciola*) snail.

luma'cone *sm* (*large*) slug; (*fig*) slowcoach (*BRIT*), slowpoke (*US*).

'lume *sm* light; (*lampada*) lamp; ~ **a olio** oil lamp; **chiedere** ~**i a qn** (*fig*) to ask sb for advice; **a** ~ **di naso** (*fig*) by rule of thumb.

lumi'cino [lumi'tʃino] *sm* small *o* faint light; **essere (ridotto) al** ~ (*fig*) to be at death's door.

lumi'era *sf* chandelier.

lumi'nare *sm* luminary.

lumi'naria *sf* (*per feste*) illuminations *pl*.

lumine'scente [luminɛʃ'ʃɛnte] *ag* luminescent.

lu'mino *sm* small light; ~ **da notte** nightlight; ~ **per i morti** candle for the dead.

luminosità *sf* brightness; (*fig: di sorriso, volto*) radiance.

lumi'noso, a *ag* (*che emette luce*) luminous; (*cielo, colore, stanza*) bright; (*sorgente*) of

light, light *cpd*; (*fig: sorriso*) bright, radiant; **insegna** ~a neon sign.
lun. *abbr* (= *lunedì*) Mon.
'**luna** *sf* moon; ~ **nuova/piena** new/full moon; **avere la** ~ to be in a bad mood; ~ **di miele** honeymoon.
'**luna park** *sm inv* amusement park, funfair.
lu'nare *ag* lunar, moon *cpd*.
lu'nario *sm* almanac; **sbarcare il** ~ to make ends meet.
lu'natico, a, ci, che *ag* whimsical, temperamental.
lunedì *sm inv* Monday; *per fraseologia vedi* **martedì**.
lun'gaggine [lun'gaddʒine] *sf* slowness; ~**i della burocrazia** red tape.
lunga'mente *av* (*a lungo*) for a long time; (*estesamente*) at length.
lun'garno *sm* embankment along the Arno.
lun'ghezza [lun'gettsa] *sf* length; ~ **d'onda** (*FISICA*) wavelength.
'**lungi** ['lundʒi] *av*: ~ **da** *prep* far from.
lungimi'rante [lundʒimi'rante] *ag* far-sighted.
'**lungo, a, ghi, ghe** *ag* long; (*lento: persona*) slow; (*diluito: caffè, brodo*) weak, watery, thin ♦ *sm* length ♦ *prep* along; ~ **3 metri** 3 metres long; **avere la barba** ~a to be unshaven; **a** ~ for a long time; **a** ~ **andare** in the long run; **di gran** ~a (*molto*) by far; **andare in** ~ *o* **per le lunghe** to drag on; **saperla** ~a to know what's what; **in** ~ **e in largo** far and wide, all over; ~ **il corso dei secoli** throughout the centuries; **navigazione di** ~ **corso** ocean-going navigation.
lungofi'ume *sm* embankment.
lungo'lago *sm* road round a lake.
lungo'mare *sm* promenade.
lungome'traggio [lungome'traddʒo] *sm* (*CINE*) feature film.
lungo'tevere *sm* embankment along the Tiber.
lu'notto *sm* (*AUT*) rear *o* back window; ~ **termico** heated rear window.
lu'ogo, ghi *sm* place; (*posto: di incidente etc*) scene, site; (*punto, passo di libro*) passage; **in** ~ **di** instead of; **in primo** ~ in the first place; **aver** ~ to take place; **dar** ~ **a** to give rise to; ~ **comune** commonplace; ~ **del delitto** scene of the crime; ~ **geometrico** locus; ~ **di nascita** birthplace; (*AMM*) place of birth; ~ **di pena** prison, penitentiary; ~ **di provenienza** place of origin.
luogote'nente *sm* (*MIL*) lieutenant.

lupacchi'otto [lupak'kjɔtto] *sm* (*ZOOL*) (wolf) cub.
lu'para *sf* sawn-off shotgun.
lu'petto *sm* (*ZOOL*) (wolf) cub; (*negli scouts*) cub scout.
'**lupo, a** *sm/f* wolf/she-wolf; **cane** ~ alsatian (dog) (*BRIT*), German shepherd (dog); **tempo da** ~**i** filthy weather.
'**luppolo** *sm* (*BOT*) hop.
'**lurido, a** *ag* filthy.
luri'dume *sm* filth.
lu'singa, ghe *sf* (*spesso al pl*) flattery *no pl*.
lusin'gare *vt* to flatter.
lusinghi'ero, a [luzin'gjero] *ag* flattering, gratifying.
lus'sare *vt* (*MED*) to dislocate.
lussazi'one [lussat'tsjone] *sf* (*MED*) dislocation.
lussembur'ghese [lussembur'gese] *ag* of (*o* from) Luxembourg ♦ *sm/f* native (*o* inhabitant) of Luxembourg.
Lussem'burgo *sm* (*stato*): **il** ~ Luxembourg ♦ *sf* (*città*) Luxembourg.
'**lusso** *sm* luxury; **di** ~ luxury *cpd*.
lussu'oso, a *ag* luxurious.
lussureggi'are [lussured'dʒare] *vi* to be luxuriant.
lus'suria *sf* lust.
lussuri'oso, a *ag* lascivious, lustful.
lus'trare *vt* to polish, shine.
lustras'carpe *sm/f inv* shoeshine.
lus'trino *sm* sequin.
'**lustro, a** *ag* shiny; (*pelliccia*) glossy ♦ *sm* shine, gloss; (*fig*) prestige, glory; (*quinquennio*) five-year period.
lute'rano, a *ag, sm/f*, Lutheran.
'**lutto** *sm* mourning; **essere in/portare il** ~ to be in/wear mourning.

M m

M, m ['emme] *sf o m inv* (*lettera*) M, m; **M come Milano** ≈ M for Mary (*BRIT*), M for Mike (*US*).
m. *abbr* = **mese**; **metro**; **miglia**; **monte**.
ma *cong* but; ~ **insomma!** for goodness sake!; ~ **no!** of course not!
'**macabro, a** *ag* gruesome, macabre.
ma'caco, chi *sm* (*ZOOL*) macaque.
macché [mak'ke] *escl* not at all!, certainly not!

macche'roni [makke'roni] *smpl* macaroni *sg.*

'macchia ['makkja] *sf* stain, spot; (*chiazza di diverso colore*) spot; splash, patch; (*tipo di boscaglia*) scrub; ~ **d'inchiostro** ink stain; **estendersi a** ~ **d'olio** (*fig*) to spread rapidly; **darsi/vivere alla** ~ (*fig*) to go into/live in hiding.

macchi'are [mak'kjare] *vt* (*sporcare*) to stain, mark; ~**rsi** *vr* (*persona*) to get o.s. dirty; (*stoffa*) to stain; to get stained *o* marked; ~**rsi di un delitto** to be guilty of a crime.

macchi'ato, a [mak'kjato] *ag* (*pelle, pelo*) spotted; ~ **di** stained with; **caffè** ~ coffee with a dash of milk.

macchi'etta [mak'kjetta] *sf* (*disegno*) sketch, caricature; (*TEAT*) caricature; (*fig: persona*) character.

'macchina ['makkina] *sf* machine; (*motore, locomotiva*) engine; (*automobile*) car; (*fig: meccanismo*) machinery; **andare in** ~ (*AUT*) to go by car; (*STAMPA*) to go to press; **salire in** ~ to get into the car; **venire in** ~ to come by car; **sala** ~**e** (*NAUT*) engine room; ~ **da cucire** sewing machine; ~ **fotografica** camera; ~ **da presa** cine *o* movie camera; ~ **da scrivere** typewriter; ~ **utensile** machine tool; ~ **a vapore** steam engine.

macchinal'mente [makkinal'mente] *av* mechanically.

macchi'nare [makki'nare] *vt* to plot.

macchi'nario [makki'narjo] *sm* machinery.

macchinazi'one [makkinat'tsjone] *sf* plot, machination.

macchi'netta [makki'netta] *sf* (*fam: caffettiera*) percolator; (*: accendino*) lighter.

macchi'nista, i [makki'nista] *sm* (*di treno*) engine-driver; (*di nave*) engineer; (*TEAT, TV*) stagehand.

macchi'noso, a [makki'noso] *ag* complex, complicated.

mace'donia [matʃe'dɔnja] *sf* fruit salad.

macel'laio [matʃel'lajo] *sm* butcher.

macel'lare [matʃel'lare] *vt* to slaughter, butcher.

macellazi'one [matʃellat'tsjone] *sf* slaughtering, butchering.

macelle'ria [matʃelle'ria] *sf* butcher's (shop).

ma'cello [ma'tʃɛllo] *sm* (*mattatoio*) slaughterhouse, abattoir (*BRIT*); (*fig*) slaughter, massacre; (*: disastro*) shambles *sg.*

mace'rare [matʃe'rare] *vt* to macerate; (*CUC*) to marinate; ~**rsi** *vr* to waste away; (*fig*): ~**rsi in** to be consumed with.

macerazi'one [matʃerat'tsjone] *sf* maceration.

ma'cerie [ma'tʃɛrje] *sfpl* rubble *sg*, debris *sg.*

'macero ['matʃero] *sm* (*operazione*) pulping; (*stabilimento*) pulping mill; **carta da** ~ paper for pulping.

machia'vellico, a, ci, che [makja'vɛlliko] *ag* (*anche fig*) Machiavellian.

ma'cigno [ma'tʃiɲɲo] *sm* (*masso*) rock, boulder.

maci'lento, a [matʃi'lɛnto] *ag* emaciated.

'macina ['matʃina] *sf* (*pietra*) millstone; (*macchina*) grinder.

macinacaffè [matʃinakaf'fɛ] *sm inv* coffee grinder.

macina'pepe [matʃina'pepe] *sm inv* peppermill.

maci'nare [matʃi'nare] *vt* to grind; (*carne*) to mince (*BRIT*), grind (*US*).

maci'nato [matʃi'nato] *sm* meal, flour; (*carne*) minced (*BRIT*) *o* ground (*US*) meat.

maci'nino [matʃi'nino] *sm* (*per caffè*) coffee grinder; (*per pepe*) peppermill; (*scherzoso: macchina*) old banger (*BRIT*), clunker (*US*).

maciul'lare [matʃul'lare] *vt* (*canapa, lino*) to brake; (*fig: braccio etc*) to crush.

'macro ... *prefisso* macro....

macrobi'otico, a *ag* macrobiotic ♦ *sf* macrobiotics *sg.*

macu'lato, a *ag* (*pelo*) spotted.

Ma'dama: palazzo ~ *sm* (*POL*) *seat of the Italian Chamber of Senators.*

made in Italy [meɪdɪ'nɪtəlɪ] *sm*: **il** ~ Italian exports *pl* (*especially fashion goods*).

Ma'dera *sf* (*GEO*) Madeira ♦ *sm inv* (*vino*) Madeira.

'madido, a *ag*: ~ (**di**) wet *o* moist (with).

Ma'donna *sf* (*REL*) Our Lady.

mador'nale *ag* enormous, huge.

'madre *sf* mother; (*matrice di bolletta*) counterfoil ♦ *ag inv* mother *cpd*; **ragazza** ~ unmarried mother; **scena** ~ (*TEAT*) principal scene; (*fig*) terrible scene.

madre'lingua *sf* mother tongue, native language.

madre'patria *sf* mother country, native land.

madre'perla *sf* mother-of-pearl.

Ma'drid *sf* Madrid.

madri'gale *sm* madrigal.

madri'leno, a *ag* of (*o* from) Madrid ♦ *sm/f* person from Madrid.

ma'drina *sf* godmother.

maestà *sf inv* majesty; **Sua M**~ **la Regina** Her Majesty the Queen.

maestosità *sf* majesty.

maes'toso, a *ag* majestic.
ma'estra *sf vedi* **maestro.**
maes'trale *sm* north-west wind.
maes'tranze [maes'trantse] *sfpl* workforce *sg.*
maes'tria *sf* mastery, skill.
ma'estro, a *sm/f* (*INS*: *anche*: ~ **di scuola** o **elementare**) primary (*BRIT*) o grade school (*US*) teacher; (*esperto*) expert ♦ *sm* (*artigiano, fig*: *guida*) master; (*MUS*) maestro ♦ *ag* (*principale*) main; (*di grande abilità*) masterly, skilful (*BRIT*), skillful (*US*); **un colpo da** ~ (*fig*) a masterly move; **muro** ~ main wall; **strada** ~**a** main road; ~**a d'asilo** nursery teacher; ~ **di ballo** dancing master; ~ **di cerimonie** master of ceremonies; ~ **d'orchestra** conductor, director (*US*); ~ **di scherma** fencing master; ~ **di sci** ski instructor.
'mafia *sf* Mafia.
mafi'oso *sm* member of the Mafia.
'maga, ghe *sf* sorceress.
ma'gagna [ma'gaɲɲa] *sf* defect, flaw, blemish; (*noia, guaio*) problem.
ma'gari *escl* (*esprime desiderio*): ~ **fosse vero!** if only it were true!, **tl piacerebbe andare in Scozia?** — ~**!** would you like to go to Scotland? — I certainly would! ♦ *av* (*anche*) even; (*forse*) perhaps.
magazzi'naggio [magaddzi'naddʒo] *sm*: (**spese di**) ~ storage charges *pl,* warehousing charges *pl.*
magazzini'ere [magaddzi'njɛre] *sm* warehouseman.
magaz'zino [magad'dzino] *sm* warehouse; **grande** ~ department store; ~ **doganale** bonded warehouse.
'maggio ['maddʒo] *sm* May; *per fraseologia vedi* **luglio.**
maggio'rana [maddʒo'rana] *sf* (*BOT*) (sweet) marjoram.
maggio'ranza [maddʒo'rantsa] *sf* majority; **nella** ~ **dei casi** in most cases.
maggio'rare [maddʒo'rare] *vt* to increase, raise.
maggiorazi'one [maddʒorat'tsjone] *sf* (*COMM*) rise, increase.
maggior'domo [maddʒor'dɔmo] *sm* butler.
maggi'ore [mad'dʒore] *ag* (*comparativo: più grande*) bigger, larger; taller; greater; (: *più vecchio: sorella, fratello*) older, elder; (: *di grado superiore*) senior; (: *più importante, MIL, MUS*) major; (*superlativo*) biggest, largest; tallest; greatest; oldest, eldest ♦ *sm/f* (*di grado*) superior; (*di età*) elder; (*MIL*) major; (: *AER*) squadron leader; **la maggior parte** the majority; **andare per la** ~ (*cantante, attore etc*) to be

very popular, be "in".
maggio'renne [maddʒo'rɛnne] *ag* of age ♦ *sm/f* person who has come of age.
maggiori'tario, a [maddʒori'tarjo] *ag* majority *cpd* ♦ (*POL*: *anche*: **sistema** ~) first-past-the-post system.
maggior'mente [maddʒor'mente] *av* much more; (*con senso superlativo*) most.
ma'gia [ma'dʒia] *sf* magic.
'magico, a, ci, che ['madʒiko] *ag* magic; (*fig*) fascinating, charming, magical.
'magio ['madʒo] *sm* (*REL*): **i re Magi** the Magi, the Three Wise Men.
magis'tero [madʒis'tero] *sm* teaching; (*fig*: *maestria*) skill; (*INS*): **Facoltà di M**~ ≈ teachers' training college.
magis'trale [madʒis'trale] *ag* primary (*BRIT*) o grade school (*US*) teachers', primary o grade school teaching *cpd*; (*abile*) skilful (*BRIT*), skillful (*US*); **istituto** ~ secondary school for the training of primary teachers.
magis'trato [madʒis'trato] *sm* magistrate.
magistra'tura [madʒistra'tura] *sf* magistrature; (*magistrati*): **la** ~ the Bench.
'maglia ['maʎʎa] *sf* stitch; (*lavoro ai ferri*) knitting *no pl*; (*tessuto, SPORT*) jersey; (*maglione*) jersey, sweater; (*di catena*) link; (*di rete*) mesh; **avviare/diminuire le** ~**e** to cast on/cast off; **lavorare a** ~~, **fare la** ~ to knit; ~ **diritta/rovescia** plain/purl.
magli'aia [maʎ'ʎaja] *sf* knitter.
maglie'ria [maʎʎe'ria] *sf* knitwear; (*negozio*) knitwear shop; **macchina per** ~ knitting machine.
magli'etta [maʎ'ʎetta] *sf* (*canottiera*) vest; (*tipo camicia*) T-shirt.
magli'ficio [maʎʎi'fitʃo] *sm* knitwear factory.
ma'glina [maʎ'ʎina] *sf* (*tessuto*) jersey.
'maglio ['maʎʎo] *sm* mallet; (*macchina*) power hammer.
magli'one [maʎ'ʎone] *sm* jersey, sweater.
'magma *sm* magma; (*fig*) mass.
ma'gnaccia [maɲ'ɲattʃa] *sm inv* (*peg*) pimp.
magnanimità [maɲɲanimi'ta] *sf* magnanimity.
ma'gnanimo, a [maɲ'ɲanimo] *ag* magnanimous.
ma'gnate [maɲ'ɲate] *sm* tycoon, magnate.
ma'gnesia [maɲ'ɲɛzja] *sf* (*CHIM*) magnesia.
ma'gnesio [maɲ'ɲɛzjo] *sm* (*CHIM*) magnesium; **al** ~ (*lampada, flash*) magnesium *cpd.*
ma'gnete [maɲ'ɲɛte] *sm* magnet.
ma'gnetico, a, ci, che [maɲ'ɲɛtiko] *ag* magnetic.

magne'tismo [maɲɲe'tizmo] *sm* magnetism.

magnetiz'zare [maɲɲetid'dzare] *vt* (*FISICA*) to magnetize; (*fig*) to mesmerize.

magne'tofono [maɲɲe'tɔfono] *sm* tape recorder.

magnifica'mente [maɲɲifika'mente] *av* magnificently, extremely well.

magnifi'cenza [maɲɲifi'tʃɛntsa] *sf* magnificence, splendour (*BRIT*), splendor (*US*).

ma'gnifico, a, ci, che [maɲ'ɲifiko] *ag* magnificent, splendid; (*ospite*) generous.

'magno, a ['maɲɲo] *ag*: **aula** ~a main hall.

ma'gnolia [maɲ'ɲɔlja] *sf* magnolia.

'mago, ghi *sm* (*stregone*) magician, wizard; (*illusionista*) magician.

ma'grezza [ma'grettsa] *sf* thinness.

'magro, a *ag* (very) thin, skinny; (*carne*) lean; (*formaggio*) low-fat; (*fig: scarso, misero*) meagre (*BRIT*), meager (*US*), poor; (*: meschino: scusa*) poor, lame; **mangiare di** ~ not to eat meat.

'mai *av* (*nessuna volta*) never; (*talvolta*) ever; **non** ... ~ never; ~ **più** never again; **come** ~? why (*o* how) on earth?; **chi/dove/quando** ~? whoever/wherever/whenever?

mai'ale *sm* (*ZOOL*) pig; (*carne*) pork.

mai'olica *sf* majolica.

maio'nese *sf* mayonnaise.

Mai'orca *sf* Majorca.

'mais *sm* maize (*BRIT*), corn (*US*).

mai'uscolo, a *ag* (*lettera*) capital ♦ *sf* capital letter ♦ *sm* capital letters *pl*; (*TIP*) upper case; **scrivere tutto (in)** ~ to write everything in capitals *o* in capital letters.

mal *av, sm vedi* **male**.

'mala *sf* (*gergo*) underworld.

malac'corto, a *ag* rash, careless.

mala'fede *sf* bad faith.

malaf'fare: di ~ *ag* (*gente*) shady, dishonest; **donna di** ~ prostitute.

mala'gevole [mala'dʒevole] *ag* difficult, hard.

mala'grazia [mala'grattsja] *sf*: **con** ~ with bad grace, impolitely.

mala'lingua, *pl* **male'lingue** *sf* gossip (*person*).

mala'mente *av* badly; (*sgarbatamente*) rudely.

malan'dato, a *ag* (*persona: di salute*) in poor health; (*: di condizioni finanziarie*) badly off; (*trascurato*) shabby.

ma'lanimo *sm* ill will, malevolence; **di** ~ unwillingly.

ma'lanno *sm* (*disgrazia*) misfortune;

(*malattia*) ailment.

mala'pena *sf*: **a** ~ hardly, scarcely.

ma'laria *sf* malaria.

ma'larico, a, ci, che *ag* malarial.

mala'sorte *sf* bad luck.

mala'ticcio, a [mala'tittʃo] *ag* sickly.

ma'lato, a *ag* ill, sick; (*gamba*) bad; (*pianta*) diseased ♦ *sm/f* sick person; (*in ospedale*) patient; **darsi** ~ (*sul lavoro etc*) to go sick.

malat'tia *sf* (*infettiva etc*) illness, disease; (*cattiva salute*) illness, sickness; (*di pianta*) disease; **mettersi in** ~ to go on sick leave; **fare una** ~ **di qc** (*fig: disperarsi*) to get in a state about sth.

malaugu'rato, a *ag* ill-fated, unlucky.

malau'gurio *sm* bad *o* ill omen; **uccello del** ~ bird of ill omen.

mala'vita *sf* underworld.

malavi'toso, a *sm/f* gangster.

mala'voglia [mala'vɔʎʎa]: **di** ~ *av* unwillingly, reluctantly.

Ma'lawi [ma'lavi] *sm*: **il** ~ Malawi.

Mala'ysia *sf* Malaysia.

malaysi'ano, a *ag, sm/f* Malaysian.

malcapi'tato, a *ag* unlucky, unfortunate ♦ *sm/f* unfortunate person.

mal'concio, a, ci, ce [mal'kontʃo] *ag* in a sorry state.

malcon'tento *sm* discontent.

malcos'tume *sm* immorality.

mal'destro, a *ag* (*inabile*) inexpert, inexperienced; (*goffo*) awkward.

maldi'cente [maldi'tʃɛnte] *ag* slanderous.

maldi'cenza [maldi'tʃɛntsa] *sf* malicious gossip.

maldis'posto, a *ag*: ~ (**verso**) ill-disposed (towards).

Mal'dive *sfpl*: **le** ~ the Maldives.

'male *av* badly ♦ *sm* (*ciò che è ingiusto, disonesto*) evil; (*danno, svantaggio*) harm; (*sventura*) misfortune; (*dolore fisico, morale*) pain, ache; **sentirsi** ~ to feel ill; **aver mal di cuore/fegato** to have a heart/liver complaint; **aver mal di denti/d'orecchi/di testa** to have toothache/earache/a headache; **aver mal di gola** to have a sore throat; **aver** ~ **ai piedi** to have sore feet; **far** ~ (*dolere*) to hurt; **far** ~ **alla salute** to be bad for one's health; **far del** ~ **a qn** to hurt *o* harm sb; **parlar** ~ **di qn** to speak ill of sb; **restare** *o* **rimanere** ~ to be sorry; to be disappointed; to be hurt; **trattar** ~ **qn** to ill-treat sb; **andare a** ~ to go off *o* bad; **come va?** — **non c'è** ~ how are you? — not bad; **di** ~ **in peggio** from bad to worse; **per** ~ **che vada** however badly things go; **non avertene a** ~, **non prendertela a** ~ don't take it to heart; **mal**

maledetto – manager

comune mezzo gaudio (*proverbio*) a trouble shared is a trouble halved; **mal d'auto** carsickness; **mal di mare** seasickness.

male'detto, a *pp di* maledire ♦ *ag* cursed, damned; (*fig fam*) damned, blasted.

male'dire *vt* to curse.

maledizi'one [maledit'tsjone] *sf* curse; ~! damn it!

maledu'cato, a *ag* rude, ill-mannered.

maleducazi'one [maledukat'tsjone] *sf* rudeness.

male'fatta *sf* misdeed.

male'ficio [male'fitʃo] *sm* witchcraft.

ma'lefico, a, ci, che *ag* (*aria, cibo*) harmful, bad; (*influsso, azione*) evil.

ma'lese *ag, sm/f* Malay(an) ♦ *sm* (*LING*) Malay.

Ma'lesia *sf* Malaya.

ma'lessere *sm* indisposition, slight illness, (*fig*) uneasiness.

malevo'lenza [malevo'lentsa] *sf* malevolence.

ma'levolo, a *ag* malevolent.

malfa'mato, a *ag* notorious.

mal'fatto, a *ag* (*persona*) deformed; (*oggetto*) badly made; (*lavoro*) badly done.

malfat'tore, 'trice *sm/f* wrongdoer.

mal'fermo, a *ag* unsteady, shaky; (*salute*) poor, delicate.

malformazi'one [malformat'tsjone] *sf* malformation.

'malga, ghe *sf* Alpine hut.

malgo'verno *sm* maladministration.

mal'grado *prep* in spite of, despite ♦ *cong* although; **mio** (*o* **tuo** *etc*) ~ against my (*o* your *etc*) will.

ma'lia *sf* spell; (*fig: fascino*) charm.

mali'ardo, a *ag* (*occhi, sorriso*) bewitching ♦ *sf* enchantress.

maligna'mente [maliɲɲa'mente] *av* maliciously.

mali'gnare [maliɲ'ɲare] *vi:* ~ **su** to malign, speak ill of.

malignità [maliɲɲi'ta] *sf inv* (*qualità*) malice, spite; (*osservazione*) spiteful remark; **con** ~ spitefully, maliciously.

ma'ligno, a [ma'liɲɲo] *ag* (*malvagio*) malicious, malignant; (*MED*) malignant.

malinco'nia *sf* melancholy, gloom.

malin'conico, a, ci, che *ag* melancholy.

malincu'ore : a ~ *av* reluctantly, unwillingly.

malinfor'mato, a *ag* misinformed.

malintenzio'nato, a [malintentsjo'nato] *ag* ill-intentioned.

malin'teso, a *ag* misunderstood; (*riguardo, senso del dovere*) mistaken, wrong ♦ *sm*

misunderstanding.

ma'lizia [ma'littsja] *sf* (*malignità*) malice; (*furbizia*) cunning; (*espediente*) trick.

malizi'oso, a [malit'tsjoso] *ag* malicious; cunning; (*vivace, birichino*) mischievous.

malle'abile *ag* malleable.

mal'loppo *sm* (*fam: refurtiva*) loot.

malme'nare *vt* to beat up; (*fig*) to ill-treat.

mal'messo, a *ag* shabby.

malnu'trito, a *ag* undernourished.

malnutrizi'one [malnutrit'tsjone] *sf* malnutrition.

'malo, a *ag:* **in** ~ **modo** badly.

ma'locchio [ma'lɔkkjo] *sm* evil eye.

ma'lora *sf* (*fam*): **andare in** ~ to go to the dogs; **va in** ~! go to hell!

ma'lore *sm* (sudden) illness.

malri'dotto, a *ag* (*abiti, scarpe, persona*) in a sorry state; (*casa, macchina*) dilapidated, in a poor state of repair.

mal'sano, a *ag* unhealthy.

malsi'curo, a *ag* unsafe.

'Malta *sf* Malta.

'malta *sf* (*EDIL*) mortar.

mal'tempo *sm* bad weather.

'malto *sm* malt.

mal'tolto *sm* ill-gotten gains *pl.*

maltratta'mento *sm* ill treatment.

maltrat'tare *vt* to ill-treat.

malu'more *sm* bad mood; (*irritabilità*) bad temper; (*discordia*) ill feeling; **di** ~ in a bad mood.

'malva *sf* (*BOT*) mallow ♦ *ag, sm inv* mauve.

mal'vagio, a, gi, gie [mal'vadʒo] *ag* wicked, evil.

malvagità [malvadʒi'ta] *sf inv* (*qualità*) wickedness; (*azione*) wicked deed.

malva'sia *sf* Italian dessert wine.

malversazi'one [malversat'tsjone] *sf* (*DIR*) embezzlement.

malves'tito, a *ag* badly dressed, ill-clad.

mal'visto, a *ag:* ~ **(da)** disliked (by), unpopular (with).

malvi'vente *sm* criminal.

malvolenti'eri *av* unwillingly, reluctantly.

malvo'lere *vt:* **farsi** ~ **da qn** to make o.s. unpopular with sb ♦ *sm:* **prendere qn a** ~ to take a dislike to sb.

'mamma *sf* mum(my) (*BRIT*), mom (*US*); ~ **mia**! my goodness!

mam'mario, a *ag* (*ANAT*) mammary.

mam'mella *sf* (*ANAT*) breast; (*di vacca, capra etc*) udder.

mam'mifero *sm* mammal.

mam'mismo *sm excessive attachment to one's mother.*

'mammola *sf* (*BOT*) violet.

'manager ['mænidʒə] *sm inv* manager.

manageri'ale [manadʒe'rjale] *ag* managerial.

ma'nata *sf* (*colpo*) slap; (*quantità*) handful.

'manca *sf* left (hand); **a destra e a** ~ left, right and centre, on all sides.

manca'mento *sm* (*di forze*) (feeling of) faintness, weakness.

man'canza [man'kantsa] *sf* lack; (*carenza*) shortage, scarcity; (*fallo*) fault; (*imperfezione*) failing, shortcoming; **per** ~ **di tempo** through lack of time; **in** ~ **di meglio** for lack of anything better; **sentire la** ~ **di qc/qn** to miss sth/sb.

man'care *vi* (*essere insufficiente*) to be lacking; (*venir meno*) to fail; (*sbagliare*) to be wrong, make a mistake; (*non esserci*) to be missing, not to be there; (*essere lontano*): ~ (**da**) to be away (from) ♦ *vt* to miss; ~ **di** to lack; ~ **a** (*promessa*) to fail to keep; **tu mi manchi** I miss you; **mancò poco che morisse** he very nearly died; **mancano ancora 10 sterline** we're still £10 short; **manca un quarto alle 6** it's a quarter to 6; **non mancherò** I won't forget, I'll make sure I do; **ci mancherebbe altro!** of course I (*o* you *etc*) will!; ~ **da casa** to be away from home; ~ **di rispetto a** *o* **verso qn** to be lacking in respect towards sb, be disrespectful towards sb; ~ **di parola** not to keep one's word, go back on one's word; **sentirsi** ~ to feel faint.

man'cato, a *ag* (*tentativo*) unsuccessful; (*artista*) failed.

manche [mãʃ] *sf inv* (*SPORT*) heat.

mancherò *etc* [manke'rɔ] *vb vedi* **mancare**.

man'chevole [man'kevole] *ag* (*insufficiente*) inadequate, insufficient.

manchevo'lezza [mankevo'lettsa] *sf* (*scorrettezza*) fault, shortcoming.

'mancia, ce ['mantʃa] *sf* tip; ~ **competente** reward.

manci'ata [man'tʃata] *sf* handful.

man'cino, a [man'tʃino] *ag* (*braccio*) left; (*persona*) left-handed; (*fig*) underhand.

'manco *av* (*nemmeno*): ~ **per sogno** *o* **per idea!** not on your life!

man'dante *sm/f* (*DIR*) principal; (*istigatore*) instigator.

manda'rancio [manda'rantʃo] *sm* clementine.

man'dare *vt* to send; (*far funzionare: macchina*) to drive; (*emettere*) to send out; (*: grido*) to give, utter, let out; ~ **avanti** (*persona*) to send ahead; (*fig: famiglia*) to provide for; (*: ditta*) to look after, run; (*: pratica*) to attend to; ~ **a chiamare qn** to send for sb; ~ **giù** to send down; (*anche*

fig) to swallow; ~ **in onda** (*RADIO, TV*) to broadcast; ~ **in rovina** to ruin; ~ **via** to send away; (*licenziare*) to fire.

manda'rino *sm* mandarin (orange); (*cinese*) mandarin.

man'data *sf* (*quantità*) lot, batch; (*di chiave*) turn; **chiudere a doppia** ~ to double-lock.

manda'tario *sm* (*DIR*) representative, agent.

man'dato *sm* (*incarico*) commission; (*DIR: provvedimento*) warrant; (*di deputato etc*) mandate; (*ordine di pagamento*) postal *o* money order; ~ **d'arresto**, ~ **di cattura** warrant for arrest; ~ **di comparizione** summons *sg*; ~ **di perquisizione** search warrant.

man'dibola *sf* mandible, jaw.

mando'lino *sm* mandolin(e).

'mandorla *sf* almond.

mandor'lato *sm* nut brittle.

'mandorlo *sm* almond tree.

'mandria *sf* herd.

mandri'ano *sm* cowherd, herdsman.

man'drino *sm* (*TECN*) mandrel.

maneg'gevole [maned'dʒevole] *ag* easy to handle.

maneggi'are [maned'dʒare] *vt* (*creta, cera*) to mould (*BRIT*), mold (*US*), work, fashion; (*arnesi, utensili*) to handle; (*: adoperare*) to use; (*fig: persone, denaro*) to handle, deal with.

ma'neggio [ma'neddʒo] *sm* moulding (*BRIT*), molding (*US*); handling; use; (*intrigo*) plot, scheme; (*per cavalli*) riding school.

ma'nesco, a, schi, sche *ag* free with one's fists.

ma'nette *sfpl* handcuffs.

manga'nello *sm* club.

manga'nese *sm* manganese.

mange'reccio, a, ci, ce [mandʒe'rettʃo] *ag* edible.

mangi'abile [man'dʒabile] *ag* edible, eatable.

mangia'dischi [mandʒa'diski] *sm inv* record player.

mangia'nastri [mandʒa'nastri] *sm inv* cassette-recorder.

mangi'are [man'dʒare] *vt* to eat; (*intaccare*) to eat into *o* away; (*CARTE, SCACCHI etc*) to take ♦ *vi* to eat ♦ *sm* eating; (*cibo*) food; (*cucina*) cooking; **fare da** ~ to do the cooking; ~**rsi le parole** to mumble; ~**rsi le unghie** to bite one's nails.

mangia'soldi [mandʒa'sɔldi] *ag inv* (*fam*): **macchinetta** ~ one-armed bandit.

mangia'toia [mandʒa'toja] *sf* feeding-trough.

man'gime [man'dʒime] sm fodder.
mangiucchi'are [mandʒuk'kjare] vt to nibble.
'mango, ghi sm mango.
ma'nia sf (PSIC) mania; (fig) obsession, craze; avere la ~ di fare qc to have a habit of doing sth; ~ di persecuzione persecution complex o mania.
mania'cale ag (PSIC) maniacal; (fanatico) fanatical.
ma'niaco, a, ci, che ag suffering from a mania; ~ (di) obsessed (by), crazy (about).
'manica, che sf sleeve; (fig: gruppo) gang, bunch; (GEO): la M~, il Canale della M~ the (English) Channel; senza ~che sleeveless; essere in ~che di camicia to be in one's shirt sleeves; essere di ~ larga/stretta to be easy-going/strict; ~ a vento (AER) wind sock.
manica'retto sm titbit (BRIT), tidbit (US).
mani'chino [mani'kino] sm (di sarto, vetrina) dummy.
'manico, ci sm handle; (MUS) neck; ~ di scopa broomstick.
mani'comio sm mental hospital; (fig) madhouse.
mani'cotto sm muff; (TECN) coupling; sleeve.
mani'cure sm o f inv manicure ♦ sf inv manicurist.
mani'era sf way, manner; (stile) style, manner; ~ e s/pl manners; in ~ che so that; in ~ da so as to; alla ~ di in o after the style of; in una ~ o nell'altra one way or another; in tutte le ~e at all costs; usare buone ~e con qn to be polite to sb; usare le ~e forti to use strong-arm tactics.
manie'rato, a ag affected.
mani'ero sm manor.
manifat'tura sf (lavorazione) manufacture; (stabilimento) factory.
manifatturi'ero, a ag manufacturing.
manifes'tante sm/f demonstrator.
manifes'tare vt to show, display; (esprimere) to express; (rivelare) to reveal, disclose ♦ vi to demonstrate; ~rsi vr to show o.s.; ~rsi amico to prove o.s. (to be) a friend.
manifestazi'one [manifestat'tsjone] sf show, display; expression; (sintomo) sign, symptom; (dimostrazione pubblica) demonstration; (cerimonia) event.
mani'festo, a ag obvious, evident ♦ sm poster, bill; (scritto ideologico) manifesto.
ma'niglia [ma'niʎʎa] sf handle; (sostegno: negli autobus etc) strap.

Ma'nila sf Manila.
manipo'lare vt to manipulate; (alterare: vino) to adulterate.
manipolazi'one [manipolat'tsjone] sf manipulation; adulteration.
manis'calco, chi sm blacksmith, farrier (BRIT).
'manna sf (REL) manna.
man'naia sf (del boia) (executioner's) axe o ax (US); (per carni) cleaver.
man'naro, a ag: lupo ~ werewolf.
'mano, i sf hand; (strato: di vernice etc) coat; a ~ by hand; cucito a ~ hand-sewn; fatto a ~ handmade; alla ~ (persona) easy-going; fuori ~ out of the way; di prima ~ (notizia) first-hand; di seconda ~ second-hand; man ~ little by little, gradually; man ~ che as; a piene ~i (fig) generously; avere le ~i bucate to spend money like water; aver le ~i in pasta to be in the know; avere qc per le ~i (progetto, lavoro) to have oth in hand; dare una ~ a qn to lend sb a hand; dare una ~ di vernice a qc to give sth a coat of paint; darsi o stringersi la ~ to shake hands; forzare la ~ to go too far; mettere ~ a qc to have a hand in sth; mettere le ~i avanti (fig) to safeguard o.s.; restare a ~i vuote to be left empty-handed; venire alle ~i to come to blows; ~i in alto! hands up!; ~i pulite vedi nota nel riquadro.
ma'nipolo sm (drappello) handful.

MANI PULITE

Mani pulite ("clean hands") is the term used to describe the judicial operation of the early 1990s which identified a number of politicians and industrialists who were implicated in bribery and corruption scandals. Evidence against them was gathered together and they were eventually brought to trial.

---

mano'dopera sf labour (BRIT), labor (US).
mano'messo, a pp di manomettere.
ma'nometro sm gauge, manometer.
mano'mettere vt (alterare) to tamper with; (aprire indebitamente) to break open illegally.
manomissi'one sf (di prove etc) tampering; (di lettera) opening.
ma'nopola sf (dell'armatura) gauntlet; (guanto) mitt; (di impugnatura) hand-grip; (pomello) knob.
manos'critto, a ag handwritten ♦ sm manuscript.
mano'vale sm labourer (BRIT), laborer (US).

mano'vella *sf* handle; (*TECN*) crank.
ma'novra *sf* manoeuvre (*BRIT*), maneuver (*US*); (*FERR*) shunting; ~**e di corridoio** palace intrigues.
mano'vrare *vt* (*veicolo*) to manoeuvre (*BRIT*), maneuver (*US*); (*macchina, congegno*) to operate; (*fig*: *persona*) to manipulate ♦ *vi* to manoeuvre.
manro'vescio [manro'vɛʃʃo] *sm* slap (*with back of hand*).
man'sarda *sf* attic.
mansi'one *sf* task, duty, job.
mansu'eto, a *ag* (*animale*) tame; (*persona*) gentle, docile.
mansue'tudine *sf* tameness; gentleness, docility.
man'tello *sm* cloak; (*fig*: *di neve etc*) blanket, mantle; (*TECN*: *involucro*) casing, shell; (*ZOOL*) coat.
mante'nere *vt* to maintain; (*adempiere*: *promesse*) to keep, abide by; (*provvedere a*) to support, maintain; ~**rsi** *vr*: ~**rsi calmo/giovane** to stay calm/young; ~ **i contatti con qn** to keep in touch with sb.
manteni'mento *sm* maintenance.
mante'nuto, a *sm/f* gigolo/kept woman.
'mantice ['mantitʃe] *sm* bellows *pl*; (*di carrozza, automobile*) hood.
'manto *sm* cloak; ~ **stradale** road surface.
'Mantova *sf* Mantua.
manto'vano, a *ag* of (*o from*) Mantua.
manu'ale *ag* manual ♦ *sm* (*testo*) manual, handbook.
manua'listico, a, ci, che *ag* textbook *cpd*.
manual'mente *av* manually, by hand.
ma'nubrio *sm* handle; (*di bicicletta etc*) handlebars *pl*; (*SPORT*) dumbbell.
manu'fatto *sm* manufactured article; ~**i** *smpl* manufactured goods.
manutenzi'one [manuten'tsjone] *sf* maintenance, upkeep; (*d'impianti*) maintenance, servicing.
'manzo ['mandzo] *sm* (*ZOOL*) steer; (*carne*) beef.
Mao'metto *sm* Mohammed.
'mappa *sf* (*GEO*) map.
mappa'mondo *sm* map of the world; (*globo girevole*) globe.
ma'rasma, i *sm* (*fig*) decay, decline.
mara'tona *sf* marathon.
'marca, che *sf* mark; (*bollo*) stamp; (*COMM*: *di prodotti*) brand; (*contrassegno, scontrino*) ticket, check; **prodotti di (gran)** ~ high-class products; ~ **da bollo** official stamp.
mar'care *vt* (*munire di contrassegno*) to mark; (*a fuoco*) to brand; (*SPORT*: *gol*) to score; (: *avversario*) to mark; (*accentuare*) to stress; ~ **visita** (*MIL*) to report sick.

mar'cato, a *ag* (*lineamenti, accento etc*) pronounced.
'Marche ['marke] *sfpl*: **le** ~ the Marches (*region of central Italy*).
marcherò *etc* [marke'rɔ] *vb vedi* **marcare**.
mar'chese, a [mar'keze] *sm/f* marquis *o* marquess/marchioness.
marchi'ano, a [mar'kjano] *ag* (*errore*) glaring, gross.
marchi'are [mar'kjare] *vt* to brand.
marchigi'ano, a [marki'dʒano] *ag* of (*o from*) the Marches.
'marchio ['markjo] *sm* (*di bestiame, COMM, fig*) brand; ~ **depositato** registered trademark; ~ **di fabbrica** trademark.
'marcia, ce ['martʃa] *sf* (*anche MUS, MIL*) march; (*funzionamento*) running; (*il camminare*) walking; (*AUT*) gear; **mettere in** ~ to start; **mettersi in** ~ to get moving; **far** ~ **indietro** (*AUT*) to reverse; (*fig*) to back-pedal; ~ **forzata** forced march; ~ **funebre** funeral march.
marciapi'ede [martʃa'pjɛde] *sm* (*di strada*) pavement (*BRIT*), sidewalk (*US*); (*FERR*) platform.
marci'are [mar'tʃare] *vi* to march; (*andare*: *treno, macchina*) to go; (*funzionare*) to run, work.
'marcio, a, ci, ce ['martʃo] *ag* (*frutta, legno*) rotten, bad; (*MED*) festering; (*fig*) corrupt, rotten ♦ *sm*: **c'è del** ~ **in questa storia** (*fig*) there's something fishy about this business; **avere torto** ~ to be utterly wrong.
mar'cire [mar'tʃire] *vi* (*andare a male*) to go bad, rot; (*suppurare*) to fester; (*fig*) to rot.
marci'ume [mar'tʃume] *sm* (*parte guasta*: *di cibi etc*) rotten part, bad part; (*di radice, pianta*) rot; (*fig*: *corruzione*) rottenness, corruption.
'marco, chi *sm* (*unità monetaria*) mark.
'mare *sm* sea; **di** ~ (*brezza, acqua, uccelli, pesce*) sea *cpd*; **in** ~ at sea; **per** ~ by sea; **sul** ~ (*barca*) on the sea; (*villaggio, località*) by *o* beside the sea; **andare al** ~ (*in vacanza etc*) to go to the seaside; **il mar Caspio** the Caspian Sea; **il mar Morto** the Dead Sea; **il mar Nero** the Black Sea; **il** ~ **del Nord** the North Sea; **il mar Rosso** the Red Sea; **il mar dei Sargassi** the Sargasso Sea; **i** ~**i del Sud** the South Seas.
ma'rea *sf* tide; **alta/bassa** ~ high/low tide.
mareggi'ata [mared'dʒata] *sf* heavy sea.
ma'remma *sf* (*GEO*) maremma, swampy coastal area.
marem'mano, a *ag* (*zona, macchia*) swampy; (*della Maremma*) of (*o* from) the Maremma.

mare'moto *sm* seaquake.

maresci'allo [mareʃ'ʃallo] *sm* (*MIL*) marshal; (: *sottufficiale*) warrant officer.

marez'zato, a [mared'dzato] *ag* (*seta etc*) watered, moiré; (*legno*) veined; (*carta*) marbled.

marga'rina *sf* margarine.

marghe'rita [marge'rita] *sf* (ox-eye) daisy, marguerite; (*di stampante*) daisy wheel.

margheri'tina [margeri'tina] *sf* daisy.

margi'nale [mardʒi'nale] *ag* marginal.

'margine ['mardʒine] *sm* margin; (*di bosco, via*) edge, border; **avere un buon ~ di tempo/denaro** to have plenty of time/money; **~ di guadagno** *o* **di utile** profit margin; **~ di sicurezza** safety margin.

mariju'ana [mæri'waːnə] *sf* marijuana.

ma'rina *sf* navy; (*costa*) (*quadro*) seascape; **~ mercantile** merchant navy (*BRIT*) *o* marine (*US*); **~ militare (M.M.)** ≈ Royal Navy (RN) (*BRIT*), Navy (*US*).

mari'naio *sm* sailor.

mari'nare *vt* (*CUC*) to marinate; **~ la scuola** to play truant.

mari'naro, a *ag* (*tradizione, popolo*) seafaring; (*CUC*) with seafood; **alla ~a** (*vestito, cappello*) sailor *cpd*; **borgo ~** district where fishing folk live.

mari'nata *sf* marinade.

ma'rino, a *ag* sea *cpd*, marine.

mario'netta *sf* puppet.

mari'tare *vt* to marry; **~rsi** *vr*: **~rsi a** *o* **con qn** to marry sb, get married to sb.

mari'tato, a *ag* married.

ma'rito *sm* husband; **prendere ~** to get married; **ragazza (in età) da ~** girl of marriageable age.

ma'rittimo, a *ag* maritime, sea *cpd*.

mar'maglia [mar'maʎʎa] *sf* mob, riff-raff.

marmel'lata *sf* jam; (*di agrumi*) marmalade.

mar'mitta *sf* (*recipiente*) pot; (*AUT*) silencer; **~ catalitica** catalytic converter.

'marmo *sm* marble.

mar'mocchio [mar'mɔkkjo] *sm* (*fam*) (little) kid.

mar'motta *sf* (*ZOOL*) marmot.

maroc'chino, a [marok'kino] *ag, sm/f* Moroccan.

Ma'rocco *sm*: **il ~** Morocco.

ma'roso *sm* breaker.

'marra *sf* hoe.

Marra'kesh [marra'keʃ] *sf* Marrakesh.

mar'rone *ag inv* brown ♦ *sm* (*BOT*) chestnut.

mar'sala *sm inv* (*vino*) Marsala (wine).

Mar'siglia [mar'siʎʎa] *sf* Marseilles.

mar'sina *sf* tails *pl*, tail coat.

mar'supio *sm* (*ZOOL*) pouch, marsupium.

mart. *abbr* (= *martedì*) Tue(s).

'Marte *sm* (*ASTR, MITOLOGIA*) Mars.

martedì *sm inv* Tuesday; **di** *o* **il ~ on** Tuesdays; **oggi è ~ 3 aprile** (the date) today is Tuesday 3rd April; **~ stavo male** I wasn't well on Tuesday; **il giornale di ~** Tuesday's newspaper; **~ grasso** Shrove Tuesday.

martel'lante *ag* (*fig: dolore*) throbbing.

martel'lare *vt* to hammer ♦ *vi* (*pulsare*) to throb; (: *cuore*) to thump.

martel'letto *sm* (*di pianoforte*) hammer; (*di macchina da scrivere*) typebar; (*di giudice, nelle vendite all'asta*) gavel; (*MED*) percussion hammer.

mar'tello *sm* hammer; (*di uscio*) knocker; **suonare a ~** (*fig: campane*) to sound the tocsin; **~ pneumatico** pneumatic drill.

marti'netto *sm* (*TECN*) jack.

martin'gala *sf* (*di giacca*) half-belt; (*di cavallo*) martingale.

'martire *sm/f* martyr.

mar'tirio *sm* martyrdom; (*fig*) agony, torture.

martori'are *vt* to torment, torture.

mar'xismo *sm* Marxism.

mar'xista, i, e *ag, sm/f* Marxist.

marza'pane [martsa'pane] *sm* marzipan.

marzi'ale [mar'tsjale] *ag* martial.

'marzo ['martso] *sm* March; *per fraseologia vedi* **luglio**.

marzo'lino, a [martso'lino] *ag* March *cpd*.

mascalzo'nata [maskaltso'nata] *sf* dirty trick.

mascal'zone [maskal'tsone] *sm* rascal, scoundrel.

mas'cara *sm inv* mascara.

mascar'pone *sm* soft cream cheese often used in desserts.

ma'scella [maʃ'ʃɛlla] *sf* (*ANAT*) jaw.

'maschera ['maskera] *sf* mask; (*travestimento*) disguise; (: *per un ballo etc*) fancy dress; (*TEAT, CINE*) usher/usherette; (*personaggio del teatro*) stock character; **in ~** (*mascherato*) masked; **ballo in ~** fancy-dress ball; **gettare la ~** (*fig*) to reveal o.s.; **~ antigas/subacquea** gas/diving mask; **~ di bellezza** face pack.

masche'rare [maske'rare] *vt* to mask; (*travestire*) to disguise; to dress up; (*fig: celare*) to hide, conceal; (*MIL*) to camouflage; **~rsi** *vr*: **~rsi da** to disguise o.s. as; to dress up as; (*fig*) to masquerade as.

masche'rina [maske'rina] *sf* (*piccola maschera*) mask; (*di animale*) patch; (*di scarpe*) toe-cap; (*AUT*) radiator grill.

mas'chile [mas'kile] *ag* masculine; (*sesso,*

popolazione) male; (*abiti*) men's; (*per ragazzi: scuola*) boys'.

'maschio, a ['maskjo] *ag* (*BIOL*) male; (*virile*) manly ♦ *sm* (*anche ZOOL, TECN*) male; (*uomo*) man; (*ragazzo*) boy; (*figlio*) son.

masco'lino, a *ag* masculine.

mas'cotte [mas'kɔt] *sf inv* mascot.

maso'chismo [mazo'kizmo] *sm* masochism.

maso'chista, i, e [mazo'kista] *ag* masochistic ♦ *sm/f* masochist.

'massa *sf* mass; (*di errori etc*): **una ~ di** heaps of, masses of; (*di gente*) mass, multitude; (*ELETTR*) earth; **in ~** (*COMM*) in bulk; (*tutti insieme*) en masse; **adunata in ~** mass meeting; **manifestazione/cultura di ~** mass demonstration/culture; **produrre in ~** to mass-produce; **la ~ (del popolo)** the masses *pl*.

massa'crante *ag* exhausting, gruelling.

massa'crare *vt* to massacre, slaughter.

mas'sacro *sm* massacre, slaughter; (*fig*) mess, disaster.

massaggi'are [massad'dʒare] *vt* to massage.

massaggia'tore, 'trice [massaddʒa'tore] *sm/f* masseur/masseuse.

mas'saggio [mas'saddʒo] *sm* massage.

mas'saia *sf* housewife.

masse'ria *sf* large farm.

masse'rizie [masse'rittsje] *sfpl* (household) furnishings.

massicci'ata [massit'tʃata] *sf* (*di strada, ferrovia*) ballast.

mas'siccio, a, ci, ce [mas'sittʃo] *ag* (*oro, legno*) solid; (*palazzo*) massive; (*corporatura*) stout ♦ *sm* (*GEO*) massif.

'massima *sf vedi* **massimo**.

massi'male *sm* maximum; (*COMM*) ceiling, limit.

'massimo, a *ag, sm* maximum ♦ *sf* (*sentenza, regola*) maxim; (*METEOR*) maximum temperature; **in linea di ~a** generally speaking; **arrivare entro il tempo ~** to arrive within the time limit; **al ~** at (the) most; **sfruttare qc al ~** to make full use of sth; **arriverò al ~ alle 5** I'll arrive at 5 at the latest; **erano presenti le ~e autorità** all the most important dignitaries were there; **il ~ della pena** (*DIR*) the maximum penalty.

mas'sivo, a *ag* (*intervento*) en masse; (*emigrazione*) mass; (*emorragia*) massive.

'masso *sm* rock, boulder.

mas'sone *sm* freemason.

massone'ria *sf* freemasonry.

mas'sonico, a, ci, che *ag* masonic.

mas'tello *sm* tub.

masti'care *vt* to chew.

'mastice ['mastitʃe] *sm* mastic; (*per vetri*) putty.

mas'tino *sm* mastiff.

masto'dontico, a, ci, che *ag* gigantic, colossal.

mastur'barsi *vr* to masturbate.

masturbazi'one [masturbat'tsjone] *sf* masturbation.

ma'tassa *sf* skein.

mate'matico, a, ci, che *ag* mathematical ♦ *sm/f* mathematician ♦ *sf* mathematics *sg*.

materas'sino *sm* mat; **~ gonfiabile** air bed.

mate'rasso *sm* mattress; **~ a molle** spring *o* interior-sprung mattress.

ma'teria *sf* (*FISICA*) matter; (*TECN, COMM*) material, matter *no pl*; (*disciplina*) subject; (*argomento*) subject matter, material; **prima di entrare in ~ ...** before discussing the matter in hand ...; **un esperto in ~ (di musica etc)** an expert on the subject (of music *etc*); **sono ignorante in ~** I know nothing about it; **~ cerebrale** cerebral matter; **~ grassa** fat; **~ grigia** (*anche fig*) grey matter; **~e plastiche** plastics; **~e prime** raw materials.

materi'ale *ag* material; (*fig: grossolano*) rough, rude ♦ *sm* material; (*insieme di strumenti etc*) equipment *no pl*, materials *pl*; **~ da costruzione** building materials *pl*.

materia'lista, i, e *ag* materialistic ♦ *sm/f* materialist.

materializ'zarsi [materjalid'dzarsi] *vr* to materialize.

material'mente *av* (*fisicamente*) materially; (*economicamente*) financially.

maternità *sf* motherhood, maternity; (*clinica*) maternity hospital; **in (congedo di) ~** on maternity leave.

ma'terno, a *ag* (*amore, cura etc*) maternal, motherly; (*nonno*) maternal; (*lingua, terra*) mother *cpd*; *vedi anche* **scuola**.

ma'tita *sf* pencil; **~e colorate** crayons; **~ per gli occhi** eyeliner (pencil).

ma'trice [ma'tritʃe] *sf* matrix; (*COMM*) counterfoil; (*fig: origine*) background.

ma'tricola *sf* (*registro*) register; (*numero*) registration number; (*nell'università*) freshman, fresher (*BRIT fam*).

ma'trigna [ma'triɲɲa] *sf* stepmother.

matrimoni'ale *ag* matrimonial, marriage *cpd*; **camera/letto ~** double room/bed.

matri'monio *sm* marriage, matrimony; (*durata*) marriage, married life; (*cerimonia*) wedding.

ma'trona *sf* (*fig*) matronly woman.

matta'toio *sm* abattoir (*BRIT*), slaughterhouse.

mat'tina *sf* morning; **la** *o* **alla** *o* **di** ~ in the morning; **di prima** ~, **la** ~ **presto** early in the morning; **dalla** ~ **alla sera** (*continuamente*) from morning to night; (*improvvisamente: cambiare*) overnight.

matti'nata *sf* morning; (*spettacolo*) matinée, afternoon performance; **in** ~ in the course of the morning; **nella** ~ in the morning; **nella tarda** ~ at the end of the morning; **nella tarda** ~ **di sabato** late on Saturday morning.

mattini'ero, a *ag*: **essere** ~ to be an early riser.

mat'tino *sm* morning; **di buon** ~ early in the morning.

'matto, a *ag* mad, crazy; (*fig: falso*) false, imitation; (: *opaco*) matt, dull ♦ *sm/f* madman/woman; **avere una voglia** ~**a di qc** to be dying for sth; **far diventare** ~ **qn** to drive sb mad *o* crazy; **una gabbia di** ~**i** (*fig*) a madhouse.

mat'tone *sm* brick; (*fig*): **questo libro/ film è un** ~ this book/film is heavy going.

matto'nella *sf* tile.

mattu'tino, a *ag* morning *cpd*.

matu'rare *vi* (*anche:* ~**rsi**) (*frutta, grano*) to ripen; (*ascesso*) to come to a head; (*fig: persona, idea, ECON*) to mature ♦ *vt* to ripen; to (make) mature; ~ **una decisione** to come to a decision.

maturità *sf* maturity; (*di frutta*) ripeness, maturity; (*INS*) school-leaving examination, ≈ GCE A-levels (*BRIT*).

ma'turo, a *ag* mature; (*frutto*) ripe, mature.

ma'tusa *sm/f inv* (*scherzoso*) old fogey.

Mauri'tania *sf*: **la** ~ Mauritania.

Mau'rizio [mau'rittsjo] *sf*: **(l'isola di)** ~ Mauritius.

mauso'leo *sm* mausoleum.

max. *abbr* (= *massimo*) max.

'maxi... *prefisso* maxi....

maxipro'cesso [maksipro'tʃɛsso] *sm vedi nota nel riquadro*.

'mazza ['mattsa] *sf* (*bastone*) club; (*martello*) sledge-hammer; (*SPORT: da golf*) club; (: *da baseball, cricket*) bat.

maz'zata [mat'tsata] *sf* (*anche fig*) heavy blow.

maz'zetta [mat'tsetta] *sf* (*di banconote etc*) bundle; (*fig*) rake-off.

'mazzo ['mattso] *sm* (*di fiori, chiavi etc*) bunch; (*di carte da gioco*) pack.

MC *sigla* = Macerata.

m.c.d. *abbr* (= *minimo comune denominatore*) lcd.

m.c.m. *abbr* (= *minimo comune multiplo*) lcm.

ME *sigla* = Messina.

me *pron* me; **sei bravo quanto** ~ you are as clever as I (am) *o* as me.

me'andro *sm* meander.

M.E.C. [mɛk] *abbr m* = **Mercato Comune Europeo**.

'Mecca *sf* (*anche fig*): **La** ~ Mecca.

meccanica'mente *av* mechanically.

mec'canico, a, ci, che *ag* mechanical ♦ *sm* mechanic ♦ *sf* mechanics *sg*; (*attività tecnologica*) mechanical engineering; (*meccanismo*) mechanism; **officina** ~**a** garage.

mecca'nismo *sm* mechanism.

meccaniz'zare [mekkanid'dzare] *vt* to mechanize.

meccanizzazi'one [mekkaniddzat'tsjone] *sf* mechanization.

mece'nate [metʃe'nate] *sm* patron.

mèche [mɛʃ] *sf inv* streak; **farsi le** ~ to have one's hair streaked.

me'daglia [me'daʎʎa] *sf* medal; ~ **d'oro** (*oggetto*) gold medal; (*persona*) gold medallist (*BRIT*) *o* medalist (*US*).

medagli'one [medaʎ'ʎone] *sm* (*ARCHIT*) medallion; (*gioiello*) locket.

me'desimo, a *ag* same; (*in persona*): **io** ~ I myself.

'media *sf vedi* **medio**.

media'mente *av* on average.

medi'ano, a *ag* median; (*valore*) mean ♦ *sm* (*CALCIO*) half-back.

medi'ante *prep* by means of.

medi'are *vt* (*fare da mediatore*) to act as mediator in; (*MAT*) to average.

medi'ato, a *ag* indirect.

media'tore, 'trice *sm/f* mediator; (*COMM*) middle man, agent; **fare da** ~ **fra** to mediate between.

mediazi'one [medjat'tsjone] *sf* mediation; (*COMM: azione, compenso*) brokerage.

medica'mento *sm* medicine, drug.

medi'care *vt* to treat; (*ferita*) to dress.

medi'cato, a *ag* (*garza, shampoo*) medicated.

medicazi'one [medikat'tsjone] *sf* treatment, medication; dressing; **fare una**

~ **a qn** to dress sb's wounds.

medi'cina [medi'tʃina] *sf* medicine; ~ **legale** forensic medicine.

medici'nale [meditʃi'nale] *ag* medicinal ♦ *sm* drug, medicine.

'medico, a, ci, che *ag* medical ♦ *sm* doctor; ~ **di bordo** ship's doctor; ~ **di famiglia** family doctor; ~ **fiscale** *doctor who examines patients signed off sick for a lengthy period by their private doctor*; ~ **generico** general practitioner, GP.

medie'vale *ag* medieval.

'medio, a *ag* average; (*punto, ceto*) middle; (*altezza, statura*) medium ♦ *sm* (*dito*) middle finger ♦ *sf* average; (*MAT*) mean; (*INS: voto*) end-of-term average; ~**e** *sfpl vedi* **scuola media inferiore; licenza** ~**a** leaving certificate awarded at the end of 3 years of secondary education; **in** ~**a** on average; **al di sopra/sotto della** ~**a** above/below average; **viaggiare ad una** ~**a di** ... to travel at an average speed of ...; **il M**~ **Oriente** the Middle East.

medi'ocre *ag* (*gen*) mediocre; (*qualità, stipendio*) poor.

mediocrità *sf* mediocrity; poorness.

medioe'vale *ag* = **medievale.**

Medio'evo *sm* Middle Ages *pl.*

medita'bondo, a *ag* thoughtful.

medi'tare *vt* to ponder over, meditate on; (*progettare*) to plan, think out ♦ *vi* to meditate.

medi'tato, a *ag* (*gen*) meditated; (*parole*) carefully-weighed; (*vendetta*) premeditated; **ben** ~ (*piano*) well worked-out, neat.

meditazi'one [meditat'tsjone] *sf* meditation.

mediter'raneo, a *ag* Mediterranean; **il** (*mare*) **M**~ the Mediterranean (Sea).

'medium *sm/f inv* medium.

me'dusa *sf* (*ZOOL*) jellyfish.

me'gafono *sm* megaphone.

mega'lomane *ag, sm/f* megalomaniac.

me'gera [me'dʒɛra] *sf* (*peg: donna*) shrew.

'meglio ['mɛʎʎo] *av, ag inv* better; (*con senso superlativo*) best ♦ *sm* (*la cosa migliore*): **il** ~ the best (thing); **faresti** ~ **ad andartene** you had better leave; **alla** ~ as best one can; **andar di bene in** ~ to get better and better; **fare del proprio** ~ to do one's best; **per il** ~ for the best; **aver la** ~ **su qn** to get the better of sb.

'mela *sf* apple; ~ **cotogna** quince.

mela'grana *sf* pomegranate.

melan'zana [melan'dzana] *sf* aubergine (*BRIT*), eggplant (*US*).

me'lassa *sf* molasses *sg*, treacle.

me'lenso, a *ag* dull, stupid.

me'lissa *sf* (*BOT*) balm.

mel'lifluo, a *ag* (*peg*) sugary, honeyed.

'melma *sf* mud, mire.

'melo *sm* apple tree.

melo'dia *sf* melody.

me'lodico, a, ci, che *ag* melodic.

melodi'oso, a *ag* melodious.

melo'dramma, i *sm* melodrama.

me'lone *sm* (musk) melon.

'membra *sfpl vedi* **membro.**

mem'brana *sf* membrane.

'membro *sm* member; (*pl(f)* ~**a**: *arto*) limb.

memo'rabile *ag* memorable.

memo'randum *sm inv* memorandum.

'memore *ag*: ~ **di** (*ricordando*) mindful of; (*riconoscente*) grateful for.

me'moria *sf* (*anche INFORM*) memory; ~**e** *sfpl* (*opera autobiografica*) memoirs; **a** ~ (*imparare, sapere*) by heart; **a** ~ **d'uomo** within living memory; ~ **di sola lettura** (*INFORM*) read-only memory; ~ **tampone** (*INFORM*) buffer.

memori'ale *sm* (*raccolta di memorie*) memoirs *pl*; (*DIR*) memorial.

memoriz'zare [memorid'dzare] *vt* (*gen*) to memorize; (*INFORM*) to store.

memorizzazi'one [memoriddzat'tsjone] *sf* memorization; storage.

'mena *sf* scheme.

mena'dito: a ~ *av* perfectly, thoroughly; **sapere qc a** ~ to have sth at one's fingertips.

mena'gramo *sm/f inv* jinx, Jonah.

me'nare *vt* to lead; (*picchiare*) to hit, beat; (*dare: colpi*) to deal; ~ **la coda** (*cane*) to wag its tail; ~ **qc per le lunghe** to drag sth out; ~ **il can per l'aia** (*fig*) to beat about (*BRIT*) o around (*US*) the bush.

mendi'cante *sm/f* beggar.

mendi'care *vt* to beg for ♦ *vi* to beg.

menefre'ghismo [menefre'gizmo] *sm* (*fam*) couldn't-care-less attitude.

me'ninge [me'nindʒe] *sf* (*MED*) meninx; **spremersi le** ~**i** to rack one's brains.

menin'gite [menin'dʒite] *sf* meningitis.

me'nisco *sm* (*ANAT, MAT, FISICA*) meniscus.

═══════════════════ *PAROLA CHIAVE*

'meno *av* **1** (*in minore misura*) less; **dovresti mangiare** ~ you should eat less, you shouldn't eat so much; **è sempre** ~ **facile** it's getting less and less easy; **ne voglio di** ~ I don't want so much

2 (*comparativo*): ~ ... **di** not as ... as, less ... than; **sono** ~ **alto di te** I'm not as tall as you (are), I'm less tall than you (are); ~ ... **che** not as ... as, less ... than; ~ **che**

mai less than ever; **è ~ intelligente che ricco** he's more rich than intelligent; **~ fumo più mangio** the less I smoke the more I eat; **~ di quanto pensassi** less than I thought

3 (*superlativo*) least; **il ~ dotato degli studenti** the least gifted of the students; **è quello che compro ~ spesso** it's the one I buy least often

4 (*MAT*) minus; **8 ~ 5** 8 minus 5, 8 take away 5; **sono le 8 ~ un quarto** it's a quarter to 8; **~ 5 gradi** 5 degrees below zero, minus 5 degrees; **mille lire in ~** a thousand lire less; **ha preso 6 ~** (*a scuola*) he scraped a pass; **centomila lire ~ le spese** a hundred thousand lire minus *o* less expenses

5 (*fraseologia*): **quanto ~ poteva telefonare** he could at least have phoned; **non so se accettare o ~** I don't know whether to accept or not; **non essere da ~ di** not to be outdone by; **fare a ~ di qc/ qn** to do without sth/sb; **non potevo fare a ~ di ridere** I couldn't help laughing; **~ male!** thank goodness!; **~ male che sei arrivato** it's a good job that you've come ♦ *ag inv* (*tempo, denaro*) less; (*errori, persone*) fewer; **ha fatto ~ errori di tutti** he made fewer mistakes than anyone, he made the fewest mistakes of all ♦ *sm inv* **1**: **il ~** (*il minimo*) the least, **parlare del più e del ~** to talk about this and that; **era il ~ che ti potesse succedere** it was the least you could have expected **2** (*MAT*) minus ♦ *prep* (*eccetto*) except (for), apart from; **tutti ~ lui** everybody apart from *o* except him; **a ~ che, a ~ di** unless; **a ~ che non piova** unless it rains; **non posso, a ~ di prendere ferie** I can't, unless I take some leave; *vedi anche* **più**.

meno'mare *vt* (*danneggiare*) to maim, disable.

meno'mato, a *ag* (*persona*) disabled ♦ *sm/f* disabled person.

menomazi'one [menomat'tsjone] *sf* disablement.

meno'pausa *sf* menopause.

'mensa *sf* (*locale*) canteen; (: *MIL*) mess; (: *nelle università*) refectory.

men'sile *ag* monthly ♦ *sm* (*periodico*) monthly (magazine); (*stipendio*) monthly salary.

mensil'mente *av* (*ogni mese*) every month; (*una volta al mese*) monthly.

'mensola *sf* bracket; (*ripiano*) shelf; (*ARCHIT*) corbel.

'menta *sf* mint; (*anche*: **~ piperita**) peppermint; (*bibita*) peppermint cordial; (*caramella*) mint, peppermint.

men'tale *ag* mental.

mentalità *sf inv* mentality.

mental'mente *av* mentally.

'mente *sf* mind; **imparare/sapere qc a ~** to learn/know sth by heart; **avere in ~ qc** to have sth in mind; **avere in ~ di fare qc** to intend to do sth; **fare venire in ~ qc a qn** to remind sb of sth; **mettersi in ~ di fare qc** to make up one's mind to do sth; **passare di ~ a qn** to slip sb's mind; **tenere a ~ qc** to bear sth in mind; **a ~ fredda** objectively; **lasciami fare ~ locale** let me think.

mente'catto, a *ag* half-witted ♦ *sm/f* halfwit, imbecile.

men'tire *vi* to lie.

men'tito, a *ag*: **sotto ~e spoglie** under false pretences (*BRIT*) *o* pretenses (*US*).

'mento *sm* chin; **doppio ~** double chin.

men'tolo *sm* menthol.

'mentre *cong* (*temporale*) while; (*avversativo*) whereas ♦ *sm*: **in quel ~** at that very moment

menù *sm inv* (set) menu; **~ turistico** standard *o* tourists' menu.

menzio'nare [mentsjo'nare] *vt* to mention.

menzi'one [men'tsjone] *sf* mention; **fare ~ di** to mention.

men'zogna [men'tsoɲɲa] *sf* lie.

menzo'gnero, a [mentsoɲ'ɲɛro] *ag* false, untrue.

mera'viglia [mera'viʎʎa] *sf* amazement, wonder; (*persona, cosa*) marvel, wonder; **a ~** perfectly, wonderfully.

meravigli'are [meraviʎ'ʎare] *vt* to amaze, astonish; **~rsi** *vr*: **~rsi (di)** to marvel (at); (*stupirsi*) to be amazed (at), be astonished (at); **mi meraviglio di te!** I'm surprised at you!; **non c'è da ~rsi** it's not surprising.

meravigli'oso, a [meraviʎ'ʎoso] *ag* wonderful, marvellous (*BRIT*), marvelous (*US*).

merc. *abbr* (= *mercoledì*) Wed.

mer'cante *sm* merchant; **~ d'arte** art dealer; **~ di cavalli** horse dealer.

mercanteggi'are [merkanted'dʒare] *vt* (*onore, voto*) to sell ♦ *vi* to bargain, haggle.

mercan'tile *ag* commercial, mercantile; (*nave, marina*) merchant *cpd* ♦ *sm* (*nave*) merchantman.

mercan'zia [merkan'tsia] *sf* merchandise, goods *pl*.

merca'tino *sm* (*rionale*) local street market; (*ECON*) unofficial stock market.

mer'cato *sm* market; **di** ~ (*economia, prezzo, ricerche*) market *cpd;* **mettere** *o* **lanciare qc sul** ~ to launch sth on the market; **a buon** ~ *ag, av* cheap; ~ **dei cambi** exchange market; **M~ Comune (Europeo)** (European) Common Market; ~ **del lavoro** labour market, job market; ~ **nero** black market; ~ **al rialzo/al ribasso** (*BORSA*) sellers'/buyers' market; ~ **a termine** futures market.

'merce ['mɛrtʃe] *sf* goods *pl,* merchandise; ~ **deperibile** perishable goods *pl.*

mercé [mer'tʃe] *sf* mercy; **essere alla** ~ **di qn** to be at sb's mercy.

merce'nario, a [mertʃe'narjo] *ag, sm* mercenary.

merce'ria [mertʃe'ria] *sf* (*articoli*) haberdashery (*BRIT*), notions *pl* (*US*); (*bottega*) haberdasher's shop (*BRIT*), notions store (*US*).

mercoledì *sm inv* Wednesday; ~ **delle Ceneri** Ash Wednesday; *vedi nota nel riquadro; per fraseologia vedi* **martedì.**

MERCOLEDÌ DELLE CENERI

In the Catholic church, **Mercoledì delle Ceneri** *signals the beginning of Lent. Churchgoers are marked on the forehead with ash from the burning of an olive branch. Ash Wednesday is traditionally a day of fasting, abstinence and repentance.*

---

mer'curio *sm* mercury.

'merda *sf* (*fam!*) shit (*!*).

me'renda *sf* afternoon snack.

meridi'ano, a *ag* (*di mezzogiorno*) midday *cpd,* noonday ♦ *sm* meridian ♦ *sf* (*orologio*) sundial.

meridio'nale *ag* southern ♦ *sm/f* southerner.

meridi'one *sm* south.

me'ringa, ghe *sf* (*CUC*) meringue.

meri'tare *vt* to deserve, merit ♦ *vb impers* (*valere la pena*): **merita andare** it is worth going; **non merita neanche parlarne** it's not worth talking about; **per quel che merita** for what it's worth.

meri'tevole *ag* worthy.

'merito *sm* merit; (*valore*) worth; **dare** ~ **a qn di** to give sb credit for; **finire a pari** ~ to finish joint first (*o second etc*); to tie; **in** ~ **a** as regards, with regard to; **entrare nel** ~ **di una questione** to go into a matter; **non so niente in** ~ I don't know anything about it.

meritocra'zia [meritokrat'tsia] *sf* meritocracy.

meri'torio, a *ag* praiseworthy.

mer'letto *sm* lace.

'merlo *sm* (*ZOOL*) blackbird; (*ARCHIT*) battlement.

mer'luzzo [mer'luttso] *sm* (*ZOOL*) cod.

'mescere ['meʃʃere] *vt* to pour (out).

meschinità [meskini'ta] *sf* wretchedness; meagreness; meanness; narrow-mindedness.

mes'chino, a [mes'kino] *ag* wretched; (*scarso*) meagre (*BRIT*), meager (*US*); (*persona: gretta*) mean; (: *limitata*) narrow-minded, petty; **fare una figura** ~**a** to cut a poor figure.

'mescita ['meʃʃita] *sf* wine shop.

mesci'uto, a [meʃ'ʃuto] *pp di* **mescere.**

mesco'lanza [mesko'lantsa] *sf* mixture.

mesco'lare *vt* to mix; (*vini, colori*) to blend; (*mettere in disordine*) to mix up, muddle up; (*carte*) to shuffle; ~**rsi** *vr* to mix; to blend; to get mixed up; (*fig*): ~**rsi in** to get mixed up in, meddle in.

'mese *sm* month; **il** ~ **scorso** last month; **il** ~ **corrente** ~ this month.

'messa *sf* (*REL*) mass; (*il mettere*): ~ **a fuoco** focusing; ~ **in moto** starting; ~ **in piega** (*acconciatura*) set; ~ **a punto** (*TECN*) adjustment; (*AUT*) tuning; (*fig*) clarification; ~ **in scena** = **messinscena.**

messagge'rie [messaddʒe'rie] *sfpl* (*ditta: di distribuzione*) distributors; (: *di trasporto*) freight company.

messag'gero [messad'dʒero] *sm* messenger.

mes'saggio [mes'saddʒo] *sm* message.

mes'sale *sm* (*REL*) missal.

'messe *sf* harvest.

Mes'sia *sm inv* (*REL*): **il** ~ the Messiah.

messi'cano, a *ag, sm/f* Mexican.

'Messico *sm:* **il** ~ Mexico; **Città del** ~ Mexico City.

messin'scena [messin'ʃɛna] *sf* (*TEAT*) production.

'messo, a *pp di* **mettere** ♦ *sm* messenger.

mestie'rante *sm/f* (*peg*) money-grubber; (: *scrittore*) hack.

mesti'ere *sm* (*professione*) job; (: *manuale*) trade; (: *artigianale*) craft; (*fig: abilità nel lavoro*) skill, technique; **di** ~ by *o* to trade; **essere del** ~ to know the tricks of the trade.

mes'tizia [mes'tittsja] *sf* sadness, melancholy.

'mesto, a *ag* sad, melancholy.

'mestola *sf* (*CUC*) ladle; (*EDIL*) trowel.

'mestolo *sm* (*CUC*) ladle.

mestru'ale *ag* menstrual.

mestruazi'one [mestruat'tsjone] *sf*

menstruation; **avere le ~i** to have one's period.

'meta *sf* destination; (*fig*) aim, goal.

metà *sf inv* half; (*punto di mezzo*) middle; **dividere qc a** *o* **per ~** to divide sth in half, halve sth; **fare a ~ (di qc con qn)** to go halves (with sb in sth); **a ~ prezzo** at half price; **a ~ settimana** midweek; **a ~ strada** halfway; **verso la ~ del mese** halfway through the month, towards the middle of the month; **dire le cose a ~** to leave some things unsaid; **fare le cose a ~** to leave things half-done; **la mia dolce ~** (*fam scherzoso*) my better half.

metabo'lismo *sm* metabolism.

meta'done *sm* methadone.

meta'fisica *sf* metaphysics *sg*.

me'tafora *sf* metaphor.

meta'forico, a, ci, che *ag* metaphorical.

me'tallico, a, ci, che *ag* (*di metallo*) metal *cpd*; (*splendore, rumore etc*) metallic.

metalliz'zato, a [metalliddzato] *ag* (*verniciatura*) metallic.

me'tallo *sm* metal; **di ~** metal *cpd*.

metallur'gia [metallur'dʒia] *sf* metallurgy.

metalmec'canico, a, ci, che *ag* engineering *cpd* ♦ *sm* engineering worker.

meta'morfosi *sf* metamorphosis.

me'tano *sm* methane.

me'teora *sf* meteor.

meteo'rite *sm* meteorite.

meteorolo'gia [meteorolo'dʒia] *sf* meteorology.

meteoro'logico, a, ci, che [meteoro'lɔdʒiko] *ag* meteorological, weather *cpd*.

meteo'rologo, a, ghi, ghe *sm/f* meteorologist.

me'ticcio, a, ci, ce [me'tittʃo] *sm/f* half-caste, half-breed.

meticolosità *sf* meticulousness.

metico'loso, a *ag* meticulous.

me'todico, a, ci, che *ag* methodical.

'metodo *sm* method; (*manuale*) tutor (*BRIT*), manual; **far qc con/senza ~** to do sth methodically/unmethodically.

me'traggio [me'traddʒo] *sm* (*SARTORIA*) length; (*CINE*) footage; **film a lungo ~** feature film; **film a corto ~** short film.

metra'tura *sf* length.

'metrico, a, ci, che *ag* metric; (*POESIA*) metrical ♦ *sf* metrics *sg*.

'metro *sm* metre (*BRIT*), meter (*US*); (*nastro*) tape measure; (*asta*) (metre) rule.

metrò *sm inv* underground (*BRIT*), subway (*US*).

metro'notte *sm inv* night security guard.

me'tropoli *sf* metropolis.

metropoli'tano, a *ag* metropolitan ♦ *sf* underground (*BRIT*), subway (*US*); **~a leggera** metro (*mainly on the surface*).

'mettere *vt* to put; (*abito*) to put on; (: *portare*) to wear; (*installare: telefono*) to put in; (*fig: provocare*): **~ fame/allegria a qn** to make sb hungry/happy; (*supporre*): **mettiamo che ...** let's suppose *o* say that **...; ~rsi** *vr* (*persona*) to put o.s.; (*oggetto*) to go; (*disporsi: faccenda*) to turn out; **~rsi a piangere/ridere** to start crying/laughing, start *o* begin to cry/laugh; **~rsi a sedere** to sit down; **~rsi al lavoro** to set to work; **~rsi a letto** to get into bed; (*per malattia*) to take to one's bed; **~rsi il cappello** to put on one's hat; **~rsi sotto** to get down to things; **~rsi in società** to set up in business; **si sono messi insieme** (*coppia*) they've started going out together (*BRIT*) *o* dating (*US*); **~rci: ~rci molta cura/molto tempo** to take a lot of care/a lot of time; **mettercela tutta** to do one's best; **ci ho messo 3 ore per venire** it's taken me 3 hours to get here; **~ un annuncio sul giornale** to place an advertisement in the paper; **~ a confronto** to compare; **~ in conto** (*somma etc*) to put on account; **~ in luce** (*problemi, errori*) to stress, highlight; **~ a tacere qn/qc** to keep sb/sth quiet; **~ su casa** to set up house; **~ su un negozio** to start a shop; **~ su peso** to put on weight; **~ via** to put away.

mez'zadro [med'dzadro] *sm* (*AGR*) sharecropper.

mezza'luna [meddza'luna], *pl* **mezze'lune** *sf* half-moon; (*dell'islamismo*) crescent; (*coltello*) (semicircular) chopping knife.

mezza'nino [meddza'nino] *sm* mezzanine (floor).

mez'zano, a [med'dzano] *ag* (*medio*) average, medium; (*figlio*) middle *cpd* ♦ *sm/f* (*intermediario*) go-between; (*ruffiano*) pimp.

mezza'notte [meddza'nɔtte] *sf* midnight.

'mezzo, a ['meddzo] *ag* half; **un ~ litro/panino** half a litre/roll ♦ *av* half-; **~ morto** half-dead ♦ *sm* (*metà*) half; (*parte centrale: di strada etc*) middle; (*per raggiungere un fine*) means *sg*; (*veicolo*) vehicle; (*nell'indicare l'ora*): **le nove e ~** half past nine; **mezzogiorno e ~** half past twelve ♦ *sf*: **la ~a** half-past twelve (in the afternoon); **~i** *smpl* (*possibilità economiche*) means; **di ~a età** middle-aged; **aver una ~a idea di fare qc** to have half a mind to do sth; **è stato un ~ scandalo** it almost caused a scandal; **un soprabito di ~a stagione** a spring (*o* autumn) coat; **a ~a**

voce in an undertone; **una volta e** ~ **più grande** one and a half times bigger; **di** ~ middle, in the middle; **andarci di** ~ (*patir danno*) to suffer; **esserci di** ~ (*ostacolo*) to be in the way; **levarsi** *o* **togliersi di** ~ to get out of the way; **mettersi di** ~ to interfere; **togliere di** ~ (*persona, cosa*) to get rid of; (*fam: uccidere*) to bump off; **non c'è una via di** ~ there's no middle course; **in** ~ **a** in the middle of; **nel bel** ~ **(di)** right in the middle (of); **per** *o* **a** ~ **di** by means of; **a** ~ **corriere** by carrier; ~**i di comunicazione di massa** mass media *pl*; ~**i pubblici** public transport *sg*; ~**i di trasporto** means of transport.

mezzogi'orno [meddzo'dʒorno] *sm* midday, noon; (*GEO*) south; **a** ~ at 12 (o'clock) *o* midday *o* noon; **il** ~ **d'Italia** southern Italy.

mez'z'ora, mez'zora [med'dzora] *sf* half-hour, half an hour.

MI *sigla* = *Milano.*

mi *pron* (*dav lo, la, li, le, ne diventa* **me**) (*oggetto*) me; (*complemento di termine*) (to) me; (*riflessivo*) myself ♦ *sm* (*MUS*) E; (*: solfeggiando la scala*) mi; ~ **aiuti?** will you help me?; **me ne ha parlato** he spoke to me about it, he told me about it; ~ **servo da solo** I'll help myself.

'mia *vedi* **mio.**

miago'lare *vi* to miaow, mew.

Mib *sigla m, ag* (= *indice borsa Milano*) Milan Stock Exchange Index.

'mica *sf* (*CHIM*) mica ♦ *av* (*fam*): **non ... ~** not ... at all; **non sono** ~ **stanco** I'm not a bit tired; **non sarà** ~ **partito?** he wouldn't have left, would he?; ~ **male** not bad.

'miccia, ce ['mittʃa] *sf* fuse.

micidi'ale [mitʃi'djale] *ag* fatal; (*dannosissimo*) deadly.

'micio, a, ci, cie ['mitʃo] *sm/f* pussy (cat).

microbiolo'gia [mikrobiolo'dʒia] *sf* microbiology.

'microbo *sm* microbe.

microcir'cuito [mikrotʃir'kuito] *sm* microcircuit.

micro'film *sm inv* microfilm.

mi'crofono *sm* microphone.

microinfor'matica *sf* microcomputing.

micro'onda *sf* microwave.

microproces'sore [mikroprotʃes'sore] *sm* microprocessor.

micros'copico, a, ci, che *ag* microscopic.

micros'copio *sm* microscope.

micro'solco, chi *sm* (*solco*) microgroove; (*disco: a 33 giri*) long-playing record, LP; (*: a 45 giri*) extended-play record, EP.

micros'pia *sf* hidden microphone, bug

(*fam*).

mi'dollo, *pl(f)* ~**a** *sm* (*ANAT*) marrow; ~ **spinale** spinal cord.

'mie, mi'ei *vedi* **mio.**

mi'ele *sm* honey.

mi'etere *vt* (*AGR*) to reap, harvest; (*fig: vite*) to take, claim.

mietitrebbia'trice [mjetitrebbja'tritʃe] *sf* combine harvester.

mieti'trice [mjeti'tritʃe] *sf* (*macchina*) harvester.

mieti'tura *sf* (*raccolto*) harvest; (*lavoro*) harvesting; (*tempo*) harvest-time.

'miglia ['miʎʎa] *sfpl di* **miglio.**

migli'aio [miʎ'ʎajo], *pl(f)* ~**a** *sm* thousand; **un** ~ **(di)** about a thousand; **a** ~**a** by the thousand, in thousands.

'miglio ['miʎʎo] *sm* (*BOT*) millet; (*pl(f)* ~**a**: *unità di misura*) mile; ~ **marino** *o* **nautico** nautical mile.

migliora'mento [miʎʎora'mento] *sm* improvement.

miglio'rare [miʎʎo'rare] *vt, vi* to improve.

migli'ore [miʎ'ʎore] *ag* (*comparativo*) better; (*superlativo*) best ♦ *sm*: **il** ~ **the** best (thing) ♦ *sm/f*: **il(la)** ~ **the best** (person); **il miglior vino di questa regione** the best wine in this area; **i** ~**i auguri** best wishes.

miglio'ria [miʎʎo'ria] *sf* improvement.

'mignolo ['miɲɲolo] *sm* (*ANAT*) little finger, pinkie; (*: dito del piede*) little toe.

mi'grare *vi* to migrate.

migrazi'one [migrat'tsjone] *sf* migration.

'mila *pl di* **mille.**

mila'nese *ag* Milanese ♦ *sm/f* person from Milan; **i** ~**i** the Milanese; **cotoletta alla** ~ (*CUC*) Wiener schnitzel; **risotto alla** ~ (*CUC*) *risotto with saffron.*

Mi'lano *sf* Milan.

miliar'dario, a *ag, sm/f* millionaire.

mili'ardo *sm* thousand million (*BRIT*), billion (*US*).

mili'are *ag*: **pietra** ~ milestone.

milio'nario, a *ag, sm/f* millionaire.

mili'one *sm* million; **un** ~ **di lire** a million lire.

mili'tante *ag, sm/f* militant.

mili'tanza [mili'tantsa] *sf* militancy.

mili'tare *vi* (*MIL*) to be a soldier, serve; (*fig: in un partito*) to be a militant ♦ *ag* military ♦ *sm* serviceman; **fare il** ~ **to do one's** military service; ~ **di carriera** regular (soldier).

milita'resco, a, schi, sche *ag* (*portamento*) military *cpd*.

'milite *sm* soldier.

mi'lizia [mi'littsja] *sf* (*corpo armato*) militia.

milizi'ano [milit'tsjano] *sm* militiaman.
millanta'tore, 'trice *sm/f* boaster.
millante'ria *sf (qualità)* boastfulness.
'mille *num (pl* **mila)** a *o* one thousand;
  diecimila ten thousand.
mille'foglie [mille'fɔʎʎe] *sm inv (CUC)* cream
  o vanilla slice.
mil'lennio *sm* millennium.
millepi'edi *sm inv* centipede.
mil'lesimo, a *ag, sm* thousandth.
milli'grammo *sm* milligram(me).
mil'lilitro *sm* millilitre *(BRIT)*, milliliter
  (US).
mil'limetro *sm* millimetre *(BRIT)*,
  millimeter *(US)*.
'milza ['miltsa] *sf (ANAT)* spleen.
mi'metico, a, ci, che *ag (arte)* mimetic;
  tuta ~a *(MIL)* camouflage.
mime'tismo *sm* camouflage.
mimetiz'zare [mimetid'dzare] *vt* to
  camouflage; **~rsi** *vr* to camouflage o.s.
'mimica *sf (arte)* mime.
'mimo *sm (attore, componimento)* mime.
mi'mosa *sf* mimosa.
min. *abbr (= minuto, minimo)* min.
'mina *sf (esplosiva)* mine; *(di matita)* lead.
mi'naccia, ce [mi'nattʃa] *sf* threat; **sotto la
  ~ di** under threat of.
minacci'are [minat'tʃare] *vt* to threaten; **~
  qn di morte** to threaten to kill sb; **~ di
  fare qc** to threaten to do sth; **minaccia di
  piovere** it looks like rain.
minacci'oso, a [minat'tʃoso] *ag*
  threatening.
mi'nare *vt (MIL)* to mine; *(fig)* to
  undermine.
mina'tore *sm* miner.
mina'torio, a *ag* threatening.
minchi'one, a [min'kjone] *(fam) ag* idiotic
  ♦ *sm/f* idiot.
mine'rale *ag, sm* mineral.
mineralo'gia [mineralo'dʒia] *sf* mineralogy.
mine'rario, a *ag (delle miniere)* mining; *(dei
  minerali)* ore *cpd.*
mi'nestra *sf* soup; **~ in brodo** noodle soup;
  ~ di verdura vegetable soup.
mines'trone *sm* thick vegetable and pasta
  soup.
mingher'lino, a [minger'lino] *ag* thin,
  slender.
'mini *ag inv* mini ♦ *sf inv* miniskirt.
minia'tura *sf* miniature.
minielabora'tore *sm* minicomputer.
mini'era *sf* mine; **~ di carbone** coalmine;
  (impresa) colliery *(BRIT)*, coalmine.
mini'gonna *sf* miniskirt.
minima'lista, i, e *ag, sm/f* minimalist.
minimiz'zare [minimid'dzare] *vt* to

minimize.
'minimo, a *ag* minimum, least, slightest;
  (piccolissimo) very small, slight; *(il più
  basso)* lowest, minimum ♦ *sm* minimum;
  al ~ at least; **girare al ~** *(AUT)* to idle; **il ~**
  indispensabile the bare minimum; **il ~
  della pena** the minimum sentence.
minis'tero *sm (POL, REL)* ministry;
  (governo) government; *(DIR)*: **Pubblico M~**
  State Prosecutor; **M~ delle Finanze**
  Ministry of Finance, ≈ Treasury.
mi'nistro *sm (POL, REL)* minister; **M~ delle
  Finanze** Minister of Finance, ≈
  Chancellor of the Exchequer *(BRIT)*.
mino'ranza [mino'rantsa] *sf* minority;
  essere in ~ to be in the minority.
mino'rato, a *ag* handicapped ♦ *sm/f*
  physically *(o* mentally) handicapped
  person.
minora'zione [minorat'tsjone] *sf* handicap.
Mi'norca *sf* Minorca.
mi'nore *ag (comparativo di piccolo)* less; *(: più piccolo)*
  smaller; *(: numero)* lower; *(: inferiore)*
  lower, inferior; *(: meno importante)*
  minor; *(: più giovane)* younger;
  (superlativo) least; smallest; lowest; least
  important; youngest ♦ *sm/f (minorenne)*
  minor, person under age; **in misura ~** to
  a lesser extent; **questo è il male ~** this is
  the lesser evil.
mino'renne *ag* under age ♦ *sm/f* minor,
  person under age.
mino'rile *ag* juvenile; **carcere ~** young
  offenders' institution; **delinquenza ~**
  juvenile delinquency.
minori'tario, a *ag* minority *cpd.*
mi'nuscolo, a *ag (scrittura, carattere)* small;
  (piccolissimo) tiny ♦ *sf* small letter ♦ *sm*
  small letters *pl*; *(TIP)* lower case; **scrivere
  tutto (in) ~** to write everything in small
  letters.
mi'nuta *sf* rough copy, draft.
mi'nuto, a *ag* tiny, minute; *(pioggia)* fine;
  (corporatura) delicate, fine; *(lavoro)*
  detailed ♦ *sm (unità di misura)* minute; **al ~**
  (COMM) retail; **avere i ~i contati** to have
  very little time.
mi'nuzia [mi'nuttsja] *sf (cura)*
  meticulousness; *(particolare)* detail.
minuziosa'mente [minuttsjosa'mente] *av*
  meticulously; in minute detail.
minuzi'oso, a [minut'tsjoso] *ag (persona,
  descrizione)* meticulous; *(esame)* minute.
'mio, 'mia, mi'ei, 'mie *det*: **il ~, la mia** *etc*
  my ♦ *pronome*: **il ~, la mia** *etc* mine ♦ *sm*:
  ho speso del ~ I spent my own money
  ♦ *sf*: **la mia** *(opinione)* my view; **i miei** my
  family; **un ~ amico** a friend of mine; **per**

amor ~ for my sake; **è dalla mia** he is on my side; **anch'io ho avuto le mie** (*disavventure*) I've had my problems too; **ne ho fatta una delle mie!** (*sciocchezze*) I've done it again!; **cerco di stare sulle mie** I try to keep myself to myself.

'miope *ag* short-sighted.

mio'pia *sf* short-sightedness, myopia; (*fig*) short-sightedness.

'mira *sf* (*anche fig*) aim; **avere una buona/ cattiva** ~ to be a good/bad shot; **prendere la** ~ to take aim; **prendere di** ~ **qn** (*fig*) to pick on sb.

mi'rabile *ag* admirable, wonderful.

mi'racolo *sm* miracle.

miraco'loso, a *ag* miraculous.

mi'raggio [mi'raddʒo] *sm* mirage.

mi'rare *vi*: ~ **a** to aim at.

mi'riade *sf* myriad.

mi'rino *sm* (*TECN*) sight; (*FOT*) viewer, viewfinder.

mir'tillo *sm* bilberry (*BRIT*), blueberry (*US*), whortleberry.

'mirto *sm* myrtle.

mi'santropo, a *sm/f* misanthropist.

mi'scela [miʃ'ʃɛla] *sf* mixture; (*di caffè*) blend.

miscel'lanea [miʃʃel'lanea] *sf* miscellany.

'mischia ['miskja] *sf* scuffle; (*RUGBY*) scrum, scrummage.

mischi'are [mis'kjare] *vt*, ~**rsi** *vr* to mix, blend.

misco'noscere [misko'noʃʃere] *vt* (*qualità, coraggio etc*) to fail to appreciate.

miscre'dente *ag* (*REL*) misbelieving; (: *incredulo*) unbelieving ♦ *sm/f* misbeliever; unbeliever.

mis'cuglio [mis'kuʎʎo] *sm* mixture, hotchpotch, jumble.

'mise *vb vedi* **mettere**.

mise'rabile *ag* (*infelice*) miserable, wretched; (*povero*) poverty-stricken; (*di scarso valore*) miserable.

mi'seria *sf* extreme poverty; (*infelicità*) misery; ~**e** *sfpl* (*del mondo etc*) misfortunes, troubles; **costare una** ~ to cost next to nothing; **piangere** ~ to plead poverty; **ridursi in** ~ to be reduced to poverty; **porca** ~**!** (*fam*) (bloody) hell!

miseri'cordia *sf* mercy, pity.

misericordi'oso, a *ag* merciful.

'misero, a *ag* miserable, wretched; (*povero*) poverty-stricken; (*insufficiente*) miserable.

mis'fatto *sm* misdeed, crime.

'misi *vb vedi* **mettere**.

mi'sogino [mi'zɔdʒino] *sm* misogynist.

'missile *sm* missile; ~ **cruise** *o* **di crociera**

cruise missile; ~ **terra-aria** surface-to-air missile.

missio'nario, a *ag*, *sm/f* missionary.

missi'one *sf* mission.

misteri'oso, a *ag* mysterious.

mis'tero *sm* mystery; **fare** ~ **di qc** to make a mystery out of sth; **quanti** ~**i!** why all the mystery?

'mistico, a, ci, che *ag* mystic(al) ♦ *sm* mystic.

mistifi'care *vt* to fool, bamboozle.

'misto, a *ag* mixed; (*scuola*) mixed, coeducational ♦ *sm* mixture; **un tessuto in** ~ **lino** a linen mix.

mis'tura *sf* mixture.

mi'sura *sf* measure; (*misurazione, dimensione*) measurement; (*taglia*) size; (*provvedimento*) measure, step; (*moderazione*) moderation; (*MUS*) time; (: *divisione*) bar; (*fig: limite*) bounds *pl*, limit; **in** ~ **di** in accordance with, according to; **nella** ~ **in cui** inasmuch as, insofar as; **in giusta** ~ moderately; **oltre** ~ beyond measure; **su** ~ made to measure; **in ugual** ~ equally, in the same way; **a** ~ **d'uomo** on a human scale; **passare la** ~ to overstep the mark, go too far; **prendere le** ~**e a qn** to take sb's measurements, measure sb; **prendere le** ~**e di qc** to measure sth; **ho preso le mie** ~**e** I've taken the necessary steps; **non ha il senso della** ~ he doesn't know when to stop; ~ **di lunghezza/capacità** measure of length/capacity; ~**e di sicurezza/ prevenzione** safety/precautionary measures.

misu'rare *vt* (*ambiente, stoffa*) to measure; (*terreno*) to survey; (*abito*) to try on; (*pesare*) to weigh; (*fig: parole etc*) to weigh up; (: *spese, cibo*) to limit ♦ *vi* to measure; ~**rsi** *vr*: ~**rsi con qn** to have a confrontation with sb; (*competere*) to compete with sb.

misu'rato, a *ag* (*ponderato*) measured; (*prudente*) cautious; (*moderato*) moderate.

misurazi'one [mizurat'tsjone] *sf* measuring; (*di terreni*) surveying.

'mite *ag* mild; (*prezzo*) moderate, reasonable.

'mitico, a, ci, che *ag* mythical.

miti'gare *vt* to mitigate, lessen; (*lenire*) to soothe, relieve; ~**rsi** *vr* (*odio*) to subside; (*tempo*) to become milder.

'mitilo *sm* mussel.

'mito *sm* myth.

mitolo'gia, 'gie [mitolo'dʒia] *sf* mythology.

mito'logico, a, ci, che [mito'lɔdʒiko] *ag* mythological.

'**mitra** *sf* (*REL*) mitre (*BRIT*), miter (*US*) ♦ *sm inv* (*arma*) sub-machine gun.
mitragli'are [mitraʎ'ʎare] *vt* to machine-gun.
mitraglia'tore, 'trice [mitraʎʎa'tore] *ag*: **fucile** *m* ~ sub-machine gun ♦ *sf* machine gun.
mitteleuro'peo, a *ag* Central European.
mit'tente *sm/f* sender.
ml *abbr* (= *millilitro*) ml.
MLD *sigla m vedi* **Movimento per la Liberazione della Donna.**
MM *abbr* = *Metropolitana Milanese.*
mm *abbr* (= *millimetro*) mm.
M.M. *abbr vedi* **marina militare.**
MN *sigla* = *Mantova.*
M/N, m/n *abbr* (= *motonave*) MV.
MO *sigla* = *Modena.*
M.O. *abbr* = **Medio Oriente.**
mo' *sm*: **a** ~ **di** *prep* like; **a** ~ **di esempio** by way of example.
'**mobile** *ag* mobile; (*parte di macchina*) moving; (*DIR: bene*) movable, personal ♦ *sm* (*arredamento*) piece of furniture; ~**i** *smpl* furniture *sg*.
mo'bilia *sf* furniture.
mobili'are *ag* (*DIR*) personal, movable.
mo'bilio *sm* = **mobilia.**
mobilità *sf* mobility.
mobili'tare *vt* to mobilize; ~ **l'opinione pubblica** to rouse public opinion.
mobilitazi'one [mobilitat'tsjone] *sf* mobilization.
mocas'sino *sm* moccasin.
mocci'oso, a [mot'tʃoso] *sm/f* (*bambino piccolo*) little kid; (*peg*) snotty-nosed kid.
'**moccolo** *sm* (*di candela*) candle end; (*fam: bestemmia*) oath; (: *moccio*) snot; **reggere il** ~ to play gooseberry (*BRIT*), act as chaperon(e).
'**moda** *sf* fashion; **alla** ~, **di** ~ fashionable, in fashion.
modalità *sf inv* formality; **seguire attentamente le** ~ **d'uso** to follow the instructions carefully; ~ **giuridiche** legal procedures; ~ **di pagamento** method of payment.
mo'della *sf* model.
model'lare *vt* (*creta*) to model, shape; ~**rsi** *vr*: ~**rsi su** to model o.s. on.
mo'dello *sm* model; (*stampo*) mould (*BRIT*), mold (*US*) ♦ *ag inv* model *cpd*.
'**modem** *sm inv* modem.
mode'nese *ag* of (*o* from) Modena.
mode'rare *vt* to moderate; ~**rsi** *vr* to restrain o.s.; ~ **la velocità** to reduce speed; ~ **i termini** to weigh one's words.
mode'rato, a *ag* moderate.

modera'tore, 'trice *sm/f* moderator.
moderazi'one [moderat'tsjone] *sf* moderation.
moderniz'zare [modernid'dzare] *vt* to bring up to date, modernize; ~**rsi** *vr* to get up to date.
mo'derno, a *ag* modern.
mo'destia *sf* modesty; ~ **a parte** ... in all modesty ..., though I say it myself ....
mo'desto, a *ag* modest.
'**modico, a, ci, che** *ag* reasonable, moderate.
mo'difica, che *sf* modification; **subire delle** ~**che** to undergo some modifications.
modifi'cabile *ag* modifiable.
modifi'care *vt* to modify, alter; ~**rsi** *vr* to alter, change.
mo'dista *sf* milliner.
'**modo** *sm* way, manner; (*mezzo*) means, way; (*occasione*) opportunity; (*LING*) mood; (*MUS*) mode; ~**i** *smpl* (*maniere*) manners; **a suo** ~, **a** ~ **suo** in his own way; **ad** *o* **in ogni** ~ anyway; **di** *o* **in** ~ **che** so that; **in** ~ **da** so as to; **in tutti i** ~**i** at all costs; (*comunque sia*) anyway; (*in ogni caso*) in any case; **in un certo qual** ~ in a way, in some ways; **in qualche** ~ somehow or other; **oltre** ~ extremely; ~ **di dire** turn of phrase; **per** ~ **di dire** so to speak; **fare a** ~ **proprio** to do as one likes; **fare le cose a** ~ to do things properly; **una persona a** ~ a well mannered person; **c'è** ~ **e** ~ **di farlo** there's a right way and a wrong way of doing it.
modu'lare *vt* to modulate ♦ *ag* modular.
modulazi'one [modulat'tsjone] *sf* modulation; ~ **di frequenza** (**FM**) frequency modulation (FM).
'**modulo** *sm* (*modello*) form; (*ARCHIT, lunare, di comando*) module; ~ **di domanda** application form; ~ **d'iscrizione** enrolment form; ~ **di versamento** deposit slip.
Moga'discio [moga'diʃʃo] *sm* Mogadishu.
'**mogano** *sm* mahogany.
'**mogio, a, gi, gie** ['mɔdʒo] *ag* down in the dumps, dejected.
'**moglie** ['moʎʎe] *sf* wife.
mo'hair [mɔ'ɛr] *sm* mohair.
mo'ine *sfpl* cajolery *sg*; (*leziosità*) affectation *sg*; **fare le** ~ **a qn** to cajole sb.
'**mola** *sf* millstone; (*utensile abrasivo*) grindstone.
mo'lare *vt* to grind ♦ *ag* (*pietra*) mill *cpd* ♦ *sm* (*dente*) molar.
'**mole** *sf* mass; (*dimensioni*) size; (*edificio grandioso*) massive structure; **una** ~ **di lavoro** masses (*BRIT*) *o* loads of work.

mo'lecola *sf* molecule.
moles'tare *vt* to bother, annoy.
mo'lestia *sf* annoyance, bother; **recar ~ a qn** to bother sb; **~e sessuali** sexual harassment *sg*.
mo'lesto, a *ag* annoying.
moli'sano, a *ag* of (*o* from) Molise.
'molla *sf* spring; **~e** *sfpl* (*per camino*) tongs; **prendere qn con le ~e** to treat sb with kid gloves.
mol'lare *vt* to release, let go; (*NAUT*) to ease; (*fig: ceffone*) to give ♦ *vi* (*cedere*) to give in; **~ gli ormeggi** (*NAUT*) to cast off; **~ la presa** to let go.
'molle *ag* soft; (*muscoli*) flabby; (*fig: debole*) weak, feeble.
molleggi'ato, a [molled'dʒato] *ag* (*letto*) sprung; (*auto*) with good suspension.
mol'leggio [mol'leddʒo] *sm* (*per veicoli*) suspension; (*elasticità*) springiness; (*GINNASTICA*) knee-bends *pl*.
mol'letta *sf* (*per capelli*) hairgrip; (*per panni stesi*) clothes peg (*BRIT*) *o* pin (*US*); **~e** *sfpl* (*per zucchero*) tongs.
mol'lezza [mol'lettsa] *sf* softness; flabbiness; weakness, feebleness; **~e** *sfpl*: **vivere nelle ~e** to live in the lap of luxury.
mol'lica, che *sf* crumb, soft part.
mol'liccio, a, ci, ce [mol'littʃo] *ag* (*terreno, impasto*) soggy; (*frutta*) soft; (*floscio: mano*) limp; (*: muscolo*) flabby.
mol'lusco, schi *sm* mollusc.
'molo *sm* jetty, pier.
mol'teplice [mol'teplitʃe] *ag* (*formato di più elementi*) complex; **~i** *pl* (*svariati: interessi, attività*) numerous, various.
molteplicità [molteplitʃi'ta] *sf* multiplicity.
moltipli'care *vt* to multiply; **~rsi** *vr* to multiply; (*richieste*) to increase in number.
moltiplicazi'one [moltiplikat'tsjone] *sf* multiplication.
molti'tudine *sf* multitude; **una ~ di** a vast number *o* a multitude of.

==================== *PAROLA CHIAVE*

'molto, a *det* (*quantità*) a lot of, much; (*numero*) a lot of, many; **~ pane/carbone** a lot of bread/coal; **~a gente** a lot of people, many people; **~i libri** a lot of books, many books; **non ho ~ tempo** I haven't got much time; **per ~ (tempo)** for a long time; **ci vuole ~ (tempo)?** will it take long?; **arriverà fra non ~** he'll arrive soon; **ne hai per ~?** will you be long?
♦ *av* **1** a lot, (very) much; **viaggia ~** he travels a lot; **non viaggia ~** he doesn't

travel much *o* a lot
2 (*intensivo: con aggettivi, avverbi*) very; (*: con participio passato*) (very) much; **~ buono** very good; **~ migliore, ~ meglio** much *o* a lot better
♦ *pron* much, a lot; **~i, e** *pron pl* many, a lot; **~i pensano che ...** many (people) think that ...; **~e sono rimaste a casa** a lot of them stayed at home; **c'era gente, ma non ~a** there were people there, but not many.

momentanea'mente *av* at the moment, at present.
momen'taneo, a *ag* momentary, fleeting.
mo'mento *sm* moment; **da un ~ all'altro** at any moment; (*all'improvviso*) suddenly; **al ~ di fare** just as I was (*o* you were *o* he was *etc*) doing; **a ~i** (*da un ~ all'altro*) any time *o* moment now; (*quasi*) nearly; **per il ~** for the time being; **dal ~ che** ever since; (*dato che*) since; **~ culminante** climax.
'monaca, che *sf* nun.
'Monaco *sf* Monaco; **~ (di Baviera)** Munich.
'monaco, ci *sm* monk.
mo'narca, chi *sm* monarch.
monar'chia [monar'kia] *sf* monarchy.
mo'narchico, a, ci, che [mo'narkiko] *ag* (*stato, autorità*) monarchic; (*partito, fede*) monarchist ♦ *sm/f* monarchist.
monas'tero *sm* (*di monaci*) monastery; (*di monache*) convent.
mo'nastico, a, ci, che *ag* monastic.
'monco, a, chi, che *ag* maimed; (*fig*) incomplete; **~ d'un braccio** one-armed.
mon'cone *sm* stump.
mon'dana *sf* prostitute.
mondanità *sf* (*frivolezza*) worldliness; **le ~** (*piaceri*) the pleasures of the world.
mon'dano, a *ag* (*anche fig*) worldly; (*dell'alta società*) society *cpd*; fashionable.
mon'dare *vt* (*frutta, patate*) to peel; (*piselli*) to shell; (*pulire*) to clean.
mondez'zaio [mondet'tsajo] *sm* rubbish (*BRIT*) *o* garbage (*US*) dump.
mondi'ale *ag* (*campionato, popolazione*) world *cpd*; (*influenza*) world-wide; **di fama ~** world famous.
'mondo *sm* world; (*grande quantità*): **un ~ di** lots of, a host of; **il gran** *o* **bel ~** high society; **per niente al ~, per nessuna cosa al ~** not for all the world; **da che ~ è ~** since time *o* the world began; **mandare qn all'altro ~** to kill sb; **mettere/venire al ~** to bring/come into the world; **vivere fuori dal ~** to be out of touch with the

real world; **(sono) cose dell'altro** ~! it's
incredible!; **com'è piccolo il** ~! it's a
small world!
mone'gasco, a, schi, sche *ag, sm/f*
Monegasque.
monelle'ria *sf* prank, naughty trick.
mo'nello, a *sm/f* street urchin; (*ragazzo
vivace*) scamp, imp.
mo'neta *sf* coin; (*ECON: valuta*) currency;
(*denaro spicciolo*) (small) change; ~ **estera**
foreign currency; ~ **legale** legal tender.
mone'tario, a *ag* monetary.
Mon'golia *sf:* **la** ~ Mongolia.
mon'golico, a, ci, che *ag* Mongolian.
mongo'lismo *sm* mongolism, Down's
syndrome.
'mongolo, a *ag* Mongolian ♦ *sm/f, sm*
Mongol, Mongolian.
mongo'loide *ag, sm/f* (*MED*) mongol.
'monito *sm* warning.
'monitor *sm inv* (*TECN, TV*) monitor.
monito'raggio [monito'raddʒo] *sm*
monitoring.
monito'rare *vt* to monitor.
mo'nocolo *sm* (*lente*) monocle, eyeglass.
monoco'lore *ag* (*POL*). **governo** ~ one-
party government.
monoga'mia *sf* monogamy.
mo'nogamo, a *ag* monogamous ♦ *sm*
monogamist.
monogra'fia *sf* monograph.
mono'gramma, i *sm* monogram.
mono'lingue *ag* monolingual.
monolo'cale *sm* ≈ studio flat.
mo'nologo, ghi *sm* monologue.
mono'pattino *sm* scooter.
mono'polio *sm* monopoly; ~ **di stato**
government monopoly.
monopoliz'zare [monopolid'dzare] *vt* to
monopolize.
mono'sillabo, a *ag* monosyllabic ♦ *sm*
monosyllable.
monoto'nia *sf* monotony.
mo'notono, a *ag* monotonous.
mono'uso *ag inv* disposable.
Mons. *abbr* (= *Monsignore*) Mgr.
monsi'gnore [monsiɲ'ɲore] *sm* (*REL: titolo*)
Your (*o* His) Grace.
mon'sone *sm* monsoon.
monta'carichi [monta'kariki] *sm inv* hoist,
goods lift.
mon'taggio [mon'taddʒo] *sm* (*TECN*)
assembly; (*CINE*) editing.
mon'tagna [mon'taɲɲa] *sf* mountain; (*zona
montuosa*): **la** ~ the mountains *pl*; **andare
in** ~ to go to the mountains; **aria/strada di**
~ mountain air/road; **casa di** ~ house in
the mountains; ~**e russe** roller coaster *sg*,

big dipper *sg* (*BRIT*).
monta'gnoso, a [montaɲ'ɲoso] *ag*
mountainous.
monta'naro, a *ag* mountain *cpd* ♦ *sm/f*
mountain dweller.
mon'tano, a *ag* mountain *cpd*.
mon'tante *sm* (*di porta*) jamb; (*di finestra*)
upright; (*CALCIO: palo*) post; (*PUGILATO*)
upper cut; (*COMM*) total amount.
mon'tare *vt* to go (*o* come) up; (*cavallo*) to
ride; (*apparecchiatura*) to set up,
assemble; (*CUC*) to whip; (*ZOOL*) to cover;
(*incastonare*) to mount, set; (*CINE*) to edit;
(*FOT*) to mount ♦ *vi* to go (*o* come) up; (*a
cavallo*): ~ **bene/male** to ride well/badly;
(*aumentare di livello, volume*) to rise; ~**rsi**
vr to become big-headed; ~ **qc** to
exaggerate sth; ~ **qn** *o* **la testa a qn** to
turn sb's head; ~**rsi la testa** to become
big-headed; ~ **in bicicletta/macchina/
treno** to get on a bicycle/ into a car/on a
train; ~ **a cavallo** to get on *o* mount a
horse; ~ **la guardia** (*MIL*) to mount guard.
monta'tura *sf* assembling *no pl*; (*di occhiali*)
frames *pl*; (*di gioiello*) mounting, setting;
(*fig*): ~ **pubblicitaria** publicity stunt.
montavi'vande *sm inv* dumbwaiter.
'monte *sm* mountain; **a** ~ upstream;
andare a ~ (*fig*) to come to nothing;
mandare a ~ **qc** (*fig*) to upset sth, cause
sth to fail; **il M**~ **Bianco** Mont Blanc; **il
M**~ **Everest** Mount Everest; ~ **di pietà**
pawnshop; ~ **premi** prize.
Monteci'torio [montetʃi'torjo] *sm:* **palazzo**
~ (*POL*) *seat of the Italian Chamber of
Deputies.*
mont'gomery [mənt'gʌməri] *sm inv* duffel
coat.
mon'tone *sm* (*ZOOL*) ram; (*anche:* **giacca di**
~) sheepskin (jacket); **carne di** ~ mutton.
montuosità *sf* mountainous nature.
montu'oso, a *ag* mountainous.
monu'mento *sm* monument.
mo'quette [mɔ'kɛt] *sf* fitted carpet.
'mora *sf* (*del rovo*) blackberry; (*del gelso*)
mulberry; (*DIR*) delay; (: *somma*) arrears
pl.
mo'rale *ag* moral ♦ *sf* (*scienza*) ethics *sg*,
moral philosophy; (*complesso di norme*)
moral standards *pl*, morality; (*condotta*)
morals *pl*; (*insegnamento morale*) moral
♦ *sm* morale; **la** ~ **della favola** the moral
of the tale; **essere giù di** ~ to be feeling
down; **aver il** ~ **alto/a terra** to be in good/
low spirits.
mora'lista, i, e *ag* moralistic ♦ *sm/f*
moralist.
moralità *sf* morality; (*condotta*) morals *pl*.

moraliz'zare [moralid'dzare] *vt* (*costumi, vita pubblica*) to set moral standards for.

moralizzazi'one [moraliddzat'tsjone] *sf* setting of moral standards.

mora'toria *sf* (*DIR*) moratorium.

morbi'dezza [morbi'dettsa] *sf* softness; smoothness; tenderness.

'morbido, a *ag* soft; (*pelle*) soft, smooth; (*carne*) tender.

mor'billo *sm* (*MED*) measles *sg*.

'morbo *sm* disease.

mor'boso, a *ag* (*fig*) morbid.

'morchia ['mɔrkja] *sf* (*residuo grasso*) dregs *pl*; oily deposit.

mor'dente *sm* (*fig*: *di satira, critica*) bite; (: *di persona*) drive.

'mordere *vt* to bite; (*addentare*) to bite into; (*corrodere*) to eat into.

mordicchi'are [mordik'kjare] *vt* (*gen*) to chew at.

mo'rente *ag* dying ♦ *sm/f* dying man/ woman.

mor'fina *sf* morphine.

mo'ria *sf* high mortality.

mori'bondo, a *ag* dying, moribund.

morige'rato, a [moridʒe'rato] *ag* of good morals.

mo'rire *vi* to die; (*abitudine, civiltà*) to die out; ~ **di dolore** to die of a broken heart; ~ **di fame** to die of hunger; (*fig*) to be starving; ~ **di freddo** to freeze to death; (*fig*) to be frozen; ~ **d'invidia** to be green with envy; ~ **di noia/paura** to be bored/ scared to death; ~ **dalla voglia di fare qc** to be dying to do sth; **fa un caldo da** ~ it's terribly hot.

mormo'rare *vi* to murmur; (*brontolare*) to grumble; **si mormora che ...** it's rumoured (*BRIT*) o rumored (*US*) that ...; **la gente mormora** people are talking.

mormo'rio *sm* murmuring; grumbling.

'moro, a *ag* dark(-haired); dark(-complexioned); **i M**~**i** *smpl* (*STORIA*) the Moors.

mo'roso, a *ag* in arrears ♦ *sm/f* (*fam: innamorato*) sweetheart.

'morsa *sf* (*TECN*) vice (*BRIT*), vise (*US*); (*fig*: *stretta*) grip.

mor'setto *sm* (*TECN*) clamp; (*ELETTR*) terminal.

morsi'care *vt* to nibble (at), gnaw (at); (*sog*: *insetto*) to bite.

'morso, a *pp di* **mordere** ♦ *sm* bite; (*di insetto*) sting; (*parte della briglia*) bit; **dare un** ~ **a qc/qn** to bite sth/sb; **i** ~**i della fame** pangs of hunger.

morta'della *sf* (*CUC*) mortadella (*type of salted pork meat*).

mor'taio *sm* mortar.

mor'tale *ag, sm* mortal.

mortalità *sf* mortality; (*STATISTICA*) mortality, death rate.

'morte *sf* death; **in punto di** ~ at death's door; **ferito a** ~ (*soldato*) mortally wounded; (*in incidente*) fatally injured; **essere annoiato a** ~ to be bored to death o to tears; **avercela a** ~ **con qn** to be bitterly resentful of sb; **avere la** ~ **nel cuore** to have a heavy heart.

mortifi'care *vt* to mortify.

'morto, a *pp di* **morire** ♦ *ag* dead ♦ *sm/f* dead man/woman; **i** ~**i** the dead; **fare il** ~ (*nell'acqua*) to float on one's back; **un** ~ **di fame** (*fig peg*) a down-and-out; **le campane suonavano a** ~ the funeral bells were tolling; *vedi anche* **Giorno dei Morti.**

mor'torio *sm* (*anche fig*) funeral.

mo'saico, ci *sm* mosaic; **l'ultimo tassello del** ~ (*fig*) the last piece of the puzzle.

'Mosca *sf* Moscow.

'mosca, sche *sf* fly; **rimanere** o **restare con un pugno di** ~**sche** (*fig*) to be left empty-handed; **non si sentiva una** ~ (*fig*) you could have heard a pin drop; ~ **cieca** blind-man's buff.

mos'cato *sm* muscatel (wine).

mosce'rino [moʃʃe'rino] *sm* midge, gnat.

mos'chea [mos'kɛa] *sf* mosque.

mos'chetto [mos'ketto] *sm* musket.

moschet'tone [mosket'tone] *sm* (*gancia*) spring clip; (*ALPINISMO*) karabiner, snaplink.

moschi'cida, i, e [moski'tʃida] *ag* fly *cpd*; **carta** ~ flypaper.

'moscio, a, sci, sce ['moʃʃo] *ag* (*fig*) lifeless; **ha la "r"** ~**a** he can't roll his "r"s.

mos'cone *sm* (*ZOOL*) bluebottle; (*barca*) pedalo; (: *a remi*) kind of pedalo with oars.

mosco'vita, i, e *ag, sm/f* Muscovite.

'mossa *sf* movement; (*nel gioco*) move; **darsi una** ~ (*fig*) to give o.s. a shake; **prendere le** ~**e da qc** to come about as the result of sth.

'mossi *etc vb vedi* **muovere.**

'mosso, a *pp di* **muovere** ♦ *ag* (*mare*) rough; (*capelli*) wavy; (*FOT*) blurred; (*ritmo, prosa*) animated.

mos'tarda *sf* mustard.

'mosto *sm* must.

'mostra *sf* exhibition, show; (*ostentazione*) show; **in** ~ on show; **far** ~ **di** (*fingere*) to pretend; **far** ~ **di sé** to show off; **mettersi in** ~ to draw attention to o.s.

mos'trare *vt* to show ♦ *vi:* ~ **di fare** to pretend to do; ~**rsi** *vr* to appear; ~ **la**

lingua to stick out one's tongue.
'**mostro** *sm* monster.
mostru'oso, a *ag* monstrous.
mo'tel *sm inv* motel.
moti'vare *vt* (*causare*) to cause;
(*giustificare*) to justify, account for.
motivazi'one [motivat'tsjone] *sf*
justification; (*PSIC*) motivation.
mo'tivo *sm* (*causa*) reason, cause;
(*movente*) motive; (*letterario*) (central)
theme; (*disegno*) motif, design; (*MUS*)
motif; **per quale ~?** why?, for what
reason?; **per ~i di salute** for health
reasons; **~i personali** personal reasons.
'**moto** *sm* (*anche FISICA*) motion;
(*movimento, gesto*) movement; (*esercizio
fisico*) exercise; (*sommossa*) rising,
revolt; (*commozione*) feeling, impulse ♦ *sf
inv* (*motocicletta*) motorbike; **fare del ~** to
take some exercise; **un ~ d'impazienza**
an impatient gesture; **mettere in ~** to set
in motion; (*AUT*) to start up.
moto'carro *sm* three wheeler van.
motoci'cletta [motot∫i'kletta] *sf*
motorcycle.
motoci'clismo [motot∫i'klizmo] *sm*
motorcycling, motorcycle racing
motoci'clista, l, e [motot∫i'klista] *sm/f*
motorcyclist.
moto'nave *sf* motor vessel.
motopesche'reccio [motopeske'rett∫o] *sm*
motor fishing vessel.
mo'tore, 'trice *ag* motor; (*TECN*) driving
♦ *sm* engine, motor ♦ *sf* (*TECN*) engine,
motor; **albero ~** drive shaft; **forza ~ trice**
driving force; **a ~** motor *cpd*, power-
driven; **~ a combustione interna/a
reazione** internal combustion/jet engine.
moto'rino *sm* moped; **~ di avviamento**
(*AUT*) starter.
motoriz'zato, a [motorid'dzato] *ag* (*truppe*)
motorized; (*persona*) having a car *o*
transport.
motorizzazi'one [motoriddzat'tsjone] *sf*
(*ufficio tecnico e organizzativo*): (**ufficio
della**) **~** road traffic office.
motos'cafo *sm* motorboat.
motove'detta *sf* motor patrol vessel.
mo'trice [mo'trit∫e] *sf vedi* **motore**.
mot'teggio [mot'tedd3o] *sm* banter.
'**motto** *sm* (*battuta scherzosa*) witty remark;
(*frase emblematica*) motto, maxim.
mountain bike *sf inv* mountain bike.
'**mouse** ['maus] *sm inv* (*INFORM*) mouse.
mo'vente *sm* motive.
mo'venza [mo'ventsa] *sf* movement.
movimen'tare *vt* to liven up.
movimen'tato, a *ag* (*festa, partita*) lively;

(*riunione*) animated; (*strada, vita*) busy;
(*soggiorno*) eventful.
movi'mento *sm* movement; (*fig*) activity,
hustle and bustle; (*MUS*) tempo,
movement; **essere sempre in ~** to be
always on the go; **fare un po' di ~**
(*esercizio fisico*) to take some exercise; **c'è
molto ~ in città** the town is very busy; **~
di capitali** movement of capital; **M~ per
la Liberazione della Donna (MLD)**
Women's Movement.
movi'ola *sf* moviola; **rivedere qc alla ~** to
see an action (*BRIT*) *o* instant (*US*) replay
of sth.
Mozam'bico [moddzam'biko] *sm:* **il ~**
Mozambique.
mozi'one [mot'tsjone] *sf* (*POL*) motion; **~
d'ordine** (*POL*) point of order.
mozzafi'ato [mottsa'fjato] *ag inv*
breathtaking.
moz'zare [mot'tsare] *vt* to cut off; (*coda*) to
dock; **~ il fiato** *o* **il respiro a qn** (*fig*) to
take sb's breath away.
mozza'rella [mottsa'rɛlla] *sf* mozzarella (*a
moist Neapolitan curd cheese*).
mozzi'cone [mottsi'kone] *sm* stub, butt,
end; (*anche*: **~ di sigaretta**) cigarette end.
'**mozzo** *sm* ['mɔddzo] (*MECCANICA*) hub;
['mottso] (*NAUT*) ship's boy; **~ di stalla**
stable boy.
mq *abbr* (= *metro quadro*) sq.m.
MS *sigla* = *Massa Carrara*.
ms. *abbr* (= *manoscritto*) ms.
M.S.I. *sigla m* (= *Movimento Sociale Italiano*)
former right-wing political party.
Mti *abbr* = *monti*.
'**mucca, che** *sf* cow.
'**mucchio** ['mukkjo] *sm* pile, heap; (*fig*): **un
~ di** lots of, heaps of.
mucil'lagine [mut∫il'ladʒine] *sf* (*BOT*)
mucilage (*green slime produced by plants
growing in water*).
'**muco, chi** *sm* mucus.
mu'cosa *sf* mucous membrane.
'**muffa** *sf* mould (*BRIT*), mold (*US*), mildew;
fare la ~ to go mouldy (*BRIT*) *o* moldy
(*US*).
mugghi'are [mug'gjare] *vi* (*fig: mare, tuono*)
to roar; (*vento*) to howl.
mug'gire [mud'dʒire] *vi* (*vacca*) to low, moo;
(*toro*) to bellow; (*fig*) to roar.
mug'gito [mud'dʒito] *sm* low, moo; bellow;
roar.
mu'ghetto [mu'getto] *sm* lily of the valley.
mu'gnaio, a [muɲ'ɲajo] *sm/f* miller.
mugo'lare *vi* (*cane*) to whimper, whine;
(*fig: persona*) to moan.
mugu'gnare [muguɲ'ɲare] *vi* (*fam*) to

mutter, mumble.

mulatti'era *sf* mule track.

mu'latto, a *ag*, *sm/f* mulatto.

muli'nare *vi* to whirl, spin (round and round).

muli'nello *sm* (*moto vorticoso*) eddy, whirl; (*di canna da pesca*) reel; (*NAUT*) windlass.

mu'lino *sm* mill; ~ **a vento** windmill.

'mulo *sm* mule.

'multa *sf* fine.

mul'tare *vt* to fine.

multico'lore *ag* multicoloured (*BRIT*), multicolored (*US*).

multi'forme *ag* (*paesaggio, attività, interessi*) varied; (*ingegno*) versatile.

multimedi'ale *ag* multimedia *cpd*.

multinazio'nale [multinattsjo'nale] *ag, sf* multinational; **forza** ~ **di pace** multinational peace-keeping force.

'multiplo, a *ag*, *sm* multiple.

multiu'tenza [multiu'tɛntsa] *sf* (*INFORM*) time sharing.

'mummia *sf* mummy.

'mungere ['mundʒere] *vt* (*anche fig*) to milk.

mungi'tura [mundʒi'tura] *sf* milking.

munici'pale [munitʃi'pale] *ag* (*gen*) municipal; **palazzo** ~ town hall; **autorità** ~**i** local authorities (*BRIT*), local government *sg*.

muni'cipio [muni'tʃipjo] *sm* town council; (*edificio*) town hall; **sposarsi in** ~ ≈ to get married in a registry office (*BRIT*), have a civil marriage.

munifi'cenza [munifi'tʃɛntsa] *sf* munificence.

mu'nifico, a, ci, che *ag* munificent, generous.

mu'nire *vt*: ~ **qc/qn di** to equip sth/sb with; ~ **di firma** (*documento*) to sign.

munizi'oni [munit'tsjoni] *sfpl* (*MIL*) ammunition *sg*.

'munsi *etc vb vedi* **mungere**.

'munto, a *pp di* **mungere**.

mu'oio *etc vb vedi* **morire**.

mu'overe *vt* to move; (*ruota, macchina*) to drive; (*sollevare: questione, obiezione*) to raise, bring up; (: *accusa*) to make, bring forward; ~**rsi** *vr* to move; ~ **causa a qn** (*DIR*) to take legal action against sb; ~ **a compassione** to move to pity; ~ **guerra a** *o* **contro qn** to wage war against sb; ~ **mari e monti** to move heaven and earth; ~ **al pianto** to move to tears; ~ **i primi passi** to take one's first steps; (*fig*) to be starting out; **muoviti!** hurry up!, get a move on!

'mura *sfpl vedi* **muro**.

mu'raglia [mu'raʎʎa] *sf* (high) wall.

mu'rale *ag* wall *cpd*; mural.

mu'rare *vt* (*persona, porta*) to wall up.

mu'rario, a *ag* building *cpd*; **arte** ~**a** masonry.

mura'tore *sm* (*con pietre*) mason; (*con mattoni*) bricklayer.

mura'tura *sf* (*lavoro murario*) masonry; **casa in** ~ (*di pietra*) stonebuilt house; (*di mattoni*) brick house.

'muro *sm* wall; ~**a** *sfpl* (*cinta cittadina*) walls; **a** ~ wall *cpd*; (*armadio etc*) built-in; **mettere al** ~ (*fucilare*) to shoot *o* execute (by firing squad); ~ **di cinta** surrounding wall; ~ **divisorio** dividing wall; ~ **del suono** sound barrier.

'musa *sf* muse.

'muschio ['muskjo] *sm* (*ZOOL*) musk; (*BOT*) moss.

musco'lare *ag* muscular, muscle *cpd*.

muscola'tura *sf* muscle structure.

'muscolo *sm* (*ANAT*) muscle.

musco'loso, a *ag* muscular.

mu'seo *sm* museum.

museru'ola *sf* muzzle.

'musica *sf* music; ~ **da ballo/camera** dance/chamber music.

musi'cale *ag* musical.

musicas'setta *sf* (pre-recorded) cassette.

musi'cista, i, e [muzi'tʃista] *sm/f* musician.

musi'comane *sm/f* music lover.

'muso *sm* muzzle; (*di auto, aereo*) nose; **tenere il** ~ to sulk.

mu'sone, a *sm/f* sulky person.

'mussola *sf* muslin.

mus(s)ul'mano, a *ag*, *sm/f* Muslim, Moslem.

'muta *sf* (*di animali*) moulting (*BRIT*), molting (*US*); (*di serpenti*) sloughing; (*per immersioni subacquee*) diving suit; (*gruppo di cani*) pack.

mu'tabile *ag* changeable.

muta'mento *sm* change.

mu'tande *sfpl* (*da uomo*) (under)pants.

mutan'dine *sfpl* (*da donna, bambino*) pants (*BRIT*), briefs; ~ **di plastica** plastic pants.

mu'tare *vt*, *vi* to change, alter.

mutazi'one [mutat'tsjone] *sf* change, alteration; (*BIOL*) mutation.

mu'tevole *ag* changeable.

muti'lare *vt* to mutilate, maim; (*fig*) to mutilate, deface.

muti'lato, a *sm/f* disabled person (*through loss of limbs*); ~ **di guerra** disabled ex-serviceman (*BRIT*) *o* war veteran (*US*).

mutilazi'one [mutilat'tsjone] *sf* mutilation.

mu'tismo *sm* (*MED*) mutism; (*atteggiamento*) (stubborn) silence.

'muto, a *ag* (*MED*) dumb; (*emozione, dolore,*

CINE) silent; (*LING*) silent, mute; (*carta geografica*) blank; ~ **per lo stupore** *etc* speechless with amazement *etc*; **ha fatto scena** ~**a** he didn't utter a word.

'**mutua** *sf* (*anche*: **cassa** ~) health insurance scheme; **medico della** ~ ≈ National Health Service doctor (*BRIT*).

mutu'are *vt* (*fig*) to borrow.

mutu'ato, a *smf* member of a health insurance scheme.

'**mutuo, a** *ag* (*reciproco*) mutual ♦ *sm* (*ECON*) (long-term) loan; ~ **ipotecario** mortgage.

N n

N, n ['ɛnne] *sf o m inv* (*lettera*) N, n; **N come Napoli** ≈ N for Nellie (*BRIT*), N for Nan (*US*).

N *abbr* (– *nord*) N.

n *abbr* (= *numero*) no.

NA *sigla* = *Napoli*.

na'babbo *sm* (*anche fig*) nabob.

'**nacchere** ['nakkere] *sfpl* castanets.

NAD *sigla m* = *nucleo anti-droga*.

na'dir *sm* (*ASTR*) nadir.

'**nafta** *sf* naphtha; (*per motori diesel*) diesel oil.

nafta'lina *sf* (*CHIM*) naphthalene; (*tarmicida*) mothballs *pl*.

'**naia** *sf* (*ZOOL*) cobra; (*MIL*) *slang term for national service*.

na'if [na'if] *ag inv* naïve.

'**nailon** *sm* = nylon.

Nai'robi *sf* Nairobi.

'**nanna** *sf* (*linguaggio infantile*): **andare a** ~ to go to beddy-byes.

'**nano, a** *ag, smf* dwarf.

napole'tano, a *ag, smf* Neapolitan ♦ *sf* (*macchinetta da caffè*) Neapolitan coffee pot.

'**Napoli** *sf* Naples.

'**nappa** *sf* tassel.

nar'ciso [nar'tʃizo] *sm* narcissus.

'**narcos** *sm inv* (*colombiano*) Colombian drug trafficker.

narco'dollari *smpl* drug money *sg*.

nar'cosi *sf* general anaesthesia, narcosis.

nar'cotico, ci *sm* narcotic.

narcotraffi'cante *smf* drug trafficker.

narco'traffico *sm* drug trade.

na'rice [na'ritʃe] *sf* nostril.

nar'rare *vt* to tell the story of, recount.

narra'tivo, a *ag* narrative ♦ *sf* (*branca letteraria*) fiction.

narra'tore, 'trice *smf* narrator.

narrazi'one [narrat'tsjone] *sf* narration; (*racconto*) story, tale.

N.A.S.A. ['naza] *sigla f* (= *National Aeronautics and Space Administration*) NASA.

na'sale *ag* nasal.

na'scente [naʃ'ʃɛnte] *ag* (*sole, luna*) rising.

'**nascere** ['naʃʃere] *vi* (*bambino*) to be born; (*pianta*) to come o spring up; (*fiume*) to rise, have its source; (*sole*) to rise; (*dente*) to come through; (*fig: derivare, conseguire*): ~ **da** to arise from, be born out of; **è nata nel 1952** she was born in 1952; **da cosa nasce cosa** one thing leads to another.

'**nascita** ['naʃʃita] *sf* birth.

nasci'turo, a [naʃʃi'turo] *smf* future child; **come si chiamerà il** ~? what's the baby going to be called?

nas'condere *vt* to hide, conceal; ~**rsi** *vr* to hide.

nascon'diglio [naskon'diʎʎo] *sm* hiding place.

nascon'dino *sm* (*gioco*) hide-and-seek.

nas'cosi *etc vb vedi* **nascondere**.

nas'costo, a *pp di* **nascondere** ♦ *ag* hidden; **di** ~ secretly.

na'sello *sm* (*ZOOL*) hake.

'**naso** *sm* nose.

Nas'sau *sf* Nassau.

'**nastro** *sm* ribbon; (*magnetico, isolante, SPORT*) tape; ~ **adesivo** adhesive tape; ~ **trasportatore** conveyor belt.

nas'turzio [nas'turtsjo] *sm* nasturtium.

na'tale *ag* of one's birth ♦ *sm* (*REL*): **N**~ Christmas; (*giorno della nascita*) birthday; ~**i** *smpl*: **di illustri/umili** ~**i** of noble/ humble birth.

natalità *sf* birth rate.

nata'lizio, a [nata'littsjo] *ag* (*del Natale*) Christmas *cpd*.

na'tante *sm* craft *inv*, boat.

'**natica, che** *sf* (*ANAT*) buttock.

na'tio, a, 'tii, 'tie *ag* native.

Natività *sf* (*REL*) Nativity.

na'tivo, a *ag, smf* native.

'**nato, a** *pp di* **nascere** ♦ *ag*: **un attore** ~ a born actor; ~**a Pieri** née Pieri.

'**N.A.T.O.** *sigla f* NATO (= *North Atlantic Treaty Organization*).

na'tura *sf* nature; **pagare in** ~ to pay in kind; ~ **morta** still life.

natu'rale *ag* natural ♦ *sm*: **al** ~ (*alimenti*) served plain; (*ritratto*) life-size; **(ma)** è ~!

(*in risposte*) of course!; **a grandezza** ~ life-size; **acqua** ~ spring water.

natura'lezza [natura'lettsa] *sf* naturalness.

natura'lista, i, e *sm/f* naturalist.

naturaliz'zare [naturalid'dzare] *vt* to naturalize.

natural'mente *av* naturally; (*certamente, si*) of course.

natu'rismo *sm* naturism, nudism.

natu'rista, i, e *ag, sm/f* naturist, nudist.

naufra'gare *vi* (*nave*) to be wrecked; (*persona*) to be shipwrecked; (*fig*) to fall through.

nau'fragio [nau'fradʒo] *sm* shipwreck; (*fig*) ruin, failure.

'naufrago, ghi *sm* castaway, shipwreck victim.

'nausea *sf* nausea; **avere la** ~ to feel sick (*BRIT*) *o* ill (*US*); **fino alla** ~ ad nauseam.

nausea'bondo, a *ag*, **nause'ante** *ag* nauseating, sickening.

nause'are *vt* to nauseate, make (feel) sick (*BRIT*) *o* ill (*US*).

'nautico, a, ci, che *ag* nautical ◆ *sf* (art of) navigation; **salone** ~ (*mostra*) boat show.

na'vale *ag* naval; **battaglia** ~ naval battle; (*gioco*) battleships *pl*.

na'vata *sf* (*anche*: ~ **centrale**) nave; (*anche*: ~ **laterale**) aisle.

'nave *sf* ship, vessel; ~ **da carico** cargo ship, freighter; ~ **cisterna** tanker; ~ **da guerra** warship; ~ **di linea** liner; ~ **passeggeri** passenger ship; ~ **portaerei** aircraft carrier; ~ **spaziale** spaceship.

na'vetta *sf* shuttle; (*servizio di collegamento*) shuttle (service).

navi'cella [navi'tʃɛlla] *sf* (*di aerostato*) gondola; ~ **spaziale** spaceship.

navi'gabile *ag* navigable.

navi'gante *sm* sailor, seaman.

navi'gare *vi* to sail; ~ **in cattive acque** (*fig*) to be in deep water; ~ **in Internet** to surf the Net.

navi'gato, a *ag* (*fig: esperto*) experienced.

naviga'tore, 'trice *sm/f* (*gen*) navigator; ~ **solitario** single-handed sailor.

navigazi'one [navigat'tsjone] *sf* navigation; **dopo una settimana di** ~ after a week at sea.

na'viglio [na'viʎʎo] *sm* fleet, ships *pl*; (*canale artificiale*) canal; ~ **da pesca** fishing fleet.

'Nazaret(h) ['naddzaret] *sf* Nazareth.

nazio'nale [nattsjo'nale] *ag* national ◆ *sf* (*SPORT*) national team.

naziona'lismo [nattsjona'lizmo] *sm* nationalism.

naziona'lista, i, e [nattsjona'lista] *ag, sm/f* nationalist.

nazionalità [nattsjonali'ta] *sf inv* nationality.

nazionaliz'zare [nattsjonalid'dzare] *vt* to nationalize.

nazionalizzazi'one [nattsjonalid-dzat'tsjone] *sf* nationalization.

nazi'one [nat'tsjone] *sf* nation.

naziskin ['naːtsiskin] *sm inv* Nazi skinhead.

na'zismo [nat'tsizmo] *sm* Nazism.

na'zista, i, e [nat'tsista] *ag, sm/f* Nazi.

NB *abbr* (= *nota bene*) NB.

N.d.A. *abbr* (= *nota dell'autore*) author's note.

N.d.D. *abbr* = *nota della direzione*.

N.d.E. *abbr* (= *nota dell'editore*) publisher's note.

N.d.R. *abbr* (= *nota della redazione*) editor's note.

'nd'rangheta [nd'rangeta] *sf* Calabrian Mafia.

N.d.T. *abbr* (= *nota del traduttore*) translator's note.

=========================== *PAROLA CHIAVE*

ne *pron* **1** (*di lui, lei, loro*) of him/her/them; about him/her/them; ~ **riconosco la voce** I recognize his (*o* her) voice

2 (*di questa, quella cosa*) of it; about it; ~ **voglio ancora** I want some more (of it *o* them); **non parliamone più!** let's not talk about it any more!

3 (*da ciò*) from this; ~ **deduco che l'avete trovato** I gather you've found it; ~ **consegue che** ... it follows therefore that ...

4 (*con valore partitivo*): **hai dei libri?** — **sì,** ~ **ho** have you any books? — yes, I have (some); **hai del pane?** — **no, non** ~ **ho** have you any bread? — no, I haven't any; **quanti anni hai?** — ~ **ho 17** how old are you? — I'm 17

◆ *av* (*moto da luogo: da lì*) from there; ~ **vengo ora** I've just come from there.

---

né *cong*: ~ ... ~ neither ... nor; ~ **l'uno** ~ **l'altro lo vuole** neither of them wants it; ~ **più** ~ **meno** no more no less; **non parla** ~ **l'italiano** ~ **il tedesco** he speaks neither Italian nor German, he doesn't speak either Italian or German; **non piove** ~ **nevica** it isn't raining or snowing.

N.E. *abbr* (= *nordest*) NE.

ne'anche [ne'anke] *av, cong* not even; **non** ... ~ not even; ~ **se volesse potrebbe venire** he couldn't come even if he wanted to; **non l'ho visto** — **neanch'io** I didn't see him — neither did I *o* I didn't either; ~ **per idea** *o* **sogno!** not on your life!; **non ci**

nebbia – nesso

penso ~! I wouldn't dream of it!; ~ **a pagarlo lo farebbe** he wouldn't do it even if you paid him.

'**nebbia** *sf* fog; (*foschia*) mist.

nebbi'oso, a *ag* foggy; misty.

nebulizza'tore [nebuliddza'tore] *sm* atomizer.

nebu'losa *sf* nebula.

nebulosità *sf* haziness.

nebu'loso, a *ag* (*atmosfera, cielo*) hazy; (*fig*) hazy, vague.

néces'saire [nesɛ'sɛr] *sm inv*: ~ **da viaggio** overnight case *o* bag.

necessaria'mente [netʃessarja'mente] *av* necessarily.

neces'sario, a [netʃes'sarjo] *ag* necessary ♦ *sm*: **fare il** ~ to do what is necessary; **lo stretto** ~ the bare essentials *pl*.

necessità [netʃessi'ta] *sf inv* necessity; (*povertà*) need, poverty; **trovarsi nella** ~ **di fare qc** to be forced *o* obliged to do sth, have to do sth.

necessi'tare [netʃessi'tare] *vt* to require ♦ *vi* (*aver bisogno*): ~ **di** to need.

necro'logio [nekro'lɔdʒo] *sm* obituary notice, (*registro*) register of deaths.

ne'fando, a *ag* infamous, wicked.

ne'fasto, a *ag* inauspicious, ill-omened.

ne'gare *vt* to deny; (*rifiutare*) to deny, refuse; ~ **di aver fatto/che** to deny having done/that.

negativa'mente *av* negatively; **rispondere** ~ to give a negative response.

nega'tivo, a *ag, sf, sm* negative.

negazi'one [negat'tsjone] *sf* negation.

negherò *etc* [nege'rɔ] *vb vedi* **negare**.

ne'gletto, a [ne'gletto] *ag* (*trascurato*) neglected.

'**negli** ['neʎʎi] *prep + det vedi* **in**.

négli'gé [negli'ʒe] *sm inv* negligee.

negli'gente [negli'dʒɛnte] *ag* negligent, careless.

negli'genza [negli'dʒɛntsa] *sf* negligence, carelessness.

negozi'abile [negot'tsjabile] *ag* negotiable.

negozi'ante [negot'tsjante] *sm/f* trader, dealer; (*bottegaio*) shopkeeper (*BRIT*), storekeeper (*US*).

negozi'are [negot'tsjare] *vt* to negotiate ♦ *vi*: ~ **in** to trade *o* deal in.

negozi'ato [negot'tsjato] *sm* negotiation.

negozia'tore, 'trice [negottsja'tore] *sm/f* negotiator.

ne'gozio [ne'gɔttsjo] *sm* (*locale*) shop (*BRIT*), store (*US*); (*affare*) (piece of) business *no pl*; (*DIR*): ~ **giuridico** legal transaction.

negri'ere, a, negri'ero, a *sm* slave trader ♦ *sm/f* (*fig*) slave driver.

'**negro, a** *ag, sm/f* Negro.

negro'mante *sm/f* necromancer.

negroman'zia [negroman'tsia] *sf* necromancy.

'**nei, nel, nell', 'nella, 'nelle, 'nello** *prep* +*det vedi* **in**.

'**nembo** *sm* (*METEOR*) nimbus.

ne'mico, a, ci, che *ag* hostile; (*MIL*) enemy *cpd* ♦ *sm/f* enemy; **essere** ~ **di** to be strongly averse *o* opposed to.

nem'meno *av, cong* = **neanche**.

'**nenia** *sf* dirge; (*motivo monotono*) monotonous tune.

'**neo** *sm* mole; (*fig*) (slight) flaw.

'**neo...** *prefisso* neo....

neofa'scista, i, e [neofaʃ'ʃista] *sm/f* neofascist.

neolo'gismo [neolo'dʒizmo] *sm* neologism

'**neon** *sm* (*chim*) neon.

neo'nato, a *ag* newborn ♦ *sm/f* newborn baby.

neozelan'dese [neoddzelan'dese] *ag* New Zealand *cpd* ♦ *sm/f* New Zealander.

Ne'pal *sm*: **il** ~ Nepal.

nepo'tismo *sm* nepotism.

nep'pure *av, cong* = **neanche**.

ner'bata *sf* (*colpo*) blow; (*sferzata*) whiplash.

'**nerbo** *sm* lash; (*fig*) strength, backbone.

nerbo'ruto, a *ag* muscular; robust.

ne'retto *sm* (*TIP*) bold type.

'**nero, a** *ag* black; (*scuro*) dark ♦ *sm* black; **nella miseria più** ~**a** in utter *o* abject poverty; **essere di umore** ~, **essere** ~ to be in a filthy mood; **mettere qc** ~ **su bianco** to put sth down in black and white; **vedere tutto** ~ to look on the ~ side (of things).

nero'fumo *sm* lampblack.

nerva'tura *sf* (*ANAT*) nervous system; (*BOT*) veining; (*ARCHIT, TECN*) rib.

'**nervo** *sm* (*ANAT*) nerve; (*BOT*) vein; **avere i** ~**i** to be on edge; **dare sui** ~**i a qn** to get on sb's nerves; **tenere/avere i** ~**i saldi** to keep/be calm; **che** ~**i!** damn (it)!

nervo'sismo *sm* (*PSIC*) nervousness; (*irritazione*) irritability.

ner'voso, a *ag* nervous; (*irritabile*) irritable ♦ *sm* (*fam*): **far venire il** ~ **a qn** to get on sb's nerves; **farsi prendere dal** ~ to let o.s. get irritated.

'**nespola** *sf* (*BOT*) medlar; (*fig*) blow, punch.

'**nespolo** *sm* medlar tree.

'**nesso** *sm* connection, link.

═══════════ *PAROLA CHIAVE*

nes'suno, a (*det: dav sm* **nessun** + *C, V,*
nessuno + *s impura, gn, pn, ps, x, z; dav sf*
nessuna + *C,* **nessun'** + *V*) *det* **1** (*non uno*)
no, *espressione negativa* + any; **non c'è**
nessun libro there isn't any book, there is
no book; **nessun altro** no one else, nobody
else; **nessun'altra cosa** nothing else; **in**
nessun luogo nowhere
2 (*qualche*) any; **hai ~a obiezione?** do you
have any objections?

♦ *pron* **1** (*non uno*) no one, nobody,
espressione negativa + any(one); (: *cosa*)
none, *espressione negativa* + any; **~ è venuto,**
non è venuto ~ nobody came
2 (*qualcuno*) anyone, anybody; **ha**
telefonato ~? did anyone phone?

netta'mente *av* clearly.
net'tare *vt* to clean ♦ *sm* ['nɛttare] nectar.
net'tezza [net'tettsa] *sf* cleanness,
cleanliness; **~ urbana** cleansing
department (*BRIT*), department of
sanitation (*US*).
'netto, a *ag* (*pulito*) clean; (*chiaro*) clear,
clear-cut; (*deciso*) definite; (*ECON*) net;
tagliare qc di ~ to cut sth clean off; **taglio**
~ col passato (*fig*) clean break with the
past.
nettur'bino *sm* dustman (*BRIT*), garbage
collector (*US*).
'neuro... *prefisso* neuro....
neurochirur'gia [neurokirur'dʒia] *sf*
neurosurgery.
neurolo'gia [neurolo'dʒia] *sf* neurology.
neuro'logico, a, ci, che [neuro'lɔdʒiko] *ag*
neurological.
neu'rologo a, gi, ghe *sm/f* neurologist.
neu'rosi *sf inv* = **nevrosi**.
neu'trale *ag* neutral.
neutralità *sf* neutrality.
neutraliz'zare [neutralid'dzare] *vt* to
neutralize.
'neutro, a *ag* neutral; (*LING*) neuter ♦ *sm*
(*LING*) neuter.
neu'trone *sm* neutron.
ne'vaio *sm* snowfield.
'neve *sf* snow; **montare a ~** (*CUC*) to whip
up; **~ carbonica** dry ice.
nevi'care *vb impers* to snow.
nevi'cata *sf* snowfall.
ne'vischio [ne'viskjo] *sm* sleet.
ne'voso, a *ag* snowy; snow-covered.
nevral'gia [nevral'dʒia] *sf* neuralgia.
ne'vralgico, a, ci, che [ne'vraldʒiko] *ag*:
punto ~ (*MED*) nerve centre; (*fig*) crucial
point.

nevras'tenico, a, ci, che *ag* (*MED*)
neurasthenic; (*fig*) hot-tempered ♦ *sm/f*
neurasthenic; hot-tempered person.
ne'vrosi *sf inv* neurosis.
ne'vrotico, a, ci, che *ag, sm/f* (*anche fig*)
neurotic.
Nia'gara *sm*: **le cascate del ~** the Niagara
Falls.
'nibbio *sm* (*ZOOL*) kite.
Nica'ragua *sm*: **il ~** Nicaragua.
nicaragu'ense *ag, sm/f* Nicaraguan.
'nicchia ['nikkja] *sf* niche; (*naturale*) cavity,
hollow; **~ di mercato** (*COMM*) niche
market.
nicchi'are [nik'kjare] *vi* to shilly-shally,
hesitate.
'nichel ['nikel] *sm* nickel.
nichi'lismo [niki'lizmo] *sm* nihilism.
Nico'sia *sf* Nicosia.
nico'tina *sf* nicotine.
nidi'ata *sf* (*di uccelli, fig: di bambini*) brood;
(*di altri animali*) litter.
nidifi'care *vi* to nest.
'nido *sm* nest ♦ *ag inv*: **asilo ~** day nursery,
crèche (*for children aged 0 to 3*); **a ~ d'ape**
(*tessuto etc*) honeycomb *cpd*.

═══════════ *PAROLA CHIAVE*

ni'ente *pron* **1** (*nessuna cosa*) nothing; **~**
può fermarlo nothing can stop him; **~ di**
~ absolutely nothing; **grazie! — di ~!**
thank you! — not at all!; **nient'altro**
nothing else; **nient'altro che** nothing but;
~ affatto not at all, not in the least; **come**
se ~ fosse as if nothing had happened;
cose da ~ trivial matters; **per ~** (*gratis,*
invano) for nothing; **non per ~, ma ...** not
for any particular reason, but ...; **poco o**
~ next to nothing; **un uomo da ~** a man
of no consequence
2 (*qualcosa*): **hai bisogno di ~?** do you
need anything?
3: **non ... ~** nothing, *espressione negativa* +
anything; **non ho visto ~** I saw nothing, I
didn't see anything; **non può farci ~** he
can't do anything about it; **(non) fa ~** (*non*
importa) it doesn't matter; **non ho ~ da**
dire I have nothing *o* haven't anything to
say

♦ *ag inv*: **~ paura!** never fear!; **e ~ scuse!**
and I don't want to hear excuses!

♦ *sm* nothing; **un bel ~** absolutely
nothing; **basta un ~ per farla piangere** the
slightest thing is enough to make her
cry; **finire in ~** to come to nothing

♦ *av* (*in nessuna misura*): **non ... ~** not ...
at all; **non è (per) ~ buono** it isn't good at
all; **non ci penso per ~** (*non ne ho nessuna*

intenzione) I wouldn't think of it; ~ **male!** not bad at all!

nientedi'meno, niente'meno *av* actually, even ♦ *escl* really!, I say!

'Niger ['nidʒer] *sm*: **il** ~ Niger; (*fiume*) the Niger.

Ni'geria [ni'dʒɛrja] *sf* Nigeria.

nigeri'ano, a [nidʒe'rjano] *ag, sm/f* Nigerian.

'Nilo *sm*: **il** ~ the Nile.

'nimbo *sm* halo.

'ninfa *sf* nymph.

nin'fea *sf* water lily.

nin'fomane *sf* nymphomaniac.

ninna'nanna *sf* lullaby.

'ninnolo *sm* (*balocco*) plaything; (*gingillo*) knick-knack.

ni'pote *sm/f* (*di zii*) nephew/niece; (*di nonni*) grandson/daughter, grandchild.

nip'ponico, a, ci, che *ag* Japanese.

niti'dezza [niti'dettsa] *sf* (*gen*) clearness; (*di stile*) clarity; (*PHOT, TV*) sharpness.

'nitido, a *ag* clear; (*immagine*) sharp, well-defined.

ni'trato *sm* nitrate.

'nitrico, a, ci, che *ag* nitric.

ni'trire *vi* to neigh.

ni'trito *sm* (*di cavallo*) neighing *no pl*; neigh; (*CHIM*) nitrite.

nitroglice'rina [nitroglitʃe'rina] *sf* nitroglycerine.

'niveo, a *ag* snow-white.

'Nizza ['nittsa] *sf* Nice.

nn *abbr* (= *numeri*) nos.

NO *sigla* = *Novara*.

no *av* (*risposta*) no; **vieni o** ~? are you coming or not?; **come** ~! of course!, certainly!; **perché** ~? why not?

N.O. *abbr* (= *nordovest*) NW.

nobil'donna *sf* noblewoman.

'nobile *ag* noble ♦ *sm/f* noble, nobleman/woman.

nobili'are *ag* noble.

nobili'tare *vt* (*anche fig*) to ennoble; ~**rsi** *vr* (*rendersi insigne*) to distinguish o.s.

nobiltà *sf* nobility; (*di azione etc*) nobleness.

nobilu'omo *sm, pl* **-u'omini** nobleman.

'nocca, che *sf* (*ANAT*) knuckle.

'noccio *etc* [*nɔttʃo*] *vb vedi* **nuocere.**

nocci'ola [not'tʃɔla] *sf* hazelnut ♦ *ag inv* (*anche*: **color** ~) hazel, light brown.

noccio'lina [nottʃo'lina] *sf* (*anche*: ~ **americana**) peanut.

'nocciolo ['nɔttʃolo] *sm* (*di frutto*) stone; (*fig*) heart, core; [not'tʃɔlo] (*albero*) hazel.

'noce ['notʃe] *sm* (*albero*) walnut tree ♦ *sf* (*frutto*) walnut; **una** ~ **di burro** (*CUC*) a knob of butter (*BRIT*), a dab of butter

(*US*); ~ **di cocco** coconut; ~ **moscata** nutmeg.

noce'pesca, sche [notʃe'pɛska] *sf* nectarine.

no'cevo *etc* [no'tʃevo] *vb vedi* **nuocere.**

noci'uto [no'tʃuto] *pp di* **nuocere.**

no'civo, a [no'tʃivo] *ag* harmful, noxious.

'nocqui *etc vb vedi* **nuocere.**

'nodo *sm* (*di cravatta, legname, NAUT*) knot; (*AUT, FERR*) junction; (*MED, ASTR, BOT*) node; (*fig: legame*) bond, tie; (: *punto centrale*) heart, crux; **avere un** ~ **alla gola** to have a lump in one's throat; **tutti i** ~**i vengono al pettine** (*proverbio*) your sins will find you out.

no'doso, a *ag* (*tronco*) gnarled.

'nodulo *sm* (*ANAT, BOT*) nodule.

'noi *pron* (*soggetto*) we; (*oggetto: per dare rilievo, con preposizione*) us; ~ **stessi(e)** we ourselves; (*oggetto*) ourselves; **da** ~ (*nel nostro paese*) in our country; **where we come from**; (*a casa nostra*) at our house.

'noia *sf* boredom; (*disturbo, impaccio*) bother *no pl*, trouble *no pl*; **avere qn/qc a** ~ not to like sb/sth; **mi è venuto a** ~ I'm tired of it; **dare** ~ **a** to annoy; **avere delle** ~**e con qn** to have trouble with sb.

nol'altri *pron* we.

noi'oso, a *ag* boring; (*fastidioso*) annoying, troublesome.

noleggi'are [noled'dʒare] *vt* (*prendere a noleggio*) to hire (*BRIT*), rent; (*dare a noleggio*) to hire out (*BRIT*), rent out; (*aereo, nave*) to charter.

noleggia'tore, 'trice [noleddʒa'tore] *sm/f* hirer (*BRIT*), renter; charterer.

no'leggio [no'leddʒo] *sm* hire (*BRIT*), rental; charter.

no'lente *ag*: **volente o** ~ whether one likes it or not, willy-nilly.

'nolo *sm* hire (*BRIT*), rental; charter; (*per trasporto merci*) freight; **prendere/dare a** ~ **qc** to hire/hire out sth (*BRIT*), rent/rent out sth.

'nomade *ag* nomadic ♦ *sm/f* nomad.

noma'dismo *sm* nomadism.

'nome *sm* name; (*LING*) noun; **in o a** ~ **di** in the name of; **di o per** ~ (*chiamato*) called, named; **conoscere qn di** ~ to know sb by name; **fare il** ~ **di qn** to name sb; **faccia pure il mio** ~ feel free to mention my name; ~ **d'arte** stage name; ~ **di battesimo** Christian name; ~ **depositato** trade name; ~ **di famiglia** surname; ~ **da ragazza** maiden name; ~ **da sposata** married name.

no'mea *sf* notoriety.

nomencla'tura *sf* nomenclature.

nomenkla'tura _sf_ (_di partito, stato_) nomenklatura.

no'mignolo [no'miɲɲolo] _sm_ nickname.

'nomina _sf_ appointment.

nomi'nale _ag_ nominal; (_LING_) noun _cpd._

nomi'nare _vt_ to name; (_eleggere_) to appoint; (_citare_) to mention; **non l'ho mai sentito** ~ I've never heard of it (_o_ him).

nomina'tivo, a _ag_ (_intestato: titolo_) registered; (: _libretto_) personal; (_LING_) nominative ♦ _sm_ (_nome_) name; (_LING_) nominative; **elenco** ~ list of names.

non _av_ not ♦ _prefisso_ non-; **grazie** — ~ **c'è di che** thank you — don't mention it; **i** ~ **credenti** the unbelievers; _vedi anche_ **affatto, appena** _etc._

nonché [non'ke] _cong_ (_tanto più, tanto meno_) let alone; (_e inoltre_) as well as.

nonconfor'mista, i, e _ag, sm/f_ nonconformist.

noncu'rante _ag_: ~ (**di**) careless (of), indifferent (to); **con fare** ~ with a nonchalant air.

noncu'ranza [nonku'rantsa] _sf_ carelessness, indifference; **un'aria di** ~ a nonchalant air.

nondi'meno _cong_ (_tuttavia_) however; (_nonostante_) nevertheless.

'nonno, a _sm/f_ grandfather/mother; (_in senso più familiare_) grandma/grandpa; ~**i** _smpl_ grandparents.

non'nulla _sm inv_: **un** ~ nothing, a trifle.

'nono, a _num_ ninth.

nonos'tante _prep_ in spite of, notwithstanding ♦ _cong_ although, even though.

non plus 'ultra _sm inv_: **il** ~ (**di**) the last word (in).

nontiscordardimé _sm inv_ (_BOT_) forget-me-not.

nord _sm_ north ♦ _ag inv_ north; (_regione_) northern; **verso** ~ north, northwards; **l'America del N**~ North America.

nor'dest _sm_ north-east.

'nordico, a, ci, che _ag_ nordic, northern European.

nor'dista, i, e _ag, sm/f_ Yankee.

nor'dovest _sm_ north-west.

Norim'berga _sf_ Nuremberg.

'norma _sf_ (_principio_) norm; (_regola_) regulation, rule; (_consuetudine_) custom, rule; **di** ~ normally; **a** ~ **di legge** according to law, as laid down by law; **al di sopra della** ~ above average, above the norm; **per sua** ~ **e regola** for your information; **proporsi una** ~ **di vita** to set o.s. rules to live by; ~**e di sicurezza** safety regulations; ~**e per l'uso**

instructions for use.

nor'male _ag_ normal.

normalità _sf_ normality.

normaliz'zare [normalid'dzare] _vt_ to normalize, bring back to normal.

normal'mente _av_ normally.

Norman'dia _sf_: **la** ~ Normandy.

nor'manno, a _ag, sm/f_ Norman.

norma'tivo, a _ag_ normative ♦ _sf_ regulations _pl._

norve'gese [norve'dʒese] _ag, sm/f, sm_ Norwegian.

Nor'vegia [nor'vɛdʒa] _sf_: **la** ~ Norway.

noso'comio _sm_ hospital.

nostal'gia [nostal'dʒia] _sf_ (_di casa, paese_) homesickness; (_del passato_) nostalgia.

nos'talgico, a, ci, che [nos'taldʒiko] _ag_ homesick; nostalgic ♦ _sm/f_ (_POL_) _person who hopes for the return of Fascism._

nos'trano, a _ag_ local; (_pianta, frutta_) home-produced.

'nostro, a _det_: **il(la)** ~(**a**) _etc_ our ♦ _pron_: **il(la)** ~(**a**) _etc_ ours ♦ _sm_: **abbiamo speso del** ~ we spent our own money ♦ _sf_: **la** ~**a** (_opinione_) our view; **i** ~**i** our family; our own people; **è dei** ~**i** he's one of us; **è dalla** ~**a** (_parte_) he's on our side; **anche noi abbiamo avuto le** ~**e** (_disavventure_) we've had our problems too; **alla** ~**a!** (_brindisi_) to us!

nos'tromo _sm_ boatswain.

'nota _sf_ (_segno_) mark; (_comunicazione scritta, MUS_) note; (_fattura_) bill; (_elenco_) list; **prendere** ~ **di qc** to note sth, make a note of sth, write sth down; (_fig: fare attenzione_) to note sth, take note of sth; **degno di** ~ noteworthy, worthy of note; ~**e caratteristiche** distinguishing marks _o_ features; ~**e a piè di pagina** footnotes.

no'tabile _ag_ notable; (_persona_) important ♦ _sm_ prominent citizen.

no'taio _sm_ notary.

no'tare _vt_ (_segnare: errori_) to mark; (_registrare_) to note (down), write down; (_rilevare, osservare_) to note, notice; **farsi** ~ to get o.s. noticed.

nota'rile _ag_: **atto** ~ legal document (_authorized by a notary_); **studio** ~ notary's office.

notazi'one [notat'tsjone] _sf_ (_MUS_) notation.

no'tevole _ag_ (_talento_) notable, remarkable; (_peso_) considerable.

no'tifica, che _sf_ notification.

notifi'care _vt_ (_DIR_): ~ **qc a qn** to notify sb of sth, give sb notice of sth.

notificazi'one [notifikat'tsjone] _sf_ notification.

no'tizia [no'tittsja] _sf_ (piece of) news _sg_;

(*informazione*) piece of information; ~**e** *sfpl* news *sg*; information *sg*.

notizi'ario [notit'tsjarjo] *sm* (*RADIO, TV, STAMPA*) news *sg*.

'noto, a *ag* (well-)known.

notorietà *sf* fame; notoriety.

no'torio, a *ag* well-known; (*peg*) notorious.

not'tambulo, a *sm/f* night-bird (*fig*).

not'tata *sf* night.

'notte *sf* night; **di** ~ at night; (*durante la* ~) in the night, during the night; **questa** ~ (*passata*) last night; (*che viene*) tonight; **nella** ~ **dei tempi** in the mists of time; **come va?** — **peggio che andar di** ~ how are things? — worse than ever; ~ **bianca** sleepless night.

notte'tempo *av* at night; during the night.

'nottola *sf* (*ZOOL*) noctule.

not'turno, a *ag* nocturnal; (*servizio, guardiano*) night *cpd* ♦ *sf* (*SPORT*) evening fixture (*BRIT*) *o* match.

nov. *abbr* (= *novembre*) Nov.

nö'vanta *num* ninety.

novan'tenne *ag, sm/f* ninety-year-old.

novan'tesimo, a *num* ninetieth.

novan'tina *sf*: **una** ~ (**di**) about ninety.

'nove *num* nine.

novecen'tesco, a, schi, sche [novetʃen'tesko] *ag* twentieth century.

nove'cento [nove'tʃento] *num* nine hundred ♦ *sm*: **il N**~ the twentieth century.

no'vella *sf* (*LETTERATURA*) short story.

novel'lino, a *ag* (*pivello*) green, inexperienced.

novel'lista, i, e *sm/f* short-story writer.

novel'listica *sf* (*arte*) short-story writing; (*insieme di racconti*) short stories *pl*.

no'vello, a *ag* (*piante, patate*) new; (*insalata, verdura*) early; (*sposo*) newly-married.

no'vembre *sm* November; *per fraseologia vedi* **luglio**.

novem'brino, a *ag* November *cpd*.

nove'mila *num* nine thousand.

noven'nale *ag* (*che dura 9 anni*) nine-year *cpd*; (*ogni 9 anni*) nine-yearly.

novi'lunio *sm* (*ASTR*) new moon.

novità *sf inv* novelty; (*innovazione*) innovation; (*cosa originale, insolita*) something new; (*notizia*) (piece of) news *sg*; **le** ~ **della moda** the latest fashions.

novizi'ato [novit'tsjato] *sm* (*REL*) novitiate; (*tirocinio*) apprenticeship.

no'vizio, a [no'vittsjo] *sm/f* (*REL*) novice; (*tirocinante*) beginner, apprentice.

nozi'one [not'tsjone] *sf* notion, idea; ~**i** *sfpl* (*rudimenti*) basic knowledge *sg*, rudiments.

nozio'nismo [nottsjo'nizmo] *sm* superficial knowledge.

nozio'nistico, a, ci, che [nottsjo'nistiko] *ag* superficial.

'nozze ['nottse] *sfpl* wedding *sg*, marriage *sg*; ~ **d'argento/d'oro** silver/golden wedding *sg*.

N.P.A. *abbr* = **nave portaerei**.

ns. *abbr* (*COMM*) = **nostro**.

NU *sigla* = Nuoro.

N.U. *sigla* (= Nazioni Unite) UN.

'nube *sf* cloud.

nubi'fragio [nubi'fradʒo] *sm* cloudburst.

'nubile *ag* (*donna*) unmarried, single.

'nuca, che *sf* nape of the neck.

nucle'are *ag* nuclear ♦ *sm*: **il** ~ nuclear energy.

'nucleo *sm* nucleus; (*gruppo*) team, unit, group; (*MIL, POLIZIA*) squad; ~ **antidroga** anti-drugs squad; **il** ~ **familiare** the family unit.

nu'dismo *sm* nudism.

nu'dista, i, e *sm/f* nudist.

nudità *sf inv* nudity, nakedness; (*di paesaggio*) bareness ♦ *sfpl* (*parti nude del corpo*) nakedness *sg*.

'nudo, a *ag* (*persona*) bare, naked, nude; (*membra*) bare, naked; (*montagna*) bare ♦ *sm* (*ARTE*) nude; **a occhio** ~ to the naked eye; **a piedi** ~**i** barefoot; **mettere a** ~ (*cuore, verità*) to lay bare; **gli ha detto** ~ **e crudo che** ... he told him bluntly that ....

'nugolo *sm*: **un** ~ **di** a whole host of.

'nulla *pron, av* = **niente** ♦ *sm*: **il** ~ nothing; **svanire nel** ~ to vanish into thin air; **basta un** ~ **per farlo arrabbiare** he gets annoyed over the slightest thing.

nulla'osta *sm inv* authorization.

nullate'nente *ag*: **essere** ~ to own nothing ♦ *sm/f* person with no property.

nullità *sf inv* nullity; (*persona*) nonentity.

'nullo, a *ag* useless, worthless; (*DIR*) null (and void); (*SPORT*): **incontro** ~ draw.

nume'rale *ag, sm* numeral.

nume'rare *vt* to number.

numera'tore *sm* (*MAT*) numerator; (*macchina*) numbering device.

numerazi'one [numerat'tsjone] *sf* numbering; (*araba, decimale*) notation.

nu'merico, a, ci, che *ag* numerical.

'numero *sm* number; (*romano, arabo*) numeral; (*di spettacolo*) act, turn; **dare i** ~**i** (*farneticare*) not to be all there; **tanto per fare** ~ **invitiamo anche lui** why don't we invite him to make up the numbers?; **ha tutti i** ~**i per riuscire** he's got what it takes to succeed; **che** ~ **tuo fratello!** your brother is a real character!; ~ **civico** house number; ~ **chiuso** (*UNIVERSITÀ*) selective entry system; ~ **doppio** (*di rivista*) issue with supplement; ~ **di scarpe** size of shoe; ~ **verde** (*TEL*) ≈ Freephone ®.

nume'roso, a *ag* numerous, many; (*folla, famiglia*) large.

numis'matica *sf* numismatics *sg*, coin collecting.

'nunzio ['nuntsjo] *sm* (*REL*) nuncio.

nu'occio *etc* ['nwɔttʃo] *vb vedi* **nuocere**.

nu'ocere ['nwɔtʃere] *vi*: ~ **a** to harm, damage; **il tentar non nuoce** (*proverbio*) there's no harm in trying.

nuoci'uto, a [nwo'tʃuto] *pp di* **nuocere**.

nu'ora *sf* daughter-in-law.

nuo'tare *vi* to swim; (*galleggiare: oggetti*) to float; ~ **a rana/sul dorso** to do the breast stroke/backstroke.

nuo'tata *sf* swim.

nuota'tore, 'trice *sm/f* swimmer.

nu'oto *sm* swimming.

nu'ova *sf vedi* **nuovo**.

nuova'mente *av* again.

Nu'ova York *sf* New York.

Nu'ova Ze'landa [-dze'landa] *sf*: **la** ~ New Zealand.

nu'ovo, a *ag* new ♦ *sf* (*notizia*) (piece of) news *sg*; **come** ~ as good as new; **di** ~ again; **fino a** ~ **ordine** until further notice; **il suo volto non mi è** ~ I know his face; **rimettere a** ~ (*cosa, macchina*) to do up like new; **anno** ~, **vita** ~**a!** it's time to turn over a new leaf!; ~ **fiammante** *o* **di zecca** brand-new; **la N**~**a Guinea** New Guinea; **la N**~**a Inghilterra** New England; **la N**~**a Scozia** Nova Scotia.

nu'trice [nu'tritʃe] *sf* wet nurse.

nutri'ente *ag* nutritious, nourishing; (*crema, balsamo*) nourishing.

nutri'mento *sm* food, nourishment.

nu'trire *vt* to feed; (*fig: sentimenti*) to harbour (*BRIT*), harbor (*US*), nurse.

nutri'tivo, a *ag* nutritional; (*alimento*) nutritious.

nu'trito, a *ag* (*numeroso*) large; (*fitto*) heavy; **ben/mal** ~ well/poorly fed.

nutrizi'one [nutrit'tsjone] *sf* nutrition.

'nuvolo, a *ag* cloudy ♦ *sf* cloud.

nuvolosità *sf* cloudiness.

nuvo'loso, a *ag* cloudy.

nuzi'ale [nut'tsjale] *ag* nuptial; wedding *cpd*.

'nylon ['nailən] *sm* nylon.

O o

O, o [ɔ] *sf o m inv* (*lettera*) O, o; ~ **come Otranto** ≈ O for Oliver (*BRIT*), O for Oboe (*US*).

o *cong* (*dav V spesso* **od**) or; ~ ... ~ either ... or; ~ **l'uno** ~ **l'altro** either (of them); ~ **meglio** or rather.

O. *abbr* (= *ovest*) W.

'oasi *sf inv* oasis.

obbedi'ente *etc vedi* **ubbidiente** *etc*.

obbiet'tare *etc vedi* **obiettare** *etc*.

obbli'gare *vt* (*costringere*): ~ **qn a fare** to force *o* oblige sb to do; (*DIR*) to bind; ~**rsi** *vr*: ~**rsi a fare** to undertake to do; ~**rsi per qn** (*DIR*) to stand surety for sb, act as guarantor for sb.

obbliga'tissimo, a *ag* (*ringraziamento*): ~! much obliged!

obbli'gato, a *ag* (*costretto, grato*) obliged; (*percorso, tappa*) set, fixed; **passaggio** ~ (*fig*) essential requirement.

obbliga'torio, a *ag* compulsory, obligatory.

obbligazi'one [obbligat'tsjone] *sf* obligation; (*COMM*) bond, debenture; ~ **dello Stato** government bond; ~**i convertibili** convertible loan stock, convertible debentures.

obbligazio'nista, i, e [obbligattsjo'nista] *sm/f* bond-holder.

'obbligo, ghi *sm* obligation; (*dovere*) duty; **avere l'**~ **di fare, essere nell'**~ **di fare** to be obliged to do; **essere d'**~ (*discorso, applauso*) to be called for; **avere degli** ~**ghi con** *o* **verso qn** to be under an obligation to sb, be indebted to sb; **le formalità d'**~ the necessary formalities.

obb.mo *abbr* = **obbligatissimo**.

ob'brobrio *sm* disgrace; (*fig*) mess, eyesore.

obe'lisco, schi *sm* obelisk.

obe'rato, a *ag*: ~ **di** (*lavoro*) overloaded *o* overburdened with; (*debiti*) crippled with.

obesità *sf* obesity.

o'beso, a *ag* obese.

obiet'tare *vt*: ~ **che** to object that; ~ **su qc** to object to sth, raise objections concerning sth.

obiettiva'mente *av* objectively.
obiettività *sf* objectivity.
obiet'tivo, a *ag* objective ♦ *sm* (*OTTICA, FOT*) lens *sg*, objective; (*MIL, fig*) objective.
obiet'tore *sm* objector; ~ **di coscienza** conscientious objector.
obiezi'one [objet'tsjone] *sf* objection.
obi'torio *sm* morgue.
o'bliquo, a *ag* oblique; (*inclinato*) slanting; (*fig*) devious, underhand; **sguardo** ~ sidelong glance.
oblite'rare *vt* (*francobollo*) to cancel; (*biglietto*) to stamp.
oblitera'trice [oblitera'tritʃe] *sf* (*anche*: **macchina** ~) cancelling machine; stamping machine.
oblò *sm inv* porthole.
o'blungo, a, ghi, ghe *ag* oblong.
'oboe *sm* oboe.
'obolo *sm* (*elemosina*) (small) offering, mite.
obsole'scenza [obsoleʃ'ʃɛntsa] *sf* (*ECON*) obsolescence.
obso'leto, a *ag* obsolete.
OC *abbr* (= *onde corte*) SW.
'oca, *pl* **'oche** *sf* goose.
o'caggine [o'kaddʒine] *sf* silliness, stupidity.
occasio'nale *ag* (*incontro*) chance; (*cliente, guadagni*) casual, occasional.
occasi'one *sf* (*caso favorevole*) opportunity; (*causa, motivo, circostanza*) occasion; (*COMM*) bargain; **all'**~ should the need arise; **alla prima** ~ at the first opportunity; **d'**~ (*a buon prezzo*) bargain *cpd*; (*usato*) secondhand.
occhi'aia [ok'kjaja] *sf* eye socket; ~**e** *sfpl* (*sotto gli occhi*) shadows (under the eyes).
occhi'ali [ok'kjali] *smpl* glasses, spectacles; ~ **da sole** sunglasses.
occhi'ata [ok'kjata] *sf* look, glance; **dare un'**~ **a** to have a look at.
occhieggi'are [okkjed'dʒare] *vi* (*apparire qua e là*) to peep (out).
occhi'ello [ok'kjɛllo] *sm* buttonhole; (*asola*) eyelet.
'occhio ['ɔkkjo] *sm* eye; ~! careful!, watch out!; **a** ~ **nudo** with the naked eye; **a quattr'**~**i** privately, in private; **avere** ~ **to** have a good eye; **chiudere un** ~ (**su**) (*fig*) to turn a blind eye (to), shut one's eyes (to); **costare un** ~ **della testa** to cost a fortune; **dare all'**~ *o* **nell'**~ **a qn** to catch sb's eye; **fare l'**~ **a qc** to get used to sth; **tenere d'**~ **qn** to keep an eye on sb; **vedere di buon/mal** ~ **qc** to look favourably/unfavourably on sth.

occhio'lino [okkjo'lino] *sm*: **fare l'**~ **a qn** to wink at sb.
occiden'tale [ottʃiden'tale] *ag* western ♦ *smlf* Westerner.
occi'dente [ottʃi'dɛnte] *sm* west; (*POL*): **l'O**~ the West; **a** ~ in the west.
oc'cipite [ot'tʃipite] *sm* back of the head, occiput (*ANAT*).
oc'cludere *vt* to block.
occlusi'one *sf* blockage, obstruction.
oc'cluso, a *pp di* **occludere**.
occor'rente *ag* necessary ♦ *sm* all that is necessary.
occor'renza [okkor'rɛntsa] *sf* necessity, need; **all'**~ in case of need.
oc'correre *vi* to be needed, be required ♦ *vb impers*: **occorre farlo** it must be done; **occorre che tu parta** you must leave, you'll have to leave; **mi occorrono i soldi** I need the money.
oc'corso, a *pp di* **occorrere**.
occulta'mento *sm* concealment.
occul'tare *vt* to hide, conceal.
oc'culto, a *ag* hidden, concealed; (*scienze, forze*) occult.
occu'pante *smlf* (*di casa*) occupier, occupant; ~ **abusivo** squatter.
occu'pare *vt* to occupy; (*manodopera*) to employ; (*ingombrare*) to occupy, take up; ~**rsi** *vr* to occupy o.s., keep o.s. busy; (*impiegarsi*) to get a job; ~**rsi di** (*interessarsi*) to take an interest in; (*prendersi cura di*) to look after, take care of.
occu'pato, a *ag* (*MIL, POL*) occupied; (*persona: affaccendato*) busy; (*posto, sedia*) taken; (*toilette, TEL*) engaged.
occupazio'nale [okkupattsjo'nale] *ag* employment *cpd*, of employment.
occupazi'one [okkupat'tsjone] *sf* occupation; (*impiego, lavoro*) job; (*ECON*) employment.
Oce'ania [otʃe'anja] *sf*: **l'**~ Oceania.
o'ceano [o'tʃɛano] *sm* ocean.
'ocra *sf* ochre.
'OCSE *sigla f* (= *Organizzazione per la Cooperazione e lo Sviluppo Economico*) OECD (= *Organization for Economic Cooperation and Development*).
ocu'lare *ag* ocular, eye *cpd*; **testimone** ~ eye witness.
ocula'tezza [okula'tettsa] *sf* caution; shrewdness.
ocu'lato, a *ag* (*attento*) cautious, prudent; (*accorto*) shrewd.
ocu'lista, i, e *smlf* eye specialist, oculist.
od *cong vedi* **o**.
'ode *sf* ode.

'**ode** *etc vb vedi* **udire**.
odi'are *vt* to hate, detest.
odi'erno, a *ag* today's, of today; (*attuale*) present; **in data** ~**a** (*formale*) today.
'**odio** *sm* hatred; **avere in** ~ **qc/qn** to hate *o* detest sth/sb.
odi'oso, a *ag* hateful, odious; **rendersi** ~ **(a)** to make o.s. unpopular (with).
'**odo** *etc vb vedi* **udire**.
odontoi'atra, i, e *sm/f* dentist, dental surgeon.
odontoia'tria *sf* dentistry.
odo'rare *vt* (*annusare*) to smell; (*profumare*) to perfume, scent ♦ *vi*: ~ **(di)** to smell (of).
odo'rato *sm* sense of smell.
o'dore *sm* smell; **gli** ~**i** *smpl* (*CUC*) (aromatic) herbs; **sentire** ~ **di qc** to smell sth; **morire in** ~ **di santità** (*REL*) to die in the odour (*BRIT*) *o* odor (*US*) of sanctity.
odo'roso, a *ag* sweet-smelling.
of'fendere *vt* to offend; (*violare*) to break, violate; (*insultare*) to insult; (*ferire*) to hurt; ~**rsi** *vr* (*con senso reciproco*) to insult one another; (*risentirsi*): ~**rsi (di)** to take offence (at), be offended (by).
offen'sivo, a *ag, sf* offensive.
offen'sore *sm* offender; (*MIL*) aggressor.
offe'rente *sm* (*in aste*): **al migliore** ~ to the highest bidder.
of'ferto, a *pp di* **offrire** ♦ *sf* offer; (*donazione, anche REL*) offering; (*in gara d'appalto*) tender; (*in aste*) bid; (*ECON*) supply; **fare un'**~**a** to make an offer; (*per appalto*) to tender; (*ad un'asta*) to bid; ~**a pubblica d'acquisto (OPA)** takeover bid; ~**a pubblica di vendita (OPV)** public offer for sale; ~**a reale** tender; "~**e d'impiego**" (*STAMPA*) "situations vacant" (*BRIT*), "help wanted" (*US*).
of'feso, a *pp di* **offendere** ♦ *ag* offended; (*fisicamente*) hurt, injured ♦ *sm/f* offended party ♦ *sf* insult, affront; (*MIL*) attack; (*DIR*) offence (*BRIT*), offense (*US*); **essere** ~ **con qn** to be annoyed with sb; **parte** ~**a** (*DIR*) plaintiff.
offi'ciare [offi'tʃare] *vi* (*REL*) to officiate.
offi'cina [offi'tʃina] *sf* workshop.
of'frire *vt* to offer; ~**rsi** *vr* (*proporsi*) to offer (o.s.), volunteer; (*occasione*) to present itself; (*esporsi*): ~**rsi a** to expose o.s. to; **ti offro da bere** I'll buy you a drink; "**offresi posto di segretaria**" "secretarial vacancy", "vacancy for secretary"; "**segretaria offresi**" "secretary seeks post".
offus'care *vt* to obscure, darken; (*fig: intelletto*) to dim, cloud; (: *fama*) to obscure, overshadow; ~**rsi** *vr* to grow dark; to cloud, grow dim; to be obscured.

of'talmico, a, ci, che *ag* ophthalmic.
oggettività [oddʒettivi'ta] *sf* objectivity.
ogget'tivo, a [oddʒet'tivo] *ag* objective.
og'getto [od'dʒetto] *sm* object; (*materia, argomento*) subject (matter); (*in lettere commerciali*): ~ ... re ...; **essere** ~ **di** (*critiche, controversia*) to be the subject of; (*odio, pietà etc*) to be the object of; **essere** ~ **di scherno** to be a laughing stock; **in** ~ **a quanto detto** (*in lettere*) as regards the matter mentioned above; ~**i preziosi** valuables, articles of value; ~**i smarriti** lost property *sg* (*BRIT*), lost and found *sg* (*US*).
'**oggi** ['ɔddʒi] *av, sm* today; ~ **stesso** today, this very day; ~ **come** ~ at present, as things stand; **dall'** ~ **al domani** from one day to the next; **a tutt'**~ up till now, till today; **le spese a tutt'**~ **sono** ... expenses to date are ...; ~ **a otto** a week today.
oggigi'orno [oddʒi'dʒorno] *av* nowadays.
o'giva [o'dʒiva] *sf* ogive, pointed arch.
OGM *sigla m* (= *organismo geneticamente modificato*) GM organism.
'**ogni** ['oɲɲi] *det* every, each; (*tutti*) all; (*con valore distributivo*) every; ~ **uomo è mortale** all men are mortal; **viene** ~ **due giorni** he comes every two days; ~ **cosa** everything; **ad** ~ **costo** at all costs, at any price; **in** ~ **luogo** everywhere; ~ **tanto** every so often; ~ **volta che** every time that.
Ognis'santi [oɲɲis'santi] *sm* All Saints' Day.
o'gnuno [oɲ'ɲuno] *pron* everyone, everybody.
'**ohi** *escl* oh!; (*esprimente dolore*) ow!
ohimè *escl* oh dear!
'**OIL** *sigla f* (= *Organizzazione Internazionale del Lavoro*) ILO.
OL *abbr* (= *onde lunghe*) LW.
O'landa *sf*: **l'**~ Holland.
olan'dese *ag* Dutch ♦ *sm* (*LING*) Dutch ♦ *sm/f* Dutchman/woman; **gli O**~**i** the Dutch.
ole'andro *sm* oleander.
ole'ato, a *ag*: **carta** ~**a** greaseproof paper (*BRIT*), wax paper (*US*).
oleo'dotto *sm* oil pipeline.
ole'oso, a *ag* oily; (*che contiene olio*) oil *cpd*.
o'lezzo [o'leddzo] *sm* fragrance.
ol'fatto *sm* sense of smell.
oli'are *vt* to oil.
olia'tore *sm* oil can, oiler.
oli'era *sf* oil cruet.
oligar'chia [oligar'kia] *sf* oligarchy.
olim'piadi *sfpl* Olympic Games.
o'limpico, a, ci, che *ag* Olympic.

'**olio** *sm* oil; (*PITTURA*): **un (quadro a)** ~ an oil painting; **sott'**~ (*CUC*) in oil; ~ **di fegato di merluzzo** cod liver oil; ~ **d'oliva** olive oil; ~ **santo** holy oil; ~ **di semi** vegetable oil; ~ **solare** suntan oil.

o'**liva** *sf* olive.

oli'**vastro, a** *ag* olive(-coloured) (*BRIT*), olive(colored) (*US*); (*carnagione*) sallow.

oli'**veto** *sm* olive grove.

o'**livo** *sm* olive tree.

'**olmo** *sm* elm.

olo'**causto** *sm* holocaust.

OLP *sigla f* (= *Organizzazione per la Liberazione della Palestina*) PLO.

oltraggi'**are** [oltrad'dʒare] *vt* to offend, insult.

ol'**traggio** [ol'traddʒo] *sm* offence (*BRIT*), offense (*US*), insult; (*DIR*): ~ **al pudore** indecent behaviour (*BRIT*) o behavior (*US*); ~ **alla corte** contempt of court.

oltraggi'**oso, a** [oltrad'dʒoso] *ag* offensive.

al'**tralpo** av beyond the Alps.

ol'**tranza** [ol'trantsa] *sf*: **a** ~ to the last, to the bitter end; **sciopero ad** ~ all-out strike.

oltran'**zismo** [oltran'tsizmo] *sm* (*POL*) extremism.

oltran'**zista, i, e** [oltran'tsista] *sm/f* (*POL*) extremist.

'**oltre** *av* (*più in là*) further; (*di più: aspettare*) longer, more ♦ *prep* (*di là da*) beyond, over, on the other side of; (*più di*) more than, over; (*in aggiunta a*) besides; (*eccetto*): ~ **a** except, apart from; ~ **a tutto** on top of all that.

oltrecor'**tina** *av* behind the Iron Curtain; **paesi d'**~ Iron Curtain countries.

oltre'**manica** *av* across the Channel.

oltre'**mare** *av* overseas.

oltre'**modo** *av* extremely, greatly.

oltreo'**ceano** [oltreo'tʃeano] *av* overseas ♦ *sm*: **paesi d'**~ overseas countries.

oltrepas'**sare** *vt* to go beyond, exceed.

oltre'**tomba** *sm inv*: **l'**~ the hereafter.

OM *abbr* (= *onde medie*) MW; (*MIL*) = *ospedale militare*.

o'**maggio** [o'maddʒo] *sm* (*dono*) gift; (*segno di rispetto*) homage, tribute; ~**i** *smpl* (*complimenti*) respects; **in** ~ (*copia, biglietto*) complimentary; **rendere** ~ **a** to pay homage o tribute to; **presentare i propri** ~**i a qn** (*formale*) to pay one's respects to sb.

'**Oman** *sm*: **l'**~ Oman.

ombeli'**cale** *ag* umbilical.

ombe'**lico, chi** *sm* navel.

'**ombra** *sf* (*zona non assolata, fantasma*) shade; (*sagoma scura*) shadow ♦ *ag inv*:

bandiera ~ flag of convenience; **governo** ~ (*POL*) shadow cabinet; **sedere all'**~ to sit in the shade; **nell'**~ (*tramare, agire*) secretly; **restare nell'**~ (*fig: persona*) to remain in obscurity; **senza** ~ **di dubbio** without the shadow of a doubt.

ombreggi'**are** [ombred'dʒare] *vt* to shade.

om'**brello** *sm* umbrella; ~ **da sole** parasol, sunshade.

ombrel'**lone** *sm* beach umbrella.

om'**bretto** *sm* eyeshadow.

om'**broso, a** *ag* shady, shaded; (*cavallo*) nervous, skittish; (*persona*) touchy, easily offended.

ome'**lette** [omə'lɛt] *sf inv* omelet(te).

ome'**lia** *sf* (*REL*) homily, sermon.

ome'**opata** *sm/f* hom(o)eopath.

omeopa'**tia** *sf* hom(o)eopathy.

omeo'**patico, a, ci, che** *ag* hom(o)eopathic ♦ *sm* hom(o)eopath.

omer'**tà** *sf* conspiracy of silence.

o'**messo, a** *pp di* omettere.

o'**mettere** *vt* to omit, leave out; ~ **di fare** to omit o fail to do.

omi'**cida, i, e** [omi'tʃida] *ag* homicidal, murderous ♦ *sm/f* murderer/murderess.

omi'**cidio** [omi'tʃidjo] *sm* murder; ~ **colposo** (*DIR*) culpable homicide; ~ **premeditato** (*DIR*) murder.

o'**misi** *etc vb vedi* omettere.

omissi'**one** *sf* omission; **reato d'**~ criminal negligence; ~ **di atti d'ufficio** negligence (*by a public employee*); ~ **di denuncia** failure to report a crime; ~ **di soccorso** (*DIR*) failure to stop and give assistance.

omogeneiz'**zato** [omodʒeneid'dzato] *sm* baby food.

omo'**geneo, a** [omo'dʒɛneo] *ag* homogeneous.

omolo'**gare** *vt* (*DIR*) to approve, recognize; (*ratificare*) to ratify.

omologazi'**one** [omologat'tsjone] *sf* approval; ratification.

o'**mologo, a, ghi, ghe** *ag* homologous, corresponding ♦ *sm/f* opposite number.

o'**monimo, a** *sm/f* namesake ♦ *sm* (*LING*) homonym.

omosessu'**ale** *ag*, *sm/f* homosexual.

O.M.S. *sigla f vedi* **Organizzazione Mondiale della Sanità**.

On. *abbr* (*POL*) = **onorevole**.

'**oncia, ce** ['ontʃa] *sf* ounce.

'**onda** *sf* wave; **mettere** o **mandare in** ~ (*RADIO, TV*) to broadcast; **andare in** ~ (*RADIO, TV*) to go on the air; ~**e corte/medie/lunghe** short/medium/long wave *sg*; **l'**~ **verde** (*AUT*) synchronized traffic lights *pl*.

on'data *sf* wave, billow; (*fig*) wave, surge; **a ~e** in waves; **~ di caldo** heatwave; **~ di freddo** cold spell *o* snap.

'onde *cong* (*affinché: con il congiuntivo*) so that, in order that; (*: con l'infinito*) so as to, in order to.

ondeggi'are [onded'dʒare] *vi* (*acqua*) to ripple; (*muoversi sulle onde: barca*) to rock, roll; (*fig: muoversi come le onde, barcollare*) to sway; (*: essere incerto*) to waver.

on'doso, a *ag* (*moto*) of the waves.

ondu'lato, a *ag* (*capelli*) wavy; (*terreno*) undulating; **cartone ~** corrugated paper; **lamiera ~a** sheet of corrugated iron.

ondula'torio, a *ag* undulating; (*FISICA*) undulatory, wave *cpd*.

ondulazi'one [ondulat'tsjone] *sf* undulation; (*acconciatura*) wave.

one'rato, a *ag:* **~ di** burdened with, loaded with.

'onere *sm* burden; **~ finanziario** financial charge; **~i fiscali** taxes.

one'roso, a *ag* (*fig*) heavy, onerous.

onestà *sf* honesty.

onesta'mente *av* honestly; fairly; virtuously; (*in verità*) honestly, frankly.

o'nesto, a *ag* (*probo, retto*) honest; (*giusto*) fair; (*casto*) chaste, virtuous.

'onice ['ɔnitʃe] *sf* onyx.

o'nirico, a, ci, che *ag* dreamlike, dream *cpd*.

onnipo'tente *ag* omnipotent.

onnipre'sente *ag* omnipresent; (*scherzoso*) ubiquitous.

onnisci'ente [onniʃ'ʃɛnte] *ag* omniscient.

onniveg'gente [onnived'dʒɛnte] *ag* all-seeing.

ono'mastico, ci *sm* name day.

onomato'pea *sf* onomatopoeia.

onomato'peico, a, ci, che *ag* onomatopoeic.

ono'ranze [ono'rantse] *sfpl* honours (*BRIT*), honors (*US*).

ono'rare *vt* to honour (*BRIT*), honor (*US*); (*far onore a*) to do credit to; **~rsi** *vr:* **~rsi di qc/di fare** to feel hono(u)red by sth/to do.

ono'rario, a *ag* honorary ♦ *sm* fee.

onora'tissimo, a *ag* (*in presentazioni*): **~!** delighted to meet you!

ono'rato, a *ag* (*reputazione, famiglia, carriera*) distinguished; **essere ~ di fare qc** to have the honour to do sth *o* of doing sth; **~ di conoscerla!** (it is) a pleasure to meet you!

o'nore *sm* honour (*BRIT*), honor (*US*); **in ~ di** in hono(u)r of; **fare gli ~i di casa** to play host (*o* hostess); **fare ~ a** to hono(u)r; (*pranzo*) to do justice to; (*famiglia*) to be a credit to; **farsi ~** to distinguish o.s.; **posto d'~** place of hono(u)r; **a onor del vero ...** to tell the truth ....

ono'revole *ag* honourable (*BRIT*), honorable (*US*) ♦ *sm/f* (*POL*) ≈ Member of Parliament (*BRIT*), ≈ Congressman/ woman (*US*).

onorifi'cenza [onorifi'tʃɛntsa] *sf* honour (*BRIT*), honor (*US*); decoration.

ono'rifico, a, ci, che *ag* honorary.

'onta *sf* shame, disgrace; **ad ~ di** despite, notwithstanding.

on'tano *sm* alder.

'O.N.U. *sigla f* (= *Organizzazione delle Nazioni Unite*) UN, UNO.

OO.PP. *abbr vedi* **opere pubbliche**.

'OPA *sigla f vedi* **offerta pubblica d'acquisto**.

o'paco, a, chi, che *ag* (*vetro*) opaque; (*metallo*) dull, matt.

o'pale *sm o f* opal.

'O.P.E.C. *sigla f* (= *Organization of Petroleum Exporting Countries*) OPEC.

'opera *sf* (*gen*) work; (*azione rilevante*) action, deed, work; (*MUS*) work; opus; (*: melodramma*) opera; (*: teatro*) opera house; (*ente*) institution, organization; **per ~ sua** thanks to him; **fare ~ di persuasione presso qn** to try to convince sb; **mettersi/essere all'~** to get down to/ be at work; **~ d'arte** work of art; **~ buffa** comic opera; **~ lirica** (grand) opera; **~ pia** religious charity; **~e pubbliche** (OO.PP.) public works; **~e di restauro/di scavo** restoration/excavation work *sg*.

ope'raio, a *ag* working-class; workers'; (*ZOOL: ape, formica*) worker *cpd* ♦ *sm/f* worker; **classe ~a** working class; **~ di fabbrica** factory worker; **~ a giornata** day labourer (*BRIT*) *o* laborer (*US*); **~ specializzato** *o* qualificato skilled worker; **~ non specializzato** semi-skilled worker.

ope'rare *vt* to carry out, make; (*MED*) to operate on ♦ *vi* to operate, work; (*rimedio*) to act, work; (*MED*) to operate; **~rsi** *vr* to occur, take place; (*MED*) to have an operation; **~rsi d'appendicite** to have one's appendix out; **~ qn d'urgenza** to perform an emergency operation on sb.

opera'tivo, a *ag* operative, operating; **piano ~** (*MIL*) plan of operations.

ope'rato *sm* (*comportamento*) actions *pl*.

opera'tore, 'trice *sm/f* operator; (*TV, CINE*) cameraman; **aperto solo agli ~i** (*COMM*) open to the trade only; **~ di borsa** dealer on the stock exchange; **~ ecologico** refuse collector; **~ economico** agent, broker; **~ del suono** sound recordist; **~ turistico** tour operator.

opera'torio, a *ag* (*MED*) operating.
operazi'one [operat'tsjone] *sf* operation.
ope'retta *sf* (*MUS*) operetta, light opera.
operosità *sf* industry.
ope'roso, a *ag* industrious, hard-working.
opi'ficio [opi'fitʃo] *sm* factory, works *pl*.
opi'nabile *ag* (*discutibile*) debatable,
questionable; **è ~** it is a matter of
opinion.
opini'one *sf* opinion; **avere il coraggio delle
proprie ~i** to have the courage of one's
convictions; **l'~ pubblica** public opinion.
opinio'nista, i, e *sm/f* (political) columnist.
op là *escl* (*per far saltare*) hup!; (*a bimbo che
è caduto*) upsy-daisy!
'oppio *sm* opium.
oppi'omane *sm/f* opium addict.
oppo'nente *ag* opposing ♦ *sm/f* opponent.
op'pongo *etc vb vedi* **opporre.**
op'porre *vt* to oppose; **opporsi** *vr*: **opporsi (a
qc)** to oppose (sth); to object (to sth); **~
resistenza/un rifiuto** to offer resistance/
to refuse.
opportu'nista, i, e *sm/f* opportunist.
opportunità *sf inv* opportunity;
(*convenienza*) opportuneness, timeliness.
oppor'tuno, a *ag* timely, opportune;
(*giusto*) right, appropriate; **a tempo ~** at
the right *o* the appropriate time.
op'posi *etc vb vedi* **opporre.**
opposi'tore, 'trice *sm/f* opposer, opponent.
opposizi'one [oppozit'tsjone] *sf* opposition;
(*DIR*) objection; **essere in netta ~** (*idee,
opinioni*) to clash, be in complete
opposition; **fare ~ a qn/qc** to oppose sb/
sth.
op'posto, a *pp di* **opporre** ♦ *ag* opposite;
(*opinioni*) conflicting ♦ *sm* opposite,
contrary; **all'~** on the contrary.
oppressi'one *sf* oppression.
oppres'sivo, a *ag* oppressive.
op'presso, a *pp di* **opprimere.**
oppres'sore *sm* oppressor.
oppri'mente *ag* (*caldo, noia*) oppressive;
(*persona*) tiresome; (: *deprimente*)
depressing.
op'primere *vt* (*premere, gravare*) to weigh
down; (*estenuare*: *sog*: *caldo*) to suffocate,
oppress; (*tiranneggiare*: *popolo*) to
oppress.
oppu'gnare [oppuɲ'ɲare] *vt* (*fig*) to refute.
op'pure *cong* or (else).
op'tare *vi*: **~ per** (*scegliere*) to opt for,
decide upon; (*BORSA*) to take (out) an
option on.
'optimum *sm inv* optimum.
opu'lento, a *ag* (*ricco*) rich, wealthy,
affluent; (: *arredamento etc*) opulent.

opu'lenza [opu'lɛntsa] *sf* (*vedi ag*) richness,
wealth, affluence; opulence.
o'puscolo *sm* booklet, pamphlet.
OPV *sigla f vedi* **offerta pubblica di vendita.**
opzio'nale [optsjo'nale] *ag* optional.
opzi'one [op'tsjone] *sf* option.
OR *sigla* = Oristano.
'ora *sf* (*60 minuti*) hour; (*momento*) time
♦ *av* (*adesso*) now; (*poco fa*): **è uscito
proprio ~** he's just gone out; (*tra poco*)
presently, in a minute; (*correlativo*):
~ ... ~ now ... now; **che ~ è?, che ~e
sono?** what time is it?; **domani a quest'~**
this time tomorrow; **non veder l'~ di fare**
to long to do, look forward to doing; **fare
le ~e piccole** to stay up till the early
hours (of the morning) *o* the small hours;
è ~ di partire it's time to go; **di buon' ~**
early; **alla buon'~!** at last!; **~ legale** *o*
estiva summer time (*BRIT*), daylight
saving time (*US*); **~ locale** local time; **~ di
pranzo** lunchtime; **~ di punta** (*AUT*) rush
hour; **d'~ in avanti** *o* **poi** from now on; **or
~** just now, a moment ago; **~ come ~**
right now, at present; **10 anni or sono** 10
years ago.
u'racolo *sm* oracle.
'orafo *sm* goldsmith.
o'rale *ag, sm* oral.
oral'mente *av* orally.
ora'mai *av* = **ormai.**
o'rario, a *ag* hourly; (*fuso, segnale*) time
cpd; (*velocità*) per hour ♦ *sm* timetable,
schedule; (*di visite etc*) hours *pl*, time(s *pl*);
~ di apertura/chiusura opening/closing
time; **~ di apertura degli sportelli** bank
opening hours; **~ elastico** *o* **flessibile**
(*INDUSTRIA*) flexitime; **~ ferroviario**
railway timetable; **~ di lavoro/d'ufficio**
working/office hours.
o'rata *sf* sea bream.
ora'tore, 'trice *sm/f* speaker; orator.
ora'torio, a *ag* oratorical ♦ *sm* (*REL*)
oratory; (*MUS*) oratorio ♦ *sf* (*arte*) oratory.
orazi'one [orat'tsjone] *sf* (*REL*) prayer;
(*discorso*) speech, oration.
or'bene *cong* so, well (then).
'orbita *sf* (*ASTR, FISICA*) orbit; (*ANAT*) (eye-)
socket.
orbi'tare *vi* to orbit.
'orbo, a *ag* blind.
'Orcadi *sfpl*: **le (isole) ~** the Orkney
Islands, the Orkneys.
or'chestra [or'kɛstra] *sf* orchestra.
orches'trale [orkes'trale] *ag* orchestral
♦ *sm/f* orchestra player.
orches'trare [orkes'trare] *vt* to orchestrate;
(*fig*) to stage-manage.

orchi'dea [orki'dεa] *sf* orchid.
'orcio ['ortʃo] *sm* jar.
'orco, chi *sm* ogre.
'orda *sf* horde.
or'digno [or'diɲɲo] *sm*: ~ **esplosivo** explosive device.
ordi'nale *ag*, *sm* ordinal.
ordina'mento *sm* order, arrangement; (*regolamento*) regulations *pl*, rules *pl*; ~ **scolastico/giuridico** education/legal system.
ordi'nanza [ordi'nantsa] *sf* (*DIR, MIL*) order; (*AMM*: *decreto*) decree; (*persona*: *MIL*) orderly, batman; **d'**~ (*MIL*) regulation *cpd*; **ufficiale d'**~ orderly; ~ **municipale** by(e)-law.
ordi'nare *vt* (*mettere in ordine*) to arrange, organize; (*COMM*) to order; (*prescrivere*: *medicina*) to prescribe; (*comandare*): ~ **a qn di fare qc** to order *o* command sb to do sth; (*REL*) to ordain.
ordi'nario, a *ag* (*comune*) ordinary; (*grossolano*) coarse, common ♦ *sm* ordinary; (*di università*) full professor.
ordina'tivo, a *ag* regulating, governing ♦ *sm* (*COMM*) order.
ordi'nato, a *ag* tidy, orderly.
ordinazi'one [ordinat'tsjone] *sf* (*COMM*) order; (*REL*) ordination; **fare un'**~ **di qc** to put in an order for sth, order sth; **eseguire qc su** ~ to make sth to order.
'ordine *sm* order; (*carattere*): **d'**~ **pratico** of a practical nature; **all'**~ (*COMM*: *assegno*) to order; **di prim'**~ first-class; **fino a nuovo** ~ until further notice; **essere in** ~ (*documenti*) to be in order; (*persona, stanza*) to be tidy; **mettere in** ~ to put in order, tidy (up); **richiamare all'**~ to call to order; **le forze dell'**~ the forces of law and order; ~ **d'acquisto** purchase order; **l'**~ **degli avvocati** ≈ the Bar; ~ **del giorno** (*di seduta*) agenda; (*MIL*) order of the day; **l'**~ **dei medici** ≈ the Medical Association; ~ **di pagamento** standing order (*BRIT*), automatic payment (*US*); **l'**~ **pubblico** law and order; ~**i** (*sacri*) (*REL*) holy orders.
or'dire *vt* (*fig*) to plot, scheme.
or'dito *sm* (*di tessuto*) warp.
orecchi'abile [orek'kjabile] *ag* (*canzone*) catchy.
orec'chino [orek'kino] *sm* earring.
o'recchio [o'rekkjo], *pl(f)* **o'recchie** *sm* (*ANAT*) ear; **avere** ~ to have a good ear (for music); **venire all'**~ **di qn** to come to sb's attention; **fare** ~**e da mercante (a)** to turn a deaf ear (to).
orecchi'oni [orek'kjoni] *smpl* (*MED*) mumps *sg*.

o'refice [o'refitʃe] *sm* goldsmith; jeweller (*BRIT*), jeweler (*US*).
orefice'ria [orefitʃe'ria] *sf* (*arte*) goldsmith's art; (*negozio*) jeweller's (shop) (*BRIT*), jewelry store (*US*).
'orfano, a *ag* orphan(ed) ♦ *sm/f* orphan; ~ **di padre/madre** fatherless/motherless.
orfano'trofio *sm* orphanage.
orga'netto *sm* barrel organ; (*fam*: *armonica a bocca*) mouth organ; (: *fisarmonica*) accordion.
or'ganico, a, ci, che *ag* organic ♦ *sm* personnel, staff.
organi'gramma, i *sm* organization chart; (*INFORM*) computer flow chart.
orga'nismo *sm* (*BIOL*) organism; (*ANAT, AMM*) body, organism.
orga'nista, i, e *sm/f* organist.
organiz'zare [organid'dzare] *vt* to organize; ~**rsi** *vr* to get organized.
organizza'tivo, a [organiddza'tivo] *ag* organizational.
organizza'tore, 'trice [organiddza'tore] *ag* organizing ♦ *sm/f* organizer.
organizzazi'one [organiddzat'tsjone] *sf* (*azione*) organizing, arranging; (*risultato*) organization; **O**~ **Mondiale della Sanità** (**O.M.S.**) World Health Organization (**WHO**).
'organo *sm* organ; (*di congegno*) part; (*portavoce*) spokesman/woman, mouthpiece; ~**i di trasmissione** (*TECN*) transmission (unit) *sg*.
or'gasmo *sm* (*FISIOL*) orgasm; (*fig*) agitation, anxiety.
'orgia, ge ['ɔrdʒa] *sf* orgy.
or'goglio [or'goʎʎo] *sm* pride.
orgogli'oso, a [orgoʎ'ʎoso] *ag* proud.
orien'tabile *ag* adjustable.
orien'tale *ag* (*paese, regione*) eastern; (*tappeti, lingua, civiltà*) oriental.
orienta'mento *sm* positioning; orientation; direction; **senso di** ~ sense of direction; **perdere l'**~ to lose one's bearings; ~ **professionale** careers guidance.
orien'tare *vt* (*situare*) to position; (*carta, bussola*) to orientate; (*fig*) to direct; ~**rsi** *vr* to find one's bearings; (*fig*: *tendere*) to tend, lean; (: *indirizzarsi*): ~**rsi verso** to take up, go in for.
orienta'tivo, a *ag* indicative, for guidance; **a scopo** ~ for guidance.
ori'ente *sm* east; **l'O**~ the East, the Orient; **il Medio/l'Estremo O**~ the Middle/Far East; **a** ~ in the east.
ori'ficio [ori'fitʃo], **ori'fizio** [ori'fittsjo] *sm* (*apertura*) opening; (: *di tubo*) mouth;

(*ANAT*) orifice.

o'rigano *sm* oregano.

origi'nale [oridʒi'nale] *ag* original; (*bizzarro*) eccentric ♦ *sm* original.

originalità [oridʒinali'ta] *sf* originality; eccentricity.

origi'nare [oridʒi'nare] *vt* to bring about, produce ♦ *vi*: ~ da to arise *o* spring from.

origi'nario, a [oridʒi'narjo] *ag* original; essere ~ di to be a native of; (*animale, pianta*) to be indigenous to, be native to.

o'rigine [o'ridʒine] *sf* origin; all'~ originally; d'~ inglese of English origin; avere ~ da to originate from; dare ~ a to give rise to.

origli'are [oriʎ'ʎare] *vi*: ~ (a) to eavesdrop (on).

o'rina *sf* urine.

ori'nale *sm* chamberpot.

ori'nare *vi* to urinate ♦ *vt* to pass.

orina'toio *sm* (public) urinal.

ori'undo, a *ag*: essere ~ di Milano *etc* to be of Milanese *etc* extraction *o* origin ♦ *sm/f* person of foreign extraction *o* origin.

orizzon'tale [oriddzon'tale] *ag* horizontal.

oriz'zonte [orid'dzonte] *sm* horizon.

ORL *sigla f* (*MED*: = *otorinolaringoiatria*) ENT.

or'lare *vt* to hem.

orla'tura *sf* (*azione*) hemming *no pl*; (*orlo*) hem.

'orlo *sm* edge, border; (*di recipiente*) rim, brim; (*di vestito etc*) hem; pieno fino all'~ full to the brim, brimful; sull'~ della pazzia/della rovina on the brink *o* verge of madness/ruin; ~ a giorno hemstitch.

'orma *sf* (*di persona*) footprint; (*di animale*) track; (*impronta, traccia*) mark, trace; seguire *o* calcare le ~e di qn to follow in sb's footsteps.

or'mai *av* by now, by this time; (*adesso*) now; (*quasi*) almost, nearly.

ormeggi'are [ormed'dʒare] *vt*, ~rsi *vr* (*NAUT*) to moor.

or'meggio [or'meddʒo] *sm* (*atto*) mooring *no pl*; (*luogo*) moorings *pl*; posto d'~ berth.

ormo'nale *ag* hormonal; (*disfunzione, cura*) hormone *cpd*; terapia ~ hormone therapy.

or'mone *sm* hormone.

ornamen'tale *ag* ornamental, decorative.

orna'mento *sm* ornament, decoration.

or'nare *vt* to adorn, decorate; ~rsi *vr*: ~rsi (di) to deck o.s. (out) (with).

or'nato, a *ag* ornate.

ornitolo'gia [ornitolo'dʒia] *sf* ornithology.

orni'tologo, a, gi, ghe *sm/f* ornithologist.

'oro *sm* gold; d'~, in ~ gold *cpd*; d'~ (*colore, occasione*) golden; (*persona*) marvellous (*BRIT*), marvelous (*US*); un affare d'~ a

real bargain; prendere qc per ~ colato to take sth as gospel (truth); ~ nero black gold; ~ zecchino pure gold.

orologe'ria [orolodʒe'ria] *sf* watchmaking *no pl*; watchmaker's (shop); clockmaker's (shop); bomba a ~ time bomb.

orologi'aio [orolo'dʒajo] *sm* watchmaker; clockmaker.

oro'logio [oro'lɔdʒo] *sm* clock; (*da tasca, da polso*) watch; ~ biologico biological clock; ~ da polso wristwatch; ~ al quarzo quartz watch; ~ a sveglia alarm clock.

o'roscopo *sm* horoscope.

or'rendo, a *ag* (*spaventoso*) horrible, awful; (*bruttissimo*) hideous.

or'ribile *ag* horrible.

'orrido, a *ag* fearful, horrid.

orripi'lante *ag* hair-raising, horrifying.

or'rore *sm* horror; avere in ~ qn/qc to loathe *o* detest sb/sth; mi fanno ~ I loathe *o* detest them.

orsacchi'otto [orsak'kjɔtto] *sm* teddy bear.

'orso *sm* bear; ~ bruno/bianco brown/polar bear.

orsù *escl* come now!

or'taggio [or'taddʒo] *sm* vegetable.

or'tensia *sf* hydrangea.

or'tica, che *sf* (stinging) nettle.

orti'caria *sf* nettle rash.

orticol'tura *sf* horticulture.

'orto *sm* vegetable garden, kitchen garden; (*AGR*) market garden (*BRIT*), truck farm (*US*); ~ botanico botanical garden(s *pl*).

orto'dosso, a *ag* orthodox.

ortofrut'ticolo, a *ag* fruit and vegetable *cpd*.

ortogo'nale *ag* perpendicular.

ortogra'fia *sf* spelling.

orto'lano, a *sm/f* (*venditore*) greengrocer (*BRIT*), produce dealer (*US*).

ortope'dia *sf* orthopaedics *sg* (*BRIT*), orthopedics *sg* (*US*).

orto'pedico, a, ci, che *ag* orthopaedic (*BRIT*), orthopedic (*US*) ♦ *sm* orthopaedic specialist (*BRIT*), orthopedist (*US*).

orzai'olo [ordza'jɔlo], orzaiu'olo [ordza'jwɔlo] *sm* (*MED*) stye.

or'zata [or'dzata] *sf* barley water.

'orzo ['ɔrdzo] *sm* barley.

'OSA *sigla f* (= *Organizzazione degli Stati Americani*) OAS (= *Organization of American States*).

o'sare *vt*, *vi* to dare; ~ fare to dare (to) do; come osi? how dare you?

oscenità [oʃʃeni'ta] *sf inv* obscenity.

o'sceno, a [oʃ'ʃɛno] *ag* obscene; (*ripugnante*) ghastly.

oscil'lare [oʃʃil'lare] *vi* (*pendolo*) to swing; (*dondolare: al vento etc*) to rock; (*variare*) to fluctuate; (*TECN*) to oscillate; (*fig*): ~ **fra** to waver between.

oscillazi'one [oʃʃillat'tsjone] *sf* oscillation; (*di prezzi, temperatura*) fluctuation.

oscura'mento *sm* darkening; obscuring; (*in tempo di guerra*) blackout.

oscu'rare *vt* to darken, obscure; (*fig*) to obscure; ~**rsi** *vr* (*cielo*) to darken, cloud over; (*persona*): **si oscurò in volto** his face clouded over.

oscurità *sf* (*vedi ag*) darkness; obscurity; gloominess.

os'curo, a *ag* dark; (*fig: incomprensibile*) obscure; (: *umile: vita, natali*) humble, obscure; (: *triste: pensiero*) gloomy, sombre ♦ *sm*: **all'**~ in the dark; **tenere qn all'**~ **di qc** to keep sb in the dark about sth.

'Oslo *sf* Oslo.

ospe'dale *sm* hospital.

ospedali'ero, a *ag* hospital *cpd*.

ospi'tale *ag* hospitable.

ospitalità *sf* hospitality.

ospi'tare *vt* to give hospitality to; (*sog: albergo*) to accommodate.

'ospite *smlf* (*persona che ospita*) host/ hostess; (*persona ospitata*) guest.

os'pizio [os'pittsjo] *sm* (*per vecchi etc*) home.

'ossa *sfpl vedi* **osso**.

os'sario *sm* (*MIL*) war memorial (*with burial place*).

ossa'tura *sf* (*ANAT*) skeletal structure, frame; (*TECN, fig*) framework.

'osseo, a *ag* bony; (*tessuto etc*) bone *cpd*.

osse'quente *ag*: ~ **alla legge** law-abiding.

os'sequio *sm* deference, respect; ~**i** *smpl* (*saluto*) respects, regards; **porgere i propri** ~**i a qn** (*formale*) to pay one's respects to sb; ~**i alla signora!** (give my) regards to your wife!

ossequi'oso, a *ag* obsequious.

osser'vanza [osser'vantsa] *sf* observance.

osser'vare *vt* to observe, watch; (*esaminare*) to examine; (*notare, rilevare*) to notice, observe; (*DIR: la legge*) to observe, respect; (*mantenere: silenzio*) to keep, observe; **far** ~ **qc a qn** to point sth out to sb.

osserva'tore, 'trice *ag* observant, perceptive ♦ *smlf* observer.

osserva'torio *sm* (*ASTR*) observatory; (*MIL*) observation post.

osservazi'one [osservat'tsjone] *sf* observation; (*di legge etc*) observance; (*considerazione critica*) observation,

remark; (*rimprovero*) reproof; **in** ~ under observation; **fare un'**~ to make a remark; to raise an objection; **fare un'**~ **a qn** to criticize sb.

ossessio'nare *vt* to obsess, haunt; (*tormentare*) to torment, harass.

ossessi'one *sf* obsession; (*seccatura*) nuisance.

osses'sivo, a *ag* obsessive, haunting; troublesome.

os'sesso, a *ag* (*spiritato*) possessed.

os'sia *cong* that is, to be precise.

ossi'buchi [ossi'buki] *smpl di* **ossobuco**.

ossi'dare *vt*, ~**rsi** *vr* to oxidize.

ossidazi'one [ossidat'tsjone] *sf* oxidization, oxidation.

'ossido *sm* oxide; ~ **di carbonio** carbon monoxide.

ossige'nare [ossidʒe'nare] *vt* to oxygenate; (*decolorare*) to bleach; **acqua ossigenata** hydrogen peroxide.

os'sigeno [os'sidʒeno] *sm* oxygen.

'osso *sm* (*pl*(*f*) **ossa** *nel senso ANAT*) bone; **d'**~ (*bottone etc*) of bone, bone *cpd*; **avere le** ~**a rotte** to be dead *o* dog tired; **bagnato fino all'**~ soaked to the skin; **essere ridotto all'**~ (*fig: magro*) to be just skin and bone; (: *senza soldi*) to be in dire straits; **rompersi l'**~ **del collo** to break one's neck; **rimetterci l'**~ **del collo** (*fig*) to ruin o.s., lose everything; **un** ~ **duro** (*persona, impresa*) a tough number; ~ **di seppia** cuttlebone.

osso'buco, *pl* ossi'buchi *sm* (*CUC*) marrowbone; (: *piatto*) *stew made with knuckle of veal in tomato sauce*.

os'suto, a *ag* bony.

ostaco'lare *vt* to block, obstruct.

os'tacolo *sm* obstacle; (*EQUITAZIONE*) hurdle, jump; **essere di** ~ **a qn/qc** (*fig*) to stand in the way of sb/sth.

os'taggio [os'taddʒo] *sm* hostage.

'oste, os'tessa *smlf* innkeeper.

osteggi'are [osted'dʒare] *vt* to oppose, be opposed to.

os'tello *sm* hostel; ~ **della gioventù** youth hostel.

osten'sorio *sm* (*REL*) monstrance.

osten'tare *vt* to make a show of, flaunt.

ostentazi'one [ostentat'tsjone] *sf* ostentation, show.

oste'ria *sf* inn.

os'tessa *sf vedi* **oste**.

os'tetrico, a, ci, che *ag* obstetric ♦ *sm* obstetrician ♦ *sf* midwife.

'ostia *sf* (*REL*) host; (*per medicinali*) wafer.

'ostico, a, ci, che *ag* difficult, tough.

os'tile *ag* hostile.

ostilità *sf* hostility ♦ *sfpl* (*MIL*) hostilities.
osti'narsi *vr* to insist, dig one's heels in; ~
  a fare to persist (obstinately) in doing.
osti'nato, a *ag* (*caparbio*) obstinate;
  (*tenace*) persistent, determined.
ostinazi'one [ostinat'tsjone] *sf* obstinacy;
  persistence.
ostra'cismo [ostra'tʃizmo] *sm* ostracism.
'ostrica, che *sf* oyster.
ostru'ire *vt* to obstruct, block.
ostruzi'one [ostrut'tsjone] *sf* obstruction,
  blockage.
ostruzio'nismo [ostruttsjo'nizmo] *sm* (*POL*)
  obstructionism; (*SPORT*) obstruction; **fare
  dell'~ a** (*progetto, legge*) to obstruct; ~
  sindacale work-to-rule (*BRIT*), slowdown
  (*US*).
o'tite *sf* ear infection.
oto'rino(laringoi'atra), i, e *smf* ear, nose
  and throat specialist.
'otre *sm* (*recipiente*) goatskin.
ott. *ubbr* (= *ottobre*) Oct.
ottago'nale *ag* octagonal.
ot'tagono *sm* octagon
ot'tano *sm* octane; **numero di** ~**i** octane
  rating.
ot'tanta *num* eighty
ottan'tenne *ug* eighty-year-old ♦ *smf*
  octogenarian.
ottan'tesimo, a *num* eightieth.
ottan'tina *sf*: **una** ~ **(di)** about eighty.
ot'tavo, a *num* eighth ♦ *sf* octave.
ottempe'ranza [ottempe'rantsa] *sf*: **in** ~ **a**
  (*AMM*) in accordance with, in compliance
  with.
ottempe'rare *vi*: ~ **a** to comply with, obey.
ottene'brare *vt* to darken; (*fig*) to cloud.
otte'nere *vt* to obtain, get; (*risultato*) to
  achieve, obtain.
'ottico, a, ci, che *ag* (*della vista*: *nervo*)
  optic; (*dell'ottica*) optical ♦ *sm* optician
  ♦ *sf* (*scienza*) optics *sg*; (*FOT*: *lenti, prismi
  etc*) optics *pl*.
otti'male *ag* optimal, optimum.
ottima'mente *av* excellently, very well.
otti'mismo *sm* optimism.
otti'mista, i, e *smf* optimist.
ottimiz'zare [ottimid'dzare] *vt* to optimize.
ottimizzazi'one [ottimiddzat'tsjone] *sf*
  optimization.
'ottimo, a *ag* excellent, very good.
'otto *num* eight.
ot'tobre *sm* October; *per fraseologia vedi*
  luglio.
otto'brino, a *ag* October *cpd*.
ottocen'tesco, a, schi, sche
  [ottotʃen'tesko] *ag* nineteenth-century.
otto'cento [otto'tʃɛnto] *num* eight hundred

  ♦ *sm*: **l'O**~ the nineteenth century.
otto'mila *num* eight thousand.
ot'tone *sm* brass; **gli** ~**i** (*MUS*) the brass.
ottuage'nario, a [ottuadʒe'narjo] *ag*, *smf*
  octogenarian.
ot'tundere *vt* (*fig*) to dull.
ottu'rare *vt* to close (up); (*dente*) to fill.
ottura'tore *sm* (*FOT*) shutter; (*nelle armi*)
  breechblock.
otturazi'one [otturat'tsjone] *sf* closing
  (up); (*dentaria*) filling.
ottusità *sf* (*vedi ag*) obtuseness; dullness.
ot'tuso, a *pp di* **ottundere** ♦ *ag* (*MAT, fig*)
  obtuse; (*suono*) dull.
o'vaia *sf*, **o'vaio** *sm* (*ANAT*) ovary.
o'vale *ag, sm* oval.
o'varico, a *ag* ovarian.
o'vatta *sf* cotton wool; (*per imbottire*)
  padding, wadding.
ovat'tare *vt* (*imbottire*) to pad; (*fig*:
  smorzare) to muffle.
ovazi'one [ovat'tsjone] *sf* ovation.
'ovest *sm* west; **a** ~ **(di)** west (of); **verso** ~
  westward(s).
o'vile *sm* pen, enclosure; **tornare all'**~ (*fig*)
  to return to the fold.
o'vino, a *ag* sheep *cpd*, ovine.
'O.V.N.I. *sigla m* (= *oggetto volante non
  identificato*) UFO.
ovulazi'one [ovulat'tsjone] *sf* ovulation.
'ovulo *sm* (*FISIOL*) ovum.
o'vunque *av* = **dovunque**.
ov'vero *cong* (*ossia*) that is, to be precise;
  (*oppure*) or (else).
ovvi'are *vi*: ~ **a** to obviate.
'ovvio, a *ag* obvious.
ozi'are [ot'tsjare] *vi* to laze around.
'ozio ['ɔttsjo] *sm* idleness; (*tempo libero*)
  leisure; **ore d'**~ leisure time; **stare in** ~ to
  be idle.
ozi'oso, a [ot'tsjoso] *ag* idle.
o'zono [od'dzɔno] *sm* ozone; **lo strato d'**~
  the ozone layer.
ozonos'fera [oddzonos'fɛra] *sf* ozone layer.

P p

P, p [pi] *sf o m inv* (*lettera*) P, p; **P come
Padova** ≈ P for Peter.
P *abbr* (= *peso*) wt; (= *posteggio*) P.
p *abbr* (= *pagina*) p.
P2 *abbr f*: **la (loggia)** ~ the P2 masonic
lodge.
PA *sigla* = *Palermo.*
P.A. *abbr* = **pubblica amministrazione.**
pa'care *vt* to calm; ~**rsi** *vr* (*tempesta,
disordini*) to subside.
paca'tezza [paka'tettsa] *sf* quietness,
calmness.
pa'cato, a *ag* quiet, calm.
'pacca, che *sf* slap.
pac'chetto [pak'ketto] *sm* packet; ~
applicativo (*INFORM*) applications
package; ~ **azionario** (*FINANZA*)
shareholding; ~ **software** (*INFORM*)
software package; ~ **turistico** package
holiday (*BRIT*) *o* tour.
pacchi'ano, a [pak'kjano] *ag* (*colori*) garish;
(*abiti, arredamento*) vulgar, garish.
'pacco, chi *sm* parcel; (*involto*) bundle; ~
postale parcel.
paccot'tiglia [pakkot'tiʎʎa] *sf* trash, junk.
'pace ['patʃe] *sf* peace; **darsi** ~ to resign
o.s.; **fare (la)** ~ **con qn** to make it up with
sb.
pachis'tano, a [pakis'tano] *ag, sm/f*
Pakistani.
pacifi'care [patʃifi'kare] *vt* (*riconciliare*) to
reconcile, make peace between; (*mettere
in pace*) to pacify.
pacificazi'one [patʃifikat'tsjone] *sf* (*vedi vt*)
reconciliation; pacification.
pa'cifico, a, ci, che [pa'tʃifiko] *ag* (*persona*)
peaceable; (*vita*) peaceful; (*fig: indiscusso*)
indisputable; (: *ovvio*) obvious, clear ♦ *sm*:
il P~, l'Oceano P~ the Pacific (Ocean).
paci'fismo [patʃi'fizmo] *sm* pacifism.
paci'fista, i, e [patʃi'fista] *sm/f* pacifist.
pa'dano, a *ag* of the Po; **la pianura** ~**a** the
Lombardy plain.
pa'della *sf* frying pan; (*per infermi*) bedpan.
padigli'one [padiʎ'ʎone] *sm* pavilion.
'Padova *sf* Padua.
pado'vano, a *ag* of (*o* from) Padua.
'padre *sm* father; ~**i** *smpl* (*antenati*)
forefathers.
Padre'terno *sm*: **il** ~ God the Father.
pa'drino *sm* godfather.
padro'nale *ag* (*scala, entrata*) main,
principal; **casa** ~ country house.
padro'nanza [padro'nantsa] *sf* command,
mastery.
padro'nato *sm*: **il** ~ the ruling class.
pa'drone, a *sm/f* master/mistress;
(*proprietario*) owner; (*datore di lavoro*)
employer; **essere** ~ **di sé** to be in control
of o.s.; ~**/a di casa** master/mistress of
the house; (*per gli inquilini*) landlord/lady.
padroneggi'are [padroned'dʒare] *vt* (*fig:
sentimenti*) to master, control; (: *materia*)
to master, know thoroughly; ~**rsi** *vr* to
control o.s.
pae'saggio [pae'zaddʒo] *sm* landscape.
paesag'gista, i, e [paezad'dʒista] *sm/f*
(*pittore*) landscape painter.
pae'sano, a *ag* country *cpd* ♦ *sm/f* villager;
countryman/woman.
pa'ese *sm* (*nazione*) country, nation; (*terra*)
country, land; (*villaggio*) village; ~ **di
provenienza** country of origin; **i P~i Bassi**
the Netherlands.
paf'futo, a *ag* chubby, plump.
'paga, ghe *sf* pay, wages *pl*; **giorno di** ~
pay day.
pa'gabile *ag* payable; ~ **alla consegna/a
vista** payable on delivery/on demand.
pa'gaia *sf* paddle.
paga'mento *sm* payment; ~ **anticipato**
payment in advance; ~ **alla consegna**
payment on delivery; ~ **all'ordine** cash
with order; **la TV a** ~ pay TV.
pa'gano, a *ag, sm/f* pagan.
pa'gare *vt* to pay; (*acquisto, fig: colpa*) to
pay for; (*contraccambiare*) to repay, pay
back ♦ *vi* to pay; **quanto l'ha pagato?** how
much did you pay for it?; ~ **con carta di
credito** to pay by credit card; ~ **in
contanti** to pay cash; ~ **di persona** (*fig*) to
suffer the consequences; **l'ho pagata cara**
(*fig*) I paid dearly for it.
pa'gella [pa'dʒella] *sf* (*INS*) school report
(*BRIT*), report card (*US*).
'paggio ['paddʒo] *sm* page(boy).
pagherò [page'rɔ] *vb vedi* **pagare** ♦ *sm inv*
IOU; ~ **cambiario** promissory note.
'pagina ['padʒina] *sf* page.
'paglia ['paʎʎa] *sf* straw; **avere la coda di** ~
(*fig*) to have a guilty conscience; **fuoco di**
~ (*fig*) flash in the pan.
pagliac'cetto [paʎʎat'tʃetto] *sm* (*per
bambini*) rompers *pl*.
pagliac'ciata [paʎʎat'tʃata] *sf* farce.
pagli'accio [paʎ'ʎattʃo] *sm* clown.

pagli'aio [paʎ'ʎajo] *sm* haystack.
paglie'riccio [paʎʎe'rittʃo] *sm* straw mattress.
paglie'rino, a [paʎʎe'rino] *ag*: **giallo ~** pale yellow.
pagli'etta [paʎ'ʎetta] *sf* (*cappello per uomo*) (straw) boater; (*per tegami etc*) steel wool.
pagli'uzza [paʎ'ʎuttsa] *sf* (blade of) straw; (*d'oro etc*) tiny particle, speck.
pa'gnotta [paɲ'ɲɔtta] *sf* round loaf.
'pago, a, ghi, ghe *ag*: **~ (di)** satisfied (with).
pa'goda *sf* pagoda.
pail'lette [pa'jɛt] *sf inv* sequin.
'paio, *pl(f)* **'paia** *sm* pair; **un ~ di occhiali** a pair of glasses; **un ~ di** (*alcuni*) a couple of; **è un altro ~ di maniche** (*fig*) that's another kettle of fish.
'paio *etc vb vedi* **parere.**
pai'olo, paiu'olo *sm* (copper) pot.
'Pakistan *sm*: **il ~** Pakistan.
pakis'tano, a *ag, sm/f* = **pachistano.**
pal. *abbr* = **palude.**
'pala *sf* shovel; (*di remo, ventilatore, elica*) blade; (*di ruota*) paddle.
palan'drana *sf* (*scherzoso: abito lungo e largo*) tent.
pa'lata *sf* shovelful; **fare soldi a ~e** to make a mint.
pala'tale *ag* (*ANAT, LING*) palatal.
pa'lato *sm* palate.
pa'lazzo [pa'lattso] *sm* (*reggia*) palace; (*edificio*) building; **~ di giustizia** courthouse; **~ dello sport** sports stadium; *vedi nota nel riquadro.*

PALAZZI

Several of the Roman palazzi now have political functions. The sixteenth-century Palazzo Chigi, in Piazza Colonna, was acquired by the state in 1919 and became the seat of the Ministry of Foreign Affairs; since 1961 it has also housed the Prime Minister's office and hosted Cabinet meetings. Palazzo Madama, another sixteenth-century building which was originally built for the Medici family, has been the home of the Senate since 1871. Palazzo di Montecitorio, completed in 1694, has housed the "Camera dei deputati" since 1870.

pal'chetto [pal'ketto] *sm* shelf.
'palco, chi *sm* (*TEAT*) box; (*tavolato*) platform, stand; (*ripiano*) layer.
palco'scenico, ci [palkoʃ'ʃɛniko] *sm* (*TEAT*) stage.

palermi'tano, a *ag* of (*o* from) Palermo ♦ *sm/f* person from Palermo.
Pa'lermo *sf* Palermo.
pale'sare *vt* to reveal, disclose; **~rsi** *vr* to reveal *o* show o.s.
pa'lese *ag* clear, evident.
Pales'tina *sf*: **la ~** Palestine.
palesti'nese *ag, sm/f* Palestinian.
pa'lestra *sf* gymnasium; (*esercizio atletico*) exercise, training; (*fig*) training ground, school.
paletot [pal'to] *sm inv* overcoat.
pa'letta *sf* spade; (*per il focolare*) shovel; (*del capostazione*) signalling disc.
pa'letto *sm* stake, peg; (*spranga*) bolt.
palin'sesto *sm* (*STORIA*) palimpsest; (*TV, RADIO*) programme (*BRIT*) *o* program (*US*) schedule.
'palio *sm* (*gara*): **il P~** horserace run at Siena; **mettere qc in ~** to offer sth as a prize; *vedi nota nel riquadro.*

PALIO

The Palio is a horse race which takes place in a number of Italian towns, the most famous being the "Palio di Siena". The Tuscan race dates back to the thirteenth century; nowadays it is usually held twice a year, on 2 July and 16 August, in the Piazza del Campo. Ten of the 17 city districts or "contrade" take part; the winner is the first horse to complete the course, whether or not it still has its rider. The race is preceded by a procession of "contrada" members in historical dress.

palis'sandro *sm* rosewood.
paliz'zata [palit'tsata] *sf* palisade.
'palla *sf* ball; (*pallottola*) bullet; **prendere la ~ al balzo** (*fig*) to seize one's opportunity.
pallaca'nestro *sf* basketball.
pallanu'oto *sf* water polo.
palla'volo *sf* volleyball.
palleggi'are [palled'dʒare] *vi* (*CALCIO*) to practise (*BRIT*) *o* practice (*US*) with the ball; (*TENNIS*) to knock up.
pallia'tivo *sm* palliative; (*fig*) stopgap measure.
'pallido, a *ag* pale.
pal'lina *sf* (*bilia*) marble.
pal'lino *sm* (*BILIARDO*) cue ball; (*BOCCE*) jack; (*proiettile*) pellet; (*pois*) dot; **bianco a ~i blu** white with blue dots; **avere il ~ di** (*fig*) to be crazy about.
pallon'cino [pallon'tʃino] *sm* balloon; (*lampioncino*) Chinese lantern.
pal'lone *sm* (*palla*) ball; (*CALCIO*) football;

(*aerostato*) balloon; **gioco del** ~ ball game.
pal'lore *sm* pallor, paleness.
pal'lottola *sf* pellet; (*proiettile*) bullet.
'palma *sf* (*ANAT*) = **palmo**; (*BOT*) palm; ~ **da datteri** date palm.
pal'mato, a *ag* (*ZOOL: piede*) webbed; (*BOT*) palmate.
pal'mipede *ag* web-footed.
pal'mizio [pal'mittsjo] *sm* (*palma*) palm tree; (*ramo*) palm.
'palmo *sm* (*ANAT*) palm; **essere alto un** ~ (*fig*) to be tiny; **restare con un** ~ **di naso** (*fig*) to be badly disappointed.
'palo *sm* (*legno appuntito*) stake; (*sostegno*) pole; **fare da o il** ~ (*fig*) to act as look-out; **saltare di** ~ **in frasca** (*fig*) to jump from one topic to another.
palom'baro *sm* diver.
pa'lombo *sm* (*pesce*) dogfish.
pal'pare *vt* to feel, finger.
'palpebra *sf* eyelid.
palpi'tare *vi* (*cuore, polso*) to beat; (: *più forte*) to pound, throb; (*fremere*) to quiver.
palpitazi'one [palpitat'tsjone] *sf* palpitation.
'palpito *sm* (*del cuore*) beat; (*fig: d'amore etc*) throb.
paltò *sm inv* overcoat.
pa'lude *sf* marsh, swamp.
palu'doso, a *ag* marshy, swampy.
pa'lustre *ag* marsh *cpd*, swamp *cpd*.
'pampino *sm* vine leaf.
pana'cea [pana'tʃɛa] *sf* panacea.
'Panama *sf* Panama; **il canale di** ~ the Panama Canal.
pana'mense *ag, sm/f* Panamanian.
'panca, che *sf* bench.
pancarrè *sm* sliced bread.
pan'cetta [pan'tʃetta] *sf* (*CUC*) bacon.
pan'chetto [pan'ketto] *sm* stool; footstool.
pan'china [pan'kina] *sf* garden seat; (*di giardino pubblico*) (park) bench.
'pancia, ce ['pantʃa] *sf* belly, stomach; **mettere o fare** ~ to be getting a paunch; **avere mal di** ~ to have stomach ache o a sore stomach.
panci'era [pan'tʃɛra] *sf* corset.
panci'olle [pan'tʃɔlle] *av*: **stare in** ~ to lounge about (*BRIT*) o around.
panci'otto [pan'tʃɔtto] *sm* waistcoat.
pan'ciuto, a [pan'tʃuto] *ag* (*persona*) potbellied; (*vaso, bottiglia*) rounded.
'pancreas *sm inv* pancreas.
'panda *sm inv* panda.
pande'monio *sm* pandemonium.
pan'doro *sm* type of sponge cake eaten at Christmas.
'pane *sm* bread; (*pagnotta*) loaf (of bread);

(*forma*): **un** ~ **di burro/cera** *etc* a pat of butter/bar of wax *etc*; **guadagnarsi il** ~ **to** earn one's living; **dire** ~ **al** ~, **vino al vino** (*fig*) to call a spade a spade; **rendere pan per focaccia** (*fig*) to give tit for tat; ~ **casereccio** homemade bread; ~ **a cassetta** sliced bread; ~ **integrale** wholemeal bread; ~ **di segale** rye bread; **pan di Spagna** sponge cake; ~ **tostato** toast.
pane'girico [pane'dʒiriko] *sm* (*fig*) panegyric.
panette'ria *sf* (*forno*) bakery; (*negozio*) baker's (shop), bakery.
panetti'ere, a *sm/f* baker.
panet'tone *sm a kind of spiced brioche with sultanas, eaten at Christmas.*
'panfilo *sm* yacht.
pan'forte *sm Sienese nougat-type delicacy.*
pangrat'tato *sm* breadcrumbs *pl*.
'panico, a, ci, che *ag, sm* panic; **essere in preda al** ~ to be panic-stricken; **lasciarsi prendere dal** ~ to panic.
pani'ere *sm* basket.
panifica'tore, trice *sm/f* bread-maker, baker.
pani'ficio [pani'fitʃo] *sm* (*forno*) bakery; (*negozio*) baker's (shop), bakery.
pa'nino *sm* roll; ~ **imbottito** filled roll; sandwich.
panino'teca, che *sf* sandwich bar.
'panna *sf* (*CUC*) cream; (*AUT*) = **panne**; ~ **di cucina** cooking cream; ~ **montata** whipped cream.
'panne [pan] *sf inv* (*AUT*) breakdown; **essere in** ~ to have broken down.
pan'nello *sm* panel; ~ **di controllo** control panel; ~ **solare** solar panel.
'panno *sm* cloth; ~**i** *smpl* (*abiti*) clothes; **mettiti nei miei** ~**i** (*fig*) put yourself in my shoes.
pan'nocchia [pan'nɔkkja] *sf* (*di mais etc*) ear.
panno'lino *sm* (*per bambini*) nappy (*BRIT*), diaper (*US*).
pano'rama, i *sm* panorama.
pano'ramico, a, ci, che *ag* panoramic; **strada** ~**a** scenic route.
pantacol'lant *smpl* leggings.
panta'loni *smpl* trousers (*BRIT*), pants (*US*), pair *sg* of trousers o pants.
pan'tano *sm* bog.
pan'tera *sf* panther.
'pantheon ['panteon] *sm inv* pantheon.
pan'tofola *sf* slipper.
panto'mima *sf* pantomime.
pan'zana [pan'tsana] *sf* fib, tall story.
pao'nazzo, a [pao'nattso] *ag* purple.

'**papa, i** sm pope.
papà sm inv dad(dy); **figlio di** ~ spoilt young man.
pa'pale ag papal.
pa'pato sm papacy.
pa'pavero sm poppy.
'**papero, a** smlf (ZOOL) gosling ♦ sf (fig) slip of the tongue, blunder.
papi'llon [papi'jɔ̃] sm inv bow tie.
pa'piro sm papyrus.
'**pappa** sf baby cereal.
pappa'gallo sm parrot; (fig: uomo) Romeo, wolf.
pappa'gorgia, ge [pappa'gɔrdʒa] sf double chin.
pappar'della sf (fig) rigmarole.
pap'pare vt (fam: anche: ~**rsi**) to gobble up.
par. abbr (= paragrafo) par.
'**para** sf: **suole di** ~ crepe soles.
parà abbr m inv (= paracadutista) para.
pa'rabola sf (MAT) parabola; (REL) parable.
para'bolico, a, ci, che ag (MAT) parabolic, vedi anche **antenna**.
para'brezza [para'breddza] sm inv (AUT) windscreen (BRIT), windshield (US).
paracadu'tare vt, ~**rsi** vr to parachute.
paraca'dute sm inv parachute.
paracadu'tismo sm parachuting.
paracadu'tista, i, e smlf parachutist; (MIL) paratrooper.
para'carro sm kerbstone (BRIT), curbstone (US).
paradi'siaco, a, ci, che ag heavenly.
para'diso sm paradise; ~ **fiscale** tax haven.
parados'sale ag paradoxical.
para'dosso sm paradox.
para'fango, ghi sm mudguard.
paraf'fina sf paraffin, paraffin wax.
parafra'sare vt to paraphrase.
pa'rafrasi sf inv paraphrase.
para'fulmine sm lightning conductor.
pa'raggi [pa'raddʒi] smpl: **nei** ~ in the vicinity, in the neighbourhood (BRIT) o neighborhood (US).
parago'nare vt: ~ **con/a** to compare with/to.
para'gone sm comparison; (esempio analogo) analogy, parallel; **reggere al** ~ to stand comparison.
pa'ragrafo sm paragraph.
paraguai'ano, a ag, smlf Paraguayan.
Paragu'ay [para'gwai] sm: **il** ~ Paraguay.
pa'ralisi sf inv paralysis.
para'litico, a, ci, che ag, smlf paralytic.
paraliz'zare [paralid'dzare] vt to paralyze.
parallela'mente av in parallel.
parallele'pipedo sm parallelepiped.
paralle'lismo sm (MAT) parallelism; (fig:

corrispondenza) similarities pl.
paral'lelo, a ag parallel ♦ sm (GEO) parallel; (comparazione): **fare un** ~ **tra** to draw a parallel between ♦ sf parallel (line); ~**e** sfpl (attrezzo ginnico) parallel bars.
para'lume sm lampshade.
para'medico, a, ci, che ag paramedical.
para'menti smpl (REL) vestments.
pa'rametro sm parameter.
paramili'tare ag paramilitary.
pa'ranco, chi sm hoist.
para'noia sf paranoia; **andare/mandare in** ~ (fam) to freak/be freaked out.
para'noico, a, ci, che ag, smlf paranoid; (fam: angosciato) freaked (out).
paranor'male ag paranormal.
para'occhi [para'ɔkki] smpl blinkers (BRIT), blinders (US).
para'petto sm parapet.
para'piglia [para'piʎʎa] sm commotion, uproar.
parapsicolo'gia [parapsikolo'dʒia] sf parapsychology.
pa'rare vt (addobbare) to adorn, deck; (proteggere) to shield, protect; (scansare: colpo) to parry, (CALCIO) to save ♦ vi: **dove vuole andare a** ~? what are you driving at?; ~**rsi** vr (presentarsi) to appear, present o.s.
parasco'lastico, a, ci, che ag (attività) extracurricular.
para'sole sm inv parasol, sunshade.
paras'sita, i sm parasite.
parassi'tario, a ag parasitic.
parasta'tale ag state-controlled.
paras'tato sm employees in the state-controlled sector.
pa'rata sf (SPORT) save; (MIL) review, parade.
pa'rati smpl hangings pl; **carta da** ~ wallpaper.
para'tia sf (di nave) bulkhead.
para'urti sm inv (AUT) bumper.
para'vento sm folding screen; **fare da** ~ **a qn** (fig) to shield sb.
par'cella [par'tʃella] sf fee.
parcheggi'are [parked'dʒare] vt to park.
par'cheggio [par'keddʒo] sm parking no pl; (luogo) car park (BRIT), parking lot (US); (singolo posto) parking space.
par'chimetro [par'kimetro] sm parking meter.
'**parco, chi** sm park; (spazio per deposito) depot; (complesso di veicoli) fleet.
'**parco, a, chi, che** ag: ~ **(in)** (sobrio) moderate (in); (avaro) sparing (with).
pa'recchio, a [pa'rekkjo] det quite a lot of; (tempo) quite a lot of, a long ♦ pron quite a

lot, quite a bit; (*tempo*) quite a while, a
long time ♦ *av* (*con ag*) quite, rather; (*con
vb*) quite a lot, quite a bit; ~**i(e)** *det pl*
quite a lot of, several ♦ *pron pl* quite a lot,
several.

pareggi'are [pared'dʒare] *vt* to make equal;
(*terreno*) to level, make level; (*bilancio,
conti*) to balance ♦ *vi* (*SPORT*) to draw.

pa'reggio [pa'reddʒo] *sm* (*ECON*) balance;
(*SPORT*) draw.

paren'tado *sm* relatives *pl*, relations *pl.*

pa'rente *smlf* relative, relation.

paren'tela *sf* (*vincolo di sangue, fig*)
relationship; (*insieme dei parenti*)
relations *pl*, relatives *pl.*

pa'rentesi *sf* (*segno grafico*) bracket,
parenthesis; (*frase incisa*) parenthesis;
(*digressione*) parenthesis, digression; **tra**
~ in brackets; (*fig*) incidentally.

pa'rere *sm* (*opinione*) opinion; (*consiglio*)
advice, opinion; **a mio** ~ in my opinion
♦ *vi* to seem, appear ♦ *vb impers*: **pare che** it
seems *o* appears that, they say that; **mi
pare che** it seems to me that; **mi pare di
si/no** I think so/don't think so; **fai come ti
pare** do as you like; **che ti pare del mio
libro?** what do you think of my book?

pa'rete *sf* wall.

'pari *ag inv* (*uguale*) equal, same; (*in giochi*)
equal; drawn, tied; (*MAT*) even ♦ *sm inv*
(*POL: di Gran Bretagna*) peer ♦ *smlf inv* peer,
equal; **copiato** ~ ~ copied word for word;
siamo ~ (*fig*) we are quits *o* even; **alla** ~
on the same level; (*BORSA*) at par;
ragazza alla ~ au pair (girl); **mettersi alla**
~ **con** to place o.s. on the same level as;
mettersi in ~ **con** to catch up with;
andare di ~ **passo con qn** to keep pace
with sb.

parifi'care *vt* (*scuola*) to recognize
officially.

parifi'cato, a *ag*: **scuola** ~**a** *officially
recognized private school.*

Pa'rigi [pa'ridʒi] *sf* Paris.

pari'gino, a [pari'dʒino] *ag, smlf* Parisian.

pa'riglia [pa'riʎʎa] *sf* pair; **rendere la** ~ to
give tit for tat.

parità *sf* parity, equality; (*SPORT*) draw,
tie.

pari'tetico, a, ci, che *ag*: **commissione** ~**a**
joint committee; **rapporto** ~ equal
relationship.

parlamen'tare *ag* parliamentary ♦ *smlf*
≈ Member of Parliament (*BRIT*),
≈ Congressman/woman (*US*) ♦ *vi* to
negotiate, parley.

parla'mento *sm* parliament; *vedi nota nel
riquadro.*

parlan'tina *sf* (*fam*) talkativeness; **avere
una buona** ~ to have the gift of the gab.

par'lare *vi* to speak, talk; (*confidare cose
segrete*) to talk ♦ *vt* to speak; ~ (**a qn**) **di** to
speak *o* talk (to sb) about; ~ **chiaro** to
speak one's mind; ~ **male di** to speak ill
of; ~ **del più e del meno** to talk of this
and that; **ne ho sentito** ~ I have heard it
mentioned; **non parliamone più** let's just
forget about it; **i dati parlano** (*fig*) the
facts speak for themselves.

par'lata *sf* (*dialetto*) dialect.

parla'tore, 'trice *smlf* speaker.

parla'torio *sm* (*di carcere etc*) visiting
room; (*REL*) parlour (*BRIT*), parlor (*US*).

parlot'tare *vi* to mutter.

parmigi'ano, a [parmi'dʒano] *ag* Parma *cpd*,
of (*o* from) Parma ♦ *sm* (*grana*) Parmesan
(cheese); **alla** ~**a** (*CUC*) with Parmesan
cheese.

paro'dia *sf* parody.

pa'rola *sf* word; (*facoltà*) speech; ~**e** *sfpl*
(*chiacchiere*) talk *sg*; **chiedere la** ~ to ask
permission to speak; **dare la** ~ **a qn** to
call on sb to speak; **dare la propria** ~ **a qn**
to give sb one's word; **mantenere la** ~ to
keep one's word; **mettere una buona** ~
per qn to put in a good word for sb;
passare dalle ~**e ai fatti** to get down to
business; **prendere la** ~ to take the floor;
rimanere senza ~**e** to be speechless;
rimangiarsi la ~ to go back on one's
word; **non ho** ~**e per ringraziarla** I don't
know how to thank you; **rivolgere la** ~ **a
qn** to speak to sb; **non è detta l'ultima** ~
that's not the end of the matter; **è una
persona di** ~ he is a man of his word; **in**
~**e povere** in plain English; ~ **d'onore**
word of honour; ~ **d'ordine** (*MIL*)
password; ~**e incrociate** crossword
(puzzle) *sg.*

paro'laccia, ce [paro'lattʃa] *sf* bad word,
swearword.

paros'sismo *sm* paroxysm.

par'quet [par'ke] *sm* parquet (flooring).

parrò *etc vb vedi* **parere.**

par'rocchia [par'rɔkkja] *sf* parish; (*chiesa*)
parish church.

parrocchi'ano, a [parrok'kjano] *sm/f* parishioner.

'**parroco, ci** *sm* parish priest.

par'rucca, che *sf* wig.

parrucchi'ere, a [parruk'kjɛre] *sm/f* hairdresser ♦ *sm* barber.

parruc'cone *sm (peg)* old fogey.

parsi'monia *sf* frugality, thrift.

parsimoni'oso, a *ag* frugal, thrifty.

'**parso, a** *pp di* parere.

'**parte** *sf* part; *(lato)* side; *(quota spettante a ciascuno)* share; *(direzione)* direction; *(POL)* party; faction; *(DIR)* party; **a ~** *ag* separate ♦ *av* separately; **scherzi a ~** joking aside; **a ~ ciò** apart from that; **inviare a ~** *(campioni etc)* to send under separate cover; **da ~** *(in disparte)* to one side, aside; **mettere/prendere da ~** to put/take aside; **d'altra ~** on the other hand; **da ~ di** *(per conto di)* on behalf of; **da ~ mia** as far as I'm concerned, as for me; **da ~ di madre** on his *(o* her *etc)* mother's side; **essere dalla ~ della ragione** to be in the right; **da ~ a ~** right through; **da qualche ~** somewhere; **da nessuna ~** nowhere; **da questa ~** *(in questa direzione)* this way; **da ogni ~** on all sides, everywhere; *(moto da luogo)* from all sides; **fare ~ di qc** to belong to sth; **prendere ~ a qc** to take part in sth; **prendere le ~ i di qn** to take sb's side; **mettere qn a ~ di qc** to inform sb of sth; **costituirsi ~ civile contro qn** *(DIR)* to associate in an action with the public prosecutor against sb; **la ~ lesa** *(DIR)* the injured party; **le ~ i in causa** the parties concerned.

parteci'pante [partetʃi'pante] *sm/f*: **~ (a)** *(a riunione, dibattito)* participant (in); *(a gara sportiva)* competitor (in); *(a concorso)* entrant (to).

parteci'pare [partetʃi'pare] *vi*: **~ a** to take part in, participate in; *(utili etc)* to share in; *(spese etc)* to contribute to; *(dolore, successo di qn)* to share (in) ♦ *vt*: **~ le nozze (a)** to announce one's wedding (to).

partecipazi'one [partetʃipat'tsjone] *sf* participation; sharing; *(ECON)* interest; **~ a banda armata** *(DIR)* belonging to an armed gang; **~ di maggioranza/ minoranza** controlling/minority interest; **~ agli utili** profit-sharing; **~ i di nozze** wedding announcement card; **ministro delle P~ i statali** *minister responsible for companies in which the state has a financial interest.*

par'tecipe [par'tetʃipe] *ag* participating; **essere ~ di** to take part in, participate in;

(gioia, dolore) to share (in); *(consapevole)* to be aware of.

parteggi'are [parted'dʒare] *vi*: **~ per** to side with, be on the side of.

par'tenza [par'tɛntsa] *sf* departure; *(SPORT)* start; **essere in ~** to be about to leave, be leaving; **passeggeri in ~ per** passengers travelling *(BRIT)* o traveling *(US)* to; **siamo tornati al punto di ~** *(fig)* we are back where we started; **falsa ~** *(anche fig)* false start.

parti'cella [parti'tʃɛlla] *sf* particle.

parti'cipio [parti'tʃipjo] *sm* participle.

partico'lare *ag (specifico)* particular; *(proprio)* personal, private; *(speciale)* special, particular; *(caratteristico)* distinctive; *(fuori dal comune)* peculiar ♦ *sm* detail, particular; **in ~** in particular, particularly; **entrare nei ~ i** to go into details.

particolareggi'ato, a [partikolared'dʒato] *ag* (extremely) detailed.

particolarità *sf inv (carattere eccezionale)* peculiarity; *(dettaglio)* particularity, detail; *(caratteristica)* characteristic, feature.

partigi'ano, a [parti'dʒano] *ag* partisan ♦ *sm (fautore)* supporter, champion; *(MIL)* partisan.

par'tire *vi* to go, leave; *(allontanarsi)* to go *(o* drive *etc)* away o off; *(petardo, colpo)* to go off; *(fig: avere inizio, SPORT)* to start; **sono partita da Roma alle 7** I left Rome at 7; **il volo parte da Ciampino** the flight leaves from Ciampino; **a ~ da** from; **la seconda a ~ da destra** the second from the right; **~ in quarta** to drive off at top speed; *(fig)* to be very enthusiastic.

par'tita *sf (COMM)* lot, consignment; *(ECON: registrazione)* entry, item; *(CARTE, SPORT: gioco)* game; *(: competizione)* match, game; **~ di caccia** hunting party; **~ IVA** VAT account; **~ semplice/doppia** *(COMM)* single-/double-entry book-keeping.

par'tito *sm (POL)* party; *(decisione)* decision, resolution; *(persona da maritare)* match; **per ~ preso** on principle; **mettere la testa a ~** to settle down.

partitocra'zia [partitokrat'tsia] *sf hijacking of institutions by the party system.*

parti'tura *sf (MUS)* score.

'**parto** *sm (MED)* labour *(BRIT)*, labor *(US)*; **sala ~** labo(u)r room; **morire di ~** to die in childbirth.

partori'ente *sf* woman in labour *(BRIT)* o labor *(US)*.

parto'rire *vt* to give birth to; *(fig)* to produce.

par'venza [par'vɛntsa] *sf* semblance.

'parvi *etc vb vedi* **parere**.

parzi'ale [par'tsjale] *ag* (*limitato*) partial; (*non obiettivo*) biased, partial.

parzialità [partsjali'ta] *sf*: ~ (**a favore di**) partiality (for), bias (towards); ~ (**contro**) bias (against).

'pascere ['paʃʃere] *vi* to graze ♦ *vt* (*brucare*) to graze on; (*far pascolare*) to graze, pasture.

pasci'uto, a [paʃ'ʃuto] *pp di* **pascere** ♦ *ag*: **ben** ~ plump.

pasco'lare *vt, vi* to graze.

'pascolo *sm* pasture.

'Pasqua *sf* Easter; **isola di** ~ Easter Island.

pas'quale *ag* Easter *cpd*.

pasqu'etta *sf* Easter Monday.

pas'sabile *ag* fairly good, passable.

pas'saggio [pas'saddʒo] *sm* passing *no pl*, passage; (*traversata*) crossing *no pl*, passage; (*luogo, prezzo della traversata, brano di libro etc*) passage; (*su veicolo altrui*) lift (*BRIT*), ride; (*SPORT*) pass; **di** ~ (*persona*) passing through; ~ **pedonale/a livello** pedestrian/level (*BRIT*) *o* grade (*US*) crossing; ~ **di proprietà** transfer of ownership.

passamane'ria *sf* braid, trimming.

passamon'tagna [passamon'taɲɲa] *sm inv* balaclava.

pas'sante *sm/f* passer-by ♦ *sm* loop.

passa'porto *sm* passport.

pas'sare *vi* (*andare*) to go; (*veicolo, pedone*) to pass (by), go by; (*fare una breve sosta: postino etc*) to come, call; (: *amico: per fare una visita*) to call *o* drop in; (*sole, aria, luce*) to get through; (*trascorrere: giorni, tempo*) to pass, go by; (*fig: proposta di legge*) to be passed; (: *dolore*) to pass, go away; (*CARTE*) to pass ♦ *vt* (*attraversare*) to cross; (*trasmettere: messaggio*): ~ **qc a qn** to pass sth on to sb; (*dare*): ~ **qc a qn** to pass sth to sb, give sb sth; (*trascorrere: tempo*) to spend; (*superare: esame*) to pass; (*triturare: verdura*) to strain; (*approvare*) to pass, approve; (*oltrepassare, sorpassare: anche fig*) to go beyond, pass; (*fig: subire*) to go through; ~ **da ... a** to pass from ... to; ~ **di padre in figlio** to be handed down *o* to pass from father to son; ~ **per** (*anche fig*) to go through; ~ **per stupido/un genio** to be taken for a fool/a genius; ~ **sopra** (*anche fig*) to pass over; ~ **attraverso** (*anche fig*) to go through; ~ **ad altro** to change the subject; (*in una riunione*) to discuss the next item; ~ **in banca/ufficio** to call (in) at the bank/ office; ~ **alla storia** to pass into history; ~

a un esame to go up (to the next class) after an exam; ~ **di moda** to go out of fashion; ~ **a prendere qc/qn** to call and pick sth/sb up; **le passo il Signor X** (*al telefono*) here is Mr X, I'm putting you through to Mr X; **farsi** ~ **per** to pass o.s. off as, pretend to be; **lasciar** ~ **qn/qc** to let sb/sth through; **col** ~ **degli anni** (*riferito al presente*) as time goes by; (*riferito al passato*) as time passed *o* went by; **il peggio è passato** the worst is over; **30 anni e passa** well over 30 years ago; ~ **una mano di vernice su qc** to give sth a coat of paint; **passarsela: come te la passi?** how are you getting on *o* along?

pas'sata *sf*: **dare una** ~ **di vernice a qc** to give sth a coat of paint; **dare una** ~ **al giornale** to have a look at the paper, skim through the paper.

passa'tempo *sm* pastime, hobby.

pas'sato, a *ag* (*scorso*) last; (*finito: gloria, generazioni*) past; (*usanze*) out of date; (*sfiorito*) faded ♦ *sm* past; (*LING*) past (tense); **l'anno** ~ last year; **nel corso degli anni** ~i over the past years; **nei tempi** ~i in the past; **sono le 8** ~**e** it's past *o* after 8 o'clock; **è acqua** ~**a** (*fig*) it's over and done with; ~ **prossimo** (*LING*) present perfect; ~ **remoto** (*LING*) past historic; ~ **di verdura** (*CUC*) vegetable purée.

passa'tutto *sm inv*, **passaver'dura** *sm inv* vegetable mill.

passeg'gero, a [passed'dʒɛro] *ag* passing ♦ *sm/f* passenger.

passeggi'are [passed'dʒare] *vi* to go for a walk; (*in veicolo*) to go for a drive.

passeggi'ata [passed'dʒata] *sf* walk; drive; (*luogo*) promenade; **fare una** ~ to go for a walk (*o* drive).

passeg'gino [passed'dʒino] *sm* pushchair (*BRIT*), stroller (*US*).

pas'seggio [pas'seddʒo] *sm* walk, stroll; (*luogo*) promenade; **andare a** ~ to go for a walk *o* a stroll.

passe'rella *sf* footbridge; (*di nave, aereo*) gangway; (*pedana*) catwalk.

'passero *sm* sparrow.

pas'sibile *ag*: ~ **di** liable to.

passio'nale *ag* (*temperamento*) passionate; **delitto** ~ crime of passion.

passi'one *sf* passion.

passività *sf* (*qualità*) passivity, passiveness; (*COMM*) liability.

pas'sivo, a *ag* passive ♦ *sm* (*LING*) passive; (*ECON*) debit; (: *complesso dei debiti*) liabilities *pl*.

'passo *sm* step; (*andatura*) pace; (*rumore*) (foot)step; (*orma*) footprint; (*passaggio,* *fig*: *brano*) passage; (*valico*) pass; **a** ~ **d'uomo** at walking pace; (*AUT*) dead slow; ~ **(a)** ~ step by step; **fare due** *o* **quattro** ~**i** to go for a walk *o* a stroll; **andare al** ~ **coi tempi** to keep up with the times; **di questo** ~ (*fig*) at this rate; **fare i primi** ~**i** (*anche fig*) to take one's first steps; **fare il gran** ~ (*fig*) to take the plunge; **fare un** ~ **falso** (*fig*) to make the wrong move; **tornare sui propri** ~**i** to retrace one's steps; "~ **carraio**" "vehicle entrance — keep clear".

'pasta *sf* (*CUC*) dough; (: *impasto per dolce*) pastry; (: *anche*: ~ **alimentare**) pasta; (*massa molle di materia*) paste; (*fig*: *indole*) nature; ~**e** *sfpl* (*pasticcini*) pastries; ~ **in brodo** noodle soup; ~ **sfoglia** puff pastry *o* paste (*US*).

pastasci'utta [pastaʃ'ʃutta] *sf* pasta.

pasteggi'are [pasted'dʒare] *vi*: ~ **a vino/ champagne** to have wine/champagne with one's meal.

pas'tella *sf* batter.

pas'tello *sm* pastel.

pas'tetta *sf* (*CUC*) = **pastella**.

pas'ticca, che *sf* = **pastiglia**.

pasticce'ria [pastitte'ria] *sf* (*pasticcini*) pastries *pl*, cakes *pl*; (*negozio*) cake shop; (*arte*) confectionery.

pasticci'are [pastit'tʃare] *vt* to mess up, make a mess of ♦ *vi* to make a mess.

pasticci'ere, a [pastit'tʃere] *sm/f* pastrycook; confectioner.

pastic'cino [pastit'tʃino] *sm* petit four.

pas'ticcio [pas'tittʃo] *sm* (*CUC*) pie; (*lavoro disordinato, imbroglio*) mess; **trovarsi nei** ~**i** to get into trouble.

pasti'ficio [pasti'fitʃo] *sm* pasta factory.

pas'tiglia [pas'tiʎʎa] *sf* pastille, lozenge.

pas'tina *sf* small pasta shapes used in soup.

pasti'naca, che *sf* parsnip.

'pasto *sm* meal; **vino da** ~ table wine.

pas'toia *sf* (*fig*): ~ **burocratica** red tape.

pas'tone *sm* (*per animali*) mash; (*peg*) overcooked stodge.

pasto'rale *ag* pastoral.

pas'tore *sm* shepherd; (*REL*) pastor, minister; (*anche*: **cane** ~) sheepdog; ~ **scozzese** (*ZOOL*) collie; ~ **tedesco** (*ZOOL*) Alsatian (dog) (*BRIT*), German shepherd (dog).

pasto'rizia [pasto'rittsja] *sf* sheep-rearing, sheep farming.

pastoriz'zare [pastorid'dzare] *vt* to pasteurize.

pas'toso, a *ag* doughy; pasty; (*fig*: *voce, colore*) mellow, soft.

pas'trano *sm* greatcoat.

pas'tura *sf* pasture.

pa'tacca, che *sf* (*distintivo*) medal, decoration; (*fig*: *macchia*) grease spot, grease mark; (: *articolo scadente*) bit of rubbish.

pa'tata *sf* potato; ~**e fritte** chips (*BRIT*), French fries.

pata'tine *sfpl* (potato) crisps (*BRIT*) *o* chips (*US*).

pata'trac *sm* (*crollo*: *anche fig*) crash.

pâté [pa'te] *sm inv* pâté; ~ **di fegato d'oca** pâté de foie gras.

pa'tella *sf* (*ZOOL*) limpet.

pa'tema, i *sm* anxiety, worry.

paten'tato, a *ag* (*munito di patente*) licensed, certified; (*fig scherzoso*: *qualificato*) utter, thorough.

pa'tente *sf* licence (*BRIT*), license (*US*); (*anche*: ~ **di guida**) driving licence (*BRIT*), driver's license (*US*).

paten'tino *sm* temporary licence (*BRIT*) *o* license (*US*).

paterna'lismo *sm* paternalism.

paterna'lista *sm* paternalist.

paterna'listico, a, ci, che *ag* paternalistic.

paternità *sf* paternity, fatherhood.

pa'terno, a *ag* (*affetto, consigli*) fatherly; (*casa, autorità*) paternal.

pa'tetico, a, ci, che *ag* pathetic; (*commovente*) moving, touching.

'pathos ['patos] *sm* pathos.

pa'tibolo *sm* gallows *sg*, scaffold.

pati'mento *sm* suffering.

'patina *sf* (*su rame etc*) patina; (*sulla lingua*) fur, coating.

pa'tire *vt, vi* to suffer.

pa'tito, a *sm/f* enthusiast, fan, lover.

patolo'gia [patolo'dʒia] *sf* pathology.

pato'logico, a, ci, che [pato'lɔdʒiko] *ag* pathological.

pa'tologo, a, gi, ghe *sm/f* pathologist.

'patria *sf* homeland; **amor di** ~ patriotism.

patri'arca, chi *sm* patriarch.

pa'trigno [pa'triɲɲo] *sm* stepfather.

patrimoni'ale *ag* (*rendita*) from property ♦ *sf* (*anche*: **imposta** ~) property tax.

patri'monio *sm* estate, property; (*fig*) heritage; **mi è costato un** ~ (*fig*) it cost me a fortune, I paid a fortune for it; ~ **spirituale/culturale** spiritual/cultural heritage; ~ **ereditario** (*fig*) hereditary characteristics *pl*; ~ **pubblico** public property.

'patrio, a, ii, ie *ag* (*di patria*) native *cpd*, of one's country; (*DIR*): ~**a potestà** parental authority; **amor** ~ love of one's country.

patri'ota, i, e *sm/f* patriot.
patri'ottico, a, ci, che *ag* patriotic.
patriot'tismo *sm* patriotism.
patroci'nare [patrotʃi'nare] *vt* (*DIR:*
difendere) to defend; (*sostenere*) to
sponsor, support.
patro'cinio [patro'tʃinjo] *sm* defence (*BRIT*),
defense (*US*); support, sponsorship.
patro'nato *sm* patronage; (*istituzione*
benefica) charitable institution *o* society.
pa'trono *sm* (*REL*) patron saint; (*socio di*
patronato) patron; (*DIR*) counsel.
'patta *sf* flap; (*dei pantaloni*) fly.
patteggia'mento [patteddʒa'mento] *sm*
(*DIR*) plea bargaining.
patteggi'are [patted'dʒare] *vt, vi* to
negotiate.
patti'naggio [patti'naddʒo] *sm* skating.
patti'nare *vi* to skate; ~ **sul ghiaccio** to
ice-skate.
pattina'tore, 'trice *sm/f* skater.
'pattino *sm* skate; (*di slitta*) runner; (*AER*)
skid; (*TECN*) sliding block; ~**i (da ghiac-**
cio) (ice) skates; ~**i in linea** rollerblades;
~**i a rotelle** roller skates.
pat'tino *sm* (*barca*) *kind of pedalo with*
oars.
pat'tista, i, e *ag* (*POL*) of Patto per l'Italia
♦ *sm/f* (*POL*) member (*o* supporter) of
Patto per l'Italia.
'patto *sm* (*accordo*) pact, agreement;
(*condizione*) term, condition; **a** ~ **che** on
condition that; **a nessun** ~ under no
circumstances; **venire** *o* **scendere a** ~**i**
(con) to come to an agreement (with); **P**~
per l'Italia (*POL*) centrist party.
pat'tuglia [pat'tuʎʎa] *sf* (*MIL*) patrol.
pattugli'are [pattuʎ'ʎare] *vt* to patrol.
pattu'ire *vt* to reach an agreement on.
pattumi'era *sf* (dust)bin (*BRIT*), ashcan
(*US*).
pa'ura *sf* fear; **aver** ~ **di/di fare/che** to be
frightened *o* afraid of/of doing/that; **far** ~
a to frighten; **per** ~ **di/che** for fear of/
that; **ho** ~ **di sì/no** I am afraid so/not.
pau'roso, a *ag* (*che fa paura*) frightening;
(*che ha paura*) fearful, timorous.
'pausa *sf* (*sosta*) break; (*nel parlare, MUS*)
pause.
paven'tato, a *ag* much-feared.
pa'vese *ag* of (*o* from) Pavia.
'pavido, a *ag* (*letterario*) fearful.
pavimen'tare *vt* (*stanza*) to floor; (*strada*)
to pave.
pavimentazi'one [pavimentat'tsjone] *sf*
flooring; paving.
pavi'mento *sm* floor.
pa'vone *sm* peacock.

pavoneggi'arsi [pavoned'dʒarsi] *vr* to strut
about, show off.
pazien'tare [pattsjen'tare] *vi* to be patient.
pazi'ente [pat'tsjɛnte] *ag, sm/f* patient.
pazi'enza [pat'tsjɛntsa] *sf* patience; **perdere**
la ~ to lose (one's) patience.
pazza'mente [pattsa'mente] *av* madly;
essere ~ **innamorato** to be madly in love.
paz'zesco, a, schi, sche [pat'tsesko] *ag*
mad, crazy.
paz'zia [pat'tsia] *sf* (*MED*) madness,
insanity; (*di azione, decisione*) madness,
folly; **è stata una** ~! it was sheer
madness!
'pazzo, a ['pattso] *ag* (*MED*) mad, insane;
(*strano*) wild, mad ♦ *sm/f* madman/woman;
~ **di** (*gioia, amore etc*) mad *o* crazy with;
~ **per qc/qn** mad *o* crazy about sth/sb;
essere ~ **da legare** to be raving mad *o* a
raving lunatic.
PC *sigla* = Piacenza.
P.C. *abbr* = **polizza di carico.**
p.c. *abbr* = *per condoglianze; per conoscenza.*
p.c.c. *abbr* (= *per copia conforme*) cc.
P.C.I. *sigla m* (= *Partito Comunista Italiano*)
former political party.
PCUS *sigla m* = *Partito Comunista dell'Unione*
Sovietica.
PD *sigla* = Padova.
P.D. *abbr* = **partita doppia.**
P.D.S. *sigla m* (= *Partito Democratico della*
Sinistra) *party originating from the P.C.I.*
PE *sigla* = Pescara.
'pecca, che *sf* defect, flaw, fault.
peccami'noso, a *ag* sinful.
pec'care *vi* to sin; (*fig*) to err.
pec'cato *sm* sin; **è un** ~ **che** it's a pity that;
che ~! what a shame *o* pity!; **un** ~ **di**
gioventù (*fig*) a youthful error *o*
indiscretion.
pecca'tore, 'trice *sm/f* sinner.
peccherò *etc* [pekke'rɔ] *vb vedi* **peccare.**
'pece ['petʃe] *sf* pitch.
pechi'nese [peki'nese] *ag, sm/f* Pekin(g)ese
(*inv*) ♦ *sm* (*anche:* **cane** ~) Pekin(g)ese *inv*,
Peke.
Pe'chino [pe'kino] *sf* Beijing, Peking.
'pecora *sf* sheep; ~ **nera** (*fig*) black sheep.
peco'raio *sm* shepherd.
peco'rella *sf* lamb; **la** ~ **smarrita** the lost
sheep; **cielo a** ~**e** (*fig: nuvole*) mackerel
sky.
peco'rino *sm* sheep's milk cheese.
pecu'lato *sm* (*DIR*) embezzlement.
peculi'are *ag*: ~ **di** peculiar to.
peculiarità *sf* peculiarity.
pecuni'ario, a *ag* financial, money *cpd*.
pe'daggio [pe'daddʒo] *sm* toll.

pedago'gia [pedago'dʒia] *sf* pedagogy, educational methods *pl*.
peda'gogico, a, ci, che [peda'gɔdʒiko] *ag* pedagogic(al).
peda'gogo, a, ghi, ghe *sm/f* pedagogue.
peda'lare *vi* to pedal; (*andare in bicicletta*) to cycle.
pe'dale *sm* pedal.
pe'dana *sf* footboard; (SPORT: *nel salto*) springboard; (: *nella scherma*) piste.
pe'dante *ag* pedantic ♦ *sm/f* pedant.
pedante'ria *sf* pedantry.
pe'data *sf* (*impronta*) footprint; (*colpo*) kick; **prendere a ~e qn/qc** to kick sb/sth.
pede'rasta, i *sm* pederast.
pe'destre *ag* prosaic, pedestrian.
pedi'atra, i, e *sm/f* paediatrician (BRIT), pediatrician (US).
pedia'tria *sf* paediatrics *sg* (BRIT), pediatrics *sg* (US).
pedi'atrico, a, ci, che *ag* pediatric.
pedi'cure *sm/f inv* chiropodist (BRIT), podiatrist (US).
pedigree *sm inv* pedigree.
pedi'luvio *sm* footbath.
pe'dina *sf* (*della dama*) draughtsman (BRIT), draftsman (US); (*fig*) pawn.
pedi'nare *vt* to shadow, tail.
pe'dofilo, a *ag, sm/f* paedophile.
pedo'nale *ag* pedestrian.
pe'done, a *sm/f* pedestrian ♦ *sm* (SCACCHI) pawn.
peeling ['piling] *sm inv* (COSMESI) facial scrub.
'peggio ['pɛddʒo] *av, ag inv* worse ♦ *sm o f*: **il** *o* **la ~** the worst; **cambiare in ~** to get *o* become worse; **alla ~** at worst, if the worst comes to the worst; **tirare avanti alla meno ~** to get along as best one can; **avere la ~** to come off worse, get the worst of it.
peggiora'mento [peddʒora'mento] *sm* worsening.
peggio'rare [peddʒo'rare] *vt* to make worse, worsen ♦ *vi* to grow worse, worsen.
peggiora'tivo, a [peddʒora'tivo] *ag* pejorative.
peggi'ore [ped'dʒore] *ag* (*comparativo*) worse; (*superlativo*) worst ♦ *sm/f*: **il(la) ~** the worst (person); **nel ~ dei casi** if the worst comes to the worst.
'pegno ['peɲɲo] *sm* (DIR) security, pledge; (*nei giochi di società*) forfeit; (*fig*) pledge, token; **dare in ~ qc** to pawn sth; **in ~ d'amicizia** as a token of friendship; **banco dei ~i** pawnshop.
pelapa'tate *sm inv* potato peeler.

pe'lare *vt* (*spennare*) to pluck; (*spellare*) to skin; (*sbucciare*) to peel; (*fig*) to make pay through the nose; **~rsi** *vr* to go bald.
pe'lato, a *ag* (*sbucciato*) peeled; (*calvo*) bald; **(pomodori) ~i** peeled tomatoes.
pel'lame *sm* skins *pl*, hides *pl*.
'pelle *sf* skin; (*di animale*) skin, hide; (*cuoio*) leather; **essere ~ ed ossa** to be skin and bone; **avere la ~ d'oca** to have goose pimples *o* goose flesh; **avere i nervi a fior di ~** to be edgy; **non stare più nella ~ dalla gioia** to be beside o.s. with delight; **lasciarci la ~** to lose one's life; **amici per la ~** firm *o* close friends.
pellegri'naggio [pellegri'naddʒo] *sm* pilgrimage.
pelle'grino, a *sm/f* pilgrim.
pelle'rossa, pelli'rossa, *pl* **pelli'rosse** *sm/f* Red Indian.
pellette'ria *sf* (*articoli*) leather goods *pl*; (*negozio*) leather goods shop.
pelli'cano *sm* pelican.
pellicce'ria [pellitt ʃe'ria] *sf* (*negozio*) furrier's (shop); (*quantità di pellicce*) furs *pl*.
pel'liccia, ce [pcl'littʃa] *sf* (*mantello di animale*) coat, fur; (*indumento*) fur coat; **~ ecologica** fake fur.
pellicci'aio [pellit'tʃajo] *sm* furrier.
pel'licola *sf* (*membrana sottile*) film, layer; (FOT, CINE) film.
pelli'rossa *sm/f* = **pellerossa**.
'pelo *sm* hair; (*pelame*) coat, hair; (*pelliccia*) fur; (*di tappeto*) pile; (*di liquido*) surface; **per un ~**: **per un ~ non ho perduto il treno** I very nearly missed the train; **c'è mancato un ~ che affogasse** he narrowly escaped drowning; **cercare il ~ nell'uovo** (*fig*) to pick holes, split hairs; **non aver ~i sulla lingua** (*fig*) to speak one's mind.
pe'loso, a *ag* hairy.
'peltro *sm* pewter.
pe'luche [pə'lyʃ] *sm* plush; **giocattoli di ~** soft toys.
pe'luria *sf* down.
'pelvi *sf inv* pelvis.
'pelvico, a, ci, che *ag* pelvic.
'pena *sf* (DIR) sentence; (*punizione*) punishment; (*sofferenza*) sadness *no pl*, sorrow; (*fatica*) trouble *no pl*, effort; (*difficoltà*) difficulty; **far ~** to be pitiful; **mi fai ~** I feel sorry for you; **essere** *o* **stare in ~ (per qc/qn)** to worry *o* be anxious (about sth/sb); **prendersi** *o* **darsi la ~ di fare** to go to the trouble of doing; **vale la ~ farlo** it's worth doing, it's worth it; **non ne vale la ~** it's not worth the effort, it's not worth it; **~ di morte** death sentence;

~ **pecuniaria** fine.

pe'nale *ag* penal ♦ *sf* (*anche*: **clausola** ~) penalty clause; **causa** ~ criminal trial; **diritto** ~ criminal law; **pagare la** ~ to pay the penalty.

pena'lista, i, e *sm/f* (*avvocato*) criminal lawyer.

penalità *sf inv* penalty.

penaliz'zare [penalid'dzare] *vt* (*SPORT*) to penalize.

penalizzazi'one [penaliddzat'tsjone] *sf* (*SPORT*) penalty.

pe'nare *vi* (*patire*) to suffer; (*faticare*) to struggle.

pen'dente *ag* hanging; leaning ♦ *sm* (*ciondolo*) pendant; (*orecchino*) drop earring.

pen'denza [pen'dɛntsa] *sf* slope, slant; (*grado d'inclinazione*) gradient; (*ECON*) outstanding account.

'pendere *vi* (*essere appeso*): ~ **da** to hang from; (*essere inclinato*) to lean; (*fig*: *incombere*): ~ **su** to hang over.

pen'dice [pen'ditʃe] *sf* (*di monte*) slope.

pen'dio, ii *sm* slope, slant; (*luogo in pendenza*) slope.

'pendola *sf* pendulum clock.

pendo'lare *ag* pendulum *cpd*, pendular ♦ *sm/f* commuter.

pendola'rismo *sm* commuting.

pendo'lino *sm* (*FERR*) high-speed tilting train.

'pendolo *sm* (*peso*) pendulum; (*anche*: **orologio a** ~) pendulum clock.

'pene *sm* penis.

pene'trante *ag* piercing, penetrating.

pene'trare *vi* to come o get in ♦ *vt* to penetrate; ~ **in** to enter; (*sog*: *proiettile*) to penetrate; (: *acqua, aria*) to go o come into.

penetrazi'one [penetrat'tsjone] *sf* penetration.

penicil'lina [penitʃil'lina] *sf* penicillin.

peninsu'lare *ag* peninsular; **l'Italia** ~ mainland Italy.

pe'nisola *sf* peninsula.

peni'tente *sm/f* penitent.

peni'tenza [peni'tɛntsa] *sf* penitence; (*punizione*) penance.

penitenzi'ario [peniten'tsjarjo] *sm* prison.

'penna *sf* (*di uccello*) feather; (*per scrivere*) pen; ~**e** *sfpl* (*CUC*) quills (*type of pasta*); ~ **a feltro/stilografica/a sfera** felt-tip/fountain/ballpoint pen.

pen'nacchio [pen'nakkjo] *sm* (*ornamento*) plume.

penna'rello *sm* felt(-tip) pen.

pennel'lare *vi* to paint.

pennel'lata *sf* brushstroke.

pen'nello *sm* brush; (*per dipingere*) (paint)brush; **a** ~ (*perfettamente*) to perfection, perfectly; ~ **per la barba** shaving brush.

Pen'nini *smpl*: **i** ~ the Pennines.

pen'nino *sm* nib.

pen'none *sm* (*NAUT*) yard; (*stendardo*) banner, standard.

pen'nuto *sm* bird.

pe'nombra *sf* half-light, dim light.

pe'noso, a *ag* painful, distressing; (*faticoso*) tiring, laborious.

pen'sare *vi* to think ♦ *vt* to think; (*inventare, escogitare*) to think out; ~ **a** to think of; (*amico, vacanze*) to think of o about; (*problema*) to think about; ~ **di fare qc** to think of doing sth; ~ **bene/male di qn** to think well/badly of sb, have a good/bad opinion of sb; **penso di sì** I think so; **penso di no** I don't think so; **a pensarci bene** ... on second thoughts (*BRIT*) o thought (*US*) ...; **non voglio nemmeno pensarci** I don't even want to think about it; **ci penso io** I'll see to o take care of it.

pen'sata *sf* (*trovata*) idea, thought.

pensa'tore, 'trice *sm/f* thinker.

pensie'rino *sm* (*dono*) little gift; (*pensiero*) **ci farò un** ~ I'll think about it.

pensi'ero *sm* thought; (*modo di pensare, dottrina*) thinking *no pl*; (*preoccupazione*) worry, care, trouble; **darsi** ~ **per qc** to worry about sth; **stare in** ~ **per qn** to be worried about sb; **un** ~ **gentile** (*anche fig*: *dono etc*) a kind thought.

pensie'roso, a *ag* thoughtful.

'pensile *ag* hanging.

pensi'lina *sf* (*in stazione*) platform roof.

pensiona'mento *sm* retirement; ~ **anticipato** early retirement.

pensio'nante *sm/f* (*presso una famiglia*) lodger; (*di albergo*) guest.

pensio'nato, a *sm/f* pensioner ♦ *sm* (*istituto*) hostel.

pensi'one *sf* (*al prestatore di lavoro*) pension; (*vitto e alloggio*) board and lodging; (*albergo*) boarding house; **andare in** ~ to retire; **mezza** ~ half board; ~ **completa** full board; ~ **d'invalidità** disablement pension; ~ **di anzianità** old-age pension.

pensio'nistico, a, ci, che *ag* pension *cpd*.

pen'soso, a *ag* thoughtful, pensive, lost in thought.

pen'tagono *sm* pentagon; **il P**~ the Pentagon.

pentag'ramma, i *sm* (*MUS*) staff, stave.

pentapar'tito *sm* (*POL*) five-party coalition government.

'**pentathlon** ['pɛntatlon] *sm* (*SPORT*) pentathlon.

Pente'coste *sf* Pentecost, Whit Sunday (*BRIT*).

penti'mento *sm* repentance, contrition.

pen'tirsi *vr*: ~ **di** to repent of; (*rammaricarsi*) to regret, be sorry for.

penti'tismo *sm* confessions from terrorists and members of organized crime rackets; vedi nota nel riquadro.

PENTITISMO

The practice of **pentitismo** *first emerged in Italy during the 1970s, a period marked by major terrorist activity. Once arrested, some members of terrorist groups would collaborate with the authorities by providing information in return for a reduced sentence, or indeed for their own reasons. In recent years it has become common practice for members of Mafia organizations to become "pentiti" and special legislation has had to be introduced to provide for the sentencing and personal protection of these informants.*

---

pen'tito, a *sm/f* ≈ supergrass (*BRIT*), terrorist/criminal who turns police informer.

'**pentola** *sf* pot; ~ **a pressione** pressure cooker.

pe'nultimo, a *ag* last but one (*BRIT*), next to last, penultimate.

pe'nuria *sf* shortage.

penzo'lare [pendzo'lare] *vi* to dangle, hang loosely.

penzo'loni [pendzo'loni] *av* dangling, hanging down; **stare** ~ to dangle, hang down.

pe'pato, a *ag* (*condito con pepe*) peppery, hot; (*fig: pungente*) sharp.

'**pepe** *sm* pepper; ~ **macinato/in grani/nero** ground/whole/black pepper.

pepero'nata *sf* stewed peppers, tomatoes and onions.

peperon'cino [peperon'tʃino] *sm* chilli pepper.

pepe'rone *sm*: ~ (**rosso**) red pepper, capsicum; ~ (**verde**) green pepper, capsicum; **rosso come un** ~ as red as a beetroot (*BRIT*), fire-engine red (*US*); ~**i ripieni** stuffed peppers.

pe'pita *sf* nugget.

=========== *PAROLA CHIAVE*

per *prep* **1** (*moto attraverso luogo*) through; **i ladri sono passati** ~ **la finestra** the thieves got in (*o* out) through the

window; **l'ho cercato** ~ **tutta la casa** I've searched the whole house *o* all over the house for it

2 (*moto a luogo*) for, to; **partire** ~ **la Germania/il mare** to leave for Germany/ the sea; **il treno** ~ **Roma** the Rome train, the train for *o* to Rome; **proseguire** ~ **Londra** to go on to London

3 (*stato in luogo*): **seduto/sdraiato** ~ **terra** sitting/lying on the ground

4 (*tempo*) for; ~ **anni/tanto tempo** for years/a long time; ~ **tutta l'estate** throughout the summer, all summer long; **lo rividi** ~ **Natale** I saw him again at Christmas; **lo faccio** ~ **lunedì** I'll do it for Monday

5 (*mezzo, maniera*) by; ~ **lettera/ferrovia/ via aerea** by letter/rail/airmail; **prendere qn** ~ **un braccio** to take sb by the arm

6 (*causa, scopo*) for; **assente** ~ **malattia** absent because of *o* through *o* owing to illness; **ottimo** ~ **il mal di gola** excellent for sore throats; ~ **abitudine** out of habit, from habit

7 (*limitazione*) for; **è troppo difficile** ~ **lui** it's too difficult for him; ~ **quel che mi riguarda** as far as I'm concerned; ~ **poco che sia** however little it may be; ~ **questa volta ti perdono** I'll forgive you this time

8 (*prezzo, misura*) for; (*distributivo*) a, per; **venduto** ~ **3 milioni** sold for 3 million; **la strada continua** ~ **3 km** the street goes on for 3 km; **1000 lire** ~ **persona** 1000 lire a *o* per person; **uno** ~ **volta** one at a time; **uno** ~ **uno** one by one; **due** ~ **parte** two either side; **5** ~ **cento** 5 per cent; **3** ~ **4 fa 12** 3 times 4 equals 12; **dividere/moltiplicare 12** ~ **4** to divide/multiply 12 by 4

9 (*in qualità di*) as; (*al posto di*) for; **avere qn** ~ **professore** to have sb as a teacher; **ti ho preso** ~ **Mario** I mistook you for Mario; **dare** ~ **morto qn** to give sb up for dead; **lo prenderanno** ~ **pazzo** they'll think he's crazy

10 (*seguito da vb: finale*): ~ **fare qc** (so as) to do sth, in order to do sth; (: *causale*): ~ **aver fatto qc** for having done sth; **studia** ~ **passare l'esame** he's studying in order to *o* (so as) to pass his exam; **l'hanno punito** ~ **aver rubato i soldi** he was punished for having stolen the money; **è abbastanza grande** ~ **andarci da solo** he's big enough to go on his own.

'**pera** *sf* pear.

pe'raltro *av* moreover, what's more.

per'bacco *escl* by Jove!

per'bene *ag inv* respectable, decent ♦ *av*

(*con cura*) properly, well.
perbe'nismo *sm* (so-called) respectability.
percentu'ale [pertʃentu'ale] *sf* percentage;
(*commissione*) commission.
perce'pire [pertʃe'pire] *vt* (*sentire*) to
perceive; (*ricevere*) to receive.
percet'tibile [pertʃet'tibile] *ag* perceptible.
percezi'one [pertʃet'tsjone] *sf* perception.

================= *PAROLA CHIAVE*

perché [per'ke] *av* why; ~ **no?** why not?; ~
non vuoi andarci? why don't you want to
go?; **spiegami** ~ **l'hai fatto** tell me why
you did it
♦ *cong* **1** (*causale*) because; **non posso
uscire** ~ **ho da fare** I can't go out because
o as I've a lot to do
2 (*finale*) in order that, so that; **te lo do** ~
tu lo legga I'm giving it to you so (that)
you can read it
3 (*consecutivo*): **è troppo forte** ~ **si possa
batterlo** he's too strong to be beaten
♦ *sm inv* reason; **il** ~ **di** the reason for; **non
c'è un vero** ~ there's no real reason for
it.

perciò [per'tʃɔ] *cong* so, for this (*o* that)
reason.
per'correre *vt* (*luogo*) to go all over;
(: *paese*) to travel up and down, go all
over; (*distanza*) to cover.
percor'ribile *ag* (*strada*) which can be
followed.
per'corso, a *pp di* **percorrere** ♦ *sm* (*tragitto*)
journey; (*tratto*) route.
per'cosso, a *pp di* **percuotere** ♦ *sf* blow.
percu'otere *vt* to hit, strike.
percussi'one *sf* percussion; **strumenti a** ~
(*MUS*) percussion instruments.
per'dente *ag* losing ♦ *sm/f* loser.
'perdere *vt* to lose; (*lasciarsi sfuggire*) to
miss; (*sprecare: tempo, denaro*) to waste;
(*mandare in rovina: persona*) to ruin ♦ *vi* to
lose; (*serbatoio etc*) to leak; ~**rsi** *vr*
(*smarrirsi*) to get lost; (*svanire*) to
disappear, vanish; **saper** ~ to be a good
loser; **lascia** ~! forget it!, never mind!;
non ho niente da ~ (*fig*) I've got nothing
to lose; **è un'occasione da non** ~ it's a
marvellous opportunity; (*affare*) it's a
great bargain; **è fatica persa** it's a waste
of effort; ~ **al gioco** to lose money
gambling; ~ **di vista qn** (*anche fig*) to lose
sight of sb; ~**rsi di vista** to lose sight of
each other; (*fig*) to lose touch; ~**rsi alla
vista** to disappear from sight; ~**rsi in
chiacchiere** to waste time talking.
perdifi'ato : **a** ~ *av* (*correre*) at

breathtaking speed; (*gridare*) at the top of
one's voice.
perdigi'orno [perdi'dʒorno] *sm/f inv* idler,
waster.
'perdita *sf* loss; (*spreco*) waste; (*fuoriuscita*)
leak; **siamo in** ~ (*COMM*) we are running
at a loss; **a** ~ **d'occhio** as far as the eye
can see.
perdi'tempo *sm/f inv* waster, idler.
perdizi'one [perdit'tsjone] *sf* (*REL*)
perdition, damnation; **luogo di** ~ place of
ill repute.
perdo'nare *vt* to pardon, forgive; (*scusare*)
to excuse, pardon; **per farsi** ~ in order to
be forgiven; **perdona la domanda ...** if
you don't mind my asking ...; **vogliate** ~
il (mio) ritardo my apologies for being
late; **un male che non perdona** an
incurable disease.
per'dono *sm* forgiveness; (*DIR*) pardon;
chiedere ~ **a qn (per)** to ask for sb's
forgiveness (for); (*scusarsi*) to apologize
to sb (for).
perdu'rare *vi* to go on, last; (*perseverare*) to
persist.
perduta'mente *av* desperately,
passionately.
per'duto, a *pp di* **perdere** ♦ *ag* (*gen*) lost;
sentirsi *o* **vedersi** ~ (*fig*) to realize the
hopelessness of one's position; **una
donna** ~**a** (*fig*) a fallen woman.
peregri'nare *vi* to wander, roam.
pe'renne *ag* eternal, perpetual, perennial;
(*BOT*) perennial.
peren'torio, a *ag* peremptory; (*definitivo*)
final.
perfetta'mente *av* perfectly; **sai** ~ **che ...**
you know perfectly well that ....
per'fetto, a *ag* perfect ♦ *sm* (*LING*) perfect
(tense).
perfeziona'mento [perfettsjona'mento] *sm*:
~ (**di**) improvement (in), perfection (of);
corso di ~ proficiency course.
perfezio'nare [perfettsjo'nare] *vt* to
improve, perfect; ~**rsi** *vr* to improve.
perfezi'one [perfet'tsjone] *sf* perfection.
perfezio'nismo [perfettsjo'nizmo] *sm*
perfectionism.
perfezio'nista, i, e [perfettsjo'nista] *sm/f*
perfectionist.
per'fidia *sf* perfidy.
'perfido, a *ag* perfidious, treacherous.
per'fino *av* even.
perfo'rare *vt* to pierce; (*MED*) to perforate;
(*banda, schede*) to punch; (*trivellare*) to
drill.
perfora'tore, 'trice *sm/f* punch-card
operator ♦ *sm* (*utensile*) punch; (*INFORM*):

~ **di schede** card punch ♦ sf (*TECN*) boring
o drilling machine; (*INFORM*) card punch.
perforazi'one [perforat'tsjone] sf piercing;
perforation; punching; drilling.
perga'mena sf parchment.
'pergola sf pergola.
pergo'lato sm pergola.
perico'lante ag precarious.
pe'ricolo sm danger; **essere fuori** ~ to be
out of danger; (*MED*) to be off the danger
list; **mettere in** ~ to endanger, put in
danger.
perico'loso, a ag dangerous.
perife'ria sf (*anche fig*) periphery; (*di città*)
outskirts pl.
peri'ferico, a, ci, che ag (*ANAT, INFORM*)
peripheral; (*zona*) outlying.
pe'rifrasi sf inv circumlocution.
pe'rimetro sm perimeter.
peri'odico, a, ci, che ag periodic(al);
(*MAT*) recurring ♦ sm periodical.
pe'riodo sm period; ~ **contabile**
accounting period; ~ **di prova** trial
period.
peripe'zie [peripet'tsie] sfpl ups and downs,
vicissitudes.
'periplo sm circumnavigation.
pe'rire vi to perish, die.
peris'copio sm periscope.
pe'rito, a ag expert, skilled ♦ sm/f expert;
(*agronomo, navale*) surveyor; **un** ~
chimico a qualified chemist.
perito'nite sf peritonitis.
pe'rizia [pe'rittsja] sf (*abilità*) ability;
(*giudizio tecnico*) expert opinion; expert's
report; ~ **psichiatrica** psychiatrist's
report.
'perla sf pearl.
per'lina sf bead.
perli'nato sm matchboarding.
perlo'meno av (*almeno*) at least.
perlopiù av (*quasi sempre*) in most cases,
usually.
perlus'trare vt to patrol.
perlustrazi'one [perlustrat'tsjone] sf patrol,
reconnaissance; **andare in** ~ to go on
patrol.
perma'loso, a ag touchy.
perma'nente ag permanent ♦ sf
permanent wave, perm.
perma'nenza [perma'nɛntsa] sf
permanence; (*soggiorno*) stay; **buona** ~!
enjoy your stay!
perma'nere vi to remain.
per'mango, per'masi etc vb vedi
permanere.
perme'abile ag permeable.
perme'are vt to permeate.

per'messo, a pp di **permettere** ♦ sm
(*autorizzazione*) permission, leave; (*dato a
militare, impiegato*) leave; (*licenza*) licence
(*BRIT*), license (*US*), permit; (*MIL: foglio*)
pass; ~?, è ~? (*posso entrare?*) may I
come in?; (*posso passare?*) excuse me; ~
di lavoro/pesca work/fishing permit.
per'mettere vt to allow, permit; ~ **a qn
qc/di fare qc** to allow sb sth/to do sth;
~**rsi** vr: ~**rsi qc/di fare qc** (*concedersi*) to
allow o.s. sth/to do sth; (*avere la
possibilità*) to afford sth/to do sth;
permettete che mi presenti let me
introduce myself, may I introduce
myself?; **mi sia permesso di sottolineare
che** ... may I take the liberty of pointing
out that ....
per'misi etc vb vedi **permettere.**
permis'sivo, a ag permissive.
'permuta sf (*DIR*) transfer; (*COMM*) trade-
in; **accettare qc in** ~ to take sth as a
trade-in; **valore di** ~ (*di macchina etc*)
trade-in value.
permu'tare vt to exchange; (*MAT*) to
permute.
per'nacchia [per'nakkja] sf (*fam*): **fare una**
~ to blow a raspberry.
per'nice [per'nitʃe] sf partridge.
pernici'oso, a [perni'tʃoso] ag pernicious.
'perno sm pivot.
pernotta'mento sm overnight stay.
pernot'tare vi to spend the night, stay
overnight.
'pero sm pear tree.
però cong (*ma*) but; (*tuttavia*) however,
nevertheless.
pero'rare vt (*DIR, fig*): ~ **la causa di qn** to
plead sb's case.
perpendico'lare ag, sf perpendicular.
perpen'dicolo sm: **a** ~ perpendicularly.
perpe'trare vt to perpetrate.
perpetu'are vt to perpetuate.
per'petuo, a ag perpetual.
perplessità sf inv perplexity.
per'plesso, a ag perplexed, puzzled.
perqui'sire vt to search.
perquisizi'one [perkwizit'tsjone] sf (*police*)
search; **mandato di** ~ search warrant.
'perse etc vb vedi **perdere.**
persecu'tore sm persecutor.
persecuzi'one [persekut'tsjone] sf
persecution.
persegu'ibile ag (*DIR*): **essere** ~ **per legge**
to be liable to prosecution.
persegu'ire vt to pursue; (*DIR*) to
prosecute.
persegui'tare vt to persecute.
perseve'rante ag persevering.

perseve'ranza [perseve'rantsa] *sf* perseverance.

perseve'rare *vi* to persevere.

'persi *etc vb vedi* **perdere**.

'Persia *sf*: **la** ~ Persia.

persi'ano, a *ag, sm/f* Persian ♦ *sf* shutter; ~**a avvolgibile** roller blind.

'persico, a, ci, che *ag*: **il golfo P**~ the Persian Gulf; **pesce** ~ perch.

per'sino *av* = **perfino**.

persis'tente *ag* persistent.

persis'tenza [persis'tɛntsa] *sf* persistence.

per'sistere *vi* to persist; ~ **a fare** to persist in doing.

persis'tito, a *pp di* **persistere**.

'perso, a *pp di* **perdere** ♦ *ag* (*smarrito*: *anche fig*) lost; (*sprecato*) wasted; **fare qc a tempo** ~ to do sth in one's spare time; ~ **per** ~ I've (*o* we've *etc*) got nothing further to lose.

per'sona *sf* person; (*qualcuno*): **una** ~ someone, somebody, *espressione interrogativa* + anyone *o* anybody; ~**e** *sfpl* people *pl*; **non c'è** ~ **che ...** there's nobody who ..., there isn't anybody who ...; **in** ~, **di** ~ in person; **per interposta** ~ through an intermediary *o* a third party; ~ **giuridica** (*DIR*) legal person.

perso'naggio [perso'naddʒo] *sm* (*persona ragguardevole*) personality, figure; (*tipo*) character, individual; (*LETTERATURA*) character.

perso'nale *ag* personal ♦ *sm* staff, personnel; (*figura fisica*) build ♦ *sf* (*mostra*) one-man (*o* one-woman) exhibition.

personalità *sf inv* personality.

personaliz'zare [personalid'dzare] *vt* (*arredamento, stile*) to personalize; (*adattare*) to customize.

personaliz'zato, a [personalid'dzato] *ag* personalized.

personal'mente *av* personally.

personifi'care *vt* to personify; (*simboleggiare*) to embody.

personificazi'one [personifikat'tsjone] *sf* (*vedi vb*) personification; embodiment.

perspi'cace [perspi'katʃe] *ag* shrewd, discerning.

perspi'cacia [perspi'katʃa] *sf* perspicacity, shrewdness.

persu'adere *vt*: ~ **qn** (**di qc/a fare**) to persuade sb (of sth/to do).

persuasi'one *sf* persuasion.

persua'sivo, a *ag* persuasive.

persu'aso, a *pp di* **persuadere**.

per'tanto *cong* (*quindi*) so, therefore.

'pertica, che *sf* pole.

perti'nace [perti'natʃe] *ag* determined;

persistent.

perti'nente *ag*: ~ (**a**) relevant (to), pertinent (to).

perti'nenza [perti'nɛntsa] *sf* (*attinenza*) pertinence, relevance; (*competenza*): **essere di** ~ **di qn** to be sb's business.

per'tosse *sf* whooping cough.

per'tugio [per'tudʒo] *sm* hole, opening.

pertur'bare *vt* to disrupt; (*persona*) to disturb, perturb.

perturbazi'one [perturbat'tsjone] *sf* disruption; disturbance.

Perù *sm*: **il** ~ Peru.

peru'gino, a [peru'dʒino] *ag* of (*o* from) Perugia.

peruvi'ano, a *ag, sm/f* Peruvian.

per'vadere *vt* to pervade.

per'vaso, a *pp di* **pervadere**.

perve'nire *vi*: ~ **a** to reach, arrive at, come to; (*venire in possesso*): **gli pervenne una fortuna** he inherited a fortune; **far** ~ **qc a** to have sth sent to.

perve'nuto, a *pp di* **pervenire**.

perversi'one *sf* perversion.

perversità *sf* perversity.

per'verso, a *ag* perverted.

perver'tire *vt* to pervert.

perver'tito, a *sm/f* pervert.

pervi'cace [pervi'katʃe] *ag* stubborn, obstinate.

pervi'cacia [pervi'katʃa] *sf* stubbornness, obstinacy.

per'vinca, che *sf* periwinkle ♦ *sm inv* (*colore*) periwinkle (blue).

p.es. *abbr* (= *per esempio*) e.g.

'pesa *sf* weighing *no pl*; weighbridge.

pe'sante *ag* heavy; (*fig*: *noioso*) dull, boring.

pesan'tezza [pesan'tettsa] *sf* (*anche fig*) heaviness; **avere** ~ **di stomaco** to feel bloated.

pesaper'sone *ag inv*: (**bilancia**) ~ (*weighing*) scales *pl*; (*automatica*) weighing machine.

pe'sare *vt* to weigh ♦ *vi* (*avere un peso*) to weigh; (*essere pesante*) to be heavy; (*fig*) to carry weight; ~ **su** (*fig*) to lie heavy on; to influence; to hang over; **mi pesa sgridarlo** I find it hard to scold him; **tutta la responsabilità pesa su di lui** all the responsibility rests on his shoulders; **è una situazione che mi pesa** it's a difficult situation for me; **il suo parere pesa molto** his opinion counts for a lot; ~ **le parole** to weigh one's words.

'pesca *sf* (*pl* **pesche**: *frutto*) peach; (*il pescare*) fishing; **andare a** ~ to go fishing; ~ **di beneficenza** (*lotteria*) lucky dip; ~

con la lenza angling; ~ subacquea underwater fishing.

pes'caggio [pes'kaddʒo] sm (NAUT) draught (BRIT), draft (US).

pes'care vt (pesce) to fish for; to catch; (qc nell'acqua) to fish out; (fig: trovare) to get hold of, find.

pesca'tore sm fisherman; (con lenza) angler.

'pesce ['peʃʃe] sm fish gen inv; P~i (dello zodiaco) Pisces; essere dei P~i to be Pisces; non saper che ~i prendere (fig) not to know which way to turn; ~ d'aprile! April Fool! vedi nota nel riquadro; ~ martello hammerhead; ~ rosso goldfish; ~ spada swordfish.

IL PESCE D'APRILE

Il pesce d'aprile is a sort of April Fool's joke, played on 1 April. Originally it took its name from a paper fish which was secretly attached to a person's back but nowadays all sorts of practical jokes are popular.

---

pesce'cane [peʃʃe'kane] sm shark.

pesche'reccio [peske'rettʃo] sm fishing boat.

pesche'ria [peske'ria] sf fishmonger's (shop) (BRIT), fish store (US).

pescherò etc [peske'rɔ] vb vedi pescare.

peschi'era [pes'kjera] sf fishpond.

pesci'vendolo, a [peʃʃi'vendolo] smf fishmonger (BRIT), fish merchant (US).

'pesco, schi sm peach tree.

pes'coso, a ug teeming with fish.

pe'seta sf peseta.

'peso sm weight; (SPORT) shot; dar ~ a qc to attach importance to sth; essere di ~ a qn (fig) to be a burden to sb; rubare sul ~ to give short weight; lo portarono via di ~ they carried him away bodily; avere due ~i e due misure (fig) to have double standards; ~ lordo/netto gross/net weight; ~ piuma/mosca/gallo/medio/ massimo (PUGILATO) feather/fly/bantam/ middle/heavyweight.

pessi'mismo sm pessimism.

pessi'mista, i, e ag pessimistic ♦ smf pessimist.

'pessimo, a ag very bad, awful; di ~a qualità of very poor quality.

pes'tare vt to tread on, trample on; (sale, pepe) to grind; (uva, aglio) to crush; (fig: picchiare): ~ qn to beat sb up; ~ i piedi to stamp one's feet; ~ i piedi a qn (anche fig) to tread on sb's toes.

'peste sf plague; (persona) nuisance, pest.

pes'tello sm pestle.

pesti'cida, i [pesti'tʃida] sm pesticide.

pes'tifero, a ag (anche fig) pestilential, pestiferous; (odore) noxious.

pesti'lenza [pesti'lɛntsa] sf pestilence; (fetore) stench.

'pesto, a ag: c'è buio ~ it's pitch dark ♦ sm (CUC) sauce made with basil, garlic, cheese and oil; occhio ~ black eye.

'petalo sm (BOT) petal.

pe'tardo sm firecracker, banger (BRIT).

petizi'one [petit'tsjone] sf petition; fare una ~ a to petition.

'peto sm (fam!) fart (!).

petro'dollaro sm petrodollar.

petrol'chimica [petrol'kimika] sf petrochemical industry.

petroli'era sf (nave) oil tanker.

petroli'ere sm (industriale) oilman; (tecnico) worker in the oil industry.

petroli'ero, a ag oil cpd.

petro'lifero, a ag oil cpd.

pe'trolio sm oil, petroleum; (per lampada, fornello) paraffin (BRIT), kerosene (US); lume a ~ oil o paraffin o kerosene lamp; ~ grezzo crude oil.

pettego'lare vi to gossip.

pettego'lezzo [pettego'leddzo] sm gossip no pl; fare ~i to gossip.

pet'tegolo, a ag gossipy ♦ sm/f gossip.

petti'nare vt to comb (the hair of); ~rsi vr to comb one's hair.

pettina'tura sf (acconciatura) hairstyle.

'pettine sm comb; (ZOOL) scallop.

petti'rosso sm robin.

'petto sm chest; (seno) breast, bust; (CUC: di carne bovina) brisket; (: di pollo etc) breast; prendere qn/qc di ~ to face up to sb/sth; a doppio ~ (abito) double-breasted.

petto'rina sf (di grembiule) bib.

petto'ruto, a ag broad-chested; full-breasted.

petu'lante ag insolent.

pe'tunia sf petunia.

'pezza ['pettsa] sf piece of cloth; (toppa) patch; (cencio) rag, cloth; (AMM): ~ d'appoggio o giustificativa voucher; trattare qn come una ~ da piedi to treat sb like a doormat.

pez'zato, a [pet'tsato] ag piebald.

pez'zente [pet'tsɛnte] sm/f beggar.

'pezzo ['pettso] sm (gen) piece; (brandello, frammento) piece, bit; (di macchina, arnese etc) part; (STAMPA) article; (di tempo): aspettare un ~ to wait quite a while o some time; andare a ~i to break into pieces; essere a ~i (oggetto) to be in

pieces *o* bits; (*fig*: *persona*) to be
shattered; **un bel ~ d'uomo** a fine figure
of a man; **abito a due** ~i two-piece suit;
essere tutto d'un ~ (*fig*) to be a man (*o*
woman) of integrity; ~ **di cronaca**
(*STAMPA*) report; ~ **grosso** (*fig*) bigwig; ~
di ricambio spare part.
P.F. *abbr* = **per favore; prossimo futuro.**
PG *sigla* = *Perugia.*
P.G. *abbr* = **procuratore generale.**
pH [pi'akka] *sm inv* (*CHIM*) pH.
PI *sigla* = *Pisa.*
P.I. *abbr* = **Pubblica Istruzione.**
pi'accio *etc* ['pjattʃo] *vb vedi* **piacere.**
pia'cente [pja'tʃɛnte] *ag* attractive,
pleasant.
pia'cere [pja'tʃere] *vi* to please; ◆ *sm*
pleasure; (*favore*) favour (*BRIT*), favor
(*US*); **una ragazza che piace** (*piacevole*) a
likeable girl; (*attraente*) an attractive girl;
~ **a: mi piace** I like it; **quei ragazzi non mi
piacciono** I don't like those boys; **gli
piacerebbe andare al cinema; il suo discorso è
piaciuto molto** his speech was well
received; *"~!"* (*nelle presentazioni*)
"pleased to meet you!"; **con** ~ certainly,
with pleasure; **per** ~ please; **fare un** ~ **a**
qn to do sb a favour; **mi fa** ~ **per lui** I am
pleased for him; **mi farebbe** ~ **rivederlo** I
would like to see him again.
pia'cevole [pja'tʃevole] *ag* pleasant,
agreeable.
piaci'mento [pjatʃi'mento] *sm*: **a** ~ (*a
volontà*) as much as one likes, at will; **lo
farà a suo** ~ he'll do it when it suits him.
piaci'uto, a [pja'tʃuto] *pp di* **piacere.**
pi'acqui *etc vb vedi* **piacere.**
pi'aga, ghe *sf* (*lesione*) sore; (*ferita: anche
fig*) wound; (*fig: flagello*) scourge, curse;
(: *persona*) pest, nuisance.
piagnis'teo [pjaɲɲis'tɛo] *sm* whining,
whimpering.
piagnuco'lare [pjaɲɲuko'lare] *vi* to
whimper.
piagnuco'lio, ii [pjaɲɲuko'lio] *sm*
whimpering.
piagnuco'loso, a [pjaɲɲuko'loso] *ag*
whiny, whimpering, moaning.
pi'alla *sf* (*arnese*) plane.
pial'lare *vt* to plane.
pialla'trice [pjalla'tritʃe] *sf* planing
machine.
pi'ana *sf* stretch of level ground; (*più
esteso*) plain.
pianeggi'ante [pjaned'dʒante] *ag* flat, level.
piane'rottolo *sm* landing.
pia'neta *sm* (*ASTR*) planet.

pi'angere ['pjandʒere] *vi* to cry, weep;
(*occhi*) to water ◆ *vt* to cry, weep;
(*lamentare*) to bewail, lament; ~ **la morte
di qn** to mourn sb's death.
pianifi'care *vt* to plan.
pianificazi'one [pjanifikat'tsjone] *sf* (*ECON*)
planning; ~ **aziendale** corporate
planning.
pia'nista, i, e *sm/f* pianist.
pi'ano, a *ag* (*piatto*) flat, level; (*MAT*) plane;
(*facile*) straightforward, simple; (*chiaro*)
clear, plain ◆ *av* (*adagio*) slowly; (*a bassa
voce*) softly; (*con cautela*) slowly,
carefully ◆ *sm* (*MAT*) plane; (*GEO*) plain;
(*livello*) level, plane; (*di edificio*) floor;
(*programma*) plan; (*MUS*) piano; **pian** ~
very slowly; (*poco a poco*) little by little;
una casa di 3 ~i a 3-storey (*BRIT*) *o* 3-
storied (*US*) house; **al** ~ **di sopra/di sotto**
on the floor above/below; **all'ultimo** ~ on
the top floor; **al** ~ **terra** on the ground
floor; **in primo/secondo** ~ (*FOT, CINE etc*)
in the foreground/background; **fare un
primo** ~ (*FOT, CINE*) to take a close-up; **di
primo** ~ (*fig*) prominent, high-ranking;
un fattore di secondo ~ a secondary *o*
minor factor; **passare in secondo** ~ to
become less important; **mettere tutto
sullo stesso** ~ to lump everything
together, give equal importance to
everything; **tutto secondo i** ~i all
according to plan; ~ **di lavoro** (*superficie*)
worktop; (*programma*) work plan; ~
regolatore (*URBANISTICA*) town-planning
scheme; ~ **stradale** road surface.
piano'forte *sm* piano, pianoforte.
piano'terra *sm inv* = **piano terra.**
pi'ansi *etc vb vedi* **piangere.**
pi'anta *sf* (*BOT*) plant; (*ANAT: anche:* ~ **del
piede**) sole (of the foot); (*grafico*) plan;
(*cartina topografica*) map; **ufficio a** ~
aperta open-plan office; **in** ~ **stabile** on
the permanent staff; ~ **stradale** street
map, street plan.
piantagi'one [pjanta'dʒone] *sf* plantation.
pianta'grane *sm/f inv* troublemaker.
pian'tare *vt* to plant; (*conficcare*) to drive *o*
hammer in; (*tenda*) to put up, pitch; (*fig:
lasciare*) to leave, desert; ~**rsi** vr: ~**rsi
davanti a qn** to plant o.s. in front of sb; ~
grane (*fig*) to cause trouble; **piantala!**
(*fam*) cut it out!
pian'tato, a *ag*: **ben** ~ (*persona*) well-built.
pianta'tore *sm* planter.
pianter'reno *sm* ground floor.
pi'anto, a *pp di* **piangere** ◆ *sm* tears *pl*,
crying.

pianto'nare *vt* to guard, watch over.
pian'tone *sm* (*vigilante*) sentry, guard; (*soldato*) orderly; (*AUT*) steering column.
pia'nura *sf* plain.
pi'astra *sf* plate; (*di pietra*) slab; (*di fornello*) hotplate; **panino alla ~ ≈** toasted sandwich; **~ di registrazione** tape deck.
pias'trella *sf* tile.
piastrel'lare *vt* to tile.
pias'trina *sf* (*ANAT*) platelet; (*MIL*) identity disc (*BRIT*) *o* tag (*US*).
piatta'forma *sf* (*anche fig*) platform; **~ continentale** (*GEO*) continental shelf; **~ girevole** (*TECN*) turntable; **~ di lancio** (*MIL*) launching pad *o* platform; **~ rivendicativa** *document prepared by the unions in an industry, setting out their claims.*
piat'tello *sm* clay pigeon; **tiro al ~** clay-pigeon shooting (*BRIT*), trapshooting.
piat'tino *sm* (*di tazza*) saucer.
pi'atto, a *ag* flat; (*fig*: *scialbo*) dull ♦ *sm* (*recipiente, vivanda*) dish; (*portata*) course; (*parte piana*) flat (part); nel umpi (*MUS*) cymbal; un ~ di minestra a plate of soup; **~ fondo** soup dish; **~ forte** main course; **~ del giorno** dish of the day, plat du jour; **~ del giradischi** turntable; **~ i gia pronti** (*CUC*) ready cooked dishes.
pi'azza ['pjattsa] *sf* square; (*COMM*) market; (*letto, lenzuolo*): **a una ~** single; **a due ~e** double; **far ~ pulita** to make a clean sweep; **mettere in ~** (*fig*: *rendere pubblico*) to make public; **scendere in ~** (*fig*) to take to the streets, demonstrate; **~ d'armi** (*MIL*) parade ground.
piazza'forte [pjattsa'fɔrte], *pl* **piazze'forti** *sf* (*MIL*) stronghold.
piaz'zale [pjat'tsale] *sm* (large) square.
piazza'mento [pjattsa'mento] *sm* (*SPORT*) place, placing.
piaz'zare [pjat'tsare] *vt* to place; (*COMM*) to market, sell; **~rsi** *vr* (*SPORT*) to be placed; **~rsi bene** to finish with the leaders *o* in a good position.
piaz'zista, i [pjat'tsista] *sm* (*COMM*) commercial traveller.
piaz'zola [pjat'tsɔla] *sf* (*AUT*) lay-by (*BRIT*), (*roadside*) stopping place.
'picca, che *sf* pike; (*CARTE*) spades; **rispondere ~che a qn** (*fig*) to give sb a flat refusal.
pic'cante *ag* hot, pungent; (*fig*) racy.
pic'carsi *vr*: **~ di fare** to pride o.s. on one's ability to do; **~ per qc** to take offence (*BRIT*) *o* offense (*US*) at sth.
picchet'taggio [pikket'taddʒo] *sm* picketing.
picchet'tare [pikket'tare] *vt* to picket.
pic'chetto [pik'ketto] *sm* (*MIL, di scioperanti*) picket.
picchi'are [pik'kjare] *vt* (*persona*: *colpire*) to hit, strike; (: *prendere a botte*) to beat (up); (*battere*) to beat; (*sbattere*) to bang ♦ *vi* (*bussare*) to knock; (: *con forza*) to bang; (*colpire*) to hit, strike; (*sole*) to beat down.
picchi'ata [pik'kjata] *sf* knock; bang; blow; (*percosse*) beating, thrashing; (*AER*) dive; **scendere in ~** to (nose-)dive.
picchiet'tare [pikkjet'tare] *vt* (*punteggiare*) to spot, dot; (*colpire*) to tap.
'picchio ['pikkjo] *sm* woodpecker.
pic'cino, a [pit'tʃino] *ag* tiny, very small.
picci'olo [pit'tʃɔlo] *sm* (*BOT*) stalk.
piccio'naia [pittʃo'naja] *sf* pigeon-loft; (*TEAT*): **la ~** the gods *sg* (*BRIT*), the gallery.
picci'one [pit'tʃone] *sm* pigeon; **pigliare due ~i con una fava** (*fig*) to kill two birds with one stone.
'picco, chi sm peak; **a ~** vertically; **colare a ~** (*NAUT, fig*) to sink.
picco'lezza [pikko'lettsa] *sf* (*dimensione*) smallness; (*fig*: *grettezza*) meanness, pettiness; (: *inezia*) trifle.
'piccolo, a *ag* small; (*oggetto, mano, di età*: *bambino*) small, little (*dav sostantivo*); (*di breve durata*: *viaggio*) short; (*fig*) mean, petty ♦ *sm/f* child, little one ♦ *sm*: **nel mio ~** in my own small way; **~ i** *smpl* (*di animale*) young *pl*; **in ~** in miniature; **la ~a borghesia** the lower middle classes; (*peg*) the petty bourgeoisie.
pic'cone *sm* pick(-axe).
pic'cozza [pik'kɔttsa] *sf* ice-axe.
pic'nic *sm inv* picnic; **fare un ~** to have a picnic.
pidies'sino, a *ag* (*POL*) of P.D.S. ♦ *sm/f* member (*o* supporter) of P.D.S.
pi'docchio [pi'dɔkkjo] *sm* louse.
pidocchi'oso, a [pidok'kjoso] *ag* (*infestato*) lousy; (*fig*: *taccagno*) mean, stingy, tight.
pidu'ista, i, e *ag* P2 *cpd* (*masonic lodge*) ♦ *sm* member of the P2 masonic lodge.
piè *sm inv*: **a ogni ~ sospinto** (*fig*) at every step; **saltare a ~ pari** (*omettere*) to skip; **a ~ di pagina** at the foot of the page; **note a ~ di pagina** footnotes.
pi'ede *sm* foot; (*di mobile*) leg; **in ~i** standing; **a ~i** on foot; **a ~i nudi** barefoot; **su due ~i** (*fig*) at once; **mettere qc in ~i** (*azienda etc*) to set sth up; **prendere ~** (*fig*) to gain ground, catch on; **puntare i ~i** (*fig*) to dig one's heels in; **sentirsi mancare la terra sotto i ~i** to feel lost; **non sta in ~i** (*persona*) he can't stand; (*fig*: *scusa etc*) it doesn't hold water; **tenere in**

~i (*persona*) to keep on his (*o* her) feet; (*fig: ditta etc*) to keep going; **a ~ libero** (*DIR*) on bail; **sul ~ di guerra** (*MIL*) ready for action; **~ di porco** crowbar.

piedipi'atti *sm inv* (*peg: poliziotto*) cop.

piedis'tallo, piedes'tallo *sm* pedestal.

pi'ega, ghe *sf* (*piegatura, GEO*) fold; (*di gonna*) pleat; (*di pantaloni*) crease; (*grinza*) wrinkle, crease; **prendere una brutta** *o* **cattiva ~** (*fig: persona*) to get into bad ways; (*: situazione*) to take a turn for the worse; **non fa una ~** (*fig: ragionamento*) it's faultless; **non ha fatto una ~** (*fig: persona*) he didn't bat an eye(lid) (*BRIT*) *o* an eye(lash) (*US*).

piega'mento *sm* folding; bending; **~ sulle gambe** (*GINNASTICA*) kneebend.

pie'gare *vt* to fold; (*braccia, gambe, testa*) to bend ♦ *vi* to bend; **~rsi** *vr* to bend; (*fig*): **~rsi (a)** to yield (to), submit (to).

piega'tura *sf* folding *no pl*; bending *no pl*; fold; bend.

piegherò *etc* [pjege'rɔ] *vb vedi* **piegare**.

pieghet'tare [pjeget'tare] *vt* to pleat.

pie'ghevole [pje'gevole] *ag* pliable, flexible; (*porta*) folding; (*fig*) yielding.

Pie'monte *sm*: **il ~** Piedmont.

piemon'tese *ag, sm/f* Piedmontese.

pi'ena *sf vedi* **pieno**.

pie'nezza [pje'nettsa] *sf* fullness.

pi'eno, a *ag* full; (*muro, mattone*) solid ♦ *sm* (*colmo*) height, peak; (*carico*) full load ♦ *sf* (*di fiume*) flood, spate; (*gran folla*) crowd, throng; **~ di** full of; **a ~e mani** abundantly; **a tempo ~** full-time; **a ~i voti** (*eleggere*) unanimously; **laurearsi a ~i voti** to graduate with full marks; **in ~ giorno** in broad daylight; **in ~ inverno** in the depths of winter; **in ~a notte** in the middle of the night; **in ~a stagione** at the height of the season; **in ~** (*completamente: sbagliare*) completely; (*colpire, centrare*) bang *o* right in the middle; **avere ~i poteri** to have full powers; **nel ~ possesso delle sue facoltà** in full possession of his faculties; **fare il ~ (di benzina)** to fill up (with petrol).

pie'none *sm*: **c'era il ~ al cinema/al teatro** the cinema/the theatre was packed.

pietà *sf* pity; (*REL*) piety; **senza ~** (*agire*) ruthlessly; (*persona*) pitiless, ruthless; **avere ~ di** (*compassione*) to pity, feel sorry for; (*misericordia*) to have pity *o* mercy on; **far ~** to arouse pity; (*peg*) to be terrible.

pie'tanza [pje'tantsa] *sf* dish, course.

pie'toso, a *ag* (*compassionevole*) pitying, compassionate; (*che desta pietà*) pitiful.

pi'etra *sf* stone; **mettiamoci una ~ sopra** (*fig*) let bygones be bygones; **~ preziosa** precious stone, gem; **~ dello scandalo** (*fig*) cause of scandal.

pie'traia *sf* (*terreno*) stony ground.

pietrifi'care *vt* to petrify; (*fig*) to transfix, paralyze.

piet'rina *sf* (*per accendino*) flint.

pie'trisco, schi *sm* crushed stone, road metal.

pi'eve *sf* parish church.

'piffero *sm* (*MUS*) pipe.

pigi'ama [pi'dʒama] *sm* pyjamas *pl*.

'pigia 'pigia ['pidʒa'pidʒa] *sm* crowd, press.

pigi'are [pi'dʒare] *vt* to press.

pigia'trice [pidʒa'tritʃe] *sf* (*macchina*) wine press.

pigi'one [pi'dʒone] *sf* rent.

pigli'are [piʎ'ʎare] *vt* to take, grab; (*afferrare*) to catch.

'piglio ['piʎʎo] *sm* look, expression.

pig'mento *sm* pigment.

pig'meo, a *sm/f* pygmy.

'pigna ['piɲɲa] *sf* pine cone.

pignole'ria [piɲɲole'ria] *sf* fastidiousness, fussiness.

pi'gnolo, a [piɲ'ɲɔlo] *ag* pernickety.

pigno'rare [piɲɲo'rare] *vt* (*DIR*) to distrain.

pigo'lare *vi* to cheep, chirp.

pigo'lio *sm* cheeping, chirping.

pigra'mente *av* lazily.

pi'grizia [pi'grittsja] *sf* laziness.

'pigro, a *ag* lazy; (*fig: ottuso*) slow, dull.

PIL *sigla m vedi* **prodotto interno lordo**.

'pila *sf* (*catasta, di ponte*) pile; (*ELETTR*) battery; (*fam: torcia*) torch (*BRIT*), flashlight; **a ~, a ~e** battery-operated.

pi'lastro *sm* pillar.

'pile ['pail] *sm inv* fleece.

'pillola *sf* pill; **prendere la ~** (*contraccettivo*) to be on the pill; **~ del giorno dopo** morning-after pill.

pi'lone *sm* (*di ponte*) pier; (*di linea elettrica*) pylon.

pi'lota, i, e *sm/f* pilot; (*AUT*) driver ♦ *ag inv* pilot *cpd*; **~ automatico** automatic pilot.

pilo'taggio [pilo'taddʒo] *sm*: **cabina di ~** flight deck.

pilo'tare *vt* to pilot; to drive.

piluc'care *vt* to nibble at.

pi'mento *sm* pimento, allspice.

pim'pante *ag* lively, full of beans.

pinaco'teca, che *sf* art gallery.

pi'neta *sf* pinewood.

ping-'pong [piŋ'pɔŋ] *sm* table tennis.

'pingue *ag* fat, corpulent.

pingu'edine *sf* corpulence.

pingu'ino *sm* (*ZOOL*) penguin.

'pinna *sf* fin; (*di pinguino, spatola di gomma*) flipper.

pin'nacolo *sm* pinnacle.

'pino *sm* pine (tree).

pi'nolo *sm* pine kernel.

'pinta *sf* pint.

'pinza ['pintsa] *sf* pliers *pl*; (*MED*) forceps *pl*; (*ZOOL*) pincer.

pinzette [pin'tsette] *sfpl* tweezers.

'pio, a, 'pii, 'pie *ag* pious; (*opere, istituzione*) charitable, charity *cpd*.

piogge'rella [pjoddʒe'rɛlla] *sf* drizzle.

pi'oggia, ge ['pjɔddʒa] *sf* rain; (*fig: di regali, fiori*) shower; (*di insulti*) hail; **sotto la** ~ in the rain; ~ **acida** acid rain.

pi'olo *sm* peg; (*di scala*) rung.

piom'bare *vi* to fall heavily; (*gettarsi con impeto*): ~ **su** to fall upon, assail ♦ *vt* (*dente*) to fill.

piomba'tura *sf* (*di dente*) filling.

piom'bino *sm* (*sigillo*) (lead) seal; (*del filo a piombo*) plummet; (*PESCA*) sinker.

pi'ombo *sm* (*CHIM*) lead; (*sigillo*) (lead) seal; (*proiettile*) (lead) shot, a ~ (*cadere*) straight down; (*muro etc*) plumb; **andare con i piedi di** ~ (*fig*) to tread carefully; **senza** ~ (*benzina*) unleaded, lead-free; **anni di** ~ (*fig*) era of terrorist outrages.

pioni'ere, a *sm/f* pioneer.

pi'oppo *sm* poplar.

pio'vano, a *ag*: **acqua** ~a rainwater.

pi'overe *vb impers* to rain ♦ *vi* (*fig: scendere dall'alto*) to rain down; (: *affluire in gran numero*): ~ **in** to pour into; **non ci piove sopra** (*fig*) there's no doubt about it.

pioviggi'nare [pjoviddʒi'nare] *vb impers* to drizzle.

piovosità *sf* rainfall.

pio'voso, a *ag* rainy.

pi'ovra *sf* octopus.

pi'ovve *etc vb vedi* piovere.

'pipa *sf* pipe.

pipì *sf* (*fam*): **fare** ~ to have a wee (wee).

pipis'trello *sm* (*ZOOL*) bat.

pi'ramide *sf* pyramid.

pi'ranha *sm inv* piranha.

pi'rata, i *sm* pirate; ~ **della strada** hit-and-run driver.

Pire'nei *smpl*: **i** ~ the Pyrenees.

pi'retro *sm* pyrethrum.

'pirico, a, ci, che *ag*: **polvere** ~a gunpowder.

pi'rite *sf* pyrite.

piro'etta *sf* pirouette.

pi'rofilo, a *ag* heat-resistant ♦ *sf* heat-resistant glass; (*tegame*) heat-resistant dish.

pi'roga, ghe *sf* dug-out canoe.

pi'romane *sm/f* arsonist.

pi'roscafo *sm* steamer, steamship.

'Pisa *sf* Pisa.

pi'sano, a *ag* Pisan.

pisci'are [piʃ'ʃare] *vi* (*fam!*) to piss (*!*), pee (*!*).

pi'scina [piʃ'ʃina] *sf* (swimming) pool.

pi'sello *sm* pea.

piso'lino *sm* nap; **fare un** ~ to have a nap.

'pista *sf* (*traccia*) track, trail; (*di stadio*) track; (*di pattinaggio*) rink; (*da sci*) run; (*AER*) runway; (*di circo*) ring; ~ **da ballo** dance floor; ~ **ciclabile** cycle lane; ~ **di lancio** launch(ing) pad; ~ **di rullaggio** (*AER*) taxiway; ~ **di volo** (*AER*) runway.

pis'tacchio [pis'takkjo] *sm* pistachio (tree); pistachio (nut).

pis'tillo *sm* (*BOT*) pistil.

pis'tola *sf* pistol, gun; ~ **a spruzzo** spray gun; ~ **a tamburo** revolver.

pis'tone *sm* piston.

pi'tocco, chi *sm* skinflint, miser.

pi'tone *sm* python.

'pittima *sf* (*fig*) bore.

pit'tore, 'trice *sm/f* painter.

pitto'resco, a, schi, sche *ag* picturesque.

pit'torico, a, ci, che *ag* of painting, pictorial.

pit'tura *sf* painting; ~ **fresca** wet paint.

pittu'rare *vt* to paint.

=========== PAROLA CHIAVE

più *av* 1 (*in maggiore quantità*) more; ~ **del solito** more than usual; **in** ~, **di** ~ more; **ne voglio di** ~ I want some more; **ci sono 3 persone in** *o* **di** ~ there are 3 more *o* extra people; **costa di** ~ it's more expensive; **una volta di** ~ once more; ~ **o meno** more or less; **né** ~ **né meno** no more, no less; **per di** ~ (*inoltre*) what's more, moreover; **è sempre** ~ **difficile** it is getting more and more difficult; **chi** ~ **chi meno hanno tutti contribuito** everybody made a contribution of some sort; ~ **dormo e** ~ **dormirei** the more I sleep the more I want to sleep

2 (*comparativo*) more; (*se monosillabo, spesso*): + ...er; ~ ... **di/che** more ... than; ~ **intelligente di lui** more intelligent than him; ~ **furbo di te** smarter than you; ~ **tardi di** ... later than ...; **lavoro** ~ **di te/di Paola** I work harder than you/than Paola; **è** ~ **fortunato che bravo** he is lucky rather than skilled; ~ **di quanto pensassi** more than I thought; ~ **che altro** mainly; ~ **che mai** more than ever

3 (*superlativo*) most; (*se monosillabico, spesso*): + ...est; **il** ~ **grande/intelligente**

the biggest/most intelligent; **è quello che compro ~ spesso** that's the one I buy most often; **al ~ presto** as soon as possible; **al ~ tardi** at the latest
4 (*negazione*): **non ... ~** no more, no longer; **non ho ~ soldi** I've got no more money, I don't have any more money; **non lavoro ~** I'm no longer working, I don't work any more; **non ce n'è ~** there isn't any left; **non c'è ~ nessuno** there's no one left; **non c'è ~ niente da fare** there's nothing more to be done; **a ~ non posso** (*gridare*) at the top of one's voice; (*correre*) as fast as one can
5 (*MAT*) plus; **4 ~ 5 fa 9** 4 plus 5 equals 9; **~ 5 gradi** 5 degrees above freezing, plus 5; **6 ~** (*a scuola*) just above a pass ♦ *prep* plus; **500.000 ~ le spese** 500,000 plus expenses; **siamo in quattro ~ il nonno** there are four of us, plus grandpa ♦ *ag inv* **1**: **~ ... (di)** more ... (than); **~ denaro/tempo** more money/time; **~ persone di quante ci aspettassimo** more people than we expected
2 (*numerosi, diversi*) several; **l'aspettai per ~ giorni** I waited for it for several days
♦ *sm* **1** (*la maggior parte*): **il ~ è fatto** most of it is done; **il ~ delle volte** more often than not, generally; **parlare del ~ e del meno** to talk about this and that
2 (*MAT*) plus (sign)
3: **i ~** the majority.

piuccheper'fetto [pjukkeper'fɛtto] *sm* (*LING*) pluperfect, past perfect.
pi'uma *sf* feather; **~e** *sfpl* down *sg*; (*piumaggio*) plumage *sg*, feathers.
piu'maggio [pju'maddʒo] *sm* plumage, feathers *pl*.
piu'mino *sm* (eider)down; (*per letto*) eiderdown; (: *tipo danese*) duvet, continental quilt; (*giacca*) quilted jacket (*with goose-feather padding*); (*per cipria*) powder puff; (*per spolverare*) feather duster.
piut'tosto *av* rather; **~ che** (*anziché*) rather than.
'piva *sf*: **con le ~e nel sacco** (*fig*) empty-handed.
pi'vello, a *sm/f* greenhorn.
'pizza ['pittsa] *sf* (*CUC*) pizza; (*CINE*) reel.
pizze'ria [pittse'ria] *sf* place where pizzas are made, sold or eaten.
pizzi'cagnolo, a [pittsi'kaɲɲolo] *sm/f* specialist grocer.
pizzi'care [pittsi'kare] *vt* (*stringere*) to nip, pinch; (*pungere*) to sting; to bite; (*MUS*) to

pluck ♦ *vi* (*prudere*) to itch, be itchy; (*cibo*) to be hot *o* spicy.
pizziche'ria [pittsike'ria] *sf* delicatessen (shop).
'pizzico, chi ['pittsiko] *sm* (*pizzicotto*) pinch, nip; (*piccola quantità*) pinch, dash; (*d'insetto*) sting; bite.
pizzi'cotto [pittsi'kɔtto] *sm* pinch, nip.
'pizzo ['pittso] *sm* (*merletto*) lace; (*barbetta*) goatee beard; (*tangente*) protection money.
pla'care *vt* to placate, soothe; **~rsi** *vr* to calm down.
'placca, che *sf* plate; (*con iscrizione*) plaque; (*anche*: **~ dentaria**) (dental) plaque.
plac'care *vt* to plate; **placcato in oro/argento** gold-/silver-plated.
pla'centa [pla'tʃɛnta] *sf* placenta.
placidità [platʃidi'ta] *sf* calm, peacefulness.
'placido, a ['platʃido] *ag* placid, calm.
plafoni'era *sf* ceiling light.
plagi'are [pla'dʒare] *vt* (*copiare*) to plagiarize; (*DIR*: *influenzare*) to coerce.
'plagio ['pladʒo] *sm* plagiarism; (*DIR*) duress.
plaid [plɛd] *sm inv* (travelling) rug (*BRIT*), lap robe (*US*).
pla'nare *vi* (*AER*) to glide.
'plancia, ce ['plantʃa] *sf* (*NAUT*) bridge; (*AUT*: *cruscotto*) dashboard.
'plancton *sm inv* plankton.
plane'tario, a *ag* planetary ♦ *sm* (*locale*) planetarium.
planis'fero *sm* planisphere.
plan'tare *sm* arch support.
'plasma *sm* plasma.
plas'mare *vt* to mould (*BRIT*), mold (*US*), shape.
'plastico, a, ci, che *ag* plastic ♦ *sm* (*rappresentazione*) relief model; (*esplosivo*): **bomba al ~** plastic bomb ♦ *sf* (*arte*) plastic arts *pl*; (*MED*) plastic surgery; (*sostanza*) plastic; **in materiale ~** plastic.
plasti'lina ® *sf* plasticine ®.
'platano *sm* plane tree.
pla'tea *sf* (*TEAT*) stalls *pl* (*BRIT*), orchestra (*US*).
plate'ale *ag* (*gesto, atteggiamento*) theatrical.
plateal'mente *av* theatrically.
'platino *sm* platinum.
pla'tonico, a, ci, che *ag* platonic.
plau'dire *vi*: **~ a** to applaud.
plau'sibile *ag* plausible.
'plauso *sm* (*fig*) approval.
'playback ['plei bæk] *sm*: **cantare in ~** to

mime.

'playboy ['pleibɔi] *sm inv* playboy.

'playmaker ['pleimeikə*] *sm/f inv* (*SPORT*) playmaker.

'play-off ['pleiɔf] *sm inv* (*SPORT*) play-off.

ple'baglia [ple'baʎʎa] *sf* (*peg*) rabble, mob.

'plebe *sf* common people.

ple'beo, a *ag* plebeian; (*volgare*) coarse, common.

plebi'scito [plebiʃ'ʃito] *sm* plebiscite.

ple'nario, a *ag* plenary.

pleni'lunio *sm* full moon.

plenipotenzi'ario, a [plenipoten'tsjarjo] *ag* plenipotentiary.

'plenum *sm inv* plenum.

'plettro *sm* plectrum.

'pleura *sf* (*ANAT*) pleura.

pleu'rite *sf* pleurisy.

P.L.I. *sigla m* (= *Partito Liberale Italiano*) *former political party*.

'plico, chi *sm* (*pacco*) parcel; **in ~ a parte** (*COMM*) under separate cover

plissé [pli se] *ag inv* plissé *cpd* ♦ *sm inv* (*anche*: **tessuto** -) plissé.

plisset'tato, a *ag* plissé *cpd*.

plo'tone *sm* (*MIL*) platoon; **~ d'esecuzione** firing squad.

'plumbeo, a *ag* leaden.

plu'rale *ag, sm* plural.

plura'lismo *sm* pluralism.

pluralità *sf* plurality; (*maggioranza*) majority.

plusva'lenza [pluzva'lɛntsa] *sf* capital gain.

plusva'lore *sm* (*ECON*) surplus.

plu'tonio *sm* plutonium.

pluvi'ale *ag* rain *cpd*.

pluvi'ometro *sm* rain gauge.

P.M. *abbr* (*POL*) = **Pubblico Ministero**; (= *Polizia Militare*) MP (= *Military Police*).

pm *abbr* = *peso molecolare*.

PN *sigla* = *Pordenone*.

pneu'matico, a, ci, che *ag* inflatable; (*TECN*) pneumatic ♦ *sm* (*AUT*) tyre (*BRIT*), tire (*US*).

PNL *sigla m vedi* **prodotto nazionale lordo**.

PO *sigla* = *Prato*.

Po *sm*: **il ~** the Po.

po' *av, sm vedi* **poco**.

P.O. *abbr* = **posta ordinaria**.

po'chezza [po'kettsa] *sf* insufficiency, shortage; (*fig*: *meschinità*) meanness, smallness.

================= *PAROLA CHIAVE*

'poco, a, chi, che *ag* (*quantità*) little, not much; (*numero*) few, not many; **~ pane/denaro/spazio** little *o* not much bread/money/space; **con ~a spesa** without

spending much; **a ~ prezzo** at a low price, cheap; **~ (tempo) fa** a short time ago; **~che persone/idee** few *o* not many people/ideas; **è un tipo di ~che parole** he's a man of few words

♦ *av* **1** (*in piccola quantità*) little, not much; (*numero limitato*) few, not many; **guadagna ~** he doesn't earn much, he earns little

2 (*con ag, av*) (a) little, not very; **è ~ più vecchia di lui** she's a little *o* slightly older than him; **è ~ socievole** he's not very sociable; **sta ~ bene** he isn't very well

3 (*tempo*): **~ dopo/prima** shortly afterwards/before; **il film dura ~** the film doesn't last very long; **ci vediamo molto ~** we don't see each other very often, we hardly ever see each other

4: **un po'** a little, a bit; **è un po' corto** it's a little *o* a bit short; **arriverà fra un po'** he'll arrive shortly *o* in a little while

5: **a dir ~** to say the least; **a ~ a ~** little by little; **per ~ non cadevo** I nearly fell; **è una cosa da ~** it's nothing, it's of no importance; **una persona da ~** a worthless person

♦ *pron* (a) little; **~chi, ~che** *pron pl* (*persone*) few (people); (*cose*) few; **ci vediamo tra ~** see you soon; **~chi lo sanno** not many people know it; **ci vuole tempo ed io ne ho ~** it takes time, and I haven't got much to spare

♦ *sm* **1** little; **vive del ~ che ha** he lives on the little he has

2: **un po'** a little; **un po' di zucchero** a little sugar; **un bel po' di denaro** quite a lot of money; **un po' per ciascuno** a bit each.

po'dere *sm* (*AGR*) farm.

pode'roso, a *ag* powerful.

podestà *sm inv* (*nel fascismo*) podestà, mayor.

'podio *sm* dais, platform; (*MUS*) podium.

po'dismo *sm* (*SPORT*: *marcia*) walking; (: *corsa*) running.

po'dista, i, e *sm/f* walker; runner.

po'ema, i *sm* poem.

poe'sia *sf* (*arte*) poetry; (*componimento*) poem.

po'eta, 'essa *sm/f* poet/poetess.

poe'tare *vi* to write poetry.

po'etico, a, ci, che *ag* poetic(al).

poggi'are [pod'dʒare] *vt* to lean, rest; (*posare*) to lay, place.

poggia'testa [poddʒa'tɛsta] *sm inv* (*AUT*) headrest.

'poggio ['pɔddʒo] *sm* hillock, knoll.

poggi'olo [pod'dʒɔlo] *sm* balcony.
'poi *av* then; (*alla fine*) finally, at last ♦ *sm*:
pensare al ~ to think of the future; **e** ~
(*inoltre*) and besides; **questa** ~ (**è bella**)
(*ironico*) that's a good one!; **d'ora in** ~
from now on; **da domani in** ~ from
tomorrow onwards.
poi'ana *sf* buzzard.
poiché [poi'ke] *cong* since, as.
pois [pwa] *sm inv* spot, (polka) dot; **a** ~
spotted, polka-dot *cpd*.
'poker *sm* poker.
po'lacco, a, chi, che *ag* Polish ♦ *sm/f*
Pole.
po'lare *ag* polar.
polariz'zare [polarid'dzare] *vt* (*anche fig*) to
polarize.
'polca, che *sf* polka.
po'lemico, a, ci, che *ag* polemic(al),
controversial ♦ *sf* controversy; **fare** ~**che**
to be contentious.
polemiz'zare [polemid'dzare] *vi*: ~ (**su qc**)
to argue (about sth).
po'lenta *sf* (*CUC*) sort *of thick porridge
made with maize flour.*
polen'tone, a *sm/f* slowcoach (*BRIT*),
slowpoke (*US*).
pole'sano, a *ag* of (*o* from) Polesine (*area
between the Po and the Adige*).
POL'FER *abbr f* = *Polizia Ferroviaria.*
'poli... *prefisso* poly....
poliambula'torio *sm* (*MED*) health clinic.
poli'clinico, ci *sm* general hospital.
poli'edro *sm* polyhedron.
poli'estere *sm* polyester.
poliga'mia *sf* polygamy.
po'ligono *sm* polygon; ~ **di tiro** rifle range.
Poli'nesia *sf*: **la** ~ Polynesia.
polinesi'ano, a *ag, sm/f* Polynesian.
'polio(mie'lite) *sf* polio(myelitis).
'polipo *sm* polyp.
polisti'rolo *sm* polystyrene.
poli'tecnico, ci *sm* postgraduate technical
college.
po'litica, che *sf vedi* politico.
politi'cante *sm/f* (*peg*) petty politician.
politiciz'zare [polititʃid'dzare] *vt* to
politicize.
po'litico, a, ci, che *ag* political ♦ *sm/f*
politician ♦ *sf* politics *sg*; (*linea di condotta*)
policy; **elezioni** ~**che** parliamentary
(*BRIT*) *o* congressional (*US*) election(s);
uomo ~ politician; **darsi alla** ~**a** to go into
politics; **fare** ~**a** (*militante*) to be a
political activist; (*come professione*) to be
in politics; **la** ~**a del governo** the
government's policies; ~**a aziendale**
company policy; ~**a estera** foreign

policy; ~**a dei prezzi** prices policy; ~**a dei
redditi** incomes policy.
poliva'lente *ag* multi-purpose.
poli'zia [polit'tsia] *sf* police; ~ **giudiziaria**
≈ Criminal Investigation Department
(CID) (*BRIT*), Federal Bureau of
Investigation (FBI) (*US*); ~ **sanitaria/
tributaria** health/tax inspectorate; ~
stradale traffic police; ~ **di stato** *vedi nota
nel riquadro.*

POLIZIA DI STATO

The remit of the **polizia di stato** *is to
maintain public order, to uphold the law, and
to prevent and investigate crime. This is a
civilian branch of the police force; male and
female officers perform similar duties. The*
polizia di stato *reports to the Minister of the
Interior.*

---

polizi'esco, a, schi, sche [polit'tsjesko] *ag*
police *cpd*; (*film, romanzo*) detective *cpd*.
polizi'otto [polit'tsjɔtto] *sm* policeman;
cane ~ police dog; **donna** ~ policewoman.
'polizza ['pɔlittsa] *sf* (*COMM*) bill; ~ **di
assicurazione** insurance policy; ~ **di
carico** bill of lading.
pol'laio *sm* henhouse.
pollai'olo, a *sm/f* poulterer (*BRIT*),
poultryman.
pol'lame *sm* poultry.
pol'lastra *sf* pullet; (*fig: ragazza*) chick.
pol'lastro *sm* (*ZOOL*) cockerel.
'pollice ['pɔllitʃe] *sm* thumb; (*unità di
misura*) inch.
'polline *sm* pollen.
polli'vendolo, a *sm/f* poulterer (*BRIT*),
poultryman.
'pollo *sm* chicken; **far ridere i** ~**i** (*situazione,
persona*) to be utterly ridiculous.
polmo'nare *ag* lung *cpd*, pulmonary.
pol'mone *sm* lung.
polmo'nite *sf* pneumonia.
'Polo *sm* (*POL*) centre-right coalition.
'polo *sm* (*GEO, FISICA*) pole; (*gioco*) polo ♦ *sf
inv* (*maglia*) polo shirt; **il P**~ **sud/nord** the
South/North Pole.
Po'lonia *sf*: **la** ~ Poland.
'polpa *sf* flesh, pulp; (*carne*) lean meat.
pol'paccio [pol'pattʃo] *sm* (*ANAT*) calf.
polpas'trello *sm* fingertip.
pol'petta *sf* (*CUC*) meatball.
polpet'tone *sm* (*CUC*) meatloaf.
'polpo *sm* octopus.
pol'poso, a *ag* fleshy.
pol'sino *sm* cuff.
'polso *sm* (*ANAT*) wrist; (*pulsazione*) pulse;

(*fig: forza*) drive, vigour (*BRIT*), vigor (*US*); **avere** ~ (*fig*) to be strong; **un uomo di** ~ a man of nerve.

pol'tiglia [pol'tiʎʎa] *sf* (*composto*) mash, mush; (*di fango e neve*) slush.

pol'trire *vi* to laze about.

pol'trona *sf* armchair; (*TEAT: posto*) seat in the front stalls (*BRIT*) *o* the orchestra (*US*).

poltron'cina [poltron'tʃina] *sf* (*TEAT*) seat in the back stalls (*BRIT*) *o* the orchestra (*US*).

pol'trone *ag* lazy, slothful.

'polvere *sf* dust; (*anche*: ~ **da sparo**) (gun)powder; (*sostanza ridotta minutissima*) powder, dust; **caffè in** ~ instant coffee; **latte in** ~ dried *o* powdered milk; **sapone in** ~ soap powder; ~ **di ferro** iron filings *pl*; ~ **d'oro** gold dust; ~ **pirica** *o* **da sparo** gunpowder.

polveri'era *sf* powder magazine.

polve'rina *sf* (*gen*, *MED*) powder; (*gergo: cocaina*) snow,

polveriz'zare [polverid'dzare] *vt* to pulverize; (*nebulizzare*) to atomize; (*fig*) to crush, pulverize; (*: record*) to smash.

polve'rone *sm* thick cloud of dust.

polve'roso, a *ag* dusty.

po'mata *sf* ointment, cream.

po'mello *sm* knob.

pomeridi'ano, a *ag* afternoon *cpd*; **nelle ore** ~**e** in the afternoon.

pome'riggio [pome'riddʒo] *sm* afternoon; **nel primo/tardo** ~ in the early/late afternoon.

'pomice ['pomitʃe] *sf* pumice.

pomici'are [pomi'tʃare] *vi* (*fam*: *sbaciucchiarsi*) to neck.

'pomo *sm* (*mela*) apple; (*ornamentale*) knob; (*di sella*) pommel; ~ **d'Adamo** (*ANAT*) Adam's apple.

pomo'doro *sm* tomato.

'pompa *sf* pump; (*sfarzo*) pomp (and ceremony); ~ **antincendio** fire hose; ~ **di benzina** petrol (*BRIT*) *o* gas (*US*) pump; (*distributore*) filling *o* gas (*US*) station; (**impresa di**) ~**e funebri** funeral parlour *sg* (*BRIT*), undertaker's *sg*, mortician's (*US*).

pom'pare *vt* to pump; (*trarre*) to pump out; (*gonfiare d'aria*) to pump up.

pompei'ano, a *ag* of (*o* from) Pompei.

pom'pelmo *sm* grapefruit.

pom'piere *sm* fireman.

pom'pon [pom'pɔn] *sm inv* pompom, pompon.

pom'poso, a *ag* pompous.

ponde'rare *vt* to ponder over, consider carefully.

ponde'roso, a *ag* (*anche fig*) weighty.

po'nente *sm* west.

'pongo, 'poni *etc vb vedi* **porre.**

'ponte *sm* bridge; (*di nave*) deck; (*: anche*: ~ **di comando**) bridge; (*impalcatura*) scaffold; **vivere sotto i** ~**i** to be a tramp; **fare il** ~ (*fig*) to take the extra day off (*between 2 public holidays*); **governo** ~ interim government; ~ **aereo** airlift; ~ **di barche** (*MIL*) pontoon bridge; ~ **di coperta** (*NAUT*) upper deck; ~ **levatoio** drawbridge; ~ **radio** radio link; ~ **sospeso** suspension bridge.

pon'tefice [pon'tefitʃe] *sm* (*REL*) pontiff.

ponti'cello [ponti'tʃello] *sm* (*di occhiali*, *MUS*) bridge.

pontifi'care *vi* (*anche fig*) to pontificate.

pontifi'cato *sm* pontificate.

pontl'ficio, a, ci, cie [ponti'fitʃo] *ag* papal; **Stato P**~ Papal State.

pon'tile *sm* jetty.

'pony ['pɔni] *sm inv* pony.

pool [puːl] *sm inv* (*consorzio*) consortium; (*organismo internazionale*) pool; (*di esperti*, *ricercatori*) team; (*antimafia*, *antidroga*) working party.

pop [pɔp] *ag inv* pop *cpd*.

'popcorn ['pɔpkɔːn] *sm inv* popcorn.

'popeline ['pɔpelin] *sm* poplin.

popò *sm inv* (*sedere*) botty.

popo'lano, a *ag* popular, of the people ♦ *sm/f* man/woman of the people.

popo'lare *ag* popular; (*quartiere*, *clientela*) working-class; (*POL*) of P.P.I. ♦ *sm/f* (*POL*) member (*o* supporter) of P.P.I. ♦ *vt* (*rendere abitato*) to populate; ~**rsi** *vr* to fill with people, get crowded; **manifestazione** ~ mass demonstration; **repubblica** ~ people's republic.

popolarità *sf* popularity.

popolazi'one [popolat'tsjone] *sf* population.

'popolo *sm* people.

popo'loso, a *ag* densely populated.

po'pone *sm* melon.

'poppa *sf* (*di nave*) stern; (*mammella*) breast; **a** ~ aft, astern.

pop'pante *sm/f* unweaned infant; (*fig: inesperto*) whippersnapper.

pop'pare *vt* to suck.

pop'pata *sf* (*allattamento*) feed.

poppa'toio *sm* (feeding) bottle.

popu'lista, i, e *ag* populist.

por'caio *sm* (*anche fig*) pigsty.

por'cata *sf* (*libro*, *film etc*) load of rubbish; **fare una** ~ **a qn** to play a dirty trick on sb.

porcel'lana [portʃel'lana] *sf* porcelain,

china; (*oggetto*) piece of porcelain.
porcel'lino, a [portʃel'lino] *sm/f* piglet; ~
d'India guinea pig.
porche'ria [porke'ria] *sf* filth, muck; (*fig*:
oscenità) obscenity; (: *azione disonesta*)
dirty trick; (: *cosa mal fatta*) rubbish.
por'chetta [por'ketta] *sf* roast sucking pig.
por'cile [por'tʃile] *sm* pigsty.
por'cino, a [por'tʃino] *ag* of pigs, pork *cpd*
♦ *sm* (*fungo*) *type of edible mushroom*.
'porco, ci *sm* pig; (*carne*) pork.
porcos'pino *sm* porcupine.
'porfido *sm* porphyry.
'porgere ['pɔrdʒere] *vt* to hand, give;
(*tendere*) to hold out.
'porno *ag inv* porn, porno.
pornogra'fia *sf* pornography.
porno'grafico, a, ci, che *ag* pornographic.
'poro *sm* pore.
po'roso, a *ag* porous.
'porpora *sf* purple.
'porre *vt* (*mettere*) to put; (*collocare*) to
place; (*posare*) to lay (down), put (down);
(*fig*: *supporre*): **poniamo (il caso) che ...**
let's suppose that ...; **porsi** *vr* (*mettersi*):
porsi a sedere/in cammino to sit down/
set off; ~ **le basi di** (*fig*) to lay the
foundations of, establish; ~ **una**
domanda a qn to ask sb a question, put
a question to sb; ~ **la propria fiducia in**
qn to place one's trust in sb; ~ **fine** *o*
termine a qc to put an end *o* a stop to sth;
posto che ... supposing that ..., on the
assumption that ...; **porsi in salvo** to save
o.s.
'porro *sm* (*BOT*) leek; (*MED*) wart.
'porsi *etc vb vedi* **porgere**.
'porta *sf* door; (*SPORT*) goal; (*INFORM*) port;
~**e** *sfpl* (*di città*) gates; **mettere qn alla** ~ **to**
throw sb out; **sbattere** *o* **chiudere la** ~ **in**
faccia a qn (*anche fig*) to slam the door in
sb's face; **trovare tutte le** ~**e chiuse** (*fig*)
to find the way barred; **a** ~**e chiuse** (*DIR*)
in camera; **l'inverno è alle** ~**e** (*fig*) winter
is upon us; **vendita** ~ **a** ~ door-to-door
selling; ~ **di servizio** tradesmen's
entrance; ~ **di sicurezza** emergency exit;
~ **stagna** watertight door.
portaba'gagli [portaba'gaʎʎi] *sm inv*
(*facchino*) porter; (*AUT, FERR*) luggage
rack.
portabandi'era *sm inv* standard bearer.
porta'borse *sm inv* (*peg*) lackey.
portabot'tiglie [portabot'tiʎʎe] *sm inv*
bottle rack.
porta'cenere [porta'tʃenere] *sm inv* ashtray.
portachi'avi [porta'kjavi] *sm inv* keyring.
porta'cipria [porta'tʃiprja] *sm inv* powder

compact.
porta'erei *sf inv* (*nave*) aircraft carrier ♦ *sm*
inv (*aereo*) aircraft transporter.
portafi'nestra, *pl* **portefi'nestre** *sf* French
window.
porta'foglio [porta'fɔʎʎo] *sm* (*busta*) wallet;
(*cartella*) briefcase; (*POL, BORSA*)
portfolio; ~ **titoli** investment portfolio.
portagi'oie [porta'dʒɔje] *sm inv*,
portagioi'elli [portadʒo'jɛlli] *sm inv*
jewellery (*BRIT*) *o* jewelry (*US*) box.
por'tale *sm* portal.
porta'lettere *sm/f inv* postman/woman
(*BRIT*), mailman/woman (*US*).
porta'mento *sm* carriage, bearing.
portamo'nete *sm inv* purse.
por'tante *ag* (*muro etc*) supporting, load-
bearing.
portan'tina *sf* sedan chair; (*per ammalati*)
stretcher.
portaog'getti [portaod'dʒɛtti] *ag inv*: **vano**
~ (*in macchina*) glove compartment.
portaom'brelli *sm inv* umbrella stand.
porta'pacchi [porta'pakki] *sm inv* (*di moto,
bicicletta*) luggage rack.
por'tare *vt* (*sostenere, sorreggere: peso,
bambino, pacco*) to carry; (*indossare: abito,
occhiali*) to wear; (: *capelli lunghi*) to have;
(*avere: nome, titolo*) to have, bear; (*recare*):
~ **qc a qn** to take (*o* bring) sth to sb; (*fig*:
sentimenti) to bear; ~**rsi** *vr* (*recarsi*) to go;
~ **avanti** (*discorso, idea*) to pursue; ~ **via**
to take away; (*rubare*) to take; ~ **i bambini**
a spasso to take the children for a walk;
~ **fortuna** to bring good luck; ~ **qc alla**
bocca to lift *o* put sth to one's lips; **porta**
bene i suoi anni he's wearing well; **dove**
porta questa strada? where does this
road lead?, where does this road take
you?; **il documento porta la tua firma** the
document has *o* bears your signature;
non gli porto rancore I don't bear him a
grudge; **la polizia si è portata sul luogo**
del disastro the police went to the scene
of the disaster.
portarit'ratti *sm inv* photo(graph) frame.
portari'viste *sm inv* magazine rack.
portasa'pone *sm inv* soap dish.
portasiga'rette *sm inv* cigarette case.
portas'pilli *sm inv* pincushion.
por'tata *sf* (*vivanda*) course; (*AUT*) carrying
(*o* loading) capacity; (*di arma*) range;
(*volume d'acqua*) (rate of) flow; (*fig: limite*)
scope, capability; (: *importanza*) impact,
import; **alla** ~ **di tutti** (*conoscenza*) within
everybody's capabilities; (*prezzo*) within
everybody's means; **a/fuori** ~ (**di**) within/
out of reach (of); **a** ~ **di mano** within

(arm's) reach; **di grande** ~ of great importance.

por'tatile *ag* portable.

por'tato, a *ag* (*incline*): ~ **a** inclined *o* apt to.

porta'tore, 'trice *sm/f* (*anche COMM*) bearer; (*MED*) carrier; **pagabile al** ~ payable to the bearer; ~ **di handicap** disabled person.

portatovagli'olo [portatovaʎ'ʌɔlo] *sm* napkin ring.

portau'ovo *sm inv* eggcup.

porta'voce [porta'votʃe] *sm/f inv* spokesman/woman.

por'tello *sm* (*di portone*) door; (*NAUT*) hatch.

portel'lone *sm* (*NAUT, AER*) hold door.

por'tento *sm* wonder, marvel.

porten'toso, a *ag* wonderful, marvellous (*BRIT*), marvelous (*US*).

porti'cato *sm* portico.

'portico, ci *sm* portico; (*riparo*) lean-to.

porti'era *sf* (*AUT*) door.

porti'ere *m* (*portinaio*) concierge, caretaker; (*di hotel*) porter; (*nel calcio*) goalkeeper.

porti'naio, a *sm/f* concierge, caretaker.

portine'ria *sf* caretaker's lodge.

'porto, a *pp di* **porgere** ♦ *sm* (*NAUT*) harbour (*BRIT*), harbor (*US*), port; (*spesa di trasporto*) carriage ♦ *sm inv* port (wine); **andare** *o* **giungere in** ~ (*fig*) to come to a successful conclusion; **condurre qc in** ~ to bring sth to a successful conclusion; ~ **d'armi** gun licence (*BRIT*) *o* license (*US*); ~ **fluviale** river port; ~ **franco** free port; ~ **marittimo** seaport; ~ **militare** naval base; ~ **pagato** carriage paid, post free *o* paid; ~ **di scalo** port of call.

Porto'gallo *sm*: **il** ~ Portugal.

porto'ghese [porto'gese] *ag, sm/f, sm* Portuguese *inv*.

por'tone *sm* main entrance, main door.

portori'cano, a *ag, sm/f* Puerto Rican.

Porto'rico *sf* Puerto Rico.

portu'ale *ag* harbour *cpd* (*BRIT*), harbor *cpd* (*US*), port *cpd* ♦ *sm* dock worker.

porzi'one [por'tsjone] *sf* portion, share; (*di cibo*) portion, helping.

'posa *sf* (*FOT*) exposure; (*atteggiamento, di modello*) pose; (*riposo*): **lavorare senza** ~ to work without a break; **mettersi in** ~ to pose; **teatro di** ~ photographic studio.

posa'cenere [posa'tʃenere] *sm inv* ashtray.

po'sare *vt* to put (down), lay (down) ♦ *vi* (*ponte, edificio, teoria*): ~ **su** to rest on; (*FOT, atteggiarsi*) to pose; ~**rsi** *vr* (*ape, aereo*) to land; (*uccello*) to alight;

(*sguardo*) to settle.

po'sata *sf* piece of cutlery; ~**e** *sfpl* cutlery *sg*.

posa'tezza [posa'tettsa] *sf* (*di persona*) composure; (*di discorso*) balanced nature.

po'sato, a *ag* steady; (*discorso*) balanced.

pos'critto *sm* postscript.

'posi *etc vb vedi* **porre**.

positiva'mente *av* positively; (*rispondere*) in the affirmative, affirmatively.

posi'tivo, a *ag* positive.

posizi'one [pozit'tsjone] *sf* position; **farsi una** ~ to make one's way in the world; **prendere** ~ (*fig*) to take a stand; **luci di** ~ (*AUT*) sidelights.

posolo'gia, 'gie [pozolo'dʒia] *sf* dosage, directions *pl* for use.

pos'porre *vt* to place after; (*differire*) to postpone, defer.

pos'posto, a *pp di* **posporre**.

posse'dere *vt* to own, possess (*qualità, virtù*) to have, possess; (*conoscere a fondo: lingua etc*) to have a thorough knowledge of; (*sog: ira etc*) to possess.

possedi'mento *sm* possession.

pos'sente *ag* strong, powerful.

posses'sivo, a *ag* possessive.

pos'sesso *sm* possession; **essere in** ~ **di qc** to be in possession of sth; **prendere** ~ **di qc** to take possession of sth; **entrare in** ~ **dell'eredità** to come into one's inheritance.

posses'sore *sm* owner.

pos'sibile *ag* possible ♦ *sm*: **fare tutto il** ~ to do everything possible; **nei limiti del** ~ as far as possible; **al più tardi** ~ as late as possible; **vieni prima** ~ come as soon as possible.

possibi'lista, i, e *ag*: **essere** ~ to keep an open mind.

possibilità *sf inv* possibility ♦ *sfpl* (*mezzi*) means; **aver la** ~ **di fare** to be in a position to do; to have the opportunity to do; **nei limiti delle nostre** ~ in so far as we can.

possibil'mente *av* if possible.

possi'dente *sm/f* landowner.

possi'edo *etc vb vedi* **possedere**.

'posso *etc vb vedi* **potere**.

post... *prefisso* post....

'posta *sf* (*servizio*) post, postal service; (*corrispondenza*) post, mail; (*ufficio postale*) post office; (*nei giochi d'azzardo*) stake; (*CACCIA*) hide (*BRIT*), blind (*US*); ~**e** *sfpl* (*amministrazione*) post office; **fare la** ~ **a qn** (*fig*) to lie in wait for sb; **la** ~ **in gioco** è **troppo alta** (*fig*) there's too much at stake; **a bella** ~ (*apposta*) on purpose;

piccola ~ (*su giornale*) letters to the editor, letters page; ~ **aerea** airmail; ~ **elettronica** electronic mail; ~ **ordinaria** ≈ second-class mail; **P~e e Telecomunicazioni (PP.TT.)** *postal and telecommunications service*; **ministro delle P~e e Telecomunicazioni** Postmaster General.

posta'giro [posta'dʒiro] *sm* post office cheque (*BRIT*) *o* check (*US*), postal giro (*BRIT*).

pos'tale *ag* postal, post office *cpd* ♦ *sm* (*treno*) mail train; (*nave*) mail boat; (*furgone*) mail van; **timbro** ~ postmark.

postazi'one [postat'tsjone] *sf* (*MIL*) emplacement.

post'bellico, a, ci, che *ag* postwar.

postda'tare *vt* to postdate.

posteggi'are [posted'dʒare] *vt, vi* to park.

posteggia'tore, 'trice [posteddʒa'tore] *sm/f* car-park attendant (*BRIT*), parking-lot attendant (*US*).

pos'teggio [pos'teddʒo] *sm* car park (*BRIT*), parking lot (*US*); (*di taxi*) rank (*BRIT*), stand (*US*).

postelegra'fonico, a, ci, che *ag* postal and telecommunications *cpd*.

'posteri *smpl* posterity *sg*; **i nostri** ~ our descendants.

posteri'ore *ag* (*dietro*) back; (*dopo*) later ♦ *sm* (*fam: sedere*) behind.

posteri'ori: a ~ *ag inv* after the event (*dopo sostantivo*) ♦ *av* looking back.

posterità *sf* posterity.

pos'ticcio, a, ci, ce [pos'tittʃo] *ag* false ♦ *sm* hairpiece.

postici'pare [postitʃi'pare] *vt* to defer, postpone.

pos'tilla *sf* marginal note.

pos'tino *sm* postman (*BRIT*), mailman (*US*).

'posto, a *pp di* **porre** ♦ *sm* (*sito, posizione*) place; (*impiego*) job; (*spazio libero*) room, space; (*di parcheggio*) space; (*sedile: al teatro, in treno etc*) seat; (*MIL*) post; **a** ~ (*in ordine*) in place, tidy; (*fig*) settled; (: *persona*) reliable; **mettere a** ~ (*riordinare*) to tidy (up), put in order; (*faccende: sistemare*) to straighten out; **prender** ~ to take a seat; **al** ~ **di** in place of; **sul** ~ on the spot; ~ **di blocco** roadblock; ~ **di lavoro** job; ~ **di polizia** police station; ~ **telefonico pubblico (P.T.P.)** public telephone; ~ **di villeggiatura** holiday (*BRIT*) *o* tourist spot; ~**i in piedi** (*TEAT, in autobus*) standing room.

postopera'torio, a *ag* (*MED*) postoperative.

pos'tribolo *sm* brothel.

post'scriptum *sm inv* postscript.

'postumo, a *ag* posthumous; (*tardivo*) belated; ~**i** *smpl* (*conseguenze*) aftereffects, consequences.

po'tabile *ag* drinkable; **acqua** ~ drinking water.

po'tare *vt* to prune.

po'tassio *sm* potassium.

pota'tura *sf* pruning.

po'tente *ag* (*nazione*) strong, powerful; (*veleno, farmaco*) potent, strong.

poten'tino, a *ag* of (*o* from) Potenza.

Po'tenza [po'tɛntsa] *sf* Potenza.

po'tenza [po'tɛntsa] *sf* power; (*forza*) strength; **all'ennesima** ~ to the nth degree; **le Grandi P~e** the Great Powers; ~ **militare** military might *o* strength.

potenzi'ale [poten'tsjale] *ag, sm* potential.

potenzia'mento [potentsja'mento] *sm* development.

potenzi'are [poten'tsjare] *vt* to develop.

═══════════════════════ *PAROLA CHIAVE*

po'tere *sm* power; **al** ~ (*partito etc*) in power; ~ **d'acquisto** purchasing power; ~ **esecutivo** executive power; ~ **giudiziario** legal power; ~ **legislativo** legislative power

♦ *vb aus* **1** (*essere in grado di*) can, be able to; **non ha potuto ripararlo** he couldn't *o* he wasn't able to repair it; **non è potuto venire** he couldn't *o* he wasn't able to come; **spiacente di non poter aiutare** sorry not to be able to help

2 (*avere il permesso*) can, may, be allowed to; **posso entrare?** can *o* may I come in?; **posso chiederti dove sei stato?** where, may I ask, have you been?

3 (*eventualità*) may, might, could; **potrebbe essere vero** it might *o* could be true; **può aver avuto un incidente** he may *o* might *o* could have had an accident; **può darsi** perhaps; **può darsi** *o* **può essere che non venga** he may *o* might not come

4 (*augurio*): **potessi almeno parlargli!** if only I could speak to him!

5 (*suggerimento*): **potresti almeno scusarti!** you could at least apologize!

♦ *vt* can, be able to; **può molto per noi** he can do a lot for us; **non ne posso più** (*per stanchezza*) I'm exhausted; (*per rabbia*) I can't take any more.

potestà *sf* (*potere*) power; (*DIR*) authority.

potrò *etc vb vedi* **potere**.

pove'raccio, a, ci, ce [pove'rattʃo] *sm/f* poor devil.

'**povero, a** *ag* poor; (*disadorno*) plain, bare ♦ *smf* poor man/woman; **i** ~**i** the poor; ~ **di** lacking in, having little; **minerale** ~ **di ferro** ore with a low iron content; **paese** ~ **di risorse** country short of *o* lacking in resources.

povertà *sf* poverty.

pozi'one [pot'tsjone] *sf* potion.

'**pozza** ['pottsa] *sf* pool.

poz'zanghera [pot'tsangera] *sf* puddle.

'**pozzo** ['pottso] *sm* well; (*cava: di carbone*) pit; (*di miniera*) shaft; ~ **nero** cesspit; ~ **petrolifero** oil well.

pp. *abbr* (= *pagine*) pp.

p.p. *abbr* (= *per procura*) pp.

P.P.I. *sigla m* (*POL*) (= *Partito Popolare Italiano*) *party originating from D.C.*

PP.SS. *abbr* = **partecipazioni statali.**

PP.TT. *abbr* = **Poste e Telecomunicazioni;** *vedi* **posta.**

PR *sigla* = *Parma* ♦ *sigla m* (*POL*) = *Partito Radicale.*

P.R. *abbr* = **piano regolatore; procuratore della Repubblica.**

'**Praga** *sf* Prague.

prag'matico, a, ci, che *ag* pragmatic.

pram'matica *sf* custom; **essere di** ~ to be customary.

pran'zare [pran'dzare] *vi* to dine, have dinner; to lunch, have lunch.

'**pranzo** ['prandzo] *sm* dinner; (*a mezzogiorno*) lunch.

'**prassi** *sf* usual procedure.

'**pratica, che** *sf* practice; (*esperienza*) experience; (*conoscenza*) knowledge, familiarity; (*tirocinio*) training, practice; (*AMM: affare*) matter, case; (: *incartamento*) file, dossier; **in** ~ (*praticamente*) in practice; **mettere in** ~ to put into practice; **fare le** ~**che per** (*AMM*) to do the paperwork for; ~ **restrittiva** restrictive practice; ~**che illecite** dishonest practices.

prati'cabile *ag* (*progetto*) practicable, feasible; (*luogo*) passable, practicable.

pratica'mente *av* (*in modo pratico*) in a practical way, practically; (*quasi*) practically, almost.

prati'cante *smf* apprentice, trainee; (*REL*) (regular) churchgoer.

prati'care *vt* to practise (*BRIT*), practice (*US*); (*SPORT: tennis etc*) to play; (: *nuoto, scherma etc*) to go in for; (*eseguire: apertura, buco*) to make; ~ **uno sconto** to give a discount.

praticità [pratitʃi'ta] *sf* practicality, practicalness; **per** ~ for practicality's sake.

'**pratico, a, ci, che** *ag* practical; ~ **di** (*esperto*) experienced *o* skilled in; (*familiare*) familiar with; **all'atto** ~ in practice; **è** ~ **del mestiere** he knows his trade; **mi è più** ~ **venire di pomeriggio** it's more convenient for me to come in the afternoon.

'**prato** *sm* meadow; (*di giardino*) lawn.

preal'larme *sm* warning (signal).

Pre'alpi *sfpl*: **le** ~ (the) Pre-Alps.

preal'pino, a *ag* of the Pre-Alps.

pre'ambolo *sm* preamble; **senza tanti** ~**i** without beating about (*BRIT*) *o* around (*US*) the bush.

preannunci'are [preannun'tʃare], **preannunzi'are** [preannun'tsjare] *vt* to give advance notice of.

preavvi'sare *vt* to give advance notice of, warn.

preav'viso *sm* notice; **telefonata con** ~ personal *o* person to person call.

pre'bellico, a, ci, che *ag* prewar *cpd*.

precari'ato *sm* temporary employment.

precarietà *sf* precariousness.

pre'cario, a *ag* precarious; (*INS*) temporary, without tenure.

precauzio'nale [prekautsjo'nale] *ag* precautionary.

precauzi'one [prekaut'tsjone] *sf* caution, care; (*misura*) precaution; **prendere** ~**i** to take precautions.

prece'dente [pretʃe'dɛnte] *ag* previous ♦ *sm* precedent; **il discorso/film** ~ the previous *o* preceding speech/film; **senza** ~**i** unprecedented; ~**i penali** (*DIR*) criminal record *sg*.

precedente'mente [pretʃedente'mente] *av* previously.

prece'denza [pretʃe'dɛntsa] *sf* priority, precedence; (*AUT*) right of way; **dare** ~ **assoluta a qc** to give sth top priority.

pre'cedere [pre'tʃɛdere] *vt* to precede, go (*o come*) before.

precet'tare [pretʃet'tare] *vt* (*lavoratori*) to order back to work (*via an injunction*).

precettazi'one [pretʃettat'tsjone] *sf* (*di lavoratori*) order to resume work.

pre'cetto [pre'tʃɛtto] *sm* precept; (*MIL*) call-up notice.

precet'tore [pretʃet'tore] *sm* (private) tutor.

precipi'tare [pretʃipi'tare] *vi* (*cadere*) to fall headlong; (*fig: situazione*) to get out of control ♦ *vt* (*gettare dall'alto in basso*) to hurl, fling; (*fig: affrettare*) to rush; ~**rsi** *vr* (*gettarsi*) to hurl *o* fling o.s.; (*affrettarsi*) to rush.

precipi'tato, a [pretʃipi'tato] *ag* hasty ♦ *sm* (*CHIM*) precipitate.

precipitazi'one [pretʃipitat'tsjone] *sf* (*METEOR*) precipitation; (*fig*) haste.

precipi'toso, a [pretʃipi'toso] *ag* (*caduta, fuga*) headlong; (*fig: avventato*) rash, reckless; (: *affrettato*) hasty, rushed.

preci'pizio [pretʃi'pittsjo] *sm* precipice; **a ~** (*fig: correre*) headlong.

pre'cipuo, a [pre'tʃipuo] *ag* principal, main.

precisa'mente [pretʃiza'mente] *av* (*gen*) precisely; (*con esattezza*) exactly.

preci'sare [pretʃi'zare] *vt* to state, specify; (*spiegare*) to explain (in detail); **vi preciseremo la data in seguito** we'll let you know the exact date later; **tengo a ~ che** ... I must point out that ....

precisazi'one [pretʃizat'tsjone] *sf* clarification.

precisi'one [pretʃi'zjone] *sf* precision; accuracy; **strumenti di ~** precision instruments.

pre'ciso, a [pre'tʃizo] *ag* (*esatto*) precise; (*accurato*) accurate, precise; (*deciso*: *idea*) precise, definite; (*uguale*): **2 vestiti ~i** 2 dresses exactly the same; **sono le 9 ~e** it's exactly 9 o'clock.

pre'cludere *vt* to block, obstruct.

pre'cluso, a *pp di* **precludere.**

pre'coce [pre'kɔtʃe] *ag* early; (*bambino*) precocious; (*vecchiaia*) premature.

precocità [prekotʃi'ta] *sf* (*di morte*) untimeliness; (*di bambino*) precociousness.

precon'cetto, a [prekon'tʃɛtto] *ag* preconceived **♦** *sm* preconceived idea, prejudice.

pre'correre *vt* to anticipate; **~ i tempi** to be ahead of one's time.

precorri'tore, 'trice *sm/f* precursor, forerunner.

pre'corso, a *pp di* **precorrere.**

precur'sore *sm* forerunner, precursor.

'preda *sf* (*bottino*) booty; (*animale, fig*) prey; **essere ~ di** to fall prey to; **essere in ~ a** to be prey to.

pre'dare *vt* to plunder.

preda'tore *sm* predator.

predeces'sore, a [predetʃes'sore] *sm/f* predecessor.

pre'della *sf* platform, dais; altar-step.

predesti'nare *vt* to predestine.

predestinazi'one [predestinat'tsjone] *sf* predestination.

pre'detto, a *pp di* **predire ♦** *ag* aforesaid, aforementioned.

'predica, che *sf* sermon; (*fig*) lecture, talking-to.

predi'care *vt, vi* to preach.

predica'tivo, a *ag* predicative.

predi'cato *sm* (*LING*) predicate.

predi'letto, a *pp di* **prediligere ♦** *ag, sm/f* favourite (*BRIT*), favorite (*US*).

predilezi'one [predilet'tsjone] *sf* fondness, partiality; **avere una ~ per qc/qn** to be partial to sth/fond of sb.

predi'ligere [predi'lidʒere] *vt* to prefer, have a preference for.

pre'dire *vt* to foretell, predict.

predis'porre *vt* to get ready, prepare; **~ qn a qc** to predispose sb to sth.

predisposizi'one [predispozit'tsjone] *sf* (*MED*) predisposition; (*attitudine*) bent, aptitude; **avere ~ alla musica** to have a bent for music.

predis'posto, a *pp di* **predisporre.**

predizi'one [predit'tsjone] *sf* prediction.

predomi'nante *ag* predominant.

predomi'nare *vi* (*prevalere*) to predominate; (*eccellere*) to excel.

predo'minio *sm* predominance; supremacy.

preesis'tente *ag* pre-existent.

pree'sistere *vi* to pre-exist.

preesis'tito, a *pp di* **preesistere.**

prefabbri'cato, a *ag* (*EDIL*) prefabricated.

prefazi'one [prefat'tsjone] *sf* preface, foreword.

prefe'renza [prefe'rɛntsa] *sf* preference; **a ~ di** rather than; **di ~** preferably, by preference; **non ho ~e** I have no preferences either way, I don't mind.

preferenzi'ale [preferen'tsjale] *ag* preferential; **corsia ~** (*AUT*) bus and taxi lane.

prefe'ribile *ag*: **~ (a)** preferable (to), better (than); **sarebbe ~ andarsene** it would be better to go.

preferibil'mente *av* preferably.

prefe'rire *vt* to prefer, like better; **~ il caffè al tè** to prefer coffee to tea, like coffee better than tea.

pre'fetto *sm* prefect.

prefet'tura *sf* prefecture.

pre'figgersi [pre'fiddʒersi] *vr*: **~rsi uno scopo** to set o.s. a goal.

prefigu'rare *vt* (*simboleggiare*) to foreshadow; (*prevedere*) to foresee.

pre'fisso, a *pp di* **prefiggersi ♦** *sm* (*LING*) prefix; (*TEL*) dialling (*BRIT*) *o* dial (*US*) code.

Preg. *abbr* = **pregiatissimo.**

pre'gare *vi* to pray **♦** *vt* (*REL*) to pray to; (*implorare*) to beg; (*chiedere*): **~ qn di fare** to ask sb to do; **farsi ~** to need coaxing *o* persuading.

pre'gevole [pre'dʒevole] *ag* valuable.

pregherò *etc* [prege'rɔ] *vb vedi* **pregare.**

preghi'era [pre'gjɛra] *sf* (*REL*) prayer; (*domanda*) request.

pregi'arsi [pre'dʒarsi] *vr*: **mi pregio di farle sapere che ...** I am pleased to inform you that ....

pregia'tissimo, a [predʒa'tissimo] *ag* (*in lettere*): ~ **Signor G. Agnelli** G. Agnelli Esquire.

pregi'ato, a [pre'dʒato] *ag* (*opera*) valuable; (*tessuto*) fine; (*valuta*) strong; **vino** ~ vintage wine.

'pregio ['prɛdʒo] *sm* (*stima*) esteem, regard; (*qualità*) (good) quality, merit; (*valore*) value, worth; **il** ~ **di questo sistema è ...** the merit of this system is ...; **oggetto di** ~ valuable object.

pregiudi'care [predʒudi'kare] *vt* to prejudice, harm, be detrimental to.

pregiudi'cato, a [predʒudi'kato] *sm/f* (*DIR*) previous offender.

pregiu'dizio [predʒu'dittsjo] *sm* (*idea errata*) prejudice; (*danno*) harm *m* *pl*.

preg'nante [pren'nante] *ag* (*fig*) pregnant, meaningful.

'pregno, a ['prenno] *ag* (*saturo*): ~ **di** full of, saturated with.

'prego *escl* (*a chi ringrazia*) don't mention it!; (*invitando qn ad accomodarsi*) please sit down!; (*invitando qn ad andare prima*) after you!

pregus'tare *vt* to look forward to.

preis'toria *sf* prehistory.

preis'torico, a, ci, che *ag* prehistoric.

pre'lato *sm* prelate.

prela'vaggio [prela'vaddʒo] *sm* pre-wash.

prelazi'one [prelat'tsjone] *sf* (*DIR*) pre-emption; **avere il diritto di** ~ **su qc** to have the first option on sth.

preleva'mento *sm* (*BANCA*) withdrawal; (*di merce*) picking up, collection.

prele'vare *vt* (*denaro*) to withdraw; (*campione*) to take; (*merce*) to pick up, collect; (*sog: polizia*) to take, capture.

preli'evo *sm* (*BANCA*) withdrawal; (*MED*): **fare un** ~ (**di**) to take a sample (of).

prelimi'nare *ag* preliminary; ~**i** *smpl* preliminary talks; preliminaries.

pre'ludere *vi*: ~ **a** (*preannunciare: crisi, guerra, temporale*) to herald, be a sign of; (*introdurre: dibattito etc*) to introduce, be a prelude to.

pre'ludio *sm* prelude.

pre'luso, a *pp di* **preludere**.

pre-ma'man [prema'mã] *sm inv* maternity dress.

prematrimoni'ale *ag* premarital.

prema'turo, a *ag* premature.

premedi'tare *vt* to premeditate, plan.

premeditazi'one [premeditat'tsjone] *sf* (*DIR*) premeditation; **con** ~ *ag* premeditated ♦ *av* with intent.

'premere *vt* to press ♦ *vi*: ~ **su** to press down on; (*fig*) to put pressure on; ~ **a** (*fig: importare*) to matter to; ~ **il grilletto** to pull the trigger.

pre'messo, a *pp di* **premettere** ♦ *sf* introductory statement, introduction; **mancano le** ~**e per una buona riuscita** we lack the basis for a successful outcome.

pre'mettere *vt* to put before; (*dire prima*) to start by saying, state first; **premetto che ...** I must say first of all that ...; **premesso che ...** given that ...; **ciò premesso ...** that having been said ....

premi'are *vt* to give a prize to; (*fig: merito, onestà*) to reward.

premiazi'one [premjat'tsjone] *sf* prize giving.

'premier ['prɛmjɛr] *sm inv* **premier**.

pre'minente *ag* pre-eminent.

'premio *sm* prize; (*ricompensa*) reward; (*COMM*) premium; (*AMM: indennità*) bonus; **in** ~ **per** as a prize (*o* reward) for; ~ **d'ingaggio** (*SPORT*) signing-on fee; ~ **di produzione** productivity bonus.

pre'misi *etc vb vedi* **premettere**.

premoni'tore, 'trice *ag* premonitory.

premonizi'one [premonit'tsjone] *sf* premonition.

premu'nirsi *vr*: ~ **di** to provide o.s. with; ~ **contro** to protect o.s. from, guard o.s. against.

pre'mura *sf* (*fretta*) haste, hurry; (*riguardo*) attention, care; **aver** ~ to be in a hurry; **far** ~ **a qn** to hurry sb; **usare ogni** ~ **nei riguardi di qn, circondare qn di** ~**e** to be very attentive to sb.

premu'roso, a *ag* thoughtful, considerate.

prena'tale *ag* antenatal.

'prendere *vt* to take; (*andare a prendere*) to get, fetch; (*ottenere*) to get; (*guadagnare*) to get, earn; (*catturare: ladro, pesce*) to catch; (*collaboratore, dipendente*) to take on; (*passeggero*) to pick up; (*chiedere: somma, prezzo*) to charge, ask; (*trattare: persona*) to handle ♦ *vi* (*colla, cemento*) to set; (*pianta*) to take; (*fuoco: nel camino*) to catch; (*voltare*): ~ **a destra** to turn (to the) right; ~**rsi** *vr* (*azzuffarsi*): ~**rsi a pugni** to come to blows; **prende qualcosa?** (*da bere, da mangiare*) would you like something to eat (*o* drink)?; **prendo un caffè** I'll have a coffee; ~ **a fare qc** to start doing sth; ~ **qn/qc per** (*scambiare*) to take sb/sth for; ~ **l'abitudine di** to get into the habit of; ~ **fuoco** to catch fire; ~ **le generalità di qn**

to take down sb's particulars; ~ **nota di** to take note of; ~ **parte a** to take part in; ~**rsi cura di qn/qc** to look after sb/sth; ~**rsi un impegno** to take on a commitment; **prendersela** (*adirarsi*) to get annoyed; (*preoccuparsi*) to get upset, worry.

prendi'sole *sm inv* sundress.

preno'tare *vt* to book, reserve.

prenotazi'one [prenotat'tsjone] *sf* booking, reservation.

'prensile *ag* prehensile.

preoccu'pante *ag* worrying.

preoccu'pare *vt* to worry; ~**rsi** *vr*: ~**rsi di qn/qc** to worry about sb/sth; ~**rsi per qn** to be anxious for sb.

preoccupazi'one [preokkupat'tsjone] *sf* worry, anxiety.

preordi'nato, a *ag* preordained.

prepa'rare *vt* to prepare; (*esame, concorso*) to prepare for; ~**rsi** *vr* (*vestirsi*) to get ready; ~**rsi a qc/a fare** to get ready *o* prepare (o.s.) for sth/to do; ~ **da mangiare** to prepare a meal.

prepara'tivi *smpl* preparations.

prepa'rato, a *ag* (*gen*) prepared; (*pronto*) ready ♦ *sm* (*prodotto*) preparation.

prepara'torio, a *ag* preparatory.

preparazi'one [preparat'tsjone] *sf* preparation; **non ha la necessaria ~ per svolgere questo lavoro** he lacks the qualifications necessary for the job.

prepensiona'mento *sm* early retirement.

preponde'rante *ag* predominant.

pre'porre *vt* to place before; (*fig*) to prefer.

preposizi'one [prepozit'tsjone] *sf* (*LING*) preposition.

pre'posto, a *pp di* **preporre**.

prepo'tente *ag* (*persona*) domineering, arrogant; (*bisogno, desiderio*) overwhelming, pressing ♦ *smf* bully.

prepo'tenza [prepo'tɛntsa] *sf* arrogance; (*comportamento*) arrogant behaviour (*BRIT*) *o* behavior (*US*).

pre'puzio [pre'puttsjo] *sm* (*ANAT*) foreskin.

preroga'tiva *sf* prerogative.

'presa *sf* taking *no pl*; catching *no pl*; (*di città*) capture; (*indurimento: di cemento*) setting; (*appiglio, SPORT*) hold; (*di acqua, gas*) (supply) point; (*ELETTR*): ~ **(di corrente)** socket; (: *al muro*) point; (*piccola quantità: di sale etc*) pinch; (*CARTE*) trick; **far ~** (*colla*) to set; **ha fatto ~ sul pubblico** (*fig*) it caught the public's imagination; **a ~ rapida** (*cemento*) quick-setting; **di forte ~** (*fig*) with wide appeal; **essere alle ~e con qc** (*fig*) to be struggling with sth;

macchina da ~ (*CINE*) cine camera (*BRIT*), movie camera (*US*); ~ **d'aria** air inlet; ~ **diretta** (*AUT*) direct drive; ~ **in giro** leg-pull (*BRIT*), joke; ~ **di posizione** stand.

pre'sagio [pre'zadʒo] *sm* omen.

presa'gire [preza'dʒire] *vt* to foresee.

presa'lario *sm* (*INS*) grant.

'presbite *ag* long-sighted.

presbiteri'ano, a *ag, smf* Presbyterian.

presbi'terio *sm* presbytery.

pre'scindere [preʃ'ʃindere] *vi*: ~ **da** to leave out of consideration; ~ **da** apart from.

pre'scisso, a [preʃ'ʃisso] *pp di* **prescindere**.

presco'lastico, a, ci, che *ag* pre-school *cpd*.

pres'critto, a *pp di* **prescrivere**.

pres'crivere *vt* to prescribe.

prescrizi'one [preskrit'tsjone] *sf* (*MED, DIR*) prescription; (*norma*) rule, regulation; **cadere in ~** (*DIR*) to become statute-barred.

'prese *etc vb vedi* **prendere**.

presen'tare *vt* to present; (*far conoscere*): ~ **qn (a)** to introduce sb (to); (*AMM*: *inoltrare*) to submit; ~**rsi** *vr* (*recarsi, farsi vedere*) to present o.s., appear; (*farsi conoscere*) to introduce o.s.; (*occasione*) to arise; ~ **qc in un'esposizione** to show *o* display sth at an exhibition; ~ **qn in società** to introduce sb into society; ~**rsi come candidato** (*POL*) to stand (*BRIT*) *o* run (*US*) as a candidate; ~**rsi bene/male** to have a good/poor appearance; **la situazione si presenta difficile** things aren't looking too good, things look a bit tricky.

presentazi'one [prezentat'tsjone] *sf* presentation; introduction.

pre'sente *ag* present; (*questo*) this ♦ *sm* present ♦ *sf* (*lettera*): **con la ~ vi comunico ... this is to inform you that ...** ♦ *smf* person present; **i ~i** those present; **aver ~ qc/qn** to remember sth/sb; **essere ~ a una riunione** to be present at *o* attend a meeting; **tener ~ qn/qc** to keep sb/sth in mind; **esclusi i ~i** present company excepted.

presenti'mento *sm* premonition.

pre'senza [pre'zɛntsa] *sf* presence; (*aspetto esteriore*) appearance; **in ~ di** in (the) presence of; **di bella ~** of good appearance; ~ **di spirito** presence of mind.

presenzi'are [prezen'tsjare] *vi*: ~ **a** to be present at, attend.

pre'sepio, pre'sepe *sm* crib.

preser'vare *vt* to protect.

preserva'tivo *sm* sheath, condom.

'presi etc vb vedi **prendere**.
'preside smlf (INS) head (teacher) (BRIT), principal (US); (di facoltà universitaria) dean.
presi'dente sm (POL) president; (di assemblea, COMM) chairman; **il P~ della Camera** (POL) ≈ the Speaker; **P~ del Consiglio (dei Ministri)** ≈ Prime Minister; **P~ della Repubblica** President of the Republic; vedi nota nel riquadro.

PRESIDENTE

The **Presidente del Consiglio**, the Italian Prime Minister, is the leader of the Government. He or she submits nominations for ministerial posts to the "Presidente della Repubblica", who then appoints them if approved. The **Presidente del Consiglio** is appointed by the "Presidente della Repubblica", in consultation with the leaders of the parliamentary parties, former heads of state, the "Presidente della Camera" and the "Presidente del Senato". The **Presidente della Repubblica** is the head of state. He or she must be an Italian citizen of at least 50 years of age, and is elected by Parliament and by three delegates from each of the Italian regions. Remaining in office for seven years, the **Presidente della Repubblica** has the power to call an election, dissolve one or both chambers of Parliament, or call a referendum.

---

presiden'tessa sf president; (moglie) president's wife; (di assemblea, COMM) chairwoman.
presi'denza [presi'dɛntsa] sf presidency; office of president; chairmanship; **assumere la ~** to become president; to take the chair; **essere alla ~** to be president (o chairman); **candidato alla ~** presidential candidate; candidate for the chairmanship.
presidenzi'ale [presidɛn'tsjale] ag presidential.
presidi'are vt to garrison.
pre'sidio sm garrison.
presi'edere vt to preside over ♦ vi: **~ a** to direct, be in charge of.
'preso, a pp di **prendere**.
'pressa sf (TECN) press.
pres'sante ag (bisogno, richiesta) urgent, pressing.
pressap'poco av about, roughly, approximately.
pres'sare vt (anche fig) to press; **~ qn con richieste** to pursue sb with demands.

pressi'one sf pressure; **far ~ su qn** to put pressure on sb; **subire forti ~i** to be under strong pressure; **~ sanguigna** blood pressure.
'presso av (vicino) nearby, close at hand ♦ prep (vicino a) near; (accanto a) beside, next to; (in casa di): **~ qn** at sb's home; (nelle lettere) care of (abbr c/o); (alle dipendenza di): **lavora ~ di noi** he works for o with us ♦ smpl: **nei ~i di** near, in the vicinity of; **ha avuto grande successo ~ i giovani** it has been a hit with young people.
pressoché [presso'ke] av nearly, almost.
pressuriz'zare [pressurid'dzare] vt to pressurize.
prestabi'lire vt to arrange beforehand, arrange in advance.
presta'nome smlf inv (peg) figurehead.
pres'tante ag good-looking
pres'tanza [pres'tantsa] sf (robust) good looks pl.
pres'tare vt: **~ (qc a qn)** to lend (sb sth o sth to sb); **~rsi** vr (offrirsi): **~rsi a fare** to offer to do; (essere adatto): **~rsi a** to lend itself to, be suitable for; **~ aiuto** to lend a hand; **~ ascolto o orecchio** to listen; **~ attenzione** to pay attention; **~ fede a qc/ qn** to give credence to sth/sb; **~ giuramento** to take an oath; **la frase si presta a molteplici interpretazioni** the phrase lends itself to numerous interpretations.
prestazi'one [prestat'tsjone] sf (TECN, SPORT) performance, **~i** sfpl (di persona: servizi) services.
prestigia'tore, 'trice [prestidʒa'tore] smlf conjurer.
pres'tigio [pres'tidʒo] sm (potere) prestige; (illusione): **gioco di ~** conjuring trick.
prestigi'oso, a [presti'dʒoso] ag prestigious.
'prestito sm lending no pl; loan; **dar in ~** to lend; **prendere in ~** to borrow; **~ bancario** bank loan; **~ pubblico** public borrowing.
'presto av (tra poco) soon; (in fretta) quickly; (di buon'ora) early; **a ~** see you soon; **~ o tardi** sooner or later; **fare ~ a fare qc** to hurry up and do sth; (non costare fatica) to have no trouble doing sth; **si fa ~ a criticare** it's easy to criticize; **è ancora ~ per decidere** it's still too early o too soon to decide.
pre'sumere vt to presume, assume.
presu'mibile ag (dati, risultati) likely.
pre'sunsi etc vb vedi **presumere**.

pre'sunto, a *pp di* **presumere** ◆ *ag*: **il** ~ **colpevole** the alleged culprit.

presuntu'oso, a *ag* presumptuous.

presunzi'one [prezun'tsjone] *sf* presumption.

presup'porre *vt* to suppose; to presuppose.

presup'posto, a *pp di* **presupporre** ◆ *sm* (*premessa*) supposition, premise; **partendo dal** ~ **che** ... assuming that ...; **mancano i** ~**i necessari** the necessary conditions are lacking.

'prete *sm* priest.

preten'dente *smf* pretender ◆ *sm* (*corteggiatore*) suitor.

pre'tendere *vt* (*esigere*) to demand, require; (*sostenere*): ~ **che** to claim that; **pretende di aver sempre ragione** he thinks he's always right.

pretenzi'oso, a [preten'tsjoso] *ag* pretentious.

preterintenzio'nale [preterintentsjo'nale] *ag* (*DIR*): **omicidio** ~ manslaughter.

pre'teso, a *pp di* **pretendere** ◆ *sf* (*esigenza*) claim, demand; (*presunzione, sfarzo*) pretentiousness; **avanzare una** ~**a** to put forward a claim *o* demand; **senza** ~**e** *ag* unpretentious ◆ *av* unpretentiously.

pre'testo *sm* pretext, excuse; **con il** ~ **di** on the pretext of.

pretestu'oso, a *ag* (*data, motivo*) used as an excuse.

pre'tore *sm* magistrate.

pre'tura *sf* (*DIR*: *sede*) magistrate's court (*BRIT*), circuit *o* superior court (*US*); (: *magistratura*) magistracy.

preva'lente *ag* prevailing.

prevalente'mente *av* mainly, for the most part.

preva'lenza [preva'lɛntsa] *sf* predominance.

preva'lere *vi* to prevail.

pre'valso, a *pp di* **prevalere**.

prevari'care *vi* (*abusare del potere*) to abuse one's power.

prevaricazi'one [prevarikat'tsjone] *sf* (*abuso di potere*) abuse of power.

preve'dere *vt* (*indovinare*) to foresee; (*presagire*) to foretell; (*considerare*) to make provision for; **nulla lasciava** ~ **che** ... there was nothing to suggest *o* to make one think that ...; **come previsto** as expected; **spese previste** anticipated expenditure; **previsto per martedì** scheduled for Tuesday.

prev'edibile *ag* predictable; **non era assolutamente** ~ **che** ... no one could have foreseen that ....

prevedibil'mente *av* as one would expect.

preve'nire *vt* (*anticipare: obiezione*) to forestall; (: *domanda*) to anticipate; (*evitare*) to avoid, prevent; (*avvertire*): ~ **qn (di)** to warn sb (of); to inform sb (of).

preventi'vare *vt* (*COMM*) to estimate.

preven'tivo, a *ag* preventive ◆ *sm* (*COMM*) estimate; **fare un** ~ to give an estimate; **bilancio** ~ budget; **carcere** ~ custody (*pending trial*).

preve'nuto, a *ag* (*mal disposto*): ~ **(contro qc/qn)** prejudiced (against sth/sb).

prevenzi'one [preven'tsjone] *sf* prevention; (*preconcetto*) prejudice.

previ'dente *ag* showing foresight; prudent.

previ'denza [previ'dɛntsa] *sf* foresight; **istituto di** ~ provident institution; ~ **sociale** social security (*BRIT*), welfare (*US*).

pre'vidi *etc vb vedi* **prevedere**.

'previo, a *ag* (*COMM*): ~ **avviso** upon notice; ~ **pagamento** upon payment.

previsi'one *sf* forecast, prediction; ~**i meteorologiche** *o* **del tempo** weather forecast *sg*.

pre'visto, a *pp di* **prevedere** ◆ *sm*: **più/meno del** ~ more/less than expected; **prima del** ~ earlier than expected.

prezi'oso, a [pret'tsjoso] *ag* precious; (*aiuto, consiglio*) invaluable ◆ *sm* jewel; valuable.

prez'zemolo [pret'tsemolo] *sm* parsley.

'prezzo ['prɛttso] *sm* price; **a** ~ **di costo** at cost, at cost price (*BRIT*); **tirare sul** ~ to bargain, haggle; **il** ~ **pattuito è 1.000.000 di lire** the agreed price is 1,000,000 lire; ~ **d'acquisto/di vendita** buying/selling price; ~ **di fabbrica** factory price; ~ **di mercato** market price; ~ **scontato** reduced price; ~ **unitario** unit price.

P.R.I. *sigla m* (= *Partito Repubblicano Italiano*) *former political party*.

prigi'one [pri'dʒone] *sf* prison.

prigio'nia [pridʒo'nia] *sf* imprisonment.

prigioni'ero, a [pridʒo'njɛro] *ag* captive ◆ *smf* prisoner.

'prima *sf vedi* **primo** ◆ *av* before; (*in anticipo*) in advance, beforehand; (*per l'addietro*) at one time, formerly; (*più presto*) sooner, earlier; (*in primo luogo*) first ◆ *cong*: ~ **di fare/che parta** before doing/he leaves; ~ **di** *prep* before; ~ **o poi** sooner or later; **due giorni** ~ two days before *o* earlier; ~ **d'ora** before now.

pri'mario, a *ag* primary; (*principale*) chief, leading, primary ◆ *smf* (*medico*) head physician, chief physician.

pri'mate *sm* (*REL, ZOOL*) primate.
prima'tista, i, e *sm/f* (*SPORT*) record holder.
pri'mato *sm* supremacy; (*SPORT*) record.
prima'vera *sf* spring.
primave'rile *ag* spring *cpd.*
primeggi'are [primed'dʒare] *vi* to excel, be one of the best.
primi'tivo, a *ag* (*gen*) primitive; (*significato*) original
pri'mizie [pri'mittsje] *sfpl* early produce *sg.*
'primo, a *ag* first; (*fig*) initial; basic; prime ♦ *sm/f* first (one) ♦ *sm* (*CUC*) first course; (*in date*): **il ~ luglio** the first of July ♦ *sf* (*TEAT*) first night; (*CINE*) première; (*AUT*) first (gear); **le ~e ore del mattino** the early hours of the morning; **di ~a mattina** early in the morning; **in ~a pagina** (*STAMPA*) on the front page; **ai ~i freddi** at the first sign of cold weather, **ai ~i di maggio** at the beginning of May; **i ~i del Novecento** the early twentieth century; **viaggiare in ~a** to travel **first** class; **per ~a cosa** firstly, **in ~ luogo** first of all, in the first place; **di prim'ordine** *o* **~a qualità** first-class, first-rate; **in un ~ tempo** *o* **momento** at first; **~a donna** leading lady; (*di opera lirica*) prima donna.
primo'genito, a [primo'dʒenito] *ag, sm/f* firstborn.
pri'mordi *smpl* beginnings.
primordi'ale *ag* primordial.
'primula *sf* primrose.
princi'pale [printʃi'pale] *ag* main, principal ♦ *sm* manager, boss; **sede ~** head office.
principal'mente [printʃipal'mente] *av* mainly, principally.
princi'pato [printʃi'pato] *sm* principality.
'principe ['printʃipe] *sm* prince; **~ ereditario** crown prince.
princi'pesco, a, schi, sche [printʃi'pesko] *ag* (*anche fig*) princely.
princi'pessa [printʃi'pessa] *sf* princess.
principi'ante [printʃi'pjante] *sm/f* beginner.
principi'are [printʃi'pjare] *vt, vi* to start, begin.
prin'cipio [prin'tʃipjo] *sm* (*inizio*) beginning, start; (*origine*) origin, cause; (*concetto, norma*) principle; **al** *o* **in ~** at first; **fin dal ~** right from the start; **per ~** on principle; **una questione di ~** a matter of principle; **una persona di sani ~i morali** a person of sound moral principles; **~ attivo** active ingredient.
pri'ore *sm* (*REL*) prior.
pri'ori: a ~ *ag inv* prior; **a priori** ♦ *av* at first glance; initially; a priori.
priorità *sf* priority; **avere la ~ (su)** to have

priority (over).
priori'tario, a *ag* having priority, of utmost importance.
'prisma, i *sm* prism.
pri'vare *vt*: **~ qn di** to deprive sb of; **~rsi** *vr*: **~rsi di** to go *o* do without.
priva'tiva *sf* (*ECON*) monopoly.
privatiz'zare [privatid'dzare] *vt* to privatize.
privatizzazi'one [privatiddzat'tsjone] *sf* privatization.
pri'vato, a *ag* private ♦ *sm/f* (*anche*: **~ cittadino**) private citizen; **in ~** in private; **diritto ~** (*DIR*) civil law; **ritirarsi a vita ~a** to withdraw from public life; **"non vendiamo a ~i"** "wholesale only".
privazi'one [privat'tsjone] *sf* privation, hardship.
privilegi'are [privile'dʒare] *vt* to favour (*BRIT*), favor (*US*).
privilegi'ato, a [privile'dʒato] *ag* (*individuo, classe*) privileged; (*trattamento, COMM: credito*) preferential; **azioni ~e** preference shares (*BRIT*), preferred stock (*US*).
privi'legio [privi'ledʒo] *sm* privilege; **avere il ~ di fare** to have the privilege of doing, be privileged to do.
'privo, a *ag*: **~ di** without, lacking.
pro *prep* for, on behalf of ♦ *sm inv* (*utilità*) advantage, benefit; **a che ~?** what's the use?; **il ~ e il contro** the pros and cons.
pro'babile *ag* probable, likely.
probabilità *sf inv* probability; **con molta ~** very probably, in all probability.
probabil'mente *av* probably.
pro'bante *ag* convincing.
pro'blema, i *sm* problem.
proble'matico, a, ci, che *ag* problematic; (*incerto*) doubtful ♦ *sf* problems *pl.*
pro'boscide [pro'bɔʃʃide] *sf* (*di elefante*) trunk.
procacci'are [prokat'tʃare] *vt* to get, obtain.
procaccia'tore [prokattʃa'tore] *sm*: **~ d'affari** sales executive.
pro'cace [pro'katʃe] *ag* (*donna, aspetto*) provocative.
pro'cedere [pro'tʃedere] *vi* to proceed; (*comportarsi*) to behave; (*iniziare*): **~ a** to start; **~ contro** (*DIR*) to start legal proceedings against; **~ oltre** to go on ahead; **prima di ~ oltre** before going any further; **gli affari procedono bene** business is going well; **bisogna ~ con cautela** we have to proceed cautiously; **non luogo a ~** (*DIR*) nonsuit.
procedi'mento [protʃedi'mento] *sm* (*modo di condurre*) procedure; (*di avvenimenti*) course; (*TECN*) process; **~ penale** (*DIR*)

criminal proceedings *pl.*
proce'dura [protʃe'dura] *sf* (*DIR*) procedure.
proces'sare [protʃes'sare] *vt* (*DIR*) to try.
processi'one [protʃes'sjone] *sf* procession.
pro'cesso [pro'tʃɛsso] *sm* (*DIR*) trial;
proceedings *pl*; (*metodo*) process; **essere
sotto** ~ to be on trial; **mettere sotto** ~
(*anche fig*) to put on trial; ~ **di
fabbricazione** manufacturing process; ~
di pace peace process.
processu'ale [protʃessu'ale] *ag* (*DIR*): **atti** ~**i**
records of a trial; **spese** ~**i** legal costs.
Proc. Gen. *abbr* = **procuratore generale.**
pro'cinto [pro'tʃinto] *sm*: **in** ~ **di fare** about
to do, on the point of doing.
pro'clama, i *sm* proclamation.
procla'mare *vt* to proclaim.
proclamazi'one [proklamat'tsjone] *sf*
proclamation, declaration.
procrasti'nare *vt* (*data*) to postpone;
(*pagamento*) to defer.
procre'are *vt* to procreate.
pro'cura *sf* (*DIR*) proxy, power of attorney;
(*ufficio*) attorney's office; **per** ~ by proxy;
la P~ della Repubblica the Public
Prosecutor's Office.
procu'rare *vt*: ~ **qc a qn** (*fornire*) to get *o*
obtain sth for sb; (*causare*: *noie etc*) to
bring *o* give sb sth.
procura'tore, 'trice *sm/f* (*DIR*) ≈ solicitor;
(*: chi ha la procura*) holder of power of
attorney; ~ **generale** (*in corte d'appello*)
public prosecutor; (*in corte di cassazione*)
Attorney General; ~ **legale** ≈ solicitor
(*BRIT*), lawyer; ~ **della Repubblica** (*in corte
d'assise, tribunale*) public prosecutor.
prodi'gare *vt* to be lavish with; ~**rsi** *vr*:
~**rsi per qn** to do all one can for sb.
pro'digio [pro'didʒo] *sm* marvel, wonder;
(*persona*) prodigy.
prodigi'oso, a [prodi'dʒoso] *ag* prodigious;
phenomenal.
'prodigo, a, ghi, ghe *ag* lavish,
extravagant.
pro'dotto, a *pp di* **produrre** ◊ *sm* product; ~
di base primary product; ~ **finale** end
product; ~ **interno lordo (PIL)** gross
domestic product (GDP); ~ **nazionale
lordo (PNL)** gross national product
(GNP); ~**i agricoli** farm produce *sg*; ~**i di
bellezza** cosmetics; ~**i chimici** chemicals.
pro'duco *etc vb vedi* **produrre.**
pro'durre *vt* to produce.
pro'dussi *etc vb vedi* **produrre.**
produttività *sf* productivity.
produt'tivo, a *ag* productive.
produt'tore, 'trice *ag* producing *cpd* ◊ *sm/f*
producer; **paese** ~ **di petrolio** oil-

producing country.
produzi'one [produt'tsjone] *sf* production;
(*rendimento*) output; ~ **in serie** mass
production.
pro'emio *sm* introduction, preface.
Prof. *abbr* (= *professore*) Prof.
profa'nare *vt* to desecrate.
pro'fano, a *ag* (*mondano*) secular, profane;
(*sacrilego*) profane.
profe'rire *vt* to utter.
profes'sare *vt* to profess; (*medicina etc*) to
practise (*BRIT*), practice (*US*).
professio'nale *ag* professional; **scuola** ~
training college.
professi'one *sf* profession; **di** ~
professional, by profession; **libera** ~
profession.
professio'nista, i, e *sm/f* professional.
profes'sore, 'essa *sm/f* (*INS*) teacher; (*: di
università*) lecturer; (*: titolare di cattedra*)
professor; ~ **d'orchestra** member of an
orchestra.
pro'feta, i *sm* prophet.
pro'fetico, a, ci, che *ag* prophetic.
profetiz'zare [profetid'dzare] *vt* to
prophesy.
profe'zia [profet'tsia] *sf* prophecy.
pro'ficuo, a *ag* useful, profitable.
profi'lare *vt* to outline; (*ornare*: *vestito*) to
edge; ~**rsi** *vr* to stand out, be silhouetted;
to loom up.
profi'lassi *sf* (*MED*) preventive treatment,
prophylaxis.
profi'lattico, a, ci, che *ag* prophylactic
◊ *sm* (*anticoncezionale*) sheath, condom.
pro'filo *sm* profile; (*breve descrizione*)
sketch, outline; **di** ~ in profile.
profit'tare *vi*: ~ **di** (*trarre profitto*) to profit
by; (*approfittare*) to take advantage of.
pro'fitto *sm* advantage, profit, benefit; (*fig*:
progresso) progress; (*COMM*) profit;
ricavare un ~ **da** to make a profit from *o*
out of; **vendere con** ~ to sell at a profit;
conto ~**i e perdite** profit and loss
account.
pro'fondere *vt* (*lodi*) to lavish; (*denaro*) to
squander; ~**rsi** *vr*: ~**rsi in** to be profuse in.
profondità *sf inv* depth.
pro'fondo, a *ag* deep; (*rancore, meditazione*)
profound ◊ *sm* depth(s *pl*); bottom; ~ **8
metri** 8 metres deep.
pro'forma *ag* routine *cpd* ◊ *sm inv* formality
◊ *av*: **fare qc** ~ to do sth as a formality.
'profugo, a, ghi, ghe *sm/f* refugee.
profu'mare *vt* to perfume ◊ *vi* to be
fragrant; ~**rsi** *vr* to put on perfume *o*
scent.
profumata'mente *av*: **pagare qc** ~ to pay

through the nose for sth.

profu'mato, a *ag* (*fiore, aria*) fragrant; (*fazzoletto, saponetta*) scented; (*pelle*) sweet-smelling; (*persona*) with perfume on.

profume'ria *sf* perfumery; (*negozio*) perfume shop.

pro'fumo *sm* (*prodotto*) perfume, scent; (*fragranza*) scent, fragrance.

profusi'one *sf* profusion; **a ~** in plenty.

pro'fuso, a *pp di* **profondere.**

progeni'tore, 'trice [prodʒeni'tore] *sm/f* ancestor.

proget'tare [prodʒet'tare] *vt* to plan; (*TECN: edificio*) to plan, design; **~ di fare qc** to plan to do sth.

progettazi'one [prodʒettat'tsjone] *sf* planning; **in corso di ~** at the planning stage.

proget'tista, i, e [prodʒet'tista] *sm/f* designer.

pro'getto [pro'dʒetto] *sm* plan; (*idea*) plan, project; **avere in ~ di fare qc** to be planning to do sth; **~ di legge** (*POL*) bill.

'prognosi ['proɲɲozi] *sf* (*MED*) prognosis; **essere in ~ riservata** to be on the danger list.

pro'gramma, i *sm* programme (*BRIT*), program (*US*); (*TV, RADIO*) program(me)s *pl*; (*INS*) syllabus, curriculum; (*INFORM*) program; **avere in ~ di fare qc** to be planning to do sth; **~ applicativo** (*INFORM*) application program.

program'mare *vt* (*TV, RADIO*) to put on; (*INFORM*) to program; (*ECON*) to plan.

programma'tore, 'trice *sm/f* (*INFORM*) computer programmer (*BRIT*) o programer (*US*).

programmazi'one [programmat'tsjone] *sf* programming (*BRIT*), programing (*US*); planning.

progre'dire *vi* to progress, make progress.

progressi'one *sf* progression.

progres'sista, i, e *ag, sm/f* progressive.

progressiva'mente *av* progressively.

progres'sivo, a *ag* progressive.

pro'gresso *sm* progress *no pl*; **fare ~i** to make progress.

proi'bire *vt* to forbid, prohibit; **~ a qn di fare qc** (*vietare*) to forbid sb to do sth; (*impedire*) to prevent sb from doing sth.

proibi'tivo, a *ag* prohibitive.

proi'bito, a *ag* forbidden; "**è ~ l'accesso**" "no admittance"; "**è ~ fumare**" "no smoking".

proibizi'one [proibit'tsjone] *sf* prohibition.

proibizio'nismo [proibittsjo'nizmo] *sm* prohibition.

proiet'tare *vt* (*gen, GEOM, CINE*) to project; (: *presentare*) to show, screen; (*luce, ombra*) to throw, cast, project.

proi'ettile *sm* projectile, bullet (*o* shell *etc*).

proiet'tore *sm* (*CINE*) projector; (*AUT*) headlamp; (*MIL*) searchlight.

proiezi'one [projet'tsjone] *sf* (*CINE*) projection; showing.

'prole *sf* children *pl*, offspring.

proletari'ato *sm* proletariat.

prole'tario, a *ag, sm/f* proletarian.

prolife'rare *vi* (*fig*) to proliferate.

pro'lifico, a, ci, che *ag* prolific.

pro'lisso, a *ag* verbose.

'prologo, ghi *sm* prologue.

pro'lunga, ghe *sf* (*di cavo elettrico etc*) extension.

prolunga'mento *sm* (*gen*) extension; (*di strada*) continuation.

prolun'gare *vt* (*discorso, attesa*) to prolong; (*linea, termine*) to extend.

pro'memoria *sm inv* memorandum.

pro'messa *sf* promise; **fare/mantenere una ~** to make/keep a promise.

pro'messo, a *pp di* **promettere.**

promet'tente *ag* promising.

pro'mettere *vt* to promise ♦ *vi* to be o look promising; **~ a qn di fare** to promise sb that one will do.

promi'nente *ag* prominent.

promi'nenza [promi'nentsa] *sf* prominence.

promiscuità *sf* promiscuousness.

pro'miscuo, a *ag:* **matrimonio ~** mixed marriage; **nome ~** (*LING*) common-gender noun.

pro'misi *etc vb vedi* **promettere.**

promon'torio *sm* promontory, headland.

pro'mosso, a *pp di* **promuovere.**

promo'tore, 'trice *sm/f* promoter, organizer.

promozio'nale [promottsjo'nale] *ag* promotional; "**vendita ~**" "special offer".

promozi'one [promot'tsjone] *sf* promotion; **~ delle vendite** sales promotion.

promul'gare *vt* to promulgate.

promulgazi'one [promulgat'tsjone] *sf* promulgation.

promu'overe *vt* to promote.

proni'pote *sm/f* (*di nonni*) great-grandchild, great-grandson/granddaughter; (*di zii*) great-nephew/niece; **~i** *smpl* (*discendenti*) descendants.

pro'nome *sm* (*LING*) pronoun.

pronomi'nale *ag* pronominal.

pronosti'care *vt* to foretell, predict.

pro'nostico, ci *sm* forecast.

pron'tezza [pron'tettsa] *sf* readiness; quickness, promptness; ~ **di riflessi** quick reflexes; ~ **di spirito/mente** readiness of wit/mind.

'pronto, a *ag* ready; (*rapido*) fast, quick, prompt; ~! (*TEL*) hello!; **essere** ~ **a fare qc** to be ready to do sth; ~ **all'ira** quick-tempered; **a** ~**a cassa** (*COMM*) cash (*BRIT*) *o* collect (*US*) on delivery; ~**a consegna** (*COMM*) prompt delivery; ~ **soccorso** first aid.

prontu'ario *sm* manual, handbook.

pro'nuncia [pro'nuntʃa] *sf* pronunciation.

pronunci'are [pronun'tʃare] *vt* (*parola, sentenza*) to pronounce; (*dire*) to utter; (*discorso*) to deliver; ~**rsi** *vr* to declare one's opinion; ~**rsi a favore di/contro** to pronounce o.s. in favour of/against; **non mi pronuncio** I'm not prepared to comment.

pronunci'ato, a [pronun'tʃato] *ag* (*spiccato*) pronounced, marked; (*sporgente*) prominent.

pro'nunzia *etc* [pro'nuntsja] = **pronuncia** *etc*.

propa'ganda *sf* propaganda.

propagan'dare *vt* (*idea*) to propagandize; (*prodotto, invenzione*) to push, plug (*fam*).

propa'gare *vt* (*FISICA, BIOL*) to propagate; (*notizia, idea, malattia*) to spread; ~**rsi** *vr* to propagate; to spread.

propagaz'ione [propagat'tsjone] *sf* (*vedi vb*) propagation; spreading.

prope'deutico, a, ci, che *ag* (*corso, trattato*) introductory.

pro'pendere *vi*: ~ **per** to favour (*BRIT*), favor (*US*), lean towards.

propensi'one *sf* inclination, propensity; **avere** ~ **a credere che** ... to be inclined to think that ....

pro'penso, a *pp di* **propendere** ♦ *ag*: **essere** ~ **a qc** to be in favour (*BRIT*) *o* favor (*US*) of sth; **essere** ~ **a fare qc** to be inclined to do sth.

propi'nare *vt* to administer.

pro'pizio, a [pro'pittsjo] *ag* favourable (*BRIT*), favorable (*US*).

pro'porre *vt* (*suggerire*): ~ **qc (a qn)** to suggest sth (to sb); (*candidato*) to put forward; (*legge, brindisi*) to propose; ~ **di fare** to suggest *o* propose doing; **proporsi di fare** to propose *o* intend to do; **proporsi una meta** to set o.s. a goal.

proporzio'nale [proportsjo'nale] *ag* proportional; **(sistema)** ~ (*POL*) proportional representation system.

proporzio'nato, a [proportsjo'nato] *ag*: ~ **a** proportionate to, proportional to; **ben** ~ well-proportioned.

proporzi'one [propor'tsjone] *sf* proportion; **in** ~ **a** in proportion to.

pro'posito *sm* (*intenzione*) intention, aim; (*argomento*) subject, matter; **a** ~ **di** regarding, with regard to; **a questo** ~ on this subject; **di** ~ (*apposta*) deliberately, on purpose; **a** ~ by the way; **capitare a** ~ (*cosa, persona*) to turn up at the right time.

proposizi'one [propozit'tsjone] *sf* (*LING*) clause; (: *periodo*) sentence.

pro'posto, a *pp di* **proporre** ♦ *sf* proposal; (*suggerimento*) suggestion; **fare una** ~**a** to put forward a proposal; **to make a** suggestion; ~**a di legge** (*POL*) bill.

propria'mente *av* (*correttamente*) properly, correctly; (*in modo specifico*) specifically; ~ **detto** in the strict sense of the word.

proprietà *sf inv* (*ciò che si possiede*) property *gen no pl*, estate; (*caratteristica*) property; (*correttezza*) correctness; **essere di** ~ **di qn** to belong to sb; ~ **edilizia** (*developed*) property; ~ **privata** private property.

proprie'tario, a *sm/f* owner; (*di albergo etc*) proprietor, owner; (*per l'inquilino*) landlord/lady; ~ **terriero** landowner.

'proprio, a *ag* (*possessivo*) own; (: *impersonale*) one's; (*esatto*) exact, correct, proper; (*senso, significato*) literal; (*LING: nome*) proper; (*particolare*): ~ **di** characteristic of, peculiar to ♦ *av* (*precisamente*) just, exactly; (*davvero*) really; (*affatto*): **non** ... ~ not ... at all ♦ *sm* (*COMM*): **mettersi in** ~ to set up on one's own; **l'ha visto con i (suoi)** ~**i occhi** he saw it with his own eyes.

propu'gnare [propuɲ'ɲare] *vt* to support.

propulsi'one *sf* propulsion; **a** ~ **atomica** atomic-powered.

propul'sore *sm* (*TECN*) propeller.

'prora *sf* (*NAUT*) bow(s *pl*), prow.

'proroga, ghe *sf* extension; postponement.

proro'gare *vt* to extend; (*differire*) to postpone, defer.

pro'rompere *vi* to burst out.

pro'rotto, a *pp di* **prorompere**.

pro'ruppi *etc vb vedi* **prorompere**.

'prosa *sf* prose; (*TEAT*): **la stagione della** ~ the theatre season; **attore di** ~ theatre actor; **compagnia di** ~ theatrical company.

pro'saico, a, ci, che *ag* (*fig*) prosaic, mundane.

pro'sciogliere [proʃ'ʃɔʎʎere] *vt* to release; (*DIR*) to acquit.

prosciogli'mento [proʃʃoʎʎi'mento] *sm*

acquittal.
prosci'olto, a [proʃ'ʃɔlto] *pp di* **prosciogliere.**
prosciu'gare [proʃʃu'gare] *vt (terreni)* to drain, reclaim; ~**rsi** *vr* to dry up.
prosci'utto [proʃ'ʃutto] *sm* ham.
pros'critto, a *pp di* **proscrivere ♦** *sm/f* exile; outlaw.
pros'crivere *vt* to exile, banish.
proscrizi'one [proskrit'tsjone] *sf (esilio)* banishment, exile.
prosecuzi'one [prosekut'tsjone] *sf* continuation.
prosegui'mento *sm* continuation; **buon** ~! all the best!
prosegu'ire *vt* to carry on with, continue ♦ *vi* to carry on, go on.
pro'selito *sm (REL, POL)* convert.
prospe'rare *vi* to thrive.
prosperità *sf* prosperity.
'prospero, a *ag (florente)* flourishing, thriving, prosperous.
prospe'roso, a *ag (robusto)* hale and hearty; (: *ragazza*) buxom.
prospet'tare *vt (esporre)* to point out, show; (*ipotesi*) to advance; (*affare*) to outline; ~**rsi** *vr* to look, appear.
prospet'tiva *sf (ARTE)* perspective; (*veduta*) view; (*fig: previsione, possibilità*) prospect.
pros'petto *sm (DISEGNO)* elevation; (*veduta*) view, prospect; (*facciata*) façade, front; (*tabella*) table; (*sommario*) summary.
prospici'ente [prospi'tʃɛnte] *ag:* ~ **qc** facing *o* overlooking sth.
prossima'mente *av* soon.
prossimità *sf* nearness, proximity; **in** ~ **di** near (to), close to; **in** ~ **delle feste natalizie** as Christmas approaches.
'prossimo, a *ag (vicino):* ~ **a** near (to), close to; (*che viene subito dopo*) next; (*parente*) close ♦ *sm* neighbour (*BRIT*), neighbor (*US*), fellow man; **nei** ~**i giorni** in the next few days; **in un** ~ **futuro** in the near future; ~ **venturo (pv)** *(AMM):* **venerdì** ~ **venturo** next Friday.
'prostata *sf* prostate (gland).
prostitu'irsi *vr* to prostitute o.s.
prosti'tuta *sf* prostitute.
prostituzi'one [prostitut'tsjone] *sf* prostitution.
pros'trare *vt (fig)* to exhaust, wear out; ~**rsi** *vr (fig)* to humble o.s.; **prostrato dal dolore** overcome *o* prostrate with grief.
prostrazi'one [prostrat'tsjone] *sf* prostration.
protago'nista, i, e *sm/f* protagonist.

pro'teggere [pro'tɛddʒere] *vt* to protect.
proteggi'slip [protɛddʒi'slip] *sm inv* panty liner.
pro'teico, a, ci, che *ag* protein *cpd;* **altamente** ~ high in protein.
prote'ina *sf* protein.
pro'tendere *vt* to stretch out.
'protesi *sf inv (MED)* prosthesis.
pro'teso, a *pp di* **protendere.**
pro'testa *sf* protest.
protes'tante *ag, sm/f* Protestant.
protes'tare *vt, vi* to protest; ~**rsi** *vr:* ~**rsi innocente** to protest one's innocence.
pro'testo *sm (DIR)* protest; **mandare una cambiale in** ~ to dishonour (*BRIT*) *o* dishonor (*US*) a bill.
protet'tivo, a *ag* protective.
pro'tetto, a *pp di* **proteggere.**
protetto'rato *sm* protectorate.
protet'tore, 'trice *sm/f* protector; (*sostenitore*) patron ♦ *ag (REL)*. **santo** ~ **patron saint, società** ~**trice dei consumatori** consumer protection society.
protezi'one [protet'tsjone] *sf* protection; (*patrocinio*) patronage; **misure di** ~ protective measures; ~ **civile** civil defence (*BRIT*) *o* defense (*US*).
protezio'nismo [protettsjo'nizmo] *sm* protectionism.
protocol'lare *vt* to register ♦ *ag* formal; of protocol.
proto'collo *sm* protocol; (*registro*) register of documents ♦ *ag inv:* **foglio** ~ foolscap; **numero di** ~ reference number.
pro'tone *sm* proton.
pro'totipo *sm* prototype.
pro'trarre *vt (prolungare)* to prolong; **protrarsi** *vr* to go on, continue.
pro'tratto, a *pp di* **protrarre.**
protube'ranza [protube'rantsa] *sf* protuberance, bulge.
Prov. *abbr (= provincia)* Prov.
'prova *sf (esperimento, cimento)* test, trial; (*tentativo*) attempt, try; (*MAT, testimonianza etc*) proof *no pl;* (*DIR*) evidence *no pl,* proof *no pl;* (*INS*) exam, test; (*TEAT*) rehearsal; (*di abito*) fitting; **a** ~ **di** (*in testimonianza di*) as proof of; **a** ~ **di fuoco** fireproof; **assumere in** ~ (*per lavoro*) to employ on a trial basis; **essere in** ~ (*persona: per lavoro*) to be on trial; **mettere alla** ~ to put to the test; **giro di** ~ test *o* trial run; **fino a** ~ **contraria** until (it's) proved otherwise; ~ **a carico/a discarico** (*DIR*) evidence for the prosecution/for the defence; ~ **documentale** (*DIR*) documentary

evidence; ~ **generale** (*TEAT*) dress rehearsal.

pro'vare *vt* (*sperimentare*) to test; (*tentare*) to try, attempt; (*assaggiare*) to try, taste; (*sperimentare in sé*) to experience; (*sentire*) to feel; (*cimentare*) to put to the test; (*dimostrare*) to prove; (*abito*) to try on; **~rsi** *vr*: **~rsi (a fare)** to try *o* attempt (to do); **~ a fare** to try *o* attempt to do.

proveni'enza [prove'njɛntsa] *sf* origin, source.

prove'nire *vi*: **~ da** to come from.

pro'venti *smpl* revenue *sg*.

prove'nuto, a *pp di* **provenire**.

Pro'venza [pro'ventsa] *sf*: **la ~** Provence.

proven'zale [proven'tsale] *ag* Provençal.

pro'verbio *sm* proverb.

pro'vetta *sf* test tube; **bambino in ~** test-tube baby.

pro'vetto, a *ag* skilled, experienced.

pro'vider [pro'vaider] *sm inv* (*INFORM*) service provider.

pro'vincia, ce *o* **cie** [pro'vintʃa] *sf* province; *vedi nota nel riquadro*.

PROVINCIA

A **Provincia** *is the autonomous political and administrative unit which is on a level between a "Comune" and a "Regione"; there are 103 in the whole of Italy. The* **Provincia** *is responsible for public health and sanitation, for the maintenance of major roads and public buildings such as schools, and for agriculture and fisheries. Situated in the "capoluogo", or chief town, each* **Provincia** *is run by a "Giunta provinciale", which is elected by the "Consiglio provinciale"; both of these bodies are presided over by a "Presidente".*

---

provinci'ale [provin'tʃale] *ag* provincial; **(strada) ~** main road (*BRIT*), highway (*US*).

pro'vino *sm* (*CINE*) screen test; (*campione*) specimen.

provo'cante *ag* (*attraente*) provocative.

provo'care *vt* (*causare*) to cause, bring about; (*eccitare: riso, pietà*) to arouse; (*irritare, sfidare*) to provoke.

provoca'tore, 'trice *sm/f* agitator ♦ *ag*: **agente ~** agent provocateur.

provoca'torio, a *ag* provocative.

provocazi'one [provokat'tsjone] *sf* provocation.

provve'dere *vi* (*disporre*): **~ (a)** to provide (for); (*prendere un provvedimento*) to take steps, act ♦ *vt*: **~ qc a qn** to supply sth to sb; **~rsi** *vr*: **~rsi di** to provide o.s. with.

provvedi'mento *sm* measure; (*di*

previdenza) precaution; **~ disciplinare** disciplinary measure.

provvedito'rato *sm* (*AMM*): **~ agli studi** divisional education offices *pl*.

provvedi'tore *sm* (*AMM*): **~ agli studi** divisional director of education.

provvi'denza [provvi'dɛntsa] *sf*: **la ~** providence.

provvidenzi'ale [provviden'tsjale] *ag* providential.

provvigi'one [provvi'dʒone] *sf* (*COMM*) commission; **lavoro/stipendio a ~** job/salary on a commission basis.

provvi'sorio, a *ag* temporary; (*governo*) temporary, provisional.

prov'vista *sf* (*riserva*) supply, stock; **fare ~ di** to stock up with.

prov'visto, a *pp di* **provvedere** ♦ *sf* provision, supply.

pro'zia [prot'tsia] *sf* great-aunt.

pro'zio, zii [prot'tsio] *sm* great-uncle.

'prua *sf* (*NAUT*) = **prora**.

pru'dente *ag* cautious, prudent; (*assennato*) sensible, wise.

pru'denza [pru'dɛntsa] *sf* prudence, caution; wisdom; **per ~** as a precaution, to be on the safe side.

'prudere *vi* to itch, be itchy.

'prugna ['pruɲɲa] *sf* plum; **~ secca** prune.

prurigi'noso, a [pruridʒi'noso] *ag* itchy.

pru'rito *sm* itchiness *no pl*; itch.

PS *sigla* = Pesaro.

P.S. *abbr* (= *postscriptum*) P.S.; (*COMM*) = **partita semplice** ♦ *sigla f vedi* **Pubblica Sicurezza**.

P.S.D.I. *sigla m* (= *Partito Socialista Democratico Italiano*) *former political party*.

pseu'donimo *sm* pseudonym.

PSI *sigla m* (*POL*) = Partito Socialista Italiano.

psica'nalisi *sf* psychoanalysis.

psicana'lista, i, e *sm/f* psychoanalyst.

psicanaliz'zare [psikanalid'dzare] *vt* to psychoanalyse.

'psiche ['psike] *sf* psyche.

psiche'delico, a, ci, che [psike'dɛliko] *ag* psychedelic.

psichi'atra, i, e [psi'kjatra] *sm/f* psychiatrist.

psichia'tria [psikja'tria] *sf* psychiatry.

psichi'atrico, a, ci, che [psi'kjatriko] *ag* (*caso*) psychiatric; (*reparto, ospedale*) psychiatric, mental.

'psichico, a, ci, che ['psikiko] *ag* psychological.

psico'farmaco, ci *sm* (*MED*) *drug used in treatment of mental conditions*.

psicolo'gia [psikolo'dʒia] *sf* psychology.

psico'logico, a, ci, che [psiko'lɔdʒiko] *ag* psychological.
psi'cologo, a, gi, ghe *sm/f* psychologist.
psico'patico, a, ci, che *ag* psychopathic ♦ *sm/f* psychopath.
psi'cosi *sf inv* (*MED*) psychosis; (*fig*) obsessive fear.
psicoso'matico, a, ci, che *ag* psychosomatic.
PT *sigla* = Pistoia.
Pt. *abbr* (*GEO*: = *punta*) Pt.
P.T. *abbr* (= *Posta e Telegrafi*) ≈ PO (= *Post Office*); (*FISCO*) = **polizia tributaria**.
P.ta *abbr* = **porta**.
P.T.P. *abbr vedi* **posto telefonico pubblico**.
pubbli'care *vt* to publish.
pubblicazi'one [pubblikat'tsjone] *sf* publication; ~ **periodica** periodical; ~**i** (**matrimoniali**) *sfpl* (marriage) banns.
pubbli'cista, i, e [pubbli'tʃista] *sm/f* (*STAMPA*) freelance journalist.
pubblicità [pubbliʧi'ta] *sf* (*diffusione*) publicity; (*attività*) advertising; (*annunci nei giornali*) advertisements *pl*; **fare ~ a qc** to advertise sth.
pubblici'tario, a [pubbliʧi'tarjo] *ag* advertising *cpd*; (*trovata, film*) publicity *cpd* ♦ *sm* advertising agent; **annuncio** *o* **avviso ~** advertisement.
'pubblico, a, ci, che *ag* public; (*statale*: *scuola etc*) state *cpd* ♦ *sm* public; (*spettatori*) audience; **in ~** in public; **la ~a amministrazione** public administration; **un ~ esercizio** a catering (*o* hotel *o* entertainment) business; **~ funzionario** civil servant; **Ministero della P~a Istruzione** ≈ Department of Education and Science (*BRIT*), ≈ Department of Health, Education and Welfare (*US*); **P~ Ministero** Public Prosecutor's Office; **la P~a Sicurezza (P.S.)** the police.
'pube *sm* (*ANAT*) pubis.
pubertà *sf* puberty.
'pudico, a, ci, che *ag* modest.
pu'dore *sm* modesty.
puericul'tura *sf* infant care.
pue'rile *ag* childish.
pu'erpera *sf* woman who has just given birth.
pugi'lato [pudʒi'lato] *sm* boxing.
'pugile ['pudʒile] *sm* boxer.
pugli'ese [puʎ'ʎese] *ag* of (*o* from) Puglia.
pugna'lare [puɲɲa'lare] *vt* to stab.
pu'gnale [puɲ'ɲale] *sm* dagger.
'pugno ['puɲɲo] *sm* fist; (*colpo*) punch; (*quantità*) fistful; **avere qn in ~** to have sb in the palm of one's hand; **tenere la situazione in ~** to have control of the

situation; **scrivere qc di proprio ~** to write sth in one's own hand.
'pulce ['pulʧe] *sf* flea.
pul'cino [pul'tʃino] *sm* chick.
pu'ledro, a *sm/f* colt/filly.
pu'leggia, ge [pu'leddʒa] *sf* pulley.
pu'lire *vt* to clean; (*lucidare*) to polish; **far ~ qc** to have sth cleaned; **~ a secco** to dry-clean.
pu'lito, a *ag* (*anche fig*) clean; (*ordinato*) neat, tidy ♦ *sf* quick clean; **avere la coscienza ~a** to have a clear conscience.
puli'tura *sf* cleaning; **~ a secco** dry-cleaning.
puli'zia [pulit'tsia] *sf* (*atto*) cleaning; (*condizione*) cleanness; **fare le ~ e** to do the cleaning, do the housework; **~ etnica** ethnic cleansing.
'pullman *sm inv* coach (*BRIT*), bus.
pul'lover *sm inv* pullover, jumper.
pullu'lare *vi* to swarm, teem.
pul'mino *sm* minibus.
'pulpito *sm* pulpit.
pul'sante *sm* (push-)button.
pul'sare *vi* to pulsate, beat.
pulsazi'one [pulsat'tsjone] *sf* beat.
pul'viscolo *sm* fine dust.
'puma *sm inv* puma.
pun'gente [pun'dʒɛnte] *ag* prickly; stinging; (*anche fig*) biting.
'pungere ['pundʒere] *vt* to prick; (*sog*: *insetto, ortica*) to sting; (: *freddo*) to bite; **~ qn sul vivo** (*fig*) to cut sb to the quick.
pungigli'one [pundʒiʎ'ʎone] *sm* sting.
pungo'lare *vt* to goad.
pu'nire *vt* to punish.
puni'tivo, a *ag* punitive.
punizi'one [punit'tsjone] *sf* punishment; (*SPORT*) penalty.
'punsi *etc vb vedi* **pungere**.
'punta *sf* point; (*parte terminale*) tip, end; (*di monte*) peak; (*di costa*) promontory; (*minima parte*) touch, trace; **in ~ di piedi** on tiptoe; **ore di ~** peak hours; **uomo di ~** (*SPORT, POL*) front-rank *o* leading man; **doppie ~e** split ends.
pun'tare *vt* (*piedi a terra, gomiti sul tavolo*) to plant; (*dirigere: pistola*) to point; (*scommettere*): **~ su** to bet on ♦ *vi* (*mirare*): **~ a** to aim at; (*avviarsi*): **~ su** to head *o* make for; (*fig: contare*): **~ su** to count *o* rely on.
puntas'pilli *sm inv* = **portaspilli**.
pun'tata *sf* (*gita*) short trip; (*scommessa*) bet; (*parte di opera*) instalment (*BRIT*), installment (*US*); **farò una ~ a Parigi** I'll pay a flying visit to Paris; **romanzo a ~e** serial.

punteggi'are [punted'dʒare] *vt* to punctuate.

punteggia'tura [punteddʒa'tura] *sf* punctuation.

pun'teggio [pun'teddʒo] *sm* score.

puntel'lare *vt* to support.

pun'tello *sm* prop, support.

punteru'olo *sm* (*TECN*) punch; (: *per stoffa*) bodkin.

pun'tiglio [pun'tiʎʎo] *sm* obstinacy, stubbornness.

puntigli'oso, a [puntiʎ'ʎoso] *ag* punctilious.

pun'tina *sf*: ~ **da disegno** drawing pin (*BRIT*), thumb tack (*US*); ~**e** *sfpl* (*AUT*) points.

pun'tino *sm* dot; **fare qc a** ~ to do sth properly; **arrivare a** ~ to arrive just at the right moment; **cotto a** ~ cooked to perfection; **mettere i** ~**i sulle "i"** (*fig*) to dot the i's and cross the t's.

'punto, a *pp di* **pungere** ♦ *sm* (*segno, macchiolina*) dot; (*LING*) full stop; (*MAT, momento, di punteggio, fig*: *argomento*) point; (*posto*) spot; (*a scuola*) mark; (*nel cucire, nella maglia, MED*) stitch ♦ *av*: **non ...** ~ **not ... at all; due** ~**i** *sm inv* (*LING*) colon; **ad un certo** ~ at a certain point; **fino ad un certo** ~ (*fig*) to a certain extent; **sul** ~ **di fare** (just) about to do; **fare il** ~ (*NAUT*) to take a bearing; **fare il** ~ **della situazione** (*analisi*) to take stock of the situation; (*riassunto*) to sum up the situation; **alle 6 in** ~ at 6 o'clock sharp *o* on the dot; **essere a buon** ~ to have reached a satisfactory stage; **mettere a** ~ to adjust; (*motore*) to tune; (*cannocchiale*) to focus; (*fig*) to settle; **venire al** ~ to come to the point; **vestito di tutto** ~ all dressed up; **di** ~ **in bianco** point-blank; ~ **d'arrivo** arrival point; ~ **cardinale** point of the compass, cardinal point; ~ **debole** weak point; ~ **esclamativo/interrogativo** exclamation/question mark; ~ **d'incontro** meeting place, meeting point; ~ **morto** standstill; ~ **nero** (*comedone*) blackhead; ~ **nevralgico** (*anche fig*) nerve centre (*BRIT*) *o* center (*US*); ~ **di partenza** (*anche fig*) starting point; ~ **di riferimento** landmark; (*fig*) point of reference; ~ **di vendita** retail outlet; ~ **e virgola** semicolon; ~ **di vista** (*fig*) point of view; ~**i di sospensione** suspension points.

puntu'ale *ag* punctual.

puntualità *sf* punctuality.

puntualiz'zare [puntualid'dzare] *vt* to make clear.

puntual'mente *av* (*gen*) on time; (*ironico*:

al solito) as usual.

pun'tura *sf* (*di ago*) prick; (*di insetto*) sting, bite; (*MED*) puncture; (: *iniezione*) injection; (*dolore*) sharp pain.

punzecchi'are [puntsek'kjare] *vt* to prick; (*fig*) to tease.

punzo'nare [puntso'nare] *vt* (*TECN*) to stamp.

pun'zone [pun'tsone] *sm* (*per metalli*) stamp, die.

può, pu'oi *vb vedi* **potere**.

'pupa *sf* doll.

pu'pazzo [pu'pattso] *sm* puppet.

pu'pillo, a *sm/f* (*DIR*) ward; (*prediletto*) favourite (*BRIT*), favorite (*US*), pet ♦ *sf* (*ANAT*) pupil.

purché [pur'ke] *cong* provided that, on condition that.

'pure *cong* (*tuttavia*) and yet, nevertheless; (*anche se*) even if ♦ *av* (*anche*) too, also; **pur di** (*al fine di*) just to; **faccia** ~! go ahead!, please do!

purè *sm*, **pu'rea** *sf* (*CUC*) purée; (: *di patate*) mashed potatoes.

pu'rezza [pu'rettsa] *sf* purity.

'purga, ghe *sf* (*MED*) purging *no pl*; purge; (*POL*) purge.

pur'gante *sm* (*MED*) purgative, purge.

pur'gare *vt* (*MED, POL*) to purge; (*pulire*) to clean.

purga'torio *sm* purgatory.

purifi'care *vt* to purify; (*metallo*) to refine.

purificazi'one [purifikat'tsjone] *sf* purification; refinement.

puri'tano, a *ag*, *sm/f* puritan.

'puro, a *ag* pure; (*acqua*) clear, limpid; (*vino*) undiluted; **di razza** ~**a** thoroughbred; **per** ~ **caso** by sheer chance, purely by chance.

puro'sangue *sm/f inv* thoroughbred.

pur'troppo *av* unfortunately.

pus *sm* pus.

pusil'lanime *ag* cowardly.

'pustola *sf* pimple.

puta'caso *av* just supposing, suppose.

puti'ferio *sm* rumpus, row.

putre'fare *vi* to putrefy, rot.

putre'fatto, a *pp di* **putrefare**.

putrefazi'one [putrefat'tsjone] *sf* putrefaction.

'putrido, a *ag* putrid, rotten.

put'tana *sf* (*fam!*) whore (*!*).

'putto *sm* cupid.

'puzza ['puttsa] *sf* = **puzzo**.

puz'zare [put'tsare] *vi* to stink; **la faccenda puzza (d'imbroglio)** the whole business stinks.

'puzzo ['puttso] *sm* stink, foul smell.

'**puzzola** ['puttsola] *sf* polecat.
puzzo'lente [puttso'lɛnte] *ag* stinking.
PV *sigla* = *Pavia*.
pv *abbr vedi* **prossimo venturo**.
P.V.C. [pivi'tʃi] *sigla m* (= *polyvinyl chloride*) PVC.
PZ *sigla* = *Potenza*.
p. zza *abbr* = **piazza**.

$$Q\,q$$

Q, q [ku] *sf o m inv* (*lettera*) Q, q; **Q come Quarto** ≈ Q for Queen.
q *abbr* (= *quintale*) q.
Qa'tar [ka'tar] *sm*: **il** ~ Qatar.
q.b. *abbr* (= *quanto basta*) as needed; **zucchero** ~ sugar to taste
Q.G. *abbr* = **quartier generale**.
Q.I. *abbr vedi* **quoziente d'intelligenza**.
qua *av* here; **in** ~ (*verso questa parte*) this way; ~ **dentro/sotto** *etc* in/under here *etc*; **da un anno in** ~ for a year now; **da quando in** ~? since when?; **per di** ~ (*passare*) this way; **al di** ~ **di** (*fiume, strada*) on this side of; *vedi* **questo**.
'**quacchero, a** ['kwakkero] *sm/f* Quaker.
qua'derno *sm* notebook; (*per scuola*) exercise book.
qua'drangolo *sm* quadrangle.
qua'drante *sm* quadrant; (*di orologio*) face.
qua'drare *vi* (*bilancio*) to balance, tally; (*fig: corrispondere*): ~ (**con**) to correspond (with) ♦ *vt* (*MAT*) to square; **far** ~ **il bilancio** to balance the books; **non mi quadra** I don't like it.
qua'drato, a *ag* square; (*fig: equilibrato*) level-headed, sensible; (: *peg*) square ♦ *sm* (*MAT*) square; (*PUGILATO*) ring; **5 al** ~ 5 squared.
quadret'tato, a *ag* (*foglio*) squared; (*tessuto*) checked.
qua'dretto *sm*: **a** ~**i** (*tessuto*) checked; (*foglio*) squared.
quadrien'nale *ag* (*che dura 4 anni*) four-year *cpd*; (*che avviene ogni 4 anni*) four-yearly.
quadri'foglio [kwadri'fɔʎʎo] *sm* four-leaf clover.
quadri'mestre *sm* (*periodo*) four-month period; (*INS*) term.
'**quadro** *sm* (*pittura*) painting, picture;

(*quadrato*) square; (*tabella*) table, chart; (*TECN*) board, panel; (*TEAT*) scene; (*fig: scena, spettacolo*) sight; (: *descrizione*) outline, description; ~**i** *smpl* (*POL*) party organizers; (*COMM*) managerial staff; (*MIL*) cadres; (*CARTE*) diamonds; **a** ~**i** (*disegno*) checked; **fare un** ~ **della situazione** to outline the situation; ~ **clinico** (*MED*) case history; ~ **di comando** control panel; ~**i intermedi** middle management *sg*.
qua'drupede *sm* quadruped.
quadrupli'care *vt* to quadruple.
'**quadruplo, a** *ag, sm* quadruple.
quaggiù [kwad'dʒu] *av* down here.
'**quaglia** ['kwaʎʎa] *sf* quail.

—————————————— *PAROLA CHIAVE*

'**qualche** ['kwalke] *det* **1** some, a few; (*in interrogative*) any; **ho comprato** ~ **libro** I've bought some *o* a few books; ~ **volta** sometimes; **hai** ~ **sigaretta?** have you any cigarettes?
2 (*uno*): **c'è** ~ **medico?** is there a doctor?; **in** ~ **modo** somehow
3 (*un certo, parecchio*) some; **un personaggio di** ~ **rilievo** a figure of some importance
4: ~ **cosa** = **qualcosa**.

qualche'duno [kwalke'duno] *pron* = **qualcuno**.
qual'cosa *pron* something; (*in espressioni interrogative*) anything; **qualcos'altro** something else; anything else; ~ **di nuovo** something new; anything new; ~ **da mangiare** something to eat; anything to eat; **c'è** ~ **che non va?** is there something *o* anything wrong?
qual'cuno *pron* (*persona*) someone, somebody; (: *in espressioni interrogative*) anyone, anybody; (*alcuni*) some; ~ **è favorevole a noi** some are on our side; **qualcun altro** someone *o* somebody else; anyone *o* anybody else.

—————————————— *PAROLA CHIAVE*

'**quale** (*spesso troncato in* **qual**) *det* **1** (*interrogativo*) what; (: *scegliendo tra due o più cose o persone*) which; ~ **uomo/denaro?** what man/money?; which man/money?; ~**i sono i tuoi programmi?** what are your plans?; ~ **stanza preferisci?** which room do you prefer?
2 (*relativo: come*): **il risultato fu** ~ **ci si aspettava** the result was as expected
3 (*in elenchi*) such as, like; **piante** ~**i l'edera** plants such as *o* like ivy

4 (*esclamativo*) what; ~ **disgrazia!** what bad luck!

5: **in un certo qual modo** in a way, in some ways; **per la qual cosa** for which reason

♦ *pron* **1** (*interrogativo*) which; ~ **dei due scegli?** which of the two do you want?

2 (*relativo*): **il(la)** ~ (*persona: soggetto*) who; (: *oggetto, con preposizione*) whom; (*cosa*) which; (*possessivo*) whose; **suo padre, il** ~ **è avvocato, ...** his father, who is a lawyer, ...; **a tutti coloro i** ~**i fossero interessati ...** to whom it may concern ...; **il signore con il** ~ **parlavo** the gentleman to whom I was speaking; **l'albergo al** ~ **ci siamo fermati** the hotel where we stayed *o* which we stayed at; **la signora della** ~ **ammiriamo la bellezza** the lady whose beauty we admire

♦ *av* (*in qualità di, come*) as; ~ **sindaco di questa città** as mayor of this town.

qua'lifica, che *sf* qualification; (*titolo*) title.

qualifi'care *vt* to qualify; (*definire*): ~ **qn/ qc come** to describe sb/sth as; ~**rsi** *vr* (*anche SPORT*) to qualify; ~**rsi a un concorso** to pass a competitive exam.

qualifica'tivo, a *ag* qualifying.

qualifi'cato, a *ag* (*dotato di qualifica*) qualified; (*esperto, abile*) skilled; **non mi ritengo** ~ **per questo lavoro** I don't think I'm qualified for this job; **è un medico molto** ~ he is a very distinguished doctor.

qualificazi'one [kwalifikat'tsjone] *sf* qualification; **gara di** ~ (*SPORT*) qualifying event.

qualità *sf inv* quality; **di ottima** *o* **prima** ~ top quality; **in** ~ **di** in one's capacity as; **in** ~ **di amica** as a friend; **articoli di ogni** ~ all sorts of goods; **controllo (di)** ~ quality control; **prodotto di** ~ quality product.

qualita'tivo, a *ag* qualitative.

qua'lora *cong* in case, if.

qual'siasi, qua'lunque *det inv* any; (*quale che sia*) whatever; (*discriminativo*) whichever; (*posposto: mediocre*) poor, indifferent; ordinary; **mettiti un vestito** ~ put on any old dress; ~ **cosa** anything; ~ **cosa accada** whatever happens; **a** ~ **costo** at any cost, whatever the cost; **l'uomo** ~ the man in the street; ~ **persona** anyone, anybody.

qualunqu'ista, i, e *smf* person indifferent to politics.

'quando *cong, av* when; ~ **sarò ricco** when I'm rich; **da** ~ (*dacché*) since;

(*interrogativo*): **da** ~ **sei qui?** how long have you been here?; **di** ~ **in** ~ from time to time; **quand'anche** even if.

quantifi'care *vt* to quantify.

quantità *sf inv* quantity; (*gran numero*): **una** ~ **di** a great deal of; a lot of; **in grande** ~ in large quantities.

quantita'tivo, a *ag* quantitative ♦ *sm* (*COMM: di merce*) amount, quantity.

━━━━━━━━━━━━━━ *PAROLA CHIAVE*

'quanto, a *det* **1** (*interrogativo: quantità*) how much; (: *numero*) how many; ~ **pane/ denaro?** how much bread/money?; ~**i libri/ragazzi?** how many books/boys?; ~ **tempo?** how long?; ~**i anni hai?** how old are you?

2 (*esclamativo*): ~**e storie!** what a lot of nonsense!; ~ **tempo sprecato!** what a waste of time!

3 (*relativo: quantità*) as much ... as; (: *numero*) as many ... as; **ho** ~ **denaro mi occorre** I have as much money as I need; **prendi** ~**i libri vuoi** take as many books as you like

♦ *pron* **1** (*interrogativo: quantità*) how much; (: *numero*) how many; (: *tempo*) how long; ~ **mi dai?** how much will you give me?; ~**i me ne hai portati?** how many did you bring me?; ~ **starai via?** how long will you be away (for)?; **da** ~ **sei qui?** how long have you been here?; ~**i ne abbiamo oggi?** what's the date today?

2 (*relativo: quantità*) as much as; (: *numero*) as many as; **farò** ~ **posso** I'll do as much as I can; **a** ~ **dice lui** according to him; **in risposta a** ~ **esposto nella sua lettera ...** in answer to the points raised in your letter; **possono venire** ~**i sono stati invitati** all those who have been invited can come

♦ *av* **1** (*interrogativo: con ag, av*) how; (: *con vb*) how much; ~ **stanco ti sembrava?** how tired did he seem to you?; ~ **corre la tua moto?** how fast can your motorbike go?; ~ **costa?** how much does it cost?; **quant'è?** how much is it?

2 (*esclamativo: con ag, av*) how; (: *con vb*) how much; ~ **sono felice!** how happy I am!; **sapessi** ~ **abbiamo camminato!** if you knew how far we've walked!; **studierò** ~ **posso** I'll study as much as *o* all I can; ~ **prima** as soon as possible; ~ **più ... tanto meno** the more ... the less; ~ **più ... tanto più** the more ... the more

3: **in** ~ (*in qualità di*) as; (*perché, per il fatto che*) as, since; **in** ~ **legale della signora** as the lady's lawyer; **non è possibile in** ~

non possiamo permettercelo it isn't possible, since we can't afford it; **(in)** ~ **a** (*per ciò che riguarda*) as for, as regards; **(in)** ~ **a lui** as far as he's concerned **4: per** ~ (*nonostante, anche se*) however; **per** ~ **si sforzi, non ce la farà** try as he may, he won't manage it; **per** ~ **sia brava, fa degli errori** however good she may be, she makes mistakes; **per** ~ **io sappia** as far as I know.

quan'tunque *cong* although, though.

qua'ranta *num* forty.

quaran'tena *sf* quarantine.

quaran'tenne *ag, smf* forty-year-old.

quaran'tennio *sm* (period of) forty years.

quaran'tesimo, a *num* fortieth.

quaran'tina *sf*: **una** ~ **(di)** about forty.

quaran'totto *sm inv* forty-eight; **fare un** ~ (*fam*) to raise hell.

Qua'resima *sf*: **la** ~ Lent.

'quarta *sf vedi* **quarto**.

quar'tetto *sm* quartet(te).

quarti'ere *sm* district, area; (*MIL*) quarters *pl*; ~ **generale (Q.G.)** headquarters *pl* (HQ); ~ **residenziale** residential area *o* district; **i** ~**i alti** the smart districts.

'quarto, a *ag* fourth ♦ *sm* fourth; (*quarta parte*) quarter ♦ *sf (AUT)* fourth (gear); (*INS: elementare*) *fourth year of primary school*; (: *superiore*) *seventh year of secondary school*; **un** ~ **di vino** a quarter-litre (*BRIT*) *o* quarter-liter (*US*) bottle of wine; **le 6 e un** ~ a quarter past (*BRIT*) *o* after (*US*) 6; ~ **d'ora** quarter of an hour; **tre** ~**i d'ora** three quarters of an hour; **le otto e tre** ~**i, le nove meno un** ~ (a) quarter to (*BRIT*) *o* of (*US*) nine; **passare un brutto** ~ **d'ora** (*fig*) to have a bad *o* nasty time of it; ~**i di finale** (*SPORT*) quarter finals.

'quarzo ['kwartso] *sm* quartz.

'quasi *av* almost, nearly ♦ *cong* (*anche*: ~ **che**) as if; **(non)** ... ~ **mai** hardly ever; ~ ~ **me ne andrei** I've half a mind to leave.

quassù *av* up here.

'quatto, a *ag* crouched, squatting; (*silenzioso*) silent; ~ ~ very quietly; stealthily.

quattordi'cenne [kwattordi'tʃɛnne] *ag, smf* fourteen-year-old.

quat'tordici [kwat'torditʃi] *num* fourteen.

quat'trini *smpl* money *sg*, cash *sg*.

'quattro *num* four; **in** ~ **e quattr'otto** in less than no time; **dirne** ~ **a qn** to give sb a piece of one's mind; **fare il diavolo a** ~ to kick up a rumpus; **fare** ~ **chiacchiere** to have a chat; **farsi in** ~ **per qn** to go out of one's way for sb, put o.s. out for sb.

quat'trocchi [kwat'trɔkki] *sm inv* (*fig fam*: *persona con occhiali*) four-eyes; **a** ~ *av* (*tra 2 persone*) face to face; (*privatamente*) in private.

quattrocen'tesco, a, schi, sche [kwattrotʃen'tesko] *ag* fifteenth-century.

quattro'cento [kwattro'tʃɛnto] *num* four hundred ♦ *sm*: **il Q**~ the fifteenth century.

quattro'mila *num* four thousand.

<hr>

PAROLA CHIAVE

'quello, a (*dav sm* **quel** + *C*, **quell'** + *V*, **quello** + *s impura, gn, pn, ps, x, z; pl* **quei** + *C*, **quegli** + *V o s impura, gn, pn, ps, x, z; dav sf* **quella** + *C*, **quell'** + *V; pl* **quelle**) *det* that; those *pl*; ~**a casa** that house; **quegli uomini** those men, **voglio** ~**a camicia (lì o là)** I want that shirt; ~ **è mio fratello** that's my brother

♦ *pron* **1** (*dimostrativo*) that (one); those (ones) *pl*; (*ciò*) that; **conosci** ~**a?** do you know her?, **prendo** ~ **bianco** I'll take the white one; **chi è** ~**?** who's that?; **prendiamo** ~ **(lì o là)** let's take that one (there); **in quel di Milano** in the Milan area *o* region

2 (*relativo*): ~ **(a) che** (*persona*) the one (who); (*cosa*) the one (which), the one (that); ~**i(e) che** (*persone*) those who; (*cose*) those which; **è lui** ~ **che non voleva venire** he's the one who didn't want to come; **ho fatto** ~ **che potevo** I did what I could; **è** ~**a che ti ho prestato** that's the one I lent you; **è proprio** ~ **che gli ho detto** that's exactly what I told him; **da** ~ **che ho sentito** from what I've heard.

'quercia, ce ['kwɛrtʃa] *sf* oak (tree); (*legno*) oak; **la Q**~(*POL*) symbol of P.D.S.

que'rela *sf* (*DIR*) (legal) action.

quere'lare *vt* to bring an action against.

que'sito *sm* question, query; problem.

'questi *pron* (*poetico*) this person.

questio'nario *sm* questionnaire.

questi'one *sf* problem, question; (*controversia*) issue; (*litigio*) quarrel; **in** ~ in question; **il caso in** ~ the matter at hand; **la persona in** ~ the person involved; **non voglio essere chiamato in** ~ I don't want to be dragged into the argument; **fuor di** ~ out of the question; **è** ~ **di tempo** it's a matter *o* question of time.

═══════════════════ *PAROLA CHIAVE*

'questo, a *det* **1** (*dimostrativo*) this; these *pl*; ~ **libro (qui** *o* **qua)** this book; **io prendo** ~ **cappotto, tu quello** I'll take this coat, you take that one; **quest'oggi** today; ~**a sera** this evening

2 (*enfatico*): **non fatemi più prendere di** ~**e paure** don't frighten me like that again

◊ *pron* (*dimostrativo*) this (one); these (ones) *pl*; (*ciò*) this; **prendo** ~ **(qui** *o* **qua)** I'll take this one; **preferisci** ~**i** *o* **quelli?** do you prefer these (ones) or those (ones)?; ~ **intendevo io** this is what I meant; ~ **non dovevi dirlo** you shouldn't have said that; **e con** ~**?** so what?; **e con** ~ **se n'è andato** and with that he left; **con tutto** ~ in spite of this, despite all this; ~ **è quanto** that's all.

ques'tore *sm public official in charge of the police in the provincial capital, reporting to the prefetto*; ≈ chief constable (*BRIT*), ≈ police commissioner (*US*).

'questua *sf* collection (of alms).

ques'tura *sf* police headquarters *pl*.

questu'rino *sm* (*fam: poliziotto*) cop.

qui *av* here; **da** *o* **di** ~ from here; **di** ~ **in avanti** from now on; **di** ~ **a poco/una settimana** in a little while/a week's time; ~ **dentro/sopra/vicino** in/up/near here; *vedi* **questo**.

quie'tanza [kwje'tantsa] *sf* receipt.

qui'ete *sf* quiet, quietness; calmness; stillness; peace; **turbare la** ~ **pubblica** (*DIR*) to disturb the peace.

qui'eto, a *ag* quiet; (*notte*) calm, still; (*mare*) calm; **l'ho fatto per il** ~ **vivere** I did it for a quiet life.

'quindi *av* then ◊ *cong* therefore, so.

quindi'cenne [kwindi't∫enne] *ag*, *sm/f* fifteen-year-old.

'quindici ['kwindit∫i] *num* fifteen; ~ **giorni** a fortnight (*BRIT*), two weeks.

quindi'cina [kwindi't∫ina] *sf* (*serie*): **una** ~ **(di)** about fifteen; **fra una** ~ **di giorni** in a fortnight (*BRIT*) *o* two weeks.

quindici'nale [kwindit∫i'nale] *ag* fortnightly (*BRIT*), semimonthly (*US*) ◊ *sm* (*rivista*) fortnightly magazine (*BRIT*), semimonthly (*US*).

quinquen'nale *ag* (*che dura 5 anni*) five-year *cpd*; (*che avviene ogni 5 anni*) five-yearly.

quin'quennio *sm* period of five years.

quinta *sf vedi* **quinto**.

quin'tale *sm* quintal (*100 kg*).

quin'tetto *sm* quintet(te).

'quinto, a *num* fifth ◊ *sf* (*AUT*) fifth (gear); (*INS: elementare*) *fifth year of primary school*; (: *superiore*) *final year of secondary school*; (*TEAT*) wing; **un** ~ **della popolazione** a fifth of the population; **tre** ~**i** three fifths; **in** ~**a pagina** on the fifth page, on page five.

qui pro quo *sm inv* misunderstanding.

Quiri'nale *sm vedi nota nel riquadro*.

┌─────────────────────────────────┐
│ **QUIRINALE** │
│ │
│ *The* **Quirinale** *takes its name from one of the* │
│ *Seven Hills of Rome on which it stands. It is the* │
│ *official residence of the "Presidente della* │
│ *Repubblica".* │
└─────────────────────────────────┘

'Quito *sf* Quito.

quiz [kwidz] *sm inv* (*domanda*) question; (*anche*: **gioco a** ~) quiz game.

'quorum *sm* quorum.

'quota *sf* (*parte*) quota, share; (*AER*) height, altitude; (*IPPICA*) odds *pl*; **prendere/ perdere** ~ (*AER*) to gain/lose height *o* altitude; ~ **imponibile** taxable income; ~ **d'iscrizione** (*INS*) enrolment fee; (*ad una gara*) entry fee; (*ad un club*) membership fee; ~ **di mercato** market share.

quo'tare *vt* (*BORSA*) to quote; (*valutare*: *anche fig*) to value; **è un pittore molto quotato** he is rated highly as a painter.

quotazi'one [kwotat'tsjone] *sf* quotation.

quotidiana'mente *av* daily, every day.

quotidi'ano, a *ag* daily; (*banale*) everyday ◊ *sm* (*giornale*) daily (paper).

quozi'ente [kwot'tsjente] *sm* (*MAT*) quotient; ~ **di crescita zero** zero growth rate; ~ **d'intelligenza (Q.I.)** intelligence quotient (IQ).

═══════════════════ ***R r***

R, r ['ɛrre] *sf o m* (*lettera*) R, r; **R come Roma** ≈ R for Robert (*BRIT*), R for Roger (*US*).

R *abbr* (*POSTA*) = **raccomandata**; (*FERR*) = **regionale**.

RA *sigla* = *Ravenna*.

ra'barbaro *sm* rhubarb.

Ra'bat *sf* Rabat.

rabberci'are [rabber'tʃare] *vt* (*anche fig*) to patch up.
'rabbia *sf* (*ira*) anger, rage; (*accanimento, furia*) fury; (*MED: idrofobia*) rabies *sg*.
rab'bino *sm* rabbi.
rabbi'oso, a *ag* angry, furious; (*facile all'ira*) quick-tempered; (*forze, acqua etc*) furious, raging; (*MED*) rabid, mad.
rabbo'nire *vt*, ~**rsi** *vr* to calm down.
rabbrivi'dire *vi* to shudder, shiver.
rabbui'arsi *vr* to grow dark.
rabdo'mante *sm* water diviner.
racc. *abbr* (*POSTA*) = **raccomandata.**
raccapez'zarsi [rakkapet'tsarsi] *vr*: **non** ~ to be at a loss.
raccapricci'ante [rakkaprit'tʃante] *ag* horrifying.
racca'priccio [rakka'prittʃo] *sm* horror.
raccatta'palle *sm inv* (*SPORT*) ballboy.
raccat'tare *vt* to pick up.
rac'chetta [rak'ketta] *sf* (*per tennis*) racket; (*per ping-pong*) bat; ~ **da neve** snowshoe; ~ **da sci** ski stick.
'racchio, a ['rakkjo] *ag* (*fam*) ugly.
racchi'udere [rak'kjudere] *vt* to contain.
racchi'uso, a [rak'kjuso] *pp di* **racchiudere.**
rac'cogliere [rak'kɔʎʎere] *vt* to collect; (*raccattare*) to pick up; (*frutti, fiori*) to pick, pluck; (*AGR*) to harvest; (*approvazione, voti*) to win; (*profughi*) to take in; (*vele*) to furl; (*capelli*) to put up; ~**rsi** *vr* to gather; (*fig*) to gather one's thoughts; to meditate; **non ha raccolto** (*allusione*) he didn't take the hint; (*frecciata*) he took no notice of it; ~ **i frutti del proprio lavoro** (*fig*) to reap the benefits of one's work; ~ **le idee** (*fig*) to gather one's thoughts.
raccogli'mento [rakkoʎʎi'mento] *sm* meditation.
raccogli'tore [rakkoʎʎi'tore] *sm* (*cartella*) folder, binder; ~ **a fogli mobili** loose-leaf binder.
rac'colto, a *pp di* **raccogliere** ♦ *ag* (*persona: pensoso*) thoughtful; (*luogo: appartato*) secluded, quiet ♦ *sm* (*AGR*) crop, harvest ♦ *sf* collecting *no pl*; collection; (*AGR*) harvesting *no pl*, gathering *no pl*; harvest, crop; **fare la** ~ **di qc** to collect sth; **chiamare a** ~**a** to gather together.
raccoman'dabile *ag* (highly) commendable; **è un tipo poco** ~ he is not to be trusted.
raccoman'dare *vt* to recommend; (*affidare*) to entrust; ~**rsi** *vr*: ~**rsi a qn** to commend o.s. to sb; ~ **a qn di fare qc** to recommend that sb does sth; ~ **a qn di non fare qc** to tell *o* warn sb not to do sth; ~ **qn a qn/alle cure di qn** to entrust sb to

sb/to sb's care; **mi raccomando!** don't forget!
raccoman'dato, a *ag* (*lettera, pacco*) recorded-delivery (*BRIT*), certified (*US*); (*candidato*) recommended ♦ *sm/f*: **essere un(a)** ~**(a) di ferro** to have friends in high places ♦ *sf* (*anche:* **lettera** ~**a**) recorded-delivery letter; ~**a con ricevuta di ritorno (Rrr)** recorded-delivery letter with advice of receipt.
raccomandazi'one [rakkomandat'tsjone] *sf* recommendation; **lettera di** ~ letter of introduction.
raccomo'dare *vt* (*riparare*) to repair, mend.
raccon'tare *vt*: ~ (**a qn**) (*dire*) to tell (sb); (*narrare*) to relate (to sb), tell (sb) about; **a me non la racconti** don't try and kid me; **cosa mi racconti di nuovo?** what's new?
rac'conto *sm* telling *no pl*, relating *no pl*; (*fatto raccontato*) story, tale; (*genere letterario*) short story; ~**i per bambini** children's stories.
raccorci'are [rakkor'tʃare] *vt* to shorten.
raccor'dare *vt* to link up, join.
rac'cordo *sm* (*TECN: giunzione*) connection, joint; (*AUT: di autostrada*) slip road (*BRIT*), entrance (*o exit*) ramp (*US*); ~ **anulare** (*AUT*) ring road (*BRIT*), beltway (*US*).
ra'chitico, a, ci, che [ra'kitiko] *ag* suffering from rickets; (*fig*) scraggy, scrawny.
rachi'tismo [raki'tizmo] *sm* (*MED*) rickets *sg*.
racimo'lare [ratʃimo'lare] *vt* (*fig*) to scrape together, glean.
'rada *sf* (natural) harbour (*BRIT*) *o* harbor (*US*).
'radar *sm inv* radar.
raddol'cire [raddol'tʃire] *vt* (*persona, carattere*) to soften; ~**rsi** *vr* (*tempo*) to grow milder; (*persona*) to soften, mellow.
raddoppia'mento *sm* doubling.
raddoppi'are *vt*, *vi* to double.
rad'doppio *sm* (*gen*) doubling; (*BILIARDO*) double; (*EQUITAZIONE*) gallop.
raddriz'zare [raddrit'tsare] *vt* to straighten; (*fig: correggere*) to put straight, correct.
'radere *vt* (*barba*) to shave off; (*mento*) to shave; (*fig: rasentare*) to graze; to skim; ~**rsi** *vr* to shave (o.s.); ~ **al suolo** to raze to the ground.
radi'ale *ag* radial.
radi'ante *ag* (*calore, energia*) radiant.
radi'are *vt* to strike off.
radia'tore *sm* radiator.
radiazi'one [radjat'tsjone] *sf* (*FISICA*) radiation; (*cancellazione*) striking off.

'radica *sf* (*BOT*): ~ **di noce** walnut (wood).
radi'cale *ag* radical ◊ *sm* (*LING*) root; (*MAT, POL*) radical.
radi'cato, a *ag* (*pregiudizio, credenza*) deep-seated, deeply-rooted.
ra'dicchio [ra'dikkjo] *sm variety of chicory.*
ra'dice [ra'ditʃe] *sf* root; **segno di** ~ (*MAT*) radical sign; **colpire alla** ~ (*fig*) to strike at the root; **mettere** ~**i** (*idee, odio etc*) to take root; (*persona*) to put down roots; ~ **quadrata** (*MAT*) square root.
'radio *sf inv* radio ◊ *sm* (*CHIM*) radium; **trasmettere per** ~ to broadcast; **stazione/ponte** ~ radio station/link; ~ **ricevente/trasmittente** receiver/transmitter.
radioabbo'nato, a *sm/f* radio subscriber.
radioama'tore, 'trice *sm/f* amateur radio operator, ham (*fam*).
radioascolta'tore, 'trice *sm/f* (radio) listener.
radioattività *sf* radioactivity.
radioat'tivo, a *ag* radioactive.
radiocoman'dare *vt* to operate by remote control.
radiocoman'dato, a *ag* remote-controlled.
radioco'mando *sm* remote control.
radiocomunicazi'one [radjokomunikat'tsjone] *sf* radio message.
radio'cronaca, che *sf* radio commentary.
radiocro'nista, i, e *sm/f* radio commentator.
radiodiffusi'one *sf* (radio) broadcasting.
radio'fonico, a, ci, che *ag* radio *cpd.*
radiogra'fare *vt* to X-ray.
radiogra'fia *sf* radiography; (*foto*) X-ray photograph.
radio'lina *sf* portable radio, transistor (radio).
radiolo'gia [radjolo'dʒia] *sf* radiology.
radi'ologo, a, gi, ghe *sm/f* radiologist.
radiorice'vente [radjoritʃe'vɛnte] *sf* (*anche*: **apparecchio** ~) receiver.
radi'oso, a *ag* radiant.
radiostazi'one [radjostat'tsjone] *sf* radio station.
radios'veglia [radjoz'veʎʎa] *sf* radio alarm.
radio'taxi *sm inv* radio taxi.
radio'tecnico, a, ci, che *ag* radio engineering *cpd* ◊ *sm* radio engineer.
radiotelegra'fista, i, e *sm/f* radiotelegrapher.
radiotera'pia *sf* radiotherapy.
radiotrasmit'tente *ag* (radio) broadcasting *cpd* ◊ *sf* (radio) broadcasting station.
'rado, a *ag* (*capelli*) sparse, thin; (*visite*)

infrequent; **di** ~ rarely; **non di** ~ not uncommonly.
radu'nare *vt*, ~**rsi** *vr* to gather, assemble.
radu'nata *sf* (*MIL*) muster.
ra'duno *sm* gathering, meeting.
ra'dura *sf* clearing.
'rafano *sm* horseradish.
raffazzo'nare [raffattso'nare] *vt* to patch up.
raf'fermo, a *ag* stale.
'raffica, che *sf* (*METEOR*) gust (of wind); ~ **di colpi** (*di fucile*) burst of gunfire.
raffigu'rare *vt* to represent.
raffigurazi'one [raffigurat'tsjone] *sf* representation, depiction.
raffi'nare *vt* to refine.
raffina'tezza [raffina'tettsa] *sf* refinement.
raffi'nato, a *ag* refined.
raffinazi'one [raffinat'tsjone] *sf* (*di sostanza*) refining; ~ **del petrolio** oil refining.
raffine'ria *sf* refinery.
raffor'zare [raffor'tsare] *vt* to reinforce.
rafforza'tivo, a [raffortsa'tivo] *ag* (*LING*) intensifying ◊ *sm* (*LING*) intensifier.
raffredda'mento *sm* cooling.
raffred'dare *vt* to cool; (*fig*) to dampen, have a cooling effect on; ~**rsi** *vr* to grow cool *o* cold; (*prendere un raffreddore*) to catch a cold; (*fig*) to cool (off).
raffred'dato, a *ag* (*MED*): **essere** ~ to have a cold.
raffred'dore *sm* (*MED*) cold.
raffron'tare *vt* to compare.
raf'fronto *sm* comparison.
'rafia *sf* (*fibra*) raffia.
raga'nella *sf* (*ZOOL*) tree frog.
ra'gazzo, a [ra'gattso] *sm/f* boy/girl; (*fam: fidanzato*) boyfriend/girlfriend; **nome da** ~**a** maiden name; ~**a madre** unmarried mother; ~**a squillo** call girl.
ragge'lare [raddʒe'lare] *vt*, *vi*, ~**rsi** *vr* to freeze.
raggi'ante [rad'dʒante] *ag* radiant, shining; ~ **di gioia** beaming *o* radiant with joy.
raggi'era [rad'dʒera] *sf* (*di ruota*) spokes *pl*; **a** ~ with a sunburst pattern.
'raggio ['raddʒo] *sm* (*di sole etc*) ray; (*MAT, distanza*) radius; (*di ruota etc*) spoke; **nel** ~ **di 20 km** within a radius of 20 km *o* a 20-km radius; **a largo** ~ (*esplorazione, incursione*) wide-ranging; ~ **d'azione** range; ~ **laser** laser beam; ~**i X** X-rays.
raggi'rare [raddʒi'rare] *vt* to take in, trick.
rag'giro [rad'dʒiro] *sm* trick.
raggi'ungere [rad'dʒundʒere] *vt* to reach; (*persona: riprendere*) to catch up (with); (*bersaglio*) to hit; (*fig: meta*) to achieve; ~

il proprio scopo to reach one's goal, achieve one's aim; ~ **un accordo** to come to o reach an agreement.

raggi'unto, a [rad'dʒunto] pp di raggiungere.

raggomito'larsi vr to curl up.

raggranel'lare vt to scrape together.

raggrin'zare [raggrin'tsare] vt, vi (anche: ~rsi) to wrinkle.

raggrin'zire [raggrin'tsire] vt = raggrinzare.

raggru'mare vt, ~rsi vr (sangue, latte) to clot.

raggruppa'mento sm (azione) grouping; (gruppo) group; (: MIL) unit.

raggrup'pare vt to group (together).

ragguagli'are [raggwaʎ'ʎare] vt (paragonare) to compare; (informare) to inform.

raggu'aglio [rag'gwaʎʎo] sm comparison; (informazione, relazione) piece of information.

ragguar'devole ag (degno di riguardo) distinguished, notable; (notevole: somma) considerevole.

'ragia ['radʒa] sf: acqua ~ turpentine.

ragiona'mento [radʒona'mento] sm reasoning no pl; argument.

ragio'nare [radʒo'nare] vi (usare la ragione) to reason; (discorrere): ~ (di) to argue (about); cerca di ~ try and be reasonable.

ragi'one [ra'dʒone] sf reason; (dimostrazione, prova) argument, reason; (diritto) right; aver ~ to be right; aver ~ di qn to get the better of sb; dare ~ a qn (sog: persona) to side with sb; (: fatto) to prove sb right; farsi una ~ di qc to accept sth, come to terms with sth; in ~ di at the rate of; a o con ~ rightly, justly; perdere la ~ to become insane; (fig) to take leave of one's senses; a ragion veduta after due consideration; per ~i di famiglia for family reasons; ~ di scambio terms of trade; ~ sociale (COMM) corporate name; ragion di stato reason of State.

ragione'ria [radʒone'ria] sf accountancy; (ufficio) accounts department.

ragio'nevole [radʒo'nevole] ag reasonable.

ragioni'ere, a [radʒo'njɛre] sm/f accountant.

ragli'are [raʎ'ʎare] vi to bray.

ragna'tela [raɲɲa'tela] sf cobweb, spider's web.

'ragno ['raɲɲo] sm spider; non cavare un ~ dal buco (fig) to draw a blank.

ragù sm inv (CUC) meat sauce (for pasta).

RAI-TV [raiti'vu] sigla f (= Radio televisione italiana) Italian Broadcasting Company.

rallegra'menti smpl congratulations.

ralle'grare vt to cheer up; ~rsi vr to cheer up; (provare allegrezza) to rejoice; ~rsi con qn to congratulate sb.

rallenta'mento sm slowing down; slackening.

rallen'tare vt, vi to slow down; ~ il passo to slacken one's pace.

rallenta'tore sm (CINE) slow-motion camera; al ~ (anche fig) in slow motion.

raman'zina [raman'dzina] sf lecture, telling-off.

ra'mare vt (superficie) to copper, coat with copper; (AGR: vite) to spray with copper sulphate.

ra'marro sm green lizard.

ra'mato, a ag (oggetto: rivestito di rame) copper-coated, coppered; (capelli, barba) coppery, copper-coloured (BRIT), copper-colored (US).

'rame sm (CHIM) copper; di ~ copper cpd; incisione su ~ copperplate.

ramifi'care vi (BOT) to put out branches; ~rsi vr (diramarsi) to branch out; (MED: tumore, vene) to ramify; ~rsi in (biforcarsi) to branch into.

ramificazi'one [ramifikat'tsjone] sf ramification.

ra'mingo, a, ghi, ghe ag (poetico): andare ~ to go wandering, wander.

ra'mino sm (CARTE) rummy.

rammari'carsi vr: ~ (di) (rincrescersi) to be sorry (about), regret; (lamentarsi) to complain (about).

ram'marico, chi sm regret.

rammen'dare vt to mend; (calza) to darn.

ram'mendo sm mending no pl; darning no pl; mend; darn.

rammen'tare vt to remember, recall; ~rsi vr: ~rsi (di qc) to remember (sth); ~ qc a qn to remind sb of sth.

rammol'lire vt to soften ♦ vi (anche: ~rsi) to go soft.

rammol'lito, a ag weak ♦ sm/f weakling.

'ramo sm branch; (di commercio) field; non è il mio ~ it's not my field o line.

ramo'scello [ramoʃ'ʃello] sm twig.

'rampa sf flight (of stairs); ~ di lancio launching pad.

rampi'cante ag (BOT) climbing.

ram'pino sm (gancio) hook; (NAUT) grapnel.

ram'pollo sm (di acqua) spring; (BOT: germoglio) shoot; (fig: discendente) descendant.

ram'pone sm harpoon; (ALPINISMO) crampon.

'rana sf frog; ~ pescatrice angler fish.

'rancido, a ['rantʃido] ag rancid.

'rancio ['rantʃo] *sm* (*MIL*) mess; **ora del** ~ mess time.

ran'core *sm* rancour (*BRIT*), rancor (*US*), resentment; **portare** ~ **a qn, provare** ~ **per** *o* **verso qn** to bear sb a grudge.

ran'dagio, a, gi, gie *o* **ge** [ran'dadʒo] *ag* (*gatto, cane*) stray.

ran'dello *sm* club, cudgel.

'rango, ghi *sm* (*grado*) rank; (*condizione sociale*) station, social standing; **persone di** ~ **inferiore** people of lower standing; **uscire dai** ~**ghi** to fall out; (*fig*) to step out of line.

Ran'gun *sf* Rangoon.

rannicchi'arsi [rannik'kjarsi] *vr* to crouch, huddle.

rannuvo'larsi *vr* to cloud over, become overcast.

ra'nocchio [ra'nɔkkjo] *sm* (edible) frog.

ranto'lare *vi* to wheeze.

ranto'lio *sm* (*il respirare affannoso*) wheezing; (: *di agonizzante*) death rattle.

'rantolo *sm* wheeze; death rattle.

ra'nuncolo *sm* (*BOT*) buttercup.

'rapa *sf* (*BOT*) turnip.

ra'pace [ra'patʃe] *ag* (*animale*) predatory; (*fig*) rapacious, grasping ♦ *sm* bird of prey.

ra'pare *vt* (*capelli*) to crop, cut very short.

'rapida *sf vedi* **rapido**.

rapida'mente *av* quickly, rapidly.

rapidità *sf* speed.

'rapido, a *ag* fast; (*esame, occhiata*) quick, rapid ♦ *sm* (*FERR*) express (train) ♦ *sf* (*di fiume*) rapid.

rapi'mento *sm* kidnapping; (*fig*) rapture.

ra'pina *sf* robbery; ~ **in banca** bank robbery; ~ **a mano armata** armed robbery.

rapi'nare *vt* to rob.

rapina'tore, 'trice *sm/f* robber.

ra'pire *vt* (*cose*) to steal; (*persone*) to kidnap; (*fig*) to enrapture, delight.

ra'pito, a *ag* (*persona*) kidnapped; (*fig: in estasi*): **ascoltare** ~ **qn** to be captivated by sb's words ♦ *sm/f* kidnapped person.

rapi'tore, 'trice *sm/f* kidnapper.

rappacifi'care [rappatʃifi'kare] *vt* (*riconciliare*) to reconcile; ~**rsi** *vr* (*uso reciproco*) to be reconciled, make it up (*fam*).

rappacificazi'one [rappatʃifikat'tsjone] *sf* reconciliation.

rappez'zare [rappet'tsare] *vt* to patch.

rappor'tare *vt* (*confrontare*) to compare; (*riprodurre*) to reproduce.

rap'porto *sm* (*resoconto*) report; (*legame*) relationship; (*MAT, TECN*) ratio; ~**i** *smpl* (*fra persone, paesi*) relations; **in** ~ **a** **quanto è successo** with regard to *o* in relation to what happened; **fare** ~ **a qn su qc** to report sth to sb; **andare a** ~ **da qn** to report to sb; **chiamare qn a** ~ (*MIL*) to summon sb; **essere in buoni/cattivi** ~**i con qn** to be on good/bad terms with sb; ~ **d'affari**, ~ **di lavoro** business relations; ~ **di compressione** (*TECN*) pressure ratio; ~ **coniugale** marital relationship; ~ **di trasmissione** (*TECN*) gear; ~**i sessuali** sexual intercourse *sg*.

rap'prendersi *vr* to coagulate, clot; (*latte*) to curdle.

rappre'saglia [rappre'saʎʎa] *sf* reprisal, retaliation.

rappresen'tante *sm/f* representative; ~ **di commercio** sales representative, sales rep (*fam*); ~ **sindacale** union delegate *o* representative.

rappresen'tanza [rapprezen'tantsa] *sf* delegation, deputation; (*COMM: ufficio, sede*) agency; **in** ~ **di qn** on behalf of sb; **spese di** ~ entertainment expenses; **macchina di** ~ official car; **avere la** ~ **di** to be the agent for; ~ **esclusiva** sole agency; **avere la** ~ **esclusiva** to be sole agent.

rappresen'tare *vt* to represent; (*TEAT*) to perform; **farsi** ~ **dal proprio legale** to be represented by one's lawyer.

rappresenta'tivo, a *ag* representative ♦ *sf* (*di partito, sindacale*) representative group; (*SPORT: squadra*) representative (team).

rappresentazi'one [rapprezentat'tsjone] *sf* representation; performing *no pl*; (*spettacolo*) performance; **prima** ~ **assoluta** world première.

rap'preso, a *pp di* **rapprendere**.

rapso'dia *sf* rhapsody.

'raptus *sm inv*: ~ **di follia** fit of madness.

rara'mente *av* seldom, rarely.

rare'fare *vt*, ~**rsi** *vr* to rarefy.

rare'fatto, a *pp di* **rarefare** ♦ *ag* rarefied.

rarefazi'one [rarefat'tsjone] *sf* rarefaction.

rarità *sf inv* rarity.

'raro, a *ag* rare.

ra'sare *vt* (*barba etc*) to shave off; (*siepi, erba*) to trim, cut; ~**rsi** *vr* to shave (o.s.).

ra'sato, a *ag* (*erba*) trimmed, cut; (*tessuto*) smooth; **avere la barba** ~**a** to be clean-shaven.

rasa'tura *sf* shave.

raschia'mento [raskja'mento] *sm* (*MED*) curettage; ~ **uterino** D and C.

raschi'are [ras'kjare] *vt* to scrape; (*macchia, fango*) to scrape off ♦ *vi* to clear one's throat.

rasen'tare *vt* (*andar rasente*) to keep close to; (*sfiorare*) to skim along (*o* over); (*fig*) to border on.

ra'sente *prep*: ~ **(a)** close to, very near.

'raso, a *pp di* **radere** ♦ *ag* (*barba*) shaved; (*capelli*) cropped; (*con misure di capacità*) level; (*pieno*: *bicchiere*) full to the brim ♦ *sm* (*tessuto*) satin; ~ **terra** close to the ground; **volare** ~ **terra** to hedgehop; **un cucchiaio** ~ a level spoonful.

ra'soio *sm* razor; ~ **elettrico** electric shaver *o* razor.

ras'pare *vt* (*levigare*) to rasp; (*grattare*) to scratch.

'raspo *sm* (*di uva*) grape stalk.

ras'segna [ras'seɲɲa] *sf* (*MIL*) inspection, review; (*esame*) inspection; (*resoconto*) review, survey; (*pubblicazione letteraria etc*) review; (*mostra*) exhibition, show; **passare in** ~ (*MIL*, *fig*) to review.

rasse'gnare [rasseɲ'ɲare] *vt*: ~ **le dimissioni** to resign, hand in one's resignation; ~**rsi** *vr* (*accettare*): ~**rsi (a qc/ a fare)** to resign o.s. (to sth/to doing).

rassegnazi'one [rasseɲɲat'tsjone] *sf* resignation.

rassere'nare *vt* (*persona*) to cheer up; ~**rsi** *vr* (*tempo*) to clear up.

rasset'tare *vt* to tidy, put in order; (*aggiustare*) to repair, mend.

rassicu'rante *ag* reassuring.

rassicu'rare *vt* to reassure; ~**rsi** *vr* to take heart, recover one's confidence.

rassicurazi'one [rassikurat'tsjone] *sf* reassurance.

rasso'dare *vt* to harden, stiffen; (*fig*) to strengthen, consolidate.

rassomigli'anza [rassomiʎ'ʎantsa] *sf* resemblance.

rassomigli'are [rassomiʎ'ʎare] *vi*: ~ **a** to resemble, look like.

rastrella'mento *sm* (*MIL*, *di polizia*) (thorough) search.

rastrel'lare *vt* to rake; (*fig*: *perlustrare*) to comb.

rastrelli'era *sf* rack; (*per piatti*) dish rack.

ras'trello *sm* rake.

'rata *sf* (*quota*) instalment, installment (*US*); **pagare a** ~**e** to pay by instal(l)ments *o* on hire purchase (*BRIT*); **comprare/vendere a** ~**e** to buy/sell on hire purchase (*BRIT*) *o* on the installment plan (*US*).

rate'ale *ag*: **pagamento** ~ payment by instal(l)ments; **vendita** ~ hire purchase (*BRIT*), installment plan (*US*).

rate'are, rateiz'zare [rateid'dzare] *vt* to

divide into instal(l)ments.

rateazi'one [rateat'tsjone] *sf* division into instal(l)ments.

'rateo *sm* (*COMM*) accrual.

ra'tifica, che *sf* ratification.

ratifi'care *vt* (*DIR*) to ratify.

'ratto *sm* (*DIR*) abduction; (*ZOOL*) rat.

rattop'pare *vt* to patch.

rat'toppo *sm* patching *no pl*; patch.

rattrap'pire *vt* to make stiff; ~**rsi** *vr* to be stiff.

rattris'tare *vt* to sadden; ~**rsi** *vr* to become sad.

rau'cedine [rau'tʃedine] *sf* hoarseness.

'rauco, a, chi, che *ag* hoarse.

rava'nello *sm* radish.

raven'nate *ag* of (*o* from) Ravenna.

ravi'oli *smpl* ravioli *sg*.

ravve'dersi *vr* to mend one's ways.

ravvi'are *vt* (*capelli*) to tidy; ~**rsi i capelli** to tidy one's hair.

ravvicina'mento [ravvitʃina'mento] *sm* (*tra persone*) reconciliation; (*POL*: *tra paesi etc*) rapprochement.

ravvici'nare [ravvitʃi'nare] *vt* (*avvicinare*): ~ **qc a** to bring sth nearer to; (*oggetti*) to bring closer together; (*fig*: *persone*) to reconcile, bring together; ~**rsi** *vr* to be reconciled.

ravvi'sare *vt* to recognize.

ravvi'vare *vt* to revive; (*fig*) to brighten up, enliven; ~**rsi** *vr* to revive; to brighten up.

Rawal'pindi [raval'pindi] *sf* Rawalpindi.

razio'cinio [rattsjo'tʃinjo] *sm* reasoning *no pl*; reason; (*buon senso*) common sense.

razio'nale [rattsjo'nale] *ag* rational.

razionalità [rattsjonali'ta] *sf* rationality; (*buon senso*) common sense.

razionaliz'zare [rattsjonalid'dzare] *vt* (*metodo, lavoro, programma*) to rationalize; (*problema, situazione*) to approach rationally.

raziona'mento [rattsjona'mento] *sm* rationing.

razio'nare [rattsjo'nare] *vt* to ration.

razi'one [rat'tsjone] *sf* ration; (*porzione*) portion, share.

'razza ['rattsa] *sf* race; (*ZOOL*) breed; (*discendenza, stirpe*) stock, race; (*sorta*) sort, kind.

raz'zia [rat'tsia] *sf* raid, foray.

razzi'ale [rat'tsjale] *ag* racial.

raz'zismo [rat'tsizmo] *sm* racism, racialism.

raz'zista, i, e [rat'tsista] *ag, smf* racist, racialist.

'razzo ['raddzo] *sm* rocket; ~ **di segnalazione** flare; ~ **vettore** vector rocket.

razzo'lare [rattso'lare] *vi* (*galline*) to scratch about.

RC *sigla* = *Reggio Calabria.*

RDT *sigla f vedi* **Repubblica Democratica Tedesca.**

RE *sigla* = *Reggio Emilia.*

re *sm inv* (*sovrano*) king; (*MUS*) D; (: *solfeggiando la scala*) re.

rea'gente [rea'dʒɛnte] *sm* reagent.

rea'gire [rea'dʒire] *vi* to react.

re'ale *ag* real; (*di, da re*) royal ♦ *sm*: **il** ~ reality; **i R**~**i** the Royal family.

rea'lismo *sm* realism.

rea'lista, i, e *sm/f* realist; (*POL*) royalist.

rea'listico, a, ci, che *ag* realistic.

realiz'zare [realid'dzare] *vt* (*progetto etc*) to realize, carry out; (*sogno, desiderio*) to realize, fulfil; (*scopo*) to achieve; (*COMM*: *titoli etc*) to realize; (*CALCIO etc*) to score; ~**rsi** *vr* to be realized.

realizzazi'one [realiddzat'tsjone] *sf* realization; fulfilment; achievement; ~ **scenica** stage production.

rea'lizzo [rea'liddzo] *sm* (*conversione in denaro*) conversion into cash; (*vendita forzata*) clearance sale.

real'mente *av* really, actually.

realtà *sf inv* reality; **in** ~ (*in effetti*) in fact; (*a dire il vero*) really.

re'ame *sm* kingdom, realm; (*fig*) realm.

re'ato *sm* offence (*BRIT*), offense (*US*).

reat'tore *sm* (*FISICA*) reactor; (*AER: aereo*) jet; (: *motore*) jet engine.

reazio'nario, a [reattsjo'narjo] *ag, sm/f* (*POL*) reactionary.

reazi'one [reat'tsjone] *sf* reaction; **motore/ aereo a** ~ jet engine/plane; **forze della** ~ reactionary forces; ~ **a catena** (*anche fig*) chain reaction.

'rebbio *sm* prong.

'rebus *sm inv* rebus; (*fig*) puzzle; enigma.

recapi'tare *vt* to deliver.

re'capito *sm* (*indirizzo*) address; (*consegna*) delivery; **ha un** ~ **telefonico?** do you have a telephone number where you can be reached?; ~ **a domicilio** home delivery (service).

re'care *vt* (*portare*) to bring; (*avere su di sé*) to carry, bear; (*cagionare*) to cause, bring; ~**rsi** *vr* to go; ~ **danno a qn** to harm sb, cause harm to sb.

re'cedere [re'tʃɛdere] *vi* to withdraw.

recensi'one [retʃen'sjone] *sf* review.

recen'sire [retʃen'sire] *vt* to review.

recen'sore, a [retʃen'sore] *sm/f* reviewer.

re'cente [re'tʃɛnte] *ag* recent; **di** ~ recently; **più** ~ latest, most recent.

recente'mente [retʃente'mente] *av* recently.

rece'pire [retʃe'pire] *vt* to understand, take in.

recessi'one [retʃes'sjone] *sf* (*ECON*) recession.

re'cesso [re'tʃɛsso] *sm* (*azione*) recession, receding; (*DIR*) withdrawal; (*luogo*) recess.

recherò *etc* [reke'rɔ] *vb vedi* **recare.**

re'cidere [re'tʃidere] *vt* to cut off, chop off.

reci'divo, a [retʃi'divo] *sm/f* (*DIR*) second (*o habitual*) offender, recidivist ♦ *sf* recidivism.

recin'tare [retʃin'tare] *vt* to enclose, fence off.

re'cinto [re'tʃinto] *sm* enclosure; (*ciò che recinge*) fence; surrounding wall.

recinzi'one [retʃin'tsjone] *sf* (*azione*) enclosure, fencing-off; (*recinto: di legno*) fence; (: *di mattoni*) wall; (: *reticolato*) wire fencing; (: *a sbarre*) railings *pl*.

recipi'ente [retʃi'pjɛnte] *sm* container.

re'ciproco, a, ci, che [re'tʃiproko] *ag* reciprocal.

re'ciso, a [re'tʃizo] *pp di* **recidere.**

'recita ['rɛtʃita] *sf* performance.

'recital ['rɛtʃital] *sm inv* recital.

reci'tare [retʃi'tare] *vt* (*poesia, lezione*) to recite; (*dramma*) to perform; (*ruolo*) to play *o* act (the part of).

recitazi'one [retʃitat'tsjone] *sf* recitation; (*di attore*) acting; **scuola di** ~ drama school.

recla'mare *vi* to complain ♦ *vt* (*richiedere*) to demand.

ré'clame [re'klam] *sf inv* advertising *no pl*; advertisement, advert (*BRIT*), ad (*fam*).

reclamiz'zare [reklamid'dzare] *vt* to advertise.

re'clamo *sm* complaint; **sporgere** ~ **a** to complain to, make a complaint to.

recli'nabile *ag* (*sedile*) reclining.

recli'nare *vt* (*capo*) to bow, lower; (*sedile*) to tilt.

reclusi'one *sf* (*DIR*) imprisonment.

re'cluso, a *sm/f* prisoner.

'recluta *sf* recruit.

recluta'mento *sm* recruitment.

reclu'tare *vt* to recruit.

re'condito, a *ag* secluded; (*fig*) secret, hidden.

'record *ag inv* record *cpd* ♦ *sm inv* record; **in tempo** ~, **a tempo di** ~ in record time; **detenere il** ~ **di** to hold the record for; ~ **mondiale** world record.

recrimi'nare *vi*: ~ (**su qc**) to complain (about sth).

recriminazi'one [rekriminat'tsjone] *sf* recrimination.

recrude'scenza [rekrudeʃ'ʃɛntsa] *sf* fresh outbreak.

recupe'rare *etc* = **ricuperare** *etc*.

re'dassi *etc vb vedi* **redigere**.

re'datto, a *pp di* **redigere**.

redat'tore, 'trice *sm/f* (*STAMPA*) editor; (*: di articolo*) writer; (*di dizionario etc*) compiler; ~ **capo** chief editor.

redazi'one [redat'tsjone] *sf* editing; writing; (*sede*) editorial office(s); (*personale*) editorial staff; (*versione*) version.

reddi'tizio, a [reddi'tittsjo] *ag* profitable.

'reddito *sm* income; (*dello Stato*) revenue; (*di un capitale*) yield; ~ **complessivo** gross income; ~ **disponibile** disposable income; ~ **fisso** fixed income; ~ **imponibile/non imponibile** taxable/non-taxable income; ~ **da lavoro** earned income; ~ **nazionale** national income; ~ **pubblico** public revenue.

re'densi *etc vb vedi* **redimere**.

re'dento, a *pp di* **redimere**.

reden'tore *sm*. **il R~** the Redeemer.

redenzi'one [reden'tsjone] *sf* redemption.

re'digere [re'didʒere] *vt* to write; (*contratto*) to draw up.

re'dimere *vt* to deliver; (*REL*) to redeem.

'redini *sfpl* reins.

redi'vivo, a *ag* returned to life, reborn.

'reduce [ˈrɛdutʃe] *ag* (*gen*): ~ **da** returning from, back from ♦ *sm/f* survivor; (*veterano*) veteran; **essere ~ da** (*esame, colloquio*) to have been through; (*malattia*) to be just over.

'refe *sm* thread.

refe'rendum *sm inv* referendum.

refe'renza [refe'rɛntsa] *sf* reference.

re'ferto *sm* medical report.

refezi'one [refet'tsjone] *sf* (*INS*) school meal.

refrat'tario, a *ag* refractory; (*fig*): **essere ~ alla matematica** to have no aptitude for mathematics.

refrige'rare [refridʒe'rare] *vt* to refrigerate; (*rinfrescare*) to cool, refresh.

refrigerazi'one [refridʒerat'tsjone] *sf* refrigeration; (*TECN*) cooling; ~ **ad acqua** (*AUT*) water-cooling.

refri'gerio [refri'dʒɛrjo] *sm*: **trovare ~** to find somewhere cool.

refur'tiva *sf* stolen goods *pl*.

Reg. *abbr* (= *reggimento*) Regt; (*AMM*) = *regolamento*.

rega'lare *vt* to give (as a present).

re'gale *ag* regal.

re'galo *sm* gift, present ♦ *ag inv*: **confezione ~** gift pack; **fare un ~ a qn** to give sb a present; **"articoli da ~"** "gifts".

re'gata *sf* regatta.

reg'gente [red'dʒɛnte] *ag* (*proposizione*) main; (*sovrano*) reigning ♦ *sm/f* regent; **principe ~** prince regent.

reg'genza [red'dʒɛntsa] *sf* regency.

'reggere [ˈrɛddʒere] *vt* (*tenere*) to hold; (*sostenere*) to support, bear, hold up; (*portare*) to carry, bear; (*resistere*) to withstand; (*dirigere: impresa*) to manage, run; (*governare*) to rule, govern; (*LING*) to take, be followed by ♦ *vi* (*resistere*): ~ **a** to stand up to, hold out against; (*sopportare*): ~ **a** to stand; (*durare*) to last; (*fig: teoria etc*) to hold water; ~**rsi** *vr* (*stare ritto*) to stand; (*fig: dominarsi*) to control o.s.; ~**rsi sulle gambe** *o* **in piedi** to stand up.

'reggia, ge [ˈreddʒa] *sf* royal palace.

reggi'calze [reddʒi'kaltse] *sm inv* suspender belt.

reggi'mento [reddʒi'mento] *sm* (*MIL*) regiment.

reggi'petto [reddʒi'pɛtto] *sm*, **reggi'seno** [reddʒi'seno] *sm* bra.

re'gia, 'gie [re'dʒia] *sf* (*TV, CINE etc*) direction.

re'gime [re'dʒime] *sm* (*POL*) regime; (*DIR: aureo, patrimoniale etc*) system; (*MED*) diet; (*TECN*) (*engine*) speed, ~ **di giri** (*di motore*) revs *pl* per minute; ~ **vegetariano** vegetarian diet.

re'gina [re'dʒina] *sf* queen.

'regio, a, gi, gie [ˈredʒo] *ag* royal.

regio'nale [redʒo'nale] *ag* regional.

regi'one [re'dʒone] *sf* (*gen*) region; (*territorio*) region, area; *vedi nota nel riquadro*.

REGIONE

The **Regione** is the biggest administrative unit in Italy. Each of the 20 **Regioni** consists of a variable number of "Province", which in turn are subdivided into "Comuni". Each of the regions has a "capoluogo", its chief province (for example, Florence is the chief province of the region of Tuscany). Five regions have special status and wider powers: Val d'Aosta, Friuli-Venezia Giulia, Trentino-Alto Adige, Sicily and Sardinia. A **Regione** is run by the "Giunta regionale", which is elected by the "Consiglio regionale"; both are presided over by a "Presidente". The "Giunta" has legislative powers within the region over the police, public health, schools, town planning and agriculture.

regista – religione

298   ITALIANO–INGLESE

re'gista, i, e [re'dʒista] *sm/f* (*TV, CINE etc*) director.

regis'trare [redʒis'trare] *vt* (*AMM*) to register; (*COMM*) to enter; (*notare*) to report, note; (*canzone, conversazione, sog: strumento di misura*) to record; (*mettere a punto*) to adjust, regulate; ~ **i bagagli** (*AER*) to check in one's luggage; ~ **i freni** (*TECN*) to adjust the brakes.

registra'tore [redʒistra'tore] *sm* (*strumento*) recorder, register; (*magnetofono*) tape recorder; ~ **di cassa** cash register; ~ **a cassette** cassette recorder; ~ **di volo** (*AER*) flight recorder, black box (*fam*).

registrazi'one [redʒistrat'tsjone] *sf* registration; entry; reporting; recording; adjustment; ~ **bagagli** (*AER*) check-in.

re'gistro [re'dʒistro] *sm* (*libro, MUS, TECN, LING*) register; (*DIR*) registry; (*COMM*): ~ (**di cassa**) ledger; **ufficio del** ~ registrar's office; ~ **di bordo** logbook; ~**i contabili** (account) books.

re'gnante [reɲ'ɲante] *ag* reigning, ruling ♦ *sm/f* ruler.

re'gnare [reɲ'ɲare] *vi* to reign, rule; (*fig*) to reign.

'regno ['reɲɲo] *sm* kingdom; (*periodo*) reign; (*fig*) realm; **il** ~ **animale/ vegetale** the animal/vegetable kingdom; **il R**~ **Unito** the United Kingdom.

'regola *sf* rule; **a** ~ **d'arte** duly; perfectly; **essere in** ~ (*dipendente*) to be a registered employee; (*fig: essere pulito*) to be clean; **fare le cose in** ~ to do things properly; **avere le carte in** ~ (*gen*) to have one's papers in order; (*fig: essere adatto*) to be the right person; **per tua (norma e)** ~ for your information; **un'eccezione alla** ~ an exception to the rule.

rego'labile *ag* adjustable.

regolamen'tare *ag* (*distanza, velocità*) regulation *cpd*, proper; (*disposizione*) statutory ♦ *vt* (*gen*) to control; **entro il tempo** ~ within the time allowed, within the prescribed time.

regola'mento *sm* (*complesso di norme*) regulations *pl*; (*di debito*) settlement; ~ **di conti** (*fig*) settling of scores.

rego'lare *ag* regular; (*velocità*) steady; (*superficie*) even; (*passo*) steady, even; (*in regola: documento*) in order ♦ *vt* to regulate, control; (*apparecchio*) to adjust, regulate; (*questione, conto, debito*) to

settle; ~**rsi** *vr* (*moderarsi*): ~**rsi nel bere/ nello spendere** to control one's drinking/ spending; (*comportarsi*) to behave, act; **presentare** ~ **domanda** to apply through the proper channels; ~ **i conti** (*fig*) to settle old scores.

regolarità *sf inv* regularity; steadiness; evenness; (*nel pagare*) punctuality.

regolariz'zare [regolarid'dzare] *vt* (*posizione*) to regularize; (*debito*) to settle.

rego'lata *sf*: **darsi una** ~ to pull o.s. together.

regola'tezza [regola'tettsa] *sf* (*ordine*) orderliness; (*moderazione*) moderation.

rego'lato, a *ag* (*ordinato*) orderly; (*moderato*) moderate.

regola'tore *sm* (*TECN*) regulator; ~ **di frequenza/di volume** frequency/volume control.

'regolo *sm* ruler; ~ **calcolatore** slide rule.

regre'dire *vi* to regress.

regressi'one *sf* regression.

re'gresso *sm* (*fig: declino*) decline.

rei'etto, a *sm/f* outcast.

reincarnazi'one [reinkarnat'tsjone] *sf* reincarnation.

reinte'grare *vt* (*produzione*) to restore; (*energie*) to recover; (*dipendente*) to reinstate.

reintegrazi'one [reintegrat'tsjone] *sf* (*di produzione*) restoration; (*di dipendente*) reinstatement.

relativa'mente *av* relatively.

relatività *sf* relativity.

rela'tivo, a *ag* relative; (*attinente*) relevant; (*rispettivo*) respective; ~ **a** (*che concerne*) relating to, concerning; (*proporzionato*) in proportion to.

rela'tore, 'trice *sm/f* (*gen*) spokesman/ woman; (*INS: di tesi*) supervisor.

re'lax [re'laks] *sm* relaxation.

relazi'one [relat'tsjone] *sf* (*fra cose, persone*) relation(ship); (*resoconto*) report, account; ~**i** *sfpl* (*conoscenze*) connections; **essere in** ~ to be connected; **mettere in** ~ (*fatti, elementi*) to make the connection between; **in** ~ **a quanto detto prima** with regard to what has already been said; **essere in buone** ~**i con qn** to be on good terms with sb; **fare una** ~ to make a report, give an account; ~**i pubbliche (RP)** public relations (PR).

rele'gare *vt* to banish; (*fig*) to relegate.

religi'one [reli'dʒone] *sf* religion.

religi'oso, a [reli'dʒoso] *ag* religious ♦ *sm/f* monk/nun.

re'liquia *sf* relic.

re'litto *sm* wreck; (*fig*) down-and-out.

re'mainder [ri'meində*] *sm inv* (*libro*) remainder.

're'make ['ri:'meik] *sm inv* (*CINE*) remake.

re'mare *vi* to row.

remini'scenze [reminiʃ'ʃɛntse] *sfpl* reminiscences.

remissi'one *sf* remission; (*deferenza*) submissiveness, compliance; ~ **del debito** remission of debt; ~ **di querela** (*DIR*) withdrawal of an action.

remissività *sf* submissiveness.

remis'sivo, a *ag* submissive, compliant.

'remo *sm* oar.

'remora *sf* (*poetico: indugio*) hesitation.

re'moto, a *ag* remote.

remune'rare *etc* = **rimunerare** *etc*.

'rena *sf* sand.

re'nale *ag* kidney *cpd*.

'rendere *vt* (*ridare*) to return, give back; (: *saluto etc*) to return; (*produrre*) to yield, bring in; (*esprimere, tradurre*) to render; (*far diventare*): ~ **qc possibile** to make sth possible ♦ *vi* (*truttare: ditta*) to be profitable; (: *investimento, campo*) to yield, be productive; ~ **grazie a qn** to thank sb; ~ **omaggio a qn** to honour sb; ~ **un servizio a qn** to do sb a service; ~ **una testimonianza** to give evidence; ~ **la visita** to pay a return visit; **non so se rendo l'idea** I don't know whether I'm making myself clear; ~**rsi utile** to make o.s. useful; ~**rsi conto di qc** to realize sth.

rendi'conto *sm* (*rapporto*) report, account; (*AMM, COMM*) statement of account.

rendi'mento *sm* (*reddito*) yield; (*di manodopera, TECN*) efficiency; (*capacità di produrre*) output; (*di studenti*) performance.

'rendita *sf* (*di individuo*) private o unearned income; (*COMM*) revenue; ~ **annua** annuity; ~ **vitalizia** life annuity.

'rene *sm* kidney.

'reni *sfpl* back *sg*.

reni'tente *ag* reluctant, unwilling; ~ **ai consigli di qn** unwilling to follow sb's advice; **essere** ~ **alla leva** (*MIL*) to fail to report for military service.

'renna *sf* reindeer *inv*.

'Reno *sm*: **il** ~ the Rhine.

'reo, a *sm/f* (*DIR*) offender.

re'parto *sm* department, section; (*MIL*) detachment; ~ **acquisti** purchasing office.

repel'lente *ag* repulsive; (*CHIM: insettifugo*): **liquido** ~ (liquid) repellant.

repen'taglio [repen'taʎʎo] *sm*: **mettere a** ~ to jeopardize, risk.

repen'tino, a *ag* sudden, unexpected.

repe'ribile *ag* available.

repe'rire *vt* to find, trace.

re'perto *sm* (*ARCHEOLOGIA*) find; (*MED*) report; (*anche*: ~ **giudiziario**) exhibit.

reper'torio *sm* (*TEAT*) repertory; (*elenco*) index, (alphabetical) list.

'replica, che *sf* repetition; reply, answer; (*obiezione*) objection; (*TEAT, CINE*) repeat performance; (*copia*) replica.

repli'care *vt* (*ripetere*) to repeat; (*rispondere*) to answer, reply.

repor'tage [rəpɔr'taʒ] *sm inv* (*STAMPA*) report.

repressi'one *sf* repression.

repres'sivo, a *ag* repressive.

re'presso, a *pp di* **reprimere**

re'primere *vt* to suppress, repress.

re'pubblica, che *sf* republic; **la R**~ **Democratica Tedesca (RDT)** the German Democratic Republic (GDR); **la R**~ **Federale Tedesca (RFT)** the Federal Republic of Germany (FRG); **la Prima/la Seconda R**~ *terms used to refer to Italy before and after the political changes resulting from the 1994 elections*; *vedi anche* **Festa della Repubblica**; **Seconda Repubblica**.

repubbli'cano, a *ag, sm/f* republican.

repu'tare *vt* to consider, judge.

reputazi'one [reputat'tsjone] *sf* reputation; **farsi una cattiva** ~ to get o.s. a bad name.

'requie *sf* rest; **dare** ~ **a qn** to give sb some peace; **senza** ~ unceasingly.

'requiem *sm inv* (*preghiera*) requiem, prayer for the dead; (*fig: ufficio funebre*) requiem.

requi'sire *vt* to requisition.

requi'sito *sm* requirement; **avere i** ~**i necessari per un lavoro** to have the necessary qualifications for a job.

requisi'toria *sf* (*DIR*) closing speech (for the prosecution).

requisizi'one [rekwizit'tsjone] *sf* requisition.

'resa *sf* (*l'arrendersi*) surrender; (*restituzione, rendimento*) return; ~ **dei conti** rendering of accounts; (*fig*) day of reckoning.

re'scindere [reʃ'ʃindere] *vt* (*DIR*) to rescind, annul.

re'scisso, a [reʃ'ʃisso] *pp di* **rescindere**.

reset'tare *vt* (*INFORM*) to reset.

'resi *etc vb vedi* **rendere**.

resi'dente *ag* resident.
resi'denza [resi'dɛntsa] *sf* residence.
residenzi'ale [residen'tsjale] *ag* residential.
re'siduo, a *ag* residual, remaining ♦ *sm* remainder; (*CHIM*) residue; ~i **industriali** industrial waste *sg*.
'resina *sf* resin.
resis'tente *ag* (*che resiste*): ~ **a** resistant to; (*forte*) strong; (*duraturo*) long-lasting, durable; ~ **all'acqua** waterproof; ~ **al caldo** heat-resistant; ~ **al fuoco** fireproof; ~ **al gelo** frost-resistant.
resis'tenza [resis'tɛntsa] *sf* (*gen, ELETTR*) resistance; (*di persona*: *fisica*) stamina, endurance; (: *mentale*) endurance, resistance; **opporre** ~ **(a)** to offer *o* put up resistance (to); (*decisione, scelta*) to show opposition (to); **la R~** *vedi nota nel riquadro*.

RESISTENZA

The Italian **Resistenza** *fought against both the Nazis and the Fascists during the Second World War. It was particularly active after the fall of the Fascist Government on 25 July 1943, throughout the German occupation and during the period of Mussolini's Republic of Salò in northern Italy. Resistance members spanned the whole political spectrum and played a vital role in the Liberation and the formation of the new democratic government.*

---

re'sistere *vi* to resist; ~ **a** to resist; (*dolore, sog: pianta*) to withstand; (*non patir danno*) to be resistant to.
resis'tito, a *pp di* **resistere**.
'reso, a *pp di* **rendere**.
reso'conto *sm* report, account.
respin'gente [respin'dʒɛnte] *sm* (*FERR*) buffer.
res'pingere [res'pindʒere] *vt* to drive back, repel; (*rifiutare: pacco, lettera*) to return; (: *invito*) to refuse; (: *proposta*) to reject, turn down; (*INS: bocciare*) to fail.
res'pinto, a *pp di* **respingere**.
respi'rare *vi* to breathe; (*fig*) to get one's breath; to breathe again ♦ *vt* to breathe (in), inhale.
respira'tore *sm* respirator.
respira'torio, a *ag* respiratory.
respirazi'one [respirat'tsjone] *sf* breathing; ~ **artificiale** artificial respiration; ~ **bocca a bocca** mouth-to-mouth resuscitation, kiss of life (*fam*).
res'piro *sm* breathing *no pl*; (*singolo atto*) breath; (*fig*) respite, rest; **mandare un** ~ **di sollievo** to give a sigh of relief;

trattenere il ~ to hold one's breath;
lavorare senza ~ to work non-stop; **di ampio** ~ (*opera, lavoro*) far-reaching.
respon'sabile *ag* responsible ♦ *sm/f* person responsible; (*capo*) person in charge; ~ **di** responsible for; (*DIR*) liable for.
responsabilità *sf inv* responsibility; (*legale*) liability; **assumere la** ~ **di** to take on the responsibility for; **affidare a qn la** ~ **di qc** to make sb responsible for sth; ~ **patrimoniale** debt liability; ~ **penale** criminal liability.
responsabiliz'zare [responsabilid'dzare] *vt*: ~ **qn** to make sb feel responsible.
res'ponso *sm* answer; (*DIR*) verdict.
'ressa *sf* crowd, throng.
'ressi *etc vb vedi* **reggere**.
res'tare *vi* (*rimanere*) to remain, stay; (*diventare*): ~ **orfano/cieco** to become *o* be left an orphan/become blind; (*trovarsi*): ~ **sorpreso** to be surprised; (*avanzare*) to be left, remain; ~ **d'accordo** to agree; **non resta più niente** there's nothing left; **restano pochi giorni** there are only a few days left; **che resti tra di noi** this is just between ourselves; ~ **in buoni rapporti** to remain on good terms; ~ **senza parole** to be left speechless.
restau'rare *vt* to restore.
restaura'tore, 'trice *sm/f* restorer.
restaurazi'one [restaurat'tsjone] *sf* (*POL*) restoration.
res'tauro *sm* (*di edifici etc*) restoration; **in** ~ under repair; **sotto** ~ (*dipinto*) being restored; **chiuso per** ~i closed for repairs.
res'tio, a, 'tii, 'tie *ag* restive; (*persona*): ~ **a** reluctant to.
restitu'ire *vt* to return, give back; (*energie, forze*) to restore.
restituzi'one [restitut'tsjone] *sf* return; (*di soldi*) repayment.
'resto *sm* remainder, rest; (*denaro*) change; (*MAT*) remainder; ~i *smpl* leftovers; (*di città*) remains; **del** ~ moreover, besides; ~i **mortali** (mortal) remains.
res'tringere [res'trindʒere] *vt* to reduce; (*vestito*) to take in; (*stoffa*) to shrink; (*fig*) to restrict, limit; ~**rsi** *vr* (*strada*) to narrow; (*stoffa*) to shrink.
restrit'tivo, a *ag* restrictive.
restrizi'one [restrit'tsjone] *sf* restriction.
resurrezi'one [resurret'tsjone] *sf* = **risurrezione**.
resusci'tare [resuʃʃi'tare] *vt, vi* = **risuscitare**.
re'tata *sf* (*PESCA*) haul, catch; **fare una** ~ **di** (*fig: persone*) to round up.
'rete *sf* net; (*di recinzione*) wire netting;

(*AUT, FERR, di spionaggio etc*) network; (*fig*) trap, snare; **segnare una** ~ (*CALCIO*) to score a goal; ~ **ferroviaria/stradale/di distribuzione** railway/road/distribution network; ~ **del letto** (sprung) bed base; ~ **da pesca** fishing net; ~ (**televisiva**) (*sistema*) network; (*canale*) channel.
reti'cente [reti'tʃɛnte] *ag* reticent.
reti'cenza [reti'tʃɛntsa] *sf* reticence.
retico'lato *sm* grid; (*rete metallica*) wire netting; (*di filo spinato*) barbed wire fence.
'**retina** *sf* (*ANAT*) retina.
re'torico, a, ci, che *ag* rhetorical ♦ *sf* rhetoric.
retribu'ire *vt* to pay; (*premiare*) to reward; **un lavoro mal retribuito** a poorly-paid job.
retribu'tivo, a *ag* pay *cpd*.
retribuzi'one [retribut'tsjone] *sf* payment; reward.
re'trivo, a *ag* (*fig*) reactionary.
'**retro** *sm inv* back ♦ *av* (*dietro*): **vedi** ~ see over(leaf).
retroattività *sf* retroactivity.
retroat'tivo, a *ag* (*DIR*: *legge*) retroactive; (*AMM*: *salario*) backdated.
retrobot'tega, ghe *sf* back shop.
retro'cedere [retro'tʃɛdere] *vi* to withdraw ♦ *vt* (*CALCIO*) to relegate; (*MIL*) to degrade; (*AMM*) to demote.
retrocessi'one [retrotʃes'sjone] *sf* (*di impiegato*) demotion.
retro'cesso, a [retro'tʃɛsso] *pp di* **retrocedere**.
retroda'tare *vt* (*AMM*) to backdate.
re'trogrado, a *ag* (*fig*) reactionary, backward-looking.
retrogu'ardia *sf* (*anche fig*) rearguard.
retro'marcia [retro'martʃa] *sf* (*AUT*) reverse; (: *dispositivo*) reverse gear.
retro'scena [retroʃ'ʃɛna] *sf inv* (*TEAT*) backstage ♦ *sm inv* (*fig*) behind-the-scenes activity.
retrospet'tivo, a *ag* retrospective ♦ *sf* (*ARTE*) retrospective (exhibition).
retros'tante *ag*: ~ (**a**) at the back (of).
retro'terra *sm* hinterland.
retro'via *sf* (*MIL*) zone behind the front; **mandare nelle** ~**e** to send to the rear.
retrovi'sore *sm* (*AUT*) (rear-view) mirror.
'**retta** *sf* (*MAT*) straight line; (*di convitto*) charge for bed and board; (*fig*: *ascolto*): **dar** ~ **a** to listen to, pay attention to.
rettango'lare *ag* rectangular.
ret'tangolo, a *ag* right-angled ♦ *sm* rectangle.
ret'tifica, che *sf* rectification, correction.

rettifi'care *vt* (*curva*) to straighten; (*fig*) to rectify, correct.
'**rettile** *sm* reptile.
retti'lineo, a *ag* rectilinear.
retti'tudine *sf* rectitude, uprightness.
'**retto, a** *pp di* **reggere** ♦ *ag* straight; (*MAT*): **angolo** ~ right angle; (*onesto*) honest, upright; (*giusto, esatto*) correct, proper, right.
ret'tore *sm* (*REL*) rector; (*di università*) ≈ chancellor.
reuma'tismo *sm* rheumatism.
Rev. *abbr* (= *Reverendo*) Rev(d).
reve'rendo, a *ag*: **il** ~ **padre Belli** the Reverend Father Belli.
reve'rente *ag* = **riverente**.
reve'renza [reve'rɛntsa] *sf* = **riverenza**.
rever'sibile *ag* reversible.
revisio'nare *vt* (*conti*) to audit; (*TECN*) to overhaul, service; (*DIR*: *processo*) to review; (*componimento*) to revise.
revisi'one *sf* auditing *no pl*; audit; servicing *no pl*; overhaul; review; revision; ~ **di bilancio** audit; ~ **di bozze** proofreading; ~ **contabile interna** internal audit.
revi'sore *sm*: ~ **di conti/bozze** auditor/proofreader.
'**revoca** *sf* revocation.
revo'care *vt* to revoke.
re'volver *sm inv* revolver.
revolve'rata *sf* revolver shot.
'**Reykjavik** [ˈreikjavik] *sf* Reykjavik.
RFT *sigla f vedi* **Repubblica Federale Tedesca**.
ri'abbia *etc vb vedi* **riavere**.
riabili'tare *vt* to rehabilitate; (*fig*) to restore to favour (*BRIT*) *o* favor (*US*).
riabilitazi'one [riabilitat'tsjone] *sf* rehabilitation.
riac'cendere [riat'tʃɛndere] *vt* (*sigaretta, fuoco, gas*) to light again; (*luce, radio, TV*) to switch on again; (*fig*: *sentimenti, interesse*) to rekindle, revive; ~**rsi** *vr* (*fuoco*) to catch again; (*luce, radio, TV*) to come back on again; (*fig*: *sentimenti*) to revive, be rekindled.
riac'ceso, a [riat'tʃeso] *pp di* **riaccendere**.
riacqui'stare *vt* (*gen*) to buy again; (*ciò che si era venduto*) to buy back; (*fig*: *buonumore, sangue freddo, libertà*) to regain; ~ **la salute** to recover (one's health); ~ **le forze** to regain one's strength.
Ri'ad *sf* Riyadh.
riaddormen'tare *vt* to put to sleep again; ~**rsi** *vr* to fall asleep again.
riallac'ciare [riallat'tʃare] *vt* (*cintura, cavo etc*) to refasten, tie up *o* fasten again; (*fig*: *rapporti, amicizia*) to resume, renew; ~**rsi**

vr: ~**rsi a** (*fig: a discorso, tema*) to resume, take up again.

rial'zare [rial'tsare] *vt* to raise, lift; (*alzare di più*) to heighten, raise; (*aumentare: prezzi*) to increase, raise ♦ *vi* (*prezzi*) to rise, increase.

rial'zato, a [rial'tsato] *ag:* **piano** ~ mezzanine, entresol.

rial'zista, i [rial'tsista] *sm* (*BORSA*) bull.

ri'alzo [ri'altso] *sm* (*di prezzi*) increase, rise; (*sporgenza*) rise; **giocare al** ~ (*BORSA*) to bull.

rian'dare *vi:* ~ (**in**), ~ (**a**) to go back (to), return (to).

riani'mare *vt* (*MED*) to resuscitate; (*fig: rallegrare*) to cheer up; (: *dar coraggio*) to give heart to; ~**rsi** *vr* to recover consciousness; to cheer up; to take heart.

rianimazi'one [rianimat'tsjone] *sf* (*MED*) resuscitation; **centro di** ~ intensive care unit.

ria'perto, a *pp di* **riaprire.**

riaper'tura *sf* reopening.

riappa'rire *vi* to reappear.

riap'parso, a *pp di* **riapparire.**

riap'pendere *vt* to rehang; (*TEL*) to hang up.

ria'prire *vt*, ~**rsi** *vr* to reopen, open again.

ri'armo *sm* (*MIL*) rearmament.

ri'arso, a *ag* (*terreno*) arid; (*gola*) parched; (*labbra*) dry.

riasset'tare *vt* (*vedi sm*) to rearrange; to reorganize.

rias'setto *sm* (*di stanza etc*) rearrangement; (*ordinamento*) reorganization.

rias'sumere *vt* (*riprendere*) to resume; (*impiegare di nuovo*) to re-employ; (*sintetizzare*) to summarize.

rias'sunto, a *pp di* **riassumere** ♦ *sm* summary.

riattac'care *vt* (*attaccare di nuovo*): ~ (**a**) (*manifesto, francobollo*) to stick back (on); (*bottone*) to sew back (on); (*quadro, chiavi*) to hang back up (on); ~ (**il telefono o il ricevitore**) to hang up (the receiver).

riatti'vare *vt* to reactivate.

ria'vere *vt* to have again; (*avere indietro*) to get back; (*riacquistare*) to recover; ~**rsi** *vr* to recover; (*da svenimento, stordimento*) to come round.

riba'dire *vt* (*fig*) to confirm.

ri'balta *sf* (*sportello*) flap; (*TEAT: proscenio*) front of the stage; (: *apparecchio d'illuminazione*) footlights *pl*; (*fig*) limelight; **tornare alla** ~ (*personaggio*) to make a comeback; (*problema*) to come up again.

ribal'tabile *ag* (*sedile*) tip-up.

ribal'tare *vt*, *vi* (*anche:* ~**rsi**) to turn over, tip over.

ribas'sare *vt* to lower, bring down ♦ *vi* to come down, fall.

ribas'sista, i *sm* (*BORSA*) bear.

ri'basso *sm* reduction, fall; **essere in** ~ (*azioni, prezzi*) to be down; (*fig: popolarità*) to be on the decline; **giocare al** ~ (*BORSA*) to bear.

ri'battere *vt* (*battere di nuovo*) to beat again; (*con macchina da scrivere*) to type again; (*palla*) to return; (*confutare*) to refute; ~ **che** to retort that.

ribattez'zare [ribatted'dzare] *vt* to rename.

ribel'larsi *vr:* ~ (**a**) to rebel (against).

ri'belle *ag* (*soldati*) rebel; (*ragazzo*) rebellious ♦ *sm/f* rebel.

ribelli'one *sf* rebellion.

'ribes *sm inv* currant; ~ **nero** blackcurrant; ~ **rosso** redcurrant.

ribol'lire *vi* (*fermentare*) to ferment; (*fare bolle*) to bubble, boil; (*fig*) to seethe.

ri'brezzo [ri'breddzo] *sm* disgust, loathing; **far** ~ **a** to disgust.

ribut'tante *ag* disgusting, revolting.

ricacci'are [rikat'tʃare] *vt* (*respingere*) to drive back; ~ **qn fuori** to throw sb out.

rica'dere *vi* to fall again; (*scendere a terra, fig: nel peccato etc*) to fall back; (*vestiti, capelli etc*) to hang (down); (*riversarsi: fatiche, colpe*): ~ **su** to fall on.

rica'duta *sf* (*MED*) relapse.

rical'care *vt* (*disegni*) to trace; (*fig*) to follow faithfully.

ricalci'trare [rikaltʃi'trare] *vi* (*cavalli, asini, muli*) to kick.

rica'mare *vt* to embroider.

ricambi'are *vt* to change again; (*contraccambiare*) to return.

ri'cambio *sm* exchange, return; (*FISIOL*) metabolism; ~**i** *smpl*, **pezzi di** ~ spare parts; ~ **della manodopera** labour turnover.

ri'camo *sm* embroidery; **senza** ~**i** (*fig*) without frills.

ricapito'lare *vt* to recapitulate, sum up.

ricapitolazi'one [rikapitolat'tsjone] *sf* recapitulation, summary.

ricari'care *vt* (*arma, macchina fotografica*) to reload; (*penna*) to refill; (*orologio, giocattolo*) to rewind; (*ELETTR*) to recharge.

ricat'tare *vt* to blackmail.

ricatta'tore, 'trice *sm/f* blackmailer.

ri'catto *sm* blackmail; **fare un** ~ **a qn** to blackmail sb; **subire un** ~ to be blackmailed.

rica'vare *vt* (*estrarre*) to draw out, extract;

(*ottenere*) to obtain, gain.
rica'vato *sm* (*di vendite*) proceeds *pl*.
ri'cavo *sm* proceeds *pl*; (*CONTABILITÀ*)
revenue.
ric'chezza [rik'kettsa] *sf* wealth; (*fig*)
richness; ~**e** *sfpl* (*beni*) wealth *sg*, riches;
~**e naturali** natural resources.
'riccio, a, ci, ce ['rittʃo] *ag* curly ♦ *sm*
(*ZOOL*) hedgehog; (: *anche*: ~ **di mare**) sea
urchin.
'ricciolo ['rittʃolo] *sm* curl.
ricci'uto, a [rit'tʃuto] *ag* curly.
'ricco, a, chi, che *ag* rich; (*persona, paese*)
rich, wealthy ♦ *sm/f* rich man/woman; **i**
~**chi** the rich; ~ **di** (*idee, illustrazioni etc*)
full of; (*risorse, fauna etc*) rich in.
ri'cerca, che [ri'tʃerka] *sf* search; (*indagine*)
investigation, inquiry; (*studio*): **la** ~
research; **una** ~ piece of research;
mettersi alla ~ **di** to go in search of, look
o search *o* hunt for; **essere alla** ~ **di** to be
searching for, be looking for; ~ **di**
mercato market research; ~ **operativa**
operational research.
ricer'care [ritʃer'kare] *vt* (*motivi, cause*) to
look for, try to determine; (*successo,*
piacere) to pursue; (*onore, gloria*) to seek.
ricerca'tezza [ritʃerka'tettsa] *sf*
(*raffinatezza*) refinement; (: *peg*)
affectation.
ricer'cato, a [ritʃer'kato] *ag* (*apprezzato*)
much sought-after; (*affettato*) studied,
affected ♦ *sm/f* (*POLIZIA*) wanted man/
woman.
ricerca'tore, 'trice [ritʃerka'tore] *sm/f* (*INS*)
researcher.
ricetrasmit'tente [ritʃetrazmit'tɛnte] *sf*
two-way radio, transceiver.
ri'cetta [ri'tʃetta] *sf* (*MED*) prescription;
(*CUC*) recipe; (*fig*: *antidoto*): ~ **contro**
remedy for.
ricet'tacolo [ritʃet'takolo] *sm* (*peg*: *luogo*
malfamato) den.
ricet'tario [ritʃet'tarjo] *sm* (*MED*)
prescription pad; (*CULIN*) recipe book.
ricetta'tore, 'trice [ritʃetta'tore] *sm/f* (*DIR*)
receiver (of stolen goods).
ricettazi'one [ritʃettat'tsjone] *sf* (*DIR*)
receiving (stolen goods).
ricet'tivo, a [ritʃet'tivo] *ag* receptive.
rice'vente [ritʃe'vɛnte] *ag* (*RADIO, TV*)
receiving ♦ *sm/f* (*COMM*) receiver.
ri'cevere [ri'tʃevere] *vt* to receive;
(*stipendio, lettera*) to get, receive;
(*accogliere*: *ospite*) to welcome; (*vedere*:
cliente, rappresentante etc) to see;
"**confermiamo di aver ricevuto tale**
merce" (*COMM*) "we acknowledge receipt

of these goods".
ricevi'mento [ritʃevi'mento] *sm* receiving
no pl; (*trattenimento*) reception; **al** ~ **della**
merce on receipt of the goods.
ricevi'tore [ritʃevi'tore] *sm* (*TECN*) receiver;
~ **delle imposte** tax collector.
ricevito'ria [ritʃevito'ria] *sf* (*FISCO*): ~ (**delle**
imposte) Inland Revenue (*BRIT*) *o*
Internal Revenue (*US*) Office; ~ **del lotto**
lottery office.
rice'vuta [ritʃe'vuta] *sf* receipt; **accusare** ~
di qc (*COMM*) to acknowledge receipt of
sth; ~ **fiscale** official receipt (for tax
purposes); ~ **di ritorno** (*POSTA*) advice of
receipt; ~ **di versamento** receipt of
payment.
ricezi'one [ritʃet'tsjone] *sf* (*RADIO, TV*)
reception.
richia'mare [rikja'mare] *vt* (*chiamare*
indietro, ritelefonare) to call back;
(*ambasciatore, truppe*) to recall;
(*rimproverare*) to reprimand; (*attirare*) to
attract, draw; ~**rsi** *vr*: ~**rsi a** (*riferirsi a*) to
refer to; ~ **qn all'ordine** to call sb to
order; **desidero** ~ **la vostra attenzione su**
... I would like to draw your attention
to ...
richi'amo [ri'kjamo] *sm* call; recall;
reprimand; attraction.
richie'dente [rikje'dɛnte] *sm/f* applicant.
richi'edere [ri'kjɛdere] *vt* to ask again for;
(*chiedere indietro*): ~ **qc** to ask for sth
back; (*chiedere*: *per sapere*) to ask; (: *per*
avere) to ask for; (*AMM*: *documenti*) to
apply for; (*esigere*) to need, require;
essere molto richiesto to be in great
demand.
richi'esto, a [ri'kjɛsto] *pp di* **richiedere** ♦ *sf*
(*domanda*) request; (*AMM*) application,
request; (*esigenza*) demand, request; **a** ~**a**
on request.
rici'claggio [ritʃi'kladdʒo] *sm* (*fig*)
laundering; ~ **di materiale** recycling; ~
di denaro sporco money laundering.
rici'clare [ritʃi'klare] *vt* (*vetro, carta, bottiglie*)
to recycle; (*fig*: *personale*) to retrain.
'ricino ['ritʃino] *sm*: **olio di** ~ castor oil.
ricogni'tore [rikoɲɲi'tore] *sm* (*AER*)
reconnaissance aircraft.
ricognizi'one [rikoɲɲit'tsjone] *sf* (*MIL*)
reconnaissance; (*DIR*) recognition,
acknowledgement.
ricolle'gare *vt* (*collegare nuovamente*: *gen*)
to join again, link again; (*connettere*: *fatti*):
~ (**a, con**) to connect (with); ~**rsi** *vr*: ~**rsi a**
(*sog*: *fatti*: *connettersi*) to be connected to;
(: *persona*: *riferirsi*) to refer to.
ri'colmo, a *ag*: ~ (**di**) (*bicchiere*) full to the

ricominciare (with); (*stanza*) full (of).

ricominci'are [rikomin'tʃare] *vt*, *vi* to start again, begin again; ~ **a fare qc** to begin doing *o* to do sth again, start doing *o* to do sth again.

ricom'pensa *sf* reward.

ricompen'sare *vt* to reward.

ricom'porsi *vr* to compose o.s., regain one's composure.

ricom'posto, a *pp di* **ricomporsi**.

riconcili'are [rikontʃi'ljare] *vt* to reconcile; ~**rsi** *vr* to be reconciled.

riconciliazi'one [rikontʃiliat'tsjone] *sf* reconciliation.

ricon'dotto, a *pp di* **ricondurre**.

ricon'durre *vt* to bring (*o* take) back.

ricon'ferma *sf* reconfirmation.

riconfer'mare *vt* to reconfirm.

ricono'scente [rikonoʃ'ʃɛnte] *ag* grateful.

ricono'scenza [rikonoʃ'ʃɛntsa] *sf* gratitude.

rico'noscere [riko'noʃʃere] *vt* to recognize; (*DIR*: *figlio, debito*) to acknowledge; (*ammettere*: *errore*) to admit, acknowledge; ~ **qn colpevole** to find sb guilty.

riconosci'mento [rikonoʃʃi'mento] *sm* recognition; acknowledgement; (*identificazione*) identification; **come** ~ **dei servizi resi** in recognition of services rendered; **documento di** ~ means of identification; **segno di** ~ distinguishing mark.

riconosci'uto, a [rikonoʃ'ʃuto] *pp di* **riconoscere**.

riconquis'tare *vt* (*MIL*) to reconquer; (*libertà, stima*) to win back.

rico'perto, a *pp di* **ricoprire**.

ricopi'are *vt* to copy.

rico'prire *vt* to re-cover; (*coprire*) to cover; (*occupare*: *carica*) to hold.

ricor'dare *vt* to remember, recall; (*richiamare alla memoria*): ~ **qc a qn** to remind sb of sth; ~**rsi** *vr*: ~**rsi (di)** to remember; ~**rsi di qc/di aver fatto** to remember sth/having done.

ri'cordo *sm* memory; (*regalo*) keepsake, souvenir; (*di viaggio*) souvenir; ~**i** *smpl* (*memorie*) memoirs.

ricor'rente *ag* recurrent, recurring.

ricor'renza [rikor'rɛntsa] *sf* recurrence; (*festività*) anniversary.

ri'correre *vi* (*ripetersi*) to recur; ~ **a** (*rivolgersi*) to turn to; (: *DIR*) to appeal to; (*servirsi di*) to have recourse to; ~ **in appello** to lodge an appeal.

ri'corso, a *pp di* **ricorrere** ♦ *sm* recurrence; (*DIR*) appeal; **far** ~ **a** = **ricorrere a**.

ricostitu'ente *ag* (*MED*): **cura** ~ tonic treatment ♦ *sm* (*MED*) tonic.

ricostitu'ire *vt* (*società*) to build up again; (*governo, partito*) to re-form; ~**rsi** *vr* (*gruppo etc*) to re-form.

ricostru'ire *vt* (*casa*) to rebuild; (*fatti*) to reconstruct.

ricostruzi'one [rikostrut'tsjone] *sf* rebuilding *no pl*; reconstruction.

ri'cotta *sf* soft white unsalted cheese made from sheep's milk.

ricove'rare *vt* to give shelter to; ~ **qn in ospedale** to admit sb to hospital.

ricove'rato, a *sm/f* patient.

ri'covero *sm* shelter, refuge; (*MIL*) shelter; (*MED*) admission (to hospital); ~ **antiaereo** air-raid shelter.

ricre'are *vt* to recreate; (*rinvigorire*) to restore; (*fig*: *distrarre*) to amuse.

ricrea'tivo, a *ag* recreational.

ricreazi'one [rikreat'tsjone] *sf* recreation, entertainment; (*INS*) break.

ri'credersi *vr* to change one's mind.

ricupe'rare *vt* (*rientrare in possesso di*) to recover, get back; (*tempo perduto*) to make up for; (*NAUT*) to salvage; (: *naufraghi*) to rescue; (*delinquente*) to rehabilitate; ~ **lo svantaggio** (*SPORT*) to close the gap.

ri'cupero *sm* (*gen*) recovery; (*di relitto etc*) salvaging; **capacità di** ~ resilience.

ricu'sare *vt* to refuse.

ridacchi'are [ridak'kjare] *vi* to snigger.

ri'dare *vt* to return, give back.

'ridda *sf* (*di ammiratori etc*) swarm; (*di pensieri*) jumble.

ri'dente *ag* (*occhi, volto*) smiling; (*paesaggio*) delightful.

'ridere *vi* to laugh; (*deridere, beffare*): ~ **di** to laugh at, make fun of; **non c'è niente da** ~, **c'è poco da** ~ it's not a laughing matter.

rides'tare *vt* (*fig*: *ricordi, passioni*) to reawaken.

ri'detto, a *pp di* **ridire**.

ridico'laggine [ridiko'laddʒine] *sf* (*di situazione*) absurdity; (*cosa detta o fatta*) nonsense *no pl*.

ridicoliz'zare [ridikolid'dzare] *vt* to ridicule.

ri'dicolo, a *ag* ridiculous, absurd ♦ *sm*: **cadere nel** ~ to become ridiculous; **rendersi** ~ to make a fool of o.s.

ridimensiona'mento *sm* reorganization; (*di fatto storico*) reappraisal.

ridimensio'nare *vt* to reorganize; (*fig*) to see in the right perspective.

ri'dire *vt* to repeat; (*criticare*) to find fault with; to object to; **trova sempre qualcosa da** ~ he always manages to find fault.

ridon'dante *ag* redundant.

ri'dosso *sm*: **a** ~ **di** (*dietro*) behind; (*contro*) against.

ri'dotto, a *pp di* **ridurre**.

ri'duco *etc vb vedi* **ridurre**.

ri'durre *vt* (*anche CHIM, MAT*) to reduce; (*prezzo, spese*) to cut, reduce; (*accorciare*: *opera letteraria*) to abridge; (: *RADIO, TV*) to adapt; **ridursi** *vr* (*diminuirsi*) to be reduced, shrink; **ridursi a** to be reduced to; **ridursi a pelle e ossa** to be reduced to skin and bone.

ri'dussi *etc vb vedi* **ridurre**.

ridut'tore *sm* (*TECN, CHIM, ELETTR*) reducer.

riduzi'one [ridut'tsjone] *sf* reduction; abridgement; adaptation.

ri'ebbi *etc vb vedi* **riavere**.

riecheg'giare [rieked'dʒare] *vi* to re-echo.

riedu'care *vt* (*persona, arto*) to re-educate; (*malato*) to rehabilitate.

rieducazi'one [riedukat'tsjone] *sf* re-education; rehabilitation; **centro di** ~ rehabilitation centre.

rie'leggere [rie'leddʒere] *vt* to re-elect.

rie'letto, *pp di* **rieleggere**.

riempi'mento *sm* filling (up).

riem'pire *vt* to fill (up); (*modulo*) to fill in *o* out; ~**rsi** *vr* to fill (up); (*mangiare troppo*) to stuff o.s.; ~ **qc di** to fill sth (up) with.

riempi'tivo, a *ag* filling ♦ *sm* (*anche fig*) filler.

rien'tranza [rien'trantsa] *sf* recess; indentation.

rien'trare *vi* (*entrare di nuovo*) to go (*o* come) back in; (*tornare*) to return; (*fare una rientranza*) to go in, curve inwards; to be indented; (*riguardare*): ~ **in** to be included among, form part of; ~ **(a casa)** to get back home; **non rientriamo nelle spese** we are not within our budget.

ri'entro *sm* (*ritorno*) return; (*di astronave*) re-entry; **è iniziato il grande** ~ (*estivo*) people are coming back from their (summer) holidays.

riepilo'gare *vt* to summarize ♦ *vi* to recapitulate.

rie'pilogo, ghi *sm* recapitulation; **fare un** ~ **di qc** to summarize sth.

rie'same *sm* re-examination.

riesami'nare *vt* to re-examine.

ri'esco *etc vb vedi* **riuscire**.

ri'essere *vi*: **ci risiamo!** (*fam*) we're back to this again!

rievo'care *vt* (*passato*) to recall; (*commemorare*: *figura, meriti*) to commemorate.

rievocazi'one [rievokat'tsjone] *sf* (*vedi vt*) recalling; commemoration.

rifaci'mento [rifatʃi'mento] *sm* (*di film*) remake; (*di opera letteraria*) rehashing.

ri'fare *vt* to do again; (*ricostruire*) to make again; (*nodo*) to tie again, do up again; (*imitare*) to imitate, copy; ~**rsi** *vr* (*risarcirsi*): ~**rsi di** to make up for; (*vendicarsi*): ~**rsi di qc su qn** to get one's own back on sb for sth; (*riferirsi*): ~**rsi a** (*periodo, fenomeno storico*) to go back to; ~ **il letto** to make the bed; ~**rsi una vita** to make a new life for o.s.

ri'fatto, a *pp di* **rifare**.

riferi'mento *sm* reference; **in** *o* **con** ~ **a** with reference to; **far** ~ **a** to refer to.

rife'rire *vt* (*riportare*) to report; (*ascrivere*): ~ **qc a** to attribute sth to ♦ *vi* to do a report; ~**rsi** *vr*: ~**rsi a** to refer to; **riferirò** I'll pass on the message.

rifi'lare *vt* (*tagliare a filo*) to trim; (*fam*: *affibbiare*): ~ **qc a qn** to palm sth off on sb.

rifi'nire *vt* to finish off, put the finishing touches to.

rifini'tura *sf* finishing touch; ~**e** *sfpl* (*di mobile, auto*) finish *sg*.

rifiu'tare *vt* to refuse; ~ **di fare** to refuse to do.

rifi'uto *sm* refusal; ~**i** *smpl* (*spazzatura*) rubbish *sg*, refuse *sg*; ~**i solidi urbani** solid urban waste *sg*.

riflessi'one *sf* (*FISICA*) reflection; (*il pensare*) thought, reflection; (*osservazione*) remark.

rifles'sivo, a *ag* (*persona*) thoughtful, reflective; (*LING*) reflexive.

ri'flesso, a *pp di* **riflettere** ♦ *sm* (*di luce, su specchio*) reflection; (*FISIOL*) reflex; (*su capelli*) light; (*fig*) effect; **di** *o* **per** ~ indirectly; **avere i** ~**i pronti** to have quick reflexes.

ri'flettere *vt* to reflect ♦ *vi* to think; ~**rsi** *vr* to be reflected; (*ripercuotersi*): ~**rsi su** to have repercussions on; ~ **su** to think over.

riflet'tore *sm* reflector; (*proiettore*) floodlight; (: *MIL*) searchlight.

ri'flusso *sm* flowing back; (*della marea*) ebb; **un'epoca di** ~ an era of nostalgia.

rifocil'larsi [rifotʃil'larsi] *vr* (*poetico*) to take refreshment.

rifondazi'one [rifondat'tsjone] *sf* (*POL*): **R**~ **Comunista** *hard left party, originating from former P.C.I.*

ri'fondere *vt* (*rimborsare*) to refund, repay; ~ **le spese a qn** to refund sb's expenses; ~ **i danni a qn** to compensate sb for damages.

ri'forma *sf* reform; (*MIL*) declaration of unfitness for service; discharge (*on* *health grounds)*; **la R~** (*REL*) the Reformation.

rifor'mare *vt* to re-form; (*cambiare, innovare*) to reform; (*MIL: recluta*) to declare unfit for service; (: *soldato*) to invalid out, discharge.

riforma'tore, 'trice *ag* reforming ♦ *sm/f* reformer.

riforma'torio *sm* (*DIR*) community home (*BRIT*), reformatory (*US*).

rifor'mista, i, e *ag, sm/f* reformist.

riforni'mento *sm* supplying, providing; restocking; (*di carburante*) refuelling; **~i** *smpl* supplies, provisions; **fare ~ di** (*viveri*) to stock up with; (*benzina*) to fill up with; **posto di ~** filling *o* gas (*US*) station.

rifor'nire *vt* (*provvedere*): **~ di** to supply *o* provide with; (*fornire di nuovo: casa etc*) to restock.

ri'frangere [ri'frandʒere] *vt* to refract.

ri'fratto, a *pp di* **rifrangere**.

rifrazi'one [rifrat'tsjone] *sf* refraction.

rifug'gire [rifud'dʒire] *vi* to escape again; (*fig*): **~ da** to shun.

rifugi'arsi [rifu'dʒarsi] *vr* to take refuge.

rifugi'ato, a [rifu'dʒato] *sm/f* refugee.

ri'fugio [ri'fudʒo] *sm* refuge, shelter; (*in montagna*) shelter; **~ antiaereo** air-raid shelter.

ri'fuso, a *pp di* **rifondere**.

'riga, ghe *sf* line; (*striscia*) stripe; (*di persone, cose*) line, row; (*regolo*) ruler; (*scriminatura*) parting; **mettersi in ~** to line up; **a ~ghe** (*foglio*) lined; (*vestito*) striped; **buttare giù due ~ghe** (*note*) to jot down a few notes; **mandami due ~ghe appena arrivi** drop me a line as soon as you arrive.

ri'gagnolo [ri'gaɲɲolo] *sm* rivulet.

ri'gare (*foglio*) to rule ♦ *vi*: **~ diritto** (*fig*) to toe the line.

riga'toni *smpl* (*CUC*) short, ridged pasta shapes.

rigatti'ere *sm* junk dealer.

riga'tura *sf* (*di pagina, quaderno*) lining, ruling; (*di fucile*) rifling.

rigene'rare [ridʒene'rare] *vt* (*gen, TECN*) to regenerate; (*forze*) to restore; (*gomma*) to retread; **~rsi** *vr* (*gen*) to regenerate; (*ramo, tumore*) to regenerate, grow again; **gomma rigenerata** retread.

rigenerazi'one [ridʒenerat'tsjone] *sf* regeneration.

riget'tare [ridʒet'tare] *vt* (*gettare indietro*) to throw back; (*fig: respingere*) to reject; (*vomitare*) to bring *o* throw up.

ri'getto [ri'dʒetto] *sm* (*anche MED*) rejection.

ri'ghello [ri'gɛllo] *sm* ruler.

righerò *etc* [rige'rɔ] *vb vedi* **rigare**.

rigi'dezza [ridʒi'dettsa], **rigidità** [ridʒidi'ta] *sf* rigidity; stiffness; severity, rigours *pl* (*BRIT*), rigors *pl* (*US*); strictness.

'rigido, a ['ridʒido] *ag* rigid, stiff; (*membra etc: indurite*) stiff; (*METEOR*) harsh, severe; (*fig*) strict.

rigi'rare [ridʒi'rare] *vt* to turn; **~rsi** *vr* to turn round; (*nel letto*) to turn over; **~ qc tra le mani** to turn sth over in one's hands; **~ il discorso** to change the subject.

'rigo, ghi *sm* line; (*MUS*) staff, stave.

rigogli'oso, a [rigoʎ'ʎoso] *ag* (*pianta*) luxuriant; (*fig: commercio, sviluppo*) thriving.

rigonfia'mento *sm* (*ANAT*) swelling; (*su legno, intonaco etc*) bulge.

ri'gonfio, a *ag* swollen; (*grembiule, sporta*): **~ di** bulging with.

ri'gore *sm* (*METEOR*) harshness, rigours *pl* (*BRIT*), rigors *pl* (*US*); (*fig*) severity, strictness; (*anche:* **calcio di ~**) penalty; **~ compulsory**; **'è di ~ l'abito da sera"** "evening dress"; **area di ~** (*CALCIO*) penalty box (*BRIT*); **a rigor di termini** strictly speaking.

rigorosità *sf* strictness; rigour (*BRIT*), rigor (*US*).

rigo'roso, a *ag* (*severo: persona, ordine*) strict; (*preciso*) rigorous.

rigover'nare *vt* to wash (up).

riguar'dare *vt* to look at again; (*considerare*) to regard, consider; (*concernere*) to regard, concern; **~rsi** *vr* (*aver cura di sé*) to look after o.s.; **per quel che mi riguarda** as far as I'm concerned; **sono affari che non ti riguardano** it's none of your business.

rigu'ardo *sm* (*attenzione*) care; (*considerazione*) regard, respect; **~ a** concerning, with regard to; **per ~ a** out of respect for; **ospite/persona di ~** very important guest/person; **non aver ~i nell'agire/nel parlare** to act/speak freely.

riguar'doso, a *ag* (*rispettoso*) respectful; (*premuroso*) considerate, thoughtful.

rigurgi'tare [rigurdʒi'tare] *vi* (*liquido*) **~ da** to gush out from; (*recipiente: traboccare*): **~ di** to overflow with.

ri'gurgito [ri'gurdʒito] *sm* (*MED*) regurgitation; (*fig: ritorno, risveglio*) revival.

rilanci'are [rilan'tʃare] *vt* (*lanciare di nuovo: gen*) to throw again; (: *moda*) to bring back; (: *prodotto*) to re-launch; **~ un'offerta** (*asta*) to make a higher bid.

ri'lancio [ri'lantʃo] *sm* (*CARTE, di offerta*) raising.

rilasci'are [rilaʃ'ʃare] *vt* (*rimettere in libertà*) to release; (*AMM: documenti*) to issue; (*intervista*) to give; ~ **delle dichiarazioni** to make a statement.

ri'lascio [ri'laʃʃo] *sm* release; issue.

rilassa'mento *sm* (*gen, MED*) relaxation.

rilas'sare *vt* to relax; ~**rsi** *vr* to relax; (*fig: disciplina*) to become slack.

rilassa'tezza [rilassa'tettsa] *sf* (*fig: di costumi, disciplina*) laxity.

rilas'sato, a *ag* (*persona, muscoli*) relaxed; (*disciplina, costumi*) lax.

rile'gare *vt* (*libro*) to bind.

rilega'tura *sf* binding.

ri'leggere [ri'leddʒere] *vt* to reread, read again; (*rivedere*) to read over.

rl'lento: a ~ *av* slowly.

ri'letto, a *pp di* **rileggere**.

rilet'tura *sf* (*vedi vt*) rereading; reading over.

rileva'mento *sm* (*topografico, statistico*) survey; (*NAUT*) bearing.

rile'vante *ag* considerable; important.

rlle'vanza [rile'vantsa] *sf* importance.

rile'vare *vt* (*ricavare*) to find; (*notare*) to notice; (*mettere in evidenza*) to point out; (*venire a conoscere: notizia*) to learn; (*raccogliere: dati*) to gather, collect; (*TOPOGRAFIA*) to survey; (*MIL*) to relieve; (*COMM*) to take over.

rilevazi'one [rilevat'tsjone] *sf* survey.

rili'evo *sm* (*ARTE, GEO*) relief; (*fig: rilevanza*) importance; (*osservazione*) point, remark; (*TOPOGRAFIA*) survey; **dar** ~ **a o mettere in** ~ **qc** (*fig*) to bring sth out, highlight sth; **di poco/nessun** ~ (*fig*) of little/no importance; **un personaggio di** ~ an important person.

rilut'tante *ag* reluctant.

rilut'tanza [rilut'tantsa] *sf* reluctance.

'rima *sf* rhyme; (*verso*) verse; **far** ~ **con** to rhyme with; **rispondere a qn per le** ~**e** to give sb tit for tat.

riman'dare *vt* to send again; (*restituire, rinviare*) to send back, return; (*differire*): ~ **qc (a)** to postpone sth *o* put sth off (till); (*fare riferimento*): ~ **qn a** to refer sb to; **essere rimandato** (*INS*) to have to resit one's exams.

ri'mando *sm* (*rinvio*) return; (*dilazione*) postponement; (*riferimento*) cross-reference.

rimaneggi'are [rimaned'dʒare] *vt* (*testo*) to reshape, recast; (*POL*) to reshuffle.

rima'nente *ag* remaining ♦ *sm* rest, remainder; **i** ~**i** (*persone*) the rest of

them, the others.

rima'nenza [rima'nentsa] *sf* rest, remainder; ~**e** *sfpl* (*COMM*) unsold stock *sg*.

rima'nere *vi* (*restare*) to remain, stay; (*avanzare*) to be left, remain; (*restare stupito*) to be amazed; (*restare, mancare*): **rimangono poche settimane a Pasqua** there are only a few weeks left till Easter; (*diventare*): ~ **vedovo** to be left a widower; (*trovarsi*): ~ **confuso/sorpreso** to be confused/surprised; **rimane da vedere se** it remains to be seen whether.

rimangi'are [riman'dʒare] *vt* to eat again; ~**rsi la parola/una promessa** (*fig*) to go back on one's word/one's promise.

ri'mango *etc vb vedi* **rimanere**.

ri'mare *vt, vi* to rhyme.

rimargi'nare [rimardʒi'nare] *vt, vi* (*anche*: ~**rsi**) to heal.

ri'masto, a *pp di* **rimanere**.

rima'sugli [rima'suʎʎi] *smpl* leftovers.

rimbal'zare [rimbal'tsare] *vi* to bounce back, rebound; (*proiettile*) to ricochet.

rim'balzo [rim'baltso] *sm* rebound; ricochet.

rimbam'bire *vi* to be in one's dotage; (*rincretinire*) to grow foolish.

rimbam'bito, a *ag* senile, gaga (*fam*); **un vecchio** ~ a doddering old man.

rimbec'care *vt* (*persona*) to answer back; (*offesa*) to return.

rimbecil'lire [rimbetʃil'lire] *vi*, ~**rsi** *vr* to become stupid.

rimboc'care *vt* (*orlo*) to turn up; (*coperta*) to tuck in; (*maniche, pantaloni*) to turn *o* roll up.

rimbom'bare *vi* to resound; (*artiglieria*) to boom; (*tuono*) to rumble.

rim'bombo *sm* (*vedi vi*) boom; rumble.

rimbor'sare *vt* to pay back, repay; ~ **qc a qn** to reimburse sb for sth.

rim'borso *sm* repayment; (*di spese, biglietto*) refund; ~ **d'imposta** tax rebate.

rimboschi'mento [rimboski'mento] *sm* reafforestation.

rimbos'chire [rimbos'kire] *vt* to reafforest.

rimbrot'tare *vt* to reproach.

rim'brotto *sm* reproach.

rimedi'are *vi*: ~ **a** to remedy ♦ *vt* (*fam: procurarsi*) to get *o* scrape together; ~ **da vivere** to scrape a living.

ri'medio *sm* (*medicina*) medicine; (*cura, fig*) remedy, cure; **porre** ~ **a qc** to remedy sth; **non c'è** ~ there's no way out, there's nothing to be done about it.

rimesco'lare *vt* to mix well, stir well; (*carte*) to shuffle; **sentirsi** ~ **il sangue** (*per* *rabbia*) to feel one's blood boil.

ri'messa *sf* (*locale: per veicoli*) garage; (: *per aerei*) hangar; (*COMM: di merce*) consignment; (: *di denaro*) remittance; (*TENNIS*) return; (*CALCIO: anche:* ~ **in gioco**) throw-in.

ri'messo, a *pp di* **rimettere**.

rimes'tare *vt* (*mescolare*) to mix well, stir well; (*fig: passato*) to drag up again.

ri'mettere *vt* (*mettere di nuovo*) to put back; (*indossare di nuovo*): ~ **qc** to put sth back on, put sth on again; (*restituire*) to return, give back; (*affidare*) to entrust; (: *decisione*) to refer; (*condonare*) to remit; (*COMM: merci*) to deliver; (: *denaro*) to remit; (*vomitare*) to bring up; (*perdere: anche:* **rimetterci**) to lose; ~**rsi** *vr:* ~**rsi a** (*affidarsi*) to trust; ~ **a nuovo** (*casa etc*) to do up (*BRIT*) *o* over (*US*); **rimetterci di tasca propria** to be out of pocket; ~**rsi al bello** (*tempo*) to clear up; ~**rsi in cammino** to set off again; ~**rsi al lavoro** to start working again; ~**rsi in salute** to get better, recover one's health.

rimi'nese *ag* of (*o* from) Rimini.

ri'misi *etc vb vedi* **rimettere**.

'rimmel ® *sm inv* mascara.

rimoderna'mento *sm* modernization.

rimoder'nare *vt* to modernize.

ri'monta *sf* (*SPORT, gen*) recovery.

rimon'tare *vt* (*meccanismo*) to reassemble; (*tenda*) to put up again ♦ *vi* (*salire di nuovo*): ~ **in** (*macchina, treno*) to get back into; (*SPORT*) to close the gap.

rimorchi'are [rimor'kjare] *vt* to tow; (*fig: ragazza*) to pick up.

rimorchia'tore [rimorkja'tore] *sm* (*NAUT*) tug(boat).

ri'morchio [ri'mɔrkjo] *sm* tow; (*veicolo*) trailer; **andare a** ~ to be towed; **prendere a** ~ to tow; **cavo da** ~ towrope; **autocarro con** ~ articulated lorry (*BRIT*), semi(trailer) (*US*).

ri'morso *sm* remorse; **avere il** ~ **di aver fatto qc** to deeply regret having done sth.

ri'mosso, a *pp di* **rimuovere**.

rimos'tranza [rimos'trantsa] *sf* protest, complaint; **fare le proprie** ~**e a qn** to remonstrate with sb.

rimozi'one [rimot'tsjone] *sf* removal; (*da un impiego*) dismissal; (*PSIC*) repression; "~ **forzata**" "illegally parked vehicles will be removed at owner's expense".

rimpas'tare *vt* (*POL: ministero*) to reshuffle.

rim'pasto *sm* (*POL*) reshuffle; ~ **ministeriale** cabinet reshuffle.

rimpatri'are *vi* to return home ♦ *vt* to repatriate.

rim'patrio *sm* repatriation.

rimpi'angere [rim'pjandʒere] *vt* to regret; (*persona*) to miss; ~ **di (non) aver fatto qc** to regret (not) having done sth.

rimpi'anto, a *pp di* **rimpiangere** ♦ *sm* regret.

rimpiat'tino *sm* hide-and-seek.

rimpiaz'zare [rimpjat'tsare] *vt* to replace.

rimpiccio'lire [rimpittʃo'lire] *vt* to make smaller ♦ *vi* (*anche:* ~**rsi**) to become smaller.

rimpin'zare [rimpin'tsare] *vt:* ~ **di** to cram *o* stuff with.

rimprove'rare *vt* to rebuke, reprimand.

rim'provero *sm* rebuke, reprimand; **di** ~ (*tono, occhiata*) reproachful; (*parole*) of reproach.

rimugi'nare [rimudʒi'nare] *vt* (*fig*) to turn over in one's mind.

rimune'rare *vt* (*retribuire*) to remunerate; (*ricompensare: sacrificio etc*) to reward; **un lavoro ben rimunerato** a well-paid job.

rimunera'tivo, a *ag* (*lavoro, attività*) remunerative, profitable.

rimunerazi'one [rimunerat'tsjone] *sf* remuneration; (*premio*) reward.

rimu'overe *vt* to remove; (*destituire*) to dismiss; (*fig: distogliere*) to dissuade.

rinascimen'tale [rinaʃʃimen'tale] *ag* Renaissance *cpd*, of the Renaissance.

Rinasci'mento [rinaʃʃi'mento] *sm:* **il** ~ the Renaissance.

ri'nascita [ri'naʃʃita] *sf* rebirth, revival.

rincal'zare [rinkal'tsare] *vt* (*palo, albero*) to support, prop up; (*lenzuola*) to tuck in.

rin'calzo [rin'kaltso] *sm* support, prop; (*rinforzo*) reinforcement; (*SPORT*) reserve (player); ~**i** *smpl* (*MIL*) reserves.

rinca'rare *vt* to increase the price of ♦ *vi* to go up, become more expensive; ~ **la dose** (*fig*) to pile it on.

rin'caro *sm:* ~ **(di)** (*prezzi, costo della vita*) increase (in); (*prodotto*) increase in the price (of).

rinca'sare *vi* to go home.

rinchi'udere [rin'kjudere] *vt* to shut (*o* lock) up; ~**rsi** *vr:* ~**rsi in** to shut o.s. up in; ~**rsi in se stesso** to withdraw into o.s.

rinchi'uso, a [rin'kjuso] *pp di* **rinchiudere**.

rincitrul'lirsi [rintʃitrul'lirsi] *vr* to grow foolish.

rin'correre *vt* to chase, run after.

rin'corso, a *pp di* **rincorrere** ♦ *sf* short run.

rin'crescere [rin'kreʃʃere] *vb impers:* **mi rincresce che/di non poter fare** I'm sorry that/I can't do, I regret that/being unable to do.

rincresci'mento [rinkreʃʃi'mento] *sm*

regret.

rincresci'uto, a [rinkreʃ'ʃuto] *pp di* **rincrescere.**

rincu'lare *vi* to draw back; (*arma*) to recoil.

rinfacci'are [rinfat'tʃare] *vt* (*fig*): ~ **qc a qn** to throw sth in sb's face.

rinfoco'lare *vt* (*fig*: *odio, passioni*) to rekindle; (: *risentimento, rabbia*) to stir up.

rinfor'zare [rinfor'tsare] *vt* to reinforce, strengthen ♦ *vi* (*anche*: ~**rsi**) to grow stronger.

rin'forzo [rin'fortso] *sm*: **mettere un** ~ **a** to strengthen; ~**i** *smpl* (*MIL*) reinforcements; **di** ~ (*asse, sbarra*) strengthening; (*esercito*) supporting; (*personale*) extra, additional.

rinfran'care *vt* to encourage, reassure.

rinfres'cante *ag* (*bibita*) refreshing.

rinfres'care *vt* (*atmosfera, temperatura*) to cool (down); (*abito, temperatura*) to freshen up ♦ *vi* (*tempo*) to grow cooler; ~**rsi** *vr* (*ristorarsi*) to refresh o.s.; (*lavarsi*) to freshen up; ~ **la memoria a qn** to refresh sb's memory.

rin'fresco, schi *sm* (*festa*) party; ~**schi** *smpl* (*cibi e bevande*) refreshments.

rin'fusa *sf*: **alla** ~ in confusion, higgledy-piggledy.

ringhi'are [rin'gjare] *vi* to growl, snarl.

ringhi'era [rin'gjera] *sf* railing; (*delle scale*) banister(s *pl*).

'ringhio ['ringjo] *sm* growl, snarl.

ringhi'oso, a [rin'gjoso] *ag* growling, snarling.

ringiova'nire [rindʒova'nire] *vt* (*sog*: *vestito, acconciatura etc*): ~ **qn** to make sb look younger; (: *vacanze etc*) to rejuvenate ♦ *vi* (*anche*: ~**rsi**) to become (*o* look) younger.

ringrazia'mento [ringrattsja'mento] *sm* thanks *pl*; **lettera/biglietto di** ~ thank you letter/card.

ringrazi'are [ringrat'tsjare] *vt* to thank; ~ **qn di qc** to thank sb for sth; ~ **qn per aver fatto qc** to thank sb for doing sth.

rinne'gare *vt* (*fede*) to renounce; (*figlio*) to disown, repudiate.

rinne'gato, a *sm/f* renegade.

rinnova'mento *sm* renewal; (*economico*) revival.

rinno'vare *vt* to renew; (*ripetere*) to repeat, renew; ~**rsi** *vr* (*fenomeno*) to be repeated, recur.

rin'novo *sm* (*di contratto*) renewal; "**chiuso per** ~ (**dei**) **locali**" (*negozio*) "closed for alterations".

rinoce'ronte [rinotʃe'ronte] *sm* rhinoceros.

rino'mato, a *ag* renowned, celebrated.

rinsal'dare *vt* to strengthen.

rinsa'vire *vi* to come to one's senses.

rinsec'chito, a [rinsek'kito] *ag* (*vecchio, albero*) thin, gaunt.

rinta'narsi *vr* (*animale*) to go into its den; (*persona*: *nascondersi*) to hide.

rintoc'care *vi* (*campana*) to toll; (*orologio*) to strike.

rin'tocco, chi *sm* toll.

rintracci'are [rintrat'tʃare] *vt* to track down; (*persona scomparsa, documento*) to trace.

rintro'nare *vi* to boom, roar ♦ *vt* (*assordare*) to deafen; (*stordire*) to stun.

rintuz'zare [rintut'tsare] *vt* (*fig*: *sentimento*) to check, repress; (: *accusa*) to refute.

ri'nuncia [ri'nuntʃa] *sf* renunciation; ~ **a** (*carica*) resignation from; (*eredità*) relinquishment of; ~ **agli atti del giudizio** (*DIR*) abandonment of a claim.

rinunci'are [rinun'tʃare] *vi*: ~ **a** to give up, renounce; ~ **a fare qc** to give up doing sth.

rinuncia'tario, a [rinuntʃa'tarjo] *ag* defeatist.

ri'nunzia *etc* [ri'nuntsja] = **rinuncia** *etc.*

rinveni'mento *sm* (*ritrovamento*) recovery; (*scoperta*) discovery; (*METALLURGIA*) tempering.

rinve'nire *vt* to find, recover; (*scoprire*) to discover, find out ♦ *vi* (*riprendere i sensi*) to come round; (*riprendere l'aspetto naturale*) to revive.

rinve'nuto, a *pp di* **rinvenire.**

rinver'dire *vi* (*bosco, ramo*) to become green again.

rinvi'are *vt* (*rimandare indietro*) to send back, return; (*differire*): ~ **qc (a)** to postpone sth *o* put sth off (till); (: *seduta*) to adjourn sth (till); (*fare un rimando*): ~ **qn a** to refer sb to; ~ **a giudizio** (*DIR*) to commit for trial.

rinvigo'rire *vt* to strengthen.

rin'vio, 'vii *sm* (*rimando*) return; (*differimento*) postponement; (: *di seduta*) adjournment; (*in un testo*) cross-reference; ~ **a giudizio** (*DIR*) indictment.

riò *etc vb vedi* **riavere.**

'Rio de Ja'neiro ['riodedʒa'neiro] *sf* Rio de Janeiro.

rio'nale *ag* (*mercato, cinema*) local, district *cpd.*

ri'one *sm* district, quarter.

riordina'mento *sm* (*di ente, azienda*) reorganization.

riordi'nare *vt* (*rimettere in ordine*) to tidy; (*riorganizzare*) to reorganize.

riorganiz'zare [riorganid'dzare] *vt* to reorganize.

riorganizzazi'one [riorganiddzat'tsjone] *sf* reorganization.

ripa'gare *vt* to repay.

ripa'rare *vt* (*proteggere*) to protect, defend; (*correggere*: *male, torto*) to make up for; (: *errore*) to put right; (*aggiustare*) to repair ♦ *vi* (*mettere rimedio*): ~ **a** to make up for; ~**rsi** *vr* (*rifugiarsi*) to take refuge *o* shelter.

ripa'rato, a *ag* (*posto*) sheltered.

riparazi'one [riparat'tsjone] *sf* (*di un torto*) reparation; (*di guasto, scarpe*) repairing *no pl*; repair; (*risarcimento*) compensation; (*INS*): **esame di** ~ resit (*BRIT*), test retake (*US*).

ri'paro *sm* (*protezione*) shelter, protection; (*rimedio*) remedy; **al** ~ **da** (*sole, vento*) sheltered from; **mettersi al** ~ to take shelter; **correre ai** ~**i** (*fig*) to take remedial action.

ripar'tire *vt* (*dividere*) to divide up; (*distribuire*) to share out, distribute ♦ *vi* to leave again; (*motore*) to start again.

ripartizi'one [ripartit'tsjone] *sf* division; sharing out, distribution; (*AMM*: *dipartimento*) department.

ripas'sare *vi* to come (*o* go) back ♦ *vt* (*scritto, lezione*) to go over (again).

ri'passo *sm* (*di lezione*) revision (*BRIT*), review (*US*).

ripensa'mento *sm* second thoughts *pl* (*BRIT*), change of mind; **avere un** ~ to have second thoughts, change one's mind.

ripen'sare *vi* to think; (*cambiare idea*) to change one's mind; (*tornare col pensiero*): ~ **a** to recall; **a ripensarci** ... on thinking it over ....

riper'correre *vt* (*itinerario*) to travel over again; (*strada*) to go along again; (*fig*: *ricordi, passato*) to go back over.

riper'corso, a *pp di* **ripercorrere**.

riper'cosso, a *pp di* **ripercuotersi**.

ripercu'otersi *vr*: ~ **su** (*fig*) to have repercussions on.

ripercussi'one *sf* (*fig*): **avere una** ~ *o* **delle** ~**i su** to have repercussions on.

ripes'care *vt* (*pesce*) to catch again; (*persona, cosa*) to fish out; (*fig*: *ritrovare*) to dig out.

ripe'tente *smf* student repeating the year, repeater (*US*).

ri'petere *vt* to repeat; (*ripassare*) to go over.

ripeti'tore *sm* (*RADIO, TV*) relay.

ripetizi'one [ripetit'tsjone] *sf* repetition; (*di lezione*) revision; ~**i** *sfpl* (*INS*) private tutoring *o* coaching *sg*; **fucile a** ~ repeating rifle.

ripetuta'mente *av* repeatedly, again and again.

ripi'ano *sm* (*GEO*) terrace; (*di mobile*) shelf.

ri'picca *sf*: **per** ~ out of spite.

'ripido, a *ag* steep.

ripiega'mento *sm* (*MIL*) retreat.

ripie'gare *vt* to refold; (*piegare più volte*) to fold (up) ♦ *vi* (*MIL*) to retreat, fall back; (*fig*: *accontentarsi*): ~ **su** to make do with; ~**rsi** *vr* to bend.

ripi'ego, ghi *sm* expedient; **una soluzione di** ~ a makeshift solution.

ripi'eno, a *ag* full; (*CUC*) stuffed; (: *panino*) filled ♦ *sm* (*CUC*) stuffing.

ri'pone, ri'pongo *etc vb vedi* **riporre**.

ri'porre *vt* (*porre al suo posto*) to put back, replace; (*mettere via*) to put away; (*fiducia, speranza*): ~ **qc in qn** to place *o* put sth in sb.

ripor'tare *vt* (*portare indietro*) to bring (*o* take) back; (*riferire*) to report; (*citare*) to quote; (*ricevere*) to receive, get; (*vittoria*) to gain; (*successo*) to have; (*MAT*) to carry; (*COMM*) to carry forward; ~**rsi** *vr*: ~**rsi a** (*anche fig*) to go back to; (*riferirsi a*) to refer to; ~ **danni** to suffer damage; **ha riportato gravi ferite** he was seriously injured.

ri'porto *sm* amount carried over; amount carried forward.

ripo'sante *ag* (*gen*) restful; (*musica, colore*) soothing.

ripo'sare *vt* (*bicchiere, valigia*) to put down; (*dare sollievo*) to rest ♦ *vi* to rest; ~**rsi** *vr* to rest; **qui riposa** ... (*su tomba*) here lies ....

ripo'sato, a *ag* (*viso, aspetto*) rested; (*mente*) fresh.

ri'posi *etc vb vedi* **riporre**.

ri'poso *sm* rest; (*MIL*): ~**!** at ease!; **a** ~ (*in pensione*) retired; **giorno di** ~ day off; **"oggi** ~**"** (*CINE, TEAT*) "no performance today"; (*ristorante*) "closed today".

ripos'tiglio [ripos'tiλλo] *sm* lumber room (*BRIT*), storage room (*US*).

ri'posto, a *pp di* **riporre** ♦ *ag* (*fig*: *senso, significato*) hidden.

ri'prendere *vt* (*prigioniero, fortezza*) to recapture; (*prendere indietro*) to take back; (*ricominciare*: *lavoro*) to resume; (*andare a prendere*) to fetch, come back for; (*assumere di nuovo*: *impiegati*) to take on again, re-employ; (*rimproverare*) to tell off; (*restringere*: *abito*) to take in; (*CINE*) to shoot; ~**rsi** *vr* to recover; (*correggersi*) to correct o.s.; ~ **a fare qc** to start doing sth again; ~ **il cammino** to set off again; ~ **i sensi** to recover consciousness; ~ **sonno**

to go back to sleep.

ripresen'tare *vt* (*certificato*) to submit again; (*domanda*) to put forward again; (*persona*) to introduce again; ~**rsi** *vr* (*ritornare: persona*) to come back; (: *occasione*) to arise again; ~**rsi a** (*esame*) to sit (*BRIT*) *o* take (*US*) again; (*concorso*) to enter again; ~**rsi come candidato** (*POL*) to stand (*BRIT*) *o* run (*US*) again (as a candidate).

ri'preso, a *pp di* **riprendere** ♦ *sf* recapture; resumption; (*economica, da malattia, emozione*) recovery; (*AUT*) acceleration *no pl*; (*TEAT, CINE*) rerun; (*CINE: presa*) shooting *no pl*; shot; (*SPORT*) second half; (: *PUGILATO*) round; **a più** ~**e** on several occasions, several times.

ripristi'nare *vt* to restore.

ri'pristino *sm* (*gen*) restoration; (*di tradizioni*) revival.

ripro'dotto, a *pp di* **riprodurre**.

ripro'durre *vt* to reproduce; **riprodursi** *vr* (*BIOL*) to reproduce; (*riformarsi*) to form again.

riprodut'tivo, a *ag* reproductive.

riprodut'tore, 'trice *ag* (*organo*) reproductive ♦ *sm*: ~ **acustico** pick-up; ~ **a cassetta** cassette player.

riproduzi'one [riprodut'tsjone] *sf* reproduction; ~ **vietata** all rights reserved.

ripro'messo, a *pp di* **ripromettersi**.

ripro'mettersi *vt* (*aspettarsi*): ~ **qc da** to expect sth from; (*intendere*): ~ **di fare qc** to intend to do sth.

ripro'porre *vt*: **riproporsi di fare qc** to intend to do sth.

ripro'posto, a *pp di* **riproporre**.

ri'prova *sf* confirmation; **a** ~ **di** as confirmation of.

ripro'vare *vt* (*provare di nuovo: gen*) to try again; (: *vestito*) to try on again; (: *sensazione*) to experience again ♦ *vi* (*tentare*): ~ **(a fare qc)** to try (to do sth) again; **riproverò più tardi** I'll try again later.

ripro'vevole *ag* reprehensible.

ripudi'are *vt* to repudiate, disown.

ri'pudio *sm* repudiation, disowning.

ripu'gnante [ripuɲ'ɲante] *ag* disgusting, repulsive.

ripu'gnanza [ripuɲ'ɲantsa] *sf* repugnance, disgust.

ripu'gnare [ripuɲ'ɲare] *vi*: ~ **a qn** to repel *o* disgust sb.

ripu'lire *vt* to clean up; (*sog: ladri*) to clean out; (*perfezionare*) to polish, refine.

ripulsi'one *sf* (*FISICA, fig*) repulsion.

ri'quadro *sm* square; (*ARCHIT*) panel.

ri'sacca, che *sf* backwash.

ri'saia *sf* paddy field.

risa'lire *vi* (*ritornare in su*) to go back up; ~ **a** (*ritornare con la mente*) to go back to; (*datare da*) to date back to, go back to.

risa'lita *sf*: **mezzi di** ~ (*SCI*) ski lifts.

risal'tare *vi* (*fig: distinguersi*) to stand out; (*ARCHIT*) to project, jut out.

ri'salto *sm* prominence; (*sporgenza*) projection; **mettere** *o* **porre in** ~ **qc** to make sth stand out.

risana'mento *sm* (*economico*) improvement; (*bonifica*) reclamation; ~ **del bilancio** reorganization of the budget; ~ **edilizio** building improvement.

risa'nare *vt* (*guarire*) to heal, cure; (*palude*) to reclaim; (*economia*) to improve; (*bilancio*) to reorganize.

risa'pere *vt*: ~ **qc** to come to know of sth.

risa'puto, a *ag*: **è** ~ **che ...** everyone knows that ..., it's common knowledge that ....

risarci'mento [risartʃi'mento] *sm*: ~ **(di)** compensation (for); **aver diritto al** ~ **dei danni** to be entitled to damages.

risar'cire [risar'tʃire] *vt* (*coso*) to pay compensation for; (*persona*): ~ **qn di qc** to compensate sb for sth; ~ **i danni a qn** to pay sb damages.

ri'sata *sf* laugh.

riscalda'mento *sm* heating; ~ **centrale** central heating.

riscal'dare *vt* (*scaldare*) to heat; (: *mani, persona*) to warm; (*minestra*) to reheat; ~**rsi** *vr* to warm up.

ris'caldo *sm* (*fam*) (slight) inflammation.

riscat'tare *vt* (*prigioniero*) to ransom, pay a ransom for; (*DIR*) to redeem; ~**rsi** *vr* (*da disonore*) to redeem o.s.

ris'catto *sm* ransom; redemption.

rischia'rare [riskja'rare] *vt* (*illuminare*) to light up; (*colore*) to make lighter; ~**rsi** *vr* (*tempo*) to clear up; (*cielo*) to clear; (*fig: volto*) to brighten up; ~**rsi la voce** to clear one's throat.

rischi'are [ris'kjare] *vt* to risk ♦ *vi*: ~ **di fare qc** to risk *o* run the risk of doing sth.

'rischio ['riskjo] *sm* risk; **a** ~ (*zona, situazione*) at risk, vulnerable; **a proprio** ~ **e pericolo** at one's own risk; **correre il** ~ **di fare qc** to run the risk of doing sth; ~ **del mestiere** occupational hazard.

rischi'oso, a [ris'kjoso] *ag* risky, dangerous.

risciac'quare [riʃʃak'kware] *vt* to rinse.

risci'acquo [riʃ'ʃakkwo] *sm* rinse.

riscon'trare *vt* (*confrontare: due cose*) to compare; (*esaminare*) to check, verify;

(*rilevare*) to find.
ris'contro *sm* comparison; check, verification; (*AMM*: *lettera di risposta*) reply; **mettere a ~** to compare; **in attesa di un vostro cortese ~** we look forward to your reply.
risco'perto, a *pp di* **riscoprire.**
risco'prire *vt* to rediscover.
riscossi'one *sf* collection.
ris'cosso, a *pp di* **riscuotere ♦** *sf* (*riconquista*) recovery, reconquest.
riscu'otere *vt* (*ritirare una somma dovuta*) to collect; (: *stipendio*) to draw, collect; (*fig*: *successo etc*) to win, earn; **~rsi** *vr*: **~rsi (da)** to shake o.s. (out of), rouse o.s. (from); **~ un assegno** to cash a cheque.
'rise *etc vb vedi* **ridere.**
risenti'mento *sm* resentment.
risen'tire *vt* to hear again; (*provare*) to feel ♦ *vi*: **~ di** to feel (*o* show) the effects of; **~rsi** *vr*: **~rsi di** *o* **per** to take offence (*BRIT*) *o* offense (*US*) at, resent.
risen'tito, a *ag* resentful.
ri'serbo *sm* reserve.
ri'serva *sf* reserve; (*di caccia, pesca*) preserve; (*restrizione, di indigeni*) reservation; **fare ~ di** (*cibo*) to get in a supply of; **tenere di ~** to keep in reserve; **con le dovute ~e** with certain reservations; **ha accettato con la ~ di potersi ritirare** he accepted with the proviso that he could pull out.
riser'vare *vt* (*tenere in serbo*) to keep, put aside; (*prenotare*) to book, reserve; **~rsi** *vr*: **~rsi di fare qc** to intend to do sth; **~rsi il diritto di fare qc** to reserve the right to do sth.
riserva'tezza [riserva'tettsa] *sf* reserve.
riser'vato, a *ag* (*prenotato, fig*: *persona*) reserved; (*confidenziale*) confidential.
'risi *etc vb vedi* **ridere.**
ri'sibile *ag* laughable.
risi'cato, a *ag* (*vittoria etc*) very narrow.
risi'edere *vi*: **~ a** *o* **in** to reside in.
'risma *sf* (*di carta*) ream; (*fig*) kind, sort.
'riso, a *pp di* **ridere ♦** *sm* (*pianta*) rice; (*pl(f)* **~a**: *il ridere*): **un ~** a laugh; **il ~** laughter; **uno scoppio di ~a** a burst of laughter.
riso'lino *sm* snigger.
risolle'vare *vt* (*sollevare di nuovo*: *testa*) to raise again, lift up again; (*fig*: *questione*) to raise again, bring up again; (: *morale*) to raise; **~rsi** *vr* (*da terra*) to rise again; (*fig*: *da malattia*) to recover; **~ le sorti di qc** to improve the chances of sth.
ri'solsi *etc vb vedi* **risolvere.**
ri'solto, a *pp di* **risolvere.**
risolu'tezza [risolu'tettsa] *sf* determination.

risolu'tivo, a *ag* (*determinante*) decisive; (*che risolve*): **arrivare ad una formula ~a** to come up with a formula to resolve a situation.
riso'luto, a *ag* determined, resolute.
risoluzi'one [risolut'tsjone] *sf* solving *no pl*; (*MAT*) solution; (*decisione, di immagine*) resolution.
ri'solvere *vt* (*difficoltà, controversia*) to resolve; (*problema*) to solve; (*decidere*): **~ di fare** to resolve to do; **~rsi** *vr* (*decidersi*): **~rsi a fare** to make up one's mind to do; (*andare a finire*): **~rsi in** to end up, turn out; **~rsi in nulla** to come to nothing.
risol'vibile *ag* solvable.
riso'nanza [riso'nantsa] *sf* resonance; **aver vasta ~** (*fig*: *fatto etc*) to be known far and wide.
riso'nare *vt, vi* = **risuonare.**
ri'sorgere [ri'sordʒere] *vi* to rise again.
risorgimen'tale [risordʒimen'tale] *ag* of the Risorgimento.
risorgi'mento [risordʒi'mento] *sm* revival; **il R~** (*STORIA*) the Risorgimento; *vedi nota nel riquadro.*

RISORGIMENTO

The **Risorgimento**, *the period stretching from the early nineteenth century to 1861 and the proclamation of the Kingdom of Italy, saw considerable upheaval and change. Political and personal freedom took on new importance as the events of the French Revolution unfolded. The* **Risorgimento** *paved the way for the unification of Italy in 1871.*

---

ri'sorsa *sf* expedient, resort; **~e** *sfpl* (*naturali, finanziarie etc*) resources; **persona piena di ~e** resourceful person.
ri'sorsi *etc vb vedi* **risorgere.**
ri'sorto, a *pp di* **risorgere.**
ri'sotto *sm* (*CUC*) risotto.
risparmi'are *vt* to save; (*non uccidere*) to spare ♦ *vi* to save; **~ qc a qn** to spare sb sth; **~ fatica/fiato** to save one's energy/breath; **risparmiati il disturbo** *o* **la fatica** (*anche ironico*) save yourself the trouble.
risparmia'tore, 'trice *sm/f* saver.
ris'parmio *sm* saving *no pl*; (*denaro*) savings *pl*.
rispecchi'are [rispek'kjare] *vt* to reflect; **~rsi** *vr* to be reflected.
rispe'dire *vt* to send back; **~ qc a qn** to send sth back to sb.
rispet'tabile *ag* respectable; (*considerevole*: *somma*) sizeable, considerable.

rispet'tare *vt* to respect; (*legge*) to obey, comply with, abide by; (*promessa*) to keep; **farsi** ~ to command respect; ~ **le distanze** to keep one's distance; ~ **i tempi** to keep to schedule; **ogni medico che si rispetti** every self-respecting doctor.

rispettiva'mente *av* respectively.

rispet'tivo, a *ag* respective.

ris'petto *sm* respect; ~**i** *smpl* (*saluti*) respects, regards; ~ **a** (*in paragone a*) compared to; (*in relazione a*) as regards, as for; ~ **(di o per)** (*norme, leggi*) observance (of), compliance (with); **portare** ~ **a qn/qc** to have *o* feel respect for sb/sth; **mancare di** ~ **a qn** to be disrespectful to sb; **con** ~ **parlando** with respect, if you will excuse my saying so; **(porga) i miei** ~**i alla signora** (give) my regards to your wife.

rispet'toso, a *ag* respectful.

risplen'dente *ag* (*giornata, sole*) bright, shining; (*occhi*) sparkling.

ris'plendere *vi* **to** shine.

rispon'dente *ag:* ~ **a** in keeping *o* conformity with.

rispon'denza [rispon'dentsa] *sf* correspondence.

ris'pondere *vi* to answer, reply; (*freni*) to respond; ~ **a** (*domanda*) to answer, reply to; (*persona*) to answer; (*invito*) to reply to; (*provocazione, sog: veicolo, apparecchio*) to respond to; (*corrispondere a*) to correspond to; (: *speranze, bisogno*) to answer; ~ **a qn di qc** (*essere responsabile*) to be answerable to sb for sth.

rispo'sarsi *vr* to get married again, remarry.

ris'posto, a *pp di* **rispondere** ♦ *sf* answer, reply; **in** ~**a a** in reply to; **dare una** ~**a** to give an answer; **diamo** ~**a alla vostra lettera del** ... in reply to your letter of ....

'rissa *sf* brawl.

ris'soso, a *ag* quarrelsome.

rist. *abbr* = **ristampa.**

ristabi'lire *vt* to re-establish, restore; (*persona: sog: riposo etc*) to restore to health; ~**rsi** *vr* to recover.

rista'gnare [ristaɲ'ɲare] *vi* (*acqua*) to become stagnant; (*sangue*) to cease flowing; (*fig: industria*) to stagnate.

ris'tagno [ris'taɲɲo] *sm* stagnation; **c'è un** ~ **delle vendite** business is slack.

ris'tampa *sf* reprinting *no pl*; reprint.

ristam'pare *vt* to reprint.

risto'rante *sm* restaurant.

risto'rare *vt* (*persona, forze*) to revive, refresh; ~**rsi** *vr* (*rifocillarsi*) to have

something to eat and drink; (*riposarsi*) to rest, have a rest.

ristora'tore, 'trice *ag* refreshing, reviving ♦ *sm* (*gestore di ristorante*) restaurateur.

ris'toro *sm* (*bevanda, cibo*) refreshment; **posto di** ~ (*FERR*) buffet, snack bar; **servizio di** ~ (*FERR*) refreshments *pl.*

ristret'tezza [ristret'tettsa] *sf* (*strettezza*) narrowness; (*fig: scarsezza*) scarcity, lack; (: *meschinità*) meanness; ~**e** *sfpl* (*povertà*) poverty *sg*.

ris'tretto, a *pp di* **restringere** ♦ *ag* (*racchiuso*) enclosed, hemmed in; (*angusto*) narrow; (*limitato*): ~ **(a)** restricted *o* limited (to); (*CUC: brodo*) thick; (: *caffè*) extra strong.

ristruttu'rare *vt* (*azienda*) to reorganize; (*edificio*) to restore; (*appartamento*) to alter; (*sog: crema, balsamo*) to repair.

ristrutturazi'one [ristrutturat'tsjone] *sf* reorganization; restoration, alteration.

risuc'chiare [risuk'kjare] *vt* to suck in.

ri'succhio [ri'sukkjo] *sm* (*di acqua*) undertow, pull; (*di aria*) suction.

risul'tare *vi* (*dimostrarsi*) to prove (to be), turn out (to be); (*riuscire*): ~ **vincitore** to emerge as the winner; ~ **da** (*provenire*) to result from, be the result of; **mi risulta che** ... I understand that ..., as far as I know ...; **(ne) risulta che** ... it follows that ...; **non mi risulta** not as far as I know.

risul'tato *sm* result.

risuo'nare *vi* (*rimbombare*) to resound.

risurrezi'one [risurret'tsjone] *sf* (*REL*) resurrection.

risusci'tare [risuʃʃi'tare] *vt* to resuscitate, restore to life; (*fig*) to revive, bring back ♦ *vi* to rise (from the dead).

risvegli'are [rizveʎ'ʎare] *vt* (*gen*) to wake up, waken; (*fig: interesse*) to stir up, arouse; (: *curiosità*) to arouse; (*fig: dall'inerzia etc*): ~ **qn (da)** to rouse sb (from); ~**rsi** *vr* to wake up, awaken; (*fig: interesse, curiosità*) to be aroused.

ris'veglio [riz'veʎʎo] *sm* waking up; (*fig*) revival.

ris'volto *sm* (*di giacca*) lapel; (*di pantaloni*) turn-up (*BRIT*), cuff (*US*); (*di manica*) cuff; (*di tasca*) flap; (*di libro*) inside flap; (*fig*) implication.

ritagli'are [ritaʎ'ʎare] *vt* (*tagliar via*) to cut out.

ri'taglio [ri'taʎʎo] *sm* (*di giornale*) cutting, clipping; (*di stoffa etc*) scrap; **nei** ~**i di tempo** in one's spare time.

ritar'dare *vi* (*persona, treno*) to be late; (*orologio*) to be slow ♦ *vt* (*rallentare*) to slow down; (*impedire*) to delay, hold up; (*diffe-*

rire) to postpone, delay; ~ **il pagamento** to defer payment.

ritarda'tario, a *sm/f* latecomer.

ritar'dato, a *ag (PSIC)* retarded.

ri'tardo *sm* delay; *(di persona aspettata)* lateness *no pl*; *(fig: mentale)* backwardness; **in** ~ late.

ri'tegno [ri'teɲɲo] *sm* restraint.

ritem'prare *vt (forze, spirito)* to restore.

rite'nere *vt (trattenere)* to hold back; *(: somma)* to deduct; *(giudicare)* to consider, believe.

ri'tengo, ri'tenni *etc vb vedi* **ritenere**.

riten'tare *vt* to try again, make another attempt at.

rite'nuta *sf (sul salario)* deduction; ~ **d'acconto** advance deduction of tax; ~ **alla fonte** *(FISCO)* taxation at source.

riterrò, riti'ene *etc vb vedi* **ritenere**.

riti'rare *vt* to withdraw; *(POL: richiamare)* to recall; *(andare a prendere: pacco etc)* to collect, pick up; ~**rsi** *vr* to withdraw; *(da un'attività)* to retire; *(stoffa)* to shrink; *(marea)* to recede; **gli hanno ritirato la patente** they disqualified him from driving *(BRIT)*, they took away his licence *(BRIT)* o license *(US)*; ~**rsi a vita privata** to withdraw from public life.

riti'rata *sf (MIL)* retreat; *(latrina)* lavatory.

riti'rato, a *ag* secluded; **fare vita** ~**a** to live in seclusion.

ri'tiro *sm (di truppe, candidati, soldi)* withdrawal; *(di pacchi)* collection; *(di passaporto)* confiscation; *(da attività)* retirement; *(luogo appartato)* retreat.

rit'mato, a *ag* rhythmic(al).

'ritmico, a, ci, che *ag* rhythmic(al).

'ritmo *sm* rhythm; *(fig)* rate; *(: della vita)* pace, tempo; **al** ~ **di** at a speed o rate of; **ballare al** ~ **di valzer** to waltz.

'rito *sm* rite; **di** ~ usual, customary.

ritoc'care *vt (disegno, fotografia)* to touch up; *(testo)* to alter.

ri'tocco, chi *sm* touching up *no pl*; alteration.

ri'torcere [ri'tɔrtʃere] *vt (filato)* to twist; *(fig: accusa, insulto)* to throw back; ~**rsi** *vr (tornare a danno di)*: ~**rsi contro** to turn against.

ritor'nare *vi* to return, go *(o* come) back; *(ripresentarsi)* to recur; *(ridiventare)*: ~ **ricco** to become rich again ♦ *vt (restituire)* to return, give back.

ritor'nello *sm* refrain.

ri'torno *sm* return; **durante il (viaggio di)** ~ on the return trip, on the way back; **al** ~ *(tornando)* on the way back; **essere di** ~ to be back; **far** ~ to return; **avere un** ~ **di**

fiamma *(AUT)* to backfire; *(fig: persona)* to be back in love again.

ritorsi'one *sf (rappresaglia)* retaliation.

ri'torto, a *pp di* **ritorcere** ♦ *ag (cotone, corda)* twisted.

ri'trarre *vt (trarre indietro, via)* to withdraw; *(distogliere: sguardo)* to turn away; *(rappresentare)* to portray, depict; *(ricavare)* to get, obtain; **ritrarsi** *vr* to move back.

ritrat'tare *vt (disdire)* to retract, take back; *(trattare nuovamente)* to deal with again.

ritrattazi'one [ritrattat'tsjone] *sf* withdrawal.

ritrat'tista, i, e *sm/f* portrait painter.

ri'tratto, a *pp di* **ritrarre** ♦ *sm* portrait.

ritro'sia *sf (riluttanza)* reluctance, unwillingness; *(timidezza)* shyness.

ri'troso, a *ag (restio)*: ~ **(a)** reluctant (to); *(schivo)* shy; **andare a** ~ to go backwards.

ritrova'mento *sm (di cadavere, oggetto smarrito etc)* finding; *(oggetto ritrovato)* find.

ritro'vare *vt* to find; *(salute)* to regain; *(persona)* to find; to meet again; ~**rsi** *vr (essere, capitare)* to find o.s.; *(raccapezzarsi)* to find one's way; *(con senso reciproco)* to meet (again).

ritro'vato *sm* discovery.

ri'trovo *sm* meeting place; ~ **notturno** night club.

'ritto, a *ag (in piedi)* standing, on one's feet; *(levato in alto)* erect, raised; *(: capelli)* standing on end; *(posto verticalmente)* upright.

ritu'ale *ag, sm* ritual.

riuni'one *sf (adunanza)* meeting; *(riconciliazione)* reunion; **essere in** ~ to be at a meeting.

riu'nire *vt (ricongiungere)* to join (together); *(riconciliare)* to reunite, bring together (again); ~**rsi** *vr (adunarsi)* to meet; *(tornare a stare insieme)* to be reunited; **siamo qui riuniti per festeggiare il vostro anniversario** we are gathered here to celebrate your anniversary.

riu'scire [riuʃ'ʃire] *vi (uscire di nuovo)* to go out again, go back out; *(aver esito: fatti, azioni)* to go, turn out; *(aver successo)* to succeed, be successful; *(essere, apparire)* to be, prove; *(raggiungere il fine)* to manage, succeed; ~ **a fare qc** to manage o be able to do sth; **questo mi riesce nuovo** this is new to me.

riu'scita [riuʃ'ʃita] *sf (esito)* result, outcome; *(buon esito)* success.

riutiliz'zare [riutilid'dzare] *vt* to use again, re-use.

'**riva** *sf* (*di fiume*) bank; (*di lago, mare*) shore; **in ~ al mare** on the (sea) shore.

ri'**vale** *ag* rival *cpd* ♦ *sm/f* rival; **non avere ~i** (*anche fig*) to be unrivalled.

rivaleggi'**are** [rivaled'dʒare] *vi* to compete, vie.

rivalità *sf* rivalry.

ri'**valsa** *sf* (*rivincita*) revenge; (*risarcimento*) compensation; **prendersi una ~ su qn** to take revenge on sb.

rivalu'**tare** *vt* (*ECON*) to revalue.

rivalutazi'**one** [rivalutat'tsjone] *sf* (*ECON*) revaluation; (*fig*) re-evaluation.

rivan'**gare** *vt* (*ricordi etc*) to dig up (again).

rive'**dere** *vt* to see again; (*ripassare*) to revise; (*verificare*) to check.

rivedrò *etc vb vedi* **rivedere**.

rive'**lare** *vt* to reveal; (*divulgare*) to reveal, disclose; (*dare indizio*) to reveal, show; **~rsi** *vr* (*manifestarsi*) to be revealed; **~rsi onesta** etc to prove to be honest *etc*.

rivela'**tore**, '**trice** *ag* revealing ♦ *sm* (*TECN*) detector; (*fig*) developer.

rivelazi'**one** [rivelat'tsjone] *sf* revelation.

ri'**vendere** *vt* (*vendere: di nuovo*) to resell, sell again; (: *al dettaglio*) to retail, sell retail.

rivendi'**care** *vt* to claim, demand. **~i salariali** wage claims.

rivendicazi'**one** [rivendikat'tsjone] *sf* claim;

ri'**vendita** *sf* (*bottega*) retailer's (shop); **~ di tabacchi** tobacconist's (shop).

rivendi'**tore**, '**trice** *sm/f* retailer; **~ autorizzato** authorized dealer.

riverbe'**rare** *vt* to reflect.

ri'**verbero** *sm* (*di luce, calore*) reflection; (*di suono*) reverberation.

rive'**rente** *ag* reverent, respectful.

rive'**renza** [rive'rɛntsa] *sf* reverence; (*inchino*) bow; curtsey.

rive'**rire** *vt* (*rispettare*) to revere; (*salutare*) to pay one's respects to.

river'**sare** *vt* (*anche fig*) to pour; **~rsi** *vr* (*fig: persone*) to pour out.

rivesti'**mento** *sm* covering; coating.

rives'**tire** *vt* to dress again; (*ricoprire*) to cover; (: *con vernice*) to coat; (*fig: carica*) to hold; **~rsi** *vr* to get dressed again; to change (one's clothes); **~ di piastrelle** to tile.

ri'**vidi** *etc vb vedi* **rivedere**.

rivi'**era** *sf* coast; **la ~ italiana** the Italian Riviera.

ri'**vincita** [ri'vintʃita] *sf* (*SPORT*) return match; (*fig*) revenge; **prendersi la ~ (su qn)** to take *o* get one's revenge (on sb).

rivis'**suto, a** *pp di* **rivivere**.

ri'**vista** *sf* review; (*periodico*) magazine,

review; (*TEAT*) revue; variety show.

ri'**visto, a** *pp di* **rivedere**.

rivitaliz'**zante** [rivitalid'dzante] *ag* revitalizing.

rivitaliz'**zare** [rivitalid'dzare] *vt* to revitalize.

ri'**vivere** *vi* (*riacquistare forza*) to come alive again; (*tornare in uso*) to be revived ♦ *vt* to relive.

'**rivo** *sm* stream.

ri'**volgere** [ri'vɔldʒere] *vt* (*attenzione, sguardo*) to turn, direct; (*parole*) to address; **~rsi** *vr* to turn round; (*fig: dirigersi per informazioni*): **~rsi a** to go and see, go and speak to; **~ un'accusa/una critica a qn** to accuse/criticize sb; **~rsi all'ufficio competente** to apply to the office concerned.

rivolgi'**mento** [rivoldʒi'mento] *sm* upheaval.

ri'**volsi** *etc vb vedi* **rivolgere**.

ri'**volta** *sf* revolt, rebellion.

rivol'**tante** *ag* revolting, disgusting.

rivol'**tare** *vt* to turn over; (*con l'interno all'esterno*) to turn inside out; (*disgustare: stomaco*) to upset, turn, (: *fig*) to revolt, disgust; **~rsi** *vr* (*ribellarsi*): **~rsi (a)** to rebel (against).

rivol'**tella** *sf* revolver.

ri'**volto, a** *pp di* **rivolgere**.

rivol'**toso, a** *ag* rebellious ♦ *sm/f* rebel.

rivoluzio'**nare** [rivoluttsjo'nare] *vt* to revolutionize.

rivoluzio'**nario, a** [rivoluttsjo'narjo] *ag, sm/f* revolutionary.

rivoluzi'**one** [rivolut'tsjone] *sf* revolution.

riz'**zare** [rit'tsare] *vt* to raise, erect; **~rsi** *vr* to stand up; (*capelli*) to stand on end; **~rsi in piedi** to stand up, get to one's feet.

RN *sigla* = *Rimini*.

RNA *sigla m* RNA (= *ribonucleic acid*).

RO *sigla* = *Rovigo*.

'**roba** *sf* stuff, things *pl*; (*possessi, beni*) belongings *pl*, things *pl*, possessions *pl*; **~ da mangiare** things to eat, food; **~ da matti!** it's sheer madness *o* lunacy!

robi'**vecchi** [robi'vɛkki] *sm/f inv* junk dealer.

'**robot** *sm inv* robot.

ro'**botica** *sf* robotics *sg*.

robus'**tezza** [robus'tettsa] *sf* (*di persona, pianta*) robustness, sturdiness; (*di edificio, ponte*) soundness.

ro'**busto, a** *ag* robust, sturdy; (*solido: catena*) strong; (: *edificio, ponte*) sound, solid; (*vino*) full-bodied.

'**rocca, che** *sf* fortress.

rocca'**forte** *sf* stronghold.

roc'**chetto** [rok'ketto] *sm* reel, spool.

'roccia, ce ['rɔttʃa] *sf* rock; **fare** ~ (*SPORT*) to go rock climbing.

roccia'tore, 'trice [rottʃa'tore] *sm/f* rock climber.

rocci'oso, a [rot'tʃoso] *ag* rocky; **le Montagne R~e** the Rocky Mountains.

'roco, a, chi, che *ag* hoarse.

ro'daggio [ro'daddʒo] *sm* running (*BRIT*) o breaking (*US*) in; **in** ~ running o breaking in; **periodo di** ~ (*fig*) period of adjustment.

'Rodano *sm*: **il** ~ the Rhone.

ro'dare *vt* (*AUT, TECN*) to run (*BRIT*) o break (*US*) in.

ro'deo *sm* rodeo.

'rodere *vt* to gnaw (at); (*distruggere poco a poco*) to eat into.

'Rodi *sf* Rhodes.

rodi'tore *sm* (*ZOOL*) rodent.

rodo'dendro *sm* rhododendron.

'rogito ['rɔdʒito] *sm* (*DIR*) (notary's) deed.

'rogna ['rɔɲɲa] *sf* (*MED*) scabies *sg*; (*di animale*) mange; (*fig*) bother, nuisance.

ro'gnone [ro'ɲɲone] *sm* (*CUC*) kidney.

ro'gnoso, a [ro'ɲɲoso] *ag* (*persona*) scabby; (*animale*) mangy; (*fig*) troublesome.

'rogo, ghi *sm* (*per cadaveri*) (funeral) pyre; (*supplizio*): **il** ~ the stake.

rol'lare *vi* (*NAUT, AER*) to roll.

rol'lino *sm* = **rullino**.

rol'lio *sm* roll(ing).

'Roma *sf* Rome.

roma'gnolo, a [roma'ɲɲɔlo] *ag* of (o from) Romagna.

roma'nesco, a, schi, sche *ag* Roman ♦ *sm* Roman dialect.

Roma'nia *sf*: **la** ~ Romania.

ro'manico, a, ci, che *ag* Romanesque.

ro'mano, a *ag, sm/f* Roman; **fare alla** ~a to go Dutch.

romantiche'ria [romantike'ria] *sf* sentimentality.

romanti'cismo [romanti'tʃizmo] *sm* romanticism.

ro'mantico, a, ci, che *ag* romantic.

ro'manza [ro'mandza] *sf* (*MUS, LETTERATURA*) romance.

roman'zare [roman'dzare] *vt* to romanticize.

roman'zesco, a, schi, sche [roman'dzesko] *ag* (*stile, personaggi*) fictional; (*fig*) storybook *cpd*.

romanzi'ere [roman'dzjere] *sm* novelist.

ro'manzo [ro'mandzo] *ag* (*LING*) romance *cpd* ♦ *sm* (*medievale*) romance; (*moderno*) novel; ~ **d'amore** love story; ~ **d'appendice** serial (story); ~ **cavalleresco** tale of chivalry; ~ **poliziesco**, ~ **giallo**

detective story; ~ **rosa** romantic novel.

rom'bare *vi* to rumble, thunder, roar.

'rombo *sm* rumble, thunder, roar; (*MAT*) rhombus; (*ZOOL*) turbot.

ro'meno, a *ag, sm/f, sm* = **rumeno.**

'rompere *vt* to break; (*conversazione, fidanzamento*) to break off ♦ *vi* to break; ~**rsi** *vr* to break; **mi rompe le scatole** (*fam*) he (o she) is a pain in the neck; ~**rsi un braccio** to break an arm.

rompi'capo *sm* worry, headache; (*indovinello*) puzzle; (*in enigmistica*) brain-teaser.

rompi'collo *sm* daredevil.

rompighi'accio [rompi'gjattʃo] *sm* (*NAUT*) icebreaker.

rompis'catole *sm/f inv* (*fam*) pest, pain in the neck.

'ronda *sf* (*MIL*) rounds *pl*, patrol.

ron'della *sf* (*TECN*) washer.

'rondine *sf* (*ZOOL*) swallow.

ron'done *sm* (*ZOOL*) swift.

ron'fare *vi* (*russare*) to snore.

ron'zare [ron'dzare] *vi* to buzz, hum.

ron'zino [ron'dzino] *sm* (*peg: cavallo*) nag.

ron'zio, ii [ron'dzio] *sm* buzzing, humming; ~ **auricolare** (*MED*) tinnitus *sg*.

'rosa *sf* rose; (*fig: gruppo*): ~ **dei candidati** list of candidates ♦ *ag inv, sm* pink.

ro'saio *sm* (*pianta*) rosebush, rose tree; (*giardino*) rose garden.

ro'sario *sm* (*REL*) rosary.

ro'sato, a *ag* pink, rosy ♦ *sm* (*vino*) rosé (wine).

ro'seo, a *ag* (*anche fig*) rosy.

ro'seto *sm* rose garden.

ro'setta *sf* (*diamante*) rose-cut diamond; (*rondella*) washer.

'rosi *vb vedi* **rodere.**

rosicchi'are [rosik'kjare] *vt* to gnaw (at); (*mangiucchiare*) to nibble (at).

rosma'rino *sm* rosemary.

'roso, a *pp di* **rodere.**

roso'lare *vt* (*CUC*) to brown.

roso'lia *sf* (*MED*) German measles *sg*, rubella.

'rospo *sm* (*ZOOL*) toad; **mandar giù** o **ingoiare un** o **il** ~ (*fig*) to swallow a bitter pill; **sputa il** ~! out with it!

ros'setto *sm* (*per labbra*) lipstick; (*per guance*) rouge.

ros'siccio, a, ci, ce [ros'sittʃo] *ag* reddish.

'rosso, a *ag, sm, sm/f* red; **diventare** ~ (**per la vergogna**) to blush o go red (with o for shame); **il mar R**~ the Red Sea; ~ **d'uovo** egg yolk.

ros'sore *sm* flush, blush.

rosticce'ria [rostittʃe'ria] *sf* shop selling

roast meat and other cooked food.
'rostro *sm* rostrum; (*becco*) beak.
ro'tabile *ag* (*percorribile*): **strada ~** roadway; (*FERR*): **materiale ~ rolling stock.**
ro'taia *sf* rut, track; (*FERR*) rail.
ro'tare *vt, vi* to rotate.
rota'tivo, a *ag* rotating, rotation *cpd.*
rotazi'one [rotat'tsjone] *sf* rotation.
rote'are *vt, vi* to whirl; **~ gli occhi** to roll one's eyes.
ro'tella *sf* small wheel; (*di mobile*) castor.
roto'calco, chi *sm* (*TIP*) rotogravure; (*rivista*) illustrated magazine.
roto'lare *vt, vi* to roll; **~rsi** *vr* to roll (about).
roto'lio *sm* rolling.
'rotolo *sm* (*di carta, stoffa*) roll; (*di corda*) coil; **andare a ~i** (*fig*) to go to rack and ruin; **mandare a ~i** (*fig*) to ruin.
ro'tondo, a *ag* round ♦ *sf* rotunda.
ro'tore *sm* rotor.
'rotta *sf* (*AER, NAUT*) course, route; (*MIL*) rout; **a ~ di collo** at breakneck speed; **essere in ~ con qn** to be on bad terms with sb; **fare ~ su** *o* **per** *o* **verso** to head for *o* towards; **cambiare ~** (*anche fig*) to change course; **in ~ di collisione** on a collision course; **ufficiale di ~** navigator, navigating officer.
rot'tame *sm* fragment, scrap, broken bit; **~i** *smpl* (*di nave, aereo etc*) wreckage *sg;* **~i di ferro** scrap iron *sg.*
'rotto, a *pp di* **rompere** ♦ *ag* broken; (*calzoni*) torn, split; (*persona: pratico, resistente*): **~ a** accustomed *o* inured to ♦ *sm:* **per il ~ della cuffia** by the skin of one's teeth; **~i** *smpl:* **20.000 lire e ~i** 20,000-odd lire.
rot'tura *sf* (*azione*) breaking *no pl;* (*di rapporti*) breaking off; (*MED*) fracture, break.
rou'lotte [ru'lɔt] *sf inv* caravan.
ro'vente *ag* red-hot.
'rovere *sm* oak.
ro'vescia [ro'veʃʃa] *sf:* **alla ~** upside-down; inside-out; **oggi mi va tutto alla ~** everything is going wrong (for me) today.
rovesci'are [roveʃ'ʃare] *vt* (*versare in giù*) to pour; (: *accidentalmente*) to spill; (*capovolgere*) to turn upside down; (*gettare a terra*) to knock down; (: *fig: governo*) to overthrow; (*piegare all'indietro: testa*) to throw back; **~rsi** *vr* (*sedia, macchina*) to overturn; (*barca*) to capsize; (*liquido*) to spill; (*fig: situazione*) to be reversed.
ro'vescio, sci [ro'veʃʃo] *sm* other side, wrong side; (*della mano*) back; (*di moneta*)

reverse; (*pioggia*) sudden downpour; (*fig*) setback; (*MAGLIA: anche:* **punto ~**) purl (stitch); (*TENNIS*) backhand (stroke); **a ~** (*sottosopra*) upside-down; (*con l'esterno all'interno*) inside-out; **capire qc a ~ to** misunderstand sth; **~ di fortuna** setback.
ro'vina *sf* ruin; **~e** *sfpl* ruins; **andare in ~** (*andare a pezzi*) to collapse; (*fig*) to go to rack and ruin; **mandare qc/qn in ~ to** ruin sth/sb.
rovi'nare *vi* to collapse, fall down ♦ *vt* (*far cadere giù: casa*) to demolish; (*danneggiare, fig*) to ruin.
rovi'nato, a *ag* ruined, damaged; (*fig: persona*) ruined.
rovi'noso, a *ag* ruinous.
rovis'tare *vt* (*casa*) to ransack; (*tasche*) to rummage in (*o* through).
'rovo *sm* (*BOT*) blackberry bush, bramble bush.
roz'zezza [rod'dzettsa] *sf* roughness, coarseness.
'rozzo, a [ˈroddzo] *ag* rough, coarse.
RP *sigla fpl vedi* **relazioni pubbliche.**
R.R. *abbr* (*POSTA*) **= ricevuta di ritorno.**
Rrr *abbr* (*POSTA*) **= raccomandata con ricevuta di ritorno.**
RSVP *abbr* (*= répondez s'il vous plaît*) RSVP.
'ruba *sf:* **andare a ~** to sell like hot cakes.
rubacu'ori *sm inv* ladykiller.
ru'bare *vt* to steal; **~ qc a qn** to steal sth from sb.
rubi'condo, a *ag* ruddy.
rubi'netto *sm* tap, faucet (*US*).
ru'bino *sm* ruby.
ru'bizzo, a [ru'bittso] *ag* lively, sprightly.
'rublo *sm* rouble.
ru'brica, che *sf* (*di giornale: colonna*) column; (: *pagina*) page; (*quadernetto*) index book; (: *per indirizzi*) address book.
'rude *ag* tough, rough.
'rudere *sm* (*rovina*) ruins *pl.*
rudimen'tale *ag* rudimentary, basic.
rudi'menti *smpl* rudiments; basic principles.
ruffi'ano *sm* pimp.
'ruga, ghe *sf* wrinkle.
'ruggine [ˈruddʒine] *sf* rust.
rug'gire [rud'dʒire] *vi* to roar.
rug'gito [rud'dʒito] *sm* roar.
rugi'ada [ru'dʒada] *sf* dew.
ru'goso, a *ag* wrinkled; (*scabro: superficie etc*) rough.
rul'lare *vi* (*tamburo, nave*) to roll; (*aereo*) to taxi.
rul'lino *sm* (*FOT*) roll of film, spool.
rul'lio, ii *sm* (*di tamburi*) roll.
'rullo *sm* (*di tamburi*) roll; (*arnese cilindrico,*

TIP) roller; ~ **compressore** steam roller;
~ **di pellicola** roll of film.
rum *sm* rum.
ru'meno, a *ag, sm/f, sm* Romanian.
rumi'nante *sm* (*ZOOL*) ruminant.
rumi'nare *vt* (*ZOOL*) to ruminate; (*fig*) to
ruminate on *o* over, chew over.
ru'more *sm*: **un** ~ a noise, a sound; **il** ~
noise; **fare** ~ to make a noise; **un** ~ **di**
passi the sound of footsteps; **la notizia ha**
fatto molto ~ (*fig*) the news aroused
great interest.
rumoreggi'are [rumored'dʒare] *vi* (*tuono*
etc) to rumble; (*fig*: *folla*) to clamour
(*BRIT*), clamor (*US*).
rumo'roso, a *ag* noisy.
ru'olo *sm* (*TEAT, fig*) role, part; (*elenco*) roll,
register, list; **di** ~ permanent, on the
permanent staff; **professore di** ~ (*INS*)
≈ lecturer with tenure; **fuori** ~
(*personale, insegnante*) temporary.
ru'ota *sf* wheel; **a** ~ (*forma*) circular; ~
anteriore/posteriore front/back wheel;
andare a ~ **libera** to freewheel; **parlare a**
~ **libera** (*fig*) to speak freely; ~ **di scorta**
spare wheel.
ruo'tare *vt, vi* = **rotare**.
'rupe *sf* cliff, rock.
ru'pestre *ag* rocky.
ru'pia *sf* rupee.
'ruppi *etc vb vedi* **rompere**.
ru'rale *ag* rural, country *cpd*.
ru'scello [ruʃ'ʃɛllo] *sm* stream.
'ruspa *sf* excavator.
rus'pante *ag* (*pollo*) free-range.
rus'sare *vi* to snore.
'Russia *sf*: **la** ~ Russia.
'russo, a *ag, sm/f, sm* Russian.
'rustico, a, ci, che *ag* country *cpd*, rural;
(*arredamento*) rustic; (*fig*) rough,
unrefined ♦ *sm* (*fabbricato*: *per attrezzi*)
shed; (*per abitazione*) farm labourer's
(*BRIT*) *o* farmhand's cottage.
'ruta *sf* (*BOT*) rue.
rut'tare *vi* to belch.
'rutto *sm* belch.
'ruvido, a *ag* rough, coarse.
ruzzo'lare [ruttso'lare] *vi* to tumble down.
ruzzo'lone [ruttso'lone] *sm* tumble, fall.
ruzzo'loni [ruttso'loni] *av*: **cadere** ~ to
tumble down; **fare le scale** ~ to tumble
down the stairs.

S s

S, s ['ɛsse] *sf o m* (*lettera*) S, s; **S come**
Savona ≈ S for Sugar.
s *abbr* (= *secondo*) sec.
S. *abbr* (= *sud*) S; (= *santo*) St.
SA *sigla* = *Salerno* ♦ *abbr vedi* **società**
anonima.
sa *vb vedi* **sapere.**
sab. *abbr* (= *sabato*) Sat.
'sabato *sm* Saturday; *per fraseologia vedi*
martedì.
'sabbia *sf* sand; ~**e mobili** quicksand(s *pl*).
sabbia'tura *sf* (*MED*) sand bath; (*TECN*)
sand-blasting; **fare le** ~**e** to take sand
baths.
sabbi'oso, a *ag* sandy.
sabo'taggio [sabo'taddʒo] *sm* sabotage.
sabo'tare *vt* to sabotage.
sabota'tore, 'trice *sm/f* saboteur.
'sacca, che *sf* bag; (*bisaccia*) haversack;
(*insenatura*) inlet; ~ **d'aria** air pocket; ~
da viaggio travelling bag.
sacca'rina *sf* saccharin(e).
sac'cente [sat'tʃɛnte] *sm/f* know-all (*BRIT*),
know-it-all (*US*).
saccheggi'are [sakked'dʒare] *vt* to sack,
plunder.
sac'cheggio [sak'keddʒo] *sm* sack(ing).
sac'chetto [sak'ketto] *sm* (small) bag;
(small) sack; ~ **di carta/di plastica**
paper/plastic bag.
'sacco, chi *sm* bag; (*per carbone etc*) sack;
(*ANAT, BIOL*) sac; (*tela*) sacking;
(*saccheggio*) sack(ing); (*fig: grande*
quantità): **un** ~ **di** lots of, heaps of;
cogliere *o* **prendere qn con le mani nel** ~
to catch sb red-handed; **vuotare il** ~ to
confess, spill the beans; **mettere qn nel** ~
to cheat sb; **colazione** *f* **al** ~ packed lunch;
~ **a pelo** sleeping bag; ~ **per i rifiuti** bin
bag (*BRIT*), garbage bag (*US*).
sacer'dote [satʃer'dote] *sm* priest.
sacer'dozio [satʃer'dɔttsjo] *sm* priesthood.
'Sacra Co'rona U'nita *sf the mafia in*
Puglia.
sacra'mento *sm* sacrament.
sa'crario *sm* memorial chapel.
sacres'tano *sm* = **sagrestano.**
sacres'tia *sf* = **sagrestia.**

sacrifi'care *vt* to sacrifice; **~rsi** *vr* to sacrifice o.s.; (*privarsi di qc*) to make sacrifices.

sacrifi'cato, a *ag* sacrificed; (*non valorizzato*) wasted; **una vita ~a** a life of sacrifice.

sacri'ficio [sakri'fitʃo] *sm* sacrifice.

sacri'legio [sacri'lɛdʒo] *sm* sacrilege.

sa'crilego, a, ghi, ghe *ag* (*REL*) sacrilegious.

'sacro, a *ag* sacred.

sacro'santo, a *ag* sacrosanct.

'sadico, a, ci, che *ag* sadistic ♦ *sm/f* sadist.

sa'dismo *sm* sadism.

sadomaso'chismo [sadomazo'kismo] *sm* sadomasochism.

sa'etta *sf* arrow; (*fulmine: anche fig*) thunderbolt.

sa'fari *sm inv* safari.

sa'gaoo [sa'gatʃɛ] *ag* shrewd, sagacious.

sa'gacia [sa'gatʃa] *sf* sagacity, shrewdness.

sag'gezza [sad'dʒettsa] *sf* wisdom.

saggi'are [sad'dʒare] *vt* (*metalli*) to assay; (*fig*) to test.

'saggio, a, gi, ge ['saddʒo] *ag* wise ♦ *sm* (*persona*) sage; (*operazione sperimentale*) test; (: *dell'oro*) assay; (*fig: prova*) proof; (*campione indicativo*) sample; (*scritto: letterario*) essay; (: *INS*) written test; **dare ~ di** to give proof of; **in ~** as a sample.

sag'gistica [sad'dʒistika] *sf* ≈ non-fiction.

Sagit'tario [sadʒit'tarjo] *sm* Sagittarius; **essere del ~** to be Sagittarius.

'sagoma *sf* (*profilo*) outline, profile; (*forma*) form, shape; (*TECN*) template; (*bersaglio*) target; (*fig: persona*) character.

'sagra *sf* festival.

sa'grato *sm* churchyard.

sagres'tano *sm* sacristan; sexton.

sagres'tia *sf* sacristy; (*culto protestante*) vestry.

Sa'hara [sa'ara] *sm*: **il (Deserto del) ~** the Sahara (Desert).

sahari'ana [saa'rjana] *sf* bush jacket.

'sai *vb vedi* **sapere**.

Sai'gon *sf* Saigon.

'saio *sm* (*REL*) habit.

'sala *sf* hall; (*stanza*) room; **~ d'aspetto** waiting room; **~ da ballo** ballroom; **~ (dei) comandi** control room; **~ per concerti** concert hall; **~ per conferenze** (*INS*) lecture hall; (*in aziende*) conference room; **~ da gioco** gaming room; **~ macchine** (*NAUT*) engine room; **~ operatoria** (*MED*) operating theatre (*BRIT*) *o* room (*US*); **~ da pranzo** dining room; **~ per ricevimenti** banqueting hall; **~ delle udienze** (*DIR*) courtroom.

sa'lace [sa'latʃe] *ag* (*spinto, piccante*) salacious, saucy; (*mordace*) cutting, biting.

sala'mandra *sf* salamander.

sa'lame *sm* salami *no pl*, salami sausage.

sala'moia *sf* (*CUC*) brine.

sa'lare *vt* to salt.

salari'ale *ag* wage *cpd*, pay *cpd*; **aumento ~** wage *o* pay increase (*BRIT*) *o* raise (*US*).

salari'ato, a *sm/f* wage-earner.

sa'lario *sm* pay, wages *pl*; **~ base** basic wage; **~ minimo garantito** guaranteed minimum wage.

salas'sare *vt* (*MED*) to bleed.

sa'lasso *sm* (*MED*) bleeding, bloodletting; (*fig: forte spesa*) drain.

sala'tino *sm* cracker, salted biscuit.

sa'lato, a *ag* (*sapore*) salty; (*CUC*) salted, salt *cpd*; (*fig: discorso etc*) biting, sharp; (: *prezzi*) steep, stiff.

sal'dare *vt* (*congiungere*) to join, bind; (*parti metalliche*) to solder; (: *con saldatura autogena*) to weld; (*conto*) to settle, pay.

salda'tore *sm* (*operaio*) solderer; welder; (*utensile*) soldering iron.

salda'trice [salda'tritʃe] *sf* (*macchina*) welder, welding machine; **~ ad arco** arc welder.

salda'tura *sf* soldering; welding; (*punto saldato*) soldered joint; weld; **~ autogena** welding; **~ dolce** soft soldering.

sal'dezza [sal'dettsa] *sf* firmness, strength.

'saldo, a *ag* (*resistente, forte*) strong, firm; (*fermo*) firm, steady, stable; (*fig*) firm, steadfast ♦ *sm* (*svendita*) sale; (*di conto*) settlement; (*ECON*) balance; **pagare a ~** to pay in full; **~ attivo** credit; **~ passivo** deficit; **~ da riportare** balance carried forward.

'sale *sm* salt; (*fig*) wit; **~i** *smpl* (*MED: da annusare*) smelling salts; **sotto ~** salted; **restare di ~** (*fig*) to be dumbfounded; **ha poco ~ in zucca** he doesn't have much sense; **~ da cucina, ~ grosso** cooking salt; **~ da tavola, ~ fino** table salt; **~i da bagno** bath salts; **~i minerali** mineral salts; **~i e tabacchi** tobacconist's (shop).

sal'gemma [sal'dʒemma] *sm* rock salt.

'salgo *etc vb vedi* **salire**.

'salice ['salitʃe] *sm* willow; **~ piangente** weeping willow.

sali'ente *ag* (*fig*) salient, main.

sali'era *sf* salt cellar.

sa'lino, a *ag* saline ♦ *sf* saltworks *sg*.

sa'lire *vi* to go (*o* come) up; (*aereo etc*) to climb, go up; (*passeggero*) to get on; (*sentiero, prezzi, livello*) to go up, rise ♦ *vt* (*scale, gradini*) to go (*o* come) up; **~ su** to climb (up); ~ **sul treno/sull'autobus** to board the train/the bus; ~ **in macchina** to get into the car; ~ **a cavallo** to mount; ~ **al potere** to rise to power; ~ **al trono** to ascend the throne; ~ **alle stelle** (*prezzi*) to rocket.

sali'scendi [saliʃˈʃendi] *sm inv* latch.

sa'lita *sf* climb, ascent; (*erta*) hill, slope; **in** ~ *ag, av* uphill.

sa'liva *sf* saliva.

'salma *sf* corpse.

sal'mastro, a *ag* (*acqua*) salt *cpd*; (*sapore*) salty ♦ *sm* (*sapore*) salty taste; (*odore*) salty smell.

salmi *sm* (*CUC*) salmi; **lepre in** ~ salmi of hare.

'salmo *sm* psalm.

sal'mone *sm* salmon.

salmo'nella *sf* salmonella.

Salo'mone: le isole ~ *sfpl* the Solomon Islands.

sa'lone *sm* (*stanza*) sitting room, lounge; (*in albergo*) lounge; (*di ricevimento*) reception room; (*su nave*) lounge, saloon; (*mostra*) show, exhibition; (*negozio: di parrucchiere*) hairdresser's (salon); ~ **dell'automobile** motor show; ~ **di bellezza** beauty salon.

salo'pette [salɔˈpɛt] *sf inv* dungarees *pl*.

salotti'ero, a *ag* mundane.

sa'lotto *sm* lounge, sitting room; (*mobilio*) lounge suite.

sal'pare *vi* (*NAUT*) to set sail; (*anche:* ~ **l'ancora**) to weigh anchor.

'salsa *sf* (*CUC*) sauce; **in tutte le** ~**e** (*fig*) in all kinds of ways; ~ **di pomodoro** tomato sauce.

sal'sedine *sf* (*del mare, vento*) saltiness; (*incrostazione*) (dried) salt.

sal'siccia, ce [salˈsittʃa] *sf* pork sausage.

salsi'era *sf* sauceboat (*BRIT*), gravy boat.

'salso *sm* saltiness.

sal'tare *vi* to jump, leap; (*esplodere*) to blow up, explode; (: *valvola*) to blow; (*venir via*) to pop off; (*non aver luogo: corso etc*) to be cancelled ♦ *vt* to jump (over), leap (over); (*fig: pranzo, capitolo*) to skip, miss (out); (*CUC*) to sauté; **far** ~ to blow up; (*serratura: forzare*) to break; **far** ~ **il banco** (*GIOCO*) to break the bank; **farsi** ~ **le cervella** to blow one's brains out; **ma che ti salta in mente?** what are you thinking of?; ~ **da un argomento all'altro** to jump from one subject to another; ~ **addosso a qn** (*aggredire*) to attack sb; ~ **fuori** to jump out, leap out; (*venire trovato*) to turn up; ~ **fuori con** (*frase, commento*) to come out with; ~ **giù da qc** to jump off sth, jump down from sth.

saltel'lare *vi* to skip; to hop.

sal'tello *sm* hop, little jump.

saltim'banco, chi *sm* acrobat.

'salto *sm* jump; (*SPORT*) jumping; (*dislivello*) drop; **fare un** ~ to jump, leap; **fare un** ~ **da qn** to pop over to sb's (place); ~ **in alto/lungo** high/long jump; ~ **con l'asta** pole vaulting; ~ **mortale** somersault; **un** ~ **di qualità** (*miglioramento*) significant improvement.

saltu'ario, a *ag* occasional, irregular.

sa'lubre *ag* healthy, salubrious.

sa'lume *sm* (*CUC*) cured pork; ~**i** *smpl* (*insaccati*) cured pork meats.

salume'ria *sf* delicatessen.

salumi'ere, a *sm/f* ≈ delicatessen owner.

salumi'ficio [salumiˈfitʃo] *sm* cured pork meat factory.

salu'tare *ag* healthy; (*fig*) salutary, beneficial ♦ *vt* (*per dire buon giorno, fig*) to greet; (*per dire addio*) to say goodbye to; (*MIL*) to salute; **mi saluti sua moglie** my regards to your wife.

sa'lute *sf* health; ~**!** (*a chi starnutisce*) bless you!; (*nei brindisi*) cheers!; **bere alla** ~ **di qn** to drink (to) sb's health; **la** ~ **pubblica** public welfare; **godere di buona** ~ to be healthy, enjoy good health.

sa'luto *sm* (*gesto*) wave; (*parola*) greeting; (*MIL*) salute; **gli ha tolto il** ~ he no longer says hello to him; **cari** ~**i, tanti** ~**i** best regards; **vogliate gradire i nostri più distinti** ~**i** yours faithfully; **i miei** ~**i alla sua signora** my regards to your wife.

'salva *sf* salvo.

salvacon'dotto *sm* (*MIL*) safe-conduct.

salva'naio *sm* moneybox, piggy bank.

salvado'regno, a [salvadoˈreɲɲo] *ag, sm/f* Salvadorean.

salva'gente [salvaˈdʒɛnte] *sm* (*NAUT*) lifebuoy; (*pl inv: stradale*) traffic island; ~ **a ciambella** lifebelt; ~ **a giubbotto** lifejacket (*BRIT*), life preserver (*US*).

salvaguar'dare *vt* to safeguard.

salvagu'ardia *sf* safeguard; **a** ~ **di** for the safeguard of.

sal'vare *vt* to save; (*trarre da un pericolo*) to rescue; (*proteggere*) to protect; ~**rsi** *vr* to save o.s.; to escape; ~ **la vita a qn** to save sb's life; ~ **le apparenze** to keep up appearances; **si salvi chi può!** every man for himself!

salva'taggio [salvaˈtaddʒo] *sm* rescue.

salva'tore, 'trice *sm/f* saviour (*BRIT*), savior (*US*).

salvazi'one [salvatˈtsjone] *sf* (*REL*) salvation.

'salve *escl* (*fam*) hi!

sal'vezza [sal'vettsa] *sf* salvation; (*sicurezza*) safety.

'salvia *sf* (*BOT*) sage.

salvi'etta *sf* napkin, serviette.

'salvo, a *ag* safe, unhurt, unharmed; (*fuori pericolo*) safe, out of danger ♦ *sm*: **in ~ safe** ♦ *prep* (*eccetto*) except; **~ che** *cong* (*a meno che*) unless; (*eccetto che*) except (that); **mettere qc in ~** to put sth in a safe place; **mettersi in ~** to reach safety; **portare qn in ~** to lead sb to safety; **~ contrordini** barring instructions to the contrary; **~ errori e omissioni** errors and omissions excepted; **~ imprevisti** barring accidents.

sam'buca *sf* (*liquore*) sambuca (*type of anisette*).

sam'buco *sm* elder (tree).

sa'nare *vt* to heal, cure; (*economia*) to put right.

sana'toria *sf* (*DIR*) act of indemnity.

sana'torio *sm* sanatorium (*BRIT*), sanitarium (*US*).

san'cire [san'tʃire] *vt* to sanction.

'sandalo *sm* (*BOT*) sandalwood; (*calzatura*) sandal.

sang'ria [san'gria] *sf* (*bibita*) sangria.

'sangue *sm* blood; **farsi cattivo ~** to fret, get worked up; **all'ultimo ~** (*duello, lotta*) to the death; **non corre buon ~ tra di loro** there's bad blood between them; **buon ~ non mente!** blood will out!; **~ freddo** (*fig*) sang-froid, calm; **a ~ freddo** in cold blood.

sangu'igno, a [san'gwiɲɲo] *ag* blood *cpd*; (*colore*) blood-red.

sangui'nante *ag* bleeding.

sangui'nare *vi* to bleed.

sangui'nario, a *ag* bloodthirsty.

sangui'noso, a *ag* bloody.

sangui'suga, ghe *sf* leech.

sanità *sf* health; (*salubrità*) healthiness; **Ministero della S~** Department of Health; **~ mentale** sanity; **~ pubblica** public health.

sani'tario, a *ag* health *cpd*; (*condizioni*) sanitary ♦ *sm* (*AMM*) doctor; **Ufficiale S~** Health Officer; (*impianti*) **~i** *smpl* bathroom *o* sanitary fittings.

San Ma'rino *sf*: **la Repubblica di ~** the Republic of San Marino.

'sanno *vb vedi* **sapere**.

'sano, a *ag* healthy; (*denti, costituzione*) healthy, sound; (*integro*) whole, unbroken; (*fig: politica, consigli*) sound; **~ di mente** sane; **di ~a pianta** completely, entirely; **~ e salvo** safe and sound.

Santi'ago *sf*: **~ (del Cile)** Santiago (de Chile).

santifi'care *vt* to sanctify; (*feste*) to observe.

san'tino *sm* holy picture.

san'tissimo, a *ag*: **il S~ Sacramento** the Holy Sacrament; **il Padre S~** (*papa*) the Holy Father.

santità *sf* sanctity; holiness; **Sua/Vostra ~** (*titolo di papa*) His/Your Holiness.

'santo, a *ag* holy; (*fig*) saintly; (*seguito da nome proprio: dav sm* **san** + *C*, **sant'** + *V*, **santo** + *s impura, gn, pn, ps, x, z*; *dav sf* **santa** + *C*, **sant'** + *V*) saint ♦ *sm/f* saint; **parole ~e!** very true!; **tutto il ~ giorno** the whole blessed day, all day long; **non c'è ~ che tenga!** that's no excuse!; **la S~a Sede** the Holy See.

san'tone *sm* holy man.

santu'ario *sm* sanctuary.

sanzio'nare [santsjo'nare] *vt* to sanction.

sanzi'one [san'tsjone] *sf* sanction, (*penale, civile*) sanction, penalty; **~i economiche** economic sanctions.

sa'pere *vt* to know; (*essere capace di*): **so nuotare** I know how to swim, I can swim ♦ *vi*: **~ di** (*aver sapore*) to taste of; (*aver odore*) to smell of ♦ *sm* knowledge; **far ~ qc a qn** to inform sb about sth, let sb know sth; **venire a ~ qc (da qn)** to find out *o* hear about sth (from sb); **non ne vuole più ~ di lei** he doesn't want to have anything more to do with her; **mi sa che non sia vero** I don't think that's true.

sapi'ente *ag* (*dotto*) learned; (*che rivela abilità*) masterly ♦ *sm/f* scholar.

sapien'tone, a *sm/f* (*peg*) know-all (*BRIT*), know-it-all (*US*).

sapi'enza [sa'pjentsa] *sf* wisdom.

sa'pone *sm* soap; **~ da barba** shaving soap; **~ da bucato** washing soap; **~ liquido** liquid soap; **~ in scaglie** soapflakes *pl*.

sapo'netta *sf* cake *o* bar *o* tablet of soap.

sa'pore *sm* taste, flavour (*BRIT*), flavor (*US*).

sapo'rito, a *ag* tasty; (*fig: arguto*) witty; (*: piccante*) racy.

sappi'amo *vb vedi* **sapere**.

saprò *etc vb vedi* **sapere**.

sapu'tello, a *sm/f* know-all (*BRIT*), know-it-all (*US*).

sarà *etc vb vedi* **essere**.

sara'banda *sf* (*fig*) uproar.

saraci'nesca, sche [saratʃi'neska] *sf* (*serranda*) rolling shutter.

sar'casmo *sm* sarcasm *no pl*; sarcastic remark.

sar'castico, a, ci, che *ag* sarcastic.

sarchi'are [sar'kjare] *vt* (*AGR*) to hoe.

sar'cofago, gi *o* **ghi** *sm* sarcophagus.

Sar'degna [sar'deɲɲa] *sf*: **la** ~ Sardinia.
sar'dina *sf* sardine.
'sardo, a *ag, sm/f* Sardinian.
sar'donico, a, ci, che *ag* sardonic.
sa'rei *etc vb vedi* **essere.**
'sarta *sf vedi* **sarto.**
'sartia *sf* (*NAUT*) stay.
sarti'ame *sm* (*NAUT*) stays *pl.*
'sarto, a *sm/f* tailor/dressmaker; ~ **d'alta moda** couturier.
sarto'ria *sf* tailor's (shop); dressmaker's (shop); (*casa di moda*) fashion house; (*arte*) couture.
sassai'ola *sf* hail of stones.
sas'sata *sf* blow with a stone; **tirare una** ~ **contro** *o* **a qc/qn** to throw a stone at sth/sb.
'sasso *sm* stone; (*ciottolo*) pebble; (*masso*) rock; **restare** *o* **rimanere di** ~ to be dumbfounded.
sassofo'nista, i, e *sm/f* saxophonist.
sas'sofono *sm* saxophone.
sas'sone *ag, sm/f, sm* Saxon.
sas'soso, a *ag* stony; pebbly.
'Satana *sm* Satan.
sa'tanico, a, ci, che *ag* satanic, fiendish.
sa'tellite *sm, ag* satellite.
'satira *sf* satire.
satireggi'are [satired'dʒare] *vt* to satirize ♦ *vi* (*fare della satira*) to be satirical; (*scrivere satire*) to write satires.
sa'tirico, a, ci, che *ag* satiric(al).
sa'tollo, a *ag* full, replete.
satu'rare *vt* to saturate.
saturazi'one [saturat'tsjone] *sf* saturation.
'saturo, a *ag* saturated; (*fig*): ~ **di** full of; ~ **d'acqua** (*terreno*) waterlogged.
'SAUB *sigla f* (= *Struttura Amministrativa Unificata di Base*) *state welfare system.*
'sauna *sf* sauna; **fare la** ~ to have *o* take a sauna.
sa'vana *sf* savannah.
'savio, a *ag* wise, sensible ♦ *sm* wise man.
Sa'voia *sf*: **la** ~ Savoy.
savoi'ardo, a *ag* of Savoy, Savoyard ♦ *sm* (*biscotto*) sponge finger.
sazi'are [sat'tsjare] *vt* to satisfy, satiate; ~**rsi** *vr* (*riempirsi di cibo*): ~**rsi (di)** to eat one's fill (of); (*fig*): ~**rsi di** to grow tired *o* weary of.
sazietà [sattsje'ta] *sf* satiety, satiation.
'sazio, a [*'*sattsjo] *ag*: ~ **(di)** sated (with), full (of); (*fig: stufo*) fed up (with), sick (of).
sbada'taggine [zbada'taddʒine] *sf* (*sventatezza*) carelessness; (*azione*) oversight.
sba'dato, a *ag* careless, inattentive.

sbadigli'are [zbadiʎ'ʎare] *vi* to yawn.
sba'diglio [zba'diʎʎo] *sm* yawn; **fare uno** ~ to yawn.
'sbafo *sm*: **a** ~ at somebody else's expense.
sbagli'are [zbaʎ'ʎare] *vt* to make a mistake in, get wrong ♦ *vi* (*fare errori*) to make a mistake (*o* mistakes), be mistaken; (*ingannarsi*) to be wrong; (*operare in modo non giusto*) to err; ~**rsi** *vr* to make a mistake, be mistaken, be wrong; ~ **la mira/strada** to miss one's aim/take the wrong road; **scusi, ho sbagliato numero** (*TEL*) sorry, I've got the wrong number; **non c'è da** ~**rsi** there can be no mistake.
sbagli'ato, a [zbaʎ'ʎato] *ag* (*gen*) wrong; (*compito*) full of mistakes; (*conclusione*) erroneous.
'sbaglio [*'*zbaʎʎo] *sm* mistake, error; (*morale*) error; **fare uno** ~ to make a mistake.
sbales'trato, a *ag* (*persona: scombussolato*) unsettled.
sbal'lare *vt* (*merce*) to unpack ♦ *vi* (*nel fare un conto*) to overestimate; (*DROGA: gergo*) to get high.
sbal'lato, a *ag* (*calcolo*) wrong; (*fam: ragionamento, persona*) screwy.
'sballo *sm* (*DROGA: gergo*) trip.
sballot'tare *vt* to toss (about).
sbalor'dire *vt* to stun, amaze ♦ *vi* to be stunned, be amazed.
sbalordi'tivo, a *ag* amazing; (*prezzo*) incredible, absurd.
sbal'zare [zbal'tsare] *vt* to throw, hurl; (*fig: da una carica*) to remove, dismiss ♦ *vi* (*balzare*) to bounce; (*saltare*) to leap, bound.
'sbalzo [*'*zbaltso] *sm* (*spostamento improvviso*) jolt, jerk; **a** ~**i** jerkily; (*fig*) in fits and starts; **uno** ~ **di temperatura** a sudden change in temperature.
sban'care *vt* (*nei giochi*) to break the bank at (*o* of); (*fig*) to ruin, bankrupt.
sbanda'mento *sm* (*NAUT*) list; (*AUT*) skid; (*fig: di persona*) confusion; **ha avuto un periodo di** ~ he went off the rails for a bit.
sban'dare *vi* (*NAUT*) to list; (*AUT*) to skid; ~**rsi** *vr* (*folla*) to disperse; (*truppe*) to scatter; (*fig: famiglia*) to break up.
sban'data *sf* (*AUT*) skid; (*NAUT*) list; **prendere una** ~ **per qn** (*fig*) to fall for sb.
sban'dato, a *sm/f* mixed-up person.
sbandie'rare *vt* (*bandiera*) to wave; (*fig*) to parade, show off.
'sbando *sm*: **essere allo** ~ to drift.
sbarac'care *vt* (*libri, piatti etc*) to clear (up).
sbaragli'are [zbaraʎ'ʎare] *vt* (*MIL*) to rout;

(*in gare sportive etc*) to beat, defeat.

sba'raglio [zba'raλλo] *sm*: **gettarsi allo ~** (*soldato*) to throw o.s. into the fray; (*fig*) to risk everything.

sbaraz'zarsi [zbarat'tsarsi] *vr*: ~ **di** to get rid of, rid o.s. of.

sbaraz'zino, a [zbarat'tsino] *ag* impish, cheeky.

sbar'bare *vt*, **~rsi** *vr* to shave.

sbarba'tello *sm* novice, greenhorn.

sbar'care *vt* (*passeggeri*) to disembark; (*merci*) to unload ♦ *vi* to disembark.

'sbarco *sm* disembarkation; unloading; (*MIL*) landing.

'sbarra *sf* bar; (*di passaggio a livello*) barrier; (*DIR*): **mettere/presentarsi alla ~** to bring/appear before the court.

sbarra'mento *sm* (*stradale*) barrier; (*diga*) dam, barrage; (*MIL*) barrage; (*POL*) cut-off point (*level of support below which a political party is excluded from representation in Parliament*).

sbar'rare *vt* (*bloccare*) to block, bar; (*cancellare: assegno*) to cross (*BRIT*); ~ **il passo** to bar the way; ~ **gli occhi** to open one's eyes wide.

sbar'rato, a *ag* (*porta*) barred; (*passaggio*) blocked, barred; (*strada*) blocked, obstructed; (*occhi*) staring; (*assegno*) crossed (*BRIT*).

'sbattere *vt* (*porta*) to bang; (*tappeti, ali, CUC*) to beat; (*urtare*) to knock, hit ♦ *vi* (*porta, finestra*) to bang; (*agitarsi: ali, vele etc*) to flap; ~ **qn fuori/in galera** to throw sb out/into prison; **me ne sbatto!** (*fam*) I don't give a damn!

sbat'tuto, a *ag* (*viso, aria*) dejected, worn out; (*uovo*) beaten.

sba'vare *vi* to dribble; (*colore*) to smear, smudge.

sbava'tura *sf* (*di persone*) dribbling; (*di lumache*) slime; (*di rossetto, vernice*) smear.

sbelli'carsi *vr*: ~ **dalle risa** to split one's sides laughing.

'sberla *sf* slap.

sber'leffo *sm*: **fare uno ~ a qn** to make a face at sb.

sbia'dire *vi* (*anche*: **~rsi**), *vt* to fade.

sbia'dito, a *ag* faded; (*fig*) colourless (*BRIT*), colorless (*US*), dull.

sbian'care *vt* to whiten; (*tessuto*) to bleach ♦ *vi* (*impallidire*) to grow pale *o* white.

sbi'eco, a, chi, che *ag* (*storto*) squint, askew; **di ~**: **guardare qn di ~** (*fig*) to look askance at sb; **tagliare una stoffa di ~** to cut material on the bias.

sbigot'tire *vt* to dismay, stun ♦ *vi* (*anche*:

~rsi) to be dismayed.

sbilanci'are [zbilan't∫are] *vt* to throw off balance; **~rsi** *vr* (*perdere l'equilibrio*) to overbalance, lose one's balance; (*fig*: *compromettersi*) to compromise o.s.

sbi'lenco, a, chi, che *ag* (*persona*) crooked, misshapen; (*fig*: *idea, ragionamento*) twisted.

sbirci'are [zbir't∫are] *vt* to cast sidelong glances at, eye.

sbirci'ata [zbir't∫ata] *sf*: **dare una ~ a qc** to glance at sth, have a look at sth.

'sbirro *sm* (*peg*) cop.

sbizzar'rirsi [zbiddzar'rirsi] *vr* to indulge one's whims.

sbloc'care *vt* to unblock, free; (*freno*) to release; (*prezzi, affitti*) to free from controls, **~rsi** *vr* (*gen*) to become unblocked; (*passaggio, strada*) to clear, become unblocked; **la situazione si è sbloccata things are moving again**.

'sblocco, chi *sm* (*vedi vt*) unblocking, freeing; release.

sboc'care *vi*: ~ **in** (*fiume*) to flow into; (*strada*) to lead into; (*persona*) to come (*out*) into; (*fig*: *concludersi*) to end (up) in.

sboc'cato, a *ag* (*persona*) foul-mouthed; (*linguaggio*) foul.

sbocci'are [zbot't∫are] *vi* (*fiore*) to bloom, open (out).

'sbocco, chi *sm* (*di fiume*) mouth; (*di strada*) end; (*di tubazione, COMM*) outlet; (*uscita: anche fig*) way out; **una strada senza ~ a dead end; siamo in una situazione senza ~chi** there's no way out of this for us.

sbocconcel'lare [zbokkont∫el'lare] *vt*: ~ (**qc**) to nibble (at sth).

sbollen'tare *vt* (*CUC*) to parboil.

sbol'lire *vi* (*fig*) to cool down, calm down.

'sbornia *sf* (*fam*): **prendersi una ~** to get plastered.

sbor'sare *vt* (*denaro*) to pay out.

sbot'tare *vi*: ~ **in una risata/per la collera** to burst out laughing/explode with anger.

sbotto'nare *vt* to unbutton, undo.

sbra'cato, a *ag* slovenly.

sbracci'arsi [zbrat't∫arsi] *vr* to wave (one's arms about).

sbracci'ato, a [zbrat't∫ato] *ag* (*camicia*) sleeveless; (*persona*) bare-armed.

sbrai'tare *vi* to yell, bawl.

sbra'nare *vt* to tear to pieces.

sbricio'lare [zbrit∫o'lare] *vt*, **~rsi** *vr* to crumble.

sbri'gare *vt* to deal with, get through; (*cliente*) to attend to, deal with; **~rsi** *vr* to hurry (up).

sbriga'tivo, a *ag* (*persona, modo*) quick, expeditious; (*giudizio*) hasty.

sbrina'mento *sm* defrosting.

sbri'nare *vt* to defrost.

sbrindel'lato, a *ag* tattered, in tatters.

sbrodo'lare *vt* to stain, dirty.

sbron'zarsi [zbron'tsarsi] *vr* (*fam*) to get sozzled.

'sbronzo, a ['zbrontso] (*fam*) *ag* sozzled ♦ *sf*: **prendersi una ~a** to get sozzled.

sbruf'fone, a *sm/f* boaster, braggart.

sbu'care *vi* (*apparire*) to pop out (*o* up).

sbucci'are [zbut't∫are] *vt* (*arancia, patata*) to peel; (*piselli*) to shell; **~rsi un ginocchio** to graze one's knee.

sbucherò *etc* [zbuke'rɔ] *vb vedi* **sbucare**.

sbudel'larsi *vr*: **~ dalle risa** to split one's sides laughing.

sbuf'fare *vi* (*persona, cavallo*) to snort; (*: ansimare*) to puff, pant; (*treno*) to puff.

'sbuffo *sm* (*di aria, fumo, vapore*) puff; **maniche a ~** puff(ed) sleeves.

sc. *abbr* (*TEAT*: = *scena*) sc.

S.C. *abbr* = **stato civile; Suprema Corte (di Cassazione).**

'scabbia *sf* (*MED*) scabies *sg*.

'scabro, a *ag* rough, harsh; (*fig*) concise, terse.

sca'broso, a *ag* (*fig*: *difficile*) difficult, thorny; (*: imbarazzante*) embarrassing; (*: sconcio*) indecent.

scacchi'era [skak'kjɛra] *sf* chessboard.

scacchiere [skak'kjɛre] *sm* (*MIL*) sector; **S~** (*in Gran Bretagna*) Exchequer.

scaccia'cani [skatt∫a'kani] *sm o f inv* pistol with blanks.

scacciapensi'eri [skatt∫apen'sjɛri] *sm inv* (*MUS*) jew's-harp.

scacci'are [skat't∫are] *vt* to chase away *o* out, drive away *o* out; **~ qn di casa** to turn sb out of the house.

'scacco, chi *sm* (*pezzo del gioco*) chessman; (*quadretto di scacchiera*) square; (*fig*) setback, reverse; **~chi** *smpl* (*gioco*) chess *sg*; **a ~chi** (*tessuto*) check(ed); **subire uno ~** (*fig*: *sconfitta*) to suffer a setback.

scacco'matto *sm* checkmate; **dare ~ a qn** (*anche fig*) to checkmate sb.

'scaddi *etc vb vedi* **scadere**.

sca'dente *ag* shoddy, of poor quality.

sca'denza [ska'dentsa] *sf* (*di cambiale, contratto*) maturity; (*di passaporto*) expiry date; **a breve/lunga ~** short-/long-term; **data di ~** expiry date; **~ a termine** fixed deadline.

sca'dere *vi* (*contratto etc*) to expire; (*debito*) to fall due; (*valore, forze, peso*) to decline,

go down.

sca'fandro *sm* (*di palombaro*) diving suit; (*di astronauta*) spacesuit.

scaffala'tura *sf* shelving, shelves *pl*.

scaf'fale *sm* shelf; (*mobile*) set of shelves.

'scafo *sm* (*NAUT, AER*) hull.

scagio'nare [skadʒo'nare] *vt* to exonerate, free from blame.

'scaglia ['skaʎʎa] *sf* (*ZOOL*) scale; (*scheggia*) chip, flake.

scagli'are [skaʎ'ʎare] *vt* (*lanciare: anche fig*) to hurl, fling; **~rsi** *vr*: **~rsi su** *o* **contro** *o* hurl *o* fling o.s. at; (*fig*) to rail at.

scagliona'mento [skaʎʎona'mento] *sm* (*MIL*) arrangement in echelons.

scaglio'nare [skaʎʎo'nare] *vt* (*pagamenti*) to space out, spread out; (*MIL*) to echelon.

scagli'one [skaʎ'ʎone] *sm* (*MIL*) echelon; (*GEO*) terrace; **a ~i** in groups.

sca'gnozzo [skaɲ'ɲɔttso] *sm* (*peg*) lackey.

'Scala *sf*: **la ~** *vedi nota nel riquadro*.

LA SCALA

Milan's **la Scala** first opened its doors in 1778 with a performance of Salieri's opera, "L'Europa riconosciuta". Built on the site of the church of Santa Maria della Scala, the theatre suffered serious damage in the bombing campaigns of 1943 but reopened in 1946 with a concert conducted by Toscanini. Enjoying world-wide renown for its opera, **la Scala** also has a famous school of classical dance.

'scala *sf* (*a gradini etc*) staircase, stairs *pl*; (*a pioli, di corda*) ladder; (*MUS, GEO, di colori, valori, fig*) scale; **~e** *sfpl* (*scalinata*) stairs; **su larga** *o* **vasta ~** on a large scale; **su piccola ~, su ~ ridotta** on a small scale; **su ~ nazionale/mondiale** on a national/worldwide scale; **in ~ di 1 a 100.000** on a scale of 1 cm to 1 km; **riproduzione in ~** reproduction to scale; **~ a chiocciola** spiral staircase; **~ a libretto** stepladder; **~ di misure** system of weights and measures; **~ mobile** escalator; (*ECON*) sliding scale; **~ mobile (dei salari)** index-linked pay scale; **~ di sicurezza** (*antincendio*) fire escape.

sca'lare *vt* (*ALPINISMO, muro*) to climb, scale; (*debito*) to scale down, reduce.

sca'lata *sf* scaling *no pl*, climbing *no pl*; (*arrampicata, fig*) climb; **dare la ~ a** (*fig*) to make a bid for.

scala'tore, 'trice *sm/f* climber.

scalca'gnato, a [skalkaɲ'ɲato] *ag* (*logoro*) worn; (*persona*) shabby.

scalci'are [skal't∫are] *vi* to kick.

scalci'nato, a [skaltʃi'nato] *ag* (*fig peg*) shabby.

scalda'bagno [skalda'baɲɲo] *sm* water heater.

scal'dare *vt* to heat; **~rsi** *vr* to warm up, heat up; (*al fuoco, al sole*) to warm o.s.; (*fig*) to get excited; **~ la sedia** (*fig*) to twiddle one's thumbs.

scaldavi'vande *sm inv* dish warmer.

scal'dino *sm* (*per mani*) hand-warmer; (*per piedi*) foot-warmer; (*per letto*) bedwarmer.

scal'fire *vt* to scratch.

scalfit'tura *sf* scratch.

scali'nata *sf* staircase.

sca'lino *sm* (*anche fig*) step; (*di scala a pioli*) rung.

scal'mana *sf* (hot) flush.

scalma'narsi *vr* (*affaticarsi*) to rush about, rush around; (*agitarsi, darsi da fare*) to get all hot and bothered; (*arrabbiarsi*) to get excited, get steamed up.

scalma'nato, a *sm/f* hothead.

'scalo *sm* (*NAUT*) slipway; (: *porto d'approdo*) port of call; (*AER*) stopover; **fare ~ (a)** (*NAUT*) to call (at), put in (at); (*AER*) to land (at), make a stop (at); **volo senza ~** non-stop flight; **~ merci** (*FERR*) goods (*BRIT*) *o* freight yard.

sca'logna [ska'loɲɲa] *sf* (*fam*) bad luck.

scalo'gnato, a [skalon'ɲato] *ag* (*fam*) unlucky.

scalop'pina *sf* (*CUC*) escalope.

scal'pello *sm* chisel.

scalpi'tare *vi* (*cavallo*) to paw the ground; (*persona*) to stamp one's feet.

scal'pore *sm* noise, row; **far ~** (*notizia*) to cause a sensation *o* a stir.

'scaltro, a *ag* cunning, shrewd.

scal'zare *vt* (*albero*) to bare the roots of; (*muro, fig: autorità*) to undermine.

'scalzo, a ['skaltso] *ag* barefoot.

scambi'are *vt* to exchange; (*confondere*): **~ qn/qc per** to take *o* mistake sb/sth for; **mi hanno scambiato il cappello** they've given me the wrong hat.

scambi'evole *ag* mutual, reciprocal.

'scambio *sm* exchange; (*COMM*) trade; (*FERR*) points *pl*; **fare (uno) ~** to make a swap; **libero ~** free trade; **~i con l'estero** foreign trade.

scamosci'ato, a [skamoʃ'ʃato] *ag* suede.

scampa'gnata [skampaɲ'ɲata] *sf* trip to the country.

scampa'nare *vi* to peal.

scam'pare *vt* (*salvare*) to rescue, save; (*evitare: morte, prigione*) to escape ♦ *vi*: **~**

(a qc) to survive (sth), escape (sth); **scamparla bella** to have a narrow escape.

'scampo *sm* (*salvezza*) escape; (*ZOOL*) prawn; **cercare ~ nella fuga** to seek safety in flight; **non c'è (via di) ~** there's no way out.

'scampolo *sm* remnant.

scanala'tura *sf* (*incavo*) channel, groove.

scandagli'are [skandaʎ'ʎare] *vt* (*NAUT*) to sound; (*fig*) to sound out; to probe.

scanda'listico, a, ci, che *ag* (*settimanale etc*) sensational.

scandaliz'zare [skandalid'dzare] *vt* to shock, scandalize; **~rsi** *vr* to be shocked.

'scandalo *sm* scandal; **dare ~** to cause a scandal.

scanda'loso, a *ag* scandalous, shocking.

Scandi'navia *sf*: **la ~** Scandinavia.

scandi'navo, a *ag*, *sm/f* Scandinavian.

scan'dire *vt* (*versi*) to scan; (*parole*) to articulate, pronounce distinctly; **~ il tempo** (*MUS*) to beat time.

scan'nare *vt* (*animale*) to butcher, slaughter; (*persona*) to cut *o* slit the throat of.

'scanno *sm* seat, bench.

scansafa'tiche [skansafa'tike] *sm/f inv* idler, loafer.

scan'sare *vt* (*rimuovere*) to move (aside), shift; (*schivare: schiaffo*) to dodge; (*sfuggire*) to avoid; **~rsi** *vr* to move aside.

scan'sia *sf* shelves *pl*; (*per libri*) bookcase.

'scanso *sm*: **a ~ di** in order to avoid, as a precaution against; **a ~ di equivoci** to avoid (any) misunderstanding.

scanti'nato *sm* basement.

scanto'nare *vi* to turn the corner; (*svignarsela*) to sneak off.

scanzo'nato, a [skantso'nato] *ag* easy-going.

scapacci'one [skapat'tʃone] *sm* clout, slap.

scapes'trato, a *ag* dissolute.

'scapito *sm* (*perdita*) loss; (*danno*) damage, detriment; **a ~ di** to the detriment of.

'scapola *sf* shoulder blade.

'scapolo *sm* bachelor.

scappa'mento *sm* (*AUT*) exhaust.

scap'pare *vi* (*fuggire*) to escape; (*andare via in fretta*) to rush off; **~ di prigione** to escape from prison; **~ di mano** (*oggetto*) to slip out of one's hands; **~ di mente a qn** to slip sb's mind; **lasciarsi ~** (*occasione, affare*) to miss, let go by; (*dettaglio*) to overlook; (*parola*) to let slip; (*prigioniero*) to let escape; **mi scappò detto** I let it slip.

scap'pata *sf* quick visit *o* call.

scappa'tella *sf* escapade.

scappa'toia *sf* way out.

scara'beo *sm* beetle.

scarabocchi'are [skarabok'kjare] *vt* to scribble, scrawl.

scara'bocchio [skara'bɔkkjo] *sm* scribble, scrawl.

scara'faggio [skara'faddʒo] *sm* cockroach.

scaraman'zia [skaraman'tsia] *sf*: **per** ~ **for** luck.

scara'muccia, ce [skara'muttʃa] *sf* skirmish.

scaraven'tare *vt* to fling, hurl.

scarce'rare [skartʃe'rare] *vt* to release (from prison).

scarcerazi'one [skartʃerat'tsjone] *sf* release (from prison).

scardi'nare *vt* to take off its hinges.

'scarica, che *sf* (*di più armi*) volley of shots; (*di sassi, pugni*) hail, shower; (*ELETTR*) discharge; ~ **di mitra** burst of machine-gun fire.

scari'care *vt* (*merci, camion etc*) to unload; (*passeggeri*) to set down; (*arma*) to unload; (: *sparare, ELETTR*) to discharge; (*sog: corso d'acqua*) to empty, pour; (*fig: liberare da un peso*) to unburden, relieve; ~**rsi** *vr* (*orologio*) to run *o* wind down; (*batteria, accumulatore*) to go flat (*BRIT*) *o* dead; (*fig: rilassarsi*) to unwind; (: *sfogarsi*) to let off steam; ~ **le proprie responsabilità su qn** to off-load one's responsibilities onto sb; ~ **la colpa addosso a qn** to blame sb; **il fulmine si scaricò su un albero the** lightning struck a tree.

scarica'tore *sm* loader; (*di porto*) docker.

'scarico, a, chi, che *ag* unloaded; (*orologio*) run down; (*batteria, accumulatore*) dead, flat (*BRIT*) ♦ *sm* (*di merci, materiali*) unloading; (*di immondizie*) dumping, tipping (*BRIT*); (: *luogo*) rubbish dump; (*TECN: deflusso*) draining; (: *dispositivo*) drain; (*AUT*) exhaust; ~ **del lavandino** waste outlet.

scarlat'tina *sf* scarlet fever.

scar'latto, a *ag* scarlet.

'scarno, a *ag* thin, bony.

'scarpa *sf* shoe; **fare le** ~**e a qn** (*fig*) to double-cross sb; ~**e da ginnastica** gym shoes; ~**e coi tacchi (alti)** high-heeled shoes; ~**e col tacco basso** low-heeled shoes; ~**e senza tacco** flat shoes; ~**e da tennis** tennis shoes.

scar'pata *sf* escarpment.

scarpi'era *sf* shoe rack.

scar'pone *sm* boot; ~**i da montagna** climbing boots; ~**i da sci** ski-boots.

scarroz'zare [skarrot'tsare] *vt* to drive around.

scarseggi'are [skarsed'dʒare] *vi* to be scarce; ~ **di** to be short of, lack.

scar'sezza [skar'settsa] *sf* scarcity, lack.

'scarso, a *ag* (*insufficiente*) insufficient, meagre (*BRIT*), meager (*US*); (*povero: annata*) poor, lean; (*INS: voto*) poor; ~ **di** lacking in; **3 chili** ~**i** just under 3 kilos, barely 3 kilos.

scartabel'lare *vt* to skim through, glance through.

scarta'faccio [skarta'fattʃo] *sm* notebook.

scarta'mento *sm* (*FERR*) gauge; ~ **normale/ridotto** standard/narrow gauge.

scar'tare *vt* (*pacco*) to unwrap; (*idea*) to reject; (*MIL*) to declare unfit for military service; (*carte da gioco*) to discard; (*CALCIO*) to dodge (past) ♦ *vi* to swerve.

'scarto *sm* (*cosa scartata, anche COMM*) reject; (*di veicolo*) swerve; (*differenza*) gap, difference; ~ **salariale** wage differential.

scar'toffie *sfpl* (*peg*) papers *pl*.

scas'sare *vt* (*fam: rompere*) to wreck.

scassi'nare *vt* to break, force.

'scasso *sm vedi* **furto**.

scate'nare *vt* (*fig*) to incite, stir up; ~**rsi** *vr* (*temporale*) to break; (*rivolta*) to break out; (*persona: infuriarsi*) to rage.

scate'nato, a *ag* wild.

'scatola *sf* box; (*di latta*) tin (*BRIT*), can; **cibi in** ~ tinned (*BRIT*) *o* canned foods; **una** ~ **di cioccolatini** a box of chocolates; **comprare qc a** ~ **chiusa** to buy sth sight unseen; ~ **cranica** cranium.

scat'tante *ag* quick off the mark; (*agile*) agile.

scat'tare *vt* (*fotografia*) to take ♦ *vi* (*congegno, molla etc*) to be released; (*balzare*) to spring up; (*SPORT*) to put on a spurt; (*fig: per l'ira*) to fly into a rage; (*legge, provvedimento*) to come into effect; ~ **in piedi** to spring to one's feet; **far** ~ to release.

'scatto *sm* (*dispositivo*) release; (: *di arma da fuoco*) trigger mechanism; (*rumore*) click; (*balzo*) jump, start; (*SPORT*) spurt; (*fig: di ira etc*) fit; (: *di stipendio*) increment; **di** ~ suddenly; **serratura a** ~ spring lock.

scatu'rire *vi* to gush, spring.

scaval'care *vt* (*ostacolo*) to pass (*o* climb) over; (*fig*) to get ahead of, overtake.

sca'vare *vt* (*terreno*) to dig; (*legno*) to hollow out; (*pozzo, galleria*) to bore; (*città sepolta etc*) to excavate.

scava'trice [skava'tritʃe] *sf* (*macchina*) excavator.

scavezza'collo [skavettsa'kɔllo] *sm* daredevil.

'**scavo** *sm* excavating *no pl*; excavation.
scazzot'tare [skattsot'tare] *vt (fam)* to beat up, give a thrashing to.
'**scegliere** ['ʃeʎʎere] *vt (gen)* to choose; *(candidato, prodotto)* to choose, select; ~ **di fare** to choose to do.
sce'icco, chi [ʃe'ikko] *sm* sheik.
'**scelgo** *etc* ['ʃelgo] *vb vedi* **scegliere**.
scelle'rato, a [ʃelle'rato] *ag* wicked, evil.
scel'lino [ʃel'lino] *sm* shilling.
'**scelto, a** ['ʃelto] *pp di* **scegliere ♦** *ag (gruppo)* carefully selected; *(frutta, verdura)* choice, top quality; *(MIL: specializzato)* crack *cpd*, highly skilled **♦** *sf* choice; *(selezione)* selection, choice; **frutta o formaggi a** ~**a** a choice of fruit or cheese; **fare una** ~**a** to make a choice, choose; **non avere** ~**a** to have no choice *o* option; **di prima** ~**a** top grade *o* quality.
sce'mare [ʃe'mare] *vt, vi* to diminish.
sce'menza [ʃe'mentsa] *sf* stupidity *no pl*; stupid thing (to do *o* say).
'**scemo, a** ['ʃemo] *ag* stupid, silly.
'**scempio** ['ʃempjo] *sm* slaughter, massacre; *(fig)* ruin; **far** ~ **di** *(fig)* to play havoc with, ruin.
'**scena** ['ʃena] *sf (gen)* scene; *(palcoscenico)* stage; **le** ~**e** *(fig: teatro)* the stage; **andare in** ~ to be staged *o* put on *o* performed; **mettere in** ~ to stage; **uscire di** ~ to leave the stage; *(fig)* to leave the scene; **fare una** ~ *(fig)* to make a scene; **ha fatto** ~ **muta** *(fig)* he didn't open his mouth.
sce'nario [ʃe'narjo] *sm* scenery; scenario.
sce'nata [ʃe'nata] *sf* row, scene.
'**scendere** ['ʃendere] *vi* to go *(o come)* down; *(strada, sole)* to go down; *(notte)* to fall; *(passeggero: fermarsi)* to get out, alight; *(fig: temperatura, prezzi)* to fall, drop **♦** *vt (scale, pendio)* to go *(o come)* down; ~ **dalle scale** to go *(o come)* down the stairs; ~ **dal treno** to get off *o* out of the train; ~ **dalla macchina** to get out of the car; ~ **da cavallo** to dismount, get off one's horse; ~ **ad un albergo** to put up *o* stay at a hotel.
sceneggi'ato [ʃened'dʒato] *sm* television drama.
sceneggia'tore, 'trice [ʃenedʒa'tore] *sm/f* script-writer.
sceneggia'tura [ʃeneddʒa'tura] *sf (TEAT)* scenario; *(CINE)* screenplay, scenario.
'**scenico, a, ci, che** ['ʃeniko] *ag* stage *cpd*.
scenogra'fia [ʃenogra'fia] *sf (TEAT)* stage design; *(CINE)* set design; *(elementi scenici)* scenery.
sce'nografo, a [ʃe'nografo] *sm/f* set

designer.
sce'riffo [ʃe'riffo] *sm* sheriff.
scervel'larsi [ʃervel'larsi] *vr:* ~ **(su qc)** to rack one's brains (over sth).
scervel'lato, a [ʃervel'lato] *ag* featherbrained, scatterbrained.
'**sceso, a** ['ʃeso] *pp di* **scendere**.
scetti'cismo [ʃetti'tʃizmo] *sm* scepticism *(BRIT)*, skepticism *(US)*.
'**scettico, a, ci, che** ['ʃettiko] *ag* sceptical *(BRIT)*, skeptical *(US)*.
'**scettro** ['ʃettro] *sm* sceptre *(BRIT)*, scepter *(US)*.
'**scheda** ['skɛda] *sf* (index) card; *(TV, RADIO)* (brief) report; ~ **a circuito stampato** printed-circuit board; ~ **elettorale** ballot paper; ~ **perforata** punch card; ~ **telefonica** phone card.
sche'dare [ske'dare] *vt (dati)* to file; *(libri)* to catalogue; *(registrare: anche POLIZIA)* to put on one's files.
sche'dario [ske'darjo] *sm* file; *(mobile)* filing cabinet.
sche'dato, a [ske'dato] *ag* with a (police) record **♦** *sm/f* person with a (police) record.
sche'dina [ske'dina] *sf* ~ pools coupon *(BRIT)*.
'**scheggia, ge** ['skeddʒa] *sf* splinter, sliver; ~ **impazzita** *(fig)* maverick.
sche'letrico, a, ci, che [ske'letriko] *ag (anche ANAT)* skeletal; *(fig: essenziale)* skeleton *cpd*.
'**scheletro** ['skɛletro] *sm* skeleton; **avere uno** ~ **nell'armadio** *(fig)* to have a skeleton in the cupboard.
'**schema, i** ['skɛma] *sm (diagramma)* diagram, sketch; *(progetto, abbozzo)* outline, plan; **ribellarsi agli** ~**i** to rebel against traditional values; **secondo gli** ~**i tradizionali** in accordance with traditional values.
sche'matico, a, ci, che [ske'matiko] *ag* schematic.
schematiz'zare [skematid'dzare] *vt* to schematize.
'**scherma** ['skerma] *sf* fencing.
scher'maglia [sker'maʎʎa] *sf (fig)* skirmish.
scher'mirsi [sker'mirsi] *vr* to defend o.s., protect o.s.
'**schermo** ['skermo] *sm* shield, screen; *(CINE, TV)* screen.
schermogra'fia [skermogra'fia] *sf* X-rays *pl*.
scher'nire [sker'nire] *vt* to mock, sneer at.
'**scherno** ['skerno] *sm* mockery, derision; **farsi** ~ **di** to sneer at; **essere oggetto di** ~ to be a laughing stock.

scher'zare [sker'tsare] vi to joke.

'scherzo ['skertso] sm joke; (tiro) trick; (MUS) scherzo; è uno ~! (una cosa facile) it's child's play!, it's easy!; per ~ for a joke o a laugh; fare un brutto ~ a qn to play a nasty trick on sb; ~i a parte seriously, joking apart.

scher'zoso, a [sker'tsoso] ag (tono, gesto) playful; (osservazione) facetious; è un tipo ~ he likes a joke.

schiaccia'noci [skjattʃa'notʃi] sm inv nutcracker.

schiacci'ante [skjat'tʃante] ag overwhelming.

schiacci'are [skjat'tʃare] vt (dito) to crush; (noci) to crack; ~ un pisolino to have a nap.

schiaffeggi'are [skjaffed'dʒare] vt to slap.

schi'affo ['skjaffo] sm slap; prendere qn a ~i to slap sb's face; uno ~ morale a slap in the face, a rebuff.

schiamaz'zare [skjamat'tsare] vi to squawk, cackle.

schia'mazzo [skja'mattso] sm (fig: chiasso) din, racket.

schian'tare [skjan'tare] vt to break, tear apart; ~rsi vr to break (up), shatter; ~rsi al suolo (aereo) to crash (to the ground).

schi'anto ['skjanto] sm (rumore) crash; tearing sound; è uno ~! (fam) it's (o he's o she's) terrific!; di ~ all of a sudden.

schia'rire [skja'rire] vt to lighten, make lighter ♦ vi (anche: ~rsi) to grow lighter; (tornar sereno) to clear, brighten up; ~rsi la voce to clear one's throat.

schia'rita [skja'rita] sf (METEOR) bright spell; (fig) improvement, turn for the better.

schiat'tare [skjat'tare] vi to burst; ~ d'invidia to be green with envy; ~ di rabbia to be beside o.s. with rage.

schiavitù [skjavi'tu] sf slavery.

schiaviz'zare [skjavid'dzare] vt to enslave.

schi'avo, a ['skjavo] sm/f slave.

schi'ena ['skjɛna] sf (ANAT) back.

schie'nale [skje'nale] sm (di sedia) back.

schi'era ['skjɛra] sf (MIL) rank; (gruppo) group, band; villette a ~ ≈ terraced houses.

schiera'mento [skjera'mento] sm (MIL, SPORT) formation; (fig) alliance.

schie'rare [skje'rare] vt (esercito) to line up, draw up, marshal; ~rsi vr to line up; (fig): ~rsi con o dalla parte di/contro qn to side with/oppose sb.

schi'etto, a ['skjɛtto] ag (puro) pure; (fig) frank, straightforward.

schi'fare [ski'fare] vt to disgust.

schi'fezza [ski'fettsa] sf: essere una ~ (cibo, bibita etc) to be disgusting; (film, libro) to be dreadful.

schifil'toso, a [skifil'toso] ag fussy, difficult.

'schifo ['skifo] sm disgust; fare ~ (essere fatto male, dare pessimi risultati) to be awful; mi fa ~ it makes me sick, it's disgusting; quel libro è uno ~ that book's rotten.

schi'foso, a [ski'foso] ag disgusting, revolting; (molto scadente) rotten, lousy.

schioc'care [skjok'kare] vt (frusta) to crack; (dita) to snap; (lingua) to click; ~ le labbra to smack one's lips.

schioppet'tata [skjoppet'tata] sf gunshot.

schi'oppo ['skjɔppo] sm rifle, gun.

schi'udere ['skjudere] vt, ~rsi vr to open.

schi'uma ['skjuma] sf foam; (di sapone) lather; (di latte) froth.

schiu'mare [skju'mare] vt to skim ♦ vi to foam.

schi'uso, a ['skjuso] pp di schiudere.

schi'vare [ski'vare] vt to dodge, avoid.

'schivo, a ['skivo] ag (ritroso) stand-offish, reserved; (timido) shy.

schizofre'nia [skiddzofre'nia] sf schizophrenia.

schizo'frenico, a, ci, che [skiddzo'frɛniko] ag schizophrenic.

schiz'zare [skit'tsare] vt (spruzzare) to spurt, squirt; (sporcare) to splash, spatter; (fig: abbozzare) to sketch ♦ vi to spurt, squirt; (saltar fuori) to dart up (o off etc); ~ via (animale, persona) to dart away; (macchina, moto) to accelerate away.

schizzi'noso, a [skittsi'noso] ag fussy, finicky.

'schizzo ['skittso] sm (di liquido) spurt; splash, spatter; (abbozzo) sketch.

sci [ʃi] sm inv (attrezzo) ski; (attività) skiing; ~ di fondo cross-country skiing, ski touring (US); ~ nautico water-skiing.

'scia, pl 'scie ['ʃia] sf (di imbarcazione) wake; (di profumo) trail.

scià [ʃa] sm inv shah.

sci'abola ['ʃabola] sf sabre (BRIT), saber (US).

scia'callo [ʃa'kallo] sm jackal; (fig peg: profittatore) shark, profiteer; (: ladro) looter.

sciac'quare [ʃak'kware] vt to rinse.

scia'gura [ʃa'gura] sf disaster, calamity.

sciagu'rato, a [ʃagu'rato] ag unfortunate; (malvagio) wicked.

scialac'quare [ʃalak'kware] vt to squander.

scia'lare [ʃa'lare] vi to throw one's money

around.

sci'albo, a [ˈʃalbo] *ag* pale, dull; (*fig*) dull, colourless (*BRIT*), colorless (*US*).

sci'alle [ˈʃalle] *sm* shawl.

sci'alo [ˈʃalo] *sm* squandering, waste.

scia'luppa [ʃaˈluppa] *sf* (*NAUT*) sloop; (*anche*): ~ **di salvataggio**) lifeboat.

scia'mare [ʃaˈmare] *vi* to swarm.

sci'ame [ˈʃame] *sm* swarm.

scian'cato, a [ʃanˈkato] *ag* lame; (*mobile*) rickety.

sci'are [ʃiˈare] *vi* to ski; **andare a** ~ to go skiing.

sci'arpa [ˈʃarpa] *sf* scarf; (*fascia*) sash.

scia'tore, 'trice [ʃiaˈtore] *smf* skier.

sciat'tezza [ʃatˈtettsa] *sf* slovenliness.

sci'atto, a [ˈʃatto] *ag* (*persona: nell'aspetto*) slovenly, unkempt; (: *nel lavoro*) sloppy, careless.

'scibile [ˈʃibile] *sm* knowledge.

scien'tifico, a, ci, che [ʃenˈtifiko] *ag* scientific; **la (polizia)** ~**a** the forensic department.

sci'enza [ˈʃentsa] *sf* science; (*sapere*) knowledge; ~**e** *sfpl* (*INS*) science *sg*; ~**e naturali** natural sciences; ~**e politiche** political science *sg*.

scienzi'ato, a [ʃenˈtsjato] *smf* scientist.

'Scilly [ˈʃilli]: **le isole** ~ *sfpl* the Scilly Isles.

'scimmia [ˈʃimmja] *sf* monkey.

scimmiot'tare [ʃimmjotˈtare] *vt* to ape, mimic.

scimpanzé [ʃimpanˈtse] *sm inv* chimpanzee.

scimu'nito, a [ʃimuˈnito] *ag* silly, idiotic.

'scindere [ˈʃindere] *vt*, ~**rsi** *vr* to split (up).

scin'tilla [ʃinˈtilla] *sf* spark.

scintil'lare [ʃintilˈlare] *vi* to spark; (*acqua, occhi*) to sparkle.

scintil'lio [ʃintilˈlio] *sm* sparkling.

scioc'care [ʃokˈkare] *vt* to shock.

scioc'chezza [ʃokˈkettsa] *sf* stupidity *no pl*; stupid *o* foolish thing; **dire** ~**e** to talk nonsense.

sci'occo, a, chi, che [ˈʃɔkko] *ag* stupid, foolish.

sci'ogliere [ˈʃɔʎʎere] *vt* (*nodo*) to untie; (*capelli*) to loosen; (*persona, animale*) to untie, release; (*fig: persona*): ~ **da** to release from; (*neve*) to melt; (*nell'acqua: zucchero etc*) to dissolve; (*fig: mistero*) to solve; (*porre fine a: contratto*) to cancel; (: *società, matrimonio*) to dissolve; (: *riunione*) to bring to an end; ~**rsi** *vr* to loosen, come untied; to melt; to dissolve; (*assemblea, corteo, duo*) to break up; ~ **i muscoli** to limber up; ~ **il ghiaccio** (*fig*) to break the ice; ~ **le vele** (*NAUT*) to set sail; ~**rsi dai legami** (*fig*) to free o.s. from all

ties.

sci'olgo *etc* [ˈʃɔlgo] *vb vedi* **sciogliere**.

sciol'tezza [ʃolˈtettsa] *sf* agility; suppleness; ease.

sci'olto, a [ˈʃɔlto] *pp di* **sciogliere** ♦ *ag* loose; (*agile*) agile, nimble; (*disinvolto*) free and easy; **essere** ~ **nei movimenti** to be supple; **versi** ~**i** (*POESIA*) blank verse.

sciope'rante [ʃopeˈrante] *smf* striker.

sciope'rare [ʃopeˈrare] *vi* to strike, go on strike.

sci'opero [ˈʃɔpero] *sm* strike; **fare** ~ to strike; **entrare in** ~ to go on *o* come out on strike; ~ **bianco** work-to-rule (*BRIT*), slowdown (*US*); ~ **della fame** hunger strike; ~ **selvaggio** wildcat strike; ~ **a singhiozzo** on-off strike; ~ **di solidarietà** sympathy strike.

sciori'nare [ʃoriˈnare] *vt* (*ostentare*) to show off, display.

scio'via [ʃioˈvia] *sf* ski lift.

sciovi'nismo [ʃoviˈnizmo] *sm* chauvinism.

sciovi'nista, i, e [ʃoviˈnista] *smf* chauvinist.

sci'pito, a [ʃiˈpito] *ag* insipid.

scip'pare [ʃipˈpare] *vt*: ~ **qn** to snatch sb's bag.

scippa'tore [ʃippaˈtore] *sm* bag-snatcher.

'scippo [ˈʃippo] *sm* bag-snatching.

sci'rocco [ʃiˈrokko] *sm* sirocco.

sci'roppo [ʃiˈroppo] *sm* syrup; ~ **per la tosse** cough syrup, cough mixture.

'scisma, i [ˈʃizma] *sm* (*REL*) schism.

scissi'one [ʃisˈsjone] *sf* (*anche fig*) split, division; (*FISICA*) fission.

'scisso, a [ˈʃisso] *pp di* **scindere**.

sciu'pare [ʃuˈpare] *vt* (*abito, libro, appetito*) to spoil, ruin; (*tempo, denaro*) to waste; ~**rsi** *vr* to get spoilt *o* ruined; (*rovinarsi la salute*) to ruin one's health.

scivo'lare [ʃivoˈlare] *vi* to slide *o* glide along; (*involontariamente*) to slip, slide.

'scivolo [ˈʃivolo] *sm* slide; (*TECN*) chute.

scivo'loso, a [ʃivoˈloso] *ag* slippery.

scle'rosi [ʃ] *sf* sclerosis.

scoc'care *vt* (*freccia*) to shoot ♦ *vi* (*guizzare*) to shoot up; (*battere: ora*) to strike.

scoccherò *etc* [skokkeˈrɔ] *vb vedi* **scoccare**.

scocci'are [skotˈtʃare] *vt* to bother, annoy; ~**rsi** *vr* to be bothered *o* annoyed.

scoccia'tore, 'trice [skottʃaˈtore] *smf* nuisance, pest (*fam*).

scoccia'tura [skottʃaˈtura] *sf* nuisance, bore.

sco'della *sf* bowl.

scodinzo'lare [skodintsoˈlare] *vi* to wag its tail.

scogli'era [skoʎˈʎera] *sf* reef; (*rupe*) cliff.

'scoglio ['skɔʎʎo] _sm (al mare)_ rock; (_fig:_ _ostacolo_) difficulty, stumbling block.

scogli'oso, a [skoʎ'ʎoso] _ag_ rocky.

scoi'attolo _sm_ squirrel.

scola'pasta _sm inv_ colander.

sco'lare _ag:_ **età** ~ school age ♦ _vt_ to drain ♦ _vi_ to drip.

scola'resca _sf_ schoolchildren _pl_, pupils _pl_.

sco'laro, a _sm/f_ pupil, schoolboy/girl.

sco'lastico, a, ci, che _ag_ (_gen_) scholastic; (_libro, anno, divisa_) school _cpd_.

scol'lare _vt_ (_staccare_) to unstick; ~**rsi** _vr_ to come unstuck.

scol'lato, a _ag_ (_vestito_) low-cut, low-necked; (_donna_) wearing a low-cut dress (_o_ blouse _etc_).

scolla'tura _sf_ neckline.

'scolo _sm_ drainage; (_sbocco_) drain; (_acqua_) waste water; **canale di** ~ drain; **tubo di** ~ drainpipe.

scolo'rire _vt_ to fade; to discolour (_BRIT_), discolor (_US_) ♦ _vi_ (_anche:_ ~**rsi**) to fade; to become discolo(u)red; (_impallidire_) to turn pale.

scol'pire _vt_ to carve, sculpt.

scombi'nare _vt_ to mess up, upset.

scombi'nato, a _ag_ confused, muddled.

scombusso'lare _vt_ to upset.

scom'messo, a _pp di_ **scommettere** ♦ _sf_ bet, wager; **fare una** ~**a** to bet.

scom'mettere _vt, vi_ to bet.

scomo'dare _vt_ to trouble, bother, disturb; (_fig: nome famoso_) to involve, drag in; ~**rsi** _vr_ to put o.s. out; ~**rsi a fare** to go to the bother _o_ trouble of doing.

scomodità _sf inv_ (_di sedia, letto etc_) discomfort; (_di orario, sistemazione etc_) inconvenience.

'scomodo, a _ag_ uncomfortable; (_sistemazione, posto_) awkward, inconvenient.

scompagi'nare [skompadʒi'nare] _vt_ to upset, throw into disorder.

scompag'nato, a [skompaɲ'ɲato] _ag_ (_calzini, guanti_) odd.

scompa'rire _vi_ (_sparire_) to disappear, vanish; (_fig_) to be insignificant.

scom'parso, a _pp di_ **scomparire** ♦ _sf_ disappearance; (_fig: morte_) passing away, death.

scomparti'mento _sm_ (_FERR_) compartment; (_sezione_) division.

scom'parto _sm_ compartment, division.

scom'penso _sm_ imbalance, lack of balance.

scompigli'are [skompiʎ'ʎare] _vt_ (_cassetto, capelli_) to mess up, disarrange; (_fig: piani_) to upset.

scom'piglio [skom'piʎʎo] _sm_ mess, confusion.

scom'porre _vt_ (_parola, numero_) to break up; (_CHIM_) to decompose; **scomporsi** _vr_ (_CHIM_) to decompose; (_fig_) to get upset, lose one's composure; **senza scomporsi** unperturbed.

scom'posto, a _pp di_ **scomporre** ♦ _ag_ (_gesto_) unseemly; (_capelli_) ruffled, dishevelled.

sco'munica, che _sf_ excommunication.

scomuni'care _vt_ to excommunicate.

sconcer'tante [skontʃer'tante] _ag_ disconcerting.

sconcer'tare [skontʃer'tare] _vt_ to disconcert, bewilder.

'sconcio, a, ci, ce ['skontʃo] _ag_ (_osceno_) indecent, obscene ♦ _sm_ (_cosa riprovevole, mal fatta_) disgrace.

sconclusio'nato, a _ag_ incoherent, illogical.

sconfes'sare _vt_ to renounce, disavow; to repudiate.

scon'figgere [skon'fiddʒere] _vt_ to defeat, overcome.

sconfi'nare _vi_ to cross the border; (_in proprietà privata_) to trespass; (_fig_): ~ **da** to stray _o_ digress from.

sconfi'nato, a _ag_ boundless, unlimited.

scon'fitto, a _pp di_ **sconfiggere** ♦ _sf_ defeat.

sconfor'tante, a _ag_ discouraging, disheartening.

sconfor'tare _vt_ to discourage, dishearten; ~**rsi** _vr_ to become discouraged, become disheartened, lose heart.

scon'forto _sm_ despondency.

sconge'lare [skondʒe'lare] _vt_ to defrost.

scongiu'rare [skondʒu'rare] _vt_ (_implorare_) to beseech, implore; (_eludere: pericolo_) to ward off, avert.

scongi'uro [skon'dʒuro] _sm_ (_esorcismo_) exorcism; **fare gli** ~**i** to touch wood (_BRIT_), knock on wood (_US_).

scon'nesso, a _ag_ (_fig: discorso_) incoherent, rambling.

sconosci'uto, a [skonoʃ'ʃuto] _ag_ unknown; new, strange ♦ _sm/f_ stranger, unknown person.

sconquas'sare _vt_ to shatter, smash.

scon'quasso _sm_ (_danno_) damage; (_fig_) confusion.

sconside'rato, a _ag_ thoughtless, rash.

sconsigli'are [skonsiʎ'ʎare] _vt:_ ~ **qc a qn** to advise sb against sth; ~ **qn dal fare qc** to advise sb not to do _o_ against doing sth.

sconso'lato, a _ag_ disconsolate.

scon'tare _vt_ (_COMM: detrarre_) to deduct; (_: debito_) to pay off; (_: cambiale_) to discount; (_pena_) to serve; (_colpa, errori_) to

pay for, suffer for.
scon'tato, a *ag* (*previsto*) foreseen, taken
for granted; (*prezzo, merce*) discounted,
at a discount; **dare per** ~ **che** to take it
for granted that.
sconten'tare *vt* to displease, dissatisfy.
sconten'tezza [skonten'tettsa] *sf*
displeasure, dissatisfaction.
scon'tento, a *ag:* ~ **(di)** discontented *o*
dissatisfied (with) ♦ *sm* discontent,
dissatisfaction.
'sconto *sm* discount; **fare** *o* **concedere uno**
~ to give a discount; **uno** ~ **del 10%** a
10% discount.
scon'trarsi *vr* (*treni etc*) to crash, collide;
(*venire ad uno scontro, fig*) to clash; ~ **con**
to crash into, collide with.
scon'trino *sm* ticket.
'scontro *sm* (*MIL, fig*) clash; (*di veicoli*)
crash, collision; ~ **a fuoco** shoot-out.
scon'troso, a *ag* sullen, surly; (*permaloso*)
touchy.
sconveni'ente *ag* unseemly, improper.
sconvol'gente [skonvol'dʒɛnte] *ag* (*notizia,
brutta esperienza*) upsetting, disturbing;
(*bellezza*) amazing; (*passione*)
overwhelming.
scon'volgere [skon'vɔldʒere] *vt* to throw
into confusion, upset; (*turbare*) to shake,
disturb, upset.
scon'volto, a *pp di* **sconvolgere** ♦ *ag*
(*persona*) distraught, very upset.
'scopa *sf* broom; (*CARTE*) *Italian card
game.*
sco'pare *vt* to sweep; (*fam!*) to bonk (*!*).
sco'pata *sf* (*fam!*) bonk (*!*).
scoperchi'are [skoper'kjare] *vt* (*pentola,
vaso*) to take the lid off, uncover; (*casa*)
to take the roof off.
sco'perto, a *pp di* **scoprire** ♦ *ag* uncovered;
(*capo*) uncovered, bare; (*macchina*) open;
(*MIL*) exposed, without cover; (*conto*)
overdrawn ♦ *sf* discovery ♦ *sm:* **allo** ~
(*dormire etc*) out in the open; **assegno** ~
uncovered cheque; **avere un conto** ~ to
be overdrawn.
'scopo *sm* aim, purpose; **a che** ~**?** what
for?; **adatto allo** ~ fit for its purpose; **allo**
~ **di fare qc** in order to do sth; **a** ~ **di**
lucro for gain *o* money; **senza** ~ (*fare,
cercare*) pointlessly.
scoppi'are *vi* (*spaccarsi*) to burst;
(*esplodere*) to explode; (*fig*) to break out;
~ **in pianto** *o* **a piangere** to burst out
crying; ~ **dalle risa** *o* **dal ridere** to split
one's sides laughing; ~ **dal caldo** to be
boiling; ~ **di salute** to be the picture of
health.

scoppiet'tare *vi* to crackle.
'scoppio *sm* explosion; (*di tuono, arma etc*)
crash, bang; (*di pneumatico*) bang; (*fig: di
guerra*) outbreak; **a** ~ **ritardato** delayed-
action; **reazione a** ~ **ritardato** delayed *o*
slow reaction; **uno** ~ **di risa** a burst of
laughter; **uno** ~ **di collera** an explosion of
anger.
sco'prire *vt* to discover; (*liberare da ciò che
copre*) to uncover; (: *monumento*) to
unveil; ~**rsi** *vr* to put on lighter clothes;
(*fig*) to give o.s. away.
scopri'tore, 'trice *sm/f* discoverer.
scoraggi'are [skorad'dʒare] *vt* to
discourage; ~**rsi** *vr* to become
discouraged, lose heart.
scor'butico, a, ci, che *ag* (*fig*)
cantankerous.
scorcia'toia [skortʃa'toja] *sf* short cut.
'scorcio ['skortʃo] *sm* (*ARTE*) foreshortening;
(*di secolo, periodo*) end, close;
panoramico vista.
scor'dare *vt* to forget; ~**rsi** *vr:* ~**rsi di qc/di**
fare to forget sth/to do.
sco'reggia [sko'reddʒa] (*fam!*) *sf* fart (*!*).
scoreggi'are [skored'dʒare] (*fam!*) *vi* to
fart (*!*).
'scorgere ['skɔrdʒere] *vt* to make out,
distinguish, see.
sco'ria *sf* (*di metalli*) slag; (*vulcanica*) scoria;
~**e radioattive** (*FISICA*) radioactive waste
sg.
'scorno *sm* ignominy, disgrace.
scorpacci'ata [skorpat'tʃata] *sf:* **fare una** ~
(di) to stuff o.s. (with), eat one's fill (of).
scorpi'one *sm* scorpion; (*dello zodiaco*): **S**~
Scorpio; **essere dello S**~ to be Scorpio.
'scorporo *sm* (*POL*) *transfer of votes aimed
at increasing the chances of
representation for minority parties.*
scorraz'zare [skorrat'tsare] *vi* to run about.
'scorrere *vt* (*giornale, lettera*) to run *o* skim
through ♦ *vi* (*liquido, fiume*) to run, flow;
(*fune*) to run; (*cassetto, porta*) to slide
easily; (*tempo*) to pass (by).
scorre'ria *sf* raid, incursion.
scorret'tezza [skorret'tettsa] *sf*
incorrectness; lack of politeness,
rudeness; unfairness; **commettere una** ~
(*essere sleale*) to be unfair.
scor'retto, a *ag* (*sbagliato*) incorrect;
(*sgarbato*) impolite; (*sconveniente*)
improper; (*sleale*) unfair; (*gioco*) foul.
scor'revole *ag* (*porta*) sliding; (*fig: stile*)
fluent, flowing.
scorri'banda *sf* (*MIL*) raid; (*escursione*) trip,
excursion.
'scorsi *etc vb vedi* **scorgere.**

'scorso, a *pp di* **scorrere** ♦ *ag* last ♦ *sf* quick
look, glance; **lo ~ mese** last month.

scor'soio, a *ag*: **nodo ~** noose.

'scorta *sf* (*di personalità, convoglio*) escort;
(*provvista*) supply, stock; **sotto la ~ di due
agenti** escorted by two policemen; **fare ~
di** to stock up with, get in a supply of; **di
~** (*materiali*) spare; **ruota di ~** spare
wheel.

scor'tare *vt* to escort.

scor'tese *ag* discourteous, rude.

scorte'sia *sf* discourtesy, rudeness;
(*azione*) discourtesy.

scorti'care *vt* to skin.

'scorto, a *pp di* **scorgere.**

'scorza ['skɔrdza] *sf* (*di albero*) bark; (*di
agrumi*) peel, skin.

sco'sceso, a [skoʃ'ʃeso] *ag* steep.

'scosso, a *pp di* **scuotere** ♦ *ag* (*turbato*)
shaken, upset ♦ *sf* jerk, jolt, shake;
(*ELETTR, fig*) shock; **prendere la ~a** to get
an electric shock; **~a di terremoto** earth
tremor.

scos'sone *sm*: **dare uno ~ a qn** to give sb a
shake; **procedere a ~i** to jolt *o* jerk along.

scos'tante *ag* (*fig*) off-putting (*BRIT*),
unpleasant.

scos'tare *vt* to move (away), shift; **~rsi** *vr*
to move away.

scostu'mato, a *ag* immoral, dissolute.

scotch [skɔtʃ] *sm inv* (*whisky*) Scotch; ®
(*nastro adesivo*) Scotch tape ®,
Sellotape ®.

scot'tante *ag* (*fig*: *urgente*) pressing;
(: *delicato*) delicate.

scot'tare *vt* (*ustionare*) to burn; (: *con
liquido bollente*) to scald ♦ *vi* to burn;
(*caffè*) to be too hot.

scotta'tura *sf* burn; scald.

'scotto, a *ag* overcooked ♦ *sm* (*fig*): **pagare
lo ~ (di)** to pay the penalty (for).

sco'vare *vt* to drive out, flush out; (*fig*) to
discover.

'Scozia ['skɔttsja] *sf*: **la ~** Scotland.

scoz'zese [skot'tsese] *ag* Scottish ♦ *sm/f*
Scot.

screan'zato, a [skrean'tsato] *ag* ill-
mannered ♦ *sm/f* boor.

scredi'tare *vt* to discredit.

scre'mare *vt* to skim.

scre'mato, a *ag* skimmed; **parzialmente ~**
semi-skimmed.

screpo'lare *vt*, **~rsi** *vr* to crack.

screpola'tura *sf* cracking *no pl*; crack.

screzi'ato, a [skret'tsjato] *ag* streaked.

'screzio ['skrɛttsjo] *sm* disagreement.

scribac'chino [skribak'kino] *sm* (*peg*:
impiegato) penpusher; (: *scrittore*) hack.

scricchio'lare [skrikkjo'lare] *vi* to creak,
squeak.

scricchio'lio [skrikkjo'lio] *sm* creaking.

'scricciolo ['skrittʃolo] *sm* wren.

'scrigno ['skriɲɲo] *sm* casket.

scrimina'tura *sf* parting.

'scrissi *etc vb vedi* **scrivere.**

'scritto, a *pp di* **scrivere** ♦ *ag* written ♦ *sm*
writing; (*lettera*) letter, note ♦ *sf*
inscription; **~i** *smpl* (*letterari etc*) work(s),
writings; **per o in ~** in writing.

scrit'toio *sm* writing desk.

scrit'tore, 'trice *sm/f* writer.

scrit'tura *sf* writing; (*COMM*) entry;
(*contratto*) contract; (*REL*): **la Sacra S~** the
Scriptures *pl*; **~e** *sfpl* (*COMM*) accounts,
books.

scrittu'rare *vt* (*TEAT, CINE*) to sign up,
engage; (*COMM*) to enter.

scriva'nia *sf* desk.

scri'vano *sm* (*amanuense*) scribe;
(*impiegato*) clerk.

scri'vente *sm/f* writer.

'scrivere *vt* to write; **come si scrive?** how is
it spelt?, how do you write it?; **~ qc a qn**
to write sth to sb; **~ qc a macchina** to
type sth; **~ a penna/matita** to write in
pen/pencil; **~ qc maiuscolo/minuscolo** to
write sth in capital/small letters.

scroc'care *vt* (*fam*) to scrounge, cadge.

scroc'cone, a *sm/f* scrounger.

'scrofa *sf* (*ZOOL*) sow.

scrol'lare *vt* to shake; **~rsi** *vr* (*anche fig*) to
give o.s. a shake; **~ le spalle/il capo** to
shrug one's shoulders/shake one's head;
~rsi qc di dosso (*ache fig*) to shake sth
off.

scrol'lata *sf* shake; **~ di spalle** shrug (of
one's shoulders).

scrosci'ante [skroʃ'ʃante] *ag* (*pioggia*)
pouring; (*fig*: *applausi*) thunderous.

scrosci'are [skroʃ'ʃare] *vi* (*pioggia*) to pour
down, pelt down; (*torrente, fig*: *applausi*) to
thunder, roar.

'scroscio ['skrɔʃʃo] *sm* pelting; thunder,
roar; (*di applausi*) burst.

scros'tare *vt* (*intonaco*) to scrape off, strip;
~rsi *vr* to peel off, flake off.

'scrupolo *sm* scruple; (*meticolosità*) care,
conscientiousness; **essere senza ~i** to be
unscrupulous.

scrupo'loso, a *ag* scrupulous;
conscientious.

scru'tare *vt* to scrutinize; (*intenzioni, causa*)
to examine, scrutinize.

scruta'tore, trice *sm/f* (*POL*) scrutineer.

scruti'nare *vt* (*voti*) to count.

scru'tinio *sm* (*votazione*) ballot; (*insieme*

delle operazioni) poll; *(INS) (meeting for)* assignment of marks at end of a term or year.

scu'cire [sku'tʃire] *vt (orlo etc)* to unpick, undo; **~rsi** *vr* to come unstitched.

scude'ria *sf* stable.

scu'detto *sm (SPORT)* (championship) shield; *(distintivo)* badge.

scu'discio [sku'diʃʃo] *sm* (riding) crop, (riding) whip.

'scudo *sm* shield; **farsi ~ di** *o* **con qc** to shield o.s. with sth; **~ aereo/missilistico** air/missile defence *(BRIT) o* defense *(US)*; **~ termico** heat shield.

sculacci'are [skulat'tʃare] *vt* to spank.

sculacci'one [skulat'tʃone] *sm* spanking.

scul'tore, 'trice *sm/f* sculptor.

scul'tura *sf* sculpture.

scu'ola *sf* school; **~ elementare** primary *(BRIT) o* grade *(US)* school *(for children from 6 to 11 years of age)*; **~ guida** driving school, **materna** nursery school *(for children aged 3 to 5);* **~ media inferiore** *first 3 years of secondary school, for children from 11 to 14 years of age;* **~ dell'obbligo** compulsory education; **~ privata/pubblica** private/state school; **~e serali** evening classes, night school *sg;* **~ tecnica** technical college; *vedi nota nel riquadro.*

> **SCUOLA**
>
> *Italian children first go to school at the age of three. They remain at the "scuola materna" until they are six, when they move on to the "scuola elementare" for another five years. After this come three years of "scuola media inferiore", the completion of which marks the end of compulsory education. Students who wish to continue their schooling attend "scuola media superiore", choosing between several types of institution which specialize in different subject areas.*

---

scu'otere *vt* to shake; **~rsi** *vr* to jump, be startled; *(fig: muoversi)* to rouse o.s., stir o.s.; *(: turbarsi)* to be shaken.

'scure *sf* axe, ax *(US)*.

scu'rire *vt* to darken, make darker.

'scuro, a *ag* dark; *(fig: espressione)* grim ♦ *sm* darkness; dark colour *(BRIT) o* color *(US)*; *(imposta)* (window) shutter; **verde/rosso** *etc* **~** dark green/red *etc.*

scur'rile *ag* scurrilous.

'scusa *sf* excuse; **~e** *sfpl* apology *sg*, apologies; **chiedere ~ a qn (per)** to apologize to sb (for); **chiedo ~** I'm sorry; *(disturbando*

etc) excuse me; **vi prego di accettare le mie ~e** please accept my apologies.

scu'sare *vt* to excuse; **~rsi** *vr:* **~rsi (di)** to apologize (for); **(mi) scusi** I'm sorry; *(per richiamare l'attenzione)* excuse me.

S.C.V. *sigla = Stato della Città del Vaticano.*

sdebi'tarsi *vt:* **~rsi (con qn di** *o* **per qc)** *(anche fig)* to repay (sb for sth).

sde'gnare [zdeɲ'ɲare] *vt* to scorn, despise; **~rsi** *vr (adirarsi)* to get angry.

sde'gnato, a [zdeɲ'ɲato] *ag* indignant, angry.

'sdegno ['zdeɲɲo] *sm* scorn, disdain.

sdegnosa'mente [zdeɲɲosa'mente] *av* scornfully, disdainfully.

sde'gnoso, a [zdeɲ'ɲoso] *ag* scornful, disdainful.

sdilin'quirsi *vr (illanguidirsi)* to become sentimental.

sdoga'nare *vt (COMM)* to clear through customs.

sdolci'nato, a [zdoltʃi'nato] *ag* mawkish, oversentimental.

sdoppia'mento *sm (CHIM: di composto)* splitting; *(PSIC):* **~ della personalità** split personality.

sdoppi'are *vt (dividere)* to divide *o* split in two.

sdrai'arsi *vr* to stretch out, lie down.

'sdraio *sm:* **sedia a ~** deck chair.

sdrammatiz'zare [zdrammatid'dzare] *vt* to play down, minimize.

sdruccio'lare [zdruttʃo'lare] *vi* to slip, slide.

sdruccio'levole [zdruttʃo'levole] *ag* slippery.

sdru'cito, a [zdru'tʃito] *ag (strappato)* torn; *(logoro)* threadbare.

================================= *PAROLA CHIAVE*

se *pron vedi* **si**
  ♦ *cong* **1** *(condizionale, ipotetica)* if; **~ nevica non vengo** I won't come if it snows; **~ fossi in te** if I were you; **sarei rimasto ~ me l'avessero chiesto** I would have stayed if they'd asked me; **non puoi fare altro ~ non telefonare** all you can do is phone; **~ mai** if, if ever; **siamo noi ~ mai che le siamo grati** it is we who should be grateful to you; **~ no** *(altrimenti)* or (else), otherwise; **~ non** *(anzi)* if not; *(tranne)* except; **~ non altro** if nothing else, at least; **~ solo** *o* **solamente** if only
  2 *(in frasi dubitative, interrogative indirette)* if, whether; **non so ~ scrivere o telefonare** I don't know whether *o* if I should write or phone.

S.E. *abbr* (= *sud-est*) SE; (= *Sua Eccellenza*) HE.

sé *pron* (*gen*) oneself; (*esso, essa, lui, lei, loro*) itself; himself; herself; themselves; ~ **stesso(a)** *pron* oneself; itself; himself; herself; ~ **stessi(e)** *pron pl* themselves; **di per ~ non è un problema** it's no problem in itself; **parlare tra ~ e ~** to talk to oneself; **va da ~ che ...** it goes without saying that ..., it's obvious that ..., it stands to reason that ...; **è un caso a ~ o a ~ stante** it's a special case; **un uomo che s'è fatto da ~** a self-made man.

S.E.A.T.O. *sigla f* (= *Southeast Asia Treaty Organization*) SEATO.

seb'bene *cong* although, though.

'sebo *sm* sebum.

sec. *abbr* (= *secolo*) c.

'SECAM *sigla m* (= *séquentiel couleur à mémoire*) SECAM.

'secca *sf vedi* secco.

secca'mente *av* (*rispondere, rifiutare*) sharply, curtly.

sec'care *vt* to dry; (*prosciugare*) to dry up; (*fig: importunare*) to annoy, bother ♦ *vi* to dry; to dry up; ~**rsi** *vr* to dry; to dry up; (*fig*) to grow annoyed; **si è seccato molto** he was very annoyed.

sec'cato, a *ag* (*fig: infastidito*) bothered, annoyed; (: *stufo*) fed up.

secca'tore, 'trice *sm/f* nuisance, bother.

secca'tura *sf* (*fig*) bother *no pl*, trouble *no pl*.

seccherò *etc* [sekke'rɔ] *vb vedi* seccare.

'secchia ['sekkja] *sf* bucket, pail.

secchi'ello [sek'kjɛllo] *sm* (*per bambini*) pail, bucket.

'secchio ['sekkjo] *sm* bucket, pail; ~ **della spazzatura** *o* **delle immondizie** dustbin (*BRIT*), garbage can (*US*).

'secco, a, chi, che *ag* dry; (*fichi, pesce*) dried; (*foglie, ramo*) withered; (*magro: persona*) thin, skinny; (*fig: risposta, modo di fare*) curt, abrupt; (: *colpo*) clean, sharp ♦ *sm* (*siccità*) drought ♦ *sf* (*del mare*) shallows *pl*; **restarci** ~ (*fig: morire sul colpo*) to drop dead; **avere la gola** ~**a** to feel dry, be parched; **lavare a** ~ to dry-clean; **tirare a** ~ (*barca*) to beach.

secen'tesco, a, schi, sche [setʃen'tesko] *ag* = seicentesco.

se'cernere [se'tʃɛrnere] *vt* to secrete.

seco'lare *ag* age-old, centuries-old; (*laico, mondano*) secular.

'secolo *sm* century; (*epoca*) age.

se'conda *sf vedi* secondo; S~ **Repubblica** *vedi nota nel riquadro.*

secondaria'mente *av* secondly.

secon'dario, a *ag* secondary; **scuola/istruzione** ~**a** secondary school/education.

secon'dino *sm* prison officer, warder (*BRIT*).

se'condo, a *ag* second ♦ *sm* second; (*di pranzo*) main course ♦ *sf* (*AUT*) second (gear); (*FERR*) second class ♦ *prep* according to; (*nel modo prescritto*) in accordance with; ~ **me** in my opinion, to my mind; ~ **la legge/quanto si era deciso** in accordance with the law/the decision taken; **di** ~**a classe** second-class; **di** ~**a mano** second-hand; **viaggiare in** ~**a** to travel second-class; **comandante** *m* **in** ~**a** second-in-command; **a** ~**a di** *prep* according to; in accordance with.

'sedano *sm* celery.

se'dare *vt* (*dolore*) to soothe; (*rivolta*) to put down, suppress.

seda'tivo, a *ag, sm* sedative.

'sede *sf* (*luogo di residenza*) (place of) residence; (*di ditta: principale*) head office; (: *secondaria*) branch (office); (*di organizzazione*) headquarters *pl*; (*di governo, parlamento*) seat; (*REL*) see; **in** ~ **di** (*in occasione di*) during; **in altra** ~ on another occasion; **in** ~ **legislativa** in legislative sitting; **prendere** ~ to take up residence; ~ **centrale** head office; ~ **sociale** registered office.

seden'tario, a *ag* sedentary.

se'dere *vi* to sit, be seated; ~**rsi** *vr* to sit down ♦ *sm* (*deretano*) bottom; **posto a** ~ seat.

'sedia *sf* chair; ~ **elettrica** electric chair; ~ **a rotelle** wheelchair.

sedi'cenne [sedi'tʃɛnne] *ag, sm/f* sixteen-year-old.

sedi'cente [sedi'tʃɛnte] *ag* self-styled.

sedi'cesimo, a [sedi'tʃɛzimo] *num* sixteenth.

'**sedici** ['seditʃi] *num* sixteen.

se'**dile** *sm* seat; (*panchina*) bench.

sedimen'**tare** *vi* to leave a sediment.

sedi'**mento** *sm* sediment.

sedizi'**one** [sedit'tsjone] *sf* revolt, rebellion.

sedizi'**oso, a** [sedit'tsjoso] *ag* seditious.

se'**dotto, a** *pp di* **sedurre.**

sedu'**cente** [sedu'tʃɛnte] *ag* seductive; (*proposta*) very attractive.

se'**durre** *vt* to seduce.

se'**duta** *sf* session, sitting; (*riunione*) meeting; **essere in** ~ to be in session, be sitting; ~ **stante** (*fig*) immediately; ~ **spiritica** seance.

sedut'**tore, 'trice** *sm/f* seducer/seductress.

seduzi'**one** [sedut'tsjone] *sf* seduction; (*fascino*) charm, appeal.

SEeO *abbr* (= *salvo errori e omissioni*) E and OE.

'**sega, ghe** *sf* saw; ~ **circolare** circular saw; ~ **a mano** handsaw.

'**segale** *sf* rye.

se'**gare** *vt* to saw; (*recidere*) to saw off.

sega'**tura** *sf* (*residuo*) sawdust.

'**seggio** ['sɛddʒo] *sm* seat; ~ **elettorale** polling station.

'**seggiola** ['sɛddʒola] *sf* chair.

seggio'**lino** [seddʒo'lino] *sm* seat; (*per bambini*) child's chair; ~ **di sicurezza** (*AUT*) child safety seat.

seggio'**lone** [seddʒo'lone] *sm* (*per bambini*) highchair.

seggio'**via** [seddʒo'via] *sf* chairlift.

seghe'**ria** [sege'ria] *sf* sawmill.

seghe'**rò** *etc* [sege'rɔ] *vb vedi* **segare.**

seghet'**tato, a** [seget'tato] *ag* serrated.

se'**ghetto** [se'getto] *sm* hacksaw.

seg'**mento** *sm* segment.

segna'**lare** [seɲɲa'lare] *vt* (*essere segno di*) to indicate, be a sign of; (*avvertire*) to signal; (*menzionare*) to indicate; (: *fatto, risultato, aumento*) to report; (: *errore, dettaglio*) to point out; (*AUT*) to signal, indicate; ~**rsi** *vr* (*distinguersi*) to distinguish o.s.; ~ **qn a qn** (*per lavoro etc*) to bring sb to sb's attention.

segnalazi'**one** [seɲɲalat'tsjone] *sf* (*azione*) signalling; (*segnale*) signal; (*annuncio*) report; (*raccomandazione*) recommendation.

se'**gnale** [seɲ'ɲale] *sm* signal; (*cartello*): ~ **stradale** road sign; ~ **acustico** acoustic *o* sound signal; ~ **d'allarme** alarm; (*FERR*) communication cord; ~ **di linea libera** (*TEL*) dialling (*BRIT*) *o* dial (*US*) tone; ~ **luminoso** light signal; ~ **di occupato** (*TEL*) engaged tone (*BRIT*), busy signal (*US*); ~

orario (*RADIO*) time signal.

segna'**letica** [seɲɲa'lɛtika] *sf* signalling, signposting; ~ **stradale** road signs *pl.*

segna'**libro** [seɲɲa'libro] *sm* bookmark(er).

segna'**punti** [seɲɲa'punti] *sm/f inv* scorer, scorekeeper.

se'**gnare** [seɲ'ɲare] *vt* to mark; (*prendere nota*) to note; (*indicare*) to indicate, mark; (*SPORT: goal*) to score; ~**rsi** *vr* (*REL*) to make the sign of the cross, cross o.s.

'**segno** ['seɲɲo] *sm* sign; (*impronta, contrassegno*) mark; (*bersaglio*) target; **fare** ~ **di sì/no** to nod (one's head)/shake one's head; **fare** ~ **a qn di fermarsi** to motion (to) sb to stop; **cogliere** *o* **colpire nel** ~ (*fig*) to hit the mark; **in** *o* **come** ~ **d'amicizia** as a mark *o* token of friendship; "~**I particolari**" (*su documento etc*) "distinguishing marks".

segre'**gare** *vt* to segregate, isolate.

segrega**zi'one** [segregat'tsjone] *sf* segregation.

se'**greta, a** *sf vedi* **segreto.**

segre'**tario, a** *sm/f* secretary; ~ **comunale** town clerk; ~ **del partito** party leader; **S**~ **di Stato** Secretary of State.

segrete'**ria** *sf* (*di ditta, scuola*) (secretary's) office; (*d'organizzazione internazionale*) secretariat; (*POL etc: carica*) office of Secretary; ~ **telefonica** answering service.

segre'**tezza** [segre'tettsa] *sf* secrecy; **notizie della massima** ~ confidential information; **in tutta** ~ in secret; (*confidenzialmente*) in confidence.

se'**greto, a** *ag* secret ♦ *sm* secret ♦ *sf* dungeon; **in** ~ in secret, secretly; **il** ~ **professionale** professional secrecy; **un** ~ **professionale** a professional secret.

segu'**ace** [se'gwatʃe] *sm/f* follower, disciple.

segu'**ente** *ag* following, next; **nel modo** ~ as follows, in the following way.

se'**gugio** [se'gudʒo] *sm* hound, hunting dog; (*fig*) private eye, sleuth.

segu'**ire** *vt* to follow; (*frequentare: corso*) to attend ♦ *vi* to follow; (*continuare: testo*) to continue; ~ **i consigli di qn** to follow *o* to take sb's advice; ~ **gli avvenimenti di attualità** to follow *o* keep up with current events; **come segue** as follows; "**segue**" "to be continued".

segui'**tare** *vt* to continue, carry on with ♦ *vi* to continue, carry on.

'**seguito** *sm* (*scorta*) suite, retinue; (*discepoli*) followers *pl*; (*serie*) sequence, series *sg*; (*continuazione*) continuation; (*conseguenza*) result; **di** ~ at a stretch, on

end; **in** ~ later on; **in** ~ **a, a** ~ **di**
following; (*a causa di*) as a result of,
owing to; **essere al** ~ **di qn** to be among
sb's suite, be one of sb's retinue; **non**
aver ~ (*conseguenze*) to have no
repercussions; **facciamo** ~ **alla lettera del**
… further to *o* in answer to your letter
of ….

'**sei** *vb vedi* **essere ♦** *num* six.

Sei'celle [sei'tʃɛlle] *sfpl*: **le** ~ the
Seychelles.

seicen'tesco, a, schi, sche [seitʃen'tesko]
ag seventeenth-century.

sei'cento [sei'tʃɛnto] *num* six hundred ♦ *sm*:
il S~ the seventeenth century.

sei'mila *num* six thousand.

'**selce** ['seltʃe] *sf* flint, flintstone.

selci'ato [sel'tʃato] *sm* cobbled surface.

selet'tivo, a *ag* selective.

selet'tore *sm* (*TECN*) selector.

selezio'nare [selettsjo'nare] *vt* to select.

selezi'one [selet'tsjone] *sf* selection; **fare**
una ~ to make a selection *o* choice.

'**sella** *sf* saddle.

sel'lare *vt* to saddle.

sel'lino *sm* saddle.

seltz *sm inv* soda (water).

'**selva** *sf* (*bosco*) wood; (*foresta*) forest.

selvag'gina [selvad'dʒina] *sf* (*animali*)
game.

sel'vaggio, a, gi, ge [sel'vaddʒo] *ag* wild;
(*tribù*) savage, uncivilized; (*fig: brutale*)
savage, brutal; (: *incontrollato: fenomeno,*
aumento etc) uncontrolled ♦ *sm/f* savage;
inflazione ~**a** runaway inflation.

sel'vatico, a, ci, che *ag* wild.

S.Em. *abbr* (= *Sua Eminenza*) HE.

se'maforo *sm* (*AUT*) traffic lights *pl*.

se'mantico, a *ag* semantic ♦ *sf* semantics
sg.

sembi'anza [sem'bjantsa] *sf* (*poetico:*
aspetto) appearance; ~**e** *sfpl* (*lineamenti*)
features; (*fig: falsa apparenza*) semblance
sg.

sem'brare *vi* to seem ♦ *vb impers*: **sembra**
che it seems that; **mi sembra che** it seems
to me that; (*penso che*) I think (that); ~ **di**
essere to seem to be; **non mi sembra**
vero! I can't believe it!

'**seme** *sm* seed; (*sperma*) semen; (*CARTE*)
suit.

se'mente *sf* seed.

semes'trale *ag* (*che dura 6 mesi*)
six-month *cpd*; (*che avviene ogni 6 mesi*)
six-monthly.

se'mestre *sm* half-year, six-month period.

'**semi** … *prefisso* semi ….

semi'cerchio [semi'tʃerkjo] *sm* semicircle.

semicondut'tore *sm* semiconductor.

semidetenzi'one [semideten'tsjone] *sf*
custodial sentence whereby individual
must spend a minimum of 10 hours per
day in prison.

semifi'nale *sf* semifinal.

semi'freddo, a *ag* (*CUC*) chilled ♦ *sm* ice-
cream cake.

semilibertà *sf custodial sentence which*
allows prisoner to study or work outside
prison for part of the day.

'**semina** *sf* (*AGR*) sowing.

semi'nare *vt* to sow.

semi'nario *sm* seminar; (*REL*) seminary.

semi'nato *sm*: **uscire dal** ~ (*fig*) to wander
off the point.

seminter'rato *sm* basement;
(*appartamento*) basement flat (*BRIT*) *o*
apartment (*US*).

semi'ologo, a, gi, ghe *sm/f* semiologist.

semi'otica *sf* semiotics *sg*.

se'mitico, a, ci, che *ag* semitic.

semivu'oto, a *ag* half-empty.

sem'mai = **se mai**.

'**semola** *sf* bran; ~ **di grano duro** durum
wheat.

semo'lato *ag*: **zucchero** ~ caster sugar.

semo'lino *sm* semolina.

'**semplice** ['semplitʃe] *ag* simple; (*di un solo*
elemento) single; **è una** ~ **formalità** it's a
mere formality.

semplice'mente [semplitʃe'mente] *av*
simply.

sempli'cistico, a, ci, che [sempli'tʃistiko]
ag simplistic.

semplicità [semplitʃi'ta] *sf* simplicity.

semplifi'care *vt* to simplify.

semplificazi'one [semplifikat'tsjone] *sf*
simplification; **fare una** ~ **di** to
simplify.

'**sempre** *av* always; (*ancora*) still; **posso** ~
tentare I can always *o* still try; **da** ~
always; **per** ~ forever; **una volta per** ~
once and for all; ~ **che** *cong* as long as,
provided (that); ~ **più** more and more; ~
meno less and less; **va** ~ **meglio** things
are getting better and better; **è** ~ **più**
giovane she gets younger and younger; **è**
~ **meglio che niente** it's better than
nothing; **è** (**pur**) ~ **tuo fratello** he is still
your brother (however); **c'è** ~ **la**
possibilità che … there's still a chance
that …, there's always the possibility
that ….

sempre'verde *ag, sm o f* (*BOT*) evergreen.

Sen. *abbr* (= *senatore*) Sen.

'**senape** *sf* (*CUC*) mustard.

se'nato *sm* senate; **il S**~ *vedi nota nel riquadro*.

SENATO

The **Senato** *is the upper house of the Italian Parliament, with similar functions to the "Camera dei deputati". Candidates must be at least 40 years of age and electors must be 25 or over. Elections are held every five years. Former heads of state become senators for life, as do five distinguished members of the public who are chosen by the head of state for their scientific, social, artistic or literary achievements. The Chamber is presided over by the "Presidente del Senato", who is elected by the senators.*

---

sena'tore, 'trice *sm/f* senator.

'Senegal *sm*: **il** ~ Senegal.

senega'lese *ag, sm/f* Senegalese *inv*.

se'nese *ag* of (*o* from) Siena.

se'nile *ag* senile.

'Senna *sf*: **la** ~ the Seine.

'senno *sm* judgment, (*common*) sense; **col** ~ **di poi** with hindsight.

sennò *av* = **se no**.

'seno *sm* (*ANAT: petto, mammella*) breast; (: *grembo, fig*) womb; (: *cavità*) sinus; (*GEO*) inlet, creek; (*MAT*) sine; **in** ~ **al partito** within the party.

sen'sale *sm* (*COMM*) agent.

sensa'tezza [sensa'tettsa] *sf* good sense, good judgment.

sen'sato, a *ag* sensible.

sensazio'nale [sensattsjo'nale] *ag* sensational.

sensazi'one [sensat'tsjone] *sf* feeling, sensation; **fare** ~ to cause a sensation, create a stir; **avere la** ~ **che** to have a feeling that.

sen'sibile *ag* sensitive; (*ai sensi*) perceptible; (*rilevante, notevole*) appreciable, noticeable; ~ **a** sensitive to.

sensibilità *sf* sensitivity.

sensibiliz'zare [sensibilid'dzare] *vt* (*fig*) to make aware, awaken.

'senso *sm* (*FISIOL, istinto*) sense; (*impressione, sensazione*) feeling, sensation; (*significato*) meaning, sense; (*direzione*) direction; ~**i** *smpl* (*coscienza*) consciousness *sg*; (*sensualità*) senses; **perdere/riprendere i** ~**i** to lose/regain consciousness; **avere** ~ **pratico** to be practical; **avere un sesto** ~ to have a sixth sense; **fare** ~ **a** (*ripugnare*) to disgust, repel; **ciò non ha** ~ that doesn't make sense; **senza** *o* **privo di** ~ meaningless; **nel** ~ **che** in the sense that; **nel vero** ~ **della parola** in the true sense

of the word; **nel** ~ **della lunghezza** lengthwise, lengthways; **nel** ~ **della larghezza** widthwise; **ho dato disposizioni in quel** ~ I've given instructions to that end *o* effect; ~ **comune** common sense; ~ **del dovere** sense of duty; **in** ~ **opposto** in the opposite direction; **in** ~ **orario/antiorario** clockwise/anticlockwise; ~ **dell'umorismo** sense of humour; **a** ~ **unico** one-way.

sensu'ale *ag* sensual; sensuous.

sensualità *sf* sensuality; sensuousness.

sen'tenza [sen'tentsa] *sf* (*DIR*) sentence; (*massima*) maxim.

sentenzi'are [senten'tsjare] *vi* (*DIR*) to pass judgment.

senti'ero *sm* path.

sentimen'tale *ag* sentimental; (*vita, avventura*) love *cpd*.

senti'mento *sm* feeling.

senti'nella *sf* sentry.

sen'tire *vt* (*percepire al tatto, fig*) to feel; (*udire*) to hear; (*ascoltare*) to listen to; (*odore*) to smell; (*avvertire con il gusto, assaggiare*) to taste ♦ *vi*: ~ **di** (*avere sapore*) to taste of; (*avere odore*) to smell of; ~**rsi** *vr* (*uso reciproco*) to be in touch; ~**rsi bene/male** to feel well/unwell *o* ill; ~**rsi di fare qc** (*essere disposto*) to feel like doing sth; ~ **la mancanza di qn** to miss sb; **ho sentito dire che** ... I have heard that ...; **a** ~ **lui** ... to hear him talk ...; **fatti** ~ keep in touch; **intendo** ~ **il mio legale** I'm going to consult my lawyer.

sentita'mente *av* sincerely; **ringraziare** ~ to thank sincerely.

sen'tito, a *ag* (*sincero*) sincere, warm; **per** ~ **dire** by hearsay.

sen'tore *sm* rumour (*BRIT*), rumor (*US*), talk; **aver** ~ **di qc** to hear about sth.

'senza ['sentsa] *prep, cong* without; ~ **dir nulla** without saying a word; ~ **dire che** ... not to mention the fact that ...; ~ **contare che** ... without considering that ...; **fare** ~ **qc** to do without sth; ~ **di me** without me; ~ **che io lo sapessi** without me *o* my knowing; ~ **amici** friendless; **senz'altro** of course, certainly; ~ **dubbio** no doubt; ~ **scrupoli** unscrupulous; **i** ~ **lavoro** the jobless, the unemployed.

senza'tetto [sentsa'tetto] *sm/f inv* homeless person; **i** ~ the homeless.

sepa'rare *vt* to separate; (*dividere*) to divide; (*tenere distinto*) to distinguish; ~**rsi** *vr* (*coniugi*) to separate, part; (*amici*) to part; ~**rsi da** (*coniuge*) to separate *o* part from; (*amico, socio*) to part company with; (*oggetto*) to part with.

separata'mente *av* separately.

sepa'rato, a *ag* (*letti, conto etc*) separate; (*coniugi*) separated.

separazi'one [separat'tsjone] *sf* separation; **~ dei beni** division of property.

séparé [sepa're] *sm inv* screen.

se'polcro *sm* sepulchre (*BRIT*), sepulcher (*US*).

se'polto, a *pp di* **seppellire.**

sepol'tura *sf* burial; **dare ~ a qn** to bury sb.

seppel'lire *vt* to bury.

'seppi *etc vb vedi* **sapere.**

'seppia *sf* cuttlefish ♦ *ag inv* sepia.

sep'pure *cong* even if.

se'quela *sf* (*di avvenimenti*) series, sequence; (*di offese, ingiurie*) string.

se'quenza [se'kwentsa] *sf* sequence.

sequenzi'ale [sekwen'tsjale] *ag* sequential.

seques'trare *vt* (*DIR*) to impound; (*rapire*) to kidnap; (*costringere in un luogo*) to keep, confine.

se'questro *sm* (*DIR*) impoundment; **~ di persona** kidnapping.

se'quoia *sf* sequoia.

'sera *sf* evening; **di ~** in the evening; **domani ~** tomorrow evening, tomorrow night; **questa ~** this evening, tonight.

se'rale *ag* evening *cpd*; **scuola ~** evening classes *pl*, night school.

se'rata *sf* evening; (*ricevimento*) party.

ser'bare *vt* to keep; (*mettere da parte*) to put aside; **~ rancore/odio verso qn** to bear sb a grudge/hate sb.

serba'toio *sm* tank; (*cisterna*) cistern.

'serbo *ag* Serbian ♦ *sm/f* Serbian, Serb ♦ *sm* (*LING*) Serbian; (*il serbare*): **mettere/tenere o avere in ~ qc** to put/keep sth aside.

serbocro'ato, a *ag, sm* Serbo-Croat.

serena'mente *av* serenely, calmly.

sere'nata *sf* (*MUS*) serenade.

serenità *sf* serenity.

se'reno, a *ag* (*tempo, cielo*) clear; (*fig*) serene, calm ♦ *sm* (*tempo*) good weather; **un fulmine a ciel ~** (*fig*) a bolt from the blue.

serg. *abbr* (= *sergente*) Sgt.

ser'gente [ser'dʒɛnte] *sm* (*MIL*) sergeant.

seri'ale *ag* (*INFORM*) serial.

seria'mente *av* (*con serietà, in modo grave*) seriously; **lavorare ~** to take one's job seriously.

'serie *sf inv* (*successione*) series *inv*; (*gruppo, collezione*: *di chiavi etc*) set; (*SPORT*) division; league; (*COMM*): **modello di ~/ fuori ~** standard/custom-built model; **in ~** in quick succession; (*COMM*) mass *cpd*; **tutta una ~ di problemi** a whole string *o*

series of problems.

serietà *sf* seriousness; reliability.

'serio, a *ag* serious; (*impiegato*) responsible, reliable; (*ditta, cliente*) reliable, dependable; **sul ~** (*davvero*) really, truly; (*seriamente*) seriously, in earnest; **dico sul ~** I'm serious; **faccio sul ~** I mean it; **prendere qc/qn sul ~** to take sth/sb seriously.

seri'oso, a *ag* (*persona, modi*): **un po' ~** a bit too serious.

ser'mone *sm* sermon.

'serpe *sf* snake; (*fig peg*) viper.

serpeggi'are [serped'dʒare] *vi* to wind; (*fig*) to spread.

ser'pente *sm* snake; **~ a sonagli** rattlesnake.

'serra *sf* greenhouse; hothouse; (*GEO*) sierra.

serra'manico *sm*: **coltello a ~** jack-knife.

ser'randa *sf* roller shutter.

ser'rare *vt* to close, shut; (*a chiave*) to lock; (*stringere*) to tighten; (*premere*: *nemico*) to close in on; **~ i pugni/i denti** to clench one's fists/teeth; **~ le file** to close ranks.

ser'rata *sf* (*INDUSTRIA*) lockout.

ser'rato, a *ag* (*veloce*): **a ritmo ~** quickly, fast.

serra'tura *sf* lock.

'serva *sf vedi* **servo.**

'server ['server] *sm inv* (*INFORM*) server.

ser'vigio [ser'vidʒo] *sm* favour (*BRIT*), favor (*US*), service.

ser'vire *vt* to serve; (*clienti: al ristorante*) to wait on; (*: al negozio*) to serve, attend to; (*fig*: *giovare*) to aid, help; (*CARTE*) to deal ♦ *vi* (*TENNIS*) to serve; (*essere utile*): **~ a qn** to be of use to sb; **~ a qc/a fare** (*utensile etc*) to be used for sth/for doing; **~ (a qn) da** to serve as (for sb); **~rsi** *vr* (*usare*): **~rsi di** to use; (*prendere*: *cibo*): **~rsi (di)** to help o.s. (to); (*essere cliente abituale*): **~rsi da** to be a regular customer at, go to; **non mi serve più** I don't need it any more; **non serve che lei vada** you don't need to go.

servitù *sf* servitude; slavery; (*personale di servizio*) servants *pl*, domestic staff.

servizi'evole [servit'tsjevole] *ag* obliging, willing to help.

ser'vizio [ser'vittsjo] *sm* service; (*al ristorante*: *sul conto*) service (charge); (*STAMPA, TV, RADIO*) report; (*da tè, caffè etc*) set, service; **~i** *smpl* (*di casa*) kitchen and bathroom; (*ECON*) services; **essere di ~** to be on duty; **fuori ~** (*telefono etc*) out of order; **~ compreso/escluso** service included/not included; **entrata di ~** service *o* tradesman's (*BRIT*) entrance;

casa con doppi ~**i** house with two bathrooms; ~ **assistenza clienti** after-sales service; ~ **civile** ≈ community service; ~ **in diretta** (*TV, RADIO*) live coverage; ~ **fotografico** (*STAMPA*) photo feature; ~ **militare** military service; ~ **d'ordine** (*POLIZIA*) police patrol; (*di manifestanti*) team of stewards (*responsible for crowd control*); ~**i segreti** secret service *sg*; ~**i di sicurezza** security forces.

'servo, a *sm/f* servant.

servo'freno *sm* (*AUT*) servo brake.

servos'terzo [servos'tɛrtso] *sm* (*AUT*) power steering.

'sesamo *sm* (*BOT*) sesame.

ses'santa *num* sixty.

sessan'tenne *ag, sm/f* sixty-year-old.

sessan'tesimo, a *num* sixtieth.

sessan'tina *sf*: **una** ~ (**di**) about sixty.

sessantot'tino, a *sm/f a person who took part in the evento of 1968.*

sessan'totto *sm vedi nota nel riquadro.*

SESSANTOTTO

Sessantotto *refers to the year 1968, when the student protest movement came into its own. Originating in France, unrest soon spread to other industrialized countries including Italy. What began as a purely student concern gradually came to include other parts of society and led to major political and social change. As a result, left-wing groups flourished, schools and universities became more democratic, and a referendum on divorce was held.*

---

sessi'one *sf* session.

'sesso *sm* sex; **il** ~ **debole/forte** the weaker/stronger sex.

sessu'ale *ag* sexual, sex *cpd*.

sessualità *sf* sexuality.

sessu'ologo, a, gi, ghe *sm/f* sexologist, sex specialist.

ses'tante *sm* sextant.

'sesto, a *num* sixth ♦ *sm*: **rimettere in** ~ (*aggiustare*) to put back in order; (*fig: persona*) to put back on his (*o* her) feet; **rimettersi in** ~ (*riprendersi*) to recover, get well; (*riassettarsi*) to tidy o.s. up.

'seta *sf* silk.

setacci'are [setat'tʃare] *vt* (*farina etc*) to sift, sieve; (*fig: zona*) to search, comb.

se'taccio [se'tattʃo] *sm* sieve; **passare al** ~ (*fig*) to search, comb.

'sete *sf* thirst; **avere** ~ to be thirsty; ~ **di potere** thirst for power.

seti'ficio [seti'fitʃo] *sm* silk factory.

'setola *sf* bristle.

sett. *abbr* (= *settembre*) Sept.

'setta *sf* sect.

set'tanta *num* seventy.

settan'tenne *ag, sm/f* seventy-year-old.

settan'tesimo, a *num* seventieth.

settan'tina *sf*: **una** ~ (**di**) about seventy.

'sette *num* seven.

settecen'tesco, a, schi, sche [settetʃen'tesko] *ag* eighteenth-century.

sette'cento [sette'tʃɛnto] *num* seven hundred ♦ *sm*: **il S**~ the eighteenth century.

set'tembre *sm* September; *per fraseologia vedi* **luglio.**

sette'mila *num* seven thousand.

settentrio'nale *ag* northern ♦ *sm/f* northerner.

settentri'one *sm* north.

'settico, a, ci, che *ag* (*MED*) septic.

setti'mana *sf* week; **la** ~ **scorsa/prossima** last/next week; **a metà** ~ in the middle of the week; ~ **bianca** winter-sports holiday.

settima'nale *ag, sm* weekly.

'settimo, a *num* seventh.

set'tore *sm* sector; ~ **privato/pubblico** private/public sector; ~ **terziario** service industries *pl*.

Se'ul *sf* Seoul.

severità *sf* severity.

se'vero, a *ag* severe.

sevizi'are [sevit'tsjare] *vt* to torture.

se'vizie [se'vittsje] *sfpl* torture *sg*.

'sexy ['sɛksi] *ag inv* sexy.

sez. *abbr* = **sezione.**

sezio'nare [settsjo'nare] *vt* to divide into sections; (*MED*) to dissect.

sezi'one [set'tsjone] *sf* section; (*MED*) dissection.

sfaccen'dato, a [sfattʃen'dato] *ag* idle.

sfaccetta'tura [sfattʃetta'tura] *sf* (*azione*) faceting; (*parte sfaccettata, fig*) facet.

sfacchi'nare [sfakki'nare] *vi* (*fam*) to toil, drudge.

sfacchi'nata [sfakki'nata] *sf* (*fam*) chore, drudgery *no pl*.

sfaccia'taggine [sfattʃa'taddʒine] *sf* insolence, cheek.

sfacci'ato, a [sfat'tʃato] *ag* (*maleducato*) cheeky, impudent; (*vistoso*) gaudy.

sfa'celo [sfa'tʃɛlo] *sm* (*fig*) ruin, collapse.

sfal'darsi *vr* to flake (off).

sfal'sare *vt* to offset.

sfa'mare *vt* (*nutrire*) to feed; (*soddisfare la fame*): ~ **qn** to satisfy sb's hunger; ~**rsi** *vr* to satisfy one's hunger, fill o.s. up.

sfarfal'lio *sm* (*CINE, TV*) flickering.

'sfarzo ['sfartso] *sm* pomp, splendour (*BRIT*), splendor (*US*).

sfar'zoso, a [sfar'tsoso] *ag* splendid, magnificent.

sfasa'mento *sm* (*ELETTR*) phase displacement; (*fig*) confusion, bewilderment.

sfa'sato, a *ag* (*ELETTR, motore*) out of phase; (*fig: persona*) confused, bewildered.

sfasci'are [sfaʃ'ʃare] *vt* (*ferita*) to unbandage; (*distruggere: porta*) to smash, shatter; ~**rsi** *vr* (*rompersi*) to smash, shatter.

sfa'tare *vt* (*leggenda*) to explode.

sfati'cato, a *sm/f* idler, loafer.

'sfatto, a *ag* (*letto*) unmade; (*orlo etc*) undone; (*gelato, neve*) melted; (*frutta*) overripe; (*riso, pasta etc*) overdone, overcooked; (*fam: persona, corpo*) flabby.

sfavil'lare *vi* to spark, send out sparks; (*risplendere*) to sparkle.

sfa'vore *sm* disfavour (*BRIT*), disfavor (*US*), disapproval.

sfavo'revole *ag* unfavourable (*BRIT*), unfavorable (*US*).

sfega'tato, a *ag* fanatical.

'sfera *sf* sphere.

'sferico, a, ci, che *ag* spherical.

sfer'rare *vt* (*fig: colpo*) to land, deal; (: *attacco*) to launch.

sfer'zante [sfer'tsante] *ag* (*critiche, parole*) stinging.

sfer'zare [sfer'tsare] *vt* to whip; (*fig*) to lash out at.

sfian'care *vt* to wear out, exhaust; ~**rsi** *vr* to exhaust o.s., wear o.s. out.

sfia'tare *vi* to allow air (*o gas etc*) to escape.

sfiata'toio *sm* blowhole; (*TECN*) vent.

sfi'brante *ag* exhausting, energy-sapping.

sfi'brare *vt* (*indebolire*) to exhaust, enervate.

sfi'brato, a *ag* exhausted, worn out.

'sfida *sf* challenge.

sfi'dante *ag* challenging ♦ *sm/f* challenger.

sfi'dare *vt* to challenge; (*fig*) to defy, brave; ~ **qn a fare qc** to challenge sb to do sth; ~ **un pericolo** to brave a danger; **sfido che ...** I dare say (that) ....

sfi'ducia [sfi'dutʃa] *sf* distrust, mistrust; **avere ~ in qn/qc** to distrust sb/sth.

sfiduci'ato, a [sfidu'tʃato] *ag* lacking confidence.

sfigu'rare *vt* (*persona*) to disfigure; (*quadro, statua*) to deface ♦ *vi* (*far cattiva figura*) to make a bad impression.

sfilacci'are [sfilat'tʃare] *vt, vi,* ~**rsi** *vr* to fray.

sfi'lare *vt* (*ago*) to unthread; (*abito, scarpe*) to slip off ♦ *vi* (*truppe*) to march past, parade; (*manifestanti*) to march; ~**rsi** *vr* (*perle etc*) to come unstrung; (*orlo, tessuto*) to fray; (*calza*) to run, ladder.

sfi'lata *sf* (*MIL*) parade; (*di manifestanti*) march; ~ **di moda** fashion show.

'sfilza ['sfiltsa] *sf* (*di case*) row; (*di errori*) series *inv*.

'sfinge ['sfindʒe] *sf* sphinx.

sfini'mento *sm* exhaustion.

sfi'nito, a *ag* exhausted.

sfio'rare *vt* to brush (against); (*argomento*) to touch upon; ~ **la velocità di 150 km/h** to touch 150 km/h.

sfio'rire *vi* to wither, fade.

'sfitto, a *ag* (*vestito*) unlet, empty.

sfo'cato, a *ag* (*FOT*) out of focus.

sfoci'are [sfo'tʃare] *vi*: ~ **in** to flow into; (*fig: malcontento*) to develop into.

sfode'rato, a *ag* (*vestito*) unlined.

sfo'gare *vt* to vent, pour out; ~**rsi** *vr* (*sfogare la propria rabbia*) to give vent to one's anger; (*confidarsi*): ~**rsi (con)** to pour out one's feelings (to); **non sfogarti su di me!** don't take your bad temper out on me!

sfoggi'are [sfod'dʒare] *vt, vi* to show off.

'sfoggio ['sfɔddʒo] *sm* show, display; **fare ~ di** to show off, display.

sfogherò *etc* [sfoge'rɔ] *vb vedi* **sfogare**.

'sfoglia ['sfɔʎʎa] *sf* sheet of pasta dough; **pasta ~** (*CUC*) puff pastry.

sfogli'are [sfoʎ'ʎare] *vt* (*libro*) to leaf through.

'sfogo, ghi *sm* outlet; (*eruzione cutanea*) rash; (*fig*) outburst; **dare ~ a** (*fig*) to give vent to.

sfolgo'rante *ag* (*luce*) blazing; (*fig: vittoria*) brilliant.

sfolgo'rare *vi* to blaze.

sfolla'gente [sfolla'dʒente] *sm inv* truncheon (*BRIT*), billy (*US*).

sfol'lare *vt* to empty, clear ♦ *vi* to disperse; ~ **da** (*città*) to evacuate.

sfol'lato, a *ag* evacuated ♦ *sm/f* evacuee.

sfol'tire *vt,* ~**rsi** *vr* to thin (out).

sfon'dare *vt* (*porta*) to break down; (*scarpe*) to wear a hole in; (*cesto, scatola*) to burst, knock the bottom out of; (*MIL*) to break through ♦ *vi* (*riuscire*) to make a name for o.s.

sfon'dato, a *ag* (*scarpe*) worn out; (*scatola*) burst; (*sedia*) broken, damaged; **essere ricco ~** to be rolling in it.

'sfondo *sm* background.

sfo'rare *vi* to overrun.

sfor'mare *vt* to put out of shape, knock out of shape; ~**rsi** *vr* to lose shape, get out of shape.

sfor'mato, a *ag* (*che ha perso forma*) shapeless ♦ *sm* (*CUC*) type of soufflé.

sfor'nare *vt* (*pane*) to take out of the oven; (*fig*) to churn out.

sfor'nito, a *ag*: ~ **di** lacking in, without; (*negozio*) out of.

sfor'tuna *sf* misfortune, ill luck *no pl*; **avere** ~ to be unlucky; **che** ~! how unfortunate!

sfortu'nato, a *ag* unlucky; (*impresa, film*) unsuccessful.

sfor'zare [sfor'tsare] *vt* to force; (*voce, occhi*) to strain; ~**rsi** *vr*: ~**rsi di** *o* **a** *o* **per fare** to try hard to do.

'sforzo ['sfɔrtso] *sm* effort; (*tensione eccessiva, TECN*) strain; **fare uno** ~ to make an effort; **essere sotto** ~ (*motore, macchina, fig: persona*) to be under stress; **'sfottere** *vt* (*fam*) to tease.

sfracel'lare [sfratʃel'lare] *vt*, ~**rsi** *vr* to smash.

sfrat'tare *vt* to evict.

'sfratto *sm* eviction; **dare lo** ~ **a qn** to give sb notice to quit.

sfrecci'are [sfret'tʃare] *vi* to shoot *o* flash past.

sfre'gare *vt* (*strofinare*) to rub; (*graffiare*) to scratch; ~**rsi le mani** to rub one's hands; ~ **un fiammifero** to strike a match.

sfregi'are [sfre'dʒare] *vt* to slash, gash; (*persona*) to disfigure; (*quadro*) to deface.

'sfregio ['sfredʒo] *sm* gash; scar; (*fig*) insult.

sfre'nato, a *ag* (*fig*) unrestrained, unbridled.

sfron'dare *vt* (*albero*) to prune, thin out; (*fig: discorso, scritto*) to prune (down).

sfronta'tezza [sfronta'tettsa] *sf* impudence, cheek.

sfron'tato, a *ag* impudent, cheeky.

sfrutta'mento *sm* exploitation.

sfrut'tare *vt* (*terreno*) to overwork, exhaust; (*miniera*) to exploit, work; (*fig: operai, occasione, potere*) to exploit.

sfrutta'tore, 'trice *sm/f* exploiter.

sfug'gente [sfud'dʒɛnte] *ag* (*fig: sguardo*) elusive; (*mento*) receding.

sfug'gire [sfud'dʒire] *vi* to escape; ~ **a** (*custode*) to escape (from); (*morte*) to escape; ~ **a qn** (*dettaglio, nome*) to escape sb; ~ **di mano a qn** to slip out of sb's hand (*o* hands); **lasciarsi** ~ **un'occasione** to let an opportunity go by; ~ **al controllo** (*macchina*) to go out of control;

(*situazione*) to be no longer under control.

sfug'gita [sfud'dʒita] *sf*: **di** ~ (*rapidamente, in fretta*) in passing.

sfu'mare *vt* (*colori, contorni*) to soften, shade off ♦ *vi* to shade (off), fade; (*fig: svanire*) to vanish, disappear; (: *speranze*) to come to nothing.

sfuma'tura *sf* shading off *no pl*; (*tonalità*) shade, tone; (*fig*) touch, hint.

sfuo'cato, a *ag* = **sfocato**.

sfuri'ata *sf* (*scatto di collera*) fit of anger; (*rimprovero*) sharp rebuke.

'sfuso, a *ag* (*caramelle etc*) loose, unpacked; (*vino*) unbottled; (*birra*) draught (*BRIT*), draft (*US*).

sg. *abbr* = **seguente**.

S.G. *abbr* = **Sua Grazia**.

sga'bello *sm* stool.

sgabuz'zino [zgabud'dzino] *sm* lumber room.

sgambet'tare *vi* to kick one's legs about.

sgam'betto *sm*: **tar lo** ~ **a qn** to trip sb up; (*fig*) to oust sb.

sganasci'arsi [zganaʃ'ʃarsi] *vr*: ~ **dalle risa** to roar with laughter.

sganci'are [zgan'tʃare] *vt* to unhook; (*chiusura*) to unfasten, undo; (*FERR*) to uncouple; (*bombe: da aereo*) to release, drop; (*fig: fam: soldi*) to fork out; ~**rsi** *vr* to come unhooked; to come unfastened, come undone; to uncouple; (*fig*): ~**rsi (da)** to get away (from).

sganghe'rato, a [zgange'rato] *ag* (*porta*) off its hinges; (*auto*) ramshackle; (*riso*) wild, boisterous.

sgar'bato, a *ag* rude, impolite.

'sgarbo *sm*: **fare uno** ~ **a qn** to be rude to sb.

sgargi'ante [zgar'dʒante] *ag* gaudy, showy.

sgar'rare *vi* (*persona*) to step out of line; (*orologio: essere avanti*) to gain; (: *essere indietro*) to lose.

'sgarro *sm* inaccuracy.

sgattaio'lare *vi* to sneak away *o* off.

sge'lare [zdʒe'lare] *vi*, *vt* to thaw.

'sghembo, a ['zgembo] *ag* (*obliquo*) slanting; (*storto*) crooked.

sghignaz'zare [zgiɲɲat'tsare] *vi* to laugh scornfully.

sghignaz'zata [zgiɲɲat'tsata] *sf* scornful laugh.

sgob'bare *vi* (*fam: scolaro*) to swot; (: *operaio*) to slog.

sgoccio'lare [zgottʃo'lare] *vt* (*vuotare*) to drain (to the last drop) ♦ *vi* (*acqua*) to drip; (*recipiente*) to drain.

'sgoccioli ['zgottʃoli] *smpl*: **essere agli** ~ (*lavoro, provviste etc*) to be nearly

finished; (*periodo*) to be nearly over;
siamo agli ~ we've nearly finished, the
end is in sight.

sgo'larsi *vr* to talk (*o* shout *o* sing) o.s.
hoarse.

sgomb(e)'rare *vt* to clear; (*andarsene da*:
stanza) to vacate; (*evacuare*) to evacuate.

'sgombero *sm vedi* **sgombro**.

'sgombro, a *ag*: ~ (**di**) clear (of), free
(from) ♦ *sm* (*ZOOL*) mackerel; (*anche*:
sgombero) clearing; vacating;
evacuation; (: *trasloco*) removal.

sgomen'tare *vt* to dismay; ~**rsi** *vr* to be
dismayed.

sgo'mento, a *ag* dismayed ♦ *sm* dismay,
consternation.

sgomi'nare *vt* (*nemico*) to rout; (*avversario*)
to defeat; (*fig*: *epidemia*) to overcome.

sgonfi'are *vt* to let down, deflate; ~**rsi** *vr* to
go down.

'sgonfio, a *ag* (*pneumatico, pallone*) flat.

'sgorbio *sm* blot; scribble.

sgor'gare *vi* to gush (out).

sgoz'zare [zgot'tsare] *vt* to cut the throat
of.

sgra'devole *ag* unpleasant, disagreeable.

sgra'dito, a *ag* unpleasant, unwelcome.

sgraffi'gnare [zgraffiɲ'ɲare] *vt* (*fam*) to
pinch, swipe.

sgrammati'cato, a *ag* ungrammatical.

sgra'nare *vt* (*piselli*) to shell; ~ **gli occhi** to
open one's eyes wide.

sgran'chirsi [zgran'kirsi] *vr* to stretch; ~ **le
gambe** to stretch one's legs.

sgranocchi'are [zgranok'kjare] *vt* to
munch.

sgras'sare *vt* to remove the grease from.

'sgravio *sm*: ~ **fiscale** *o* **contributivo** tax
relief.

sgrazi'ato, a [zgrat'tsjato] *ag* clumsy,
ungainly.

sgreto'lare *vt* to cause to crumble; ~**rsi** *vr*
to crumble.

sgri'dare *vt* to scold.

sgri'data *sf* scolding.

sguai'ato, a *ag* coarse, vulgar.

sguai'nare *vt* to draw, unsheathe.

sgual'cire [zgwal'tʃire] *vt* to crumple (up),
crease.

sgual'drina *sf* (*peg*) slut.

sgu'ardo *sm* (*occhiata*) look, glance;
(*espressione*) look (in one's eye); **dare uno**
~ **a qc** to glance at sth, cast a glance *o* an
eye over sth; **alzare** *o* **sollevare lo** ~ to
raise one's eyes, look up; **cercare qc/qn
con lo** ~ to look (a)round for sth/sb.

'sguattero, a *sm/f* scullery boy/maid.

sguaz'zare [zgwat'tsare] *vi* (*nell'acqua*) to

splash about; (*nella melma*) to wallow; ~
nell'oro to be rolling in money.

sguinzagli'are [zgwintsaʎ'ʎare] *vt* to let off
the leash; (*fig*: *persona*): ~ **qn dietro a qn**
to set sb on sb.

sgusci'are [zguʃ'ʃare] *vt* to shell ♦ *vi*
(*sfuggire di mano*) to slip; ~ **via** to slip *o*
slink away.

'shaker ['ʃeikə*] *sm inv* (cocktail) shaker.

'shampoo ['ʃampo] *sm inv* shampoo.

shoc'care [ʃok'kare] *vt* = **shockare**.

shock [ʃɔk] *sm inv* shock.

shoc'kare [ʃok'kare] *vt* to shock.

SI *sigla* = **Siena**.

══════════════ **PAROLA CHIAVE**

si (*dav lo, la, li, le, ne diventa* **se**) *pron* **1**
(*riflessivo*: *maschile*) himself; (: *femminile*)
herself; (: *neutro*) itself; (: *impersonale*)
oneself; (: *pl*) themselves; **lavarsi** to wash
(oneself); ~ **è tagliato** he has cut himself;
~ **credono importanti** they think a lot of
themselves

2 (*con complemento oggetto*): **lavarsi le
mani** to wash one's hands; **sporcarsi i
pantaloni** to get one's trousers dirty; ~
sta lavando i capelli he (*o* she) is washing
his (*o* her) hair

3 (*reciproco*) one another, each other; **si
amano** they love one another *o* each
other

4 (*passivo*): ~ **ripara facilmente** it is
easily repaired; **affittasi camera** room to
let

5 (*impersonale*): ~ **dice che ... they** *o*
people say that ...; ~ **vede che è vecchio**
one *o* you can see that it's old; **non** ~ **fa
credito** we do not give credit; **ci** ~ **sbaglia
facilmente** it's easy to make a mistake

6 (*noi*) we; **tra poco** ~ **parte** we're
leaving soon.

sì *av* yes ♦ *sm*: **non mi aspettavo un** ~ I
didn't expect him (*o* her *etc*) to say yes;
per me è ~ I should think so, I expect so;
saranno stati ~ **e no in 20** there must
have been about 20 of them; **uno** ~ **e uno
no** every other one; **un giorno** ~ **e uno no**
every other day; **dire di** ~ to say yes;
spero/penso di ~ I hope/think so; **fece di**
~ **col capo** he nodded (his head); **e** ~ **che**
... and to think that ....

'sia *cong*: ~ ... ~ (*o* ... *o*): ~ **che lavori,** ~ **che
non lavori** whether he works or not;
(*tanto ... quanto*): **verranno** ~ **Luigi** ~ **suo
fratello** both Luigi and his brother will be
coming.

'sia *etc vb vedi* **essere**.

SIAE *sigla f* = *Società Italiana Autori ed Editori.*
Si'am *sm:* **il** ~ Siam.
sia'mese *ag, sm/f* siamese *inv.*
si'amo *vb vedi* **essere.**
Si'beria *sf:* **la** ~ Siberia.
siberi'ano, a *ag, sm/f* Siberian.
sibi'lare *vi* to hiss; (*fischiare*) to whistle.
'sibilo *sm* hiss; whistle.
si'cario *sm* hired killer.
sicché [sik'ke] *cong* (*perciò*) so (that), therefore; (*e quindi*) (and) so.
siccità [sittʃi'ta] *sf* drought.
sic'come *cong* since, as.
Si'cilia [si'tʃilja] *sf:* **la** ~ Sicily.
sicili'ano, a [sitʃi'ljano] *ag, sm/f* Sicilian.
sico'moro *sm* sycamore.
'siculo, a *ag, sm/f* Sicilian.
si'cura *sf* (*di arma, spilla*) safety catch; (*di portiera*) safety lock.
sicura'mente *av* certainly.
sicu'rezza [siku'rettsa] *sf* safety, security; confidence; certainty; **di** ~ safety *cpd*; **la** ~ **stradale** road safety; **avere la** ~ **di qc** to be sure *o* certain of sth; **lo so con** ~ I am quite certain; **ha risposto con molta** ~ he answered very confidently.
si'curo, a *ag* safe; (*ben difeso*) secure; (*fiducioso*) confident; (*certo*) sure, certain; (*notizia, amico*) reliable; (*esperto*) skilled ♦ *av* (*anche:* **di** ~) certainly ♦ *sm:* **andare sul** ~ to play safe, **essere/mettere al** ~ to be safe/put in a safe place; ~ **di sé** self-confident, sure of o.s.; **sentirsi** ~ to feel safe *o* secure; **essere** ~ **di/che** to be sure of/that; **da fonte** ~**a** from reliable sources.
siderur'gia [siderur'dʒia] *sf* iron and steel industry.
side'rurgico, a, ci, che [side'rurdʒiko] *ag* iron and steel *cpd.*
'sidro *sm* cider.
si'edo *etc vb vedi* **sedere.**
si'epe *sf* hedge.
si'ero *sm* (*MED*) serum; ~ **antivipera** snake bite serum; ~ **del latte** whey.
sieronegatività *sf inv* HIV-negative status.
sieronega'tivo, a *ag* HIV-negative ♦ *sm/f* HIV-negative person.
sieropositività *sf inv* HIV-positive status.
sieroposi'tivo, a *ag* HIV-positive ♦ *sm/f* HIV-positive person.
si'erra *sf* (*GEO*) sierra.
Si'erra Le'one *sf:* **la** ~ Sierra Leone.
si'esta *sf* siesta, (afternoon) nap.
si'ete *vb vedi* **essere.**
si'filide *sf* syphilis.
si'fone *sm* siphon.

Sig. *abbr* (= *signore*) Mr.
siga'retta *sf* cigarette.
'sigaro *sm* cigar.
Sigg. *abbr* (= *signori*) Messrs.
sigil'lare [sidʒil'lare] *vt* to seal.
si'gillo [si'dʒillo] *sm* seal.
'sigla *sf* (*iniziali*) initials *pl*; (*abbreviazione*) acronym, abbreviation; ~ **automobilistica** *abbreviation of province on vehicle number plate*; ~ **musicale** signature tune.
si'glare *vt* to initial.
Sig.na *abbr* (= *signorina*) Miss.
signifi'care [siɲɲifi'kare] *vt* to mean; **cosa significa?** what does this mean?
significa'tivo, a [siɲɲifika'tivo] *ag* significant.
signifi'cato [siɲɲifi'kato] *sm* meaning.
si'gnora [siɲ'ɲora] *sf* lady; **la** ~ **X** Mrs ['mɪsɪz] X; **buon giorno S**~**/Signore/ Signorina** good morning; (*deferente*) good morning Madam/Sir/Madam; (*quando si conosce il nome*) good morning Mrs/Mr/ Miss X; **Gentile S**~**/Signore/Signorina** (*in una lettera*) Dear Madam/Sir/Madam; **Gentile** (*o Cara*) **S**~ **Rossi** Dear Mrs Rossi; **Gentile S**~ **Anna Rossi** (*sulle buste*) Mrs Anna Rossi; **il signor Rossi e** ~ Mr Rossi and his wife; ~**e e signori** ladies and gentlemen; **le presento la mia** ~ may I introduce my wife?
si'gnore [siɲ'ɲore] *sm* gentleman; (*padrone*) lord, master; (*REL*): **il S**~ the Lord; **il signor X** Mr ['mɪstə*] X; **signor Presidente** Mr Chairman; **Gentile** (*o Caro*) **Signor Rossi** (*in lettere*) Dear Mr Rossi; **Gentile Signor Paolo Rossi** (*sulle buste*) Mr Paolo Rossi; **i** ~**i Bianchi** (*coniugi*) Mr and Mrs Bianchi; *vedi anche* **signora.**
signo'ria [siɲɲo'ria] *sf* (*STORIA*) seignory, signoria; **S**~ **Vostra** (*S.V.*) (*AMM*) you.
signo'rile [siɲɲo'rile] *ag* refined.
signorilità [siɲɲorili'ta] *sf* (*raffinatezza*) refinement; (*eleganza*) elegance.
signo'rina [siɲɲo'rina] *sf* young lady; **la** ~ **X** Miss X; **Gentile** (*o Cara*) **S**~ **Rossi** (*in lettere*) Dear Miss Rossi; **Gentile S**~ **Anna Rossi** (*sulle buste*) Miss Anna Rossi; *vedi anche* **signora.**
signo'rino [siɲɲo'rino] *sm* young master.
Sig.ra *abbr* (= *signora*) Mrs.
silenzia'tore [silentsja'tore] *sm* silencer.
si'lenzio [si'lɛntsjo] *sm* silence; **fare** ~ to be quiet, stop talking; **far passare qc sotto** ~ to keep quiet about sth, hush sth up.
silenzi'oso, a [silen'tsjoso] *ag* silent, quiet.
'silice [silitʃe] *sf* silica.
si'licio [si'litʃo] *sm* silicon; **piastrina di** ~

silicon chip.
sili'cone *sm* silicone.
'sillaba *sf* syllable.
silu'rare *vt* to torpedo; (*fig: privare del comando*) to oust.
si'luro *sm* torpedo.
simbi'osi *sf* (*BIOL, fig*) symbiosis.
simboleggi'are [simboled'dʒare] *vt* to symbolize.
sim'bolico, a, ci, che *ag* symbolic(al).
simbo'lismo *sm* symbolism.
'simbolo *sm* symbol.
simi'lare *ag* similar.
'simile *ag* (*analogo*) similar; (*di questo tipo*): **un uomo ~** such a man, a man like this ♦ *sm* (*persona*) fellow man; **libri ~i** such books; **~ a** similar to; **non ho mai visto niente di ~** I've never seen anything like that; **è insegnante o qualcosa di ~** he's a teacher or something like that; **vendono vasi e ~i** they sell vases and things like that; **i suoi ~i** one's fellow men; one's peers.
simili'tudine *sf* (*LING*) simile.
simme'tria *sf* symmetry.
sim'metrico, a, ci, che *ag* symmetric(al).
simpa'tia *sf* (*qualità*) pleasantness; (*inclinazione*) liking; **avere ~ per qn** to like sb, have a liking for sb; **con ~** (*su lettera etc*) with much affection.
sim'patico, a, ci, che *ag* (*persona*) nice, pleasant, likeable; (*casa, albergo etc*) nice, pleasant.
simpatiz'zante [simpatid'dzante] *smf* sympathizer.
simpatiz'zare [simpatid'dzare] *vi:* **~ con** to take a liking to.
sim'posio *sm* symposium.
simu'lacro *sm* (*monumento, statua*) image; (*fig*) semblance.
simu'lare *vt* to sham, simulate; (*TECN*) to simulate.
simulazi'one [simulat'tsjone] *sf* shamming; simulation.
simul'taneo, a *ag* simultaneous.
sin. *abbr* (= *sinistra*) L.
sina'goga, ghe *sf* synagogue.
sincera'mente [sintʃera'mente] *av* (*gen*) sincerely; (*francamente*) honestly, sincerely.
since'rarsi [sintʃe'rarsi] *vr:* **~ (di qc)** to make sure (of sth).
sincerità [sintʃeri'ta] *sf* sincerity.
sin'cero, a [sin'tʃero] *ag* (*genuino*) sincere; (*onesto*) genuine.
'sincope *sf* syncopation; (*MED*) blackout.
sincro'nia *sf* (*di movimento*) synchronism.
sin'cronico, a, ci, che *ag* synchronic.

sincroniz'zare [sinkronid'dzare] *vt* to synchronize.
sinda'cale *ag* (trade-)union *cpd*.
sindaca'lista, i, e *smf* trade unionist.
sinda'care *vt* (*controllare*) to inspect; (*fig: criticare*) to criticize.
sinda'cato *sm* (*di lavoratori*) (trade) union; **~ dei datori di lavoro** employers' association.
'sindaco, ci *sm* mayor.
'sindrome *sf* (*MED*) syndrome.
siner'gia, gie [siner'dʒia] *sf* (*anche fig*) synergy.
sinfo'nia *sf* (*MUS*) symphony.
sin'fonico, a, ci, che *ag* symphonic; (*orchestra*) symphony *cpd*.
singa'lese *ag, smf, sm* Sin(g)halese *inv*.
Singa'pore *sf* Singapore.
singhioz'zare [singjot'tsare] *vi* to sob; to hiccup.
singhi'ozzo [sin'gjottso] *sm* (*di pianto*) sob; (*MED*) hiccup; **avere il ~** to have the hiccups; **a ~** (*fig*) by fits and starts.
singo'lare *ag* (*insolito*) remarkable, singular; (*LING*) singular ♦ *sm* (*LING*) singular; (*TENNIS*): **~ maschile/femminile** men's/women's singles.
singolar'mente *av* (*separatamente*) individually, one at a time; (*in modo strano*) strangely, peculiarly, oddly.
'singolo, a *ag* single, individual ♦ *sm* (*persona*) individual; (*TENNIS*) = **singolare**; **ogni ~ individuo** each individual; **camera ~a** a single room.
sinis'trato, a *ag* damaged ♦ *smf* disaster victim; **zona ~a** disaster area.
si'nistro, a *ag* left, left-hand; (*fig*) sinister ♦ *sm* (*incidente*) accident ♦ *sf* (*POL*) left (wing); **a ~a** on the left; (*direzione*) to the left; **a ~a di** to the left of; **di ~a** left-wing; **tenere la ~a** to keep to the left; **guida a ~a** left-hand drive.
'sino *prep* = **fino**.
si'nonimo, a *ag* synonymous ♦ *sm* synonym; **~ di** synonymous with.
sin'tassi *sf* syntax.
sin'tattico, a, ci, che *ag* syntactic.
'sintesi *sf* synthesis; (*riassunto*) summary, résumé; **in ~** in brief, in short.
sin'tetico, a, ci, che *ag* synthetic; (*conciso*) brief, concise.
sintetiz'zare [sintetid'dzare] *vt* to synthesize; (*riassumere*) to summarize.
sintetizza'tore [sintetiddza'tore] *sm* (*MUS*) synthesizer; **~ di voce** voice synthesizer.
sinto'matico, a, ci, che *ag* symptomatic.
'sintomo *sm* symptom.
sinto'nia *sf* (*RADIO*) tuning; **essere in ~ con**

qn (*fig*) to be on the same wavelength as sb.

sintoniz'zare [sintonid'dzare] *vt* to tune (in); ~**rsi** *vr*: ~**rsi su** to tune in to.

sintonizza'tore [sintoniddza'tore] *sm* tuner.

sinu'oso, a *ag* (*strada*) winding.

sinu'site *sf* sinusitis.

SIP *sigla f* (= *Società Italiana per l'esercizio telefonico*) *Italian telephone company.*

si'pario *sm* (*TEAT*) curtain.

si'rena *sf* (*apparecchio*) siren; (*nella mitologia, fig*) siren, mermaid; ~ **d'allarme** (*per incendio*) fire alarm; (*per furto*) burglar alarm.

'Siria *sf*: **la** ~ Syria.

siri'ano, a *ag, sm/f* Syrian.

si'ringa, ghe *sf* syringe.

'sisma, i *sm* earthquake.

'SISMI *sigla m* (= *Servizio per l'Informazione e la Sicurezza Militari*) *military security service.*

'sismico, a, ci, che *ag* seismic; (*zona*) earthquake *cpd*.

sis'mografo *sm* seismograph.

sissi'gnore [sissin'nore] *av* (*a un superiore*) yes, sir; (*enfatico*) yes indeed, of course.

sis'tema, i *sm* system; (*metodo*) method, way; **trovare il** ~ **per fare qc** to find a way to do sth; ~ **decimale/metrico** decimal/metric system; ~ **operativo** (*INFORM*) operating system; ~ **solare** solar system; ~ **di vita** way of life.

siste'mare *vt* (*mettere a posto*) to tidy, put in order; (*risolvere: questione*) to sort out, settle; (*procurare un lavoro a*) to find a job for; (*dare un alloggio a*) to settle, find accommodation (*BRIT*) *o* accommodations (*US*) for; ~**rsi** *vr* (*problema*) to be settled; (*persona: trovare alloggio*) to find accommodation(s); (: *trovarsi un lavoro*) to get fixed up with a job; **ti sistemo io!** I'll soon sort you out!; ~ **qn in un albergo** to fix sb up with a hotel.

sistematica'mente *av* systematically.

siste'matico, a, ci, che *ag* systematic.

sistemazi'one [sistemat'tsjone] *sf* arrangement, order; settlement; employment; accommodation (*BRIT*), accommodations (*US*).

'sito, a *ag* (*AMM*) situated ♦ *sm* (*letterario*) place; ~ **Internet** website.

situ'are *vt* to site, situate.

situ'ato, a *ag*: ~ **a/su** situated at/on.

situazi'one [situat'tsjone] *sf* situation; **vista la sua** ~ **familiare** given your family situation *o* circumstances; **nella sua** ~ in your position *o* situation; **mi trovo in una** ~ **critica** I'm in a very difficult position.

'skai ® *sm* Leatherette ®.

ski-lift [ski'lift] *sm inv* ski lift.

ski pass [ski'pɑːs] *sm inv* ski pass.

slacci'are [zlat'tʃare] *vt* to undo, unfasten.

slanci'arsi [zlan'tʃarsi] *vr* to dash, fling o.s.

slanci'ato, a [zlan'tʃato] *ag* slender.

'slancio ['zlantʃo] *sm* dash, leap; (*fig*) surge; **in uno** ~ **d'affetto** in a burst *o* rush of affection; **di** ~ impetuously.

sla'vato, a *ag* faded, washed out; (*fig: viso, occhi*) pale, colourless (*BRIT*), colorless (*US*).

sla'vina *sf* snowslide.

'slavo, a *ag* Slav(onic), Slavic.

sle'ale *ag* disloyal; (*concorrenza etc*) unfair.

slealtà *sf* disloyalty; unfairness.

sle'gare *vt* to untie.

slip *sm inv* (*mutandine*) briefs *pl*; (*da bagno: per uomo*) (swimming) trunks *pl*; (: *per donna*) bikini bottoms *pl*.

'slitta *sf* sledge; (*trainata*) sleigh.

slitta'mento *sm* slipping; skidding; postponement; ~ **salariale** wage drift.

slit'tare *vi* to slip, slide; (*AUT*) to skid; (*incontro, conferenza*) to be put off, be postponed.

s.l.m. *abbr* (= *sul livello del mare*) a.s.l.

slo'gare *vt* (*MED*) to dislocate; (: *caviglia, polso*) to sprain.

sloga'tura *sf* dislocation; sprain.

sloggi'are [zlod'dʒare] *vt* (*inquilino*) to turn out; (*nemico*) to drive out, dislodge ♦ *vi* to move out.

Slo'vacchia [zlo'vakkja] *sf* Slovakia.

slo'vacco, a, ci, che *ag, sm/f* Slovak, Slovakian; **la Repubblica S~a** the Slovak Republic.

Slo'venia *sf* Slovenia.

slo'veno, a *ag, sm/f* Slovene, Slovenian ♦ *sm* (*LING*) Slovene.

S.M. *abbr* (*MIL*) = **Stato Maggiore**; (= *Sua Maestà*) HM.

smac'cato, a *ag* (*fig*) excessive.

smacchi'are [zmak'kjare] *vt* to remove stains from.

smacchia'tore [zmakkja'tore] *sm* stain remover.

'smacco, chi *sm* humiliating defeat.

smagli'ante [zmaʎ'ʎante] *ag* brilliant, dazzling.

smagli'are [zmaʎ'ʎare] *vt*, ~**rsi** *vr* (*calza*) to ladder.

smaglia'tura [zmaʎʎa'tura] *sf* (*su maglia, calza*) ladder (*BRIT*), run; (*MED: sulla pelle*) stretch mark.

sma'grire *vt* to make thin ♦ *vi* to get *o* grow thin, lose weight.

sma'grito, a *ag*: **essere** ~ to have lost a lot

of weight.

smalizi'ato, a [smalit'tsjato] *ag* shrewd, cunning.

smal'tare *vt* to enamel; (*ceramica*) to glaze; (*unghie*) to varnish.

smalti'mento *sm* (*di rifiuti*) disposal.

smal'tire *vt* (*merce*) to sell off; (*rifiuti*) to dispose of; (*cibo*) to digest; (*peso*) to lose; (*rabbia*) to get over; ~ **la sbornia** to sober up.

'smalto *sm* (*anche di denti*) enamel; (*per ceramica*) glaze; ~ **per unghie** nail varnish.

smance'rie [zmantʃe'rie] *sfpl* mawkishness *sg*.

'smania *sf* agitation, restlessness; (*fig*): ~ **di** thirst for, craving for; **avere la** ~ **addosso** to have the fidgets; **avere la** ~ **di fare** to long *o* yearn to do.

smani'are *vi* (*agitarsi*) to be restless *o* agitated; (*fig*): ~ **di fare** to long *o* yearn to do.

smantella'mento *sm* dismantling.

smantel'lare *vt* to dismantle.

smar'carsi *vr* (*SPORT*) to get free of marking.

smargi'asso [zmar'dʒasso] *sm* show-off.

smarri'mento *sm* loss; (*fig*) bewilderment; dismay.

smar'rire *vt* to lose; (*non riuscire a trovare*) to mislay; ~**rsi** *vr* (*perdersi*) to lose one's way, get lost; (: *oggetto*) to go astray.

smar'rito, a *ag* (*oggetto*) lost; (*fig: confuso: persona*) bewildered, nonplussed; (: *sguardo*) bewildered; **ufficio oggetti** ~**i** lost property office (*BRIT*), lost and found (*US*).

smasche'rare [zmaske'rare] *vt* to unmask.

SME *abbr* = *Stato Maggiore Esercito* ♦ *sigla m* (= *Sistema Monetario Europeo*) EMS (= *European Monetary System*).

smem'brare *vt* (*gruppo, partito etc*) to split; ~**rsi** *vr* to split up.

smemo'rato, a *ag* forgetful.

smen'tire *vt* (*negare*) to deny; (*testimonianza*) to refute; (*reputazione*) to give the lie to; ~**rsi** *vr* to be inconsistent.

smen'tita *sf* denial; refutation.

sme'raldo *sm, ag inv* emerald.

smerci'are [zmer'tʃare] *vt* (*COMM*) to sell; (: *svendere*) to sell off.

'smercio ['zmɛrtʃo] *sm* sale; **avere poco/ molto** ~ to have poor/good sales.

smerigli'ato, a [zmeriʎ'ʎato] *ag*: **carta** ~**a** emery paper; **vetro** ~ frosted glass.

sme'riglio [zme'riʎʎo] *sm* emery.

'smesso, a *pp di* **smettere** ♦ *ag*: **abiti** *mpl* ~**i** cast-offs.

'smettere *vt* to stop; (*vestiti*) to stop wearing ♦ *vi* to stop, cease; ~ **di fare** to stop doing.

smidol'lato, a *ag* spineless ♦ *sm/f* spineless person.

smilitarizzazi'one [zmilitariddzat'tsjone] *sf* demilitarization.

'smilzo, a ['zmiltso] *ag* thin, lean.

sminu'ire *vt* to diminish, lessen; (*fig*) to belittle; ~ **l'importanza di qc** to play sth down.

sminuz'zare [zminut'tsare] *vt* to break into small pieces; to crumble.

'smisi *etc vb vedi* **smettere**.

smista'mento *sm* (*di posta*) sorting; (*FERR*) shunting.

smis'tare *vt* (*pacchi etc*) to sort; (*FERR*) to shunt.

smisu'rato, a *ag* boundless, immeasurable; (*grandissimo*) immense, enormous.

smitiz'zare [zmitid'dzare] *vt* to debunk.

smobili'tare *vt* to demobilize.

smobilitazi'one [zmobilitat'tsjone] *sf* demobilization.

smobi'lizzo [zmobi'liddzo] *sm* (*COMM*) disinvestment.

smo'dato, a *ag* excessive, unrestrained.

smode'rato, a *ag* immoderate.

smog [zmɔg] *sm inv* smog.

'smoking ['smoukiŋ] *sm inv* dinner jacket (*BRIT*), tuxedo (*US*).

smon'tare *vt* (*mobile, macchina etc*) to take to pieces, dismantle; (*fig: scoraggiare*) to dishearten ♦ *vi* (*scendere: da cavallo*) to dismount; (: *da treno*) to get off; (*terminare il lavoro*) to stop (work); ~**rsi** *vr* to lose heart; to lose one's enthusiasm.

'smorfia *sf* grimace; (*atteggiamento lezioso*) simpering; **fare** ~**e** to make faces; to simper.

smorfi'oso, a *ag* simpering.

'smorto, a *ag* (*viso*) pale, wan; (*colore*) dull.

smor'zare [zmor'tsare] *vt* (*suoni*) to deaden; (*colori*) to tone down; (*luce*) to dim; (*sete*) to quench; (*entusiasmo*) to dampen; ~**rsi** *vr* (*suono, luce*) to fade; (*entusiasmo*) to dampen.

'smosso, a *pp di* **smuovere**.

smotta'mento *sm* landslide.

'smunto, a *ag* haggard, pinched.

smu'overe *vt* to move, shift; (*fig: commuovere*) to move; (: *dall'inerzia*) to rouse, stir; ~**rsi** *vr* to move, shift.

smus'sare *vt* (*angolo*) to round off, smooth; (*lama etc*) to blunt; ~**rsi** *vr* to become blunt.

s.n. *abbr* = *senza numero*.

snatu'rato, a *ag* inhuman, heartless.

snazionaliz'zare [znattsjonalid'dzare] *vt* to denationalize.

snelli'mento *sm* (*di traffico*) speeding up; (*di procedura*) streamlining.

snel'lire *vt* (*persona*) to make slim; (*traffico*) to speed up; (*procedura*) to streamline; ~rsi *vr* (*persona*) to (get) slim; (*traffico*) to speed up.

'snello, a *ag* (*agile*) agile; (*svelto*) slender, slim.

sner'vante *ag* (*attesa, lavoro*) exasperating.

sner'vare *vt* to enervate, wear out; ~rsi *vr* to become enervated.

sni'dare *vt* to drive out, flush out.

snob'bare *vt* to snub.

sno'bismo *sm* snobbery.

snocclo'lare [znott∫o'lare] *vt* (*frutta*) to stone; (*fig: orazioni*) to rattle off; (*: verità*) to blab; (*: fam: soldi*) to shell out.

sno'dabile *ag* (*lampada*) adjustable; (*tubo, braccio*) hinged; rasoio con tootina swivel-head razor.

sno'dare *vt* to untie, undo; (*rendere agile, mobile*) to loosen; ~rsi *vr* to come loose; (*articolarsi*) to bend; (*strada, flume*) to wind

SO *sigla* = Sondrio.

so *vb vedi* sapere.

S.O. *abbr* (= *sudovest*) SW.

so'ave *ag* (*voce, maniera*) gentle; (*volto*) delicate, sweet; (*musica*) soft, sweet; (*profumo*) delicate.

soavità *sf* gentleness; delicacy; sweetness; softness.

sobbal'zare [sobbal'tsare] *vi* to jolt, jerk; (*trasalire*) to jump, start.

sob'balzo [sob'baltso] *sm* jerk, jolt; jump, start.

sobbar'carsi *vr*: ~ a to take on, undertake.

sob'borgo, ghi *sm* suburb.

sobil'lare *vt* to stir up, incite.

'sobrio, a *ag* sober.

Soc. *abbr* (= *società*) Soc.

socchi'udere [sok'kjudere] *vt* (*porta*) to leave ajar; (*occhi*) to half-close.

socchi'uso, a [sok'kjuso] *pp di* socchiudere ♦ *ag* (*porta, finestra*) ajar; (*occhi*) half-closed.

soc'combere *vi* to succumb, give way.

soc'correre *vt* to help, assist.

soccorri'tore, 'trice *sm/f* rescuer.

soc'corso, a *pp di* soccorrere ♦ *sm* help, aid, assistance; ~i *smpl* relief *sg*, aid *sg*; prestare ~ a qn to help *o* assist sb; venire in ~ di qn to help sb, come to sb's aid; operazioni di ~ rescue operations; ~ stradale breakdown service.

socialdemo'cratico, a, ci, che [sot∫aldemo'kratiko] *sm/f* Social Democrat.

soci'ale [so't∫ale] *ag* social; (*di associazione*) club *cpd*, association *cpd*.

socia'lismo [sot∫a'lizmo] *sm* socialism.

socia'lista, i, e [sot∫a'lista] *ag, sm/f* socialist.

socializ'zare [sot∫alid'dzare] *vi* to socialize.

società [sot∫e'ta] *sf inv* society; (*sportiva*) club; (*COMM*) company; in ~ con qn in partnership with sb; mettersi in ~ con qn to go into business with sb; l'alta ~ high society; ~ anonima (SA) ≈ limited (*BRIT*) *o* incorporated (*US*) company; ~ per azioni (S.p.A.) joint-stock company; ~ di comodo shell company; ~ fiduciaria trust company; ~ di mutuo soccorso friendly society (*BRIT*), benefit society (*US*); ~ a responsabilità limitata (S.r.l.) *type of* limited liability company.

soci'evole [so't∫evole] *ag* sociable.

socievo'lezza [sot∫evo'lettsa] *sf* sociableness.

'socio ['sot∫o] *sm* (*DIR, COMM*) partner; (*membro di associazione*) member.

sociolo'gia [sot∫olo'dʒia] *sf* sociology.

soci'ologo, a, gi, ghe [so't∫ologo] *sm/f* sociologist.

'soda *sf* (*CHIM*) soda; (*acqua gassata*) soda (water).

soda'lizio [soda'littsjo] *sm* association, society.

soddisfa'cente [soddisfa't∫ente] *ag* satisfactory.

soddis'fare *vt, vi*: ~ a to satisfy; (*impegno*) to fulfil; (*debito*) to pay off; (*richiesta*) to meet, comply with; (*offesa*) to make amends for.

soddis'fatto, a *pp di* soddisfare ♦ *ag* satisfied, pleased; essere ~ di to be satisfied *o* pleased with.

soddisfazi'one [soddisfat'tsjone] *sf* satisfaction.

'sodio *sm* (*CHIM*) sodium.

'sodo, a *ag* firm, hard ♦ *sm*: venire al ~ to come to the point ♦ *av* (*picchiare, lavorare*) hard; dormire ~ to sleep soundly.

sofà *sm inv* sofa.

soffe'renza [soffe'rentsa] *sf* suffering; (*COMM*): in ~ unpaid.

sof'ferto, a *pp di* soffrire ♦ *ag* (*vittoria*) hard-fought; (*distacco, decisione*) painful.

soffi'are *vt* to blow; (*notizia, segreto*) to whisper ♦ *vi* to blow; (*sbuffare*) to puff (and blow); ~rsi il naso to blow one's nose; ~ qc/qn a qn (*fig*) to pinch *o* steal sth/sb from sb; ~ via qc to blow sth away.

soffi'ata *sf* (*fam*) tip-off; fare una ~ alla

polizia to tip off the police.

'soffice ['sɔffitʃe] *ag* soft.

soffi'etto *sm* (*MUS*, *per fuoco*) bellows *pl*; porta a ~ folding door.

'soffio *sm* (*di vento*) breath; (*di fumo*) puff; (*MED*) murmur.

soffi'one *sm* (*BOT*) dandelion.

sof'fitta *sf* attic.

sof'fitto *sm* ceiling.

soffo'cante *ag* suffocating, stifling.

soffo'care *vi* (*anche:* ~rsi) to suffocate, choke ♦ *vt* to suffocate, choke; (*fig*) to stifle, suppress.

soffocazi'one [soffokat'tsjone] *sf* suffocation.

sof'friggere [sof'friddʒere] *vt* to fry lightly.

sof'frire *vt* to suffer, endure; (*sopportare*) to bear, stand ♦ *vi* to suffer; to be in pain; ~ (di) qc (*MED*) to suffer from sth.

sof'fritto, a *pp di* soffriggere ♦ *sm* (*CUC*) *fried mixture of herbs, bacon and onions.*

sof'fuso, a *ag* (*di luce*) suffused.

So'fia *sf* (*GEO*) Sofia.

sofisti'care *vt* (*vino*, *cibo*) to adulterate.

sofisti'cato, a *ag* sophisticated; (*vino*) adulterated.

sofisticazi'one [sofistikat'tsjone] *sf* adulteration.

'software ['sɔftwɛə] *sm*: ~ applicativo applications package.

sogget'tivo, a [soddʒet'tivo] *ag* subjective.

sog'getto, a [sod'dʒetto] *ag*: ~ a (*sottomesso*) subject to; (*esposto: a variazioni, danni etc*) subject *o* liable to ♦ *sm* subject; ~ a tassa taxable; recitare a ~ (*TEAT*) to improvise.

soggezi'one [soddʒet'tsjone] *sf* subjection; (*timidezza*) awe; avere ~ di qn to be ill at ease in sb's presence.

sogghi'gnare [soggiɲ'ɲare] *vi* to sneer.

sog'ghigno [sog'giɲɲo] *sm* sneer.

soggia'cere [soddʒa'tʃere] *vi*: ~ a to be subjected to.

soggio'gare [soddʒo'gare] *vt* to subdue, subjugate.

soggior'nare [soddʒor'nare] *vi* to stay.

soggi'orno [sod'dʒorno] *sm* (*invernale, marino*) stay; (*stanza*) living room.

soggi'ungere [sod'dʒundʒere] *vt* to add.

soggi'unto, a [sod'dʒunto] *pp di* soggiungere

'soglia ['sɔʎʎa] *sf* doorstep; (*anche fig*) threshold.

'sogliola ['sɔʎʎola] *sf* (*ZOOL*) sole.

so'gnante [soɲ'ɲante] *ag* dreamy.

so'gnare [soɲ'ɲare] *vt*, *vi* to dream; ~ a occhi aperti to daydream.

sogna'tore, 'trice [soɲɲa'tore] *sm/f*

dreamer.

'sogno ['soɲɲo] *sm* dream.

'soia *sf* (*BOT*) soya.

sol *sm* (*MUS*) G; (: *solfeggiando la scala*) so(h).

so'laio *sm* (*soffitta*) attic.

sola'mente *av* only, just.

so'lare *ag* solar, sun *cpd.*

sol'care *vt* (*terreno, fig: mari*) to plough (*BRIT*), plow (*US*).

'solco, chi *sm* (*scavo, fig: ruga*) furrow; (*incavo*) rut, track; (*di disco*) groove; (*scia*) wake.

sol'dato *sm* soldier; ~ di leva conscript; ~ semplice private.

'soldo *sm* (*fig*): non avere un ~ to be penniless; non vale un ~ it's not worth a penny; ~i *smpl* (*denaro*) money *sg.*

'sole *sm* sun; (*luce*) sun(light); (*tempo assolato*) sun(shine); prendere il ~ to sunbathe; il S~ che ride (*POL*) *symbol of the Italian Green party.*

soleggi'ato, a [soled'dʒato] *ag* sunny.

so'lenne *ag* solemn.

solennità *sf* solemnity; (*festività*) holiday, feast day.

so'lere *vt*: ~ fare qc to be in the habit of doing sth ♦ *vb impers*: come suole accadere as is usually the case, as usually happens; come si suol dire as they say.

so'lerte *ag* diligent.

so'lerzia [so'lɛrtsja] *sf* diligence.

so'letta *sf* (*per scarpe*) insole.

sol'fato *sm* sulphate (*BRIT*), sulfate (*US*).

sol'forico, a, ci, che *ag* sulphuric (*BRIT*), sulfuric (*US*); acido ~ sulphuric *o* sulfuric acid.

sol'furo *sm* sulphur (*BRIT*), sulfur (*US*).

soli'dale *ag* in agreement; essere ~ con qn (*essere d'accordo*) to be in agreement with sb; (*appoggiare*) to be behind sb.

solidarietà *sf* solidarity.

solidifi'care *vt*, *vi* (*anche:* ~rsi) to solidify.

solidità *sf* solidity.

'solido, a *ag* solid; (*forte, robusto*) sturdy, solid; (*fig: ditta*) sound, solid ♦ *sm* (*MAT*) solid.

soli'loquio *sm* soliloquy.

so'lista, i, e *ag* solo ♦ *sm/f* soloist.

solita'mente *av* usually, as a rule.

soli'tario, a *ag* (*senza compagnia*) solitary, lonely; (*solo, isolato*) solitary, lone; (*deserto*) lonely ♦ *sm* (*gioiello, gioco*) solitaire.

'solito, a *ag* usual; essere ~ fare to be in the habit of doing; di ~ usually; più tardi del ~ later than usual; come al ~ as usual; siamo alle ~e! (*fam*) here we go again!

soli'tudine *sf* solitude.

sollaz'zare [sollat'tsare] *vt* to entertain; ~**rsi** *vr* to amuse o.s.

sol'lazzo [sol'lattso] *sm* amusement.

solleci'tare [solletʃi'tare] *vt* (*lavoro*) to speed up; (*persona*) to urge on; (*chiedere con insistenza*) to press for, request urgently; (*stimolare*): ~ **qn a fare** to urge sb to do; (*TECN*) to stress.

sollecitazi'one [solletʃitat'tsjone] *sf* entreaty, request; (*fig*) incentive; (*TECN*) stress; **lettera di** ~ (*COMM*) reminder.

sol'lecito, a [sol'letʃito] *ag* prompt, quick ♦ *sm* (*COMM*) reminder; ~ **di pagamento** payment reminder.

solleci'tudine [solletʃi'tudine] *sf* promptness, speed.

solleti'care *vt* to tickle.

sol'letico *sm* tickling; **soffrire il** ~ to be ticklish.

solleva'mento *sm* raising; lifting; (*ribellione*) revolt; **pesi** (*sport*) weight-lifting.

solle'vare *vt* to lift, raise; (*fig: persona: alleggerire*): ~ (**da**) to relieve (of); (*: dar conforto*) to comfort, relieve; (*: questione*) to raise, (*: far insorgere*) to stir (to revolt); ~**rsi** *vr* to rise; (*fig: riprendersi*) to recover; (*: ribellarsi*) to rise up; ~**rsi da terra** (*persona*) to get up from the ground; (*aereo*) to take off; **sentirsi sollevato** to feel relieved.

solli'evo *sm* relief; (*conforto*) comfort; **con mio grande** ~ to my great relief.

'solo, a *ag* alone; (*in senso spirituale: isolato*) lonely; (*unico*): **un** ~ **libro** only one book, a single book; (*con ag numerale*): **veniamo noi tre** ~**i** just *o* only the three of us are coming ♦ *av* (*soltanto*) only, just; ~ **che** *cong* but; **è il** ~ **proprietario** he's the sole proprietor; **l'incontrò due** ~**e volte** he only met him twice; **non** ~ ... **ma anche** not only ... but also; **fare qc da** ~ to do sth (all) by oneself; **vive (da)** ~ he lives on his own; **possiamo vederci da** ~**i?** can I see you in private?

sol'stizio [sol'stittsjo] *sm* solstice.

sol'tanto *av* only.

so'lubile *ag* (*sostanza*) soluble; **caffè** ~ instant coffee.

soluzi'one [solut'tsjone] *sf* solution; **senza** ~ **di continuità** uninterruptedly.

sol'vente *ag, sm* solvent; ~ **per unghie** nail polish remover; ~ **per vernici** paint remover.

sol'venza [sol'vɛntsa] *sf* (*COMM*) solvency.

'soma *sf* load, burden; **bestia da** ~ beast of burden.

So'malia *sf*: **la** ~ Somalia.

'somalo, a *ag, sm/f, sm* Somali.

so'maro *sm* ass, donkey.

so'matico, a, ci, che *ag* somatic.

somigli'anza [somiʎ'ʎantsa] *sf* resemblance.

somigli'are [somiʎ'ʎare] *vi*: ~ **a** to be like, resemble; (*nell'aspetto fisico*) to look like; ~**rsi** *vr* to be (*o* look) alike.

'somma *sf* (*MAT*) sum; (*di denaro*) sum (of money); (*complesso di varie cose*) whole amount, sum total; **tirare le** ~**e** (*fig*) to sum up; **tirate le** ~**e** (*fig*) all things considered.

som'mare *vt* to add up; (*aggiungere*) to add; **tutto sommato** all things considered.

som'mario, a *ag* (*racconto, indagine*) brief; (*giustizia*) summary ♦ *sm* summary.

som'mergere [som'mɛrdʒere] *vt* to submerge.

sommer'gibile [sommer'dʒibile] *sm* submarine.

som'merso, a *pp di* **sommergere**.

som'messo, a *ag* (*voce*) soft, subdued.

somminis'trare *vt* to give, administer.

sommità *sf inv* summit, top; (*fig*) height.

'sommo, a *ag* highest; (*rispetto*) highest, greatest; (*poeta, artista*) great, outstanding ♦ *sm* (*fig*) height; **per** ~**i capi** in short, in brief.

som'mossa *sf* uprising.

sommozza'tore [sommottsa'tore] *sm* (deep-sea) diver; (*MIL*) frogman.

so'naglio [so'naʎʎo] *sm* (*di mucche etc*) bell; (*per bambini*) rattle.

so'nante *ag*: **denaro** *o* **moneta** ~ (ready) cash.

so'nare *etc* = **suonare** *etc*.

'sonda *sf* (*MED, METEOR, AER*) probe; (*MINERALOGIA*) drill ♦ *ag inv*: **pallone** *m* ~ weather balloon.

son'daggio [son'daddʒo] *sm* sounding; probe; boring, drilling; (*indagine*) survey; ~ **d'opinioni** opinion poll.

son'dare *vt* (*NAUT*) to sound; (*atmosfera, piaga*) to probe; (*MINERALOGIA*) to bore, drill; (*fig: opinione etc*) to survey, poll.

so'netto *sm* sonnet.

son'nambulo, a *sm/f* sleepwalker.

sonnecchi'are [sonnek'kjare] *vi* to doze, nod.

sonnel'lino *sm* nap.

son'nifero *sm* sleeping drug (*o* pill).

'sonno *sm* sleep; **aver** ~ to be sleepy; **prendere** ~ to fall asleep.

sonno'lento, a *ag* sleepy, drowsy;

(*movimenti*) sluggish.
sonno'lenza [sonno'lɛntsa] *sf* sleepiness, drowsiness.
'sono *vb vedi* **essere.**
sonoriz'zare [sonorid'dzare] *vt* (*LING*) to voice; (*CINE*) to add a sound-track to.
so'noro, a *ag* (*ambiente*) resonant; (*voce*) sonorous, ringing; (*onde, film*) sound *cpd* ♦ *sm*: **il ~** (*CINE*) the talkies *pl.*
sontu'oso, a *ag* sumptuous.
so'pire *vt* (*fig: dolore, tensione*) to soothe.
so'pore *sm* drowsiness.
sopo'rifero, a *ag* soporific.
soppe'rire *vi*: **~ a** to provide for; **~ alla mancanza di qc** to make up for the lack of sth.
soppe'sare *vt* to weigh in one's hand(s), feel the weight of; (*fig*) to weigh up.
soppian'tare *vt* to supplant.
soppi'atto *av*: **di ~** secretly; furtively.
soppor'tabile *ag* tolerable, bearable.
soppor'tare *vt* (*reggere*) to support; (*subire: perdita, spese*) to bear, sustain; (*soffrire: dolore*) to bear, endure; (*sog: cosa: freddo*) to withstand; (: *persona: freddo, vino*) to take; (*tollerare*) to put up with, tolerate.
sopportazi'one [sopportat'tsjone] *sf* patience; **avere spirito di ~, avere capacità di ~** to be long-suffering.
soppressi'one *sf* abolition; withdrawal; suppression; deletion; elimination, liquidation.
sop'presso, a *pp di* **sopprimere.**
sop'primere *vt* (*carica, privilegi etc*) to abolish, do away with; (*servizio*) to withdraw; (*pubblicazione*) to suppress; (*parola, frase*) to delete; (*uccidere*) to eliminate, liquidate.
'sopra *prep* (*gen*) on; (*al di sopra di, più in alto di*) above; over; (*riguardo a*) on, about ♦ *av* on top; (*attaccato, scritto*) on it; (*al di sopra*) above; (*al piano superiore*) upstairs; **donne ~ i 30 anni** women over 30 (years of age); **100 metri ~ il livello del mare** 100 metres above sea level; **5 gradi ~ lo zero** 5 degrees above zero; **abito di ~** I live upstairs; **essere al di ~ di ogni sospetto** to be above suspicion; **per i motivi ~ illustrati** for the above-mentioned reasons, for the reasons shown above; **dormirci ~** (*fig*) to sleep on it; **passar ~ a qc** (*anche fig*) to pass over sth.
so'prabito *sm* overcoat.
sopraccen'nato, a [sopratt'ʃen'nato] *ag* above-mentioned.
soprac'ciglio [soprat'tʃiʎʎo], *pl*(*f*) **soprac'ciglia** *sm* eyebrow.
sopracco'perta *sf* (*di letto*) bedspread; (*di*

libro) jacket.
soprad'detto, a *ag* aforesaid.
sopraf'fare *vt* to overcome, overwhelm.
sopraf'fatto, a *pp di* **sopraffare.**
sopraffazi'one [sopraffat'tsjone] *sf* overwhelming, overpowering.
sopraf'fino, a *ag* (*pranzo, vino*) excellent; (*fig*) masterly.
sopraggi'ungere [soprad'dʒundʒere] *vi* (*giungere all'improvviso*) to arrive (unexpectedly); (*accadere*) to occur (unexpectedly).
sopraggi'unto, a [soprad'dʒunto] *pp di* **sopraggiungere.**
soprallu'ogo, ghi *sm* (*di esperti*) inspection; (*di polizia*) on-the-spot investigation.
sopram'mobile *sm* ornament.
soprannatu'rale *ag* supernatural.
sopran'nome *sm* nickname.
soprannomi'nare *vt* to nickname.
sopran'numero *av*: **in ~** in excess.
so'prano, a *sm/f* (*persona*) soprano ♦ *sm* (*voce*) soprano.
soprappensi'ero *av* lost in thought.
soprappiù *sm* surplus, extra; **in ~** extra, surplus; (*per giunta*) besides, in addition.
sopras'salto *sm*: **di ~** with a start, with a jump.
soprasse'dere *vi*: **~ a** to delay, put off.
soprat'tassa *sf* surtax.
soprat'tutto *av* (*anzitutto*) above all; (*specialmente*) especially.
sopravvalu'tare *vt* (*persona, capacità*) to overestimate.
sopravve'nire *vi* to arrive, appear; (*fatto*) to occur.
soprav'vento *sm*: **avere/prendere il ~ su qn** to have/get the upper hand over sb.
sopravvis'suto, a *pp di* **sopravvivere** ♦ *sm/f* survivor.
sopravvi'venza [sopravvi'vɛntsa] *sf* survival.
soprav'vivere *vi* to survive; (*continuare a vivere*): **~ (in)** to live on (in); **~ a** (*incidente etc*) to survive; (*persona*) to outlive.
soprele'vata *sf* (*di strada, ferrovia*) elevated section.
soprinten'dente *sm/f* supervisor; (*statale: di belle arti etc*) keeper.
soprinten'denza [soprinten'dɛntsa] *sf* supervision; (*ente*): **~ alle Belle Arti** government department responsible for monuments and artistic treasures.
soprin'tendere *vi*: **~ a** to superintend, supervise.
soprin'teso, a *pp di* **soprintendere.**
so'pruso *sm* abuse of power; **subire un ~**

to be abused.

soq'quadro *sm*: **mettere a** ~ **to** turn upside-down.

sor'betto *sm* sorbet, water ice (*BRIT*).

sor'bire *vt* to sip; (*fig*) to put up with.

'sorcio ['sortʃo] *sm* mouse.

'sordido, a *ag* sordid; (*fig: gretto*) stingy.

sor'dina *sf*: **in** ~ softly; (*fig*) on the sly.

sordità *sf* deafness.

'sordo, a *ag* deaf; (*rumore*) muffled; (*dolore*) dull; (*lotta*) silent, hidden; (*odio, rancore*) veiled ♦ *sm/f* deaf person.

sordo'muto, a *ag* deaf-and-dumb ♦ *sm/f* deaf-mute.

so'rella *sf* sister.

sorel'lastra *sf* stepsister.

sor'gente [sor'dʒɛnte] *sf* (*acqua che sgorga*) spring; (*di fiume, FISICA, fig*) source; **acqua di** ~ spring water; ~ **di calore** source of heat; ~ **termale** thermal spring.

'sorgere ['sordʒere] *vi* to rise; (*scaturire*) to spring, rise; (*fig: difficoltà*) to arise ♦ *sm*: **al ~ del sole** at sunrise.

sori'ano, a *ag, sm/f* tabby.

sormon'tare *vt* (*fig*) to overcome, surmount.

sorni'one, a *ag* sly.

sorpas'sare *vt* (*AUT*) to overtake; (*fig*) to surpass; (: *eccedere*) to exceed, go beyond; ~ **in altezza** to be higher than; (*persona*) to be taller than.

sorpas'sato, a *ag* (*metodo, moda*) outmoded, old-fashioned; (*macchina*) obsolete.

sor'passo *sm* (*AUT*) overtaking.

sorpren'dente *ag* surprising; (*eccezionale, inaspettato*) astonishing, amazing.

sor'prendere *vt* (*cogliere: in flagrante etc*) to catch; (*stupire*) to surprise; ~**rsi** *vr*: ~**rsi (di)** to be surprised (at).

sor'preso, a *pp di* **sorprendere** ♦ *sf* surprise; **fare una** ~**a a qn** to give sb a surprise; **prendere qn di** ~**a** to take sb by surprise *o* unawares.

sor'reggere [sor'reddʒere] *vt* to support, hold up; (*fig*) to sustain.

sor'retto, a *pp di* **sorreggere**.

sor'ridere *vi* to smile.

sor'riso, a *pp di* **sorridere** ♦ *sm* smile.

sor'sata *sf* gulp; **bere a** ~**e** to gulp.

sorseggi'are [sorsed'dʒare] *vt* to sip.

'sorsi *etc vb vedi* **sorgere**.

'sorso *sm* sip; **d'un** ~, **in un** ~ **solo** at one gulp.

'sorta *sf* sort, kind; **di** ~ whatever, of any kind at all; **ogni** ~ **di** all sorts of; **di ogni** ~ of every kind.

'sorte *sf* (*fato*) fate, destiny; (*evento fortuito*)

chance; **tirare a** ~ to draw lots; **tentare la** ~ to try one's luck.

sorteggi'are [sorted'dʒare] *vt* to draw for.

sor'teggio [sor'teddʒo] *sm* draw.

sorti'legio [sorti'lɛdʒo] *sm* witchcraft *no pl*; (*incantesimo*) spell; **fare un** ~ **a qn** to cast a spell on sb.

sor'tire *vt* (*ottenere*) to produce.

sor'tita *sf* (*MIL*) sortie.

'sorto, a *pp di* **sorgere**.

sorvegli'ante [sorveʎ'ʎante] *sm/f* (*di carcere*) guard, warder (*BRIT*); (*di fabbrica etc*) supervisor.

sorvegli'anza [sorveʎ'ʎantsa] *sf* watch; supervision; (*POLIZIA, MIL*) surveillance.

sorvegli'are [sorveʎ'ʎare] *vt* (*bambino, bagagli, prigioniero*) to watch, keep an eye on; (*malato*) to watch over; (*territorio, casa*) to watch *o* keep watch over; (*lavori*) to supervise.

sorvo'lare *vt* (*territorio*) to fly over ♦ *vi*: ~ **su** (*fig*) to skim over.

S.O.S. *sigla m* mayday, SOS.

'sosia *sm inv* double.

sos'pendere *vt* (*appendere*) to hang (up); (*interrompere, privare di una carica*) to suspend; (*rimandare*) to defer; ~ **un quadro al muro/un lampadario al soffitto** to hang a picture on the wall/a chandelier from the ceiling; ~ **qn dal suo incarico** to suspend sb from office.

sospensi'one *sf* (*anche CHIM, AUT*) suspension; deferment; ~ **condizionale della pena** (*DIR*) suspended sentence.

sos'peso, a *pp di* **sospendere** ♦ *ag* (*appeso*): ~ **a** a hanging on (*o* from); (*treno, autobus*) cancelled; **in** ~ in abeyance; (*conto*) outstanding; **tenere in** ~ (*fig*) to keep in suspense; **col fiato** ~ with bated breath.

sospet'tare *vt* to suspect ♦ *vi*: ~ **di** to suspect; (*diffidare*) to be suspicious of.

sos'petto, a *ag* suspicious ♦ *sm* suspicion; **destare** ~**i** to arouse suspicion.

sospet'toso, a *ag* suspicious.

sos'pingere [sos'pindʒere] *vt* to drive, push.

sos'pinto, a *pp di* **sospingere**.

sospi'rare *vi* to sigh ♦ *vt* to long for, yearn for.

sos'piro *sm* sigh; ~ **di sollievo** sigh of relief.

'sosta *sf* (*fermata*) stop, halt; (*pausa*) pause, break; **senza** ~ non-stop, without a break.

sostanti'vato, a *ag* (*LING*): **aggettivo** ~ adjective used as a noun.

sostan'tivo *sm* noun, substantive.

sos'tanza [sos'tantsa] *sf* substance; ~**e** *sfpl*

(*ricchezze*) wealth *sg*, possessions; **in** ~ in short, to sum up; **la** ~ **del discorso** the essence of the speech.

sostanzi'ale [sostan'tsjale] *ag* substantial.

sostanzi'oso, a [sostan'tsjoso] *ag* (*cibo*) nourishing, substantial.

sos'tare *vi* (*fermarsi*) to stop (for a while), stay; (*fare una pausa*) to take a break.

sos'tegno [sos'teɲɲo] *sm* support; **a** ~ **di** in support of; **muro di** ~ supporting wall.

soste'nere *vt* to support; (*prendere su di sé*) to take on, bear; (*resistere*) to withstand, stand up to; (*affermare*): ~ **che** to maintain that; ~**rsi** *vr* to hold o.s. up, support o.s.; (*fig*) to keep up one's strength; ~ **qn** (*moralmente*) to be a support to sb; (*difendere*) to stand up for sb, take sb's part; ~ **gli esami** to sit exams; ~ **il confronto** to bear *o* stand comparison.

soste'nibile *ag* (*tesi*) tenable; (*spese*) bearable; (*sviluppo*) sustainable.

sosteni'tore, 'trice *sm/f* supporter.

sostenta'mento *sm* maintenance, support; **mezzi di** ~ means of support.

soste'nuto, a *ag* (*stile*) elevated; (*velocità, ritmo*) sustained; (*prezzo*) high ♦ *sm/f*: **fare il(la)** ~**(a)** to be standoffish, keep one's distance.

sostitu'ire *vt* (*mettere al posto di*): ~ **qn/qc a** to substitute sb/sth for; (*prendere il posto di*) to replace, take the place of.

sostitu'tivo, a *ag* (*AMM*: *documento, certificato*) equivalent.

sosti'tuto, a *sm/f* substitute; ~ **procuratore della Repubblica** (*DIR*) deputy public prosecutor.

sostituzi'one [sostitut'tsjone] *sf* substitution; **in** ~ **di** as a substitute for, in place of.

sotta'ceti [sotta'tʃeti] *smpl* pickles.

sot'tana *sf* (*sottoveste*) underskirt; (*gonna*) skirt; (*REL*) soutane, cassock.

sot'tecchi [sot'tekki] *av*: **guardare di** ~ **to** steal a glance at.

sotter'fugio [sotter'fudʒo] *sm* subterfuge.

sotter'raneo, a *ag* underground ♦ *sm* cellar.

sotter'rare *vt* to bury.

sottigli'ezza [sottiʎ'ʎettsa] *sf* thinness; slimness; (*fig*: *acutezza*) subtlety; shrewdness; ~**e** *sfpl* (*pedanteria*) quibbles.

sot'tile *ag* thin; (*figura, caviglia*) thin, slim, slender; (*fine*: *polvere, capelli*) fine; (*fig*: *leggero*) light; (: *vista*) sharp, keen; (: *olfatto*) fine, discriminating; (: *mente*) subtle; shrewd ♦ *sm*: **non andare per il** ~ not to mince matters.

sottiliz'zare [sottilid'dzare] *vi* to split hairs.

sottin'tendere *vt* (*intendere qc non espresso*) to understand; (*implicare*) to imply; **lasciare** ~ **che** to let it be understood that.

sottin'teso, a *pp di* **sottintendere** ♦ *sm* allusion; **parlare senza** ~**i** to speak plainly.

'sotto *prep* (*gen*) under; (*più in basso di*) below ♦ *av* underneath, beneath; below; (*al piano inferiore*): (**al piano**) **di** ~ downstairs; ~ **il monte** at the foot of the mountain; ~ **la pioggia/il sole** in the rain/sun(shine); **tutti quelli** ~ **i 18 anni** all those under 18 (years of age) (*BRIT*) *o* under age 18 (*US*); ~ **il livello del mare** below sea level; ~ **il chilo** under *o* less than a kilo; **ha 5 impiegati** ~ **di sé** he has 5 clerks under him; **siamo** ~ **Natale/Pasqua** it's nearly Christmas/Easter; ~ **un certo punto di vista** in a sense; ~ **forma di** in the form of; ~ **falso nome** under a false name; ~ **terra** underground; ~ **voce** in a low voice; **chiuso** ~ **vuoto** vacuum packed.

sotto'banco *av* (*di nascosto*: *vendere, comprare*) under the counter; (*agire*) in an underhand way.

sottobicchi'ere [sottobik'kjɛre] *sm* mat, coaster.

sotto'bosco, schi *sm* undergrowth *no pl*.

sotto'braccio [sotto'brattʃo] *av* by the arm; **prendere qn** ~ to take sb by the arm; **camminare** ~ **a qn** to walk arm in arm with sb.

sottochi'ave [sotto'kjave] *av* under lock and key.

sottoco'perta *av* (*NAUT*) below deck.

sotto'costo *av* below cost (price).

sottocu'taneo, a *ag* subcutaneous.

sottoes'posto, a *ag* (*fotografia, pellicola*) underexposed.

sotto'fondo *sm* background; ~ **musicale** background music.

sotto'gamba *av*: **prendere qc** ~ not to take sth seriously.

sotto'gonna *sf* underskirt.

sottogo'verno *sm* political patronage.

sotto'gruppo *sm* subgroup; (*di partito*) faction.

sottoline'are *vt* to underline; (*fig*) to emphasize, stress.

sot't'olio *av, ag inv* in oil.

sotto'mano *av* (*a portata di mano*) within reach, to hand; (*di nascosto*) secretly.

sottoma'rino, a *ag* (*flora*) submarine; (*cavo, navigazione*) underwater ♦ *sm* (*NAUT*) submarine.

sotto'messo, a *pp di* **sottomettere** ♦ *ag* submissive.
sotto'mettere *vt* to subdue, subjugate; **~rsi** *vr* to submit.
sottomissi'one *sf* submission.
sottopas'saggio [sottopas'saddʒo] *sm* (*AUT*) underpass; (*pedonale*) subway, underpass.
sotto'porre *vt* (*costringere*) to subject; (*fig*: *presentare*) to submit; **sottoporsi** *vr* to submit; **sottoporsi a** (*subire*) to undergo.
sotto'posto, a *pp di* **sottoporre**.
sottopro'dotto *sm* by-product.
sottoproduzi'one [sottoprodut'tsjone] *sf* underproduction.
sottoproletari'ato *sm*: **il ~** the underprivileged class.
sot'tordine *av*: **passare in ~** to become of minor importance.
sottos'cala *sm inv* (*ripostiglio*) cupboard (*BRIT*) *o* closet (*US*) under the stairs; (*stanza*) room under the stairs.
sottos'critto, a *pp di* **sottoscrivere** ♦ *sm/f*: **io ~, il ~** the undersigned.
sottos'crivere *vt* to sign ♦ *vi*: **~ a** to subscribe to.
sottoscrizi'one [sottoskrit'tsjone] *sf* signing; subscription.
sottosegre'tario *sm*: **S~ di Stato** undersecretary of state (*BRIT*), assistant secretary of state (*US*).
sotto'sopra *av* upside-down.
sottos'tante *ag* (*piani*) lower; **nella valle ~** in the valley below.
sottos'tare *vi*: **~ a** (*assoggettarsi a*) to submit to; (: *richieste*) to give in to; (*subire*: *prova*) to undergo.
sottosu'olo *sm* subsoil.
sottosvilup'pato, a *ag* underdeveloped.
sottosvi'luppo *sm* underdevelopment.
sottote'nente *sm* (*MIL*) second lieutenant.
sotto'terra *av* underground.
sotto'tetto *sm* attic.
sotto'titolo *sm* subtitle.
sottovalu'tare *vt* (*persona, prova*) to underestimate, underrate.
sotto'vento *av* (*NAUT*) leeward(s) ♦ *ag inv* (*lato*) leeward, lee.
sotto'veste *sf* underskirt.
sotto'voce [sotto'votʃe] *av* in a low voice.
sottovu'oto *av*: **confezionare ~** to vacuum-pack ♦ *ag*: **confezione *f* ~** vacuum pack.
sot'trarre *vt* (*MAT*) to subtract, take away; **sottrarsi** *vr*: **sottrarsi a** (*sfuggire*) to escape; (*evitare*) to avoid; **~ qn/qc a** (*togliere*) to remove sb/sth from; (*salvare*) to save *o* rescue sb/sth from; **~ qc a qn**

(*rubare*) to steal sth from sb; **sottratte le spese** once expenses have been deducted.
sot'tratto, a *pp di* **sottrarre**.
sottrazi'one [sottrat'tsjone] *sf* (*MAT*) subtraction; (*furto*) removal.
sottuffici'ale [sottuffi'tʃale] *sm* (*MIL*) non-commissioned officer; (*NAUT*) petty officer.
soufflé [su'fle] *sm inv* (*CUC*) soufflé.
souve'nir [suv(ə)'nir] *sm inv* souvenir.
so'vente *av* often.
soverchi'are [sover'kjare] *vt* to overpower, overwhelm.
soverchie'ria [soverkje'ria] *sf* (*prepotenza*) abuse (of power).
sovi'etico, a, ci, che *ag* Soviet ♦ *sm/f* Soviet citizen.
sovrabbon'dante *ag* overabundant.
sovrabbon'danza [sovrabbon'dantsa] *sf* overabundance; **in ~** in eccess.
sovraccari'care *vt* to overload.
sovrac'carico, a, chi, che *ag*: **~ (di)** overloaded (with) ♦ *sm* excess load, **~ di lavoro** extra work.
sovraesposizi'one [sovraespozit'tsjone] *sf* (*FOT*) overexposure.
sovraffol'lato, a *ag* overcrowded.
sovraimmagazzi'nare [sovraimmagaddzi-'nare] *vt* to overstock.
sovranità *sf* sovereignty; (*fig*: *superiorità*) supremacy.
sovrannatu'rale *ag* = **soprannaturale**.
so'vrano, a *ag* sovereign; (*fig*: *sommo*) supreme ♦ *sm/f* sovereign, monarch.
sovrappopolazi'one [sovrappopolat'tsjone] *sf* overpopulation.
sovrap'porre *vt* to place on top of, put on top of; (*FOT, GEOM*) to superimpose; **sovrapporsi** *vr* (*fig*: *aggiungersi*) to be added; (*FOT*) to be superimposed.
sovrapposizi'one [sovrapposit'tsjone] *sf* superimposition.
sovrap'posto, a *pp di* **sovrapporre**.
sovrapproduzi'one [sovrapprodut'tsjone] *sf* overproduction.
sovras'tante *ag* overhanging; (*fig*) imminent.
sovras'tare *vi*: **~ a** *vt* (*vallata, fiume*) to overhang; (*fig*) to hang over, threaten.
sovrastrut'tura *sf* superstructure.
sovrecci'tare [sovrettʃi'tare] *vt* to overexcite.
sovrimpressi'one *sf* (*FOT, CINE*) double exposure; **immagini in ~** superimposed images.
sovrinten'dente *etc* = **soprintendente** *etc*.

sovru'mano, a *ag* superhuman.

sovve'nire *vi* (*venire in mente*): ~ **a** to occur to.

sovvenzio'nare [sovventsjo'nare] *vt* to subsidize.

sovvenzi'one [sovven'tsjone] *sf* subsidy, grant.

sovver'sivo, a *ag* subversive.

sovverti'mento *sm* subversion, undermining.

sovver'tire *vt* (*POL: ordine, stato*) to subvert, undermine.

'sozzo, a ['sottso] *ag* filthy, dirty.

SP *sigla* = *La Spezia.*

S.P. *abbr* = **strada provinciale;** *vedi* **provinciale.**

S.p.A. *abbr vedi* **società per azioni.**

spac'care *vt* to split, break; (*legna*) to chop; (*fig*) to divide; **~rsi** *vr* to split, break.

spacca'tura *sf* split.

spaccherò [spakke'rɔ] *etc vb vedi* **spaccare.**

spacci'are [spat'tʃare] *vt* (*vendere*) to sell (off); (*mettere in circolazione*) to circulate; (*droga*) to peddle, push; **~rsi** *vr*: **~rsi per** (*farsi credere*) to pass o.s. off as, pretend to be.

spacci'ato, a [spat'tʃato] *ag* (*fam: malato, fuggiasco*): **essere ~** to be done for.

spaccia'tore, 'trice [spattʃa'tore] *sm/f* (*di droga*) pusher; (*di denaro falso*) dealer.

'spaccio ['spattʃo] *sm* (*di merce rubata, droga*): ~ **(di)** trafficking (in); (*di denaro falso*): ~ **(di)** passing (of); (*vendita*) sale; (*bottega*) shop.

'spacco, chi *sm* (*fenditura*) split, crack; (*strappo*) tear; (*di gonna*) slit.

spac'cone *sm/f* boaster, braggart.

'spada *sf* sword.

spadroneggi'are [spadroned'dʒare] *vi* to swagger.

spae'sato, a *ag* disorientated, lost.

spaghet'tata [spaget'tata] *sf* spaghetti meal.

spa'ghetti [spa'getti] *smpl* (*CUC*) spaghetti *sg*.

'Spagna ['spaɲɲa] *sf*: **la ~** Spain.

spa'gnolo, a [spaɲ'ɲɔlo] *ag* Spanish ♦ *sm/f* Spaniard ♦ *sm* (*LING*) Spanish; **gli S~i** the Spanish.

'spago, ghi *sm* string, twine; **dare ~ a qn** (*fig*) to let sb have his (*o* her) way.

spai'ato, a *ag* (*calza, guanto*) odd.

spalan'care *vt*, **~rsi** *vr* to open wide.

spa'lare *vt* to shovel.

'spalla *sf* shoulder; (*fig: TEAT*) stooge; **~e** *sfpl* (*dorso*) back; **di ~e** from behind; **seduto alle mie ~e** sitting behind me; **prendere/colpire qn alle ~e** to take/hit sb from behind; **mettere qn con le ~e al muro** (*fig*) to put sb with his (*o* her) back to the wall; **vivere alle ~e di qn** (*fig*) to live off sb.

spal'lata *sf* (*urto*) shove *o* push with the shoulder; **dare una ~ a qc** to give sth a push *o* shove with one's shoulder.

spalleggi'are [spalled'dʒare] *vt* to back up, support.

spal'letta *sf* (*parapetto*) parapet.

spalli'era *sf* (*di sedia etc*) back; (*di letto: da capo*) head(board); (: *da piedi*) foot(board); (*GINNASTICA*) wall bars *pl.*

spal'lina *sf* (*MIL*) epaulette; (*di sottoveste, maglietta*) strap; **senza ~e** strapless.

spal'mare *vt* to spread.

'spalti *smpl* (*di stadio*) terraces (*BRIT*), ≈ bleachers (*US*).

'spandere *vt* to spread; (*versare*) to pour (out); **~rsi** *vr* to spread; **~ lacrime** to shed tears.

'spanto, a *pp di* **spandere.**

spa'rare *vt* to fire ♦ *vi* (*far fuoco*) to fire; (*tirare*) to shoot; ~ **a qn/qc** to shoot sb/sth, fire at sb/sth.

spa'rato *sm* (*di camicia*) dicky.

spara'tore *sm* gunman.

spara'toria *sf* exchange of shots.

sparecchi'are [sparek'kjare] *vt*: ~ **(la tavola)** to clear the table.

spa'reggio [spa'reddʒo] *sm* (*SPORT*) play-off.

'spargere ['spardʒere] *vt* (*sparpagliare*) to scatter; (*versare: vino*) to spill; (: *lacrime, sangue*) to shed; (*diffondere*) to spread; (*emanare*) to give off (*o* out); **~rsi** *vr* (*voce, notizia*) to spread; (*persone*) to scatter; **si è sparsa una voce sul suo conto** there is a rumour going round about him.

spargi'mento [spardʒi'mento] *sm* scattering; spilling; shedding; ~ **di sangue** bloodshed.

spa'rire *vi* to disappear, vanish; ~ **dalla circolazione** (*fig fam*) to lie low, keep a low profile.

sparizi'one [sparit'tsjone] *sf* disappearance.

spar'lare *vi*: ~ **di** to run down, speak ill of.

'sparo *sm* shot.

sparpagli'are [sparpaʎ'ʎare] *vt*, **~rsi** *vr* to scatter.

'sparso, a *pp di* **spargere** ♦ *ag* scattered; (*sciolto*) loose; **in ordine ~** (*MIL*) in open order.

sparti'acque *sm* (*GEO*) watershed.

sparti'neve *sm inv* snowplough (*BRIT*), snowplow (*US*).

spar'tire *vt* (*eredità, bottino*) to share out;

(*avversari*) to separate.
spar'tito *sm* (*MUS*) score.
sparti'traffico *sm inv* (*AUT*) central reservation (*BRIT*), median (strip) (*US*).
spartizi'one [spartit'tsjone] *sf* division.
spa'ruto, a *ag* (*viso etc*) haggard.
sparvi'ero *sm* (*ZOOL*) sparrowhawk.
spasi'mante *sm* suitor.
spasi'mare *vi* to be in agony; ~ **di fare** (*fig*) to yearn to do; ~ **per qn** to be madly in love with sb.
'spasimo *sm* pang.
'spasmo *sm* (*MED*) spasm.
spas'modico, a, ci, che *ag* (*angoscioso*) agonizing; (*MED*) spasmodic.
spas'sarsela *vi* to enjoy o.s., have a good time.
spassio'nato, a *ag* dispassionate, impartial.
'spasso *sm* (*divertimento*) amusement, enjoyment; **andare a** ~ to go out for a walk; **essere a** ~ (*fig*) to be out of work; **mandare qn a** ~ (*fig*) to give sb the sack.
spas'soso, a *ag* amusing, entertaining.
'spastico, a, ci, che *ag, sm/f* spastic.
'spatola *sf* spatula.
spau'racchio [spau'rakkjo] *sm* scarecrow.
spau'rire *vt* to frighten, terrify.
spavalde'ria *sf* boldness, arrogance.
spa'valdo, a *ag* arrogant, bold.
spaventa'passeri *sm inv* scarecrow.
spaven'tare *vt* to frighten, scare; ~**rsi** *vr* to become frightened, become scared.
spa'vento *sm* fear, fright; **far** ~ **a qn** to give sb a fright.
spaven'toso, a *ag* frightening, terrible; (*fig fam*) tremendous, fantastic.
spazi'ale [spat'tsjale] *ag* (*volo, nave, tuta*) space *cpd*; (*ARCHIT, GEOM*) spatial.
spazia'tura [spattsja'tura] *sf* (*TIP*) spacing.
spazien'tire [spattsjen'tire] *vi* (*anche*: ~**rsi**) to lose one's patience.
'spazio ['spattsjo] *sm* space; (*posto*) room, space; **fare** ~ **per qc/qn** to make room for sth/sb; **nello** ~ **di un'ora** within an hour, in the space of an hour; **dare** ~ **a** (*fig*) to make room for; ~ **aereo** airspace.
spazi'oso, a [spat'tsjoso] *ag* spacious.
spazzaca'mino [spattsaka'mino] *sm* chimney sweep.
spazza'neve [spattsa'neve] *sm inv* (*spartineve, SCI*) snowplough (*BRIT*), snowplow (*US*).
spaz'zare [spat'tsare] *vt* to sweep; (*foglie etc*) to sweep up; (*cacciare*) to sweep away.
spazza'tura [spattsa'tura] *sf* sweepings *pl*; (*immondizia*) rubbish.

spaz'zino [spat'tsino] *sm* street sweeper.
'spazzola ['spattsola] *sf* brush; **capelli a** ~ crew cut *sg*; ~ **per abiti** clothesbrush; ~ **da capelli** hairbrush.
spazzo'lare [spattso'lare] *vt* to brush.
spazzo'lino [spattso'lino] *sm* (*small*) brush; ~ **da denti** toothbrush.
specchi'arsi [spek'kjarsi] *vr* to look at o.s. in a mirror; (*riflettersi*) to be mirrored, be reflected.
specchi'era [spek'kjɛra] *sf* large mirror; (*mobile*) dressing table.
specchi'etto [spek'kjetto] *sm* (*tabella*) table, chart; ~ **da borsetta** pocket mirror; ~ **retrovisore** (*AUT*) rear-view mirror.
'specchio ['spekkjo] *sm* mirror; (*tabella*) table, chart; **uno** ~ **d'acqua** a sheet of water.
speci'ale [spe'tʃale] *ag* special; **in special modo** especially; **inviato** ~ (*RADIO, TV, STAMPA*) special correspondent; **offerta** ~ special offer; **poteri/leggi** ~**i** (*POL*) emegency powers/legislation.
specia'lista, i, e [spetʃa'lista] *sm/f* specialist.
specia'listico, a, ci, che [spetʃa'listiko] *ag* (*conoscenza, preparazione*) specialized.
specialità [spetʃali'ta] *sf inv* speciality; (*branca di studio*) special field, speciality.
specializ'zare [spetʃalid'dzare] *vt* (*industria*) to make more specialized; ~**rsi** *vr*: ~**rsi** (**in**) to specialize (in).
specializ'zato, a [spetʃalid'dzato] *ag* (*manodopera*) skilled; **operaio non** ~ semiskilled worker; **essere** ~ **in** to be a specialist in.
specializzazi'one [spetʃaliddzat'tsjone] *sf* specialization; **prendere la** ~ **in** to specialize in.
special'mente [spetʃal'mente] *av* especially, particularly.
'specie ['spɛtʃe] *sf inv* (*BIOL, BOT, ZOOL*) species *inv*; (*tipo*) kind, sort ♦ *av* especially, particularly; **una** ~ **di** a kind of; **fare** ~ **a qn** to surprise sb; **la** ~ **umana** mankind.
spe'cifica, che [spe'tʃifika] *sf* specification.
specifi'care [spetʃifi'kare] *vt* to specify, state.
specificata'mente [spetʃifikata'mente] *av* in detail.
spe'cifico, a, ci, che [spe'tʃifiko] *ag* specific.
speck [ʃpɛk] *sm inv* kind of smoked ham.
specu'lare *vi*: ~ **su** (*COMM*) to speculate in; (*sfruttare*) to exploit; (*meditare*) to speculate on.

specula'tore, 'trice *sm/f* (*COMM*) speculator.

speculazi'one [spekulat'tsjone] *sf* speculation.

spe'dire *vt* to send; (*COMM*) to dispatch, forward; ~ **per posta** to post (*BRIT*), mail (*US*); ~ **per mare** to ship.

spedita'mente *av* quickly; **camminare** ~ to walk at a brisk pace.

spe'dito, a *ag* (*gen*) quick; **con passo** ~ at a brisk pace.

spedizi'one [spedit'tsjone] *sf* sending; (*collo*) consignment; (*scientifica etc*) expedition; (*COMM*) forwarding; shipping; **fare una** ~ to send a consignment; **agenzia di** ~ forwarding agency; **spese di** ~ postal charges; (*COMM*) forwarding charges.

spedizioni'ere [spedittsjo'njɛre] *sm* forwarding agent, shipping agent.

'spegnere ['spɛɲɲere] *vt* (*fuoco, sigaretta*) to put out, extinguish; (*apparecchio elettrico*) to turn *o* switch off; (*gas*) to turn off; (*fig: suoni, passioni*) to stifle; (*debito*) to extinguish; ~**rsi** *vr* to go out; to go off; (*morire*) to pass away.

speleolo'gia [speleolo'dʒia] *sf* (*studio*) speleology; (*pratica*) potholing (*BRIT*), speleology.

spele'ologo, a, gi, ghe *sm/f* speleologist; potholer.

spel'lare *vt* (*scuoiare*) to skin; (*scorticare*) to graze; ~**rsi** *vr* to peel.

spendacci'one, a [spendat'tʃone] *sm/f* spendthrift.

'spendere *vt* to spend; ~ **una buona parola per qn** (*fig*) to put in a good word for sb.

'spengo *etc vb vedi* **spegnere.**

spen'nare *vt* to pluck.

'spensi *etc vb vedi* **spegnere.**

spensiera'tezza [spensjera'tettsa] *sf* carefreeness, lightheartedness.

spensie'rato, a *ag* carefree.

'spento, a *pp di* **spegnere** ♦ *ag* (*suono*) muffled; (*colore*) dull; (*sigaretta*) out; (*civiltà, vulcano*) extinct.

spe'ranza [spe'rantsa] *sf* hope; **nella** ~ **di rivederti** hoping to see *o* in the hope of seeing you again; **pieno di** ~**e** hopeful; **senza** ~ (*situazione*) hopeless; (*amare*) without hope.

speran'zoso, a [speran'tsoso] *ag* hopeful.

spe'rare *vt* to hope for ♦ *vi:* ~ **in** to trust in; ~ **che/di fare** to hope that/to do; **lo spero, spero di sì** I hope so; **tutto fa** ~ **per il meglio** everything leads one to hope for the best.

sper'duto, a *ag* (*isolato*) out-of-the-way;

(*persona*: smarrita, a disagio) lost.

spergi'uro, a [sper'dʒuro] *sm/f* perjurer ♦ *sm* perjury.

sperico'lato, a *ag* fearless, daring; (*guidatore*) reckless.

sperimen'tale *ag* experimental; **fare qc in via** ~ to try sth out.

sperimen'tare *vt* to experiment with, test; (*fig*) to test, put to the test.

sperimentazi'one [sperimentat'tsjone] *sf* experimentation.

'sperma, i *sm* (*BIOL*) sperm.

spermato'zoo, i [spermatod'dzɔo] *sm* spermatozoon.

spe'rone *sm* spur.

sperpe'rare *vt* to squander.

'sperpero *sm* (*di denaro*) squandering, waste; (*di cibo, materiali*) waste.

'spesa *sf* (*soldi spesi*) expense; (*costo*) cost; (*acquisto*) purchase; (*fam: acquisto del cibo quotidiano*) shopping; ~**e** *sfpl* expenses; (*COMM*) costs; charges; **ridurre le** ~**e** (*gen*) to cut down; (*COMM*) to reduce expenditure; **fare la** ~ to do the shopping; **fare le** ~**e di qc** (*fig*) to pay the price for sth; **a** ~**e di** (*a carico di*) at the expense of; **con la modica** ~ **di un milione di lire** for the modest sum *o* outlay of one million lire; ~ **pubblica** public expenditure; ~**e accessorie** incidental expenses; ~**e generali** overheads; ~**e di gestione** operating expenses; ~**e d'impianto** initial outlay; ~**e legali** legal costs; ~**e di manutenzione**, ~**e di mantenimento** maintenance costs; ~**e postali** postage *sg*; ~**e di sbarco e sdoganamento** landing charges; ~**e di trasporto** handling charge; ~**e di viaggio** travelling (*BRIT*) *o* traveling (*US*) expenses.

spe'sare *vt:* **viaggio tutto spesato** all-expenses-paid trip.

'speso, a *pp di* **spendere.**

'spesso, a *ag* (*fitto*) thick; (*frequente*) frequent ♦ *av* often; ~**e volte** frequently, often.

spes'sore *sm* thickness; **ha uno** ~ **di 20 cm** it is 20 cm thick.

Spett. *abbr vedi* **spettabile.**

spet'tabile *ag* (*abbr:* **Spett.**: *in lettere*): ~ **ditta X** Messrs X and Co; **avvertiamo la** ~ **clientela** ... we inform our customers ....

spettaco'lare *ag* spectacular.

spet'tacolo *sm* (*rappresentazione*) performance, show; (*vista, scena*) sight; **dare** ~ **di sé** to make an exhibition *o* a spectacle of o.s.

spettaco'loso, a *ag* spectacular.

spet'tanza [spet'tantsa] *sf* (*competenza*)

concern; **non è di mia** ~ it's no concern of mine.

spet'tare *vi*: ~ **a** (*decisione*) to be up to; (*stipendio*) to be due to; **spetta a lei decidere** it's up to you to decide.

spetta'tore, 'trice *sm/f* (*CINE, TEAT*) member of the audience; (*di avvenimento*) onlooker, witness.

spettego'lare *vi* to gossip.

spetti'nare *vt*: ~ **qn** to ruffle sb's hair; ~**rsi** *vr* to get one's hair in a mess.

spet'trale *ag* spectral, ghostly.

'spettro *sm* (*fantasma*) spectre (*BRIT*), specter (*US*); (*FISICA*) spectrum.

'spezie ['spɛttsje] *sfpl* (*CUC*) spices.

spez'zare [spet'tsare] *vt* (*rompere*) to break; (*fig: interrompere*) to break up; ~**rsi** *vr* to break.

spezza'tino [spettsa'tino] *sm* (*CUC*) stew.

spez'zato, a [spet'tsato] *ag* (*unghia, ramo, braccio*) broken ♦ *sm* (*abito maschile*) coordinated jacket and trousers (*BRIT*) *o* pants (*US*); **fare orarlo** ~ to work a split shift.

spezzet'tare [spettset'tare] *vt* to break up (*o* chop) into small pieces.

spez'zino, a [spet'tsino] *ag* of (*o* from) La Spezia.

spez'zone [spet'tsone] *sm* (*CINE*) clip.

'spia *sf* spy; (*confidente della polizia*) informer; (*ELETTR*) indicating light; warning light; (*fessura*) peephole; (*fig: sintomo*) sign, indication; ~ **dell'olio** (*AUT*) oil warning light.

spiacci'care [spjattʃi'kare] *vt* to squash, crush.

spia'cente [spja'tʃɛnte] *ag* sorry; **essere ~ di qc/di fare qc** to be sorry about sth/for doing sth; **siamo ~i di dovervi annunciare che** ... we regret to announce that ....

spia'cevole [spja'tʃevole] *ag* unpleasant, disagreeable.

spi'aggia, ge ['spjaddʒa] *sf* beach.

spia'nare *vt* (*terreno*) to level, make level; (*edificio*) to raze to the ground; (*pasta*) to roll out; (*rendere liscio*) to smooth (out).

spi'ano *sm*: **a tutto** ~ (*lavorare*) non-stop, without a break; (*spendere*) lavishly.

spian'tato, a *ag* penniless, ruined.

spi'are *vt* to spy on; (*occasione etc*) to watch *o* wait for.

spi'ata *sf* tip-off.

spiattel'lare *vt* (*fam: verità, segreto*) to blurt out.

spi'azzo ['spjattso] *sm* open space; (*radura*) clearing.

spic'care *vt* (*assegno, mandato di cattura*) to issue ♦ *vi* (*risaltare*) to stand out; ~ **il volo** to fly off; (*fig*) to spread one's wings; ~ **un balzo** to jump, leap.

spic'cato, a *ag* (*marcato*) marked, strong; (*notevole*) remarkable.

spiccherò *etc* [spikke'rɔ] *vb vedi* **spiccare**.

'spicchio ['spikkjo] *sm* (*di agrumi*) segment; (*di aglio*) clove; (*parte*) piece, slice.

spicci'are [spit'tʃare] *vt* (*faccenda, impegno*) to finish off; ~**rsi** *vr* (*fare in fretta*) to hurry up, get a move on.

'spiccio, a, ci, ce ['spittʃo] *ag* (*modi, mezzi*) quick; **andare per le** ~**ce** to be quick off the mark, waste no time.

spiccio'lata [spittʃo'lata] *av*: **alla** ~ in dribs and drabs, a few at a time.

'spicciolo, a ['spittʃolo] *ag*: **moneta** ~**a**, ~**i** *smpl* (small) change.

'spicco, chi *sm*: **fare** ~ to stand out; **di** ~ outstanding, prominent; (*tema*) main, principal.

spie'dino *sm* (*utensile*) skewer, (*cibo*) kebab.

spi'edo *sm* (*CUC*) spit; **pollo allo** ~ spit-roasted chicken.

spiega'mento *sm* (*MIL*): ~ **di forze** deployment of forces.

spie'gare *vt* (*far capire*) to explain; (*tovaglia*) to unfold; (*vele*) to unfurl; ~**rsi** *vr* to explain o.s., make o.s. clear; ~ **qc a qn** to explain sth to sb; **il problema si spiega** one can understand the problem; **non mi spiego come** ... I can't understand how ....

spiegazi'one [spjegat'tsjone] *sf* explanation; **avere una** ~ **con qn** to have it out with sb.

spiegaz'zare [spjegat'tsare] *vt* to crease, crumple.

spiegherò *etc* [spjege'rɔ] *vb vedi* **spiegare**.

spie'tato, a *ag* ruthless, pitiless.

spiffe'rare *vt* (*fam*) to blurt out, blab.

'spiffero *sm* draught (*BRIT*), draft (*US*).

'spiga, ghe *sf* (*BOT*) ear.

spigli'ato, a [spiʎ'ʎato] *ag* self-possessed, self-confident.

spigo'lare *vt* (*anche fig*) to glean.

'spigolo *sm* corner; (*GEOM*) edge.

spigo'loso, a *ag* (*mobile*) angular; (*persona, carattere*) difficult.

'spilla *sf* brooch; (*da cravatta, cappello*) pin.

spil'lare *vt* (*vino, fig*) to tap; ~ **denaro/ notizie a qn** to tap sb for money/ information.

'spillo *sm* pin; (*spilla*) brooch; **tacco a** ~ stiletto heel (*BRIT*), spike heel (*US*); ~ **di sicurezza** *o* **da balia** safety pin; ~ **di sicurezza** (*MIL*) (safety) pin.

spilorce'ria [spilort'ʃe'ria] *sf* meanness,

stinginess.

spi'lorcio, a, ci, ce [spi'lortʃo] *ag* mean, stingy.

spilun'gone *sm/f* beanpole.

'spina *sf* (*BOT*) thorn; (*ZOOL*) spine, prickle; (*di pesce*) bone; (*ELETTR*) plug; (*di botte*) bunghole; **birra alla** ~ draught beer; **stare sulle** ~**e** (*fig*) to be on tenterhooks; ~ **dorsale** (*ANAT*) backbone.

spi'nacio [spi'natʃo] *sm* spinach *no pl*; (*CUC*): ~**i** spinach *sg*.

spi'nale *ag* (*ANAT*) spinal.

spi'nato, a *ag* (*fornito di spine*): **filo** ~ barbed wire; (*tessuto*) herringbone *cpd*.

spi'nello *sm* (*DROGA*: *gergo*) joint.

'spingere ['spindʒere] *vt* to push; (*condurre*: *anche fig*) to drive; (*stimolare*): ~ **qn a fare** to urge *o* press sb to do; ~**rsi** *vr* (*inoltrarsi*) to push on, carry on; ~**rsi troppo lontano** (*anche fig*) to go too far.

'spino *sm* (*BOT*) thorn bush.

spi'noso, a *ag* thorny, prickly.

'spinsi *etc vb vedi* **spingere**.

spinte'rogeno [spinte'rodʒeno] *sm* (*AUT*) coil ignition.

'spinto, a *pp di* **spingere** ♦ *sf* (*urto*) push; (*FISICA*) thrust; (*fig*: *stimolo*) incentive, spur; (: *appoggio*) string-pulling *no pl*; **dare una** ~**a a qn** (*fig*) to pull strings for sb.

spinto'nare *vt* to shove, push.

spin'tone *sm* push, shove.

spio'naggio [spio'naddʒo] *sm* espionage, spying.

spion'cino [spion'tʃino] *sm* peephole.

spi'one, a *sm/f* (*spia*) informer; (*ragazzino, collega*) telltale, sneak.

spio'nistico, a, ci, che *ag* (*organizzazione*) spy *cpd*; **rete** ~**a** spy ring.

spi'overe *vi* (*scorrere*) to flow down; (*ricadere*) to hang down, fall.

'spira *sf* coil.

spi'raglio [spi'raʎʎo] *sm* (*fessura*) chink, narrow opening; (*raggio di luce, fig*) glimmer, gleam.

spi'rale *sf* spiral; (*contraccettivo*) coil; **a** ~ spiral(-shaped); ~ **inflazionistica** inflationary spiral.

spi'rare *vi* (*vento*) to blow; (*morire*) to expire, pass away.

spiri'tato, a *ag* possessed; (*fig*: *persona, espressione*) wild.

spiri'tismo *sm* spiritualism.

'spirito *sm* (*REL, CHIM, disposizione d'animo, di legge etc, fantasma*) spirit; (*pensieri, intelletto*) mind; (*arguzia*) wit; (*umorismo*) humour, wit; **in buone condizioni di** ~ in the right frame of mind; **è una persona di** ~ he has a sense of humour (*BRIT*) *o*

humor (*US*); **battuta di** ~ joke; ~ **di classe** class consciousness; **non ha** ~ **di parte** he never takes sides; **lo S**~ **Santo** the Holy Spirit *o* Ghost.

spirito'saggine [spirito'saddʒine] *sf* witticism; (*peg*) wisecrack.

spiri'toso, a *ag* witty.

spiritu'ale *ag* spiritual.

splen'dente *ag* (*giornata*) bright, sunny; (*occhi*) shining; (*pavimento*) shining, gleaming.

'splendere *vi* to shine.

'splendido, a *ag* splendid; (*splendente*) shining; (*sfarzoso*) magnificent, splendid.

splen'dore *sm* splendour (*BRIT*), splendor (*US*); (*luce intensa*) brilliance, brightness.

spodes'tare *vt* to deprive of power; (*sovrano*) to depose.

'spoglia ['spoʎʎa] *sf vedi* **spoglio**.

spogli'are [spoʎ'ʎare] *vt* (*svestire*) to undress; (*privare, fig*: *depredare*): ~ **qn di qc** to deprive sb of sth; (*togliere ornamenti: anche fig*): ~ **qn/qc di** to strip sb/sth of; ~**rsi** *vr* to undress, strip; ~**rsi di** (*ricchezze etc*) to deprive o.s. of, give up; (*pregiudizi*) to rid o.s. of.

spoglia'rello [spoʎʎa'rɛllo] *sm* striptease.

spoglia'toio [spoʎʎa'tojo] *sm* dressing room; (*di scuola etc*) cloakroom; (*SPORT*) changing room.

'spoglio, a ['spoʎʎo] *ag* (*pianta, terreno*) bare; (*privo*): ~ **di** stripped of; lacking in, without ♦ *sm* (*di voti*) counting ♦ *sf* (*ZOOL*) skin, hide; (: *di rettile*) slough; ~**e** *sfpl* (*salma*) remains; (*preda*) spoils, booty *sg*.

'spola *sf* shuttle; (*bobina*) spool; **fare la** ~ (**fra**) to go to and fro *o* shuttle (between).

spo'letta *sf* (*CUCITO*: *bobina*) spool; (*di bomba*) fuse.

spol'pare *vt* to strip the flesh off.

spolve'rare *vt* (*anche CUC*) to dust; (*con spazzola*) to brush; (*con battipanni*) to beat; (*fig*: *mangiare*) to polish off ♦ *vi* to dust.

spolve'rino *sm* (*soprabito*) dust coat.

'sponda *sf* (*di fiume*) bank; (*di mare, lago*) shore; (*bordo*) edge.

sponsoriz'zare [sponsorid'dzare] *vt* to sponsor.

sponsorizzazi'one [sponsoriddzat'tsjone] *sf* sponsorship.

spontanea'mente *av* (*comportarsi*) naturally; (*agire*) spontaneously; (*reagire*) instinctively, spontaneously.

spon'taneo, a *ag* spontaneous; (*persona*) unaffected, natural; **di sua** ~**a volontà** of his own free will.

spopo'lare *vt* to depopulate ♦ *vi* (*attirare folla*) to draw the crowds; ~**rsi** *vr* to become depopulated.

spo'radico, a, ci, che *ag* sporadic.

sporcacci'one, a [sporkat'tʃone] *sm/f* (*peg*) pig, filthy person.

spor'care *vt* to dirty, make dirty; (*fig*) to sully, soil; ~**rsi** *vr* to get dirty.

spor'cizia [spor'tʃittsja] *sf* (*stato*) dirtiness; (*sudiciume*) dirt, filth; (*fig: cosa oscena*) obscenity.

'sporco, a, chi, che *ag* dirty, filthy; **avere la coscienza** ~**a** to have a guilty conscience.

spor'genza [spor'dʒɛntsa] *sf* projection.

'sporgere ['spɔrdʒere] *vt* to put out, stretch out ♦ *vi* (*venire in fuori*) to stick out; ~**rsi** *vr* to lean out; ~ **querela contro qn** (*DIR*) to take legal action against sb.

'sporsi *etc vb vedi* **sporgere**.

sport *sm inv* sport.

'sporta *sf* shopping bag.

spor'tello *sm* (*di treno, auto etc*) door; (*di banca, ufficio*) window, counter; ~ **automatico** (*BANCA*) cash dispenser, automated telling machine.

spor'tivo, a *ag* (*gara, giornale*) sports *cpd*; (*persona*) sporty; (*abito*) casual; (*spirito, atteggiamento*) sporting ♦ *sm/f* sportsman/ woman; **campo** ~ playing field; **giacca** ~**a** sports (*BRIT*) *o* sport (*US*) jacket.

'sporto, a *pp di* **sporgere**.

'sposa *sf* bride; (*moglie*) wife; **abito** *o* **vestito da** ~ wedding dress.

sposa'lizio [spoza'littsjo] *sm* wedding.

spo'sare *vt* to marry; (*fig: idea, fede*) to espouse; ~**rsi** *vr* to get married, marry; ~**rsi con qn** to marry sb, get married to sb.

spo'sato, a *ag* married.

'sposo *sm* (bride)groom; (*marito*) husband; **gli** ~**i** the newlyweds.

spos'sante *ag* exhausting.

spossa'tezza [spossa'tettsa] *sf* exhaustion.

spos'sato, a *ag* exhausted, weary.

sposta'mento *sm* movement, change of position.

spos'tare *vt* to move, shift; (*cambiare: orario*) to change; ~**rsi** *vr* to move; **hanno spostato la partenza di qualche giorno** they postponed *o* put off their departure by a few days.

spot [spɔt] *sm inv* (*faretto*) spotlight, spot; (*TV*) advert, commercial, ad.

'spranga, ghe *sf* (*sbarra*) bar; (*catenaccio*) bolt.

spran'gare *vt* to bar; to bolt.

spray ['sprai] *sm inv* (*dispositivo, sostanza*) spray ♦ *ag inv* (*bombola, confezione*) spray *cpd*.

'sprazzo ['sprattso] *sm* (*di sole etc*) flash; (*fig: di gioia etc*) burst.

spre'care *vt* to waste; ~**rsi** *vr* (*persona*) to waste one's energy.

'spreco, chi *sm* waste.

spre'gevole [spre'dʒevole] *ag* contemptible, despicable.

'spregio ['spredʒo] *sm* scorn, disdain.

spregiudi'cato, a [spredʒudi'kato] *ag* unprejudiced, unbiased; (*peg*) unscrupulous.

'spremere *vt* to squeeze; ~**rsi le meningi** (*fig*) to rack one's brains.

spre'muta *sf* fresh fruit juice; ~ **d'arancia** fresh orange juice.

sprez'zante [spret'tsante] *ag* scornful, contemptuous.

'sprezzo ['sprettso] *sm* contempt, scorn, disdain.

sprigio'nare [spridʒo'nare] *vt* to give off, emit; ~**rsi** *vr to* emanato; (*uscire con impeto*) to burst out.

spriz'zare [sprit'tsare] *vt, vi* to spurt; ~ **gioia/salute** to be bursting with joy/ health.

sprofon'dare *vi* to sink; (*casa*) to collapse; (*suolo*) to give way, subside; ~**rsi** *vr*: ~**rsi in** (*poltrona*) to sink into; (*fig*) to become immersed *o* absorbed in.

sproloqui'are *vi* to ramble on.

spro'loquio *sm* rambling speech.

spro'nare *vt* to spur (on).

'sprone *sm* (*sperone, fig*) spur.

sproporzio'nato, a [sproportsjo'nato] *ag* disproportionate, out of all proportion.

sproporzi'one [spropor'tsjone] *sf* disproportion.

sproposi'tato, a *ag* (*lettera, discorso*) full of mistakes; (*fig: costo*) excessive, enormous.

spro'posito *sm* blunder; **a** ~ at the wrong time; (*rispondere, parlare*) irrelevantly.

sprovve'duto, a *ag* inexperienced, naïve.

sprov'visto, a *ag* (*mancante*): ~ **di** lacking in, without; **ne siamo** ~**i** (*negozio*) we are out of it (*o* them); **alla** ~**a** unawares.

spruz'zare [sprut'tsare] *vt* (*a nebulizzazione*) to spray; (*aspergere*) to sprinkle; (*inzaccherare*) to splash.

spruzza'tore [spruttsa'tore] *sm* (*per profumi*) spray, atomizer; (*per biancheria*) sprinkler, spray.

'spruzzo ['spruttso] *sm* spray; splash; **verniciatura a** ~ spray painting.

spudora'tezza [spudora'tettsa] *sf* shamelessness.

spudo'rato, a *ag* shameless.

'spugna ['spuɲɲa] *sf* (*ZOOL*) sponge;

(*tessuto*) towelling.

spu'gnoso, a [spuɲ'ɲoso] *ag* spongy.

spulci'are [spul'tʃare] *vt* (*animali*) to rid of fleas; (*fig*: *testo, compito*) to examine thoroughly.

'spuma *sf* (*schiuma*) foam; (*bibita*) fizzy drink.

spu'mante *sm* sparkling wine.

spumeggi'ante [spumed'dʒante] *ag* (*vino, fig*) sparkling; (*birra, mare*) foaming.

spu'mone *sm* (*CUC*) mousse.

spun'tare *sm*: **allo ~ del sole** at sunrise; **allo ~ del giorno** at daybreak ♦ *vt* (*coltello*) to break the point of; (*capelli*) to trim; (*elenco*) to tick off (*BRIT*), check off (*US*) ♦ *vi* (*uscire: germogli*) to sprout; (: *capelli*) to begin to grow; (: *denti*) to come through; (*apparire*) to appear (suddenly); ~**rsi** *vr* to become blunt, lose its point; **spuntarla** (*fig*) to make it, win through.

spun'tino *sm* snack.

'spunto *sm* (*TEAT, MUS*) cue; (*fig*) starting point; **dare lo ~ a** to give rise to; **prendere ~ da qc** to take sth as one's starting point.

spur'gare *vt* (*fogna*) to clean, clear; ~**rsi** *vr* (*MED*) to expectorate.

spu'tare *vt* to spit out; (*fig*) to belch (out) ♦ *vi* to spit.

'sputo *sm* spittle *no pl*, spit *no pl*.

sputta'nare *vt* (*fam*) to bad-mouth.

'squadra *sf* (*strumento*) (set) square; (*gruppo*) team, squad; (*di operai*) gang, squad; (*MIL*) squad; (: *AER, NAUT*) squadron; (*SPORT*) team; **lavoro a ~e** teamwork; **~ mobile/del buon costume** (*POLIZIA*) flying/vice squad.

squa'drare *vt* to square, make square; (*osservare*) to look at closely.

squa'driglia [skwa'driʎʎa] *sf* (*AER*) flight; (*NAUT*) squadron.

squa'drone *sm* squadron.

squagli'arsi [skwaʎ'ʎarsi] *vr* to melt; (*fig*) to sneak off.

squa'lifica, che *sf* disqualification.

squalifi'care *vt* to disqualify.

'squallido, a *ag* wretched, bleak.

squal'lore *sm* wretchedness, bleakness.

'squalo *sm* shark.

'squama *sf* scale.

squa'mare *vt* to scale; ~**rsi** *vr* to flake *o* peel (off).

squarcia'gola [skwartʃa'gola]: **a ~** *av* at the top of one's voice.

squarci'are [skwar'tʃare] *vt* (*muro, corpo*) to rip open; (*tessuto*) to rip; (*fig*: *tenebre, silenzio*) to split; (: *nuvole*) to pierce.

'squarcio ['skwartʃo] *sm* (*ferita*) gash; (*in lenzuolo, abito*) rip; (*in un muro*) breach; (*in una nave*) hole; (*brano*) passage, excerpt; **uno ~ di sole** a burst of sunlight.

squar'tare *vt* to quarter, cut up; (*cadavere*) to dismember.

squattri'nato, a *ag* penniless ♦ *sm/f* pauper.

squili'brare *vt* to unbalance.

squili'brato, a *ag* (*PSIC*) unbalanced ♦ *sm/f* deranged person.

squi'librio *sm* (*differenza, sbilancio*) imbalance; (*PSIC*) derangement.

squil'lante *ag* (*suono*) shrill, sharp; (*voce*) shrill.

squil'lare *vi* (*campanello, telefono*) to ring (out); (*tromba*) to blare.

'squillo *sm* ring, ringing *no pl*; blare ♦ *sf inv* (*anche*: **ragazza ~**) call girl.

squi'sito, a *ag* exquisite; (*cibo*) delicious; (*persona*) delightful.

squit'tire *vi* (*uccello*) to squawk; (*topo*) to squeak.

SR *sigla* = Siracusa.

sradi'care *vt* to uproot; (*fig*) to eradicate.

sragio'nare [zradʒo'nare] *vi* to talk nonsense, rave.

sregola'tezza [zregola'tettsa] *sf* (*nel mangiare, bere*) lack of moderation; (*di vita*) dissoluteness, dissipation.

srego'lato, a *ag* (*senza ordine: vita*) disorderly; (*smodato*) immoderate; (*dissoluto*) dissolute.

Sri 'Lanka [sri'lanka] *sm*: **il ~** Sri Lanka.

S.r.l. *abbr vedi* **società a responsabilità limitata.**

sroto'lare *vt*, ~**rsi** *vr* to unroll.

SS *sigla* = Sassari.

S.S. *abbr* (*REL*) = Sua Santità; Santa Sede; santi, santissimo; (*AUT*) = **strada statale**; *vedi* **statale.**

S.S.N. *abbr* (= *Servizio Sanitario Nazionale*) ≈ NHS.

sta *etc vb vedi* **stare.**

'stabbio *sm* (*recinto*) pen, fold; (*di maiali*) pigsty; (*letame*) manure.

'stabile *ag* stable, steady; (*tempo: non variabile*) settled; (*TEAT: compagnia*) resident ♦ *sm* (*edificio*) building; **teatro ~** civic theatre.

stabili'mento *sm* (*edificio*) establishment; (*fabbrica*) plant, factory; **~ balneare** bathing establishment; **~ tessile** textile mill.

stabi'lire *vt* to establish; (*fissare: prezzi, data*) to fix; (*decidere*) to decide; ~**rsi** *vr* (*prendere dimora*) to settle; **resta stabilito**

che ... it is agreed that ....

stabilità *sf* stability.

stabiliz'zare [stabilid'dzare] *vt* to stabilize.

stabilizza'tore [stabiliddza'tore] *sm* stabilizer; (*fig*) stabilizing force.

stabilizzazi'one [stabilidzat'tsjone] *sf* stabilization.

stacano'vista, i, e *sm/f* (*ironico*) eager beaver.

stac'care *vt* (*levare*) to detach, remove; (*separare: anche fig*) to separate, divide; (*strappare*) to tear off (*o* out); (*scandire: parole*) to pronounce clearly; (*SPORT*) to leave behind; ~**rsi** *vr* (*bottone etc*) to come off; (*scostarsi*): ~**rsi (da)** to move away (from); (*fig: separarsi*): ~**rsi da** to leave; **non ~ gli occhi da qn** not to take one's eyes off sb; ~ **la televisione/il telefono** to disconnect the television/the phone; ~ **un assegno** to write a cheque.

staccio'nata [stattʃo'nata] *sf* (*gen*) fence, (*IPPICA*) hurdle.

'stacco, chi *sm* (*intervallo*) gap; (: *tra due scene*) break; (*differenza*) difference; (*SPORT: nel salto*) takeoff.

sta'dera *sf* lever scales *pl*.

'stadio *sm* (*SPORT*) stadium; (*periodo, fase*) phase, stage.

'staffa *sf* (*di sella, TECN*) stirrup; **perdere le ~e** (*fig*) to fly off the handle.

staf'fetta *sf* (*messo*) dispatch rider; (*SPORT*) relay race.

stagflazi'one [stagflat'tsjone] *sf* (*ECON*) stagflation.

stagio'nale [stadʒo'nale] *ag* seasonal ♦ *sm/f* seasonal worker.

stagio'nare [stadʒo'nare] *vt* (*legno*) to season; (*formaggi, vino*) to mature.

stagio'nato, a [stadʒo'nato] *ag* (*vedi vb*) seasoned; matured; (*scherzoso: attempato*) getting on in years.

stagi'one [sta'dʒone] *sf* season; **alta/bassa ~** high/low season.

stagli'arsi [staʎ'ʎarsi] *vr* to stand out, be silhouetted.

sta'gnante [staɲ'ɲante] *ag* stagnant.

sta'gnare [staɲ'ɲare] *vt* (*vaso, tegame*) to tin-plate; (*barca, botte*) to make watertight; (*sangue*) to stop ♦ *vi* to stagnate.

sta'gnino [staɲ'ɲino] *sm* tinsmith.

'stagno, a ['staɲɲo] *ag* (*a tenuta d'acqua*) watertight; (*a tenuta d'aria*) airtight ♦ *sm* (*acquitrino*) pond; (*CHIM*) tin.

sta'gnola [staɲ'ɲɔla] *sf* tinfoil.

stalag'mite *sf* stalagmite.

stalat'tite *sf* stalactite.

stali'nismo *sm* (*POL*) Stalinism.

'stalla *sf* (*per bovini*) cowshed; (*per cavalli*) stable.

stalli'ere *sm* groom, stableboy.

'stallo *sm* stall, seat; (*SCACCHI*) stalemate; (*AER*) stall; **situazione di ~** (*fig*) stalemate.

stal'lone *sm* stallion.

sta'mani, stamat'tina *av* this morning.

stam'becco, chi *sm* ibex.

stam'berga, ghe *sf* hovel.

'stampa *sf* (*TIP, FOT: tecnica*) printing; (*impressione, copia fotografica*) print; (*insieme di quotidiani, giornalisti etc*): **la ~** the press; **andare in ~** to go to press; **mandare in ~** to pass for press; **errore di ~** printing error; **prova di ~** print sample; **libertà di ~** freedom of the press; "**~e**" "printed matter".

stam'pante *sf* (*INFORM*) printer; ~ **seriale/termica** serial/thermal printer.

stam'pare *vt* to print; (*pubblicare*) to publish, (*coniare*) to strike, coin; (*imprimere: anche fig*) to impress.

stampa'tello *sm* block letters *pl*.

stam'pato, a *ag* printed ♦ *sm* (*opuscolo*) leaflet; (*modulo*) form; ~**i** *smpl* printed matter *sg*.

stam'pella *sf* crutch.

stampigli'are [stampiʎ'ʎare] *vt* to stamp.

stampiglia'tura [stampiʎʎa'tura] *sf* (*atto*) stamping; (*marchio*) stamp.

'stampo *sm* mould; (*fig: indole*) type, kind, sort.

sta'nare *vt* to drive out.

stan'care *vt* to tire, make tired; (*annoiare*) to bore; (*infastidire*) to annoy; ~**rsi** *vr* to get tired, tire o.s. out; ~**rsi (di)** (*stufarsi*) to grow weary (of), grow tired (of).

stan'chezza [stan'kettsa] *sf* tiredness, fatigue.

'stanco, a, chi, che *ag* tired; ~ **di** tired of, fed up with.

stand [stand] *sm inv* (*in fiera*) stand.

'standard ['standard] *sm inv* (*livello*) standard.

standardiz'zare [standardid'dzare] *vt* to standardize.

stan'dista, i, e *sm/f* (*in una fiera etc*) person responsible for a stand.

'stanga, ghe *sm* bar; (*di carro*) shaft.

stan'gare *vt* (*fig: cliente*) to overcharge; (: *studente*) to fail.

stan'gata *sf* (*colpo: anche fig*) blow; (*cattivo risultato*) poor result; (*CALCIO*) shot.

stan'ghetta [stan'getta] *sf* (*di occhiali*) leg; (*MUS, di scrittura*) bar.

'stanno *vb vedi* **stare**.

sta'notte *av* tonight; (*notte passata*) last night.

'**stante** *prep* owing to, because of; **a sé ~** (*appartamento, casa*) independent, separate.
stan'tio, a, 'tii, 'tie *ag* stale; (*burro*) rancid; (*fig*) old.
stan'tuffo *sm* piston.
'**stanza** ['stantsa] *sf* room; (*POESIA*) stanza; **essere di ~ a** (*MIL*) to be stationed in; **~ da bagno** bathroom; **~ da letto** bedroom.
stanzia'mento [stantsja'mento] *sm* allocation.
stanzi'are [stan'tsjare] *vt* to allocate.
stan'zino [stan'tsino] *sm* (*ripostiglio*) storeroom; (*spogliatoio*) changing room (*BRIT*), locker room (*US*).
stap'pare *vt* to uncork; (*tappo a corona*) to uncap.
star [star] *sf* (*attore, attrice etc*) star.
'**stare** *vi* (*restare in un luogo*) to stay, remain; (*abitare*) to stay, live; (*essere situato*) to be, be situated; (*anche: ~ in piedi*) to stand; (*essere, trovarsi*) to be; (*dipendere*): **se stesse in me** if it were up to me, if it depended on me; (*seguito da gerundio*): **sta studiando** he's studying; **~ per fare qc** to be about to do sth; **starci** (*esserci spazio*): **nel baule non ci sta più niente** there's no more room in the boot; (*accettare*): **ci stai?** is that okay with you?; **~ a** (*attenersi a*) to follow, stick to; (*seguito dall'infinito*): **~ a sentire** to listen; **staremo a vedere** let's wait and see; **stiamo a discutere** we're talking; (*toccare a*): **sta a te giocare** it's your turn to play; **sta a te decidere** it's up to you to decide; **~ a qn** (*abiti etc*) to fit sb; **queste scarpe mi stanno strette** these shoes are tight for me; **il rosso ti sta bene** red suits you; **come sta?** how are you?; **io sto bene/male** I'm very well/not very well; **~ fermo** to keep *o* stay still; **~ seduto** to sit, be sitting; **~ zitto** to keep quiet; **stando così le cose** given the situation; **stando a ciò che dice lui** according to him *o* to his version.
starnaz'zare [starnat'tsare] *vi* to squawk.
starnu'tire *vi* to sneeze.
star'nuto *sm* sneeze.
sta'sera *av* this evening, tonight.
'**stasi** *sf* (*MED, fig*) stasis.
sta'tale *ag* state *cpd*, government *cpd* ♦ *sm/f* state employee; (*nell'amministrazione*) ≈ civil servant; **bilancio ~** national budget; **strada ~** ≈ main road.
stataliz'zare [statalid'dzare] *vt* to nationalize, put under state control.
'**statico, a, ci, che** *ag* (*ELETTR, fig*) static.
sta'tista, i *sm* statesman.

sta'tistico, a, ci, che *ag* statistical ♦ *sf* statistic; (*scienza*) statistics *sg*; **fare una ~a** to carry out a statistical examination.
'**stato, a** *pp di* **essere, stare** ♦ *sm* (*condizione*) state, condition; (*POL*) state; (*DIR*) status; **essere in ~ d'accusa** (*DIR*) to be committed for trial; **essere in ~ d'arresto** (*DIR*) to be under arrest; **essere in ~ interessante** to be pregnant; **~ d'assedio/d'emergenza** state of siege/ emergency; **~ civile** (*AMM*) marital status; **~ di famiglia** (*AMM*) *certificate giving details of a household and its dependents*; **~ maggiore** (*MIL*) general staff; **~ patrimoniale** (*COMM*) statement of assets and liabilities; **gli S~i Uniti (d'America)** the United States (of America).
'**statua** *sf* statue.
statuni'tense *ag* United States *cpd*, of the United States.
sta'tura *sf* (*ANAT*) height; (*fig*) stature; **essere alto/basso di ~** to be tall/short *o* small.
sta'tuto *sm* (*DIR*) statute; **regione a ~ speciale** *Italian region with political autonomy in certain matters*; **~ della società** (*COMM*) articles *pl* of association.
sta'volta *av* this time.
staziona'mento [stattsjona'mento] *sm* (*AUT*) parking; (: *sosta*) waiting; **freno di ~** handbrake.
stazio'nare [stattsjo'nare] *vi* (*veicoli*) to be parked.
stazio'nario, a [stattsjo'narjo] *ag* stationary; (*fig*) unchanged.
stazi'one [stat'tsjone] *sf* station; (*balneare, invernale etc*) resort; **~ degli autobus** bus station; **~ balneare** seaside resort; **~ climatica** health resort; **~ ferroviaria** railway (*BRIT*) *o* railroad (*US*) station; **~ invernale** winter sports resort; **~ di lavoro** work station; **~ di polizia** police station (*in small town*); **~ di servizio** service *o* petrol (*BRIT*) *o* filling station; **~ termale** spa.
'**stazza** ['stattsa] *sf* tonnage.
st. civ. *abbr* = **stato civile**.
'**stecca, che** *sf* stick; (*di ombrello*) rib; (*di sigarette*) carton; (*MED*) splint; (*stonatura*): **fare una ~** to sing (*o* play) a wrong note.
stec'cato *sm* fence.
stec'chito, a [stek'kito] *ag* dried up; (*persona*) skinny; **lasciar ~ qn** (*fig*) to leave sb flabbergasted; **morto ~** stone dead.
'**stella** *sf* star; **~ alpina** (*BOT*) edelweiss; **~ cadente** *o* **filante** shooting star; **~ di mare**

(*ZOOL*) starfish.
stel'lato, a *ag* (*cielo, notte*) starry.
'stelo *sm* stem; (*asta*) rod; **lampada a** ~ standard lamp (*BRIT*), floor lamp.
'stemma, i *sm* coat of arms.
'stemmo *vb vedi* **stare**.
stempe'rare *vt* (*calce, colore*) to dissolve.
stempi'ato, a *ag* with a receding hairline.
stempia'tura *sf* receding hairline.
sten'dardo *sm* standard.
'stendere *vt* (*braccia, gambe*) to stretch (out); (*tovaglia*) to spread (out); (*bucato*) to hang out; (*mettere a giacere*) to lay (down); (*spalmare: colore*) to spread; (*mettere per iscritto*) to draw up; ~**rsi** *vr* (*coricarsi*) to stretch out, lie down; (*estendersi*) to extend, stretch.
stendibianche'ria [stendibjanke'ria] *sm inv* clotheshorse.
stendi'toio *sm* (*locale*) drying room; (*stendibiancheria*) clotheshorse,
stenodattilografi'a *sf* shorthand typing (*BRIT*), stenography (*US*).
stenodatti'lografo, a *smf* shorthand typist (*BRIT*), stenographer (*US*).
stenogra'fare *vt* to take down in shorthand.
stenogra'fia *sf* shorthand.
ste'nografo, a *smf* stenographer.
sten'tare *vi*: ~ **a fare** to find it hard to do, have difficulty doing.
sten'tato, a *ag* (*compito, stile*) laboured (*BRIT*), labored (*US*); (*sorriso*) forced.
'stento *sm* (*fatica*) difficulty; ~**i** *smpl* (*privazioni*) hardship *sg*, privation *sg*; **a** ~ *av* with difficulty, barely.
'steppa *sf* steppe.
'sterco *sm* dung.
stereofo'nia *sf* stereophony.
'stereo('fonico, a, ci, che) *ag* stereo(phonic).
stereoti'pato, a *ag* stereotyped.
stere'otipo *sm* stereotype; **pensare per** ~**i** to think in clichés.
'sterile *ag* sterile; (*terra*) barren; (*fig*) futile, fruitless.
sterilità *sf* sterility.
steriliz'zare [sterilid'dzare] *vt* to sterilize.
sterilizzazi'one [steriliddzat'tsjone] *sf* sterilization.
ster'lina *sf* pound (sterling).
stermi'nare *vt* to exterminate, wipe out.
stermi'nato, a *ag* immense, endless.
ster'minio *sm* extermination, destruction; **campo di** ~ death camp.
'sterno *sm* (*ANAT*) breastbone.
ster'paglia [ster'paʎʎa] *sf* brushwood.
'sterpo *sm* dry twig.

ster'rare *vt* to excavate.
ster'zare [ster'tsare] *vt, vi* (*AUT*) to steer.
'sterzo ['stɛrtso] *sm* steering; (*volante*) steering wheel.
'steso, a *pp di* **stendere**.
'stessi *etc vb vedi* **stare**.
'stesso, a *ag* same; (*rafforzativo: in persona, proprio*): **il re** ~ the king himself *o* in person ♦ *pron*: **lo(la)** ~**(a)** the same (one); **quello** ~ **giorno** that very day; **i suoi** ~**i avversari lo ammirano** even his enemies admire him; **fa lo** ~ it doesn't matter; **parto lo** ~ I'm going all the same; **per me è lo** ~ it's all the same to me, it doesn't matter to me; **io, tu** *etc*.
ste'sura *sf* (*azione*) drafting *no pl*, drawing up *no pl*; (*documento*) draft.
stetos'copio *sm* stethoscope.
'stetti *etc vb vedi* **stare**.
'stia *sf* hutch.
'stie *etc vb vedi* **stare**.
'stigma, i *sm* stigma.
'stigmate *sfpl* (*REL*) stigmata.
sti'lare *vt* to draw up, draft.
'stile *sm* style; (*classe*) style, class; (*SPORT*): ~ **libero** freestyle; **mobili in** ~ period furniture; **in grande** ~ in great style; **è proprio nel suo** ~ (*fig*) it's just like him.
sti'lismo *sm* concern for style.
sti'lista, i, e *smf* designer.
sti'listico, a, ci, che *ag* stylistic.
stiliz'zato, a [stilid'dzato] *ag* stylized.
stil'lare *vi* (*trasudare*) to ooze; (*gocciolare*) to drip.
stilli'cidio [stilli'tʃidjo] *sm* (*fig*) continual pestering (*o moaning etc*).
stilo'grafica, che *sf* (*anche*: **penna** ~) fountain pen.
Stim. *abbr* = **stimata**.
'stima *sf* esteem; valuation; assessment, estimate; **avere** ~ **di qn** to have respect for sb; **godere della** ~ **di qn** to enjoy sb's respect; **fare la** ~ **di qc** to estimate the value of sth.
sti'mare *vt* (*persona*) to esteem, hold in high regard; (*terreno, casa etc*) to value; (*stabilire in misura approssimativa*) to estimate, assess; (*ritenere*): ~ **che** to consider that; ~**rsi fortunato** to consider o.s. (to be) lucky.
Stim.ma *abbr* = **stimatissima**.
stimo'lante *ag* stimulating ♦ *sm* (*MED*) stimulant.
stimo'lare *vt* to stimulate; (*incitare*): ~ **qn (a fare)** to spur sb on (to do).
stimolazi'one [stimolat'tsjone] *sf* stimulation.
'stimolo *sm* (*anche fig*) stimulus.

'stinco, chi *sm* shin; shinbone.

'stingere ['stindʒere] *vt, vi* (*anche*: ~**rsi**) to fade.

'stinto, a *pp di* **stingere.**

sti'pare *vt* to cram, pack; ~**rsi** *vr* (*accalcarsi*) to crowd, throng.

stipendi'are *vt* (*pagare*) to pay (a salary to).

stipendi'ato, a *ag* salaried ♦ *sm/f* salaried worker.

sti'pendio *sm* salary.

'stipite *sm* (*di porta, finestra*) jamb.

stipu'lare *vt* (*redigere*) to draw up.

stipulazi'one [stipulat'tsjone] *sf* (*di contratto*: *stesura*) drafting; (: *firma*) signing.

stiracchi'are [stirak'kjare] *vt* (*fig: significato di una parola*) to stretch, force; ~**rsi** *vr* (*persona*) to stretch.

stira'mento *sm* (*MED*) sprain.

sti'rare *vt* (*abito*) to iron; (*distendere*) to stretch; (*strappare: muscolo*) to strain; ~**rsi** *vr* (*fam*) to stretch (o.s.).

stira'tura *sf* ironing.

'stirpe *sf* birth, stock; descendants *pl.*

stiti'chezza [stiti'kettsa] *sf* constipation.

'stitico, a, ci, che *ag* constipated.

'stiva *sf* (*di nave*) hold.

sti'vale *sm* boot.

stiva'letto *sm* ankle boot.

sti'vare *vt* to stow, load.

'stizza ['stittsa] *sf* anger, vexation.

stiz'zire [stit'tsire] *vt* to irritate ♦ *vi*, ~**rsi** *vr* to become irritated, become vexed.

stiz'zoso, a [stit'tsoso] *ag* (*persona*) quick-tempered, irascible; (*risposta*) angry.

stocca'fisso *sm* stockfish, dried cod.

Stoc'carda *sf* Stuttgart.

stoc'cata *sf* (*colpo*) stab, thrust; (*fig*) gibe, cutting remark.

Stoc'colma *sf* Stockholm.

stock [stɔk] *sm inv* (*COMM*) stock.

'stoffa *sf* material, fabric; (*fig*): **aver la** ~ **di** to have the makings of; **avere della** ~ to have what it takes.

stoi'cismo [stoi'tʃizmo] *sm* stoicism.

'stoico, a, ci, che *ag* stoic(al).

sto'ino *sm* doormat.

'stola *sf* stole.

stol'tezza [stol'tettsa] *sf* stupidity; (*azione*) foolish action.

'stolto, a *ag* stupid, foolish.

'stomaco, chi *sm* stomach; **dare di** ~ to vomit, be sick.

sto'nare *vt* to sing (*o* play) out of tune ♦ *vi* to be out of tune, sing (*o* play) out of tune; (*fig*) to be out of place, jar; (: *colori*) to clash.

sto'nato, a *ag* (*persona*) off-key; (*strumento*) off-key, out of tune.

stona'tura *sf* (*suono*) false note.

stop *sm inv* (*TELEGRAFIA*) stop; (*AUT*: *cartello*) stop sign; (: *fanalino d'arresto*) brake-light (*BRIT*), stoplight.

'stoppa *sf* tow.

'stoppia *sf* (*AGR*) stubble.

stop'pino *sm* (*di candela*) wick; (*miccia*) fuse.

'storcere ['stɔrtʃere] *vt* to twist; ~**rsi** *vr* to writhe, twist; ~ **il naso** (*fig*) to turn up one's nose; ~**rsi la caviglia** to twist one's ankle.

stordi'mento *sm* (*gen*) dizziness; (*da droga*) stupefaction.

stor'dire *vt* (*intontire*) to stun, daze; ~**rsi** *vr*: ~**rsi col bere** to dull one's senses with drink.

stor'dito, a *ag* stunned; (*sventato*) scatterbrained, heedless.

'storia *sf* (*scienza, avvenimenti*) history; (*racconto, bugia*) story; (*faccenda, questione*) business *no pl*; (*pretesto*) excuse, pretext; ~**e** *sfpl* (*smancerie*) fuss *sg*; **passare alla** ~ to go down in history; **non ha fatto** ~**e** he didn't make a fuss.

storicità [storitʃi'ta] *sf* historical authenticity.

'storico, a, ci, che *ag* historic(al) ♦ *sm/f* historian.

storiogra'fia *sf* historiography.

stori'one *sm* (*ZOOL*) sturgeon.

stor'mire *vi* to rustle.

'stormo *sm* (*di uccelli*) flock.

stor'nare *vt* (*COMM*) to transfer.

stor'nello *sm* kind of folk song.

'storno *sm* starling.

storpi'are *vt* to cripple, maim; (*fig: parole*) to mangle; (: *significato*) to twist.

storpia'tura *sf* (*fig: di parola*) twisting, distortion.

'storpio, a *ag* crippled, maimed.

'storsi *etc vb vedi* **storcere.**

'storto, a *pp di* **storcere** ♦ *ag* (*chiodo*) twisted, bent; (*gamba, quadro*) crooked; (*fig: ragionamento*) false, wrong ♦ *sf* (*distorsione*) sprain, twist; (*recipiente*) retort ♦ *av*: **guardare** ~ **qn** (*fig*) to look askance at sb; **andar** ~ to go wrong.

sto'viglie [sto'viʎʎe] *sfpl* dishes *pl*, crockery.

str. *abbr* (*GEO*) = **stretto.**

'strabico, a, ci, che *ag* squint-eyed; (*occhi*) squint.

strabili'ante *ag* astonishing, amazing.

strabili'are *vi* to astonish, amaze.

stra'bismo *sm* squinting.

strabuz'zare [strabud'dzare] *vt:* ~ **gli occhi** to open one's eyes wide.

stra'carico, a, chi, che *ag* overloaded.

strac'chino [strak'kino] *sm type of soft cheese.*

stracci'are [strat't∫are] *vt* to tear.

'straccio, a, ci, ce ['strattʃo] *ag:* **carta** ~**a** waste paper ♦ *sm* rag; (*per pulire*) cloth, duster.

stracci'one, a [strat'tʃone] *sm/f* ragamuffin.

stracci'vendolo [strattʃi'vendolo] *sm* ragman.

'stracco, a, chi, che *ag:* ~ **(morto)** exhausted, dead tired.

stra'cotto, a *ag* overcooked ♦ *sm* (*CUC*) beef stew.

'strada *sf* road; (*di città*) street; (*cammino, via, fig*) way; ~ **facendo** on the way, **tre ore di** ~ **(a piedi)/(in macchina)** three hours' walk/drive; **essere sulla buona** ~ (*nella vita*) to be on the right road o path; (*con indagine etc*) to be on the right track; **essere fuori** ~ (*fig*) to be on the wrong track; **fare** ~ **a qn** to show sb the way; **fare** o **farsi** ~ (*fig: persona*) to get on in life; **portare qn sulla cattiva** ~ to lead sb astray; **donna di** ~ (*fig peg*) streetwalker; **ragazzo di** ~ (*fig peg*) street urchin; ~ **ferrata** railway (*BRIT*), railroad (*US*); ~ **principale** main road; ~ **senza uscita** dead end, cul-de-sac.

stra'dale *ag* road *cpd*; (*polizia, regolamento*) traffic *cpd*.

stra'dario *sm* street guide.

stra'dino *sm* road worker.

strafalci'one [strafal'tʃone] *sm* blunder, howler.

stra'fare *vi* to overdo it.

stra'fatto, a *pp di* strafare.

stra'foro: di ~ *av* (*di nascosto*) on the sly.

strafot'tente *ag:* **è** ~ he doesn't give a damn, he couldn't care less.

strafot'tenza [strafot'tɛntsa] *sf* arrogance.

'strage ['stradʒe] *sf* massacre, slaughter.

stra'grande *ag:* **la** ~ **maggioranza** the overwhelming majority.

stralci'are [stral'tʃare] *vt* to remove.

'stralcio ['straltʃo] *sm* (*COMM*): **vendere in** ~ to sell off (at bargain prices) ♦ *ag inv:* **legge** ~ abridged version of an act.

stralu'nato, a *ag* (*occhi*) rolling; (*persona*) beside o.s., very upset.

stramaz'zare [stramat'tsare] *vi* to fall heavily.

strambe'ria *sf* eccentricity.

'strambo, a *ag* strange, queer.

strampa'lato, a *ag* odd, eccentric.

strana'mente *av* oddly, strangely; **e lui,** ~,

ha **accettato** and, surprisingly, he agreed.

stra'nezza [stra'nettsa] *sf* strangeness.

strango'lare *vt* to strangle; ~**rsi** *vr* to choke.

strani'ero, a *ag* foreign ♦ *sm/f* foreigner.

stra'nito, a *ag* dazed.

'strano, a *ag* strange, odd.

straordi'nario, a *ag* extraordinary; (*treno etc*) special ♦ *sm* (*lavoro*) overtime.

strapaz'zare [strapat'tsare] *vt* to ill-treat; ~**rsi** *vr* to tire o.s. out, overdo things.

strapaz'zato, a [strapat'tsato] *ag:* **uova** ~**e** scrambled eggs.

stra'pazzo [stra'pattso] *sm* strain, fatigue; **da** ~ (*fig*) third-rate.

strapi'eno, a *ag* full to overflowing.

strapi'ombo *sm* overhanging rock; **a** ~ overhanging.

strapo'tere *sm* excessive power.

strappa'lacrime *ag inv* (*film*). **romanzo** (o **film** *etc*) ~ tear-jerker.

strap'pare *vt* (*gen*) to tear, rip; (*pagina etc*) to tear off, tear out; (*sradicare*) to pull up; (*togliere*): ~ **qc a qn** to snatch sth from sb; (*fig*) to wrest sth from sb; ~**rsi** *vr* (*lacerarsi*) to rip, tear; (*rompersi*) to break; ~**rsi un muscolo** to tear a muscle.

strap'pato, a *ag* torn, ripped.

'strappo *sm* (*strattone*) pull, tug; (*lacerazione*) tear, rip; (*fig fam: passaggio*) lift (*BRIT*), ride (*US*); **fare uno** ~ **alla regola** to make an exception to the rule; ~ **muscolare** torn muscle.

strapun'tino *sm* jump o foldaway seat.

strari'pare *vi* to overflow.

Stras'burgo *sf* Strasbourg.

strasci'care [straʃʃi'kare] *vt* to trail; (*piedi*) to drag; ~ **le parole** to drawl.

'strascico, chi ['straʃʃiko] *sm* (*di abito*) train; (*conseguenza*) after-effect.

strata'gemma, i [strata'dʒɛmma] *sm* stratagem.

stra'tega, ghi *sm* strategist.

strate'gia, 'gie [strate'dʒia] *sf* strategy.

stra'tegico, a, ci, che [stra'tɛdʒiko] *ag* strategic.

'strato *sm* layer; (*rivestimento*) coat, coating; (*GEO, fig*) stratum; (*METEOR*) stratus.

stratos'fera *sf* stratosphere.

strat'tone *sm* tug, jerk; **dare uno** ~ **a qc** to tug o jerk sth, give sth a tug o jerk.

stravac'cato, a *ag* sprawling.

strava'gante *ag* odd, eccentric.

strava'ganza [strava'gantsa] *sf* eccentricity.

stra'vecchio, a [stra'vɛkkjo] *ag* very old.

strave'dere _vi:_ ~ **per qn** to dote on sb.

stra'visto, a _pp di_ **stravedere**.

stra'vizio [stra'vittsjo] _sm_ excess.

stra'volgere [stra'vɔldʒere] _vt_ (_volto_) to contort; (_fig: animo_) to trouble deeply; (: _verità_) to twist, distort.

stra'volto, a _pp di_ **stravolgere** ♦ _ag_ (_persona_: _per stanchezza etc_) in a terrible state; (: _per sofferenza_) distraught.

strazi'ante [strat'tsjante] _ag_ (_scena_) harrowing; (_urlo_) bloodcurdling; (_dolore_) excruciating.

strazi'are [strat'tsjare] _vt_ to torture, torment.

'strazio ['strattsjo] _sm_ torture; (_fig: cosa fatta male_): **essere uno** ~ to be appalling; **fare** ~ **di** (_corpo, vittima_) to mutilate.

'strega, ghe _sf_ witch.

stre'gare _vt_ to bewitch.

stre'gone _sm_ (_mago_) wizard; (_di tribù_) witch doctor.

stregone'ria _sf_ (_pratica_) witchcraft; **fare una** ~ to cast a spell.

'stregua _sf:_ **alla** ~ **di** by the same standard as.

stre'mare _vt_ to exhaust.

'stremo _sm:_ **essere allo** ~ to be at the end of one's tether.

'strenna _sf:_ ~ **natalizia** (_regalo_) Christmas present; (_libro_) book published for the Christmas market.

'strenuo, a _ag_ brave, courageous.

strepi'tare _vi_ to yell and shout.

'strepito _sm_ (_di voci, folla_) clamour (_BRIT_), clamor (_US_); (_di catene_) clanking, rattling.

strepi'toso, a _ag_ clamorous, deafening; (_fig: successo_) resounding.

stres'sante _ag_ stressful.

stres'sare _vt_ to put under stress.

stres'sato, a _ag_ under stress.

'stretta _sf vedi_ **stretto**.

stretta'mente _av_ tightly; (_rigorosamente_) strictly.

stret'tezza [stret'tettsa] _sf_ narrowness; ~**e** _sfpl_ (_povertà_) poverty _sg_, straitened circumstances.

'stretto, a _pp di_ **stringere** ♦ _ag_ (_corridoio, limiti_) narrow; (_gonna, scarpe, nodo, curva_) tight; (_intimo: parente, amico_) close; (_rigoroso: osservanza_) strict; (_preciso: significato_) precise, exact ♦ _sm_ (_braccio di mare_) strait ♦ _sf_ (_di mano_) grasp; (_finanziaria_) squeeze; (_fig: dolore, turbamento_) pang; **a denti** ~**i** with clenched teeth; **lo** ~ **necessario** the bare minimum; **una** ~**a di mano** a handshake; **una** ~**a al cuore** a sudden sadness; **essere alle** ~**e** to have one's back to the wall.

stret'toia _sf_ bottleneck; (_fig_) tricky situation.

stri'ato, a _ag_ streaked.

stria'tura _sf_ (_atto_) streaking; (_effetto_) streaks _pl_.

stric'nina _sf_ strychnine.

'strida _sfpl_ screaming _sg_.

stri'dente _ag_ strident.

'stridere _vi_ (_porta_) to squeak; (_animale_) to screech, shriek; (_colori_) to clash.

'strido, _pl(f)_ **strida** _sm_ screech, shriek.

stri'dore _sm_ screeching, shrieking.

'stridulo, a _ag_ shrill.

'striglia ['striʎʎa] _sf_ currycomb.

strigli'are [striʎ'ʎare] _vt_ (_cavallo_) to curry.

strigli'ata [striʎ'ʎata] _sf_ (_di cavallo_) currying; (_fig_): **dare una** ~ **a qn** to give sb a scolding.

stril'lare _vt, vi_ to scream, shriek.

'strillo _sm_ scream, shriek.

stril'lone _sm_ newspaper seller.

strimin'zito, a [strimin'tsito] _ag_ (_misero_) shabby; (_molto magro_) skinny.

strimpel'lare _vt_ (_MUS_) to strum.

'stringa, ghe _sf_ lace; (_INFORM_) string.

strin'gare _vt_ (_fig: discorso_) to condense.

strin'gato, a _ag_ (_fig_) concise.

'stringere ['strindʒere] _vt_ (_avvicinare due cose_) to press (together), squeeze (together); (_tenere stretto_) to hold tight, clasp, clutch; (_pugno, mascella, denti_) to clench; (_labbra_) to compress; (_avvitare_) to tighten; (_abito_) to take in; (_sog: scarpe_) to pinch, be tight for; (_fig: concludere: patto_) to make; (: _accelerare: passo_) to quicken ♦ _vi_ (_incalzare_) to be pressing; ~**rsi** _vr_ (_accostarsi_): ~**rsi a** to press o.s. up against; ~ **la mano a qn** to shake sb's hand; ~ **gli occhi** to screw up one's eyes; ~ **amicizia con qn** to make friends with sb; **stringi stringi** in conclusion; **il tempo stringe** time is short.

'strinsi _etc vb vedi_ **stringere**.

'striscia, sce ['striʃʃa] _sf_ (_di carta, tessuto etc_) strip; (_riga_) stripe; ~**sce** (_pedonali_) zebra crossing _sg_; **a** ~**sce** striped.

strisci'ante [striʃ'ʃante] _ag_ (_fig peg_) unctuous; (_ECON: inflazione_) creeping.

strisci'are [striʃ'ʃare] _vt_ (_piedi_) to drag; (_muro, macchina_) to graze ♦ _vi_ to crawl, creep.

'striscio ['striʃʃo] _sm_ graze; (_MED_) smear; **colpire di** ~ to graze.

strisci'one [striʃ'ʃone] _sm_ banner.

strito'lare _vt_ to grind.

striz'zare [strit'tsare] _vt_ (_arancia_) to squeeze; (_panni_) to wring (out); ~ **l'occhio** to wink.

striz'zata [strit'tsata] *sf*: **dare una ~ a qc** to give sth a wring; **una ~ d'occhio** a wink.
'**strofa** *sf*, '**strofe** *sf inv* strophe.
strofi'naccio [strofi'nattʃo] *sm* duster, cloth; (*per piatti*) dishcloth; (*per pavimenti*) floorcloth.
strofi'nare *vt* to rub.
stron'care *vt* to break off; (*fig: ribellione*) to suppress, put down; (*: film, libro*) to tear to pieces.
'**stronzo** ['strontso] *sm* (*sterco*) turd; (*fig faml: persona*) shit (*!*).
stropicci'are [stropit'tʃare] *vt* to rub.
stroz'zare [strot'tsare] *vt* (*soffocare*) to choke, strangle; **~rsi** *vr* to choke.
strozza'tura [strottsa'tura] *sf* (*restringimento*) narrowing; (*di strada etc*) bottleneck.
stroz'zino, a [strot'tsino] *sm/f* (*usuraio*) usurer; (*fig*) shark.
struc'care *vt* to remove make-up from; **~rsi** *vr* to remove one's make-up.
'**struggere** ['struddʒere] *vt* (*fig*) to consume; **~rsi** *vr* (*fig*): **~rsi di** to be consumed with.
struggi'mento [struddʒi'mento] *sm* (*desiderio*) yearning.
strumen'tale *ag* (*MUS*) instrumental.
strumentaliz'zare [strumentalid'dzare] *vt* to exploit, use to one's own ends.
strumentalizzazi'one [strumentaliddzat'tsjone] *sf* exploitation.
strumentazi'one [strumentat'tsjone] *sf* (*MUS*) orchestration; (*TECN*) instrumentation.
stru'mento *sm* (*arnese, fig*) instrument, tool; (*MUS*) instrument; **~ a corda** *o* **ad arco/a fiato** string(ed)/wind instrument.
'**strussi** *etc vb vedi* **struggere**.
'**strutto** *sm* lard.
strut'tura *sf* structure.
struttu'rare *vt* to structure.
'**struzzo** ['struttso] *sm* ostrich; **fare lo ~, fare la politica dello ~** to bury one's head in the sand.
stuc'care *vt* (*muro*) to plaster; (*vetro*) to putty; (*decorare con stucchi*) to stucco.
stucca'tore, 'trice *sm/f* plasterer; (*artista*) stucco worker.
stuc'chevole [stuk'kevole] *ag* nauseating; (*fig*) tedious, boring.
'**stucco, chi** *sm* plaster; (*da vetri*) putty; (*ornamentale*) stucco; **rimanere di ~** (*fig*) to be dumbfounded.
stu'dente, 'essa *sm/f* student; (*scolaro*) pupil, schoolboy/girl.
studen'tesco, a, schi, sche *ag* student *cpd*.
studi'are *vt* to study; **~rsi** *vr* (*sforzarsi*): **~rsi**

di fare to try *o* endeavour (*BRIT*) *o* endeavor (*US*) to do.
studi'ato, a *ag* (*modi, sorriso*) affected.
'**studio** *sm* studying; (*ricerca, saggio, stanza*) study; (*di professionista*) office; (*di artista, CINE, TV, RADIO*) studio; (*di medico*) surgery (*BRIT*), office (*US*); **~i** *smpl* (*INS*) studies; **alla fine degli ~i** at the end of one's course (of studies); **secondo recenti ~i, appare che ...** recent research indicates that ...; **la proposta è allo ~** the proposal is under consideration; **~ legale** lawyer's office.
studi'oso, a *ag* studious, hardworking ♦ *sm/f* scholar.
'**stufa** *sf* stove; **~ elettrica** electric fire *o* heater; **~ a legna/carbone** wood-burning/coal stove.
stu'fare *vt* (*CUC*) to stew; (*fig fam*) to bore.
stu'fato *sm* (*CUC*) stew.
'**stufo, a** *ag* (*fam*): **essere ~ di** to be fed up with, be sick and tired of.
stu'oia *sf* mat.
stu'olo *sm* crowd, host.
stupefa'cente [stupefa'tʃente] *ag* stunning, astounding ♦ *sm* drug, narcotic.
stupe'fare *vt* to stun, astound.
stupe'fatto, a *pp di* **stupefare**.
stupefazi'one [stupefat'tsjone] *sf* astonishment.
stu'pendo, a *ag* marvellous, wonderful.
stupi'daggine [stupi'daddʒine] *sf* stupid thing (to do *o* say).
stupidità *sf* stupidity.
'**stupido, a** *ag* stupid.
stu'pire *vt* to amaze, stun ♦ *vi* (*anche: ~rsi*): **~ (di)** to be amazed (at), be stunned (by); **non c'è da ~rsi** that's not surprising.
stu'pore *sm* amazement, astonishment.
stu'prare *vt* to rape.
stupra'tore *sm* rapist.
'**stupro** *sm* rape.
stu'rare *vt* (*lavandino*) to clear.
stuzzica'denti [stuttsika'dɛnti] *sm* toothpick.
stuzzi'cante [stuttsi'kante] *ag* (*gen*) stimulating; (*appetitoso*) appetizing.
stuzzi'care [stuttsi'kare] *vt* (*ferita etc*) to poke (at), prod (at); (*fig*) to tease; (*: appetito*) to whet; (*: curiosità*) to stimulate; **~ i denti** to pick one's teeth.

================== *PAROLA CHIAVE*

su (*su + il* = **sul**, *su + lo* = **sullo**, *su + l'* = **sull'**, *su + la* = **sulla**, *su + i* = **sui**, *su + gli* = **sugli**, *su + le* = **sulle**) *prep* **1** (*gen*) on; (*moto*) on(to); (*in cima a*) on (top of); **mettilo sul tavolo** put it on the table;

salire sul treno to get on the train; **un paesino sul mare** a village by the sea; **è sulla destra** it's on the right; **cento metri sul livello del mare** a hundred metres above sea level; **fecero rotta** ~ **Palermo** they set out for Palermo; **sul vestito portava un golf rosso** she was wearing a red sweater over her dress 2 (*argomento*) about, on; **un libro** ~ **Cesare** a book on *o* about Caesar 3 (*circa*) about; **costerà sui 3 milioni** it will cost about 3 million; **una ragazza sui 17 anni** a girl of about 17 (years of age) 4: ~ **misura** made to measure; ~ **ordinazione** to order; ~ **richiesta** on request; **3 casi** ~ **dieci** 3 cases out of 10 ♦ *av* 1 (*in alto, verso l'alto*) up; **vieni** ~ **come on up; guarda** ~ **look up; andare** ~ **e giù** to go up and down; ~ **le mani!** hands up!; **in** ~ (*verso l'alto*) up(wards); (*in poi*) onwards; **vieni** ~ **da me?** are you going to come up?; **dai 20 anni in** ~ from the age of 20 onwards 2 (*addosso*) on; **cos'hai** ~**?** what have you got on? ♦ *escl* **come on!;** ~ **avanti, muoviti!** come on, hurry up!; ~ **coraggio!** come on, cheer up!

'sua *vedi* **suo.**
sua'dente *ag* persuasive.
sub *sm/f inv* skin-diver.
su'bacqueo, a *ag* underwater ♦ *sm* skin-diver.
subaffit'tare *vt* to sublet.
subaf'fitto *sm* (*contratto*) sublet.
subal'terno, a *ag, sm* subordinate; (*MIL*) subaltern.
subappal'tare *vt* to subcontract.
subap'palto *sm* subcontract.
sub'buglio [sub'buʎʎo] *sm* confusion, turmoil; **essere/mettere in** ~ to be in/ throw into a turmoil.
sub'conscio, a [sub'kɔnʃo], **subcosci'ente** [subkoʃ'ʃɛnte] *ag, sm* subconscious.
'subdolo, a *ag* underhand, sneaky.
suben'trare *vi:* ~ **a qn in qc** to take over sth from sb; **sono subentrati altri problemi** other problems arose.
su'bire *vt* to suffer, endure.
subis'sare *vt* (*fig*): ~ **di** to overwhelm with, load with.
subi'taneo, a *ag* sudden.
'subito *av* immediately, at once, straight away.
subli'mare *vt* (*PSIC*) to sublimate; (*CHIM*) to sublime.

su'blime *ag* sublime.
sublo'care *vt* to sublease.
sublocazi'one [sublokat'tsjone] *sf* sublease.
subnor'male *ag* subnormal ♦ *sm/f* mentally handicapped person.
subodo'rare *vt* (*insidia etc*) to smell, suspect.
subordi'nare *vt* to subordinate.
subordi'nato, a *ag* subordinate; (*dipendente*): ~ **a** dependent on, subject to.
subordinazi'one [subordinat'tsjone] *sf* subordination.
su'bordine *sm:* **in** ~ secondarily.
subur'bano, a *ag* suburban.
succe'daneo [suttʃe'daneo] *sm* substitute.
suc'cedere [sut'tʃɛdere] *vi* (*prendere il posto di qn*): ~ **a** to succeed; (*venire dopo*): ~ **a** to follow; (*accadere*) to happen; ~**rsi** *vr* to follow each other; ~ **al trono** to succeed to the throne; **sono cose che succedono** these things happen.
successi'one [suttʃes'sjone] *sf* succession; **tassa di** ~ death duty (*BRIT*), inheritance tax (*US*).
successiva'mente [suttʃessiva'mente] *av* subsequently.
succes'sivo, a [suttʃes'sivo] *ag* successive; **il giorno** ~ the following day; **in un momento** ~ subsequently.
suc'cesso, a [sut'tʃɛsso] *pp di* **succedere** ♦ *sm* (*esito*) outcome; (*buona riuscita*) success; **di** ~ (*libro, personaggio*) successful; **avere** ~ (*persona*) to be successful; (*idea*) to be well received.
succes'sore [suttʃes'sore] *sm* successor.
succhi'are [suk'kjare] *vt* to suck (up).
succhi'otto [suk'kjɔtto] *sm* dummy (*BRIT*), pacifier (*US*), comforter (*US*).
suc'cinto, a [sut'tʃinto] *ag* (*discorso*) succinct; (*abito*) brief.
'succo, chi *sm* juice; (*fig*) essence, gist; ~ **di frutta/pomodoro** fruit/tomato juice.
suc'coso, a *ag* juicy; (*fig*) pithy.
'succube *sm/f* victim; **essere** ~ **di qn** to be dominated by sb.
succur'sale *sf* branch (office).
sud *sm* south ♦ *ag inv* south; (*regione*) southern; **verso** ~ south, southwards; **l'Italia del S**~ Southern Italy; **l'America del S**~ South America.
Su'dafrica *sm:* **il** ~ South Africa.
sudafri'cano, a *ag, sm/f* South African.
Suda'merica *sm:* **il** ~ South America.
sudameri'cano, a *ag, sm/f* South American.
Su'dan *sm:* **il** ~ (the) Sudan.
suda'nese *ag, sm/f* Sudanese *inv.*
su'dare *vi* to perspire, sweat; ~ **freddo** to

come out in a cold sweat.

su'dato, a *ag (persona, mani)* sweaty; *(fig: denaro)* hard-earned ♦ *sf (anche fig)* sweat; **una vittoria ~a** a hard-won victory; **ho fatto una bella ~a per finirlo in tempo** it was a real sweat to get it finished in time.

sud'detto, a *ag* above-mentioned.

suddi'tanza [suddi'tantsa] *sf* subjection; *(cittadinanza)* citizenship.

sud'dito, a *sm/f* subject.

suddi'videre *vt* to subdivide.

suddivisi'one *sf* subdivision.

suddi'viso, a *pp di* **suddividere**.

su'dest *sm* south-east; **vento di ~** south-easterly wind; **il ~ asiatico** South-East Asia.

sudice'ria [sudit∫e'ria] *sf (qualità)* filthiness, dirtiness; *(cosa sporca)* dirty thing.

'sudicio, a, ci, ce ['sudit∫o] *ag* dirty, filthy.

sudici'ume [sudit∫ume] *sm* dirt, filth.

su'dore *sm* perspiration, sweat.

su'dovest *sm* south-west; **vento di ~** south-westerly wind.

'sue *vedi* **suo**.

'Suez ['suez] *sm*: **il Canale di ~** the Suez Canal.

suffici'ente [suffi't∫ente] *ag* enough, sufficient; *(borioso)* self-important; *(INS)* satisfactory.

sufficiente'mente [suffit∫ente'mente] *av* sufficiently, enough; *(guadagnare, darsi da fare)* enough.

suffici'enza [suffi't∫entsa] *sf (INS)* pass mark; **con un'aria di ~** *(fig)* with a condescending air; **a ~** enough; **ne ho avuto a ~!** I've had enough of this!

suf'fisso *sm (LING)* suffix.

suffra'gare *vt* to support.

suf'fragio [suf'fradʒo] *sm (voto)* vote; **~ universale** universal suffrage.

suggel'lare [suddʒel'lare] *vt (fig)* to seal.

suggeri'mento [suddʒeri'mento] *sm* suggestion; *(consiglio)* piece of advice, advice *no pl*; **dietro suo ~** on his advice.

sugge'rire [suddʒe'rire] *vt (risposta)* to tell; *(consigliare)* to advise; *(proporre)* to suggest; *(TEAT)* to prompt; **~ a qn di fare qc** to suggest to sb that he (*o* she) do sth.

suggeri'tore, 'trice [suddʒeri'tore] *sm/f (TEAT)* prompter.

suggestio'nare [suddʒestjo'nare] *vt* to influence.

suggesti'one [suddʒes'tjone] *sf (PSIC)* suggestion; *(istigazione)* instigation.

sugges'tivo, a [suddʒes'tivo] *ag (paesaggio)* evocative; *(teoria)* interesting, attractive.

'sughero ['sugero] *sm* cork.

'sugli ['suʎʎi] *prep +det vedi* **su**.

'sugo, ghi *sm (succo)* juice; *(di carne)* gravy; *(condimento)* sauce; *(fig)* gist, essence.

su'goso, a *ag (frutto)* juicy; *(fig: articolo etc)* pithy.

'sui *prep +det vedi* **su**.

sui'cida, i, e [sui't∫ida] *ag* suicidal ♦ *sm/f* suicide.

suici'darsi [suit∫i'darsi] *vr* to commit suicide.

sui'cidio [sui't∫idjo] *sm* suicide.

su'ino, a *ag*: **carne ~a** pork ♦ *sm* pig; **~i** *smpl* swine *pl*.

sul, sull', 'sulla, 'sulle, 'sullo *prep + det vedi* **su**.

sulfa'midico, a, ci, che *ag, sm (MED)* sulphonamide.

sulta'nina *sf*: **(uva) ~** sultana.

sul'tano, a *sm/f* sultan/sultana.

Su'matra *sf* Sumatra.

'summit ['summit] *sm inv* summit.

S.U.N.I.A. *sigla m (= sindacato unitario nazionale inquilini e assegnatari)* national association of tenants.

sunnomi'nato, a *ag* aforesaid *cpd*.

'sunto *sm* summary.

'suo, 'sua, 'sue, su'oi *det*: **il ~, la sua** *etc (di lui)* his; *(di lei)* her; *(di esso)* its; *(con valore indefinito)* one's, his/her; *(forma di cortesia: anche:* **S~**) your ♦ *pron*: **il ~, la sua** *etc* his; hers; yours ♦ *sm*: **ha speso del ~** he (*o* she *etc*) spent his (*o her etc*) own money ♦ *sf*: **la ~a** *(opinione)* his (*o her etc*) view; **i suoi** *(parenti)* his (*o her etc*) family; **un ~ amico** a friend of his (*o hers etc*); **è dalla ~a** he's on his (*o her etc*) side; **anche lui ha avuto le ~e** *(disavventure)* he's had his problems too; **sta sulle ~e** he keeps himself to himself.

su'ocero, a ['swɔt∫ero] *sm/f* father/mother-in-law; **i ~i** *smpl* father- and mother-in-law.

su'oi *vedi* **suo**.

su'ola *sf (di scarpa)* sole.

su'olo *sm (terreno)* ground; *(terra)* soil.

suo'nare *vt (MUS)* to play; *(campana)* to ring; *(ore)* to strike; *(clacson, allarme)* to sound ♦ *vi* to play; *(telefono, campana)* to ring; *(ore)* to strike; *(clacson, fig: parole)* to sound.

suo'nato, a *ag (compiuto)*: **ha cinquant'anni ~i** he is well over fifty.

suona'tore, 'trice *sm/f* player; **~ ambulante** street musician.

suone'ria *sf* alarm.

su'ono *sm* sound.

su'ora *sf (REL)* nun; **Suor Maria** Sister

Maria.

'**super** *ag inv*: (benzina) ~ ≈ four-star (petrol) (*BRIT*), premium (*US*).

supera'mento *sm* (*di ostacolo*) overcoming; (*di montagna*) crossing.

supe'rare *vt* (*oltrepassare*: *limite*) to exceed, surpass; (*attraversare*: *fiume*) to cross; (*sorpassare*: *veicolo*) to overtake; (*fig*: *essere più bravo di*) to surpass, outdo; (*: difficoltà*) to overcome; (*: esame*) to get through; ~ **qn in altezza/peso** to be taller/heavier than sb; **ha superato la cinquantina** he's over fifty (years of age); ~ **i limiti di velocità** to exceed the speed limit; **stavolta ha superato se stesso** this time he has surpassed himself.

supe'rato, a *ag* outmoded.

supe'rattico, ci *sm* penthouse.

su'perbia *sf* pride.

su'perbo, a *ag* proud; (*fig*) magnificent, superb.

supercondut'tore *sm* superconductor.

superena'lotto *sm* Italian national lottery.

superfici'ale [superfi't∫ale] *ag* superficial.

superficialità [superfit∫ali'ta] *sf* superficiality.

super'ficie, ci [super'fit∫e] *sf* surface; **tornare in** ~ (*a galla*) to return to the surface; (*problemi*) to resurface; ~ **alare** (*AER*) wing area; ~ **velica** (*NAUT*) sail area.

su'perfluo, a *ag* superfluous.

superi'ora *sf* (*REL*: *anche*: **madre** ~) mother superior.

superi'ore *ag* (*piano, arto, classi*) upper; (*più elevato*: *temperatura, livello*): ~ (**a**) higher (than); (*migliore*): ~ (**a**) superior (to) ♦ *sf/pl*: **le** ~**i** (*INS*) *vedi* **scuola media superiore; il corso** ~ **di un fiume** the upper reaches of a river; **scuola media** ~ ≈ senior comprehensive school (*BRIT*); ≈ senior high (school) (*US*).

superiorità *sf* superiority.

superla'tivo, a *ag, sm* superlative.

superla'voro *sm* overwork.

super'market [super'market] *sm inv* = **supermercato.**

supermer'cato *sm* supermarket.

super'nova *sf* supernova.

superpo'tenza [superpo'tentsa] *sf* (*POL*) superpower.

super'sonico, a, ci, che *ag* supersonic.

su'perstite *ag* surviving ♦ *sm/f* survivor.

superstizi'one [superstit'tsjone] *sf* superstition.

superstizi'oso, a [superstit'tsjoso] *ag* superstitious.

super'strada *sf* ≈ expressway.

supervisi'one *sf* supervision.

supervi'sore *sm* supervisor.

su'pino, a *ag* supine; **accettazione** ~**a** (*fig*) blind acceptance.

suppel'lettile *sf* furnishings *pl*.

suppergiù [supper'dʒu] *av* more or less, roughly.

suppl. *abbr* (= *supplemento*) supp(l).

supplemen'tare *ag* extra; (*treno*) relief *cpd*; (*entrate*) additional.

supple'mento *sm* supplement.

sup'plente *ag* temporary; (*insegnante*) supply *cpd* (*BRIT*), substitute *cpd* (*US*) ♦ *sm/f* temporary member of staff; supply (*o* substitute) teacher.

supp'lenza [sup'plɛntsa] *sf*: **fare** ~ to do supply (*BRIT*) *o* substitute (*US*) teaching.

supple'tivo, a *ag* (*gen*) supplementary; (*sessione d'esami*) extra.

'**supplica, che** *sf* (*preghiera*) plea; (*domanda scritta*) petition, request.

suppli'care *vt* to implore, beseech.

suppli'chevole [suppli'kevole] *ag* imploring.

sup'plire *vi*: ~ **a** to make up for.

sup'plizio [sup'plittsjo] *sm* torture.

sup'pongo, sup'poni *etc vb vedi* **supporre.**

sup'porre *vt* to suppose; **supponiamo che** … let's *o* just suppose that ….

sup'porto *sm* (*sostegno*) support.

supposizi'one [suppozit'tsjone] *sf* supposition.

sup'posta *sf* (*MED*) suppository.

sup'posto, a *pp di* **supporre.**

suppu'rare *vi* to suppurate.

supre'mazia [supremat'tsia] *sf* supremacy.

su'premo, a *ag* supreme; **S~a Corte (di Cassazione)** Supreme Court.

surclas'sare *vt* to outclass.

surge'lare [surdʒe'lare] *vt* to (deep-)freeze.

surge'lato, a [surdʒe'lato] *ag* (deep-)frozen ♦ *smpl*: **i** ~**i** frozen food *sg*.

surme'nage [syrmə'naʒ] *sm* (*fisico*) overwork; (*mentale*) mental strain; (*SPORT*) overtraining.

sur'plus *sm inv* (*ECON*) surplus; ~ **di manodopera** overmanning.

surre'ale *ag* surrealistic.

surriscalda'mento *sm* (*gen, TECN*) overheating.

surriscal'dare *vt* to overheat.

surro'gato *sm* substitute.

suscet'tibile [su∫∫et'tibile] *ag* (*sensibile*) touchy, sensitive; (*soggetto*): ~ **di miglioramento** that can be improved, open to improvement.

suscettibilità [su∫∫ettibili'ta] *sf* touchiness; **urtare la** ~ **di qn** to hurt sb's feelings.

susci'tare [suʃʃi'tare] *vt* to provoke, arouse.
su'sina *sf* plum.
su'sino *sm* plum (tree).
sussegu'ire *vt* to follow; **~rsi** *vr* to follow one another.
sussidi'ario, a *ag* subsidiary; (*treno*) relief *cpd*; (*fermata*) extra.
sus'sidio *sm* subsidy; (*aiuto*) aid; **~i didattici/audiovisivi** teaching/audiovisual aids; **~ di disoccupazione** unemployment benefit (*BRIT*) *o* benefits (*US*); **~ per malattia** sickness benefit.
sussi'ego *sm* haughtiness; **con aria di ~** haughtily.
sussis'tenza [sussis'tɛntsa] *sf* subsistence.
sus'sistere *vi* to exist; (*essere fondato*) to be valid *o* sound.
sussul'tare *vi* to shudder.
sus'sulto *sm* start.
sussur'rare *vt, vi* to whisper, murmur; **si sussurra che** it's rumoured (*BRIT*) *o* rumored (*US*) that ....
sus'surro *sm* whisper, murmur.
su'tura *sf* (*MED*) suture.
sutu'rare *vt* to stitch up, suture.
suv'via *escl* come on!
SV *sigla* = *Savona*.
S.V. *abbr vedi* **Signoria Vostra**.
sva'gare *vt* (*divertire*) to amuse; (*distrarre*): **~ qn** to take sb's mind off things; **~rsi** *vr* to amuse o.s.; to take one's mind off things.
sva'gato, a *ag* (*persona*) absent-minded; (*scolaro*) inattentive.
'svago, ghi *sm* (*riposo*) relaxation; (*ricreazione*) amusement; (*passatempo*) pastime.
svaligi'are [zvali'dʒare] *vt* to rob, burgle (*BRIT*), burglarize (*US*).
svaligia'tore, 'trice [zvalidʒa'tore] *sm/f* (*di banca*) robber; (*di casa*) burglar.
svalu'tare *vt* (*ECON*) to devalue; (*fig*) to belittle; **~rsi** *vr* (*ECON*) to be devalued.
svalutazi'one [zvalutat'tsjone] *sf* devaluation.
svam'pito, a *ag* absent-minded ♦ *sm/f* absent-minded person.
sva'nire *vi* to disappear, vanish.
sva'nito, a *ag* (*fig: persona*) absent-minded.
svantaggi'ato, a [zvantad'dʒato] *ag* at a disadvantage.
svan'taggio [zvan'taddʒo] *sm* disadvantage; (*inconveniente*) drawback, disadvantage; **tornerà a suo ~** it will work against you.
svantaggi'oso, a [zvantad'dʒoso] *ag* disadvantageous; **è un'offerta ~a per me** it's not in my interest to accept this

offer; **è un prezzo ~** it is not an attractive price.
svapo'rare *vi* to evaporate.
svapo'rato, a *ag* (*bibita*) flat.
svari'ato, a *ag* (*vario, diverso*) varied; (*numeroso*) various.
'svastica, che *sf* swastika.
sve'dese *ag* Swedish ♦ *sm/f* Swede ♦ *sm* (*LING*) Swedish.
'sveglia ['zveʎʎa] *sf* waking up; (*orologio*) alarm (clock); **suonare la ~** (*MIL*) to sound the reveille; **~ telefonica** alarm call.
svegli'are [zveʎ'ʎare] *vt* to wake up; (*fig*) to awaken, arouse; **~rsi** *vr* to wake up; (*fig*) to be revived, reawaken.
'sveglio, a ['zveʎʎo] *ag* awake; (*fig*) alert, quick-witted.
sve'lare *vt* to reveal.
svel'tezza [zvel'tettsa] *sf* (*gen*) speed; (*mentale*) quick-wittedness.
svel'tire *vt* (*gen*) to speed up, (*procedura*) to streamline.
'svelto, a *ag* (*passo*) quick; (*mente*) quick, alert; (*linea*) slim, slender; **alla ~a** quickly.
'svendere *vt* to sell off, clear.
'svendita *sf* (*COMM*) (clearance) sale.
sve'nevole *ag* mawkish.
'svengo *etc vb vedi* **svenire**.
sveni'mento *sm* fainting fit, faint.
sve'nire *vi* to faint.
sven'tare *vt* to foil, thwart.
sventa'tezza [zventa'tettsa] *sf* (*distrazione*) absent-mindedness; (*mancanza di prudenza*) rashness.
sven'tato, a *ag* (*distratto*) scatterbrained; (*imprudente*) rash.
'sventola *sf* (*colpo*) slap; **orecchie a ~** sticking-out ears.
svento'lare *vt, vi* to wave, flutter.
sven'trare *vt* to disembowel.
sven'tura *sf* misfortune.
sventu'rato, a *ag* unlucky, unfortunate.
sve'nuto, a *pp di* **svenire**.
svergo'gnare [zvergoɲ'ɲare] *vt* to shame.
svergo'gnato, a [zvergoɲ'ɲato] *ag* shameless ♦ *sm/f* shameless person.
sver'nare *vi* to spend the winter.
sverrò *etc vb vedi* **svenire**.
sves'tire *vt* to undress; **~rsi** *vr* to get undressed.
'Svezia ['zvettsja] *sf*: **la ~** Sweden.
svez'zare [zvet'tsare] *vt* to wean.
svi'are *vt* to divert; (*fig*) to lead astray; **~rsi** *vr* to go astray.
svico'lare *vi* to slip down an alley; (*fig*) to sneak off.
svi'gnarsela [zviɲ'ɲarsela] *vr* to slip away,

sneak off.

svili'mento *sm* debasement.

svi'lire *vt* to debase.

svilup'pare *vt*, **~rsi** *vr* to develop.

svi'luppo *sm* development; (*di industria*) expansion; **in via di ~** in the process of development; **paesi in via di ~** developing countries.

svinco'lare *vt* to free, release; (*merce*) to clear.

'svincolo *sm* (*COMM*) clearance; (*stradale*) motorway (*BRIT*) *o* expressway (*US*) intersection.

svisce'rare [zviʃʃe'rare] *vt* (*fig: argomento*) to examine in depth.

svisce'rato, a [zviʃʃe'rato] *ag* (*amore, odio*) passionate.

'svista *sf* oversight.

svi'tare *vt* to unscrew.

'Svizzera ['zvittsera] *sf*: **la ~** Switzerland.

'svizzero, a ['zvittsero] *ag, sm/f* Swiss.

svoglia'tezza [zvoʎʎa'tettsa] *sf* listlessness; indolence.

svogli'ato, a [zvoʎ'ʎato] *ag* listless; (*pigro*) lazy, indolent.

svolaz'zare [zvolat'tsare] *vi* to flutter.

'svolgere ['zvɔldʒere] *vt* to unwind; (*srotolare*) to unroll; (*fig: argomento*) to develop; (: *piano, programma*) to carry out; **~rsi** *vr* to unwind; to unroll; (*fig: aver luogo*) to take place; (: *procedere*) to go on; **tutto si è svolto secondo i piani** everything went according to plan.

svolgi'mento [zvoldʒi'mento] *sm* development; carrying out; (*andamento*) course.

'svolsi *etc vb vedi* **svolgere**.

'svolta *sf* (*atto*) turning *no pl*; (*curva*) turn, bend; (*fig*) turning-point; **essere ad una ~ nella propria vita** to be at a crossroads in one's life.

svol'tare *vi* to turn.

'svolto, a *pp di* **svolgere**.

svuo'tare *vt* to empty (out).

'Swaziland ['swadziland] *sm*: **lo ~** Swaziland.

T t

T, t [ti] *sf o m inv* (*lettera*) T, t; **T come Taranto** ≈ T for Tommy.

T *abbr* = **tabaccheria**.

t *abbr* = **tara**; **tonnellata**.

TA *sigla* = *Taranto*.

tabac'caio, a *sm/f* tobacconist.

tabacche'ria [tabakke'ria] *sf* tobacconist's (shop).

tabacchi'era [tabak'kjɛra] *sf* snuffbox.

ta'bacco, chi *sm* tobacco.

ta'bella *sf* (*tavola*) table; (*elenco*) list; **~ di marcia** schedule; **~ dei prezzi** price list.

tabel'lone *sm* (*per pubblicità*) billboard; (*per informazioni*) notice board (*BRIT*), bulletin board (*US*); (: *in stazione*) timetable board.

taber'nacolo *sm* tabernacle.

tabù *ag, sm inv* taboo.

'tabula 'rasa *sf* tabula rasa; **fare ~** (*fig*) to make a clean sweep.

tabu'lare *vt* to tabulate.

tabu'lato *sm* (*INFORM*) printout.

tabula'tore *sm* tabulator.

TAC *sigla f* (*MED*: = *Tomografia Assiale Computerizzata*) CAT.

'tacca, che *sf* notch, nick; **di mezza ~** (*fig*) mediocre.

taccagne'ria [takkaɲɲe'ria] *sf* meanness, stinginess.

tac'cagno, a [tak'kaɲɲo] *ag* mean, stingy.

tac'cheggio [tak'keddʒo] *sm* shoplifting.

tac'chino [tak'kino] *sm* turkey.

'taccia, ce ['tattʃa] *sf* bad reputation.

tacci'are [tat'tʃare] *vt*: **~ qn di** (*vigliaccheria etc*) to accuse sb of.

'taccio *etc* ['tattʃo] *vb vedi* **tacere**.

'tacco, chi *sm* heel.

taccu'ino *sm* notebook.

ta'cere [ta'tʃere] *vi* to be silent *o* quiet; (*smettere di parlare*) to fall silent ♦ *vt* to keep to oneself, say nothing about; **far ~ qn** to make sb be quiet; (*fig*) to silence sb; **mettere a ~ qc** to hush sth up.

tachicar'dia [takikar'dia] *sf* (*MED*) tachycardia.

ta'chimetro [ta'kimetro] *sm* speedometer.

'tacito, a ['tatʃito] *ag* silent; (*sottinteso*) tacit, unspoken.

taci'turno, a [tatʃi'turno] *ag* taciturn.

taci'uto, a [ta't∫uto] *pp di* **tacere**.
'tacqui *etc vb vedi* **tacere**.
ta'fano *sm* horsefly.
taffe'ruglio [taffe'ruʎʎo] *sm* brawl, scuffle.
taffettà *sm* taffeta.
'taglia ['taʎʎa] *sf* (*statura*) height; (*misura*) size; (*riscatto*) ransom; (*ricompensa*) reward; **~e forti** (*ABBIGLIAMENTO*) outsize.
taglia'boschi [taʎʎa'bɔski] *sm inv* woodcutter.
taglia'carte [taʎʎa'karte] *sm inv* paperknife.
taglia'legna [taʎʎa'leɲɲa] *sm inv* woodcutter.
tagli'ando [taʎ'ʎando] *sm* coupon.
tagli'are [taʎ'ʎare] *vt* to cut; (*recidere, interrompere*) to cut off; (*intersecare*) to cut across, intersect; (*carne*) to carve; (*vini*) to blend ♦ *vi* to cut; (*prendere una scorciatoia*) to take a short-cut; **~ la strada a qn** to cut across in front of sb; **~ corto** (*fig*) to cut short.
taglia'telle [taʎʎa'tɛlle] *sfpl* tagliatelle *pl*.
tagli'ato, a [taʎ'ʎato] *ag*: **essere ~ per qc** (*fig*) to be cut out for sth.
taglia'unghie [taʎʎa'ungje] *sm inv* nail clippers *pl*.
tagli'ente [taʎ'ʎɛnte] *ag* sharp.
tagli'ere [taʎ'ʎɛre] *sm* chopping board; (*per il pane*) bread board.
'taglio ['taʎʎo] *sm* (*anche fig*) cut; (*azione*) cutting *no pl*; (*di carne*) piece, (*di stoffa*) length; (*di vini*) blending; **di ~** on edge, edgeways; **banconote di piccolo/grosso ~** notes of small/large denomination; **un bel ~ di capelli** a nice haircut *o* hairstyle; **pizza al ~** pizza by the slice.
tagli'one [taʎ'ʎone] *sm*: **la legge del ~** the concept of an eye for an eye and a tooth for a tooth.
tagliuz'zare [taʎʎut'tsare] *vt* to cut into small pieces.
Ta'hiti [ta'iti] *sf* Tahiti.
tailan'dese *ag, sm/f, sm* Thai.
Tai'landia *sf*: **la ~** Thailand.
tai'lleur [ta'jœr] *sm inv* lady's suit.
Tai'wan [tai'wan] *sm*: **il ~** Taiwan.
'talco *sm* talcum powder.

================ *PAROLA CHIAVE*

'tale *det* **1** (*simile, così grande*) such; **un(a) ~ ... such (a) ...; non accetto ~i discorsi** I won't allow such talk; **è di una ~ arroganza** he is so arrogant; **fa una ~ confusione!** he makes such a mess!
2 (*persona o cosa indeterminata*) such-and-such; **il giorno ~ all'ora ~** on such-and-such a day at such-and-such a time; **la tal persona** that person; **ha telefonato**

---

una ~ Giovanna somebody called Giovanna phoned
3 (*nelle similitudini*): **~ ... ~ like ... like; ~ padre ~ figlio** like father, like son; **hai il vestito ~ quale il mio** your dress is just *o* exactly like mine
♦ *pron* (*indefinito: persona*): **un(a) ~** someone; **quel** (*o* **quella**) **~** that person, that man (*o* woman); **il tal dei ~i** what's-his-name.

---

ta'lento *sm* talent.
talis'mano *sm* talisman.
talk-'show [tɔlk'∫o] *sm inv* talk *o* chat show.
tallo'nare *vt* to pursue; **~ il pallone** (*CALCIO, RUGBY*) to heel the ball.
tallon'cino [tallon't∫ino] *sm* counterfoil (*BRIT*), stub; **~ del prezzo** (*di medicinali*) tear-off tag.
tal'lone *sm* heel.
tal'mente *av* so.
ta'lora *av* = **talvolta**.
'talpa *sf* (*anche fig*) mole.
tal'volta *av* sometimes, at times.
tambu'rello *sm* tambourine.
tambu'rino *sm* drummer boy.
tam'buro *sm* drum; **freni a ~** drum brakes; **a ~ battente** (*fig*) immediately, at once.
Ta'migi [ta'midʒi] *sm*: **il ~** the Thames.
tampona'mento *sm* (*AUT*) collision; **~ a catena** pile-up.
tampo'nare *vt* (*otturare*) to plug; (*urtare: macchina*) to crash *o* ram into.
tam'pone *sm* (*MED*) wad, pad; (*per timbri*) ink-pad; (*respingente*) buffer; **~ assorbente** tampon.
'tamtam *sm inv* (*fig*) grapevine.
'tana *sf* lair, den; (*fig*) den, hideout.
'tanfo *sm* stench.
tan'gente [tan'dʒɛnte] *ag* (*MAT*): **~ a** tangential to ♦ *sf* tangent; (*quota*) share; (*denaro estorto*) rake-off (*fam*), cut.
tangen'topoli [tandʒen'tɔpoli] *sf* (*POL, MEDIA*) Bribesville; *vedi nota nel riquadro*.

TANGENTOPOLI

Tangentopoli *refers to the corruption scandal of the early 1990s which involved a large number of politicians from all parties, including government ministers, as well as leading industrialists and business people. Subsequent investigations unearthed a complex series of illegal payments and bribes involving both public and private money. The scandal began in Milan, which came to be known as* **Tangentopoli***, or "Bribesville".*

tangenzi'ale [tandʒen'tsjale] *sf* (*strada*) bypass.

'Tangeri ['tandʒeri] *sf* Tangiers.

tan'gibile [tan'dʒibile] *ag* tangible.

tangibil'mente [tandʒibil'mente] *av* tangibly.

'tango, ghi *sm* tango.

'tanica, che *sf* jerry can.

tan'nino *sm* tannin.

tan'tino: un ~ *av* (*un po'*); a little, a bit; (*alquanto*) rather.

═══════════ *PAROLA CHIAVE*

'tanto, a *det* **1** (*molto: quantità*) a lot of, much; (*: numero*) a lot of, many; ~ **pane/ latte** a lot of bread/milk; ~ **tempo** a lot of time, a long time; ~**i auguri!** all the best!; ~**e grazie** many thanks; ~ **persone** a lot of people, many people; ~**e volte** many times, often; **ogni** ~**i chilometri** every so many kilometres

2: (*così* ~: *quantità*) so much, such a lot of; (*: numero*) so many, such a lot of; ~**a fatica per niente!** a lot of trouble for nothing!; **ha** ~ **coraggio che ...** he's got so much courage that ..., he's so brave that ...; **ho aspettato per** ~ **tempo** I waited so long *o* for such a long time

3: ~ ... **quanto** (*quantità*) as much ... as; (*numero*) as many ... as; **ho** ~**a pazienza quanta ne hai tu** I have as much patience as you have *o* as you; **ha** ~**i amici quanti nemici** he has as many friends as he has enemies

♦ *pron* **1** (*molto*) much, a lot; (*così* ~) so much, such a lot; ~**i, e** many, a lot; so many, such a lot; **credevo ce ne fosse** ~ I thought there was (such) a lot, I thought there was plenty; **una persona come** ~**e a** person just like any other; **è passato** ~ (*tempo*) it's been so long; **è** ~ **che aspetto** I've been waiting for a long time; ~ **di guadagnato!** so much the better!

2: ~ **quanto** (*denaro*) as much as; (*cioccolatini*) as many as; **ne ho** ~ **quanto basta** I have as much as I need; **due volte** ~ twice as much

3 (*indeterminato*) so much; ~ **per l'affitto,** ~ **per il gas** so much for the rent, so much for the gas; **costa un** ~ **al metro** it costs so much per metre; **di** ~ **in** ~, **ogni** ~ every so often; ~ **vale che ...** I (*o* we *etc*) may as well ...; ~ **meglio!** so much the better!; ~ **peggio per lui!** so much the worse for him!; **se** ~ **mi dà** ~ if that's how things are; **guardare qc con** ~ **d'occhi** to gaze wide-eyed at sth

♦ *av* **1** (*molto*) very; **vengo** ~ **volentieri** I'd be very glad to come; **non ci vuole** ~ **a capirlo** it doesn't take much to understand it

2 (*così* ~: *con ag, av*) so; (*: con vb*) so much, such a lot; **è** ~ **bella!** she's so beautiful!; **non urlare** ~ **(forte)** don't shout so much; **sto** ~ **meglio adesso** I'm so much better now; **era** ~ **bella da non credere** she was incredibly beautiful; ~ ... **che** so ... (that); ~ ... **da** so ... as

3: ~ ... **quanto** as ... as; **conosco** ~ **Carlo quanto suo padre** I know both Carlo and his father; **non è poi** ~ **complicato quanto sembra** it's not as difficult as it seems; **è** ~ **bella quanto buona** she is as good as she is beautiful; ~ **più insisti,** ~ **più non mollerà** the more you insist, the more stubborn he'll be; **quanto più ...** ~ **meno** the more ... the less; **quanto più lo conosco** ~ **meno mi piace** the better I know him the less I like him

4 (*solamente*) just; ~ **per cambiare/ scherzare** just for a change/a joke; **una volta** ~ for once

5 (*a lungo*) (for) long

♦ *cong* after all; **non insistere,** ~ **è inutile** don't keep on, it's no use; **lascia stare,** ~ **è troppo tardi** forget it, it's too late.

Tanza'nia [tandza'nia] *sf*: **la** ~ Tanzania.

tapi'oca *sf* tapioca.

ta'piro *sm* (*ZOOL*) tapir.

'tappa *sf* (*luogo di sosta, fermata*) stop, halt; (*parte di un percorso*) stage, leg; (*SPORT*) lap; **a** ~**e** in stages; **bruciare le** ~**e** (*fig*) to be a whizz kid.

tappa'buchi [tappa'buki] *sm inv* stopgap; **fare da** ~ to act as a stopgap.

tap'pare *vt* to plug, stop up; (*bottiglia*) to cork; ~**rsi il naso** to hold one's nose; ~**rsi le orecchie** to turn a deaf ear; ~**rsi gli occhi** to turn a blind eye.

tappa'rella *sf* rolling shutter.

tappe'tino *sm* (*per auto*) car mat; ~ **antiscivolo** (*da bagno*) non-slip mat.

tap'peto *sm* carpet; (*anche*: **tappetino**) rug; (*di tavolo*) cloth; (*SPORT*): **andare al** ~ to go down for the count; **mettere sul** ~ (*fig*) to bring up for discussion.

tappez'zare [tappet'tsare] *vt* (*con carta*) to paper; (*rivestire*): ~ **qc (di)** to cover sth (with).

tappezze'ria [tappettse'ria] *sf* (*arredamento*) soft furnishings *pl*; (*carta da parati*) wall covering; (*di automobile*) upholstery; **far da** ~ (*fig*) to be a wallflower.

tappezzi'ere [tappet'tsjɛre] *sm* upholsterer.

'tappo *sm* stopper; (*in sughero*) cork; ~ **a**

corona bottle top; ~ **a vite** screw top.
TAR *sigla m* = *Tribunale Amministrativo Regionale*.
'**tara** *sf* (*peso*) tare; (*MED*) hereditary defect; (*difetto*) flaw.
taran'tella *sf* tarantella.
ta'rantola *sf* tarantula.
ta'rare *vt* (*COMM*) to tare; (*TECN*) to calibrate.
ta'rato, a *ag* (*COMM*) tared; (*MED*) with a hereditary defect.
tara'tura *sf* (*COMM*) taring; (*TECN*) calibration.
tarchi'ato, a [tar'kjato] *ag* stocky, thickset.
tar'dare *vi* to be late ♦ *vt* to delay; ~ **a fare** to delay doing.
'**tardi** *av* late; **più** ~ later (on); **al più** ~ at the latest; **sul** ~ (*verso sera*) late in the day; **far** ~ to be late; (*restare alzato*) to stay up late.
tar'divo, a *ag* (*primavera*) late; (*rimedio*) belated, tardy; (*fig: bambino*) retarded.
'**tardo, a** *ag* (*lento, fig: ottuso*) slow; (*tempo: avanzato*) late.
tar'dona *sf* (*peg*): **essere una** ~ to be mutton dressed as lamb.
'**targa, ghe** *sf* plate; (*AUT*) number (*BRIT*) *o* license (*US*) plate; *vedi anche* **circolazione**.
tar'gare *vt* (*AUT*) to register.
targ'hetta [tar'getta] *sf* (*con nome: su porta*) nameplate; (: *su bagaglio*) name tag.
ta'riffa *sf* (*gen*) rate, tariff; (*di trasporti*) fare; (*elenco*) price list; tariff; **la** ~ **in vigore** the going rate; ~ **normale/ridotta** standard/reduced rate; (*su mezzi di trasporto*) full/concessionary fare; ~ **salariale** wage rate; ~ **unica** flat rate; ~**e doganali** customs rates *o* tariff; ~**e postali/telefoniche** postal/telephone charges.
tarif'fario, ii *ag*: **aumento** ~ increase in charges *o* rates ♦ *sm* tariff, table of charges.
'**tarlo** *sm* woodworm.
'**tarma** *sf* moth.
tarmi'cida, i [tarmi'tʃida] *ag*, *sm* moth-killer.
ta'rocco, chi *sm* tarot card; ~**chi** *smpl* (*gioco*) tarot *sg*.
tar'pare *vt* (*fig*): ~ **le ali a qn** to clip sb's wings.
tartagli'are [tartaʎ'ʎare] *vi* to stutter, stammer.
'**tartaro, a** *ag*, *sm* (*in tutti i sensi*) tartar.
tarta'ruga, ghe *sf* tortoise; (*di mare*) turtle; (*materiale*) tortoiseshell.
tartas'sare *vt* (*fam*): ~ **qn** to give sb the

works; ~ **qn a un esame** to give sb a grilling at an exam.
tar'tina *sf* canapé.
tar'tufo *sm* (*BOT*) truffle.
'**tasca, sche** *sf* pocket; **da** ~ pocket *cpd*; **fare i conti in** ~ **a qn** (*fig*) to meddle in sb's affairs.
tas'cabile *ag* (*libro*) pocket *cpd*.
tasca'pane *sm* haversack.
tas'chino [tas'kino] *sm* breast pocket.
Tas'mania *sf*: **la** ~ Tasmania.
'**tassa** *sf* (*imposta*) tax; (*doganale*) duty; (*per iscrizione: a scuola etc*) fee; ~ **di circolazione/di soggiorno** road/tourist tax.
tas'sametro *sm* taximeter.
tas'sare *vt* to tax; to levy a duty on.
tassa'tivo, a *ag* peremptory.
tassazi'one [tassat'tsjone] *sf* taxation; **soggetto a** ~ taxable.
tas'sello *sm* (*di legno, pietra*) plug; (*assaggio*) wedge.
tassì *sm inv* = **taxi**.
tas'sista, i, e *smlf* taxi driver.
'**tasso** *sm* (*di natalità, d'interesse etc*) rate; (*BOT*) yew; (*ZOOL*) badger; ~ **di cambio/ d'interesse** rate of exchange/interest; ~ **di crescita** growth rate.
tas'tare *vt* to feel; ~ **il terreno** (*fig*) to see how the land lies.
tasti'era *sf* keyboard.
tastie'rino *sm*: ~ **numerico** numeric keypad.
'**tasto** *sm* key; (*tatto*) touch, feel; **toccare un** ~ **delicato** (*fig*) to touch on a delicate subject; **toccare il** ~ **giusto** (*fig*) to strike the right note; ~ **funzione** (*INFORM*) function key; ~ **delle maiuscole** (*su macchina da scrivere etc*) shift key.
tas'toni *av*: **procedere (a)** ~ to grope one's way forward.
'**tata** *sf* (*linguaggio infantile*) nanny.
'**tattico, a, ci, che** *ag* tactical ♦ *sf* tactics *pl*.
'**tatto** *sm* (*senso*) touch; (*fig*) tact; **duro al** ~ hard to the touch; **aver** ~ to be tactful, have tact.
tatu'aggio [tatu'addʒo] *sm* tattooing; (*disegno*) tattoo.
tatu'are *vt* to tattoo.
tauma'turgico, a, ci, che [tauma'turdʒiko] *ag* (*fig*) miraculous.
ta'verna *sf* (*osteria*) tavern.
'**tavola** *sf* table; (*asse*) plank, board; (*lastra*) tablet; (*quadro*) panel (painting); (*illustrazione*) plate; ~ **calda** snack bar; ~ **pieghevole** folding table.
tavo'lata *sf* company at table.
tavo'lato *sm* boarding; (*pavimento*) wooden

floor.

tavo'letta *sf* tablet, bar; **a** ~ (*AUT*) flat out.

tavo'lino *sm* small table; (*scrivania*) desk; ~ **da tè/gioco** coffee/card table; **mettersi a** ~ to get down to work; **decidere qc a** ~ (*fig*) to decide sth on a theoretical level.

'tavolo *sm* table; ~ **da disegno** drawing board; ~ **da lavoro** desk; (*TECN*) workbench; ~ **operatorio** (*MED*) operating table.

tavo'lozza [tavo'lɔttsa] *sf* (*ARTE*) palette.

'taxi *sm inv* taxi.

'tazza ['tattsa] *sf* cup; ~ **da caffè/tè** coffee/tea cup; **una** ~ **di caffè/tè** a cup of coffee/tea.

taz'zina [tat'tsina] *sf* coffee cup.

TBC *abbr f* (= *tubercolosi*) TB.

TCI *sigla m* = *Touring Club Italiano*.

TE *sigla* = *Teramo*.

te *pron* (*soggetto: in forme comparative, oggetto*) you.

tè *sm inv* tea; (*trattenimento*) tea party.

tea'trale *ag* theatrical.

te'atro *sm* theatre; ~ **comico** comedy; ~ **di posa** film studio.

'tecnico, a, ci, che *ag* technical ♦ *sm/f* technician ♦ *sf* technique; (*tecnologia*) technology.

tecnolo'gia [teknolo'dʒia] *sf* technology; **alta** ~ high technology, hi-tech.

tecno'logico, a, ci, che [tekno'lɔdʒiko] *ag* technological.

te'desco, a, schi, sche *ag, sm/f, sm* German; ~ **orientale/occidentale** East/West German.

tedi'are *vt* (*infastidire*) to bother, annoy; (*annoiare*) to bore.

'tedio *sm* tedium, boredom.

tedi'oso, a *ag* tedious, boring.

te'game *sm* (*CUC*) pan; **al** ~ fried.

'teglia ['teʎʎa] *sf* (*CUC: per dolci*) (baking) tin (*BRIT*), cake pan (*US*); (: *per arrosti*) (roasting) tin.

'tegola *sf* tile.

Teh'ran *sf* Tehran.

tei'era *sf* teapot.

te'ina *sf* (*CHIM*) theine.

tel. *abbr* (= *telefono*) tel.

'tela *sf* (*tessuto*) cloth; (*per vele, quadri*) canvas; (*dipinto*) canvas, painting; **di** ~ (*calzoni*) (heavy) cotton *cpd*; (*scarpe, borsa*) canvas *cpd*; ~ **cerata** oilcloth; ~ **di ragno** spider's web.

te'laio *sm* (*apparecchio*) loom; (*struttura*) frame.

Tel A'viv *sf* Tel Aviv.

tele... *prefisso* tele....

teleabbo'nato *sm* television licence holder.

tele'camera *sf* television camera.

telecoman'dare *vt* to operate by remote control.

teleco'mando *sm* remote control; (*dispositivo*) remote-control device.

telecomunicazi'oni [telekomunikat'tsjoni] *sfpl* telecommunications.

teleconfe'renza *sf* teleconferencing.

tele'cronaca, che *sf* television report.

telecro'nista, i, e *sm/f* (television) commentator.

tele'ferica, che *sf* cableway.

tele'film *sm inv* television film.

telefo'nare *vi* to telephone, ring; (*fare una chiamata*) to make a phone call ♦ *vt* to telephone; ~ **a qn** to telephone sb, phone *o* ring *o* call sb (up).

telefo'nata *sf* (telephone) call; ~ **urbana/interurbana** local/long-distance call; ~ **a carico del destinatario** reverse-charge (*BRIT*) *o* collect (*US*) call; ~ **con preavviso** person-to-person call.

telefonica'mente *av* by (tele)phone.

tele'fonico, a, ci, che *ag* (tele)phone *cpd*.

telefo'nino *sm* (*cellulare*) mobile phone.

telefo'nista, i, e *sm/f* telephonist; (*d'impresa*) switchboard operator.

te'lefono *sm* telephone; **avere il** ~ to be on the (tele)phone; ~ **a gettoni** ≈ pay phone; ~ **azzurro** ≈ Childline; ~ **interno** internal phone; ~ **pubblico** public phone, call box (*BRIT*); ~ **rosa** ≈ rape crisis.

telegior'nale [teledʒor'nale] *sm* television news (programme).

telegra'fare *vt, vi* to telegraph, cable.

tele'grafico, a, ci, che *ag* telegraph *cpd*, telegraphic.

telegra'fista, i, e *sm/f* telegraphist.

te'legrafo *sm* telegraph; (*ufficio*) telegraph office.

tele'gramma, i *sm* telegram.

telela'voro *sm* teleworking.

tele'matica *sf* data transmission; telematics *sg*.

teleno'vela *sf* soap opera.

teleobiet'tivo *sm* telephoto lens *sg*.

telepa'tia *sf* telepathy.

tele'quiz [tele'kwits] *sm inv* (*TV*) game show.

teles'chermo [teles'kɛrmo] *sm* television screen.

teles'copio *sm* telescope.

telescri'vente *sf* teleprinter (*BRIT*), teletypewriter (*US*).

teleselet'tivo, a *ag*: **prefisso** ~ dialling code (*BRIT*), dial code (*US*).

teleselezi'one [teleselet'tsjone] *sf* direct dialling.

telespetta'tore, 'trice *sm/f* (television) viewer.

tele'text *sm inv* teletext.

tele'video *sm videotext service.*

televisi'one *sf* television; ~ **digitale** digital TV; *vedi nota nel riquadro.*

TELEVISIONE

Three state-owned channels, RAI 1, 2 and 3, and a large number of private companies broadcast television programmes in Italy. Some of the latter function at purely local level, while others are regional; some form part of a network, while others remain independent. As a public corporation, RAI reports to the Post and Telecommunications Ministry. Both RAI and the private-sector channels compete for advertising revenues.

---

televi'sore *sm* television set.

'telex *sm inv* telex.

'telo *sm* length of cloth.

te'lone *sm (per merci etc)* tarpaulin; *(sipario)* drop curtain.

'tema, i *sm* theme; *(INS)* essay.

te'matica *sf* basic themes *pl.*

teme'rario, a *ag* rash, reckless.

te'mere *vt* to fear, be afraid of; *(essere sensibile a: freddo, calore)* to be sensitive to ♦ *vi* to be afraid; *(essere preoccupato)*: ~ **per** to worry about, fear for; ~ **di/che** to be afraid of/that.

'tempera *sf (pittura)* tempera; *(dipinto)* painting in tempera.

temperama'tite *sm inv* pencil sharpener.

tempera'mento *sm* temperament.

tempe'rante *ag* moderate.

tempe'rare *vt (aguzzare)* to sharpen; *(fig)* to moderate, control, temper.

tempe'rato, a *ag* moderate, temperate; *(clima)* temperate.

tempera'tura *sf* temperature; ~ **ambiente** room temperature.

tempe'rino *sm* penknife.

tem'pesta *sf* storm; ~ **di sabbia/neve** sand/snowstorm.

tempes'tare *vt (percuotere)*: ~ **qn di colpi** to rain blows on sb; *(bombardare)*: ~ **qn di domande** to bombard sb with questions; *(ornare)* to stud.

tempes'tivo, a *ag* timely.

tempes'toso, a *ag* stormy.

'tempia *sf (ANAT)* temple.

'tempio *sm (edificio)* temple.

tem'pismo *sm* sense of timing.

tem'pistiche [tem'pistike] *sfpl (COMM)* time

and motion.

'tempo *sm (METEOR)* weather; *(cronologico)* time; *(epoca)* time, times *pl*; *(di film, gioco: parte)* part; *(MUS)* time; *(: battuta)* beat; *(LING)* tense; **un** ~ once; **da** ~ for a long time now; ~ **fa** some time ago; **poco** ~ **dopo** not long after; **a** ~ **e luogo** at the right time and place; **ogni cosa a suo** ~ we'll *(o* you'll *etc)* deal with it in due course; **al** ~ **stesso** *o* **a un** ~ at the same time; **per** ~ early; **per qualche** ~ for a while; **trovare il** ~ **di fare qc** to find the time to do sth; **aver fatto il proprio** ~ to have had its *(o* his *etc)* day; **primo/ secondo** ~ *(TEAT)* first/second part; *(SPORT)* first/second half; **rispettare i** ~**i** to keep to the timetable; **stringere i** ~**i** to speed things up; **con i** ~**i che corrono** these days; **in questi ultimi** ~**i** of late; **ai miei** ~**i** in my day; ~ **di cottura** cooking time; **in** ~ **utile** in due time *o* course; ~**i di esecuzione** *(COMM)* time scale *sg*; ~**i di lavorazione** *(COMM)* throughput time *sg*; ~**i morti** *(COMM)* downtime *sg*, idle time *sg*.

tempo'rale *ag* temporal ♦ *sm (METEOR)* (thunder)storm.

tempora'lesco, a, schi, sche *ag* stormy.

tempo'raneo, a *ag* temporary.

temporeggi'are [tempored'dʒare] *vi* to play for time, temporize.

'tempra *sf (TECN: atto)* tempering, hardening; *(: effetto)* temper; *(fig: costituzione fisica)* constitution; *(: intellettuale)* temperament.

tem'prare *vt* to temper.

te'nace [te'natʃe] *ag* strong, tough; *(fig)* tenacious.

te'nacia [te'natʃa] *sf* tenacity.

te'naglie [te'naʎʎe] *sfpl* pincers *pl.*

'tenda *sf (riparo)* awning; *(di finestra)* curtain; *(per campeggio etc)* tent.

ten'daggio [ten'daddʒo] *sm* curtaining, curtains *pl*, drapes *pl (US).*

ten'denza [ten'dentsa] *sf* tendency; *(orientamento)* trend; **avere** ~ **a** *o* **per qc** to have a bent for sth; ~ **al rialzo/ribasso** *(BORSA)* upward/downward trend.

tendenziosità [tendentsjosi'ta] *sf* tendentiousness.

tendenzi'oso, a [tenden'tsjoso] *ag* tendentious, bias(s)ed.

'tendere *vt (allungare al massimo)* to stretch, draw tight; *(porgere: mano)* to hold out; *(fig: trappola)* to lay, set ♦ *vi*: ~ **a qc/a fare** to tend towards sth/to do; **tutti i nostri sforzi sono tesi a ...** all our efforts are geared towards ...; ~ **l'orecchio** to prick up one's ears; **il tempo tende al caldo** the weather is getting hot; **un blu che tende al verde** a greenish blue.

ten'dina *sf* curtain.

'tendine *sm* tendon, sinew.

ten'done *sm* (*da circo*) big top.

ten'dopoli *sf inv* (large) camp.

'tenebre *sfpl* darkness *sg*.

tene'broso, a *ag* dark, gloomy.

te'nente *sm* lieutenant.

te'nere *vt* to hold; (*conservare, mantenere*) to keep; (*ritenere, considerare*) to consider; (*spazio: occupare*) to take up, occupy; (*seguire: strada*) to keep to; (*dare: lezione, conferenza*) to give ♦ *vi* to hold; (*colori*) to be fast; (*dare importanza*): ~ **a** to care about; ~ **a fare** to want to do, be keen to do; ~**rsi** *vr* (*stare in una determinata posizione*) to stand; (*stimarsi*) to consider o.s.; (*aggrapparsi*): ~**rsi a** to hold on to; (*attenersi*): ~**rsi a** to stick to; ~ **in gran conto** *o* **considerazione qn** to have a high regard for sb, think highly of sb; ~ **conto di qc** to take sth into consideration; ~ **presente qc** to bear sth in mind; **non ci sono scuse che tengano** I'll take no excuses; ~**rsi per la mano** (*uso reciproco*) to hold hands; ~**rsi in piedi** to stay on one's feet.

tene'rezza [tene'rettsa] *sf* tenderness.

'tenero, a *ag* tender; (*pietra, cera, colore*) soft; (*fig*) tender, loving ♦ *sm*: **tra quei due c'è del** ~ there's a romance budding between those two.

'tengo *etc vb vedi* **tenere.**

'tenia *sf* tapeworm.

'tenni *etc vb vedi* **tenere.**

'tennis *sm* tennis; ~ **da tavolo** table tennis.

ten'nista, i, e *sm/f* tennis player.

te'nore *sm* (*tono*) tone; (*MUS*) tenor; ~ **di vita** way of life; (*livello*) standard of living.

tensi'one *sf* tension; **ad alta** ~ (*ELETTR*) high-voltage *cpd*, high-tension *cpd*.

tentaco'lare *ag* tentacular; (*fig: città*) magnet-like.

ten'tacolo *sm* tentacle.

ten'tare *vt* (*indurre*) to tempt; (*provare*): ~ **qc/di fare** to attempt *o* try sth/to do; ~ **la sorte** to try one's luck.

tenta'tivo *sm* attempt.

tentazi'one [tentat'tsjone] *sf* temptation; **aver la** ~ **di fare** to be tempted to do.

tentenna'mento *sm* (*fig*) hesitation, wavering; **dopo molti** ~**i** after much hesitation.

tenten'nare *vi* to shake, be unsteady; (*fig*) to hesitate, waver ♦ *vt*: ~ **il capo** to shake

one's head.

ten'toni *av*: **andare a** ~ (*anche fig*) to grope one's way.

'tenue *ag* (*sottile*) fine; (*colore*) soft; (*fig*) slender, slight.

te'nuta *sf* (*capacità*) capacity; (*divisa*) uniform; (*abito*) dress; (*AGR*) estate; **a** ~ **d'aria** airtight; ~ **di strada** roadholding power; **in** ~ **da lavoro** in one's working clothes; **in** ~ **da sci** in a skiing outfit.

teolo'gia [teolo'dʒia] *sf* theology.

teo'logico, a, ci, che [teo'lɔdʒiko] *ag* theological.

te'ologo, gi *sm* theologian.

teo'rema, i *sm* theorem.

teo'ria *sf* theory; **in** ~ in theory, theoretically.

te'orico, a, ci, che *ag* theoretic(al) ♦ *sm* theorist, theoretician; **a livello** ~, **in linea** ~**a** theoretically.

teoriz'zare [teorid'dzare] *vt* to theorize.

'tepido, a *ag* = **tiepido**.

te'pore *sm* warmth.

'teppa *sf* mob, hooligans *pl*.

tep'paglia [tep'paʎʎa] *sf* hooligans *pl*.

tep'pismo *sm* hooliganism.

tep'pista, i *sm* hooligan.

tera'peutico, a, ci, che *ag* therapeutic.

tera'pia *sf* therapy; ~ **di gruppo** group therapy.

tera'pista, i, e *sm/f* therapist.

tergicris'tallo [terdʒikris'tallo] *sm* windscreen (*BRIT*) *o* windshield (*US*) wiper.

tergiver'sare [terdʒiver'sare] *vi* to shilly-shally.

'tergo *sm*: **a** ~ behind; **vedi a** ~ please turn over.

'terital ® *sm inv* Terylene ®.

ter'male *ag* thermal.

'terme *sfpl* thermal baths.

'termico, a, ci, che *ag* thermal; **centrale** ~**a** thermal power station.

termi'nale *ag* (*fase, parte*) final; (*MED*) terminal ♦ *sm* terminal; **tratto** ~ (*di fiume*) lower reaches *pl*.

termi'nare *vt* to end; (*lavoro*) to finish ♦ *vi* to end.

terminazi'one [terminat'tsjone] *sf* (*fine*) end; (*LING*) ending; ~**i nervose** (*ANAT*) nerve endings.

'termine *sm* term; (*fine, estremità*) end; (*di territorio*) boundary, limit; **fissare un** ~ to set a deadline; **portare a** ~ **qc** to bring sth to a conclusion; **contratto a** ~ (*COMM*) forward contract; **a breve/lungo** ~ short-/long-term; **ai** ~**i di legge** by law; **in altri** ~**i** in other words; **parlare senza**

mezzi ~**i** to talk frankly, not to mince one's words.
terminolo'gia [terminolo'dʒia] *sf* terminology.
'**termite** *sf* termite.
termoco'perta *sf* electric blanket.
ter'mometro *sm* thermometer.
termonucle'are *ag* thermonuclear.
'**termos** *sm inv* = **thermos.**
termosi'fone *sm* radiator; **(riscaldamento a)** ~ central heating.
ter'mostato *sm* thermostat.
'**terna** *sf* set of three; *(lista di tre nomi)* list of three candidates.
'**terno** *sm* (*al lotto etc*) (set of) three winning numbers; **vincere un** ~ **al lotto** *(fig)* to hit the jackpot.
'**terra** *sf* (*gen, ELETTR*) earth; (*sostanza*) soil, earth; (*opposto al mare*) land *no pl*; (*regione, paese*) land; (*argilla*) clay; ~**e** *sfpl* (*possedimento*) lands, land *sg*; **a o per** ~ (*stato*) on the ground (*a fluor*), (*moto*) to the ground, down; **mettere a** ~ (*ELETTR*) to earth; **essere a** ~ *(fig: depresso)* to be at rock bottom; **via** ~ (*viaggiare*) by land, overland; **strada in** ~ **battuta** dirt track; ~ **di nessuno** no man's land; **la T**~ Santa the Holy Land; ~ **di Siena** sienna; ~ ~ (*fig: persona, argomento*) prosaic, pedestrian.
'**terra-'aria** *ag inv* (*MIL*) ground-to-air.
terra'cotta *sf* terracotta; **vasellame di** ~ earthenware.
terra'ferma *sf* dry land, terra firma; (*continente*) mainland.
ter'raglia [ter'raʎʎa] *sf* pottery; ~**e** *pl* (*oggetti*) crockery *sg*, earthenware *sg*.
Terra'nova *sf*: **la** ~ Newfoundland.
terrapi'eno *sm* embankment, bank.
'**terra-'terra** *ag inv* (*MIL*) surface-to-surface.
ter'razza [ter'rattsa] *sf*, **ter'razzo** [ter'rattso] *sm* terrace.
terremo'tato, a *ag* (*zona*) devastated by an earthquake ♦ *sm/f* earthquake victim.
terre'moto *sm* earthquake.
ter'reno, a *ag* (*vita, beni*) earthly ♦ *sm* (*suolo, fig*) ground; (*COMM*) land *no pl*, plot (of land); site; (*SPORT, MIL*) field; **perdere** ~ (*anche fig*) to lose ground; **un** ~ **montuoso** a mountainous terrain; ~ **alluvionale** (*GEO*) alluvial soil.
'**terreo, a** *ag* (*viso, colorito*) wan.
ter'restre *ag* (*superficie*) of the earth, earth's; (*di terra: battaglia, animale*) land *cpd*; (*REL*) earthly, worldly.
ter'ribile *ag* terrible, dreadful.
ter'riccio [ter'rittʃo] *sm* soil.
terri'ero, a *ag*: **proprietà** ~**a** landed

property; **proprietario** ~ landowner.
terrifi'cante *ag* terrifying.
ter'rina *sf* (*zuppiera*) tureen.
territori'ale *ag* territorial.
terri'torio *sm* territory.
ter'rone, a *sm/f derogatory term used by Northern Italians to describe Southern Italians.*
ter'rore *sm* terror; **avere il** ~ **di qc** to be terrified of sth.
terro'rismo *sm* terrorism.
terro'rista, i, e *sm/f* terrorist.
terroriz'zare [terrorid'dzare] *vt* to terrorize.
'**terso, a** *ag* clear.
ter'zetto [ter'tsetto] *sm* (*MUS*) trio, terzetto; (*di persone*) trio.
terzi'ario, a [ter'tsjarjo] *ag* (*GEO, ECON*) tertiary.
ter'zino [ter'tsino] *sm* (*CALCIO*) fullback, back.
'**terzo, a** [ˈtɛrtso] *ag* **third** ♦ *sm* (*frazione*) third; (*DIR*) third party ♦ *sf* (*gen*) third; (*AUT*) third (gear); (*di trasporti*) third class; (*SCOL: elementare*) third year *at primary school*; (*: media*) third year *at secondary school*; (*: superiore*) sixth year *at secondary school*; ~**i** *smpl* (*altri*) others, other people; **agire per conto di** ~**i** to act on behalf of a third party; **assicurazione contro** ~**i** third-party insurance (*BRIT*), liability insurance (*US*); **la** ~**a età** old age; **il** ~ **mondo** the Third World; **di terz'ordine** third rate; **la** ~**a pagina** (*STAMPA*) the Arts page.
'**tesa** *sf* brim; **a larghe** ~**e** wide-brimmed.
'**teschio** [ˈtɛskjo] *sm* skull.
'**tesi** *sf inv* thesis; ~ **di laurea** degree thesis.
'**tesi** *etc vb vedi* **tendere.**
'**teso, a** *pp di* **tendere** ♦ *ag* (*tirato*) taut, tight; (*fig*) tense.
tesore'ria *sf* treasury.
tesori'ere *sm* treasurer.
te'soro *sm* treasure; **il Ministero del T**~ the Treasury; **far** ~ **dei consigli di qn** to take sb's advice to heart.
'**tessera** *sf* (*documento*) card; (*di abbonato*) season ticket; (*di giornalista*) pass; **ha la** ~ **del partito** he's a party member.
tesse'rare *vt* (*iscrivere*) to give a membership card to.
tesse'rato, a *sm/f* (*di società sportiva etc*) (fully paid-up) member; (*POL*) (card-carrying) member.
'**tessere** *vt* to weave; ~ **le lodi di qn** (*fig*) to sing sb's praises.
'**tessile** *ag, sm* textile.
tessi'tore, 'trice *sm/f* weaver.
tessi'tura *sf* weaving.

tes'suto *sm* fabric, material; (*BIOL*) tissue; (*fig*) web.

'testa *sf* head; (*di cose: estremità, parte anteriore*) head, front; **5.000 lire a ~ 5,000** lire apiece *o* a head *o* per person; **a ~ alta** with one's head held high; **a ~ bassa** (*correre*) headlong; (*con aria dimessa*) with head bowed; **di ~** *ag* (*vettura etc*) front; **dare alla ~** to go to one's head; **fare di ~ propria** to go one's own way; **in ~** (*SPORT*) in the lead; **essere in ~ alla classifica** (*corridore*) to be number one; (*squadra*) to be at the top of the league table; (*disco*) to be top of the charts, be number one; **essere alla ~ di qc** (*società*) to be the head of; (*esercito*) to be at the head of; **tenere ~ a qn** (*nemico etc*) to stand up to sb; **una ~ d'aglio** a bulb of garlic; **~ o croce?** heads or tails?; **avere la ~ dura** to be stubborn; **~ di serie** (*TENNIS*) seed, seeded player.

'testa-'coda *sm inv* (*AUT*) spin.

testamen'tario, a *ag* (*DIR*) testamentary; **le sue disposizioni ~e** the provisions of his will.

testa'mento *sm* (*atto*) will, testament; **l'Antico/il Nuovo T~** (*REL*) the Old/New Testament.

testar'daggine [testar'daddʒine] *sf* stubbornness, obstinacy.

tes'tardo, a *ag* stubborn, pig-headed.

tes'tare *vt* to test.

tes'tata *sf* (*parte anteriore*) head; (*intestazione*) heading; **missile a ~ nucleare** missile with a nuclear warhead.

'teste *sm/f* witness.

tes'ticolo *sm* testicle.

testi'era *sf* (*del letto*) headboard; (*di cavallo*) headpiece.

testi'mone *sm/f* (*DIR*) witness; **fare da ~ alle nozze di qn** to be a witness at sb's wedding; **~ oculare** eye witness.

testimoni'anza [testimo'njantsa] *sf* (*atto*) deposition; (*effetto*) evidence; (*fig: prova*) proof; **accusare qn di falsa ~** to accuse sb of perjury; **rilasciare una ~** to give evidence.

testimoni'are *vt* to testify; (*fig*) to bear witness to, testify to ♦ *vi* to give evidence, testify; **~ il vero** to tell the truth; **~ il falso** to perjure o.s.

tes'tina *sf* (*di giradischi, registratore*) head.

'testo *sm* text; **fare ~** (*opera, autore*) to be authoritative; (*fig: dichiarazione*) to carry weight.

testoste'rone *sm* testosterone.

testu'ale *ag* textual; **le sue parole ~i** his (*o* her) actual words.

tes'tuggine [tes'tuddʒine] *sf* tortoise; (*di mare*) turtle.

'tetano *sm* (*MED*) tetanus.

'tetro, a *ag* gloomy.

'tetta *sf* (*fam*) boob, tit.

tetta'rella *sf* teat.

'tetto *sm* roof; **abbandonare il ~ coniugale** to desert one's family; **~ a cupola** dome.

tet'toia *sf* roofing; canopy.

'Tevere *sm*: **il ~** the Tiber.

TG [tid'dʒi] *abbr m* (= *telegiornale*) TV news *sg.*

'thermos ® ['tɛrmos] *sm inv* vacuum *o* Thermos ® flask.

'thriller ['θrilə], **'thrilling** ['θriliŋ] *sm inv* thriller.

ti *pron* (*dav lo, la, li, le, ne diventa* **te**) (*oggetto*) you; (*complemento di termine*) (to) you; (*riflessivo*) yourself; **~ aiuto?** can I give you a hand?; **te lo ha dato?** did he give it to you?; **~ sei lavato?** have you washed?

ti'ara *sf* (*REL*) tiara.

'Tibet *sm*: **il ~** Tibet.

tibe'tano, a *ag, sm/f* Tibetan.

'tibia *sf* tibia, shinbone.

tic *sm inv* tic, (nervous) twitch; (*fig*) mannerism.

ticchet'tio [tikket'tio] *sm* (*di macchina da scrivere*) clatter; (*di orologio*) ticking; (*della pioggia*) patter.

'ticchio ['tikkjo] *sm* (*ghiribizzo*) whim; (*tic*) tic, (nervous) twitch.

'ticket *sm inv* (*MED*) prescription charge (*BRIT*).

ti'ene *etc vb vedi* **tenere**.

ti'epido, a *ag* lukewarm, tepid.

ti'fare *vi*: **~ per** to be a fan of; (*parteggiare*) to side with.

'tifo *sm* (*MED*) typhus; (*fig*): **fare il ~ per** to be a fan of.

tifoi'dea *sf* typhoid.

ti'fone *sm* typhoon.

ti'foso, a *sm/f* (*SPORT etc*) fan.

tight ['tait] *sm inv* morning suit.

'tiglio ['tiʎʎo] *sm* lime (tree), linden (tree).

'tigna ['tiɲɲa] *sf* (*MED*) ringworm.

ti'grato, a *ag* striped.

'tigre *sf* tiger.

tilt *sm*: **andare in ~** (*fig*) to go haywire.

tim'ballo *sm* (*strumento*) kettledrum; (*CUC*) timbale.

tim'brare *vt* to stamp; (*annullare: francobolli*) to postmark; **~ il cartellino** to clock in.

'timbro *sm* stamp; (*MUS*) timbre, tone.

timi'dezza [timi'dettsa] *sf* shyness, timidity.

'timido, a *ag* shy, timid.

'timo *sm* thyme.

ti'mone *sm* (*NAUT*) rudder.
timoni'ere *sm* helmsman.
timo'rato, a *ag* conscientious; ~ **di Dio** God-fearing.
ti'more *sm* (*paura*) fear; (*rispetto*) awe; **avere** ~ **di qc/qn** (*paura*) to be afraid of sth/sb.
timo'roso, a *ag* timid, timorous.
'timpano *sm* (*ANAT*) eardrum; (*MUS*): ~**i** kettledrums, timpani.
'tinca, che *sf* (*ZOOL*) tench.
ti'nello *sm* small dining room.
'tingere ['tindʒere] *vt* to dye.
'tino *sm* vat.
ti'nozza [ti'nɔttsa] *sf* tub.
'tinsi *etc vb vedi* **tingere**.
'tinta *sf* (*materia colorante*) dye; (*colore*) colour (*BRIT*), color (*US*), shade.
tinta'rella *sf* (*fam*) (sun)tan.
tintin'nare *vi* to tinkle.
tintin'nio *sm* tinkling.
'tinto, a *pp di* **tingere**.
tinto'ria *sf* (*officina*) dyeworks *sg*; (*lavasecco*) dry cleaner's (shop).
tin'tura *sf* (*operazione*) dyeing; (*colorante*) dye; ~ **di iodio** tincture of iodine.
'tipico, a, ci, che *ag* typical.
'tipo *sm* type; (*genere*) kind, type; (*fam*) chap, fellow; **vestiti di tutti i** ~**i** all kinds of clothes; **sul** ~ **di questo** of this sort; **sei un bel** ~**!** you're a fine one!
tipogra'fia *sf* typography.
tipo'grafico, a, ci, che *ag* typographic(al).
ti'pografo *sm* typographer.
tip 'tap [tip'tap] *sm* (*ballo*) tap dancing.
T.I.R. *sigla m* (= *Transports Internationaux Routiers*) International Heavy Goods Vehicle).
'tira e 'molla *sm inv* tug-of-war.
ti'raggio [ti'raddʒo] *sm* (*di camino etc*) draught (*BRIT*), draft (*US*).
Ti'rana *sf* Tirana.
tiranneggi'are [tiranned'dʒare] *vt* to tyrannize.
tiran'nia *sf* tyranny.
ti'ranno, a *ag* tyrannical ♦ *sm* tyrant.
ti'rante *sm* (*NAUT, di tenda etc*) guy; (*EDIL*) brace.
tirapi'edi *sm/f inv* hanger-on.
tira'pugni [tira'puɲɲi] *sm inv* knuckle-duster.
ti'rare *vt* (*gen*) to pull; (*estrarre*): ~ **qc da** to take *o* pull sth out of; to get sth out of; to extract sth from; (*chiudere: tenda etc*) to draw, pull; (*tracciare, disegnare*) to draw, trace; (*lanciare: sasso, palla*) to throw; (*stampare*) to print; (*pistola, freccia*) to fire ♦ *vi* (*pipa, camino*) to draw; (*vento*) to

blow; (*abito*) to be tight; (*fare fuoco*) to fire; (*fare del tiro, CALCIO*) to shoot; ~ **qn da parte** to take *o* draw sb aside; ~ **un sospiro (di sollievo)** to heave a sigh (of relief); ~ **a indovinare** to take a guess; ~ **sul prezzo** to bargain; ~ **avanti** *vi* to struggle on ♦ *vt* (*famiglia*) to provide for; (*ditta*) to look after; ~ **fuori** to take out, pull out; ~ **giù** to pull down; ~ **su** to pull up; (*capelli*) to put up; (*fig: bambino*) to bring up; ~**rsi indietro** to move back; (*fig*) to back out; ~**rsi su** to pull o.s. up; (*fig*) to cheer o.s. up.
ti'rato, a *ag* (*teso*) taut; (*fig: teso, stanco*) drawn.
tira'tore *sm* gunman; **un buon** ~ a good shot; ~ **scelto** marksman.
tira'tura *sf* (*azione*) printing; (*di libro*) (print) run; (*di giornale*) circulation.
tirchie'ria [tirkje'ria] *sf* meanness, stinginess.
'tirchio, a ['tirkjo] *ag* mean, stingy.
tiri'tera *sf* drivel, hot air.
'tiro *sm* shooting *no pl*, firing *no pl*; (*colpo, sparo*) shot; (*di palla: lancio*) throwing *no pl*; throw; (*fig*) trick; **essere a** ~ to be in range; **giocare un brutto** ~ *o* **un** ~ **mancino a qn** to play a dirty trick on s.b.; **cavallo da** ~ draught (*BRIT*) *o* draft (*US*) horse; ~ **a segno** target shooting; (*luogo*) shooting range.
tiroci'nante [tirotʃi'nante] *ag, sm/f* apprentice (*cpd*); trainee (*cpd*).
tiro'cinio [tiro'tʃinjo] *sm* apprenticeship; (*professionale*) training.
ti'roide *sf* thyroid (gland).
tiro'lese *ag, sm/f* Tyrolean, Tyrolese *inv*.
Ti'rolo *sm*: **il** ~ the Tyrol.
tir'rennico, a, ci, che *ag* Tyrrhenian.
Tir'reno *sm*: **il (mar)** ~ the Tyrrhenian Sea.
ti'sana *sf* herb tea.
'tisi *sf* (*MED*) consumption.
'tisico, a, ci, che *ag* (*MED*) consumptive; (*fig: gracile*) frail ♦ *sm/f* consumptive (person).
ti'tanico, a, ci, che *ag* gigantic, enormous.
ti'tano *sm* (*MITOLOGIA, fig*) titan.
tito'lare *ag* appointed; (*sovrano*) titular ♦ *sm/f* incumbent; (*proprietario*) owner; (*CALCIO*) regular player.
tito'lato, a *ag* (*persona*) titled.
'titolo *sm* title; (*di giornale*) headline; (*diploma*) qualification; (*COMM*) security; (: *azione*) share; **a che** ~**?** for what reason?; **a** ~ **di amicizia** out of friendship; **a** ~ **di cronaca** for your information; **a** ~ **di premio** as a prize; ~ **di credito** share; ~ **obbligazionario** bond; ~ **al portatore**

bearer bond; ~ **di proprietà** title deed; ~**i di stato** government securities; ~**i di testa** (*CINE*) credits.

titu'bante *ag* hesitant, irresolute.

tivù *sf inv* (*fam*) telly (*BRIT*), TV.

'tizio, a ['tittsjo] *sm/f* fellow, chap.

tiz'zone [tit'tsone] *sm* brand.

T.M.G. *abbr* (= *tempo medio di Greenwich*) GMT.

TN *sigla* = *Trento*.

TNT *sigla m* (= *trinitrotoluolo*) TNT.

TO *sigla* = *Torino*.

toast [toust] *sm inv* toasted sandwich.

toc'cante *ag* touching.

toc'care *vt* to touch; (*tastare*) to feel; (*fig: riguardare*) to concern; (: *commuovere*) to touch, move; (: *pungere*) to hurt, wound; (: *far cenno a: argomento*) to touch on, mention ♦ *vi:* ~ **a** (*accadere*) to happen to; (*spettare*) to be up to; **tocca a te difenderci** it's up to you to defend us; **a chi tocca?** whose turn is it?; **mi toccò pagare** I had to pay; ~ **il fondo** (*in acqua*) to touch the bottom; (*fig*) to touch rock bottom; ~ **con mano** (*fig*) to find out for o.s.; ~ **qn sul vivo** to cut sb to the quick.

tocca'sana *sm inv* cure-all, panacea.

toccherò *etc* [tokke'rɔ] *vb vedi* **toccare**.

'tocco, chi *sm* touch; (*ARTE*) stroke, touch.

toe'letta *sf* = **toilette**.

'toga, ghe *sf* toga; (*di magistrato, professore*) gown.

'togliere ['tɔʎʎere] *vt* (*rimuovere*) to take away (o off), remove; (*riprendere, non concedere più*) to take away, remove; (*MAT*) to take away, subtract; (*liberare*) to free; ~ **qc a qn** to take sth (away) from sb; **ciò non toglie che ...** nevertheless ..., be that as it may ...; ~**rsi il cappello** to take off one's hat.

'Togo *sm:* **il** ~ Togo.

toilette [twa'lɛt] *sf inv* (*gabinetto*) toilet; (*cosmesi*) make-up; (*abbigliamento*) gown, dress; (*mobile*) dressing table; **fare** ~ to get made up, make o.s. beautiful.

'Tokyo *sf* Tokyo.

to'letta *sf* = **toilette**.

'tolgo *etc vb vedi* **togliere**.

tolle'rante *ag* tolerant.

tolle'ranza [tolle'rantsa] *sf* tolerance; **casa di** ~ brothel.

tolle'rare *vt* to tolerate; **non tollero repliche** I won't stand for objections; **non sono tollerati i ritardi** lateness will not be tolerated.

To'losa *sf* Toulouse.

'tolsi *etc vb vedi* **togliere**.

'tolto, a *pp di* **togliere**.

to'maia *sf* (*di scarpa*) upper.

'tomba *sf* tomb.

tom'bale *ag:* **pietra** ~ tombstone, gravestone.

tom'bino *sm* manhole cover.

'tombola *sf* (*gioco*) tombola; (*ruzzolone*) tumble.

'tomo *sm* volume.

tomogra'fia *sf* (*MED*) tomography; ~ **assiale computerizzata** computerized axial tomography.

'tonaca, che *sf* (*REL*) habit.

to'nare *vi* = **tuonare**.

'tondo, a *ag* round.

'tonfo *sm* splash; (*rumore sordo*) thud; (*caduta*): **fare un** ~ to take a tumble.

'tonico, a, ci, che *ag* tonic ♦ *sm* tonic; (*cosmetico*) toner.

tonifi'cante *ag* invigorating, bracing.

tonifi'care *vt* (*muscoli, pelle*) to tone up; (*irrobustire*) to invigorate, brace.

ton'nara *sf* tuna-fishing nets *pl*.

ton'nato, a *ag* (*CUC*): **salsa** ~**a** tuna fish sauce; **vitello** ~ veal with tuna fish sauce.

tonnel'laggio [tonnel'laddʒo] *sm* (*NAUT*) tonnage.

tonnel'lata *sf* ton.

'tonno *sm* tuna (fish).

'tono *sm* (*gen, MUS*) tone; (*di colore*) shade, tone; **rispondere a** ~ (*a proposito*) to answer to the point; (*nello stesso modo*) to answer in kind; (*per le rime*) to answer back.

ton'silla *sf* tonsil.

tonsil'lite *sf* tonsillitis.

ton'sura *sf* tonsure.

'tonto, a *ag* dull, stupid ♦ *sm/f* blockhead, dunce; **fare il finto** ~ to play dumb.

top [tɔp] *sm inv* (*vertice, camicetta*) top.

to'paia *sf* (*di topo*) mousehole; (*di ratto*) rat's nest; (*fig: casa etc*) hovel, dump.

to'pazio [to'pattsjo] *sm* topaz.

topi'cida, i [topi'tʃida] *sm* rat poison.

'topless ['tɔplis] *sm inv* topless bathing costume.

'topo *sm* mouse; ~ **d'albergo** (*fig*) hotel thief; ~ **di biblioteca** (*fig*) bookworm.

topogra'fia *sf* topography.

topog'rafico, a, ci, che *ag* topographic, topographical.

to'ponimo *sm* place name.

'toppa *sf* (*serratura*) keyhole; (*pezza*) patch.

to'race [to'ratʃe] *sm* chest.

'torba *sf* peat.

'torbido, a *ag* (*liquido*) cloudy; (: *fiume*) muddy; (*fig*) dark; troubled ♦ *sm:* **pescare nel** ~ (*fig*) to fish in troubled waters.

'torcere ['tɔrtʃere] *vt* to twist; (*biancheria*) to

wring (out); ~**rsi** *vr* to twist, writhe; **dare del filo da** ~ **a qn** to make life *o* things difficult for sb.

torchi'are [tor'kjare] *vt* to press.

'**torchio** ['tɔrkjo] *sm* press; **mettere qn sotto il** ~ (*fig fam*: *interrogare*) to grill sb; ~ **tipografico** printing press.

'**torcia, ce** ['tɔrtʃa] *sf* torch; ~ **elettrica** torch (*BRIT*), flashlight (*US*).

torci'collo [tortʃi'kɔllo] *sm* stiff neck.

'**tordo** *sm* thrush.

to'rero *sm* bullfighter, toreador.

tori'nese *ag* of (*o* from) Turin ♦ *sm/f* person from Turin.

To'rino *sf* Turin.

tor'menta *sf* snowstorm.

tormen'tare *vt* to torment; ~**rsi** *vr* to fret, worry o.s.

tor'mento *sm* torment.

torna'conto *sm* advantage, benefit.

tor'nado *sm* tornado.

tor'nante *sm* hairpin bend (*BRIT*) *o* curve (*US*).

tor'nare *vi* to return, go (*o* come) back; (*ridiventare: anche fig*) to become (again); (*riuscire giusto, esatto: conto*) to work out; (*risultare*) to turn out (to be), prove (to be); ~ **al punto di partenza** to start again; ~ **a casa** to go (*o* come) home; **i conti tornano** the accounts balance; ~ **utile** to prove *o* turn out (to be) useful.

torna'sole *sm inv* litmus.

tor'neo *sm* tournament.

'**tornio** *sm* lathe.

tor'nire *vt* (*TECN*) to turn (on a lathe); (*fig*) to shape, polish.

tor'nito, a *ag* (*gambe, caviglie*) well-shaped.

'**toro** *sm* bull; (*dello zodiaco*): **T**~ Taurus; **essere del T**~ to be Taurus.

tor'pedine *sf* torpedo.

torpedini'era *sf* torpedo boat.

tor'pore *sm* torpor.

'**torre** *sf* tower; (*SCACCHI*) rook, castle; ~ **di controllo** (*AER*) control tower.

torrefazi'one [torrefat'tsjone] *sf* roasting.

torreggi'are [torred'dʒare] *vi*: ~ (**su**) to tower (over).

tor'rente *sm* torrent.

torren'tizio, a [torren'tittsjo] *ag* torrential.

torrenzi'ale [torren'tsjale] *ag* torrential.

tor'retta *sf* turret.

'**torrido, a** *ag* torrid.

torri'one *sm* keep.

tor'rone *sm* nougat.

'**torsi** *etc vb vedi* **torcere.**

torsi'one *sf* twisting; (*TECN*) torsion.

'**torso** *sm* torso, trunk; (*ARTE*) torso; **a** ~ **nudo** bare-chested.

'**torsolo** *sm* (*di cavolo etc*) stump; (*di frutta*) core.

'**torta** *sf* cake.

tortel'lini *smpl* (*CUC*) tortellini.

torti'era *sf* cake tin (*BRIT*), cake pan (*US*).

'**torto, a** *pp di* **torcere** ♦ *ag* (*ritorto*) twisted; (*storto*) twisted, crooked ♦ *sm* (*ingiustizia*) wrong; (*colpa*) fault; **a** ~ wrongly; **a** ~ **o a ragione** rightly or wrongly; **aver** ~ to be wrong; **fare un** ~ **a qn** to wrong sb; **essere/passare dalla parte del** ~ to be/put o.s. in the wrong; **lui non ha tutti i** ~**i** there's something in what he says.

'**tortora** *sf* turtle dove.

tortu'oso, a *ag* (*strada*) twisting; (*fig*) tortuous.

tor'tura *sf* torture.

tortu'rare *vt* to torture.

'**torvo, a** *ag* menacing, grim.

tosa'erba *sm o f inv* (lawn)mower.

to'sare *vt* (*pecora*) **to** shear; (*cane*) to clip; (*siepe*) to clip, trim.

tosa'tura *sf* (*di pecore*) shearing; (*di cani*) clipping; (*di siepi*) trimming, clipping.

Tos'cana *sf*: **la** ~ Tuscany.

tos'cano, a *ag*, *sm/f* Tuscan ♦ *sm* (*anche*: **sigaro** ~) *strong Italian cigar.*

'**tosse** *sf* cough.

tossicità [tossitʃi'ta] *sf* toxicity.

'**tossico, a, ci, che** *ag* toxic.

tossicodipen'dente *sm/f* drug addict.

tossicodipen'denza [tossikodipen'dentsa] *sf* drug addiction.

tossi'comane *sm/f* drug addict.

tossicoma'nia *sf* drug addiction.

tos'sina *sf* toxin.

tos'sire *vi* to cough.

tosta'pane *sm inv* toaster.

tos'tare *vt* to toast; (*caffè*) to roast.

tosta'tura *sf* (*di pane*) toasting; (*di caffè*) roasting.

'**tosto, a** *ag*: **faccia** ~**a** cheek ♦ *av* at once, immediately; ~ **che** as soon as.

to'tale *ag, sm* total.

totalità *sf*: **la** ~ **di** all of, the total amount (*o* number) of; **the whole +** *sg*.

totali'tario, a *ag* totalitarian; (*totale*) complete, total; **adesione** ~**a** complete support.

totalita'rismo *sm* (*POL*) totalitarianism.

totaliz'zare [totalid'dzare] *vt* to total; (*SPORT: punti*) to score.

totalizza'tore [totaliddza'tore] *sm* (*TECN*) totalizator; (*IPPICA*) totalizator, tote (*fam*).

to'tip *sm gambling pool betting on horse racing.*

toto'calcio [toto'kaltʃo] *sm gambling pool betting on football results,* ≈ (football) pools *pl* (*BRIT*).

tou'pet [tu'pɛ] *sm inv* toupee.

tour [tur] *sm inv* (*giro*) tour; (*CICLISMO*) tour de France.

tour de 'force ['tur də 'fɔrs] *sm inv* (*SPORT: anche fig*) tour de force.

tour'née [tur'ne] *sf* tour; **essere in** ~ to be on tour.

to'vaglia [to'vaʎʎa] *sf* tablecloth.

tovagli'olo [tovaʎ'ʎɔlo] *sm* napkin.

'tozzo, a ['tɔttso] *ag* squat ♦ *sm*: ~ **di pane** crust of bread.

TP *sigla* = *Trapani*.

TR *sigla* = *Terni*.

Tr *abbr* (*COMM*) = **tratta**.

tra *prep* (*di due persone, cose*) between; (*di più persone, cose*) among(st); (*tempo: entro*) within, in; **prendere qn** ~ **le braccia** to take sb in one's arms; **litigano** ~ (**di**) **loro** they're fighting amongst themselves; ~ **5 giorni** in 5 days' time; ~ **breve** *o* **poco** soon; ~ **sé e sé** (*parlare etc*) to oneself; **sia detto** ~ **noi** ... between you and me ...; ~ **una cosa e l'altra** what with one thing and another.

trabal'lante *ag* shaky.

trabal'lare *vi* to stagger, totter.

tra'biccolo *sm* (*peg: auto*) old banger (*BRIT*), jalopy.

traboc'care *vi* to overflow.

traboc'chetto [trabok'ketto] *sm* (*fig*) trap ♦ *ag inv* trap *cpd*; **domanda** ~ trick question.

traca'gnotto, a [trakaɲ'ɲɔtto] *ag* dumpy ♦ *sm/f* dumpy person.

tracan'nare *vt* to gulp down.

'traccia, ce ['trattʃa] *sf* (*segno, striscia*) trail, track; (*orma*) tracks *pl*; (*residuo, testimonianza*) trace, sign; (*abbozzo*) outline; **essere sulle** ~**ce di qn** to be on sb's trail.

tracci'are [trat'tʃare] *vt* to trace, mark (out); (*disegnare*) to draw; (*fig: abbozzare*) to outline; ~ **un quadro della situazione** to outline the situation.

tracci'ato [trat'tʃato] *sm* (*grafico*) layout, plan; ~ **di gara** (*SPORT*) race route.

tra'chea [tra'kɛa] *sf* windpipe, trachea.

tra'colla *sf* shoulder strap; **portare qc a** ~ to carry sth over one's shoulder; **borsa a** ~ shoulder bag.

tra'collo *sm* (*fig*) collapse, ruin; ~ **finanziario** crash; **avere un** ~ (*MED*) to have a setback; (*COMM*) to collapse.

traco'tante *ag* overbearing, arrogant.

traco'tanza [trako'tantsa] *sf* arrogance.

trad. *abbr* = **traduzione**.

tradi'mento *sm* betrayal; (*DIR, MIL*)

treason; **a** ~ by surprise; **alto** ~ high treason.

tra'dire *vt* to betray; (*coniuge*) to be unfaithful to; (*doveri: mancare*) to fail in; (*rivelare*) to give away, reveal; **ha tradito le attese di tutti** he let everyone down.

tradi'tore, 'trice *sm/f* traitor.

tradizio'nale [tradittsjo'nale] *ag* traditional.

tradizi'one [tradit'tsjone] *sf* tradition.

tra'dotto, a *pp di* **tradurre** ♦ *sf* (*MIL*) troop train.

tra'durre *vt* to translate; (*spiegare*) to render, convey; (*DIR*): ~ **qn in carcere/tribunale** to take sb to prison/court; ~ **in cifre** to put into figures; ~ **in atto** (*fig*) to put into effect.

tradut'tore, 'trice *sm/f* translator.

traduzi'one [tradut'tsjone] *sf* translation; (*DIR*) transfer.

'trae *vb vedi* **trarre**.

tra'ente *sm/f* (*ECON*) drawer.

trafe'lato, a *ag* out of breath.

traffi'cante *sm/f* dealer; (*peg*) trafficker.

traffi'care *vi* (*commerciare*): ~ (**in**) to trade (in), deal (in); (*affaccendarsi*) to busy o.s. ♦ *vt* (*peg*) to traffic in.

traffi'cato, a *ag* (*strada, zona*) busy.

'traffico, ci *sm* traffic; (*commercio*) trade, traffic; ~ **aereo/ferroviario** air/rail traffic; ~ **di droga** drug trafficking; ~ **stradale** traffic.

tra'figgere [tra'fiddʒere] *vt* to run through, stab; (*fig*) to pierce.

tra'fila *sf* procedure.

trafi'letto *sm* (*di giornale*) short article.

tra'fitto, a *pp di* **trafiggere**.

trafo'rare *vt* to bore, drill.

tra'foro *sm* (*azione*) boring, drilling; (*galleria*) tunnel.

trafu'gare *vt* to purloin.

tra'gedia [tra'dʒɛdja] *sf* tragedy.

'traggo *etc vb vedi* **trarre**.

traghet'tare [traget'tare] *vt* to ferry.

tra'ghetto [tra'getto] *sm* crossing; (*barca*) ferry(boat).

tragicità [tradʒitʃi'ta] *sf* tragedy.

'tragico, a, ci, che ['tradʒiko] *ag* tragic ♦ *sm* (*autore*) tragedian; **prendere tutto sul** ~ (*fig*) to take everything far too seriously.

tragi'comico, a, ci, che [tradʒi'kɔmiko] *ag* tragicomic.

tra'gitto [tra'dʒitto] *sm* (*passaggio*) crossing; (*viaggio*) journey.

tragu'ardo *sm* (*SPORT*) finishing line; (*fig*) goal, aim.

'trai *etc vb vedi* **trarre**.

traiet'toria *sf* trajectory.

trai'nante *ag* (*cavo, fune*) towing; (*fig: persona, settore*) driving.
trai'nare *vt* to drag, haul; (*rimorchiare*) to tow.
'training ['treinin(g)] *sm inv* training.
'traino *sm* (*carro*) wagon; (*slitta*) sledge; (*carico*) load.
tralasci'are [tralaʃ'ʃare] *vt* (*studi*) to neglect; (*dettagli*) to leave out, omit.
'tralcio ['traltʃo] *sm* (*BOT*) shoot.
tra'liccio [tra'littʃo] *sm* (*tela*) ticking; (*struttura*) trellis; (*ELETTR*) pylon.
tram *sm inv* tram (*BRIT*), streetcar (*US*).
'trama *sf* (*filo*) weft, woof; (*fig: argomento, maneggio*) plot.
traman'dare *vt* to pass on, hand down.
tra'mare *vt* (*fig*) to scheme, plot.
tram'busto *sm* turmoil.
trames'tio *sm* bustle.
tramez'zino [tramed'dzino] *sm* sandwich.
tra'mezzo [tra'meddzo] *sm* partition.
'tramite *prep* through ♦ *sm* means *pl*; **agire/fare da** ~ to act as/be a go-between.
tramon'tana *sf* (*METEOR*) north wind.
tramon'tare *vi* to set, go down.
tra'monto *sm* setting; (*del sole*) sunset.
tramor'tire *vi* to faint ♦ *vt* to stun.
trampo'lino *sm* (*per tuffi*) springboard, diving board; (*per lo sci*) ski-jump.
'trampolo *sm* stilt.
tramu'tare *vt*: ~ **in** to change into, turn into.
trance [trains] *sf inv* (*di medium*) trance; **cadere in** ~ to fall into a trance.
'trancia, ce ['trantʃa] *sf* slice; (*cesoia*) shearing machine.
tranci'are [tran'tʃare] *vt* (*TECN*) to shear.
'trancio ['trantʃo] *sm* slice.
tra'nello *sm* trap; **tendere un** ~ **a qn** to set a trap for sb.
trangugi'are [trangu'dʒare] *vt* to gulp down.
'tranne *prep* except (for), but (for); ~ **che** *cong* unless; **tutti i giorni** ~ **il venerdì** every day except *o* with the exception of Friday.
tranquil'lante *sm* (*MED*) tranquillizer.
tranquillità *sf* calm, stillness; quietness; peace of mind.
tranquilliz'zare [trankwillid'dzare] *vt* to reassure.
tran'quillo, a *ag* calm, quiet; (*bambino, scolaro*) quiet; (*sereno*) with one's mind at rest; **sta'** ~ don't worry.
transat'lantico, a, ci, che *ag* transatlantic ♦ *sm* transatlantic liner; (*POL*) corridor used as a meeting place by members of the lower chamber of the Italian Parliament; *vedi nota nel riquadro*.

TRANSATLANTICO

The **transatlantico** is a room in the Palazzo di Montecitorio which is used by "deputati" between parliamentary sessions for relaxation and conversation. It is also used for media interviews and press conferences.

tran'satto, a *pp di* **transigere**.
transazi'one [transat'tsjone] *sf* (*DIR*) settlement; (*COMM*) transaction, deal.
tran'senna *sf* barrier.
tran'setto *sm* transept.
transiberi'ano, a *ag* trans-Siberian.
tran'sigere [tran'sidʒere] *vi* (*DIR*) to reach a settlement; (*venire a patti*) to compromise, come to an agreement.
tran'sistor *sm inv*, **transis'tore** *sm* transistor.
transi'tabile *ag* passable.
transi'tare *vi* to pass.
transi'tivo, a *ag* transitive.
'transito *sm* transit; **di** ~ (*merci*) in transit; (*stazione*) transit *cpd*; **"divieto di** ~**"** "no entry"; **"**~ **interrotto"** "road closed".
transi'torio, a *ag* transitory, transient; (*provvisorio*) provisional.
transizi'one [transit'tsjone] *sf* transition.
tran 'tran *sm* routine; **il solito** ~ the same old routine.
tran'via *sf* tramway (*BRIT*), streetcar line (*US*).
tranvi'ario, a *ag* tram *cpd* (*BRIT*), streetcar *cpd* (*US*); **linea** ~**a** tramline, streetcar line.
tranvi'ere *sm* (*conducente*) tram driver (*BRIT*), streetcar driver (*US*); (*bigliettaio*) tram *o* streetcar conductor.
trapa'nare *vt* (*TECN*) to drill.
'trapano *sm* (*utensile*) drill; (: *MED*) trepan.
trapas'sare *vt* to pierce.
trapas'sato *sm* (*LING*) past perfect.
tra'passo *sm* passage; ~ **di proprietà** (*di case*) conveyancing; (*di auto etc*) legal transfer.
trape'lare *vi* to leak, drip; (*fig*) to leak out.
tra'pezio [tra'pettsjo] *sm* (*MAT*) trapezium; (*attrezzo ginnico*) trapeze.
trape'zista, i, e [trapet'tsista] *sm/f* trapeze artist.
trapian'tare *vt* to transplant.
trapi'anto *sm* transplanting; (*MED*) transplant.
'trappola *sf* trap.
tra'punta *sf* quilt.
'trarre *vt* to draw, pull; (*prendere, tirare fuori*) to take (out), draw; (*derivare*) to

obtain; ~ **beneficio** *o* **profitto da qc** to benefit from sth; ~ **le conclusioni** to draw one's own conclusions; ~ **esempio da qn** to follow sb's example; ~ **guadagno** to make a profit; ~ **qn d'impaccio** to get sb out of an awkward situation; ~ **origine da qc** to have its origins *o* originate in sth; ~ **in salvo** to rescue.

trasa'lire *vi* to start, jump.

trasan'dato, a *ag* shabby.

trasbor'dare *vt* to transfer; (*NAUT*) to tran(s)ship ♦ *vi* (*NAUT*) to change ship; (*AER*) to change plane; (*FERR*) to change (trains).

trascenden'tale [traʃʃendenˈtale] *ag* transcendental.

tra'scendere [traʃˈʃendere] *vt* (*FILOSOFIA, REL*) to transcend; (*fig: superare*) to surpass, go beyond.

tra'sceso, a [traʃˈʃeso] *pp di* **trascendere**.

trasci'nare [traʃʃiˈnare] *vt* to drag; ~**rsi** *vr* to drag o.s. along; (*fig*) to drag on.

tras'correre *vt* (*tempo*) to spend, pass ♦ *vi* to pass.

tras'corso, a *pp di* **trascorrere** ♦ *ag* past ♦ *sm* mistake.

tras'critto, a *pp di* **trascrivere**.

tras'crivere *vt* to transcribe.

trascrizi'one [traskritˈtsjone] *sf* transcription.

trascu'rare *vt* to neglect; (*non considerare*) to disregard.

trascura'tezza [traskuraˈtettsa] *sf* carelessness, negligence.

trascu'rato, a *ag* (*casa*) neglected; (*persona*) careless, negligent.

traseco'lato, a *ag* astounded, amazed.

trasferi'mento *sm* transfer; (*trasloco*) removal, move.

trasfe'rire *vt* to transfer; ~**rsi** *vr* to move.

tras'ferta *sf* transfer; (*indennità*) travelling expenses *pl*; (*SPORT*) away game.

trasfigu'rare *vt* to transfigure.

trasfor'mare *vt* to transform, change.

trasforma'tore *sm* transformer.

trasformazi'one [trasformatˈtsjone] *sf* transformation.

trasfusi'one *sf* (*MED*) transfusion.

trasgre'dire *vt* to break, infringe; (*ordini*) to disobey.

trasgressi'one *sf* breaking, infringement; disobeying.

trasgres'sivo, a *ag* (*personaggio, atteggiamento*) rule-breaking.

trasgres'sore, trasgredi'trice [trazgrediˈtritʃe] *sm/f* (*DIR*) transgressor.

tras'lato, a *ag* metaphorical, figurative.

traslo'care *vt* to move, transfer; ~**rsi** *vr* to move.

tras'loco, chi *sm* removal.

tras'messo, a *pp di* **trasmettere**.

tras'mettere *vt* (*passare*): ~ **qc a qn** to pass sth on to sb; (*mandare*) to send; (*TECN, TEL, MED*) to transmit; (*TV, RADIO*) to broadcast.

trasmetti'tore *sm* transmitter.

trasmissi'one *sf* (*gen, FISICA, TECN*) transmission; (*passaggio*) transmission, passing on; (*TV, RADIO*) broadcast.

trasmit'tente *sf* transmitting *o* broadcasting station.

traso'gnato, a [trasoɲˈɲato] *ag* dreamy.

traspa'rente *ag* transparent.

traspa'renza [traspaˈrɛntsa] *sf* transparency; **guardare qc in** ~ to look at sth against the light.

traspa'rire *vi* to show (through).

tras'parso, a *pp di* **trasparire**.

traspi'rare *vi* to perspire; (*fig*) to come to light, leak out.

traspirazi'one [traspiratˈtsjone] *sf* perspiration.

tras'porre *vt* to transpose.

traspor'tare *vt* to carry, move; (*merce*) to transport, convey; **lasciarsi** ~ (**da qc**) (*fig*) to let o.s. be carried away (by sth).

tras'porto *sm* transport; (*fig*) rapture, passion; **con** ~ passionately; **compagnia di** ~ carriers *pl*; (*per strada*) hauliers *pl* (*BRIT*), haulers *pl* (*US*); **mezzi di** ~ means of transport; **nave/aereo da** ~ transport ship/aircraft *inv*; ~ (**funebre**) funeral procession; ~ **marittimo/aereo** sea/air transport; ~ **stradale** (road) haulage; **i** ~**i pubblici** public transport.

tras'posto, a *pp di* **trasporre**.

'trassi *etc vb vedi* **trarre**.

trastul'lare *vt* to amuse; ~**rsi** *vr* to amuse o.s.

tras'tullo *sm* game.

trasu'dare *vi* (*filtrare*) to ooze; (*sudare*) to sweat ♦ *vt* to ooze with.

trasver'sale *ag* (*taglio, sbarra*) cross(-); (*retta*) transverse; **via** ~ side street.

trasvo'lare *vt* to fly over.

'tratta *sf* (*ECON*) draft; (*di persone*): **la** ~ **delle bianche** the white slave trade; ~ **documentaria** documentary bill of exchange.

tratta'mento *sm* treatment; (*servizio*) service; **ricevere un buon** ~ (*cliente*) to get good service; ~ **di bellezza** beauty treatment; ~ **di fine rapporto** (*COMM*) severance pay.

trat'tare *vt* (*gen*) to treat; (*commerciare*) to

deal in; (*svolgere: argomento*) to discuss, deal with; (*negoziare*) to negotiate ♦ *vi:* ~ **di** to deal with; ~ **con** (*persona*) to deal with; **si tratta di** ... it's about ...; **si tratterebbe solo di poche ore** it would just be a matter of a few hours.

tratta'tiva *sf* negotiation; ~**e** *sfpl* (*tra governi, stati*) talks; **essere in** ~ **con** to be in negotiation with.

trat'tato *sm* (*testo*) treatise; (*accordo*) treaty; ~ **commerciale** trade agreement; ~ **di pace** peace treaty.

trattazi'one [trattat'tsjone] *sf* treatment.

tratteggi'are [tratted'dʒare] *vt* (*disegnare: a tratti*) to sketch, outline; (*: col tratteggio*) to hatch.

trat'teggio [trat'teddʒo] *sm* hatching.

tratte'nere *vt* (*far rimanere: persona*) to detain; (*tenere, frenare, reprimere*) to hold back, keep back; (*astenersi dal consegnare*) to hold, keep; (*detrarre: somma*) to deduct; ~**rsi** *vr* (*astenersi*) to restrain o.s., stop o.s.; (*soffermarsi*) to stay, remain; **sono stato trattenuto in ufficio** I was delayed at the office.

tratteni'mento *sm* entertainment; (*festa*) party.

tratte'nuta *sf* deduction.

trat'tino *sm* dash; (*in parole composte*) hyphen.

'tratto, a *pp di* **trarre** ♦ *sm* (*di penna, matita*) stroke; (*parte*) part, piece; (*di strada*) stretch; (*di mare, cielo*) expanse; (*di tempo*) period (of time); ~**i** *smpl* (*caratteristiche*) features; (*modo di fare*) ways, manners; **a un** ~, **d'un** ~ suddenly.

trat'tore *sm* tractor.

tratto'ria *sf* (small) restaurant.

'trauma, i *sm* trauma; ~ **cranico** concussion.

trau'matico, a, ci, che *ag* traumatic.

traumatiz'zare [traumatid'dzare] *vt* (*MED*) to traumatize; (*fig: impressionare*) to shock.

tra'vaglio [tra'vaʎʎo] *sm* (*angoscia*) pain, suffering; (*MED*) pains *pl*; ~ **di parto** labour pains.

trava'sare *vt* to pour; (*vino*) to decant.

tra'vaso *sm* pouring; decanting.

trava'tura *sf* beams *pl*.

'trave *sf* beam.

tra'veggole *sfpl:* **avere le** ~ to be seeing things.

tra'versa *sf* (*trave*) crosspiece; (*via*) sidestreet; (*FERR*) sleeper (*BRIT*), (railroad) tie (*US*); (*CALCIO*) crossbar.

traver'sare *vt* to cross.

traver'sata *sf* crossing; (*AER*) flight, trip.

traver'sie *sfpl* mishaps, misfortunes.

traver'sina *sf* (*FERR*) sleeper (*BRIT*), (railroad) tie (*US*).

tra'verso, a *ag* oblique; **di** ~ *ag* askew ♦ *av* sideways; **andare di** ~ (*cibo*) to go down the wrong way; **messo di** ~ sideways on; **guardare di** ~ to look askance at; **via** ~**a** side road; **ottenere qc per vie** ~**e** (*fig*) to obtain sth in an underhand way.

travesti'mento *sm* disguise.

traves'tire *vt* to disguise; ~**rsi** *vr* to disguise o.s.

traves'tito *sm* transvestite.

travi'are *vt* (*fig*) to lead astray.

travi'sare *vt* (*fig*) to distort, misrepresent.

travol'gente [travol'dʒente] *ag* overwhelming.

tra'volgere [tra'vɔldʒere] *vt* to sweep away, carry away; (*fig*) to overwhelm.

tra'volto, a *pp di* **travolgere**.

trazi'one [trat'tsjone] *sf* traction; ~ **anteriore/posteriore** (*AUT*) front-wheel/rear-wheel drive.

tre *num* three.

tre'alberi *sm inv* (*NAUT*) three-master.

'trebbia *sf* (*AGR: operazione*) threshing; (*: stagione*) threshing season.

trebbi'are *vt* to thresh.

trebbia'trice [trebbja'tritʃe] *sf* threshing machine.

trebbia'tura *sf* threshing.

'treccia, ce ['trettʃa] *sf* plait, braid; **lavorato a** ~**ce** (*pullover etc*) cable-knit.

trecen'tesco, a, schi, sche [tretʃen'tesko] *ag* fourteenth-century.

tre'cento [tre'tʃento] *num* three hundred ♦ *sm:* **il T**~ the fourteenth century.

tredi'cenne [tredi'tʃenne] *ag, sm/f* thirteen-year-old.

tredi'cesimo, a [tredi'tʃezimo] *num* thirteenth ♦ *sf* Christmas bonus of a month's pay.

'tredici ['treditʃi] *num* thirteen ♦ *sm inv:* **fare** ~ (*TOTOCALCIO*) to win the pools (*BRIT*).

'tregua *sf* truce; (*fig*) respite; **senza** ~ nonstop, without stopping, uninterruptedly.

tre'mante *ag* trembling, shaking.

tre'mare *vi* to tremble, shake; ~ **di** (*freddo etc*) to shiver o tremble with; (*paura, rabbia*) to shake o tremble with.

trema'rella *sf* shivers *pl*.

tremen'tina *sf* turpentine.

tre'mila *num* three thousand.

'tremito *sm* trembling *no pl*; shaking *no pl*; shivering *no pl*.

tremo'lare *vi* to tremble; (*luce*) to flicker; (*foglie*) to quiver.

tremo'lio *sm* (*vedi vi*) tremble; flicker; quiver.

tre'more *sm* tremor.

'treno *sm* train; (*AUT*): ~ **di gomme** set of tyres; ~ **locale/diretto/espresso** local/ fast/express train; ~ **merci** goods (*BRIT*) *o* freight train; ~ **rapido** express (train) (*for which supplement must be paid*); ~ **straordinario** special train; ~ **viaggiatori** passenger train; *vedi nota nel riquadro.*

TRENI

There are several different types of train in Italy. "Regionali" and "interregionali" are local trains which stop at every small town and village; the former operate within regional boundaries, while the latter may cross them. "Diretti" are ordinary trains for which passengers do not pay a supplement; the main difference from "espressi" is that the latter are long-distance and mainly run at night. "Intercity" and "eurocity" are faster and entail a supplement. "Rapidi" only contain first-class seats, and the high-speed "pendolino", which offers both first- and second-class travel, runs between the major cities.

'trenta *num* thirty ♦ *sm inv* (*INS*): ~ **e lode** full marks plus distinction *o* cum laude.

tren'tenne *ag, sm/f* thirty-year-old.

tren'tennio *sm* period of thirty years.

tren'tesimo, a *num* thirtieth.

tren'tina *sf*: **una** ~ (**di**) thirty or so, about thirty.

tren'tino, a *ag* of (*o* from) Trento.

trepi'dante *ag* anxious.

trepi'dare *vi* to be anxious; ~ **per qn** to be anxious about sb.

'trepido, a *ag* anxious.

treppi'ede *sm* tripod; (*CUC*) trivet.

tre'quarti *sm inv* three-quarter-length coat.

'tresca, sche *sf* (*fig*) intrigue; (: *relazione amorosa*) affair.

'trespolo *sm* trestle.

trevigi'ano, a [trevi'dʒano] *ag* of (*o* from) Treviso.

triango'lare *ag* triangular.

tri'angolo *sm* triangle.

tribo'lare *vi* (*patire*) to suffer; (*fare fatica*) to have a lot of trouble.

tribolazi'one [tribolat'tsjone] *sf* suffering, tribulation.

tri'bordo *sm* (*NAUT*) starboard.

tribù *sf inv* tribe.

tri'buna *sf* (*podio*) platform; (*in aule etc*) gallery; (*di stadio*) stand; ~ **della stampa/ riservata al pubblico** press/public gallery.

tribu'nale *sm* court; **presentarsi** *o* **comparire in** ~ to appear in court; ~ **militare** military tribunal; ~ **supremo** supreme court.

tribu'tare *vt* to bestow; ~ **gli onori dovuti a qn** to pay tribute to sb.

tribu'tario, a *ag* (*imposta*) fiscal, tax *cpd*; (*GEO*): **essere** ~ **di** to be a tributary of.

tri'buto *sm* tax; (*fig*) tribute.

tri'checo, chi [tri'kɛko] *sm* (*ZOOL*) walrus.

tri'ciclo [tri'tʃiklo] *sm* tricycle.

trico'lore *ag* three-coloured (*BRIT*), three-colored (*US*) ♦ *sm* tricolo(u)r; (*bandiera italiana*) Italian flag.

tri'dente *sm* trident.

trien'nale *ag* (*che dura 3 anni*) three-year *cpd*; (*che avviene ogni 3 anni*) three-yearly.

tri'ennio *sm* period of three years.

tries'tino, a *ag* of (*o* from) Trieste.

tri'fase *ag* (*ELETTR*) three-phase.

tri'foglio [tri'fɔʎʎo] *sm* clover.

trifo'lato, a *ag* (*CUC*) *cooked in oil, garlic and parsley.*

'triglia ['triʎʎa] *sf* red mullet.

trigonome'tria *sf* trigonometry.

tril'lare *vi* (*MUS*) to trill.

'trillo *sm* trill.

tri'mestre *sm* period of three months; (*INS*) term, quarter (*US*); (*COMM*) quarter.

trimo'tore *sm* (*AER*) three-engined plane.

'trina *sf* lace.

trin'cea [trin'tʃea] *sf* trench.

trince'rare [trintʃe'rare] *vt* to entrench.

trinci'are [trin'tʃare] *vt* to cut up.

'Trinidad *sm*: ~ **e Tobago** Trinidad and Tobago.

Trinità *sf* (*REL*) Trinity.

'trio, *pl* 'trii *sm* trio.

trion'fale *ag* triumphal, triumphant.

trion'fante *ag* triumphant.

trion'fare *vi* to triumph, win; ~ **su** to triumph over, overcome.

tri'onfo *sm* triumph.

tripli'care *vt* to triple.

'triplice ['triplitʃe] *ag* triple; **in** ~ **copia** in triplicate.

'triplo, a *ag* triple, treble ♦ *sm*: **il** ~ (**di**) three times as much (as); **la spesa è** ~**a** it costs three times as much.

'tripode *sm* tripod.

'Tripoli *sf* Tripoli.

'trippa *sf* (*CUC*) tripe.

tri'pudio *sm* triumph, jubilation; (*fig*: *di colori*) galaxy.

tris *sm inv* (*CARTE*): ~ **d'assi/di re** *etc* three aces/kings *etc*.

'triste *ag* sad; (*luogo*) dreary, gloomy.

tris'tezza [tris'tettsa] *sf* sadness;

gloominess.

'**tristo, a** *ag* (*cattivo*) wicked, evil; (*meschino*) sorry, poor.

trita'carne *sm inv* mincer, grinder (*US*).

trita'ghiaccio [trita'gjattʃo] *sm inv* ice crusher.

tri'tare *vt* to mince, grind (*US*).

trita'tutto *sm inv* mincer, grinder (*US*).

'**trito, a** *ag* (*tritato*) minced, ground (*US*); ~ **e ritrito** (*idee, argomenti, frasi*) trite, hackneyed.

tri'tolo *sm* trinitrotoluene.

tri'tone *sm* (*ZOOL*) newt.

'**trittico, ci** *sm* (*ARTE*) triptych.

tritu'rare *vt* to grind.

tri'vella *sf* drill.

trivel'lare *vt* to drill.

trivellazi'one [trivellat'tsjone] *sf* drilling; **torre di** ~ derrick.

trivi'ale *ag* vulgar, low.

trivialità *sf inv* (*volgarità*) coarseness, crudeness; (: *osservazione*) coarse *o* crude remark.

tro'feo *sm* trophy.

'**trogolo** *sm* (*per maiali*) trough.

'**troia** *sf* (*ZOOL*) sow; (*fig peg*) whore.

'**tromba** *sf* (*MUS*) trumpet; (*AUT*) horn; ~ **d'aria** whirlwind; ~ **delle scale** stairwell.

trombet'tista, i, e *sm/f* trumpeter, trumpet (player).

trom'bone *sm* trombone.

trom'bosi *sf* thrombosis.

tron'care *vt* to cut off; (*spezzare*) to break off.

'**tronco, a, chi, che** *ag* cut off; broken off; (*LING*) truncated ♦ *sm* (*BOT, ANAT*) trunk; (*fig: tratto*) section; (: *pezzo: di lancia*) stump; **licenziare qn in** ~ (*fig*) to fire sb on the spot.

troneggi'are [troned'dʒare] *vi*: ~ (**su**) to tower (over).

'**tronfio, a** *ag* conceited.

'**trono** *sm* throne.

tropi'cale *ag* tropical.

'**tropico, ci** *sm* tropic; ~ **del Cancro/Capricorno** Tropic of Cancer/Capricorn; **i** ~**ci** the tropics.

=========== *PAROLA CHIAVE*

'**troppo, a** *det* (*in eccesso: quantità*) too much; (: *numero*) too many; **ho messo** ~ **zucchero** I put too much sugar in; **c'era** ~**a gente** there were too many people ♦ *pron* (*in eccesso: quantità*) too much; (: *numero*) too many; **ne hai messo** ~ you've put in too much; **meglio** ~**i che pochi** better too many than too few ♦ *av* (*eccessivamente: con ag, av*) too; (: *con*

vb) too much; ~ **amaro/tardi** too bitter/late; **lavora** ~ he works too much; ~ **buono da parte tua!** (*anche ironico*) you're too kind!; **di** ~ too much; too many; **qualche tazza di** ~ a few cups too many; **3000 lire di** ~ 3000 lire too much; **essere di** ~ to be in the way.

'**trota** *sf* trout.

trot'tare *vi* to trot.

trotterel'lare *vi* to trot along; (*bambino*) to toddle.

'**trotto** *sm* trot.

'**trottola** *sf* spinning top.

tro'vare *vt* to find; (*giudicare*): **trovo che** I **find** *o* think that; ~**rsi** *vr* (*reciproco: incontrarsi*) to meet; (*essere, stare*) to be; (*arrivare, capitare*) to find o.s.; **andare a** ~ **qn** to go and see sb; ~ **qn colpevole** to find sb guilty; **trovo giusto/sbagliato che** ... I think/don't think it's right that ...; ~**rsi bene/male** (*in un luogo, con qn*) to get on well/badly; ~**rsi d'accordo con qn** to be in agreement with sb.

tro'vata *sf* good idea; ~ **pubblicitaria** advertising gimmick.

trova'tello, a *sm/f* foundling.

truc'care *vt* (*falsare*) to fake; (*attore etc*) to make up; (*travestire*) to disguise; (*SPORT*) to fix; (*AUT*) to soup up; ~**rsi** *vr* to make up (one's face).

trucca'tore, 'trice *sm/f* (*CINE, TEAT*) make-up artist.

'**trucco, chi** *sm* trick; (*cosmesi*) make-up; **i** ~**chi del mestiere** the tricks of the trade.

'**truce** ['trutʃe] *ag* fierce.

truci'dare [trutʃi'dare] *vt* to slaughter.

truci'olo ['trutʃolo] *sm* shaving.

'**truffa** *sf* fraud, swindle.

truf'fare *vt* to swindle, cheat.

truffa'tore, 'trice *sm/f* swindler, cheat.

'**truppa** *sf* troop.

TS *sigla* = Trieste.

tu *pron* you; ~ **stesso(a)** you yourself; **dare del** ~ **a qn** to address sb as "tu"; **trovarsi a** ~ **per** ~ **con qn** to find o.s. face to face with sb.

'**tua** *vedi* **tuo**.

'**tuba** *sf* (*MUS*) tuba; (*cappello*) top hat.

tu'bare *vi* to coo.

tuba'tura *sf*, **tubazi'one** [tubat'tsjone] *sf* piping *no pl*, pipes *pl*.

tuberco'losi *sf* tuberculosis.

'**tubero** *sm* (*BOT*) tuber.

tu'betto *sm* tube.

tu'bino *sm* (*cappello*) bowler (*BRIT*), derby (*US*); (*abito da donna*) sheath dress.

'**tubo** *sm* tube; (*per conduttore*) pipe; ~

digerente (*ANAT*) alimentary canal, digestive tract; ~ **di scappamento** (*AUT*) exhaust pipe.

tubo'lare *ag* tubular ♦ *sm* tubeless tyre (*BRIT*) *o* tire (*US*).

'tue *vedi* **tuo.**

tuf'fare *vt* to plunge; (*intingere*) to dip; ~**rsi** *vr* to plunge, dive.

tuffa'tore, 'trice *sm/f* (*SPORT*) diver.

'tuffo *sm* dive; (*breve bagno*) dip.

tu'gurio *sm* hovel.

tuli'pano *sm* tulip.

'tulle *sm* (*tessuto*) tulle.

tume'fare *vt* to cause to swell; ~**rsi** *vr* to swell.

'tumido, a *ag* swollen.

tu'more *sm* (*MED*) tumour (*BRIT*), tumor (*US*).

tumulazi'one [tumulat'tsjone] *sf* burial.

tu'multo *sm* uproar, commotion; (*sommossa*) riot; (*fig*) turmoil.

tumultu'oso, a *ag* rowdy, unruly; (*fig*) turbulent, stormy.

tungs'teno *sm* tungsten.

'tunica, che *sf* tunic.

'Tunisi *sf* Tunis.

Tuni'sia *sf*: **la** ~ Tunisia.

tuni'sino, a *ag*, *sm/f* Tunisian.

'tunnel *sm inv* tunnel.

'tuo, 'tua, tu'oi, 'tue *det*: **il** ~, **la tua** *etc* your ♦ *pron*: **il** ~, **la tua** *etc* yours ♦ *sm*: **hai speso del** ~? did you spend your own money? ♦ *sf*: **la** ~**a** (*opinione*) your view; **i tuoi** (*genitori, famiglia*) your family; **una** ~**a amica** a friend of yours; **è dalla** ~**a** he is on your side; **alla** ~**a!** (*brindisi*) your health!; **ne hai fatta una delle** ~**e!** (*sciocchezze*) you've done it again!

tuo'nare *vi* to thunder; **tuona** it is thundering, there's some thunder.

tu'ono *sm* thunder.

tu'orlo *sm* yolk.

tu'racciolo [tu'rattʃolo] *sm* cap, top; (*di sughero*) cork.

tu'rare *vt* to stop, plug; (*con sughero*) to cork; ~**rsi il naso** to hold one's nose.

'turba *sf* (*folla*) crowd, throng; (: *peg*) mob; ~**e** *sfpl* disorder(s); **soffrire di** ~**e psichiche** to suffer from a mental disorder.

turba'mento *sm* disturbance; (*di animo*) anxiety, agitation.

tur'bante *sm* turban.

tur'bare *vt* to disturb, trouble; ~ **la quiete pubblica** (*DIR*) to disturb the peace.

tur'bina *sf* turbine.

turbi'nare *vi* to whirl.

'turbine *sm* whirlwind; ~ **di neve** swirl of snow; ~ **di polvere/sabbia** dust/sandstorm.

turbi'noso, a *ag* (*vento, danza etc*) whirling.

turbo'lento, a *ag* turbulent; (*ragazzo*) boisterous, unruly.

turbo'lenza [turbo'lɛntsa] *sf* turbulence.

turboreat'tore *sm* turbojet engine.

tur'chese [tur'kese] *ag*, *sm*, *sf* turquoise.

Tur'chia [tur'kia] *sf*: **la** ~ Turkey.

tur'chino, a [tur'kino] *ag* deep blue.

'turco, a, chi, che *ag* Turkish ♦ *sm/f* Turk/Turkish woman ♦ *sm* (*LING*) Turkish; **parlare** ~ (*fig*) to talk double Dutch.

'turgido, a ['turdʒido] *ag* swollen.

tu'rismo *sm* tourism.

tu'rista, i, e *sm/f* tourist.

tu'ristico, a, ci, che *ag* tourist *cpd*.

tur'nista, i, e *sm/f* shift worker.

'turno *sm* turn; (*di lavoro*) shift; **di** ~ (*soldato, medico, custode*) on duty; **a** ~ (*rispondere*) in turn; (*lavorare*) in shifts; **fare a** ~ **a fare qc** to take turns to do sth; **è il suo** ~ it's your (*o* his *etc*) turn.

'turpe *ag* filthy, vile.

turpi'loquio *sm* obscene language.

'tuta *sf* overalls *pl*; (*SPORT*) tracksuit; ~ **mimetica** (*MIL*) camouflage clothing; ~ **spaziale** spacesuit; ~ **subacquea** wetsuit.

tu'tela *sf* (*DIR: di minore*) guardianship; (: *protezione*) protection; (*difesa*) defence (*BRIT*), defense (*US*); ~ **dell'ambiente** environmental protection; ~ **del consumatore** consumer protection.

tute'lare *vt* to protect, defend ♦ *ag* (*DIR*): **giudice** ~ *judge with responsibility for guardianship cases.*

tu'tore, 'trice *sm/f* (*DIR*) guardian.

tutta'via *cong* nevertheless, yet.

═══════════════════ *PAROLA CHIAVE*

'tutto, a *det* **1** (*intero*) all; ~ **il latte** all the milk; ~**a la notte** all night, the whole night; ~ **il libro** the whole book; ~**a una bottiglia** a whole bottle; **in** ~ **il mondo** all over the world

2 (*pl, collettivo*) all; every; ~**i i libri** all the books; ~**e le notti** every night; ~**i i venerdì** every Friday; ~**i gli uomini** all the men; (*collettivo*) all men; ~**e le volte che** every time (that); ~**i e due** both *o* each of us (*o* them *o* you); ~**i e cinque** all five of us (*o* them *o* you)

3 (*completamente*): **era** ~**a sporca** she was all dirty; **tremava** ~ he was trembling all over; **è** ~**a sua madre** she's just *o* exactly like her mother

4: **a tutt'oggi** so far, up till now; **a** ~**a velocità** at full *o* top speed

♦ *pron* **1** (*ogni cosa*) everything, all; (*qualsiasi cosa*) anything; **ha mangiato** ~ he's eaten everything; **dimmi** ~ tell me all about it; ~ **compreso** all included, all-in (*BRIT*); ~ **considerato** all things considered; **con** ~ **che** (*malgrado*) although; **del** ~ completely; **10.000 lire in** ~ 10,000 lire in all; **in** ~ **eravamo 50** there were 50 of us in all; **in** ~ **e per** ~ completely; **il che è** ~ **dire** and that's saying a lot **2**: ~**i, e** (*ognuno*) all, everybody; **vengono** ~**i** they are all coming, everybody's coming; ~**i sanno che** everybody knows that; ~**i quanti** all and sundry ♦ *av* (*completamente*) entirely, quite; **è** ~ **il contrario** it's quite the opposite; **tutt'al più: saranno stati tutt'al più una cinquantina** there were about fifty of them at (the very) most; **tutt'al più possiamo prendere un treno** if the worst comes to the worst we can take a train; **tutt'altro** on the contrary; **è tutt'altro che felice** he's anything but happy; **tutt'intorno** all around; **tutt'a un tratto** suddenly ♦ *sm*: **il** ~ the whole lot, all of it; **il** ~ **si è svolto senza incidenti** it all went off without incident; **il** ~ **le costerà due milioni** the whole thing will cost you two million.

tutto'fare *ag inv*: **domestica** ~ general maid; **ragazzo** ~ office boy ♦ *sm/f inv* handyman/woman.
tut'tora *av* still.
tutù *sm inv* tutu, ballet skirt.
TV [ti'vu] *sf inv* (= *televisione*) TV ♦ *sigla* = *Treviso*.

U u

U, u [u] *sf o m inv* (*lettera*) U, u; **U come Udine** ≈ U for Uncle; **inversione ad U** U-turn.
ub'bia *sf* (*letterario*) irrational fear.
ubbidi'ente *ag* obedient.
ubbidi'enza [ubbi'djɛntsa] *sf* obedience.
ubbi'dire *vi* to obey; ~ **a** to obey; (*sog: veicolo, macchina*) to respond to.
ubicazi'one [ubikat'tsjone] *sf* site, location.
ubiquità *sf*: **non ho il dono dell'**~ I can't be

everywhere at once.
ubria'care *vt*: ~ **qn** to get sb drunk; (*sog: alcool*) to make sb drunk; (*fig*) to make sb's head spin *o* reel; ~**rsi** *vr* to get drunk; ~**rsi di** (*fig*) to become intoxicated with.
ubria'chezza [ubria'kettsa] *sf* drunkenness.
ubri'aco, a, chi, che *ag, sm/f* drunk.
ubria'cone *sm* drunkard.
uccellagi'one [uttʃella'dʒone] *sf* bird catching.
uccelli'era [uttʃel'ljɛra] *sf* aviary.
uccel'lino [uttʃel'lino] *sm* baby bird, chick.
uc'cello [ut'tʃello] *sm* bird.
uc'cidere [ut'tʃidere] *vt* to kill; ~**rsi** *vr* (*suicidarsi*) to kill o.s.; (*perdere la vita*) to be killed.
uccisi'one [uttʃi'zjone] *sf* killing.
uc'ciso, a [ut'tʃizo] *pp di* **uccidere**.
ucci'sore [uttʃi'zore] *sm* killer.
U'craina *sf* Ukraine.
u'craino, a *ag, sm/f* Ukrainian.
UD *sigla* = *Udine*.
U.D.C. *sigla f* (*POL*: = *Unione di Centro*) *centre party*.
u'dente *sm/f*: **i non udenti** the hard of hearing.
udi'enza [u'djɛntsa] *sf* audience; (*DIR*) hearing; **dare** ~ **(a)** to grant an audience (to); ~ **a porte chiuse** hearing in camera.
u'dire *vt* to hear.
udi'tivo, a *ag* auditory.
u'dito *sm* (sense of) hearing.
udi'tore, 'trice *sm/f* listener; (*INS*) unregistered student (*attending lectures*).
udi'torio *sm* (*persone*) audience.
UE *sigla f* (= *Unione Europea*) EU.
UEFA *sigla f* UEFA (= *Union of European Football Associations*).
UEM *sigla f* (*Unione economica e monetaria*) EMU.
'uffa *escl* tut!
uffici'ale [uffi'tʃale] *ag* official ♦ *sm* (*AMM*) official, officer; (*MIL*) officer; **pubblico** ~ public official; ~ **giudiziario** clerk of the court; ~ **di marina** naval officer; ~ **sanitario** health inspector; ~ **di stato civile** registrar.
ufficializ'zare [uffitʃalid'dzare] *vt* to make official.
uf'ficio [uf'fitʃo] *sm* (*gen*) office; (*dovere*) duty; (*mansione*) task, function, job; (*agenzia*) agency, bureau; (*REL*) service; **d'**~ *ag* office *cpd*; official ♦ *av* officially; **provvedere d'**~ to act officially; **convocare d'**~ (*DIR*) to summons; **difensore** *o* **avvocato d'**~ (*DIR*) court-appointed counsel for the defence; ~ **brevetti** patent office; ~ **di collocamento**

employment office; ~ **informazioni** information bureau; ~ **oggetti smarriti** lost property office (*BRIT*), lost and found (*US*); ~ **postale** post office; ~ **vendite/del personale** sales/personnel department.

uffici'oso, a [uffi'tʃoso] *ag* unofficial.

'UFO *sm inv* (= *unidentified flying object*) UFO.

'ufo: a ~ *av* free, for nothing.

U'ganda *sf*: l'~ Uganda.

'uggia ['uddʒa] *sf* (*noia*) boredom; (*fastidio*) bore; **avere/prendere qn in** ~ to dislike/ take a dislike to sb.

uggi'oso, a [ud'dʒoso] *ag* tiresome; (*tempo*) dull.

'ugola *sf* uvula.

uguagli'anza [ugwaʎ'ʎantsa] *sf* equality.

uguagli'are [ugwaʎ'ʎare] *vt* to make equal; (*essere uguale*) to equal, be equal to; (*livellare*) to level; ~**rsi** *vr*: ~**rsi a** *o* **con qn** (*paragonarsi*) to compare o.s. to sb.

ugu'ale *ag* equal; (*identico*) identical, the same; (*uniforme*) level, even ♦ *av*: **costano** ~ they cost the same; **sono bravi** ~ they're equally good.

ugual'mente *av* equally; (*lo stesso*) all the same.

U.I. *abbr* = *uso interno*.

UIL *sigla f* (= *Unione Italiana del Lavoro*) trade union *federation*.

'ulcera ['ultʃera] *sf* ulcer.

ulcerazi'one [ultʃerat'tsjone] *sf* ulceration.

u'liva *etc* = *oliva etc*.

U'livo *sm* (*POL*) *centre-left coalition*.

ulteri'ore *ag* further.

ultima'mente *av* lately, of late.

ulti'mare *vt* to finish, complete.

ulti'matum *sm inv* ultimatum.

ulti'missime *sfpl* latest news *sg*.

'ultimo, a *ag* (*finale*) last; (*estremo*) farthest, utmost; (*recente: notizia, moda*) latest; (*fig: sommo, fondamentale*) ultimate ♦ *sm/f* last (one); **fino all'**~ to the last, until the end; **da** ~, **in** ~ in the end; **per** ~ (*entrare, arrivare*) last; **abitare all'**~ **piano** to live on the top floor; **in** ~**a pagina** (*di giornale*) on the back page; **negli** ~**i tempi** recently; **all'**~ **momento** at the last minute; ... **la vostra lettera del 7 aprile** ~ **scorso** ... your letter of April 7th last; **in** ~**a analisi** in the final *o* last analysis; **in** ~ **luogo** finally.

ultrà *sm/f* ultra.

ultrasi'nistra *sf* (*POL*) extreme left.

ultrasu'ono *sm* ultrasound.

ultravio'letto, a *ag* ultraviolet.

ulu'lare *vi* to howl.

ulu'lato *sm* howling *no pl*; howl.

umana'mente *av* (*con umanità*) humanely; (*nei limiti delle capacità umane*) humanly.

uma'nesimo *sm* humanism.

umanità *sf* humanity.

umani'tario, a *ag* humanitarian.

umaniz'zare [umanid'dzare] *vt* to humanize.

u'mano, a *ag* human; (*comprensivo*) humane.

umbi'lico *sm* = *ombelico*.

'umbro, a *ag* of (*o* from) Umbria.

umet'tare *vt* to dampen, moisten.

umi'diccio, a, ci, ce [umi'dittʃo] *ag* (*terreno*) damp; (*mano*) moist, clammy.

umidifi'care *vt* to humidify.

umidifica'tore *sm* humidifier.

umidità *sf* dampness; moistness; humidity.

'umido, a *ag* damp; (*mano, occhi*) moist; (*clima*) humid ♦ *sm* dampness, damp; **carne in** ~ stew.

'umile *ag* humble.

umili'ante *ag* humiliating.

umili'are *vt* to humiliate; ~**rsi** *vr* to humble o.s.

umiliazi'one [umiljat'tsjone] *sf* humiliation.

umiltà *sf* humility, humbleness.

u'more *sm* (*disposizione d'animo*) mood; (*carattere*) temper; **di buon/cattivo** ~ in a good/bad mood.

umo'rismo *sm* humour (*BRIT*), humor (*US*); **avere il senso dell'**~ to have a sense of humo(u)r.

umo'rista, i, e *sm/f* humorist.

umo'ristico, a, ci, che *ag* humorous, funny.

un, un', una *vedi* **uno**.

u'nanime *ag* unanimous.

unanimità *sf* unanimity; **all'**~ unanimously.

'una 'tantum *ag* one-off *cpd* ♦ *sf* (*imposta*) one-off tax.

unci'nato, a [untʃi'nato] *ag* (*amo*) barbed; (*ferro*) hooked; **croce** ~**a** swastika.

un'cino [un'tʃino] *sm* hook.

undi'cenne [undi'tʃɛnne] *ag, sm/f* eleven-year-old.

undi'cesimo, a [undi'tʃɛzimo] eleventh.

'undici ['unditʃi] *num* eleven.

U'NESCO *sigla f* (= *United Nations Educational, Scientific and Cultural Organization*) UNESCO.

'ungere ['undʒere] *vt* to grease, oil; (*REL*) to anoint; (*fig*) to flatter, butter up; ~**rsi** *vr* (*sporcarsi*) to get covered in grease; ~**rsi con la crema** to put on cream.

unghe'rese [unge'rese] *ag, sm/f, sm* Hungarian.

Unghe'ria [unge'ria] *sf*: l'~ Hungary.

'unghia ['ungja] *sf* (*ANAT*) nail; (*di animale*) claw; (*di rapace*) talon; (*di cavallo*) hoof; **pagare sull'**~ (*fig*) to pay on the nail
unghi'ata [un'gjata] *sf* (*graffio*) scratch.
ungu'ento *sm* ointment.
unica'mente *av* only.
'UNICEF ['unitʃɛf] *sigla m* (= *United Nations International Children's Emergency Fund*) UNICEF.
'unico, a, ci, che *ag* (*solo*) only; (*ineguagliabile*) unique; (*singolo: binario*) single; **è figlio** ~ he's an only child; **atto** ~ (*TEAT*) one-act play; **agente** ~ (*COMM*) sole agent.
uni'corno *sm* unicorn.
unifi'care *vt* to unite, unify; (*sistemi*) to standardize.
unificazi'one [unifikat'tsjone] *sf* unification; standardization.
unifor'mare *vt* (*terreno, superficie*) to level; ~**rsi** *vr*: ~**rsi a** to conform to; ~ **qc a** to adjust *o* relate sth to.
uni'forme *ag* uniform; (*superficie*) even ♦ *sf* (*divisa*) uniform; **alta** ~ dress uniform.
uniformità *sf* uniformity, evenness.
unilate'rale *ag* one-sided; (*DIR, POL*) unilateral.
uninomi'nale *ag* (*POL: collegio, sistema*) single-candidate *cpd*.
uni'one *sf* union; (*fig: concordia*) unity, harmony; **U~ economica e monetaria** economic and monetary union; **U~ Europea** European Union; **l'U~ Sovietica** the Soviet Union.
u'nire *vt* to unite; (*congiungere*) to join, connect; (*: ingredienti, colori*) to combine; (*in matrimonio*) to unite, join together; ~**rsi** *vr* to unite; (*in matrimonio*) to be joined together; ~ **qc a** to unite sth with; to join *o* connect sth with; to combine sth with; ~**rsi a** (*gruppo, società*) to join.
u'nisono *sm*: **all'**~ in unison.
unità *sf inv* (*unione, concordia*) unity; (*MAT, MIL, COMM, di misura*) unit; ~ **centrale (di elaborazione)** (*INFORM*) central processing unit; ~ **disco** (*INFORM*) disk drive; ~ **monetaria** monetary unit.
uni'tario, a *ag* unitary; **prezzo** ~ price per unit.
u'nito, a *ag* (*paese*) united; (*amici, famiglia*) close; **in tinta** ~**a** plain, self-coloured (*BRIT*), self-colored (*US*).
univer'sale *ag* universal; general.
universalità *sf* universality.
universal'mente *av* universally.
università *sf inv* university.
universi'tario, a *ag* university *cpd* ♦ *sm/f* (*studente*) university student; (*insegnante*)

academic, university lecturer.
uni'verso *sm* universe.
u'nivoco, a, ci, che *ag* unambiguous.

══════════ *PAROLA CHIAVE*

'uno, a (*dav sm* **un** + *C, V,* **uno** + *s impura, gn, pn, ps, x, z; dav sf* **un'** + *V,* **una** + *C*) *det*
1 a; (*dav vocale*) an; **un bambino** a child; ~**a strada** a street; ~ **zingaro** a gypsy
2 (*intensivo*): **ho avuto** ~**a paura!** I got such a fright!
♦ *pron* **1** one; **ce n'è** ~ **qui** there's one here; **prendine** ~ take one (of them); **l'**~ **o l'altro** either (of them); **l'**~ **e l'altro** both (of them); **aiutarsi l'un l'altro** to help one another; **sono entrati l'**~ **dopo l'altro** they came in one after the other; **a** ~ **a** ~ one by one; **metà per** ~ half each
2 (*un tale*) someone, somebody; **ho incontrato** ~ **che ti conosce** I met somebody who knows you
3 (*con valore impersonale*) one, you; **se** ~ **vuole** if one wants, if you want; **cosa fa** ~ **in quella situazione?** what does one do in that situation?
♦ *num* one; ~**a mela e due pere** one apple and two pears; ~ **più** ~ **fa due** one plus one equals two, one and one are two
♦ *sf*: **è l'**~**a** it's one (o'clock).

'unsi *etc vb vedi* **ungere**.
'unto, a *pp di* **ungere** ♦ *ag* greasy, oily ♦ *sm* grease.
untu'oso, a *ag* greasy, oily.
unzi'one [un'tsjone] *sf*: **l'Estrema U~** (*REL*) Extreme Unction.
u'omo, *pl* **u'omini** *sm* man; **da** ~ (*abito, scarpe*) men's, for men; **a memoria d'**~ since the world began; **a passo d'**~ at walking pace; ~ **d'affari** businessman; ~ **d'azione** man of action; ~ **di fiducia** right-hand man; ~ **di mondo** man of the world; ~ **di paglia** stooge; **l'**~ **della strada** the man in the street.
u'opo *sm*: **all'**~ if necessary.
u'ovo, *pl*(*f*) **u'ova** *sm* egg; **cercare il pelo nell'**~ (*fig*) to split hairs; ~ **affogato** *o* **in camicia** poached egg; ~ **bazzotto/sodo** soft-/hard-boiled egg; ~ **alla coque** boiled egg; ~ **di Pasqua** Easter egg; ~ **al tegame** *o* **all'occhio di bue** fried egg; **uova strapazzate** scrambled eggs.
ura'gano *sm* hurricane.
U'rali *smpl*: **gli** ~, **i Monti** ~ the Urals, the Ural Mountains.
u'ranio *sm* uranium.
urba'nesimo *sm* urbanization.
urba'nista, i, e *sm/f* town planner.

urba'nistica *sf* town planning.

urbanità *sf* urbanity.

ur'bano, a *ag* urban, city *cpd*, town *cpd*; (*TEL*: *chiamata*) local; (*fig*) urbane.

ur'gente [ur'dʒɛnte] *ag* urgent.

ur'genza [ur'dʒɛntsa] *sf* urgency; **in caso d'~** in (case of) an emergency; **d'~** *ag* emergency ♦ *av* urgently, as a matter of urgency; **non c'è ~** there's no hurry; **questo lavoro va fatto con ~** this work is urgent.

'urgere ['urdʒere] *vi* to be needed urgently.

u'rina *etc* = **orina** *etc*.

ur'lare *vi* (*persona*) to scream, yell; (*animale, vento*) to howl ♦ *vt* to scream, yell.

'urlo, *pl*(*m*) **'urli,** *pl*(*f*) **'urla** *sm* scream, yell; howl.

'urna *sf* urn; (*elettorale*) ballot box; **andare alle ~e** to go to the polls.

urrà *escl* hurrah!

U.R.S.S. *sigla f* (= *Unione delle Repubbliche Socialiste Sovietiche*): **l'~** the USSR.

ur'tare *vt* to bump into, knock against; (*fig*: *irritare*) to annoy ♦ *vi*: **~ contro** *o* **in** to bump into, knock against; (*fig*: *imbattersi*) to come up against; **~rsi** *vr* (*reciproco*: *scontrarsi*) to collide; (: *fig*) to clash; (*irritarsi*) to get annoyed.

'urto *sm* (*colpo*) knock, bump; (*scontro*) crash, collision; (*fig*) clash; **terapia d'~** (*MED*) shock treatment.

uruguai'ano, a *ag, sm/f* Uruguayan.

Urugu'ay *sm*: **l'~** Uruguay.

u.s. *abbr* = **ultimo scorso**.

'USA *smpl*: **gli ~** the USA.

u'sanza [u'zantsa] *sf* custom; (*moda*) fashion.

u'sare *vt* to use, employ ♦ *vi* (*essere di moda*) to be fashionable; (*servirsi*): **~ di** to use; (: *diritto*) to exercise; (*essere solito*): **~ fare** to be in the habit of doing, be accustomed to doing ♦ *vb impers*: **qui usa così** it's the custom round here; **~ la massima cura nel fare qc** to exercise great care when doing sth.

u'sato, a *ag* used; (*consumato*) worn; (*di seconda mano*) used, second-hand ♦ *sm* second-hand goods *pl*.

u'scente [uʃ'ʃɛnte] *ag* (*AMM*) outgoing.

usci'ere [uʃ'ʃɛre] *sm* usher.

'uscio ['uʃʃo] *sm* door.

u'scire [uʃ'ʃire] *vi* (*gen*) to come out; (*partire, andare a passeggio, a uno spettacolo etc*) to go out; (*essere sorteggiato: numero*) to come up; **~ da** (*gen*) to leave; (*posto*) to go (*o* come) out of, leave; (*solco, vasca etc*) to come out of; (*muro*) to stick out of;

(*competenza etc*) to be outside; (*infanzia, adolescenza*) to leave behind; (*famiglia nobile etc*) to come from; **~ da** *o* **di casa** to go out; (*fig*) to leave home; **~ in automobile** to go out in the car, go for a drive; **~ di strada** (*AUT*) to go off *o* leave the road.

u'scita [uʃ'ʃita] *sf* (*passaggio, varco*) exit, way out; (*per divertimento*) outing; (*ECON*: *somma*) expenditure; (*fig*: *battuta*) witty remark; **"vietata l'~"** "no exit"; **~ di sicurezza** emergency exit.

usi'gnolo [uziɲ'ɲɔlo] *sm* nightingale.

U.S.L. [uzl] *sigla f* (= *unità sanitaria locale*) local health centre.

'uso *sm* (*utilizzazione*) use; (*esercizio*) practice (*BRIT*), practise (*US*); (*abitudine*) custom; **fare ~ di qc** to use sth; **con l'~** with practice; **a ~ di** for (the use of); **d'~** (*corrente*) in use; **fuori ~** out of use; **essere in ~** to be in common *o* current use.

ustio'nare *vt* to burn; **~rsi** *vr* to burn o.s.

usti'one *sf* burn.

usu'ale *ag* common, everyday.

usufru'ire *vi*: **~ di** (*giovarsi di*) to take advantage of, make use of.

usu'frutto *sm* (*DIR*) usufruct.

u'sura *sf* usury; (*logoramento*) wear (and tear).

usu'raio *sm* usurer.

usur'pare *vt* to usurp.

usurpa'tore, 'trice *sm/f* usurper.

uten'sile *sm* tool, implement ♦ *ag*: **macchina ~** machine tool; **~i da cucina** kitchen utensils.

utensile'ria *sf* (*utensili*) tools *pl*; (*reparto*) tool room.

u'tente *sm/f* user; (*di gas etc*) consumer; (*del telefono*) subscriber; **~ finale** end user.

'utero *sm* uterus, womb; **~ in affitto** host womb.

'utile *ag* useful ♦ *sm* (*vantaggio*) advantage, benefit; (*ECON*: *profitto*) profit; **rendersi ~** to be helpful; **in tempo ~** per in time for; **unire l'~ al dilettevole** to combine business with pleasure; **partecipare agli ~i** (*ECON*) to share in the profits.

utilità *sf* usefulness *no pl*; use; (*vantaggio*) benefit; **essere di grande ~** to be very useful.

utili'tario, a *ag* utilitarian ♦ *sf* (*AUT*) economy car.

utiliz'zare [utilid'dzare] *vt* to use, make use of, utilize.

utilizzazi'one [utiliddzat'tsjone] *sf* utilization, use.

uti'lizzo [uti'liddzo] *sm* (*AMM*) utilization; (*BANCA: di credito*) availment.
util'mente *av* usefully, profitably.
uto'pia *sf* utopia; **è pura ~ that's** sheer utopianism.
uto'pistico, a, ci, che *ag* utopian.
UVA *abbr* = *ultravioletto prossimo*.
'uva *sf* grapes *pl*; **~ passa** raisins *pl*; **~ spina** gooseberry.

V v

V, v [vi, vu] *sf o m inv* (*lettera*) V, v; **V come Venezia** ≈ V for Victor.
V *abbr* (= *volt*) V.
v. *abbr* (= *vedi, verso, versetto*) v.
VA *sigla* = *Varese*.
va, va' *vb vedi* **andare**.
va'cante *ag* vacant.
va'canza |va'kantsa| *sf* (*l'essere vacante*) vacancy; (*riposo, ferie*) holiday(s *pl*) (*BRIT*), vacation (*US*); (*giorno di permesso*) day off, holiday; **~e** *sfpl* (*periodo di ferie*) holidays, vacation *sg*; **essere/andare in ~** to be/go on holiday o vacation; **far ~** to have a holiday; **~e estive** summer holiday(s) o vacation.
'vacca, che *sf* cow.
vacci'nare [vattʃi'nare] *vt* to vaccinate; **farsi ~** to have a vaccination, get vaccinated.
vaccinazi'one [vattʃinat'tsjone] *sf* vaccination.
vac'cino [vat'tʃino] *sm* (*MED*) vaccine.
vacil'lante [vatʃil'lante] *ag* (*edificio, vecchio*) shaky, unsteady; (*fiamma*) flickering; (*salute, memoria*) shaky, failing.
vacil'lare [vatʃil'lare] *vi* to sway; (*fiamma*) to flicker; (*fig: memoria, coraggio*) to be failing, falter.
'vacuo, a *ag* (*fig*) empty, vacuous ♦ *sm* vacuum.
'vado *etc vb vedi* **andare**.
vagabon'daggio [vagabon'daddʒo] *sm* wandering, roaming; (*DIR*) vagrancy.
vagabon'dare *vi* to roam, wander.
vaga'bondo, a *sm/f* tramp, vagrant; (*fannullone*) idler, loafer.
va'gare *vi* to wander.
vagheggi'are [vaged'dʒare] *vt* to long for, dream of.

vagherò *etc* [vage'rɔ] *vb vedi* **vagare**.
va'ghezza [va'gettsa] *sf* vagueness.
va'gina [va'dʒina] *sf* vagina.
va'gire [va'dʒire] *vi* to whimper.
va'gito [va'dʒito] *sm* cry, wailing.
'vaglia ['vaʎʎa] *sm inv* money order; **~ cambiario** promissory note; **~ postale** postal order.
vagli'are [vaʎ'ʎare] *vt* to sift; (*fig*) to weigh up.
'vaglio ['vaʎʎo] *sm* sieve; **passare al ~** (*fig*) to examine closely.
'vago, a, ghi, ghe *ag* vague.
va'gone *sm* (*FERR: per passeggeri*) carriage (*BRIT*), car (*US*); (: *per merci*) truck, wagon; **~ letto** sleeper, sleeping car; **~ ristorante** dining o restaurant car.
'vai *vb vedi* **andare**.
vai'olo *sm* smallpox.
val. *abbr* = **valuta**.
va'langa, ghe *sf* avalanche.
va'lente *ag* able, talented.
va'lenza [va'lɛntsa] *sf* (*fig: significato*) content; (*CHIM*) valency.
va'lere *vi* (*avere forza, potenza*) to have influence; (*essere valido*) to be valid; (*avere vigore, autorità*) to hold, apply; (*essere capace: poeta, studente*) to be good, be able ♦ *vt* (*prezzo, sforzo*) to be worth; (*corrispondere*) to correspond to; (*procurare*): **~ qc a qn** to earn sb sth; **~rsi** *vr*: **~rsi di** to make use of, take advantage of; **far ~** (*autorità etc*) to assert; **far ~ le proprie ragioni** to make o.s. heard; **farsi ~** to make o.s. appreciated o respected; **vale a dire** that is to say; **~ la pena** to be worth the effort o worth it; **l'uno vale l'altro** the one is as good as the other, they amount to the same thing; **non vale niente** it's worthless; **~rsi dei consigli di qn** to take sb's advice, act upon sb's advice.
valeri'ana *sf* (*BOT, MED*) valerian.
va'levole *ag* valid.
'valgo *etc vb vedi* **valere**.
vali'care *vt* to cross.
'valico, chi *sm* (*passo*) pass.
validità *sf* validity.
'valido, a *ag* valid; (*rimedio*) effective; (*persona*) worthwhile; **essere di ~ aiuto a qn** to be a great help to sb.
valige'ria [validʒe'ria] *sf* (*assortimento*) leather goods *pl*; (*fabbrica*) leather goods factory; (*negozio*) leather goods shop.
va'ligia, gie o **ge** [va'lidʒa] *sf* (*suit*)case; **fare le ~gie** to pack (up); **~ diplomatica** diplomatic bag.
val'lata *sf* valley.

'**valle** *sf* valley; **a ~** (*di fiume*) downstream; **scendere a ~** to go downhill.

val'letto *sm* valet.

valligi'ano, a [valli'dʒano] *sm/f* inhabitant of a valley.

va'lore *sm* (*gen, COMM*) value; (*merito*) merit, worth; (*coraggio*) valour (*BRIT*), valor (*US*), courage; (*FINANZA: titolo*) security; **~i** *smpl* (*oggetti preziosi*) valuables; **crescere/diminuire di ~** to go up/down in value, gain/lose in value; **è di gran ~** it's worth a lot, it's very valuable; **privo di ~** worthless; **~ contabile** book value; **~ effettivo** real value; **~ nominale** *o* **facciale** nominal value; **~ di realizzo** break-up value; **~ di riscatto** surrender value; **~i bollati** (revenue) stamps.

valoriz'zare [valorid'dzare] *vt* (*terreno*) to develop; (*fig*) to make the most of.

valo'roso, a *ag* courageous.

'**valso, a** *pp di* **valere.**

va'luta *sf* currency, money; (*BANCA*): **~ 15 gennaio** interest to run from January 15th; **~ estera** foreign currency.

valu'tare *vt* (*casa, gioiello, fig*) to value; (*stabilire: peso, entrate, fig*) to estimate.

valu'tario, a *ag* (*FINANZA: norme*) currency *cpd.*

valutazi'one [valutat'tsjone] *sf* valuation; estimate.

'**valva** *sf* (*ZOOL, BOT*) valve.

'**valvola** *sf* (*TECN, ANAT*) valve; (*ELETTR*) fuse; **~ a farfalla del carburatore** (*AUT*) throttle; **~ di sicurezza** safety valve.

'**valzer** ['valtser] *sm inv* waltz.

vam'pata *sf* (*di fiamma*) blaze; (*di calore*) blast; (: *al viso*) flush.

vam'piro *sm* vampire.

vana'gloria *sf* boastfulness.

van'dalico, a, ci, che *ag* vandal *cpd;* **atto ~** act of vandalism.

vanda'lismo *sm* vandalism.

'**vandalo** *sm* vandal.

vaneggia'mento [vanedddʒa'mento] *sm* raving, delirium.

vaneggi'are [vaned'dʒare] *vi* to rave.

va'nesio, a *ag* vain, conceited.

'**vanga, ghe** *sf* spade.

van'gare *vt* to dig.

van'gelo [van'dʒɛlo] *sm* gospel.

vanifi'care *vt* to nullify.

va'niglia [va'niʎʎa] *sf* vanilla.

vanigli'ato, a [vaniʎ'ʎato] *ag:* **zucchero ~** (*CUC*) vanilla sugar.

vanità *sf* vanity; (*di promessa*) emptiness; (*di sforzo*) futility.

vani'toso, a *ag* vain, conceited.

'**vanno** *vb vedi* **andare.**

'**vano, a** *ag* vain **♦** *sm* (*spazio*) space; (*apertura*) opening; (*stanza*) room; **il ~ della porta** the doorway; **il ~ portabagagli** (*AUT*) the boot (*BRIT*), the trunk (*US*).

van'taggio [van'tadddʒo] *sm* advantage; **trarre ~ da qc** to benefit from sth; **essere/portarsi in ~** (*SPORT*) to be in/take the lead.

vantaggi'oso, a [vantad'dʒoso] *ag* advantageous, favourable (*BRIT*), favorable (*US*).

van'tare *vt* to praise, speak highly of; **~rsi** *vr:* **~rsi (di/di aver fatto)** to boast *o* brag (about/about having done).

vante'ria *sf* boasting.

'**vanto** *sm* boasting; (*merito*) virtue, merit; (*gloria*) pride.

'**vanvera** *sf:* **a ~** haphazardly; **parlare a ~** to talk nonsense.

va'pore *sm* vapour (*BRIT*), vapor (*US*); (*anche:* **~ acqueo**) steam; (*nave*) steamer; **a ~** (*turbina etc*) steam *cpd;* **al ~** (*CUC*) steamed.

vapo'retto *sm* steamer.

vapori'era *sf* (*FERR*) steam engine.

vaporiz'zare [vaporid'dzare] *vt* to vaporize.

vaporizza'tore [vaporiddza'tore] *sm* spray.

vaporizzazi'one [vaporiddzat'tsjone] *sf* vaporization.

vapo'roso, a *ag* (*tessuto*) filmy; (*capelli*) soft and full.

va'rare *vt* (*NAUT, fig*) to launch; (*DIR*) to pass.

var'care *vt* to cross.

'**varco, chi** *sm* passage; **aprirsi un ~ tra la folla** to push one's way through the crowd.

vare'china [vare'kina] *sf* bleach.

vari'abile *ag* variable; (*tempo, umore*) changeable, variable **♦** *sf* (*MAT*) variable.

vari'ante *sf* (*gen*) variation, change; (*di piano*) modification; (*LING*) variant; (*SPORT*) alternative route.

vari'are *vt, vi* to vary; **~ di opinione** to change one's mind.

variazi'one [varjat'tsjone] *sf* variation, change; (*MUS*) variation; **una ~ di programma** a change of plan.

va'rice [va'ritʃe] *sf* varicose vein.

vari'cella [vari'tʃella] *sf* chickenpox.

vari'coso, a *ag* varicose.

varie'gato, a *ag* variegated.

varietà *sf inv* variety **♦** *sm inv* variety show.

'**vario, a** *ag* varied; (*parecchi: col sostantivo al pl*) various; (*mutevole: umore*) changeable; **~e** *sfpl:* **~e ed eventuali** (*nell'ordine del giorno*) any other business.

vario'pinto, a *ag* multicoloured (*BRIT*),

multicolored (*US*).

'**varo** *sm* (*NAUT, fig*) launch; (*di leggi*) passing.

varrò *etc vb vedi* **valere.**

Var'savia *sf* Warsaw.

va'saio *sm* potter.

'**vasca, sche** *sf* basin; (*anche:* ~ **da bagno**) bathtub, bath.

va'scello [vaʃ'ʃɛllo] *sm* (*NAUT*) vessel, ship.

vas'chetta [vas'ketta] *sf* (*per gelato*) tub; (*per sviluppare fotografie*) dish.

vase'lina *sf* vaseline.

vasel'lame *sm* (*stoviglie*) crockery; (: *di porcellana*) china; ~ **d'oro/d'argento** gold/silver plate.

'**vaso** *sm* (*recipiente*) pot; (: *barattolo*) jar; (: *decorativo*) vase; (*ANAT*) vessel; ~ **da fiori** vase; (*per piante*) flowerpot.

vas'sallo *sm* vassal.

vas'soio *sm* tray.

vastità *sf* vastness.

'**vasto, a** *ag* vast, immense; **di** ~**e proporzioni** (*incendio*) huge; (*fenomeno, rivolta*) widespread; **su** ~**a scala** on a vast o huge scale.

Vati'cano *sm*: **il** ~ the Vatican; **la Città del** ~ the Vatican City.

VB *sigla* = *Vibo Valenza.*

VC *sigla* = *Vercelli.*

VE *sigla* = *Venezia* ♦ *abbr* = *Vostra Eccellenza.*

ve *pron, av vedi* **vi.**

vecchi'aia [vek'kjaja] *sf* old age.

'**vecchio, a** [ˈvɛkkjo] *ag* old ♦ *sm/f* old man/woman; **i** ~**i** the old; **è un mio** ~ **amico** he's an old friend of mine; **è un uomo** ~ **stile** o **stampo** he's an old-fashioned man; **è** ~ **del mestiere** he's an old hand at the job.

'**vece** [ˈvetʃe] *sf*: **in** ~ **di** in the place of, for; **fare le** ~**i di qn** to take sb's place; **firma del padre o di chi ne fa le** ~**i** signature of the father or guardian.

ve'dere *vt, vi* to see; ~**rsi** *vr* to meet, see one another; ~ **di fare qc** to see (to it) that sth is done, make sure that sth is done; **far** ~ **qc a qn** to show sb sth; **farsi** ~ to show o.s.; (*farsi vivo*) to show one's face; **farsi** ~ **da un medico** to go and see a doctor; **modo di** ~ outlook, view of things; **vedi pagina 8** (*rimando*) see page 8; **è da** ~ **se** ... it remains to be seen whether ...; **non vedo la ragione di farlo** I can't see any reason to do it; **si era visto costretto a** ... he found himself forced to ...; **non (ci) si vede** (*è buio etc*) you can't see a thing; **ci vediamo domani!** see you tomorrow!; **non lo posso** ~ (*fig*) I can't stand him.

ve'detta *sf* (*sentinella, posto*) look-out; (*NAUT*) patrol boat.

ve'dette [vəˈdɛt] *sf inv* (*attrice*) star.

'**vedovo, a** *sm/f* widower/widow; **rimaner** ~ to be widowed.

vedrò *etc vb vedi* **vedere.**

ve'duta *sf* view; **di larghe** o **ample** ~ **e** broad-minded; **di** ~**e limitate** narrow-minded.

vee'mente *ag* (*discorso, passione*) vehement; (*assalto*) vigorous; (*passione*) overwhelming.

vee'menza [veeˈmɛntsa] *sf* vehemence; **con** ~ vehemently.

vege'tale [vedʒeˈtale] *ag, sm* vegetable.

vege'tare [vedʒeˈtare] *vi* (*fig*) to vegetate.

vegetari'ano, a [vedʒetaˈrjano] *ag, sm/f* vegetarian.

vegeta'tivo, a *ag* vegetative.

vegetazi'one [vedʒetatˈtsjone] *sf* vegetation.

'**vegeto, a** [ˈvɛdʒeto] *ag* (*pianta*) thriving; (*persona*) strong, vigorous.

veg'gente [vedˈdʒɛnte] *sm/f* (*indovino*) clairvoyant.

'**veglia** [ˈveʎʎa] *sf* (*sorveglianza*) watch; (*trattenimento*) evening gathering; **tra la** ~ **e il sonno** half awake; **fare la** ~ **a un malato** to watch over a sick person; ~ **funebre** wake.

vegli'ardo, a [veʎˈʎardo] *sm/f* venerable old man/woman.

vegli'are [veʎˈʎare] *vi* to stay o sit up; (*stare vigile*) to watch; to keep watch ♦ *vt* (*malato, morto*) to watch over, sit up with.

vegli'one [veʎˈʎone] *sm* ball, dance.

ve'icolo *sm* vehicle; ~ **spaziale** spacecraft *inv*.

'**vela** *sf* (*NAUT: tela*) sail; (*sport*) sailing; **tutto va a gonfie** ~**e** (*fig*) everything is going perfectly.

ve'lare *vt* to veil; ~**rsi** *vr* (*occhi, luna*) to mist over; (*voce*) to become husky; ~**rsi il viso** to cover one's face (with a veil).

ve'lato, a *ag* veiled.

vela'tura *sf* (*NAUT*) sails *pl*.

veleggi'are [veledˈdʒare] *vi* to sail; (*AER*) to glide.

ve'leno *sm* poison.

vele'noso, a *ag* poisonous.

ve'letta *sf* (*di cappello*) veil.

veli'ero *sm* sailing ship.

ve'lina *sf* (*anche:* **carta** ~: *per imballare*) tissue paper; (: *per copie*) flimsy paper; (*copia*) carbon copy.

ve'lista, i, e *sm/f* yachtsman/woman.

ve'livolo *sm* aircraft.

velleità *sf inv* vain ambition, vain desire.

vellei'tario, a *ag* unrealistic.

'vello *sm* fleece.

vellu'tato, a *ag* (*stoffa, pesca, colore*) velvety; (*voce*) mellow.

vel'luto *sm* velvet; ~ **a coste** cord.

'velo *sm* veil; (*tessuto*) voile.

ve'loce [ve'lotʃe] *ag* fast, quick ♦ *av* fast, quickly.

velo'cista, i, e [velo'tʃista] *sm/f* (*SPORT*) sprinter.

velocità [velotʃi'ta] *sf* speed; **a forte** ~ at high speed; ~ **di crociera** cruising speed.

ve'lodromo *sm* velodrome.

ven. *abbr* (*REL*) = **venerabile**; (= *venerdì*) Fri.

'vena *sf* (*gen*) vein; (*filone*) vein, seam; (*fig: ispirazione*) inspiration; (: *umore*) mood; **essere in** ~ **di qc** to be in the mood for sth.

ve'nale *ag* (*prezzo, valore*) market *cpd*; (*fig*) venal; mercenary.

venalità *sf* venality.

ve'nato, a *ag* (*marmo*) veined, streaked; (*legno*) grained.

vena'torio, a *ag* hunting; **la stagione** ~**a** the hunting season.

vena'tura *sf* (*di marmo*) vein, streak; (*di legno*) grain.

ven'demmia *sf* (*raccolta*) grape harvest; (*quantità d'uva*) grape crop, grapes *pl*; (*vino ottenuto*) vintage.

vendemmi'are *vt* to harvest ♦ *vi* to harvest the grapes.

'vendere *vt* to sell; ~ **all'ingrosso/al dettaglio** *o* **minuto** to sell wholesale/retail; ~ **all'asta** to auction, sell by auction; **"vendesi" "for sale"**.

ven'detta *sf* revenge.

vendi'care *vt* to avenge; ~**rsi** *vr*: ~**rsi (di)** to avenge o.s. (for); (*per rancore*) to take one's revenge (for); ~**rsi su qn** to revenge o.s. on sb.

vendica'tivo, a *ag* vindictive.

'vendita *sf* sale; **la** ~ (*attività*) selling; (*smercio*) sales *pl*; **in** ~ on sale; **mettere in** ~ to put on sale; **in** ~ **presso** on sale at; **contratto di** ~ sales agreement; **reparto** ~**e** sales department; ~ **all'asta** sale by auction; ~ **al dettaglio** *o* **minuto** retail; ~ **all'ingrosso** wholesale.

vendi'tore, 'trice *sm/f* seller, vendor; (*gestore di negozio*) trader, dealer.

ven'duto, a *ag* (*merce*) sold; (*fig: corrotto*) corrupt.

ve'nefico, a, ci, che *ag* poisonous.

vene'rabile *ag*, **vene'rando, a** *ag* venerable.

vene'rare *vt* to venerate.

venerazi'one [venerat'tsjone] *sf* veneration.

venerdì *sm inv* Friday; **V~ Santo** Good Friday; *per fraseologia vedi* **martedì**.

'Venere *sm*, *sf* Venus.

ve'nereo, a *ag* venereal.

'veneto, a *ag* of (*o* from) the Veneto.

'veneto-giuli'ano, a ['venetodʒu'ljano] *ag* of (*o* from) Venezia-Giulia.

Ve'nezia [ve'nɛttsja] *sf* Venice.

venezi'ano, a [venet'tsjano] *ag*, *sm/f* Venetian.

Venezu'ela [venettsu'ela] *sm*: **il** ~ Venezuela.

venezue'lano, a [venettsue'lano] *ag*, *sm/f* Venezuelan.

'vengo *etc vb vedi* **venire**.

veni'ale *ag* venial.

ve'nire *vi* to come; (*riuscire: dolce, fotografia*) to turn out; (*come ausiliare: essere*): **viene ammirato da tutti** he is admired by everyone; ~ **da** to come from; **quanto viene?** how much does it cost?; **far** ~ (*mandare a chiamare*) to send for; (*medico*) to call, send for; ~ **a capo di qc** to unravel sth, sort sth out; ~ **al dunque** *o* **nocciolo** *o* **fatto** to come to the point; ~ **fuori** to come out; ~ **giù** to come down; ~ **meno** (*svenire*) to faint; ~ **meno a qc** not to fulfil sth; ~ **su** to come up; ~ **via** to come away; ~ **a sapere qc** to learn sth; ~ **a trovare qn** to come and see sb; **negli anni a** ~ in the years to come, in future; **è venuto il momento di …** the time has come to ….

'venni *etc vb vedi* **venire**.

ven'taglio [ven'taʎʎo] *sm* fan.

ven'tata *sf* gust (of wind).

venten'nale *ag* (*che dura 20 anni*) twenty-year *cpd*; (*che ricorre ogni 20 anni*) which takes place every twenty years.

ven'tenne *ag*, *sm/f* twenty-year-old.

ven'tennio *sm* period of twenty years; **il** ~ **fascista** the Fascist period.

ven'tesimo, a *num* twentieth.

'venti *num* twenty.

venti'lare *vt* (*stanza*) to air, ventilate; (*fig: idea, proposta*) to air.

venti'lato, a *ag* (*camera, zona*) airy; **poco** ~ airless.

ventila'tore *sm* fan; (*su parete, finestra*) ventilator, fan.

ventilazi'one [ventilat'tsjone] *sf* ventilation.

ven'tina *sf*: **una** ~ **(di)** around twenty, twenty or so.

ventiquat'tr'ore *sfpl* (*periodo*) twenty-four hours ♦ *sf inv* (*SPORT*) twenty-four-hour race; (*valigetta*) overnight case.

venti'sette *num* twenty-seven; **il** ~ (*giorno di paga*) (monthly) pay day.

ventitré *num* twenty-three ♦ *sfpl*: **portava il cappello sulle** ~ he wore his hat at a jaunty angle.

'**vento** *sm* wind; **c'è** ~ it's windy; **un colpo di** ~ a gust of wind; **contro** ~ against the wind; ~ **contrario** (*NAUT*) headwind.

'**ventola** *sf* (*AUT*, *TECN*) fan.

ven'tosa *sf* (*ZOOL*) sucker; (*di gomma*) suction pad.

ven'toso, a *ag* windy.

ven'totto *num* twenty-eight.

'**ventre** *sm* stomach.

ven'triloquo *sm* ventriloquist.

ven'tuno *num* twenty-one.

ven'tura *sf*: **andare alla** ~ to trust to luck; **soldato di** ~ mercenary.

ven'turo, a *ag* next, coming.

ve'nuto, a *pp di* **venire** ♦ *sm/f*: **il(la) primo(a) ~ -(a)** the first person who comes along ♦ *sf* coming, arrival.

ver. *abbr* – **versamento**.

'**vera** *sf* wedding ring.

ve'race [ve'ratʃe] *ag* (*testimone*) truthful; (*testimonianza*) accurate; (*cibi*) real, genuine.

vera'mente *av* really.

ve'randa *sf* veranda(h).

ver'bale *ag* verbal ♦ *sm* (*di riunione*) minutes *pl*; **accordo** ~ verbal agreement; **mettere a** ~ to place in the minutes *o* on record.

'**verbo** *sm* (*LING*) verb; (*parola*) word; (*REL*): **il V~** the Word.

ver'boso, a *ag* verbose, wordy.

ver'dastro, a *ag* greenish.

'**verde** *ag*, *sm* green; ~ **bottiglia/oliva** *ag inv* bottle/olive green; **benzina** ~ lead-free *o* unleaded petrol; **i V~i** (*POL*) the Greens; **essere al** ~ (*fig*) to be broke.

verdeggi'ante [verded'dʒante] *ag* green, verdant.

verde'rame *sm* verdigris.

ver'detto *sm* verdict.

ver'dura *sf* vegetables *pl*.

vere'condia *sf* modesty.

vere'condo, a *ag* modest.

'**verga, ghe** *sf* rod.

ver'gato, a *ag* (*foglio*) ruled.

vergi'nale [verdʒi'nale] *ag* virginal.

'**vergine** ['verdʒine] *sf* virgin; (*dello zodiaco*): **V~** Virgo ♦ *ag* virgin; (*ragazza*): **essere** ~ to be a virgin; **essere della V~** (*dello zodiaco*) to be Virgo; **pura lana** ~ pure new wool; **olio** ~ **d'oliva** unrefined olive oil.

verginità [verdʒini'ta] *sf* virginity.

ver'gogna [ver'goɲɲa] *sf* shame; (*timidezza*) shyness, embarrassment.

vergo'gnarsi [vergoɲ'ɲarsi] *vr*: ~ (**di**) to be *o* feel ashamed (of); to be shy (about), be embarrassed (about).

vergo'gnoso, a [vergoɲ'ɲoso] *ag* ashamed; (*timido*) shy, embarrassed; (*causa di vergogna: azione*) shameful.

veridicità [veriditʃi'ta] *sf* truthfulness.

ve'ridico, a, ci, che *ag* truthful.

ve'rifica, che *sf* checking *no pl*; check; **fare una** ~ **di** (*freni*, *testimonianza*, *firma*) to check; ~ **contabile** (*FINANZA*) audit.

verifi'care *vt* (*controllare*) to check; (*confermare*) to confirm, bear out; (*FINANZA*) to audit.

verità *sf inv* truth; **a dire la** ~, **per la** ~ truth to tell, actually.

veriti'ero, a *ag* (*che dice la verità*) truthful; (*conforme a verità*) true.

'**verme** *sm* worm.

vermi'celli [vermi'tʃelli] *smpl* vermicelli *sg*.

ver'miglio [ver'miʎʎo] *sm* vermilion, scarlet.

'**vermut** *sm inv* vermouth.

ver'nacolo *sm* vernacular.

ver'nice [ver'nitʃe] *sf* (*colorazione*) paint; (*trasparente*) varnish; (*pelle*) patent leather; "~ **fresca**" "wet paint".

vernici'are [verni'tʃare] *vt* to paint; to varnish.

vernicia'tura [vernitʃa'tura] *sf* painting; varnishing.

'**vero, a** *ag* (*veridico: fatti*, *testimonianza*) true; (*autentico*) real ♦ *sm* (*verità*) truth; (*realtà*) (real) life; **un** ~ **e proprio delinquente** a real criminal, an out and out criminal; **tant'è** ~ **che** ... so much so that ...; **a onor del** ~, **a dire il** ~ to tell the truth.

Ve'rona *sf* Verona.

vero'nese *ag* of (*o* from) Verona.

vero'simile *ag* likely, probable.

verrò *etc vb vedi* **venire**.

ver'ruca, che *sf* wart.

versa'mento *sm* (*pagamento*) payment; (*deposito di denaro*) deposit.

ver'sante *sm* slopes *pl*, side.

ver'sare *vt* (*fare uscire: vino, farina*) to pour (out); (*spargere: lacrime, sangue*) to shed; (*rovesciare*) to spill; (*ECON*) to pay; (: *depositare*) to deposit, pay in ♦ *vi*: ~ **in gravi difficoltà** to find o.s. with serious problems; ~**rsi** *vr* (*rovesciarsi*) to spill; (*fiume, folla*): ~**rsi (in)** to pour (into).

versa'tile *ag* versatile.

versatilità *sf* versatility.

ver'sato, a *ag*: ~ **in** to be (well-)versed in.

ver'setto *sm* (*REL*) verse.

versi'one *sf* version; (*traduzione*) translation.

'verso *sm* (*di poesia*) verse, line; (*di animale, uccello, venditore ambulante*) cry; (*direzione*) direction; (*modo*) way; (*di foglio di carta*) verso; (*di moneta*) reverse; ~**i** *smpl* (*poesia*) verse *sg*; **per un ~ o per l'altro** one way or another; **prendere qn/ qc per il ~ giusto** to approach sb/sth the right way; **rifare il ~ a qn** (*imitare*) to mimic sb; **non c'è ~ di persuaderlo** there's no way of persuading him, he can't be persuaded ♦ *prep* (*in direzione di*) toward(s); (*nei pressi di*) near, around (about); (*in senso temporale*) about, around; (*nei confronti di*) for; ~ **di me** towards me; ~ **l'alto** upwards; ~ **il basso** downwards; ~ **sera** towards evening.

'vertebra *sf* vertebra.

verte'brale *ag* vertebral; **colonna ~** spinal column, spine.

verte'brato, a *ag*, *sm* vertebrate.

ver'tenza [ver'tɛntsa] *sf* (*lite*) lawsuit, case; (*sindacale*) dispute.

'vertere *vi*: ~ **su** to deal with, be about.

verti'cale *ag*, *sf* vertical.

'vertice ['vɛrtitʃe] *sm* summit, top; (*MAT*) vertex; **conferenza al ~** (*POL*) summit conference.

ver'tigine [ver'tidʒine] *sf* dizziness *no pl*; dizzy spell; (*MED*) vertigo; **avere le ~i** to feel dizzy.

vertigi'noso, a [vertidʒi'noso] *ag* (*altezza*) dizzy; (*fig*) breathtakingly high (*o* deep *etc*).

'verza ['vɛrdza] *sf* Savoy cabbage.

ve'scica, che [veʃ'ʃika] *sf* (*ANAT*) bladder; (*MED*) blister.

vesco'vile *ag* episcopal.

'vescovo *sm* bishop.

'vespa *sf* wasp; ((R): *veicolo*) (motor) scooter.

ves'paio *sm* wasps' nest; **suscitare un ~** (*fig*) to stir up a hornets' nest.

vespasi'ano *sm* urinal.

'vespro *sm* (*REL*) vespers *pl*.

ves'sare *vt* to oppress.

vessazi'one [vessat'tsjone] *sf* oppression.

ves'sillo *sm* standard; (*bandiera*) flag.

ves'taglia [ves'taʎʎa] *sf* dressing gown, robe (*US*).

'veste *sf* garment; (*rivestimento*) covering; (*qualità, facoltà*) capacity; ~**i** *sfpl* clothes, clothing *sg*; **in ~ ufficiale** (*fig*) in an official capacity; **in ~ di** in the guise of, as; ~ **da camera** dressing gown, robe

(*US*); ~ **editoriale** layout.

vesti'ario *sm* wardrobe, clothes *pl*; **capo di ~** article of clothing, garment.

ves'tibolo *sm* (*entrance*) hall.

ves'tigia [ves'tidʒa] *sfpl* (*tracce*) vestiges; traces; (*rovine*) ruins, remains.

ves'tire *vt* (*bambino, malato*) to dress; (*avere indosso*) to have on, wear; ~**rsi** *vr* to dress, get dressed; ~**rsi da** (*negozio, sarto*) to buy *o* get one's clothes at.

ves'tito, a *ag* dressed ♦ *sm* garment; (*da donna*) dress; (*da uomo*) suit; ~**i** *smpl* (*indumenti*) clothes; ~ **di bianco** dressed in white.

Ve'suvio *sm*: **il ~** Vesuvius.

vete'rano, a *ag*, *sm/f* veteran.

veteri'nario, a *ag* veterinary ♦ *sm* veterinary surgeon (*BRIT*), veterinarian (*US*), vet ♦ *sf* veterinary medicine.

'veto *sm inv* veto; **porre il ~ a qc** to veto sth.

ve'traio *sm* glassmaker; (*per finestre*) glazier.

ve'trato, a *ag* (*porta, finestra*) glazed; (*che contiene vetro*) glass *cpd* ♦ *sf* glass door (*o* window); (*di chiesa*) stained glass window; **carta ~a** sandpaper.

vetre'ria *sf* (*stabilimento*) glassworks *sg*; (*oggetti di vetro*) glassware.

ve'trina *sf* (*di negozio*) (shop) window; (*armadio*) display cabinet.

vetri'nista, i, e *sm/f* window dresser.

ve'trino *sm* slide.

vetri'olo *sm* vitriol.

'vetro *sm* glass; (*per finestra, porta*) pane (of glass); ~ **blindato** bulletproof glass; ~ **infrangibile** shatterproof glass; ~ **di sicurezza** safety glass; **i ~i di Murano** Murano glassware *sg*.

ve'troso, a *ag* vitreous.

'vetta *sf* peak, summit, top.

vet'tore *sm* (*MAT, FISICA*) vector; (*chi trasporta*) carrier.

vetto'vaglie [vetto'vaʎʎe] *sfpl* supplies.

vet'tura *sf* (*carrozza*) carriage; (*FERR*) carriage (*BRIT*), car (*US*); (*auto*) car (*BRIT*), automobile (*US*); ~ **di piazza** hackney carriage.

vettu'rino *sm* coach driver, coachman.

vezzeggi'are [vettsedd'dʒare] *vt* to fondle, caress.

vezzeggia'tivo [vettseddʒa'tivo] *sm* (*LING*) term of endearment.

'vezzo ['vettso] *sm* habit; ~**i** *smpl* (*smancerie*) affected ways; (*leggiadria*) charms.

vez'zoso, a [vet'tsoso] *ag* (*grazioso*) charming, pretty; (*lezioso*) affected.

V.F. *abbr* = **vigili del fuoco.**

V.G. *abbr* = *Vostra Grazia*.
VI *sigla* = *Vicenza*.
vi (*dav lo, la, li, le, ne diventa* **ve**) *pron*
(*oggetto*) you; (*complemento di termine*)
(to) you; (*riflessivo*) yourselves; (*reciproco*)
each other ♦ *av* (*lì*) there; (*qui*) here; (*per
questo/quel luogo*) through here/there; ~
è/sono there is/are.
'via *sf* (*gen*) way; (*strada*) street; (*sentiero,
pista*) path, track; (*AMM: procedimento*)
channels *pl* ♦ *prep* (*passando per*) via, by
way of ♦ *av* away ♦ *escl* go away!; (*suvvia*)
come on!; (*SPORT*) go! ♦ *sm* (*SPORT*)
starting signal; **per** ~ **di** (*a causa di*)
because of, on account of; **in** *o* **per** ~ **on**
the way; **in** ~ **di guarigione** (*fig*) on the
road to recovery; **per** ~ **aerea** by air;
(*lettere*) by airmail; ~ **satellite** by
satellite; **andare/essere** ~ to go/be away;
~ ~ (*pian piano*) gradually; ~ ~ **lattea**
mano a mano) as; **e** ~ **dicendo, e** ~ **di
questo passo** and so on (and so forth);
dare il ~ (*SPORT*) to give the starting
signal; **dare il** ~ **a un progetto** to give the
green light to a project; **hanno dato il** ~
ai lavori they've begun *o* started work; **in**
~ **amichevole** in a friendly manner;
comporre una disputa in ~ **amichevole**
(*DIR*) to settle a dispute out of court; **in** ~
eccezionale as an exception; **in** ~ **privata**
o **confidenziale** (*dire etc*) in confidence; **in**
~ **provvisoria** provisionally; **V~ lattea**
(*ASTR*) Milky Way; ~ **di mezzo** middle
course; **non c'è** ~ **di scampo** *o* **d'uscita**
there's no way out; ~**e di comunicazione**
communication routes.
viabilità *sf* (*di strada*) practicability; (*rete
stradale*) roads *pl*, road network.
via'dotto *sm* viaduct.
viaggi'are [viad'dʒare] *vi* to travel; **le merci
viaggiano via mare** the goods go *o* are
sent by sea.
viaggia'tore, 'trice [viadd'ʒa'tore] *ag*
travelling (*BRIT*), traveling (*US*) ♦ *sm*
traveller (*BRIT*), traveler (*US*);
(*passeggero*) passenger.
vi'aggio [vi'addʒo] *sm* travel(ling); (*tragitto*)
journey, trip; **buon** ~! have a good trip!;
~ **d'affari** business trip; ~ **di nozze**
honeymoon; ~ **organizzato** package tour
o holiday.
vi'ale *sm* avenue.
vian'dante *sm/f* vagrant.
vi'atico, ci *sm* (*REL*) viaticum; (*fig*)
encouragement.
via'vai *sm* coming and going, bustle.
vi'brare *vi* to vibrate; (*agitarsi*): ~ (**di**) to
quiver (with).

vibra'tore *sm* vibrator.
vibrazi'one [vibrat'tsjone] *sf* vibration.
vi'cario *sm* (*apostolico etc*) vicar.
'vice ['vitʃe] *sm/f* deputy ♦ *prefisso* vice.
vice'console [vitʃe'kɔnsole] *sm* vice-consul.
vicediret'tore, 'trice [vitʃediret'tore] *sm/f*
assistant manager/manageress; (*di
giornale etc*) deputy editor.
vi'cenda [vi'tʃenda] *sf* event; ~**e** *sfpl* (*sorte*)
fortunes; **a** ~ in turn; **con alterne** ~**e** with
mixed fortunes.
vicen'devole [vitʃen'devole] *ag* mutual,
reciprocal.
vicen'tino, a [vitʃen'tino] *ag* of (*o* from)
Vicenza.
vicepresi'dente [vitʃepresi'dɛnte] *sm* vice-
president, vice-chairman.
vice'versa [vitʃe'vɛrsa] *av* vice versa; **da
Roma a Pisa e** ~ from Rome to Pisa and
back.
vi'chingo, a ghi, ghe [vi'kinga] *ag, sm/f*
Viking.
vici'nanza [vitʃi'nantsa] *sf* nearness,
closeness; ~**e** *sfpl* (*paraggi*)
neighbourhood (*BRIT*), neighborhood (*US*),
vicinity.
vici'nato [vitʃi'nato] *sm* neighbourhood
(*BRIT*), neighborhood (*US*); (*vicini*)
neighbo(u)rs *pl*.
vi'cino, a [vi'tʃino] *ag* (*gen*) near; (*nello
spazio*) near, nearby; (*accanto*) next; (*nel
tempo*) near, close at hand ♦ *sm/f*
neighbour (*BRIT*), neighbor (*US*) ♦ *av* near,
close; **da** ~ (*guardare*) close up;
(*esaminare, seguire*) closely; (*conoscere*)
well, intimately; ~ **a** *prep* near (to), close
to; (*accanto a*) beside; **mi sono stati molto
~i** (*fig*) they were very supportive
towards me; ~ **di casa** neighbo(u)r.
vicissi'tudini [vitʃissi'tudini] *sfpl* trials and
tribulations.
'vicolo *sm* alley; ~ **cieco** blind alley.
'video *sm inv* (*TV: schermo*) screen.
video'camera *sf* camcorder.
videocas'setta *sf* videocassette.
videogi'oco, chi [video'dʒɔko] *sm* video
game.
videoregistra'tore [videoredʒistra'tore] *sm*
(*apparecchio*) video (recorder).
video'teca, che *sf* video shop.
videotermi'nale *sm* visual display unit.
'vidi *etc vb vedi* **vedere**.
vidi'mare *vt* (*AMM*) to authenticate.
vidimazi'one [vidimat'tsjone] *sf* (*AMM*)
authentication.
Vi'enna *sf* Vienna.
vien'nese *ag, sm/f* Viennese *inv*.
vie'tare *vt* to forbid; (*AMM*) to prohibit;

(*libro*) to ban; ~ **a qn di fare** to forbid sb to do; to prohibit sb from doing.

vie'tato, a *ag* (*vedi vb*) forbidden; prohibited; banned; "~ **fumare/ l'ingresso**" "no smoking/admittance"; ~ **ai minori di 14/18 anni** prohibited to children under 14/18; "**senso ~**" (*AUT*) "no entry"; "**sosta ~a**" (*AUT*) "no parking".

Viet'nam *sm*: **il ~** Vietnam.

vietna'mita, i, e *ag, sm/f, sm* Vietnamese *inv*.

vi'gente [vi'dʒɛnte] *ag* in force.

'vigere ['vidʒere] *vi* (*difettivo: si usa solo alla terza persona*) to be in force; **in casa mia vige l'abitudine di ...** at home we are in the habit of ....

vigi'lante [vidʒi'lante] *ag* vigilant, watchful.

vigi'lanza [vidʒi'lantsa] *sf* vigilance; (*sorveglianza: di operai, alunni*) supervision; (: *di sospetti, criminali*) surveillance.

vigi'lare [vidʒi'lare] *vt* to watch over, keep an eye on; ~ **che** to make sure that, see to it that.

vigi'lato, a [vidʒi'lato] *sm/f* (*DIR*) person under police surveillance.

vigila'trice [vidʒila'tritʃe] *sf*: ~ **d'infanzia** nursery-school teacher; ~ **scolastica** school health officer.

'vigile ['vidʒile] *ag* watchful ♦ *sm* (*anche:* ~ **urbano**) policeman (*in towns*); ~ **del fuoco** fireman; *vedi nota nel riquadro*.

VIGILI URBANI

The **vigili urbani** *are a municipal police force attached to the "Comune". Their duties involve everyday aspects of life such as traffic, public works and services, and commerce.*

vigi'lessa [vidʒi'lessa] *sf* (traffic) policewoman.

vi'gilia [vi'dʒilja] *sf* (*giorno antecedente*) eve; **la ~ di Natale** Christmas Eve.

vigliacche'ria [viʎʎakke'ria] *sf* cowardice.

vigli'acco, a, chi, che [viʎ'ʎakko] *ag* cowardly ♦ *sm/f* coward.

'vigna ['viɲɲa] *sf*, **vi'gneto** [viɲ'ɲeto] *sm* vineyard.

vi'gnetta [viɲ'ɲetta] *sf* cartoon.

vi'gore *sm* vigour (*BRIT*), vigor (*US*); (*DIR*): **essere/entrare in ~** to be in/come into force; **non è più in ~** it is no longer in force, it no longer applies.

vigo'roso, a *ag* vigorous.

'vile *ag* (*spregevole*) low, mean, base; (*codardo*) cowardly.

vili'pendere *vt* to despise, scorn.

vili'pendio *sm* contempt, scorn.

vili'peso, a *pp di* **vilipendere**.

'villa *sf* villa.

vil'laggio [vil'laddʒo] *sm* village; ~ **turistico** holiday village.

villa'nia *sf* rudeness, lack of manners; **fare** (*o* **dire**) **una ~ a qn** to be rude to sb.

vil'lano, a *ag* rude, ill-mannered ♦ *sm/f* boor.

villeggi'ante [villed'dʒante] *sm/f* holiday-maker (*BRIT*), vacationer (*US*).

villeggi'are [villed'dʒare] *vi* to holiday, spend one's holidays, vacation (*US*).

villeggia'tura [villeddʒa'tura] *sf* holiday(s *pl*) (*BRIT*), vacation (*US*); **luogo di ~** (holiday) resort.

vil'letta *sf*, **vil'lino** *sm* small house (with a garden), cottage.

vil'loso, a *ag* hairy.

viltà *sf* cowardice *no pl*; (*gesto*) cowardly act.

Vimi'nale *sm vedi nota nel riquadro*.

VIMINALE

The **Viminale**, *which takes its name from one of the famous Seven Hills of Rome on which it stands, is home to the Ministry of the Interior.*

'vimine *sm* wicker; **mobili di ~i** wicker furniture *sg*.

vi'naio *sm* wine merchant.

'vincere ['vintʃere] *vt* (*in guerra, al gioco, a una gara*) to defeat, beat; (*premio, guerra, partita*) to win; (*fig*) to overcome, conquer ♦ *vi* to win; ~ **qn in** (*abilità, bellezza*) to surpass sb in.

'vincita ['vintʃita] *sf* win; (*denaro vinto*) winnings *pl*.

vinci'tore, 'trice [vintʃi'tore] *sm/f* winner; (*MIL*) victor.

vinco'lante *ag* binding.

vinco'lare *vt* to bind; (*COMM: denaro*) to tie up.

vinco'lato, a *ag*: **deposito ~** (*COMM*) fixed deposit.

'vincolo *sm* (*fig*) bond, tie; (*DIR*) obligation.

vi'nicolo, a *ag* wine *cpd*; **regione ~a** wine-producing area.

vinificazi'one [vinifikat'tsjone] *sf* wine-making.

'vino *sm* wine; ~ **bianco/rosso** white/red wine.

'vinsi *etc vb vedi* **vincere**.

'vinto, a *pp di* **vincere** ♦ *ag*: **darla ~a a qn** to let sb have his (*o* her) way; **darsi per ~** to give up, give in.

vi'ola *sf* (*BOT*) violet; (*MUS*) viola ♦ *ag, sm inv* (*colore*) purple.

vio'lare *vt* (*chiesa*) to desecrate, violate; (*giuramento, legge*) to violate.

violazi'one [violat'tsjone] *sf* desecration; violation; ~ **di domicilio** (*DIR*) breaking and entering.

violen'tare *vt* to use violence on; (*donna*) to rape.

vio'lento, a *ag* violent.

vio'lenza [vio'lɛntsa] *sf* violence; ~ **carnale** rape.

vio'letto, a *ag, sm* (*colore*) violet ♦ *sf* (*BOT*) violet.

violi'nista, i, e *smf* violinist.

vio'lino *sm* violin.

violoncel'lista, i, e [violontʃel'lista] *smf* cellist, cello player.

violon'cello [violon'tʃɛllo] *sm* cello.

vi'ottolo *sm* path, track.

VIP *smf inv* (= *Very Important Person*) VIP.

'vipera *sf* viper, adder.

vi'raggio [vi'raddʒo] *sm* (*NAUT, AER*) turn; (*FOT*) toning.

vi'rale *ag* viral.

vi'rare *vi* (*NAUT*) to come about; (*AER*) to turn; (*FOT*) to tone; ~ **di bordo** to change course.

vi'rata *sf* coming about; turning; change of course.

'virgola *sf* (*LING*) comma; (*MAT*) point.

virgo'lette *sfpl* inverted commas, quotation marks.

vi'rile *ag* (*proprio dell'uomo*) masculine; (*non puerile, da uomo*) manly, virile.

virilità *sf* masculinity; manliness; (*sessuale*) virility.

virtù *sf inv* virtue; **in** *o* **per** ~ **di** by virtue of, by.

virtu'ale *ag* virtual.

virtu'oso, a *ag* virtuous ♦ *smf* (*MUS etc*) virtuoso.

viru'lento, a *ag* virulent.

'virus *sm inv* virus.

visa'gista, i, e [viza'dʒista] *smf* beautician.

visce'rale [viʃʃe'rale] *ag* (*MED*) visceral; (*fig*) profound, deep-rooted.

'viscere ['viʃʃere] *sm* (*ANAT*) internal organ ♦ *sfpl* (*di animale*) entrails *pl*; (*fig*) depths *pl*, bowels *pl*.

'vischio ['viskjo] *sm* (*BOT*) mistletoe; (*pania*) birdlime.

vischi'oso, a [vis'kjoso] *ag* sticky.

viscidità [viʃʃidi'ta] *sf* sliminess.

'viscido, a ['viʃʃido] *ag* slimy.

vis'conte, 'essa *smf* viscount/viscountess.

viscosità *sf* viscosity.

vis'coso, a *ag* viscous.

vi'sibile *ag* visible.

visi'bilio *sm*: **andare in** ~ to go into raptures.

visibilità *sf* visibility.

visi'era *sf* (*di elmo*) visor; (*di berretto*) peak.

visio'nare *vt* (*gen*) to look at, examine; (*CINE*) to screen.

visio'nario, a *ag, smf* visionary.

visi'one *sf* vision; **prendere** ~ **di qc** to examine sth, look sth over; **prima/seconda** ~ (*CINE*) first/second showing.

'visita *sf* visit; (*MED*) visit, call; (*: esame*) examination; **far** ~ **a qn, andare in** ~ **da qn** to visit sb, pay sb a visit; **in** ~ **ufficiale in Italia** on an official visit to Italy; **orario di** ~**e** (*ospedale*) visiting hours; ~ **di controllo** (*MED*) checkup; ~ **a domicilio** house call; ~ **guidata** guided tour; ~ **sanitaria** sanitary inspection.

visi'tare *vt* to visit; (*MED*) to visit, call on; (*: esaminare*) to examine.

visita'tore, 'trice *smf* visitor.

vi'sivo, a *ag* visual.

'viso *sm* face; **fare buon** ~ **a cattivo gioco** to make the best of things.

vi'sone *sm* mink.

vi'sore *sm* (*FOT*) viewer.

'vispo, a *ag* quick, lively.

'vissi *etc vb vedi* **vivere**.

vis'suto, a *pp di* **vivere** ♦ *ag* (*aria, modo di fare*) experienced.

'vista *sf* (*facoltà*) (eye)sight; (*fatto di vedere*): **la** ~ **di** the sight of; (*veduta*) view; **con** ~ **sul lago** with a view over the lake; **sparare a** ~ to shoot on sight; **pagabile a** ~ payable on demand; **in** ~ in sight; **avere in** ~ **qc** to have sth in view; **mettersi in** ~ to draw attention to o.s.; (*peg*) to show off; **perdere qn di** ~ to lose sight of sb; (*fig*) to lose touch with sb; **far** ~ **di fare** to pretend to do; **a** ~ **d'occhio** as far as the eye can see; (*fig*) before one's very eyes.

vis'tare *vt* to approve; (*AMM: passaporto*) to visa.

'visto, a *pp di* **vedere** ♦ *sm* visa; ~ **che** *cong* seeing (that); ~ **d'ingresso/di transito** entry/transit visa; ~ **permanente/di soggiorno** permanent/tourist visa.

vis'toso, a *ag* gaudy, garish; (*ingente*) considerable.

visu'ale *ag* visual.

visualiz'zare [vizualid'dzare] *vt* to visualize.

visualizza'tore [vizualiddza'tore] *sm* (*INFORM*) visual display unit, VDU.

visualizzazi'one [vizualiddzat'tsjone] *sf* (*INFORM*) display.

'**vita** *sf* life; (*ANAT*) waist; **essere in** ~ to be alive; **pieno di** ~ full of life; **a** ~ for life; **membro a** ~ life member.
vi'tale *ag* vital.
vitalità *sf* vitality.
vita'lizio, a [vita'littsjo] *ag* life *cpd* ♦ *sm* life annuity.
vita'mina *sf* vitamin.
'**vite** *sf* (*BOT*) vine; (*TECN*) screw; **giro di** ~ (*anche fig*) turn of the screw.
vi'tello *sm* (*ZOOL*) calf; (*carne*) veal; (*pelle*) calfskin.
vi'ticcio [vi'tittʃo] *sm* (*BOT*) tendril.
viticol'tore *sm* wine grower.
viticol'tura *sf* wine growing.
'**vitreo, a** *ag* vitreous; (*occhio, sguardo*) glassy.
'**vittima** *sf* victim.
vitti'mismo *sm* self-pity.
'**vitto** *sm* food; (*in un albergo etc*) board; ~ **e alloggio** board and lodging.
vit'toria *sf* victory.
vittori'ano, a *ag* Victorian.
vittori'oso, a *ag* victorious.
vitupe'rare *vt* to rail at *o* against.
vi'uzza [vi'uttsa] *sf* (*in città*) alley.
'**viva** *escl*: ~ **il re!** long live the king!
vivacchi'are [vivak'kjare] *vi* to scrape a living.
vi'vace [vi'vatʃe] *ag* (*vivo, animato*) lively; (*: mente*) lively, sharp; (*colore*) bright.
vivacità [vivatʃi'ta] *sf* liveliness; brightness.
vivaciz'zare [vivatʃid'dzare] *vt* to liven up.
vi'vaio *sm* (*di pesci*) hatchery; (*AGR*) nursery.
viva'mente *av* (*commuoversi*) deeply, profoundly; (*ringraziare etc*) sincerely, warmly.
vi'vanda *sf* food; (*piatto*) dish.
vi'vente *ag* living, alive; **i** ~**i** the living.
'**vivere** *vi* to live ♦ *vt* to live; (*passare: brutto momento*) to live through, go through; (*sentire: gioie, pene di qn*) to share ♦ *sm* life; (*anche*: **modo di** ~) way of life; ~**i** *smpl* food *sg*, provisions; ~ **di** to live on.
vi'veur [vi'vœr] *sm inv* pleasure-seeker.
'**vivido, a** *ag* (*colore*) vivid, bright.
vivifi'care *vt* to enliven, give life to; (*piante etc*) to revive.
vivisezi'one [viviset'tsjone] *sf* vivisection.
'**vivo, a** *ag* (*vivente*) alive, living; (*fig*) lively; (*: colore*) bright, brilliant ♦ *sm*: **entrare nel** ~ **di una questione** to get to the heart of a matter; **i** ~**i** the living; **esperimenti su animali** ~**i** experiments on live *o* living animals; ~ **e vegeto** hale and hearty; **farsi** ~ (*fig*) to show one's face; to

keep in touch; **con** ~ **rammarico** with deep regret; **congratulazioni vivissime** heartiest congratulations; **con i più** ~**i ringraziamenti** with deepest *o* warmest thanks; **ritrarre dal** ~ to paint from life; **pungere qn nel** ~ (*fig*) to cut sb to the quick.
vivrò *etc vb vedi* **vivere**.
vizi'are [vit'tsjare] *vt* (*bambino*) to spoil; (*corrompere moralmente*) to corrupt; (*DIR*) to invalidate.
vizi'ato, a [vit'tsjato] *ag* spoilt; (*aria, acqua*) polluted; (*DIR*) invalid, invalidated.
'**vizio** ['vittsjo] *sm* (*morale*) vice; (*cattiva abitudine*) bad habit; (*imperfezione*) flaw, defect; (*errore*) fault, mistake; ~ **di forma** legal flaw *o* irregularity; ~ **procedurale** procedural error.
vizi'oso, a [vit'tsjoso] *ag* depraved; (*inesatto*) incorrect, wrong; **circolo** ~ vicious circle.
V.le *abbr* = **viale**.
vocabo'lario *sm* (*dizionario*) dictionary; (*lessico*) vocabulary.
vo'cabolo *sm* word.
vo'cale *ag* vocal ♦ *sf* vowel.
vocazi'one [vokat'tsjone] *sf* vocation; (*fig*) natural bent.
'**voce** ['votʃe] *sf* voice; (*diceria*) rumour (*BRIT*), rumor (*US*); (*di un elenco, in bilancio*) item; (*di dizionario*) entry; **parlare a alta/bassa** ~ to speak in a loud/low *o* soft voice; **fare la** ~ **grossa** to raise one's voice; **dar** ~ **a qc** to voice sth, give voice to sth; **a gran** ~ in a loud voice, loudly; **te lo dico a** ~ I'll tell you when I see you; **a una** ~ unanimously; **aver** ~ **in capitolo** (*fig*) to have a say in the matter; ~**i di corridoio** rumours.
voci'are [vo'tʃare] *vi* to shout, yell.
vocife'rante [votʃife'rante] *ag* noisy.
vo'cio [vo'tʃio] *sm* shouting.
'**vodka** *sf inv* vodka.
'**voga** *sf* (*NAUT*) rowing; (*usanza*): **essere in** ~ to be in fashion *o* in vogue.
vo'gare *vi* to row.
voga'tore, 'trice *sm/f* oarsman/woman ♦ *sm* rowing machine.
vogherò *etc* [voge'rɔ] *vb vedi* **vogare**.
'**voglia** ['vɔʎʎa] *sf* desire, wish; (*macchia*) birthmark; **aver** ~ **di qc/di fare** to feel like sth/like doing; (*più forte*) to want sth/ to do; **di buona** ~ willingly.
'**voglio** *etc* ['vɔʎʎo] *vb vedi* **volere**.
vogli'oso, a [voʎ'ʎoso] *ag* (*sguardo etc*) longing; (*più forte*) full of desire.
'**voi** *pron* you; ~ **stessi(e)** you yourselves.
voi'altri *pron* you.

vol. *abbr* (= *volume*) vol.
vo'lano *sm* (*SPORT*) shuttlecock; (*TECN*) flywheel.
vo'lant [vɔ'lã] *sm inv* frill.
vo'lante *ag* flying ♦ *sm* (steering) wheel ♦ *sf* (*POLIZIA: anche*: **squadra** ~) flying squad.
volanti'naggio [volanti'naddʒo] *sm* leafleting.
volanti'nare *vt* (*distribuire volantini*) to leaflet, hand out leaflets.
volan'tino *sm* leaflet.
vo'lare *vi* (*uccello, aereo, fig*) to fly; (*cappello*) to blow away *o* off, fly away *o* off; ~ **via** to fly away *o* off.
vo'lata *sf* flight; (*d'uccelli*) flock, flight; (*corsa*) rush; (*SPORT*) final sprint; **passare di** ~ **da qn** to drop in on sb briefly.
vo'latile *ag* (*CHIM*) volatile ♦ *sm* (*ZOOL*) bird.
volatiliz'zarsi [volatilid'dzarsi] *vr* (*CHIM*) to volatilize; (*fig*) to vanish, disappear.
vo'lente *ag*: **verrai** ~ **o nolente** you'll come whether you like it or not.
volente'roso, a *ag* willing, keen.
volenti'eri *av* willingly; "~" "with pleasure", "I'd be glad to".

==================== *PAROLA CHIAVE*

vo'lere *sm* will, wish(es); **contro il** ~ **di** against the wishes of; **per** ~ **di qn** in obedience to sb's will *o* wishes
♦ *vt* **1** (*esigere, desiderare*) to want; ~ **fare qc** to want to do sth; ~ **che qn faccia qc** to want sb to do sth; **vorrei andarmene** I'd like to go; **vorrei che se ne andasse** I'd like him to go; **vorrei quello lì!** I'd like that one; **volevo parlartene** I meant to talk to you about it; **come vuoi** as you like; **la vogliono al telefono** there's a call for you; **che tu lo voglia o no** whether you like it or not; **vuoi un caffè?** would you like a coffee?; **senza** ~ (*inavvertitamente*) without meaning to, unintentionally; **te la sei voluta** you asked for it; **la tradizione vuole che** ... custom requires that ...; **la leggenda vuole che** ... legend has it that ...
2 (*consentire*): **vogliate attendere, per piacere** please wait; **vogliamo andare?** shall we go?; **vuole essere così gentile da** ...? would you be so kind as to ...?; **non ha voluto ricevermi** he wouldn't see me
3: **volerci** (*essere necessario: materiale, attenzione*) to be needed; (: *tempo*) to take; **quanta farina ci vuole per questa torta?** how much flour do you need for this cake?; **ci vuole un'ora per arrivare a Venezia** it takes an hour to get to Venice; **è quel che ci vuole** it's just what is

needed
4: **voler bene a qn** (*amore*) to love sb; (*affetto*) to be fond of, like sb very much; **voler male a qn** to dislike sb; **volerne a qn** to bear sb a grudge; **voler dire** to mean; **voglio dire** ... I mean ...; **volevo ben dire!** I thought as much!

vol'gare *ag* vulgar.
volgarità *sf* vulgarity.
volgariz'zare [volgarid'dzare] *vt* to popularize.
volgar'mente *av* (*in modo volgare*) vulgarly, coarsely; (*del popolo*) commonly, popularly.
'volgere ['vɔldʒere] *vt* to turn ♦ *vi* to turn; (*tendere*): ~ **a: il tempo volge al brutto/al bello** the weather is breaking/is setting fair; **un rosso che volge al viola** a red verging on purple; **~rsi** *vr* to turn; ~ **al peggio** to take a turn for the worse; **al termine** to draw to an end.
'volgo *sm* common people.
voli'era *sf* aviary.
voli'tivo, a *ag* strong-willed.
'volli *etc vb vedi* **volere**.
'volo *sm* flight; **ci sono due ore di** ~ **da Londra a Milano** it's a two-hour flight between London and Milan; **al** ~: **colpire qc al** ~ to hit sth as it flies past; **prendere al** ~ (*autobus, treno*) to catch at the last possible moment; (*palla*) to catch as it flies past; (*occasione*) to seize; **capire al** ~ to understand straight away; **veduta a** ~ **d'uccello** bird's-eye view; ~ **di linea** scheduled flight.
volontà *sf inv* will; **a** ~ (*mangiare, bere*) as much as one likes; **buona/cattiva** ~ goodwill/lack of goodwill; **le sue ultime** ~ (*testamento*) his last will and testament *sg*.
volontaria'mente *av* voluntarily.
volontari'ato *sm* (*MIL*) voluntary service; (*lavoro*) voluntary work.
volon'tario, a *ag* voluntary ♦ *sm* (*MIL*) volunteer.
'volpe *sf* fox.
vol'pino, a *ag* (*pelo, coda*) fox's; (*aspetto, astuzia*) fox-like ♦ *sm* (*cane*) Pomeranian.
vol'pone, a *smf* (*fig*) old fox.
'volsi *etc vb vedi* **volgere**.
volt *sm inv* (*ELETTR*) volt.
'volta *sf* (*momento, circostanza*) time; (*turno, giro*) turn; (*curva*) turn, bend; (*ARCHIT*) vault; (*direzione*): **partire alla** ~ **di** to set off for; **a mia** (*o* **tua** *etc*) ~ in turn; **una** ~ once; **una** ~ **sola** only once; **c'era una** ~ once upon a time there was; **le cose di**

una ~ the things of the past; **due ~e**
twice; **tre ~e** three times; **una cosa per ~**
one thing at a time; **una ~ o l'altra** one of
these days; **una ~ per tutte** once and for
all; **una ~ tanto** just for once; **lo facciamo
un'altra ~** we'll do it another time *o* some
other time; **a ~e** at times, sometimes; **di
~ in ~** from time to time; **una ~ che**
(*temporale*) once; (*causale*) since; **3 ~e 4** 3
times 4; **ti ha dato di ~ il cervello?** have
you gone out of your mind?

volta'faccia [volta'fattʃa] *sm inv* (*fig*) volte-
face.

vol'taggio [vol'taddʒo] *sm* (*ELETTR*) voltage.

vol'tare *vt* to turn; (*girare: moneta*) to turn
over; (*rigirare*) to turn round ♦ *vi* to turn;
~rsi *vr* to turn; to turn over; to turn
round.

voltas'tomaco *sm* nausea; (*fig*) disgust.

volteggi'are [volted'dʒare] *vi* (*volare*) to
circle; (*in equitazione*) to do trick riding;
(*in ginnastica*) to vault.

'volto, a *pp di* **volgere** ♦ *ag* (*inteso a*): **il mio
discorso è ~ a spiegare ...** in my speech I
intend to explain ... ♦ *sm* face.

vo'lubile *ag* changeable, fickle.

vo'lume *sm* volume.

volumi'noso, a *ag* voluminous, bulky.

vo'luta *sf* (*gen*) spiral; (*ARCHIT*) volute.

voluttà *sf* sensual pleasure *o* delight.

voluttu'oso, a *ag* voluptuous.

vomi'tare *vt, vi* to vomit.

'vomito *sm* vomit; **ho il ~** I feel sick.

'vongola *sf* clam.

vo'race [vo'ratʃe] *ag* voracious, greedy.

voracità [vorat'ʃita] *sf* voracity,
voraciousness.

vo'ragine [vo'radʒine] *sf* abyss, chasm.

vorrò *etc vb vedi* **volere**.

'vortice ['vɔrtitʃe] *sm* whirl, vortex; (*fig*)
whirl.

vorti'coso, a *ag* whirling.

'vostro, a *det*: **il(la) ~(a)** *etc* your ♦ *pron*:
il(la) ~(a) *etc* yours ♦ *sm*: **avete speso del
~?** did you spend your own money? ♦ *sf*:
la ~a (*opinione*) your view; **i ~i** (*famiglia*)
your family; **un ~ amico** a friend of
yours; **è dei ~i, è dalla ~a** he's on your
side; **l'ultima ~a** (*COMM: lettera*) your
most recent letter; **alla ~a!** (*brindisi*)
here's to you!, your health!

vo'tante *sm/f* voter.

vo'tare *vi* to vote ♦ *vt* (*sottoporre a
votazione*) to take a vote on; (*approvare*) to
vote for; (*REL*): **~ qc a** to dedicate sth to;
~rsi *vr* to devote o.s. to.

votazi'one [votat'tsjone] *sf* vote, voting; **~i**
sfpl (*POL*) votes; (*INS*) marks.

'voto *sm* (*POL*) vote; (*INS*) mark (*BRIT*),
grade (*US*); (*REL*) vow; (: *offerta*) votive
offering; **aver ~i belli/brutti** (*INS*) to get
good/bad marks *o* grades; **prendere i ~i**
to take one's vows; **~ di fiducia** vote of
confidence.

V.P. *abbr* (= *vicepresidente*) VP.

VR *sigla* = Verona.

v.r. *abbr* (= *vedi retro*) PTO.

V.S. *abbr* = *Vostra Santità, Vostra Signoria*.

vs. *abbr* (= *vostro*) yr.

v.s. *abbr* = *vedi sopra*.

VT *sigla* = Viterbo.

V.U. *abbr* = **vigile urbano**.

vul'canico, a, ci, che *ag* volcanic.

vulcanizzazi'one [vulkaniddzat'tsjone] *sf*
vulcanization.

vul'cano *sm* volcano.

vulne'rabile *ag* vulnerable.

vulnerabilità *sf* vulnerability.

vu'oi, vu'ole *vb vedi* **volere**.

vuo'tare *vt*, **~rsi** *vr* to empty.

vu'oto, a *ag* empty; (*fig: privo*): **~ di** (*senso
etc*) devoid of ♦ *sm* empty space, gap;
(*spazio in bianco*) blank; (*FISICA*) vacuum;
(*fig: mancanza*) gap, void; **a mani ~e**
empty-handed; **assegno a ~** dud cheque
(*BRIT*), bad check (*US*); **~ d'aria** air
pocket; **"~ a perdere"** "no deposit"; **"~ a
rendere"** "returnable bottle".

v.v. *abbr* (= *vostro*) yr.

W w

W, w ['dɔppjovu] *sf o m inv* (*lettera*) W, w; **W
come Washington** ≈ W for William.

W *abbr* = **viva, evviva**.

'wafer ['vafer] *sm inv* (*CUC, ELETTR*) wafer.

wagon-'lit [vagɔ̃'li] *sm inv* (*FERR*) sleeping
car.

'walkman ® ['wɔːkmən] *sm inv* Walkman ®.

'water 'closet ['wɔːtə'klɔzit] *sm inv* toilet,
lavatory.

watt [vat] *sm inv* (*ELETTR*) watt.

wat'tora [vat'tora] *sm inv* (*ELETTR*) watt-
hour.

WC *sm inv* WC.

'weekend ['wiːkend] *sm inv* weekend.

'western ['wɛstern] *ag* (*CINE*) cowboy *cpd*
♦ *sm inv* western, cowboy film; **~
all'italiana** spaghetti western.

'**whisky** ['wiski] *sm inv* whisky.
'**windsurf** ['windsə:f] *sm inv* (*tavola*)
windsurfer, sailboard; (*sport*)
windsurfing.
'**würstel** ['vyrstəl] *sm inv* frankfurter.

Xx

X, x [iks] *sf o m inv* (*lettera*) X, x; **X come**
Xeres ≈ X for Xmas.
xenofo'bia [ksenofo'bia] *sf* xenophobia.
xe'nofobo, a [kse'nɔfobo] *ag* xenophobic
♦ *sm/f* xenophobe.
'**xeres** ['ksɛres] *sm inv* sherry.
xero'copia [ksɛro'kɔpja] *sf* xerox ®,
photocopy.
xerocopi'are [kseroko'pjare] *vt* to
photocopy.
xi'lofono [ksi'lɔfono] *sm* xylophone.

Yy

Y, y ['ipsilon] *sf o m inv* (*lettera*) Y, y; **Y come**
Yacht ≈ Y for Yellow (*BRIT*), Y for Yoke
(*US*).
yacht [jɔt] *sm inv* yacht.
'**yankee** ['jæŋki] *sm/f inv* Yank, Yankee.
Y.C.I. *abbr* = *Yacht Club d'Italia*.
'**Yemen** ['jemen] *sm*: **lo** ~ Yemen.
yen [jen] *sm inv* (*moneta*) yen.
'**yiddish** ['jidiʃ] *ag inv, sm inv* Yiddish.
'**yoga** ['jɔga] *ag inv, sm* yoga (*cpd*).
yogurt ['jɔgurt] *sm inv* yog(h)urt.

Zz

Z, z ['dzɛta] *sf o m inv* (*lettera*) Z, z; **Z come**
Zara ≈ Z for Zebra.
zabai'one [dzaba'jone] *sm dessert made of*
egg yolks, sugar and marsala.
zaf'fata [tsaf'fata] *sf* (*tanfo*) stench.
zaffe'rano [dzaffe'rano] *sm* saffron.
zaf'firo [dzaf'firo] *sm* sapphire.
'**zagara** ['dzagara] *sf* orange blossom.
'**zaino** ['dzaino] *sm* rucksack.
Za'ire [dza'ire] *sm*: **lo** ~ Zaire.
'**Zambia** ['dzambja] *sm*: **lo** ~ Zambia.
'**zampa** ['tsampa] *sf* (*di animale: gamba*) leg;
(*: piede*) paw; **a quattro** ~**e** on all fours;
~**e di gallina** (*calligrafia*) scrawl; (*rughe*)
crow's feet.
zam'pata [tsam'pata] *sf* (*di cane, gatto*) blow
with a paw.
zampet'tare [tsampet'tare] *vi* to scamper.
zampil'lare [tsampil'lare] *vi* to gush, spurt.
zam'pillo [tsam'pillo] *sm* gush, spurt.
zam'pino [tsam'pino] *sm* paw; **qui c'è sotto**
il suo ~ (*fig*) he's had a hand in this.
zam'pogna [tsam'poɲɲa] *sf instrument*
similar to bagpipes.
'**zanna** ['tsanna] *sf* (*di elefante*) tusk; (*di*
carnivori) fang.
zan'zara [dzan'dzara] *sf* mosquito.
zanzari'era [dzandza'rjera] *sf* mosquito net.
'**zappa** ['tsappa] *sf* hoe.
zap'pare [tsap'pare] *vt* to hoe.
zappa'tura [tsappa'tura] *sf* (*AGR*) hoeing.
'**zapping** ['tsapiŋ] *sm* (*TV*) channel-hopping.
zar, za'rina [tsar, tsa'rina] *sm/f* tsar/tsarina.
'**zattera** ['dzattera] *sf* raft.
za'vorra [dza'vɔrra] *sf* ballast.
'**zazzera** ['tsattsera] *sf* shock of hair.
'**zebra** ['dzɛbra] *sf* zebra; ~**e** *sfpl* (*AUT*) zebra
crossing *sg* (*BRIT*), crosswalk *sg* (*US*).
ze'brato, a [dze'brato] *ag* with black and
white stripes; **strisce** ~**e,**
attraversamento ~ (*AUT*) zebra crossing
(*BRIT*), crosswalk (*US*).
'**zecca, che** ['tsekka] *sf* (*ZOOL*) tick; (*officina*
di monete) mint.
zec'chino [tsek'kino] *sm* gold coin; **oro** ~
pure gold.
ze'lante [dze'lante] *ag* zealous.
'**zelo** ['dzɛlo] *sm* zeal.

'zenit ['dzɛnit] *sm* zenith.
'zenzero ['dzendzero] *sm* ginger.
'zeppa ['tseppa] *sf* wedge.
'zeppo, a ['tseppo] *ag*: ~ **di** crammed *o* packed with.
zer'bino [dzer'bino] *sm* doormat.
'zero ['dzɛro] *sm* zero, nought; **vincere per tre a** ~ (*SPORT*) to win three-nil.
'zeta ['dzɛta] *sm o f* zed, (the letter) z.
'zia ['tsia] *sf* aunt.
zibel'lino [dzibel'lino] *sm* sable.
zi'gano, a [tsi'gano] *ag*, *sm/f* gypsy.
'zigomo ['dzigomo] *sm* cheekbone.
zigri'nare [dzigri'nare] *vt* (*gen*) to knurl; (*pellame*) to grain; (*monete*) to mill.
zig'zag [dzig'dzag] *sm inv* zigzag; **andare a** ~ to zigzag.
Zim'babwe [tsim'babwe] *sm*: **lo** ~ Zimbabwe.
zim'bello [dzim'bɛllo] *sm* (*oggetto di burle*) laughing-stock.
'zinco ['dzinko] *sm* zinc.
zinga'resco, a, schi, sche [dzinga'resko] *ag* gypsy *cpd*.
'zingaro, a ['dzingaro] *sm/f* gipsy.
'zio ['tsio], *pl* **'zii** *sm* uncle; **zii** *smpl* (*zio e zia*) uncle and aunt.
zi'tella [dzi'tɛlla] *sf* spinster; (*peg*) old maid.
zit'tire [tsit'tire] *vt* to silence, hush *o* shut up ♦ *vi* to hiss.
'zitto, a ['tsitto] *ag* quiet, silent; **sta'** ~! be quiet!
ziz'zania [dzid'dzanja] *sf* (*BOT*) darnel; (*fig*) discord; **gettare** *o* **seminare** ~ to sow discord.
'zoccolo ['tsɔkkolo] *sm* (*calzatura*) clog; (*di cavallo etc*) hoof; (*ARCHIT*) plinth; (*di parete*) skirting (board); (*di armadio*) base.
zodia'cale [dzodia'kale] *ag* zodiac *cpd*; **segno** ~ sign of the zodiac.
zo'diaco [dzo'diako] *sm* zodiac.
zolfa'nello [tsolfa'nɛllo] *sm* (*sulphur*) match.
'zolfo ['tsolfo] *sm* sulphur (*BRIT*), sulfur (*US*).
'zolla ['dzolla] *sf* clod (of earth).
zol'letta [dzol'letta] *sf* sugar lump.
'zona ['dzɔna] *sf* zone, area; ~ **di depressione** (*METEOR*) trough of low pressure; ~ **erogena** erogenous zone; ~ **pedonale** pedestrian precinct; ~ **verde** (*di abitato*) green area.

'zonzo ['dzondzo]: **a** ~ *av*: **andare a** ~ to wander about, stroll about.
'zoo ['dzɔo] *sm inv* zoo.
zoolo'gia [dzoolo'dʒia] *sf* zoology.
zoo'logico, a, ci, che [dzoo'lɔdʒiko] *ag* zoological.
zo'ologo, a, gi, ghe [dzo'ɔlogo] *sm/f* zoologist.
zoosa'fari [dzoosa'fari] *sm inv* safari park.
zoo'tecnico, a, ci, che [dzoo'tɛkniko] *ag* zootechnical; **il patrimonio** ~ **di un paese** a country's livestock resources.
zoppi'care [tsoppi'kare] *vi* to limp; (*fig*: *mobile*) to be shaky, rickety.
'zoppo, a ['tsɔppo] *ag* lame; (*fig*: *mobile*) shaky, rickety.
zoti'cone [dzoti'kone] *sm* lout.
zu'ava [dzu'ava] *sf*: **pantaloni** *mpl* **alla** ~ knickerbockers.
'zucca, che ['tsukka] *sf* (*BOT*) marrow (*BRIT*), vegetable marrow (*US*); pumpkin; (*scherzoso*) head.
zucche'rare [tsukke'rare] *vt* to put sugar in.
zucche'rato, a [tsukke'rato] *ag* sweet, sweetened.
zuccheri'era [tsukke'rjɛra] *sf* sugar bowl.
zuccheri'ficio [tsukkeri'fitʃo] *sm* sugar refinery.
zucche'rino, a [tsukke'rino] *ag* sugary, sweet.
'zucchero ['tsukkero] *sm* sugar; ~ **di canna** cane sugar; ~ **caramellato** caramel; ~ **filato** candy floss, cotton candy (*US*); ~ **a velo** icing sugar (*BRIT*), confectioner's sugar (*US*).
zucche'roso, a [tsukke'roso] *ag* sugary.
zuc'china [tsuk'kina] *sf*, **zuc'chino** [tsuk'kino] *sm* courgette (*BRIT*), zucchini (*US*).
zuc'cotto [tsuk'kɔtto] *sm* ice-cream sponge.
'zuffa ['tsuffa] *sf* brawl.
zufo'lare [tsufo'lare] *vt*, *vi* to whistle.
'zufolo ['tsufolo] *sm* (*MUS*) flageolet.
'zuppa ['tsuppa] *sf* soup; (*fig*) mixture, muddle; ~ **inglese** (*CUC*) dessert made with sponge cake, custard and chocolate, ≈ trifle (*BRIT*).
zuppi'era [tsup'pjɛra] *sf* soup tureen.
'zuppo, a ['tsuppo] *ag*: ~ (**di**) drenched (with), soaked (with).
Zu'rigo [dzu'rigo] *sf* Zurich.

English-Italian
Inglese-Italiano

Aa

A, a [eɪ] n (*letter*) A, a *form inv*; (*SCOL: mark*)
≈ 10 (*ottimo*); (*MUS*): **A** la m; **A for Andrew,**
(*US*) **A for Able** ≈ A come Ancona;
from A to Z dall'A alla Z; **A road** n (*BRIT
AUT*) ≈ strada statale; **A shares** npl (*BRIT
STOCK EXCHANGE*) azioni fpl senza diritto
di voto; **A to Z** ® n stradario.

================================ *KEYWORD*

a [ə] (*before vowel or silent h:* **an**) *indef art* **1**
un (uno +s *impure, gn, pn, ps, x, z*), f una
(un' +*vowel*); ~ **book** un libro; ~ **mirror**
uno specchio; **an apple** una mela; **she's** ~
doctor è medico
2 (*instead of the number "one"*) un(o), f
una; ~ **year ago** un anno fa; ~ **hundred/
thousand pounds** cento/mille sterline
3 (*in expressing ratios, prices etc*) a, per; **3**
~ **day/week** 3 al giorno/alla settimana; **10
km an hour** 10 km all'ora; **£5** ~ **person** 5
sterline a persona *or* per persona.

a. *abbr* = **acre.**
AA n abbr (*BRIT*: = *Automobile Association*)
≈ A.C.I. m (= *Automobile Club d'Italia*);
(*US*: = *Associate in/of Arts*) titolo di studio;
(= *Alcoholics Anonymous*) A.A. f
(= *Anonima Alcolisti*); (*MIL*) = **anti-aircraft.**
AAA n abbr (= *American Automobile
Association*) ≈ A.C.I. m (= *Automobile
Club d'Italia*); (*BRIT*) = *Amateur Athletics
Association.*
A & R n abbr (*MUS*) = *artists and repertoire*; ~
man talent scout m inv.
AAUP n abbr (= *American Association of
University Professors*) *associazione dei
professori universitari.*
AB abbr (*BRIT*) *see* **able-bodied seaman;**

(*Canada*) = *Alberta.*
aback [ə'bæk] *adv*: **to be taken** ~ essere
sbalordito(a).
abacus, pl **abaci** ['æbəkəs, -saɪ] n
pallottoliere m, abaco.
abandon [ə'bændən] vt abbandonare ♦ n
abbandono; **to** ~ **ship** abbandonare la
nave.
abandoned [ə'bændənd] adj (*child, house
etc*) abbandonato(a); (*unrestrained:
manner*) disinvolto(a).
abase [ə'beɪs] vt: **to** ~ **o.s. (so far as to do)**
umiliarsi *or* abbassarsi (al punto di fare).
abashed [ə'bæʃt] adj imbarazzato(a).
abate [ə'beɪt] vi calmarsi.
abatement [ə'beɪtmənt] n (*of pollution,
noise*) soppressione f, eliminazione f;
noise ~ **society** associazione f per la lotta
contro i rumori.
abattoir ['æbətwɑ:*] n (*BRIT*) mattatoio.
abbey ['æbɪ] n abbazia, badia.
abbot ['æbət] n abate m.
abbreviate [ə'bri:vɪeɪt] vt abbreviare.
abbreviation [əbri:vɪ'eɪʃən] n
abbreviazione f.
ABC n abbr (= *American Broadcasting
Company*) *rete televisiva americana.*
abdicate ['æbdɪkeɪt] vt abdicare a ♦ vi
abdicare.
abdication [æbdɪ'keɪʃən] n abdicazione f.
abdomen ['æbdəmən] n addome m.
abdominal [æb'dɔmɪnl] adj addominale.
abduct [æb'dʌkt] vt rapire.
abduction [æb'dʌkʃən] n rapimento.
Aberdonian [æbə'dəʊnɪən] adj di Aberdeen
♦ n abitante m/f di Aberdeen; originario/a
di Aberdeen.
aberration [æbə'reɪʃən] n aberrazione f.

abet [ə'bɛt] *vt see* aid.
abeyance [ə'beɪəns] *n*: **in** ~ in sospeso.
abhor [əb'hɔː*] *vt* aborrire.
abhorrent [əb'hɔrənt] *adj* odioso(a).
abide [ə'baɪd] *vt* sopportare.
▶**abide by** *vt fus* conformarsi a.
abiding [ə'baɪdɪŋ] *adj* (*memory etc*)
persistente, duraturo(a).
ability [ə'bɪlɪtɪ] *n* abilità *f inv*; **to the best of
my** ~ con il massimo impegno.
abject ['æbdʒɛkt] *adj* (*poverty*) abietto(a);
(*apology*) umiliante; (*coward*) indegno(a),
vile.
ablaze [ə'bleɪz] *adj* in fiamme; ~ **with light**
risplendente di luce.
able ['eɪbl] *adj* capace; **to be** ~ **to do sth**
essere capace di fare qc, poter fare qc.
able-bodied ['eɪbl'bɔdɪd] *adj* robusto(a).
able-bodied seaman (AB) *n* (*BRIT*)
marinaio scelto.
ably ['eɪblɪ] *adv* abilmente.
ABM *n abbr* (= *anti-ballistic missile*) ABM *m*.
abnormal [æb'nɔːməl] *adj* anormale.
abnormality [æbnɔː'mælɪtɪ] *n* (*condition*)
anormalità; (*instance*) anomalia.
aboard [ə'bɔːd] *adv* a bordo ♦ *prep* a bordo
di; ~ **the train** in *or* sul treno.
abode [ə'bəud] *n* (*old*) dimora; (*LAW*)
domicilio, dimora; **of no fixed** ~ senza
fissa dimora.
abolish [ə'bɔlɪʃ] *vt* abolire.
abolition [æbəu'lɪʃən] *n* abolizione *f*.
abominable [ə'bɔmɪnəbl] *adj* abominevole.
aborigine [æbə'rɪdʒɪnɪ] *n* aborigeno/a.
abort [ə'bɔːt] *vt* (*MED, fig*) abortire;
(*COMPUT*) interrompere l'esecuzione di.
abortion [ə'bɔːʃən] *n* aborto; **to have an** ~
avere un aborto, abortire.
abortionist [ə'bɔːʃənɪst] *n* abortista *m/f*.
abortive [ə'bɔːtɪv] *adj* abortivo(a).
abound [ə'baund] *vi* abbondare; **to** ~ **in**
abbondare di.

========================= **KEYWORD**

about [ə'baut] *adv* **1** (*approximately*) circa,
quasi; ~ **a hundred/thousand** un
centinaio/migliaio, circa cento/mille; **it
takes** ~ **10 hours** ci vogliono circa 10 ore;
at ~ **2 o'clock** verso le 2; **I've just** ~
finished ho quasi finito; **it's** ~ **here** è qui
intorno, è qui vicino
2 (*referring to place*) qua e là, in giro; **to
leave things lying** ~ lasciare delle cose in
giro; **to run** ~ correre qua e là; **to walk** ~
camminare; **is Paul** ~? (*BRIT*) hai visto
Paul in giro?; **it's the other way** ~ (*BRIT*) è
il contrario
3: **to be** ~ **to do sth** stare per fare qc; **I'm**

not ~ **to do all that for nothing** non ho
intenzione di fare tutto questo per niente
♦ *prep* **1** (*relating to*) su, di; **a book** ~
London un libro su Londra; **what is it** ~?
di che si tratta?; (*book, film etc*) di cosa
tratta?; **we talked** ~ **it** ne abbiamo
parlato; **do something** ~ **it**! fai qualcosa!;
what *or* **how** ~ **doing this?** che ne dici di
fare questo?
2 (*referring to place*): **to walk** ~ **the town**
camminare per la città; **her clothes were
scattered** ~ **the room** i suoi vestiti erano
sparsi *or* in giro per tutta la stanza.

about-face [ə'baut'feɪs] *n*, **about-turn**
[ə'baut'təːn] *n* (*MIL*) dietro front *m inv*.
above [ə'bʌv] *adv, prep* sopra; **mentioned** ~
suddetto; **costing** ~ **£10** più caro di 10
sterline; **he's not** ~ **a bit of blackmail** non
rifuggirebbe dal ricatto; ~ **all** soprattutto.
aboveboard [ə'bʌv'bɔːd] *adj* aperto(a);
onesto(a).
abrasion [ə'breɪʒən] *n* abrasione *f*.
abrasive [ə'breɪzɪv] *adj* abrasivo(a).
abreast [ə'brɛst] *adv* di fianco; **3** ~ per 3 di
fronte; **to keep** ~ **of** tenersi aggiornato
su.
abridge [ə'brɪdʒ] *vt* ridurre.
abroad [ə'brɔːd] *adv* all'estero; **there is a
rumour** ~ **that** ... (*fig*) si sente dire in
giro che ..., circola la voce che ....
abrupt [ə'brʌpt] *adj* (*steep*) erto(a); (*sudden*)
improvviso(a); (*gruff, blunt*) brusco(a).
abscess ['æbsɪs] *n* ascesso.
abscond [əb'skɔnd] *vi* scappare.
absence ['æbsəns] *n* assenza; **in the** ~ **of**
(*person*) in assenza di; (*thing*) in
mancanza di.
absent ['æbsənt] *adj* assente; **to be** ~
without leave (AWOL) (*MIL etc*) essere
assente ingiustificato.
absentee [æbsən'tiː] *n* assente *m/f*.
absenteeism [æbsən'tiːɪzəm] *n*
assenteismo.
absent-minded ['æbsənt'maɪndɪd] *adj*
distratto(a).
absent-mindedness ['æbsənt'maɪndɪdnɪs]
n distrazione *f*.
absolute ['æbsəluːt] *adj* assoluto(a).
absolutely [æbsə'luːtlɪ] *adv* assolutamente.
absolve [əb'zɔlv] *vt*: **to** ~ **sb (from)** (*sin etc*)
assolvere qn (da); **to** ~ **sb from** (*oath*)
sciogliere qn da.
absorb [əb'sɔːb] *vt* assorbire; **to be** ~**ed in
a book** essere immerso(a) in un libro.
absorbent [əb'sɔːbənt] *adj* assorbente.
absorbent cotton *n* (*US*) cotone *m* idrofilo.
absorbing [əb'sɔːbɪŋ] *adj* avvincente, molto

interessante.

absorption [əb'sɔːpʃən] *n* assorbimento.

abstain [əb'steɪn] *vi*: **to ~ (from)** astenersi (da).

abstemious [əb'stiːmɪəs] *adj* astemio(a).

abstention [əb'stɛnʃən] *n* astensione *f*.

abstinence ['æbstɪnəns] *n* astinenza.

abstract ['æbstrækt] *adj* astratto(a) ♦ *n* (*summary*) riassunto ♦ *vt* [æb'strækt] estrarre.

absurd [əb'sɜːd] *adj* assurdo(a).

absurdity [əb'sɜːdɪtɪ] *n* assurdità *f inv*.

ABTA ['æbtə] *n abbr* = Association of British Travel Agents.

Abu Dhabi ['æbuː'dɑːbɪ] *n* Abu Dhabi *f*.

abundance [ə'bʌndəns] *n* abbondanza.

abundant [ə'bʌndənt] *adj* abbondante.

abuse *n* [ə'bjuːs] abuso; (*insults*) ingiurie *fpl* ♦ *vt* [ə'bjuːz] abusare di; **open to ~** che si presta ad abusi.

abusive [ə'bjuːsɪv] *adj* ingiurioso(a).

abysmal [ə'bɪzməl] *adj* spaventoso(n)

abyss [ə'bɪs] *n* abisso.

AC *n abbr* (*US*) = **athletic club.**

a/c *abbr* (*BANKING etc*: = account, account current) c.

academic [ækə'dɛmɪk] *adj* accademico(a); (*pej: Issue*) puramente formale ♦ *n* universitario/a.

academic year *n* anno accademico.

academy [ə'kædəmɪ] *n* (*learned body*) accademia; (*school*) scuola privata; **military/naval ~** scuola militare/navale; **~ of music** conservatorio.

ACAS ['eɪkæs] *n abbr* (*BRIT*: = Advisory, Conciliation and Arbitration Service) comitato governativo per il miglioramento della contrattazione collettiva.

accede [æk'siːd] *vi*: **to ~ to** (*request*) accedere a; (*throne*) ascendere a.

accelerate [æk'sɛləreɪt] *vt, vi* accelerare.

acceleration [æksɛlə'reɪʃən] *n* accelerazione *f*.

accelerator [æk'sɛləreɪtə*] *n* acceleratore *m*.

accent ['æksɛnt] *n* accento.

accentuate [æk'sɛntjueɪt] *vt* (*syllable*) accentuare; (*need, difference etc*) accentuare, mettere in risalto *or* in evidenza.

accept [ək'sɛpt] *vt* accettare.

acceptable [ək'sɛptəbl] *adj* accettabile.

acceptance [ək'sɛptəns] *n* accettazione *f*; **to meet with general ~** incontrare il favore *or* il consenso generale.

access ['æksɛs] *n* accesso ♦ *vt* (*COMPUT*) accedere a; **to have ~ to** avere accesso a;

the burglars gained ~ through a window i ladri sono riusciti a penetrare da *or* attraverso una finestra.

accessible [æk'sɛsəbl] *adj* accessibile.

accession [æk'sɛʃən] *n* (*addition*) aggiunta; (*to library*) accessione *f*, acquisto; (*of king*) ascesa *or* salita al trono.

accessory [æk'sɛsərɪ] *n* accessorio; **toilet accessories** *npl* (*BRIT*) articoli *mpl* da toilette.

access road *n* strada d'accesso; (*to motorway*) raccordo di entrata.

access time *n* (*COMPUT*) tempo di accesso.

accident ['æksɪdənt] *n* incidente *m*; (*chance*) caso; **to meet with** *or* **to have an ~** avere un incidente; **~s at work** infortuni *mpl* sul lavoro; **by ~** per caso.

accidental [æksɪ'dɛntl] *adj* accidentale.

accidentally [æksɪ'dɛntəlɪ] *adv* per caso.

accident insurance *n* assicurazione *f* contro gli infortuni

accident-prone ['æksɪdənt'prəun] *adj*: **he's very ~** è un vero passaguai.

acclaim [ə'kleɪm] *vt* acclamare ♦ *n* acclamazione *f*.

acclamation [æklə'meɪʃən] *n* (*approval*) acclamazione *f*; (*applause*) applauso.

acclimatize [ə'klaɪmətaɪz], (*US*) **acclimate** [ə'klaɪmeɪt] *vt*: **to become ~d** acclimatarsi.

accolade ['ækəleɪd] *n* encomio.

accommodate [ə'kɔmədeɪt] *vt* alloggiare; (*oblige, help*) favorire; **this car ~s 4 people comfortably** quest'auto può trasportare comodamente 4 persone.

accommodating [ə'kɔmədeɪtɪŋ] *adj* compiacente.

accommodation, (*US*) **accommodations** [əkɔmə'deɪʃən(z)] *n(pl)* alloggio; **seating ~** (*BRIT*) posti a sedere; **"~ to let"** (*BRIT*) "camere in affitto"; **have you any ~?** avete posto?

accompaniment [ə'kʌmpənɪmənt] *n* accompagnamento.

accompanist [ə'kʌmpənɪst] *n* (*MUS*) accompagnatore/trice.

accompany [ə'kʌmpənɪ] *vt* accompagnare.

accomplice [ə'kʌmplɪs] *n* complice *m/f*.

accomplish [ə'kʌmplɪʃ] *vt* compiere; (*achieve*) ottenere.

accomplished [ə'kʌmplɪʃt] *adj* (*person*) esperto(a).

accomplishment [ə'kʌmplɪʃmənt] *n* compimento; (*thing achieved*) risultato; **~s** *npl* (*skills*) doti *fpl*.

accord [ə'kɔːd] *n* accordo ♦ *vt* accordare; **of his own ~** di propria iniziativa; **with one ~** all'unanimità, di comune accordo.

accordance [ə'kɔːdəns] *n*: **in ~ with** in

conformità con.

according [ə'kɔːdɪŋ]: ~ **to** *prep* secondo; **it went ~ to plan** è andata secondo il previsto.

accordingly [ə'kɔːdɪŋlɪ] *adv* in conformità.

accordion [ə'kɔːdɪən] *n* fisarmonica.

accost [ə'kɔst] *vt* avvicinare.

account [ə'kaunt] *n* (*COMM*) conto; (*report*) descrizione *f*; ~**s** *npl* (*COMM*) conti; "*~* **payee only**" (*BRIT*) "assegno non trasferibile"; **to keep an ~ of** tenere nota di; **to bring sb to ~ for sth/for having done sth** chiedere a qn di render conto di qc/per aver fatto qc; **by all ~s** a quanto si dice; **of little ~** di poca importanza; **on ~** in acconto; **to buy sth on ~** comprare qc a credito; **on no ~** per nessun motivo; **on ~ of** a causa di; **to take into ~, take ~ of** tener conto di.

▸**account for** *vt fus* (*explain*) spiegare; giustificare; **all the children were ~ed for** nessun bambino mancava all'appello.

accountability [ə'kauntə'bɪlɪtɪ] *n* responsabilità.

accountable [ə'kauntəbl] *adj* responsabile; **to be held ~ for sth** dover rispondere di qc.

accountancy [ə'kauntənsɪ] *n* ragioneria.

accountant [ə'kauntənt] *n* ragioniere/a.

accounting [ə'kauntɪŋ] *n* contabilità.

accounting period *n* esercizio finanziario, periodo contabile.

account number *n* numero di conto.

account payable *n* conto passivo.

account receivable *n* conto da esigere.

accredited [ə'krɛdɪtɪd] *adj* accreditato(a).

accretion [ə'kriːʃən] *n* accrescimento.

accrue [ə'kruː] *vi* (*mount up*) aumentare; **to ~ to** derivare a; ~**d charges** ratei *mpl* passivi; ~**d interest** interesse *m* maturato.

accumulate [ə'kjuːmjuleɪt] *vt* accumulare ♦ *vi* accumularsi.

accumulation [əkjuːmju'leɪʃən] *n* accumulazione *f*.

accuracy ['ækjurəsɪ] *n* precisione *f*.

accurate ['ækjurɪt] *adj* preciso(a).

accurately ['ækjurɪtlɪ] *adv* precisamente.

accusation [ækju'zeɪʃən] *n* accusa.

accusative [ə'kjuːzətɪv] *n* (*LING*) accusativo.

accuse [ə'kjuːz] *vt* accusare.

accused [ə'kjuːzd] *n* accusato/a.

accuser [ə'kjuːzə*] *n* accusatore/trice.

accustom [ə'kʌstəm] *vt* abituare; **to ~ o.s. to sth** abituarsi a qc.

accustomed [ə'kʌstəmd] *adj* (*usual*) abituale; ~ **to** abituato(a) a.

AC/DC *abbr* (= *alternating current/direct current*) c.a./c.c.

ACE [eɪs] *n abbr* = *American Council on Education*.

ace [eɪs] *n* asso; **within an ~ of** (*BRIT*) a un pelo da.

acerbic [ə'səːbɪk] *adj* (*also fig*) acido(a).

acetate ['æsɪteɪt] *n* acetato.

ache [eɪk] *n* male *m*, dolore *m* ♦ *vi* (*be sore*) far male, dolere; (*yearn*): **to ~ to do sth** morire dalla voglia di fare qc; **I've got stomach ~** *or* (*US*) **a stomach ~** ho mal di stomaco; **my head ~s** mi fa male la testa; **I'm aching all over** mi duole dappertutto.

achieve [ə'tʃiːv] *vt* (*aim*) raggiungere; (*victory, success*) ottenere; (*task*) compiere.

achievement [ə'tʃiːvmənt] *n* compimento; successo.

Achilles heel [ə'kɪliːz-] *n* tallone *m* d'Achille.

acid ['æsɪd] *adj* acido(a) ♦ *n* acido.

acidity [ə'sɪdɪtɪ] *n* acidità.

acid rain *n* pioggia acida.

acid test *n* (*fig*) prova del fuoco.

acknowledge [ək'nɔlɪdʒ] *vt* riconoscere; (*letter: also*: ~ **receipt of**) accusare ricevuta di.

acknowledgement [ək'nɔlɪdʒmənt] *n* riconoscimento; (*of letter*) conferma; ~**s** (*in book*) ringraziamenti *mpl*.

ACLU *n abbr* (= *American Civil Liberties Union*) *unione americana per le libertà civili*.

acme ['ækmɪ] *n* culmine *m*, acme *m*.

acne ['æknɪ] *n* acne *f*.

acorn ['eɪkɔːn] *n* ghianda.

acoustic [ə'kuːstɪk] *adj* acustico(a); *see also* **acoustics**.

acoustic coupler [-'kʌplə*] *n* (*COMPUT*) accoppiatore *m* acustico.

acoustics [ə'kuːstɪks] *n, npl* acustica.

acquaint [ə'kweɪnt] *vt*: **to ~ sb with sth** far sapere qc a qn; **to be ~ed with** (*person*) conoscere.

acquaintance [ə'kweɪntəns] *n* conoscenza; (*person*) conoscente *m/f*; **to make sb's ~** fare la conoscenza di qn.

acquiesce [ækwɪ'ɛs] *vi* (*agree*): **to ~ (in)** acconsentire (a).

acquire [ə'kwaɪə*] *vt* acquistare.

acquired [ə'kwaɪəd] *adj* acquisito(a); **it's an ~ taste** è una cosa che si impara ad apprezzare.

acquisition [ækwɪ'zɪʃən] *n* acquisto.

acquisitive [ə'kwɪzɪtɪv] *adj* a cui piace accumulare le cose.

acquit [ə'kwɪt] *vt* assolvere; **to ~ o.s. well**

comportarsi bene.

acquittal [ə'kwɪtl] n assoluzione f.

acre ['eɪkə*] n acro (= 4047 m²).

acreage ['eɪkərɪdʒ] n superficie f in acri.

acrid ['ækrɪd] adj (smell) acre, pungente; (fig) pungente.

acrimonious [ækrɪ'məunɪəs] adj astioso(a).

acrobat ['ækrəbæt] n acrobata m/f.

acrobatic [ækrə'bætɪk] adj acrobatico(a).

acrobatics [ækrə'bætɪks] n acrobatica ♦ npl acrobazie fpl.

Acropolis [ə'krɔpəlɪs] n: the ~ l'Acropoli f.

across [ə'krɔs] prep (on the other side) dall'altra parte di; (crosswise) attraverso ♦ adv dall'altra parte; in larghezza; **to walk ~ (the road)** attraversare (la strada); **to take sb ~ the road** far attraversare la strada a qn; ~ **from** di fronte a; **the lake is 12 km ~** il lago ha una larghezza di 12 km or è largo 12 km; **to get sth ~ to sb** (fig) far capire qc a qn.

acrylic [ə'krɪlɪk] adj acrilico(a) ♦ n acrilico.

ACT n abbr (= American College Test) esame di ammissione a college.

act [ækt] n atto; (in music-hall etc) numero; (LAW) decreto ♦ vi agire; (THEAT) recitare; (pretend) fingere ♦ vt (part) recitare; **to catch sb in the ~** cogliere qn in flagrante or sul fatto; **it's only an ~** è tutta scena, è solo una messinscena; ~ **of God** (LAW) calamità f inv naturale; **to ~ Hamlet** (BRIT) recitare la parte di Amleto; **to ~ the fool** (BRIT) fare lo stupido; **to ~ as** agire da; **it ~s as a deterrent** serve da deterrente; ~**ing in my capacity as chairman, I …** in qualità di presidente, io ….

▶**act on** vt: **to ~ on sth** agire in base a qc.

▶**act out** vt (event) ricostruire; (fantasies) dare forma concreta a.

acting ['æktɪŋ] adj che fa le funzioni di ♦ n (of actor) recitazione f; (activity): **to do some ~** fare del teatro (or del cinema); **he is the ~ manager** fa le veci del direttore.

action ['ækʃən] n azione f; (MIL) combattimento; (LAW) processo; **to take ~** agire; **to put a plan into ~** realizzare un piano; **out of ~** fuori combattimento; (machine etc) fuori servizio; **killed in ~** (MIL) ucciso in combattimento; **to bring an ~ against sb** (LAW) intentare causa contro qn.

action replay n (BRIT TV) replay m inv.

activate ['æktɪveɪt] vt (mechanism) fare funzionare; (CHEM, PHYSICS) rendere attivo(a).

active ['æktɪv] adj attivo(a); **to play an ~ part in** partecipare attivamente a.

active duty (AD) n (US MIL) = **active service**.

actively ['æktɪvlɪ] adv attivamente.

active partner n (COMM) socio effettivo.

active service n (BRIT MIL): **to be on ~** prestar servizio in zona di operazioni.

activist ['æktɪvɪst] n attivista m/f.

activity [æk'tɪvɪtɪ] n attività f inv.

activity holiday n vacanza attiva (in bici, a cavallo, in barca a vela ecc.).

actor ['æktə*] n attore m.

actress ['æktrɪs] n attrice f.

actual ['æktjuəl] adj reale, vero(a).

actually ['æktjuəlɪ] adv veramente; (even) addirittura.

actuary ['æktjuərɪ] n attuario/a.

actuate ['æktjueɪt] vt attivare.

acuity [ə'kjuːɪtɪ] n acutezza.

acumen ['ækjumən] n acume m; **business ~** fiuto negli affari.

acupuncture ['ækjupʌŋktʃə*] n agopuntura.

AD uav abbr (= Anno Domini) d. C. ♦ n abbr (US MIL) see **active duty**.

ad [æd] n abbr = **advertisement**.

adamant ['ædəmənt] adj irremovibile.

Adam's apple ['ædəmz-] n pomo di Adamo.

adapt [ə'dæpt] vt adattare ♦ vi: **to ~ (to)** adattarsi (a).

adaptability [ədæptə'bɪlɪtɪ] n adattabilità.

adaptable [ə'dæptəbl] adj (device) adattabile; (person) che sa adattarsi.

adaptation [ædæp'teɪʃən] n adattamento.

adapter, adaptor [ə'dæptə*] n (ELEC) adattatore m.

ADC n abbr (MIL) = aide-de-camp; (US: = Aid to Dependent Children) sussidio per figli a carico.

add [æd] vt aggiungere; (figures) addizionare ♦ vi: **to ~ to** (increase) aumentare.

▶**add on** vt aggiungere.

▶**add up** vt (figures) addizionare ♦ vi (fig): **it doesn't ~ up** non ha senso; **it doesn't ~ up to much** non è un granché.

adder ['ædə*] n vipera.

addict ['ædɪkt] n tossicomane m/f; (fig) fanatico/a; **heroin ~** eroinomane m/f; **drug ~** tossicodipendente m/f, tossicomane m/f.

addicted [ə'dɪktɪd] adj: **to be ~ to** (drink etc) essere dedito(a) a; (fig: football etc) essere tifoso(a) di.

addiction [ə'dɪkʃən] n (MED) tossicomania.

adding machine ['ædɪŋ-] n addizionatrice f.

addition [ə'dɪʃən] n addizione f; **in ~** inoltre; **in ~ to** oltre.

additional [ə'dɪʃənl] adj supplementare.

additive ['ædɪtɪv] n additivo.

address [ə'drɛs] n (gen, COMPUT) indirizzo; (talk) discorso ♦ vt indirizzare; (speak to) fare un discorso a; **form of** ~ (gen) formula di cortesia; (in letters) formula d'indirizzo or di intestazione; **to** ~ **o.s. to sth** indirizzare le proprie energie verso qc; **absolute/relative** ~ (COMPUT) indirizzo assoluto/relativo.

address book n rubrica.

addressee [ædrɛ'siː] n destinatario/a.

Aden ['eɪdən] n: **the Gulf of** ~ il golfo di Aden.

adenoids ['ædɪnɔɪdz] npl adenoidi fpl.

adept ['ædɛpt] adj: ~ **at** esperto(a) in.

adequate ['ædɪkwɪt] adj (description, reward) adeguato(a); (amount) sufficiente; **to feel** ~ **to a task** sentirsi all'altezza di un compito.

adequately ['ædɪkwɪtlɪ] adv adeguatamente; sufficientemente.

adhere [əd'hɪə*] vi: **to** ~ **to** aderire a; (fig: rule, decision) seguire.

adhesion [əd'hiːʒən] n adesione f.

adhesive [əd'hiːzɪv] adj adesivo(a) ♦ n adesivo; ~ **tape** (BRIT: for parcels etc) nastro adesivo; (US: MED) cerotto adesivo.

ad hoc [æd'hɔk] adj (decision) ad hoc inv; (committee) apposito(a).

ad infinitum ['ædɪnfɪ'naɪtəm] adv all'infinito.

adjacent [ə'dʒeɪsənt] adj adiacente; ~ **to** accanto a.

adjective ['ædʒɛktɪv] n aggettivo.

adjoin [ə'dʒɔɪn] vt essere contiguo(a) or attiguo(a) a.

adjoining [ə'dʒɔɪnɪŋ] adj accanto inv, adiacente ♦ prep accanto a.

adjourn [ə'dʒəːn] vt rimandare, aggiornare; (US: end) sospendere ♦ vi sospendere la seduta; (PARLIAMENT) sospendere i lavori; (go) spostarsi; **to** ~ **a meeting till the following week** aggiornare or rinviare un incontro alla settimana seguente; **they** ~**ed to the pub** (col) si sono trasferiti al pub.

adjournment [ə'dʒəːnmənt] n rinvio, aggiornamento; sospensione f.

Adjt abbr (MIL) = **adjutant**.

adjudicate [ə'dʒuːdɪkeɪt] vt (contest) giudicare; (claim) decidere su.

adjudication [ədʒuːdɪ'keɪʃən] n decisione f.

adjust [ə'dʒʌst] vt aggiustare; (COMM) rettificare ♦ vi: **to** ~ **(to)** adattarsi (a).

adjustable [ə'dʒʌstəbl] adj regolabile.

adjuster [ə'dʒʌstə*] n see **loss adjuster**.

adjustment [ə'dʒʌstmənt] n adattamento; (of prices, wages) aggiustamento.

adjutant ['ædʒətənt] n aiutante m.

ad-lib [æd'lɪb] vt, vi improvvisare ♦ n improvvisazione f ♦ adv: **ad lib** a piacere, a volontà.

adman ['ædmæn] n (col) pubblicitario/a.

admin [æd'mɪn] n abbr (col) = **administration**.

administer [əd'mɪnɪstə*] vt amministrare; (justice) somministrare.

administration [ədmɪnɪs'treɪʃən] n amministrazione f; **the A**~ (US) il Governo.

administrative [əd'mɪnɪstrətɪv] adj amministrativo(a).

administrator [əd'mɪnɪstreɪtə*] n amministratore/trice.

admirable ['ædmərəbl] adj ammirevole.

admiral ['ædmərəl] n ammiraglio.

Admiralty ['ædmərəltɪ] n (BRIT: also: ~ Board) Ministero della Marina.

admiration [ædmə'reɪʃən] n ammirazione f.

admirer [əd'maɪərə*] n ammiratore/trice.

admiring [əd'maɪərɪŋ] adj (glance etc) di ammirazione.

admissible [əd'mɪsəbl] adj ammissibile.

admission [əd'mɪʃən] n ammissione f; (to exhibition, night club etc) ingresso; (confession) confessione f; **by his own** ~ per sua ammissione; "~ **free**", "**free** ~" "ingresso gratuito".

admit [əd'mɪt] vt ammettere; far entrare; (agree) riconoscere; "**children not** ~**ted**" "vietato l'ingresso ai bambini"; **this ticket** ~**s two** questo biglietto è valido per due persone; **I must** ~ **that** ... devo ammettere or confessare che ....

► **admit of** vt fus lasciare adito a.

► **admit to** vt fus riconoscere.

admittance [əd'mɪtəns] n ingresso; "**no** ~" "vietato l'ingresso".

admittedly [əd'mɪtɪdlɪ] adv bisogna pur riconoscere (che).

admonish [əd'mɔnɪʃ] vt ammonire.

ad nauseam [æd'nɔːzɪæm] adv fino alla nausea, a non finire.

ado [ə'duː] n: **without (any) more** ~ senza più indugi.

adolescence [ædəu'lɛsns] n adolescenza.

adolescent [ædəu'lɛsnt] adj, n adolescente (m/f).

adopt [ə'dɔpt] vt adottare.

adopted [ə'dɔptɪd] adj adottivo(a).

adoption [ə'dɔpʃən] n adozione f.

adore [ə'dɔː*] vt adorare.

adoring [ə'dɔːrɪŋ] adj adorante; **his** ~ **wife** sua moglie che lo adora.

adoringly [ə'dɔːrɪŋlɪ] adv con adorazione.

adorn [ə'dɔːn] vt ornare.

adornment [ə'dɔːnmənt] *n* ornamento.

ADP *n abbr see* **automatic data processing.**

adrenalin [ə'drɛnəlɪn] *n* adrenalina; **it gets the ~ going** ti dà una carica.

Adriatic (Sea) [eɪdrɪ'ætɪk-] *n* Adriatico.

adrift [ə'drɪft] *adv* alla deriva; **to come ~** (*boat*) andare alla deriva; (*wire, rope etc*) essersi staccato(a) *or* sciolto(a).

adroit [ə'drɔɪt] *adj* abile, destro(a).

ADT *abbr* (*US:* = *Atlantic Daylight Time*) *ora legale di New York.*

adult ['ædʌlt] *n* adulto/a.

adult education *n* scuola per adulti.

adulterate [ə'dʌltəreɪt] *vt* adulterare.

adulterer [ə'dʌltərə*] *n* adultero.

adulteress [ə'dʌltərɪs] *n* adultera.

adultery [ə'dʌltərɪ] *n* adulterio.

adulthood ['ædʌlthud] *n* età adulta.

advance [əd'vɑːns] *n* avanzamento; (*money*) anticipo ♦ *vt* avanzare; (*date, money*) anticipare ♦ *vi* avanzare; **in ~** in anticipo; **to make ~s to sb** (*gen*) fare degli approcci a qn; (*amorously*) fare delle avances a qn.

advanced [əd'vɑːnst] *adj* avanzato(a); (*SCOL: studies*) superiore; **~ in years** avanti negli anni.

advancement [əd'vɑːnsmənt] *n* avanzamento.

advance notice *n* preavviso.

advantage [əd'vɑːntɪdʒ] *n* (*also TENNIS*) vantaggio; **to take ~ of** approfittarsi di; **it's to our ~** è nel nostro interesse, torna a nostro vantaggio.

advantageous [ædvən'teɪdʒəs] *adj* vantaggioso(a).

advent ['ædvənt] *n* avvento; **A~** (*REL*) Avvento.

Advent calendar *n* calendario dell'Avvento.

adventure [əd'vɛntʃə*] *n* avventura.

adventure playground *n* area attrezzata di giochi per bambini con funi, strutture in legno etc.

adventurous [əd'vɛntʃərəs] *adj* avventuroso(a).

adverb ['ædvɜːb] *n* avverbio.

adversary ['ædvəsərɪ] *n* avversario/a.

adverse ['ædvɜːs] *adj* avverso(a); **in ~ circumstances** nelle avversità; **~ to** contrario(a) a.

adversity [əd'vɜːsɪtɪ] *n* avversità.

advert ['ædvɜːt] *n abbr* (*BRIT*) = **advertisement.**

advertise ['ædvətaɪz] *vi* (*vt*) fare pubblicità *or* réclame (a); fare un'inserzione (per vendere); **to ~ for** (*staff*) cercare tramite annuncio.

advertisement [əd'vɜːtɪsmənt] *n* (*COMM*) réclame *f inv*, pubblicità *f inv*; (*in classified ads*) inserzione *f*.

advertiser ['ædvətaɪzə*] *n* azienda che reclamizza un prodotto; (*in newspaper*) inserzionista *m/f*.

advertising ['ædvətaɪzɪŋ] *n* pubblicità.

advertising agency *n* agenzia pubblicitaria *or* di pubblicità.

advertising campaign *n* campagna pubblicitaria.

advice [əd'vaɪs] *n* consigli *mpl*; (*notification*) avviso; **piece of ~** consiglio; **to ask (sb) for ~** chiedere il consiglio (di qn), chiedere un consiglio (a qn); **legal ~** consulenza legale.

advice note *n* (*BRIT*) avviso di spedizione.

advisable [əd'vaɪzəbl] *adj* consigliabile.

advise [əd'vaɪz] *vt* consigliare; **to ~ sb of sth** informare qn di qc; **to ~ sb against sth/against doing sth** sconsigliare qu u qn/a qn di fare qc; **you will be well/ill ~d to go** fareste bene/male ad andare.

advisedly [əd'vaɪzɪdlɪ] *adv* (*deliberately*) deliberatamente.

adviser [əd'vaɪzə*] *n* consigliere/a; (*in business*) consulente *m/f*, consigliere/a.

advisory [əd'vaɪzərɪ] *adj* consultivo(a); **in an ~ capacity** in veste di consulente.

advocate *n* ['ædvəkɪt] (*upholder*) sostenitore/trice ♦ *vt* ['ædvəkeɪt] propugnare; **to be an ~ of** essere a favore di.

advt. *abbr* = **advertisement.**

AEA *n abbr* (*BRIT:* = *Atomic Energy Authority*) *ente di controllo sulla ricerca e lo sviluppo dell'energia atomica.*

AEC *n abbr* (*US:* = *Atomic Energy Commission*) *ente di controllo sulla ricerca e lo sviluppo dell'energia atomica.*

Aegean (Sea) [iː'dʒiːən-] *n* (*mare m*) Egeo.

aegis ['iːdʒɪs] *n*: **under the ~ of** sotto gli auspici di.

aeon ['iːən] *n* eternità *f inv*.

aerial ['ɛərɪəl] *n* antenna ♦ *adj* aereo(a).

aerobatics ['ɛərəu'bætɪks] *npl* acrobazia aerea *sg*; (*stunts*) acrobazie *fpl* aeree.

aerobics [ɛə'rəubɪks] *n* aerobica.

aerodrome ['ɛərədrəum] *n* (*BRIT*) aerodromo.

aerodynamic ['ɛərəudaɪ'næmɪk] *adj* aerodinamico(a).

aeronautics [ɛərə'nɔːtɪks] *n* aeronautica.

aeroplane ['ɛərəpleɪn] *n* aeroplano.

aerosol ['ɛərəsɔl] *n* aerosol *m inv*.

aerospace industry ['ɛərəuspeɪs-] *n* industria aerospaziale.

aesthetic [ɪs'θɛtɪk] adj estetico(a).
afar [ə'fɑː*] adv lontano; **from** ~ da lontano.
AFB n abbr (US) = Air Force Base.
AFDC n abbr (US: = Aid to Families with Dependent Children) ≈ A.F. (= assegni familiari).
affable ['æfəbl] adj affabile.
affair [ə'fɛə*] n affare m; (also: **love** ~) relazione f amorosa; ~**s** (business) affari; **the Watergate** ~ il caso Watergate.
affect [ə'fɛkt] vt toccare; (feign) fingere.
affectation [æfɛk'teɪʃən] n affettazione f.
affected [ə'fɛktɪd] adj affettato(a).
affection [ə'fɛkʃən] n affezione f.
affectionate [ə'fɛkʃənɪt] adj affettuoso(a).
affectionately [ə'fɛkʃənɪtlɪ] adv affettuosamente.
affidavit [æfɪ'deɪvɪt] n (LAW) affidavit m inv.
affiliated [ə'fɪlɪeɪtɪd] adj affiliato(a); ~ **company** filiale f.
affinity [ə'fɪnɪtɪ] n affinità f inv.
affirm [ə'fəːm] vt affermare, asserire.
affirmation [æfə'meɪʃən] n affermazione f.
affirmative [ə'fəːmətɪv] adj affermativo(a)
♦ n: **in the** ~ affermativamente.
affix [ə'fɪks] vt apporre; attaccare.
afflict [ə'flɪkt] vt affliggere.
affliction [ə'flɪkʃən] n afflizione f.
affluence ['æfluəns] n ricchezza.
affluent ['æfluənt] adj ricco(a); **the** ~ **society** la società del benessere.
afford [ə'fɔːd] vt permettersi; (provide) fornire; **I can't** ~ **the time** non ho veramente il tempo; **can we** ~ **a car?** possiamo permetterci un'automobile?
affordable [ə'fɔːdəbl] adj (che ha un prezzo) abbordabile.
affray [ə'freɪ] n (BRIT LAW) rissa.
affront [ə'frʌnt] n affronto.
affronted [ə'frʌntɪd] adj insultato(a).
Afghan ['æfgæn] adj, n afgano(a).
Afghanistan [æf'gænɪstɑːn] n Afganistan m.
afield [ə'fiːld] adv: **far** ~ lontano.
AFL-CIO n abbr (= American Federation of Labor and Congress of Industrial Organizations) confederazione sindacale.
afloat [ə'fləʊt] adj, adv a galla.
afoot [ə'fut] adv: **there is something** ~ si sta preparando qualcosa.
aforementioned [ə'fɔːmenʃənd] adj suddetto(a).
aforesaid [ə'fɔːsɛd] adj suddetto(a).
afraid [ə'freɪd] adj impaurito(a); **to be** ~ **of** aver paura di; **to be** ~ **of doing** or **to do** aver paura di fare; **I am** ~ **that I'll be late** mi dispiace, ma farò tardi; **I'm** ~ **so!** ho paura di sì!, temo proprio di sì!; **I'm** ~

not no, mi dispiace, purtroppo no.
afresh [ə'frɛʃ] adv di nuovo.
Africa ['æfrɪkə] n Africa.
African ['æfrɪkən] adj, n africano(a).
Afrikaans [æfrɪ'kɑːns] n afrikaans m.
Afrikaner [æfrɪ'kɑːnə*] n africander m inv.
Afro-American ['æfrəʊə'mɛrɪkən] adj afroamericano(a).
AFT n abbr (= American Federation of Teachers) sindacato degli insegnanti.
aft [ɑːft] adv a poppa, verso poppa.
after ['ɑːftə*] prep, adv dopo; ~ **dinner** dopo cena; **the day** ~ **tomorrow** dopodomani; **what/who are you** ~? che/chi cerca?; **the police are** ~ **him** è ricercato dalla polizia; ~ **you!** prima lei!, dopo di lei!; ~ **all** dopo tutto.
afterbirth ['ɑːftəbəːθ] n placenta.
aftercare ['ɑːftəkɛə*] n (BRIT MED) assistenza medica post-degenza.
after-effects ['ɑːftərɪfɛkts] npl conseguenze fpl; (of illness) postumi mpl.
afterlife ['ɑːftəlaɪf] n vita dell'al di là.
aftermath ['ɑːftəmæθ] n conseguenze fpl; **in the** ~ **of** nel periodo dopo.
afternoon ['ɑːftə'nuːn] n pomeriggio; **good** ~! buon giorno!
afters ['ɑːftəz] n (BRIT col: dessert) dessert m inv.
after-sales service [ɑːftə'seɪlz-] n servizio assistenza clienti.
after-shave (lotion) ['ɑːftəʃeɪv-] n dopobarba m inv.
aftershock ['ɑːftəʃɔk] n scossa di assestamento.
aftersun ['ɑːftəsʌn] adj: ~ **(lotion/cream)** (lozione f/crema) doposole m inv.
aftertaste ['ɑːftəteɪst] n retrogusto.
afterthought ['ɑːftəθɔːt] n: **as an** ~ come aggiunta.
afterwards ['ɑːftəwədz] adv dopo.
again [ə'gɛn] adv di nuovo; **to begin/see** ~ ricominciare/rivedere; **he opened it** ~ l'ha aperto di nuovo, l'ha riaperto; **not** ... ~ **non** ... più; ~ **and** ~ ripetutamente; **now and** ~ di tanto in tanto, a volte.
against [ə'gɛnst] prep contro; ~ **a blue background** su uno sfondo azzurro; **leaning** ~ **the desk** appoggiato alla scrivania; **(as)** ~ (BRIT) in confronto a.
age [eɪdʒ] n età f inv ♦ vt, vi invecchiare; **what** ~ **is he?** quanti anni ha?; **he is 20 years of** ~ ha 20 anni; **under** ~ minorenne; **to come of** ~ diventare maggiorenne; **it's been** ~**s since** ... sono secoli che ....
aged ['eɪdʒd] adj: ~ **10** di 10 anni; **the** ~ ['eɪdʒɪd] npl (elderly) gli anziani.

age group n generazione f; **the 40 to 50** ~ le persone fra i 40 e i 50 anni.

ageing ['eɪdʒɪŋ] adj che diventa vecchio(a); **an** ~ **filmstar** una diva stagionata.

ageless ['eɪdʒlɪs] adj senza età.

age limit n limite m d'età.

agency ['eɪdʒənsɪ] n agenzia; **through** or **by the** ~ **of** grazie a.

agenda [ə'dʒɛndə] n ordine m del giorno; **on the** ~ all'ordine del giorno.

agent ['eɪdʒənt] n agente m.

aggravate ['ægrəveɪt] vt aggravare, peggiorare; (annoy) esasperare.

aggravation [ægrə'veɪʃən] n peggioramento; esasperazione f.

aggregate ['ægrɪgeɪt] n aggregato; **on** ~ (SPORT) con punteggio complessivo.

aggression [ə'grɛʃən] n aggressione f.

aggressive [ə'grɛsɪv] adj aggressivo(a).

aggressiveness [ə'grɛsɪvnɪs] n aggressività.

aggressor [ə'grɛsə*] n aggressore m.

aggrieved [ə'griːvd] adj addolorato(a).

aggro ['ægrəu] n (col: behaviour) aggressività f inv; (: hassle) rottura.

aghast [ə'gɑːst] adj sbigottito(a).

agile ['ædʒaɪl] adj agile.

agility [ə'dʒɪlɪtɪ] n agilità f inv.

agitate ['ædʒɪteɪt] vt turbare; agitare ♦ vi: **to** ~ **for** agitarsi per.

agitator ['ædʒɪteɪtə*] n agitatore/trice.

AGM n abbr see **annual general meeting**.

agnostic [æg'nɒstɪk] adj, n agnostico(a).

ago [ə'gəu] adv: **2 days** ~ 2 giorni fa; **not long** ~ poco tempo fa; **as long** ~ **as 1960** già nel 1960; **how long** ~? quanto tempo fa?

agog [ə'gɒg] adj: **(all)** ~ **(for)** ansioso(a) (di), impaziente (di).

agonize ['ægənaɪz] vi: **to** ~ **(over)** angosciarsi (per).

agonizing ['ægənaɪzɪŋ] adj straziante.

agony ['ægənɪ] n agonia; **I was in** ~ avevo dei dolori atroci.

agony aunt n (BRIT col) chi tiene la rubrica della posta del cuore.

agony column n posta del cuore.

agree [ə'griː] vt (price) pattuire ♦ vi: **to** ~ **(with)** essere d'accordo (con); (LING) concordare (con); **to** ~ **to sth/to do sth** accettare qc/di fare qc; **to** ~ **that** (admit) ammettere che; **to** ~ **on sth** accordarsi su qc; **it was** ~d **that ...** è stato deciso (di comune accordo) che ...; **garlic doesn't** ~ **with me** l'aglio non mi va.

agreeable [ə'griːəbl] adj gradevole; (willing) disposto(a); **are you** ~ **to this?** è d'accordo con questo?

agreed [ə'griːd] adj (time, place) stabilito(a); **to be** ~ essere d'accordo.

agreement [ə'griːmənt] n accordo; **in** ~ d'accordo; **by mutual** ~ di comune accordo.

agricultural [ægrɪ'kʌltʃərəl] adj agricolo(a).

agriculture ['ægrɪkʌltʃə*] n agricoltura.

aground [ə'graund] adv: **to run** ~ arenarsi.

ahead [ə'hɛd] adv avanti; davanti; ~ **of** davanti a; (fig: schedule etc) in anticipo su; ~ **of time** in anticipo; **go** ~! avanti!; **go right** or **straight** ~ tiri diritto; **they were (right)** ~ **of us** erano (proprio) davanti a noi.

AI n abbr = Amnesty International; (COMPUT) see **artificial intelligence**.

AIB n abbr (BRIT: = Accident Investigation Bureau) ufficio d'inchiesta per incidenti aerei e simili.

AID n abbr = artificial insemination by donor; (US: = Agency for International Development) A.I.D. f.

aid [eɪd] n aiuto ♦ vt aiutare; **with the** ~ **of** con l'aiuto di; **in** ~ **of** a favore di; **to** ~ **and abet** (LAW) essere complice di.

aide [eɪd] n (person) aiutante m.

aide-de-camp (ADC) ['eɪddə'kɒŋ] n (MIL) aiutante m di campo.

AIDS [eɪdz] n abbr (= acquired immune or immuno-deficiency syndrome) A.I.D.S. f.

AIH n abbr = artificial insemination by husband.

ailing ['eɪlɪŋ] adj sofferente; (fig: economy, industry etc) in difficoltà.

ailment ['eɪlmənt] n indisposizione f.

aim [eɪm] vt: **to** ~ **sth at** (gun) mirare qc a, puntare qc a; (camera, remark) rivolgere qc a; (missile) lanciare qc contro; (blow etc) tirare qc a ♦ vi (also: **to take** ~) prendere la mira ♦ n mira; **to** ~ **at** mirare; **to** ~ **to do** aver l'intenzione di fare.

aimless ['eɪmlɪs] adj, **aimlessly** ['eɪmlɪslɪ] adv senza scopo.

ain't [eɪnt] (col) = **am not**; **aren't**; **isn't**.

air [ɛə*] n aria ♦ vt (room, bed) arieggiare; (clothes) far prendere aria a; (idea, grievance) esprimere pubblicamente, manifestare; (views) far conoscere ♦ cpd (currents) d'aria; (attack) aereo(a); **by** ~ (travel) in aereo; **to be on the** ~ (RADIO, TV: station) trasmettere; (: programme) essere in onda.

air bag n airbag m inv.

air base n base f aerea.

airbed ['ɛəbɛd] n (BRIT) materassino.

airborne ['ɛəbɔːn] adj (plane) in volo; (troops) aerotrasportato(a); **as soon as**

the plane was ~ appena l'aereo ebbe decollato.

air cargo *n* carico trasportato per via aerea.

air-conditioned ['ɛəkən'dɪʃənd] *adj* con *or* ad aria condizionata.

air conditioning *n* condizionamento d'aria.

air-cooled ['ɛəkuːld] *adj* raffreddato(a) ad aria.

aircraft ['ɛəkrɑːft] *n* (*pl inv*) apparecchio.

aircraft carrier *n* portaerei *f inv.*

air cushion *n* cuscino gonfiabile; (*TECH*) cuscino d'aria.

airfield ['ɛəfiːld] *n* campo d'aviazione.

Air Force *n* aviazione *f* militare.

air freight *n* spedizione *f* di merci per via aerea; (*goods*) carico spedito per via aerea.

airgun ['ɛəgʌn] *n* fucile *m* ad aria compressa.

air hostess *n* hostess *f inv.*

airily ['ɛərɪlɪ] *adv* con disinvoltura.

airing ['ɛərɪŋ] *n*: **to give an** ~ **to** (*linen*) far prendere aria a; (*room*) arieggiare; (*fig: ideas etc*) ventilare.

air letter *n* (*BRIT*) aerogramma *m.*

airlift ['ɛəlɪft] *n* ponte *m* aereo.

airline ['ɛəlaɪn] *n* linea aerea.

airliner ['ɛəlaɪnə*] *n* aereo di linea.

airlock ['ɛəlɔk] *n* cassa d'aria.

air mail *n* posta aerea; **by** ~ per via *or* posta aerea.

air mattress *n* materassino gonfiabile.

airplane ['ɛəpleɪn] *n* (*US*) aeroplano.

air pocket *n* vuoto d'aria.

airport ['ɛəpɔːt] *n* aeroporto.

air raid *n* incursione *f* aerea.

air rifle *n* fucile *m* ad aria compressa.

airsick ['ɛəsɪk] *adj*: **to be** ~ soffrire di mal d'aereo.

airspace ['ɛəspeɪs] *n* spazio aereo.

airspeed ['ɛəspiːd] *n* velocità *f inv* di crociera (*AER*).

airstrip ['ɛəstrɪp] *n* pista d'atterraggio.

air terminal *n* air-terminal *m inv.*

airtight ['ɛətaɪt] *adj* ermetico(a).

air time *n* (*RADIO*) spazio radiofonico; (*TV*) spazio televisivo.

air traffic control *n* controllo del traffico aereo.

air traffic controller *n* controllore *m* del traffico aereo.

airway ['ɛəweɪ] *n* (*AVIAT*) rotte *fpl* aeree; (*ANAT*) vie *fpl* respiratorie.

airy ['ɛərɪ] *adj* arioso(a); (*manners*) noncurante.

aisle [aɪl] *n* (*of church*) navata laterale;

navata centrale; (*of plane*) corridoio.

aisle seat *n* (*on plane*) posto sul corridoio.

ajar [ə'dʒɑː*] *adj* socchiuso(a).

AK *abbr* (*US*) = *Alaska.*

aka *abbr* (= *also known as*) alias.

akin [ə'kɪn] *prep* simile a.

AL *abbr* (*US*) = *Alabama.*

Ala. *abbr* (*US*) = *Alabama.*

à la carte [ɑːlɑː'kɑːt] *adv* alla carta.

alacrity [ə'lækrɪtɪ] *n*: **with** ~ con prontezza.

alarm [ə'lɑːm] *n* allarme *m* ♦ *vt* allarmare.

alarm clock *n* sveglia.

alarmed [ə'lɑːmd] *adj* (*person*) allarmato(a); (*house, car etc*) dotato(a) di allarme.

alarming [ə'lɑːmɪŋ] *adj* allarmante, preoccupante.

alarmingly [ə'lɑːmɪŋlɪ] *adv* in modo allarmante; ~ **close** pericolosamente vicino.

alarmist [ə'lɑːmɪst] *n* allarmista *m/f.*

alas [ə'læs] *excl* ohimè!, ahimè!

Alas. *abbr* (*US*) = *Alaska.*

Alaska [ə'læskə] *n* Alasca.

Albania [æl'beɪnɪə] *n* Albania.

Albanian [æl'beɪnɪən] *adj* albanese ♦ *n* albanese *m/f*; (*LING*) albanese *m.*

albatross ['ælbətrɔs] *n* albatro, albatros *m inv.*

albeit [ɔːl'biːɪt] *conj* sebbene + *sub*, benché + *sub.*

album ['ælbəm] *n* album *m inv*; (*L.P.*) 33 giri *m inv*, L.P. *m inv.*

albumen ['ælbjumɪn] *n* albume *m.*

alchemy ['ælkɪmɪ] *n* alchimia.

alcohol ['ælkəhɔl] *n* alcool *m.*

alcohol-free ['ælkəhɔl'friː] *adj* analcolico(a).

alcoholic [ælkə'hɔlɪk] *adj* alcolico(a) ♦ *n* alcolizzato/a.

alcoholism ['ælkəhɔlɪzəm] *n* alcolismo.

alcove ['ælkəuv] *n* alcova.

Ald. *abbr* = *alderman.*

alderman ['ɔːldəmən] *n* consigliere *m* comunale.

ale [eɪl] *n* birra.

alert [ə'lɔːt] *adj* vivo(a); (*watchful*) vigile ♦ *n* allarme *m* ♦ *vt*: **to** ~ **sb (to sth)** avvisare qn (di qc), avvertire qn (di qc); **to** ~ **sb to the dangers of sth** mettere qn in guardia contro qc; **on the** ~ all'erta.

Aleutian Islands [ə'luːʃən-] *npl* isole *fpl* Aleutine.

A level *n* (*BRIT*) diploma di studi superiori.

Alexandria [ælɪg'zændrɪə] *n* Alessandria (d'Egitto).

alfresco [æl'freskəu] *adj, adv* all'aperto.

algebra ['ældʒɪbrə] *n* algebra.

Algeria [æl'dʒɪərɪə] *n* Algeria.

Algerian [æl'dʒɪərɪən] *adj, n* algerino(a).

Algiers [æl'dʒɪəz] n Algeri f.
algorithm ['ælgərɪðəm] n algoritmo.
alias ['eɪlɪəs] adv alias ♦ n pseudonimo, falso
nome m.
alibi ['ælɪbaɪ] n alibi m inv.
alien ['eɪlɪən] n straniero/a ♦ adj: ~ **(to)**
estraneo(a) (a).
alienate ['eɪlɪəneɪt] vt alienare.
alienation [eɪlɪə'neɪʃən] n alienazione f.
alight [ə'laɪt] adj acceso(a) ♦ vi scendere;
(bird) posarsi.
align [ə'laɪn] vt allineare.
alignment [ə'laɪnmənt] n allineamento; **out
of** ~ **(with)** non allineato (con).
alike [ə'laɪk] adj simile ♦ adv allo stesso
modo; **to look** ~ assomigliarsi; **winter
and summer** ~ sia d'estate che d'inverno.
alimony ['ælɪmənɪ] n (payment) alimenti
mpl.
alive [ə'laɪv] adj vivo(a); (active) attivo(a); ~
with pieno(a) di; ~ **to** conscio(a) di.
alkali ['ælkəlaɪ] n alcali m inv.

─────────── KEYWORD ───────────

all [ɔ:l] adj tutto(a); ~ **day** tutto il giorno; ~
night tutta la notte; ~ **men** tutti gli
uomini; ~ **five girls** tutt'e cinque le
ragazze; ~ **five came** sono venuti tutti e
cinque; ~ **the books** tutti i libri, ~ **the
food** tutto il cibo; ~ **the time** tutto il
tempo; (always) sempre; ~ **his life** tutta la
vita; **for** ~ **their efforts** nonostante tutti i
loro sforzi
♦ pron **1** tutto(a); **is that** ~? non c'è altro?;
(in shop) basta così?; ~ **of them** tutti(e); ~
of it tutto(a); **I ate it** ~, **I ate** ~ **of it** l'ho
mangiato tutto; ~ **of us went** tutti noi
siamo andati; ~ **of the boys went** tutti i
ragazzi sono andati
2 (in phrases): **above** ~ soprattutto; **after**
~ dopotutto; **at** ~: **not at** ~ (in answer to
question) niente affatto; (in answer to
thanks) prego!, di niente!, s'immagini!;
I'm not at ~ **tired** non sono affatto stanco;
anything at ~ **will do** andrà bene
qualsiasi cosa; ~ **in** ~ tutto sommato
♦ adv: ~ **alone** tutto(a) solo(a); **to be/feel** ~
in (BRIT col) essere/sentirsi sfinito(a) or
distrutto(a); ~ **out** adv: **to go** ~ **out**
mettercela tutta; **it's not as hard as** ~
that non è poi così difficile; ~ **the more/
the better** tanto più/meglio; ~ **but** quasi;
the score is two ~ il punteggio è di due a
due or è due pari.

────────────────────────

allay [ə'leɪ] vt (fears) dissipare.
all clear n (MIL) cessato allarme m inv; (fig)
okay m.

allegation [ælɪ'geɪʃən] n asserzione f.
allege [ə'lɛdʒ] vt asserire; **he is** ~**d to have
said** ... avrebbe detto che ....
alleged [ə'lɛdʒd] adj presunto(a).
allegedly [ə'lɛdʒɪdlɪ] adv secondo quanto si
asserisce.
allegiance [ə'li:dʒəns] n fedeltà.
allegory ['ælɪgərɪ] n allegoria.
all-embracing ['ɔ:lɪm'breɪsɪŋ] adj
universale.
allergic [ə'lɔ:dʒɪk] adj: ~ **to** allergico(a) a.
allergy ['ælədʒɪ] n allergia.
alleviate [ə'li:vɪeɪt] vt alleviare.
alley ['ælɪ] n vicolo; (in garden) vialetto.
alleyway ['ælɪweɪ] n vicolo.
alliance [ə'laɪəns] n alleanza.
allied ['ælaɪd] adj alleato(a).
alligator ['ælɪgeɪtəʳ] n alligatore m.
all-important ['ɔ:lɪm'pɔ:tənt] adj
importantissimo(a).
all-in ['ɔ:lɪn] adj (BRIT: also adv: charge) tutto
compreso.
all-in wrestling n (BRIT) lotta americana.
alliteration [əlɪtə'reɪʃən] n allitterazione f.
all-night ['ɔ:l'naɪt] adj aperto(a) (or che
dura) tutta la notte.
allocate ['æləkeɪt] vt (share out) distribuire;
(duties, sum, time): **to** ~ **sth to** assegnare
qc a; **to** ~ **sth for** stanziare qc per.
allocation [æləu'keɪʃən] n: ~ **(of money)**
stanziamento.
allot [ə'lɔt] vt (share out) spartire; **to** ~ **sth
to** (time) dare qc a; (duties) assegnare qc
a; **in the** ~**ted time** nel tempo fissato or
prestabilito.
allotment [ə'lɔtmənt] n (share) spartizione
f; (garden) lotto di terra.
all-out ['ɔ:laut] adj (effort etc) totale ♦ adv: **to
go all out for** mettercela tutta per.
allow [ə'lau] vt (practice, behaviour)
permettere; (sum to spend etc) accordare;
(sum, time estimated) dare; (concede): **to** ~
that ammettere che; **to** ~ **sb to do**
permettere a qn di fare; **he is** ~**ed to (do
it)** lo può fare; **smoking is not** ~**ed** è
vietato fumare, non è permesso fumare;
we must ~ **3 days for the journey**
dobbiamo calcolare 3 giorni per il
viaggio.
►**allow for** vt fus tener conto di.
allowance [ə'lauəns] n (money received)
assegno; (for travelling, accommodation)
indennità f inv; (TAX) detrazione f di
imposta; **to make** ~**(s) for** tener conto di;
(person) scusare.
alloy ['ælɔɪ] n lega.
all right adv (feel, work) bene; (as answer)
va bene.

all-round ['ɔːl'raund] *adj* completo(a).
all-rounder [ɔːl'raundə*] *n* (*BRIT*): **to be a good** ~ essere bravo(a) in tutto.
allspice ['ɔːlspais] *n* pepe *m* della Giamaica.
all-time ['ɔːl'taim] *adj* (*record*) assoluto(a).
allude [ə'luːd] *vi*: **to** ~ **to** alludere a.
alluring [ə'ljuəriŋ] *adj* seducente.
allusion [ə'luːʒən] *n* allusione *f*.
alluvium [ə'luːviəm] *n* materiale *m* alluvionale.
ally *n* ['ælai] alleato ♦ *vt* [ə'lai]: **to** ~ **o.s. with** allearsi con.
almighty [ɔːl'maiti] *adj* onnipotente.
almond ['ɑːmənd] *n* mandorla.
almost ['ɔːlməust] *adv* quasi; **he** ~ **fell** per poco non è caduto.
alms [ɑːmz] *n* elemosina.
aloft [ə'lɔft] *adv* in alto; (*NAUT*) sull'alberatura.
alone [ə'ləun] *adj*, *adv* solo(a); **to leave sb** ~ lasciare qn in pace; **to leave sth** ~ lasciare stare qc; **let** ~ ... figuriamoci poi ..., tanto meno ....
along [ə'lɔŋ] *prep* lungo ♦ *adv*: **is he coming** ~**?** viene con noi?; **he was limping** ~ veniva zoppicando; ~ **with** insieme con.
alongside [ə'lɔŋ'said] *prep* accanto a; lungo ♦ *adv* accanto; (*NAUT*) sottobordo; **we brought our boat** ~ (*of a pier/shore etc*) abbiamo accostato la barca (al molo/alla riva *etc*).
aloof [ə'luːf] *adj* distaccato(a) ♦ *adv* a distanza, in disparte; **to stand** ~ tenersi a distanza *or* in disparte.
aloofness [ə'luːfnis] *n* distacco, riserbo.
aloud [ə'laud] *adv* ad alta voce.
alphabet ['ælfəbɛt] *n* alfabeto.
alphabetical [ælfə'bɛtikəl] *adj* alfabetico(a); **in** ~ **order** in ordine alfabetico.
alphanumeric [ælfənjuː'mɛrik] *adj* alfanumerico(a).
alpine ['ælpain] *adj* alpino(a); ~ **hut** rifugio alpino; ~ **pasture** pascolo alpestre; ~ **skiing** sci alpino.
Alps [ælps] *npl*: **the** ~ le Alpi.
already [ɔːl'rɛdi] *adv* già.
alright ['ɔːl'rait] *adv* (*BRIT*) = **all right**.
Alsatian [æl'seiʃən] *n* (*BRIT*: *dog*) pastore *m* tedesco, (*cane m*) lupo.
also ['ɔːlsəu] *adv* anche.
Alta. *abbr* (*Canada*) = Alberta.
altar ['ɔltə*] *n* altare *m*.
alter ['ɔltə*] *vt*, *vi* alterare.
alteration [ɔltə'reiʃən] *n* modificazione *f*, alterazione *f*; ~**s** (*SEWING*, *ARCHIT*) modifiche *fpl*; **timetable subject to** ~ orario soggetto a variazioni.

altercation [ɔːltə'keiʃən] *n* alterco, litigio.
alternate *adj* [ɔl'təːnit] alterno(a) ♦ *vi* ['ɔltəːneit] alternare; **on** ~ **days** ogni due giorni.
alternately [ɔl'təːnitli] *adv* alternatamente.
alternating current ['ɔltəneitiŋ-] *n* corrente *f* alternata.
alternative [ɔl'təːnətiv] *adj* (*solutions*) alternativo(a); (*solution*) altro(a) ♦ *n* (*choice*) alternativa; (*other possibility*) altra possibilità.
alternatively [ɔl'təːnətivli] *adv* altrimenti, come alternativa.
alternative medicine *n* medicina alternativa.
alternator ['ɔltəneitə*] *n* (*AUT*) alternatore *m*.
although [ɔːl'ðəu] *conj* benché + *sub*, sebbene + *sub*.
altitude ['æltitjuːd] *n* altitudine *f*.
alto ['æltəu] *n* contralto.
altogether [ɔːltə'gɛðə*] *adv* del tutto, completamente; (*on the whole*) tutto considerato; (*in all*) in tutto; **how much is that** ~**?** quant'è in tutto?
altruism ['æltruizəm] *n* altruismo.
altruistic [æltru'istik] *adj* altruistico(a).
aluminium [ælju'miniəm], (*US*) **aluminum** [ə'luːminəm] *n* alluminio.
always ['ɔːlweiz] *adv* sempre.
Alzheimer's ['æltshaiməz] *n* (*also*: ~ **disease**) morbo di Alzheimer.
AM *abbr* (= *amplitude modulation*) AM ♦ *n abbr* (= *Assembly Member*) deputato gallese.
am [æm] *vb see* **be**.
a.m. *adv abbr* (= *ante meridiem*) della mattina.
AMA *n abbr* = *American Medical Association*.
amalgam [ə'mælgəm] *n* amalgama *m*.
amalgamate [ə'mælgəmeit] *vt* amalgamare ♦ *vi* amalgamarsi.
amalgamation [əmælgə'meiʃən] *n* amalgamazione *f*; (*COMM*) fusione *f*.
amass [ə'mæs] *vt* ammassare.
amateur ['æmətə*] *n* dilettante *m/f* ♦ *adj* (*SPORT*) dilettante; ~ **dramatics** *n* filodrammatica.
amateurish ['æmətəriʃ] *adj* (*pej*) da dilettante.
amaze [ə'meiz] *vt* stupire; **to be** ~**d** (**at**) essere sbalordito(a) (da).
amazement [ə'meizmənt] *n* stupore *m*.
amazing [ə'meiziŋ] *adj* sorprendente, sbalorditivo(a); (*bargain*, *offer*) sensazionale.
amazingly [ə'meiziŋli] *adv* incredibilmente, sbalorditivamente.
Amazon ['æməzən] *n* (*MYTHOLOGY*)

Amazzone *f*; (*river*): **the** ~ il Rio delle Amazzoni ♦ *cpd* (*basin, jungle*) amazzonico(a).

Amazonian [æmə'zəunɪən] *adj* amazzonico(a).

ambassador [æm'bæsədə*] *n* ambasciatore/trice.

amber ['æmbə*] *n* ambra; **at** ~ (*BRIT AUT*) giallo.

ambidextrous [æmbɪ'dɛkstrəs] *adj* ambidestro(a).

ambience ['æmbɪəns] *n* ambiente *m*.

ambiguity [æmbɪ'gjuɪtɪ] *n* ambiguità *f inv*.

ambiguous [æm'bɪgjuəs] *adj* ambiguo(a).

ambition [æm'bɪʃən] *n* ambizione *f*; **to achieve one's** ~ realizzare le proprie aspirazioni *or* ambizioni.

ambitious [æm'bɪʃəs] *adj* ambizioso(a).

ambivalent [æm'bɪvələnt] *adj* ambivalente.

amble ['æmbl] *vi* (*gen*: **to** ~ **along**) camminare tranquillamente.

ambulance ['æmbjuləns] *n* ambulanza.

ambush ['æmbuʃ] *n* imboscata ♦ *vt* fare un'imboscata a.

ameba [ə'mi:bə] *n* (*US*) = **amoeba**.

ameliorate [ə'mi:lɪəreɪt] *vt* migliorare.

amen ['ɑ:'mɛn] *excl* così sia, amen.

amenable [ə'mi:nəbl] *adj*: ~ **to** (*advice etc*) ben disposto(a) a.

amend [ə'mɛnd] *vt* (*law*) emendare; (*text*) correggere ♦ *vi* emendarsi; **to make ~s** fare ammenda.

amendment [ə'mɛndmənt] *n* emendamento; correzione *f*.

amenities [ə'mi:nɪtɪz] *npl* attrezzature *fpl* ricreative e culturali.

amenity [ə'mi:nɪtɪ] *n* amenità *f inv*.

America [ə'mɛrɪkə] *n* America.

American [ə'mɛrɪkən] *adj*, *n* americano(a).

americanize [ə'mɛrɪkənaɪz] *vt* americanizzare.

amethyst ['æmɪθɪst] *n* ametista.

Amex ['æmɛks] *n abbr* = *American Stock Exchange*.

amiable ['eɪmɪəbl] *adj* amabile, gentile.

amicable ['æmɪkəbl] *adj* amichevole.

amicably ['æmɪkəblɪ] *adv*: **to part** ~ lasciarsi senza rancori.

amid(st) [ə'mɪd(st)] *prep* fra, tra, in mezzo a.

amiss [ə'mɪs] *adj*, *adv*: **there's something** ~ c'è qualcosa che non va bene; **don't take it** ~ non avertene a male.

ammo ['æməu] *n abbr* (*col*) = **ammunition**.

ammonia [ə'məunɪə] *n* ammoniaca.

ammunition [æmju'nɪʃən] *n* munizioni *fpl*; (*fig*) arma.

ammunition dump *n* deposito di

munizioni.

amnesia [æm'ni:zɪə] *n* amnesia.

amnesty ['æmnɪstɪ] *n* amnistia; **to grant an** ~ **to** concedere l'amnistia a, amnistiare.

Amnesty International *n* Amnesty International *f*.

amoeba, (*US*) **ameba** [ə'mi:bə] *n* ameba.

amok [ə'mɔk] *adv*: **to run** ~ diventare pazzo(a) furioso(a).

among(st) [ə'mʌŋ(st)] *prep* fra, tra, in mezzo a.

amoral [eɪ'mɔrəl] *adj* amorale.

amorous ['æmərəs] *adj* amoroso(a).

amorphous [ə'mɔ:fəs] *adj* amorfo(a).

amortization [əmɔːtaɪ'zeɪʃən] *n* (*COMM*) ammortamento.

amount [ə'maunt] *n* (*sum of money*) somma; (*of bill etc*) importo; (*quantity*) quantità *f inv* ♦ *vi*: **to** ~ **to** (*total*) ammontare a; (*be same as*) essere come; **this ~s to a refusal** questo equivale a un rifiuto.

amp(ère) ['æmp(ɛə*)] *n* ampere *m inv*; **a 13** ~ **plug** una spina con fusibile da 13 ampere.

ampersand ['æmpəsænd] *n* e *f* commerciale.

amphetamine [æm'fɛtəmi:n] *n* anfetamina.

amphibian [æm'fɪbɪən] *n* anfibio.

amphibious [æm'fɪbɪəs] *adj* anfibio(a).

amphitheatre, (*US*) **amphitheater** ['æmfɪθɪətə*] *n* anfiteatro.

ample ['æmpl] *adj* ampio(a); spazioso(a); (*enough*): **this is** ~ questo è più che sufficiente; **to have** ~ **time/room** avere assai tempo/posto.

amplifier ['æmplɪfaɪə*] *n* amplificatore *m*.

amplify ['æmplɪfaɪ] *vt* amplificare.

amply ['æmplɪ] *adv* ampiamente.

ampoule, (*US*) **ampule** ['æmpu:l] *n* (*MED*) fiala.

amputate ['æmpjuteɪt] *vt* amputare.

amputee [æmpju'ti:] *n* mutilato/a, chi ha subito un'amputazione.

Amsterdam [æmstə'dæm] *n* Amsterdam *f*.

amt *abbr* = **amount**.

amuck [ə'mʌk] *adv* = **amok**.

amuse [ə'mju:z] *vt* divertire; **to** ~ **o.s. with sth/by doing sth** divertirsi con qc/a fare qc; **to be ~d at** essere divertito da; **he was not ~d** non l'ha trovato divertente.

amusement [ə'mju:zmənt] *n* divertimento; **much to my** ~ con mio grande spasso.

amusement arcade *n* sala giochi (*solo con macchinette a gettoni*).

amusement park *n* luna park *m inv*.

amusing [ə'mju:zɪŋ] *adj* divertente.

an [æn, ən, n] *indef art see* **a**.

ANA *n abbr* = *American Newspaper*

Association; _American Nurses Association._

anachronism [ə'nækrənɪzəm] _n_ anacronismo.

anaemia [ə'niːmɪə] _n_ anemia.

anaemic [ə'niːmɪk] _adj_ anemico(a).

anaesthetic [ænɪs'θetɪk] _adj_ anestetico(a) ♦ _n_ anestetico; **local/general** ~ anestesia locale/totale; **under the** ~ sotto anestesia.

anaesthetist [æ'niːsθɪtɪst] _n_ anestesista _m/f._

anagram ['ænəgræm] _n_ anagramma _m._

anal ['eɪnl] _adj_ anale.

analgesic [ænæl'dʒiːsɪk] _adj_ analgesico(a) ♦ _n_ analgesico.

analogous [ə'næləgəs] _adj_: ~ **to** _or_ **with** analogo(a) a.

analog(ue) ['ænəlɔg] _adj_ (_watch, computer_) analogico(a).

analogy [ə'nælədʒɪ] _n_ analogia; **to draw an** ~ **between** fare un'analogia tra.

analyse ['ænəlaɪz] _vt_ (_BRIT_) analizzare.

analysis, _pl_ **analyses** [ə'næləsɪs, -siːz] _n_ analisi _f inv;_ **in the last** ~ in ultima analisi.

analyst ['ænəlɪst] _n_ (_political_ ~ _etc_) analista _m/f;_ (_US_) (psic)analista _m/f._

analytic(al) [ænə'lɪtɪk(l)] _adj_ analitico(a).

analyze ['ænəlaɪz] _vt_ (_US_) = **analyse**.

anarchic [æ'nɑːkɪk] _adj_ anarchico(a).

anarchist ['ænəkɪst] _adj, n_ anarchico(a).

anarchy ['ænəkɪ] _n_ anarchia.

anathema [ə'næθɪmə] _n:_ **it is** ~ **to him** non ne vuol neanche sentir parlare.

anatomical [ænə'tɒmɪkl] _adj_ anatomico(a).

anatomy [ə'nætəmɪ] _n_ anatomia.

ANC _n abbr_ = _African National Congress._

ancestor ['ænsɪstə*] _n_ antenato/a.

ancestral [æn'sestrəl] _adj_ avito(a).

ancestry ['ænsɪstrɪ] _n_ antenati _mpl;_ ascendenza.

anchor ['æŋkə*] _n_ ancora ♦ _vi_ (_also:_ **to drop** ~) gettare l'ancora ♦ _vt_ ancorare; **to weigh** ~ salpare _or_ levare l'ancora.

anchorage ['æŋkərɪdʒ] _n_ ancoraggio.

anchor man _n_ (_TV, RADIO_) anchorman _m inv._

anchor woman _n_ (_TV, RADIO_) anchorwoman _f inv._

anchovy ['æntʃəvɪ] _n_ acciuga.

ancient ['eɪnʃənt] _adj_ antico(a); (_fig_) anziano(a); ~ **monument** monumento storico.

ancillary [æn'sɪlərɪ] _adj_ ausiliario(a).

and [ænd] _conj_ e (_often_ ed _before vowel_); ~ **so on** e così via; **try** ~ **do it** prova a farlo; **come** ~ **sit here** vieni a sedere qui; **better** ~ **better** sempre meglio; **more** ~ **more** sempre di più.

Andes ['ændiːz] _npl:_ **the** ~ le Ande.

Andorra [æn'dɔːrə] _n_ Andorra.

anecdote ['ænɪkdəut] _n_ aneddoto.

anemia [ə'niːmɪə] _etc_ = **anaemia** _etc._

anemone [ə'nemənɪ] _n_ (_BOT_) anemone _m;_ (_sea_ ~) anemone _m_ di mare, attinia.

anesthetic [ænɪs'θetɪk] _etc_ = **anaesthetic** _etc._

anew [ə'njuː] _adv_ di nuovo.

angel ['eɪndʒəl] _n_ angelo.

angel dust _n_ _sedativo usato a scopo allucinogeno._

anger ['æŋgə*] _n_ rabbia ♦ _vt_ arrabbiare.

angina [æn'dʒaɪnə] _n_ angina pectoris.

angle ['æŋgl] _n_ angolo ♦ _vi:_ **to** ~ **for** (_fig_) cercare di avere; **from their** ~ dal loro punto di vista.

angler ['æŋglə*] _n_ pescatore _m_ con la lenza.

Anglican ['æŋglɪkən] _adj, n_ anglicano(a).

anglicize ['æŋglɪsaɪz] _vt_ anglicizzare.

angling ['æŋglɪŋ] _n_ pesca con la lenza.

Anglo- ['æŋgləu] _prefix_ anglo...; ~**Italian** _adj, n_ italobritannico(a).

Anglo-Saxon ['æŋgləu'sæksən] _adj, n_ anglosassone (_m/f_).

Angola [æŋ'gəulə] _n_ Angola.

Angolan [æŋ'gəulən] _adj, n_ angolano(a).

angrily ['æŋgrɪlɪ] _adv_ con rabbia.

angry ['æŋgrɪ] _adj_ arrabbiato(a), furioso(a); **to be** ~ **with sb/at sth** essere in collera con qn/per qc; **to get** ~ arrabbiarsi; **to make sb** ~ fare arrabbiare qn.

anguish ['æŋgwɪʃ] _n_ angoscia.

anguished ['æŋgwɪʃt] _adj_ angosciato(a), pieno(a) d'angoscia.

angular ['æŋgjulə*] _adj_ angolare.

animal ['ænɪml] _adj, n_ animale (_m_).

animal rights _npl_ diritti _mpl_ degli animali.

animate _vt_ ['ænɪmeɪt] animare ♦ _adj_ ['ænɪmɪt] animato(a).

animated ['ænɪmeɪtɪd] _adj_ animato(a).

animation [ænɪ'meɪʃən] _n_ animazione _f._

animosity [ænɪ'mɒsɪtɪ] _n_ animosità.

aniseed ['ænɪsiːd] _n_ semi _mpl_ di anice.

Ankara ['æŋkərə] _n_ Ankara.

ankle ['æŋkl] _n_ caviglia.

ankle socks _npl_ calzini _mpl._

annex _n_ ['æneks] (_also:_ _BRIT:_ **annexe**) edificio annesso ♦ _vt_ [ə'neks] annettere.

annexation [ænɛk'seɪʃən] _n_ annessione _f._

annihilate [ə'naɪəleɪt] _vt_ annientare.

annihilation [ənaɪə'leɪʃən] _n_ annientamento.

anniversary [ænɪ'vɜːsərɪ] _n_ anniversario.

anniversary dinner _n_ cena commemorativa.

annotate ['ænəuteɪt] _vt_ annotare.

announce [ə'nauns] _vt_ annunciare; **he** ~**d that he wasn't going** ha dichiarato che

non (ci) sarebbe andato.
announcement [ə'naunsmənt] n annuncio;
(*letter, card*) partecipazione *f*; **I'd like to
make an** ~ ho una comunicazione da fare.
announcer [ə'naunsə*] n (*RADIO, TV*:
between programmes) annunciatore/trice;
(: *in a programme*) presentatore/trice.
annoy [ə'nɔɪ] *vt* dare fastidio a; **to be ~ed
(at sth/with sb)** essere seccato *or* irritato
(per qc/con qn); **don't get ~ed!** non
irritarti!
annoyance [ə'nɔɪəns] n fastidio; (*cause of*
~) noia.
annoying [ə'nɔɪɪŋ] *adj* irritante,
seccante.
annual ['ænjuəl] *adj* annuale ♦ n (*BOT*)
pianta annua; (*book*) annuario.
annual general meeting (AGM) n (*BRIT*)
assemblea generale.
annually ['ænjuəlɪ] *adv* annualmente.
annual report n relazione *f* annuale.
annuity [ə'njuːɪtɪ] n annualità *f inv*; **life** ~
vitalizio.
annul [ə'nʌl] *vt* annullare; (*law*) rescindere.
annulment [ə'nʌlmənt] n annullamento;
rescissione *f*.
annum ['ænəm] n *see* **per annum**.
Annunciation [ənʌnsɪ'eɪʃən] n
Annunciazione *f*.
anode ['ænəud] n anodo.
anoint [ə'nɔɪnt] *vt* ungere.
anomalous [ə'nɔmələs] *adj* anomalo(a).
anomaly [ə'nɔməlɪ] n anomalia.
anon. [ə'nɔn] *abbr* = **anonymous**.
anonymity [ænə'nɪmɪtɪ] n anonimato.
anonymous [ə'nɔnɪməs] *adj* anonimo(a); **to
remain** ~ mantenere l'anonimato.
anorak ['ænəræk] n giacca a vento.
anorexia [ænə'rɛksɪə] n (*also*: ~ **nervosa**)
anoressia.
anorexic [ænə'rɛksɪk] *adj, n* anoressico(a).
another [ə'nʌðə*] *adj*: ~ **book** (*one more*)
un altro libro, ancora un libro; (*a
different one*) un altro libro ♦ *pron* un
altro(un'altra), ancora uno(a); ~ **drink?**
ancora qualcosa da bere?; **in** ~ **5 years**
fra altri 5 anni; *see also* **one.**
ANSI n *abbr* (= *American National Standards
Institution*) Istituto americano di
standardizzazione.
answer ['ɑːnsə*] n risposta; soluzione *f* ♦ *vi*
rispondere ♦ *vt* (*reply to*) rispondere a;
(*problem*) risolvere; (*prayer*) esaudire; **in**
~ **to your letter** in risposta alla sua
lettera; **to** ~ **the phone** rispondere (al
telefono); **to** ~ **the bell** rispondere al
campanello; **to** ~ **the door** aprire la
porta.

▶**answer back** *vi* ribattere.
▶**answer for** *vt fus* essere responsabile di.
▶**answer to** *vt fus* (*description*)
corrispondere a.
answerable ['ɑːnsərəbl] *adj*: ~ **(to sb/for
sth)** responsabile (verso qn/di qc); **I am** ~
to no one non devo rispondere a
nessuno.
answering machine ['ɑːnsərɪŋ-] n
segreteria (telefonica) automatica.
ant [ænt] n formica.
ANTA n *abbr* = *American National Theater and
Academy.*
antagonism [æn'tægənɪzəm] n
antagonismo.
antagonist [æn'tægənɪst] n antagonista *m/f*.
antagonistic [æntægə'nɪstɪk] *adj*
antagonistico(a).
antagonize [æn'tægənaɪz] *vt* provocare
l'ostilità di.
Antarctic [æn'ɑːktɪk] n: **the** ~ l'Antartide *f*
♦ *adj* antartico(a).
Antarctica [æn'ɑːktɪkə] n Antartide *f*.
Antarctic Circle n Circolo polare
antartico.
Antarctic Ocean n Oceano antartico.
ante ['æntɪ] n (*CARDS, fig*): **to up the** ~
alzare la posta in palio.
ante... ['æntɪ] *prefix* anti..., ante..., pre....
anteater ['ænti:tə*] n formichiere *m*.
antecedent [æntɪ'siːdənt] n antecedente *m*,
precedente *m*.
antechamber ['æntɪtʃeɪmbə*] n
anticamera.
antelope ['æntɪləup] n antilope *f*.
antenatal ['æntɪ'neɪtl] *adj* prenatale.
antenatal clinic n assistenza medica
preparto.
antenna, *pl* **antennae** [æn'tɛnə, -niː] n
antenna.
anthem ['ænθəm] n antifona; **national** ~
inno nazionale.
ant-hill ['ænthɪl] n formicaio.
anthology [æn'θɔlədʒɪ] n antologia.
anthropologist [ænθrə'pɔlədʒɪst] n
antropologo/a.
anthropology [ænθrə'pɔlədʒɪ] n
antropologia.
anti- ['æntɪ] *prefix* anti....
anti-aircraft ['æntɪ'ɛəkrɑːft] *adj*
antiaereo(a).
anti-aircraft defence n difesa antiaerea.
antiballistic ['æntɪbə'lɪstɪk] *adj*
antibalistico(a).
antibiotic ['æntɪbaɪ'ɔtɪk] *adj* antibiotico(a)
♦ n antibiotico.
antibody ['æntɪbɔdɪ] n anticorpo.
anticipate [æn'tɪsɪpeɪt] *vt* prevedere;

pregustare; (*wishes, request*) prevenire;
as ~d come previsto; **this is worse than I**
~d è peggio di quel che immaginavo *or*
pensavo.
anticipation [æntɪsɪ'peɪʃən] *n* anticipazione
f; (*expectation*) aspettative *fpl*; **thanking
you in** ~ vi ringrazio in anticipo.
anticlimax ['æntɪ'klaɪmæks] *n*: **it was an** ~
fu una completa delusione.
anticlockwise ['æntɪ'klɔkwaɪz] *adj* in senso
antiorario.
antics ['æntɪks] *npl* buffonerie *fpl*.
anticyclone ['æntɪ'saɪkləun] *n* anticiclone
m.
antidote ['æntɪdəut] *n* antidoto.
antifreeze ['æntɪfriːz] *n* anticongelante *m*.
antihistamine [æntɪ'hɪstəmɪn] *n*
antistaminico.
Antilles [æn'tɪliːz] *npl*: **the** ~ le Antille.
antipathy [æn'tɪpəθɪ] *n* antipatia.
antiperspirant ['æntɪ'pəːspərənt] *adj*
antitraspirante.
Antipodean [æntɪpə'diːən] *adj* degli
Antipodi.
Antipodes [æn'tɪpədiːz] *npl*: **the** ~ gli
Antipodi.
antiquarian [æntɪ'kwɛərɪən] *adj*: ~
bookshop libreria antiquaria ♦ *n*
antiquario/a.
antiquated ['æntɪkweɪtɪd] *adj* antiquato(a).
antique [æn'tiːk] *n* antichità *f inv* ♦ *adj*
antico(a).
antique dealer *n* antiquario/a.
antique shop *n* negozio d'antichità.
antiquity [æn'tɪkwɪtɪ] *n* antichità *f inv*.
anti-semitic ['æntɪsɪ'mɪtɪk] *adj*
antisemitico(a), antisemita.
anti-semitism ['æntɪ'sɛmɪtɪzəm] *n*
antisemitismo.
antiseptic [æntɪ'sɛptɪk] *adj* antisettico(a)
♦ *n* antisettico.
antisocial ['æntɪ'səuʃəl] *adj* asociale;
(*against society*) antisociale.
antitank [æntɪ'tæŋk] *adj* anticarro *inv*.
antithesis, *pl* **antitheses** [æn'tɪθɪsɪs, -siːz]
n antitesi *f inv*; (*contrast*) carattere *m*
antitetico.
anti-trust [æntɪ'trʌst] *adj* (*COMM*): ~
legislation legislazione *f* antitrust *inv*.
antlers ['æntləz] *npl* palchi *mpl*.
Antwerp ['æntwəːp] *n* Anversa.
anus ['eɪnəs] *n* ano.
anvil ['ænvɪl] *n* incudine *f*.
anxiety [æŋ'zaɪətɪ] *n* ansia; (*keenness*): ~ **to
do** smania di fare.
anxious ['æŋkʃəs] *adj* ansioso(a),
inquieto(a); (*keen*): ~ **to do/that**
impaziente di fare/che + *sub*; **I'm very** ~

about you sono molto preoccupato *or* in
pensiero per te.
anxiously ['æŋkʃəslɪ] *adv* ansiosamente,
con ansia.

═══════════════════════ **KEYWORD**

any ['ɛnɪ] *adj* **1** (*in questions etc*): **have you** ~
butter? hai del burro?, hai un po' di
burro?; **have you** ~ **children?** hai
bambini?; **if there are** ~ **tickets left** se ci
sono ancora (dei) biglietti, se c'è ancora
qualche biglietto
2 (*with negative*): **I haven't** ~ **money/
books** non ho soldi/libri; **without** ~
difficulty senza nessuna *or* alcuna
difficoltà
3 (*no matter which*) qualsiasi, qualunque;
choose ~ **book you like** scegli un libro
qualsiasi
4 (*in phrases*): **in** ~ **case** in ogni caso; ~
day now da un giorno all'altro; **at** ~
moment in qualsiasi momento, da un
momento all'altro; **at** ~ **rate** ad ogni
modo
♦ *pron* **1** (*in questions, with negative*): **have
you got** ~**?** ne hai?; **can** ~ **of you sing?**
qualcuno di voi sa cantare?; **I haven't** ~
(of them) non ne ho
2 (*no matter which one(s)*): **take** ~ **of those
books (you like)** prendi uno qualsiasi di
quei libri
♦ *adv* **1** (*in questions etc*): **do you want** ~
more soup/sandwiches? vuoi ancora un
po' di minestra/degli altri panini?; **are
you feeling** ~ **better?** ti senti meglio?
2 (*with negative*): **I can't hear him** ~ **more**
non lo sento più; **don't wait** ~ **longer** non
aspettare più.

═══════════════════════════════════

anybody ['ɛnɪbɔdɪ] *pron* qualsiasi persona;
(*in interrogative sentences*) qualcuno; (*in
negative sentences*): **I don't see** ~ non vedo
nessuno.
anyhow ['ɛnɪhau] *adv* in qualsiasi modo;
(*haphazard*) come capita; **I shall go** ~ ci
andrò lo stesso *or* comunque.
anyone ['ɛnɪwʌn] *pron* = **anybody**.
anyplace ['ɛnɪpleɪs] *pron* (*US col*)
= **anywhere**.
anything ['ɛnɪθɪŋ] *pron* qualsiasi cosa; (*in
interrogative sentences*) qualcosa; (*in
negative sentences*) non ... niente, non ...
nulla; ~ **else?** (*in shop*) basta (così)?; **it
can cost** ~ **between £15 and £20** può
costare qualcosa come 15 o 20 sterline.
anytime ['ɛnɪtaɪm] *adv* in qualunque
momento; quando vuole.
anyway ['ɛnɪweɪ] *adv* in *or* ad ogni modo.

anywhere ['ɛnɪwɛə*] adv da qualsiasi parte; (in interrogative sentences) da qualche parte; **I don't see him** ~ non lo vedo da nessuna parte; ~ **in the world** dovunque nel mondo.

Anzac ['ænzæk] n abbr (= Australia-New Zealand Army Corps) A.N.Z.A.C. m.

Anzac Day n see boxed note.

ANZAC DAY

L'**Anzac Day** è una festa nazionale australiana e neozelandese che cade il 25 aprile e commemora il famoso sbarco delle forze armate congiunte dei due paesi a Gallipoli nel 1915, durante la prima guerra mondiale.

---

apart [ə'pɑːt] adv (to one side) a parte; (separately) separatamente; **with one's legs** ~ con le gambe divaricate; **10 miles/a long way** ~ a 10 miglia di distanza/molto lontani l'uno dall'altro; **they are living** ~ sono separati; ~ **from** prep a parte, eccetto.

apartheid [ə'pɑːteɪt] n apartheid f.

apartment [ə'pɑːtmənt] n (US) appartamento; ~**s** npl appartamento ammobiliato.

apartment building n (US) stabile m, caseggiato.

apathetic [æpə'θɛtɪk] adj apatico(a).

apathy ['æpəθɪ] n apatia.

APB n abbr (US: = all points bulletin: police expression) espressione della polizia che significa "trovate e arrestate il sospetto".

ape [eɪp] n scimmia ♦ vt scimmiottare.

Apennines ['æpənaɪnz] npl: **the** ~ gli Apennini.

aperitif [ə'pɛrɪtiːf] n aperitivo.

aperture ['æpətʃjuə*] n apertura.

APEX ['eɪpɛks] n abbr (AVIAT: = advance purchase excursion) APEX m inv.

apex ['eɪpɛks] n apice m.

aphrodisiac [æfrəʊ'dɪzɪæk] adj afrodisiaco(a) ♦ n afrodisiaco.

API n abbr = American Press Institute.

apiece [ə'piːs] adv ciascuno(a).

aplomb [ə'plɔm] n disinvoltura.

APO n abbr (US: = Army Post Office) ufficio postale dell'esercito.

apocalypse [ə'pɔkəlɪps] n apocalisse f.

apolitical [eɪpə'lɪtɪkl] adj apolitico(a).

apologetic [əpɔlə'dʒɛtɪk] adj (tone, letter) di scusa; **to be very** ~ **about** scusarsi moltissimo di.

apologetically [əpɔlə'dʒɛtɪkəlɪ] adv per scusarsi.

apologize [ə'pɔlədʒaɪz] vi: **to** ~ **(for sth to sb)** scusarsi (di qc a qn), chiedere scusa (a qn per qc).

apology [ə'pɔlədʒɪ] n scuse fpl; **please accept my apologies** la prego di accettare le mie scuse.

apoplectic [æpə'plɛktɪk] adj (MED) apoplettico(a); ~ **with rage** (col) livido(a) per la rabbia.

apoplexy ['æpəplɛksɪ] n apoplessia.

apostle [ə'pɔsl] n apostolo.

apostrophe [ə'pɔstrəfɪ] n (sign) apostrofo.

appal [ə'pɔːl] vt atterrire; sgomentare.

Appalachian Mountains [æpə'leɪʃən-] npl: **the** ~ i Monti Appalachi.

appalling [ə'pɔːlɪŋ] adj spaventoso(a); **she's an** ~ **cook** è un disastro come cuoca.

apparatus [æpə'reɪtəs] n apparato.

apparel [ə'pærl] n (US) abbigliamento, confezioni fpl.

apparent [ə'pærənt] adj evidente.

apparently [ə'pærəntlɪ] adv evidentemente, a quanto pare.

apparition [æpə'rɪʃən] n apparizione f.

appeal [ə'piːl] vi (LAW) appellarsi alla legge ♦ n (LAW) appello; (request) richiesta; (charm) attrattiva; **to** ~ **for** chiedere (con insistenza); **to** ~ **to** (subj: person) appellarsi a; (: thing) piacere a; **to** ~ **to sb for mercy** chiedere pietà a qn; **it doesn't** ~ **to me** mi dice poco; **right of** ~ diritto d'appello.

appealing [ə'piːlɪŋ] adj (moving) commovente; (attractive) attraente.

appear [ə'pɪə*] vi apparire; (LAW) comparire; (publication) essere pubblicato(a); (seem) sembrare; **it would** ~ **that** sembra che; **to** ~ **in Hamlet** recitare nell'Amleto; **to** ~ **on TV** presentarsi in televisione.

appearance [ə'pɪərəns] n apparizione f; (look, aspect) aspetto; **to put in** or **make an** ~ fare atto di presenza; **by order of** ~ (THEAT) in ordine di apparizione; **to keep up** ~**s** salvare le apparenze; **to all** ~**s** a giudicar dalle apparenze.

appease [ə'piːz] vt calmare, appagare.

appeasement [ə'piːzmənt] n (POL) appeasement m inv.

append [ə'pɛnd] vt (COMPUT) aggiungere in coda.

appendage [ə'pɛndɪdʒ] n aggiunta.

appendicitis [əpɛndɪ'saɪtɪs] n appendicite f.

appendix, pl **appendices** [ə'pɛndɪks, -siːz] n appendice f; **to have one's** ~ **out** operarsi or farsi operare di appendicite.

appetite ['æpɪtaɪt] n appetito; **that walk has given me an** ~ la passeggiata mi ha messo appetito.

appetizer ['æpɪtaɪzə*] *n* (*food*) stuzzichino; (*drink*) aperitivo.

appetizing ['æpɪtaɪzɪŋ] *adj* appetitoso(a).

applaud [ə'plɔːd] *vt, vi* applaudire.

applause [ə'plɔːz] *n* applauso.

apple ['æpl] *n* mela; (*also:* ~ **tree**) melo; **the** ~ **of one's eye** la pupilla dei propri occhi.

apple turnover *n* sfogliatella alle mele.

appliance [ə'plaɪəns] *n* apparecchio; **electrical** ~**s** elettrodomestici *mpl*.

applicable [ə'plɪkəbl] *adj* applicabile; **to be** ~ **to** essere valido per; **the law is** ~ **from January** la legge entrerà in vigore in gennaio.

applicant ['æplɪkənt] *n* candidato/a; (*ADMIN*: *for benefit etc*) chi ha fatto domanda *or* richiesta.

application [æplɪ'keɪʃən] *n* applicazione *f*; (*for a job, a grant etc*) domanda; **on** ~ su richiesta.

application form *n* modulo di domanda.

application program *n* (*COMPUT*) programma applicativo.

applications package *n* (*COMPUT*) software *m inv* applicativo.

applied [ə'plaɪd] *adj* applicato(a); ~ **arts** arti *fpl* applicate.

apply [ə'plaɪ] *vt*: **to** ~ (**to**) (*paint, ointment*) dare (a); (*theory, technique*) applicare (a) ♦ *vi*: **to** ~ **to** (*ask*) rivolgersi a; (*be suitable for, relevant to*) riguardare, riferirsi a; **to** ~ (**for**) (*permit, grant, job*) fare domanda (per); **to** ~ **the brakes** frenare; **to** ~ **o.s. to** dedicarsi a.

appoint [ə'pɔɪnt] *vt* nominare.

appointee [əpɔɪn'tiː] *n* incaricato/a.

appointment [ə'pɔɪntmənt] *n* nomina; (*arrangement to meet*) appuntamento; **by** ~ su *or* per appuntamento; **to make an** ~ **with sb** prendere un appuntamento con qn; (*PRESS*): "~**s** (**vacant**)" "offerte *fpl* di impiego".

apportion [ə'pɔːʃən] *vt* attribuire.

appraisal [ə'preɪzl] *n* valutazione *f*.

appraise [ə'preɪz] *vt* (*value*) valutare, fare una stima di; (*situation etc*) fare il bilancio di.

appreciable [ə'priːʃəbl] *adj* apprezzabile.

appreciably [ə'priːʃəblɪ] *adv* notevolmente, sensibilmente.

appreciate [ə'priːʃɪeɪt] *vt* (*like*) apprezzare; (*be grateful for*) essere riconoscente di; (*be aware of*) rendersi conto di ♦ *vi* (*COMM*) aumentare; **I** ~**d your help** ti sono grato per l'aiuto.

appreciation [əpriːʃɪ'eɪʃən] *n* apprezzamento; (*FINANCE*) aumento del

valore.

appreciative [ə'priːʃɪətɪv] *adj* (*person*) sensibile; (*comment*) elogiativo(a).

apprehend [æprɪ'hɛnd] *vt* (*arrest*) arrestare; (*understand*) comprendere.

apprehension [æprɪ'hɛnʃən] *n* (*fear*) inquietudine *f*.

apprehensive [æprɪ'hɛnsɪv] *adj* apprensivo(a).

apprentice [ə'prɛntɪs] *n* apprendista *m/f* ♦ *vt*: **to be** ~**d to** lavorare come apprendista presso.

apprenticeship [ə'prɛntɪsʃɪp] *n* apprendistato; **to serve one's** ~ fare il proprio apprendistato *or* tirocinio.

appro. ['æprəu] *abbr* (*BRIT COMM*: *col*) = **approval.**

approach [ə'prəutʃ] *vi* avvicinarsi ♦ *vt* (*come near*) avvicinarsi a; (*ask, apply to*) rivolgersi a; (*subject, passer-by*) avvicinare ♦ *n* approccio; accesso; (*to problem*) modo di affrontare; **to** ~ **sb about sth** rivolgersi a qn per qc.

approachable [ə'prəutʃəbl] *adj* accessibile.

approach road *n* strada d'accesso.

approbation [æprə'beɪʃən] *n* approvazione *f*, benestare *m*.

appropriate *vt* [ə'prəuprɪeɪt] (*take*) appropriarsi di ♦ *adj* [ə'prəuprɪt] appropriato(a); adatto(a); **it would not be** ~ **for me to comment** non sta a me fare dei commenti.

appropriately [ə'prəuprɪtlɪ] *adv* in modo appropriato.

appropriation [əprəuprɪ'eɪʃən] *n* stanziamento.

approval [ə'pruːvəl] *n* approvazione *f*; **on** ~ (*COMM*) in prova, in esame; **to meet with sb's** ~ soddisfare qn, essere di gradimento di qn.

approve [ə'pruːv] *vt, vi* approvare.
▶**approve of** *vt fus* approvare.

approved school *n* (*BRIT*: *old*) riformatorio.

approvingly [ə'pruːvɪŋlɪ] *adv* in approvazione.

approx. *abbr* = **approximately.**

approximate *adj* [ə'prɒksɪmɪt] approssimativo(a) ♦ *vt* [ə'prɒksɪmeɪt] essere un'approssimazione di, avvicinarsi a.

approximately [ə'prɒksɪmətlɪ] *adv* circa.

approximation [əprɒksɪ'meɪʃən] *n* approssimazione *f*.

apr *n abbr* (= *annual percentage rate*) tasso di percentuale annuo.

Apr. *abbr* (= *April*) apr.

apricot ['eɪprɪkɔt] *n* albicocca.

April ['eɪprəl] n aprile m; ~ **fool!** pesce d'aprile!; *for phrases see also* **July.**
April Fools' Day n *see boxed note.*

APRIL FOOLS' DAY

April Fools' Day *è il primo aprile, il giorno degli scherzi e delle burle. Il nome deriva dal fatto che, se una persona cade nella trappola che gli è stata tesa, fa la figura del* **fool**, *cioè dello sciocco. Di recente gli scherzi stanno diventando sempre più elaborati, e persino i giornalisti a volte inventano vicende incredibili per burlarsi dei lettori.*

---

apron ['eɪprən] n grembiule m; (*AVIAT*) area di stazionamento.
apse [æps] n (*ARCHIT*) abside f.
APT n abbr (*BRIT*: = advanced passenger train) treno ad altissima velocità.
apt [æpt] adj (*suitable*) adatto(a); (*able*) capace; (*likely*): **to be** ~ **to do** avere tendenza a fare.
Apt. abbr = **apartment.**
aptitude ['æptɪtjuːd] n abilità f inv.
aptitude test n test m inv attitudinale.
aptly ['æptlɪ] adv appropriatamente, in modo adatto.
aqualung ['ækwəlʌŋ] n autorespiratore m.
aquarium [ə'kwɛərɪəm] n acquario.
Aquarius [ə'kwɛərɪəs] n Acquario; **to be** ~ essere dell'Acquario.
aquatic [ə'kwætɪk] adj acquatico(a).
aqueduct ['ækwɪdʌkt] n acquedotto.
AR abbr (*US*) = Arkansas.
ARA n abbr (*BRIT*) = Associate of the Royal Academy.
Arab ['ærəb] adj, n arabo(a).
Arabia [ə'reɪbɪə] n Arabia.
Arabian [ə'reɪbɪən] adj arabo(a).
Arabian Desert n Deserto arabico.
Arabian Sea n mare m Arabico.
Arabic ['ærəbɪk] adj arabico(a) ♦ n arabo.
Arabic numerals npl numeri arabi mpl, numerazione f araba.
arable ['ærəbl] adj arabile.
ARAM n abbr (*BRIT*) = Associate of the Royal Academy of Music.
arbitrary ['ɑːbɪtrərɪ] adj arbitrario(a).
arbitrate ['ɑːbɪtreɪt] vi arbitrare.
arbitration [ɑːbɪ'treɪʃən] n (*LAW*) arbitrato; (*INDUSTRY*) arbitraggio.
arbitrator ['ɑːbɪtreɪtə*] n arbitro.
ARC n abbr (= American Red Cross) C.R.I. f (= Croce Rossa Italiana).
arc [ɑːk] n arco.
arcade [ɑː'keɪd] n portico; (*passage with shops*) galleria.

arch [ɑːtʃ] n arco; (*of foot*) arco plantare ♦ vt inarcare ♦ prefix: ~(-) grande (*before n*); per eccellenza.
archaeological [ɑːkɪə'lɔdʒɪkəl] adj archeologico(a).
archaeologist [ɑːkɪ'ɔlədʒɪst] n archeologo/a.
archaeology [ɑːkɪ'ɔlədʒɪ] n archeologia.
archaic [ɑː'keɪɪk] adj arcaico(a).
archangel ['ɑːkeɪndʒəl] n arcangelo.
archbishop [ɑːtʃ'bɪʃəp] n arcivescovo.
arched [ɑːtʃt] adj arcuato(a), ad arco.
arch-enemy ['ɑːtʃ'enɪmɪ] n arcinemico/a.
archeology [ɑːkɪ'ɔlədʒɪ] etc = **archaeology** etc.
archer ['ɑːtʃə*] n arciere m.
archery ['ɑːtʃərɪ] n tiro all'arco.
archetypal ['ɑːkɪtaɪpəl] adj tipico(a).
archipelago [ɑːkɪ'pɛlɪgəu] n arcipelago.
architect ['ɑːkɪtɛkt] n architetto.
architectural [ɑːkɪ'tɛktʃərəl] adj architettonico(a).
architecture ['ɑːkɪtɛktʃə*] n architettura.
archive file n (*COMPUT*) file m inv di archivio.
archives ['ɑːkaɪvz] npl archivi mpl.
archivist ['ɑːkɪvɪst] n archivista m/f.
archway ['ɑːtʃweɪ] n arco.
ARCM n abbr (*BRIT*) = Associate of the Royal College of Music.
Arctic ['ɑːktɪk] adj artico(a) ♦ n: **the** ~ l'Artico.
Arctic Circle n Circolo polare artico.
Arctic Ocean n Oceano artico.
ARD n abbr (*US MED*) = acute respiratory disease.
ardent ['ɑːdənt] adj ardente.
ardour, (*US*) **ardor** ['ɑːdə*] n ardore m.
arduous ['ɑːdjuəs] adj arduo(a).
are [ɑː*] vb see **be.**
area ['ɛərɪə] n (*GEOM*) area; (*zone*) zona; (: *smaller*) settore m; **dining** ~ zona pranzo; **the London** ~ la zona di Londra.
area code n (*US TEL*) prefisso.
arena [ə'riːnə] n arena.
aren't [ɑːnt] = **are not.**
Argentina [ɑːdʒən'tiːnə] n Argentina.
Argentinian [ɑːdʒən'tɪnɪən] adj, n argentino(a).
arguable ['ɑːgjuəbl] adj discutibile; **it is** ~ **whether ...** è una cosa discutibile se ... + sub.
arguably ['ɑːgjuəblɪ] adv: **it is** ~ ... si può sostenere che sia ....
argue ['ɑːgjuː] vi (*quarrel*) litigare; (*reason*) ragionare ♦ vt (*debate: case, matter*) dibattere; **to** ~ **that** sostenere che; **to** ~ **about sth (with sb)** litigare per or a

proposito di qc (con qn).
argument ['ɑːgjumənt] *n (reasons)*
argomento; *(quarrel)* lite *f*; *(debate)*
discussione *f*; ~ **for/against** argomento a
or in favore di/contro.
argumentative [ɑːgjuˈmɛntətɪv] *adj*
litigioso(a).
aria ['ɑːrɪə] *n* aria.
ARIBA *n abbr (BRIT)* = *Associate of the Royal
Institute of British Architects.*
arid ['ærɪd] *adj* arido(a).
aridity [əˈrɪdɪtɪ] *n* aridità.
Aries ['ɛərɪz] *n* Ariete *m*; **to be** ~ essere
dell'Ariete.
arise, *pt* **arose**, *pp* **arisen** [əˈraɪz, əˈrəʊz,
əˈrɪzn] *vi* alzarsi; *(opportunity, problem)*
presentarsi; **to** ~ **from** risultare da;
should the need ~ dovesse presentarsi la
necessità, in caso di necessità.
aristocracy [ærɪsˈtɒkrəsɪ] *n* aristocrazia.
aristocrat ['ærɪstəkræt] *n* aristocratico/a.
aristocratic [ærɪstəˈkrætɪk] *adj*
aristocratico(a).
arithmetic [əˈrɪθmətɪk] *n* aritmetica.
arithmetical [ærɪθˈmɛtɪkəl] *adj*
aritmetico(a).
Ariz. *abbr (US)* = *Arizona.*
ark [ɑːk] *n*: **Noah's A**~ l'arca di Noè.
Ark. *abbr (US)* = *Arkansas.*
arm [ɑːm] *n* braccio; *(MIL: branch)* arma ♦ *vt*
armare; ~ **in** ~ a braccetto; *see also* **arms.**
armaments ['ɑːməmənts] *npl (weapons)*
armamenti *mpl.*
armband ['ɑːmbænd] *n* bracciale *m.*
armchair ['ɑːmtʃɛə*] *n* poltrona.
armed [ɑːmd] *adj* armato(a).
armed forces *npl* forze *fpl* armate.
armed robbery *n* rapina a mano armata.
Armenia [ɑːˈmiːnɪə] *n* Armenia.
Armenian [ɑːˈmiːnɪən] *adj* armeno(a) ♦ *n*
armeno/a; *(LING)* armeno.
armful ['ɑːmful] *n* bracciata.
armistice ['ɑːmɪstɪs] *n* armistizio.
armour, *(US)* **armor** ['ɑːmə*] *n* armatura;
(also: ~-plating) corazza, blindatura; *(MIL:
tanks)* mezzi *mpl* blindati.
armo(u)red car *n* autoblinda *f inv.*
armo(u)ry ['ɑːmərɪ] *n* arsenale *m.*
armpit ['ɑːmpɪt] *n* ascella.
armrest ['ɑːmrɛst] *n* bracciolo.
arms [ɑːmz] *npl (weapons)* armi *fpl*;
(HERALDRY) stemma *m.*
arms control *n* controllo degli armamenti.
arms race *n* corsa agli armamenti.
army ['ɑːmɪ] *n* esercito.
aroma [əˈrəʊmə] *n* aroma.
aromatherapy [ərəʊməˈθɛrəpɪ] *n*
aromaterapia.

aromatic [ærəˈmætɪk] *adj* aromatico(a).
arose [əˈrəʊz] *pt of* **arise.**
around [əˈraʊnd] *adv* attorno, intorno ♦ *prep*
intorno a; *(fig: about)*: ~ **£5/3 o'clock** circa
5 sterline/le 3; **is he** ~? è in giro?
arousal [əˈrauzəl] *n (sexual etc)* eccitazione
f; *(awakening)* risveglio.
arouse [əˈrauz] *vt (sleeper)* svegliare;
(curiosity, passions) suscitare.
arrange [əˈreɪndʒ] *vt* sistemare;
(programme) preparare ♦ *vi*: **we have** ~**d**
for a taxi to pick you up la faremo venire
a prendere da un taxi; **it was** ~**d that** ... è
stato deciso *or* stabilito che ...; **to** ~ **to do**
sth mettersi d'accordo per fare qc.
arrangement [əˈreɪndʒmənt] *n*
sistemazione *f*; *(plans etc)*: ~**s** progetti
mpl, piani *mpl*; **by** ~ su richiesta; **to come**
to an ~ **(with sb)** venire ad un accordo
(con qn), mettersi d'accordo *or*
accordarsi (con qn); **I'll make** ~**s for you**
to be met darò disposizioni *or* istruzioni
perché ci sia qualcuno ad incontrarla.
arrant ['ærənt] *adj*: ~ **nonsense** colossali
sciocchezze *fpl.*
array [əˈreɪ] *n* fila; *(COMPUT)* array *m inv*,
insiemi *mpl.*
arrears [əˈrɪəz] *npl* arretrati *mpl*; **to be in** ~
with one's rent essere in arretrato con
l'affitto.
arrest [əˈrɛst] *vt* arrestare; *(sb's attention)*
attirare ♦ *n* arresto; **under** ~ in arresto.
arresting [əˈrɛstɪŋ] *adj (fig)* che colpisce.
arrival [əˈraɪvəl] *n* arrivo; *(person)*
arrivato/a; **new** ~ nuovo venuto.
arrive [əˈraɪv] *vi* arrivare.
▶**arrive at** *vt fus* arrivare a.
arrogance ['ærəgəns] *n* arroganza.
arrogant ['ærəgənt] *adj* arrogante.
arrow ['ærəu] *n* freccia.
arse [ɑːs] *n (BRIT col!)* culo(*!*).
arsenal ['ɑːsɪnl] *n* arsenale *m.*
arsenic ['ɑːsnɪk] *n* arsenico.
arson ['ɑːsn] *n* incendio doloso.
art [ɑːt] *n* arte *f*; *(craft)* mestiere *m*; **work of**
~ opera d'arte; *see also* **arts.**
artefact, *(US)* **artifact** ['ɑːtɪfækt] *n*
manufatto.
arterial [ɑːˈtɪərɪəl] *adj (ANAT)* arterioso(a);
(road etc) di grande comunicazione; ~
roads le (grandi *or* principali) arterie.
artery ['ɑːtərɪ] *n* arteria.
artful ['ɑːtful] *adj* furbo(a).
art gallery *n* galleria d'arte.
arthritis [ɑːˈθraɪtɪs] *n* artrite *f.*
artichoke ['ɑːtɪtʃəuk] *n* carciofo; **Jerusalem**
~ topinambur *m inv.*
article ['ɑːtɪkl] *n* articolo; ~**s** *npl (BRIT LAW:*

training) contratto di tirocinio; ~s of clothing indumenti *mpl.*

articles of association *npl* (*COMM*) statuto sociale.

articulate *adj* [ɑː'tɪkjulɪt] (*person*) che si esprime forbitamente; (*speech*) articolato(a) ♦ *vi* [ɑː'tɪkjuleɪt] articolare.

articulated lorry *n* (*BRIT*) autotreno.

artifact ['ɑːtɪfækt] *n* (*US*) = artefact.

artifice ['ɑːtɪfɪs] *n* (*cunning*) abilità, destrezza; (*trick*) artificio.

artificial [ɑːtɪ'fɪʃəl] *adj* artificiale.

artificial insemination [-ɪnsɛmɪ'neɪʃən] *n* fecondazione *f* artificiale.

artificial intelligence (AI) *n* intelligenza artificiale (IA).

artificial respiration *n* respirazione *f* artificiale.

artillery [ɑː'tɪlərɪ] *n* artiglieria.

artisan ['ɑːtɪzæn] *n* artigiano/a.

artist ['ɑːtɪst] *n* artista *m/f.*

artistic [ɑː'tɪstɪk] *adj* artistico(a).

artistry ['ɑːtɪstrɪ] *n* arte *f*

artless ['ɑːtlɪs] *adj* semplice, ingenuo(a).

arts [ɑːts] *npl* (*SCOL*) lettere *fpl.*

art school *n* scuola d'arte.

artwork ['ɑːtwɔːk] *n* materiale *m* illustrativo.

ARV *n abbr* (= *American Revised Version*) *traduzione della Bibbia.*

AS *n abbr* (*US SCOL*: = *Associate in/of Sciences*) *titolo di studio* ♦ *abbr* (*US*) = *American Samoa.*

========================= KEYWORD

as [æz] *conj* 1 (*referring to time*) mentre; ~ the years went by col passare degli anni; he came in ~ I was leaving arrivò mentre stavo uscendo; ~ from tomorrow da domani

2 (*in comparisons*): ~ big ~ grande come; twice ~ big ~ due volte più grande di; ~ much/many ~ tanto quanto/tanti quanti; ~ soon ~ possible prima possibile

3 (*since, because*) dal momento che, siccome

4 (*referring to manner, way*) come; big ~ it is grande com'è; much ~ I like them, ... per quanto mi siano simpatici, ...; do ~ you wish fa' come vuoi; ~ she said come ha detto lei

5 (*concerning*): ~ for *or* to that per quanto riguarda *or* quanto a quello

6: ~ if *or* though come se; he looked ~ if he was ill sembrava stare male; *see also* long; such; well

♦ *prep*: he works ~ a driver fa l'autista; ~ chairman of the company, he ... come

presidente della compagnia, lui ...; he gave me it ~ a present me lo ha regalato.

ASA *n abbr* (= *American Standards Association*) *associazione per la normalizzazione.*

a.s.a.p. *abbr* (= *as soon as possible*) prima possibile.

asbestos [æz'bɛstəs] *n* asbesto, amianto.

ascend [ə'sɛnd] *vt* salire.

ascendancy [ə'sɛndənsɪ] *n* ascendente *m.*

ascendant [ə'sɛndənt] *n*: to be in the ~ essere in auge.

ascension [ə'sɛnʃən] *n*: the A~ (*REL*) l'Ascensione *f.*

Ascension Island *n* isola dell'Ascensione.

ascent [ə'sɛnt] *n* salita.

ascertain [æsə'teɪn] *vt* accertare.

ascetic [ə'sɛtɪk] *adj* ascetico(a).

asceticism [ə'sɛtɪsɪzəm] *n* ascetismo.

ASCII ['æskiː] *n abbr* (= *American Standard Code for Information Interchange*) ASCII *m.*

ascribe [ə'skraɪb] *vt*: to ~ sth to attribuire qc a.

ASCU *n abbr* (*US*) = *Association of State Colleges and Universities.*

ASE *n abbr* = *American Stock Exchange.*

ASH [æʃ] *n abbr* (*BRIT*: = *Action on Smoking and Health*) *iniziativa contro il fumo.*

ash [æʃ] *n* (*dust*) cenere *f*; ~ (tree) frassino.

ashamed [ə'ʃeɪmd] *adj* vergognoso(a); to be ~ of vergognarsi di; to be ~ (of o.s.) for having done vergognarsi di aver fatto.

ashen ['æʃən] *adj* (*pale*) livido(a).

ashore [ə'ʃɔː*] *adv* a terra; to go ~ sbarcare.

ashtray ['æʃtreɪ] *n* portacenere *m.*

Ash Wednesday *n* Mercoledì *m inv* delle Ceneri.

Asia Minor *n* Asia minore.

Asian ['eɪʃən] *adj*, *n* asiatico(a).

Asiatic [eɪsɪ'ætɪk] *adj* asiatico(a).

aside [ə'saɪd] *adv* da parte ♦ *n* a parte *m*; to take sb ~ prendere qn da parte; ~ from (*as well as*) oltre a; (*except for*) a parte.

ask [ɑːsk] *vt* (*request*) chiedere; (*question*) domandare; (*invite*) invitare; to ~ about sth informarsi su *or* di qc; to ~ sb sth/sb to do sth chiedere qc a qn/a qn di fare qc; to ~ sb about sth chiedere a qn di qc; to ~ (sb) a question fare una domanda (a qn); to ~ sb the time chiedere l'ora a qn; to ~ sb out to dinner invitare qn a mangiare fuori; you should ~ at the information desk dovreste rivolgervi all'ufficio informazioni.

▶ask after *vt fus* chiedere di.

▶ask for vt fus chiedere; it's just ~ing for trouble or for it è proprio (come) andarsele a cercare.

askance [ə'skɑːns] adv: to look ~ at sb guardare qn di traverso.

askew [ə'skjuː] adv di traverso, storto.

asking price ['ɑːskɪŋ-] n prezzo di partenza.

asleep [ə'sliːp] adj addormentato(a); to be ~ dormire; to fall ~ addormentarsi.

ASLEF ['æzlɛf] n abbr (BRIT: = Associated Society of Locomotive Engineers and Firemen) sindacato dei conducenti dei treni e dei macchinisti.

asp [æsp] n cobra m inv egiziano.

asparagus [əs'pærəgəs] n asparagi mpl.

asparagus tips npl punte fpl d'asparagi.

ASPCA n abbr (= American Society for the Prevention of Cruelty to Animals) ≈ E.N.P.A. m (Ente Nazionale per la Protezione degli Animali).

aspect ['æspɛkt] n aspetto.

aspersions [əs'pəːʃənz] npl: to cast ~ on diffamare.

asphalt ['æsfælt] n asfalto.

asphyxiate [æs'fɪksɪeɪt] vt asfissiare.

asphyxiation [æsfɪksɪ'eɪʃən] n asfissia.

aspiration [æspə'reɪʃən] n aspirazione f.

aspire [əs'paɪə*] vi: to ~ to aspirare a.

aspirin ['æsprɪn] n aspirina.

aspiring [əs'paɪərɪŋ] adj aspirante.

ass [æs] n asino; (US col!) culo(!).

assail [ə'seɪl] vt assalire.

assailant [ə'seɪlənt] n assalitore m.

assassin [ə'sæsɪn] n assassino.

assassinate [ə'sæsɪneɪt] vt assassinare.

assassination [əsæsɪ'neɪʃən] n assassinio.

assault [ə'sɔːlt] n (MIL) assalto; (gen: attack) aggressione f; (LAW): ~ (and battery) minacce e vie di fatto fpl ♦ vt assaltare; aggredire; (sexually) violentare.

assemble [ə'sɛmbl] vt riunire; (TECH) montare ♦ vi riunirsi.

assembly [ə'sɛmblɪ] n (meeting) assemblea; (construction) montaggio.

assembly language n (COMPUT) linguaggio assemblativo.

assembly line n catena di montaggio.

assent [ə'sɛnt] n assenso, consenso ♦ vi assentire; to ~ (to sth) approvare (qc).

assert [ə'səːt] vt asserire; (insist on) far valere; to ~ o.s. farsi valere.

assertion [ə'səːʃən] n asserzione f.

assertive [ə'səːtɪv] adj che sa imporsi.

assess [ə'sɛs] vt valutare.

assessment [ə'sɛsmənt] n valutazione f; (judgment): ~ (of) giudizio (su).

assessor [ə'sɛsə*] n perito; funzionario del fisco.

asset ['æsɛt] n vantaggio; (person) elemento prezioso; ~s npl (COMM) beni mpl; disponibilità fpl; attivo.

asset-stripping ['æsɛt'strɪpɪŋ] n (COMM) acquisto di una società in fallimento con lo scopo di rivenderne le attività.

assiduous [ə'sɪdjuəs] adj assiduo(a).

assign [ə'saɪn] vt: to ~ (to) (task) assegnare (a); (resources) riservare (a); (cause, meaning) attribuire (a); to ~ a date to sth fissare la data di qc.

assignment [ə'saɪnmənt] n compito.

assimilate [ə'sɪmɪleɪt] vt assimilare.

assimilation [əsɪmɪ'leɪʃən] n assimilazione f.

assist [ə'sɪst] vt assistere, aiutare.

assistance [ə'sɪstəns] n assistenza, aiuto.

assistant [ə'sɪstənt] n assistente m/f; (BRIT: also: shop ~) commesso/a.

assistant manager n vicedirettore m.

assizes [ə'saɪzɪz] npl assise fpl.

associate [ə'səʊʃɪɪt] adj associato(a); (member) aggiunto(a) ♦ n collega m/f; (in business) socio/a ♦ vb [ə'səʊʃɪeɪt] vt associare ♦ vi: to ~ with sb frequentare qn.

associated company [ə'səʊsɪ'eɪtɪd-] n società collegata.

associate director n amministratore m aggiunto.

association [əsəʊsɪ'eɪʃən] n associazione f; in ~ with in collaborazione con.

association football n (BRIT) (gioco del) calcio.

assorted [ə'sɔːtɪd] adj assortito(a); in ~ sizes in diverse taglie.

assortment [ə'sɔːtmənt] n assortimento.

Asst. abbr = assistant.

assuage [ə'sweɪdʒ] vt alleviare.

assume [ə'sjuːm] vt supporre; (responsibilities etc) assumere; (attitude, name) prendere.

assumed name n nome m falso.

assumption [ə'sʌmpʃən] n supposizione f, ipotesi f inv; on the ~ that ... partendo dal presupposto che ....

assurance [ə'ʃʊərəns] n assicurazione f; (self-confidence) fiducia in se stesso; I can give you no ~s non posso assicurarle or garantirle niente.

assure [ə'ʃʊə*] vt assicurare.

assured [ə'ʃʊəd] adj (confident) sicuro(a); (certain: promotion etc) assicurato(a).

AST abbr (US: = Atlantic Standard Time) ora invernale di New York.

asterisk ['æstərɪsk] n asterisco.

astern [ə'stəːn] adv a poppa.

asteroid ['æstərɔɪd] n asteroide m.
asthma ['æsmə] n asma.
asthmatic [æs'mætɪk] adj, n asmatico(a).
astigmatism [ə'stɪgmətɪzəm] n
astigmatismo.
astir [ə'stəː*] adv in piedi; (excited) in
fermento.
astonish [ə'stɔnɪʃ] vt stupire.
astonishing [ə'stɔnɪʃɪŋ] adj sorprendente,
stupefacente; I find it ~ that ... mi
stupisce che ....
astonishingly [ə'stɔnɪʃɪŋlɪ] adv
straordinariamente, incredibilmente.
astonishment [ə'stɔnɪʃmənt] n stupore m;
to my ~ con mia gran meraviglia, con
mio grande stupore.
astound [ə'staund] vt sbalordire.
astray [ə'streɪ] adv: to go ~ smarrirsi; (fig)
traviarsi; to go ~ in one's calculations
sbagliare i calcoli.
astride [ə'straɪd] adv a cavalcioni ♦ prep a
cavalcioni di.
astringent [əs'trɪndʒənt] adj, n astringente
(m).
astrologer [əs'trɔlədʒə*] n astrologo/a.
astrology [əs'trɔlədʒɪ] n astrologia.
astronaut ['æstrənɔːt] n astronauta m/f.
astronomer [əs'trɔnəmə*] n astronomo/a.
astronomical [æstrə'nɔmɪkl] adj
astronomico(a).
astronomy [əs'trɔnəmɪ] n astronomia.
astrophysics ['æstrou'fɪzɪks] n astrofisica.
astute [əs'tjuːt] adj astuto(a).
asunder [ə'sʌndə*] adv: to tear ~
strappare.
ASV n abbr (= American Standard Version)
traduzione della Bibbia.
asylum [ə'saɪləm] n asilo; (lunatic ~)
manicomio; to seek political ~ chiedere
asilo politico.
asymmetric(al) [eɪsɪ'mɛtrɪk(əl)] adj
asimmetrico(a).

=============== **KEYWORD**

at [æt] prep **1** (referring to position, direction)
a; ~ the top in cima; ~ the desk al banco,
alla scrivania; ~ home/school a casa/
scuola; ~ Paolo's da Paolo; ~ the baker's
dal panettiere; to look ~ sth guardare qc;
to throw sth ~ sb lanciare qc a qn
2 (referring to time) a; ~ 4 o'clock alle 4; ~
night di notte; ~ Christmas a Natale; ~
times a volte
3 (referring to rates, speed etc) a; ~ £1 a
kilo a 1 sterlina al chilo; two ~ a time
due alla volta, due per volta; ~ 50 km/h a
50 km/h; ~ full speed a tutta velocità
4 (referring to manner): ~ a stroke d'un

solo colpo; ~ peace in pace
5 (referring to activity): to be ~ work
essere al lavoro; to play ~ cowboys
giocare ai cowboy; to be good ~ sth/
doing sth essere bravo in qc/a fare qc
6 (referring to cause): shocked/surprised/
annoyed ~ sth colpito da/sorpreso da/
arrabbiato per qc; I went ~ his
suggestion ci sono andato dietro suo
consiglio.

ate [eɪt] pt of eat.
atheism ['eɪθɪɪzəm] n ateismo.
atheist ['eɪθɪɪst] n ateo/a.
Athenian [ə'θiːnɪən] adj, n ateniese (m/f).
Athens ['æθɪnz] n Atene f.
athlete ['æθliːt] n atleta m/f.
athletic [æθ'lɛtɪk] adj atletico(a).
athletics [æθ'lɛtɪks] n atletica.
Atlantic [ət'læntɪk] adj atlantico(a) ♦ n: the
~ (Ocean) l'Atlantico, l'Oceano Atlantico.
atlas ['ætləs] n atlante m.
Atlas Mountains npl: the ~ i Monti
dell'Atlante.
A.T.M. abbr (= automated telling machine)
cassa automatica prelievi, sportello
automatico.
atmosphere ['ætməsfɪə*] n atmosfera; (air)
aria.
atmospheric [ætməs'fɛrɪk] adj
atmosferico(a).
atmospherics [ætməs'fɛrɪks] npl (RADIO)
scariche fpl.
atoll ['ætɔl] n atollo.
atom ['ætəm] n atomo.
atomic [ə'tɔmɪk] adj atomico(a).
atom(ic) bomb n bomba atomica.
atomizer ['ætəmaɪzə*] n atomizzatore m.
atone [ə'təun] vi: to ~ for espiare.
atonement [ə'təunmənt] n espiazione f.
ATP n abbr = Association of Tennis
Professionals.
atrocious [ə'trəuʃəs] adj atroce,
pessimo(a).
atrocity [ə'trɔsɪtɪ] n atrocità f inv.
atrophy ['ætrəfɪ] n atrofia ♦ vi atrofizzarsi.
attach [ə'tætʃ] vt attaccare; (document,
letter) allegare; (MIL: troops) assegnare; to
be ~ed to sb/sth (to like) essere
affezionato(a) a qn/qc; the ~ed letter la
lettera acclusa or allegata.
attaché [ə'tæʃeɪ] n addetto.
attaché case n valigetta per documenti.
attachment [ə'tætʃmənt] n (tool)
accessorio; (love): ~ (to) affetto (per).
attack [ə'tæk] vt attaccare; (task etc)
iniziare; (problem) affrontare ♦ n attacco;
(also: heart ~) infarto.

attacker [ə'tækə*] n aggressore m, assalitore/trice.
attain [ə'teɪn] vt (also: **to ~ to**) arrivare a, raggiungere.
attainments [ə'teɪnmənts] npl cognizioni fpl.
attempt [ə'tɛmpt] n tentativo ♦ vt tentare; **~ed murder** (LAW) tentato omicidio; **to make an ~ on sb's life** attentare alla vita di qn; **he made no ~ to help** non ha (neanche) tentato or cercato di aiutare.
attend [ə'tɛnd] vt frequentare; (meeting, talk) andare a; (patient) assistere.
▶ **attend to** vt fus (needs, affairs etc) prendersi cura di; (customer) occuparsi di.
attendance [ə'tɛndəns] n (being present) presenza; (people present) gente f presente.
attendant [ə'tɛndənt] n custode m/f; persona di servizio ♦ adj concomitante.
attention [ə'tɛnʃən] n attenzione f; **~s** premure fpl, attenzioni fpl; **~!** (MIL) attenti!; **at ~** (MIL) sull'attenti; **for the ~ of** (ADMIN) per l'attenzione di; **it has come to my ~ that ...** sono venuto a conoscenza (del fatto) che ....
attentive [ə'tɛntɪv] adj attento(a); (kind) premuroso(a).
attentively [ə'tɛntɪvlɪ] adv attentamente.
attenuate [ə'tɛnjueɪt] vt attenuare ♦ vi attenuarsi.
attest [ə'tɛst] vi: **to ~ to** attestare.
attic ['ætɪk] n soffitta.
attire [ə'taɪə*] n abbigliamento.
attitude ['ætɪtjuːd] n (behaviour) atteggiamento; (posture) posa; (view): **~ (to)** punto di vista (nei confronti di).
attorney [ə'tɜːnɪ] n (US: lawyer) avvocato; (having proxy) mandatario; **power of ~** procura.
Attorney General n (BRIT) Procuratore m Generale; (US) Ministro della Giustizia.
attract [ə'trækt] vt attirare.
attraction [ə'trækʃən] n (gen pl: pleasant things) attrattiva; (PHYSICS, fig: towards sth) attrazione f.
attractive [ə'træktɪv] adj attraente; (idea, offer, price) allettante, interessante.
attribute n ['ætrɪbjuːt] attributo ♦ vt [ə'trɪbjuːt]: **to ~ sth to** attribuire qc a.
attrition [ə'trɪʃən] n: **war of ~** guerra di logoramento.
Atty. Gen. abbr = **Attorney General**.
atypical [eɪ'tɪpɪkl] adj atipico(a).
aubergine ['əubəʒiːn] n melanzana.
auburn ['ɔːbən] adj tizianesco(a).
auction ['ɔːkʃən] n (also: **sale by ~**) asta ♦ vt

(also: **to sell by ~**) vendere all'asta; (also: **to put up for ~**) mettere all'asta.
auctioneer [ɔːkʃə'nɪə*] n banditore m.
auction room n sala dell'asta.
audacious [ɔː'deɪʃəs] adj (bold) audace; (impudent) sfrontato(a).
audacity [ɔː'dæsɪtɪ] n audacia.
audible ['ɔːdɪbl] adj udibile.
audience ['ɔːdɪəns] n (people) pubblico; spettatori mpl; ascoltatori mpl; (interview) udienza.
audio-typist ['ɔːdɪəu'taɪpɪst] n dattilografo/a che trascrive da nastro.
audiovisual [ɔːdɪəu'vɪzjuəl] adj audiovisivo(a); **~ aids** sussidi mpl audiovisivi.
audit ['ɔːdɪt] n revisione f, verifica f ♦ vt rivedere, verificare.
audition [ɔː'dɪʃən] n (THEAT) audizione f; (CINE) provino ♦ vi fare un'audizione (or un provino).
auditor ['ɔːdɪtə*] n revisore m.
auditorium [ɔːdɪ'tɔːrɪəm] n sala, auditorio.
Aug. abbr (= August) ago., ag.
augment [ɔːg'mɛnt] vt, vi aumentare.
augur ['ɔːgə*] vt (be a sign of) predire ♦ vi: **it ~s well** promette bene.
August ['ɔːgəst] n agosto; for phrases see also **July**.
august [ɔː'gʌst] adj augusto(a).
aunt [ɑːnt] n zia.
auntie, aunty ['ɑːntɪ] n zietta.
au pair ['əu'pɛə*] n (also: **~ girl**) (ragazza f) alla pari inv.
aura ['ɔːrə] n aura.
auspices ['ɔːspɪsɪz] npl: **under the ~ of** sotto gli auspici di.
auspicious [ɔːs'pɪʃəs] adj propizio(a).
austere [ɔs'tɪə*] adj austero(a).
austerity [ɔs'tɛrɪtɪ] n austerità f inv.
Australasia [ɔstrə'leɪzɪə] n Australasia.
Australia [ɔs'treɪlɪə] n Australia.
Australian [ɔs'treɪlɪən] adj, n australiano(a).
Austria ['ɔstrɪə] n Austria.
Austrian ['ɔstrɪən] adj, n austriaco(a).
AUT n abbr (BRIT: = Association of University Teachers) associazione dei docenti universitari.
authentic [ɔː'θɛntɪk] adj autentico(a).
authenticate [ɔː'θɛntɪkeɪt] vt autenticare.
authenticity [ɔːθɛn'tɪsɪtɪ] n autenticità.
author ['ɔːθə*] n autore/trice.
authoritarian [ɔːθɔrɪ'tɛərɪən] adj autoritario(a).
authoritative [ɔː'θɔrɪtətɪv] adj (account etc) autorevole; (manner) autoritario(a).
authority [ɔː'θɔrɪtɪ] n autorità f inv; (permission) autorizzazione f; **the**

authorities *npl* le autorità; **to have ~ to do sth** avere l'autorizzazione a fare *or* il diritto di fare qc.

authorization [ɔːθəraɪˈzeɪʃən] *n* autorizzazione *f*.

authorize [ˈɔːθəraɪz] *vt* autorizzare.

authorized capital *n* capitale *m* nominale.

authorship [ˈɔːθəʃɪp] *n* paternità (*letteraria* etc).

autistic [ɔːˈtɪstɪk] *adj* autistico(a).

auto [ˈɔːtəu] *n* (*US*) auto *f inv*.

autobiography [ɔːtəbaɪˈɔgrəfɪ] *n* autobiografia.

autocratic [ɔːtəˈkrætɪk] *adj* autocratico(a).

Autocue ® [ˈɔːtəukjuː] *n* (*BRIT*) gobbo (*TV*).

autograph [ˈɔːtəgrɑːf] *n* autografo ♦ *vt* firmare.

autoimmune [ɔːtəuɪˈmjuːn] *adj* autoimmune.

automat [ˈɔːtəmæt] *n* (*US*) tavola calda fornita esclusivamente di distributori automatici.

automated [ˈɔːtəmeɪtɪd] *adj* automatizzato(a).

automatic [ɔːtəˈmætɪk] *adj* automatico(a) ♦ *n* (*gun*) arma automatica; (*car*) automobile *f* con cambio automatico; (*washing machine*) lavatrice *f* automatica.

automatically [ɔːtəˈmætɪklɪ] *adv* automaticamente.

automatic data processing (ADP) *n* elaborazione *f* automatica dei dati (EAD).

automation [ɔːtəˈmeɪʃən] *n* automazione *f*.

automaton, *pl* **automata** [ɔːˈtɒmətən, -tə] *n* automa *m*.

automobile [ˈɔːtəməbiːl] *n* (*US*) automobile *f*.

autonomous [ɔːˈtɒnəməs] *adj* autonomo(a).

autopsy [ˈɔːtɒpsɪ] *n* autopsia.

autumn [ˈɔːtəm] *n* autunno.

auxiliary [ɔːgˈzɪlɪərɪ] *adj* ausiliario(a) ♦ *n* ausiliare *m/f*.

AV *n abbr* (= *Authorized Version*) traduzione inglese della Bibbia ♦ *abbr* = **audiovisual**.

Av. *abbr* = **avenue**.

avail [əˈveɪl] *vt*: **to ~ o.s. of** servirsi di; approfittarsi di ♦ *n*: **to no ~** inutilmente.

availability [əveɪləˈbɪlɪtɪ] *n* disponibilità.

available [əˈveɪləbl] *adj* disponibile; **every ~ means** tutti i mezzi disponibili; **to make sth ~ to sb** mettere qc a disposizione di qn; **is the manager ~?** è libero il direttore?

avalanche [ˈævəlɑːnʃ] *n* valanga.

avant-garde [ˈævɑ̃ŋˈgɑːd] *adj* d'avanguardia.

avarice [ˈævərɪs] *n* avarizia.

avaricious [ævəˈrɪʃəs] *adj* avaro(a).

avdp. *abbr* (= *avoirdupois*) sistema ponderale anglosassone basato su libbra, oncia e multipli.

Ave. *abbr* = **avenue**.

avenge [əˈvɛndʒ] *vt* vendicare.

avenue [ˈævənjuː] *n* viale *m*.

average [ˈævərɪdʒ] *n* media ♦ *adj* medio(a) ♦ *vt* (*also*: **~ out at**) aggirarsi in media su; essere in media di; **on ~** in media; **above/below (the) ~** sopra/sotto la media.

averse [əˈvɜːs] *adj*: **to be ~ to sth/doing** essere contrario(a) a qc/a fare; **I wouldn't be ~ to a drink** non avrei nulla in contrario a bere qualcosa.

aversion [əˈvɜːʃən] *n* avversione *f*.

avert [əˈvɜːt] *vt* evitare, prevenire; (*one's eyes*) distogliere.

aviary [ˈeɪvɪərɪ] *n* voliera, uccelliera.

aviation [eɪvɪˈeɪʃən] *n* aviazione *f*.

avid [ˈævɪd] *adj* avido(a).

avidly [ˈævɪdlɪ] *adv* avidamente.

avocado [ævəˈkɑːdəu] *n* (*also: BRIT*: **~ pear**) avocado *m inv*.

avoid [əˈvɔɪd] *vt* evitare.

avoidable [əˈvɔɪdəbl] *adj* evitabile.

avoidance [əˈvɔɪdəns] *n* l'evitare *m*.

avowed [əˈvaud] *adj* dichiarato(a).

AVP *n abbr* (*US*) = *assistant vice-president*.

AWACS [ˈeɪwæks] *n abbr* (= *airborne warning and control system*) sistema di allarme e controllo in volo.

await [əˈweɪt] *vt* aspettare; **~ing attention** (*COMM: letter*) in attesa di risposta; (: *order*) in attesa di essere evaso; **long ~ed** tanto atteso(a).

awake [əˈweɪk] *adj* sveglio(a) ♦ *vb* (*pt* **awoke** [əˈwəuk], *pp* **awoken** [əˈwəukən] *or* **awaked**) *vt* svegliare ♦ *vi* svegliarsi; **~ to** consapevole di.

awakening [əˈweɪknɪŋ] *n* risveglio.

award [əˈwɔːd] *n* premio; (*LAW*) decreto ♦ *vt* assegnare; (*LAW: damages*) decretare.

aware [əˈwɛə*] *adj*: **~ of** (*conscious*) conscio(a) di; (*informed*) informato(a) di; **to become ~ of** accorgersi di; **politically/socially ~** politicamente/socialmente preparato; **I am fully ~ that …** mi rendo perfettamente conto che ….

awareness [əˈwɛənɪs] *n* consapevolezza; coscienza; **to develop people's ~ (of)** sensibilizzare la gente (a).

awash [əˈwɔʃ] *adj*: **~ (with)** inondato(a) (da).

away [əˈweɪ] *adj*, *adv* via; lontano(a); **two kilometres ~** a due chilometri di distanza; **two hours ~ by car** a due ore di

distanza in macchina; **the holiday was
two weeks** ~ mancavano due settimane
alle vacanze; ~ **from** lontano da; **he's** ~
for a week è andato via per una
settimana; **he's** ~ **in Milan** è (andato) a
Milano; **to take** ~ *vt* portare via; **he was
working/pedalling** *etc* ~ *la particella indica
la continuità e l'energia dell'azione*: lavorava/
pedalava *etc* più che poteva; **to fade/
wither** *etc* ~ *la particella rinforza l'idea della
diminuzione*.
away game *n* (*SPORT*) partita fuori casa.
awe [ɔː] *n* timore *m*.
awe-inspiring ['ɔːɪnspaɪərɪŋ], **awesome**
['ɔːsəm] *adj* imponente.
awestruck ['ɔːstrʌk] *adj* sgomento(a).
awful ['ɔːfəl] *adj* terribile; **an** ~ **lot of**
(*people, cars, dogs*) un numero incredibile
di; (*jam, flowers*) una quantità incredibile
di.
awfully ['ɔːflɪ] *adv* (*very*) terribilmente.
awhile [ə'waɪl] *adv* (per) un po'.
awkward ['ɔːkwəd] *adj* (*clumsy*) goffo(a);
(*inconvenient*) scomodo(a); (*embarrassing*)
imbarazzante; (*difficult*) delicato(a),
difficile.
awkwardness ['ɔːkwədnɪs] *n* goffaggine *f*;
scomodità; imbarazzo; delicatezza,
difficoltà.
awl ['ɔːl] *n* punteruolo.
awning ['ɔːnɪŋ] *n* (*of tent*) veranda; (*of shop,
hotel etc*) tenda.
awoke [ə'wəuk] *pt of* **awake**.
awoken [ə'wəukən] *pp of* **awake**.
AWOL ['eɪwɔl] *abbr* (*MIL etc*) *see* **absent
without leave**.
awry [ə'raɪ] *adv* di traverso ◆ *adj* storto(a);
to go ~ andare a monte.
axe, (*US*) **ax** [æks] *n* scure *f* ◆ *vt* (*project etc*)
abolire; (*jobs*) sopprimere; **to have an** ~
to grind (*fig*) fare i propri interessi *or* il
proprio tornaconto.
axiom ['æksɪəm] *n* assioma *m*.
axiomatic [æksɪəu'mætɪk] *adj*
assiomatico(a).
axis, *pl* **axes** ['æksɪs, -siːz] *n* asse *m*.
axle ['æksl] *n* (*also*: ~-**tree**) asse *m*.
ay(e) [aɪ] *excl* (*yes*) sì.
AYH *n abbr* = **American Youth Hostels**.
AZ *abbr* (*US*) = **Arizona**.
azalea [ə'zeɪlɪə] *n* azalea.
Azerbaijan [æzəbaɪ'dʒɑːn] *n* Azerbaigian *m*.
Azerbaijani [æzəbaɪ'dʒɑːnɪ], **Azeri** [ə'zɛərɪ]
adj, n azerbaigiano(a), azero(a).
Azores [ə'zɔːz] *npl*: **the** ~ le Azzorre.
AZT *n abbr* (= *azidothymidine*) AZT *m*.
Aztec ['æztɛk] *adj, n* azteco(a).
azure ['eɪʒə*] *adj* azzurro(a).

B b

B, b [biː] *n* (*letter*) B, b *f or m inv*; (*SCOL*: mark)
≈ 8 (*buono*); (*MUS*): **B** si *m*; **B for
Benjamin**, (*US*) **B for Baker** ≈ B come
Bologna; **B road** *n* (*BRIT AUT*) ≈ strada
secondaria.
b. *abbr* = **born**.
BA *n abbr* = **British Academy**; (*SCOL*) *see*
Bachelor of Arts.
babble ['bæbl] *vi* cianciare; mormorare ◆ *n*
ciance *fpl*; mormorio.
babe [beɪb] *n* (*col*): **she's a real** ~ è uno
schianto di ragazza.
baboon [bə'buːn] *n* babbuino.
baby ['beɪbɪ] *n* bambino/a.
baby carriage *n* (*US*) carrozzina.
babyhood ['beɪbɪhud] *n* prima infanzia.
babyish ['beɪbɪʃ] *adj* infantile.
baby-minder ['beɪbɪ'maɪndə*] *n* (*BRIT*)
bambinaia (*che tiene i bambini mentre la
madre lavora*).
baby-sit ['beɪbɪsɪt] *vi* fare il (*or* la)
babysitter.
baby-sitter ['beɪbɪsɪtə*] *n* baby-sitter *m/f
inv*.
bachelor ['bætʃələ*] *n* scapolo; **B**~ **of Arts/
Science (BA/BSc)** ≈ laureato/a in lettere/
scienze; **B**~ **of Arts/Science degree (BA/
BSc)** *n* ≈ laurea in lettere/scienze; *see
boxed note*.

BACHELOR'S DEGREE

Il **Bachelor's Degree** *è il riconoscimento che
viene conferito a chi ha completato un corso di
laurea di tre o quattro anni all'università. I
Bachelor's degree più importanti sono il "BA"
(Bachelor of Arts), il "BSc" (Bachelor of
Science), il "BEd" (Bachelor of Education), e il
"LLB" (Bachelor of Laws); vedi anche* **Master's
degree, doctorate**.

---

bachelor party *n* (*US*) festa di addio al
celibato.
back [bæk] *n* (*of person, horse*) dorso,
schiena; (*of hand*) dorso; (*of house, car*)
didietro; (*of train*) coda; (*of chair*)
schienale *m*; (*of page*) rovescio;
(*FOOTBALL*) difensore *m*; ~ **to front**

all'incontrario; **to break the ~ of a job**
(*BRIT*) fare il grosso *or* il peggio di un
lavoro; **to have one's ~ to the wall** (*fig*)
essere *or* trovarsi con le spalle al muro
♦ *vt* (*financially*) finanziare; (*candidate*: *also*:
~ **up**) appoggiare; (*horse*: *at races*)
puntare su; (*car*) guidare a marcia
indietro ♦ *vi* indietreggiare; (*car etc*) fare
marcia indietro ♦ *adj* (*in compounds*)
posteriore, di dietro; arretrato(a); ~
seats/wheels (*AUT*) sedili *mpl*/ruote *fpl*
posteriori; ~ **payments/rent** arretrati
mpl; ~ **garden/room** giardino/stanza sul
retro (della casa); **to take a ~ seat** (*fig*)
restare in secondo piano ♦ *adv* (*not
forward*) indietro; (*returned*): **he's ~** è
tornato; **when will you be ~?** quando
torni?; **he ran ~** tornò indietro di corsa;
(*restitution*): **throw the ball ~** ritira la
palla; **can I have it ~?** posso riaverlo?;
(*again*): **he called ~** ha richiamato.
► **back down** *vi* (*fig*) fare marcia indietro.
► **back on to** *vt fus*: **the house ~s on to the
golf course** il retro della casa dà sul
campo da golf.
► **back out** *vi* (*of promise*) tirarsi indietro.
► **back up** *vt* (*support*) appoggiare,
sostenere; (*COMPUT*) fare una copia di
riserva di.
backache ['bækeɪk] *n* mal *m* di schiena.
back benches *npl posti in Parlamento
occupati dai backbencher; see boxed note.*

BACK BENCHES

*Nella "House of Commons", una delle camere
del Parlamento britannico, sono chiamati* **back
benches** *gli scanni dove siedono i
"backbencher", parlamentari che non hanno
incarichi né al governo né all'opposizione.
Nelle file davanti ad essi siedono i
"frontbencher"; vedi anche* **front bench.**

---

backbencher ['bæk'bentʃə*] *n* (*BRIT*)
*parlamentare che non ha incarichi né al
governo né all opposizione.*
backbiting ['bækbaɪtɪŋ] *n* maldicenza.
backbone ['bækbəun] *n* spina dorsale; **the
~ of the organization** l'anima
dell'organizzazione.
backchat ['bæktʃæt] *n* (*BRIT col*)
impertinenza.
backcloth ['bækklɔθ] *n* (*BRIT*) scena di
sfondo.
backcomb ['bækkəum] *vt* (*BRIT*) cotonare.
backdate [bæk'deɪt] *vt* (*letter*) retrodatare;
~**d pay rise** aumento retroattivo.
backdrop ['bækdrɔp] *n* = **backcloth.**

backer ['bækə*] *n* sostenitore/trice; (*COMM*)
fautore *m*.
backfire ['bæk'faɪə*] *vi* (*AUT*) dar ritorni di
fiamma; (*plans*) fallire.
backgammon ['bækgæmən] *n* tavola reale.
background ['bækgraund] *n* sfondo; (*of
events*, *COMPUT*) background *m inv*; (*basic
knowledge*) base *f*; (*experience*) esperienza
♦ *cpd* (*noise*, *music*) di fondo; ~ **reading**
letture *fpl* sull'argomento; **family ~**
ambiente *m* familiare.
backhand ['bækhænd] *n* (*TENNIS*: *also*: ~
stroke) rovescio.
backhanded [bæk'hændɪd] *adj* (*fig*)
ambiguo(a).
backhander ['bækhændə*] *n* (*BRIT*: *bribe*)
bustarella.
backing [bækɪŋ] *n* (*COMM*) finanziamento;
(*MUS*) accompagnamento; (*fig*) appoggio.
backlash ['bæklæʃ] *n* contraccolpo,
ripercussione *f*.
backlog ['bæklɔg] *n*: ~ **of work** lavoro
arretrato.
back number *n* (*of magazine etc*) numero
arretrato.
backpack ['bækpæk] *n* zaino.
backpacker ['bækpækə*] *n chi viaggia con
zaino e sacco a pelo.*
back pay *n* arretrato di paga.
backpedal ['bækpedl] *vi* pedalare
all'indietro; (*fig*) far marcia indietro.
backseat driver ['bæksiːt-] *n passeggero
che dà consigli non richiesti al guidatore.*
backside [bæk'saɪd] *n* (*col*) sedere *m*.
backslash ['bækslæʃ] *n* backslash *m inv*,
barra obliqua inversa.
backslide ['bækslaɪd] *vi* ricadere.
backspace ['bækspeɪs] *vi* (*in typing*) battere
il tasto di ritorno.
backstage [bæk'steɪdʒ] *adv* nel retroscena.
back street *n* vicolo.
backstroke ['bækstrəuk] *n* nuoto sul dorso.
backtrack ['bæktræk] *vi* = **backpedal.**
backup ['bækʌp] *adj* (*train*, *plane*)
supplementare; (*COMPUT*) di riserva ♦ *n*
(*support*) appoggio, sostegno; (*COMPUT*:
also: ~ **file**) file *m inv* di riserva.
backward ['bækwəd] *adj* (*movement*)
indietro *inv*; (*person*) tardivo(a); (*country*)
arretrato(a); ~ **and forward movement**
movimento avanti e indietro.
backwards ['bækwədz] *adv* indietro; (*fall*,
walk) all'indietro; **to know sth ~** *or* (*US*) ~
and forwards (*col*) sapere qc a menadito.
backwater ['bækwɔːtə*] *n* (*fig*) posto
morto.
back yard *n* cortile *m* sul retro.
bacon ['beɪkən] *n* pancetta.

bacteria [bæk'tɪərɪə] *npl* batteri *mpl*.
bacteriology [bæktɪərɪ'ɔlədʒɪ] *n* batteriologia.
bad [bæd] *adj* cattivo(a); (*child*) cattivello(a); (*meat, food*) andato(a) a male; **his ~ leg** la sua gamba malata; **to go ~** (*meat, food*) andare a male; **to have a ~ time of it** passarsela male; **I feel ~ about it** (*guilty*) mi sento un po' in colpa; **~ debt** credito difficile da recuperare; **~ faith** malafede *f*.
baddie, baddy ['bædɪ] *n* (*col*: CINE *etc*) cattivo/a.
bade [bæd] *pt of* bid.
badge [bædʒ] *n* insegna; (*of policeman*) stemma *m*; (*stick-on*) adesivo.
badger ['bædʒə*] *n* tasso ♦ *vt* tormentare.
badly ['bædlɪ] *adv* (*work, dress etc*) male; **things are going ~** le cose vanno male; **~ wounded** gravemente ferito; **he needs it ~** ne ha gran bisogno; **~ off** *adj* povero(a).
bad-mannered [bæd'mænəd] *adj* maleducato(a), sgarbato(a).
badminton ['bædmɪntən] *n* badminton *m*.
bad-tempered [bæd'tɛmpəd] *adj* irritabile; (*in bad mood*) di malumore.
baffle ['bæfl] *vt* (*puzzle*) confondere.
baffling ['bæflɪŋ] *adj* sconcertante.
bag [bæg] *n* sacco; (*handbag etc*) borsa; (*of hunter*) carniere *m*; bottino ♦ *vt* (*col*: *take*) mettersi in tasca; prendersi; **~s of** (*col*: *lots of*) un sacco di; **to pack one's ~s** fare le valigie; **~s under the eyes** borse sotto gli occhi.
bagful ['bægful] *n* sacco (pieno).
baggage ['bægɪdʒ] *n* bagagli *mpl*.
baggage allowance *n* peso bagaglio consentito.
baggage car *n* (US) bagagliaio.
baggage claim *n* ritiro bagagli.
baggy ['bægɪ] *adj* largo(a), sformato(a).
Baghdad [bæg'dæd] *n* Bagdad *f*.
bag lady *n* (*col*) stracciona, barbona.
bagpipes ['bægpaɪps] *npl* cornamusa.
bag-snatcher ['bægsnætʃə*] *n* (BRIT) scippatore/trice.
Bahamas [bə'hɑːməz] *npl*: **the ~** le isole Bahama.
Bahrain [bɑː'reɪn] *n* Bahrein *m*.
bail [beɪl] *n* cauzione *f* ♦ *vt* (*prisoner: gen*: **to grant ~ to**) concedere la libertà provvisoria su cauzione a; (NAUT: *also*: **~ out**) *see* bale out; **to be released on ~** essere rilasciato(a) su cauzione.
▶**bail out** *vt* (*prisoner*) ottenere la libertà provvisoria su cauzione di; (*fig*) tirare fuori dai guai ♦ *vi see* bale out.
bailiff ['beɪlɪf] *n* usciere *m*; fattore *m*.

bait [beɪt] *n* esca ♦ *vt* (*hook*) innescare; (*trap*) munire di esca; (*fig*) tormentare.
bake [beɪk] *vt* cuocere al forno ♦ *vi* cuocersi al forno.
baked beans *npl* fagioli *mpl* all'uccelletto.
baked potato *n* patata (con la buccia) cotta al forno.
baker ['beɪkə*] *n* fornaio/a, panettiere/a.
bakery ['beɪkərɪ] *n* panetteria.
baking ['beɪkɪŋ] *n* cottura (al forno).
baking powder *n* lievito in polvere.
baking tin *n* stampo, tortiera.
baking tray *n* teglia.
balaclava [bælə'klɑːvə] *n* (*also*: **~ helmet**) passamontagna *m inv*.
balance ['bæləns] *n* equilibrio; (COMM: *sum*) bilancio; (*scales*) bilancia ♦ *vt* tenere in equilibrio; (*pros and cons*) soppesare; (*budget*) far quadrare; (*account*) pareggiare; (*compensate*) contrappesare; **~ of trade/payments** bilancia commerciale/dei pagamenti; **~ brought forward** saldo riportato; **~ carried forward** saldo da riportare; **to ~ the books** fare il bilancio.
balanced ['bælənst] *adj* (*personality, diet*) equilibrato(a).
balance sheet *n* bilancio.
balcony ['bælkənɪ] *n* balcone *m*.
bald [bɔːld] *adj* calvo(a).
baldness ['bɔːldnɪs] *n* calvizie *f*.
bale [beɪl] *n* balla.
▶**bale out** *vt* (NAUT: *water*) vuotare; (: *boat*) aggottare ♦ *vi* (*of a plane*) gettarsi col paracadute.
Balearic [bælɪ'ærɪk] *adj*: **the ~ Islands** le (isole) Baleari.
baleful ['beɪlful] *adj* funesto(a).
balk [bɔːlk] *vi*: **to ~ (at)** tirarsi indietro (davanti a); (*horse*) recalcitrare (davanti a).
Balkan ['bɔːlkən] *adj* balcanico(a) ♦ *n*: **the ~s** i Balcani.
ball [bɔːl] *n* palla; (*football*) pallone *m*; (*for golf*) pallina; (*dance*) ballo; **to play ~ (with sb)** giocare a palla (con qn); (*fig*) stare al gioco (di qn); **to be on the ~** (*fig*: *competent*) essere in gamba; (: *alert*) stare all'erta; **to start the ~ rolling** (*fig*) fare la prima mossa; **the ~ is in your court** (*fig*) a lei la prossima mossa; *see also* balls.
ballad ['bæləd] *n* ballata.
ballast ['bæləst] *n* zavorra.
ball bearing *n* cuscinetto a sfere.
ball cock *n* galleggiante *m*.
ballerina [bælə'riːnə] *n* ballerina.
ballet ['bæleɪ] *n* balletto.
ballet dancer *n* ballerino/a.
ballistic [bə'lɪstɪk] *adj* balistico(a).
ballistics [bə'lɪstɪks] *n* balistica.

balloon [bə'luːn] n pallone m; (in comic strip) fumetto ♦ vi gonfiarsi.

balloonist [bə'luːnɪst] n aeronauta m/f.

ballot ['bælət] n scrutinio.

ballot box n urna (per le schede).

ballot paper n scheda.

ballpark ['bɔːlpɑːk] n (US) stadio di baseball.

ballpark figure n (col) cifra approssimativa.

ball-point pen ['bɔːlpɔɪnt-] n penna a sfera.

ballroom ['bɔːlrum] n sala da ballo.

balls [bɔːlz] npl (col!) coglioni mpl (!).

balm [bɑːm] n balsamo.

balmy ['bɑːmɪ] adj (breeze, air) balsamico(a); (BRIT col) = **barmy**.

BALPA ['bælpə] n abbr (= British Airline Pilots' Association) sindacato dei piloti.

balsam ['bɔːlsəm] n balsamo.

balsa (wood) ['bɔːlsə-] n (legno di) balsa.

Baltic ['bɔːltɪk] adj, n: **the ~ (Sea)** il (mar) Baltico.

balustrade [bæləs'treɪd] n balaustrata.

bamboo [bæm'buː] n bambù m

bamboozle [bæm'buːzl] vt (col) infinocchiare.

ban [bæn] n interdizione f ♦ vt interdire; **he was ~ned from driving** (BRIT) gli hanno ritirato la patente.

banal [bə'nɑːl] adj banale.

banana [bə'nɑːnə] n banana.

band [bænd] n banda; (at a dance) orchestra; (MIL) fanfara.

▶**band together** vi collegarsi.

bandage ['bændɪdʒ] n benda.

Band-Aid ® ['bændeɪd] n (US) cerotto.

bandit ['bændɪt] n bandito.

bandstand ['bændstænd] n palco dell'orchestra.

bandwagon ['bændwægən] n: **to jump on the ~** (fig) seguire la corrente.

bandy ['bændɪ] vt (jokes, insults) scambiare.

▶**bandy about** vt far circolare.

bandy-legged ['bændɪ'lɛgɪd] adj dalle gambe storte.

bane [beɪn] n: **it (or he etc) is the ~ of my life** è la mia rovina.

bang [bæŋ] n botta; (of door) lo sbattere; (blow) colpo ♦ vt battere (violentemente); (door) sbattere ♦ vi scoppiare; sbattere; **to ~ at the door** picchiare alla porta; **to ~ into sth** sbattere contro qc ♦ adv: **to be ~ on time** (BRIT col) spaccare il secondo; see also **bangs**.

banger ['bæŋə*] n (BRIT: car. also: **old ~**) macinino; (BRIT col: sausage) salsiccia; (firework) mortaretto.

Bangkok ['bæŋkɔk] n Bangkok f.

Bangladesh [bɑːŋglə'dɛʃ] n Bangladesh m.

bangle ['bæŋgl] n braccialetto.

bangs [bæŋz] npl (US: fringe) frangia, frangetta.

banish ['bænɪʃ] vt bandire.

banister(s) ['bænɪstə(z)] n(pl) ringhiera.

banjo, ~es or **~s** ['bændʒəu] n banjo m inv.

bank [bæŋk] n (for money) banca, banco; (of river, lake) riva, sponda; (of earth) banco.

▶**bank on** vt fus contare su.

bank account n conto in banca.

bank balance n saldo; **a healthy ~** un solido conto in banca.

bank card n = **banker's card**.

bank charges npl (BRIT) spese fpl bancarie.

bank draft n assegno circolare or bancario.

banker ['bæŋkə*] n banchiere m; **~'s card** (BRIT) carta f assegni inv; **~'s order** (BRIT) ordine m di banca.

bank giro n bancogiro.

bank holiday n (BRIT) giorno di festa; see boxed note.

banking ['bæŋkɪŋ] n attività bancaria; professione f di banchiere.

banking hours npl orario di sportello.

bank loan n prestito bancario.

bank manager n direttore m di banca.

banknote ['bæŋknəut] n banconota.

bank rate n tasso bancario.

bankrupt ['bæŋkrʌpt] adj, n fallito(a); **to go ~** fallire.

bankruptcy ['bæŋkrʌptsɪ] n fallimento.

bank statement n estratto conto.

banner ['bænə*] n bandiera.

bannister(s) ['bænɪstə(z)] n(pl) = **banister(s)**.

banns [bænz] npl pubblicazioni fpl di matrimonio.

banquet ['bæŋkwɪt] n banchetto.

bantam-weight ['bæntəmweɪt] n peso gallo.

banter ['bæntə*] n scherzi mpl bonari.

baptism ['bæptɪzəm] *n* battesimo.
Baptist ['bæptɪst] *adj*, *n* battista (*m/f*).
baptize [bæp'taɪz] *vt* battezzare.
bar [bɑː*] *n* barra; (*of window etc*) sbarra; (*of chocolate*) tavoletta; (*pub*) bar *m inv*; (*counter*: *in pub*) banco; (*MUS*) battuta ♦ *vt* (*road, window*) sbarrare; (*person*) escludere; (*activity*) interdire; ~ **of soap** saponetta; **the B~** (*LAW*) l'Ordine *m* degli avvocati; **behind** ~**s** (*prisoner*) dietro le sbarre; ~ **none** senza eccezione.
Barbados [bɑː'beɪdɔs] *n* Barbados *fsg*.
barbaric [bɑː'bærɪk], **barbarous** ['bɑːbərəs] *adj* barbaro(a); barbarico(a).
barbecue ['bɑːbɪkjuː] *n* barbecue *m inv*.
barbed wire ['bɑːbd-] *n* filo spinato.
barber ['bɑːbə*] *n* barbiere *m*.
barbiturate [bɑː'bɪtjurɪt] *n* barbiturico.
Barcelona [bɑːsɪ'ləunə] *n* Barcellona.
bar chart *n* diagramma *m* di frequenza.
bar code *n* codice *m* a barre.
bare [bɛə*] *adj* nudo(a) ♦ *vt* scoprire, denudare; (*teeth*) mostrare; **the** ~ **essentials** lo stretto necessario.
bareback ['bɛəbæk] *adv* senza sella.
barefaced ['bɛəfeɪst] *adj* sfacciato(a).
barefoot ['bɛəfut] *adj*, *adv* scalzo(a).
bareheaded [bɛə'hɛdɪd] *adj*, *adv* a capo scoperto.
barely ['bɛəlɪ] *adv* appena.
Barents Sea ['bærənts-] *n*: **the** ~ il mar di Barents.
bargain ['bɑːgɪn] *n* (*transaction*) contratto; (*good buy*) affare *m* ♦ *vi* (*haggle*) tirare sul prezzo; (*trade*) contrattare; **into the** ~ per giunta.
▶**bargain for** *vt fus* (*col*): **to** ~ **for sth** aspettarsi qc; **he got more than he** ~**ed for** gli è andata peggio di quel che si aspettasse.
bargaining ['bɑːgənɪŋ] *n* contrattazione *f*.
bargaining position *n*: **to be in a weak/strong** ~ non avere/avere potere contrattuale.
barge [bɑːdʒ] *n* chiatta.
▶**barge in** *vi* (*walk in*) piombare dentro; (*interrupt talk*) intromettersi a sproposito.
▶**barge into** *vt fus* urtare contro.
baritone ['bærɪtəun] *n* baritono.
barium meal ['bɛərɪəm-] *n* (pasto di) bario.
bark [bɑːk] *n* (*of tree*) corteccia; (*of dog*) abbaio ♦ *vi* abbaiare.
barley ['bɑːlɪ] *n* orzo.
barley sugar *n* zucchero d'orzo.
barmaid ['bɑːmeɪd] *n* cameriera al banco.
barman ['bɑːmən] *n* barista *m*.
barmy ['bɑːmɪ] *adj* (*BRIT col*) tocco(a).

barn [bɑːn] *n* granaio; (*for animals*) stalla.
barnacle ['bɑːnəkl] *n* cirripede *m*.
barn owl *n* barbagianni *m inv*.
barometer [bə'rɔmɪtə*] *n* barometro.
baron ['bærən] *n* barone *m*; (*fig*) magnate *m*; **the oil** ~**s** i magnati del petrolio; **the press** ~**s** i baroni della stampa.
baroness ['bærənɪs] *n* baronessa.
baronet ['bærənɪt] *n* baronetto.
barrack ['bærək] *vt* (*BRIT*): **to** ~ **sb** subissare qn di grida e fischi.
barracks ['bærəks] *npl* caserma.
barrage ['bærɑːʒ] *n* (*MIL*) sbarramento; **a** ~ **of questions** una raffica di *or* un fuoco di fila di domande.
barrel ['bærəl] *n* barile *m*; (*of gun*) canna.
barrel organ *n* organetto a cilindro.
barren ['bærən] *adj* sterile; (*soil*) arido(a).
barricade [bærɪ'keɪd] *n* barricata ♦ *vt* barricare.
barrier ['bærɪə*] *n* barriera; (*BRIT*: *also*: **crash** ~) guardrail *m inv*.
barrier cream *n* (*BRIT*) crema protettiva.
barring ['bɑːrɪŋ] *prep* salvo.
barrister ['bærɪstə*] *n* (*BRIT*) avvocato; *see boxed note*.

BARRISTER

Il **barrister** *è un membro della più prestigiosa delle due branche della professione legale (l'altra è quella dei "solicitor"); la sua funzione è quella di rappresentare i propri clienti in tutte le corti ("magistrates' court", "crown court" e "Court of Appeal"), generalmente seguendo le istruzioni del caso preparate dai "solicitor".*

---

barrow ['bærəu] *n* (*cart*) carriola.
barstool ['bɑːstuːl] *n* sgabello.
Bart. *abbr* (*BRIT*) = **baronet**.
bartender ['bɑːtɛndə*] *n* (*US*) barista *m*.
barter ['bɑːtə*] *n* baratto ♦ *vt*: **to** ~ **sth for** barattare qc con.
base [beɪs] *n* base *f* ♦ *adj* vile ♦ *vt*: **to** ~ **sth on** basare qc su; **to** ~ **at** (*troops*) mettere di stanza a; **coffee-**~**d** a base di caffè; **a Paris-**~**d firm** una ditta con sede centrale a Parigi; **I'm** ~**d in London** sono di base *or* ho base a Londra.
baseball ['beɪsbɔːl] *n* baseball *m*.
baseboard ['beɪsbɔːd] *n* (*US*) zoccolo, battiscopa *m inv*.
base camp *n* campo *m* base *inv*.
Basel [bɑːl] *n* = **Basle**.
baseline ['beɪslaɪn] *n* (*TENNIS*) linea di fondo.
basement ['beɪsmənt] *n* seminterrato; (*of shop*) sotterraneo.

base rate n tasso di base.
bases ['beisi:z] npl of **basis**; ['beisiz] npl of **base**.
bash [bæʃ] vt (col) picchiare ♦ n: **I'll have a ~ (at it)** (BRIT col) ci proverò; **~ed in** adj sfondato(a).
► **bash up** vt (col: car) sfasciare; (: BRIT: person) riempire di or prendere a botte.
bashful ['bæʃful] adj timido(a).
bashing ['bæʃɪŋ] n: **Paki-/queer-~** atti mpl di violenza contro i pachistani/gli omosessuali.
BASIC ['beisik] n (COMPUT) BASIC m.
basic ['beisik] adj (principles, precautions, rules) elementare; (salary) base inv (after n).
basically ['beisikli] adv fondamentalmente, sostanzialmente.
basic rate n (of tax) aliquota minima.
basil ['hæzl] n basilico.
basin ['beisn] n (vessel, also GEO) bacino; (also: **wash~**) lavabo; (BRIT: for food) terrina.
basis, pl **bases** ['beisis, -si:z] n base f; **on the ~ of what you've said** in base alle sue asserzioni.
bask [bɑ:sk] vi: **to ~ in the sun** crogiolarsi al sole.
basket ['bɑ:skit] n cesta; (smaller) cestino; (with handle) paniere m.
basketball ['bɑ:skitbɔ:l] n pallacanestro f.
basketball player n cestista m/f.
Basle [bɑ:l] n Basilea.
basmati rice [bəz'mæti-] n riso basmati.
Basque [bæsk] adj, n basco(a).
bass [beis] n (MUS) basso.
. **bass clef** n chiave f di basso.
bassoon [bə'su:n] n fagotto.
bastard ['bɑ:stəd] n bastardo/a; (col!) stronzo (!).
baste [beist] vt (CULIN) ungere con grasso; (SEWING) imbastire.
bastion ['bæstiən] n bastione m; (fig) baluardo.
bat [bæt] n pipistrello; (for baseball etc) mazza; (BRIT: for table tennis) racchetta; **off one's own ~** di propria iniziativa ♦ vt: **he didn't ~ an eyelid** non battè ciglio.
batch [bætʃ] n (of bread) infornata; (of papers) cumulo; (of applicants, letters) gruppo; (of work) sezione f; (of goods) partita, lotto.
batch processing n (COMPUT) elaborazione f a blocchi.
bated ['beitid] adj: **with ~ breath** col fiato sospeso.
bath [bɑ:θ, pl bɑ:ðz] n bagno; (bathtub) vasca da bagno ♦ vt far fare il bagno a; **to**

have a ~ fare un bagno; see also **baths**.
bathchair ['bɑ:θtʃɛə*] n (BRIT) poltrona a rotelle.
bathe [beið] vi fare il bagno ♦ vt bagnare; (wound etc) lavare.
bather ['beiðə*] n bagnante m/f.
bathing ['beiðɪŋ] n bagni mpl.
bathing cap n cuffia da bagno.
bathing costume, (US) **bathing suit** n costume m da bagno.
bathmat ['bɑ:θmæt] n tappetino da bagno.
bathrobe ['bɑ:θrəub] n accappatoio.
bathroom ['bɑ:θrum] n stanza da bagno.
baths [bɑ:ðz] npl bagni mpl pubblici.
bath towel n asciugamano da bagno.
bathtub ['bɑ:θtʌb] n (vasca da) bagno.
batman ['bætmən] n (BRIT MIL) attendente m.
baton ['bætən] n bastone m; (MUS) bacchetta.
battalion [bə'tæliən] n battaglione m.
batten ['bætən] n (CARPENTRY) assicella, correntino; (for flooring) tavola per pavimenti m; (NAUT) serretta; (: on sail) stecca.
► **batten down** vt (NAUT): **to ~ down the hatches** chiudere i boccaporti.
batter ['bætə*] vt battere ♦ n pastetta.
battered ['bætəd] adj (hat) sformato(a); (pan) ammaccato(a); **~ wife/baby** consorte f/bambino(a) maltrattato(a).
battering ram ['bætərɪŋ-] n ariete m.
battery ['bætəri] n batteria; (of torch) pila.
battery charger n caricabatterie m inv.
battle ['bætl] n battaglia ♦ vi battagliare, lottare; **to fight a losing ~** (fig) battersi per una causa persa; **that's half the ~** (col) è già una mezza vittoria.
battle dress n uniforme f da combattimento.
battlefield ['bætlfi:ld] n campo di battaglia.
battlements ['bætlmənts] npl bastioni mpl.
battleship ['bætlʃip] n nave f da guerra.
batty ['bæti] adj (col: person) svitato(a), strambo(a); (: behaviour, idea) strampalato(a).
bauble ['bɔ:bl] n ninnolo.
baud [bɔ:d] n (COMPUT) baud m inv.
baulk [bɔ:lk] vi = **balk**.
bauxite ['bɔ:ksait] n bauxite f.
Bavaria [bə'vɛəriə] n Bavaria.
Bavarian [bə'vɛəriən] adj, n bavarese (m/f).
bawdy ['bɔ:di] adj piccante.
bawl [bɔ:l] vi urlare.
bay [bei] n (of sea) baia; (BRIT: for parking) piazzola di sosta; (loading) piazzale m di (sosta e) carico; **to hold sb at ~** tenere qn a bada.

bay leaf *n* foglia d'alloro.
bayonet ['beɪənɪt] *n* baionetta.
bay tree *n* alloro.
bay window *n* bovindo.
bazaar [bə'zɑː*] *n* bazar *m inv*; vendita di beneficenza.
bazooka [bə'zuːkə] *n* bazooka *m inv*.
BB *n abbr* (*BRIT*: = *Boys' Brigade*) *organizzazione giovanile a fine educativo.*
B & B *n abbr see* **bed and breakfast**.
BBB *n abbr* (*US*: = *Better Business Bureau*) *organismo per la difesa dei consumatori.*
BBC *n abbr* = *British Broadcasting Corporation*; *see boxed note.*

BBC

La BBC è l'azienda statale che fornisce il servizio radiofonico e televisivo in Gran Bretagna. Pur dovendo rispondere al Parlamento del proprio operato, la BBC non è soggetta al controllo dello stato per scelte e programmi, anche perché si autofinanzia con il ricavato dei canoni d'abbonamento. La BBC fornisce anche un servizio di informazione internazionale, il "BBC World Service", trasmesso in tutto il mondo.

BBE *n abbr* (*US*: = *Benevolent and Protective Order of Elks*) *organizzazione filantropica.*
BC *adv abbr* (= *before Christ*) a.C. ♦ *abbr* (*Canada*) = *British Columbia.*
BCG *n abbr* (= *Bacillus Calmette-Guérin*) *vaccino antitubercolare.*
BD *n abbr* (= *Bachelor of Divinity*) *titolo di studio.*
B/D *abbr* = **bank draft**.
BDS *n abbr* (= *Bachelor of Dental Surgery*) *titolo di studio.*

=============== *KEYWORD*

be [biː] (*pt* **was, were**, *pp* **been**) *aux vb* **1** (*with present participle*: *forming continuous tenses*): **what are you doing?** che fai?, che stai facendo?; **they're coming tomorrow** vengono domani; **I've been waiting for her for hours** sono ore che l'aspetto
2 (*with pp*: *forming passives*) essere; **to ~ killed** essere *or* venire ucciso(a); **the box had been opened** la scatola era stata aperta; **the thief was nowhere to ~ seen** il ladro non si trovava da nessuna parte
3 (*in tag questions*): **it was fun, wasn't it?** è stato divertente, no?; **he's good-looking, isn't he?** è un bell'uomo, vero?; **she's back, is she?** così è tornata, eh?
4 (+*to* +*infinitive*): **the house is to ~ sold**

abbiamo (*or* hanno *etc*) intenzione di vendere casa; **you're to ~ congratulated for all your work** dovremo farvi i complimenti per tutto il vostro lavoro; **am I to understand that …?** devo dedurre che …?; **he's not to open it** non deve aprirlo; **he was to have come yesterday** sarebbe dovuto venire ieri
♦ *vb* +*complement* **1** (*gen*) essere; **I'm English** sono inglese; **I'm tired** sono stanco(a); **I'm hot/cold** ho caldo/freddo; **he's a doctor** è medico; **2 and 2 are 4** 2 più 2 fa 4; **~ careful!** sta attento!; **~ good** sii buono; **if I were you …** se fossi in te …
2 (*of health*) stare; **how are you?** come sta?; **he's very ill** sta molto male
3 (*of age*): **how old are you?** quanti anni hai?; **I'm sixteen (years old)** ho sedici anni
4 (*cost*) costare; **how much was the meal?** quant'era *or* quanto costava il pranzo?; **that'll ~ £5, please** (sono) 5 sterline, per favore
♦ *vi* **1** (*exist, occur etc*) essere, esistere; **the best singer that ever was** il migliore cantante mai esistito *or* di tutti tempi; **~ that as it may** comunque sia, sia come sia; **so ~ it** sia pure, e sia
2 (*referring to place*) essere, trovarsi; **I won't ~ here tomorrow** non ci sarò domani; **Edinburgh is in Scotland** Edimburgo si trova in Scozia
3 (*referring to movement*): **where have you been?** dove sei stato?; **I've been to China** sono stato in Cina
♦ *impers vb* **1** (*referring to time, distance*) essere; **it's 5 o'clock** sono le 5; **it's the 28th of April** è il 28 aprile; **it's 10 km to the village** di qui al paese sono 10 km
2 (*referring to the weather*) fare; **it's too hot/cold** fa troppo caldo/freddo; **it's windy** c'è vento
3 (*emphatic*): **it's me** sono io; **it's only me** sono solo io; **it was Maria who paid the bill** è stata Maria che ha pagato il conto.

B/E *abbr* = **bill of exchange**.
beach [biːtʃ] *n* spiaggia ♦ *vt* tirare in secco.
beach buggy *n* dune buggy *f inv*.
beachcomber ['biːtʃkəumə*] *n* vagabondo (che s'aggira sulla spiaggia).
beachwear ['biːtʃwɛə*] *n* articoli *mpl* da spiaggia.
beacon ['biːkən] *n* (*lighthouse*) faro; (*marker*) segnale *m*; (*radio* ~) radiofaro.
bead [biːd] *n* perlina; (*of dew, sweat*) goccia; **~s** (*necklace*) collana.
beady ['biːdɪ] *adj*: **~ eyes** occhi *mpl* piccoli e

penetranti.

beagle ['bi:gl] n cane m da lepre.

beak [bi:k] n becco.

beaker ['bi:kə*] n coppa.

beam [bi:m] n trave f; (of light) raggio; (RADIO) fascio (d'onde) ♦ vi brillare; (smile): to ~ at sb rivolgere un radioso sorriso a qn; **to drive on full** or **main** ~ or (US) **high** ~ guidare con gli abbaglianti accesi.

beaming ['bi:mɪŋ] adj (sun, smile) raggiante.

bean [bi:n] n fagiolo; (of coffee) chicco.

beanpole ['bi:npəul] n (col) spilungone/a.

beansprouts ['bi:nsprauts] npl germogli mpl di soia.

bear [bɛə*] n orso; (STOCK EXCHANGE) ribassista m/f ♦ vb (pt **bore**, pp **borne** [bɔ:*, bɔ:n]) vt (gen) portare; (produce: fruit) produrre, dare; (: traces, signs) mostrare; (COMM: interest) fruttare; (endure) sopportare ♦ vi: **to** ~ **right/left** piegare a destra/sinistra; **to** ~ **the responsibility of** assumersi la responsabilità di; **to** ~ **comparison with** reggere al paragone con; **I can't** ~ **him** non lo posso soffrire or sopportare; **to bring pressure to** ~ **on sb** fare pressione su qn.

▶**bear out** vt (theory, suspicion) confermare, convalidare.

▶**bear up** vi farsi coraggio; **he bore up well under the strain** ha sopportato bene lo stress.

▶**bear with** vt fus (sb's moods, temper) sopportare (con pazienza); ~ **with me a minute** solo un attimo, prego.

bearable ['bɛərəbl] adj sopportabile.

beard [bɪəd] n barba.

bearded ['bɪədɪd] adj barbuto(a).

bearer ['bɛərə*] n portatore m; (of passport) titolare m/f.

bearing ['bɛərɪŋ] n portamento; (connection) rapporto; (ball) ~s npl cuscinetti mpl a sfere; **to take a** ~ fare un rilevamento; **to find one's** ~s orientarsi.

beast [bi:st] n bestia.

beastly ['bi:stlɪ] adj meschino(a); (weather) da cani.

beat [bi:t] n colpo; (of heart) battito; (MUS) tempo; battuta; (of policeman) giro ♦ vt (pt **beat**, pp **beaten**) battere; **off the** ~**en track** fuori mano; **to** ~ **about the bush** menare il cane per l'aia; **to** ~ **time** battere il tempo; **that** ~**s everything!** (col) questo è il colmo!

▶**beat down** vt (door) abbattere, buttare giù; (price) far abbassare; (seller) far scendere ♦ vi (rain) scrosciare; (sun)

picchiare.

▶**beat off** vt respingere.

▶**beat up** vt (col: person) picchiare.

beater ['bi:tə*] n (for eggs, cream) frullino.

beating ['bi:tɪŋ] n botte fpl; (defeat) batosta; **to take a** ~ prendere una (bella) batosta.

beat-up [bi:t'ʌp] adj (col) scassato(a).

beautician [bju:'tɪʃən] n estetista m/f.

beautiful ['bju:tɪful] adj bello(a).

beautify ['bju:tɪfaɪ] vt abbellire.

beauty ['bju:tɪ] n bellezza; (concept) bello; **the** ~ **of it is that** ... il bello è che ....

beauty contest n concorso di bellezza.

beauty queen n miss f inv, reginetta di bellezza.

beauty salon n istituto di bellezza.

beauty sleep n: **to get one's** ~ farsi un sonno ristoratore.

beauty spot n neo; (BRIT: TOURISM) luogo pittoresco.

beaver ['bi:və*] n castoro.

becalmed [bɪ'ka:md] adj in bonaccia.

became [bɪ'keɪm] pt of **become**.

because [bɪ'kɔz] conj perché; ~ **of** prep a causa di.

beck [bɛk] n: **to be at sb's** ~ **and call** essere a completa disposizione di qn.

beckon ['bɛkən] vt (also: ~ **to**) chiamare con un cenno.

become [bɪ'kʌm] vt (irreg: like **come**) diventare; **to** ~ **fat/thin** ingrassarsi/ dimagrire; **to** ~ **angry** arrabbiarsi; **it became known that** ... si è venuto a sapere che ...; **what has** ~ **of him?** che gli è successo?

becoming [bɪ'kʌmɪŋ] adj (behaviour) che si conviene; (clothes) grazioso(a).

BEd n abbr (= Bachelor of Education) laurea con abilitazione all'insegnamento.

bed [bɛd] n letto; (of flowers) aiuola; (of coal, clay) strato; (of sea, lake) fondo; **to go to** ~ andare a letto.

▶**bed down** vi sistemarsi (per dormire).

bed and breakfast (B & B) n (terms) camera con colazione; (place) ≈ pensione f familiare; see boxed note.

BED AND BREAKFAST

I **bed and breakfast**, anche **B & B**, sono piccole pensioni a conduzione familiare, in case private o fattorie, dove si affittano camere e viene servita al mattino la tradizionale colazione all'inglese. Queste graziose pensioni offrono un servizio di camera con prima colazione, appunto "bed and breakfast", a prezzi più contenuti rispetto agli alberghi.

bedbug ['bɛdbʌg] *n* cimice *f*.
bedclothes ['bɛdkləuðz] *npl* coperte e lenzuola *fpl*.
bedcover ['bɛdkʌvə*] *n* copriletto.
bedding ['bɛdɪŋ] *n* coperte e lenzuola *fpl*.
bedevil [bɪ'dɛvl] *vt* (*person*) tormentare; (*plans*) ostacolare continuamente.
bedfellow ['bɛdfɛləu] *n*: **they are strange ~s** (*fig*) fanno una coppia ben strana.
bedlam ['bɛdləm] *n* baraonda.
bedpan ['bɛdpæn] *n* padella.
bedpost ['bɛdpəust] *n* colonnina del letto.
bedraggled [bɪ'drægld] *adj* sbrindellato(a); (*wet*) fradicio(a).
bedridden ['bɛdrɪdən] *adj* costretto(a) a letto.
bedrock ['bɛdrɔk] *n* (*GEO*) basamento; (*fig*) fatti *mpl* di base.
bedroom ['bɛdrum] *n* camera da letto.
Beds *abbr* (*BRIT*) = *Bedfordshire*.
bed settee *n* divano *m* letto *inv*.
bedside ['bɛdsaɪd] *n*: **at sb's ~** al capezzale di qn.
bedside lamp *n* lampada da comodino.
bedsit(ter) ['bɛdsɪt(ə*)] *n* (*BRIT*) monolocale *m*.
bedspread ['bɛdsprɛd] *n* copriletto.
bedtime ['bɛdtaɪm] *n*: **it's ~** è ora di andare a letto.
bee [biː] *n* ape *f*; **to have a ~ in one's bonnet (about sth)** avere la fissazione (di qc).
beech [biːtʃ] *n* faggio.
beef [biːf] *n* manzo.
►beef up *vt* (*col*) rinforzare.
beefburger ['biːfbəːgə*] *n* hamburger *m inv*.
beefeater ['biːfiːtə*] *n* *guardia della Torre di Londra*.
beehive ['biːhaɪv] *n* alveare *m*.
bee-keeping ['biːkiːpɪŋ] *n* apicoltura.
beeline ['biːlaɪn] *n*: **to make a ~ for** buttarsi a capo fitto verso.
been [biːn] *pp of* **be**.
beep [biːp] *n* (*of horn*) colpo di clacson; (*of phone etc*) segnale *m* (acustico), bip *m inv* ♦ *vi* suonare.
beeper ['biːpə*] *n* (*of doctor etc*) cercapersone *m inv*.
beer [bɪə*] *n* birra.
beer belly *n* (*col*) stomaco da bevitore.
beer can *n* lattina di birra.
beetle ['biːtl] *n* scarafaggio; coleottero.
beetroot ['biːtruːt] *n* (*BRIT*) barbabietola.
befall [bɪ'fɔːl] *vi(vt)* (*irreg*: *like* **fall**) accadere (a).
befit [bɪ'fɪt] *vt* addirsi a.
before [bɪ'fɔː*] *prep* (*in time*) prima di; (*in space*) davanti a ♦ *conj* prima che + *sub*; prima di ♦ *adv* prima; **~ going** prima di andare; **~ she goes** prima che vada; **the week ~** la settimana prima; **I've seen it ~** l'ho già visto; **I've never seen it ~** è la prima volta che lo vedo.
beforehand [bɪ'fɔːhænd] *adv* in anticipo.
befriend [bɪ'frɛnd] *vt* assistere; mostrarsi amico a.
befuddled [bɪ'fʌdld] *adj* confuso(a).
beg [bɛg] *vi* chiedere l'elemosina ♦ *vt* chiedere in elemosina; (*favour*) chiedere; (*entreat*) pregare; **I ~ your pardon** (*apologising*) mi scusi; (*not hearing*) scusi?; **this ~s the question of ...** questo presuppone che sia già risolto il problema di ....
began [bɪ'gæn] *pt of* **begin**.
beggar ['bɛgə*] *n* (*also*: **~man**, **~woman**) mendicante *m/f*.
begin, *pt* **began,** *pp* **begun** [bɪ'gɪn, bɪ'gæn, bɪ'gʌn] *vt*, *vi* cominciare; **to ~ doing** *or* **to do sth** incominciare *or* iniziare a fare qc; **I can't ~ to thank you** non so proprio come ringraziarla; **to ~ with, I'd like to know ...** tanto per cominciare vorrei sapere ...; **~ning from Monday** a partire da lunedì.
beginner [bɪ'gɪnə*] *n* principiante *m/f*.
beginning [bɪ'gɪnɪŋ] *n* inizio, principio; **right from the ~** fin dall'inizio.
begrudge [bɪ'grʌdʒ] *vt*: **to ~ sb sth** dare qc a qn a malincuore; invidiare qn per qc.
beguile [bɪ'gaɪl] *vt* (*enchant*) incantare.
beguiling [bɪ'gaɪlɪŋ] *adj* (*charming*) allettante; (*deluding*) ingannevole.
begun [bɪ'gʌn] *pp of* **begin**.
behalf [bɪ'hɑːf] *n*: **on ~ of**, (*US*) **in ~ of** per conto di; a nome di.
behave [bɪ'heɪv] *vi* comportarsi; (*well*: *also*: **~ o.s.**) comportarsi bene.
behaviour, (*US*) **behavior** [bɪ'heɪvjə*] *n* comportamento, condotta.
behead [bɪ'hɛd] *vt* decapitare.
beheld [bɪ'hɛld] *pt*, *pp of* **behold**.
behind [bɪ'haɪnd] *prep* dietro; (*followed by pronoun*) dietro di; (*time*) in ritardo con ♦ *adv* dietro; in ritardo ♦ *n* didietro; **we're ~ them in technology** siamo più indietro *or* più arretrati di loro nella tecnica; **~ the scenes** dietro le quinte; **to be ~ (schedule) with sth** essere indietro con qc; (*payments*) essere in arretrato con qc; **to leave sth ~** dimenticare di prendere qc.
behold [bɪ'həuld] *vt* (*irreg*: *like* **hold**) vedere, scorgere.

beige [beɪʒ] adj beige inv.
Beijing [beɪ'dʒɪŋ] n Pechino f.
being ['biːɪŋ] n essere m; **to come into ~** cominciare ad esistere.
Beirut [beɪ'ruːt] n Beirut f.
Belarus ['bɛlærus] n Bielorussia.
Belarussian [bɛlə'rʌʃən] adj bielorusso(a) ♦ n bielorusso/a; (LING) bielorusso.
belated [bɪ'leɪtɪd] adj tardo(a).
belch [bɛltʃ] vi ruttare ♦ vt (gen: ~ out: smoke etc) eruttare.
beleaguered [bɪ'liːɡəd] adj (city) assediato(a); (army) accerchiato(a); (fig) assillato(a).
Belfast ['bɛlfɑːst] n Belfast f.
belfry ['bɛlfrɪ] n campanile m.
Belgian ['bɛldʒən] adj, n belga (m/f).
Belgium ['bɛldʒəm] n Belgio.
Belgrade ['bɛl'ɡreɪd] n Belgrado f.
belie [bɪ'laɪ] vt smentire; (give false impression of) nascondere.
belief [bɪ'liːf] n (opinion) opinione f, convinzione f; (trust, faith) fede f; (acceptance as true) credenza; **in the ~ that** nella convinzione che; **it's beyond ~** è incredibile.
believe [bɪ'liːv] vt, vi credere; **to ~ in** (God) credere in; (ghosts) credere a; (method) avere fiducia in; **I don't ~ in corporal punishment** sono contrario alle punizioni corporali; **he is ~d to be abroad** si pensa (che) sia all'estero.
believer [bɪ'liːvə*] n (REL) credente m/f; (in idea, activity): **to be a ~ in** credere in.
belittle [bɪ'lɪtl] vt sminuire.
Belize [bɛ'liːz] n Belize m.
bell [bɛl] n campana; (small, on door, electric) campanello; **that rings a ~** (fig) mi ricorda qualcosa.
bell-bottoms ['bɛlbɒtəmz] npl calzoni mpl a zampa d'elefante.
bellboy ['bɛlbɔɪ], (US) **bellhop** ['bɛlhɒp] n ragazzo d'albergo, fattorino d'albergo.
belligerent [bɪ'lɪdʒərənt] adj (at war) belligerante; (fig) bellicoso(a).
bellow ['bɛləʊ] vi muggire; (cry) urlare (a squarciagola) ♦ vt (orders) urlare (a squarciagola).
bellows ['bɛləʊz] npl soffietto m.
bell push n (BRIT) pulsante m del campanello.
belly ['bɛlɪ] n pancia.
bellyache ['bɛleɪk] n mal m di pancia ♦ vi (col) mugugnare.
bellybutton ['bɛlɪbʌtn] n ombelico.
bellyful ['bɛlɪful] n (col): **to have had a ~ of** (fig) averne piene le tasche (di).
belong [bɪ'lɒŋ] vi: **to ~ to** appartenere a;

(club etc) essere socio di; **this book ~s here** questo libro va qui.
belongings [bɪ'lɒŋɪŋz] npl cose fpl, roba; **personal ~** effetti mpl personali.
Belorussia [bɛləʊ'rʌʃə] n Bielorussia.
Belorussian [bɛləʊ'rʌʃən] adj, n = **Belarussian**.
beloved [bɪ'lʌvɪd] adj adorato(a).
below [bɪ'ləʊ] prep sotto, al di sotto di ♦ adv sotto, di sotto; giù; **see ~** vedi sotto or oltre; **temperatures ~ normal** temperature al di sotto del normale.
belt [bɛlt] n cintura; (TECH) cinghia ♦ vt (thrash) picchiare ♦ vi (BRIT col) filarsela; **industrial ~** zona industriale.
▸ **belt out** vt (song) cantare a squarciagola.
▸ **belt up** vi (BRIT col) chiudere la boccaccia.
beltway ['bɛltweɪ] n (US AUT) circonvallazione f; (: motorway) autostrada.
bemoan [bɪ'məʊn] vt lamentare.
bemused [bɪ'mjuːzd] adj perplesso(a), stupito(a).
bench [bɛntʃ] n panca; (in workshop) banco; **the B~** (LAW) la Corte.
bench mark n banco di prova.
bend [bɛnd] vb (pt, pp **bent** [bɛnt]) vt curvare; (leg, arm) piegare ♦ vi curvarsi; piegarsi ♦ n (BRIT: in road) curva; (in pipe, river) gomito.
▸ **bend down** vi chinarsi.
▸ **bend over** vi piegarsi.
bends [bɛndz] npl (MED) embolia.
beneath [bɪ'niːθ] prep sotto, al di sotto di; (unworthy of) indegno(a) di ♦ adv sotto, di sotto.
benefactor ['bɛnɪfæktə*] n benefattore m.
benefactress ['bɛnɪfæktrɪs] n benefattrice f.
beneficial [bɛnɪ'fɪʃl] adj che fa bene; **~ to** che giova a.
beneficiary [bɛnɪ'fɪʃərɪ] n (LAW) beneficiario/a.
benefit ['bɛnɪfɪt] n beneficio, vantaggio; (allowance of money) indennità f inv ♦ vt far bene a ♦ vi: **he'll ~ from it** ne trarrà beneficio or profitto.
benefit performance n spettacolo di beneficenza.
Benelux ['bɛnɪlʌks] n Benelux m.
benevolent [bɪ'nɛvələnt] adj benevolo(a).
BEng n abbr (= Bachelor of Engineering) laurea in ingegneria.
benign [bɪ'naɪn] adj benevolo(a); (MED) benigno(a).
bent [bɛnt] pt, pp of **bend** ♦ n inclinazione f ♦ adj (wire, pipe) piegato(a), storto(a); (col: dishonest) losco(a); **to be ~ on** essere

deciso(a) a.

bequeath [bɪ'kwiːð] *vt* lasciare in eredità.

bequest [bɪ'kwɛst] *n* lascito.

bereaved [bɪ'riːvd] *adj* in lutto ♦ *npl*: **the ~** i familiari in lutto.

bereavement [bɪ'riːvmənt] *n* lutto.

beret ['bɛreɪ] *n* berretto.

Bering Sea ['bɛrɪŋ-] *n*: **the ~** il mar di Bering.

berk [bəːk] *n* (*BRIT col!*) coglione/a (*!*).

Berks *abbr* (*BRIT*) = Berkshire.

Berlin [bəː'lɪn] *n* Berlino *f*; **East/West ~** Berlino est/ovest.

berm [bəːm] *n* (*US AUT*) corsia d'emergenza.

Bermuda [bəː'mjuːdə] *n* le Bermude.

Bermuda shorts *npl* bermuda *mpl*.

Bern [bəːn] *n* Berna *f*.

berry ['bɛrɪ] *n* bacca.

berserk [bə'səːk] *adj*: **to go ~** montare su tutte le furie.

berth [bəːθ] *n* (*bed*) cuccetta; (*for ship*) ormeggio ♦ *vi* (*in harbour*) entrare in porto; (*at anchor*) gettare l'ancora; **to give sb a wide ~** (*fig*) tenersi alla larga da qn.

beseech, *pt, pp* **besought** [bɪ'siːtʃ, bɪ'sɔːt] *vt* implorare.

beset, *pt, pp* **beset** [bɪ'sɛt] *vt* assalire ♦ *adj*: **a policy ~ with dangers** una politica irta *or* piena di pericoli.

besetting [bɪ'sɛtɪŋ] *adj*: **his ~ sin** il suo più grande difetto.

beside [bɪ'saɪd] *prep* accanto a; (*compared with*) rispetto a, in confronto a; **to be ~ o.s. (with anger)** essere fuori di sé; **that's ~ the point** non c'entra.

besides [bɪ'saɪdz] *adv* inoltre, per di più ♦ *prep* oltre a; (*except*) a parte.

besiege [bɪ'siːdʒ] *vt* (*town*) assediare; (*fig*) tempestare.

besotted [bɪ'sɔtɪd] *adj* (*BRIT*): **~ with** infatuato(a) di.

besought [bɪ'sɔːt] *pt, pp of* **beseech**.

bespectacled [bɪ'spɛktɪkld] *adj* occhialuto(a).

bespoke [bɪ'spəuk] *adj* (*BRIT: garment*) su misura; **~ tailor** sarto.

best [bɛst] *adj* migliore ♦ *adv* meglio; **the ~ thing to do is ...** la cosa migliore da fare *or* farsi è ...; **the ~ part of** (*quantity*) la maggior parte di; **at ~** tutt'al più; **to make the ~ of sth** cavare il meglio possibile da qc; **to do one's ~** fare del proprio meglio; **to the ~ of my knowledge** per quel che ne so; **to the ~ of my ability** al massimo delle mie capacità; **he's not exactly patient at the ~ of times** non è mai molto paziente.

best-before date *n* (*COMM*) data limite d'utilizzo *or* di consumo.

best man *n* testimone *m* dello sposo.

bestow [bɪ'stəu] *vt*: **to ~ sth on sb** conferire qc a qn.

bestseller ['bɛst'sɛlə*] *n* bestseller *m inv*.

bet [bɛt] *n* scommessa ♦ *vt, vi* (*pt, pp* **bet** *or* **betted**) scommettere; **it's a safe ~** (*fig*) è molto probabile.

Bethlehem ['bɛθlɪhɛm] *n* Betlemme *f*.

betray [bɪ'treɪ] *vt* tradire.

betrayal [bɪ'treɪəl] *n* tradimento.

better ['bɛtə*] *adj* migliore ♦ *adv* meglio ♦ *vt* migliorare ♦ *n*: **to get the ~ of** avere la meglio su; **you had ~ do it** è meglio che lo faccia; **he thought ~ of it** cambiò idea; **to get ~** migliorare; **a change for the ~** un cambiamento in meglio; **that's ~!** così va meglio!; **I had ~ go** dovrei andare; **~ off** *adj* più ricco(a); (*fig*): **you'd be ~ off this way** starebbe meglio così.

betting ['bɛtɪŋ] *n* scommesse *fpl*.

betting shop *n* (*BRIT*) ufficio dell'allibratore.

between [bɪ'twiːn] *prep* tra ♦ *adv* in mezzo, nel mezzo; **the road ~ here and London** la strada da qui a Londra; **we only had £5 ~ us** fra tutti e due avevamo solo 5 sterline.

bevel ['bɛvl] *n* (*also*: **~(led) edge**) profilo smussato.

beverage ['bɛvərɪdʒ] *n* bevanda.

bevy ['bɛvɪ] *n*: **a ~ of** una banda di.

bewail [bɪ'weɪl] *vt* lamentare.

beware [bɪ'wɛə*] *vt, vi*: **to ~ (of)** stare attento(a) (a).

bewildered [bɪ'wɪldəd] *adj* sconcertato(a), confuso(a).

bewildering [bɪ'wɪldərɪŋ] *adj* sconcertante, sbalorditivo(a).

bewitching [bɪ'wɪtʃɪŋ] *adj* affascinante.

beyond [bɪ'jɔnd] *prep* (*in space*) oltre; (*exceeding*) al di sopra di ♦ *adv* di là; **~ doubt** senza dubbio; **~ repair** irreparabile.

b/f *abbr see* **brought forward**.

bhp *n abbr* (*AUT*: = brake horsepower*) c.v. (= *cavallo vapore*).

bi... [baɪ] *prefix* bi....

biannual [baɪ'ænjuəl] *adj* semestrale.

bias ['baɪəs] *n* (*prejudice*) pregiudizio; (*preference*) preferenza.

bias(s)ed ['baɪəst] *adj* parziale; **to be ~ against** essere prevenuto(a) contro.

biathlon [baɪ'æθlən] *n* biathlon *m*.

bib [bɪb] *n* bavaglino.

Bible ['baɪbl] *n* Bibbia.

bibliography [bɪblɪ'ɔgrəfɪ] n bibliografia.
bicarbonate of soda [baɪ'kɑːbənɪt-] n bicarbonato (di sodio).
bicentenary [baɪsɛn'tiːnərɪ], **bicentennial** [baɪsɛn'tɛnɪəl] n bicentenario.
biceps ['baɪsɛps] n bicipite m.
bicker ['bɪkə*] vi bisticciare.
bicycle ['baɪsɪkl] n bicicletta.
bicycle path n, **bicycle track** n sentiero ciclabile.
bicycle pump n pompa della bicicletta.
bid [bɪd] n offerta; (attempt) tentativo ♦ vb (pt **bade** [bæd] or **bid**, pp **bidden** ['bɪdn] or **bid**) vi fare un'offerta ♦ vt fare un'offerta di; **to ~ sb good day** dire buon giorno a qn.
bidder ['bɪdə*] n: **the highest ~** il maggior offerente.
bidding ['bɪdɪŋ] n offerte fpl.
bide [baɪd] vt: **to ~ one's time** aspettare il momento giusto.
bidet ['biːdeɪ] n bidè m inv.
bidirectional ['baɪdɪ rɛkʃənl] adj bidirezionale.
biennial [baɪ'ɛnɪəl] adj biennale ♦ n (pianta) biennale f.
bier [bɪə*] n bara.
bifocals [baɪ'fəuklz] npl occhiali mpl bifocali.
big [bɪg] adj grande; grosso(a); **my ~ brother** mio fratello maggiore; **to do things in a ~ way** fare le cose in grande.
bigamy ['bɪgəmɪ] n bigamia.
big dipper [-'dɪpə*] n montagne fpl russe, otto m inv volante.
big end n (AUT) testa di biella.
biggish ['bɪgɪʃ] adj (see big) piuttosto grande; piuttosto grosso(a); **a ~ rent** un affitto piuttosto alto.
bigheaded ['bɪg'hɛdɪd] adj presuntuoso(a).
big-hearted ['bɪg'hɑːtɪd] adj generoso(a).
bigot ['bɪgət] n persona gretta.
bigoted ['bɪgətɪd] adj gretto(a).
bigotry ['bɪgətrɪ] n grettezza.
big toe n alluce m.
big top n tendone m del circo.
big wheel n (at fair) ruota (panoramica).
bigwig ['bɪgwɪg] n (col) pezzo grosso.
bike [baɪk] n bici f inv.
bikini [bɪ'kiːnɪ] n bikini m inv.
bilateral [baɪ'lætərl] adj bilaterale.
bile [baɪl] n bile f.
bilingual [baɪ'lɪŋgwəl] adj bilingue.
bilious ['bɪlɪəs] adj biliare; (fig) bilioso(a).
bill [bɪl] n (in hotel, restaurant) conto; (COMM) fattura; (for gas, electricity) bolletta, conto; (POL) atto; (US: banknote) banconota; (notice) avviso; (THEAT): **on the ~** in

cartellone; (of bird) becco ♦ vt mandare il conto a; **may I have the ~ please?** posso avere il conto per piacere?; **"stick or post no ~s"** "divieto di affissione"; **to fit** or **fill the ~** (fig) fare al caso; **~ of exchange** cambiale f, tratta; **~ of lading** polizza di carico; **~ of sale** atto di vendita.
billboard ['bɪlbɔːd] n tabellone m.
billet ['bɪlɪt] n alloggio ♦ vt (troops etc) alloggiare.
billfold ['bɪlfəuld] n (US) portafoglio.
billiards ['bɪljədz] n biliardo.
billion ['bɪljən] n (BRIT) bilione m; (US) miliardo.
billow ['bɪləu] n (of smoke) nuvola; (of sail) rigonfiamento ♦ vi (smoke) alzarsi in volute; (sail) gonfiarsi.
bills payable (B/P, b.p.) npl effetti mpl passivi.
bills receivable (B/R, b.r.) npl effetti mpl attivi.
billy goat ['bɪlɪgəut] n caprone m, becco.
bimbo ['bɪmbəu] n (col) pollastrella, svampitella.
bin [bɪn] n bidone m; (BRIT: also: **dust~**) pattumiera; (: also: **litter ~**) cestino.
binary ['baɪnərɪ] adj binario(a).
bind, pt, pp **bound** [baɪnd, baund] vt legare; (oblige) obbligare.
▶**bind over** vt (LAW) dare la condizionale a.
▶**bind up** vt (wound) fasciare, bendare; **to be bound up in** (work, research etc) essere completamente assorbito da; **to be bound up with** (person) dedicarsi completamente a.
binder ['baɪndə*] n (file) classificatore m.
binding ['baɪndɪŋ] n (of book) legatura ♦ adj (contract) vincolante.
binge [bɪndʒ] n (col): **to go on a ~** fare baldoria.
bingo ['bɪŋgəu] n gioco simile alla tombola.
bin liner n sacchetto per l'immondizia.
binoculars [bɪ'nɔkjuləz] npl binocolo.
biochemistry [baɪəu'kɛmɪstrɪ] n biochimica.
biodegradable ['baɪəudɪ'greɪdəbl] adj biodegradabile.
biodiversity ['baɪəudaɪ'vəːsɪtɪ] n biodiversità f inv.
biofuel ['baɪəufjuəl] n carburante m biologico.
biographer [baɪ'ɔgrəfə*] n biografo/a.
biographic(al) [baɪə'græfɪk(l)] adj biografico(a).
biography [baɪ'ɔgrəfɪ] n biografia.
biological [baɪə'lɔdʒɪkl] adj biologico(a).
biological clock n orologio biologico.

biologist [baɪ'ɒlədʒɪst] n biologo/a.
biology [baɪ'ɒlədʒɪ] n biologia.
biophysics [baɪəu'fɪzɪks] n biofisica.
biopic ['baɪəupɪk] n film m inv biografia inv.
biosphere ['baɪəusfɪə*] n biosfera.
biopsy ['baɪɒpsɪ] n biopsia.
biotechnology [baɪəutɛk'nɒlədʒɪ] n biotecnologia.
birch [bəːtʃ] n betulla.
bird [bəːd] n uccello; (BRIT col: girl) bambola.
bird of prey n (uccello) rapace m.
bird's-eye view ['bəːdzaɪ-] n vista panoramica.
bird watcher n ornitologo/a dilettante.
Biro ® ['baɪrəu] n biro ® f inv.
birth [bəːθ] n nascita; **to give ~ to** dare alla luce; (fig) dare inizio a.
birth certificate n certificato di nascita.
birth control n controllo delle nascite; contraccezione f.
birthday ['bəːθdeɪ] n compleanno.
birthmark ['bəːθmɑːk] n voglia.
birthplace ['bəːθpleɪs] n luogo di nascita.
birth rate n indice m di natalità.
Biscay ['bɪskeɪ] n: **the Bay of ~** il golfo di Biscaglia.
biscuit ['bɪskɪt] n (BRIT) biscotto; (US) panino al latte.
bisect [baɪ'sɛkt] vt tagliare in due (parti); (MATH) bisecare.
bisexual ['baɪ'sɛksjuəl] adj, n bisessuale (m/f).
bishop ['bɪʃəp] n vescovo; (CHESS) alfiere m.
bistro ['biːstrəu] n bistrò m inv.
bit [bɪt] pt of **bite ♦** n pezzo; (of tool) punta; (of horse) morso; (COMPUT) bit m inv; (US: coin) ottavo di dollaro; **a ~ of** un po' di; **a ~ mad/dangerous** un po' matto/pericoloso; **~ by** ~ a poco a poco; **to do one's ~** fare la propria parte; **to come to ~s** (break) andare a pezzi; **bring all your ~s and pieces** porta tutte le tue cose.
bitch [bɪtʃ] n (dog) cagna; (col!) puttana (!).
bite [baɪt] vt, vi (pt **bit** [bɪt], pp **bitten** ['bɪtn]) mordere ♦ n morso; (insect ~) puntura; (mouthful) boccone m; **let's have a ~ (to eat)** mangiamo un boccone; **to ~ one's nails** mangiarsi le unghie.
biting ['baɪtɪŋ] adj pungente.
bit part n (THEAT) particina.
bitten ['bɪtn] pp of **bite**.
bitter ['bɪtə*] adj amaro(a); (wind, criticism) pungente; (icy: weather) gelido(a) ♦ n (BRIT: beer) birra amara; **to the ~ end** a oltranza.
bitterly ['bɪtəlɪ] adv (disappoint, complain,

weep) amaramente; (oppose, criticise) aspramente; (jealous) profondamente; **it's ~ cold** fa un freddo gelido.
bitterness ['bɪtənɪs] n amarezza; gusto amaro.
bittersweet ['bɪtəswiːt] adj agrodolce.
bitty ['bɪtɪ] adj (BRIT col) frammentario(a).
bitumen ['bɪtjumɪn] n bitume m.
bivouac ['bɪvuæk] n bivacco.
bizarre [bɪ'zɑː*] adj bizzarro(a).
bk abbr = **bank; book**.
BL n abbr (= Bachelor of Law(s), Bachelor of Letters) titolo di studio; (US: = Bachelor of Literature) titolo di studio.
bl abbr = **bill of lading**.
blab [blæb] vi parlare troppo ♦ vt (also: ~ out) spifferare.
black [blæk] adj nero(a) ♦ n nero; (person): **B~** negro/a ♦ vt (BRIT INDUSTRY) boicottare; **~ coffee** caffè m inv nero; **to give sb a ~ eye** fare un occhio nero a qn; **in the ~** (in credit) in attivo; **there it is in ~ and white** (fig) eccolo nero su bianco; **~ and blue** adj tutto(a) pesto(a).
►black out vi (faint) svenire.
black belt n (SPORT) cintura nera; (US: area): **the ~** zona abitata principalmente da negri.
blackberry ['blækbərɪ] n mora.
blackbird ['blækbəːd] n merlo.
blackboard ['blækbɔːd] n lavagna.
black box n (AVIAT) scatola nera.
Black Country n (BRIT): **the ~** zona carbonifera del centro dell'Inghilterra.
blackcurrant [blæk'kʌrənt] n ribes m inv.
black economy n (BRIT) economia sommersa.
blacken ['blækn] vt annerire.
Black Forest n: **the ~** la Foresta Nera.
blackhead ['blækhɛd] n punto nero, comedone m.
black hole n (ASTRON) buco nero.
black ice n strato trasparente di ghiaccio.
blackjack ['blækdʒæk] n (CARDS) ventuno; (US: truncheon) manganello.
blackleg ['blæklɛg] n (BRIT) crumiro.
blacklist ['blæklɪst] n lista nera ♦ vt mettere sulla lista nera.
blackmail ['blækmeɪl] n ricatto ♦ vt ricattare.
blackmailer ['blækmeɪlə*] n ricattatore/trice.
black market n mercato nero.
blackout ['blækaut] n oscuramento; (fainting) svenimento; (TV) interruzione f delle trasmissioni.
black pepper n pepe m nero.
Black Sea n: **the ~** il mar Nero.

black sheep n pecora nera.
blacksmith ['blæksmɪθ] n fabbro ferraio.
black spot n (AUT) luogo famigerato per
gli incidenti.
bladder ['blædə*] n vescica.
blade [bleɪd] n lama; (of oar) pala; ~ of
grass filo d'erba.
blame [bleɪm] n colpa ♦ vt: **to** ~ **sb/sth for
sth** dare la colpa di qc a qn/qc; **who's to**
~? chi è colpevole?; **I'm not to** ~ non è
colpa mia.
blameless ['bleɪmlɪs] adj irreprensibile.
blanch [blɑ:ntʃ] vi (person) sbiancare in
viso ♦ vt (CULIN) scottare.
bland [blænd] adj mite; (taste) blando(a).
blank [blæŋk] adj bianco(a); (look)
distratto(a) ♦ n spazio vuoto; (cartridge)
cartuccia a salve; **to draw a** ~ (fig) non
aver nessun risultato.
blank cheque, (US) **blank check** n
assegno in bianco; **to give sb a** ~ **to do**
(fig) dare carta bianca a qn per fare.
blanket ['blæŋkɪt] n coperta ♦ adj
(statement, agreement) globale.
blanket cover n: **to give** ~ (subj: insurance
policy) coprire tutti i rischi.
blare [blɛə*] vi strombettare; (radio)
suonare a tutto volume.
blasé ['blɑ:zeɪ] adj blasé inv.
blasphemous ['blæsfɪməs] adj blasfemo(a).
blasphemy ['blæsfɪmɪ] n bestemmia.
blast [blɑ:st] n (of wind) raffica; (of air,
steam) getto; (bomb ~) esplosione f ♦ vt
far saltare ♦ excl (BRIT col) mannaggia!;
(at) full ~ a tutta forza.
▶**blast off** vi (SPACE) essere lanciato(a).
blast-off ['blɑ:stɔf] n (SPACE) lancio.
blatant ['bleɪtənt] adj flagrante.
blatantly ['bleɪtəntlɪ] adv: **it's** ~ **obvious** è
lampante.
blaze [bleɪz] n (fire) incendio; (glow: of fire,
sun etc) bagliore m; (fig) vampata ♦ vi (fire)
ardere, fiammeggiare; (fig) infiammarsi
♦ vt: **to** ~ **a trail** (fig) tracciare una via
nuova; **in a** ~ **of publicity** circondato da
grande pubblicità.
blazer ['bleɪzə*] n blazer m inv.
bleach [bli:tʃ] n (also: household ~)
varechina ♦ vt (material) candeggiare.
bleached ['bli:tʃt] adj (hair) decolorato(a).
bleachers ['bli:tʃəz] npl (US) posti mpl di
gradinata.
bleak [bli:k] adj (prospect, future) tetro(a);
(landscape) desolato(a); (weather)
gelido(a); (smile) pallido(a).
bleary-eyed ['blɪərɪ'aɪd] adj dagli occhi
offuscati.
bleat [bli:t] vi belare.

bleed, pt, pp **bled** [bli:d, blɛd] vt
dissanguare; (brakes, radiator) spurgare
♦ vi sanguinare; **my nose is** ~**ing** mi viene
fuori sangue dal naso.
bleep [bli:p] n breve segnale m acustico,
bip m inv ♦ vi suonare ♦ vt (doctor)
chiamare con il cercapersone.
bleeper ['bli:pə*] n (of doctor etc)
cercapersone m inv.
blemish ['blɛmɪʃ] n macchia.
blend [blɛnd] n miscela ♦ vt mescolare ♦ vi
(colours etc) armonizzare.
blender ['blɛndə*] n (CULIN) frullatore m.
bless, pt, pp **blessed** or **blest** [blɛs, blɛst] vt
benedire; ~ **you!** (sneezing) salute!; **to be**
~**ed with** godere di.
blessed ['blɛsɪd] adj (REL: holy)
benedetto(a); (happy) beato(a); **every** ~
day tutti i santi giorni.
blessing ['blɛsɪŋ] n benedizione f; fortuna;
to count one's ~**s** ringraziare Iddio,
ritenersi fortunato; **it was a** ~ **in disguise**
in fondo è stato un bene.
blest [blɛst] pt, pp of **bless**.
blew [blu:] pt of **blow**.
blight [blaɪt] n (of plants) golpe f ♦ vt (hopes
etc) deludere; (life) rovinare.
blimey ['blaɪmɪ] excl (BRIT col) accidenti!
blind [blaɪnd] adj cieco(a) ♦ n (for window)
avvolgibile m; (Venetian ~) veneziana ♦ vt
accecare; **to turn a** ~ **eye** (on or to)
chiudere un occhio (su).
blind alley n vicolo cieco.
blind corner n (BRIT) svolta cieca.
blind date n appuntamento combinato (tra
due persone che non si conoscono).
blinders ['blaɪndəz] npl (US) = **blinkers**.
blindfold ['blaɪndfəuld] n benda ♦ adj, adv
bendato(a) ♦ vt bendare gli occhi a.
blinding ['blaɪndɪŋ] adj (flash, light)
accecante; (pain) atroce.
blindly ['blaɪndlɪ] adv ciecamente.
blindness ['blaɪndnɪs] n cecità.
blind spot n (AUT etc) punto cieco; (fig)
punto debole.
blink [blɪŋk] vi battere gli occhi; (light)
lampeggiare ♦ n: **to be on the** ~ (col)
essere scassato(a).
blinkers ['blɪŋkəz] npl (BRIT) paraocchi mpl.
blinking ['blɪŋkɪŋ] adj (BRIT col): **this** ~ ...
questo(a) maledetto(a) ....
blip [blɪp] n (on radar etc) segnale m
intermittente; (on graph) piccola
variazione f; (fig) momentanea battuta
d'arresto.
bliss [blɪs] n estasi f.
blissful ['blɪsfəl] adj (event, day)
stupendo(a), meraviglioso(a); (smile)

beato(a); **in ~ ignorance** nella (più) beata ignoranza.

blissfully ['blɪsfəlɪ] *adj (sigh, smile)* beatamente; **~ happy** magnificamente felice.

blister ['blɪstə*] *n (on skin)* vescica; *(on paintwork)* bolla ♦ *vi (paint)* coprirsi di bolle.

blithe [blaɪð] *adj* gioioso(a), allegro(a).

blithely ['blaɪðlɪ] *adv* allegramente.

blithering ['blɪðərɪŋ] *adj (col):* **this ~ idiot** questa razza d'idiota.

BLit(t) *n abbr (= Bachelor of Literature) titolo di studio.*

blitz [blɪts] *n* blitz *m*; **to have a ~ on sth** *(fig)* prendere d'assalto qc.

blizzard ['blɪzəd] *n* bufera di neve.

BLM *n abbr (US: = Bureau of Land Management)* ≈ il demanio.

bloated ['bləʊtɪd] *adj* gonfio(a).

blob [blɒb] *n (drop)* goccia; *(stain, spot)* macchia.

bloc [blɒk] *n (POL)* blocco.

block [blɒk] *n (gen, COMPUT)* blocco; *(in pipes)* ingombro; *(toy)* cubo; *(of buildings)* isolato ♦ *vt (gen, COMPUT)* bloccare; **~ of flats** caseggiato; **3 ~s from here** a 3 isolati di distanza da qui; **mental ~** blocco mentale.

►**block up** *vt* bloccare; *(pipe)* ingorgare, intasare.

blockade [blɒ'keɪd] *n* blocco ♦ *vt* assediare.

blockage ['blɒkɪdʒ] *n* ostacolo.

block and tackle *n (TECH)* paranco.

block booking *n* prenotazione *f* in blocco.

blockbuster ['blɒkbʌstə*] *n* libro *or* film *etc* sensazionale.

block capitals *npl* stampatello.

blockhead ['blɒkhɛd] *n* testa di legno.

block letters *npl* stampatello.

block release *n (BRIT) periodo pagato concesso al tirocinante per effettuare studi superiori.*

block vote *n (BRIT)* voto per delega.

bloke [bləʊk] *n (BRIT col)* tizio.

blond [blɒnd] *n (man)* biondo ♦ *adj* biondo(a).

blonde [blɒnd] *n (woman)* bionda ♦ *adj* biondo(a).

blood [blʌd] *n* sangue *m*; **new ~** *(fig)* nuova linfa.

blood bank *n* banca del sangue.

blood count *n* conteggio di globuli rossi e bianchi.

bloodcurdling ['blʌdkə:dlɪŋ] *adj* raccapricciante, da far gelare il sangue.

blood donor *n* donatore/trice di sangue.

blood group *n* gruppo sanguigno.

bloodhound ['blʌdhaʊnd] *n* segugio.

bloodless ['blʌdlɪs] *adj (pale)* smorto(a), esangue; *(coup)* senza spargimento di sangue.

bloodletting ['blʌdlɛtɪŋ] *n (MED)* salasso; *(fig)* spargimento di sangue.

blood poisoning *n* setticemia.

blood pressure *n* pressione *f* sanguigna; **to have high/low ~** avere la pressione alta/bassa.

bloodshed ['blʌdʃɛd] *n* spargimento di sangue.

bloodshot ['blʌdʃɒt] *adj:* **~ eyes** occhi iniettati di sangue.

bloodstained ['blʌdsteɪnd] *adj* macchiato(a) di sangue.

bloodstream ['blʌdstri:m] *n* flusso del sangue.

blood test *n* analisi *f inv* del sangue.

bloodthirsty ['blʌdθə:stɪ] *adj* assetato(a) di sangue.

blood transfusion *n* trasfusione *f* di sangue.

blood type *n* gruppo sanguigno.

blood vessel *n* vaso sanguigno.

bloody ['blʌdɪ] *adj* sanguinoso(a); *(BRIT col!):* **this ~ ...** questo maledetto ...; **a ~ awful day** *(col!)* una giornata di merda *(!)*; **~ good** *(col!)* maledettamente buono.

bloody-minded ['blʌdɪ'maɪndɪd] *adj (BRIT col)* indisponente.

bloom [blu:m] *n* fiore *m* ♦ *vi* essere in fiore.

blooming ['blu:mɪŋ] *adj (col):* **this ~ ...** questo(a) dannato(a) ....

blossom ['blɒsəm] *n* fiore *m*; *(with pl sense)* fiori *mpl* ♦ *vi* essere in fiore; **to ~ into** *(fig)* diventare.

blot [blɒt] *n* macchia ♦ *vt* macchiare; **to be a ~ on the landscape** rovinare il paesaggio; **to ~ one's copy book** *(fig)* farla grossa.

►**blot out** *vt (memories)* cancellare; *(view)* nascondere; *(nation, city)* annientare.

blotchy ['blɒtʃɪ] *adj (complexion)* coperto(a) di macchie.

blotter ['blɒtə*] *n* tampone *m* (di carta assorbente).

blotting paper ['blɒtɪŋ-] *n* carta assorbente.

blotto ['blɒtəʊ] *adj (col)* sbronzo(a).

blouse [blaʊz] *n* camicetta.

blow [bləʊ] *n* colpo ♦ *vb (pt* **blew**, *pp* **blown** [blu:, bləʊn]) *vi* soffiare ♦ *vt (fuse)* far saltare; **to come to ~s** venire alle mani; **to ~ one's nose** soffiarsi il naso; **to ~ a whistle** fischiare.

►**blow away** *vi* volare via ♦ *vt* portare via.

►**blow down** *vt* abbattere.

►**blow off** *vt* far volare via; **to ~ off course**

far uscire di rotta.

▶**blow out** *vi* scoppiare.

▶**blow over** *vi* calmarsi.

▶**blow up** *vi* saltare in aria ♦ *vt* far saltare in aria; (*tyre*) gonfiare; (*PHOT*) ingrandire.

blow-dry ['bləʊdraɪ] *n* (*hairstyle*) messa in piega a föhn ♦ *vt* asciugare con il föhn.

blowlamp ['bləʊlæmp] *n* (*BRIT*) lampada a benzina per saldare.

blown [bləʊn] *pp of* **blow**.

blowout ['bləʊaʊt] *n* (*of tyre*) scoppio; (*col: big meal*) abbuffata.

blowtorch ['bləʊtɔːtʃ] *n* lampada a benzina per saldare.

blowzy ['blaʊzɪ] *adj* trasandato(a).

BLS *n abbr* (*US*) = *Bureau of Labor Statistics*.

blubber ['blʌbə*] *n* grasso di balena ♦ *vi* (*pej*) piangere forte.

bludgeon ['blʌdʒən] *vt* prendere a randellate.

blue [bluː] *adj* azzurro(a), celeste; (*darker*) blu *inv*; ~ **film/joke** film/barzelletta pornografico(a); (**only**) **once in a** ~ **moon** a ogni morte di papa; **out of the** ~ (*fig*) all'improvviso; *see also* **blues**.

blue baby *n* neonato cianotico.

bluebell ['bluːbɛl] *n* giacinto di bosco.

bluebottle ['bluːbɔtl] *n* moscone *m*.

blue cheese *n* formaggio tipo gorgonzola.

blue-chip ['bluːtʃɪp] *adj*: ~ **investment** investimento sicuro.

blue-collar worker ['bluːkɔlə*-] *n* operaio/a.

blue jeans *npl* blue-jeans *mpl*.

blueprint ['bluːprɪnt] *n* cianografia, (*fig*): ~ (**for**) formula (di).

blues [bluːz] *npl*: **the** ~ (*MUS*) il blues; **to have the** ~ (*col: feeling*) essere a terra.

bluff [blʌf] *vi* bluffare ♦ *n* bluff *m inv*; (*promontory*) promontorio scosceso ♦ *adj* (*person*) brusco(a); **to call sb's** ~ mettere alla prova il bluff di qn.

blunder ['blʌndə*] *n* abbaglio ♦ *vi* prendere un abbaglio; **to** ~ **into sb/sth** andare a sbattere contro qn/qc.

blunt [blʌnt] *adj* (*edge*) smussato(a); (*point*) spuntato(a); (*knife*) che non taglia; (*person*) brusco(a) ♦ *vt* smussare; spuntare; **this pencil is** ~ questa matita non ha più la punta; ~ **instrument** (*LAW*) corpo contundente.

bluntly ['blʌntlɪ] *adv* (*speak*) senza mezzi termini.

bluntness ['blʌntnɪs] *n* (*of person*) brutale franchezza.

blur [bləː*] *n* cosa offuscata ♦ *vt* offuscare.

blurb [bləːb] *n* trafiletto pubblicitario.

blurred [bləːd] *adj* (*photo*) mosso(a); (*TV*)

sfuocato(a).

blurt out [bləːt-] *vt* lasciarsi sfuggire.

blush [blʌʃ] *vi* arrossire ♦ *n* rossore *m*.

blusher ['blʌʃə*] *n* fard *m inv*.

bluster ['blʌstə*] *n* spacconate *fpl*; (*threats*) vuote minacce *fpl* ♦ *vi* fare lo spaccone; minacciare a vuoto.

blustering ['blʌstərɪŋ] *adj* (*tone etc*) da spaccone.

blustery ['blʌstərɪ] *adj* (*weather*) burrascoso(a).

Blvd *abbr* = *boulevard*.

BM *n abbr* = *British Museum*; (*SCOL*): = *Bachelor of Medicine*) titolo di studio.

BMA *n abbr* = *British Medical Association*.

BMJ *n abbr* = *British Medical Journal*.

BMus *n abbr* (= *Bachelor of Music*) titolo di studio.

BMX *n abbr* (= *bicycle motorcross*) BMX *f inv*; ~ **bike** mountain bike *f inv* per cross.

BO *n abbr* (*col*: = *body odour*) odori *mpl* sgradevoli (del corpo); (*US*) = **box office**.

boar [bɔː*] *n* cinghiale *m*.

board [bɔːd] *n* tavola; (*on wall*) tabellone *m*; (*for chess etc*) scacchiera; (*committee*) consiglio, comitato; (*in firm*) consiglio d'amministrazione; (*NAUT, AVIAT*): **on** ~ a bordo ♦ *vt* (*ship*) salire a bordo di; (*train*) salire su; **full** ~ (*BRIT*) pensione *f* completa; **half** ~ (*BRIT*) mezza pensione; ~ **and lodging** vitto e alloggio; **above** ~ (*fig*) regolare; **across the** ~ (*fig*) *adv* per tutte le categorie ♦ *adj* generale; **to go by the** ~ venir messo(a) da parte.

▶**board up** *vt* (*door*) chiudere con assi.

boarder ['bɔːdə*] *n* pensionante *m/f*; (*SCOL*) convittore/trice.

board game *n* gioco da tavolo.

boarding card ['bɔːdɪŋ-] *n* (*AVIAT, NAUT*) carta d'imbarco.

boarding house *n* pensione *f*.

boarding party *n* squadra di ispezione (*del carico di una nave*).

boarding pass *n* (*BRIT*) = **boarding card**.

boarding school *n* collegio.

board meeting *n* riunione *f* di consiglio.

board room *n* sala del consiglio.

boardwalk ['bɔːdwɔːk] *n* (*US*) passeggiata a mare.

boast [bəʊst] *vi*: **to** ~ (**about** *or* **of**) vantarsi (di) ♦ *vt* vantare ♦ *n* vanteria; vanto.

boastful ['bəʊstful] *adj* vanaglorioso(a).

boastfulness ['bəʊstfulnɪs] *n* vanagloria.

boat [bəʊt] *n* nave *f*; (*small*) barca; **to go by** ~ andare in barca *or* in nave; **we're all in the same** ~ (*fig*) siamo tutti nella stessa barca.

boater ['bəʊtə*] *n* (*hat*) paglietta.

boating ['bəʊtɪŋ] *n* canottaggio.
boat people *n* boat people *mpl.*
boatswain ['bəʊsn] *n* nostromo.
bob [bɔb] *vi* (*boat, cork on water: also:* ~ **up and down**) andare su e giù ♦ *n* (*BRIT col*) = **shilling**.
▶**bob up** *vi* saltare fuori.
bobbin ['bɔbɪn] *n* bobina; (*of sewing machine*) rocchetto.
bobby ['bɔbɪ] *n* (*BRIT col*) ≈ poliziotto.
bobsleigh ['bɔbsleɪ] *n* bob *m inv.*
bode [bəʊd] *vi:* **to** ~ **well/ill** (**for**) essere di buon/cattivo auspicio (per).
bodice ['bɔdɪs] *n* corsetto.
bodily ['bɔdɪlɪ] *adj* (*comfort, needs*) materiale; (*pain*) fisico(a) ♦ *adv* (*carry*) in braccio; (*lift*) di peso.
body ['bɔdɪ] *n* corpo; (*of car*) carrozzeria; (*of plane*) fusoliera; (*organization*) associazione *f*, organizzazione *f*; (*quantity*) quantità *f inv*; (*of speech, document*) parte *f* principale; (*also:* ~ **stocking**) body *m inv*; **in a** ~ in massa; **ruling** ~ direttivo; **a wine with** ~ un vino corposo.
body blow *n* (*fig*) duro colpo.
body-building ['bɔdɪ'bɪldɪŋ] *n* culturismo.
bodyguard ['bɔdɪgɑːd] *n* guardia del corpo.
body language *n* linguaggio del corpo.
body repairs *npl* (*AUT*) lavori *mpl* di carrozzeria.
body search *n* perquisizione *f* personale; **to submit to** *or* **undergo a** ~ essere sottoposto(a) a perquisizione personale.
bodywork ['bɔdɪwɜːk] *n* carrozzeria.
boffin ['bɔfɪn] *n* scienziato.
bog [bɔg] *n* palude *f* ♦ *vt:* **to get** ~ged **down** (*fig*) impantanarsi.
bogey ['bəʊgɪ] *n* (*worry*) spauracchio; (*also:* ~ **man**) babau *m inv.*
boggle ['bɔgl] *vi:* **the mind** ~s è incredibile.
Bogotá [bəʊgə'tɑː] *n* Bogotà *f.*
bogus ['bəʊgəs] *adj* falso(a); finto(a).
Bohemia [bəʊ'hiːmɪə] *n* Boemia.
Bohemian [bəʊ'hiːmɪən] *adj, n* boemo(a).
boil [bɔɪl] *vt, vi* bollire ♦ *n* (*MED*) foruncolo; **to come to the** *or* (*US*) **a** ~ raggiungere l'ebollizione; **to bring to the** *or* (*US*) **a** ~ portare a ebollizione; ~ed **egg** uovo alla coque; ~ed **potatoes** patate *fpl* bollite *or* lesse.
▶**boil down** *vi* (*fig*): **to** ~ **down to** ridursi a.
▶**boil over** *vi* traboccare (bollendo).
boiler ['bɔɪlə*] *n* caldaia.
boiler suit *n* (*BRIT*) tuta.
boiling ['bɔɪlɪŋ] *adj* bollente; **I'm** ~ (**hot**) (*col*) sto morendo di caldo.

boiling point *n* punto di ebollizione.
boil-in-the-bag [bɔɪlɪnðə'bæg] *adj* (*rice etc*) da bollire nel sacchetto.
boisterous ['bɔɪstərəs] *adj* chiassoso(a).
bold [bəʊld] *adj* audace; (*child*) impudente; (*outline*) chiaro(a); (*colour*) deciso(a).
boldness ['bəʊldnɪs] *n* audacia; impudenza.
bold type *n* (*TYP*) neretto, grassetto.
Bolivia [bə'lɪvɪə] *n* Bolivia.
Bolivian [bə'lɪvɪən] *adj, n* boliviano(a).
bollard ['bɔləd] *n* (*NAUT*) bitta; (*BRIT AUT*) colonnina luminosa.
bolshy ['bɔlʃɪ] *adj* (*BRIT col*) piantagrane, ribelle; **to be in a** ~ **mood** essere in vena di piantar grane.
bolster ['bəʊlstə*] *n* capezzale *m.*
▶**bolster up** *vt* sostenere.
bolt [bəʊlt] *n* chiavistello; (*with nut*) bullone *m* ♦ *adv:* ~ **upright** diritto(a) come un fuso ♦ *vt* serrare; (*food*) mangiare in fretta ♦ *vi* scappare via; **a** ~ **from the blue** (*fig*) un fulmine a ciel sereno.
bomb [bɔm] *n* bomba ♦ *vt* bombardare.
bombard [bɔm'bɑːd] *vt* bombardare.
bombardment [bɔm'bɑːdmənt] *n* bombardamento.
bombastic [bɔm'bæstɪk] *adj* ampolloso(a).
bomb disposal *n:* ~ **expert** artificiere *m;* ~ **unit** corpo degli artificieri.
bomber ['bɔmə*] *n* bombardiere *m;* (*terrorist*) dinamitardo/a.
bombing ['bɔmɪŋ] *n* bombardamento.
bomb scare *n* stato di allarme (*per sospetta presenza di una bomba*).
bombshell ['bɔmʃel] *n* (*fig*) notizia bomba.
bomb site *n* luogo bombardato.
bona fide ['bəʊnə'faɪdɪ] *adj* sincero(a); (*offer*) onesto(a).
bonanza [bə'nænzə] *n* cuccagna.
bond [bɔnd] *n* legame *m;* (*binding promise, FINANCE*) obbligazione *f;* **in** ~ (*of goods*) in attesa di sdoganamento.
bondage ['bɔndɪdʒ] *n* schiavitù *f.*
bonded warehouse ['bɔndɪd-] *n* magazzino doganale.
bone [bəʊn] *n* osso; (*of fish*) spina, lisca ♦ *vt* disossare; togliere le spine a.
bone china *n* porcellana fine.
bone-dry ['bəʊn'draɪ] *adj* asciuttissimo(a).
bone idle *adj:* **to be** ~ essere un(a) fannullone(a).
bone marrow *n* midollo osseo.
boner ['bəʊnə*] *n* (*US*) gaffe *f inv.*
bonfire ['bɔnfaɪə*] *n* falò *m inv.*
bonk [bɔŋk] *vt, vi* (*hum, col*) scopare (*!*).
bonkers ['bɔŋkəz] *adj* (*BRIT col*) suonato(a).
Bonn [bɔn] *n* Bonn *f.*
bonnet ['bɔnɪt] *n* cuffia; (*BRIT: of car*)

cofano.

bonny ['bɒnɪ] adj (esp Scottish) bello(a), carino(a).

bonus ['bəʊnəs] n premio; (on wages) gratifica.

bony ['bəʊnɪ] adj (thin: person) ossuto(a), angoloso(a); (arm, face, MED: tissue) osseo(a); (meat) pieno(a) di ossi; (fish) pieno(a) di spine.

boo [buː] excl ba! ♦ vt fischiare ♦ n fischio.

boob [buːb] n (col: breast) tetta; (: BRIT: mistake) gaffe f inv.

booby prize ['buːbɪ-] n premio per il peggior contendente.

booby trap ['buːbɪ-] n trabocchetto; (bomb) congegno che esplode al contatto.

booby-trapped ['buːbɪtræpt] adj: a ~ car una macchina con dell'esplosivo a bordo.

book [buk] n libro; (of stamps etc) blocchetto ♦ vt (ticket, seat, room) prenotare; (driver) multare; (football player) ammonire; ~s npl (COMM) conti mpl; to keep the ~s (COMM) tenere la contabilità; by the ~ secondo le regole; to throw the ~ at sb incriminare qn seriamente or con tutte le aggravanti.

►**book in** vi (BRIT: at hotel) prendere una camera.

►**book up** vt riservare, prenotare; the hotel is ~ed up l'albergo è al completo; all seats are ~ed up è tutto esaurito.

bookable ['bukəbl] adj: seats are ~ si possono prenotare i posti.

bookcase ['bukkeɪs] n scaffale m.

book ends npl reggilibri mpl.

booking ['bukɪŋ] n (BRIT) prenotazione f.

booking office n (BRIT) biglietteria.

book-keeping ['buk'kiːpɪŋ] n contabilità.

booklet ['buklɪt] n opuscolo, libretto.

bookmaker ['bukmeɪkə*] n allibratore m.

bookseller ['buksɛlə*] n libraio.

bookshelf ['bukʃɛlf] n mensola (per libri); **bookshelves** npl (bookcase) libreria.

bookshop ['bukʃɔp] n libreria.

bookstall ['bukstɔːl] n bancarella di libri.

bookstore ['bukstɔː*] n = **bookshop**.

book token n buono m libri inv.

book value n valore m contabile.

bookworm ['bukwəːm] n (fig) topo di biblioteca.

boom [buːm] n (noise) rimbombo; (busy period) boom m inv ♦ vi rimbombare; andare a gonfie vele.

boomerang ['buːməræŋ] n boomerang m inv ♦ vi (fig) avere effetto contrario; to ~ on sb (fig) ritorcersi contro qn.

boom town n città f inv in rapidissima espansione.

boon [buːn] n vantaggio.

boorish ['buərɪʃ] adj maleducato(a).

boost [buːst] n spinta ♦ vt spingere; (increase: sales, production) incentivare; to give a ~ to (morale) tirar su; it gave a ~ to his confidence è stata per lui un'iniezione di fiducia.

booster ['buːstə*] n (ELEC) amplificatore m; (TV) amplificatore m di segnale; (also: ~ rocket) razzo vettore; (MED) richiamo.

booster seat n (AUT: for children) seggiolino di sicurezza.

boot [buːt] n stivale m; (ankle ~) stivaletto; (for hiking) scarpone m da montagna; (for football etc) scarpa; (BRIT: of car) portabagagli m inv ♦ vt (COMPUT) inizializzare; to ~ (in addition) per giunta, in più; to give sb the ~ (col) mettere qn alla porta.

booth [buːð] n (at fair) baraccone m; (of cinema, telephone etc) cabina, (also: voting ~) cabina (elettorale).

bootleg ['buːtlɛg] adj di contrabbando; ~ record registrazione f pirata inv.

booty ['buːtɪ] n bottino.

booze [buːz] (col) n alcool m ♦ vi trincare.

boozer ['buːzə*] n (col: person) beone m; (BRIT col: pub) osteria.

border ['bɔːdə*] n orlo; margine m; (of a country) frontiera; the B~ la frontiera tra l'Inghilterra e la Scozia; the B~s la zona di confine tra l'Inghilterra e la Scozia.

►**border on** vt fus confinare con.

borderline ['bɔːdəlaɪn] n (fig) linea di demarcazione ♦ adj: ~ case caso limite.

bore [bɔː*] pt of bear ♦ vt (hole) perforare; (person) annoiare ♦ n (person) seccatore/ trice; (of gun) calibro; he's ~d to tears or ~d to death or ~d stiff è annoiato a morte, si annoia da morire.

boredom ['bɔːdəm] n noia.

boring ['bɔːrɪŋ] adj noioso(a).

born [bɔːn] adj: to be ~ nascere; I was ~ in 1960 sono nato nel 1960; ~ blind cieco dalla nascita; a ~ comedian un comico nato.

born-again [bɔːnə'gɛn] adj: ~ Christian convertito(a) alla chiesa evangelica.

borne [bɔːn] pp of bear.

Borneo ['bɔːnɪəu] n Borneo.

borough ['bʌrə] n comune m.

borrow ['bɒrəu] vt: to ~ sth (from sb) prendere in prestito qc (da qn); may I ~ your car? può prestarmi la macchina?

borrower ['bɒrəuə*] n (gen) chi prende a prestito; (ECON) mutuatario/a.

borrowing ['bɒrəuɪŋ] n prestito.

borstal ['bɔːstl] n (BRIT) riformatorio.

Bosnia ['bɔznɪə] n Bosnia.
Bosnia-Herzegovina
['bɔznɪəhɛrzə'gəuviːnə] n (also: **Bosnia-Hercegovina**) Bosnia-Erzegovina.
Bosnian ['bɔznɪən] adj, n bosniaco(a).
bosom ['buzəm] n petto; (fig) seno.
bosom friend n amico/a del cuore.
boss [bɔs] n capo ♦ vt (also: ~ **about** or **around**) comandare a bacchetta; **stop ~ing everyone about!** smettila di dare ordini a tutti!
bossy ['bɔsɪ] adj prepotente.
bosun ['bəusn] n nostromo.
botanical [bə'tænɪkl] adj botanico(a).
botanist ['bɔtənɪst] n botanico/a.
botany ['bɔtənɪ] n botanica.
botch [bɔtʃ] vt fare un pasticcio di.
both [bəuθ] adj entrambi(e), tutt'e due
♦ pron: ~ (**of them**) entrambi(e) ♦ adv: **they sell ~ meat and poultry** vendono insieme la carne ed il pollame; ~ **of us went, we ~ went** ci siamo andati tutt'e due.
bother ['bɔðə*] vt (worry) preoccupare; (annoy) infastidire ♦ vi (gen: ~ o.s.) preoccuparsi ♦ n: **it is a ~ to have to do è** una seccatura dover fare ♦ excl uffa!, accidenti!; **to ~ doing sth** darsi la pena di fare qc; **I'm sorry to ~ you** mi dispiace disturbarla; **please don't ~** non si scomodi; **it's no ~** non c'è problema.
Botswana [bɔt'swɑːnə] n Botswana m.
bottle ['bɔtl] n bottiglia; (of perfume, shampoo etc) flacone m; (baby's) biberon m inv ♦ vt imbottigliare; ~ **of wine/milk** bottiglia di vino/latte; **wine/milk** ~ bottiglia da vino/del latte.
►**bottle up** vt contenere.
bottle bank n contenitore m per la raccolta del vetro.
bottle-fed ['bɔtlfɛd] adj allattato(a) artificialmente.
bottleneck ['bɔtlnɛk] n ingorgo.
bottle-opener ['bɔtləupnə*] n apribottiglie m inv.
bottom ['bɔtəm] n fondo; (of mountain, tree, hill) piedi mpl; (buttocks) sedere m ♦ adj più basso(a); ultimo(a); **at the ~ of** in fondo a; **to get to the ~ of sth** (fig) andare al fondo di or in fondo a qc.
bottomless ['bɔtəmlɪs] adj senza fondo.
bottom line n: **the ~ is ...** in ultima analisi ....
botulism ['bɔtjulɪzəm] n botulismo.
bough [bau] n ramo.
bought [bɔːt] pt, pp of **buy**.
boulder ['bəuldə*] n masso (tondeggiante).
boulevard ['buːlvɑːd] n viale m.
bounce [bauns] vi (ball) rimbalzare;

(cheque) essere restituito(a) ♦ vt far rimbalzare ♦ n (rebound) rimbalzo; **to ~ in entrare** di slancio or con foga; **he's got plenty of ~** (fig) è molto esuberante.
bouncer ['baunsə*] n buttafuori m inv.
bouncy castle ® ['baunsɪ-] n grande castello gonfiabile per giocare.
bound [baund] pt, pp of **bind** ♦ n (gen pl) limite m; (leap) salto ♦ vt (leap) saltare; (limit) delimitare ♦ adj: **to be ~ to do sth** (obliged) essere costretto(a) a fare qc; **he's ~ to fail** (likely) è certo di fallire; ~ **for** diretto(a) a; **out of ~s** il cui accesso è vietato.
boundary ['baundrɪ] n confine m.
boundless ['baundlɪs] adj illimitato(a).
bountiful ['bauntɪful] adj (person) munifico(a); (God) misericordioso(a); (supply) abbondante.
bounty ['bauntɪ] n (generosity) liberalità, munificenza; (reward) taglia.
bounty hunter n cacciatore m di taglie.
bouquet ['bukeɪ] n bouquet m inv.
bourbon ['buəbən] n (US: also: ~ **whiskey**) bourbon m inv.
bourgeois ['buəʒwɑː] adj, n borghese (m/f).
bout [baut] n periodo; (of malaria etc) attacco; (BOXING etc) incontro.
boutique [buː'tiːk] n boutique f inv.
bow¹ [bəu] n nodo; (weapon) arco; (MUS) archetto; (NAUT: also: ~**s**) prua.
bow² [bau] n (with body) inchino ♦ vi inchinarsi; (yield): **to ~ to** or **before** sottomettersi a; **to ~ to the inevitable** rassegnarsi all'inevitabile.
bowels [bauəlz] npl intestini mpl; (fig) viscere fpl.
bowl [bəul] n (for eating) scodella; (for washing) bacino; (ball) boccia; (of pipe) fornello; (US: stadium) stadio ♦ vi (CRICKET) servire (la palla); see also **bowls**.
►**bowl over** vt (fig) sconcertare.
bow-legged ['bəu'lɛgɪd] adj dalle gambe storte.
bowler ['bəulə*] n giocatore m di bocce; (CRICKET) giocatore che serve la palla; (BRIT: also: ~ **hat**) bombetta.
bowling ['bəulɪŋ] n (game) gioco delle bocce; bowling m.
bowling alley n pista da bowling.
bowling green n campo di bocce.
bowls [bəulz] n gioco delle bocce.
bow tie n cravatta a farfalla.
box [bɔks] n scatola; (also: **cardboard** ~) (scatola di) cartone m; (crate; also for money) cassetta; (THEAT) palco; (BRIT AUT) area d'incrocio ♦ vi fare pugilato ♦ vt mettere in (una) scatola; (SPORT)

combattere contro.
boxer ['bɔksə*] n (person) pugile m; (dog)
boxer m inv.
boxing ['bɔksɪŋ] n (SPORT) pugilato.
Boxing Day n (BRIT) ≈ Santo Stefano; see
boxed note.

BOXING DAY

Il **Boxing Day** è il primo giorno
infrasettimanale dopo Natale e cade
generalmente il 26 di dicembre. Prende il nome
dall'usanza di donare pacchi regalo natalizi, un
tempo chiamati "Christmas boxes", a fornitori,
dipendenti e così via.

---

boxing gloves npl guantoni mpl da pugile.
boxing ring n ring m inv.
box number n (for advertisements) casella.
box office n biglietteria.
box room n ripostiglio.
boy [bɔɪ] n ragazzo; (small) bambino; (son)
figlio; (servant) servo.
boycott ['bɔɪkɔt] n boicottaggio ♦ vt
boicottare.
boyfriend ['bɔɪfrɛnd] n ragazzo.
boyish ['bɔɪɪʃ] adj di or da ragazzo.
Bp abbr = bishop.
BR abbr see British Rail.
bra [brɑː] n reggipetto, reggiseno.
brace [breɪs] n sostegno; (on teeth)
apparecchio correttore; (tool) trapano;
(TYP: also: ~ bracket) graffa ♦ vt
rinforzare, sostenere; **to ~ o.s.** (fig) farsi
coraggio; see also braces.
bracelet ['breɪslɪt] n braccialetto.
braces ['breɪsɪz] npl (BRIT) bretelle fpl.
bracing ['breɪsɪŋ] adj invigorante.
bracken ['brækən] n felce f.
bracket ['brækɪt] n (TECH) mensola; (group)
gruppo; (TYP) parentesi f inv ♦ vt mettere
fra parentesi; (fig: also: ~ **together**)
mettere insieme; **in ~s** tra parentesi;
round/square ~s parentesi tonde/quadre;
income ~ fascia di reddito.
brag [bræg] vi vantarsi.
braid [breɪd] n (trimming) passamano; (of
hair) treccia.
Braille [breɪl] n braille m.
brain [breɪn] n cervello; **~s** npl cervella fpl;
he's got ~s è intelligente.
brainchild ['breɪntʃaɪld] n creatura,
creazione f.
braindead ['breɪndɛd] adj (MED) che ha
subito morte cerebrale.
brainless ['breɪnlɪs] adj deficiente,
stupido(a).
brainstorm ['breɪnstɔːm] n (fig) attacco di

pazzia; (US) = brainwave.
brainwash ['breɪnwɔʃ] vt fare un lavaggio
di cervello a.
brainwave ['breɪnweɪv] n lampo di genio.
brainy ['breɪnɪ] adj intelligente.
braise [breɪz] vt brasare.
brake [breɪk] n (on vehicle) freno ♦ vt, vi
frenare.
brake light n (fanalino dello) stop m inv.
brake pedal n pedale m del freno.
bramble ['bræmbl] n rovo; (fruit) mora.
bran [bræn] n crusca.
branch [brɑːntʃ] n ramo; (COMM)
succursale f, filiale f ♦ vi diramarsi.
►**branch out** vi: **to ~ out into**
intraprendere una nuova attività nel
ramo di.
branch line n (RAIL) linea secondaria.
branch manager n direttore m di filiale.
brand [brænd] n marca ♦ vt (cattle) marcare
(a ferro rovente); (fig: pej): **to ~ sb a
communist** etc definire qn come
comunista etc.
brandish ['brændɪʃ] vt brandire.
brand name n marca.
brand-new ['brænd'njuː] adj nuovo(a) di
zecca.
brandy ['brændɪ] n brandy m inv.
brash [bræʃ] adj sfacciato(a).
brass [brɑːs] n ottone m; **the ~** (MUS) gli
ottoni.
brass band n fanfara.
brassière ['bræsɪə*] n reggipetto,
reggiseno.
brass tacks npl: **to get down to ~** (col)
venire al sodo.
brat [bræt] n (pej) marmocchio, monello/a.
bravado [brə'vɑːdəu] n spavalderia.
brave [breɪv] adj coraggioso(a) ♦ n
guerriero m pellerossa inv ♦ vt affrontare.
bravery ['breɪvərɪ] n coraggio.
bravo [brɑː'vəu] excl bravo!, bene!
brawl [brɔːl] n rissa ♦ vi azzuffarsi.
brawn [brɔːn] n muscolo; (meat) carne f di
testa di maiale.
brawny ['brɔːnɪ] adj muscoloso(a).
bray [breɪ] n raglio ♦ vi ragliare.
brazen ['breɪzn] adj svergognato(a) ♦ vt: **to
~ it out** fare lo sfacciato.
brazier ['breɪzɪə*] n braciere m.
Brazil [brə'zɪl] n Brasile m.
Brazilian [brə'zɪljən] adj, n brasiliano(a).
Brazil nut n noce f del Brasile.
breach [briːtʃ] vt aprire una breccia in ♦ n
(gap) breccia, varco; (estrangement)
rottura; (of duty) abuso; (breaking): **~ of
contract** rottura di contratto; **~ of the
peace** violazione f dell'ordine pubblico; **~**

of trust abuso di fiducia.

bread [brɛd] *n* pane *m*; (*col*: *money*) grana; **to earn one's daily** ~ guadagnarsi il pane; **to know which side one's** ~ **is buttered on** saper fare i propri interessi; ~ **and butter** *n* pane e burro; (*fig*) mezzi *mpl* di sussistenza.

breadbin ['brɛdbɪn] *n* (*BRIT*) cassetta *f* portapane *inv*.

breadboard ['brɛdbɔːd] *n* tagliere *m* (*per il pane*); (*COMPUT*) pannello per esperimenti.

breadbox ['brɛdbɔks] *n* (*US*) cassetta *f* portapane *inv*.

breadcrumbs ['brɛdkrʌmz] *npl* briciole *fpl*; (*CULIN*) pangrattato.

breadline ['brɛdlaɪn] *n*: **to be on the** ~ avere appena denaro per vivere.

breadth [brɛtθ] *n* larghezza.

breadwinner ['brɛdwɪnə*] *n chi guadagna il pane per tutta la famiglia.*

break [breɪk] *vb* (*pt* **broke** [brəuk], *pp* **broken** ['brəukən]) *vt* rompere; (*law*) violare; (*promise*) mancare a ♦ *vi* rompersi; (*weather*) cambiare ♦ *n* (*gap*) breccia; (*fracture*) rottura; (*rest, also SCOL*) intervallo; (: *short*) pausa; (*chance*) possibilità *f inv*; (*holiday*) vacanza; **to** ~ **one's leg** *etc* rompersi la gamba *etc*; **to** ~ **a record** battere un primato; **to** ~ **the news to sb** comunicare per primo la notizia a qn; **to** ~ **with sb** (*fig*) rompere con qn; **to** ~ **even** *vi* coprire le spese; **to** ~ **free** *or* **loose** liberarsi; **without a** ~ senza una pausa; **to have** *or* **take a** ~ (*few minutes*) fare una pausa; (*holiday*) prendere un po' di riposo; **a lucky** ~ un colpo di fortuna.

▶**break down** *vt* (*figures, data*) analizzare; (*door etc*) buttare giù, abbattere; (*resistance*) stroncare ♦ *vi* crollare; (*MED*) avere un esaurimento (nervoso); (*AUT*) guastarsi.

▶**break in** *vt* (*horse etc*) domare ♦ *vi* (*burglar*) fare irruzione.

▶**break into** *vt fus* (*house*) fare irruzione in.

▶**break off** *vi* (*speaker*) interrompersi; (*branch*) troncarsi ♦ *vt* (*talks, engagement*) rompere.

▶**break open** *vt* (*door etc*) sfondare.

▶**break out** *vi* evadere; **to** ~ **out in spots** coprirsi di macchie.

▶**break through** *vi*: **the sun broke through** il sole ha fatto capolino tra le nuvole ♦ *vt* (*defences, barrier*) sfondare, penetrare in; (*crowd*) aprirsi un varco in *or* tra, aprirsi un passaggio in *or* tra.

▶**break up** *vi* (*partnership*) sciogliersi; (*friends*) separarsi ♦ *vt* fare in pezzi, spaccare; (*fight etc*) interrompere, far cessare; (*marriage*) finire.

breakable ['breɪkəbl] *adj* fragile; ~**s** *npl* oggetti *mpl* fragili.

breakage ['breɪkɪdʒ] *n* rottura; **to pay for** ~**s** pagare i danni.

breakaway ['breɪkəweɪ] *adj* (*group etc*) scissionista, dissidente.

break-dancing ['breɪkdɑːnsɪŋ] *n* breakdance *f*.

breakdown ['breɪkdaun] *n* (*AUT*) guasto; (*in communications*) interruzione *f*; (*MED*: *also*: **nervous** ~) esaurimento nervoso; (*of payments etc*) resoconto.

breakdown service *n* (*BRIT*) servizio riparazioni.

breakdown van *n* carro *m* attrezzi *inv*.

breaker ['breɪkə*] *n* frangente *m*.

breakeven ['breɪk'iːvn] *cpd*: ~ **chart** diagramma *m* del punto di rottura *or* pareggio; ~ **point** punto di rottura *or* pareggio.

breakfast ['brɛkfəst] *n* colazione *f*.

breakfast cereal *n* fiocchi *mpl* d'avena *or* di mais *etc*.

break-in ['breɪkɪn] *n* irruzione *f*.

breaking point ['breɪkɪŋ-] *n* punto di rottura.

breakthrough ['breɪkθruː] *n* (*MIL*) breccia; (*fig*) passo avanti.

break-up ['breɪkʌp] *n* (*of partnership, marriage*) rottura.

break-up value *n* (*COMM*) valore *m* di realizzo.

breakwater ['breɪkwɔːtə*] *n* frangiflutti *m inv*.

breast [brɛst] *n* (*of woman*) seno; (*chest*) petto.

breast-feed ['brɛstfiːd] *vt, vi* (*irreg*: *like* **feed**) allattare (al seno).

breast pocket *n* taschino.

breast-stroke ['brɛststrəuk] *n* nuoto a rana.

breath [brɛθ] *n* fiato; **out of** ~ senza fiato; **to go out for a** ~ **of air** andare a prendere una boccata d'aria.

Breathalyser ® ['brɛθəlaɪzə*] *n* alcoltest *m inv*.

breathe [briːð] *vt, vi* respirare; **I won't** ~ **a word about it** non fiaterò.

▶**breathe in** *vi* inspirare ♦ *vt* respirare.

▶**breathe out** *vt, vi* espirare.

breather ['briːðə*] *n* attimo di respiro.

breathing ['briːðɪŋ] *n* respiro, respirazione *f*.

breathing space *n* (*fig*) attimo di respiro.

breathless ['brɛθlɪs] *adj* senza fiato; (*with*

excitement) con il fiato sospeso.
breath-taking ['brɛθteɪkɪŋ] *adj*
sbalorditivo(a).
breath test *n* ≈ prova del palloncino.
-bred [brɛd] *suffix*: **to be well/ill~** essere ben
educato(a)/maleducato(a).
breed [briːd] *vb* (*pt, pp* **bred** [brɛd]) *vt*
allevare; (*fig: hate, suspicion*) generare,
provocare ♦ *vi* riprodursi ♦ *n* razza,
varietà *f inv*.
breeder ['briːdə*] *n* (*PHYSICS: also:* ~
reactor) reattore *m* autofertilizzante.
breeding ['briːdɪŋ] *n* riproduzione *f*;
allevamento.
breeze [briːz] *n* brezza.
breeze block *n* (*BRIT*) *mattone composto
di scorie di coke.*
breezy ['briːzɪ] *adj* arioso(a); allegro(a).
Breton ['brɛtən] *adj*, *n* brettone (*m/f*).
brevity ['brɛvɪtɪ] *n* brevità.
brew [bruː] *vt* (*tea*) fare un infuso di; (*beer*)
fare; (*plot*) tramare ♦ *vi* (*tea*) ooùere in
infusione; (*beer*) essere in
fermentazione; (*fig*) bollire in pentola.
brewer ['bruːə*] *n* birraio.
brewery ['bruːərɪ] *n* fabbrica di birra.
briar ['braɪə*] *n* (*thorny bush*) rovo; (*wild
rose*) rosa selvatica.
bribe [braɪb] *n* bustarella ♦ *vt* comprare; **to
~ sb to do sth** pagare qn sottobanco
perché faccia qc.
bribery ['braɪbərɪ] *n* corruzione *f*.
bric-a-brac ['brɪkəbræk] *n* bric-a-brac *m*.
brick [brɪk] *n* mattone *m*.
bricklayer ['brɪkleɪə*] *n* muratore *m*.
brickwork ['brɪkwəːk] *n* muratura in
mattoni.
brickworks ['brɪkwəːks] *n* fabbrica di
mattoni.
bridal ['braɪdl] *adj* nuziale; ~ **party** corteo
nuziale.
bride [braɪd] *n* sposa.
bridegroom ['braɪdgruːm] *n* sposo.
bridesmaid ['braɪdzmeɪd] *n* damigella
d'onore.
bridge [brɪdʒ] *n* ponte *m*; (*NAUT*) ponte di
comando; (*of nose*) dorso; (*CARDS,
DENTISTRY*) bridge *m inv* ♦ *vt* (*river*) fare un
ponte sopra; (*gap*) colmare.
bridging loan ['brɪdʒɪŋ-] *n* (*BRIT*)
anticipazione *f* sul mutuo.
bridle ['braɪdl] *n* briglia ♦ *vt* tenere a freno;
(*horse*) mettere la briglia a ♦ *vi* (*in anger
etc*) adombrarsi, adontarsi.
bridle path *n* sentiero (per cavalli).
brief [briːf] *adj* breve ♦ *n* (*LAW*) comparsa
♦ *vt* (*MIL etc*) dare istruzioni a; **in ~ ...** in
breve ..., a farla breve ...; **to ~ sb (about**

sth) mettere qn al corrente (di qc); *see
also* **briefs**.
briefcase ['briːfkeɪs] *n* cartella.
briefing ['briːfɪŋ] *n* istruzioni *fpl*.
briefly ['briːflɪ] *adv* (*speak, visit*)
brevemente; (*glimpse*) di sfuggita.
briefness ['briːfnɪs] *n* brevità.
briefs [briːfs] *npl* mutande *fpl*.
Brig. *abbr* = **brigadier**.
brigade [brɪ'geɪd] *n* (*MIL*) brigata.
brigadier [brɪgə'dɪə*] *n* generale *m* di
brigata.
bright [braɪt] *adj* luminoso(a); (*person*)
sveglio(a); (*colour*) vivace; **to look on the
~ side** vedere il lato positivo delle cose.
brighten ['braɪtn] (*also:* ~ **up**) *vt* (*room*)
rendere luminoso(a); rallegrare ♦ *vi*
schiarirsi; (*person*) rallegrarsi.
brightly ['braɪtlɪ] *adv* (*shine*) vivamente,
intensamente; (*smile*) radiosamente; (*talk*)
con animazione.
brill [brɪl] *excl* (*BRIT col*) stupendo!,
fantastico!
brilliance ['brɪljəns] *n* splendore *m*; (*fig: of
person*) genialità, talento.
brilliant ['brɪljənt] *adj* brillante; (*sunshine*)
sfolgorante.
brim [brɪm] *n* orlo.
brimful ['brɪm'ful] *adj* pieno(a) *or* colmo(a)
fino all'orlo; (*fig*) pieno(a).
brine [braɪn] *n* acqua salmastra; (*CULIN*)
salamoia.
bring, *pt, pp* **brought** [brɔːt] *vt* portare;
to ~ sth to an end mettere fine a qc; **I
can't ~ myself to sack him** non so
risolvermi a licenziarlo.
▶**bring about** *vt* causare.
▶**bring back** *vt* riportare.
▶**bring down** *vt* (*lower*) far scendere;
(*shoot down*) abbattere; (*government*) far
cadere.
▶**bring forward** *vt* portare avanti; (*in time*)
anticipare; (*BOOK-KEEPING*) riportare.
▶**bring in** *vt* (*person*) fare entrare; (*object*)
portare; (*POL: bill*) presentare;
(: *legislation*) introdurre; (*LAW: verdict*)
emettere; (*produce: income*) rendere.
▶**bring off** *vt* (*task, plan*) portare a
compimento; (*deal*) concludere.
▶**bring out** *vt* (*meaning*) mettere in
evidenza; (*new product*) lanciare; (*book*)
pubblicare, fare uscire.
▶**bring round** *or* **to** *vt* (*unconscious person*)
far rinvenire.
▶**bring up** *vt* allevare; (*question*)
introdurre.
brink [brɪŋk] *n* orlo; **on the ~ of doing sth**
sul punto di fare qc; **she was on the ~ of**

tears era lì lì per piangere.

brisk [brɪsk] *adj* (*person, tone*) spiccio(a), sbrigativo(a); (: *abrupt*) brusco(a); (*wind*) fresco(a); (*trade etc*) vivace, attivo(a); **to go for a ~ walk** fare una camminata di buon passo; **business is ~** gli affari vanno bene.

bristle ['brɪsl] *n* setola ♦ *vi* rizzarsi; **bristling with** irto(a) di.

bristly ['brɪslɪ] *adj* (*chin*) ispido(a); (*beard, hair*) irsuto(a), setoloso(a).

Brit [brɪt] *n abbr* (*col*: = *British person*) britannico/a.

Britain ['brɪtən] *n* Gran Bretagna.

British ['brɪtɪʃ] *adj* britannico(a); **the ~** *npl* i Britannici; **the ~ Isles** *npl* le Isole Britanniche.

British Rail (BR) *n compagnia ferroviaria britannica*, ≈ Ferrovie *fpl* dello Stato (F.S.).

British Summer Time *n* ora legale (*in Gran Bretagna*).

Briton ['brɪtən] *n* britannico/a.

Brittany ['brɪtənɪ] *n* Bretagna.

brittle ['brɪtl] *adj* fragile.

Br(o) *abbr* (*REL*) = **brother**.

broach [brəutʃ] *vt* (*subject*) affrontare.

broad [brɔːd] *adj* largo(a); (*distinction*) generale; (*accent*) spiccato(a) ♦ *n* (*US col*) bellona; **~ hint** allusione *f* esplicita; **in ~ daylight** in pieno giorno; **the ~ outlines** le grandi linee.

broad bean *n* fava.

broadcast ['brɔːdkɑːst] *n* trasmissione *f* ♦ *vb* (*pt, pp* **broadcast**) *vt* trasmettere per radio (*or* per televisione) ♦ *vi* fare una trasmissione.

broadcaster ['brɔːdkɑːstə*] *n* annunciatore/trice radiotelevisivo(a) (*or* radiofonico(a)).

broadcasting ['brɔːdkɑːstɪŋ] *n* radiodiffusione *f*; televisione *f*.

broaden ['brɔːdn] *vt* allargare ♦ *vi* allargarsi.

broadly ['brɔːdlɪ] *adv* (*fig*) in generale.

broad-minded ['brɔːd'maɪndɪd] *adj* di mente aperta.

broadsheet ['brɔːdʃiːt] *n* (*BRIT*) giornale *m* (*si contrappone al tabloid che è di formato più piccolo*).

broccoli ['brɔkəlɪ] *n* (*BOT*) broccolo; (*CULIN*) broccoli *mpl*.

brochure ['brəuʃjuə*] *n* dépliant *m inv*.

brogue [brəug] *n* (*shoe*) scarpa rozza in cuoio; (*accent*) accento irlandese.

broil [brɔɪl] *vt* cuocere a fuoco vivo.

broke [brəuk] *pt of* **break** ♦ *adj* (*col*) squattrinato(a); **to go ~** fare fallimento.

broken ['brəukən] *pp of* **break** ♦ *adj* (*gen*) rotto(a); (*stick, promise, vow*) spezzato(a); (*marriage*) fallito(a); **he comes from a ~ home** i suoi sono divisi; **in ~ French/English** in un francese/inglese stentato.

broken-down ['brəukən'daun] *adj* (*car*) in panne, rotto(a); (*machine*) guasto(a), fuori uso; (*house*) abbandonato(a), in rovina.

broken-hearted ['brəukən'hɑːtɪd] *adj*: **to be ~** avere il cuore spezzato.

broker ['brəukə*] *n* agente *m*.

brokerage ['brəukərɪdʒ] *n* (*COMM*) commissione *f* di intermediazione.

brolly ['brɔlɪ] *n* (*BRIT col*) ombrello.

bronchitis [brɔŋ'kaɪtɪs] *n* bronchite *f*.

bronze [brɔnz] *n* bronzo.

bronzed [brɔnzd] *adj* abbronzato(a).

brooch [brəutʃ] *n* spilla.

brood [bruːd] *n* covata ♦ *vi* (*hen*) covare; (*person*) rimuginare.

broody ['bruːdɪ] *adj* (*fig*) cupo(a) e taciturno(a).

brook [bruk] *n* ruscello.

broom [brum] *n* scopa.

broomstick ['brumstɪk] *n* manico di scopa.

Bros. *abbr* (*COMM*: = *brothers*) F.lli (= *Fratelli*).

broth [brɔθ] *n* brodo.

brothel ['brɔθl] *n* bordello.

brother ['brʌðə*] *n* fratello.

brotherhood ['brʌðəhud] *n* fratellanza; confraternità *f inv*.

brother-in-law ['brʌðərɪnlɔː] *n* cognato.

brotherly ['brʌðəlɪ] *adj* fraterno(a).

brought [brɔːt] *pt, pp of* **bring**.

brought forward (b/f) *adj* (*COMM*) riportato(a).

brow [brau] *n* fronte *f*; (*rare, gen*: *eye~*) sopracciglio; (*of hill*) cima.

browbeat ['braubiːt] *vt* intimidire.

brown [braun] *adj* bruno(a), marrone; (*hair*) castano(a) ♦ *n* (*colour*) color *m* bruno *or* marrone ♦ *vt* (*CULIN*) rosolare; **to go ~** (*person*) abbronzarsi; (*leaves*) ingiallire.

brown bread *n* pane *m* integrale, pane nero.

brownie ['braunɪ] *n* giovane esploratrice *f*.

brown paper *n* carta da pacchi *or* da imballaggio.

brown rice *n* riso greggio.

brown sugar *n* zucchero greggio.

browse [brauz] *vi* (*animal*) brucare; (*in bookshop etc*) curiosare ♦ *n*: **to have a ~ (around)** dare un'occhiata (in giro); **to ~ through a book** sfogliare un libro.

browser ['brauzə*] *n* (*COMPUT*) browser *sm inv*.

bruise [bruːz] n ammaccatura; (on person) livido ♦ vt ammaccare; (leg etc) farsi un livido a; (fig: feelings) urtare ♦ vi (fruit) ammaccarsi.

Brum [brʌm] n abbr, **Brummagem** ['brʌmədʒəm] n (col) = Birmingham.

Brummie ['brʌmɪ] n (col) abitante m/f di Birmingham; originario/a di Birmingham.

brunch [brʌntʃ] n ricca colazione consumata in tarda mattinata.

brunette [bruːˈnɛt] n bruna.

brunt [brʌnt] n: **the ~ of** (attack, criticism etc) il peso maggiore di.

brush [brʌʃ] n spazzola; (quarrel) schermaglia ♦ vt spazzolare; (gen: ~ past, ~ against) sfiorare; **to have a ~ with sb** (verbally) avere uno scontro con qn; (physically) venire a diverbio or alle mani con qn; **to have a ~ with the police** avere delle noie con la polizia.

►**brush aside** vt scostare.

►**brush up** vt (knowledge) rinfrescare.

brushed [brʌʃt] adj (TECH: steel, chrome etc) sabbiato(a); (nylon, denim etc) pettinato(a).

brush-off ['brʌʃɔf] n: **to give sb the ~** dare il ben servito a qn.

brushwood ['brʌʃwud] n macchia.

brusque [bruːsk] adj (person, manner) brusco(a); (tone) secco(a).

Brussels ['brʌslz] n Bruxelles f.

Brussels sprout n cavolo di Bruxelles.

brutal ['bruːtl] adj brutale.

brutality [bruːˈtælɪtɪ] n brutalità.

brutalize ['bruːtəlaɪz] vt (harden) abbrutire; (ill-treat) brutalizzare.

brute [bruːt] n bestia; **by ~ force** con la forza, a viva forza.

brutish ['bruːtɪʃ] adj da bruto.

BS n abbr (US: = Bachelor of Science) titolo di studio.

bs abbr = bill of sale.

BSA n abbr (US) = Boy Scouts of America.

BSc n abbr see **Bachelor of Science**.

BSE n abbr (= bovine spongiform encephalopathy) encefalite f bovina spongiforme.

BSI n abbr (= British Standards Institution) associazione per la normalizzazione.

BST abbr (= British Summer Time) ora legale.

Bt. abbr (BRIT) = baronet.

btu n abbr (= British thermal unit) Btu m (= 1054.2 joules).

bubble ['bʌbl] n bolla ♦ vi ribollire; (sparkle, fig) essere effervescente.

bubble bath n bagno m schiuma inv.

bubblejet printer ['bʌbldʒɛt-] n stampante f a getto d'inchiostro.

bubbly ['bʌblɪ] adj (also fig) frizzante ♦ n (col) (champagne) spumante m.

Bucharest [buːkəˈrɛst] n Bucarest f.

buck [bʌk] n maschio (di camoscio, caprone, coniglio etc); (US col) dollaro ♦ vi sgroppare; **to pass the ~ (to sb)** scaricare (su di qn) la propria responsabilità.

►**buck up** vi (cheer up) rianimarsi ♦ vt: **to ~ one's ideas up** mettere la testa a partito.

bucket ['bʌkɪt] n secchio ♦ vi (BRIT col): **the rain is ~ing (down)** piove a catinelle.

Buckingham Palace ['bʌkɪŋəm-] n see boxed note.

BUCKINGHAM PALACE

Buckingham Palace è la residenza ufficiale a Londra del sovrano britannico, Costruita nel 1703 per il duca di Buckingham, fu acquistata nel 1762 dal re Giorgio III e ricostruita tra il 1821 e il 1838 sotto la guida dell'architetto John Nash. All'inizio del Novecento alcune sue parti sono state ulteriormente modificate.

---

buckle ['bʌkl] n fibbia ♦ vt affibbiare; (warp) deformare.

►**buckle down** vi mettersi sotto.

Bucks [bʌks] abbr (BRIT) = Buckinghamshire.

bud [bʌd] n gemma; (of flower) boccio ♦ vi germogliare; (flower) sbocciare.

Budapest [bjuːdəˈpɛst] n Budapest f.

Buddha ['budə] n Budda m.

Buddhism ['budɪzəm] n buddismo.

Buddhist ['budɪst] adj, n buddista (m/f).

budding ['bʌdɪŋ] adj (flower) in boccio; (poet etc) in erba.

buddy ['bʌdɪ] n (US) compagno.

budge [bʌdʒ] vt scostare ♦ vi spostarsi.

budgerigar ['bʌdʒərɪgɑː*] n pappagallino.

budget ['bʌdʒɪt] n bilancio preventivo ♦ vi: **to ~ for sth** fare il bilancio per qc; **I'm on a tight ~** devo contare la lira; **she works out her ~ every month** fa il preventivo delle spese ogni mese.

budgie ['bʌdʒɪ] n = **budgerigar**.

Buenos Aires ['bweɪnɔsˈaɪrɪz] n Buenos Aires f.

buff [bʌf] adj color camoscio inv ♦ n (enthusiast) appassionato/a.

buffalo, pl ~ or ~es ['bʌfələu] n bufalo; (US) bisonte m.

buffer ['bʌfə*] n respingente m; (COMPUT) memoria tampone, buffer m inv.

buffer state n stato cuscinetto.

buffer zone n zona f cuscinetto inv.

buffet n ['bufeɪ] (*food, BRIT: bar*) buffet m inv
♦ vt ['bʌfɪt] schiaffeggiare; scuotere;
urtare.
buffet car n (*BRIT RAIL*) ≈ servizio ristoro.
buffet lunch n pranzo in piedi.
buffoon [bə'fuːn] n buffone m.
bug [bʌg] n (*insect*) cimice f; (: *gen*) insetto;
(*fig: germ*) virus m inv; (*spy device*)
microfono spia; (*COMPUT*) bug m inv,
errore m nel programma ♦ vt mettere
sotto controllo; (*room*) installare
microfoni spia in; (*annoy*) scocciare; **I've
got the travel** ~ (*fig*) mi è presa la mania
dei viaggi.
bugbear ['bʌgbeə*] n spauracchio.
bugger ['bʌgə*] (*col!*) n bastardo (*!*) ♦ vb: ~
off! vaffanculo! (*!*); ~ (**it**)! merda! (*!*).
bugle ['bjuːgl] n tromba.
build [bɪld] n (*of person*) corporatura ♦ vt
(*pt, pp* **built** [bɪlt]) costruire.
▶**build on** vt fus (*fig*) prendere il via da.
▶**build up** vt (*establish: business*) costruire;
(: *reputation*) fare, consolidare; (*increase:
production*) allargare, incrementare;
don't ~ **your hopes up too soon** non
sperarci troppo.
builder ['bɪldə*] n costruttore m.
building ['bɪldɪŋ] n costruzione f; edificio;
(*also:* ~ **trade**) edilizia.
building contractor n costruttore m,
imprenditore m (edile).
building industry n industria edilizia.
building site n cantiere m di costruzione.
building society n *società immobiliare e
finanziaria*; *see boxed note.*

BUILDING SOCIETY

Le **building society** *sono società immobiliari
e finanziarie che forniscono anche numerosi
servizi bancari ai clienti che vi investono i
risparmi. Chi ha bisogno di un prestito per
l'acquisto di una casa si rivolge in genere ad
una* **building society**.

---

building trade n = **building industry**.
build-up ['bɪldʌp] n (*of gas etc*) accumulo;
(*publicity*): **to give sb/sth a good** ~ fare
buona pubblicità a qn/qc.
built [bɪlt] pt, pp of **build**; **well-~** robusto(a).
built-in ['bɪlt'ɪn] adj (*cupboard*) a muro;
(*device*) incorporato(a).
built-up area ['bɪltʌp-] n abitato.
bulb [bʌlb] n (*BOT*) bulbo; (*ELEC*) lampadina.
Bulgaria [bʌl'geəriə] n Bulgaria.
Bulgarian [bʌl'geəriən] adj bulgaro(a) ♦ n
bulgaro/a; (*LING*) bulgaro.
bulge [bʌldʒ] n rigonfiamento; (*in birth rate,*

sales) punta ♦ vi essere protuberante *or*
rigonfio(a); **to be bulging with** essere
pieno(a) *or* zeppo(a) di.
bulimia [bə'lɪmɪə] n bulimia.
bulk [bʌlk] n massa, volume m; **the** ~ **of** il
grosso di; (**to buy**) **in** ~ (comprare) in
grande quantità.
bulk buying n acquisto di merce in
grande quantità.
bulk carrier n grossa nave f da carico.
bulkhead ['bʌlkhed] n paratia.
bulky ['bʌlkɪ] adj grosso(a); voluminoso(a).
bull [bul] n toro; (*STOCK EXCHANGE*) rialzista
m/f; (*REL*) bolla (papale).
bulldog ['buldɔg] n bulldog m inv.
bulldoze ['buldəuz] vt aprire *or* spianare
col bulldozer; **I was ~d into doing it** (*fig
col*) mi ci hanno costretto con la
prepotenza.
bulldozer ['buldəuzə*] n bulldozer m inv.
bullet ['bulɪt] n pallottola.
bulletin ['bulɪtɪn] n bollettino.
bulletin board n (*COMPUT*) bulletin board
m inv.
bullet-proof ['bulɪtpruːf] adj a prova di
proiettile; ~ **vest** giubbotto
antiproiettile.
bullfight ['bulfaɪt] n corrida.
bullfighter ['bulfaɪtə*] n torero.
bullfighting ['bulfaɪtɪŋ] n tauromachia.
bullion ['buljən] n oro in lingotti.
bullock ['bulək] n giovenco.
bullring ['bulrɪŋ] n arena (per corride).
bull's-eye ['bulzaɪ] n centro del bersaglio.
bullshit ['bulʃɪt] (*col!*) excl, n stronzate fpl (*!*)
♦ vi raccontare stronzate (*!*) ♦ vt
raccontare stronzate a (*!*).
bully ['bulɪ] n prepotente m ♦ vt angariare;
(*frighten*) intimidire.
bullying ['bulɪŋ] n prepotenze fpl.
bum [bʌm] n (*col: backside*) culo; (*tramp*)
vagabondo/a; (*US: idler*) fannullone/a.
▶**bum around** vi (*col*) fare il vagabondo.
bumblebee ['bʌmblbiː] n (*ZOOL*) bombo.
bumf [bʌmf] n (*col: forms etc*) scartoffie fpl.
bump [bʌmp] n (*blow*) colpo; (*jolt*) scossa;
(*noise*) botto; (*on road etc*) protuberanza;
(*on head*) bernoccolo ♦ vt battere; (*car*)
urtare, sbattere.
▶**bump along** vi procedere sobbalzando.
▶**bump into** vt fus scontrarsi con; (*col:
meet*) imbattersi in, incontrare per caso.
bumper ['bʌmpə*] n (*BRIT*) paraurti m inv
♦ adj: ~ **harvest** raccolto eccezionale.
bumper cars npl (*US*) autoscontri mpl.
bumph [bʌmf] n = **bumf**.
bumptious ['bʌmpʃəs] adj presuntuoso(a).
bumpy ['bʌmpɪ] adj (*road*) dissestato(a);

bun–bury

(*journey, flight*) movimentato(a).
bun [bʌn] *n* focaccia; (*of hair*) crocchia.
bunch [bʌntʃ] *n* (*of flowers, keys*) mazzo; (*of bananas*) ciuffo; (*of people*) gruppo; ~ **of grapes** grappolo d'uva.
bundle ['bʌndl] *n* fascio ♦ *vt* (*also:* ~ **up**) legare in un fascio; (*put*): **to ~ sth/sb into** spingere qc/qn in.
► **bundle off** *vt* (*person*) mandare via in gran fretta.
► **bundle out** *vt* far uscire (senza tante cerimonie).
bun fight *n* (*BRIT: col*) tè *m inv* (*ricevimento*).
bung [bʌŋ] *n* tappo ♦ *vt* (*BRIT: throw: also:* ~ **into**) buttare; (*also:* ~ **up**: *pipe, hole*) tappare, otturare; **my nose is ~ed up** (*col*) ho il naso otturato.
bungalow ['bʌŋɡələu] *n* bungalow *m inv.*
bungee jumping ['bʌndʒiː'dʒʌmpɪŋ] *n salto nel vuoto da ponti, grattacieli etc con un cavo fissato alla caviglia.*
bungle ['bʌŋɡl] *vt* abborracciare.
bunion ['bʌnjən] *n* callo (al piede).
bunk [bʌŋk] *n* cuccetta.
► **bunk off** *vi* (*BRIT col*): **to ~ off school** marinare la scuola; **I'll ~ off at 3 this afternoon** oggi me la filo dal lavoro alle 3.
bunk beds *npl* letti *mpl* a castello.
bunker ['bʌŋkə*] *n* (*coal store*) ripostiglio per il carbone; (*MIL, GOLF*) bunker *m inv.*
bunny ['bʌnɪ] *n* (*also:* ~ **rabbit**) coniglietto.
bunny hill *n* (*US SKI*) pista per principianti.
bunting ['bʌntɪŋ] *n* pavesi *mpl*, bandierine *fpl.*
buoy [bɔɪ] *n* boa.
► **buoy up** *vt* tenere a galla; (*fig*) sostenere.
buoyancy ['bɔɪənsɪ] *n* (*of ship*) galleggiabilità.
buoyant ['bɔɪənt] *adj* galleggiante; (*fig*) vivace; (*COMM: market*) sostenuto(a); (*prices, currency*) stabile.
burden ['bəːdn] *n* carico, fardello ♦ *vt* caricare; (*oppress*) opprimere; **to be a ~ to sb** essere di peso a qn.
bureau, *pl* ~**x** ['bjuərəu, -z] *n* (*BRIT: writing desk*) scrivania; (*US: chest of drawers*) cassettone *m*; (*office*) ufficio, agenzia.
bureaucracy [bjuə'rɔkrəsɪ] *n* burocrazia.
bureaucrat ['bjuərəkræt] *n* burocrate *m/f.*
bureaucratic [bjuərə'krætɪk] *adj* burocratico(a).
burgeon ['bəːdʒən] *vi* svilupparsi rapidamente.
burger ['bəːɡə*] *n* hamburger *m inv.*
burglar ['bəːɡlə*] *n* scassinatore *m.*
burglar alarm *n* antifurto *m inv.*
burglarize ['bəːɡləraɪz] *vt* (*US*) svaligiare.
burglary ['bəːɡlərɪ] *n* furto con scasso.

burgle ['bəːɡl] *vt* svaligiare.
burial ['berɪəl] *n* sepoltura.
burial ground *n* cimitero.
burly ['bəːlɪ] *adj* robusto(a).
Burma ['bəːmə] *n* Birmania; *see* **Myanmar.**
Burmese [bəː'miːz] *adj* birmano(a) ♦ *n* (*pl inv*) birmano/a; (*LING*) birmano.
burn [bəːn] *vt, vi* (*pt, pp* **burned** *or* **burnt** [bəːnt]) bruciare ♦ *n* bruciatura, scottatura; (*MED*) ustione *f*; **I've ~t myself!** mi sono bruciato!; **the cigarette ~t a hole in her dress** si è fatta un buco nel vestito con la sigaretta.
► **burn down** *vt* distruggere col fuoco.
► **burn out** *vt* (*subj: writer etc*): **to ~ o.s. out** esaurirsi.
burner ['bəːnə*] *n* fornello.
burning ['bəːnɪŋ] *adj* (*building, forest*) in fiamme; (*issue, question*) scottante.
burnish ['bəːnɪʃ] *vt* brunire.
Burns' Night *n* *see boxed note*

BURNS' NIGHT

Burns' Night *è la festa celebrata il 25 gennaio per commemorare il poeta scozzese Robert Burns (1759–1796). Gli scozzesi festeggiano questa data con una cena a base di "haggis" e "whisky", spesso al suono di una cornamusa; durante la cena vengono recitate le poesie di Robert Burns e vengono letti discorsi alla sua memoria.*

---

burnt [bəːnt] *pt, pp of* **burn.**
burp [bəːp] (*col*) *n* rutto ♦ *vi* ruttare.
burrow ['bʌrəu] *n* tana ♦ *vt* scavare.
bursar ['bəːsə*] *n* economo/a; (*BRIT: student*) borsista *m/f.*
bursary ['bəːsərɪ] *n* (*BRIT*) borsa di studio.
burst [bəːst] *vb* (*pt, pp* **burst**) *vt* far scoppiare *or* esplodere ♦ *vi* esplodere; (*tyre*) scoppiare ♦ *n* scoppio; (*also:* ~ **pipe**) rottura nel tubo, perdita; ~ **of energy/ laughter** scoppio d'energia/di risa; **a ~ of applause** uno scroscio d'applausi; **a ~ of speed** uno scatto (di velocità); ~ **blood vessel** rottura di un vaso sanguigno; **the river has ~ its banks** il fiume ha rotto gli argini *or* ha straripato; **to ~ into flames/ tears** scoppiare in fiamme/lacrime; **to be ~ing with** essere pronto a scoppiare di; **to ~ out laughing** scoppiare a ridere; **to ~ open** *vi* aprirsi improvvisamente; (*door*) spalancarsi.
► **burst into** *vt fus* (*room etc*) irrompere in.
► **burst out of** *vt fus* precipitarsi fuori da.
bury ['berɪ] *vt* seppellire; **to ~ one's face in one's hands** nascondere la faccia tra le

mani; **to ~ one's head in the sand** (*fig*) fare (la politica del)lo struzzo; **to ~ the hatchet** (*fig*) seppellire l'ascia di guerra.
bus, ~**es** [bʌs, 'bʌsɪz] *n* autobus *m inv*.
bus boy *n* (*US*) aiuto *inv* cameriere/a.
bush [buʃ] *n* cespuglio; (*scrub land*) macchia.
bushed [buʃt] *adj* (*col*) distrutto(a).
bushel ['buʃl] *n* staio.
bushfire ['buʃfaɪə*] *n grande incendio in aperta campagna*.
bushy ['buʃɪ] *adj* (*plant, tail, beard*) folto(a); (*eyebrows*) irsuto(a).
busily ['bɪzɪlɪ] *adv* con impegno, alacremente.
business ['bɪznɪs] *n* (*matter*) affare *m*; (*trading*) affari *mpl*; (*firm*) azienda; (*job, duty*) lavoro; **to be away on ~** essere andato via per affari; **I'm here on ~** sono qui per affari; **to do ~ with sb** fare affari con qn; **he's in the insurance ~** lavora nel campo delle assicurazioni; **it's none of my ~** questo non mi riguarda; **he means ~** non scherza.
business address *n* indirizzo di lavoro *or* d'ufficio.
business card *n* biglietto da visita della ditta.
businesslike ['bɪznɪslaɪk] *adj* serio(a); efficiente.
businessman ['bɪznɪsmən] *n* uomo d'affari.
business trip *n* viaggio d'affari.
businesswoman ['bɪznɪswumən] *n* donna d'affari.
busker ['bʌskə*] *n* (*BRIT*) suonatore/trice ambulante.
bus lane *n* (*BRIT*) corsia riservata agli autobus.
bus shelter *n* pensilina (*alla fermata dell'autobus*).
bus station *n* stazione *f* delle autolinee, autostazione *f*.
bus stop *n* fermata d'autobus.
bust [bʌst] *n* (*ART*) busto; (*bosom*) seno ♦ *adj* (*broken*) rotto(a) ♦ *vt* (*col: POLICE: arrest*) pizzicare, beccare; **to go ~** fallire.
bustle ['bʌsl] *n* movimento, attività ♦ *vi* darsi da fare.
bustling ['bʌslɪŋ] *adj* (*person*) indaffarato(a); (*shop, street*) animato(a); (*town*) animato(a).
bust-up ['bʌstʌp] *n* (*BRIT col*) lite *f*.
busty ['bʌstɪ] *adj* (*col*) tettone(a).
busy ['bɪzɪ] *adj* occupato(a); (*shop, street*) molto frequentato(a) ♦ *vt*: **to ~ o.s.** darsi da fare; **he's a ~ man** (*normally*) è un uomo molto occupato; (*temporarily*) ha molto da fare, è molto occupato.
busybody ['bɪzɪbɔdɪ] *n* ficcanaso *m/f inv*.

busy signal *n* (*US*) segnale *m* di occupato.

══════════ *KEYWORD*

but [bʌt] *conj* ma; **I'd love to come, ~ I'm busy** vorrei tanto venire, ma ho da fare
♦ *prep* (*apart from, except*) eccetto, tranne, meno; **nothing ~** nient'altro che; **he was nothing ~ trouble** non dava altro che guai; **no-one ~ him** solo lui; **no-one ~ him can do it** nessuno può farlo tranne lui; **the last ~ one** (*BRIT*) il(la) penultimo(a); **~ for you/your help** se non fosse per te/per il tuo aiuto; **anything ~ that** tutto ma non questo; **anything ~ finished** tutt'altro che finito
♦ *adv* (*just, only*) solo, soltanto; **she's ~ a child** è solo una bambina; **had I ~ known** se solo avessi saputo; **I can ~ try** tentar non nuoce; **all ~ finished** quasi finito.

butane ['bju:teɪn] *n* (*also:* **~ gas**) butano.
butch [butʃ] *adj* (*woman: pej*) mascolino(a); (*man*) macho *inv*.
butcher ['butʃə*] *n* macellaio ♦ *vt* macellare; **~'s (shop)** macelleria.
butler ['bʌtlə*] *n* maggiordomo.
butt [bʌt] *n* (*cask*) grossa botte *f*; (*thick end*) estremità *f inv* più grossa; (*of gun*) calcio; (*of cigarette*) mozzicone *m*; (*BRIT fig: target*) oggetto ♦ *vt* cozzare.
►**butt in** *vi* (*interrupt*) interrompere.
butter ['bʌtə*] *n* burro ♦ *vt* imburrare.
buttercup ['bʌtəkʌp] *n* ranuncolo.
butter dish *n* burriera.
butterfingers ['bʌtəfɪŋgəz] *n* (*col*) mani *fpl* di ricotta.
butterfly ['bʌtəflaɪ] *n* farfalla; (*SWIMMING: also:* **~ stroke**) (nuoto a) farfalla.
buttocks ['bʌtəks] *npl* natiche *fpl*.
button ['bʌtn] *n* bottone *m* ♦ *vt* (*also:* **~ up**) abbottonare ♦ *vi* abbottonarsi.
buttonhole ['bʌtnhəul] *n* asola, occhiello ♦ *vt* (*person*) attaccar bottone a.
buttress ['bʌtrɪs] *n* contrafforte *m*.
buxom ['bʌksəm] *adj* formoso(a).
buy [baɪ] *vt* (*pt, pp* **bought** [bɔːt]) comprare, acquistare ♦ *n*: **a good/bad ~** un buon/cattivo acquisto *or* affare; **to ~ sb sth/sth from sb** comprare qc per qc/a qn; **to ~ sb a drink** offrire da bere a qn.
►**buy back** *vt* riprendersi, prendersi indietro.
►**buy in** *vt* (*BRIT: goods*) far provvista di.
►**buy into** *vt fus* (*BRIT COMM*) acquistare delle azioni di.
►**buy off** *vt* (*col: bribe*) comprare.
►**buy out** *vt* (*business*) rilevare.
►**buy up** *vt* accaparrare.

buyer ['baɪə*] *n* compratore/trice; ~'s
market mercato favorevole ai
compratori.
buy-out ['baɪaut] *n* (*COMM*) acquisto di una
società da parte dei suoi dipendenti.
buzz [bʌz] *n* ronzio; (*col*: phone call) colpo di
telefono ♦ *vi* ronzare ♦ *vt* (call on intercom)
chiamare al citofono; (: with buzzer)
chiamare col cicalino; (*AVIAT*: plane,
building) passare rasente; **my head is
~ing** mi gira la testa.
►**buzz off** *vi* (*BRIT col*) filare, levarsi di
torno.
buzzard ['bʌzəd] *n* poiana.
buzzer ['bʌzə*] *n* cicalino.
buzz word *n* (*col*) termine *m* in voga.

===================== *KEYWORD*

by [baɪ] *prep* **1** (referring to cause, agent) da;
killed ~ lightning ucciso da un fulmine;
surrounded ~ a fence circondato da uno
steccato; **a painting ~ Picasso** un quadro
di Picasso
2 (referring to method, manner, means): ~
bus/car/train in autobus/macchina/treno,
con l'autobus/la macchina/il treno; **to pay
~ cheque** pagare con (un) assegno; ~
moonlight al chiaro di luna; ~ **saving
hard, he …** risparmiando molto, lui …
3 (via, through) per; **we came ~ Dover**
siamo venuti via Dover
4 (close to, past) accanto a; **the house ~
the river** la casa sul fiume; **a holiday ~
the sea** una vacanza al mare; **she sat ~
his bed** si sedette accanto al suo letto;
she rushed ~ me mi è passata accanto
correndo; **I go ~ the post office every day**
passo davanti all'ufficio postale ogni
giorno
5 (not later than) per, entro; ~ **4 o'clock**
per or entro le 4; ~ **this time tomorrow**
domani a quest'ora; ~ **the time I got here
it was too late** quando sono arrivato era
ormai troppo tardi
6 (during): ~ **day/night** di giorno/notte
7 (amount) a; ~ **the kilo** a chili; **paid ~
the hour** pagato all'ora; **to increase ~ the
hour** aumentare di ora in ora; **one ~ one**
uno per uno; **little ~ little** a poco a poco
8 (MATH, measure): **to divide/multiply ~ 3**
dividere/moltiplicare per 3; **a room 3
metres ~ 4** una stanza di 3 metri per 4;
it's broader ~ a metre è un metro più
largo, è più largo di un metro
9 (according to) per; **to play ~ the rules**
attenersi alle regole; **it's all right ~ me**
per me va bene
10: (all) ~ **oneself** (tutto(a)) solo(a); **he did**

it (all) ~ himself lo ha fatto (tutto) da solo
11: ~ **the way** a proposito; **this wasn't my
idea ~ the way** tra l'altro l'idea non è
stata mia
♦ *adv* **1** see **go**; **pass** etc
2: ~ **and** ~ (in past) poco dopo; (in future)
fra breve; ~ **and large** nel complesso.

bye(-bye) ['baɪ('baɪ)] *excl* ciao!,
arrivederci!
by(e)-law ['baɪlɔ:] *n* legge *f* locale.
by-election ['baɪɪlɛkʃən] *n* (*BRIT*) elezione *f*
straordinaria; see boxed note.

BY-ELECTION

Una **by-election** in Gran Bretagna e in alcuni
paesi del Commonwealth è un'elezione che si
tiene per coprire un posto in Parlamento resosi
vacante, a governo ancora in carica. È
importante in quanto serve a misurare il
consenso degli elettori in vista delle successive
elezioni politiche.

Byelorussia [bjɛləu'rʌʃə] *n* Bielorussia,
Belorussia.
Byelorussian [bjɛləu'rʌʃən] *adj, n* =
Belarussian.
bygone ['baɪgɔn] *adj* passato(a) ♦ *n*: **let ~s
be ~s** mettiamoci una pietra sopra.
bypass ['baɪpɑ:s] *n* circonvallazione *f*;
(*MED*) by-pass *m inv* ♦ *vt* fare una
deviazione intorno a.
by-product ['baɪprɔdʌkt] *n* sottoprodotto;
(fig) conseguenza secondaria.
byre ['baɪə*] *n* (*BRIT*) stalla.
bystander ['baɪstændə*] *n* spettatore/trice.
byte [baɪt] *n* (*COMPUT*) byte *m inv*.
byway ['baɪweɪ] *n* strada secondaria.
byword ['baɪwə:d] *n*: **to be a ~ for** essere
sinonimo di.
by-your-leave ['baɪjɔ:'li:v] *n*: **without so
much as a ~** senza nemmeno chiedere il
permesso.

Cc

C, c [siː] *n* (*letter*) C, c *f or m inv*; (*SCOL: mark*)
≈ 6 (*sufficiente*); (*MUS*): **C** do; ~ **for Charlie**
≈ C come Como.

C *abbr* (= *Celsius, centigrade*) C.

c. *abbr* (= *century*) sec.; (= *circa*) c; (*US etc*)
= **cent(s)**.

CA *abbr* = **Central America**; (*US*) = *California*
♦ *n abbr* (*BRIT*) *see* **chartered accountant**.

ca. *abbr* (= *circa*) ca.

c/a *abbr* = **capital account; credit account;
current account**.

CAA *n abbr* (*BRIT*: = *Civil Aviation Authority*,
US: = *Civil Aeronautics Authority*)
*organismo di controllo e di sviluppo
dell'aviazione civile*.

CAB *n abbr* (*BRIT*: = *Citizens' Advice Bureau*)
*organizzazione per la tutela del
consumatore*.

cab [kæb] *n* taxi *m inv*; (*of train, truck*) cabina;
(*horsedrawn*) carrozza.

cabaret ['kæbəreɪ] *n* cabaret *m inv*.

cabbage ['kæbɪdʒ] *n* cavolo.

cabbie, cabby ['kæbɪ] *n* (*col*), **cab driver** *n*
tassista *m/f*.

cabin ['kæbɪn] *n* capanna; (*on ship*) cabina.

cabin cruiser *n* cabinato.

cabinet ['kæbɪnɪt] *n* (*POL*) consiglio dei
ministri; (*furniture*) armadietto; (*also*:
display ~) vetrinetta; **cocktail ~** mobile *m*
bar *inv*.

cabinet-maker ['kæbɪnɪt'meɪkə*] *n*
stipettaio.

cabinet minister *n* ministro (*membro del
Consiglio*).

cable ['keɪbl] *n* cavo; fune *f*; (*TEL*)
cablogramma *m* ♦ *vt* telegrafare.

cable-car ['keɪblkɑː*] *n* funivia.

cablegram ['keɪblgræm] *n* cablogramma *m*.

cable railway *n* funicolare *f*.

cable television *n* televisione *f* via cavo.

cache [kæʃ] *n* nascondiglio; **a ~ of food** *etc*
un deposito segreto di viveri *etc*.

cackle ['kækl] *vi* schiamazzare.

cactus, *pl* **cacti** ['kæktəs, -taɪ] *n* cactus *m inv*.

CAD *n abbr* (= *computer-aided design*)
progettazione *f* con l'ausilio
dell'elaboratore.

caddie ['kædɪ] *n* caddie *m inv*.

cadet [kə'dɛt] *n* (*MIL*) cadetto; **police ~**
allievo poliziotto.

cadge [kædʒ] *vt* (*col*) scroccare; **to ~ a
meal (off sb)** scroccare un pranzo (a qn).

cadre ['kædrɪ] *n* quadro.

Caesarean, (*US*) **Cesarean** [siː'zɛərɪən] *adj*:
~ **(section)** (taglio) cesareo.

CAF *abbr* (*BRIT*: = *cost and freight*) Caf *m*.

café ['kæfeɪ] *n* caffè *m inv*.

cafeteria [kæfɪ'tɪərɪə] *n* self-service *m inv*.

caffein(e) ['kæfiːn] *n* caffeina.

cage [keɪdʒ] *n* gabbia ♦ *vt* mettere in
gabbia.

cagey ['keɪdʒɪ] *adj* (*col*) chiuso(a);
guardingo(a).

cagoule [kə'guːl] *n* K-way ® *m inv*.

cahoots [kə'huːts] *n*: **to be in ~ (with sb)**
essere in combutta (con qn).

CAI *n abbr* (= *computer-aided instruction*)
istruzione *f* assistita dall'elaboratore.

Cairo ['kaɪərəʊ] *n* il Cairo.

cajole [kə'dʒəʊl] *vt* allettare.

cake [keɪk] *n* torta; ~ **of soap** saponetta; **it's
a piece of ~** (*col*) è una cosa da nulla; **he
wants to have his ~ and eat it (too)** (*fig*)
vuole la botte piena e la moglie ubriaca.

caked [keɪkt] *adj*: ~ **with** incrostato(a) di.

cake shop *n* pasticceria.

Cal. *abbr* (*US*) = *California*.

calamitous [kə'læmɪtəs] *adj* disastroso(a).

calamity [kə'læmɪtɪ] *n* calamità *f inv*.

calcium ['kælsɪəm] *n* calcio.

calculate ['kælkjuleɪt] *vt* calcolare;
(*estimate: chances, effect*) valutare.

▶**calculate on** *vt fus*: **to ~ on sth/on doing
sth** contare su qc/di fare qc.

calculated ['kælkjuleɪtɪd] *adj* calcolato(a),
intenzionale; **a ~ risk** un rischio
calcolato.

calculating ['kælkjuleɪtɪŋ] *adj*
calcolatore(trice).

calculation [kælkju'leɪʃən] *n* calcolo.

calculator ['kælkjuleɪtə*] *n* calcolatrice *f*.

calculus ['kælkjuləs] *n* calcolo; **integral/
differential ~** calcolo integrale/
differenziale.

calendar ['kæləndə*] *n* calendario.

calendar year *n* anno civile.

calf, *pl* **calves** [kɑːf, kɑːvz] *n* (*of cow*)
vitello; (*of other animals*) piccolo; (*also*:
~**skin**) (pelle *f* di) vitello; (*ANAT*)
polpaccio.

caliber ['kælɪbə*] *n* (*US*) = **calibre**.

calibrate ['kælɪbreɪt] *vt* (*gun etc*) calibrare;
(*scale of measuring instrument*) tarare.

calibre, (*US*) **caliber** ['kælɪbə*] *n* calibro.

calico ['kælɪkəʊ] *n* tela grezza, cotone *m*
grezzo; (*US*) cotonina stampata.

Calif. *abbr* (*US*) = *California*.
California [kælɪ'fɔːnɪə] *n* California.
calipers ['kælɪpəz] *npl* (*US*) = **callipers**.
call [kɔːl] *vt* (*gen*, *also TEL*) chiamare;
(*announce: flight*) annunciare; (*meeting,
strike*) indire, proclamare ♦ *vi* chiamare;
(*visit: also*: ~ **in**, ~ **round**) passare ♦ *n* (*shout*)
grido, urlo; *visita;* (*summons: for flight etc*)
chiamata; (*fig: lure*) richiamo; (*also*:
telephone ~) telefonata; **to be on** ~ essere
a disposizione; **to make a** ~ telefonare,
fare una telefonata; **please give me a** ~ **at 7**
per piacere mi chiami alle 7; **to pay a** ~ **on
sb** fare (una) visita a qn; **there's not much** ~
for these items non c'è molta richiesta
di questi articoli; **she's** ~**ed Jane** si
chiama Jane; **who is** ~**ing?** (*TEL*) chi
parla?; **London** ~**ing** (*RADIO*) qui Londra.
► **call at** *vt fus* (*subj: ship*) fare scalo a; (*:
train*) fermarsi a.
► **call back** *vi* (*return*) ritornare; (*TEL*)
ritelefonare, richiamare ♦ *vt* (*TEL*)
ritelefonare a, richiamare.
► **call for** *vt fus* (*demand: action etc*)
richiedere; (*collect: person*) passare a
prendere; (*: goods*) ritirare.
► **call in** *vt* (*doctor, expert, police*) chiamare,
far venire.
► **call off** *vt* (*meeting, race*) disdire; (*deal*)
cancellare; (*dog*) richiamare; **the strike
was** ~**ed off** lo sciopero è stato revocato.
► **call on** *vt fus* (*visit*) passare da; (*request*):
to ~ **on sb to do** chiedere a qn di fare.
► **call out** *vi* urlare ♦ *vt* (*doctor, police,
troops*) chiamare.
► **call up** *vt* (*MIL*) richiamare.
Callanetics ® [kælə'nɛtɪks] *nsg* tipo di
ginnastica basata sulla ripetizione di
piccoli movimenti.
callbox ['kɔːlbɔks] *n* (*BRIT*) cabina
telefonica.
call centre *n* centre informazioni
telefoniche.
caller ['kɔːlə*] *n* persona che chiama;
visitatore/trice; **hold the line,** ~**!** (*TEL*)
rimanga in linea, signore (*or* signora)!
call girl *n* ragazza *f* squillo *inv*.
call-in ['kɔːlɪn] *n* (*US*) = **phone-in**.
calling ['kɔːlɪŋ] *n* vocazione *f*.
calling card *n* (*US*) biglietto da visita.
callipers, (*US*) **calipers** ['kælɪpəz] *npl* (*MED*)
gambale *m*; (*MATH*) calibro.
callous ['kæləs] *adj* indurito(a), insensibile.
callow ['kæləu] *adj* immaturo(a).
calm [kɑːm] *adj* calmo(a) ♦ *n* calma ♦ *vt*
calmare.
► **calm down** *vi* calmarsi ♦ *vt* calmare.
calmly ['kɑːmlɪ] *adv* con calma.

calmness ['kɑːmnɪs] *n* calma.
Calor gas ® ['kælə*-] *n* (*BRIT*) butano.
calorie ['kælərɪ] *n* caloria; **low-~ product**
prodotto a basso contenuto di calorie.
calve [kɑːv] *vi* figliare.
calves [kɑːvz] *npl of* **calf**.
CAM *n abbr* (= *computer-aided
manufacturing*) fabbricazione *f* con
l'ausilio dell'elaboratore.
camber ['kæmbə*] *n* (*of road*) bombatura.
Cambodia [kæm'bəudjə] *n* Cambogia.
Cambodian [kæm'bəudɪən] *adj, n*
cambogiano(a).
Cambs *abbr* (*BRIT*) = *Cambridgeshire*.
camcorder ['kæmkɔːdə*] *n* videocamera.
came [keɪm] *pt of* **come**.
camel ['kæməl] *n* cammello.
cameo ['kæmɪəu] *n* cammeo.
camera ['kæmərə] *n* macchina fotografica;
(*CINE, TV*) telecamera; (*also*: **cine~, movie**
~) cinepresa; **in** ~ a porte chiuse.
cameraman ['kæmərəmæn] *n* cameraman
m inv.
Cameroon, Cameroun ['kæməruːn] *n*
Camerun *m*.
camouflage ['kæməflɑːʒ] *n* camuffamento;
(*MIL*) mimetizzazione *f* ♦ *vt* camuffare;
mimetizzare.
camp [kæmp] *n* campeggio; (*MIL*) campo ♦
vi campeggiare; accamparsi; **to go** ~**ing**
andare in campeggio.
campaign [kæm'peɪn] *n* (*MIL, POL etc*)
campagna ♦ *vi*: **to** ~ **(for/against)** (*also fig*)
fare una campagna (per/contro).
campaigner [kæm'peɪnə*] *n*: ~ **for** fautore/
trice di; ~ **against** oppositore/trice di.
campbed ['kæmp'bɛd] *n* (*BRIT*) brandina.
camper ['kæmpə*] *n* campeggiatore/trice.
camping ['kæmpɪŋ] *n* campeggio.
camp(ing) site *n* campeggio.
campus ['kæmpəs] *n* campus *m inv*.
camshaft ['kæmʃɑːft] *n* albero a camme.
can [kæn] *aux vb see next headword* ♦ *n* (*of milk*)
scatola; (*of oil*) bidone *m*; (*of water*) tanica;
(*tin*) scatola ♦ *vt* mettere in scatola; **a** ~ **of
beer** una lattina di birra; **to carry the** ~
(*BRIT col*) prendere la colpa.

====================================== *KEYWORD*

can [kæn] (*negative* **cannot, can't**; *conditional
and pt* **could**) *aux vb* **1** (*be able to*) potere; **I
~'t go any further** non posso andare
oltre; **you** ~ **do it if you try** sei in grado di
farlo — basta provarci; **I'll help you all I
~** ti aiuterò come potrò; **I** ~'t **see you** non
ti vedo; ~ **you hear me?** mi senti?, riesci
a sentirmi?

2 (*know how to*) sapere, essere capace di;

I ~ **swim** so nuotare; ~ **you speak French?** parla francese? **3** (*may*) potere; **could I have a word with you?** posso parlarle un momento? **4** (*expressing disbelief, puzzlement etc*): **it** ~'**t be true!** non può essere vero!; **what CAN he want?** cosa può mai volere? **5** (*expressing possibility, suggestion etc*): **he could be in the library** può darsi che sia in biblioteca; **they could have forgotten** potrebbero essersene dimenticati; **she could have been delayed** può aver avuto un contrattempo.

Canada ['kænədə] *n* Canada *m*.
Canadian [kə'neɪdɪən] *adj, n* canadese (*m/f*).
canal [kə'næl] *n* canale *m*.
canary [kə'nɛərɪ] *n* canarino.
Canary Islands, Canaries [kə'nɛərɪz] *npl*: **the** ~ le (isole) Canarie.
Canberra ['kænbərə] *n* Camberra.
cancel ['kænsəl] *vt* annullare; (*train*) sopprimere; (*cross out*) cancellare.
▶**cancel out** *vt* (*MATH*) semplificare; (*fig*) annullare; **they** ~ **each other out** (*also fig*) si annullano a vicenda.
cancellation [kænsə'leɪʃən] *n* annullamento; soppressione *f*; cancellazione *f*; (*TOURISM*) prenotazione *f* annullata.
cancer ['kænsə*] *n* cancro; **C**~ (*sign*) Cancro; **to be C**~ essere del Cancro.
cancerous ['kænsərəs] *adj* canceroso(a).
cancer patient *n* malato/a di cancro.
cancer research *n* ricerca sul cancro.
C and F *abbr* (*BRIT*: = *cost and freight*) Caf *m*.
candid ['kændɪd] *adj* onesto(a).
candidacy ['kændɪdəsɪ] *n* candidatura.
candidate ['kændɪdeɪt] *n* candidato/a.
candidature ['kændɪdətʃə*] *n* (*BRIT*) = **candidacy**.
candied ['kændɪd] *adj* candito(a); ~ **apple** (*US*) mela caramellata.
candle ['kændl] *n* candela.
candlelight ['kændl'laɪt] *n*: **by** ~ a lume di candela.
candlestick ['kændlstɪk] *n* (*also*: **candle holder**) bugia; (*bigger, ornate*) candeliere *m*.
candour, (*US*) **candor** ['kændə*] *n* sincerità.
candy ['kændɪ] *n* zucchero candito; (*US*) caramella; caramelle *fpl*.
candy-floss ['kændɪflɔs] *n* (*BRIT*) zucchero filato.
candy store *n* (*US*) ≈ pasticceria.
cane [keɪn] *n* canna; (*for baskets, chairs etc*) bambù *m*; (*SCOL*) verga; (*for walking*)

bastone *m* (da passeggio) ♦ *vt* (*BRIT SCOL*) punire a colpi di verga.
canine ['kænaɪn] *adj* canino(a).
canister ['kænɪstə*] *n* scatola metallica.
cannabis ['kænəbɪs] *n* canapa indiana.
canned ['kænd] *adj* (*food*) in scatola; (*col*: *recorded*: *music*) registrato(a); (*BRIT col*: *drunk*) sbronzo(a); (*US col*: *worker*) licenziato(a).
cannibal ['kænɪbəl] *n* cannibale *m/f*.
cannibalism ['kænɪbəlɪzəm] *n* cannibalismo.
cannon, *pl* ~ *or* ~**s** ['kænən] *n* (*gun*) cannone *m*.
cannonball ['kænənbɔ:l] *n* palla di cannone.
cannon fodder *n* carne *f* da macello.
cannot ['kænɔt] = **can not**.
canny ['kænɪ] *adj* furbo(a).
canoe [kə'nu:] *n* canoa; (*SPORT*) canotto.
canoeing [kə'nu:ɪŋ] *n* (*sport*) canottaggio.
canoeist [kə'nu:ɪst] *n* canottiere *m*.
canon ['kænən] *n* (*clergyman*) canonico; (*standard*) canone *m*.
canonize ['kænənaɪz] *vt* canonizzare.
can opener [-'əupnə*] *n* apriscatole *m inv*.
canopy ['kænəpɪ] *n* baldacchino.
cant [kænt] *n* gergo ♦ *vt* inclinare ♦ *vi* inclinarsi.
can't [kænt] = **can not**.
Cantab. *abbr* (*BRIT*: = *cantabrigiensis*) *of* Cambridge.
cantankerous [kæn'tæŋkərəs] *adj* stizzoso(a).
canteen [kæn'ti:n] *n* mensa; (*BRIT*: *of cutlery*) portaposate *m inv*.
canter ['kæntə*] *n* piccolo galoppo ♦ *vi* andare al piccolo galoppo.
cantilever ['kæntɪli:və*] *n* trave *f* a sbalzo.
canvas ['kænvəs] *n* tela; **under** ~ (*camping*) sotto la tenda; (*NAUT*) sotto la vela.
canvass ['kænvəs] *vt* (*COMM*: *district*) fare un'indagine di mercato in; (: *citizens, opinions*) fare un sondaggio di; (*POL*: *district*) fare un giro elettorale di; (: *person*) fare propaganda elettorale a.
canvasser ['kænvəsə*] *n* (*COMM*) agente *m* viaggiatore, piazzista *m*; (*POL*) propagandista *m/f* (elettorale).
canvassing ['kænvəsɪŋ] *n* sollecitazione *f*.
canyon ['kænjən] *n* canyon *m inv*.
CAP *n abbr* (= *Common Agricultural Policy*) PAC *f*.
cap [kæp] *n* (*also FOOTBALL*) berretto; (*of pen*) coperchio; (*of bottle*) tappo; (*for swimming*) cuffia; (*BRIT*: *contraceptive*: *also*: **Dutch** ~) diaframma *m* ♦ *vt* tappare; (*outdo*) superare; ~**ped with** ricoperto(a) di; **and to** ~ **it all, he** ... (*BRIT*) e per

completare l'opera, lui ....

capability [keɪpə'bɪlɪtɪ] n capacità f inv, abilità f inv.

capable ['keɪpəbl] adj capace; ~ of capace di; suscettibile di.

capacious [kə'peɪʃəs] adj capace.

capacity [kə'pæsɪtɪ] n capacità f inv; (of lift etc) capienza; in his ~ as nella sua qualità di; to work at full ~ lavorare al massimo delle proprie capacità; this work is beyond my ~ questo lavoro supera le mie possibilità; filled to ~ pieno zeppo; in an advisory ~ a titolo consultativo.

cape [keɪp] n (garment) cappa; (GEO) capo.

Cape of Good Hope n Capo di Buona Speranza.

caper ['keɪpə*] n (CULIN: also: ~s) cappero; (leap) saltello; (escapade) birichinata.

Cape Town n Città del Capo.

capita ['kæpɪtə] see **per capita**.

capital ['kæpɪtl] n (also: ~ city) capitale f; (money) capitale m; (also: ~ letter) (lettera) maiuscola.

capital account n conto capitale.

capital allowance n ammortamento fiscale.

capital assets npl capitale m fisso.

capital expenditure n spese fpl in capitale.

capital gains tax n imposta sulla plusvalenza.

capital goods n beni mpl d'investimento, beni mpl capitali.

capital-intensive ['kæpɪtlɪn'tensɪv] adj ad alta intensità di capitale.

capitalism ['kæpɪtəlɪzəm] n capitalismo.

capitalist ['kæpɪtəlɪst] adj, n capitalista (m/f).

capitalize ['kæpɪtəlaɪz] vt (provide with capital) capitalizzare.

▶**capitalize on** vt fus (fig) trarre vantaggio da.

capital punishment n pena capitale.

capital transfer tax n (BRIT) imposta sui trasferimenti di capitali.

Capitol ['kæpɪtl] n: **the** ~ il Campidoglio; see boxed note.

CAPITOL

Il **Capitol** è l'edificio che ospita le riunioni del Congresso degli Stati Uniti. È situato sull'omonimo colle, "Capitol Hill", a Washington DC. In molti stati americani il termine Capitol viene usato per indicare l'edificio dove si riuniscono i rappresentanti dello stato.

---

capitulate [kə'pɪtjuleɪt] vi capitolare.

capitulation [kəpɪtju'leɪʃən] n capitolazione f.

capricious [kə'prɪʃəs] adj capriccioso(a).

Capricorn ['kæprɪkɔːn] n Capricorno; to be ~ essere del Capricorno.

caps [kæps] abbr = **capital letters**.

capsize [kæp'saɪz] vt capovolgere ♦ vi capovolgersi.

capstan ['kæpstən] n argano.

capsule ['kæpsjuːl] n capsula.

Capt. abbr (= captain) Cap.

captain ['kæptɪn] n capitano ♦ vt capitanare.

caption ['kæpʃən] n leggenda.

captivate ['kæptɪveɪt] vt avvincere.

captive ['kæptɪv] adj, n prigioniero(a).

captivity [kæp'tɪvɪtɪ] n prigionia; in ~ (animal) in cattività.

captor ['kæptə*] n (lawful) chi ha catturato; (unlawful) rapitore m.

capture ['kæptʃə*] vt catturare, prendere; (attention) attirare ♦ n cattura; (data ~) registrazione f or rilevazione f di dati.

car [kɑː*] n macchina, automobile f; (US RAIL) carrozza; by ~ in macchina.

carafe [kə'ræf] n caraffa.

carafe wine n (in restaurant) ≈ vino sfuso.

caramel ['kærəməl] n caramello.

carat ['kærət] n carato; 18 ~ gold oro a 18 carati.

caravan ['kærəvæn] n roulotte f inv.

caravan site n (BRIT) campeggio per roulotte.

caraway ['kærəweɪ] n: ~ seed seme m di cumino.

carbohydrates [kɑːbəu'haɪdreɪts] npl (foods) carboidrati mpl.

car bomb n ordigno esplosivo collocato in una macchina; a ~ went off yesterday ieri è esplosa un'autobomba.

carbon ['kɑːbən] n carbonio.

carbonated ['kɑːbəneɪtəd] adj (drink) gassato(a).

carbon copy n copia f carbone inv.

carbon dioxide [-daɪ'ɔksaɪd] n diossido di carbonio.

carbon paper n carta carbone.

carbon ribbon n nastro carbonato.

car boot sale n mercatino dell'usato dove la merce viene esposta nel bagagliaio delle macchine.

carburettor, (US) **carburetor** [kɑːbju'retə*] n carburatore m.

carcass ['kɑːkəs] n carcassa.

carcinogenic [kɑːsɪnə'dʒenɪk] adj cancerogeno(a).

card [kɑːd] n carta; (thin cardboard)

cartoncino; (*visiting* ~ *etc*) biglietto;
(*membership* ~) tessera; (*Christmas* ~ *etc*)
cartolina; **to play ~s** giocare a carte.
cardamom ['kɑːdəməm] *n* cardamomo.
cardboard ['kɑːdbɔːd] *n* cartone *m*.
cardboard box *n* (scatola di) cartone *m*.
cardboard city *n luogo dove dormono in
scatole di cartone emarginati senzatetto.*
card-carrying member ['kɑːd'kærɪŋ-] *n*
tesserato/a.
card game *n* gioco di carte.
cardiac ['kɑːdɪæk] *adj* cardiaco(a).
cardigan ['kɑːdɪgən] *n* cardigan *m inv.*
cardinal ['kɑːdɪnl] *adj, n* cardinale (*m*).
card index *n* schedario.
cardphone ['kɑːdfəun] *n* telefono a scheda
(magnetica).
cardsharp ['kɑːdʃɑːp] *n* baro.
card vote *n* (*BRIT*) voto (palese) per
delega.
CARE [kɛə*] *n abbr* = *Cooperative for
American Relief Everywhere.*
care [kɛə*] *n* cura, attenzione *f*; (*worry*)
preoccupazione *f* ♦ *vi*: **to** ~ **about**
interessarsi di; **would you** ~ **to/for ...?** le
piacerebbe ...?; **I wouldn't** ~ **to do it** non
lo vorrei fare; **in sb's** ~ alle cure di qn; **to
take** ~ fare attenzione; **to take** ~ **of**
curarsi di; (*details, arrangements*)
occuparsi di; **I don't** ~ non me ne
importa; **I couldn't** ~ **less** non me ne
importa un bel niente; ~ **of (c/o)** (*on
letter*) presso; "**with** ~" "fragile"; **the
child has been taken into** ~ il bambino è
stato preso in custodia.
▶**care for** *vt fus* aver cura di; (*like*) voler
bene a.
careen [kə'riːn] *vi* (*ship*) sbandare ♦ *vt*
carenare.
career [kə'rɪə*] *n* carriera; (*occupation*)
professione *f* ♦ *vi* (*also*: ~ **along**) andare di
(gran) carriera.
career girl *n* donna dedita alla carriera.
careers officer *n* consulente *m/f*
d'orientamento professionale.
carefree ['kɛəfriː] *adj* sgombro(a) di
preoccupazioni.
careful ['kɛəful] *adj* attento(a); (*cautious*)
cauto(a); **(be)** ~! attenzione!; **he's very** ~
with his money bada molto alle spese.
carefully ['kɛəfəlɪ] *adv* con cura;
cautamente.
careless ['kɛəlɪs] *adj* negligente; (*remark*)
privo(a) di tatto.
carelessly ['kɛəlɪslɪ] *adv* negligentemente;
senza tatto; (*without thinking*)
distrattamente.
carelessness ['kɛəlɪsnɪs] *n* negligenza;

mancanza di tatto.
carer ['kɛərə*] *n chi si occupa di un
familiare anziano o invalido.*
caress [kə'rɛs] *n* carezza ♦ *vt* accarezzare.
caretaker ['kɛəteɪkə*] *n* custode *m*.
caretaker government *n* (*BRIT*) governo
m ponte *inv.*
car-ferry ['kɑːfɛrɪ] *n* traghetto.
cargo, ~es ['kɑːgəu] *n* carico.
cargo boat *n* cargo.
cargo plane *n* aereo di linea da carico.
car hire *n* (*BRIT*) autonoleggio.
Caribbean [kærɪ'biːən] *adj* caraibico(a); **the
~ (Sea)** il Mar dei Caraibi.
caricature ['kærɪkətjuə*] *n* caricatura.
caring ['kɛərɪŋ] *adj* (*person*) premuroso(a);
(*society, organization*) umanitario(a).
carnage ['kɑːnɪdʒ] *n* carneficina.
carnal ['kɑːnl] *adj* carnale.
carnation [kɑː'neɪʃən] *n* garofano.
carnival ['kɑːnɪvəl] *n* (*public celebration*)
carnevale *m*; (*US*: *funfair*) luna park *m inv.*
carnivorous [kɑː'nɪvərəs] *adj* carnivoro(a).
carol ['kærəl] *n*: (**Christmas**) ~ canto di
Natale.
carouse [kə'rauz] *vi* far baldoria.
carousel [kærə'sɛl] *n* (*US*) giostra.
carp [kɑːp] *n* (*fish*) carpa.
▶**carp at** *vt fus* trovare a ridire su.
car park *n* parcheggio.
carpenter ['kɑːpɪntə*] *n* carpentiere *m*.
carpentry ['kɑːpɪntrɪ] *n* carpenteria.
carpet ['kɑːpɪt] *n* tappeto; (*BRIT*: *fitted* ~)
moquette *f inv* ♦ *vt* coprire con tappeto.
carpet bombing *n* bombardamento a
tappeto.
carpet slippers *npl* pantofole *fpl.*
carpet sweeper *n* scopatappeti *m inv.*
car phone *n* telefonino per auto.
car rental *n* (*US*) autonoleggio.
carriage ['kærɪdʒ] *n* vettura; (*of goods*)
trasporto; (*of typewriter*) carrello;
(*bearing*) portamento; ~ **forward** porto
assegnato; ~ **free** franco di porto; ~ **paid**
porto pagato.
carriage return *n* (*on typewriter etc*) leva
(*or* tasto) del ritorno a capo.
carriageway ['kærɪdʒweɪ] *n* (*BRIT*: *part of
road*) carreggiata.
carrier ['kærɪə*] *n* (*of disease*) portatore/
trice; (*COMM*) impresa di trasporti;
(*NAUT*) portaerei *f inv.*
carrier bag *n* (*BRIT*) sacchetto.
carrier pigeon *n* colombo viaggiatore.
carrion ['kærɪən] *n* carogna.
carrot ['kærət] *n* carota.
carry ['kærɪ] *vt* (*subj*: *person*) portare;
(: *vehicle*) trasportare; (*a motion, bill*) far

passare; (involve: responsibilities etc)
comportare; (COMM: goods) tenere;
(: interest) avere; (MATH: figure) riportare
♦ vi (sound) farsi sentire; this loan carries
10% interest questo prestito è sulla base
di un interesse del 10%; to be carried
away (fig) farsi trascinare.
►carry forward vt (MATH, COMM)
riportare.
►carry on vi: to ~ on with sth/doing
continuare qc/a fare ♦ vt mandare avanti.
►carry out vt (orders) eseguire;
(investigation) svolgere; (accomplish etc:
plan) realizzare; (perform, implement: idea,
threat) mettere in pratica.
carrycot ['kærɪkɔt] n (BRIT) culla portabile.
carry-on [kærɪ'ɔn] n (col: fuss) casino,
confusione f; (: annoying behaviour): I've
had enough of your ~! mi hai proprio
scocciato!
cart [kɑːt] n carro ♦ vt (col) trascinare,
scarrozzare.
carte blanche ['kɑːt'blɒnʃ] n: to give sb ~
dare carta bianca a qn.
cartel [kɑː'tɛl] n (COMM) cartello.
cartilage ['kɑːtɪlɪdʒ] n cartilagine f.
cartographer [kɑː'tɔgrəfə*] n cartografo/a.
cartography [kɑː'tɔgrəfi] n cartografia.
carton ['kɑːtən] n (box) scatola di cartone;
(of yogurt) cartone m; (of cigarettes)
stecca.
cartoon [kɑː'tuːn] n (in newspaper etc)
vignetta; (CINE, TV) cartone m animato;
(ART) cartone.
cartoonist [kɑː'tuːnɪst] n vignettista m/f,
cartonista m/f.
cartridge ['kɑːtrɪdʒ] n (for gun, pen)
cartuccia; (for camera) caricatore m;
(music tape) cassetta; (of record player)
testina.
cartwheel ['kɑːtwiːl] n: to turn a ~ (SPORT
etc) fare la ruota.
carve [kɑːv] vt (meat) trinciare; (wood,
stone) intagliare.
►carve up vt (meat) tagliare; (fig: country)
suddividere.
carving ['kɑːvɪŋ] n (in wood etc) scultura.
carving knife n trinciante m.
car wash n lavaggio auto.
Casablanca [kæsə'blæŋkə] n Casablanca.
cascade [kæs'keɪd] n cascata ♦ vi scendere
a cascata.
case [keɪs] n caso; (LAW) causa, processo;
(box) scatola; (also: suit~) valigia; (TYP):
lower/upper ~ (carattere m) minuscolo/
maiuscolo; to have a good ~ avere
pretese legittime; there's a strong ~ for
reform ci sono validi argomenti a favore

della riforma; in ~ of in caso di; in ~ he
caso mai lui; just in ~ in caso di bisogno.
case history n (MED) cartella clinica.
case study n studio di un caso.
cash [kæʃ] n (coins, notes) soldi mpl, denaro;
(col: money) quattrini mpl ♦ vt incassare;
to pay (in) ~ pagare in contanti; to be
short of ~ essere a corto di soldi; ~ with
order/on delivery (COD) (COMM)
pagamento all'ordinazione/alla consegna.
►cash in vt (insurance policy etc) riscuotere,
riconvertire.
►cash in on vt fus: to ~ in on sth sfruttare
qc.
cash account n conto m cassa inv.
cash-and-carry ['kæʃənd'kærɪ] n cash and
carry m inv.
cashbook ['kæʃbuk] n giornale m di cassa.
cash box n cassetta per il denaro
spicciolo.
cash card n carta per prelievi automatici.
cash desk n (BRIT) cassa.
cash discount n sconto per contanti.
cash dispenser n sportello automatico.
cashew [kæ'ʃuː] n (also: ~ nut) anacardio
cash flow n cash-flow m inv, liquidità f inv.
cashier [kæ'ʃɪə*] n cassiere/a ♦ vt (esp MIL)
destituire.
cashmere ['kæʃmɪə*] n cachemire m.
cash payment n pagamento in contanti.
cash price n prezzo per contanti.
cash register n registratore m di cassa.
cash sale n vendita per contanti.
casing ['keɪsɪŋ] n rivestimento.
casino [kə'siːnəu] n casinò m inv.
cask [kɑːsk] n botte f.
casket ['kɑːskɪt] n cofanetto; (US: coffin)
bara.
Caspian Sea ['kæspɪən-] n: the ~ il mar
Caspio.
casserole ['kæsərəul] n casseruola; (food):
chicken ~ pollo in casseruola.
cassette [kæ'sɛt] n cassetta.
cassette deck n piastra di registrazione.
cassette player n riproduttore m a
cassette.
cassette recorder n registratore m a
cassette.
cast [kɑːst] vt (pt, pp cast) (throw) gettare;
(shed) perdere; spogliarsi di; (metal)
gettare, fondere ♦ n (THEAT) complesso di
attori; (mould) forma; (also: plaster ~)
ingessatura; (THEAT): to ~ sb as Hamlet
scegliere qn per la parte di Amleto; to ~
one's vote votare, dare il voto.
►cast aside vt (reject) mettere da parte.
►cast off vi (NAUT) salpare; (KNITTING)
diminuire, calare ♦ vt (NAUT)

disormeggiare; (*KNITTING*) diminuire, calare.
►**cast on** *vt* (*KNITTING*) avviare ♦ *vi* avviare (le maglie).
castanets [kæstə'nɛts] *npl* castagnette *fpl*.
castaway ['kɑːstəwəɪ] *n* naufrago/a.
caste [kɑːst] *n* casta.
caster sugar ['kɑːstə-] *n* zucchero semolato.
casting vote ['kɑːstɪŋ-] *n* (*BRIT*) voto decisivo.
cast iron *n* ghisa ♦ *adj*: **cast-iron** (*fig: will, alibi*) di ferro, d'acciaio.
castle ['kɑːsl] *n* castello; (*fortified*) rocca.
castor ['kɑːstə*] *n* (*wheel*) rotella.
castor oil *n* olio di ricino.
castrate [kæs'treɪt] *vt* castrare.
casual ['kæʒjul] *adj* (*by chance*) casuale, fortuito(a); (*irregular: work etc*) avventizio(a); (*unconcerned*) noncurante, indifferente; ~ **wear** casual *m*.
casual labour *n* manodopera avventizia.
casually ['kæʒjulɪ] *adv* con disinvoltura; (*by chance*) casualmente.
casualty ['kæʒjultɪ] *n* ferito/a; (*dead*) morto/a, vittima; **heavy casualties** *npl* grosse perdite *fpl*.
casualty ward *n* (*BRIT*) pronto soccorso.
cat [kæt] *n* gatto.
catacombs ['kætəkuːmz] *npl* catacombe *fpl*.
catalogue, (*US*) **catalog** ['kætəlɔg] *n* catalogo ♦ *vt* catalogare.
catalyst ['kætəlɪst] *n* catalizzatore *m*.
catalytic converter [kætə'lɪtɪkkən'vəːtə*] *n* marmitta catalitica, catalizzatore *m*.
catapult ['kætəpʌlt] *n* catapulta; fionda.
cataract ['kætərækt] *n* (*also MED*) cateratta.
catarrh [kə'tɑː*] *n* catarro.
catastrophe [kə'tæstrəfɪ] *n* catastrofe *f*.
catastrophic [kætə'strɔfɪk] *adj* catastrofico(a).
catcall ['kætkɔːl] *n* (*at meeting etc*) fischio.
catch [kætʃ] *vb* (*pt, pp* **caught** [kɔːt]) *vt* (*train, thief, cold*) acchiappare; (*ball*) afferrare; (*person: by surprise*) sorprendere; (*understand*) comprendere; (*get entangled*) impigliare ♦ *vi* (*fire*) prendere ♦ *n* (*fish etc caught*) retata, presa; (*trick*) inganno; (*TECH*) gancio; **to** ~ **sb's attention** *or* **eye** attirare l'attenzione di qn; **to** ~ **fire** prendere fuoco; **to** ~ **sight of** scorgere.
►**catch on** *vi* (*become popular*) affermarsi, far presa; (*understand*): **to** ~ **on (to sth)** capire (qc).
►**catch out** *vt* (*BRIT fig: with trick question*) cogliere in fallo.
►**catch up** *vi* mettersi in pari ♦ *vt* (*also:* ~ **up with**) raggiungere.

catching ['kætʃɪŋ] *adj* (*MED*) contagioso(a).
catchment area ['kætʃmənt-] *n* (*BRIT SCOL*) circoscrizione *f* scolare; (*GEO*) bacino pluviale.
catch phrase *n* slogan *m inv*; frase *f* fatta.
catch-22 ['kætʃtwɛntɪ'tuː] *n*: **it's a** ~ **situation** non c'è via d'uscita.
catchy ['kætʃɪ] *adj* orecchiabile.
catechism ['kætɪkɪzəm] *n* catechismo.
categoric(al) [kætɪ'gɔrɪk(l)] *adj* categorico(a).
categorize ['kætɪgəraɪz] *vt* categorizzare.
category ['kætɪgərɪ] *n* categoria.
cater ['keɪtə*] *vi* (*gen:* ~ **for**) provvedere da mangiare (per).
►**cater for** *vt fus* (*BRIT: needs*) provvedere a; (*: consumers*) incontrare i gusti di.
caterer ['keɪtərə*] *n* fornitore *m*.
catering ['keɪtərɪŋ] *n* approvvigionamento.
catering trade *n* settore *m* ristoranti.
caterpillar ['kætəpɪlə*] *n* (*ZOOL*) bruco ♦ *cpd* (*vehicle*) cingolato(a); ~ **track** cingolo.
cat flap *n* gattaiola.
cathedral [kə'θiːdrəl] *n* cattedrale *f*, duomo.
cathode ['kæθəud] *n* catodo.
cathode ray tube *n* tubo a raggi catodici.
catholic ['kæθəlɪk] *adj* universale; aperto(a); eclettico(a); **C**~ *adj*, *n* (*REL*) cattolico(a).
CAT scanner [kæt-] *n* (*MED*: = *computerized axial tomography scanner*) (rilevatore *m* per la) TAC *f inv*.
cat's-eye ['kæts'aɪ] *n* (*BRIT AUT*) catarifrangente *m*.
catsup ['kætsəp] *n* (*US*) ketchup *m inv*.
cattle ['kætl] *npl* bestiame *m*, bestie *fpl*.
catty ['kætɪ] *adj* maligno(a), dispettoso(a).
catwalk ['kætwɔːk] *n* passerella.
Caucasian [kɔː'keɪzɪən] *adj*, *n* caucasico(a).
caucus ['kɔːkəs] *n* (*US POL*) (riunione *f* del) comitato elettorale; (*BRIT POL: group*) comitato di dirigenti; *see boxed note.*

CAUCUS

Caucus *è il termine usato, specialmente negli Stati Uniti, per indicare una riunione informale dei rappresentanti di spicco di un partito politico che precede una riunione ufficiale. Con uso estensivo, la parola indica il nucleo direttivo di un partito politico.*

---

caught [kɔːt] *pt, pp of* **catch**.
cauliflower ['kɔlɪflauə*] *n* cavolfiore *m*.
cause [kɔːz] *n* causa ♦ *vt* causare; **there is no** ~ **for concern** non c'è ragione di preoccuparsi; **to** ~ **sb to do sth** far fare qc a qn; **to** ~ **sth to be done** far fare qc.

causeway ['kɔːzweɪ] n strada rialzata.
caustic ['kɔːstɪk] adj caustico(a).
caution ['kɔːʃən] n prudenza; (warning) avvertimento ♦ vt ammonire.
cautious ['kɔːʃəs] adj cauto(a), prudente.
cautiously ['kɔːʃəslɪ] adv prudentemente.
cautiousness ['kɔːʃəsnɪs] n cautela.
cavalier [kævə'lɪə*] n (knight) cavaliere m ♦ adj (pej: offhand) brusco(a).
cavalry ['kævəlrɪ] n cavalleria.
cave [keɪv] n caverna, grotta ♦ vi: **to go caving** fare speleologia.
▶**cave in** vi (roof etc) crollare.
caveman ['keɪvmæn] n uomo delle caverne.
cavern ['kævən] n caverna.
caviar(e) ['kævɪɑː*] n caviale m.
cavity ['kævɪtɪ] n cavità f inv.
cavity wall insulation n isolamento per pareti a intercapedine.
cavort [kə'vɔːt] vi far capriole.
cayenne (pepper) [keɪ'ɛn-] n pepe m di Caienna.
CB n abbr (BRIT: = Companion (of the Order) of the Bath) titolo; (= Citizens' Band (Radio)) C.B. m; ~ **radio (set)** baracchino.
CBC n abbr = Canadian Broadcasting Corporation.
CBE n abbr (BRIT: = Companion (of the Order) of the British Empire) titolo.
CBI n abbr (= Confederation of British Industry) ≈ CONFINDUSTRIA (= Confederazione Generale dell'Industria Italiana).
CBS n abbr (US) = Columbia Broadcasting System.
CC abbr (BRIT) = county council.
cc abbr (= cubic centimetre) cc; (on letter etc) = carbon copy.
CCA n abbr (US: = Circuit Court of Appeals) corte f d'appello itinerante.
CCTV n abbr = closed-circuit television.
CCU n abbr (US: = coronary care unit) unità coronarica.
CD n abbr (= compact disk) compact disc m inv; ~ **player** lettore m CD; (MIL) = Civil Defence (Corps) (BRIT), Civil Defense (US) ♦ abbr (BRIT: = Corps Diplomatique) C.D.
CDC n abbr (US) = center for disease control.
CD-I ® n CD-I m inv, compact disc m inv interattivo.
Cdr. abbr (= commander) Com.
CD-ROM ['siː'diːrɔm] n abbr (= compact disc read-only memory) CD-ROM m inv.
CDT abbr (US: = Central Daylight Time) ora legale del centro.
CDW n abbr see collision damage waiver.
cease [siːs] vt, vi cessare.

ceasefire ['siːsfaɪə*] n cessate il fuoco m inv.
ceaseless ['siːslɪs] adj incessante.
CED n abbr (US) = Committee for Economic Development.
cedar ['siːdə*] n cedro.
cede [siːd] vt cedere.
CEEB n abbr (US: = College Entrance Examination Board) commissione f per l'esame di ammissione al college.
ceilidh ['keɪlɪ] n festa con musiche e danze popolari scozzesi o irlandesi.
ceiling ['siːlɪŋ] n soffitto; (fig: upper limit) tetto, limite m massimo.
celebrate ['sɛlɪbreɪt] vt, vi celebrare.
celebrated ['sɛlɪbreɪtɪd] adj celebre.
celebration [sɛlɪ'breɪʃən] n celebrazione f.
celebrity [sɪ'lɛbrɪtɪ] n celebrità f inv.
celeriac [sə'lɛrɪæk] n sedano m rapa inv.
celery ['sɛlərɪ] n sedano.
celestial [sɪ'lɛstɪəl] adj celeste.
celibacy ['sɛlɪbəsɪ] n celibato.
cell [sɛl] n cella; (BIOL) cellula; (ELEC) elemento (di batteria).
cellar ['sɛlə*] n sottosuolo, cantina.
cellist ['tʃɛlɪst] n violoncellista m/f.
cello ['tʃɛləu] n violoncello.
cellophane ® ['sɛləfeɪn] n cellophane ® m.
cellphone ['sɛlfəun] n cellulare m.
cellular ['sɛljulə*] adj cellulare.
celluloid ['sɛljulɔɪd] n celluloide f.
cellulose ['sɛljuləus] n cellulosa.
Celsius ['sɛlsɪəs] adj Celsius inv.
Celt [kɛlt, sɛlt] n celta m/f.
Celtic ['kɛltɪk, 'sɛltɪk] adj celtico(a) ♦ n (LING) celtico.
cement [sə'mɛnt] n cemento ♦ vt cementare.
cement mixer n betoniera.
cemetery ['sɛmɪtrɪ] n cimitero.
cenotaph ['sɛnətɑːf] n cenotafio.
censor ['sɛnsə*] n censore m ♦ vt censurare.
censorship ['sɛnsəʃɪp] n censura.
censure ['sɛnʃə*] vt censurare.
census ['sɛnsəs] n censimento.
cent [sɛnt] n (US: coin) centesimo (= 1:100 di un dollaro); see also per cent.
centenary [sɛn'tiːnərɪ], **centennial** [sɛn'tɛnɪəl] n centenario.
center ['sɛntə*] n, vt (US) = centre.
centigrade ['sɛntɪgreɪd] adj centigrado(a).
centilitre, (US) **centiliter** ['sɛntɪliːtə*] n centilitro.
centimetre, (US) **centimeter** ['sɛntɪmiːtə*] n centimetro.
centipede ['sɛntɪpiːd] n centopiedi m inv.
central ['sɛntrəl] adj centrale.
Central African Republic n Repubblica

centrafricana.
Central America *n* America centrale.
central heating *n* riscaldamento centrale.
centralize ['sɛntrəlaɪz] *vt* accentrare.
central processing unit (CPU) *n*
(*COMPUT*) unità *f inv* centrale di
elaborazione.
central reservation *n* (*BRIT AUT*) banchina
f spartitraffico *inv*.
centre, (*US*) **center** ['sɛntə*] *n* centro ♦ *vt*
(*concentrate*): **to ~ (on)** concentrare (su).
centrefold, (*US*) **centerfold** ['sɛntəfəuld] *n*
(*PRESS*) poster *m* (all'interno di rivista).
centre-forward ['sɛntə'fɔ:wəd] *n* (*SPORT*)
centroavanti *m inv*.
centre-half ['sɛntə'hɑ:f] *n* (*SPORT*)
centromediano.
centrepiece, (*US*) **centerpiece** ['sɛntəpi:s]
n centrotavola *m*; (*fig*) punto centrale.
centre spread *n* (*BRIT*) pubblicità a doppia
pagina.
centre-stage [sɛntə'steɪdʒ] *n*: **to take ~**
porsi al centro dell'attenzione.
centrifugal [sɛn'trɪfjugəl] *adj* centrifugo(a).
centrifuge ['sɛntrɪfju:ʒ] *n* centrifuga.
century ['sɛntjurɪ] *n* secolo; **in the
twentieth ~** nel ventesimo secolo.
CEO *n abbr* (*US*) *see* **chief executive officer.**
ceramic [sɪ'ræmɪk] *adj* ceramico(a).
cereal ['si:rɪəl] *n* cereale *m*.
cerebral ['sɛrɪbrəl] *adj* cerebrale.
ceremonial [sɛrɪ'məunɪəl] *n* cerimoniale *m*;
(*rite*) rito.
ceremony ['sɛrɪmənɪ] *n* cerimonia; **to stand
on ~** fare complimenti.
cert [sə:t] *n* (*BRIT col*): **it's a dead ~** non c'è
alcun dubbio.
certain ['sə:tən] *adj* certo(a); **to make ~ of**
assicurarsi di; **for ~** per certo, di sicuro.
certainly ['sə:tənlɪ] *adv* certamente, certo.
certainty ['sə:təntɪ] *n* certezza.
certificate [sə'tɪfɪkɪt] *n* certificato; diploma
m.
certified letter ['sə:tɪfaɪd-] *n* (*US*) lettera
raccomandata.
certified public accountant (CPA)
['sə:tɪfaɪd-] *n* (*US*) ≈ commercialista *m/f*.
certify ['sə:tɪfaɪ] *vt* certificare ♦ *vi*: **to ~ to**
attestare a.
cervical ['sə:vɪkl] *adj*: **~ cancer** cancro della
cervice, tumore *m* al collo dell'utero; **~
smear** Pap-test *m inv*.
cervix ['sə:vɪks] *n* cervice *f*.
Cesarean [si:'zɛərɪən] *adj, n* (*US*) =
Caesarean.
cessation [sə'seɪʃən] *n* cessazione *f*;
arresto.
cesspit ['sɛspɪt] *n* pozzo nero.

CET *abbr* (= *Central European Time*) *fuso
orario.*
Ceylon [sɪ'lɔn] *n* Ceylon *f*.
cf. *abbr* (= *compare*) cfr.
c/f *abbr* (*COMM*) = *carried forward.*
CFC *n abbr* (= *chlorofluorocarbon*) CFC *m inv*.
CG *n abbr* (*US*) = **coastguard.**
cg *abbr* (= *centigram*) cg.
CH *n abbr* (*BRIT*: = *Companion of Honour*)
titolo.
ch *abbr* (*BRIT*) = **central heating.**
ch. *abbr* (= *chapter*) cap.
Chad [tʃæd] *n* Chad *m*.
chafe [tʃeɪf] *vt* fregare, irritare ♦ *vi* (*fig*): **to
~ against** scontrarsi con.
chaffinch ['tʃæfɪntʃ] *n* fringuello.
chagrin ['ʃægrɪn] *n* disappunto, dispiacere
m.
chain [tʃeɪn] *n* catena ♦ *vt* (*also*: **~ up**)
incatenare.
chain reaction *n* reazione *f* a catena.
chain-smoke ['tʃeɪnsməuk] *vi* fumare una
sigaretta dopo l'altra.
chain store *n* negozio a catena.
chair [tʃɛə*] *n* sedia; (*armchair*) poltrona; (*of
university*) cattedra ♦ *vt* (*meeting*)
presiedere; **the ~** (*US*: *electric* **~**) la sedia
elettrica.
chairlift ['tʃɛəlɪft] *n* seggiovia.
chairman ['tʃɛəmən] *n* presidente *m*.
chairperson ['tʃɛəpə:sn] *n* presidente/essa.
chairwoman ['tʃɛəwumən] *n*
presidentessa.
chalet ['ʃæleɪ] *n* chalet *m inv*.
chalice ['tʃælɪs] *n* calice *m*.
chalk [tʃɔ:k] *n* gesso.
▶**chalk up** *vt* scrivere col gesso; (*fig*:
success) ottenere; (: *victory*) riportare.
challenge ['tʃælɪndʒ] *n* sfida ♦ *vt* sfidare;
(*statement, right*) mettere in dubbio; **to ~
sb to a fight/game** sfidare qn a battersi/
ad una partita; **to ~ sb to do** sfidare qn a
fare.
challenger ['tʃælɪndʒə*] *n* (*SPORT*) sfidante
m/f.
challenging ['tʃælɪndʒɪŋ] *adj* sfidante;
(*remark, look*) provocatorio(a).
chamber ['tʃeɪmbə*] *n* camera; **~ of
commerce** camera di commercio.
chambermaid ['tʃeɪmbəmeɪd] *n* cameriera.
chamber music *n* musica da camera.
chamberpot ['tʃeɪmbəpɔt] *n* vaso da notte.
chameleon [kə'mi:lɪən] *n* camaleonte *m*.
chamois ['ʃæmwɑ:] *n* camoscio.
chamois leather ['ʃæmɪ-] *n* pelle *f* di
camoscio.
champagne [ʃæm'peɪn] *n* champagne *m inv*.
champers ['ʃæmpəz] *nsg* (*col*) sciampagna.

champion ['tʃæmpɪən] n campione/essa; (of cause) difensore m ♦ vt difendere.

championship ['tʃæmpɪənʃɪp] n campionato.

chance [tʃɑːns] n caso; (opportunity) occasione f; (likelihood) possibilità f inv ♦ vt: **to ~ it** rischiare, provarci ♦ adj fortuito(a); **there is little ~ of his coming** è molto improbabile che venga; **to take a ~** rischiare; **by ~** per caso; **it's the ~ of a lifetime** è un'occasione unica; **the ~s are that ...** probabilmente ..., è probabile che ... + sub; **to ~ to do sth** (formal: happen) fare per caso qc.

►**chance (up)on** vt fus (person) incontrare per caso, imbattersi in; (thing) trovare per caso.

chancel ['tʃɑːnsəl] n coro.

chancellor ['tʃɑːnsələ*] n cancelliere m; (of university) rettore m (onorario); **C~ of the Exchequer** (BRIT) Cancelliere m dello Scacchiere.

chandelier [ʃændə'lɪə*] n lampadario.

change [tʃeɪndʒ] vt cambiare; (transform): **to ~ sb into** trasformare qn in ♦ vi cambiarsi; (be transformed): **to ~ into** trasformarsi in ♦ n cambiamento; (money) resto; **to ~ one's mind** cambiare idea; **to ~ gear** (AUT) cambiare (marcia); **she ~d into an old skirt** si è cambiata e ha messo una vecchia gonna; **a ~ of clothes** un cambio (di vestiti); **for a ~** tanto per cambiare; **small ~** spiccioli mpl, moneta; **keep the ~** tenga il resto; **can you give me ~ for £1?** mi può cambiare una sterlina?

changeable ['tʃeɪndʒəbl] adj (weather) variabile; (person) mutevole.

change machine n distributore m automatico di monete.

changeover ['tʃeɪndʒəʊvə*] n cambiamento, passaggio.

changing ['tʃeɪndʒɪŋ] adj che cambia; (colours) cangiante.

changing room n (BRIT: in shop) camerino; (: SPORT) spogliatoio.

channel ['tʃænl] n canale m; (of river, sea) alveo ♦ vt canalizzare; (fig: interest, energies): **to ~ into** concentrare su, indirizzare verso; **through the usual ~s** per le solite vie; **the (English) C~** la Manica; **green/red ~** (CUSTOMS) uscita "niente da dichiarare"/"merci da dichiarare".

channel-hopping ['tʃænl,hɒpɪŋ] n (TV) zapping m.

Channel Islands npl: **the ~** le Isole Normanne.

Channel Tunnel n: **the ~** il tunnel della Manica.

chant [tʃɑːnt] n canto; salmodia; (of crowd) slogan m inv ♦ vt cantare; salmodiare; **the demonstrators ~ed their disapproval** i dimostranti lanciavano slogan di protesta.

chaos ['keɪɒs] n caos m.

chaos theory n teoria del caos.

chaotic [keɪ'ɒtɪk] adj caotico(a).

chap [tʃæp] n (BRIT col: man) tipo ♦ vt (skin) screpolare; **old ~** vecchio mio.

chapel ['tʃæpl] n cappella.

chaperone ['ʃæpərəun] n accompagnatore/trice ♦ vt accompagnare.

chaplain ['tʃæplɪn] n cappellano.

chapped [tʃæpt] adj (skin, lips) screpolato(a).

chapter ['tʃæptə*] n capitolo.

char [tʃɑː*] vt (burn) carbonizzare ♦ vi (BRIT: cleaner) lavorare come domestica (a ore) ♦ n (BRIT) = **charlady**.

character ['kærɪktə*] n (gen, COMPUT) carattere m; (in novel, film) personaggio; (eccentric) originale m; **a person of good ~** una persona a modo.

character code n (COMPUT) codice m di carattere.

characteristic ['kærɪktə'rɪstɪk] adj caratteristico(a) ♦ n caratteristica; **~ of** tipico(a) di.

characterize ['kærɪktəraɪz] vt caratterizzare; (describe): **to ~ (as)** descrivere (come).

charade [ʃə'rɑːd] n sciarada.

charcoal ['tʃɑːkəul] n carbone m di legna.

charge [tʃɑːdʒ] n accusa; (cost) prezzo; (of gun, battery, MIL: attack) carica ♦ vt (gun, battery, MIL: enemy) caricare; (customer) fare pagare a; (sum) fare pagare; (LAW): **to ~ sb (with)** accusare qn (di) ♦ vi (gen with: up, along etc) lanciarsi; **~s** npl: **bank ~s** commissioni fpl bancarie; **labour ~s** costi mpl del lavoro; **to ~ in/out** precipitarsi dentro/fuori; **to ~ up/down** lanciarsi su/giù per; **is there a ~?** c'è da pagare?; **there's no ~** non c'è niente da pagare; **extra ~** supplemento; **to take ~ of** incaricarsi di; **to be in ~ of** essere responsabile per; **to have ~ of sb** aver cura di qn; **how much do you ~ for this repair?** quanto chiede per la riparazione?; **to ~ an expense (up) to sb** addebitare una spesa a qn; **~ it to my account** lo metta or addebiti sul mio conto.

charge account n conto.

charge card n carta di credito commerciale.

chargé d'affaires [ˈʃɑːʒeɪdæˈfɛə*] n incaricato d'affari.
chargehand [ˈtʃɑːdʒhænd] n (*BRIT*) caposquadra *m/f*.
charger [ˈtʃɑːdʒə*] n (*also:* **battery** ~) caricabatterie *m inv*; (*old: warhorse*) destriero.
chariot [ˈtʃærɪət] n carro.
charitable [ˈtʃærɪtəbl] adj caritatevole.
charity [ˈtʃærɪtɪ] n carità; (*organization*) opera pia.
charlady [ˈtʃɑːleɪdɪ] n (*BRIT*) domestica a ore.
charlatan [ˈʃɑːlətən] n ciarlatano.
charm [tʃɑːm] n fascino; (*on bracelet*) ciondolo ♦ vt affascinare, incantare.
charm bracelet n braccialetto con ciondoli.
charming [ˈtʃɑːmɪŋ] adj affascinante.
chart [tʃɑːt] n tabella; grafico; (*map*) carta nautica; (*weather* ~) carta del tempo ♦ vt fare una carta nautica di; (*sales, progress*) tracciare il grafico di; **to be in the** ~**s** (*record, pop group*) essere in classifica.
charter [ˈtʃɑːtə*] vt (*plane*) noleggiare ♦ n (*document*) carta; **on** ~ a nolo.
chartered accountant (CA) [ˈtʃɑːtəd-] n (*BRIT*) ragioniere/a professionista.
charter flight n volo *m* charter *inv*.
charwoman [ˈtʃɑːwumən] n = **charlady**.
chase [tʃeɪs] vt inseguire; (*also:* ~ **away**) cacciare ♦ n caccia.
►**chase down** vt (*US*) = **chase up**.
►**chase up** vt (*BRIT: person*) scovare; (: *information*) scoprire, raccogliere.
chasm [ˈkæzəm] n abisso.
chassis [ˈʃæsɪ] n telaio.
chastened [ˈtʃeɪsnd] adj abbattuto(a), provato(a).
chastening [ˈtʃeɪsnɪŋ] adj che fa riflettere.
chastise [tʃæsˈtaɪz] vt punire, castigare.
chastity [ˈtʃæstɪtɪ] n castità.
chat [tʃæt] vi (*also:* **have a** ~) chiacchierare ♦ n chiacchierata.
►**chat up** vt (*BRIT col: girl*) abbordare.
chatline [ˈtʃætlaɪn] n chatline *f*.
chat show n (*BRIT*) talk show *m inv*, conversazione *f* televisiva.
chattel [ˈtʃætl] n see **goods**.
chatter [ˈtʃætə*] vi (*person*) ciarlare ♦ n ciarle *fpl*; **her teeth were** ~**ing** batteva i denti.
chatterbox [ˈtʃætəbɔks] n chiacchierone/a.
chattering classes [ˈtʃætərɪŋ-] npl: **the** ~ (*col, pej*) ≈ gli intellettuali da salotto.
chatty [ˈtʃætɪ] adj (*style*) familiare; (*person*) chiacchierino(a).
chauffeur [ˈʃəufə*] n autista *m*.

chauvinism [ˈʃəuvɪnɪzəm] n (*also:* **male** ~) maschilismo; (*nationalism*) sciovinismo.
chauvinist [ˈʃəuvɪnɪst] n (*also:* **male** ~) maschilista *m*; (*nationalist*) sciovinista *m/f*.
chauvinistic [ʃəuvɪˈnɪstɪk] adj sciovinistico(a).
ChE abbr = *chemical engineer.*
cheap [tʃiːp] adj a buon mercato; (*reduced: fare, ticket*) ridotto(a); (*joke*) grossolano(a); (*poor quality*) di cattiva qualità ♦ adv a buon mercato; ~**er** meno caro; ~ **day return** biglietto giornaliero ridotto di andata e ritorno; ~ **money** denaro a basso tasso di interesse.
cheapen [ˈtʃiːpn] vt ribassare; (*fig*) avvilire.
cheaply [ˈtʃiːplɪ] adv a buon prezzo, a buon mercato.
cheat [tʃiːt] vi imbrogliare; (*at school*) copiare ♦ vt ingannare; (*rob*) defraudare ♦ n imbroglione *m*; copione *m*; (*trick*) inganno; **he's been** ~**ing on his wife** ha tradito sua moglie.
cheating [ˈtʃiːtɪŋ] n imbrogliare *m*; copiare *m*.
check [tʃɛk] vt verificare; (*passport, ticket*) controllare; (*halt*) fermare; (*restrain*) contenere ♦ vi (*official etc*) informarsi ♦ n verifica; controllo; (*curb*) freno; (*bill*) conto; (*pattern: gen pl*) quadretti *mpl*; (*US*) = **cheque** ♦ adj (*also:* ~**ed**: *pattern, cloth*) a scacchi, a quadretti; **to** ~ **with sb** chiedere a qn; **to keep a** ~ **on sb/sth** controllare qn/qc.
►**check in** vi (*in hotel*) registrare; (*at airport*) presentarsi all'accettazione ♦ vt (*luggage*) depositare.
►**check off** vt segnare.
►**check out** vi (*from hotel*) saldare il conto ♦ vt (*luggage*) ritirare; (*investigate: story*) controllare, verificare; (: *person*) prendere informazioni su.
►**check up** vi: **to** ~ **up (on sth)** investigare (qc); **to** ~ **up on sb** informarsi sul conto di qn.
checkbook [ˈtʃɛkbuk] n (*US*) = **chequebook**.
checkered [ˈtʃɛkəd] adj (*US*) = **chequered**.
checkers [ˈtʃɛkəz] n (*US*) dama.
check guarantee card n (*US*) carta *f* assegni *inv*.
check-in [ˈtʃɛkɪn] n (*also:* ~ **desk**: *at airport*) check-in *m inv*, accettazione *f* (*bagagli inv*).
checking account [ˈtʃɛkɪŋ-] n (*US*) conto corrente.
checklist [ˈtʃɛklɪst] n lista di controllo.
checkmate [ˈtʃɛkmeɪt] n scaccomatto.
checkout [ˈtʃɛkaut] n (*in supermarket*)

cassa.
checkpoint ['tʃɛkpɔɪnt] n posto di blocco.
checkroom ['tʃɛkrum] n (US) deposito m
bagagli inv.
checkup ['tʃɛkʌp] n (MED) controllo
medico.
cheek [tʃiːk] n guancia; (impudence) faccia
tosta.
cheekbone ['tʃiːkbəun] n zigomo.
cheeky ['tʃiːkɪ] adj sfacciato(a).
cheep [tʃiːp] n (of bird) pigolio ♦ vi pigolare.
cheer [tʃɪə*] vt applaudire; (gladden)
rallegrare ♦ vi applaudire ♦ n (gen pl)
applausi mpl; evviva mpl; ~s! salute!
►**cheer on** vt (person etc) incitare.
►**cheer up** vi rallegrarsi, farsi animo ♦ vt
rallegrare.
cheerful ['tʃɪəful] adj allegro(a).
cheerfulness ['tʃɪəfulnɪs] n allegria.
cheerio ['tʃɪərɪ'əu] excl (BRIT) ciao!
cheerleader ['tʃɪəliːdə*] n cheerleader f inv.
cheerless ['tʃɪəlɪs] adj triste.
cheese [tʃiːz] n formaggio.
cheeseboard ['tʃiːzbɔːd] n piatto del (or
per il) formaggio.
cheeseburger ['tʃiːzbəːgə*] n
cheeseburger m inv.
cheesecake ['tʃiːzkeɪk] n specie di torta di
ricotta, a volte con frutta.
cheetah ['tʃiːtə] n ghepardo.
chef [ʃɛf] n capocuoco.
chemical ['kɛmɪkl] adj chimico(a) ♦ n
prodotto chimico.
chemical engineering n ingegneria
chimica.
chemist ['kɛmɪst] n (BRIT: pharmacist)
farmacista m/f; (scientist) chimico/a; ~'s
shop n (BRIT) farmacia.
chemistry ['kɛmɪstrɪ] n chimica.
chemotherapy [kiːməu'θɛrəpɪ] n
chemioterapia.
cheque, (US) check [tʃɛk] n assegno; **to
pay by** ~ pagare per assegno or con un
assegno.
chequebook, (US) checkbook ['tʃɛkbuk] n
libretto degli assegni.
cheque card n (BRIT) carta f assegni inv.
chequered, (US) checkered ['tʃɛkəd] adj
(fig) movimentato(a).
cherish ['tʃɛrɪʃ] vt aver caro; (hope etc)
nutrire.
cheroot [ʃə'ruːt] n sigaro spuntato.
cherry ['tʃɛrɪ] n ciliegia.
Ches abbr (BRIT) = Cheshire.
chess [tʃɛs] n scacchi mpl.
chessboard ['tʃɛsbɔːd] n scacchiera.
chessman ['tʃɛsmæn] n pezzo degli
scacchi.

chessplayer ['tʃɛspleɪə*] n scacchista m/f.
chest [tʃɛst] n petto; (box) cassa; **to get sth
off one's** ~ (col) sputare il rospo; ~ **of
drawers** cassettone m.
chest measurement n giro m torace inv.
chestnut ['tʃɛsnʌt] n castagna; (also: ~ tree)
castagno ♦ adj castano(a).
chesty ['tʃɛstɪ] adj: ~ **cough** tosse f
bronchiale.
chew [tʃuː] vt masticare.
chewing gum ['tʃuːɪŋ-] n chewing gum m.
chic [ʃiːk] adj elegante.
chick [tʃɪk] n pulcino; (US col) pollastrella.
chicken ['tʃɪkɪn] n pollo; (col: coward)
coniglio.
►**chicken out** vi (col) avere fifa; **to** ~ **out
of sth** tirarsi indietro da qc per fifa or
paura.
chicken feed n (fig) miseria.
chickenpox ['tʃɪkɪnpɔks] n varicella.
chickpea ['tʃɪkpiː] n cece m.
chicory ['tʃɪkərɪ] n cicoria.
chide [tʃaɪd] vt rimproverare.
chief [tʃiːf] n capo ♦ adj principale; **C~ of
Staff** (MIL) Capo di Stato Maggiore.
chief constable n (BRIT) ≈ questore m.
**chief executive, (US) chief executive
officer (CEO)** n direttore m generale.
chiefly ['tʃiːflɪ] adv per lo più, soprattutto.
chiffon ['ʃɪfɔn] n chiffon m inv.
chilblain ['tʃɪlbleɪn] n gelone m.
child, pl ~**ren** [tʃaɪld, 'tʃɪldrən] n
bambino/a.
child abuse n molestie fpl a minori.
child abuser [-ə'bjuːzə*] n molestatore/
trice di bambini.
child benefit n (BRIT) ≈ assegni mpl
familiari.
childbirth ['tʃaɪldbəːθ] n parto.
childhood ['tʃaɪldhud] n infanzia.
childish ['tʃaɪldɪʃ] adj puerile.
childless ['tʃaɪldlɪs] adj senza figli.
childlike ['tʃaɪldlaɪk] adj fanciullesco(a).
child minder n (BRIT) bambinaia.
child prodigy n bambino m prodigio inv.
children ['tʃɪldrən] npl of **child**.
children's home n istituto per l'infanzia.
Chile ['tʃɪlɪ] n Cile m.
Chilean ['tʃɪlɪən] adj, n cileno(a).
chill [tʃɪl] n freddo; (MED) infreddatura ♦
adj freddo(a), gelido(a) ♦ vt raffreddare;
(CULIN) mettere in fresco; "**serve** ~**ed**"
"servire fresco".
►**chill out** vi (esp US: col) darsi una
calmata.
chilli, (US) chili ['tʃɪlɪ] n peperoncino.
chilling ['tʃɪlɪŋ] adj agghiacciante; (wind)
gelido(a).

chilly ['tʃɪlɪ] *adj* freddo(a), fresco(a); (*sensitive to cold*) freddoloso(a); **to feel** ~ sentirsi infreddolito(a).

chime [tʃaɪm] *n* carillon *m inv* ♦ *vi* suonare, scampanare.

chimney ['tʃɪmnɪ] *n* camino.

chimney sweep *n* spazzacamino.

chimpanzee [tʃɪmpæn'ziː] *n* scimpanzé *m inv*.

chin [tʃɪn] *n* mento.

China ['tʃaɪnə] *n* Cina.

china ['tʃaɪnə] *n* porcellana.

Chinese [tʃaɪ'niːz] *adj* cinese ♦ *n* (*pl inv*) cinese *m/f*; (*LING*) cinese *m*.

chink [tʃɪŋk] *n* (*opening*) fessura; (*noise*) tintinnio.

chip [tʃɪp] *n* (*gen pl: CULIN*) patatina fritta; (*: US: also: **potato** ~) patatina; (*of wood, glass, stone*) scheggia; (*in gambling*) fiche *f inv*; (*COMPUT: **micro**~) chip *m inv* ♦ *vt* (*cup, plate*) scheggiare; **when the ~s are down** (*fig*) al momento critico.

▶**chip in** *vi* (*col: contribute*) contribuire; (*: interrupt*) intromettersi.

chipboard ['tʃɪpbɔːd] *n* agglomerato.

chipmunk ['tʃɪpmʌŋk] *n* tamia *m* striato.

chippings ['tʃɪpɪŋz] *npl*: **loose** ~ brecciame *m*.

chip shop *n* (*BRIT*) see boxed note.

CHIP SHOP

I **chip shop**, anche chiamati "fish-and-chip shop", sono friggitorie che vendono principalmente filetti di pesce impanati e patatine fritte che un tempo venivano serviti ai clienti avvolti in carta di giornale.

---

chiropodist [kɪ'rɔpədɪst] *n* (*BRIT*) pedicure *m/f inv*.

chiropody [kɪ'rɔpədɪ] *n* (*BRIT*) mestiere *m* di callista.

chirp [tʃəːp] *n* cinguettio; (*of crickets*) cri cri *m* ♦ *vi* cinguettare.

chirpy ['tʃəːpɪ] *adj* (*col*) frizzante.

chisel ['tʃɪzl] *n* cesello.

chit [tʃɪt] *n* biglietto.

chitchat ['tʃɪttʃæt] *n* (*col*) chiacchiere *fpl*.

chivalrous ['ʃɪvəlrəs] *adj* cavalleresco(a).

chivalry ['ʃɪvəlrɪ] *n* cavalleria; cortesia.

chives [tʃaɪvz] *npl* erba cipollina.

chloride ['klɔːraɪd] *n* cloruro.

chlorinate ['klɔrɪneɪt] *vt* clorare.

chlorine ['klɔːriːn] *n* cloro.

chock-a-block ['tʃɔkə'blɔk], **chockfull** ['tʃɔk'ful] *adj* pieno(a) zeppo(a).

chocolate ['tʃɔklɪt] *n* (*substance*) cioccolato, cioccolata; (*drink*) cioccolata; (*a sweet*) cioccolatino.

choice [tʃɔɪs] *n* scelta ♦ *adj* scelto(a); **a wide** ~ un'ampia scelta; **I did it by** *or* **from** ~ l'ho fatto di mia volontà *or* per mia scelta.

choir ['kwaɪə*] *n* coro.

choirboy ['kwaɪəbɔɪ] *n* corista *m* fanciullo.

choke [tʃəuk] *vi* soffocare ♦ *vt* soffocare; (*block*) ingombrare ♦ *n* (*AUT*) valvola dell'aria.

cholera ['kɔlərə] *n* colera *m*.

cholesterol [kə'lɛstərɔl] *n* colesterolo.

choose, *pt* chose, *pp* chosen [tʃuːz, tʃəuz, 'tʃəuzn] *vt* scegliere; **to** ~ **to do** decidere di fare; **preferire fare; to** ~ **between** scegliere tra; **to** ~ **from** scegliere da *or* tra.

choosy ['tʃuːzɪ] *adj*: (**to be**) ~ (fare lo(la)) schizzinoso(a).

chop [tʃɔp] *vt* (*wood*) spaccare; (*CULIN: also:* ~ **up**) tritare ♦ *n* colpo netto; (*CULIN*) costoletta; **to get the** ~ (*BRIT col: project*) essere bocciato(a); (*: person: be sacked*) essere licenziato(a); *see also* **chops**.

▶**chop down** *vt* (*tree*) abbattere.

choppy ['tʃɔpɪ] *adj* (*sea*) mosso(a).

chops [tʃɔps] *npl* (*jaws*) mascelle *fpl*.

chopsticks ['tʃɔpstɪks] *npl* bastoncini *mpl* cinesi.

choral ['kɔːrəl] *adj* corale.

chord [kɔːd] *n* (*MUS*) accordo.

chore [tʃɔː*] *n* faccenda; **household** ~**s** faccende *fpl* domestiche.

choreographer [kɔrɪ'ɔgrəfə*] *n* coreografo/a.

choreography [kɔrɪ'ɔgrəfɪ] *n* coreografia.

chorister ['kɔrɪstə*] *n* corista *m/f*.

chortle ['tʃɔːtl] *vi* ridacchiare.

chorus ['kɔːrəs] *n* coro; (*repeated part of song, also fig*) ritornello.

chose [tʃəuz] *pt of* **choose**.

chosen ['tʃəuzn] *pp of* **choose**.

chowder ['tʃaudə*] *n* zuppa di pesce.

Christ [kraɪst] *n* Cristo.

christen ['krɪsn] *vt* battezzare.

christening ['krɪsnɪŋ] *n* battesimo.

Christian ['krɪstɪən] *adj, n* cristiano(a).

Christianity [krɪstɪ'ænɪtɪ] *n* cristianesimo.

Christian name *n* nome *m* di battesimo.

Christmas ['krɪsməs] *n* Natale *m*; **happy** *or* **merry** ~! Buon Natale!

Christmas card *n* cartolina di Natale.

Christmas Day *n* il giorno di Natale.

Christmas Eve *n* la vigilia di Natale.

Christmas Island *n* isola di Christmas.

Christmas tree *n* albero di Natale.

chrome [krəum] *n* = **chromium**.

chromium ['krəumɪəm] *n* cromo; (*also:* ~

plating) cromatura.
chromosome ['krəuməsəum] n cromosoma m.
chronic ['krɔnɪk] adj cronico(a); (fig: liar, smoker) incallito(a).
chronicle ['krɔnɪkl] n cronaca.
chronological [krɔnə'lɔdʒɪkl] adj cronologico(a).
chrysanthemum [krɪ'sænθəməm] n crisantemo.
chubby ['tʃʌbɪ] adj paffuto(a).
chuck [tʃʌk] vt buttare, gettare; **to ~ (up or in)** (BRIT: job, person) piantare.
▶**chuck out** vt buttar fuori.
chuckle ['tʃʌkl] vi ridere sommessamente.
chuffed [tʃʌft] adj (col): **to be ~ about sth** essere arcicontento(a) di qc.
chug [tʃʌg] vi (also: ~ along: train) muoversi sbuffando.
chum [tʃʌm] n compagno/a.
chump [tʃʌmp] n (col) idiota m/f.
chunk [tʃʌŋk] n pezzo; (of bread) tocco.
chunky [tʃʌŋkɪ] adj (furniture etc) basso(a) e largo(a); (person) ben piantato(a); (knitwear) di lana grossa.
Chunnel ['tʃʌnəl] n = Channel Tunnel.
church [tʃəːtʃ] n chiesa; **the C~ of England** la Chiesa anglicana.
churchyard ['tʃəːtʃjɑːd] n sagrato.
churlish ['tʃəːlɪʃ] adj rozzo(a), sgarbato(a).
churn [tʃəːn] n (for butter) zangola; (also: milk ~) bidone m.
▶**churn out** vt sfornare.
chute [ʃuːt] n cascata; (also: rubbish ~) canale m di scarico; (BRIT: children's slide) scivolo.
chutney ['tʃʌtnɪ] n salsa piccante (di frutta, zucchero e spezie).
CIA n abbr (US: = Central Intelligence Agency) C.I.A. f.
CID n abbr (BRIT) see **Criminal Investigation Department**.
cider ['saɪdə*] n sidro.
CIF abbr (= cost, insurance and freight) C.I.F. m.
cigar [sɪ'gɑː*] n sigaro.
cigarette [sɪgə'rɛt] n sigaretta.
cigarette case n portasigarette m inv.
cigarette end n mozzicone m.
cigarette holder n bocchino.
C-in-C abbr see **commander-in-chief**.
cinch [sɪntʃ] n (col): **it's a ~** è presto fatto; (sure thing) è una cosa sicura.
cinder ['sɪndə*] n cenere f.
Cinderella [sɪndə'rɛlə] n Cenerentola.
cine-camera ['sɪnɪ'kæmərə] n (BRIT) cinepresa.
cine-film ['sɪnɪfɪlm] n (BRIT) pellicola.

cinema ['sɪnəmə] n cinema m inv.
cine-projector ['sɪnɪprə'dʒɛktə*] n (BRIT) proiettore m.
cinnamon ['sɪnəmən] n cannella.
cipher ['saɪfə*] n cifra; (fig: faceless employee etc) persona di nessun conto; **in ~** in codice.
circa ['səːkə] prep circa.
circle ['səːkl] n cerchio; (of friends etc) circolo; (in cinema) galleria ♦ vi girare in circolo ♦ vt (surround) circondare; (move round) girare intorno a.
circuit ['səːkɪt] n circuito.
circuit board n (COMPUT) tavola dei circuiti.
circuitous [səː'kjuɪtəs] adj indiretto(a).
circular ['səːkjulə*] adj circolare ♦ n (letter) circolare f; (as advertisement) volantino pubblicitario.
circulate ['səːkjuleɪt] vi circolare; (person: socially) girare e andare un po' dla tutti ♦ vt far circolare.
circulating capital ['səːkjuleɪtɪŋ-] n (COMM) capitale m d'esercizio.
circulation [səːkju'leɪʃən] n circolazione f; (of newspaper) tiratura.
circumcise ['səːkəmsaɪz] vt circoncidere.
circumference [sə'kʌmfərəns] n circonferenza.
circumflex ['səːkəmflɛks] n (also: ~ accent) accento circonflesso.
circumscribe ['səːkəmskraɪb] vt circoscrivere; (fig: limit) limitare.
circumspect ['səːkəmspɛkt] adj circospetto(a).
circumstances ['səːkəmstənsɪz] npl circostanze fpl; (financial condition) condizioni fpl finanziarie; **in the ~s** date le circostanze; **under no ~s** per nessun motivo.
circumstantial ['səːkəm'stænʃəl] adj (report, statement) circostanziato(a), dettagliato(a); **~ evidence** prova indiretta.
circumvent [səːkəm'vɛnt] vt (rule etc) aggirare.
circus ['səːkəs] n circo; (also: C~: in place names) piazza (di forma circolare).
cirrhosis [sɪ'rəusɪs] n (also: ~ of the liver) cirrosi f inv (epatica).
CIS n abbr (= Commonwealth of Independent States) CSI f.
cissy ['sɪsɪ] n = **sissy**.
cistern ['sɪstən] n cisterna; (in toilet) serbatoio d'acqua.
citation [saɪ'teɪʃən] n citazione f.
cite [saɪt] vt citare.
citizen ['sɪtɪzn] n (POL) cittadino/a;

(*resident*): **the ~s of this town** gli abitanti di questa città.

Citizens' Advice Bureau n (*BRIT*) organizzazione di volontari che offre gratuitamente assistenza legale e finanziaria.

citizenship ['sɪtɪznʃɪp] n cittadinanza.

citric ['sɪtrɪk] *adj*: **~ acid** acido citrico.

citrus fruit ['sɪtrəs-] n agrume m.

city ['sɪtɪ] n città f inv; **the C~** la Città di Londra (*centro commerciale*).

city centre n centro della città.

City Hall n (*US*) ≈ Comune m.

City Technology College n (*BRIT*) istituto tecnico superiore (*finanziato dall'industria*).

civic ['sɪvɪk] *adj* civico(a).

civic centre n (*BRIT*) centro civico.

civil ['sɪvɪl] *adj* civile; (*polite*) educato(a), gentile.

civil disobedience n disubbidienza civile.

civil engineer n ingegnere m civile.

civil engineering n ingegneria civile.

civilian [sɪ'vɪlɪən] *adj*, n borghese (m/f).

civilization [sɪvɪlaɪ'zeɪʃən] n civiltà f inv.

civilized ['sɪvɪlaɪzd] *adj* civilizzato(a); (*fig*) cortese.

civil law n codice m civile; (*study*) diritto civile.

civil liberties npl libertà fpl civili.

civil rights npl diritti mpl civili.

civil servant n impiegato/a statale.

Civil Service n amministrazione f statale.

civil war n guerra civile.

civvies ['sɪvɪz] npl (*col*): **in ~** in borghese.

cl abbr (= centilitre) cl.

clad [klæd] *adj*: **~ (in)** vestito(a) (di).

claim [kleɪm] vt (*rights etc*) rivendicare; (*damages*) richiedere; (*assert*) sostenere, pretendere ♦ vi (*for insurance*) fare una domanda d'indennizzo ♦ n rivendicazione f; pretesa; (*right*) diritto; **to ~ that/to be** sostenere che/di essere; (**insurance**) **~** domanda d'indennizzo; **to put in a ~ for** sth fare una richiesta di qc.

claimant ['kleɪmənt] n (*ADMIN, LAW*) richiedente m/f.

claim form n (*gen*) modulo di richiesta; (*for expenses*) modulo di rimborso spese.

clairvoyant [klɛə'vɔɪənt] n chiaroveggente m/f.

clam [klæm] n vongola.

▶**clam up** vi (*col*) azzittirsi.

clamber ['klæmbə*] vi arrampicarsi.

clammy ['klæmɪ] *adj* (*weather*) caldo(a) umido(a); (*hands*) viscido(a).

clamour, (*US*) **clamor** ['klæmə*] n (*noise*) clamore m; (*protest*) protesta ♦ vi: **to ~ for** sth chiedere a gran voce qc.

clamp [klæmp] n pinza; morsa ♦ vt ammorsare.

▶**clamp down** vt fus (*fig*): **to ~ down (on)** dare un giro di vite (a).

clampdown ['klæmpdaun] n stretta, giro di vite; **a ~ on sth/sb** un giro di vite a qc/qn.

clan [klæn] n clan m inv.

clandestine [klæn'dɛstɪn] *adj* clandestino(a).

clang [klæŋ] n fragore m, suono metallico.

clanger ['klæŋə*] n: **to drop a ~** (*BRIT col*) fare una gaffe.

clansman ['klænzmən] n membro di un clan.

clap [klæp] vi applaudire ♦ vt: **to ~ one's hands** battere le mani ♦ n: **a ~ of thunder** un tuono.

clapping ['klæpɪŋ] n applausi mpl.

claptrap ['klæptræp] n (*col*) stupidaggini fpl.

claret ['klærət] n vino di Bordeaux.

clarification [klærɪfɪ'keɪʃən] n (*fig*) chiarificazione f, chiarimento.

clarify ['klærɪfaɪ] vt chiarificare, chiarire.

clarinet [klærɪ'nɛt] n clarinetto.

clarity ['klærɪtɪ] n chiarezza.

clash [klæʃ] n frastuono; (*fig*) scontro ♦ vi (*MIL, fig: have an argument*) scontrarsi; (*colours*) stridere; (*dates, events*) coincidere.

clasp [klɑːsp] n fermaglio, fibbia ♦ vt stringere.

class [klɑːs] n classe f; (*group, category*) tipo, categoria ♦ vt classificare.

class-conscious ['klɑːskɔnʃəs] *adj* che ha coscienza di classe.

class consciousness n coscienza di classe.

classic ['klæsɪk] *adj* classico(a) ♦ n classico.

classical ['klæsɪkəl] *adj* classico(a).

classics ['klæsɪks] npl (*SCOL*) studi mpl umanistici.

classification [klæsɪfɪ'keɪʃən] n classificazione f.

classified ['klæsɪfaɪd] *adj* (*information*) segreto(a), riservato(a); **~ ads** annunci economici.

classify ['klæsɪfaɪ] vt classificare.

classless society ['klɑːslɪs-] n società f inv senza distinzioni di classe.

classmate ['klɑːsmeɪt] n compagno/a di classe.

classroom ['klɑːsrum] n aula.

clatter ['klætə*] n acciottolio; scalpitio ♦ vi acciottolare; scalpitare.

clause [klɔːz] n clausola; (*LING*) proposizione f.

claustrophobia [klɔːstrə'fəubɪə] n
claustrofobia.
claustrophobic [klɔːstrə'fəubɪk] adj
claustrofobico(a).
claw [klɔː] n tenaglia; (of bird of prey)
artiglio; (of lobster) pinza ♦ vt graffiare;
afferrare.
olay [klɛɪ] n argilla.
clean [kliːn] adj pulito(a); (clear, smooth)
netto(a) ♦ vt pulire ♦ adv: **he ~ forgot** si è
completamente dimenticato; **to come ~**
(col: admit guilt) confessare; **to have a ~**
driving licence or (US) **record** non aver
mai preso contravvenzioni; **to ~ one's**
teeth (BRIT) lavarsi i denti.
▸**clean off** vt togliere.
▸**clean out** vt ripulire.
▸**clean up** vi far pulizia ♦ vt (also fig)
ripulire; (fig: make profit): **to ~ up on** fare
una barca di soldi con.
clean-cut ['kliːn'kʌt] adj (man) curato(a);
(situation etc) ben definito(a).
cleaner ['kliːnə*] n (person) uomo/donna
delle pulizie; (also: **dry ~**) tintore/a;
(product) smacchiatore m.
cleaning ['kliːnɪŋ] n pulizia
cleaning lady n donna delle pulizie.
cleanliness ['klɛnlɪnɪs] n pulizia.
cleanly ['kliːnlɪ] adv in modo netto.
cleanse [klɛnz] vt pulire; purificare.
cleanser ['klɛnzə*] n detergente m;
(cosmetic) latte m detergente.
clean-shaven ['kliːn'ʃeɪvn] adj sbarbato(a).
cleansing department ['klɛnzɪŋ-] n (BRIT)
nettezza urbana.
clean sweep n: **to make a ~ (of)** fare
piazza pulita (di).
clean-up ['kliːnʌp] n pulizia.
clear [klɪə*] adj chiaro(a); (road, way)
libero(a); (profit, majority) netto(a) ♦ vt
sgombrare; liberare; (site, woodland)
spianare; (COMM: goods) liquidare; (LAW:
suspect) discolpare; (obstacle) superare;
(cheque) fare la compensazione di ♦ vi
(weather) rasserenarsi; (fog) andarsene
♦ adv: **~ of** distante da ♦ n: **to be in the ~**
(out of debt) essere in attivo; (out of
suspicion) essere a posto; (out of danger)
essere fuori pericolo; **to ~ the table**
sparecchiare (la tavola); **to ~ one's**
throat schiarirsi la gola; **to ~ a profit**
avere un profitto netto; **to make o.s. ~**
spiegarsi bene; **to make it ~ to sb that ...**
far capire a qn che ...; **I have a ~ day**
tomorrow (BRIT) non ho impegni domani;
to keep ~ of sb/sth tenersi lontano da
qn/qc, stare alla larga da qn/qc.
▸**clear off** vi (col: leave) svignarsela.

▸**clear up** vi schiarirsi ♦ vt mettere in
ordine; (mystery) risolvere.
clearance ['klɪərəns] n (removal) sgombro;
(free space) spazio; (permission)
autorizzazione f, permesso.
clearance sale n vendita di liquidazione.
clear-cut ['klɪə'kʌt] adj ben delineato(a),
distinto(a).
clearing ['klɪərɪŋ] n radura; (BRIT BANKING)
clearing m.
clearing bank n (BRIT) banca che fa uso
della camera di compensazione.
clearing house n (COMM) camera di
compensazione.
clearly ['klɪəlɪ] adv chiaramente.
clearway ['klɪəweɪ] n (BRIT) strada con
divieto di sosta.
cleavage ['kliːvɪdʒ] n (of woman)
scollatura.
cleaver ['kliːvə*] n mannaia.
clef [klɛf] n (MUS) chiave f.
cleft [klɛft] n (in rock) crepa, fenditura.
clemency ['klɛmənsɪ] n clemenza.
clement ['klɛmənt] adj (weather) mite,
clemente.
clench [klɛntʃ] vt stringere.
clergy ['kləːdʒɪ] n clero.
clergyman ['kləːdʒɪmən] n ecclesiastico.
clerical ['klɛrɪkl] adj d'impiegato; (REL)
clericale.
clerk [klɑːk, (US) kləːrk] n impiegato/a; (US:
salesman/woman) commesso/a; **C~ of the**
Court (LAW) cancelliere m.
clever ['klɛvə*] adj (mentally) intelligente;
(deft, skilful) abile; (device, arrangement)
ingegnoso(a).
cleverly ['klɛvəlɪ] adv abilmente.
clew [kluː] n (US) = **clue.**
cliché ['kliːʃeɪ] n cliché m inv.
click [klɪk] vi scattare ♦ vt: **to ~ one's**
tongue schioccare la lingua; **to ~ one's**
heels battere i tacchi.
client ['klaɪənt] n cliente m/f.
clientele [kliːɑːn'tɛl] n clientela.
cliff [klɪf] n scogliera scoscesa, rupe f.
cliffhanger ['klɪfhæŋə*] n (TV, fig) episodio
(or situazione etc) ricco(a) di suspense.
climactic [klaɪ'mæktɪk] adj culminante.
climate ['klaɪmɪt] n clima m.
climax ['klaɪmæks] n culmine m; (of play etc)
momento più emozionante; (sexual ~)
orgasmo.
climb [klaɪm] vi salire; (clamber)
arrampicarsi; (plane) prendere quota ♦ vt
salire; (CLIMBING) scalare ♦ n salita;
arrampicata; scalata; **to ~ over a wall**
scavalcare un muro.
▸**climb down** vi scendere; (BRIT fig) far

marcia indietro.

climbdown ['klaɪmdaun] *n* (*BRIT*) ritirata.

climber ['klaɪmə*] *n* (*also*: **rock** ~) rocciatore/trice; alpinista *m/f*.

climbing ['klaɪmɪŋ] *n* (*also*: **rock** ~) alpinismo.

clinch [klɪntʃ] *vt* (*deal*) concludere.

clincher ['klɪntʃə*] *n* (*col*): **that was the** ~ quello è stato il fattore decisivo.

cling, *pt*, *pp* **clung** [klɪŋ, klʌŋ] *vi*: **to** ~ (**to**) tenersi stretto(a) (a); (*of clothes*) aderire strettamente (a).

clingfilm ['klɪŋfɪlm] *n* pellicola trasparente (*per alimenti*).

clinic ['klɪnɪk] *n* clinica; (*session*) seduta; serie *f* di sedute.

clinical ['klɪnɪkəl] *adj* clinico(a); (*fig*) freddo(a), distaccato(a).

clink [klɪŋk] *vi* tintinnare.

clip [klɪp] *n* (*for hair*) forcina; (*also*: **paper** ~) graffetta; (*BRIT*: *also*: **bulldog** ~) fermagli *m inv*; (*holding hose etc*) anello d'attacco ♦ *vt* (*also*: ~ **together**: *papers*) attaccare insieme; (*hair, nails*) tagliare; (*hedge*) tosare.

clippers ['klɪpəz] *npl* macchinetta per capelli; (*also*: **nail** ~) forbicine *fpl* per le unghie.

clipping ['klɪpɪŋ] *n* (*from newspaper*) ritaglio.

clique [kliːk] *n* cricca.

cloak [kləuk] *n* mantello ♦ *vt* avvolgere.

cloakroom ['kləukrum] *n* (*for coats etc*) guardaroba *m inv*; (*BRIT*: *W.C.*) gabinetti *mpl*.

clock [klɔk] *n* orologio; (*of taxi*) tassametro; **around the** ~ ventiquatt'ore su ventiquattro; **to sleep round the** ~ *or* **the** ~ **round** dormire un giorno intero; **to work against the** ~ lavorare in gara col tempo; **30,000 on the** ~ (*BRIT AUT*) 30.000 sul contachilometri.

▶**clock in, clock on** *vi* (*BRIT*) timbrare il cartellino (all'entrata).

▶**clock off, clock out** *vi* (*BRIT*) timbrare il cartellino (all'uscita).

▶**clock up** *vt* (*miles, hours etc*) fare.

clockwise ['klɔkwaɪz] *adv* in senso orario.

clockwork ['klɔkwəːk] *n* movimento *or* meccanismo a orologeria ♦ *adj* (*toy, train*) a molla.

clog [klɔg] *n* zoccolo ♦ *vt* intasare ♦ *vi* intasarsi, bloccarsi.

cloister ['klɔɪstə*] *n* chiostro.

clone [kləun] *n* clone *m*.

close *adj*, *adv and derivatives* [kləus] *adj* vicino(a); (*writing, texture*) fitto(a); (*watch*) stretto(a); (*examination*) attento(a);

(*weather*) afoso(a) ♦ *adv* vicino, dappresso; ~ **to** *prep* vicino a; ~ **by**, ~ **at hand** qui (*or* lì) vicino; **how** ~ **is Edinburgh to Glasgow?** quanto dista Edimburgo da Glasgow?; **a** ~ **friend** un amico intimo; **to have a** ~ **shave** (*fig*) scamparla bella; **at** ~ **quarters** da vicino

♦ *vb*, *n and derivatives* [kləuz] *vt* chiudere; (*bargain, deal*) concludere ♦ *vi* (*shop etc*) chiudere; (*lid, door etc*) chiudersi; (*end*) finire ♦ *n* (*end*) fine *f*; **to bring sth to a** ~ terminare qc.

▶**close down** *vt* chiudere (definitivamente) ♦ *vi* cessare (definitivamente).

▶**close in** *vi* (*hunters*) stringersi attorno; (*evening, night, fog*) calare; **to** ~ **in on sb** accerchiare qn; **the days are closing in** le giornate si accorciano.

▶**close off** *vt* (*area*) chiudere.

closed [kləuzd] *adj* chiuso(a).

closed-circuit ['kləuzd'səːkɪt] *adj*: ~ **television** televisione *f* a circuito chiuso.

closed shop *n* azienda o fabbrica che impiega solo aderenti ai sindacati.

close-knit ['kləus'nɪt] *adj* (*family, community*) molto unito(a).

closely ['kləuslɪ] *adv* (*examine, watch*) da vicino; **we are** ~ **related** siamo parenti stretti; **a** ~ **guarded secret** un assoluto segreto.

close season ['kləuz-] *n* (*FOOTBALL*) periodo di vacanza del campionato; (*HUNTING*) stagione *f* di chiusura (*di caccia, pesca etc*).

closet ['klɔzɪt] *n* (*cupboard*) armadio.

close-up ['kləusʌp] *n* primo piano.

closing ['kləuzɪŋ] *adj* (*stages, remarks*) conclusivo(a), finale; ~ **price** (*STOCK EXCHANGE*) prezzo di chiusura.

closing time *n* orario di chiusura.

closure ['kləuʒə*] *n* chiusura.

clot [klɔt] *n* (*also*: **blood** ~) coagulo; (*col*: *idiot*) scemo/a ♦ *vi* coagularsi.

cloth [klɔθ] *n* (*material*) tessuto, stoffa; (*BRIT*: *also*: **tea**~) strofinaccio; (*also*: **table**~) tovaglia.

clothe [kləuð] *vt* vestire.

clothes [kləuðz] *npl* abiti *mpl*, vestiti *mpl*; **to put one's** ~ **on** vestirsi; **to take one's** ~ **off** togliersi i vestiti, svestirsi.

clothes brush *n* spazzola per abiti.

clothes line *n* corda (per stendere il bucato).

clothes peg, (*US*) **clothes pin** *n* molletta.

clothing ['kləuðɪŋ] *n* = **clothes**.

clotted cream ['klɔtɪd-] *n* (*BRIT*) panna rappresa.

cloud [klaud] n nuvola; (of dust, smoke, gas) nube f ♦ vt (liquid) intorbidire; **to ~ the issue** distogliere dal problema; **every ~ has a silver lining** (proverb) non tutto il male vien per nuocere.

►**cloud over** vi rannuvolarsi; (fig) offuscarsi.

cloudburst ['klaudbɔːst] n acquazzone m.

cloud-cuckoo-land ['klaud'kuku:'lænd] n (BRIT) mondo dei sogni.

cloudy ['klaudɪ] adj nuvoloso(a); (liquid) torbido(a).

clout [klaut] n (blow) colpo; (fig) influenza ♦ vt dare un colpo a.

clove [kləuv] n chiodo di garofano; **~ of garlic** spicchio d'aglio.

clover ['kləuvə*] n trifoglio.

cloverleaf ['kləuvəli:f] n foglia di trifoglio; (AUT) raccordo (a quadrifoglio).

clown [klaun] n pagliaccio ♦ vi (also: ~ about, ~ around) fare il pagliaccio.

cloying ['klɔɪɪŋ] adj (taste, smell) nauseabondo(a).

club [klʌb] n (society) club m inv, circolo; (weapon, GOLF) mazza ♦ vt bastonare ♦ vi: **to ~ together** associarsi; **~s** npl (CARDS) fiori mpl.

club car n (US RAIL) carrozza or vagone m ristorante.

club class n (AVIAT) classe f club.

clubhouse ['klʌbhaus] n sede f del circolo.

club soda n (US) = soda.

cluck [klʌk] vi chiocciare.

clue [kluː] n indizio; (in crosswords) definizione f; **I haven't a ~** non ho la minima idea.

clued up, (US) **clued in** [kluːd-] adj (col) (ben) informato(a).

clump [klʌmp] n: **~ of trees** folto d'alberi.

clumsy ['klʌmzɪ] adj (person) goffo(a), maldestro(a); (object) malfatto(a), mal costruito(a).

clung [klʌŋ] pt, pp of **cling**.

cluster ['klʌstə*] n gruppo ♦ vi raggrupparsi.

clutch [klʌtʃ] n (grip, grasp) presa, stretta; (AUT) frizione f ♦ vt afferrare, stringere forte; **to ~ at** aggrapparsi a.

clutter ['klʌtə*] vt (also: ~ up) ingombrare ♦ n confusione f, disordine m.

CM abbr (US POST) = North Marianna Islands.

cm abbr (= centimetre) cm.

CNAA n abbr (BRIT: = Council for National Academic Awards) organizzazione che conferisce premi accademici.

CND n abbr = Campaign for Nuclear Disarmament.

CO n abbr (= commanding officer) Com.;

(BRIT) = Commonwealth Office ♦ abbr (US) = Colorado.

Co. abbr = **county**; (= company) C., C.ia.

c/o abbr (= care of) c/o.

coach [kəutʃ] n (bus) pullman m inv; (horse-drawn, of train) carrozza; (SPORT) allenatore/trice ♦ vt allenare.

coach trip n viaggio in pullman.

coagulate [kəu'ægjuleɪt] vt coagulare ♦ vi coagularsi.

coal [kəul] n carbone m.

coalface ['kəulfeɪs] n fronte f.

coalfield ['kəulfiːld] n bacino carbonifero.

coalition [kəuə'lɪʃən] n coalizione f.

coalman ['kəulmən] n negoziante m di carbone.

coalmine ['kəulmaɪn] n miniera di carbone.

coalminer ['kəulmaɪnə*] n minatore m.

coalmining ['kəulmaɪnɪŋ] n estrazione f del carbone.

coarse [kɔːs] adj (salt, sand etc) grosso(n)· (cloth, person) rozzo(a); (vulgar: character, laugh) volgare.

coast [kəust] n costa ♦ vi (with cycle etc) scendere a ruota libera.

coastal ['kəustəl] adj costiero(a).

coaster ['kəustə*] n (NAUT) nave f da cabotaggio; (for glass) sottobicchiere m.

coastguard ['kəustgaːd] n guardia costiera.

coastline ['kəustlaɪn] n linea costiera.

coat [kəut] n cappotto; (of animal) pelo; (of paint) mano f ♦ vt coprire; **~ of arms** n stemma m.

coat hanger n attaccapanni m inv.

coating ['kəutɪŋ] n rivestimento.

co-author ['kəu'ɔ:θə*] n coautore/trice.

coax [kəuks] vt indurre (con moine).

cob [kɔb] n see **corn**.

cobbler ['kɔblə*] n calzolaio.

cobbles ['kɔblz], **cobblestones** ['kɔblstəunz] npl ciottoli mpl.

COBOL ['kəubɔl] n COBOL m.

cobra ['kəubrə] n cobra m inv.

cobweb ['kɔbwɛb] n ragnatela.

cocaine [kə'keɪn] n cocaina.

cock [kɔk] n (rooster) gallo; (male bird) maschio ♦ vt (gun) armare; **to ~ one's ears** (fig) drizzare le orecchie.

cock-a-hoop [kɔkə'hu:p] adj euforico(a).

cockerel ['kɔkərəl] n galletto.

cock-eyed ['kɔkaɪd] adj (fig) storto(a); strampalato(a).

cockle ['kɔkl] n cardio.

cockney ['kɔknɪ] n cockney m/f inv (abitante dei quartieri popolari dell'East End di Londra).

cockpit ['kɔkpɪt] n abitacolo.

cockroach ['kɔkrəutʃ] *n* blatta.
cocktail ['kɔkteɪl] *n* cocktail *m inv*; **prawn** ~, (*US*) **shrimp** ~ cocktail *m inv* di gamberetti.
cocktail cabinet *n* mobile *m* bar *inv*.
cocktail party *n* cocktail *m inv*.
cocktail shaker *n* shaker *m inv*.
cocky ['kɔkɪ] *adj* spavaldo(a), arrogante.
cocoa ['kəukəu] *n* cacao.
coconut ['kəukənʌt] *n* noce *f* di cocco.
cocoon [kə'ku:n] *n* bozzolo.
COD *abbr see* **cash on delivery, collect on delivery.**
cod [kɔd] *n* merluzzo.
code [kəud] *n* codice *m*; ~ **of behaviour** regole *fpl* di condotta; ~ **of practice** codice professionale.
codeine ['kəudi:n] *n* codeina.
codger ['kɔdʒə*] *n* (*BRIT col*): **an old** ~ un simpatico nonnetto.
codicil ['kɔdɪsɪl] *n* codicillo.
codify ['kəudɪfaɪ] *vt* codificare.
cod-liver oil ['kɔdlɪvə*-] *n* olio di fegato di merluzzo.
co-driver ['kəu'draɪvə*] *n* (*in race*) copilota *m*; (*of lorry*) secondo autista *m*.
co-ed ['kəu'ed] *adj abbr* = **coeducational** ♦ *n abbr* (*US: female student*) *studentessa presso un'università mista*; (*BRIT: school*) scuola mista.
coeducational ['kəuɛdju'keɪʃənl] *adj* misto(a).
coerce [kəu'ə:s] *vt* costringere.
coercion [kəu'ə:ʃən] *n* coercizione *f*.
coexistence ['kəuɪg'zɪstəns] *n* coesistenza.
C. of C. *n abbr* = **chamber of commerce.**
C of E *abbr* = **Church of England.**
coffee ['kɔfɪ] *n* caffè *m inv*; **white** ~, (*US*) ~ **with cream** caffellatte *m*.
coffee bar *n* (*BRIT*) caffè *m inv*.
coffee bean *n* grano *or* chicco di caffè.
coffee break *n* pausa per il caffè.
coffeecake ['kɔfɪkeɪk] *n* (*US*) panino dolce all'uva.
coffee cup *n* tazzina da caffè.
coffeepot ['kɔfɪpɔt] *n* caffettiera.
coffee table *n* tavolino da tè.
coffin ['kɔfɪn] *n* bara.
C of I *abbr* = **Church of Ireland.**
C of S *abbr* = **Church of Scotland.**
cog [kɔg] *n* dente *m*.
cogent ['kəudʒənt] *adj* convincente.
cognac ['kɔnjæk] *n* cognac *m inv*.
cogwheel ['kɔgwi:l] *n* ruota dentata.
cohabit [kəu'hæbɪt] *vi* (*formal*): **to** ~ (**with sb**) coabitare (con qn).
coherent [kəu'hɪərənt] *adj* coerente.
cohesion [kəu'hi:ʒən] *n* coesione *f*.

cohesive [kəu'hi:sɪv] *adj* (*fig*) unificante, coesivo(a).
COI *n abbr* (*BRIT*) = *Central Office of Information.*
coil [kɔɪl] *n* rotolo; (*one loop*) anello; (*AUT, ELEC*) bobina; (*contraceptive*) spirale *f*; (*of smoke*) filo ♦ *vt* avvolgere.
coin [kɔɪn] *n* moneta ♦ *vt* (*word*) coniare.
coinage ['kɔɪnɪdʒ] *n* sistema *m* monetario.
coin-box ['kɔɪnbɔks] *n* (*BRIT*) cabina telefonica.
coincide [kəuɪn'saɪd] *vi* coincidere.
coincidence [kəu'ɪnsɪdəns] *n* combinazione *f*.
coin-operated ['kɔɪn'ɔpəreɪtɪd] *adj* (*machine*) (che funziona) a monete.
Coke ® [kəuk] *n* (*Coca-Cola*) coca *f inv*.
coke [kəuk] *n* coke *m*.
Col. *abbr* = **colonel**; (*US*) = *Colorado.*
COLA *n abbr* (*US*: = *cost-of-living adjustment*) ≈ scala mobile.
colander ['kɔləndə*] *n* colino.
cold [kəuld] *adj* freddo(a) ♦ *n* freddo; (*MED*) raffreddore *m*; **it's** ~ fa freddo; **to be** ~ aver freddo; **to catch** ~ prendere freddo; **to catch a** ~ prendere un raffreddore; **in** ~ **blood** a sangue freddo; **to have** ~ **feet** avere i piedi freddi; (*fig*) aver la fifa; **to give sb the** ~ **shoulder** ignorare qn.
cold-blooded [kəuld'blʌdɪd] *adj* (*ZOOL*) a sangue freddo.
cold cream *n* crema emolliente.
coldly ['kəuldlɪ] *adv* freddamente.
cold sore *n* erpete *m*.
cold sweat *n*: **to be in a** ~ (**about sth**) sudare freddo (per qc).
cold turkey *n* (*col*): **to go** ~ avere la scimmia (*drogato*).
Cold War *n*: **the** ~ la guerra fredda.
coleslaw ['kəulslɔ:] *n insalata di cavolo bianco.*
colic ['kɔlɪk] *n* colica.
colicky ['kɔlɪkɪ] *adj* che soffre di coliche.
collaborate [kə'læbəreɪt] *vi* collaborare.
collaboration [kəlæbə'reɪʃən] *n* collaborazione *f*.
collaborator [kə'læbəreɪtə*] *n* collaboratore/trice.
collage [kɔ'lɑ:ʒ] *n* (*ART*) collage *m inv*.
collagen ['kɔlədʒən] *n* collageno.
collapse [kə'læps] *vi* (*gen*) crollare; (*government*) cadere; (*MED*) avere un collasso; (*plans*) fallire ♦ *n* crollo; caduta; collasso; fallimento.
collapsible [kə'læpsəbl] *adj* pieghevole.
collar ['kɔlə*] *n* (*of coat, shirt*) colletto; (*for dog*) collare *m*; (*TECH*) anello, fascetta ♦ *vt* (*col: person, object*) beccare.

collarbone ['kɔləbəun] n clavicola.
collate [kɔ'leɪt] vt collazionare.
collateral [kɔ'lætərəl] n garanzia.
collation [kɔ'leɪʃən] n collazione f.
colleague ['kɔliːɡ] n collega m/f.
collect [kɔ'lɛkt] vt (gen) raccogliere; (as a hobby) fare collezione di; (BRIT: call for) prendere; (money owed, pension) riscuotere; (donations, subscriptions) fare una colletta di ♦ vi (people) adunarsi, riunirsi; (rubbish etc) ammucchiarsi ♦ adv (US TEL): to call ~ fare una chiamata a carico del destinatario; to ~ one's thoughts raccogliere le idee; ~ on delivery (COD) (US COMM) pagamento alla consegna.
collected [kə'lɛktɪd] adj: ~ works opere fpl raccolte.
collection [kə'lɛkʃən] n collezione f; raccolta; (for money) colletta; (POST) levata.
collective [kə'lɛktɪv] adj collettivo(a) ♦ n collettivo.
collective bargaining n trattative fpl (sindacali) collettive.
collector [kə'lɛktə*] n collezionista m/f; (of taxes) esattore m; ~'s item or piece pezzo da collezionista.
college ['kɔlɪdʒ] n (BRIT, US SCOL) college m inv; (of technology, agriculture etc) istituto superiore; (body) collegio; ~ of education ≈ facoltà f inv di Magistero.
collide [kə'laɪd] vi: to ~ (with) scontrarsi (con).
collie ['kɔlɪ] n (dog) collie m inv.
colliery ['kɔlɪərɪ] n (BRIT) miniera di carbone.
collision [kə'lɪʒən] n collisione f, scontro; to be on a ~ course (also fig) essere in rotta di collisione.
collision damage waiver (CDW) n (INSURANCE) copertura per i danni alla vettura.
colloquial [kə'ləukwɪəl] adj familiare.
collusion [kə'luːʒən] n collusione f; in ~ with in accordo segreto con.
Colo. abbr (US) = Colorado.
Cologne [kə'ləun] n Colonia.
cologne [kə'ləun] n (also: eau de ~) acqua di colonia.
Colombia [kə'lɔmbɪə] n Colombia.
Colombian [kə'lɔmbɪən] adj, n colombiano(a).
colon ['kəulən] n (sign) due punti mpl; (MED) colon m inv.
colonel ['kɔːnl] n colonnello.
colonial [kə'ləunɪəl] adj coloniale.
colonize ['kɔlənaɪz] vt colonizzare.

colony ['kɔlənɪ] n colonia.
color etc [ˈkʌlə*] (US) = colour etc.
Colorado beetle [kɔlə'rɑːdəu-] n dorifora.
colossal [kə'lɔsl] adj colossale.
colour, (US) **color** ['kʌlə*] n colore m ♦ vt colorare; (tint, dye) tingere; (fig: affect) influenzare ♦ vi arrossire ♦ cpd (film, photograph, television) a colori; ~s npl (of party, club) emblemi mpl.
colo(u)r bar n discriminazione f razziale (in locali etc).
colo(u)r-blind ['kʌləblaɪnd] adj daltonico(a).
colo(u)red ['kʌləd] adj colorato(a); (photo) a colori ♦ n: ~s gente f di colore.
colo(u)r film n (for camera) pellicola a colori.
colo(u)rful ['kʌləful] adj pieno(a) di colore, a vivaci colori; (personality) colorato(a).
colo(u)ring ['kʌlərɪŋ] n colorazione f; (complexion) colorito.
colo(u)r scheme combinazione f di colori.
colour supplement n (BRIT PRESS) supplemento a colori.
colo(u)r television n televisione f a colori.
colt [kəult] n puledro.
column ['kɔləm] n colonna; (fashion ~, sports ~ etc) rubrica; **the editorial** ~ l'articolo di fondo.
columnist ['kɔləmnɪst] n articolista m/f.
coma ['kəumə] n coma m inv.
comb [kəum] n pettine m ♦ vt (hair) pettinare; (area) battere a tappeto.
combat ['kɔmbæt] n combattimento ♦ vt combattere, lottare contro.
combination [kɔmbɪ'neɪʃən] n combinazione f.
combination lock n serratura a combinazione.
combine vb [kəm'baɪn] vt (one quality with another): to ~ sth with sth unire qc a qc ♦ vi unirsi; (CHEM) combinarsi ♦ n ['kɔmbaɪn] lega; (ECON) associazione f; a ~d effort uno sforzo collettivo.
combine (harvester) n mietitrebbia.
combo ['kɔmbəu] n (JAZZ etc) gruppo.
combustible [kəm'bʌstɪbl] adj combustibile.
combustion [kəm'bʌstʃən] n combustione f.
come, pt **came,** pp **come** [kʌm, keɪm] vi venire; (arrive) venire, arrivare; ~ with me vieni con me; we've just ~ from Paris siamo appena arrivati da Parigi; nothing came of it non è saltato fuori niente; to ~ into sight or view apparire; to ~ to (decision etc) raggiungere; to ~ undone/

loose slacciarsi/allentarsi; **coming!** vengo!; **if it ~s to it** nella peggiore delle ipotesi.

▶**come about** *vi* succedere.

▶**come across** *vt fus* trovare per caso; **to ~ across well/badly** fare una buona/cattiva impressione.

▶**come along** *vi* (*pupil, work*) fare progressi; **~ along!** avanti!, andiamo!, forza!

▶**come apart** *vi* andare in pezzi; (*become detached*) staccarsi.

▶**come away** *vi* venire via; (*become detached*) staccarsi.

▶**come back** *vi* ritornare; (*reply: col*): **can I ~ back to you on that one?** possiamo riparlarne più tardi?

▶**come by** *vt fus* (*acquire*) ottenere; procurarsi.

▶**come down** *vi* scendere; (*prices*) calare; (*buildings*) essere demolito(a).

▶**come forward** *vi* farsi avanti; presentarsi.

▶**come from** *vt fus* venire da; provenire da.

▶**come in** *vi* entrare.

▶**come in for** *vt fus* (*criticism etc*) ricevere.

▶**come into** *vt fus* (*money*) ereditare.

▶**come off** *vi* (*button*) staccarsi; (*stain*) andar via; (*attempt*) riuscire.

▶**come on** *vi* (*lights, electricity*) accendersi; (*pupil, undertaking*) fare progressi; **~ on!** avanti!, andiamo!, forza!

▶**come out** *vi* uscire; (*strike*) entrare in sciopero.

▶**come over** *vt fus*: **I don't know what's ~ over him!** non so cosa gli sia successo!

▶**come round** *vi* (*after faint, operation*) riprendere conoscenza, rinvenire.

▶**come through** *vi* (*survive*) sopravvivere, farcela; **the call came through** ci hanno passato la telefonata.

▶**come to** *vi* rinvenire ♦ *vt* (*add up to: amount*): **how much does it ~ to?** quanto costa?, quanto viene?

▶**come under** *vt fus* (*heading*) trovarsi sotto; (*influence*) cadere sotto, subire.

▶**come up** *vi* venire su.

▶**come up against** *vt fus* (*resistance, difficulties*) urtare contro.

▶**come up to** *vt fus* arrivare (fino) a; **the film didn't ~ up to our expectations** il film ci ha delusi.

▶**come up with** *vt fus*: **he came up with an idea** venne fuori con un'idea.

▶**come upon** *vt fus* trovare per caso.

comeback ['kʌmbæk] *n* (*THEAT etc*) ritorno; (*reaction*) reazione *f*; (*response*) risultato, risposta.

COMECON ['kɔmɪkɔn] *n abbr* (= *Council for Mutual Economic Aid*) COMECON *m*.

comedian [kə'miːdɪən] *n* comico.

comedienne [kəmiːdɪ'ɛn] *n* attrice *f* comica.

comedown ['kʌmdaun] *n* rovescio.

comedy ['kɔmɪdɪ] *n* commedia.

comet ['kɔmɪt] *n* cometa.

comeuppance [kʌm'ʌpəns] *n*: **to get one's ~** ricevere ciò che si merita.

comfort ['kʌmfət] *n* comodità *f inv*, benessere *m*; (*solace*) consolazione *f*, conforto ♦ *vt* consolare, confortare; *see also* **comforts**.

comfortable ['kʌmfətəbl] *adj* comodo(a); (*income, majority*) più che sufficiente; **I don't feel very ~ about it** non mi sento molto tranquillo.

comfortably ['kʌmfətəblɪ] *adv* (*sit*) comodamente; (*live*) bene.

comforter ['kʌmfətə*] *n* (*US*) trapunta.

comforts ['kʌmfəts] *npl* comforts *mpl*, comodità *fpl*.

comfort station *n* (*US*) gabinetti *mpl*.

comic ['kɔmɪk] *adj* comico(a) ♦ *n* comico; (*magazine*) giornaletto.

comical ['kɔmɪkl] *adj* divertente, buffo(a).

comic strip *n* fumetto.

coming ['kʌmɪŋ] *n* arrivo ♦ *adj* (*next*) prossimo(a); (*future*) futuro(a); **in the ~ weeks** nelle prossime settimane.

coming(s) and going(s) *n*(*pl*) andirivieni *m inv*.

Comintern ['kɔmɪntəːn] *n* KOMINTERN *m*.

comma ['kɔmə] *n* virgola.

command [kə'mɑːnd] *n* ordine *m*, comando; (*MIL: authority*) comando; (*mastery*) padronanza; (*COMPUT*) command *m inv*, comando ♦ *vt* comandare; **to ~ sb to do** ordinare a qn di fare; **to have/take ~ of** avere/prendere il comando di; **to have at one's ~** (*money, resources etc*) avere a propria disposizione.

command economy *n* = **planned economy**.

commandeer [kɔmən'dɪə*] *vt* requisire.

commander [kə'mɑːndə*] *n* capo; (*MIL*) comandante *m*.

commander-in-chief (C-in-C) [kə'mɑːndər-ɪn't ʃiːf] *n* (*MIL*) comandante *m* in capo.

commanding [kə'mɑːndɪŋ] *adj* (*appearance*) imponente; (*voice, tone*) autorevole; (*lead, position*) dominante.

commanding officer *n* comandante *m*.

commandment [kə'mɑːndmənt] *n* (*REL*) comandamento.

command module n (SPACE) modulo di comando.

commando [kə'mɑːndəu] n commando m inv; membro di un commando.

commemorate [kə'mɛməreɪt] vt commemorare.

commemoration [kəmɛmə'reɪʃən] n commemorazione f.

commemorative [kə'mɛmərətɪv] adj commemorativo(a).

commence [kə'mɛns] vt, vi cominciare.

commend [kə'mɛnd] vt lodare; raccomandare.

commendable [kə'mɛndəbl] adj lodevole.

commendation [kɔmɛn'deɪʃən] n lode f; (for bravery etc) raccomandazione f; encomio.

commensurate [kə'mɛnʃərɪt] adj: ~ with proporzionato(a) a.

comment ['kɔmɛnt] n commento ♦ vi: to ~ (on) fare commenti (su); to ~ that osservare che; "no ~" "niente da dire".

commentary ['kɔməntərɪ] n commentario; (SPORT) radiocronaca; telecronaca.

commentator ['kɔməntɛɪtə*] n commentatore/trice; (SPORT) radiocronista m/f; telecronista m/f.

commerce ['kɔmɜːs] n commercio.

commercial [kə'mɜːʃəl] adj commerciale ♦ n (TV: also: ~ break) pubblicità f inv.

commercial bank n banca commerciale.

commercial college n ≈ istituto commerciale.

commercialism [kə'mɜːʃəlɪzəm] n affarismo.

commercial television n televisione f commerciale.

commercial traveller n commesso viaggiatore.

commercial vehicle n veicolo commerciale.

commiserate [kə'mɪzəreɪt] vi: to ~ with condolersi con.

commission [kə'mɪʃən] n commissione f; (for salesman) commissione, provvigione f ♦ vt (MIL) nominare (al comando); (work of art) commissionare; **I get 10%** ~ ricevo il 10% sulle vendite; **out of** ~ (NAUT) in disarmo; (machine) fuori uso; **to** ~ **sb to do sth** incaricare qn di fare qc; **to** ~ **sth from sb** (painting etc) commissionare qc a qn; ~ **of inquiry** (BRIT) commissione f d'inchiesta.

commissionaire [kəmɪʃə'nɛə*] n (BRIT: at shop, cinema etc) portiere m in livrea.

commissioner [kə'mɪʃənə*] n commissionario; (POLICE) questore m.

commit [kə'mɪt] vt (act) commettere; (to sb's care) affidare; **to** ~ **o.s. (to do)** impegnarsi (a fare); **to** ~ **suicide** suicidarsi; **to** ~ **sb for trial** rinviare qn a giudizio.

commitment [kə'mɪtmənt] n impegno.

committed [kə'mɪtɪd] adj (writer) impegnato(a); (Christian) convinto(a).

committee [kə'mɪtɪ] n comitato; **to be on a** ~ far parte di un comitato or di una commissione.

committee meeting n riunione f di comitato or di commissione.

commodity [kə'mɔdɪtɪ] n prodotto, articolo; (food) derrata.

commodity exchange n borsa f merci inv.

common ['kɔmən] adj comune; (pej) volgare; (usual) normale ♦ n terreno comune; **in** ~ in comune; **in** ~ **use** di uso comune; **it's** ~ **knowledge that** è di dominio pubblico che; **to the** ~ **good** nell'interesse generale, per il bene comune; see also **Commons**.

common cold n: **the** ~ il raffreddore.

common denominator n denominatore m comune.

commoner ['kɔmənə*] n cittadino/a (non nobile).

common ground n (fig) terreno comune.

common land n terreno di uso pubblico.

common law n diritto consuetudinario.

common-law ['kɔmənlɔː] adj: ~ **wife** convivente f more uxorio.

commonly ['kɔmənlɪ] adv comunemente, usualmente.

Common Market n Mercato Comune.

commonplace ['kɔmənpleɪs] adj banale, ordinario(a).

commonroom ['kɔmənrum] n sala di riunione; (SCOL) sala dei professori.

Commons ['kɔmənz] npl (BRIT POL): **the (House of)** ~ la Camera dei Comuni.

common sense n buon senso.

Commonwealth ['kɔmənwɛlθ] n: **the** ~ il Commonwealth; see boxed note.

COMMONWEALTH

Il **Commonwealth** è un'associazione di stati sovrani indipendenti e di alcuni territori annessi che facevano parte dell'antico Impero Britannico. Attualmente gli stati del Commonwealth riconoscono ancora il proprio capo di stato nel sovrano britannico e i loro rappresentanti si riuniscono per discutere questioni di comune interesse.

commotion [kə'məʊʃən] *n* confusione *f*, tumulto.

communal ['kɔmjuːnl] *adj* (*life*) comunale; (*for common use*) pubblico(a).

commune *n* ['kɔmjuːn] (*group*) comune *f* ♦ *vi* [kə'mjuːn]: **to ~ with** mettersi in comunione con.

communicate [kə'mjuːnɪkeɪt] *vt* comunicare, trasmettere ♦ *vi*: **to ~ (with)** comunicare (con).

communication [kəmjuːnɪ'keɪʃən] *n* comunicazione *f*.

communication cord *n* (*BRIT*) segnale *m* d'allarme.

communications network *n* rete *f* delle comunicazioni.

communications satellite *n* satellite *m* per telecomunicazioni.

communicative [kə'mjuːnɪkətɪv] *adj* (*gen*) loquace.

communion [kə'mjuːnɪən] *n* (*also:* **Holy C~**) comunione *f*.

communiqué [kə'mjuːnɪkeɪ] *n* comunicato.

communism ['kɔmjunɪzəm] *n* comunismo.

communist ['kɔmjunɪst] *adj, n* comunista (*m/f*).

community [kə'mjuːnɪtɪ] *n* comunità *f inv*.

community centre *n* circolo ricreativo.

community chest *n* (*US*) fondo di beneficenza.

community health centre *n* centro socio-sanitario.

community home *n* (*BRIT*) riformatorio.

community service *n* (*BRIT*) ≈ lavoro sostitutivo.

community spirit *n* spirito civico.

commutation ticket [kɔmjuː'teɪʃən-] *n* (*US*) biglietto di abbonamento.

commute [kə'mjuːt] *vi* fare il pendolare ♦ *vt* (*LAW*) commutare.

commuter [kə'mjuːtə*] *n* pendolare *m/f*.

compact *adj* [kəm'pækt] compatto(a) ♦ *n* ['kɔmpækt] (*also:* **powder ~**) portacipria *m inv*.

compact disc *n* compact disc *m inv*; **~ player** lettore *m* CD *inv*.

companion [kəm'pænjən] *n* compagno/a.

companionship [kəm'pænjənʃɪp] *n* compagnia.

companionway [kəm'pænjənweɪ] *n* (*NAUT*) scala.

company ['kʌmpənɪ] *n* (*also* COMM, MIL, THEAT) compagnia; **he's good ~** è di buona compagnia; **we have ~** abbiamo ospiti; **to keep sb ~** tenere compagnia a qn; **to part ~ with** separarsi da; **Smith and C~** Smith e soci.

company car *n* macchina (di proprietà) della ditta.

company director *n* amministratore *m*, consigliere *m* di amministrazione.

company secretary *n* (*BRIT COMM*) segretario/a generale.

comparable ['kɔmpərəbl] *adj* comparabile.

comparative [kəm'pærətɪv] *adj* (*freedom, cost*) relativo(a); (*adjective, adverb etc*) comparativo(a); (*literature*) comparato(a).

comparatively [kəm'pærətɪvlɪ] *adv* relativamente.

compare [kəm'pɛə*] *vt*: **to ~ sth/sb with/to** confrontare qc/qn con/a ♦ *vi*: **to ~ (with)** reggere il confronto (con); **~d with** *or* **to** a paragone di, rispetto a; **how do the prices ~?** che differenza di prezzo c'è?

comparison [kəm'pærɪsn] *n* confronto; **in ~ (with)** a confronto (di).

compartment [kəm'pɑːtmənt] *n* compartimento; (*RAIL*) scompartimento.

compass ['kʌmpəs] *n* bussola; (**a pair of**) **~es** (*MATH*) compasso; **within the ~ of** entro i limiti di.

compassion [kəm'pæʃən] *n* compassione *f*.

compassionate [kəm'pæʃənɪt] *adj* compassionevole; **on ~ grounds** per motivi personali.

compassionate leave *n* congedo straordinario (*per gravi motivi di famiglia*).

compatibility [kəmpætɪ'bɪlɪtɪ] *n* compatibilità.

compatible [kəm'pætɪbl] *adj* compatibile.

compel [kəm'pɛl] *vt* costringere, obbligare.

compelling [kəm'pɛlɪŋ] *adj* (*fig: argument*) irresistibile.

compendium [kəm'pɛndɪəm] *n* compendio.

compensate ['kɔmpənseɪt] *vt* risarcire ♦ *vi*: **to ~ for** compensare.

compensation [kɔmpən'seɪʃən] *n* compensazione *f*; (*money*) risarcimento.

compère ['kɔmpɛə*] *n* presentatore/trice.

compete [kəm'piːt] *vi* (*take part*) concorrere; (*vie*): **to ~ (with)** fare concorrenza (a).

competence ['kɔmpɪtəns] *n* competenza.

competent ['kɔmpɪtənt] *adj* competente.

competing [kəm'piːtɪŋ] *adj* (*theories, ideas*) opposto(a); (*companies*) in concorrenza; **three ~ explanations (of)** tre spiegazioni contrastanti tra di loro (di).

competition [kɔmpɪ'tɪʃən] *n* gara, concorso; (*SPORT*) gara; (*ECON*) concorrenza; **in ~ with** in concorrenza con.

competitive [kəm'pɛtɪtɪv] *adj* (*sports*) agonistico(a); (*person*) che ha spirito di competizione; (*ECON*) concorrenziale.

competitive examination *n* concorso.

competitor [kəm'pɛtɪtə*] n concorrente m/f.
compile [kəm'paɪl] vt compilare.
complacency [kəm'pleɪsnsɪ] n compiacenza di sé.
complacent [kəm'pleɪsnt] adj compiaciuto(a) di sé.
complain [kəm'pleɪn] vi: **to ~ (about)** lagnarsi (di); (in shop etc) reclamare (per).
▶**complain of** vt fus (MED) accusare.
complaint [kəm'pleɪnt] n lamento; reclamo; (MED) malattia.
complement n ['kɔmplɪmənt] complemento; (especially of ship's crew etc) effettivo ♦ vt ['kɔmplɪmɛnt] (enhance) accompagnarsi bene a.
complementary [kɔmplɪ'mɛntərɪ] adj complementare.
complete [kəm'pliːt] adj completo(a) ♦ vt completare; (a form) riempire; **it's a ~ disaster** è un vero disastro.
completely [kəm'pliːtlɪ] adv completamente.
completion [kəm'pliːʃən] n completamento; **to be nearing ~** essere in fase di completamento; **on ~ of contract** alla firma del contratto.
complex ['kɔmplɛks] adj complesso(a) ♦ n (PSYCH, buildings etc) complesso.
complexion [kəm'plɛkʃən] n (of face) carnagione f; (of event etc) aspetto.
complexity [kəm'plɛksɪtɪ] n complessità f inv.
compliance [kəm'plaɪəns] n acquiescenza; **in ~ with** (orders, wishes etc) in conformità con.
compliant [kəm'plaɪənt] adj acquiescente, arrendevole.
complicate ['kɔmplɪkeɪt] vt complicare.
complicated ['kɔmplɪkeɪtɪd] adj complicato(a).
complication [kɔmplɪ'keɪʃən] n complicazione f.
compliment n ['kɔmplɪmənt] complimento ♦ vt ['kɔmplɪmɛnt] fare un complimento a; **~s** npl complimenti mpl; rispetti mpl; **to pay sb a ~** fare un complimento a qn; **to ~ sb (on sth/on doing sth)** congratularsi or complimentarsi con qn (per qc/per aver fatto qc).
complimentary [kɔmplɪ'mɛntərɪ] adj complimentoso(a), elogiativo(a); (free) in omaggio.
complimentary ticket n biglietto d'omaggio.
compliments slip n cartoncino della società.
comply [kəm'plaɪ] vi: **to ~ with** assentire a;

conformarsi a.
component [kəm'pəunənt] adj, n componente (m).
compose [kəm'pəuz] vt comporre; **to ~ o.s.** ricomporsi; **~d of** composto(a) di.
composed [kəm'pəuzd] adj calmo(a).
composer [kəm'pəuzə*] n (MUS) compositore/trice.
composite ['kɔmpəzɪt] adj composito(a); (MATH) composto(a).
composition [kɔmpə'zɪʃən] n composizione f.
compost ['kɔmpɔst] n composta, concime m.
composure [kəm'pəuʒə*] n calma.
compound ['kɔmpaund] n (CHEM, LING) composto; (enclosure) recinto ♦ adj composto(a) ♦ vt (fig: problem, difficulty) peggiorare.
compound fracture n frattura esposta.
compound interest n interesse m composto.
comprehend [kɔmprɪ'hɛnd] vt comprendere, capire.
comprehension [kɔmprɪ'hɛnʃən] n comprensione f.
comprehensive [kɔmprɪ'hɛnsɪv] adj comprensivo(a).
comprehensive insurance policy n polizza multi-rischio inv.
comprehensive (school) n (BRIT) scuola secondaria aperta a tutti.
compress vt [kəm'prɛs] comprimere ♦ n ['kɔmprɛs] (MED) compressa.
compression [kəm'prɛʃən] n compressione f.
comprise [kəm'praɪz] vt (also: **be ~d of**) comprendere.
compromise ['kɔmprəmaɪz] n compromesso ♦ vt compromettere ♦ vi venire a un compromesso ♦ cpd (decision, solution) di compromesso.
compulsion [kəm'pʌlʃən] n costrizione f; **under ~** sotto pressioni.
compulsive [kəm'pʌlsɪv] adj (PSYCH) incontrollabile; **he's a ~ smoker** non riesce a controllarsi nel fumare.
compulsory [kəm'pʌlsərɪ] adj obbligatorio(a).
compulsory purchase n espropriazione f.
compunction [kəm'pʌŋkʃən] n scrupolo; **to have no ~ about doing sth** non farsi scrupoli a fare qc.
computer [kəm'pjuːtə*] n computer m inv, elaboratore m elettronico.
computer game n computer game m inv.
computerization [kəmpjuːtəraɪ'zeɪʃən] n computerizzazione f.

computerize [kəm'pju:təraɪz] *vt* computerizzare.
computer language *n* linguaggio *m* macchina *inv.*
computer literate *adj*: **to be ~** essere in grado di usare il computer.
computer peripheral *n* unità periferica.
computer program *n* programma *m* di computer.
computer programmer *n* programmatore/trice.
computer programming *n* programmazione *f* di computer.
computer science *n* informatica.
computer scientist *n* informatico/a.
computing [kəm'pju:tɪŋ] *n* informatica.
comrade ['kɔmrɪd] *n* compagno/a.
comradeship ['kɔmrɪdʃɪp] *n* cameratismo.
comsat ['kɔmsæt] *n abbr* = **communications satellite.**
con [kɔn] *vt* (*col*) truffare ♦ *n* truffa; **to ~ sb into doing sth** indurre qn a fare qc con raggiri.
concave ['kɔn'keɪv] *adj* concavo(a).
conceal [kən'si:l] *vt* nascondere.
concede [kən'si:d] *vt* concedere ♦ *vi* fare una concessione.
conceit [kən'si:t] *n* presunzione *f*, vanità.
conceited [kən'si:tɪd] *adj* presuntuoso(a), vanitoso(a).
conceivable [kən'si:vəbl] *adj* concepibile; **it is ~ that** ... può anche darsi che ....
conceivably [kən'si:vəblɪ] *adv*: **he may ~ be right** può anche darsi che abbia ragione.
conceive [kən'si:v] *vt* concepire ♦ *vi* concepire un bambino; **to ~ of sth/of doing sth** immaginare qc/di fare qc.
concentrate ['kɔnsəntreɪt] *vi* concentrarsi ♦ *vt* concentrare.
concentration [kɔnsən'treɪʃən] *n* concentrazione *f*.
concentration camp *n* campo di concentramento.
concentric [kɔn'sɛntrɪk] *adj* concentrico(a).
concept ['kɔnsept] *n* concetto.
conception [kən'sepʃən] *n* concezione *f*; (*idea*) idea, concetto.
concern [kən'sə:n] *n* affare *m*; (*COMM*) azienda, ditta; (*anxiety*) preoccupazione *f* ♦ *vt* riguardare; **to be ~ed (about)** preoccuparsi (di); **to be ~ed with** occuparsi di; **as far as I am ~ed** per quanto mi riguarda; **"to whom it may ~"** "a tutti gli interessati"; **the department ~ed** (*under discussion*) l'ufficio in questione; (*relevant*) l'ufficio competente.
concerning [kən'sə:nɪŋ] *prep* riguardo a, circa.

concert ['kɔnsət] *n* concerto; **in ~ di** concerto.
concerted [kən'sə:tɪd] *adj* concertato(a).
concert hall *n* sala da concerti.
concertina [kɔnsə'ti:nə] *n* piccola fisarmonica ♦ *vi* ridursi come una fisarmonica.
concerto [kən'tʃə:təu] *n* concerto.
concession [kən'sɛʃən] *n* concessione *f*.
concessionaire [kənsɛʃə'nɛə*] *n* concessionario.
concessionary [kən'sɛʃənərɪ] *adj* (*ticket, fare*) a prezzo ridotto.
conciliation [kənsɪlɪ'eɪʃən] *n* conciliazione *f*.
conciliatory [kən'sɪlɪətrɪ] *adj* conciliativo(a).
concise [kən'saɪs] *adj* conciso(a).
conclave ['kɔnkleɪv] *n* riunione *f* segreta; (*REL*) conclave *m*.
conclude [kən'klu:d] *vt* concludere ♦ *vi* (*speaker*) concludere; (*events*): **to ~ (with)** concludersi (con).
concluding [kən'klu:dɪŋ] *adj* (*remarks etc*) conclusivo(a), finale.
conclusion [kən'klu:ʒən] *n* conclusione *f*; **to come to the ~ that** ... concludere che ..., arrivare alla conclusione che ....
conclusive [kən'klu:sɪv] *adj* conclusivo(a).
concoct [kən'kɔkt] *vt* inventare.
concoction [kən'kɔkʃən] *n* (*food, drink*) miscuglio.
concord ['kɔnkɔ:d] *n* (*harmony*) armonia, concordia; (*treaty*) accordo.
concourse ['kɔnkɔ:s] *n* (*hall*) atrio.
concrete ['kɔnkri:t] *n* calcestruzzo ♦ *adj* concreto(a); (*CONSTR*) di calcestruzzo.
concrete mixer *n* betoniera.
concur [kən'kə:*] *vi* concordare.
concurrently [kən'kʌrntlɪ] *adv* simultaneamente.
concussion [kən'kʌʃən] *n* (*MED*) commozione *f* cerebrale.
condemn [kən'dem] *vt* condannare.
condemnation [kɔndem'neɪʃən] *n* condanna.
condensation [kɔnden'seɪʃən] *n* condensazione *f*.
condense [kən'dens] *vi* condensarsi ♦ *vt* condensare.
condensed milk *n* latte *m* condensato.
condescend [kɔndɪ'send] *vi* condiscendere; **to ~ to do sth** degnarsi di fare qc.
condescending [kɔndɪ'sendɪŋ] *adj* condiscendente.
condition [kən'dɪʃən] *n* condizione *f*; (*disease*) malattia ♦ *vt* condizionare, regolare; **in good/poor ~** in buone/cattive condizioni; **to have a heart ~**

soffrire di (mal di) cuore; **weather** ~**s** condizioni meteorologiche; **on** ~ **that** a condizione che + *sub*, a condizione di.
conditional [kən'dɪʃənl] *adj* condizionale; **to be** ~ **upon** dipendere da.
conditioner [kən'dɪʃənə*] *n* (*for hair*) balsamo.
condo ['kɔndəu] *n abbr* (*US col*) = **condominium**.
condolences [kən'dəulənsɪz] *npl* condoglianze *fpl*.
condom ['kɔndəm] *n* preservativo.
condominium [kɔndə'mɪnɪəm] *n* (*US*) condominio.
condone [kən'dəun] *vt* condonare.
conducive [kən'djuːsɪv] *adj*: ~ **to** favorevole a.
conduct *n* ['kɔndʌkt] condotta ♦ *vt* [kən'dʌkt] condurre; (*manage*) dirigere; amministrare; (*MUS*) dirigere; **to** ~ **o.s.** comportarsi.
conductor [kən'dʌktə*] *n* (*of orchestra*) direttore *m* d'orchestra; (*on bus*) bigliettaio; (*US RAIL*) controllore *m*; (*ELEC*) conduttore *m*.
conductress [kən'dʌktrɪs] *n* (*on bus*) bigliettaia
conduit ['kɔndɪt] *n* condotto; tubo.
cone [kəun] *n* cono; (*BOT*) pigna.
confectioner [kən'fɛkʃənə*] *n*: ~'**s (shop)** ≈ pasticceria.
confectionery [kən'fɛkʃənərɪ] *n* dolciumi *mpl*.
confederate [kən'fɛdərɪt] *adj* confederato(a) ♦ *n* (*pej*) complice *m/f*; (*US HISTORY*) confederato.
confederation [kənfɛdə'reɪʃən] *n* confederazione *f*.
confer [kən'fəː*] *vt*: **to** ~ **sth on** conferire qc a ♦ *vi* conferire; **to** ~ **(with sb about sth)** consultarsi (con qn su qc).
conference ['kɔnfərns] *n* congresso; **to be in** ~ essere in riunione.
conference room *n* sala *f* conferenze *inv*.
confess [kən'fɛs] *vt* confessare, ammettere ♦ *vi* confessarsi.
confession [kən'fɛʃən] *n* confessione *f*.
confessional [kən'fɛʃənl] *n* confessionale *m*.
confessor [kən'fɛsə*] *n* confessore *m*.
confetti [kən'fɛtɪ] *n* coriandoli *mpl*.
confide [kən'faɪd] *vi*: **to** ~ **in** confidarsi con.
confidence ['kɔnfɪdns] *n* confidenza; (*trust*) fiducia; (*also*: **self-**~) sicurezza di sé; **to tell sb sth in strict** ~ dire qc a qn in via strettamente confidenziale; **to have (every)** ~ **that** ... essere assolutamente certo(a) che ...; **motion of no** ~ mozione *f*

di sfiducia.
confidence trick *n* truffa.
confident ['kɔnfɪdənt] *adj* sicuro(a); (*also*: **self-**~) sicuro(a) di sé.
confidential [kɔnfɪ'dɛnʃəl] *adj* riservato(a); (*secretary*) particolare.
confidentiality ['kɔnfɪdɛnʃɪ'ælɪtɪ] *n* riservatezza, carattere *m* confidenziale.
configuration [kən'fɪgju'reɪʃən] *n* (*COMPUT*) configurazione *f*.
confine [kən'faɪn] *vt* limitare; (*shut up*) rinchiudere; **to** ~ **o.s. to doing sth** limitarsi a fare qc; *see also* **confines.**
confined [kən'faɪnd] *adj* (*space*) ristretto(a).
confinement [kən'faɪnmənt] *n* prigionia; (*MIL*) consegna; (*MED*) parto.
confines ['kɔnfaɪnz] *npl* confini *mpl*.
confirm [kən'fəːm] *vt* confermare; (*REL*) cresimare.
confirmation [kɔnfə'meɪʃən] *n* conferma; cresima.
confirmed [kən'fəːmd] *adj* inveterato(a).
confiscate ['kɔnfɪskeɪt] *vt* confiscare.
confiscation [kɔnfɪs'keɪʃən] *n* confisca.
conflagration [kɔnflə'greɪʃən] *n* conflagrazione *f*.
conflict *n* ['kɔnflɪkt] conflitto ♦ *vi* [kən'flɪkt] essere in conflitto.
conflicting [kən'flɪktɪŋ] *adj* contrastante; (*reports, evidence, opinions*) contraddittorio(a).
conform [kən'fɔːm] *vi*: **to** ~ **(to)** conformarsi (a).
conformist [kən'fɔːmɪst] *n* conformista *m/f*.
confound [kən'faund] *vt* confondere; (*amaze*) sconcertare.
confounded [kən'faundɪd] *adj* maledetto(a).
confront [kən'frʌnt] *vt* confrontare; (*enemy, danger*) affrontare.
confrontation [kɔnfrən'teɪʃən] *n* scontro.
confrontational [kɔnfrən'teɪʃənəl] *adj* polemico(a), aggressivo(a).
confuse [kən'fjuːz] *vt* imbrogliare; (*one thing with another*) confondere.
confused [kən'fjuːzd] *adj* confuso(a); **to get** ~ confondersi.
confusing [kən'fjuːzɪŋ] *adj* che fa confondere.
confusion [kən'fjuːʒən] *n* confusione *f*.
congeal [kən'dʒiːl] *vi* (*blood*) congelarsi.
congenial [kən'dʒiːnɪəl] *adj* (*person*) simpatico(a); (*place, work, company*) piacevole.
congenital [kən'dʒɛnɪtl] *adj* congenito(a).
conger eel ['kɔngər-] *n* grongo.
congested [kən'dʒɛstɪd] *adj* congestionato(a); (*telephone lines*)

sovraccarico(a).
congestion [kənˈdʒɛstʃən] *n* congestione *f*.
conglomerate [kənˈglɔmərɪt] *n* (*COMM*)
conglomerato.
conglomeration [kənglɔməˈreɪʃən] *n*
conglomerazione *f*.
Congo [ˈkɔŋgəu] *n* Congo.
congratulate [kənˈgrætjuleɪt] *vt*: **to ~ sb
(on)** congratularsi con qn (per *or* di).
congratulations [kəngrætjuˈleɪʃənz] *npl*: **~
(on)** congratulazioni *fpl* (per) ♦ *excl*
congratulazioni!, rallegramenti!
congregate [ˈkɔŋgrɪgeɪt] *vi* congregarsi,
riunirsi.
congregation [kɔŋgrɪˈgeɪʃən] *n*
congregazione *f*.
congress [ˈkɔŋgrɛs] *n* congresso; (*US POL*):
C~ il Congresso; *see boxed note.*

CONGRESS

Il **Congress** *è l'assemblea statunitense che si
riunisce a Washington D.C. nel "Capitol" per
elaborare e discutere le leggi federali. È
costituita dalla "House of Representatives"
(435 membri, eletti nei vari stati in base al
numero degli abitanti) e dal "Senate" (100
senatori, due per ogni stato). Sia i membri della
"House of Representatives" che quelli del
"Senate" sono eletti direttamente dal popolo.*

---

congressman [ˈkɔŋgrɛsmən] *n* (*US*)
membro del Congresso.
congresswoman [ˈkɔŋgrɛswumən] *n* (*US*)
(donna) membro del Congresso.
conical [ˈkɔnɪkl] *adj* conico(a).
conifer [ˈkɔnɪfə*] *n* conifero.
coniferous [kəˈnɪfərəs] *adj* di conifere.
conjecture [kənˈdʒɛktʃə*] *n* congettura
♦ *vt, vi* congetturare.
conjugal [ˈkɔndʒugl] *adj* coniugale.
conjugate [ˈkɔndʒugeɪt] *vt* coniugare.
conjugation [kɔndʒəˈgeɪʃən] *n*
coniugazione *f*.
conjunction [kənˈdʒʌŋkʃən] *n* congiunzione
f; **in ~ with** in accordo con, insieme con.
conjunctivitis [kɔndʒʌŋktɪˈvaɪtɪs] *n*
congiuntivite *f*.
conjure [ˈkʌndʒə*] *vi* fare giochi di
prestigio.
▶**conjure up** *vt* (*ghost, spirit*) evocare;
(*memories*) rievocare.
conjurer [ˈkʌndʒərə*] *n* prestigiatore/trice,
prestidigitatore/trice.
conjuring trick [ˈkʌndʒərɪŋ-] *n* gioco di
prestigio.
conker [ˈkɔŋkə*] *n* (*BRIT col*) castagna
(d'ippocastano).

conk out [kɔŋk-] *vi* (*col*) andare in panne.
conman [ˈkɔnmæn] *n* truffatore *m*.
Conn. *abbr* (*US*) = Connecticut.
connect [kəˈnɛkt] *vt* connettere, collegare;
(*ELEC*) collegare; (*fig*) associare ♦ *vi*
(*train*): **to ~ with** essere in coincidenza
con; **to be ~ed with** aver rapporti con;
essere imparentato(a) con; **I am trying to
~ you** (*TEL*) sto cercando di darle la linea.
connection [kəˈnɛkʃən] *n* relazione *f*,
rapporto; (*ELEC*) connessione *f*; (*TEL*)
collegamento; (*train etc*) coincidenza; **in ~
with** con riferimento a, a proposito di;
what is the ~ between them? in che
modo sono legati?; **business ~s** rapporti
d'affari; **to miss/get one's ~** (*train etc*)
perdere/prendere la coincidenza.
connexion [kəˈnɛkʃən] *n* (*BRIT*) =
connection.
conning tower [ˈkɔnɪŋ-] *n* torretta di
comando.
connive [kəˈnaɪv] *vi*: **to ~ at** essere
connivente in.
connoisseur [kɔnɪˈsə:*] *n* conoscitore/
trice.
connotation [kɔnəˈteɪʃən] *n* connotazione *f*.
connubial [kəˈnjuːbɪəl] *adj* coniugale.
conquer [ˈkɔŋkə*] *vt* conquistare; (*feelings*)
vincere.
conqueror [ˈkɔŋkərə*] *n* conquistatore *m*.
conquest [ˈkɔŋkwɛst] *n* conquista.
cons [kɔnz] *npl see* **pro**; **convenience**.
conscience [ˈkɔnʃəns] *n* coscienza; **in all ~**
onestamente, in coscienza.
conscientious [kɔnʃɪˈɛnʃəs] *adj*
coscienzioso(a).
conscientious objector *n* obiettore *m* di
coscienza.
conscious [ˈkɔnʃəs] *adj* consapevole; (*MED*)
conscio(a); (*deliberate: insult, error*)
intenzionale, voluto(a); **to become ~ of
sth/that** rendersi conto di qc/che.
consciousness [ˈkɔnʃəsnɪs] *n*
consapevolezza; (*MED*) coscienza; **to
lose/regain ~** perdere/riprendere
coscienza.
conscript [ˈkɔnskrɪpt] *n* coscritto.
conscription [kənˈskrɪpʃən] *n* coscrizione *f*.
consecrate [ˈkɔnsɪkreɪt] *vt* consacrare.
consecutive [kənˈsɛkjutɪv] *adj*
consecutivo(a); **on 3 ~ occasions** 3 volte
di fila.
consensus [kənˈsɛnsəs] *n* consenso; **the ~
of opinion** l'opinione *f* unanime *or*
comune.
consent [kənˈsɛnt] *n* consenso ♦ *vi*: **to ~ (to)**
acconsentire (a); **age of ~** età legale
(per avere rapporti sessuali); **by**

common ~ di comune accordo.
consenting adults [kən'sɛntɪŋ-] npl adulti mpl consenzienti.
consequence ['kɔnsɪkwəns] n conseguenza, risultato; importanza; **in** ~ di conseguenza.
consequently ['kɔnsɪkwəntlɪ] adv di conseguenza, dunque.
conservation [kɔnsə'veɪʃən] n conservazione f; (also: **nature** ~) tutela dell'ambiente; **energy** ~ risparmio energetico.
conservationist [kɔnsə'veɪʃənɪst] n fautore/trice della tutela dell'ambiente.
conservative [kən'sɔ:vətɪv] adj conservatore(trice); (cautious) cauto(a); **C** ~ adj, n (BRIT POL) conservatore(trice); **the C~ Party** il partito conservatore.
conservatory [kən'sɔ:vətrɪ] n (greenhouse) serra.
conserve [kən'sɔ:v] vt conservare ♦ n conserva.
consider [kən'sɪdə*] vt considerare; (take into account) tener conto di; **to** ~ **doing sth** considerare la possibilità di fare qc; **all things** ~**ed** tutto sommato or considerato; ~ **yourself lucky** puoi dirti fortunato.
considerable [kən'sɪdərəbl] adj considerevole, notevole.
considerably [kən'sɪdərəblɪ] adv notevolmente, decisamente.
considerate [kən'sɪdərɪt] adj premuroso(a).
consideration [kənsɪdə'reɪʃən] n considerazione f; (reward) rimunerazione f; **out of** ~ **for** per riguardo a; **under** ~ in esame; **my first** ~ **is my family** il mio primo pensiero è per la mia famiglia.
considered [kən'sɪdəd] adj: **it is my** ~ **opinion that** ... dopo lunga riflessione il mio parere è che ....
considering [kən'sɪdərɪŋ] prep in considerazione di; ~ **(that)** se si considera (che).
consign [kən'saɪn] vt consegnare; (send: goods) spedire.
consignee [kɔnsaɪ'ni:] n consegnatario/a, destinatario/a.
consignment [kən'saɪnmənt] n consegna; spedizione f.
consignment note n (COMM) nota di spedizione.
consist [kən'sɪst] vi: **to** ~ **of** constare di, essere composto(a) di.
consistency [kən'sɪstənsɪ] n consistenza; (fig) coerenza.
consistent [kən'sɪstənt] adj coerente; (constant) costante; ~ **with** compatibile

con.
consolation [kɔnsə'leɪʃən] n consolazione f.
console vt [kən'səul] consolare ♦ n ['kɔnsəul] quadro di comando.
consolidate [kən'sɔlɪdeɪt] vt consolidare.
consols ['kɔnsɔlz] npl (STOCK EXCHANGE) titoli mpl del debito consolidato.
consommé [kən'sɔmeɪ] n consommé m inv, brodo ristretto.
consonant ['kɔnsənənt] n consonante f.
consort ['kɔnsɔ:t] n consorte m/f; **prince** ~ principe m consorte ♦ vi (often pej): **to** ~ **with sb** frequentare qn.
consortium [kən'sɔ:tɪəm] n consorzio.
conspicuous [kən'spɪkjuəs] adj cospicuo(a); **to make o.s.** ~ farsi notare.
conspiracy [kən'spɪrəsɪ] n congiura, cospirazione f.
conspiratorial [kənspɪrə'tɔ:rɪəl] adj cospiratorio(a).
conspire [kən'spaɪə*] vi congiurare, cospirare.
constable ['kʌnstəbl] n (BRIT: also: **police** ~) ≈ poliziotto, agente m di polizia.
constabulary [kən'stæbjulərɪ] n forze fpl dell'ordine.
constant ['kɔnstənt] adj costante; continuo(a).
constantly ['kɔnstəntlɪ] adv costantemente; continuamente.
constellation [kɔnstə'leɪʃən] n costellazione f.
consternation [kɔnstə'neɪʃən] n costernazione f.
constipated ['kɔnstɪpeɪtɪd] adj stitico(a).
constipation [kɔnstɪ'peɪʃən] n stitichezza.
constituency [kən'stɪtjuənsɪ] n collegio elettorale; (people) elettori mpl (del collegio); see boxed note.

CONSTITUENCY

Con il termine **constituency** viene indicato sia un collegio elettorale che i suoi elettori. In Gran Bretagna ogni collegio elegge un rappresentante che in seguito incontra regolarmente i propri elettori in riunioni chiamate "surgery" per discutere questioni di interesse locale.

---

constituency party n sezione f locale (del partito).
constituent [kən'stɪtjuənt] n elettore/trice; (part) elemento componente.
constitute ['kɔnstɪtju:t] vt costituire.
constitution [kɔnstɪ'tju:ʃən] n costituzione f.
constitutional [kɔnstɪ'tju:ʃənl] adj costituzionale.

constitutional monarchy *n* monarchia costituzionale.
constrain [kən'streɪn] *vt* costringere.
constrained [kən'streɪnd] *adj* costretto(a).
constraint [kən'streɪnt] *n* (*restraint*) limitazione *f*, costrizione *f*; (*embarrassment*) imbarazzo, soggezione *f*.
constrict [kən'strɪkt] *vt* comprimere; opprimere.
construct [kən'strʌkt] *vt* costruire.
construction [kən'strʌkʃən] *n* costruzione *f*; (*fig: interpretation*) interpretazione *f*; **under** ~ in costruzione.
construction industry *n* edilizia, industria edile.
constructive [kən'strʌktɪv] *adj* costruttivo(a).
construe [kən'struː] *vt* interpretare.
consul ['kɔnsl] *n* console *m*.
consulate ['kɔnsjulɪt] *n* consolato.
consult [kən'sʌlt] *vt*: **to** ~ **sb (about sth)** consultare qn (su *or* riguardo a qc).
consultancy [kən'sʌltənsɪ] *n* consulenza.
consultancy fee *n* onorario di consulenza.
consultant [kən'sʌltənt] *n* (*MED*) consulente *m* medico; (*other specialist*) consulente ♦ *cpd*: ~ **engineer** *n* ingegnere *m* consulente; ~ **paediatrician** *n* specialista *m/f* in pediatria; **legal/ management** ~ consulente legale/ gestionale.
consultation [kɔnsəl'teɪʃən] *n* consultazione *f*; (*MED, LAW*) consulto; **in** ~ **with** consultandosi con.
consultative [kən'sʌltətɪv] *adj* di consulenza.
consulting room [kən'sʌltɪŋ-] *n* (*BRIT*) ambulatorio.
consume [kən'sjuːm] *vt* consumare.
consumer [kən'sjuːmə*] *n* consumatore/ trice; (*of electricity, gas etc*) utente *m/f*.
consumer credit *n* credito al consumatore.
consumer durables *npl* prodotti *mpl* di consumo durevole.
consumer goods *npl* beni *mpl* di consumo.
consumerism [kən'sjuːmərɪzəm] *n* (*consumer protection*) tutela del consumatore; (*ECON*) consumismo.
consumer society *n* società dei consumi.
consumer watchdog *n* comitato di difesa dei consumatori.
consummate ['kɔnsʌmeɪt] *vt* consumare.
consumption [kən'sʌmpʃən] *n* consumo; (*MED*) consunzione *f*; **not fit for human** ~ non commestibile.
cont. *abbr* (= *continued*) segue.
contact ['kɔntækt] *n* contatto; (*person*)

conoscenza ♦ *vt* mettersi in contatto con; **to be in** ~ **with sb/sth** essere in contatto con qn/qc; **business** ~**s** contatti *mpl* d'affari.
contact lenses *npl* lenti *fpl* a contatto.
contagious [kən'teɪdʒəs] *adj* contagioso(a).
contain [kən'teɪn] *vt* contenere; **to** ~ **o.s.** contenersi.
container [kən'teɪnə*] *n* recipiente *m*; (*for shipping etc*) container *m*.
containerize [kən'teɪnəraɪz] *vt* mettere in container.
container ship *n* nave *f* container *inv*.
contaminate [kən'tæmɪneɪt] *vt* contaminare.
contamination [kəntæmɪ'neɪʃən] *n* contaminazione *f*.
cont'd *abbr* (= *continued*) segue.
contemplate ['kɔntəmpleɪt] *vt* contemplare; (*consider*) pensare a (*or* di).
contemplation [kɔntəm'pleɪʃən] *n* contemplazione *f*.
contemporary [kən'tempərərɪ] *adj* contemporaneo(a); (*design*) moderno(a) ♦ *n* contemporaneo/a; (*of the same age*) coetaneo/a.
contempt [kən'tempt] *n* disprezzo; ~ **of court** (*LAW*) oltraggio alla Corte.
contemptible [kən'temptəbl] *adj* spregevole, vergognoso(a).
contemptuous [kən'temptjuəs] *adj* sdegnoso(a).
contend [kən'tend] *vt*: **to** ~ **that** sostenere che ♦ *vi*: **to** ~ **with** lottare contro; **he has a lot to** ~ **with** ha un sacco di guai.
contender [kən'tendə*] *n* contendente *m/f*; concorrente *m/f*.
content [kən'tent] *adj* contento(a), soddisfatto(a) ♦ *vt* contentare, soddisfare ♦ *n* ['kɔntent] contenuto; ~**s** *npl* contenuto; (*of barrel etc: capacity*) capacità *f inv*; (**table of**) ~**s** indice *m*; **to be** ~ **with** essere contento di; **to** ~ **o.s. with sth/with doing sth** accontentarsi di qc/di fare qc.
contented [kən'tentɪd] *adj* contento(a), soddisfatto(a).
contentedly [kən'tentɪdlɪ] *adv* con soddisfazione.
contention [kən'tenʃən] *n* contesa; (*assertion*) tesi *f inv*; **bone of** ~**pomo della discordia.
contentious [kən'tenʃəs] *adj* polemico(a).
contentment [kən'tentmənt] *n* contentezza.
contest *n* ['kɔntest] lotta; (*competition*) gara, concorso ♦ *vt* [kən'test] contestare; (*LAW*) impugnare; (*compete for*) contendere.

contestant [kən'tɛstənt] *n* concorrente *m/f*; (*in fight*) avversario/a.
context ['kɔntɛkst] *n* contesto; **in/out of** ~ nel/fuori dal contesto.
continent ['kɔntɪnənt] *n* continente *m*; **the** C~ (*BRIT*) l'Europa continentale; **on the** C~ in Europa.
continental [kɔntɪ'nɛntl] *adj* continentale ♦ *n* (*BRIT*) abitante *m/f* dell'Europa continentale.
continental breakfast *n* colazione *f* all'europea.
continental quilt *n* (*BRIT*) piumino.
contingency [kən'tɪndʒənsɪ] *n* eventualità *f* *inv*.
contingency plan *n* misura d'emergenza.
contingent [kən'tɪndʒənt] *n* contingenza ♦ *adj*: **to be** ~ **upon** dipendere da.
continual [kən'tɪnjuəl] *adj* continuo(a).
continually [kən'tɪnjuəlɪ] *adv* di continuo.
continuation [kəntɪnju'eɪʃən] *n* continuazione *f*; (*after interruption*) ripresa; (*of story*) seguito.
continue [kən'tɪnjuː] *vi* continuare ♦ *vt* continuare; (*start again*) riprendere; **to be** ~**d** (*story*) continua; **-d on page 10** segue *or* continua a pagina 10.
continuing education [kən'tɪnjuɪŋ-] *n* corsi *mpl* per adulti.
continuity [kɔntɪ'njuːɪtɪ] *n* continuità; (*CINE*) (ordine *m* della) sceneggiatura.
continuity girl *n* (*CINE*) segretaria di edizione.
continuous [kən'tɪnjuəs] *adj* continuo(a), ininterrotto(a); ~ **performance** (*CINE*) spettacolo continuato; ~ **stationery** (*COMPUT*) carta a moduli continui.
continuously [kən'tɪnjuəslɪ] *adv* (*repeatedly*) continuamente; (*uninterruptedly*) ininterrottamente.
contort [kən'tɔːt] *vt* contorcere.
contortion [kən'tɔːʃən] *n* contorcimento; (*of acrobat*) contorsione *f*.
contortionist [kən'tɔːʃənɪst] *n* contorsionista *m/f*.
contour ['kɔntuə*] *n* contorno, profilo; (*also*: ~ **line**) curva di livello.
contraband ['kɔntrəbænd] *n* contrabbando ♦ *adj* di contrabbando.
contraception [kɔntrə'sɛpʃən] *n* contraccezione *f*.
contraceptive [kɔntrə'sɛptɪv] *adj* contraccettivo(a) ♦ *n* contraccettivo.
contract *n* ['kɔntrækt] contratto ♦ *cpd* ['kɔntrækt] (*price, date*) del contratto; (*work*) a contratto ♦ *vi* [kən'trækt] (*COMM*): **to** ~ **to do sth** fare un contratto per fare qc; (*become smaller*) contrarre; **to be**

under ~ **to do sth** aver stipulato un contratto per fare qc; ~ **of employment** contratto di lavoro.
►**contract in** *vi* impegnarsi (con un contratto); (*BRIT ADMIN*) scegliere di pagare i contributi per una pensione.
►**contract out** *vi*: **to** ~ **out (of)** ritirarsi (da); (*BRIT ADMIN*) (*scegliere di*) non pagare i contributi per una pensione.
contraction [kən'trækʃən] *n* contrazione *f*.
contractor [kən'træktə*] *n* imprenditore *m*.
contractual [kən'træktjuəl] *adj* contrattuale.
contradict [kɔntrə'dɪkt] *vt* contraddire.
contradiction [kɔntrə'dɪkʃən] *n* contraddizione *f*; **to be in** ~ **with** discordare con.
contradictory [kɔntrə'dɪktərɪ] *adj* contraddittorio(a).
contralto [kən'træltəu] *n* contralto.
contraption [kən'træpʃən] *n* (*pej*) aggeggio.
contrary ['kɔntrərɪ] *adj* contrario(a); (*unfavourable*) avverso(a), contrario(a); [kən'trɛərɪ] (*perverse*) bisbetico(a) ♦ *n* contrario; **on the** ~ al contrario; **unless you hear to the** ~ a meno che non si disdica; ~ **to what we thought** a differenza di *or* contrariamente a quanto pensavamo.
contrast *n* ['kɔntrɑːst] contrasto ♦ *vt* [kən'trɑːst] mettere in contrasto; **in** ~ **to** *or* **with** a differenza di, contrariamente a.
contrasting [kən'trɑːstɪŋ] *adj* contrastante, di contrasto.
contravene [kɔntrə'viːn] *vt* contravvenire.
contravention [kɔntrə'vɛnʃən] *n*: ~ **(of)** contravvenzione *f* (a), infrazione *f* (di).
contribute [kən'trɪbjuːt] *vi* contribuire ♦ *vt*: **to** ~ **£10/an article** to dare 10 sterline/un articolo a; **to** ~ **to** contribuire a; (*newspaper*) scrivere per; (*discussion*) partecipare a.
contribution [kɔntrɪ'bjuːʃən] *n* contribuzione *f*.
contributor [kən'trɪbjutə*] *n* (*to newspaper*) collaboratore/trice.
contributory [kən'trɪbjutərɪ] *adj* (*cause*) che contribuisce; **it was a** ~ **factor in ...** quello ha contribuito a ....
contributory pension scheme *n* (*BRIT*) sistema di pensionamento finanziato congiuntamente dai contributi del lavoratore e del datore di lavoro.
contrite ['kɔntraɪt] *adj* contrito(a).
contrivance [kən'traɪvəns] *n* congegno; espediente *m*.
contrive [kən'traɪv] *vt* inventare;

escogitare ♦ *vi*: **to ~ to do** fare in modo di fare.

control [kən'trəul] *vt* dominare; (*firm, operation etc*) dirigere; (*check*) controllare; (*disease, fire*) arginare, limitare ♦ *n* controllo; **~s** *npl* comandi *mpl*; **to take ~ of** assumere il controllo di; **to be in ~ of** aver autorità su; essere responsabile di; controllare; **to ~ o.s.** controllarsi; **everything is under ~** tutto è sotto controllo; **the car went out of ~** la macchina non rispondeva ai comandi; **circumstances beyond our ~** circostanze *fpl* che non dipendono da noi.

control key *n* (*COMPUT*) tasto di controllo.

controlled substance [kən'trəuld-] *n* sostanza stupefacente.

controller [kən'trəulə*] *n* controllore *m*.

controlling interest [kən'trəuliŋ-] *n* (*COMM*) maggioranza delle azioni.

control panel *n* (*on aircraft, ship, TV etc*) quadro dei comandi.

control point *n* punto di controllo.

control room *n* (*NAUT*, *MIL*) sala di comando; (*RADIO, TV*) sala di regia.

control tower *n* (*AVIAT*) torre *f* di controllo.

control unit *n* (*COMPUT*) unità *f inv* di controllo.

controversial [kɔntrə'vəːʃl] *adj* controverso(a), polemico(a).

controversy ['kɔntrəvəːsɪ] *n* controversia, polemica.

conurbation [kɔnəː'beɪʃən] *n* conurbazione *f*.

convalesce [kɔnvə'lɛs] *vi* rimettersi in salute.

convalescence [kɔnvə'lɛsns] *n* convalescenza.

convalescent [kɔnvə'lɛsnt] *adj, n* convalescente (*m/f*).

convector [kən'vɛktə*] *n* convettore *m*.

convene [kən'viːn] *vt* convocare; (*meeting*) organizzare ♦ *vi* convenire, adunarsi.

convenience [kən'viːnɪəns] *n* comodità *f inv*; **at your ~** a suo comodo; **at your earliest ~** (*COMM*) appena possibile; **all modern ~s**, (*BRIT*) **all mod cons** tutte le comodità moderne.

convenience foods *npl* cibi *mpl* precotti.

convenient [kən'viːnɪənt] *adj* conveniente, comodo(a); **if it is ~ to you** se per lei va bene, se non la incomoda.

conveniently [kən'viːnɪəntlɪ] *adv* (*happen*) a proposito; (*situated*) in un posto comodo.

convent ['kɔnvənt] *n* convento.

convention [kən'vɛnʃən] *n* convenzione *f*; (*meeting*) convegno.

conventional [kən'vɛnʃənl] *adj* convenzionale.

convent school *n* scuola retta da suore.

converge [kən'vəːdʒ] *vi* convergere.

conversant [kən'vəːsnt] *adj*: **to be ~ with** essere al corrente di; essere pratico(a) di.

conversation [kɔnvə'seɪʃən] *n* conversazione *f*.

conversational [kɔnvə'seɪʃənl] *adj* non formale; (*COMPUT*) conversazionale; **~ Italian** l'italiano parlato.

conversationalist [kɔnvə'seɪʃnəlɪst] *n* conversatore/trice.

converse *n* ['kɔnvəːs] contrario, opposto ♦ *vi* [kən'vəːs]: **to ~ (with sb about sth)** conversare (con qn su qc).

conversely [kɔn'vəːslɪ] *adv* al contrario

conversion [kən'vəːʃən] *n* conversione *f*; (*BRIT: of house*) trasformazione *f*, rimodernamento.

conversion table *n* tavola di equivalenze.

convert *vt* [kən'vəːt] (*REL, COMM*) convertire; (*alter*) trasformare ♦ *n* ['kɔnvəːt] convertito/a.

convertible [kən'vəːtəbl] *n* macchina decappottabile.

convex ['kɔnvɛks] *adj* convesso(a).

convey [kən'veɪ] *vt* trasportare; (*thanks*) comunicare; (*idea*) dare.

conveyance [kən'veɪəns] *n* (*of goods*) trasporto; (*vehicle*) mezzo di trasporto.

conveyancing [kən'veɪənsɪŋ] *n* (*LAW*) redazione *f* di transazioni di proprietà.

conveyor belt *n* nastro trasportatore.

convict *vt* [kən'vɪkt] dichiarare colpevole ♦ *n* ['kɔnvɪkt] carcerato/a.

conviction [kən'vɪkʃən] *n* condanna; (*belief*) convinzione *f*.

convince [kən'vɪns] *vt*: **to ~ sb (of sth/that)** convincere qn (di qc/che).

convincing [kən'vɪnsɪŋ] *adj* convincente.

convincingly [kən'vɪnsɪŋlɪ] *adv* in modo convincente.

convivial [kən'vɪvɪəl] *adj* allegro(a).

convoluted ['kɔnvəluːtɪd] *adj* (*shape*) attorcigliato(a), avvolto(a); (*argument*) involuto(a).

convoy ['kɔnvɔɪ] *n* convoglio.

convulse [kən'vʌls] *vt* sconvolgere; **to be ~d with laughter** contorcersi dalle risa.

convulsion [kən'vʌlʃən] *n* convulsione *f*.

coo [kuː] *vi* tubare.

cook [kuk] *vt* cucinare, cuocere; (*meal*) preparare ♦ *vi* cuocere; (*person*) cucinare ♦ *n* cuoco/a.

►**cook up** *vt* (*col: excuse, story*) improvvisare, inventare.

cookbook ['kukbuk] n = **cookery book**.
cooker ['kukə*] n fornello, cucina.
cookery book n (BRIT) libro di cucina.
cookie ['kukı] n (US) biscotto.
cooking ['kukıŋ] n cucina ♦ cpd (apples, chocolate) da cuocere; (utensils, salt, foil) da cucina.
cookout ['kukaut] n (US) pranzo (cucinato) all'aperto.
cool [ku:l] adj fresco(a); (not afraid) calmo(a); (unfriendly) freddo(a); (impertinent) sfacciato(a) ♦ vt raffreddare, rinfrescare ♦ vi raffreddarsi, rinfrescarsi; **it's ~** (weather) fa fresco; **to keep sth ~** or **in a ~ place** tenere qc in fresco.
▶**cool down** vi raffreddarsi; (fig: person, situation) calmarsi.
coolant ['ku:lənt] n (liquido) refrigerante m.
cool box, (US) **cooler** ['ku:lə*] n borsa termica.
cooling ['ku:lıŋ] adj (breeze) fresco(a).
cooling tower n torre f di raffreddamento.
coolly ['ku:lı] adv (calmly) con calma, tranquillamente; (audaciously) come se niente fosse; (unenthusiastically) freddamente.
coolness ['ku:lnıs] n freschezza; sangue m freddo, calma.
coop [ku:p] n stia ♦ vt: **to ~ up** (fig) rinchiudere.
co-op ['kəuɔp] n abbr (= cooperative (society)) coop f.
cooperate [kəu'ɔpəreıt] vi cooperare, collaborare.
cooperation [kəuɔpə'reıʃən] n cooperazione f, collaborazione f.
cooperative [kəu'ɔpərətıv] adj cooperativo(a) ♦ n cooperativa.
coopt [kəu'ɔpt] vt: **to ~ sb into sth** cooptare qn per qc.
coordinate vt [kəu'ɔ:dıneıt] coordinare ♦ n [kəu'ɔ:dınət] (MATH) coordinata; **~s** npl (clothes) coordinati mpl.
coordination [kəuɔ:dı'neıʃən] n coordinazione f.
coot [ku:t] n folaga.
co-ownership [kəu'əunəʃıp] n comproprietà.
cop [kɔp] n (col) sbirro.
cope [kəup] vi farcela; **to ~ with** (problems) far fronte a.
Copenhagen [kəupən'heıgən] n Copenhagen f.
copier ['kɔpıə*] n (also: **photo~**) (foto)copiatrice f.

co-pilot ['kəupaılət] n secondo pilota m.
copious ['kəupıəs] adj copioso(a), abbondante.
copper ['kɔpə*] n rame m; (col: policeman) sbirro; **~s** npl spiccioli mpl.
coppice ['kɔpıs], **copse** [kɔps] n bosco ceduo.
copulate ['kɔpjuleıt] vi accoppiarsi.
copy ['kɔpı] n copia; (book etc) esemplare m; (material: for printing) materiale m, testo ♦ vt (gen, COMPUT) copiare; (imitate) imitare; **rough/fair ~** brutta/bella (copia); **to make good ~** (fig) fare notizia.
▶**copy out** vt ricopiare, trascrivere.
copycat ['kɔpıkæt] n (pej) copione m.
copyright ['kɔpıraıt] n diritto d'autore; **~ reserved** tutti i diritti riservati.
copy typist n dattilografo/a.
copywriter ['kɔpıraıtə*] n redattore m pubblicitario.
coral ['kɔrəl] n corallo.
coral reef n barriera corallina.
Coral Sea n: **the ~** il mar dei Coralli.
cord [kɔ:d] n corda; (ELEC) filo; (fabric) velluto a coste; **~s** npl (trousers) calzoni mpl (di velluto) a coste.
cordial ['kɔ:dıəl] adj, n cordiale (m).
cordless ['kɔ:dlıs] adj senza cavo.
cordon ['kɔ:dn] n cordone m.
▶**cordon off** vt fare cordone intorno a.
corduroy ['kɔ:dərɔı] n fustagno.
CORE [kɔ:*] n abbr (US) = Congress of Racial Equality.
core [kɔ:*] n (of fruit) torsolo; (TECH) centro; (of earth, nuclear reactor) nucleo; (of problem etc) cuore m, nocciolo ♦ vt estrarre il torsolo da; **rotten to the ~** marcio fino al midollo.
Corfu [kɔ:'fu:] n Corfù f.
coriander [kɔrı'ændə*] n coriandolo.
cork [kɔ:k] n sughero; (of bottle) tappo.
corkage ['kɔ:kıdʒ] n somma da pagare se il cliente porta il proprio vino.
corked [kɔ:kt], (US) **corky** ['kɔ:kı] adj (wine) che sa di tappo.
corkscrew ['kɔ:kskru:] n cavatappi m inv.
cormorant ['kɔ:mərnt] n cormorano.
Corn abbr (BRIT) = **Cornwall**.
corn [kɔ:n] n (BRIT: wheat) grano; (US: maize) granturco; (on foot) callo; **~ on the cob** (CULIN) pannocchia cotta.
cornea ['kɔ:nıə] n cornea.
corned beef ['kɔ:nd-] n carne f di manzo in scatola.
corner ['kɔ:nə*] n angolo; (AUT) curva; (FOOTBALL: also: **~ kick**) corner m inv, calcio d'angolo ♦ vt intrappolare; mettere con le spalle al muro; (COMM: market)

accaparrare ♦ *vi* prendere una curva; **to cut** ~**s** (*fig*) prendere una scorciatoia.

corner flag *n* (*FOOTBALL*) bandierina d'angolo.

corner kick *n* (*FOOTBALL*) calcio d'angolo.

cornerstone ['kɔːnəstəun] *n* pietra angolare.

cornet ['kɔːnɪt] *n* (*MUS*) cornetta; (*BRIT: of ice-cream*) cono.

cornflakes ['kɔːnfleɪks] *npl* fiocchi *mpl* di granturco.

cornflour ['kɔːnflauə*] *n* (*BRIT*) ≈ fecola di patate.

cornice ['kɔːnɪs] *n* cornicione *m*; cornice *f*.

Cornish ['kɔːnɪʃ] *adj* della Cornovaglia.

corn oil *n* olio di mais.

cornstarch ['kɔːnstɑːtʃ] *n* (*US*) = **cornflour**.

cornucopia [kɔːnjuːkəupɪə] *n* grande abbondanza.

Cornwall ['kɔːnwəl] *n* Cornovaglia.

corny ['kɔːnɪ] *adj* (*col*) trito(a).

corollary [kəˈrɔlərɪ] *n* corollario.

coronary ['kɔrənərɪ] *n*: ~ **(thrombosis)** trombosi *f* coronaria.

coronation [kɔrəˈneɪʃən] *n* incoronazione *f*.

coroner ['kɔrənə*] *n magistrato incaricato di indagare la causa di morte in circostanze sospette.*

coronet ['kɔrənɪt] *n* diadema *m*.

Corp. *abbr* = **corporation**.

corporal ['kɔːpərl] *n* caporalmaggiore *m* ♦ *adj*: ~ **punishment** pena corporale.

corporate ['kɔːpərɪt] *adj* comune; (*COMM*) costituito(a) (in corporazione).

corporate hospitality *n* omaggi *mpl* ai clienti (*come biglietti per spettacoli, cene etc*).

corporate identity, corporate image *n* (*of organization*) immagine *f* di marca.

corporation [kɔːpəˈreɪʃən] *n* (*of town*) consiglio comunale; (*COMM*) ente *m*.

corporation tax *n* ≈ imposta societaria.

corps [kɔː*], *pl* **corps** [kɔːz] *n* corpo; **press** ~ ufficio *m* stampa *inv*.

corpse [kɔːps] *n* cadavere *m*.

corpuscle ['kɔːpʌsl] *n* corpuscolo.

corral [kəˈrɑːl] *n* recinto.

correct [kəˈrɛkt] *adj* (*accurate*) corretto(a), esatto(a); (*proper*) corretto(a) ♦ *vt* correggere; **you are** ~ ha ragione.

correction [kəˈrɛkʃən] *n* correzione *f*.

correlate ['kɔrɪleɪt] *vt* mettere in correlazione ♦ *vi*: **to** ~ **with** essere in rapporto con.

correlation [kɔrɪˈleɪʃən] *n* correlazione *f*.

correspond [kɔrɪsˈpɔnd] *vi* corrispondere.

correspondence [kɔrɪsˈpɔndəns] *n* corrispondenza.

correspondence course *n* corso per corrispondenza.

correspondent [kɔrɪsˈpɔndənt] *n* corrispondente *m/f*.

corridor ['kɔrɪdɔː*] *n* corridoio.

corroborate [kəˈrɔbəreɪt] *vt* corroborare, confermare.

corrode [kəˈrəud] *vt* corrodere ♦ *vi* corrodersi.

corrosion [kəˈrəuʒən] *n* corrosione *f*.

corrosive [kəˈrəuzɪv] *adj* corrosivo(a).

corrugated ['kɔrəgeɪtɪd] *adj* increspato(a); ondulato(a).

corrugated iron *n* lamiera di ferro ondulata.

corrupt [kəˈrʌpt] *adj* corrotto(a) ♦ *vt* corrompere; ~ **practices** (*dishonesty, bribery*) pratiche *fpl* illecite.

corruption [kəˈrʌpʃən] *n* corruzione *f*.

corset ['kɔːsɪt] *n* busto.

Corsica ['kɔːsɪkə] *n* Corsica.

Corsican ['kɔːsɪkən] *adj*, *n* corso(a).

cortège [kɔːˈteɪʒ] *n* corteo.

cortisone ['kɔːtɪzəun] *n* cortisone *m*.

coruscating ['kɔrəskeɪtɪŋ] *adj* scintillante.

c.o.s. *abbr* (= *cash on shipment*) pagamento alla spedizione.

cosh [kɔʃ] *n* (*BRIT*) randello (corto).

cosignatory [kəuˈsɪgnətərɪ] *n* cofirmatario/a.

cosiness ['kəuzɪnɪs] *n* intimità.

cos lettuce ['kɔs-] *n* lattuga romana.

cosmetic [kɔzˈmɛtɪk] *n* cosmetico ♦ *adj* (*preparation*) cosmetico(a); (*surgery*) estetico(a); (*fig: reforms*) ornamentale.

cosmic ['kɔzmɪk] *adj* cosmico(a).

cosmonaut ['kɔzmənɔːt] *n* cosmonauta *m/f*.

cosmopolitan [kɔzməˈpɔlɪtn] *adj* cosmopolita.

cosmos ['kɔzmɔs] *n* cosmo.

cosset ['kɔsɪt] *vt* vezzeggiare.

cost [kɔst] *n* costo ♦ *vb* (*pt*, *pp* **cost**) *vi* costare ♦ *vt* stabilire il prezzo di; ~**s** *npl* (*LAW*) spese *fpl*; **it** ~**s £5/too much** costa 5 sterline/troppo; **it** ~ **him his life/job** gli costò la vita/il suo lavoro; **how much does it** ~? quanto costa?, quanto viene?; **what will it** ~ **to have it repaired?** quanto costerà farlo riparare?; ~ **of living** costo della vita; **at all** ~**s** a ogni costo.

cost accountant *n* analizzatore *m* dei costi.

co-star ['kəustɑː*] *n attore/trice della stessa importanza del protagonista.*

Costa Rica ['kɔstəˈriːkə] *n* Costa Rica.

cost centre *n* centro di costo.

cost control *n* controllo dei costi.

cost-effective ['kɔstɪˈfɛktɪv] *adj* (*gen*)

conveniente, economico(a); (*COMM*) redditizio(a), conveniente.

cost-effectiveness ['kɔstɪ'fɛktɪvnɪs] *n* convenienza.

costing ['kɔstɪŋ] *n* (determinazione *f* dei) costi *mpl*.

costly ['kɔstlɪ] *adj* costoso(a), caro(a).

cost-of-living ['kɔstəv'lɪvɪŋ] *adj*: ~ **allowance** indennità *f inv* di contingenza; ~ **index** indice *m* della scala mobile.

cost price *n* (*BRIT*) prezzo all'ingrosso.

costume ['kɔstjuːm] *n* costume *m*; (*lady's suit*) tailleur *m inv*; (*BRIT*: *also*: **swimming** ~) costume da bagno.

costume jewellery *n* bigiotteria.

cosy, (*US*) **cozy** ['kəuzɪ] *adj* intimo(a); (*room, atmosphere*) accogliente.

cot [kɔt] *n* (*BRIT*: *child's*) lettino; (*US*: *folding bed*) brandina.

cot death *n* improvvisa e inspiegabile morte nel sonno di un neonato.

Cotswolds ['kɔtswəuldz] *npl*: **the** ~ *zona* collinare del Gloucestershire.

cottage ['kɔtɪdʒ] *n* cottage *m inv*.

cottage cheese *n* fiocchi *mpl* di latte magro.

cottage industry *n* industria artigianale basata sul lavoro a cottimo.

cottage pie *n* piatto a base di carne macinata in sugo e purè di patate.

cotton ['kɔtn] *n* cotone *m*; ~ **dress** *etc* vestito *etc* di cotone.

▶ **cotton on** *vi* (*col*): **to** ~ **on (to sth)** afferrare (qc).

cotton wool *n* (*BRIT*) cotone *m* idrofilo.

couch [kautʃ] *n* sofà *m inv*; (*in doctor's surgery*) lettino ♦ *vt* esprimere.

couchette [kuː'ʃɛt] *n* cuccetta.

couch potato *n* (*col*) pigrone/a teledipendente.

cough [kɔf] *vi* tossire ♦ *n* tosse *f*.

cough drop *n* pasticca per la tosse.

cough mixture, cough syrup *n* sciroppo per la tosse.

could [kud] *pt of* **can**.

couldn't ['kudnt] = **could not**.

council ['kaunsl] *n* consiglio; **city** *or* **town** ~ consiglio comunale; **C~ of Europe** Consiglio d'Europa.

council estate *n* (*BRIT*) quartiere *m* di case popolari.

council house *n* (*BRIT*) casa popolare.

council housing *n* alloggi *mpl* popolari.

councillor ['kaunsələ*] *n* consigliere/a.

council tax *n* (*BRIT*) tassa comunale sulla proprietà.

counsel ['kaunsl] *n* avvocato; consultazione *f* ♦ *vt*: **to** ~ **sth/sb to do sth** consigliare

qc/a qn di fare qc; ~ **for the defence/the prosecution** avvocato difensore/di parte civile.

counsellor, (*US*) **counselor** ['kaunslə*] *n* consigliere/a; (*US*: *lawyer*) avvocato/essa.

count [kaunt] *vt, vi* contare ♦ *n* conto; (*nobleman*) conte *m*; **to** ~ **(up) to 10** contare fino a 10; **to** ~ **the cost of** calcolare il costo di; **not** ~**ing the children** senza contare i bambini; **10** ~**ing him** 10 compreso lui; ~ **yourself lucky** considerati fortunato; **it** ~**s for very little** non conta molto, non ha molta importanza; **to keep** ~ **of sth** tenere il conto di qc.

▶ **count on** *vt fus* contare su; **to** ~ **on doing sth** contare di fare qc.

▶ **count up** *vt* addizionare.

countdown ['kauntdaun] *n* conto alla rovescia.

countenance ['kauntɪnəns] *n* volto, aspetto ♦ *vt* approvare.

counter ['kauntə*] *n* banco; (*position: in post office, bank*) sportello; (*in game*) gettone *m*; (*TECH*) contatore *m* ♦ *vt* opporsi a; (*blow*) parare ♦ *adv*: ~ **to** contro; in opposizione a; **to buy under the** ~ (*fig*) comprare sottobanco; **to** ~ **sth with sth/by doing sth** rispondere a qc con qc/facendo qc.

counteract [kauntər'ækt] *vt* agire in opposizione a; (*poison etc*) annullare gli effetti di.

counterattack ['kauntərətæk] *n* contrattacco ♦ *vi* contrattaccare.

counterbalance ['kauntəbæləns] *vt* contrappesare.

counter-clockwise ['kauntə'klɔkwaɪz] *adv* in senso antiorario.

counter-espionage [kauntər'ɛspɪənɑːʒ] *n* controspionaggio.

counterfeit ['kauntəfɪt] *n* contraffazione *f*, falso ♦ *vt* contraffare, falsificare ♦ *adj* falso(a).

counterfoil ['kauntəfɔɪl] *n* matrice *f*.

counterintelligence ['kauntərɪn'tɛlɪdʒəns] *n* = **counter-espionage**.

countermand ['kauntəmɑːnd] *vt* annullare.

countermeasure ['kauntəmɛʒə*] *n* contromisura.

counteroffensive ['kauntərə'fɛnsɪv] *n* controffensiva.

counterpane ['kauntəpeɪn] *n* copriletto *m inv*.

counterpart ['kauntəpɑːt] *n* (*of document etc*) copia; (*of person*) corrispondente *m/f*.

counterproductive ['kauntəprə'dʌktɪv] *adj* controproducente.

countersign ['kauntəsaın] *vt* controfirmare.
countersink ['kauntəsıŋk] *vt* (*hole*) svasare.
countess ['kauntıs] *n* contessa.
countless ['kauntlıs] *adj* innumerevole.
countrified ['kʌntrıfaıd] *adj* rustico(a)
country ['kʌntrı] *n* paese *m*; (*native land*) patria; (*as opposed to town*) campagna; (*region*) regione *f*; **in the** ~ in campagna; **mountainous** ~ territorio montagnoso.
country and western (music) *n* musica country e western, country *m*.
country dancing *n* (*BRIT*) danza popolare.
country house *n* villa in campagna.
countryman ['kʌntrımən] *n* (*national*) compatriota *m*; (*rural*) contadino.
countryside ['kʌntrısaıd] *n* campagna.
country-wide ['kʌntrı'waıd] *adj* diffuso(a) in tutto il paese ♦ *adv* in tutto il paese.
county ['kauntı] *n* contea.
county council *n* (*BRIT*) consiglio di contea.
county town *n* (*BRIT*) capoluogo.
coup, ~**s** [ku:, -z] *n* (*also:* ~ **d'état**) colpo di Stato; (*triumph*) bel colpo.
coupé [ku:'peı] *n* coupé *m inv*.
couple ['kʌpl] *n* coppia ♦ *vt* (*carriages*) agganciare; (*TECH*) accoppiare; (*ideas, names*) associare; **a** ~ **of** un paio di.
couplet ['kʌplıt] *n* distico.
coupling ['kʌplıŋ] *n* (*RAIL*) agganciamento.
coupon ['ku:pɔn] *n* (*voucher*) buono; (*COMM*) coupon *m inv*.
courage ['kʌrıdʒ] *n* coraggio.
courageous [kə'reıdʒəs] *adj* coraggioso(a).
courgette [kuə'ʒet] *n* (*BRIT*) zucchina.
courier ['kurıə*] *n* corriere *m*; (*for tourists*) guida.
course [kɔ:s] *n* corso; (*of ship*) rotta; (*for golf*) campo; (*part of meal*) piatto; **first** ~ primo piatto; **of** ~ *adv* senz'altro, naturalmente; **(no) of** ~ **not!** certo che no!, no di certo!; **in the** ~ **of the next few days** nel corso dei prossimi giorni; **in due** ~ a tempo debito; ~ **(of action)** modo d'agire; **the best** ~ **would be to** ... la cosa migliore sarebbe ...; **we have no other** ~ **but to** ... non possiamo far altro che ...; ~ **of lectures** corso di lezioni; **a** ~ **of treatment** (*MED*) una cura.
court [kɔ:t] *n* corte *f*; (*TENNIS*) campo ♦ *vt* (*woman*) fare la corte a; (*fig: favour, popularity*) cercare di conquistare; (: *death, disaster*) sfiorare, rasentare; **out of** ~ (*LAW: settle*) in via amichevole; **to take to** ~ citare in tribunale; **C**~ **of Appeal** corte d'appello.
courteous ['kɔ:tıəs] *adj* cortese.
courtesan [kɔ:tı'zæn] *n* cortigiana.

courtesy ['kə:təsı] *n* cortesia; **by** ~ **of** per gentile concessione di.
courtesy bus *n* navetta gratuita (*di hotel, aeroporto*).
courtesy car *n* vettura sostitutiva.
courtesy light *n* (*AUT*) luce *f* interna.
court-house ['kɔ:thaus] *n* (*US*) palazzo di giustizia.
courtier ['kɔ:tıə*] *n* cortigiano/a.
courtmartial, pl courtsmartial ['kɔ:t'mɑ:ʃəl] *n* corte *f* marziale.
courtroom ['kɔ:trum] *n* tribunale *m*.
court shoe *n* scarpa *f* décolleté *inv*.
courtyard ['kɔ:tjɑ:d] *n* cortile *m*.
cousin ['kʌzn] *n* cugino/a.
cove [kəuv] *n* piccola baia.
covenant ['kʌvənənt] *n* accordo ♦ *vt*: **to** ~ **to do sth** impegnarsi (per iscritto) a fare qc.
Coventry ['kɔvəntrı] *n*: **to send sb to** ~ (*fig*) dare l'ostracismo a qn.
cover ['kʌvə*] *vt* (*gen*) coprire; (*distance*) coprire, percorrere; (*PRESS: report on*) fare un servizio su ♦ *n* (*of pan*) coperchio; (*over furniture*) fodera; (*of book*) copertina; (*shelter*) riparo; (*COMM, INSURANCE*) copertura; **to take** ~ mettersi al coperto; **under** ~ al riparo; **under** ~ **of darkness** protetto dall'oscurità; **under separate** ~ (*COMM*) a parte, in plico separato; **£10 will** ~ **everything** 10 sterline saranno sufficienti.
►**cover up** *vt* (*child, object*): **to** ~ **up (with)** coprire (di); (*fig: hide: truth, facts*) nascondere ♦ *vi*: **to** ~ **up for sb** (*fig*) coprire qn.
coverage ['kʌvərıdʒ] *n* (*PRESS, TV, RADIO*): **to give full** ~ **to** fare un ampio servizio su.
coveralls ['kʌvərɔ:lz] *npl* (*US*) tuta.
cover charge *n* coperto.
covering ['kʌvərıŋ] *n* copertura.
covering letter, (*US*) **cover letter** *n* lettera d'accompagnamento.
cover note *n* (*INSURANCE*) polizza (di assicurazione) provvisoria.
cover price *n* prezzo di copertina.
covert ['kʌvət] *adj* nascosto(a); (*glance*) di sottecchi, furtivo(a).
cover-up ['kʌvərʌp] *n* occultamento (di informazioni).
covet ['kʌvıt] *vt* bramare.
cow [kau] *n* vacca ♦ *cpd* femmina ♦ *vt* intimidire; ~ **elephant** *n* elefantessa.
cowardice ['kauədıs] *n* vigliaccheria.
cowardly ['kauədlı] *adj* vigliacco(a).
cowboy ['kaubɔı] *n* cow-boy *m inv*.
cower ['kauə*] *vi* acquattarsi.

cowshed ['kauʃɛd] n stalla.
cowslip ['kauslɪp] n (BOT) primula (odorata).
coxswain ['kɔksn] n (abbr: **cox**) timoniere m.
coy [kɔɪ] adj falsamente timido(a).
coyote [kɔɪ'əutɪ] n coyote m inv.
cozy ['kəuzɪ] adj (US) = **cosy**.
CP n abbr (= Communist Party) P.C. m.
cp. abbr (= compare) cfr.
c/p abbr (BRIT) = **carriage paid**.
CPA n abbr (US) see **certified public accountant**.
CPI n abbr (US: = Consumer Price Index) indice dei prezzi al consumo.
Cpl. abbr = **corporal**.
CP/M n abbr (= Control Program for Microcomputers) CP/M m.
c.p.s. abbr (= characters per second) c.p.s.
CPSA n abbr (BRIT: = Civil and Public Services Association) sindacato dei servizi pubblici.
CPU n abbr see **central processing unit**.
cr. abbr = **credit; creditor**.
crab [kræb] n granchio.
crab apple n mela selvatica.
crack [kræk] n (split, slit) fessura, crepa; incrinatura; (noise) schiocco; (: of gun) scoppio; (joke) battuta; (col: attempt): **to have a ~ at sth** tentare qc; (DRUGS) crack m inv ♦ vt spaccare; incrinare; (whip) schioccare; (nut) schiacciare; (case, mystery: solve) risolvere; (code) decifrare ♦ cpd (athlete) di prim'ordine; **to ~ jokes** (col) dire battute, scherzare; **to get ~ing** (col) darsi una mossa.
▶**crack down on** vt fus prendere serie misure contro, porre freno a.
▶**crack up** vi crollare.
crackdown ['krækdaun] n repressione f.
cracked [krækt] adj (col) matto(a).
cracker ['krækə*] n cracker m inv; (firework) petardo; (Christmas ~) mortaretto natalizio (con sorpresa); **a ~ of a ...** (BRIT col) un(a) ... formidabile; **he's ~s** (BRIT col) è tocco.
crackle ['krækl] vi crepitare.
crackling ['kræklɪŋ] n crepitio; (on radio, telephone) disturbo; (of pork) cotenna croccante (del maiale).
crackpot ['krækpɔt] n (col) imbecille m/f con idee assurde, assurdo/a.
cradle ['kreɪdl] n culla ♦ vt (child) tenere fra le braccia; (object) reggere tra le braccia.
craft [krɑ:ft] n mestiere m; (cunning) astuzia; (boat) naviglio.
craftsman ['krɑ:ftsmən] n artigiano.
craftsmanship ['krɑ:ftsmənʃɪp] n abilità.

crafty ['krɑ:ftɪ] adj furbo(a), astuto(a).
crag [kræg] n roccia.
cram [kræm] vt (fill): **to ~ sth with** riempire qc di; (put): **to ~ sth into** stipare qc in.
cramming ['kræmɪŋ] n (fig: pej) sgobbare m.
cramp [kræmp] n crampo ♦ vt soffocare, impedire.
cramped [kræmpt] adj ristretto(a).
crampon ['kræmpən] n (CLIMBING) rampone m.
cranberry ['krænbərɪ] n mirtillo.
crane [kreɪn] n gru f inv ♦ vt, vi: **to ~ forward, to ~ one's neck** allungare il collo.
cranium, pl crania ['kreɪnɪəm, 'kreɪnɪə] n cranio.
crank [kræŋk] n manovella; (person) persona stramba.
crankshaft ['kræŋkʃɑ:ft] n albero a gomiti.
cranky ['kræŋkɪ] adj eccentrico(a); (bad-tempered): **to be ~** avere i nervi.
cranny ['krænɪ] n see **nook**.
crap [kræp] n (col!) fesserie fpl; **to have a ~** cacare (!).
crappy ['kræpɪ] adj (col) di merda (!).
crash [kræʃ] n fragore m; (of car) incidente m; (of plane) caduta; (of business) fallimento; (STOCK EXCHANGE) crollo ♦ vt fracassare ♦ vi (plane) fracassarsi; (car) avere un incidente; (two cars) scontrarsi; (fig) fallire, andare in rovina; **to ~ into** scontrarsi con; **he ~ed the car into a wall** andò a sbattere contro un muro con la macchina.
crash barrier n (BRIT AUT) guardrail m inv.
crash course n corso intensivo.
crash helmet n casco.
crash landing n atterraggio di fortuna.
crass [kræs] adj crasso(a).
crate [kreɪt] n gabbia.
crater ['kreɪtə*] n cratere m.
cravat(e) [krə'væt] n fazzoletto da collo.
crave [kreɪv] vi: **to ~ for** desiderare ardentemente.
craving ['kreɪvɪŋ] n: **~ (for)** (for food, cigarettes etc) (gran) voglia (di).
crawl [krɔ:l] vi strisciare carponi; (child) andare a gattoni; (vehicle) avanzare lentamente ♦ n (SWIMMING) crawl m; **to ~ to sb** (col: suck up) arruffianarsi qn.
crawler lane ['krɔ:lə*-] n (BRIT AUT) corsia riservata al traffico lento.
crayfish ['kreɪfɪʃ] n (pl inv) gambero (d'acqua dolce).
crayon ['kreɪən] n matita colorata.
craze [kreɪz] n mania.
crazed [kreɪzd] adj (look, person) folle, pazzo(a); (pottery, glaze) incrinato(a).

crazy ['kreɪzɪ] *adj* matto(a); **to go** ~ uscir di senno, impazzire; **to be** ~ **about sb** (*col: keen*) essere pazzo di qn; **to be** ~ **about sth** andare matto per qc.
crazy paving *n* (*BRIT*) lastricato a mosaico irregolare.
creak [kriːk] *vi* cigolare, scricchiolare.
cream [kriːm] *n* crema; (*fresh*) panna ♦ *adj* (*colour*) color crema *inv*; **whipped** ~ panna montata.
▶**cream off** *vt* (*best talents, part of profits*) portarsi via.
cream cake *n* torta alla panna.
cream cheese *n* formaggio fresco.
creamery ['kriːmərɪ] *n* (*shop*) latteria; (*factory*) caseificio.
creamy ['kriːmɪ] *adj* cremoso(a).
crease [kriːs] *n* grinza; (*deliberate*) piega ♦ *vt* sgualcire ♦ *vi* sgualcirsi.
crease-resistant ['kriːsrɪzɪstənt] *adj* ingualcibile.
create [kriːˈeɪt] *vt* creare; (*fuss, noise*) fare.
creation [kriːˈeɪʃən] *n* creazione *f*.
creative [kriːˈeɪtɪv] *adj* creativo(a).
creativity [kriːeɪˈtɪvɪtɪ] *n* creatività.
creator [kriːˈeɪtə*] *n* creatore/trice.
creature ['kriːtʃə*] *n* creatura.
crèche, creche [krɛʃ] *n* asilo infantile.
credence ['kriːdns] *n* credenza, fede *f*.
credentials [krɪˈdɛnʃlz] *npl* (*papers*) credenziali *fpl*; (*letters of reference*) referenze *fpl*.
credibility [krɛdɪˈbɪlɪtɪ] *n* credibilità.
credible ['krɛdɪbl] *adj* credibile; (*witness, source*) attendibile.
credit ['krɛdɪt] *n* credito; onore *m*; (*SCOL: esp US*) *certificato del compimento di una parte del corso universitario* ♦ *vt* (*COMM*) accreditare; (*believe: also:* **give** ~ **to**) credere, prestar fede a; **to** ~ **£5 to sb** accreditare 5 sterline a qn; **to** ~ **sb with sth** (*fig*) attribuire qc a qn; **on** ~ a credito; **to one's** ~ a proprio onore; **to take the** ~ **for** farsi il merito di; **to be in** ~ (*person*) essere creditore(trice); (*bank account*) essere coperto(a); **he's a** ~ **to his family** fa onore alla sua famiglia; *see also* **credits**.
creditable ['krɛdɪtəbl] *adj* che fa onore, degno(a) di lode.
credit account *n* conto di credito.
credit agency *n* (*BRIT*) agenzia di analisi di credito.
credit balance *n* saldo attivo.
credit bureau *n* (*US*) agenzia di analisi di credito.
credit card *n* carta di credito.
credit control *n* controllo dei crediti.

credit facilities *npl* agevolazioni *fpl* creditizie.
credit limit *n* limite *m* di credito.
credit note *n* (*BRIT*) nota di credito.
creditor ['krɛdɪtə*] *n* creditore/trice.
credits ['krɛdɪts] *npl* (*CINE*) titoli *mpl*.
credit transfer *n* bancogiro, postagiro.
creditworthy ['krɛdɪt'wəːðɪ] *adj* autorizzabile al credito.
credulity [krɪˈdjuːlɪtɪ] *n* credulità.
creed [kriːd] *n* credo; dottrina.
creek [kriːk] *n* insenatura; (*US*) piccolo fiume *m*.
creel ['kriːl] *n* cestino per il pesce; (*also:* **lobster** ~) nassa.
creep [kriːp] *vi* (*pt, pp* **crept** [krɛpt]) avanzare furtivamente (*or* pian piano); (*plant*) arrampicarsi ♦ *n* (*col*): **he's a** ~ è un tipo viscido; **it gives me the** ~**s** (*col*) mi fa venire la pelle d'oca; **to** ~ **up on sb** avvicinarsi quatto quatto a qn; (*fig: old age etc*) cogliere qn alla sprovvista.
creeper ['kriːpə*] *n* pianta rampicante.
creepers ['kriːpəz] *npl* (*US: rompers*) tutina.
creepy ['kriːpɪ] *adj* (*frightening*) che fa accapponare la pelle.
creepy-crawly ['kriːpɪ'krɔːlɪ] *n* (*col*) bestiolina, insetto.
cremate [krɪˈmeɪt] *vt* cremare.
cremation [krɪˈmeɪʃən] *n* cremazione *f*.
crematorium, *pl* **crematoria** [krɛməˈtɔːrɪəm, -ˈtɔːrɪə] *n* forno crematorio.
creosote ['krɪəsəut] *n* creosoto.
crêpe [kreɪp] *n* crespo.
crêpe bandage *n* (*BRIT*) fascia elastica.
crêpe paper *n* carta crespa.
crêpe sole *n* suola di para.
crept [krɛpt] *pt, pp of* **creep**.
crescendo [krɪˈʃɛndəu] *n* crescendo.
crescent ['krɛsnt] *n* (*shape*) mezzaluna; (*street*) strada semicircolare.
cress [krɛs] *n* crescione *m*.
crest [krɛst] *n* cresta; (*of helmet*) pennacchiera; (*of coat of arms*) cimiero.
crestfallen ['krɛstfɔːlən] *adj* mortificato(a).
Crete ['kriːt] *n* Creta.
crevasse [krɪˈvæs] *n* crepaccio.
crevice ['krɛvɪs] *n* fessura, crepa.
crew [kruː] *n* equipaggio; (*CINE*) troupe *f inv*; (*gang*) banda, compagnia.
crew-cut ['kruːkʌt] *n*: **to have a** ~ avere i capelli a spazzola.
crew-neck ['kruːnɛk] *n* girocollo.
crib [krɪb] *n* culla; (*REL*) presepio ♦ *vt* (*col*) copiare.
cribbage ['krɪbɪdʒ] *n* tipo di gioco di carte.
crick [krɪk] *n* crampo; ~ **in the neck**

torcicollo.

cricket ['krɪkɪt] n (insect) grillo; (game) cricket m.

cricketer ['krɪkɪtə*] n giocatore m di cricket.

crime [kraɪm] n (in general) criminalità; (instance) crimine m, delitto.

crime wave n ondata di criminalità.

criminal ['krɪmɪnl] adj, n criminale (m/f); **C~ Investigation Department (CID)** ≈ polizia giudiziaria.

crimp [krɪmp] vt arricciare.

crimson ['krɪmzn] adj color cremisi inv.

cringe [krɪndʒ] vi acquattarsi; (fig) essere servile.

crinkle ['krɪŋkl] vt arricciare, increspare.

cripple ['krɪpl] n zoppo/a ♦ vt azzoppare; (ship, plane) avariare; (production, exports) rovinare; **~d with arthritis** sciancato(a) per l'artrite.

crippling ['krɪplɪŋ] adj (taxes, debts) esorbitante; (disease) molto debilitante.

crisis, pl **crises** ['kraɪsɪs, -siːz] n crisi f inv.

crisp [krɪsp] adj croccante; (fig) frizzante; vivace; deciso(a).

crisps [krɪsps] npl (BRIT) patatine fpl fritte.

criss-cross ['krɪskrɔs] adj incrociato(a) ♦ vt incrociarsi.

criterion, pl **criteria** [kraɪ'tɪərɪən, -'tɪərɪə] n criterio.

critic ['krɪtɪk] n critico/a.

critical ['krɪtɪkl] adj critico(a); **to be ~ of sb/sth** criticare qn/qc, essere critico verso qn/qc.

critically ['krɪtɪklɪ] adv criticamente; **~ ill** gravemente malato.

criticism ['krɪtɪsɪzəm] n critica.

criticize ['krɪtɪsaɪz] vt criticare.

critique [krɪ'tiːk] n critica, saggio critico.

croak [krəuk] vi gracchiare.

Croat ['krəuæt] adj, n = **Croatian**.

Croatia [krəu'eɪʃə] n Croazia.

Croatian [krəu'eɪʃən] adj croato(a) ♦ n croato/a; (LING) croato.

crochet ['krəuʃeɪ] n lavoro all'uncinetto.

crock [krɔk] n coccio; (col: person: also: **old ~**) rottame m; (: car etc) caffettiera, rottame m.

crockery ['krɔkərɪ] n vasellame m; (plates, cups etc) stoviglie fpl.

crocodile ['krɔkədaɪl] n coccodrillo.

crocus ['krəukəs] n croco.

croft [krɔft] n (BRIT) piccolo podere m.

crofter ['krɔftə*] n (BRIT) affittuario di un piccolo podere.

crone [krəun] n strega.

crony ['krəunɪ] n (col) amicone/a.

crook [kruk] n truffatore m; (of shepherd)

bastone m.

crooked ['krukɪd] adj curvo(a), storto(a); (person, action) disonesto(a).

crop [krɔp] n raccolto; (produce) coltivazione f; (of bird) gozzo, ingluvie f ♦ vt (cut: hair) tagliare, rapare; (subj: animals: grass) brucare.

►**crop up** vi presentarsi.

cropper ['krɔpə*] n: **to come a ~** (col) fare fiasco.

crop spraying n spruzzatura di antiparassitari.

croquet ['krəukeɪ] n croquet m.

croquette [krə'kɛt] n crocchetta.

cross [krɔs] n croce f; (BIOL) incrocio ♦ vt (street etc) attraversare; (arms, legs, BIOL) incrociare; (cheque) sbarrare; (thwart: person, plan) contrastare, ostacolare ♦ vi: **the boat ~es from ... to ...** la barca fa la traversata da ... a ... ♦ adj di cattivo umore; **to ~ o.s.** fare il segno della croce bgnarsi, **we have a ~ed line** (BRIT: on telephone) c'è un'interferenza; **they've got their lines ~ed** (fig) si sono fraintesi; **to be/get ~ with sb (about sth)** essere arrabbiato(a)/arrabbiarsi con qn (per qc).

►**cross out** vt cancellare.

►**cross over** vi attraversare.

crossbar ['krɔsbɑː*] n traversa.

crossbow ['krɔsbəu] n balestra.

crossbreed ['krɔsbriːd] n incrocio.

cross-Channel ferry ['krɔs'tʃænl-] n traghetto che attraversa la Manica.

cross-check ['krɔstʃɛk] n controprova ♦ vi fare una controprova.

crosscountry (race) [krɔs'kʌntrɪ-] n cross-country m inv.

cross-dressing [krɔs'drɛsɪŋ] n travestitismo.

cross-examination ['krɔsɪgzæmɪ'neɪʃən] n (LAW) controinterrogatorio.

cross-examine ['krɔsɪg'zæmɪn] vt (LAW) sottoporre a controinterrogatorio.

cross-eyed ['krɔsaɪd] adj strabico(a).

crossfire ['krɔsfaɪə*] n fuoco incrociato.

crossing ['krɔsɪŋ] n incrocio; (sea-passage) traversata; (also: **pedestrian ~**) passaggio pedonale.

crossing point n valico di frontiera.

cross-purposes ['krɔs'pə:pəsɪz] npl: **to be at ~ with sb** (misunderstand) fraintendere qn; **to talk at ~** fraintendersi.

cross-question [krɔs'kwɛstʃən] vt (LAW) = **cross-examine**; (fig) sottoporre ad un interrogatorio.

cross-reference ['krɔsrɛfərəns] n rinvio, rimando.

crossroads ['krɔsrəudz] _n_ incrocio.
cross section _n_ (_BIOL_) sezione _f_
trasversale; (_in population_) settore _m_
rappresentativo.
crosswalk ['krɔswɔːk] _n_ (_US_) strisce _fpl_
pedonali, passaggio pedonale.
crosswind ['krɔswɪnd] _n_ vento di traverso.
crosswise ['krɔswaɪz] _adv_ di traverso.
crossword ['krɔswəːd] _n_ cruciverba _m inv._
crotch [krɔtʃ] _n_ (_ANAT_) inforcatura; (_of
garment_) pattina.
crotchet ['krɔtʃɪt] _n_ (_MUS_) semiminima.
crotchety ['krɔtʃɪtɪ] _adj_ (_person_)
burbero(a).
crouch [krautʃ] _vi_ acquattarsi;
rannicchiarsi.
croup [kruːp] _n_ (_MED_) crup _m._
crouton ['kruːtɔn] _n_ crostino.
crow [krəu] _n_ (_bird_) cornacchia; (_of cock_)
canto del gallo ♦ _vi_ (_cock_) cantare; (_fig_)
vantarsi; cantar vittoria.
crowbar ['krəubɑː*] _n_ piede _m_ di porco.
crowd [kraud] _n_ folla ♦ _vt_ affollare, stipare
♦ _vi_ affollarsi; ~**s of people** un sacco di
gente.
crowded ['kraudɪd] _adj_ affollato(a); ~ **with**
stipato(a) di.
crowd scene _n_ (_CINE, THEAT_) scena di
massa.
crown [kraun] _n_ corona; (_of head_) calotta
cranica; (_of hat_) cocuzzolo; (_of hill_) cima
♦ _vt_ incoronare; (_tooth_) incapsulare; **and
to ~ it all** ... (_fig_) e per giunta ..., e come
se non bastasse ...; _see boxed note._

CROWN COURT

_Nel sistema legale inglese, la **crown court** è
un tribunale penale che si sposta da una città
all'altra. È formata da una giuria e presieduta
da un giudice. Vi si discutono i reati più gravi,
mentre dei reati minori si occupano le
"magistrates' court", presiedute da un giudice
di pace, ma senza giuria. È il giudice di pace
che decide se passare o meno un caso alla
crown court._

---

crowning ['kraunɪŋ] _adj_ (_achievement, glory_)
supremo(a).
crown jewels _npl_ gioielli _mpl_ della Corona.
crown prince _n_ principe _m_ ereditario.
crow's-feet ['krəuzfiːt] _npl_ zampe _fpl_ di
gallina.
crow's-nest ['krəuznɛst] _n_ (_on sailing-ship_)
coffa.
crucial ['kruːʃl] _adj_ cruciale, decisivo(a); ~
to essenziale per.
crucifix ['kruːsɪfɪks] _n_ crocifisso.

crucifixion [kruːsɪ'fɪkʃən] _n_ crocifissione _f._
crucify ['kruːsɪfaɪ] _vt_ crocifiggere, mettere
in croce; (_fig_) distruggere, fare a pezzi.
crude [kruːd] _adj_ (_materials_) greggio(a); non
raffinato(a); (_fig: basic_) crudo(a),
primitivo(a); (: _vulgar_) rozzo(a),
grossolano(a).
crude (oil) _n_ (petrolio) greggio.
cruel ['kruəl] _adj_ crudele.
cruelty ['kruəltɪ] _n_ crudeltà _f inv._
cruet ['kruːɪt] _n_ ampolla.
cruise [kruːz] _n_ crociera ♦ _vi_ andare a
velocità di crociera; (_taxi_) circolare.
cruise missile _n_ missile _m_ cruise _inv._
cruiser ['kruːzə*] _n_ incrociatore _m._
cruising speed ['kruːzɪŋ-] _n_ velocità _f inv_ di
crociera.
crumb [krʌm] _n_ briciola.
crumble ['krʌmbl] _vt_ sbriciolare ♦ _vi_
sbriciolarsi; (_plaster etc_) sgretolarsi;
(_land, earth_) franare; (_building, fig_)
crollare.
crumbly ['krʌmblɪ] _adj_ friabile.
crummy ['krʌmɪ] _adj_ (_col: cheap_) di infima
categoria; (: _depressed_) giù _inv._
crumpet ['krʌmpɪt] _n_ specie di _frittella._
crumple ['krʌmpl] _vt_ raggrinzare,
spiegazzare.
crunch [krʌntʃ] _vt_ sgranocchiare;
(_underfoot_) scricchiolare ♦ _n_ (_fig_) punto _or_
momento cruciale.
crunchy ['krʌntʃɪ] _adj_ croccante.
crusade [kruː'seɪd] _n_ crociata ♦ _vi_ (_fig_): **to ~
for/against** fare una crociata per/contro.
crusader [kruː'seɪdə*] _n_ crociato; (_fig_): ~
(for) sostenitore/trice (di).
crush [krʌʃ] _n_ folla; (_love_): **to have a ~ on
sb** avere una cotta per qn; (_drink_): **lemon
~** spremuta di limone ♦ _vt_ schiacciare;
(_crumple_) sgualcire; (_grind, break up: garlic,
ice_) tritare; (: _grapes_) pigiare.
crushing ['krʌʃɪŋ] _adj_ schiacciante.
crust [krʌst] _n_ crosta.
crustacean [krʌs'teɪʃən] _n_ crostaceo.
crusty ['krʌstɪ] _adj_ (_bread_) croccante;
(_person_) brontolone(a).
crutch [krʌtʃ] _n_ (_MED_) gruccia; (_support_)
sostegno; (_also:_ **crotch**) pattina.
crux [krʌks] _n_ nodo.
cry [kraɪ] _vi_ piangere; (_shout: also:_ ~ **out**)
urlare ♦ _n_ urlo, grido; (_of animal_) verso; **to
~ for help** gridare aiuto; **what are you
~ing about?** perché piangi?; **she had a
good ~** si è fatta un bel pianto; **it's a far
~ from** ... (_fig_) è tutt'un'altra cosa da ....
▶**cry off** _vi_ ritirarsi.
crying ['kraɪɪŋ] _adj_ (_fig_) palese; urgente.
crypt [krɪpt] _n_ cripta.

cryptic ['krɪptɪk] *adj* ermetico(a).

crystal ['krɪstl] *n* cristallo.

crystal-clear ['krɪstl'klɪə*] *adj* cristallino(a); (*fig*) chiaro(a) (come il sole).

crystallize ['krɪstəlaɪz] *vi* cristallizzarsi ♦ *vt* (*fig*) concretizzare, concretare; ~**d fruits** (*BRIT*) frutta candita.

CSA *n abbr* (*US*) = Confederate States of America; (*BRIT*: = Child Support Agency) *istituto a difesa dei figli di coppie separate, che si adopera affinché venga rispettato l'obbligo del mantenimento.*

CSC *n abbr* (= Civil Service Commission) *commissione per il reclutamento dei funzionari statali.*

CSE *n abbr* (*BRIT old*: = Certificate of Secondary Education) *diploma di istruzione superiore.*

CS gas *n* (*BRIT*) *tipo di gas lacrimogeno.*

CST *abbr* (*US*: = central standard time) *fuso orario.*

CT *abbr* (*US*) = Connecticut.

ct *abbr* = **carat**.

CTC *n abbr* (*BRIT*: = city technology college) *istituto tecnico superiore.*

cu. *abbr* = **cubic**.

cub [kʌb] *n* cucciolo; (*also*: ~ **scout**) lupetto.

Cuba ['kju:bə] *n* Cuba.

Cuban ['kju:bən] *adj*, *n* cubano(a).

cubbyhole ['kʌbɪhəʊl] *n* angolino.

cube [kju:b] *n* cubo ♦ *vt* (*MATH*) elevare al cubo.

cube root *n* radice *f* cubica.

cubic ['kju:bɪk] *adj* cubico(a); ~ **metre** *etc* metro *etc* cubo; ~ **capacity** (*AUT*) cilindrata.

cubicle ['kju:bɪkl] *n* scompartimento separato; cabina.

cuckoo ['kuku:] *n* cucù *m inv*.

cuckoo clock *n* orologio a cucù.

cucumber ['kju:kʌmbə*] *n* cetriolo.

cud [kʌd] *n*: **to chew the** ~ ruminare.

cuddle ['kʌdl] *vt* abbracciare, coccolare ♦ *vi* abbracciarsi.

cuddly ['kʌdlɪ] *adj* da coccolare.

cudgel ['kʌdʒl] *n* randello ♦ *vt*: **to** ~ **one's brains** scervellarsi, spremere le meningi.

cue [kju:] *n* stecca; (*THEAT etc*) segnale *m*.

cuff [kʌf] *n* (*of shirt, coat etc*) polsino; (*US*: on trousers*) = **turnup**; (*blow*) schiaffo ♦ *vt* dare uno schiaffo a; **off the** ~ *adv* improvvisando.

cufflink ['kʌflɪŋk] *n* gemello.

cu. ft. *abbr* = **cubic feet**.

cu. in. *abbr* = **cubic inches**.

cuisine [kwɪ'zi:n] *n* cucina.

cul-de-sac ['kʌldəsæk] *n* vicolo cieco.

culinary ['kʌlɪnərɪ] *adj* culinario(a).

cull [kʌl] *vt* (*kill selectively: animals*) selezionare e abbattere.

culminate ['kʌlmɪneɪt] *vi*: **to** ~ **in** culminare con.

culmination [kʌlmɪ'neɪʃən] *n* culmine *m*.

culottes [kju:'lɔts] *npl* gonna *f* pantalone *inv*.

culpable ['kʌlpəbl] *adj* colpevole.

culprit ['kʌlprɪt] *n* colpevole *m/f*.

cult [kʌlt] *n* culto.

cult figure *n* idolo.

cultivate ['kʌltɪveɪt] *vt* (*also fig*) coltivare.

cultivation [kʌltɪ'veɪʃən] *n* coltivazione *f*.

cultural ['kʌltʃərəl] *adj* culturale.

culture ['kʌltʃə*] *n* (*also fig*) cultura.

cultured ['kʌltʃəd] *adj* colto(a).

cumbersome ['kʌmbəsəm] *adj* ingombrante.

cumin ['kʌmɪn] *n* (*spice*) cumino.

cumulative ['kju:mjʊlətɪv] *adj* cumulativo(a).

cunning ['kʌnɪŋ] *n* astuzia, furberia ♦ *adj* astuto(a), furbo(a); (*clever: device, idea*) ingegnoso(a).

cunt [kʌnt] (*col!*) *n* figa (*!*); (*insult*) stronzo/a (*!*).

cup [kʌp] *n* tazza; (*prize*) coppa; **a** ~ **of tea** una tazza di tè.

cupboard ['kʌbəd] *n* armadio.

cup final *n* (*BRIT FOOTBALL*) finale *f* di coppa.

Cupid ['kju:pɪd] *n* Cupido; (*figurine*). c~ cupido.

cupidity [kju:'pɪdɪtɪ] *n* cupidigia.

cupola ['kju:pələ] *n* cupola.

cuppa ['kʌpə] *n* (*BRIT col*) tazza di tè.

cup-tie ['kʌptaɪ] *n* (*BRIT FOOTBALL*) partita di coppa.

curable ['kjʊərəbl] *adj* curabile.

curate ['kjʊərɪt] *n* cappellano.

curator [kjʊə'reɪtə*] *n* direttore *m* (*di museo etc*).

curb [kə:b] *vt* tenere a freno; (*expenditure*) limitare ♦ *n* freno; (*US*) = **kerb**.

curd cheese [kə:d-] *n* cagliata.

curdle ['kə:dl] *vi* cagliare.

curds [kə:dz] *npl* latte *m* cagliato.

cure [kjʊə*] *vt* guarire; (*CULIN*) trattare; affumicare; essiccare ♦ *n* rimedio; **to be** ~**d of sth** essere guarito(a) da qc.

cure-all ['kjʊərɔ:l] *n* (*also fig*) panacea, toccasana *m inv*.

curfew ['kə:fju:] *n* coprifuoco.

curio ['kjʊərɪəʊ] *n* curiosità *f inv*.

curiosity [kjʊərɪ'ɔsɪtɪ] *n* curiosità.

curious ['kjʊərɪəs] *adj* curioso(a); **I'm** ~

about him m'incuriosisce.
curiously ['kjuərɪəslɪ] *adv* con curiosità;
(*strangely*) stranamente; ~ **enough,** ... per
quanto possa sembrare strano, ...
curl [kəːl] *n* riccio; (*of smoke etc*) anello ♦ *vt*
ondulare; (*tightly*) arricciare ♦ *vi*
arricciarsi.
►**curl up** *vi* avvolgersi a spirale;
rannicchiarsi.
curler ['kəːlə*] *n* bigodino; (*SPORT*)
giocatore/trice di curling.
curlew ['kəːluː] *n* chiurlo.
curling ['kəːlɪŋ] *n* (*SPORT*) curling *m*.
curling tongs, (*US*) **curling irons** *npl* (*for
hair*) arricciacapelli *m inv*.
curly ['kəːlɪ] *adj* ricciuto(a).
currant ['kʌrnt] *n* uva passa.
currency ['kʌrnsɪ] *n* moneta; **foreign** ~
divisa estera; **to gain** ~ (*fig*) acquistare
larga diffusione.
current ['kʌrnt] *adj* corrente; (*tendency,
price, event*) attuale ♦ *n* corrente *f*; **in** ~
use in uso corrente, d'uso comune; **the** ~
issue of a magazine l'ultimo numero di
una rivista; **direct/alternating** ~ (*ELEC*)
corrente continua/alternata.
current account *n* (*BRIT*) conto corrente.
current affairs *npl* attualità *fpl*.
current assets (*COMM*) attivo realizzabile
e disponibile.
current liabilities *npl* (*COMM*) passività *fpl*
correnti.
currently ['kʌrntlɪ] *adv* attualmente.
curriculum, *pl* ~**s** *or* **curricula**
[kə'rɪkjuləm, -lə] *n* curriculum *m inv*.
curriculum vitae (CV) [-'viːtaɪ] *n*
curriculum vitae *m inv*.
curry ['kʌrɪ] *n* curry *m inv* ♦ *vt*: **to** ~ **favour
with** cercare di attirarsi i favori di;
chicken ~ pollo al curry.
curry powder *n* curry *m*.
curse [kəːs] *vt* maledire ♦ *vi* bestemmiare
♦ *n* maledizione *f*; bestemmia.
cursor ['kəːsə*] *n* (*COMPUT*) cursore *m*.
cursory ['kəːsərɪ] *adj* superficiale.
curt [kəːt] *adj* secco(a).
curtail [kəː'teɪl] *vt* (*visit etc*) accorciare;
(*expenses etc*) ridurre, decurtare.
curtain ['kəːtn] *n* tenda; (*THEAT*) sipario; **to
draw the** ~**s** (*together*) chiudere *or* tirare
le tende; (*apart*) aprire le tende.
curtain call *n* (*THEAT*) chinata alla ribalta.
curts(e)y ['kəːtsɪ] *n* inchino, riverenza ♦ *vi*
fare un inchino *or* una riverenza.
curvature ['kəːvətʃə*] *n* curvatura.
curve [kəːv] *n* curva ♦ *vt* curvare ♦ *vi*
curvarsi; (*road*) fare una curva.
curved [kəːvd] *adj* curvo(a).

cushion ['kuʃən] *n* cuscino ♦ *vt* (*shock*) fare
da cuscinetto a.
cushy ['kuʃɪ] *adj* (*col*): **a** ~ **job** un lavoro di
tutto riposo; **to have a** ~ **time**
spassarsela.
custard ['kʌstəd] *n* (*for pouring*) crema.
custard powder *n* (*BRIT*) crema
pasticcera in polvere.
custodial sentence [kʌs'təudɪəl-] *n*
condanna a pena detentiva.
custodian [kʌs'təudɪən] *n* custode *m/f*; (*of
museum etc*) soprintendente *m/f*.
custody ['kʌstədɪ] *n* (*of child*) custodia; (*for
offenders*) arresto; **to take sb into** ~
mettere qn in detenzione preventiva; **in
the** ~ **of** alla custodia di.
custom ['kʌstəm] *n* costume *m*, usanza;
(*LAW*) consuetudine *f*; (*COMM*) clientela;
see also **customs**.
customary ['kʌstəmərɪ] *adj* consueto(a); **it
is** ~ **to do** è consuetudine fare.
custom-built ['kʌstəm'bɪlt] *adj see* **custom-
made.**
customer ['kʌstəmə*] *n* cliente *m/f*; **he's an
awkward** ~ (*col*) è un tipo
incontentabile.
customer profile *n* profilo del cliente.
customized ['kʌstəmaɪzd] *adj*
personalizzato(a); (*car*) fuoriserie *inv*.
custom-made ['kʌstəm'meɪd] *adj* (*clothes*)
fatto(a) su misura; (*other goods*: *also*:
custom-built) fatto(a) su ordinazione.
customs ['kʌstəmz] *npl* dogana; **to go
through (the)** ~ passare la dogana.
Customs and Excise *n* (*BRIT*) Ufficio Dazi
e Dogana.
customs officer *n* doganiere *m*.
cut [kʌt] *vb* (*pt, pp* **cut**) *vt* tagliare; (*shape,
make*) intagliare; (*reduce*) ridurre; (*col*:
avoid: *class, lecture, appointment*) saltare
♦ *vi* tagliare; (*intersect*) tagliarsi ♦ *n* taglio;
(*in salary etc*) riduzione *f*; **cold** ~**s** *npl* (*US*)
affettati *mpl*; **power** ~ mancanza di
corrente elettrica; **to** ~ **one's finger**
tagliarsi un dito; **to get one's hair** ~ farsi
tagliare i capelli; **to** ~ **a tooth** mettere un
dente; **to** ~ **sb/sth short** interrompere
qn/qc; **to** ~ **sb dead** ignorare qn
completamente.
►**cut back** *vt* (*plants*) tagliare; (*production,
expenditure*) ridurre.
►**cut down** *vt* (*tree*) abbattere;
(*consumption, expenses*) ridurre; **to** ~ **sb
down to size** (*fig*) sgonfiare *or*
ridimensionare qn.
►**cut down on** *vt fus* ridurre.
►**cut in** *vi* (*interrupt conversation*): **to** ~ **in
(on)** intromettersi (in); (*AUT*) tagliare la

strada (a).
►**cut off** *vt* tagliare; (*fig*) isolare; **we've been** ~ **off** (*TEL*) è caduta la linea.
►**cut out** *vt* tagliare; (*picture*) ritagliare.
►**cut up** *vt* (*gen*) tagliare; (*chop: food*) sminuzzare.
cut-and-dried ['kʌtən'draɪd] *adj* (*also*: **cut-and-dry**) assodato(a).
cutback ['kʌtbæk] *n* riduzione *f.*
cute [kjuːt] *adj* grazioso(a); (*clever*) astuto(a).
cut glass *n* cristallo.
cuticle ['kjuːtɪkl] *n* (*on nail*) pellicina, cuticola.
cutlery ['kʌtlərɪ] *n* posate *fpl.*
cutlet ['kʌtlɪt] *n* costoletta.
cutoff ['kʌtɔf] *n* (*also*: ~ **point**) limite *m.*
cutoff switch *n* interruttore *m.*
cutout ['kʌtaut] *n* (*switch*) interruttore *m*; (*paper, cardboard figure*) ritaglio.
cut-price ['kʌt'praɪs], (*US*) **cut-rate** ['kʌt'reɪt] *adj* a prezzo ridotto.
cutthroat ['kʌtθrəut] *n* assassino ♦ *adj*: ~ **competition** concorrenza spietata.
cutting ['kʌtɪŋ] *adj* tagliente; (*fig*) pungente ♦ *n* (*BRIT: PRESS*) ritaglio (di giornale); (: *RAIL*) trincea; (*CINE*) montaggio.
cutting edge *n* (*of knife*) taglio, filo; **on** *or* **at the** ~ **of sth** all'avanguardia di qc.
cut-up ['kʌtʌp] *adj* stravolto(a).
CV *n abbr see* **curriculum vitae.**
C & W *n abbr* = **country and western** (**music**).
cwt. *abbr* = **hundredweight.**
cyanide ['saɪənaɪd] *n* cianuro.
cybercafé ['saɪbə,kæfeɪ] *n* cybercaffè *m inv*
cybernetics [saɪbə'nɛtɪks] *n* cibernetica.
cyclamen ['sɪkləmən] *n* ciclamino.
cycle ['saɪkl] *n* ciclo; (*bicycle*) bicicletta ♦ *vi* andare in bicicletta.
cycle path *n* percorso ciclabile.
cycle race *n* gara *or* corsa ciclistica.
cycle rack *n* portabiciclette *m inv.*
cycle track *n* percorso ciclabile; (*in velodrome*) pista.
cycling ['saɪklɪŋ] *n* ciclismo; **to go on a** ~ **holiday** (*BRIT*) fare una vacanza in bicicletta.
cyclist ['saɪklɪst] *n* ciclista *m/f.*
cyclone ['saɪkləun] *n* ciclone *m.*
cygnet ['sɪgnɪt] *n* cigno giovane.
cylinder ['sɪlɪndə*] *n* cilindro.
cylinder capacity *n* cilindrata.
cylinder head *n* testata.
cylinder head gasket *n* guarnizione *f* della testata del cilindro.
cymbals ['sɪmblz] *npl* cembali *mpl.*
cynic ['sɪnɪk] *n* cinico/a.

cynical ['sɪnɪkl] *adj* cinico(a).
cynicism ['sɪnɪsɪzəm] *n* cinismo.
CYO *n abbr* (*US*) = *Catholic Youth Organization.*
cypress ['saɪprɪs] *n* cipresso.
Cypriot ['sɪprɪət] *adj, n* cipriota (*m/f*).
Cyprus ['saɪprəs] *n* Cipro.
cyst [sɪst] *n* cisti *f inv.*
cystitis [sɪ'staɪtɪs] *n* cistite *f.*
CZ *n abbr* (*US*: = *Canal Zone*) *zona del Canale di Panama.*
czar [zɑː*] *n* zar *m inv.*
Czech [tʃɛk] *adj* ceco(a) ♦ *n* ceco/a; (*LING*) ceco; **the** ~ **Republic** la Repubblica Ceca.
Czechoslovak [tʃɛkə'sləuvæk] *adj, n* = **Czechoslovakian.**
Czechoslovakia [tʃɛkəslə'vækɪə] *n* Cecoslovacchia.
Czechoslovakian [tʃɛkəslə'vækɪən] *adj, n* cecoslovacco(a).

D d

D, d [diː] *n* (*letter*) D, d *f or m inv*; (*MUS*): **D** re *m*; **D for David**, (*US*) **D for Dog** ≈ D come Domodossola.
D *abbr* (*US POL*) = **democrat(ic).**
d *abbr* (*BRIT*: *old*) = **penny.**
d. *abbr* = **died.**
DA *n abbr* (*US*) *see* **district attorney.**
dab [dæb] *vt* (*eyes, wound*) tamponare; (*paint, cream*) applicare (con leggeri colpetti); **a** ~ **of paint** un colpetto di vernice.
dabble ['dæbl] *vi*: **to** ~ **in** occuparsi (da dilettante) di.
Dacca ['dækə] *n* Dacca *f.*
dachshund ['dækshund] *n* bassotto.
dad, daddy [dæd, 'dædɪ] *n* babbo, papà *m inv.*
daddy-long-legs [dædɪ'lɔŋlɛgz] *n* tipula, zanzarone *m.*
daffodil ['dæfədɪl] *n* trombone *m*, giunchiglia.
daft [dɑːft] *adj* sciocco(a); **to be** ~ **about sb** perdere la testa per qn; **to be** ~ **about sth** andare pazzo per qc.
dagger ['dægə*] *n* pugnale *m.*
dahlia ['deɪljə] *n* dalia.
daily ['deɪlɪ] *adj* quotidiano(a), giornaliero(a) ♦ *n* quotidiano; (*BRIT*:

servant) donna di servizio ♦ *adv* tutti i giorni; **twice** ~ due volte al giorno.
dainty ['deɪntɪ] *adj* delicato(a), grazioso(a).
dairy ['dɛərɪ] *n* (*shop*) latteria; (*on farm*) caseificio ♦ *cpd* caseario(a).
dairy cow *n* mucca da latte.
dairy farm *n* caseificio.
dairy produce *n* latticini *mpl*.
dais ['deɪɪs] *n* pedana, palco.
daisy ['deɪzɪ] *n* margherita.
daisy wheel *n* (*on printer*) margherita.
daisy-wheel printer ['deɪzɪwiːl-] *n* stampante *f* a margherita.
Dakar ['dækə*] *n* Dakar *f*.
dale [deɪl] *n* valle *f*.
dally ['dælɪ] *vi* trastullarsi.
dalmatian [dæl'meɪʃən] *n* (*dog*) dalmata *m*.
dam [dæm] *n* diga; (*reservoir*) bacino artificiale ♦ *vt* sbarrare; costruire dighe su.
damage ['dæmɪdʒ] *n* danno, danni *mpl*; (*fig*) danno ♦ *vt* danneggiare; (*fig*) recar danno a; ~ **to property** danni materiali.
damages ['dæmɪdʒɪz] *npl* (*LAW*) danni *mpl*; **to pay £5000 in** ~ pagare 5000 sterline di indennizzo.
damaging ['dæmɪdʒɪŋ] *adj*: ~ (**to**) nocivo(a) (a).
Damascus [də'mɑːskəs] *n* Damasco *f*.
dame [deɪm] *n* (*title*, *US col*) donna; (*THEAT*) vecchia signora (*ruolo comico di donna recitato da un uomo*).
damn [dæm] *vt* condannare; (*curse*) maledire ♦ *n* (*col*): **I don't give a** ~ non me ne importa un fico ♦ *adj* (*col*): **this** ~ ... questo maledetto ...; ~ (**it**)! accidenti!
damnable ['dæmnəbl] *adj* (*col: behaviour*) vergognoso(a); (: *weather*) schifoso(a).
damnation [dæm'neɪʃən] *n* (*REL*) dannazione *f* ♦ *excl* (*col*) dannazione!, diavolo!
damning ['dæmɪŋ] *adj* (*evidence*) schiacciante.
damp [dæmp] *adj* umido(a) ♦ *n* umidità, umido ♦ *vt* (*also*: ~**en**) (*cloth*, *rag*) inumidire, bagnare; (*enthusiasm etc*) spegnere.
dampcourse ['dæmpkɔːs] *n* strato *m* isolante antiumido *inv*.
damper ['dæmpə*] *n* (*MUS*) sordina; (*of fire*) valvola di tiraggio; **to put a** ~ **on sth** (*fig*: *atmosphere*) gelare; (: *enthusiasm*) far sbollire.
dampness ['dæmpnɪs] *n* umidità, umido.
damson ['dæmzən] *n* susina damaschina.
dance [dɑːns] *n* danza, ballo; (*ball*) ballo ♦ *vi* ballare; **to** ~ **about** saltellare.
dance hall *n* dancing *m inv*, sala da ballo.

dancer ['dɑːnsə*] *n* danzatore/trice; (*professional*) ballerino/a.
dancing ['dɑːnsɪŋ] *n* danza, ballo.
D and C *n abbr* (*MED*: = *dilation and curettage*) raschiamento.
dandelion ['dændɪlaɪən] *n* dente *m* di leone.
dandruff ['dændrəf] *n* forfora.
dandy ['dændɪ] *n* dandy *m inv*, elegantone *m* ♦ *adj* (*US col*) fantastico(a).
Dane [deɪn] *n* danese *m/f*.
danger ['deɪndʒə*] *n* pericolo; **there is a** ~ **of fire** c'è pericolo di incendio; **in** ~ in pericolo; **out of** ~ fuori pericolo; **he was in** ~ **of falling** rischiava di cadere.
danger list *n* (*MED*): **on the** ~ **list** in prognosi riservata.
dangerous ['deɪndʒrəs] *adj* pericoloso(a).
dangerously ['deɪndʒrəslɪ] *adv*: ~ **ill** in pericolo di vita.
danger zone *n* area di pericolo.
dangle ['dæŋgl] *vt* dondolare; (*fig*) far balenare ♦ *vi* pendolare.
Danish ['deɪnɪʃ] *adj* danese ♦ *n* (*LING*) danese *m*.
Danish pastry *n* dolce *m* di pasta sfoglia.
dank [dæŋk] *adj* freddo(a) e umido(a).
Danube ['dænjuːb] *n*: **the** ~ il Danubio.
dapper ['dæpə*] *adj* lindo(a).
Dardanelles [dɑːdə'nɛlz] *npl* Dardanelli *mpl*.
dare [dɛə*] *vt*: **to** ~ **sb to do** sfidare qn a fare ♦ *vi*: **to** ~ (**to**) **do sth** osare fare qc; **I** ~**n't tell him** (*BRIT*) non oso dirglielo; **I** ~ **say he'll turn up** immagino che spunterà.
daredevil ['dɛədɛvl] *n* scavezzacollo *m/f*.
Dar-es-Salaam ['dɑːrɛssə'lɑːm] *n* Dar-es-Salaam *f*.
daring ['dɛərɪŋ] *adj* audace, ardito(a).
dark [dɑːk] *adj* (*night*, *room*) buio(a), scuro(a); (*colour*, *complexion*) scuro(a); (*fig*) cupo(a), tetro(a), nero(a) ♦ *n*: **in the** ~ al buio; **it is/is getting** ~ è/si sta facendo buio; **in the** ~ **about** (*fig*) all'oscuro di; **after** ~ a notte fatta; ~ **chocolate** cioccolata amara.
darken ['dɑːkən] *vt* (*room*) oscurare; (*photo*, *painting*) far scuro(a) ♦ *vi* oscurarsi; imbrunirsi.
dark glasses *npl* occhiali *mpl* scuri.
dark horse *n* (*fig*) incognita.
darkly ['dɑːklɪ] *adv* (*gloomily*) cupamente, con aria cupa; (*in a sinister way*) minacciosamente.
darkness ['dɑːknɪs] *n* oscurità, buio.
darkroom ['dɑːkruːm] *n* camera oscura.
darling ['dɑːlɪŋ] *adj* caro(a) ♦ *n* tesoro.
darn [dɑːn] *vt* rammendare.
dart [dɑːt] *n* freccetta ♦ *vi*: **to** ~ **towards** (*also*: **make a** ~ **towards**) precipitarsi

verso; **to ~ along** passare come un razzo; **to ~ away** guizzare via; *see also* **darts**.
dartboard ['dɑːtbɔːd] *n* bersaglio (per freccette).
darts [dɑːts] *n* tiro al bersaglio (con freccette).
dash [dæʃ] *n* (*sign*) lineetta; (*small quantity: of liquid*) goccio, goccino; (: *of soda*) spruzzo ♦ *vt* (*missile*) gettare; (*hopes*) infrangere ♦ *vi*: **to ~ towards** (*also*: **make a ~ towards**) precipitarsi verso.
▶**dash away** *vi* scappare via.
dashboard ['dæʃbɔːd] *n* cruscotto.
dashing ['dæʃɪŋ] *adj* ardito(a).
dastardly ['dæstədlɪ] *adj* vile.
DAT *n abbr* (= *digital audio tape*) cassetta *f* digitale audio *inv*.
data ['deɪtə] *npl* dati *mpl*.
database ['deɪtəbeɪs] *n* database *m*, base *f* di dati.
data capture *n* registrazione *f or* rilevazione *f* di dati.
data processing *n* elaborazione *f* (elettronica) dei dati.
data transmission *n* trasmissione *f* di dati.
date [deɪt] *n* data; (*appointment*) appuntamento; (*fruit*) dattero ♦ *vt* datare; (*col: girl etc*) uscire con; **what's the ~ today?** quanti ne abbiamo oggi?; **~ of birth** data di nascita; **closing ~** scadenza, termine *m*; **to ~** *adv* fino a oggi; **out of ~** scaduto(a); (*old-fashioned*) passato(a) di moda; **up to ~** moderno(a); aggiornato(a); **to bring up to ~** (*correspondence, information*) aggiornare; (*method*) modernizzare; (*person*) aggiornare, mettere al corrente; **~d the 13th** datato il 13; **thank you for your letter ~d 5th July** *or* (*US*) **July 5th** la ringrazio per la sua lettera in data 5 luglio.
dated ['deɪtɪd] *adj* passato(a) di moda.
dateline ['deɪtlaɪn] *n* linea del cambiamento di data.
date rape *n stupro perpetrato da persona conosciuta.*
date stamp *n* timbro datario.
daub [dɔːb] *vt* imbrattare.
daughter ['dɔːtə*] *n* figlia.
daughter-in-law ['dɔːtərɪnlɔː] *n* nuora.
daunt [dɔːnt] *vt* intimidire.
daunting ['dɔːntɪŋ] *adj* non invidiabile.
dauntless ['dɔːntlɪs] *adj* intrepido(a).
dawdle ['dɔːdl] *vi* bighellonare; **to ~ over one's work** gingillarsi con il lavoro.
dawn [dɔːn] *n* alba ♦ *vi* (*day*) spuntare; (*fig*) venire in mente; **at ~** all'alba; **from ~ to dusk** dall'alba al tramonto; **it ~ed on him**

that ... gli è venuto in mente che ....
dawn chorus *n* (*BRIT*) coro mattutino degli uccelli.
day [deɪ] *n* giorno; (*as duration*) giornata; (*period of time, age*) tempo, epoca; **the ~ before** il giorno avanti *or* prima; **the ~ after, the following ~** il giorno dopo, il giorno seguente; **the ~ before yesterday** l'altroieri; **the ~ after tomorrow** dopodomani; **(on) that ~** quel giorno; **(on) the ~ that ...** il giorno che *or* in cui ...; **to work an 8-hour ~** avere una giornata lavorativa di 8 ore; **by ~** di giorno; **~ by ~** giorno per giorno; **paid by the ~** pagato(a) a giornata; **these ~s, in the present ~** di questi tempi, oggigiorno.
daybook ['deɪbuk] *n* (*BRIT*) brogliaccio.
day boy *n* (*SCOL*) alunno esterno.
daybreak ['deɪbreɪk] *n* spuntar *m* del giorno.
day care centre *n* scuola materna.
daydream ['deɪdriːm] *n* sogno a occhi aperti ♦ *vi* sognare a occhi aperti.
day girl *n* (*SCOL*) alunna esterna.
daylight ['deɪlaɪt] *n* luce *f* del giorno.
daylight robbery *n*: **it's ~!** (*BRIT col*) è un vero furto!
Daylight Saving Time *n* (*US*) ora legale.
day release *n*: **to be on ~** *avere un giorno di congedo alla settimana per formazione professionale.*
day return (ticket) *n* (*BRIT*) biglietto giornaliero di andata e ritorno.
day shift *n* turno di giorno.
daytime ['deɪtaɪm] *n* giorno.
day-to-day ['deɪtə'deɪ] *adj* (*routine*) quotidiano(a); (*expenses*) giornaliero(a); **on a ~ basis** a giornata.
day trip *n* gita (di un giorno).
day tripper *n* gitante *m/f*.
daze [deɪz] *vt* (*subj: drug*) inebetire; (: *blow*) stordire ♦ *n*: **in a ~** inebetito(a); stordito(a).
dazzle ['dæzl] *vt* abbagliare.
dazzling ['dæzlɪŋ] *adj* (*light*) abbagliante; (*colour*) violento(a); (*smile*) smagliante.
dB *abbr* (= *decibel*) db.
DC *abbr* (*ELEC*: = *direct current*) c.c.; (*US*) = **District of Columbia**.
DCC ® *n abbr* = *digital compact cassette*.
DD *n abbr* (= *Doctor of Divinity*) titolo di studio.
dd. *abbr* (*COMM*) = *delivered*.
D/D *abbr* = *direct debit*.
D-day ['diːdeɪ] *n giorno dello sbarco alleato in Normandia.*
DDS *n abbr* (*US*: = *Doctor of Dental Science*; *Doctor of Dental Surgery*) *titoli di studio.*

DDT n abbr (= dichlorodiphenyl trichloroethane) D.D.T. m.
DE abbr (US) = Delaware.
DEA n abbr (US: = Drug Enforcement Administration) ≈ squadra narcotici.
deacon ['diːkən] n diacono.
dead [dɛd] adj morto(a); (numb) intirizzito(a) ♦ adv assolutamente, perfettamente; **the** ~ npl i morti; **he was shot** ~ fu colpito a morte; ~ **on time** in perfetto orario; ~ **tired** stanco(a) morto(a); **to stop** ~ fermarsi in tronco; **the line has gone** ~ (TEL) è caduta la linea.
dead beat adj (col) stanco(a) morto(a).
deaden ['dɛdn] vt (blow, sound) ammortire; (make numb) intirizzire.
dead end n vicolo cieco.
dead-end ['dɛdɛnd] adj: **a** ~ **job** un lavoro senza sbocchi.
dead heat n (SPORT): **to finish in a** ~ finire alla pari.
dead-letter office [dɛd'lɛtə-] n ufficio della posta in giacenza.
deadline ['dɛdlaɪn] n scadenza; **to work to a** ~ avere una scadenza.
deadlock ['dɛdlɔk] n punto morto.
dead loss n (col): **to be a** ~ (person, thing) non valere niente.
deadly ['dɛdlɪ] adj mortale; (weapon, poison) micidiale ♦ adv: ~ **dull** di una noia micidiale.
deadpan ['dɛdpæn] adj a faccia impassibile.
Dead Sea n: **the** ~ il mar Morto.
deaf [dɛf] adj sordo(a); **to turn a** ~ **ear to sth** fare orecchi da mercante a qc.
deaf-aid ['dɛfeɪd] n apparecchio per la sordità.
deaf-and-dumb ['dɛfən'dʌm] adj (person) sordomuto(a); (alphabet) dei sordomuti.
deafen ['dɛfn] vt assordare.
deafening ['dɛfnɪŋ] adj fragoroso(a), assordante.
deaf-mute ['dɛfmjuːt] n sordomuto/a.
deafness ['dɛfnɪs] n sordità.
deal [diːl] n accordo; (business ~) affare m ♦ vt (pt, pp **dealt** [dɛlt]) (blow, cards) dare; **to strike a** ~ **with sb** fare un affare con qn; **it's a** ~! (col) affare fatto!; **he got a bad/fair** ~ **from them** l'hanno trattato male/bene; **a good** ~ **of, a great** ~ **of** molto(a).
▶**deal in** vt fus (COMM) occuparsi di.
▶**deal with** vt fus (COMM) fare affari con, trattare con; (handle) occuparsi di; (be about: book etc) trattare di.
dealer ['diːlə*] n commerciante m/f.
dealership ['diːləʃɪp] n rivenditore m.

dealings ['diːlɪŋz] npl rapporti mpl; (in goods, shares) transazioni fpl.
dealt [dɛlt] pt, pp of **deal**.
dean [diːn] n (REL) decano; (SCOL) preside m di facoltà (or di collegio).
dear [dɪə*] adj caro(a) ♦ n: **my** ~ caro mio/cara mia; ~ **me!** Dio mio!; **D**~ **Sir/Madam** (in letter) Egregio Signore/Egregia Signora; **D**~ **Mr/Mrs X** Gentile Signor/Signora X.
dearly ['dɪəlɪ] adv (love) moltissimo; (pay) a caro prezzo.
dear money n (COMM) denaro ad alto interesse.
dearth [dəːθ] n scarsità, carestia.
death [dɛθ] n morte f; (ADMIN) decesso.
deathbed ['dɛθbɛd] n letto di morte.
death certificate n atto di decesso.
death duty n (BRIT) imposta or tassa di successione.
deathly ['dɛθlɪ] adj di morte ♦ adv come un cadavere.
death penalty n pena di morte.
death rate n indice m di mortalità.
death row [-rəu] n (US): **to be on** ~ essere nel braccio della morte.
death sentence n condanna a morte.
death squad n squadra della morte.
deathtrap ['dɛθtræp] n trappola mortale.
deb [dɛb] n abbr (col) = **debutante**.
debacle [deɪ'baːkl] n (defeat) disfatta; (collapse) sfacelo.
debar [dɪ'baː*] vt: **to** ~ **sb from a club** etc escludere qn da un club etc; **to** ~ **sb from doing** vietare a qn di fare.
debase [dɪ'beɪs] vt (currency) adulterare; (person) degradare.
debatable [dɪ'beɪtəbl] adj discutibile; **it is** ~ **whether ...** è in dubbio se ....
debate [dɪ'beɪt] n dibattito ♦ vt dibattere, discutere ♦ vi (consider): **to** ~ **whether** riflettere se.
debauchery [dɪ'bɔːtʃərɪ] n dissolutezza.
debenture [dɪ'bɛntʃə*] n (COMM) obbligazione f.
debilitate [dɪ'bɪlɪteɪt] vt debilitare.
debit ['dɛbɪt] n debito ♦ vt: **to** ~ **a sum to sb** or **to sb's account** addebitare una somma a qn.
debit balance n saldo debitore.
debit note n nota di addebito.
debonair [dɛbə'nɛə*] adj gioviale e disinvolto(a).
debrief [diː'briːf] vt chiamare a rapporto (a operazione ultimata).
debriefing [diː'briːfɪŋ] n rapporto.
debris ['dɛbriː] n detriti mpl.
debt [dɛt] n debito; **to be in** ~ essere

indebitato(a); ~s of £5000 debiti per 5000 sterline; bad ~ debito insoluto.

debt collector n agente m di recupero crediti.

debtor ['detə*] n debitore/trice.

debug [diː'bʌg] vt (COMPUT) localizzare e rimuovere errori in.

debunk [diː'bʌŋk] vt (col: theory) demistificare; (: claim) smentire; (: person, institution) screditare.

debut ['deɪbjuː] n debutto.

debutante ['debjutɑːnt] n debuttante f.

Dec. abbr (= December) dic.

decade ['dekeɪd] n decennio.

decadence ['dekədəns] n decadenza.

decadent ['dekədənt] adj decadente.

de-caff ['diːkæf] n (col) decaffeinato.

decaffeinated [diː'kæfɪneɪtɪd] adj decaffeinato(a).

decamp [diː'kæmp] vi (col) filarsela, levare le tende.

decant [dɪ'kænt] vt (wine) travasare.

decanter [dɪ'kæntə*] n caraffa.

decarbonize [diː'kɑːbənaɪz] vt (AUT) decarburare.

decathlon [dɪ'kæθlən] n decathlon m.

decay [dɪ'keɪ] n decadimento; imputridimento; (fig) rovina; (also: tooth ~) carie f ♦ vi (rot) imputridire; (fig) andare in rovina.

decease [dɪ'siːs] n decesso.

deceased [dɪ'siːst] n: the ~ il(la) defunto(a).

deceit [dɪ'siːt] n inganno.

deceitful [dɪ'siːtful] adj ingannevole, perfido(a).

deceive [dɪ'siːv] vt ingannare; to ~ o.s. illudersi, ingannarsi.

decelerate [diː'seləreɪt] vt, vi rallentare.

December [dɪ'sembə*] n dicembre m; for phrases see also July.

decency ['diːsənsɪ] n decenza.

decent ['diːsənt] adj decente; they were very ~ about it si sono comportati da signori riguardo a ciò.

decently ['diːsəntlɪ] adv (respectably) decentemente, convenientemente; (kindly) gentilmente.

decentralization [diːsentrəlaɪ'zeɪʃən] n decentramento.

decentralize [diː'sentrəlaɪz] vt decentrare.

deception [dɪ'sepʃən] n inganno.

deceptive [dɪ'septɪv] adj ingannevole.

decibel ['desɪbel] n decibel m inv.

decide [dɪ'saɪd] vt (person) far prendere una decisione a; (question, argument) risolvere, decidere ♦ vi decidere, decidersi; to ~ to do/that decidere di

fare/che; to ~ on decidere per; to ~ against doing sth decidere di non fare qc.

decided [dɪ'saɪdɪd] adj (resolute) deciso(a); (clear, definite) netto(a), chiaro(a).

decidedly [dɪ'saɪdɪdlɪ] adv indubbiamente; decisamente.

deciding [dɪ'saɪdɪŋ] adj decisivo(a).

deciduous [dɪ'sɪdjuəs] adj deciduo(a).

decimal ['desɪməl] adj, n decimale (m); to 3 ~ places al terzo decimale.

decimalize ['desɪməlaɪz] vt (BRIT) convertire al sistema metrico decimale.

decimal point n ≈ virgola.

decimate ['desɪmeɪt] vt decimare.

decipher [dɪ'saɪfə*] vt decifrare.

decision [dɪ'sɪʒən] n decisione f; to make a ~ prendere una decisione.

decisive [dɪ'saɪsɪv] adj (victory, factor) decisivo(a); (influence) determinante; (manner, person) risoluto(a), deciso(a); (reply) deciso(a), categorico(a).

deck [dek] n (NAUT) ponte m; (of cards) mazzo; (of bus): top ~ imperiale m; to go up on ~ salire in coperta; below ~ sotto coperta; cassette ~ piastra (di registrazione); record ~ piatto (giradischi).

deckchair ['dektʃeə*] n sedia a sdraio.

deck hand n marinaio.

declaration [deklə'reɪʃən] n dichiarazione f.

declare [dɪ'kleə*] vt dichiarare.

declassify [diː'klæsɪfaɪ] vt rendere accessibile al pubblico.

decline [dɪ'klaɪn] n (decay) declino; (lessening) ribasso ♦ vt declinare; rifiutare ♦ vi declinare; diminuire; ~ in living standards abbassamento del tenore di vita; to ~ to do sth rifiutar(si) di fare qc.

declutch [diː'klʌtʃ] vi (BRIT) premere la frizione.

decode [diː'kəud] vt decifrare.

decoder [diː'kəudə*] n (COMPUT, TV) decodificatore m.

decompose [diːkəm'pəuz] vi decomporre.

decomposition [diːkɔmpə'zɪʃən] n decomposizione f.

decompression [diːkəm'preʃən] n decompressione f.

decompression chamber n camera di decompressione.

decongestant [diːkən'dʒestənt] n decongestionante m.

decontaminate [diːkən'tæmɪneɪt] vt decontaminare.

decontrol [diːkən'trəul] vt (trade) liberalizzare; (prices) togliere il controllo governativo a.

decor ['deɪkɔ:*] *n* decorazione *f.*
decorate ['dɛkəreɪt] *vt* (*adorn, give a medal to*) decorare; (*paint and paper*) pitturare e tappezzare.
decoration [dɛkə'reɪʃən] *n* decorazione *f.*
decorative ['dɛkərətɪv] *adj* decorativo(a).
decorator ['dɛkəreɪtə*] *n* decoratore/trice.
decorum [dɪ'kɔ:rəm] *n* decoro.
decoy ['di:kɔɪ] *n* zimbello; **they used him as a ~ for the enemy** l'hanno usato come esca per il nemico.
decrease *n* ['di:kri:s] diminuzione *f* ♦ *vt, vi* [di:'kri:s] diminuire; **to be on the ~** essere in diminuzione.
decreasing [di:'kri:sɪŋ] *adj* sempre meno *inv.*
decree [dɪ'kri:] *n* decreto ♦ *vt:* **to ~ (that)** decretare (che + *sub*); **~ absolute** sentenza di divorzio definitiva; **~ nisi** [-'naɪsaɪ] sentenza provvisoria di divorzio.
decrepit [dɪ'krɛpɪt] *adj* decrepito(a); (*building*) cadente.
decry [dɪ'kraɪ] *vt* condannare, deplorare.
dedicate ['dɛdɪkeɪt] *vt* consacrare; (*book etc*) dedicare.
dedicated ['dɛdɪkeɪtɪd] *adj* coscienzioso(a); (*COMPUT*) specializzato(a), dedicato(a).
dedication [dɛdɪ'keɪʃən] *n* (*devotion*) dedizione *f*; (*in book*) dedica.
deduce [dɪ'dju:s] *vt* dedurre.
deduct [dɪ'dʌkt] *vt:* **to ~ sth (from)** dedurre qc (da); (*from wage etc*) trattenere qc (da).
deduction [dɪ'dʌkʃən] *n* (*deducting*) deduzione *f*; (*from wage etc*) trattenuta; (*deducing*) deduzione *f*, conclusione *f.*
deed [di:d] *n* azione *f*, atto; (*LAW*) atto; **~ of covenant** atto di donazione.
deem [di:m] *vt* (*formal*) giudicare, ritenere; **to ~ it wise to do** ritenere prudente fare.
deep [di:p] *adj* profondo(a) ♦ *adv:* **~ in snow** affondato(a) nella neve; **spectators stood 20 ~** c'erano 20 file di spettatori; **knee-~ in water** in acqua fino alle ginocchia; **4 metres ~** profondo(a) 4 metri; **he took a ~ breath** fece un respiro profondo.
deepen ['di:pn] *vt* (*hole*) approfondire ♦ *vi* approfondirsi; (*darkness*) farsi più intenso(a).
deep-freeze [di:p'fri:z] *n* congelatore *m* ♦ *vt* congelare.
deep-fry ['di:p'fraɪ] *vt* friggere in olio abbondante.
deeply ['di:plɪ] *adv* profondamente; **to regret sth ~** rammaricarsi sinceramente di qc.
deep-rooted ['di:p'ru:tɪd] *adj* (*prejudice*) profondamente radicato(a); (*affection*)

profondo(a); (*habit*) inveterato(a).
deep-sea diver ['di:p'si:-] *n* palombaro.
deep-sea diving *n* immersione *f* in alto mare.
deep-sea fishing *n* pesca d'alto mare.
deep-seated ['di:p'si:tɪd] *adj* (*beliefs*) radicato(a).
deep-set ['di:pset] *adj* (*eyes*) infossato(a).
deer [dɪə*] *n* (*pl inv*): **the ~** i cervidi (*ZOOL*); **(red) ~** cervo; **(fallow) ~** daino; **(roe) ~** capriolo.
deerskin ['dɪəskɪn] *n* pelle *f* di daino.
deerstalker ['dɪəstɔ:kə*] *n* berretto da cacciatore.
deface [dɪ'feɪs] *vt* imbrattare.
defamation [dɛfə'meɪʃən] *n* diffamazione *f.*
defamatory [dɪ'fæmətərɪ] *adj* diffamatorio(a).
default [dɪ'fɔ:lt] *vi* (*LAW*) essere contumace; (*gen*) essere inadempiente ♦ *n* (*COMPUT: also:* **~ value**) default *m inv*; **by ~** (*LAW*) in contumacia; (*SPORT*) per abbandono; **to ~ on a debt** non onorare un debito.
defaulter [dɪ'fɔ:ltə*] *n* (*on debt*) inadempiente *m/f.*
default option *n* (*COMPUT*) opzione *f* di default.
defeat [dɪ'fi:t] *n* sconfitta ♦ *vt* (*team, opponents*) sconfiggere; (*fig: plans, efforts*) frustrare.
defeatism [dɪ'fi:tɪzəm] *n* disfattismo.
defeatist [dɪ'fi:tɪst] *adj, n* disfattista (*m/f*).
defecate ['dɛfəkeɪt] *vi* defecare.
defect *n* ['di:fɛkt] difetto ♦ *vi* [dɪ'fɛkt]: **to ~ to the enemy/the West** passare al nemico/all'Ovest; **physical ~** difetto fisico; **mental ~** anomalia mentale.
defective [dɪ'fɛktɪv] *adj* difettoso(a).
defector [dɪ'fɛktə*] *n* rifugiato(a) politico/a.
defence, (*US*) **defense** [dɪ'fɛns] *n* difesa; **in ~ of** in difesa di; **the Ministry of D~**, (*US*) **the Department of Defense** il Ministero della Difesa; **witness for the ~** teste *m/f* a difesa.
defenceless [dɪ'fɛnslɪs] *adj* senza difesa.
defend [dɪ'fɛnd] *vt* difendere; (*decision, action*) giustificare; (*opinion*) sostenere.
defendant [dɪ'fɛndənt] *n* imputato/a.
defender [dɪ'fɛndə*] *n* difensore/a.
defending champion *n* (*SPORT*) campione/essa in carica.
defending counsel *n* (*LAW*) avvocato difensore.
defense [dɪ'fɛns] *n* (*US*) = **defence.**
defensive [dɪ'fɛnsɪv] *adj* difensivo(a) ♦ *n* difensiva; **on the ~** sulla difensiva.

defer [dɪ'fəː*] vt (postpone) differire, rinviare ♦ vi (submit): **to** ~ **to sb/sth** rimettersi a qn/qc.

deference ['dɛfərəns] n deferenza; riguardo; **out of** or **in** ~ **to** per riguardo a.

defiance [dɪ'faɪəns] n sfida; **in** ~ **of a** dispetto di.

defiant [dɪ'faɪənt] adj (attitude) di sfida; (person) ribelle.

defiantly [dɪ'faɪəntlɪ] adv con aria di sfida.

deficiency [dɪ'fɪʃənsɪ] n deficienza; carenza; (COMM) ammanco.

deficiency disease n malattia da carenza.

deficient [dɪ'fɪʃənt] adj deficiente; insufficiente; **to be** ~ **in** mancare di.

deficit ['dɛfɪsɪt] n disavanzo.

defile vb [dɪ'faɪl] vt contaminare ♦ vi sfilare ♦ n ['diːfaɪl] gola, stretta.

define [dɪ'faɪn] vt (gen, COMPUT) definire.

definite ['dɛfɪnɪt] adj (fixed) definito(a), preciso(a); (clear, obvious) ben definito(a), esatto(a); (LING) determinativo(a); **he was** ~ **about it** ne era sicuro.

definitely ['dɛfɪnɪtlɪ] adv indubbiamente.

definition [dɛfɪ'nɪʃən] n definizione f.

definitive [dɪ'fɪnɪtɪv] adj definitivo(a).

deflate [diː'fleɪt] vt sgonfiare; (ECON) deflazionare; (pompous person) fare abbassare la cresta a.

deflation [diː'fleɪʃən] n (ECON) deflazione f.

deflationary [diː'fleɪʃənrɪ] adj (ECON) deflazionistico(a).

deflect [dɪ'flɛkt] vt deflettere, deviare.

defog ['diː'fɔg] vt (US AUT) sbrinare.

defogger ['diː'fɔgə*] n (US AUT) sbrinatore m.

deform [dɪ'fɔːm] vt deformare.

deformed [dɪ'fɔːmd] adj deforme.

deformity [dɪ'fɔːmɪtɪ] n deformità f inv.

defraud [dɪ'frɔːd] vt: **to** ~ (of) defraudare (di).

defray [dɪ'freɪ] vt: **to** ~ **sb's expenses** sostenere le spese di qn.

defrost [diː'frɔst] vt (fridge) disgelare; (frozen food) scongelare.

deft [dɛft] adj svelto(a), destro(a).

defunct [dɪ'fʌŋkt] adj defunto(a).

defuse [diː'fjuːz] vt disinnescare; (fig) distendere.

defy [dɪ'faɪ] vt sfidare; (efforts etc) resistere a; (refuse to obey: person) rifiutare di obbedire a.

degenerate vi [dɪ'dʒɛnəreɪt] degenerare ♦ adj [dɪ'dʒɛnərɪt] degenere.

degradation [dɛgrə'deɪʃən] n degradazione f.

degrade [dɪ'greɪd] vt degradare.

degrading [dɪ'greɪdɪŋ] adj degradante.

degree [dɪ'griː] n grado; (SCOL) laurea (universitaria); **10** ~**s below freezing** 10 gradi sotto zero; **a (first)** ~ **in maths** una laurea in matematica; **a considerable** ~ **of risk** una grossa percentuale di rischio; **by** ~**s** (gradually) gradualmente, a poco a poco; **to some** ~, **to a certain** ~ fino a un certo punto, in certa misura.

dehydrated [diːhaɪ'dreɪtɪd] adj disidratato(a); (milk, eggs) in polvere.

dehydration [diːhaɪ'dreɪʃən] n disidratazione f.

de-ice [diː'aɪs] vt (windscreen) disgelare.

de-icer ['diːaɪsə*] n sbrinatore m.

deign [deɪn] vi: **to** ~ **to do** degnarsi di fare.

deity ['diːɪtɪ] n divinità f inv; dio/dea.

déjà vu [deɪʒɑː'vuː] n déjà vu m inv.

dejected [dɪ'dʒɛktɪd] adj abbattuto(a), avvilito(a).

dejection [dɪ'dʒɛkʃən] n abbattimento, avvilimento.

Del. abbr (US) = Delaware.

del. abbr = **delete**.

delay [dɪ'leɪ] vt (journey, operation) ritardare, rinviare; (travellers, trains) ritardare; (payment) differire ♦ n ritardo; **without** ~ senza ritardo.

delayed-action [dɪ'leɪd'ækʃən] adj a azione ritardata.

delectable [dɪ'lɛktəbl] adj delizioso(a).

delegate n ['dɛlɪgɪt] delegato/a ♦ vt ['dɛlɪgeɪt] delegare; **to** ~ **sth to sb/sb to do sth** delegare qc a qn/qn a fare qc.

delegation [dɛlɪ'geɪʃən] n delegazione f; (of work etc) delega.

delete [dɪ'liːt] vt (gen, COMPUT) cancellare.

Delhi ['dɛlɪ] n Delhi f.

deli ['dɛlɪ] n = **delicatessen**.

deliberate adj [dɪ'lɪbərɪt] (intentional) intenzionale; (slow) misurato(a) ♦ vi [dɪ'lɪbəreɪt] deliberare, riflettere.

deliberately [dɪ'lɪbərɪtlɪ] adv (on purpose) deliberatamente.

deliberation [dɪlɪbə'reɪʃən] n (consideration) riflessione f; (discussion) discussione f, deliberazione f.

delicacy ['dɛlɪkəsɪ] n delicatezza.

delicate ['dɛlɪkɪt] adj delicato(a).

delicately ['dɛlɪkɪtlɪ] adv (gen) delicatamente; (act, express) con delicatezza.

delicatessen [dɛlɪkə'tɛsn] n ≈ salumeria.

delicious [dɪ'lɪʃəs] adj delizioso(a), squisito(a).

delight [dɪ'laɪt] n delizia, gran piacere m ♦ vt dilettare; **it is a** ~ **to the eyes** è un piacere guardarlo; **to take** ~ **in** divertirsi a; **to be the** ~ **of** essere la gioia di.

delighted [dɪ'laɪtɪd] *adj*: ~ **(at** *or* **with sth)** contentissimo(a) (di qc), felice (di qc); **to be ~ to do sth/that** essere felice di fare qc/che + *sub*; **I'd be ~** con grande piacere.

delightful [dɪ'laɪtful] *adj* (*person, place, meal*) delizioso(a); (*smile, manner*) incantevole.

delimit [diː'lɪmɪt] *vt* delimitare.

delineate [dɪ'lɪnɪeɪt] *vt* delineare.

delinquency [dɪ'lɪŋkwənsɪ] *n* delinquenza.

delinquent [dɪ'lɪŋkwənt] *adj, n* delinquente (*m/f*).

delirious [dɪ'lɪrɪəs] *adj* (*MED, fig*) delirante, in delirio; **to be ~** delirare; (*fig*) farneticare.

delirium [dɪ'lɪrɪəm] *n* delirio.

deliver [dɪ'lɪvə*] *vt* (*mail*) distribuire; (*goods*) consegnare; (*speech*) pronunciare; (*free*) liberare; (*MED*) far partorire; **to ~ a message** fare un'ambasciata; **to ~ the goods** (*fig*) partorire.

deliverance [dɪ'lɪvrəns] *n* liberazione *f*.

delivery [dɪ'lɪvərɪ] *n* distribuzione *f*; consegna; (*of speaker*) dizione *f*; (*MED*) parto; **to take ~ of** prendere in consegna.

delivery note *n* bolla di consegna.

delivery van, (*US*) **delivery truck** *n* furgoncino (per le consegne).

delta ['dɛltə] *n* delta *m*.

delude [dɪ'luːd] *vt* deludere, illudere.

deluge ['dɛljuːdʒ] *n* diluvio ♦ *vt* (*fig*): **to ~ (with)** subissare (di), inondare (di).

delusion [dɪ'luːʒən] *n* illusione *f*.

de luxe [də'lʌks] *adj* di lusso.

delve [dɛlv] *vi*: **to ~ into** frugare in; (*subject*) far ricerche in.

Dem. *abbr* (*US POL*) = **democrat(ic).**

demagogue ['dɛməgɒg] *n* demagogo.

demand [dɪ'mɑːnd] *vt* richiedere ♦ *n* richiesta; (*ECON*) domanda; **to ~ sth (from** *or* **of sb)** pretendere qc (da qn), esigere qc (da qn); **in ~** ricercato(a), richiesto(a); **on ~** a richiesta.

demand draft *n* (*COMM*) tratta a vista.

demanding [dɪ'mɑːndɪŋ] *adj* (*boss*) esigente; (*work*) impegnativo(a).

demarcation [diːmɑː'keɪʃən] *n* demarcazione *f*.

demarcation dispute *n* (*INDUSTRY*) controversia settoriale (*or* di categoria).

demean [dɪ'miːn] *vt*: **to ~ o.s.** umiliarsi.

demeanour, (*US*) **demeanor** [dɪ'miːnə*] *n* comportamento; contegno.

demented [dɪ'mɛntɪd] *adj* demente, impazzito(a).

demilitarized zone [diː'mɪlɪtəraɪzd-] *n* zona smilitarizzata.

demise [dɪ'maɪz] *n* decesso.

demist [diː'mɪst] *vt* (*BRIT AUT*) sbrinare.

demister [diː'mɪstə*] *n* (*BRIT AUT*) sbrinatore *m*.

demo ['dɛməʊ] *n* *abbr* (*col*) = **demonstration.**

demobilize [diː'məʊbɪlaɪz] *vt* smobilitare.

democracy [dɪ'mɒkrəsɪ] *n* democrazia.

democrat ['dɛməkræt] *n* democratico/a.

democratic [dɛmə'krætɪk] *adj* democratico(a); **the D~ Party** (*US*) il partito democratico.

demography [dɪ'mɒgrəfɪ] *n* demografia.

demolish [dɪ'mɒlɪʃ] *vt* demolire.

demolition [dɛmə'lɪʃən] *n* demolizione *f*.

demon ['diːmən] *n* (*also fig*) demonio ♦ *cpd*: **a ~ squash player** un mago dello squash; **a ~ driver** un guidatore folle.

demonstrate ['dɛmənstreɪt] *vt* dimostrare, provare ♦ *vi*: **to ~ (for/against)** dimostrare (per/contro), manifestare (per/contro).

demonstration [dɛmən'streɪʃən] *n* dimostrazione *f*; (*POL*) manifestazione *f*, dimostrazione; **to hold a ~** (*POL*) tenere una manifestazione, fare una dimostrazione.

demonstrative [dɪ'mɒnstrətɪv] *adj* dimostrativo(a).

demonstrator ['dɛmənstreɪtə*] *n* (*POL*) dimostrante *m/f*; (*COMM: sales person*) dimostratore/trice; (: *car, computer etc*) modello per dimostrazione.

demoralize [dɪ'mɒrəlaɪz] *vt* demoralizzare.

demote [dɪ'məʊt] *vt* far retrocedere.

demotion [dɪ'məʊʃən] *n* retrocessione *f*, degradazione *f*.

demur [dɪ'mə:*] *vi* (*formal*): **to ~ (at)** sollevare obiezioni (a *or* su) ♦ *n*: **without ~** senza obiezioni.

demure [dɪ'mjʊə*] *adj* contegnoso(a).

demurrage [dɪ'mʌrɪdʒ] *n* diritti *mpl* di immagazzinaggio; spese *fpl* di controstallia.

den [dɛn] *n* tana, covo.

denationalization ['diːnæʃnəlaɪ'zeɪʃən] *n* denazionalizzazione *f*.

denationalize [diː'næʃnəlaɪz] *vt* snazionalizzare.

denial [dɪ'naɪəl] *n* diniego; rifiuto.

denier ['dɛnɪə*] *n* denaro (*di filati, calze*).

denigrate ['dɛnɪgreɪt] *vt* denigrare.

denim ['dɛnɪm] *n* tessuto di cotone ritorto; *see also* **denims.**

denim jacket *n* giubbotto di jeans.

denims ['dɛnɪmz] *npl* blue jeans *mpl*.

denizen ['dɛnɪzən] *n* (*inhabitant*) abitante *m/f*; (*foreigner*) straniero(a) naturalizzato(a).

Denmark ['dɛnmɑːk] n Danimarca.

denomination [dɪnɔmɪ'neɪʃən] n (money) valore m; (REL) confessione f.

denominator [dɪ'nɔmɪneɪtə*] n denominatore m.

denote [dɪ'nəut] vt denotare.

denounce [dɪ'nauns] vt denunciare.

dense [dɛns] adj fitto(a); (stupid) ottuso(a), duro(a).

densely ['dɛnslɪ] adv: ~ **wooded** fittamente boscoso(a); ~ **populated** densamente popolato(a).

density ['dɛnsɪtɪ] n densità f inv; **single/ double** ~ **disk** (COMPUT) disco a singola/ doppia densità di registrazione.

dent [dɛnt] n ammaccatura ♦ vt (also: **make a** ~ **in**) ammaccare; (fig) intaccare.

dental ['dɛntl] adj dentale.

dental floss [-flɔs] n filo interdentale.

dental surgeon n medico/a dentista.

dentist ['dɛntɪst] n dentista m/f; (surgery) (BRIT) gabinetto dentistico.

dentistry ['dɛntɪstrɪ] n odontoiatria.

denture(s) ['dɛntʃə(z)] n(pl) dentiera.

denunciation [dɪnʌnsɪ'eɪʃən] n denuncia.

deny [dɪ'naɪ] vt negare; (refuse) rifiutare; **he denies having said it** nega di averlo detto.

deodorant [diː'əudərənt] n deodorante m.

depart [dɪ'pɑːt] vi partire; **to** ~ **from** (leave) allontanarsi da, partire da; (fig) deviare da.

departed [dɪ'pɑːtɪd] adj estinto(a) ♦ n: **the** ~ il caro estinto/la cara estinta.

department [dɪ'pɑːtmənt] n (COMM) reparto; (SCOL) sezione f, dipartimento; (POL) ministero; **that's not my** ~ (also fig) questo non è di mia competenza; **D~ of State** (US) Dipartimento di Stato.

departmental [diːpɑːt'mɛntl] adj (dispute) settoriale; (meeting) di sezione; ~ **manager** caporeparto m/f.

department store n grande magazzino.

departure [dɪ'pɑːtʃə*] n partenza; (fig): ~ **from** deviazione f da; **a new** ~ una novità.

departure lounge n sala d'attesa.

depend [dɪ'pɛnd] vi: **to** ~ **(up)on** dipendere da; (rely on) contare su; (be dependent on) dipendere (economicamente) da, essere a carico di; **it** ~**s** dipende; ~**ing on the result** ... a seconda del risultato ....

dependable [dɪ'pɛndəbl] adj fidato(a); (car etc) affidabile.

dependant [dɪ'pɛndənt] n persona a carico.

dependence [dɪ'pɛndəns] n dipendenza.

dependent [dɪ'pɛndənt] adj: **to be** ~ **(on)** (gen) dipendere (da); (child, relative) essere a carico (di) ♦ n = **dependant**.

depict [dɪ'pɪkt] vt (in picture) dipingere; (in words) descrivere.

depilatory [dɪ'pɪlətərɪ] n (also: ~ **cream**) crema depilatoria.

depleted [dɪ'pliːtɪd] adj diminuito(a).

deplorable [dɪ'plɔːrəbl] adj deplorevole, lamentevole.

deplore [dɪ'plɔː*] vt deplorare.

deploy [dɪ'plɔɪ] vt dispiegare.

depopulate [diː'pɔpjuleɪt] vt spopolare.

depopulation ['diːpɔpju'leɪʃən] n spopolamento.

deport [dɪ'pɔːt] vt deportare; espellere.

deportation [diːpɔː'teɪʃən] n deportazione f.

deportation order n foglio di via obbligatorio.

deportee [diːpɔː'tiː] n deportato/a.

deportment [dɪ'pɔːtmənt] n portamento.

depose [dɪ'pəuz] vt deporre.

deposit [dɪ'pɔzɪt] n (COMM, GEO) deposito, (of ore, oil) giacimento; (CHEM) sedimento; (part payment) acconto; (for hired goods etc) cauzione f ♦ vt depositare; dare in acconto; (luggage etc) mettere or lasciare in deposito; **to put down a** ~ **of £50** versare una caparra di 50 sterline.

deposit account n conto vincolato.

depositor [dɪ'pɔzɪtə*] n depositante m/f.

depository [dɪ'pɔzɪtərɪ] n (person) depositario/a; (place) deposito.

depot ['dɛpəu] n deposito.

depraved [dɪ'preɪvd] adj depravato(a).

depravity [dɪ'prævɪtɪ] n depravazione f.

deprecate ['dɛprɪkeɪt] vt deprecare.

deprecating ['dɛprɪkeɪtɪŋ] adj (disapproving) di biasimo; (apologetic): **a** ~ **smile** un sorriso di scusa.

depreciate [dɪ'priːʃeɪt] vt svalutare ♦ vi svalutarsi.

depreciation [dɪpriːʃɪ'eɪʃən] n svalutazione f.

depress [dɪ'prɛs] vt deprimere; (press down) premere.

depressant [dɪ'prɛsnt] n (MED) sedativo.

depressed [dɪ'prɛst] adj (person) depresso(a), abbattuto(a); (area) depresso(a); (COMM: market, trade) stagnante, in ribasso; **to get** ~ deprimersi.

depressing [dɪ'prɛsɪŋ] adj deprimente.

depression [dɪ'prɛʃən] n depressione f.

deprivation [dɛprɪ'veɪʃən] n privazione f; (state) indigenza; (PSYCH) carenza affettiva.

deprive [dɪ'praɪv] vt: **to** ~ **sb of** privare qn di.

deprived [dɪ'praɪvd] adj disgraziato(a).

dept. *abbr* = **department.**

depth [dεpθ] *n* profondità *f inv*; **at a ~ of 3 metres** a una profondità di 3 metri, a 3 metri di profondità; **in the ~s of** nel profondo di; nel cuore di; **in the ~s of winter** in pieno inverno; **to study sth in ~** studiare qc in profondità; **to be out of one's ~** ~ (*BRIT*: *swimmer*) essere dove non si tocca; (*fig*) non sentirsi all'altezza della situazione.

depth charge *n* carica di profondità.

deputation [dεpju'teɪʃən] *n* deputazione *f*, delegazione *f*.

deputize ['dεpjutaɪz] *vi*: **to ~ for** svolgere le funzioni di.

deputy ['dεpjutɪ] *n* (*replacement*) supplente *m/f*; (*second in command*) vice *m/f* ♦ *cpd*: **~ chairman** vicepresidente *m*; **~ head** (*SCOL*) vicepreside *m/f*; **~ leader** (*BRIT POL*) sottosegretario.

derail [dɪ'reɪl] *vt* far deragliare; **to be ~ed** deragliare.

derailment [dɪ'reɪlmənt] *n* deragliamento.

deranged [dɪ'reɪndʒd] *adj*: **to be (mentally) ~** essere pazzo(a).

derby ['dɜːbɪ] *n* (*US*) bombetta.

Derbys *abbr* (*BRIT*) = **Derbyshire.**

deregulate [diː'rεgjuleɪt] *vt* eliminare la regolamentazione di.

deregulation ['diːrεgju'leɪʃən] *n* eliminazione *f* della regolamentazione.

derelict ['dεrɪlɪkt] *adj* abbandonato(a).

deride [dɪ'raɪd] *vt* deridere.

derision [dɪ'rɪʒən] *n* derisione *f*.

derisive [dɪ'raɪsɪv] *adj* di derisione.

derisory [dɪ'raɪsərɪ] *adj* (*sum*) irrisorio(a).

derivation [dεrɪ'veɪʃən] *n* derivazione *f*.

derivative [dɪ'rɪvətɪv] *n* derivato ♦ *adj* derivato(a).

derive [dɪ'raɪv] *vt*: **to ~ sth from** derivare qc da; trarre qc da ♦ *vi*: **to ~ from** derivare da.

dermatitis [dɜːmə'taɪtɪs] *n* dermatite *f*.

dermatology [dɜːmə'tɔlədʒɪ] *n* dermatologia.

derogatory [dɪ'rɔgətərɪ] *adj* denigratorio(a).

derrick ['dεrɪk] *n* gru *f inv*; (*for oil*) derrick *m inv*.

derv [dɜːv] *n* (*BRIT*) gasolio.

DES *n abbr* (*BRIT*: = *Department of Education and Science*) ≈ ministero della Pubblica Istruzione.

desalination [diːsælɪ'neɪʃən] *n* desalinizzazione *f*, dissalazione *f*.

descend [dɪ'sεnd] *vt*, *vi* discendere, scendere; **to ~ from** discendere da; **in ~ing order of importance** in ordine decrescente d'importanza.

▶**descend on** *vt fus* (*subj*: *enemy, angry person*) assalire, piombare su; (: *misfortune*) arrivare addosso a; (: *fig*: *gloom, silence*) scendere su; **visitors ~ed (up)on us** ci sono arrivate visite tra capo e collo.

descendant [dɪ'sεndənt] *n* discendente *m/f*.

descent [dɪ'sεnt] *n* discesa; (*origin*) discendenza, famiglia.

describe [dɪs'kraɪb] *vt* descrivere.

description [dɪs'krɪpʃən] *n* descrizione *f*; (*sort*) genere *m*, specie *f*; **of every ~** di ogni genere e specie.

descriptive [dɪs'krɪptɪv] *adj* descrittivo(a).

desecrate ['dεsɪkreɪt] *vt* profanare.

desert *n* ['dεzət] deserto ♦ *vb* [dɪ'zɜːt] *vt* lasciare, abbandonare ♦ *vi* (*MIL*) disertare; *see also* **deserts.**

deserter [dɪ'zɜːtə*] *n* disertore *m*.

desertion [dɪ'zɜːʃən] *n* diserzione *f*.

desert island *n* isola deserta.

deserts [dɪ'zɜːts] *npl*: **to get one's just ~** avere ciò che si merita.

deserve [dɪ'zɜːv] *vt* meritare.

deservedly [dɪ'zɜːvɪdlɪ] *adv* meritatamente, giustamente.

deserving [dɪ'zɜːvɪŋ] *adj* (*person*) meritevole, degno(a); (*cause*) meritorio(a).

desiccated ['dεsɪkeɪtɪd] *adj* essiccato(a).

design [dɪ'zaɪn] *n* (*sketch*) disegno; (: *of dress, car*) modello; (*layout, shape*) linea; (*pattern*) fantasia; (*COMM*) disegno tecnico; (*intention*) intenzione *f* ♦ *vt* disegnare; progettare; **to have ~s on** aver mire su; **well-~ed** ben concepito(a); **industrial ~** disegno industriale.

designate *vt* ['dεzɪgneɪt] designare ♦ *adj* ['dεzɪgnɪt] designato(a).

designation [dεzɪg'neɪʃən] *n* designazione *f*.

designer [dɪ'zaɪnə*] *n* (*TECH*) disegnatore/ trice, progettista *m/f*; (*of furniture*) designer *m/f inv*; (*fashion ~*) disegnatore/ trice di moda; (*of theatre sets*) scenografo/a.

desirability [dɪzaɪərə'bɪlɪtɪ] *n* desiderabilità; vantaggio.

desirable [dɪ'zaɪərəbl] *adj* desiderabile; **it is ~ that** è opportuno che + *sub*.

desire [dɪ'zaɪə*] *n* desiderio, voglia ♦ *vt* desiderare, volere; **to ~ sth/to do sth/ that** desiderare qc/di fare qc/che + *sub*.

desirous [dɪ'zaɪərəs] *adj*: **~ of** desideroso(a) di.

desk [dεsk] *n* (*in office*) scrivania; (*for pupil*) banco; (*BRIT*: *in shop, restaurant*) cassa; (*in* *hotel*) ricevimento; (*at airport*) accettazione *f.*

desk job *n* lavoro d'ufficio.

desktop computer ['dɛsktɔp-] *n* personal *m inv*, personal computer *m inv*.

desktop publishing *n* desktop publishing *m.*

desolate ['dɛsəlɪt] *adj* desolato(a).

desolation [dɛsə'leɪʃən] *n* desolazione *f.*

despair [dɪs'pɛə*] *n* disperazione *f* ♦ *vi*: **to ~ of** disperare di; **in ~** disperato(a).

despatch [dɪs'pætʃ] *n, vt* = **dispatch.**

desperate ['dɛspərɪt] *adj* disperato(a); (*measures*) estremo(a); (*fugitive*) capace di tutto; **we are getting ~** siamo sull'orlo della disperazione.

desperately ['dɛspərɪtlɪ] *adv* disperatamente; (*very*) terribilmente, estremamente; **~ ill** in pericolo di vita.

desperation [dɛspə'reɪʃən] *n* disperazione *f*; **in ~** per disperazione.

despicable [dɪs'pɪkəbl] *adj* disprezzabile.

despise [dɪs'paɪz] *vt* disprezzare, sdegnare.

despite [dɪs'paɪt] *prep* malgrado, a dispetto di, nonostante.

despondent [dɪs'pɔndənt] *adj* abbattuto(a), scoraggiato(a).

despot ['dɛspɔt] *n* despota *m.*

dessert [dɪ'zɜːt] *n* dolce *m*; frutta.

dessertspoon [dɪ'zɜːtspuːn] *n* cucchiaio da dolci.

destabilize [diː'steɪbɪlaɪz] *vt* privare di stabilità; (*fig*) destabilizzare.

destination [dɛstɪ'neɪʃən] *n* destinazione *f.*

destine ['dɛstɪn] *vt* destinare.

destined ['dɛstɪnd] *adj*: **to be ~ to do sth** essere destinato(a) a fare qc; **~ for London** diretto a Londra, con destinazione Londra.

destiny ['dɛstɪnɪ] *n* destino.

destitute ['dɛstɪtjuːt] *adj* indigente, bisognoso(a); **~ of** privo(a) di.

destroy [dɪs'trɔɪ] *vt* distruggere.

destroyer [dɪs'trɔɪə*] *n* (*NAUT*) cacciatorpediniere *m.*

destruction [dɪs'trʌkʃən] *n* distruzione *f.*

destructive [dɪs'trʌktɪv] *adj* distruttivo(a).

desultory ['dɛsəltərɪ] *adj* (*reading*) disordinato(a); (*conversation*) sconnesso(a); (*contact*) saltuario(a), irregolare.

detach [dɪ'tætʃ] *vt* staccare, distaccare.

detachable [dɪ'tætʃəbl] *adj* staccabile.

detached [dɪ'tætʃt] *adj* (*attitude*) distante.

detached house *n* villa.

detachment [dɪ'tætʃmənt] *n* (*MIL*) distaccamento; (*fig*) distacco.

detail ['diːteɪl] *n* particolare *m*, dettaglio;

(*MIL*) piccolo distaccamento ♦ *vt* dettagliare, particolareggiare; (*MIL*): **to ~ sb (for)** assegnare qn (a); **in ~** nei particolari; **to go into ~(s)** scendere nei particolari.

detailed ['diːteɪld] *adj* particolareggiato(a).

detain [dɪ'teɪn] *vt* trattenere; (*in captivity*) detenere.

detainee [diːteɪ'niː] *n* detenuto/a.

detect [dɪ'tɛkt] *vt* scoprire, scorgere; (*MED, POLICE, RADAR etc*) individuare.

detection [dɪ'tɛkʃən] *n* scoperta; individuazione *f*; **crime ~** indagini *fpl* criminali; **to escape ~** (*criminal*) eludere le ricerche; (*mistake*) passare inosservato(a).

detective [dɪ'tɛktɪv] *n* investigatore/trice; **private ~** investigatore *m* privato.

detective story *n* giallo.

detector [dɪ'tɛktə*] *n* rivelatore *m.*

détente [deɪ'taːnt] *n* distensione *f.*

detention [dɪ'tɛnʃən] *n* detenzione *f*; (*SCOL*) permanenza forzata per punizione.

deter [dɪ'tɜː*] *vt* dissuadere.

detergent [dɪ'tɜːdʒənt] *n* detersivo.

deteriorate [dɪ'tɪərɪəreɪt] *vi* deteriorarsi.

deterioration [dɪtɪərɪə'reɪʃən] *n* deterioramento.

determination [dɪtɜːmɪ'neɪʃən] *n* determinazione *f.*

determine [dɪ'tɜːmɪn] *vt* determinare; **to ~ to do sth** decidere di fare qc.

determined [dɪ'tɜːmɪnd] *adj* (*person*) risoluto(a), deciso(a); **to be ~ to do sth** essere determinato *or* deciso a fare qc; **a ~ effort** uno sforzo di volontà.

deterrence [dɪ'tɛrəns] *n* deterrenza.

deterrent [dɪ'tɛrənt] *n* deterrente *m*; **to act as a ~** fungere da deterrente.

detest [dɪ'tɛst] *vt* detestare.

detestable [dɪ'tɛstəbl] *adj* detestabile, abominevole.

detonate ['dɛtəneɪt] *vi* detonare ♦ *vt* far detonare.

detonator ['dɛtəneɪtə*] *n* detonatore *m.*

detour ['diːtuə*] *n* deviazione *f.*

detract [dɪ'trækt] *vt*: **to ~ from** detrarre da.

detractor [dɪ'træktə*] *n* detrattore/trice.

detriment ['dɛtrɪmənt] *n*: **to the ~ of** a detrimento di; **without ~ to** senza danno a.

detrimental [dɛtrɪ'mɛntl] *adj*: **~ to** dannoso(a) a, nocivo(a) a.

deuce [djuːs] *n* (*TENNIS*) quaranta pari *m inv.*

devaluation [diːvæljuː'eɪʃən] *n* svalutazione *f.*

devalue ['diː'væljuː] *vt* svalutare.

devastate ['dɛvəsteɪt] *vt* devastare; **he was ~d by the news** la notizia fu per lui un colpo terribile.
devastating ['dɛvəsteɪtɪŋ] *adj* devastatore(trice).
devastation [dɛvə'steɪʃən] *n* devastazione *f*.
develop [dɪ'vɛləp] *vt* sviluppare; (*habit*) prendere (gradualmente) ♦ *vi* svilupparsi; (*facts, symptoms*: *appear*) manifestarsi, rivelarsi; **to ~ a taste for sth** imparare a gustare qc; **to ~ into** diventare.
developer [dɪ'vɛləpə*] *n* (*PHOT*) sviluppatore *m*; **property ~** costruttore *m* (edile).
developing country [dɪ'vɛləpɪŋ-] *n* paese *m* in via di sviluppo.
development [dɪ'vɛləpmənt] *n* sviluppo.
development area *n* area di sviluppo industriale.
deviant ['diːvɪənt] *adj* deviante.
deviate ['diːvɪeɪt] *vi*: **to ~ (from)** deviare (da).
deviation [diːvɪ'eɪʃən] *n* deviazione *f*.
device [dɪ'vaɪs] *n* (*apparatus*) congegno; (*explosive* ~) ordigno esplosivo.
devil ['dɛvl] *n* diavolo; demonio.
devilish ['dɛvlɪʃ] *adj* diabolico(a).
devil-may-care ['dɛvlmeɪ'kɛə*] *adj* impudente.
devil's advocate *n*: **to play ~** fare l'avvocato del diavolo.
devious ['diːvɪəs] *adj* (*means*) indiretto(a), tortuoso(a); (*person*) subdolo(a).
devise [dɪ'vaɪz] *vt* escogitare, concepire.
devoid [dɪ'vɔɪd] *adj*: **~ of** privo(a) di.
devolution [diːvə'luːʃən] *n* (*POL*) decentramento.
devolve [dɪ'vɔlv] *vi*: **to ~ (up)on** ricadere su.
devote [dɪ'vəut] *vt*: **to ~ sth to** dedicare qc a.
devoted [dɪ'vəutɪd] *adj* devoto(a); **to be ~ to** essere molto attaccato(a) a.
devotee [dɛvəu'tiː] *n* (*REL*) adepto/a; (*MUS, SPORT*) appassionato/a.
devotion [dɪ'vəuʃən] *n* devozione *f*, attaccamento; (*REL*) atto di devozione, preghiera.
devour [dɪ'vauə*] *vt* divorare.
devout [dɪ'vaut] *adj* pio(a), devoto(a).
dew [djuː] *n* rugiada.
dexterity [dɛks'tɛrɪtɪ] *n* destrezza.
dext(e)rous ['dɛkstrəs] *adj* (*skilful*) destro(a), abile; (*movement*) agile.
dg *abbr* (= *decigram*) dg.
DH *n abbr* = **Department of Health**; *see*

health.
DHSS *n abbr* (*BRIT*: *old*) = *Department of Health and Social Security.*
diabetes [daɪə'biːtiːz] *n* diabete *m*.
diabetic [daɪə'bɛtɪk] *adj* diabetico(a); (*chocolate, jam*) per diabetici ♦ *n* diabetico/a.
diabolical [daɪə'bɔlɪkl] *adj* diabolico(a); (*col*: *dreadful*) infernale, atroce.
diaeresis [daɪ'ɛrɪsɪs] *n* dieresi *f inv*.
diagnose [daɪəg'nəuz] *vt* diagnosticare.
diagnosis, *pl* **diagnoses** [daɪəg'nəusɪs, -siːz] *n* diagnosi *f inv*.
diagonal [daɪ'ægənl] *adj*, *n* diagonale (*f*).
diagram ['daɪəgræm] *n* diagramma *m*.
dial ['daɪəl] *n* quadrante *m*; (*on telephone*) disco combinatore ♦ *vt* (*number*) fare; **to ~ a wrong number** sbagliare numero; **can I ~ London direct?** si può chiamare Londra in teleselezione?
dial. *abbr* = **dialect**.
dialect ['daɪəlɛkt] *n* dialetto.
dialling code ['daɪəlɪŋ-], (*US*) **area code** *n* prefisso.
dialling tone ['daɪəlɪŋ-], (*US*) **dial tone** *n* segnale *m* di linea libera.
dialogue ['daɪəlɔg] *n* dialogo.
dialysis [daɪ'ælɪsɪs] *n* dialisi *f*.
diameter [daɪ'æmɪtə*] *n* diametro.
diametrically [daɪə'mɛtrɪklɪ] *adv*: **~ opposed (to)** diametralmente opposto(a) (a).
diamond ['daɪəmənd] *n* diamante *m*; (*shape*) rombo; **~s** *npl* (*CARDS*) quadri *mpl*.
diamond ring *n* anello di brillanti; (*with one diamond*) anello con brillante.
diaper ['daɪəpə*] *n* (*US*) pannolino.
diaphragm ['daɪəfræm] *n* diaframma *m*.
diarrhoea, (*US*) **diarrhea** [daɪə'riːə] *n* diarrea.
diary ['daɪərɪ] *n* (*daily account*) diario; (*book*) agenda; **to keep a ~** tenere un diario.
diatribe ['daɪətraɪb] *n* diatriba.
dice [daɪs] *n* (*pl inv*) dado ♦ *vt* (*CULIN*) tagliare a dadini.
dicey ['daɪsɪ] *adj* (*col*): **it's a bit ~** è un po' un rischio.
dichotomy [daɪ'kɔtəmɪ] *n* dicotomia.
dickhead ['dɪkhɛd] *n* (*BRIT col!*) testa *m* di cazzo(*!*).
Dictaphone ® ['dɪktəfəun] *n* dittafono.
dictate *vt* [dɪk'teɪt] dettare ♦ *vi*: **to ~ to** (*person*) dare ordini a, dettar legge a ♦ *n* ['dɪkteɪt] dettame *m*; **I won't be ~d to** non ricevo ordini.
dictation [dɪk'teɪʃən] *n* dettato; (*to secretary etc*) dettatura; **at ~ speed** a velocità di dettatura.

dictator [dɪk'teɪtə*] n dittatore m.
dictatorship [dɪk'teɪtəʃɪp] n dittatura.
diction ['dɪkʃən] n dizione f.
dictionary ['dɪkʃənrɪ] n dizionario.
did [dɪd] pt of do.
didactic [daɪ'dæktɪk] adj didattico(a).
didn't = did not.
die [daɪ] n (pl: dies) conio; matrice f; stampo ♦ vi morire; **to be dying** star morendo; **to be dying for sth/to do sth** morire dalla voglia di qc/di fare qc; **to ~ (of or from)** morire di qc.
▶**die away** vi spegnersi a poco a poco.
▶**die down** vi abbassarsi.
▶**die out** vi estinguersi.
diehard ['daɪhɑːd] n reazionario/a.
diesel ['diːzl] n diesel m.
diesel engine n motore m diesel inv.
diesel fuel, diesel oil n gasolio (per motori diesel).
diet ['daɪət] n alimentazione f; (restricted food) dieta ♦ vi (also: **be on a ~**) stare a dieta; **to live on a ~ of** nutrirsi di.
dietician [daɪə'tɪʃən] n dietologo/a.
differ ['dɪfə*] vi: **to ~ from sth** differire da qc; essere diverso(a) da qc; **to ~ from sb over sth** essere in disaccordo con qn su qc.
difference ['dɪfrəns] n differenza; (quarrel) screzio; **it makes no ~ to me** per me è lo stesso; **to settle one's ~s** risolvere la situazione.
different ['dɪfrənt] adj diverso(a).
differential [dɪfə'renʃəl] n (AUT, wages) differenziale m.
differentiate [dɪfə'renʃɪeɪt] vi differenziarsi; **to ~ between** discriminare fra, fare differenza fra.
differently ['dɪfrəntlɪ] adv diversamente.
difficult ['dɪfɪkəlt] adj difficile; **~ to understand** difficile da capire.
difficulty ['dɪfɪkəltɪ] n difficoltà f inv; **to have difficulties with** (police, landlord etc) avere noie con; **to be in ~** essere or trovarsi in difficoltà.
diffidence ['dɪfɪdəns] n mancanza di sicurezza.
diffident ['dɪfɪdənt] adj sfiduciato(a).
diffuse adj [dɪ'fjuːs] diffuso(a) ♦ vt [dɪ'fjuːz] diffondere, emanare.
dig [dɪg] vb (pt, pp dug [dʌg]) vt (hole) scavare; (garden) vangare ♦ vi scavare ♦ n (prod) gomitata; (fig) frecciata; (ARCHAEOLOGY) scavo, scavi mpl; **to ~ into** (snow, soil) scavare; **to ~ into one's pockets for sth** frugarsi le tasche cercando qc; **to ~ one's nails into** conficcare le unghie in; see also **digs**.

▶**dig in** vi (col: eat) attaccare a mangiare; (also: ~ **o.s. in**: MIL) trincerarsi; (: fig) insediarsi, installarsi ♦ vt (compost) interrare; (knife, claw) affondare; **to ~ in one's heels** (fig) impuntarsi.
▶**dig out** vt (survivors, car from snow) tirar fuori (scavando); estrarre (scavando).
▶**dig up** vt scavare; (tree etc) sradicare.
digest [daɪ'dʒest] vt digerire.
digestible [dɪ'dʒestəbl] adj digeribile.
digestion [dɪ'dʒestʃən] n digestione f.
digestive [dɪ'dʒestɪv] adj digestivo(a); **~ system** apparato digerente.
digit ['dɪdʒɪt] n cifra; (finger) dito.
digital ['dɪdʒɪtəl] adj digitale.
digital compact cassette n piastra digitale per CD.
digital TV n televisione f digitale.
dignified ['dɪgnɪfaɪd] adj dignitoso(a).
dignitary ['dɪgnɪtərɪ] n dignitario.
dignity ['dɪgnɪtɪ] n dignità.
digress [daɪ'gres] vi: **to ~ from** divagare da.
digression [daɪ'greʃən] n digressione f.
digs [dɪgz] npl (BRIT col) camera ammobiliata.
dilapidated [dɪ'læpɪdeɪtɪd] adj cadente.
dilate [daɪ'leɪt] vt dilatare ♦ vi dilatarsi.
dilatory ['dɪlətərɪ] adj dilatorio(a).
dilemma [daɪ'lemə] n dilemma m; **to be in a ~** essere di fronte a un dilemma.
diligent ['dɪlɪdʒənt] adj diligente.
dill [dɪl] n aneto.
dilly-dally ['dɪlɪdælɪ] vi gingillarsi.
dilute [daɪ'luːt] vt diluire; (with water) annacquare ♦ adj diluito(a).
dim [dɪm] adj (light, eyesight) debole; (memory, outline) vago(a); (stupid) ottuso(a) ♦ vt (light: also: US AUT) abbassare; **to take a ~ view of sth** non vedere di buon occhio qc.
dime [daɪm] n (US) = 10 cents.
dimension [dɪ'menʃən] n dimensione f.
-dimensional [dɪ'menʃənl] adj suffix: **two~** bi-dimensionale.
diminish [dɪ'mɪnɪʃ] vt, vi diminuire.
diminished [dɪ'mɪnɪʃt] adj: **~ responsibility** (LAW) incapacità d'intendere e di volere.
diminutive [dɪ'mɪnjutɪv] adj minuscolo(a) ♦ n (LING) diminutivo.
dimly ['dɪmlɪ] adv debolmente; indistintamente.
dimmer ['dɪmə*] n (also: ~ **switch**) dimmer m inv, interruttore m a reostato; **~s** (US AUT) anabbaglianti mpl; (: parking lights) luci fpl di posizione.
dimple ['dɪmpl] n fossetta.
dim-witted ['dɪm'wɪtɪd] adj (col) sciocco(a).
din [dɪn] n chiasso, fracasso ♦ vt: **to ~ sth**

into sb (*col*) ficcare qc in testa a qn.
dine [daɪn] *vi* pranzare.
diner ['daɪnə*] *n* (*person: in restaurant*)
cliente *m*; (*RAIL*) carrozza *or* vagone *m*
ristorante; (*US: eating place*) tavola calda.
dinghy ['dɪŋgɪ] *n* battello pneumatico;
(*also*: **sailing** ~) dinghy *m inv*.
dingy ['dɪndʒɪ] *adj* grigio(a).
dining area ['daɪnɪŋ-] *n* zona pranzo *inv*.
dining car *n* vagone *m* ristorante.
dining room *n* sala da pranzo.
dinner ['dɪnə*] *n* pranzo; (*evening meal*)
cena; (*public*) banchetto; ~**'s ready!** a
tavola!
dinner jacket *n* smoking *m inv*.
dinner party *n* cena.
dinner service *n* servizio da tavola.
dinner time *n* ora di pranzo (*or* cena).
dinosaur ['daɪnəsɔ:*] *n* dinosauro.
dint [dɪnt] *n*: **by** ~ **of (doing) sth** a forza di
(fare) qc.
diocese ['daɪəsɪs] *n* diocesi *f inv*.
dioxide [daɪ'ɔksaɪd] *n* biossido.
dip [dɪp] *n* (*slope*) discesa; (*in sea*) bagno
◆ *vt* immergere, bagnare; (*BRIT AUT: lights*)
abbassare ◆ *vi* (*road*) essere in pendenza;
(*bird, plane*) abbassarsi.
Dip. *abbr* (*BRIT*) = **diploma**.
diphtheria [dɪf'θɪərɪə] *n* difterite *f*.
diphthong ['dɪfθɔŋ] *n* dittongo.
diploma [dɪ'pləumə] *n* diploma *m*.
diplomacy [dɪ'pləuməsɪ] *n* diplomazia.
diplomat ['dɪpləmæt] *n* diplomatico.
diplomatic [dɪplə'mætɪk] *adj*
diplomatico(a); **to break off** ~ **relations**
rompere le relazioni diplomatiche.
diplomatic corps *n* corpo diplomatico.
diplomatic immunity *n* immunità *f inv*
diplomatica.
dipstick ['dɪpstɪk] *n* (*AUT*) indicatore *m* di
livello dell'olio.
dipswitch ['dɪpswɪtʃ] *n* (*BRIT AUT*) levetta
dei fari.
dire [daɪə*] *adj* terribile; estremo(a).
direct [daɪ'rɛkt] *adj* diretto(a); (*manner,
person*) franco(a), esplicito(a) ◆ *vt*
dirigere; **to** ~ **sb to do sth** dare direttive
a qn di fare qc; **can you** ~ **me to ...?** mi
può indicare la strada per ...?
direct cost *n* (*COMM*) costo diretto.
direct current *n* (*ELEC*) corrente *f*
continua.
direct debit *n* (*BANKING*) addebito
effettuato per ordine di un cliente di
banca.
direct dialling *n* (*TEL*) ≈ teleselezione *f*.
direct hit *n* (*MIL*) colpo diretto.
direction [dɪ'rɛkʃən] *n* direzione *f*; (*of play,*

film, programme) regia; ~**s** *npl* (*advice*)
chiarimenti *mpl*; (*instructions: to a place*)
indicazioni *fpl*; ~**s for use** istruzioni *fpl*; **to
ask for** ~**s** chiedere la strada; **sense of** ~
senso dell'orientamento; **in the** ~ **of** in
direzione di.
directive [dɪ'rɛktɪv] *n* direttiva, ordine *m*; **a
government** ~ una disposizione
governativa.
direct labour *n* manodopera diretta.
directly [dɪ'rɛktlɪ] *adv* (*in straight line*)
direttamente; (*at once*) subito.
direct mail *n* pubblicità diretta.
direct mailshot *n* (*BRIT*) materiale *m*
pubblicitario ad approccio diretto.
directness [daɪ'rɛktnɪs] *n* (*of person, speech*)
franchezza.
director [dɪ'rɛktə*] *n* direttore/trice;
amministratore/trice; (*THEAT, CINE, TV*)
regista *m/f*; **D**~ **of Public Prosecutions
(DPP)** (*BRIT*) ≈ Procuratore *m* della
Repubblica.
directory [dɪ'rɛktərɪ] *n* elenco; (*street* ~)
stradario; (*trade* ~) repertorio del
commercio; (*COMPUT*) directory *m inv*.
directory enquiries, (*US*) **directory
assistance** *n* (*TEL*) servizio informazioni,
informazioni *fpl* elenco abbonati.
dirt [dɜ:t] *n* sporcizia; immondizia; **to treat
sb like** ~ trattare qn come uno straccio.
dirt-cheap ['dɜ:t'tʃi:p] *adj* da due soldi.
dirt road *n* strada non asfaltata.
dirty ['dɜ:tɪ] *adj* sporco(a) ◆ *vt* sporcare; ~
story storia oscena; ~ **trick** brutto
scherzo.
disability [dɪsə'bɪlɪtɪ] *n* invalidità *f inv*;
(*LAW*) incapacità *f inv*.
disability allowance *n* pensione *f*
d'invalidità.
disable [dɪs'eɪbl] *vt* (*subj: illness, accident*)
rendere invalido(a); (*tank, gun*) mettere
fuori uso.
disabled [dɪs'eɪbld] *adj* invalido(a);
(*maimed*) mutilato(a); (*through illness, old
age*) inabile.
disadvantage [dɪsəd'vɑ:ntɪdʒ] *n*
svantaggio.
disadvantaged [dɪsəd'vɑ:ntɪdʒd] *adj*
(*person*) svantaggiato(a).
disadvantageous [dɪsædvɑ:n'teɪdʒəs] *adj*
svantaggioso(a).
disaffected [dɪsə'fɛktɪd] *adj*: ~ (**to** *or*
towards) scontento(a) di, insoddisfatto(a)
di.
disaffection [dɪsə'fɛkʃən] *n* malcontento,
insoddisfazione *f*.
disagree [dɪsə'gri:] *vi* (*differ*) discordare;
(*be against, think otherwise*): **to** ~ (**with**)

essere in disaccordo (con), dissentire (da); **I ~ with you** non sono d'accordo con lei; **garlic ~s with me** l'aglio non mi va.
disagreeable [dɪsə'griːəbl] adj sgradevole; (person) antipatico(a).
disagreement [dɪsə'griːmənt] n disaccordo; (quarrel) dissapore m; **to have a ~ with sb** litigare con qn.
disallow ['dɪsə'lau] vt respingere; (BRIT FOOTBALL: goal) annullare.
disappear [dɪsə'pɪə*] vi scomparire.
disappearance [dɪsə'pɪərəns] n scomparsa.
disappoint [dɪsə'pɔɪnt] vt deludere.
disappointed [dɪsə'pɔɪntɪd] adj deluso(a).
disappointing [dɪsə'pɔɪntɪŋ] adj deludente.
disappointment [dɪsə'pɔɪntmənt] n delusione f.
disapproval [dɪsə'pruːvəl] n disapprovazione f.
disapprove [dɪsə'pruːv] vi: **to ~ of** disapprovare.
disapproving [dɪsə'pruːvɪŋ] adj di disapprovazione.
disarm [dɪs'aːm] vt disarmare.
disarmament [dɪs'aːməmənt] n disarmo.
disarming [dɪs'aːmɪŋ] adj (smile) disarmante.
disarray [dɪsə'reɪ] n: **in ~** (troops) in rotta; (thoughts) confuso(a); (clothes) in disordine; **to throw into ~** buttare all'aria.
disaster [dɪ'zaːstə*] n disastro.
disaster area n zona disastrata.
disastrous [dɪ'zaːstrəs] adj disastroso(a).
disband [dɪs'bænd] vt sbandare; (MIL) congedare ♦ vi sciogliersi.
disbelief ['dɪsbə'liːf] n incredulità; **in ~** incredulo(a).
disbelieve ['dɪsbə'liːv] vt (person, story) non credere a, mettere in dubbio; **I don't ~ you** vorrei poterle credere.
disc [dɪsk] n disco.
disc. abbr (COMM) = **discount**.
discard [dɪs'kaːd] vt (old things) scartare; (fig) abbandonare.
disc brake n freno a disco.
discern [dɪ'səːn] vt discernere, distinguere.
discernible [dɪ'səːnəbl] adj percepibile.
discerning [dɪ'səːnɪŋ] adj perspicace.
discharge vt [dɪs'tʃaːdʒ] (duties) compiere; (settle: debt) pagare, estinguere; (ELEC, waste etc) scaricare; (MED) emettere; (patient) dimettere; (employee) licenziare; (soldier) congedare; (defendant) liberare ♦ n ['dɪstʃaːdʒ] (ELEC) scarica; (MED, of gas, chemicals) emissione f; (vaginal ~) perdite fpl (bianche); (dismissal) licenziamento; congedo; liberazione f; **to ~ one's gun**

fare fuoco.
discharged bankrupt [dɪs'tʃaːdʒd-] n fallito cui il tribunale ha concesso la riabilitazione.
disciple [dɪ'saɪpl] n discepolo.
disciplinary ['dɪsɪplɪnərɪ] adj disciplinare; **to take ~ action against sb** prendere un provvedimento disciplinare contro qn.
discipline ['dɪsɪplɪn] n disciplina ♦ vt disciplinare; (punish) punire; **to ~ o.s. to do sth** imporsi di fare qc.
disc jockey (DJ) n disc jockey m inv.
disclaim [dɪs'kleɪm] vt negare, smentire.
disclaimer [dɪs'kleɪmə*] n smentita; **to issue a ~** pubblicare una smentita.
disclose [dɪs'kləuz] vt rivelare, svelare.
disclosure [dɪs'kləuʒə*] n rivelazione f.
disco ['dɪskəu] n abbr = **discothèque**.
discolour, (US) **discolor** [dɪs'kʌlə*] vt scolorire; (sth white) ingiallire ♦ vi sbiadire, scolorirsi; (sth white) ingiallire.
discolo(u)ration [dɪskʌlə'reɪʃən] n scolorimento.
discolo(u)red [dɪs'kʌləd] adj scolorito(a); ingiallito(a).
discomfort [dɪs'kʌmfət] n disagio; (lack of comfort) scomodità f inv.
disconcert [dɪskən'səːt] vt sconcertare.
disconnect [dɪskə'nɛkt] vt sconnettere, staccare; (ELEC, RADIO) staccare; (gas, water) chiudere.
disconnected [dɪskə'nɛktɪd] adj (speech, thought) sconnesso(a).
disconsolate [dɪs'kɔnsəlɪt] adj sconsolato(a).
discontent [dɪskən'tɛnt] n scontentezza.
discontented [dɪskən'tɛntɪd] adj scontento(a).
discontinue [dɪskən'tɪnjuː] vt smettere, cessare; "**~d**" (COMM) "sospeso".
discord ['dɪskɔːd] n disaccordo; (MUS) dissonanza.
discordant [dɪs'kɔːdənt] adj discordante; dissonante.
discothèque ['dɪskəutɛk] n discoteca.
discount n ['dɪskaunt] sconto ♦ vt [dɪs'kaunt] scontare; (report etc) non badare a; **at a ~** con uno sconto; **to give sb a ~ on sth** fare uno sconto a qn su qc; **~ for cash** sconto m cassa inv.
discount house n (FINANCE) casa di sconto, discount house f inv; (COMM: also: **discount store**) discount m inv.
discount rate n tasso di sconto.
discourage [dɪs'kʌrɪdʒ] vt scoraggiare; (dissuade, deter) tentare di dissuadere.
discouragement [dɪs'kʌrɪdʒmənt] n (dissuasion) disapprovazione f;

(*depression*) scoraggiamento; **to act as a** ~ **to** ostacolare.

discouraging [dɪs'kʌrɪdʒɪŋ] *adj* scoraggiante.

discourteous [dɪs'kɔːtɪəs] *adj* scortese.

discover [dɪs'kʌvə*] *vt* scoprire.

discovery [dɪs'kʌvərɪ] *n* scoperta.

discredit [dɪs'kredɪt] *vt* screditare; mettere in dubbio ♦ *n* discredito.

discreet [dɪ'skriːt] *adj* discreto(a).

discreetly [dɪ'skriːtlɪ] *adv* con discrezione.

discrepancy [dɪ'skrepənsɪ] *n* discrepanza.

discretion [dɪ'skreʃən] *n* discrezione *f*; **use your own** ~ giudichi lei.

discretionary [dɪs'kreʃənərɪ] *adj* (*powers*) discrezionale.

discriminate [dɪ'skrɪmɪneɪt] *vi*: **to** ~ **between** distinguere tra; **to** ~ **against** discriminare contro.

discriminating [dɪs'krɪmɪneɪtɪŋ] *adj* (*ear, taste*) fine, giudizioso(a); (*person*) esigente; (*tax, duty*) discriminante.

discrimination [dɪskrɪmɪ'neɪʃən] *n* discriminazione *f*; (*judgement*) discernimento; **racial/sexual** ~ discriminazione razziale/sessuale.

discus ['dɪskəs] *n* disco.

discuss [dɪ'skʌs] *vt* discutere; (*debate*) dibattere.

discussion [dɪ'skʌʃən] *n* discussione *f*; **under** ~ in discussione.

disdain [dɪs'deɪn] *n* disdegno.

disease [dɪ'ziːz] *n* malattia.

diseased [dɪ'ziːzd] *adj* malato(a).

disembark [dɪsɪm'bɑːk] *vt, vi* sbarcare.

disembarkation [dɪsɛmbɑː'keɪʃən] *n* sbarco.

disembodied [dɪsɪm'bɔdɪd] *adj* disincarnato(a).

disembowel [dɪsɪm'bauəl] *vt* sbudellare, sventrare.

disenchanted [dɪsɪn'tʃɑːntɪd] *adj* disincantato(a); ~ (**with**) deluso(a) (da).

disenfranchise [dɪsɪn'fræntʃaɪz] *vt* privare del diritto di voto; (*COMM*) revocare una condizione di privilegio commerciale a.

disengage [dɪsɪn'geɪdʒ] *vt* disimpegnare; (*TECH*) distaccare; (*AUT*) disinnestare.

disentangle [dɪsɪn'tæŋgl] *vt* sbrogliare.

disfavour, (*US*) **disfavor** [dɪs'feɪvə*] *n* sfavore *m*; disgrazia.

disfigure [dɪs'fɪgə*] *vt* sfigurare.

disgorge [dɪs'gɔːdʒ] *vt* (*subj: river*) riversare.

disgrace [dɪs'greɪs] *n* vergogna; (*disfavour*) disgrazia ♦ *vt* disonorare, far cadere in disgrazia.

disgraceful [dɪs'greɪsful] *adj* scandaloso(a),

vergognoso(a).

disgruntled [dɪs'grʌntld] *adj* scontento(a), di cattivo umore.

disguise [dɪs'gaɪz] *n* travestimento ♦ *vt* travestire; (*voice*) contraffare; (*feelings etc*) mascherare; **to** ~ **o.s. as** travestirsi da; **in** ~ travestito(a); **there's no disguising the fact that** ... non si può nascondere (il fatto) che ....

disgust [dɪs'gʌst] *n* disgusto, nausea ♦ *vt* disgustare, far schifo a.

disgusting [dɪs'gʌstɪŋ] *adj* disgustoso(a).

dish [dɪʃ] *n* piatto; **to do** *or* **wash the** ~**es** fare i piatti.

▶**dish out** *vt* (*food*) servire; (*advice*) elargire; (*money*) tirare fuori; (*exam papers*) distribuire.

▶**dish up** *vt* (*food*) servire; (*facts, statistics*) presentare.

dishcloth ['dɪʃklɔθ] *n* strofinaccio dei piatti.

dishearten [dɪs'hɑːtn] *vt* scoraggiare.

dishevelled, (*US*) **disheveled** [dɪ'ʃevəld] *adj* arruffato(a); scapigliato(a).

dishonest [dɪs'ɔnɪst] *adj* disonesto(a).

dishonesty [dɪs'ɔnɪstɪ] *n* disonestà.

dishonour, (*US*) **dishonor** [dɪs'ɔnə*] *n* disonore *m*.

dishono(u)rable [dɪs'ɔnərəbl] *adj* disonorevole.

dish soap *n* (*US*) detersivo liquido (per stoviglie).

dishtowel ['dɪʃtauəl] *n* strofinaccio dei piatti.

dishwasher ['dɪʃwɔʃə*] *n* lavastoviglie *f inv*; (*person*) sguattero/a.

dishy ['dɪʃɪ] *adj* (*BRIT col*) figo(a).

disillusion [dɪsɪ'luːʒən] *vt* disilludere, disingannare ♦ *n* disillusione *f*; **to become** ~**ed** (**with**) perdere le illusioni (su).

disillusionment [dɪsɪ'luːʒənmənt] *n* disillusione *f*.

disincentive [dɪsɪn'sentɪv] *n*: **to act as a** ~ (**to**) agire da freno (su); **to be a** ~ **to** scoraggiare.

disinclined [dɪsɪn'klaɪnd] *adj*: **to be** ~ **to do sth** essere poco propenso(a) a fare qc.

disinfect [dɪsɪn'fekt] *vt* disinfettare.

disinfectant [dɪsɪn'fektənt] *n* disinfettante *m*.

disinflation [dɪsɪn'fleɪʃən] *n* disinflazione *f*.

disinformation [dɪsɪnfə'meɪʃən] *n* disinformazione *f*.

disinherit [dɪsɪn'herɪt] *vt* diseredare.

disintegrate [dɪs'ɪntɪgreɪt] *vi* disintegrarsi.

disinterested [dɪs'ɪntrəstɪd] *adj* disinteressato(a).

disjointed [dɪs'dʒɔɪntɪd] *adj* sconnesso(a).

disk [dɪsk] n (COMPUT) disco; **single-/ double-sided** ~ disco m monofaccia inv/a doppia faccia.

disk drive n disk drive m inv, unità f inv a dischi magnetici.

disk operating system (DOS) n sistema m operativo a disco.

diskette [dɪs'kɛt] n (COMPUT) dischetto.

dislike [dɪs'laɪk] n antipatia, avversione f ♦ vt: **he ~s it** non gli piace; **I ~ the idea** l'idea non mi va; **to take a ~ to sb/sth** prendere in antipatia qn/qc.

dislocate ['dɪsləkeɪt] vt (MED) slogare; (fig) disorganizzare; **he ~d his shoulder** si è lussato una spalla.

dislodge [dɪs'lɔdʒ] vt rimuovere, staccare; (enemy) sloggiare.

disloyal [dɪs'lɔɪəl] adj sleale.

dismal ['dɪzml] adj triste, cupo(a).

dismantle [dɪs'mæntl] vt smantellare, smontare; (fort, warship) disarmare.

dismast [dɪs'mɑːst] vt disalberare.

dismay [dɪs'meɪ] n costernazione f ♦ vt sgomentare; **much to my** ~ con mio gran stupore.

dismiss [dɪs'mɪs] vt congedare; (employee) licenziare; (idea) scacciare; (LAW) respingere ♦ vi (MIL) rompere i ranghi.

dismissal [dɪs'mɪsəl] n congedo; licenziamento.

dismount [dɪs'maunt] vi scendere ♦ vt (rider) disarcionare.

disobedience [dɪsə'biːdɪəns] n disubbidienza.

disobedient [dɪsə'biːdɪənt] adj disubbidiente.

disobey [dɪsə'beɪ] vt disubbidire; (rule) trasgredire.

disorder [dɪs'ɔːdə*] n disordine m; (rioting) tumulto; (MED) disturbo; **civil** ~ disordini mpl interni.

disorderly [dɪs'ɔːdəlɪ] adj disordinato(a); tumultuoso(a).

disorderly conduct n (LAW) comportamento atto a turbare l'ordine pubblico.

disorganize [dɪs'ɔːgənaɪz] vt disorganizzare.

disorganized [dɪs'ɔːgənaɪzd] adj (person, life) disorganizzato(a); (system, meeting) male organizzato(a).

disorientated [dɪs'ɔːrɪɛnteɪtɪd] adj disorientato(a).

disown [dɪs'əun] vt ripudiare.

disparaging [dɪs'pærɪdʒɪŋ] adj spregiativo(a), sprezzante; **to be** ~ **about sb/sth** denigrare qn/qc.

disparate ['dɪspərɪt] adj disparato(a).

disparity [dɪs'pærɪtɪ] n disparità f inv.

dispassionate [dɪs'pæʃənət] adj calmo(a), freddo(a); imparziale.

dispatch [dɪs'pætʃ] vt spedire, inviare; (deal with: business) sbrigare ♦ n spedizione f, invio; (MIL, PRESS) dispaccio.

dispatch department n reparto spedizioni.

dispatch rider n (MIL) corriere m, portaordini m inv.

dispel [dɪs'pɛl] vt dissipare, scacciare.

dispensary [dɪs'pɛnsərɪ] n farmacia; (in chemist's) dispensario.

dispense [dɪs'pɛns] vt distribuire, amministrare; (medicine) preparare e dare; **to** ~ **sb from** dispensare qn da; ►**dispense with** vt fus fare a meno di; (make unnecessary) rendere superfluo(a).

dispenser [dɪs'pɛnsə*] n (container) distributore m.

dispensing chemist n (BRIT) farmacista m/f.

dispersal [dɪs'pəːsl] n dispersione f.

disperse [dɪs'pəːs] vt disperdere; (knowledge) disseminare ♦ vi disperdersi.

dispirited [dɪs'pɪrɪtɪd] adj scoraggiato(a), abbattuto(a).

displace [dɪs'pleɪs] vt spostare.

displaced person n (POL) profugo/a.

displacement [dɪs'pleɪsmənt] n spostamento.

display [dɪs'pleɪ] n mostra; esposizione f; (of feeling etc) manifestazione f; (military ~) parata (militare); (computer ~) display m inv; (pej) ostentazione f ♦ vt mostrare; (goods) esporre; (results) affiggere; (departure times) indicare; **on** ~ (gen) in mostra; (goods) in vetrina.

display advertising n pubblicità tabellare.

displease [dɪs'pliːz] vt dispiacere a, scontentare; ~**d with** scontento(a) di.

displeasure [dɪs'plɛʒə*] n dispiacere m.

disposable [dɪs'pəuzəbl] adj (pack etc) a perdere; (income) disponibile; ~ **nappy** (BRIT) pannolino di carta.

disposal [dɪs'pəuzl] n (of rubbish) evacuazione f; distruzione f; (of property etc: by selling) vendita; (: by giving away) cessione f; **at one's** ~ alla sua disposizione; **to put sth at sb's** ~ mettere qc a disposizione di qn.

dispose [dɪs'pəuz] vt disporre; ►**dispose of** vt fus (time, money) disporre di; (COMM: sell) vendere; (unwanted goods) sbarazzarsi di; (problem) eliminare.

disposed [dɪs'pəuzd] adj: ~ **to do** disposto(a) a fare.

disposition [dɪspə'zɪʃən] *n* disposizione *f*;
(*temperament*) carattere *m*.

dispossess ['dɪspə'zɛs] *vt*: **to** ~ **sb (of)**
spossessare qn (di).

disproportion [dɪsprə'pɔ:ʃən] *n*
sproporzione *f*.

disproportionate [dɪsprə'pɔ:ʃənət] *adj*
sproporzionato(a).

disprove [dɪs'pru:v] *vt* confutare.

dispute [dɪs'pju:t] *n* disputa; (*also*:
industrial ~) controversia (sindacale) ♦ *vt*
contestare; (*matter*) discutere; (*victory*)
disputare; **to be in** *or* **under** ~ (*matter*)
essere in discussione; (*territory*) essere
oggetto di contesa.

disqualification [dɪskwɔlɪfɪ'keɪʃən] *n*
squalifica; ~ (**from driving**) (*BRIT*) ritiro
della patente.

disqualify [dɪs'kwɔlɪfaɪ] *vt* (*SPORT*)
squalificare; **to** ~ **sb from sth/from doing**
rendere qn incapace a qc/a fare;
squalificare qn da qc/da fare; **to** ~ **sb**
from driving (*BRIT*) ritirare la patente a
qn.

disquiet [dɪs'kwaɪət] *n* inquietudine *f*.

disquieting [dɪs'kwaɪətɪŋ] *adj* inquietante,
allarmante.

disregard [dɪsrɪ'gɑːd] *vt* non far caso a, non
badare a ♦ *n* (*indifference*): ~ (**for**)
(*feelings*) insensibilità (a), indifferenza
(verso); (*danger*) noncuranza (di);
(*money*) disprezzo (di).

disrepair [dɪsrɪ'pɛə*] *n* cattivo stato; **to fall**
into ~ (*building*) andare in rovina; (*street*)
deteriorarsi.

disreputable [dɪs'rɛpjutəbl] *adj* (*person*) di
cattiva fama; (*area*) malfamato(a), poco
raccomandabile.

disrepute ['dɪsrɪ'pju:t] *n* disonore *m*,
vergogna; **to bring into** ~ rovinare la
reputazione di.

disrespectful [dɪsrɪ'spɛktful] *adj* che manca
di rispetto.

disrupt [dɪs'rʌpt] *vt* (*meeting*, *lesson*)
disturbare, interrompere; (*public*
transport) creare scompiglio in; (*plans*)
scombussolare.

disruption [dɪs'rʌpʃən] *n* disordine *m*;
interruzione *f*.

disruptive [dɪs'rʌptɪv] *adj* (*influence*)
negativo(a), deleterio(a); (*strike action*)
paralizzante.

dissatisfaction [dɪssætɪs'fækʃən] *n*
scontentezza, insoddisfazione *f*.

dissatisfied [dɪs'sætɪsfaɪd] *adj*: ~ (**with**)
scontento(a) *or* insoddisfatto(a) (di).

dissect [dɪ'sɛkt] *vt* sezionare; (*fig*)
sviscerare.

disseminate [dɪ'sɛmɪneɪt] *vt* disseminare.

dissent [dɪ'sɛnt] *n* dissenso.

dissenter [dɪ'sɛntə*] *n* (*REL*, *POL etc*)
dissidente *m/f*.

dissertation [dɪsə'teɪʃən] *n* (*SCOL*) tesi *f inv*,
dissertazione *f*.

disservice [dɪs'sə:vɪs] *n*: **to do sb a** ~ fare
un cattivo servizio a qn.

dissident ['dɪsɪdnt] *adj* dissidente; (*speech*,
voice) di dissenso ♦ *n* dissidente *m/f*.

dissimilar [dɪ'sɪmɪlə*] *adj*: ~ (**to**) dissimile
or diverso(a) (da).

dissipate ['dɪsɪpeɪt] *vt* dissipare.

dissipated ['dɪsɪpeɪtɪd] *adj* dissipato(a).

dissociate [dɪ'səuʃɪeɪt] *vt* dissociare; **to** ~
o.s. from dichiarare di non avere niente a
che fare con.

dissolute ['dɪsəlu:t] *adj* dissoluto(a),
licenzioso(a).

dissolve [dɪ'zɔlv] *vt* dissolvere, sciogliere;
(*COMM*, *POL*, *marriage*) sciogliere ♦ *vi*
dissolversi, sciogliersi; (*fig*) svanire.

dissuade [dɪ'sweɪd] *vt*: **to** ~ **sb (from)**
dissuadere qn (da).

distaff side ['dɪstɑːf-] *n ramo femminile di*
una famiglia.

distance ['dɪstns] *n* distanza; **in the** ~ **in**
lontananza; **what's the** ~ **to London?**
quanto dista Londra?; **it's within walking**
~ ci si arriva a piedi; **at a** ~ **of 2 metres** a
2 metri di distanza.

distant ['dɪstnt] *adj* lontano(a), distante;
(*manner*) riservato(a), freddo(a).

distaste [dɪs'teɪst] *n* ripugnanza.

distasteful [dɪs'teɪstful] *adj* ripugnante,
sgradevole.

Dist. Atty. *abbr* (*US*) = **district attorney**.

distemper [dɪs'tɛmpə*] *n* (*paint*) tempera;
(*of dogs*) cimurro.

distend [dɪs'tɛnd] *vt* dilatare ♦ *vi* dilatarsi.

distended [dɪs'tɛndɪd] *adj* (*stomach*)
dilatato(a).

distil, (*US*) **distill** [dɪs'tɪl] *vt* distillare.

distillery [dɪs'tɪlərɪ] *n* distilleria.

distinct [dɪs'tɪŋkt] *adj* distinto(a);
(*preference*, *progress*) definito(a); **as** ~
from a differenza di.

distinction [dɪs'tɪŋkʃən] *n* distinzione *f*; (*in*
exam) lode *f*; **to draw a** ~ **between** fare
distinzione tra; **a writer of** ~ uno
scrittore di notevoli qualità.

distinctive [dɪs'tɪŋktɪv] *adj* distintivo(a).

distinctly [dɪs'tɪŋktlɪ] *adv* distintamente;
(*remember*) chiaramente; (*unhappy*, *better*)
decisamente.

distinguish [dɪs'tɪŋgwɪʃ] *vt* distinguere;
discernere ♦ *vi*: **to** ~ (**between**)
distinguere (tra); **to** ~ **o.s.** distinguersi.

distinguished [dɪs'tɪŋgwɪʃt] adj (eminent) eminente; (career) brillante; (refined) distinto(a), signorile.

distinguishing [dɪs'tɪŋgwɪʃɪŋ] adj (feature) distinto(a), caratteristico(a).

distort [dɪs'tɔːt] vt (also fig) distorcere; (account, news) falsare; (TECH) deformare.

distortion [dɪs'tɔːʃən] n (gen) distorsione f; (of truth etc) alterazione f; (of facts) travisamento; (TECH) deformazione f.

distract [dɪs'trækt] vt distrarre.

distracted [dɪs'træktɪd] adj distratto(a).

distraction [dɪs'trækʃən] n distrazione f; **to drive sb to** ~ spingere qn alla pazzia.

distraught [dɪs'trɔːt] adj stravolto(a).

distress [dɪs'trɛs] n angoscia; (pain) dolore m ♦ vt affliggere; **in** ~ (ship etc) in pericolo, in difficoltà; **~ed area** (BRIT) zona sinistrata.

distressing [dɪs'trɛsɪŋ] adj doloroso(a), penoso(a).

distress signal n segnale m di pericolo.

distribute [dɪs'trɪbjuːt] vt distribuire.

distribution [dɪstrɪ'bjuːʃən] n distribuzione f.

distribution cost n costo di distribuzione.

distributor [dɪs'trɪbjutə*] n distributore m; (COMM) concessionario.

district ['dɪstrɪkt] n (of country) regione f; (of town) quartiere m; (ADMIN) distretto.

district attorney (DA) n (US) ≈ sostituto procuratore m della Repubblica.

district council n organo di amministrazione locale; see boxed note.

DISTRICT COUNCIL

In Inghilterra e in Galles, il **district council** è l'organo amministrativo responsabile di ciascun "district". È finanziato tramite una tassa locale e riceve un contributo da parte del governo. I **district councils** vengono eletti a livello locale ogni quattro anni.

---

district nurse n (BRIT) infermiera di quartiere.

distrust [dɪs'trʌst] n diffidenza, sfiducia ♦ vt non aver fiducia in.

distrustful [dɪs'trʌstful] adj diffidente.

disturb [dɪs'təːb] vt disturbare; (inconvenience) scomodare; **sorry to** ~ **you** scusi se la disturbo.

disturbance [dɪs'təːbəns] n disturbo; (political etc) tumulto; (by drunks etc) disordini mpl; ~ **of the peace** disturbo della quiete pubblica; **to cause a** ~

provocare disordini.

disturbed [dɪs'təːbd] adj turbato(a); **to be emotionally** ~ avere problemi emotivi; **to be mentally** ~ essere malato(a) di mente.

disturbing [dɪs'təːbɪŋ] adj sconvolgente.

disuse [dɪs'juːs] n: **to fall into** ~ cadere in disuso.

disused [dɪs'juːzd] adj abbandonato(a).

ditch [dɪtʃ] n fossa ♦ vt (col) piantare in asso.

dither ['dɪðə*] vi vacillare.

ditto ['dɪtəu] adv idem.

divan [dɪ'væn] n divano.

divan bed n divano letto inv.

dive [daɪv] n tuffo; (of submarine) immersione f; (AVIAT) picchiata; (pej) buco ♦ vi tuffarsi.

diver ['daɪvə*] n tuffatore/trice; (deep-sea ~) palombaro.

diverge [daɪ'vəːdʒ] vi divergere.

divergent [daɪ'vəːdʒənt] adj divergente.

diverse [daɪ'vəːs] adj vario(a).

diversification [daɪvəːsɪfɪ'keɪʃən] n diversificazione f.

diversify [daɪ'vəːsɪfaɪ] vt diversificare.

diversion [daɪ'vəːʃən] n (BRIT AUT) deviazione f; (distraction) distrazione f.

diversionary tactics [daɪ'vəːʃənrɪ-] npl tattica fsg diversiva.

diversity [daɪ'vəːsɪtɪ] n diversità f inv, varietà f inv.

divert [daɪ'vəːt] vt (traffic, river) deviare; (train, plane) dirottare; (amuse) divertire.

divest [daɪ'vɛst] vt: **to** ~ **sb of** spogliare qn di.

divide [dɪ'vaɪd] vt dividere; (separate) separare ♦ vi dividersi; **to** ~ (**between** or **among**) dividere (tra), ripartire (tra); **40** ~**d by 5** 40 diviso 5.

► **divide out** vt: **to** ~ **out (between** or **among)** (sweets etc) distribuire (tra); (tasks) distribuire or ripartire (tra).

divided [dɪ'vaɪdɪd] adj (country) diviso(a); (opinions) discordi.

divided highway n (US) strada a doppia carreggiata.

divided skirt n gonna f pantalone inv.

dividend ['dɪvɪdɛnd] n dividendo.

dividend cover n rapporto dividendo profitti.

dividers [dɪ'vaɪdəz] npl compasso a punte fisse.

divine [dɪ'vaɪn] adj divino(a) ♦ vt (future) divinare, predire; (truth) indovinare; (water, metal) individuare tramite radioestesia.

diving ['daɪvɪŋ] n tuffo.

diving board n trampolino.

diving suit *n* scafandro.
divinity [dɪ'vɪnɪtɪ] *n* divinità *f inv*; teologia.
division [dɪ'vɪʒən] *n* divisione *f*; separazione *f*; (*BRIT FOOTBALL*) serie *f inv*; ~ **of labour** divisione *f* del lavoro.
divisive [dɪ'vaɪsɪv] *adj* che è causa di discordia.
divorce [dɪ'vɔːs] *n* divorzio ♦ *vt* divorziare da.
divorced [dɪ'vɔːst] *adj* divorziato(a).
divorcee [dɪvɔː'siː] *n* divorziato/a.
divot ['dɪvət] *n* (*GOLF*) zolla di terra (*sollevata accidentalmente*).
divulge [daɪ'vʌldʒ] *vt* divulgare, rivelare.
D.I.Y. *adj*, *n abbr* (*BRIT*) *see* **do-it-yourself.**
dizziness ['dɪzɪnɪs] *n* vertigini *fpl*.
dizzy ['dɪzɪ] *adj* (*height*) vertiginoso(a); **to make sb** ~ far girare la testa a qn; **to feel** ~ avere il capogiro; **I feel** ~ mi gira la testa, ho il capogiro.
DJ *n abbr see* **disc jockey.**
d.j. *n abbr* = **dinner jacket.**
Djakarta [dʒə'kɑːtə] *n* Giakarta.
DJIA *n abbr* (*US STOCK EXCHANGE*: = *Dow-Jones Industrial Average*) indice *m* Dow-Jones.
dl *abbr* (= *decilitre*) dl.
DLit(t) *n abbr* = *Doctor of Literature*; *Doctor of Letters*.
DLO *n abbr* = **dead-letter office.**
dm *abbr* (= *decimetre*) dm.
DMus *n abbr* = *Doctor of Music*.
DMZ *n abbr* (= *demilitarized zone*) zona smilitarizzata.
DNA *n abbr* (= *deoxyribonucleic acid*) DNA *m*.

=========================== *KEYWORD*

do [duː] (*pt* **did**, *pp* **done**) *n* (*col*: *party etc*) festa; **it was rather a grand** ~ è stato un ricevimento piuttosto importante
♦ *vb* **1** (*in negative constructions*) *non tradotto*; **I don't understand** non capisco
2 (*to form questions*) *non tradotto*; **didn't you know?** non lo sapevi?; **why didn't you come?** perché non sei venuto?
3 (*for emphasis, in polite expressions*): **she does seem rather late** sembra essere piuttosto in ritardo; **I DO wish I could …** magari potessi …; **but I DO like it!** sì che mi piace!; ~ **sit down** si accomodi la prego, prego si sieda; ~ **take care!** mi raccomando, stai attento!
4 (*used to avoid repeating vb*): **she swims better than I** ~ lei nuota meglio di me; ~ **you agree?** — **yes, I** ~**/no, I don't** sei d'accordo? — sì/no; **she lives in Glasgow** — **so** ~ **I** lei vive a Glasgow — anch'io; **he asked me to help him and I did** mi ha

chiesto di aiutarlo ed io l'ho fatto; **they come here often** — ~ **they?** vengono qui spesso — ah sì?, davvero?
5 (*in question tags*): **you like him, don't you?** ti piace, vero?; **I don't know him,** ~ **I?** non lo conosco, vero?
♦ *vt* (*gen, carry out, perform etc*) fare; **what are you** ~**ing tonight?** che fai stasera?; **what can I** ~ **for you?** (*in shop*) desidera?; **I'll** ~ **all I can** farò tutto il possibile; **to** ~ **the cooking** cucinare; **to** ~ **the washing-up** fare i piatti; **to** ~ **one's teeth** lavarsi i denti; **to** ~ **one's hair/nails** farsi i capelli/le unghie; **the car was** ~**ing 100** la macchina faceva i 100 all'ora; **how** ~ **you like your steak done?** come preferisce la bistecca?; **well done** ben cotto(a)
♦ *vi* **1** (*act, behave*) fare; ~ **as I** ~ faccia come me, faccia come faccio io; **what did he** ~ **with the cat?** che ne ha fatto del gatto?
2 (*get on, fare*) andare; **he's** ~**ing well/badly at school** va bene/male a scuola; **how** ~ **you** ~? piacere!
3 (*suit*) andare bene; **this room will** ~ questa stanza va bene
4 (*be sufficient*) bastare; **will £10** ~? basteranno 10 sterline?; **that'll** ~ basta così; **that'll** ~! (*in annoyance*) ora basta!; **to make** ~ **(with)** arrangiarsi (con)
▶**do away with** *vt fus* (*kill*) far fuori; (*abolish*) abolire
▶**do for** *vt fus* (*BRIT col*: *clean for*) fare i servizi per
▶**do out of** *vt fus*: **to** ~ **sb out of sth** fregare qc a qn
▶**do up** *vt* (*laces*) allacciare; (*dress, buttons*) abbottonare; (*renovate*: *room, house*) rimettere a nuovo, rifare; **to** ~ **o.s. up** farsi bello(a)
▶**do with** *vt fus* (*need*) aver bisogno di; **I could** ~ **with some help/a drink** un aiuto/un bicchierino non guasterebbe; **it could** ~ **with a wash** una lavata non gli farebbe male; (*be connected*): **what has it got to** ~ **with you?** e tu che c'entri?; **I won't have anything to** ~ **with it** non voglio avere niente a che farci; **it has to** ~ **with money** si tratta di soldi
▶**do without** *vi* fare senza ♦ *vt fus* fare a meno di.

do. *abbr* = **ditto.**
DOA *abbr* (= *dead on arrival*) morto(a) durante il trasporto.
d.o.b. *abbr* = *date of birth*.
doc [dɔk] *n* (*col*) dottore/essa.
docile ['dəusaɪl] *adj* docile.

dock [dɔk] n bacino; (wharf) molo; (LAW) banco degli imputati ♦ vi entrare in bacino ♦ vt (pay etc) decurtare.
dock dues npl diritti mpl di banchina.
docker ['dɔkə*] n scaricatore m.
docket ['dɔkɪt] n (on parcel etc) etichetta, cartellino.
dockyard ['dɔkjɑːd] n cantiere m navale.
doctor ['dɔktə*] n medico, dottore/essa; (PhD etc) dottore/essa ♦ vt (interfere with: food, drink) adulterare; (: text, document) alterare, manipolare; ~'s office (US) gabinetto medico, ambulatorio; D~ of Philosophy (PhD) dottorato di ricerca; (person) titolare m/f di un dottorato di ricerca.
doctorate ['dɔktərɪt] n dottorato; see boxed note.

DOCTORATE

Il **doctorate** è il riconoscimento accademico più prestigioso in tutti i campi del sapere e viene conferito in seguito alla presentazione di una tesi originale di fronte ad una commissione di esperti. Generalmente tale tesi è un compendio del lavoro svolto durante più anni di studi; vedi anche **Bachelor's degree**, **Master's degree**.

---

doctrine ['dɔktrɪn] n dottrina.
docudrama [dɔkju'drɑːmə] n (TV) ricostruzione f filmata.
document n ['dɔkjumənt] documento ♦ vt ['dɔkjument] documentare.
documentary [dɔkju'mɛntərɪ] adj documentario(a); (evidence) documentato(a) ♦ n documentario.
documentation [dɔkjumən'teɪʃən] n documentazione f.
DOD n abbr (US) = Department of Defense; see defence.
doddering ['dɔdərɪŋ] adj traballante.
doddery ['dɔdərɪ] adj malfermo(a).
doddle ['dɔdl] n: it's a ~ (col) è un gioco da ragazzi.
dodge [dɔdʒ] n trucco; schivata ♦ vt schivare, eludere ♦ vi scansarsi; (SPORT) fare una schivata; to ~ out of the way scansarsi; to ~ through the traffic destreggiarsi nel traffico.
dodgems ['dɔdʒəmz] npl (BRIT) autoscontri mpl.
dodgy ['dɔdʒɪ] adj (col: uncertain) rischioso(a); (untrustworthy) sospetto(a).
DOE n abbr (BRIT: = Department of the Environment) ≈ Ministero dell'Ambiente; (US) = Department of Energy; see energy.

doe [dəu] n (deer) femmina di daino; (rabbit) coniglia.
does [dʌz] see do.
doesn't ['dʌznt] = does not.
dog [dɔg] n cane m ♦ vt (follow closely) pedinare; (fig: memory etc) perseguitare; to go to the ~s (person) ridursi male, lasciarsi andare; (nation etc) andare in malora.
dog biscuits npl biscotti mpl per cani.
dog collar n collare m di cane; (fig) collarino.
dog-eared ['dɔgɪəd] adj (book) con orecchie.
dog food n cibo per cani.
dogged ['dɔgɪd] adj ostinato(a), tenace.
doggie, doggy ['dɔgɪ] n (col) cane m, cagnolino.
doggy bag n sacchetto per gli avanzi (da portare a casa).
dogma ['dɔgmə] n dogma m.
dogmatic [dɔg'mætɪk] adj dogmatico(a).
do-gooder [duː'gudə*] n (col pej): to be a ~ fare il filantropo.
dogsbody ['dɔgzbɔdɪ] n (BRIT) factotum m inv.
doily ['dɔɪlɪ] n centrino di carta sottopiatto.
doing ['duːɪŋ] n: this is your ~ è opera tua, sei stato tu; ~s npl attività fpl.
do-it-yourself (DIY) ['duːɪtjɔː'sɛlf] n il far da sé.
doldrums ['dɔldrəmz] npl (fig): to be in the ~ essere giù; (business) attraversare un momento difficile.
dole [dəul] n (BRIT) sussidio di disoccupazione; to be on the ~ vivere del sussidio.
►**dole out** vt distribuire.
doleful ['dəulful] adj triste, doloroso(a).
doll [dɔl] n bambola.
►**doll up** vt: to ~ o.s. up farsi bello(a).
dollar ['dɔlə*] n dollaro.
dollop ['dɔləp] n (of food) cucchiaiata.
dolly ['dɔlɪ] n bambola.
dolphin ['dɔlfɪn] n delfino.
domain [də'meɪn] n dominio; (fig) campo, sfera.
dome [dəum] n cupola.
domestic [də'mɛstɪk] adj (duty, happiness, animal) domestico(a); (policy, affairs, flights) nazionale; (news) dall'interno.
domesticated [də'mɛstɪkeɪtɪd] adj addomesticato(a); (person) casalingo(a).
domesticity [dəumɛs'tɪsɪtɪ] n vita di famiglia.
domestic servant n domestico/a.
domicile ['dɔmɪsaɪl] n domicilio.
dominant ['dɔmɪnənt] adj dominante.

dominate ['dɔmɪneɪt] *vt* dominare.
domination [dɔmɪ'neɪʃən] *n* dominazione *f*.
domineering [dɔmɪ'nɪərɪŋ] *adj* dispotico(a), autoritario(a).
Dominican Republic [də'mɪnɪkən-] *n* Repubblica Dominicana.
dominion [də'mɪnɪən] *n* dominio; sovranità; (*BRIT POL*) dominion *m inv*.
domino, ~es ['dɔmɪnəu] *n* domino; *~es n* (*game*) gioco del domino.
don [dɔn] *n* (*BRIT*) docente *m/f* universitario(a) ♦ *vt* indossare.
donate [də'neɪt] *vt* donare.
donation [də'neɪʃən] *n* donazione *f*.
done [dʌn] *pp of* do.
donkey ['dɔŋkɪ] *n* asino.
donkey-work ['dɔŋkɪwə:k] *n* (*BRIT col*) lavoro ingrato.
donor ['dəunə*] *n* donatore/trice.
donor card *n* tessera di donatore di organi.
don't [dəunt] *vb* = do not.
donut ['dəunʌt] *n* (*US*) = **doughnut**.
doodle ['du:dl] *n* scarabocchio ♦ *vi* scarabocchiare.
doom [du:m] *n* destino; rovina ♦ *vt*: **to be ~ed** (**to failure**) essere predestinato(a) (a fallire).
doomsday ['du:mzdeɪ] *n* il giorno del Giudizio.
door [dɔ:*] *n* porta; (*of vehicle*) sportello, portiera; **from ~ to ~** di porta in porta.
doorbell ['dɔ:bɛl] *n* campanello.
door handle *n* maniglia.
doorman ['dɔ:mæn] *n* (*in hotel*) portiere *m* in livrea; (*in block of flats*) portinaio.
doormat ['dɔ:mæt] *n* stuoia della porta.
doorstep ['dɔ:stɛp] *n* gradino della porta.
door-to-door ['dɔ:tə'dɔ:*] *adj*: **~ selling** vendita porta a porta.
doorway ['dɔ:weɪ] *n* porta; **in the ~** nel vano della porta.
dope [dəup] *n* (*col: drugs*) roba; (: *information*) dati *mpl* ♦ *vt* (*horse etc*) drogare.
dopey ['dəupɪ] *adj* (*col*) inebetito(a).
dormant ['dɔ:mənt] *adj* inattivo(a); (*fig*) latente.
dormer ['dɔ:mə*] *n* (*also*: **~ window**) abbaino.
dormice ['dɔ:maɪs] *npl of* **dormouse**.
dormitory ['dɔ:mɪtrɪ] *n* dormitorio; (*US: hall of residence*) casa dello studente.
dormouse, *pl* **dormice** ['dɔ:maus, -maɪs] *n* ghiro.
Dors *abbr* (*BRIT*) = Dorset.
DOS [dɔs] *n abbr see* **disk operating system**.
dosage ['dəusɪdʒ] *n* (*on medicine bottle*) posologia.
dose [dəus] *n* dose *f*; (*BRIT: bout*) attacco ♦ *vt*: **to ~ sb with sth** somministrare qc a qn; **a ~ of flu** una bella influenza.
dosser ['dɔsə*] *n* (*BRIT col*) barbone/a.
doss house ['dɔs-] *n* (*BRIT*) asilo notturno.
dossier ['dɔsɪeɪ] *n* dossier *m inv*.
DOT *n abbr* (*US*) = **Department of Transportation**; *see* **transportation**.
dot [dɔt] *n* punto; macchiolina ♦ *vt*: **~ted with** punteggiato(a) di; **on the ~** in punto.
dot command *n* (*COMPUT*) dot command *m inv*.
dote [dəut]: **to ~ on** *vt fus* essere infatuato(a) di.
dot-matrix printer [dɔt'meɪtrɪks-] *n* stampante *f* a matrice a punti.
dotted line ['dɔtɪd-] *n* linea punteggiata; **to sign on the ~** firmare (nell'apposito spazio); (*fig*) accettare.
dotty ['dɔtɪ] *adj* (*col*) strambo(a).
double ['dʌbl] *adj* doppio(a) ♦ *adv* (*fold*) in due, doppio; (*twice*): **to cost ~** (**sth**) costare il doppio (di qc) ♦ *n* sosia *m inv*; (*CINE*) controfigura ♦ *vt* raddoppiare; (*fold*) piegare doppio *or* in due ♦ *vi* raddoppiarsi; **spelt with a ~ "l"** scritto con due elle *or* con doppia elle; **~ five two six (5526)** (*BRIT TEL*) cinque cinque due sei; **on the ~,** (*BRIT*) **at the ~** a passo di corsa; **to ~ as** (*have two uses etc*) funzionare *or* servire anche da; *see also* **doubles**.
▶**double back** *vi* (*person*) tornare sui propri passi.
▶**double up** *vi* (*bend over*) piegarsi in due; (*share room*) dividere la stanza.
double bass *n* contrabbasso.
double bed *n* letto matrimoniale.
double-breasted ['dʌbl'brɛstɪd] *adj* a doppio petto.
double-check ['dʌbl'tʃɛk] *vt, vi* ricontrollare.
double-clutch ['dʌbl'klʌtʃ] *vi* (*US*) fare la doppietta.
double cream *n* (*BRIT*) doppia panna.
doublecross ['dʌbl'krɔs] *vt* fare il doppio gioco con.
doubledecker ['dʌbl'dɛkə*] *n* autobus *m inv* a due piani.
double declutch *vi* (*BRIT*) fare la doppietta.
double exposure *n* (*PHOT*) sovrimpressione *f*.
double glazing *n* (*BRIT*) doppi vetri *mpl*.
double-page ['dʌblpeɪdʒ] *adj*: **~ spread** pubblicità a doppia pagina.
double parking *n* parcheggio in doppia

double room – doz.

fila.
double room n camera per due.
doubles ['dʌblz] n (TENNIS) doppio.
double time n tariffa doppia per lavoro straordinario.
double whammy [-'wæmɪ] n doppia mazzata (fig).
doubly ['dʌblɪ] adv doppiamente.
doubt [daut] n dubbio ♦ vt dubitare di; **to ~ that** dubitare che + sub; **without a** ~ senza dubbio; **beyond** ~ fuor di dubbio; **I ~ it very much** ho i miei dubbi, nutro seri dubbi in proposito.
doubtful ['dautful] adj dubbioso(a), incerto(a); (person) equivoco(a); **to be ~ about sth** avere dei dubbi su qc, non essere convinto di qc; **I'm a bit ~** non ne sono sicuro.
doubtless ['dautlɪs] adv indubbiamente.
dough [dəu] n pasta, impasto; (col: money) grana.
doughnut, (US) **donut** ['dəunʌt] n bombolone m.
dour [duə*] adj arcigno(a).
douse [daus] vt (with water) infradiciare; (flames) spegnere.
dove [dʌv] n colomba/a
Dover ['dəuvə*] n Dover f.
dovetail ['dʌvteɪl] n: ~ **joint** incastro a coda di rondine ♦ vi (fig) combaciare.
dowager ['dauədʒə*] n vedova titolata.
dowdy ['daudɪ] adj trasandato(a), malvestito(a).
Dow-Jones average ['dau'dʒəunz-] n (US) indice m Dow-Jones.
down [daun] n (fluff) piumino; (hill) collina, colle m ♦ adv giù, di sotto ♦ prep giù per ♦ vt (col: drink) scolarsi; ~ **there** laggiù, là in fondo; ~ **here** quaggiù; **I'll be ~ in a minute** scendo tra un minuto; **the price of meat is** ~ il prezzo della carne è sceso; **I've got it ~ in my diary** ce l'ho sulla mia agenda; **to pay £2** ~ dare 2 sterline in acconto or di anticipo; **I've been** ~ **with flu** sono stato a letto con l'influenza; **England is two goals** ~ l'Inghilterra sta perdendo per due goal; **to** ~ **tools** (BRIT) incrociare le braccia; ~ **with X!** abbasso X!
down-and-out ['daunəndaut] n (tramp) barbone m.
down-at-heel ['daunət'hiːl] adj scalcagnato(a); (fig) trasandato(a).
downbeat ['daunbiːt] n (MUS) tempo in battere ♦ adj (col) volutamente distaccato(a).
downcast ['daunkɑːst] adj abbattuto(a).
downer ['daunə*] n (col: drug) farmaco

depressivo; **to be on a** ~ (depressed) essere giù.
downfall ['daunfɔːl] n caduta; rovina.
downgrade ['daungreɪd] vt (job, hotel) declassare; (employee) degradare.
downhearted [daun'hɑːtɪd] adj scoraggiato(a).
downhill ['daun'hɪl] adv verso il basso ♦ n (SKI: also: ~ **race**) discesa libera; **to go** ~ andare in discesa; (business) andare a rotoli.
Downing Street ['daunɪŋ-] n: **lo** ~ residenza del primo ministro inglese; see boxed note.

download ['daunləud] vt (COMPUT) trasferire (per esempio da un grosso calcolatore ad un microcalcolatore).
down-market ['daun'mɑːkɪt] adj rivolto(a) ad una fascia di mercato inferiore.
down payment n acconto.
downplay ['daunpleɪ] vt (US) minimizzare.
downpour ['daunpɔː*] n scroscio di pioggia.
downright ['daunraɪt] adj franco(a); (refusal) assoluto(a).
downsize ['daunsaɪz] vt (workforce) ridurre.
Down's syndrome n sindrome f di Down.
downstairs ['daun'stɛəz] adv di sotto; al piano inferiore; **to come** ~, **go** ~ scendere giù.
downstream ['daun'striːm] adv a valle.
downtime ['dauntaɪm] n (COMM) tempi mpl morti.
down-to-earth ['dauntu'əːθ] adj pratico(a).
downtown ['daun'taun] adv in città ♦ adj (US): ~ **Chicago** il centro di Chicago.
downtrodden ['dauntrɔdn] adj oppresso(a).
down under adv agli antipodi.
downward ['daunwəd] adj in giù, in discesa; **a** ~ **trend** una diminuzione progressiva.
downward(s) ['daunwəd(z)] adv in giù, in discesa.
dowry ['dauri] n dote f.
doz. abbr = **dozen**.

doze [dəuz] *vi* sonnecchiare.
▶**doze off** *vi* appisolarsi.
dozen ['dʌzn] *n* dozzina; **a** ~ **books** una dozzina di libri; **80p a** ~ 80 pence la dozzina; ~**s of times** centinaia *or* migliaia di volte.
DPh, DPhil *n abbr* (= *Doctor of Philosophy*) ≈ dottorato di ricerca.
DPP *n abbr* (*BRIT*) *see* **Director of Public Prosecutions.**
DPT *n abbr* (*MED*: = *diphtheria, pertussis, tetanus*) *vaccino.*
DPW *n abbr* (*US*: = *Department of Public Works*) ≈ Ministero dei Lavori Pubblici.
Dr, Dr. *abbr* (= *doctor*) Dr, Dott./Dott.ssa.
dr *abbr* (*COMM*) = **debtor.**
Dr. *abbr* (*in street names*) = **drive.**
drab [dræb] *adj* tetro(a), grigio(a).
draft [drɑːft] *n* abbozzo; (*COMM*) tratta; (*US MIL*) contingente *m*; (: *call-up*) leva ♦ *vt* abbozzare; (*document, report*) stendere (in versione preliminare); *see also* **draught.**
drag [dræg] *vt* trascinare; (*river*) dragare ♦ *vi* trascinarsi ♦ *n* (*AVIAT, NAUT*) resistenza (aerodinamica); (*col: person*) noioso/a; (: *task*) noia; (*women's clothing*): **in** ~ travestito (da donna).
▶**drag away** *vt*: **to** ~ **away (from)** tirare via (da).
▶**drag on** *vi* tirar avanti lentamente.
dragnet ['drægnɛt] *n* giacchio; (*fig*) rastrellamento.
dragon ['drægən] *n* drago.
dragonfly ['drægənflaɪ] *n* libellula.
dragoon [drə'guːn] *n* (*cavalryman*) dragone *m* ♦ *vt*: **to** ~ **sb into doing sth** (*BRIT*) costringere qn a fare qc.
drain [dreɪn] *n* canale *m* di scolo; (*for sewage*) fogna; (*on resources*) salasso ♦ *vt* (*land, marshes*) prosciugare; (*vegetables*) scolare; (*reservoir etc*) vuotare ♦ *vi* (*water*) defluire; **to feel** ~**ed** sentirsi svuotato(a), sentirsi sfinito(a).
drainage ['dreɪnɪdʒ] *n* prosciugamento; fognatura.
draining board ['dreɪnɪŋ-], **drainboard** (*US*) ['dreɪnbɔːd] *n* piano del lavello.
drainpipe ['dreɪnpaɪp] *n* tubo di scarico.
drake [dreɪk] *n* maschio dell'anatra.
dram [dræm] *n* bicchierino (di whisky *etc*).
drama ['drɑːmə] *n* (*art*) dramma *m*, teatro; (*play*) commedia; (*event*) dramma.
dramatic [drə'mætɪk] *adj* drammatico(a).
dramatically [drə'mætɪklɪ] *adv* in modo spettacolare.
dramatist ['dræmətɪst] *n* drammaturgo/a.
dramatize ['dræmətaɪz] *vt* (*events etc*) drammatizzare; (*adapt: novel: for TV*)

ridurre *or* adattare per la televisione; (: *for cinema*) ridurre *or* adattare per lo schermo.
drank [dræŋk] *pt of* **drink.**
drape [dreɪp] *vt* drappeggiare; *see also* **drapes.**
draper ['dreɪpə*] *n* (*BRIT*) negoziante *m/f* di stoffe.
drapes [dreɪps] *npl* (*US*) tende *fpl.*
drastic ['dræstɪk] *adj* drastico(a).
drastically ['dræstɪklɪ] *adv* drasticamente.
draught, (*US*) **draft** [drɑːft] *n* corrente *f* d'aria; (*NAUT*) pescaggio; **on** ~ (*beer*) alla spina; *see also* **draughts.**
draught beer *n* birra alla spina.
draughtboard ['drɑːftbɔːd] *n* scacchiera.
draughts [drɑːfts] *n* (*BRIT*) (gioco della) dama.
draughtsman, (*US*) **draftsman** ['drɑːftsmən] *n* disegnatore *m.*
draughtsmanship, (*US*) **draftsmanship** ['drɑːftsmənʃɪp] *n* disegno tecnico; (*skill*) arte *f* del disegno.
draw [drɔː] *vb* (*pt* **drew,** *pp* **drawn** [druː, drɔːn]) *vt* tirare; (*attract*) attirare; (*picture*) disegnare; (*line, circle*) tracciare; (*money*) ritirare; (*formulate: conclusion*) trarre, ricavare; (: *comparison, distinction*): **to** ~ **(between)** fare (tra) ♦ *vi* (*SPORT*) pareggiare ♦ *n* (*SPORT*) pareggio; (*in lottery*) estrazione *f*; (*attraction*) attrazione *f*; **to** ~ **to a close** avvicinarsi alla conclusione; **to** ~ **near** *vi* avvicinarsi.
▶**draw back** *vi*: **to** ~ **back (from)** indietreggiare (di fronte a), tirarsi indietro (di fronte a).
▶**draw in** *vi* (*BRIT: car*) accostarsi; (: *train*) entrare in stazione.
▶**draw on** *vt* (*resources*) attingere a; (*imagination, person*) far ricorso a.
▶**draw out** *vi* (*lengthen*) allungarsi ♦ *vt* (*money*) ritirare.
▶**draw up** *vi* (*stop*) arrestarsi, fermarsi ♦ *vt* (*document*) compilare; (*plans*) formulare.
drawback ['drɔːbæk] *n* svantaggio, inconveniente *m.*
drawbridge ['drɔːbrɪdʒ] *n* ponte *m* levatoio.
drawee [drɔː'iː] *n* trattario.
drawer [drɔː*] *n* cassetto; ['drɔːə*] (*of cheque*) riscuotitore/trice.
drawing ['drɔːɪŋ] *n* disegno.
drawing board *n* tavola da disegno.
drawing pin *n* (*BRIT*) puntina da disegno.
drawing room *n* salotto.
drawl [drɔːl] *n* pronuncia strascicata.
drawn [drɔːn] *pp of* **draw** ♦ *adj* (*haggard: with tiredness*) tirato(a); (: *with pain*)

contratto(a) (dal dolore).

drawstring ['drɔːstrɪŋ] n laccio (per stringere maglie, sacche etc).

dread [drɛd] n terrore m ♦ vt tremare all'idea di.

dreadful ['drɛdful] adj terribile; **I feel** ~! (ill) mi sento uno straccio!; (ashamed) vorrei scomparire (dalla vergogna)!

dream [driːm] n sogno ♦ vt, vi (pt, pp **dreamed** or **dreamt** [drɛmt]) sognare; **to have a** ~ **about sb/sth** fare un sogno su qn/qc; **sweet** ~**s!** sogni d'oro!
▶**dream up** vt (reason, excuse) inventare; (plan, idea) escogitare.

dreamer ['driːmə*] n sognatore/trice.

dreamt [drɛmt] pt, pp of **dream**.

dreamy ['driːmɪ] adj (look, voice) sognante; (person) distratto(a), sognatore(trice).

dreary ['drɪərɪ] adj tetro(a); monotono(a).

dredge [drɛdʒ] vt dragare.
▶**dredge up** vt tirare alla superficie; (fig: unpleasant facts) rivangare.

dredger ['drɛdʒə*] n draga; (BRIT: also: **sugar** ~) spargizucchero m inv.

dregs [drɛgz] npl feccia.

drench [drɛntʃ] vt inzuppare; ~**ed to the skin** bagnato(a) fino all'osso, bagnato(a) fradicio(a).

dress [drɛs] n vestito; (clothing) abbigliamento ♦ vt vestire; (wound) fasciare; (food) condire; preparare; (shop window) allestire ♦ vi vestirsi; **to** ~ **o.s., to get** ~**ed** vestirsi; **she** ~**es very well** veste molto bene.
▶**dress up** vi vestirsi a festa; (in fancy dress) vestirsi in costume.

dress circle n prima galleria.

dress designer n disegnatore/trice di moda.

dresser ['drɛsə*] n (THEAT) assistente m/f del camerino; (also: **window** ~) vetrinista m/f; (furniture) credenza.

dressing ['drɛsɪŋ] n (MED) benda; (CULIN) condimento.

dressing gown n (BRIT) vestaglia.

dressing room n (THEAT) camerino; (SPORT) spogliatoio.

dressing table n toilette f inv.

dressmaker ['drɛsmeɪkə*] n sarta.

dressmaking ['drɛsmeɪkɪŋ] n sartoria; confezioni fpl per donna.

dress rehearsal n prova generale.

dress shirt n camicia da sera.

dressy ['drɛsɪ] adj (col) elegante.

drew [druː] pt of **draw**.

dribble ['drɪbl] vi gocciolare; (baby) sbavare; (FOOTBALL) dribblare ♦ vt dribblare.

dried [draɪd] adj (fruit, beans) secco(a); (eggs, milk) in polvere.

drier ['draɪə*] n = **dryer**.

drift [drɪft] n (of current etc) direzione f; forza; (of sand, snow) cumulo; (general meaning) senso ♦ vi (boat) essere trasportato(a) dalla corrente; (sand, snow) ammucchiarsi; **to catch sb's** ~ capire dove qn vuole arrivare; **to let things** ~ lasciare che le cose vadano come vogliono; **to** ~ **apart** (friends) perdersi di vista; (lovers) allontanarsi l'uno dall'altro.

drifter ['drɪftə*] n persona che fa una vita da zingaro.

driftwood ['drɪftwud] n resti mpl della mareggiata.

drill [drɪl] n trapano; (MIL) esercitazione f ♦ vt trapanare; (soldiers) esercitare, addestrare; (pupils: in grammar) fare esercitare ♦ vi (for oil) fare trivellazioni.

drilling ['drɪlɪŋ] n (for oil) trivellazione f.

drilling rig n (on land) torre f di perforazione; (at sea) piattaforma (per trivellazioni subacquee).

drily ['draɪlɪ] adv = **dryly**.

drink [drɪŋk] n bevanda, bibita ♦ vt, vi (pt **drank**, pp **drunk** [dræŋk, drʌŋk]) bere; **to have a** ~ bere qualcosa; **a** ~ **of water** un bicchier d'acqua; **would you like something to** ~? vuole qualcosa da bere?; **we had** ~**s before lunch** abbiamo preso l'aperitivo.
▶**drink in** vt (subj: person: fresh air) aspirare; (: story) ascoltare avidamente; (: sight) ammirare, bersi con gli occhi.

drinkable ['drɪŋkəbl] adj (not poisonous) potabile; (palatable) bevibile.

drink-driving ['drɪŋk'draɪvɪŋ] n guida in stato di ebbrezza.

drinker ['drɪŋkə*] n bevitore/trice.

drinking ['drɪŋkɪŋ] n (drunkenness) il bere, alcoolismo.

drinking fountain n fontanella.

drinking water n acqua potabile.

drip [drɪp] n goccia; (~ping) sgocciolio; (MED) fleboclisi f inv; (col: spineless person) lavativo ♦ vi gocciolare; (washing) sgocciolare; (wall) trasudare.

drip-dry ['drɪp'draɪ] adj (shirt) che non si stira.

drip-feed ['drɪpfiːd] vt alimentare mediante fleboclisi.

dripping ['drɪpɪŋ] n (CULIN) grasso d'arrosto ♦ adj: ~ **wet** fradicio(a).

drive [draɪv] n passeggiata or giro in macchina; (also: ~**way**) viale m d'accesso; (energy) energia; (PSYCH) impulso;

bisogno; (*push*) sforzo eccezionale; campagna; (*SPORT*) drive *m inv*; (*TECH*) trasmissione *f*; (*COMPUT*: *also*: **disk** ~) disk drive *m inv*, unità *f inv* a dischi magnetici ♦ *vb* (*pt* **drove**, *pp* **driven** [drəuv, 'drɪvn]) *vt* (*vehicle*) guidare; (*nail*) piantare; (*push*) cacciare, spingere; (*TECH*: *motor*) azionare; far funzionare ♦ *vi* (*AUT*: *at controls*) guidare; (: *travel*) andare in macchina; **to go for a** ~ andare a fare un giro in macchina; **it's 3 hours'** ~ **from London** è a 3 ore di macchina da Londra; **left-/right-hand** ~ (*AUT*) guida a sinistra/destra; **front-/rear-wheel** ~ (*AUT*) trazione *f* anteriore/posteriore; **to** ~ **sb to (do) sth** spingere qn a (fare) qc; **he** ~**s a taxi** fa il tassista; **to** ~ **at 50 km an hour** guidare *or* andare a 50 km all'ora.
▶**drive at** *vt fus* (*fig*: *intend, mean*) mirare a, voler dire.
▶**drive on** *vi* proseguire, andare (più) avanti ♦ *vt* (*incite, encourage*) sospingere, spingere.
drive-by ['draɪvbaɪ] *n* (*also*: ~ **shooting**) sparatoria dalla macchina; **he was killed in a** ~ **shooting** lo hanno ammazzato sparandogli da una macchina in corsa.
drive-in ['draɪvɪn] *adj, n* (*esp US*) drive-in (*m inv*).
drive-in window *n* (*US*) sportello di drive-in.
drivel ['drɪvl] *n* (*col*: *nonsense*) ciance *fpl*.
driven ['drɪvn] *pp of* **drive**.
driver ['draɪvə*] *n* conducente *m/f*; (*of taxi*) tassista *m*; (*of bus*) autista *m*.
driver's license *n* (*US*) patente *f* di guida.
driveway ['draɪvweɪ] *n* viale *m* d'accesso.
driving ['draɪvɪŋ] *adj*: ~ **rain** pioggia sferzante ♦ *n* guida.
driving force *n* forza trainante.
driving instructor *n* istruttore/trice di scuola guida.
driving lesson *n* lezione *f* di guida.
driving licence *n* (*BRIT*) patente *f* di guida.
driving school *n* scuola *f* guida *inv*.
driving test *n* esame *m* di guida.
drizzle ['drɪzl] *n* pioggerella ♦ *vi* piovigginare.
droll [drəul] *adj* buffo(a).
dromedary ['drɒmədərɪ] *n* dromedario.
drone [drəun] *n* ronzio; (*male bee*) fuco ♦ *vi* (*bee, aircraft, engine*) ronzare; (*also*: ~ **on**: *person*) continuare a parlare (in modo monotono); (: *voice*) continuare a ronzare.
drool [druːl] *vi* sbavare; **to** ~ **over sb/sth** (*fig*) andare in estasi per qn/qc.
droop [druːp] *vi* abbassarsi; languire.
drop [drɒp] *n* goccia; (*fall*: *in price*) calo,

ribasso; (: *in salary*) riduzione *f*, taglio; (*also*: **parachute** ~) lancio; (*steep incline*) salto ♦ *vt* lasciar cadere; (*voice, eyes, price*) abbassare; (*set down from car*) far scendere ♦ *vi* cascare; (*decrease*: *wind, temperature, price, voice*) calare; (*numbers, attendance*) diminuire; ~**s** *npl* (*MED*) gocce *fpl*; **cough** ~**s** pastiglie *fpl* per la tosse; **a** ~ **of 10%** un calo del 10%; **to** ~ **sb a line** mandare due righe a qn; **to** ~ **anchor** gettare l'ancora.
▶**drop in** *vi* (*col*: *visit*): **to** ~ **in (on)** fare un salto (da), passare (da).
▶**drop off** *vi* (*sleep*) addormentarsi ♦ *vt*: **to** ~ **sb off** far scendere qn.
▶**drop out** *vi* (*withdraw*) ritirarsi; (*student etc*) smettere di studiare.
droplet ['drɒplɪt] *n* gocciolina.
dropout ['drɒpaut] *n* (*from society/university*) chi ha abbandonato (la società/gli studi).
dropper ['drɒpə*] *n* (*MED etc*) contagocce *m inv*.
droppings ['drɒpɪŋz] *npl* sterco.
dross [drɒs] *n* scoria; scarto.
drought [draut] *n* siccità *f inv*.
drove [drəuv] *pt of* **drive** ♦ *n*: ~**s of people** una moltitudine di persone.
drown [draun] *vt* affogare; (*also*: ~ **out**: *sound*) coprire ♦ *vi* affogare.
drowse [drauz] *vi* sonnecchiare.
drowsy ['drauzɪ] *adj* sonnolento(a), assonnato(a).
drudge [drʌdʒ] *n* (*person*) uomo/donna di fatica; (*job*) faticaccia.
drudgery ['drʌdʒərɪ] *n* fatica improba; **housework is sheer** ~ le faccende domestiche sono alienanti.
drug [drʌg] *n* farmaco; (*narcotic*) droga ♦ *vt* drogare; **he's on** ~**s** si droga; (*MED*) segue una cura.
drug abuser [-ə'bjuːzə*] *n* chi fa uso di droghe.
drug addict *n* tossicomane *m/f*.
druggist ['drʌgɪst] *n* (*US*) farmacista *m/f*.
drug peddler *n* spacciatore/trice di droga.
drugstore ['drʌgstɔː*] *n* (*US*) negozio di generi vari e di articoli di farmacia con un bar.
drum [drʌm] *n* tamburo; (*for oil, petrol*) fusto ♦ *vt*: **to** ~ **one's fingers on the table** tamburellare con le dita sulla tavola; ~**s** *npl* (*MUS*) batteria.
▶**drum up** *vt* (*enthusiasm, support*) conquistarsi.
drummer ['drʌmə*] *n* batterista *m/f*.
drum roll *n* rullio di tamburi.
drumstick ['drʌmstɪk] *n* (*MUS*) bacchetta; (*chicken leg*) coscia di pollo.

drunk [drʌŋk] *pp of* **drink** ♦ *adj* ubriaco(a); ebbro(a) ♦ *n* ubriacone/a; **to get ~** ubriacarsi, prendere una sbornia.
drunkard ['drʌŋkəd] *n* ubriacone/a.
drunken ['drʌŋkən] *adj* ubriaco(a); da ubriaco; **~ driving** guida in stato di ebbrezza.
drunkenness ['drʌŋkənnɪs] *n* ubriachezza; ebbrezza.
dry [draɪ] *adj* secco(a); (*day, clothes, fig: humour*) asciutto(a); (*uninteresting: lecture, subject*) poco avvincente ♦ *vt* seccare; (*clothes, hair, hands*) asciugare ♦ *vi* asciugarsi; **on ~ land** sulla terraferma; **to ~ one's hands/hair/eyes** asciugarsi le mani/i capelli/gli occhi.
► **dry up** *vi* seccarsi; (*source of supply*) esaurirsi; (*fig: imagination etc*) inaridirsi; (*fall silent: speaker*) azzittirsi.
dry-clean [draɪ'kliːn] *vt* pulire *or* lavare a secco.
dry-cleaner s [draɪ'kliːnəz] *n* lavasecco *m inv*.
dry-cleaning [draɪ'kliːnɪŋ] *n* pulitura a secco.
dry dock *n* (*NAUT*) bacino di carenaggio.
dryer ['draɪə*] *n* (*for hair*) föhn *m inv*, asciugacapelli *m inv*; (*for clothes*) asciugabiancheria *m inv*.
dry goods *npl* (*COMM*) tessuti *mpl* e mercerie *fpl*.
dry goods store *n* (*US*) negozio di stoffe.
dry ice *n* ghiaccio secco.
dryly ['draɪlɪ] *adv* con fare asciutto.
dryness ['draɪnɪs] *n* secchezza; (*of ground*) aridità.
dry rot *n* fungo del legno.
dry run *n* (*fig*) prova.
dry ski slope *n* pista artificiale.
DSc *n abbr* (= *Doctor of Science*) *titolo di studio.*
DSS *n abbr* (*BRIT*) = **Department of Social Security;** *see* **social security.**
DST *abbr* (*US*) = **Daylight Saving Time.**
DT *n abbr* (*COMPUT*) = **data transmission.**
DTI *n abbr* (*BRIT*) = **Department of Trade and Industry;** *see* **trade.**
DTP *n abbr* = **desktop publishing.**
DT's *n abbr* (*col*) = *delirium tremens.*
dual ['djuəl] *adj* doppio(a).
dual carriageway *n* (*BRIT*) strada a doppia carreggiata.
dual-control ['djuəlkən'trəul] *adj* con doppi comandi.
dual nationality *n* doppia nazionalità.
dual-purpose ['djuəl'pəːpəs] *adj* a doppio uso.
dubbed [dʌbd] *adj* (*CINE*) doppiato(a);

(*nicknamed*) soprannominato(a).
dubious ['djuːbɪəs] *adj* dubbio(a); (*character, manner*) ambiguo(a), equivoco(a); **I'm very ~ about it** ho i miei dubbi in proposito.
Dublin ['dʌblɪn] *n* Dublino *f.*
Dubliner ['dʌblɪnə*] *n* dublinese *m/f.*
duchess ['dʌtʃɪs] *n* duchessa.
duck [dʌk] *n* anatra ♦ *vi* abbassare la testa ♦ *vt* spingere sotto (acqua).
duckling ['dʌklɪŋ] *n* anatroccolo.
duct [dʌkt] *n* condotto; (*ANAT*) canale *m.*
dud [dʌd] *n* (*shell*) proiettile *m* che fa cilecca; (*object, tool*): **it's a ~** è inutile, non funziona ♦ *adj* (*BRIT: cheque*) a vuoto; (*note, coin*) falso(a).
due [djuː] *adj* dovuto(a); (*expected*) atteso(a); (*fitting*) giusto(a) ♦ *n* dovuto ♦ *adv*: **~ north** diritto verso nord; **~s** *npl* (*for club, union*) quota; (*in harbour*) diritti *mpl* di porto; **in ~ course** a tempo debito; **finally**; **~ to** dovuto a; à causa di; **the rent's ~ on the 30th** l'affitto scade il 30; **the train is ~ at 8** il treno è atteso per le 8; **she is ~ back tomorrow** dovrebbe essere di ritorno domani; **I am ~ 6 days' leave** mi spettano 6 giorni di ferie.
due date *n* data di scadenza.
duel ['djuəl] *n* duello.
duet [djuː'ɛt] *n* duetto.
duff [dʌf] *adj* (*BRIT col*) barboso(a).
duffelbag, duffle bag ['dʌflbæg] *n* sacca da viaggio di tela.
duffelcoat, duffle coat ['dʌflkəut] *n* montgomery *m inv.*
duffer ['dʌfə*] *n* (*col*) schiappa.
dug [dʌg] *pt, pp of* **dig.**
dugout ['dʌgaut] *n* (*FOOTBALL*) panchina.
duke [djuːk] *n* duca *m.*
dull [dʌl] *adj* (*boring*) noioso(a); (*slow-witted*) ottuso(a); (*sound, pain*) sordo(a); (*weather, day*) fosco(a), scuro(a); (*blade*) smussato(a) ♦ *vt* (*pain, grief*) attutire; (*mind, senses*) intorpidire.
duly ['djuːlɪ] *adv* (*on time*) a tempo debito; (*as expected*) debitamente.
dumb [dʌm] *adj* muto(a); (*stupid*) stupido(a); **to be struck ~** (*fig*) ammutolire, restare senza parole.
dumbbell ['dʌmbɛl] *n* (*SPORT*) manubrio, peso.
dumbfounded [dʌm'faundɪd] *adj* stupito(a), stordito(a).
dummy ['dʌmɪ] *n* (*tailor's model*) manichino; (*SPORT*) finto; (*BRIT: for baby*) tettarella ♦ *adj* falso(a), finto(a).
dummy run *n* giro di prova.
dump [dʌmp] *n* mucchio di rifiuti; (*place*)

luogo di scarico; (*MIL*) deposito; (*COMPUT*) scaricamento, dump *m inv* ♦ *vt* (*put down*) scaricare; mettere giù; (*get rid of*) buttar via; (*COMM*: *goods*) svendere; (*COMPUT*) scaricare; **to be (down) in the** ~**s** (*col*) essere giù di corda.

dumping ['dʌmpɪŋ] *n* (*ECON*) dumping *m*; (*of rubbish*): "**no** ~" "vietato lo scarico".

dumpling ['dʌmplɪŋ] *n specie di gnocco.*

dumpy ['dʌmpɪ] *adj* tracagnotto(a).

dunce [dʌns] *n* asino.

dune [djuːn] *n* duna.

dung [dʌŋ] *n* concime *m.*

dungarees [dʌŋgə'riːz] *npl* tuta.

dungeon ['dʌndʒən] *n* prigione *f* sotterranea.

dunk [dʌŋk] *vt* inzuppare.

duo ['djuːəu] *n* (*gen*, *MUS*) duo *m inv.*

duodenal [djuːəu'diːnl] *adj* (*ulcer*) duodenale.

duodenum [djuːəu'diːnəm] *n* duodeno.

dupe [djuːp] *vt* gabbare, ingannare.

duplex ['djuːplɛks] *n* (*US*: *also*: ~ **apartment**) appartamento su due piani.

duplicate *n* ['djuːplɪkət] doppio; (*copy of letter etc*) duplicato ♦ *vt* ['djuːplɪkeɪt] raddoppiare; (*on machine*) ciclostilare ♦ *adj* (*copy*) conforme, esattamente uguale; **in** ~ in duplice copia; ~ **key** duplicato (della chiave).

duplicating machine ['djuːplɪkeɪtɪŋ-], **duplicator** ['djuːplɪkeɪtə*] *n* duplicatore *m.*

duplicity [djuː'plɪsɪtɪ] *n* doppiezza, duplicità.

Dur. *abbr* (*BRIT*) = *Durham.*

durability [djuərə'bɪlɪtɪ] *n* durevolezza; resistenza.

durable ['djuərəbl] *adj* durevole; (*clothes, metal*) resistente.

duration [djuə'reɪʃən] *n* durata.

duress [djuə'rɛs] *n*: **under** ~ sotto costrizione.

Durex ® ['djuərɛks] *n* (*BRIT*) preservativo.

during ['djuərɪŋ] *prep* durante, nel corso di.

dusk [dʌsk] *n* crepuscolo.

dusky ['dʌskɪ] *adj* scuro(a).

dust [dʌst] *n* polvere *f* ♦ *vt* (*furniture*) spolverare; (*cake etc*): **to** ~ **with** cospargere con.

▶**dust off** *vt* rispolverare.

dustbin ['dʌstbɪn] *n* (*BRIT*) pattumiera.

duster ['dʌstə*] *n* straccio per la polvere.

dust jacket *n* sopraccoperta.

dustman ['dʌstmən] *n* (*BRIT*) netturbino.

dustpan ['dʌstpæn] *n* pattumiera.

dusty ['dʌstɪ] *adj* polveroso(a).

Dutch [dʌtʃ] *adj* olandese ♦ *n* (*LING*)

olandese *m* ♦ *adv*: **to go** ~ *or* **d**~ fare alla romana; **the** ~ gli Olandesi.

Dutch auction *n* asta all'olandese.

Dutchman ['dʌtʃmən], **Dutchwoman** ['dʌtʃwumən] *n* olandese *m/f.*

dutiable ['djuːtɪəbl] *adj* soggetto(a) a dazio.

dutiful ['djuːtɪful] *adj* (*child*) rispettoso(a); (*husband*) premuroso(a); (*employee*) coscienzioso(a).

duty ['djuːtɪ] *n* dovere *m*; (*tax*) dazio, tassa; **duties** *npl* mansioni *fpl*; **on** ~ di servizio; (*MED*: *in hospital*) di guardia; **off** ~ libero(a), fuori servizio; **to make it one's** ~ **to do sth** assumersi l'obbligo di fare qc; **to pay** ~ **on sth** pagare il dazio su qc.

duty-free ['djuːtɪ'friː] *adj* esente da dazio; ~ **shop** duty free *m inv.*

duty officer *n* (*MIL etc*) ufficiale *m* di servizio.

duvet ['duːveɪ] *n* piumino, piumone *m.*

DV *abbr* (= *Deo volente*) D.V.

DVLA *n abbr* (= *Driver and Vehicle Licensing Authority*) ≈ I.M.C.T.C. *m* (= *Ispettorato Generale della Motorizzazione Civile e dei Trasporti in Concessione*).

DVLC *n abbr* (*BRIT*: = *Driver and Vehicle Licensing Office*) ≈ I.M.C.T.C. *m.*

DVM *n abbr* (*US*: = *Doctor of Veterinary Medicine*) *titolo di studio.*

dwarf [dwɔːf] *n* nano/a ♦ *vt* far apparire piccolo.

dwell, *pt*, *pp* **dwelt** [dwɛl, dwɛlt] *vi* dimorare.

▶**dwell on** *vt fus* indugiare su.

dweller ['dwɛlə*] *n* abitante *m/f*; **city** ~ cittadino/a.

dwelling ['dwɛlɪŋ] *n* dimora.

dwelt [dwɛlt] *pt*, *pp of* **dwell.**

dwindle ['dwɪndl] *vi* diminuire, decrescere.

dwindling ['dwɪndlɪŋ] *adj* (*strength, interest*) che si affievolisce; (*resources, supplies*) in diminuzione.

dye [daɪ] *n* colore *m*; (*chemical*) colorante *m*, tintura ♦ *vt* tingere; **hair** ~ tinta per capelli.

dyestuffs ['daɪstʌfs] *npl* coloranti *mpl.*

dying ['daɪɪŋ] *adj* morente, moribondo(a).

dyke [daɪk] *n* diga; (*channel*) canale *m* di scolo; (*causeway*) sentiero rialzato.

dynamic [daɪ'næmɪk] *adj* dinamico(a).

dynamics [daɪ'næmɪks] *n or npl* dinamica.

dynamite ['daɪnəmaɪt] *n* dinamite *f* ♦ *vt* far saltare con la dinamite.

dynamo ['daɪnəməu] *n* dinamo *f inv.*

dynasty ['dɪnəstɪ] *n* dinastia.

dysentery ['dɪsntrɪ] *n* dissenteria.

dyslexia [dɪs'lɛksɪə] *n* dislessia.

dyslexic [dɪs'lɛksɪk] *adj, n* dislessico(a).

dyspepsia [dɪs'pɛpsɪə] *n* dispepsia.
dystrophy ['dɪstrəfɪ] *n* distrofia; **muscular**
~ distrofia muscolare.

E e

E, e [iː] *n* (*letter*) E, e *f or m inv*; (*MUS*): **E** mi *m*;
E for Edward, (*US*) **E for Easy** ≈ E come
Empoli.
E *abbr* (= *east*) E ♦ *n abbr* (= *Ecstasy*) ecstasy
f inv.
E111 *n abbr* (*also*: **form** ~) E111 (*modulo CEE
per rimborso spese mediche*).
ea, *abbr* = **each.**
E.A. *n abbr* (*US*) = *educational age.*
each [iːtʃ] *adj* ogni, ciascuno(a) ♦ *pron*
ciascuno(a), ognuno(a); ~ **one** ognuno(a);
~ **other** si (*or* ci *etc*); **they hate** ~ **other** si
odiano (l'un l'altro); **you are jealous of** ~
other siete gelosi l'uno dell'altro; ~ **day**
ogni giorno; **they have 2 books** ~ hanno 2
libri ciascuno; **they cost £5** ~ costano 5
sterline l'uno; ~ **of us** ciascuno *or* ognuno
di noi.
eager ['iːgə*] *adj* impaziente;
desideroso(a); ardente; (*keen: pupil*)
appassionato(a), attento(a); **to be** ~ **to do
sth** non veder l'ora di fare qc; essere
desideroso di fare qc; **to be** ~ **for** essere
desideroso di, aver gran voglia di.
eagle ['iːgl] *n* aquila.
E and OE *abbr* (= *errors and omissions
excepted*) S.E.O.
ear [ɪə*] *n* orecchio; (*of corn*) pannocchia;
up to the ~**s in debt** nei debiti fino al
collo.
earache ['ɪəreɪk] *n* mal *m* d'orecchi.
eardrum ['ɪədrʌm] *n* timpano.
earful ['ɪəful] *n*: **to give sb an** ~ fare una
ramanzina a qn.
earl [əːl] *n* conte *m*.
earlier ['əːlɪə*] *adj* (*date etc*) anteriore;
(*edition etc*) precedente, anteriore ♦ *adv*
prima; **I can't come any** ~ non posso
venire prima.
early ['əːlɪ] *adv* presto, di buon'ora; (*ahead
of time*) in anticipo ♦ *adj* precoce;
anticipato(a); che si fa vedere di
buon'ora; (*man*) primitivo(a); (*Christians,
settlers*) primo(a); ~ **in the morning/
afternoon** nelle prime ore del mattino/del

pomeriggio; **you're** ~! sei in anticipo!;
have an ~ **night/start** vada a letto/parta
presto; **in the** ~ *or* ~ **in the spring/19th
century** all'inizio della primavera/
dell'Ottocento; **she's in her** ~ **forties** ha
appena passato la quarantina; **at your
earliest convenience** (*COMM*) non appena
possibile.
early retirement *n* ritiro anticipato.
early warning system *n* sistema *m* del
preallarme.
earmark ['ɪəmɑːk] *vt*: **to** ~ **sth for** destinare
qc a.
earn [əːn] *vt* guadagnare; (*rest, reward*)
meritare; (*COMM: yield*) maturare; **to** ~
one's living guadagnarsi da vivere; **this
~ed him much praise, he** ~**ed much
praise for this** si è attirato grandi lodi per
questo.
earned income *n* reddito da lavoro.
earnest ['əːnɪst] *adj* serio(a) ♦ *n* (*also*: ~
money) caparra; **in** ~ *adv* sul serio.
earnings ['əːnɪŋz] *npl* guadagni *mpl*; (*of
company etc*) proventi *mpl*; (*salary*)
stipendio.
ear, nose and throat specialist *n*
otorinolaringoiatra *m/f*.
earphones ['ɪəfəunz] *npl* cuffia.
earplugs ['ɪəplʌgz] *npl* tappi *mpl* per le
orecchie.
earring ['ɪərɪŋ] *n* orecchino.
earshot ['ɪəʃɒt] *n*: **out of/within** ~ fuori
portata/a portata d'orecchio.
earth [əːθ] *n* (*gen, also BRIT ELEC*) terra; (*of
fox etc*) tana ♦ *vt* (*BRIT ELEC*) mettere a
terra.
earthenware ['əːθənwɛə*] *n* terracotta;
stoviglie *fpl* di terracotta ♦ *adj* di
terracotta.
earthly ['əːθlɪ] *adj* terreno(a); ~ **paradise**
paradiso terrestre; **there is no** ~ **reason
to think** ... non vi è ragione di pensare....
earthquake ['əːθkweɪk] *n* terremoto.
earth-shattering ['əːθʃætərɪŋ] *adj*
stupefacente.
earth tremor *n* scossa sismica.
earthworks ['əːθwəːks] *npl* lavori *mpl* di
sterro.
earthworm ['əːθwəːm] *n* lombrico.
earthy ['əːθɪ] *adj* (*fig*) grossolano(a).
earwax ['ɪəwæks] *n* cerume *m*.
earwig ['ɪəwɪg] *n* forbicina.
ease [iːz] *n* agio, comodo ♦ *vt* (*soothe*)
calmare; (*loosen*) allentare ♦ *vi* (*situation*)
allentarsi, distendersi; **life of** ~ vita
comoda; **with** ~ senza difficoltà; **at** ~ a
proprio agio; (*MIL*) a riposo; **to feel at** ~/
ill at ~ sentirsi a proprio agio/a disagio;

to ~ sth out/in tirare fuori/infilare qc con delicatezza; facilitare l'uscita/ l'entrata di qc.

▶**ease off, ease up** *vi* diminuire; (*slow down*) rallentarsi; (*fig*) rilassarsi.

easel ['i:zl] *n* cavalletto.

easily ['i:zɪlɪ] *adv* facilmente.

easiness ['i:zɪnɪs] *n* facilità, semplicità; (*of manners*) disinvoltura.

east [i:st] *n* est *m* ♦ *adj* dell'est ♦ *adv* a oriente; **the E~** l'Oriente *m*; (*POL*) i Paesi dell'Est.

Easter ['i:stə*] *n* Pasqua ♦ *adj* (*holidays*) pasquale, di Pasqua.

Easter egg *n* uovo di Pasqua.

Easter Island *n* isola di Pasqua.

easterly ['i:stəlɪ] *adj* dall'est, d'oriente.

Easter Monday *n* Pasquetta.

eastern ['i:stən] *adj* orientale, d'oriente; **E~ Europe** l'Europa orientale; **the E~ bloc** (*POL*) i Paesi dell'Est.

Easter Sunday *n* domenica di Pasqua.

East Germany *n* Germania dell'Est.

eastward(s) ['i:stwəd(z)] *adv* verso est, verso levante.

easy ['i:zɪ] *adj* facile; (*manner*) disinvolto(a); (*carefree: life*) agiato(a), tranquillo(a) ♦ *adv*: **to take it** *or* **things ~** prendersela con calma; **I'm ~** (*col*) non ho problemi; **easier said than done** tra il dire e il fare c'è di mezzo il mare; **payment on ~ terms** (*COMM*) facilitazioni *fpl* di pagamento.

easy chair *n* poltrona.

easy-going ['i:zɪ'gəʊɪŋ] *adj* accomodante.

eat, *pt* **ate**, *pp* **eaten** [i:t, eɪt, 'i:tn] *vt* mangiare.

▶**eat away** *vt* (*subj: sea*) erodere; (: *acid*) corrodere.

▶**eat away at, eat into** *vt fus* rodere.

▶**eat out** *vi* mangiare fuori.

▶**eat up** *vt* (*meal etc*) finire di mangiare; **it ~s up electricity** consuma un sacco di corrente.

eatable ['i:təbl] *adj* mangiabile; (*safe to eat*) commestibile.

eaten ['i:tn] *pp of* **eat**.

eau de Cologne ['əʊdəkə'ləʊn] *n* acqua di colonia.

eaves [i:vz] *npl* gronda.

eavesdrop ['i:vzdrɔp] *vi*: **to ~** (**on a conversation**) origliare (una conversazione).

ebb [ɛb] *n* riflusso ♦ *vi* rifluire; (*fig: also: ~ away*) declinare; **~ and flow** flusso e riflusso; **to be at a low ~** (*fig: person, spirits*) avere il morale a terra; (: *business*) andar male.

ebony ['ɛbənɪ] *n* ebano.

ebullient [ɪ'bʌlɪənt] *adj* esuberante.

EC *n abbr* (= *European Community*) CE (= *Comunità Europea*).

ECB *n abbr* (= *European Central Bank*) BCE *f*

eccentric [ɪk'sɛntrɪk] *adj, n* eccentrico(a).

ecclesiastic [ɪkli:zɪ'æstɪk] *n* ecclesiastico.

ecclesiastic(al) [ɪkli:zɪ'æstɪk(əl)] *adj* ecclesiastico(a).

ECG *n abbr see* **electrocardiogram**.

ECGD *n abbr* (= *Export Credits Guarantee Department*) *servizio di garanzia finanziaria per l'esportazione.*

echo, **~es** ['ɛkəʊ] *n* eco *m or f* ♦ *vt* ripetere; fare eco a ♦ *vi* echeggiare; dare un eco.

éclair ['eɪkleə*] *n* ≈ bignè *m inv*.

eclipse [ɪ'klɪps] *n* eclissi *f inv* ♦ *vt* eclissare.

ECM *n abbr* (*US*: = *European Common Market*) MEC *m*.

eco... ['i:kəʊ] *prefix* eco....

eco-friendly [i:kəʊ'frɛndlɪ] *adj* ecologico(a).

ecological [i:kə'lɔdʒɪkəl] *adj* ecologico(a).

ecologist [ɪ'kɔlədʒɪst] *n* ecologo/a.

ecology [ɪ'kɔlədʒɪ] *n* ecologia.

economic [i:kə'nɔmɪk] *adj* economico(a); (*profitable: price*) vantaggioso(a); (*business*) che rende.

economical [i:kə'nɔmɪkəl] *adj* economico(a); (*person*) economo(a).

economically [i:kə'nɔmɪklɪ] *adv* con economia; (*regarding economics*) dal punto di vista economico.

economics [i:kə'nɔmɪks] *n* economia ♦ *npl* aspetto *or* lato economico.

economist [ɪ'kɔnəmɪst] *n* economista *m/f*.

economize [ɪ'kɔnəmaɪz] *vi* risparmiare, fare economia.

economy [ɪ'kɔnəmɪ] *n* economia; **economies of scale** (*COMM*) economie *fpl* di scala.

economy class *n* (*AVIAT etc*) classe *f* turistica.

economy size *n* confezione *f* economica.

ecosystem ['i:kəʊsɪstəm] *n* ecosistema *m*.

eco-tourism [i:kəʊ'tʊərɪzəm] *n* ecoturismo.

ECSC *n abbr* (= *European Coal & Steel Community*) C.E.C.A. *f* (= *Comunità Europea del Carbone e dell'Acciaio*).

ecstasy ['ɛkstəsɪ] *n* estasi *f inv*; **to go into ecstasies over** andare in estasi davanti a; **E~** (*drug*) ecstasy *f inv*.

ecstatic [ɛks'tætɪk] *adj* estatico(a), in estasi.

ECT *n abbr see* **electroconvulsive therapy**.

ECU, ecu ['eɪkju:] *n abbr* (= *European Currency Unit*) ECU *f inv*, ecu *f inv*.

Ecuador ['ɛkwədɔ:*] *n* Ecuador *m*.

ecumenical [i:kju'mɛnɪkl] *adj*

ecumenico(a).
eczema ['ɛksɪmə] *n* eczema *m*.
eddy ['ɛdɪ] *n* mulinello.
edge [ɛdʒ] *n* margine *m*; (*of table, plate, cup*) orlo; (*of knife etc*) taglio ♦ *vt* bordare ♦ *vi*: **to ~ away from** sgattaiolare da; **to ~ past** passar rasente; **to ~ forward** avanzare a poco a poco; **on ~** (*fig*) = **edgy**; **to have the ~ on** essere in vantaggio su.
edgeways ['ɛdʒweɪz] *adv* di fianco; **he couldn't get a word in ~** non riuscì a dire una parola.
edging ['ɛdʒɪŋ] *n* bordo.
edgy ['ɛdʒɪ] *adj* nervoso(a).
edible ['ɛdɪbl] *adj* commestibile; (*meal*) mangiabile.
edict ['iːdɪkt] *n* editto.
edifice ['ɛdɪfɪs] *n* edificio.
edifying ['ɛdɪfaɪɪŋ] *adj* edificante.
Edinburgh ['ɛdɪnbərə] *n* Edimburgo *f*.
edit ['ɛdɪt] *vt* curare; (*newspaper, magazine*) dirigere; (*COMPUT*) correggere e modificare, editare.
edition [ɪ'dɪʃən] *n* edizione *f*.
editor ['ɛdɪtə*] *n* (*in newspaper*) redattore/trice, redattore/trice capo; (*of ob's work*) curatore/trice; (*film ~*) responsabile *m/f* del montaggio.
editorial [ɛdɪ'tɔːrɪəl] *adj* redazionale, editoriale ♦ *n* editoriale *m*; **the ~ staff** la redazione.
EDP *n abbr see* **electronic data processing**.
EDT *abbr* (*US*: = *Eastern Daylight Time*) *ora legale di New York*.
educate ['ɛdjukeɪt] *vt* istruire; educare.
educated guess ['ɛdjukeɪtɪd-] *n* ipotesi *f* ben fondata.
education [ɛdju'keɪʃən] *n* (*teaching*) insegnamento; istruzione *f*; (*knowledge, culture*) cultura; (*SCOL: subject etc*) pedagogia; **primary** *or* (*US*) **elementary/secondary ~** scuola primaria/secondaria.
educational [ɛdju'keɪʃənl] *adj* pedagogico(a); scolastico(a); istruttivo(a); **~ technology** tecnologie *fpl* applicate alla didattica.
Edwardian [ɛd'wɔːdɪən] *adj* edoardiano(a).
EE *abbr* = **electrical engineer**.
EEC *n abbr* (= *European Economic Community*) C.E.E. *f* (= *Comunità Economica Europea*).
EEG *n abbr see* **electroencephalogram**.
eel [iːl] *n* anguilla.
EENT *n abbr* (*US MED*) = *eye, ear, nose and throat*.
EEOC *n abbr* (*US*) = **Equal Employment Opportunity Commission**.
eerie ['ɪərɪ] *adj* che fa accapponare la pelle.

EET *abbr* (= *Eastern European Time*) *fuso orario*.
effect [ɪ'fɛkt] *n* effetto ♦ *vt* effettuare; **to take ~** (*law*) entrare in vigore; (*drug*) fare effetto; **to have an ~ on sb/sth** avere *or* produrre un effetto su qn/qc; **to put into ~** (*plan*) attuare; **in ~** effettivamente; **his letter is to the ~ that ...** il contenuto della sua lettera è che ...; *see also* **effects**.
effective [ɪ'fɛktɪv] *adj* efficace; (*striking: display, outfit*) che fa colpo; **~ date** data d'entrata in vigore; **to become ~** (*law*) entrare in vigore.
effectively [ɪ'fɛktɪvlɪ] *adv* (*efficiently*) efficacemente; (*strikingly*) ad effetto; (*in reality*) di fatto; (*in effect*) in effetti.
effectiveness [ɪ'fɛktɪvnɪs] *n* efficacia.
effects [ɪ'fɛkts] *npl* (*THEAT*) effetti *mpl* scenici; (*property*) effetti *mpl*.
effeminate [ɪ'fɛmɪnɪt] *adj* effeminato(a).
effervescent [ɛfə'vɛsnt] *adj* effervescente.
efficacy ['ɛfɪkəsɪ] *n* efficacia.
efficiency [ɪ'fɪʃənsɪ] *n* efficienza; rendimento effettivo.
efficiency apartment *n* (*US*) miniappartamento.
efficient [ɪ'fɪʃənt] *adj* efficiente; (*remedy, product, system*) efficace; (*machine, car*) che ha un buon rendimento.
efficiently [ɪ'fɪʃəntlɪ] *adv* efficientemente; efficacemente.
effigy ['ɛfɪdʒɪ] *n* effigie *f*.
effluent ['ɛfluənt] *n* effluente *m*.
effort ['ɛfət] *n* sforzo; **to make an ~ to do sth** sforzarsi di fare qc.
effortless ['ɛfətlɪs] *adj* senza sforzo, facile.
effrontery [ɪ'frʌntərɪ] *n* sfrontatezza.
effusive [ɪ'fjuːsɪv] *adj* (*person*) espansivo(a); (*welcome, letter*) caloroso(a); (*thanks, apologies*) interminabile.
EFL *n abbr* (*SCOL*) = *English as a foreign language*.
EFTA ['ɛftə] *n abbr* (= *European Free Trade Association*) E.F.T.A. *f*.
e.g. *adv abbr* (= *exempli gratia: for example*) p.es.
egalitarian [ɪgælɪ'tɛərɪən] *adj* egualitario(a).
egg [ɛg] *n* uovo.
▶**egg on** *vt* incitare.
eggcup ['ɛgkʌp] *n* portauovo *m inv*.
eggplant ['ɛgplɑːnt] *n* (*esp US*) melanzana.
eggshell ['ɛgʃɛl] *n* guscio d'uovo ♦ *adj* (*colour*) guscio d'uovo *inv*.
egg-timer ['ɛgtaɪmə*] *n* clessidra (*per misurare il tempo di cottura delle uova*).
egg white *n* albume *m*, bianco d'uovo.

egg yolk n tuorlo, rosso (d'uovo).
ego ['i:gəu] n ego m inv.
egoism ['εgəuizəm] n egoismo.
egoist ['εgəuist] n egoista m/f.
egotism ['εgəutizəm] n egotismo.
egotist ['εgəutist] n egotista m/f.
ego trip n: **to be on an ~** gasarsi.
Egypt ['i:dʒipt] n Egitto.
Egyptian [i'dʒipfən] adj, n egiziano(a).
eiderdown ['aidədaun] n piumino.
eight [eit] num otto.
eighteen ['ei'ti:n] num diciotto.
eighth [eitθ] num ottavo(a).
eighty [eiti] num ottanta.
Eire ['εərə] n Repubblica d'Irlanda.
EIS n abbr (= Educational Institute of Scotland) principale sindacato degli insegnanti in Scozia.
either ['aiðə*] adj l'uno(a) o l'altro(a); (both, each) ciascuno(a); **on ~ side** su ciascun lato ♦ pron: **~ (of them)** (o) l'uno(a) o l'altro(a); **I don't like ~** non mi piace né l'uno né l'altro ♦ adv neanche; **no, I don't ~** no, neanch'io ♦ conj: **~ good or bad** o buono o cattivo; **I haven't seen ~ one or the other** non ho visto né l'uno né l'altro.
ejaculation [idʒækju'leifən] n (PHYSIOL) eiaculazione f.
eject [i'dʒεkt] vt espellere; lanciare ♦ vi (pilot) catapultarsi.
ejector seat [i'dʒεktə-] n sedile m eiettabile.
eke [i:k]: **to ~ out** vt far durare; aumentare.
EKG n abbr (US) = electrocardiogram.
el [εl] n abbr (US col) see elevated railroad.
elaborate adj [i'læbərit] elaborato(a), minuzioso(a) ♦ vb [i'læbəreit] vt elaborare ♦ vi entrare in dettagli.
elapse [i'læps] vi trascorrere, passare.
elastic [i'læstik] adj elastico(a) ♦ n elastico.
elastic band n (BRIT) elastico.
elasticity [ilæs'tisiti] n elasticità.
elated [i'leitid] adj pieno(a) di gioia.
elation [i'leifən] n gioia.
elbow ['εlbəu] n gomito ♦ vt: **to ~ one's way through the crowd** farsi largo tra la folla a gomitate.
elbow grease n: **to use a bit of ~** usare un po' di olio di gomiti.
elbowroom ['εlbəurum] n spazio.
elder ['εldə*] adj maggiore, più vecchio(a) ♦ n (tree) sambuco; **one's ~s** i più anziani.
elderly ['εldəli] adj anziano(a) ♦ npl: **the ~** gli anziani.
elder statesman n anziano uomo politico in pensione, ma ancora influente; (of company) anziano/a consigliere/a.

eldest ['εldist] adj, n: **the ~ (child)** il(la) maggiore (dei bambini).
elect [i'lεkt] vt eleggere; (choose): **to ~ to do** decidere di fare ♦ adj: **the president ~** il presidente designato.
election [i'lεkfən] n elezione f; **to hold an ~** indire un'elezione.
election campaign n campagna elettorale.
electioneering [ilεkfə'niəriŋ] n propaganda elettorale.
elector [i'lεktə*] n elettore/trice.
electoral [i'lεktərəl] adj elettorale.
electoral college n collegio elettorale.
electoral roll n (BRIT) registro elettorale.
electoral system n sistema m elettorale.
electorate [i'lεktərit] n elettorato.
electric [i'lεktrik] adj elettrico(a).
electrical [i'lεktrikəl] adj elettrico(a).
electrical engineer n ingegnere m elettrotecnico.
electrical failure n guasto all'impianto elettrico.
electric blanket n coperta elettrica.
electric chair n sedia elettrica.
electric cooker n cucina elettrica.
electric current n corrente f elettrica.
electric fire n (BRIT) stufa elettrica.
electrician [ilεk'trifən] n elettricista m.
electricity [ilεk'trisiti] n elettricità; **to switch on/off the ~** attaccare/staccare la corrente.
electricity board n (BRIT) ente m regionale per l'energia elettrica.
electric light n luce f elettrica.
electric shock n scossa (elettrica).
electrify [i'lεktrifai] vt (RAIL) elettrificare; (audience) elettrizzare.
electro... [i'lεktrəu] prefix elettro....
electrocardiogram (ECG) [i'lεktrə-'ka:diəgræm] n elettrocardiogramma m.
electro-convulsive therapy (ECT) [i'lεktrəkən'vΛlsiv-] n elettroshockterapia.
electrocute [i'lεktrəkju:t] vt fulminare.
electrode [i'lεktrəud] n elettrodo.
electroencephalogram (EEG) [i'lεktrəuεn'sεfələgræm] n (MED) elettroencefalogramma m (EEG).
electrolysis [ilεk'trɔlisis] n elettrolisi f.
electromagnetic [i'lεktrəumæg'nεtik] n elettromagnetico(a).
electron [i'lεktrɔn] n elettrone m.
electronic [ilεk'trɔnik] adj elettronico(a); see also electronics.
electronic data processing (EDP) n elaborazione f elettronica di dati.
electronic mail n posta elettronica.
electronics [ilεk'trɔniks] n elettronica.

electron microscope n microscopio elettronico.
electroplated [ɪ'lɛktrəu'pleɪtɪd] adj galvanizzato(a).
electrotherapy [ɪ'lɛktrəu'θɛrəpɪ] n elettroterapia.
elegance ['ɛlɪgəns] n eleganza.
elegant ['ɛlɪgənt] adj elegante.
element ['ɛlɪmənt] n elemento; (of heater, kettle etc) resistenza.
elementary [ɛlɪ'mɛntərɪ] adj elementare.
elementary school n (US) see boxed note.

ELEMENTARY SCHOOL

L'**elementary school**, negli Stati Uniti e in Canada, è un istituto scolastico dove i bambini ricevono un'istruzione per un periodo che va dai 6 agli 8 anni. Negli Stati Uniti si chiama · anche "grade school" o "grammar school".

---

elephant ['ɛlɪfənt] n elefante/essa.
elevate ['ɛlɪveɪt] vt elevare.
elevated railroad (cl) n (US) (ferrovia) soprelevata.
elevation [ɛlɪ'veɪʃən] n elevazione f; (height) altitudine f.
elevator ['ɛlɪveɪtə*] n elevatore m; (US: lift) ascensore m.
eleven [ɪ'lɛvn] num undici.
elevenses [ɪ'lɛvnzɪz] npl (BRIT) caffè m a metà mattina.
eleventh [ɪ'lɛvnθ] adj undicesimo(a); **at the ~ hour** (fig) all'ultimo minuto.
elf, pl **elves** [ɛlf, ɛlvz] n elfo.
elicit [ɪ'lɪsɪt] vt: **to ~ (from)** trarre (da), cavare fuori (da); **to ~ sth (from sb)** strappare qc (a qn).
eligible ['ɛlɪdʒəbl] adj eleggibile; (for membership) che ha i requisiti; **to be ~ for a pension** essere pensionabile.
eliminate [ɪ'lɪmɪneɪt] vt eliminare.
elimination [ɪlɪmɪ'neɪʃən] n eliminazione f; **by process of ~** per eliminazione.
élite [eɪ'liːt] n élite f inv.
elitist [eɪ'liːtɪst] adj (pej) elitario(a).
elixir [ɪ'lɪksə*] n elisir m inv.
Elizabethan [ɪlɪzə'biːθən] n elisabettiano(a).
ellipse [ɪ'lɪps] n ellisse f.
elliptical [ɪ'lɪptɪkl] adj ellittico(a).
elm [ɛlm] n olmo.
elocution [ɛlə'kjuːʃən] n elocuzione f.
elongated ['iːlɔŋgeɪtɪd] adj allungato(a).
elope [ɪ'ləup] vi (lovers) scappare.
eloquence ['ɛləkwəns] n eloquenza.
eloquent ['ɛləkwənt] adj eloquente.
else [ɛls] adv altro; **something ~**

qualcos'altro; **somewhere ~** altrove; **everywhere ~** in qualsiasi altro luogo; **where ~?** in quale altro luogo?; **little ~** poco altro; **everyone ~** tutti gli altri; **nothing ~** nient'altro; **or ~** (otherwise) altrimenti; **is there anything ~ I can do?** posso fare qualcos'altro?
elsewhere [ɛls'wɛə*] adv altrove.
ELT n abbr (SCOL) = English Language Teaching.
elucidate [ɪ'luːsɪdeɪt] vt delucidare.
elude [ɪ'luːd] vt eludere.
elusive [ɪ'luːsɪv] adj elusivo(a); (answer) evasivo(a); **he is very ~** è proprio inafferrabile or irraggiungibile.
elves [ɛlvz] npl of **elf**.
emaciated [ɪ'meɪsɪeɪtɪd] adj emaciato(a).
E-mail, e-mail ['iːmeɪl] n abbr (= electronic mail) posta elettronica ♦ vt: **to ~ sb** comunicare con qn mediante posta elettronica.
emanate ['ɛməneɪt] vi: **to ~ from** emanare da.
emancipate [ɪ'mænsɪpeɪt] vt emancipare.
emancipation [ɪmænsɪ'peɪʃən] n emancipazione f.
emasculate [ɪ'mæskjuleɪt] vt (fig) rendere impotente.
embalm [ɪm'baːm] vt imbalsamare.
embankment [ɪm'bæŋkmənt] n (of road, railway) massicciata; (riverside) argine m; (dyke) diga.
embargo [ɪm'baːgəu] n (pl ~es: COMM, NAUT) embargo ♦ vt mettere l'embargo su; **to put an ~ on sth** mettere l'embargo su qc.
embark [ɪm'baːk] vi: **to ~ (on)** imbarcarsi (su) ♦ vt imbarcare; **to ~ on** (fig) imbarcarsi in; (journey) intraprendere.
embarkation [ɛmbaː'keɪʃən] n imbarco.
embarkation card n carta d'imbarco.
embarrass [ɪm'bærəs] vt imbarazzare; **to be ~ed** essere imbarazzato(a).
embarrassing [ɪm'bærəsɪŋ] adj imbarazzante.
embarrassment [ɪm'bærəsmənt] n imbarazzo.
embassy ['ɛmbəsɪ] n ambasciata; **the Italian E~** l'ambasciata d'Italia.
embed [ɪm'bɛd] vt conficcare; incastrare.
embellish [ɪm'bɛlɪʃ] vt abbellire; **to ~ (with)** (fig: story, truth) infiorare (con).
embers ['ɛmbəz] npl braci fpl.
embezzle [ɪm'bɛzl] vt appropriarsi indebitamente di.
embezzlement [ɪm'bɛzlmənt] n appropriazione f indebita.

embezzler [ɪm'bɛzlə*] n malversatore/trice.

embitter [ɪm'bɪtə*] vt amareggiare; inasprire.

emblem ['ɛmbləm] n emblema m.

embodiment [ɪm'bɔdɪmənt] n personificazione f, incarnazione f.

embody [ɪm'bɔdɪ] vt (features) racchiudere, comprendere; (ideas) dar forma concreta a, esprimere.

embolden [ɪm'bəuldn] vt incitare.

embolism ['ɛmbəlɪzəm] n embolia.

embossed [ɪm'bɔst] adj in rilievo; goffrato(a); ~ **with** ... con in rilievo ....

embrace [ɪm'breɪs] vt abbracciare; (include) comprendere ♦ vi abbracciarsi ♦ n abbraccio.

embroider [ɪm'brɔɪdə*] vt ricamare; (fig: story) abbellire.

embroidery [ɪm'brɔɪdərɪ] n ricamo.

embroil [ɪm'brɔɪl] vt: **to become ~ed (in sth)** restare invischiato(a) (in qc).

embryo ['ɛmbrɪəu] n (also fig) embrione m.

emcee [ɛm'siː] n abbr = **master of ceremonies.**

emend [ɪ'mɛnd] vt (text) correggere, emendare.

emerald ['ɛmərəld] n smeraldo.

emerge [ɪ'məːdʒ] vi apparire, sorgere; **it ~s that** (BRIT) risulta che.

emergence [ɪ'məːdʒəns] n apparizione f; (of nation) nascita.

emergency [ɪ'məːdʒənsɪ] n emergenza; **in an ~** in caso di emergenza; **to declare a state of ~** dichiarare lo stato di emergenza.

emergency exit n uscita di sicurezza.

emergency landing n atterraggio forzato.

emergency lane n (US AUT) corsia d'emergenza.

emergency road service n (US) servizio riparazioni.

emergency service n servizio di pronto intervento.

emergency stop n (BRIT AUT) frenata improvvisa.

emergent [ɪ'məːdʒənt] adj: ~ **nation** paese m in via di sviluppo.

emery board ['ɛmərɪ-] n limetta di carta smerigliata.

emery paper n carta smerigliata.

emetic [ɪ'mɛtɪk] n emetico.

emigrant ['ɛmɪgrənt] n emigrante m/f.

emigrate ['ɛmɪgreɪt] vi emigrare.

emigration [ɛmɪ'greɪʃən] n emigrazione f.

émigré ['ɛmɪgreɪ] n emigrato/a.

eminence ['ɛmɪnəns] n eminenza.

eminent ['ɛmɪnənt] adj eminente.

eminently ['ɛmɪnəntlɪ] adv assolutamente, perfettamente.

emirate [ɛ'mɪərɪt] n emirato.

emission [ɪ'mɪʃən] n (of gas, radiation) emissione f.

emit [ɪ'mɪt] vt emettere.

emolument [ɪ'mɔljumənt] n (often pl: formal) emolumento.

emotion [ɪ'məuʃən] n emozione f; (love, jealousy etc) sentimento.

emotional [ɪ'məuʃənl] adj (person) emotivo(a); (scene) commovente; (tone, speech) carico(a) d'emozione.

emotionally [ɪ'məuʃnəlɪ] adv (behave, be involved) sentimentalmente; (speak) con emozione; ~ **disturbed** con turbe emotive.

emotive [ɪ'məutɪv] adj emotivo(a); ~ **power** capacità di commuovere.

empathy ['ɛmpəθɪ] n immedesimazione f; **to feel ~ with sb** immedesimarsi con i sentimenti di qn.

emperor ['ɛmpərə*] n imperatore m.

emphasis, pl **-ases** ['ɛmfəsɪs, -siːz] n enfasi f inv; importanza; **to lay** or **place ~ on sth** (fig) mettere in risalto or in evidenza qc; **the ~ is on sport** si dà molta importanza allo sport.

emphasize ['ɛmfəsaɪz] vt (word, point) sottolineare; (feature) mettere in evidenza.

emphatic [ɪm'fætɪk] adj (strong) vigoroso(a); (unambiguous, clear) netto(a); categorico(a).

emphatically [ɪm'fætɪkəlɪ] adv vigorosamente; nettamente.

emphysema [ɛmfɪ'siːmə] n (MED) enfisema m.

empire ['ɛmpaɪə*] n impero.

empirical [ɛm'pɪrɪkl] adj empirico(a).

employ [ɪm'plɔɪ] vt (make use of: thing, method, person) impiegare, servirsi di; (give job to) dare lavoro a, impiegare; **he's ~ed in a bank** lavora in banca.

employee [ɪmplɔɪ'iː] n impiegato/a.

employer [ɪm'plɔɪə*] n principale m/f, datore m di lavoro.

employment [ɪm'plɔɪmənt] n impiego; **to find ~** trovare impiego or lavoro; **without ~** disoccupato(a); **place of ~** posto di lavoro.

employment agency n agenzia di collocamento.

employment exchange n (BRIT) ufficio m collocamento inv.

empower [ɪm'pauə*] vt: **to ~ sb to do** concedere autorità a qn di fare.

empress ['ɛmprɪs] n imperatrice f.

emptiness ['ɛmptɪnɪs] n vuoto.

empty ['ɛmptɪ] adj vuoto(a); (street, area) deserto(a); (threat, promise) vano(a) ♦ n (bottle) vuoto ♦ vt vuotare ♦ vi vuotarsi; (liquid) scaricarsi; **on an ~ stomach** a stomaco vuoto

empty-handed [ɛmptɪ'hændɪd] adj a mani vuote.

empty-headed [ɛmptɪ'hɛdɪd] adj sciocco(a).

EMS n abbr (= European Monetary System) S.M.E. m.

EMT n abbr = emergency medical technician.

EMU n abbr (= European Monetary Union) Unità f monetaria europea; (= economic and monetary union) UEM f.

emulate ['ɛmjuleɪt] vt emulare.

emulsion [ɪ'mʌlʃən] n emulsione f; (also: ~ paint) colore m a tempera.

enable [ɪ'neɪbl] vt: **to ~ sb to do** permettere a qn di fare.

enact [ɪn'ækt] vt (law) emanare; (play, scene) rappresentare.

enamel [ɪ'næməl] n smalto.

enamel paint n vernice f a smalto.

enamoured [ɪ'næməd] adj: **~ of** innamorato(a) di.

encampment [ɪn'kæmpmənt] n accampamento.

encased [ɪn'keɪst] adj: **~ in** racchiuso(a) in; rivestito(a) di.

enchant [ɪn'tʃɑːnt] vt incantare; (subj: magic spell) catturare.

enchanting [ɪn'tʃɑːntɪŋ] adj incantevole, affascinante.

encircle [ɪn'sɜːkl] vt accerchiare.

encl(l). abbr (on letters etc: = enclosed, enclosure) all., alleg.

enclose [ɪn'kləuz] vt (land) circondare, recingere; (letter etc): **to ~ (with)** allegare (con); **please find ~d** trovi qui accluso.

enclosure [ɪn'kləuʒə*] n recinto; (COMM) allegato.

encoder [ɪn'kəudə*] n (COMPUT) codificatore m.

encompass [ɪn'kʌmpəs] vt comprendere.

encore [ɔŋ'kɔː*] excl, n bis (m inv).

encounter [ɪn'kauntə*] n incontro ♦ vt incontrare.

encourage [ɪn'kʌrɪdʒ] vt incoraggiare; (industry, growth etc) favorire; **to ~ sb to do sth** incoraggiare qn a fare qc.

encouragement [ɪn'kʌrɪdʒmənt] n incoraggiamento.

encouraging [ɪn'kʌrɪdʒɪŋ] adj incoraggiante.

encroach [ɪn'krəutʃ] vi: **to ~ (up)on** (rights)

usurpare; (time) abusare di; (land) oltrepassare i limiti di.

encrusted [ɪn'krʌstɪd] adj: **~ with** incrostato(a) di.

encumbered [ɪn'kʌmbəd] adj: **to be ~ (with)** essere carico(a) di.

encyclop(a)edia [ɛnsaɪkləu'piːdɪə] n enciclopedia.

end [ɛnd] n fine f; (aim) fine m; (of table) bordo estremo; (of line, rope etc) estremità f inv; (of pointed object) punta; (of town) parte f ♦ vt finire; (also: **bring to an ~, put an ~ to**) mettere fine a ♦ vi finire; **from ~ to ~** da un'estremità all'altra; **to come to an ~** arrivare alla fine, finire; **to be at an ~** essere finito; **in the ~** alla fine; **at the ~ of the street** in fondo alla strada; **at the ~ of the day** (BRIT fig) in fin dei conti; **on ~** (object) ritto(a); **to stand on ~** (hair) rizzarsi; **for 5 hours on ~** per 5 ore di fila; **for hours on ~** per ore e ore; **to this ~, with this ~ in view** a questo fine; **to ~ (with)** concludere (con).

▶ **end up** vi: **to ~ up in** finire in.

endanger [ɪn'deɪndʒə*] vt mettere in pericolo; **an ~ed species** una specie in via di estinzione.

endear [ɪn'dɪə*] vt: **to ~ o.s. to sb** accattivarsi le simpatie di qn.

endearing [ɪn'dɪərɪŋ] adj accattivante.

endearment [ɪn'dɪəmənt] n: **to whisper ~s** sussurrare tenerezze; **term of ~** vezzeggiativo, parola affettuosa.

endeavour, (US) endeavor [ɪn'dɛvə*] n sforzo, tentativo ♦ vi: **to ~ to do** cercare or sforzarsi di fare.

endemic [ɛn'dɛmɪk] adj endemico(a).

ending ['ɛndɪŋ] n fine f, conclusione f; (LING) desinenza.

endive ['ɛndaɪv] n (curly) indivia (riccia); (smooth, flat) indivia belga.

endless ['ɛndlɪs] adj senza fine; (patience, resources) infinito(a); (possibilities) illimitato(a).

endorse [ɪn'dɔːs] vt (cheque) girare; (approve) approvare, appoggiare.

endorsee [ɪndɔː'siː] n giratario/a.

endorsement [ɪn'dɔːsmənt] n (approval) approvazione f; (signature) firma; (BRIT: on driving licence) contravvenzione registrata sulla patente.

endorser [ɪn'dɔːsə*] n girante m/f.

endow [ɪn'dau] vt (prize) istituire; (hospital) fondare; (provide with money) devolvere denaro a; (equip): **to ~ with** fornire di, dotare di.

endowment [ɪn'daumənt] n istituzione f;

fondazione *f*; (*amount*) donazione *f*.
endowment mortgage *n* mutuo che viene ripagato sotto forma di un'assicurazione a vita.
endowment policy *n* polizza-vita mista.
end product *n* (*INDUSTRY*) prodotto finito; (*fig*) risultato.
end result *n* risultato finale.
endurable [ɪn'djuərəbl] *adj* sopportabile.
endurance [ɪn'djuərəns] *n* resistenza; pazienza.
endurance test *n* prova di resistenza.
endure [ɪn'djuə*] *vt* sopportare, resistere a ♦ *vi* durare.
enduring [ɪn'djuərɪŋ] *adj* duraturo(a).
end user *n* (*COMPUT*) consumatore(trice) effettivo(a).
enema ['ɛnɪmə] *n* (*MED*) clistere *m*.
enemy ['ɛnəmɪ] *adj*, *n* nemico(a); **to make an ~ of sb** inimicarsi qn.
energetic [ɛnə'dʒɛtɪk] *adj* energico(a); attivo(a).
energy ['ɛnədʒɪ] *n* energia; **Department of E~** Ministero dell'Energia.
energy crisis *n* crisi *f* energetica.
energy-saving ['ɛnədʒɪ'seɪvɪŋ] *adj* (*policy*) del risparmio energetico; (*device*) che risparmia energia.
enervating ['ɛnə:veɪtɪŋ] *adj* debilitante.
enforce [ɪn'fɔ:s] *vt* (*LAW*) applicare, far osservare.
enforced [ɪn'fɔ:st] *adj* forzato(a).
enfranchise [ɪn'fræntʃaɪz] *vt* (*give vote to*) concedere il diritto di voto a; (*set free*) affrancare.
engage [ɪn'ɡeɪdʒ] *vt* (*hire*) assumere; (*lawyer*) incaricare; (*attention, interest*) assorbire; (*MIL*) attaccare; (*TECH*): **to ~ gear/the clutch** innestare la marcia/la frizione ♦ *vi* (*TECH*) ingranare; **to ~ in** impegnarsi in; **he is ~d in research/a survey** si occupa di ricerca/di un'inchiesta; **to ~ sb in conversation** attaccare conversazione con qn.
engaged [ɪn'ɡeɪdʒd] *adj* (*BRIT: busy, in use*) occupato(a); (*betrothed*) fidanzato(a); **to get ~** fidanzarsi.
engaged tone *n* (*BRIT TEL*) segnale *m* di occupato.
engagement [ɪn'ɡeɪdʒmənt] *n* impegno, obbligo; appuntamento; (*to marry*) fidanzamento; (*MIL*) combattimento; **I have a previous ~** ho già un impegno.
engagement ring *n* anello di fidanzamento.
engaging [ɪn'ɡeɪdʒɪŋ] *adj* attraente.
engender [ɪn'dʒɛndə*] *vt* produrre, causare.

engine ['ɛndʒɪn] *n* (*AUT*) motore *m*; (*RAIL*) locomotiva.
engine driver *n* (*BRIT: of train*) macchinista *m*.
engineer [ɛndʒɪ'nɪə*] *n* ingegnere *m*; (*BRIT: for domestic appliances*) tecnico; (*US RAIL*) macchinista *m*; **civil/mechanical ~** ingegnere civile/meccanico.
engineering [ɛndʒɪ'nɪərɪŋ] *n* ingegneria ♦ *cpd* (*works, factory, worker etc*) metalmeccanico(a).
engine failure *n* guasto al motore.
engine trouble *n* panne *f*.
England ['ɪŋɡlənd] *n* Inghilterra.
English ['ɪŋɡlɪʃ] *adj* inglese ♦ *n* (*LING*) inglese *m*; **the ~** *npl* gli Inglesi; **to be an ~ speaker** essere anglofono(a).
English Channel *n*: **the ~** il Canale della Manica.
Englishman ['ɪŋɡlɪʃmən], **Englishwoman** ['ɪŋɡlɪʃwumən] *n* inglese *m/f*.
English-speaking ['ɪŋɡlɪʃspi:kɪŋ] *adj* di lingua inglese.
engrave [ɪn'ɡreɪv] *vt* incidere.
engraving [ɪn'ɡreɪvɪŋ] *n* incisione *f*.
engrossed [ɪn'ɡrəust] *adj*: **~ in** assorbito(a) da, preso(a) da.
engulf [ɪn'ɡʌlf] *vt* inghiottire.
enhance [ɪn'hɑ:ns] *vt* accrescere; (*position, reputation*) migliorare.
enigma [ɪ'nɪɡmə] *n* enigma *m*.
enigmatic [ɛnɪɡ'mætɪk] *adj* enigmatico(a).
enjoy [ɪn'dʒɔɪ] *vt* godere; (*have: success, fortune*) avere; (*have benefit of: health*) godere (di); **I ~ dancing** mi piace ballare; **to ~ o.s.** godersela, divertirsi.
enjoyable [ɪn'dʒɔɪəbl] *adj* piacevole.
enjoyment [ɪn'dʒɔɪmənt] *n* piacere *m*, godimento.
enlarge [ɪn'lɑ:dʒ] *vt* ingrandire ♦ *vi*: **to ~ on** (*subject*) dilungarsi su.
enlarged [ɪn'lɑ:dʒd] *adj* (*edition*) ampliato(a); (*MED: organ, gland*) ingrossato(a).
enlargement [ɪn'lɑ:dʒmənt] *n* (*PHOT*) ingrandimento.
enlighten [ɪn'laɪtn] *vt* illuminare; dare chiarimenti a.
enlightened [ɪn'laɪtnd] *adj* illuminato(a).
enlightening [ɪn'laɪtnɪŋ] *adj* istruttivo(a).
enlightenment [ɪn'laɪtnmənt] *n* progresso culturale; chiarimenti *mpl*; (*HISTORY*): **the E~** l'Illuminismo.
enlist [ɪn'lɪst] *vt* arruolare; (*support*) procurare ♦ *vi* arruolarsi; **~ed man** (*US MIL*) soldato semplice.
enliven [ɪn'laɪvn] *vt* (*people*) rallegrare; (*events*) ravvivare.

enmity ['ɛnmɪtɪ] *n* inimicizia.
ennoble [ɪ'nəubl] *vt* nobilitare; (*with title*) conferire un titolo nobiliare a.
enormity [ɪ'nɔːmɪtɪ] *n* enormità *f inv.*
enormous [ɪ'nɔːməs] *adj* enorme.
enormously [ɪ'nɔːməslɪ] *adv* enormemente.
enough [ɪ'nʌf] *adj, n*: ~ **time/books** assai tempo/libri; **have you got** ~? nc ha abbastanza *or* a sufficienza? ♦ *adv*: **big** ~ abbastanza grande; **he has not worked** ~ non ha lavorato abbastanza; ~! basta!; **it's hot** ~ (**as it is**)! fa abbastanza caldo così!; **will £5 be** ~? bastano 5 sterline?; **that's** ~ basta; **I've had** ~! non ne posso più!; **he was kind** ~ **to lend me the money** è stato così gentile da prestarmi i soldi; ... **which, funnily** ~ ... che, strano a dirsi.
enquire [ɪn'kwaɪə*] *vt, vi* – **inquire.**
enrage [ɪn'reɪdʒ] *vt* fare arrabbiare.
enrich [ɪn'rɪtʃ] *vt* arricchire.
enrol, (US) enroll [ɪn'rəul] *vt* iscrivere; (*at university*) immatricolare ♦ *vi* iscriversi.
enrol(l)ment [ɪn'rəulmənt] *n* iscrizione *f.*
en route [ɔn'ruːt] *adv*: ~ **for/from/to** in viaggio per/da/a.
ensconced [ɪn'skɔnst] *adj*: ~ **in** ben sistemato(a) in.
ensemble [ãːn'sãːmbl] *n* (*MUS*) ensemble *m inv.*
enshrine [ɪn'ʃraɪn] *vt* conservare come una reliquia.
ensign *n* (*NAUT*) ['ɛnsən] bandiera; (*MIL*) ['ɛnsaɪn] portabandiera *m inv.*
enslave [ɪn'sleɪv] *vt* fare schiavo.
ensue [ɪn'sjuː] *vi* seguire, risultare.
ensure [ɪn'ʃuə*] *vt* assicurare; garantire; **to** ~ **that** assicurarsi che.
ENT *n abbr* (*MED*: = *Ear, Nose & Throat*) O.R.L.
entail [ɪn'teɪl] *vt* comportare.
entangle [ɪn'tæŋgl] *vt* (*thread etc*) impigliare; **to become** ~**d in sth** (*fig*) rimanere impegolato in qc.
enter ['ɛntə*] *vt* (*gen*) entrare in; (*club*) associarsi a; (*profession*) intraprendere; (*army*) arruolarsi in; (*competition*) partecipare a; (*sb for a competition*) iscrivere; (*write down*) registrare; (*COMPUT*: *data*) introdurre, inserire ♦ *vi* entrare.
► **enter for** *vt fus* iscriversi a.
► **enter into** *vt fus* (*explanation*) cominciare a dare; (*debate*) partecipare a; (*agreement*) concludere; (*negotiations*) prendere parte a.
► **enter (up)on** *vt fus* cominciare.
enteritis [ɛntə'raɪtɪs] *n* enterite *f.*
enterprise ['ɛntəpraɪz] *n* (*undertaking,*

company) impresa; (*spirit*) iniziativa.
enterprising ['ɛntəpraɪzɪŋ] *adj* intraprendente.
entertain [ɛntə'teɪn] *vt* divertire; (*invite*) ricevere; (*idea, plan*) nutrire.
entertainer [ɛntə'teɪnə*] *n* comico/a.
entertaining [ɛntə'teɪnɪŋ] *adj* divertente
♦ *n*: **to do a lot of** ~ avere molti ospiti.
entertainment [ɛntə'teɪnmənt] *n* (*amusement*) divertimento; (*show*) spettacolo.
entertainment allowance *n* spese *fpl* di rappresentanza.
enthral [ɪn'θrɔːl] *vt* affascinare, avvincere.
enthralled [ɪn'θrɔːld] *adj* affascinato(a).
enthralling [ɪn'θrɔːlɪŋ] *adj* avvincente.
enthuse [ɪn'θuːz] *vi*: **to** ~ (**about** *or* **over**) entusiasmarsi (per).
enthusiasm [ɪn'θuːzɪæzəm] *n* entusiasmo.
enthusiast [ɪn'θuːzɪæst] *n* entusiasta *m/f*; **a jazz etc** ~ un appassionato di jazz *etc.*
enthusiastic [ɪnθuːzɪ'æstɪk] *adj* entusiasta, entusiastico(a); **to be** ~ **about sth/sb** essere appassionato di qc/entusiasta di qn.
entice [ɪn'taɪs] *vt* allettare, sedurre.
enticing [ɪn'taɪsɪŋ] *adj* allettante.
entire [ɪn'taɪə*] *adj* intero(a).
entirely [ɪn'taɪəlɪ] *adv* completamente, interamente.
entirety [ɪn'taɪərətɪ] *n*: **in its** ~ nel suo complesso.
entitle [ɪn'taɪtl] *vt* (*give right*): **to** ~ **sb to sth/to do** dare diritto a qn a qc/a fare.
entitled [ɪn'taɪtld] *adj* (*book*) che si intitola; **to be** ~ **to sth/to do sth** avere diritto a qc/a fare qc.
entity ['ɛntɪtɪ] *n* entità *f inv.*
entrails ['ɛntreɪlz] *npl* interiora *fpl.*
entrance *n* ['ɛntrns] entrata, ingresso; (*of person*) entrata ♦ *vt* [ɪn'trɑːns] incantare, rapire; **to gain** ~ **to** (*university etc*) essere ammesso a.
entrance examination *n* (*to school*) esame *m* di ammissione.
entrance fee *n* tassa d'iscrizione; (*to museum etc*) prezzo d'ingresso.
entrance ramp *n* (*US AUT*) rampa di accesso.
entrancing [ɪn'trɑːnsɪŋ] *adj* incantevole.
entrant ['ɛntrnt] *n* partecipante *m/f*; concorrente *m/f*; (*BRIT*: *in exam*) candidato/a.
entreat [ɛn'triːt] *vt* supplicare.
entreaty [ɪn'triːtɪ] *n* supplica, preghiera.
entrée ['ɔntreɪ] *n* (*CULIN*) prima portata.
entrenched [ɛn'trɛntʃt] *adj* radicato(a).
entrepreneur ['ɔntrəprə'nɜː*] *n*

imprenditore *m*.
entrepreneurial ['ɔntrəprə'nəːrɪəl] *adj* imprenditoriale.
entrust [ɪn'trʌst] *vt*: **to ~ sth to** affidare qc a.
entry ['entrɪ] *n* entrata; (*way in*) entrata, ingresso; (*in dictionary*) voce *f*; (*in diary, ship's log*) annotazione *f*; (*in account book, ledger, list*) registrazione *f*; **"no ~"** "vietato l'ingresso"; (*AUT*) "divieto di accesso"; **single/double ~ book-keeping** partita semplice/doppia.
entry form *n* modulo d'iscrizione.
entry phone *n* (*BRIT*) citofono.
entwine [ɪn'twaɪn] *vt* intrecciare.
E number *n* sigla di *additivo alimentare*.
enumerate [ɪ'njuːməreɪt] *vt* enumerare.
enunciate [ɪ'nʌnsɪeɪt] *vt* enunciare; pronunciare.
envelop [ɪn'vɛləp] *vt* avvolgere, avviluppare.
envelope ['ɛnvələup] *n* busta.
enviable ['ɛnvɪəbl] *adj* invidiabile.
envious ['ɛnvɪəs] *adj* invidioso(a).
environment [ɪn'vaɪərənmənt] *n* ambiente *m*; **Department of the E~** (*BRIT*) ≈ Ministero dell'Ambiente.
environmental [ɪnvaɪərən'mɛntl] *adj* ecologico(a); ambientale; **~ studies** (*in school etc*) ecologia.
environmentalist [ɪn'vaɪərən'mɛntəlɪst] *n* studioso/a della protezione dell'ambiente.
environmentally [ɪnvaɪərən'mɛntəlɪ] *adv*: **~ sound/friendly** che rispetta l'ambiente.
Environmental Protection Agency (EPA) *n* (*US*) ≈ Ministero dell'Ambiente.
envisage [ɪn'vɪzɪdʒ] *vt* immaginare; prevedere.
envision [ɪn'vɪʒən] *vt* concepire, prevedere.
envoy ['ɛnvɔɪ] *n* inviato/a.
envy ['ɛnvɪ] *n* invidia ♦ *vt* invidiare; **to ~ sb sth** invidiare qn per qc.
enzyme ['ɛnzaɪm] *n* enzima *m*.
EPA *n abbr* (*US*) *see* **Environmental Protection Agency**.
ephemeral [ɪ'fɛmərəl] *adj* effimero(a).
epic ['ɛpɪk] *n* poema *m* epico ♦ *adj* epico(a).
epicentre, (*US*) **epicenter** ['ɛpɪsɛntə*] *n* epicentro.
epidemic [ɛpɪ'dɛmɪk] *n* epidemia.
epilepsy ['ɛpɪlɛpsɪ] *n* epilessia.
epileptic [ɛpɪ'lɛptɪk] *adj, n* epilettico(a).
epilogue ['ɛpɪlɔg] *n* epilogo.
Epiphany [ɪ'pɪfənɪ] *n* Epifania.
episcopal [ɪ'pɪskəpəl] *adj* episcopale.
episode ['ɛpɪsəud] *n* episodio.

epistle [ɪ'pɪsl] *n* epistola.
epitaph ['ɛpɪtɑːf] *n* epitaffio.
epithet ['ɛpɪθɛt] *n* epiteto.
epitome [ɪ'pɪtəmɪ] *n* epitome *f*; quintessenza.
epitomize [ɪ'pɪtəmaɪz] *vt* (*fig*) incarnare.
epoch ['iːpɔk] *n* epoca.
epoch-making ['iːpɔkmeɪkɪŋ] *adj* che fa epoca.
eponymous [ɪ'pɔnɪməs] *adj* dello stesso nome.
equable ['ɛkwəbl] *adj* uniforme; (*climate*) costante; (*character*) equilibrato(a).
equal ['iːkwl] *adj, n* uguale (*m/f*) ♦ *vt* uguagliare; **~ to** (*task*) all'altezza di.
equality [iː'kwɔlɪtɪ] *n* uguaglianza.
equalize ['iːkwəlaɪz] *vt, vi* pareggiare.
equalizer ['iːkwəlaɪzə*] *n* punto del pareggio.
equally ['iːkwəlɪ] *adv* ugualmente; **they are ~ clever** sono intelligenti allo stesso modo.
Equal Opportunities Commission, (*US*) **Equal Employment Opportunity Commission** *n commissione contro discriminazioni sessuali o razziali nel mondo del lavoro*.
equal(s) sign *n* segno d'uguaglianza.
equanimity [ɛkwə'nɪmɪtɪ] *n* serenità.
equate [ɪ'kweɪt] *vt*: **to ~ sth with** considerare qc uguale a; (*compare*) paragonare qc con; **to ~ A to B** mettere in equazione A e B.
equation [ɪ'kweɪʃən] *n* (*MATH*) equazione *f*.
equator [ɪ'kweɪtə*] *n* equatore *m*.
Equatorial Guinea [ɛkwə'tɔːrɪəl-] *n* Guinea Equatoriale.
equestrian [ɪ'kwɛstrɪən] *adj* equestre ♦ *n* cavaliere/amazzone.
equilibrium [iːkwɪ'lɪbrɪəm] *n* equilibrio.
equinox ['iːkwɪnɔks] *n* equinozio.
equip [ɪ'kwɪp] *vt* equipaggiare, attrezzare; **to ~ sb/sth with** fornire qn/qc di; **~ped with** (*machinery etc*) dotato(a) di; **he is well ~ped for the job** ha i requisiti necessari per quel lavoro.
equipment [ɪ'kwɪpmənt] *n* attrezzatura; (*electrical etc*) apparecchiatura.
equitable ['ɛkwɪtəbl] *adj* equo(a), giusto(a).
equities ['ɛkwɪtɪz] *npl* (*BRIT COMM*) azioni *fpl* ordinarie.
equity ['ɛkwɪtɪ] *n* equità.
equity capital *n* capitale *m* azionario.
equivalent [ɪ'kwɪvələnt] *adj, n* equivalente (*m*); **to be ~ to** equivalere a.
equivocal [ɪ'kwɪvəkl] *adj* equivoco(a); (*open to suspicion*) dubbio(a).
equivocate [ɪ'kwɪvəkeɪt] *vi* esprimersi in

modo equivoco.

equivocation [ɪkwɪvə'keɪʃən] *n* parole *fpl* equivoche.

ER *abbr* (*BRIT*) = Elizabeth Regina.

ERA *n abbr* (*US POL*) = Equal Rights Amendment.

era ['ɪərə] *n* era, età *f inv.*

eradicate [ɪ'rædɪkeɪt] *vt* sradicare.

erase [ɪ'reɪz] *vt* cancellare.

eraser [ɪ'reɪzə*] *n* gomma.

erect [ɪ'rɛkt] *adj* eretto(a) ♦ *vt* costruire; (*monument, tent*) alzare.

erection [ɪ'rɛkʃən] *n* (*also PHYSIOL*) erezione *f*; (*of building*) costruzione *f*; (*of machinery*) montaggio.

ergonomics [ɔːgə'nɔmɪks] *n* ergonomia.

ERISA *n abbr* (*US*: = Employee Retirement Income Security Act*) legge relativa al pensionamento statale.

Eritrea [ɛrɪ'treɪə] *n* Eritrea.

ERM *n abbr* (= Exchange Rate Mechanism) meccanismo dei tassi di cambio.

ermine ['ɔːmɪn] *n* ermellino.

ERNIE ['ɔːnɪ] *n abbr* (*BRIT*: = Electronic Random Number Indicator Equipment) sistema che seleziona i numeri vincenti di buoni del Tesoro.

erode [ɪ'rəud] *vt* erodere; (*metal*) corrodere.

erogenous zone [ɪ'rɔdʒənəs-] *n* zona erogena.

erosion [ɪ'rəuʒən] *n* crosione *f.*

erotic [ɪ'rɔtɪk] *adj* erotico(a).

eroticism [ɪ'rɔtɪsɪzəm] *n* erotismo.

err [ɔː*] *vi* errare; (*REL*) peccare.

errand ['ɛrənd] *n* commissione *f*; **to run ~s** fare commissioni; **~ of mercy** atto di carità.

errand boy *n* fattorino.

erratic [ɪ'rætɪk] *adj* imprevedibile; (*person, mood*) incostante.

erroneous [ɪ'rəunɪəs] *adj* erroneo(a).

error ['ɛrə*] *n* errore *m*; **typing/spelling ~** errore di battitura/di ortografia; **in ~** per errore; **~s and omissions excepted** salvo errori ed omissioni.

error message *n* (*COMPUT*) messaggio di errore.

erstwhile ['ɔːstwaɪl] *adv* allora, un tempo ♦ *adj* di allora.

erudite ['ɛrjudaɪt] *adj* erudito(a).

erupt [ɪ'rʌpt] *vi* erompere; (*volcano*) mettersi (*or* essere) in eruzione.

eruption [ɪ'rʌpʃən] *n* eruzione *f*; (*of anger, violence*) esplosione *f.*

ESA *n abbr* (= European Space Agency) ESA *f.*

escalate ['ɛskəleɪt] *vi* intensificarsi; (*costs*) salire.

escalation [ɛskə'leɪʃən] *n* escalation *f*; (*of prices*) aumento.

escalation clause *n* clausola di revisione.

escalator ['ɛskəleɪtə*] *n* scala mobile.

escapade [ɛskə'peɪd] *n* scappatella; avventura.

escape [ɪ'skeɪp] *n* evasione *f*; fuga; (*of gas etc*) fuga, fuoriuscita ♦ *vi* fuggire; (*from jail*) evadere, scappare; (*fig*) sfuggire; (*leak*) uscire ♦ *vt* sfuggire a; **to ~ from sb** sfuggire a qn; **to ~ to** (*another place*) fuggire in; (*freedom, safety*) fuggire verso; **to ~ notice** passare inosservato(a).

escape artist *n* mago della fuga.

escape clause *n* clausola scappatoia.

escapee [ɪskeɪ'piː] *n* evaso/a.

escape hatch *n* (*in submarine, space rocket*) portello di sicurezza.

escape key *n* (*COMPUT*) tasto di escape, tasto per cambio di codice.

escape route *n* percorso della fuga.

escapism [ɪs'keɪpɪzəm] *n* evasione *f* (dalla realtà).

escapist [ɪs'keɪpɪst] *adj* d'evasione ♦ *n* persona che cerca di evadere dalla realtà.

escapologist [ɛskə'pɔlədʒɪst] *n* (*BRIT*) = escape artist.

escarpment [ɪs'kɑːpmənt] *n* scarpata.

eschew [ɪs'tʃuː] *vt* evitare.

escort *n* ['ɛskɔːt] scorta; (*to dance etc*): **her ~** il suo cavaliere; **his ~** la sua dama ♦ *vt* [ɪ'skɔːt] scortare; accompagnare.

escort agency *n* agenzia di hostess.

Eskimo ['ɛskɪməu] *adj* eschimese ♦ *n* eschimese *m/f*; (*LING*) eschimese *m.*

ESL *n abbr* (*SCOL*) = English as a Second Language.

esophagus [iː'sɔfəgəs] *n* (*US*) = oesophagus.

esoteric [ɛsəu'tɛrɪk] *adj* esoterico(a).

ESP *n abbr see* extrasensory perception; (*SCOL*) = English for Special Purposes.

esp. *abbr* (= especially) spec.

especially [ɪ'spɛʃlɪ] *adv* specialmente; (*above all*) soprattutto; (*specifically*) espressamente; (*particularly*) particolarmente.

espionage ['ɛspɪɑːʒ] *n* spionaggio.

esplanade [ɛsplə'neɪd] *n* lungomare *m.*

espouse [ɪ'spauz] *vt* abbracciare.

Esquire [ɪ'skwaɪə*] *n* (*BRIT*: *abbr* Esq.): **J. Brown, ~** Signor J. Brown.

essay ['ɛseɪ] *n* (*SCOL*) composizione *f*; (*LITERATURE*) saggio.

essence ['ɛsns] *n* essenza; **in ~** in sostanza;

speed is of the ~ la velocità è di estrema importanza.
essential [ɪ'sɛnʃəl] *adj* essenziale; (*basic*) fondamentale ♦ *n* elemento essenziale; **it is** ~ **that** è essenziale che + *sub*.
essentially [ɪ'sɛnʃəlɪ] *adv* essenzialmente.
EST *abbr* (*US*: = *Eastern Standard Time*) *fuso orario.*
est. *abbr* = *established*; *estimate(d).*
establish [ɪ'stæblɪʃ] *vt* stabilire; (*business*) mettere su; (*one's power etc*) confermare; (*prove*: *fact, identity, sb's innocence*) dimostrare.
establishment [ɪs'tæblɪʃmənt] *n* stabilimento; (*business*) azienda; **the E~** la classe dirigente; l'establishment *m*; **a teaching** ~ un istituto d'istruzione.
estate [ɪ'steɪt] *n* proprietà *f inv*; (*LAW*) beni *mpl*, patrimonio; (*BRIT*: *also*: **housing** ~) complesso edilizio.
estate agency *n* (*BRIT*) agenzia immobiliare.
estate agent *n* (*BRIT*) agente *m* immobiliare.
estate car *n* (*BRIT*) giardiniera.
esteem [ɪ'stiːm] *n* stima ♦ *vt* considerare; stimare; **I hold him in high** ~ gode di tutta la mia stima.
esthetic [ɪs'θɛtɪk] *adj* (*US*) = **aesthetic.**
estimate *n* ['ɛstɪmət] stima; (*COMM*) preventivo ♦ *vb* ['ɛstɪmeɪt] *vt* stimare, valutare ♦ *vi* (*BRIT COMM*): **to** ~ **for** fare il preventivo per; **to give sb an** ~ **of** fare a qn una valutazione approssimativa (*or* un preventivo) di; **at a rough** ~ approssimativamente.
estimation [ɛstɪ'meɪʃən] *n* stima; opinione *f*; **in my** ~ a mio giudizio, a mio avviso.
Estonia [ɛ'stəunɪə] *n* Estonia.
Estonian [ɛ'stəunɪən] *adj* estone *inv* ♦ *n* estone *m/f*; (*LING*) estone *m*.
estranged [ɪ'streɪndʒd] *adj* separato(a).
estrangement [ɪs'treɪndʒmənt] *n* alienazione *f*.
estrogen ['iːstrəudʒən] *n* (*US*) = **oestrogen.**
estuary ['ɛstjuərɪ] *n* estuario.
ET *abbr* (*US*: = *Eastern Time*) *fuso orario*
ETA *n abbr* (= *estimated time of arrival*) ora di arrivo prevista.
et al. *abbr* (= *et alii*: *and others*) ed altri.
etc. *abbr* (= *et cetera*) ecc., etc.
etch [ɛtʃ] *vt* incidere all'acquaforte.
etching ['ɛtʃɪŋ] *n* acquaforte *f*.
ETD *n abbr* (= *estimated time of departure*) ora di partenza prevista.
eternal [ɪ'təːnl] *adj* eterno(a).
eternity [ɪ'təːnɪtɪ] *n* eternità.
ether ['iːθə*] *n* etere *m*.

ethereal [ɪ'θɪərɪəl] *adj* etereo(a).
ethical ['ɛθɪkl] *adj* etico(a), morale.
ethics ['ɛθɪks] *n* etica ♦ *npl* morale *f*.
Ethiopia [iːθɪ'əupɪə] *n* Etiopia.
Ethiopian [iːθɪ'əupɪən] *adj, n* etiope (*m/f*).
ethnic ['ɛθnɪk] *adj* etnico(a).
ethnic cleansing [-'klɛnzɪŋ] *n* pulizia etnica.
ethnic minority *n* minoranza etnica.
ethnology [ɛθ'nɔlədʒɪ] *n* etnologia.
ethos ['iːθɔs] *n* (*of culture, group*) norma di vita.
etiquette ['ɛtɪkɛt] *n* etichetta.
ETV *n abbr* (*US*) = *Educational Television.*
etymology [ɛtɪ'mɔlədʒɪ] *n* etimologia.
EU *n abbr* (= *European Union*) UE *f*.
eucalyptus [juːkə'lɪptəs] *n* eucalipto.
eulogy ['juːlədʒɪ] *n* elogio.
euphemism ['juːfəmɪzəm] *n* eufemismo.
euphemistic [juːfə'mɪstɪk] *adj* eufemistico(a).
euphoria [juː'fɔːrɪə] *n* euforia.
Eurasia [juə'reɪʃə] *n* Eurasia.
Eurasian [juə'reɪʃən] *adj, n* eurasiano(a).
Euratom [juə'rætəm] *n abbr* (= *European Atomic Energy Community*) EURATOM *f*.
euro ['juərəu] *n* (*currency*) euro *m inv*.
Euro- ['juərəu] *prefix* euro-.
Eurocheque ['juərəutʃɛk] *n* eurochèque *m inv*.
Eurocrat ['juərəukræt] *n* eurocrate *m/f*.
Eurodollar ['juərəudɔlə*] *n* eurodollaro.
Euroland ['juərəu,lænd] *n* Eurolandia.
Europe ['juərəp] *n* Europa.
European [juərə'piːən] *adj, n* europeo(a).
European Court of Justice *n* Corte *f* di Giustizia della Comunità Europea.
Euro-sceptic ['juərəuskɛptɪk] *n* euroscettico/a.
euthanasia [juːθə'neɪzɪə] *n* eutanasia.
evacuate [ɪ'vækjueɪt] *vt* evacuare.
evacuation [ɪvækju'eɪʃən] *n* evacuazione *f*.
evacuee [ɪvækju'iː] *n* sfollato/a.
evade [ɪ'veɪd] *vt* eludere; (*duties etc*) sottrarsi a.
evaluate [ɪ'væljueɪt] *vt* valutare.
evangelist [ɪ'vændʒəlɪst] *n* evangelista *m*.
evangelize [ɪ'vændʒəlaɪz] *vt* evangelizzare.
evaporate [ɪ'væpəreɪt] *vi* evaporare ♦ *vt* far evaporare.
evaporated milk *n* latte *m* concentrato.
evaporation [ɪvæpə'reɪʃən] *n* evaporazione *f*.
evasion [ɪ'veɪʒən] *n* evasione *f*.
evasive [ɪ'veɪsɪv] *adj* evasivo(a).
eve [iːv] *n*: **on the** ~ **of** alla vigilia di.
even ['iːvn] *adj* regolare; (*number*) pari *inv* ♦ *adv* anche, perfino; ~ **if**, ~ **though** anche

se; ~ **more** ancora di più; **he loves her** ~ **more** la ama anche di più; ~ **faster** ancora più veloce; ~ **so** ciò nonostante; **not** ~ ... nemmeno ...; **to break** ~ finire in pari *or* alla pari; **to get** ~ **with sb** dare la pari a qn.

▶**even out** *vi* pareggiare.

even-handed ['iːvn'hændɪd] *adj* imparziale, equo(a).

evening ['iːvnɪŋ] *n* sera; (*as duration, event*) serata; **in the** ~ la sera; **this** ~ stasera, questa sera; **tomorrow/yesterday** ~ domani/ieri sera.

evening class *n* corso serale.

evening dress *n* (*woman's*) abito da sera; **in** ~ (*man*) in abito scuro; (*woman*) in abito lungo.

evenly ['iːvənlɪ] *adv* (*distribute, space, spread*) uniformemente; (*divide*) in parti uguali.

evensong ['iːvnsɒŋ] *n* ≈ vespro.

event [ɪ'vɛnt] *n* avvenimento; (*SPORT*) gara; **in the** ~ **of** in caso di; **at all** ~**s** (*BRIT*), **in any** ~ in ogni caso; **in the** ~ in realtà, di fatto; **in the course of** ~**s** nel corso degli eventi.

eventful [ɪ'vɛntful] *adj* denso(a) di eventi.

eventing [ɪ'vɛntɪŋ] *n* (*HORSERIDING*) concorso ippico.

eventual [ɪ'vɛntʃuəl] *adj* finale.

eventuality [ɪventʃu'ælɪtɪ] *n* possibilità *f inv*, eventualità *f inv*.

eventually [ɪ'vɛntʃuəlɪ] *adv* finalmente.

ever ['ɛvə*] *adv* mai; (*at all times*) sempre; **for** ~ per sempre; **the best** ~ il migliore che ci sia mai stato; **hardly** ~ non ... quasi mai; **did you** ~ **meet him?** l'ha mai incontrato?; **have you** ~ **been there?** c'è mai stato?; ~ **so pretty** così bello(a); **thank you** ~ **so much** grazie mille; **yours** ~ (*BRIT: in letters*) sempre tuo; ~ **since** *adv* da allora ♦ *conj* sin da quando.

Everest ['ɛvərɪst] *n* (*also*: **Mount** ~) Everest *m*.

evergreen ['ɛvəgriːn] *n* sempreverde *m*.

everlasting [ɛvə'lɑːstɪŋ] *adj* eterno(a).

every ['ɛvrɪ] *adj* ogni; ~ **day** tutti i giorni, ogni giorno; ~ **other/third day** ogni due/tre giorni; ~ **other car** una macchina su due; ~ **now and then** ogni tanto, di quando in quando; **I have** ~ **confidence in him** ho piena fiducia in lui.

everybody ['ɛvrɪbɔdɪ] *pron* ognuno, tutti *pl*; ~ **else** tutti gli altri; ~ **knows about it** lo sanno tutti.

everyday ['ɛvrɪdeɪ] *adj* quotidiano(a); di ogni giorno; (*use, occurrence, experience*) comune; (*expression*) di uso corrente.

everyone ['ɛvrɪwʌn] = **everybody**.

everything ['ɛvrɪθɪŋ] *pron* tutto, ogni cosa; ~ **is ready** è tutto pronto; **he did** ~ **possible** ha fatto tutto il possibile.

everywhere ['ɛvrɪwɛə*] *adv* in ogni luogo, dappertutto; (*wherever*) ovunque; ~ **you go you meet** ... ovunque si vada si trova ....

evict [ɪ'vɪkt] *vt* sfrattare.

eviction [ɪ'vɪkʃən] *n* sfratto.

eviction notice *n* avviso di sfratto.

evidence ['ɛvɪdəns] *n* (*proof*) prova; (*of witness*) testimonianza; (*sign*): **to show** ~ **of** dare segni di; **to give** ~ deporre; **in** ~ (*obvious*) in evidenza; in vista.

evident ['ɛvɪdənt] *adj* evidente.

evidently ['ɛvɪdəntlɪ] *adv* evidentemente.

evil ['iːvl] *adj* cattivo(a), maligno(a) ♦ *n* male *m*.

evince [ɪ'vɪns] *vt* manifestare.

evocative [ɪ'vɔkətɪv] *adj* evocativo(a).

evoke [ɪ'vəuk] *vt* evocare; (*admiration*) suscitare.

evolution [iːvə'luːʃən] *n* evoluzione *f*.

evolve [ɪ'vɔlv] *vt* elaborare ♦ *vi* svilupparsi, evolversi.

ewe [juː] *n* pecora.

ex- [ɛks] *prefix* ex; (*out of*): **the price** ~ **works** il prezzo franco fabbrica.

exacerbate [ɪk'sæsəbeɪt] *vt* (*pain*) aggravare; (*fig: relations, situation*) esacerbare, esasperare.

exact [ɪg'zækt] *adj* esatto(a) ♦ *vt*: **to** ~ **sth** (**from**) estorcere qc (da); esigere qc (da).

exacting [ɪg'zæktɪŋ] *adj* esigente; (*work*) faticoso(a).

exactitude [ɪg'zæktɪtjuːd] *n* esattezza, precisione *f*.

exactly [ɪg'zæktlɪ] *adv* esattamente; ~! esatto!

exaggerate [ɪg'zædʒəreɪt] *vt, vi* esagerare.

exaggeration [ɪgzædʒə'reɪʃən] *n* esagerazione *f*.

exalt [ɪg'zɔːlt] *vt* esaltare; elevare.

exalted [ɪg'zɔːltɪd] *adj* (*rank, person*) elevato(a); (*elated*) esaltato(a).

exam [ɪg'zæm] *n abbr* (*SCOL*) = **examination**.

examination [ɪgzæmɪ'neɪʃən] *n* (*SCOL*) esame *m*; (*MED*) controllo; **to take** *or* (*BRIT*) **sit an** ~ sostenere *or* dare un esame; **the matter is under** ~ la questione è all'esame.

examine [ɪg'zæmɪn] *vt* esaminare; (*SCOL: orally, LAW: person*) interrogare; (*inspect: machine, premises*) ispezionare; (*luggage, passport*) controllare; (*MED*) visitare.

examiner [ɪg'zæmɪnə*] *n* esaminatore/trice.

example [ɪg'zɑːmpl] *n* esempio; **for** ~ ad *or* per esempio; **to set a good/bad** ~ dare il buon/cattivo esempio.
exasperate [ɪg'zɑːspəreɪt] *vt* esasperare; ~**d by** (*or* at *or* with) esasperato da.
exasperating [ɪg'zɑːspəreɪtɪŋ] *adj* esasperante.
exasperation [ɪgzɑːspə'reɪʃən] *n* esasperazione *f*.
excavate ['ɛkskəveɪt] *vt* scavare.
excavation [ɛkskə'veɪʃən] *n* escavazione *f*.
excavator ['ɛkskəveɪtə*] *n* scavatore *m*, scavatrice *f*.
exceed [ɪk'siːd] *vt* superare; (*one's powers, time limit*) oltrepassare.
exceedingly [ɪk'siːdɪŋlɪ] *adv* eccessivamente.
excel [ɪk'sɛl] *vi* eccellere ♦ *vt* sorpassare; **to** ~ **o.s.** (*BRIT*) superare se stesso.
excellence ['ɛksələns] *n* eccellenza.
Excellency ['ɛksələnsɪ] *n*: **His** ~ Sua Eccellenza.
excellent ['ɛksələnt] *adj* eccellente.
except [ɪk'sɛpt] *prep* (*also*: ~ **for**, ~**ing**) salvo, all'infuori di, eccetto ♦ *vt* escludere; ~ **if/when** salvo se/quando; ~ **that** salvo che.
exception [ɪk'sɛpʃən] *n* eccezione *f*; **to take** ~ **to** trovare a ridire su; **with the** ~ **of** ad eccezione di.
exceptional [ɪk'sɛpʃənl] *adj* eccezionale.
excerpt ['ɛksəːpt] *n* estratto.
excess [ɪk'sɛs] *n* eccesso; **in** ~ **of** al di sopra di.
excess baggage *n* bagaglio in eccedenza.
excess fare *n* supplemento.
excessive [ɪk'sɛsɪv] *adj* eccessivo(a).
excess supply *n* eccesso di offerta.
exchange [ɪks'tʃeɪndʒ] *n* scambio; (*also*: **telephone** ~) centralino ♦ *vt*: **to** ~ (**for**) scambiare (con); **in** ~ **for** in cambio di; **foreign** ~ (*COMM*) cambio.
exchange control *n* controllo sui cambi.
exchange market *n* mercato dei cambi.
exchange rate *n* tasso di cambio.
Exchequer [ɪks'tʃɛkə*] *n*: **the** ~ (*BRIT*) lo Scacchiere, ≈ il ministero delle Finanze.
excisable [ɪk'saɪzəbl] *adj* soggetto(a) a dazio.
excise *n* ['ɛksaɪz] imposta, dazio ♦ *vt* [ɛk'saɪz] recidere.
excise duties *npl* dazi *mpl*.
excitable [ɪk'saɪtəbl] *adj* eccitabile.
excite [ɪk'saɪt] *vt* eccitare; **to get** ~**d** eccitarsi.
excitement [ɪk'saɪtmənt] *n* eccitazione *f*; agitazione *f*.
exciting [ɪk'saɪtɪŋ] *adj* avventuroso(a);

(*film, book*) appassionante.
excl. *abbr* (= *excluding, exclusive (of)*) escl.
exclaim [ɪk'skleɪm] *vi* esclamare.
exclamation [ɛksklə'meɪʃən] *n* esclamazione *f*.
exclamation mark *n* punto esclamativo.
exclude [ɪk'skluːd] *vt* escludere.
excluding [ɪk'skluːdɪŋ] *prep*: ~ **VAT** IVA esclusa.
exclusion [ɪk'skluːʒən] *n* esclusione *f*; **to the** ~ **of** escludendo.
exclusion clause *n* clausola di esclusione.
exclusion zone *n* area interdetta.
exclusive [ɪk'skluːsɪv] *adj* esclusivo(a); (*club*) selettivo(a); (*district*) snob *inv* ♦ *adv* (*COMM*) non compreso; ~ **of VAT** IVA esclusa; ~ **of postage** spese postali escluse; ~ **of service** servizio escluso; **from 1st to 15th March** ~ dal 1° al 15 marzo esclusi; ~ **rights** *npl* (*COMM*) diritti *mpl* esclusivi.
exclusively [ɪk'skluːsɪvlɪ] *adv* esclusivamente.
excommunicate [ɛkskə'mjuːnɪkeɪt] *vt* scomunicare.
excrement ['ɛkskrəmənt] *n* escremento.
excruciating [ɪk'skruːʃɪeɪtɪŋ] *adj* straziante, atroce.
excursion [ɪk'skəːʃən] *n* escursione *f*, gita.
excursion ticket *n* biglietto a tariffa escursionistica.
excusable [ɪk'skjuːzəbl] *adj* scusabile.
excuse *n* [ɪk'skjuːs] scusa ♦ *vt* [ɪk'skjuːz] scusare; (*justify*) giustificare; **to make** ~**s for sb** trovare giustificazioni per qn; **to** ~ **sb from** (*activity*) dispensare qn da; ~ **me!** mi scusi!; **now if you will** ~ **me**, ... ora, mi scusi ma ...; **to** ~ **o.s. (for (doing) sth)** giustificarsi (per (aver fatto) qc).
ex-directory ['ɛksdɪ'rɛktərɪ] *adj* (*BRIT*): ~ **(phone) number** numero non compreso nell'elenco telefonico.
execrable ['ɛksɪkrəbl] *adj* (*gen*) pessimo(a); (*manners*) esecrabile.
execute ['ɛksɪkjuːt] *vt* (*prisoner*) giustiziare; (*plan etc*) eseguire.
execution [ɛksɪ'kjuːʃən] *n* esecuzione *f*.
executioner [ɛksɪ'kjuːʃnə*] *n* boia *m inv*.
executive [ɪg'zɛkjutɪv] *n* (*COMM*) dirigente *m*; (*POL*) esecutivo ♦ *adj* esecutivo(a); (*secretary*) di direzione; (*offices, suite*) della direzione; (*car, plane*) dirigenziale; (*position, job, duties*) direttivo(a).
executive director *n* amministratore/trice.
executor [ɪg'zɛkjutə*] *n* esecutore(trice) testamentario(a).
exemplary [ɪg'zɛmplərɪ] *adj* esemplare.

exemplify [ɪg'zɛmplɪfaɪ] *vt* esemplificare.

exempt [ɪg'zɛmpt] *adj*: ~ **(from)** (*person: from tax*) esentato(a) (da); (: *from military service etc*) esonerato(a) (da); (*goods*) esente (da) ♦ *vt*: **to ~ sb from** esentare qn da.

exemption [ɪg'zɛmpʃən] *n* esenzione *f*.

exercise ['ɛksəsaɪz] *n* esercizio ♦ *vt* esercitare; (*dog*) portar fuori ♦ *vi* (*also*: **take ~**) fare del movimento *or* moto.

exercise bike *n* cyclette ® *f inv*.

exercise book *n* quaderno.

exert [ɪg'zəːt] *vt* esercitare; (*strength, force*) impiegare; **to ~ o.s.** sforzarsi.

exertion [ɪg'zəːʃən] *n* sforzo.

ex gratia ['ɛks'greɪʃə] *adj*: ~ **payment** gratifica.

exhale [ɛks'heɪl] *vt, vi* espirare.

exhaust [ɪg'zɔːst] *n* (*also*: ~ **fumes**) scappamento; (*also*: ~ **pipe**) tubo di scappamento ♦ *vt* esaurire; **to ~ o.s.** sfiancarsi.

exhausted [ɪg'zɔːstɪd] *adj* esaurito(a).

exhausting [ɪg'zɔːstɪŋ] *adj* estenuante.

exhaustion [ɪg'zɔːstʃən] *n* esaurimento; **nervous ~** sovraffaticamento mentale.

exhaustive [ɪg'zɔːstɪv] *adj* esauriente.

exhibit [ɪg'zɪbɪt] *n* (*ART*) oggetto esposto; (*LAW*) documento *or* oggetto esibito ♦ *vt* esporre; (*courage, skill*) dimostrare.

exhibition [ɛksɪ'bɪʃən] *n* mostra, esposizione *f*; (*of rudeness etc*) spettacolo; **to make an ~ of o.s.** dare spettacolo di sé.

exhibitionist [ɛksɪ'bɪʃənɪst] *n* esibizionista *m/f*.

exhibitor [ɪg'zɪbɪtə*] *n* espositore/trice.

exhilarating [ɪg'zɪləreɪtɪŋ] *adj* esilarante; stimolante.

exhilaration [ɪgzɪlə'reɪʃən] *n* esaltazione *f*, ebbrezza.

exhort [ɪg'zɔːt] *vt* esortare.

exile ['ɛksaɪl] *n* esilio; (*person*) esiliato/a ♦ *vt* esiliare; **in ~** in esilio.

exist [ɪg'zɪst] *vi* esistere.

existence [ɪg'zɪstəns] *n* esistenza; **to be in ~** esistere.

existentialism [ɛgzɪs'tɛnʃəlɪzəm] *n* esistenzialismo.

existing [ɪg'zɪstɪŋ] *adj* (*laws, regime*) attuale.

exit ['ɛksɪt] *n* uscita ♦ *vi* (*COMPUT, THEAT*) uscire.

exit poll *n* exit poll *m inv*, sondaggio all'uscita dei seggi.

exit ramp *n* (*US AUT*) rampa di uscita.

exit visa *n* visto d'uscita.

exodus ['ɛksədəs] *n* esodo.

ex officio ['ɛksə'fɪʃɪəu] *adj, adv* d'ufficio.

exonerate [ɪg'zɒnəreɪt] *vt*: **to ~ from** discolpare da.

exorbitant [ɪg'zɔːbɪtənt] *adj* (*price*) esorbitante; (*demands*) spropositato(a).

exorcize ['ɛksɔːsaɪz] *vt* esorcizzare.

exotic [ɪg'zɒtɪk] *adj* esotico(a).

expand [ɪk'spænd] *vt* (*chest, economy etc*) sviluppare; (*market, operations*) espandere; (*influence*) estendere; (*horizons*) allargare ♦ *vi* svilupparsi; (*also gas*) espandersi; (*metal*) dilatarsi; **to ~ on** (*notes, story etc*) ampliare.

expanse [ɪk'spæns] *n* distesa, estensione *f*.

expansion [ɪk'spænʃən] *n* (*gen*) espansione *f*; (*of town, economy*) sviluppo; (*of metal*) dilatazione *f*.

expansionism [ɪk'spænʃənɪzəm] *n* espansionismo.

expansionist [ɪk'spænʃənɪst] *adj* espansionistico(a).

expatriate *n* [ɛks'pætrɪət] espatriato/a ♦ *vt* [ɛks'pætrɪeɪt] espatriare.

expect [ɪk'spɛkt] *vt* (*anticipate*) prevedere, aspettarsi, prevedere *or* aspettarsi che + *sub*; (*count on*) contare su, (*hope for*) sperare; (*require*) richiedere, esigere; (*suppose*) supporre; (*await, also baby*) aspettare ♦ *vi*: **to be ~ing** essere in stato interessante; **to ~ sb to do** aspettarsi che qn faccia; **to ~ to do sth** pensare *or* contare di fare qc; **as ~ed** come previsto; **I ~ so** credo di sì.

expectancy [ɪk'spɛktənsɪ] *n* attesa; **life ~** probabilità *fpl* di vita.

expectant [ɪk'spɛktənt] *adj* pieno(a) di aspettative.

expectantly [ɪk'spɛktəntlɪ] *adv* (*look, listen*) con un'aria d'attesa.

expectant mother *n* gestante *f*.

expectation [ɛkspɛk'teɪʃən] *n* aspettativa; speranza; **in ~ of** in previsione di; **against** *or* **contrary to all ~(s)** contro ogni aspettativa; **to come** *or* **live up to sb's ~s** rispondere alle attese di qn.

expedience, expediency [ɪk'spiːdɪəns, ɪk'spiːdɪənsɪ] *n* convenienza; **for the sake of ~** per una questione di comodità.

expedient [ɪk'spiːdɪənt] *adj* conveniente; vantaggioso(a) ♦ *n* espediente *m*.

expedite ['ɛkspədaɪt] *vt* sbrigare; facilitare.

expedition [ɛkspə'dɪʃən] *n* spedizione *f*.

expeditionary force [ɛkspə'dɪʃənərɪ-] *n* corpo di spedizione.

expeditious [ɛkspə'dɪʃəs] *adj* sollecito(a), rapido(a).

expel [ɪk'spɛl] *vt* espellere.

expend [ɪk'spɛnd] *vt* spendere; (*use up*) consumare.

expendable [ɪk'spɛndəbl] *adj* sacrificabile.

expenditure [ɪk'spɛndɪtʃə*] *n* spesa; (*of time, effort*) dispendio.

expense [ɪk'spɛns] *n* spesa; (*high cost*) costo; ~s *npl* (*COMM*) spese *fpl*, indennità *fpl*; **to go to the** ~ **of** sobbarcarsi la spesa di; **at great** ~ con grande impiego di mezzi; **at the** ~ **of** a spese di.

expense account *n* conto *m* spese *inv*.

expensive [ɪk'spɛnsɪv] *adj* caro(a), costoso(a); **she has** ~ **tastes** le piacciono le cose costose.

experience [ɪk'spɪərɪəns] *n* esperienza ♦ *vt* (*pleasure*) provare; (*hardship*) soffrire; **to learn by** ~ imparare per esperienza.

experienced [ɪk'spɪərɪənst] *adj* che ha esperienza.

experiment *n* [ɪk'spɛrɪmənt] esperimento, esperienza ♦ *vi* [ɪk'spɛrɪmɛnt] fare esperimenti; **to perform** *or* **carry out an** ~ fare un esperimento; **as an** ~ a titolo di esperimento; **to** ~ **with a new vaccine** sperimentare un nuovo vaccino.

experimental [ɪksperɪ'mɛntl] *adj* sperimentale; **at the** ~ **stage** in via di sperimentazione.

expert ['ɛkspəːt] *adj, n* esperto(a); ~ **witness** (*LAW*) esperto/a; ~ **in** *or* **at doing sth** esperto nel fare qc; **an** ~ **on sth** un esperto di qc.

expertise [ɛkspəː'tiːz] *n* competenza.

expire [ɪk'spaɪə*] *vi* (*period of time, licence*) scadere.

expiry [ɪk'spaɪərɪ] *n* scadenza.

explain [ɪk'spleɪn] *vt* spiegare.

▶**explain away** *vt* dar ragione di.

explanation [ɛksplə'neɪʃən] *n* spiegazione *f*; **to find an** ~ **for sth** trovare la spiegazione di qc.

explanatory [ɪk'splænətrɪ] *adj* esplicativo(a).

expletive [ɪk'spliːtɪv] *n* imprecazione *f*.

explicit [ɪk'splɪsɪt] *adj* esplicito(a); (*definite*) netto(a).

explode [ɪk'spləud] *vi* esplodere ♦ *vt* (*fig: theory*) demolire; **to** ~ **a myth** distruggere un mito.

exploit *n* ['ɛksplɔɪt] impresa ♦ *vt* [ɪk'splɔɪt] sfruttare.

exploitation [ɛksplɔɪ'teɪʃən] *n* sfruttamento.

exploration [ɛksplə'reɪʃən] *n* esplorazione *f*.

exploratory [ɪk'splɔrətrɪ] *adj* (*fig: talks*) esplorativo(a); ~ **operation** (*MED*) intervento d'esplorazione.

explore [ɪk'splɔ:*] *vt* esplorare; (*possibilities*) esaminare.

explorer [ɪk'splɔːrə*] *n* esploratore/trice.

explosion [ɪk'spləuʒən] *n* esplosione *f*.

explosive [ɪk'spləusɪv] *adj* esplosivo(a) ♦ *n* esplosivo.

exponent [ɪk'spəunənt] *n* esponente *m/f*.

export *vt* [ɛk'spɔːt] esportare ♦ *n* ['ɛkspɔːt] esportazione *f*; articolo di esportazione ♦ *cpd* d'esportazione.

exportation [ɛkspɔː'teɪʃən] *n* esportazione *f*.

exporter [ɪk'spɔːtə*] *n* esportatore *m*.

export licence *n* licenza d'esportazione.

expose [ɪk'spəuz] *vt* esporre; (*unmask*) smascherare; **to** ~ **o.s.** (*LAW*) oltraggiare il pudore.

exposed [ɪk'spəuzd] *adj* (*land, house*) esposto(a); (*ELEC: wire*) scoperto(a); (*pipe, beam*) a vista.

exposition [ɛkspə'zɪʃən] *n* esposizione *f*.

exposure [ɪk'spəuʒə*] *n* esposizione *f*; (*PHOT*) posa; (*MED*) assideramento; **to die of** ~ morire assiderato(a).

exposure meter *n* esposimetro.

expound [ɪk'spaund] *vt* esporre; (*theory, text*) spiegare.

express [ɪk'sprɛs] *adj* (*definite*) chiaro(a), espresso(a); (*BRIT: letter etc*) espresso *inv* ♦ *n* (*train*) espresso ♦ *adv*: **to send sth** ~ spedire qc per espresso ♦ *vt* esprimere; **to** ~ **o.s.** esprimersi.

expression [ɪk'sprɛʃən] *n* espressione *f*.

expressionism [ɪk'sprɛʃənɪzəm] *n* espressionismo.

expressive [ɪk'sprɛsɪv] *adj* espressivo(a).

expressly [ɪk'sprɛslɪ] *adv* espressamente.

expressway [ɪk'sprɛsweɪ] *n* (*US*) autostrada che attraversa la città.

expropriate [ɛks'prəuprɪeɪt] *vt* espropriare.

expulsion [ɪk'spʌlʃən] *n* espulsione *f*.

exquisite [ɛk'skwɪzɪt] *adj* squisito(a).

ex-serviceman ['ɛks'səːvɪsmən] *n* ex combattente *m*.

ext. *abbr* (*TEL:* = *extension*) int. (= *interno*).

extemporize [ɪk'stɛmpəraɪz] *vi* improvvisare.

extend [ɪk'stɛnd] *vt* (*visit*) protrarre; (*road, deadline*) prolungare; (*building*) ampliare; (*offer*) offrire, porgere; (*COMM: credit*) accordare ♦ *vi* (*land*) estendersi.

extension [ɪk'stɛnʃən] *n* (*of road, term*) prolungamento; (*of contract, deadline*) proroga; (*building*) annesso; (*to wire, table*) prolunga; (*telephone*) interno; (: *in private house*) apparecchio supplementare; ~ **3718** (*TEL*) interno 3718.

extension cable *n* (*ELEC*) prolunga.

extensive [ɪk'stɛnsɪv] *adj* esteso(a), ampio(a); (*damage*) su larga scala; (*alterations*) notevole; (*inquiries*) esauriente; (*use*) grande.

extensively [ɪk'stɛnsɪvlɪ] *adv* (*altered, damaged etc*) radicalmente; **he's travelled** ~ ha viaggiato molto.

extent [ɪk'stɛnt] *n* estensione *f*; (*of knowledge, activities, power*) portata; (*degree: of damage, loss*) proporzioni *fpl*; **to some** ~ fino a un certo punto; **to a certain/large** ~ in certa/larga misura; **to what** ~? fino a che punto?; **to such an** ~ **that** ... a tal punto che ....

extenuating [ɪk'stɛnjueɪtɪŋ] *adj:* ~ **circumstances** attenuanti *fpl*.

exterior [ɛk'stɪərɪə*] *adj* esteriore, esterno(a) ♦ *n* esteriore *m*, esterno; aspetto (esteriore).

exterminate [ɪk'stə:mɪneɪt] *vt* sterminare.

extermination [ɪkstə:mɪ'neɪʃən] *n* sterminio

external [ɛk'stə:nl] *adj* esterno(a), esteriore ♦ *n*: **the** ~**s** le apparenze; **for** ~ **use only** (*MED*) solo per uso esterno; ~ **affairs** (*POL*) affari *mpl* esteri.

externally [ɛk'stə:nəlɪ] *adv* esternamente.

extinct [ɪk'stɪŋkt] *adj* estinto(a).

extinction [ɪk'stɪŋkʃən] *n* estinzione *f*.

extinguish [ɪk'stɪŋgwɪʃ] *vt* estinguere.

extinguisher [ɪk'stɪŋgwɪʃə*] *n* estintore *m*.

extol, (*US*) **extoll** [ɪk'stəul] *vt* (*merits, virtues*) magnificare; (*person*) celebrare.

extort [ɪk'stɔ:t] *vt*: **to** ~ **sth (from)** estorcere qc (da).

extortion [ɪk'stɔ:ʃən] *n* estorsione *f*.

extortionate [ɪk'stɔ:ʃənɪt] *adj* esorbitante.

extra ['ɛkstrə] *adj* extra *inv*, supplementare ♦ *adv* (*in addition*) di più ♦ *n* supplemento; (*THEAT*) comparso; **wine will cost** ~ il vino è extra; ~ **large sizes** taglie *fpl* forti.

extra... ['ɛkstrə] *prefix* extra....

extract *vt* [ɪk'strækt] estrarre; (*money, promise*) strappare ♦ *n* ['ɛkstrækt] estratto; (*passage*) brano.

extraction [ɪk'strækʃən] *n* estrazione *f*; (*descent*) origine *f*.

extractor fan [ɪk'stræktə*-] *n* aspiratore *m*.

extracurricular [ɛkstrəkə'rɪkjulə*] *adj* (*SCOL*) parascolastico(a).

extradite ['ɛkstrədaɪt] *vt* estradare.

extradition [ɛkstrə'dɪʃən] *n* estradizione *f*.

extramarital [ɛkstrə'mærɪtl] *adj* extraconiugale.

extramural [ɛkstrə'mjuərl] *adj* fuori dell'università.

extraneous [ɛk'streɪnɪəs] *adj:* ~ **to** estraneo(a) a.

extraordinary [ɪk'strɔ:dnrɪ] *adj* straordinario(a); **the** ~ **thing is that** ... la cosa strana è che ....

extraordinary general meeting *n* assemblea straordinaria.

extrapolation [ɪkstræpə'leɪʃən] *n* estrapolazione *f*.

extrasensory perception (ESP) [ɛkstrə'sɛnsərɪ-] *n* percezione *f* extrasensoriale.

extra time *n* (*FOOTBALL*) tempo supplementare.

extravagance [ɪk'strævəgəns] *n* (*excessive spending*) sperpero; (*thing bought*) stravaganza.

extravagant [ɪk'strævəgənt] *adj* stravagante; (*in spending: person*) prodigo(a); (: *tastes*) dispendioso(a)

extreme [ɪk'stri:m] *adj* estremo(a) ♦ *n* estremo; ~**s of temperature** eccessivi sbalzi *mpl* di temperatura; **the** ~ **left/right** (*POL*) l'estrema sinistra/destra.

extremely [ɪk'stri:mlɪ] *adv* estremamente.

extremist [ɪk'stri:mɪst] *adj, n* estremista (*m/f*).

extremity [ɪk'strɛmɪtɪ] *n* estremità *f inv*.

extricate ['ɛkstrɪkeɪt] *vt*: **to** ~ **sth (from)** districare qc (da).

extrovert ['ɛkstrəvə:t] *n* estroverso/a.

exuberance [ɪg'zu:bərəns] *n* esuberanza.

exuberant [ɪg'zju:bərənt] *adj* esuberante.

exude [ɪg'zju:d] *vt* trasudare; (*fig*) emanare.

exult [ɪg'zʌlt] *vi* esultare, gioire.

exultant [ɪg'zʌltənt] *adj* (*person, smile*) esultante; (*shout, expression*) di giubilo.

exultation [ɛgzʌl'teɪʃən] *n* giubilo; **in** ~ per la gioia.

eye [aɪ] *n* occhio; (*of needle*) cruna ♦ *vt* osservare; **to keep an** ~ **on** tenere d'occhio; **in the public** ~ esposto(a) al pubblico; **as far as the** ~ **can see** a perdita d'occhio; **with an** ~ **to doing sth** (*BRIT*) con l'idea di far qc; **to have an** ~ **for sth** avere occhio per qc; **there's more to this than meets the** ~ non è così semplice come sembra.

eyeball ['aɪbɔ:l] *n* globo dell'occhio.

eyebath ['aɪbɑ:θ] *n* occhino.

eyebrow ['aɪbrau] *n* sopracciglio.

eyebrow pencil *n* matita per le sopracciglia.

eye-catching ['aɪkætʃɪŋ] *adj* che colpisce l'occhio.

eye cup *n* (*US*) = **eyebath**.

eyedrops ['aɪdrɒps] *npl* gocce *fpl* oculari, collirio.

eyeful ['aɪful] *n*: **to get an** ~ **(of sth)** (*col*) avere l'occasione di dare una bella sbirciata (a qc).

eyeglass ['aɪglɑːs] *n* monocolo.

eyelash ['aɪlæʃ] *n* ciglio.

eyelet ['aɪlɪt] *n* occhiello.

eye-level ['aɪlɛvl] *adj* all'altezza degli occhi.

eyelid ['aɪlɪd] *n* palpebra.

eyeliner ['aɪlaɪnə*] *n* eye-liner *m inv*.

eye-opener ['aɪəupnə*] *n* rivelazione *f*.

eyeshadow ['aɪʃædəu] *n* ombretto.

eyesight ['aɪsaɪt] *n* vista.

eyesore ['aɪsɔː*] *n* pugno nell'occhio.

eyestrain ['aɪstreɪn] *n*: **to get** ~ stancarsi gli occhi.

eye-tooth, *pl* **-teeth** ['aɪtuːθ, -tiːθ] *n* canino superiore; **to give one's eye-teeth for sth/to do sth** (*fig*) dare non so che cosa per qc/per fare qc.

eyewash ['aɪwɔʃ] *n* collirio; (*fig*) sciocchezze *fpl*.

eye witness *n* testimone *m/f* oculare.

eyrie ['ɪərɪ] *n* nido (d'aquila).

Ff

F, f [ɛf] *n* (*letter*) F, f *f or m inv*; (*MUS*): F fa *m*; **F for Frederick,** (*US*) **F for Fox** ≈ F come Firenze.

F. *abbr* (= *Fahrenheit*) F.

FA *n abbr* (*BRIT*) = *Football Association*.

FAA *n abbr* (*US*) = *Federal Aviation Administration*.

fable ['feɪbl] *n* favola.

fabric ['fæbrɪk] *n* stoffa, tessuto; (*ARCHIT*) struttura.

fabricate ['fæbrɪkeɪt] *vt* fabbricare.

fabrication [fæbrɪ'keɪʃən] *n* fabbricazione *f*.

fabric ribbon *n* (*for typewriter*) dattilonastro di tessuto.

fabulous ['fæbjuləs] *adj* favoloso(a); (*col: super*) favoloso(a), fantastico(a).

façade [fə'sɑːd] *n* facciata; (*fig*) apparenza.

face [feɪs] *n* faccia, viso, volto; (*expression*) faccia; (*grimace*) smorfia; (*of clock*) quadrante *m*; (*of building*) facciata; (*side, surface*) faccia; (*of mountain, cliff*) parete *f* ♦ *vt* fronteggiare; (*fig*) affrontare; ~ **down** (*person*) bocconi; (*object*) a faccia in giù; **to lose/save** ~ perdere/salvare la faccia; **to pull a** ~ fare una smorfia; **in**

the ~ **of** (*difficulties etc*) di fronte a; **on the** ~ **of it** a prima vista; **to** ~ **the fact that ...** riconoscere *or* ammettere che ....

▶**face up to** *vt fus* affrontare, far fronte a.

face cloth *n* (*BRIT*) guanto di spugna.

face cream *n* crema per il viso.

faceless ['feɪslɪs] *adj* anonimo(a).

face lift *n* lifting *m inv*; (*of façade etc*) ripulita.

face powder *n* cipria.

face-saving ['feɪs'seɪvɪŋ] *adj* che salva la faccia.

facet ['fæsɪt] *n* faccetta, sfaccettatura; (*fig*) sfaccettatura.

facetious [fə'siːʃəs] *adj* faceto(a).

face-to-face ['feɪstə'feɪs] *adv* faccia a faccia.

face value ['feɪs'væljuː] *n* (*of coin*) valore *m* facciale *or* nominale; **to take sth at** ~ (*fig*) giudicare qc dalle apparenze.

facia ['feɪʃɪə] *n* = **fascia**.

facial ['feɪʃəl] *adj* facciale ♦ *n* trattamento del viso.

facile ['fæsaɪl] *adj* facile; superficiale.

facilitate [fə'sɪlɪteɪt] *vt* facilitare.

facility [fə'sɪlɪtɪ] *n* facilità; **facilities** *npl* attrezzature *fpl*; **credit facilities** facilitazioni *fpl* di credito.

facing ['feɪsɪŋ] *n* (*of wall etc*) rivestimento; (*SEWING*) paramontura.

facsimile [fæk'sɪmɪlɪ] *n* facsimile *m inv*.

facsimile machine *n* telecopiatrice *f*.

fact [fækt] *n* fatto; **in** ~ infatti; **to know for a** ~ **that ...** sapere per certo che ...; **the** ~ **(of the matter) is that ...** la verità è che ...; **the** ~**s of life** (*sex*) i fatti riguardanti la vita sessuale; (*fig*) le realtà della vita.

fact-finding ['fæktfaɪndɪŋ] *adj*: **a** ~ **tour/ mission** un viaggio/una missione d'inchiesta.

faction ['fækʃən] *n* fazione *f*.

factional ['fækʃənl] *adj*: ~ **fighting** scontri *mpl* tra fazioni.

factor ['fæktə*] *n* fattore *m*; (*COMM: company*) organizzazione specializzata nell'incasso di crediti per conto terzi; (*: agent*) agente *m* depositario ♦ *vi* incassare crediti per conto terzi; **human** ~ elemento umano; **safety** ~ coefficiente *m* di sicurezza.

factory ['fæktərɪ] *n* fabbrica, stabilimento.

factory farming *n* (*BRIT*) allevamento su scala industriale.

factory floor *n*: **the** ~ (*workers*) gli operai; (*area*) il reparto produzione; **on the** ~ nel reparto produzione.

factory ship *n* nave *f* fattoria *inv*.

factual ['fæktjuəl] *adj* che si attiene ai fatti.

faculty ['fækəltɪ] n facoltà f inv; (US: teaching staff) corpo insegnante.

fad [fæd] n mania; capriccio.

fade [feɪd] vi sbiadire, sbiadirsi; (light, sound, hope) attenuarsi, affievolirsi; (flower) appassire.

►**fade in** vt (picture) aprire in dissolvenza; (sound) aumentare gradualmente d'intensità.

►**fade out** vt (picture) chiudere in dissolvenza; (sound) diminuire gradualmente d'intensità.

faeces, (US) **feces** ['fiːsiːz] npl feci fpl.

fag [fæg] n (BRIT col: cigarette) cicca; (: chore) sfacchinata; (US col: homosexual) frocio.

fag end n (BRIT col) mozzicone m.

fagged out ['fægd-] adj (BRIT col) stanco(a) morto(a).

fail [feɪl] vt (exam) non superare; (candidate) bocciare; (subj: courage, memory) mancare a ♦ vi fallire; (student) essere respinto(a); (supplies) mancare, (eyesight, health, light: also: be ~ing) venire a mancare; (brakes) non funzionare; to ~ to do sth (neglect) mancare di fare qc; (be unable) non riuscire a fare qc; without ~ senza fallo; certamente.

failing ['feɪlɪŋ] n difetto ♦ prep in mancanza di; ~ that se questo non è possibile.

failsafe ['feɪlseɪf] adj (device etc) di sicurezza.

failure ['feɪljə*] n fallimento; (person) fallito/a; (mechanical etc) guasto; (in exam) insuccesso, bocciatura; (of crops) perdita; his ~ to come il fatto che non sia venuto; it was a complete ~ è stato un vero fiasco.

faint [feɪnt] adj debole; (recollection) vago(a); (mark) indistinto(a); (smell, breeze, trace) leggero(a) ♦ vi svenire; to feel ~ sentirsi svenire.

faintest ['feɪntɪst] adj: I haven't the ~ idea non ho la più pallida idea.

faint-hearted [feɪnt'haːtɪd] adj pusillanime.

faintly ['feɪntlɪ] adv debolmente; vagamente.

faintness ['feɪntnɪs] n debolezza.

fair [fɛə*] adj (person, decision) giusto(a), equo(a); (hair etc) biondo(a); (skin, complexion) bianco(a); (weather) bello(a), clemente; (good enough) assai buono(a); (sizeable) bello(a) ♦ adv: to play ~ giocare correttamente ♦ n fiera; (BRIT: funfair) luna park m inv; (also: trade ~) fiera campionaria; it's not ~! non è giusto!; a ~ amount of un bel po' di.

fair copy n bella copia.

fair game n: to be ~ (person) essere bersaglio legittimo.

fairground ['fɛəgraund] n luna park m inv.

fair-haired [fɛə'hɛəd] adj (person) biondo(a).

fairly ['fɛəlɪ] adv equamente; (quite) abbastanza.

fairness ['fɛənɪs] n equità, giustizia; in all ~ per essere giusti, a dire il vero.

fair play n correttezza.

fairy ['fɛərɪ] n fata.

fairy godmother n fata buona.

fairy lights npl (BRIT) lanternine fpl colorate.

fairy tale n fiaba.

faith [feɪθ] n fede f; (trust) fiducia; (sect) religione f, fede f; to have ~ in sb/sth avere fiducia in qn/qc.

faithful ['feɪθful] adj fedele.

faithfully ['feɪθfəlɪ] adv fedelmente; yours ~ (BRIT: in letters) distinti saluti.

faith healer n guaritore/trice.

fake [feɪk] n imitazione f; (picture) falso; (person) impostore/a ♦ adj falso(a) ♦ vt (accounts) falsificare; (illness) fingere; (painting) contraffare; his illness is a ~ fa finta di essere malato.

falcon ['fɔːlkən] n falco, falcone m.

Falkland Islands ['fɔːlklənd-] npl: the ~ le isole Falkland.

fall [fɔːl] n caduta; (decrease) diminuzione f, calo; (in temperature) abbassamento; (in price) ribasso; (US: autumn) autunno ♦ vi (pt fell, pp fallen [fɛl, 'fɔːlən]) cadere; (temperature, price) abbassare; a ~ of earth uno smottamento; a ~ of snow (BRIT) una nevicata; to ~ in love (with sb/sth) innamorarsi (di qn/qc); to ~ short of (sb's expectations) non corrispondere a; to ~ flat vi (on one's face) cadere bocconi; (joke) fare cilecca; (plan) fallire; see also falls.

►**fall apart** vi cadere a pezzi.

►**fall back** vi indietreggiare; (MIL) ritirarsi.

►**fall back on** vt fus ripiegare su; to have sth to ~ back on avere qc di riserva.

►**fall behind** vi rimanere indietro; (fig: with payments) essere in arretrato.

►**fall down** vi (person) cadere; (building, hopes) crollare.

►**fall for** vt fus (person) prendere una cotta per; to ~ for a trick (or a story etc) cascarci.

►**fall in** vi crollare; (MIL) mettersi in riga.

►**fall in with** vt fus (sb's plans etc) trovarsi d'accordo con.

►**fall off** vi cadere; (diminish) diminuire, abbassarsi.

►**fall out** *vi* (*friends etc*) litigare.

►**fall over** *vi* cadere.

►**fall through** *vi* (*plan, project*) fallire.

fallacy ['fæləsɪ] *n* errore *m*.

fallback ['fɔːlbæk] *adj*: ~ **position** posizione *f* di ripiego.

fallen ['fɔːlən] *pp of* **fall**.

fallible ['fælɪbl] *adj* fallibile.

falling ['fɔːlɪŋ] *adj*: ~ **market** (*COMM*) mercato in ribasso.

falling-off ['fɔːlɪŋ'ɔf] *n* calo.

fallopian tube [fə'ləupɪən-] *n* (*ANAT*) tuba di Falloppio.

fallout ['fɔːlaut] *n* fall-out *m*.

fallout shelter *n* rifugio antiatomico.

fallow ['fæləu] *adj* incolto(a); a maggese.

falls [fɔːlz] *npl* (*waterfall*) cascate *fpl*.

false [fɔːls] *adj* falso(a); **under** ~ **pretences** con l'inganno.

false alarm *n* falso allarme *m*.

falsehood ['fɔːlshud] *n* menzogna.

falsely ['fɔːlslɪ] *adv* (*accuse*) a torto.

false teeth *npl* (*BRIT*) denti *mpl* finti.

falsify ['fɔːlsɪfaɪ] *vt* falsificare; (*figures*) alterare.

falter ['fɔːltə*] *vi* esitare, vacillare.

fame [feɪm] *n* fama, celebrità.

familiar [fə'mɪlɪə*] *adj* familiare; (*common*) comune; (*close*) intimo(a); **to be** ~ **with** (*subject*) conoscere; **to make o.s.** ~ **with** familiarizzarsi con; **to be on** ~ **terms with** essere in confidenza con.

familiarity [fəmɪlɪ'ærɪtɪ] *n* familiarità; intimità.

familiarize [fə'mɪlɪəraɪz] *vt*: **to** ~ **sb with sth** far conoscere qc a qn.

family ['fæmɪlɪ] *n* famiglia.

family allowance *n* (*BRIT*) assegni *mpl* familiari.

family business *n* impresa familiare.

family credit *n* (*BRIT*) ≈ assegni *mpl* familiari.

family doctor *n* medico di famiglia.

family life *n* vita familiare.

family man *n* padre *m* di famiglia.

family planning clinic *n* consultorio familiare.

family tree *n* albergo genealogico.

famine ['fæmɪn] *n* carestia.

famished ['fæmɪʃt] *adj* affamato(a); **I'm** ~! (*col*) ho una fame da lupo!

famous ['feɪməs] *adj* famoso(a).

famously ['feɪməslɪ] *adv* (*get on*) a meraviglia.

fan [fæn] *n* (*folding*) ventaglio; (*machine*) ventilatore *m*; (*person*) ammiratore/trice; (*SPORT*) tifoso/a ♦ *vt* far vento a; (*fire, quarrel*) alimentare.

►**fan out** *vi* spargersi (a ventaglio).

fanatic [fə'nætɪk] *n* fanatico/a.

fanatical [fə'nætɪkl] *adj* fanatico(a).

fan belt *n* cinghia del ventilatore.

fancied ['fænsɪd] *adj* immaginario(a).

fanciful ['fænsɪful] *adj* fantasioso(a); (*object*) di fantasia.

fan club *n* fan club *m inv*.

fancy ['fænsɪ] *n* immaginazione *f*, fantasia; (*whim*) capriccio ♦ *cpd* (di) fantasia *inv* ♦ *vt* (*feel like, want*) aver voglia di; (*imagine*) immaginare, credere; **to take a** ~ **to** incapricciarsi di; **it took** *or* **caught my** ~ mi è piaciuto; **when the** ~ **takes him** quando ne ha voglia; **to** ~ **that** immaginare che; **he fancies her** gli piace.

fancy dress *n* costume *m* (per maschera).

fancy-dress ball *n* ballo in maschera.

fancy goods *npl* articoli *mpl* di ogni genere.

fanfare ['fænfɛə*] *n* fanfara.

fanfold paper ['fænfəuld-] *n* carta a moduli continui.

fang [fæŋ] *n* zanna; (*of snake*) dente *m*.

fan heater *n* (*BRIT*) stufa ad aria calda.

fanlight ['fænlaɪt] *n* lunetta.

fanny ['fænɪ] *n* (*BRIT col!*) figa(*!*); (*US col*) culo(*!*).

fantasize ['fæntəsaɪz] *vi* fantasticare, sognare.

fantastic [fæn'tæstɪk] *adj* fantastico(a).

fantasy ['fæntəsɪ] *n* fantasia, immaginazione *f*; fantasticheria; chimera.

fanzine ['fænziːn] *n* rivista specialistica (*per appassionati*).

FAO *n abbr* (= *Food and Agriculture Organization*) FAO *f*.

FAQ *abbr* (= *free alongside quay*) franco lungo banchina.

far [fɑː*] *adj*: **the** ~ **side/end** l'altra parte/ l'altro capo; **the** ~ **left/right** (*POL*) l'estrema sinistra/destra ♦ *adv* lontano; **is it** ~ **to London?** è lontana Londra?; **it's not** ~ (**from here**) non è lontano (da qui); ~ **away**, ~ **off** lontano, distante; ~ **better** assai migliore; ~ **from** lontano da; **by** ~ di gran lunga; **as** ~ **back as the 13th century** già nel duecento; **go as** ~ **as the farm** vada fino alla fattoria; **as** ~ **as I know** per quel che so; **as** ~ **as possible** nei limiti del possibile; **how** ~ **have you got with your work?** dov'è arrivato con il suo lavoro?

faraway ['fɑːrəweɪ] *adj* lontano(a); (*voice, look*) assente.

farce [fɑːs] *n* farsa.

farcical ['fɑːsɪkəl] *adj* farsesco(a).

fare [fɛə*] n (on trains, buses) tariffa; (in taxi) prezzo della corsa; (food) vitto, cibo ♦ vi passarsela.

Far East n: the ~ l'Estremo Oriente m.

farewell [fɛə'wɛl] excl, n addio ♦ cpd (party etc) d'addio.

far-fetched ['fɑː'fɛtʃt] adj (explanation) stiracchiato(a), forzato(a); (idea, scheme, story) inverosimile.

farm [fɑːm] n fattoria, podere m ♦ vt coltivare.

▶**farm out** vt (work) dare in consegna.

farmer ['fɑːmə*] n coltivatore/trice; agricoltore/trice.

farmhand ['fɑːmhænd] n bracciante m agricolo.

farmhouse ['fɑːmhaus] n fattoria.

farming ['fɑːmɪŋ] n agricoltura; **intensive** ~ coltura intensiva; **sheep** ~ allevamento di pecore.

farm labourer n = **farmhand**.

farmland ['fɑːmlænd] n terreno da coltivare.

farm produce n prodotti mpl agricoli.

farm worker n = **farmhand**.

farmyard ['fɑːmjɑːd] n aia.

Faroe Islands ['fɛərəu-], **Faroes** ['fɛərəuz] npl: **the** ~ le isole Faeroer.

far-reaching ['fɑː'riːtʃɪŋ] adj di vasta portata.

far-sighted ['fɑː'saɪtɪd] adj presbite; (fig) lungimirante.

fart [fɑːt] (col!) n scoreggia(!) ♦ vi scoreggiare (!).

farther ['fɑːðə*] adv più lontano ♦ adj più lontano(a).

farthest ['fɑːðɪst] superlative of **far**.

FAS abbr (BRIT: = free alongside ship) franco banchina nave.

fascia ['feɪʃɪə] n (AUT) cruscotto.

fascinate ['fæsɪneɪt] vt affascinare.

fascinating ['fæsɪneɪtɪŋ] adj affascinante.

fascination [fæsɪ'neɪʃən] n fascino.

fascism ['fæʃɪzəm] n fascismo.

fascist ['fæʃɪst] adj, n fascista (m/f).

fashion ['fæʃən] n moda; (manner) maniera, modo ♦ vt foggiare, formare; **in** ~ alla moda; **out of** ~ passato(a) di moda; **after a** ~ (finish, manage etc) così così; **in the Greek** ~ alla greca.

fashionable ['fæʃənəbl] adj alla moda, di moda; (writer) di grido.

fashion designer n disegnatore/trice di moda.

fashion show n sfilata di moda.

fast [fɑːst] adj rapido(a), svelto(a), veloce; (clock): **to be** ~ andare avanti; (dye, colour) solido(a) ♦ adv rapidamente; (stuck,

held) saldamente ♦ n digiuno ♦ vi digiunare; ~ **asleep** profondamente addormentato; **as** ~ **as I can** più in fretta possibile; **my watch is 5 minutes** ~ il mio orologio va avanti di 5 minuti; **to make a boat** ~ (BRIT) ormeggiare una barca.

fasten ['fɑːsn] vt chiudere, fissare; (coat) abbottonare, allacciare ♦ vi chiudersi, fissarsi; abbottonarsi, allacciarsi.

▶**fasten (up)on** vt fus (idea) cogliere al volo.

fastener ['fɑːsnə*], **fastening** ['fɑːsnɪŋ] n fermaglio, chiusura; (BRIT: zip ~) chiusura lampo.

fast food n fast food m inv.

fastidious [fæs'tɪdɪəs] adj esigente, difficile.

fast lane n (AUT) ≈ corsia di sorpasso.

fat [fæt] adj grasso(a) ♦ n grasso; **to live off the** ~ **of the land** vivere nel lusso, avere ogni ben di Dio.

fatal ['feɪtl] adj fatale; mortale; disastroso(a).

fatalism ['feɪtəlɪzəm] n fatalismo.

fatality [fə'tælɪtɪ] n (road death etc) morto/a, vittima.

fatally ['feɪtəlɪ] adv a morte.

fate [feɪt] n destino; (of person) sorte f; **to meet one's** ~ trovare la morte.

fated ['feɪtɪd] adj (governed by fate) destinato(a); (person, project etc) destinato(a) a finire male.

fateful ['feɪtful] adj fatidico(a).

fat-free ['fæt'friː] adj senza grassi.

father ['fɑːðə*] n padre m.

Father Christmas n Babbo Natale.

fatherhood ['fɑːðəhuːd] n paternità.

father-in-law ['fɑːðərɪnlɔː] n suocero.

fatherland ['fɑːðəlænd] n patria.

fatherly ['fɑːðəlɪ] adj paterno(a).

fathom ['fæðəm] n braccio (= 1828 mm) ♦ vt (mystery) penetrare, sondare.

fatigue [fə'tiːg] n stanchezza; (MIL) corvé f; **metal** ~ fatica del metallo.

fatness ['fætnɪs] n grassezza.

fatten ['fætn] vt, vi ingrassare; **chocolate is** ~**ing** la cioccolata fa ingrassare.

fatty ['fætɪ] adj (food) grasso(a) ♦ n (col) ciccione/a.

fatuous ['fætjuəs] adj fatuo(a).

faucet ['fɔːsɪt] n (US) rubinetto.

fault [fɔːlt] n colpa; (TENNIS) fallo; (defect) difetto; (GEO) faglia ♦ vt criticare; **it's my** ~ è colpa mia; **to find** ~ **with** trovare da ridire su; **at** ~ in fallo; **generous to a** ~ eccessivamente generoso.

faultless ['fɔːltlɪs] adj perfetto(a); senza difetto; impeccabile.

faulty ['fɔːltɪ] *adj* difettoso(a).

fauna ['fɔːnə] *n* fauna.

faux pas [fəu'pɑː] *n* gaffe *f inv*.

favour, (*US***) favor** ['feɪvə*] *n* favore *m* ♦ *vt* (*proposition*) favorire, essere favorevole a; (*pupil etc*) favorire; (*team, horse*) dare per vincente; **to do sb a** ~ fare un favore *or* una cortesia a qn; **in** ~ **of** in favore di; **to be in** ~ **of sth/of doing sth** essere favorevole a qc/a fare qc; **to find** ~ **with sb** (*subj: person*) entrare nelle buone grazie di qn; (*: suggestion*) avere l'approvazione di qn.

favo(u)rable ['feɪvərəbl] *adj* favorevole.

favo(u)rably ['feɪvərəblɪ] *adv* favorevolmente.

favo(u)rite ['feɪvrɪt] *adj, n* favorito(a).

favo(u)ritism ['feɪvrɪtɪzəm] *n* favoritismo.

fawn [fɔːn] *n* daino ♦ *adj* (*also*: ~-**coloured**) marrone chiaro *inv* ♦ *vi*: **to** ~ (**up**)**on** adulare servilmente.

fax [fæks] *n* (*document, machine*) facsimile *m inv* ♦ *vt* teletrasmettere, spedire in facsimile.

FBI *n abbr* (*US*: = *Federal Bureau of Investigation*) FBI *f*.

FCC *n abbr* (*US*) = *Federal Communications Commission*.

FCO *n abbr* (*BRIT*: = *Foreign and Commonwealth Office*) ≈ Ufficio affari esteri.

FD *n abbr* (*US*) = **fire department**.

FDA *n abbr* (*US*) = *Food and Drug Administration*.

FE *n abbr* = **further education**.

fear [fɪə*] *n* paura, timore *m* ♦ *vt* aver paura di, temere ♦ *vi*: **to** ~ **for** temere per, essere in ansia per; ~ **of heights** vertigini *fpl*; **for** ~ **of** per paura di; **to** ~ **that** avere paura di (*or* che + *sub*), temere di (*or* che + *sub*).

fearful ['fɪəful] *adj* pauroso(a); (*sight, noise*) terribile, spaventoso(a); (*frightened*): **to be** ~ **of** temere.

fearfully ['fɪəfəlɪ] *adv* (*timidly*) timorosamente; (*col: very*) terribilmente, spaventosamente.

fearless ['fɪəlɪs] *adj* intrepido(a), senza paura.

fearsome ['fɪəsəm] *adj* (*opponent*) formidabile, terribile; (*sight*) terrificante.

feasibility [fiːzə'bɪlɪtɪ] *n* praticabilità.

feasibility study *n* studio delle possibilità di realizzazione.

feasible ['fiːzəbl] *adj* fattibile, realizzabile.

feast [fiːst] *n* festa, banchetto; (*REL: also*: ~ **day**) festa ♦ *vi* banchettare; **to** ~ **on** godersi, gustare.

feat [fiːt] *n* impresa, fatto insigne.

feather ['fɛðə*] *n* penna ♦ *cpd* (*mattress, bed, pillow*) di piume ♦ *vt*: **to** ~ **one's nest** (*fig*) arricchirsi.

feather-weight ['fɛðəweɪt] *n* peso *m* piuma *inv*.

feature ['fiːtʃə*] *n* caratteristica; (*article*) articolo ♦ *vt* (*subj: film*) avere come protagonista ♦ *vi* figurare; ~**s** *npl* (*of face*) fisionomia; **a** (**special**) ~ **on sth/sb** un servizio speciale su qc/qn; **it** ~**d prominently in ...** ha avuto un posto di prima importanza in ....

feature film *n* film *m inv* principale.

featureless ['fiːtʃəlɪs] *adj* anonimo(a), senza caratteri distinti.

Feb. [fɛb] *abbr* (= *February*) feb.

February ['fɛbruərɪ] *n* febbraio; *for phrases see also* **July**.

feces ['fiːsiːz] *npl* (*US*) = **faeces**.

feckless ['fɛklɪs] *adj* irresponsabile, incosciente.

Fed [fɛd] *abbr* (*US*) = **federal; federation**.

fed [fɛd] *pt, pp of* **feed**; **to be** ~ **up** essere stufo(a).

Fed. [fɛd] *n abbr* (*US col*) = **Federal Reserve Board**.

federal ['fɛdərəl] *adj* federale.

Federal Republic of Germany (FRG) *n* Repubblica Federale Tedesca (RFT).

Federal Reserve Board (Fed.) *n* (*US*) *organo di controllo del sistema bancario statunitense*.

Federal Trade Commission (FTC) *n* (*US*) *organismo di protezione contro le pratiche commerciali abusive*.

federation [fɛdə'reɪʃən] *n* federazione *f*.

fee [fiː] *n* pagamento; (*of doctor, lawyer*) onorario; (*for examination*) tassa d'esame; **school** ~**s** tasse *fpl* scolastiche; **entrance** ~, **membership** ~ quota d'iscrizione; **for a small** ~ per una somma modesta.

feeble ['fiːbl] *adj* debole.

feeble-minded [fiːbl'maɪndɪd] *adj* deficiente.

feed [fiːd] *n* (*of baby*) pappa ♦ *vt* (*pt, pp* **fed** [fɛd]) nutrire; (*horse etc*) dare da mangiare a; (*fire, machine*) alimentare ♦ *vi* (*baby, animal*) mangiare; **to** ~ **material into sth** introdurre materiale in qc; **to** ~ **data/information into sth** inserire dati/informazioni in qc.

▶**feed back** *vt* (*results*) riferire.

▶**feed on** *vt fus* nutrirsi di.

feedback ['fiːdbæk] *n* feed-back *m*; (*from person*) reazioni *fpl*.

feeder ['fiːdə*] *n* (*bib*) bavaglino.

feeding bottle ['fiːdɪŋ-] *n* (*BRIT*) biberon *m*

inv.

feel [fi:l] *n* sensazione *f*; (*sense of touch*) tatto; (*of substance*) consistenza ♦ *vt* (*pt, pp* **felt** [fɛlt]) toccare; palpare; tastare; (*cold, pain, anger*) sentire; (*grief*) provare; (*think, believe*): **to ~ (that)** pensare che; **I ~ that you ought to do it** penso che dovreste farlo; **to ~ hungry/cold** aver fame/freddo; **to ~ lonely/better** sentirsi solo/meglio; **I don't ~ well** non mi sento bene; **to ~ sorry for** dispiacersi per; **it ~s soft** è morbido al tatto; **it ~s colder out here** sembra più freddo qui fuori; **it ~s like velvet** sembra velluto (al tatto); **to ~ like** (*want*) aver voglia di; **to ~ about** *or* **around for** cercare a tastoni; **to ~ about** *or* **around in one's pocket for** frugarsi in tasca per cercare; **I'm still ~ing my way** (*fig*) sto ancora tastando il terreno; **to get the ~ of sth** (*fig*) abituarsi a qc.

feeler ['fi:lə*] *n* (*of insect*) antenna; **to put out ~s** (*fig*) fare un sondaggio.

feeling ['fi:lɪŋ] *n* sensazione *f*; sentimento; (*impression*) senso, impressione *f*; **to hurt sb's ~s** offendere qn; **what are your ~s about the matter?** che cosa ne pensa?; **my ~ is that** ... ho l'impressione che ...; **I got the ~ that** ... ho avuto l'impressione che ...; **~s ran high about it** la cosa aveva provocato grande eccitazione.

fee-paying school ['fi:peɪɪŋ-] *n* scuola privata.

feet [fi:t] *npl of* **foot**.

feign [feɪn] *vt* fingere, simulare.

felicitous [fɪ'lɪsɪtəs] *adj* felice.

fell [fɛl] *pt of* **fall** ♦ *vt* (*tree*) abbattere; (*person*) atterrare ♦ *adj*: **with one ~ blow** con un colpo terribile; **at one ~ swoop** in un colpo solo ♦ *n* (*BRIT: mountain*) monte *m*; (*: moorland*): **the ~s** la brughiera.

fellow ['fɛləu] *n* individuo, tipo; (*comrade*) compagno; (*of learned society*) membro; (*of university*) ≈ docente *m/f* ♦ *cpd*: **their ~ prisoners/students** i loro compagni di prigione/studio.

fellow citizen *n* concittadino/a.

fellow countryman *n* compatriota *m*.

fellow feeling *n* simpatia.

fellow men *npl* simili *mpl*.

fellowship ['fɛləuʃɪp] *n* associazione *f*; compagnia; (*SCOL*) specie di borsa di studio universitaria.

fellow traveller *n* compagno/a di viaggio; (*POL*) simpatizzante *m/f*.

fell-walking ['fɛlwɔ:kɪŋ] *n* (*BRIT*) passeggiate *fpl* in montagna.

felon ['fɛlən] *n* (*LAW*) criminale *m/f*.

felony ['fɛlənɪ] *n* (*LAW*) reato, crimine *m*.

felt [fɛlt] *pt, pp of* **feel** ♦ *n* feltro.

felt-tip pen ['fɛlttɪp-] *n* pennarello.

female ['fi:meɪl] *n* (*ZOOL*) femmina; (*pej: woman*) donna, femmina ♦ *adj* femminile; (*BIOL, ELEC*) femmina *inv*; **male and ~ students** studenti e studentesse.

female impersonator *n* (*THEAT*) attore comico che fa parti da donna.

feminine ['fɛmɪnɪn] *adj, n* femminile (*m*).

femininity [fɛmɪ'nɪnɪtɪ] *n* femminilità.

feminism ['fɛmɪnɪzəm] *n* femminismo.

feminist ['fɛmɪnɪst] *n* femminista *m/f*.

fen [fɛn] *n* (*BRIT*): **the F~s** la regione delle Fen.

fence [fɛns] *n* recinto; (*SPORT*) ostacolo; (*col: person*) ricettatore/trice ♦ *vt* (*also: ~ in*) recingere ♦ *vi* schermire; **to sit on the ~** (*fig*) rimanere neutrale.

fencing ['fɛnsɪŋ] *n* (*SPORT*) scherma.

fend [fɛnd] *vi*: **to ~ for o.s.** arrangiarsi.

▶**fend off** *vt* (*attack, attacker*) respingere, difendersi da; (*blow*) parare; (*awkward question*) eludere.

fender ['fɛndə*] *n* parafuoco; (*US*) parafango; paraurti *m inv*.

fennel ['fɛnl] *n* finocchio.

ferment *vi* [fə'mɛnt] fermentare ♦ *n* ['fə:mɛnt] agitazione *f*, eccitazione *f*.

fermentation [fə:mɛn'teɪʃən] *n* fermentazione *f*.

fern [fə:n] *n* felce *f*.

ferocious [fə'rəuʃəs] *adj* feroce.

ferocity [fə'rɔsɪtɪ] *n* ferocità.

ferret ['fɛrɪt] *n* furetto.

▶**ferret about, ferret around** *vi* frugare.

▶**ferret out** *vt* (*person*) scovare, scoprire; (*secret, truth*) scoprire.

ferry ['fɛrɪ] *n* (*small*) traghetto; (*large: also: ~boat*) nave *f* traghetto *inv* ♦ *vt* traghettare; **to ~ sth/sb across** *or* **over** traghettare qc/qn da una parte all'altra.

ferryman ['fɛrɪmən] *n* traghettatore *m*.

fertile ['fə:taɪl] *adj* fertile; (*BIOL*) fecondo(a); **~ period** periodo di fecondità.

fertility [fə'tɪlɪtɪ] *n* fertilità; fecondità.

fertility drug *n* farmaco fecondativo.

fertilize ['fə:tɪlaɪz] *vt* fertilizzare; fecondare.

fertilizer ['fə:tɪlaɪzə*] *n* fertilizzante *m*.

fervent ['fə:vənt] *adj* ardente, fervente.

fervour, (*US*) **fervor** ['fə:və*] *n* fervore *m*, ardore *m*.

fester ['fɛstə*] *vi* suppurare.

festival ['fɛstɪvəl] *n* (*REL*) festa; (*ART, MUS*) festival *m inv*.

festive ['fɛstɪv] *adj* di festa; **the ~ season** (*BRIT: Christmas*) il periodo delle feste.

festivities [fɛs'tɪvɪtɪz] *npl* festeggiamenti *mpl.*

festoon [fɛ'stuːn] *vt*: **to ~ with** ornare di; decorare con.

fetch [fɛtʃ] *vt* andare a prendere; (*sell for*) essere venduto(a) per; **how much did it ~?** a *or* per quanto lo ha venduto?

▶**fetch up** *vi* (*BRIT*) andare a finire.

fetching ['fɛtʃɪŋ] *adj* attraente.

fête [feɪt] *n* festa.

fetid ['fɛtɪd] *adj* fetido(a).

fetish ['fɛtɪʃ] *n* feticcio.

fetter ['fɛtə*] *vt* (*person*) incatenare; (*horse*) legare; (*fig*) ostacolare.

fetters ['fɛtəz] *npl* catene *fpl.*

fettle ['fɛtl] *n* (*BRIT*): **in fine ~** in gran forma.

fetus ['fiːtəs] *n* (*US*) = **foetus.**

feud [fjuːd] *n* contesa, lotta ♦ *vi* essere in lotta; **a family ~** una lite in famiglia.

feudal ['fjuːdl] *adj* feudale.

feudalism ['fjuːdəlɪzəm] *n* feudalesimo.

fever ['fiːvə*] *n* febbre *f*; **he has a ~** ha la febbre.

feverish ['fiːvərɪʃ] *adj* (*also fig*) febbrile; (*person*) febbricitante.

few [fjuː] *adj* pochi(e) ♦ *pron* alcuni(e); **~ succeed** pochi ci riescono; **they were ~** erano pochi; **a ~ ...** qualche ...; **I know a ~** ne conosco alcuni; **a good ~, quite a ~** parecchi; **in the next ~ days** nei prossimi giorni; **in the past ~ days** negli ultimi giorni, in questi ultimi giorni; **every ~ days/months** ogni due o tre giorni/mesi; **a ~ more days** qualche altro giorno.

fewer ['fjuːə*] *adj* meno *inv*; meno numerosi(e) ♦ *pron* meno; **they are ~ now** adesso ce ne sono di meno.

fewest ['fjuːɪst] *adj* il minor numero di.

FFA *n abbr* = *Future Farmers of America.*

FH *abbr* (*BRIT*) = *fire hydrant.*

FHA *n abbr* (*US*) = *Federal Housing Administration.*

fiancé [fɪ'ɑːŋseɪ] *n* fidanzato.

fiancée [fɪ'ɑːŋseɪ] *n* fidanzata.

fiasco [fɪ'æskəu] *n* fiasco.

fib [fɪb] *n* piccola bugia.

fibre, (*US*) **fiber** ['faɪbə*] *n* fibra.

fibreboard, (*US*) **fiberboard** ['faɪbəbɔːd] *n* pannello di fibre.

fibre-glass, (*US*) **fiber-glass** ['faɪbəglɑːs] *n* fibra di vetro.

fibrositis [faɪbrə'saɪtɪs] *n* cellulite *f.*

FICA *n abbr* (*US*) = *Federal Insurance Contributions Act.*

fickle ['fɪkl] *adj* incostante, capriccioso(a).

fiction ['fɪkʃən] *n* narrativa; (*sth made up*) finzione *f.*

fictional ['fɪkʃənl] *adj* immaginario(a).

fictionalize ['fɪkʃənəlaɪz] *vt* romanzare.

fictitious [fɪk'tɪʃəs] *adj* fittizio(a).

fiddle ['fɪdl] *n* (*MUS*) violino; (*cheating*) imbroglio; truffa ♦ *vt* (*BRIT: accounts*) falsificare, falsare; **tax ~** frode *f* fiscale; **to work a ~** fare un imbroglio.

▶**fiddle with** *vt fus* gingillarsi con.

fiddler ['fɪdlə*] *n* violinista *m/f.*

fiddly ['fɪdlɪ] *adj* (*task*) da certosino; (*object*) complesso(a).

fidelity [fɪ'dɛlɪtɪ] *n* fedeltà; (*accuracy*) esattezza.

fidget ['fɪdʒɪt] *vi* agitarsi.

fidgety ['fɪdʒɪtɪ] *adj* agitato(a).

fiduciary [fɪ'duːʃɪərɪ] *n* fiduciario.

field [fiːld] *n* (*gen, COMPUT*) campo; **to lead the ~** (*SPORT, COMM*) essere in testa, essere al primo posto; **to have a ~ day** (*fig*) divertirsi, spassarsela.

field glasses *npl* binocolo (da campagna).

field hospital *n* ospedale *m* da campo.

field marshal (FM) *n* feldmaresciallo.

fieldwork ['fiːldwəːk] *n* ricerche *fpl* esterne; (*ARCHEOLOGY, GEO*) lavoro sul campo.

fiend [fiːnd] *n* demonio.

fiendish ['fiːndɪʃ] *adj* demoniaco(a).

fierce [fɪəs] *adj* (*look, fighting*) fiero(a); (*wind*) furioso(a); (*attack*) feroce; (*enemy*) acerrimo(a).

fiery ['faɪərɪ] *adj* ardente; infocato(a).

FIFA ['fiːfə] *n abbr* (= *Fédération Internationale de Football Association*) F.I.F.A. *f.*

fifteen [fɪf'tiːn] *num* quindici.

fifth [fɪfθ] *num* quinto(a).

fiftieth ['fɪftɪɪθ] *num* cinquantesimo(a).

fifty ['fɪftɪ] *num* cinquanta.

fifty-fifty ['fɪftɪ'fɪftɪ] *adj, adv*: **to go ~ with sb** fare a metà con qn; **we have a ~ chance of success** abbiamo una probabilità su due di successo.

fig [fɪg] *n* fico.

fight [faɪt] *n* zuffa, rissa; (*MIL*) battaglia, combattimento; (*against cancer etc*) lotta ♦ *vb* (*pt, pp* **fought** [fɔːt]) *vt* combattere; (*cancer, alcoholism*) lottare contro, combattere; (*LAW: case*) difendere ♦ *vi* battersi, combattere; (*quarrel*): **to ~ (with sb)** litigare (con qn); (*fig*): **to ~ (for/against)** lottare (per/contro).

▶**fight back** *vi* difendersi; (*SPORT, after illness*) riprendersi ♦ *vt* (*tears*) ricacciare.

▶**fight down** *vt* (*anger, anxiety*) vincere; (*urge*) reprimere.

▶**fight off** *vt* (*attack, attacker*) respingere; (*disease, sleep, urge*) lottare contro.

▶**fight out** *vt*: **to ~ it out** risolvere la

fighter – find

questione a pugni.
fighter ['faɪtə*] n combattente m; (plane)
aeroplano da caccia.
fighter-bomber ['faɪtəbɔmə*] n
cacciabombardiere m.
fighter pilot n pilota m di caccia.
fighting ['faɪtɪŋ] n combattimento; (in
streets) scontri mpl.
figment ['fɪgmənt] n: **a ~ of the
imagination** un parto della fantasia.
figurative ['fɪgjurətɪv] adj figurato(a).
figure ['fɪgə*] n (DRAWING, GEOM, person)
figura; (number, cipher) cifra; (body,
outline) forma ♦ vi (appear) figurare; (US:
make sense) spiegarsi; essere logico(a)
♦ vt (US: think, calculate) pensare,
immaginare; **public ~** personaggio
pubblico; **~ of speech** figura retorica.
►**figure on** vt fus (US) contare su.
►**figure out** vt riuscire a capire; calcolare.
figurehead ['fɪgəhɛd] n (NAUT) polena; (pej)
prestanome m/f inv.
figure skating n pattinaggio artistico.
Fiji (Islands) ['fi:dʒi:-] n(pl) le (isole) Figi.
filament ['fɪləmənt] n filamento.
filch [fɪltʃ] vt (col: steal) grattare.
file [faɪl] n (tool) lima; (for nails) limetta;
(dossier) incartamento; (in cabinet)
scheda; (folder) cartellina; (for loose leaf)
raccoglitore m; (row) fila; (COMPUT)
archivio, file m inv ♦ vt (nails, wood)
limare; (papers) archiviare; (LAW: claim)
presentare ♦ vi: **to ~ in/out** entrare/
uscire in fila; **to ~ past** marciare in fila
davanti a; **to ~ a suit against sb** intentare
causa contro qn.
file name n (COMPUT) nome m del file.
filibuster ['fɪlɪbʌstə*] (esp US POL) n (also:
~er) ostruzionista m/f ♦ vi fare
ostruzionismo.
filing ['faɪlɪŋ] n archiviare m; see also **filings**.
filing cabinet n casellario.
filing clerk n archivista m/f.
filings ['faɪlɪŋz] npl limatura.
Filipino [fɪlɪ'pi:nəu] n filippino/a; (LING)
tagal m.
fill [fɪl] vt riempire; (tooth) otturare; (job)
coprire; (supply: order, requirements, need)
soddisfare ♦ n: **to eat one's ~** mangiare a
sazietà; **we've already ~ed that vacancy**
abbiamo già assunto qualcuno per quel
posto.
►**fill in** vt (hole) riempire; (form) compilare;
(details, report) completare ♦ vi: **to ~ in for
sb** sostituire qn; **to ~ sb in on sth** (col)
mettere qn al corrente di qc.
►**fill out** vt (form, receipt) riempire.
►**fill up** vt riempire ♦ vi (AUT) fare il pieno;

~ it up, please (AUT) mi faccia il pieno,
per piacere.
fillet ['fɪlɪt] n filetto.
fillet steak n bistecca di filetto.
filling ['fɪlɪŋ] n (CULIN) impasto, ripieno;
(for tooth) otturazione f.
filling station n stazione f di rifornimento.
fillip ['fɪlɪp] n incentivo, stimolo.
filly ['fɪlɪ] n puledra.
film [fɪlm] n (CINE) film m inv; (PHOT)
pellicola; (thin layer) velo ♦ vt (scene)
filmare.
film script n copione m.
film star n divo/a dello schermo.
filmstrip ['fɪlmstrɪp] n filmina.
film studio n studio cinematografico.
Filofax ® ['faɪləufæks] n agenda ad anelli.
filter ['fɪltə*] n filtro ♦ vt filtrare.
►**filter in, filter through** vi (news)
trapelare.
filter coffee n caffè m da passare al filtro.
filter lane n (BRIT AUT) corsia di svincolo.
filter tip n filtro.
filth [fɪlθ] n sporcizia; (fig) oscenità.
filthy ['fɪlθɪ] adj lordo(a), sozzo(a);
(language) osceno(a).
fin [fɪn] n (of fish) pinna.
final ['faɪnl] adj finale, ultimo(a);
definitivo(a) ♦ n (SPORT) finale f; **~s** npl
(SCOL) esami mpl finali; **~ demand**
ingiunzione f di pagamento.
finale [fɪ'nɑ:lɪ] n finale m.
finalist ['faɪnəlɪst] n (SPORT) finalista m/f.
finality [faɪ'nælɪtɪ] n irrevocabilità; **with an
air of ~** con risolutezza.
finalize ['faɪnəlaɪz] vt mettere a punto.
finally ['faɪnəlɪ] adv (lastly) alla fine;
(eventually) finalmente; (once and for all)
definitivamente.
finance [faɪ'næns] n finanza; (funds) fondi
mpl, capitale m ♦ vt finanziare; **~s** npl
finanze fpl.
financial [faɪ'nænʃəl] adj finanziario(a); **~
statement** estratto conto finanziario.
financially [faɪ'nænʃəlɪ] adv
finanziariamente.
financial year n anno finanziario, esercizio
finanziario.
financier [faɪ'nænsɪə*] n finanziatore m.
find [faɪnd] vt (pt, pp **found** [faund]) trovare;
(lost object) ritrovare ♦ n trovata,
scoperta; **to ~ (some) difficulty in doing
sth** trovare delle difficoltà nel fare qc; **to
~ sb guilty** (LAW) giudicare qn colpevole.
►**find out** vt informarsi di; (truth, secret)
scoprire; (person) cogliere in fallo ♦ vi: **to
~ out about** informarsi su; (by chance)
venire a sapere.

findings ['faɪndɪŋz] *npl* (*LAW*) sentenza, conclusioni *fpl*; (*of report*) conclusioni.

fine [faɪn] *adj* bello(a); ottimo(a); (*thin, subtle*) fine ♦ *adv* (*well*) molto bene; (*small*) finemente ♦ *n* (*LAW*) multa ♦ *vt* (*LAW*) multare; **he's** ~ sta bene; **the weather is** ~ il tempo è bello; **you're doing** ~ te la cavi benissimo; **to cut it** ~ (*of time, money*) farcela per un pelo.

fine arts *npl* belle arti *fpl*.

finely ['faɪnlɪ] *adv* (*splendidly*) in modo stupendo; (*chop*) finemente; (*adjust*) con precisione.

fine print *n*: **the** ~ i caratteri minuti.

finery ['faɪnərɪ] *n* abiti *mpl* eleganti.

finesse [fɪ'nɛs] *n* finezza.

fine-tooth comb ['faɪntuːθ-] *n*: **to go through sth with a** ~ (*fig*) passare qc al setaccio.

finger ['fɪŋgə*] *n* dito ♦ *vt* toccare, tastare.

fingernail ['fɪŋgəneɪl] *n* unghia.

fingerprint ['fɪŋgəprɪnt] *n* impronta digitale ♦ *vt* (*person*) prendere le impronte digitali di.

fingerstall ['fɪŋgəstɔːl] *n* ditale *m*.

fingertip ['fɪŋgətɪp] *n* punta del dito; **to have sth at one's** ~**s** (*fig*) avere qc sulla punta delle dita.

finicky ['fɪnɪkɪ] *adj* esigente, pignolo(a); minuzioso(a).

finish ['fɪnɪʃ] *n* fine *f*; (*SPORT: place*) traguardo; (*polish etc*) finitura ♦ *vt* finire; (*use up*) esaurire ♦ *vi* finire; (*session*) terminare; **to** ~ **doing sth** finire di fare qc; **to** ~ **first/second** (*SPORT*) arrivare primo/secondo; **she's** ~**ed with him** ha chiuso con lui.

▶**finish off** *vt* compiere; (*kill*) uccidere.

▶**finish up** *vi, vt* finire.

finished ['fɪnɪʃt] *adj* (*product*) finito(a); (*performance*) perfetto(a); (*col: tired*) sfinito(a).

finishing line ['fɪnɪʃɪŋ-] *n* linea d'arrivo.

finishing school *n* scuola privata di perfezionamento (*per signorine*).

finishing touches *npl* ultimi ritocchi *mpl*.

finite ['faɪnaɪt] *adj* limitato(a); (*verb*) finito(a).

Finland ['fɪnlənd] *n* Finlandia.

Finn [fɪn] *n* finlandese *m/f*.

Finnish ['fɪnɪʃ] *adj* finlandese ♦ *n* (*LING*) finlandese *m*.

fiord [fjɔːd] *n* fiordo.

fir [fəː*] *n* abete *m*.

fire [faɪə*] *n* fuoco; incendio ♦ *vt* (*discharge*): **to** ~ **a gun** scaricare un fucile; (*fig*) infiammare; (*dismiss*) licenziare ♦ *vi* sparare, far fuoco; **on** ~ in fiamme;

insured against ~ assicurato contro gli incendi; **electric/gas** ~ stufa elettrica/a gas; **to set** ~ **to sth, set sth on** ~ dar fuoco a qc, incendiare qc; **to be/come under** ~ (*from*) essere/finire sotto il fuoco *or* il tiro (di).

fire alarm *n* allarme *m* d'incendio.

firearm ['faɪərɑːm] *n* arma da fuoco.

fire brigade *n* (*BRIT*) (corpo dei) pompieri *mpl*.

fire chief *n* (*US*) = **fire master**.

fire department *n* (*US*) = **fire brigade**.

fire door *n* porta *f* rompifuoco *inv*.

fire drill *n* esercitazione *f* antincendio.

fire engine *n* autopompa.

fire escape *n* scala di sicurezza.

fire extinguisher *n* estintore *m*.

fireguard ['faɪəgɑːd] *n* (*BRIT*) parafuoco.

fire hazard *n*: **that's a** ~ comporta rischi in caso d'incendio.

fire hydrant *n* idrante *m*.

fire insurance *n* assicurazione *f* contro gli incendi.

fireman ['faɪəmən] *n* pompiere *m*.

fire master *n* (*BRIT*) comandante *m* dei vigili del fuoco.

fireplace ['faɪəpleɪs] *n* focolare *m*.

fireplug ['faɪəplʌg] *n* (*US*) = **fire hydrant**.

fire practice *n* = **fire drill**.

fireproof ['faɪəpruːf] *adj* resistente al fuoco.

fire regulations *npl* norme *fpl* antincendio.

fire screen *n* parafuoco.

fireside ['faɪəsaɪd] *n* angolo del focolare.

fire station *n* caserma dei pompieri.

firewood ['faɪəwud] *n* legna.

firework ['faɪəwɜːk] *n* fuoco d'artificio.

firing ['faɪərɪŋ] *n* (*MIL*) spari *mpl*, tiro.

firing line *n* linea del fuoco; **to be in the** ~ (*fig*) essere sotto tiro.

firing squad *n* plotone *m* d'esecuzione.

firm [fəːm] *adj* fermo(a); (*offer, decision*) definitivo(a) ♦ *n* ditta, azienda; **to be a** ~ **believer in sth** credere fermamente in qc.

firmly ['fəːmlɪ] *adv* fermamente.

firmness ['fəːmnɪs] *n* fermezza.

first [fəːst] *adj* primo(a) ♦ *adv* (*before others*) il primo, la prima; (*before other things*) per primo; (*for the first time*) per la prima volta; (*when listing reasons etc*) per prima cosa ♦ *n* (*person: in race*) primo/a; (*BRIT SCOL*) laurea con lode; (*AUT*) prima; **at** ~ dapprima, all'inizio; ~ **of all** prima di tutto; **in the** ~ **instance** prima di tutto, in primo luogo; **I'll do it** ~ **thing tomorrow** lo farò per prima cosa domani; **from the (very)** ~ fin dall'inizio, fin dal primo momento; **the** ~ **of January** il primo (di) gennaio.

first aid n pronto soccorso.
first-aid kit ['fəːst'eɪd-] n cassetta pronto soccorso.
first-class ['fəːst'klɑːs] adj di prima classe.
first-class mail n ≈ espresso.
first-hand ['fəːst'hænd] adj di prima mano; diretto(a).
first lady n (US) moglie f del presidente.
firstly ['fəːstlɪ] adv in primo luogo.
first name n nome m di battesimo.
first night n (THEAT) prima.
first-rate ['fəːst'reɪt] adj di prima qualità, ottimo(a).
first-time buyer ['fəːsttaɪm-] n acquirente m/f di prima casa.
First World War n: **the** ~ la prima guerra mondiale.
fir tree n abete m.
FIS n abbr (BRIT: = Family Income Supplement) ≈ A.F. (= assegni familiari).
fiscal ['fɪskəl] adj fiscale; ~ **year** anno fiscale.
fish [fɪʃ] n (pl inv) pesce m ♦ vt, vi pescare; **to** ~ **a river** pescare in un fiume; **to go** ~**ing** andare a pesca.
▶**fish out** vt (from water) ripescare; (from box etc) tirare fuori.
fish-and-chip shop [fɪʃən'tʃɪp-] n ≈ friggitoria; see **chip shop.**
fishbone ['fɪʃbəun] n lisca, spina.
fisherman ['fɪʃəmən] n pescatore m.
fishery ['fɪʃərɪ] n zona da pesca.
fish factory n (BRIT) fabbrica per la lavorazione del pesce.
fish farm n vivaio.
fish fingers npl (BRIT) bastoncini mpl di pesce (surgelati).
fish hook n amo.
fishing boat ['fɪʃɪŋ-] n barca da pesca.
fishing industry n industria della pesca.
fishing line n lenza.
fishing net n rete f da pesca.
fishing rod n canna da pesca.
fishing tackle n attrezzatura da pesca.
fish market n mercato del pesce.
fishmonger ['fɪʃmʌŋgə*] n pescivendolo; ~**'s (shop)** pescheria.
fish slice n (BRIT) posata per servire il pesce.
fish sticks npl (US) = **fish fingers.**
fishy ['fɪʃɪ] adj (fig) sospetto(a).
fission ['fɪʃən] n fissione f; **atomic/nuclear** ~ fissione atomica/nucleare.
fissure ['fɪʃə*] n fessura.
fist [fɪst] n pugno.
fistfight ['fɪstfaɪt] n scazzottata.
fit [fɪt] adj (MED, SPORT) in forma; (proper) adatto(a), appropriato(a); conveniente

♦ vt (subj: clothes) stare bene a; (match: facts etc) concordare con; (: description) corrispondere a; (adjust) aggiustare; (put in, attach) mettere, installare; (equip) fornire, equipaggiare ♦ vi (clothes) stare bene; (parts) andare bene, adattarsi; (in space, gap) entrare ♦ n (MED) attacco; ~ **to** in grado di; ~ **for** adatto(a) a; degno(a) di; **to keep** ~ tenersi in forma; ~ **for work** (after illness) in grado di riprendere il lavoro; **do as you think** or **see** ~ faccia come meglio crede; **this dress is a tight/ good** ~ questo vestito è stretto/sta bene; ~ **of anger/enthusiasm** accesso d'ira/ d'entusiasmo; **to have a** ~ (MED) avere un attacco di convulsioni; (col) andare su tutte le furie; **by** ~**s and starts** a sbalzi.
▶**fit in** vi accordarsi; adattarsi ♦ vt (object) far entrare; (fig: appointment, visitor) trovare il tempo per; **to** ~ **in with sb's plans** adattarsi ai progetti di qn.
▶**fit out** vt (BRIT: also: ~ **up**) equipaggiare.
fitful ['fɪtful] adj saltuario(a).
fitment ['fɪtmənt] n componibile m.
fitness ['fɪtnɪs] n (MED) forma fisica; (of remark) appropriatezza.
fitted ['fɪtɪd] adj: ~ **carpet** moquette f inv; ~ **cupboards** armadi mpl a muro; ~ **kitchen** (BRIT) cucina componibile.
fitter ['fɪtə*] n aggiustatore m or montatore m meccanico; (DRESSMAKING) sarto/a.
fitting ['fɪtɪŋ] adj appropriato(a) ♦ n (of dress) prova; (of piece of equipment) montaggio, aggiustaggio; see also **fittings.**
fitting room n (in shop) camerino.
fittings ['fɪtɪŋz] npl impianti mpl.
five [faɪv] num cinque.
five-day week ['faɪvdeɪ-] n settimana di 5 giorni (lavorativi).
fiver ['faɪvə*] n (col: BRIT) biglietto da cinque sterline; (: US) biglietto da cinque dollari.
fix [fɪks] vt fissare; (mend) riparare; (make ready: meal, drink) preparare ♦ n: **to be in a** ~ essere nei guai; **the fight was a** ~ (col) l'incontro è stato truccato.
▶**fix up** vt (arrange: date, meeting) fissare, stabilire; **to** ~ **sb up with sth** procurare qc a qn.
fixation [fɪk'seɪʃən] n (PSYCH, fig) fissazione f, ossessione f.
fixed [fɪkst] adj (prices etc) fisso(a); **there's a** ~ **charge** c'è una quota fissa; **how are you** ~ **for money?** (col) a soldi come stai?
fixed assets npl beni mpl patrimoniali.
fixture ['fɪkstʃə*] n impianto (fisso); (SPORT) incontro (del calendario sportivo).

fizz [fɪz] *vi* frizzare.
fizzle ['fɪzl] *vi* frizzare; (*also*: ~ **out**: *enthusiasm, interest*) smorzarsi, svanire; (: *plan*) fallire.
fizzy ['fɪzɪ] *adj* frizzante; gassato(a).
fjord [fjɔːd] *n* = **fiord**.
FL, Fla. *abbr* (*US*) = *Florida*.
flabbergasted ['flæbəɡɑːstɪd] *adj* sbalordito(a).
flabby ['flæbɪ] *adj* flaccido(a).
flag [flæɡ] *n* bandiera; (*also*: ~**stone**) pietra da lastricare ♦ *vi* stancarsi; affievolirsi; ~ **of convenience** bandiera di convenienza.
▶**flag down** *vt* fare segno (di fermarsi) a.
flagon ['flæɡən] *n* bottiglione *m*.
flagpole ['flæɡpəul] *n* albero.
flagrant ['fleɪɡrənt] *adj* flagrante.
flag stop *n* (*US*: *for bus*) fermata facoltativa, fermata a richiesta.
flair [flɛə*] *n* (*for business etc*) fiuto; (*for languages etc*) facilità.
flak [flæk] *n* (*MIL*) fuoco d'artiglieria; (*col*: *criticism*) critiche *fpl*.
flake [fleɪk] *n* (*of rust, paint*) scaglia; (*of snow, soap powder*) fiocco ♦ *vi* (*also*: ~ **off**) sfaldarsi.
flaky ['fleɪkɪ] *adj* (*paintwork*) scrostato(a); (*skin*) squamoso(a); ~ **pastry** (*CULIN*) pasta sfoglia.
flamboyant [flæm'bɔɪənt] *adj* sgargiante.
flame [fleɪm] *n* fiamma; **old** ~ (*col*) vecchia fiamma.
flamingo [flə'mɪŋɡəu] *n* fenicottero, fiammingo.
flammable ['flæməbl] *adj* infiammabile.
flan [flæn] *n* (*BRIT*) flan *m inv*.
Flanders ['flɑːndəz] *n* Fiandre *fpl*.
flange [flændʒ] *n* flangia; (*on wheel*) suola.
flank [flæŋk] *n* fianco.
flannel ['flænl] *n* (*BRIT*: *also*: **face** ~) guanto di spugna; (*fabric*) flanella; ~**s** *npl* pantaloni *mpl* di flanella.
flannelette [flænə'lɛt] *n* flanella di cotone.
flap [flæp] *n* (*of pocket*) patta; (*of envelope*) lembo; (*AVIAT*) flap *m inv* ♦ *vt* (*wings*) battere ♦ *vi* (*sail, flag*) sbattere; (*col*: *also*: **be in a** ~) essere in agitazione.
flapjack ['flæpdʒæk] *n* (*US*: *pancake*) frittella; (*BRIT*: *biscuit*) biscotto di avena.
flare [flɛə*] *n* razzo; (*in skirt etc*) svasatura.
▶**flare up** *vi* andare in fiamme; (*fig*: *person*) infiammarsi di rabbia; (: *revolt*) scoppiare.
flared ['flɛəd] *adj* (*trousers*) svasato(a).
flash [flæʃ] *n* vampata; (*also*: **news** ~) notizia *f* lampo *inv*; (*PHOT*) flash *m inv*; (*US*: *torch*) torcia elettrica, lampadina tascabile ♦ *vt* accendere e spegnere;

(*send*: *message*) trasmettere; (*flaunt*) ostentare ♦ *vi* brillare; (*light on ambulance, eyes etc*) lampeggiare; **in a** ~ in un lampo; ~ **of inspiration** lampo di genio; **to** ~ **one's headlights** lampeggiare; **he** ~**ed by** *or* **past** ci passò davanti come un lampo.
flashback ['flæʃbæk] *n* flashback *m inv*.
flashbulb ['flæʃbʌlb] *n* cubo *m* flash *inv*.
flash card *n* (*SCOL*) scheda didattica.
flashcube ['flæʃkjuːb] *n* flash *m inv*.
flasher ['flæʃə*] *n* (*AUT*) lampeggiatore *m*.
flashlight ['flæʃlaɪt] *n* (*torch*) lampadina tascabile.
flashpoint ['flæʃpɔɪnt] *n* punto di infiammabilità; (*fig*) livello critico.
flashy ['flæʃɪ] *adj* (*pej*) vistoso(a).
flask [flɑːsk] *n* fiasco; (*CHEM*) beuta; (*also*: **vacuum** ~) thermos ® *m inv*.
flat [flæt] *adj* piatto(a); (*tyre*) sgonfio(a), a terra; (*battery*) scarico(a); (*denial*) netto(a); (*MUS*) bemolle *inv*; (: *voice*) stonato(a); (: *instrument*) scordato(a) ♦ *n* (*BRIT*: *rooms*) appartamento; (*MUS*) bemolle *m*; (*AUT*) pneumatico sgonfio ♦ *adv*: (**to work**) ~ **out** (lavorare) a più non posso; ~ **rate of pay** tariffa unica di pagamento.
flat-footed ['flæt'futɪd] *adj*: **to be** ~ avere i piedi piatti.
flatly ['flætlɪ] *adv* categoricamente, nettamente.
flatmate ['flætmeɪt] *n* (*BRIT*): **he's my** ~ divide l'appartamento con me.
flatness ['flætnɪs] *n* (*of land*) assenza di rilievi.
flat-screen ['flætskriːn] *adj* a schermo piatto.
flatten ['flætn] *vt* (*also*: ~ **out**) appiattire; (*house, city*) abbattere, radere al suolo.
flatter ['flætə*] *vt* lusingare; (*show to advantage*) donare a.
flatterer ['flætərə*] *n* adulatore/trice.
flattering ['flætərɪŋ] *adj* lusinghiero(a); (*clothes etc*) che dona, che abbellisce.
flattery ['flætərɪ] *n* adulazione *f*.
flatulence ['flætjuləns] *n* flatulenza.
flaunt [flɔːnt] *vt* fare mostra di.
flavour, (*US*) flavor ['fleɪvə*] *n* gusto, sapore *m* ♦ *vt* insaporire, aggiungere sapore a; **vanilla-**~**ed** al gusto di vaniglia.
flavo(u)ring ['fleɪvərɪŋ] *n* essenza (artificiale).
flaw [flɔː] *n* difetto.
flawless ['flɔːlɪs] *adj* senza difetti.
flax [flæks] *n* lino.
flaxen ['flæksən] *adj* biondo(a).
flea [fliː] *n* pulce *f*.
flea market *n* mercato delle pulci.

fleck [flɛk] n (of mud, paint, colour) macchiolina; (of dust) granello ♦ vt (with blood, mud etc) macchiettare; **brown ~ed with white** marrone screziato di bianco.

fled [flɛd] pt, pp of **flee**.

fledg(e)ling ['flɛdʒlɪŋ] n uccellino.

flee, pt, pp **fled** [fliː, flɛd] vt fuggire da ♦ vi fuggire, scappare.

fleece [fliːs] n vello; (garment) pile sm inv ♦ vt (col) pelare.

fleecy ['fliːsɪ] adj (blanket) soffice; (cloud) come ovatta.

fleet [fliːt] n flotta; (of lorries etc) convoglio; (of cars) parco.

fleeting ['fliːtɪŋ] adj fugace; (visit) volante.

Flemish ['flɛmɪʃ] adj fiammingo(a) ♦ n (LING) fiammingo; **the ~** npl i Fiamminghi.

flesh [flɛʃ] n carne f; (of fruit) polpa.

flesh wound n ferita superficiale.

flew [fluː] pt of **fly**.

flex [flɛks] n filo (flessibile) ♦ vt flettere; (muscles) contrarre.

flexibility [flɛksɪ'bɪlɪtɪ] n flessibilità.

flexible ['flɛksəbl] adj flessibile.

flexitime ['flɛksɪtaɪm] n orario flessibile.

flick [flɪk] n colpetto; see also **flicks**.

►**flick through** vt fus sfogliare.

flicker ['flɪkə*] vi tremolare ♦ n tremolio; **a ~ of light** un breve bagliore.

flick knife n (BRIT) coltello a serramanico.

flicks npl: **the ~** (col) il cine.

flier ['flaɪə*] n aviatore m.

flight [flaɪt] n volo; (escape) fuga; (also: ~ of steps) scalinata; **to take ~** darsi alla fuga; **to put to ~** mettere in fuga.

flight attendant n (US) steward m, hostess f inv.

flight crew n equipaggio.

flight deck n (AVIAT) cabina di controllo; (NAUT) ponte m di comando.

flight path n (of aircraft) rotta di volo; (of rocket, projectile) traiettoria.

flight recorder n registratore m di volo.

flimsy ['flɪmzɪ] adj (fabric) inconsistente; (excuse) meschino(a).

flinch [flɪntʃ] vi ritirarsi; **to ~ from** tirarsi indietro di fronte a.

fling, pt, pp **flung** [flɪŋ, flʌŋ] vt lanciare, gettare ♦ n (love affair) avventura.

flint [flɪnt] n selce f; (in lighter) pietrina.

flip [flɪp] n colpetto ♦ vt dare un colpetto a; (US: pancake) far saltare (in aria) ♦ vi: **to ~ for sth** (US) fare a testa e croce per qc.

►**flip through** vt fus (book, records) dare una scorsa a.

flippant ['flɪpənt] adj senza rispetto, irriverente.

flipper ['flɪpə*] n pinna.

flip side n (of record) retro.

flirt [flɜːt] vi flirtare ♦ n civetta.

flirtation [flɜː'teɪʃən] n flirt m inv.

flit [flɪt] vi svolazzare.

float [fləut] n galleggiante m; (in procession) carro; (sum of money) somma ♦ vi galleggiare; (bather) fare il morto; (COMM: currency) fluttuare ♦ vt far galleggiare; (loan, business) lanciare; **to ~ an idea** ventilare un'idea.

floating ['fləutɪŋ] adj a galla; **~ vote** voto oscillante; **~ voter** elettore m indeciso.

flock [flɔk] n gregge m; (of people) folla; (of birds) stormo.

floe [fləu] n (also: **ice ~**) banchisa.

flog [flɔg] vt flagellare.

flood [flʌd] n alluvione f; (of words, tears etc) diluvio ♦ vt inondare, allagare; (AUT: carburettor) ingolfare; **in ~** in pieno; **to ~ the market** (COMM) inondare il mercato.

flooding ['flʌdɪŋ] n inondazione f.

floodlight ['flʌdlaɪt] n riflettore m ♦ vt illuminare a giorno.

floodlit ['flʌdlɪt] pt, pp of **floodlight** ♦ adj illuminato(a) a giorno.

flood tide n alta marea, marea crescente.

floodwater ['flʌdwɔːtə*] n acque fpl (di inondazione).

floor [flɔː*] n pavimento; (storey) piano; (of sea, valley) fondo; (fig: at meeting): **the ~** il pubblico ♦ vt pavimentare; (knock down) atterrare; (baffle) confondere; (silence) far tacere; **on the ~** sul pavimento, per terra; **ground ~**, (US) **first ~** pianterreno; **first ~**, (US) **second ~** primo piano; **top ~** ultimo piano; **to have the ~** (speaker) prendere la parola.

floorboard ['flɔːbɔːd] n tavellone m di legno.

flooring ['flɔːrɪŋ] n (floor) pavimento; (material) materiale m per pavimentazioni.

floor lamp n (US) lampada a stelo.

floor show n spettacolo di varietà.

floorwalker ['flɔːwɔːkə*] n (esp US) ispettore m di reparto.

flop [flɔp] n fiasco ♦ vi (fail) far fiasco.

floppy ['flɔpɪ] adj floscio(a), molle ♦ n (COMPUT) = **floppy disk**; **~ hat** cappello floscio.

floppy disk n floppy disk m inv.

flora ['flɔːrə] n flora.

floral ['flɔːrl] adj floreale.

Florence ['flɔrəns] n Firenze f.

Florentine ['flɔrəntaɪn] adj fiorentino(a).

florid ['flɔrɪd] adj (complexion) florido(a); (style) fiorito(a).

florist ['flɔrɪst] n fioraio/a; **at the ~'s (shop)**

dal fioraio.

flotation [fləu'teɪʃən] *n* (*COMM*) lancio.

flounce [flauns] *n* balzo.

▶**flounce out** *vi* uscire stizzito(a).

flounder ['flaundə*] *vi* annaspare ♦ *n* (*ZOOL*) passera di mare.

flour ['flauə*] *n* farina.

flourish ['flʌrɪʃ] *vi* fiorire ♦ *vt* brandire ♦ *n* abbellimento; svolazzo; (*of trumpets*) fanfara.

flourishing ['flʌrɪʃɪŋ] *adj* prosperoso(a), fiorente.

flout [flaut] *vt* (*order*) contravvenire a; (*convention*) sfidare.

flow [fləu] *n* flusso; circolazione *f*; (*of river, also ELEC*) corrente *f* ♦ *vi* fluire; (*traffic, blood in veins*) circolare; (*hair*) scendere.

flow chart *n* schema *m* di flusso.

flow diagram *n* organigramma *m*.

flower ['flauə*] *n* fiore *m* ♦ *vi* fiorire; **in ~** in fiore.

flower bed *n* aiuola.

flowerpot ['flauəpɔt] *n* vaso da fiori.

flowery ['flauərɪ] *adj* fiorito(a).

flown [fləun] *pp of* **fly**.

flu [fluː] *n* influenza.

fluctuate ['flʌktjueɪt] *vi* fluttuare, oscillare.

fluctuation [flʌktju'eɪʃən] *n* fluttuazione *f*, oscillazione *f*.

flue [fluː] *n* canna fumaria.

fluency ['fluːənsɪ] *n* facilità, scioltezza; **his ~ in English** la sua scioltezza nel parlare l'inglese.

fluent ['fluːənt] *adj* (*speech*) facile, sciolto(a); **he's a ~ speaker/reader** si esprime/legge senza difficoltà; **he speaks ~ Italian, he's ~ in Italian** parla l'italiano correntemente.

fluently ['fluːəntlɪ] *adv* con facilità; correntemente.

fluff [flʌf] *n* lanugine *f*.

fluffy ['flʌfɪ] *adj* lanuginoso(a); (*toy*) di peluche.

fluid ['fluːɪd] *adj* fluido(a) ♦ *n* fluido; (*in diet*) liquido.

fluid ounce *n* (*BRIT*) = 0.028 l; 0.05 pints.

fluke [fluːk] *n* (*col*) colpo di fortuna.

flummox ['flʌməks] *vt* rendere perplesso(a).

flung [flʌŋ] *pt*, *pp of* **fling**.

flunky ['flʌŋkɪ] *n* tirapiedi *m/f inv*.

fluorescent [fluə'rɛsnt] *adj* fluorescente.

fluoride ['fluəraɪd] *n* fluoruro.

fluorine ['fluəriːn] *n* fluoro.

flurry ['flʌrɪ] *n* (*of snow*) tempesta; **a ~ of activity/excitement** una febbre di attività/un'improvvisa agitazione.

flush [flʌʃ] *n* rossore *m*; (*fig*) ebbrezza ♦ *vt*

ripulire con un getto d'acqua; (*also*: ~ **out**: *birds*) far alzare in volo; (: *animals, fig*: *criminal*) stanare ♦ *vi* arrossire ♦ *adj*: ~ **with** a livello di, pari a; ~ **against** aderente a; **hot ~es** (*MED*) vampate *fpl* di calore; **to ~ the toilet** tirare l'acqua.

flushed [flʌʃt] *adj* tutto(a) rosso(a).

fluster ['flʌstə*] *n* agitazione *f*.

flustered ['flʌstəd] *adj* sconvolto(a).

flute [fluːt] *n* flauto.

flutter ['flʌtə*] *n* agitazione *f*; (*of wings*) frullio ♦ *vi* (*bird*) battere le ali.

flux [flʌks] *n*: **in a state of ~** in continuo mutamento.

fly [flaɪ] *n* (*insect*) mosca; (*on trousers: also*: **flies**) bracchetta ♦ *vb* (*pt* **flew**, *pp* **flown** [fluː, fləun]) *vt* pilotare; (*passengers, cargo*) trasportare (in aereo); (*distances*) percorrere ♦ *vi* volare; (*passengers*) andare in aereo; (*escape*) fuggire; (*flag*) sventolare; **to ~ open** spalancarsi all'improvviso; **to ~ off the handle** perdere le staffe, uscire dai gangheri.

▶**fly away** *vi* volar via.

▶**fly in** *vi* (*plane*) arrivare; (*person*) arrivare in aereo.

▶**fly off** *vi* volare via.

▶**fly out** *vi* (*plane*) partire; (*person*) partire in aereo.

fly-fishing ['flaɪfɪʃɪŋ] *n* pesca con la mosca.

flying ['flaɪɪŋ] *n* (*activity*) aviazione *f*; (*action*) volo ♦ *adj*: ~ **visit** visita volante; **with ~ colours** con risultati brillanti; **he doesn't like ~** non gli piace viaggiare in aereo.

flying buttress *n* arco rampante.

flying picket *n* picchetto (*proveniente da fabbriche non direttamente coinvolte nello sciopero*).

flying saucer *n* disco volante.

flying squad *n* (*POLICE*) (squadra) volante *f*.

flying start *n*: **to get off to a ~ start** partire come un razzo.

flyleaf ['flaɪliːf] *n* risguardo.

flyover ['flaɪəuvə*] *n* (*BRIT*: *bridge*) cavalcavia *m inv*.

flypast ['flaɪpɑːst] *n* esibizione *f* della pattuglia aerea.

flysheet ['flaɪʃiːt] *n* (*for tent*) sopratetto.

flyweight ['flaɪweɪt] *n* (*SPORT*) peso *m* mosca *inv*.

flywheel ['flaɪwiːl] *n* volano.

FM *abbr see* **frequency modulation**; (*BRIT MIL*) *see* **Field Marshal**.

FMB *n abbr* (*US*) = *Federal Maritime Board*.

FMCS *n abbr* (*US*: = *Federal Mediation and Conciliation Services*) organismo di *conciliazione in caso di conflitti sul lavoro.*

FO *n abbr* (*BRIT*) *see* **Foreign Office.**

foal [fəul] *n* puledro.

foam [fəum] *n* schiuma ♦ *vi* schiumare.

foam rubber *n* gommapiuma ®.

FOB *abbr* (= *free on board*) franco a bordo.

fob [fɔb] *vt*: **to ~ sb off with** appioppare qn con; sbarazzarsi di qn con ♦ *n* (*also*: **watch ~**: *chain*) catena per orologio; (*: band of cloth*) nastro per orologio.

foc *abbr* (*BRIT*) = **free of charge.**

focal ['fəukəl] *adj* focale.

focal point *n* punto focale.

focus ['fəukəs] *n* (*pl* ~**es**) fuoco; (*of interest*) centro ♦ *vt* (*field glasses etc*) mettere a fuoco; (*light rays*) far convergere ♦ *vi*: **to ~ on** (*with camera*) mettere a fuoco; (*person*) fissare lo sguardo su; **in ~** a fuoco; **out of ~** sfocato(a).

fodder ['fɔdə*] *n* foraggio.

FOE *n abbr* (= *Friends of the Earth*) Amici mpl della Terra, (*US*: = *Fraternal Order of Eagles*) organizzazione filantropica.

foe [fəu] *n* nemico.

foetus, (*US*) **fetus** ['fiːtəs] *n* feto.

fog [fɔg] *n* nebbia.

fogbound ['fɔgbaund] *adj* fermo(a) a causa della nebbia.

foggy ['fɔgɪ] *adj* nebbioso(a); **it's ~** c'è nebbia.

fog lamp, (*US*) **fog light** *n* (*AUT*) faro *m* antinebbia *inv*.

foible ['fɔɪbl] *n* debolezza, punto debole.

foil [fɔɪl] *vt* confondere, frustrare ♦ *n* lamina di metallo; (*also*: **kitchen ~**) foglio di alluminio; (*FENCING*) fioretto; **to act as a ~ to** (*fig*) far risaltare.

foist [fɔɪst] *vt*: **to ~ sth on sb** rifilare qc a qn.

fold [fəuld] *n* (*bend, crease*) piega; (*AGR*) ovile *m*; (*fig*) gregge *m* ♦ *vt* piegare; **to ~ one's arms** incrociare le braccia.

►**fold up** *vi* (*map etc*) piegarsi; (*business*) crollare ♦ *vt* (*map etc*) piegare, ripiegare.

folder ['fəuldə*] *n* (*for papers*) cartella; cartellina; (*binder*) raccoglitore *m*.

folding ['fəuldɪŋ] *adj* (*chair, bed*) pieghevole.

foliage ['fəulɪɪdʒ] *n* fogliame *m*.

folk [fəuk] *npl* gente *f* ♦ *cpd* popolare; ~**s** *npl* famiglia.

folklore ['fəuklɔ:*] *n* folclore *m*.

folk music *n* musica folk *inv*.

folk singer *n* cantante *m/f* folk *inv*.

folksong ['fəuksɔŋ] *n* canto popolare.

follow ['fɔləu] *vt* seguire ♦ *vi* seguire; (*result*) conseguire, risultare; **to ~ sb's advice** seguire il consiglio di qn; **I don't**

quite ~ you non ti capisco *or* seguo affatto; **to ~ in sb's footsteps** seguire le orme di qn; **it ~s that ...** ne consegue che ...; **he ~ed suit** lui ha fatto lo stesso.

►**follow on** *vi* (*continue*): **to ~ on from** seguire.

►**follow out** *vt* (*implement: idea, plan*) eseguire, portare a termine.

►**follow through** *vt* = **follow out.**

►**follow up** *vt* (*victory*) sfruttare; (*letter, offer*) fare seguito a; (*case*) seguire.

follower ['fɔləuə*] *n* seguace *m/f*, discepolo/a.

following ['fɔləuɪŋ] *adj* seguente, successivo(a) ♦ *n* seguito, discepoli *mpl*.

follow-up ['fɔləuʌp] *n* seguito.

folly ['fɔlɪ] *n* pazzia, follia.

fond [fɔnd] *adj* (*memory, look*) tenero(a), affettuoso(a); **to be ~ of** volere bene a; **she's ~ of swimming** le piace nuotare.

fondle ['fɔndl] *vt* accarezzare.

fondly ['fɔndlɪ] *adv* (*lovingly*) affettuosamente; (*naively*): **he ~ believed that ...** ha avuto l'ingenuità di credere che ....

fondness ['fɔndnɪs] *n* affetto; ~ (**for sth**) predilezione *f* (per qc).

font [fɔnt] *n* (*REL*) fonte *m* (battesimale); (*TYP*) stile *m* di carattere.

food [fu:d] *n* cibo.

food chain *n* catena alimentare.

food mixer *n* frullatore *m*.

food poisoning *n* intossicazione *f* alimentare.

food processor *n* tritatutto *m inv* elettrico.

food stamp *n* (*US*) buono alimentare dato agli indigenti.

foodstuffs ['fu:dstʌfs] *npl* generi *fpl* alimentari.

fool [fu:l] *n* sciocco/a; (*HISTORY: of king*) buffone *m*; (*CULIN*) frullato ♦ *vt* ingannare ♦ *vi* (*gen*: ~ **around**) fare lo sciocco; **to make a ~ of sb** prendere in giro qn; **to make a ~ of o.s.** coprirsi di ridicolo; **you can't ~ me** non mi inganna.

►**fool about, fool around** *vi* (*waste time*) perdere tempo.

foolhardy ['fu:lha:dɪ] *adj* avventato(a).

foolish ['fu:lɪʃ] *adj* scemo(a), stupido(a); imprudente.

foolishly ['fu:lɪʃlɪ] *adv* stupidamente.

foolishness ['fu:lɪʃnɪs] *n* stupidità.

foolproof ['fu:lpru:f] *adj* (*plan etc*) sicurissimo(a).

foolscap ['fu:lskæp] *n* carta protocollo.

foot [fut] *n* (*pl* **feet** [fi:t]) piede *m*; (*measure*) piede (= *304 mm; 12 inches*); (*of animal*) zampa; (*of page, stairs etc*) fondo ♦ *vt* (*bill*)

pagare; **on** ~ a piedi; **to put one's** ~
down (*AUT*) schiacciare l'acceleratore;
(*say no*) imporsi; **to find one's feet**
ambientarsi.
footage ['futɪdʒ] *n* (*CINE: length*) ≈
metraggio; (: *material*) sequenza.
foot and mouth (disease) *n* afta
epizootica.
football ['fuːtbɔːl] *n* pallone *m*; (*sport: BRIT*)
calcio; (: *US*) football *m* americano.
footballer ['fuːtbɔːlə*] *n* (*BRIT*) = **football
player.**
football ground *n* campo di calcio.
football match *n* (*BRIT*) partita di calcio.
football player *n* (*BRIT*) calciatore *m*; (*US*)
giocatore *m* di football americano.
footbrake ['fuːtbreɪk] *n* freno a pedale.
footbridge ['fuːtbrɪdʒ] *n* passerella.
foothills ['fuːthɪlz] *npl* contrafforti *fpl*.
foothold ['futhəuld] *n* punto d'appoggio.
footing ['futɪŋ] *n* (*fig*) posizione *f*; **to lose
one's** ~ mettere un piede in fallo; **on an
equal** ~ in condizioni di parità.
footlights ['futlaɪts] *npl* luci *fpl* della
ribalta.
footman ['futmən] *n* lacchè *m inv.*
footnote ['futnəut] *n* nota (a piè di pagina).
footpath ['futpɑːθ] *n* sentiero; (*in street*)
marciapiede *m.*
footprint ['futprɪnt] *n* orma, impronta.
footrest ['futrest] *n* poggiapiedi *m inv.*
footsie ['futsɪ] *n* (*col*): **to play** ~ **with sb**
fare piedino a qn.
Footsie (index) ['futsɪ-] *n* (*col*) = *Financial
Times Stock Exchange 100 Index.*
footsore ['futsɔː*] *adj*: **to be** ~ avere mal di
piedi.
footstep ['futstep] *n* passo.
footwear ['futwɛə*] *n* calzatura.
FOR *abbr* (= *free on rail*) franco vagone.

========= *KEYWORD*

for [fɔː*] *prep* **1** (*indicating destination,
intention, purpose*) per; **the train** ~ **London**
il treno per Londra; **he went** ~ **the paper**
è andato a prendere il giornale; **it's time**
~ **lunch** è ora di pranzo; **what's it** ~? a
che serve?; **what** ~? (*why*) perché?
2 (*on behalf of, representing*) per; **to work**
~ **sb/sth** lavorare per qn/qc; **I'll ask him**
~ **you** glielo chiederò a nome tuo; **G** ~
George G come George
3 (*because of*) per, a causa di; ~ **this
reason** per questo motivo
4 (*with regard to*) per; **it's cold** ~ **July** è
freddo per luglio; ~ **everyone who voted
yes, 50 voted no** per ogni voto a favore
ce n'erano 50 contro

5 (*in exchange for*) per; **I sold it** ~ **£5** l'ho
venduto per 5 sterline
6 (*in favour of*) per, a favore di; **are you** ~
or against us? sei con noi o contro di
noi?; **I'm all** ~ **it** sono completamente a
favore
7 (*referring to distance, time*) per; **there are
roadworks** ~ **5 km** ci sono lavori in corso
per 5 km; **he was away** ~ **2 years** è stato
via per 2 anni; **she will be away** ~ **a
month** starà via un mese; **it hasn't rained**
~ **3 weeks** non piove da 3 settimane; **can
you do it** ~ **tomorrow?** può farlo per
domani?
8 (*with infinitive clauses*): **it is not** ~ **me to
decide** non sta a me decidere; **it would be
best** ~ **you to leave** sarebbe meglio che
lei se ne andasse; **there is still time** ~ **you
to do it** ha ancora tempo per farlo; ~ **this
to be possible** ... perché ciò sia possibile
...
9 (*in spite of*) nonostante; ~ **all his
complaints, he's very fond of her**
nonostante tutte le sue lamentele, le
vuole molto bene
♦ *conj* (*since, as: rather formal*) dal
momento che, poiché.

forage ['fɔrɪdʒ] *vi* foraggiare.
forage cap *n* bustina.
foray ['fɔreɪ] *n* incursione *f.*
forbad(e) [fə'bæd] *pt of* **forbid.**
forbearing [fɔː'bɛərɪŋ] *adj* paziente,
tollerante.
forbid, *pt* **forbad(e)**, *pp* **forbidden** [fə'bɪd,
-'bæd, -'bɪdn] *vt* vietare, interdire; **to** ~ **sb
to do sth** proibire a qn di fare qc.
forbidding [fə'bɪdɪŋ] *adj* arcigno(a),
d'aspetto minaccioso.
force [fɔːs] *n* forza ♦ *vt* forzare; (*obtain by
~: smile, confession) strappare; **the F~s**
npl (*BRIT*) le forze armate; **in** ~ (*in large
numbers*) in gran numero; (*law*) in vigore;
to come into ~ entrare in vigore; **a** ~ **5
wind** un vento forza 5; **to join** ~**s** unire le
forze; **the sales** ~ (*COMM*) l'effettivo dei
rappresentanti; **to** ~ **sb to do sth**
costringere qn a fare qc.
►**force back** *vt* (*crowd, enemy*) respingere;
(*tears*) ingoiare.
►**force down** *vt* (*food*) sforzarsi di
mangiare.
forced [fɔːst] *adj* forzato(a).
force-feed ['fɔːsfiːd] *vt* sottoporre ad
alimentazione forzata.
forceful ['fɔːsful] *adj* forte, vigoroso(a).
forcemeat ['fɔːsmiːt] *n* (*BRIT CULIN*) ripieno.
forceps ['fɔːsɪps] *npl* forcipe *m.*

forcibly ['fɔːsəblɪ] *adv* con la forza;
(*vigorously*) vigorosamente.
ford [fɔːd] *n* guado ♦ *vt* guadare.
fore [fɔː*] *n*: **to the** ~ in prima linea; **to
come to the** ~ mettersi in evidenza.
forearm ['fɔːrɑːm] *n* avambraccio.
forebear ['fɔːbɛə*] *n* antenato.
foreboding [fɔː'bəudɪŋ] *n* presagio di male.
forecast ['fɔːkɑːst] *n* previsione *f*; (*weather
~*) previsioni *fpl* del tempo ♦ *vt* (*irreg*: *like
cast*) prevedere.
foreclose [fɔː'kləuz] *vt* (*LAW: also:* ~ **on**)
sequestrare l'immobile ipotecato di.
foreclosure [fɔː'kləuʒə*] *n* sequestro di
immobile ipotecato.
forecourt ['fɔːkɔːt] *n* (*of garage*) corte *f*
esterna.
forefathers ['fɔːfɑːðəz] *npl* antenati *mpl*, avi
mpl.
forefinger ['fɔːfɪŋgə*] *n* (dito) indice *m*.
forefront ['fɔːfrʌnt] *n*: **in the** ~ **of**
all'avanguardia di.
forego [fɔː'gəu] *vt* = **forgo**.
foregoing ['fɔːgəuɪŋ] *adj* precedente.
foregone ['fɔːgɒn] *pp of* **forego** ♦ *adj*: **it's a** ~
conclusion è una conclusione scontata.
foreground ['fɔːgraund] *n* primo piano
♦ *cpd* (*COMPUT*) foreground *inv*, di primo
piano.
forehand ['fɔːhænd] *n* (*TENNIS*) diritto.
forehead ['fɒrɪd] *n* fronte *f*.
foreign ['fɒrən] *adj* straniero(a); (*trade*)
estero(a).
foreign body *n* corpo estraneo.
foreign currency *n* valuta estera.
foreigner ['fɒrənə*] *n* straniero/a.
foreign exchange *n* cambio di valuta;
(*currency*) valuta estera.
foreign exchange market *n* mercato
delle valute.
foreign exchange rate *n* cambio.
foreign investment *n* investimento
all'estero.
foreign minister *n* ministro degli Affari
esteri.
Foreign Office (FO) *n* (*BRIT*) Ministero
degli Esteri.
foreign secretary *n* (*BRIT*) ministro degli
Affari esteri.
foreleg ['fɔːlɛg] *n* zampa anteriore.
foreman ['fɔːmən] *n* caposquadra *m*; (*LAW:
of jury*) portavoce *m* della giuria.
foremost ['fɔːməust] *adj* principale; più in
vista ♦ *adv*: **first and** ~ innanzitutto.
forename ['fɔːneɪm] *n* nome *m* di
battesimo.
forensic [fə'rɛnsɪk] *adj*: ~ **medicine**
medicina legale; ~ **expert** esperto della

(polizia) scientifica.
foreplay ['fɔːpleɪ] *n* preliminari *mpl*.
forerunner ['fɔːrʌnə*] *n* precursore *m*.
foresee, *pt* **foresaw**, *pp* **foreseen** [fɔː'siː,
-'sɔː, -'siːn] *vt* prevedere.
foreseeable [fɔː'siːəbl] *adj* prevedibile.
foreseen [fɔː'siːn] *pp of* **foresee**.
foreshadow [fɔː'ʃædəu] *vt* presagire, far
prevedere.
foreshorten [fɔː'ʃɔːtn] *vt* (*figure, scene*)
rappresentare in scorcio.
foresight ['fɔːsaɪt] *n* previdenza.
foreskin ['fɔːskɪn] *n* (*ANAT*) prepuzio.
forest ['fɒrɪst] *n* foresta.
forestall [fɔː'stɔːl] *vt* prevenire.
forestry ['fɒrɪstrɪ] *n* silvicoltura.
foretaste ['fɔːteɪst] *n* pregustazione *f*.
foretell, *pt*, *pp* **foretold** [fɔː'tɛl, -'təuld] *vt*
predire.
forethought ['fɔːθɔːt] *n* previdenza.
foretold [fɔː'təuld] *pt*, *pp of* **foretell**.
forever [fə'rɛvə*] *adv* per sempre; (*fig*)
sempre, di continuo.
forewarn [fɔː'wɔːn] *vt* avvisare in
precedenza.
forewent [fɔː'wɛnt] *pt of* **forego**.
foreword ['fɔːwəːd] *n* prefazione *f*.
forfeit ['fɔːfɪt] *n* ammenda, pena ♦ *vt*
perdere; (*one's happiness, health*) giocarsi.
forgave [fə'geɪv] *pt of* **forgive**.
forge [fɔːdʒ] *n* fucina ♦ *vt* falsificare;
(*signature*) contraffare, falsificare;
(*wrought iron*) fucinare, foggiare.
▶**forge ahead** *vi* tirare avanti.
forger ['fɔːdʒə*] *n* contraffattore *m*.
forgery ['fɔːdʒərɪ] *n* falso; (*activity*)
contraffazione *f*.
forget, *pt* **forgot**, *pp* **forgotten** [fə'gɛt, -'gɒt,
-'gɒtn] *vt*, *vi* dimenticare.
forgetful [fə'gɛtful] *adj* di corta memoria;
~ **of** dimentico(a) di.
forgetfulness [fə'gɛtfulnɪs] *n*
smemoratezza; (*oblivion*) oblio.
forget-me-not [fə'gɛtmɪnɒt] *n*
nontiscordardimé *m inv*.
forgive, *pt* **forgave**, *pp* **forgiven** [fə'gɪv,
-'geɪv, -'gɪvn] *vt* perdonare; **to** ~ **sb for
sth/for doing sth** perdonare qc a qn/a qn
di aver fatto qc.
forgiveness [fə'gɪvnɪs] *n* perdono.
forgiving [fə'gɪvɪŋ] *adj* indulgente.
forgo, *pt* **forwent**, *pp* **forgone** [fɔː'gəu,
-'wɛnt, -'gɒn] *vt* rinunciare a.
forgot [fə'gɒt] *pt of* **forget**.
forgotten [fə'gɒtn] *pp of* **forget**.
fork [fɔːk] *n* (*for eating*) forchetta; (*for
gardening*) forca; (*of roads*) bivio; (*of
railways*) inforcazione *f* ♦ *vi* (*road*)

biforcarsi.
►**fork out** (*col: pay*) *vt* sborsare ♦ *vi* pagare.
forked [fɔːkt] *adj* (*lightning*) a zigzag.
fork-lift truck [ˈfɔːklɪft-] *n* carrello
elevatore.
forlorn [fəˈlɔːn] *adj* (*person*) sconsolato(a);
(*deserted: cottage*) abbandonato(a);
(*desperate: attempt*) disperato(a).
form [fɔːm] *n* forma; (*SCOL*) classe *f*;
(*questionnaire*) modulo ♦ *vt* formare;
(*circle, queue etc*) fare; **in the ~ of** a forma
di, sotto forma di; **to be in good ~**
(*SPORT*, *fig*) essere in forma; **in top ~** in
gran forma; **to ~ part of sth** far parte di
qc.
formal [ˈfɔːməl] *adj* (*offer, receipt*) vero(a) e
proprio(a); (*person*) cerimonioso(a);
(*occasion, dinner*) formale, ufficiale; (*ART,
PHILOSOPHY*) formale; **~ dress** abito da
cerimonia; (*evening dress*) abito da sera.
formality [fɔːˈmælɪtɪ] *n* formalità *f inv*.
formalize [ˈfɔːməlaɪz] *vt* rendere ufficiale.
formally [ˈfɔːməlɪ] *adv* ufficialmente;
formalmente; cerimoniosamente; **to be ~
invited** ricevere un invito ufficiale.
format [ˈfɔːmæt] *n* formato ♦ *vt* (*COMPUT*)
formattare.
formation [fɔːˈmeɪʃən] *n* formazione *f*.
formative [ˈfɔːmətɪv] *adj*: **~ years** anni *mpl*
formativi.
former [ˈfɔːmə*] *adj* vecchio(a) (*before n*),
ex *inv* (*before n*); **the ~ president** l'ex
presidente; **the ~ ... the latter** quello ...
questo; **the ~ Yugoslavia/Soviet Union**
l'ex Jugoslavia/Unione Sovietica.
formerly [ˈfɔːməlɪ] *adv* in passato.
form feed *n* (*on printer*) alimentazione *f*
modulo.
formidable [ˈfɔːmɪdəbl] *adj* formidabile.
formula [ˈfɔːmjulə] *n* formula; **F~ One**
(*AUT*) formula uno.
formulate [ˈfɔːmjuleɪt] *vt* formulare.
fornicate [ˈfɔːnɪkeɪt] *vi* fornicare.
forsake, *pt* **forsook,** *pp* **forsaken** [fəˈseɪk,
-ˈsuk, -ˈseɪkən] *vt* abbandonare.
fort [fɔːt] *n* forte *m*; **to hold the ~** (*fig*)
prendere le redini (della situazione).
forte [ˈfɔːtɪ] *n* forte *m*.
forth [fɔːθ] *adv* in avanti; **to go back and ~**
andare avanti e indietro; **and so ~** e così
via.
forthcoming [fɔːθˈkʌmɪŋ] *adj* prossimo(a);
(*character*) aperto(a), comunicativo(a).
forthright [ˈfɔːθraɪt] *adj* franco(a),
schietto(a).
forthwith [fɔːθˈwɪθ] *adv* immediatamente,
subito.
fortieth [ˈfɔːtɪɪθ] *num* quarantesimo(a).

fortification [fɔːtɪfɪˈkeɪʃən] *n* fortificazione
f.
fortified wine *n* vino ad alta gradazione
alcolica.
fortify [ˈfɔːtɪfaɪ] *vt* fortificare.
fortitude [ˈfɔːtɪtjuːd] *n* forza d'animo.
fortnight [ˈfɔːtnaɪt] *n* (*BRIT*) quindici giorni
mpl, due settimane *fpl*; **it's a ~ since ...**
sono due settimane da quando ....
fortnightly [ˈfɔːtnaɪtlɪ] *adj* bimensile ♦ *adv*
ogni quindici giorni.
FORTRAN [ˈfɔːtræn] *n* FORTRAN *m*.
fortress [ˈfɔːtrɪs] *n* fortezza, rocca.
fortuitous [fɔːˈtjuːɪtəs] *adj* fortuito(a).
fortunate [ˈfɔːtʃənɪt] *adj* fortunato(a); **he is
~ to have ...** ha la fortuna di avere ...; **it
is ~ that** è una fortuna che + *sub*.
fortunately [ˈfɔːtʃənɪtlɪ] *adv*
fortunatamente.
fortune [ˈfɔːtʃən] *n* fortuna; **to make a ~**
farsi una fortuna.
fortuneteller [ˈfɔːtʃəntɛlə*] *n* indovino/a.
forty [ˈfɔːtɪ] *num* quaranta.
forum [ˈfɔːrəm] *n* foro; (*fig*) luogo di
pubblica discussione.
forward [ˈfɔːwəd] *adj* (*movement, position*)
in avanti; (*not shy*) sfacciato(a); (*COMM:
delivery, sales, exchange*) a termine ♦ *n*
(*SPORT*) avanti *m inv* ♦ *vt* (*letter*) inoltrare;
(*parcel, goods*) spedire; (*fig*) promuovere,
appoggiare; **to move ~** avanzare; **"please
~"** "si prega di inoltrare"; **~ planning**
programmazione *f* in anticipo.
forward(s) [ˈfɔːwəd(z)] *adv* avanti.
forwent [fɔːˈwɛnt] *pt of* **forgo**.
fossil [ˈfɔsl] *adj, n* fossile (*m*); **~ fuel**
combustibile *m* fossile.
foster [ˈfɔstə*] *vt* incoraggiare, nutrire;
(*child*) avere in affidamento.
foster brother *n* fratellastro.
foster child *n* bambino(a) preso(a) in
affidamento.
foster mother *n* madre *f* affidataria.
fought [fɔːt] *pt, pp of* **fight**.
foul [faul] *adj* (*smell, food*) cattivo(a);
(*weather*) brutto(a), orribile; (*language*)
osceno(a); (*deed*) infame ♦ *n* (*FOOTBALL*)
fallo ♦ *vt* sporcare; (*football player*)
commettere un fallo su; (*entangle: anchor,
propeller*) impigliarsi in.
foul play *n* (*SPORT*) gioco scorretto; **~ is
not suspected** si è scartata l'ipotesi del
delitto (*or* dell'attentato *etc*).
found [faund] *pt, pp of* **find** ♦ *vt* (*establish*)
fondare.
foundation [faunˈdeɪʃən] *n* (*act*) fondazione
f; (*base*) base *f*; (*also: ~ cream*) fondo
tinta; **~s** *npl* (*of building*) fondamenta *fpl*;

to lay the ~s gettare le fondamenta.
foundation stone n prima pietra.
founder ['faundə*] n fondatore/trice ♦ vi affondare.
founding ['faundɪŋ] adj: ~ **fathers** (US) padri mpl fondatori; ~ **member** socio fondatore.
foundry ['faundrɪ] n fonderia.
fount [faunt] n fonte f; (TYP) stile m di carattere.
fountain ['fauntɪn] n fontana.
fountain pen n penna stilografica.
four [fɔ:*] num quattro; **on all ~s** a carponi.
four-letter word ['fɔ:letə-] n parolaccia.
four-poster ['fɔ:'pəustə*] n (also: ~ **bed**) letto a quattro colonne.
foursome ['fɔ:səm] n partita a quattro; uscita in quattro.
fourteen ['fɔ:ti:n] num quattordici.
fourth [fɔ:θ] num quarto(a) ♦ n (AUT: also: ~ **gear**) quarta.
four-wheel drive ['fɔ:wi:l-] n (AUT): **with ~ ~** a quattro ruote motrici.
fowl [faul] n pollame m; volatile m.
fox [fɔks] n volpe f ♦ vt confondere.
fox fur n volpe f, pelliccia di volpe.
foxglove ['fɔksglʌv] n (BOT) digitale f.
fox-hunting ['fɔkshʌntɪŋ] n caccia alla volpe.
foyer ['fɔɪeɪ] n atrio; (THEAT) ridotto.
FP n abbr (BRIT) = former pupil; (US) = fireplug.
FPA n abbr (BRIT: = Family Planning Association) ≈ A.I.E.D. f (= Associazione Italiana Educazione Demografica).
Fr. abbr (REL) = father; friar.
fr. abbr (= franc) fr.
fracas ['fræka:] n rissa, lite f.
fraction ['frækʃən] n frazione f.
fractionally ['frækʃnəlɪ] adv un tantino, minimamente.
fractious ['frækʃəs] adj irritabile.
fracture ['fræktʃə*] n frattura ♦ vt fratturare.
fragile ['frædʒaɪl] adj fragile.
fragment ['frægmənt] n frammento.
fragmentary ['frægməntərɪ] adj frammentario(a).
fragrance ['freɪgrəns] n fragranza, profumo.
fragrant ['freɪgrənt] adj fragrante, profumato(a).
frail [freɪl] adj debole, delicato(a).
frame [freɪm] n (of building) armatura; (of human, animal) ossatura, corpo; (of picture) cornice f; (of door, window) telaio; (of spectacles: also: ~s) montatura ♦ vt (picture) incorniciare; **to ~ sb** (col)

incastrare qn; ~ **of mind** stato d'animo.
framework ['freɪmwɔ:k] n struttura.
France [frɑ:ns] n Francia.
franchise ['fræntʃaɪz] n (POL) diritto di voto; (COMM) concessione f.
franchisee [fræntʃaɪ'zi:] n concessionaria.
franchiser ['fræntʃaɪzə*] n concedente m.
frank [fræŋk] adj franco(a), aperto(a) ♦ vt (letter) affrancare.
Frankfurt ['fræŋkfə:t] n Francoforte f.
frankfurter ['fræŋkfə:tə*] n würstel m inv.
franking machine ['fræŋkɪŋ-] n macchina affrancatrice.
frankly ['fræŋklɪ] adv francamente, sinceramente.
frankness ['fræŋknɪs] n franchezza.
frantic ['fræntɪk] adj (activity, pace) frenetico(a); (desperate: need, desire) pazzo(a), sfrenato(a); (: search) affannoso(a); (person) fuori di sé.
frantically ['fræntɪklɪ] adv freneticamente, affannosamente.
fraternal [frə'tə:nl] adj fraterno(a).
fraternity [frə'tə:nɪtɪ] n (club) associazione f, (spirit) fratellanza.
fraternize ['frætənaɪz] vi fraternizzare.
fraud [frɔ:d] n truffa; (LAW) frode f; (person) impostore/a.
fraudulent ['frɔ:djulənt] adj fraudolento(a).
fraught [frɔ:t] adj (tense) teso(a); ~ **with** pieno(a) di, intriso(a) da.
fray [freɪ] n baruffa ♦ vt logorare ♦ vi logorarsi; **to return to the ~** tornare nella mischia; **tempers were getting ~ed** cominciavano ad innervosirsi; **her nerves were ~ed** aveva i nervi a pezzi.
FRB n abbr (US) = Federal Reserve Board.
FRCM n abbr (BRIT) = Fellow of the Royal College of Music.
FRCO n abbr (BRIT) = Fellow of the Royal College of Organists.
FRCP n abbr (BRIT) = Fellow of the Royal College of Physicians.
FRCS n abbr (BRIT) = Fellow of the Royal College of Surgeons.
freak [fri:k] n fenomeno, mostro; (col: enthusiast) fanatico/a ♦ adj (storm, conditions) anormale; (victory) inatteso(a).
▶**freak out** vi (col) andare fuori di testa.
freakish ['fri:kɪʃ] adj (result, appearance) strano(a), bizzarro(a); (weather) anormale.
freckle ['frekl] n lentiggine f.
free [fri:] adj libero(a); (gratis) gratuito(a); (liberal) generoso(a) ♦ vt (prisoner, jammed person) liberare; (jammed object) districare; ~ **(of charge)** gratuitamente; **admission ~** entrata libera; **to give sb a**

~ **hand** dare carta bianca a qn; ~ **and easy** rilassato.

freebie ['fri:bɪ] *n* (*col*): **it's a** ~ è in omaggio.

freedom ['fri:dəm] *n* libertà.

freedom fighter *n* combattente *m/f* per la libertà.

free enterprise *n* liberalismo economico.

Freefone ® ['fri:fəʊn] *n* (*BRIT*) ≈ numero verde.

free-for-all ['fri:fərɔ:l] *n* parapiglia *m* generale.

free gift *n* regalo, omaggio.

freehold ['fri:həʊld] *n* proprietà assoluta.

free kick *n* (*SPORT*) calcio libero.

freelance ['fri:lɑ:ns] *adj* indipendente; ~ **work** collaborazione *f* esterna.

freeloader ['fri:ləʊdə*] *n* (*pej*) scroccone/a.

freely ['fri:lɪ] *adv* liberamente; (*liberally*) liberalmente.

free-market economy [fri:'mɑ:kɪt-] *n* economia di libero mercato.

freemason ['fri:meɪsn] *n* massone *m*.

freemasonry ['fri:meɪsnrɪ] *n* massoneria.

freepost ['fri:pəʊst] *n* affrancatura a carica del destinatario.

free-range ['fri:'reɪndʒ] *adj* (*eggs*) di gallina ruspante.

free sample *n* campione *m* gratuito.

free speech *n* libertà di parola.

freestyle ['fri:staɪl] *n* (*in swimming*) stile *m* libero.

free trade *n* libero scambio.

freeway ['fri:weɪ] *n* (*US*) superstrada.

freewheel [fri:'wi:l] *vi* andare a ruota libera.

freewheeling [fri:'wi:lɪŋ] *adj* a ruota libera.

free will *n* libero arbitrio; **of one's own** ~ di spontanea volontà.

freeze [fri:z] *vb* (*pt* **froze**, *pp* **frozen** [frəʊz, 'frəʊzn]) *vi* gelare ♦ *vt* gelare; (*food*) congelare; (*prices, salaries*) bloccare ♦ *n* gelo; blocco.

▶**freeze over** *vi* (*lake, river*) ghiacciarsi; (*windows, windscreen*) coprirsi di ghiaccio.

▶**freeze up** *vi* gelarsi.

freeze-dried ['fri:zdraɪd] *adj* liofilizzato(a).

freezer ['fri:zə*] *n* congelatore *m*.

freezing ['fri:zɪŋ] *adj*: **I'm** ~ mi sto congelando ♦ *n* (*also*: ~ **point**) punto di congelamento; **3 degrees below** ~ 3 gradi sotto zero.

freight [freɪt] *n* (*goods*) merce *f*, merci *fpl*; (*money charged*) spese *fpl* di trasporto; ~ **forward** spese a carico del destinatario; ~ **inward** spese di trasporto sulla merce in entrata.

freight car *n* (*US*) carro *m* merci *inv*.

freighter ['freɪtə*] *n* (*NAUT*) nave *f* da carico.

freight forwarder [-'fɔ:wədə*] *n* spedizioniere *m*.

freight train *n* (*US*) treno *m* merci *inv*.

French [frɛntʃ] *adj* francese ♦ *n* (*LING*) francese *m*; **the** ~ *npl* i Francesi.

French bean *n* fagiolino.

French Canadian *adj*, *n* franco-canadese (*m/f*).

French dressing *n* (*CULIN*) condimento per insalata.

French fried potatoes, (*US*) **French fries** *npl* patate *fpl* fritte.

French Guiana [-gaɪ'ænə] *n* Guiana francese.

French loaf *n* ≈ filoncino.

Frenchman ['frɛntʃmən] *n* francese *m*.

French Riviera *n*: **the** ~ la Costa Azzurra.

French stick *n* baguette *f inv*.

French window *n* portafinestra.

Frenchwoman ['frɛntʃwumən] *n* francese *f*.

frenetic [frə'nɛtɪk] *adj* frenetico(a).

frenzy ['frɛnzɪ] *n* frenesia.

frequency ['fri:kwənsɪ] *n* frequenza.

frequency modulation (FM) *n* modulazione *f* di frequenza (F.M.).

frequent *adj* ['fri:kwənt] frequente ♦ *vt* [frɪ'kwɛnt] frequentare.

frequently ['fri:kwəntlɪ] *adv* frequentemente, spesso.

fresco ['frɛskəʊ] *n* affresco.

fresh [frɛʃ] *adj* fresco(a); (*new*) nuovo(a); (*cheeky*) sfacciato(a); **to make a** ~ **start** cominciare da capo.

freshen ['frɛʃən] *vi* (*wind, air*) rinfrescare.

▶**freshen up** *vi* rinfrescarsi.

freshener ['frɛʃnə*] *n*: **skin** ~ tonico rinfrescante; **air** ~ deodorante *m* per ambienti.

fresher ['frɛʃə*] *n* (*BRIT SCOL*: *col*) = **freshman**.

freshly ['frɛʃlɪ] *adv* di recente, di fresco.

freshman ['frɛʃmən] *n* (*SCOL*) matricola.

freshness ['frɛʃnɪs] *n* freschezza.

freshwater ['frɛʃwɔ:tə*] *adj* (*fish*) d'acqua dolce.

fret [frɛt] *vi* agitarsi, affliggersi.

fretful ['frɛtful] *adj* (*child*) irritabile.

Freudian ['frɔɪdɪən] *adj* freudiano(a); ~ **slip** lapsus *m inv* freudiano.

FRG *n abbr see* **Federal Republic of Germany**.

Fri. *abbr* (= *Friday*) ven.

friar ['fraɪə*] *n* frate *m*.

friction ['frɪkʃən] *n* frizione *f*, attrito.

friction feed *n* (*on printer*) trascinamento ad attrito.

Friday ['fraɪdɪ] n venerdì m inv; for phrases see also **Tuesday**.
fridge [frɪdʒ] n (BRIT) frigo, frigorifero.
fridge-freezer ['frɪdʒ'friːzə*] n freezer m inv.
fried [fraɪd] pt, pp of **fry ♦** adj fritto(a); ~ **egg** uovo fritto.
friend [frɛnd] n amico/a; **to make ~s with** fare amicizia con.
friendliness ['frɛndlɪnɪs] n amichevolezza.
friendly ['frɛndlɪ] adj amichevole ♦ n (also: ~ **match**) partita amichevole; **to be ~ with** essere amico di; **to be ~ to** essere cordiale con.
friendly fire n fuoco amico.
friendship ['frɛndʃɪp] n amicizia.
frieze [friːz] n fregio.
frigate ['frɪgɪt] n (NAUT: modern) fregata.
fright [fraɪt] n paura, spavento; **to take ~** spaventarsi; **she looks a ~!** guarda com'è conciata!
frighten ['fraɪtn] vt spaventare, far paura a.
▶**frighten away, frighten off** vt (birds, children etc) scacciare (facendogli paura).
frightened ['fraɪtnd] adj; **to be ~ (of)** avere paura (di).
frightening ['fraɪtnɪŋ] adj spaventoso(a), pauroso(a).
frightful ['fraɪtful] adj orribile.
frightfully ['fraɪtfulɪ] adv terribilmente; **I'm ~ sorry** mi dispiace moltissimo.
frigid ['frɪdʒɪd] adj (woman) frigido(a).
frigidity [frɪ'dʒɪdɪtɪ] n frigidità.
frill [frɪl] n balza; **without ~s** (fig) senza fronzoli.
frilly ['frɪlɪ] adj (clothes, lampshade) pieno(a) di fronzoli.
fringe [frɪndʒ] n frangia; (edge: of forest etc) margine m; (fig): **on the ~** al margine.
fringe benefits npl vantaggi mpl.
fringe theatre n teatro d'avanguardia.
Frisbee ® ['frɪzbɪ] n frisbee ® m inv.
frisk [frɪsk] vt perquisire.
frisky ['frɪskɪ] adj vivace, vispo(a).
fritter ['frɪtə*] n frittella.
▶**fritter away** vt sprecare.
frivolity [frɪ'vɔlɪtɪ] n frivolezza.
frivolous ['frɪvələs] adj frivolo(a).
frizzy ['frɪzɪ] adj crespo(a).
fro [frəʊ] adv: **to and ~** avanti e indietro.
frock [frɔk] n vestito.
frog [frɔg] n rana; **to have a ~ in one's throat** avere la voce rauca.
frogman ['frɔgmən] n uomo m rana inv.
frogmarch ['frɔgmɑːtʃ] vt (BRIT): **to ~ sb in/out** portar qn dentro/fuori con la forza.

frolic ['frɔlɪk] vi sgambettare.

═══════════════ KEYWORD

from [frɔm] prep **1** (indicating starting place, origin etc) da; **where do you come ~?, where are you ~?** da dove viene?, di dov'è?; **where has he come ~?** da dove arriva?; ~ **London to Glasgow** da Londra a Glasgow; **a letter ~ my sister** una lettera da mia sorella; **tell him ~ me that …** gli dica da parte mia che …
2 (indicating time) da; ~ **one o'clock to** or **until** or **till two** dall'una alle due; **(as) ~ Friday** a partire da venerdì; ~ **January (on)** da gennaio, a partire da gennaio
3 (indicating distance) da; **the hotel is 1 km ~ the beach** l'albergo è a 1 km dalla spiaggia
4 (indicating price, number etc) da; ~ **a pound** da una sterlina in su; **prices range ~ £10 to £50** i prezzi vanno dalle 10 alle 50 sterline
5 (indicating difference) da; **he can't tell red ~ green** non sa distinguere il rosso dal verde
6 (because of, on the basis of): ~ **what he says** da quanto dice lui; **weak ~ hunger** debole per la fame.

frond [frɔnd] n fronda.
front [frʌnt] n (of house, dress) davanti m inv; (of train) testa; (of book) copertina; (promenade: also: sea ~) lungomare m; (MIL, POL, METEOR) fronte m; (fig: appearances) fronte f ♦ adj primo(a); anteriore, davanti inv ♦ vi: **to ~ onto sth** dare su qc, guardare verso qc; **in ~ (of)** davanti (a).
frontage ['frʌntɪdʒ] n facciata.
frontal ['frʌntl] adj frontale.
front bench n posti in Parlamento occupati dai frontbencher; see boxed note.

FRONT BENCH

Nel Parlamento britannico, si chiamano **front bench** gli scanni della "House of Commons" che si trovano alla sinistra e alla destra dello "Speaker" davanti ai "back benches". I **front bench** sono occupati dai "frontbencher", parlamentari che ricoprono una carica di governo o che fanno parte dello "shadow cabinet" dell'opposizione.

---

frontbencher ['frʌnt'bɛntʃə*] n (BRIT) parlamentare con carica al governo o all'opposizione.
front desk n (US: in hotel) reception f inv; (:

at doctor's) accettazione *f*.

front door *n* porta d'entrata; (*of car*) sportello anteriore.

frontier ['frʌntɪə*] *n* frontiera.

frontispiece ['frʌntɪspiːs] *n* frontespizio.

front page *n* prima pagina.

front room *n* (*BRIT*) salotto.

front runner *n* (*fig*) favorito/a.

front-wheel drive ['frʌntwiːl-] *n* trasmissione *f* anteriore.

frost [frɔst] *n* gelo; (*also:* **hoar~**) brina.

frostbite ['frɔstbaɪt] *n* congelamento.

frosted ['frɔstɪd] *adj* (*glass*) smerigliato(a); (*US: cake*) glassato(a).

frosting ['frɔstɪŋ] *n* (*US: on cake*) glassa.

frosty ['frɔstɪ] *adj* (*window*) coperto(a) di ghiaccio; (*welcome*) gelido(a).

froth ['frɔθ] *n* spuma; schiuma.

frown [fraun] *n* cipiglio ♦ *vi* accigliarsi.

▶**frown on** *vt fus* (*fig*) disapprovare.

froze [frəuz] *pt of* **freeze**.

frozen ['frəuzn] *pp of* **freeze** ♦ *adj* (*food*) congelato(a); (*COMM: assets*) bloccato(a).

FRS *n abbr* (*BRIT*) = *Fellow of the Royal Society*; (*US:* = *Federal Reserve System*) *sistema bancario degli Stati Uniti*.

frugal ['fruːgəl] *adj* frugale; (*person*) economo(a).

fruit [fruːt] *n* (*pl inv*) frutto; (*collectively*) frutta.

fruiterer ['fruːtərə*] *n* fruttivendolo; **at the ~'s (shop)** dal fruttivendolo.

fruit fly *n* mosca della frutta.

fruitful ['fruːtful] *adj* fruttuoso(a); (*plant*) fruttifero(a); (*soil*) fertile.

fruition [fruː'ɪʃən] *n*: **to come to ~** realizzarsi.

fruit juice *n* succo di frutta.

fruitless ['fruːtlɪs] *adj* (*fig*) vano(a), inutile.

fruit machine *n* (*BRIT*) macchina *f* mangiasoldi *inv*.

fruit salad *n* macedonia.

frump [frʌmp] *n*: **to feel a ~** sentirsi infagottato(a).

frustrate [frʌs'treɪt] *vt* frustrare.

frustrated [frʌs'treɪtɪd] *adj* frustrato(a).

frustrating [frʌs'treɪtɪŋ] *adj* (*job*) frustrante; (*day*) disastroso(a).

frustration [frʌs'treɪʃən] *n* frustrazione *f*.

fry, *pt, pp* **fried** [fraɪ, -d] *vt* friggere ♦ *npl*: **the small ~** i pesci piccoli.

frying pan ['fraɪŋ-] *n* padella.

FT *n abbr* (*BRIT*: = *Financial Times*) giornale finanziario; **the ~ index** l'indice FT.

ft. *abbr* = **foot**, **feet**.

FTC *n abbr* (*US*) *see* **Federal Trade Commission**.

FT-SE 100 Index *n abbr* = *Financial Times Stock Exchange 100 Index*.

fuchsia ['fjuːʃə] *n* fucsia.

fuck [fʌk] *vt*, *vi* (*col!*) fottere (*!*); ~ **off!** vaffanculo! (*!*).

fuddled ['fʌdld] *adj* (*muddled*) confuso(a); (*col: tipsy*) brillo(a).

fuddy-duddy ['fʌdɪdʌdɪ] *n* (*pej*) parruccone *m*.

fudge [fʌdʒ] *n* (*CULIN*) specie di caramella a base di latte, burro e zucchero ♦ *vt* (*issue, problem*) evitare.

fuel [fjuəl] *n* (*for heating*) combustibile *m*; (*for propelling*) carburante *m* ♦ *vt* (*furnace etc*) alimentare; (*aircraft, ship etc*) rifornire di carburante.

fuel oil *n* nafta.

fuel pump *n* (*AUT*) pompa del carburante.

fuel tank *n* deposito *m* nafta *inv*; (*on vehicle*) serbatoio (della benzina).

fug [fʌg] *n* (*BRIT*) aria viziata.

fugitive ['fjuːdʒɪtɪv] *n* fuggitivo/a, profugo/a; (*from prison*) evaso/a.

fulfil, (*US*) **fulfill** [ful'fɪl] *vt* (*function*) compiere; (*order*) eseguire; (*wish, desire*) soddisfare, appagare.

fulfilled [ful'fɪld] *adj* (*person*) realizzato(a), soddisfatto(a).

fulfil(l)ment [ful'fɪlmənt] *n* (*of wishes*) soddisfazione *f*, appagamento.

full [ful] *adj* pieno(a); (*details, skirt*) ampio(a); (*price*) intero(a) ♦ *adv*: **to know ~ well that** sapere benissimo che; ~ (**up**) (*hotel etc*) al completo; **I'm ~ (up)** sono pieno; **a ~ two hours** due ore intere; **at ~ speed** a tutta velocità; **in ~** per intero; **to pay in ~** pagare tutto; ~ **name** nome *m* e cognome *m*; ~ **employment** piena occupazione; ~ **fare** tariffa completa.

fullback ['fulbæk] *n* (*RUGBY, FOOTBALL*) terzino.

full-blooded ['ful'blʌdɪd] *adj* (*vigorous: attack*) energico(a); (*virile: male*) virile.

full-cream ['ful'kriːm] *adj*: ~ **milk** (*BRIT*) latte *m* intero.

full-grown ['ful'grəun] *adj* maturo(a).

full-length ['ful'leŋθ] *adj* (*portrait*) in piedi; (*film*) a lungometraggio.

full moon *n* luna piena.

full-scale ['fulskeɪl] *adj* (*plan, model*) in grandezza naturale; (*search, retreat*) su vasta scala.

full-sized ['ful'saɪzd] *adj* (*portrait etc*) a grandezza naturale.

full stop *n* punto.

full-time ['ful'taɪm] *adj*, *adv* (*work*) a tempo pieno ♦ *n* (*SPORT*) fine *f* partita.

fully ['fulɪ] *adv* interamente, pienamente, completamente; (*at least*): ~ **as big**

almeno così grosso.

fully-fledged ['fulɪ'fledʒd] *adj* (*bird*) adulto(a); (*fig*: *teacher, member etc*) a tutti gli effetti.

fulsome ['fulsəm] *adj* (*pej*: *praise*) esagerato(a), eccessivo(a); (: *manner*) insincero.

fumble ['fʌmbl] *vi* brancolare, andare a tentoni ♦ *vt* (*ball*) lasciarsi sfuggire.

▶**fumble with** *vt fus* trafficare.

fume [fju:m] *vi* essere furioso(a); ~**s** *npl* esalazioni *fpl*, vapori *mpl*.

fumigate ['fju:mɪgeɪt] *vt* suffumicare.

fun [fʌn] *n* divertimento, spasso; **to have** ~ divertirsi; **for** ~ per scherzo; **it's not much** ~ non è molto divertente; **to make** ~ **of** prendersi gioco di.

function ['fʌŋkʃən] *n* funzione *f*; cerimonia, ricevimento ♦ *vi* funzionare; **to** ~ **as** fungere da, funzionare da.

functional ['fʌŋkʃənl] *adj* funzionale.

function key *n* (*COMPUT*) tasto di funzioni.

fund [fʌnd] *n* fondo, cassa; (*source*) fondo; (*store*) riserva; ~**s** *npl* (*money*) fondi *mpl*.

fundamental [fʌndə'mentl] *adj* fondamentale; ~**s** *npl* basi *fpl*.

fundamentalism [fʌndə'mentəlɪzəm] *n* fondamentalismo.

fundamentalist [fʌndə'mentəlɪst] *n* fondamentalista *m/f*.

fundamentally [fʌndə'mentəlɪ] *adv* essenzialmente, fondamentalmente.

funding ['fʌndɪŋ] *n* finanziamento.

fund-raising ['fʌndreɪzɪŋ] *n* raccolta di fondi.

funeral ['fju:nərəl] *n* funerale *m*.

funeral director *n* impresario di pompe funebri.

funeral parlour *n* impresa di pompe funebri.

funeral service *n* ufficio funebre.

funereal [fju:'nɪərɪəl] *adj* funereo(a), lugubre.

fun fair *n* luna park *m inv*.

fungus, *pl* **fungi** ['fʌŋgəs, -gaɪ] *n* fungo; (*mould*) muffa.

funicular [fju:'nɪkjulə*] *adj* (*also*: ~ **railway**) funicolare *f*.

funky ['fʌŋkɪ] *adj* (*music*) funky *inv*; (*col*: *excellent*) figo(a).

funnel ['fʌnl] *n* imbuto; (*of ship*) ciminiera.

funnily ['fʌnɪlɪ] *adv* in modo divertente; (*oddly*) stranamente.

funny ['fʌnɪ] *adj* divertente, buffo(a); (*strange*) strano(a), bizzarro(a).

funny bone *n* osso cubitale.

fun run *n* marcia non competitiva.

fur [fə:*] *n* pelo; pelliccia; pelle *f*; (*BRIT*: *in*

kettle etc) deposito calcare.

fur coat *n* pelliccia.

furious ['fjuərɪəs] *adj* furioso(a); (*effort*) accanito(a); (*argument*) violento(a).

furiously ['fjuərɪəslɪ] *adv* furiosamente; accanitamente.

furl [fə:l] *vt* (*sail*) piegare.

furlong ['fə:lɒŋ] *n* = 201.17 *m* (*termine ippico*).

furlough ['fə:ləu] *n* (*US*) congedo, permesso.

furnace ['fə:nɪs] *n* fornace *f*.

furnish ['fə:nɪʃ] *vt* ammobiliare; (*supply*) fornire; ~**ed flat** *or* (*US*) **apartment** appartamento ammobiliato.

furnishings ['fə:nɪʃɪŋz] *npl* mobili *mpl*, mobilia.

furniture ['fə:nɪtʃə*] *n* mobili *mpl*; **piece of** ~ mobile *m*.

furore [fjuə'rɔ:rɪ] *n* (*protests*) scalpore *m*; (*enthusiasm*) entusiasmo.

furrier [ˈfʌrɪə*] *n* pellicciaio/a.

furrow ['fʌrəu] *n* solco ♦ *vt* (*forehead*) segnare di rughe.

furry ['fə:rɪ] *adj* (*animal*) peloso(a); (*toy*) di peluche.

further ['fə:ðə*] *adj* supplementare, altro(a); nuovo(a); più lontano(a) ♦ *adv* più lontano; (*more*) di più; (*moreover*) inoltre ♦ *vt* favorire, promuovere; **until** ~ **notice** fino a nuovo avviso; **how much** ~ **is it?** quanto manca or dista?; ~ **to your letter of** ... (*COMM*) con riferimento alla vostra lettera del ...; **to** ~ **one's interests** fare i propri interessi.

further education *n* ≈ corsi *mpl* di formazione.

furthermore [fə:ðə'mɔ:*] *adv* inoltre, per di più.

furthermost ['fə:ðəməust] *adj* più lontano(a).

furthest ['fə:ðɪst] *superlative of* **far**.

furtive ['fə:tɪv] *adj* furtivo(a).

fury ['fjuərɪ] *n* furore *m*.

fuse, (*US*) **fuze** [fju:z] *n* fusibile *m*; (*for bomb etc*) miccia, spoletta ♦ *vt* fondere; (*ELEC*): **to** ~ **the lights** far saltare i fusibili ♦ *vi* fondersi; **a** ~ **has blown** è saltato un fusibile.

fuse box *n* cassetta dei fusibili.

fuselage ['fju:zəla:ʒ] *n* fusoliera.

fuse wire *n* filo (di fusibile).

fusillade [fju:zɪ'leɪd] *n* scarica di fucileria; (*fig*) fuoco di fila, serie *f inv* incalzante.

fusion ['fju:ʒən] *n* fusione *f*.

fuss [fʌs] *n* chiasso, trambusto, confusione *f*; (*complaining*) storie *fpl* ♦ *vt* (*person*) infastidire, scocciare ♦ *vi* agitarsi; **to**

make a ~ fare delle storie; **to make a ~ of sb** coprire qn di attenzioni.

▶**fuss over** *vt fus* (*person*) circondare di premure.

fusspot ['fʌspɔt] *n* (*col*): **he's such a ~** fa sempre tante storie.

fussy ['fʌsɪ] *adj* (*person*) puntiglioso(a), esigente; che fa le storie; (*dress*) carico(a) di fronzoli; (*style*) elaborato(a); **I'm not ~** (*col*) per me è lo stesso.

fusty ['fʌstɪ] *adj* (*pej: archaic*) stantio(a); (: *smell*) che sa di stantio.

futile ['fjuːtaɪl] *adj* futile.

futility [fjuː'tɪlɪtɪ] *n* futilità.

futon ['fuːtɔn] *n* futon *m inv*, letto giapponese.

future ['fjuːtʃə*] *adj* futuro(a) ♦ *n* futuro, avvenire *m*; (*LING*) futuro; **in ~** in futuro; **in the near ~** in un prossimo futuro; **in the immediate ~** nell'immediato futuro.

futures ['fjuːtʃəz] *npl* (*COMM*) operazioni *fpl* a termine.

futuristic [fjuːtʃə'rɪstɪk] *adj* futuristico(a).

fuze [fjuːz] *n*, *vt*, *vi* (*US*) = **fuse**.

fuzzy ['fʌzɪ] *adj* (*PHOT*) indistinto(a), sfocato(a); (*hair*) crespo(a).

fwd. *abbr* = **forward**.

fwy *abbr* (*US*) = **freeway**.

FY *abbr* = **fiscal year.**

FYI *abbr* = **for your information.**

Gg

G, g [dʒiː] *n* (*letter*) G, g *f or m inv*; (*MUS*): **G** sol *m*; **G for George** ≈ G come Genova.

G *n abbr* (*BRIT SCOL: mark:* = *good*) ≈ buono; (*US CINE:* = *general audience*) per tutti.

g *abbr* (= *gram; gravity*) g.

G7 *n abbr* (*POL:* = *Group of Seven*) G7 *mpl*.

GA *abbr* (*US POST*) = *Georgia.*

gab [gæb] *n* (*col*): **to have the gift of the ~** avere parlantina.

gabble ['gæbl] *vi* borbottare; farfugliare.

gaberdine [gæbə'diːn] *n* gabardine *m inv*.

gable ['geɪbl] *n* frontone *m*.

Gabon [gə'bɔn] *n* Gabon *m*.

gad about [gæd-] *vi* (*col*) svolazzare (qua e là).

gadget ['gædʒɪt] *n* aggeggio.

Gaelic ['geɪlɪk] *adj* gaelico(a) ♦ *n* (*language*) gaelico.

gaffe [gæf] *n* gaffe *f inv*.

gaffer ['gæfə*] *n* (*BRIT col*) capo.

gag [gæg] *n* bavaglio; (*joke*) facezia, scherzo ♦ *vt* (*prisoner etc*) imbavagliare ♦ *vi* (*choke*) soffocare.

gaga ['gɑːgɑː] *adj*: **to go ~** rimbambirsi.

gage [geɪdʒ] *n*, *vt* (*US*) = **gauge.**

gaiety ['geɪɪtɪ] *n* gaiezza.

gaily ['geɪlɪ] *adv* allegramente.

gain [geɪn] *n* guadagno, profitto ♦ *vt* guadagnare ♦ *vi* (*watch*) andare avanti; **~ in/by** aumentare di/con; **to ~ 3lbs (in weight)** aumentare di 3 libbre; **to ~ ground** guadagnare terreno.

▶**gain (up)on** *vt fus* accorciare le distanze da, riprendere.

gainful ['geɪnful] *adj* profittevole, lucrativo(a).

gainfully ['geɪnfəlɪ] *adv*: **to be ~ employed** avere un lavoro retribuito.

gainsay [geɪn'seɪ] *vt irreg* (*like* **say**) contraddire; negare.

gait [geɪt] *n* andatura.

gal. *abbr* = **gallon.**

gala ['gɑːlə] *n* gala; **swimming ~** manifestazione *f* di nuoto.

Galapagos Islands [gə'læpəgəs-] *npl*: **the ~** le isole Galapagos.

galaxy ['gæləksɪ] *n* galassia.

gale [geɪl] *n* vento forte; burrasca; **~ force 10** vento forza 10.

gall [gɔːl] *n* (*ANAT*) bile *f*; (*fig: impudence*) fegato, faccia ♦ *vt* urtare (i nervi a).

gall. *abbr* = **gallon.**

gallant ['gælənt] *adj* valoroso(a); (*towards ladies*) galante, cortese.

gallantry ['gæləntrɪ] *n* valore *m* militare; galanteria, cortesia.

gall bladder ['gɔːl-] *n* cistifellea.

galleon ['gælɪən] *n* galeone *m*.

gallery ['gælərɪ] *n* galleria; loggia; (*for spectators*) tribuna; (*in theatre*) loggione *m*, balconata; (*also:* **art ~**: *state-owned*) museo; (: *private*) galleria.

galley ['gælɪ] *n* (*ship's kitchen*) cambusa; (*ship*) galea; (*also:* **~ proof**) bozza in colonna.

Gallic ['gælɪk] *adj* gallico(a); (*French*) francese.

galling ['gɔːlɪŋ] *adj* irritante.

gallon ['gælən] *n* gallone *m* (*BRIT:* = *4.543 l; 8 pints; US* = *3.785 l*).

gallop ['gæləp] *n* galoppo ♦ *vi* galoppare; **~ing inflation** inflazione *f* galoppante.

gallows ['gæləuz] *n* forca.

gallstone ['gɔːlstəun] *n* calcolo biliare.

Gallup Poll ['gæləp-] *n* sondaggio a campione.

galore [gə'lɔ:*] *adv* a iosa, a profusione.
galvanize ['gælvənaɪz] *vt* galvanizzare; **to
~ sb into action** (*fig*) galvanizzare qn,
spronare qn all'azione.
Gambia ['gæmbɪə] *n* Gambia *m*.
gambit ['gæmbɪt] *n* (*fig*): (**opening**) ~ prima
mossa.
gamble ['gæmbl] *n* azzardo, rischio
calcolato ♦ *vt, vi* giocare; **to ~ on** (*fig*)
giocare su; **to ~ on the Stock Exchange**
giocare in Borsa.
gambler ['gæmblə*] *n* giocatore/trice
d'azzardo.
gambling ['gæmblɪŋ] *n* gioco d'azzardo.
gambol ['gæmbəl] *vi* saltellare.
game [geɪm] *n* gioco; (*event*) partita;
(*HUNTING*) selvaggina ♦ *adj* coraggioso(a);
(*ready*): **to be ~ (for sth/to do)** essere
pronto(a) (a qc/a fare); **~s** *npl* (*SCOL*)
attività *fpl* sportive; **big ~** selvaggina
grossa.
game bird *n* uccello selvatico.
gamekeeper ['geɪmki:pə*] *n* guardacaccia
m inv.
gamely ['geɪmlɪ] *adv* coraggiosamente.
game reserve *n* riserva di caccia.
games console *n* console *f inv* dei
videogame.
gameshow ['geɪmʃəu] *n* gioco a premi.
gamesmanship ['geɪmzmənʃɪp] *n* abilità.
gaming ['geɪmɪŋ] *n* gioco d'azzardo.
gammon ['gæmən] *n* (*bacon*) quarto di
maiale; (*ham*) prosciutto affumicato.
gamut ['gæmət] *n* gamma.
gang [gæŋ] *n* banda, squadra ♦ *vi*: **to ~ up
on sb** far combutta contro qn.
Ganges ['gændʒi:z] *n*: **the ~** il Gange.
gangland ['gæŋlænd] *adj* della malavita; **~
killer** sicario.
gangling ['gæŋglɪŋ] *adj* allampanato(a).
gangly ['gæŋglɪ] *adj* = **gangling**.
gangplank ['gæŋplæŋk] *n* passerella.
gangrene ['gæŋgri:n] *n* cancrena.
gangster ['gæŋstə*] *n* gangster *m inv*.
gangway ['gæŋweɪ] *n* passerella; (*BRIT: of
bus*) passaggio.
gantry ['gæntrɪ] *n* (*for crane, railway signal*)
cavalletto; (*for rocket*) torre *f* di lancio.
GAO *n abbr* (*US*: = *General Accounting Office*)
≈ Corte *f* dei Conti.
gaol [dʒeɪl] *n, vt* (*BRIT*) = **jail**.
gap [gæp] *n* buco; (*in time*) intervallo; (*fig*)
lacuna; vuoto.
gape [geɪp] *vi* restare a bocca aperta.
gaping ['geɪpɪŋ] *adj* (*hole*) squarciato(a).
garage ['gærɑ:ʒ] *n* garage *m inv*.
garb [gɑ:b] *n* abiti *mpl*, veste *f*.
garbage ['gɑ:bɪdʒ] *n* immondizie *fpl*, rifiuti

mpl; (*fig: film, book*) porcheria, robaccia; (:
nonsense) fesserie *fpl*.
garbage can *n* (*US*) bidone *m* della
spazzatura.
garbage collector *n* (*US*) spazzino/a.
garbage disposal unit *n* tritarifiuti *m inv*.
garbage truck *n* (*US*) camion *m inv* della
spazzatura.
garbled ['gɑ:bld] *adj* deformato(a);
ingarbugliato(a).
garden ['gɑ:dn] *n* giardino ♦ *vi* lavorare nel
giardino; **~s** *npl* (*public*) giardini pubblici;
(*private*) parco.
garden centre *n* vivaio.
garden city *n* (*BRIT*) città *f inv* giardino *inv*.
gardener ['gɑ:dnə*] *n* giardiniere/a.
gardening ['gɑ:dnɪŋ] *n* giardinaggio.
gargle ['gɑ:gl] *vi* fare gargarismi ♦ *n*
gargarismo.
gargoyle ['gɑ:gɔɪl] *n* gargouille *f inv*.
garish ['gɛərɪʃ] *adj* vistoso(a).
garland ['gɑ:lənd] *n* ghirlanda; corona.
garlic ['gɑ:lɪk] *n* aglio.
garment ['gɑ:mənt] *n* indumento.
garner ['gɑ:nə*] *vt* ammucchiare,
raccogliere.
garnish ['gɑ:nɪʃ] *vt* guarnire.
garret ['gærɪt] *n* soffitta.
garrison ['gærɪsn] *n* guarnigione *f* ♦ *vt*
guarnire.
garrulous ['gærjuləs] *adj* ciarliero(a),
loquace.
garter ['gɑ:tə*] *n* giarrettiera; (*US:
suspender*) gancio (di reggicalze).
garter belt *n* (*US*) reggicalze *m inv*.
gas [gæs] *n* gas *m inv*; (*used as anaesthetic*)
etere *m*; (*US: gasoline*) benzina ♦ *vt*
asfissiare con il gas; (*MIL*) gasare.
gas cooker *n* (*BRIT*) cucina a gas.
gas cylinder *n* bombola del gas.
gaseous ['gæsɪəs] *adj* gassoso(a).
gas fire *n* (*BRIT*) radiatore *m* a gas.
gas-fired ['gæsfaɪəd] *adj* (alimentato(a)) a
gas.
gash [gæʃ] *n* sfregio ♦ *vt* sfregiare.
gasket ['gæskɪt] *n* (*AUT*) guarnizione *f*.
gas mask *n* maschera *f* antigas *inv*.
gas meter *n* contatore *m* del gas.
gasoline ['gæsəli:n] *n* (*US*) benzina.
gasp [gɑ:sp] *vi* ansare, boccheggiare; (*in
surprise*) restare senza fiato.
▶**gasp out** *vt* dire affannosamente.
gas ring *n* fornello a gas.
gas station *n* (*US*) distributore *m* di
benzina.
gas stove *n* cucina a gas.
gassy ['gæsɪ] *adj* gassoso(a).
gas tank *n* (*US AUT*) serbatoio (di benzina).

gas tap n (*on cooker*) manopola del gas; (*on pipe*) rubinetto del gas.
gastric ['gæstrɪk] *adj* gastrico(a).
gastric ulcer n ulcera gastrica.
gastroenteritis ['gæstrəuɛntə'raɪtɪs] n gastroenterite f.
gastronomy [gæs'trɒnəmɪ] n gastronomia.
gasworks ['gæswəːks] n or npl impianto di produzione del gas.
gate [geɪt] n cancello; (*of castle, town*) porta; (*at airport*) uscita; (*at level crossing*) barriera.
gâteau, pl ~**x** ['gætəu, -z] n torta.
gatecrash ['geɪtkræʃ] vt partecipare senza invito a.
gatecrasher ['geɪtkræʃə*] n intruso(a), ospite m/f non invitato(a).
gatehouse ['geɪthaus] n casetta del custode (*all'entrata di un parco*).
gateway ['geɪtweɪ] n porta.
gather ['gæðə*] vt (*flowers, fruit*) cogliere; (*pick up*) raccogliere; (*assemble*) radunare; raccogliere; (*understand*) capire ♦ vi (*assemble*) radunarsi; (*dust*) accumularsi; (*clouds*) addensarsi; **to ~ speed** acquistare velocità; **to ~ (from/ that)** comprendere (da/che), dedurre (da/che); **as far as I can ~** da quel che ho potuto capire.
gathering ['gæðərɪŋ] n adunanza.
GATT [gæt] n abbr (= General Agreement on Tariffs and Trade) G.A.T.T. m.
gauche [gəuʃ] adj goffo(a), maldestro(a).
gaudy ['gɔːdɪ] adj vistoso(a).
gauge [geɪdʒ] n (*standard measure*) calibro; (*RAIL*) scartamento; (*instrument*) indicatore m ♦ vt misurare; (*fig: sb's capabilities, character*) valutare, stimare; **to ~ the right moment** calcolare il momento giusto; **petrol ~,** (*US*) **gas ~** indicatore m or spia della benzina.
gaunt [gɔːnt] adj scarno(a); (*grim, desolate*) desolato(a).
gauntlet ['gɔːntlɪt] n (*fig*): **to run the ~ through an angry crowd** passare sotto il fuoco di una folla ostile; **to throw down the ~** gettare il guanto.
gauze [gɔːz] n garza.
gave [geɪv] pt of **give**.
gawky ['gɔːkɪ] adj goffo(a), sgraziato(a).
gawp [gɔːp] vi: **to ~ at** guardare a bocca aperta.
gay [geɪ] adj (*person*) gaio(a), allegro(a); (*colour*) vivace, vivo(a); (*col*) omosessuale.
gaze [geɪz] n sguardo fisso ♦ vi: **to ~ at** guardare fisso.
gazelle [gə'zɛl] n gazzella.

gazette [gə'zɛt] n (*newspaper*) gazzetta; (*official publication*) gazzetta ufficiale.
gazetteer [gæzə'tɪə*] n (*book*) dizionario dei nomi geografici; (*section of book*) indice m dei nomi geografici.
gazump [gə'zʌmp] vt (*BRIT*): **to ~ sb** *nella compravendita di immobili, venire meno all'impegno preso con un acquirente accettando un'offerta migliore fatta da altri.*
GB abbr (= Great Britain) GB.
GBH n abbr (*BRIT LAW: col*) see **grievous bodily harm**.
GC n abbr (*BRIT*: = George Gross) decorazione al valore.
GCE n abbr (*BRIT*: = General Certificate of Education) ≈ diploma m di maturità.
GCHQ n abbr (*BRIT*: = Government Communications Headquarters*) centro per l'intercettazione delle telecomunicazioni straniere.
GCSE n abbr (*BRIT*: = General Certificate of Secondary Education) diploma di istruzione secondaria conseguito a 16 anni in Inghilterra e Galles.
Gdns. abbr = gardens.
GDP n abbr = gross domestic product.
GDR n abbr see **German Democratic Republic**.
gear [gɪə*] n attrezzi mpl, equipaggiamento; (*belongings*) roba; (*TECH*) ingranaggio; (*AUT*) marcia ♦ vt (*fig: adapt*) adattare; **top** or (*US*) **high/low/ bottom ~** quarta (or quinta)/ seconda/ prima; **in ~** in marcia; **out of ~** in folle; **our service is ~ed to meet the needs of the disabled** la nostra organizzazione risponde espressamente alle esigenze degli handicappati.
▶**gear up** vi: **to ~ up (to do)** prepararsi (a fare).
gear box n scatola del cambio.
gear lever, (*US*) **gear shift** n leva del cambio.
GED n abbr (*US SCOL*) = general educational development.
geese [giːs] npl of **goose**.
geezer ['giːzə*] n (*BRIT col*) tizio.
Geiger counter ['gaɪgə-] n geiger m inv.
gel [dʒɛl] n gel m inv.
gelatin(e) ['dʒɛlətiːn] n gelatina.
gelignite ['dʒɛlɪgnaɪt] n nitroglicerina.
gem [dʒɛm] n gemma.
Gemini ['dʒɛmɪnaɪ] n Gemelli mpl; **to be ~** essere dei Gemelli.
gen [dʒɛn] n (*BRIT col*): **to give sb the ~ on sth** mettere qn al corrente di qc.
Gen. abbr (*MIL*: = General) Gen.

gen. *abbr* (= *general, generally*) gen.
gender ['dʒɛndə*] *n* genere *m*.
gene [dʒiːn] *n* (*BIOL*) gene *m*.
genealogy [dʒiːnɪ'ælədʒɪ] *n* genealogia.
general ['dʒɛnərl] *n* generale *m* ♦ *adj* generale; **in** ~ in genere; **the** ~ **public** il grande pubblico.
general anaesthetic *n* anestesia totale.
general delivery *n* (*US*) fermo posta *m*.
general election *n* elezioni *fpl* generali.
generalization ['dʒɛnrəlaɪ'zeɪʃən] *n* generalizzazione *f*.
generalize ['dʒɛnrəlaɪz] *vi* generalizzare.
generally ['dʒɛnrəlɪ] *adv* generalmente.
general manager *n* direttore *m* generale.
general practitioner (GP) *n* medico generico; **who's your GP?** qual'è il suo medico di fiducia?
general strike *n* sciopero generale.
generate ['dʒɛnəreɪt] *vt* generare.
generation [dʒɛnə'reɪʃən] *n* generazione *f*; (*of electricity etc*) produzione *f*.
generator ['dʒɛnəreɪtə*] *n* generatore *m*.
generic [dʒɪ'nɛrɪk] *adj* generico(a).
generosity [dʒɛnə'rɔsɪtɪ] *n* generosità.
generous ['dʒɛnərəs] *adj* generoso(a); (*copious*) abbondante.
genesis ['dʒɛnɪsɪs] *n* genesi *f*.
genetic [dʒɪ'nɛtɪk] *adj* genetico(a); ~ **engineering** ingegneria genetica.
genetic fingerprinting [-fɪŋgəprɪntɪŋ] *n* rilevamento delle impronte genetiche.
genetics [dʒɪ'nɛtɪks] *n* genetica.
Geneva [dʒɪ'niːvə] *n* Ginevra; **Lake** ~ il lago di Ginevra.
genial ['dʒiːnɪəl] *adj* geniale, cordiale.
genitals ['dʒɛnɪtlz] *npl* genitali *mpl*.
genitive ['dʒɛnɪtɪv] *n* genitivo.
genius ['dʒiːnɪəs] *n* genio.
Genoa ['dʒɛnəuə] *n* Genova.
genocide ['dʒɛnəusaɪd] *n* genocidio.
Genoese [dʒɛnəu'iːz] *adj*, *n* (*pl inv*) genovese (*m/f*).
gent [dʒɛnt] *n* *abbr* (*BRIT col*) = **gentleman**.
genteel [dʒɛn'tiːl] *adj* raffinato(a), distinto(a).
gentle ['dʒɛntl] *adj* delicato(a); (*person*) dolce.
gentleman ['dʒɛntlmən] *n* signore *m*; (*well-bred man*) gentiluomo; ~**'s agreement** impegno sulla parola.
gentlemanly ['dʒɛntlmənlɪ] *adj* da gentiluomo.
gentleness ['dʒɛntlnɪs] *n* delicatezza; dolcezza.
gently ['dʒɛntlɪ] *adv* delicatamente.
gentry ['dʒɛntrɪ] *n* nobiltà minore.

gents [dʒɛnts] *n* W.C. *m* (per signori).
genuine ['dʒɛnjuɪn] *adj* autentico(a); sincero(a).
genuinely ['dʒɛnjuɪnlɪ] *adv* genuinamente.
geographer [dʒɪ'ɔgrəfə*] *n* geografo/a.
geographic(al) [dʒɪə'græfɪk(l)] *adj* geografico(a).
geography [dʒɪ'ɔgrəfɪ] *n* geografia.
geological [dʒɪə'lɔdʒɪkl] *adj* geologico(a).
geologist [dʒɪ'ɔlədʒɪst] *n* geologo/a.
geology [dʒɪ'ɔlədʒɪ] *n* geologia.
geometric(al) [dʒɪə'mɛtrɪk(l)] *adj* geometrico(a).
geometry [dʒɪ'ɔmətrɪ] *n* geometria.
Geordie ['dʒɔːdɪ] *n* (*col*) abitante *m/f* del Tyneside; originario/a del Tyneside.
Georgia ['dʒɔːdʒə] *n* Georgia.
Georgian ['dʒɔːdʒən] *adj* georgiano(a) ♦ *n* georgiano/a; (*LING*) georgiano.
geranium [dʒɪ'reɪnɪəm] *n* geranio.
geriatric [dʒɛrɪ'ætrɪk] *adj* geriatrico(a).
germ [dʒəːm] *n* (*MED*) microbo; (*BIOL, fig*) germe *m*.
German ['dʒəːmən] *adj* tedesco(a) ♦ *n* tedesco/a; (*LING*) tedesco.
German Democratic Republic (GDR) *n* Repubblica Democratica Tedesca (R.D.T.).
germane [dʒəː'meɪn] *adj* (*formal*): **to be** ~ **to** **sth** essere attinente a qc.
German measles *n* rosolia.
Germany ['dʒəːmənɪ] *n* Germania.
germination [dʒəːmɪ'neɪʃən] *n* germinazione *f*.
germ warfare *n* guerra batteriologica.
gerrymandering ['dʒɛrɪmændərɪŋ] *n* manipolazione *f* dei distretti elettorali.
gestation [dʒɛs'teɪʃən] *n* gestazione *f*.
gesticulate [dʒɛs'tɪkjuleɪt] *vi* gesticolare.
gesture ['dʒɛstʃə*] *n* gesto; **as a** ~ **of** **friendship** in segno d'amicizia.

———————————— *KEYWORD*

get [gɛt] (*pt, pp* **got**, (*US*) *pp* **gotten**) *vi* **1** (*become, be*) diventare, farsi; **to** ~ **drunk** ubriacarsi; **to** ~ **killed** venire *or* rimanere ucciso(a); **it's** ~**ting late** si sta facendo tardi; **to** ~ **old** invecchiare; **to** ~ **paid** venire pagato(a); **to** ~ **ready** prepararsi; **to** ~ **shaved** farsi la barba; **to** ~ **tired** stancarsi; **to** ~ **washed** lavarsi **2** (*go*): **to** ~ **to/from** andare a/da; **to** ~ **home** arrivare *or* tornare a casa; **how did you** ~ **here?** come sei venuto?; **he got across the bridge** ha attraversato il

ponte; **he got under the fence** è passato sotto il recinto
3 (*begin*) mettersi a, cominciare a; **to ~ to know sb** incominciare a conoscere qn; **let's ~ going** *or* **started** muoviamoci
4 (*modal aux vb*): **you've got to do it** devi farlo
♦ *vt* **1**: **to ~ sth done** (*do*) fare qc; (*have done*) far fare qc; **to ~ sth/sb ready** preparare qc/qn; **to ~ one's hair cut** tagliarsi *or* farsi tagliare i capelli; **to ~ sb to do sth** far fare qc a qn
2 (*obtain: money, permission, results*) ottenere; (*find: job, flat*) trovare; (*fetch: person, doctor*) chiamare; (: *object*) prendere; **to ~ sth for sb** prendere *or* procurare qc a qn; **~ me Mr Jones, please** (*TEL*) mi passi il signor Jones, per favore; **can I ~ you a drink?** le posso offrire da bere?
3 (*receive: present, letter, prize*) ricevere; (*acquire: reputation*) farsi; **how much did you ~ for the painting?** quanto le hanno dato per il quadro?
4 (*catch*) prendere; (*hit: target etc*) colpire; **to ~ sb by the arm/throat** afferrare qn per un braccio/alla gola; **~ him!** prendetelo!; **he really ~s me** (*fig: annoy*) mi dà proprio sui nervi
5 (*take, move*) portare; **to ~ sth to sb** far avere qc a qn; **do you think we'll ~ it through the door?** pensi che riusciremo a farlo passare per la porta?
6 (*catch, take: plane, bus etc*) prendere; **he got the last bus** ha preso l'ultimo autobus; **she got the morning flight to Milan** ha preso il volo per Milano del mattino
7 (*understand*) afferrare; (*hear*) sentire; **I've got it!** ci sono arrivato!, ci sono!; **I'm sorry, I didn't ~ your name** scusi, non ho capito (*or* sentito) come si chiama
8 (*have, possess*): **to have got** avere; **how many have you got?** quanti ne ha?
▶**get about** *vi* muoversi; (*news*) diffondersi
▶**get across** *vt*: **to ~ acròss (to)** (*message, meaning*) comunicare (a) ♦ *vi*: **to ~ across to** (*subj: speaker*) comunicare con
▶**get along** *vi* (*agree*) andare d'accordo; (*depart*) andarsene; (*manage*) = **get by**
▶**get at** *vt fus* (*attack*) prendersela con; (*reach*) raggiungere, arrivare a; **what are you ~ting at?** dove vuoi arrivare?
▶**get away** *vi* partire, andarsene; (*escape*) scappare
▶**get away with** *vt fus*: **he'll never ~ away with it!** non riuscirà a farla franca!

▶**get back** *vi* (*return*) ritornare, tornare ♦ *vt* riottenere, riavere; **to ~ back to** (*start again*) ritornare a; (*contact again*) rimettersi in contatto con
▶**get back at** *vt fus* (*col*): **to ~ back at sb (for sth)** rendere pan per focaccia a qn (per qc)
▶**get by** *vi* (*pass*) passare; (*manage*) farcela; **I can ~ by in Dutch** mi arrangio in olandese
▶**get down** *vi*, *vt fus* scendere ♦ *vt* far scendere; (*depress*) buttare giù
▶**get down to** *vt fus* (*work*) mettersi a (fare); **to ~ down to business** venire al dunque
▶**get in** *vi* entrare; (*train*) arrivare; (*arrive home*) ritornare, tornare ♦ *vt* (*bring in: harvest*) raccogliere; (: *coal, shopping, supplies*) fare provvista di; (*insert*) far entrare, infilare
▶**get into** *vt fus* entrare in; **to ~ into a rage** incavolarsi; **to ~ into bed** mettersi a letto
▶**get off** *vi* (*from train etc*) scendere; (*depart: person, car*) andare via; (*escape*) cavarsela ♦ *vt* (*remove: clothes, stain*) levare; (*send off*) spedire; (*have as leave: days, time*): **we got 2 days off** abbiamo avuto 2 giorni liberi ♦ *vt fus* (*train, bus*) scendere da; **to ~ off to a good start** (*fig*) cominciare bene
▶**get on** *vi*: **how did you ~ on?** com'è andata?; **he got on quite well** ha fatto bene, (gli) è andata bene; **to ~ on (with sb)** andare d'accordo (con qn); **how are you ~ting on?** come va la vita? ♦ *vt fus* montare in; (*horse*) montare su
▶**get on to** *vt fus* (*BRIT col: contact: on phone etc*) contattare, rintracciare; (: *deal with*) occuparsi di
▶**get out** *vi* uscire; (*of vehicle*) scendere ♦ *vt* tirar fuori, far uscire; **to ~ out (of)** (*money from bank etc*) ritirare (da)
▶**get out of** *vt fus* uscire da; (*duty etc*) evitare; **what will you ~ out of it?** cosa ci guadagni?
▶**get over** *vt fus* (*illness*) riaversi da; (*communicate: idea etc*) comunicare, passare; **let's ~ it over (with)** togliamoci il pensiero
▶**get round** *vt fus* aggirare; (*fig: person*) rigirare ♦ *vi*: **to ~ round to doing sth** trovare il tempo di fare qc
▶**get through** *vi* (*TEL*) avere la linea ♦ *vt fus* (*finish: work*) sbrigare; (: *book*) finire
▶**get through to** *vt fus* (*TEL*) parlare a
▶**get together** *vi* riunirsi ♦ *vt* raccogliere; (*people*) adunare
▶**get up** *vi* (*rise*) alzarsi ♦ *vt fus* salire su

per
►**get up to** vt fus (reach) raggiungere; (prank etc) fare.

getaway ['gɛtəweɪ] n fuga.
getaway car n macchina per la fuga.
get-together ['gɛttəgɛðə*] n (piccola) riunione f; (party) festicciola.
get-up ['gɛtʌp] n (col: outfit) tenuta.
get-well card [gɛt'wɛl-] n cartolina di auguri di pronta guarigione.
geyser ['giːzə*] n scaldabagno; (GEO) geyser m inv.
Ghana ['gɑːnə] n Ghana m.
Ghanaian [gɑː'neɪən] adj, n ganaense (m/f).
ghastly ['gɑːstlɪ] adj orribile, orrendo(a).
gherkin ['gəːkɪn] n cetriolino.
ghetto ['gɛtəu] n ghetto.
ghetto blaster [-'blɑːstə*] n maxistereo portatile.
ghost [gəust] n fantasma m, spettro ♦ vt (book) fare lo scrittore ombra per.
ghostly ['gəustlɪ] adj spettrale.
ghostwriter ['gəustraɪtə*] n scrittore/trice ombra inv.
ghoul [guːl] n vampiro che si nutre di cadaveri.
ghoulish ['guːlɪʃ] adj (tastes etc) macabro(a).
GHQ n abbr (MIL: = general headquarters) ≈ comando di Stato maggiore.
GI n abbr (US col: = government issue) G.I. m, soldato americano.
giant ['dʒaɪənt] n gigante/essa ♦ adj gigante, enorme; ~ **(size) packet** confezione f gigante.
giant killer n (SPORT) piccola squadra che riesce a batterne una importante.
gibber ['dʒɪbə*] vi (monkey) squittire confusamente; (idiot) farfugliare.
gibberish ['dʒɪbərɪʃ] n parole fpl senza senso.
gibe [dʒaɪb] n frecciata ♦ vi: **to ~ at** lanciare frecciate a.
giblets ['dʒɪblɪts] npl frattaglie fpl.
Gibraltar [dʒɪ'brɔːltə*] n Gibilterra.
giddiness ['gɪdɪnɪs] n vertigine f.
giddy ['gɪdɪ] adj (dizzy): **to be ~** aver le vertigini; (height) vertiginoso(a); **I feel ~** mi gira la testa.
gift [gɪft] n regalo; (donation, ability) dono; (COMM: also: **free ~**) omaggio; **to have a ~ for sth** (talent) avere il dono di qc.
gifted ['gɪftɪd] adj dotato(a).
gift token, gift voucher n buono (acquisto).
gig [gɪg] n (col: of musician) serata.
gigabyte [giːgəbaɪt] n gigabyte m inv.

gigantic [dʒaɪ'gæntɪk] adj gigantesco(a).
giggle ['gɪgl] vi ridere scioccamente ♦ n risolino (sciocco).
GIGO ['gaɪgəu] abbr (COMPUT: col: = garbage in, garbage out) qualità di input = qualità di output.
gild [gɪld] vt dorare.
gill [dʒɪl] n (measure) = 0.25 pints (BRIT = 0.148 l; US = 0.118 l).
gills [gɪlz] npl (of fish) branchie fpl.
gilt [gɪlt] n doratura ♦ adj dorato(a).
gilt-edged ['gɪltɛdʒd] adj (stocks, securities) della massima sicurezza.
gimlet ['gɪmlɪt] n succhiello.
gimmick ['gɪmɪk] n trucco; **sales ~** trovata commerciale.
gin [dʒɪn] n (liquor) gin m inv.
ginger ['dʒɪndʒə*] n zenzero.
►**ginger up** vt scuotere; animare.
ginger ale, ginger beer n bibita gassosa allo zenzero.
gingerbread ['dʒɪndʒəbrɛd] n pan m di zenzero.
ginger group n (BRIT) gruppo di pressione.
ginger-haired ['dʒɪndʒə'hɛəd] adj rossiccio(a).
gingerly ['dʒɪndʒəlɪ] adv cautamente.
gingham ['gɪŋəm] n percalle m a righe (or quadretti).
ginseng ['dʒɪnsɛŋ] n ginseng m.
gipsy ['dʒɪpsɪ] n zingaro/a ♦ adj degli zingari.
giraffe [dʒɪ'rɑːf] n giraffa.
girder ['gəːdə*] n trave f.
girdle ['gəːdl] n (corset) guaina.
girl [gəːl] n ragazza; (young unmarried woman) signorina; (daughter) figlia, figliola; **a little ~** una bambina.
girlfriend ['gəːlfrɛnd] n (of girl) amica; (of boy) ragazza.
girlish ['gəːlɪʃ] adj da ragazza.
Girl Scout n (US) Giovane Esploratrice f.
Giro ['dʒaɪrəu] n: **the National ~** (BRIT) ≈ la or il Bancoposta.
giro ['dʒaɪrəu] n (bank ~) versamento bancario; (post office ~) postagiro.
girth [gəːθ] n circonferenza; (of horse) cinghia.
gist [dʒɪst] n succo.
give [gɪv] n (of fabric) elasticità ♦ vb (pt **gave**, pp **given** [geɪv, 'gɪvn]) vt dare ♦ vi cedere; **to ~ sb sth, ~ sth to sb** dare qc a qn; **to ~ a cry/sigh** emettere un grido/ sospiro; **how much did you ~ for it?** quanto (l')hai pagato?; **12 o'clock, ~ or take a few minutes** mezzogiorno, minuto più minuto meno; **to ~ way** vi cedere;

(*BRIT AUT*) dare la precedenza.
▶**give away** *vt* dare via; (*give free*) fare dono di; (*betray*) tradire; (*disclose*) rivelare; (*bride*) condurre all'altare.
▶**give back** *vt* rendere.
▶**give in** *vi* cedere ♦ *vt* consegnare.
▶**give off** *vt* emettere.
▶**give out** *vt* distribuire; annunciare ♦ *vi* (*be exhausted*: *supplies*) esaurirsi, venir meno; (*fail*: *engine*) fermarsi; (: *strength*) mancare.
▶**give up** *vi* rinunciare ♦ *vt* rinunciare a; **to ~ up smoking** smettere di fumare; **to ~ o.s. up** arrendersi.
give-and-take [gɪvən'teɪk] *n* (*col*) elasticità (da ambo le parti), concessioni *fpl* reciproche.
giveaway ['gɪvəweɪ] *n* (*col*): **her expression was a ~** le si leggeva tutto in volto; **the exam was a ~**! l'esame è stato uno scherzo! ♦ *cpd*: **~ prices** prezzi stracciati.
given ['gɪvn] *pp of* **give** ♦ *adj* (*fixed*: *time, amount*) dato(a), determinato(a) ♦ *conj*: **~ (that)** ... dato che ...; **~ the circumstances** ... date le circostanze ....
glacial ['gleɪsɪəl] *adj* glaciale.
glacier ['glæsɪə*] *n* ghiacciaio.
glad [glæd] *adj* lieto(a), contento(a); **to be ~ about sth/that** essere contento *or* lieto di qc/che + *sub*; **I was ~ of his help** gli sono stato grato del suo aiuto.
gladden ['glædn] *vt* rallegrare, allietare.
glade [gleɪd] *n* radura.
gladioli [glædɪ'əʊlaɪ] *npl* gladioli *mpl*.
gladly ['glædlɪ] *adv* volentieri.
glamorous ['glæmərəs] *adj* (*gen*) favoloso(a); (*person*) affascinante, seducente; (*occasion*) brillante, elegante.
glamour ['glæmə*] *n* fascino.
glance [glɑːns] *n* occhiata, sguardo ♦ *vi*: **to ~ at** dare un'occhiata a.
▶**glance off** *vt fus* (*bullet*) rimbalzare su.
glancing ['glɑːnsɪŋ] *adj* (*blow*) che colpisce di striscio.
gland [glænd] *n* ghiandola.
glandular ['glændjʊlə*] *adj*: **~ fever** (*BRIT*) mononucleosi *f*.
glare [glɛə*] *n* riverbero, luce *f* abbagliante; (*look*) sguardo furioso ♦ *vi* abbagliare; **to ~ at** guardare male.
glaring ['glɛərɪŋ] *adj* (*mistake*) madornale.
glasnost ['glæznɒst] *n* glasnost *f*.
glass [glɑːs] *n* (*substance*) vetro; (*tumbler*) bicchiere *m*; (*also*: **looking ~**) specchio; *see also* **glasses**.
glass-blowing ['glɑːsbləʊɪŋ] *n* soffiatura del vetro.
glass ceiling *n* (*fig*) barriera invisibile.

glasses ['glɑːsɪz] *npl* (*spectacles*) occhiali *mpl*.
glass fibre *n* fibra di vetro.
glasshouse ['glɑːshaʊs] *n* serra.
glassware ['glɑːswɛə*] *n* vetrame *m*.
glassy ['glɑːsɪ] *adj* (*eyes*) vitreo(a).
Glaswegian [glæs'wiːdʒən] *adj* di Glasgow ♦ *n* abitante *m/f* di Glasgow; originario/a di Glasgow.
glaze [gleɪz] *vt* (*door*) fornire di vetri; (*pottery*) smaltare; (*CULIN*) glassare ♦ *n* smalto; glassa.
glazed ['gleɪzd] *adj* (*eye*) vitreo(a); (*tiles, pottery*) smaltato(a).
glazier ['gleɪzɪə*] *n* vetraio.
gleam [gliːm] *n* barlume *m*; raggio ♦ *vi* luccicare; **a ~ of hope** un barlume di speranza.
gleaming ['gliːmɪŋ] *adj* lucente.
glean [gliːn] *vt* (*information*) racimolare.
glee [gliː] *n* allegrezza, gioia.
gleeful ['gliːfʊl] *adj* allegro(a), gioioso(a).
glen [glɛn] *n* valletta.
glib [glɪb] *adj* dalla parola facile; facile.
glide [glaɪd] *vi* scivolare; (*AVIAT, birds*) planare ♦ *n* scivolata; planata.
glider ['glaɪdə*] *n* (*AVIAT*) aliante *m*.
gliding ['glaɪdɪŋ] *n* (*AVIAT*) volo a vela.
glimmer ['glɪmə*] *vi* luccicare ♦ *n* barlume *m*.
glimpse [glɪmps] *n* impressione *f* fugace ♦ *vt* vedere di sfuggita; **to catch a ~ of** vedere di sfuggita.
glint [glɪnt] *n* luccichio ♦ *vi* luccicare.
glisten ['glɪsn] *vi* luccicare.
glitter ['glɪtə*] *vi* scintillare ♦ *n* scintillio.
glitz [glɪts] *n* (*col*) vistosità, chiassosità.
gloat [gləʊt] *vi*: **to ~ (over)** gongolare di piacere (per).
global ['gləʊbl] *adj* globale; (*world-wide*) mondiale.
global warming *n* riscaldamento dell'atmosfera terrestre.
globe [gləʊb] *n* globo, sfera.
globetrotter ['gləʊbtrɒtə*] *n* giramondo *m/f inv*.
globule ['glɒbjuːl] *n* (*ANAT*) globulo; (*of water etc*) gocciolina.
gloom [gluːm] *n* oscurità, buio; (*sadness*) tristezza, malinconia.
gloomy ['gluːmɪ] *adj* fosco(a), triste; **to feel ~** sentirsi giù *or* depresso.
glorification [glɔːrɪfɪ'keɪʃən] *n* glorificazione *f*.
glorify ['glɔːrɪfaɪ] *vt* glorificare; celebrare, esaltare.
glorious ['glɔːrɪəs] *adj* glorioso(a); magnifico(a).

glory ['glɔːrɪ] n gloria; splendore m ♦ vi: **to** ~ **in** gloriarsi di or in.
glory hole n (col) ripostiglio.
Glos abbr (BRIT) = Gloucestershire.
gloss [glɔs] n (shine) lucentezza; (also: ~ paint) vernice f a olio.
►**gloss over** vt fus scivolare su.
glossary ['glɔsərɪ] n glossario.
glossy ['glɔsɪ] adj lucente ♦ n (also: ~ magazine) rivista di lusso.
glove [glʌv] n guanto.
glove compartment n (AUT) vano portaoggetti.
glow [gləu] vi ardere; (face) essere luminoso(a) ♦ n bagliore m; (of face) colorito acceso.
glower ['glauə*] vi: **to** ~ **(at sb)** guardare (qn) in cagnesco.
glowing ['gləuɪŋ] adj (fire) ardente; (complexion) luminoso(a); (fig: report, description etc) entusiasta.
glow-worm ['gləuwəːm] n lucciola.
glucose ['gluːkəus] n glucosio.
glue [gluː] n colla ♦ vt incollare.
glue-sniffing ['gluːsnɪfɪŋ] n sniffare m (colla).
glum [glʌm] adj abbattuto(a).
glut [glʌt] n eccesso ♦ vt saziare; (market) saturare.
glutinous ['gluːtɪnəs] adj colloso(a), appiccicoso(a).
glutton ['glʌtn] n ghiottone/a; **a** ~ **for work** un(a) patito(a) del lavoro.
gluttonous ['glʌtənəs] adj ghiotto(a), goloso(a).
gluttony ['glʌtənɪ] n ghiottoneria; (sin) gola.
glycerin(e) ['glɪsəriːn] n glicerina.
GM abbr (= genetically modified) geneticamente modificato.
gm abbr = gram.
GMAT n abbr (US: = Graduate Management Admissions Test) esame di ammissione all'ultimo biennio di scuola superiore.
GMT abbr (= Greenwich Mean Time) T.M.G.
gnarled [nɑːld] adj nodoso(a).
gnash [næʃ] vt: **to** ~ **one's teeth** digrignare i denti.
gnat [næt] n moscerino.
gnaw [nɔː] vt rodere.
gnome [nəum] n gnomo.
GNP n abbr = gross national product.
go [gəu] vb (pt **went**, pp **gone** [wɛnt, gɔn]) vi andare; (depart) partire, andarsene; (work) funzionare; (break etc) cedere; (be sold): **to** ~ **for £10** essere venduto per 10 sterline; (fit, suit): **to** ~ **with** andare bene con; (become): **to** ~ **pale** diventare pallido(a); **to** ~ **mouldy** ammuffire ♦ n (pl ~es): **to have a** ~ (at) provare; **to be on the** ~ essere in moto; **whose** ~ **is it?** a chi tocca?; **to** ~ **by car/on foot** andare in macchina/a piedi; **he's** ~ing **to do** sta per fare; **to** ~ **for a walk** andare a fare una passeggiata; **to** ~ **dancing/shopping** andare a ballare/fare la spesa; **to** ~ **looking for sb/sth** andare in cerca di qn/qc; **to** ~ **to sleep** addormentarsi; **to** ~ **and see sb, to** ~ **to see sb** andare a trovare qn; **how is it** ~ing? come va (la vita)?; **how did it** ~? com'è andato?; **to** ~ **round the back/by the shop** passare da dietro/davanti al negozio; **my voice has gone** m'è andata via la voce; **the cake is all gone** il dolce è finito tutto; **I'll take whatever is** ~ing (BRIT) prendo quello che c'è; ... **to** ~ (US: food) ... da portar via; **the money will** ~ **towards our holiday** questi soldi li mettiamo per la vacanza
►**go about** vi (also: ~ **around**) aggirarsi; (: rumour) correre, circolare ♦ vt fus: **how do I** ~ **about this?** qual'è la prassi per questo?; **to** ~ **about one's business** occuparsi delle proprie faccende.
►**go after** vt fus (pursue) correr dietro a, rincorrere; (job, record etc) mirare a.
►**go against** vt fus (be unfavourable to) essere contro; (be contrary to) andare contro.
►**go ahead** vi andare avanti; ~ **ahead!** faccia pure!
►**go along** vi andare, avanzare ♦ vt fus percorrere; **to** ~ **along with** (accompany) andare con, accompagnare; (agree with: idea) sottoscrivere, appoggiare.
►**go away** vi partire, andarsene.
►**go back** vi tornare, ritornare; (go again) andare di nuovo.
►**go back on** vt fus (promise) non mantenere.
►**go by** vi (years, time) scorrere ♦ vt fus attenersi a, seguire (alla lettera); prestar fede a.
►**go down** vi scendere; (ship) affondare; (sun) tramontare ♦ vt fus scendere; **that should** ~ **down well with him** dovrebbe incontrare la sua approvazione.
►**go for** vt fus (fetch) andare a prendere; (like) andar matto(a) per; (attack) attaccare; saltare addosso a.
►**go in** vi entrare.
►**go in for** vt fus (competition) iscriversi a; (be interested in) interessarsi di.
►**go into** vt fus entrare in; (investigate) indagare, esaminare; (embark on) lanciarsi in.

▶**go off** *vi* partire, andar via; (*food*) guastarsi; (*explode*) esplodere, scoppiare; (*lights etc*) spegnersi; (*event*) passare ♦ *vt fus*: **I've gone off chocolate** la cioccolata non mi piace più; **the gun went off** il fucile si scaricò; **the party went off well** la festa è andata *or* è riuscita bene; **to ~ off to sleep** addormentarsi.

▶**go on** *vi* continuare; (*happen*) succedere; (*lights*) accendersi ♦ *vt fus* (*be guided by*: *evidence etc*) basarsi su, fondarsi su; **to ~ on doing** continuare a fare; **what's ~ing on here?** che succede *or* che sta succedendo qui?

▶**go on at** *vt fus* (*nag*) assillare.

▶**go on with** *vt fus* continuare, proseguire.

▶**go out** *vi* uscire; (*fire, light*) spegnersi; (*ebb*: *tide*) calare; **to ~ out with sb** uscire con qn.

▶**go over** *vi* (*ship*) ribaltarsi ♦ *vt fus* (*check*) esaminare; **to ~ over sth in one's mind** pensare bene a qc.

▶**go round** *vi* (*circulate*: *news, rumour*) circolare; (*revolve*) girare; (*visit*): **to ~ round (to sb's)** passare (da qn); (*make a detour*): **to ~ round (by)** passare (per); (*suffice*) bastare (per tutti).

▶**go through** *vt fus* (*town etc*) attraversare; (*search through*) frugare in; (*examine*: *list, book*) leggere da capo a fondo; (*perform*) fare.

▶**go through with** *vt fus* (*plan, crime*) mettere in atto, eseguire; **I couldn't ~ through with it** non sono riuscito ad andare fino in fondo.

▶**go under** *vi* (*sink*: *ship*) affondare, colare a picco; (: *person*) andare sotto; (*fig*: *business, firm*) fallire.

▶**go up** *vi* salire ♦ *vt fus* salire su per; **to ~ up in flames** andare in fiamme.

▶**go without** *vt fus* fare a meno di.

goad [gəud] *vt* spronare.

go-ahead ['gəuəhɛd] *adj* intraprendente ♦ *n*: **to give sb/sth the ~** dare l'okay a qn/qc.

goal [gəul] *n* (*SPORT*) gol *m*, rete *f*; (: *place*) porta; (*fig*: *aim*) fine *m*, scopo.

goal difference *n* differenza *f* reti *inv*.

goalie ['gəuli] *n* (*col*) portiere *m*.

goalkeeper ['gəulki:pə*] *n* portiere *m*.

goalpost ['gəulpəust] *n* palo (della porta).

goat [gəut] *n* capra.

gobble ['gɔbl] *vt* (*also*: **~ down, ~ up**) ingoiare.

go-between ['gəubɪtwi:n] *n* intermediario/a.

Gobi Desert ['gəubɪ-] *n*: **the ~** il Deserto dei Gobi.

goblet ['gɔblɪt] *n* calice *m*, coppa.

goblin ['gɔblɪn] *n* folletto.

go-cart ['gəukɑ:t] *n* go-kart *m inv* ♦ *cpd*: **~ racing** *n* kartismo.

god [gɔd] *n* dio; **G~** Dio.

god-awful [gɔd'ɔːfəl] *adj* (*col*) di merda (*!*).

godchild ['gɔdtʃaɪld] *n* figlioccio/a.

goddamn(ed) ['gɔddæm(d)] (*esp US*: *col*) *excl*: **goddamn!** porca miseria! ♦ *adj* fottuto(a) (*!*), maledetto(a) ♦ *adv* maledettamente.

goddaughter ['gɔddɔːtə*] *n* figlioccia.

goddess ['gɔdɪs] *n* dea.

godfather ['gɔdfɑːðə*] *n* padrino.

god-fearing ['gɔdfɪərɪŋ] *adj* timorato(a) di Dio.

god-forsaken ['gɔdfəseɪkən] *adj* desolato(a), sperduto(a).

godmother ['gɔdmʌðə*] *n* madrina.

godparents ['gɔdpɛərənts] *npl*: **the ~** il padrino e la madrina.

godsend ['gɔdsɛnd] *n* dono del cielo.

godson ['gɔdsʌn] *n* figlioccio.

goes [gəuz] *vb see* **go**.

gofer ['gəufə*] *n* (*col*) tuttofare *m/f*, tirapiedi *m/f inv*.

go-getter ['gəugɛtə*] *n* arrivista *m/f*.

goggle ['gɔgl] *vi*: **to ~ (at)** stare con gli occhi incollati *or* appicciccati (a *or* addosso a).

goggles ['gɔglz] *npl* occhiali *mpl* (di protezione).

going ['gəuɪŋ] *n* (*conditions*) andare *m*, stato del terreno ♦ *adj*: **the ~ rate** la tariffa in vigore; **a ~ concern** un'azienda avviata; **it was slow ~** si andava a rilento.

going-over [gəuɪŋ'əuvə*] *n* (*col*) controllata; (*violent attack*) pestaggio.

goings-on ['gəuɪŋz'ɔn] *npl* (*col*) fatti *mpl* strani, cose *fpl* strane.

go-kart ['gəukɑːt] *n* = **go-cart**.

gold [gəuld] *n* oro ♦ *adj* d'oro; (*reserves*) aureo(a).

golden ['gəuldən] *adj* (*made of gold*) d'oro; (*gold in colour*) dorato(a).

golden age *n* età d'oro.

golden handshake *n* (*BRIT*) gratifica di fine servizio.

golden rule *n* regola principale.

goldfish ['gəuldfɪʃ] *n* pesce *m* dorato *or* rosso.

gold leaf *n* lamina d'oro.

gold medal *n* (*SPORT*) medaglia d'oro.

goldmine ['gəuldmaɪn] *n* miniera d'oro.

gold-plated ['gəuld'pleɪtɪd] *adj* placcato(a) oro *inv*.

goldsmith ['gəuldsmɪθ] *n* orefice *m*, orafo.

gold standard *n* tallone *m* aureo.

golf [gɔlf] *n* golf *m*.
golf ball *n* pallina da golf.
golf club *n* circolo di golf; (*stick*) bastone *m* or mazza da golf.
golf course *n* campo di golf.
golfer ['gɔlfə*] *n* giocatore/trice di golf.
golfing ['gɔlfɪŋ] *n* il giocare a golf.
gondola ['gɔndələ] *n* gondola.
gondolier [gɔndə'lɪə*] *n* gondoliere *m*.
gone [gɔn] *pp of* go.
goner ['gɔnə*] *n* (*col*): **I thought you were a** ~ pensavo che ormai fossi spacciato.
gong [gɔŋ] *n* gong *m inv*.
good [gud] *adj* buono(a); (*kind*) buono(a), gentile; (*child*) bravo(a) ♦ *n* bene *m*; ~! bene!, ottimo!; **to be** ~ **at** essere bravo(a) in; **it's** ~ **for you** fa bene; **it's a** ~ **thing you were there** meno male che c'era; **she is** ~ **with children/her hands** ci sa fare coi bambini/è abile nei lavori manuali; **to feel** ~ sentirsi bene; **it's** ~ **to see you** che piacere vederla; **he's up to no** ~ ne sta combinando qualcuna; **it's no** ~ **complaining** brontolare non serve a niente; **for the common** ~ nell'interesse generale, per il bene comune; **for** ~ (*for ever*) per sempre, definitivamente; **would you be** ~ **enough to** ...? avrebbe la gentilezza di ...?; **that's very** ~ **of you** è molto gentile da parte sua; **is this any** ~? (*will it do?*) va bene questo?; (*what's it like?*) com'è?; **a** ~ **deal (of)** molto(a), una buona quantità (di); **a** ~ **many** molti(e); ~ **morning!** buon giorno!; ~ **afternoon/ evening!** buona sera!; ~ **night!** buona notte!; *see also* **goods**.
goodbye [gud'baɪ] *excl* arrivederci!; **to say** ~ **to** (*person*) salutare.
good faith *n* buona fede.
good-for-nothing ['gudfənʌθɪŋ] *n* buono/a a nulla, vagabondo/a.
Good Friday *n* Venerdì Santo.
good-humoured [gud'hjuːməd] *adj* (*person*) di buon umore; (*remark, joke*) bonario(a).
good-looking [gud'lukɪŋ] *adj* bello(a).
good-natured [gud'neɪtʃəd] *adj* (*person*) affabile; (*discussion*) amichevole, cordiale.
goodness ['gudnɪs] *n* (*of person*) bontà; **for** ~ **sake!** per amor di Dio!; ~ **gracious!** santo cielo!, mamma mia!
goods [gudz] *npl* (*COMM etc*) merci *fpl*, articoli *mpl*; ~ **and chattels** beni *mpl* e effetti *mpl*.
goods train *n* (*BRIT*) treno *m* merci *inv*.
goodwill [gud'wɪl] *n* amicizia, benevolenza; (*COMM*) avviamento.

goody-goody ['gudɪgudɪ] *n* (*pej*) santarellino/a.
gooey ['guːɪ] *adj* (*BRIT col*: sticky) appiccicoso(a); (*cake, dessert*) troppo zuccherato(a).
goose, *pl* **geese** [guːs, giːs] *n* oca.
gooseberry ['guzbərɪ] *n* uva spina; **to play** ~ (*BRIT*) tenere la candela.
gooseflesh ['guːsfleʃ] *n*, **goosepimples** ['guːspɪmplz] *npl* pelle *f* d'oca.
goose step *n* (*MIL*) passo dell'oca.
GOP *n abbr* (*US POL*: col: = Grand Old Party) partito repubblicano.
gopher ['gəufə*] *n* = **gofer**.
gore [gɔː*] *vt* incornare ♦ *n* sangue *m* (coagulato).
gorge [gɔːdʒ] *n* gola ♦ *vt*: **to** ~ **o.s. (on)** ingozzarsi (di).
gorgeous ['gɔːdʒəs] *adj* magnifico(a).
gorilla [gə'rɪlə] *n* gorilla *m inv*.
gormless ['gɔːmlɪs] *adj* (*BRIT col*) tonto(a), (*: stronger*) deficiente.
gorse [gɔːs] *n* ginestrone *m*.
gory ['gɔːrɪ] *adj* sanguinoso(a).
go-slow ['gəu'sləu] *n* (*BRIT*) rallentamento dei lavori (*per agitazione sindacale*).
gospel ['gɔspl] *n* vangelo.
gossamer ['gɔsəmə*] *n* (*cobweb*) fili *mpl* della Madonna or di ragnatela; (*light fabric*) stoffa sottilissima.
gossip ['gɔsɪp] *n* chiacchiere *fpl*; pettegolezzi *mpl*; (*person*) pettegolo/a ♦ *vi* chiacchierare; (*maliciously*) pettegolare; **a piece of** ~ un pettegolezzo.
gossip column *n* cronaca mondana.
got [gɔt] *pt, pp of* get.
Gothic ['gɔθɪk] *adj* gotico(a).
gotten ['gɔtn] (*US*) *pp of* get.
gouge [gaudʒ] *vt* (*also*: ~ **out**: *hole etc*) scavare; (*: initials*) scolpire; (*: sb's eyes*) cavare.
gourd [guəd] *n* zucca.
gourmet ['guəmeɪ] *n* buongustaio/a.
gout [gaut] *n* gotta.
govern ['gʌvən] *vt* governare; (*LING*) reggere.
governess ['gʌvənɪs] *n* governante *f*.
governing ['gʌvənɪŋ] *adj* (*POL*) al potere, al governo; ~ **body** consiglio di amministrazione.
government ['gʌvnmənt] *n* governo; (*BRIT*: *ministers*) ministero ♦ *cpd* statale; **local** ~ amministrazione *f* locale.
governmental [gʌvn'mɛntl] *adj* governativo(a).
government housing *n* (*US*) alloggi *mpl* popolari.
government stock *n* titoli *mpl* di stato.

governor ['gʌvənə*] n (of state, bank) governatore m; (of school, hospital) amministratore m; (BRIT: of prison) direttore/trice.

Govt abbr = **government**.

gown [gaun] n vestito lungo; (of teacher, judge) toga.

GP n abbr (MED) see **general practitioner**.

GPMU n abbr (BRIT) = Graphical, Paper and Media Union.

GPO n abbr (BRIT: old) = General Post Office; (US: = Government Printing Office) ≈ Poligrafici dello Stato.

gr. abbr (COMM) = **gross**.

grab [græb] vt afferrare, arraffare; (property, power) impadronirsi di ♦ vi: **to ~ at** tentare disperatamente di afferrare.

grace [greɪs] n grazia; (graciousness) garbo, cortesia ♦ vt onorare; **5 days' ~** dilazione f di 5 giorni; **to say ~** dire il benedicite; **with a good/bad ~** volentieri/ malvolentieri; **his sense of humour is his saving ~** il suo senso dell'umorismo è quello che lo salva.

graceful ['greɪsful] adj elegante, aggraziato(a).

gracious ['greɪʃəs] adj grazioso(a); misericordioso(a) ♦ excl: **(good) ~!** madonna (mia)!

gradation [grə'deɪʃən] n gradazione f.

grade [greɪd] n (COMM) qualità f inv; classe f; categoria; (in hierarchy) grado; (US SCOL) voto; classe; (gradient) pendenza, gradiente m ♦ vt classificare; ordinare; graduare; **to make the ~** (fig) farcela.

grade crossing n (US) passaggio a livello.

grade school n (US) scuola elementare or primaria.

gradient ['greɪdɪənt] n pendenza, gradiente m.

gradual ['grædjuəl] adj graduale.

gradually ['grædjuəlɪ] adv man mano, a poco a poco.

graduate n ['grædjuɪt] laureato/a; (US SCOL) diplomato/a, licenziato/a ♦ vi ['grædjueɪt] laurearsi.

graduated pension ['grædjueɪtɪd-] n pensione calcolata sugli ultimi stipendi.

graduation [grædju'eɪʃən] n cerimonia del conferimento della laurea; (US SCOL) consegna dei diplomi.

graffiti [grə'fi:tɪ] npl graffiti mpl.

graft [grɑ:ft] n (AGR, MED) innesto ♦ vt innestare; **hard ~** (col) duro lavoro.

grain [greɪn] n (no pl: cereals) cereali mpl; (US: corn) grano; (of sand) granello; (of wood) venatura; **it goes against the ~**

(fig) va contro la mia (or la sua etc) natura.

gram [græm] n grammo.

grammar ['græmə*] n grammatica.

grammar school n (BRIT) ≈ liceo; (US) ≈ scuola elementare.

grammatical [grə'mætɪkl] adj grammaticale.

gramme [græm] n = **gram**.

gramophone ['græməfəun] n (BRIT) grammofono.

granary ['grænərɪ] n granaio.

grand [grænd] adj grande, magnifico(a); grandioso(a) ♦ n (col: thousand) mille dollari mpl (or sterline fpl).

grandchild, pl **-children** ['græntʃaɪld, -tʃɪldrən] n nipote m.

granddad ['grændæd] n (col) nonno.

granddaughter ['grændɔ:tə*] n nipote f.

grandeur ['grændjə*] n (of style, house) splendore m; (of occasion, scenery etc) grandiosità, maestà.

grandfather ['grændfɑ:ðə*] n nonno.

grandiose ['grændɪəus] adj grandioso(a); (pej) pomposo(a).

grand jury n (US) giuria (formata da 12 a 23 membri).

grandma ['grænmɑ:] n (col) nonna.

grandmother ['grænmʌðə*] n nonna.

grandpa ['grænpɑ:] n (col) = **granddad**.

grandparent ['grænpεərənt] n nonno/a.

grand piano n pianoforte m a coda.

Grand Prix ['grɑ:'pri:] n (AUT) Gran Premio, Grand Prix m inv.

grandson ['grænsʌn] n nipote m.

grandstand ['grændstænd] n (SPORT) tribuna.

grand total n somma complessiva.

granite ['grænɪt] n granito.

granny ['grænɪ] n (col) nonna.

grant [grɑ:nt] vt accordare; (a request) accogliere; (admit) ammettere, concedere ♦ n (SCOL) borsa; (ADMIN) sussidio, sovvenzione f; **to take sth for ~ed** dare qc per scontato.

granulated ['grænjuleɪtɪd] adj: **~ sugar** zucchero cristallizzato.

granule ['grænju:l] n granello.

grape [greɪp] n chicco d'uva, acino; **a bunch of ~s** un grappolo d'uva.

grapefruit ['greɪpfru:t] n pompelmo.

grapevine ['greɪpvaɪn] n vite f; **I heard it on the ~** (fig) me l'ha detto l'uccellino.

graph [grɑ:f] n grafico.

graphic ['græfɪk] adj grafico(a); (vivid) vivido(a); see also **graphics**.

graphic designer n grafico/a.

graphic equalizer n equalizzatore m

grafico.
graphics ['græfɪks] n (art, process) grafica; (pl: drawings) illustrazioni fpl.
graphite ['græfaɪt] n grafite f.
graph paper n carta millimetrata.
grapple ['græpl] vi: to ~ with essere alle prese con.
grappling iron ['græplɪŋ-] n (NAUT) grappino.
grasp [grɑːsp] vt afferrare ♦ n (grip) presa; (fig) potere m; comprensione f; **to have sth within one's** ~ avere qc a portata di mano; **to have a good** ~ **of** (subject) avere una buona padronanza di.
►**grasp at** vt fus (rope etc) afferrarsi a, aggrapparsi a; (fig: opportunity) non farsi sfuggire, approfittare di.
grasping ['grɑːspɪŋ] adj avido(a).
grass [grɑːs] n erba; (pasture) pascolo, prato; (BRIT col: informer) informatore/trice; (ex-terrorist) pentito/a.
grasshopper ['grɑːshɒpə] n cavalletta.
grassland ['grɑːslænd] n prateria.
grass roots npl (fig) base f.
grass snake n natrice f.
grassy ['grɑːsɪ] adj erboso(a).
grate [greɪt] n graticola (del focolare) ♦ vi cigolare, stridere ♦ vt (CULIN) grattugiare.
grateful ['greɪtful] adj grato(a), riconoscente.
gratefully ['greɪtfulɪ] adv con gratitudine.
grater ['greɪtə*] n grattugia.
gratification [grætɪfɪ'keɪʃən] n soddisfazione f.
gratify ['grætɪfaɪ] vt appagare; (whim) soddisfare.
gratifying ['grætɪfaɪɪŋ] adj gradito(a); soddisfacente.
grating ['greɪtɪŋ] n (iron bars) grata ♦ adj (noise) stridente, stridulo(a).
gratitude ['grætɪtjuːd] n gratitudine f.
gratuitous [grə'tjuːɪtəs] adj gratuito(a).
gratuity [grə'tjuːɪtɪ] n mancia.
grave [greɪv] n tomba ♦ adj grave, serio(a).
gravedigger ['greɪvdɪgə*] n becchino.
gravel ['grævl] n ghiaia.
gravely ['greɪvlɪ] adv gravemente, solennemente; ~ **ill** in pericolo di vita.
gravestone ['greɪvstəun] n pietra tombale.
graveyard ['greɪvjɑːd] n cimitero.
gravitate ['grævɪteɪt] vi gravitare.
gravity ['grævɪtɪ] n (all senses) gravità.
gravy ['greɪvɪ] n intingolo della carne; salsa.
gravy boat n salsiera.
gravy train n: **the** ~ (col) l'albero della cuccagna.

gray [greɪ] adj (US) = **grey**.
graze [greɪz] vi pascolare, pascere ♦ vt (touch lightly) sfiorare; (scrape) escoriare ♦ n (MED) escoriazione f.
grazing ['greɪzɪŋ] n pascolo.
grease [griːs] n (fat) grasso; (lubricant) lubrificante m ♦ vt ingrassare; lubrificare; **to** ~ **the skids** (US: fig) spianare la strada.
grease gun n ingrassatore m.
greasepaint ['griːspeɪnt] n cerone m.
greaseproof paper ['griːspruːf-] n (BRIT) carta oleata.
greasy ['griːsɪ] adj grasso(a); untuoso(a); (BRIT: road, surface) scivoloso(a); (hands, clothes) unto(a).
great [greɪt] adj grande; (pain, heat) forte, intenso(a); (col) magnifico(a), meraviglioso(a); **they're** ~ **friends** sono grandi amici; **the** ~ **thing is that** ... il bello è che ...; **it was** ~! è stato fantastico!; **we had a** ~ **time** ci siamo divertiti un mondo.
Great Barrier Reef n: **the** ~ la Grande Barriera Corallina.
Great Britain n Gran Bretagna.
great-grandchild, pl **-children** [greɪt'græntʃaɪld, -tʃɪldrən] n pronipote m/f.
great-grandfather [greɪt'grændfɑːðə*] n bisnonno.
great-grandmother [greɪt'grænmʌðə*] n bisnonna.
Great Lakes npl: **the** ~ i Grandi Laghi.
greatly ['greɪtlɪ] adv molto.
greatness ['greɪtnɪs] n grandezza.
Grecian ['griːʃən] adj greco(a).
Greece [griːs] n Grecia.
greed [griːd] n (also: ~iness) avarizia; (for food) golosità, ghiottoneria.
greedily ['griːdɪlɪ] adv avidamente; golosamente.
greedy ['griːdɪ] adj avido(a); goloso(a), ghiotto(a).
Greek [griːk] adj greco(a) ♦ n greco/a; (LING) greco; **ancient/modern** ~ greco antico/moderno.
green [griːn] adj (also POL) verde; (inexperienced) inesperto(a), ingenuo(a) ♦ n verde m; (stretch of grass) prato; (also: **village** ~) ≈ piazza del paese; ~**s** npl (vegetables) verdura; (of golf course) green m inv; **to have** ~ **fingers** or (US) **a** ~ **thumb** (fig) avere il pollice verde; **the G**~ **Party** (BRIT POL) i Verdi.
green belt n (round town) cintura di verde.
green card n (AUT) carta verde.
greenery ['griːnərɪ] n verde m.
greenfly ['griːnflaɪ] n afide f.
greengage ['griːngeɪdʒ] n susina Regina

Claudia.

greengrocer ['gri:ngrəusə*] n (BRIT) fruttivendolo/a, erbivendolo/a.

greenhouse ['gri:nhaus] n serra.

greenhouse effect n: the ~ l'effetto serra.

greenhouse gas n gas m inv responsabile dell'effetto serra.

greenish ['gri:nɪʃ] adj verdastro(a).

Greenland ['gri:nlənd] n Groenlandia.

Greenlander ['gri:nləndə*] n groenlandese m/f.

green light n: to give sb the ~ dare via libera a qn.

green pepper n peperone m verde.

greet [gri:t] vt salutare.

greeting ['gri:tɪŋ] n saluto; **Christmas/ birthday** ~s auguri mpl di Natale/di compleanno; **Season's** ~s Buone Feste.

greeting(s) card n cartolina d'auguri.

gregarious [grə'gɛərɪəs] adj gregario(a); socievole.

grenade [grə'neɪd] n (also: **hand** ~) granata.

grew [gru:] pt of **grow**.

grey [greɪ] adj grigio(a); **to go** ~ diventar grigio.

greyhound ['greɪhaund] n levriere m.

grid [grɪd] n grata; (ELEC) rete f; (US AUT) area d'incrocio.

griddle ['grɪdl] n piastra.

gridiron ['grɪdaɪən] n graticola.

gridlock ['grɪdlɔk] n (traffic jam) paralisi f inv del traffico.

grief [gri:f] n dolore m; **to come to** ~ (plan) naufragare; (person) finire male.

grievance ['gri:vəns] n doglianza, lagnanza; (cause for complaint) motivo di risentimento.

grieve [gri:v] vi addolorarsi, soffrire ♦ vt addolorare; **to** ~ **for sb** compiangere qn; (dead person) piangere qn.

grievous bodily harm (GBH) ['gri:vəs-] n (LAW) aggressione f.

grill [grɪl] n (on cooker) griglia ♦ vt (BRIT) cuocere ai ferri; (question) interrogare senza sosta; ~**ed meat** carne f ai ferri or alla griglia.

grille [grɪl] n grata; (AUT) griglia.

grill(room) ['grɪl(rum)] n rosticceria.

grim [grɪm] adj sinistro(a); brutto(a).

grimace [grɪ'meɪs] n smorfia ♦ vi fare smorfie.

grime [graɪm] n sudiciume m.

grimy ['graɪmɪ] adj sudicio(a).

grin [grɪn] n sorriso smagliante ♦ vi: **to** ~ **(at)** sorridere (a), fare un gran sorriso (a).

grind [graɪnd] vb (pt, pp **ground** [graund]) vt macinare; (US: meat) tritare, macinare; (make sharp) arrotare; (polish: gem, lens) molare ♦ vi (car gears) grattare ♦ n (work) sgobbata; **to** ~ **one's teeth** digrignare i denti; **to** ~ **to a halt** (vehicle) arrestarsi con uno stridio di freni; (fig: talks, scheme) insabbiarsi; (: work, production) cessare del tutto; **the daily** ~ (col) il trantran quotidiano.

grinder ['graɪndə*] n (machine: for coffee) macinino.

grindstone ['graɪndstəun] n: **to keep one's nose to the** ~ darci sotto.

grip [grɪp] n presa; (holdall) borsa da viaggio ♦ vt afferrare; **to come to** ~s **with** affrontare; cercare di risolvere; **to** ~ **the road** (tyres) far presa sulla strada; (car) tenere bene la strada; **to lose one's** ~ perdere or allentare la presa; (fig) perdere la grinta.

gripe [graɪp] n (MED) colica; (col: complaint) lagna ♦ vi (col) brontolare.

gripping ['grɪpɪŋ] adj avvincente.

grisly ['grɪzlɪ] adj macabro(a), orrido(a).

grist [grɪst] n (fig): **it's (all)** ~ **to the mill** tutto aiuta.

gristle ['grɪsl] n cartilagine f.

grit [grɪt] n ghiaia; (courage) fegato ♦ vt (road) coprire di sabbia; **to** ~ **one's teeth** stringere i denti; **I've got a piece of** ~ **in my eye** ho un bruscolino nell'occhio.

grits [grɪts] npl (US) macinato grosso (di avena etc).

grizzle ['grɪzl] vi (BRIT) piagnucolare.

grizzly ['grɪzlɪ] n (also: ~ **bear**) orso grigio, grizzly m inv.

groan [grəun] n gemito ♦ vi gemere.

grocer ['grəusə*] n negoziante m di generi alimentari; ~**'s (shop)** negozio di alimentari.

groceries ['grəusərɪz] npl provviste fpl.

grocery ['grəusərɪ] n (shop) (negozio di) alimentari.

grog [grɔg] n grog m inv.

groggy ['grɔgɪ] adj barcollante.

groin [grɔɪn] n inguine m.

groom [gru:m] n palafreniere m; (also: **bride**~) sposo ♦ vt (horse) strigliare; (fig): **to** ~ **sb for** avviare qn a.

groove [gru:v] n scanalatura, solco.

grope [grəup] vi andare a tentoni; **to** ~ **for sth** cercare qc a tastoni.

gross [grəus] adj grossolano(a); (COMM) lordo(a) ♦ n (pl inv) (twelve dozen) grossa ♦ vt (COMM) incassare, avere un incasso lordo di.

gross domestic product (GDP) n

prodotto interno lordo (P.I.L.).
grossly ['grəuslı] *adv* (*greatly*) molto.
gross national product (GNP) *n*
prodotto nazionale lordo (P.N.L.).
grotesque [grəu'tɛsk] *adj* grottesco(a).
grotto ['grɔtəu] *n* grotta.
grotty ['grɔtı] *adj* (*BRIT col*) squallido(a).
grouch [grautʃ] (*col*) *vi* brontolare ♦ *n*
(*person*) brontolone/a.
ground [graund] *pt, pp of* **grind** ♦ *adj* (*coffee
etc*) macinato(a) ♦ *n* suolo, terra; (*land*)
terreno; (*SPORT*) campo; (*reason: gen pl*)
ragione *f*; (*US: also*: ~ **wire**) (presa a)
terra ♦ *vt* (*plane*) tenere a terra; (*US ELEC*)
mettere la presa a terra a ♦ *vi* (*ship*)
arenarsi; ~**s** *npl* (*of coffee etc*) fondi *mpl*;
(*gardens etc*) terreno, giardini *mpl*; **on/to
the** ~ per/a terra; **below** ~ sottoterra;
common ~ terreno comune; **to gain/lose**
~ guadagnare/perdere terreno; **he
covered a lot of** ~ **in his lecture** ha
toccato molti argomenti nel corso della
conferenza.
ground cloth *n* (*US*) = **groundsheet**.
ground control *n* (*AVIAT, SPACE*) base *f* di
controllo.
ground floor *n* pianterreno.
grounding ['graundıŋ] *n* (*in education*) basi
fpl.
groundless ['graundlıs] *adj* infondato(a).
groundnut ['graundnʌt] *n* arachide *f*.
ground rent *n* (*BRIT*) canone *m* di affitto di
un terreno.
ground rules *npl* regole *fpl* fondamentali.
groundsheet ['graundʃi:t] *n* (*BRIT*) telone *m*
impermeabile.
groundsman ['graundzmən], (*US*)
groundskeeper ['graundzki:pə*] *n*
(*SPORT*) custode *m* (di campo sportivo).
ground staff *n* personale *m* di terra.
groundswell ['graundswɛl] *n* maremoto;
(*fig*) movimento.
ground-to-air ['graundtu'ɛə*] *adj* terra-aria
inv.
ground-to-ground ['graundə'graund] *adj*: ~
missile missile *m* terra-terra.
groundwork ['graundwə:k] *n* preparazione
f.
group [gru:p] *n* gruppo; (*MUS: pop* ~)
complesso, gruppo ♦ *vt* raggruppare ♦ *vi*
raggrupparsi.
groupie ['gru:pı] *n* groupie *m/f inv*, fan *m/f inv*
scatenato(a).
group therapy *n* terapia di gruppo.
grouse [graus] *n* (*pl inv*) (*bird*) tetraone *m*
♦ *vi* (*complain*) brontolare.
grove [grəuv] *n* boschetto.
grovel ['grɔvl] *vi* (*fig*): **to** ~ **(before)**

strisciare (di fronte a).
grow, *pt* **grew**, *pp* **grown** [grəu, gru:, grəun]
vi crescere; (*increase*) aumentare;
(*become*): **to** ~ **rich/weak** arricchirsi/
indebolirsi ♦ *vt* coltivare, far crescere; **to**
~ **tired of waiting** stancarsi di aspettare.
▶**grow apart** *vi* (*fig*) estraniarsi.
▶**grow away from** *vt fus* (*fig*) allontanarsi
da, staccarsi da.
▶**grow on** *vt fus*: **that painting is** ~**ing on
me** quel quadro più lo guardo più mi
piace.
▶**grow out of** *vt fus* (*clothes*) diventare
troppo grande per indossare; (*habit*)
perdere (col tempo); **he'll** ~ **out of it** gli
passerà.
▶**grow up** *vi* farsi grande, crescere.
grower ['grəuə*] *n* coltivatore/trice.
growing ['grəuıŋ] *adj* (*fear, amount*)
crescente; ~ **pains** (*also fig*) problemi *mpl*
di crescita.
growl [graul] *vi* ringhiare.
grown [grəun] *pp of* **grow** ♦ *adj* adulto(a),
maturo(a).
grown-up [grəun'ʌp] *n* adulto/a, grande *m/f*.
growth [grəuθ] *n* crescita, sviluppo; (*what
has grown*) crescita; (*MED*) escrescenza,
tumore *m*.
growth rate *n* tasso di crescita.
GRSM *n abbr* (*BRIT*) = *Graduate of the Royal
Schools of Music*.
grub [grʌb] *n* larva; (*col: food*) roba (da
mangiare).
grubby ['grʌbı] *adj* sporco(a).
grudge [grʌdʒ] *n* rancore *m* ♦ *vt*: **to** ~ **sb sth**
dare qc a qn di malavoglia; invidiare qc
a qn; **to bear sb a** ~ **(for)** serbar rancore a
qn (per).
grudgingly ['grʌdʒıŋlı] *adv* di malavoglia,
di malincuore.
gruelling, (*US*) **grueling** ['gruəlıŋ] *adj*
estenuante.
gruesome ['gru:səm] *adj* orribile.
gruff [grʌf] *adj* rozzo(a).
grumble ['grʌmbl] *vi* brontolare, lagnarsi.
grumpy ['grʌmpı] *adj* stizzito(a).
grunge [grʌndʒ] *n* (*MUS*) grunge *m inv*;
(*style*) moda *f* grunge *inv*.
grunt [grʌnt] *vi* grugnire ♦ *n* grugnito.
G-string ['dʒi:strıŋ] *n* (*garment*) tanga *m inv*.
GSUSA *n abbr* = *Girl Scouts of the United
States of America*.
GT *abbr* (*AUT*: = *gran turismo*) GT.
GU *abbr* (*US POST*) = *Guam*.
guarantee [gærən'ti:] *n* garanzia ♦ *vt*
garantire; **he can't** ~ **(that)** **he'll come**
non può garantire che verrà.
guarantor [gærən'tɔ:*] *n* garante *m/f*.

guard [gɑːd] *n* guardia; (*protection*) riparo, protezione *f*; (*BOXING*) difesa; (*one man*) guardia, sentinella; (*BRIT RAIL*) capotreno; (*safety device*: *on machine*) schermo protettivo; (*also*: **fire ~**) parafuoco ♦ *vt* fare la guardia a; **to ~** (**against** *or* **from**) proteggere (da), salvaguardare (da); **to be on one's ~** (*fig*) stare in guardia.

►**guard against** *vi*: **to ~ against doing sth** guardarsi dal fare qc.

guard dog *n* cane *m* da guardia.

guarded ['gɑːdɪd] *adj* (*fig*) cauto(a), guardingo(a).

guardian ['gɑːdɪən] *n* custode *m*; (*of minor*) tutore/trice.

guard's van *n* (*BRIT RAIL*) vagone *m* di servizio.

Guatemala [gwɑːtə'mɑːlə] *n* Guatemala *m*.

Guernsey ['gɜːnzɪ] *n* Guernesey *f*.

guerrilla [gə'rɪlə] *n* guerrigliero.

guerrilla warfare *n* guerriglia.

guess [gɛs] *vi* indovinare ♦ *vt* indovinare; (*US*) credere, pensare ♦ *n* congettura; **to take** *or* **have a ~** cercare di indovinare; **my ~ is that ...** suppongo che ...; **to keep sb ~ing** tenere qn in sospeso *or* sulla corda; **I ~ you're right** mi sa che hai ragione.

guesstimate ['gɛstɪmɪt] *n* (*col*) stima approssimativa.

guesswork ['gɛswɜːk] *n*: **I got the answer by ~** ho azzeccato la risposta.

guest [gɛst] *n* ospite *m/f*; (*in hotel*) cliente *m/f*; **be my ~** (*col*) fai come (se fossi) a casa tua.

guest-house ['gɛsthaus] *n* pensione *f*.

guest room *n* camera degli ospiti.

guff [gʌf] *n* (*col*) stupidaggini *fpl*, assurdità *fpl*.

guffaw [gʌ'fɔː] *n* risata sonora ♦ *vi* scoppiare in una risata sonora.

guidance ['gaɪdəns] *n* guida, direzione *f*; **marriage/vocational ~** consulenza matrimoniale/per l'avviamento professionale.

guide [gaɪd] *n* (*person*, *book etc*) guida; (*also*: **girl ~**) giovane esploratrice *f* ♦ *vt* guidare; **to be ~d by sb/sth** farsi *or* lasciarsi guidare da qn/qc.

guidebook ['gaɪdbuk] *n* guida.

guided missile *n* missile *m* telecomandato.

guide dog *n* (*BRIT*) cane *m* guida *inv*.

guidelines ['gaɪdlaɪnz] *npl* (*fig*) indicazioni *fpl*, linee *fpl* direttive.

guild [gɪld] *n* arte *f*, corporazione *f*; associazione *f*.

guildhall ['gɪldhɔːl] *n* (*BRIT*) palazzo municipale.

guile [gaɪl] *n* astuzia.

guileless ['gaɪllɪs] *adj* candido(a).

guillotine ['gɪlətiːn] *n* ghigliottina.

guilt [gɪlt] *n* colpevolezza.

guilty ['gɪltɪ] *adj* colpevole; **to feel ~ (about)** sentirsi in colpa (per); **to plead ~/not ~** dichiararsi colpevole/innocente.

Guinea ['gɪnɪ] *n*: **Republic of ~** Repubblica di Guinea.

guinea ['gɪnɪ] *n* (*BRIT*) ghinea (= *21 shillings: valuta ora fuori uso*).

guinea pig *n* cavia.

guise [gaɪz] *n* maschera.

guitar [gɪ'tɑː*] *n* chitarra.

guitarist [gɪ'tɑːrɪst] *n* chitarrista *m/f*.

gulch [gʌltʃ] *n* (*US*) burrone *m*.

gulf [gʌlf] *n* golfo; (*abyss*) abisso; **the (Persian) G~** il Golfo Persico.

Gulf States *npl*: **the ~** i paesi del Golfo Persico.

Gulf Stream *n*: **the ~** la corrente del Golfo.

gull [gʌl] *n* gabbiano.

gullet ['gʌlɪt] *n* gola.

gullibility [gʌlɪ'bɪlɪtɪ] *n* semplicioneria.

gullible ['gʌlɪbl] *adj* credulo(a).

gully ['gʌlɪ] *n* burrone *m*; gola; canale *m*.

gulp [gʌlp] *vi* deglutire; (*from emotion*) avere il nodo in gola ♦ *vt* (*also*: **~ down**) tracannare, inghiottire ♦ *n* (*of liquid*) sorso; (*of food*) boccone *m*; **in ~ or at one ~** in un sorso, d'un fiato.

gum [gʌm] *n* (*ANAT*) gengiva; (*glue*) colla; (*sweet*) gelatina di frutta; (*also*: **chewing-~**) chewing-gum *m* ♦ *vt* incollare.

►**gum up** *vt*: **to ~ up the works** (*col*) mettere il bastone tra le ruote.

gumboil ['gʌmbɔɪl] *n* ascesso (dentario).

gumboots ['gʌmbuːts] *npl* (*BRIT*) stivali *mpl* di gomma.

gumption ['gʌmpʃən] *n* buon senso, senso pratico.

gun [gʌn] *n* fucile *m*; (*small*) pistola, rivoltella; (*rifle*) carabina; (*shotgun*) fucile da caccia; (*cannon*) cannone *m* ♦ *vt* (*also*: **~ down**) abbattere a colpi di pistola *or* fucile; **to stick to one's ~s** (*fig*) tener duro.

gunboat ['gʌnbəut] *n* cannoniera.

gun dog *n* cane *m* da caccia.

gunfire ['gʌnfaɪə*] *n* spari *mpl*.

gung-ho ['gʌŋ'həu] *adj* (*col*) stupidamente entusiasta.

gunk [gʌŋk] *n* porcherie *fpl*.

gunman ['gʌnmən] *n* bandito armato.

gunner ['gʌnə*] *n* artigliere *m*.

gunpoint ['gʌnpɔɪnt] *n*: **at ~** sotto minaccia

di fucile.
gunpowder ['gʌnpaudə*] n polvere f da
sparo.
gunrunning ['gʌnrʌnɪŋ] n contrabbando
d'armi.
gunshot ['gʌnʃɔt] n sparo; **within** ~ **a**
portata di fucile.
gunsmith ['gʌnsmɪθ] n armaiolo.
gurgle ['gɔːgl] n gorgoglio ♦ vi gorgogliare.
guru ['guruː] n guru m inv.
gush [gʌʃ] n fiotto, getto ♦ vi sgorgare; (fig)
abbandonarsi ad effusioni.
gushing ['gʌʃɪŋ] adj che fa smancerie.
gusset ['gʌsɪt] n gherone m; (in tights, pants)
rinforzo.
gust [gʌst] n (of wind) raffica.
gusto ['gʌstəu] n entusiasmo.
gusty ['gʌstɪ] adj (wind) a raffiche; (day)
tempestoso(a).
gut [gʌt] n intestino, budello; (MUS etc)
minugia; ~**s** npl (col: innards) budella fpl;
(: of animals) interiora fpl; (courage) fegato
♦ vt (poultry, fish) levare le interiora a,
sventrare; (building) svuotare; (: subj: fire)
divorare l'interno di; **to hate sb's** ~**s**
odiare qn a morte.
gut reaction n reazione f istintiva.
gutsy ['gʌtsɪ] adj (col: style) che ha
mordente; (plucky) coraggioso(a).
gutted ['gʌtɪd] adv (col: upset) scioccato(a).
gutter ['gʌtə*] n (of roof) grondaia; (in
street) cunetta.
gutter press n: **the** ~ la stampa
scandalistica.
guttural ['gʌtərl] adj gutturale.
guy [gaɪ] n (also: ~**rope**) cavo or corda di
fissaggio; (col: man) tipo, elemento;
(figure) effigie di Guy Fawkes.
Guyana [gaɪ'ænə] n Guayana f.
Guy Fawkes' Night [-'fɔːks-] n (BRIT) see
boxed note.

GUY FAWKES' NIGHT

Durante la notte del 5 novembre, la **Guy
Fawkes' Night**, che commemora il fallimento
della Congiura delle Polveri contro Giacomo I
nel 1605, vengono lanciati fuochi d'artificio e
viene bruciata l'effigie di Guy Fawkes, uno dei
cospiratori.

---

guzzle ['gʌzl] vi gozzovigliare ♦ vt
trangugiare.
gym [dʒɪm] n (also: **gymnasium**) palestra;
(also: **gymnastics**) ginnastica.
gymkhana [dʒɪm'kɑːnə] n gimkana.
gymnasium [dʒɪm'neɪzɪəm] n palestra.
gymnast ['dʒɪmnæst] n ginnasta m/f.

gymnastics [dʒɪm'næstɪks] n, npl
ginnastica.
gym shoes npl scarpe fpl da ginnastica.
gym slip n (BRIT) grembiule m da scuola
(per ragazze).
gynaecologist, (US) **gynecologist**
[gaɪnɪ'kɔlədʒɪst] n ginecologo/a.
gynaecology, (US) **gynecology**
[gaɪnə'kɔlədʒɪ] n ginecologia.
gypsy ['dʒɪpsɪ] n = **gipsy**.
gyrate [dʒaɪ'reɪt] vi girare.
gyroscope ['dʒaɪərəskəup] n giroscopio.

H h

H, h [eɪtʃ] n (letter) H, h f or m inv; **H for
Harry**, (US) **H for How** ≈ H come Hotel.
habeas corpus ['heɪbɪəs'kɔːpəs] n (LAW)
habeas corpus m inv.
haberdashery ['hæbədæʃərɪ] n merceria.
habit ['hæbɪt] n abitudine f; (costume) abito;
(REL) tonaca; **to get out of/into the** ~ **of
doing sth** perdere/prendere l'abitudine
di fare qc.
habitable ['hæbɪtəbl] adj abitabile.
habitat ['hæbɪtæt] n habitat m inv.
habitation [hæbɪ'teɪʃən] n abitazione f.
habitual [hə'bɪtjuəl] adj abituale; (drinker,
liar) inveterato(a).
habitually [hə'bɪtjuəlɪ] adv abitualmente, di
solito.
hack [hæk] vt tagliare, fare a pezzi ♦ n (cut)
taglio; (blow) colpo; (old horse) ronzino;
(pej: writer) negro.
hacker ['hækə*] n (COMPUT) pirata m
informatico.
hackles ['hæklz] npl: **to make sb's** ~ **rise**
(fig) rendere qn furioso.
hackney cab ['hæknɪ-] n carrozza a nolo.
hackneyed ['hæknɪd] adj comune, trito(a).
hacksaw ['hæksɔː] n seghetto (per
metallo).
had [hæd] pt, pp of **have**.
haddock ['hædək] n eglefino.
hadn't ['hædnt] = **had not**.
haematology, (US) **hematology**
[hiːmə'tɔlədʒɪ] n ematologia.
haemoglobin, (US) **hemoglobin**
[hiːməu'gləubɪn] n emoglobina.
haemophilia, (US) **hemophilia**
[hiːməu'fɪlɪə] n emofilia.

haemorrhage, (*US*) **hemorrhage** ['hemərɪdʒ] *n* emorragia.
haemorrhoids, (*US*) **hemorrhoids** ['heməroɪdz] *npl* emorroidi *fpl.*
hag [hæg] *n* (*ugly*) befana; (*nasty*) megera; (*witch*) strega.
haggard ['hægəd] *adj* smunto(a).
haggis ['hægɪs] *n* (*Scottish*) *insaccato a base di frattaglie di pecora e avena.*
haggle ['hægl] *vi*: **to ~** (*over*) contrattare (su); (*argue*) discutere (su).
haggling ['hæglɪŋ] *n* contrattazioni *fpl.*
Hague [heɪg] *n*: **The ~** L'Aia.
hail [heɪl] *n* grandine *f* ♦ *vt* (*call*) chiamare; (*greet*) salutare ♦ *vi* grandinare; **to ~** (**as**) acclamare (come); **he ~s from Scotland** viene dalla Scozia.
hailstone ['heɪlstəun] *n* chicco di grandine.
hailstorm ['heɪlstɔːm] *n* grandinata.
hair [hɛə*] *n* capelli *mpl*; (*single hair: on head*) capello; (: *on body*) pelo; **to do one's ~** pettinarsi.
hairbrush ['hɛəbrʌʃ] *n* spazzola per capelli.
haircut ['hɛəkʌt] *n* taglio di capelli; **I need a ~** devo tagliarmi i capelli.
hairdo ['hɛəduː] *n* acconciatura.
hairdresser ['hɛədrɛsə*] *n* parrucchiere/a.
hair-dryer ['hɛədraɪə*] *n* asciugacapelli *m inv.*
-haired [hɛəd] *suffix*: **fair/long~** dai capelli biondi/lunghi.
hairgrip ['hɛəgrɪp] *n* forcina.
hairline ['hɛəlaɪn] *n* attaccatura dei capelli.
hairline fracture *n* incrinatura.
hair oil *n* brillantina.
hairpiece ['hɛəpiːs] *n* toupet *m inv.*
hairpin ['hɛəpɪn] *n* forcina.
hairpin bend, (*US*) **hairpin curve** *n* tornante *m.*
hair-raising ['hɛəreɪzɪŋ] *adj* orripilante.
hair remover *n* crema depilatoria.
hair spray *n* lacca per capelli.
hairstyle ['hɛəstaɪl] *n* pettinatura, acconciatura.
hairy ['hɛərɪ] *adj* irsuto(a); peloso(a); (*col: frightening*) spaventoso(a).
Haiti ['heɪtɪ] *n* Haiti *f.*
hake, *pl* **~** *or* **~s** [heɪk] *n* nasello.
halcyon ['hælsɪən] *adj* sereno(a).
hale [heɪl] *adj*: **~ and hearty** che scoppia di salute.
half [hɑːf] *n* (*pl* **halves** [hɑːvz]) mezzo, metà *f inv*; (*SPORT: of match*) tempo; (: *of ground*) metà campo ♦ *adj* mezzo(a) ♦ *adv* a mezzo, a metà; **~ an hour** mezz'ora; **~ a dozen** mezza dozzina; **~ a pound** mezza libbra; **two and a ~** due e mezzo; **a week and a ~** una settimana e mezza; **~ (of it)** la metà;

~ (of) la metà di; **~ the amount of** la metà di; **to cut sth in ~** tagliare qc in due; **~ empty/closed** mezzo vuoto/chiuso, semivuoto/semichiuso; **~ past 3** le 3 e mezza; **to go halves (with sb)** fare a metà (con qn).
half-back ['hɑːfbæk] *n* (*SPORT*) mediano.
half-baked [hɑːf'beɪkt] *adj* (*fig col: idea, scheme*) mal combinato(a), che non sta in piedi.
half-breed ['hɑːfbriːd] *n* = **half-caste.**
half-brother ['hɑːfbrʌðə*] *n* fratellastro.
half-caste ['hɑːfkɑːst] *n* meticcio/a.
half-hearted [hɑːf'hɑːtɪd] *adj* tiepido(a).
half-hour [hɑːf'auə*] *n* mezz'ora.
half-mast ['hɑːf'mɑːst] *n*: **at ~** (*flag*) a mezz'asta.
halfpenny ['heɪpnɪ] *n* mezzo penny *m inv.*
half-price ['hɑːf'praɪs] *adj* a metà prezzo ♦ *adv* (*also*: **at ~**) a metà prezzo.
half term *n* (*BRIT SCOL*) vacanza a *or* di metà trimestre.
half-time [hɑːf'taɪm] *n* (*SPORT*) intervallo.
halfway [hɑːf'weɪ] *adv* a metà strada; **to meet sb ~** (*fig*) arrivare a un compromesso con qn.
halfway house *n* (*hostel*) *ostello dove possono alloggiare temporaneamente ex detenuti*; (*fig*) via di mezzo.
half-wit ['hɑːfwɪt] *n* (*col*) idiota *m/f.*
half-yearly [hɑːf'jɪəlɪ] *adv* semestralmente, ogni sei mesi ♦ *adj* semestrale.
halibut ['hælɪbət] *n* (*pl inv*) ippoglosso.
halitosis [hælɪ'təusɪs] *n* alitosi *f.*
hall [hɔːl] *n* sala, salone *m*; (*entrance way*) entrata; (*corridor*) corridoio; (*mansion*) grande villa, maniero; **~ of residence** *n* (*BRIT*) casa dello studente.
hallmark ['hɔːlmɑːk] *n* marchio di garanzia; (*fig*) caratteristica.
hallo [hə'ləu] *excl* = **hello.**
Hallowe'en ['hæləu'iːn] *n* vigilia d'Ognissanti; *see boxed note.*

HALLOWE'EN

*Secondo la tradizione anglosassone, durante la notte di **Hallowe'en**, il 31 di ottobre, è possibile vedere le streghe e i fantasmi. Negli Stati Uniti e in Scozia i bambini, travestiti da fantasmi e con in mano lanterne ricavate da zucche, vanno di porta in porta e raccolgono dolci e piccoli doni.*

---

hallucination [həluːsɪ'neɪʃən] *n* allucinazione *f.*
hallucinogenic [həluːsɪnəu'dʒenɪk] *adj* allucinogeno(a).

hallway ['hɔːlweɪ] n ingresso; corridoio.
halo ['heɪləʊ] n (of saint etc) aureola; (of sun) alone m.
halt [hɔːlt] n fermata ♦ vt fermare ♦ vi fermarsi; **to call a ~ (to sth)** (fig) mettere or porre fine (a qc).
halter ['hɔːltə*] n (for horse) cavezza.
halterneck ['hɔːltənɛk] adj allacciato(a) dietro il collo.
halve [hɑːv] vt (apple etc) dividere a metà; (expense) ridurre di metà.
halves [hɑːvz] npl of half.
ham [hæm] n prosciutto; (col: also: radio ~) radioamatore/trice; (also: ~ actor) attore/trice senza talento.
Hamburg ['hæmbɔːg] n Amburgo f.
hamburger ['hæmbɔːgə*] n hamburger m inv.
ham-fisted ['hæm'fɪstɪd], (US) **ham-handed** ['hæm'hændɪd] adj maldestro(a).
hamlet ['hæmlɪt] n paesetto.
hammer ['hæmə*] n martello ♦ vt martellare; (fig) sconfiggere duramente ♦ vi (at door) picchiare; **to ~ a point home to sb** cacciare un'idea in testa a qn.
▶**hammer out** vt (metal) spianare (a martellate); (fig: solution, agreement) mettere a punto.
hammock ['hæmək] n amaca.
hamper ['hæmpə*] vt impedire ♦ n cesta.
hamster ['hæmstə*] n criceto.
hamstring ['hæmstrɪŋ] n (ANAT) tendine m del ginocchio.
hand [hænd] n mano f; (of clock) lancetta; (handwriting) scrittura; (at cards) mano; (: game) partita; (worker) operaio/a; (measurement: of horse) ≈ dieci centimetri ♦ vt dare, passare; **to give sb a ~** dare una mano a qn; **at ~** a portata di mano; **in ~** a disposizione; (work) in corso; **we have the matter in ~** ci stiamo occupando della cosa; **we have the situation in ~** abbiamo la situazione sotto controllo; **to be on ~** (person) essere disponibile; (emergency services) essere pronto(a) a intervenire; **to ~** (information etc) a portata di mano; **to force sb's ~** forzare la mano a qn; **to have a free ~** avere carta bianca; **to have in one's ~** (also fig) avere in mano or in pugno; **on the one ~ ..., on the other ~** da un lato ..., dall'altro.
▶**hand down** vt passare giù; (tradition, heirloom) tramandare; (US: sentence, verdict) emettere.
▶**hand in** vt consegnare.
▶**hand out** vt (leaflets) distribuire; (advice) elargire.

▶**hand over** vt passare; cedere.
▶**hand round** vt (BRIT: information, papers) far passare; (distribute: chocolates etc) far girare; (subj: hostess) offrire.
handbag ['hændbæg] n borsetta.
hand baggage n bagaglio a mano.
handball ['hændbɔːl] n pallamano f.
handbasin ['hændbeɪsn] n lavandino.
handbook ['hændbʊk] n manuale m.
handbrake ['hændbreɪk] n freno a mano.
hand cream n crema per le mani.
handcuffs ['hændkʌfs] npl manette fpl.
handful ['hændfʊl] n manciata, pugno.
hand-held ['hænd'hɛld] adj portatile.
handicap ['hændɪkæp] n handicap m inv ♦ vt handicappare; **to be mentally ~ped** essere un handicappato mentale; **to be physically ~ped** essere handicappato.
handicraft ['hændɪkrɑːft] n lavoro d'artigiano.
handiwork ['hændɪwɜːk] n lavorazione f a mano; **this looks like his ~** (pej) qui c'è il suo zampino.
handkerchief ['hæŋkətʃɪf] n fazzoletto.
handle ['hændl] n (of door etc) maniglia; (of cup etc) ansa; (of knife etc) impugnatura; (of saucepan) manico; (for winding) manovella ♦ vt toccare, maneggiare; manovrare; (deal with) occuparsi di; (treat: people) trattare; **"~ with care"** "fragile".
handlebar(s) ['hændlbɑː(z)] n(pl) manubrio.
handling ['hændlɪŋ] n (AUT) maneggevolezza; (of issue) modo di affrontare.
handling charges npl commissione f per la prestazione; (for goods) spese fpl di trasporto; (BANKING) spese fpl bancarie.
hand-luggage ['hændlʌgɪdʒ] n bagagli mpl a mano.
handmade [hænd'meɪd] adj fatto(a) a mano; (biscuits etc) fatto(a) in casa.
handout ['hændaʊt] n (leaflet) volantino; (press ~) comunicato stampa.
hand-picked [hænd'pɪkt] adj (produce) scelto(a), selezionato(a); (staff etc) scelto(a).
handrail ['hændreɪl] n (on staircase etc) corrimano m.
handset ['hændsɛt] n (TEL) ricevitore m.
handshake ['hændʃeɪk] n stretta di mano; (COMPUT) colloquio.
handsome ['hænsəm] adj bello(a); (reward) generoso(a); (profit, fortune) considerevole.
hands-on ['hændz'ɔn] adj: **~ experience** esperienza diretta or pratica.
handstand ['hændstænd] n: **to do a ~** fare

la verticale.
hand-to-mouth ['hændtə'mauθ] *adj*
(*existence*) precario(a).
handwriting ['hændraɪtɪŋ] *n* scrittura.
handwritten ['hændrɪtn] *adj* scritto(a) a
mano, manoscritto(a).
handy ['hændɪ] *adj* (*person*) bravo(a); (*close
at hand*) a portata di mano; (*convenient*)
comodo(a); (*useful: machine etc*)
pratico(a), utile; **to come in** ~ servire.
handyman ['hændɪmæn] *n* tuttofare *m inv*;
tools for the ~ arnesi per il fatelo-da-voi.
hang, *pt, pp* **hung** [hæŋ, hʌŋ] *vt* appendere;
(*criminal: pt, pp* **hanged**) impiccare ♦ *vi*
pendere; (*hair*) scendere; (*drapery*)
cadere; **to get the** ~ **of (doing)** sth (*col*)
cominiciare a capire (come si fa) qc.
▶**hang about** *vi* bighellonare, ciondolare.
▶**hang back** *vi* (*hesitate*): **to** ~ **back (from
doing)** essere riluttante (a fare).
▶**hang on** *vi* (*wait*) aspettare ♦ *vt fus*
(*depend on: decision etc*) dipendere da; **to**
~ **on to** (*keep hold of*) aggrapparsi a,
attaccarsi a; (*keep*) tenere.
▶**hang out** *vt* (*washing*) stendere (fuori);
(*col: live*) stare ♦ *vi* penzolare, pendere.
▶**hang together** *vi* (*argument etc*) stare in
piedi.
▶**hang up** *vi* (*TEL*) riattaccare ♦ *vt*
appendere; **to** ~ **up on sb** (*TEL*) metter
giù il ricevitore a qn.
hangar ['hæŋə*] *n* hangar *m inv*.
hangdog ['hæŋdɔg] *adj* (*guilty: look,
expression*) da cane bastonato.
hanger ['hæŋə*] *n* gruccia.
hanger-on [hæŋər'ɔn] *n* parassita *m*.
hang-glider ['hæŋglaɪdə*] *n* deltaplano.
hang-gliding ['hæŋglaɪdɪŋ] *n* volo col
deltaplano.
hanging ['hæŋɪŋ] *n* (*execution*)
impiccagione *f*.
hangman ['hæŋmən] *n* boia *m*, carnefice *m*.
hangover ['hæŋəuvə*] *n* (*after drinking*)
postumi *mpl* di sbornia.
hang-up ['hæŋʌp] *n* complesso.
hank [hæŋk] *n* matassa.
hanker ['hæŋkə*] *vi*: **to** ~ **after** bramare.
hankering ['hæŋkərɪŋ] *n*: **to have a** ~ **for
sth/to do sth** avere una gran voglia di
qc/di fare qc.
hankie, hanky ['hæŋkɪ] *n abbr =
handkerchief*.
Hants *abbr* (*BRIT*) = Hampshire.
haphazard [hæp'hæzəd] *adj* a casaccio, alla
carlona.
hapless ['hæplɪs] *adj* disgraziato(a);
(*unfortunate*) sventurato(a).
happen ['hæpən] *vi* accadere, succedere;

she ~ed **to be free** per caso era libera; **if
anything** ~ed **to him** se dovesse
succedergli qualcosa; **as it** ~s guarda
caso; **what's** ~ing? cosa succede?, cosa
sta succedendo?
▶**happen (up)on** *vt fus* capitare su.
happening ['hæpnɪŋ] *n* avvenimento.
happily ['hæpɪlɪ] *adv* felicemente;
fortunatamente.
happiness ['hæpɪnɪs] *n* felicità,
contentezza.
happy ['hæpɪ] *adj* felice, contento(a); ~
with (*arrangements etc*) soddisfatto(a) di;
yes, I'd be ~ **to** (certo,) con piacere, (ben)
volentieri; ~ **birthday!** buon
compleanno!; ~ **Christmas/New Year!**
buon Natale/anno!
happy-go-lucky ['hæpɪgəu'lʌkɪ] *adj*
spensierato(a).
happy hour *n* orario in cui i *pub* hanno
prezzi ridotti.
harangue [hə'ræŋ] *vt* arringare.
harass ['hærəs] *vt* molestare.
harassed ['hærəst] *adj* assillato(a).
harassment ['hærəsmənt] *n* molestia.
harbour, (*US*) **harbor** ['hɑːbə*] *n* porto ♦ *vt*
dare rifugio a; (*retain: grudge etc*) covare,
nutrire.
harbo(u)r dues *npl* diritti *mpl* portuali.
harbo(u)r master *n* capitano di porto.
hard [hɑːd] *adj* duro(a) ♦ *adv* (*work*) sodo;
(*think, try*) bene; **to look** ~ **at** guardare
fissamente; esaminare attentamente; **to
drink** ~ bere forte; ~ **luck!** peccato!; **no** ~
feelings! senza rancore!; **to be** ~ **of
hearing** essere duro(a) d'orecchio; **to be**
~ **on sb** essere severo con qn; **to be** ~
done by essere trattato(a)
ingiustamente; **I find it** ~ **to believe that**
... stento *or* faccio fatica a credere che ...
+ *sub*.
hard-and-fast ['hɑːdən'fɑːst] *adj* ferreo(a).
hardback ['hɑːdbæk] *n* libro rilegato.
hardboard ['hɑːdbɔːd] *n* legno
precompresso.
hard-boiled egg ['hɑːd'bɔɪld-] *n* uovo sodo.
hard cash *n* denaro in contanti.
hard copy *n* (*COMPUT*) hard copy *f inv*,
terminale *m* di stampa.
hard-core ['hɑːd'kɔː*] *adj* (*pornography*)
hardcore *inv*; (*supporters*) irriducibile.
hard court *n* (*TENNIS*) campo in terra
battuta.
hard disk *n* (*COMPUT*) hard disk *m inv*, disco
rigido.
harden ['hɑːdn] *vt* indurire; (*steel*)
temprare; (*fig: determination*) rafforzare
♦ *vi* (*substance*) indurirsi.

hardened ['hɑːdnd] *adj* (*criminal*) incallito(a); **to be ~ to sth** essere (diventato) insensibile a qc.

hard graft *n*: **by sheer ~** lavorando da matti.

hard-headed ['hɑːd'hɛdɪd] *adj* pratico(a).

hard-hearted ['hɑːd'hɑːtɪd] *adj* che non si lascia commuovere, dal cuore duro.

hard-hitting ['hɑːd'hɪtɪŋ] *adj* molto duro(a); **a ~ documentary** un documentario *m* verità *inv*.

hard labour *n* lavori forzati *mpl*.

hardliner [hɑːd'laɪnə*] *n* fautore/trice della linea dura.

hard-luck story [hɑːd'lʌk-] *n* storia lacrimosa (*con un fine ben preciso*).

hardly ['hɑːdlɪ] *adv* (*scarcely*) appena, a mala pena; **it's ~ the case** non è proprio il caso; **~ anyone/anywhere** quasi nessuno/da nessuna parte; **I can ~ believe it** stento a crederci.

hardness ['hɑːdnɪs] *n* durezza.

hard-nosed ['hɑːd'nəuzd] *adj* (*people*) con i piedi per terra.

hard-pressed ['hɑːd'prɛst] *adj* in difficoltà.

hard sell *n* (*COMM*) intensa campagna promozionale.

hardship ['hɑːdʃɪp] *n* avversità *f inv*; privazioni *fpl*.

hard shoulder *n* (*BRIT AUT*) corsia d'emergenza.

hard-up [hɑːd'ʌp] *adj* (*col*) al verde.

hardware ['hɑːdwɛə*] *n* ferramenta *fpl*; (*COMPUT*) hardware *m*.

hardware shop *n* (negozio di) ferramenta *fpl*.

hard-wearing [hɑːd'wɛərɪŋ] *adj* resistente, robusto(a).

hard-won ['hɑːd'wʌn] *adj* sudato(a).

hard-working [hɑːd'wəːkɪŋ] *adj* lavoratore(trice).

hardy ['hɑːdɪ] *adj* robusto(a); (*plant*) resistente al gelo.

hare [hɛə*] *n* lepre *f*.

hare-brained ['hɛəbreɪnd] *adj* folle; scervellato(a).

harelip ['hɛəlɪp] *n* (*MED*) labbro leporino.

harem [hɑː'riːm] *n* harem *m inv*.

hark back [hɑːk-] *vi*: **to ~ back to** (*former days*) rievocare; (*earlier occasion*) ritornare a *or* su.

harm [hɑːm] *n* male *m*; (*wrong*) danno ♦ *vt* (*person*) fare male a; (*thing*) danneggiare; **to mean no ~** non avere l'intenzione d'offendere; **out of ~'s way** al sicuro; **there's no ~ in trying** tentar non nuoce.

harmful ['hɑːmful] *adj* dannoso(a).

harmless ['hɑːmlɪs] *adj* innocuo(a);

inoffensivo(a).

harmonic [hɑː'mɔnɪk] *adj* armonico(a).

harmonica [hɑː'mɔnɪkə] *n* armonica.

harmonics [hɑː'mɔnɪks] *npl* armonia.

harmonious [hɑː'məunɪəs] *adj* armonioso(a).

harmonium [hɑː'məunɪəm] *n* armonium *m inv*.

harmonize ['hɑːmənaɪz] *vt, vi* armonizzare.

harmony ['hɑːmənɪ] *n* armonia.

harness ['hɑːnɪs] *n* bardatura, finimenti *mpl* ♦ *vt* (*horse*) bardare; (*resources*) sfruttare.

harp [hɑːp] *n* arpa ♦ *vi*: **to ~ on about** insistere tediosamente su.

harpist ['hɑːpɪst] *n* arpista *m/f*.

harpoon [hɑː'puːn] *n* arpione *m*.

harpsichord ['hɑːpsɪkɔːd] *n* clavicembalo.

harrow ['hærəu] *n* (*AGR*) erpice *m*.

harrowing ['hærəuɪŋ] *adj* straziante.

harry ['hærɪ] *vt* (*MIL*) saccheggiare; (*person*) assillare.

harsh [hɑːʃ] *adj* (*hard*) duro(a); (*severe*) severo(a); (*unpleasant: sound*) rauco(a); (: *colour*) chiassoso(a); violento(a).

harshly ['hɑːʃlɪ] *adv* duramente; severamente.

harshness ['hɑːʃnɪs] *n* durezza; severità.

harvest ['hɑːvɪst] *n* raccolto; (*of grapes*) vendemmia ♦ *vt* fare il raccolto di, raccogliere; vendemmiare ♦ *vi* fare il raccolto; vendemmiare.

harvester ['hɑːvɪstə*] *n* (*machine*) mietitrice *f*; (*also*: **combine ~**) mietitrebbia; (*person*) mietitore/trice.

has [hæz] *see* **have**.

has-been ['hæzbiːn] *n* (*col: person*): **he's/she's a ~** ha fatto il suo tempo.

hash [hæʃ] *n* (*CULIN*) specie di spezzatino fatto con carne già cotta; (*fig: mess*) pasticcio ♦ *n abbr* (*col*) = **hashish**.

hashish ['hæʃɪʃ] *n* hascisc *m*.

hasn't ['hæznt] = **has not**.

hassle ['hæsl] *n* (*col*) sacco di problemi.

haste [heɪst] *n* fretta.

hasten ['heɪsn] *vt* affrettare ♦ *vi* affrettarsi; **I ~ to add that ...** mi preme di aggiungere che ....

hastily ['heɪstɪlɪ] *adv* in fretta, precipitosamente.

hasty ['heɪstɪ] *adj* affrettato(a), precipitoso(a).

hat [hæt] *n* cappello.

hatbox ['hætbɔks] *n* cappelliera.

hatch [hætʃ] *n* (*NAUT: also*: **~way**) boccaporto; (*BRIT: also*: **service ~**) portello di servizio ♦ *vi* schiudersi ♦ *vt* covare; (*fig: scheme, plot*) elaborare, mettere a punto.

hatchback ['hætʃbæk] *n* (*AUT*) tre (*or*

cinque) porte *f inv.*
hatchet ['hætʃɪt] *n* accetta.
hatchet job *n (col)* attacco spietato; **to do a ~ on sb** fare a pezzi qn.
hatchet man *n (col)* tirapiedi *m inv,* scagnozzo.
hate [heɪt] *vt* odiare, detestare ♦ *n* odio; **to ~ to do** *or* **doing** detestare fare; **I ~ to trouble you, but ...** mi dispiace disturbarla, ma ....
hateful ['heɪtful] *adj* odioso(a), detestabile.
hatred ['heɪtrɪd] *n* odio.
hat trick *n (BRIT SPORT, also fig)*: **to get a ~** segnare tre punti consecutivi *(or* vincere per tre volte consecutive).
haughty ['hɔːtɪ] *adj* altero(a), arrogante.
haul [hɔːl] *vt* trascinare, tirare ♦ *n (of fish)* pescata; *(of stolen goods etc)* bottino.
haulage ['hɔːlɪdʒ] *n* trasporto; autotrasporto.
haulage contractor *n (BRIT: firm)* impresa di trasporti; *(: person)* autotrasportatore *m.*
haulier ['hɔːlɪə*], *(US)* **hauler** ['hɔːlə*] *n* autotrasportatore *m.*
haunch [hɔːntʃ] *n* anca; **a ~ of venison** una coscia di cervo.
haunt [hɔːnt] *vt (subj: fear)* pervadere; *(: person)* frequentare ♦ *n* rifugio; **a ghost ~s this house** questa casa è abitata da un fantasma.
haunted ['hɔːntɪd] *adj (castle etc)* abitato(a) dai fantasmi *or* dagli spiriti; *(look)* ossessionato(a), tormentato(a).
haunting ['hɔːntɪŋ] *adj (sight, music)* ossessionante, che perseguita.
Havana [hə'vænə] *n* l'Avana.

============= *KEYWORD*

have [hæv] *(pt, pp had) aux vb* **1** *(gen)* avere; essere; **to ~ arrived/gone** essere arrivato(a)/andato(a); **to ~ eaten/slept** avere mangiato/dormito; **he has been kind/promoted** è stato gentile/promosso; **having finished** *or* **when he had finished, he left** dopo aver finito, se n'è andato
2 *(in tag questions)*: **you've done it, ~n't you?** l'hai fatto, (non è) vero?; **he hasn't done it, has he?** non l'ha fatto, vero?
3 *(in short answers and questions)*: **you've made a mistake — no I ~n't/so I ~** ha fatto un errore — ma no, niente affatto/ sì, è vero; **we ~n't paid — yes we ~!** non abbiamo pagato — ma sì che abbiamo pagato!; **I've been there before, ~ you?** ci sono già stato, e lei?
♦ *modal aux vb (be obliged)*: **to ~ (got) to do sth** dover fare qc; **I ~n't got** *or* **I don't ~**

to wear glasses non ho bisogno di portare gli occhiali; **I had better leave** è meglio che io vada
♦ *vt* **1** *(possess, obtain)* avere; **he has (got) blue eyes/dark hair** ha gli occhi azzurri/i capelli scuri; **you got** *or* **do you ~ a car/phone?** ha la macchina/il telefono?; **may I ~ your address?** potrebbe darmi il suo indirizzo?; **you can ~ it for £5** te lo do per 5 sterline
2 *(+noun: take, hold etc)*: **to ~ a bath** fare un bagno; **to ~ breakfast** fare colazione; **to ~ a cigarette** fumare una sigaretta; **to ~ dinner** cenare; **to ~ a drink** bere qualcosa; **to ~ lunch** pranzare; **to ~ a party** dare *or* fare una festa; **to ~ an operation** avere *or* subire un'operazione; **to ~ a swim** fare una nuotata; **I'll ~ a coffee** prendo un caffè; **let me ~ a try** fammi *or* lasciami provare
3: **to ~ sth done** far fare qc; **to ~ one's hair cut** tagliarsi *or* farsi tagliare i capelli; **he had a suit made** si fece fare un abito; **to ~ sb do sth** far fare qc a qn; **he had me phone his boss** mi ha fatto telefonare al suo capo
4 *(experience, suffer)* avere; **to ~ a cold/ flu** avere il raffreddore/l'influenza; **she had her bag stolen** le hanno rubato la borsa
5 *(phrases)*: **you've been had!** ci sei cascato!; **I won't ~ it!** *(accept)* non mi sta affatto bene!; *see also* **haves**
▶**have in** *vt*: **to ~ it in for sb** *(col)* avercela con qn
▶**have on** *vt (garment)* avere addosso; *(be busy with)* avere da fare; **I don't ~ any money on me** non ho soldi con me; **~ you anything on tomorrow?** *(BRIT)* ha qualcosa in programma per domani?; **to ~ sb on** *(BRIT col)* prendere in giro qn
▶**have out** *vt*: **to ~ it out with sb** *(settle a problem etc)* mettere le cose in chiaro con qn.

haven ['heɪvn] *n* porto; *(fig)* rifugio.
haversack ['hævəsæk] *n* zaino.
haves [hævz] *npl (col)*: **the ~ and the have- nots** gli abbienti e i non abbienti.
havoc ['hævək] *n* confusione *f,* subbuglio; **to play ~ with sth** scombussolare qc; **to wreak ~ on sth** mettere in subbuglio qc.
Hawaii [hə'waiiː] *n* le Hawaii.
Hawaiian [hə'waɪjən] *adj* hawaiano(a) ♦ *n* hawaiano/a; *(LING)* lingua hawaiana.
hawk [hɔːk] *n* falco ♦ *vt (goods for sale)* vendere per strada.
hawker ['hɔːkə*] *n* venditore *m* ambulante.

hawkish ['hɔːkɪʃ] *adj* violento(a).
hawthorn ['hɔːθɔːn] *n* biancospino.
hay [heɪ] *n* fieno.
hay fever *n* febbre *f* da fieno.
haystack ['heɪstæk] *n* pagliaio.
haywire ['heɪwaɪə*] *adj* (*col*): **to go** ~
perdere la testa; impazzire.
hazard ['hæzəd] *n* (*chance*) azzardo; (*risk*)
pericolo, rischio ♦ *vt* (*one's life*) rischiare,
mettere a repentaglio; (*remark*)
azzardare; **to be a health/fire** ~ essere
pericoloso per la salute/in caso
d'incendio; **to** ~ **a guess** tirare a
indovinare.
hazardous ['hæzədəs] *adj* pericoloso(a),
rischioso(a).
hazard pay *n* (*US*) indennità di rischio.
hazard warning lights *npl* (*AUT*) luci *fpl* di
emergenza.
haze [heɪz] *n* foschia.
hazel ['heɪzl] *n* (*tree*) nocciolo ♦ *adj* (*eyes*)
(color) nocciola *inv*.
hazelnut ['heɪzlnʌt] *n* nocciola.
hazy ['heɪzɪ] *adj* fosco(a); (*idea*) vago(a);
(*photograph*) indistinto(a).
H-bomb ['eɪtʃbɔm] *n* bomba H.
h & c *abbr* (*BRIT*) = **hot and cold** (*water*).
HE *abbr* = **high explosive**; (*REL, DIPLOMACY*: =
His (*or Her*) *Excellency*) S.E.
he [hiː] *pron* lui, egli; **it is** ~ **who** ... è lui che
...; **here** ~ **is** eccolo; ~**-bear** *etc* orso *etc*
maschio.
head [hɛd] *n* testa, capo; (*leader*) capo; (*on
tape recorder, computer etc*) testina ♦ *vt*
(*list*) essere in testa a; (*group*) essere a
capo di; ~**s** (**or tails**) testa (o croce), pari
(o dispari); ~ **first** a capofitto; ~ **over
heels in love** pazzamente innamorato(a);
£10 a *or* **per** ~ 10 sterline a testa; **to sit at
the** ~ **of the table** sedersi a capotavola;
to have a ~ **for business** essere tagliato
per gli affari; **to have no** ~ **for heights**
soffrire di vertigini; **to lose/keep one's** ~
perdere/non perdere la testa; **to come to
a** ~ (*fig: situation etc*) precipitare; **to** ~ **the
ball** (*SPORT*) dare di testa alla palla.
▶**head for** *vt fus* dirigersi verso.
▶**head off** *vt* (*threat, danger*) sventare.
headache ['hɛdeɪk] *n* mal *m* di testa; **to
have a** ~ aver mal di testa.
headband ['hɛdbænd] *n* fascia per i capelli.
headboard ['hɛdbɔːd] *n* testiera (del letto).
head cold *n* raffreddore *m* di testa.
headdress ['hɛddrɛs] *n* (*of Indian etc*)
copricapo; (*of bride*) acconciatura.
headed notepaper ['hɛdɪd-] *n* carta
intestata.
header ['hɛdə*] *n* (*BRIT col: FOOTBALL*) colpo

di testa; (: *fall*) caduta di testa.
head-first ['hɛd'fɔːst] *adv* a testa in giù;
(*fig*) senza pensare.
headhunt ['hɛdhʌnt] *vt*: **to be** ~**ed** avere
un'offerta di lavoro da un cacciatore di
teste.
headhunter ['hɛdhʌntə*] *n* cacciatore *m* di
teste.
heading ['hɛdɪŋ] *n* titolo; intestazione *f*.
headlamp ['hɛdlæmp] *n* (*BRIT*) = **headlight**.
headland ['hɛdlənd] *n* promontorio.
headlight ['hɛdlaɪt] *n* fanale *m*.
headline ['hɛdlaɪn] *n* titolo.
headlong ['hɛdlɔŋ] *adv* (*fall*) a capofitto;
(*rush*) precipitosamente.
headmaster [hɛd'mɑːstə*] *n* preside *m*.
headmistress [hɛd'mɪstrɪs] *n* preside *f*.
head office *n* sede *f* (centrale).
head-on [hɛd'ɔn] *adj* (*collision*) frontale.
headphones ['hɛdfəunz] *npl* cuffia.
headquarters (HQ) [hɛd'kwɔːtəz] *npl*
ufficio centrale; (*MIL*) quartiere *m*
generale.
head-rest ['hɛdrɛst] *n* poggiacapo.
headroom ['hɛdrum] *n* (*in car*) altezza
dell'abitacolo; (*under bridge*) altezza
limite.
headscarf ['hɛdskɑːf] *n* foulard *m inv*.
headset ['hɛdsɛt] *n* = **headphones**.
headstone ['hɛdstəun] *n* (*on grave*) lapide *f*,
pietra tombale.
headstrong ['hɛdstrɔŋ] *adj* testardo(a).
head waiter *n* capocameriere *m*.
headway ['hɛdweɪ] *n*: **to make** ~ fare
progressi *or* passi avanti.
headwind ['hɛdwɪnd] *n* controvento.
heady ['hɛdɪ] *adj* che dà alla testa;
inebriante.
heal [hiːl] *vt, vi* guarire.
health [hɛlθ] *n* salute *f*; **Department of H**~
≈ Ministero della Sanità.
health care *n* assistenza sanitaria.
health centre *n* (*BRIT*) poliambulatorio.
health food(s) *n(pl)* alimenti *mpl* integrali.
health hazard *n* pericolo per la salute.
Health Service *n*: **the** ~ (*BRIT*) ≈ il
Servizio Sanitario Statale.
healthy ['hɛlθɪ] *adj* (*person*) in buona salute;
(*climate*) salubre; (*food*) salutare; (*attitude
etc*) sano(a); (*economy*) florido(a); (*bank
balance*) solido(a).
heap [hiːp] *n* mucchio ♦ *vt* ammucchiare;
~**s** (**of**) (*col: lots*) un sacco (di), un
mucchio (di); **to** ~ **favours/praise/gifts**
etc **on sb** ricolmare qn di favori/lodi/
regali *etc*.
hear, *pt, pp* **heard** [hɪə*, hɜːd] *vt* sentire;
(*news*) ascoltare; (*lecture*) assistere a;

(*LAW: case*) esaminare ♦ *vi* sentire; **to ~ about** sentire parlare di; (*have news of*) avere notizie di; **did you ~ about the move?** ha sentito del trasloco?; **to ~ from sb** ricevere notizie da qn.

▶**hear out** *vt* ascoltare senza interrompere.

hearing ['hɪərɪŋ] *n* (*sense*) udito; (*of witnesses*) audizione *f*; (*of a case*) udienza; **to give sb a ~** dare ascolto a qn.

hearing aid *n* apparecchio acustico.

hearsay ['hɪəseɪ] *n* dicerie *fpl*, chiacchiere *fpl*; **by ~** *adv* per sentito dire.

hearse [hə:s] *n* carro funebre.

heart [hɑ:t] *n* cuore *m*; **~s** *npl* (*CARDS*) cuori *mpl*; **at ~** in fondo; **by ~** (*learn, know*) a memoria; **to take ~** farsi coraggio *or* animo; **to lose ~** perdere coraggio, scoraggiarsi; **to have a weak ~** avere il cuore debole; **to set one's ~ on sth/on doing sth** tenere molto a qc/a fare qc; **the ~ of the matter** il nocciolo della questione.

heartache ['hɑ:teɪk] *n* pene *fpl*, dolori *mpl*.

heart attack *n* attacco di cuore.

heartbeat ['hɑ:tbi:t] *n* battito del cuore.

heartbreak ['hɑ:tbreɪk] *n* immenso dolore *m*.

heartbreaking ['hɑ:tbreɪkɪŋ] *adj* straziante.

heartbroken ['hɑ:tbrəukən] *adj* affranto(a); **to be ~** avere il cuore spezzato.

heartburn ['hɑ:tbə:n] *n* bruciore *m* di stomaco.

-hearted ['hɑ:tɪd] *suffix*: **a kind~ person** una persona molto gentile.

heartening ['hɑ:tnɪŋ] *adj* incoraggiante.

heart failure *n* (*MED*) arresto cardiaco.

heartfelt ['hɑ:tfɛlt] *adj* sincero(a).

hearth [hɑ:θ] *n* focolare *m*.

heartily ['hɑ:tɪlɪ] *adv* (*laugh*) di cuore; (*eat*) di buon appetito; (*agree*) in pieno, completamente; **to be ~ sick of** (*BRIT*) essere veramente stufo di, essere arcistufo di.

heartland ['hɑ:tlænd] *n* zona centrale; **Italy's industrial ~** il cuore dell'industria italiana.

heartless ['hɑ:tlɪs] *adj* senza cuore, insensibile; crudele.

heartstrings ['hɑ:tstrɪŋz] *npl*: **to tug at sb's ~** toccare il cuore a qn, toccare qn nel profondo.

heart-throb ['hɑ:tθrɔb] *n* rubacuori *m inv*.

heart-to-heart ['hɑ:ttə'hɑ:t] *adj*, *adv* a cuore aperto.

heart transplant *n* trapianto del cuore.

heartwarming ['hɑ:twɔ:mɪŋ] *adj* confortante, che scalda il cuore.

hearty ['hɑ:tɪ] *adj* caloroso(a); robusto(a); sano(a); vigoroso(a).

heat [hi:t] *n* calore *m*; (*fig*) ardore *m*; fuoco; (*SPORT: also:* **qualifying ~**) prova eliminatoria; (*ZOOL*): **in** *or* (*BRIT*) **on ~** in calore ♦ *vt* scaldare.

▶**heat up** *vi* (*liquids*) scaldarsi; (*room*) riscaldarsi ♦ *vt* riscaldare.

heated ['hi:tɪd] *adj* riscaldato(a); (*fig*) appassionato(a); acceso(a), eccitato(a).

heater ['hi:tə*] *n* stufa; radiatore *m*.

heath [hi:θ] *n* (*BRIT*) landa.

heathen ['hi:ðn] *adj*, *n* pagano(a).

heather ['hɛðə*] *n* erica.

heating ['hi:tɪŋ] *n* riscaldamento.

heat-resistant ['hi:trɪzɪstənt] *adj* termoresistente.

heat-seeking ['hi:tsi:kɪŋ] *adj* che cerca fonti di calore.

heatstroke ['hi:tstrəuk] *n* colpo di sole.

heatwave ['hi:tweɪv] *n* ondata di caldo.

heave [hi:v] *vt* sollevare (con forza) ♦ *vi* sollevarsi ♦ *n* (*push*) grande spinta; **to ~ a sigh** emettere *or* mandare un sospiro.

▶**heave to** (*pt, pp* **hove**) *vi* (*NAUT*) mettersi in cappa.

heaven ['hɛvn] *n* paradiso, cielo; **~ forbid!** Dio ce ne guardi!; **for ~'s sake!** (*pleading*) per amor del cielo!, per carità!; (*protesting*) santo cielo!, in nome del cielo!; **thank ~!** grazie al cielo!

heavenly ['hɛvnlɪ] *adj* divino(a), celeste.

heavily ['hɛvɪlɪ] *adv* pesantemente; (*drink, smoke*) molto.

heavy ['hɛvɪ] *adj* pesante; (*sea*) grosso(a); (*rain*) forte; (*drinker, smoker*) gran (*before noun*); **it's ~ going** è una gran fatica; **~ industry** industria pesante.

heavy cream *n* (*US*) doppia panna.

heavy-duty ['hɛvɪ'dju:tɪ] *adj* molto resistente.

heavy goods vehicle (HGV) *n* (*BRIT*) veicolo per trasporti pesanti.

heavy-handed ['hɛvɪ'hændɪd] *adj* (*clumsy, tactless*) pesante.

heavy metal *n* (*MUS*) heavy metal *m*.

heavy-set ['hɛvɪ'sɛt] *adj* (*esp US*) tarchiato(a).

heavyweight ['hɛvɪweɪt] *n* (*SPORT*) peso massimo.

Hebrew ['hi:bru:] *adj* ebreo(a) ♦ *n* (*LING*) ebraico.

Hebrides ['hɛbrɪdi:z] *npl*: **the ~** le Ebridi.

heck [hɛk] (*col*) *excl*: **oh ~!** oh no! ♦ *n*: **a ~ of a lot of** un gran bel po' di.

heckle ['hɛkl] *vt* interpellare e dare noia a (*un oratore*).

heckler ['hɛklə*] *n* agitatore/trice.

hectare ['hɛktɑ:*] n (BRIT) ettaro.
hectic ['hɛktɪk] adj movimentato(a); (busy) frenetico(a).
hector ['hɛktə*] vt usare le maniere forti con.
he'd [hi:d] = he would; he had.
hedge [hɛdʒ] n siepe f ♦ vi essere elusivo(a); **as a ~ against inflation** per cautelarsi contro l'inflazione; **to ~ one's bets** (fig) coprirsi dai rischi.
▶**hedge in** vt recintare con una siepe.
hedgehog ['hɛdʒhɔg] n riccio.
hedgerow ['hɛdʒrəu] n siepe f.
hedonism ['hi:dənɪzəm] n edonismo.
heed [hi:d] vt (also: **take ~ of**) badare a, far conto di ♦ n: **to pay (no) ~ to, to take (no) ~ of** (non) ascoltare, (non) tener conto di.
heedless ['hi:dlɪs] adj sbadato(a).
heel [hi:l] n (ANAT) calcagno; (of shoe) tacco ♦ vt (shoe) rifare i tacchi a; **to bring to ~** addomesticare; **to take to one's ~s** (col) darsela a gambe, alzare i tacchi.
hefty ['hɛftɪ] adj (person) solido(a); (parcel) pesante; (piece, price) grosso(a).
heifer ['hɛfə*] n giovenca.
height [haɪt] n altezza; (high ground) altura; (fig: of glory) apice m; (: of stupidity) colmo; **what ~ are you?** quanto sei alto?; **of average ~** di statura media; **to be afraid of ~s** soffrire di vertigini; **it's the ~ of fashion** è l'ultimo grido della moda.
heighten ['haɪtn] vt innalzare; (fig) accrescere.
heinous ['heɪnəs] adj nefando(a), atroce.
heir [ɛə*] n erede m.
heir apparent n erede m/f legittimo(a).
heiress ['ɛərɛs] n erede f.
heirloom ['ɛəlu:m] n mobile m (or gioiello or quadro) di famiglia.
heist [haɪst] n (US col) rapina.
held [hɛld] pt, pp of **hold**.
helicopter ['hɛlɪkɔptə*] n elicottero.
heliport ['hɛlɪpɔːt] n eliporto.
helium ['hi:lɪəm] n elio.
hell [hɛl] n inferno; **a ~ of a ...** (col) un(a) maledetto(a) ...; **oh ~!** (col) porca miseria!, accidenti!
he'll [hi:l] = he will, he shall.
hell-bent [hɛl'bɛnt] adj (col): **to be ~ on doing sth** voler fare qc a tutti i costi.
hellish ['hɛlɪʃ] adj infernale.
hello [hə'ləu] excl buon giorno!; ciao!; (to sb one addresses as "tu"); (surprise) ma guarda!
helm [hɛlm] n (NAUT) timone m.
helmet ['hɛlmɪt] n casco.
helmsman ['hɛlmzmən] n timoniere m.
help [hɛlp] n aiuto; (charwoman) donna di

servizio; (assistant etc) impiegato/a ♦ vt aiutare; **~!** aiuto!; **with the ~ of** con l'aiuto di; **to be of ~ to sb** essere di aiuto or essere utile a qn; **to ~ sb (to) do sth** aiutare qn a far qc; **can I ~ you?** (in shop) desidera?; **~ yourself (to bread)** si serva (del pane); **I can't ~ saying** non posso evitare di dire, he can't ~ it non ci può far niente.
helper ['hɛlpə*] n aiutante m/f, assistente m/f.
helpful ['hɛlpful] adj di grande aiuto; (useful) utile.
helping ['hɛlpɪŋ] n porzione f.
helping hand n: **to give sb a ~** dare una mano a qn.
helpless ['hɛlplɪs] adj impotente; debole; (baby) indifeso(a).
helplessly ['hɛlplɪslɪ] adv (watch) senza poter fare nulla.
helpline ['hɛlplaɪn] n ≈ telefono amico; (COMM) servizio di informazioni a pagamento.
Helsinki ['hɛlsɪŋkɪ] n Helsinki f.
helter-skelter ['hɛltə'skɛltə*] n (BRIT: in funfair) scivolo (a spirale).
hem [hɛm] n orlo ♦ vt fare l'orlo a.
▶**hem in** vt cingere; **to feel ~med in** (fig) sentirsi soffocare.
he-man ['hi:mæn] n (col) fusto.
hematology [hi:mə'tɔlədʒɪ] n (US) = **haematology**.
hemisphere ['hɛmɪsfɪə*] n emisfero.
hemlock ['hɛmlɔk] n cicuta.
hemoglobin [hi:məu'gləubɪn] n (US) = **haemoglobin**.
hemophilia [hi:məu'fɪlɪə] n (US) = **haemophilia**.
hemorrhage n (US) = **haemorrhage**.
hemorrhoids ['hɛmərɔɪdz] npl (US) = **haemorrhoids**.
hemp [hɛmp] n canapa.
hen [hɛn] n gallina; (female bird) femmina.
hence [hɛns] adv (therefore) dunque; **2 years ~** di qui a 2 anni.
henceforth [hɛns'fɔːθ] adv d'ora in poi.
henchman ['hɛntʃmən] n (pej) caudatario.
henna ['hɛnə] n henna.
hen night n (col) addio al nubilato.
hen party n (col) festa di sole donne.
henpecked ['hɛnpɛkt] adj dominato dalla moglie.
hepatitis [hɛpə'taɪtɪs] n epatite f.
her [hə:*] pron (direct) la, l' + vowel; (indirect) le; (stressed, after prep) lei; see note at **she** ♦ adj il(la) suo(a), i(le) suoi(sue); **I see ~** la vedo; **give ~ a book** le dia un libro; **after ~** dopo (di)

lei.
herald ['hɛrəld] *n* araldo ♦ *vt* annunciare.
heraldic [hɛ'rældɪk] *adj* araldico(a).
heraldry ['hɛrəldrɪ] *n* araldica.
herb [hɜːb] *n* erba; ~s *npl* (*CULIN*) erbette *fpl*.
herbaceous [hɜː'beɪʃəs] *adj* erbaceo(a).
herbal ['hɜːbəl] *adj* di erbe; ~ **tea** tisana.
herbicide ['hɜːbɪsaɪd] *n* erbicida *m*.
herd [hɜːd] *n* mandria; (*of wild animals, swine*) branco ♦ *vt* (*drive, gather: animals*) guidare; (: *people*) radunare; ~**ed together** ammassati (come bestie).
here [hɪə*] *adv* qui, qua ♦ *excl* ehi!; ~! (*at roll call*) presente!; ~ **is**, ~ **are** ecco; ~**'s my sister** ecco mia sorella; ~ **she is** eccola; ~ **she comes** eccola che viene; **come** ~! vieni qui!; ~ **and there** qua e là.
hereabouts ['hɪərəbauts] *adv* da queste parti.
hereafter [hɪər'ɑːftə*] *adv* in futuro; dopo questo ♦ *n*: **the** ~ l'al di là *m*.
hereby [hɪə'baɪ] *adv* (*in letter*) con la presente.
hereditary [hɪ'rɛdɪtrɪ] *adj* ereditario(a).
heredity [hɪ'rɛdɪtɪ] *n* eredità.
heresy ['hɛrəsɪ] *n* eresia.
heretic ['hɛrətɪk] *n* eretico/a.
heretical [hɪ'rɛtɪkl] *adj* eretico(a).
herewith [hɪə'wɪð] *adv* qui accluso.
heritage ['hɛrɪtɪdʒ] *n* eredità; (*of country, nation*) retaggio; **our national** ~ il nostro patrimonio nazionale.
hermetically [hɜː'mɛtɪklɪ] *adv* ermeticamente; ~ **sealed** ermeticamente chiuso.
hermit ['hɜːmɪt] *n* eremita *m*.
hernia ['hɜːnɪə] *n* ernia.
hero, ~**es** ['hɪərəu] *n* eroe *m*.
heroic [hɪ'rəuɪk] *adj* eroico(a).
heroin ['hɛrəuɪn] *n* eroina (*droga*).
heroin addict *n* eroinomane *m/f*.
heroine ['hɛrəuɪn] *n* eroina (*donna*).
heroism ['hɛrəuɪzəm] *n* eroismo.
heron ['hɛrən] *n* airone *m*.
hero worship *n* divismo.
herring ['hɛrɪŋ] *n* aringa.
hers [hɜːz] *pron* il(la) suo(a), i(le) suoi(sue); **a friend of** ~ un suo amico; **this is** ~ questo è (il) suo.
herself [hɜː'sɛlf] *pron* (*reflexive*) si; (*emphatic*) lei stessa; (*after prep*) se stessa, sé.
Herts *abbr* (*BRIT*) = Hertfordshire.
he's [hiːz] = **he is**; **he has**.
hesitant ['hɛzɪtənt] *adj* esitante, indeciso(a); **to be** ~ **about doing sth** esitare a fare qc.

hesitate ['hɛzɪteɪt] *vi*: **to** ~ (**about/to do**) esitare (su/a fare); **don't** ~ **to ask (me)** non aver timore *or* paura di chiedermelo.
hesitation [hɛzɪ'teɪʃən] *n* esitazione *f*; **I have no** ~ **in saying (that)** ... non esito a dire che ....
hessian ['hɛsɪən] *n* tela di canapa.
heterogeneous [hɛtərəu'dʒiːnɪəs] *adj* eterogeneo(a).
heterosexual [hɛtərəu'sɛksjuəl] *adj*, *n* eterosessuale (*m/f*).
het up [hɛt'ʌp] *adj* agitato(a).
HEW *n abbr* (*US*: = Department of Health, Education and Welfare*) ministero della sanità, della pubblica istruzione e della previdenza sociale.
hew [hjuː] *vt* tagliare (con l'accetta).
hex [hɛks] (*US*) *n* stregoneria ♦ *vt* stregare.
hexagon ['hɛksəgən] *n* esagono.
hexagonal [hɛk'sægənl] *adj* esagonale.
hey [heɪ] *excl* ehi!
heyday ['heɪdeɪ] *n*: **the** ~ **of** i bei giorni di, l'età d'oro di.
HF *n abbr* (= high frequency) AF.
HGV *n abbr see* **heavy goods vehicle**.
HI *abbr* (*US*) = Hawaii.
hi [haɪ] *excl* ciao!
hiatus [haɪ'eɪtəs] *n* vuoto; (*LING*) iato.
hibernate ['haɪbəneɪt] *vi* ibernare.
hibernation [haɪbə'neɪʃən] *n* letargo, ibernazione *f*.
hiccough, hiccup ['hɪkʌp] *vi* singhiozzare ♦ *n* singhiozzo; **to have (the)** ~**s** avere il singhiozzo.
hick [hɪk] *n* (*US col*) buzzurro/a.
hid [hɪd] *pt of* **hide**.
hidden ['hɪdn] *pp of* **hide** ♦ *adj* nascosto(a); **there are no** ~ **extras** è veramente tutto compreso nel prezzo; ~ **agenda** programma *m* occulto.
hide [haɪd] *n* (*skin*) pelle *f* ♦ *vb* (*pt* **hid**, *pp* **hidden** [hɪd, 'hɪdn]) *vt*: **to** ~ **sth (from sb)** nascondere qc (a qn) ♦ *vi*: **to** ~ (**from sb**) nascondersi (da qn).
hide-and-seek ['haɪdən'siːk] *n* rimpiattino.
hideaway ['haɪdəweɪ] *n* nascondiglio.
hideous ['hɪdɪəs] *adj* laido(a); orribile.
hide-out ['haɪdaut] *n* nascondiglio.
hiding ['haɪdɪŋ] *n* (*beating*) bastonata; **to be in** ~ (*concealed*) tenersi nascosto(a).
hiding place *n* nascondiglio.
hierarchy ['haɪərɑːkɪ] *n* gerarchia.
hieroglyphic [haɪərə'glɪfɪk] *adj* geroglifico(a); ~**s** *npl* geroglifici *mpl*.
hi-fi ['haɪ'faɪ] *adj*, *n abbr* (= high fidelity) hi-fi (*m*) *inv*.
higgledy-piggledy ['hɪgldɪ'pɪgldɪ] *adv* alla rinfusa.

high [haɪ] adj alto(a); (speed, respect, number) grande; (wind) forte; (BRIT CULIN: meat, game) frollato(a); (: spoilt) andato(a) a male; (col: on drugs) fatto(a); (: on drink) su di giri ♦ adv alto, in alto ♦ n: **exports have reached a new** ~ le esportazioni hanno toccato un nuovo record; **20m** ~ alto(a) 20m; **to pay a** ~ **price for sth** pagare (molto) caro qc.

highball ['haɪbɔːl] n (US: drink) whisky (or brandy) e soda con ghiaccio.

highboy ['haɪbɔɪ] n (US) cassettone m.

highbrow ['haɪbrau] adj, n intellettuale (m/f).

highchair ['haɪtʃɛə*] n seggiolone m.

high-class ['haɪ'klɑːs] adj (neighbourhood) elegante; (hotel) di prim'ordine; (person) di gran classe; (food) raffinato(a).

High Court n alta corte f; see boxed note.

HIGH COURT

Nel sistema legale inglese e gallese, la **High Court** e la "Court of Appeal" compongono la "Supreme Court of Judicature". In Scozia, invece, la **High Court** è la corte che si occupa dei reati più gravi e corrisponde alla "crown court" inglese.

---

higher ['haɪə*] adj (form of life, study etc) superiore ♦ adv più in alto, più in su.

higher education n istruzione f superiore, istruzione universitaria.

highfalutin [haɪfə'luːtɪn] adj (col) pretenzioso(a).

high finance n alta finanza.

high-flier, high-flyer [haɪ'flaɪə*] n (giovane) promessa f (fig).

high-flying [haɪ'flaɪɪŋ] adj (fig) promettente.

high-handed [haɪ'hændɪd] adj prepotente.

high-heeled [haɪ'hiːld] adj a tacchi alti.

highjack ['haɪdʒæk] vt, n = **hijack**.

high jump n (SPORT) salto in alto.

highlands ['haɪləndz] npl zona montuosa; **the H~** le Highlands scozzesi.

high-level ['haɪlɛvl] adj (talks etc, COMPUT) ad alto livello.

highlight ['haɪlaɪt] n (fig: of event) momento culminante ♦ vt mettere in evidenza; ~**s** npl (in hair) colpi mpl di sole.

highlighter ['haɪlaɪtə*] n (pen) evidenziatore m.

highly ['haɪlɪ] adv molto; ~ **paid** pagato molto bene; **to speak** ~ **of** parlare molto bene di.

highly-strung ['haɪlɪ'strʌŋ] adj teso(a) di nervi, eccitabile.

highness ['haɪnɪs] n altezza; **Her H~** Sua Altezza.

high-pitched [haɪ'pɪtʃt] adj acuto(a).

high point n: **the** ~ il momento più importante.

high-powered ['haɪ'pauəd] adj (engine) molto potente, ad alta potenza; (fig: person) di prestigio.

high-pressure ['haɪprɛʃə*] adj ad alta pressione; (fig) aggressivo(a).

high-rise block ['haɪraɪz-] n palazzone m.

high school n (BRIT) scuola secondaria; (US) istituto d'istruzione secondaria; see boxed note.

HIGH SCHOOL

Negli Stati Uniti la **high school** è un istituto di istruzione secondaria. Si suddivide in "junior high school" (dal settimo al nono anno di corso) e "senior high school" (dal decimo al dodicesimo), dove vengono impartiti sia insegnamenti accademici che di formazione professionale. In Gran Bretagna molte scuole secondarie si chiamano **high school**; vedi anche **elementary school**.

---

high season n (BRIT) alta stagione.

high spirits npl buonumore m, euforia; **to be in** ~ essere euforico(a).

high street n (BRIT) strada principale.

highway ['haɪweɪ] n strada maestra; **the information** ~ l'autostrada telematica.

Highway Code n (BRIT) codice m della strada.

highwayman ['haɪweɪmən] n bandito.

hijack ['haɪdʒæk] vt dirottamento; (also: ~**ing**) pirateria aerea.

hijacker ['haɪdʒækə*] n dirottatore/trice.

hike [haɪk] vi fare un'escursione a piedi ♦ n escursione f a piedi; (col: in prices etc) aumento ♦ vt (col) aumentare.

hiker ['haɪkə*] n escursionista m/f.

hiking ['haɪkɪŋ] n escursioni fpl a piedi.

hilarious [hɪ'lɛərɪəs] adj che fa schiantare dal ridere.

hilarity [hɪ'lærɪtɪ] n ilarità.

hill [hɪl] n collina, colle m; (fairly high) montagna; (on road) salita.

hillbilly ['hɪlbɪlɪ] n (US) montanaro/a dal sud degli Stati Uniti; (pej) zotico/a.

hillside ['hɪlsaɪd] n fianco della collina.

hill start n (AUT) partenza in salita.

hilly ['hɪlɪ] adj collinoso(a); montagnoso(a).

hilt [hɪlt] n (fig): **to the** ~ fino in fondo.

him [hɪm] pron (direct) lo, l' + vowel; (indirect) gli; (stressed, after prep) lui; **I see** ~ lo vedo; **give** ~ **a book** gli dia un libro; **after** ~ dopo (di) lui.

Himalayas [hɪmə'leɪəz] _npl_: **the ~** l'Himalaia _m_.

himself [hɪm'sɛlf] _pron_ (_reflexive_) si; (_emphatic_) lui stesso; (_after prep_) se stesso, sé.

hind [haɪnd] _adj_ posteriore ♦ _n_ cerva.

hinder ['hɪndə*] _vt_ ostacolare; (_delay_) tardare; (_prevent_): **to ~ sb from doing** impedire a qn di fare.

hindquarters ['haɪndkwɔːtəz] _npl_ (_ZOOL_) posteriore _m_.

hindrance ['hɪndrəns] _n_ ostacolo, impedimento.

hindsight ['haɪndsaɪt] _n_ senno di poi; **with the benefit of ~** con il senno di poi.

Hindu ['hɪnduː] _n_ indù _m/f inv_.

hinge [hɪndʒ] _n_ cardine _m_ ♦ _vi_ (_fig_): **to ~ on** dipendere da.

hint [hɪnt] _n_ accenno, allusione _f_; (_advice_) consiglio ♦ _vt_: **to ~ that** lasciar capire che ♦ _vi_: **to ~ at** accennare a; **to drop a ~** lasciar capire; **give me a ~** (_clue_) dammi almeno un'idea, dammi un'indicazione.

hip [hɪp] _n_ anca, fianco; (_BOT_) frutto della rosa canina.

hip flask _n_ fiaschetta da liquore tascabile.

hip hop _n_ hip-hop _m_.

hippie ['hɪpɪ] _n_ hippy _m/f inv_.

hip pocket _n_ tasca posteriore dei calzoni.

hippopotamus, _pl_ **~es** _or_ **hippopotami** [hɪpə'pɔtəməs, -'pɔtəmaɪ] _n_ ippopotamo.

hippy ['hɪpɪ] _n_ = **hippie**.

hire ['haɪə*] _vt_ (_BRIT_: _car, equipment_) noleggiare; (_worker_) assumere, dare lavoro a ♦ _n_ nolo, noleggio; **for ~** da nolo; (_taxi_) libero(a); **on ~** a nolo.

▶**hire out** _vt_ noleggiare, dare a nolo _or_ noleggio, affittare.

hire(d) car _n_ (_BRIT_) macchina a nolo.

hire purchase (HP) _n_ (_BRIT_) acquisto (_or_ vendita) rateale; **to buy sth on ~** comprare qc a rate.

his [hɪz] _adj, pron_ il(la) suo(sua), i(le) suoi(sue); **this is ~** questo è (il) suo.

hiss [hɪs] _vi_ fischiare; (_cat, snake_) sibilare ♦ _n_ fischio; sibilo.

histogram ['hɪstəgræm] _n_ istogramma _m_.

historian [hɪ'stɔːrɪən] _n_ storico/a.

historic(al) [hɪ'stɔrɪk(l)] _adj_ storico(a).

history ['hɪstərɪ] _n_ storia; **there's a long ~ of that illness in his family** ci sono molti precedenti (della malattia) nella sua famiglia.

histrionics [hɪstrɪ'ɔnɪks] _n_ istrionismo.

hit [hɪt] _vt_ (_pt, pp_ **hit**) colpire, picchiare; (_knock against_) battere; (_reach: target_) raggiungere; (_collide with: car_) urtare contro; (_fig: affect_) colpire; (_find: problem_)

incontrare ♦ _n_ colpo; (_success, song_) successo; **to ~ the headlines** far titolo; **to ~ the road** (_col_) mettersi in cammino; **to ~ it off with sb** andare molto d'accordo con qn.

▶**hit back** _vi_: **to ~ back at sb** restituire il colpo a qn.

▶**hit out at** _vt fus_ sferrare dei colpi contro; (_fig_) attaccare.

▶**hit (up)on** _vt fus_ (_answer_) imbroccare, azzeccare; (_solution_) trovare (per caso).

hit-and-run driver ['hɪtænd'rʌn-] _n_ pirata _m_ della strada.

hitch [hɪtʃ] _vt_ (_fasten_) attaccare; (_also: ~ up_) tirare su ♦ _n_ (_difficulty_) intoppo, difficoltà _f inv_; **technical ~** difficoltà tecnica; **to ~ a lift** fare l'autostop.

▶**hitch up** _vt_ (_horse, cart_) attaccare.

hitch-hike ['hɪtʃhaɪk] _vi_ fare l'autostop.

hitch-hiker ['hɪtʃhaɪkə*] _n_ autostoppista _m/f_.

hi-tech ['haɪtɛk] _adj_ high-tech _inv_, a tecnologia avanzata.

hitherto ['hɪðə'tuː] _adv_ finora.

hit list _n_ libro nero.

hitman ['hɪtmæn] _n_ (_col_) sicario.

hit-or-miss ['hɪtə'mɪs] _adj_ casuale; **it's ~ whether ...** è in dubbio se ...; **the service in this hotel is very ~** il servizio dell'albergo lascia a desiderare.

hit parade _n_ hit-parade _f_.

HIV _n abbr_ (= _human immunodeficiency virus_) virus _m inv_ di immunodeficienza; **~-negative/-positive** sieronegativo(a)/ sieropositivo(a).

hive [haɪv] _n_ alveare _m_; **the shop was a ~ of activity** (_fig_) c'era una grande attività nel negozio.

▶**hive off** _vt_ (_col_) separare.

hl _abbr_ (= _hectolitre_) hl.

HM _abbr_ (= _His (or Her) Majesty_) S.M. (= _Sua Maestà_).

HMG _abbr_ (_BRIT_) = _His (or Her) Majesty's Government_.

HMI _n abbr_ (_BRIT SCOL_: = _His (or Her) Majesty's Inspector_) ≈ ispettore _m_ scolastico.

HMO _n abbr_ (_US_: = _health maintenance organization_) _organo per la salvaguardia della salute pubblica_.

HMS _abbr_ (_BRIT_) = _His (or Her) Majesty's Ship_.

HMSO _n abbr_ (_BRIT_: = _His (or Her) Majesty's Stationery Office_) ≈ Poligrafici _mpl_ dello Stato.

HNC _n abbr_ (_BRIT_: = _Higher National Certificate_) _diploma di istituto tecnico o professionale_.

HND _n abbr_ (_BRIT_: = _Higher National Diploma_)

diploma in materie tecniche equivalente ad una laurea.

hoard [hɔːd] n (of food) provviste fpl; (of money) gruzzolo ♦ vt ammassare.

hoarding ['hɔːdɪŋ] n (BRIT) tabellone m per affissioni.

hoarfrost ['hɔːfrɔst] n brina.

hoarse [hɔːs] adj rauco(a).

hoax [həuks] n scherzo; falso allarme.

hob [hɔb] n piastra (con fornelli).

hobble ['hɔbl] vi zoppicare.

hobby ['hɔbɪ] n hobby m inv, passatempo.

hobby-horse ['hɔbɪhɔːs] n cavallo a dondolo; (fig) chiodo fisso.

hobnail(ed) boots ['hɔbneɪl(d)-] n scarponi mpl chiodati.

hobnob ['hɔbnɔb] vi: **to ~ (with)** mescolarsi (con).

hobo ['həubəu] n (US) vagabondo.

hock [hɔk] n (BRIT: wine) vino del Reno; (of animal, CULIN) garretto; (col): **to be in ~** avere debiti.

hockey ['hɔkɪ] n hockey m.

hocus-pocus ['həukəs'pəukəs] n (trickery) trucco; (words: of magician) abracadabra m inv; (: jargon) parolone fpl.

hod [hɔd] n (TECH) cassetta per portare i mattoni.

hodgepodge ['hɔdʒpɔdʒ] n = **hotchpotch**.

hoe [həu] n zappa ♦ vt (ground) zappare.

hog [hɔg] n maiale m ♦ vt (fig) arraffare; **to go the whole ~** farlo fino in fondo.

Hogmanay [hɔgmə'neɪ] n (SCOTTISH) ≈ San Silvestro.

hogwash ['hɔgwɔʃ] n (col) stupidaggini fpl.

hoist [hɔɪst] n paranco ♦ vt issare.

hoity-toity [hɔɪtɪ'tɔɪtɪ] adj (col) altezzoso(a).

hold [həuld] vb (pt, pp **held** [hɛld]) vt tenere; (contain) contenere; (keep back) trattenere; (believe) mantenere; considerare; (possess) avere, possedere; detenere ♦ vi (withstand pressure) tenere; (be valid) essere valido(a) ♦ n presa; (fig) potere m; (NAUT) stiva; **~ the line!** (TEL) resti in linea!; **to ~ office** (POL) essere in carica; **to ~ sb responsible for sth** considerare or ritenere qn responsabile di qc; **to ~ one's own** (fig) difendersi bene; **he ~s the view that ...** è del parere che ...; **to ~ firm** or **fast** resistere bene, tenere; **to catch** or **get (a) ~ of** afferrare; **to get ~ of** (fig) trovare; **to get ~ of o.s.** trattenersi.

▶**hold back** vt trattenere; (secret) tenere celato(a); **to ~ sb back from doing sth** impedire a qn di fare qc.

▶**hold down** vt (person) tenere a terra;

(job) tenere.

▶**hold forth** vi fare or tenere una concione.

▶**hold off** vt tener lontano ♦ vi (rain): **if the rain ~s off** se continua a non piovere.

▶**hold on** vi tener fermo; (wait) aspettare; **~ on!** (TEL) resti in linea!

▶**hold on to** vt fus tenersi stretto(a) a; (keep) conservare.

▶**hold out** vt offrire ♦ vi (resist): **to ~ out (against)** resistere (a).

▶**hold over** vt (meeting etc) rimandare, rinviare.

▶**hold up** vt (raise) alzare; (support) sostenere; (delay) ritardare; (traffic) rallentare; (rob: bank) assaltare.

holdall ['həuldɔːl] n (BRIT) borsone m.

holder ['həuldə*] n (of ticket, title) possessore/posseditrice; (of office etc) incaricato/a; (of passport, post) titolare; (of record) detentore/trice.

holding ['həuldɪŋ] n (share) azioni fpl, titoli mpl; (farm) podere m, tenuta.

holding company n holding f inv.

holdup ['həuldʌp] n (robbery) rapina a mano armata; (delay) ritardo; (BRIT: in traffic) blocco.

hole [həul] n buco, buca ♦ vt bucare; **~ in the heart** (MED) morbo blu; **to pick ~s in** (fig) trovare da ridire su.

▶**hole up** vi nascondersi, rifugiarsi.

holiday ['hɔlədɪ] n vacanza; (from work) ferie fpl; (day off) giorno di vacanza; (public) giorno festivo; **to be on ~** essere in vacanza; **tomorrow is a ~** domani è festa.

holiday camp n (BRIT: for children) colonia (di villeggiatura); (also: **holiday centre**) ≈ villaggio (di vacanze).

holiday-maker ['hɔlədmeɪkə*] n (BRIT) villeggiante m/f.

holiday pay n stipendio delle ferie.

holiday resort n luogo di villeggiatura.

holiday season n stagione f delle vacanze.

holiness ['həulɪnɪs] n santità.

holistic [həu'lɪstɪk] adj olistico(a).

Holland ['hɔlənd] n Olanda.

holler ['hɔlə*] vi gridare, urlare.

hollow ['hɔləu] adj cavo(a), vuoto(a); (fig) falso(a); vano(a) ♦ n cavità f inv; (in land) valletta, depressione f.

▶**hollow out** vt scavare.

holly ['hɔlɪ] n agrifoglio.

hollyhock ['hɔlɪhɔk] n malvone m.

holocaust ['hɔləkɔːst] n olocausto.

hologram ['hɔləgræm] n ologramma m.

hols [hɔlz] npl: **the ~** le vacanze.

holster ['həulstə*] n fondina (di pistola).

holy ['həulɪ] *adj* santo(a); (*bread*)
benedetto(a); (*ground*) consacrato(a); **the**
H~ Father il Santo Padre.
Holy Communion *n* la Santa Comunione.
Holy Ghost, Holy Spirit *n* Spirito Santo.
Holy Land *n*: **the ~** la Terra Santa.
holy orders *npl* ordini *mpl* (sacri).
homage ['hɔmɪdʒ] *n* omaggio; **to pay ~ to**
rendere omaggio a.
home [həum] *n* casa; (*country*) patria;
(*institution*) casa, ricovero ♦ *cpd* (*life*)
familiare; (*cooking etc*) casalingo(a);
(*ECON, POL*) nazionale, interno(a); (*SPORT:*
team) di casa; (: *match, win*) in casa ♦ *adv* a
casa; in patria; (*right in*: *nail etc*) fino in
fondo; **at ~** a casa; **to go** (*or* **come**) **~**
tornare a casa (*or* in patria); **it's near my**
~ è vicino a casa mia; **make yourself at ~**
si metta a suo agio.
▶**home in on** *vt fus* (*missiles*) dirigersi
(automaticamente) verso.
home address *n* indirizzo di casa.
home-brew [həum'bru:] *n* birra *or* vino
fatto(a) in casa.
homecoming ['həumkʌmɪŋ] *n* ritorno.
home computer *n* home computer
m inv.
Home Counties *npl* contee *fpl* intorno a
Londra.
home economics *n* economia domestica.
home ground *n* (*fig*): **to be on ~** essere
sul proprio terreno.
home-grown [həum'grəun] *adj* nostrano(a),
di produzione locale.
home help *n* (*BRIT*) *collaboratore*
familiare per persone bisognose
stipendiato dal comune.
homeland ['həumlænd] *n* patria.
homeless ['həumlɪs] *adj* senza tetto;
spatriato(a); **the ~** *npl* i senzatetto.
home loan *n* prestito con garanzia
immobiliare.
homely ['həumlɪ] *adj* semplice, alla buona;
accogliente.
home-made [həum'meɪd] *adj* casalingo(a).
Home Office *n* (*BRIT*) ministero degli
Interni.
homeopathy *etc* [həumɪ'ɔpəθɪ] (*US*) =
homoeopathy *etc.*
home page *n* (*COMPUT*) home page *f inv.*
home rule *n* autogoverno.
Home Secretary *n* (*BRIT*) ministro degli
Interni.
homesick ['həumsɪk] *adj*: **to be ~** avere la
nostalgia.
homestead ['həumstɛd] *n* fattoria e
terreni.
home town *n* città *f inv* natale.

home truth *n*: **to tell sb a few ~s** dire a qn
qualche amara verità.
homeward ['həumwəd] *adj* (*journey*) di
ritorno.
homeward(s) ['həumwəd(z)] *adv* verso
casa.
homework ['həumwə:k] *n* compiti *mpl* (per
casa).
homicidal [hɔmɪ'saɪdl] *adj* omicida.
homicide ['hɔmɪsaɪd] *n* (*US*) omicidio.
homily ['hɔmɪlɪ] *n* omelia.
homing ['həumɪŋ] *adj* (*device, missile*)
autocercante; **~ pigeon** piccione *m*
viaggiatore.
homoeopath, (*US*) homeopath
['həumɪəupæθ] *n* omeopatico.
homoeopathic, (*US*) homeopathic
['həumɪəu'pæθɪk] *adj* omeopatico(a).
homoeopathy, (*US*) homeopathy
[həumɪ'ɔpəθɪ] *n* omeopatia.
homogeneous [hɔməu'dʒi:nɪəs] *adj*
omogeneo(a).
homogenize [hə'mɔdʒənaɪz] *vt*
omogenizzare.
homosexual [hɔməu'sɛksjuəl] *adj, n*
omosessuale (*m/f*).
Hon. *abbr* = **honourable; honorary.**
Honduras [hɔn'djuərəs] *n* Honduras *m.*
hone [həun] *vt* (*sharpen*) affilare; (*fig*)
affinare.
honest ['ɔnɪst] *adj* onesto(a); sincero(a); **to**
be quite ~ with you ... se devo dirle la
verità ....
honestly ['ɔnɪstlɪ] *adv* onestamente;
sinceramente.
honesty ['ɔnɪstɪ] *n* onestà.
honey ['hʌnɪ] *n* miele *m*; (*US col*) tesoro,
amore *m.*
honeycomb ['hʌnɪkəum] *n* favo ♦ *vt* (*fig*):
~ed with tunnels *etc* pieno(a) di gallerie
etc.
honeymoon ['hʌnɪmu:n] *n* luna di miele,
viaggio di nozze.
honeysuckle ['hʌnɪsʌkl] *n* caprifoglio.
Hong Kong ['hɔŋ'kɔŋ] *n* Hong Kong *f.*
honk [hɔŋk] *n* (*AUT*) colpo di clacson ♦ *vi*
suonare il clacson.
Honolulu [hɔnə'lu:lu:] *n* Honolulu *f.*
honorary ['ɔnərərɪ] *adj* onorario(a); (*duty,*
title) onorifico(a).
honour, (*US*) honor ['ɔnə*] *vt* onorare ♦ *n*
onore *m*; **in ~ of** in onore di.
hono(u)rable ['ɔnərəbl] *adj* onorevole.
hono(u)r-bound ['ɔnə'baund] *adj*: **to be ~**
to do dover fare per una questione di
onore.
hono(u)rs degree *n* (*SCOL*) *laurea* (*con*
corso di studi di 4 o 5 anni); *see boxed note.*

HONOURS DEGREE

*Il corso universitario di studi che porta al conferimento del "Bachelor's degree" può avere una durata diversa a seconda del profitto dello studente. Dopo quattro o cinque anni di corso si ottiene l'*honours degree*, il riconoscimento più alto, che, abbreviato in* Hons.*, viene posto dopo il titolo ottenuto (ad esempio BA Hons); vedi anche* ordinary degree*.*

honours list *n* (*BRIT*) elenco ufficiale dei destinati al conferimento di onorificenze; *see boxed note.*

HONOURS LIST

La honours list *è un elenco di cittadini britannici e del Commonwealth che si sono distinti in campo imprenditoriale, militare, sportivo, ecc, meritando il conferimento di un titolo o di una decorazione da parte del sovrano. Ogni anno vengono redatte dal primo ministro due* honours list*, una a Capodanno o una in occasione del compleanno del sovrano.*

Hons. [ɔnz] *abbr* (*SCOL*) = **hono(u)rs degree**.
hood [hud] *n* cappuccio; (*BRIT AUT*) capote *f*; (*US AUT*) cofano; (*col*) malvivente *m/f*.
hooded ['hudɪd] *adj* (*robber*) mascherato(a).
hoodlum ['hu:dləm] *n* malvivente *m/f*.
hoodwink ['hudwɪŋk] *vt* infinocchiare.
hoof, *pl* ~**s** *or* **hooves** [hu:f, hu:vz] *n* zoccolo.
hook [huk] *n* gancio; (*for fishing*) amo ♦ *vt* uncinare; (*dress*) agganciare; **to be** ~**ed on** (*col*) essere fanatico di; ~**s and eyes** gancetti; **by** ~ **or by crook** in un modo o nell'altro.
▶**hook up** *vt* (*RADIO, TV etc*) allacciare, collegare.
hooligan ['hu:lɪgən] *n* giovinastro, teppista *m*.
hooliganism ['hu:lɪgənɪzəm] *n* teppismo.
hoop [hu:p] *n* cerchio.
hoot [hu:t] *vi* (*AUT*) suonare il clacson; (*owl*) gufare ♦ *n* colpo di clacson; **to** ~ **with laughter** farsi una gran risata.
hooter ['hu:tə*] *n* (*AUT*) clacson *m inv*; (*NAUT, at factory*) sirena.
hoover ® ['hu:və*] *n* (*BRIT*) aspirapolvere *m inv* ♦ *vt* pulire con l'aspirapolvere.
hooves [hu:vz] *npl of* **hoof**.
hop [hɔp] *vi* saltellare, saltare; (*on one foot*) saltare su una gamba ♦ *n* salto; ~**s** *npl* luppoli *mpl*.

hope [həup] *vt*, *vi* sperare ♦ *n* speranza; **I** ~ **so/not** spero di sì/no.
hopeful ['həupful] *adj* (*person*) pieno(a) di speranza; (*situation*) promettente; **I'm** ~ **that she'll manage to come** ho buone speranze che venga.
hopefully ['həupfulɪ] *adv* con speranza; ~ **he will recover** speriamo che si riprenda.
hopeless ['həuplɪs] *adj* senza speranza, disperato(a); (*useless*) inutile.
hopelessly ['həuplɪslɪ] *adv* (*live etc*) senza speranza; (*involved, complicated*) spaventosamente; (*late*) disperatamente, irrimediabilmente; **I'm** ~ **confused/lost** sono completamente confuso/perso.
hopper ['hɔpə*] *n* (*chute*) tramoggia.
horde [hɔ:d] *n* orda.
horizon [hə'raɪzn] *n* orizzonte *m*.
horizontal [hɔrɪ'zɔntl] *adj* orizzontale.
hormone ['hɔ:məun] *n* ormone *m*.
hormone replacement therapy *n* terapia ormonale (*usata in menopausa*).
horn [hɔ:n] *n* corno; (*AUT*) clacson *m inv*.
horned [hɔ:nd] *adj* (*animal*) cornuto(a).
hornet ['hɔ:nɪt] *n* calabrone *m*.
horny ['hɔ:nɪ] *adj* corneo(a); (*hands*) calloso(a).
horoscope ['hɔrəskəup] *n* oroscopo.
horrendous [hə'rendəs] *n* orrendo(a).
horrible ['hɔrɪbl] *adj* orribile, tremendo(a).
horrid ['hɔrɪd] *adj* orrido(a); (*person*) antipatico(a).
horrific [hə'rɪfɪk] *adj* (*accident*) spaventoso(a); (*film*) orripilante.
horrify ['hɔrɪfaɪ] *vt* lasciare inorridito(a).
horrifying ['hɔrɪfaɪɪŋ] *adj* terrificante.
horror ['hɔrə*] *n* orrore *m*.
horror film *n* film *m inv* dell'orrore.
horror-struck ['hɔrəstrʌk], **horror-stricken** ['hɔrəstrɪkn] *adj* inorridito (a).
hors d'œuvre [ɔ:'də:vrə] *n* antipasto.
horse [hɔ:s] *n* cavallo.
horseback ['hɔ:sbæk]: **on** ~ *adj*, *adv* a cavallo.
horsebox ['hɔ:sbɔks] *n* carro *or* furgone *m* per il trasporto dei cavalli.
horse chestnut *n* ippocastano.
horse-drawn ['hɔ:sdrɔ:n] *adj* tirato(a) da cavallo.
horsefly ['hɔ:sflaɪ] *n* tafano, mosca cavallina.
horseman ['hɔ:smən] *n* cavaliere *m*.
horseplay ['hɔ:spleɪ] *n* giochi *mpl* scatenati.
horsepower (hp) ['hɔ:spauə*] *n* cavallo (vapore) (c/v).
horse-racing ['hɔ:sreɪsɪŋ] *n* ippica.
horseradish ['hɔ:srædɪʃ] *n* rafano.
horseshoe ['hɔ:sʃu:] *n* ferro di cavallo.

horse show n concorso ippico, gare fpl ippiche.

horse-trading ['hɔːstreɪdɪŋ] n mercanteggiamento.

horse trials npl = horse show.

horsewhip ['hɔːswɪp] vt frustare.

horsewoman ['hɔːswumən] n amazzone f.

horsey ['hɔːsɪ] adj (col: person) che adora i cavalli; (appearance) cavallino(a), da cavallo.

horticulture ['hɔːtɪkʌltʃə*] n orticoltura.

hose [həuz] n (also: ~pipe) tubo; (also: garden ~) tubo per annaffiare.

▶**hose down** vt lavare con un getto d'acqua.

hosepipe ['həuzpaɪp] n see hose.

hosiery ['həuzɪərɪ] n (in shop) (reparto di) calze fpl e calzini mpl.

hospice ['hɔspɪs] n ricovero, ospizio.

hospitable [hɔ'spɪtəbl] adj ospitale.

hospital ['hɔspɪtl] n ospedale m; in ~, (US) in the ~ all'ospedale.

hospitality [hɔspɪ'tælɪtɪ] n ospitalità.

hospitalize ['hɔspɪtəlaɪz] vt ricoverare (in or all'ospedale).

host [həust] n ospite m; (TV, RADIO) presentatore/trice; (REL) ostia; (large number): **a ~ of** una schiera di ♦ vt (TV programme, games) presentare.

hostage ['hɔstɪdʒ] n ostaggio/a.

host country n paese m ospite, paese che ospita.

hostel ['hɔstl] n ostello; (for students, nurses etc) pensionato; (for homeless people) ospizio, ricovero; (also: youth ~) ostello della gioventù.

hostelling ['hɔstəlɪŋ] n: **to go (youth) ~** passare le vacanze negli ostelli della gioventù.

hostess ['həustɪs] n ospite f; (AVIAT) hostess f inv; (in nightclub) entraineuse f inv.

hostile ['hɔstaɪl] adj ostile.

hostility [hɔ'stɪlɪtɪ] n ostilità f inv.

hot [hɔt] adj caldo(a); (as opposed to only warm) molto caldo(a); (spicy) piccante; (fig) accanito(a); ardente; violento(a), focoso(a); **to be ~** (person) aver caldo; (thing) essere caldo(a); (METEOR) far caldo.

▶**hot up** (BRIT col) vi (situation) farsi più teso(a); (party) scaldarsi ♦ vt (pace) affrettare; (engine) truccare.

hot-air balloon [hɔt'ɛə-] n mongolfiera.

hotbed ['hɔtbɛd] n (fig) focolaio.

hotchpotch ['hɔtʃpɔtʃ] n (BRIT) pot-pourri m.

hot dog n hot dog m inv.

hotel [həu'tɛl] n albergo.

hotelier [həu'tɛljeɪ] n albergatore/trice.

hotel industry n industria alberghiera.

hotel room n camera d'albergo.

hot flush n (BRIT) scalmana, caldana.

hotfoot ['hɔtfut] adv di gran carriera.

hothead ['hɔthɛd] n (fig) testa calda.

hotheaded [hɔt'hɛdɪd] adj focoso(a), eccitabile.

hothouse ['hɔthaus] n serra.

hot line n (POL) telefono rosso.

hotly ['hɔtlɪ] adv violentemente.

hotplate ['hɔtpleɪt] n fornello; piastra riscaldante.

hotpot ['hɔtpɔt] n (BRIT CULIN) stufato.

hot potato n (BRIT col) patata bollente; **to drop sb/sth like a ~** mollare subito qn/qc.

hot seat n (fig) posto che scotta.

hot spot n (fig) zona calda.

hot spring n sorgente f termale.

hot-tempered [hɔt'tɛmpəd] adj irascibile.

hot-water bottle [hɔt'wɔːtə-] n borsa dell'acqua calda.

hot-wire ['hɔtwaɪə*] vt (col: car) avviare mettendo in contatto i fili dell'accensione.

hound [haund] vt perseguitare ♦ n segugio; **the ~s** la muta.

hour ['auə*] n ora; **at 30 miles an ~** a 30 miglia all'ora; **lunch ~** intervallo di pranzo; **to pay sb by the ~** pagare qn a ore.

hourly ['auəlɪ] adj (ad) ogni ora; (rate) orario(a) ♦ adv ogni ora; **~ paid** adj pagato(a) a ore.

house n [haus] (pl ~s ['hauzɪz]) (also: firm) casa; (POL) camera; (THEAT) sala; pubblico; spettacolo ♦ vt [hauz] (person) ospitare; **at (or to) my ~** a casa mia; **the H~ (of Commons/Lords)** (BRIT) la Camera dei Comuni/Lords; **the H~ (of Representatives)** (US) ≈ la Camera dei Deputati; **on the ~** (fig) offerto(a) dalla casa.

house arrest n arresti mpl domiciliari.

houseboat ['hausbəut] n house boat f inv.

housebound ['hausbaund] adj confinato(a) in casa.

housebreaking ['hausbreɪkɪŋ] n furto con scasso.

house-broken ['hausbrəukn] adj (US) = house-trained.

housecoat ['hauskəut] n vestaglia.

household ['haushəuld] n famiglia, casa.

householder ['haushəuldə*] n padrone/a di casa; (head of house) capofamiglia m/f.

household name n nome m che tutti conoscono.

househunting ['haushʌntɪŋ] n: **to go ~**

mettersi a cercar casa.

housekeeper ['hauski:pə*] n governante f.

housekeeping ['hauski:pɪŋ] n (work) governo della casa; (also: ~ **money**) soldi mpl per le spese di casa; (COMPUT) ausilio.

houseman ['hausmən] n (BRIT MED) ≈ interno.

house-owner ['hausəunə*] n possessore m/f di casa.

house plant n pianta da appartamento.

house-proud ['hauspraud] adj che è maniaco(a) della pulizia.

house-to-house ['haustə'haus] adj (collection) di porta in porta; (search) casa per casa.

house-train ['haustreɪn] vt (pet animal) addestrare a non sporcare in casa.

house-trained ['haustreɪnd] adj (BRIT: animal) che non sporca in casa.

house-warming party ['hauswɔ:mɪŋ-] n festa per inaugurare la casa nuova.

housewife ['hauswaɪf] n massaia, casalinga.

housework ['hauswə:k] n faccende fpl domestiche.

housing ['hauzɪŋ] n alloggio ♦ cpd (problem, shortage) degli alloggi.

housing association n cooperativa edilizia.

housing benefit n (BRIT) contributo abitativo (ad affittuari e a coloro che comprano una casa).

housing conditions npl condizioni fpl di abitazione.

housing development, (BRIT) housing estate n zona residenziale con case popolari e/o private.

hovel ['hɔvl] n casupola.

hover ['hɔvə*] vi (bird) librarsi; (helicopter) volare a punto fisso; **to ~ round sb** aggirarsi intorno a qn.

hovercraft ['hɔvəkrɑ:ft] n hovercraft m inv.

hoverport ['hɔvəpɔ:t] n porto per hovercraft.

how [hau] adv come; ~ **are you?** come sta?; ~ **do you do?** piacere!, molto lieto!; ~ **far is it to ...?** quanto è lontano ...?; ~ **long have you been here?** da quanto tempo sta qui?; ~ **lovely!** che bello!; ~ **many?** quanti(e)?; ~ **much?** quanto(a)?; ~ **many people/much milk?** quante persone/ quanto latte?; ~ **old are you?** quanti anni ha?; ~**'s life?** (col) come va (la vita)?; ~ **about a drink?** che ne diresti di andare a bere qualcosa?; ~ **is it that ...?** com'è che ... + sub?

however [hau'evə*] adv in qualsiasi modo or maniera che; (+ adjective) per quanto

+ sub; (in questions) come ♦ conj comunque, però.

howitzer ['hauɪtsə*] n (MIL) obice m.

howl [haul] n ululato ♦ vi ululare.

howler ['haulə*] n marronata.

howling ['haulɪŋ] adj: **a ~ wind** or **gale** un vento terribile.

HP n abbr (BRIT) see **hire purchase**.

hp abbr (AUT) see **horsepower**.

HQ n abbr (= headquarters) Q.G.

HR n abbr (US) = **House of Representatives**.

HRH abbr (= His (or Her) Royal Highness) S.A.R.

hr(s) abbr (= hour(s)) h.

HRT n abbr = **hormone replacement therapy**.

HS abbr (US) = **high school**.

HST abbr (= Hawaiian Standard Time) fuso orario.

HT abbr (= high tension) A.T.

hub [hʌb] n (of wheel) mozzo; (fig) fulcro.

hubbub ['hʌbʌb] n baccano.

hubcap ['hʌbkæp] n (AUT) coprimozzo.

HUD n abbr (US) = Department of Housing and Urban Development.

huddle ['hʌdl] vi: **to ~ together** rannicchiarsi l'uno contro l'altro.

hue [hju:] n tinta; ~ **and cry** n clamore m.

huff [hʌf] n: **in a ~** stizzito(a); **to take the ~** mettere il broncio.

huffy ['hʌfɪ] adj (col) stizzito(a), indispettito(a).

hug [hʌg] vt abbracciare; (shore, kerb) stringere ♦ n abbraccio, stretta; **to give sb a ~** abbracciare qn.

huge [hju:dʒ] adj enorme, immenso(a).

hulk [hʌlk] n carcassa.

hulking ['hʌlkɪŋ] adj: ~ **(great)** grosso(a) e goffo(a).

hull [hʌl] n (of ship) scafo.

hullabaloo [hʌləbə'lu:] n (col: noise) fracasso.

hullo [hə'ləu] excl = **hello**.

hum [hʌm] vt (tune) canticchiare ♦ vi canticchiare; (insect, plane, tool) ronzare ♦ n (also ELEC) ronzio; (of traffic, machines) rumore m; (of voices etc) mormorio, brusio.

human ['hju:mən] adj umano(a) ♦ n (also: ~ **being**) essere m umano.

humane [hju:'meɪn] adj umanitario(a).

humanism ['hju:mənɪzəm] n umanesimo.

humanitarian [hju:mænɪ'tɛərɪən] adj umanitario(a).

humanity [hju:'mænɪtɪ] n umanità; **the humanities** gli studi umanistici.

humanly ['hju:mənlɪ] adv umanamente.

humanoid ['hju:mənɔɪd] adj che sembra

umano(a) ♦ *n* umanoide *m/f*.
human rights *npl* diritti *mpl* dell'uomo.
humble ['hʌmbl] *adj* umile, modesto(a) ♦ *vt* umiliare.
humbly ['hʌmblɪ] *adv* umilmente, modestamente.
humbug ['hʌmbʌg] *n* inganno; sciocchezze *fpl*; (*BRIT: sweet*) caramella alla menta.
humdrum ['hʌmdrʌm] *adj* monotono(a), tedioso(a).
humid ['hju:mɪd] *adj* umido(a).
humidifier [hju:'mɪdɪfaɪə*] *n* umidificatore *m*.
humidity [hju:'mɪdɪtɪ] *n* umidità.
humiliate [hju:'mɪlɪeɪt] *vt* umiliare.
humiliation [hju:mɪlɪ'eɪʃən] *n* umiliazione *f*.
humility [hju:'mɪlɪtɪ] *n* umiltà.
humorist ['hju:mərɪst] *n* umorista *m/f*.
humorous ['hju:mərəs] *adj* umoristico(a); (*person*) buffo(a).
humour, (*US***) humor** ['hju:mə*] *n* umore *m* ♦ *vt* (*person*) compiacere; (*sb's whims*) assecondare; **sense of** ~ senso dell'umorismo; **to be in a good/bad** ~ essere di buon/cattivo umore.
humo(u)rless ['hju:məlɪs] *adj* privo(a) di umorismo.
hump [hʌmp] *n* gobba.
humpback ['hʌmpbæk] *n* schiena d'asino; (*BRIT: also*: ~ **bridge**) ponte *m* a schiena d'asino.
humus ['hju:məs] *n* humus *m*.
hunch [hʌntʃ] *n* gobba; (*premonition*) intuizione *f*; **I have a** ~ **that** ho la vaga impressione che.
hunchback ['hʌntʃbæk] *n* gobbo/a.
hunched [hʌntʃt] *adj* incurvato(a).
hundred ['hʌndrəd] *num* cento; **about a** ~ **people** un centinaio di persone; ~**s of people** centinaia *fpl* di persone; **I'm a** ~ **per cent sure** sono sicuro al cento per cento.
hundredweight ['hʌndrɪdweɪt] *n* (*BRIT*) = *50.8 kg*; *112 lb*; (*US*) = *45.3 kg*, *100 lb*.
hung [hʌŋ] *pt, pp of* **hang**.
Hungarian [hʌŋ'gɛərɪən] *adj* ungherese ♦ *n* ungherese *m/f*; (*LING*) ungherese *m*.
Hungary ['hʌŋgərɪ] *n* Ungheria.
hunger ['hʌŋgə*] *n* fame *f* ♦ *vi*: **to** ~ **for** desiderare ardentemente.
hunger strike *n* sciopero della fame.
hungover [hʌŋ'əuvə*] *adj* (*col*): **to be** ~ avere i postumi della sbornia.
hungrily ['hʌŋgrəlɪ] *adv* voracemente; (*fig*) avidamente.
hungry ['hʌŋgrɪ] *adj* affamato(a); **to be** ~ aver fame; ~ **for** (*fig*) assetato di.
hung up *adj* (*col*) complessato(a).

hunk [hʌŋk] *n* bel pezzo.
hunt [hʌnt] *vt* (*seek*) cercare; (*SPORT*) cacciare ♦ *vi* andare a caccia ♦ *n* caccia.
▶**hunt down** *vt* scovare.
hunter ['hʌntə*] *n* cacciatore *m*; (*BRIT: horse*) cavallo da caccia.
hunting ['hʌntɪŋ] *n* caccia.
hurdle ['hə:dl] *n* (*SPORT, fig*) ostacolo.
hurl [hə:l] *vt* lanciare con violenza.
hurling ['hə:lɪŋ] *n* (*SPORT*) hurling *m*.
hurly-burly ['hə:lɪ'bə:lɪ] *n* chiasso, baccano.
hurrah, hurray [hu'rɑ:, hu'reɪ] *excl* urra!, evviva!
hurricane ['hʌrɪkən] *n* uragano.
hurried ['hʌrɪd] *adj* affrettato(a); (*work*) fatto(a) in fretta.
hurriedly ['hʌrɪdlɪ] *adv* in fretta.
hurry ['hʌrɪ] *n* fretta ♦ *vi* affrettarsi ♦ *vt* (*person*) affrettare; (*work*) far in fretta; **to be in a** ~ aver fretta; **to do sth in a** ~ fare qc in fretta; **to** ~ **in/out** entrare/uscire in fretta; **to** ~ **back/home** affrettarsi a tornare indietro/a casa.
▶**hurry along** *vi* camminare in fretta.
▶**hurry away, hurry off** *vi* andarsene in fretta.
▶**hurry up** *vi* sbrigarsi.
hurt [hə:t] *vb* (*pt, pp* **hurt**) *vt* (*cause pain to*) far male a; (*injure, fig*) ferire; (*business, interests etc*) colpire, danneggiare ♦ *vi* far male ♦ *adj* ferito(a); **I** ~ **my arm** mi sono fatto male al braccio; **where does it** ~**?** dove ti fa male?
hurtful ['hə:tful] *adj* (*remark*) che ferisce.
hurtle ['hə:tl] *vt* scagliare ♦ *vi*: **to** ~ **past/down** passare/scendere a razzo.
husband ['hʌzbənd] *n* marito.
hush [hʌʃ] *n* silenzio, calma ♦ *vt* zittire; ~**!** zitto(a)!
▶**hush up** *vt* (*fact*) cercare di far passare sotto silenzio.
hush-hush ['hʌʃ'hʌʃ] *adj* (*col*) segretissimo(a).
husk [hʌsk] *n* (*of wheat*) cartoccio; (*of rice, maize*) buccia.
husky ['hʌskɪ] *adj* roco(a) ♦ *n* cane *m* eschimese.
hustings ['hʌstɪŋz] *npl* (*BRIT POL*) comizi *mpl* elettorali.
hustle ['hʌsl] *vt* spingere, incalzare ♦ *n* pigia pigia *m inv*; ~ **and bustle** trambusto.
hut [hʌt] *n* rifugio; (*shed*) ripostiglio.
hutch [hʌtʃ] *n* gabbia.
hyacinth ['haɪəsɪnθ] *n* giacinto.
hybrid ['haɪbrɪd] *adj* ibrido(a) ♦ *n* ibrido.
hydrant ['haɪdrənt] *n* (*also*: **fire** ~) idrante *m*.
hydraulic [haɪ'drɔlɪk] *adj* idraulico(a).

hydraulics [haɪˈdrɔlɪks] *n* idraulica.
hydrochloric [haɪdrəˈklɔrɪk] *adj*: ~ **acid** acido cloridrico.
hydroelectric [haɪdrəʊˈlɛktrɪk] *adj* idroelettrico(a).
hydrofoil [ˈhaɪdrəfɔɪl] *n* aliscafo.
hydrogen [ˈhaɪdrədʒən] *n* idrogeno.
hydrogen bomb *n* bomba all'idrogeno.
hydrophobia [haɪdrəˈfəʊbɪə] *n* idrofobia.
hydroplane [ˈhaɪdrəʊpleɪn] *n* idrovolante *m*.
hyena [haɪˈiːnə] *n* iena.
hygiene [ˈhaɪdʒiːn] *n* igiene *f*.
hygienic [haɪˈdʒiːnɪk] *adj* igienico(a).
hymn [hɪm] *n* inno; cantica.
hype [haɪp] *n* (*col*) clamorosa pubblicità.
hyperactive [haɪpərˈæktɪv] *adj* iperattivo(a).
hypermarket [ˈhaɪpəmɑːkɪt] *n* (*BRIT*) ipermercato.
hypertension [haɪpəˈtɛnʃən] *n* (*MED*) ipertensione *f*.
hypertext [ˈhaɪpətɛkst] *n* (*COMPUT*) ipertesto.
hyphen [ˈhaɪfn] *n* trattino.
hypnosis [hɪpˈnəʊsɪs] *n* ipnosi *f*.
hypnotic [hɪpˈnɒtɪk] *adj* ipnotico(a).
hypnotism [ˈhɪpnətɪzəm] *n* ipnotismo.
hypnotist [ˈhɪpnətɪst] *n* ipnotizzatore/trice.
hypnotize [ˈhɪpnətaɪz] *vt* ipnotizzare.
hypoallergenic [haɪpəʊæləˈdʒɛnɪk] *adj* ipoallergico(a).
hypochondriac [haɪpəˈkɒndrɪæk] *n* ipocondriaco/a.
hypocrisy [hɪˈpɒkrɪsɪ] *n* ipocrisia.
hypocrite [ˈhɪpəkrɪt] *n* ipocrita *m/f*.
hypocritical [hɪpəˈkrɪtɪkl] *adj* ipocrita.
hypodermic [haɪpəˈdəːmɪk] *adj* ipodermico(a) ♦ *n* (*syringe*) siringa ipodermica.
hypotenuse [haɪˈpɒtɪnjuːz] *n* ipotenusa.
hypothermia [haɪpəʊˈθəːmɪə] *n* ipotermia.
hypothesis, *pl* **hypotheses** [haɪˈpɒθɪsɪs, -siːz] *n* ipotesi *f inv*.
hypothetical [haɪpəʊˈθɛtɪkl] *adj* ipotetico(a).
hysterectomy [hɪstəˈrɛktəmɪ] *n* isterectomia.
hysteria [hɪˈstɪərɪə] *n* isteria.
hysterical [hɪˈstɛrɪkl] *adj* isterico(a); **to become ~** avere una crisi isterica.
hysterics [hɪˈstɛrɪks] *npl* accesso di isteria; (*laughter*) attacco di riso; **to have ~** avere una crisi isterica.

I i

I, i [aɪ] *n* (*letter*) I, i *f or m inv*; **I for Isaac**, (*US*) **I for Item** ≈ I come Imola.
I [aɪ] *pron* io ♦ *abbr* (= *island, isle*) Is.
IA *abbr* (*US*) = Iowa.
IAEA *n abbr* = **International Atomic Energy Agency**.
IBA *n abbr* (*BRIT*: = *Independent Broadcasting Authority*) organo di controllo sulle reti televisive.
Iberian [aɪˈbɪərɪən] *adj* iberico(a).
Iberian Peninsula *n*: **the ~** la Penisola iberica.
IBEW *n abbr* (*US*: = *International Brotherhood of Electrical Workers*) associazione internazionale degli elettrotecnici.
ib(id). [ˈɪb(ɪd)] *abbr* (= *ibidem: from the same source*) ibid.
i/c *abbr* (*BRIT*) = **in charge**.
ICBM *n abbr* (= *intercontinental ballistic missile*) ICBM *m inv*.
ICC *n abbr* (= *International Chamber of Commerce*) C.C.I. *f*; (*US*: = *Interstate Commerce Commission*) commissione per il commercio tra gli stati degli USA.
ice [aɪs] *n* ghiaccio; (*on road*) gelo ♦ *vt* (*cake*) glassare; (*drink*) ghiacciare ♦ *vi* (*also*: ~ **over**) ghiacciare; (*also*: ~ **up**) gelare; **to keep sth on** ~ (*fig*: plan, project) mettere da parte (per il momento), accantonare.
Ice Age *n* era glaciale.
ice axe *n* piccozza da ghiaccio.
iceberg [ˈaɪsbəːg] *n* iceberg *m inv*; **tip of the ~** (*also fig*) punta dell'iceberg.
icebox [ˈaɪsbɒks] *n* (*US*) frigorifero; (*BRIT*) reparto ghiaccio; (*insulated box*) frigo portatile.
icebreaker [ˈaɪsbreɪkə*] *n* rompighiaccio *m inv*.
ice bucket *n* secchiello del ghiaccio.
ice-cap [ˈaɪskæp] *n* calotta polare.
ice-cold [aɪsˈkəʊld] *adj* gelato(a).
ice cream *n* gelato.
ice-cream soda *n* (gelato) affogato al seltz.
ice cube *n* cubetto di ghiaccio.
iced [aɪst] *adj* (*drink*) ghiacciato(a); (*coffee, tea*) freddo(a); (*cake*) glassato(a).

ice hockey n hockey m su ghiaccio.
Iceland ['aɪslənd] n Islanda.
Icelander ['aɪsləndə*] n islandese m/f.
Icelandic [aɪs'lændɪk] adj islandese ♦ n (LING) islandese m.
ice lolly n (BRIT) ghiacciolo.
ice pick n piccone m per ghiaccio.
ice rink n pista di pattinaggio.
ice-skate ['aɪsskeɪt] n pattino da ghiaccio ♦ vi pattinare sul ghiaccio.
ice-skating ['aɪsskeɪtɪŋ] n pattinaggio sul ghiaccio.
icicle ['aɪsɪkl] n ghiacciolo.
icing ['aɪsɪŋ] n (AVIAT etc) patina di ghiaccio; (CULIN) glassa.
icing sugar n zucchero a velo.
ICJ n abbr see **International Court of Justice.**
icon ['aɪkɔn] n icona; (COMPUT) immagine f.
ICR n abbr (US) = Institute for Cancer Research.
ICRC n abbr (= International Committee of the Red Cross) CICR m.
ICU n abbr see **intensive care unit.**
icy ['aɪsɪ] adj ghiacciato(a); (weather, temperature) gelido(a).
ID abbr (US) = Idaho.
I'd [aɪd] = I would; I had.
Ida. abbr (US) = Idaho.
ID card n = identity card.
IDD n abbr (BRIT TEL: = International direct dialling) teleselezione f internazionale.
idea [aɪ'dɪə] n idea; good ~! buon'idea!; to have an ~ that ... aver l'impressione che ...; I haven't the least ~ non ne ho la minima idea.
ideal [aɪ'dɪəl] adj, n ideale (m).
idealist [aɪ'dɪəlɪst] n idealista m/f.
ideally [aɪ'dɪəlɪ] adv perfettamente, assolutamente; ~ the book should have ... l'ideale sarebbe che il libro avesse ....
identical [aɪ'dɛntɪkl] adj identico(a).
identification [aɪdɛntɪfɪ'keɪʃən] n identificazione f; means of ~ carta d'identità.
identify [aɪ'dɛntɪfaɪ] vt identificare ♦ vi: to ~ with identificarsi con.
Identikit ® [aɪ'dɛntɪkɪt] n: ~ (picture) identikit m inv.
identity [aɪ'dɛntɪtɪ] n identità f inv.
identity card n carta d'identità.
identity parade n (BRIT) confronto all'americana.
ideological [aɪdɪə'lɔdʒɪkəl] adj ideologico(a).
ideology [aɪdɪ'ɔlədʒɪ] n ideologia.
idiocy ['ɪdɪəsɪ] n idiozia.
idiom ['ɪdɪəm] n idioma m; (phrase) espressione f idiomatica.
idiomatic [ɪdɪə'mætɪk] adj idiomatico(a).
idiosyncrasy [ɪdɪəu'sɪŋkrəsɪ] n idiosincrasia.
idiot ['ɪdɪət] n idiota m/f.
idiotic [ɪdɪ'ɔtɪk] adj idiota.
idle ['aɪdl] adj inattivo(a); (lazy) pigro(a), ozioso(a); (unemployed) disoccupato(a); (question, pleasures) ozioso(a) ♦ vi (engine) girare al minimo; to lie ~ stare fermo, non funzionare.
▶**idle away** vt (time) sprecare, buttar via.
idleness ['aɪdlnɪs] n ozio; pigrizia.
idler ['aɪdlə*] n ozioso/a, fannullone/a.
idle time n tempi mpl morti.
idol ['aɪdl] n idolo.
idolize ['aɪdəlaɪz] vt idoleggiare.
idyllic [ɪ'dɪlɪk] adj idillico(a).
i.e. abbr (= id est: that is) cioè.
if [ɪf] conj se ♦ n: there are a lot of ~s and buts ci sono molti se e ma; I'd be pleased ~ you could do it sarei molto contento se potesse farlo; ~ necessary se (è) necessario; ~ only he were here se solo fosse qui; ~ only to show him my gratitude se non altro per esprimergli la mia gratitudine.
iffy ['ɪfɪ] adj (col) incerto(a).
igloo ['ɪgluː] n igloo m inv.
ignite [ɪg'naɪt] vt accendere ♦ vi accendersi.
ignition [ɪg'nɪʃən] n (AUT) accensione f; to switch on/off the ~ accendere/spegnere il motore.
ignition key n (AUT) chiave f dell'accensione.
ignoble [ɪg'nəubl] adj ignobile.
ignominious [ɪgnə'mɪnɪəs] adj vergognoso(a), ignominioso(a).
ignoramus [ɪgnə'reɪməs] n ignorante m/f.
ignorance ['ɪgnərəns] n ignoranza; to keep sb in ~ of sth tenere qn all'oscuro di qc.
ignorant ['ɪgnərənt] adj ignorante; to be ~ of (subject) essere ignorante in; (events) essere ignaro(a) di.
ignore [ɪg'nɔː*] vt non tener conto di; (person, fact) ignorare.
ikon ['aɪkɔn] n = icon.
IL abbr (US) = Illinois.
ILA n abbr (US: = International Longshoremen's Association) associazione internazionale degli scaricatori di porto.
ill [ɪl] adj (sick) malato(a); (bad) cattivo(a) ♦ n male m; to take or be taken ~ ammalarsi; to feel ~ star male; to speak/think ~ of sb parlar/pensar male di qn.
I'll [aɪl] = I will, I shall.

III. *abbr* (*US*) = *Illinois.*

ill-advised [ɪləd'vaɪzd] *adj* (*decision*) poco giudizioso(a); (*person*) mal consigliato(a).

ill-at-ease [ɪlət'iːz] *adj* a disagio.

ill-considered [ɪlkən'sɪdəd] *adj* (*plan*) avventato(a).

ill-disposed [ɪldɪs'pəuzd] *adj*: **to be ~ towards sb/sth** essere maldisposto(a) verso qn/qc *or* nei riguardi di qn/qc.

illegal [ɪ'liːgl] *adj* illegale.

illegally [ɪ'liːgəlɪ] *adv* illegalmente.

illegible [ɪ'lɛdʒɪbl] *adj* illeggibile.

illegitimate [ɪlɪ'dʒɪtɪmət] *adj* illegittimo(a).

ill-fated [ɪl'feɪtɪd] *adj* nefasto(a).

ill-favoured, (*US*) **ill-favored** [ɪl'feɪvəd] *adj* sgraziato(a), brutto(a).

ill feeling *n* rancore *m.*

ill-gotten ['ɪlgɔtn] *adj*: **~ gains** maltolto.

ill health *n* problemi *mpl* di salute.

illicit [ɪ'lɪsɪt] *adj* illecito(a).

ill-informed [ɪlɪn'fɔːmd] *adj* (*judgement, speech*) pieno(a) di inesattezze; (*person*) male informato(a).

illiterate [ɪ'lɪtərət] *adj* analfabeta, illetterato(a); (*letter*) scorretto(a).

ill-mannered [ɪl'mænəd] *adj* maleducato(a), sgarbato(a).

illness ['ɪlnɪs] *n* malattia.

illogical [ɪ'lɔdʒɪkl] *adj* illogico(a).

ill-suited [ɪl'suːtɪd] *adj* (*couple*) mal assortito(a); **he is ~ to the job** è inadatto a quel lavoro.

ill-timed [ɪl'taɪmd] *adj* intempestivo(a), inopportuno(a).

ill-treat [ɪl'triːt] *vt* maltrattare.

ill-treatment [ɪl'triːtmənt] *n* maltrattamenti *mpl.*

illuminate [ɪ'luːmɪneɪt] *vt* illuminare; **~d sign** insegna luminosa.

illuminating [ɪ'luːmɪneɪtɪŋ] *adj* chiarificatore(trice).

illumination [ɪluːmɪ'neɪʃən] *n* illuminazione *f.*

illusion [ɪ'luːʒən] *n* illusione *f*; **to be under the ~ that** avere l'impressione che.

illusive [ɪ'luːsɪv], **illusory** [ɪ'luːsərɪ] *adj* illusorio(a).

illustrate ['ɪləstreɪt] *vt* illustrare.

illustration [ɪlə'streɪʃən] *n* illustrazione *f.*

illustrator ['ɪləstreɪtə*] *n* illustratore/trice.

illustrious [ɪ'lʌstrɪəs] *adj* illustre.

ill will *n* cattiva volontà.

ILO *n abbr* (= *International Labour Organization*) OIL *f.*

ILWU *n abbr* (*US*: = *International Longshoremen's and Warehousemen's Union*) sindacato internazionale degli scaricatori di porto e magazzinieri.

I'm [aɪm] = **I am.**

image ['ɪmɪdʒ] *n* immagine *f*; (*public face*) immagine (pubblica).

imagery ['ɪmɪdʒərɪ] *n* immagini *fpl.*

imaginable [ɪ'mædʒɪnəbl] *adj* immaginabile, che si possa immaginare.

imaginary [ɪ'mædʒɪnərɪ] *adj* immaginario(a).

imagination [ɪmædʒɪ'neɪʃən] *n* immaginazione *f*, fantasia.

imaginative [ɪ'mædʒɪnətɪv] *adj* immaginoso(a).

imagine [ɪ'mædʒɪn] *vt* immaginare.

imbalance [ɪm'bæləns] *n* squilibrio.

imbecile ['ɪmbəsiːl] *n* imbecille *m/f.*

imbue [ɪm'bjuː] *vt*: **to ~ sth with** impregnare qc di.

IMF *n abbr see* **International Monetary Fund.**

imitate ['ɪmɪteɪt] *vt* imitare.

imitation [ɪmɪ'teɪʃən] *n* imitazione *f.*

imitator ['ɪmɪteɪtə*] *n* imitatore/trice.

immaculate [ɪ'mækjulət] *adj* immacolato(a); (*dress, appearance*) impeccabile.

immaterial [ɪmə'tɪərɪəl] *adj* immateriale, indifferente; **it is ~ whether** poco importa se *or* che + *sub.*

immature [ɪmə'tjuə*] *adj* immaturo(a).

immaturity [ɪmə'tjuərɪtɪ] *n* immaturità, mancanza di maturità.

immeasurable [ɪ'mɛʒərəbl] *adj* incommensurabile.

immediacy [ɪ'miːdɪəsɪ] *n* immediatezza.

immediate [ɪ'miːdɪət] *adj* immediato(a).

immediately [ɪ'miːdɪətlɪ] *adv* (*at once*) subito, immediatamente; **~ next to** proprio accanto a.

immense [ɪ'mɛns] *adj* immenso(a); enorme.

immensity [ɪ'mɛnsɪtɪ] *n* (*of size, difference*) enormità; (*of problem etc*) vastità.

immerse [ɪ'məːs] *vt* immergere.

immersion heater [ɪ'məːʃən-] *n* (*BRIT*) scaldaacqua *m inv* a immersione.

immigrant ['ɪmɪgrənt] *n* immigrante *m/f*; (*already established*) immigrato/a.

immigration [ɪmɪ'greɪʃən] *n* immigrazione *f.*

immigration authorities *npl* ufficio stranieri.

immigration laws *npl* leggi *fpl* relative all'immigrazione.

imminent ['ɪmɪnənt] *adj* imminente.

immobile [ɪ'məubaɪl] *adj* immobile.

immobilize [ɪ'məubɪlaɪz] *vt* immobilizzare.

immoderate [ɪ'mɔdərɪt] *adj* (*person*) smodato(a), sregolato(a); (*opinion, reaction, demand*) eccessivo(a).

immodest [ɪ'mɔdɪst] *adj* (*indecent*)

indecente, impudico(a); (*boasting*)
presuntuoso(a).
immoral [ɪ'mɔrl] *adj* immorale.
immorality [ɪmɔ'rælɪtɪ] *n* immoralità.
immortal [ɪ'mɔːtl] *adj, n* immortale (*m/f*).
immortalize [ɪ'mɔːtəlaɪz] *vt* rendere
immortale.
immovable [ɪ'muːvəbl] *adj* (*object*) non
movibile; (*person*) irremovibile.
immune [ɪ'mjuːn] *adj*: ~ (**to**) immune (da).
immune system *n* sistema *m*
immunitario.
immunity [ɪ'mjuːnɪtɪ] *n* (*also fig: of*
diplomat) immunità; **diplomatic** ~
immunità diplomatica.
immunization [ɪmjunaɪ'zeɪʃən] *n*
immunizzazione *f*.
immunize ['ɪmjunaɪz] *vt* immunizzare.
imp [ɪmp] *n* folletto, diavoletto; (*child*)
diavoletto.
impact ['ɪmpækt] *n* impatto.
impair [ɪm'pɛə*] *vt* danneggiare.
impaired [ɪm'pɛəd] *adj* indebolito(a).
-impaired [ɪm'pɛəd] *suffix*: **visually**~
videoleso(a).
impale [ɪm'peɪl] *vt* impalare.
impart [ɪm'pɑːt] *vt* (*make known*)
comunicare; (*bestow*) impartire.
impartial [ɪm'pɑːʃl] *adj* imparziale.
impartiality [ɪmpɑːʃɪ'ælɪtɪ] *n* imparzialità.
impassable [ɪm'pɑːsəbl] *adj* insuperabile;
(*road*) impraticabile.
impasse [æm'pɑːs] *n* impasse *f inv*.
impassioned [ɪm'pæʃənd] *adj*
appassionato(a).
impassive [ɪm'pæsɪv] *adj* impassibile.
impatience [ɪm'peɪʃəns] *n* impazienza.
impatient [ɪm'peɪʃənt] *adj* impaziente; **to**
get *or* **grow** ~ perdere la pazienza.
impeach [ɪm'piːtʃ] *vt* accusare, attaccare;
(*public official*) mettere sotto accusa.
impeachment [ɪm'piːtʃmənt] *n* (*LAW*)
imputazione *f*.
impeccable [ɪm'pɛkəbl] *adj* impeccabile.
impecunious [ɪmpɪ'kjuːnɪəs] *adj* povero(a).
impede [ɪm'piːd] *vt* impedire.
impediment [ɪm'pɛdɪmənt] *n* impedimento;
(*also*: **speech** ~) difetto di pronuncia.
impel [ɪm'pɛl] *vt* (*force*): **to** ~ **sb** (**to do sth**)
costringere *or* obbligare qn (a fare qc).
impending [ɪm'pɛndɪŋ] *adj* imminente.
impenetrable [ɪm'pɛnɪtrəbl] *adj*
impenetrabile.
imperative [ɪm'pɛrətɪv] *adj* imperativo(a);
necessario(a), urgente; (*voice*)
imperioso(a) ♦ *n* (*LING*) imperativo.
imperceptible [ɪmpə'sɛptɪbl] *adj*
impercettibile.

imperfect [ɪm'pəːfɪkt] *adj* imperfetto(a);
(*goods etc*) difettoso(a) ♦ *n* (*LING*: *also*: ~
tense) imperfetto.
imperfection [ɪmpə'fɛkʃən] *n*
imperfezione *f*; (*flaw*) difetto.
imperial [ɪm'pɪərɪəl] *adj* imperiale;
(*measure*) legale.
imperialism [ɪm'pɪərɪəlɪzəm] *n*
imperialismo.
imperil [ɪm'pɛrɪl] *vt* mettere in pericolo.
imperious [ɪm'pɪərɪəs] *adj* imperioso(a).
impersonal [ɪm'pəːsənl] *adj* impersonale.
impersonate [ɪm'pəːsəneɪt] *vt*
impersonare; (*THEAT*) imitare.
impersonation [ɪmpəːsə'neɪʃən] *n* (*LAW*)
usurpazione *f* d'identità; (*THEAT*)
imitazione *f*.
impersonator [ɪm'pəːsəneɪtə*] *n* (*gen*,
THEAT) imitatore/trice.
impertinence [ɪm'pəːtɪnəns] *n*
impertinenza.
impertinent [ɪm'pəːtɪnənt] *adj*
impertinente.
imperturbable [ɪmpə'təːbəbl] *adj*
imperturbabile.
impervious [ɪm'pəːvɪəs] *adj* impermeabile;
(*fig*): ~ **to** insensibile a; impassibile di
fronte a.
impetuous [ɪm'pɛtjuəs] *adj* impetuoso(a),
precipitoso(a).
impetus ['ɪmpətəs] *n* impeto.
impinge [ɪm'pɪndʒ]: **to** ~ **on** *vt fus* (*person*)
colpire; (*rights*) ledere.
impish ['ɪmpɪʃ] *adj* malizioso(a),
birichino(a).
implacable [ɪm'plækəbl] *adj* implacabile.
implant [ɪm'plɑːnt] *vt* (*MED*) innestare; (*fig*:
idea, principle) inculcare.
implausible [ɪm'plɔːzɪbl] *adj* non plausibile.
implement *n* ['ɪmplɪmənt] attrezzo; (*for*
cooking) utensile *m* ♦ *vt* ['ɪmplɪmɛnt]
effettuare.
implicate ['ɪmplɪkeɪt] *vt* implicare.
implication [ɪmplɪ'keɪʃən] *n* implicazione *f*;
by ~ implicitamente.
implicit [ɪm'plɪsɪt] *adj* implicito(a);
(*complete*) completo(a).
implicitly [ɪm'plɪsɪtlɪ] *adv* implicitamente.
implore [ɪm'plɔː*] *vt* implorare.
imply [ɪm'plaɪ] *vt* insinuare; suggerire.
impolite [ɪmpə'laɪt] *adj* scortese.
imponderable [ɪm'pɒndərəbl] *adj*
imponderabile.
import *vt* [ɪm'pɔːt] importare ♦ *n* ['ɪmpɔːt]
(*COMM*) importazione *f*; (*meaning*)
significato, senso ♦ *cpd* (*duty, licence etc*)
d'importazione.
importance [ɪm'pɔːtns] *n* importanza; **to be**

of great/little ~ importare molto/poco, essere molto/poco importante.

important [ɪm'pɔːtnt] *adj* importante; **it's not** ~ non ha importanza; **it is** ~ **that** è importante che + *sub*.

importantly [ɪm'pɔːtəntlɪ] *adv* (*pej*) con (un'aria d')importanza; **but, more** ~, ... ma, quel che più conta *or* importa, ...

importation [ɪmpɔː'teɪʃən] *n* importazione *f*.

imported [ɪm'pɔːtɪd] *adj* importato(a).

importer [ɪm'pɔːtə*] *n* importatore/trice.

impose [ɪm'pəuz] *vt* imporre ♦ *vi*: **to** ~ **on sb** sfruttare la bontà di qn.

imposing [ɪm'pəuzɪŋ] *adj* imponente.

imposition [ɪmpə'zɪʃən] *n* imposizione *f*; **to be an** ~ **on** (*person*) abusare della gentilezza di.

impossibility [ɪmpɔsə'bɪlɪtɪ] *n* impossibilità.

impossible [ɪm'pɔsɪbl] *adj* impossibile; **it is** ~ **for me to leave now** mi è impossibile venir via adesso.

impostor [ɪm'pɔstə*] *n* impostore/a.

impotence ['ɪmpətns] *n* impotenza.

impotent ['ɪmpətnt] *adj* impotente.

impound [ɪm'paund] *vt* confiscare.

impoverished [ɪm'pɔvərɪʃt] *adj* impoverito(a).

impracticable [ɪm'præktɪkəbl] *adj* impraticabile.

impractical [ɪm'præktɪkl] *adj* non pratico(a).

imprecise [ɪmprɪ'saɪs] *adj* impreciso(a).

impregnable [ɪm'prɛgnəbl] *adj* (*fortress*) inespugnabile; (*fig*) inoppugnabile; irrefutabile.

impregnate ['ɪmprɛgneɪt] *vt* impregnare; (*fertilize*) fecondare.

impresario [ɪmprɪ'sɑːrɪəu] *n* impresario/a.

impress [ɪm'prɛs] *vt* impressionare; (*mark*) imprimere, stampare; **to** ~ **sth on sb** far capire qc a qn.

impression [ɪm'prɛʃən] *n* impressione *f*; **to be under the** ~ **that** avere l'impressione che; **to make a good/bad** ~ **on sb** fare una buona/cattiva impressione a *or* su qn.

impressionable [ɪm'prɛʃnəbl] *adj* impressionabile.

impressionist [ɪm'prɛʃənɪst] *n* impressionista *m/f*.

impressive [ɪm'prɛsɪv] *adj* impressionante.

imprint ['ɪmprɪnt] *n* (*PUBLISHING*) sigla editoriale.

imprinted [ɪm'prɪntɪd] *adj*: ~ **on** impresso(a) in.

imprison [ɪm'prɪzn] *vt* imprigionare.

imprisonment [ɪm'prɪznmənt] *n* imprigionamento.

improbable [ɪm'prɔbəbl] *adj* improbabile; (*excuse*) inverosimile.

impromptu [ɪm'prɔmptjuː] *adj* improvvisato(a) ♦ *adv* improvvisando, così su due piedi.

improper [ɪm'prɔpə*] *adj* scorretto(a); (*unsuitable*) inadatto(a), improprio(a); sconveniente, indecente.

impropriety [ɪmprə'praɪətɪ] *n* sconvenienza; (*of expression*) improprietà.

improve [ɪm'pruːv] *vt* migliorare ♦ *vi* migliorare; (*pupil etc*) fare progressi. ►**improve (up)on** *vt fus* (*offer*) aumentare.

improvement [ɪm'pruːvmənt] *n* miglioramento; progresso; **to make** ~**s to** migliorare, apportare dei miglioramenti a.

improvisation [ɪmprəvaɪ'zeɪʃən] *n* improvvisazione *f*.

improvise ['ɪmprəvaɪz] *vt, vi* improvvisare.

imprudence [ɪm'pruːdns] *n* imprudenza.

imprudent [ɪm'pruːdnt] *adj* imprudente.

impudence ['ɪmpjudns] *n* impudenza.

impudent ['ɪmpjudnt] *adj* impudente, sfacciato(a).

impugn [ɪm'pjuːn] *vt* impugnare.

impulse ['ɪmpʌls] *n* impulso; **to act on** ~ agire d'impulso *or* impulsivamente.

impulse buy *n* acquisto fatto d'impulso.

impulsive [ɪm'pʌlsɪv] *adj* impulsivo(a).

impunity [ɪm'pjuːnɪtɪ] *n*: **with** ~ impunemente.

impure [ɪm'pjuə*] *adj* impuro(a).

impurity [ɪm'pjuərɪtɪ] *n* impurità *f inv*.

IN *abbr* (*US*) = *Indiana*.

===================== KEYWORD

in [ɪn] *prep* **1** (*indicating place, position*) in; ~ **the house/garden** in casa/giardino; ~ **the box** nella scatola; ~ **the fridge** nel frigorifero; **I have it** ~ **my hand** ce l'ho in mano; ~ **town/the country** in città/ campagna; ~ **school** a scuola; ~ **here/ there** qui/lì dentro

2 (*with place names: of town, region, country*): ~ **London** a Londra; ~ **England** in Inghilterra; ~ **the United States** negli Stati Uniti; ~ **Yorkshire** nello Yorkshire

3 (*indicating time: during, in the space of*) in; ~ **spring/summer** in primavera/ estate; ~ **1988** nel 1988; ~ **May** in *or* a maggio; **I'll see you** ~ **July** ci vediamo a luglio; ~ **the afternoon** nel pomeriggio; **at 4 o'clock** ~ **the afternoon** alle 4 del pomeriggio; **I did it** ~ **3 hours/days** l'ho

fatto in 3 ore/giorni; **I'll see you** ~ **2 weeks** *or* ~ **2 weeks' time** ci vediamo tra 2 settimane; **once** ~ **a hundred years** una volta ogni cento anni
4 (*indicating manner etc*) a; ~ **a loud/soft voice** a voce alta/bassa; ~ **pencil** a matita; ~ **English/French** in inglese/francese; ~ **writing** per iscritto; **the boy** ~ **the blue shirt** il ragazzo con la camicia blu
5 (*indicating circumstances*): ~ **the sun** al sole; ~ **the shade** all'ombra; ~ **the rain** sotto la pioggia; **a rise** ~ **prices** un aumento dei prezzi
6 (*indicating mood, state*): ~ **tears** in lacrime; ~ **anger** per la rabbia; ~ **despair** disperato(a); ~ **good condition** in buono stato, in buone condizioni; **to live** ~ **luxury** vivere nel lusso
7 (*with ratios, numbers*): **1** ~ **10** 1 su 10; **20 pence** ~ **the pound** 20 pence per sterlina; **they lined up** ~ **twos** si misero in fila per due; ~ **hundreds** a centinaia
8 (*referring to people, works*) in; **the disease is common** ~ **children** la malattia è comune nei bambini; ~ **(the works of) Dickens** in Dickens, nelle opere di Dickens
9 (*indicating profession etc*) in; **to be** ~ **teaching** fare l'insegnante, insegnare; **to be** ~ **publishing** lavorare nell'editoria
10 (*after superlative*) di; **the best** ~ **the class** il migliore della classe
11 (*with present participle*): ~ **saying this** dicendo questo, nel dire questo
12: ~ **that** *conj* poiché
♦ *adv*: **to be** ~ (*person: at home, work*) esserci; (*train, ship, plane*) essere arrivato(a); (*in fashion*) essere di moda; **their party is** ~ il loro partito è al potere; **to ask sb** ~ invitare qn ad entrare; **to run/limp** *etc* ~ entrare di corsa/ zoppicando *etc*
♦ *n*: **the** ~**s and outs of the problem** tutti gli aspetti del problema.

in., ins *abbr* = **inch(es)**.
inability [ɪnə'bɪlɪtɪ] *n* inabilità, incapacità; ~ **to pay** impossibilità di pagare.
inaccessible [ɪnək'sɛsɪbl] *adj* inaccessibile.
inaccuracy [ɪn'ækjurəsɪ] *n* inaccuratezza; inesattezza; imprecisione *f*.
inaccurate [ɪn'ækjurət] *adj* inaccurato(a); (*figures*) inesatto(a); (*translation*) impreciso(a).
inaction [ɪn'ækʃən] *n* inazione *f*.
inactivity [ɪnæk'tɪvɪtɪ] *n* inattività.
inadequacy [ɪn'ædɪkwəsɪ] *n* insufficienza.
inadequate [ɪn'ædɪkwət] *adj* insufficiente.

inadmissible [ɪnəd'mɪsəbl] *adj* inammissibile.
inadvertent [ɪnəd'vɜːtənt] *adj* involontario(a).
inadvertently [ɪnəd'vɜːtntlɪ] *adv* senza volerlo.
inadvisable [ɪnəd'vaɪzəbl] *adj* sconsigliabile.
inane [ɪ'neɪn] *adj* vacuo(a), stupido(a).
inanimate [ɪn'ænɪmət] *adj* inanimato(a).
inapplicable [ɪn'æplɪkəbl] *adj* inapplicabile.
inappropriate [ɪnə'prəuprɪət] *adj* disadatto(a); (*word, expression*) improprio(a).
inapt [ɪn'æpt] *adj* maldestro(a); fuori luogo.
inaptitude [ɪn'æptɪtjuːd] *n* improprietà.
inarticulate [ɪnɑː'tɪkjulət] *adj* (*person*) che si esprime male; (*speech*) inarticolato(a).
inasmuch as [ɪnəz'mʌtʃæz] *adv* in quanto che; (*seeing that*) poiché.
inattention [ɪnə'tenʃən] *n* mancanza di attenzione.
inattentive [ɪnə'tentɪv] *adj* disattento(a), distratto(a); negligente.
inaudible [ɪn'ɔːdɪbl] *adj* che non si riesce a sentire.
inaugural [ɪ'nɔːgjurəl] *adj* inaugurale.
inaugurate [ɪ'nɔːgjureɪt] *vt* inaugurare; (*president, official*) insediare.
inauguration [ɪnɔːgju'reɪʃən] *n* inaugurazione *f*; insediamento in carica.
inauspicious [ɪnɔːs'pɪʃəs] *adj* poco propizio(a).
in-between [ɪnbɪ'twiːn] *adj* fra i (*or* le) due.
inborn [ɪn'bɔːn] *adj* (*feeling*) innato(a); (*defect*) congenito(a).
inbred [ɪn'brɛd] *adj* innato(a); (*family*) connaturato(a).
inbreeding [ɪn'briːdɪŋ] *n* incrocio ripetuto di animali consanguinei; unioni *fpl* fra consanguinei.
Inc. *abbr see* **incorporated**.
Inca [ˈɪŋkə] *adj* (*also:* ~**n**) inca *inv* ♦ *n* inca *m/f inv*.
incalculable [ɪn'kælkjuləbl] *adj* incalcolabile.
incapability [ɪnkeɪpə'bɪlɪtɪ] *n* incapacità.
incapable [ɪn'keɪpəbl] *adj*: ~ **(of doing sth)** incapace (di fare qc).
incapacitate [ɪnkə'pæsɪteɪt] *vt*: **to** ~ **sb from doing** rendere qn incapace di fare.
incapacitated [ɪnkə'pæsɪteɪtɪd] *adj* (*LAW*) inabilitato(a).
incapacity [ɪnkə'pæsɪtɪ] *n* incapacità.
incarcerate [ɪn'kɑːsəreɪt] *vt* imprigionare.
incarnate *adj* [ɪn'kɑːnɪt] incarnato(a) ♦ *vt* [ˈɪnkɑːneɪt] incarnare.
incarnation [ɪnkɑː'neɪʃən] *n* incarnazione *f*.

incendiary [ɪn'sɛndɪərɪ] *adj* incendiario(a)
♦ *n* (*bomb*) bomba incendiaria.
incense *n* ['ɪnsɛns] incenso ♦ *vt* [ɪn'sɛns]
(*anger*) infuriare.
incense burner *n* incensiere *m*.
incentive [ɪn'sɛntɪv] *n* incentivo.
incentive scheme *n* piano di
incentivazione.
inception [ɪn'sɛpʃən] *n* inizio, principio.
incessant [ɪn'sɛsnt] *adj* incessante.
incessantly [ɪn'sɛsntlɪ] *adv* di continuo,
senza sosta.
incest ['ɪnsɛst] *n* incesto.
inch [ɪntʃ] *n* pollice *m* (= *25 mm*; *12 in a
foot*); **within an** ~ **of** a un pelo da; **he
wouldn't give an** ~ (*fig*) non ha ceduto di
un millimetro.
▸**inch forward** *vi* avanzare pian piano.
inch tape *n* (*BRIT*) metro a nastro (da
sarto).
incidence ['ɪnsɪdns] *n* incidenza.
incident ['ɪnsɪdnt] *n* incidente *m*; (*in book*)
episodio.
incidental [ɪnsɪ'dɛntl] *adj* accessorio(a),
d'accompagnamento; (*unplanned*)
incidentale; ~ **to** marginale a; ~
expenses *npl* spese *fpl* accessorie.
incidentally [ɪnsɪ'dɛntəlɪ] *adv* (*by the way*) a
proposito.
incidental music *n* sottofondo (musicale),
musica di sottofondo.
incident room *n* (*POLICE*) centrale *f* delle
operazioni (*per indagini*).
incinerate [ɪn'sɪnəreɪt] *vt* incenerire.
incinerator [ɪn'sɪnəreɪtə*] *n* inceneritore *m*.
incipient [ɪn'sɪpɪənt] *adj* incipiente.
incision [ɪn'sɪʒən] *n* incisione *f*.
incisive [ɪn'saɪsɪv] *adj* incisivo(a); tagliante;
acuto(a).
incisor [ɪn'saɪzə*] *n* incisivo.
incite [ɪn'saɪt] *vt* incitare.
incl. *abbr* = **including, inclusive (of)**.
inclement [ɪn'klɛmənt] *adj* inclemente.
inclination [ɪnklɪ'neɪʃən] *n* inclinazione *f*.
incline *n* ['ɪnklaɪn] pendenza, pendio ♦ *vb*
[ɪn'klaɪn] *vt* inclinare ♦ *vi*: **to** ~ **to** tendere
a; **to be** ~**d to do** tendere a fare; essere
propenso(a) a fare; **to be well** ~**d
towards sb** essere ben disposto(a) verso
qn.
include [ɪn'kluːd] *vt* includere,
comprendere; **the tip is/is not** ~**d** la
mancia è compresa/esclusa.
including [ɪn'kluːdɪŋ] *prep* compreso(a),
incluso(a); ~ **tip** mancia compresa,
compresa la mancia.
inclusion [ɪn'kluːʒən] *n* inclusione *f*.
inclusive [ɪn'kluːsɪv] *adj* incluso(a),

compreso(a); **£50**, ~ **of all surcharges** 50
sterline, incluse tutte le soprattasse.
inclusive terms *npl* (*BRIT*) prezzo tutto
compreso.
incognito [ɪnkɔg'niːtəu] *adv* in incognito.
incoherent [ɪnkəu'hɪərənt] *adj* incoerente.
income ['ɪnkʌm] *n* reddito; **gross/net** ~
reddito lordo/netto; ~ **and expenditure
account** conto entrate ed uscite.
income support *n* (*BRIT*) sussidio di
indigenza *or* povertà.
income tax *n* imposta sul reddito.
income tax inspector *n* ispettore *m* delle
imposte dirette.
income tax return *n* dichiarazione *f*
annuale dei redditi.
incoming ['ɪnkʌmɪŋ] *adj* (*passengers*) in
arrivo; (*government, tenant*) subentrante;
~ **tide** marea montante.
incommunicado [ɪnkəmjunɪ'kɑːdəu] *adj*: **to
hold sb** ~ tenere qn in segregazione.
incomparable [ɪn'kɔmpərəbl] *adj*
incomparabile.
incompatible [ɪnkəm'pætɪbl] *adj*
incompatibile.
incompetence [ɪn'kɔmpɪtns] *n*
incompetenza, incapacità.
incompetent [ɪn'kɔmpɪtnt] *adj*
incompetente, incapace.
incomplete [ɪnkəm'pliːt] *adj* incompleto(a).
incomprehensible [ɪnkɔmprɪ'hɛnsɪbl] *adj*
incomprensibile.
inconceivable [ɪnkən'siːvəbl] *adj*
inimmaginabile.
inconclusive [ɪnkən'kluːsɪv] *adj*
improduttivo(a); (*argument*) poco
convincente.
incongruous [ɪn'kɔŋgruəs] *adj* poco
appropriato(a); (*remark, act*)
incongruo(a).
inconsequential [ɪnkɔnsɪ'kwɛnʃl] *adj* senza
importanza.
inconsiderable [ɪnkən'sɪdərəbl] *adj*: **not** ~
non trascurabile.
inconsiderate [ɪnkən'sɪdərət] *adj*
sconsiderato(a).
inconsistency [ɪnkən'sɪstənsɪ] *n* (*of actions
etc*) incongruenza; (*of work*) irregolarità;
(*of statement etc*) contraddizione *f*.
inconsistent [ɪnkən'sɪstnt] *adj* incoerente;
poco logico(a); contraddittorio(a); ~ **with**
in contraddizione con.
inconsolable [ɪnkən'səuləbl] *adj*
inconsolabile.
inconspicuous [ɪnkən'spɪkjuəs] *adj*
incospicuo(a); (*colour*) poco appariscente;
(*dress*) dimesso(a); **to make o.s.** ~
cercare di passare inosservato(a).

inconstant [ɪn'kɔnstnt] *adj* incostante.
incontinence [ɪn'kɔntɪnəns] *n* incontinenza.
incontinent [ɪn'kɔntɪnənt] *adj* incontinente.
incontrovertible [ɪnkɔntrə'vəːtəbl] *adj* incontrovertibile.
inconvenience [ɪnkən'viːnjəns] *n* inconveniente *m*; (*trouble*) disturbo ♦ *vt* disturbare; **to put sb to great** ~ creare degli inconvenienti a qn.
inconvenient [ɪnkən'viːnjənt] *adj* scomodo(a); **that time is very** ~ **for me** quell'ora mi è molto scomoda, non è un'ora adatta per me.
incorporate [ɪn'kɔːpəreɪt] *vt* incorporare; (*contain*) contenere.
incorporated [ɪn'kɔːpəreɪtɪd] *adj*: ~ **company** (*US*: *abbr* **Inc.**) società *f inv* registrata.
incorrect [ɪnkə'rɛkt] *adj* scorretto(a); (*statement*) impreciso(a).
incorrigible [ɪn'kɔrɪdʒəbl] *adj* incorreggibile.
incorruptible [ɪnkə'rʌptɪbl] *adj* incorruttibile.
increase *n* ['ɪnkriːs] aumento ♦ *vi* [ɪn'kriːs] aumentare; **to be on the** ~ essere in aumento; **an** ~ **of £5/10%** un aumento di 5 sterline/del 10%.
increasing [ɪn'kriːsɪŋ] *adj* (*number*) crescente.
increasingly [ɪn'kriːsɪŋlɪ] *adv* sempre più.
incredible [ɪn'krɛdɪbl] *adj* incredibile.
incredulous [ɪn'krɛdjuləs] *adj* incredulo(a).
increment ['ɪnkrɪmənt] *n* aumento, incremento.
incriminate [ɪn'krɪmɪneɪt] *vt* compromettere.
incriminating [ɪn'krɪmɪneɪtɪŋ] *adj* incriminante.
incubate ['ɪnkjubeɪt] *vt* (*eggs*) covare ♦ *vi* (*egg*) essere in incubazione; (*disease*) avere un'incubazione.
incubation [ɪnkju'beɪʃən] *n* incubazione *f*.
incubation period *n* (periodo di) incubazione *f*.
incubator ['ɪnkjubeɪtə*] *n* incubatrice *f*.
inculcate ['ɪnkʌlkeɪt] *vt*: **to** ~ **sth in sb** inculcare qc a qn, instillare qc a qn.
incumbent [ɪn'kʌmbənt] *adj*: **it is** ~ **on him to do** ... è suo dovere fare ... ♦ *n* titolare *m/f*.
incur [ɪn'kəː*] *vt* (*expenses*) incorrere; (*debt*) contrarre; (*loss*) subire; (*anger, risk*) esporsi a.
incurable [ɪn'kjuərəbl] *adj* incurabile.
incursion [ɪn'kəːʃən] *n* incursione *f*.
Ind. *abbr* (*US*) = *Indiana*.
indebted [ɪn'dɛtɪd] *adj*: **to be** ~ **to sb (for)**

essere obbligato(a) verso qn (per).
indecency [ɪn'diːsnsɪ] *n* indecenza.
indecent [ɪn'diːsnt] *adj* indecente.
indecent assault *n* (*BRIT*) aggressione *f* a scopo di violenza sessuale.
indecent exposure *n* atti *mpl* osceni in luogo pubblico.
indecipherable [ɪndɪ'saɪfərəbl] *adj* indecifrabile.
indecision [ɪndɪ'sɪʒən] *n* indecisione *f*.
indecisive [ɪndɪ'saɪsɪv] *adj* indeciso(a); (*discussion*) non decisivo(a).
indeed [ɪn'diːd] *adv* infatti; veramente; **yes** ~**!** certamente!
indefatigable [ɪndɪ'fætɪgəbl] *adj* infaticabile, instancabile.
indefensible [ɪndɪ'fɛnsəbl] *adj* (*conduct*) ingiustificabile.
indefinable [ɪndɪ'faɪnəbl] *adj* indefinibile.
indefinite [ɪn'dɛfɪnɪt] *adj* indefinito(a); (*answer*) vago(a); (*period, number*) indeterminato(a).
indefinitely [ɪn'dɛfɪnɪtlɪ] *adv* (*wait*) indefinitamente.
indelible [ɪn'dɛlɪbl] *adj* indelebile.
indelicate [ɪn'dɛlɪkɪt] *adj* (*tactless*) indelicato(a), privo(a) di tatto; (*not polite*) sconveniente.
indemnify [ɪn'dɛmnɪfaɪ] *vt* indennizzare.
indemnity [ɪn'dɛmnɪtɪ] *n* (*insurance*) assicurazione *f*; (*compensation*) indennità, indennizzo.
indent [ɪn'dɛnt] *vt* (*TYP*: *text*) far rientrare dal margine.
indentation [ɪndɛn'teɪʃən] *n* dentellatura; (*TYP*) rientranza; (*dent*) tacca.
indented [ɪn'dɛntɪd] *adj* (*TYP*) rientrante.
indenture [ɪn'dɛntʃə*] *n* contratto *m* formazione *inv*.
independence [ɪndɪ'pɛndns] *n* indipendenza.
Independence Day *n* (*US*) *see boxed note*.

INDEPENDENCE DAY

*Negli Stati Uniti il 4 luglio si festeggia l'***Independence Day***, il giorno in cui è stata firmata, nel 1776, la Dichiarazione di Indipendenza con la quale tredici colonie britanniche dichiaravano la propria autonomia dalla Gran Bretagna e la propria appartenenza agli Stati Uniti d'America.*

---

independent [ɪndɪ'pɛndnt] *adj* indipendente.
independently [ɪndɪ'pɛndntlɪ] *adv* indipendentemente; separatamente; ~ **of** indipendentemente da.

in-depth ['ɪn'dɛpθ] *adj* approfondito(a).
indescribable [ɪndɪ'skraɪbəbl] *adj* indescrivibile.
indestructible [ɪndɪ'strʌktəbl] *adj* indistruttibile.
indeterminate [ɪndɪ'tə:mɪnɪt] *adj* indeterminato(a).
index ['ɪndɛks] *n* (*pl* ~**es**: *in book*) indice *m*; (: *in library etc*) catalogo; (*pl* **indices** ['ɪndɪsi:z]: *ratio, sign*) indice *m*.
index card *n* scheda.
index finger *n* (dito) indice *m*.
index-linked ['ɪndɛks'lɪŋkt], (*US*) **indexed** ['ɪndɛkst] *adj* legato(a) al costo della vita.
India ['ɪndɪə] *n* India.
Indian ['ɪndɪən] *adj, n* indiano(a).
Indian ink *n* inchiostro di china.
Indian Ocean *n*: **the** ~ l'Oceano Indiano.
Indian Summer *n* (*fig*) estate *f* di San Martino.
India paper *n* carta d'India, carta bibbia.
India rubber *n* caucciù *m*
indicate ['ɪndɪkeɪt] *vt* indicare ♦ *vi* (*BRIT AUT*): **to** ~ **left/right** mettere la freccia a sinistra/a destra.
indication [ɪndɪ'keɪʃən] *n* indicazione *f*, segno.
indicative [ɪn'dɪkətɪv] *adj* indicativo(a) ♦ *n* (*LING*) indicativo; **to be** ~ **of sth** essere indicativo(a) *or* un indice di qc.
indicator ['ɪndɪkeɪtə*] *n* (*sign*) segno; (*AUT*) indicatore *m* di direzione, freccia.
indices ['ɪndɪsi:z] *npl of* **index**.
indict [ɪn'daɪt] *vt* accusare.
indictable [ɪn'daɪtəbl] *adj* passibile di pena; ~ **offence** atto che costituisce reato.
indictment [ɪn'daɪtmənt] *n* accusa.
indifference [ɪn'dɪfrəns] *n* indifferenza.
indifferent [ɪn'dɪfrənt] *adj* indifferente; (*poor*) mediocre.
indigenous [ɪn'dɪdʒɪnəs] *adj* indigeno(a).
indigestible [ɪndɪ'dʒɛstɪbl] *adj* indigeribile.
indigestion [ɪndɪ'dʒɛstʃən] *n* indigestione *f*.
indignant [ɪn'dɪgnənt] *adj*: ~ (**at sth/with sb**) indignato(a) (per qc/contro qn).
indignation [ɪndɪg'neɪʃən] *n* indignazione *f*.
indignity [ɪn'dɪgnɪtɪ] *n* umiliazione *f*.
indigo ['ɪndɪgəu] *adj, n* indaco (*inv*).
indirect [ɪndɪ'rɛkt] *adj* indiretto(a).
indirectly [ɪndɪ'rɛktlɪ] *adv* indirettamente.
indiscreet [ɪndɪ'skri:t] *adj* indiscreto(a); (*rash*) imprudente.
indiscretion [ɪndɪ'skrɛʃən] *n* indiscrezione *f*; imprudenza.
indiscriminate [ɪndɪ'skrɪmɪnət] *adj* (*person*) che non sa discernere; (*admiration*) cieco(a); (*killings*) indiscriminato(a).
indispensable [ɪndɪ'spɛnsəbl] *adj* indispensabile.
indisposed [ɪndɪ'spəuzd] *adj* (*unwell*) indisposto(a).
indisposition [ɪndɪspə'zɪʃən] *n* (*illness*) indisposizione *f*.
indisputable [ɪndɪ'spju:təbl] *adj* incontestabile, indiscutibile.
indistinct [ɪndɪ'stɪŋkt] *adj* indistinto(a); (*memory, noise*) vago(a).
indistinguishable [ɪndɪ'stɪŋgwɪʃəbl] *adj* indistinguibile.
individual [ɪndɪ'vɪdjuəl] *n* individuo ♦ *adj* individuale; (*characteristic*) particolare, originale.
individualist [ɪndɪ'vɪdjuəlɪst] *n* individualista *m/f*.
individuality [ɪndɪvɪdju'ælɪtɪ] *n* individualità.
individually [ɪndɪ'vɪdjuəlɪ] *adv* singolarmente, uno(a) per uno(a).
indivisible [ɪndɪ'vɪzɪbl] *adj* indivisibile.
Indochina ['ɪndəu'tʃaɪnə] *n* Indocina.
indoctrinate [ɪn'dɔktrɪneɪt] *vt* indottrinare.
indoctrination [ɪndɔktrɪ'neɪʃən] *n* indottrinamento.
indolent ['ɪndələnt] *adj* indolente.
Indonesia [ɪndəu'ni:zɪə] *n* Indonesia.
Indonesian [ɪndəu'ni:zɪən] *adj, n* indonesiano(a); (*LING*) indonesiano.
indoor ['ɪndɔ:*] *adj* da interno; (*plant*) d'appartamento; (*swimming pool*) coperto(a); (*sport, games*) fatto(a) al coperto.
indoors [ɪn'dɔ:z] *adv* all'interno; (*at home*) in casa.
indubitable [ɪn'dju:bɪtəbl] *adj* indubitabile.
induce [ɪn'dju:s] *vt* persuadere; (*bring about*) provocare; **to** ~ **sb to do sth** persuadere qn a fare qc.
inducement [ɪn'dju:smənt] *n* incitamento; (*incentive*) stimolo, incentivo.
induct [ɪn'dʌkt] *vt* insediare; (*fig*) iniziare.
induction [ɪn'dʌkʃən] *n* (*MED: of birth*) parto indotto.
induction course *n* (*BRIT*) corso di avviamento.
indulge [ɪn'dʌldʒ] *vt* (*whim*) compiacere, soddisfare; (*child*) viziare ♦ *vi*: **to** ~ **in sth** concedersi qc; abbandonarsi a qc.
indulgence [ɪn'dʌldʒəns] *n* lusso (che uno si permette); (*leniency*) indulgenza.
indulgent [ɪn'dʌldʒənt] *adj* indulgente.
industrial [ɪn'dʌstrɪəl] *adj* industriale; (*injury*) sul lavoro; (*dispute*) di lavoro.
industrial action *n* azione *f* rivendicativa.
industrial estate *n* zona industriale.
industrialist [ɪn'dʌstrɪəlɪst] *n* industriale *m*.
industrialize [ɪn'dʌstrɪəlaɪz] *vt*

industrializzare.
industrial park n (*US*) zona industriale.
industrial relations *npl* relazioni *fpl* industriali.
industrial tribunal n (*BRIT*) ≈ Tribunale *m* Amministrativo Regionale.
industrial unrest n (*BRIT*) agitazione *f* (sindacale).
industrious [ɪn'dʌstrɪəs] *adj* industrioso(a), assiduo(a).
industry ['ɪndəstrɪ] n industria; (*diligence*) operosità.
inebriated [ɪ'niːbrɪeɪtɪd] *adj* ubriaco(a).
inedible [ɪn'ɛdɪbl] *adj* immangiabile; non commestibile.
ineffective [ɪnɪ'fɛktɪv] *adj* inefficace.
ineffectual [ɪnɪ'fɛktʃuəl] *adj* inefficace; incompetente.
inefficiency [ɪnɪ'fɪʃənsɪ] n inefficienza.
inefficient [ɪnɪ'fɪʃənt] *adj* inefficiente.
inelegant [ɪn'ɛlɪgənt] *adj* poco elegante.
ineligible [ɪn'ɛlɪdʒɪbl] *adj* (*candidate*) ineleggibile; **to be ~ for sth** non avere il diritto a qc.
inept [ɪ'nɛpt] *adj* inetto(a).
ineptitude [ɪ'nɛptɪtjuːd] n inettitudine *f*, stupidità.
inequality [ɪnɪ'kwɔlɪtɪ] n ineguaglianza.
inequitable [ɪn'ɛkwɪtəbl] *adj* iniquo(a).
ineradicable [ɪnɪ'rædɪkəbl] *adj* inestirpabile.
inert [ɪ'nɜːt] *adj* inerte.
inertia [ɪ'nɜːʃə] n inerzia.
inertia-reel seat belt [ɪ'nɜːʃə'riːl-] n cintura di sicurezza con arrotolatore.
inescapable [ɪnɪ'skeɪpəbl] *adj* inevitabile.
inessential [ɪnɪ'sɛnʃl] *adj* non essenziale.
inestimable [ɪn'ɛstɪməbl] *adj* inestimabile, incalcolabile.
inevitable [ɪn'ɛvɪtəbl] *adj* inevitabile.
inevitably [ɪn'ɛvɪtəblɪ] *adv* inevitabilmente; **as ~ happens** ... come immancabilmente succede ....
inexact [ɪnɪg'zækt] *adj* inesatto(a).
inexcusable [ɪnɪks'kjuːzəbl] *adj* imperdonabile.
inexhaustible [ɪnɪg'zɔːstɪbl] *adj* inesauribile; (*person*) instancabile.
inexorable [ɪn'ɛksərəbl] *adj* inesorabile.
inexpensive [ɪnɪk'spɛnsɪv] *adj* poco costoso(a).
inexperience [ɪnɪk'spɪərɪəns] n inesperienza.
inexperienced [ɪnɪk'spɪərɪənst] *adj* inesperto(a), senza esperienza; **to be ~ in sth** essere poco pratico di qc.
inexplicable [ɪnɪk'splɪkəbl] *adj* inesplicabile.

inexpressible [ɪnɪk'sprɛsəbl] *adj* inesprimibile.
inextricable [ɪnɪk'strɪkəbl] *adj* inestricabile.
infallibility [ɪnfælə'bɪlɪtɪ] n infallibilità.
infallible [ɪn'fælɪbl] *adj* infallibile.
infamous ['ɪnfəməs] *adj* infame.
infamy ['ɪnfəmɪ] n infamia.
infancy ['ɪnfənsɪ] n infanzia.
infant ['ɪnfənt] n bambino/a.
infantile ['ɪnfəntaɪl] *adj* infantile.
infant mortality n mortalità infantile.
infantry ['ɪnfəntrɪ] n fanteria.
infantryman ['ɪnfəntrɪmən] n fante *m*.
infant school n (*BRIT*) scuola elementare (*per bambini dall'età di 5 a 7 anni*).
infatuated [ɪn'fætjueɪtɪd] *adj*: **~ with** infatuato(a) di; **to become ~ (with sb)** infatuarsi (di qn).
infatuation [ɪnfætju'eɪʃən] n infatuazione *f*.
infect [ɪn'fɛkt] *vt* infettare; **~ed with** (*illness*) affetto(a) da; **to become ~ed** (*wound*) infettarsi.
infection [ɪn'fɛkʃən] n infezione *f*.
infectious [ɪn'fɛkʃəs] *adj* (*disease*) infettivo(a), contagioso(a); (*person, laughter*) contagioso(a).
infer [ɪn'fɜː*] *vt*: **to ~ (from)** dedurre (da), concludere (da).
inference ['ɪnfərəns] n deduzione *f*, conclusione *f*.
inferior [ɪn'fɪərɪə*] *adj* inferiore; (*goods*) di qualità scadente ♦ n inferiore *m/f*; (*in rank*) subalterno/a; **to feel ~** sentirsi inferiore.
inferiority [ɪnfɪərɪ'ɔrətɪ] n inferiorità.
inferiority complex n complesso di inferiorità.
infernal [ɪn'fɜːnl] *adj* infernale.
inferno [ɪn'fɜːnəu] n inferno.
infertile [ɪn'fɜːtaɪl] *adj* sterile.
infertility [ɪnfɜː'tɪlɪtɪ] n sterilità.
infested [ɪn'fɛstɪd] *adj*: **~ (with)** infestato(a) (di).
infidelity [ɪnfɪ'dɛlɪtɪ] n infedeltà.
in-fighting ['ɪnfaɪtɪŋ] n lotte *fpl* intestine.
infiltrate ['ɪnfɪltreɪt] *vt* (*troops etc*) far penetrare; (*enemy line etc*) infiltrare ♦ *vi* infiltrarsi.
infinite ['ɪnfɪnɪt] *adj* infinito(a); **an ~ amount of time/money** un'illimitata quantità di tempo/denaro.
infinitely ['ɪnfɪnɪtlɪ] *adv* infinitamente.
infinitesimal [ɪnfɪnɪ'tɛsɪməl] *adj* infinitesimale.
infinitive [ɪn'fɪnɪtɪv] n infinito.
infinity [ɪn'fɪnɪtɪ] n infinità; (*also MATH*) infinito.
infirm [ɪn'fɜːm] *adj* infermo(a).
infirmary [ɪn'fɜːmərɪ] n ospedale *m*; (*in*

school, factory) infermeria.
infirmity [ɪn'fɔːmɪtɪ] *n* infermità *f inv.*
inflamed [ɪn'fleɪmd] *adj* infiammato(a).
inflammable [ɪn'flæməbl] *adj* infiammabile.
inflammation [ɪnflə'meɪʃən] *n*
infiammazione *f.*
inflammatory [ɪn'flæmətərɪ] *adj (speech)*
incendiario(a).
inflatable [ɪn'fleɪtəbl] *adj* gonfiabile.
inflate [ɪn'fleɪt] *vt (tyre, balloon)* gonfiare;
(fig) esagerare; gonfiare; **to ~ the**
currency far ricorso all'inflazione.
inflated [ɪn'fleɪtɪd] *adj (style)* gonfio(a);
(value) esagerato(a).
inflation [ɪn'fleɪʃən] *n (ECON)* inflazione *f.*
inflationary [ɪn'fleɪʃənɔrɪ] *adj*
inflazionistico(a).
inflexible [ɪn'flɛksɪbl] *adj* inflessibile,
rigido(a).
inflict [ɪn'flɪkt] *vt:* **to ~ on** infliggere a.
infliction [ɪn'flɪkʃən] *n* inflizione *f;* afflizione
f.
in-flight ['ɪnflaɪt] *adj* a bordo.
inflow ['ɪnfləʊ] *n* afflusso.
influence ['ɪnfluəns] *n* influenza ♦ *vt*
influenzare; **under the ~ of** sotto
l'influenza di; **under the ~ of drink** sotto
l'influenza *or* l'effetto dell'alcool.
influential [ɪnflu'ɛnʃl] *adj* influente.
influenza [ɪnflu'ɛnzə] *n (MED)* influenza.
influx ['ɪnflʌks] *n* afflusso.
inform [ɪn'fɔːm] *vt:* **to ~ sb (of)** informare
qn (di) ♦ *vi:* **to ~ on sb** denunciare qn; **to**
~ sb about mettere qn al corrente di.
informal [ɪn'fɔːml] *adj (person, manner)* alla
buona, semplice; *(visit, discussion)*
informale; *(invitation)* non ufficiale;
"**dress ~**" "non è richiesto l'abito
scuro"; **~ language** linguaggio
colloquiale.
informality [ɪnfɔː'mælɪtɪ] *n* semplicità,
informalità; carattere *m* non ufficiale.
informally [ɪn'fɔːməlɪ] *adv* senza cerimonie;
(invite) in modo non ufficiale.
informant [ɪn'fɔːmənt] *n* informatore/trice.
informatics [ɪnfəː'mætɪks] *n* informatica.
information [ɪnfə'meɪʃən] *n* informazioni
fpl; particolari *mpl;* **to get ~ on** informarsi
su; **a piece of ~** un'informazione; **for your**
~ a titolo d'informazione, per sua
informazione.
information bureau *n* ufficio *m*
informazioni *inv.*
information processing *n* elaborazione *f*
delle informazioni.
information retrieval *n* ricupero delle
informazioni.
information superhighway *n* autostrada

informatica.
information technology (IT) *n*
informatica.
informative [ɪn'fɔːmətɪv] *adj* istruttivo(a).
informed [ɪn'fɔːmd] *adj (observer)* (ben)
informato(a); **an ~ guess** un'ipotesi
fondata.
informer [ɪn'fɔːmə*] *n* informatore/trice.
infra dig ['ɪnfrə'dɪg] *adj abbr (col: = infra*
dignitatem: beneath one's dignity)
indecoroso(a).
infra-red [ɪnfrə'rɛd] *adj* infrarosso(a).
infrastructure ['ɪnfrəstrʌktʃə*] *n*
infrastruttura.
infrequent [ɪn'friːkwənt] *adj* infrequente,
raro(a).
infringe [ɪn'frɪndʒ] *vt* infrangere ♦ *vi:* **to ~**
on calpestare.
infringement [ɪn'frɪndʒmənt] *n:* **~ (of)**
infrazione *f* (di).
infuriate [ɪn'fjuərɪeɪt] *vt* rendere furioso(a).
infuriating [ɪn'fjuərɪeɪtɪŋ] *adj* molto
irritante.
infuse [ɪn'fjuːz] *vt (with courage,*
enthusiasm): **to ~ sb with sth** infondere
qc a qn, riempire qn di qc.
infusion [ɪn'fjuːʒən] *n (tea etc)* infuso,
infusione *f.*
ingenious [ɪn'dʒiːnjəs] *adj* ingegnoso(a).
ingenuity [ɪndʒɪ'njuːɪtɪ] *n* ingegnosità.
ingenuous [ɪn'dʒɛnjuəs] *adj* ingenuo(a).
ingot ['ɪŋgət] *n* lingotto.
ingrained [ɪn'greɪnd] *adj* radicato(a).
ingratiate [ɪn'greɪʃɪeɪt] *vt:* **to ~ o.s. with sb**
ingraziarsi qn.
ingratiating [ɪn'greɪʃɪeɪtɪŋ] *adj (smile,*
speech) suadente, cattivante; *(person)*
compiacente.
ingratitude [ɪn'grætɪtjuːd] *n* ingratitudine *f.*
ingredient [ɪn'griːdɪənt] *n* ingrediente *m;*
elemento.
ingrowing ['ɪngrəʊɪŋ], **ingrown** ['ɪngrəʊn]
adj: **~ (toe)nail** unghia incarnita.
inhabit [ɪn'hæbɪt] *vt* abitare.
inhabitable [ɪn'hæbɪtəbl] *adj* abitabile.
inhabitant [ɪn'hæbɪtnt] *n* abitante *m/f.*
inhale [ɪn'heɪl] *vt* inalare ♦ *vi (in smoking)*
aspirare.
inhaler [ɪn'heɪlə*] *n* inalatore *m.*
inherent [ɪn'hɪərənt] *adj:* **~ (in or to)**
inerente (a).
inherently [ɪn'hɪərəntlɪ] *adv (easy, difficult)*
di per sé; **~ lazy** pigro di natura.
inherit [ɪn'hɛrɪt] *vt* ereditare.
inheritance [ɪn'hɛrɪtəns] *n* eredità.
inhibit [ɪn'hɪbɪt] *vt (PSYCH)* inibire; **to ~ sb**
from doing impedire a qn di fare.
inhibited [ɪn'hɪbɪtɪd] *adj (person)* inibito(a).

inhibiting [ɪn'hɪbɪtɪŋ] *adj* che inibisce.
inhibition [ɪnhɪ'bɪʃən] *n* inibizione *f*.
inhospitable [ɪnhɔs'pɪtəbl] *adj* inospitale.
in-house ['ɪn'haus] *adj* effettuato(a) da personale interno, interno(a) ♦ *adv* (*training*) all'interno dell'azienda.
inhuman [ɪn'hjuːmən] *adj* inumano(a), disumano(a).
inhumane [ɪnhjuː'meɪn] *adj* inumano(a), disumano(a).
inimitable [ɪ'nɪmɪtəbl] *adj* inimitabile.
iniquity [ɪ'nɪkwɪtɪ] *n* iniquità *f inv*.
initial [ɪ'nɪʃl] *adj* iniziale ♦ *n* iniziale *f* ♦ *vt* siglare; ~s *npl* iniziali *fpl*; (*as signature*) sigla.
initialize [ɪ'nɪʃəlaɪz] *vt* (*COMPUT*) inizializzare.
initially [ɪ'nɪʃəlɪ] *adv* inizialmente, all'inizio.
initiate [ɪ'nɪʃɪeɪt] *vt* (*start*) avviare; intraprendere; iniziare; (*person*) iniziare; **to ~ sb into sth** iniziare qn a qc; **to ~ proceedings against sb** (*LAW*) intentare causa a *or* contro qn.
initiation [ɪnɪʃɪ'eɪʃən] *n* iniziazione *f*.
initiative [ɪ'nɪʃətɪv] *n* iniziativa; **to take the ~** prendere l'iniziativa.
inject [ɪn'dʒɛkt] *vt* (*liquid*) iniettare; (*person*) fare una puntura a; (*fig: money*): **to ~ into** immettere in.
injection [ɪn'dʒɛkʃən] *n* iniezione *f*, puntura; **to have an ~** farsi fare un'iniezione *or* una puntura.
injudicious [ɪndʒu'dɪʃəs] *adj* poco saggio(a).
injunction [ɪn'dʒʌŋkʃən] *n* (*LAW*) ingiunzione *f*, intimazione *f*.
injure ['ɪndʒə*] *vt* ferire; (*wrong*) fare male *or* torto a; (*damage: reputation etc*) nuocere a; (*feelings*) offendere; **to ~ o.s.** farsi male.
injured ['ɪndʒəd] *adj* (*person, leg etc*) ferito(a); (*tone, feelings*) offeso(a); **~ party** (*LAW*) parte *f* lesa.
injurious [ɪn'dʒuərɪəs] *adj*: **~ (to)** nocivo(a) (a), pregiudizievole (per).
injury ['ɪndʒərɪ] *n* ferita; (*wrong*) torto; **to escape without ~** rimanere illeso.
injury time *n* (*SPORT*) tempo di ricupero.
injustice [ɪn'dʒʌstɪs] *n* ingiustizia; **you do me an ~** mi fa un torto, è ingiusto verso di me.
ink [ɪŋk] *n* inchiostro.
ink-jet printer ['ɪŋkdʒɛt-] *n* stampante *f* a getto d'inchiostro.
inkling ['ɪŋklɪŋ] *n* sentore *m*, vaga idea.
inkpad ['ɪŋkpæd] *n* tampone *m*, cuscinetto per timbri.
inky ['ɪŋkɪ] *adj* macchiato(a) *or* sporco(a) d'inchiostro.

inlaid ['ɪnleɪd] *adj* incrostato(a); (*table etc*) intarsiato(a).
inland *adj* ['ɪnlənd] interno(a) ♦ *adv* [ɪn'lænd] all'interno; ~ **waterways** canali e fiumi *mpl* navigabili.
Inland Revenue *n* (*BRIT*) Fisco.
in-laws ['ɪnlɔːz] *npl* suoceri *mpl*; famiglia del marito (*or* della moglie).
inlet ['ɪnlɛt] *n* (*GEO*) insenatura, baia.
inlet pipe *n* (*TECH*) tubo d'immissione.
inmate ['ɪnmeɪt] *n* (*in prison*) carcerato/a; (*in asylum*) ricoverato/a.
inmost ['ɪnməust] *adj* più profondo(a), più intimo(a).
inn [ɪn] *n* locanda.
innards ['ɪnədz] *npl* (*col*) interiora *fpl*, budella *fpl*.
innate [ɪ'neɪt] *adj* innato(a).
inner ['ɪnə*] *adj* interno(a), interiore.
inner city *n* centro di una zona urbana.
innermost ['ɪnəməust] *adj* = **inmost**.
inner tube *n* camera d'aria.
innings ['ɪnɪŋz] *n* (*CRICKET*) turno di battuta; (*BRIT fig*): **he has had a good ~** ha avuto molto dalla vita.
innocence ['ɪnəsns] *n* innocenza.
innocent ['ɪnəsnt] *adj* innocente.
innocuous [ɪ'nɔkjuəs] *adj* innocuo(a).
innovation [ɪnəu'veɪʃən] *n* innovazione *f*.
innuendo, ~es [ɪnju'ɛndəu] *n* insinuazione *f*.
innumerable [ɪ'njuːmrəbl] *adj* innumerevole.
inoculate [ɪ'nɔkjuleɪt] *vt*: **to ~ sb with sth/against sth** inoculare qc a qn/qn contro qc.
inoculation [ɪnɔkju'leɪʃən] *n* inoculazione *f*.
inoffensive [ɪnə'fɛnsɪv] *adj* inoffensivo(a), innocuo(a).
inopportune [ɪn'ɔpətjuːn] *adj* inopportuno(a).
inordinate [ɪ'nɔːdɪnɪt] *adj* eccessivo(a).
inordinately [ɪ'nɔːdɪnətlɪ] *adv* smoderatamente.
inorganic [ɪnɔː'gænɪk] *adj* inorganico(a).
in-patient ['ɪnpeɪʃənt] *n* ricoverato/a.
input ['ɪnput] *n* (*ELEC*) energia, potenza; (*of machine*) alimentazione *f*; (*of computer*) input *m* ♦ *vt* (*COMPUT*) inserire, introdurre.
inquest ['ɪnkwɛst] *n* inchiesta.
inquire [ɪn'kwaɪə*] *vi* informarsi ♦ *vt* domandare, informarsi di *or* su; **to ~ about** informarsi di *or* su, chiedere informazioni su; **to ~ when/where/whether** informarsi di quando/su dove/se.
▶**inquire after** *vt fus* (*person*) chiedere di;

(sb's health) informarsi di.

►**inquire into** vt fus indagare su, fare delle indagini or ricerche su.

inquiring [ɪn'kwaɪərɪŋ] adj (mind) inquisitivo(a).

inquiry [ɪn'kwaɪərɪ] n domanda; (LAW) indagine f, investigazione f; **to hold an ~ into sth** fare un'inchiesta su qc.

inquiry desk n (BRIT) banco delle informazioni.

inquiry office n (BRIT) ufficio m informazioni inv.

inquisition [ɪnkwɪ'zɪʃən] n inquisizione f, inchiesta; (REL): **the I~** l'Inquisizione.

inquisitive [ɪn'kwɪzɪtɪv] adj curioso(a).

inroads ['ɪnrəudz] npl: **to make ~ into** (savings, supplies) intaccare (seriamente).

insane [ɪn'seɪn] adj matto(a), pazzo(a); (MED) alienato(a).

insanitary [ɪn'sænɪtərɪ] adj insalubre.

insanity [ɪn'sænɪtɪ] n follia; (MED) alienazione f mentale.

insatiable [ɪn'seɪʃəbl] adj insaziabile.

inscribe [ɪn'skraɪb] vt iscrivere; (book etc): **to ~ (to sb)** dedicare (a qn).

inscription [ɪn'skrɪpʃən] n iscrizione f; (in book) dedica.

inscrutable [ɪn'skruːtəbl] adj imperscrutabile.

inseam ['ɪnsiːm] n (US): **~ measurement** lunghezza interna.

insect ['ɪnsɛkt] n insetto.

Insect bite n puntura or morsicatura di insetto.

insecticide [ɪn'sɛktɪsaɪd] n insetticida m.

insect repellent n insettifugo.

insecure [ɪnsɪ'kjuə*] adj malsicuro(a); (person) insicuro(a).

insecurity [ɪnsɪ'kjuərɪtɪ] n mancanza di sicurezza.

insensible [ɪn'sɛnsɪbl] adj insensibile; (unconscious) privo(a) di sensi.

insensitive [ɪn'sɛnsɪtɪv] adj insensibile.

insensitivity [ɪnsɛnsɪ'tɪvɪtɪ] n mancanza di sensibilità.

inseparable [ɪn'sɛprəbl] adj inseparabile.

insert vt [ɪn'səːt] inserire, introdurre ♦ n ['ɪnsəːt] inserto.

insertion [ɪn'səːʃən] n inserzione f.

in-service ['ɪnsəːvɪs] adj (course, training) dopo l'assunzione.

inshore [ɪn'ʃɔː*] adj costiero(a) ♦ adv presso la riva; verso la riva.

inside ['ɪnsaɪd] n interno, parte f interiore; (of road: BRIT) sinistra; (: US, in Europe etc) destra ♦ adj interno(a), interiore ♦ adv dentro, all'interno ♦ prep dentro, all'interno di; (of time): **~ 10 minutes**

entro 10 minuti; **~s** npl (col) ventre m; **~ out** adv alla rovescia; **to turn sth ~ out** rivoltare qc; **to know sth ~ out** conoscere qc a fondo; **~ information** informazioni fpl riservate; **~ story** storia segreta.

inside forward n (SPORT) mezzala, interno.

inside lane n (AUT) corsia di marcia.

inside leg measurement n (BRIT) lunghezza interna.

insider [ɪn'saɪdə*] n uno(a) che ha le mani in pasta.

insider dealing, insider trading n (STOCK EXCHANGE) insider trading m inv.

insidious [ɪn'sɪdɪəs] adj insidioso(a).

insight ['ɪnsaɪt] n acume m, perspicacia; (glimpse, idea) percezione f; **to gain or get an ~ into sth** potersi render conto di qc.

insignia [ɪn'sɪgnɪə] npl insegne fpl.

insignificant [ɪnsɪg'nɪfɪknt] adj insignificante.

insincere [ɪnsɪn'sɪə*] adj insincero(a).

insincerity [ɪnsɪn'sɛrɪtɪ] n falsità, insincerità.

insinuate [ɪn'sɪnjueɪt] vt insinuare.

insinuation [ɪnsɪnju'eɪʃən] n insinuazione f.

insipid [ɪn'sɪpɪd] adj insipido(a), insulso(a).

Insist [ɪn'sɪst] vi insistere; **to ~ on doing** insistere per fare; **to ~ that** insistere perché + sub; (claim) sostenere che.

insistence [ɪn'sɪstəns] n insistenza.

insistent [ɪn'sɪstənt] adj insistente.

insofar [ɪnsəu'faː*] conj: **~ as** in quanto.

insole ['ɪnsəul] n soletta; (fixed part of shoe) tramezza.

insolence ['ɪnsələns] n insolenza.

insolent ['ɪnsələnt] adj insolente.

insoluble [ɪn'sɔljubl] adj insolubile.

insolvency [ɪn'sɔlvənsɪ] n insolvenza.

insolvent [ɪn'sɔlvənt] adj insolvente.

insomnia [ɪn'sɔmnɪə] n insonnia.

insomniac [ɪn'sɔmnɪæk] n chi soffre di insonnia.

inspect [ɪn'spɛkt] vt ispezionare; (BRIT: ticket) controllare.

inspection [ɪn'spɛkʃən] n ispezione f; controllo.

inspector [ɪn'spɛktə*] n ispettore/trice; controllore m.

inspiration [ɪnspə'reɪʃən] n ispirazione f.

inspire [ɪn'spaɪə*] vt ispirare.

inspired [ɪn'spaɪəd] adj (writer, book etc) ispirato(a); **in an ~ moment** in un momento d'ispirazione.

inspiring [ɪn'spaɪərɪŋ] adj stimolante.

inst. [ɪnst] abbr (BRIT COMM: = instant) c.m. (=corrente mese).

instability [ɪnstə'bɪlɪtɪ] *n* instabilità.
install [ɪn'stɔːl] *vt* installare.
installation [ɪnstə'leɪʃən] *n* installazione *f*.
installment plan *n* (*US*) acquisto a rate.
installment, (*US*) **installment**
[ɪn'stɔːlmənt] *n* rata; (*of TV serial etc*)
puntata; **to pay in** ~**s** pagare a rate.
instance ['ɪnstəns] *n* esempio, caso; **for** ~
per *or* ad esempio; **in that** ~ in quel caso;
in the first ~ in primo luogo.
instant ['ɪnstənt] *n* istante *m*, attimo ♦ *adj*
immediato(a); urgente; (*coffee, food*) in
polvere; **the 10th** ~ il 10 corrente (mese).
instantaneous [ɪnstən'teɪnɪəs] *adj*
istantaneo(a).
instantly ['ɪnstəntlɪ] *adv* immediatamente,
subito.
instant replay *n* (*US TV*) replay *m inv*.
instead [ɪn'stɛd] *adv* invece; ~ **of** invece di;
~ **of sb** al posto di qn.
instep ['ɪnstɛp] *n* collo del piede; (*of shoe*)
collo della scarpa.
instigate ['ɪnstɪgeɪt] *vt* (*rebellion, strike,
crime*) istigare a; (*new ideas etc*)
promuovere.
instigation [ɪnstɪ'geɪʃən] *n* istigazione *f*; **at
sb's** ~ per *or* in seguito al suggerimento
di qn.
instil [ɪn'stɪl] *vt*: **to** ~ **(into)** inculcare (in).
instinct ['ɪnstɪŋkt] *n* istinto.
instinctive [ɪn'stɪŋktɪv] *adj* istintivo(a).
instinctively [ɪn'stɪŋktɪvlɪ] *adv* per istinto.
institute ['ɪnstɪtjuːt] *n* istituto ♦ *vt* istituire,
stabilire; (*inquiry*) avviare; (*proceedings*)
iniziare.
institution [ɪnstɪ'tjuːʃən] *n* istituzione *f*;
istituto (d'istruzione); istituto
(psichiatrico).
institutional [ɪnstɪ'tjuːʃənl] *adj*
istituzionale; ~ **care** assistenza presso un
istituto.
instruct [ɪn'strʌkt] *vt* istruire; **to** ~ **sb in
sth** insegnare qc a qn; **to** ~ **sb to do** dare
ordini a qn di fare.
instruction [ɪn'strʌkʃən] *n* istruzione *f*; ~**s**
(for use) istruzioni per l'uso.
instruction book *n* libretto di istruzioni.
instructive [ɪn'strʌktɪv] *adj* istruttivo(a).
instructor [ɪn'strʌktə*] *n* istruttore/trice;
(*for skiing*) maestro/a.
instrument ['ɪnstrumənt] *n* strumento.
instrumental [ɪnstru'mɛntl] *adj* (*MUS*)
strumentale; **to be** ~ **in sth/in doing sth**
avere un ruolo importante in qc/nel fare
qc.
instrumentalist [ɪnstru'mɛntəlɪst] *n*
strumentista *m/f*.
instrument panel *n* quadro *m*

portastrumenti *inv*.
insubordinate [ɪnsə'bɔːdənɪt] *adj*
insubordinato(a).
insubordination [ɪnsəbɔːdə'neɪʃən] *n*
insubordinazione *f*.
insufferable [ɪn'sʌfrəbl] *adj* insopportabile.
insufficient [ɪnsə'fɪʃənt] *adj* insufficiente.
insufficiently [ɪnsə'fɪʃəntlɪ] *adv* in modo
insufficiente.
insular ['ɪnsjulə*] *adj* insulare; (*person*) di
mente ristretta.
insulate ['ɪnsjuleɪt] *vt* isolare.
insulating tape ['ɪnsjuleɪtɪŋ-] *n* nastro
isolante.
insulation [ɪnsju'leɪʃən] *n* isolamento.
insulin ['ɪnsjulɪn] *n* insulina.
insult *n* ['ɪnsʌlt] insulto, affronto ♦ *vt*
[ɪn'sʌlt] insultare.
insulting [ɪn'sʌltɪŋ] *adj* offensivo(a),
ingiurioso(a).
insuperable [ɪn'sjuːprəbl] *adj*
insormontabile, insuperabile.
insurance [ɪn'ʃuərəns] *n* assicurazione *f*;
fire/life ~ assicurazione contro gli
incendi/sulla vita; **to take out** ~ **(against)**
fare un'assicurazione (contro),
assicurarsi (contro).
insurance agent *n* agente *m*
d'assicurazioni.
insurance broker *n* broker *m inv*
d'assicurazioni.
insurance policy *n* polizza
d'assicurazione.
insurance premium *n* premio
assicurativo.
insure [ɪn'ʃuə*] *vt* assicurare; **to** ~ **sb** *or*
sb's life assicurare qn sulla vita; **to be** ~**d
for £5000** essere assicurato per 5000
sterline.
insured [ɪn'ʃuəd] *n*: **the** ~ l'assicurato/a.
insurer [ɪn'ʃuərə*] *n* assicuratore/trice.
insurgent [ɪn'sɔːdʒənt] *adj* ribelle ♦ *n*
insorto/a, rivoltoso/a.
insurmountable [ɪnsə'mauntəbl] *adj*
insormontabile.
insurrection [ɪnsə'rɛkʃən] *n* insurrezione *f*.
intact [ɪn'tækt] *adj* intatto(a).
intake ['ɪnteɪk] *n* (*TECH*) immissione *f*; (*of
food*) consumo; (*of pupils etc*) afflusso.
intangible [ɪn'tændʒɪbl] *adj* intangibile.
integral ['ɪntɪgrəl] *adj* integrale; (*part*)
integrante.
integrate ['ɪntɪgreɪt] *vt* integrare.
integrated circuit *n* (*COMPUT*) circuito
integrato.
integration [ɪntɪ'greɪʃən] *n* integrazione *f*;
racial ~ integrazione razziale.
integrity [ɪn'tɛgrɪtɪ] *n* integrità.

intellect ['ɪntəlɛkt] n intelletto.
intellectual [ɪntə'lɛktjuəl] adj, n intellettuale (m/f).
intelligence [ɪn'tɛlɪdʒəns] n intelligenza; (MIL etc) informazioni fpl.
intelligence quotient (IQ) n quoziente m d'intelligenza (Q.I.).
Intelligence Service n servizio segreto.
intelligence test n test m inv d'intelligenza.
intelligent [ɪn'tɛlɪdʒənt] adj intelligente.
intelligible [ɪn'tɛlɪdʒɪbl] adj intelligibile.
intemperate [ɪn'tɛmpərət] adj immoderato(a); (drinking too much) intemperante nel bere.
intend [ɪn'tɛnd] vt (gift etc): to ~ sth for destinare qc a; to ~ to do aver l'intenzione di fare.
intended [ɪn'tɛndɪd] adj (insult) intenzionale; (effect) voluto(a); (journey, route) progettato(a).
intense [ɪn'tɛns] adj intenso(a); (person) di forti sentimenti.
intensely [ɪn'tɛnslɪ] adv intensamente; profondamente.
intensify [ɪn'tɛnsɪfaɪ] vt intensificare.
intensity [ɪn'tɛnsɪtɪ] n intensità.
intensive [ɪn'tɛnsɪv] adj intensivo(a).
intensive care n terapia intensiva; ~ **unit** (**ICU**) n reparto terapia intensiva.
intent [ɪn'tɛnt] n intenzione f ♦ adj: ~ (**on**) intento(a) (a), immerso(a) (in); **to all ~s and purposes** a tutti gli effetti; **to be ~ on doing sth** essere deciso a fare qc.
intention [ɪn'tɛnʃən] n intenzione f.
intentional [ɪn'tɛnʃənl] adj intenzionale, deliberato(a).
intentionally [ɪn'tɛnʃənlɪ] adv apposta.
intently [ɪn'tɛntlɪ] adv attentamente.
inter [ɪn'tə:*] vt sotterrare.
interact [ɪntər'ækt] vi agire reciprocamente, interagire.
interaction [ɪntər'ækʃən] n azione f reciproca, interazione f.
interactive [ɪntər'æktɪv] adj interattivo(a).
intercede [ɪntə'si:d] vi: to ~ (**with sb/on behalf of sb**) intercedere (presso qn/a favore di qn).
intercept [ɪntə'sɛpt] vt intercettare; (person) fermare.
interception [ɪntə'sɛpʃən] n intercettamento.
interchange n ['ɪntətʃeɪndʒ] (exchange) scambio; (on motorway) incrocio pluridirezionale ♦ vt [ɪntə'tʃeɪndʒ] scambiare; sostituire l'uno(a) per l'altro(a).
interchangeable [ɪntə'tʃeɪndʒəbl] adj intercambiabile.

intercity [ɪntə'sɪtɪ] adj: ~ (**train**) ≈ (treno) rapido.
intercom ['ɪntəkɔm] n interfono.
interconnect [ɪntəkə'nɛkt] vi (rooms) essere in comunicazione.
intercontinental ['ɪntəkɔntɪ'nɛntl] adj intercontinentale.
intercourse ['ɪntəkɔːs] n rapporti mpl; (sexual ~) rapporti sessuali.
interdependent [ɪntədɪ'pɛndənt] adj interdipendente.
interest ['ɪntrɪst] n interesse m; (COMM: stake, share) interessi mpl ♦ vt interessare; **compound/simple** ~ interesse composto/semplice; **business** ~**s** attività fpl commerciali; **British** ~**s in the Middle East** gli interessi (commerciali) britannici nel Medio Oriente.
interested ['ɪntrɪstɪd] adj interessato(a); **to be** ~ **in** interessarsi di.
interest-free ['ɪntrɪst'friː] adj senza interesse.
interesting ['ɪntrɪstɪŋ] adj interessante.
interest rate n tasso di interesse.
interface ['ɪntəfeɪs] n (COMPUT) interfaccia.
interfere [ɪntə'fɪə*] vi: to ~ (**in**) (quarrel, other people's business) immischiarsi (in); **to** ~ **with** (object) toccare; (plans) ostacolare; (duty) interferire con.
interference [ɪntə'fɪərəns] n interferenza.
interfering [ɪntə'fɪərɪŋ] adj invadente.
interim ['ɪntərɪm] adj provvisorio(a) ♦ n: **in the** ~ nel frattempo; ~ **dividend** (COMM) acconto di dividendo.
interior [ɪn'tɪərɪə*] n interno; (of country) entroterra ♦ adj interiore, interno(a).
interior decorator, interior designer n decoratore/trice (d'interni).
interjection [ɪntə'dʒɛkʃən] n interiezione f.
interlock [ɪntə'lɔk] vi ingranarsi ♦ vt ingranare.
interloper ['ɪntələupə*] n intruso/a.
interlude ['ɪntəluːd] n intervallo; (THEAT) intermezzo.
intermarry [ɪntə'mærɪ] vi imparentarsi per mezzo di matrimonio; sposarsi tra parenti.
intermediary [ɪntə'miːdɪərɪ] n intermediario/a.
intermediate [ɪntə'miːdɪət] adj intermedio(a); (SCOL: course, level) medio(a).
interment [ɪn'tə:mənt] n (formal) inumazione f.
interminable [ɪn'tə:mɪnəbl] adj interminabile.
intermission [ɪntə'mɪʃən] n pausa; (THEAT,

CINE) intermissione *f*, intervallo.
intermittent [ɪntə'mɪtnt] *adj* intermittente.
intermittently [ɪntə'mɪtntlɪ] *adv* a
intermittenza.
intern *vt* [ɪn'tə:n] internare ♦ *n* ['ɪntə:n] (*US*)
medico interno.
internal [ɪn'tə:nl] *adj* interno(a); ~ **injuries**
lesioni *fpl* interne.
internally [ɪn'tə:nəlɪ] *adv* all'interno; "**not
to be taken** ~" "per uso esterno".
Internal Revenue (Service) (IRS) *n* (*US*)
Fisco.
international [ɪntə'næʃənl] *adj*
internazionale ♦ *n* (*BRIT SPORT*) partita
internazionale.
**International Atomic Energy Agency
(IAEA)** *n* Agenzia Internazionale per
l'Energia Atomica (IAEA).
International Court of Justice (ICJ) *n*
Corte *f* Internazionale di Giustizia.
international date line *n* linea del
cambiamento di data.
internationally [ɪntə'næʃnəlɪ] *adv* a livello
internazionale.
International Monetary Fund (IMF) *n*
Fondo monetario internazionale (F.M.I.).
international relations *npl* rapporti *mpl*
internazionali.
internecine [ɪntə'ni:saɪn] *adj* sanguinoso(a).
internee [ɪntə'ni:] *n* internato/a.
Internet ['ɪntə,nɛt] *n*: **the** ~ Internet *f*.
internment [ɪn'tə:nmənt] *n* internamento.
interplay ['ɪntəpleɪ] *n* azione e reazione *f*.
Interpol ['ɪntəpɔl] *n* Interpol *f*.
interpret [ɪn'tə:prɪt] *vt* interpretare ♦ *vi*
fare da interprete.
interpretation [ɪntə:prɪ'teɪʃən] *n*
interpretazione *f*.
interpreter [ɪn'tə:prɪtə*] *n* interprete *m/f*.
interpreting [ɪn'tə:prɪtɪŋ] *n* (*profession*)
interpretariato.
interrelated [ɪntərɪ'leɪtɪd] *adj* correlato(a).
interrogate [ɪn'tɛrəugeɪt] *vt* interrogare.
interrogation [ɪntɛrəu'geɪʃən] *n* interrogazione *f*; (*of suspect etc*) interrogatorio.
interrogative [ɪntə'rɔgətɪv] *adj*
interrogativo(a) ♦ *n* (*LING*) interrogativo.
interrogator [ɪn'tɛrəgeɪtə*] *n* interrogante
m/f.
interrupt [ɪntə'rʌpt] *vt* interrompere.
interruption [ɪntə'rʌpʃən] *n* interruzione *f*.
intersect [ɪntə'sɛkt] *vt* intersecare ♦ *vi*
(*roads*) intersecarsi.
intersection [ɪntə'sɛkʃən] *n* intersezione *f*;
(*of roads*) incrocio.
intersperse [ɪntə'spə:s] *vt*: **to** ~ **with**
costellare di.
intertwine [ɪntə'twaɪn] *vt* intrecciare ♦ *vi*

intrecciarsi.
interval ['ɪntəvl] *n* intervallo; (*BRIT SCOL*)
ricreazione *f*, intervallo; **bright** ~**s** (*in
weather*) schiarite *fpl*; **at** ~**s** a intervalli.
intervene [ɪntə'vi:n] *vi* (*time*) intercorrere;
(*event, person*) intervenire.
intervention [ɪntə'vɛnʃən] *n* intervento.
interview ['ɪntəvju:] *n* (*RADIO, TV etc*)
intervista; (*for job*) colloquio ♦ *vt*
intervistare; avere un colloquio con.
interviewee [ɪntəvju'i:] *n* (*TV*)
intervistato/a; (*for job*) chi si presenta ad
un colloquio di lavoro.
interviewer ['ɪntəvju:ə*] *n* intervistatore/
trice.
intestate [ɪn'tɛsteɪt] *adj* intestato(a).
intestinal [ɪn'tɛstɪnl] *adj* intestinale.
intestine [ɪn'tɛstɪn] *n* intestino; **large/small**
~ intestino crasso/tenue.
intimacy ['ɪntɪməsɪ] *n* intimità.
intimate *adj* ['ɪntɪmət] intimo(a);
(*knowledge*) profondo(a) ♦ *vt* ['ɪntɪmeɪt]
lasciar capire.
intimately ['ɪntɪmɪtlɪ] *adv* intimamente.
intimation [ɪntɪ'meɪʃən] *n* annuncio.
intimidate [ɪn'tɪmɪdeɪt] *vt* intimidire,
intimorire.
intimidation [ɪntɪmɪ'deɪʃən] *n*
intimidazione *f*.
into ['ɪntu] *prep* dentro, in; **come** ~ **the
house** vieni dentro la casa; ~ **pieces** a
pezzi; ~ **Italian** in italiano; **to change
pounds** ~ **dollars** cambiare delle sterline
in dollari.
intolerable [ɪn'tɔlərəbl] *adj* intollerabile.
intolerance [ɪn'tɔlərns] *n* intolleranza.
intolerant [ɪn'tɔlərnt] *adj*: ~ **(of)**
intollerante (di).
intonation [ɪntəu'neɪʃən] *n* intonazione *f*.
intoxicate [ɪn'tɔksɪkeɪt] *vt* inebriare.
intoxicated [ɪn'tɔksɪkeɪtɪd] *adj* inebriato(a).
intoxication [ɪntɔksɪ'keɪʃən] *n* ebbrezza.
intractable [ɪn'træktəbl] *adj* intrattabile;
(*illness*) difficile da curare; (*problem*)
insolubile.
intranet ['ɪntrənɛt] *n* Intranet *f*.
intransigence [ɪn'trænsɪdʒəns] *n*
intransigenza.
intransigent [ɪn'trænsɪdʒənt] *adj*
intransigente.
intransitive [ɪn'trænsɪtɪv] *adj*
intransitivo(a).
intra-uterine device (IUD) [ɪntrə'-
ju:təraɪn-]*n* dispositivo intrauterino (IUD).
intravenous [ɪntrə'vi:nəs] *adj*
endovenoso(a).
in-tray ['ɪntreɪ] *n* raccoglitore *m* per le
carte in arrivo.

intrepid [ɪn'trɛpɪd] *adj* intrepido(a).
intricacy ['ɪntrɪkəsɪ] *n* complessità *f inv.*
intricate ['ɪntrɪkət] *adj* intricato(a), complicato(a).
intrigue [ɪn'triːg] *n* intrigo ♦ *vt* affascinare ♦ *vi* complottare, tramare.
intriguing [ɪn'triːgɪŋ] *adj* affascinante.
intrinsic [ɪn'trɪnsɪk] *adj* intrinseco(a).
introduce [ɪntrə'djuːs] *vt* introdurre; **to ~ sb (to sb)** presentare qn (a qn); **to ~ sb to** *(pastime, technique)* iniziare qn a; **may I ~ ...?** permette che le presenti ...?
introduction [ɪntrə'dʌkʃən] *n* introduzione *f*; *(of person)* presentazione *f*; **a letter of ~** una lettera di presentazione.
introductory [ɪntrə'dʌktərɪ] *adj* introduttivo(a); **an ~ offer** un'offerta di lancio; **~ remarks** osservazioni *fpl* preliminari.
introspection [ɪntrəu'spɛkʃən] *n* introspezione *f*.
introspective [ɪntrəu'spɛktɪv] *adj* introspettivo(a).
introvert ['ɪntrəuvɜːt] *adj, n* introverso(a).
intrude [ɪn'truːd] *vi* *(person)* intromettersi; **to ~ on** *(person)* importunare; **~ on** *or* **into** *(conversation)* intromettersi in; **am I intruding?** disturbo?
intruder [ɪn'truːdə*] *n* intruso/a.
intrusion [ɪn'truːʒən] *n* intrusione *f*.
intrusive [ɪn'truːsɪv] *adj* importuno(a).
intuition [ɪntjuː'ɪʃən] *n* intuizione *f*.
intuitive [ɪn'tjuːɪtɪv] *adj* intuitivo(a); dotato(a) di intuito.
inundate ['ɪnʌndeɪt] *vt*: **to ~ with** inondare di.
inure [ɪn'juə*] *vt*: **to ~ (to)** assuefare (a).
invade [ɪn'veɪd] *vt* invadere.
invader [ɪn'veɪdə*] *n* invasore *m.*
invalid *n* ['ɪnvəlɪd] malato/a; *(with disability)* invalido/a ♦ *adj* [ɪn'vælɪd] *(not valid)* invalido(a), non valido(a).
invalidate [ɪn'vælɪdeɪt] *vt* invalidare.
invalid chair *n* *(BRIT)* sedia a rotelle.
invaluable [ɪn'væljuəbl] *adj* prezioso(a); inestimabile.
invariable [ɪn'vɛərɪəbl] *adj* costante, invariabile.
invariably [ɪn'vɛərɪəblɪ] *adv* invariabilmente; **she is ~ late** è immancabilmente in ritardo.
invasion [ɪn'veɪʒən] *n* invasione *f.*
invective [ɪn'vɛktɪv] *n* invettiva.
inveigle [ɪn'viːgl] *vt*: **to ~ sb into (doing) sth** circuire qn per (fargli fare) qc.
invent [ɪn'vɛnt] *vt* inventare.
invention [ɪn'vɛnʃən] *n* invenzione *f.*
inventive [ɪn'vɛntɪv] *adj* inventivo(a).

inventiveness [ɪn'vɛntɪvnɪs] *n* inventiva.
inventor [ɪn'vɛntə*] *n* inventore *m.*
inventory ['ɪnvəntrɪ] *n* inventario.
inventory control *n* *(COMM)* controllo delle giacenze.
inverse [ɪn'vɜːs] *adj* inverso(a) ♦ *n* inverso, contrario; **in ~ proportion (to)** in modo inversamente proporzionale (a).
inversely [ɪn'vɜːslɪ] *adv* inversamente.
invert [ɪn'vɜːt] *vt* invertire; *(object)* rovesciare.
invertebrate [ɪn'vɜːtɪbrɪt] *n* invertebrato.
inverted commas [ɪn'vɜːtɪd-] *npl* *(BRIT)* virgolette *fpl.*
invest [ɪn'vɛst] *vt* investire; *(fig: time, effort)* impiegare; *(endow)*: **to ~ sb with sth** investire qn di qc ♦ *vi* fare investimenti; **to ~ in** investire in, fare (degli) investimenti in; *(acquire)* comprarsi.
investigate [ɪn'vɛstɪgeɪt] *vt* investigare, indagare; *(crime)* fare indagini su.
investigation [ɪnvɛstɪ'geɪʃən] *n* investigazione *f*; *(of crime)* indagine *f.*
investigative [ɪn'vɛstɪgətɪv] *adj*: **~ journalism** giornalismo investigativo.
investigator [ɪn'vɛstɪgeɪtə*] *n* investigatore/trice; **a private ~** un investigatore privato, un detective.
investiture [ɪn'vɛstɪtʃə*] *n* investitura.
investment [ɪn'vɛstmənt] *n* investimento.
investment income *n* reddito da investimenti.
investment trust *n* fondo comune di investimento.
investor [ɪn'vɛstə*] *n* investitore/trice; *(shareholder)* azionista *m/f.*
inveterate [ɪn'vɛtərət] *adj* inveterato(a).
invidious [ɪn'vɪdɪəs] *adj* odioso(a); *(task)* spiacevole.
invigilate [ɪn'vɪdʒɪleɪt] *vt, vi* *(BRIT SCOL)* sorvegliare.
invigilator [ɪn'vɪdʒɪleɪtə*] *n* *(BRIT)* chi sorveglia agli esami.
invigorating [ɪn'vɪgəreɪtɪŋ] *adj* stimolante; vivificante.
invincible [ɪn'vɪnsɪbl] *adj* invincibile.
inviolate [ɪn'vaɪələt] *adj* inviolato(a).
invisible [ɪn'vɪzɪbl] *adj* invisibile.
invisible assets *npl* *(BRIT)* beni *mpl* immateriali.
invisible ink *n* inchiostro simpatico.
invisible mending *n* rammendo invisibile.
invitation [ɪnvɪ'teɪʃən] *n* invito; **by ~ only** esclusivamente su *or* per invito; **at sb's ~** dietro invito di qn.
invite [ɪn'vaɪt] *vt* invitare; *(opinions etc)* sollecitare; *(trouble)* provocare; **to ~ sb**

(to do) invitare qn (a fare); **to ~ sb to dinner** invitare qn a cena.
►**invite out** *vt* invitare fuori.
►**invite over** *vt* invitare (a casa).
inviting [ɪn'vaɪtɪŋ] *adj* invitante, attraente.
invoice ['ɪnvɔɪs] *n* fattura ♦ *vt* fatturare; **to ~ sb for goods** inviare a qn la fattura per le *or* delle merci.
invoke [ɪn'vəuk] *vt* invocare.
involuntary [ɪn'vɔləntrɪ] *adj* involontario(a).
involve [ɪn'vɔlv] *vt* (*entail*) richiedere, comportare; (*associate*): **to ~ sb (in)** implicare qn (in); coinvolgere qn (in); **to involve o.s. in sth** (*politics etc*) impegnarsi in qc.
involved [ɪn'vɔlvd] *adj* involuto(a), complesso(a); **to feel ~** sentirsi coinvolto(a); **to become ~ with sb** (*socially*) legarsi a qn; (*emotionally*) legarsi sentimentalmente a qn.
involvement [ɪn'vɔlvmənt] *n* implicazione *f*; coinvolgimento; impegno; partecipazione *f*.
invulnerable [ɪn'vʌlnərəbl] *adj* invulnerabile.
inward ['ɪnwəd] *adj* (*movement*) verso l'interno; (*thought, feeling*) interiore, intimo(a); *see also* **inward(s)**.
inwardly ['ɪnwədlɪ] *adv* (*feel, think etc*) nell'intimo, entro di sé.
inward(s) ['ɪnwəd(z)] *adv* verso l'interno.
I/O *abbr* (*COMPUT*: = *input/output*) I/O.
IOC *n abbr* (= *International Olympic Committee*) CIO *m* (= *Comitato Internazionale Olimpico*).
iodine ['aɪəudiːn] *n* iodio.
IOM *abbr* (*BRIT*) = *Isle of Man*.
ion ['aɪən] *n* ione *m*.
Ionian Sea [aɪ'əunɪən-] *n*: **the ~** il mare Ionio.
ioniser ['aɪənaɪzə*] *n* ionizzatore *m*.
iota [aɪ'əutə] *n* (*fig*) briciolo.
IOU *n abbr* (= *I owe you*) pagherò *m inv*.
IOW *abbr* (*BRIT*) = *Isle of Wight*.
IPA *n abbr* (= *International Phonetic Alphabet*) I.P.A. *m*.
IQ *n abbr* = **intelligence quotient**.
IRA *n abbr* (= *Irish Republican Army*) I.R.A. *f*; (*US*) = *individual retirement account*.
Iran [ɪ'rɑːn] *n* Iran *m*.
Iranian [ɪ'reɪnɪən] *adj* iraniano(a) ♦ *n* iraniano/a; (*LING*) iranico.
Iraq [ɪ'rɑːk] *n* Iraq *m*.
Iraqi [ɪ'rɑːkɪ] *adj* iracheno(a) ♦ *n* iracheno/a.
irascible [ɪ'ræsɪbl] *adj* irascibile.
irate [aɪ'reɪt] *adj* irato(a).

Ireland ['aɪələnd] *n* Irlanda; **Republic of ~** Repubblica d'Irlanda, Eire *f*.
iris, ~es ['aɪrɪs, -ɪz] *n* iride *f*; (*BOT*) giaggiolo, iride.
Irish ['aɪrɪʃ] *adj* irlandese ♦ *npl*: **the ~** gli Irlandesi.
Irishman ['aɪrɪʃmən] *n* irlandese *m*.
Irish Sea *n*: **the ~** il mar d'Irlanda.
Irishwoman ['aɪrɪʃwumən] *n* irlandese *f*.
irk [əːk] *vt* seccare.
irksome ['əːksəm] *adj* seccante.
IRN *n abbr* (= *Independent Radio News*) *agenzia d'informazioni per la radio*.
IRO *n abbr* (*US*: = *International Refugee Organization*) O.I.R. *f* (= *Organizzazione Internazionale per i Rifugiati*).
iron ['aɪən] *n* ferro; (*for clothes*) ferro da stiro ♦ *adj* di *or* in ferro ♦ *vt* (*clothes*) stirare; *see also* **irons**.
►**iron out** *vt* (*crease*) appianare; (*fig*) spianare; far sparire.
Iron Curtain *n*: **the ~** la cortina di ferro.
iron foundry *n* fonderia.
ironic(al) [aɪ'rɔnɪk(l)] *adj* ironico(a).
ironically [aɪ'rɔnɪklɪ] *adv* ironicamente.
ironing ['aɪənɪŋ] *n* (*act*) stirare *m*; (*clothes*) roba da stirare.
ironing board *n* asse *f* da stiro.
iron lung *n* (*MED*) polmone *m* d'acciaio.
ironmonger ['aɪənmʌŋgə*] *n* (*BRIT*) negoziante *m* in ferramenta; **~'s (shop)** *n* negozio di ferramenta.
iron ore *n* minerale *m* di ferro.
irons ['aɪənz] *npl* (*chains*) catene *fpl*.
ironworks ['aɪənwəːks] *n* ferriera.
irony ['aɪrənɪ] *n* ironia.
irrational [ɪ'ræʃənl] *adj* irrazionale; irragionevole; illogico(a).
irreconcilable [ɪrekən'saɪləbl] *adj* irreconciliabile; (*opinion*): **~ with** inconciliabile con.
irredeemable [ɪrɪ'diːməbl] *adj* (*COMM*) irredimibile.
irrefutable [ɪrɪ'fjuːtəbl] *adj* irrefutabile.
irregular [ɪ'regjulə*] *adj* irregolare.
irregularity [ɪregju'lærɪtɪ] *n* irregolarità *f inv*.
irrelevance [ɪ'reləvəns] *n* inappropriatezza.
irrelevant [ɪ'reləvənt] *adj* non pertinente.
irreligious [ɪrɪ'lɪdʒəs] *adj* irreligioso(a).
irreparable [ɪ'reprəbl] *adj* irreparabile.
irreplaceable [ɪrɪ'pleɪsəbl] *adj* insostituibile.
irrepressible [ɪrɪ'presəbl] *adj* irrefrenabile.
irreproachable [ɪrɪ'prəutʃəbl] *adj* irreprensibile.
irresistible [ɪrɪ'zɪstɪbl] *adj* irresistibile.
irresolute [ɪ'rezəluːt] *adj* irresoluto(a),

indeciso(a).

irrespective [ɪrɪ'spektɪv]: ~ **of** prep senza riguardo a.

irresponsible [ɪrɪ'spɔnsɪbl] adj irresponsabile.

irretrievable [ɪrɪ'triːvəbl] adj (object) irrecuperabile; (loss) irreparabile.

irreverent [ɪ'revərnt] adj irriverente.

irrevocable [ɪ'revəkəbl] adj irrevocabile.

irrigate ['ɪrɪgeɪt] vt irrigare.

irrigation [ɪrɪ'geɪʃən] n irrigazione f.

irritable ['ɪrɪtəbl] adj irritabile.

irritant ['ɪrɪtənt] n sostanza irritante.

irritate ['ɪrɪteɪt] vt irritare.

irritation [ɪrɪ'teɪʃən] n irritazione f.

IRS n abbr (US) see **Internal Revenue Service**.

is [ɪz] vb see **be**.

ISBN n abbr (= International Standard Book Number) I.S.B.N. m.

Islam ['ɪzlɑːm] n Islam m.

island ['aɪlənd] n isola; (also: traffic ~) salvagente m.

islander ['aɪləndə*] n isolano/a.

isle [aɪl] n isola.

isn't ['ɪznt] = **is not**.

isolate ['aɪsəleɪt] vt isolare.

isolated ['aɪsəleɪtɪd] adj isolato(a).

isolation [aɪsə'leɪʃən] n isolamento.

isotope ['aɪsəʊtəʊp] n isotopo.

Israel ['ɪzreɪl] n Israele m.

Israeli [ɪz'reɪlɪ] adj, n israeliano(a).

issue ['ɪʃuː] n questione f, problema m; (outcome) esito, risultato; (of banknotes etc) emissione f; (of newspaper etc) numero; (offspring) discendenza ♦ vt (rations, equipment) distribuire; (orders) dare; (book) pubblicare; (banknotes, cheques, stamps) emettere ♦ vi: **to** ~ **(from)** uscire (da), venir fuori (da); **at** ~ in gioco, in discussione; **to avoid the** ~ evitare la discussione; **to take** ~ **with sb (over sth)** prendere posizione contro qn (riguardo a qc); **to confuse** or **obscure the** ~ confondere le cose; **to make an** ~ **of sth** fare un problema di qc; **to** ~ **sth to sb,** ~ **sb with sth** consegnare qc a qn.

Istanbul [ɪstæn'buːl] n Istanbul f.

isthmus ['ɪsməs] n istmo.

IT n abbr see **information technology**.

=========== KEYWORD

it [ɪt] pron **1** (specific: subject) esso(a) (mostly omitted in Italian); (: direct object) lo(la), l'; (: indirect object) gli(le); **where's my book?** — ~**'s on the table** dov'è il mio libro? — è sulla tavola; **what is** ~? che cos'è?; (what's the matter?) cosa c'è?; **where is** ~?

dov'è?; **I can't find** ~ non lo (or la) trovo; **give** ~ **to me** dammelo (or dammela); **about/from/of** ~ ne; **I spoke to him about** ~ gliene ho parlato; **what did you learn from** ~? quale insegnamento ne hai tratto?; **I'm proud of** ~ ne sono fiero; **in/to/at** ~ ci; **did you go to** ~? ci sei andato?; **I wasn't at** ~ non c'ero; **above/over** ~ sopra; **below/under** ~ sotto; **in front of/behind** ~ lì davanti/dietro

2 (impers): ~**'s raining** piove; ~**'s Friday tomorrow** domani è venerdì; ~**'s 6 o'clock** sono le 6; ~**'s 2 hours on the train** sono or ci vogliono 2 ore di treno; **who is** ~? — ~**'s me** chi è? — sono io.

Italian [ɪ'tæljən] adj italiano(a) ♦ n italiano/a; (LING) italiano; **the** ~**s** gli Italiani.

italic [ɪ'tælɪk] adj corsivo(a); ~**s** npl corsivo.

Italy ['ɪtəlɪ] n Italia.

ITC n abbr (BRIT: = Independent Television Commission) organo di controllo sulle reti televisive.

itch [ɪtʃ] n prurito ♦ vi (person) avere il prurito; (part of body) prudere; **to be** ~**ing to do** non veder l'ora di fare.

itchy ['ɪtʃɪ] adj che prude; **my back is** ~ ho prurito alla schiena.

it'd ['ɪtd] = **it would; it had**.

item ['aɪtəm] n articolo; (on agenda) punto; (in programme) numero; (also: news ~) notizia; ~**s of clothing** capi mpl di abbigliamento.

itemize ['aɪtəmaɪz] vt specificare.

itemized bill ['aɪtəmaɪzd-] n conto dettagliato.

itinerant [ɪ'tɪnərənt] adj ambulante.

itinerary [aɪ'tɪnərərɪ] n itinerario.

it'll ['ɪtl] = **it will, it shall**.

ITN n abbr (BRIT: = Independent Television News) agenzia d'informazioni per la televisione.

its [ɪts] adj, pron il(la) suo(a), i(le) suoi(sue).

it's [ɪts] = **it is; it has**.

itself [ɪt'self] pron (emphatic) esso(a) stesso(a); (reflexive) si.

ITV n abbr (BRIT: = Independent Television) rete televisiva indipendente; see boxed note.

ITV

La **ITV** è un'azienda televisiva privata che comprende una serie di emittenti regionali, la prima delle quali è stata aperta nel 1955. Si autofinanzia tramite la pubblicità ed è sottoposta al controllo di un ente ufficiale, la "ITC"; vedi anche **BBC**.

IUD *n abbr* = **intra-uterine device**.
I've [aɪv] = **I have**.
ivory ['aɪvərɪ] *n* avorio.
Ivory Coast *n* Costa d'Avorio.
ivory tower *n* torre *f* d'avorio.
ivy ['aɪvɪ] *n* edera.
Ivy League *n* (*US*) *see boxed note*.

IVY LEAGUE

Ivy League *è il termine usato per indicare le otto università più prestigiose degli Stati Uniti nordorientali (Brown, Columbia, Cornell, Dartmouth College, Harvard, Princeton, University of Pennsylvania e Yale).*

J j

J, j [dʒeɪ] *n* (*letter*) J, j *f or m inv*; **J for Jack,** (*US*) **J for Jig** ≈ J come Jersey.
JA *n abbr see* **judge advocate**.
J/A *abbr see* **joint account**.
jab [dʒæb] *vt*: **to ~ sth into** affondare *or* piantare qc dentro ♦ *vi*: **to ~ at** dare colpi a ♦ *n* colpo; (*MED*: *col*) puntura.
jabber ['dʒæbə*] *vt, vi* borbottare.
jack [dʒæk] *n* (*AUT*) cricco; (*BOWLS*) boccino, pallino; (*CARDS*) fante *m*.
▶**jack in** *vt* (*col*) mollare.
▶**jack up** *vt* sollevare sul cricco; (*raise: prices etc*) alzare.
jackal ['dʒækl] *n* sciacallo.
jackass ['dʒækæs] *n* (*also fig*) asino, somaro.
jackdaw ['dʒækdɔ:] *n* taccola.
jacket ['dʒækɪt] *n* giacca; (*of book*) copertura; **potatoes in their ~s** (*BRIT*) patate *fpl* con la buccia.
jacket potato *n patata cotta al forno con la buccia.*
jack-in-the-box ['dʒækɪndəbɔks] *n* scatola a sorpresa (con pupazzo a molla).
jack-knife ['dʒæknaɪf] *vi*: **the lorry ~d** l'autotreno si è piegato su se stesso.
jack-of-all-trades [dʒækəv'ɔ:ltreɪdz] *n* uno che fa un po' di tutto.
jack plug *n* (*BRIT*) jack plug *f inv*.
jackpot ['dʒækpɔt] *n* primo premio (in denaro).
Jacuzzi ® [dʒə'ku:zɪ] *n* vasca per idromassaggio Jacuzzi ®.
jade [dʒeɪd] *n* (*stone*) giada.
jaded ['dʒeɪdɪd] *adj* sfinito(a), spossato(a).
jagged ['dʒægɪd] *adj* sbocconcellato(a); (*cliffs etc*) frastagliato(a).
jaguar ['dʒægjuə*] *n* giaguaro.
jail [dʒeɪl] *n* prigione *f* ♦ *vt* mandare in prigione.
jailbird ['dʒeɪlbə:d] *n* avanzo di galera.
jailbreak ['dʒeɪlbreɪk] *n* evasione *f*.
jailer ['dʒeɪlə*] *n* custode *m* del carcere.
jalopy [dʒə'lɔpɪ] *n* (*col*) macinino.
jam [dʒæm] *n* marmellata; (*of shoppers etc*) ressa; (*also*: **traffic ~**) ingorgo ♦ *vt* (*passage etc*) ingombrare, ostacolare; (*mechanism, drawer etc*) bloccare; (*RADIO*) disturbare con interferenze ♦ *vi* (*mechanism, sliding part*) incepparsi, bloccarsi; (*gun*) incepparsi; **to get sb out of a ~** tirare qn fuori dai pasticci; **to ~ sth into** forzare qc dentro; infilare qc a forza dentro; **the telephone lines are ~med** le linee sono sovraccariche.
Jamaica [dʒə'meɪkə] *n* Giamaica.
Jamaican [dʒə'meɪkən] *adj, n* giamaicano(a).
jamb [dʒæm] *n* stipite *m*.
jam-packed [dʒæm'pækt] *adj*: **~ (with)** pieno(a) zeppo(a) (di), strapieno(a) (di).
jam session *n* improvvisazione *f* jazzistica.
Jan. *abbr* (= *January*) gen., genn.
jangle ['dʒæŋgl] *vi* risuonare; (*bracelet*) tintinnare.
janitor ['dʒænɪtə*] *n* (*caretaker*) portiere *m*; (*SCOL*) bidello.
January ['dʒænjuərɪ] *n* gennaio; *for phrases see also* **July**.
Japan [dʒə'pæn] *n* Giappone *m*.
Japanese [dʒæpə'ni:z] *adj* giapponese ♦ *n* (*pl inv*) giapponese *m/f*; (*LING*) giapponese *m*.
jar [dʒɑ:*] *n* (*container*) barattolo, vasetto ♦ *vi* (*sound*) stridere; (*colours etc*) stonare ♦ *vt* (*shake*) scuotere.
jargon ['dʒɑ:gən] *n* gergo.
jarring ['dʒɑ:rɪŋ] *adj* (*sound, colour*) stonato(a).
Jas. *abbr* = **James**.
jasmin(e) ['dʒæzmɪn] *n* gelsomino.
jaundice ['dʒɔ:ndɪs] *n* itterizia.
jaundiced ['dʒɔ:ndɪst] *adj* (*fig*) invidioso(a) e critico(a).
jaunt [dʒɔ:nt] *n* gita.
jaunty ['dʒɔ:ntɪ] *adj* vivace; disinvolto(a), spigliato(a).
Java ['dʒɑ:və] *n* Giava.
javelin ['dʒævlɪn] *n* giavellotto.

jaw [dʒɔ:] n mascella; ~s (TECH: of vice etc) morsa.
jawbone ['dʒɔ:bəun] n mandibola.
jay [dʒeɪ] n ghiandaia.
jaywalker ['dʒeɪwɔ:kə*] n pedone(a) indisciplinato(a).
jazz [dʒæz] n jazz m.
▶**jazz up** vt rendere vivace.
jazz band n banda f jazz inv.
jazzy ['dʒæzɪ] adj vistoso(a), chiassoso(a).
JCB ® n scavatrice f.
JCS n abbr (US) = Joint Chiefs of Staff.
JD n abbr (US: = Doctor of Laws) titolo di studio; (: = Justice Department) ministero della Giustizia.
jealous ['dʒeləs] adj geloso(a).
jealously ['dʒeləslɪ] adv (enviously) con gelosia; (watchfully) gelosamente.
jealousy ['dʒeləsɪ] n gelosia.
jeans [dʒi:nz] npl (blue-)jeans mpl.
Jeep ® [dʒi:p] n jeep m inv.
jeer [dʒɪə*] vi: to ~ (at) fischiare, beffeggiare; see also **jeers**.
jeering ['dʒɪərɪŋ] adj (crowd) che urla e fischia ♦ n fischi mpl; parole fpl di scherno.
jeers ['dʒɪəz] npl fischi mpl.
jelly ['dʒelɪ] n gelatina.
jellyfish ['dʒelɪfɪʃ] n medusa.
jeopardize ['dʒepədaɪz] vt mettere in pericolo.
jeopardy ['dʒepədɪ] n: in ~ in pericolo.
jerk [dʒə:k] n sobbalzo, scossa; sussulto; (col) povero scemo ♦ vt dare una scossa a ♦ vi (vehicles) sobbalzare.
jerkin ['dʒə:kɪn] n giubbotto.
jerky ['dʒə:kɪ] adj a scatti; a sobbalzi.
jerry-built ['dʒerɪbɪlt] adj fatto(a) di cartapesta.
jerry can ['dʒerɪ-] n tanica.
Jersey ['dʒə:zɪ] n Jersey m.
jersey ['dʒə:zɪ] n maglia, jersey m.
Jerusalem [dʒə'ru:sələm] n Gerusalemme f.
jest [dʒest] n scherzo; in ~ per scherzo.
jester ['dʒestə*] n (HISTORY) buffone m.
Jesus ['dʒi:zəs] n Gesù m; ~ **Christ** Gesù Cristo.
jet [dʒet] n (of gas, liquid) getto; (AUT) spruzzatore m; (AVIAT) aviogetto.
jet-black ['dʒet'blæk] adj nero(a) come l'ebano, corvino(a).
jet engine n motore m a reazione.
jet lag n (problemi mpl dovuti allo) sbalzo dei fusi orari.
jetsam ['dʒetsəm] n relitti mpl di mare.
jet-setter ['dʒetsetə*] n membro del jet set.
jettison ['dʒetɪsn] vt gettare in mare.
jetty ['dʒetɪ] n molo.
Jew [dʒu:] n ebreo.

jewel ['dʒu:əl] n gioiello.
jeweller, (US) **jeweler** ['dʒu:ələ*] n orefice m, gioielliere/a; ~'s **(shop)** n oreficeria, gioielleria.
jewellery, (US) **jewelry** ['dʒu:əlrɪ] n gioielli mpl.
Jewess ['dʒu:ɪs] n ebrea.
Jewish ['dʒu:ɪʃ] adj ebreo(a), ebraico(a).
JFK n abbr (US) = John Fitzgerald Kennedy International Airport.
jib [dʒɪb] n (NAUT) fiocco; (of crane) braccio ♦ vi (horse) impennarsi; to ~ at doing sth essere restio a fare qc.
jibe [dʒaɪb] n beffa.
jiffy ['dʒɪfɪ] n (col): in a ~ in un batter d'occhio.
jig [dʒɪg] n (dance, tune) giga.
jigsaw ['dʒɪgsɔ:] n (tool) sega da traforo; (also: ~ puzzle) puzzle m inv.
jilt [dʒɪlt] vt piantare in asso.
jingle ['dʒɪŋgl] n (advert) sigla pubblicitaria ♦ vi tintinnare, scampanellare.
jingoism ['dʒɪŋgəuɪzəm] n sciovinismo.
jinx [dʒɪŋks] n (col) iettatura; (person) iettatore/trice.
jitters ['dʒɪtəz] npl (col): to get the ~ aver fifa.
jittery ['dʒɪtərɪ] adj (col) teso(a), agitato(a); to be ~ aver fifa.
jiujitsu [dʒu:'dʒɪtsu:] n jujitsu m.
job [dʒɔb] n lavoro; (employment) impiego, posto; a part-time/full-time ~ un lavoro a mezza giornata/a tempo pieno; that's not my ~ non è compito mio; he's only doing his ~ non fa che il suo dovere; it's a good ~ that ... meno male che ...; just the ~! proprio ... quello che ci vuole!
jobber ['dʒɔbə*] n (BRIT STOCK EXCHANGE) intermediario tra agenti di cambio.
jobbing ['dʒɔbɪŋ] adj (BRIT: workman) a ore, a giornata.
Jobcentre ['dʒɔbsentə*] n ufficio di collocamento.
job creation scheme n progetto per la creazione di nuovi posti di lavoro.
job description n caratteristiche fpl (di un lavoro).
jobless ['dʒɔblɪs] adj senza lavoro, disoccupato(a) ♦ npl: the ~ i senza lavoro.
job lot n partita di articoli disparati.
job satisfaction n soddisfazione f nel lavoro.
job security n sicurezza del posto di lavoro.
job specification n caratteristiche fpl (di un lavoro).
Jock [dʒɔk] n (col) termine colloquiale per chiamare uno scozzese.

jockey ['dʒɔkɪ] *n* fantino, jockey *m inv* ♦ *vi*: **to ~ for position** manovrare per una posizione di vantaggio.

jockey box *n* (*US AUT*) vano portaoggetti.

jockstrap ['dʒɔkstræp] *n* conchiglia (*per atleti*).

jocular ['dʒɔkjulə*] *adj* gioviale; scherzoso(a).

jog [dʒɔg] *vt* urtare ♦ *vi* (*SPORT*) fare footing, fare jogging; **to ~** (*meet*) **along** trottare; (*fig*) andare avanti pian piano; **to ~ sb's memory** stimolare la memoria di qn.

jogger ['dʒɔgə*] *n* persona che fa footing *or* jogging.

jogging ['dʒɔgɪŋ] *n* footing *m*, jogging *m*.

john [dʒɔn] *n* (*US col*): **the ~** il gabinetto.

join [dʒɔɪn] *vt* unire, congiungere; (*become member of*) iscriversi a; (*meet*) raggiungere; riunirsi a ♦ *vi* (*roads, rivers*) confluire ♦ *n* giuntura; **to ~ forces (with)** allearsi (con *or* a); (*fig*) mettersi insieme (a); **will you ~ us for dinner?** viene a cena con noi?; **I'll ~ you later** vi raggiungo più tardi.

▶**join in** *vt fus* unirsi a, prendere parte a, partecipare a ♦ *vi* partecipare.

▶**join up** *vi* arruolarsi.

joiner ['dʒɔɪnə*] *n* falegname *m*.

joinery ['dʒɔɪnərɪ] *n* falegnameria.

joint [dʒɔɪnt] *n* (*TECH*) giuntura; giunto; (*ANAT*) articolazione *f*, giuntura; (*BRIT CULIN*) arrosto; (*col: place*) locale *m* ♦ *adj* comune; (*responsibility*) collettivo(a); (*committee*) misto(a).

joint account (J/A) *n* (*at bank etc*) conto in comune.

jointly ['dʒɔɪntlɪ] *adv* in comune, insieme.

joint ownership *n* comproprietà.

joint-stock company ['dʒɔɪntstɔk-] *n* società *f inv* per azioni.

joist [dʒɔɪst] *n* trave *f*.

joke [dʒəuk] *n* scherzo; (*funny story*) barzelletta ♦ *vi* scherzare; **to play a ~ on** fare uno scherzo a.

joker ['dʒəukə*] *n* buffone/a, burlone/a; (*CARDS*) matta, jolly *m inv*.

joking ['dʒəukɪŋ] *n* scherzi *mpl*.

jollity ['dʒɔlɪtɪ] *n* allegria.

jolly ['dʒɔlɪ] *adj* allegro(a), gioioso(a) ♦ *adv* (*BRIT col*) veramente, proprio ♦ *vt* (*BRIT*): **to ~ sb along** cercare di tenere qn su (di morale); **~ good!** (*BRIT*) benissimo!

jolt [dʒəult] *n* scossa, sobbalzo ♦ *vt* urtare.

Jordan ['dʒɔːdən] *n* (*country*) Giordania; (*river*) Giordano.

Jordanian [dʒɔː'deɪnɪən] *adj*, *n* giordano(a).

joss stick ['dʒɔs-] *n* bastoncino d'incenso.

jostle ['dʒɔsl] *vt* spingere coi gomiti ♦ *vi* farsi spazio coi gomiti.

jot [dʒɔt] *n*: **not one ~** nemmeno un po'.

▶**jot down** *vt* annotare in fretta, buttare giù.

jotter ['dʒɔtə*] *n* (*BRIT*) quaderno; blocco.

journal ['dʒəːnl] *n* (*newspaper*) giornale *m*; (*periodical*) rivista; (*diary*) diario.

journalese [dʒəːnə'liːz] *n* (*pej*) stile *m* giornalistico.

journalism ['dʒəːnəlɪzəm] *n* giornalismo.

journalist ['dʒəːnəlɪst] *n* giornalista *m/f*.

journey ['dʒəːnɪ] *n* viaggio; (*distance covered*) tragitto; **a 5-hour ~** un viaggio *or* un tragitto di 5 ore.

jovial ['dʒəuvɪəl] *adj* gioviale, allegro(a).

jowl [dʒaul] *n* mandibola; guancia.

joy [dʒɔɪ] *n* gioia.

joyful ['dʒɔɪful], **joyous** ['dʒɔɪəs] *adj* gioioso(a), allegro(a).

joyride ['dʒɔɪraɪd] *n*: **to go for a ~** rubare una macchina per farsi un giro.

joyrider ['dʒɔɪraɪdə*] *n* chi ruba una macchina per andare a farsi un giro.

joystick ['dʒɔɪstɪk] *n* (*AVIAT*) barra di comando; (*COMPUT*) joystick *m inv*.

JP *n abbr see* **Justice of the Peace**.

Jr. *abbr* = **junior**.

JTPA *n abbr* (*US*: = *Job Training Partnership Act*) piano governativo di parziale sovvenzione per l'addestramento sul lavoro di apprendisti.

jubilant ['dʒuːbɪlnt] *adj* giubilante; trionfante.

jubilation [dʒuːbɪ'leɪʃən] *n* giubilo.

jubilee ['dʒuːbɪliː] *n* giubileo; **silver ~** venticinquesimo anniversario.

judge [dʒʌdʒ] *n* giudice *m/f* ♦ *vt* giudicare; (*consider*) ritenere; (*estimate: weight, size etc*) calcolare, valutare ♦ *vi*: **judging** *or* **to ~ by his expression** a giudicare dalla sua espressione; **as far as I can ~** a mio giudizio; **I ~d it necessary to inform him** ho ritenuto necessario informarlo.

judge advocate (JA) *n* (*MIL*) magistrato militare.

judg(e)ment ['dʒʌdʒmənt] *n* giudizio; (*punishment*) punizione *f*; **in my ~** a mio giudizio; **to pass ~ (on)** (*LAW*) pronunciare un giudizio (su); (*fig*) dare giudizi affrettati (su).

judicial [dʒuː'dɪʃl] *adj* giudiziale, giudiziario(a).

judiciary [dʒuː'dɪʃɪərɪ] *n* magistratura.

judicious [dʒuː'dɪʃəs] *adj* giudizioso(a).

judo ['dʒuːdəu] *n* judo.

jug [dʒʌg] *n* brocca, bricco.

jugged hare [dʒʌgd-] *n* (*BRIT*) lepre *f* in salmì.

juggernaut ['dʒʌgənɔːt] n (BRIT: huge truck) bestione m.
juggle ['dʒʌgl] vi fare giochi di destrezza.
juggler ['dʒʌglə*] n giocoliere/a.
Jugoslav ['juːgəu'slɑːv] adj, n = **Yugoslav**.
jugular ['dʒʌgjulə*] adj: ~ **(vein)** vena giugulare.
juice [dʒuːs] n succo; (of meat) sugo; **we've run out of** ~ (col: petrol) siamo rimasti a secco.
juicy ['dʒuːsɪ] adj succoso(a).
jukebox ['dʒuːkbɔks] n juke-box m inv.
Jul. abbr (= July) lug., lu.
July [dʒuː'laɪ] n luglio; **the first of** ~ il primo luglio; **(on) the eleventh of** ~ l'undici luglio; **in the month of** ~ nel mese di luglio; **at the beginning/end of** ~ all'inizio/alla fine di luglio; **in the middle of** ~ a metà luglio; **during** ~ durante (il mese di) luglio; **in** ~ **of next year** a luglio dell'anno prossimo; **each** or **every** ~ ogni anno a luglio; ~ **was wet this year** ha piovuto molto a luglio quest'anno.
jumble ['dʒʌmbl] n miscuglio ♦ vt (also: ~ **up**, ~ **together**) mischiare, mettere alla rinfusa.
jumble sale n ≈ vendita di beneficenza; see boxed note.

JUMBLE SALE

La **jumble sale** è un mercatino dove vengono venduti vari oggetti, per lo più di seconda mano; viene organizzata in chiese, scuole o circoli ricreativi. I proventi delle vendite vengono devoluti in beneficenza o usati per una giusta causa.

---

jumbo ['dʒʌmbəu] adj: ~ **jet** jumbo-jet m inv; ~ **size** formato gigante.
jump [dʒʌmp] vi saltare, balzare; (start) sobbalzare; (increase) rincarare ♦ vt saltare ♦ n salto, balzo; sobbalzo; (SHOWJUMPING) salto; (fence) ostacolo; **to** ~ **the queue** (BRIT) passare davanti agli altri (in una coda).
▶**jump about** vi fare salti, saltellare.
▶**jump at** vt fus (fig) cogliere or afferrare al volo; **he** ~**ed at the offer** si affrettò ad accettare l'offerta.
▶**jump down** vi saltare giù.
▶**jump up** vi saltare in piedi.
jumped-up ['dʒʌmptʌp] adj (BRIT pej) presuntuoso(a).
jumper ['dʒʌmpə*] n (BRIT: pullover) maglia; (US: pinafore dress) scamiciato; (SPORT) saltatore/trice.
jump leads, (US) **jumper cables** npl cavi

mpl per batteria.
jump-start ['dʒʌmpstɑːt] vt (car) far partire spingendo; (fig) dare una spinta a, rimettere in moto.
jump suit n tuta.
jumpy ['dʒʌmpɪ] adj nervoso(a), agitato(a).
Jun. abbr (= June) giu.
Jun., Junr abbr = **junior**.
junction ['dʒʌŋkʃən] n (BRIT: of roads) incrocio; (of rails) nodo ferroviario.
juncture ['dʒʌŋktʃə*] n: **at this** ~ in questa congiuntura.
June [dʒuːn] n giugno; for phrases see also July.
jungle ['dʒʌŋgl] n giungla.
junior ['dʒuːnɪə*] adj, n: **he's** ~ **to me (by 2 years), he's my** ~ **(by 2 years)** è più giovane di me (di 2 anni); **he's** ~ **to me** (seniority) è al di sotto di me, ho più anzianità di lui.
junior high school n (US) scuola media (da 12 a 15 anni).
junior minister n (BRIT POL) ministro che non fa parte del Cabinet.
junior partner n socio meno anziano.
junior school n (BRIT) scuola elementare (da 8 a 11 anni).
juniper ['dʒuːnɪpə*] n: ~ **berry** bacca di ginepro.
junk [dʒʌŋk] n (rubbish) chincaglia; (ship) giunca ♦ vt disfarsi di.
junk bond n (COMM) titolo m spazzatura inv.
junk dealer n rigattiere m.
junket ['dʒʌŋkɪt] n (CULIN) giuncata; (BRIT col: also: ~**ing**): **to go on a** ~, **go** ~**ing** fare bisboccia.
junk food n porcherie fpl, cibo a scarso valore nutritivo.
junkie ['dʒʌŋkɪ] n (col) drogato/a.
junk mail n posta f spazzatura inv.
junk room n (US) ripostiglio.
junk shop n chincaglieria.
junta ['dʒʌntə] n giunta.
Jupiter ['dʒuːpɪtə*] n (planet) Giove m.
jurisdiction [dʒuərɪs'dɪkʃən] n giurisdizione f; **it falls** or **comes within/outside our** ~ è/ non è di nostra competenza.
jurisprudence [dʒuərɪs'pruːdəns] n giurisprudenza.
juror ['dʒuərə*] n giurato/a.
jury ['dʒuərɪ] n giuria.
jury box n banco della giuria.
juryman ['dʒuərɪmən] n = **juror**.
just [dʒʌst] adj giusto(a) ♦ adv: **he's** ~ **done it/left** lo ha appena fatto/è appena partito; ~ **as I expected** proprio come me

lo aspettavo; ~ **right** proprio giusto; ~ **2 o'clock** le 2 precise; **we were** ~ **going** stavamo uscendo; **I was** ~ **about to phone** stavo proprio per telefonare; ~ **as he was leaving** proprio mentre se ne stava andando; **it was** ~ **before/enough/ here** era poco prima/appena assai/ proprio qui; **it's** ~ **me** sono solo io; **it's** ~ **a mistake** non è che uno sbaglio; ~ **missed/caught** appena perso/preso; ~ **listen to this!** senta un po' questo!; ~ **ask someone the way** basta che tu chieda la strada a qualcuno; **it's** ~ **as good** è altrettanto buono; **it's** ~ **as well you didn't go** per fortuna non ci sei andato; **not** ~ **now** non proprio adesso; ~ **a minute!, ~ one moment!** un attimo!

justice ['dʒʌstɪs] n giustizia; **Lord Chief J~** (BRIT) presidente m della Corte d'Appello; **this photo doesn't do you** ~ questa foto non ti fa giustizia.

Justice of the Peace (JP) n giudice m conciliatore.

justifiable [dʒʌstɪ'faɪəbl] adj giustificabile.

justifiably [dʒʌstɪ'faɪəblɪ] adv legittimamente, con ragione.

justification [dʒʌstɪfɪ'keɪʃən] n giustificazione f; (TYP) giustezza.

justify ['dʒʌstɪfaɪ] vt giustificare; (TYP etc) allineare, giustificare; **to be justified in doing sth** avere ragione di fare qc.

justly ['dʒʌstlɪ] adv giustamente.

justness ['dʒʌstnɪs] n giustezza.

jut [dʒʌt] vi (also: ~ **out**) sporgersi.

jute [dʒuːt] n iuta.

juvenile ['dʒuːvənaɪl] adj giovane, giovanile; (court) dei minorenni; (books) per ragazzi ♦ n giovane m/f, minorenne m/f.

juvenile delinquency n delinquenza minorile.

juvenile delinquent n delinquente m/f minorenne.

juxtapose ['dʒʌkstəpəuz] vt giustapporre.

juxtaposition [dʒʌkstəpə'zɪʃən] n giustapposizione f.

Kk

K, k [keɪ] n (letter) K, k f or m inv; **K for King** ≈ K come Kursaal.

K n abbr (= one thousand) mille ♦ abbr (BRIT: = Knight) titolo; (= kilobyte) K.

kaftan ['kæftæn] n caffettano.

Kalahari Desert [kælə'hɑːrɪ-] n Deserto di Calahari.

kale [keɪl] n cavolo verde.

kaleidoscope [kə'laɪdəskəup] n caleidoscopio.

kamikaze [kæmɪ'kɑːzɪ] adj da kamikaze.

Kampala [kæm'pɑːlə] n Kampala f.

Kampuchea [kæmpu'tʃɪə] n Kampuchea f.

kangaroo [kæŋgə'ruː] n canguro.

Kans. abbr (US) = Kansas.

kaput [kə'put] adj (col) kaputt inv.

karaoke [kɑːrə'əukɪ] n karaoke m inv.

karate [kə'rɑːtɪ] n karate m.

Kashmir [kæʃ'mɪə*] n Kashmir m.

Kazakhstan [kæzæk'stɑːn] n Kazakistan m.

KC n abbr (BRIT LAW: = King's Counsel) avvocato della Corona; see also **QC**.

kd abbr (US: = knocked down) da montare.

kebab [kə'bæb] n spiedino.

keel [kiːl] n chiglia; **on an even** ~ (fig) in uno stato normale.

▶**keel over** vi (NAUT) capovolgersi; (person) crollare.

keen [kiːn] adj (interest, desire) vivo(a); (eye, intelligence) acuto(a); (competition) serrato(a); (edge) affilato(a); (eager) entusiasta; **to be** ~ **to do** or **on doing sth** avere una gran voglia di fare qc; **to be** ~ **on sth** essere appassionato(a) di qc; **to be** ~ **on sb** avere un debole per qn; **I'm not** ~ **on going** non mi va di andare.

keenly ['kiːnlɪ] adv (enthusiastically) con entusiasmo; (acutely) vivamente; in modo penetrante.

keenness ['kiːnnɪs] n (eagerness) entusiasmo.

keep [kiːp] vb (pt, pp **kept** [kɛpt]) vt tenere; (hold back) trattenere; (feed: one's family etc) mantenere, sostentare; (a promise) mantenere; (chickens, bees, pigs etc) allevare ♦ vi (food) mantenersi; (remain: in a certain state or place) restare ♦ n (of *castle*) maschio; (*food etc*): **enough for his** ~ abbastanza per vitto e alloggio; **to** ~ **doing sth** continuare a fare qc; fare qc di continuo; **to** ~ **sb from doing/sth from happening** impedire a qn di fare/che qc succeda; **to** ~ **sb busy/a place tidy** tenere qn occupato(a)/un luogo in ordine; **to** ~ **sb waiting** far aspettare qn; **to** ·· **an appointment** andare ad un appuntamento; **to** ~ **a record** *or* **note of sth** prendere nota di qc; **to** ~ **sth to o.s.** tenere qc per sé; **to** ~ **sth (back) from sb** celare qc a qn; **to** ~ **time** (*clock*) andar bene; ~ **the change** tenga il resto; *see also* **keeps**.

▶**keep away** *vt*: **to** ~ **sth/sb away from sb** tenere qc/qn lontano da qn ♦ *vi*: **to** ~ **away (from)** stare lontano (da).

▶**keep back** *vt* (*crowds, tears, money*) trattenere ♦ *vi* tenersi indietro.

▶**keep down** *vt* (*control: prices, spending*) contenere, ridurre, (inflati, food) trattenere, ritenere ♦ *vi* tenersi giù, stare giù.

▶**keep in** *vt* (*invalid, child*) tenere a casa; (*SCOL*) trattenere a scuola ♦ *vi* (*col*): **to** ~ **in with sb** tenersi buono qn.

▶**keep off** *vt* (*dog, person*) tenere lontano da ♦ *vi* stare alla larga; ~ **your hands off!** non toccare!, giù le mani!; "~ **off the grass**" "non calpestare l'erba".

▶**keep on** *vi* continuare; **to** ~ **on doing** continuare a fare.

▶**keep out** *vt* tener fuori ♦ *vi* restare fuori; "~ **out**" "vietato l'accesso".

▶**keep up** *vi* mantenersi ♦ *vt* continuare, mantenere; **to** ~ **up with** tener dietro a, andare di pari passo con; (*work etc*) farcela a seguire; **to** ~ **up with sb** (*in race etc*) mantenersi al passo con qn.

keeper ['ki:pə*] *n* custode *m/f*, guardiano/a.

keep-fit [ki:p'fɪt] *n* ginnastica.

keeping ['ki:pɪŋ] *n* (*care*) custodia; **in** ~ **with** in armonia con; in accordo con.

keeps [ki:ps] *n*: **for** ~ (*col*) per sempre.

keepsake ['ki:pseɪk] *n* ricordo.

keg [kɛg] *n* barilotto.

Ken. *abbr* (*US*) = Kentucky.

kennel ['kɛnl] *n* canile *m*.

Kenya ['kɛnjə] *n* Kenia *m*.

Kenyan ['kɛnjən] *adj, n* Keniano(a), Keniota (*m/f*).

kept [kɛpt] *pt, pp of* **keep.**

kerb [kə:b] *n* (*BRIT*) orlo del marciapiede.

kerb crawler [-'krɔ:lə*] *n* chi va in macchina in cerca di una prostituta.

kernel ['kə:nl] *n* nocciolo.

kerosene ['kɛrəsi:n] *n* cherosene *m*.

ketchup ['kɛtʃəp] *n* ketchup *m inv*.

kettle ['kɛtl] *n* bollitore *m*.

kettle drum *n* timpano.

key [ki:] *n* (*gen, MUS*) chiave *f*; (*of piano, typewriter*) tasto; (*on map*) leg(g)enda ♦ *cpd* (*vital: position, industry etc*) chiave *inv*.

▶**key in** *vt* (*text*) introdurre da tastiera.

keyboard ['ki:bɔ:d] *n* tastiera ♦ *vt* (*text*) comporre su tastiera.

keyboarder ['ki:bɔ:də*] *n* dattilografo(a).

keyed up [ki:d'ʌp] *adj*: **to be** ~ essere agitato(a).

keyhole ['ki:həʊl] *n* buco della serratura.

keyhole surgery *n* chirurgia mininvasiva.

keynote ['ki:nəʊt] *n* (*MUS*) tonica; (*fig*) nota dominante.

keypad ['ki:pæd] *n* tastierino numerico.

key ring *n* portachiavi *m inv*.

keystroke ['ki:strəʊk] *n* battuta (di un tasto).

kg *abbr* (= *kilogram*) Kg.

KGB *n abbr* KGB *m*.

khaki ['kɑ:kɪ] *adj, n* cachi (*m*).

kibbutz [kɪ'bʊts] *n* kibbutz *m inv*.

kick [kɪk] *vt* calciare, dare calci a ♦ *vi* (*horse*) tirar calci ♦ *n* calcio; (*of rifle*) contraccolpo; (*thrill*): **he does it for** ~**s** lo fa giusto per il piacere di farlo.

▶**kick around** *vi* (*col*) essere in giro.

▶**kick off** *vi* (*SPORT*) dare il primo calcio.

kick-off ['kɪkɔf] *n* (*SPORT*) calcio d'inizio.

kick-start ['kɪkstɑ:t] *n* (*also*: ~**er**) pedale *m* d'avviamento.

kid [kɪd] *n* ragazzino/a; (*animal, leather*) capretto ♦ *vi* (*col*) scherzare ♦ *vt* (*col*) prendere in giro.

kid gloves *npl*: **to treat sb with** ~ trattare qn coi guanti.

kidnap ['kɪdnæp] *vt* rapire, sequestrare.

kidnapper ['kɪdnæpə*] *n* rapitore/trice.

kidnapping ['kɪdnæpɪŋ] *n* sequestro (di persona).

kidney ['kɪdnɪ] *n* (*ANAT*) rene *m*; (*CULIN*) rognone *m*.

kidney bean *n* fagiolo borlotto.

kidney machine *n* rene *m* artificiale.

Kilimanjaro [kɪlɪmən'dʒɑ:rəʊ] *n*: **Mount** ~ il monte Kilimangiaro.

kill [kɪl] *vt* uccidere, ammazzare; (*fig*) sopprimere; sopraffare; ammazzare ♦ *n* uccisione *f*; **to** ~ **time** ammazzare il tempo.

▶**kill off** *vt* sterminare; (*fig*) eliminare, soffocare.

killer ['kɪlə*] *n* uccisore *m*, killer *m inv*; assassino/a.

killer instinct *n*: **to have a/the** ~ essere

spietato(a).

killing ['kılıŋ] *n* assassinio; (*massacre*) strage *f*; (*col*): **to make a ~** fare un bel colpo.

kill-joy ['kıldʒɔı] *n* guastafeste *m/f inv*.

kiln [kıln] *n* forno.

kilo ['ki:ləu] *n abbr* (= *kilogram*) chilo.

kilobyte ['kıləbaıt] *n* kilobyte *m inv*.

kilogram(me) ['kıləugræm] *n* chilogrammo.

kilometre, (*US*) **kilometer** ['kıləmi:tə*] *n* chilometro.

kilowatt ['kıləuwɔt] *n* chilowatt *m inv*.

kilt [kılt] *n* gonnellino scozzese.

kilter ['kıltə*] *n*: **out of ~** fuori fase.

kimono [kı'məunəu] *n* chimono.

kin [kın] *n see* **next of kin, kith**.

kind [kaınd] *adj* gentile, buono(a) ♦ *n* sorta, specie *f*; (*species*) genere *m*; **to be two of a ~** essere molto simili; **would you be ~ enough to …?**, **would you be so ~ as to …?** sarebbe così gentile da …?; **it's very ~ of you (to do)** è molto gentile da parte sua (di fare); **in ~** (*COMM*) in natura; (*fig*): **to repay sb in ~** ripagare qn della stessa moneta.

kindergarten ['kındəgɑ:tn] *n* giardino d'infanzia.

kind-hearted [kaınd'hɑ:tıd] *adj* di buon cuore.

kindle ['kındl] *vt* accendere, infiammare.

kindling ['kındlıŋ] *n* frasche *fpl*, ramoscelli *mpl*.

kindly ['kaındlı] *adj* pieno(a) di bontà, benevolo(a) ♦ *adv* con bontà, gentilmente; **will you ~ …** vuole … per favore; **he didn't take it ~** se l'è presa a male.

kindness ['kaındnıs] *n* bontà, gentilezza.

kindred ['kındrıd] *adj* imparentato(a); **~ spirit** spirito affine.

kinetic [kı'nεtık] *adj* cinetico(a).

king [kıŋ] *n* re *m inv*.

kingdom ['kıŋdəm] *n* regno, reame *m*.

kingfisher ['kıŋfıʃə*] *n* martin *m inv* pescatore.

kingpin ['kıŋpın] *n* (*TECH, fig*) perno.

king-size(d) ['kıŋsaız(d)] *adj* super *inv*; gigante; (*cigarette*) extra lungo(a).

kink [kıŋk] *n* (*of rope*) attorcigliamento; (*in hair*) ondina; (*fig*) aberrazione *f*.

kinky ['kıŋkı] *adj* (*fig*) eccentrico(a); dai gusti particolari.

kinship ['kınʃıp] *n* parentela.

kinsman ['kınzmən] *n* parente *m*.

kinswoman ['kınzwumən] *n* parente *f*.

kiosk ['ki:ɔsk] *n* edicola, chiosco; (*BRIT: also*: **telephone ~**) cabina (telefonica); (: *also*: **newspaper ~**) edicola.

kipper ['kıpə*] *n* aringa affumicata.

Kirghizia [kə:'gızıə] *n* Kirghizistan.

kiss [kıs] *n* bacio ♦ *vt* baciare; **to ~ (each other)** baciarsi; **to ~ sb goodbye** congedarsi da qn con un bacio; **~ of life** (*BRIT*) respirazione *f* bocca a bocca.

kissagram ['kısəgræm] *n servizio di recapito a domicilio di messaggi e baci augurali.*

kit [kıt] *n* equipaggiamento, corredo; (*set of tools etc*) attrezzi *mpl*; (*for assembly*) scatola di montaggio; **tool ~** cassetta *or* borsa degli attrezzi.

▶**kit out** *vt* (*BRIT*) attrezzare, equipaggiare.

kitbag ['kıtbæg] *n* zaino; sacco militare.

kitchen ['kıtʃın] *n* cucina.

kitchen garden *n* orto.

kitchen sink *n* acquaio.

kitchen unit *n* (*BRIT*) elemento da cucina.

kitchenware ['kıtʃınwεə*] *n* stoviglie *fpl*; utensili *mpl* da cucina.

kite [kaıt] *n* (*toy*) aquilone *m*; (*ZOOL*) nibbio.

kith [kıθ] *n*: **~ and kin** amici e parenti *mpl*.

kitten ['kıtn] *n* gattino/a, micino/a.

kitty ['kıtı] *n* (*money*) fondo comune.

kiwi fruit ['ki:wi:-] *n* kiwi *m inv*.

KKK *n abbr* (*US*) = **Ku Klux Klan**.

Kleenex ® ['kli:nεks] *n* fazzolettino di carta.

kleptomaniac [klεptəu'meınıæk] *n* cleptomane *m/f*.

km *abbr* (= *kilometre*) km.

km/h *abbr* (= *kilometres per hour*) km/h.

knack [næk] *n*: **to have a ~ (for doing)** avere una pratica (per fare); **to have the ~ of** avere l'abilità di; **there's a ~ to doing this** c'è un trucco per fare questo.

knackered ['nækəd] *adj* (*col*) fuso(a).

knapsack ['næpsæk] *n* zaino, sacco da montagna.

knave [neıv] *n* (*CARDS*) fante *m*.

knead [ni:d] *vt* impastare.

knee [ni:] *n* ginocchio.

kneecap ['ni:kæp] *n* rotula ♦ *vt* gambizzare.

knee-deep ['ni:'di:p] *adj*: **the water was ~** l'acqua ci arrivava alle ginocchia.

kneel [ni:l] *vi* (*pt, pp* **knelt** [nεlt]) inginocchiarsi.

kneepad ['ni:pæd] *n* ginocchiera.

knell [nεl] *n* rintocco.

knelt [nεlt] *pt, pp of* **kneel**.

knew [nju:] *pt of* **know**.

knickers ['nıkəz] *npl* (*BRIT*) mutandine *fpl*.

knick-knack ['nıknæk] *n* ninnolo.

knife [naıf] *n* (*pl* **knives**) coltello ♦ *vt* accoltellare, dare una coltellata a; **~, fork and spoon** coperto.

knife edge *n*: **to be on a ~** (*fig*) essere appeso(a) a un filo.

knight [naɪt] n cavaliere m; (CHESS) cavallo.

knighthood ['naɪthud] n cavalleria; (title): **to get a** ~ essere fatto cavaliere.

knit [nɪt] vt fare a maglia; (fig): **to ~ together** unire ♦ vi lavorare a maglia; (broken bones) saldarsi.

knitted ['nɪtɪd] adj lavorato(a) a maglia.

knitting ['nɪtɪŋ] n lavoro a maglia.

knitting machine n macchina per maglieria.

knitting needle n ferro (da calza).

knitting pattern n modello (per maglia).

knitwear ['nɪtwɛə*] n maglieria.

knives [naɪvz] npl of knife.

knob [nɔb] n bottone m; manopola; (BRIT): **a** ~ **of butter** una noce di burro.

knobbly ['nɔblɪ], (US) **knobby** ['nɔbɪ] adj (wood, surface) nodoso(a); (knee) ossuto(a).

knock [nɔk] vt (strike) colpire; urtare; (fig: col) criticare ♦ vi (engine) battere; (at door etc): **to** ~ **at/on** bussare a ♦ n bussata; colpo, botta; **he ~ed at the door** ha bussato alla porta; **to** ~ **a nail into sth** conficcare un chiodo in qc.

►**knock down** vt abbattere; (pedestrian) investire; (price) abbassare.

►**knock off** vi (col: finish) smettere (di lavorare) ♦ vt (strike off) far cadere; (col: steal) sgraffignare, grattare; **to** ~ **off £10** fare uno sconto di 10 sterline.

►**knock out** vt stendere; (BOXING) mettere K.O., mettere fuori combattimento.

►**knock over** vt (object) far cadere; (pedestrian) investire.

knockdown ['nɔkdaun] adj (price) fortemente scontato(a).

knocker ['nɔkə*] n (on door) battente m.

knocking ['nɔkɪŋ] n colpi mpl.

knock-kneed [nɔk'niːd] adj che ha le gambe ad x.

knockout ['nɔkaut] n (BOXING) knock out m inv.

knockout competition n (BRIT) gara ad eliminazione.

knock-up ['nɔkʌp] n (TENNIS etc) palleggio; **to have a** ~ palleggiare.

knot [nɔt] n nodo ♦ vt annodare; **to tie a** ~ fare un nodo.

knotty ['nɔtɪ] adj (fig) spinoso(a).

know [nəu] vt (pt **knew**, pp **known** [njuː, nəun]) sapere; (person, author, place) conoscere ♦ vi sapere; **to** ~ **that** ... sapere che ...; **to** ~ **how to do** sapere fare; **to get to** ~ **sth** venire a sapere qc; **I** ~ **nothing about it** non ne so niente; **I don't** ~ **him** non lo conosco; **to** ~ **right from wrong**

distinguere il bene dal male; **as far as I** ~ ... che io sappia ..., per quanto io ne sappia ...; **yes, I** ~ sì, lo so; **I don't** ~ non lo so.

know-all ['nəuɔːl] n (BRIT pej) sapientone/a.

know-how ['nəuhau] n tecnica; pratica.

knowing ['nəuɪŋ] adj (look etc) d'intesa.

knowingly ['nəuɪŋlɪ] adv consapevolmente; di complicità.

know-it-all ['nəuɪtɔːl] n (US) = know-all.

knowledge ['nɔlɪdʒ] n consapevolezza; (learning) conoscenza, sapere m; **to have no** ~ **of** ignorare, non sapere; **not to my** ~ che io sappia, no; **to have a working** ~ **of Italian** avere una conoscenza pratica dell'italiano; **without my** ~ a mia insaputa; **it is common** ~ **that** ... è risaputo che ...; **it has come to my** ~ **that** ... sono venuto a sapere che ....

knowledgeable ['nɔlɪdʒəbl] adj ben informato(a).

known [nəun] pp of know ♦ adj (thief, facts) noto(a); (expert) riconosciuto(a).

knuckle ['nʌkl] n nocca.

►**knuckle down** vi (col): **to** ~ **down to some hard work** mettersi sotto a lavorare.

►**knuckle under** vi (col) cedere.

knuckleduster ['nʌkldʌstə*] n tirapugni m inv.

KO abbr (= knock out) n K.O. m ♦ vt mettere K.O.

koala [kəu'ɑːlə] n (also: ~ **bear**) koala m inv.

kook [kuːk] n (US col) svitato/a.

Koran [kɔ'rɑːn] n Corano.

Korea [kə'riːə] n Corea; **North/South** ~ Corea del Nord/Sud.

Korean [kə'riːən] adj, n coreano(a).

kosher ['kəuʃə*] adj kasher inv.

kowtow ['kau'tau] vi: **to** ~ **to sb** mostrarsi ossequioso(a) verso qn.

Kremlin ['krɛmlɪn] n: **the** ~ il Cremlino.

KS abbr (US) = Kansas.

Kt abbr (BRIT: = Knight) titolo.

Kuala Lumpur ['kwɑːlə'lumpuə*] n Kuala Lumpur f.

kudos ['kjuːdɔs] n gloria, fama.

Kurd [kəːd] n curdo/a.

Kuwait [ku'weɪt] n Kuwait m.

Kuwaiti [ku'weɪtɪ] adj, n kuwaitiano(a).

kw abbr (= kilowatt) kw.

KY, Ky. abbr (US) = Kentucky.

L l

L, l [ɛl] n (*letter*) L, l f or m inv; **L for Lucy,** (*US*) **L for Love** ≈ L come Livorno.
L abbr (= *lake*) l; (= *large*) taglia grande; (= *left*) sin.; (*BRIT AUT*) = **learner**.
l abbr (= *litre*) l.
LA n abbr (*US*) = *Los Angeles* ♦ abbr (*US*) = *Louisiana*.
La. abbr (*US*) = *Louisiana*.
lab [læb] n abbr (= *laboratory*) laboratorio.
Lab. abbr (*Canada*) = *Labrador*.
label ['leɪbl] n etichetta, cartellino; (*brand: of record*) casa ♦ vt etichettare; classificare.
labor etc ['leɪbə*] (*US*) = **labour** etc.
laboratory [lə'bɒrətərɪ] n laboratorio.
Labor Day n (*US*) festa del lavoro; *see boxed note.*

LABOR DAY

*Negli Stati Uniti e nel Canada il **Labor Day**, la festa del lavoro, cade il primo lunedì di settembre, contrariamente a quanto accade nella maggior parte dei paesi europei dove tale celebrazione ha luogo il primo maggio.*

---

laborious [lə'bɔːrɪəs] adj laborioso(a).
labor union n (*US*) sindacato.
Labour ['leɪbə*] n (*BRIT POL: also:* **the ~ Party**) il partito laburista, i laburisti.
labour, (*US*) **labor** ['leɪbə*] n (*task*) lavoro; (*workmen*) manodopera; (*MED*) travaglio del parto, doglie fpl ♦ vi: **to ~ (at)** lavorare duro (a); **to be in ~** (*MED*) avere le doglie.
labo(u)r camp n campo dei lavori forzati.
labo(u)r cost n costo del lavoro.
labo(u)r dispute n conflitto tra lavoratori e datori di lavoro.
labo(u)red ['leɪbəd] adj (*breathing*) affaticato(a); (*style*) elaborato(a), pesante.
labo(u)rer ['leɪbərə*] n manovale m; (*on farm*) lavoratore m agricolo.
labo(u)r force n manodopera.
labo(u)r-intensive [leɪbərɪn'tɛnsɪv] adj che assorbe molta manodopera.
labo(u)r market n mercato del lavoro.
labo(u)r pains npl doglie fpl.
labo(u)r relations npl relazioni fpl

industriali.
labo(u)r-saving ['leɪbəseɪvɪŋ] adj che fa risparmiare fatica or lavoro.
labo(u)r unrest n agitazioni fpl degli operai.
labyrinth ['læbɪrɪnθ] n labirinto.
lace [leɪs] n merletto, pizzo; (*of shoe etc*) laccio ♦ vt (*shoe*) allacciare; (*drink: with spirits*) correggere.
lacemaking ['leɪsmeɪkɪŋ] n fabbricazione f dei pizzi or dei merletti.
laceration [læsə'reɪʃən] n lacerazione f.
lace-up ['leɪsʌp] adj (*shoes etc*) con i lacci, con le stringhe.
lack [læk] n mancanza, scarsità ♦ vt mancare di; **through** or **for ~ of** per mancanza di; **to be ~ing (in)** mancare di.
lackadaisical [lækə'deɪzɪkl] adj disinteressato(a), noncurante.
lackey ['lækɪ] n (*also fig*) lacchè m inv.
lacklustre, (*US*) **lackluster** ['læklʌstə*] adj (*surface*) opaco(a); (*style*) scialbo(a); (*eyes*) spento(a).
laconic [lə'kɒnɪk] adj laconico(a).
lacquer ['lækə*] n lacca; **hair ~** lacca per (i) capelli.
lacy ['leɪsɪ] adj (*like lace*) che sembra un pizzo.
lad [læd] n ragazzo, giovanotto; (*BRIT: in stable etc*) mozzo or garzone m di stalla.
ladder ['lædə*] n scala; (*BRIT: in tights*) smagliatura ♦ vt smagliare ♦ vi smagliarsi.
laden ['leɪdn] adj: **~ (with)** carico(a) or caricato(a) (di); **fully ~** (*truck, ship*) a pieno carico.
ladle ['leɪdl] n mestolo.
lady ['leɪdɪ] n signora; **L~ Smith** lady Smith; **the ladies' (toilets)** i gabinetti per signore; **a ~ doctor** una dottoressa.
ladybird ['leɪdɪbɜːd], (*US*) **ladybug** ['leɪdɪbʌg] n coccinella.
lady-in-waiting ['leɪdɪɪn'weɪtɪŋ] n dama di compagnia.
ladykiller ['leɪdɪkɪlə*] n dongiovanni m inv.
ladylike ['leɪdɪlaɪk] adj da signora.
ladyship ['leɪdɪʃɪp] n: **your L~** signora contessa etc.
lag [læg] n = **time ~** ♦ vi (*also:* ~ **behind**) trascinarsi ♦ vt (*pipes*) rivestire di materiale isolante.
lager ['lɑːgə*] n lager m inv.
lager lout n (*BRIT col*) giovinastro ubriaco.
lagging ['lægɪŋ] n rivestimento di materiale isolante.
lagoon [lə'guːn] n laguna.
Lagos ['leɪgɔs] n Lagos f.
laid [leɪd] pt, pp of **lay**.

laid-back [leɪd'bæk] adj (col) rilassato(a).
lain [leɪn] pp of **lie**.
lair [lɛə*] n covo, tana.
laissez-faire [lɛseɪ'fɛə*] n liberismo.
laity ['leɪətɪ] n laici mpl.
lake [leɪk] n lago.
Lake District n: **the** ~ (BRIT) la regione dei laghi.
lamb [læm] n agnello.
lamb chop n cotoletta d'agnello.
lambskin ['læmskɪn] n (pelle fd')agnello.
lambswool ['læmzwul] n lamb's wool m.
lame [leɪm] adj zoppo(a); ~ **duck** (fig: person) persona inetta; (: firm) azienda traballante.
lamely ['leɪmlɪ] adv (fig) in modo poco convincente.
lament [lə'mɛnt] n lamento ♦ vt lamentare, piangere.
lamentable ['læməntəbl] adj doloroso(a); deplorevole.
laminated ['læmɪneɪtɪd] adj laminato(a).
lamp [læmp] n lampada.
lamplight ['læmplaɪt] n: **by** ~ a lume della lampada.
lampoon [læm'puːn] n satira.
lamppost ['læmppəust] n lampione m.
lampshade ['læmpʃeɪd] n paralume m.
lance [lɑːns] n lancia ♦ vt (MED) incidere.
lance corporal n (BRIT) caporale m.
lancet ['lɑːnsɪt] n (MED) bisturi m inv.
Lancs [læŋks] abbr (BRIT) = Lancashire.
land [lænd] n (as opposed to sea) terra (ferma); (country) paese m; (soil) terreno; (estate) terreni mpl, terre fpl ♦ vi (from ship) sbarcare; (AVIAT) atterrare; (fig: fall) cadere ♦ vt (obtain) acchiappare; (passengers) sbarcare; (goods) scaricare; **to go/travel by** ~ andare/viaggiare per via di terra; **to own** ~ possedere dei terreni, avere delle proprietà (terriere); **to** ~ **on one's feet** cadere in piedi; (fig: to be lucky) cascar bene.
▶**land up** vi andare a finire.
landed gentry ['lændɪd-] n proprietari mpl terrieri.
landfill site ['lændfɪl-] n discarica dove i rifiuti vengono sepolti.
landing ['lændɪŋ] n (from ship) sbarco; (AVIAT) atterraggio; (of staircase) pianerottolo.
landing card n carta di sbarco.
landing craft n mezzo da sbarco.
landing gear n (AVIAT) carrello d'atterraggio.
landing stage n pontile m da sbarco.
landing strip n pista d'atterraggio.
landlady ['lændleɪdɪ] n padrona or

proprietaria di casa.
landlocked ['lændlɒkt] adj senza sbocco sul mare.
landlord ['lændlɔːd] n padrone m or proprietario di casa; (of pub etc) oste m.
landlubber ['lændlʌbə*] n marinaio d'acqua dolce.
landmark ['lændmɑːk] n punto di riferimento; (fig) pietra miliare.
landowner ['lændəunə*] n proprietario(a) terriero(a).
landscape ['lænskeɪp] n paesaggio.
landscape architect, landscape gardener n paesaggista m/f.
landscape painting n (ART) paesaggistica.
landslide ['lændslaɪd] n (GEO) frana; (fig: POL) valanga.
lane [leɪn] n (in country) viottolo; (in town) stradetta; (AUT, in race) corsia; **shipping** ~ rotta (marittima).
language ['læŋgwɪdʒ] n lingua; (way one speaks) linguaggio; **bad** ~ linguaggio volgare.
language laboratory n laboratorio linguistico.
languid ['læŋgwɪd] adj languente; languido(a).
languish ['læŋgwɪʃ] vi languire.
lank [læŋk] adj (hair) liscio(a) e opaco(a).
lanky ['læŋkɪ] adj allampanato(a).
lanolin(e) ['lænəlɪn] n lanolina.
lantern ['læntn] n lanterna.
Laos [lauz] n Laos m.
lap [læp] n (of track) giro; (of body): **in** or **on one's** ~ in grembo ♦ vt (also: ~ **up**) papparsi, leccare ♦ vi (waves) sciabordare.
▶**lap up** vt (fig: compliments, attention) bearsi di.
La Paz [læ'pæz] n La Paz f.
lapdog ['læpdɒg] n cane m da grembo.
lapel [lə'pɛl] n risvolto.
Lapland ['læplænd] n Lapponia.
Lapp [læp] adj lappone ♦ n lappone m/f; (LING) lappone m.
lapse [læps] n lapsus m inv; (longer) caduta; (fault) mancanza; (in behaviour) scorrettezza ♦ vi (law, act) cadere; (ticket, passport) scadere; **to** ~ **into bad habits** pigliare cattive abitudini; ~ **of time** spazio di tempo; **a** ~ **of memory** un vuoto di memoria.
laptop ['læptɒp] n (also: ~ **computer**) laptop m inv.
larceny ['lɑːsənɪ] n furto.
lard [lɑːd] n lardo.
larder ['lɑːdə*] n dispensa.

large [lɑːdʒ] *adj* grande; (*person, animal*) grosso(a) ♦ *adv*: **by and ~** generalmente; **at ~** (*free*) in libertà; (*generally*) in generale; nell'insieme; **to make ~r** ingrandire; **a ~ number of people** molta gente; **on a ~ scale** su vasta scala.

largely ['lɑːdʒlɪ] *adv* in gran parte.

large-scale ['lɑːdʒ'skeɪl] *adj* (*map, drawing etc*) in grande scala; (*reforms, business activities*) su vasta scala.

lark [lɑːk] *n* (*bird*) allodola; (*joke*) scherzo, gioco.

▶**lark about** *vi* fare lo stupido.

larva [ˈlɑːvə], *pl* **larvae** [ˈlɑːvə, -iː] *n* larva.

laryngitis [lærɪnˈdʒaɪtɪs] *n* laringite *f*.

larynx [ˈlærɪŋks] *n* laringe *f*.

lasagne [ləˈzænjə] *n* lasagne *fpl*.

lascivious [ləˈsɪvɪəs] *adj* lascivo(a).

laser [ˈleɪzə*] *n* laser *m*.

laser beam *n* raggio *m* laser *inv*.

laser printer *n* stampante *f* laser *inv*.

lash [læʃ] *n* frustata; (*also:* **eye~**) ciglio ♦ *vt* frustare; (*tie*) legare.

▶**lash down** *vt* assicurare (con corde) ♦ *vi* (*rain*) scrosciare.

▶**lash out** *vi*: **to ~ out (at** *or* **against sb/sth)** attaccare violentemente (qn/qc); **to ~ out (on sth)** (*col: spend*) spendere un sacco di soldi (per qc).

lashing [ˈlæʃɪŋ] *n* (*beating*) frustata, sferzata; **~s of** (*BRIT col*) un mucchio di, una montagna di.

lass [læs] *n* ragazza.

lasso [læˈsuː] *n* laccio ♦ *vt* acchiappare con il laccio.

last [lɑːst] *adj* ultimo(a); (*week, month, year*) scorso(a), passato(a) ♦ *adv* per ultimo ♦ *vi* durare; **~ week** la settimana scorsa; **~ night** ieri sera, la notte scorsa; **at ~** finalmente, alla fine; **~ but one** penultimo(a); **the ~ time** l'ultima volta; **it ~s (for) 2 hours** dura 2 ore.

last-ditch [ˈlɑːstˈdɪtʃ] *adj* ultimo(a) e disperato(a).

lasting [ˈlɑːstɪŋ] *adj* durevole.

lastly [ˈlɑːstlɪ] *adv* infine, per finire, per ultimo.

last-minute [ˈlɑːstmɪnɪt] *adj* fatto(a) (*or* preso(a)) all'ultimo momento.

latch [lætʃ] *n* serratura a scatto.

▶**latch on to** *vt fus* (*cling to: person*) attaccarsi a, appiccicarsi a; (*: idea*) afferrare, capire.

latchkey [ˈlætʃkiː] *n* chiave *f* di casa.

late [leɪt] *adj* (*not on time*) in ritardo; (*far on in day etc*) tardi *inv*; tardo(a); (*recent*) recente, ultimo(a); (*former*) ex; (*dead*) defunto(a) ♦ *adv* tardi; (*behind time,*

schedule*) in ritardo; **to be (10 minutes) ~** essere in ritardo (di 10 minuti); **to work ~** lavorare fino a tardi; **~ in life** in età avanzata; **of ~** di recente; **in the ~ afternoon** nel tardo pomeriggio; **in ~ May** verso la fine di maggio; **the ~ Mr X** il defunto Signor X.

latecomer [ˈleɪtkʌmə*] *n* ritardatario/a.

lately [ˈleɪtlɪ] *adv* recentemente.

lateness [ˈleɪtnɪs] *n* (*of person*) ritardo; (*of event*) tardezza, ora tarda.

latent [ˈleɪtnt] *adj* latente; **~ defect** vizio occulto.

later [ˈleɪtə*] *adj* (*date etc*) posteriore; (*version etc*) successivo(a) ♦ *adv* più tardi; **~ on today** oggi più tardi.

lateral [ˈlætərl] *adj* laterale.

latest [ˈleɪtɪst] *adj* ultimo(a), più recente; **at the ~** al più tardi; **the ~ news** le ultime notizie.

latex [ˈleɪtɛks] *n* latice *m*.

lath, **~s** [læθ, læðz] *n* assicella.

lathe [leɪð] *n* tornio.

lather [ˈlɑːðə*] *n* schiuma di sapone ♦ *vt* insaponare ♦ *vi* far schiuma.

Latin [ˈlætɪn] *n* latino ♦ *adj* latino(a).

Latin America *n* America Latina.

Latin American *adj* sudamericano(a).

latitude [ˈlætɪtjuːd] *n* latitudine *f*; (*fig: freedom*) libertà d'azione.

latrine [ləˈtriːn] *n* latrina.

latter [ˈlætə*] *adj* secondo(a); più recente ♦ *n*: **the ~** quest'ultimo, il secondo.

latterly [ˈlætəlɪ] *adv* recentemente, negli ultimi tempi.

lattice [ˈlætɪs] *n* traliccio; graticolato.

lattice window *n* finestra con vetrata a losanghe.

Latvia [ˈlætvɪə] *n* Lettonia.

Latvian [ˈlætvɪən] *adj* lettone *inv* ♦ *n* lettone *m/f*; (*LING*) lettone *m*.

laudable [ˈlɔːdəbl] *adj* lodevole.

laudatory [ˈlɔːdətrɪ] *adj* elogiativo(a).

laugh [lɑːf] *n* risata ♦ *vi* ridere.

▶**laugh at** *vt fus* (*misfortune etc*) ridere di; **I ~ed at his joke** la sua barzelletta mi fece ridere.

▶**laugh off** *vt* prendere alla leggera.

laughable [ˈlɑːfəbl] *adj* ridicolo(a).

laughing [ˈlɑːfɪŋ] *adj* (*face*) ridente; **this is no ~ matter** non è una cosa da ridere.

laughing gas *n* gas *m* esilarante.

laughing stock *n*: **the ~ of** lo zimbello di.

laughter [ˈlɑːftə*] *n* riso; risate *fpl*.

launch [lɔːntʃ] *n* (*of rocket, product etc*) lancio; (*of new ship*) varo; (*boat*) scialuppa; (*also:* **motor ~**) lancia ♦ *vt* (*rocket, product*) lanciare; (*ship, plan*)

varare.
►**launch out** vi: **to ~ out (into)** lanciarsi
(in).
launching ['lɔːntʃɪŋ] n lancio; varo.
launch(ing) pad n rampa di lancio.
launder ['lɔːndə*] vt lavare e stirare.
Launderette ® [lɔːn'drɛt], (US)
Laundromat ® ['lɔːndrəmæt] n
lavanderia (automatica).
laundry ['lɔːndrɪ] n lavanderia; (clothes)
biancheria; **to do the ~** fare il bucato.
laureate ['lɔːrɪət] adj see **poet laureate**.
laurel ['lɔrl] n lauro, alloro; **to rest on one's
~s** riposare or dormire sugli allori.
Lausanne [ləu'zæn] n Losanna.
lava ['lɑːvə] n lava.
lavatory ['lævətərɪ] n gabinetto.
lavatory paper n (BRIT) carta igienica.
lavender ['lævəndə*] n lavanda.
lavish ['lævɪʃ] adj abbondante; sontuoso(a);
(giving freely): **~ with** prodigo(a) di,
largo(a) in ♦ vt. **to ~ sth on sb/stn**
profondere qc a qn/qc.
lavishly ['lævɪʃlɪ] adv (give, spend)
generosamente; (furnished)
sontuosamente, lussuosamente.
law [lɔː] n legge f; **against the ~** contro la
legge; **to study ~** studiare diritto; **to go
to ~** (BRIT) ricorrere alle vie legali; **civil/
criminal ~** diritto civile/penale.
law-abiding ['lɔːəbaɪdɪŋ] adj ubbidiente
alla legge.
law and order n l'ordine m pubblico.
lawbreaker ['lɔːbreɪkə*] n violatore/trice
della legge.
law court n tribunale m, corte f di
giustizia.
lawful ['lɔːful] adj legale.
lawfully ['lɔːfəlɪ] adv legalmente.
lawless ['lɔːlɪs] adj senza legge; illegale.
Law Lords npl ≈ Corte f Suprema.
lawmaker ['lɔːmeɪkə*] n legislatore m.
lawn [lɔːn] n tappeto erboso.
lawnmower ['lɔːnməuə*] n tosaerba m or f
inv.
lawn tennis n tennis m su prato.
law school n facoltà f inv di legge.
law student n studente/essa di legge.
lawsuit ['lɔːsuːt] n processo, causa; **to
bring a ~ against** intentare causa a.
lawyer ['lɔːjə*] n (consultant, with company)
giurista m/f; (for sales, wills etc) ≈ notaio;
(partner, in court) ≈ avvocato/essa.
lax [læks] adj (conduct) rilassato(a); (person:
careless) negligente; (: on discipline)
permissivo(a).
laxative ['læksətɪv] n lassativo.
laxity ['læksɪtɪ] n rilassatezza; negligenza.

lay [leɪ] pt of **lie** ♦ adj laico(a); secolare ♦ vt
(pt, pp **laid** [leɪd]) posare, mettere; (eggs)
fare; (trap) tendere; (plans) fare,
elaborare; **to ~ the table** apparecchiare
la tavola; **to ~ the facts/one's proposals
before sb** presentare i fatti/delle
proposte a qn; **to get laid** (col!) scopare
(!); essere scopato(a) (!).
►**lay aside, lay by** vt mettere da parte.
►**lay down** vt mettere giù; **to ~ down the
law** (fig) dettar legge.
►**lay in** vt fare una scorta di.
►**lay into** vt fus (col: attack, scold) aggredire.
►**lay off** vt (workers) licenziare.
►**lay on** vt (water, gas) installare, mettere;
(provide: meal etc) fornire; (paint)
applicare.
►**lay out** vt (design) progettare; (display)
presentare; (spend) sborsare.
►**lay up** vt (to store) accumulare; (ship)
mettere in disarmo; (subj: illness)
costringere a letto.
layabout ['leɪəbaut] n sfaccendato/a,
fannullone/a.
lay-by ['leɪbaɪ] n (BRIT) piazzola (di sosta).
lay days npl (NAUT) stallie fpl.
layer ['leɪə*] n strato.
layette [leɪ'ɛt] n corredino (per neonato).
layman ['leɪmən] n laico; profano.
lay-off ['leɪɔf] n sospensione f,
licenziamento.
layout ['leɪaut] n lay-out m inv, disposizione
f; (PRESS) impaginazione f.
laze [leɪz] vi oziare.
laziness ['leɪzɪnɪs] n pigrizia.
lazy ['leɪzɪ] adj pigro(a).
lb. abbr (= libra: pound) lb.
lbw abbr (CRICKET: = leg before wicket) fallo
dovuto al fatto che il giocatore ha la
gamba davanti alla porta.
LC n abbr (US) = Library of Congress.
lc abbr (TYP) = **lower case**.
L/C abbr = **letter of credit**.
LCD n abbr see **liquid crystal display**.
Ld abbr (BRIT: = lord) titolo.
LDS n abbr (= Licentiate in Dental Surgery)
specializzazione dopo la laurea;
(= Latter-day Saints) Chiesa di Gesù Cristo
dei Santi dell'Ultimo Giorno.
LEA n abbr (BRIT: = local education authority)
≈ Provveditorato degli Studi.
lead [liːd] n (front position) posizione f di
testa; (distance, time ahead) vantaggio;
(clue) indizio; (ELEC) filo (elettrico); (for
dog) guinzaglio; (THEAT) parte f
principale; [lɛd] (metal) piombo; (in pencil)
mina ♦ vb (pt, pp **led** [lɛd]) vt menare,
guidare, condurre; (induce) indurre; (be

leader of) essere a capo di; (: *orchestra*: BRIT) essere il primo violino di; (: *US*) dirigere; (*SPORT*) essere in testa a ♦ *vi* condurre, essere in testa; **to be in the ~** (*SPORT*) essere in testa; **to take the ~** (*SPORT*) passare in testa; (*fig*) prendere l'iniziativa; **to ~ to** menare a; condurre a; portare a; **to ~ astray** sviare; **to ~ sb to believe that ...** far credere a qn che ...; **to ~ sb to do sth** portare qn a fare qc.
►**lead away** *vt* condurre via.
►**lead back** *vt* riportare, ricondurre.
►**lead off** *vt* portare ♦ *vi* partire da.
►**lead on** *vt* (*tease*) tenere sulla corda.
►**lead on to** *vt* (*induce*) portare a.
►**lead up to** *vt fus* portare a; (*fig*) preparare la strada per.
leaded ['lɛdɪd] *adj* (*petrol*) con piombo; **~ windows** vetrate *fpl* (artistiche).
leaden ['lɛdn] *adj* di piombo.
leader ['liːdə*] *n* capo; leader *m inv*; (*in newspaper*) articolo di fondo; **they are ~s in their field** (*fig*) sono all'avanguardia nel loro campo; **the L~ of the House** (*BRIT*) il capo della maggioranza ministeriale.
leadership ['liːdəʃɪp] *n* direzione *f*; **under the ~ of ...** sotto la direzione *or* guida di ...; **qualities of ~** qualità *fpl* di un capo.
lead-free ['lɛdfriː] *adj* senza piombo.
leading ['liːdɪŋ] *adj* primo(a); principale; **a ~ question** una domanda tendenziosa; **~ role** ruolo principale.
leading lady *n* (*THEAT*) prima attrice.
leading light *n* (*person*) personaggio di primo piano.
leading man *n* (*THEAT*) primo attore.
lead pencil [lɛd-] *n* matita con la mina di grafite.
lead poisoning [lɛd-] *n* saturnismo.
lead time [liːd-] *n* (*COMM*) tempo di consegna.
lead weight [lɛd-] *n* piombino, piombo.
leaf [liːf] *n* (*pl* **leaves**) foglia; (*of table*) ribalta; **to turn over a new ~** (*fig*) cambiar vita; **to take a ~ out of sb's book** (*fig*) prendere esempio da qn.
►**leaf through** *vt* (*book*) sfogliare.
leaflet ['liːflɪt] *n* dépliant *m inv*; (*POL, REL*) volantino.
leafy ['liːfɪ] *adj* ricco(a) di foglie.
league [liːg] *n* lega; (*FOOTBALL*) campionato; **to be in ~ with** essere in lega con.
league table *n* classifica.
leak [liːk] *n* (*out*) fuga; (*in*) infiltrazione *f*; (*fig*: *of information*) fuga di notizie ♦ *vi* (*roof, bucket*) perdere; (*liquid*) uscire; (*shoes*) lasciar passare l'acqua ♦ *vt* (*liquid*) spandere; (*information*) divulgare.

►**leak out** *vi* uscire; (*information*) trapelare.
leakage ['liːkɪdʒ] *n* (*of water, gas etc*) perdita.
leaky ['liːkɪ] *adj* (*pipe, bucket, roof*) che perde; (*shoe*) che lascia passare l'acqua; (*boat*) che fa acqua.
lean [liːn] *adj* magro(a) ♦ *n* (*of meat*) carne *f* magra ♦ *vb* (*pt, pp* **leaned** *or* **leant** [lɛnt]) *vt*: **to ~ sth on** appoggiare qc su ♦ *vi* (*slope*) pendere; (*rest*): **to ~ against** appoggiarsi contro; essere appoggiato(a) a; **to ~ on** appoggiarsi a.
►**lean back** *vi* sporgersi indietro.
►**lean forward** *vi* sporgersi in avanti.
►**lean out** *vi*: **to ~ out (of)** sporgersi (da).
►**lean over** *vi* inclinarsi.
leaning ['liːnɪŋ] *n*: **~ (towards)** propensione *f* (per) ♦ *adj* inclinato(a), pendente; **the L~ Tower of Pisa** la torre (pendente) di Pisa.
leant [lɛnt] *pt, pp of* **lean**.
lean-to ['liːntuː] *n* (*roof*) tettoia; (*building*) edificio con tetto appoggiato ad altro edificio.
leap [liːp] *n* salto, balzo ♦ *vi* (*pt, pp* **leaped** *or* **leapt** [lɛpt]) saltare, balzare; **to ~ at an offer** afferrare al volo una proposta.
►**leap up** *vi* (*person*) alzarsi d'un balzo, balzare su.
leapfrog ['liːpfrɔg] *n* gioco della cavallina ♦ *vi*: **to ~ over sb/sth** saltare (alla cavallina) qn/qc.
leapt [lɛpt] *pt, pp of* **leap**.
leap year *n* anno bisestile.
learn, *pt, pp* **learned** *or* **learnt** [ləːn, -t] *vt, vi* imparare; **to ~ how to do sth** imparare a fare qc; **to ~ that ...** apprendere che ...; **to ~ about sth** (*SCOL*) studiare qc; (*hear*) apprendere qc; **we were sorry to ~ that it was closing down** la notizia della chiusura ci ha fatto dispiacere.
learned ['ləːnɪd] *adj* erudito(a), dotto(a).
learner ['ləːnə*] *n* principiante *m/f*; apprendista *m/f*; **he's a ~ (driver)** (*BRIT*) sta imparando a guidare.
learning ['ləːnɪŋ] *n* erudizione *f*, sapienza.
learnt [ləːnt] *pt, pp of* **learn**.
lease [liːs] *n* contratto d'affitto ♦ *vt* affittare; **on ~** in affitto.
►**lease back** *vt* effettuare un lease-back *inv*.
leaseback ['liːsbæk] *n* lease-back *m inv*.
leasehold ['liːshəʊld] *n* (*contract*) contratto di affitto (*a lungo termine con responsabilità simili a quelle di un proprietario*) ♦ *adj* in affitto.
leash [liːʃ] *n* guinzaglio.
least [liːst] *adj*: **the ~ + noun** il(la) più piccolo(a), il(la) minimo(a); (*smallest*

amount of) il(la) meno ♦ *adv*: **the ~ + *adjective*: the ~ beautiful girl** la ragazza meno bella; **the ~ expensive** il(la) meno caro(a); **I have the ~ money** ho meno denaro di tutti; **at ~** almeno; **not in the ~** affatto, per nulla.

leather ['lɛðə*] *n* (*soft*) pelle *f*; (*hard*) cuoio ♦ *cpd* di *or* in pelle; di cuoio; **~ goods** pelletteria, pelletterie *fpl*.

leave [li:v] *vb* (*pt, pp* **left** [lɛft]) *vt* lasciare; (*go away from*) partire da ♦ *vi* partire, andarsene ♦ *n* (*time off*) congedo; (*MIL, also: consent*) licenza; **to be left** rimanere; **there's some milk left over** c'è rimasto del latte; **to take one's ~** of congedarsi di; **he's already left for the airport** è già uscito per andare all'aeroporto; **to ~ school** finire la scuola; **~ it to me!** ci penso io!, lascia fare a me!; **on ~** in congedo; **on ~ of absence** in permesso; (*public employee*) in congedo; (*MIL*) in licenza.

▶ **leave behind** *vt* (*also fig*) lasciare indietro; (*forget*) dimenticare.

▶ **leave off** *vt* non mettere; (*BRIT col: stop*): **to ~ off doing sth** smetterla *or* piantarla di fare qc.

▶ **leave on** *vt* lasciare su; (*light, fire, cooker*) lasciare acceso(a).

▶ **leave out** *vt* omettere, tralasciare.

leaves [li:vz] *npl of* **leaf**.

leavetaking ['li:vteɪkɪŋ] *n* commiato, addio.

Lebanese [lɛbə'ni:z] *adj, n* (*pl inv*) libanese (*m/f*).

Lebanon ['lɛbənən] *n* Libano.

lecherous ['lɛtʃərəs] *adj* lascivo(a), lubrico(a).

lectern ['lɛktə:n] *n* leggio.

lecture ['lɛktʃə*] *n* conferenza; (*SCOL*) lezione *f* ♦ *vi* fare conferenze; fare lezioni; (*reprove*) rimproverare, fare una ramanzina a; **to ~ on** fare una conferenza su; **to give a ~ (on)** (*BRIT*) fare una conferenza (su); fare lezione (su).

lecture hall *n* aula magna.

lecturer ['lɛktʃərə*] *n* (*speaker*) conferenziere/a; (*BRIT: at university*) professore/essa, docente *m/f*; **assistant ~** (*BRIT*) ≈ professore(essa) associato(a); **senior ~** (*BRIT*) ≈ professore(essa) ordinario(a).

lecture theatre *n* = **lecture hall**.

LED *n abbr* (*ELEC*: = *light-emitting diode*) diodo a emissione luminosa.

led [lɛd] *pt, pp of* **lead**.

ledge [lɛdʒ] *n* (*of window*) davanzale *m*; (*on wall etc*) sporgenza; (*of mountain*) cornice *f*, cengia.

ledger ['lɛdʒə*] *n* libro maestro, registro.

lee [li:] *n* lato sottovento; **in the ~ of a** ridosso di, al riparo di.

leech [li:tʃ] *n* sanguisuga.

leek [li:k] *n* porro.

leer [lɪə*] *vi*: **to ~ at sb** gettare uno sguardo voglioso (*or* maligno) su qn.

leeward ['li:wəd] *adj* sottovento *inv* ♦ *n* lato sottovento; **to ~** sottovento.

leeway ['li:weɪ] *n* (*fig*): **to have some ~** avere una certa libertà di agire.

left [lɛft] *pt, pp of* **leave** ♦ *adj* sinistro(a) ♦ *adv* a sinistra ♦ *n* sinistra; **on the ~, to the ~** a sinistra; **the L~** (*POL*) la sinistra.

left-hand drive ['lɛfthænd-] *n* (*BRIT*) guida a sinistra.

left-handed [lɛft'hændɪd] *adj* mancino(a); **~ scissors** forbici *fpl* per mancini.

left-hand side ['lɛfthænd-] *n* lato *or* fianco sinistro.

leftie ['lɛftɪ] *n*: **a ~** (*col*) uno/a di sinistra.

leftist ['lɛftɪst] *adj* (*POL*) di sinistra.

left-luggage (office) [lɛft'lʌgɪdʒ-] *n* deposito *m* bagagli *inv*.

left-overs ['lɛftəuvəz] *npl* avanzi *mpl*, resti *mpl*.

left wing *n* (*MIL, SPORT*) ala sinistra; (*POL*) sinistra ♦ *adj*: **left-wing** (*POL*) di sinistra.

left-winger [lɛft'wɪŋə*] *n* (*POL*) uno/a di sinistra; (*SPORT*) ala sinistra.

lefty ['lɛftɪ] *n* = **leftie**.

leg [lɛg] *n* gamba; (*of animal*) zampa; (*of furniture*) piede *m*; (*CULIN: of chicken*) coscia; (*of journey*) tappa; **1st/2nd ~** (*SPORT*) partita di andata/ritorno; **~ of lamb** (*CULIN*) cosciotto d'agnello; **to stretch one's ~s** sgranchirsi le gambe.

legacy ['lɛgəsɪ] *n* eredità *f inv*; (*fig*) retaggio.

legal ['li:gl] *adj* legale; **to take ~ action** *or* **proceedings against sb** intentare un'azione legale contro qn, far causa a qn.

legal adviser *n* consulente *m/f* legale.

legality [lɪ'gælɪtɪ] *n* legalità.

legalize ['li:gəlaɪz] *vt* legalizzare.

legally ['li:gəlɪ] *adv* legalmente; **~ binding** legalmente vincolante.

legal tender *n* moneta legale.

legation [lɪ'geɪʃən] *n* legazione *f*.

legend ['lɛdʒənd] *n* leggenda.

legendary ['lɛdʒəndərɪ] *adj* leggendario(a).

-legged ['lɛgɪd] *suffix*: **two~** a due gambe (*or* zampe), bipede.

leggings ['lɛgɪŋz] *npl* ghette *fpl*.

leggy ['lɛgɪ] *adj* dalle gambe lunghe.

legibility [lɛdʒɪ'bɪlɪtɪ] *n* leggibilità.

legible ['lɛdʒəbl] *adj* leggibile.

legibly ['lɛdʒəblɪ] *adv* in modo leggibile.

legion ['li:dʒən] *n* legione *f*.
legionnaire [li:dʒə'neə*] *n* legionario; ~'s **disease** morbo del legionario.
legislate ['lɛdʒɪsleɪt] *vi* legiferare.
legislation [lɛdʒɪs'leɪʃən] *n* legislazione *f*; **a piece of** ~ una legge.
legislative ['lɛdʒɪslətɪv] *adj* legislativo(a).
legislator ['lɛdʒɪsleɪtə*] *n* legislatore/trice.
legislature ['lɛdʒɪslətʃə*] *n* corpo legislativo.
legitimacy [lɪ'dʒɪtɪməsɪ] *n* legittimità.
legitimate [lɪ'dʒɪtɪmət] *adj* legittimo(a).
legitimize [lɪ'dʒɪtɪmaɪz] *vt* (*gen*) legalizzare, rendere legale; (*child*) legittimare.
legless ['lɛglɪs] *adj* (*BRIT col*) sbronzo(a), fatto(a).
leg-room ['lɛgruːm] *n* spazio per le gambe.
Leics *abbr* (*BRIT*) = *Leicestershire*.
leisure ['lɛʒə*] *n* agio, tempo libero; ricreazioni *fpl*; **at** ~ all'agio; **a proprio comodo.**
leisure centre *n* centro di ricreazione.
leisurely ['lɛʒəlɪ] *adj* tranquillo(a); fatto(a) con comodo *or* senza fretta.
leisure suit *n* (*BRIT*) tuta (da ginnastica).
lemon ['lɛmən] *n* limone *m*.
lemonade [lɛmə'neɪd] *n* limonata.
lemon cheese, lemon curd *n* crema di limone (*che si spalma sul pane etc*).
lemon juice *n* succo di limone.
lemon squeezer *n* spremiagrumi *m inv*.
lemon tea *n* tè *m inv* al limone.
lend, *pt, pp* **lent** [lɛnd, lɛnt] *vt*: **to** ~ **sth (to sb)** prestare qc (a qn); **to** ~ **a hand** dare una mano.
lender ['lɛndə*] *n* prestatore/trice.
lending library ['lɛndɪŋ-] *n* biblioteca circolante.
length [lɛŋθ] *n* lunghezza; (*section: of road, pipe etc*) pezzo, tratto; ~ **of time** periodo (di tempo); **what** ~ **is it?** quant'è lungo?; **it is 2 metres in** ~ è lungo 2 metri; **to fall full** ~ cadere lungo disteso; **at** ~ (*at last*) finalmente, alla fine; (*lengthily*) a lungo; **to go to any** ~(s) **to do sth** fare qualsiasi cosa pur di *or* per fare qc.
lengthen ['lɛŋθən] *vt* allungare, prolungare ♦ *vi* allungarsi.
lengthways ['lɛŋθweɪz] *adv* per il lungo.
lengthy ['lɛŋθɪ] *adj* molto lungo(a).
leniency ['li:nɪənsɪ] *n* indulgenza, clemenza.
lenient ['li:nɪənt] *adj* indulgente, clemente.
leniently ['li:nɪəntlɪ] *adv* con indulgenza.
lens [lɛnz] *n* lente *f*; (*of camera*) obiettivo.
Lent [lɛnt] *n* Quaresima.
lent [lɛnt] *pt, pp of* **lend**.

lentil ['lɛntl] *n* lenticchia.
Leo ['li:əu] *n* Leone *m*; **to be** ~ essere del Leone.
leopard ['lɛpəd] *n* leopardo.
leotard ['li:ətɑːd] *n* calzamaglia.
leper ['lɛpə*] *n* lebbroso/a.
leper colony *n* lebbrosario.
leprosy ['lɛprəsɪ] *n* lebbra.
lesbian ['lɛzbɪən] *n* lesbica ♦ *adj* lesbico(a).
lesion ['li:ʒən] *n* (*MED*) lesione *f*.
Lesotho [lɪ'su:tu] *n* Lesotho *m*.
less [lɛs] *adj, pron, adv* meno; ~ **than you/ ever** meno di lei/che mai; ~ **than half** meno della metà; ~ **and** ~ sempre meno; **the** ~ **he works** ... meno lavora ...; ~ **than £1/a kilo/3 metres** meno di una sterlina/ un chilo/3 metri; ~ **5%** meno il 5%.
lessee [lɛ'si:] *n* affittuario/a, locatario/a.
lessen ['lɛsn] *vi* diminuire, attenuarsi ♦ *vt* diminuire, ridurre.
lesser ['lɛsə*] *adj* minore, più piccolo(a); **to a** ~ **extent** *or* **degree** in grado *or* misura minore.
lesson ['lɛsn] *n* lezione *f*; **a maths** ~ una lezione di matematica; **to give** ~s **in** dare *or* impartire lezioni di; **it taught him a** ~ (*fig*) gli è servito di lezione.
lessor ['lɛsɔ:*, lɛ'sɔ:*] *n* locatore/trice.
lest [lɛst] *conj* per paura di + *infinitive*, per paura che + *sub*.
let, *pt, pp* **let** [lɛt] *vt* lasciare; (*BRIT: lease*) dare in affitto; **to** ~ **sb do sth** lasciar fare qc a qn, lasciare che qn faccia qc; **to** ~ **sb know sth** far sapere qc a qn; **to** ~ **sb have sth** dare qc a qn; **he** ~ **me go** mi ha lasciato andare; ~ **the water boil and ...** fate bollire l'acqua e ...; ~'s **go** andiamo; ~ **him come** lo lasci venire; "**to** ~" "affittasi".
►**let down** *vt* (*lower*) abbassare; (*dress*) allungare; (*hair*) sciogliere; (*disappoint*) deludere; (*BRIT: tyre*) sgonfiare.
►**let go** *vi* mollare ♦ *vt* mollare; (*allow to go*) lasciare andare.
►**let in** *vt* lasciare entrare; (*visitor etc*) far entrare; **what have you** ~ **yourself in for?** in che guai *or* pasticci sei andato a cacciarti?
►**let off** *vt* (*allow to go*) lasciare andare; (*firework etc*) far partire; (*smell etc*) emettere; (*subj: taxi driver, bus driver*) far scendere; **to** ~ **off steam** (*fig col*) sfogarsi, scaricarsi.
►**let on** *vi* (*col*): **to** ~ **on that** ... lasciar capire che ....
►**let out** *vt* lasciare uscire; (*dress*) allargare; (*scream*) emettere; (*rent out*) affittare, dare in affitto.

▶**let up** vi diminuire.
let-down ['lɛtdaun] n (disappointment)
delusione f.
lethal ['liːθl] adj letale, mortale.
lethargic [lɛ'θɑːdʒɪk] adj letargico(a).
lethargy ['lɛθədʒɪ] n letargia.
letter ['lɛtə*] n lettera; ~**s** npl (LITERATURE)
lettere; **small/capital** ~ lettera
minuscola/maiuscola; ~ **of credit** lettera
di credito; **documentary** ~ **of credit**
lettera di credito documentata.
letter bomb n lettera esplosiva.
letterbox ['lɛtəbɔks] n buca delle lettere.
letterhead ['lɛtəhɛd] n intestazione f.
lettering ['lɛtərɪŋ] n iscrizione f; caratteri
mpl.
letter-opener ['lɛtərəupnə*] n tagliacarte m
inv.
letterpress ['lɛtəprɛs] n (method)
rilievografia.
letter quality n (of printer) qualità di
stampa.
letters patent npl brevetto di invenzione.
lettuce ['lɛtɪs] n lattuga, insalata.
let-up ['lɛtʌp] n (col) interruzione f.
leukaemia, (US) **leukemia** [luː'kiːmɪə] n
leucemia.
level ['lɛvl] adj piatto(a), piano(a);
orizzontale ♦ n livello; (also: **spirit** ~)
livella (a bolla d'aria) ♦ vt livellare,
spianare; (gun) puntare (verso);
(accusation): **to** ~ (**against**) lanciare (a or
contro) ♦ vi (col): **to** ~ **with sb** essere
franco(a) con qn; **to be** ~ **with** essere alla
pari di; **a** ~ **spoonful** (CULIN) un cucchiaio
raso; **to draw** ~ **with** (team) mettersi alla
pari di; (runner, car) affiancarsi a; **A** ~**s**
npl (BRIT) ≈ esami mpl di maturità; **O** ~**s**
npl (BRIT: formerly) diploma di istruzione
secondaria conseguito a 16 anni in
Inghilterra e Galles, ora sostituito dal
GCSE; **on the** ~ piatto(a); (fig) onesto(a).
▶**level off, level out** vi (prices etc)
stabilizzarsi; (ground) diventare
pianeggiante; (aircraft) volare in quota.
level crossing n (BRIT) passaggio a livello.
level-headed [lɛvl'hɛdɪd] adj
equilibrato(a).
levelling, (US) **leveling** ['lɛvlɪŋ] adj
(process, effect) di livellamento.
level playing field n: **to compete on a** ~
(fig) competere ad armi pari.
lever ['liːvə*] n leva ♦ vt: **to** ~ **up/out**
sollevare/estrarre con una leva.
leverage ['liːvərɪdʒ] n: ~ (**on** or **with**)
ascendente m (su).
levity ['lɛvɪtɪ] n leggerezza, frivolità.
levy ['lɛvɪ] n tassa, imposta ♦ vt imporre.

lewd [luːd] adj osceno(a), lascivo(a).
lexicographer [lɛksɪ'kɔgrəfə*] n
lessicografo/a.
lexicography [lɛksɪ'kɔgrəfɪ] n lessicografia.
LGV n abbr (= Large Goods Vehicle)
automezzo pesante.
LI abbr (US) = Long Island.
liabilities [laɪə'bɪlətɪz] npl debiti mpl; (on
balance sheet) passivo.
liability [laɪə'bɪlətɪ] n responsabilità f inv;
(handicap) peso.
liable ['laɪəbl] adj (subject): ~ **to** soggetto(a)
a; passibile di; (responsible): ~ (**for**)
responsabile (di); (likely): ~ **to do**
propenso(a) a fare; **to be** ~ **to a fine**
essere passibile di multa.
liaise [liː'eɪz] vi: **to** ~ (**with**) mantenere i
contatti (con).
liaison [liː'eɪzɔn] n relazione f; (MIL)
collegamento.
liar ['laɪə*] n bugiardo/a.
libel ['laɪbl] n libello, diffamazione f ♦ vt
diffamare.
libellous, (US) **libelous** ['laɪbləs] adj
diffamatorio(a).
liberal ['lɪbərl] adj liberale; (generous): **to be**
~ **with** distribuire liberalmente ♦ n (POL):
L~ liberale m/f.
Liberal Democrat n liberal-
democratico(a).
liberality [lɪbə'rælɪtɪ] n (generosity)
generosità, liberalità.
liberalize ['lɪbərəlaɪz] vt liberalizzare.
liberal-minded [lɪbərl'maɪndɪd] adj
tollerante.
liberate ['lɪbəreɪt] vt liberare.
liberation [lɪbə'reɪʃən] n liberazione f.
liberation theology n teologia della
liberazione.
Liberia [laɪ'bɪərɪə] n Liberia.
Liberian [laɪ'bɪərɪən] adj, n liberiano(a).
liberty ['lɪbətɪ] n libertà f inv; **at** ~ **to do**
libero(a) di fare; **to take the** ~ **of**
prendersi la libertà di, permettersi di.
libido [lɪ'biːdəu] n libido f.
Libra ['liːbrə] n Bilancia; **to be** ~ essere
della Bilancia.
librarian [laɪ'brɛərɪən] n bibliotecario/a.
library ['laɪbrərɪ] n biblioteca.
library book n libro della biblioteca.
libretto [lɪ'brɛtəu] n libretto.
Libya ['lɪbɪə] n Libia.
Libyan ['lɪbɪən] adj, n libico(a).
lice [laɪs] npl of **louse**.
licence, (US) **license** ['laɪsns] n
autorizzazione f, permesso; (COMM)
licenza; (RADIO, TV) canone m,
abbonamento; (also: **driving** ~, (US)

driver's ~) patente *f* di guida; (*excessive freedom*) licenza; **import** ~ licenza di importazione; **produced under** ~ prodotto su licenza.

licence number *n* (*BRIT AUT*) numero di targa.

license ['laɪsns] *n* (*US*) = **licence** ♦ *vt* dare una licenza a; (*car*) pagare la tassa di circolazione *or* il bollo di.

licensed ['laɪsnst] *adj* (*for alcohol*) che ha la licenza di vendere bibite alcoliche.

licensed trade *n* commercio di bevande alcoliche con licenza speciale.

licensee [laɪsən'siː] *n* (*BRIT*: *of pub*) detentore/trice di autorizzazione alla vendita di bevande alcoliche.

license plate *n* (*esp US AUT*) targa (automobilistica).

licentious [laɪ'sɛnʃəs] *adj* licenzioso(a).

lichen ['laɪkən] *n* lichene *m*.

lick [lɪk] *vt* leccare; (*col*: *defeat*) suonarle a, stracciare ♦ *n* leccata; **a** ~ **of paint** una passata di vernice.

licorice ['lɪkərɪs] *n* = **liquorice**.

lid [lɪd] *n* coperchio; **to take the** ~ **off sth** (*fig*) smascherare qc.

lido ['laɪdəu] *n* piscina all'aperto; (*part of the beach*) lido, stabilimento balneare.

lie [laɪ] *n* bugia, menzogna ♦ *vi* mentire, dire bugie; (*pt* **lay**, *pp* **lain** [leɪ, leɪn]) (*rest*) giacere, star disteso(a); (*in grave*) giacere, riposare; (*of object*: *be situated*) trovarsi, essere; **to tell** ~**s** raccontare *or* dire bugie; **to** ~ **low** (*fig*) latitare.

▶**lie about, lie around** *vi* (*things*) essere in giro; (*person*) bighellonare.

▶**lie back** *vi* stendersi.

▶**lie down** *vi* stendersi, sdraiarsi.

▶**lie up** *vi* (*hide*) nascondersi.

Liechtenstein ['lɪktənstaɪn] *n* Liechtenstein *m*.

lie detector *n* macchina della verità.

lie-down ['laɪdaun] *n* (*BRIT*): **to have a** ~ sdraiarsi, riposarsi.

lie-in ['laɪɪn] *n* (*BRIT*): **to have a** ~ rimanere a letto.

lieu [luː] *n*: **in** ~ **of** invece di, al posto di.

Lieut. *abbr* (= *lieutenant*) Ten.

lieutenant [lɛf'tɛnənt, (*US*) luː'tɛnənt] *n* tenente *m*.

lieutenant-colonel [lɛf'tɛnənt'kəːnl, (*US*) luː'tɛnənt'kəːnl] *n* tenente colonnello.

life [laɪf] *n* (*pl* **lives**) vita ♦ *cpd* di vita; della vita; a vita; **country/city** ~ vita di campagna/di città; **to be sent to prison for** ~ essere condannato all'ergastolo; **true to** ~ fedele alla realtà; **to paint from** ~ dipingere dal vero.

life annuity *n* rendita vitalizia.

life assurance *n* (*BRIT*) = **life insurance**.

lifebelt ['laɪfbɛlt] *n* (*BRIT*) salvagente *m*.

lifeblood ['laɪfblʌd] *n* (*fig*) linfa vitale.

lifeboat ['laɪfbəut] *n* scialuppa di salvataggio.

life expectancy *n* durata media della vita.

lifeguard ['laɪfgaːd] *n* bagnino.

life imprisonment *n* ergastolo.

life insurance *n* assicurazione *f* sulla vita.

life jacket *n* giubbotto di salvataggio.

lifeless ['laɪflɪs] *adj* senza vita.

lifelike ['laɪflaɪk] *adj* che sembra vero(a); rassomigliante.

lifeline ['laɪflaɪn] *n* cavo di salvataggio.

lifelong ['laɪflɔŋ] *adj* per tutta la vita.

life preserver *n* (*US*) salvagente *m*; giubbotto di salvataggio; (*BRIT*) sfollagente *m inv*.

lifer ['laɪfə*] *n* (*col*) ergastolano/a.

life-raft ['laɪfrɑːft] *n* zattera di salvataggio.

life-saver ['laɪfseɪvə*] *n* bagnino.

life sentence *n* (condanna all')ergastolo.

life-sized ['laɪfsaɪzd] *adj* a grandezza naturale.

life span *n* (durata della) vita.

life style *n* stile *m* di vita.

life support system *n* (*MED*) respiratore *m* automatico.

lifetime ['laɪftaɪm] *n*: **in his** ~ durante la sua vita; **in a** ~ nell'arco della vita; **in tutta la vita**; **the chance of a** ~ un'occasione unica.

lift [lɪft] *vt* sollevare, levare; (*steal*) prendere, rubare ♦ *vi* (*fog*) alzarsi ♦ *n* (*BRIT*: *elevator*) ascensore *m*; **to give sb a** ~ (*BRIT*) dare un passaggio a qn.

▶**lift off** *vt* togliere ♦ *vi* (*rocket*) partire; (*helicopter*) decollare.

▶**lift out** *vt* tirar fuori; (*troops, evacuees etc*) far evacuare per mezzo di elicotteri (*or* aerei).

▶**lift up** *vt* sollevare, alzare.

lift-off ['lɪftɔf] *n* decollo.

ligament ['lɪgəmənt] *n* legamento.

light [laɪt] *n* luce, lume *m*; (*daylight*) luce, giorno; (*lamp*) lampada; (*AUT*: *rear* ~) luce di posizione; (: *headlamp*) fanale *m*; (*for cigarette etc*): **have you got a** ~? ha da accendere? ♦ *vt* (*pt, pp* **lighted** *or* **lit** [lɪt]) (*candle, cigarette, fire*) accendere; (*room*) illuminare ♦ *adj* (*room, colour*) chiaro(a); (*not heavy, also fig*) leggero(a) ♦ *adv* (*travel*) con poco bagaglio; ~**s** *npl* (*AUT*: *traffic* ~**s**) semaforo; **in the** ~ **of** alla luce di; **to turn the** ~ **on/off** accendere/spegnere la luce; **to come to** ~ venire in luce; **to cast** *or* **shed** *or* **throw** ~ **on**

gettare luce su; **to make ~ of sth** (*fig*) prendere alla leggera qc, non dar peso a qc.

►**light up** *vi* illuminarsi ♦ *vt* illuminare.

light bulb *n* lampadina.

lighten ['laitn] *vi* schiarirsi ♦ *vt* (*give light to*) illuminare; (*make lighter*) schiarire; (*make less heavy*) alleggerire.

lighter ['laitə*] *n* (*also:* **cigarette ~**) accendino; (*boat*) chiatta.

light-fingered [lait'fiŋgəd] *adj* lesto(a) di mano.

light-headed ['lait'hɛdid] *adj* stordito(a).

light-hearted ['lait'hɑːtid] *adj* gioioso(a), gaio(a).

lighthouse ['laithaus] *n* faro.

lighting ['laitiŋ] *n* illuminazione *f*.

lighting-up time ['laitiŋʌp-] *n* (*BRIT*) *orario per l'accensione delle luci.*

lightly ['laitli] *adv* leggermente; **to get off ~** cavarsela a buon mercato.

light meter *n* (*PHOT*) esposimetro.

lightness ['laitnis] *n* chiarezza; (*in weight*) leggerezza.

lightning ['laitniŋ] *n* lampo, fulmine *m*; **a flash of ~** un lampo, un fulmine.

lightning conductor, (US) lightning rod *n* parafulmine *m*.

lightning strike *n* (*BRIT*) sciopero *m* lampo *inv*.

light pen *n* penna luminosa.

lightship ['laitʃip] *n* battello *m* faro *inv*.

lightweight ['laitweit] *adj* (*suit*) leggero(a); (*boxer*) peso leggero *inv*.

light year ['laitjiə*] *n* anno *m* luce *inv*.

Ligurian [li'gjuəriən] *adj*, *n* ligure (*m/f*).

like [laik] *vt* (*person*) volere bene a; (*activity, object, food*): **I ~ swimming/that book/chocolate** mi piace nuotare/quel libro/il cioccolato ♦ *prep* come ♦ *adj* simile, uguale ♦ *n*: **the ~** uno(a) uguale; **I would ~, I'd ~** mi piacerebbe, vorrei; **would you ~ a coffee?** gradirebbe un caffè?; **if you ~** se vuoi; **to be/look ~ sb/sth** somigliare a qn/qc; **what's he ~?** che tipo è?, com'è?; **what's the weather ~?** che tempo fa?; **that's just ~ him** è proprio da lui; **something ~ that** qualcosa del genere; **I feel ~ a drink** avrei voglia di bere qualcosa; **there's nothing ~ …** non c'è niente di meglio di *or* niente come …; **his ~s and dislikes** i suoi gusti.

likeable ['laikəbl] *adj* simpatico(a).

likelihood ['laiklihud] *n* probabilità; **in all ~** con ogni probabilità, molto probabilmente.

likely ['laikli] *adj* probabile; plausibile; **he's ~ to leave** probabilmente partirà, è

probabile che parta; **not ~!** (*col*) neanche per sogno!

like-minded ['laik'maindid] *adj* che pensa allo stesso modo.

liken ['laikən] *vt*: **to ~ sth to** paragonare qc a.

likeness ['laiknis] *n* (*similarity*) somiglianza.

likewise ['laikwaiz] *adv* similmente, nello stesso modo.

liking ['laikiŋ] *n*: **~ (for)** simpatia (per); debole *m* (per); **to be to sb's ~** essere di gusto *or* gradimento di qn; **to take a ~ to sb** prendere qn in simpatia.

lilac ['lailək] *n* lilla *m inv* ♦ *adj* lilla *inv*.

Lilo ® ['lailəu] *n* materasso gonfiabile.

lilt [lilt] *n* cadenza.

lilting ['liltiŋ] *adj* melodioso(a).

lily ['lili] *n* giglio; **~ of the valley** mughetto.

Lima ['liːmə] *n* Lima.

limb [lim] *n* membro; **to be out on a ~** (*fig*) sentirsi spaesato *or* tagliato fuori.

limber ['limbə*]: **to ~ up** *vi* riscaldarsi i muscoli.

limbo ['limbəu] *n*: **to be in ~** (*fig*) essere lasciato(a) nel dimenticatoio.

lime [laim] *n* (*tree*) tiglio; (*fruit*) limetta; (*GEO*) calce *f*.

lime juice *n* succo di limetta.

limelight ['laimlait] *n*: **in the ~** (*fig*) alla ribalta, in vista.

limerick ['limərik] *n* poesiola umoristica di cinque versi.

limestone ['laimstəun] *n* pietra calcarea; (*GEO*) calcare *m*.

limit ['limit] *n* limite *m* ♦ *vt* limitare; **weight/speed ~** limite di peso/di velocità; **within ~s** entro certi limiti.

limitation [limi'teiʃən] *n* limitazione *f*, limite *m*.

limited ['limitid] *adj* limitato(a), ristretto(a); **~ edition** edizione *f* a bassa tiratura.

limited (liability) company (Ltd) *n* (*BRIT*) ≈ società *f inv* a responsabilità limitata (S.R.L.).

limitless ['limitlis] *adj* illimitato(a).

limousine ['liməziːn] *n* limousine *f inv*.

limp [limp] *n*: **to have a ~** zoppicare ♦ *vi* zoppicare ♦ *adj* floscio(a), flaccido(a).

limpet ['limpit] *n* patella.

limpid ['limpid] *adj* (*poet*) limpido(a).

linchpin ['lintʃpin] *n* acciarino, bietta; (*fig*) perno.

Lincs *abbr* (*BRIT*) = Lincolnshire.

line [lain] *n* (*gen, COMM*) linea; (*rope*) corda; (*wire*) filo; (*of poem*) verso; (*row, series*) fila, riga; coda ♦ *vt* (*clothes*): **to ~ (with)** foderare (di); (*box*): **to ~ (with)** rivestire *or* foderare (di); (*subj: trees, crowd*) fiancheggiare; **to cut in** ~ (*US*) passare avanti; **in his** ~ **of business** nel suo ramo (di affari); **on the right** ~**s** sulla buona strada; **a new** ~ **in cosmetics** una nuova linea di cosmetici; **hold the** ~ **please** (*BRIT TEL*) resti in linea per cortesia; **to be in** ~ **for sth** (*fig*) essere in lista per qc; **in** ~ **with** d'accordo con, in linea con; **to bring sth into** ~ **with sth** mettere qc al passo con qc; **to draw the** ~ **at (doing) sth** (*fig*) rifiutarsi di fare qc; **to take the** ~ **that** ... essere del parere che ....

▶**line up** *vi* allinearsi, mettersi in fila ♦ *vt* mettere in fila; **to have sth** ~**d up** avere qc in programma; **to have sb** ~**d up** avere qn in mente.

linear ['lɪnɪə*] *adj* lineare.

lined [laɪnd] *adj* (*paper*) a righe, rigato(a); (*face*) rugoso(a); (*clothes*) foderato(a).

line feed *n* (*COMPUT*) avanzamento di una interlinea.

linen ['lɪnɪn] *n* biancheria, panni *mpl*; (*cloth*) tela di lino.

line printer *n* stampante *f* parallela.

liner ['laɪnə*] *n* nave *f* di linea; **dustbin** ~ sacchetto per la pattumiera.

linesman ['laɪnzmən] *n* guardalinee *m inv*, segnalinee *m inv*.

line-up ['laɪnʌp] *n* allineamento, fila; (*also*: **police** ~) confronto all'americana; (*SPORT*) formazione *f* di gioco.

linger ['lɪŋgə*] *vi* attardarsi; indugiare; (*smell, tradition*) persistere.

lingerie ['lænʒəriː] *n* biancheria intima (femminile).

lingering ['lɪŋgərɪŋ] *adj* lungo(a); persistente; (*death*) lento(a).

lingo, ~es ['lɪŋgəu] *n* (*pej*) gergo.

linguist ['lɪŋgwɪst] *n* linguista *m/f*; poliglotta *m/f*.

linguistic [lɪŋ'gwɪstɪk] *adj* linguistico(a).

linguistics [lɪŋ'gwɪstɪks] *n* linguistica.

lining ['laɪnɪŋ] *n* fodera; (*TECH*) rivestimento (interno); (*of brake*) guarnizione *f*.

link [lɪŋk] *n* (*of a chain*) anello; (*connection*) legame *m*, collegamento ♦ *vt* collegare, unire, congiungere; **rail** ~ collegamento ferroviario; *see also* **links**.

▶**link up** *vt* collegare, unire ♦ *vi* riunirsi; associarsi.

links [lɪŋks] *npl* pista *or* terreno da golf.

link-up ['lɪŋkʌp] *n* legame *m*; (*of roads*) nodo; (*of spaceships*) aggancio; (*RADIO, TV*) collegamento.

linoleum [lɪ'nəuliəm] *n* linoleum *m inv*.

linseed oil ['lɪnsiːd-] *n* olio di semi di lino.

lint [lɪnt] *n* garza.

lintel ['lɪntl] *n* architrave *f*.

lion ['laɪən] *n* leone *m*.

lion cub *n* leoncino.

lioness ['laɪənɪs] *n* leonessa.

lip [lɪp] *n* labbro; (*of cup etc*) orlo; (*insolence*) sfacciataggine *f*.

liposuction ['lɪpəusʌkʃən] *n* liposuzione *f*.

lipread ['lɪpriːd] *vi* leggere sulle labbra.

lip salve *n* burro di cacao.

lip service *n*: **to pay** ~ **to sth** essere favorevole a qc solo a parole.

lipstick ['lɪpstɪk] *n* rossetto.

liquefy ['lɪkwɪfaɪ] *vt* liquefare ♦ *vi* liquefarsi.

liqueur [lɪ'kjuə*] *n* liquore *m*.

liquid ['lɪkwɪd] *n* liquido ♦ *adj* liquido(a).

liquid assets *npl* attività *fpl* liquide, crediti *mpl* liquidi.

liquidate ['lɪkwɪdeɪt] *vt* liquidare.

liquidation [lɪkwɪ'deɪʃən] *n* liquidazione *f*; **to go into** ~ andare in liquidazione.

liquidator ['lɪkwɪdeɪtə*] *n* liquidatore *m*.

liquid crystal display (LCD) *n* visualizzazione *f* a cristalli liquidi.

liquidity [lɪ'kwɪdɪtɪ] *n* (*COMM*) liquidità.

liquidize ['lɪkwɪdaɪz] *vt* (*BRIT CULIN*) passare al frullatore.

liquidizer ['lɪkwɪdaɪzə*] *n* (*BRIT CULIN*) frullatore *m* (a brocca).

liquor ['lɪkə*] *n* alcool *m*.

liquorice ['lɪkərɪs] *n* liquirizia.

Lisbon ['lɪzbən] *n* Lisbona.

lisp [lɪsp] *n* difetto nel pronunciare le sibilanti.

lissom ['lɪsəm] *adj* leggiadro(a).

list [lɪst] *n* lista, elenco; (*of ship*) sbandamento ♦ *vt* (*write down*) mettere in lista; fare una lista di; (*enumerate*) elencare; (*COMPUT*) stampare (un prospetto di) ♦ *vi* (*ship*) sbandare; **shopping** ~ lista *or* nota della spesa.

listed building ['lɪstəd-] *n* (*ARCHIT*) edificio sotto la protezione delle Belle Arti.

listed company *n* società quotata in Borsa.

listen ['lɪsn] *vi* ascoltare; **to** ~ **to** ascoltare.

listener ['lɪsnə*] *n* ascoltatore/trice.

listeria [lɪs'tɪərɪə] *n* listeria.

listing ['lɪstɪŋ] *n* (*COMPUT*) lista stampata.

listless ['lɪstlɪs] *adj* svogliato(a); apatico(a).

listlessly ['lɪstlɪslɪ] *adv* svogliatamente; apaticamente.

list price *n* prezzo di listino.

lit [lɪt] *pt, pp of* **light**.

litany ['lɪtənɪ] *n* litania.

liter ['liːtə*] *n* (*US*) = **litre**.

literacy ['lɪtərəsɪ] *n* il sapere leggere e

scrivere.

literacy campaign n lotta contro l'analfabetismo.

literal ['lɪtərl] adj letterale.

literally ['lɪtərəlɪ] adv alla lettera, letteralmente.

literary ['lɪtərərɪ] adj letterario(a).

literate ['lɪtərɪt] adj che sa leggere e scrivere.

literature ['lɪtərɪtʃə*] n letteratura; (brochures etc) materiale m.

lithe [laɪð] adj agile, snello(a).

lithography [lɪ'θɔɡrəfɪ] n litografia.

Lithuania [lɪθju'eɪnɪə] n Lituania.

Lithuanian [lɪθju'eɪnɪən] adj lituano(a) ♦ n lituano/a; (LING) lituano.

litigate ['lɪtɪɡeɪt] vt muovere causa a ♦ vi litigare.

litigation [lɪtɪ'ɡeɪʃən] n causa.

litmus ['lɪtməs] n: ~ **paper** cartina di tornasole.

litre, (US) **liter** ['li:tə*] n litro.

litter ['lɪtə*] n (rubbish) rifiuti mpl; (young animals) figliata ♦ vt sparpagliare; lasciare rifiuti in; ~-**ed with** coperto(a) di.

litter bin n (BRIT) cestino per rifiuti.

litter lout, (US) **litterbug** ['lɪtəbʌɡ] n persona che butta per terra le cartacce o i rifiuti.

little ['lɪtl] adj (small) piccolo(a); (not much) poco(a) ♦ adv poco; **a** ~ un po' (di); **a** ~ **milk** un po' di latte; **with** ~ **difficulty** senza fatica or difficoltà; ~ **by** ~ a poco a poco; **as** ~ **as possible** il meno possibile; **for a** ~ **while** per un po'; **to make** ~ **of** dare poca importanza a; ~ **finger** mignolo.

little-known ['lɪtl'nəun] adj poco noto(a).

liturgy ['lɪtədʒɪ] n liturgia.

live vi [lɪv] vivere; (reside) vivere, abitare ♦ adj [laɪv] (animal) vivo(a); (issue) scottante, d'attualità; (wire) sotto tensione; (broadcast) diretto(a); (ammunition: not blank) carico(a); (unexploded) inesploso(a); **to** ~ **in London** abitare a Londra; **to** ~ **together** vivere insieme, convivere.

▶**live down** vt far dimenticare (alla gente).

▶**live in** vi essere interno(a); avere vitto e alloggio.

▶**live off** vi (land, fish etc) vivere di; (pej: parents etc) vivere alle spalle or a spese di.

▶**live on** vt fus (food) vivere di ♦ vi sopravvivere, continuare a vivere; **to** ~ **on £50 a week** vivere con 50 sterline la settimana.

▶**live out** vi (BRIT: students) essere esterno(a) ♦ vt: **to** ~ **out one's days** or **life** trascorrere gli ultimi anni.

▶**live up** vt: **to** ~ **it up** (col) fare la bella vita.

▶**live up to** vt fus tener fede a, non venir meno a.

live-in ['lɪvɪn] adj (col: partner) convivente; (servant) che vive in casa; **he has a** ~ **girlfriend** la sua ragazza vive con lui.

livelihood ['laɪvlɪhud] n mezzi mpl di sostentamento.

liveliness ['laɪvlɪnəs] n vivacità.

lively ['laɪvlɪ] adj vivace, vivo(a).

liven up ['laɪvn-] vt (room etc) ravvivare; (discussion, evening) animare.

liver ['lɪvə*] n fegato.

liverish ['lɪvərɪʃ] adj che soffre di mal di fegato; (fig) scontroso(a).

Liverpudlian [lɪvə'pʌdlɪən] adj di Liverpool ♦ n abitante m/f di Liverpool; originario/a di Liverpool.

livery ['lɪvərɪ] n livrea.

lives [laɪvz] npl of **life**.

livestock ['laɪvstɔk] n bestiame m.

live wire [laɪv-] n (col: fig): **to be a** ~ essere pieno(a) di vitalità.

livid ['lɪvɪd] adj livido(a); (furious) livido(a) di rabbia, furibondo(a).

living ['lɪvɪŋ] adj vivo(a), vivente ♦ n: **to earn** or **make a** ~ guadagnarsi la vita; **cost of** ~ costo della vita, carovita m; **within** ~ **memory** a memoria d'uomo.

living conditions npl condizioni fpl di vita.

living expenses npl spese fpl di mantenimento.

living room n soggiorno.

living standards npl tenore m di vita.

living wage n salario sufficiente per vivere.

lizard ['lɪzəd] n lucertola.

llama ['lɑːmə] n lama m inv.

LLB n abbr (= Bachelor of Laws) ≈ laurea in legge.

LLD n abbr (= Doctor of Laws) titolo di studio.

LMT abbr (US: = Local Mean Time) tempo medio locale.

load [ləud] n (weight) peso; (ELEC, TECH, thing carried) carico ♦ vt: **to** ~ **(with)** (lorry, ship) caricare (di); (gun, camera) caricare (con); **a** ~ **of,** ~**s of** (fig) un sacco di; **to** ~ **a program** (COMPUT) caricare un programma.

loaded ['ləudɪd] adj (dice) falsato(a); (question, word) capzioso(a); (col: rich) pieno(a) di soldi.

loading bay ['ləudɪŋ-] n piazzola di carico.

loaf [ləuf] n (pl **loaves**) pane m, pagnotta ♦ vi (also: ~ **about**, ~ **around**) bighellonare.
loam [ləum] n terra di marna.
loan [ləun] n prestito ♦ vt dare in prestito; **on** ~ in prestito.
loan account n conto dei prestiti.
loan capital n capitale m di prestito.
loan shark n (col: pej) strozzino(a).
loath [ləuθ] adj: **to be** ~ **to do** essere restio(a) a fare.
loathe [ləuð] vt detestare, aborrire.
loathing ['ləuðɪŋ] n aborrimento, disgusto.
loathsome ['ləuðsəm] adj (gen) ripugnante; (person) detestabile, odioso(a).
loaves [ləuvz] npl of **loaf**.
lob [lɔb] vt (ball) lanciare.
lobby ['lɔbɪ] n atrio, vestibolo; (POL: pressure group) gruppo di pressione ♦ vt fare pressione su.
lobbyist ['lɔbɪɪst] n appartenente m/f ad un gruppo di pressione.
lobe [ləub] n lobo.
lobster ['lɔbstə*] n aragosta.
lobster pot n nassa per aragoste.
local ['ləukl] adj locale ♦ n (BRIT: pub) ≈ bar m inv all'angolo; **the** ~**s** npl la gente della zona.
local anaesthetic n anestesia locale.
local authority n autorità locale.
local call n (TEL) telefonata urbana.
local government n amministrazione f locale.
locality [ləu'kælɪtɪ] n località f inv; (position) posto, luogo.
localize ['ləukəlaɪz] vt localizzare.
locally ['ləukəlɪ] adv da queste parti; nel vicinato.
locate [ləu'keɪt] vt (find) trovare; (situate) collocare.
location [ləu'keɪʃən] n posizione f; **on** ~ (CINE) all'esterno.
loch [lɔx] n lago.
lock [lɔk] n (of door, box) serratura; (of canal) chiusa; (of hair) ciocca, riccio ♦ vt (with key) chiudere a chiave; (immobilize) bloccare ♦ vi (door etc) chiudersi; (wheels) bloccarsi, incepparsi; ~ **stock and barrel** (fig) in blocco; **on full** ~ (BRIT AUT) a tutto sterzo.
►**lock away** vt (valuables) tenere (rinchiuso(a)) al sicuro; (criminal) metter dentro.
►**lock out** vt chiudere fuori; **to** ~ **workers out** fare una serrata.
►**lock up** vi chiudere tutto (a chiave).
locker ['lɔkə*] n armadietto.
locket ['lɔkɪt] n medaglione m.
lockjaw ['lɔkdʒɔː] n tetano.

lockout ['lɔkaut] n (INDUSTRY) serrata.
locksmith ['lɔksmɪθ] n magnano.
lock-up ['lɔkʌp] n (prison) prigione f; (cell) guardina; (also: ~ **garage**) box m inv.
locomotive [ləukə'məutɪv] n locomotiva.
locum ['ləukəm] n (MED) medico sostituto.
locust ['ləukəst] n locusta.
lodge [lɔdʒ] n casetta, portineria; (FREEMASONRY) loggia ♦ vi (person): **to** ~ (**with**) essere a pensione (presso or da) ♦ vt (appeal etc) presentare, fare; **to** ~ **a complaint** presentare un reclamo; **to** ~ (**itself**) **in/between** piantarsi dentro/fra.
lodger ['lɔdʒə*] n affittuario/a; (with room and meals) pensionante m/f.
lodging ['lɔdʒɪŋ] n alloggio; see also **board**; **lodgings**.
lodging house n (BRIT) casa con camere in affitto.
lodgings ['lɔdʒɪŋz] npl camera d'affitto; camera ammobiliata.
loft [lɔft] n soffitta; (AGR) granaio; (US) appartamento ricavato da solaio (or granaio etc).
lofty ['lɔftɪ] adj alto(a); (haughty) altezzoso(a); (sentiments, aims) nobile.
log [lɔg] n (of wood) ceppo; (book) = **logbook** ♦ n abbr = **logarithm** ♦ vt registrare.
►**log in**, **log on** vi (COMPUT) aprire una sessione (con codice di riconoscimento).
►**log off**, **log out** vi (COMPUT) terminare una sessione.
logarithm ['lɔgərɪðm] n logaritmo.
logbook ['lɔgbuk] n (NAUT, AVIAT) diario di bordo; (AUT) libretto di circolazione; (of lorry driver) registro di viaggio; (of events, movement of goods etc) registro.
log cabin n capanna di tronchi.
log fire n fuoco di legna.
logger ['lɔgə*] n boscaiolo, taglialegna m inv.
loggerheads ['lɔgəhɛdz] npl: **at** ~ (**with**) ai ferri corti (con).
logic ['lɔdʒɪk] n logica.
logical ['lɔdʒɪkəl] adj logico(a).
logically ['lɔdʒɪkəlɪ] adv logicamente.
logistics [lɔ'dʒɪstɪks] n logistica.
logjam ['lɔgdʒæm] n: **to break the** ~ superare l'impasse.
logo ['ləugəu] n logo m inv.
loin [lɔɪn] n (CULIN) lombata; ~**s** npl reni fpl.
loin cloth n perizoma m.
loiter ['lɔɪtə*] vi attardarsi; **to** ~ (**about**) indugiare, bighellonare.
loll [lɔl] vi (also: ~ **about**) essere stravaccato(a).
lollipop ['lɔlɪpɔp] n lecca lecca m inv.

lollipop man, lollipop lady n (BRIT) see boxed note.

LOLLIPOP MAN/LADY

In Gran Bretagna il **lollipop man** e la **lollipop lady** sono persone incaricate di regolare il traffico in prossimità delle scuole e di aiutare i bambini ad attraversare la strada; usano una paletta la cui forma ricorda quella di un lecca lecca, in inglese, appunto, "lollipop".

---

lollop ['lɔləp] vi (BRIT) camminare (or correre) goffamente.

lolly ['lɔlı] (col) n lecca lecca m inv; (also: **ice ~**) ghiacciolo; (money) grana.

Lombardy ['lɔmbədɪ] n Lombardia.

London ['lʌndən] n Londra.

Londoner ['lʌndənə*] n londinese m/f.

lone [ləun] adj solitario(a).

loneliness ['ləunlɪnɪs] n solitudine.

lonely ['ləunlɪ] adj solitario(a), (place) isolato(a); **to feel ~** sentirsi solo(a).

lonely hearts adj: **~ ads, ~ column** messaggi mpl personali.

lone parent n (unmarried: mother) ragazza madre; (: father) ragazzo padre; (divorced) genitore m divorziato(a); (widowed) genitore rimasto vedovo.

loner ['ləunə*] n solitario/a.

lonesome ['ləunsəm] adj solo(a).

long [lɔŋ] adj lungo(a) ♦ adv a lungo, per molto tempo ♦ n: **the ~ and the short of it is that ...** (fig) a farla breve ... ♦ vi: **to ~ for sth/to do** desiderare qc/di fare; non veder l'ora di aver qc/di fare; **he had ~ understood that ...** aveva capito da molto tempo che ...; **how ~ is this river/course?** quanto è lungo questo fiume/corso?; **6 metres ~** lungo 6 metri; **6 months ~** che dura 6 mesi, di 6 mesi; **all night ~** tutta la notte; **he no ~er comes** non viene più; **~ before** molto tempo prima; **before ~** (+ future) presto, fra poco; (+ past) poco tempo dopo; **~ ago** molto tempo fa; **don't be ~!** faccia presto!; **I shan't be ~** non ne avrò per molto; **at ~ last** finalmente; **in the ~ run** alla fin fine; **so** or **as ~ as** sempre che + sub.

long-distance [lɔŋ'dɪstəns] adj (race) di fondo; (call) interurbano(a).

long-haired ['lɔŋ'hɛəd] adj (person) dai capelli lunghi; (animal) dal pelo lungo.

longhand ['lɔŋhænd] n scrittura normale.

longing ['lɔŋɪŋ] n desiderio, voglia, brama ♦ adj di desiderio; pieno(a) di nostalgia.

longingly ['lɔŋɪŋlɪ] adv con desiderio.

longitude ['lɔŋgɪtjuːd] n longitudine f.

long johns [-dʒɔnz] npl mutande fpl lunghe.

long jump n salto in lungo.

long-lost ['lɔŋlɔst] adj perduto(a) da tempo.

long-playing ['lɔŋpleɪɪŋ] adj: **~ record (LP)** (disco) 33 giri m inv.

long-range [lɔŋ'reɪndʒ] adj a lunga portata; (weather forecast) a lungo termine.

longshoreman ['lɔŋʃɔːmən] n (US) scaricatore m (di porto), portuale m.

long-sighted [lɔŋ'saɪtɪd] adj (BRIT) presbite; (fig) lungimirante.

long-standing ['lɔŋstændɪŋ] adj di vecchia data.

long-suffering [lɔŋ'sʌfərɪŋ] adj estremamente paziente; infinitamente tollerante.

long-term ['lɔŋtəːm] adj a lungo termine.

long wave n (RADIO) onde fpl lunghe.

long-winded [lɔŋ'wɪndɪd] adj prolisso(a), interminabile.

loo [luː] n (BRIT col) W.C. m inv, cesso.

loofah ['luːfə] n luffa.

look [luk] vi guardare; (seem) sembrare, parere; (building etc): **to ~ south/on to the sea** dare a sud/sul mare ♦ n sguardo; (appearance) aspetto, aria; **~s** npl aspetto; bellezza; **to ~ like** assomigliare a; **to ~ ahead** guardare avanti; **it ~s about 4 metres long** sarà lungo un 4 metri; **it ~s all right to me** a me pare che vada bene; **to have a ~ at sth** dare un'occhiata a qc; **to have a ~ for sth** cercare qc.

►**look after** vt fus occuparsi di, prendersi cura di; (keep an eye on) guardare, badare a.

►**look around** vi guardarsi intorno.

►**look at** vt fus guardare.

►**look back** vi: **to ~ back at sth/sb** voltarsi a guardare qc/qn; **to ~ back on** (event, period) ripensare a.

►**look down on** vt fus (fig) guardare dall'alto, disprezzare.

►**look for** vt fus cercare.

►**look forward to** vt fus non veder l'ora di; **I'm not ~ing forward to it** non ne ho nessuna voglia; **~ing forward to hearing from you** (in letter) aspettando tue notizie.

►**look in** vi: **to ~ in on sb** (visit) fare un salto da qn.

►**look into** vt fus (matter, possibility) esaminare.

►**look on** vi fare da spettatore.

►**look out** vi (beware): **to ~ out (for)** stare in guardia (per).

►**look out for** vt fus cercare; (watch out for): **to ~ out for sb/sth** guardare se arriva qn/qc.

►**look over** vt (essay) dare un'occhiata a,

riguardare; (*town, building*) vedere; (*person*) esaminare.

▶**look round** *vi* (*turn*) girarsi, voltarsi; (*in shops*) dare un'occhiata; **to ~ round for sth** guardarsi intorno cercando qc.

▶**look through** *vt fus* (*papers, book*) scorrere; (*telescope*) guardare attraverso.

▶**look to** *vt fus* stare attento(a) a; (*rely on*) contare su.

▶**look up** *vi* alzare gli occhi; (*improve*) migliorare ♦ *vt* (*word*) cercare; (*friend*) andare a trovare.

▶**look up to** *vt fus* avere rispetto per.

look-out ['lukaut] *n* posto d'osservazione; guardia; **to be on the ~ (for)** stare in guardia (per).

look-up table ['lukʌp-] *n* (*COMPUT*) tabella di consultazione.

LOOM *n abbr* (*US:* = *Loyal Order of Moose*) *organizzazione filantropica.*

loom [luːm] *n* telaio ♦ *vi* sorgere; (*fig*) minacciare.

loony ['luːnɪ] *adj, n* (*col*) pazzo(a).

loop [luːp] *n* cappio; (*COMPUT*) anello.

loophole ['luːphəul] *n* via d'uscita; scappatoia.

loose [luːs] *adj* (*knot*) sciolto(a); (*screw*) allentato(a); (*stone*) cadente; (*clothes*) ampio(a), largo(a); (*animal*) in libertà, scappato(a); (*life, morals*) dissoluto(a); (*discipline*) allentato(a); (*thinking*) poco rigoroso(a), vago(a) ♦ *vt* (*untie*) sciogliere; (*slacken*) allentare; (*free*) liberare; (*BRIT: arrow*) scoccare; ~ **connection** (*ELEC*) filo che fa contatto; **to be at a ~ end** *or* (*US*) **at ~ ends** (*fig*) non saper che fare; **to tie up ~ ends** (*fig*) avere ancora qualcosa da sistemare.

loose change *n* spiccioli *mpl*, moneta.

loose-fitting ['luːsfɪtɪŋ] *adj* ampio(a).

loose-leaf ['luːsliːf] *adj:* ~ **binder** *or* **folder** raccoglitore *m*.

loose-limbed [luːs'lɪmd] *adj* snodato(a), agile.

loosely ['luːslɪ] *adv* lentamente, approssimativamente.

loosely-knit ['luːslɪ'nɪt] *adj* non rigidamente strutturato(a).

loosen ['luːsn] *vt* sciogliere.

▶**loosen up** *vi* (*before game*) sciogliere i muscoli, scaldarsi; (*col: relax*) rilassarsi.

loot [luːt] *n* bottino ♦ *vt* saccheggiare.

looter ['luːtə*] *n* saccheggiatore/trice.

looting ['luːtɪŋ] *n* saccheggio.

lop [lɒp] *vt* (*also:* ~ **off**) tagliare via, recidere.

lop-sided ['lɒp'saɪdɪd] *adj* non

equilibrato(a), asimmetrico(a).

lord [lɔːd] *n* signore *m*; **L~ Smith** lord Smith; **the L~** (*REL*) il Signore; **the (House of) L~s** (*BRIT*) la Camera dei Lord.

lordly ['lɔːdlɪ] *adj* nobile, maestoso(a); (*arrogant*) altero(a).

lordship ['lɔːdʃɪp] *n* (*BRIT*): **your L~** Sua Eccellenza.

lore [lɔː*] *n* tradizioni *fpl*.

lorry ['lɒrɪ] *n* (*BRIT*) camion *m inv*.

lorry driver *n* (*BRIT*) camionista *m*.

lose, *pt, pp* **lost** [luːz, lɒst] *vt* perdere; (*pursuers*) distanziare ♦ *vi* perdere; **to ~ (time)** (*clock*) ritardare; **to ~ no time (in doing sth)** non perdere tempo (a fare qc); **to get lost** (*person*) perdersi, smarrirsi; (*object*) andare perso *or* perduto.

loser ['luːzə*] *n* perdente *m/f*; **to be a good/ bad** ~ saper/non saper perdere.

loss [lɒs] *n* perdita; **to cut one's ~es** rimetterci il meno possibile; **to make a ~** subire una perdita; **to sell sth at a ~** vendere qc in perdita; **to be at a ~** essere perplesso(a); **to be at a ~ to explain sth** non saper come fare a spiegare qc.

loss adjuster *n* (*INSURANCE*) responsabile *m/f* della valutazione dei danni.

loss leader *n* (*COMM*) articolo a prezzo ridottissimo per attirare la clientela.

lost [lɒst] *pt, pp of* **lose** ♦ *adj* perduto(a); ~ **in thought** immerso *or* perso nei propri pensieri; ~ **and found property** *n* (*US*) oggetti *mpl* smarriti; ~ **and found** *n* (*US*) ufficio oggetti smarriti.

lost property *n* (*BRIT*) oggetti *mpl* smarriti; ~ **office** *or* **department** ufficio oggetti smarriti.

lot [lɒt] *n* (*at auctions*) lotto; (*destiny*) destino, sorte *f*; **the** ~ tutto(a) quanto(a); tutti(e) quanti(e); **a** ~ molto; **a** ~ **of** una gran quantità di, un sacco di; **~s of** molto(a); **to draw ~s (for sth)** tirare a sorte (per qc).

lotion ['ləuʃən] *n* lozione *f*.

lottery ['lɒtərɪ] *n* lotteria.

loud [laud] *adj* forte, alto(a); (*gaudy*) vistoso(a), sgargiante ♦ *adv* (*speak etc*) forte; **out** ~ ad alta voce.

loudhailer [laud'heɪlə*] *n* (*BRIT*) portavoce *m inv*.

loudly ['laudlɪ] *adv* fortemente, ad alta voce.

loudspeaker [laud'spiːkə*] *n* altoparlante *m*.

lounge [laundʒ] *n* salotto, soggiorno; (*of hotel*) salone *m*; (*of airport*) sala d'attesa ♦ *vi* oziare; starsene colle mani in mano.

lounge bar *n* bar *m inv* con servizio a

tavolino.
lounge suit *n* (*BRIT*) completo da uomo.
louse [laus] *n* (*pl* **lice**) pidocchio.
▶**louse up** *vt* (*col*) rovinare.
lousy ['lauzɪ] *adj* (*fig*) orrendo(a), schifoso(a).
lout [laut] *n* zoticone *m*.
louvre, (*US*) **louver** ['luːvə*] *adj* (*door, window*) con apertura a gelosia.
lovable ['lʌvəbl] *adj* simpatico(a), carino(a); amabile.
love [lʌv] *n* amore *m* ♦ *vt* amare; voler bene a; **to ~ to do: I ~ to do** mi piace fare; **I'd ~ to come** mi piacerebbe molto venire; **to be in ~ with** essere innamorato(a) di; **to fall in ~ with** innamorarsi di; **to make ~** fare l'amore; **~ at first sight** amore a prima vista, colpo di fulmine; **to send one's ~ to sb** mandare i propri saluti a qn; **~ from Anne, ~,** Anne con affetto, Anne; "**15 ~**" (*TENNIS*) "15 a zero".
love affair *n* relazione *f*.
love child *n* figlio/a dell'amore.
loved ones [lʌvd-] *npl*: **my ~** i miei cari.
love-hate relationship ['lʌv'heɪt-] *n* rapporto amore-odio *inv*.
love letter *n* lettera d'amore.
love life *n* vita sentimentale.
lovely ['lʌvlɪ] *adj* bello(a); (*delicious: smell, meal*) buono(a); **we had a ~ time** ci siamo divertiti molto.
lover ['lʌvə*] *n* amante *m/f*; (*amateur*): **a ~ of** un(un')amante di; un(un')appassionato(a) di.
lovesick ['lʌvsɪk] *adj* malato(a) d'amore.
lovesong ['lʌvsɒŋ] *n* canzone *f* d'amore.
loving ['lʌvɪŋ] *adj* affettuoso(a), amoroso(a), tenero(a).
low [ləu] *adj* basso(a) ♦ *adv* in basso ♦ *n* (*METEOR*) depressione *f* ♦ *vi* (*cow*) muggire; **to feel ~** sentirsi giù; **to reach a new** *or* **an all-time ~** toccare il livello più basso *or* il minimo; **to turn (down) ~** *vt* abbassare.
low-alcohol [ləu'ælkəhɒl] *adj* a basso contenuto alcolico.
lowbrow ['ləubrau] *adj* (*person*) senza pretese intellettuali.
low-calorie ['ləu'kælərɪ] *adj* a basso contenuto calorico.
low-cut ['ləukʌt] *adj* (*dress*) scollato(a).
low-down ['ləudaun] *adj* (*mean*) ignobile ♦ *n* (*col*): **he gave me the ~ on it** mi ha messo al corrente dei fatti.
lower ['ləuə*] *adj, adv comparative of* **low** ♦ *vt* (*gen*) calare; (*reduce: price*) abbassare, ridurre; (*resistance*) indebolire.
lower case *n* minuscolo.

low-fat ['ləu'fæt] *adj* magro(a).
low-key ['ləu'kiː] *adj* moderato(a); (*operation*) condotto(a) con discrezione.
lowland ['ləulənd] *n* bassopiano, pianura.
low-level ['ləulevl] *adj* a basso livello; (*flying*) a bassa quota.
low-loader ['ləuləudə*] *n* camion *m* a pianale basso.
lowly ['ləulɪ] *adj* umile, modesto(a).
low-lying [ləu'laɪɪŋ] *adj* a basso livello.
low-paid [ləu'peɪd] *adj* mal pagato(a).
low-rise ['ləuraɪz] *adj* di altezza contenuta.
low-tech ['ləu'tɛk] *adj* a basso contenuto tecnologico.
loyal ['lɔɪəl] *adj* fedele, leale.
loyalist ['lɔɪəlɪst] *n* lealista *m/f*.
loyalty ['lɔɪəltɪ] *n* fedeltà, lealtà.
loyalty card *n* carta che offre sconti a clienti abituali.
lozenge ['lɒzɪndʒ] *n* (*MED*) pastiglia; (*GEOM*) losanga.
LP *n abbr* (= *long-playing record*) LP *m*.
L-plate *n* = contrassegno P principiante; *see boxed note*.

L-PLATE
Le **L-plate** sono delle tabelle bianche con una L rossa che in Gran Bretagna i guidatori principianti, "*learners*", in possesso di una "*provisional licence*" che corrisponde al nostro foglio rosa, devono applicare davanti e dietro alla loro autovettura finché non ottengono la patente.

LPN *n abbr* (*US*: = *Licensed Practical Nurse*) ≈ infermiera diplomata.
LRAM *n abbr* (*BRIT*: = *Licentiate of the Royal Academy of Music*) specializzazione dopo la laurea.
LSD *n abbr* (= *lysergic acid diethylamide*) L.S.D. *m*; (*BRIT*: = *pounds, shillings and pence*) sistema monetario in vigore in Gran Bretagna fino al 1971.
LSE *n abbr* = *London School of Economics*.
LT *abbr* (*ELEC*: = *low tension*) B.T.
Lt. *abbr* (= *lieutenant*) Ten.
Ltd *abbr* (*COMM*) = **limited**.
lubricant ['luːbrɪkənt] *n* lubrificante *m*.
lubricate ['luːbrɪkeɪt] *vt* lubrificare.
lucid ['luːsɪd] *adj* lucido(a).
lucidity [luː'sɪdɪtɪ] *n* lucidità.
luck [lʌk] *n* fortuna, sorte *f*; **bad ~** sfortuna, mala sorte; **good ~** (buona) fortuna; **to be in ~** essere fortunato(a); **to be out of ~** essere sfortunato(a).
luckily ['lʌkɪlɪ] *adv* fortunatamente, per fortuna.

luckless ['lʌklɪs] *adj* sventurato(a).
lucky ['lʌkɪ] *adj* fortunato(a); (*number etc*) che porta fortuna.
lucrative ['lu:krətɪv] *adj* lucrativo(a), lucroso(a), profittevole.
ludicrous ['lu:dɪkrəs] *adj* ridicolo(a), assurdo(a).
ludo ['lu:dəu] *n* ≈ gioco dell'oca.
lug [lʌg] *vt* trascinare.
luggage ['lʌgɪdʒ] *n* bagagli *mpl*.
luggage rack *n* portabagagli *m inv*.
luggage van, (*US*) **luggage car** *n* (*RAIL*) bagagliaio.
lugubrious [lu'gu:brɪəs] *adj* lugubre.
lukewarm ['lu:kwɔ:m] *adj* tiepido(a).
lull [lʌl] *n* intervallo di calma ♦ *vt* (*child*) cullare; (*person, fear*) acquietare, calmare.
lullaby ['lʌləbaɪ] *n* ninnananna.
lumbago [lʌm'beɪgəu] *n* lombaggine *f*.
lumber ['lʌmbə*] *n* roba vecchia ♦ *vt* (*BRIT col*): **to ~ sb with sth/sb** affibbiare *or* rifilare qc/qn a qn ♦ *vi* (*also:* ~ **about,** ~ **along**) muoversi pesantemente.
lumberjack ['lʌmbədʒæk] *n* boscaiolo.
lumber room *n* (*BRIT*) sgabuzzino.
lumber yard *n* segheria.
luminous ['lu:mɪnəs] *adj* luminoso(a).
lump [lʌmp] *n* pezzo; (*in sauce*) grumo; (*swelling*) gonfiore *m* ♦ *vt* (*also:* ~ **together**) riunire, mettere insieme.
lump sum *n* somma globale.
lumpy ['lʌmpɪ] *adj* (*sauce*) grumoso(a).
lunacy ['lu:nəsɪ] *n* demenza, follia, pazzia.
lunar ['lu:nə*] *adj* lunare.
lunatic ['lu:nətɪk] *adj, n* pazzo(a), matto(a).
lunatic asylum *n* manicomio.
lunch [lʌntʃ] *n* pranzo, colazione *f*; **to invite sb to** *or* **for ~** invitare qn a pranzo *or* a colazione.
lunch break *n* intervallo del pranzo.
luncheon ['lʌntʃən] *n* pranzo.
luncheon meat *n* ≈ mortadella.
luncheon voucher *n* buono *m* pasto *inv*.
lunch hour *n* = lunch break.
lunchtime ['lʌntʃtaɪm] *n* ora di pranzo.
lung [lʌŋ] *n* polmone *m*.
lung cancer *n* cancro del polmone.
lunge [lʌndʒ] *vi* (*also:* ~ **forward**) fare un balzo in avanti; **to ~ at sb** balzare su qn.
lupin ['lu:pɪn] *n* lupino.
lurch [lə:tʃ] *vi* vacillare, barcollare ♦ *n* scatto improvviso; **to leave sb in the ~** piantare in asso qn.
lure [luə*] *n* richiamo; lusinga ♦ *vt* attirare (con l'inganno).
lurid ['luərɪd] *adj* sgargiante; (*details etc*) impressionante.

lurk [lə:k] *vi* stare in agguato.
luscious ['lʌʃəs] *adj* succulento(a); delizioso(a).
lush [lʌʃ] *adj* lussureggiante.
lust [lʌst] *n* lussuria; cupidigia; desiderio; (*fig*): ~ **for** sete *f* di.
►**lust after** *vt fus* bramare, desiderare.
luster ['lʌstə*] *n* (*US*) = lustre.
lustful ['lʌstful] *adj* lascivo(a), voglioso(a).
lustre, (*US*) **luster** ['lʌstə*] *n* lustro, splendore *m*.
lusty ['lʌstɪ] *adj* vigoroso(a), robusto(a).
lute [lu:t] *n* liuto.
Luxembourg ['lʌksəmbə:g] *n* (*state*) Lussemburgo *m*; (*city*) Lussemburgo *f*.
luxuriant [lʌg'zjuərɪənt] *adj* lussureggiante.
luxurious [lʌg'zjuərɪəs] *adj* sontuoso(a), di lusso.
luxury ['lʌkʃərɪ] *n* lusso ♦ *cpd* di lusso.
LV *n abbr* (*BRIT*) = luncheon voucher.
LW *abbr* (*RADIO*: = *long wave*) O.L.
Lycra ® ['laɪkrə] *n* lycra ® *f inv*.
lying ['laɪɪŋ] *n* bugie *fpl*, menzogne *fpl* ♦ *adj* (*statement, story*) falso(a); (*person*) bugiardo(a).
lynch [lɪntʃ] *vt* linciare.
lynx [lɪŋks] *n* lince *f*.
Lyons ['laɪənz] *n* Lione *f*.
lyre ['laɪə*] *n* lira.
lyric ['lɪrɪk] *adj* lirico(a); ~**s** *npl* (*of song*) parole *fpl*.
lyrical ['lɪrɪkl] *adj* lirico(a).
lyricism ['lɪrɪsɪzəm] *n* lirismo.

M m

M, m [ɛm] *n* (*letter*) M, m *f or* m *inv*; **M for Mary,** (*US*) **M for Mike** ≈ M come Milano.
M *n abbr* (*BRIT*: = *motorway*): **the M8** ≈ l'A8 ♦ *abbr* (= *medium*) taglia media.
m *abbr* (= *metre*) m; = **mile; million**.
MA *n abbr* (*SCOL*) *see* **Master of Arts;** (*US*) = *military academy* ♦ (*US*) = *Massachusetts*.
mac [mæk] *n* (*BRIT*) impermeabile *m*.
macabre [mə'kɑːbrə] *adj* macabro(a).
macaroni [mækə'rəunɪ] *n* maccheroni *mpl*.
macaroon [mækə'ru:n] *n* amaretto (*biscotto*).
mace [meɪs] *n* mazza; (*spice*) macis *m or f*.
Macedonia [mæsɪ'dəunɪə] *n* Macedonia.
Macedonian [mæsɪ'dəunɪən] *adj* macedone

♦ *n* macedone *m/f*; (*LING*) macedone *m*.
machinations [mækɪ'neɪʃənz] *npl*
macchinazioni *fpl*, intrighi *mpl*.
machine [mə'ʃiːn] *n* macchina ♦ *vt* (*dress etc*) cucire a macchina; (*TECH*) lavorare (a macchina).
machine code *n* (*COMPUT*) codice *m* di macchina, codice assoluto.
machine gun *n* mitragliatrice *f*.
machine language *n* (*COMPUT*) linguaggio *m* macchina *inv*.
machine-readable [mə'ʃiːnriːdəbl] *adj* (*COMPUT*) leggibile dalla macchina.
machinery [mə'ʃiːnərɪ] *n* macchinario, macchine *fpl*; (*fig*) macchina.
machine shop *n* officina meccanica.
machine tool *n* macchina utensile.
machine washable *adj* lavabile in lavatrice.
machinist [mə'ʃiːnɪst] *n* macchinista *m/f*.
macho ['mætʃəu] *adj* macho *inv*.
mackerel ['mækrəl] *n* (*pl inv*) sgombro.
mackintosh ['mækɪntɔʃ] *n* impermeabile *m*.
macro... ['mækrəu] *prefix* macro....
macroeconomics ['mækrəuiːkə'nɔmɪks] *n* macroeconomia.
mad [mæd] *adj* matto(a), pazzo(a); (*foolish*) sciocco(a); (*angry*) furioso(a); **to go ~** impazzire, diventar matto; **~ (at or with sb)** furibondo(a) (con qn); **to be ~ (keen) about** *or* **on sth** (*col*) andar pazzo *or* matto per qc.
madam ['mædəm] *n* signora; **M~ Chairman** Signora Presidentessa.
madcap ['mædkæp] *adj* (*col*) senza senso, assurdo(a).
mad cow disease *n* encefalite *f* bovina spongiforme.
madden ['mædn] *vt* fare infuriare.
maddening ['mædnɪŋ] *adj* esasperante.
made [meɪd] *pt*, *pp* of **make**.
Madeira [mə'dɪərə] *n* (*GEO*) Madera; (*wine*) madera *m*.
made-to-measure ['meɪdtə'mɛʒə*] *adj* (*BRIT*) fatto(a) su misura.
madhouse ['mædhaus] *n* (*also fig*) manicomio.
madly ['mædlɪ] *adv* follemente; (*love*) alla follia.
madman ['mædmən] *n* pazzo, alienato.
madness ['mædnɪs] *n* pazzia.
Madrid [mə'drɪd] *n* Madrid *f*.
Mafia ['mæfɪə] *n* mafia *f*.
mag. [mæg] *n* abbr (*BRIT col*) = **magazine** (*PRESS*).
magazine [mægə'ziːn] *n* (*PRESS*) rivista; (*MIL: store*) magazzino, deposito; (*of firearm*) caricatore *m*.

maggot ['mægət] *n* baco, verme *m*.
magic ['mædʒɪk] *n* magia ♦ *adj* magico(a).
magical ['mædʒɪkəl] *adj* magico(a).
magician [mə'dʒɪʃən] *n* mago/a.
magistrate ['mædʒɪstreɪt] *n* magistrato; giudice *m/f*.
magistrates' court *n* see **crown court**.
magnanimous [mæg'nænɪməs] *adj* magnanimo(a).
magnate ['mægneɪt] *n* magnate *m*.
magnesium [mæg'niːzɪəm] *n* magnesio.
magnet ['mægnɪt] *n* magnete *m*, calamita.
magnetic [mæg'nɛtɪk] *adj* magnetico(a).
magnetic disk *n* (*COMPUT*) disco magnetico.
magnetic tape *n* nastro magnetico.
magnetism ['mægnɪtɪzəm] *n* magnetismo.
magnification [mægnɪfɪ'keɪʃən] *n* ingrandimento.
magnificence [mæg'nɪfɪsns] *n* magnificenza.
magnificent [mæg'nɪfɪsnt] *adj* magnifico(a).
magnify ['mægnɪfaɪ] *vt* ingrandire.
magnifying glass ['mægnɪfaɪɪŋ-] *n* lente *f* d'ingrandimento.
magnitude ['mægnɪtjuːd] *n* grandezza; importanza.
magnolia [mæg'nəulɪə] *n* magnolia.
magpie ['mægpaɪ] *n* gazza.
mahogany [mə'hɔgənɪ] *n* mogano ♦ *cpd* di *or* in mogano.
maid [meɪd] *n* domestica; (*in hotel*) cameriera; **old ~** (*pej*) vecchia zitella.
maiden ['meɪdn] *n* fanciulla ♦ *adj* (*aunt etc*) nubile; (*speech*, *voyage*) inaugurale.
maiden name *n* nome *m* nubile *or* da ragazza.
mail [meɪl] *n* posta ♦ *vt* spedire (per posta); **by ~** per posta.
mailbox ['meɪlbɔks] *n* (*US*) cassetta delle lettere; (*COMPUT*) mailbox *f inv*.
mailing list ['meɪlɪŋ-] *n* elenco d'indirizzi.
mailman ['meɪlmæn] *n* (*US*) portalettere *m inv*, postino.
mail-order ['meɪlɔːdə*] *n* vendita (*or* acquisto) per corrispondenza ♦ *cpd*: **~ firm** *or* **house** ditta di vendita per corrispondenza.
mailshot ['meɪlʃɔt] *n* mailing *m inv*.
mail train *n* treno postale.
mail truck *n* (*US AUT*) = **mail van**.
mail van *n* (*BRIT*: *AUT*) furgone *m* postale; (:*RAIL*) vagone *m* postale.
maim [meɪm] *vt* mutilare.
main [meɪn] *adj* principale ♦ *n* (*pipe*) conduttura principale; **the ~s** (*ELEC*) la linea principale; **~s operated** *adj* che funziona a elettricità; **in the ~** nel

complesso, nell'insieme.

main course *n* (*CULIN*) piatto principale, piatto forte.

mainframe ['meɪnfreɪm] *n* (*also*: ~ **computer**) mainframe *m inv*.

mainland ['meɪnlənd] *n* continente *m*.

mainline ['meɪnlaɪn] *adj* (*RAIL*) della linea principale ♦ *vb* (*drugs slang*) *vt* bucarsi di ♦ *vi* bucarsi.

main line *n* (*RAIL*) linea principale.

mainly ['meɪnlɪ] *adv* principalmente, soprattutto.

main road *n* strada principale.

mainstay ['meɪnsteɪ] *n* (*fig*) sostegno principale.

mainstream ['meɪnstriːm] *n* (*fig*) corrente *f* principale.

maintain [meɪn'teɪn] *vt* mantenere; (*affirm*) sostenere; **to ~ that …** sostenere che ….

maintenance ['meɪntənəns] *n* manutenzione *f*; (*alimony*) alimenti *mpl*.

maintenance contract *n* contratto di manutenzione.

maintenance order *n* (*LAW*) obbligo degli alimenti.

maisonette [meɪzə'nɛt] *n* (*BRIT*) appartamento a due piani.

maize [meɪz] *n* granturco, mais *m*.

Maj. *abbr* (*MIL*) = **major**.

majestic [mə'dʒɛstɪk] *adj* maestoso(a).

majesty ['mædʒɪstɪ] *n* maestà *f inv*.

major ['meɪdʒə*] *n* (*MIL*) maggiore *m* ♦ *adj* (*greater*, *MUS*) maggiore; (*in importance*) principale, importante ♦ *vi* (*US SCOL*): **to ~ (in)** specializzarsi (in); **a ~ operation** (*MED*) una grossa operazione.

Majorca [mə'jɔːkə] *n* Maiorca.

major general *n* (*MIL*) generale *m* di divisione.

majority [mə'dʒɔrɪtɪ] *n* maggioranza ♦ *cpd* (*verdict*) maggioritario(a).

majority holding *n* (*COMM*): **to have a ~** essere maggiore azionista.

make [meɪk] *vt* (*pt*, *pp* **made** [meɪd]) fare; (*manufacture*) fare, fabbricare; (*cause to be*): **to ~ sb sad** *etc* rendere qn triste *etc*; (*force*): **to ~ sb do sth** costringere qn a fare qc, far fare qc a qn; (*equal*): **2 and 2 ~ 4** 2 più 2 fa 4 ♦ *n* fabbricazione *f*; (*brand*) marca; **to ~ it** (*in time etc*) arrivare; (*succeed*) farcela; **what time do you ~ it?** che ora fai?; **to ~ good** *vi* (*succeed*) aver successo ♦ *vt* (*deficit*) colmare; (*losses*) compensare; **to ~ do with** arrangiarsi con.

▶**make for** *vt fus* (*place*) avviarsi verso.

▶**make off** *vi* svignarsela.

▶**make out** *vt* (*write out*) scrivere;

(*understand*) capire; (*see*) distinguere; (: *numbers*) decifrare; (*claim*, *imply*): **to ~ out (that)** voler far credere (che); **to ~ out a case for sth** presentare delle valide ragioni in favore di qc.

▶**make over** *vt* (*assign*): **to ~ over (to)** passare (a), trasferire (a).

▶**make up** *vt* (*invent*) inventare; (*parcel*) fare ♦ *vi* conciliarsi; (*with cosmetics*) truccarsi; **to be made up of** essere composto di *or* formato da.

▶**make up for** *vt fus* compensare; ricuperare.

make-believe ['meɪkbɪliːv] *n*: **a world of ~** un mondo di favole; **it's just ~** è tutta un'invenzione.

maker ['meɪkə*] *n* fabbricante *m*; creatore/trice, autore/trice.

makeshift ['meɪkʃɪft] *adj* improvvisato(a).

make-up ['meɪkʌp] *n* trucco.

make-up bag *n* borsa del trucco.

make-up remover *n* struccatore *m*.

making ['meɪkɪŋ] *n* (*fig*): **in the ~** in formazione; **he has the ~s of an actor** ha la stoffa dell'attore.

maladjusted [mælə'dʒʌstɪd] *adj* disadattato(a).

maladroit [mælə'drɔɪt] *adj* maldestro(a).

malaise [mæ'leɪz] *n* malessere *m*.

malaria [mə'lɛərɪə] *n* malaria.

Malawi [mə'lɑːwɪ] *n* Malawi *m*.

Malay [mə'leɪ] *adj* malese ♦ *n* malese *m/f*; (*LING*) malese *m*.

Malaya [mə'leɪə] *n* Malesia.

Malayan [mə'leɪən] *adj*, *n* = **Malay**.

Malaysia [mə'leɪzɪə] *n* Malaysia.

Malaysian [mə'leɪzɪən] *adj*, *n* malaysiano(a).

Maldives ['mɔːldaɪvz] *npl*: **the ~** le (isole) Maldive.

male [meɪl] *n* (*BIO*, *ELEC*) maschio ♦ *adj* (*gen*, *sex*) maschile; (*animal*, *child*) maschio(a); **~ and female students** studenti e studentesse.

male chauvinist *n* maschilista *m*.

male nurse *n* infermiere *m*.

malevolence [mə'lɛvələns] *n* malevolenza.

malevolent [mə'lɛvələnt] *adj* malevolo(a).

malfunction [mæl'fʌŋkʃən] *n* funzione *f* difettosa.

malice ['mælɪs] *n* malevolenza.

malicious [mə'lɪʃəs] *adj* malevolo(a); (*LAW*) doloso(a).

malign [mə'laɪn] *vt* malignare su; calunniare.

malignant [mə'lɪgnənt] *adj* (*MED*) maligno(a).

malingerer [mə'lɪŋgərə*] *n* scansafatiche *m/f inv*.

mall [mɔːl] n (also: **shopping** ~) centro commerciale.
malleable ['mælɪəbl] adj malleabile.
mallet ['mælɪt] n maglio.
malnutrition [mælnjuː'trɪʃən] n denutrizione f.
malpractice [mæl'præktɪs] n prevaricazione f; negligenza.
malt [mɔːlt] n malto ♦ cpd (whisky) di malto.
Malta ['mɔːltə] n Malta.
Maltese [mɔːl'tiːz] adj, n (pl inv) maltese (m/f); (LING) maltese m.
maltreat [mæl'triːt] vt maltrattare.
mammal ['mæml] n mammifero.
mammoth ['mæməθ] n mammut m inv ♦ adj enorme, gigantesco(a).
man [mæn] n (pl **men**) uomo; (CHESS) pezzo; (DRAUGHTS) pedina ♦ vt fornire d'uomini; stare a; essere di servizio a.
Man. abbr (Canada) = Manitoba
manacles ['mænəklz] npl manette fpl.
manage ['mænɪdʒ] vi farcela ♦ vt (be in charge of) occuparsi di; (shop, restaurant) gestire; **to** ~ **without sth/sb** fare a meno di qc/qn; **to** ~ **to do sth** riuscire a far qc.
manageable ['mænɪdʒəbl] adj maneggevole; (task etc) fattibile.
management ['mænɪdʒmənt] n amministrazione f, direzione f; gestione f; (persons: of business, firm) dirigenti mpl; (: of hotel, shop, theatre) direzione f; **"under new** ~" "sotto nuova gestione".
management accounting n contabilità di gestione.
management consultant n consulente m/f aziendale.
manager ['mænɪdʒə*] n direttore m; (of shop, restaurant) gerente m; (of artist) manager m inv; **sales** ~ direttore m delle vendite.
manageress [mænɪdʒə'res] n direttrice f; gerente f.
managerial [mænə'dʒɪərɪəl] adj dirigenziale.
managing director (MD) ['mænɪdʒɪŋ-] n amministratore m delegato.
Mancunian [mæn'kjuːnɪən] adj di Manchester ♦ n abitante m/f di Manchester; originario/a di Manchester.
mandarin ['mændərɪn] n (person, fruit) mandarino.
mandate ['mændeɪt] n mandato.
mandatory ['mændətərɪ] adj obbligatorio(a); ingiuntivo(a).
mandolin(e) ['mændəlɪn] n mandolino.
mane [meɪn] n criniera.
maneuver [mə'nuːvə*] etc (US) = manoeuvre etc.

manful ['mænful] adj coraggioso(a), valoroso(a).
manfully ['mænfəlɪ] adv valorosamente.
manganese [mæŋgə'niːz] n manganese m.
mangetout ['mɔnʒ'tuː] n pisello dolce, taccola.
mangle ['mæŋgl] vt straziare; mutilare ♦ n strizzatoio.
mango, ~**es** ['mæŋgəu] n mango.
mangrove ['mæŋgrəuv] n mangrovia.
mangy ['meɪndʒɪ] adj rognoso(a).
manhandle ['mænhændl] vt (treat roughly) malmenare; (move by hand: goods) spostare a mano.
manhole ['mænhəul] n botola stradale.
manhood ['mænhud] n età virile; virilità.
man-hour ['mænauə*] n ora di lavoro.
manhunt ['mænhʌnt] n caccia all'uomo.
mania ['meɪnɪə] n mania.
maniac ['meɪnɪæk] n maniaco/a.
manic ['mænɪk] adj maniacale.
manic-depressive ['mænɪkdɪ'presɪv] adj maniaco-depressivo(a) ♦ n persona affetta da mania depressiva.
manicure ['mænɪkjuə*] n manicure f inv.
manicure set n trousse f inv della manicure.
manifest ['mænɪfest] vt manifestare ♦ adj manifesto(a), palese ♦ n (AVIAT, NAUT) manifesto.
manifestation [mænɪfes'teɪʃən] n manifestazione f.
manifesto [mænɪ'festəu] n manifesto.
manifold ['mænɪfəuld] adj molteplice ♦ n (AUT etc): **exhaust** ~ collettore m di scarico.
Manila [mə'nɪlə] n Manila.
manil(l)a [mə'nɪlə] adj (paper, envelope) manilla inv.
manipulate [mə'nɪpjuleɪt] vt (tool) maneggiare; (controls) azionare; (limb, facts) manipolare.
manipulation [mənɪpju'leɪʃən] n maneggio m; capacità di azionare; manipolazione f.
mankind [mæn'kaɪnd] n umanità, genere m umano.
manliness ['mænlɪnɪs] n virilità.
manly ['mænlɪ] adj virile; coraggioso(a).
man-made ['mæn'meɪd] adj sintetico(a); artificiale.
manna ['mænə] n manna.
mannequin ['mænɪkɪn] n (dummy) manichino; (fashion model) indossatrice f.
manner ['mænə*] n maniera, modo; ~**s** npl maniere fpl; **(good)** ~**s** buona educazione f, buone maniere; **bad** ~**s** maleducazione f; **all** ~ **of** ogni sorta di.

mannerism ['mænərızəm] *n* vezzo, tic *m inv*.
mannerly ['mænəlɪ] *adj* educato(a), civile.
manoeuvrable, (*US*) **maneuverable**
[mə'nuːvrəbl] *adj* facile da manovrare;
(*car*) maneggevole.
manoeuvre, (*US*) **maneuver** [mə'nuːvə*]
vt manovrare ♦ *vi* far manovre ♦ *n*
manovra; **to** ~ **sb into doing sth**
costringere abilmente qn a fare qc.
manor ['mænə*] *n* (*also:* ~ **house**) maniero.
manpower ['mænpauə*] *n* manodopera.
Manpower Services Commission
(MSC) *n* (*BRIT*) *ente nazionale per
l'occupazione*.
manservant, *pl* **menservants**
['mænsə:vənt, 'mɛn-] *n* domestico.
mansion ['mænʃən] *n* casa signorile.
manslaughter ['mænslɔːtə*] *n* omicidio
preterintenzionale.
mantelpiece ['mæntlpiːs] *n* mensola del
caminetto.
mantle ['mæntl] *n* mantello.
man-to-man ['mæntə'mæn] *adj, adv* da
uomo a uomo.
Mantua ['mæntjuə] *n* Mantova.
manual ['mænjuəl] *adj, n* manuale (*m*).
manual worker *n* manovale *m*.
manufacture [mænju'fæktʃə*] *vt*
fabbricare ♦ *n* fabbricazione *f*,
manifattura.
manufactured goods *npl* manufatti *mpl*.
manufacturer [mænju'fæktʃərə*] *n*
fabbricante *m*.
manufacturing industries
[mænju'fæktʃərɪŋ-] *npl* industrie *fpl*
manifatturiere.
manure [mə'njuə*] *n* concime *m*.
manuscript ['mænjuskrɪpt] *n* manoscritto.
many ['mɛnɪ] *adj* molti(e) ♦ *pron* molti(e),
un gran numero; **a great** ~ moltissimi(e),
un gran numero (di); ~ **a** ... molti(e) ...,
più di un(a) ...; **too** ~ **difficulties** troppe
difficoltà; **twice as** ~ due volte tanto;
how ~? quanti(e)?
Maori ['maurɪ] *adj, n* maori (*m/f*) *inv*.
map [mæp] *n* carta (geografica) ♦ *vt* fare
una carta di.
▶**map out** *vt* tracciare un piano di; (*fig:
career, holiday, essay*) pianificare.
maple ['meɪpl] *n* acero.
mar [mɑː*] *vt* sciupare.
Mar. *abbr* (= *March*) mar.
marathon ['mærəθən] *n* maratona ♦ *adj:* **a** ~
session una seduta fiume.
marathon runner *n* maratoneta *m/f*.
marauder [mə'rɔːdə*] *n* saccheggiatore *m*;
predatore *m*.
marble ['mɑːbl] *n* marmo; (*toy*) pallina,

bilia; ~**s** *n* (*game*) palline, bilie.
March [mɑːtʃ] *n* marzo; *for phrases see also*
July.
march [mɑːtʃ] *vi* marciare; sfilare ♦ *n*
marcia; (*demonstration*) dimostrazione *f*;
to ~ **into a room** entrare a passo deciso
in una stanza.
marcher ['mɑːtʃə*] *n* dimostrante *m/f*.
marching ['mɑːtʃɪŋ] *n:* **to give sb his** ~
orders (*fig*) dare il benservito a qn.
march-past ['mɑːtʃpɑːst] *n* sfilata.
mare [mɛə*] *n* giumenta.
marg. [mɑːdʒ] *n abbr* (*col*) = **margarine**.
margarine [mɑːdʒə'riːn] *n* margarina.
margin ['mɑːdʒɪn] *n* margine *m*.
marginal ['mɑːdʒɪnl] *adj* marginale; ~ **seat**
(*POL*) *seggio elettorale ottenuto con una
stretta maggioranza*.
marginally ['mɑːdʒɪnəlɪ] *adv* (*bigger, better*)
lievemente, di poco; (*different*) un po'.
marigold ['mærɪɡəuld] *n* calendola.
marijuana [mærɪ'wɑːnə] *n* marijuana.
marina [mə'riːnə] *n* marina.
marinade *n* [mærɪ'neɪd] marinata ♦ *vt*
['mærɪneɪd] = **marinate**.
marinate ['mærɪneɪt] *vt* marinare.
marine [mə'riːn] *adj* (*animal, plant*)
marino(a); (*forces, engineering*)
marittimo(a) ♦ *n* fante *m* di marina; (*US*)
marine *m inv*.
marine insurance *n* assicurazione *f*
marittima.
marital ['mærɪtl] *adj* maritale, coniugale; ~
status stato coniugale.
maritime ['mærɪtaɪm] *adj* marittimo(a).
maritime law *n* diritto marittimo.
marjoram ['mɑːdʒərəm] *n* maggiorana.
mark [mɑːk] *n* segno; (*stain*) macchia; (*of
skid etc*) traccia; (*BRIT SCOL*) voto; (*SPORT*)
bersaglio; (*currency*) marco; (*BRIT TECH*):
M~ 2/3 1a/2a serie *f* ♦ *vt* segnare; (*stain*)
macchiare; (*BRIT SCOL*) dare un voto a;
correggere; (*SPORT: player*) marcare;
punctuation ~**s** segni di punteggiatura;
to be quick off the ~ (**in doing**) (*fig*) non
perdere tempo (per fare); **up to the** ~ (*in
efficiency*) all'altezza; **to** ~ **time** segnare il
passo.
▶**mark down** *vt* (*reduce: prices, goods*)
ribassare, ridurre.
▶**mark off** *vt* (*tick off*) spuntare, cancellare.
▶**mark out** *vt* delimitare.
▶**mark up** *vt* (*price*) aumentare.
marked ['mɑːkt] *adj* spiccato(a), chiaro(a).
markedly ['mɑːkɪdlɪ] *adv* visibilmente,
notevolmente.
marker ['mɑːkə*] *n* (*sign*) segno; (*bookmark*)
segnalibro.

market ['mɑːkɪt] n mercato ♦ vt (COMM)
mettere in vendita; (promote) lanciare sul
mercato; **to play the** ~ giocare or
speculare in borsa; **to be on the** ~ essere
(messo) in vendita or in commercio;
open ~ mercato libero.

marketable ['mɑːkɪtəbl] adj
commercializzabile.

market analysis n analisi f di mercato.

market day n giorno di mercato.

market demand n domanda del mercato.

market economy n economia di mercato.

market forces npl forze fpl di mercato.

market garden n (BRIT) orto industriale.

marketing ['mɑːkɪtɪŋ] n marketing m.

marketplace ['mɑːkɪtpleɪs] n (piazza del)
mercato; (world of trade) piazza, mercato.

market price n prezzo di mercato.

market research n indagine f or ricerca di
mercato.

market value n valore m di mercato.

marking ['mɑːkɪŋ] n (on animal) marcatura
di colore; (on road) segnaletica
orizzontale.

marksman ['mɑːksmən] n tiratore m scelto.

marksmanship ['mɑːksmənʃɪp] n abilità
nel tiro.

mark-up ['mɑːkʌp] n (COMM: margin)
margine m di vendita; (: increase)
aumento.

marmalade ['mɑːməleɪd] n marmellata
d'arance.

maroon [mə'ruːn] vt (fig): **to be ~ed (in** or
at) essere abbandonato(a) (in) ♦ adj
bordeaux inv.

marquee [mɑː'kiː] n padiglione m.

marquess, marquis ['mɑːkwɪs] n
marchese m.

Marrakech, Marrakesh [mærə'kɛʃ] n
Marrakesh f.

marriage ['mærɪdʒ] n matrimonio.

marriage bureau n agenzia matrimoniale.

marriage certificate n certificato di
matrimonio.

**marriage guidance, (US) marriage
counseling** n consulenza matrimoniale.

marriage of convenience n matrimonio
di convenienza.

married ['mærɪd] adj sposato(a); (life, love)
coniugale, matrimoniale.

marrow ['mærəu] n midollo; (vegetable)
zucca.

marry ['mærɪ] vt sposare, sposarsi con;
(subj: father, priest etc) dare in matrimonio
♦ vi (also: **get married**) sposarsi.

Mars [mɑːz] n (planet) Marte m.

Marseilles [mɑː'seɪlz] n Marsiglia.

marsh [mɑːʃ] n palude f.

marshal ['mɑːʃl] n maresciallo; (US: fire ~)
capo; (: police ~) capitano; (for
demonstration, meeting) membro del
servizio d'ordine ♦ vt adunare.

marshalling yard ['mɑːʃlɪŋ-] n scalo
smistamento.

marshmallow [mɑːʃ'mæləu] n (BOT) altea;
(sweet) caramella soffice e gommosa.

marshy ['mɑːʃɪ] adj paludoso(a).

marsupial [mɑː'suːpɪəl] adj, n marsupiale
(m).

martial ['mɑːʃl] adj marziale.

martial arts npl arti fpl marziali.

martial law n legge f marziale.

Martian ['mɑːʃən] n marziano/a.

martin ['mɑːtɪn] n (also: **house** ~)
balestruccio.

martyr ['mɑːtə*] n martire m/f ♦ vt
martirizzare.

martyrdom ['mɑːtədəm] n martirio.

marvel ['mɑːvl] n meraviglia ♦ vi; **to** ~ **(at)**
meravigliarsi (di).

marvellous, (US) marvelous ['mɑːvələs]
adj meraviglioso(a).

Marxism ['mɑːksɪzəm] n marxismo.

Marxist ['mɑːksɪst] adj, n marxista (m/f).

marzipan ['mɑːzɪpæn] n marzapane m.

mascara [mæs'kɑːrə] n mascara m inv.

mascot ['mæskət] n mascotte f inv.

masculine ['mæskjulɪn] adj maschile ♦ n
genere m maschile.

masculinity [mæskju'lɪnɪtɪ] n mascolinità.

MASH [mæʃ] n abbr (US MIL: = mobile army
surgical hospital) ospedale di campo di
unità mobile dell'esercito.

mash [mæʃ] vt (CULIN) passare,
schiacciare.

mashed [mæʃt] adj; ~ **potatoes** purè m di
patate.

mask [mɑːsk] n (gen, ELEC) maschera ♦ vt
mascherare.

masochism ['mæsəkɪzəm] n masochismo.

masochist ['mæsəkɪst] n masochista m/f.

mason ['meɪsn] n (also: **stone**~)
scalpellino; (also: **free**~) massone m.

masonic [mə'sɔnɪk] adj massonico(a).

masonry ['meɪsnrɪ] n muratura.

masquerade [mæskə'reɪd] n ballo in
maschera; (fig) mascherata ♦ vi: **to** ~ **as**
farsi passare per.

mass [mæs] n moltitudine f, massa;
(PHYSICS) massa; (REL) messa ♦ vi
ammassarsi; **the ~es** le masse; **to go to** ~
andare a or alla messa.

Mass. abbr (US) = Massachusetts.

massacre ['mæsəkə*] n massacro ♦ vt
massacrare.

massage ['mæsɑːʒ] n massaggio ♦ vt

massaggiare.
masseur [mæ'sə:*] *n* massaggiatore *m*.
masseuse [mæ'sə:z] *n* massaggiatrice *f*.
massive ['mæsɪv] *adj* enorme,
massiccio(a).
mass market *n* mercato di massa.
mass media *npl* mass media *mpl*.
mass meeting *n* riunione *f* generale;
(*huge*) adunata popolare.
mass-produce ['mæsprə'dju:s] *vt* produrre
in serie.
mass production *n* produzione *f* in serie.
mast [mɑ:st] *n* albero; (*RADIO, TV*) pilone *m*
(a traliccio).
mastectomy [mæs'tɛktəmɪ] *n*
mastectomia.
master ['mɑ:stə*] *n* padrone *m*; (*ART etc,
teacher: in primary school*) maestro; (: *in
secondary school*) professore *m*; (*title for
boys*): **M~ X** Signorino X ♦ *vt* domare;
(*learn*) imparare a fondo; (*understand*)
conoscere a fondo; ~ **of ceremonies (MC)**
n maestro di cerimonie; **M~'s degree** *n see
boxed note*.

MASTER'S DEGREE

Il **Master's degree** *è il riconoscimento che
viene conferito a chi segue un corso di
specializzazione dopo aver conseguito un
"Bachelor's degree". Vi sono diversi tipi di
Master's Degree; i più comuni sono il "Master
of Arts (MA)" e il "Master of Science (MSc)"
che si ottengono dopo aver seguito un corso e
aver presentato una tesi originale. Per il
"Master of Letters (MLitt)" e il "Master of
Philosophy (MPhil)" è invece sufficiente
presentare la tesi; vedi anche* **doctorate**.

---

master disk *n* (*COMPUT*) disco *m* master
inv, disco principale.
masterful ['mɑ:stəful] *adj* autoritario(a),
imperioso(a).
master key *n* chiave *f* maestra.
masterly ['mɑ:stəlɪ] *adj* magistrale.
mastermind ['mɑ:stəmaɪnd] *n* mente *f*
superiore ♦ *vt* essere il cervello di.
masterpiece ['mɑ:stəpi:s] *n* capolavoro.
master plan *n* piano generale.
master stroke *n* colpo maestro.
mastiff ['mæstɪf] *n* mastino inglese.
masturbate ['mæstəbeɪt] *vi* masturbare.
masturbation [mæstə'beɪʃən] *n*
masturbazione *f*.
mat [mæt] *n* stuoia; (*also*: **door~**) stoino,
zerbino ♦ *adj* = **matt**.
match [mætʃ] *n* fiammifero; (*game*) partita,
incontro; (*fig*) uguale *m/f*; matrimonio;

partito ♦ *vt* intonare; (*go well with*) andare
benissimo con; (*equal*) uguagliare ♦ *vi*
intonarsi; **to be a good** ~ andare bene.
▶**match up** *vt* intonare.
matchbox ['mætʃbɔks] *n* scatola per
fiammiferi.
matching ['mætʃɪŋ] *adj* ben assortito(a).
matchless ['mætʃlɪs] *adj* senza pari.
mate [meɪt] *n* compagno/a di lavoro; (*col:
friend*) amico/a; (*animal*) compagno/a; (*in
merchant navy*) secondo ♦ *vi* accoppiarsi
♦ *vt* accoppiare.
material [mə'tɪərɪəl] *n* (*substance*) materiale
m, materia; (*cloth*) stoffa ♦ *adj* materiale;
(*important*) essenziale; ~**s** *npl* (*equipment
etc*) materiali *mpl*; occorrente *m*.
materialistic [mətɪərɪə'lɪstɪk] *adj*
materialistico(a).
materialize [mə'tɪərɪəlaɪz] *vi*
materializzarsi, realizzarsi.
materially [mə'tɪərɪəlɪ] *adv* dal punto di
vista materiale; sostanzialmente.
maternal [mə'tə:nl] *adj* materno(a).
maternity [mə'tə:nɪtɪ] *n* maternità ♦ *cpd* di
maternità; (*clothes*) pre-maman *inv*.
maternity benefit *n* sussidio di
maternità.
maternity hospital *n* ≈ clinica ostetrica.
matey ['meɪtɪ] *adj* (*BRIT col*) amicone(a).
math. [mæθ] *n abbr* (*US*) = **mathematics**.
mathematical [mæθə'mætɪkl] *adj*
matematico(a).
mathematician [mæθəmə'tɪʃən] *n*
matematico/a.
mathematics [mæθə'mætɪks] *n*
matematica.
maths [mæθs] *n abbr* (*BRIT*) = **mathematics**.
matinée ['mætɪneɪ] *n* matinée *f inv*.
mating ['meɪtɪŋ] *n* accoppiamento.
mating call *n* chiamata all'accoppiamento.
mating season *n* stagione *f* degli amori.
matriarchal [meɪtrɪ'ɑ:kl] *adj* matriarcale.
matrices ['meɪtrɪsi:z] *npl of* **matrix**.
matriculation [mətrɪkju'leɪʃən] *n*
immatricolazione *f*.
matrimonial [mætrɪ'məunɪəl] *adj*
matrimoniale, coniugale.
matrimony ['mætrɪmənɪ] *n* matrimonio.
matrix, *pl* **matrices** ['meɪtrɪks, 'meɪtrɪsi:z] *n*
matrice *f*.
matron ['meɪtrən] *n* (*in hospital*)
capoinfermiera; (*in school*) infermiera.
matronly ['meɪtrənlɪ] *adj* da matrona.
matt [mæt] *adj* opaco(a).
matted ['mætɪd] *adj* ingarbugliato(a).
matter ['mætə*] *n* questione *f*; (*PHYSICS*)
materia, sostanza; (*content*) contenuto;
(*MED: pus*) pus *m* ♦ *vi* importare; **it doesn't**

~ non importa; (*I don't mind*) non fa niente; **what's the** ~**?** che cosa c'è?; **no** ~ **what** qualsiasi cosa accada; **that's another** ~ quello è un altro affare; **as a** ~ **of course** come cosa naturale; **as a** ~ **of fact** in verità; **it's a** ~ **of habit** è una questione di abitudine; **printed** ~ stampe *fpl*; **reading** ~ (*BRIT*) qualcosa da leggere.

matter-of-fact [mætərəv'fækt] *adj* prosaico(a).

matting ['mætɪŋ] *n* stuoia.

mattress ['mætrɪs] *n* materasso.

mature [mə'tjuə*] *adj* maturo(a); (*cheese*) stagionato(a) ♦ *vi* maturare; stagionare; (*COMM*) scadere.

mature student *n* studente universitario che ha più di 25 anni.

maturity [mə'tjuərɪtɪ] *n* maturità.

maudlin ['mɔːdlɪn] *adj* lacrimoso(a).

maul [mɔːl] *vt* lacerare.

Mauritania [mɔrɪ'teɪnɪə] *n* Mauritania.

Mauritius [mə'rɪʃəs] *n* Maurizio.

mausoleum [mɔːsə'lɪəm] *n* mausoleo.

mauve [məuv] *adj* malva *inv*.

maverick ['mævərɪk] *n* (*fig*) chi sta fuori del branco.

mawkish ['mɔːkɪʃ] *adj* sdolcinato(a), insipido(a).

max. *abbr* = maximum.

maxim ['mæksɪm] *n* massima.

maxima ['mæksɪmə] *npl of* **maximum**.

maximize ['mæksɪmaɪz] *vt* (*profits etc*) massimizzare; (*chances*) aumentare al massimo.

maximum ['mæksɪməm] *adj* massimo(a) ♦ *n* (*pl* **maxima**) massimo.

May [meɪ] *n* maggio; *for phrases see also* **July**.

may [meɪ] *vi* (*conditional*: **might**) (*indicating possibility*): **he** ~ **come** può darsi che venga; (*be allowed to*): ~ **I smoke?** posso fumare?; ~ **I sit here?** le dispiace se mi siedo qua?; (*wishes*): ~ **God bless you!** Dio la benedica!; **he might be there** può darsi che ci sia; **he might come** potrebbe venire, può anche darsi che venga; **I might as well go** potrei anche andarmene; **you might like to try** forse le piacerebbe provare.

maybe ['meɪbiː] *adv* forse, può darsi; ~ **he'll** ... può darsi che lui ... +*sub*, forse lui ...; ~ **not** forse no, può darsi di no.

mayday ['meɪdeɪ] *n* S.O.S. *m*, mayday *m inv*.

May Day *n* il primo maggio.

mayhem ['meɪhɛm] *n* cagnara.

mayonnaise [meɪə'neɪz] *n* maionese *f*.

mayor [mɛə*] *n* sindaco.

mayoress ['mɛərɛs] *n* sindaco (*donna*); moglie *f* del sindaco.

maypole ['meɪpəul] *n* palo ornato di fiori attorno a cui si danza durante la festa di maggio.

maze [meɪz] *n* labirinto, dedalo.

MB *abbr* (*COMPUT*) = megabyte; (*Canada*) = Manitoba.

MBA *n abbr* (= *Master of Business Administration*) titolo di studio.

MBBS, MBChB *n abbr* (*BRIT*: = *Bachelor of Medicine and Surgery*) titolo di studio.

MBE *n abbr* (*BRIT*: = *Member of the Order of the British Empire*) titolo.

MC *n abbr see* **master of ceremonies**; (*US*: = *Member of Congress*) membro del Congresso.

MCAT *n abbr* (*US*: = *Medical College Admissions Test*) esame di ammissione a studi superiori di medicina.

MCP *n abbr* (*BRIT col*: = *male chauvinist pig*) sporco maschilista *m*.

MD *n abbr* (= *Doctor of Medicine*) titolo di studio; (*COMM*) see **managing director** ♦ *abbr* (*US*) = Maryland.

Md. *abbr* (*US*) = Maryland.

MDT *abbr* (*US*: = *Mountain Daylight Time*) ora legale delle Montagne Rocciose.

ME *abbr* (*US*) = Maine ♦ *n abbr* (*MED*: = *myalgic encephalomyelitis*) sindrome *f* da affaticamento cronico; (*US*) see **medical examiner**.

me [miː] *pron* mi, m' + *vowel*; (*stressed, after prep*) me; **it's** ~ sono io; **it's for** ~ è per me.

meadow ['mɛdəu] *n* prato.

meagre, (*US*) **meager** ['miːgə*] *adj* magro(a).

meal [miːl] *n* pasto; (*flour*) farina; **to go out for a** ~ mangiare fuori.

meals on wheels *n* (*BRIT*) distribuzione *f* di pasti caldi a domicilio (*per persone malate o anziane*).

mealtime ['miːltaɪm] *n* l'ora di mangiare.

mealy-mouthed ['miːlɪmauðd] *adj* che parla attraverso eufemismi.

mean [miːn] *adj* (*with money*) avaro(a), gretto(a); (*unkind*) meschino(a), maligno(a); (*US*: *vicious*: *animal*) cattivo(a); (: *person*) perfido(a); (*average*) medio(a) ♦ *vt* (*pt*, *pp* **meant** [mɛnt]) (*signify*) significare, voler dire; (*intend*): **to** ~ **to do** aver l'intenzione di fare ♦ *n* mezzo; (*MATH*) media; **to be meant for** essere destinato(a) a; **do you** ~ **it?** dice sul serio?; **what do you** ~**?** che cosa vuol dire?; *see also* **means**.

meander [mɪ'ændə*] *vi* far meandri; (*fig*) divagare.

meaning ['miːnɪŋ] *n* significato, senso.

meaningful ['miːnɪŋful] *adj* significativo(a); (*relationship*) valido(a).
meaningless ['miːnɪŋlɪs] *adj* senza senso.
meanness ['miːnnɪs] *n* avarizia; meschinità.
means [miːnz] *npl* mezzi *mpl*; **by ~ of** per mezzo di; (*person*) a mezzo di; **by all ~** ma certo, prego.
means test *n* (*ADMIN*) accertamento dei redditi (*per una persona che ha chiesto un aiuto finanziario*).
meant [mɛnt] *pt, pp of* **mean**.
meantime ['miːntaɪm], **meanwhile** ['miːnwaɪl] *adv* (*also*: **in the ~**) nel frattempo.
measles ['miːzlz] *n* morbillo.
measly ['miːzlɪ] *adj* (*col*) miserabile.
measurable ['mɛʒərəbl] *adj* misurabile.
measure ['mɛʒə*] *vt, vi* misurare ♦ *n* misura; (*ruler*) metro; **a litre ~** una misura da un litro; **some ~ of success** un certo successo; **to take ~s to do sth** prendere provvedimenti per fare qc.
▶**measure up** *vi*: **to ~ up (to)** dimostrarsi *or* essere all'altezza (di).
measured ['mɛʒəd] *adj* misurato(a).
measurement ['mɛʒəmənt] *n* (*act*) misurazione *f*; (*measure*) misura; **chest/ hip ~** giro petto/fianchi; **to take sb's ~s** prendere le misure di qn.
meat [miːt] *n* carne *f*; **cold ~s** (*BRIT*) affettati *mpl*; **crab ~** polpa di granchio.
meatball ['miːtbɔːl] *n* polpetta di carne.
meat pie *n* torta salata in pasta frolla con ripieno di carne.
meaty ['miːtɪ] *adj* che sa di carne; (*fig*) sostanzioso(a); (*of person*) corpulento(a); (*of part of body*) carnoso(a); **~ meal** pasto a base di carne.
Mecca ['mɛkə] *n* La Mecca; (*fig*): **a ~ (for)** la Mecca (di).
mechanic [mɪ'kænɪk] *n* meccanico; *see also* **mechanics**.
mechanical [mɪ'kænɪkəl] *adj* meccanico(a).
mechanical engineering *n* (*science*) ingegneria meccanica; (*industry*) costruzioni *fpl* meccaniche.
mechanics [mɪ'kænɪks] *n* meccanica ♦ *npl* meccanismo.
mechanism ['mɛkənɪzəm] *n* meccanismo.
mechanization [mɛkənaɪ'zeɪʃən] *n* meccanizzazione *f*.
MEd *n abbr* (= *Master of Education*) titolo di studio.
medal ['mɛdl] *n* medaglia.
medallion [mɪ'dælɪən] *n* medaglione *m*.
medallist, (*US*) **medalist** ['mɛdəlɪst] *n* (*SPORT*) vincitore/trice di medaglia.

meddle ['mɛdl] *vi*: **to ~ in** immischiarsi in, mettere le mani in; **to ~ with** toccare.
meddlesome ['mɛdlsəm], **meddling** ['mɛdlɪŋ] *adj* (*interfering*) che mette il naso dappertutto; (*touching things*) che tocca tutto.
media ['miːdɪə] *npl* (*PRESS, RADIO, TV*) media *mpl*; (*means*) *pl of* **medium**.
media circus *n* carrozzone *m* dell'informazione.
mediaeval [mɛdɪ'iːvl] *adj* = **medieval**.
median ['miːdɪən] *n* (*US: also*: **~ strip**) banchina *f* spartitraffico *inv*.
media research *n* sondaggio tra gli utenti dei mass media.
mediate ['miːdɪeɪt] *vi* interporsi; fare da mediatore/trice.
mediation [miːdɪ'eɪʃən] *n* mediazione *f*.
mediator ['miːdɪeɪtə*] *n* mediatore/trice.
Medicaid ['mɛdɪkeɪd] *n* (*US*) assistenza *medica ai poveri*.
medical ['mɛdɪkl] *adj* medico(a); **~ (examination)** visita medica.
medical certificate *n* certificato medico.
medical examiner (ME) *n* (*US*) medico *incaricato di indagare la causa di morte in circostanze sospette*.
medical student *n* studente/essa di medicina.
Medicare ['mɛdɪkɛə*] *n* (*US*) assistenza *medica agli anziani*.
medicated ['mɛdɪkeɪtɪd] *adj* medicato(a).
medication [mɛdɪ'keɪʃən] *n* (*drugs etc*) medicinali *mpl*, farmaci *mpl*.
medicinal [mɛ'dɪsɪnl] *adj* medicinale.
medicine ['mɛdsɪn] *n* medicina.
medicine chest *n* armadietto farmaceutico.
medicine man *n* stregone *m*.
medieval [mɛdɪ'iːvl] *adj* medievale.
mediocre [miːdɪ'əukə*] *adj* mediocre.
mediocrity [miːdɪ'ɔkrɪtɪ] *n* mediocrità.
meditate ['mɛdɪteɪt] *vi*: **to ~ (on)** meditare (su).
meditation [mɛdɪ'teɪʃən] *n* meditazione *f*.
Mediterranean [mɛdɪtə'reɪnɪən] *adj* mediterraneo(a); **the ~ (Sea)** il (mare) Mediterraneo.
medium ['miːdɪəm] *adj* medio(a) ♦ *n* (*pl* **media**: *means*) mezzo; (*pl* **mediums**: *person*) medium *m inv*; **the happy ~** una giusta via di mezzo; *see also* **media**.
medium-dry ['miːdɪəm'draɪ] *adj* demisec *inv*.
medium-sized ['miːdɪəmsaɪzd] *adj* (*tin etc*) di grandezza media; (*clothes*) di taglia media.
medium wave *n* (*RADIO*) onde *fpl* medie.

medley ['mɛdlɪ] n selezione f.

meek [miːk] adj dolce, umile.

meet, pt, pp **met** [miːt, mɛt] vt incontrare; (for the first time) fare la conoscenza di; (fig) affrontare; far fronte a; soddisfare; raggiungere ♦ vi incontrarsi; (in session) riunirsi; (join: objects) unirsi ♦ n (BRIT HUNTING) raduno (dei partecipanti alla caccia alla volpe); (US SPORT) raduno (sportivo); **I'll ~ you at the station** verrò a prenderla alla stazione; **pleased to ~ you!** lieto di conoscerla!, piacere!

► **meet up** vi: **to ~ up with sb** incontrare qn.

► **meet with** vt fus incontrare; **he met with an accident** ha avuto un incidente.

meeting ['miːtɪŋ] n incontro; (session: of club etc) riunione f; (interview) intervista; (formal) colloquio; (SPORT: rally) raduno; **she's at a ~** (COMM) è in riunione; **to call a ~** convocare una riunione.

meeting place n luogo d'incontro.

megabyte ['mɛgəbaɪt] n megabyte m inv.

megalomaniac [mɛgələu'meɪnɪæk] n megalomane m/f.

megaphone ['mɛgəfəun] n megafono.

megawatt ['mɛgəwɔt] n megawatt m inv.

melancholy ['mɛlənkəlɪ] n malinconia ♦ adj malinconico(a).

mellow ['mɛləu] adj (wine, sound) ricco(a); (person, light) dolce; (colour) caldo(a); (fruit) maturo(a) ♦ vi (person) addolcirsi.

melodious [mɪ'ləudɪəs] adj melodioso(a).

melodrama ['mɛləudrɑːmə] n melodramma m.

melodramatic [mɛlədrə'mætɪk] adj melodrammatico(a).

melody ['mɛlədɪ] n melodia.

melon ['mɛlən] n melone m.

melt [mɛlt] vi (gen) sciogliersi, struggersi; (metals) fondersi; (fig) intenerirsi ♦ vt sciogliere, struggere; fondere; (person) commuovere; **~ed butter** burro fuso.

► **melt away** vi sciogliersi completamente.

► **melt down** vt fondere.

meltdown ['mɛltdaun] n melt-down m inv.

melting point ['mɛltɪŋ-] n punto di fusione.

melting pot ['mɛltɪŋ-] n (fig) crogiolo; **to be in the ~** essere ancora in discussione.

member ['mɛmbə*] n membro; (of club) socio/a, iscritto/a; (of political party) iscritto/a; **~ country/state** n paese m/stato membro; **M~ of Parliament (MP)** n (BRIT) deputato; **M~ of the European Parliament (MEP)** n eurodeputato; **M~ of the House of Representatives (MHR)** n (US) membro della Camera dei Rappresentanti.

membership ['mɛmbəʃɪp] n iscrizione f;

(numero d')iscritti mpl, membri mpl.

membership card n tessera (di iscrizione).

membrane ['mɛmbreɪn] n membrana.

memento [mə'mɛntəu] n ricordo.

memo ['mɛməu] n appunto; (COMM etc) comunicazione f di servizio.

memoir ['mɛmwɑː*] n memoria; **~s** npl memorie fpl, ricordi mpl.

memo pad n blocchetto per appunti.

memorable ['mɛmərəbl] adj memorabile.

memorandum, pl **memoranda** [mɛmə'rændəm, -də] n appunto; (COMM etc) comunicazione f di servizio; (DIPLOMACY) memorandum m inv.

memorial [mɪ'mɔːrɪəl] n monumento commemorativo ♦ adj commemorativo(a).

Memorial Day n (US) see boxed note.

memorize ['mɛməraɪz] vt imparare a memoria.

memory ['mɛmərɪ] n (gen, COMPUT) memoria; (recollection) ricordo; **in ~ of** in memoria di; **to have a good/bad ~** aver buona/ cattiva memoria; **loss of ~** amnesia.

men [mɛn] npl of **man**.

menace ['mɛnɪs] n minaccia; (col: nuisance) peste f ♦ vt minacciare; **a public ~** un pericolo pubblico.

menacing ['mɛnɪsɪŋ] adj minaccioso(a).

menagerie [mɪ'nædʒərɪ] n serraglio.

mend [mɛnd] vt aggiustare, riparare; (darn) rammendare ♦ n rammendo; **on the ~** in via di guarigione.

mending ['mɛndɪŋ] n rammendo; (items to be mended) roba da rammendare.

menial ['miːnɪəl] adj da servo; umile.

meningitis [mɛnɪn'dʒaɪtɪs] n meningite f.

menopause ['mɛnəupɔːz] n menopausa.

menservants ['mɛnsəːvənts] npl of **manservant**.

men's room n: **the ~** (esp US) la toilette degli uomini.

menstruate ['mɛnstrueɪt] vi mestruare.

menstruation [mɛnstru'eɪʃən] n mestruazione f.

menswear ['mɛnzwɛə*] n abbigliamento maschile.

mental ['mɛntl] adj mentale; **~ illness**

malattia mentale.
mental hospital *n* ospedale *m*
psichiatrico.
mentality [mɛn'tælɪtɪ] *n* mentalità *f inv.*
mentally ['mɛntlɪ] *adv:* **to be** ~
handicapped essere minorato psichico.
menthol ['mɛnθɔl] *n* mentolo.
mention ['mɛnʃən] *n* menzione *f* ♦ *vt*
menzionare, far menzione di; **don't** ~ **it!**
non c'è di che!, prego!; **I need hardly** ~
that ... inutile dire che ...; **not to** ~,
without ~**ing** per non parlare di, senza
contare.
mentor ['mɛntɔ:*] *n* mentore *m.*
menu ['mɛnju:] *n* (*set* ~, *COMPUT*) menù *m*
inv; (*printed*) carta.
menu-driven ['mɛnju:drɪvn] *adj* (*COMPUT*)
guidato(a) da menù.
MEP *n abbr see* **Member of the European
Parliament.**
mercantile ['mɜ:kəntaɪl] *adj* mercantile;
(*law*) commerciale.
mercenary ['mɜ:sɪnərɪ] *adj* venale ♦ *n*
mercenario.
merchandise ['mɜ:tʃəndaɪz] *n* merci *fpl* ♦ *vt*
commercializzare.
merchandiser ['mɜ:tʃəndaɪzə*] *n*
merchandiser *m inv.*
merchant ['mɜ:tʃənt] *n* (*trader*)
commerciante *m;* (*shopkeeper*) negoziante
m; **timber/wine** ~ negoziante di legno/
vino.
merchant bank *n* (*BRIT*) banca d'affari.
merchantman ['mɜ:tʃəntmən] *n*
mercantile *m.*
merchant navy, (*US*) **merchant marine**
n marina mercantile.
merciful ['mɜ:sɪful] *adj* pietoso(a),
clemente.
mercifully ['mɜ:sɪflɪ] *adv* con clemenza;
(*fortunately*) per fortuna.
merciless ['mɜ:sɪlɪs] *adj* spietato(a).
mercurial [mɜ:'kjuərɪəl] *adj* (*unpredictable*)
volubile.
mercury ['mɜ:kjurɪ] *n* mercurio.
mercy ['mɜ:sɪ] *n* pietà; (*REL*) misericordia;
to have ~ **on sb** aver pietà di qn; **at the** ~
of alla mercè di.
mercy killing *n* eutanasia.
mere [mɪə*] *adj* semplice; **by a** ~ **chance**
per mero caso.
merely ['mɪəlɪ] *adv* semplicemente, non ...
che.
merge [mɜ:dʒ] *vt* unire; (*COMPUT: files, text*)
fondere ♦ *vi* fondersi, unirsi; (*COMM*)
fondersi.
merger ['mɜ:dʒə*] *n* (*COMM*) fusione *f.*
meridian [mə'rɪdɪən] *n* meridiano.

meringue [mə'ræŋ] *n* meringa.
merit ['mɛrɪt] *n* merito, valore *m* ♦ *vt*
meritare.
meritocracy [mɛrɪ'tɔkrəsɪ] *n* meritocrazia.
mermaid ['mɜ:meɪd] *n* sirena.
merriment ['mɛrɪmənt] *n* gaiezza, allegria.
merry ['mɛrɪ] *adj* gaio(a), allegro(a); **M~
Christmas!** Buon Natale!
merry-go-round ['mɛrɪgəuraund] *n*
carosello.
mesh [mɛʃ] *n* maglia; rete *f* ♦ *vi* (*gears*)
ingranarsi; **wire** ~ rete metallica.
mesmerize ['mɛzməraɪz] *vt* ipnotizzare;
affascinare.
mess [mɛs] *n* confusione *f,* disordine *m;* (*fig*)
pasticcio; (*MIL*) mensa; **to be (in) a** ~
(*house, room*) essere in disordine (*or*
molto sporco); (*fig: marriage, life*) essere
un caos; **to be/get o.s. in a** ~ (*fig*) essere/
cacciarsi in un pasticcio.
▶**mess about, mess around** *vi* (*col*)
trastullarsi.
▶**mess about** *or* **around with** *vt fus* (*col*)
gingillarsi con; (*plans*) fare un pasticcio
di.
▶**mess up** *vt* sporcare; fare un pasticcio
di; rovinare.
message ['mɛsɪdʒ] *n* messaggio; **to get the**
~ (*fig col*) capire l'antifona.
message switching *n* (*COMPUT*)
smistamento messaggi.
messenger ['mɛsɪndʒə*] *n* messaggero/a.
Messiah [mɪ'saɪə] *n* Messia *m.*
Messrs, Messrs. ['mɛsəz] *abbr* (*on letters:*
= *messieurs*) Spett.
messy ['mɛsɪ] *adj* sporco(a); disordinato(a);
(*confused: situation etc*) ingarbugliato(a).
Met [mɛt] *n abbr* (*US*) = *Metropolitan Opera.*
met [mɛt] *pt, pp of* **meet** ♦ *adj abbr*
(= *meteorological*): **the M~ Office** l'Ufficio
Meteorologico.
metabolism [mɛ'tæbəlɪzəm] *n*
metabolismo.
metal ['mɛtl] *n* metallo ♦ *vt* massicciare.
metallic
[mɛ'tælɪk] *adj* metallico(a).
metallurgy [mɛ'tælədʒɪ] *n* metallurgia.
metalwork ['mɛtlwɜ:k] *n* (*craft*) lavorazione
f del metallo.
metamorphosis, *pl* **-phoses**
[mɛtə'mɔ:fəsɪs, -i:z] *n* metamorfosi *f inv.*
metaphor ['mɛtəfə*] *n* metafora.
metaphysics [mɛtə'fɪzɪks] *n* metafisica.
mete [mi:t]: **to** ~ **out** *vt fus* infliggere.
meteor ['mi:tɪə*] *n* meteora.
meteoric [mi:tɪ'ɔrɪk] *adj* (*fig*) fulmineo(a).
meteorite ['mi:tɪəraɪt] *n* meteorite *m.*
meteorological [mi:tɪərə'lɔdʒɪkl] *adj*

meteorologico(a).
meteorology [miːtɪə'rɔlədʒɪ] n
meteorologia.
meter ['miːtə*] n (*instrument*) contatore m;
(*parking* ~) parchimetro; (*US*) = **metre**.
methane ['miːθeɪn] n metano.
method ['mɛθəd] n metodo; ~ **of payment**
modo *or* modalità *f inv* di pagamento.
methodical [mɪ'θɔdɪkl] *adj* metodico(a).
Methodist ['mɛθədɪst] *adj*, n metodista
(*m/f*).
methylated spirits ['mɛθɪleɪtɪd-] n (*BRIT*:
also: **meths**) alcool m denaturato.
meticulous [mɛ'tɪkjuləs] *adj* meticoloso(a).
metre, (*US*) **meter** ['miːtə*] n metro.
metric ['mɛtrɪk] *adj* metrico(a); **to go** ~
adottare il sistema metrico decimale.
metrical ['mɛtrɪkl] *adj* metrico(a).
metrication [mɛtrɪ'keɪʃən] n conversione *f*
al sistema metrico.
metric system n sistema m metrico
decimale.
metric ton n tonnellata.
metronome ['mɛtrənəum] n metronomo.
metropolis [mɪ'trɔpəlɪs] n metropoli *f inv.*
metropolitan [mɛtrə'pɔlɪtən] *adj*
metropolitano(a).
Metropolitan Police n (*BRIT*): **the** ~ la
polizia di Londra.
mettle ['mɛtl] n coraggio.
mew [mjuː] *vi* (*cat*) miagolare.
mews [mjuːz] n (*BRIT*): ~ **flat**
*appartamentino ricavato da una vecchia
scuderia.*
Mexican ['mɛksɪkən] *adj*, n messicano(a).
Mexico ['mɛksɪkəu] n Messico.
Mexico City n Città del Messico.
mezzanine ['mɛtsəniːn] n mezzanino.
MFA n abbr (*US*: = *Master of Fine Arts*) *titolo
di studio.*
mfr abbr = **manufacture; manufacturer**.
mg abbr (= *milligram*) mg.
Mgr abbr (= *Monseigneur, Monsignor*)
mons.; (*COMM*) = **manager**.
MHR n abbr (*US*) see **Member of the House of
Representatives**.
MHz abbr (= *megahertz*) MHz.
MI abbr (*US*) = *Michigan*.
MI5 n abbr (*BRIT*: = *Military Intelligence 5*)
agenzia di controspionaggio.
MI6 n abbr (*BRIT*: = *Military Intelligence 6*)
agenzia di spionaggio.
MIA abbr = **missing in action**.
miaow [miː'au] *vi* miagolare.
mice [maɪs] *npl of* **mouse**.
Mich. abbr (*US*) = *Michigan*.
microbe ['maɪkrəub] n microbio.
microbiology [maɪkrəubaɪ'ɔlədʒɪ] n

microbiologia.
microchip ['maɪkrəutʃɪp] n microcircuito
integrato, chip m inv.
microcomputer [maɪkrəukəm'pjuːtə*] n
microcomputer m inv.
microcosm ['maɪkrəukɔzəm] n
microcosmo.
microeconomics [maɪkrəuiːkə'nɔmɪks] n
microeconomia.
microfiche ['maɪkrəufiːʃ] n microfiche *f inv*.
microfilm ['maɪkrəufɪlm] n microfilm m inv
♦ *vt* microfilmare.
microlight ['maɪkrəulaɪt] n aereo m biposto
inv.
micrometer [maɪ'krɔmɪtə*] n micrometro,
palmer m inv.
microphone ['maɪkrəfəun] n microfono.
microprocessor [maɪkrəu'prəusɛsə*] n
microprocessore m.
microscope ['maɪkrəskəup] n microscopio;
under the ~ al microscopio.
microscopic [maɪkrə'skɔpɪk] *adj*
microscopico(a).
microwave ['maɪkrəuweɪv] n (*also*: ~ **oven**)
forno a microonde.
mid [mɪd] *adj*: ~ **May** metà maggio; ~
afternoon metà pomeriggio; **in** ~ **air** a
mezz'aria; **he's in his** ~ **thirties** avrà circa
trentacinque anni.
midday [mɪd'deɪ] n mezzogiorno.
middle ['mɪdl] n mezzo; centro; (*waist*) vita
♦ *adj* di mezzo; **I'm in the** ~ **of reading it**
sto proprio leggendolo ora; **in the** ~ **of
the night** nel mezzo della notte.
middle age n mezza età.
middle-aged [mɪdl'eɪdʒd] *adj* di mezza età.
Middle Ages *npl*: **the** ~ il Medioevo.
middle class *adj* (*also*: **middle-class**)
≈ borghese ♦ n: **the** ~(**es**) ≈ la borghesia.
Middle East n: **the** ~ il Medio Oriente.
middleman ['mɪdlmæn] n intermediario;
agente m rivenditore.
middle management n quadri *mpl*
intermedi.
middle name n secondo nome m.
middle-of-the-road ['mɪdləvðə'rəud] *adj*
moderato(a).
middleweight ['mɪdlweɪt] n (*BOXING*) peso
medio.
middling ['mɪdlɪŋ] *adj* medio(a).
midge [mɪdʒ] n moscerino.
midget ['mɪdʒɪt] n nano/a.
midi system ['mɪdɪ-] n (*hi-fi*) compatto.
Midlands ['mɪdləndz] *npl* contee del centro
dell'Inghilterra.
midnight ['mɪdnaɪt] n mezzanotte *f*; **at** ~ a
mezzanotte.
midriff ['mɪdrɪf] n diaframma m.

midst [mɪdst] *n*: **in the ~ of** in mezzo a.
midsummer [mɪd'sʌmə*] *n* mezza *or* piena estate *f*.
midway [mɪd'weɪ] *adj, adv*: **~ (between)** a mezza strada (fra).
midweek [mɪd'wiːk] *adv, adj* a metà settimana.
midwife, *pl* **midwives** ['mɪdwaɪf, -vz] *n* levatrice *f*.
midwifery ['mɪdwɪfərɪ] *n* ostetrica.
midwinter [mɪd'wɪntə*] *n* pieno inverno.
miffed [mɪft] *adj* (*col*) seccato(a).
might [maɪt] *vb see* **may** ♦ *n* potere *m*, forza.
mighty ['maɪtɪ] *adj* forte, potente ♦ *adv* (*col*) molto.
migraine ['miːɡreɪn] *n* emicrania.
migrant ['maɪɡrənt] *n* (*bird, animal*) migratore *m*; (*person*) migrante *m/f*; nomade *m/f* ♦ *adj* migratore(trice); nomade; (*worker*) emigrato(a).
migrate [maɪ'ɡreɪt] *vi* migrare.
migration [maɪ'ɡreɪʃən] *n* migrazione *f*.
mike [maɪk] *n abbr* (= *microphone*) microfono.
Milan [mɪ'læn] *n* Milano *f*.
mild [maɪld] *adj* mite; (*person, voice*) dolce; (*flavour*) delicato(a); (*illness*) leggero(a) ♦ *n* birra leggera.
mildew ['mɪldjuː] *n* muffa.
mildly ['maɪldlɪ] *adv* mitemente; dolcemente; delicatamente; leggermente; **to put it ~** a dire poco.
mildness ['maɪldnɪs] *n* mitezza; dolcezza; delicatezza; non gravità.
mile [maɪl] *n* miglio; **to do 20 ~s per gallon** ≈ usare 14 litri per cento chilometri.
mileage ['maɪlɪdʒ] *n* distanza in miglia, ≈ chilometraggio.
mileage allowance *n* rimborso per miglio.
mileometer [maɪ'lɔmɪtə*] *n* (*BRIT*) = **milometer**.
milestone ['maɪlstəun] *n* pietra miliare.
milieu ['miːljəː] *n* ambiente *m*.
militant ['mɪlɪtnt] *adj, n* militante (*m/f*).
militarism ['mɪlɪtərɪzəm] *n* militarismo.
militaristic [mɪlɪtə'rɪstɪk] *adj* militaristico(a).
military ['mɪlɪtərɪ] *adj* militare ♦ *n*: **the ~** i militari, l'esercito.
military service *n* servizio militare.
militate ['mɪlɪteɪt] *vi*: **to ~ against** essere d'ostacolo a.
militia [mɪ'lɪʃə] *n* milizia.
milk [mɪlk] *n* latte *m* ♦ *vt* (*cow*) mungere; (*fig*) sfruttare.
milk chocolate *n* cioccolato al latte.
milk float *n* (*BRIT*) furgone *m* del lattaio.

milking ['mɪlkɪŋ] *n* mungitura.
milkman ['mɪlkmən] *n* lattaio.
milk shake *n* frappé *m inv*.
milk tooth *n* dente *m* di latte.
milk truck *n* (*US*) = **milk float**.
milky ['mɪlkɪ] *adj* lattiginoso(a); (*colour*) latteo(a).
Milky Way *n* Via Lattea.
mill [mɪl] *n* mulino; (*small: for coffee, pepper etc*) macinino; (*factory*) fabbrica; (*spinning ~*) filatura ♦ *vt* macinare ♦ *vi* (*also*: **~ about**) formicolare.
millennium, *pl* **~s** *or* **millennia** [mɪ'lenɪəm, -'lenɪə] *n* millennio.
millennium bug *n* baco di fine millennio.
miller ['mɪlə*] *n* mugnaio.
millet ['mɪlɪt] *n* miglio.
milli... ['mɪlɪ] *prefix* milli....
milligram(me) ['mɪlɪɡræm] *n* milligrammo.
millilitre, (*US***) milliliter** ['mɪlɪliːtə*] *n* millilitro.
millimetre, (*US***) millimeter** ['mɪlɪmiːtə*] *n* millimetro.
milliner ['mɪlɪnə*] *n* modista.
millinery ['mɪlɪnərɪ] *n* modisteria.
million ['mɪljən] *n* milione *m*.
millionaire [mɪljə'nɛə*] *n* milionario, ≈ miliardario.
millipede ['mɪlɪpiːd] *n* millepiedi *m inv*.
millstone ['mɪlstəun] *n* macina.
millwheel ['mɪlwiːl] *n* ruota di mulino.
milometer [maɪ'lɔmɪtə*] *n* ≈ contachilometri *m inv*.
mime [maɪm] *n* mimo ♦ *vt, vi* mimare.
mimic ['mɪmɪk] *n* imitatore/trice ♦ *vt* (*subj: comedian*) imitare; (: *animal, person*) scimmiottare.
mimicry ['mɪmɪkrɪ] *n* imitazioni *fpl*; (*ZOOL*) mimetismo.
Min. *abbr* (*BRIT POL*: = *ministry*) Min.
min. *abbr* (= *minute, minimum*) min.
minaret [mɪnə'rɛt] *n* minareto.
mince [mɪns] *vt* tritare, macinare ♦ *vi* (*in walking*) camminare a passettini ♦ *n* (*BRIT CULIN*) carne *f* tritata; **he does not ~ (his) words** parla chiaro e tondo.
mincemeat ['mɪnsmiːt] *n frutta secca tritata per uso in pasticceria.*
mince pie *n specie di torta con frutta secca.*
mincer ['mɪnsə*] *n* tritacarne *m inv*.
mincing ['mɪnsɪŋ] *adj* lezioso(a).
mind [maɪnd] *n* mente *f* ♦ *vt* (*attend to, look after*) badare a, occuparsi di; (*be careful*) fare attenzione a, stare attento(a) a; (*object to*): **I don't ~ the noise** il rumore non mi dà alcun fastidio; **do you ~ if ...?**

le dispiace se ...?; **I don't** ~ non m'importa; ~ **you,** ... sì, però va detto che ...; **never** ~ non importa, non fa niente; **it is on my** ~ mi preoccupa; **to change one's** ~ cambiare idea; **to be in two** ~**s about sth** essere incerto su qc; **to my** ~ secondo me, a mio parere; **to be out of one's** ~ essere uscito(a) di mente; **to keep sth in** ~ non dimenticare qc; **to bear sth in** ~ tener presente qc; **to have sb/sth in** ~ avere in mente qn/qc; **to have in** ~ **to do** aver l'intenzione di fare; **it went right out of my** ~ mi è completamente passato di mente, me ne sono completamente dimenticato; **to bring** or **call sth to** ~ riportare or richiamare qc alla mente; **to make up one's** ~ decidersi; "~ **the step**" "attenzione allo scalino".

mind-boggling ['maɪndbɔglɪŋ] adj (col) sconcertante.

-minded ['maɪndɪd] adj: fair~ imparziale, **an industrially**~ **nation** una nazione orientata verso l'industria.

minder ['maɪndə*] n (child -) bambinaia; (bodyguard) guardia del corpo.

mindful ['maɪndful] adj: ~ **of** attento(a) a; memore di.

mindless ['maɪndlɪs] adj idiota; (violence, crime) insensato(a).

mine [maɪn] pron il(la) mio(a), pl i(le) miei(mie); **this book is** ~ questo libro è mio ♦ n miniera; (explosive) mina ♦ vt (coal) estrarre; (ship, beach) minare.

mine detector n rivelatore m di mine.

minefield ['maɪnfiːld] n campo minato.

miner ['maɪnə*] n minatore m.

mineral ['mɪnərəl] adj minerale ♦ n minerale m; ~**s** npl (BRIT: soft drinks) bevande fpl gasate.

mineralogy [mɪnə'rælədʒɪ] n mineralogia.

mineral water n acqua minerale.

minesweeper ['maɪnswiːpə*] n dragamine m inv.

mingle ['mɪŋgl] vt mescolare, mischiare ♦ vi: **to** ~ **with** mescolarsi a, mischiarsi con.

mingy ['mɪndʒɪ] adj (col: amount) misero(a); (: person) spilorcio(a).

miniature ['mɪnətʃə*] adj in miniatura ♦ n miniatura.

minibus ['mɪnɪbʌs] n minibus m inv.

minicab ['mɪnɪkæb] n (BRIT) ≈ taxi m inv.

minicomputer ['mɪnɪkəm'pjuːtə*] n minicomputer m inv.

minim ['mɪnɪm] n (MUS) minima.

minima ['mɪnɪmə] npl of **minimum.**

minimal ['mɪnɪml] adj minimo(a).

minimalist ['mɪnɪməlɪst] adj, n minimalista (m/f).

minimize ['mɪnɪmaɪz] vt minimizzare.

minimum ['mɪnɪməm] n (pl **minima**) minimo ♦ adj minimo(a); **to reduce to a** ~ ridurre al minimo; ~ **wage** salario minimo garantito.

minimum lending rate (MLR) n (BRIT) ≈ tasso ufficiale di sconto (T.U.S.).

mining ['maɪnɪŋ] n industria mineraria ♦ adj minerario(a); di minatori.

minion ['mɪnjən] n (pej) caudatario; favorito/a.

mini-series ['mɪnɪsɪəriːz] n miniserie f inv.

miniskirt ['mɪnɪskəːt] n minigonna.

minister ['mɪnɪstə*] n (BRIT POL) ministro; (REL) pastore m ♦ vi: **to** ~ **to sb** assistere qn; **to** ~ **to sb's needs** provvedere ai bisogni di qn.

ministerial [mɪnɪs'tɪərɪəl] adj (BRIT POL) ministeriale.

ministry ['mɪnɪstrɪ] n (BRIT POL) ministero; (REL): **to go into the** ~ diventare pastore.

mink [mɪŋk] n visone m.

mink coat n pelliccia di visone.

Minn. abbr (US) = Minnesota.

minnow ['mɪnəu] n pesciolino d'acqua dolce.

minor ['maɪnə*] adj minore, di poca importanza; (MUS) minore ♦ n (LAW) minorenne m/f.

Minorca [mɪ'nɔːkə] n Minorca.

minority [maɪ'nɔrɪtɪ] n minoranza; **to be in a** ~ essere in minoranza.

minster ['mɪnstə*] n cattedrale f (annessa a monastero).

minstrel ['mɪnstrəl] n giullare m, menestrello.

mint [mɪnt] n (plant) menta; (sweet) pasticca di menta ♦ vt (coins) battere; **the (Royal) M**~, (US) **the (US) M**~ la Zecca; **in** ~ **condition** come nuovo(a) di zecca.

mint sauce n salsa di menta.

minuet [mɪnju'ɛt] n minuetto.

minus ['maɪnəs] n (also: ~ **sign**) segno meno ♦ prep meno.

minuscule ['mɪnəskjuːl] adj minuscolo(a).

minute adj [maɪ'njuːt] minuscolo(a); (detail) minuzioso(a) ♦ n ['mɪnɪt] minuto; (official record) processo verbale, resoconto sommario; ~**s** npl verbale m, verbali mpl; **it is 5** ~**s past 3** sono le 3 e 5 (minuti); **wait a** ~**!** (aspetta) un momento!; **at the last** ~ all'ultimo momento; **up to the** ~ ultimissimo; modernissimo; **in** ~ **detail** minuziosamente.

minute book n libro dei verbali.

minute hand n lancetta dei minuti.

minutely [maɪ'njuːtlɪ] *adv* (*by a small amount*) di poco; (*in detail*) minuziosamente.

minutiae [mɪ'njuːʃiiː] *npl* minuzie *fpl*.

miracle ['mɪrəkl] *n* miracolo.

miraculous [mɪ'rækjuləs] *adj* miracoloso(a).

mirage ['mɪrɑːʒ] *n* miraggio.

mire ['maɪə*] *n* pantano, melma.

mirror ['mɪrə*] *n* specchio ♦ *vt* rispecchiare, riflettere.

mirror image *n* immagine *f* speculare.

mirth [mɔːθ] *n* gaiezza.

misadventure [mɪsəd'vɛntʃə*] *n* disavventura; **death by** ~ (*BRIT*) morte *f* accidentale.

misanthropist [mɪ'zænθrəpɪst] *n* misantropo/a.

misapply [mɪsə'plaɪ] *vt* impiegare male.

misapprehension ['mɪsæprɪ'hɛnʃən] *n* malinteso.

misappropriate [mɪsə'prəuprɪeɪt] *vt* appropriarsi indebitamente di.

misappropriation ['mɪsəprəuprɪ'eɪʃən] *n* appropriazione *f* indebita.

misbehave [mɪsbɪ'heɪv] *vi* comportarsi male.

misbehaviour, (*US*) **misbehavior** [mɪsbɪ'heɪvjə*] *n* comportamento scorretto.

misc. *abbr* = **miscellaneous**.

miscalculate [mɪs'kælkjuleɪt] *vt* calcolare male.

miscalculation ['mɪskælkju'leɪʃən] *n* errore *m* di calcolo.

miscarriage ['mɪskærɪdʒ] *n* (*MED*) aborto spontaneo; ~ **of justice** errore *m* giudiziario.

miscarry [mɪs'kærɪ] *vi* (*MED*) abortire; (*fail: plans*) andare a monte, fallire.

miscellaneous [mɪsɪ'leɪnɪəs] *adj* (*items*) vario(a); (*selection*) misto(a); ~ **expenses** spese varie.

miscellany [mɪ'sɛlənɪ] *n* raccolta.

mischance [mɪs'tʃɑːns] *n*: **by (some)** ~ per sfortuna.

mischief ['mɪstʃɪf] *n* (*naughtiness*) birichineria; (*harm*) male *m*, danno; (*maliciousness*) malizia.

mischievous ['mɪstʃɪvəs] *adj* (*naughty*) birichino(a); (*harmful*) dannoso(a).

misconception [mɪskən'sɛpʃən] *n* idea sbagliata.

misconduct [mɪs'kɔndʌkt] *n* cattiva condotta; **professional** ~ reato professionale.

misconstrue [mɪskən'struː] *vt* interpretare male.

miscount [mɪs'kaunt] *vt, vi* contare male.

misdeed [mɪs'diːd] *n* (*old*) misfatto.

misdemeanour, (*US*) **misdemeanor** [mɪsdɪ'miːnə*] *n* misfatto; infrazione *f*.

misdirect [mɪsdɪ'rɛkt] *vt* mal indirizzare.

miser ['maɪzə*] *n* avaro.

miserable ['mɪzərəbl] *adj* infelice; (*wretched*) miserabile; (*weather*) deprimente; **to feel** ~ sentirsi avvilito *or* giù di morale.

miserably ['mɪzərəblɪ] *adv* (*fail, live, pay*) miseramente; (*smile, answer*) tristemente.

miserly ['maɪzəlɪ] *adj* avaro(a).

misery ['mɪzərɪ] *n* (*unhappiness*) tristezza; (*pain*) sofferenza; (*wretchedness*) miseria.

misfire [mɪs'faɪə*] *vi* far cilecca; (*car engine*) perdere colpi.

misfit ['mɪsfɪt] *n* (*person*) spostato/a.

misfortune [mɪs'fɔːtʃən] *n* sfortuna.

misgiving(s) [mɪs'gɪvɪŋ(z)] *n(pl)* dubbi *mpl*, sospetti *mpl*; **to have** ~**s about sth** essere diffidente *or* avere dei dubbi per quanto riguarda qc.

misguided [mɪs'gaɪdɪd] *adj* sbagliato(a); poco giudizioso(a).

mishandle [mɪs'hændl] *vt* (*treat roughly*) maltrattare; (*mismanage*) trattare male.

mishap ['mɪshæp] *n* disgrazia.

mishear [mɪs'hɪə*] *vt, vi irreg* capire male.

mishmash ['mɪʃmæʃ] *n* (*col*) minestrone *m*, guazzabuglio.

misinform [mɪsɪn'fɔːm] *vt* informare male.

misinterpret [mɪsɪn'təːprɪt] *vt* interpretare male.

misinterpretation ['mɪsɪntə:prɪ'teɪʃən] *n* errata interpretazione *f*.

misjudge [mɪs'dʒʌdʒ] *vt* giudicare male.

mislay [mɪs'leɪ] *vt irreg* smarrire.

mislead [mɪs'liːd] *vt irreg* sviare.

misleading [mɪs'liːdɪŋ] *adj* ingannevole.

misled [mɪs'lɛd] *pt, pp of* **mislead**.

mismanage [mɪs'mænɪdʒ] *vt* gestire male; trattare male.

mismanagement [mɪs'mænɪdʒmənt] *n* cattiva amministrazione *f*.

misnomer [mɪs'nəumə*] *n* termine *m* sbagliato *or* improprio.

misogynist [mɪ'sɔdʒɪnɪst] *n* misogino.

misplace [mɪs'pleɪs] *vt* smarrire; collocare fuori posto; **to be** ~**d** (*trust etc*) essere malriposto(a).

misprint ['mɪsprɪnt] *n* errore *m* di stampa.

mispronounce [mɪsprə'nauns] *vt* pronunziare male.

misquote [mɪs'kwəut] *vt* citare erroneamente.

misread [mɪs'riːd] *vt irreg* leggere male.

misrepresent [mɪsreprɪ'zɛnt] *vt* travisare.

Miss [mɪs] n Signorina; **Dear ~ Smith** Cara Signorina; (*more formal*) Gentile Signorina.

miss [mɪs] vt (*fail to get*) perdere; (*appointment, class*) mancare a; (*escape, avoid*) evitare; (*notice loss of*: *money etc*) accorgersi di non avere più; (*regret the absence of*): **I ~ him/it** sento la sua mancanza, lui/esso mi manca ♦ vi mancare ♦ n (*shot*) colpo mancato; (*fig*): **that was a near ~** c'è mancato poco; **the bus just ~ed the wall** l'autobus per un pelo non è andato a finire contro il muro; **you're ~ing the point** non capisce.

▶**miss out** vt (*BRIT*) omettere.

▶**miss out on** vt fus (*fun, party*) perdersi; (*chance, bargain*) lasciarsi sfuggire.

Miss. abbr (*US*) = Mississippi.

missal ['mɪsl] n messale m.

misshapen [mɪs'ʃeɪpən] adj deforme.

missile ['mɪsaɪl] n (*AVIAT*) missile m; (*object thrown*) proiettile m

missile base n base f missilistica.

missile launcher n lancia-missili m inv.

missing ['mɪsɪŋ] adj perso(a), smarrito(a); **to go ~** sparire; **~ person** scomparso/a, disperso/a; **~ in action** (*MIL*) disperso/a.

mission ['mɪʃən] n missione f; **on a ~ to sb** in missione da qn.

missionary ['mɪʃənrɪ] n missionario/a.

misspell [mɪs'spel] vt (*irreg*: *like* **spell**) sbagliare l'ortografia di.

misspent [mɪs'spent] adj: **his ~ youth** la sua gioventù sciupata.

mist [mɪst] n nebbia, foschia ♦ vi (*also*: ~ **over**, ~ **up**) annebbiarsi; (*BRIT*: *windows*) appannarsi.

mistake [mɪs'teɪk] n sbaglio, errore m ♦ vt (*irreg*: *like* **take**) sbagliarsi di; fraintendere; **to ~ for** prendere per; **by ~** per sbaglio; **to make a ~** (*in writing, calculating etc*) fare uno sbaglio *or* un errore; **to make a ~ about sb/sth** sbagliarsi sul conto di qn/su qc.

mistaken [mɪs'teɪkən] pp of **mistake** ♦ adj (*idea etc*) sbagliato(a); **to be ~** sbagliarsi.

mistaken identity n errore m di persona.

mistakenly [mɪs'teɪkənlɪ] adv per errore.

mister ['mɪstə*] n (*col*) signore m; *see* **Mr.**

mistletoe ['mɪsltəu] n vischio.

mistook [mɪs'tuk] pt of **mistake**.

mistranslation [mɪstræns'leɪʃən] n traduzione f errata.

mistreat [mɪs'triːt] vt maltrattare.

mistress ['mɪstrɪs] n padrona; (*lover*) amante f; (*BRIT SCOL*) insegnante f.

mistrust [mɪs'trʌst] vt diffidare di ♦ n: **~ (of)** diffidenza (nei confronti di).

mistrustful [mɪs'trʌstful] adj: **~ (of)** diffidente (nei confronti di).

misty ['mɪstɪ] adj nebbioso(a), brumoso(a).

misty-eyed ['mɪstɪ'aɪd] adj trasognato(a).

misunderstand [mɪsʌndə'stænd] vt, vi irreg capire male, fraintendere.

misunderstanding [mɪsʌndə'stændɪŋ] n malinteso, equivoco.

misunderstood [mɪsʌndə'stud] pt, pp of **misunderstand**.

misuse n [mɪs'juːs] cattivo uso; (*of power*) abuso ♦ vt [mɪs'juːz] far cattivo uso di; abusare di.

MIT n abbr (*US*) = Massachusetts Institute of Technology.

mite [maɪt] n (*small quantity*) bricciolo; (*BRIT*: *small child*): **poor ~!** povera creaturina!

miter ['maɪtə*] n (*US*) = **miter**.

mitigate ['mɪtɪgeɪt] vt mitigare; (*suffering*) alleviare; **mitigating circumstances** circostanze fpl attenuanti.

mitigation [mɪtɪ'geɪʃən] n mitigazione f; alleviamento.

mitre, (*US*) **miter** ['maɪtə*] n mitra; (*CARPENTRY*) giunto ad angolo retto.

mitt(en) ['mɪt(n)] n mezzo guanto; manopola.

mix [mɪks] vt mescolare ♦ vi mescolarsi ♦ n mescolanza; preparato; **to ~ sth with sth** mischiare qc a qc; **to ~ business with pleasure** unire l'utile al dilettevole; **cake ~** preparato per torta.

▶**mix in** vt (*eggs etc*) incorporare.

▶**mix up** vt mescolare; (*confuse*) confondere; **to be ~ed up in sth** essere coinvolto in qc.

mixed [mɪkst] adj misto(a).

mixed-ability ['mɪkstə'bɪlɪtɪ] adj (*class etc*) con alunni di capacità diverse.

mixed bag n miscuglio, accozzaglia; **it's a ~** c'è un po' di tutto.

mixed blessing n: **it's a ~** ha i suoi lati positivi e negativi.

mixed doubles npl (*SPORT*) doppio misto.

mixed economy n economia mista.

mixed grill n (*BRIT*) misto alla griglia.

mixed marriage n matrimonio misto.

mixed-up [mɪkst'ʌp] adj (*confused*) confuso(a).

mixer ['mɪksə*] n (*for food*: *electric*) frullatore m; (: *hand*) frullino; (*person*): **he is a good ~** è molto socievole.

mixer tap n miscelatore m.

mixture ['mɪkstʃə*] n mescolanza; (*blend*: *tobacco etc*) miscela; (*MED*) sciroppo.

mix-up ['mɪksʌp] n confusione f.

MK abbr (*BRIT TECH*) = **mark**.

mk abbr = **mark** (*currency*).

mkt *abbr* = **market**.

MLitt *n abbr* (= *Master of Literature, Master of Letters*) *titolo di studio*.

MLR *n abbr* (*BRIT*) *see* **minimum lending rate**.

mm *abbr* (= *millimetre*) mm.

MN *abbr* (*BRIT*) = **Merchant Navy**; (*US*) = *Minnesota*.

MO *n abbr* = *medical officer*, (*US col*: = *modus operandi*) modo d'agire ♦ *abbr* (*US*) = *Missouri*.

m.o. *abbr* = **money order**.

moan [mǝun] *n* gemito ♦ *vi* gemere; (*col: complain*): **to** ~ (**about**) lamentarsi (di).

moaner ['mǝunǝ*] *n* (*col*) uno/a che si lamenta sempre.

moaning ['mǝunɪŋ] *n* gemiti *mpl*.

moat [mǝut] *n* fossato.

mob [mɔb] *n* folla; (*disorderly*) calca; (*pej*): **the** ~ la plebaglia ♦ *vt* accalcarsi intorno a.

mobile ['mǝubaɪl] *adj* mobile ♦ *n* (*ART*) mobile *m inv*; **applicants must be** ~ (*BRIT*) i candidati devono essere disposti a viaggiare.

mobile home *n* grande roulotte *f inv* (*utilizzata come domicilio*).

mobile phone *n* telefonino.

mobile shop *n* (*BRIT*) negozio ambulante.

mobility [mǝu'bɪlɪtɪ] *n* mobilità; (*of applicant*) disponibilità a viaggiare.

mobilize ['mǝubɪlaɪz] *vt* mobilitare ♦ *vi* mobilitarsi.

moccasin ['mɔkǝsɪn] *n* mocassino.

mock [mɔk] *vt* deridere, burlarsi di ♦ *adj* falso/a.

mockery ['mɔkǝrɪ] *n* derisione *f*; **to make a** ~ **of** rendere ridicolo.

mocking ['mɔkɪŋ] *adj* derisorio(a).

mockingbird ['mɔkɪŋbǝːd] *n* mimo (*uccello*).

mock-up ['mɔkʌp] *n* modello dimostrativo; abbozzo.

MOD *n abbr* (*BRIT*) = **Ministry of Defence**; *see* **defence**.

mod cons ['mɔd'kɔnz] *npl abbr* (*BRIT*) = **modern conveniences**.

mode [mǝud] *n* modo; (*of transport*) mezzo; (*COMPUT*) modalità *f inv*.

model ['mɔdl] *n* modello; (*person: for fashion*) indossatore/trice; (: *for artist*) modello/a ♦ *vt* modellare ♦ *vi* fare l'indossatore (*or* l'indossatrice) ♦ *adj* (*small-scale: railway etc*) in miniatura; (*child, factory*) modello *inv*; **to** ~ **clothes** presentare degli abiti; **to** ~ **sb/sth on** modellare qn/qc su.

modem ['mǝudɛm] *n* modem *m inv*.

moderate ['mɔdǝrɪt] *adj* moderato(a) ♦ *n*

(*POL*) moderato/a ♦ *vb* ['mɔdǝreɪt] *vi* moderarsi, placarsi ♦ *vt* moderare.

moderately ['mɔdǝrɪtlɪ] *adv* (*act*) con moderazione; (*expensive, difficult*) non troppo; (*pleased, happy*) abbastanza, discretamente; ~ **priced** a prezzo modico.

moderation [mɔdǝ'reɪʃǝn] *n* moderazione *f*, misura; **in** ~ in quantità moderata, con moderazione.

moderator ['mɔdǝreɪtǝ*] *n* moderatore/ trice; (*REL*) moderatore in importanti riunioni ecclesiastiche.

modern ['mɔdǝn] *adj* moderno(a); ~ **conveniences** comodità *fpl* moderne; ~ **languages** lingue *fpl* moderne.

modernization [mɔdǝnaɪ'zeɪʃǝn] *n* rimodernamento, modernizzazione *f*.

modernize ['mɔdǝnaɪz] *vt* modernizzare.

modest ['mɔdɪst] *adj* modesto(a).

modesty ['mɔdɪstɪ] *n* modestia.

modicum ['mɔdɪkǝm] *n*: **a** ~ **of** un minimo di.

modification [mɔdɪfɪ'keɪʃǝn] *n* modificazione *f*; **to make** ~**s** fare *or* apportare delle modifiche.

modify ['mɔdɪfaɪ] *vt* modificare.

modish ['mǝudɪʃ] *adj* (*liter*) à la page *inv*.

Mods [mɔdz] *n abbr* (*BRIT*: = *Honour Moderations*) *esame all'università di Oxford*.

modular ['mɔdjulǝ*] *adj* (*filing, unit*) modulare.

modulate ['mɔdjuleɪt] *vt* modulare.

modulation [mɔdju'leɪʃǝn] *n* modulazione *f*.

module ['mɔdjuːl] *n* modulo.

Mogadishu [mɔgǝ'dɪʃuː] *n* Mogadiscio *f*.

mogul ['mǝugl] *n* (*fig*) magnate *m*, pezzo grosso; (*SKI*) cunetta.

MOH *n abbr* (*BRIT*: = *Medical Officer of Health*) ≈ ufficiale *m* sanitario.

mohair ['mǝuhɛǝ*] *n* mohair *m*.

Mohammed [mǝu'hæmɪd] *n* Maometto.

moist [mɔɪst] *adj* umido(a).

moisten ['mɔɪsn] *vt* inumidire.

moisture ['mɔɪstʃǝ*] *n* umidità; (*on glass*) goccioline *fpl* di vapore.

moisturize ['mɔɪstʃǝraɪz] *vt* (*skin*) idratare.

moisturizer ['mɔɪstʃǝraɪzǝ*] *n* idratante *f*.

molar ['mǝulǝ*] *n* molare *m*.

molasses [mǝu'læsɪz] *n* molassa.

mold [mǝuld] *etc* (*US*) = **mould** *etc*.

Moldavia [mɔl'deɪvɪǝ], **Moldova** [mɔl'dǝuvǝ] *n* Moldavia.

Moldavian [mɔl'deɪvɪǝn], **Moldovan** [mɔl'dǝuvǝn] *adj* moldavo(a).

mole [mǝul] *n* (*animal*) talpa; (*spot*) neo.

molecule ['mɔlɪkjuːl] *n* molecola.

molehill ['mǝulhɪl] *n* cumulo di terra sulla

tana di una talpa.
molest [məu'lɛst] *vt* molestare.
mollusc, (*US*) **mollusk** ['mɔləsk] *n*
mollusco.
mollycoddle ['mɔlɪkɔdl] *vt* coccolare,
vezzeggiare.
Molotov cocktail ['mɔlətɔf-] *n* (bottiglia)
Molotov *f inv.*
molt [məult] *vi* (*US*) = **moult.**
molten ['məultən] *adj* fuso(a).
mom [mɔm] *n* (*US*) = **mum.**
moment ['məumənt] *n* momento, istante *m*;
importanza; **at the** ~ al momento, in
questo momento; **for the** ~ per il
momento, per ora; **in a** ~ tra un
momento; "**one** ~ **please**" (*TEL*) "attenda,
prego".
momentarily ['məuməntərɪlɪ] *adv* per un
momento; (*US*: *very soon*) da un momento
all'altro.
momentary ['məuməntərɪ] *adj*
momentaneo(a), passeggero(a).
momentous [məu'mɛntɔs] *adj* di grande
importanza.
momentum [məu'mɛntəm] *n* velocità
acquisita, slancio; (*PHYSICS*) momento; **to**
gather ~ aumentare di velocità; (*fig*)
prendere *or* guadagnare terreno.
mommy ['mɔmɪ] *n* (*US*) mamma.
Mon. *abbr* (= *Monday*) lun.
Monaco ['mɔnəkəu] *n* Monaco *f.*
monarch ['mɔnək] *n* monarca *m.*
monarchist ['mɔnəkɪst] *n* monarchico/a.
monarchy ['mɔnəkɪ] *n* monarchia.
monastery ['mɔnəstərɪ] *n* monastero.
monastic [mə'næstɪk] *adj* monastico(a).
Monday ['mʌndɪ] *n* lunedì *m inv; for phrases*
see also **Tuesday.**
Monegasque [mɔnə'gæsk] *adj*, *n*
monegasco(a).
monetarist ['mʌnɪtərɪst] *n* monetarista *m/f.*
monetary ['mʌnɪtərɪ] *adj* monetario(a).
money ['mʌnɪ] *n* denaro, soldi *mpl*; **to make**
~ (*person*) fare (i) soldi; (*business*)
rendere; **danger** ~ (*BRIT*) indennità di
rischio; **I've got no** ~ **left** non ho più
neanche una lira.
moneyed ['mʌnɪd] *adj* ricco(a).
moneylender ['mʌnɪlɛndə*] *n* prestatore *m*
di denaro.
moneymaker ['mʌnɪmeɪkə*] *n* (*BRIT col*:
business) affare *m* d'oro.
moneymaking ['mʌnɪmeɪkɪŋ] *adj* che rende
(bene *or* molto), lucrativo(a).
money market *n* mercato monetario.
money order *n* vaglia *m inv.*
money-spinner ['mʌnɪspɪnə*] *n* (*col*)
miniera d'oro (*fig*).

money supply *n* liquidità monetaria.
Mongol ['mɔŋgəl] *n* mongolo/a; (*LING*)
mongolo.
mongol ['mɔŋgəl] *adj*, *n* (*MED*) mongoloide
(*m/f*).
Mongolia [mɔŋ'gəulɪə] *n* Mongolia.
Mongolian [mɔŋ'gəulɪən] *adj* mongolico(a)
♦ *n* mongolo/a; (*LING*) mongolo.
mongoose ['mɔŋguːs] *n* mangusta.
mongrel ['mʌŋgrəl] *n* (*dog*) cane *m*
bastardo.
monitor ['mɔnɪtə*] *n* (*BRIT SCOL*) capoclasse
m/f; (*US SCOL*) chi sorveglia agli esami;
(*TV*, *COMPUT*) monitor *m inv* ♦ *vt*
controllare; (*foreign station*) ascoltare le
trasmissioni di.
monk [mʌŋk] *n* monaco.
monkey ['mʌŋkɪ] *n* scimmia.
monkey business *n* (*col*) scherzi *mpl.*
monkey nut *n* (*BRIT*) nocciolina
americana.
monkey wrench *n* chiave *f* a rullino.
mono ['mɔnəu] *adj* mono *inv*; (*broadcast*) in
mono.
mono... ['mɔnəu] *prefix* mono....
monochrome ['mɔnəkrəum] *adj*
monocromo(a).
monocle ['mɔnəkl] *n* monocolo.
monogamous [mə'nɔgəməs] *adj*
monogamo(a).
monogamy [mə'nɔgəmɪ] *n* monogamia.
monogram ['mɔnəgræm] *n* monogramma
m.
monolith ['mɔnəlɪθ] *n* monolito.
monologue ['mɔnəlɔg] *n* monologo.
monoplane ['mɔnəupleɪn] *n* monoplano.
monopolize [mə'nɔpəlaɪz] *vt*
monopolizzare.
monopoly [mə'nɔpəlɪ] *n* monopolio;
Monopolies and Mergers Commission
(*BRIT*) commissione *f* antimonopoli.
monorail ['mɔnəureɪl] *n* monorotaia.
monosodium glutamate (MSG)
[mɔnə'səudɪəm'gluːtəmeɪt] *n* glutammato di
sodio.
monosyllabic [mɔnəsɪ'læbɪk] *adj*
monosillabico(a); (*person*) che parla a
monosillabi.
monosyllable ['mɔnəsɪləbl] *n* monosillabo.
monotone ['mɔnətəun] *n* pronunzia (*or*
voce *f*) monotona; **to speak in a** ~ parlare
con voce monotona.
monotonous [mə'nɔtənəs] *adj*
monotono(a).
monotony [mə'nɔtənɪ] *n* monotonia.
monoxide [mɔ'nɔksaɪd] *n*: **carbon** ~ ossido
di carbonio.
monsoon [mɔn'suːn] *n* monsone *m.*

monster ['mɒnstə*] *n* mostro.
monstrosity [mɒn'strɒsɪtɪ] *n* mostruosità *f* *inv.*
monstrous ['mɒnstrəs] *adj* mostruoso(a).
Mont. *abbr* (*US*) = *Montana.*
montage [mɒn'tɑːʒ] *n* montaggio.
Mont Blanc [mɔ̃blɑ̃] *n* Monte *m* Bianco.
month [mʌnθ] *n* mese *m*; **300 dollars a** ~ 300 dollari al mese; **every** ~ (*happen*) tutti i mesi; (*pay*) mensilmente, ogni mese.
monthly ['mʌnθlɪ] *adj* mensile ♦ *adv* al mese; ogni mese ♦ *n* (*magazine*) rivista mensile; **twice** ~ due volte al mese.
monument ['mɒnjumənt] *n* monumento.
monumental [mɒnju'mɛntl] *adj* monumentale; (*fig*) colossale.
monumental mason *n* lapidario.
moo [muː] *vi* muggire, mugghiare.
mood [muːd] *n* umore *m*; **to be in a good/ bad** ~ essere di buon/cattivo umore; **to be in the** ~ **for** essere disposto(a) a, aver voglia di.
moody ['muːdɪ] *adj* (*variable*) capriccioso(a), lunatico(a); (*sullen*) imbronciato(a).
moon [muːn] *n* luna.
moonbeam ['muːnbiːm] *n* raggio di luna.
moon landing *n* allunaggio.
moonlight ['muːnlaɪt] *n* chiaro di luna ♦ *vi* fare del lavoro nero.
moonlighting ['muːnlaɪtɪŋ] *n* lavoro nero.
moonlit ['muːnlɪt] *adj* illuminato(a) dalla luna; **a** ~ **night** una notte rischiarata dalla luna.
moonshot ['muːnʃɒt] *n* lancio sulla luna.
moonstruck ['muːnstrʌk] *adj* lunatico(a).
moony ['muːnɪ] *adj* (*eyes*) sognante.
Moor [muə*] *n* moro/a.
moor [muə*] *n* brughiera ♦ *vt* (*ship*) ormeggiare ♦ *vi* ormeggiarsi.
moorings ['muərɪŋz] *npl* (*chains*) ormeggi *mpl*; (*place*) ormeggio.
Moorish ['muərɪʃ] *adj* moresco(a).
moorland ['muələnd] *n* brughiera.
moose [muːs] *n* (*pl inv*) alce *m*.
moot [muːt] *vt* sollevare ♦ *adj*: ~ **point** punto discutibile.
mop [mɒp] *n* lavapavimenti *m* *inv*; (*also*: ~ **of hair**) zazzera ♦ *vt* lavare con lo straccio; **to** ~ **one's brow** asciugarsi la fronte.
▶**mop up** *vt* asciugare con uno straccio.
mope [məup] *vi* fare il broncio.
▶**mope about, mope around** *vi* trascinarsi *or* aggirarsi con aria avvilita.
moped ['məupɛd] *n* (*BRIT*) ciclomotore *m*.

MOR *adj* *abbr* (*MUS*: = *middle-of-the-road*): ~ **music** musica leggera.
moral ['mɒrəl] *adj* morale ♦ *n* morale *f*; ~**s** *npl* moralità.
morale [mɒ'rɑːl] *n* morale *m*.
morality [mə'rælɪtɪ] *n* moralità.
moralize ['mɒrəlaɪz] *vi*: **to** ~ (**about**) fare il (*or* la) moralista (riguardo), moraleggiare (riguardo).
morally ['mɒrəlɪ] *adv* moralmente.
moral victory *n* vittoria morale.
morass [mə'ræs] *n* palude *f*, pantano.
moratorium [mɔrə'tɔːrɪəm] *n* moratoria.
morbid ['mɔːbɪd] *adj* morboso(a).

═══════════════════════════ *KEYWORD*

more [mɔː*] *adj* **1** (*greater in number etc*) più; ~ **people/letters than we expected** più persone/lettere di quante ne aspettavamo; **I have** ~ **wine/money than you** ho più vino/soldi di te; **I have** ~ **wine than beer** ho più vino che birra
2 (*additional*) altro(a), ancora; **do you want (some)** ~ **tea?** vuole dell'altro tè?, vuole ancora del tè?; **I have no** *or* **I don't have any** ~ **money** non ho più soldi
♦ *pron* **1** (*greater amount*) più; ~ **than 10** più di 10; **it cost** ~ **than we expected** è costato più di quanto ci aspettassimo; **and what's** ~ ... e per di più ...
2 (*further or additional amount*) ancora; **is there any** ~? ce n'è ancora?; **there's no** ~ non ce n'è più; **a little** ~ ancora un po';
many/much ~ molti(e)/molto(a) di più
♦ *adv*: ~ **dangerous/easily (than)** più pericoloso/facilmente (di); ~ **and** ~ sempre di più; ~ **and** ~ **difficult** sempre più difficile; ~ **or less** più o meno; ~ **than ever** più che mai; **once** ~ ancora (una volta), un'altra volta; **no** ~, **not any** ~ non ... più; **I have no** ~ **money, I haven't any** ~ **money** non ho più soldi.

moreover [mɔː'rəuvə*] *adv* inoltre, di più.
morgue [mɔːg] *n* obitorio.
MORI ['mɔːrɪ] *n* *abbr* (*BRIT*: = *Market & Opinion Research Institute*) *istituto di sondaggio.*
moribund ['mɔrɪbʌnd] *adj* moribondo(a).
morning ['mɔːnɪŋ] *n* mattina, mattino; (*duration*) mattinata; **in the** ~ la mattina; **this** ~ stamattina; **7 o'clock in the** ~ le 7 di or della mattina.
morning-after pill ['mɔːnɪŋ'ɑːftə-] *n* pillola del giorno dopo.
morning sickness *n* nausee *fpl* mattutine.
Moroccan [mə'rɔkən] *adj*, *n* marocchino(a).
Morocco [mə'rɔkəu] *n* Marocco.

moron ['mɔːrɔn] n deficiente m/f.
moronic [mə'rɔnɪk] adj deficiente.
morose [mə'rəus] adj cupo(a), tetro(a).
morphine ['mɔːfiːn] n morfina.
morris dancing ['mɔrɪs-] n (BRIT) antica danza tradizionale inglese.
Morse [mɔːs] n (also: ~ **code**) alfabeto Morse.
morsel ['mɔːsl] n boccone m.
mortal ['mɔːtl] adj, n mortale (m).
mortality [mɔː'tælɪtɪ] n mortalità.
mortality rate n tasso di mortalità.
mortar ['mɔːtə*] n (CONSTR) malta; (dish) mortaio.
mortgage ['mɔːgɪdʒ] n ipoteca; (in house buying) mutuo ipotecario ♦ vt ipotecare; **to take out a** ~ contrarre un mutuo (or un'ipoteca).
mortgage company n (US) società f inv immobiliare.
mortgagee [mɔːgɪ'dʒiː] n creditore m ipotecario.
mortgagor ['mɔːgɪdʒə*] n debitore m ipotecario.
mortician [mɔː'tɪʃən] n (US) impresario di pompe funebri.
mortified ['mɔːtɪfaɪd] adj umiliato(a).
mortise lock ['mɔːtɪs-] n serratura incastrata.
mortuary ['mɔːtjuərɪ] n camera mortuaria; obitorio.
mosaic [məu'zeɪɪk] n mosaico.
Moscow ['mɔskəu] n Mosca.
Moslem ['mɔzləm] adj, n = **Muslim**.
mosque [mɔsk] n moschea.
mosquito, ~**es** [mɔs'kiːtəu] n zanzara.
mosquito net n zanzariera.
moss [mɔs] n muschio.
mossy ['mɔsɪ] adj muscoso(a).
most [məust] adj la maggior parte di; il più di ♦ pron la maggior parte ♦ adv più; (work, sleep etc) di più; (very) molto, estremamente; **the** ~ (also: + adjective) il(la) più; ~ **fish** la maggior parte dei pesci; ~ **of** la maggior parte di; ~ **of them** quasi tutti; **I saw** ~ ho visto più io; **at the (very)** ~ al massimo; **to make the** ~ **of** trarre il massimo vantaggio da.
mostly ['məustlɪ] adv per lo più.
MOT n abbr (BRIT: = Ministry of Transport): **the** ~ (**test**) revisione obbligatoria degli autoveicoli.
motel [məu'tɛl] n motel m inv.
moth [mɔθ] n farfalla notturna; tarma.
mothball ['mɔθbɔːl] n pallina di naftalina.
moth-eaten ['mɔθiːtn] adj tarmato(a).
mother ['mʌðə*] n madre f ♦ vt (care for) fare da madre a.

mother board n (COMPUT) scheda madre.
motherhood ['mʌðəhud] n maternità.
mother-in-law ['mʌðərɪnlɔː] n suocera.
mother-of-pearl [mʌðərəv'pəːl] n madreperla.
mother's help n bambinaia.
mother-to-be [mʌðətə'biː] n futura mamma.
mother tongue n madrelingua.
mothproof ['mɔθpruːf] adj antitarmico(a).
motif [məu'tiːf] n motivo.
motion ['məuʃən] n movimento, moto; (gesture) gesto; (at meeting) mozione f; (BRIT: also: **bowel** ~) evacuazione f ♦ vt, vi: **to** ~ (**to**) **sb to do** fare cenno a qn di fare; **to be in** ~ (vehicle) essere in moto; **to set in** ~ avviare; **to go through the** ~**s of doing sth** (fig) fare qc pro forma.
motionless ['məuʃənlɪs] adj immobile.
motion picture n film m inv.
motivate ['məutɪveɪt] vt (act, decision) dare origine a, motivare; (person) spingere.
motivated ['məutɪveɪtɪd] adj motivato(a).
motivation [məutɪ'veɪʃən] n motivazione f.
motive ['məutɪv] n motivo ♦ adj motore(trice); **from the best** ~**s** con le migliori intenzioni.
motley ['mɔtlɪ] adj eterogeneo(a), molto vario(a).
motor ['məutə*] n motore m; (BRIT col: vehicle) macchina ♦ adj motore(trice).
motorbike ['məutəbaɪk] n moto f inv.
motorboat ['məutəbəut] n motoscafo.
motorcade ['məutəkeɪd] n corteo di macchine.
motorcar ['məutəkɑː] n automobile f.
motorcoach ['məutəkəutʃ] n (BRIT) pullman m inv.
motorcycle ['məutəsaɪkl] n motocicletta.
motorcyclist ['məutəsaɪklɪst] n motociclista m/f.
motoring ['məutərɪŋ] n (BRIT) turismo automobilistico ♦ adj (accident) d'auto, automobilistico(a); (offence) di guida; ~ **holiday** vacanza in macchina.
motorist ['məutərɪst] n automobilista m/f.
motorize ['məutəraɪz] vt motorizzare.
motor oil n olio lubrificante.
motor racing n (BRIT) corse fpl automobilistiche.
motor scooter n motorscooter m inv.
motor vehicle n autoveicolo.
motorway ['məutəweɪ] n (BRIT) autostrada.
mottled ['mɔtld] adj chiazzato(a), marezzato(a).
motto, ~**es** ['mɔtəu] n motto.
mould, (US) mold [məuld] n forma, stampo; (mildew) muffa ♦ vt formare; (fig)

foggiare.
mo(u)lder ['məuldə*] vi (decay) ammuffire.
mo(u)lding ['məuldıŋ] n (ARCHIT)
modanatura.
mo(u)ldy ['məuldı] adj ammuffito(a).
moult, (US) **molt** [məult] vi far la muta.
mound [maund] n rialzo, collinetta.
mount [maunt] n monte m, montagna;
(horse) cavalcatura; (for jewel etc)
montatura ♦ vt montare; (horse) montare
a; (exhibition) organizzare; (attack)
sferrare, condurre; (picture, stamp)
sistemare ♦ vi salire; (get on a horse)
montare a cavallo; (also: ~ up)
aumentare.
mountain ['mauntın] n montagna ♦ cpd di
montagna; **to make a ~ out of a molehill**
fare di una mosca un elefante.
mountain bike n mountain bike f inv.
mountaineer [mauntı'nıə*] n alpinista m/f.
mountaineering [mauntı'nıərıŋ] n
alpinismo; **to go ~** fare dell'alpinismo.
mountainous ['mauntınəs] adj
montagnoso(a).
mountain range n catena montuosa.
mountain rescue team n ≈ squadra di
soccorso alpino.
mountainside ['mauntınsaıd] n fianco della
montagna.
mounted ['mauntıd] adj a cavallo.
mourn [mɔ:n] vt piangere, lamentare ♦ vi:
to ~ (for sb) piangere (la morte di qn).
mourner ['mɔ:nə*] n parente m/f (or amico/
a) del defunto.
mourning ['mɔ:nıŋ] n lutto ♦ cpd (dress) da
lutto; **in ~** in lutto.
mouse, pl **mice** [maus, maıs] n topo;
(COMPUT) mouse m inv.
mousetrap ['maustræp] n trappola per i
topi.
moussaka [mu'sɑ:kə] n moussaka.
mousse [mu:s] n mousse f inv.
moustache [məs'tɑ:ʃ] n baffi mpl.
mousy ['mausı] adj (person) timido(a); (hair)
né chiaro(a) né scuro(a).
mouth, ~s [mauθ, -ðz] n bocca; (of river)
bocca, foce f; (opening) orifizio.
mouthful ['mauθful] n boccata.
mouth organ n armonica.
mouthpiece ['mauθpi:s] n (MUS) bocchino;
(TEL) microfono; (of breathing apparatus)
boccaglio; (person) portavoce m/f.
mouth-to-mouth ['mauθtə'mauθ] adj: ~
resuscitation respirazione f bocca a
bocca.
mouthwash ['mauθwɔʃ] n collutorio.
mouth-watering ['mauθwɔ:tərıŋ] adj che
fa venire l'acquolina in bocca.

movable ['mu:vəbl] adj mobile.
move [mu:v] n (movement) movimento; (in
game) mossa; (: turn to play) turno;
(change of house) trasloco ♦ vt muovere,
spostare; (emotionally) commuovere;
(POL: resolution etc) proporre ♦ vi (gen)
muoversi, spostarsi; (traffic) circolare;
(also: ~ house) cambiar casa, traslocare;
to ~ towards andare verso; **to ~ sb to do
sth** indurre or spingere qn a fare qc; **to
get a ~ on** affrettarsi, sbrigarsi; **to be
~d** (emotionally) essere commosso(a).
► **move about, move around** vi (fidget)
agitarsi; (travel) viaggiare.
► **move along** vi muoversi avanti.
► **move away** vi allontanarsi, andarsene.
► **move back** vi indietreggiare; (return)
ritornare.
► **move forward** vi avanzare ♦ vt avanzare,
spostare in avanti; (people) far avanzare.
► **move in** vi (to a house) entrare (in una
nuova casa).
► **move off** vi partire.
► **move on** vi riprendere la strada ♦ vt
(onlookers) far circolare.
► **move out** vi (of house) sgombrare.
► **move over** vi spostarsi.
► **move up** vi avanzare.
movement ['mu:vmənt] n (gen)
movimento; (gesture) gesto; (of stars,
water, physical) moto; ~ (of the bowels)
(MED) evacuazione f.
mover ['mu:və*] n proponente m/f.
movie ['mu:vı] n film m inv; **the ~s** il
cinema.
movie camera n cinepresa.
moviegoer ['mu:vıgəuə*] n (US)
frequentatore/trice di cinema.
moving ['mu:vıŋ] adj mobile; (causing
emotion) commovente; (instigating)
animatore(trice).
mow, pt **mowed,** pp **mowed** or **mown**
[məu, -n] vt falciare; (grass) tagliare.
► **mow down** vt falciare.
mower ['məuə*] n (also: **lawn ~**) tagliaerba
m inv.
mown [məun] pp of **mow**.
Mozambique [məuzəm'bi:k] n Mozambico.
MP n abbr = Military Police; (Canada)
= Mounted Police; (BRIT) see **Member of
Parliament**.
mpg n abbr = miles per gallon (30 mpg = 9.4
l. per 100 km).
mph n abbr = miles per hour (60 mph = 96
km/h).
MPhil n abbr (US: = Master of Philosophy)
titolo di studio.
MPS n abbr (BRIT) = Member of the

Pharmaceutical Society.

Mr, Mr. ['mɪstə*] *n*: ~ **X** Signor X, Sig. X.

MRC *n abbr* (*BRIT*: = *Medical Research Council*) *ufficio governativo per la ricerca medica in Gran Bretagna e nel Commonwealth.*

MRCP *n abbr* (*BRIT*) = *Member of the Royal College of Physicians.*

MRCS *n abbr* (*BRIT*) = *Member of the Royal College of Surgeons.*

MRCVS *n abbr* (*BRIT*) = *Member of the Royal College of Veterinary Surgeons.*

Mrs, Mrs. ['mɪsɪz] *n*: ~ **X** Signora X, Sig.ra X.

MS *n abbr* (*US*: = *Master of Science*) *titolo di studio*; (= *manuscript*) ms; (*MED*) = **multiple sclerosis** ♦ *abbr* (*US*) = *Mississippi*.

Ms, Ms. [mɪz] *n* (= *Miss or Mrs*): ~ **X** ≈ Signora X, Sig.ra X.

MSA *n abbr* (*US*: = *Master of Science in Agriculture*) *titolo di studio*.

MSc *n abbr see* **Master of Science.**

MSG *abbr see* **monosodium glutamate.**

MSP *n abbr* = *Member of the Scottish Parliament.*

MST *abbr* (*US*: – *Mountain Standard Time*) *ora invernale delle Montagne Rocciose.*

MSW *n abbr* (*US*: = *Master of Social Work*) *titolo di studio.*

MT *n abbr* = *machine translation* ♦ (*US*) = *Montana.*

Mt *abbr* (*GEO*: = *mount*) M.

mth *abbr* (= *month*) m.

MTV *n abbr* = **music television.**

================= *KEYWORD*

much [mʌtʃ] *adj, pron* molto(a); **he's done so ~ work** ha lavorato così tanto; **I have as ~ money as you** ho tanti soldi quanti ne hai tu; **how ~ is it?** quant'è?; **it's not ~** non è tanto; **it costs too ~** costa troppo; **as ~ as you want** quanto vuoi

♦ *adv* **1** (*greatly*) molto, tanto; **thank you very ~** molte grazie; **I like it very/so ~** mi piace moltissimo/così tanto; **~ to my amazement** con mio enorme stupore; **he's very ~ the gentleman** è il vero gentiluomo; **I read as ~ as I can** leggo quanto posso; **as ~ as you** tanto quanto te

2 (*by far*) molto; **it's ~ the biggest company in Europe** è di gran lunga la più grossa società in Europa

3 (*almost*) grossomodo, praticamente; **they're ~ the same** sono praticamente uguali.

lo stupido; (: *waste time*) gingillarsi; (*tinker*) armeggiare.

▶**muck in** *vi* (*BRIT col*) mettersi insieme.

▶**muck out** *vt* (*stable*) pulire.

▶**muck up** *vt* (*col: dirty*) sporcare; (: *spoil*) rovinare.

muckraking ['mʌkreɪkɪŋ] *n* (*fig col*) caccia agli scandali ♦ *adj* scandalistico(a).

mucky ['mʌkɪ] *adj* (*dirty*) sporco(a), lordo(a).

mucus ['mjuːkəs] *n* muco.

mud [mʌd] *n* fango.

muddle ['mʌdl] *n* confusione *f*, disordine *m*; pasticcio ♦ *vt* (*also*: ~ **up**) mettere sottosopra; confondere; **to be in a ~** (*person*) non riuscire a raccapezzarsi; **to get in a ~** (*while explaining*) imbrogliarsi.

▶**muddle along** *vi* andare avanti a casaccio.

▶**muddle through** *vi* cavarsela alla meno peggio.

muddle-headed [mʌdl'hɛdɪd] *adj* (*person*) confusionario(a).

muddy ['mʌdɪ] *adj* fangoso(a).

mud flats *npl* distesa fangosa.

mudguard ['mʌdɡɑːd] *n* parafango.

mudpack ['mʌdpæk] *n* maschera di fango.

mud-slinging ['mʌdslɪŋɪŋ] *n* (*fig*) infangamento.

muesli ['mjuːzlɪ] *n* müsli *m inv*.

muff [mʌf] *n* manicotto ♦ *vt* (*shot, catch etc*) mancare, sbagliare; **to ~ it** sbagliare tutto.

muffin ['mʌfɪn] *n* specie di pasticcino soffice da tè.

muffle ['mʌfl] *vt* (*sound*) smorzare, attutire; (*against cold*) imbacuccare.

muffled ['mʌfld] *adj* smorzato(a), attutito(a).

muffler ['mʌflə*] *n* (*scarf*) sciarpa (pesante); (*US AUT*) marmitta; (*on motorbike*) silenziatore *m*.

mufti ['mʌftɪ] *n*: **in ~** in borghese.

mug [mʌɡ] *n* (*cup*) tazzone *m*; (*for beer*) boccale *m*; (*col: face*) muso; (: *fool*) scemo/a ♦ *vt* (*assault*) assalire; **it's a ~'s game** (*BRIT*) è proprio (una cosa) da fessi.

▶**mug up** *vt* (*BRIT col: also*: ~ **up on**) studiare bene.

mugger ['mʌɡə*] *n* aggressore *m*.

mugging ['mʌɡɪŋ] *n* aggressione *f* (a scopo di rapina).

muggins ['mʌɡɪnz] *n* (*col*) semplicione/a, sprovveduto/a.

muggy ['mʌɡɪ] *adj* afoso(a).

mug shot *n* (*col*) foto *f inv* segnaletica.

mulatto, ~es [mjuː'lætəu] *n* mulatto/a.

mulberry ['mʌlbərɪ] *n* (*fruit*) mora (di gelso); (*tree*) gelso, moro.

muck [mʌk] *n* (*mud*) fango; (*dirt*) sporcizia.

▶**muck about, muck around** *vi* (*col*) fare

mule [mju:l] n mulo.
mull [mʌl]: **to ~ over** vt rimuginare.
mulled [mʌld] adj: **~ wine** vino caldo.
multi... ['mʌltɪ] prefix multi....
multi-access [mʌltɪ'æksɛs] adj (COMPUT) ad accesso multiplo.
multicoloured, (US) **multicolored** ['mʌltɪkʌləd] adj multicolore, variopinto(a).
multifarious [mʌltɪ'fɛərɪəs] adj molteplice, svariato(a).
multilateral [mʌltɪ'lætərəl] adj (POL) multilaterale.
multi-level ['mʌltɪlɛvl] adj (US) = **multistorey**.
multimillionaire [mʌltɪmɪljə'nɛə*] n multimiliardario/a.
multinational [mʌltɪ'næʃənl] adj, n multinazionale (f).
multiple ['mʌltɪpl] adj multiplo(a); molteplice ♦ n multiplo; (BRIT: also: ~ store) grande magazzino che fa parte di una catena.
multiple choice n esercizi mpl a scelta multipla.
multiple crash n serie f inv di incidenti a catena.
multiple sclerosis n sclerosi f a placche.
multiplex ['mʌltɪplɛks] n (also: ~ cinema) cinema m inv multisale inv.
multiplication [mʌltɪplɪ'keɪʃən] n moltiplicazione f.
multiplication table n tavola pitagorica.
multiplicity [mʌltɪ'plɪsɪtɪ] n molteplicità.
multiply ['mʌltɪplaɪ] vt moltiplicare ♦ vi moltiplicarsi.
multiracial [mʌltɪ'reɪʃəl] adj multirazziale.
multistorey ['mʌltɪ'stɔːrɪ] adj (BRIT: building, car park) a più piani.
multitude ['mʌltɪtjuːd] n moltitudine f.
mum [mʌm] n (BRIT) mamma ♦ adj: **to keep ~** non aprire bocca; **~'s the word!** acqua in bocca!
mumble ['mʌmbl] vt, vi borbottare.
mumbo jumbo ['mʌmbəu-] n (col) parole fpl incomprensibili.
mummify ['mʌmɪfaɪ] vt mummificare.
mummy ['mʌmɪ] n (BRIT: mother) mamma; (embalmed) mummia.
mumps [mʌmps] n orecchioni mpl.
munch [mʌntʃ] vt, vi sgranocchiare.
mundane [mʌn'deɪn] adj terra a terra inv.
Munich ['mjuːnɪk] n Monaco f (di Baviera).
municipal [mjuː'nɪsɪpl] adj municipale.
municipality [mjuːnɪsɪ'pælɪtɪ] n municipio.
munitions [mjuː'nɪʃənz] npl munizioni fpl.
mural ['mjuərəl] n dipinto murale.
murder ['mɜːdə*] n assassinio, omicidio

♦ vt assassinare; **to commit ~** commettere un omicidio.
murderer ['mɜːdərə*] n omicida m, assassino.
murderess ['mɜːdərɪs] n omicida f, assassina.
murderous ['mɜːdərəs] adj micidiale.
murk [mɜːk] n oscurità, buio.
murky ['mɜːkɪ] adj tenebroso(a), buio(a).
murmur ['mɜːmə*] n mormorio ♦ vt, vi mormorare; **heart ~** (MED) soffio al cuore.
MusB(ac) n abbr (= Bachelor of Music) titolo di studio.
muscle ['mʌsl] n muscolo.
▶**muscle in** vi immischiarsi.
muscular ['mʌskjulə*] adj muscolare; (person, arm) muscoloso(a).
muscular dystrophy n distrofia muscolare.
MusD(oc) n abbr (= Doctor of Music) titolo di studio.
muse [mjuːz] vi meditare, sognare ♦ n musa.
museum [mjuː'zɪəm] n museo.
mush [mʌʃ] n pappa.
mushroom ['mʌʃrum] n fungo ♦ vi (fig) svilupparsi rapidamente.
mushy ['mʌʃɪ] adj (of food) spappolato(a); (sentimental) sdolcinato(a).
music ['mjuːzɪk] n musica.
musical ['mjuːzɪkəl] adj musicale ♦ n (show) commedia musicale.
music(al) box n carillon m inv.
musical chairs n gioco delle sedie (in cui bisogna sedersi non appena cessa la musica); (fig) scambio delle poltrone.
musical instrument n strumento musicale.
music centre n impianto m stereo inv monoblocco inv.
music hall n teatro di varietà.
musician [mjuː'zɪʃən] n musicista m/f.
music stand n leggio.
musk [mʌsk] n muschio.
musket ['mʌskɪt] n moschetto.
muskrat ['mʌskræt] n topo muschiato.
musk rose n (BOT) rosa muschiata.
Muslim ['mʌzlɪm] adj, n musulmano(a).
muslin ['mʌzlɪn] n mussola.
musquash ['mʌskwɔʃ] n (fur) rat musqué m inv.
mussel ['mʌsl] n cozza.
must [mʌst] aux vb (obligation): **I ~ do it** devo farlo; (probability): **he ~ be there by now** dovrebbe essere arrivato ormai; **I ~ have made a mistake** devo essermi sbagliato ♦ n: **this programme/trip is a ~**

è un programma/viaggio da non perdersi.
mustache ['mʌstæʃ] n (US) = **moustache**.
mustard ['mʌstəd] n senape f, mostarda.
mustard gas n iprite f.
muster ['mʌstə*] vt radunare; (also: ~ up: strength, courage) fare appello a.
mustiness ['mʌstɪnɪs] n odor di muffa or di stantio.
mustn't ['mʌsnt] = **must not**.
musty ['mʌstɪ] adj che sa di muffa or di rinchiuso.
mutant ['mjuːtənt] adj, n mutante (m).
mutate [mjuː'teɪt] vi subire una mutazione.
mutation [mjuː'teɪʃən] n mutazione f.
mute [mjuːt] adj, n muto(a).
muted ['mjuːtɪd] adj (noise) attutito(a), smorzato(a); (criticism) attenuato(a); (MUS) in sordina; (: trumpet) con sordina.
mutilate ['mjuːtɪleɪt] vt mutilare.
mutilation [mjuːtɪ'leɪʃən] n mutilazione f.
mutinous ['mjuːtɪnəs] adj (troops) ammutinato(n)· (attitude) ribelle.
mutiny ['mjuːtɪnɪ] n ammutinamento ♦ vi ammutinarsi.
mutter ['mʌtə*] vt, vi borbottare, brontolare.
mutton ['mʌtn] n carne f di montone.
mutual ['mjuːtʃuəl] adj mutuo(a), reciproco(a).
mutually ['mjuːtʃuəlɪ] adv reciprocamente.
Muzak ® ['mjuːzæk] n (often pej) musica di sottofondo.
muzzle ['mʌzl] n muso; (protective device) museruola; (of gun) bocca ♦ vt mettere la museruola a.
MV abbr (= motor vessel) M/N, m/n.
MVP n abbr (US SPORT: = most valuable player) titolo ottenuto da sportivo.
MW abbr (RADIO: = medium wave) O.M.
my [maɪ] adj il(la) mio(a), pl i(le) miei(mie).
Myanmar ['maɪænmɑː*] n Myanma.
myopic [maɪ'ɔpɪk] adj miope.
myriad ['mɪrɪəd] n miriade f.
myself [maɪ'sɛlf] pron (reflexive) mi; (emphatic) io stesso(a); (after prep) me.
mysterious [mɪs'tɪərɪəs] adj misterioso(a).
mystery ['mɪstərɪ] n mistero.
mystery story n racconto del mistero.
mystic ['mɪstɪk] adj, n mistico(a).
mystical ['mɪstɪkəl] adj mistico(a).
mystify ['mɪstɪfaɪ] vt mistificare; (puzzle) confondere.
mystique [mɪs'tiːk] n fascino.
myth [mɪθ] n mito.
mythical ['mɪθɪkl] adj mitico(a).
mythological [mɪθə'lɔdʒɪkl] adj mitologico(a).

mythology [mɪ'θɔlədʒɪ] n mitologia.

N n

N, n [ɛn] n (letter) N, n f or m inv; **N for Nellie**, (US) **N for Nan** ≈ N come Napoli.
N abbr (= north) N.
NA n abbr (US: = Narcotics Anonymous) associazione in aiuto dei tossicodipendenti; (US) = National Academy.
n/a abbr (= not applicable) non pertinente; (COMM etc) = no account.
NAACP n abbr (US) = National Association for the Advancement of Coloured People.
NAAFI ['næfɪ] n abbr (BRIT: = Navy, Army & Air Force Institute) organizzazione che gestisce negozi, mense ecc. per il personale militare.
nab [næb] vt (col) beccare, acchiappare.
NACU n abbr (US) = National Association of Colleges and Universities.
nadir ['neɪdɪə*] n (ASTRONOMY) nadir m; (fig) punto più basso.
nag [næg] n (pej: horse) ronzino; (person) brontolone/a ♦ vt tormentare ♦ vi brontolare in continuazione.
nagging ['nægɪŋ] adj (doubt, pain) persistente ♦ n brontolii mpl, osservazioni fpl continue.
nail [neɪl] n (human) unghia; (metal) chiodo ♦ vt inchiodare; **to ~ sb down to a date/ price** costringere qn a un appuntamento/ ad accettare un prezzo; **to pay cash on the ~** (BRIT) pagare a tamburo battente.
nailbrush ['neɪlbrʌʃ] n spazzolino da or per unghie.
nailfile ['neɪlfaɪl] n lima da or per unghie.
nail polish n smalto da or per unghie.
nail polish remover n acetone m, solvente m.
nail scissors npl forbici fpl da or per unghie.
nail varnish n (BRIT) = **nail polish**.
Nairobi [naɪ'rəubɪ] n Nairobi f.
naïve [naɪ'iːv] adj ingenuo(a).
naïveté [nɑːiː'vteɪ], **naivety** [naɪ'iːvtɪ] n ingenuità f inv.
naked ['neɪkɪd] adj nudo(a); **with the ~ eye** a occhio nudo.
nakedness ['neɪkɪdnɪs] n nudità.

NAM n abbr (US) = National Association of Manufacturers.

name [neɪm] n nome m; (reputation) nome, reputazione f ♦ vt (baby etc) chiamare; (person, object) identificare; (price, date) fissare; **by** ~ di nome; **she knows them all by** ~ li conosce tutti per nome; **in the** ~ **of** in nome di; **what's your** ~? come si chiama?; **my** ~ **is Peter** mi chiamo Peter; **to take sb's** ~ **and address** prendere nome e indirizzo di qn; **to make a** ~ **for o.s.** farsi un nome; **to get (o.s.) a bad** ~ farsi una cattiva fama or una brutta reputazione; **to call sb** ~**s** insultare qn.

name dropping n menzionare qualcuno per fare bella figura.

nameless ['neɪmlɪs] adj senza nome.

namely ['neɪmlɪ] adv cioè.

nameplate ['neɪmpleɪt] n (on door etc) targa.

namesake ['neɪmseɪk] n omonimo.

nan bread [nɑːn-] n tipo di pane indiano poco lievitato di forma allungata.

nanny ['nænɪ] n bambinaia.

nanny goat n capra.

nap [næp] n (sleep) pisolino; (of cloth) peluria ♦ vi: **to be caught** ~**ping** essere preso alla sprovvista; **to have a** ~ schiacciare un pisolino.

NAPA n abbr (US: = National Association of Performing Artists) associazione nazionale degli artisti di palcoscenico.

napalm ['neɪpɑːm] n napalm m.

nape [neɪp] n: ~ **of the neck** nuca.

napkin ['næpkɪn] n tovagliolo; (BRIT: for baby) pannolino.

Naples ['neɪplz] n Napoli f.

Napoleonic [nəpəʊlɪ'ɒnɪk] adj napoleonico(a).

nappy ['næpɪ] n (BRIT) pannolino.

nappy liner n (BRIT) fogliettino igienico.

narcissistic [nɑːsɪ'sɪstɪk] adj narcisistico(a).

narcissus, pl **narcissi** [nɑː'sɪsəs, -saɪ] n narciso.

narcotic [nɑː'kɒtɪk] n (MED) narcotico; ~**s** npl (drugs) narcotici, stupefacenti mpl.

nark [nɑːk] vt (BRIT col) scocciare.

narrate [nə'reɪt] vt raccontare, narrare.

narration [nə'reɪʃən] n narrazione f.

narrative ['nærətɪv] n narrativa ♦ adj narrativo(a).

narrator [nə'reɪtə*] n narratore/trice.

narrow ['nærəʊ] adj stretto(a); (resources, means) limitato(a), modesto(a); (fig): **to take a** ~ **view of** avere una visione limitata di ♦ vi restringersi; **to have a** ~ **escape** farcela per un pelo; **to** ~ **sth**

down to ridurre qc a.

narrow gauge adj (RAIL) a scartamento ridotto.

narrowly ['nærəʊlɪ] adv: **Maria** ~ **escaped drowning** per un pelo Maria non è affogata; **he** ~ **missed hitting the cyclist** per poco non ha investito il ciclista.

narrow-minded [nærəʊ'maɪndɪd] adj meschino(a).

NAS n abbr (US) = National Academy of Sciences.

NASA ['næsə] n abbr (US: = National Aeronautics and Space Administration) N.A.S.A. f.

nasal ['neɪzl] adj nasale.

Nassau ['næsɔː] n Nassau f.

nastily ['nɑːstɪlɪ] adv con cattiveria.

nastiness ['nɑːstɪnɪs] n (of person, remark) cattiveria; (: spitefulness) malignità.

nasturtium [nəs'təːʃəm] n cappuccina, nasturzio (indiano).

nasty ['nɑːstɪ] adj (person, remark) cattivo(a); (: spiteful) maligno(a); (smell, wound, situation) brutto(a); **to turn** ~ (situation) mettersi male; (weather) guastarsi; (person) incattivirsi; **it's a** ~ **business** è una brutta faccenda, è un brutto affare.

NAS/UWT n abbr (BRIT: = National Association of Schoolmasters/Union of Women Teachers) sindacato di insegnanti in Inghilterra e Galles.

nation ['neɪʃən] n nazione f.

national ['næʃənl] adj nazionale ♦ n cittadino/a.

national anthem n inno nazionale.

National Curriculum n (BRIT) ≈ programma m scolastico ministeriale (in Inghilterra e Galles).

national debt n debito pubblico.

national dress n costume m nazionale.

National Guard n (US) milizia nazionale (volontaria, in ogni stato).

National Health Service (NHS) n (BRIT) servizio nazionale di assistenza sanitaria, ≈ S.A.U.B. f.

National Insurance n (BRIT) ≈ Previdenza Sociale.

nationalism ['næʃnəlɪzəm] n nazionalismo.

nationalist ['næʃnəlɪst] adj, n nazionalista (m/f).

nationality [næʃə'nælɪtɪ] n nazionalità f inv.

nationalization [næʃnəlaɪ'zeɪʃən] n nazionalizzazione f.

nationalize ['næʃnəlaɪz] vt nazionalizzare.

nationally ['næʃnəlɪ] adv a livello nazionale.

national park n parco nazionale.

national press n stampa a diffusione

nazionale.
National Security Council n (US)
consiglio nazionale di sicurezza.
national service n (MIL) servizio militare.
National Trust n sovrintendenza ai beni
culturali e ambientali; see boxed note.

NATIONAL TRUST

Fondato nel 1895, il **National Trust** è
un'organizzazione che si occupa della tutela e
salvaguardia di edifici e monumenti di
interesse storico e di territori di interesse
ambientale.

---

nation-wide ['neɪʃənwaɪd] adj diffuso(a) in
tutto il paese ♦ adv in tutto il paese.
native ['neɪtɪv] n abitante m/f del paese; (in
colonies) indigeno/a ♦ adj indigeno(a);
(country) natio(a); (ability) innato(a); **a ~
of Russia** un nativo della Russia; **a ~
speaker of French** una persona di
madrelingua francese; **~ language**
madrelingua.
Native American n discendente di tribù
dell'America settentrionale.
Nativity [nə'tɪvɪtɪ] n (REL): **the ~** la
Natività.
nativity play n recita sulla Natività.
NATO ['neɪtəu] n abbr (= North Atlantic
Treaty Organization) N.A.T.O. f.
natter ['nætə*] (BRIT col) vi chiacchierare
♦ n chiacchierata.
natural ['nætʃrəl] adj naturale; (ability)
innato(a); (manner) semplice; **death from
~ causes** (LAW) morte f per cause
naturali.
natural childbirth n parto indolore.
natural gas n gas m metano.
natural history n storia naturale.
naturalist ['nætʃrəlɪst] n naturalista m/f.
naturalization [nætʃrəlaɪ'zeɪʃən] n
naturalizzazione f; acclimatazione f.
naturalize ['nætʃrəlaɪz] vt: **to be ~d**
(person) naturalizzarsi.
naturally ['nætʃrəlɪ] adv naturalmente; (by
nature: gifted) di natura.
naturalness ['nætʃrəlnɪs] n naturalezza.
natural resources npl risorse fpl naturali.
natural selection n selezione f naturale.
natural wastage n (INDUSTRY)
diminuzione f di manodopera (per
pensionamento, decesso etc).
nature ['neɪtʃə*] n natura; (character)
natura, indole f; **by ~** di natura;
documents of a confidential ~ documenti
mpl di natura privata.
-natured ['neɪtʃəd] suffix: **ill~**

maldisposto(a).
nature reserve n (BRIT) parco naturale.
nature trail n percorso tracciato in parchi
nazionali ecc con scopi educativi.
naturist ['neɪtʃərɪst] n naturista m/f.
naught [nɔːt] n = **nought**.
naughtiness ['nɔːtɪnɪs] n cattiveria.
naughty ['nɔːtɪ] adj (child) birichino(a),
cattivello(a); (story, film) spinto(a).
nausea ['nɔːsɪə] n (MED) nausea; (fig:
disgust) schifo.
nauseate ['nɔːsɪeɪt] vt nauseare; far schifo
a.
nauseating ['nɔːsɪeɪtɪŋ] adj nauseante; (fig)
disgustoso(a).
nauseous ['nɔːsɪəs] adj nauseabondo(a);
(feeling sick): **to be ~** avere la nausea.
nautical ['nɔːtɪkl] adj nautico(a).
nautical mile n miglio nautico or marino.
naval ['neɪvl] adj navale.
naval officer n ufficiale m di marina.
nave [neɪv] n navata centrale.
navel ['neɪvl] n ombelico.
navigable ['nævɪgəbl] adj navigabile.
navigate ['nævɪgeɪt] vt percorrere
navigando ♦ vi navigare; (AUT) fare da
navigatore.
navigation [nævɪ'geɪʃən] n navigazione f.
navigator ['nævɪgeɪtə*] n (NAUT, AVIAT)
ufficiale m di rotta; (explorer) navigatore
m; (AUT) copilota m/f.
navvy ['nævɪ] n manovale m.
navy ['neɪvɪ] n marina; **Department of the
N~** (US) Ministero della Marina.
navy(-blue) ['neɪvɪ('bluː)] adj blu scuro inv.
Nazareth ['næzərɪθ] n Nazareth f.
Nazi ['nɑːtsɪ] adj, n nazista (m/f).
NB abbr (= nota bene) N.B.; (Canada) = New
Brunswick.
NBA n abbr (US: = National Basketball
Association) ≈ F.I.P. f (= Federazione
Italiana Pallacanestro); = National Boxing
Association.
NBC n abbr (US: = National Broadcasting
Company) compagnia nazionale di
radiodiffusione.
NBS n abbr (US: = National Bureau of
Standards) ufficio per la normalizzazione.
NC abbr (COMM etc: = no charge) gratis; (US)
= North Carolina.
NCC n abbr (= Nature Conservancy Council)
organismo di protezione dei beni
naturali; (US) = National Council of
Churches.
NCCL n abbr (BRIT: = National Council for Civil
Liberties) associazione per la difesa delle
libertà civili.
NCO n abbr see **non-commissioned**.

ND, N. Dak. *abbr* (*US*) = *North Dakota.*
NE *abbr* (*US*) = *Nebraska*; *New England.*
NEA *n abbr* (*US*) = *National Education Association.*
neap [niːp] *n* (*also*: ~**tide**) marea di quadratura.
Neapolitan [nɪə'pɔlɪtən] *adj, n* napoletano(a).
near [nɪə*] *adj* vicino(a); (*relation*) prossimo(a) ♦ *adv* vicino ♦ *prep* (*also*: ~ **to**) vicino a, presso; (*time*) verso ♦ *vt* avvicinarsi a; **to come** ~ avvicinarsi; ~ **here/there** qui/lì vicino; **£25,000 or** ~**est offer** (*BRIT*) 25.000 sterline trattabili; **in the** ~ **future** in un prossimo futuro; **the building is** ~**ing completion** il palazzo è quasi terminato *or* ultimato.
nearby [nɪə'baɪ] *adj* vicino(a) ♦ *adv* vicino.
Near East *n*: **the** ~ il Medio Oriente.
nearer ['nɪərə*] *adj* più vicino(a) ♦ *adv* più vicino.
nearly ['nɪəlɪ] *adv* quasi; **not** ~ non ... affatto; **I** ~ **lost it** per poco non lo perdevo; **she was** ~ **crying** era lì lì per piangere.
near miss *n*: **that was a** ~ c'è mancato poco.
nearness ['nɪənɪs] *n* vicinanza.
nearside ['nɪəsaɪd] *n* (*right-hand drive*) lato sinistro; (*left-hand drive*) lato destro ♦ *adj* sinistro(a); destro(a).
near-sighted [nɪə'saɪtɪd] *adj* miope.
neat [niːt] *adj* (*person, room*) ordinato(a); (*work*) pulito(a); (*solution, plan*) ben indovinato(a), azzeccato(a); (*spirits*) liscio(a).
neatly ['niːtlɪ] *adv* con ordine; (*skilfully*) abilmente.
neatness ['niːtnɪs] *n* (*tidiness*) ordine *m*; (*skilfulness*) abilità.
Nebr. *abbr* (*US*) = *Nebraska.*
nebulous ['nɛbjuləs] *adj* nebuloso(a); (*fig*) vago(a).
necessarily ['nɛsɪsrɪlɪ] *adv* necessariamente; **not** ~ non è detto, non necessariamente.
necessary ['nɛsɪsrɪ] *adj* necessario(a); **if** ~ se necessario.
necessitate [nɪ'sɛsɪteɪt] *vt* rendere necessario(a).
necessity [nɪ'sɛsɪtɪ] *n* necessità *f inv*; **in case of** ~ in caso di necessità.
neck [nɛk] *n* collo; (*of garment*) colletto ♦ *vi* (*col*) pomiciare, sbaciucchiarsi; ~ **and** ~ testa a testa; **to stick one's** ~ **out** (*col*) rischiare (forte).
necklace ['nɛklɪs] *n* collana.
neckline ['nɛklaɪn] *n* scollatura.

necktie ['nɛktaɪ] *n* (*esp US*) cravatta.
nectar ['nɛktə*] *n* nettare *m*.
nectarine ['nɛktərɪn] *n* nocepesca.
NEDC *n abbr* (*BRIT*: = *National Economic Development Council*) ≈ C.N.E.L. *m* (= *Consiglio Nazionale dell'Economia e del Lavoro*).
Neddy ['nɛdɪ] *n abbr* (*BRIT col*) = **NEDC**.
née [neɪ] *adj*: ~ **Scott** nata Scott.
need [niːd] *n* bisogno ♦ *vt* aver bisogno di; **I** ~ **to do it** lo devo fare, bisogna che io lo faccia; **you don't** ~ **to go** non deve andare, non c'è bisogno che lei vada; **a signature is** ~**ed** occorre *or* ci vuole una firma; **to be in** ~ **of, have** ~ **of** aver bisogno di; **£10 will meet my immediate** ~**s** 10 sterline mi basteranno per le necessità più urgenti; **in case of** ~ in caso di bisogno *or* necessità; **there's no** ~ **for** ... non c'è bisogno *or* non occorre che ...; **there's no** ~ **to do** ... non occorre fare ...; **the** ~**s of industry** le esigenze dell'industria.
needle ['niːdl] *n* ago; (*on record player*) puntina ♦ *vt* punzecchiare.
needlecord ['niːdlkɔːd] *n* (*BRIT*) velluto a coste sottili.
needless ['niːdlɪs] *adj* inutile; ~ **to say,** ... inutile dire che ....
needlessly ['niːdlɪslɪ] *adv* inutilmente.
needlework ['niːdlwəːk] *n* cucito.
needn't ['niːdnt] = **need not.**
needy ['niːdɪ] *adj* bisognoso(a).
negation [nɪ'geɪʃən] *n* negazione *f*.
negative ['nɛgətɪv] *n* (*PHOT*) negativa, negativo; (*ELEC*) polo negativo; (*LING*) negazione *f* ♦ *adj* negativo(a); **to answer in the** ~ rispondere negativamente *or* di no.
negative equity *n situazione in cui l'ammontare del mutuo su un immobile supera il suo valore sul mercato.*
neglect [nɪ'glɛkt] *vt* trascurare ♦ *n* (*of person, duty*) negligenza; **state of** ~ stato di abbandono; **to** ~ **to do sth** trascurare *or* tralasciare di fare qc.
neglected [nɪ'glɛktɪd] *adj* trascurato(a).
neglectful [nɪ'glɛktful] *adj* (*gen*) negligente; **to be** ~ **of sb/sth** trascurare qn/qc.
negligee ['nɛglɪʒeɪ] *n* négligé *m inv*.
negligence ['nɛglɪdʒəns] *n* negligenza.
negligent ['nɛglɪdʒənt] *adj* negligente.
negligently ['nɛglɪdʒəntlɪ] *adv* con negligenza.
negligible ['nɛglɪdʒɪbl] *adj* insignificante, trascurabile.
negotiable [nɪ'gəuʃɪəbl] *adj* negoziabile; (*cheque*) trasferibile; (*road*) transitabile.
negotiate [nɪ'gəuʃɪeɪt] *vi* negoziare ♦ *vt*

(*COMM*) negoziare; (*obstacle*) superare; (*bend in road*) prendere; **to ~ with sb for sth** trattare con qn per ottenere qc.
negotiating table [nɪ'gəʊʃɪeɪtɪŋ-] *n* tavolo delle trattative.
negotiation [nɪgəʊʃɪ'eɪʃən] *n* trattativa; (*POL*) negoziato; **to enter into ~s with sb** entrare in trattative (*or* intavolare i negoziati) con qn.
negotiator [nɪ'gəʊʃɪeɪtə*] *n* negoziatore/trice.
Negress ['niːgrɪs] *n* negra.
Negro ['niːgrəʊ] *adj, n* (*pl* **~es**) negro(a).
neigh [neɪ] *vi* nitrire.
neighbour, (*US*) **neighbor** ['neɪbə*] *n* vicino/a.
neighbo(u)rhood ['neɪbəhud] *n* vicinato.
neighbourhood watch *n* (*BRIT: also:* ~ **scheme**) *sistema di vigilanza reciproca in un quartiere.*
neighbo(u)ring ['neɪbərɪŋ] *adj* vicino(a).
neighbo(u)rly ['neɪbəlɪ] *adj*: **he is a ~ person** è un buon vicino.
neither ['naɪðə*] *adj, pron* né l'uno(a) né l'altro(a), nessuno(a) dei(delle) due ♦ *conj* neanche, nemmeno, neppure ♦ *adv*: ~ **good nor bad né buono né cattivo; I didn't move and ~ did Claude** io non mi mossi e nemmeno Claude; **... ~ did I refuse ...,** ma non ho nemmeno rifiutato.
neo... ['niːəʊ] *prefix* neo....
neolithic [niːəʊ'lɪθɪk] *adj* neolitico(a).
neologism [nɪ'ɔlədʒɪzəm] *n* neologismo.
neon ['niːɔn] *n* neon *m*.
neon light *n* luce *f* al neon.
neon sign *n* insegna al neon.
Nepal [nɪ'pɔːl] *n* Nepal *m*.
nephew ['nevjuː] *n* nipote *m*.
nepotism ['nɛpətɪzəm] *n* nepotismo.
nerd [nəːd] *n* (*col*) sfigato/a, povero(a) fesso/a.
nerve [nəːv] *n* nervo; (*fig*) coraggio; (*impudence*) faccia tosta; **he gets on my ~s** mi dà ai nervi, mi fa venire i nervi; **a fit of ~s** una crisi di nervi; **to lose one's ~** (*self-confidence*) perdere fiducia in se stesso; **I lost my ~** (*courage*) mi è mancato il coraggio.
nerve centre *n* (*ANAT*) centro nervoso; (*fig*) cervello, centro vitale.
nerve gas *n* gas *m* nervino.
nerve-racking ['nəːvrækɪŋ] *adj* che spezza i nervi.
nervous ['nəːvəs] *adj* nervoso(a).
nervous breakdown *n* esaurimento nervoso.
nervously ['nəːvəslɪ] *adv* nervosamente.
nervousness ['nəːvəsnɪs] *n* nervosismo.

nervous wreck *n*: **to be a ~** (*col*) essere nevrastenico(a).
nervy ['nəːvɪ] *adj* agitato(a), nervoso(a).
nest [nɛst] *n* nido; ~ **of tables** tavolini *mpl* cicogna *inv.*
nest egg *n* (*fig*) gruzzolo.
nestle ['nɛsl] *vi* accoccolarsi.
nestling ['nɛslɪŋ] *n* uccellino di nido.
net [nɛt] *n* rete *f*; (*fabric*) tulle *m*; **the N~** (*Internet*) Internet *f* ♦ *adj* netto(a) ♦ *vt* (*subj: person*) ricavare un utile netto di; (*deal, sale*) dare un utile netto di; ~ **of tax** netto, al netto di tasse; **he earns £10,000 ~ per year** guadagna 10.000 sterline nette all'anno.
netball ['nɛtbɔːl] *n specie di pallacanestro.*
net curtains *npl* tende *fpl* di tulle.
Netherlands ['nɛðələndz] *npl*: **the ~** i Paesi Bassi.
net profit *n* utile *m* netto.
nett [nɛt] *adj* = **net**.
netting ['nɛtɪŋ] *n* (*for fence etc*) reticolato; (*fabric*) tulle *m*.
nettle ['nɛtl] *n* ortica.
network ['nɛtwəːk] *n* rete *f*.
neuralgia [njʊə'rældʒə] *n* nevralgia.
neurological [njʊərə'lɔdʒɪkl] *adj* neurologico(a).
neurosis, *pl* **neuroses** [njʊə'rəʊsɪs, -siːz] *n* nevrosi *f inv.*
neurotic [njʊə'rɔtɪk] *adj, n* nevrotico(a).
neuter ['njuːtə*] *adj* neutro(a) ♦ *n* neutro ♦ *vt* (*cat etc*) castrare.
neutral ['njuːtrəl] *adj* neutro(a); (*person, nation*) neutrale ♦ *n* (*AUT*): **in ~** in folle.
neutrality [njuː'trælɪtɪ] *n* neutralità.
neutralize ['njuːtrəlaɪz] *vt* neutralizzare.
Nev. *abbr* (*US*) = *Nevada.*
never ['nevə*] *adv* (non...) mai; ~ **again** mai più; **I'll ~ go there again** non ci vado più; ~ **in my life** mai in vita mia; *see also* **mind.**
never-ending [nevər'endɪŋ] *adj* interminabile.
nevertheless [nevəðə'lɛs] *adv* tuttavia, ciò nonostante, ciò nondimeno.
new [njuː] *adj* nuovo(a); (*brand new*) nuovo(a) di zecca; **as good as ~** come nuovo.
New Age *adj, n* New Age (*f*) *inv.*
newborn ['njuːbɔːn] *adj* neonato(a).
newcomer ['njuːkʌmə*] *n* nuovo(a) venuto(a).
new-fangled ['njuːfæŋgld] *adj* (*pej*) stramoderno(a).
new-found ['njuːfaund] *adj* nuovo(a).
Newfoundland ['njuːfənlənd] *n* Terranova.
New Guinea *n* Nuova Guinea.

newly ['nju:lɪ] *adv* di recente.
newly-weds ['nju:lɪwɛdz] *npl* sposini *mpl*, sposi *mpl* novelli.
new moon *n* luna nuova.
newness ['nju:nɪs] *n* novità.
news [nju:z] *n* notizie *fpl*; (*RADIO*) giornale *m* radio; (*TV*) telegiornale *m*; **a piece of** ~ una notizia; **good/bad** ~ buone/cattive notizie; **financial** ~ (*PRESS*) pagina economica e finanziaria; (*RADIO*, *TV*) notiziario economico.
news agency *n* agenzia di stampa.
newsagent ['nju:zeɪdʒənt] *n* (*BRIT*) giornalaio.
news bulletin *n* (*RADIO*, *TV*) notiziario.
newscaster ['nju:zkɑːstə*] *n* (*RADIO*, *TV*) annunciatore/trice.
newsdealer ['nju:zdi:lə*] *n* (*US*) = **newsagent**.
newsflash ['nju:zflæʃ] *n* notizia *f* lampo *inv*.
newsletter ['nju:zlɛtə*] *n* bollettino (*di ditta, associazione*).
newspaper ['nju:zpeɪpə*] *n* giornale *m*; **daily** ~ quotidiano; **weekly** ~ settimanale *m*.
newsprint ['nju:zprɪnt] *n* carta da giornale.
newsreader ['nju:zri:də*] *n* = **newscaster**.
newsreel ['nju:zri:l] *n* cinegiornale *m*.
newsroom ['nju:zrum] *n* (*PRESS*) redazione *f*; (*RADIO*, *TV*) studio.
news stand *n* edicola.
newsworthy ['nju:zwɔ:ðɪ] *adj* degno(a) di menzione (*per radio, TV ecc*); **to be** ~ fare notizia.
newt [nju:t] *n* tritone *m*.
new town *n* (*BRIT*) *nuovo centro urbano creato con fondi pubblici.*
New Year *n* Anno Nuovo; **Happy** ~! Buon Anno!; **to wish sb a happy** ~ augurare Buon Anno a qn.
New Year's Day *n* il Capodanno.
New Year's Eve *n* la vigilia di Capodanno.
New York [-'jɔ:k] *n* New York *f*, Nuova York *f*; (*also*: ~ **State**) stato di New York.
New Zealand [-'zi:lənd] *n* Nuova Zelanda ♦ *adj* neozelandese.
New Zealander [-'zi:ləndə*] *n* neozelandese *m/f*.
next [nɛkst] *adj* prossimo(a) ♦ *adv* accanto; (*in time*) dopo; ~ **to** *prep* accanto a; ~ **to nothing** quasi niente; ~ **time** *adv* la prossima volta; ~ **week** la settimana prossima; **the** ~ **week** la settimana dopo *or* seguente; **the week after** ~ fra due settimane; **the** ~ **day** il giorno dopo, l'indomani; ~ **year** l'anno prossimo *or* venturo; **"turn to the** ~ **page"** "vedi pagina seguente"; **who's** ~? a chi tocca?;

when do we meet ~? quando ci rincontriamo?
next door *adv* accanto.
next of kin *n* parente *m/f* prossimo(a).
NF *n abbr* (*BRIT POL*: = National Front) *partito di estrema destra* ♦ *abbr* (*Canada*) = **Newfoundland**.
NFL *n abbr* (*US*) = National Football League.
Nfld. *abbr* (*Canada*) = **Newfoundland**.
NG *abbr* (*US*) = **National Guard**.
NGO *n abbr* (*US*) = non-governmental organization.
NH *abbr* (*US*) = New Hampshire.
NHL *n abbr* (*US*: = National Hockey League) ≈ F.I.H.P. *f* (= Federazione Italiana Hockey e Pattinaggio).
NHS *n abbr* (*BRIT*) *see* **National Health Service**.
NI *abbr* = **Northern Ireland**; (*BRIT*) = **National Insurance**.
Niagara Falls [naɪ'ægərə-] *npl*: **the** ~ le cascate del Niagara.
nib [nɪb] *n* (*of pen*) pennino.
nibble ['nɪbl] *vt* mordicchiare.
Nicaragua [nɪkə'rægjuə] *n* Nicaragua *m*.
Nicaraguan [nɪkə'rægjuən] *adj, n* nicaraguense (*m/f*).
Nice [ni:s] *n* Nizza.
nice [naɪs] *adj* (*holiday, trip*) piacevole; (*flat, picture*) bello(a); (*person*) simpatico(a), gentile; (*taste, smell, meal*) buono(a); (*distinction, point*) sottile.
nice-looking ['naɪslukɪŋ] *adj* bello(a).
nicely ['naɪslɪ] *adv* bene; **that will do** ~ andrà benissimo.
niceties ['naɪsɪtɪz] *npl* finezze *fpl*.
nick [nɪk] *n* tacca ♦ *vt* intaccare; tagliare; (*col: steal*) rubare; (: *BRIT: arrest*) beccare; **in the** ~ **of time** appena in tempo; **in good** ~ (*BRIT col*) decente, in buono stato; **to** ~ **o.s.** farsi un taglietto.
nickel ['nɪkl] *n* nichel *m*; (*US*) *moneta da cinque centesimi di dollaro.*
nickname ['nɪkneɪm] *n* soprannome *m* ♦ *vt* soprannominare.
Nicosia [nɪkə'si:ə] *n* Nicosia.
nicotine ['nɪkəti:n] *n* nicotina.
nicotine patch *n* cerotto antifumo (*a base di nicotina*).
niece [ni:s] *n* nipote *f*.
nifty ['nɪftɪ] *adj* (*col: car, jacket*) chic *inv*; (: *gadget, tool*) ingegnoso(a).
Niger ['naɪdʒə*] *n* Niger *m*.
Nigeria [naɪ'dʒɪərɪə] *n* Nigeria.
Nigerian [naɪ'dʒɪərɪən] *adj, n* nigeriano(a).
niggardly ['nɪgədlɪ] *adj* (*person*) tirchio(a), spilorcio(a); (*allowance, amount*) misero(a).

nigger ['nɪgə*] n (col!: highly offensive) negro/a.

niggle ['nɪgl] vt assillare ♦ vi fare il(la) pignolo(a).

niggling ['nɪglɪŋ] adj pignolo(a); (detail) insignificante; (doubt, pain) persistente.

night [naɪt] n notte f; (evening) sera; **at** ~ la notte; la sera; **by** ~ di notte; **in the** ~, **during the** ~ durante la notte; **the** ~ **before last** l'altro ieri notte; l'altro ieri sera.

night-bird ['naɪtbɜːd] n uccello notturno; (fig) nottambulo/a.

nightcap ['naɪtkæp] n bicchierino prima di andare a letto.

night club n locale m notturno.

nightdress ['naɪtdrɛs] n camicia da notte.

nightfall ['naɪtfɔːl] n crepuscolo.

nightie ['naɪtɪ] n camicia da notte.

nightingale ['naɪtɪŋgeɪl] n usignolo.

night life n vita notturna.

nightly ['naɪtlɪ] adj di ogni notte or sera; (by night) notturno(a) ♦ adv ogni notte or sera.

nightmare ['naɪtmɛə*] n incubo.

night porter n portiere m di notte.

night safe n cassa continua.

night school n scuola serale.

nightshade ['naɪtʃeɪd] n: **deadly** ~ (BOT) belladonna.

nightshift ['naɪtʃɪft] n turno di notte.

night-time ['naɪttaɪm] n notte f.

night watchman n guardiano notturno.

nihilism ['naɪɪlɪzəm] n nichilismo.

nil [nɪl] n nulla m; (SPORT) zero.

Nile [naɪl] n: **the** ~ il Nilo.

nimble ['nɪmbl] adj agile.

nine [naɪn] num nove.

nineteen [naɪn'tiːn] num diciannove.

ninety ['naɪntɪ] num novanta.

ninth [naɪnθ] num nono(a).

nip [nɪp] vt pizzicare ♦ vi (BRIT col): **to** ~ **out/down/up** fare un salto fuori/giù/di sopra ♦ n (pinch) pizzico; (drink) goccio, bicchierino.

nipple ['nɪpl] n (ANAT) capezzolo.

nippy ['nɪpɪ] adj (weather) pungente; (BRIT: car, person) svelto(a).

nit [nɪt] n (of louse) lendine m; (col: idiot) cretino/a, scemo/a.

nit-pick ['nɪtpɪk] vi (col) cercare il pelo nell'uovo.

nitrogen ['naɪtrədʒən] n azoto.

nitroglycerin(e) [naɪtrəu'glɪsəriːn] n nitroglicerina.

nitty-gritty ['nɪtɪ'grɪtɪ] n (col): **to get down to the** ~ venire al sodo.

nitwit ['nɪtwɪt] n (col) scemo/a.

NJ abbr (US) = New Jersey.

NLF n abbr (= National Liberation Front) ≈ F.L.N. m.

NLQ abbr (= near letter quality) qualità quasi di corrispondenza.

NLRB n abbr (US: = National Labor Relations Board) organismo per la tutela dei lavoratori.

NM, N. Mex. abbr (US) = New Mexico.

════════════════════════ KEYWORD

no [nəu] adv (opposite of "yes") no; **are you coming?** — ~ **(I'm not)** viene? — no (non vengo); **would you like some more?** — ~ **thank you** ne vuole ancora un po'? — no, grazie; **I have** ~ **more wine** non ho più vino

♦ adj (not any) nessuno(a); **I have** ~ **money/time/books** non ho soldi/tempo/ libri; ~ **student would have done it** nessuno studente lo avrebbe fatto; **there is** ~ **reason to believe ...** non c'è nessuna ragione per crederci ...; "~ **parking**" "divieto di sosta"; "~ **smoking**" "vietato fumare"; "~ **entry**" "ingresso vietato"; "~ **dogs**" "vietato l'accesso ai cani"

♦ n (pl ~es) no m inv; **I won't take** ~ **for an answer** non accetterò un rifiuto.

─────────────────────────────

no. abbr (= number) n.

nobble ['nɔbl] vt (BRIT col: bribe: person) comprare, corrompere; (: person to speak to, criminal) bloccare, beccare; (RACING: horse, dog) drogare.

Nobel prize [nəu'bɛl-] n premio Nobel.

nobility [nəu'bɪlɪtɪ] n nobiltà.

noble ['nəubl] adj, n nobile (m).

nobleman ['nəublmən] n nobile m, nobiluomo.

nobly ['nəublɪ] adv (selflessly) generosamente.

nobody ['nəubədɪ] pron nessuno.

no-claims bonus ['nəukleɪmz-] n bonus malus m inv.

nocturnal [nɔk'təːnl] adj notturno(a).

nod [nɔd] vi accennare col capo, fare un cenno; (sleep) sonnecchiare ♦ vt: **to** ~ **one's head** fare di sì col capo ♦ n cenno; **they** ~**ded their agreement** accennarono di sì col capo.

▶**nod off** vi assopirsi.

no-fly zone [nəu'flaɪ-] n zona di interdizione aerea.

noise [nɔɪz] n rumore m; (din, racket) chiasso.

noiseless ['nɔɪzlɪs] adj silenzioso(a).

noisily ['nɔɪzɪlɪ] adv rumorosamente.

noisy ['nɔɪzɪ] adj (street, car) rumoroso(a); (person) chiassoso(a).

nomad ['nəumæd] *n* nomade *m/f*.
nomadic [nəu'mædɪk] *adj* nomade.
no man's land *n* terra di nessuno.
nominal ['nɔmɪnl] *adj* nominale.
nominate ['nɔmɪneɪt] *vt* (*propose*) proporre come candidato; (*elect*) nominare.
nomination [nɔmɪ'neɪʃən] *n* nomina; candidatura.
nominee [nɔmɪ'niː] *n* persona nominata; candidato/a.
non... [nɔn] *prefix* non....
non-alcoholic ['nɔnælkə'hɔlɪk] *adj* analcolico(a).
non-breakable [nɔn'breɪkəbl] *adj* infrangibile.
nonce word ['nɔns-] *n* parola coniata per l'occasione.
nonchalant ['nɔnʃələnt] *adj* incurante, indifferente.
non-commissioned [nɔnkə'mɪʃnd] *adj*: ~ **officer (NCO)** sottufficiale *m*.
non-committal [nɔnkə'mɪtl] *adj* evasivo(a).
nonconformist [nɔnkən'fɔːmɪst] *n* anticonformista *m/f*; (*BRIT REL*) dissidente *m/f* ♦ *adj* anticonformista.
non-contributory [nɔnkən'trɪbjutərɪ] *adj*: ~ **pension scheme** *or* (*US*) **plan** *sistema di pensionamento con i contributi interamente a carico del datore di lavoro*.
non-cooperation ['nɔnkəuɔpə'reɪʃən] *n* non cooperazione *f*, non collaborazione *f*.
nondescript ['nɔndɪskrɪpt] *adj* qualunque *inv*.
none [nʌn] *pron* (*not one thing*) niente; (*not one person*) nessuno(a); ~ **of you** nessuno(a) di voi; **I have** ~ non ne ho nemmeno uno; **I have** ~ **left** non ne ho più; ~ **at all** proprio niente; (*not one*) nemmeno uno; **he's** ~ **the worse for it** non ne ha risentito.
nonentity [nɔ'nentɪtɪ] *n* persona insignificante.
non-essential [nɔnɪ'senʃl] *adj* non essenziale ♦ *n*: ~**s** superfluo, cose *fpl* superflue.
nonetheless ['nʌnðə'les] *adv* nondimeno.
non-event [nɔnɪ'vent] *n* delusione *f*.
non-executive [nɔnɪg'zekjutɪv] *adj*: ~ **director** direttore *m* senza potere esecutivo.
non-existent [nɔnɪg'zɪstənt] *adj* inesistente.
non-fiction [nɔn'fɪkʃən] *n* saggistica.
non-flammable [nɔn'flæməbl] *adj* ininfiammabile.
non-intervention ['nɔnɪntə'venʃən] *n* non intervento.

no-no ['nəunəu] *n*: **it's a** ~! (*undesirable*) è inaccettabile!; (*forbidden*) non si può fare!
non obst. *abbr* (= *non obstante*: *notwithstanding*) nonostante.
no-nonsense [nəu'nɔnsəns] *adj* che va al sodo.
non-payment [nɔn'peɪmənt] *n* mancato pagamento.
nonplussed [nɔn'plʌst] *adj* sconcertato(a).
non-profit-making [nɔn'prɔfɪtmeɪkɪŋ] *adj* senza scopo di lucro.
nonsense ['nɔnsəns] *n* sciocchezze *fpl*; ~! che sciocchezze!, che assurdità!; **it is** ~ **to say that** ... è un'assurdità *or* non ha senso dire che ....
nonsensical [nɔn'sensɪkl] *adj* assurdo(a), ridicolo(a).
non-shrink [nɔn'ʃrɪŋk] *adj* (*BRIT*) irrestringibile.
non-skid [nɔn'skɪd] *adj* antisdrucciolo(a).
non-smoker ['nɔn'sməukə*] *n* non fumatore/trice.
non-starter [nɔn'stɑːtə*] *n*: **it's a** ~ è fallito in partenza.
non-stick ['nɔn'stɪk] *adj* antiaderente, antiadesivo(a).
non-stop ['nɔn'stɔp] *adj* continuo(a); (*train, bus*) direttissimo(a) ♦ *adv* senza sosta.
non-taxable [nɔn'tæksəbl] *adj*: ~ **income** reddito non imponibile.
non-U [nɔn'juː] *adj abbr* (*BRIT col*) = *non-upper class*.
non-volatile [nɔn'vɔlətaɪl] *adj*: ~ **memory** (*COMPUT*) memoria permanente.
non-voting [nɔn'vəutɪŋ] *adj*: ~ **shares** azioni *fpl* senza diritto di voto.
non-white ['nɔn'waɪt] *adj* di colore ♦ *n* persona di colore.
noodles ['nuːdlz] *npl* taglierini *mpl*.
nook [nuk] *n*: ~**s and crannies** angoli *mpl*.
noon [nuːn] *n* mezzogiorno.
no one ['nəuwʌn] *pron* = **nobody**.
noose [nuːs] *n* nodo scorsoio, cappio; (*hangman's*) cappio.
nor [nɔː*] *conj* = **neither** ♦ *adv see* **neither**.
Norf *abbr* (*BRIT*) = Norfolk.
norm [nɔːm] *n* norma.
normal ['nɔːml] *adj* normale ♦ *n*: **to return to** ~ tornare alla normalità.
normality [nɔː'mælɪtɪ] *n* normalità.
normally ['nɔːməlɪ] *adv* normalmente.
Normandy ['nɔːməndɪ] *n* Normandia.
north [nɔːθ] *n* nord *m*, settentrione *m* ♦ *adj* nord *inv*, del nord, settentrionale ♦ *adv* verso nord.
North Africa *n* Africa del Nord.
North African *adj*, *n* nordafricano(a).

North America n America del Nord.
North American adj, n nordamericano(a).
Northants [nɔː'θænts] abbr (BRIT)
= Northamptonshire.
northbound ['nɔːθbaund] adj (traffic)
diretto(a) a nord; (carriageway) nord inv.
Northd abbr (BRIT) = Northumberland.
north-east [nɔːθ'iːst] n nord-est m.
northerly ['nɔːðəlɪ] adj (wind) del nord;
(direction) verso nord.
northern ['nɔːðən] adj del nord,
settentrionale.
Northern Ireland n Irlanda del Nord.
North Pole n: the ~ il Polo Nord.
North Sea n: the ~ il mare del Nord.
North Sea oil n petrolio del mare del
Nord.
northward(s) ['nɔːθwəd(z)] adv verso nord.
north-west [nɔːθ'wɛst] n nord-ovest m.
Norway ['nɔːweɪ] n Norvegia.
Norwegian [nɔː'wiːdʒən] adj norvegese ♦ n
norvegese m/f; (LING) norvegese m.
nos. abbr (= numbers) nn.
nose [nəuz] n naso; (of animal) muso ♦ vi
(also: ~ one's way) avanzare cautamente;
to pay through the ~ **(for sth)** (col) pagare
(qc) un occhio della testa.
▶**nose about, nose around** vi aggirarsi.
nosebleed ['nəuzbliːd] n emorragia nasale.
nose-dive ['nəuzdaɪv] n picchiata.
nose drops npl gocce fpl per il naso.
nosey ['nəuzɪ] adj curioso(a).
nostalgia [nɔs'tældʒɪə] n nostalgia.
nostalgic [nɔs'tældʒɪk] adj nostalgico(a).
nostril ['nɔstrɪl] n narice f; (of horse) frogia.
nosy ['nəuzɪ] adj = **nosey.**
not [nɔt] adv non; ~ **at all** niente affatto;
(after thanks) prego, s'immagini; **you must**
~ **or** mustn't **do this** non deve fare
questo; **he isn't** ... egli non è ...; **I hope** ~
spero di no.
notable ['nəutəbl] adj notevole.
notably ['nəutəblɪ] adv notevolmente; (in
particular) in particolare.
notary ['nəutərɪ] n (also: ~ **public**) notaio.
notation [nəu'teɪʃən] n notazione f.
notch [nɔtʃ] n tacca.
▶**notch up** vt (score, victory) marcare,
segnare.
note [nəut] n nota; (letter, banknote)
biglietto ♦ vt prendere nota di; **to take** ~
of prendere nota di; **to take** ~**s** prendere
appunti; **to compare** ~**s** (fig) scambiarsi
le impressioni; **of** ~ eminente,
importante; **just a quick** ~ **to let you**
know ... ti scrivo solo due righe per
informarti ....
notebook ['nəutbuk] n taccuino; (for

shorthand) bloc-notes m inv.
note-case ['nəutkeɪs] n (BRIT) portafoglio.
noted ['nəutɪd] adj celebre.
notepad ['nəutpæd] n bloc-notes m inv,
blocchetto.
notepaper ['nəutpeɪpə*] n carta da lettere.
noteworthy ['nəutwəːðɪ] adj degno(a) di
nota, importante.
nothing ['nʌθɪŋ] n nulla m, niente m; **he**
does ~ non fa niente; ~ **new** niente di
nuovo; **for** ~ (free) per niente; ~ **at all**
proprio niente.
notice ['nəutɪs] n avviso; (of leaving)
preavviso; (BRIT: review: of play etc)
critica, recensione f ♦ vt notare,
accorgersi di; **to take** ~ **of** fare
attenzione a; **to bring sth to sb's** ~ far
notare qc a qn; **to give sb** ~ **of sth**
avvisare qn di qc; **to give** ~, **hand in**
one's ~ (subj: employee) licenziarsi;
without ~ senza preavviso; **at short** ~
con un breve preavviso; **until further** ~
fino a nuovo avviso; **advance** ~
preavviso; **to escape** or **avoid** ~ passare
inosservato; **it has come to my** ~ **that** ...
sono venuto a sapere che ....
noticeable ['nəutɪsəbl] adj evidente.
notice board n (BRIT) tabellone m per
affissi.
notification [nəutɪfɪ'keɪʃən] n annuncio;
notifica; denuncia.
notify ['nəutɪfaɪ] vt: **to** ~ **sth to sb** notificare
qc a qn; **to** ~ **sb of sth** avvisare qn di qc;
(police) denunciare qc a qn.
notion ['nəuʃən] n idea; (concept) nozione f.
notions ['nəuʃənz] npl (US: haberdashery)
merceria.
notoriety [nəutə'raɪətɪ] n notorietà.
notorious [nəu'tɔːrɪəs] adj famigerato(a).
notoriously [nəu'tɔːrɪəslɪ] adv
notoriamente.
Notts [nɔts] abbr (BRIT) = Nottinghamshire.
notwithstanding [nɔtwɪθ'stændɪŋ] adv
nondimeno ♦ prep nonostante, malgrado.
nougat ['nuːgɑː] n torrone m.
nought [nɔːt] n zero.
noun [naun] n nome m, sostantivo.
nourish ['nʌrɪʃ] vt nutrire.
nourishing ['nʌrɪʃɪŋ] adj nutriente.
nourishment ['nʌrɪʃmənt] n nutrimento.
Nov. abbr (= November) nov.
Nova Scotia ['nəuvə'skəuʃə] n Nuova
Scozia.
novel ['nɔvl] n romanzo ♦ adj nuovo(a).
novelist ['nɔvəlɪst] n romanziere/a.
novelty ['nɔvəltɪ] n novità f inv.
November [nəu'vɛmbə*] n novembre m; for
phrases see also **July.**

novice ['nɔvɪs] *n* principiante *m/f*; (*REL*) novizio/a.
NOW [nau] *n abbr* (*US*: = National Organization for Women) ≈ U.D.I. *f* (= *Unione Donne Italiane*).
now [nau] *adv* ora, adesso ♦ *conj*: ~ (that) adesso che, ora che; **right** ~ subito; **by** ~ ormai; **just** ~: **that's the fashion just** ~ è la moda del momento; **I saw her just** ~ l'ho vista proprio adesso; **I'll read it just** ~ lo leggo subito; ~ **and then**, ~ **and again** ogni tanto; **from** ~ **on** da ora in poi; **in 3 days from** ~ fra 3 giorni; **between** ~ **and Monday** da qui a lunedì, entro lunedì; **that's all for** ~ per ora basta.
nowadays ['nauədeɪz] *adv* oggidì.
nowhere ['nəuwɛə*] *adv* in nessun luogo, da nessuna parte; ~ **else** in nessun altro posto.
no-win situation [nəu'wɪn-] *n*: **to be in a** ~ aver perso in partenza.
noxious ['nɔkʃəs] *adj* nocivo(a).
nozzle ['nɔzl] *n* (*of hose etc*) boccaglio.
NP *n abbr* = notary public.
NS *abbr* (*Canada*) = **Nova Scotia**.
NSC *n abbr* (*US*) = **National Security Council.**
NSF *n abbr* (*US*) = National Science Foundation.
NSPCC *n abbr* (*BRIT*) = National Society for the Prevention of Cruelty to Children.
NSW *abbr* (*Australia*) = New South Wales.
NT *n abbr* (= *New Testament*) N.T. ♦ *abbr* (*Canada*) = Northwest Territories.
nth [ɛnθ] *adj*: **for the** ~ **time** (*col*) per l'ennesima volta.
nuance ['nju:ɑ̃:ns] *n* sfumatura.
nubile ['nju:baɪl] *adj* nubile; (*attractive*) giovane e desiderabile.
nuclear ['nju:klɪə*] *adj* nucleare; (*warfare*) atomico(a).
nuclear disarmament *n* disarmo nucleare.
nuclear family *n* famiglia nucleare.
nuclear-free zone ['nju:klɪə'fri:-] *n* zona denuclearizzata.
nucleus, *pl* **nuclei** ['nju:klɪəs, 'nju:klɪaɪ] *n* nucleo.
NUCPS *n abbr* (*BRIT*) = National Union of Civil and Public Servants.
nude [nju:d] *adj* nudo(a) ♦ *n* (*ART*) nudo; **in the** ~ tutto(a) nudo(a).
nudge [nʌdʒ] *vt* dare una gomitata a.
nudist ['nju:dɪst] *n* nudista *m/f*.
nudity ['nju:dɪtɪ] *n* nudità.
nugget ['nʌgɪt] *n* pepita.
nuisance ['nju:sns] *n*: **it's a** ~ è una seccatura; **he's a** ~ lui dà fastidio; **what a**

~! che seccatura!
NUJ *n abbr* (*BRIT*: = National Union of Journalists*) sindacato nazionale dei giornalisti.
nuke [nju:k] *n* (*col*) bomba atomica.
null [nʌl] *adj*: ~ **and void** nullo(a).
nullify ['nʌlɪfaɪ] *vt* annullare.
NUM *n abbr* (*BRIT*: = National Union of Mineworkers*) sindacato nazionale dei dipendenti delle miniere.
numb [nʌm] *adj* intorpidito(a) ♦ *vt* intorpidire; ~ **with** (*fear*) paralizzato(a) da; (*grief*) impietrito(a) da; ~ **with cold** intirizzito(a) (dal freddo).
number ['nʌmbə*] *n* numero ♦ *vt* numerare; (*include*) contare; **a** ~ **of** un certo numero di; **telephone** ~ numero di telefono; **wrong** ~ (*TEL*) numero sbagliato; **the staff** ~**s 20** gli impiegati sono in 20.
numbered account ['nʌmbəd-] *n* (*in bank*) conto numerato.
number plate *n* (*BRIT AUT*) targa.
Number Ten *n* (*BRIT*: = 10 Downing Street*) residenza del Primo Ministro del Regno Unito.
numbness ['nʌmnɪs] *n* intorpidimento; (*due to cold*) intirizzimento.
numbskull ['nʌmskʌl] *n* (*col*) imbecille *m/f*, idiota *m/f*.
numeral ['nju:mərəl] *n* numero, cifra.
numerate ['nju:mərɪt] *adj* (*BRIT*): **to be** ~ saper far di conto.
numerical [nju:'mɛrɪkl] *adj* numerico(a).
numerous ['nju:mərəs] *adj* numeroso(a).
nun [nʌn] *n* suora, monaca.
nunnery ['nʌnərɪ] *n* convento.
nuptial ['nʌpʃəl] *adj* nuziale.
nurse [nə:s] *n* infermiere/a; (*also*: ~**maid**) bambinaia ♦ *vt* (*patient, cold*) curare; (*baby*: *BRIT*) cullare; (: *US*) allattare, dare il latte a; (*hope*) nutrire.
nursery ['nə:sərɪ] *n* (*room*) camera dei bambini; (*institution*) asilo; (*for plants*) vivaio.
nursery rhyme *n* filastrocca.
nursery school *n* scuola materna.
nursery slope *n* (*BRIT SKI*) pista per principianti.
nursing ['nə:sɪŋ] *n* (*profession*) professione *f* di infermiere (*or* di infermiera) ♦ *adj* (*mother*) che allatta.
nursing home *n* casa di cura.
nurture ['nə:tʃə*] *vt* allevare; nutrire.
NUS *n abbr* (*BRIT*: = National Union of Students*) sindacato nazionale degli studenti.
NUT *n abbr* (*BRIT*: = National Union of Teachers*) sindacato nazionale degli

insegnanti.

nut [nʌt] n (of metal) dado; (fruit) noce f (or nocciola or mandorla etc) ♦ adj (chocolate etc) alla nocciola etc; **he's ~s** (col) è matto.

nutcase ['nʌtkeɪs] n (col) mattarello/a.

nutcrackers ['nʌtkrækəz] npl schiaccianoci m inv.

nutmeg ['nʌtmɛg] n noce f moscata.

nutrient ['njuːtrɪənt] adj nutriente ♦ n sostanza nutritiva.

nutrition [njuː'trɪʃən] n nutrizione f.

nutritionist [njuː'trɪʃənɪst] n nutrizionista m/f.

nutritious [njuː'trɪʃəs] adj nutriente.

nutshell ['nʌtʃɛl] n guscio di noce; **in a ~** in poche parole.

nutty ['nʌtɪ] adj di noce (or nocciola or mandorla etc); (BRIT col) tocco(a), matto(a).

nuzzle ['nʌzl] vi: **to ~ up to** strofinare il muso contro.

NV abbr (US) = Nevada.

NWT abbr (Canada) = Northwest Territories.

NY abbr (US) = New York.

NYC abbr (US) = New York City.

nylon ['naɪlɔn] n nailon m, ~s npl calze fpl di nailon.

nymph [nɪmf] n ninfa.

nymphomaniac [nɪmfəu'meɪnɪæk] adj, n ninfomane (f).

NYSE abbr (US) = New York Stock Exchange.

Oo

O, o [əu] n (letter) O, o f or m inv; (US SCOL: = outstanding) ≈ ottimo; (number: TEL etc) zero; **O for Oliver,** (US) **O for Oboe** ≈ O come Otranto.

oaf [əuf] n zoticone m.

oak [əuk] n quercia ♦ cpd di quercia.

OAP n abbr (BRIT) see old-age pensioner.

oar [ɔː*] n remo; **to put or shove one's ~ in** (fig col) intromettersi.

oarsman ['ɔːzmən], **oarswoman** ['ɔːzwumən] n rematore/trice.

OAS n abbr (= Organization of American States) O.S.A. f (= Organizzazione degli Stati Americani).

oasis, pl **oases** [əu'eɪsɪs, əu'eɪsiːz] n oasi f inv.

oath [əuθ] n giuramento; (swear word) bestemmia; **to take the ~** giurare; **on ~** (BRIT) or **under ~** sotto giuramento.

oatmeal ['əutmiːl] n farina d'avena.

oats [əuts] npl avena.

OAU n abbr (= Organization of African Unity) O.A.U. f.

obdurate ['ɔbdjurɪt] adj testardo(a); incallito(a); ostinato(a), irremovibile.

OBE n abbr (BRIT: = Order of the British Empire) titolo.

obedience [ə'biːdɪəns] n ubbidienza; **in ~ to** conformemente a.

obedient [ə'biːdɪənt] adj ubbidiente; **to be ~ to sb/sth** ubbidire a qn/qc.

obelisk ['ɔbɪlɪsk] n obelisco.

obese [əu'biːs] adj obeso(a).

obesity [əu'biːsɪtɪ] n obesità.

obey [ə'beɪ] vt ubbidire a; (instructions, regulations) osservare ♦ vi ubbidire.

obituary [ə'bɪtjuərɪ] n necrologia.

object n ['ɔbdʒɪkt] oggetto; (purpose) scopo, intento; (LING) complemento oggetto ♦ vi [əb'dʒɛkt]: **to ~ to** (attitude) disapprovare; (proposal) protestare contro, sollevare delle obiezioni contro; **I ~!** mi oppongo!; **he ~ed that ...** obiettò che ...; **do you ~ to my smoking?** la disturba se fumo?; **what's the ~ of doing that?** a che serve farlo?; **expense is no ~** non si bada a spese.

objection [əb'dʒɛkʃən] n obiezione f; (drawback) inconveniente m; **if you have no ~** se non ha obiezioni; **to make or raise an ~** sollevare un'obiezione.

objectionable [əb'dʒɛkʃənəbl] adj antipatico(a); (smell) sgradevole; (language) scostumato(a).

objective [əb'dʒɛktɪv] n obiettivo ♦ adj obiettivo(a).

objectivity [ɔbdʒɪk'tɪvɪtɪ] n obiettività.

object lesson n: **~ (in)** dimostrazione f (di).

objector [əb'dʒɛktə*] n oppositore/trice.

obligation [ɔblɪ'geɪʃən] n obbligo, dovere m; (debt) obbligo (di riconoscenza); **"without ~"** "senza impegno"; **to be under an ~ to sb/to do sth** essere in dovere verso qn/di fare qc.

obligatory [ə'blɪgətərɪ] adj obbligatorio(a).

oblige [ə'blaɪdʒ] vt (force): **to ~ sb to do** costringere qn a fare; (do a favour) fare una cortesia a; **to be ~d to sb for sth** essere grato a qn per qc; **anything to ~!** (col) questo e altro!

obliging [ə'blaɪdʒɪŋ] adj servizievole, compiacente.

oblique [ə'bliːk] adj obliquo(a); (allusion)

indiretto(a) ♦ n (*BRIT TYP*): ~ **(stroke)** barra.
obliterate [ə'blıtəreıt] vt cancellare.
oblivion [ə'blıvıən] n oblio.
oblivious [ə'blıvıəs] adj: ~ **of** incurante di; inconscio(a) di.
oblong ['ɔblɔŋ] adj oblungo(a) ♦ n rettangolo.
obnoxious [əb'nɔkʃəs] adj odioso(a); (*smell*) disgustoso(a), ripugnante.
o.b.o. abbr (*US*: = or best offer: in classified ads) o al miglior offerente.
oboe ['əubəu] n oboe m.
obscene [əb'siːn] adj osceno(a).
obscenity [əb'senıtı] n oscenità f inv.
obscure [əb'skjuə*] adj oscuro(a) ♦ vt oscurare; (*hide: sun*) nascondere.
obscurity [əb'skjuərıtı] n oscurità; (*obscure point*) punto oscuro; (*lack of fame*) anonimato.
obsequious [əb'siːkwıəs] adj ossequioso(a).
observable [əb'zəːvəbl] adj osservabile; (*appreciable*) notevole.
observance [əb'zəːvns] n osservanza; **religious** ~s pratiche fpl religiose.
observant [əb'zəːvnt] adj attento(a).
observation [ɔbzə'veıʃən] n osservazione f; (*by police etc*) sorveglianza.
observation post n (*MIL*) osservatorio.
observatory [əb'zəːvətrı] n osservatorio.
observe [əb'zəːv] vt osservare.
observer [əb'zəːvə*] n osservatore/trice.
obsess [əb'ses] vt ossessionare; **to be ~ed by** or **with sb/sth** essere ossessionato da qn/qc.
obsession [əb'seʃən] n ossessione f.
obsessive [əb'sesıv] adj ossessivo(a).
obsolescence [ɔbsə'lesns] n obsolescenza; **built-in** or **planned** ~ (*COMM*) obsolescenza programmata.
obsolescent [ɔbsə'lesnt] adj obsolescente.
obsolete ['ɔbsəliːt] adj obsoleto(a); (*word*) desueto(a).
obstacle ['ɔbstəkl] n ostacolo.
obstacle race n corsa agli ostacoli.
obstetrician [ɔbstə'trıʃən] n ostetrico/a.
obstetrics [ɔb'stetrıks] n ostetrica.
obstinacy ['ɔbstınəsı] n ostinatezza.
obstinate ['ɔbstınıt] adj ostinato(a).
obstreperous [əb'strepərəs] adj turbolento(a).
obstruct [əb'strʌkt] vt (*block*) ostruire, ostacolare; (*halt*) fermare; (*hinder*) impedire.
obstruction [əb'strʌkʃən] n ostruzione f; ostacolo.
obstructive [əb'strʌktıv] adj ostruttivo(a); che crea impedimenti.

obtain [əb'teın] vt ottenere ♦ vi essere in uso; **to** ~ **sth (for o.s.)** procurarsi qc.
obtainable [əb'teınəbl] adj ottenibile.
obtrusive [əb'truːsıv] adj (*person*) importuno(a); (*smell*) invadente; (*building etc*) imponente e invadente.
obtuse [əb'tjuːs] adj ottuso(a).
obverse ['ɔbvəːs] n opposto, inverso.
obviate ['ɔbvıeıt] vt ovviare a, evitare.
obvious ['ɔbvıəs] adj ovvio(a), evidente.
obviously ['ɔbvıəslı] adv ovviamente; ~! certo!; ~ **not!** certo che no!; **he was** ~ **not drunk** si vedeva che non era ubriaco; **he was not** ~ **drunk** non si vedeva che era ubriaco.
OCAS n abbr = Organization of Central American States.
occasion [ə'keıʒən] n occasione f; (*event*) avvenimento ♦ vt cagionare; **on that** ~ in quell'occasione, quella volta; **to rise to the** ~ mostrarsi all'altezza della situazione.
occasional [ə'keıʒənl] adj occasionale; **I smoke an** ~ **cigarette** ogni tanto fumo una sigaretta.
occasionally [ə'keıʒənəlı] adv ogni tanto; **very** ~ molto raramente.
occasional table n tavolino.
occult [ɔ'kʌlt] adj occulto(a) ♦ n: **the** ~ l'occulto.
occupancy ['ɔkjupənsı] n occupazione f.
occupant ['ɔkjupənt] n occupante m/f; (*of boat, car etc*) persona a bordo.
occupation [ɔkju'peıʃən] n occupazione f; (*job*) mestiere m, professione f; **unfit for** ~ (*house*) inabitabile.
occupational [ɔkju'peıʃənl] adj (*disease*) professionale; (*hazard*) del mestiere; ~ **accident** infortunio sul lavoro.
occupational guidance n (*BRIT*) orientamento professionale.
occupational pension scheme n sistema pensionistico programmato dal datore di lavoro.
occupational therapy n ergoterapia.
occupier ['ɔkjupaıə*] n occupante m/f.
occupy ['ɔkjupaı] vt occupare; **to** ~ **o.s. by doing** occuparsi a fare; **to be occupied with sth/in doing sth** essere preso da qc/ occupato a fare qc.
occur [ə'kəː*] vi accadere; (*difficulty, opportunity*) capitare; (*phenomenon, error*) trovarsi; **to** ~ **to sb** venire in mente a qn.
occurrence [ə'kʌrəns] n caso, fatto; presenza.
ocean ['əuʃən] n oceano; ~s **of** (*col*) un sacco di.
ocean bed n fondale m oceanico.

ocean-going [ˈəuʃəngəuɪŋ] *adj* d'alto mare.
Oceania [əuʃɪˈɑːnɪə] *n* Oceania.
ocean liner *n* transatlantico.
ochre, (*US*) **ocher** [ˈəukə*] *adj* ocra *inv*.
o'clock [əˈklɔk] *adv*: **it is one** ~ è l'una; **it is
5** ~ sono le 5.
OCR *n abbr see* **optical character reader;
optical character recognition.**
Oct. *abbr* (= *October*) ott.
octagonal [ɔkˈtægənl] *adj* ottagonale.
octane [ˈɔkteɪn] *n* ottano; **high-~ petrol** *or*
(*US*) **gas** benzina ad alto numero di
ottani.
octave [ˈɔktɪv] *n* ottavo.
October [ɔkˈtəubə*] *n* ottobre *m*; *for phrases
see also* **July.**
octogenarian [ɔktəudʒɪˈnɛərɪən] *n*
ottuagenario/a.
octopus [ˈɔktəpəs] *n* polpo, piovra.
odd [ɔd] *adj* (*strange*) strano(a), bizzarro(a);
(*number*) dispari *inv*; (*left over*) in più; (*not
of a set*) spaiato(a); **60** ~ 60 e oltre, **at
times** di tanto in tanto; **the ~ one out**
l'eccezione *f*.
oddball [ˈɔdbɔːl] *n* (*col*) eccentrico/a.
oddity [ˈɔdɪtɪ] *n* bizzarria; (*person*)
originale *m/f*.
odd-job man [ɔdˈdʒɔb-] *n* tuttofare *m inv*.
odd jobs *npl* lavori *mpl* occasionali.
oddly [ˈɔdlɪ] *adv* stranamente.
oddments [ˈɔdmənts] *npl* (*BRIT COMM*)
rimanenze *fpl*.
odds [ɔdz] *npl* (*in betting*) quota; **the ~ are
against his coming** c'è poca probabilità
che venga; **it makes no** ~ non importa; **at
~** in contesa; **to succeed against all the ~**
riuscire contro ogni aspettativa; **~ and
ends** avanzi *mpl*.
odds-on [ɔdzˈɔn] *adj* (*col*) probabile; **~
favourite** (*RACING*) favorito(a).
ode [əud] *n* ode *f*.
odious [ˈəudɪəs] *adj* odioso(a), ripugnante.
odometer [ɔˈdɔmɪtə*] *n* odometro.
odour, (*US*) **odor** [ˈəudə*] *n* odore *m*.
odo(u)rless [ˈəudəlɪs] *adj* inodoro(a).
OECD *n abbr* (= *Organization for Economic
Cooperation and Development*) O.C.S.E. *f*
(= *Organizzazione per la Cooperazione e lo
Sviluppo Economico*).
oesophagus, (*US*) **esophagus** [iːˈsɔfəgəs]
n esofago.
oestrogen, (*US*) **estrogen** [ˈiːstrəudʒən] *n*
estrogeno.

═══════════════ *KEYWORD*

of [ɔv, əv] *prep* **1** (*gen*) di; **a boy ~ 10** un
ragazzo di 10 anni; **a friend ~ ours** un
nostro amico; **that was kind ~ you** è stato
molto gentile da parte sua
2 (*expressing quantity, amount, dates etc*)
di; **a kilo ~ flour** un chilo di farina; **how
much ~ this do you need?** quanto gliene
serve?; **there were four ~ them** (*people*)
erano in quattro; (*objects*) ce n'erano
quattro; **three ~ us went** tre di noi sono
andati; **the 5th ~ July** il 5 luglio; **a quarter
~ 4** (*US*) le 4 meno un quarto
3 (*from, out of*) di, in; **made ~ wood**
(fatto) di *or* in legno.

═══════════════ *KEYWORD*

off [ɔf] *adv* **1** (*distance, time*): **it's a long way
~** è lontano; **the game is 3 days ~** la
partita è tra 3 giorni
2 (*departure, removal*) via; **to go ~ to
Paris** andarsene a Parigi; **I must be ~**
devo andare via; **to take ~ one's coat**
togliersi il cappotto; **the button came ~** il
bottone è venuto via *or* si è staccato; **10%
~** con lo sconto del 10%
3 (*not at work*): **to have a day ~** avere un
giorno libero; **to be ~ sick** essere assente
per malattia
♦ *adj* (*engine*) spento(a); (*tap*) chiuso(a);
(*cancelled*) sospeso(a); (*BRIT: food*)
andato(a) a male; **to be well/badly ~**
essere/non essere benestante; **the lid was
~** non c'era il coperchio; **I'm afraid the
chicken is ~** (*BRIT: not available*) purtroppo
il pollo è finito; **on the ~ chance** nel caso;
to have an ~ day non essere in forma;
that's a bit ~, isn't it? (*fig col*) non è molto
carino, vero?
♦ *prep* **1** (*motion, removal etc*) da; (*distant
from*) a poca distanza da; **a street ~ the
square** una strada che parte dalla piazza;
5km ~ the road a 5km dalla strada; **~ the
coast** al largo della costa; **a house ~ the
main road** una casa che non è sulla
strada principale
2: to be ~ meat non mangiare più la
carne.

offal [ˈɔfl] *n* (*CULIN*) frattaglie *fpl*.
offbeat [ˈɔfbiːt] *adj* eccentrico(a).
off-centre, (*US*) **off-center** [ɔfˈsentə*] *adj*
storto(a), fuori centro.
off-colour [ˈɔfˈkʌlə*] *adj* (*BRIT: ill*) malato(a),
indisposto(a); **to feel ~** sentirsi poco
bene.
offence, (*US*) **offense** [əˈfɛns] *n* (*LAW*)
contravvenzione *f*; (: *more serious*) reato;
to give ~ to offendere; **to take ~ at**
offendersi per; **to commit an ~**
commettere un reato.

offend [ə'fɛnd] *vt* (*person*) offendere ♦ *vi*: **to ~ against** (*law, rule*) trasgredire.
offender [ə'fɛndə*] *n* delinquente *m/f*; (*against regulations*) contravventore/trice.
offending [ə'fɛndɪŋ] *adj* (*often hum*): **the ~ word/object** la parola incriminata/ l'oggetto incriminato.
offense [ə'fɛns] *n* (*US*) = **offence**.
offensive [ə'fɛnsɪv] *adj* offensivo(a); (*smell etc*) sgradevole, ripugnante ♦ *n* (*MIL*) offensiva.
offer ['ɔfə*] *n* offerta, proposta ♦ *vt* offrire; "**on ~**" (*COMM*) "in offerta speciale"; **to make an ~ for sth** fare un'offerta per qc; **to ~ sth to sb, ~ sb sth** offrire qc a qn; **to ~ to do sth** offrirsi di fare qc.
offering ['ɔfərɪŋ] *n* offerta.
offhand [ɔf'hænd] *adj* disinvolto(a), noncurante ♦ *adv* all'improvviso; **I can't tell you ~** non posso dirglielo su due piedi.
office ['ɔfɪs] *n* (*place*) ufficio; (*position*) carica; **doctor's ~** (*US*) ambulatorio; **to take ~** entrare in carica; **through his good ~s** con il suo prezioso aiuto; **O~ of Fair Trading** (*BRIT*) *organismo di protezione contro le pratiche commerciali abusive*.
office automation *n* automazione *f* d'ufficio, burotica.
office bearer *n* (*of club etc*) membro dell'amministrazione.
office block, (*US*) **office building** *n* complesso di uffici.
office boy *n* garzone *m*.
office hours *npl* orario d'ufficio; (*US MED*) orario di visite.
office manager *n* capoufficio *m/f*.
officer ['ɔfɪsə*] *n* (*MIL etc*) ufficiale *m*; (*of organization*) funzionario; (*also*: **police ~**) agente *m* di polizia.
office work *n* lavoro d'ufficio.
office worker *n* impiegato/a d'ufficio.
official [ə'fɪʃl] *adj* (*authorized*) ufficiale ♦ *n* ufficiale *m*; (*civil servant*) impiegato/a statale; funzionario.
officialdom [ə'fɪʃəldəm] *n* burocrazia.
officially [ə'fɪʃəlɪ] *adv* ufficialmente.
official receiver *n* curatore *m* fallimentare.
officiate [ə'fɪʃɪeɪt] *vi* (*REL*) ufficiare; **to ~ as Mayor** esplicare le funzioni di sindaco; **to ~ at a marriage** celebrare un matrimonio.
officious [ə'fɪʃəs] *adj* invadente.
offing ['ɔfɪŋ] *n*: **in the ~** (*fig*) in vista.
off-key [ɔf'kiː] *adj* stonato(a) ♦ *adv* fuori tono.
off-licence ['ɔflaɪsns] *n* (*BRIT*) spaccio di

bevande alcoliche; *see boxed note.*

OFF-LICENCE

In Gran Bretagna e in Irlanda, gli **off-licence** *sono esercizi pubblici specializzati nella vendita strettamente regolamentata di bevande alcoliche, per la quale è necessario avere un'apposita licenza. In genere sono aperti fino a tarda sera.*

---

off-limits [ɔf'lɪmɪts] *adj* (*esp US*) in cui vige il divieto d'accesso.
off line *adj, adv* (*COMPUT*) off line *inv*, fuori linea; (*: switched off*) spento(a).
off-load ['ɔfləud] *vt* scaricare.
off-peak ['ɔf'piːk] *adj* (*ticket etc*) a tariffa ridotta; (*time*) non di punta.
off-putting ['ɔfputɪŋ] *adj* (*BRIT*) un po' scostante.
off-season ['ɔfsiːzn] *adj, adv* fuori stagione.
offset ['ɔfsɛt] *vt irreg* (*counteract*) contro-bilanciare ♦ *n* (*also*: **~ printing**) offset *m*.
offshoot ['ɔfʃuːt] *n* (*fig*) diramazione *f*.
offshore [ɔf'ʃɔː*] *adj* (*breeze*) di terra; (*island*) vicino alla costa; (*fishing*) costiero(a); **~ oilfield** giacimento petrolifero in mare aperto.
offside ['ɔf'saɪd] *adj* (*SPORT*) fuori gioco; (*AUT: with right-hand drive*) destro(a); (*: with left-hand drive*) sinistro(a) ♦ *n* destra; sinistra.
offspring ['ɔfsprɪŋ] *n* prole *f*, discendenza.
offstage [ɔf'steɪdʒ] *adv* dietro le quinte.
off-the-cuff [ɔfðə'kʌf] *adv* improvvisando.
off-the-job ['ɔfðə'dʒɔb] *adj*: **~ training** addestramento fuori sede.
off-the-peg ['ɔfðə'pɛg], (*US*) **off-the-rack** ['ɔfðə'ræk] *adv* prêt-à-porter.
off-the-record ['ɔfðə'rɛkɔːd] *adj* ufficioso(a) ♦ *adv* in via ufficiosa.
off-white ['ɔfwaɪt] *adj* bianco sporco *inv*.
Ofgas ['ɔfgæs] *n abbr* (*BRIT: Office of Gas Supply*) *organo indipendente di controllo per la tutela dei consumatori.*
Oftel ['ɔftɛl] *n abbr* (*BRIT: Office of Telecommunications*) *organo indipendente di controllo per la tutela dei consumatori.*
often ['ɔfn] *adv* spesso; **how ~ do you go?** quanto spesso ci va?; **as ~ as not** quasi sempre.
Ofwat ['ɔfwɔt] *n abbr* (*BRIT: = Office of Water Services*) *in Inghilterra e Galles, organo indipendente di controllo per la tutela dei consumatori.*
ogle ['əugl] *vt* occhieggiare.
ogre ['əugə*] *n* orco.

OH *abbr* (*US*) = *Ohio*.

oh [əu] *excl* oh!

OHMS *abbr* (*BRIT*) = *On His (or Her) Majesty's Service*.

oil [ɔɪl] *n* olio; (*petroleum*) petrolio; (*for central heating*) nafta ♦ *vt* (*machine*) lubrificare.

oilcan ['ɔɪlkæn] *n* oliatore *m* a mano; (*for storing*) latta da olio.

oil change *n* cambio dell'olio.

oilfield ['ɔɪfiːld] *n* giacimento petrolifero.

oil filter *n* (*AUT*) filtro dell'olio.

oil-fired ['ɔɪlfaɪəd] *adj* a nafta.

oil gauge *n* indicatore *m* del livello dell'olio.

oil industry *n* industria del petrolio.

oil level *n* livello dell'olio.

oil painting *n* quadro a olio.

oil refinery *n* raffineria di petrolio.

oil rig *n* derrick *m inv*; (*at sea*) piattaforma per trivellazioni subacquee.

oilskins ['ɔɪlskɪnz] *npl* indumenti *mpl* di tela cerata.

oil slick *n* chiazza d'olio.

oil tanker *n* petroliera.

oil well *n* pozzo petrolifero.

oily ['ɔɪlɪ] *adj* unto(a), oleoso(a); (*food*) untuoso(a).

ointment ['ɔɪntmənt] *n* unguento.

OK *abbr* (*US*) = *Oklahoma*.

O.K., okay [əu'keɪ] *excl* d'accordo! ♦ *vt* approvare ♦ *n*: **to give sth one's ~** approvare qc ♦ *adj*: **is it ~?, are you ~?** tutto bene?; **it's ~ with** *or* **by me** per me va bene; **are you ~ for money?** sei a posto coi soldi?

Okla. *abbr* (*US*) = *Oklahoma*.

old [əuld] *adj* vecchio(a); (*ancient*) antico(a), vecchio(a); (*person*) vecchio(a), anziano(a); **how ~ are you?** quanti anni ha?; **he's 10 years ~** ha 10 anni; **~er brother/sister** fratello/sorella maggiore; **any ~ thing will do** va bene qualsiasi cosa.

old age *n* vecchiaia.

old-age pensioner (OAP) ['əuldeɪdʒ-] *n* (*BRIT*) pensionato/a.

old-fashioned ['əuld'fæʃnd] *adj* antiquato(a), fuori moda; (*person*) all'antica.

old maid *n* zitella.

old people's home *n* ricovero per anziani.

old-style ['əuldstaɪl] *adj* (di) vecchio stampo *inv*.

old-time ['əuldtaɪm] *adj* di una volta.

old-timer [əuld'taɪmə*] *n* veterano/a.

old wives' tale *n* vecchia superstizione *f*.

O levels *npl* (*BRIT*: *formerly*) diploma di istruzione secondaria conseguito a 16 anni in Inghilterra e Galles, ora sostituito dal GCSE.

olive ['ɔlɪv] *n* (*fruit*) oliva; (*tree*) olivo ♦ *adj* (*also*: **~-green**) verde oliva *inv*.

olive oil *n* olio d'oliva.

Olympic [əu'lɪmpɪk] *adj* olimpico(a); **the ~ Games, the ~s** i giochi olimpici, le Olimpiadi.

OM *n abbr* (*BRIT*: = *Order of Merit*) titolo.

O & M *abbr* = *organization and method*.

Oman [əu'mɑːn] *n* Oman *m*.

OMB *n abbr* (*US*: = *Office of Management and Budget*) servizio di consulenza al Presidente in materia di bilancio.

omelet(te) ['ɔmlɪt] *n* omelette *f inv*; **ham/cheese ~** omelette al prosciutto/al formaggio.

omen ['əumən] *n* presagio, augurio.

ominous ['ɔmɪnəs] *adj* minaccioso(a); (*event*) di malaugurio.

omission [əu'mɪʃən] *n* omissione *f*.

omit [əu'mɪt] *vt* omettere; **to ~ to do sth** tralasciare *or* trascurare di fare qc.

omnivorous [ɔm'nɪvərəs] *adj* onnivoro(a).

ON *abbr* (*Canada*) = *Ontario*.

────────── *KEYWORD*

on [ɔn] *prep* **1** (*indicating position*) su; **~ the wall** sulla parete; **~ the left** a *or* sulla sinistra; **I haven't any money ~ me** non ho soldi con me

2 (*indicating means, method, condition etc*): **~ foot** a piedi; **~ the train/plane** in treno/aereo; **~ the telephone** al telefono; **~ the radio/television** alla radio/televisione; **to be ~ drugs** drogarsi; **~ holiday** in vacanza; **he's ~ £16,000 a year** guadagna 16.000 sterline all'anno; **this round's ~ me** questo giro lo offro io

3 (*referring to time*): **~ Friday** venerdì; **~ Fridays** il *or* di venerdì; **~ June 20th** il 20 giugno; **~ Friday, June 20th** venerdì, 20 giugno; **a week ~ Friday** venerdì a otto; **his arrival** al suo arrivo; **~ seeing this** vedendo ciò

4 (*about, concerning*) su, di; **information ~ train services** informazioni sui collegamenti ferroviari; **a book ~ Goldoni/physics** un libro su Goldoni/di *or* sulla fisica

♦ *adv* **1** (*referring to dress, covering*): **to have one's coat ~** avere indosso il cappotto; **to put one's coat ~** mettersi il

cappotto; **what's she got** ~**?** cosa
indossa?; **she put her boots/gloves/hat** ~
si mise gli stivali/i guanti/il cappello;
screw the lid ~ **tightly** avvita bene il
coperchio
2 (*further, continuously*): **to walk** ~**, go** ~
etc continuare, proseguire; **to read** ~
continuare a leggere; ~ **and off** ogni
tanto; **from that day** ~ da quel giorno in
poi; **it was well** ~ **in the evening** era sera
inoltrata
♦ *adj* **1** (*in operation: machine, TV, light*)
acceso(a); (: *tap*) aperto(a); (: *brake*)
inserito(a); **is the meeting still** ~**?** (*in
progress*) la riunione è ancora in corso?;
(*not cancelled*) è confermato l'incontro?;
there's a good film ~ **at the cinema** danno
un buon film al cinema; **when is the film**
~**?** quando c'è questo film?; **my father's
always** ~ **at me to get a job** (*col*) mio
padre mi tormenta sempre perché trovi
un lavoro
2 (*col*): **that's not** ~**!** (*not acceptable*) non
si fa così!; (*not possible*) non se ne parla
neanche!

ONC *n abbr* (*BRIT*: = *Ordinary National
Certificate*) *diploma in materie tecniche a
livello di maturità.*
once [wʌns] *adv* una volta ♦ *conj* non
appena, quando; ~ **he had left/it was
done** dopo che se n'era andato/fu fatto; **at**
~ subito; (*simultaneously*) a un tempo; **all
at** ~ (tutto) ad un tratto; ~ **a week** una
volta alla settimana; ~ **more** ancora una
volta; **I knew him** ~ un tempo *or* in
passato lo conoscevo; ~ **and for all** una
volta per sempre; ~ **upon a time there
was** … c'era una volta ….
oncoming ['ɔnkʌmɪŋ] *adj* (*traffic*) che viene
in senso opposto.
OND *n abbr* (*BRIT*: = *Ordinary National
Diploma*) *diploma in materie tecniche
conseguito dopo un corso biennale.*

========== KEYWORD ==========

one [wʌn] *num* uno(a); ~ **hundred and fifty**
centocinquanta; ~ **day** un giorno; **it's** ~
(o'clock) è l'una; **to be** ~ **up on sb** essere
avvantaggiato(a) rispetto a qn; **to be at** ~
(with sb) andare d'accordo (con qn)
♦ *adj* **1** (*sole*) unico(a); **the** ~ **book which**
l'unico libro che; **the** ~ **man who** l'unico
che
2 (*same*) stesso(a); **they came in the** ~
car sono venuti nella stessa macchina
♦ *pron* **1**: **this** ~ questo(a); **that** ~
quello(a); **which** ~ **do you want?** quale

vuole?; **I've already got** ~**/a red** ~ ne ho
già uno/uno rosso; ~ **by** ~ uno per uno
2: ~ **another** l'un l'altro; **to look at** ~
another guardarsi; **to help** ~ **another**
aiutarsi l'un l'altro *or* a vicenda
3 (*impersonal*) si; ~ **never knows** non si
sa mai; **to cut** ~**'s finger** tagliarsi un dito;
to express ~**'s opinion** esprimere la
propria opinione; ~ **needs to eat** bisogna
mangiare.

one-armed bandit ['wʌnɑːmd-] *n* slot-
machine *f inv.*
one-day excursion ['wʌndeɪ-] *n* (*US*)
biglietto giornaliero di andata e ritorno.
One-hundred share index ['wʌnhʌndrəd-]
n indice borsistico del Financial Times.
one-man ['wʌn'mæn] *adj* (*business*)
diretto(a) *etc* da un solo uomo.
one-man band *n suonatore ambulante
con vari strumenti.*
one-off [wʌn'ɔf] (*BRIT col*) *n* fatto
eccezionale ♦ *adj* eccezionale.
one-parent family ['wʌnpɛərənt-] *n*
famiglia monogenitore.
one-piece ['wʌnpiːs] *adj* (*bathing suit*)
intero(a).
onerous ['ɔnərəs] *adj* (*task, duty*)
gravoso(a); (*responsibility*) pesante.
oneself [wʌn'sɛlf] *pron* si; (*after prep*) sé, se
stesso(a); **to do sth (by)** ~ fare qc da sé.
one-shot [wʌn'ʃɔt] *n* (*US*) = **one-off.**
one-sided [wʌn'saɪdɪd] *adj* (*decision, view*)
unilaterale; (*judgement, account*) parziale;
(*game, contest*) impari *inv.*
one-time ['wʌntaɪm] *adj* ex *inv.*
one-to-one ['wʌntəwʌn] *adj* (*relationship*)
univoco(a).
one-upmanship [wʌn'ʌpmənʃɪp] *n*: **the art
of** ~ l'arte *f* di primeggiare.
one-way ['wʌnweɪ] *adj* (*street, traffic*) a
senso unico.
ongoing ['ɔngəʊɪŋ] *adj* in corso; in
attuazione.
onion ['ʌnjən] *n* cipolla.
on line *adj* (*COMPUT*) on line *inv*, in linea;
(: *switched on*) acceso(a).
onlooker ['ɔnlʊkə*] *n* spettatore/trice.
only ['əʊnlɪ] *adv* solo, soltanto ♦ *adj* solo(a),
unico(a) ♦ *conj* solo che, ma; **an** ~ **child** un
figlio unico; **not** ~ non solo; **I** ~ **took one**
ne ho preso soltanto uno, non ne ho preso
che uno; **I saw her** ~ **yesterday** l'ho vista
appena ieri; **I'd be** ~ **too pleased to help**
sarei proprio felice di essere d'aiuto; **I
would come,** ~ **I'm very busy** verrei
volentieri, solo che sono molto occupato.
ono *abbr* = **or nearest offer**; *see* **near.**

onset ['ɔnsɛt] *n* inizio; (*of winter*) arrivo.
onshore ['ɔnʃɔ:*] *adj* (*wind*) di mare.
onslaught ['ɔnslɔ:t] *n* attacco, assalto.
Ont. *abbr* (*Canada*) = *Ontario*.
on-the-job ['ɔnðə'dʒɔb] *adj*: ~ **training** addestramento in sede.
onto ['ɔntu] *prep* su, sopra.
onus ['əunəs] *n* onere *m*, peso; **the ~ is upon him to prove it** sta a lui dimostrarlo.
onward(s) ['ɔnwəd(z)] *adv* (*move*) in avanti; **from this time ~** d'ora in poi.
onyx ['ɔnɪks] *n* onice *f*.
oops [ups] *excl* ops! (*esprime rincrescimento per un piccolo contrattempo*); **~-a-daisy!** oplà!
ooze [u:z] *vi* stillare.
opacity [əu'pæsɪtɪ] *n* opacità.
opal ['əupl] *n* opale *m or f*.
opaque [əu'peɪk] *adj* opaco(a).
OPEC ['əupɛk] *n abbr* (= *Organization of Petroleum-Exporting Countries*) O.P.E.C. *f*.
open ['əupn] *adj* aperto(a); (*road*) libero(a); (*meeting*) pubblico(a); (*admiration*) evidente, franco(a); (*question*) insoluto(a); (*enemy*) dichiarato(a) ♦ *vt* aprire ♦ *vi* (*eyes, door, debate*) aprirsi; (*flower*) sbocciare; (*shop, bank, museum*) aprire; (*book etc: commence*) cominciare; **in the ~ (air)** all'aperto; **the ~ sea** il mare aperto, l'alto mare; ~ **ground** (*among trees*) radura; (*waste ground*) terreno non edificato; **to have an ~ mind (on sth)** non avere ancora deciso (su qc).
▶**open on to** *vt fus* (*subj: room, door*) dare su.
▶**open out** *vt* aprire ♦ *vi* aprirsi.
▶**open up** *vt* aprire; (*blocked road*) sgombrare ♦ *vi* aprirsi.
open-air [əupn'ɛə*] *adj* all'aperto.
open-and-shut ['əupnən'ʃʌt] *adj*: ~ **case** caso indubbio.
open day *n* (*BRIT*) giornata di apertura al pubblico.
open-ended [əupn'ɛndɪd] *adj* (*fig*) aperto(a), senza limiti.
opener ['əupnə*] *n* (*also*: **can ~**, **tin ~**) apriscatole *m inv*.
open-heart [əupn'hɑ:t] *adj*: ~ **surgery** chirurgia a cuore aperto.
opening ['əupnɪŋ] *n* apertura; (*opportunity*) occasione *f*, opportunità *f inv*; sbocco; (*job*) posto vacante.
opening night *n* (*THEAT*) prima.
open learning *n sistema educativo secondo il quale lo studente ha maggior controllo e gestione delle modalità di apprendimento.*
openly ['əupnlɪ] *adv* apertamente.

open-minded [əupn'maɪndɪd] *adj* che ha la mente aperta.
open-necked ['əupnnɛkt] *adj* col collo slacciato.
openness ['əupnnɪs] *n* (*frankness*) franchezza, sincerità.
open-plan ['əupn'plæn] *adj* senza pareti divisorie.
open prison *n istituto di pena dove viene data maggiore libertà ai detenuti.*
open sandwich *n* canapè *m inv*.
open shop *n fabbrica o ditta dove sono accolti anche operai non iscritti ai sindacati.*
Open University *n* (*BRIT*) *see boxed note.*

OPEN UNIVERSITY

La **Open University (OU)**, *fondata in Gran Bretagna nel 1969, organizza corsi universitari per corrispondenza, basati anche su lezioni che vengono trasmesse dalla BBC per radio e per televisione o su corsi estivi.*

---

opera ['ɔpərə] *n* opera.
opera glasses *npl* binocolo da teatro.
opera house *n* opera.
opera singer *n* cantante *m/f* d'opera *or* lirico(a).
operate ['ɔpəreɪt] *vt* (*machine*) azionare, far funzionare; (*system*) usare ♦ *vi* funzionare; (*drug, person*) agire; **to ~ on sb (for)** (*MED*) operare qn (di).
operatic [ɔpə'rætɪk] *adj* dell'opera, lirico(a).
operating ['ɔpəreɪtɪŋ] *adj* (*COMM: costs etc*) di gestione; (*MED*) operatorio(a).
operating room *n* (*US*) = **operating theatre**.
operating system *n* (*COMPUT*) sistema *m* operativo.
operating theatre *n* (*MED*) sala operatoria.
operation [ɔpə'reɪʃən] *n* operazione *f*; **to be in ~** (*machine*) essere in azione *or* funzionamento; (*system*) essere in vigore; **to have an ~ (for)** (*MED*) essere operato(a) (di).
operational [ɔpə'reɪʃənl] *adj* operativo(a); (*COMM*) di gestione, d'esercizio; (*ready for use or action*) in attività, in funzione.
operative ['ɔpərətɪv] *adj* (*measure*) operativo(a) ♦ *n* (*in factory*) operaio/a; **the ~ word** la parola chiave.
operator ['ɔpəreɪtə*] *n* (*of machine*) operatore/trice; (*TEL*) centralinista *m/f*.
operetta [ɔpə'rɛtə] *n* operetta.
ophthalmologist [ɔfθæl'mɔlədʒɪst] *n*

oftalmologo/a.
opinion [ə'pɪnjən] *n* opinione *f*, parere *m*; **in my** ~ secondo me, a mio avviso; **to seek a second** ~ (*MED etc*) consultarsi con un altro medico *etc*.
opinionated [ə'pɪnjəneɪtɪd] *adj* dogmatico(a).
opinion poll *n* sondaggio di opinioni.
opium ['əʊpɪəm] *n* oppio.
opponent [ə'pəʊnənt] *n* avversario/a.
opportune ['ɔpətjuːn] *adj* opportuno(a).
opportunist [ɔpə'tjuːnɪst] *n* opportunista *m/f*.
opportunity [ɔpə'tjuːnɪtɪ] *n* opportunità *f inv*, occasione *f*; **to take the** ~ **to do** *or* **of doing** cogliere l'occasione per fare.
oppose [ə'pəʊz] *vt* opporsi a; **~d to** contrario(a) a; **as** ~**d to** in contrasto con.
opposing [ə'pəʊzɪŋ] *adj* opposto(a); (*team*) avversario(a).
opposite ['ɔpəzɪt] *adj* opposto(a); (*house etc*) di fronte ♦ *adv* di fronte, dirimpetto ♦ *prep* di fronte a ♦ *n* opposto, contrario; (*of word*) contrario; **"see** ~ **page"** "vedere pagina a fronte".
opposite number *n* controparte *f*, corrispondente *m/f*.
opposite sex *n*: **the** ~ l'altro sesso.
opposition [ɔpə'zɪʃən] *n* opposizione *f*.
oppress [ə'prɛs] *vt* opprimere.
oppression [ə'prɛʃən] *n* oppressione *f*.
oppressive [ə'prɛsɪv] *adj* oppressivo(a).
opprobrium [ə'prəʊbrɪəm] *n* (*formal*) obbrobrio.
opt [ɔpt] *vi*: **to** ~ **for** optare per; **to** ~ **to do** scegliere di fare; **to** ~ **out of** (*BRIT: of NHS*) scegliere di non far più parte di; (*of agreement, arrangement*) scegliere di non partecipare a.
optical ['ɔptɪkl] *adj* ottico(a).
optical character reader/recognition (OCR) *n* lettore *m* ottico/lettura ottica di caratteri.
optical fibre *n* fibra ottica.
optician [ɔp'tɪʃən] *n* ottico.
optics ['ɔptɪks] *n* ottica.
optimism ['ɔptɪmɪzəm] *n* ottimismo.
optimist ['ɔptɪmɪst] *n* ottimista *m/f*.
optimistic [ɔptɪ'mɪstɪk] *adj* ottimistico(a).
optimum ['ɔptɪməm] *adj* ottimale.
option ['ɔpʃən] *n* scelta; (*SCOL*) materia facoltativa; (*COMM*) opzione *f*; **to keep one's** ~**s open** (*fig*) non impegnarsi; **I have no** ~ non ho scelta.
optional ['ɔpʃənl] *adj* facoltativo(a); (*COMM*) a scelta; ~ **extra** optional *m inv*.
opulence ['ɔpjuləns] *n* opulenza.
opulent ['ɔpjulənt] *adj* opulento(a).

OR *abbr* (*US*) = *Oregon*.
or [ɔː*] *conj* o, oppure; (*with negative*): **he hasn't seen** ~ **heard anything** non ha visto né sentito niente; ~ **else** se no, altrimenti; oppure.
oracle ['ɔrəkl] *n* oracolo.
oral ['ɔːrəl] *adj* orale ♦ *n* esame *m* orale.
orange ['ɔrɪndʒ] *n* (*fruit*) arancia ♦ *adj* arancione.
orangeade [ɔrɪndʒ'eɪd] *n* aranciata.
oration [ɔː'reɪʃən] *n* orazione *f*.
orator ['ɔrətə*] *n* oratore/trice.
oratorio [ɔrə'tɔːrɪəu] *n* oratorio.
orb [ɔːb] *n* orbe *m*.
orbit ['ɔːbɪt] *n* orbita ♦ *vt* orbitare intorno a; **to be in/go into** ~ (**round**) essere/entrare in orbita (attorno a).
orbital ['ɔːbɪtl] *n* (*also*: ~ **motorway**) raccordo anulare.
orchard ['ɔːtʃəd] *n* frutteto; **apple** ~ meleto.
orchestra ['ɔːkɪstrə] *n* orchestra; (*US: seating*) platea.
orchestral [ɔː'kɛstrəl] *adj* orchestrale; (*concert*) sinfonico(a).
orchestrate ['ɔːkɪstreɪt] *vt* (*MUS, fig*) orchestrare.
orchid ['ɔːkɪd] *n* orchidea.
ordain [ɔː'deɪn] *vt* (*REL*) ordinare; (*decide*) decretare.
ordeal [ɔː'diːl] *n* prova, travaglio.
order ['ɔːdə*] *n* ordine *m*; (*COMM*) ordinazione *f* ♦ *vt* ordinare; **to** ~ **sb to do** ordinare a qn di fare; **in** ~ in ordine; (*of document*) in regola; **in** ~ **of size** in ordine di grandezza; **in** ~ **to do** per fare; **in** ~ **that** affinché +*sub*; **a machine in working** ~ una macchina che funziona bene; **to be out of** ~ (*machine, toilets*) essere guasto(a); (*telephone*) essere fuori servizio; **to place an** ~ **for sth with sb** ordinare qc a qn; **to the** ~ **of** (*BANKING*) all'ordine di; **to be under** ~**s to do sth** avere l'ordine di fare qc; **a point of** ~ una questione di procedura; **to be on** ~ essere stato ordinato; **made to** ~ fatto su commissione; **the lower** ~**s** (*pej*) i ceti inferiori.
order book *n* copiacommissioni *m inv*.
order form *n* modulo d'ordinazione.
orderly ['ɔːdəlɪ] *n* (*MIL*) attendente *m* ♦ *adj* (*room*) in ordine; (*mind*) metodico(a); (*person*) ordinato(a), metodico(a).
order number *n* numero di ordinazione.
ordinal ['ɔːdɪnl] *adj* (*number*) ordinale.
ordinary ['ɔːdnrɪ] *adj* normale, comune; (*pej*) mediocre ♦ *n*: **out of the** ~ diverso dal solito, fuori dell'ordinario.

ordinary degree n laurea (con corso di studi di 3 anni); see boxed note.

ORDINARY DEGREE

Il corso universitario di studi che porta al conferimento del "Bachelor's degree" può avere una durata diversa, a seconda del profitto dello studente. Chi non è interessato a proseguire gli studi oltre tre anni di corso può optare per l'**ordinary degree**; vedi anche **honours degree**.

---

ordinary seaman (OS) n (BRIT) marinaio semplice.
ordinary shares npl azioni fpl ordinarie.
ordination [ɔːdɪ'neɪʃən] n ordinazione f.
ordnance ['ɔːdnəns] n (MIL: unit) (reparto di) sussistenza.
Ordnance Survey map n (BRIT) ≈ carta topografica dell'IGM.
ore [ɔː*] n minerale m grezzo.
Oreg(on) abbr (US) = Oregon.
organ ['ɔːgən] n organo.
organic [ɔː'gænɪk] adj organico(a).
organism ['ɔːgənɪzəm] n organismo.
organist ['ɔːgənɪst] n organista m/f.
organization [ɔːgənaɪ'zeɪʃən] n organizzazione f.
organize ['ɔːgənaɪz] vt organizzare; **to get** ~**d** organizzarsi.
organized crime ['ɔːgənaɪzd-] n criminalità organizzata.
organized labour ['ɔːgənaɪzd-] n manodopera organizzata.
organizer ['ɔːgənaɪzə*] n organizzatore/trice.
orgasm ['ɔːgæzəm] n orgasmo.
orgy ['ɔːdʒɪ] n orgia.
Orient ['ɔːrɪənt] n: **the** ~ l'Oriente m.
oriental [ɔːrɪ'entl] adj, n orientale (m/f).
orientate ['ɔːrɪənteɪt] vt orientare.
orifice ['ɔrɪfɪs] n orifizio.
origin ['ɔrɪdʒɪn] n origine f; **country of** ~ paese m d'origine.
original [ə'rɪdʒɪnl] adj originale; (earliest) originario(a) ♦ n originale m.
originality [ərɪdʒɪ'nælɪtɪ] n originalità.
originally [ə'rɪdʒɪnəlɪ] adv (at first) all'inizio.
originate [ə'rɪdʒɪneɪt] vi: **to** ~ **from** venire da, essere originario(a) di; (suggestion) provenire da; **to** ~ **in** nascere in; (custom) avere origine in.
originator [ə'rɪdʒɪneɪtə*] n iniziatore/trice.
Orkneys ['ɔːknɪz] npl: **the** ~ (also: **the Orkney Islands**) le (isole) Orcadi.
ornament ['ɔːnəmənt] n ornamento; (trinket) ninnolo.

ornamental [ɔːnə'mentl] adj ornamentale.
ornamentation [ɔːnəmen'teɪʃən] n decorazione f, ornamento.
ornate [ɔː'neɪt] adj molto ornato(a).
ornithologist [ɔːnɪ'θɔlədʒɪst] n ornitologo/a.
ornithology [ɔːnɪ'θɔlədʒɪ] n ornitologia.
orphan ['ɔːfn] n orfano/a ♦ vt: **to be** ~**ed** diventare orfano.
orphanage ['ɔːfənɪdʒ] n orfanotrofio.
orthodox ['ɔːθədɔks] adj ortodosso(a).
orthopaedic, (US) **orthopedic** [ɔːθə'piːdɪk] adj ortopedico(a).
OS abbr (BRIT: = Ordnance Survey) ≈ IGM m (= Istituto Geografico Militare); (: NAUT) see **ordinary seaman**; (: DRESS) = **outsize**.
O/S abbr = **out of stock**.
oscillate ['ɔsɪleɪt] vi oscillare.
OSHA n abbr (US: = Occupational Safety and Health Administration) amministrazione per la sicurezza e la salute sul lavoro.
Oslo ['ɔsləu] n Oslo f.
ostensible [ɔs'tensɪbl] adj preteso(a); apparente.
ostensibly [ɔs'tensɪblɪ] adv all'apparenza.
ostentation [ɔsten'teɪʃən] n ostentazione f.
ostentatious [ɔsten'teɪʃəs] adj pretenzioso(a); ostentato(a).
osteopath ['ɔstɪəpæθ] n specialista m/f di osteopatia.
ostracize ['ɔstrəsaɪz] vt dare l'ostracismo a.
ostrich ['ɔstrɪtʃ] n struzzo.
OT abbr (= Old Testament) V.T.
OTB n abbr (US: = off-track betting) puntate effettuate fuori dagli ippodromi.
OTE abbr (= on-target earnings) stipendio compreso le commissioni.
other ['ʌðə*] adj altro(a) ♦ pron: **the** ~ l'altro(a); **the** ~**s** gli altri; **the** ~ **day** l'altro giorno; **some** ~ **people have still to arrive** (alcuni) altri devono ancora arrivare; **some actor or** ~ un certo attore; **somebody or** ~ qualcuno; ~ **than** altro che; a parte; **the car was none** ~ **than Roberta's** la macchina era proprio di Roberta.
otherwise ['ʌðəwaɪz] adv, conj altrimenti; **an** ~ **good piece of work** un lavoro comunque buono.
OTT abbr (col) = **over the top**; see **top**.
otter ['ɔtə*] n lontra.
OU n abbr (BRIT) see **Open University**.
ouch [autʃ] excl ohi!, ahi!
ought [ɔːt] pt **ought** aux vb: **I** ~ **to do it** dovrei farlo; **this** ~ **to have been corrected** questo avrebbe dovuto essere corretto; **he** ~ **to win** dovrebbe vincere; **you** ~ **to go and see it** dovreste andare a

vederlo, fareste bene ad andarlo a vedere.
ounce [auns] *n* oncia (= *28.35 g; 16 in a pound*).
our [auə*] *adj* il(la) nostro(a), *pl* i(le) nostri(e).
ours [auəz] *pron* il(la) nostro(a), *pl* i(le) nostri(e).
ourselves [auə'sɛlvz] *pron pl* (*reflexive*) ci; (*after preposition*) noi stessi(e); (*emphatic*) noi stessi(e); **we did it (all) by** ~ l'abbiamo fatto (tutto) da soli.
oust [aust] *vt* cacciare, espellere.

================= *KEYWORD*

out [aut] *adv* (*gen*) fuori; ~ **here/there** qui/là fuori; **to speak** ~ **loud** parlare forte; **to have a night** ~ uscire una sera; **to be** ~ **and about** *or* (*US*) **around again** essere di nuovo in piedi; **the boat was 10 km** ~ la barca era a 10 km dalla costa; **the journey** ~ l'andata; **3 days** ~ **from Plymouth** a 3 giorni da Plymouth
♦ *adj*: **to be** ~ (*gen*) essere fuori; (*unconscious*) aver perso i sensi; (*style, singer*) essere fuori moda; **before the week was** ~ prima che la settimana fosse finita; **to be** ~ **to do sth** avere intenzione di fare qc; **he's** ~ **for all he can get** sta cercando di trarne il massimo profitto; **to be** ~ **in one's calculations** aver sbagliato i calcoli
♦ **out of** *prep* **1** (*outside, beyond*) fuori di; **to go** ~ **of the house** uscire di casa; **to look** ~ **of the window** guardare fuori dalla finestra
2 (*because of*) per; ~ **of pity** per pietà; ~ **of boredom** per noia
3 (*origin*) da; **made** ~ **of wood** (fatto) di *or* in legno; **to drink** ~ **of a cup** bere da una tazza
4 (*from among*): ~ **of 10** su 10
5 (*without*) senza; ~ **of petrol** senza benzina; **it's** ~ **of stock** (*COMM*) è esaurito.

outage ['autɪdʒ] *n* (*esp US: power failure*) interruzione *f or* mancanza di corrente elettrica.
out-and-out ['autəndaut] *adj* vero(a) e proprio(a).
outback ['autbæk] *n* zona isolata; (*in Australia*) interno, entroterra.
outbid, *pt*, *pp* **outbid** [aut'bɪd] *vt* fare un'offerta più alta di.
outboard ['autbɔːd] *n*: ~ (**motor**) (motore *m*) fuoribordo.
outbound ['autbaund] *adj*: ~ (**for** *or* **from**) in

partenza (per *or* da).
outbreak ['autbreɪk] *n* scoppio; epidemia.
outbuilding ['autbɪldɪŋ] *n* dipendenza.
outburst ['autbɜːst] *n* scoppio.
outcast ['autkɑːst] *n* esule *m/f*; (*socially*) paria *m inv*.
outclass [aut'klɑːs] *vt* surclassare.
outcome ['autkʌm] *n* esito, risultato.
outcrop ['autkrɔp] *n* affioramento.
outcry ['autkraɪ] *n* protesta, clamore *m*.
outdated [aut'deɪtɪd] *adj* (*custom, clothes*) fuori moda; (*idea*) sorpassato(a).
outdistance [aut'dɪstəns] *vt* distanziare.
outdo [aut'duː] *vt irreg* sorpassare.
outdoor [aut'dɔː*] *adj* all'aperto.
outdoors [aut'dɔːz] *adv* fuori; all'aria aperta.
outer ['autə*] *adj* esteriore; ~ **suburbs** estrema periferia.
outer space *n* spazio cosmico.
outfit ['autfɪt] *n* equipaggiamento; (*clothes*) abito; (*col: organization*) organizzazione *f*.
outfitter ['autfɪtə*] *n* (*BRIT*): "**(gent's)** ~**s**" "confezioni da uomo".
outgoing ['autgəuɪŋ] *adj* (*president, tenant*) uscente; (*means of transport*) in partenza; (*character*) socievole.
outgoings ['autgəuɪŋz] *npl* (*BRIT: expenses*) spese *fpl*.
outgrow [aut'grəu] *vt irreg* (*clothes*) diventare troppo grande per.
outhouse ['authaus] *n* costruzione *f* annessa.
outing ['autɪŋ] *n* gita; escursione *f*.
outlandish [aut'lændɪʃ] *adj* strano(a).
outlast [aut'lɑːst] *vt* sopravvivere a.
outlaw ['autlɔː] *n* fuorilegge *m/f* ♦ *vt* (*person*) mettere fuori della legge; (*practice*) proscrivere.
outlay ['autleɪ] *n* spesa.
outlet ['autlɛt] *n* (*for liquid etc*) sbocco, scarico; (*for emotion*) sfogo; (*for goods*) sbocco, mercato; (*also*: **retail** ~) punto di vendita; (*US ELEC*) presa di corrente.
outline ['autlaɪn] *n* contorno, profilo; (*summary*) abbozzo, grandi linee *fpl*.
outlive [aut'lɪv] *vt* sopravvivere a.
outlook ['autluk] *n* prospettiva, vista.
outlying ['autlaɪɪŋ] *adj* periferico(a).
outmanoeuvre, (*US*) **outmaneuver** [autmə'nuːvə*] *vt* (*rival etc*) superare in strategia.
outmoded [aut'məudɪd] *adj* passato(a) di moda; antiquato(a).
outnumber [aut'nʌmbə*] *vt* superare in numero.
out-of-court [autəv'kɔːt] *adj* extragiudiziale ♦ *adv* (*settle*) senza

ricorrere al tribunale.
out-of-date [autəv'deɪt] *adj* (*passport, ticket*) scaduto(a); (*theory, idea*) sorpassato(a); superato(a); (*custom*) antiquato(a); (*clothes*) fuori moda.
out-of-the-way ['autəvðə'weɪ] *adj* (*remote*) fuori mano; (*unusual*) originale, insolito(a).
outpatient ['autpeɪʃənt] *n* paziente *m/f* esterno(a).
outpost ['autpəust] *n* avamposto.
outpouring ['autpɔːrɪŋ] *n* (*fig*) torrente *m*.
output ['autput] *n* produzione *f*; (*COMPUT*) output *m inv* ♦ *vt* emettere.
outrage ['autreɪdʒ] *n* oltraggio; scandalo ♦ *vt* oltraggiare.
outrageous [aut'reɪdʒəs] *adj* oltraggioso(a).
outrider ['autraɪdə*] *n* (*on motorcycle*) battistrada *m inv*.
outright *adv* [aut'raɪt] completamente; schiettamente; apertamente; sul colpo ♦ *adj* ['autraɪt] completo(a); schietto(a) e netto(a).
outrun [aut'rʌn] *vt irreg* superare (nella corsa).
outset ['autset] *n* inizio.
outshine [aut'ʃaɪn] *vt irreg* (*fig*) eclissare.
outside [aut'saɪd] *n* esterno, esteriore *m* ♦ *adj* esterno(a), esteriore; (*remote, unlikely*). **an ~ chance** una vaga possibilità ♦ *adv* fuori, all'esterno ♦ *prep* fuori di, all'esterno di; **at the ~** (*fig*) al massimo; **~ left/right** *n* (*FOOTBALL*) ala sinistra/destra.
outside broadcast *n* (*RADIO, TV*) trasmissione *f* in esterno.
outside lane *n* (*AUT*) corsia di sorpasso.
outside line *n* (*TEL*) linea esterna.
outsider [aut'saɪdə*] *n* (*in race etc*) outsider *m inv*; (*stranger*) straniero/a.
outsize ['autsaɪz] *adj* enorme; (*clothes*) per taglie forti.
outskirts ['autskɔːts] *npl* sobborghi *mpl*.
outsmart [aut'smɑːt] *vt* superare in astuzia.
outspoken [aut'spəukən] *adj* molto franco(a).
outspread ['autspred] *adj* (*wings*) aperto(a).
outstanding [aut'stændɪŋ] *adj* eccezionale, di rilievo; (*unfinished*) non completo(a); non evaso(a); non regolato(a); **your account is still ~** deve ancora saldare il conto.
outstay [aut'steɪ] *vt*: **to ~ one's welcome** diventare un ospite sgradito.
outstretched [aut'stretʃt] *adj* (*hand*) teso(a); (*body*) disteso(a).
outstrip [aut'strɪp] *vt* (*also fig*) superare.

out-tray ['auttreɪ] *n* raccoglitore *m* per le carte da spedire.
outvote [aut'vəut] *vt*: **to ~ sb (by)** avere la maggioranza rispetto a qn (per); **to ~ sth (by)** respingere qc (per).
outward ['autwəd] *adj* (*sign, appearances*) esteriore; (*journey*) d'andata.
outwardly ['autwədlɪ] *adv* esteriormente; in apparenza.
outweigh [aut'weɪ] *vt* avere maggior peso di.
outwit [aut'wɪt] *vt* superare in astuzia.
oval ['əuvl] *adj, n* ovale (*m*).
Oval Office *n* (*US*) see boxed note.

OVAL OFFICE

*L'***Oval Office** *è una grande stanza di forma ovale nella "White House", la Casa Bianca, dove ha sede l'ufficio del Presidente degli Stati Uniti. Spesso il termine è usato per indicare la stessa presidenza degli Stati Uniti.*

---

ovarian [əu'vɛərɪən] *adj* ovarico(a).
ovary ['əuvərɪ] *n* ovaia.
ovation [əu'veɪʃən] *n* ovazione *f*.
oven ['ʌvn] *n* forno.
ovenproof ['ʌvnpruːf] *adj* da forno.
oven-ready ['ʌvnredɪ] *adj* pronto(a) da infornare.
ovenware ['ʌvnwɛə*] *n* vasellame *m* da mettere in forno.
over ['əuvə*] *adv* al di sopra; (*excessively*) molto, troppo ♦ *adj* (*or adv*) (*finished*) finito(a), terminato(a); (*too much*) troppo; (*remaining*) che avanza ♦ *prep* su; sopra; (*above*) al di sopra di; (*on the other side of*) di là di; (*more than*) più di; (*during*) durante; **~ here** qui; **~ there** là; **all ~** (*everywhere*) dappertutto; (*finished*) tutto(a) finito(a); **~ and (again)** più e più volte; **~ and above** oltre (a); **to ask sb ~** invitare qn (a passare); **now ~ to our Rome correspondent** diamo ora la linea al nostro corrispondente da Roma; **the world ~** in tutto il mondo; **she's not ~ intelligent** (*BRIT*) non è troppo intelligente; **they fell out ~ money** litigarono per una questione di denaro.
over... ['əuvə*] *prefix*: **~abundant** sovrabbondante.
overact [əuvər'ækt] *vi* (*THEAT*) esagerare *or* strafare la propria parte.
overall *adj, n* ['əuvərɔːl] *adj* totale ♦ *n* (*BRIT*) grembiule *m* ♦ *adv* [əuvər'ɔːl] nell'insieme, complessivamente; **~s** *npl* tuta (da lavoro).
overall majority *n* maggioranza assoluta.

overanxious [əuvər'æŋkʃəs] *adj* troppo ansioso(a).

overawe [əuvər'ɔ:] *vt* intimidire.

overbalance [əuvə'bæləns] *vi* perdere l'equilibrio.

overbearing [əuvə'bɛərɪŋ] *adj* imperioso(a), prepotente.

overboard ['əuvəbɔ:d] *adv* (*NAUT*) fuori bordo, in acqua; **to go ~ for sth** (*fig*) impazzire per qc.

overbook [əuvə'buk] *vt* sovrapprenotare.

overcapitalize [əuvə'kæpɪtəlaɪz] *vt* sovraccapitalizzare.

overcast ['əuvəkɑ:st] *adj* coperto(a).

overcharge [əuvə'tʃɑ:dʒ] *vt*: **to ~ sb for sth** far pagare troppo caro a qn per qc.

overcoat ['əuvəkəut] *n* soprabito, cappotto.

overcome [əuvə'kʌm] *vt irreg* superare; sopraffare; **~ with grief** sopraffatto(a) dal dolore.

overconfident [əuvə'kɔnfɪdənt] *adj* troppo sicuro(a) (di sé), presuntuoso(a).

overcrowded [əuvə'kraudɪd] *adj* sovraffollato(a).

overcrowding [əuvə'kraudɪŋ] *n* sovraffollamento; (*in bus*) calca.

overdo [əuvə'du:] *vt irreg* esagerare; (*overcook*) cuocere troppo; **to ~ it, to ~ things** (*work too hard*) lavorare troppo.

overdose ['əuvədəus] *n* dose *f* eccessiva.

overdraft ['əuvədrɑːft] *n* scoperto (di conto).

overdrawn [əuvə'drɔːn] *adj* (*account*) scoperto(a).

overdrive ['əuvədraɪv] *n* (*AUT*) overdrive *m inv*.

overdue [əuvə'dju:] *adj* in ritardo; (*recognition*) tardivo(a); (*bill*) insoluto(a); **that change was long ~** quel cambiamento ci voleva da tempo.

overemphasis [əuvər'ɛmfəsɪs] *n*: **~ on sth** importanza eccessiva data a qc.

overemphasize [əuvər'ɛmfəsaɪz] *vt* dare un'importanza eccessiva a.

overestimate [əuvər'ɛstɪmeɪt] *vt* sopravvalutare.

overexcited [əuvərɪk'saɪtɪd] *adj* sovraeccitato(a).

overexertion [əuvərɪg'zəːʃən] *n* logorio (fisico).

overexpose [əuvərɪk'spəuz] *vt* (*PHOT*) sovraesporre.

overflow *vi* [əuvə'fləu] traboccare ♦ *n* ['əuvəfləu] eccesso; (*also:* ~ **pipe**) troppopieno.

overfly [əuvə'flaɪ] *vt irreg* sorvolare.

overgenerous [əuvə'dʒɛnərəs] *adj* troppo generoso(a).

overgrown [əuvə'grəun] *adj* (*garden*) ricoperto(a) di vegetazione; **he's just an ~ schoolboy** è proprio un bambinone.

overhang [əuvə'hæŋ] *irreg vt* sporgere da ♦ *vi* sporgere.

overhaul *vt* [əuvə'hɔ:l] revisionare ♦ *n* ['əuvəhɔ:l] revisione *f*.

overhead *adv* [əuvə'hɛd] di sopra ♦ *adj* ['əuvəhɛd] aereo(a); (*lighting*) verticale ♦ *n* (*US*) = **overheads**.

overheads ['əuvəhɛdz] *npl* (*BRIT*) spese *fpl* generali.

overhear [əuvə'hɪə*] *vt irreg* sentire (per caso).

overheat [əuvə'hi:t] *vi* surriscaldarsi.

overjoyed [əuvə'dʒɔɪd] *adj* pazzo(a) di gioia.

overkill ['əuvəkɪl] *n* (*fig*) strafare *m*.

overland ['əuvəlænd] *adj, adv* per via di terra.

overlap *vi* [əuvə'læp] sovrapporsi ♦ *n* ['əuvəlæp] sovrapposizione *f*.

overleaf [əuvə'li:f] *adv* a tergo.

overload [əuvə'ləud] *vt* sovraccaricare.

overlook [əuvə'luk] *vt* (*have view of*) dare su; (*miss*) trascurare; (*forgive*) passare sopra a.

overlord ['əuvələːd] *n* capo supremo.

overmanning [əuvə'mænɪŋ] *n* eccedenza di manodopera.

overnight *adv* [əuvə'naɪt] (*happen*) durante la notte; (*fig*) tutto ad un tratto ♦ *adj* ['əuvənaɪt] di notte; fulmineo(a); **he stayed there ~** ci ha passato la notte; **if you travel ~ ...** se viaggia di notte ...; **he'll be away ~** passerà la notte fuori.

overpass ['əuvəpɑːs] *n* cavalcavia *m inv*.

overpay [əuvə'peɪ] *vt*: **to ~ sb by £50** pagare 50 sterline in più a qn.

overplay [əuvə'pleɪ] *vt* dare troppa importanza a; **to ~ one's hand** sopravvalutare la propria posizione.

overpower [əuvə'pauə*] *vt* sopraffare.

overpowering [əuvə'pauərɪŋ] *adj* irresistibile; (*heat, stench*) soffocante.

overproduction ['əuvəprə'dʌkʃən] *n* sovrapproduzione *f*.

overrate [əuvə'reɪt] *vt* sopravvalutare.

overreach [əuvə'ri:tʃ] *vt*: **to ~ o.s.** volere strafare.

overreact [əuvəri:'ækt] *vi* reagire in modo esagerato.

override [əuvə'raɪd] *vt* (*irreg: like* **ride**) (*order, objection*) passar sopra a; (*decision*) annullare.

overriding [əuvə'raɪdɪŋ] *adj* preponderante.

overrule [əuvə'ru:l] *vt* (*decision*) annullare; (*claim*) respingere.

overrun [əuvə'rʌn] *vt irreg* (*MIL: country etc*) invadere; (*time limit etc*) superare, andare al di là di ♦ *vi* protrarsi; **the town is ~ with tourists** la città è invasa dai turisti.

overseas [əuvə'si:z] *adv* oltremare; (*abroad*) all'estero ♦ *adj* (*trade*) estero(a); (*visitor*) straniero(a).

oversee [əuvə'si:] *vt irreg* sorvegliare.

overseer ['əuvəsiə*] *n* (*in factory*) caposquadra *m*.

overshadow [əuvə'ʃædəu] *vt* (*fig*) eclissare.

overshoot [əuvə'ʃu:t] *vt irreg* superare.

oversight ['əuvəsait] *n* omissione *f*, svista; **due to an ~** per una svista.

oversimplify [əuvə'simplifai] *vt* rendere troppo semplice.

oversleep [əuvə'sli:p] *vi irreg* dormire troppo a lungo.

overspend [əuvə'spɛnd] *vi irreg* spendere troppo; **we have overspent by 5000 dollars** abbiamo speso 5000 dollari di troppo.

overspill ['əuvəspil] *n* eccedenza di popolazione.

overstaffed [əuvə'sta:ft] *adj*: **to be ~** avere troppo personale.

overstate [əuvə'steit] *vt* esagerare.

overstatement [əuvə'steitmənt] *n* esagerazione *f*.

overstay [əuvə'stei] *vt*: **to ~ one's welcome** trattenersi troppo a lungo (come ospite).

overstep [əuvə'stɛp] *vt*: **to ~ the mark** superare ogni limite.

overstock [əuvə'stɔk] *vt* sovrapprovvigionare, sovraimmagazzinare.

overstretched [əuvə'strɛtʃt] *adj* sovraccarico(a); (*budget*) arrivato(a) al limite.

overstrike *n* ['əuvəstraik] (*on printer*) sovrapposizione *f* (di caratteri) ♦ *vt irreg* [əuvə'straik] sovrapporre.

overt [əu'və:t] *adj* palese.

overtake [əuvə'teik] *vt irreg* sorpassare.

overtaking [əuvə'teikiŋ] *n* (*AUT*) sorpasso.

overtax [əuvə'tæks] *vt* (*ECON*) imporre tasse eccessive a, tassare eccessivamente; (*fig: strength, patience*) mettere alla prova, abusare di; **to ~ o.s.** chiedere troppo alle proprie forze.

overthrow [əuvə'θrəu] *vt irreg* (*government*) rovesciare.

overtime ['əuvətaim] *n* (*lavoro*) straordinario; **to do** *or* **work ~** fare lo straordinario.

overtime ban *n* rifiuto sindacale a fare gli straordinari.

overtone ['əuvətəun] *n* (*also*: **~s**) sfumatura.

overture ['əuvətʃuə*] *n* (*MUS*) ouverture *f inv*; (*fig*) approccio.

overturn [əuvə'tə:n] *vt* rovesciare ♦ *vi* rovesciarsi.

overview ['əuvəvju:] *n* visione *f* d'insieme.

overweight [əuvə'weit] *adj* (*person*) troppo grasso(a); (*luggage*) troppo pesante.

overwhelm [əuvə'wɛlm] *vt* sopraffare; sommergere; schiacciare.

overwhelming [əuvə'wɛlmiŋ] *adj* (*victory*) schiacciante; (*desire*) irresistibile; **one's ~ impression is of heat** l'impressione dominante è quella di caldo.

overwhelmingly [əuvə'wɛlmiŋli] *adv* in massa.

overwork [əuvə'wə:k] *vt* far lavorare troppo ♦ *vi* lavorare troppo, strapazzarsi.

overwrite [əuvə'rait] *vt* (*COMPUT*) ricoprire.

overwrought [əuvə'rɔ:t] *adj* molto agitato(a).

ovulation [ɔvju'leiʃən] *n* ovulazione *f*.

owe [əu] *vt* dovere; **to ~ sb sth, to ~ sth to sb** dovere qc a qn.

owing to ['əuiŋtu:] *prep* a causa di.

owl [aul] *n* gufo.

own [əun] *adj* proprio(a) ♦ *vt* possedere ♦ *vi* (*BRIT*): **to ~ to sth** ammettere qc; **to ~ to having done sth** ammettere di aver fatto qc; **a room of my ~** la mia propria camera; **to get one's ~ back** vendicarsi; **on one's ~** tutto(a) solo(a); **can I have it for my (very) ~?** posso averlo tutto per me?; **to come into one's ~** mostrare le proprie qualità.

▶**own up** *vi* confessare.

own brand *n* (*COMM*) etichetta propria.

owner ['əunə*] *n* proprietario/a.

owner-occupier ['əunər'ɔkjupaiə*] *n* proprietario/a della casa in cui abita.

ownership ['əunəʃip] *n* possesso; **it's under new ~** ha un nuovo proprietario.

own goal *n* (*also fig*) autogol *m inv*.

ox [ɔks], *pl* **oxen** [ɔks, 'ɔksn] *n* bue *m*.

Oxbridge ['ɔksbridʒ] *n* le *università di Oxford e/o Cambridge*; *see boxed note*.

OXBRIDGE

La parola **Oxbridge** *deriva dalla fusione dei nomi* Ox(ford) *e* (Cam)bridge *e fa riferimento a queste due antiche università e a coloro che le frequentano o le hanno frequentate.*

Oxfam ['ɔksfæm] *n abbr* (*BRIT*: = *Oxford Committee for Famine Relief*) *organizzazione per aiuti al terzo mondo.*

oxide ['ɔksaɪd] n ossido.
Oxon. ['ɔksn] abbr (BRIT: = Oxoniensis) = of Oxford.
oxtail ['ɔksteɪl] n: ~ **soup** minestra di coda di bue.
oxyacetylene ['ɔksɪə'sɛtɪliːn] adj ossiacetilenico(a); ~ **burner,** ~ **lamp** cannello ossiacetilenico.
oxygen ['ɔksɪdʒən] n ossigeno.
oxygen mask n maschera ad ossigeno.
oxygen tent n tenda ad ossigeno.
oyster ['ɔɪstə*] n ostrica.
oz. abbr = **ounce.**
ozone ['əuzəun] n ozono.

P p

P, p [piː] n (letter) P, p f or m inv; **P for Peter** ≈ P come Padova.
P abbr = **president; prince.**
p abbr (= page) p; (BRIT) = **penny, pence.**
PA n abbr see **personal assistant; public address system** ♦ abbr (US) = **Pennsylvania.**
pa [pɑː] n (col) papà m inv, babbo.
p.a. abbr = **per annum.**
PAC n abbr (US) = political action committee.
pace [peɪs] n passo; (speed) passo; velocità ♦ vi: **to** ~ **up and down** camminare su e giù; **to keep** ~ **with** camminare di pari passo a; (events) tenersi al corrente di; **to put sb through his** ~**s** (fig) mettere qn alla prova; **to set the** ~ (running) fare l'andatura; (fig) dare il la or il tono.
pacemaker ['peɪsmeɪkə*] n (MED) pacemaker m inv, stimolatore m cardiaco; (SPORT) chi fa l'andatura.
pacific [pə'sɪfɪk] adj pacifico(a) ♦ n: **the P**~ **(Ocean)** il Pacifico, l'Oceano Pacifico.
pacification [pæsɪfɪ'keɪʃən] n pacificazione f.
pacifier ['pæsɪfaɪə*] n (US: dummy) succhiotto, ciuccio (col).
pacifist ['pæsɪfɪst] n pacifista m/f.
pacify ['pæsɪfaɪ] vt pacificare; (soothe) calmare.
pack [pæk] n (packet) pacco; (COMM) confezione f; (US: of cigarettes) pacchetto; (of goods) balla; (of hounds) muta; (of wolves) branco; (of thieves etc) banda; (of cards) mazzo ♦ vt (goods) impaccare, imballare; (in suitcase etc) mettere; (box)

riempire; (cram) stipare, pigiare; (press down) tamponare; turare; (COMPUT) comprimere, impaccare ♦ vi: **to** ~ (one's bags) fare la valigia; **to send sb** ~**ing** (col) spedire via qn.
▶**pack in** (BRIT col) vi (watch, car) guastarsi ♦ vt mollare, piantare; ~ **it in!** piantala!
▶**pack off** vt (person) spedire.
▶**pack up** vi (BRIT col: machine) guastarsi; (: person) far fagotto ♦ vt (belongings, clothes) mettere in una valigia; (goods, presents) imballare.
package ['pækɪdʒ] n pacco; balla; (also: ~ **deal**) pacchetto; forfait m inv ♦ vt (goods) confezionare.
package holiday n (BRIT) vacanza organizzata.
package tour n viaggio organizzato.
packaging ['pækɪdʒɪŋ] n confezione f, imballo.
packed [pækt] adj (crowded) affollato(a); ~ **lunch** (BRIT) pranzo al sacco.
packer ['pækə*] n (person) imballatore/ trice.
packet ['pækɪt] n pacchetto.
packet switching [-swɪtʃɪŋ] n (COMPUT) commutazione f di pacchetto.
pack ice ['pækaɪs] n banchisa.
packing ['pækɪŋ] n imballaggio.
packing case n cassa da imballaggio.
pact [pækt] n patto, accordo; trattato.
pad [pæd] n blocco; (for inking) tampone m; (col: flat) appartamentino ♦ vt imbottire ♦ vi: **to** ~ **about/in** etc camminare/entrare etc a passi felpati.
padded cell ['pædɪd-] n cella imbottita.
padding ['pædɪŋ] n imbottitura; (fig) riempitivo.
paddle ['pædl] n (oar) pagaia ♦ vi sguazzare ♦ vt (boat) fare andare a colpi di pagaia.
paddle steamer n battello a ruote.
paddling pool ['pædlɪŋ-] n piscina per bambini.
paddock ['pædək] n recinto; paddock m inv.
paddy ['pædɪ] n (also: ~ **field**) risaia.
padlock ['pædlɔk] n lucchetto ♦ vt chiudere con il lucchetto.
padre ['pɑːdrɪ] n cappellano.
Padua ['pædʒuə] n Padova.
paediatrician, (US) **pediatrician** [piːdɪə'trɪʃən] n pediatra m/f.
paediatrics, (US) **pediatrics** [piːdɪ'ætrɪks] n pediatria.
paedophile, (US) **pedophile** ['piːdəufaɪl] adj, n pedofilo(a).
pagan ['peɪɡən] adj, n pagano(a).
page [peɪdʒ] n pagina; (also: ~ **boy**) fattorino; (: at wedding) paggio ♦ vt (in

hotel etc) (*far*) chiamare.
pageant ['pædʒənt] *n* spettacolo storico;
grande cerimonia.
pageantry ['pædʒəntrɪ] *n* pompa.
page break *n* interruzione *f* di pagina.
pager ['peɪdʒə*] *n* cicalino, cercapersone
m.
paginate ['pædʒɪneɪt] *vt* impaginare.
pagination [pædʒɪ'neɪʃən] *n* impaginazione
f.
pagoda [pə'gəʊdə] *n* pagoda.
paid [peɪd] *pt, pp of* **pay** ♦ *adj* (*work, official*)
rimunerato(a); **to put ~ to** (*BRIT*) mettere
fine a.
paid-up ['peɪdʌp], (*US*) **paid in** ['peɪdɪn] *adj*
(*member*) che ha pagato la sua quota;
(*share*) interamente pagato(a); **~ capital**
capitale *m* interamente versato.
pail [peɪl] *n* secchio.
pain [peɪn] *n* dolore *m*; **to be in ~** soffrire,
aver male; **to have a ~ in** aver male *or* un
dolore a; **to take ~s to do** mettercela
tutta per fare; **on ~ of death** sotto pena
di morte.
pained [peɪnd] *adj* addolorato(a), afflitto(a).
painful ['peɪnful] *adj* doloroso(a), che fa
male; (*difficult*) difficile, penoso(a).
painfully ['peɪnfəlɪ] *adv* (*fig: very*) fin troppo.
painkiller ['peɪnkɪlə*] *n* antalgico,
antidolorifico.
painstaking ['peɪnzteɪkɪŋ] *adj* sollecito(a).
paint [peɪnt] *n* (*for house etc*) tinta, vernice
f; (*ART*) colore *m* ♦ *vt* (*ART, walls*)
dipingere; (*door etc*) verniciare; **a tin of ~**
un barattolo di tinta *or* vernice; **to ~ the
door blue** verniciare la porta di azzurro;
to ~ in oils dipingere a olio.
paintbox ['peɪntbɒks] *n* scatola di colori.
paintbrush ['peɪntbrʌʃ] *n* pennello.
painter ['peɪntə*] *n* (*artist*) pittore *m*;
(*decorator*) imbianchino.
painting ['peɪntɪŋ] *n* (*activity: of artist*)
pittura; (: *of decorator*) imbiancatura;
verniciatura; (*picture*) dipinto, quadro.
paint-stripper ['peɪntstrɪpə*] *n* prodotto
sverniciante.
paintwork ['peɪntwɔːk] *n* (*BRIT*) tinta; (: *of
car*) vernice *f*.
pair [pɛə*] *n* (*of shoes, gloves etc*) paio; (*of
people*) coppia; duo *m inv*; **a ~ of scissors/
trousers** un paio di forbici/pantaloni.
▶**pair off** *vi*: **to ~ off (with sb)** fare coppia
(con qn).
pajamas [pə'dʒɑːməz] *npl* (*US*) pigiama *m*.
Pakistan [pɑːkɪ'stɑːn] *n* Pakistan *m*.
Pakistani [pɑːkɪ'stɑːnɪ] *adj, n* pakistano(a).
PAL [pæl] *n abbr* (*TV*: = *phase alternation line*)
PAL *m*.

pal [pæl] *n* (*col*) amico/a, compagno/a.
palace ['pæləs] *n* palazzo.
palatable ['pælɪtəbl] *adj* gustoso(a).
palate ['pælɪt] *n* palato.
palatial [pə'leɪʃəl] *adj* sontuoso(a),
sfarzoso(a).
palaver [pə'lɑːvə*] *n* chiacchiere *fpl*; storie
fpl.
pale [peɪl] *adj* pallido(a) ♦ *vi* impallidire ♦ *n*:
to be beyond the ~ aver oltrepassato
ogni limite; **to grow** *or* **turn ~** (*person*)
diventare pallido(a), impallidire; **to ~
into insignificance (beside)** perdere
d'importanza (nei confronti di); **~ blue**
azzurro *or* blu pallido *inv*.
paleness ['peɪlnɪs] *n* pallore *m*.
Palestine ['pælɪstaɪn] *n* Palestina.
Palestinian [pælɪs'tɪnɪən] *adj, n* palestinese
(*m/f*).
palette ['pælɪt] *n* tavolozza.
paling ['peɪlɪŋ] *n* (*stake*) palo; (*fence*)
palizzata.
palisade [pælɪ'seɪd] *n* palizzata.
pall [pɔːl] *n* (*of smoke*) cappa ♦ *vi*: **to ~ (on)**
diventare noioso(a) (a).
pallet ['pælɪt] *n* (*for goods*) paletta.
pallid ['pælɪd] *adj* pallido(a), smorto(a).
pallor ['pælə*] *n* pallore *m*.
pally ['pælɪ] *adj* (*col*) amichevole.
palm [pɑːm] *n* (*ANAT*) palma, palmo; (*also:
~ tree*) palma ♦ *vt*: **to ~ sth off on sb** (*col*)
rifilare qc a qn.
palmist ['pɑːmɪst] *n* chiromante *m/f*.
Palm Sunday *n* Domenica delle Palme.
palpable ['pælpəbl] *adj* palpabile.
palpitation [pælpɪ'teɪʃən] *n* palpitazione *f*;
to have ~s avere le palpitazioni.
paltry ['pɔːltrɪ] *adj* derisorio(a);
insignificante.
pamper ['pæmpə*] *vt* viziare, accarezzare.
pamphlet ['pæmflət] *n* dépliant *m inv*
(*political etc*) volantino, manifestino.
pan [pæn] *n* (*also:* **sauce~**) casseruola;
(*also: frying ~*) padella ♦ *vi* (*CINE*) fare una
panoramica; **to ~ for gold** (lavare le
sabbie aurifere per) cercare l'oro.
panacea [pænə'sɪə] *n* panacea.
panache [pə'næʃ] *n* stile *m*.
Panama ['pænəmɑː] *n* Panama *m*.
Panama Canal *n* canale *m* di Panama.
Panamanian [pænə'meɪnɪən] *adj, n*
panamense (*m/f*).
pancake ['pænkeɪk] *n* frittella.
Pancake Day *n* (*BRIT*) martedì *m* grasso.
pancake roll *n* crêpe ripiena di verdure
alla cinese.
pancreas ['pæŋkrɪəs] *n* pancreas *m inv*.
panda ['pændə] *n* panda *m inv*.

panda car *n* (*BRIT*) auto *f* della polizia.
pandemonium [pændɪ'məʊnɪəm] *n* pandemonio.
pander ['pændə*] *vi*: **to** ~ **to** lusingare; concedere tutto a.
p & h *abbr* (*US*: = *postage and handling*) affrancatura e trasporto.
P & L *abbr* (= *profit and loss*) P.P.
p & p *abbr* (*BRIT*: = *postage and packing*) affrancatura ed imballaggio.
pane [peɪn] *n* vetro.
panel ['pænl] *n* (*of wood, cloth etc*) pannello; (*RADIO, TV*) giuria.
panel game *n* (*BRIT*) quiz *m inv* a squadre.
panelling, (*US*) **paneling** ['pænəlɪŋ] *n* rivestimento a pannelli.
panellist, (*US*) **panelist** ['pænəlɪst] *n* partecipante *m/f* (al quiz, alla tavola rotonda *etc*).
pang [pæŋ] *n*: **to feel** ~**s of remorse** essere torturato(a) dal rimorso; ~**s of hunger** spasimi *mpl* della fame; ~**s of conscience** morsi *mpl* di coscienza.
panhandler ['pænhændlə*] *n* (*US col*) accattone/a.
panic ['pænɪk] *n* panico ♦ *vi* perdere il sangue freddo.
panic buying [-baɪɪŋ] *n* accaparramento.
panicky ['pænɪkɪ] *adj* (*person*) pauroso(a).
panic-stricken ['pænɪkstrɪkən] *adj* (*person*) in preda al panico; (*look*) terrorizzato(a).
pannier ['pænɪə*] *n* (*on bicycle*) borsa.
panorama [pænə'rɑːmə] *n* panorama *m*.
panoramic [pænə'ræmɪk] *adj* panoramico(a).
pansy ['pænzɪ] *n* (*BOT*) viola del pensiero.
pant [pænt] *vi* ansare.
panther ['pænθə*] *n* pantera.
panties ['pæntɪz] *npl* slip *m*, mutandine *fpl*.
pantihose ['pæntɪhəʊz] *n* (*US*) collant *m inv*.
panto ['pæntəʊ] *n* (*BRIT col*) *see* **pantomime**.
pantomime ['pæntəmaɪm] *n* (*at Christmas*) spettacolo natalizio; (*tecnica*) pantomima; *see boxed note*.

PANTOMIME

*In Gran Bretagna la **pantomime** (abbreviata in **panto**) è una sorta di libera interpretazione delle favole più conosciute che vengono messe in scena nei teatri durante il periodo natalizio. Gli attori principali sono la dama, "dame", che è un uomo vestito da donna, il protagonista, "principal boy", che è una donna travestita da uomo, e il cattivo, "villain". È uno spettacolo per tutta la famiglia, che prevede la partecipazione del pubblico.*

---

pantry ['pæntrɪ] *n* dispensa.
pants [pænts] *npl* (*BRIT*) mutande *fpl*, slip *m*; (*US*: *trousers*) pantaloni *mpl*.
pantsuit ['pæntsuːt] *n* (*US*) completo *m or* tailleur *m inv* pantalone *inv*.
papacy ['peɪpəsɪ] *n* papato.
papal ['peɪpəl] *adj* papale, pontificio(a).
paparazzi [pæpə'rætsiː] *npl* paparazzi *mpl*.
paper ['peɪpə*] *n* carta; (*also*: **wall**~) carta da parati, tappezzeria; (*also*: **news**~) giornale *m*; (*study, article*) saggio; (*exam*) prova scritta ♦ *adj* di carta ♦ *vt* tappezzare; **a piece of** ~ (*odd bit*) un pezzo di carta; (*sheet*) un foglio (di carta); **to put sth down on** ~ mettere qc per iscritto; *see also* **papers**.
paper advance *n* (*on printer*) avanzamento della carta.
paperback ['peɪpəbæk] *n* tascabile *m*; edizione *f* economica ♦ *adj*: ~ **edition** edizione *f* tascabile.
paper bag *n* sacchetto di carta.
paperboy ['peɪpəbɔɪ] *n* (*selling*) strillone *m*; (*delivering*) ragazzo che recapita i giornali.
paper clip *n* graffetta, clip *f inv*.
paper handkerchief *n* fazzolettino di carta.
paper mill *n* cartiera.
paper money *n* cartamoneta, moneta cartacea.
paper profit *n* utile *m* teorico.
papers ['peɪpəz] *npl* (*also*: **identity** ~) carte *fpl*, documenti *mpl*.
paper shop *n* (*BRIT*) giornalaio (*negozio*).
paperweight ['peɪpəweɪt] *n* fermacarte *m inv*.
paperwork ['peɪpəwəːk] *n* lavoro amministrativo.
papier-mâché ['pæpɪeɪ'mæʃeɪ] *n* cartapesta.
paprika ['pæprɪkə] *n* paprica.
Pap test, Pap smear ['pæp-] *n* (*MED*) pap-test *m inv*.
par [pɑː*] *n* parità, pari *f*; (*GOLF*) norma; **on a** ~ **with** alla pari con; **at/above/ below** ~ (*COMM*) alla/sopra la/sotto la pari; **above/below** ~ (*gen, GOLF*) al di sopra/al di sotto della norma; **to feel below** *or* **under** *or* **not up to** ~ non sentirsi in forma.
parable ['pærəbl] *n* parabola (*REL*).
parabola [pə'ræbələ] *n* parabola (*MATH*).
parachute ['pærəʃuːt] *n* paracadute *m inv* ♦ *vi* scendere col paracadute.
parachute jump *n* lancio col paracadute.

parachutist ['pærəʃuːtɪst] *n* paracadutista *m/f*.

parade [pə'reɪd] *n* parata; (*inspection*) rivista, rassegna ♦ *vt* (*fig*) fare sfoggio di ♦ *vi* sfilare in parata; **a fashion ~** (*BRIT*) una sfilata di moda.

parade ground *n* piazza d'armi.

paradise ['pærədaɪs] *n* paradiso.

paradox ['pærədɔks] *n* paradosso.

paradoxical [pærə'dɔksɪkl] *adj* paradossale.

paradoxically [pærə'dɔksɪklɪ] *adv* paradossalmente.

paraffin ['pærəfɪn] *n* (*BRIT*): **~ (oil)** paraffina; **liquid ~** olio di paraffina.

paraffin heater *n* (*BRIT*) stufa al cherosene.

paraffin lamp *n* (*BRIT*) lampada al cherosene.

paragon ['pærəgən] *n* modello di perfezione *or* di virtù.

paragraph ['pærəgrɑːf] *n* paragrafo; **to begin a new ~** andare a capo.

Paraguay ['pærəgwaɪ] *n* Paraguay *m*.

Paraguayan [pærə'gwaɪən] *adj, n* paraguaiano(a).

parallel ['pærəlɛl] *adj* (*also COMPUT*) parallelo(a); (*fig*) analogo(a) ♦ *n* (*line*) parallela; (*fig, GEO*) parallelo; **~ (with** *or* **to)** parallelo(a) (a).

paralysis, *pl* **paralyses** [pə'rælɪsɪs, -siːz] *n* paralisi *f inv*.

paralytic [pærə'lɪtɪk] *adj* paralitico(a); (*BRIT col: drunk*) ubriaco(a) fradicio(a).

paralyze ['pærəlaɪz] *vt* paralizzare.

paramedic [pærə'mɛdɪk] *n* paramedico.

parameter [pə'ræmɪtə*] *n* parametro.

paramilitary [pærə'mɪlɪtərɪ] *adj* paramilitare.

paramount ['pærəmaunt] *adj*: **of ~ importance** di capitale importanza.

paranoia [pærə'nɔɪə] *n* paranoia.

paranoid ['pærənɔɪd] *adj* paranoico(a).

paranormal [pærə'nɔːml] *adj* paranormale.

paraphernalia [pærəfə'neɪlɪə] *n* attrezzi *mpl*, roba.

paraphrase ['pærəfreɪz] *vt* parafrasare.

paraplegic [pærə'pliːdʒɪk] *n* paraplegico(a).

parapsychology [pærəsaɪ'kɔlədʒɪ] *n* parapsicologia.

parasite ['pærəsaɪt] *n* parassita *m*.

parasol ['pærəsɔl] *n* parasole *m inv*.

paratrooper ['pærətruːpə*] *n* paracadutista *m* (*soldato*).

parcel ['pɑːsl] *n* pacco, pacchetto ♦ *vt* (*also: ~ up*) impaccare.

▶**parcel out** *vt* spartire.

parcel bomb *n* (*BRIT*) pacchetto esplosivo.

parcel post *n* servizio pacchi.

parch [pɑːtʃ] *vt* riardere.

parched ['pɑːtʃt] *adj* (*person*) assetato(a).

parchment ['pɑːtʃmənt] *n* pergamena.

pardon ['pɑːdn] *n* perdono; grazia ♦ *vt* perdonare; (*LAW*) graziare; **~! scusi!; ~ me!** mi scusi!; **I beg your ~!** scusi!; **(I beg your) ~?, (***US***) ~ me?** prego?

pare [pɛə*] *vt* (*BRIT: nails*) tagliarsi; (*: fruit etc*) sbucciare, pelare.

parent ['pɛərənt] *n* padre *m* (*or* madre *f*); **~s** *npl* genitori *mpl*.

parentage ['pɛərəntɪdʒ] *n* natali *mpl*; **of unknown ~** di genitori sconosciuti.

parental [pə'rɛntl] *adj* dei genitori.

parent company *n* società madre *f inv*.

parenthesis, *pl* **parentheses** [pə'rɛnθɪsɪs, -siːz] *n* parentesi *f inv*; **in parentheses** fra parentesi.

parenthood ['pɛərənthud] *n* paternità *or* maternità.

parenting ['pɛərəntɪŋ] *n* mestiere *m* di genitore.

Paris ['pærɪs] *n* Parigi *f*.

parish ['pærɪʃ] *n* parrocchia; (*civil*) ≈ municipio ♦ *adj* parrocchiale.

parish council *n* (*BRIT*) ≈ consiglio comunale.

parishioner [pə'rɪʃənə*] *n* parrocchiano/a.

Parisian [pə'rɪzɪən] *adj, n* parigino(a).

parity ['pærɪtɪ] *n* parità.

park [pɑːk] *n* parco; (*public*) giardino pubblico ♦ *vt, vi* parcheggiare.

parka ['pɑːkə] *n* eskimo.

parking ['pɑːkɪŋ] *n* parcheggio; **"no ~"** "sosta vietata".

parking lights *npl* luci *fpl* di posizione.

parking lot *n* (*US*) posteggio, parcheggio.

parking meter *n* parchimetro.

parking offence *n* (*BRIT*) infrazione *f* al divieto di sosta.

parking place *n* posto di parcheggio.

parking ticket *n* multa per sosta vietata.

parking violation *n* (*US*) = **parking offence**.

Parkinson's ['pɑːkɪnsənz] *n* (*also: ~ disease*) morbo di Parkinson.

parkway ['pɑːkweɪ] *n* viale *m*.

parlance ['pɑːləns] *n*: **in common/modern ~** nel gergo *or* linguaggio comune/moderno.

parliament ['pɑːləmənt] *n* parlamento; *see boxed note*.

PARLIAMENT

Nel Regno Unito il Parlamento, the
Parliament, _è formato da due camere: la_
"House of Commons", e la "House of Lords".
Nella "House of Commons" siedono 650
parlamentari, chiamati "MP", eletti per
votazione diretta del popolo nelle rispettive
circoscrizioni elettorali, le "constituency". Le
sessioni del Parlamento sono presiedute e
moderate dal presidente della Camera, lo
"Speaker". Alla "House of Lords", i cui poteri
sono più limitati, si accede tramite nomina o
carica ereditaria e non per elezione.

---

parliamentary [pɑːlə'mɛntərɪ] _adj_
parlamentare.
parlour, (_US_) **parlor** ['pɑːlə*] _n_ salotto.
parlous ['pɑːləs] _adj_ periglioso(a).
Parmesan [pɑːmɪ'zæn] _n_ parmigiano.
parochial [pə'rəʊkɪəl] _adj_ parrocchiale;
(_pej_) provinciale.
parody ['pærədɪ] _n_ parodia.
parole [pə'rəʊl] _n_: **on** ~ in libertà per buona
condotta.
paroxysm ['pærəksɪzəm] _n_ (_MED_)
parossismo; (_of anger, laughter, coughing_)
convulso; (_of grief_) attacco.
parquet ['pɑːkeɪ] _n_: ~ **floor(ing)** parquet _m_.
parrot ['pærət] _n_ pappagallo.
parrot fashion _adv_ in modo pappagallesco.
parsimonious [pɑːsɪ'məʊnɪəs] _adj_
parsimonioso(a).
parsley ['pɑːslɪ] _n_ prezzemolo.
parsnip ['pɑːsnɪp] _n_ pastinaca.
parson ['pɑːsn] _n_ prete _m_; (_Church of_
England) parroco.
part [pɑːt] _n_ parte _f_; (_of machine_) pezzo;
(_THEAT etc_) parte, ruolo; (_MUS_) voce _f_;
parte ♦ _adj_ in parte ♦ _adv_ = **partly** ♦ _vt_
separare ♦ _vi_ (_people_) separarsi; (_roads_)
dividersi; **to take** ~ **in** prendere parte a;
to take sb's ~ parteggiare per qn; **on his**
~ da parte sua; **for my** ~ per parte mia;
for the most ~ in generale; nella maggior
parte dei casi; **for the better** ~ **of the day**
per la maggior parte della giornata; **to**
be ~ **and parcel of** essere parte
integrante di; **to take sth in good/bad** ~
prendere bene/male qc; ~ **of speech**
(_LING_) parte del discorso.
▶**part with** _vt fus_ separarsi da; rinunciare a.
partake [pɑː'teɪk] _vi irreg_ (_formal_): **to** ~ **of**
sth consumare qc, prendere qc.
part exchange _n_ (_BRIT_): **in** ~ in pagamento
parziale.
partial ['pɑːʃl] _adj_ parziale; **to be** ~ **to**

avere un debole per.
partially ['pɑːʃəlɪ] _adv_ in parte.
participant [pɑː'tɪsɪpənt] _n_: ~ (**in**)
partecipante _m/f_ (a).
participate [pɑː'tɪsɪpeɪt] _vi_: **to** ~ (**in**)
prendere parte (a), partecipare (a).
participation [pɑːtɪsɪ'peɪʃən] _n_
partecipazione _f_.
participle ['pɑːtɪsɪpl] _n_ participio.
particle ['pɑːtɪkl] _n_ particella.
particular [pə'tɪkjʊlə*] _adj_ particolare;
speciale; (_fussy_) difficile; meticoloso(a);
~**s** _npl_ particolari _mpl_, dettagli _mpl_;
(_information_) informazioni _fpl_; **in** ~ in
particolare, particolarmente; **to be very**
~ **about** essere molto pignolo(a) su; **I'm**
not ~ per me va bene tutto.
particularly [pə'tɪkjʊləlɪ] _adv_
particolarmente; in particolare.
parting ['pɑːtɪŋ] _n_ separazione _f_; (_BRIT_: _in_
hair) scriminatura ♦ _adj_ d'addio; ~ **shot**
(_fig_) battuta finale.
partisan [pɑːtɪ'zæn] _n_ partigiano/a ♦ _adj_
partigiano(a); di parte.
partition [pɑː'tɪʃən] _n_ (_POL_) partizione _f_;
(_wall_) tramezzo.
partly ['pɑːtlɪ] _adv_ parzialmente; in parte.
partner ['pɑːtnə*] _n_ (_COMM_) socio/a; (_SPORT_)
compagno/a; (_at dance_) cavaliere/dama.
partnership ['pɑːtnəʃɪp] _n_ associazione _f_;
(_COMM_) società _f inv_; **to go into** ~ (**with**)
mettersi in società (con), associarsi (a).
part payment _n_ acconto.
partridge ['pɑːtrɪdʒ] _n_ pernice _f_.
part-time ['pɑːt'taɪm] _adj_, _adv_ a orario
ridotto, part-time (_inv_).
part-timer ['pɑːt'taɪmə*] _n_ (_also_: **part-time**
worker) lavoratore/trice part-time.
party ['pɑːtɪ] _n_ (_POL_) partito; (_team_)
squadra; gruppo; (_LAW_) parte _f_;
(_celebration_) ricevimento; serata; festa;
dinner ~ cena; **to give** _or_ **throw a** ~ dare
una festa _or_ un party; **to be a** ~ **to a**
crime essere coinvolto in un reato.
party line _n_ (_POL_) linea del partito; (_TEL_)
duplex _m inv_.
party piece _n_: **to do one's** ~ (_BRIT col_)
esibirsi nel proprio pezzo forte a una
festa, cena etc.
party political broadcast _n_ comunicato
radiotelevisivo di propaganda.
pass [pɑːs] _vt_ (_gen_) passare; (_place_) passare
davanti a; (_exam_) promuovere; (_overtake,_
surpass) sorpassare, superare; (_approve_)
approvare ♦ _vi_ passare; (_SCOL_) essere
promosso(a) ♦ _n_ (_permit_) lasciapassare _m_
inv; permesso; (_in mountains_) passo, gola;

(*SPORT*) passaggio; (*SCOL*: *also*: ~ **mark**):
to get a ~ prendere la sufficienza; **to** ~
for passare per; **could you** ~ **the**
vegetables round? potrebbe far passare i
contorni?; **to make a** ~ **at sb** (*col*) fare
delle proposte *or* delle avances a qn;
things have come to a pretty ~ (*BRIT*)
ecco a cosa siamo arrivati.
▶**pass away** *vi* morire.
▶**pass by** *vi* passare ♦ *vt* trascurare.
▶**pass down** *vt* (*customs, inheritance*)
tramandare, trasmettere.
▶**pass on** *vi* (*die*) spegnersi, mancare ♦ *vt*
(*hand on*): **to** ~ **on (to)** (*news, information,
object*) passare (a); (*cold, illness*)
attaccare (a); (*benefits*) trasmettere (a);
(*price rises*) riversare (su).
▶**pass out** *vi* svenire; (*BRIT MIL*) uscire
dall'accademia.
▶**pass over** *vi* (*die*) spirare ♦ *vt* lasciare da
parte.
▶**pass up** *vt* (*opportunity*) lasciarsi
sfuggire, perdere.
passable ['pɑːsəbl] *adj* (*road*) praticabile;
(*work*) accettabile.
passage ['pæsɪdʒ] *n* (*gen*) passaggio; (*also*:
~**way**) corridoio; (*in book*) brano, passo;
(*by boat*) traversata.
passenger ['pæsɪndʒə*] *n* passeggero/a.
passer-by [pɑːsə'baɪ] *n* passante *m/f*.
passing ['pɑːsɪŋ] *adj* (*fig*) fuggevole; **to
mention sth in** ~ accennare a qc di
sfuggita.
passing place *n* (*AUT*) piazzola (di sosta).
passion ['pæʃən] *n* passione *f*; amore *m*; **to
have a** ~ **for sth** aver la passione di *or*
per qc.
passionate ['pæʃənɪt] *adj* appassionato(a).
passion fruit *n* frutto della passione.
passive ['pæsɪv] *adj* (*also LING*) passivo(a).
passive smoking *n* fumo passivo.
passkey ['pɑːskiː] *n* passe-partout *m inv*.
Passover ['pɑːsəuvə*] *n* Pasqua ebraica.
passport ['pɑːspɔːt] *n* passaporto.
passport control *n* controllo *m* passaporti
inv.
passport office *n* ufficio *m* passaporti
inv.
password ['pɑːswəːd] *n* parola d'ordine.
past [pɑːst] *prep* (*further than*) oltre, di là di;
dopo; (*later than*) dopo ♦ *adv*: **to run** ~
passare di corsa; **to walk** ~ passare ♦ *adj*
passato(a); (*president etc*) ex *inv* ♦ *n*
passato; **quarter/half** ~ **four** le quattro e
un quarto/e mezzo; **ten/twenty** ~ **four** le
quattro e dieci/venti; **he's** ~ **forty** ha più
di quarant'anni; **it's** ~ **midnight** è
mezzanotte passata; **for the** ~ **few days**

da qualche giorno; **in questi ultimi
giorni**; **for the** ~ **3 days** negli ultimi 3
giorni; **in the** ~ in *or* nel passato; (*LING*) al
passato; **I'm** ~ **caring** non me ne importa
più nulla; **to be** ~ **it** (*BRIT col*: *person*)
essere finito(a).
pasta ['pæstə] *n* pasta.
paste [peɪst] *n* (*glue*) colla; (*CULIN*) pâté *m
inv*; pasta ♦ *vt* collare; **tomato** ~
concentrato di pomodoro.
pastel ['pæstl] *adj* pastello *inv*.
pasteurized ['pæstəraɪzd] *adj*
pastorizzato(a).
pastille ['pæstl] *n* pastiglia.
pastime ['pɑːstaɪm] *n* passatempo.
past master *n* (*BRIT*): **to be a** ~ **at** essere
molto esperto(a) in.
pastor ['pɑːstə*] *n* pastore *m*.
pastoral ['pɑːstərl] *adj* pastorale.
pastry ['peɪstrɪ] *n* pasta.
pasture ['pɑːstʃə*] *n* pascolo.
pasty *n* ['pæstɪ] pasticcio di carne ♦ *adj*
['peɪstɪ] pastoso(a), (*complexion*)
pallido(a).
pat [pæt] *vt* accarezzare, dare un colpetto
(affettuoso) a ♦ *n*: **a** ~ **of butter** un
panetto di burro; **to give sb/o.s. a** ~ **on
the back** (*fig*) congratularsi *or*
compiacersi di qn/se stesso; **he knows
it (off)** ~, (*US*) **he has it down** ~ lo
conosce *or* sa a menadito.
patch [pætʃ] *n* (*of material*) toppa; (*spot*)
macchia; (*of land*) pezzo ♦ *vt* (*clothes*)
rattoppare; **a bad** ~ (*BRIT*) un brutto
periodo.
▶**patch up** *vt* rappezzare.
patchwork ['pætʃwəːk] *n* patchwork *m*.
patchy ['pætʃɪ] *adj* irregolare.
pate [peɪt] *n*: **a bald** ~ una testa pelata.
pâté ['pæteɪ] *n* pâté *m inv*.
patent ['peɪtnt] *n* brevetto ♦ *vt* brevettare
♦ *adj* patente, manifesto(a).
patent leather *n* cuoio verniciato.
patently ['peɪtntlɪ] *adv* palesemente.
patent medicine *n* specialità *f inv*
medicinale.
patent office *n* ufficio brevetti.
paternal [pə'təːnl] *adj* paterno(a).
paternity [pə'təːnɪtɪ] *n* paternità.
paternity suit *n* (*LAW*) causa di
riconoscimento della paternità.
path [pɑːθ] *n* sentiero, viottolo; viale *m*;
(*fig*) via, strada; (*of planet, missile*)
traiettoria.
pathetic [pə'θetɪk] *adj* (*pitiful*) patetico(a);
(*very bad*) penoso(a).
pathological [pæθə'lɔdʒɪkl] *adj*
patologico(a).

pathologist [pə'θɔlədʒɪst] n patologo/a.
pathology [pə'θɔlədʒɪ] n patologia.
pathos ['peɪθɔs] n pathos m.
pathway ['pɑːθweɪ] n sentiero, viottolo.
patience ['peɪʃns] n pazienza; (*BRIT CARDS*) solitario; **to lose one's** ~ spazientirsi.
patient ['peɪʃnt] n paziente *m/f*; malato/a
♦ *adj* paziente; **to be** ~ **with sb** essere paziente *or* aver pazienza con qn.
patiently ['peɪʃntlɪ] *adv* pazientemente.
patio ['pætɪəu] n terrazza.
patriot ['peɪtrɪət] n patriota *m/f*.
patriotic [pætrɪ'ɔtɪk] *adj* patriottico(a).
patriotism ['pætrɪətɪzəm] n patriottismo.
patrol [pə'trəul] n pattuglia ♦ *vt* pattugliare; **to be on** ~ fare la ronda; essere in ricognizione; essere in perlustrazione.
patrol boat n guardacoste *m inv.*
patrol car n autoradio *f inv* (della polizia).
patrolman [pə'trəulmən] n (*US*) poliziotto.
patron ['peɪtrən] n (*in shop*) cliente *m/f*; (*of charity*) benefattore/trice; ~ **of the arts** mecenate *m/f*.
patronage ['pætrənɪdʒ] n patronato.
patronize ['pætrənaɪz] *vt* essere cliente abituale di; (*fig*) trattare con condiscendenza.
patronizing ['pætrənaɪzɪŋ] *adj* condiscendente.
patron saint n patrono.
patter ['pætə*] n picchiettio; (*sales talk*) propaganda di vendita ♦ *vi* picchiettare.
pattern ['pætən] n modello; (*SEWING etc*) modello (di carta), cartamodello; (*design*) disegno, motivo; (*sample*) campione *m*; **behaviour** ~**s** tipi *mpl* di comportamento.
patterned ['pætənd] *adj* a disegni, a motivi; (*material*) fantasia *inv.*
paucity ['pɔːsɪtɪ] n scarsità.
paunch [pɔːntʃ] n pancione *m.*
pauper ['pɔːpə*] n indigente *m/f*; ~**'s grave** fossa comune.
pause [pɔːz] n pausa ♦ *vi* fare una pausa, arrestarsi; **to** ~ **for breath** fermarsi un attimo per riprender fiato.
pave [peɪv] *vt* pavimentare; **to** ~ **the way for** aprire la via a.
pavement ['peɪvmənt] n (*BRIT*) marciapiede *m*; (*US*) pavimentazione *f* stradale.
pavilion [pə'vɪlɪən] n padiglione *m*; tendone *m*; (*SPORT*) *edificio annesso ad un campo sportivo.*
paving ['peɪvɪŋ] n pavimentazione *f.*
paving stone n lastra di pietra.
paw [pɔː] n zampa ♦ *vt* dare una zampata a; (*subj: person: pej*) palpare.
pawn [pɔːn] n pegno; (*CHESS*) pedone *m*; (*fig*) pedina ♦ *vt* dare in pegno.

pawnbroker ['pɔːnbrəukə*] n prestatore *m* su pegno.
pawnshop ['pɔːnʃɔp] n monte *m* di pietà.
pay [peɪ] n (*gen*) paga ♦ *vb* (*pt, pp* **paid** [peɪd]) *vt* pagare; (*be profitable to: also fig*) convenire a ♦ *vi* pagare; (*be profitable*) rendere; **to** ~ **attention** (**to**) fare attenzione (a); **I paid £5 for that record** quel disco l'ho pagato 5 sterline; **how much did you** ~ **for it?** quanto l'ha pagato?; **to** ~ **one's way** pagare la propria parte; (*company*) coprire le spese; **to** ~ **dividends** (*fig*) dare buoni frutti.
▶**pay back** *vt* rimborsare.
▶**pay for** *vt fus* pagare.
▶**pay in** *vt* versare.
▶**pay off** *vt* (*debts*) saldare; (*creditor*) pagare; (*mortgage*) estinguere; (*workers*) licenziare ♦ *vi* (*scheme*) funzionare; (*patience*) dare dei frutti; **to** ~ **sth off in instalments** pagare qc a rate.
▶**pay out** *vt* (*money*) sborsare, tirar fuori; (*rope*) far allentare.
▶**pay up** *vt* saldare.
payable ['peɪəbl] *adj* pagabile; **to make a cheque** ~ **to sb** intestare un assegno a (nome di) qn.
pay award n aumento salariale.
pay day n giorno di paga.
PAYE n abbr (*BRIT*: = *pay as you earn*) *pagamento di imposte tramite ritenute alla fonte.*
payee [peɪ'iː] n beneficiario/a.
pay envelope n (*US*) busta *f* paga *inv.*
paying ['peɪɪŋ] *adj*: ~ **guest** ospite *m/f* pagante, pensionante *m/f.*
payload ['peɪləud] n carico utile.
payment ['peɪmənt] n pagamento; **advance** ~ (*part sum*) anticipo, acconto; (*total sum*) pagamento anticipato; **deferred** ~, ~ **by instalments** pagamento dilazionato *or* a rate; **in** ~ **for, in** ~ **of** in pagamento di; **on** ~ **of £5** dietro pagamento di 5 sterline.
pay packet n (*BRIT*) busta *f* paga *inv.*
payphone ['peɪfəun] n cabina telefonica.
payroll ['peɪrəul] n ruolo (organico); **to be on a firm's** ~ far parte del personale di una ditta.
pay slip n (*BRIT*) foglio *m* paga *inv.*
pay station n (*US*) cabina telefonica.
PBS n abbr (*US*: = *Public Broadcasting Service*) *servizio che collabora alla realizzazione di programmi per la rete televisiva nazionale.*
PBX abbr (= *private branch exchange*) *sistema telefonico con centralino.*
PC n abbr see **personal computer**; (*BRIT*) see

police constable ♦ abbr (BRIT) = **Privy Councillor** ♦ adj abbr = **politically correct.**
pc abbr = **per cent**; (= postcard) C.P.
p/c abbr = **petty cash.**
PCB n abbr see **printed circuit board.**
pcm abbr = per calendar month.
PD n abbr (US) = **police department.**
pd abbr = **paid.**
PDQ abbr (col) = pretty damn quick.
PDSA n abbr (BRIT: = People's Dispensary for Sick Animals) assistenza veterinaria gratuita.
PDT abbr (US: = Pacific Daylight Time) ora legale del Pacifico.
PE n abbr (= physical education) ed. fisica
♦ abbr (Canada) = Prince Edward Island.
pea [pi:] n pisello.
peace [pi:s] n pace f; (calm) calma, tranquillità; **to be at** ~ **with sb/sth** essere in pace con qn/qc; **to keep the** ~ (subj: policeman) mantenere l'ordine pubblico; (: citizen) rispettare l'ordine pubblico.
peaceable ['pi:səbl] adj pacifico(a).
peaceful ['pi:sful] adj pacifico(a), calmo(a).
peacekeeping ['pi:ski:pɪŋ] n mantenimento della pace; ~ **force** forza di pace.
peace offering n (fig) dono in segno di riconciliazione.
peach [pi:tʃ] n pesca.
peacock ['pi:kɔk] n pavone m.
peak [pi:k] n (of mountain) cima, vetta; (mountain itself) picco; (fig) massimo; (: of career) acme f.
peak-hour ['pi:kauə*] adj (traffic etc) delle ore di punta.
peak hours npl ore fpl di punta.
peak period n periodo di punta.
peak rate n tariffa massima.
peaky ['pi:kɪ] adj (BRIT col) sbattuto(a).
peal [pi:l] n (of bells) scampanio, carillon m inv; ~**s of laughter** scoppi mpl di risa.
peanut ['pi:nʌt] n arachide f, nocciolina americana.
peanut butter n burro di arachidi.
pear [pɛə*] n pera.
pearl [pə:l] n perla.
peasant ['pɛznt] n contadino/a.
peat [pi:t] n torba.
pebble ['pɛbl] n ciottolo.
peck [pɛk] vt (also: ~ **at**) beccare; (: food) mangiucchiare ♦ n colpo di becco; (kiss) bacetto.
pecking order ['pɛkɪŋ-] n (fig) ordine m gerarchico.
peckish ['pɛkɪʃ] adj (BRIT col): **I feel** ~ ho un languorino.
peculiar [pɪ'kju:lɪə*] adj strano(a), bizzarro(a); (particular: importance,

qualities) particolare; ~ **to** tipico(a) di, caratteristico(a) di.
peculiarity [pɪkju:lɪ'ærɪtɪ] n peculiarità f inv; (oddity) bizzarria.
pecuniary [pɪ'kju:nɪərɪ] adj pecuniario(a).
pedal ['pɛdl] n pedale m ♦ vi pedalare.
pedal bin n (BRIT) pattumiera a pedale.
pedantic [pɪ'dæntɪk] adj pedantesco(a).
peddle ['pɛdl] vt (goods) andare in giro a vendere; (drugs) spacciare; (gossip) mettere in giro.
peddler ['pɛdlə*] n venditore m ambulante.
pedestal ['pɛdəstl] n piedestallo.
pedestrian [pɪ'dɛstrɪən] n pedone/a ♦ adj pedonale; (fig) prosaico(a), pedestre.
pedestrian crossing n (BRIT) passaggio pedonale.
pedestrian precinct n (BRIT) zona pedonale.
pediatrics [pi:dɪ'ætrɪks] n (US) = **paediatrics.**
pedigree [ˈpɛdɪɡriː] n stirpe f; (of animal) pedigree m inv ♦ cpd (animal) di razza.
pedlar ['pɛdlə*] n = **peddler.**
pee [pi:] vi (col) pisciare.
peek [pi:k] vi guardare furtivamente.
peel [pi:l] n buccia; (of orange, lemon) scorza ♦ vt sbucciare ♦ vi (paint etc) staccarsi.
▶**peel back** vt togliere, levare.
peeler [pi:lə*] n: **potato** ~ sbucciapatate m inv.
peelings ['pi:lɪŋz] npl bucce fpl.
peep [pi:p] n (BRIT: look) sguardo furtivo, sbirciata; (sound) pigolio ♦ vi (BRIT) guardare furtivamente.
▶**peep out** vi (BRIT) mostrarsi furtivamente.
peephole ['pi:phəul] n spioncino.
peer [pɪə*] vi: **to** ~ **at** scrutare ♦ n (noble) pari m inv; (equal) pari m/f inv, uguale m/f.
peerage ['pɪərɪdʒ] n dignità di pari; pari mpl.
peerless ['pɪəlɪs] adj impareggiabile, senza pari.
peeved [pi:vd] adj stizzito(a).
peevish ['pi:vɪʃ] adj stizzoso(a).
peg [pɛg] n (tent ~) picchetto; (for coat etc) attaccapanni m inv; (BRIT: also: **clothes** ~) molletta ♦ vt (clothes) appendere con le mollette; (BRIT: groundsheet) fissare con i picchetti; (fig: prices, wages) fissare, stabilizzare; **off the** ~ confezionato(a).
pejorative [pɪ'dʒɔrətɪv] adj peggiorativo(a).
Pekin [pi:'kɪn], **Peking** [pi:'kɪŋ] n Pechino f.
pekin(g)ese [pi:kɪ'ni:z] n pechinese m.
pelican ['pɛlɪkən] n pellicano.
pelican crossing n (BRIT AUT)

attraversamento pedonale con semaforo a controllo manuale.
pellet ['pɛlɪt] *n* pallottola, pallina.
pell-mell ['pɛl'mɛl] *adv* disordinatamente.
pelmet ['pɛlmɪt] *n* mantovana; cassonetto.
pelt [pɛlt] *vt*: **to ~ sb (with)** bombardare qn (con) ♦ *vi* (*rain*) piovere a dirotto ♦ *n* pelle *f*.
pelvis ['pɛlvɪs] *n* pelvi *f inv*, bacino.
pen [pɛn] *n* penna; (*for sheep*) recinto; (*US col: prison*) galera; **to put ~ to paper** prendere la penna in mano.
penal ['piːnl] *adj* penale.
penalize ['piːnəlaɪz] *vt* punire; (*SPORT*) penalizzare; (*fig*) svantaggiare.
penal servitude [-'səːvɪtjuːd] *n* lavori *mpl* forzati.
penalty ['pɛnltɪ] *n* penalità *f inv*; sanzione *f* penale; (*fine*) ammenda; (*SPORT*) penalizzazione *f*; (*FOOTBALL: also*: ~ **kick**) calcio di rigore.
penalty area *n* (*BRIT SPORT*) area di rigore.
penalty clause *n* penale *f*.
penalty kick *n* (*FOOTBALL*) calcio di rigore.
penalty shoot-out [-'ʃuːtaut] *n* (*FOOTBALL*) rigori *mpl*.
penance ['pɛnəns] *n* penitenza.
pence [pɛns] *npl* (*BRIT*) *of* **penny**.
penchant ['pãːʃãːŋ] *n* debole *m*.
pencil ['pɛnsl] *n* matita ♦ *vt* (*also*: ~ **in**) scrivere a matita.
pencil case *n* astuccio per matite.
pencil sharpener *n* temperamatite *m inv*.
pendant ['pɛndnt] *n* pendaglio.
pending ['pɛndɪŋ] *prep* in attesa di ♦ *adj* in sospeso.
pendulum ['pɛndjuləm] *n* pendolo.
penetrate ['pɛnɪtreɪt] *vt* penetrare.
penetrating ['pɛnɪtreɪtɪŋ] *adj* penetrante.
penetration [pɛnɪ'treɪʃən] *n* penetrazione *f*.
penfriend ['pɛnfrɛnd] *n* (*BRIT*) corrispondente *m/f*.
penguin ['pɛŋgwɪn] *n* pinguino.
penicillin [pɛnɪ'sɪlɪn] *n* penicillina.
peninsula [pə'nɪnsjulə] *n* penisola.
penis ['piːnɪs] *n* pene *m*.
penitence ['pɛnɪtns] *n* penitenza.
penitent ['pɛnɪtnt] *adj* penitente.
penitentiary [pɛnɪ'tɛnʃərɪ] *n* (*US*) carcere *m*.
penknife ['pɛnnaɪf] *n* temperino.
Penn(a). *abbr* (*US*) = *Pennsylvania.*
pen name *n* pseudonimo.
pennant ['pɛnənt] *n* banderuola.
penniless ['pɛnɪlɪs] *adj* senza un soldo.
Pennines ['pɛnaɪnz] *npl*: **the ~** i Pennini.
penny, *pl* **pennies** *or* **pence** ['pɛnɪ, 'pɛnɪz, pɛns] *n* penny *m* (*pl* pence); (*US*)

centesimo.
penpal ['pɛnpæl] *n* corrispondente *m/f*.
penpusher ['pɛnpuʃə*] *n* (*pej*) scribacchino/a.
pension ['pɛnʃən] *n* pensione *f*.
▶**pension off** *vt* mandare in pensione.
pensionable ['pɛnʃənəbl] *adj* (*person*) che ha diritto a una pensione, pensionabile; (*age*) pensionabile.
pensioner ['pɛnʃənə*] *n* (*BRIT*) pensionato/a.
pension fund *n* fondo pensioni.
pensive ['pɛnsɪv] *adj* pensoso(a).
pentagon ['pɛntəgən] *n* pentagono; **the P~** (*US POL*) il Pentagono; *see boxed note.*

Pentecost ['pɛntɪkɔst] *n* Pentecoste *f*.
penthouse ['pɛnthaus] *n* appartamento (di lusso) nell'attico.
pent-up ['pɛntʌp] *adj* (*feelings*) represso(a).
penultimate [pɪ'nʌltɪmət] *adj* penultimo(a).
penury ['pɛnjurɪ] *n* indigenza.
people ['piːpl] *npl* gente *f*; persone *fpl*; (*citizens*) popolo ♦ *n* (*nation, race*) popolo ♦ *vt* popolare; **old ~** i vecchi; **young ~** i giovani; **~ at large** il grande pubblico; **a man of the ~** un uomo del popolo; **4/ several ~ came** 4/parecchie persone sono venute; **the room was full of ~** la stanza era piena di gente; **~ say that ...** si dice *or* la gente dice che ....
PEP [pɛp] *n* = **personal equity plan**.
pep [pɛp] *n* (*col*) dinamismo.
▶**pep up** *vt* vivacizzare; (*food*) rendere più gustoso(a).
pepper ['pɛpə*] *n* pepe *m*; (*vegetable*) peperone *m* ♦ *vt* pepare.
peppermint ['pɛpəmɪnt] *n* (*plant*) menta peperita; (*sweet*) pasticca di menta.
pepperoni [pɛpə'rəunɪ] *n* salsiccia piccante.
pepperpot ['pɛpəpɔt] *n* pepaiola.
peptalk ['pɛptɔːk] *n* (*col*) discorso di incoraggiamento.
per [pəː*] *prep* per; a; **~ hour** all'ora; **~ kilo** *etc* il chilo *etc*; **~ day** al giorno; **~ week** alla settimana; **~ person** a testa, a *or* per persona; **as ~ your instructions** secondo le vostre istruzioni.

per annum *adv* all'anno.
per capita *adj, adv* pro capite.
perceive [pə'siːv] *vt* percepire; (*notice*) accorgersi di.
per cent *adv* per cento; **a 20 ~ discount** uno sconto del 20 per cento.
percentage [pə'sɛntɪdʒ] *n* percentuale *f;* **on a ~ basis** a percentuale.
percentage point *n* punto percentuale.
perceptible [pə'sɛptɪbl] *adj* percettibile.
perception [pə'sɛpʃən] *n* percezione *f;* sensibilità; perspicacia.
perceptive [pə'sɛptɪv] *adj* percettivo(a); perspicace.
perch [pɔːtʃ] *n* (*fish*) pesce *m* persico; (*for bird*) sostegno, ramo ♦ *vi* appollaiarsi.
percolate ['pɔːkəleɪt] *vt* filtrare.
percolator ['pɔːkəleɪtə*] *n* caffettiera a pressione; caffettiera elettrica.
percussion [pə'kʌʃən] *n* percussione *f;* (*MUS*) strumenti *mpl* a percussione.
peremptory [pə'rɛmptərɪ] *adj* perentorio(a).
perennial [pə'rɛnɪəl] *adj* perenne ♦ *n* pianta perenne.
perfect *adj, n* ['pɔːfɪkt] *adj* perfetto(a) ♦ *n* (*also: ~ tense*) perfetto, passato prossimo ♦ *vt* [pə'fɛkt] perfezionare; mettere a punto; **he's a ~ stranger to me** mi è completamente sconosciuto.
perfection [pə'fɛkʃən] *n* perfezione *f.*
perfectionist [pə'fɛkʃənɪst] *n* perfezionista *m/f.*
perfectly ['pɔːfɪktlɪ] *adv* perfettamente; **I'm ~ happy with the situation** sono completamente soddisfatta della situazione; **you know ~ well** sa benissimo.
perforate ['pɔːfəreɪt] *vt* perforare.
perforated ulcer ['pɔːfəreɪtɪd-] *n* (*MED*) ulcera perforata.
perforation [pɔːfə'reɪʃən] *n* perforazione *f;* (*line of holes*) dentellatura.
perform [pə'fɔːm] *vt* (*carry out*) eseguire, fare; (*symphony etc*) suonare; (*play, ballet*) dare; (*opera*) fare ♦ *vi* suonare; recitare.
performance [pə'fɔːməns] *n* esecuzione *f;* (*at theatre etc*) rappresentazione *f,* spettacolo; (*of an artist*) interpretazione *f;* (*of player etc*) performance *f;* (*of car, engine*) prestazione *f;* **the team put up a good ~** la squadra ha giocato una bella partita.
performer [pə'fɔːmə*] *n* artista *m/f.*
performing [pə'fɔːmɪŋ] *adj* (*animal*) ammaestrato(a).
performing arts *npl:* **the ~** le arti dello spettacolo.

perfume ['pɔːfjuːm] *n* profumo ♦ *vt* profumare.
perfunctory [pə'fʌŋktərɪ] *adj* superficiale, per la forma.
perhaps [pə'hæps] *adv* forse; **~ he'll come** forse verrà, può darsi che venga; **~ so/ not** forse sì/no, può darsi di sì/di no.
peril ['pɛrɪl] *n* pericolo.
perilous ['pɛrɪləs] *adj* pericoloso(a).
perilously ['pɛrɪləslɪ] *adv:* **they came ~ close to being caught** sono stati a un pelo dall'esser presi.
perimeter [pə'rɪmɪtə*] *n* perimetro.
perimeter wall *n* muro di cinta.
period ['pɪərɪəd] *n* periodo; (*HISTORY*) epoca; (*SCOL*) lezione *f;* (*full stop*) punto; (*US FOOTBALL*) tempo; (*MED*) mestruazioni *fpl* ♦ *adj* (*costume, furniture*) d'epoca; **for a ~ of three weeks** per un periodo di *or* per la durata di tre settimane; **the holiday ~** (*BRIT*) il periodo delle vacanze.
periodic [pɪərɪ'ɔdɪk] *adj* periodico(a).
periodical [pɪərɪ'ɔdɪkl] *adj* periodico(a) ♦ *n* periodico.
periodically [pɪərɪ'ɔdɪklɪ] *adv* periodicamente.
period pains *npl* (*BRIT*) dolori *mpl* mestruali.
peripatetic [pɛrɪpə'tɛtɪk] *adj* (*salesman*) ambulante; (*BRIT: teacher*) peripatetico(a).
peripheral [pə'rɪfərəl] *adj* periferico(a) ♦ *n* (*COMPUT*) unità *f inv* periferica.
periphery [pə'rɪfərɪ] *n* periferia.
periscope ['pɛrɪskəup] *n* periscopio.
perish ['pɛrɪʃ] *vi* perire, morire; (*decay*) deteriorarsi.
perishable ['pɛrɪʃəbl] *adj* deperibile.
perishables ['pɛrɪʃəblz] *npl* merci *fpl* deperibili.
perishing ['pɛrɪʃɪŋ] *adj* (*BRIT col*): **it's ~ (cold)** fa un freddo da morire.
peritonitis [pɛrɪtə'naɪtɪs] *n* peritonite *f.*
perjure ['pɔːdʒə*] *vt:* **to ~ o.s.** spergiurare.
perjury ['pɔːdʒərɪ] *n* (*LAW: in court*) falso giuramento; (*breach of oath*) spergiuro.
perk [pɔːk] *n* vantaggio.
▶**perk up** *vi* (*cheer up*) rianimarsi.
perky ['pɔːkɪ] *adj* (*cheerful*) vivace, allegro(a).
perm [pɔːm] *n* (*for hair*) permanente *f* ♦ *vt:* **to have one's hair ~ed** farsi fare la permanente.
permanence ['pɔːmənəns] *n* permanenza.
permanent ['pɔːmənənt] *adj* permanente; (*job, position*) fisso(a); (*dye, ink*) indelebile; **~ address** residenza fissa; **I'm not ~ here** non sono fisso qui.
permanently ['pɔːmənəntlɪ] *adv*

definitivamente.
permeable ['pɜːmɪəbl] *adj* permeabile.
permeate ['pɜːmɪeɪt] *vi* penetrare ♦ *vt*
permeare.
permissible [pə'mɪsɪbl] *adj* permissibile,
ammissibile.
permission [pə'mɪʃən] *n* permesso; **to give**
sb ~ **to do sth** dare a qn il permesso di
fare qc.
permissive [pə'mɪsɪv] *adj* tollerante; **the** ~
society la società permissiva.
permit *n* ['pɜːmɪt] permesso; (*entrance*
pass) lasciapassare *m* ♦ *vt*, *vi* [pə'mɪt]
permettere; **fishing** ~ licenza di pesca; **to**
~ **sb to do** permettere a qn di fare, dare
il permesso a qn di fare; **weather** ~**ting**
tempo permettendo.
permutation [pɜːmjuˈteɪʃən] *n*
permutazione *f*.
pernicious [pə'nɪʃəs] *adj* pernicioso(a),
nocivo(a).
pernickety [pə'nɪkɪtɪ] *adj* (*col: person*)
pignolo(a); (*: task*) da certosino.
perpendicular [pɜːpən'dɪkjulə*] *adj, n*
perpendicolare (*f*).
perpetrate ['pɜːpɪtreɪt] *vt* perpetrare,
commettere.
perpetual [pə'petjuəl] *adj* perpetuo(a).
perpetuate [pə'petjueɪt] *vt* perpetuare.
perpetuity [pɜːpɪ'tjuːɪtɪ] *n*: **in** ~ in
perpetuo.
perplex [pə'pleks] *vt* lasciare perplesso(a).
perplexing [pə'pleksɪŋ] *adj* che lascia
perplesso(a).
perquisites ['pɜːkwɪzɪts] *npl* (*also*: **perks**)
benefici *mpl* collaterali.
persecute ['pɜːsɪkjuːt] *vt* perseguitare.
persecution [pɜːsɪ'kjuːʃən] *n* persecuzione
f.
perseverance [pɜːsɪ'vɪərəns] *n*
perseveranza.
persevere [pɜːsɪ'vɪə*] *vi* perseverare.
Persia ['pɜːʃə] *n* Persia.
Persian ['pɜːʃən] *adj* persiano(a) ♦ *n* (*LING*)
persiano; **the (~) Gulf** il Golfo Persico.
Persian cat *n* gatto persiano.
persist [pə'sɪst] *vi*: **to** ~ (**in doing**)
persistere (nel fare); ostinarsi (a
fare).
persistence [pə'sɪstəns] *n* persistenza;
ostinazione *f*.
persistent [pə'sɪstənt] *adj* persistente;
ostinato(a); (*lateness, rain*) continuo(a); ~
offender (*LAW*) delinquente *m/f* abituale.
persnickety [pə'snɪkɪtɪ] *adj* (*US col*)
= **pernickety**.
person ['pɜːsn] *n* persona; **in** ~ di *or* in
persona, personalmente; **on** *or* **about**

one's ~ (*weapon*) su di sé; (*money*) con
sé; **a** ~ **to** ~ **call** (*TEL*) una chiamata con
preavviso.
personable ['pɜːsnəbl] *adj* di bell'aspetto.
personal ['pɜːsnl] *adj* personale;
individuale; ~ **belongings**, ~ **effects**
oggetti *mpl* d'uso personale; **a** ~ **interview**
un incontro privato.
personal allowance *n* (*TAX*) quota del
reddito non imponibile.
personal assistant (PA) *n* segretaria
personale.
personal call *n* (*TEL*) chiamata con
preavviso.
personal column *n* messaggi *mpl*
personali.
personal computer (PC) *n* personal
computer *m inv*.
personal details *npl* dati *mpl* personali.
personal equity plan *n* (*FINANCE*) *fondo di*
investimento azionario con agevolazioni
fiscali destinato al piccolo risparmiatore.
personal identification number (PIN) *n*
(*COMPUT, BANKING*) numero di codice
segreto.
personality [pɜːsə'nælɪtɪ] *n* personalità *f*
inv.
personally ['pɜːsnəlɪ] *adv* personalmente.
personal organizer *n* agenda; (*electronic*)
agenda elettronica.
personal property *n* beni *mpl* personali.
personal stereo *n* walkman ® *m inv*.
personify [pɜː'sɒnɪfaɪ] *vt* personificare.
personnel [pɜːsə'nel] *n* personale *m*.
personnel department *n* ufficio del
personale.
personnel manager *n* direttore/trice del
personale.
perspective [pə'spektɪv] *n* prospettiva; **to**
get sth into ~ ridimensionare qc.
Perspex ® ['pɜːspeks] *n* (*BRIT*) *tipo di resina*
termoplastica.
perspicacity [pɜːspɪ'kæsɪtɪ] *n* perspicacia.
perspiration [pɜːspɪ'reɪʃən] *n* traspirazione
f, sudore *m*.
perspire [pə'spaɪə*] *vi* traspirare.
persuade [pə'sweɪd] *vt*: **to** ~ **sb to do sth**
persuadere qn a fare qc; **to** ~ **sb of sth/**
that persuadere qn di qc/che.
persuasion [pə'sweɪʒən] *n* persuasione *f*;
(*creed*) convinzione *f*, credo.
persuasive [pə'sweɪsɪv] *adj* persuasivo(a).
pert [pɜːt] *adj* (*bold*) sfacciato(a),
impertinente; (*hat*) spiritoso(a).
pertaining [pɜː'teɪnɪŋ]: ~ **to** *prep* che
riguarda.
pertinent ['pɜːtɪnənt] *adj* pertinente.
perturb [pə'tɜːb] *vt* turbare.

perturbing [pə'tə:bɪŋ] adj inquietante.
Peru [pə'ru:] n Perù m.
perusal [pə'ru:zl] n attenta lettura.
Peruvian [pə'ru:vjən] adj, n peruviano(a).
pervade [pə'veɪd] vt pervadere.
pervasive [pə:'veɪsɪv] adj (smell)
penetrante; (influence) dilagante; (gloom, feelings) diffuso(a).
perverse [pə'və:s] adj perverso(a).
perversion [pə'və:ʃən] n pervertimento, perversione f.
perversity [pə'və:sɪtɪ] n perversità.
pervert n ['pə:və:t] pervertito/a ♦ vt [pə'və:t] pervertire.
pessimism ['pɛsɪmɪzəm] n pessimismo.
pessimist ['pɛsɪmɪst] n pessimista m/f.
pessimistic [pɛsɪ'mɪstɪk] adj
pessimistico(a).
pest [pɛst] n animale m (or insetto)
pestifero; (fig) peste f.
pest control n disinfestazione f.
pester ['pɛstə*] vt tormentare, molestare.
pesticide ['pɛstɪsaɪd] n pesticida m.
pestilence ['pɛstɪləns] n pestilenza.
pestle ['pɛsl] n pestello.
pet [pɛt] n animale m domestico; (favourite)
favorito/a ♦ vt accarezzare ♦ vi (col) fare
il petting; ~ **lion** etc leone m etc
ammaestrato.
petal ['pɛtl] n petalo.
peter ['pi:tə*]: **to ~ out** vi esaurirsi;
estinguersi.
petite [pə'ti:t] adj piccolo(a) e
aggraziato(a).
petition [pə'tɪʃən] n petizione f ♦ vi
richiedere; **to ~ for divorce** presentare
un'istanza di divorzio.
pet name n (BRIT) nomignolo.
petrified ['pɛtrɪfaɪd] adj (fig) morto(a) di
paura.
petrify ['pɛtrɪfaɪ] vt pietrificare; (fig)
terrorizzare.
petrochemical [pɛtrə'kɛmɪkl] adj
petrolchimico(a).
petrodollars ['pɛtrəudɔləz] npl petrodollari
mpl.
petrol ['pɛtrəl] n (BRIT) benzina.
petrol bomb n (BRIT) (bottiglia) molotov
f inv.
petrol can n (BRIT) tanica per benzina.
petrol engine n (BRIT) motore m a benzina.
petroleum [pə'trəuliəm] n petrolio.
petroleum jelly n vaselina.
petrol pump n (BRIT: in car, at garage)
pompa di benzina.
petrol station n (BRIT) stazione f di
rifornimento.
petrol tank n (BRIT) serbatoio della

benzina.
petticoat ['pɛtɪkəut] n sottana.
pettifogging ['pɛtɪfɔgɪŋ] adj cavilloso(a).
pettiness ['pɛtɪnɪs] n meschinità.
petty ['pɛtɪ] adj (mean) meschino(a);
(unimportant) insignificante.
petty cash n piccola cassa.
petty officer n sottufficiale m di marina.
petulant ['pɛtjulənt] adj irritabile.
pew [pju:] n panca (di chiesa).
pewter ['pju:tə*] n peltro.
Pfc abbr (US MIL) = private first class.
PG n abbr (CINE: = parental guidance)
consenso dei genitori richiesto.
PGA n abbr (= Professional Golfers
Association) associazione dei giocatori di
golf professionisti.
PH n abbr (US MIL: = Purple Heart)
decorazione per ferite riportate in
guerra.
PHA n abbr (US: = Public Housing
Administration) amministrazione per
l'edilizia pubblica.
phallic ['fælɪk] adj fallico(a).
phantom ['fæntəm] n fantasma m.
Pharaoh ['fɛərəu] n faraone m.
pharmaceutical [fɑ:mə'sju:tɪkl] adj
farmaceutico(a) ♦ n: ~**s** prodotti mpl
farmaceutici.
pharmacist ['fɑ:məsɪst] n farmacista m/f.
pharmacy ['fɑ:məsɪ] n farmacia.
phase [feɪz] n fase f, periodo ♦ vt: **to ~ sth
in/out** introdurre/eliminare qc
progressivamente.
PhD n abbr = Doctor of Philosophy.
pheasant ['fɛznt] n fagiano.
phenomenon, pl **phenomena**
[fə'nɔmɪnən, -nə] n fenomeno.
phew [fju:] excl uff!
phial ['faɪəl] n fiala.
philanderer [fɪ'lændərə*] n donnaiolo.
philanthropic [fɪlən'θrɔpɪk] adj
filantropico(a).
philanthropist [fɪ'lænθrəpɪst] n filantropo.
philatelist [fɪ'lætəlɪst] n filatelico/a.
philately [fɪ'lætəlɪ] n filatelia.
Philippines ['fɪlɪpi:nz] npl (also: Philippine
Islands): **the ~** le Filippine.
philosopher [fɪ'lɔsəfə*] n filosofo/a.
philosophical [fɪlə'sɔfɪkl] adj filosofico(a).
philosophy [fɪ'lɔsəfɪ] n filosofia.
phlegm [flɛm] n flemma.
phlegmatic [flɛg'mætɪk] adj flemmatico(a).
phobia ['fəubjə] n fobia.
phone [fəun] n telefono ♦ vt telefonare a
♦ vi telefonare; **to be on the ~** avere il
telefono; (be calling) essere al telefono.
▶**phone back** vt, vi richiamare.

phone book *n* guida del telefono, elenco telefonico.
phone box, phone booth *n* cabina telefonica.
phone call *n* telefonata.
phonecard ['fəunkɑːd] *n* scheda telefonica.
phone-in ['fəunɪn] *n* (*BRIT RADIO, TV*) *trasmissione radiofonica o televisiva con intervento telefonico degli ascoltatori.*
phone tapping [-tæpɪŋ] *n* intercettazioni *fpl* telefoniche.
phonetics [fə'nɛtɪks] *n* fonetica.
phoney ['fəunɪ] *adj* falso(a), fasullo(a) ♦ *n* (*person*) ciarlatano.
phonograph ['fəunəgrɑːf] *n* (*US*) giradischi *m inv.*
phony ['fəunɪ] *adj, n* = **phoney**.
phosphate ['fɔsfeɪt] *n* fosfato.
phosphorus ['fɔsfərəs] *n* fosforo.
photo ['fəutəu] *n* foto *f inv.*
photo... ['fəutəu] *prefix* foto....
photocall ['fəutəukɔːl] *n convocazione di fotoreporter a scopo pubblicitario.*
photocopier ['fəutəukɔpɪə*] *n* fotocopiatrice *f.*
photocopy ['fəutəukɔpɪ] *n* fotocopia ♦ *vt* fotocopiare.
photoelectric [fəutəuɪ'lɛktrɪk] *adj:* ~ **cell** cellula fotoelettrica.
Photofit ® ['fəutəufɪt] *n* photofit *m inv.*
photogenic [fəutəu'dʒɛnɪk] *adj* fotogenico(a).
photograph ['fəutəgræf] *n* fotografia ♦ *vt* fotografare; **to take a** ~ **of sb** fare una fotografia a *or* fotografare qn.
photographer [fə'tɔgrəfə*] *n* fotografo.
photographic [fəutə'græfɪk] *adj* fotografico(a).
photography [fə'tɔgrəfɪ] *n* fotografia.
photo opportunity *n opportunità di scattare delle foto ad un personaggio importante.*
Photostat ® ['fəutəustæt] *n* fotocopia.
photosynthesis [fəutəu'sɪnθəsɪs] *n* fotosintesi *f.*
phrase [freɪz] *n* espressione *f*; (*LING*) locuzione *f*; (*MUS*) frase *f* ♦ *vt* esprimere; (*letter*) redigere.
phrasebook ['freɪzbuk] *n* vocabolarietto.
physical ['fɪzɪkl] *adj* fisico(a); ~ **examination** visita medica; ~ **education** educazione *f* fisica; ~ **exercises** ginnastica.
physically [fɪzɪklɪ] *adv* fisicamente.
physician [fɪ'zɪʃən] *n* medico.
physicist ['fɪzɪsɪst] *n* fisico.
physics ['fɪzɪks] *n* fisica.
physiological [fɪzɪə'lɔdʒɪkəl] *adj* fisiologico(a).
physiology [fɪzɪ'ɔlədʒɪ] *n* fisiologia.
physiotherapist [fɪzɪəu'θɛrəpɪst] *n* fisioterapista *m/f.*
physiotherapy [fɪzɪəu'θɛrəpɪ] *n* fisioterapia.
physique [fɪ'ziːk] *n* fisico.
pianist ['piːənɪst] *n* pianista *m/f.*
piano [pɪ'ænəu] *n* pianoforte *m.*
piano accordion *n* (*BRIT*) fisarmonica (a tastiera).
piccolo ['pɪkələu] *n* ottavino.
pick [pɪk] *n* (*tool: also:* ~**-axe**) piccone *m* ♦ *vt* scegliere; (*gather*) cogliere; (*scab, spot*) grattarsi ♦ *vi:* **to** ~ **and choose** scegliere con cura; **take your** ~ scelga; **the** ~ **of** il fior fiore di; **to** ~ **one's nose** mettersi le dita nel naso; **to** ~ **one's teeth** stuzzicarsi i denti; **to** ~ **sb's brains** farsi dare dei suggerimenti da qn; **to** ~ **pockets** borseggiare; **to** ~ **a fight/quarrel with sb** attaccar rissa/briga con qn; **to** ~ **one's way through** attraversare stando ben attento a dove mettere i piedi.
▶**pick off** *vt* (*kill*) abbattere.
▶**pick on** *vt fus* (*person*) avercela con.
▶**pick out** *vt* scegliere; (*distinguish*) distinguere.
▶**pick up** *vi* (*improve*) migliorarsi ♦ *vt* raccogliere; (*collect*) passare a prendere; (*AUT: give lift to*) far salire; (*learn*) imparare; (*RADIO, TV, TEL*) captare; **to** ~ **o.s. up** rialzarsi; **to** ~ **up where one left off** riprendere dal punto in cui ci si era fermati; **to** ~ **up speed** acquistare velocità.
pickaxe, (*US*) **pickax** ['pɪkæks] *n* piccone *m.*
picket ['pɪkɪt] *n* (*in strike*) scioperante *m/f* che fa parte di un picchetto; picchetto ♦ *vt* picchettare.
picket line *n* cordone *m* degli scioperanti.
pickings ['pɪkɪŋz] *npl* (*pilferings*): **there are good** ~ **to be had here** qui ci sono buone possibilità di intascare qualcosa sottobanco.
pickle ['pɪkl] *n* (*also:* ~**s**: *as condiment*) sottaceti *mpl*; (*fig*): **in a** ~ nei pasticci ♦ *vt* mettere sottaceto; mettere in salamoia.
pick-me-up ['pɪkmiːʌp] *n* tiramisù *m inv.*
pickpocket ['pɪkpɔkɪt] *n* borsaiolo.
pickup ['pɪkʌp] *n* (*BRIT: on record player*) pick-up *m inv*; (*small truck: also:* ~ **truck,** ~ **van**) camioncino.
picnic ['pɪknɪk] *n* picnic *m inv* ♦ *vi* fare un picnic.
picnicker ['pɪknɪkə*] *n* chi partecipa a un picnic.

pictorial [pɪk'tɔːrɪəl] *adj* illustrato(a).

picture ['pɪktʃə*] *n* quadro; (*painting*) pittura; (*photograph*) foto(grafia); (*drawing*) disegno; (*TV*) immagine *f*; (*film*) film *m inv* ♦ *vt* raffigurarsi; **the ~s** (*BRIT*) il cinema; **to take a ~ of sb/sth** fare una foto a qn/di qc; **we get a good ~ here** (*TV*) la ricezione qui è buona; **the overall ~** il quadro generale; **to put sb in the ~** mettere qn al corrente.

picture book *n* libro illustrato.

picturesque [pɪktʃə'rɛsk] *adj* pittoresco(a).

picture window *n* finestra panoramica.

piddling ['pɪdlɪŋ] *adj* (*col*) insignificante.

pidgin English ['pɪdʒɪn-] *n inglese semplificato misto ad elementi indigeni.*

pie [paɪ] *n* torta; (*of meat*) pasticcio.

piebald ['paɪbɔːld] *adj* pezzato(a).

piece [piːs] *n* pezzo; (*of land*) appezzamento; (*DRAUGHTS etc*) pedina; (*item*): **a ~ of furniture/advice** un mobile/consiglio ♦ *vt*: **to ~ together** mettere insieme; **in ~s** (*broken*) in pezzi, (*not yet assembled*) smontato(a); **to take to ~s** smontare; **~ by** poco alla volta; **a 10p ~** (*BRIT*) una moneta da 10 pence; **a six-band** un complesso di sei strumentisti; **in one ~** (*object*) intatto; **to get back all in one ~** (*person*) tornare a casa incolume *or* sano e salvo; **to say one's ~** dire la propria.

piecemeal ['piːsmiːl] *adv* pezzo a pezzo, a spizzico.

piece rate *n* tariffa a cottimo.

piecework ['piːswəːk] *n* (lavoro a) cottimo.

pie chart *n* grafico a torta.

Piedmont ['piːdmɔnt] *n* Piemonte *m*.

pier [pɪə*] *n* molo; (*of bridge etc*) pila.

pierce [pɪəs] *vt* forare; (*with arrow etc*) trafiggere; **to have one's ears ~d** farsi fare i buchi per gli orecchini.

piercing ['pɪəsɪŋ] *adj* (*cry*) acuto(a).

piety ['paɪətɪ] *n* pietà, devozione *f*.

piffling ['pɪflɪŋ] *adj* insignificante.

pig [pɪg] *n* maiale *m*, porco.

pigeon ['pɪdʒən] *n* piccione *m*.

pigeonhole ['pɪdʒənhəul] *n* casella ♦ *vt* classificare.

pigeon-toed ['pɪdʒən'təud] *adj* che cammina con i piedi in dentro.

piggy bank ['pɪgɪ-] *n* salvadanaio.

pigheaded ['pɪg'hɛdɪd] *adj* caparbio(a), cocciuto(a).

piglet ['pɪglɪt] *n* porcellino.

pigment ['pɪgmənt] *n* pigmento.

pigmentation [pɪgmən'teɪʃən] *n* pigmentazione *f*.

pigmy ['pɪgmɪ] *n* = **pygmy**.

pigskin ['pɪgskɪn] *n* cinghiale *m*.

pigsty ['pɪgstaɪ] *n* porcile *m*.

pigtail ['pɪgteɪl] *n* treccina.

pike [paɪk] *n* (*spear*) picca; (*fish*) luccio.

pilchard ['pɪltʃəd] *n specie di sardina.*

pile [paɪl] *n* (*pillar, of books*) pila; (*heap*) mucchio; (*of carpet*) pelo ♦ *vb* (*also*: **~ up**) *vt* ammucchiare ♦ *vi* ammucchiarsi; **in a ~** ammucchiato; *see also* **piles**.

▶**pile on** *vt*: **to ~ it on** (*col*) esagerare, drammatizzare.

piles [paɪlz] *npl* (*MED*) emorroidi *fpl*.

pileup ['paɪlʌp] *n* (*AUT*) tamponamento a catena.

pilfer ['pɪlfə*] *vt* rubacchiare ♦ *vi* fare dei furtarelli.

pilfering ['pɪlfərɪŋ] *n* rubacchiare *m*.

pilgrim ['pɪlgrɪm] *n* pellegrino/a.

pilgrimage ['pɪlgrɪmɪdʒ] *n* pellegrinaggio.

pill [pɪl] *n* pillola; **to be on the ~** prendere la pillola.

pillage ['pɪlɪdʒ] *vt* saccheggiare.

pillar ['pɪlə*] *n* colonna.

pillar box *n* (*BRIT*) cassetta delle lettere (a colonnina).

pillion ['pɪljən] *n* (*of motor cycle*) sellino posteriore; **to ride ~** viaggiare dietro.

pillory ['pɪlərɪ] *n* berlina ♦ *vt* mettere alla berlina.

pillow ['pɪləu] *n* guanciale *m*.

pillowcase ['pɪləukeɪs], **pillowslip** ['pɪləuslɪp] *n* federa.

pilot ['paɪlət] *n* pilota *m/f* ♦ *cpd* (*scheme etc*) pilota *inv* ♦ *vt* pilotare.

pilot boat *n* pilotina.

pilot light *n* fiammella di sicurezza.

pimento [pɪ'mɛntəu] *n* peperoncino.

pimp [pɪmp] *n* mezzano.

pimple ['pɪmpl] *n* foruncolo.

pimply ['pɪmplɪ] *adj* foruncoloso(a).

PIN *n abbr see* **personal identification number**.

pin [pɪn] *n* spillo; (*TECH*) perno; (*BRIT: drawing ~*) puntina da disegno; (*BRIT ELEC: of plug*) spinotto ♦ *vt* attaccare con uno spillo; **~s and needles** formicolio; **to ~ sb against/to** inchiodare qn contro/a; **to ~ sth on sb** (*fig*) addossare la colpa di qc a qn.

▶**pin down** *vt* (*fig*): **to ~ sb down** obbligare qn a pronunziarsi; **there's something strange here but I can't quite ~ it down** c'è qualcosa di strano qua ma non riesco a capire cos'è.

pinafore ['pɪnəfɔː*] *n* grembiule *m* (senza maniche).

pinafore dress *n* scamiciato.

pinball ['pɪnbɔːl] *n* flipper *m inv*.

pincers ['pɪnsəz] *npl* pinzette *fpl*.
pinch [pɪntʃ] *n* pizzicotto, pizzico ♦ *vt* pizzicare; (*col: steal*) grattare ♦ *vi* (*shoe*) stringere; **at a ~** in caso di bisogno; **to feel the ~** (*fig*) trovarsi nelle ristrettezze.
pinched [pɪntʃt] *adj* (*drawn*) dai lineamenti tirati; (*short*): **~ for money/space** a corto di soldi/di spazio; **~ with cold** raggrinzito dal freddo.
pincushion ['pɪnkuʃən] *n* puntaspilli *m inv*.
pine [paɪn] *n* (*also*: **~ tree**) pino ♦ *vi*: **to ~ for** struggersi dal desiderio di.
▶**pine away** *vi* languire.
pineapple ['paɪnæpl] *n* ananas *m inv*.
pine cone *n* pigna.
pine needles *npl* aghi *mpl* di pino.
ping [pɪŋ] *n* (*noise*) tintinnio.
Ping-Pong ® ['pɪŋpɔŋ] *n* ping-pong ® *m*.
pink [pɪŋk] *adj* rosa *inv* ♦ *n* (*colour*) rosa *m inv*; (*BOT*) garofano.
pinking shears ['pɪŋkɪŋ-] *n* forbici *fpl* a zigzag.
pin money *n* (*BRIT*) denaro per le piccole spese.
pinnacle ['pɪnəkl] *n* pinnacolo.
pinpoint ['pɪnpɔɪnt] *vt* indicare con precisione.
pinstripe ['pɪnstraɪp] *n* stoffa gessata; (*also*: **~ suit**) gessato.
pint [paɪnt] *n* pinta (*BRIT* = 0.57 *l*; *US* = 0.47 *l*); (*BRIT col: of beer*) ≈ birra piccola.
pinup ['pɪnʌp] *n* pin-up girl *f inv*.
pioneer [paɪə'nɪə*] *n* pioniere/a ♦ *vt* essere un pioniere in.
pious ['paɪəs] *adj* pio(a).
pip [pɪp] *n* (*seed*) seme *m*; (*time signal on radio*) segnale *m* orario.
pipe [paɪp] *n* tubo; (*for smoking*) pipa; (*MUS*) piffero ♦ *vt* portare per mezzo di tubazione; **~s** *npl* (*also*: **bag~s**) cornamusa (scozzese).
▶**pipe down** *vi* (*col*) calmarsi.
pipe cleaner *n* scovolino.
piped music [paɪpt-] *n* musica di sottofondo.
pipe dream *n* vana speranza.
pipeline ['paɪplaɪn] *n* conduttura; (*for oil*) oleodotto; (*for natural gas*) metanodotto; **it is in the ~** (*fig*) è in arrivo.
piper ['paɪpə*] *n* piffero; suonatore/trice di cornamusa.
pipe tobacco *n* tabacco da pipa.
piping ['paɪpɪŋ] *adv*: **~ hot** bollente.
piquant ['pi:kənt] *adj* (*sauce*) piccante; (*conversation*) stimolante.
pique [pi:k] *n* picca.
piracy ['paɪərəsɪ] *n* pirateria.
pirate ['paɪərət] *n* pirata *m* ♦ *vt* (*record,*

video, book) riprodurre abusivamente.
pirate radio *n* (*BRIT*) radio pirata *f inv*.
pirouette [pɪru'ɛt] *n* piroetta ♦ *vi* piroettare.
Pisces ['paɪsi:z] *n* Pesci *mpl*; **to be ~** essere dei Pesci.
piss [pɪs] *vi* (*col!*) pisciare; **~ off!** vaffanculo! (*!*).
pissed [pɪst] *adj* (*BRIT col: drunk*) ubriaco(a) fradicio(a).
pistol ['pɪstl] *n* pistola.
piston ['pɪstən] *n* pistone *m*.
pit [pɪt] *n* buca, fossa; (*also: coal ~*) miniera; (*also: orchestra ~*) orchestra ♦ *vt*: **to ~ sb against sb** opporre qn a qn; **~s** *npl* (*AUT*) box *m*; **to ~ o.s. against** opporsi a.
pitapat ['pɪtə'pæt] *adv* (*BRIT*): **to go ~** (*heart*) palpitare, battere forte; (*rain*) picchiettare.
pitch [pɪtʃ] *n* (*throw*) lancia; (*MUS*) tono; (*of voice*) altezza; (*fig: degree*) grado, punto; (*also: sales ~*) discorso di vendita, imbonimento; (*BRIT SPORT*) campo; (*NAUT*) beccheggio; (*tar*) pece *f* ♦ *vt* (*throw*) lanciare ♦ *vi* (*fall*) cascare; (*NAUT*) beccheggiare; **to ~ a tent** piantare una tenda; **at this ~** a questo ritmo.
pitch-black [pɪtʃ'blæk] *adj* nero(a) come la pece.
pitched battle [pɪtʃt-] *n* battaglia campale.
pitcher ['pɪtʃə*] *n* brocca.
pitchfork ['pɪtʃfɔ:k] *n* forcone *m*.
piteous ['pɪtɪəs] *adj* pietoso(a).
pitfall ['pɪtfɔ:l] *n* trappola.
pith [pɪθ] *n* (*of plant*) midollo; (*of orange*) parte *f* interna della scorza; (*fig*) essenza, succo; vigore *m*.
pithead ['pɪthɛd] *n* (*BRIT*) imbocco della miniera.
pithy ['pɪθɪ] *adj* conciso(a); vigoroso(a).
pitiable ['pɪtɪəbl] *adj* pietoso(a).
pitiful ['pɪtɪful] *adj* (*touching*) pietoso(a); (*contemptible*) miserabile.
pitifully ['pɪtɪfəlɪ] *adv* pietosamente; **it's ~ obvious** è penosamente chiaro.
pitiless ['pɪtɪlɪs] *adj* spietato(a).
pittance ['pɪtns] *n* miseria, magro salario.
pitted ['pɪtɪd] *adj*: **~ with** (*potholes*) pieno(a) di; (*chickenpox*) butterato(a) da.
pity ['pɪtɪ] *n* pietà ♦ *vt* aver pietà di, compatire, commiserare; **to have** *or* **take ~ on sb** aver pietà di qn; **it is a ~ that you can't come** è un peccato che non possa venire; **what a ~!** che peccato!
pitying ['pɪtɪɪŋ] *adj* compassionevole.
pivot ['pɪvət] *n* perno ♦ *vi* impernarsi.
pixel ['pɪksl] *n* (*COMPUT*) pixel *m inv*.

pixie ['pɪksɪ] n folletto.
pizza ['piːtsə] n pizza.
placard ['plækɑːd] n affisso.
placate [plə'keɪt] vt placare, calmare.
placatory [plə'keɪtərɪ] adj conciliante.
place [pleɪs] n posto, luogo; (proper position, rank, seat) posto; (house) casa, alloggio; (home): **at/to his ~** a casa sua; (in street names): **Laurel P~** via dei Lauri ♦ vt (object) posare, mettere; (identify) riconoscere; individuare; (goods) piazzare; **to take ~** aver luogo; succedere; **out of ~** (not suitable) inopportuno(a); **I feel rather out of ~ here** qui mi sento un po' fuori posto; **in the first ~** in primo luogo; **to change ~s with sb** scambiare il posto con qn; **to put sb in his ~** (fig) mettere a posto qn, mettere qn al suo posto; **from ~ to ~** da un posto all'altro; **all over the ~** dappertutto; **he's going ~s** (fig col) si sta facendo strada; **it is not my ~ to do it** non sta a me farlo; **how are you ~d next week?** com'è messo la settimana prossima?; **to ~ an order with sb (for)** (COMM) fare un'ordinazione a qn (di).
placebo [plə'siːbəu] n placebo m inv.
place mat n sottopiatto; (in linen etc) tovaglietta.
placement ['pleɪsmənt] n collocamento; (job) lavoro.
place name n toponimo.
placenta [plə'sɛntə] n placenta.
placid ['plæsɪd] adj placido(a), calmo(a).
placidity [plə'sɪdɪtɪ] n placidità.
plagiarism ['pleɪdʒərɪzəm] n plagio.
plagiarist ['pleɪdʒərɪst] n plagiario/a.
plagiarize ['pleɪdʒəraɪz] vt plagiare.
plague [pleɪg] n peste f ♦ vt tormentare; **to ~ sb with questions** assillare qn di domande.
plaice [pleɪs] n (pl inv) pianuzza.
plaid [plæd] n plaid m inv.
plain [pleɪn] adj (clear) chiaro(a), palese; (simple) semplice; (frank) franco(a), aperto(a); (not handsome) bruttino(a); (without seasoning etc) scondito(a); naturale; (in one colour) tinta unita inv ♦ adv francamente, chiaramente ♦ n pianura; **to make sth ~ to sb** far capire chiaramente qc a qn; **in ~ clothes** (police) in borghese.
plain chocolate n cioccolato fondente.
plainly ['pleɪnlɪ] adv chiaramente; (frankly) francamente.
plainness ['pleɪnnɪs] n semplicità.
plain speaking n: **there has been some ~ between the two leaders** i due leader si

sono parlati chiaro.
plaintiff ['pleɪntɪf] n attore/trice.
plaintive ['pleɪntɪv] adj (voice, song) lamentoso(a); (look) struggente.
plait [plæt] n treccia ♦ vt intrecciare; **to ~ one's hair** farsi una treccia (or le trecce).
plan [plæn] n pianta; (scheme) progetto, piano ♦ vt (think in advance) progettare; (prepare) organizzare; (intend) avere in progetto ♦ vi: **to ~ (for)** far piani or progetti (per); **to ~ to do** progettare di fare, avere l'intenzione di fare; **how long do you ~ to stay?** quanto conta di restare?
plane [pleɪn] n (AVIAT) aereo; (tree) platano; (tool) pialla; (ART, MATH etc) piano ♦ adj piano(a), piatto(a) ♦ vt (with tool) piallare.
planet ['plænɪt] n pianeta m.
planetarium [plænɪ'tɛərɪəm] n planetario.
plank [plæŋk] n tavola, asse f.
plankton ['plæŋktən] n plancton m.
planned economy [plænd-] n economia pianificata.
planner ['plænə*] n pianificatore/trice; (chart) calendario; **town** or (US) **city ~** urbanista m/f.
planning ['plænɪŋ] n progettazione f; (POL, ECON) pianificazione f; **family ~** pianificazione delle nascite.
planning permission n (BRIT) permesso di costruzione.
plant [plɑːnt] n pianta; (machinery) impianto; (factory) fabbrica ♦ vt piantare; (bomb) mettere.
plantation [plæn'teɪʃən] n piantagione f.
plant pot n (BRIT) vaso (di fiori).
plaque [plæk] n placca.
plasma ['plæzmə] n plasma m.
plaster ['plɑːstə*] n intonaco; (also: **~ of Paris**) gesso; (BRIT: also: **sticking ~**) cerotto ♦ vt intonacare; ingessare; (cover): **to ~ with** coprire di; (col: mud etc) impiastricciare; **in ~** (BRIT: leg etc) ingessato(a).
plasterboard ['plɑːstəbɔːd] n lastra di cartone ingessato.
plaster cast n (MED) ingessatura, gesso; (model, statue) modello in gesso.
plastered ['plɑːstəd] adj (col) ubriaco(a) fradicio(a).
plasterer ['plɑːstərə*] n intonacatore m.
plastic ['plæstɪk] n plastica ♦ adj (made of plastic) di or in plastica; (flexible) plastico(a), malleabile; (art) plastico(a).
plastic bag n sacchetto di plastica.
plastic bullet n pallottola di plastica.
plastic explosive n esplosivo al plastico.
plasticine ® ['plæstɪsiːn] n plastilina ®.

plastic surgery n chirurgia plastica.

plate [pleɪt] n (dish) piatto; (sheet of metal) lamiera; (PHOT) lastra; (TYP) cliché m inv; (in book) tavola; (on door) targa, targhetta; (AUT: number ~) targa; (dishes): **gold** ~ vasellame m d'oro; **silver** ~ argenteria.

plateau, ~s or ~x ['plætəu, -z] n altipiano.

plateful ['pleɪtful] n piatto.

plate glass n vetro piano.

platen ['plætən] n (on typewriter, printer) rullo.

plate rack n scolapiatti m inv.

platform ['plætfɔːm] n (stage, at meeting) palco; (BRIT: on bus) piattaforma; (RAIL) marciapiede m; **the train leaves from** ~ **7** il treno parte dal binario 7.

platform ticket n (BRIT) biglietto d'ingresso ai binari.

platinum ['plætɪnəm] n platino.

platitude ['plætɪtjuːd] n luogo comune.

platoon [plə'tuːn] n plotone m.

platter ['plætə*] n piatto.

plaudits ['plɔːdɪts] npl plauso.

plausible ['plɔːzɪbl] adj plausibile, credibile; (person) convincente.

play [pleɪ] n gioco; (THEAT) commedia ♦ vt (game) giocare a; (team, opponent) giocare contro; (instrument, piece of music) suonare; (play, part) interpretare ♦ vi giocare; suonare; recitare; **to bring** or **call into** ~ (plan) mettere in azione; (emotions) esprimere; ~ **on words** gioco di parole; **to** ~ **a trick on sb** fare uno scherzo a qn; **they're** ~**ing at soldiers** stanno giocando ai soldati; **to** ~ **for time** (fig) cercare di guadagnar tempo; **to** ~ **into sb's hands** (fig) fare il gioco di qn.

▶**play about, play around** vi (person) divertirsi; **to** ~ **about** or **around with** (fiddle with) giocherellare con; (idea) accarezzare.

▶**play along** vi: **to** ~ **along with** (fig: person) stare al gioco di; (: plan, idea) fingere di assecondare ♦ vt (fig): **to** ~ **sb along** tenere qn in sospeso.

▶**play back** vt riascoltare, risentire.

▶**play down** vt minimizzare.

▶**play on** vt fus (sb's feelings, credulity) giocare su; **to** ~ **on sb's nerves** dare sui nervi a qn.

▶**play up** vi (cause trouble) fare i capricci.

playact ['pleɪækt] vi fare la commedia.

playboy ['pleɪbɔɪ] n playboy m inv.

played-out ['pleɪd'aut] adj spossato(a).

player ['pleɪə*] n giocatore/trice; (THEAT) attore/trice; (MUS) musicista m/f.

playful ['pleɪful] adj giocoso(a).

playgoer ['pleɪgəuə*] n assiduo(a) frequentatore(trice) di teatri.

playground ['pleɪgraund] n (in school) cortile m per la ricreazione; (in park) parco m giochi inv.

playgroup ['pleɪgruːp] n giardino d'infanzia.

playing card ['pleɪɪŋ-] n carta da gioco.

playing field ['pleɪɪŋ-] n campo sportivo.

playmaker ['pleɪmeɪkə*] n (SPORT) playmaker m inv.

playmate ['pleɪmeɪt] n compagno/a di gioco.

play-off ['pleɪɔf] n (SPORT) bella.

playpen ['pleɪpɛn] n box m inv.

playroom ['pleɪruːm] n stanza dei giochi.

plaything ['pleɪθɪŋ] n giocattolo.

playtime ['pleɪtaɪm] n (SCOL) ricreazione f.

playwright ['pleɪraɪt] n drammaturgo/a.

plc abbr (BRIT) see **public limited company**.

plea [pliː] n (request) preghiera, domanda; (excuse) scusa; (LAW) (argomento di) difesa.

plea bargaining n (LAW) patteggiamento.

plead [pliːd] vt patrocinare; (give as excuse) addurre a pretesto ♦ vi (LAW) perorare la causa; (beg): **to** ~ **with sb** implorare qn; **to** ~ **for sth** implorare qc; **to** ~ **guilty/not guilty** (defendant) dichiararsi colpevole/innocente.

pleasant ['plɛznt] adj piacevole, gradevole.

pleasantly ['plɛzntlɪ] adv piacevolmente.

pleasantry ['plɛzntrɪ] n (joke) scherzo; (polite remark): **to exchange pleasantries** scambiarsi i convenevoli.

please [pliːz] vt piacere a ♦ vi (think fit): **do as you** ~ faccia come le pare; ~**!** per piacere!; **my bill,** ~ il conto, per piacere; ~ **yourself!** come ti (or le) pare!; ~ **don't cry!** ti prego, non piangere!

pleased [pliːzd] adj (happy) felice, lieto(a); ~ (**with**) (satisfied) contento(a) (di); **we are** ~ **to inform you that** ... abbiamo il piacere di informarla che ...; ~ **to meet you!** piacere!

pleasing ['pliːzɪŋ] adj piacevole, che fa piacere.

pleasurable ['plɛʒərəbl] adj molto piacevole, molto gradevole.

pleasure ['plɛʒə*] n piacere m; **with** ~ con piacere, volentieri; **"it's a** ~**"** "prego"; **is this trip for business or** ~**?** è un viaggio d'affari o di piacere?

pleasure cruise n crociera.

pleat [pliːt] n piega.

plebiscite ['plɛbɪsɪt] n plebiscito.

plebs [plɛbz] npl (pej) plebe f.

plectrum ['plɛktrəm] n plettro.

pledge [plɛdʒ] n pegno; (*promise*) promessa ♦ vt impegnare; promettere; **to ~ support for sb** impegnarsi a sostenere qn; **to ~ sb to secrecy** far promettere a qn di mantenere il segreto.

plenary ['pli:nərɪ] *adj* plenario(a); **in ~ session** in seduta plenaria.

plentiful ['plɛntɪful] *adj* abbondante, copioso(a).

plenty ['plɛntɪ] n abbondanza; **~ of** tanto(a), molto(a); un'abbondanza di; **we've got ~ of time to get there** abbiamo un sacco di tempo per arrivarci.

pleurisy ['pluərɪsɪ] n pleurite f.

Plexiglas ® ['plɛksɪglɑːs] n (*US*) plexiglas ® m.

pliable ['plaɪəbl] *adj* flessibile; (*person*) malleabile.

pliers ['plaɪəz] *npl* pinza.

plight [plaɪt] n situazione f critica.

plimsolls ['plɪmsəlz] *npl* (*BRIT*) scarpe *fpl* da tennis.

plinth [plɪnθ] n plinto; piedistallo.

PLO n abbr (= Palestine Liberation Organization) O.L.P. f.

plod [plɔd] vi camminare a stento; (*fig*) sgobbare.

plodder ['plɔdə*] n sgobbone m.

plodding ['plɔdɪŋ] *adj* lento(a) e pesante.

plonk [plɔŋk] (*col*) n (*BRIT*: wine) vino da poco ♦ vt: **to ~ sth down** buttare giù qc bruscamente.

plot [plɔt] n congiura, cospirazione f; (*of story, play*) trama; (*of land*) lotto ♦ vt (*mark out*) fare la pianta di; rilevare; (: *diagram etc*) tracciare; (*conspire*) congiurare, cospirare ♦ vi congiurare; **a vegetable ~** (*BRIT*) un orticello.

plotter ['plɔtə*] n cospiratore/trice; (*COMPUT*) plotter m inv, tracciatore m di curve.

plough, (US) plow [plau] n aratro ♦ vt (*earth*) arare.

►**plough back** vt (*COMM*) reinvestire.

►**plough through** vt fus (*snow etc*) procedere a fatica in.

ploughing, (US) plowing ['plauɪŋ] n aratura.

ploughman, (US) plowman ['plaumən] n aratore m; **~'s lunch** (*BRIT*) semplice pasto a base di pane e formaggio.

ploy [plɔɪ] n stratagemma m.

pluck [plʌk] vt (*fruit*) cogliere; (*musical instrument*) pizzicare; (*bird*) spennare ♦ n coraggio, fegato; **to ~ one's eyebrows** depilarsi le sopracciglia; **to ~ up courage** farsi coraggio.

plucky ['plʌkɪ] *adj* coraggioso(a).

plug [plʌg] n tappo; (*ELEC*) spina; (*AUT*: also: **spark(ing) ~**) candela ♦ vt (*hole*) tappare; (*col: advertise*) spingere; **to give sb/sth a ~** fare pubblicità a qn/qc.

►**plug in** (*ELEC*) vi inserire la spina ♦ vt attaccare a una presa.

plughole ['plʌghəul] n (*BRIT*) scarico.

plum [plʌm] n (*fruit*) susina ♦ cpd: **~ job** (*col*) impiego ottimo or favoloso.

plumage ['plu:mɪdʒ] n piume *fpl*, piumaggio.

plumb [plʌm] *adj* verticale ♦ n piombo ♦ *adv* (*exactly*) esattamente ♦ vt sondare.

►**plumb in** vt (*washing machine*) collegare all'impianto idraulico.

plumber ['plʌmə*] n idraulico.

plumbing ['plʌmɪŋ] n (*trade*) lavoro di idraulico; (*piping*) tubature *fpl*.

plumbline ['plʌmlaɪn] n filo a piombo.

plume [plu:m] n piuma, penna; (*decorative*) pennacchio.

plummet ['plʌmɪt] vi cadere a piombo.

plump [plʌmp] *adj* grassoccio(a) ♦ vt: **to ~ sth (down) on** lasciar cadere qc di peso su.

►**plump for** vt fus (*col*) decidersi per.

►**plump up** vt sprimacciare.

plunder ['plʌndə*] n saccheggio ♦ vt saccheggiare.

plunge [plʌndʒ] n tuffo ♦ vt immergere ♦ vi (*dive*) tuffarsi; (*fall*) cadere, precipitare; **to take the ~** (*fig*) saltare il fosso; **to ~ a room into darkness** far piombare una stanza nel buio.

plunger ['plʌndʒə*] n (*for blocked sink*) sturalavandini m inv.

plunging ['plʌndʒɪŋ] *adj* (*neckline*) profondo(a).

pluperfect [plu:'pə:fɪkt] n piuccheperfetto.

plural ['pluərl] *adj*, n plurale (m).

plus [plʌs] n (*also*: **~ sign**) segno più ♦ prep più ♦ *adj* (*MATH, ELEC*) positivo(a); **ten/ twenty ~** più di dieci/venti; **it's a ~** (*fig*) è un vantaggio.

plus fours *npl* calzoni *mpl* alla zuava.

plush [plʌʃ] *adj* lussuoso(a) ♦ n felpa.

plutonium [plu:'təunɪəm] n plutonio.

ply [plaɪ] n (*of wool*) capo; (*of wood*) strato ♦ vt (*tool*) maneggiare; (*a trade*) esercitare ♦ vi (*ship*) fare il servizio; **three ~ (wool)** lana a tre capi; **to ~ sb with drink** dare da bere continuamente a qn.

plywood ['plaɪwud] n legno compensato.

PM n abbr (*BRIT*) see **prime minister**.

p.m. *adv abbr* (= post meridiem) del pomeriggio.

PMS n abbr (= premenstrual syndrome) sindrome f premestruale.

PMT *n abbr* (= *premenstrual tension*) sindrome *f* premestruale.
pneumatic [nju:'mætɪk] *adj* pneumatico(a); ~ **drill** martello pneumatico.
pneumonia [nju:'məʊnɪə] *n* polmonite *f*.
PO *n abbr* (= *Post Office*) ≈ P.T. (= *Poste e Telegrafi*) ♦ *abbr* (*NAUT*) = **petty officer**.
po *abbr* = **postal order**.
POA *n abbr* (*BRIT*: = *Prison Officers' Association*) *sindacato delle guardie carcerarie.*
poach [pəʊtʃ] *vt* (*cook*) affogare; (*steal*) cacciare (*or* pescare) di frodo ♦ *vi* fare il bracconiere.
poached [pəʊtʃt] *adj* (*egg*) affogato(a).
poacher ['pəʊtʃə*] *n* bracconiere *m*.
poaching ['pəʊtʃɪŋ] *n* caccia (*or* pesca) di frodo.
PO box *n abbr see* **post office box**.
pocket ['pɔkɪt] *n* tasca ♦ *vt* intascare; **to be out of** ~ rimetterci; **to be £5 in/out of** ~ (*BRIT*) trovarsi con 5 sterline in più/in meno; **air** ~ vuoto d'aria.
pocketbook ['pɔkɪtbuk] *n* (*wallet*) portafoglio; (*notebook*) taccuino; (*US: handbag*) busta.
pocket knife *n* temperino.
pocket money *n* paghetta, settimana.
pockmarked ['pɔkmɑ:kt] *adj* (*face*) butterato(a).
pod [pɔd] *n* guscio ♦ *vt* sgusciare.
podgy ['pɔdʒɪ] *adj* grassoccio(a).
podiatrist [pɔ'di:ətrɪst] *n* (*US*) callista *m/f*.
podiatry [pɔ'di:ətrɪ] *n* (*US*) mestiere *m* di callista.
podium ['pəʊdɪəm] *n* podio.
POE *n abbr* = *port of embarkation*; *port of entry*.
poem ['pəʊɪm] *n* poesia.
poet ['pəʊɪt] *n* poeta/essa.
poetic [pəʊ'ɛtɪk] *adj* poetico(a).
poet laureate *n* (*BRIT*) poeta *m* laureato; *see boxed note.*

POET LAUREATE

*In Gran Bretagna un **poet laureate** è un poeta che riceve un vitalizio dalla casa reale britannica e che ha l'incarico di scrivere delle poesie commemorative in occasione delle festività ufficiali.*

---

poetry ['pəʊɪtrɪ] *n* poesia.
poignant ['pɔɪnjənt] *adj* struggente.
point [pɔɪnt] *n* (*gen*) punto; (*tip: of needle etc*) punta; (*BRIT ELEC: also:* **power** ~) presa (di corrente); (*in time*) punto, momento; (*SCOL*) voto; (*main idea,*

important part) nocciolo; (*also:* **decimal** ~): **2 ~ 3 (2.3)** 2 virgola 3 (2,3) ♦ *vt* (*show*) indicare; (*gun etc*): **to ~ sth at** puntare qc contro ♦ *vi* mostrare a dito; ~**s** *npl* (*AUT*) puntine *fpl*; (*RAIL*) scambio; **to ~ to** indicare; (*fig*) dimostrare; **to make a ~** fare un'osservazione; **to get the ~** capire; **to come to the ~** venire al fatto; **when it comes to the ~** quando si arriva al dunque; **to be on the ~ of doing sth** essere sul punto di *or* stare (proprio) per fare qc; **to be beside the ~** non entrarci; **to make a ~ of doing sth** non mancare di fare qc; **there's no ~ (in doing)** è inutile (fare); **in ~ of fact** a dire il vero; **that's the whole ~!** precisamente!, sta tutto lì!; **you've got a ~ there!** giusto!, ha ragione!; **the train stops at Carlisle and all** ~**s south** si ferma a Carlisle e in tutte le stazioni a sud di Carlisle; **good** ~**s** vantaggi *mpl*; (*of person*) qualità *fpl*; ~ **of departure** (*also fig*) punto di partenza; ~ **of order** mozione *f* d'ordine; ~ **of sale** (*COMM*) punto di vendita; ~ **of view** punto di vista.
▶**point out** *vt* far notare.
point-blank ['pɔɪnt'blæŋk] *adv* (*also:* **at** ~ **range**) a bruciapelo; (*fig*) categoricamente.
pointed ['pɔɪntɪd] *adj* (*shape*) aguzzo(a), appuntito(a); (*remark*) specifico(a).
pointedly ['pɔɪntɪdlɪ] *adv* in maniera inequivocabile.
pointer ['pɔɪntə*] *n* (*stick*) bacchetta; (*needle*) lancetta; (*clue*) indizio; (*advice*) consiglio; (*dog*) pointer *m*, cane *m* da punta.
pointless ['pɔɪntlɪs] *adj* inutile, vano(a).
poise [pɔɪz] *n* (*balance*) equilibrio; (*of head, body*) portamento; (*calmness*) calma ♦ *vt* tenere in equilibrio; **to be** ~**d for** (*fig*) essere pronto(a) a.
poison ['pɔɪzn] *n* veleno ♦ *vt* avvelenare.
poisoning ['pɔɪznɪŋ] *n* avvelenamento.
poisonous ['pɔɪznəs] *adj* velenoso(a); (*fumes*) venefico(a), tossico(a); (*ideas, literature*) pernicioso(a); (*rumours, individual*) perfido(a).
poke [pəʊk] *vt* (*fire*) attizzare; (*jab with finger, stick etc*) punzecchiare; (*put*): **to ~ sth in(to)** spingere qc dentro ♦ *n* (*jab*) colpetto; (*with elbow*) gomitata; **to ~ one's head out of the window** mettere la testa fuori dalla finestra; **to ~ fun at sb** prendere in giro qn.
▶**poke about** *vi* frugare.
poker ['pəʊkə*] *n* attizzatoio; (*CARDS*) poker *m*.
poker-faced ['pəʊkə'feɪst] *adj* dal viso

impassibile.
poky ['pəukı] *adj* piccolo(a) e stretto(a).
Poland ['pəulənd] *n* Polonia.
polar ['pəulə*] *adj* polare.
polar bear *n* orso bianco.
polarize ['pəulərɑız] *vt* polarizzare.
Pole [pəul] *n* polacco/a.
pole [pəul] *n* (*of wood*) palo; (*ELEC, GEO*) polo.
poleaxe, (*US*) **poleax** ['pəulæks] *vt* (*fig*) stendere.
pole bean *n* (*US*) fagiolino.
polecat ['pəulkæt] *n* puzzola; (*US*) moffetta.
Pol. Econ. ['pɔlıkɔn] *n abbr* = *political economy.*
polemic [pə'lɛmık] *n* polemica.
pole star *n* stella polare.
pole vault *n* salto con l'asta.
police [pə'liːs] *n* polizia ♦ *vt* mantenere l'ordine in; (*streets, city, frontier*) presidiare; **a large number of** ~ wore hurt molti poliziotti sono rimasti feriti.
police car *n* macchina della polizia.
police constable (PC) *n* (*BRIT*) agente *m* di polizia.
police department *n* (*US*) dipartimento di polizia.
police force *n* corpo di polizia, polizia.
policeman [pə'liːsmən] *n* poliziotto, agente *m* di polizia.
police officer *n* = **police constable.**
police record *n*: **to have a** ~ avere precedenti penali.
police state *n* stato di polizia.
police station *n* posto di polizia.
policewoman [pə'liːswumən] *n* donna *f* poliziotto *inv.*
policy ['pɔlısı] *n* politica, (*of newspaper, company*) linea di condotta, prassi *f inv*; (*also:* **insurance** ~) polizza (d'assicurazione); **to take out a** ~ (*INSURANCE*) stipulare una polizza di assicurazione.
policy holder *n* assicurato/a.
policy-making ['pɔlısımeıkıŋ] *n* messa a punto di programmi.
polio ['pəulıəu] *n* polio *f.*
Polish ['pəulıʃ] *adj* polacco(a) ♦ *n* (*LING*) polacco.
polish ['pɔlıʃ] *n* (*for shoes*) lucido; (*for floor*) cera; (*for nails*) smalto; (*shine*) lucentezza, lustro; (*fig: refinement*) raffinatezza ♦ *vt* lucidare; (*fig: improve*) raffinare.
▶**polish off** *vt* (*work*) sbrigare; (*food*) mangiarsi.
polished ['pɔlıʃt] *adj* (*fig*) raffinato(a).
polite [pə'laıt] *adj* cortese; **it's not** ~ **to do**

that non è educato *or* buona educazione fare questo.
politely [pə'laıtlı] *adv* cortesemente.
politeness [pə'laıtnıs] *n* cortesia.
politic ['pɔlıtık] *adj* diplomatico(a).
political [pə'lıtıkl] *adj* politico(a).
political asylum *n* asilo politico.
politically [pə'lıtıklı] *adv* politicamente.
politically correct *adj* politicamente corretto(a).
politician [pɔlı'tıʃən] *n* politico.
politics ['pɔlıtıks] *n* politica ♦ *npl* idee *fpl* politiche.
polka ['pɔlkə] *n* polca.
polka dot *n* pois *m inv.*
poll [pəul] *n* scrutinio; (*votes cast*) voti *mpl*; (*also:* **opinion** ~) sondaggio (d'opinioni) ♦ *vt* ottenere; **to go to the** ~**s** (*voters*) andare alle urne; (*government*) indire le elezioni.
pollen ['pɔlən] *n* polline *m.*
pollen count *n* tasso di polline nell'aria.
pollination [pɔlı'neıʃən] *n* impollinazione *f.*
polling ['pəulıŋ] *n* (*BRIT POL*) votazione *f*, votazioni *fpl*; (*TEL*) interrogazione *f* ciclica.
polling booth *n* (*BRIT*) cabina elettorale.
polling day *n* (*BRIT*) giorno delle elezioni.
polling station *n* (*BRIT*) sezione *f* elettorale.
pollster ['pəulstə*] *n* chi esegue sondaggi d'opinione.
poll tax *n* (*BRIT*) *imposta locale sulla persona fisica* (*non più in vigore*).
pollutant [pə'luːtənt] *n* sostanza inquinante.
pollute [pə'luːt] *vt* inquinare.
pollution [pə'luːʃən] *n* inquinamento.
polo ['pəuləu] *n* polo.
polo neck *n* collo alto; (*also:* ~ **sweater**) dolcevita ♦ *adj* a collo alto.
poly ['pɔlı] *n abbr* (*BRIT*) = **polytechnic.**
poly bag *n* (*BRIT col*) borsa di plastica.
polyester [pɔlı'estə*] *n* poliestere *m.*
polygamy [pə'lıgəmı] *n* poligamia.
polygraph ['pɔlıgrɑːf] *n* macchina della verità.
Polynesia [pɔlı'niːzıə] *n* Polinesia.
Polynesian [pɔlı'niːzıən] *adj, n* polinesiano(a).
polyp ['pɔlıp] *n* (*MED*) polipo.
polystyrene [pɔlı'stɑırıːn] *n* polistirolo.
polytechnic [pɔlı'tɛknık] *n* (*college*) istituto superiore ad indirizzo tecnologico.
polythene ['pɔlıθıːn] *n* politene *m.*
polythene bag *n* borsa di plastica.
polyurethane ['pɔlı'juərıθeın] *n* poliuretano.

pomegranate ['pɒmɪgrænɪt] n melagrana.
pommel ['pɒml] n pomo ♦ vt = **pummel.**
pomp [pɒmp] n pompa, fasto.
pompom ['pɒmpɒm] n pompon m inv.
pompous ['pɒmpəs] adj pomposo(a); (person) pieno(a) di boria.
pond [pɒnd] n stagno; (in park) laghetto.
ponder ['pɒndə*] vi riflettere, meditare ♦ vt ponderare, riflettere su.
ponderous ['pɒndərəs] adj ponderoso(a), pesante.
pong [pɒŋ] (BRIT col) n puzzo ♦ vi puzzare.
pontiff ['pɒntɪf] n pontefice m.
pontificate [pɒn'tɪfɪkeɪt] vi (fig): to ~ (about) pontificare (su).
pontoon [pɒn'tuːn] n pontone m; (BRIT CARDS) ventuno.
pony ['pəʊnɪ] n pony m inv.
ponytail ['pəʊnɪteɪl] n coda di cavallo.
pony trekking [-trɛkɪŋ] n (BRIT) escursione f a cavallo.
poodle ['puːdl] n barboncino, barbone m.
pooh-pooh [puː'puː] vt deridere.
pool [puːl] n (of rain) pozza; (pond) stagno; (artificial) vasca; (also: **swimming** ~) piscina; (sth shared) fondo comune; (COMM: consortium) pool m inv; (US: monopoly trust) trust m inv; (billiards) specie di biliardo a buca ♦ vt mettere in comune; **typing** ~, (US) **secretary** ~ servizio comune di dattilografia; **to do the (football)** ~s ≈ fare la schedina, giocare al totocalcio.
poor [puə*] adj povero(a); (mediocre) mediocre, cattivo(a) ♦ npl: **the** ~ i poveri.
poorly ['puəlɪ] adv poveramente; (badly) male ♦ adj indisposto(a), malato(a).
pop [pɒp] n (noise) schiocco; (MUS) musica pop; (US col: father) babbo; (col: drink) bevanda gasata ♦ vt (put) mettere (in fretta) ♦ vi scoppiare; (cork) schioccare; **she** ~**ped her head out** (of the window) sporse fuori la testa.
▶**pop in** vi passare.
▶**pop out** vi fare un salto fuori.
▶**pop up** vi apparire, sorgere.
pop concert n concerto m pop inv.
popcorn ['pɒpkɔːn] n pop-corn m.
pope [pəʊp] n papa m.
poplar ['pɒplə*] n pioppo.
poplin ['pɒplɪn] n popeline f.
popper ['pɒpə*] n (BRIT) bottone m automatico, bottone a pressione.
poppy ['pɒpɪ] n papavero.
poppycock ['pɒpɪkɒk] n (col) scempiaggini fpl.
Popsicle ® ['pɒpsɪkl] n (US) ghiacciolo.
populace ['pɒpjuləs] n popolo.

popular ['pɒpjulə*] adj popolare; (fashionable) in voga; **to be** ~ **(with)** (person) essere benvoluto(a) or ben visto(a) (da); (decision) essere gradito(a) (a); **a** ~ **song** una canzone di successo.
popularity [pɒpju'lærɪtɪ] n popolarità.
popularize ['pɒpjuləraɪz] vt divulgare; (science) volgarizzare.
populate ['pɒpjuleɪt] vt popolare.
population [pɒpju'leɪʃən] n popolazione f.
population explosion n forte espansione f demografica.
populous ['pɒpjuləs] adj popolato(a).
porcelain ['pɔːslɪn] n porcellana.
porch [pɔːtʃ] n veranda.
porcupine ['pɔːkjupaɪn] n porcospino.
pore [pɔː*] n poro ♦ vi: **to** ~ **over** essere immerso(a) in.
pork [pɔːk] n carne f di maiale.
pork chop n braciola or costoletta di maiale.
porn [pɔːn] (col) n pornografia ♦ adj porno inv.
pornographic [pɔːnə'græfɪk] adj pornografico(a).
pornography [pɔː'nɒgrəfɪ] n pornografia.
porous ['pɔːrəs] adj poroso(a).
porpoise ['pɔːpəs] n focena.
porridge ['pɒrɪdʒ] n porridge m.
port1 [pɔːt] n porto; (opening in ship) portello; (NAUT: left side) babordo; (COMPUT) porta; **to** ~ (NAUT) a babordo; ~ **of call** (porto di) scalo.
port2 [pɔːt] n (wine) porto.
portable ['pɔːtəbl] adj portatile.
portal ['pɔːtl] n portale m.
portcullis [pɔːt'kʌlɪs] n saracinesca.
portent ['pɔːtent] n presagio.
porter ['pɔːtə*] n (for luggage) facchino, portabagagli m inv; (doorkeeper) portiere m, portinaio; (US RAIL) addetto ai vagoni letto.
portfolio [pɔːt'fəʊlɪəu] n (POL: office; ECON) portafoglio; (of artist) raccolta dei propri lavori.
porthole ['pɔːthəʊl] n oblò m inv.
portico ['pɔːtɪkəʊ] n portico.
portion ['pɔːʃən] n porzione f.
portly ['pɔːtlɪ] adj corpulento(a).
portrait ['pɔːtreɪt] n ritratto.
portray [pɔː'treɪ] vt fare il ritratto di; (character on stage) rappresentare; (in writing) ritrarre.
portrayal ['pɔːtreɪəl] n ritratto; rappresentazione f.
Portugal ['pɔːtjugl] n Portogallo.
Portuguese [pɔːtju'giːz] adj portoghese ♦ n (pl inv) portoghese m/f; (LING) portoghese m.

Portuguese man-of-war [-mænəv'wɔː*] n (jellyfish) medusa.

pose [pəuz] n posa ♦ vi posare; (pretend): **to ~ as** atteggiarsi a, posare a ♦ vt porre; **to strike a ~** mettersi in posa.

poser ['pəuzə*] n domanda difficile; (person) = **poseur**.

poseur [pəu'zəː*] n (pej) persona affettata.

posh [pɔʃ] adj (col) elegante; (family) per bene ♦ adv (col): **to talk ~** parlare in modo snob.

position [pə'zɪʃən] n posizione f; (job) posto ♦ vt mettere in posizione, collocare; **to be in a ~ to do sth** essere nella posizione di fare qc.

positive ['pɔzɪtɪv] adj positivo(a); (certain) sicuro(a), certo(a); (definite) preciso(a); definitivo(a).

posse ['pɔsɪ] n (US) drappello.

possess [pə'zɛs] vt possedere; **like one ~ed** come un ossesso; **whatever can have ~ed you?** cosa ti ha preso?

possession [pə'zɛʃən] n possesso; (object) bene m; **to take ~ of sth** impossessarsi or impadronirsi di qc.

possessive [pə'zɛsɪv] adj possessivo(a).

possessiveness [pə'zɛsɪvnɪs] n possessività.

possessor [pə'zɛsə*] n possessore/ posseditrice.

possibility [pɔsɪ'bɪlɪtɪ] n possibilità f inv; **he's a ~ for the part** è uno dei candidati per la parte.

possible ['pɔsɪbl] adj possibile; **it is ~ to do it** è possibile farlo; **if ~** se possibile; **as big as ~** il più grande possibile; **as far as ~** nei limiti del possibile.

possibly ['pɔsɪblɪ] adv (perhaps) forse; **if you ~ can** se le è possibile; **I cannot ~ come** proprio non posso venire.

post [pəust] n (BRIT: mail, letters, delivery) posta; (: collection) levata; (job, situation) posto; (pole) palo; (trading ~) stazione f commerciale ♦ vt (BRIT: send by post) impostare; (MIL) appostare; (notice) affiggere; (BRIT: appoint): **to ~ to** assegnare a; **by ~** (BRIT) per posta; **by return of ~** (BRIT) a giro di posta; **to keep sb ~ed** tenere qn al corrente.

post... [pəust] prefix post...; **~-1990** dopo il 1990.

postage ['pəustɪdʒ] n affrancatura.

postage stamp n francobollo.

postal ['pəustəl] adj postale.

postal order n vaglia m inv postale.

postbag ['pəustbæg] n (BRIT) sacco postale, sacco della posta.

postbox ['pəustbɔks] n cassetta delle lettere.

postcard ['pəustkɑːd] n cartolina.

postcode ['pəustkəud] n (BRIT) codice m (di avviamento) postale.

postdate ['pəust'deɪt] vt (cheque) postdatare.

poster ['pəustə*] n manifesto, affisso.

poste restante [pəust'rɛstɑ̃ːnt] n (BRIT) fermo posta m.

posterior [pɔs'tɪərɪə*] n (col) deretano, didietro.

posterity [pɔs'tɛrɪtɪ] n posterità.

poster paint n tempera.

post exchange (PX) n (US MIL) spaccio militare.

post-free [pəust'friː] adj, adv (BRIT) franco di porto.

postgraduate ['pəust'grædjuət] n laureato/a che continua gli studi.

posthumous ['pɔstjuməs] adj postumo(a).

posthumously ['pɔstjuməslɪ] adv dopo la mia (or sua etc) morte.

posting ['pəustɪŋ] n (BRIT) incarico.

postman ['pəustmən] n postino.

postmark ['pəustmɑːk] n bollo or timbro postale.

postmaster ['pəustmɑːstə*] n direttore m di un ufficio postale.

Postmaster General n ≈ ministro delle Poste.

postmistress ['pəustmɪstrɪs] n direttrice f di un ufficio postale.

post-mortem [pəust'mɔːtəm] n autopsia; (fig) analisi f inv a posteriori.

postnatal ['pəust'neɪtl] adj post-parto inv.

post office n (building) ufficio postale; (organization) poste fpl.

post office box (PO box) n casella postale (C.P.).

post-paid ['pəust'peɪd] adj già affrancato(a).

postpone [pəust'pəun] vt rinviare.

postponement [pəust'pəunmənt] n rinvio.

postscript ['pəustskrɪpt] n poscritto.

postulate ['pɔstjuleɪt] vt postulare.

posture ['pɔstʃə*] n portamento, (pose) posa, atteggiamento ♦ vi posare.

postwar ['pəust'wɔː*] adj del dopoguerra.

posy ['pəuzɪ] n mazzetto di fiori.

pot [pɔt] n (for cooking) pentola; casseruola; (for plants, jam) vaso; (piece of pottery) ceramica; (col: marijuana) erba ♦ vt (plant) piantare in vaso; **to go to ~** (col) andare in malora; **~s of** (BRIT col) un sacco di.

potash ['pɔtæʃ] n potassa.

potassium [pə'tæsɪəm] n potassio.

potato, ~es [pə'teɪtəu] n patata.

potato crisps, (US) **potato chips** npl

patatine *fpl*.
potato flour *n* fecola di patate.
potato peeler *n* sbucciapatate *m inv*.
potbellied ['pɔtbɛlɪd] *adj* (*from overeating*) panciuto(a); (*from malnutrition*) dal ventre gonfio.
potency ['pəutnsɪ] *n* potenza; (*of drink*) forza.
potent ['pəutnt] *adj* potente, forte.
potentate ['pəutnteɪt] *n* potentato.
potential [pə'tɛnʃl] *adj* potenziale ♦ *n* possibilità *fpl*; **to have** ~ essere promettente.
potentially [pə'tɛnʃəlɪ] *adv* potenzialmente.
pothole ['pɔthəul] *n* (*in road*) buca; (*BRIT: underground*) marmitta.
potholer ['pɔthəulə*] *n* (*BRIT*) speleologo/a.
potholing ['pɔthəulɪŋ] *n* (*BRIT*): **to go** ~ fare la speleologia.
potion ['pəuʃən] *n* pozione *f*.
potluck [pɔt'lʌk] *n*: **to take** ~ tentare la sorte.
potpourri [pəu'puriː] *n* (*dried petals etc*) miscuglio di petali essiccati profumati; (*fig*) pot-pourri *m inv*.
pot roast *n* brasato.
potshot ['pɔtʃɔt] *n*: **to take ~s at** tirare a casaccio contro.
potted ['pɔtɪd] *adj* (*food*) in conserva; (*plant*) in vaso; (*fig: shortened*) condensato(a).
potter ['pɔtə*] *n* vasaio ♦ *vi* (*BRIT*): **to** ~ **around, ~ about** lavoracchiare; **to** ~ **round the house** sbrigare con calma le faccende di casa; ~**'s wheel** tornio (da vasaio).
pottery ['pɔtərɪ] *n* ceramiche *fpl*; **a piece of** ~ una ceramica.
potty ['pɔtɪ] *adj* (*BRIT col: mad*) tocco(a) ♦ *n* (*child's*) vasino.
potty-trained ['pɔtɪtreɪnd] *adj* che ha imparato a farla nel vasino.
pouch [pautʃ] *n* borsa; (*ZOOL*) marsupio.
pouf(fe) [puːf] *n* (*stool*) pouf *m inv*.
poultice ['pəultɪs] *n* impiastro, cataplasma *m*.
poultry ['pəultrɪ] *n* pollame *m*.
poultry farm *n* azienda avicola.
poultry farmer *n* pollicoltore/trice.
pounce [pauns] *vi*: **to** ~ (**on**) balzare addosso (a), piombare (su) ♦ *n* balzo.
pound [paund] *n* (*weight*: = 453g, 16 ounces) libbra; (*money*: = 100 pence) (lira) sterlina; (*for dogs*) canile *m* municipale ♦ *vt* (*beat*) battere; (*crush*) pestare, polverizzare ♦ *vi* (*beat*) battere, martellare; **half a** ~ mezza libbra; **a five-** ~ **note** una banconota da cinque sterline.

pounding ['paundɪŋ] *n*: **to take a** ~ (*fig*) prendere una batosta.
pound sterling *n* sterlina.
pour [pɔː*] *vt* versare ♦ *vi* riversarsi; (*rain*) piovere a dirotto.
▶**pour away, pour off** *vt* vuotare.
▶**pour in** *vi* (*people*) entrare in fiotto; **to come ~ing in** (*water*) entrare a fiotti; (*letters*) arrivare a valanghe; (*cars, people*) affluire in gran quantità.
▶**pour out** *vi* (*people*) riversarsi fuori ♦ *vt* vuotare; versare.
pouring ['pɔːrɪŋ] *adj*: ~ **rain** pioggia torrenziale.
pout [paut] *vi* sporgere le labbra; fare il broncio.
poverty ['pɔvətɪ] *n* povertà, miseria.
poverty line *n* soglia di povertà.
poverty-stricken ['pɔvətɪstrɪkən] *adj* molto povero(a), misero(a).
poverty trap *n* (*BRIT*) circolo vizioso della povertà.
POW *n abbr* = **prisoner of war**.
powder ['paudə*] *n* polvere *f* ♦ *vt* spolverizzare; (*face*) incipriare; ~**ed milk** latte *m* in polvere; **to** ~ **one's nose** incipriarsi il naso; (*euphemism*) andare alla toilette.
powder compact *n* portacipria *m inv*.
powder keg *n* (*fig: area*) polveriera; (*: situation*) situazione *f* esplosiva.
powder puff *n* piumino della cipria.
powder room *n* toilette *f inv* (per signore).
powdery ['paudərɪ] *adj* polveroso(a).
power ['pauə*] *n* (*strength*) potenza, forza; (*ability, POL: of party, leader*) potere *m*; (*MATH*) potenza; (*ELEC*) corrente *f* ♦ *vt* fornire di energia; azionare; **to be in** ~ essere al potere; **to do all in one's** ~ **to help sb** fare tutto quello che si può per aiutare qn; **the world ~s** le grandi potenze; **mental ~s** capacità *fpl* mentali.
powerboat ['pauəbəut] *n* (*BRIT*) motobarca, imbarcazione *f* a motore.
power cut *n* (*BRIT*) interruzione *f* or mancanza di corrente.
powered ['pauəd] *adj*: ~ **by** azionato(a) da; **nuclear-~ submarine** sottomarino a propulsione atomica.
power failure *n* guasto alla linea elettrica.
powerful ['pauəful] *adj* potente, forte.
powerhouse ['pauəhaus] *n* (*fig: person*) persona molto dinamica; **a ~ of ideas** una miniera di idee.
powerless ['pauəlɪs] *adj* impotente, senza potere.
power line *n* linea elettrica.
power of attorney *n* procura.

power point n (BRIT) presa di corrente.
power station n centrale f elettrica.
power steering n (AUT: also: **power-assisted steering**) servosterzo.
powwow ['pauwau] n riunione f.
pp abbr (= pages) pp.; (= per procurationem: by proxy): ~ **J. Smith** per il Signor J. Smith.
PPE n abbr (BRIT SCOL: = philosophy, politics and economics) corso di laurea.
PPS n abbr (BRIT: = parliamentary private secretary) parlamentare che assiste un ministro; = post postscriptum.
PQ abbr (Canada) = Province of Quebec.
PR n abbr see **proportional representation**; **public relations** ♦ abbr (US) = Puerto Rico.
Pr. abbr = prince.
practicability [præktɪkə'bɪlɪtɪ] n praticabilità.
practicable ['præktɪkəbl] adj (scheme) praticabile.
practical ['præktɪkl] adj pratico(a).
practicality [præktɪ'kælɪtɪ] n (of plan) fattibilità; (of person) senso pratico; **practicalities** dettagli mpl pratici.
practical joke n beffa.
practically ['præktɪklɪ] adv (almost) quasi, praticamente.
practice ['præktɪs] n pratica; (of profession) esercizio; (at football etc) allenamento; (business) gabinetto; clientela ♦ vt, vi (US) = **practise; in** ~ (in reality) in pratica; **out of** ~ fuori esercizio; **2 hours' piano** ~ 2 ore di esercizio al pianoforte; **it's common** ~ è d'uso; **to put sth into** ~ mettere qc in pratica; **target** ~ pratica di tiro.
practice match n partita di allenamento.
practise, (US) **practice** ['præktɪs] vt (work at: piano, one's backhand etc) esercitarsi a; (train for: skiing, running etc) allenarsi a; (a sport, religion) praticare; (method) usare; (profession) esercitare ♦ vi esercitarsi; (train) allenarsi; **to** ~ **for a match** allenarsi per una partita.
practised ['præktɪst] adj (BRIT: person) esperto(a); (: performance) da virtuoso(a); (: liar) matricolato(a); **with a** ~ **eye** con occhio esperto.
practising ['præktɪsɪŋ] adj (Christian etc) praticante; (lawyer) che esercita la professione; (homosexual) attivo(a).
practitioner [præk'tɪʃənə*] n professionista m/f; (MED) medico.
pragmatic [præg'mætɪk] adj prammatico(a).
Prague [prɑːg] n Praga.
prairie ['prɛərɪ] n prateria.

praise [preɪz] n elogio, lode f ♦ vt elogiare, lodare.
praiseworthy ['preɪzwɜːðɪ] adj lodevole.
pram [præm] n (BRIT) carrozzina.
prance [prɑːns] vi (horse) impennarsi.
prank [præŋk] n burla.
prat [præt] n (BRIT col) cretino/a.
prattle ['prætl] vi cinguettare.
prawn [prɔːn] n gamberetto.
pray [preɪ] vi pregare.
prayer [prɛə*] n preghiera.
prayer book n libro di preghiere.
pre... [priː] prefix pre...; **~-1970** prima del 1970.
preach [priːtʃ] vt, vi predicare; **to** ~ **at sb** fare la predica a qn.
preacher ['priːtʃə*] n predicatore/trice; (US: minister) pastore m.
preamble [prɪ'æmbl] n preambolo.
prearranged [priːə'reɪndʒd] adj organizzato(a) in anticipo.
precarious [prɪ'kɛərɪəs] adj precario(a).
precaution [prɪ'kɔːʃən] n precauzione f.
precautionary [prɪ'kɔːʃənərɪ] adj (measure) precauzionale.
precede [prɪ'siːd] vt, vi precedere.
precedence ['prɛsɪdəns] n precedenza; **to take** ~ **over** avere la precedenza su.
precedent ['prɛsɪdənt] n precedente m; **to establish** or **set a** ~ creare un precedente.
preceding [prɪ'siːdɪŋ] adj precedente.
precept ['priːsɛpt] n precetto.
precinct ['priːsɪŋkt] n (round cathedral) recinto; (US: district) circoscrizione f; **~s** npl (neighbourhood) dintorni mpl, vicinanze fpl; **pedestrian** ~ zona pedonale; **shopping** ~ (BRIT) centro commerciale.
precious ['prɛʃəs] adj prezioso(a) ♦ adv (col): ~ **little/few** ben poco/pochi; **your** ~ **dog** (ironic) il suo amatissimo cane.
precipice ['prɛsɪpɪs] n precipizio.
precipitate adj [prɪ'sɪpɪtɪt] (hasty) precipitoso(a) ♦ vt [prɪ'sɪpɪteɪt] accelerare.
precipitation [prɪsɪpɪ'teɪʃən] n precipitazione f.
precipitous [prɪ'sɪpɪtəs] adj (steep) erto(a), ripido(a).
précis, pl **précis** ['preɪsiː, -z] n riassunto.
precise [prɪ'saɪs] adj preciso(a).
precisely [prɪ'saɪslɪ] adv precisamente; **~!** appunto!
precision [prɪ'sɪʒən] n precisione f.
preclude [prɪ'kluːd] vt precludere, impedire; **to** ~ **sb from doing** impedire a qn di fare.
precocious [prɪ'kəʊʃəs] adj precoce.

preconceived [pri:kən'si:vd] *adj* (*idea*) preconcetto(a).
preconception [pri:kən'sɛpʃən] *n* preconcetto.
precondition [pri:kən'dɪʃən] *n* condizione *f* necessaria.
precursor [pri:'kə:sə*] *n* precursore *m*.
predate [pri:'deɪt] *vt* (*precede*) precedere.
predator ['prɛdətə*] *n* predatore *m*.
predatory ['prɛdətərɪ] *adj* predatore(trice).
predecessor ['pri:dɪsɛsə*] *n* predecessore/a.
predestination [pri:dɛstɪ'neɪʃən] *n* predestinazione *f*.
predetermine [pri:dɪ'tə:mɪn] *vt* predeterminare.
predicament [prɪ'dɪkəmənt] *n* situazione *f* difficile.
predicate ['prɛdɪkɪt] *n* (*LING*) predicativo.
predict [prɪ'dɪkt] *vt* predire.
predictable [prɪ'dɪktəbl] *adj* prevedibile.
predictably [prɪ'dɪktəblɪ] *adv* (*behave, react*) in modo prevedibile; ~ **she didn't arrive** come era da prevedere, non è arrivata.
prediction [prɪ'dɪkʃən] *n* predizione *f*.
predispose [pri:dɪs'pəuz] *vt* predisporre.
predominance [prɪ'dɔmɪnəns] *n* predominanza.
predominant [prɪ'dɔmɪnənt] *adj* predominante.
predominantly [prɪ'dɔmɪnəntlɪ] *adv* in maggior parte; soprattutto.
predominate [prɪ'dɔmɪneɪt] *vi* predominare.
pre-eminent [prɪ'ɛmɪnənt] *adj* preminente.
pre-empt [prɪ'ɛmpt] *vt* acquistare per diritto di prelazione; (*fig*) anticipare.
pre-emptive [prɪ'ɛmptɪv] *adj*: ~ **strike** azione *f* preventiva.
preen [pri:n] *vt*: **to** ~ **itself** (*bird*) lisciarsi le penne; **to** ~ **o.s.** agghindarsi.
prefab ['pri:fæb] *n* casa prefabbricata.
prefabricated [pri:'fæbrikeɪtɪd] *adj* prefabbricato(a).
preface ['prɛfəs] *n* prefazione *f*.
prefect ['pri:fɛkt] *n* (*BRIT: in school*) studente/essa con funzioni disciplinari; (*in Italy*) prefetto.
prefer [prɪ'fə:*] *vt* preferire; (*LAW: charges, complaint*) sporgere; (: *action*) intentare; **to** ~ **coffee to tea** preferire il caffè al tè.
preferable ['prɛfrəbl] *adj* preferibile.
preferably ['prɛfrəblɪ] *adv* preferibilmente.
preference ['prɛfrəns] *n* preferenza; **in** ~ **to sth** piuttosto che qc.
preference shares *npl* (*BRIT*) azioni *fpl*

privilegiate.
preferential [prɛfə'rɛnʃəl] *adj* preferenziale; ~ **treatment** trattamento di favore.
preferred stock [prɪ'fə:d-] *npl* (*US*) = **preference shares**.
prefix ['pri:fɪks] *n* prefisso.
pregnancy ['prɛgnənsɪ] *n* gravidanza.
pregnancy test *n* test *m inv* di gravidanza.
pregnant ['prɛgnənt] *adj* incinta *adj f*; (*animal*) gravido(a); (*fig: remark, pause*) significativo(a); **3 months** ~ incinta di 3 mesi.
prehistoric ['pri:hɪs'tɔrɪk] *adj* preistorico(a).
prehistory [pri:'hɪstərɪ] *n* preistoria.
prejudge [pri:'dʒʌdʒ] *vt* pregiudicare.
prejudice ['prɛdʒudɪs] *n* pregiudizio; (*harm*) torto, danno ♦ *vt* pregiudicare, ledere; (*bias*): **to** ~ **sb in favour of/against** disporre bene/male qn verso.
prejudiced ['prɛdʒudɪst] *adj* (*person*) pieno(a) di pregiudizi; (*view*) prevenuto(a); **to be** ~ **against sb/sth** essere prevenuto contro qn/qc.
prelate ['prɛlət] *n* prelato.
preliminaries [prɪ'lɪmɪnərɪz] *npl* preliminari *mpl*.
preliminary [prɪ'lɪmɪnərɪ] *adj* preliminare.
prelude ['prɛlju:d] *n* preludio.
premarital ['pri:'mærɪtl] *adj* prematrimoniale.
premature ['prɛmətʃuə*] *adj* prematuro(a); (*arrival*) (molto) anticipato(a); **you are being a little** ~ è un po' troppo precipitoso.
premeditated [pri:'mɛdɪteɪtɪd] *adj* premeditato(a).
premeditation [pri:mɛdɪ'teɪʃən] *n* premeditazione *f*.
premenstrual tension [pri:'mɛnstruəl-] *n* (*MED*) tensione *f* premestruale.
premier ['prɛmɪə*] *adj* primo(a) ♦ *n* (*POL*) primo ministro.
première ['prɛmɪɛə*] *n* prima.
premise ['prɛmɪs] *n* premessa.
premises ['prɛmɪsɪz] *npl* locale *m*; **on the** ~ sul posto; **business** ~ locali commerciali.
premium ['pri:mɪəm] *n* premio; **to be at a** ~ (*fig: housing etc*) essere ricercatissimo; **to sell at a** ~ (*shares*) vendere sopra la pari.
premium bond *n* (*BRIT*) obbligazione *f* a premio.
premium deal *n* (*COMM*) offerta speciale.

premium gasoline n (US) super f.

premonition [prɛmə'nɪʃən] n premonizione
f.

preoccupation [priːɔkju'peɪʃən] n
preoccupazione f.

preoccupied [priː'ɔkjupaɪd] adj
preoccupato(a).

prep [prɛp] n abbr (SCOL: = preparation)
studio ♦ adj abbr: ~ **school** = **preparatory
school**.

prepackaged [priː'pækɪdʒd] adj già
impacchettato(a).

prepaid [priː'peɪd] adj pagato(a) in anticipo;
(envelope) affrancato(a).

preparation [prɛpə'reɪʃən] n preparazione
f; ~**s** npl (for trip, war) preparativi mpl; **in** ~
for sth in vista di qc.

preparatory [prɪ'pærətərɪ] adj
preparatorio(a); ~ **to sth/to doing sth**
prima di qc/di fare qc.

preparatory school n (BRIT) scuola
elementare privata; (US) scuola
superiore privata; ⇒ box seguente.

PREPARATORY SCHOOL

In Gran Bretagna, la **prep(aratory) school** è
una scuola, generalmente privata, frequentata
da bambini dai 7 ai 13 anni in vista
dell'iscrizione alla "public school". Negli Stati
Uniti, invece, è una scuola superiore privata
che prepara i ragazzi che si iscriveranno al
"college".

---

prepare [prɪ'pɛə*] vt preparare ♦ vi: **to** ~
for prepararsi a.

prepared [prɪ'pɛəd] adj: ~ **for** preparato(a)
a; ~ **to** pronto(a) a; **to be** ~ **to help sb**
(willing) essere disposto or pronto ad
aiutare qn.

preponderance [prɪ'pɔndərns] n
preponderanza.

preposition [prɛpə'zɪʃən] n preposizione f.

prepossessing [priːpə'zɛsɪŋ] adj
simpatico(a), attraente.

preposterous [prɪ'pɔstərəs] adj assurdo(a).

prerecord ['priːrɪ'kɔːd] vt registrare in
anticipo; ~**ed broadcast** trasmissione f
registrata; ~**ed cassette** (musi)cassetta.

prerequisite [priː'rɛkwɪzɪt] n requisito
indispensabile.

prerogative [prɪ'rɔgətɪv] n prerogativa.

presbyterian [prɛzbɪ'tɪərɪən] adj, n
presbiteriano(a).

presbytery ['prɛzbɪtərɪ] n presbiterio.

preschool ['priː'skuːl] adj (age)
prescolastico(a); (child) in età
prescolastica.

prescribe [prɪ'skraɪb] vt prescrivere; (MED)
ordinare; ~**d books** (BRIT SCOL) testi mpl
in programma.

prescription [prɪ'skrɪpʃən] n prescrizione f;
(MED) ricetta; **to make up** or (US) **fill a** ~
preparare or fare una ricetta; "**only
available on** ~" "ottenibile solo dietro
presentazione di ricetta medica".

prescription charges npl (BRIT) ticket m
inv.

prescriptive [prɪ'skrɪptɪv] adj normativo(a).

presence ['prɛzns] n presenza; ~ **of mind**
presenza di spirito.

present ['prɛznt] adj presente; (wife,
residence, job) attuale ♦ n regalo; (also: ~
tense) tempo presente ♦ vt [prɪ'zɛnt]
presentare; (give): **to** ~ **sb with sth**
offrire qc a qn; **to be** ~ **at** essere
presente a; **those** ~ i presenti; **at** ~ al
momento; **to make sb a** ~ **of sth** regalare
qc a qn.

presentable [prɪ'zɛntəbl] adj presentabile.

presentation [prɛzn'teɪʃən] n
presentazione f; (gift) regalo, dono;
(ceremony) consegna ufficiale; **on** ~ **of
the voucher** dietro presentazione del
buono.

present-day ['prɛzntdeɪ] adj attuale.

presenter [prɪ'zɛntə*] n (BRIT RADIO, TV)
presentatore/trice.

presently ['prɛzntlɪ] adv (soon) fra poco,
presto; (at present) al momento; (US: now)
adesso, ora.

preservation [prɛzə'veɪʃən] n
preservazione f, conservazione f.

preservative [prɪ'zəːvətɪv] n conservante
m.

preserve [prɪ'zəːv] vt (keep safe)
preservare, proteggere; (maintain)
conservare; (food) mettere in conserva
♦ n (for game, fish) riserva; (often pl: jam)
marmellata; (: fruit) frutta sciroppata.

preside [prɪ'zaɪd] vi presiedere.

presidency ['prɛzɪdənsɪ] n presidenza; (US:
of company) direzione f.

president ['prɛzɪdənt] n presidente m; (US:
of company) direttore/trice generale.

presidential [prɛzɪ'dɛnʃl] adj presidenziale.

press [prɛs] n (tool, machine) pressa; (for
wine) torchio; (newspapers) stampa; (for
crowd) folla ♦ vt (push) premere, pigiare;
(doorbell) suonare; (squeeze) spremere;
(: hand) stringere; (clothes: iron) stirare;
(pursue) incalzare; (insist): **to** ~ **sth on sb**
far accettare qc da qn; (urge, entreat): **to**
~ **sb to do** or **into doing sth** fare
pressione su qn affinché faccia qc ♦ vi
premere; accalcare; **to go to** ~

(*newspaper*) andare in macchina; **to be in the** ~ (*in the newspapers*) essere sui giornali; **we are** ~**ed for time** ci manca il tempo; **to** ~ **for sth** insistere per avere qc; **to** ~ **sb for an answer** insistere perché qn risponda; **to** ~ **charges against sb** (*LAW*) sporgere una denuncia contro qn.

▶**press ahead** *vi*: **to** ~ **ahead (with)** andare avanti (con).

▶**press on** *vi* continuare.

press agency *n* agenzia di stampa.

press clipping *n* ritaglio di giornale.

press conference *n* conferenza stampa.

press cutting *n* = **press clipping**.

press-gang ['prɛsgæŋ] *vt*: **to** ~ **sb into doing sth** costringere qn a viva forza a fare qc.

pressing ['prɛsɪŋ] *adj* urgente ♦ *n* stiratura.

press officer *n* addetto/a stampa *inv*.

press release *n* comunicato stampa.

press stud *n* (*BRIT*) bottone *m* a pressione.

press-up ['prɛsʌp] *n* (*BRIT*) flessione *f* sulle braccia.

pressure ['prɛʃə*] *n* pressione *f* ♦ *vt* = **to put** ~ **on**; **high/low** ~ alta/bassa pressione; **to put** ~ **on sb** fare pressione su qn.

pressure cooker *n* pentola a pressione.

pressure gauge *n* manometro.

pressure group *n* gruppo di pressione.

pressurize ['prɛʃəraɪz] *vt* pressurizzare; (*fig*): **to** ~ **sb (into doing sth)** fare delle pressioni su qn (per costringerlo a fare qc).

pressurized ['prɛʃəraɪzd] *adj* pressurizzato(a).

Prestel ® ['prɛstɛl] *n* Videotel ® *m inv*.

prestige [prɛs'tiːʒ] *n* prestigio.

prestigious [prɛs'tɪdʒəs] *adj* prestigioso(a).

presumably [prɪ'zjuːməblɪ] *adv* presumibilmente; ~ **he did it** penso *or* presumo che l'abbia fatto.

presume [prɪ'zjuːm] *vt* supporre; **to** ~ **to do** (*dare*) permettersi di fare.

presumption [prɪ'zʌmpʃən] *n* presunzione *f*; (*boldness*) audacia.

presumptuous [prɪ'zʌmpʃəs] *adj* presuntuoso(a).

presuppose [priːsə'pəuz] *vt* presupporre.

pre-tax [priː'tæks] *adj* al lordo d'imposta.

pretence, (*US*) **pretense** [prɪ'tɛns] *n* (*claim*) pretesa; (*pretext*) pretesto, scusa; **to make a** ~ **of doing** far finta di fare; **on** *or* **under the** ~ **of doing sth** con il pretesto *or* la scusa di fare qc; **she is devoid of all** ~ non si nasconde dietro false apparenze.

pretend [prɪ'tɛnd] *vt* (*feign*) fingere ♦ *vi* far finta; (*claim*): **to** ~ **to sth** pretendere a qc; **to** ~ **to do** far finta di fare.

pretense [prɪ'tɛns] *n* (*US*) = **pretence**.

pretension [prɪ'tɛnʃən] *n* (*claim*) pretesa; **to have no** ~**s to sth/to being sth** non avere la pretesa di avere qc/di essere qc.

pretentious [prɪ'tɛnʃəs] *adj* pretenzioso(a).

preterite ['prɛtərɪt] *n* preterito.

pretext ['priːtɛkst] *n* pretesto; **on** *or* **under the** ~ **of doing sth** col pretesto di fare qc.

pretty ['prɪtɪ] *adj* grazioso(a), carino(a) ♦ *adv* abbastanza, assai.

prevail [prɪ'veɪl] *vi* (*win, be usual*) prevalere; (*persuade*): **to** ~ (**up)on sb to do** persuadere qn a fare.

prevailing [prɪ'veɪlɪŋ] *adj* dominante.

prevalent ['prɛvələnt] *adj* (*belief*) predominante; (*customs*) diffuso(a); (*fashion*) corrente; (*disease*) comune.

prevarication [prɪværɪ'keɪʃən] *n* tergiversazione *f*.

prevent [prɪ'vɛnt] *vt* prevenire; **to** ~ **sb from doing** impedire a qn di fare.

preventable [prɪ'vɛntəbl] *adj* evitabile.

preventative [prɪ'vɛntətɪv] *adj* preventivo(a).

prevention [prɪ'vɛnʃən] *n* prevenzione *f*.

preventive [prɪ'vɛntɪv] *adj* preventivo(a).

preview ['priːvjuː] *n* (*of film*) anteprima.

previous ['priːvɪəs] *adj* precedente; anteriore; **I have a** ~ **engagement** ho già (preso) un impegno; ~ **to doing** prima di fare.

previously ['priːvɪəslɪ] *adv* prima.

prewar ['priː'wɔː*] *adj* anteguerra *inv*.

prey [preɪ] *n* preda ♦ *vi*: **to** ~ **on** far preda di; **it was** ~**ing on his mind** gli rodeva la mente.

price [praɪs] *n* prezzo; (*BETTING: odds*) quotazione *f* ♦ *vt* (*goods*) fissare il prezzo di; valutare; **what is the** ~ **of ...?** quanto costa ...?; **to go up** *or* **rise in** ~ salire *or* aumentare di prezzo; **to put a** ~ **on sth** valutare *or* stimare qc; **he regained his freedom, but at a** ~ ha riconquistato la sua libertà, ma a caro prezzo; **what** ~ **his promises now?** (*BRIT*) a che valgono ora le sue promesse?; **to be** ~**d out of the market** (*article*) essere così caro da diventare invendibile; (*producer, nation*) non poter sostenere la concorrenza.

price control *n* controllo dei prezzi.

price-cutting ['praɪskʌtɪŋ] *n* riduzione *f* dei prezzi.

priceless ['praɪslɪs] *adj* di valore

inestimabile; (*col*: *amusing*) impagabile,
spassosissimo(a).
price list *n* listino (dei) prezzi.
price range *n* gamma di prezzi; **it's within
my** ~ rientra nelle mie possibilità.
price tag *n* cartellino del prezzo.
price war *n* guerra dei prezzi.
pricey ['praɪsɪ] *adj* (*col*) caruccio(a).
prick [prɪk] *n* puntura ♦ *vt* pungere; **to** ~ **up
one's ears** drizzare gli orecchi.
prickle ['prɪkl] *n* (*of plant*) spina; (*sensation*)
pizzicore *m*.
prickly ['prɪklɪ] *adj* spinoso(a); (*fig*: *person*)
permaloso(a); ~ **heat** sudamina.
pride [praɪd] *n* orgoglio; superbia ♦ *vt*: **to** ~
o.s. on essere orgoglioso(a) di; vantarsi
di; **to take (a)** ~ **in** tenere molto a; essere
orgoglioso di; **to take a** ~ **in doing** andare
orgoglioso di fare; **to have** ~ **of place**
(*BRIT*) essere al primo posto.
priest [priːst] *n* prete *m*, sacerdote *m*.
priestess ['priːstɪs] *n* sacerdotessa.
priesthood ['priːsthud] *n* sacerdozio.
prig [prɪg] *n*: **he's a** ~ è compiaciuto di se
stesso.
prim [prɪm] *adj* pudico(a); contegnoso(a).
primacy ['praɪməsɪ] *n* primato.
prima facie ['praɪmə'feɪʃɪ] *adj*: **to have a** ~
case (*LAW*) presentare una causa in
apparenza fondata.
primal ['praɪməl] *adj* primitivo(a).
primarily ['praɪmərɪlɪ] *adv* principalmente.
primary ['praɪmərɪ] *adj* primario(a); (*first in
importance*) primo(a) ♦ *n* (*US*: *election*)
primarie *fpl*; *see boxed note*.

---

primary colour *n* colore *m* fondamentale.
primary school *n* (*BRIT*) scuola
elementare; *see boxed note*.

---

primate *n* (*REL*: ['praɪmɪt], *ZOOL*: ['praɪmeɪt])
primate *m*.
prime [praɪm] *adj* primario(a),
fondamentale; (*excellent*) di prima qualità
♦ *n*: **in the** ~ **of life** nel fiore della vita ♦ *vt*
(*gun*) innescare; (*pump*) adescare; (*fig*)
mettere al corrente.
prime minister (PM) *n* primo ministro.
primer ['praɪmə*] *n* (*book*) testo
elementare; (*paint*) vernice *f* base *inv*.
prime time *n* (*RADIO*, *TV*) fascia di
massimo ascolto.
primeval [praɪ'miːvl] *adj* primitivo(a).
primitive ['prɪmɪtɪv] *adj* primitivo(a).
primrose ['prɪmrəuz] *n* primavera.
primus (stove) ® ['praɪməs-] *n* (*BRIT*)
fornello a petrolio.
prince [prɪns] *n* principe *m*.
prince charming *n* principe *m* azzurro.
princess [prɪn'sɛs] *n* principessa.
principal ['prɪnsɪpl] *adj* principale ♦ *n* (*of
school, college etc*) preside *m/f*; (*money*)
capitale *m*; (*in play*) protagonista *m/f*.
principality [prɪnsɪ'pælɪtɪ] *n* principato.
principally ['prɪnsɪplɪ] *adv* principalmente.
principle ['prɪnsɪpl] *n* principio;
in ~ in linea di principio; **on** ~ per
principio.
print [prɪnt] *n* (*mark*) impronta; (*letters*)
caratteri *mpl*; (*fabric*) tessuto stampato;
(*ART*, *PHOT*) stampa ♦ *vt* imprimere;
(*publish*) stampare, pubblicare; (*write in
capitals*) scrivere in stampatello; **out of** ~
esaurito(a).
▶**print out** *vt* (*COMPUT*) stampare.
printed circuit board (PCB) [prɪntɪd-] *n*
circuito stampato.
printed matter [prɪntɪd-] *n* stampe *fpl*.
printer ['prɪntə*] *n* tipografo; (*machine*)
stampante *m*.
printhead ['prɪnthɛd] *n* testa di stampa.
printing ['prɪntɪŋ] *n* stampa.
printing press *n* macchina tipografica.
print-out ['prɪntaut] *n* tabulato.
print wheel *n* margherita.
prior ['praɪə*] *adj* precedente ♦ *n* (*REL*)
priore *m*; ~ **to doing** prima di fare;
without ~ **notice** senza preavviso; **to
have a** ~ **claim to sth** avere un diritto di
precedenza su qc.
priority [praɪ'ɔrɪtɪ] *n* priorità *f inv*,
precedenza; **to have** *or* **take** ~ **over sth**
avere la precedenza su qc.
priory ['praɪərɪ] *n* monastero.
prise [praɪz] *vt*: **to** ~ **open** forzare.
prism ['prɪzəm] *n* prisma *m*.
prison ['prɪzn] *n* prigione *f*.
prison camp *n* campo di prigionia.

prisoner ['prɪznə*] *n* prigioniero/a; **to take sb ~ far** prigioniero qn; **the ~ at the bar** l'accusato, l'imputato; **~ of war** prigioniero/a di guerra.

prissy ['prɪsɪ] *adj* per benino.

pristine ['prɪstiːn] *adj* originario(a); intatto(a); puro(a).

privacy ['prɪvəsɪ] *n* solitudine *f*, intimità.

private ['praɪvɪt] *adj* privato(a); personale ♦ *n* soldato semplice; **"~"** (*on envelope*) "riservata"; **in ~** in privato; **in (his) ~ life** nella vita privata; **he is a very ~ person** è una persona molto riservata; **~ hearing** (*LAW*) udienza a porte chiuse; **to be in ~ practice** essere medico non convenzionato (con la mutua).

private enterprise *n* iniziativa privata.

private eye *n* investigatore *m* privato.

private limited company *n* (*BRIT*) società per azioni non quotata in Borsa.

privately ['praɪvɪtlɪ] *adv* in privato; (*within o.s.*) dentro di sé.

private parts *npl* (*ANAT*) parti *fpl* intime.

private property *n* proprietà privata.

private school *n* scuola privata.

privation [praɪ'veɪʃən] *n* (*state*) privazione *f*; (*hardship*) privazioni *fpl*, stenti *mpl*.

privatize ['praɪvɪtaɪz] *vt* privatizzare.

privet ['prɪvɪt] *n* ligustro.

privilege ['prɪvɪlɪdʒ] *n* privilegio.

privileged ['prɪvɪlɪdʒd] *adj* privilegiato(a); **to be ~ to do sth** avere il privilegio *or* l'onore di fare qc.

privy ['prɪvɪ] *adj*: **to be ~ to** essere al corrente di.

Privy Council *n* (*BRIT*) Consiglio della Corona; *see boxed note.*

PRIVY COUNCIL

Il **Privy Council**, *un gruppo di consiglieri del re, era il principale organo di governo durante il regno dei Tudor e degli Stuart. Col tempo ha perso la sua importanza e oggi è un organo senza potere effettivo formato da ministri e altre personalità politiche ed ecclesiastiche.*

Privy Councillor *n* (*BRIT*) Consigliere *m* della Corona.

prize [praɪz] *n* premio ♦ *adj* (*example, idiot*) perfetto(a); (*bull, novel*) premiato(a) ♦ *vt* apprezzare, pregiare.

prize-fighter ['praɪzfaɪtə*] *n* pugile *m* (*che si batte per conquistare un premio*).

prize giving *n* premiazione *f*.

prize money *n* soldi *mpl* del premio.

prizewinner ['praɪzwɪnə*] *n* premiato/a.

prizewinning ['praɪzwɪnɪŋ] *adj* vincente;

(*novel, essay etc*) premiato(a).

PRO *n abbr* = **public relations officer.**

pro [prəʊ] *n* (*SPORT*) professionista *m/f*; **the ~s and cons** il pro e il contro.

pro- [prəʊ] *prefix* (*in favour of*) filo...; **~Soviet** *adj* filosovietico(a).

pro-active [prəʊ'æktɪv] *adj*: **to be ~** agire d'iniziativa.

probability [prɔbə'bɪlɪtɪ] *n* probabilità *f inv*; **in all ~** con ogni probabilità.

probable ['prɔbəbl] *adj* probabile; **it is ~/ hardly ~ that ...** è probabile/poco probabile che ... + *sub.*

probably ['prɔbəblɪ] *adv* probabilmente.

probate ['prəʊbɪt] *n* (*LAW*) omologazione *f* (*di un testamento*).

probation [prə'beɪʃən] *n* (*in employment*) periodo di prova; (*LAW*) libertà vigilata; (*REL*) probandato; **on ~** (*employee*) in prova; (*LAW*) in libertà vigilata.

probationary [prəʊ'beɪʃənərɪ] *adj*: **~ period** periodo di prova.

probe [prəʊb] *n* (*MED, SPACE*) sonda; (*enquiry*) indagine *f*, investigazione *f* ♦ *vt* sondare, esplorare; indagare.

probity ['prəʊbɪtɪ] *n* probità.

problem ['prɔbləm] *n* problema *m*; **to have ~s with the car** avere dei problemi con la macchina; **what's the ~?** che cosa c'è?; **I had no ~ in finding her** non mi è stato difficile trovarla; **no ~!** ma certamente!, non c'è problema!

problematic [prɔblə'mætɪk] *adj* problematico(a).

problem-solving ['prɔbləmsɔlvɪŋ] *n* risoluzione *f* di problemi.

procedure [prə'siːdʒə*] *n* (*ADMIN, LAW*) procedura; (*method*) metodo.

proceed [prə'siːd] *vi* (*go forward*) avanzare, andare avanti; (*go about it*) procedere; (*continue*): **to ~ (with)** continuare; **to ~ to** andare a; passare a; **to ~ to do** mettersi a fare; **to ~ against sb** (*LAW*) procedere contro qn; **I am not sure how to ~** non so bene come fare.

proceedings [prə'siːdɪŋz] *npl* misure *fpl*; (*LAW*) procedimento; (*meeting*) riunione *f*; (*records*) rendiconti *mpl*; atti *mpl*.

proceeds ['prəʊsiːdz] *npl* profitto, incasso.

process ['prəʊsɛs] *n* processo; (*method*) metodo, sistema *m* ♦ *vt* trattare; (*information*) elaborare ♦ *vi* [prə'sɛs] (*BRIT formal: go in procession*) sfilare, procedere in corteo; **we are in the ~ of moving to ...** stiamo per trasferirci a ....

processed cheese, (*US*) **process cheese** *n* formaggio fuso.

processing ['prəʊsɛsɪŋ] *n* trattamento;

elaborazione f.
procession [prə'sɛʃən] n processione f,
corteo; **funeral** ~ corteo funebre.
pro-choice [prəu'tʃɔɪs] adj per la libertà di
scelta di gravidanza.
proclaim [prə'kleɪm] vt proclamare,
dichiarare.
proclamation [prɔklə'meɪʃən] n
proclamazione f.
proclivity [prə'klɪvɪtɪ] n tendenza,
propensione f.
procrastination [prəukræstɪ'neɪʃən] n
procrastinazione f.
procreation [prəukrɪ'eɪʃən] n procreazione
f.
Procurator Fiscal ['prɔkjureɪtə-] n
(Scottish) procuratore m.
procure [prə'kjuə*] vt (for o.s.) procurarsi;
(for sb) procurare.
procurement [prə'kjuəmənt] n
approvvigionamento.
prod [prɔd] vt dare un colpetto a ♦ n (push,
jab) colpetto.
prodigal ['prɔdɪgl] adj prodigo(a).
prodigious [prə'dɪdʒəs] adj prodigioso(a).
prodigy ['prɔdɪdʒɪ] n prodigio.
produce n ['prɔdjuːs] (AGR) prodotto,
prodotti mpl ♦ vt [prə'djuːs] produrre; (to
show) esibire, mostrare; (proof of identity)
produrre, fornire; (cause) cagionare,
causare; (THEAT) mettere in scena.
producer [prə'djuːsə*] n (THEAT) direttore/
trice; (AGR, CINE) produttore m.
product ['prɔdʌkt] n prodotto.
production [prə'dʌkʃən] n produzione f;
(THEAT) messa in scena; **to put into** ~
mettere in produzione.
production agreement n (US) accordo
sui tempi di produzione.
production line n catena di lavorazione.
production manager n production
manager m inv, direttore m della
produzione.
productive [prə'dʌktɪv] adj produttivo(a).
productivity [prɔdʌk'tɪvɪtɪ] n produttività.
productivity agreement n (BRIT) accordo
sui tempi di produzione.
productivity bonus n premio di
produzione.
Prof. abbr (= professor) Prof.
profane [prə'feɪn] adj profano(a); (language)
empio(a).
profess [prə'fɛs] vt professare; **I do not** ~
to be an expert non pretendo di essere un
esperto.
professed [prə'fɛst] adj (self-declared)
dichiarato(a).
profession [prə'fɛʃən] n professione f; **the**

~**s** le professioni liberali.
professional [prə'fɛʃənl] n (SPORT)
professionista m/f ♦ adj professionale;
(work) da professionista; **he's a** ~ **man** è
un professionista; **to take** ~ **advice**
consultare un esperto.
professionalism [prə'fɛʃnəlɪzəm] n
professionismo.
professionally [prə'fɛʃnəlɪ] adv
professionalmente, in modo
professionale; (SPORT: play) come
professionista; **I only know him** ~ con lui
ho solo rapporti di lavoro.
professor [prə'fɛsə*] n professore m
(titolare di una cattedra); (US: teacher)
professore/essa.
professorship [prə'fɛsəʃɪp] n cattedra.
proffer ['prɔfə*] vt (remark) profferire;
(apologies) porgere, presentare; (one's
hand) porgere.
proficiency [prə'fɪʃənsɪ] n competenza,
abilità.
proficient [prə'fɪʃənt] adj competente,
abile.
profile ['prəufaɪl] n profilo; **to keep a low** ~
(fig) cercare di passare inosservato or di
non farsi notare troppo; **to maintain a
high** ~ mettersi in mostra.
profit ['prɔfɪt] n profitto; beneficio ♦ vi: **to** ~
(**by** or **from**) approfittare (di); ~ **and loss
account** conto perdite e profitti; **to make
a** ~ realizzare un profitto; **to sell sth at a**
~ vendere qc con un utile.
profitability [prɔfɪtə'bɪlɪtɪ] n redditività.
profitable ['prɔfɪtəbl] adj redditizio(a); (fig:
beneficial) vantaggioso(a); (: meeting, visit)
fruttuoso(a).
profit centre n centro di profitto.
profiteering [prɔfɪ'tɪərɪŋ] n (pej) affarismo.
profit-making ['prɔfɪtmeɪkɪŋ] adj a scopo di
lucro.
profit margin n margine m di profitto.
profit-sharing ['prɔfɪtʃɛərɪŋ] n
compartecipazione f agli utili.
profits tax n (BRIT) imposta sugli utili.
profligate ['prɔflɪgɪt] adj (dissolute:
behaviour) dissipato(a); (: person)
debosciato(a); (extravagant): **he's very** ~
with his money è uno che sperpera i suoi
soldi.
pro forma ['prəu'fɔːmə] adv: ~ **invoice**
fattura proforma.
profound [prə'faund] adj profondo(a).
profuse [prə'fjuːs] adj infinito(a),
abbondante.
profusely [prə'fjuːslɪ] adv con grande
effusione.
profusion [prə'fjuːʒən] n profusione f,

abbondanza.

progeny ['prɔdʒɪnɪ] *n* progenie *f*; discendenti *mpl.*

programme, (*US*) **program** ['prəugræm] *n* programma *m* ♦ *vt* programmare.

program(m)er ['prəugræmə*] *n* programmatore/trice.

program(m)ing ['prəugræmɪŋ] *n* programmazione *f.*

program(m)ing language *n* linguaggio di programmazione.

progress *n* ['prəugrɛs] progresso ♦ *vi* [prə'grɛs] (*go forward*) avanzare, procedere; (*in time*) procedere; (*also*: **make ~**) far progressi; **in ~** in corso.

progression [prə'grɛʃən] *n* progressione *f.*

progressive [prə'grɛsɪv] *adj* progressivo(a); (*person*) progressista.

progressively [prə'grɛsɪvlɪ] *adv* progressivamente.

progress report *n* (*MED*) bollettino medico; (*ADMIN*) rendiconto dei lavori.

prohibit [prə'hɪbɪt] *vt* proibire, vietare; **to ~ sb from doing sth** vietare *or* proibire a qn di fare qc; "**smoking ~ed**" "vietato fumare".

prohibition [prəuɪ'bɪʃən] *n* (*US*) proibizionismo.

prohibitive [prə'hɪbɪtɪv] *adj* (*price etc*) proibitivo(a).

project *n* ['prɔdʒɛkt] (*plan*) piano; (*venture*) progetto; (*SCOL*) studio, ricerca ♦ *vb* [prə'dʒɛkt] *vt* proiettare ♦ *vi* (*stick out*) sporgere.

projectile [prə'dʒɛktaɪl] *n* proiettile *m.*

projection [prə'dʒɛkʃən] *n* proiezione *f*; sporgenza.

projectionist [prə'dʒɛkʃənɪst] *n* (*CINE*) proiezionista *m/f.*

projection room *n* (*CINE*) cabina *or* sala di proiezione.

projector [prə'dʒɛktə*] *n* proiettore *m.*

proletarian [prəulɪ'tɛərɪən] *adj, n* proletario(a).

proletariat [prəulɪ'tɛərɪət] *n* proletariato.

pro-life [prəu'laɪf] *adj* per il diritto alla vita.

proliferate [prə'lɪfəreɪt] *vi* proliferare.

proliferation [prəlɪfə'reɪʃən] *n* proliferazione *f.*

prolific [prə'lɪfɪk] *adj* prolifico(a).

prologue, (*US*) **prolog** ['prəulɔg] *n* prologo.

prolong [prə'lɔŋ] *vt* prolungare.

prom [prɔm] *n abbr* = **promenade, promenade concert;** (*US: ball*) ballo studentesco; *see boxed note.*

PROM

In Gran Bretagna i **Prom** (= *promenade concert) sono concerti di musica classica, i più noti dei quali sono quelli eseguiti nella Royal Albert Hall a Londra. Prendono il nome dal fatto che in origine il pubblico li ascoltava stando in piedi o passeggiando. Negli Stati Uniti, invece, con* **prom** *si intende il ballo studentesco di un'università o di un college.*

---

promenade [prɔmə'nɑːd] *n* (*by sea*) lungomare *m.*

promenade concert *n* concerto (*con posti in piedi*).

promenade deck *n* (*NAUT*) ponte *m* di passeggiata.

prominence ['prɔmɪnəns] *n* prominenza; importanza.

prominent ['prɔmɪnənt] *adj* (*standing out*) prominente; (*important*) importante; **he is ~ in the field of ...** è un'autorità nel campo di ....

prominently ['prɔmɪnəntlɪ] *adv* (*display, set*) ben in vista; **he figured ~ in the case** ha avuto una parte di primo piano nella faccenda.

promiscuity [prɔmɪs'kjuːɪtɪ] *n* (*sexual*) rapporti *mpl* multipli.

promiscuous [prə'mɪskjuəs] *adj* (*sexually*) di facili costumi.

promise ['prɔmɪs] *n* promessa ♦ *vt, vi* promettere; **to make sb a ~** fare una promessa a qn; **a young man of ~** un giovane promettente; **to ~ (sb) to do sth** promettere (a qn) di fare qc.

promising ['prɔmɪsɪŋ] *adj* promettente.

promissory note ['prɔmɪsərɪ-] *n* pagherò *m inv.*

promontory ['prɔməntrɪ] *n* promontorio.

promote [prə'məut] *vt* promuovere; (*venture, event*) organizzare; (*product*) lanciare, reclamizzare; **the team was ~d to the second division** (*BRIT FOOTBALL*) la squadra è stata promossa in serie B.

promoter [prə'məutə*] *n* (*of sporting event*) organizzatore/trice; (*of cause etc*) sostenitore/trice.

promotion [prə'məuʃən] *n* promozione *f.*

prompt [prɔmpt] *adj* rapido(a), svelto(a); puntuale; (*reply*) sollecito(a) ♦ *adv* (*punctually*) in punto ♦ *n* (*COMPUT*) guida ♦ *vt* incitare; provocare; (*THEAT*) suggerire a; **at 8 o'clock ~** alle 8 in punto; **to ~ sb to do** spingere qn a fare.

prompter ['prɔmptə*] *n* (*THEAT*) suggeritore *m.*

promptly ['promptlɪ] adv prontamente; puntualmente.

promptness ['promptnɪs] n prontezza; puntualità.

prone [prəun] adj (lying) prono(a); ~ **to** propenso(a) a, incline a; **to be** ~ **to illness** essere soggetto(a) a malattie; **she is** ~ **to burst into tears if** ... può facilmente scoppiare in lacrime se ....

prong [prɒŋ] n rebbio, punta.

pronoun ['prəunaun] n pronome m.

pronounce [prə'nauns] vt pronunziare ♦ vi: **to** ~ **(up)on** pronunziare su; **they** ~**d him unfit to drive** lo hanno dichiarato inabile alla guida.

pronounced [prə'naunst] adj (marked) spiccato(a).

pronouncement [prə'naunsmənt] n dichiarazione f.

pronunciation [prənʌnsɪ'eɪʃən] n pronunzia.

proof [pruːf] n prova; (of book) bozza; (PHOT) provino; (of alcohol): **70%** ~ ≈ 40° in volume ♦ vt (tent, anorak) impermeabilizzare ♦ adj: ~ **against** a prova di.

proofreader ['pruːfriːdə*] n correttore/ trice di bozze.

prop [prɒp] n sostegno, appoggio ♦ vt (also: ~ **up**) sostenere, appoggiare; (lean): **to** ~ **sth against** appoggiare qc contro or a.

Prop. abbr (COMM) = **proprietor**.

propaganda [prɒpə'gændə] n propaganda.

propagation [prɒpə'geɪʃən] n propagazione f.

propel [prə'pɛl] vt spingere (in avanti), muovere.

propeller [prə'pɛlə*] n elica.

propelling pencil [prə'pɛlɪŋ-] n (BRIT) matita a mina.

propensity [prə'pɛnsɪtɪ] n tendenza.

proper ['prɒpə*] adj (suited, right) adatto(a), appropriato(a); (seemly) decente; (authentic) vero(a); (col: real) n + vero(a) e proprio(a); **to go through the** ~ **channels** (ADMIN) seguire la regolare procedura.

properly ['prɒpəlɪ] adv decentemente; (really, thoroughly) veramente.

proper noun n nome m proprio.

property ['prɒpətɪ] n (things owned) beni mpl; (land, building, CHEM etc) proprietà f inv.

property developer n (BRIT) costruttore m edile.

property owner n proprietario/a.

property tax n imposta patrimoniale.

prophecy ['prɒfɪsɪ] n profezia.

prophesy ['prɒfɪsaɪ] vt predire, profetizzare.

prophet ['prɒfɪt] n profeta m.

prophetic [prə'fɛtɪk] adj profetico(a).

proportion [prə'pɔːʃən] n proporzione f; (share) parte f ♦ vt proporzionare, commisurare; **to be in/out of** ~ **to** or **with sth** essere in proporzione/sproporzionato rispetto a qc; **to see sth in** ~(fig) dare il giusto peso a qc.

proportional [prə'pɔːʃənl] adj proporzionale.

proportional representation (PR) n rappresentanza proporzionale.

proportionate [prə'pɔːʃənɪt] adj proporzionato(a).

proposal [prə'pəuzl] n proposta; (plan) progetto; (of marriage) proposta di matrimonio.

propose [prə'pəuz] vt proporre, suggerire ♦ vi fare una proposta di matrimonio; **to** ~ **to do** proporsi di fare, aver l'intenzione di fare.

proposer [prə'pəuzə*] n (BRIT: of motion) proponente m/f.

proposition [prɒpə'zɪʃən] n proposizione f; (proposal) proposta; **to make sb a** ~ proporre qualcosa a qn.

propound [prə'paund] vt proporre, presentare.

proprietary [prə'praɪətərɪ] adj: ~ **article** prodotto con marchio deposited; ~ **brand** marchio di fabbrica.

proprietor [prə'praɪətə*] n proprietario/a.

propriety [prə'praɪətɪ] n (seemliness) decoro, rispetto delle convenienze sociali.

propulsion [prə'pʌlʃən] n propulsione f.

pro rata [prəu'rɑːtə] adv in proporzione.

prosaic [prəu'zeɪɪk] adj prosaico(a).

Pros. Atty. abbr (US) = **prosecuting attorney**.

proscribe [prə'skraɪb] vt proscrivere.

prose [prəuz] n prosa; (SCOL: translation) traduzione f dalla madrelingua.

prosecute ['prɒsɪkjuːt] vt intentare azione contro.

prosecuting attorney ['prɒsɪkjuːtɪŋ-] n (US) ≈ procuratore m.

prosecution [prɒsɪ'kjuːʃən] n (LAW) azione f giudiziaria; (accusing side) accusa.

prosecutor ['prɒsɪkjuːtə*] n (also: public ~) ≈ procuratore m della Repubblica.

prospect n ['prɒspɛkt] prospettiva; (hope) speranza ♦ vb [prə'spɛkt] vt esplorare ♦ vi: **to** ~ **for gold** cercare l'oro; **there is every** ~ **of an early victory** tutto lascia prevedere una rapida vittoria; see also **prospects**.

prospecting [prə'spɛktɪŋ] n prospezione f.

prospective [prə'spɛktɪv] *adj* (*buyer*) probabile; (*legislation, son-in-law*) futuro(a).
prospector [prə'spɛktə*] *n* prospettore *m*; **gold** ~ cercatore *m* d'oro.
prospects ['prɔspɛkts] *npl* (*for work etc*) prospettive *fpl*.
prospectus [prə'spɛktəs] *n* prospetto, programma *m*.
prosper ['prɔspə*] *vi* prosperare.
prosperity [prɔ'spɛrɪtɪ] *n* prosperità.
prosperous ['prɔspərəs] *adj* prospero(a).
prostate ['prɔsteɪt] *n* (*also:* ~ **gland**) prostata, ghiandola prostatica.
prostitute ['prɔstɪtjuːt] *n* prostituta; **male** ~ uomo che si prostituisce.
prostitution [prɔstɪ'tjuːʃən] *n* prostituzione *f*.
prostrate *adj* ['prɔstreɪt] prostrato(a) ♦ *vt* [prɔ'streɪt]: **to** ~ **o.s.** (*before sb*) prostrarsi.
protagonist [prə'tægənɪst] *n* protagonista *m/f*.
protect [prə'tɛkt] *vt* proteggere, salvaguardare.
protection [prə'tɛkʃən] *n* protezione *f*; **to be under sb's** ~ essere sotto la protezione di qn.
protectionism [prə'tɛkʃənɪzəm] *n* protezionismo.
protection racket *n* racket *m inv*.
protective [prə'tɛktɪv] *adj* protettivo(a); ~ **custody** (*LAW*) protezione *f*.
protector [prə'tɛktə*] *n* protettore/trice.
protégé ['prəutɪʒeɪ] *n* protetto.
protégée ['prəutɪʒeɪ] *n* protetta.
protein ['prəutiːn] *n* proteina.
pro tem [prəu'tɛm] *adv abbr* (= *pro tempore*: *for the time being*) pro tempore.
protest *n* ['prəutɛst] protesta ♦ *vt, vi* [prə'tɛst] protestare; **to do sth under** ~ fare qc protestando; **to** ~ **against/about** protestare contro/per.
Protestant ['prɔtɪstənt] *adj, n* protestante (*m/f*).
protester, protestor [prə'tɛstə*] *n* (*in demonstration*) dimostrante *m/f*.
protest march *n* marcia di protesta.
protocol ['prəutəkɔl] *n* protocollo.
prototype ['prəutətaɪp] *n* prototipo.
protracted [prə'træktɪd] *adj* tirato(a) per le lunghe.
protractor [prə'træktə*] *n* (*GEOM*) goniometro.
protrude [prə'truːd] *vi* sporgere.
protuberance [prə'tjuːbərəns] *n* sporgenza.
proud [praud] *adj* fiero(a), orgoglioso(a); (*pej*) superbo(a); **to be** ~ **to do sth** essere onorato(a) di fare qc; **to do sb** ~ non far

mancare nulla a qn; **to do o.s.** ~ trattarsi bene.
proudly ['praudlɪ] *adv* con orgoglio, fieramente.
prove [pruːv] *vt* provare, dimostrare ♦ *vi*: **to** ~ **correct** *etc* risultare vero(a) *etc*; **to** ~ **o.s.** mostrare le proprie capacità; **to** ~ **o.s./itself (to be) useful** *etc* mostrarsi *or* rivelarsi utile *etc*; **he was** ~**d right in the end** alla fine i fatti gli hanno dato ragione.
Provence [prɔvɑ̃s] *n* Provenza.
proverb ['prɔvəːb] *n* proverbio.
proverbial [prə'vəːbɪəl] *adj* proverbiale.
provide [prə'vaɪd] *vt* fornire, provvedere; **to** ~ **sb with sth** fornire *or* provvedere qn di qc; **to be** ~**d with** essere dotato *or* munito di.
▶**provide for** *vt fus* provvedere a.
provided [prə'vaɪdɪd] *conj*: ~ **(that)** purché + *sub*, a condizione che + *sub*.
Providence ['prɔvɪdəns] *n* Provvidenza.
providing [prə'vaɪdɪŋ] *conj* purché + *sub*, a condizione che + *sub*.
province ['prɔvɪns] *n* provincia.
provincial [prə'vɪnʃəl] *adj* provinciale.
provision [prə'vɪʒən] *n* (*supply*) riserva; (*supplying*) provvista; rifornimento; (*stipulation*) condizione *f*; ~**s** *npl* (*food*) provviste *fpl*; **to make** ~ **for** (*one's family, future*) pensare a; **there's no** ~ **for this in the contract** il contratto non lo prevede.
provisional [prə'vɪʒənl] *adj* provvisorio(a) ♦ *n*: **P**~ (*Irish POL*) provisional *m inv*.
provisional licence *n* (*BRIT AUT*) ≈ foglio *m* rosa *inv*.
provisionally [prə'vɪʒnəlɪ] *adv* provvisoriamente; (*appoint*) a titolo provvisorio.
proviso [prə'vaɪzəu] *n* condizione *f*; **with the** ~ **that** a condizione che + *sub*, a patto che + *sub*.
Provo ['prɔvəu] *n abbr* (*col*) = **Provisional**.
provocation [prɔvə'keɪʃən] *n* provocazione *f*.
provocative [prə'vɔkətɪv] *adj* (*aggressive*) provocatorio(a); (*thought-provoking*) stimolante; (*seductive*) provocante.
provoke [prə'vəuk] *vt* provocare; incitare; **to** ~ **sb to sth/to do** *or* **into doing sth** spingere qn a qc/a fare qc.
provoking [prə'vəukɪŋ] *adj* irritante, esasperante.
provost ['prɔvəst] *n* (*BRIT: of university*) rettore *m*; (*Scottish*) sindaco.
prow [prau] *n* prua.
prowess ['prauɪs] *n* prodezza; **his** ~ **as a footballer** le sue capacità di calciatore.

prowl [praul] *vi* (*also*: ~ **about**, ~ **around**) aggirarsi furtivamente ♦ *n*: **on the** ~ **in** cerca di preda.

prowler ['praulə*] *n* tipo sospetto (*che s'aggira con l'intenzione di rubare, aggredire etc*).

proximity [prɔk'sɪmɪtɪ] *n* prossimità.

proxy ['prɔksɪ] *n* procura; **by** ~ per procura.

PRP *n abbr* (= *performance related pay*) retribuzione *f* commensurata al rendimento.

prude [pruːd] *n* puritano/a.

prudence ['pruːdns] *n* prudenza.

prudent ['pruːdnt] *adj* prudente.

prudish ['pruːdɪʃ] *adj* puritano(a).

prune [pruːn] *n* prugna secca ♦ *vt* potare.

pry [praɪ] *vi*: **to** ~ **into** ficcare il naso in.

PS *n abbr* (= *postscript*) P.S.

psalm [saːm] *n* salmo.

PSAT *n abbr* (*US*) = *Preliminary Scholastic Aptitude Test*.

PSBR *n abbr* (*BRIT* = *public sector borrowing requirement*) *fabbisogno di prestiti per il settore pubblico*.

pseud ['sjuːd] *n* (*BRIT col: intellectually*) intellettualoide *m/f*; (: *socially*) snob *m/f inv*.

pseudo- ['sjuːdəu] *prefix* pseudo....

pseudonym ['sjuːdənɪm] *n* pseudonimo.

PST *abbr* (*US*: = *Pacific Standard Time*) *ora invernale del Pacifico*.

PSV *n abbr* (*BRIT*) *see* **public service vehicle**.

psyche ['saɪkɪ] *n* psiche *f*.

psychedelic [saɪkɪ'delɪk] *adj* psichedelico(a).

psychiatric [saɪkɪ'ætrɪk] *adj* psichiatrico(a).

psychiatrist [saɪ'kaɪətrɪst] *n* psichiatra *m/f*.

psychiatry [saɪ'kaɪətrɪ] *n* psichiatria.

psychic ['saɪkɪk] *adj* (*also*: ~**al**) psichico(a); (*person*) dotato(a) di qualità telepatiche.

psycho ['saɪkəu] *n* (*col*) folle *m/f*.

psychoanalyse [saɪkəu'ænəlaɪz] *vt* psicanalizzare.

psychoanalysis, *pl* **-ses** [saɪkəuə'nælɪsɪs, -siːz] *n* psicanalisi *f inv*.

psychoanalyst [saɪkəu'ænəlɪst] *n* psicanalista *m/f*.

psychological [saɪkə'lɔdʒɪkl] *adj* psicologico(a).

psychologist [saɪ'kɔlədʒɪst] *n* psicologo/a.

psychology [saɪ'kɔlədʒɪ] *n* psicologia.

psychopath ['saɪkəupæθ] *n* psicopatico/a.

psychosis, *pl* **psychoses** [saɪ'kəusɪs, -siːz] *n* psicosi *f inv*.

psychosomatic [saɪkəusə'mætɪk] *adj* psicosomatico(a).

psychotherapy [saɪkəu'θerəpɪ] *n* psicoterapia.

psychotic [saɪ'kɔtɪk] *adj*, *n* psicotico(a).

PT *n abbr* (*BRIT*: = *physical training*) ed. fisica.

pt *abbr* (= *pint*; *point*) pt.

Pt. *abbr* (*in place names*: = *Point*) Pt.

PTA *n abbr* (= *Parent-Teacher Association*) *associazione genitori e insegnanti*.

Pte. *abbr* (*BRIT MIL*) = **private**.

PTO *abbr* (= *please turn over*) v.r. (= *vedi retro*).

PTV *n abbr* (*US*) = *pay television*, *public television*.

pub [pʌb] *n abbr* (= *public house*) pub *m inv*; *see boxed note*.

PUB

In Gran Bretagna e in Irlanda i **pub** *sono locali dove vengono servite bibite alcoliche ed analcoliche e dove è anche possibile mangiare. Sono punti di ritrovo dove spesso si può giocare a biliardo, a freccette o guardare la televisione. Le leggi che regolano la vendita degli alcolici sono molto severe in Gran Bretagna e quindi gli orari di apertura e di chiusura vengono osservati scrupolosamente.*

---

pub crawl *n*: **to go on a** ~ (*BRIT col*) fare il giro dei pub.

puberty ['pjuːbətɪ] *n* pubertà.

pubic ['pjuːbɪk] *adj* pubico(a), del pube.

public ['pʌblɪk] *adj* pubblico(a) ♦ *n* pubblico; **in** ~ in pubblico; **the general** ~ il pubblico; **to make sth** ~ render noto *or* di pubblico dominio qc; **to be** ~ **knowledge** essere di dominio pubblico; **to go** ~ (*COMM*) emettere le azioni sul mercato.

public address system (PA) *n* impianto di amplificazione.

publican ['pʌblɪkən] *n* (*BRIT*) gestore *m* (*or* proprietario) di un pub.

publication [pʌblɪ'keɪʃən] *n* pubblicazione *f*.

public company *n* ≈ società *f inv* per azioni (*costituita tramite pubblica sottoscrizione*).

public convenience *n* (*BRIT*) gabinetti *mpl*.

public holiday *n* (*BRIT*) giorno festivo, festa nazionale.

public house *n* (*BRIT*) pub *m inv*.

publicity [pʌb'lɪsɪtɪ] *n* pubblicità.

publicize ['pʌblɪsaɪz] *vt* fare (della) pubblicità a, reclamizzare.

public limited company (plc) *n* ≈ società per azioni a responsabilità limitata (*quotata in Borsa*).

publicly ['pʌblɪklɪ] *adv* pubblicamente.

public opinion *n* opinione *f* pubblica.

public ownership *n* proprietà pubblica *or*

sociale; **to be taken into** ~ essere statalizzato(a).
public prosecutor *n* pubblico ministero; ~**'s office** ufficio del pubblico ministero.
public relations *n* pubbliche relazioni *fpl*.
public relations officer *n* addetto/a alle pubbliche relazioni.
public school *n* (*BRIT*) scuola privata; (*US*) scuola statale; *see boxed note.*

PUBLIC SCHOOL

*In Inghilterra le **public school** sono scuole o collegi privati di istruzione secondaria, spesso di un certo prestigio. In Scozia e negli Stati Uniti, invece, le **public school** sono scuole pubbliche gratuite amministrate dallo stato.*

---

public sector *n* settore *m* pubblico.
public service vehicle (PSV) *n* (*BRIT*) mezzo pubblico.
public-spirited [pʌblɪk'spɪrɪtɪd] *adj* che ha senso civico.
public transport, (*US*) **public transportation** *n* mezzi *mpl* pubblici.
public utility *n* servizio pubblico.
public works *npl* lavori *mpl* pubblici.
publish ['pʌblɪʃ] *vt* pubblicare.
publisher ['pʌblɪʃə*] *n* editore *m*; (*firm*) casa editrice.
publishing ['pʌblɪʃɪŋ] *n* (*industry*) editoria; (*of a book*) pubblicazione *f*.
publishing company *n* casa *or* società editrice.
puce [pjuːs] *adj* color pulce *inv*.
puck [pʌk] *n* (*ICE HOCKEY*) disco.
pucker ['pʌkə*] *vt* corrugare.
pudding ['pudɪŋ] *n* budino; (*dessert*) dolce *m*; **black** ~, (*US*) **blood** ~ sanguinaccio; **rice** ~ budino di riso.
puddle ['pʌdl] *n* pozza, pozzanghera.
puerile ['pjuərail] *adj* puerile.
Puerto Rico ['pwəːtəu'riːkəu] *n* Portorico.
puff [pʌf] *n* sbuffo; (*also*: **powder** ~) piumino ♦ *vt* (*also*: ~ **out**: *sails, cheeks*) gonfiare ♦ *vi* uscire a sbuffi; (*pant*) ansare; **to** ~ **out smoke** mandar fuori sbuffi di fumo.
puffed [pʌft] *adj* (*col: out of breath*) senza fiato.
puffin ['pʌfɪn] *n* puffino.
puff pastry, (*US*) **puff paste** *n* pasta sfoglia.
puffy ['pʌfɪ] *adj* gonfio(a).
pugnacious [pʌg'neɪʃəs] *adj* combattivo(a).
pull [pul] *n* (*tug*) strattone *m*, tirata; (*of moon, magnet, the sea etc*) attrazione *f*; (*fig*) influenza ♦ *vt* tirare; (*muscle*)

strappare, farsi uno strappo a ♦ *vi* tirare; **to give sth a** ~ tirare su qc; **to** ~ **a face** fare una smorfia; **to** ~ **to pieces** fare a pezzi; **to** ~ **one's punches** (*BOXING*) risparmiare l'avversario; **not to** ~ **one's punches** (*fig*) non avere peli sulla lingua; **to** ~ **one's weight** dare il proprio contributo; **to** ~ **o.s. together** ricomporsi, riprendersi; **to** ~ **sb's leg** prendere in giro qn; **to** ~ **strings (for sb)** muovere qualche pedina (per qn).
▶**pull about** *vt* (*BRIT: handle roughly: object*) strapazzare; (: *person*) malmenare.
▶**pull apart** *vt* (*break*) fare a pezzi.
▶**pull down** *vt* (*house*) demolire; (*tree*) abbattere.
▶**pull in** *vi* (*AUT: at the kerb*) accostarsi; (*RAIL*) entrare in stazione.
▶**pull off** *vt* (*deal etc*) portare a compimento.
▶**pull out** *vi* partire; (*withdraw*) ritirarsi; (*AUT: come out of line*) spostarsi sulla mezzeria ♦ *vt* staccare; far uscire; (*withdraw*) ritirare.
▶**pull over** *vi* (*AUT*) accostare.
▶**pull round** *vi* (*unconscious person*) rinvenire; (*sick person*) ristabilirsi.
▶**pull through** *vi* farcela.
▶**pull up** *vi* (*stop*) fermarsi ♦ *vt* (*uproot*) sradicare; (*stop*) fermare.
pulley ['pulɪ] *n* puleggia, carrucola.
pull-out ['pulaut] *n* inserto ♦ *cpd* staccabile.
pullover ['puləuvə*] *n* pullover *m inv*.
pulp [pʌlp] *n* (*of fruit*) polpa; (*for paper*) pasta per carta; (*magazines, books*) stampa di qualità e di tono scadenti; **to reduce sth to** ~ spappolare qc.
pulpit ['pulpɪt] *n* pulpito.
pulsate [pʌl'seɪt] *vi* battere, palpitare.
pulse [pʌls] *n* polso; **to feel** *or* **take sb's** ~ sentire *or* tastare il polso a qn.
pulses ['pʌlsəz] *npl* (*CULIN*) legumi *mpl*.
pulverize ['pʌlvəraɪz] *vt* polverizzare.
puma ['pjuːmə] *n* puma *m inv*.
pumice (stone) ['pʌmɪs-] *n* (pietra) pomice *f*.
pummel ['pʌml] *vt* dare pugni a.
pump [pʌmp] *n* pompa; (*shoe*) scarpetta ♦ *vt* pompare; (*fig: col*) far parlare; **to** ~ **sb for information** cercare di strappare delle informazioni a qn.
▶**pump up** *vt* gonfiare.
pumpkin ['pʌmpkɪn] *n* zucca.
pun [pʌn] *n* gioco di parole.
punch [pʌntʃ] *n* (*blow*) pugno; (*fig: force*) forza; (*tool*) punzone *m*; (*drink*) ponce *m* ♦ *vt* (*hit*): **to** ~ **sb/sth** dare un pugno a qn/qc; **to** ~ **a hole (in)** fare un buco (in).

▶**punch in** vi (US) timbrare il cartellino (all'entrata).

▶**punch out** vi (US) timbrare il cartellino (all'uscita).

punch-drunk ['pʌntʃdrʌŋk] adj (BRIT) stordito(a).

punch(ed) card ['pʌntʃ(t)-] n scheda perforata.

punch line n (of joke) battuta finale.

punch-up ['pʌntʃʌp] n (BRIT col) rissa.

punctual ['pʌŋktjuəl] adj puntuale.

punctuality [pʌŋktju'ælɪtɪ] n puntualità.

punctually [pʌŋktjuəlɪ] adv puntualmente; **it will start ~ at 6** comincerà alle 6 precise or in punto.

punctuate ['pʌŋktjueɪt] vt punteggiare.

punctuation [pʌŋktju'eɪʃən] n interpunzione f, punteggiatura.

punctuation mark n segno d'interpunzione.

puncture ['pʌŋktʃə*] n (BRIT) foratura ♦ vt forare; **to have a ~** (AUT) forare (una gomma).

pundit ['pʌndɪt] n sapientone/a.

pungent ['pʌndʒənt] adj piccante; (fig) mordace, caustico(a).

punish ['pʌnɪʃ] vt punire; **to ~ sb for sth/ for doing sth** punire qn per qc/per aver fatto qc.

punishable ['pʌnɪʃəbl] adj punibile.

punishing ['pʌnɪʃɪŋ] adj (fig: exhausting) sfiancante.

punishment ['pʌnɪʃmənt] n punizione f; (fig col): **to take a lot of ~** (boxer) incassare parecchi colpi; (car) essere messo(a) a dura prova.

punk [pʌŋk] n (person: also: ~ **rocker**) punk m/f inv; (music: also: ~ **rock**) musica punk, punk rock m; (US col: hoodlum) teppista m.

punt [pʌnt] n (boat) barchino; (FOOTBALL) colpo a volo; (Irish) sterlina irlandese ♦ vi (BRIT: bet) scommettere.

punter ['pʌntə*] n (BRIT: gambler) scommettitore/trice.

puny ['pjuːnɪ] adj gracile.

pup [pʌp] n cucciolo/a.

pupil ['pjuːpl] n allievo/a; (ANAT) pupilla.

puppet ['pʌpɪt] n burattino.

puppet government n governo fantoccio.

puppy ['pʌpɪ] n cucciolo/a, cagnolino/a.

purchase ['pəːtʃɪs] n acquisto, compera; (grip) presa ♦ vt comprare; **to get a ~ on** (grip) trovare un appoggio su.

purchase order n ordine m d'acquisto, ordinazione f.

purchase price n prezzo d'acquisto.

purchaser ['pəːtʃɪsə*] n compratore/trice.

purchase tax n (BRIT) tassa d'acquisto.

purchasing power ['pəːtʃɪsɪŋ-] n potere m d'acquisto.

pure [pjuə*] adj puro(a); **a ~ wool jumper** un golf di pura lana; **it's laziness ~ and simple** è pura pigrizia.

purebred ['pjuəbred] adj di razza pura.

purée ['pjuəreɪ] n purè m inv.

purely ['pjuəlɪ] adv puramente.

purge [pəːdʒ] n (MED) purga; (POL) epurazione f ♦ vt purgare; (fig) epurare.

purification [pjuərɪfɪ'keɪʃən] n purificazione f.

purify ['pjuərɪfaɪ] vt purificare.

purist ['pjuərɪst] n purista m/f.

puritan ['pjuərɪtən] adj, n puritano(a).

puritanical [pjuərɪ'tænɪkl] adj puritano(a).

purity ['pjuərɪtɪ] n purità.

purl [pəːl] n punto rovescio ♦ vt lavorare a rovescio.

purloin [pəː'lɔɪn] vt rubare.

purple ['pəːpl] adj di porpora; viola inv.

purport [pəː'pɔːt] vi: **to ~ to be/do** pretendere di essere/fare.

purpose ['pəːpəs] n intenzione f, scopo; **on ~** apposta, di proposito; **for illustrative ~s** a titolo illustrativo; **for teaching ~s** per l'insegnamento; **for the ~s of this meeting** agli effetti di questa riunione; **to no ~** senza nessun risultato, inutilmente.

purpose-built ['pəːpəs'bɪlt] adj (BRIT) costruito(a) allo scopo.

purposeful ['pəːpəsful] adj deciso(a), risoluto(a).

purposely ['pəːpəslɪ] adv apposta.

purr [pəː*] n fusa fpl ♦ vi fare le fusa.

purse [pəːs] n borsellino; (US: handbag) borsetta, borsa ♦ vt contrarre.

purser ['pəːsə*] n (NAUT) commissario di bordo.

purse snatcher [-'snætʃə*] n (US) scippatore m.

pursue [pə'sjuː] vt inseguire; essere alla ricerca di; (inquiry, matter) approfondire.

pursuer [pə'sjuːə*] n inseguitore/trice.

pursuit [pə'sjuːt] n inseguimento; (occupation) occupazione f, attività f inv; **in (the) ~ of sth** alla ricerca di qc; **scientific ~s** ricerche fpl scientifiche.

purveyor [pə'veɪə*] n fornitore/trice.

pus [pʌs] n pus m.

push [puʃ] n spinta; (effort) grande sforzo; (drive) energia ♦ vt spingere; (button) premere; (thrust): **to ~ sth (into)** ficcare qc (in); (fig) fare pubblicità a ♦ vi spingere; premere; **to ~ a door open/ shut** aprire/chiudere una porta con una spinta or spingendola; **to be ~ed for time/money** essere a corto di tempo/

soldi; **she is ~ing 50** (*col*) va per i 50; **to ~ for** (*better pay, conditions etc*) fare pressione per ottenere; *"~"* (*on door*) "spingere"; (*on bell*) "suonare"; **at a ~** (*BRIT col*) in caso di necessità.
▶**push aside** *vt* scostare.
▶**push in** *vi* introdursi a forza.
▶**push off** *vi* (*col*) filare.
▶**push on** *vi* (*continue*) continuare.
▶**push over** *vt* far cadere.
▶**push through** *vt* (*measure*) far approvare.
▶**push up** *vt* (*total, prices*) far salire.
push-bike ['pʊʃbaɪk] *n* (*BRIT*) bicicletta.
push-button ['pʊʃbʌtn] *adj* a pulsante.
pushchair ['pʊʃtʃɛə*] *n* passeggino.
pusher ['pʊʃə*] *n* (*also:* **drug ~**) spacciatore/trice (di droga).
pushover ['pʊʃəʊvə*] *n* (*col*): **it's a ~** è un lavoro da bambini.
push-up ['pʊʃʌp] *n* (*US*) flessione *f* sulle braccia.
pushy ['pʊʃɪ] *adj* (*pej*) troppo intraprendente.
puss, pussy(-cat) [pʊs, 'pʊsɪ(kæt)] *n* micio.
put, *pt, pp* **put** [pʊt] *vt* mettere, porre; (*say*) dire, esprimere; (*a question*) fare; (*estimate*) stimare ◆ *adv:* **to stay ~** non muoversi; **to ~ sb to bed** mettere qn a letto; **to ~ sb in a good/bad mood** mettere qn di buon/cattivo umore; **to ~ sb to a lot of trouble** scomodare qn; **to ~ a lot of time into sth** dedicare molto tempo a qc; **to ~ money on a horse** scommettere su un cavallo; **how shall I ~ it?** come dire?; **I ~ it to you that ...** (*BRIT*) io sostengo che ....
▶**put about** *vi* (*NAUT*) virare di bordo ◆ *vt* (*rumour*) diffondere.
▶**put across** *vt* (*ideas etc*) comunicare, far capire.
▶**put aside** *vt* (*lay down: book etc*) mettere da una parte, posare; (*save*) mettere da parte; (*in shop*) tenere da parte.
▶**put away** *vt* (*clothes, toys etc*) mettere via.
▶**put back** *vt* (*replace*) rimettere (a posto); (*postpone*) rinviare; (*delay*) ritardare; (*set back: watch, clock*) mettere indietro; **this will ~ us back 10 years** questo ci farà tornare indietro di 10 anni.
▶**put by** *vt* (*money*) mettere da parte.
▶**put down** *vt* (*parcel etc*) posare, mettere giù; (*pay*) versare; (*in writing*) mettere per iscritto; (*suppress: revolt etc*) reprimere, sopprimere; (*attribute*) attribuire.
▶**put forward** *vt* (*ideas*) avanzare,

proporre; (*date*) anticipare.
▶**put in** *vt* (*application, complaint*) presentare.
▶**put in for** *vt fus* (*job*) far domanda per; (*promotion*) far domanda di.
▶**put off** *vt* (*postpone*) rimandare, rinviare; (*discourage*) dissuadere.
▶**put on** *vt* (*clothes, lipstick etc*) mettere; (*light etc*) accendere; (*play etc*) mettere in scena; (*concert, exhibition etc*) allestire, organizzare; (*extra bus, train etc*) mettere in servizio; (*food, meal*) servire; (*brake*) mettere; (*assume: accent, manner*) affettare; (*col: tease*) prendere in giro; (*inform, indicate*): **to ~ sb on to sb/sth** indicare qn/qc a qn; **to ~ on weight** ingrassare; **to ~ on airs** darsi delle arie.
▶**put out** *vt* mettere fuori; (*one's hand*) porgere; (*light etc*) spegnere; (*person: inconvenience*) scomodare; (*dislocate: shoulder, knee*) lussarsi; (*: back*) farsi uno strappo a ◆ *vi* (*NAUT*): **to ~ out to sea** prendere il largo; **to ~ out from Plymouth** partire da Plymouth.
▶**put through** *vt* (*caller*) mettere in comunicazione; (*call*) passare; **~ me through to Miss Blair** mi passi la signorina Blair.
▶**put together** *vt* mettere insieme, riunire; (*assemble: furniture*) montare; (*: meal*) improvvisare.
▶**put up** *vt* (*raise*) sollevare, alzare; (*pin up*) affiggere; (*hang*) appendere; (*build*) costruire, erigere; (*increase*) aumentare; (*accommodate*) alloggiare; (*incite*): **to ~ sb up to doing sth** istigare qn a fare qc; **to ~ sth up for sale** mettere in vendita qc.
▶**put upon** *vt fus:* **to be ~ upon** (*imposed on*) farsi mettere sotto i piedi.
▶**put up with** *vt fus* sopportare.
putrid ['pjuːtrɪd] *adj* putrido(a).
putt [pʌt] *vt* (*ball*) colpire leggermente ◆ *n* colpo leggero.
putter ['pʌtə*] *n* (*GOLF*) putter *m inv* ◆ *vi* (*US*) = **potter**.
putting green ['pʌtɪŋ-] *n* green *m inv*; campo da putting.
putty ['pʌtɪ] *n* stucco.
put-up ['pʊtʌp] *adj:* **~ job** montatura.
puzzle ['pʌzl] *n* enigma *m*, mistero; (*jigsaw*) puzzle *m* ◆ *vt* confondere, rendere perplesso(a) ◆ *vi* scervellarsi; **to be ~d about sth** domandarsi il perché di qc; **to ~ over** (*sb's actions*) cercare di capire; (*mystery, problem*) cercare di risolvere.
puzzling ['pʌzlɪŋ] *adj* (*question*) poco chiaro(a); (*attitude, set of instructions*) incomprensibile.

PVC *n abbr* (= *polyvinyl chloride*) P.V.C. *m*.
Pvt. *abbr* (*US MIL*) = **private**.
PW *n abbr* (*US*) = **prisoner of war**.
pw *abbr* = *per week*.
PX *n abbr* (*US MIL*) *see* **post exchange**.
pygmy ['pɪgmɪ] *n* pigmeo/a.
pyjamas, (*US*) **pajamas** [pə'dʒɑːməz] *npl*
pigiama *m*; **a pair of** ~ un pigiama.
pylon ['paɪlən] *n* pilone *m*.
pyramid ['pɪrəmɪd] *n* piramide *f*.
Pyrenees [pɪrə'niːz] *npl*: **the** ~ i Pirenei.
Pyrex ® ['paɪrɛks] *n* Pirex ® *m inv* ♦ *cpd*: ~
dish pirofila.
python ['paɪθən] *n* pitone *m*.

$$Q\,q$$

Q, q [kjuː] *n* (*letter*) Q, q *f or m inv*; **Q for
Queen** ≈ Q come Quarto.
Qatar [kæ'tɑː*] *n* Qatar *m*.
QC *n abbr* (*BRIT*: = *Queen's Counsel*)
avvocato della Corona.
QED *abbr* (= *quod erat demonstrandum*) qed.
QM *n abbr see* **quartermaster**.
q.t. *n abbr* (*col*: = *quiet*): **on the** ~ di
nascosto.
qty *abbr* = **quantity**.
quack [kwæk] *n* (*of duck*) qua qua *m inv*; (*pej*:
doctor) ciarlatano/a.
quad [kwɔd] *n abbr* = **quadrangle;
quadruple; quadruplet**.
quadrangle ['kwɔdræŋgl] *n* (*MATH*)
quadrilatero; (*courtyard*) cortile *m*.
quadruped ['kwɔdruped] *n* quadrupede *m*.
quadruple [kwɔ'drupl] *adj* quadruplo(a) ♦ *n*
quadruplo ♦ *vt* quadruplicare ♦ *vi*
quadruplicarsi.
quadruplet [kwɔ'druːplɪt] *n* uno/a di
quattro gemelli.
quagmire ['kwægmaɪə*] *n* pantano.
quail [kweɪl] *n* (*ZOOL*) quaglia ♦ *vi*: **to** ~ **at**
or **before** perdersi d'animo davanti a.
quaint [kweɪnt] *adj* bizzarro(a); (*old-
fashioned*) antiquato(a) e pittoresco(a).
quake [kweɪk] *vi* tremare ♦ *n abbr*
= **earthquake**.
Quaker ['kweɪkə*] *n* quacchero/a.
qualification [kwɔlɪfɪ'keɪʃən] *n* (*degree etc*)
qualifica, titolo; (*ability*) competenza,
qualificazione *f*; (*limitation*) riserva,
restrizione *f*; **what are your** ~**s?** quali

sono le sue qualifiche?
qualified ['kwɔlɪfaɪd] *adj* qualificato(a);
(*able*) competente, qualificato(a); (*limited*)
condizionato(a); ~ **for/to do**
qualificato(a) per/per fare; **he's not** ~ **for
the job** non ha i requisiti necessari per
questo lavoro; **it was a** ~ **success** è stato
un successo parziale.
qualify ['kwɔlɪfaɪ] *vt* abilitare; (*limit*:
statement) modificare, precisare ♦ *vi*: **to** ~
(**as**) qualificarsi (come); **to** ~ (**for**)
acquistare i requisiti necessari (per);
(*SPORT*) qualificarsi (per *or* a); **to** ~ **as an
engineer** diventare un perito tecnico.
qualifying ['kwɔlɪfaɪɪŋ] *adj* (*exam*) di
ammissione; (*round*) eliminatorio(a).
qualitative ['kwɔlɪtətɪv] *adj* qualitativo(a).
quality ['kwɔlɪtɪ] *n* qualità *f inv* ♦ *cpd* di
qualità; **of good** ~ di buona qualità; **of
poor** ~ scadente; ~ **of life** qualità della
vita.
quality control *n* controllo di qualità.
quality papers *npl*, **quality press** *n* (*BRIT*):
the ~ la stampa d'informazione; *see boxed
note*.

qualm [kwɑːm] *n* dubbio; scrupolo; **to have**
~**s about sth** avere degli scrupoli per qc.
quandary ['kwɔndrɪ] *n*: **in a** ~ in un
dilemma.
quango ['kwæŋgəu] *n abbr* (*BRIT*: = *quasi-
autonomous non-governmental organization*)
*commissione consultiva di nomina
governativa*.
quantifiable ['kwɔntɪfaɪəbl] *adj*
quantificabile.
quantitative ['kwɔntɪtətɪv] *adj*
quantitativo(a).
quantity ['kwɔntɪtɪ] *n* quantità *f inv*; **in** ~ in
grande quantità.
quantity surveyor *n* (*BRIT*) geometra *m*
(*specializzato nel calcolare la quantità e il
costo del materiale da costruzione*).
quantum leap ['kwɔntəm-] *n* (*fig*) enorme
cambiamento.
quarantine ['kwɔrntiːn] *n* quarantena.
quark [kwɑːk] *n* quark *m inv*.

quarrel ['kwɔrl] *n* lite *f*, disputa ♦ *vi* litigare; **to have a ~ with sb** litigare con qn; **I've no ~ with him** non ho niente contro di lui; **I can't ~ with that** non ho niente da ridire su questo.

quarrelsome ['kwɔrəlsəm] *adj* litigioso(a).

quarry ['kwɔrɪ] *n* (*for stone*) cava; (*animal*) preda ♦ *vt* (*marble etc*) estrarre.

quart [kwɔːt] *n* due pinte *fpl*, ≈ litro.

quarter ['kwɔːtə*] *n* quarto; (*of year*) trimestre *m*; (*district*) quartiere *m*; (*US, Canada: 25 cents*) quarto di dollaro, 25 centesimi ♦ *vt* dividere in quattro; (*MIL*) alloggiare; **~s** *npl* alloggio; (*MIL*) alloggi *mpl*, quadrato; **a ~ of an hour** un quarto d'ora; **it's a ~ to 3**, (*US*) **it's a ~ of 3** sono le 3 meno un quarto, manca un quarto alle 3; **it's a ~ past 3**, (*US*) **it's a ~ after 3** sono le 3 e un quarto; **from all ~s** da tutte la parti *or* direzioni; **at close ~s** a distanza ravvicinata.

quarterback ['kwɔːtəbæk] *n* (*US FOOTBALL*) quarterback *m inv*.

quarter-deck ['kwɔːtədɛk] *n* (*NAUT*) cassero.

quarter final *n* quarto di finale.

quarterly ['kwɔːtəlɪ] *adj* trimestrale ♦ *adv* trimestralmente ♦ *n* periodico trimestrale.

quartermaster (QM) ['kwɔːtəmɑːstə*] *n* (*MIL*) furiere *m*.

quartet(te) [kwɔː'tɛt] *n* quartetto.

quarto ['kwɔːtəu] *adj, n* in quarto (*m*) *inv*.

quartz [kwɔːts] *n* quarzo ♦ *cpd* di quarzo; (*watch, clock*) al quarzo.

quash [kwɔʃ] *vt* (*verdict*) annullare.

quasi- ['kweɪzaɪ] *prefix* quasi + *noun*; quasi, pressoché + *adjective*.

quaver ['kweɪvə*] *n* (*BRIT MUS*) croma ♦ *vi* tremolare.

quay [kiː] *n* (*also:* **~side**) banchina.

Que. *abbr* (*Canada*) = **Quebec**.

queasy ['kwiːzɪ] *adj* (*stomach*) delicato(a); **to feel ~** aver la nausea.

Quebec [kwɪ'bɛk] *n* Quebec *m*.

queen [kwiːn] *n* (*gen*) regina; (*CARDS etc*) regina, donna.

queen mother *n* regina madre.

Queen's speech *n* (*BRIT*) *see boxed note*.

QUEEN'S SPEECH

*Durante la sessione di apertura del Parlamento britannico il sovrano legge un discorso redatto dal primo ministro, il **Queen's speech** (se si tratta della regina), che contiene le linee generali del nuovo programma politico.*

---

queer [kwɪə*] *adj* strano(a), curioso(a); (*suspicious*) dubbio(a), sospetto(a); (*BRIT: sick*): **I feel ~** mi sento poco bene ♦ *n* (*col*) finocchio.

quell [kwɛl] *vt* domare.

quench [kwɛntʃ] *vt* (*flames*) spegnere; **to ~ one's thirst** dissetarsi.

querulous ['kwɛruləs] *adj* querulo(a).

query ['kwɪərɪ] *n* domanda, questione *f*; (*doubt*) dubbio ♦ *vt* mettere in questione; (*disagree with, dispute*) contestare.

quest [kwɛst] *n* cerca, ricerca.

question ['kwɛstʃən] *n* domanda, questione *f* ♦ *vt* (*person*) interrogare; (*plan, idea*) mettere in questione *or* in dubbio; **to ask sb a ~, put a ~ to sb** fare una domanda a qn; **to bring** *or* **call sth into ~** mettere in dubbio qc; **the ~ is** ... il problema è ...; **it's a ~ of doing** si tratta di fare; **there's some ~ of doing** c'è chi suggerisce di fare; **beyond ~** fuori di dubbio; **out of the ~** fuori discussione, impossibile.

questionable ['kwɛstʃənəbl] *adj* discutibile.

questioner ['kwɛstʃənə*] *n* interrogante *m/f*.

questioning ['kwɛstʃənɪŋ] *adj* interrogativo(a) ♦ *n* interrogatorio.

question mark *n* punto interrogativo.

questionnaire [kwɛstʃə'nɛə*] *n* questionario.

queue [kjuː] *n* coda, fila ♦ *vi* fare la coda; **to jump the ~** passare davanti agli altri (in una coda).

quibble ['kwɪbl] *vi* cavillare.

quick [kwɪk] *adj* rapido(a), veloce; (*reply*) pronto(a); (*mind*) pronto(a), acuto(a) ♦ *adv* rapidamente, presto ♦ *n*: **cut to the ~** (*fig*) toccato(a) sul vivo; **be ~!** fa presto!; **to be ~ to act** agire prontamente; **she was ~ to see that** ... ha visto subito che ....

quicken ['kwɪkn] *vt* accelerare, affrettare; (*rouse*) animare, stimolare ♦ *vi* accelerarsi, affrettarsi.

quick fix *n* soluzione *f* tampone *inv*.

quicklime ['kwɪklaɪm] *n* calce *f* viva.

quickly ['kwɪklɪ] *adv* rapidamente, velocemente; **we must act ~** dobbiamo agire tempestivamente.

quickness ['kwɪknɪs] *n* rapidità; prontezza; acutezza.

quicksand ['kwɪksænd] *n* sabbie *fpl* mobili.

quickstep ['kwɪkstɛp] *n* tipo di ballo simile al fox-trot.

quick-tempered [kwɪk'tɛmpəd] *adj* che si arrabbia facilmente.

quick-witted [kwɪk'wɪtɪd] *adj* pronto(a) d'ingegno.

quid [kwɪd] *n* (*pl inv*: *BRIT col*) sterlina.

quid pro quo ['kwɪdprəu'kwəu] *n*

contraccambio.
quiet ['kwaɪət] *adj* tranquillo(a), quieto(a); (*reserved*) quieto(a), taciturno(a); (*ceremony*) semplice; (*not noisy: engine*) silenzioso(a); (*not busy: day*) calmo(a), tranquillo(a); (*colour*) discreto(a) ♦ *n* tranquillità, calma ♦ *vt, vi* (*US*) = **quieten**; **keep ~!** sta zitto!; **on the ~** di nascosto; **I'll have a ~ word with him** gli dirò due parole in privato; **business is ~ at this time of year** questa è la stagione morta.
quieten ['kwaɪətn] (*BRIT: also*: **~ down**) *vi* calmarsi, chetarsi ♦ *vt* calmare, chetare.
quietly ['kwaɪətlɪ] *adv* tranquillamente, calmamente; silenziosamente.
quietness ['kwaɪətnɪs] *n* tranquillità, calma; silenzio.
quill [kwɪl] *n* penna d'oca.
quilt [kwɪlt] *n* trapunta, **continental ~** piumino.
quin [kwɪn] *n abbr* = **quintuplet**.
quince [kwɪns] *n* (*mela*) cotogna; (*tree*) cotogno.
quinine [kwɪ'niːn] *n* chinino.
quintet(te) [kwɪn'tɛt] *n* quintetto.
quintuplet [kwɪn'tjuːplɪt] *n* uno/a di cinque gemelli.
quip [kwɪp] *n* battuta di spirito.
quire ['kwaɪə*] *n* ventesima parte di una risma.
quirk [kwəːk] *n* ghiribizzo; **by some ~ of fate** per un capriccio della sorte.
quit, *pt, pp* **quit** *or* **quitted** [kwɪt] *vt* lasciare, partire da ♦ *vi* (*give up*) mollare; (*resign*) dimettersi; **to ~ doing** smettere di fare; **~ stalling!** (*US col*) non tirarla per le lunghe!; **notice to ~** (*BRIT*) preavviso (*dato all'inquilino*).
quite [kwaɪt] *adv* (*rather*) assai; (*entirely*) completamente, del tutto; **I ~ understand** capisco perfettamente; **~ a few of them** non pochi di loro; **~ (so)!** esatto!; **~ new** proprio nuovo; **that's not ~ right** non è proprio esatto; **she's ~ pretty** è piuttosto carina.
Quito ['kiːtəu] *n* Quito *m*.
quits [kwɪts] *adj*: **~ (with)** pari (con); **let's call it ~** adesso siamo pari.
quiver ['kwɪvə*] *vi* tremare, fremere ♦ *n* (*for arrows*) faretra.
quiz [kwɪz] *n* (*game*) quiz *m inv*; indovinello ♦ *vt* interrogare.
quizzical ['kwɪzɪkəl] *adj* enigmatico(a).
quoits [kwɔɪts] *npl* gioco degli anelli.
quorum ['kwɔːrəm] *n* quorum *m*.
quota ['kwəutə] *n* quota.
quotation [kwəu'teɪʃən] *n* citazione *f*; (*of shares etc*) quotazione *f*; (*estimate*)

preventivo.
quotation marks *npl* virgolette *fpl*.
quote [kwəut] *n* citazione *f* ♦ *vt* (*sentence*) citare; (*price*) dare, indicare, fissare; (*shares*) quotare ♦ *vi*: **to ~ from** citare; **to ~ for a job** dare un preventivo per un lavoro; **~s** *npl* (*col*) = **quotation marks**; **in ~s** tra virgolette; **~ ... unquote** (*in dictation*) aprire le virgolette ... chiudere le virgolette.
quotient ['kwəuʃənt] *n* quoziente *m*.
qv *abbr* (= *quod vide: which see*) v.
qwerty keyboard ['kwəːtɪ-] *n* tastiera qwerty *inv*.

R r

R, r [ɑː*] *n* (*letter*) R, r *f or m inv*; **R for Robert**, (*US*) **R for Roger** ≈ R come Roma.
R *abbr* (= *Réaumur* (*scale*)) R; (= *river*) F; (= *right*) D; (*US CINE*: = *restricted*) ≈ vietato; (*US POL*) = **republican**; (*BRIT*) = *Rex, Regina*.
RA *n abbr* (*BRIT*) = *Royal Academy, Royal Academician* ♦ *abbr* = **rear admiral**.
RAAF *n abbr* = *Royal Australian Air Force*.
Rabat [rə'bɑːt] *n* Rabat *f*.
rabbi ['ræbaɪ] *n* rabbino.
rabbit ['ræbɪt] *n* coniglio ♦ *vi*: **to ~ (on)** (*BRIT*) blaterare.
rabbit hole *n* tana di coniglio.
rabbit hutch *n* conigliera.
rabble ['ræbl] *n* (*pej*) canaglia, plebaglia.
rabid ['ræbɪd] *adj* rabbioso(a); (*fig*) fanatico(a).
rabies ['reɪbiːz] *n* rabbia.
RAC *n abbr* (*BRIT*: = *Royal Automobile Club*) ≈ A.C.I. *m* (= *Automobile Club d'Italia*).
raccoon [rə'kuːn] *n* procione *m*.
race [reɪs] *n* razza; (*competition, rush*) corsa ♦ *vt* (*person*) gareggiare (in corsa) con; (*horse*) far correre; (*engine*) imballare ♦ *vi* correre; **the human ~** la razza umana; **he ~d across the road** ha attraversato la strada di corsa; **to ~ in/ out** *etc* precipitarsi dentro/fuori *etc*.
race car *n* (*US*) = **racing car**.
race car driver *n* (*US*) = **racing driver**.
racecourse ['reɪskɔːs] *n* campo di corse, ippodromo.

racehorse ['reɪshɔːs] *n* cavallo da corsa.
race relations *npl* rapporti razziali.
racetrack ['reɪstræk] *n* pista.
racial ['reɪʃl] *adj* razziale.
racial discrimination *n* discriminazione *f* razziale.
racialism ['reɪʃəlɪzəm] *n* razzismo.
racialist ['reɪʃəlɪst] *adj, n* razzista (*m/f*).
racing ['reɪsɪŋ] *n* corsa.
racing car *n* (*BRIT*) macchina da corsa.
racing driver *n* (*BRIT*) corridore *m* automobilista.
racism ['reɪsɪzəm] *n* razzismo.
racist ['reɪsɪst] *adj, n* (*pej*) razzista (*m/f*).
rack [ræk] *n* rastrelliera; (*also*: **luggage ~**) rete *f*, portabagagli *m inv*; (*also*: **roof ~**) portabagagli ♦ *vt* torturare, tormentare; **magazine ~** portariviste *m inv*; **shoe ~** scarpiera; **toast ~** portatoast *m inv*; **to go to ~ and ruin** (*building*) andare in rovina; (*business*) andare in malora *or* a catafascio; **to ~ one's brains** scervellarsi.
▶**rack up** *vt* accumulare.
racket ['rækɪt] *n* (*for tennis*) racchetta; (*noise*) fracasso, baccano; (*swindle*) imbroglio, truffa; (*organized crime*) racket *m inv*.
racketeer [rækɪ'tɪə*] *n* (*US*) trafficante *m/f*.
racoon [rə'kuːn] *n* = **raccoon**.
racquet ['rækɪt] *n* racchetta.
racy ['reɪsɪ] *adj* brioso(a); piccante.
RADA ['rɑːdə] *n abbr* (*BRIT*) = *Royal Academy of Dramatic Art*.
radar ['reɪdɑː*] *n* radar *m* ♦ *cpd* radar *inv*.
radar trap *n* controllo della velocità con radar.
radial ['reɪdɪəl] *adj* (*also*: **~-ply**) radiale.
radiance ['reɪdɪəns] *n* splendore *m*, radiosità.
radiant ['reɪdɪənt] *adj* raggiante; (*PHYSICS*) radiante.
radiate ['reɪdɪeɪt] *vt* (*heat*) irraggiare, irradiare ♦ *vi* (*lines*) irradiarsi.
radiation [reɪdɪ'eɪʃən] *n* irradiamento; (*radioactive*) radiazione *f*.
radiation sickness *n* malattia da radiazioni.
radiator ['reɪdɪeɪtə*] *n* radiatore *m*.
radiator cap *n* tappo del radiatore.
radiator grill *n* (*AUT*) mascherina, calandra.
radical ['rædɪkl] *adj* radicale.
radii ['reɪdɪaɪ] *npl of* **radius**.
radio ['reɪdɪəu] *n* radio *f inv* ♦ *vt* (*information*) trasmettere per radio; (*one's position*) comunicare via radio; (*person*) chiamare

via radio ♦ *vi*: **to ~ to sb** comunicare via radio con qn; **on the ~** alla radio.
radio... ['reɪdɪəu] *prefix* radio....
radioactive ['reɪdɪəu'æktɪv] *adj* radioattivo(a).
radioactivity ['reɪdɪəuæk'tɪvɪtɪ] *n* radioattività.
radio announcer *n* annunciatore/trice della radio.
radio-controlled ['reɪdɪəukən'trəuld] *adj* radiocomandato(a), radioguidato(a).
radiographer [reɪdɪ'ɔɡrəfə*] *n* radiologo/a (*tecnico*).
radiography [reɪdɪ'ɔɡrəfɪ] *n* radiografia.
radiologist [reɪdɪ'ɔlədʒɪst] *n* radiologo/a (*medico*).
radiology [reɪdɪ'ɔlədʒɪ] *n* radiologia.
radio station *n* stazione *f* radio *inv*.
radio taxi *n* radiotaxi *m inv*.
radiotelephone ['reɪdɪəu'tɛlɪfəun] *n* radiotelefono.
radiotherapist ['reɪdɪəu'θɛrəpɪst] *n* radioterapista *m/f*.
radiotherapy ['reɪdɪəu'θɛrəpɪ] *n* radioterapia.
radish ['rædɪʃ] *n* ravanello.
radium ['reɪdɪəm] *n* radio.
radius, *pl* **radii** ['reɪdɪəs, -ɪaɪ] *n* raggio; (*ANAT*) radio; **within a ~ of 50 miles** in un raggio di 50 miglia.
RAF *n abbr* (*BRIT*) *see* **Royal Air Force**.
raffia ['ræfɪə] *n* rafia.
raffish ['ræfɪʃ] *adj* dal look trasandato.
raffle ['ræfl] *n* lotteria ♦ *vt* (*object*) mettere in palio.
raft [rɑːft] *n* zattera.
rafter ['rɑːftə*] *n* trave *f*.
rag [ræɡ] *n* straccio, cencio; (*pej*: *newspaper*) giornalaccio; (*for charity*) *iniziativa studentesca a scopo benefico* ♦ *vt* (*BRIT*) prendere in giro; **~s** *npl* stracci *mpl*, brandelli *mpl*; **in ~s** stracciato.
rag-and-bone man ['ræɡən'bəun-] *n* straccivendolo.
ragbag ['ræɡbæɡ] *n* (*fig*) guazzabuglio.
rag doll *n* bambola di pezza.
rage [reɪdʒ] *n* (*fury*) collera, furia ♦ *vi* (*person*) andare su tutte le furie; (*storm*) infuriare; **it's all the ~** fa furore; **to fly into a ~** andare *or* montare su tutte le furie.
ragged ['ræɡɪd] *adj* (*edge*) irregolare; (*cuff*) logoro(a); (*appearance*) pezzente.
raging ['reɪdʒɪŋ] *adj* (*all senses*) furioso(a); **in a ~ temper** su tutte le furie.
rag trade *n* (*col*): **the ~** l'abbigliamento.

rag week *n* (*BRIT*) *see boxed note.*

RAG WEEK

Durante il **rag week***, gli studenti universitari organizzano vari spettacoli e manifestazioni i cui proventi vengono devoluti in beneficenza.*

---

raid [reɪd] *n* (*MIL*) incursione *f*; (*criminal*) rapina; (*by police*) irruzione *f* ♦ *vt* fare un'incursione in; rapinare; fare irruzione in.

raider ['reɪdə*] *n* rapinatore/trice; (*plane*) aeroplano da incursione.

rail [reɪl] *n* (*on stair*) ringhiera; (*on bridge, balcony*) parapetto; (*of ship*) battagliola; (*for train*) rotaia; ~**s** *npl* binario, rotaie *fpl*; **by** ~ per ferrovia, in treno.

railcard ['reɪlkɑːd] *n* (*BRIT*) tessera di riduzione ferroviaria.

railing(s) ['reɪlɪŋ(z)] *n*(*pl*) ringhiere *fpl*.

railway ['reɪlweɪ], (*US*) **railroad** ['reɪlrəud] *n* ferrovia.

railway engine *n* (*BRIT*) locomotiva.

railway line *n* (*BRIT*) linea ferroviaria.

railwayman ['reɪlweɪmən] *n* (*BRIT*) ferroviere *m*.

railway station *n* (*BRIT*) stazione *f* ferroviaria.

rain [reɪn] *n* pioggia ♦ *vi* piovere; **in the** ~ sotto la pioggia; **it's** ~**ing** piove; **it's** ~**ing cats and dogs** piove a catinelle.

rainbow ['reɪnbəu] *n* arcobaleno.

raincoat ['reɪnkəut] *n* impermeabile *m*.

raindrop ['reɪndrɔp] *n* goccia di pioggia.

rainfall ['reɪnfɔːl] *n* pioggia; (*measurement*) piovosità.

rainforest ['reɪnfɔrɪst] *n* foresta pluviale *or* equatoriale.

rainproof ['reɪnpruːf] *adj* impermeabile.

rainstorm ['reɪnstɔːm] *n* pioggia torrenziale.

rainwater ['reɪnwɔːtə*] *n* acqua piovana.

rainy ['reɪnɪ] *adj* piovoso(a).

raise [reɪz] *n* aumento ♦ *vt* (*lift*) alzare, sollevare; (*build*) erigere; (*increase*) aumentare; (*a protest, doubt, question*) sollevare; (*cattle, family*) allevare; (*crop*) coltivare; (*army, funds*) raccogliere; (*loan*) ottenere; (*end: siege, embargo*) togliere; **to** ~ **one's voice** alzare la voce; **to** ~ **sb's hopes** accendere le speranze di qn; **to** ~ **one's glass to sb/sth** brindare a qn/qc; **to** ~ **a laugh/a smile** far ridere/sorridere.

raisin ['reɪzn] *n* uva secca.

Raj [rɑːdʒ] *n*: **the** ~ l'impero britannico (*in India*).

rajah ['rɑːdʒə] *n* ragià *m inv*.

rake [reɪk] *n* (*tool*) rastrello; (*person*) libertino ♦ *vt* (*garden*) rastrellare; (*with machine gun*) spazzare ♦ *vi*: **to** ~ **through** (*fig: search*) frugare tra.

rake-off ['reɪkɔf] *n* (*col*) parte *f* percentuale.

rakish ['reɪkɪʃ] *adj* dissoluto(a); disinvolto(a).

rally ['rælɪ] *n* (*POL etc*) riunione *f*; (*AUT*) rally *m inv*; (*TENNIS*) scambio ♦ *vt* riunire, radunare ♦ *vi* raccogliersi, radunarsi; (*sick person, STOCK EXCHANGE*) riprendersi.

▶**rally round** *vt fus* raggrupparsi intorno a; venire in aiuto di.

rallying point ['rælɪŋ-] *n* (*POL, MIL*) punto di riunione, punto di raduno.

RAM [ræm] *n abbr* (*COMPUT*: = *random access memory*) RAM *f*.

ram [ræm] *n* montone *m*, ariete *m*; (*device*) ariete ♦ *vt* conficcare; (*crash into*) cozzare, sbattere contro; percuotere; speronare.

ramble ['ræmbl] *n* escursione *f* ♦ *vi* (*pej: also:* ~ **on**) divagare.

rambler ['ræmblə*] *n* escursionista *m/f*.

rambling ['ræmblɪŋ] *adj* (*speech*) sconnesso(a); (*BOT*) rampicante; (*house*) tutto(a) nicchie e corridoi.

rambunctious [ræm'bʌŋkʃəs] *adj* (*US*) = **rumbustious**.

RAMC *n abbr* (*BRIT*) = *Royal Army Medical Corps*.

ramification [ræmɪfɪ'keɪʃən] *n* ramificazione *f*.

ramp [ræmp] *n* rampa; (*AUT*) dosso artificiale.

rampage [ræm'peɪdʒ] *n*: **to go on the** ~ scatenarsi in modo violento ♦ *vi*: **they went rampaging through the town** si sono scatenati in modo violento per la città.

rampant ['ræmpənt] *adj* (*disease etc*) che infierisce.

rampart ['ræmpɑːt] *n* bastione *m*.

ram raiding [-reɪdɪŋ] *n* il rapinare un negozio sfondandone la vetrina con un veicolo rubato.

ramshackle ['ræmʃækl] *adj* (*house*) cadente; (*car etc*) sgangherato(a).

ran [ræn] *pt of* **run**.

ranch [rɑːntʃ] *n* ranch *m inv*.

rancid ['rænsɪd] *adj* rancido(a).

rancour, (*US*) **rancor** ['ræŋkə*] *n* rancore *m*.

R&B *n abbr* = *rhythm and blues*.

R&D *n abbr see* **research and development**.

random ['rændəm] *adj* fatto(a) *or* detto(a) per caso; (*COMPUT, MATH*) casuale ♦ *n*: **at** ~ a casaccio.

random access *n* (*COMPUT*) accesso

casuale.

randy ['rændɪ] *adj* (*col*) arrapato(a); lascivo(a).

rang [ræŋ] *pt of* **ring**.

range [reɪndʒ] *n* (*of mountains*) catena; (*of missile, voice*) portata; (*of products*) gamma; (*MIL: also*: **shooting** ~) campo di tiro; (*also*: **kitchen** ~) fornello, cucina economica ♦ *vt* (*place*) disporre, allineare; (*roam*) vagare per ♦ *vi*: **to ~ over** coprire; **to ~ from ... to** andare da ... a; **price ~** gamma di prezzi; **do you have anything else in this price ~?** ha nient'altro su *or* di questo prezzo?; **within** (**firing**) ~ a portata di tiro; ~**d left/right** (*text*) allineato(a) a destra/sinistra.

ranger ['reɪndʒə*] *n* guardia forestale.

Rangoon [ræŋ'guːn] *n* Rangun *f*.

rank [ræŋk] *n* fila; (*MIL*) grado; (*BRIT: also*: **taxi** ~) posteggio di taxi ♦ *vi*: **to ~ among** essere nel numero di ♦ *adj* (*smell*) puzzolente; (*hypocrisy, injustice*) vero(a) e proprio(a); **the ~s** (*MIL*) la truppa; **the ~ and file** (*fig*) la gran massa; **to close ~s** (*MIL, fig*) serrare i ranghi; **I ~ him sixth** gli do il sesto posto, lo metto al sesto posto.

rankle ['ræŋkl] *vi*: **to ~** (**with sb**) bruciare (a qn).

rank outsider *n* outsider *m/f inv*.

ransack ['rænsæk] *vt* rovistare; (*plunder*) saccheggiare.

ransom ['rænsəm] *n* riscatto; **to hold sb to ~** (*fig*) esercitare pressione su qn.

rant [rænt] *vi* vociare.

ranting ['ræntɪŋ] *n* vociare *m*.

rap [ræp] *n* (*noise*) colpetti *mpl*; (*at a door*) bussata ♦ *vt* dare dei colpetti a; bussare a.

rape [reɪp] *n* violenza carnale, stupro ♦ *vt* violentare.

rape(seed) oil ['reɪp(siːd)-] *n* olio di ravizzone.

rapid ['ræpɪd] *adj* rapido(a).

rapidity [rə'pɪdɪtɪ] *n* rapidità.

rapidly ['ræpɪdlɪ] *adv* rapidamente.

rapids ['ræpɪdz] *npl* (*GEO*) rapida.

rapist ['reɪpɪst] *n* violentatore *m*.

rapport [ræ'pɔː*] *n* rapporto.

rapt [ræpt] *adj* (*attention*) rapito(a), profondo(a); **to be ~ in contemplation** essere in estatica contemplazione.

rapture ['ræptʃə*] *n* estasi *f inv*; **to go into ~s over** andare in sollucchero per.

rapturous ['ræptʃərəs] *adj* estatico(a).

rare [rɛə*] *adj* raro(a); (*CULIN: steak*) al sangue; **it is ~ to find that ...** capita di rado *or* raramente che ... + *sub*.

rarebit ['rɛəbɪt] *n see* **Welsh rarebit**.

rarefied ['rɛərɪfaɪd] *adj* (*air, atmosphere*) rarefatto(a).

rarely ['rɛəlɪ] *adv* raramente.

raring ['rɛərɪŋ] *adj*: **to be ~ to go** (*col*) non veder l'ora di cominciare.

rarity ['rɛərɪtɪ] *n* rarità *f inv*.

rascal ['rɑːskl] *n* mascalzone *m*.

rash [ræʃ] *adj* imprudente, sconsiderato(a) ♦ *n* (*MED*) eruzione *f*; **to come out in a ~** avere uno sfogo.

rasher ['ræʃə*] *n* fetta sottile (di lardo *or* prosciutto).

rasp [rɑːsp] *n* (*tool*) lima ♦ *vt* (*speak: also*: ~ **out**) gracchiare.

raspberry ['rɑːzbərɪ] *n* lampone *m*.

raspberry bush *n* lampone *m* (*pianta*).

rasping ['rɑːspɪŋ] *adj* stridulo(a).

Rastafarian [ræstə'fɛərɪən] *adj, n* rastafariano(a).

rat [ræt] *n* ratto.

ratable ['reɪtəbl] *adj* = **rateable**.

ratchet ['rætʃɪt] *n*: ~ **wheel** ruota dentata.

rate [reɪt] *n* (*proportion*) tasso, percentuale *f*; (*speed*) velocità *f inv*; (*price*) tariffa ♦ *vt* valutare; stimare; **to ~ sb/sth as** valutare qn/qc come; **to ~ sb/sth among** annoverare qn/qc tra; **to ~ sb/sth highly** stimare molto qn/qc; **at a ~ of 60 kph** alla velocità di 60 km all'ora; ~ **of exchange** tasso di cambio; ~ **of flow** flusso medio; ~ **of growth** tasso di crescita; ~ **of return** tasso di rendimento; **pulse ~** frequenza delle pulsazioni; *see also* **rates**.

rateable value ['reɪtəbl-] *n* (*BRIT*) valore *m* imponibile (agli effetti delle imposte comunali).

ratepayer ['reɪtpeɪə*] *n* (*BRIT*) contribuente *m/f* (che paga le imposte comunali).

rates [reɪts] *npl* (*BRIT*) imposte *fpl* comunali.

rather ['rɑːðə*] *adv* piuttosto; (*somewhat*) abbastanza; (*to some extent*) un po'; **it's ~ expensive** è piuttosto caro; (*too much*) è un po' caro; **there's ~ a lot** ce n'è parecchio; **I would** *or* **I'd ~ go** preferirei andare; **I had ~ go** farei meglio ad andare; **I'd ~ not leave** preferirei non partire; **or ~** (*more accurately*) anzi, per essere (più) precisi; **I ~ think he won't come** credo proprio che non verrà.

ratification [rætɪfɪ'keɪʃən] *n* ratificazione *f*.

ratify ['rætɪfaɪ] *vt* ratificare.

rating ['reɪtɪŋ] *n* classificazione *f*; punteggio di merito; (*NAUT: category*) classe *f*; (*: sailor: BRIT*) marinaio semplice.

ratings ['reɪtɪŋz] *npl* (*RADIO, TV*) indice *m* di ascolto.

ratio ['reɪʃɪəu] *n* proporzione *f*; **in the ~ of 2**

to 1 in rapporto di 2 a 1.
ration ['ræʃən] n razione f ♦ vt razionare.
rational ['ræʃənl] adj razionale,
ragionevole; (solution, reasoning)
logico(a).
rationale [ræʃə'nɑːl] n fondamento logico;
giustificazione f.
rationalization [ræʃnəlaɪ'zeɪʃən] n
razionalizzazione f.
rationalize ['ræʃnəlaɪz] vt razionalizzare.
rationally ['ræʃnəlɪ] adv razionalmente;
logicamente.
rationing ['ræʃnɪŋ] n razionamento.
ratpack ['rætpæk] n (BRIT col) stampa
scandalistica.
rat poison n veleno per topi.
rat race n carrierismo, corsa al successo.
rattan [ræ'tæn] n malacca.
rattle ['rætl] n tintinnio; (louder) rumore m
di ferraglia; (object of baby) sonaglino;
(: of sports fan) raganella ♦ vi risuonare,
tintinnare; fare un rumore di ferraglia
♦ vt agitare; far tintinnare; (col:
disconcert) sconcertare.
rattlesnake ['rætlsneɪk] n serpente m a
sonagli.
ratty ['rætɪ] adj (col) incavolato(a).
raucous ['rɔːkəs] adj sguaiato(a).
raucously ['rɔːkəslɪ] adv sguaiatamente.
raunchy ['rɔːntʃɪ] adj (col: person)
allupato(a); (: voice, song) libidinoso(a).
ravage ['rævɪdʒ] vt devastare.
ravages ['rævɪdʒɪz] npl danni mpl.
rave [reɪv] vi (in anger) infuriarsi; (with
enthusiasm) andare in estasi; (MED)
delirare ♦ n: a ~ (party) un rave ♦ adj
(scene, culture, music) del fenomeno rave
♦ cpd: ~ review (col) critica entusiastica.
raven ['reɪvən] n corvo.
ravenous ['rævənəs] adj affamato(a).
ravine [rə'viːn] n burrone m.
raving ['reɪvɪŋ] adj: ~ lunatic pazzo(a)
furioso(a).
ravings ['reɪvɪŋz] npl vaneggiamenti mpl.
ravioli [rævɪ'əʊlɪ] n ravioli mpl.
ravish ['rævɪʃ] vt (delight) estasiare.
ravishing ['rævɪʃɪŋ] adj incantevole.
raw [rɔː] adj (uncooked) crudo(a); (not
processed) greggio(a); (sore) vivo(a);
(inexperienced) inesperto(a); **to get a ~
deal** (col: bad bargain) prendere un
bidone; (: harsh treatment) venire trattato
ingiustamente.
Rawalpindi [rɔːl'pɪndɪ] n Rawalpindi f.
raw material n materia prima.
ray [reɪ] n raggio.
rayon ['reɪɔn] n raion m.
raze [reɪz] vt radere, distruggere; (also: ~

to the ground) radere al suolo.
razor ['reɪzə*] n rasoio.
razor blade n lama di rasoio.
razzle(-dazzle) ['ræzl('dæzl)] n (BRIT col): **to
be/go on the ~** darsi alla pazza gioia.
razzmatazz ['ræzmə'tæz] n (col) clamore m.
RC abbr = **Roman Catholic.**
RCAF n abbr = Royal Canadian Air Force.
RCMP n abbr = Royal Canadian Mounted
Police.
RCN n abbr = Royal Canadian Navy.
RD abbr (US POST) = rural delivery.
Rd abbr = road.
RDC n abbr (BRIT) see **rural district council.**
RE n abbr (BRIT MIL: = Royal Engineers)
≈ G.M. (= Genio Militare); (BRIT) =
religious education.
re [riː] prep con riferimento a.
reach [riːtʃ] n portata; (of river etc) tratto
♦ vt raggiungere; arrivare a ♦ vi
stendersi; (stretch out hand: also: ~ **down**,
over, **across etc**) allungare una
mano; **out of/within ~** (object) fuori/a
portata di mano; **within easy ~ (of)** (place)
a breve distanza (di), vicino (a); **to ~ sb
by phone** contattare qn per telefono; **can
I ~ you at your hotel?** la posso contattare
al suo albergo?
►**reach out** vi: **to ~ out for** stendere la
mano per prendere.
react [riː'ækt] vi reagire.
reaction [riː'ækʃən] n reazione f.
reactionary [riː'ækʃənrɪ] adj, n
reazionario(a).
reactor [riː'æktə*] n reattore m.
read, pt, pp **read** [riːd, rɛd] vi leggere ♦ vt
leggere; (understand) intendere,
interpretare; (study) studiare; **do you ~
me?** (TEL) mi ricevete?; **to take sth as
read** (fig) dare qc per scontato.
►**read out** vt leggere ad alta voce.
►**read over** vt rileggere attentamente.
►**read through** vt (quickly) dare una
scorsa a; (thoroughly) leggere da cima a
fondo.
►**read up** vt, **read up on** vt fus studiare
bene.
readable ['riːdəbl] adj leggibile; che si
legge volentieri.
reader ['riːdə*] n lettore/trice; (book) libro
di lettura; (BRIT: at university) professore
con funzioni preminenti di ricerca.
readership ['riːdəʃɪp] n (of paper etc)
numero di lettori.
readily ['rɛdɪlɪ] adv volentieri; (easily)
facilmente.
readiness ['rɛdɪnɪs] n prontezza; **in ~**
(prepared) pronto(a).

reading ['ri:dɪŋ] n lettura; (*understanding*) interpretazione f; (*on instrument*) indicazione f.

reading lamp n lampada da studio.

reading room n sala di lettura.

readjust [ri:ə'dʒʌst] vt raggiustare ♦ vi (*person*): **to ~ (to)** riadattarsi (a).

ready ['rɛdɪ] adj pronto(a); (*willing*) pronto(a), disposto(a); (*quick*) rapido(a); (*available*) disponibile ♦ n: **at the ~** (*MIL*) pronto a sparare; (*fig*) tutto(a) pronto(a); **~ for use** pronto per l'uso; **to be ~ to do sth** essere pronto a fare qc; **to get ~** vi prepararsi ♦ vt preparare.

ready cash n denaro in contanti.

ready-cooked [rɛdɪ'kukt] adj già cotto(a).

ready-made [rɛdɪ'meɪd] adj prefabbricato(a); (*clothes*) confezionato(a).

ready reckoner [-'rɛkənə*] n (*BRIT*) prontuario di calcolo.

ready-to-wear [rɛdɪtə'wɛə*] adj prêt-à-porter inv.

reagent [ri:'eɪdʒənt] n: **chemical ~** reagente m chimico.

real [rɪəl] adj reale; vero(a) ♦ adv (*US col*: *very*) veramente, proprio; **in ~ terms** in realtà; **in ~ life** nella realtà.

real ale n birra ad effervescenza naturale.

real estate n beni mpl immobili.

realism ['rɪəlɪzəm] n (*also ART*) realismo.

realist ['rɪəlɪst] n realista m/f.

realistic [rɪə'lɪstɪk] adj realistico(a).

reality [ri:'ælɪtɪ] n realtà f inv; **in ~** in realtà, in effetti.

realization [rɪəlaɪ'zeɪʃən] n (*awareness*) presa di coscienza; (*of hopes, project etc*) realizzazione f.

realize ['rɪəlaɪz] vt (*understand*) rendersi conto di; (*a project, COMM: asset*) realizzare; **I ~ that** ... mi rendo conto or capisco che ....

really ['rɪəlɪ] adv veramente, davvero.

realm [rɛlm] n reame m, regno.

real time n (*COMPUT*) tempo reale.

Realtor ® ['rɪəltɔ:*] n (*US*) agente m immobiliare.

ream [ri:m] n risma; **~s** (*fig col*) pagine e pagine fpl.

reap [ri:p] vt mietere; (*fig*) raccogliere.

reaper ['ri:pə*] n (*machine*) mietitrice f.

reappear [ri:ə'pɪə*] vi ricomparire, riapparire.

reappearance [ri:ə'pɪərəns] n riapparizione f.

reapply [ri:ə'plaɪ] vi: **to ~ for** fare un'altra domanda per.

reappraisal [ri:ə'preɪzl] n riesame m.

rear [rɪə*] adj di dietro; (*AUT: wheel etc*) posteriore ♦ n didietro, parte f posteriore ♦ vt (*cattle, family*) allevare ♦ vi (*also: ~ up: animal*) impennarsi.

rear admiral n contrammiraglio.

rear-engined ['rɪər'ɛndʒɪnd] adj (*AUT*) con motore posteriore.

rearguard ['rɪəgɑːd] n retroguardia.

rearm [ri:'ɑːm] vt, vi riarmare.

rearmament [ri:'ɑːməmənt] n riarmo.

rearrange [ri:ə'reɪndʒ] vt riordinare.

rear-view mirror ['rɪəvjuː-] n (*AUT*) specchio retrovisivo.

reason ['ri:zn] n ragione f; (*cause, motive*) ragione, motivo ♦ vi: **to ~ with sb** far ragionare qn; **to have ~ to think** avere motivi per pensare; **it stands to ~ that** è ovvio che; **the ~ for/why** la ragione or il motivo di/per cui; **with good ~** a ragione; **all the more ~ why you should not sell it** ragione di più per non venderlo.

reasonable ['ri:znəbl] adj ragionevole; (*not bad*) accettabile.

reasonably ['ri:znəblɪ] adv ragionevolmente; **one can ~ assume that** ... uno può facilmente supporre che ....

reasoned ['ri:znd] adj (*argument*) ponderato(a).

reasoning ['ri:znɪŋ] n ragionamento.

reassemble [ri:ə'sɛmbl] vt riunire; (*machine*) rimontare.

reassert [ri:ə'sɔːt] vt riaffermare.

reassurance [ri:ə'ʃuərəns] n rassicurazione f.

reassure [ri:ə'ʃuə*] vt rassicurare; **to ~ sb of** rassicurare qn di or su.

reassuring [ri:ə'ʃuərɪŋ] adj rassicurante.

reawakening [ri:ə'weɪknɪŋ] n risveglio.

rebate ['ri:beɪt] n rimborso.

rebel n ['rɛbl] ribelle m/f ♦ vi [rɪ'bɛl] ribellarsi.

rebellion [rɪ'bɛljən] n ribellione f.

rebellious [rɪ'bɛljəs] adj ribelle.

rebirth [ri:'bɔːθ] n rinascita.

rebound vi [rɪ'baund] (*ball*) rimbalzare ♦ n ['ri:baund] rimbalzo.

rebuff [rɪ'bʌf] n secco rifiuto ♦ vt respingere.

rebuild [ri:'bɪld] vt irreg ricostruire.

rebuke [rɪ'bju:k] n rimprovero ♦ vt rimproverare.

rebut [rɪ'bʌt] vt rifiutare.

rebuttal [rɪ'bʌtl] n rifiuto.

recalcitrant [rɪ'kælsɪtrənt] adj recalcitrante.

recall [rɪ'kɔːl] vt (*gen, COMPUT*) richiamare; (*remember*) ricordare, richiamare alla mente ♦ n richiamo; **beyond ~**

irrevocabile.

recant [rɪ'kænt] *vi* ritrattarsi; (*REL*) fare abiura.

recap ['riːkæp] *n* ricapitolazione *f* ♦ *vt* ricapitolare ♦ *vi* riassumere.

recapture [riː'kæptʃə*] *vt* riprendere; (*atmosphere*) ricreare.

recd. *abbr* = *received*.

recede [rɪ'siːd] *vi* allontanarsi; ritirarsi; calare.

receding [rɪ'siːdɪŋ] *adj* (*forehead, chin*) sfuggente; **he's got a ~ hairline** è stempiato.

receipt [rɪ'siːt] *n* (*document*) ricevuta; (*act of receiving*) ricevimento; **to acknowledge ~ of** accusare ricevuta di; **we are in ~ of** ... abbiamo ricevuto ....

receipts [rɪ'siːts] *npl* (*COMM*) introiti *mpl*.

receivable [rɪ'siːvəbl] *adj* (*COMM*) esigibile; (*: owed*) dovuto(a).

receive [rɪ'siːv] *vt* ricevere; (*guest*) ricevere, accogliere, " d with thanks (*COMM*) "per quietanza".

Received Pronunciation (RP) *n* (*BRIT*) *see boxed note.*

RECEIVED PRONUNCIATION

Si chiama **Received Pronunciation (RP)** *l'accento dell'inglese parlato in alcune parti del sud-est dell'Inghilterra. In esso si identifica l'inglese "standard" delle classi colte, privo di inflessioni regionali e adottato tradizionalmente dagli annunciatori della BBC. È anche l'accento standard dell'inglese insegnato come lingua straniera.*

---

receiver [rɪ'siːvə*] *n* (*TEL*) ricevitore *m*; (*RADIO*) apparecchio ricevente; (*of stolen goods*) ricettatore/trice; (*LAW*) curatore *m* fallimentare.

receivership [rɪ'siːvəʃɪp] *n* curatela; **to go into ~** andare in amministrazione controllata.

recent ['riːsnt] *adj* recente; **in ~ years** negli ultimi anni.

recently ['riːsntlɪ] *adv* recentemente; **as ~ as** ... soltanto ...; **until ~** fino a poco tempo fa.

receptacle [rɪ'sɛptɪkl] *n* recipiente *m*.

reception [rɪ'sɛpʃən] *n* (*gen*) ricevimento; (*welcome*) accoglienza; (*TV*) ricezione *f*.

reception centre *n* (*BRIT*) centro di raccolta.

reception desk *n* (*in hotel*) reception *f inv*; (*in hospital, at doctor's*) accettazione *f*; (*in large building, offices*) portineria.

receptionist [rɪ'sɛpʃənɪst] *n* receptionist *m/f*

inv.

receptive [rɪ'sɛptɪv] *adj* ricettivo(a).

recess [rɪ'sɛs] *n* (*in room*) alcova; (*POL etc: holiday*) vacanze *fpl*; (*US LAW: short break*) sospensione *f*; (*US SCOL*) intervallo.

recession [rɪ'sɛʃən] *n* (*ECON*) recessione *f*.

recharge [riː'tʃɑːdʒ] *vt* (*battery*) ricaricare.

rechargeable ['riː'tʃɑːdʒəbl] *adj* ricaricabile.

recipe ['rɛsɪpɪ] *n* ricetta.

recipient [rɪ'sɪpɪənt] *n* beneficiario/a; (*of letter*) destinatario/a.

reciprocal [rɪ'sɪprəkl] *adj* reciproco(a).

reciprocate [rɪ'sɪprəkeɪt] *vt* ricambiare.

recital [rɪ'saɪtl] *n* recital *m inv*; concerto (di solista).

recite [rɪ'saɪt] *vt* (*poem*) recitare.

reckless ['rɛkləs] *adj* (*driver etc*) spericolato(a); (*spender*) incosciente.

recklessly ['rɛkləslɪ] *adv* in modo spericolato; da incosciente.

reckon ['rɛkən] *vt* (*count*) calcolare; (*consider*) considerare, stimare; (*think*): **I ~ that** ... penso che ... ♦ *vi* contare, calcolare; **to ~ without sb/sth** non tener conto di qn/qc; **he is somebody to be ~ed with** è uno da non sottovalutare.

▶**reckon on** *vt fus* contare su.

reckoning ['rɛknɪŋ] *n* conto; stima; **the day of ~** il giorno del giudizio.

reclaim [rɪ'kleɪm] *vt* (*land*) bonificare; (*demand back*) richiedere, reclamare.

recline [rɪ'klaɪn] *vi* stare sdraiato(a).

reclining [rɪ'klaɪnɪŋ] *adj* (*seat*) ribaltabile.

recluse [rɪ'kluːs] *n* eremita *m*, recluso/a.

recognition [rɛkəg'nɪʃən] *n* riconoscimento; **to gain ~** essere riconosciuto(a); **in ~ of** or come segno di riconoscimento per; **transformed beyond ~** irriconoscibile.

recognizable ['rɛkəgnaɪzəbl] *adj*: **~ (by)** riconoscibile (a or da).

recognize ['rɛkəgnaɪz] *vt*: **to ~ (by/as)** riconoscere (a or da/come).

recoil [rɪ'kɔɪl] *vi* (*gun*) rinculare; (*spring*) balzare indietro; (*person*): **to ~ (from)** indietreggiare (davanti a) ♦ *n* (*of gun*) rinculo.

recollect [rɛkə'lɛkt] *vt* ricordare.

recollection [rɛkə'lɛkʃən] *n* ricordo; **to the best of my ~** per quello che mi ricordo.

recommend [rɛkə'mɛnd] *vt* raccomandare; (*advise*) consigliare; **she has a lot to ~ her** ha molti elementi a suo favore.

recommendation [rɛkəmɛn'deɪʃən] *n* raccomandazione *f*; consiglio.

recommended retail price (RRP) [rɛkə'mɛndɪd-] *n* (*BRIT*) prezzo

raccomandato al dettaglio.
recompense ['rɛkəmpɛns] *vt*
ricompensare; (*compensate*) risarcire ♦ *n*
ricompensa; risarcimento.
reconcilable ['rɛkənsaɪləbl] *adj* conciliabile.
reconcile ['rɛkənsaɪl] *vt* (*two people*)
riconciliare; (*two facts*) conciliare,
quadrare; **to** ~ **o.s. to** rassegnarsi a.
reconciliation [rɛkənsɪlɪ'eɪʃən] *n*
riconciliazione *f*; conciliazione *f*.
recondition [riːkən'dɪʃən] *vt* rimettere a
nuovo; rifare.
reconnaissance [rɪ'kɔnɪsns] *n* (*MIL*)
ricognizione *f*.
reconnoitre, (*US*) **reconnoiter**
[rɛkə'nɔɪtə*] (*MIL*) *vt* fare una ricognizione
di ♦ *vi* fare una ricognizione.
reconsider [riːkən'sɪdə*] *vt* riconsiderare.
reconstitute [riː'kɔnstɪtjuːt] *vt* ricostituire.
reconstruct [riːkən'strʌkt] *vt* ricostruire.
reconstruction [riːkən'strʌkʃən] *n*
ricostruzione *f*.
reconvene [riːkən'viːn] *vt* riconvocare ♦ *vi*
radunarsi.
record *n* ['rɛkɔːd] ricordo, documento; (*of
meeting etc*) nota, verbale *m*; (*register*)
registro; (*file*) pratica, dossier *m inv*;
(*COMPUT*) record *m inv*, registrazione *f*;
(*also*: **police** ~) fedina penale sporca;
(*MUS*: *disc*) disco; (*SPORT*) record *m inv*,
primato ♦ *vt* [rɪ'kɔːd] (*set down*) prendere
nota di; (*relate*) raccontare; (*COMPUT,
MUS*: *song etc*) registrare; **public** ~**s**
archivi *mpl*; **Italy's excellent** ~ **i** brillanti
successi italiani; **in** ~ **time** a tempo di
record; **to keep a** ~ **of** tener nota di; **to
set the** ~ **straight** mettere le cose in
chiaro; **off the** ~ *adj* ufficioso(a) ♦ *adv*
ufficiosamente; **he is on** ~ **as saying that**
... ha dichiarato pubblicamente che ....
record card *n* (*in file*) scheda.
recorded delivery letter [rɪ'kɔːdɪd-] *n*
(*BRIT POST*) lettera raccomandata.
recorder [rɪ'kɔːdə*] *n* (*LAW*) avvocato che
funge da giudice; (*MUS*) flauto diritto.
record holder *n* (*SPORT*) primatista *m/f*.
recording [rɪ'kɔːdɪŋ] *n* (*MUS*) registrazione
f.
recording studio *n* studio di
registrazione.
record player *n* giradischi *m inv*.
recount [rɪ'kaunt] *vt* raccontare, narrare.
re-count *n* ['riːkaunt] (*POL*: *of votes*) nuovo
conteggio ♦ *vt* [riː'kaunt] ricontare.
recoup [rɪ'kuːp] *vt* ricuperare; **to** ~ **one's
losses** ricuperare le perdite, rifarsi.
recourse [rɪ'kɔːs] *n*: **to have** ~ **to** ricorrere
a.

recover [rɪ'kʌvə*] *vt* ricuperare ♦ *vi* (*from
illness*) rimettersi (in salute), ristabilirsi;
(*country, person*: *from shock*) riprendersi.
re-cover [riː'kʌvə*] *vt* (*chair etc*) ricoprire.
recovery [rɪ'kʌvərɪ] *n* ricupero;
ristabilimento; ripresa.
recreate [riːkrɪ'eɪt] *vt* ricreare.
recreation [rɛkrɪ'eɪʃən] *n* ricreazione *f*;
svago.
recreational [rɛkrɪ'eɪʃənəl] *adj*
ricreativo(a).
recreational drug *n droga usata
saltuariamente.*
recreational vehicle (RV) *n* (*US*) camper
m inv.
recrimination [rɪkrɪmɪ'neɪʃən] *n*
recriminazione *f*.
recruit [rɪ'kruːt] *n* recluta ♦ *vt* reclutare.
recruitment [rɪ'kruːtmənt] *n* reclutamento.
rectangle ['rɛktæŋgl] *n* rettangolo.
rectangular [rɛk'tæŋgjulə*] *adj*
rettangolare.
rectify ['rɛktɪfaɪ] *vt* (*error*) rettificare;
(*omission*) riparare.
rector ['rɛktə*] *n* (*REL*) parroco (*anglicano*);
(*in Scottish universities*) *personalità eletta
dagli studenti per rappresentarli.*
rectory ['rɛktərɪ] *n* presbiterio.
rectum ['rɛktəm] *n* (*ANAT*) retto.
recuperate [rɪ'kjuːpəreɪt] *vi* ristabilirsi.
recur [rɪ'kə:*] *vi* riaccadere; (*idea,
opportunity*) riapparire; (*symptoms*)
ripresentarsi.
recurrence [rɪ'kʌrəns] *n* ripresentarsi *m*;
riapparizione *f*.
recurrent [rɪ'kʌrənt] *adj* ricorrente.
recurring [rɪ'kʌrɪŋ] *adj* (*MATH*) periodico(a).
recycle [riː'saɪkl] *vt* riciclare.
red [rɛd] *n* rosso; (*POL*: *pej*) rosso/a ♦ *adj*
rosso(a); **in the** ~ (*account*) scoperto;
(*business*) in deficit.
red alert *n* allarme *m* rosso.
red-blooded ['rɛd'blʌdɪd] *adj* (*col*)
gagliardo(a).
red-brick university ['rɛdbrɪk-] *n* (*BRIT*)
*università di recente formazione; see boxed
note.*

RED-BRICK UNIVERSITY

*In Gran Bretagna, con **red-brick university**
(letteralmente, università di mattoni rossi) si
indicano le università di recente formazione,
cioè quelle istituite tra la fine dell'Ottocento e i
primi del Novecento, per contraddistinguerle
dalle università più antiche, i cui edifici sono di
pietra; vedi anche **Oxbridge.***

red carpet treatment n cerimonia col gran pavese.

Red Cross n Croce f Rossa.

redcurrant ['rɛdkʌrənt] n ribes m inv.

redden ['rɛdn] vt arrossare ♦ vi arrossire.

reddish ['rɛdɪʃ] adj rossiccio(a).

redecorate [riː'dɛkəreɪt] vt tinteggiare (e tappezzare) di nuovo.

redeem [rɪ'diːm] vt (debt) riscattare; (sth in pawn) ritirare; (fig, also REL) redimere.

redeemable [rɪ'diːməbl] adj con diritto di riscatto; redimibile.

redeeming [rɪ'diːmɪŋ] adj (feature) che salva.

redefine [riːdɪ'faɪn] vt ridefinire.

redemption [rɪ'dɛmpʃən] n (REL) redenzione f; **past** or **beyond** ~ irrecuperabile.

redeploy [riːdɪ'plɔɪ] vt (MIL) riorganizzare lo schieramento di; (resources) riorganizzare.

redeployment [riːdɪ'plɔɪmənt] n riorganizzazione f.

redevelop [riːdɪ'vɛləp] vt ristrutturare.

redevelopment [riːdɪ'vɛləpmənt] n ristrutturazione f.

red-handed [rɛd'hændɪd] adj: **to be caught** ~ essere preso(a) in flagrante or con le mani nel sacco.

redhead ['rɛdhɛd] n rosso/a.

red herring n (fig) falsa pista.

red-hot [rɛd'hɔt] adj arroventato(a).

redirect [riːdaɪ'rɛkt] vt (mail) far seguire.

redistribute [riːdɪ'strɪbjuːt] vt ridistribuire.

red-letter day ['rɛdlɛtə-] n giorno memorabile.

red light n: **to go through a** ~ (AUT) passare col rosso.

red-light district [rɛd'laɪt-] n quartiere m luce rossa inv.

red meat n carne f rossa.

redness ['rɛdnɪs] n rossore m; (of hair) rosso.

redo [riː'duː] vt irreg rifare.

redolent ['rɛdələnt] adj: ~ **of** che sa di; (fig) che ricorda.

redouble [riː'dʌbl] vt: **to** ~ **one's efforts** raddoppiare gli sforzi.

redraft [riː'drɑːft] vt fare una nuova stesura di.

redress [rɪ'drɛs] n riparazione f ♦ vt riparare; **to** ~ **the balance** ristabilire l'equilibrio.

Red Sea n: **the** ~ il mar Rosso.

redskin ['rɛdskɪn] n pellerossa m/f.

red tape n (fig) burocrazia.

reduce [rɪ'djuːs] vt ridurre; (lower) ridurre, abbassare; "~ **speed now**" (AUT) "rallentare"; **to** ~ **sth by/to** ridurre qc di/a; **to** ~ **sb to silence/despair/tears** ridurre qn al silenzio/alla disperazione/in lacrime.

reduced [rɪ'djuːst] adj (decreased) ridotto(a); **at a** ~ **price** a prezzo ribassato or ridotto; "**greatly** ~ **prices**" "grandi ribassi".

reduction [rɪ'dʌkʃən] n riduzione f; (of price) ribasso; (discount) sconto.

redundancy [rɪ'dʌndənsɪ] n licenziamento (per eccesso di personale); **compulsory** ~ licenziamento; **voluntary** ~ forma di cassa integrazione volontaria.

redundancy payment n (BRIT) indennità f inv di licenziamento.

redundant [rɪ'dʌndnt] adj (BRIT: worker) licenziato(a); (detail, object) superfluo(a); **to make** ~ (BRIT) licenziare (per eccesso di personale).

reed [riːd] n (BOT) canna; (MUS: of clarinet etc) ancia.

re-educate [riː'ɛdjukeɪt] vt rieducare.

reedy ['riːdɪ] adj (voice, instrument) acuto(a).

reef [riːf] n (at sea) scogliera; **coral** ~ barriera corallina.

reek [riːk] vi: **to** ~ **(of)** puzzare (di).

reel [riːl] n bobina, rocchetto; (TECH) aspo; (FISHING) mulinello; (CINE) rotolo ♦ vt (TECH) annaspare; (also: ~ **up**) avvolgere ♦ vi (sway) barcollare, vacillare; **my head is** ~**ing** mi gira la testa.

▶**reel off** vt snocciolare.

re-election [riːɪ'lɛkʃən] n rielezione f.

re-enter [riː'ɛntə*] vt rientrare in.

re-entry [riː'ɛntrɪ] n rientro.

re-export vt [riːɪk'spɔːt] riesportare ♦ n [riː'ɛkspɔːt] merce f riesportata, riesportazione f.

ref [rɛf] n abbr (col: = referee) arbitro.

ref. abbr (COMM: = with reference to) sogg.

refectory [rɪ'fɛktərɪ] n refettorio.

refer [rɪ'fəː*] vt: **to** ~ **sth to** (dispute, decision) deferire qc a; **to** ~ **sb to** (inquirer: for information) indirizzare qn a; (reader: to text) rimandare qn a; **he** ~**red me to the manager** mi ha detto di rivolgermi al direttore.

▶**refer to** vt fus (allude to) accennare a; (apply to) riferire a; (consult) rivolgersi a; ~**ring to your letter** (COMM) in riferimento alla Vostra lettera.

referee [rɛfə'riː] n arbitro; (TENNIS) giudice m di gara; (BRIT: for job application)

referenza ♦ vt arbitrare.
reference ['rɛfrəns] n riferimento;
(*mention*) menzione f, allusione f; (*for job
application: letter*) referenza; lettera di
raccomandazione; (: *person*) referenza;
(*in book*) rimando; **with ~ to** riguardo a;
(*COMM: in letter*) in *or* con riferimento a;
"please quote this ~" (*COMM*) "si prega
di far riferimento al numero di
protocollo".
reference book n libro di consultazione.
reference library n biblioteca per la
consultazione.
reference number n (*COMM*) numero di
riferimento.
referendum, pl **referenda** [rɛfə'rɛndəm,
-də] n referendum m inv.
referral [rɪ'fəːrəl] n deferimento; (*MED*)
richiesta (di visita specialistica).
refill vt [riː'fɪl] riempire di nuovo; (*pen,
lighter etc*) ricaricare ♦ n ['riːfɪl] (*for pen
etc*) ricambio.
refine [rɪ'faɪn] vt raffinare.
refined [rɪ'faɪnd] adj raffinato(a).
refinement [rɪ'faɪnmənt] n (*of person*)
raffinatezza.
refinery [rɪ'faɪnərɪ] n raffineria.
refit n ['riːfɪt] (*NAUT*) raddobbo ♦ vt [riː'fɪt]
(*ship*) raddobbare.
reflate [riː'fleɪt] vt (*economy*) rilanciare.
reflation [riː'fleɪʃən] n rilancio.
reflationary [riː'fleɪʃənərɪ] adj nuovamente
inflazionario(a).
reflect [rɪ'flɛkt] vt (*light, image*) riflettere;
(*fig*) rispecchiare ♦ vi (*think*) riflettere,
considerare.
▶**reflect on** vt fus (*discredit*) rispecchiarsi
su.
reflection [rɪ'flɛkʃən] n riflessione f; (*image*)
riflesso; (*criticism*): ~ **on** giudizio su;
attacco a; **on ~** pensandoci sopra.
reflector [rɪ'flɛktə*] n (*also AUT*)
catarifrangente m.
reflex ['riːflɛks] adj riflesso(a) ♦ n riflesso.
reflexive [rɪ'flɛksɪv] adj (*LING*) riflessivo(a).
reform [rɪ'fɔːm] n riforma ♦ vt riformare.
reformat [riː'fɔːmæt] vt (*COMPUT*)
riformattare.
Reformation [rɛfə'meɪʃən] n: **the ~** la
Riforma.
reformatory [rɪ'fɔːmətərɪ] n (*US*)
riformatorio.
reformed [rɪ'fɔːmd] adj cambiato(a) (per il
meglio).
reformer [rɪ'fɔːmə*] n riformatore/trice.
refrain [rɪ'freɪn] vi: **to ~ from doing**
trattenersi dal fare ♦ n ritornello.
refresh [rɪ'frɛʃ] vt rinfrescare; (*subj: food,
sleep*) ristorare.
refresher course [rɪ'frɛʃə-] n (*BRIT*) corso
di aggiornamento.
refreshing [rɪ'frɛʃɪŋ] adj (*drink*)
rinfrescante; (*sleep*) riposante,
ristoratore(trice); (*change etc*) piacevole;
(*idea, point of view*) originale.
refreshment [rɪ'frɛʃmənt] n (*eating, resting
etc*) ristoro; ~**(s)** rinfreschi mpl.
refrigeration [rɪfrɪdʒə'reɪʃən] n
refrigerazione f.
refrigerator [rɪ'frɪdʒəreɪtə*] n frigorifero.
refuel [riː'fjuəl] vt rifornire (di carburante)
♦ vi far rifornimento (di carburante).
refuge ['rɛfjuːdʒ] n rifugio; **to take ~ in**
rifugiarsi in.
refugee [rɛfju'dʒiː] n rifugiato/a, profugo/a.
refugee camp n campo (di) profughi.
refund n ['riːfʌnd] rimborso ♦ vt [rɪ'fʌnd]
rimborsare.
refurbish [riː'fəːbɪʃ] vt rimettere a nuovo.
refurnish [riː'fəːnɪʃ] vt ammobiliare di
nuovo.
refusal [rɪ'fjuːzəl] n rifiuto; **to have first ~
on sth** avere il diritto d'opzione su qc.
refuse n ['rɛfjuːs] rifiuti mpl ♦ vt, vi [rɪ'fjuːz]
rifiutare; **to ~ to do sth** rifiutare *or*
rifiutarsi di fare qc.
refuse collection n raccolta di rifiuti.
refuse disposal n sistema m di scarico dei
rifiuti.
refusenik [rɪ'fjuːznɪk] n *ebreo a cui il
governo sovietico impediva di lasciare il
paese.*
refute [rɪ'fjuːt] vt confutare.
regain [rɪ'geɪn] vt riguadagnare;
riacquistare, ricuperare.
regal ['riːgl] adj regale.
regale [rɪ'geɪl] vt: **to ~ sb with sth**
intrattenere qn con qc.
regalia [rɪ'geɪlɪə] n insegne fpl reali.
regard [rɪ'gɑːd] n riguardo, stima ♦ vt
considerare, stimare; **to give one's ~s to**
porgere i suoi saluti a; (**kind**) ~**s** cordiali
saluti; **as ~s, with ~ to** riguardo a.
regarding [rɪ'gɑːdɪŋ] prep riguardo a, per
quanto riguarda.
regardless [rɪ'gɑːdlɪs] adv lo stesso; ~ **of**
a dispetto di, nonostante.
regatta [rɪ'gætə] n regata.
regency ['riːdʒənsɪ] n reggenza.
regenerate [rɪ'dʒɛnəreɪt] vt rigenerare;
(*feelings, enthusiasm*) far rinascere ♦ vi
rigenerarsi; rinascere.
regent ['riːdʒənt] n reggente m.
reggae ['rɛgeɪ] n reggae m.
régime [reɪ'ʒiːm] n regime m.
regiment n ['rɛdʒɪmənt] reggimento ♦ vt

['rɛdʒɪmɛnt] irreggimentare.
regimental [rɛdʒɪ'mɛntl] *adj* reggimentale.
regimentation [rɛdʒɪmɛn'teɪʃən] *n*
irreggimentazione *f*.
region ['riːdʒən] *n* regione *f*; **in the** ~ **of** (*fig*)
all'incirca di.
regional ['riːdʒənl] *adj* regionale.
regional development *n* sviluppo
regionale.
register ['rɛdʒɪstə*] *n* registro; (*also:*
electoral ~) lista elettorale ♦ *vt*
registrare; (*vehicle*) immatricolare;
(*luggage*) spedire assicurato(a); (*letter*)
assicurare; (*subj: instrument*) segnare ♦ *vi*
iscriversi; (*at hotel*) firmare il registro;
(*make impression*) entrare in testa; **to** ~ **a**
protest fare un esposto; **to** ~ **for a course**
iscriversi a un corso.
registered ['rɛdʒɪstəd] *adj* (*design*)
depositato(a); (*BRIT: letter*) assicurato(a);
(*student, voter*) iscritto(a).
registered company *n* società iscritta al
registro.
registered nurse *n* (*US*) infermiere(a)
diplomato(a).
registered office *n* sede *f* legale.
registered trademark *n* marchio
depositato.
registrar ['rɛdʒɪstrɑː*] *n* ufficiale *m* di stato
civile; segretario.
registration [rɛdʒɪs'treɪʃən] *n* (*act*)
registrazione *f*; iscrizione *f*; (*AUT: also:* ~
number) numero di targa.
registry ['rɛdʒɪstrɪ] *n* ufficio del registro.
registry office *n* (*BRIT*) anagrafe *f*; **to get**
married in a ~ ≈ sposarsi in municipio.
regret [rɪ'grɛt] *n* rimpianto, rincrescimento
♦ *vt* rimpiangere; **I** ~ **that I/he cannot**
help mi rincresce di non poter aiutare/
che lui non possa aiutare; **we** ~ **to inform**
you that ... siamo spiacenti di informarla
che ....
regretfully [rɪ'grɛtfəlɪ] *adv* con
rincrescimento.
regrettable [rɪ'grɛtəbl] *adj* deplorevole.
regrettably [rɪ'grɛtəblɪ] *adv* purtroppo,
sfortunatamente.
regroup [riː'gruːp] *vt* raggruppare ♦ *vi*
raggrupparsi.
regt *abbr* (= *regiment*) Reg.
regular ['rɛgjulə*] *adj* regolare; (*usual*)
abituale, normale; (*listener, reader*) fedele;
(*soldier*) dell'esercito regolare; (*COMM:*
size) normale ♦ *n* (*client etc*) cliente *m/f*
abituale.
regularity [rɛgju'lærɪtɪ] *n* regolarità *f inv*.
regularly ['rɛgjuləlɪ] *adv* regolarmente.
regulate ['rɛgjuleɪt] *vt* regolare.

regulation [rɛgju'leɪʃən] *n* (*rule*) regola,
regolamento; (*adjustment*) regolazione *f*
♦ *cpd* (*MIL*) di ordinanza.
rehabilitate [riːə'bɪlɪteɪt] *vt* (*criminal, drug*
addict, invalid) ricuperare, reinserire.
rehabilitation ['riːəbɪlɪ'teɪʃən] *n* (*see vb*)
ricupero, reinserimento.
rehash [riː'hæʃ] *vt* (*col*) rimaneggiare.
rehearsal [rɪ'həːsəl] *n* prova; **dress** ~ prova
generale.
rehearse [rɪ'həːs] *vt* provare.
rehouse [riː'hauz] *vt* rialloggiare.
reign [reɪn] *n* regno ♦ *vi* regnare.
reigning ['reɪnɪŋ] *adj* (*monarch*) regnante;
(*champion*) attuale.
reimburse [riːɪm'bəːs] *vt* rimborsare.
rein [reɪn] *n* (*for horse*) briglia; **to give sb**
free ~ (*fig*) lasciare completa libertà a
qn.
reincarnation [riːɪnkɑː'neɪʃən] *n*
reincarnazione *f*.
reindeer ['reɪndɪə*] *n* (*pl inv*) renna.
reinforce [riːɪn'fɔːs] *vt* rinforzare.
reinforced concrete [riːɪn'fɔːst-] *n*
cemento armato.
reinforcement [riːɪn'fɔːsmənt] *n* (*action*)
rinforzamento; ~**s** *npl* (*MIL*) rinforzi *mpl*.
reinstate [riːɪn'steɪt] *vt* reintegrare.
reinstatement [riːɪn'steɪtmənt] *n*
reintegrazione *f*.
reissue [riː'ɪʃjuː] *vt* (*book*) ristampare,
ripubblicare; (*film*) distribuire di nuovo.
reiterate [riː'ɪtəreɪt] *vt* reiterare, ripetere.
reject *n* ['riːdʒɛkt] (*COMM*) scarto ♦ *vt*
[rɪ'dʒɛkt] rifiutare, respingere; (*COMM:*
goods) scartare.
rejection [rɪ'dʒɛkʃən] *n* rifiuto.
rejoice [rɪ'dʒɔɪs] *vi*: **to** ~ (**at** *or* **over**)
provare diletto (in).
rejoinder [rɪ'dʒɔɪndə*] *n* (*retort*) replica.
rejuvenate [rɪ'dʒuːvəneɪt] *vt* ringiovanire.
rekindle [riː'kɪndl] *vt* riaccendere.
relapse [rɪ'læps] *n* (*MED*) ricaduta.
relate [rɪ'leɪt] *vt* (*tell*) raccontare; (*connect*)
collegare ♦ *vi*: **to** ~ **to** (*refer to*) riferirsi a;
(*get on with*) stabilire un rapporto con.
related [rɪ'leɪtɪd] *adj* imparentato(a);
collegato(a), connesso(a); ~ **to**
imparentato(a) con; collegato(a) *or*
connesso(a) con.
relating [rɪ'leɪtɪŋ]: ~ **to** *prep* che riguarda,
rispetto a.
relation [rɪ'leɪʃən] *n* (*person*) parente *m/f*;
(*link*) rapporto, relazione *f*; **in** ~ **to** con
riferimento a; **diplomatic/international**
~**s** rapporti diplomatici/internazionali; **to**
bear a ~ **to** corrispondere a.
relationship [rɪ'leɪʃənʃɪp] *n* rapporto;

(_personal ties_) rapporti _mpl_, relazioni _fpl_; (_also_: **family** ~) legami _mpl_ di parentela; (_affair_) relazione _f_; **they have a good** ~ vanno molto d'accordo.

relative ['rɛlətɪv] _n_ parente _m/f_ ♦ _adj_ relativo(a); (_respective_) rispettivo(a).

relatively ['rɛlətɪvlɪ] _adv_ relativamente; (_fairly, rather_) abbastanza.

relax [rɪ'læks] _vi_ rilasciarsi; (_person_: _unwind_) rilassarsi ♦ _vt_ rilasciare; (_mind, person_) rilassare; ~! (_calm down_) calma!

relaxation [riːlæk'seɪʃən] _n_ rilasciamento; rilassamento; (_entertainment_) ricreazione _f_, svago.

relaxed [rɪ'lækst] _adj_ rilasciato(a); rilassato(a).

relaxing [rɪ'læksɪŋ] _adj_ rilassante.

relay ['riːleɪ] _n_ (_SPORT_) corsa a staffetta ♦ _vt_ (_message_) trasmettere.

release [rɪ'liːs] _n_ (_from prison_) rilascio; (_from obligation_) liberazione _f_; (_of gas etc_) emissione _f_; (_of film etc_) distribuzione _f_; (_record_) disco; (_device_) disinnesto ♦ _vt_ (_prisoner_) rilasciare; (_from obligation, wreckage etc_) liberare; (_book, film_) fare uscire; (_news_) rendere pubblico(a); (_gas etc_) emettere; (_TECH_: catch, spring etc) disinnestare; (_let go_) rilasciare; lasciar andare; sciogliere; **to** ~ **one's grip** mollare la presa; **to** ~ **the clutch** (_AUT_) staccare la frizione.

relegate ['rɛləgeɪt] _vt_ relegare; (_SPORT_): **to be** ~**d** essere retrocesso(a).

relent [rɪ'lɛnt] _vi_ cedere.

relentless [rɪ'lɛntlɪs] _adj_ implacabile.

relevance ['rɛləvəns] _n_ pertinenza; ~ **of sth to sth** rapporto tra qc e qc.

relevant ['rɛləvənt] _adj_ pertinente; (_chapter_) in questione; ~ **to** pertinente a.

reliability [rɪlaɪə'bɪlɪtɪ] _n_ (_of person_) serietà; (_of machine_) affidabilità.

reliable [rɪ'laɪəbl] _adj_ (_person, firm_) fidato(a), che dà affidamento; (_method_) sicuro(a); (_machine_) affidabile.

reliably [rɪ'laɪəblɪ] _adv_: **to be** ~ **informed** sapere da fonti sicure.

reliance [rɪ'laɪəns] _n_: ~ (**on**) dipendenza (da).

reliant [rɪ'laɪənt] _adj_: **to be** ~ **on sth/sb** dipendere da qc/qn.

relic ['rɛlɪk] _n_ (_REL_) reliquia; (_of the past_) resto.

relief [rɪ'liːf] _n_ (_from pain, anxiety_) sollievo; (_help, supplies_) soccorsi _mpl_; (_of guard_) cambio; (_ART, GEO_) rilievo; **by way of light** ~ come diversivo.

relief map _n_ carta in rilievo.

relief road _n_ (_BRIT_) circonvallazione _f_.

relieve [rɪ'liːv] _vt_ (_pain, patient_) sollevare; (_bring help_) soccorrere; (_take over from_: _gen_) sostituire; (: _guard_) rilevare; **to** ~ **sb of sth** (_load_) alleggerire qn di qc; **to** ~ **sb of his command** (_MIL_) esonerare qn dal comando; **to** ~ **o.s.** (_euphemism_) fare i propri bisogni.

relieved [rɪ'liːvd] _adj_ sollevato(a); **to be** ~ **that** ... essere sollevato(a) (dal fatto) che ...; **I'm** ~ **to hear it** mi hai tolto un peso con questa notizia.

religion [rɪ'lɪdʒən] _n_ religione _f_.

religious [rɪ'lɪdʒəs] _adj_ religioso(a).

religious education _n_ religione _f_.

relinquish [rɪ'lɪŋkwɪʃ] _vt_ abbandonare; (_plan, habit_) rinunziare a.

relish ['rɛlɪʃ] _n_ (_CULIN_) condimento; (_enjoyment_) gran piacere _m_ ♦ _vt_ (_food etc_) godere; **to** ~ **doing** adorare fare.

relive [riː'lɪv] _vt_ rivivere.

reload [riː'ləud] _vt_ ricaricare.

relocate [riːləu'keɪt] _vt_ (_business_) trasferire ♦ _vi_: **to** ~ **in** trasferire la propria sede a.

reluctance [rɪ'lʌktəns] _n_ riluttanza.

reluctant [rɪ'lʌktənt] _adj_ riluttante, mal disposto(a); **to be** ~ **to do sth** essere restio a fare qc.

reluctantly [rɪ'lʌktəntlɪ] _adv_ di mala voglia, a malincuore.

rely [rɪ'laɪ]: **to** ~ **on** _vt fus_ contare su; (_be dependent_) dipendere da.

remain [rɪ'meɪn] _vi_ restare, rimanere; **to** ~ **silent** restare in silenzio; **I** ~, **yours faithfully** (_BRIT_: _in letters_) distinti saluti.

remainder [rɪ'meɪndə*] _n_ resto; (_COMM_) rimanenza.

remaining [rɪ'meɪnɪŋ] _adj_ che rimane.

remains [rɪ'meɪnz] _npl_ resti _mpl_.

remand [rɪ'mɑːnd] _n_: **on** ~ in detenzione preventiva ♦ _vt_: **to** ~ **in custody** rinviare in carcere; trattenere a disposizione della legge.

remand home _n_ (_BRIT_) riformatorio, casa di correzione.

remark [rɪ'mɑːk] _n_ osservazione _f_ ♦ _vt_ osservare, dire; (_notice_) notare ♦ _vi_: **to** ~ **on sth** fare dei commenti su qc.

remarkable [rɪ'mɑːkəbl] _adj_ notevole; eccezionale.

remarry [riː'mærɪ] _vi_ risposarsi.

remedial [rɪ'miːdɪəl] _adj_ (_tuition, classes_) di riparazione.

remedy ['rɛmədɪ] _n_: ~ (**for**) rimedio (per) ♦ _vt_ rimediare a.

remember [rɪ'mɛmbə*] _vt_ ricordare, ricordarsi di; **I** ~ **seeing it**, **I** ~ **having seen it** (mi) ricordo di averlo visto; **she** ~**ed to do it** si è ricordata di farlo; ~ **me**

to your wife and children! saluti sua moglie e i bambini da parte mia!
remembrance [rɪ'mɛmbrəns] *n* memoria; ricordo.
Remembrance Sunday *n* (*BRIT*) *see boxed note*.

REMEMBRANCE SUNDAY

Nel Regno Unito, la domenica più vicina all'11 di novembre, data in cui fu firmato l'armistizio con la Germania nel 1918, ricorre il **Remembrance Sunday**, *giorno in cui vengono commemorati i caduti in guerra. In questa occasione molti portano un papavero di carta appuntato al petto in segno di rispetto.*

remind [rɪ'maɪnd] *vt*: **to ~ sb of sth** ricordare qc a qn; **to ~ sb to do** ricordare a qn di fare; **that ~s me!** a proposito!
reminder [rɪ'maɪndə*] *n* richiamo; (*note etc*) promemoria *m inv*
reminisce [rɛmɪ'nɪs] *vi*: **to ~ (about)** abbandonarsi ai ricordi (di).
reminiscences [rɛmɪ'nɪsnsɪz] *npl* reminiscenze *fpl*, memorie *fpl*.
reminiscent [rɛmɪ'nɪsnt] *adj*: **~ of** che fa pensare a, che richiama.
remiss [rɪ'mɪs] *adj* negligente; **it was ~ of me** è stata una negligenza da parte mia.
remission [rɪ'mɪʃən] *n* remissione *f*; (*of fee*) esonero.
remit [rɪ'mɪt] *vt* rimettere.
remittance [rɪ'mɪtəns] *n* rimessa.
remnant ['rɛmnənt] *n* resto, avanzo; **~s** *npl* (*COMM*) scampoli *mpl*; fine *f* serie.
remonstrate ['rɛmənstreɪt] *vi* protestare; **to ~ with sb about sth** fare le proprie rimostranze a qn circa qc.
remorse [rɪ'mɔːs] *n* rimorso.
remorseful [rɪ'mɔːsful] *adj* pieno(a) di rimorsi.
remorseless [rɪ'mɔːslɪs] *adj* spietato(a).
remote [rɪ'məut] *adj* remoto(a), lontano(a); (*person*) distaccato(a); **there is a ~ possibility that** ... c'è una vaga possibilità che ... + *sub*.
remote control *n* telecomando.
remote-controlled [rɪ'məutkən'trəuld] *adj* telecomandato(a).
remotely [rɪ'məutlɪ] *adv* remotamente; (*slightly*) vagamente.
remould ['riːməuld] *n* (*BRIT*: *tyre*) gomma rivestita.
removable [rɪ'muːvəbl] *adj* (*detachable*) staccabile.
removal [rɪ'muːvəl] *n* (*taking away*) rimozione *f*; soppressione *f*; (*from house*) trasloco; (*from office*: *sacking*) destituzione *f*; (*MED*) ablazione *f*.
removal man *n* (*BRIT*) addetto ai traslochi.
removal van *n* (*BRIT*) furgone *m* per traslochi.
remove [rɪ'muːv] *vt* togliere, rimuovere; (*employee*) destituire; (*stain*) far sparire; (*doubt, abuse*) sopprimere, eliminare; **first cousin once ~d** cugino di secondo grado.
remover [rɪ'muːvə*] *n* (*for paint*) prodotto sverniciante; (*for varnish*) solvente *m*; **make-up ~** struccatore *m*.
remunerate [rɪ'mjuːnəreɪt] *vt* rimunerare.
remuneration [rɪmjuːnə'reɪʃən] *n* rimunerazione *f*.
Renaissance [rə'neɪsəns] *n*: **the ~** il Rinascimento.
rename [riː'neɪm] *vt* ribattezzare.
rend, *pt*, *pp* **rent** [rɛnd, rɛnt] *vt* lacerare.
render ['rɛndə*] *vt* rendere; (*CULIN*: *fat*) struggere.
rendering ['rɛndərɪŋ] *n* (*MUS etc*) interpretazione *f*.
rendez-vous ['rɔndɪvuː] *n* appuntamento; (*place*) luogo d'incontro; (*meeting*) incontro ♦ *vi* ritrovarsi; (*spaceship*) effettuare un rendez-vous.
rendition [rɛn'dɪʃən] *n* (*MUS*) interpretazione *f*.
renegade ['rɛnɪgeɪd] *n* rinnegato/a.
renew [rɪ'njuː] *vt* rinnovare; (*negotiations*) riprendere.
renewable [rɪ'njuːəbl] *adj* riutilizzabile; **~ energy, ~s** fonti *mpl* di energia rinnovabile.
renewal [rɪ'njuːəl] *n* rinnovamento; ripresa.
renounce [rɪ'nauns] *vt* rinunziare a; (*disown*) ripudiare.
renovate ['rɛnəveɪt] *vt* rinnovare; (*art work*) restaurare.
renovation [rɛnə'veɪʃən] *n* rinnovamento; restauro.
renown [rɪ'naun] *n* rinomanza.
renowned [rɪ'naund] *adj* rinomato(a).
rent [rɛnt] *pt*, *pp of* **rend** ♦ *n* affitto ♦ *vt* (*take for rent*) prendere in affitto; (*car, TV*) noleggiare, prendere a noleggio; (*also*: **~ out**) dare in affitto; (*car, TV*) noleggiare, dare a noleggio.
rental ['rɛntl] *n* (*cost*: *on TV, telephone*) abbonamento; (: *on car*) nolo, noleggio.
rent boy *n* (*BRIT col*) giovane prostituto.
renunciation [rɪnʌnsɪ'eɪʃən] *n* rinnegamento; (*self-denial*) rinunzia.
reopen [riː'əupən] *vt* riaprire.
reopening [riː'əupnɪŋ] *n* riapertura.

reorder [riː'ɔːdə*] *vt* ordinare di nuovo; (*rearrange*) riorganizzare.
reorganize [riː'ɔːgənaɪz] *vt* riorganizzare.
Rep *abbr* (*US POL*) = **representative; republican.**
rep [rɛp] *n abbr* (*COMM*: = *representative*) rappresentante *m/f*; (*THEAT*: = *repertory*) teatro di repertorio.
repair [rɪ'pɛə*] *n* riparazione *f* ♦ *vt* riparare; **in good/bad** ~ in buona/cattiva condizione; **under** ~ in riparazione.
repair kit *n* corredo per riparazioni.
repair man *n* riparatore *m*.
repair shop *n* (*AUT etc*) officina.
repartee [rɛpɑː'tiː] *n* risposta pronta.
repast [rɪ'pɑːst] *n* (*formal*) pranzo.
repatriate [riː'pætrɪeɪt] *vt* rimpatriare.
repay [riː'peɪ] *vt irreg* (*money, creditor*) rimborsare, ripagare; (*sb's efforts*) ricompensare.
repayment [riː'peɪmənt] *n* rimborsamento; ricompensa.
repeal [rɪ'piːl] *n* (*of law*) abrogazione *f*; (*of sentence*) annullamento ♦ *vt* abrogare; annullare.
repeat [rɪ'piːt] *n* (*RADIO, TV*) replica ♦ *vt* ripetere; (*pattern*) riprodurre; (*promise, attack, also COMM: order*) rinnovare ♦ *vi* ripetere.
repeatedly [rɪ'piːtɪdlɪ] *adv* ripetutamente, spesso.
repeat order *n* (*COMM*): **to place a** ~ (**for**) rinnovare l'ordinazione (di).
repel [rɪ'pɛl] *vt* respingere.
repellent [rɪ'pɛlənt] *adj* repellente ♦ *n*: **insect** ~ prodotto *m* anti-insetti *inv*; **moth** ~ anti-tarmico.
repent [rɪ'pɛnt] *vi*: **to** ~ (**of**) pentirsi (di).
repentance [rɪ'pɛntəns] *n* pentimento.
repercussion [riːpə'kʌʃən] *n* (*consequence*) ripercussione *f*.
repertoire ['rɛpətwɑː*] *n* repertorio.
repertory ['rɛpətərɪ] *n* (*also*: ~ **theatre**) teatro di repertorio.
repertory company *n* compagnia di repertorio.
repetition [rɛpɪ'tɪʃən] *n* ripetizione *f*; (*COMM*: *of order etc*) rinnovo.
repetitious [rɛpɪ'tɪʃəs] *adj* (*speech*) pieno(a) di ripetizioni.
repetitive [rɪ'pɛtɪtɪv] *adj* (*movement*) che si ripete; (*work*) monotono(a); (*speech*) pieno(a) di ripetizioni.
replace [rɪ'pleɪs] *vt* (*put back*) rimettere a posto; (*take the place of*) sostituire; (*TEL*): *"*~ **the receiver"** "riattaccare".
replacement [rɪ'pleɪsmənt] *n* rimessa; sostituzione *f*; (*person*) sostituto/a.

replacement part *n* pezzo di ricambio.
replay ['riːpleɪ] *n* (*of match*) partita ripetuta; (*of tape, film*) replay *m inv*.
replenish [rɪ'plɛnɪʃ] *vt* (*glass*) riempire; (*stock etc*) rifornire.
replete [rɪ'pliːt] *adj*: ~ (**with**) ripieno(a) (di); (*well-fed*) sazio(a) (di).
replica ['rɛplɪkə] *n* replica, copia.
reply [rɪ'plaɪ] *n* risposta ♦ *vi* rispondere; **in** ~ **in risposta; there's no** ~ (*TEL*) non risponde (nessuno).
reply coupon *n* buono di risposta.
report [rɪ'pɔːt] *n* rapporto; (*PRESS etc*) cronaca; (*BRIT*: *also*: **school** ~) pagella ♦ *vt* riportare; (*PRESS etc*) fare una cronaca su; (*bring to notice*: *occurrence*) segnalare; (: *person*) denunciare ♦ *vi* (*make a report*) fare un rapporto (*or* una cronaca); (*present o.s.*): **to** ~ (**to sb**) presentarsi (a qn); **to** ~ (**on**) fare un rapporto (su); **it is** ~**ed that** si dice che; **it is** ~**ed from Berlin that** ... ci è stato riferito da Berlino che ....
report card *n* (*US, Scottish*) pagella.
reportedly [rɪ'pɔːtɪdlɪ] *adv*: **she is** ~ **living in Spain** si dice che vive in Spagna.
reported speech [rɪ'pɔːtɪd-] *n* (*LING*) discorso indiretto.
reporter [rɪ'pɔːtə*] *n* (*PRESS*) cronista *m/f*; reporter *m inv*; (*RADIO*) radiocronista *m/f*; (*TV*) telecronista *m/f*.
repose [rɪ'pəuz] *n*: **in** ~ in riposo.
repossess [riːpə'zɛs] *vt* rientrare in possesso di.
repossession order [riːpə'zɛʃən-] *n* ordine *m* di espropriazione.
reprehensible [rɛprɪ'hɛnsɪbl] *adj* riprensibile.
represent [rɛprɪ'zɛnt] *vt* rappresentare.
representation [rɛprɪzɛn'teɪʃən] *n* rappresentazione *f*; ~**s** *npl* (*protest*) protesta.
representative [rɛprɪ'zɛntətɪv] *n* rappresentativo/a; (*COMM*) rappresentante *m* (di commercio); (*US: POL*) deputato/a ♦ *adj*: ~ (**of**) rappresentativo(a) (di).
repress [rɪ'prɛs] *vt* reprimere.
repression [rɪ'prɛʃən] *n* repressione *f*.
repressive [rɪ'prɛsɪv] *adj* repressivo(a).
reprieve [rɪ'priːv] *n* (*LAW*) sospensione *f* dell'esecuzione della condanna; (*fig*) dilazione *f* ♦ *vt* sospendere l'esecuzione della condanna a; accordare una dilazione a.
reprimand ['rɛprɪmɑːnd] *n* rimprovero ♦ *vt* rimproverare, redarguire.
reprint ['riːprɪnt] *n* ristampa ♦ *vt*

ristampare.

reprisal [rɪ'praɪzl] n rappresaglia; **to take** ~**s** fare delle rappresaglie.

reproach [rɪ'prəʊtʃ] n rimprovero ♦ vt: **to** ~ **sb with sth** rimproverare qn di qc; **beyond** ~ irreprensibile.

reproachful [rɪ'prəʊtʃful] adj di rimprovero.

reproduce [riːprə'djuːs] vt riprodurre ♦ vi riprodursi.

reproduction [riːprə'dʌkʃən] n riproduzione f.

reproductive [riːprə'dʌktɪv] adj riproduttore(trice); riproduttivo(a).

reproof [rɪ'pruːf] n riprovazione f.

reprove [rɪ'pruːv] vt (action) disapprovare; (person): **to** ~ **(for)** biasimare (per).

reproving [rɪ'pruːvɪŋ] adj di disapprovazione.

reptile ['reptaɪl] n rettile m.

Repub. abbr (US POL) = **republican.**

republic [rɪ'pʌblɪk] n repubblica

republican [rɪ'pʌblɪkən] adj, n repubblicano(a).

repudiate [rɪ'pjuːdɪeɪt] vt ripudiare.

repugnant [rɪ'pʌgnənt] adj ripugnante.

repulse [rɪ'pʌls] vt respingere.

repulsion [rɪ'pʌlʃən] n ripulsione f.

repulsive [rɪ'pʌlsɪv] adj ripugnante, ripulsivo(a).

reputable ['repjutəbl] adj di buona reputazione; (occupation) rispettabile.

reputation [repju'teɪʃən] n reputazione f; **he has a** ~ **for being awkward** ha la fama di essere un tipo difficile.

repute [rɪ'pjuːt] n reputazione f.

reputed [rɪ'pjuːtɪd] adj reputato(a); **to be** ~ **to be rich/intelligent** etc essere ritenuto(a) ricco(a)/intelligente etc.

reputedly [rɪ'pjuːtɪdlɪ] adv secondo quanto si dice.

request [rɪ'kwest] n domanda; (formal) richiesta ♦ vt: **to** ~ **(of** or **from sb)** chiedere (a qn); **at the** ~ **of** su richiesta di; **"you are** ~**ed not to smoke"** "si prega di non fumare".

request stop n (BRIT: for bus) fermata facoltativa or a richiesta.

requiem ['rekwɪəm] n requiem m or f inv.

require [rɪ'kwaɪə*] vt (need: subj: person) aver bisogno di; (: thing, situation) richiedere; (want) volere; esigere; (order) obbligare; **to** ~ **sb to do sth/sth of sb** esigere che qn faccia qc/qc da qn; **what qualifications are** ~**d?** che requisiti ci vogliono?; ~**d by law** prescritto dalla legge; **if** ~**d** in caso di bisogno.

required [rɪ'kwaɪəd] adj richiesto(a).

requirement [rɪ'kwaɪəmənt] n (need) esigenza; (condition) requisito; **to meet sb's** ~**s** soddisfare le esigenze di qn.

requisite ['rekwɪzɪt] n cosa necessaria ♦ adj necessario(a); **toilet** ~**s** articoli mpl da toletta.

requisition [rekwɪ'zɪʃən] n: ~ **(for)** richiesta (di) ♦ vt (MIL) requisire.

reroute [riː'ruːt] vt (train etc) deviare.

resale ['riːseɪl] n rivendita.

resale price maintenance (RPM) n prezzo minimo di vendita imposto.

rescind [rɪ'sɪnd] vt annullare; (law) abrogare; (judgement) rescindere.

rescue ['reskjuː] n salvataggio; (help) soccorso ♦ vt salvare; **to come/go to sb's** ~ venire/andare in aiuto a or di qn.

rescue party n squadra di salvataggio.

rescuer ['reskjuə*] n salvatore/trice.

research [rɪ'səːtʃ] n ricerca, ricerche fpl ♦ vt fare ricerche su ♦ vi: **to** ~ **(into sth)** fare ricerca (su qc), **a piece of** ~ un lavoro di ricerca; ~ **and development (R&D)** ricerca e sviluppo.

researcher [rɪ'səːtʃə*] n ricercatore/trice.

research work n ricerche fpl.

resell [riː'sel] vt irreg rivendere.

resemblance [rɪ'zembləns] n somiglianza; **to bear a strong** ~ **to** somigliare moltissimo a.

resemble [rɪ'zembl] vt assomigliare a.

resent [rɪ'zent] vt risentirsi di.

resentful [rɪ'zentful] adj pieno(a) di risentimento.

resentment [rɪ'zentmənt] n risentimento.

reservation [rezə'veɪʃən] n (booking) prenotazione f; (doubt) dubbio; (protected area) riserva; (BRIT AUT: also: **central** ~) spartitraffico m inv; **to make a** ~ **(in an hotel/a restaurant/on a plane)** prenotare (una camera/una tavola/un posto); **with** ~**s** (doubts) con le dovute riserve.

reservation desk n (US: in hotel) reception f inv.

reserve [rɪ'zəːv] n riserva ♦ vt (seats etc) prenotare; ~**s** npl (MIL) riserve fpl; **in** ~ in serbo.

reserve currency n valuta di riserva.

reserved [rɪ'zəːvd] adj (shy) riservato(a); (seat) prenotato(a).

reserve price n (BRIT) prezzo di riserva, prezzo m base inv.

reserve team n (BRIT SPORT) seconda squadra.

reservist [rɪ'zəːvɪst] n (MIL) riservista m.

reservoir ['rezəvwɑː*] n serbatoio; (artificial lake) bacino idrico.

reset [riː'set] vt (COMPUT) azzerare.

reshape [riː'ʃeɪp] *vt* (*policy*) ristrutturare.
reshuffle [riː'ʃʌfl] *n*: **Cabinet** ~ (*POL*) rimpasto governativo.
reside [rɪ'zaɪd] *vi* risiedere.
residence ['rɛzɪdəns] *n* residenza; **to take up** ~ prendere residenza; **in** ~ (*queen etc*) in sede; (*doctor*) fisso.
residence permit *n* (*BRIT*) permesso di soggiorno.
resident ['rɛzɪdənt] *n* (*gen, COMPUT*) residente *m/f*; (*in hotel*) cliente *m/f* fisso(a) ♦ *adj* residente.
residential [rɛzɪ'dɛnʃəl] *adj* di residenza; (*area*) residenziale.
residue ['rɛzɪdjuː] *n* resto; (*CHEM, PHYSICS*) residuo.
resign [rɪ'zaɪn] *vt* (*one's post*) dimettersi da ♦ *vi*: **to** ~ (**from**) dimettersi (da), dare le dimissioni (da); **to** ~ **o.s. to** rassegnarsi a.
resignation [rɛzɪg'neɪʃən] *n* dimissioni *fpl*; rassegnazione *f*; **to tender one's** ~ dare le dimissioni.
resilience [rɪ'zɪlɪəns] *n* (*of material*) elasticità, resilienza; (*of person*) capacità di recupero.
resilient [rɪ'zɪlɪənt] *adj* elastico(a); (*person*) che si riprende facilmente.
resin ['rɛzɪn] *n* resina.
resist [rɪ'zɪst] *vt* resistere a.
resistance [rɪ'zɪstəns] *n* resistenza.
resistant [rɪ'zɪstənt] *adj*: ~ (**to**) resistente (a).
resolute ['rɛzəluːt] *adj* risoluto(a).
resolution [rɛzə'luːʃən] *n* (*resolve*) fermo proposito, risoluzione *f*; (*determination*) risolutezza; (*on screen*) risoluzione *f*; **to make a** ~ fare un proposito.
resolve [rɪ'zɔlv] *n* risoluzione *f* ♦ *vi* (*decide*): **to** ~ **to do** decidere di fare ♦ *vt* (*problem*) risolvere.
resolved [rɪ'zɔlvd] *adj* risoluto(a).
resonance ['rɛzənəns] *n* risonanza.
resonant ['rɛzənənt] *adj* risonante.
resort [rɪ'zɔːt] *n* (*town*) stazione *f*; (*place*) località *f inv*; (*recourse*) ricorso ♦ *vi*: **to** ~ **to** far ricorso a; **seaside/winter sports** ~ stazione *f* balneare/di sport invernali; **as a last** ~ come ultima risorsa.
resound [rɪ'zaund] *vi*: **to** ~ (**with**) risonare (di).
resounding [rɪ'zaundɪŋ] *adj* risonante.
resource [rɪ'sɔːs] *n* risorsa; ~**s** *npl* risorse *fpl*; **natural** ~**s** risorse naturali; **to leave sb to his** (*or* **her**) **own** ~**s** (*fig*) lasciare che qn si arrangi (per conto suo).
resourceful [rɪ'sɔːsful] *adj* pieno(a) di risorse, intraprendente.

resourcefulness [rɪ'sɔːsfəlnɪs] *n* intraprendenza.
respect [rɪs'pɛkt] *n* rispetto; (*point, detail*): **in some** ~**s** sotto certi aspetti ♦ *vt* rispettare; ~**s** *npl* ossequi *mpl*; **to have** *or* **show** ~ **for** aver rispetto per; **out of** ~ **for** per rispetto *or* riguardo a; **with** ~ **to** rispetto a, riguardo a; **in** ~ **of** quanto a; **in this** ~ per questo riguardo; **with (all) due** ~ **I** ... con rispetto parlando, io ....
respectability [rɪspɛktə'bɪlɪtɪ] *n* rispettabilità.
respectable [rɪs'pɛktəbl] *adj* rispettabile; (*quite big: amount etc*) considerevole; (*quite good: player, result etc*) niente male *inv*.
respectful [rɪs'pɛktful] *adj* rispettoso(a).
respective [rɪs'pɛktɪv] *adj* rispettivo(a).
respectively [rɪs'pɛktɪvlɪ] *adv* rispettivamente.
respiration [rɛspɪ'reɪʃən] *n* respirazione *f*.
respirator ['rɛspɪreɪtə*] *n* respiratore *m*.
respiratory ['rɛspərətərɪ] *adj* respiratorio(a).
respite ['rɛspaɪt] *n* respiro, tregua.
resplendent [rɪs'plɛndənt] *adj* risplendente.
respond [rɪs'pɔnd] *vi* rispondere.
respondent [rɪs'pɔndənt] *n* (*LAW*) convenuto/a.
response [rɪs'pɔns] *n* risposta; **in** ~ **to** in risposta a.
responsibility [rɪspɔnsɪ'bɪlɪtɪ] *n* responsabilità *f inv*; **to take** ~ **for sth/sb** assumersi *or* prendersi la responsabilità di qc/per qn.
responsible [rɪs'pɔnsɪbl] *adj* (*liable*): ~ (**for**) responsabile (di); (*trustworthy*) fidato(a); (*job*) di (grande) responsabilità; **to be** ~ **to sb (for sth)** dover rispondere a qn (di qc).
responsibly [rɪs'pɔnsəblɪ] *adv* responsabilmente.
responsive [rɪs'pɔnsɪv] *adj* che reagisce.
rest [rɛst] *n* riposo; (*stop*) sosta, pausa; (*MUS*) pausa; (*support*) appoggio, sostegno; (*remainder*) resto, avanzi *mpl* ♦ *vi* riposarsi; (*remain*) rimanere, restare; (*be supported*): **to** ~ **on** appoggiarsi su ♦ *vt* (*lean*): **to** ~ **sth on/against** appoggiare qc su/contro; **to set sb's mind at** ~ tranquillizzare qn; **the** ~ **of them** gli altri; **to** ~ **one's eyes** *or* **gaze on** posare lo sguardo su; ~ **assured that ...** stia tranquillo che ...; **it** ~**s with him to decide** sta a lui decidere.
restart [riː'stɑːt] *vt* (*engine*) rimettere in marcia; (*work*) ricominciare.
restaurant ['rɛstərɔŋ] *n* ristorante *m*.

restaurant car n (BRIT) vagone m ristorante.
rest cure n cura del riposo.
restful ['restful] adj riposante.
rest home n casa di riposo.
restitution [restɪ'tjuːʃən] n (act) restituzione f; (reparation) riparazione f.
restive ['restɪv] adj agitato(a), impaziente; (horse) restio(a).
restless ['restlɪs] adj agitato(a), irrequieto(a); **to get** ~ spazientirsi.
restlessly ['restlɪslɪ] adv in preda all'agitazione.
restock [riː'stɔk] vt rifornire.
restoration [restə'reɪʃən] n restauro; restituzione f.
restorative [rɪ'stɔrətɪv] adj corroborante, ristorativo(a) ♦ n ricostituente m.
restore [rɪ'stɔː*] vt (building) restaurare; (sth stolen) restituire; (peace, health) ristorare.
restorer [rɪs'tɔːrə*] n (ART etc) restauratore/trice.
restrain [rɪs'treɪn] vt (feeling) contenere, frenare; (person): **to** ~ **(from doing)** trattenere (dal fare).
restrained [rɪs'treɪnd] adj (style) contenuto(a), sobrio(a); (manner) riservato(a).
restraint [rɪs'treɪnt] n (restriction) limitazione f; (moderation) ritegno; **wage** ~ restrizioni fpl salariali.
restrict [rɪs'trɪkt] vt restringere, limitare.
restricted area [rɪs'trɪktɪd-] n (AUT) zona a velocità limitata.
restriction [rɪs'trɪkʃən] n restrizione f, limitazione f.
restrictive [rɪs'trɪktɪv] adj restrittivo(a).
restrictive practices npl (INDUSTRY) pratiche restrittive di produzione.
rest room n (US) toletta.
restructure [riː'strʌktʃə*] vt ristrutturare.
result [rɪ'zʌlt] n risultato ♦ vi: **to** ~ **in** avere per risultato; **as a** ~ **(of)** in or di conseguenza (a), in seguito (a); **to** ~ **(from)** essere una conseguenza (di), essere causato(a) (da).
resultant [rɪ'zʌltənt] adj risultante, conseguente.
resume [rɪ'zjuːm] vt, vi (work, journey) riprendere; (sum up) riassumere.
résumé ['reɪzjuːmeɪ] n riassunto; (US: curriculum vitae) curriculum vitae m inv.
resumption [rɪ'zʌmpʃən] n ripresa.
resurgence [rɪ'səːdʒəns] n rinascita.
resurrection [rezə'rekʃən] n risurrezione f.
resuscitate [rɪ'sʌsɪteɪt] vt (MED) risuscitare.

resuscitation [rɪsʌsɪ'teɪʃən] n rianimazione f.
retail ['riːteɪl] n (vendita al) minuto ♦ cpd al minuto ♦ vt vendere al minuto ♦ vi: **to** ~ **at** essere in vendita al pubblico al prezzo di.
retailer ['riːteɪlə*] n commerciante m/f al minuto, dettagliante m/f.
retail outlet n punto di vendita al dettaglio.
retail price n prezzo al minuto.
retail price index n indice m dei prezzi al consumo.
retain [rɪ'teɪn] vt (keep) tenere, serbare.
retainer [rɪ'teɪnə*] n (servant) servitore m; (fee) onorario.
retaliate [rɪ'tælɪeɪt] vi: **to** ~ **(against)** vendicarsi (di); **to** ~ **on sb** fare una rappresaglia contro qn.
retaliation [rɪtælɪ'eɪʃən] n rappresaglie fpl; **in** ~ **for** per vendicarsi di.
retaliatory [rɪ'tælɪətɔrɪ] adj di rappresaglia, di ritorsione.
retarded [rɪ'tɑːdɪd] adj ritardato(a); (also: **mentally** ~) tardo(a) (di mente).
retch [retʃ] vi aver conati di vomito.
retentive [rɪ'tentɪv] adj ritentivo(a).
rethink ['riː'θɪŋk] vt ripensare.
reticence ['retɪsns] n reticenza.
reticent ['retɪsnt] adj reticente.
retina ['retɪnə] n retina.
retinue ['retɪnjuː] n seguito, scorta.
retire [rɪ'taɪə*] vi (give up work) andare in pensione; (withdraw) ritirarsi, andarsene; (go to bed) andare a letto, ritirarsi.
retired [rɪ'taɪəd] adj (person) pensionato(a).
retirement [rɪ'taɪəmənt] n pensione f.
retirement age n età del pensionamento.
retiring [rɪ'taɪərɪŋ] adj (person) riservato(a); (departing: chairman) uscente.
retort [rɪ'tɔːt] n (reply) rimbecco; (container) storta ♦ vi rimbeccare.
retrace [riː'treɪs] vt ricostruire; **to** ~ **one's steps** tornare sui propri passi.
retract [rɪ'trækt] vt (statement) ritrattare; (claws, undercarriage, aerial) ritrarre, ritirare ♦ vi ritrarsi.
retractable [rɪ'træktəbl] adj retrattile.
retrain [riː'treɪn] vt (worker) riaddestrare.
retraining [rɪ'treɪnɪŋ] n riaddestramento.
retread vt [riː'tred] (AUT: tyre) rigenerare ♦ n ['riːtred] gomma rigenerata.
retreat [rɪ'triːt] n ritirata; (place) rifugio ♦ vi battere in ritirata; (flood) ritirarsi; **to beat a hasty** ~ (fig) battersela.
retrial [riː'traɪəl] n nuovo processo.
retribution [retrɪ'bjuːʃən] n castigo.
retrieval [rɪ'triːvəl] n ricupero.

retrieve [rɪˈtriːv] *vt* (*sth lost*) ricuperare, ritrovare; (*situation, honour*) salvare; (*COMPUT*) ricuperare.
retriever [rɪˈtriːvə*] *n* cane *m* da riporto.
retroactive [rɛtrəuˈæktɪv] *adj* retroattivo(a).
retrograde [ˈrɛtrəugreɪd] *adj* retrogrado(a).
retrospect [ˈrɛtrəspɛkt] *n*: **in ~** guardando indietro.
retrospective [rɛtrəˈspɛktɪv] *adj* retrospettivo(a); (*law*) retroattivo(a) ♦ *n* (*ART*) retrospettiva.
return [rɪˈtəːn] *n* (*going or coming back*) ritorno; (*of sth stolen etc*) restituzione *f*; (*COMM: from land, shares*) profitto, reddito; (: *of merchandise*) resa; (*report*) rapporto; (*reward*): **in ~** (**for**) in cambio (di) ♦ *cpd* (*journey, match*) di ritorno; (*BRIT: ticket*) di andata e ritorno ♦ *vi* tornare, ritornare ♦ *vt* rendere, restituire; (*bring back*) riportare; (*send back*) mandare indietro; (*put back*) rimettere; (*POL: candidate*) eleggere; **~s** *npl* (*COMM*) incassi *mpl*; profitti *mpl*; **by ~ of post** a stretto giro di posta; **many happy ~s (of the day)!** auguri!, buon compleanno!
returnable [rɪˈtəːnəbl] *adj*: **~ bottle** vuoto a rendere.
returner [rɪˈtəːnə*] *n donna che ritorna al lavoro dopo la maternità.*
returning officer [rɪˈtəːnɪŋ-] *n* (*BRIT POL*) *funzionario addetto all'organizzazione delle elezioni in un distretto.*
return key *n* (*COMPUT*) tasto di ritorno.
reunion [riːˈjuːnɪən] *n* riunione *f*.
reunite [riːjuːˈnaɪt] *vt* riunire.
rev [rɛv] *n abbr* (= *revolution*: *AUT*) giro ♦ *vb* (*also*: **~ up**) *vt* imballare ♦ *vi* imballarsi.
revaluation [riːvæljuˈeɪʃən] *n* rivalutazione *f*.
revamp [ˈriːˈvæmp] *vt* rinnovare; riorganizzare.
rev counter *n* contagiri *m inv*.
Rev(d). *abbr* = **reverend**.
reveal [rɪˈviːl] *vt* (*make known*) rivelare, svelare; (*display*) rivelare, mostrare.
revealing [rɪˈviːlɪŋ] *adj* rivelatore(trice); (*dress*) scollato(a).
reveille [rɪˈvælɪ] *n* (*MIL*) sveglia.
revel [ˈrɛvl] *vi*: **to ~ in sth/in doing** dilettarsi di qc/a fare.
revelation [rɛvəˈleɪʃən] *n* rivelazione *f*.
reveller [ˈrɛvlə*] *n* festaiolo/a.
revelry [ˈrɛvlrɪ] *n* baldoria.
revenge [rɪˈvɛndʒ] *n* vendetta; (*in game etc*) rivincita ♦ *vt* vendicare; **to take ~** vendicarsi; **to get one's ~ (for sth)** vendicarsi (di qc).

revengeful [rɪˈvɛndʒful] *adj* vendicatore(trice); vendicativo(a).
revenue [ˈrɛvənjuː] *n* reddito.
reverberate [rɪˈvəːbəreɪt] *vi* (*sound*) rimbombare; (*light*) riverberarsi.
reverberation [rɪvəːbəˈreɪʃən] *n* (*of light, sound*) riverberazione *f*.
revere [rɪˈvɪə*] *vt* venerare.
reverence [ˈrɛvərəns] *n* venerazione *f*, riverenza.
Reverend [ˈrɛvərənd] *adj* (*in titles*) reverendo(a).
reverent [ˈrɛvərənt] *adj* riverente.
reverie [ˈrɛvərɪ] *n* fantasticheria.
reversal [rɪˈvəːsl] *n* capovolgimento.
reverse [rɪˈvəːs] *n* contrario, opposto; (*back*) rovescio; (*AUT: also*: **~ gear**) marcia indietro ♦ *adj* (*order*) inverso(a); (*direction*) opposto(a) ♦ *vt* (*turn*) invertire, rivoltare; (*change*) capovolgere, rovesciare; (*LAW: judgement*) cassare ♦ *vi* (*BRIT AUT*) fare marcia indietro; **in ~ order** in ordine inverso; **to go into ~** fare marcia indietro.
reverse-charge call *n* (*BRIT TEL*) telefonata con addebito al ricevente.
reverse video *n* reverse video *m*.
reversible [rɪˈvəːsəbl] *adj* (*garment*) double-face *inv*; (*procedure*) reversibile.
reversing lights [rɪˈvəːsɪŋ-] *npl* (*BRIT AUT*) luci *fpl* per la retromarcia.
reversion [rɪˈvəːʃən] *n* ritorno.
revert [rɪˈvəːt] *vi*: **to ~ to** tornare a.
review [rɪˈvjuː] *n* rivista; (*of book, film*) recensione *f* ♦ *vt* passare in rivista; fare la recensione di; **to come under ~** essere preso in esame.
reviewer [rɪˈvjuːə*] *n* recensore/a.
revile [rɪˈvaɪl] *vt* insultare.
revise [rɪˈvaɪz] *vt* (*manuscript*) rivedere, correggere; (*opinion*) emendare, modificare; (*study: subject, notes*) ripassare; **~d edition** edizione riveduta.
revision [rɪˈvɪʒən] *n* revisione *f*; ripasso; (*revised version*) versione *f* riveduta e corretta.
revitalize [riːˈvaɪtəlaɪz] *vt* ravvivare.
revival [rɪˈvaɪvəl] *n* ripresa; ristabilimento; (*of faith*) risveglio.
revive [rɪˈvaɪv] *vt* (*person*) rianimare; (*custom*) far rivivere; (*hope, courage*) ravvivare; (*play, fashion*) riesumare ♦ *vi* (*person*) rianimarsi; (*hope*) ravvivarsi; (*activity*) riprendersi.
revoke [rɪˈvəuk] *vt* revocare; (*promise, decision*) rinvenire su.
revolt [rɪˈvəult] *n* rivolta, ribellione *f* ♦ *vi* rivoltarsi, ribellarsi; **to ~ (against sb/**

sth) ribellarsi (a qn/qc).
revolting [rɪ'vəultɪŋ] *adj* ripugnante.
revolution [rɛvə'luːʃən] *n* rivoluzione *f*; (*of wheel etc*) rivoluzione, giro.
revolutionary [rɛvə'luːʃənrɪ] *adj, n* rivoluzionario(a).
revolutionize [rɛvə'luːʃənaɪz] *vt* rivoluzionare.
revolve [rɪ'vɔlv] *vi* girare.
revolver [rɪ'vɔlvə*] *n* rivoltella.
revolving [rɪ'vɔlvɪŋ] *adj* girevole.
revolving door *n* porta girevole.
revue [rɪ'vjuː] *n* (*THEAT*) rivista.
revulsion [rɪ'vʌlʃən] *n* ripugnanza.
reward [rɪ'wɔːd] *n* ricompensa, premio ♦ *vt*: **to ~ (for)** ricompensare (per).
rewarding [rɪ'wɔːdɪŋ] *adj* (*fig*) soddisfacente; **financially ~** conveniente dal punto di vista economico.
rewind [riː'waɪnd] *vt irreg* (*watch*) ricaricare; (*ribbon etc*) riavvolgere.
rewire [riː'waɪə*] *vt* (*house*) rifare l'impianto elettrico di.
reword [riː'wəːd] *vt* formulare *or* esprimere con altre parole.
rewrite [riː'raɪt] *vt irreg* riscrivere.
Reykjavik ['reɪkjəviːk] *n* Reykjavik *f*.
RFD *abbr* (*US POST*) = rural free delivery.
Rh *abbr* (= rhesus) Rh.
rhapsody ['ræpsədɪ] *n* (*MUS*) rapsodia; (*fig*) elogio stravagante.
rhesus negative ['riːsəs-] *adj* (*MED*) Rh-negativo(a).
rhesus positive *adj* (*MED*) Rh-positivo(a).
rhetoric ['rɛtərɪk] *n* retorica.
rhetorical [rɪ'tɔrɪkl] *adj* retorico(a).
rheumatic [ruː'mætɪk] *adj* reumatico(a).
rheumatism ['ruːmətɪzəm] *n* reumatismo.
rheumatoid arthritis ['ruːmətɔɪd-] *n* artrite *f* reumatoide.
Rhine [raɪn] *n*: **the ~** il Reno.
rhinestone ['raɪnstəun] *n* diamante *m* falso.
rhinoceros [raɪ'nɔsərəs] *n* rinoceronte *m*.
Rhodes [rəudz] *n* Rodi *f*.
Rhodesia [rəu'diːʒə] *n* Rhodesia.
Rhodesian [rəu'diːʒən] *adj, n* Rhodesiano(a).
rhododendron [rəudə'dɛndrn] *n* rododendro.
Rhone [rəun] *n*: **the ~** il Rodano.
rhubarb ['ruːbaːb] *n* rabarbaro.
rhyme [raɪm] *n* rima; (*verse*) poesia ♦ *vi*: **to ~ (with)** fare rima (con); **without ~ or reason** senza capo né coda.
rhythm ['rɪðm] *n* ritmo.
rhythmic(al) ['rɪðmɪk(əl)] *adj* ritmico(a).
rhythmically ['rɪðmɪkəlɪ] *adv* con ritmo.
rhythm method *n* metodo Ogino-Knauss.

RI *abbr* (*US POST*) = Rhode Island ♦ *n abbr* (*BRIT*) = religious instruction.
rib [rɪb] *n* (*ANAT*) costola ♦ *vt* (*tease*) punzecchiare.
ribald ['rɪbəld] *adj* licenzioso(a), volgare.
ribbed [rɪbd] *adj* (*knitting*) a coste.
ribbon ['rɪbən] *n* nastro; **in ~s** (*torn*) a brandelli.
rice [raɪs] *n* riso.
ricefield ['raɪsfiːld] *n* risaia.
rice pudding *n* budino di riso.
rich [rɪtʃ] *adj* ricco(a); (*clothes*) sontuoso(a); **the ~** *npl* i ricchi; **~es** *npl* ricchezze *fpl*; **to be ~ in sth** essere ricco di qc.
richly ['rɪtʃlɪ] *adv* riccamente; (*dressed*) sontuosamente; (*deserved*) pienamente.
rickets ['rɪkɪts] *n* rachitismo.
rickety ['rɪkɪtɪ] *adj* zoppicante.
rickshaw ['rɪkʃɔː] *n* risciò *m inv*.
ricochet ['rɪkəʃeɪ] *n* rimbalzo ♦ *vi* rimbalzare.
rid [rɪd], *pt, pp* **rid** [rɪd] *vt*: **to ~ sb of** sbarazzare *or* liberare qn di; **to get ~ of** sbarazzarsi di.
riddance ['rɪdns] *n*: **good ~!** che liberazione!
ridden ['rɪdn] *pp of* ride.
riddle ['rɪdl] *n* (*puzzle*) indovinello ♦ *vt*: **to be ~d with** essere crivellato(a) di.
ride [raɪd] *n* (*on horse*) cavalcata; (*outing*) passeggiata; (*distance covered*) cavalcata; corsa ♦ *vb* (*pt* **rode**, *pp* **ridden** [rəud, 'rɪdn]) *vi* (*as sport*) cavalcare; (*go somewhere: on horse, bicycle*) andare (a cavallo *or* in bicicletta *etc*); (*journey: on bicycle, motorcycle, bus*) andare, viaggiare ♦ *vt* (*a horse*) montare, cavalcare; **to go for a ~** andare a fare una cavalcata; andare a fare un giro; **can you ~ a bike?** sai andare in bicicletta?; **we rode all day/all the way** abbiamo cavalcato tutto il giorno/per tutto il tragitto; **to ~ a horse/bicycle/camel** montare a cavallo/in bicicletta/in groppa a un cammello; **to ~ at anchor** (*NAUT*) essere alla fonda; **horse/car ~** passeggiata in macchina; **to take sb for a ~** (*fig*) prendere in giro qn; fregare qn.
▶**ride out** *vt*: **to ~ out the storm** (*fig*) mantenersi a galla.
rider ['raɪdə*] *n* cavalcatore/trice; (*jockey*) fantino; (*on bicycle*) ciclista *m/f*; (*on motorcycle*) motociclista *m/f*; (*in document*) clausola addizionale, aggiunta.
ridge [rɪdʒ] *n* (*of hill*) cresta; (*of roof*) colmo; (*of mountain*) giogo; (*on object*) riga (in rilievo).
ridicule ['rɪdɪkjuːl] *n* ridicolo ♦ *vt* mettere in

ridicolo; **to hold sb/sth up to** ~ mettere in ridicolo qn/qc.

ridiculous [rɪ'dɪkjʊləs] *adj* ridicolo(a).

riding ['raɪdɪŋ] *n* equitazione *f*.

riding school *n* scuola d'equitazione.

rife [raɪf] *adj* diffuso(a); **to be** ~ **with** abbondare di.

riffraff ['rɪfræf] *n* canaglia, gentaglia.

rifle ['raɪfl] *n* carabina ♦ *vt* vuotare.

▸**rifle through** *vt fus* frugare.

rifle range *n* campo di tiro; (*at fair*) tiro a segno.

rift [rɪft] *n* fessura, crepatura; (*fig: disagreement*) incrinatura.

rig [rɪg] *n* (*also:* **oil** ~: **on land**) derrick *m inv*; (: *at sea*) piattaforma di trivellazione ♦ *vt* (*election etc*) truccare.

▸**rig out** *vt* (*BRIT*) attrezzare; (*pej*) abbigliare, agghindare.

▸**rig up** *vt* allestire.

rigging ['rɪgɪŋ] *n* (*NAUT*) attrezzatura.

right [raɪt] *adj* giusto(a); (*suitable*) appropriato(a); (*not left*) destro(a) ♦ *n* (*title, claim*) diritto; (*not left*) destra ♦ *adv* (*answer*) correttamente; (*not on the left*) a destra ♦ *vt* raddrizzare; (*fig*) riparare ♦ *excl* bene!; **the** ~ **time** l'ora esatta; **to be** ~ (*person*) aver ragione; (*answer*) essere giusto(a) *or* corretto(a); **to get sth** ~ far giusto qc; **you did the** ~ **thing** ha fatto bene; **let's get it** ~ **this time!** cerchiamo di farlo bene stavolta!; **to put a mistake** ~ (*BRIT*) correggere un errore; ~ **now** proprio adesso; subito; ~ **away** subito; ~ **before/after** subito prima/dopo; **to go** ~ **to the end of sth** andare fino in fondo a qc; ~ **against the wall** proprio contro il muro; ~ **ahead** sempre diritto; proprio davanti; ~ **in the middle** proprio nel mezzo; **by** ~**s** di diritto; **on the** ~, **to the** ~ a destra; ~ **and wrong** il bene e il male; **to have a** ~ **to sth** aver diritto a qc; **film** ~**s** diritti di riproduzione cinematografica; ~ **of way** diritto di passaggio; (*AUT*) precedenza.

right angle *n* angolo retto.

righteous ['raɪtʃəs] *adj* retto(a), virtuoso(a); (*anger*) giusto(a), giustificato(a).

righteousness ['raɪtʃəsnɪs] *n* rettitudine *f*, virtù *f*.

rightful ['raɪtful] *adj* (*heir*) legittimo(a).

rightfully ['raɪtfəlɪ] *adv* legittimamente.

right-handed [raɪt'hændɪd] *adj* (*person*) che adopera la mano destra.

right-hand man ['raɪthænd-] *n* braccio destro (*fig*).

right-hand side *n* lato destro.

rightly ['raɪtlɪ] *adv* bene, correttamente; (*with reason*) a ragione; **if I remember** ~ se mi ricordo bene.

right-minded [raɪt'maɪndɪd] *adj* sensato(a).

rights issue *n* (*STOCK EXCHANGE*) emissione *f* di azioni riservate agli azionisti.

right wing *n* (*MIL, SPORT*) ala destra; (*POL*) destra ♦ *adj*: **right-wing** (*POL*) di destra.

right-winger [raɪt'wɪŋə*] *n* (*POL*) uno/a di destra; (*SPORT*) ala destra.

rigid ['rɪdʒɪd] *adj* rigido(a); (*principle*) rigoroso(a).

rigidity [rɪ'dʒɪdɪtɪ] *n* rigidità.

rigidly ['rɪdʒɪdlɪ] *adv* rigidamente.

rigmarole ['rɪgmərəul] *n* tiritera; commedia.

rigor ['rɪgə*] *n* (*US*) = **rigour**.

rigor mortis ['rɪgə'mɔːtɪs] *n* rigidità cadaverica.

rigorous ['rɪgərəs] *adj* rigoroso(a).

rigorously ['rɪgərəslɪ] *adv* rigorosamente.

rigour, (*US*) **rigor** ['rɪgə*] *n* rigore *m*.

rig-out ['rɪgaut] *n* (*BRIT col*) tenuta.

rile [raɪl] *vt* irritare, seccare.

rim [rɪm] *n* orlo; (*of spectacles*) montatura; (*of wheel*) cerchione *m*.

rimless ['rɪmlɪs] *adj* (*spectacles*) senza montatura.

rimmed [rɪmd] *adj* bordato(a); cerchiato(a).

rind [raɪnd] *n* (*of bacon*) cotenna; (*of lemon etc*) scorza.

ring [rɪŋ] *n* anello; (*also:* **wedding** ~) fede *f*; (*of people, objects*) cerchio; (*of spies*) giro; (*of smoke etc*) spirale *f*; (*arena*) pista, arena; (*for boxing*) ring *m inv*; (*sound of bell*) scampanio; (*telephone call*) colpo di telefono ♦ *vb* (*pt* **rang**, *pp* **rung** [ræŋ, rʌŋ]) *vi* (*person, bell, telephone*) suonare; (*also:* ~ **out**: *voice, words*) risuonare; (*TEL*) telefonare ♦ *vt* (*BRIT TEL*: *also:* ~ **up**) telefonare a; **to give sb a** ~ (*TEL*) dare un colpo di telefono a qn; **that has the** ~ **of truth about it** questo ha l'aria d'essere vero; **to** ~ **the bell** suonare il campanello; **the name doesn't** ~ **a bell (with me)** questo nome non mi dice niente.

▸**ring back** *vt, vi* (*BRIT TEL*) richiamare.

▸**ring off** *vi* (*BRIT TEL*) mettere giù, riattaccare.

ring binder *n* classificatore *m* a anelli.

ring finger *n* anulare *m*.

ringing ['rɪŋɪŋ] *n* (*of bell*) scampanio; (: *louder*) scampanellata; (*of telephone*) squillo; (*in ears*) fischio, ronzio.

ringing tone *n* (*BRIT TEL*) segnale *m* di libero.

ringleader ['rɪŋliːdə*] *n* (*of gang*)

capobanda *m.*

ringlets ['rɪŋlɪts] *npl* boccoli *mpl.*

ring road *n* (*BRIT*) raccordo anulare.

rink [rɪŋk] *n* (*also*: **ice** ~) pista di pattinaggio; (*for roller-skating*) pista di pattinaggio (a rotelle).

rinse [rɪns] *n* risciacquatura; (*hair tint*) cachet *m inv* ♦ *vt* sciacquare.

Rio (de Janeiro) ['riːəu(dədʒə'nɪərəu)] *n* Rio de Janeiro *f.*

riot ['raɪət] *n* sommossa, tumulto ♦ *vi* tumultuare; **a** ~ **of colours** un'orgia di colori; **to run** ~ creare disordine.

rioter ['raɪətə*] *n* dimostrante *m/f* (*durante dei disordini*).

riot gear *n*: **in** ~ in assetto di guerra.

riotous ['raɪətəs] *adj* tumultuoso(a); che fa crepare dal ridere.

riotously ['raɪətəslɪ] *adv*: ~ **funny** che fa crepare dal ridere.

riot police *n* ≈ la Celere.

RIP *abbr* (= *rest in peace*) R.I.P.

rip [rɪp] *n* strappo ♦ *vt* strappare ♦ *vi* strapparsi.

►**rip up** *vt* stracciare.

ripcord ['rɪpkɔːd] *n* cavo di spiegamento.

ripe [raɪp] *adj* (*fruit*) maturo(a); (*cheese*) stagionato(a).

ripen ['raɪpən] *vt* maturare ♦ *vi* maturarsi; stagionarsi.

ripeness ['raɪpnɪs] *n* maturità.

rip-off ['rɪpɔf] *n* (*col*): **it's a** ~! è un furto!

riposte [rɪ'pɔst] *n* risposta per le rime.

ripple ['rɪpl] *n* increspamento, ondulazione *f*; mormorio ♦ *vi* incresparsi ♦ *vt* increspare.

rise [raɪz] *n* (*slope*) salita, pendio; (*hill*) altura; (*increase: in wages*) aumento; (: *in prices, temperature*) rialzo, aumento; (*fig*: *to power etc*) ascesa ♦ *vi* (*pt* **rose**, *pp* **risen** [rəuz, 'rɪzn]) alzarsi, levarsi; (*prices*) aumentare; (*waters, river*) crescere; (*sun, wind*) levarsi; (*also*: ~ **up**: *rebel*) insorgere; ribellarsi; **to give** ~ **to** provocare, dare origine a; **to** ~ **to the occasion** dimostrarsi all'altezza della situazione.

rising ['raɪzɪŋ] *adj* (*increasing: number*) sempre crescente; (*prices*) in aumento; (*tide*) montante; (*sun, moon*) nascente, che sorge ♦ *n* (*uprising*) sommossa.

rising damp *n* infiltrazioni *fpl* d'umidità.

rising star *n* (*also fig*) astro nascente.

risk [rɪsk] *n* rischio ♦ *vt* rischiare; **to take** *or* **run the** ~ **of doing** correre il rischio di fare; **at** ~ in pericolo; **at one's own** ~ a proprio rischio e pericolo; **fire/health** ~ rischio d'incendio/per la salute; **I'll** ~ **it** ci proverò lo stesso.

risk capital *n* capitale *m* di rischio.

risky ['rɪskɪ] *adj* rischioso(a).

risqué ['riːskeɪ] *adj* (*joke*) spinto(a).

rissole ['rɪsəul] *n* crocchetta.

rite [raɪt] *n* rito; **last** ~**s** l'estrema unzione.

ritual ['rɪtjuəl] *adj, n* rituale (*m*).

rival ['raɪvl] *n* rivale *m/f*; (*in business*) concorrente *m/f* ♦ *adj* rivale; che fa concorrenza ♦ *vt* essere in concorrenza con; **to** ~ **sb/sth in** competere con qn/qc in.

rivalry ['raɪvlrɪ] *n* rivalità; concorrenza.

river ['rɪvə*] *n* fiume *m* ♦ *cpd* (*port, traffic*) fluviale; **up/down** ~ a monte/valle.

riverbank ['rɪvəbæŋk] *n* argine *m.*

riverbed ['rɪvəbɛd] *n* alveo (fluviale).

riverside ['rɪvəsaɪd] *n* sponda del fiume.

rivet ['rɪvɪt] *n* ribattino, rivetto ♦ *vt* ribadire; (*fig*) concentrare, fissare.

riveting ['rɪvɪtɪŋ] *adj* (*fig*) avvincente.

Riviera [rɪvɪ'ɛərə] *n*: **the (French)** ~ la Costa Azzurra; **the Italian** ~ la Riviera.

Riyadh [rɪ'juːd] *n* Riad *f.*

RMT *n abbr* (= *Rail, Maritime and Transport*) *sindacato dei Ferrovieri, Marittimi e Trasportatori.*

RN *n abbr* (*BRIT*) = **Royal Navy**; (*US*) = **registered nurse**.

RNA *n abbr* (= *ribonucleic acid*) R.N.A. *m.*

RNLI *n abbr* (*BRIT*: = *Royal National Lifeboat Institution*) *associazione volontaria che organizza e dispone di scialuppe di salvataggio.*

RNZAF *n abbr* = *Royal New Zealand Air Force.*

RNZN *n abbr* = *Royal New Zealand Navy.*

road [rəud] *n* strada; (*small*) cammino; (*in town*) via; **main** ~ strada principale; **major/minor** ~ strada con/senza diritto di precedenza; **it takes 4 hours by** ~ sono 4 ore di macchina (*or* in camion *etc*); **on the** ~ **to success** sulla via del successo; "~ **up**" (*BRIT*) "attenzione: lavori in corso".

road accident *n* incidente *m* stradale.

roadblock ['rəudblɔk] *n* blocco stradale.

road haulage *n* autotrasporti *mpl.*

roadhog ['rəudhɔg] *n* pirata *m* della strada.

road map *n* carta stradale.

road rage *n* aggressività al volante.

road safety *n* sicurezza sulle strade.

roadside ['rəudsaɪd] *n* margine *m* della strada; **by the** ~ a lato della strada.

roadsign ['rəudsaɪn] *n* cartello stradale.

roadsweeper ['rəudswiːpə*] *n* (*BRIT*: *person*) spazzino.

road user *n* utente *m/f* della strada.

roadway ['rəudweɪ] *n* carreggiata.

roadworks ['rəudwɔːks] *npl* lavori *mpl* stradali.

roadworthy ['rəudwəːðɪ] *adj* in buono stato di marcia.

roam [rəum] *vi* errare, vagabondare ♦ *vt* vagare per.

roar [rɔː*] *n* ruggito; (*of crowd*) tumulto; (*of thunder, storm*) muggito ♦ *vi* ruggire; tumultuare; muggire; **to ~ with laughter** scoppiare dalle risa.

roaring ['rɔːrɪŋ] *adj*: **a ~ fire** un bel fuoco; **to do a ~ trade** fare affari d'oro; **a ~ success** un successo strepitoso.

roast [rəust] *n* arrosto ♦ *vt* (*meat*) arrostire.

roast beef *n* arrosto di manzo.

roasting ['rəustɪŋ] *n* (*col*): **to give sb a ~** dare una lavata di capo a qn.

rob [rɔb] *vt* (*person*) rubare; (*bank*) svaligiare; **to ~ sb of sth** derubare qn di qc; (*fig: deprive*) privare qn di qc.

robber ['rɔbə*] *n* ladro; (*armed*) rapinatore *m*.

robbery ['rɔbərɪ] *n* furto; rapina.

robe [rəub] *n* (*for ceremony etc*) abito; (*also:* **bath~**) accappatoio ♦ *vt* vestire.

robin ['rɔbɪn] *n* pettirosso.

robot ['rəubɔt] *n* robot *m inv*.

robotics ['rəubɔtɪks] *n* robotica.

robust [rəu'bʌst] *adj* robusto(a); (*material*) solido(a).

rock [rɔk] *n* (*substance*) roccia; (*boulder*) masso; roccia; (*in sea*) scoglio; (*BRIT: sweet*) zucchero candito ♦ *vt* (*swing gently: cradle*) dondolare; (: *child*) cullare; (*shake*) scrollare, far tremare ♦ *vi* dondolarsi; oscillare; **on the ~s** (*drink*) col ghiaccio; (*ship*) sugli scogli; (*marriage etc*) in crisi; **to ~ the boat** (*fig*) piantare grane.

rock and roll *n* rock and roll *m*.

rock-bottom ['rɔk'bɔtəm] *n* (*fig*) stremo; **to reach** *or* **touch ~** (*price*) raggiungere il livello più basso; (*person*) toccare il fondo.

rock climber *n* rocciatore/trice, scalatore/trice.

rock climbing *n* roccia.

rockery ['rɔkərɪ] *n* giardino roccioso.

rocket ['rɔkɪt] *n* razzo; (*MIL*) razzo, missile *m* ♦ *vi* (*prices*) salire alle stelle.

rocket launcher [-lɔːntʃə*] *n* lanciarazzi *m inv*.

rock face *n* parete *f* della roccia.

rock fall *n* caduta di massi.

rocking chair ['rɔkɪŋ-] *n* sedia a dondolo.

rocking horse *n* cavallo a dondolo.

rocky ['rɔkɪ] *adj* (*hill*) roccioso(a); (*path*) sassoso(a); (*unsteady: table*) traballante.

Rocky Mountains *npl*: **the ~** le Montagne Rocciose.

rod [rɔd] *n* (*metallic, TECH*) asta; (*wooden*) bacchetta; (*also:* **fishing ~**) canna da pesca.

rode [rəud] *pt of* **ride**.

rodent ['rəudnt] *n* roditore *m*.

rodeo ['rəudɪəu] *n* rodeo.

roe [rəu] *n* (*species: also:* **~ deer**) capriolo; (*of fish: also:* **hard ~**) uova *fpl* di pesce; **soft ~** latte *m* di pesce.

roe deer *n* (*species*) capriolo; (*female deer: pl inv*) capriolo femmina.

rogue [rəug] *n* mascalzone *m*.

roguish ['rəugɪʃ] *adj* birbantesco(a).

role [rəul] *n* ruolo.

role model *n* modello (di comportamento).

role-play ['rəulpleɪ], **role-playing** ['rəulpleɪɪŋ] *n* il recitare un ruolo, role-playing *m inv*.

roll [rəul] *n* rotolo; (*of banknotes*) mazzo; (*also:* **bread ~**) panino; (*register*) lista; (*sound: of drums etc*) rullo; (*movement: of ship*) rullio ♦ *vt* rotolare; (*also:* **~ up**: *string*) aggomitolare; (*also:* **~ out**: *pastry*) stendere ♦ *vi* rotolare; (*wheel*) girare; **cheese ~** panino al formaggio.

▶**roll about, roll around** *vi* rotolare qua e là; (*person*) rotolarsi.

▶**roll by** *vi* (*time*) passare.

▶**roll in** *vi* (*mail, cash*) arrivare a bizzeffe.

▶**roll over** *vi* rivoltarsi.

▶**roll up** *vi* (*col: arrive*) arrivare ♦ *vt* (*carpet, cloth, map*) arrotolare; (*sleeves*) rimboccare; **to ~ o.s. up into a ball** raggomitolarsi.

roll call *n* appello.

rolled gold [rəuld-] *adj* d'oro laminato.

roller ['rəulə*] *n* rullo; (*wheel*) rotella.

rollerblades ['rəuləbleɪdz] *npl* pattini *mpl* in linea.

roller blind *n* (*BRIT*) avvolgibile *m*.

roller coaster *n* montagne *fpl* russe.

roller skates *npl* pattini *mpl* a rotelle.

rollicking ['rɔlɪkɪŋ] *adj* allegro(a) e chiassoso(a).

rolling ['rəulɪŋ] *adj* (*landscape*) ondulato(a).

rolling pin *n* matterello.

rolling stock *n* (*RAIL*) materiale *m* rotabile.

roll-on-roll-off ['rəulɔn'rəulɔf] *adj* (*BRIT: ferry*) roll-on roll-off *inv*.

roly-poly ['rəulɪ'pəulɪ] *n* (*BRIT CULIN*) rotolo di pasta con ripieno di marmellata.

ROM [rɔm] *n abbr* (*COMPUT:* = *read-only memory*) ROM *f*.

Roman ['rəumən] *adj, n* romano(a).

Roman Catholic *adj, n* cattolico(a).

romance [rə'mæns] *n* storia (*or* avventura *or* film *m inv*) romantico(a); (*charm*) poesia; (*love affair*) idillio.

Romanesque [rəumə'nɛsk] adj romanico(a).
Romania [rəu'meɪnɪə] n Romania.
Romanian [rəu'meɪnɪən] adj romeno(a) ♦ n romeno/a; (LING) romeno.
Roman numeral n numero romano.
romantic [rə'mæntɪk] adj romantico(a); sentimentale.
romanticism [rə'mæntɪsɪzəm] n romanticismo.
Romany ['rɔmənɪ] adj zingaresco(a) ♦ n (person) zingaro/a; (LING) lingua degli zingari.
Rome [rəum] n Roma.
romp [rɔmp] n gioco chiassoso ♦ vi (also: ~ about) giocare chiassosamente; to ~ home (horse) vincere senza difficoltà, stravincere.
rompers ['rɔmpəz] npl pagliaccetto.
rondo ['rɔndəu] n (MUS) rondò m inv.
roof [ruːf] n tetto; (of tunnel, cave) volta ♦ vt coprire (con un tetto); ~ of the mouth palato.
roof garden n giardino pensile.
roofing ['ruːfɪŋ] n materiale m per copertura.
roof rack n (AUT) portabagagli m inv.
rook [ruk] n (bird) corvo nero; (CHESS) torre f ♦ vt (cheat) truffare, spennare.
rookie ['rukɪ] n (col: esp MIL) pivellino/a.
room [ruːm] n (in house) stanza, camera; (in school etc) sala; (space) posto, spazio; ~s npl (lodging) alloggio; "~s to let", (US) "~s for rent" "si affittano camere"; is there ~ for this? c'è spazio per questo?, ci sta anche questo?; to make ~ for sb far posto a qn; there is ~ for improvement si potrebbe migliorare.
rooming house ['ruːmɪŋ-] n (US) casa in cui si affittano camere o appartamentini ammobiliati.
roommate ['ruːmmeɪt] n compagno/a di stanza.
room service n servizio da camera.
room temperature n temperatura ambiente.
roomy ['ruːmɪ] adj spazioso(a); (garment) ampio(a).
roost [ruːst] n appollaiato ♦ vi appollaiarsi.
rooster ['ruːstə*] n gallo.
root [ruːt] n radice f ♦ vt (plant, belief) far radicare; to take ~ (plant) attecchire, prendere; (idea) far presa; the ~ of the problem is that ... il problema deriva dal fatto che ....
▶**root about** vi (fig) frugare.
▶**root for** vt fus (col) fare il tifo per.
▶**root out** vt estirpare.

root beer n (US) bibita dolce a base di estratti di erbe e radici.
rope [rəup] n corda, fune f; (NAUT) cavo ♦ vt (box) legare; (climbers) legare in cordata; to ~ sb in (fig) coinvolgere qn; to know the ~s (fig) conoscere i trucchi del mestiere.
rope ladder n scala di corda.
ropey ['rəupɪ] adj (col) scadente, da quattro soldi; to feel ~ (ill) sentirsi male.
rosary ['rəuzərɪ] n rosario; roseto.
rose [rəuz] pt of **rise** ♦ n rosa; (also: ~ bush) rosaio; (on watering can) rosetta ♦ adj rosa inv.
rosé ['rəuzeɪ] n vino rosato.
rosebed ['rəuzbɛd] n roseto.
rosebud ['rəuzbʌd] n bocciolo di rosa.
rosebush ['rəuzbuʃ] n rosaio.
rosemary ['rəuzmərɪ] n rosmarino.
rosette [rəu'zɛt] n coccarda.
ROSPA ['rɔspə] n abbr (BRIT: = Royal Society for the Prevention of Accidents) ≈ E.N.P.I. m (= Ente Nazionale Prevenzione Infortuni).
roster ['rɔstə*] n: **duty** ~ ruolino di servizio.
rostrum ['rɔstrəm] n tribuna.
rosy ['rəuzɪ] adj roseo(a).
rot [rɔt] n (decay) putrefazione f; (col: nonsense) stupidaggini fpl ♦ vt, vi imputridire, marcire; dry/wet ~ funghi parassiti del legno; to stop the ~ (BRIT fig) salvare la situazione.
rota ['rəutə] n tabella dei turni; on a ~ basis a turno.
rotary ['rəutərɪ] adj rotante.
rotate [rəu'teɪt] vt (revolve) far girare; (change round: crops) avvicendare; (: jobs) fare a turno ♦ vi (revolve) girare.
rotating [rəu'teɪtɪŋ] adj (movement) rotante.
rotation [rəu'teɪʃən] n rotazione f; in ~ a turno, in rotazione.
rote [rəut] n: to learn sth by ~ imparare qc a memoria.
rotor ['rəutə*] n rotore m.
rotten ['rɔtn] adj (decayed) putrido(a), marcio(a); (: teeth) cariato(a); (dishonest) corrotto(a); (col: bad) brutto(a); (: action) vigliacco(a); to feel ~ (ill) sentirsi proprio male.
rotting ['rɔtɪŋ] adj in putrefazione.
rotund [rəu'tʌnd] adj grassoccio(a); tondo(a).
rouble, (US) **ruble** ['ruːbl] n rublo.
rouge [ruːʒ] n belletto.
rough [rʌf] adj aspro(a); (person, manner: coarse) rozzo(a), aspro(a); (: violent) brutale; (district) malfamato(a); (weather) cattivo(a); (plan) abbozzato(a); (guess)

approssimativo(a) ♦ *n* (*GOLF*) macchia; ~ **estimate** approssimazione *f*; **to** ~ **it** far vita dura; **to play** ~ far il gioco pesante; **to sleep** ~ (*BRIT*) dormire all'addiaccio; **to feel** ~ (*BRIT*) sentirsi male; **to have a** ~ **time (of it)** passare un periodaccio; **the sea is** ~ **today** c'è mare grosso oggi.

►**rough out** *vt* (*draft*) abbozzare.

roughage ['rʌfɪdʒ] *n* alimenti *mpl* ricchi di cellulosa.

rough-and-ready ['rʌfən'rɛdɪ] *adj* rudimentale.

rough-and-tumble ['rʌfən'tʌmbl] *n* zuffa.

roughcast ['rʌfkɑːst] *n* intonaco grezzo.

rough copy, rough draft *n* brutta copia.

roughen ['rʌfn] *vt* (*a surface*) rendere ruvido(a).

rough justice *n* giustizia sommaria.

roughly ['rʌflɪ] *adv* (*handle*) rudemente, brutalmente; (*make*) grossolanamente; (*approximately*) approssimativamente; ~ **speaking** grosso modo, ad occhio e croce.

roughness ['rʌfnɪs] *n* asprezza; rozzezza; brutalità.

roughshod ['rʌfʃɔd] *adv*: **to ride** ~ **over** (*person*) mettere sotto i piedi; (*objection*) passare sopra a.

rough work *n* (*at school etc*) brutta copia.

roulette [ruː'lɛt] *n* roulette *f*.

Roumania *etc* [ruː'meɪnɪə] = **Romania** *etc*.

round [raund] *adj* rotondo(a) ♦ *n* tondo, cerchio; (*BRIT*: *of toast*) fetta; (*duty*: *of policeman, milkman etc*) giro; (: *of doctor*) visite *fpl*; (*game*: *of cards, in competition*) partita; (*BOXING*) round *m inv*; (*of talks*) serie *f inv* ♦ *vt* (*corner*) girare; (*bend*) prendere; (*cape*) doppiare ♦ *prep* intorno a ♦ *adv*: **right** ~, **all** ~ tutt'attorno; **the long way** ~ il giro più lungo; **all the year** ~ tutto l'anno; **in** ~ **figures** in cifra tonda; **it's just** ~ **the corner** (*also fig*) è dietro l'angolo; **to ask sb** ~ invitare qn (a casa propria); **I'll be** ~ **at 6 o'clock** ci sarò alle 6; **to go** ~ fare il giro; **to go** ~ **to sb's (house)** andare da qn; **to go** ~ **an obstacle** aggirare un ostacolo; **go** ~ **the back** passi da dietro; **to go** ~ **a house** visitare una casa; **enough to go** ~ abbastanza per tutti; **she arrived** ~ (**about**) **noon** è arrivata intorno a mezzogiorno; ~ **the clock** 24 ore su 24; **to go the** ~**s** (*illness*) diffondersi; (*story*) circolare, passare di bocca in bocca; **the daily** ~ (*fig*) la routine quotidiana; ~ **of ammunition** cartuccia; ~ **of applause** applausi *mpl*; ~ **of drinks** giro di bibite; ~ **of sandwiches** (*BRIT*) sandwich *m inv*.

►**round off** *vt* (*speech etc*) finire.

►**round up** *vt* radunare; (*criminals*) fare una retata di; (*prices*) arrotondare.

roundabout ['raundəbaut] *n* (*BRIT AUT*) rotatoria; (*at fair*) giostra ♦ *adj* (*route, means*) indiretto(a).

rounded ['raundɪd] *adj* arrotondato(a); (*style*) armonioso(a).

rounders ['raundəz] *npl* (*game*) gioco simile al baseball.

roundly ['raundlɪ] *adv* (*fig*) chiaro e tondo.

round robin *n* (*SPORT*: *also*: ~ **tournament**) ≈ torneo all'italiana.

round-shouldered [raund'ʃəuldəd] *adj* dalle spalle tonde.

round trip *n* (viaggio di) andata e ritorno.

roundup ['raundʌp] *n* raduno; (*of criminals*) retata; **a** ~ **of the latest news** un sommario *or* riepilogo delle ultime notizie.

rouse [rauz] *vt* (*wake up*) svegliare; (*stir up*) destare; provocare; risvegliare.

rousing ['rauzɪŋ] *adj* (*speech, applause*) entusiastico(a).

rout [raut] *n* (*MIL*) rotta ♦ *vt* mettere in rotta.

route [ruːt] *n* itinerario; (*of bus*) percorso; (*of trade, shipping*) rotta; "**all** ~**s**" (*AUT*) "tutte le direzioni"; **the best** ~ **to London** la strada migliore per andare a Londra; **en** ~ **for** in viaggio verso; **en** ~ **from ... to** viaggiando da ... a.

route map *n* (*BRIT*: *for journey*) cartina di itinerario; (*for trains etc*) pianta dei collegamenti.

routine [ruː'tiːn] *adj* (*work*) corrente, abituale; (*procedure*) solito(a) ♦ *n* (*pej*) routine *f*, tran tran *m*; (*THEAT*) numero; (*COMPUT*) sottoprogramma *m*; **daily** ~ orario quotidiano; ~ **procedure** prassi *f*.

roving ['rəuvɪŋ] *adj* (*life*) itinerante.

roving reporter *n* reporter *m inv* volante.

row¹ [rəu] *n* (*line*) riga, fila; (*KNITTING*) ferro; (*behind one another*: *of cars, people*) fila ♦ *vi* (*in boat*) remare; (*as sport*) vogare ♦ *vt* (*boat*) manovrare a remi; **in a** ~ (*fig*) di fila.

row² [rau] *n* (*noise*) baccano, chiasso; (*dispute*) lite *f* ♦ *vi* litigare; **to make a** ~ far baccano; **to have a** ~ litigare.

rowboat ['rəubəut] *n* (*US*) barca a remi.

rowdiness ['raudɪnɪs] *n* baccano; (*fighting*) zuffa.

rowdy ['raudɪ] *adj* chiassoso(a); turbolento(a) ♦ *n* teppista *m/f*.

rowdyism ['raudɪɪzəm] *n* teppismo.

rowing ['rəuɪŋ] *n* canottaggio.

rowing boat n (BRIT) barca a remi.
royal ['rɔɪəl] adj reale.
Royal Academy n (BRIT) see boxed note.

ROYAL ACADEMY

L'Accademia Reale d'Arte britannica, **Royal Academy (of the Arts)**, è un'istituzione fondata nel 1768 al fine di incoraggiare la pittura, la scultura e l'architettura. Ogni anno organizza una mostra estiva d'arte contemporanea.

Royal Air Force (RAF) n (BRIT) aeronautica militare britannica.
royal blue adj blu reale inv.
royalist ['rɔɪəlɪst] adj, n realista (m/f).
Royal Navy (RN) n (BRIT) marina militare britannica.
royalty ['rɔɪəltɪ] n (royal persons) (membri mpl della) famiglia reale; (payment: to author) diritti mpl d'autore; (: to inventor) diritti di brevetto.
RP n abbr (BRIT: = received pronunciation) pronuncia standard.
RPM abbr = resale price maintenance.
rpm abbr (= revolutions per minute) giri/min.
RR abbr (US = railroad) Ferr.
R&R n abbr (US MIL: = rest and recreation) permesso per militari.
RRP n abbr (BRIT) see recommended retail price.
RSA n abbr (BRIT) = Royal Society of Arts; Royal Scottish Academy.
RSI n abbr (MED: = repetitive strain injury) lesione al braccio tipica di violinisti e terminalisti.
RSPB n abbr (BRIT: = Royal Society for the Protection of Birds) ≈ L.I.P.U. f (= Lega Italiana Protezione Uccelli).
RSPCA n abbr (BRIT: = Royal Society for the Prevention of Cruelty to Animals) ≈ E.N.P.A. m (= Ente Nazionale per la Protezione degli Animali).
RSVP abbr (= répondez s'il vous plaît) R.S.V.P.
RTA n abbr (= road traffic accident) incidente m stradale.
Rt Hon. abbr (BRIT: = Right Honourable) ≈ On. (= Onorevole).
Rt Rev. abbr (= Right Reverend) Rev.
rub [rʌb] n (with cloth) fregata, strofinata; (on person) frizione f, massaggio ♦ vt fregare, strofinare; frizionare; **to ~ sb up** or (US) **~ sb the wrong way** lisciare qn contro pelo.
▶**rub down** vt (body) strofinare, frizionare; (horse) strigliare.

▶**rub in** vt (ointment) far penetrare (massaggiando or frizionando).
▶**rub off** vi andare via; **to ~ off on** lasciare una traccia su.
▶**rub out** vt cancellare ♦ vi cancellarsi.
rubber ['rʌbə*] n gomma.
rubber band n elastico.
rubber bullet n pallottola di gomma.
rubber plant n ficus m inv.
rubber ring n (for swimming) ciambella.
rubber stamp n timbro di gomma.
rubber-stamp [rʌbə'stæmp] vt (fig) approvare senza discussione.
rubbery ['rʌbərɪ] adj gommoso(a).
rubbish ['rʌbɪʃ] n (from household) immondizie fpl, rifiuti mpl; (fig: pej) cose fpl senza valore; robaccia; (nonsense) sciocchezze fpl ♦ vt (col) sputtanare.
rubbish bin n (BRIT) pattumiera.
rubbish dump n luogo di scarico.
rubbishy ['rʌbɪʃɪ] adj (BRIT col) scadente, che non vale niente.
rubble ['rʌbl] n macerie fpl; (smaller) pietrisco.
ruble ['ruːbl] n (US) = rouble.
ruby ['ruːbɪ] n rubino.
RUC n abbr (BRIT: = Royal Ulster Constabulary) forza di polizia dell'Irlanda del Nord.
rucksack ['rʌksæk] n zaino.
ructions ['rʌkʃənz] npl putiferio, finimondo.
rudder ['rʌdə*] n timone m.
ruddy ['rʌdɪ] adj (face) fresco(a); (col: damned) maledetto(a).
rude [ruːd] adj (impolite: person) scortese, rozzo(a); (: word, manners) grossolano(a), rozzo(a); (shocking) indecente; **to be ~ to sb** essere maleducato con qn.
rudely ['ruːdlɪ] adv scortesemente; grossolanamente.
rudeness ['ruːdnɪs] n scortesia; grossolanità.
rudiment ['ruːdɪmənt] n rudimento.
rudimentary [ruːdɪ'mɛntərɪ] adj rudimentale.
rue [ruː] vt pentirsi amaramente di.
rueful ['ruːful] adj mesto(a), triste.
ruff [rʌf] n gorgiera.
ruffian ['rʌfɪən] n briccone m, furfante m.
ruffle ['rʌfl] vt (hair) scompigliare; (clothes, water) increspare; (fig: person) turbare.
rug [rʌg] n tappeto; (BRIT: for knees) coperta.
rugby ['rʌgbɪ] n (also: ~ football) rugby m.
rugged ['rʌgɪd] adj (landscape) aspro(a); (features, determination) duro(a); (character) brusco(a).
rugger ['rʌgə*] n (col) rugby m.

ruin ['ruːɪn] *n* rovina ♦ *vt* rovinare; (*spoil: clothes*) sciupare; ~s *npl* rovine *fpl*, ruderi *mpl*; **in** ~**s** in rovina.

ruination [ruːɪ'neɪʃən] *n* rovina.

ruinous ['ruːɪnəs] *adj* rovinoso(a); (*expenditure*) inverosimile.

rule [ruːl] *n* (*gen*) regola; (*regulation*) regolamento, regola; (*government*) governo; (*dominion etc*): **under British** ~ sotto la sovranità britannica ♦ *vt* (*country*) governare; (*person*) dominare; (*decide*) decidere ♦ *vi* regnare; decidere; (*LAW*) dichiarare; **to** ~ **against/in favour of/on** (*LAW*) pronunciarsi a sfavore di/in favore di/su; **it's against the** ~**s** è contro le regole *or* il regolamento; **by** ~ **of thumb** a lume di naso; **as a** ~ normalmente, di regola.

▶**rule out** *vt* escludere; **murder cannot be** ~**d out** non si esclude che si tratti di omicidio.

ruled [ruːld] *adj* (*paper*) vergato(a).

ruler ['ruːlə*] *n* (*sovereign*) sovrano/a; (*leader*) capo (dello Stato); (*for measuring*) regolo, riga.

ruling ['ruːlɪŋ] *adj* (*party*) al potere; (*class*) dirigente ♦ *n* (*LAW*) decisione *f*.

rum [rʌm] *n* rum *m* ♦ *adj* (*BRIT col*) strano(a).

Rumania *etc* [ruː'meɪnɪə] = **Romania** *etc*.

rumble ['rʌmbl] *n* rimbombo; brontolio ♦ *vi* rimbombare; (*stomach, pipe*) brontolare.

rumbustious [rʌm'bʌstʃəs] *adj* (*person*): **to be** ~ essere un terremoto.

rummage ['rʌmɪdʒ] *vi* frugare.

rumour, (*US*) **rumor** ['ruːmə*] *n* voce *f* ♦ *vt*: **it is** ~**ed that** corre voce che.

rump [rʌmp] *n* (*of animal*) groppa.

rumple ['rʌmpl] *vt* (*hair*) arruffare, scompigliare; (*clothes*) spiegazzare, sgualcire.

rump steak *n* bistecca di girello.

rumpus ['rʌmpəs] *n* (*col*) baccano; (: *quarrel*) rissa; **to kick up a** ~ fare un putiferio.

run [rʌn] *n* corsa; (*outing*) gita (in macchina); (*distance travelled*) percorso, tragitto; (*series*) serie *f inv*; (*THEAT*) periodo di rappresentazione; (*SKI*) pista ♦ *vb* (*pt* **ran**, *pp* **run** [ræn, rʌn]) *vt* (*operate: business*) gestire, dirigere; (: *competition, course*) organizzare; (: *hotel*) gestire; (: *house*) governare; (*COMPUT: program*) eseguire; (*water, bath*) far scorrere; (*force through: rope, pipe*): **to** ~ **sth through** far passare qc attraverso; (*to pass: hand, finger*): **to** ~ **sth over** passare qc su ♦ *vi* correre; (*pass: road etc*) passare; (*work: machine, factory*) funzionare, andare; (*bus,*

train: operate) far servizio; (: *travel*) circolare; (*continue: play, contract*) durare; (*slide: drawer, flow: river, bath*) scorrere; (*colours, washing*) stemperarsi; (*in election*) presentarsi come candidato; **to go for a** ~ andare a correre; (*in car*) fare un giro (in macchina); **to break into a** ~ mettersi a correre; **a** ~ **of luck** un periodo di fortuna; **to have the** ~ **of sb's house** essere libero di andare e venire in casa di qn; **there was a** ~ **on ...** c'era una corsa a ...; **in the long** ~ alla lunga; in fin dei conti; **in the short** ~ sulle prime; **on the** ~ in fuga; **to make a** ~ **for it** scappare, tagliare la corda; **I'll** ~ **you to the station** la porto alla stazione; **to** ~ **a risk** correre un rischio; **to** ~ **errands** andare a fare commissioni; **the train** ~**s between Gatwick and Victoria** il treno collega Gatwick alla stazione Victoria; **the bus** ~**s every 20 minutes** c'è un autobus ogni 20 minuti; **it's very cheap to** ~ comporta poche spese; **to** ~ **on petrol** *or* (*US*) **gas/on diesel/off batteries** andare a benzina/a diesel/a batterie; **to** ~ **for the bus** fare una corsa per prendere l'autobus; **to** ~ **for president** presentarsi come candidato per la presidenza; **their losses ran into millions** le loro perdite hanno raggiunto i milioni; **to be** ~ **off one's feet** (*BRIT*) doversi fare in quattro.

▶**run about** *vi* (*children*) correre qua e là.

▶**run across** *vt fus* (*find*) trovare per caso.

▶**run away** *vi* fuggire.

▶**run down** *vi* (*clock*) scaricarsi ♦ *vt* (*AUT*) investire; (*criticize*) criticare; (*BRIT: reduce: production*) ridurre gradualmente; (: *factory, shop*) rallentare l'attività di; **to be** ~ **down** (*battery*) essere scarico(a); (*person*) essere giù (di corda).

▶**run in** *vt* (*BRIT: car*) rodare, fare il rodaggio di.

▶**run into** *vt fus* (*meet: person*) incontrare per caso; (: *trouble*) incontrare, trovare; (*collide with*) andare a sbattere contro; **to** ~ **into debt** trovarsi nei debiti.

▶**run off** *vi* fuggire ♦ *vt* (*water*) far defluire; (*copies*) fare.

▶**run out** *vi* (*person*) uscire di corsa; (*liquid*) colare; (*lease*) scadere; (*money*) esaurirsi.

▶**run out of** *vt fus* rimanere a corto di; **I've** ~ **out of petrol** *or* (*US*) **gas** sono rimasto senza benzina.

▶**run over** *vt* (*AUT*) investire, mettere sotto ♦ *vt fus* (*revise*) rivedere.

▶**run through** *vt fus* (*instructions*) dare una scorsa a.

▶**run up** *vt* (*debt*) lasciar accumulare; **to ~ up against** (*difficulties*) incontrare.
runaround ['rʌnəraund] *n* (*col*): **to give sb the ~** far girare a vuoto qn.
runaway ['rʌnəweɪ] *adj* (*person*) fuggiasco(a); (*horse*) in libertà; (*truck*) fuori controllo; (*inflation*) galoppante.
rundown ['rʌndaun] *n* (*BRIT: of industry etc*) riduzione *f* graduale dell'attività di.
rung [rʌŋ] *pp of* **ring** ♦ *n* (*of ladder*) piolo.
run-in ['rʌnɪn] *n* (*col*) scontro.
runner ['rʌnə*] *n* (*in race*) corridore *m*; (*on sledge*) pattino; (*for drawer etc, carpet*) guida.
runner bean *n* (*BRIT*) fagiolino.
runner-up [rʌnər'ʌp] *n* secondo(a) arrivato(a).
running ['rʌnɪŋ] *n* corsa; direzione *f*; organizzazione *f*; funzionamento ♦ *adj* (*water*) corrente; (*commentary*) simultaneo(a); **6 days ~** 6 giorni di seguito; **to be in/out of the ~ for sth** essere/non essere più in lizza per qc.
running costs *npl* (*of business*) costi *mpl* d'esercizio; (*of car*) spese *fpl* di mantenimento.
running head *n* (*TYP, WORD PROCESSING*) testata, titolo corrente.
running mate *n* (*US POL*) candidato alla vicepresidenza.
runny ['rʌnɪ] *adj* che cola.
run-off ['rʌnɔf] *n* (*in contest, election*) confronto definitivo; (*extra race*) spareggio.
run-of-the-mill ['rʌnəvðə'mɪl] *adj* solito(a), banale.
runt [rʌnt] *n* (*also pej*) omuncolo; (*ZOOL*) animale *m* più piccolo del normale.
run-through ['rʌnθruː] *n* prova.
run-up ['rʌnʌp] *n* (*BRIT*): **~ to sth** periodo che precede qc.
runway ['rʌnweɪ] *n* (*AVIAT*) pista (di decollo).
rupture ['rʌptʃə*] *n* (*MED*) ernia ♦ *vt*: **to ~ o.s.** farsi venire un'ernia.
rural ['ruərl] *adj* rurale.
rural district council (RDC) *n* (*BRIT*) consiglio (amministrativo) di distretto rurale.
ruse [ruːz] *n* trucco.
rush [rʌʃ] *n* corsa precipitosa; (*of crowd*) afflusso; (*hurry*) furia, fretta; (*current*) flusso; (*BOT*) giunco ♦ *vt* mandare or spedire velocemente; (*attack: town etc*) prendere d'assalto ♦ *vi* precipitarsi; **is there any ~ for this?** è urgente?; **we've had a ~ of orders** abbiamo avuto una valanga di ordinazioni; **I'm in a ~ (to do)**

ho fretta *or* premura (di fare); **gold ~** corsa all'oro; **to ~ sth off** spedire con urgenza qc; **don't ~ me!** non farmi fretta!
▶**rush through** *vt* (*meal*) mangiare in fretta; (*book*) dare una scorsa frettolosa a; (*town*) attraversare in fretta; (*COMM: order*) eseguire d'urgenza ♦ *vt fus* (*work*) sbrigare frettolosamente.
rush hour *n* ora di punta.
rush job *n* (*urgent*) lavoro urgente.
rush matting *n* stuoia.
rusk [rʌsk] *n* fetta biscottata.
Russia ['rʌʃə] *n* Russia.
Russian ['rʌʃən] *adj* russo(a) ♦ *n* russo/a; (*LING*) russo.
rust [rʌst] *n* ruggine *f* ♦ *vi* arrugginirsi.
rustic ['rʌstɪk] *adj* rustico(a) ♦ *n* (*pej*) cafone/a.
rustle ['rʌsl] *vi* frusciare ♦ *vt* (*paper*) far frusciare; (*US: cattle*) rubare.
rustproof ['rʌstpruːf] *adj* inossidabile.
rustproofing ['rʌstpruːfɪŋ] *n* trattamento antiruggine.
rusty ['rʌstɪ] *adj* arrugginito(a).
rut [rʌt] *n* solco; (*ZOOL*) fregola; **to be in a ~** (*fig*) essersi fossilizzato(a).
rutabaga [ruːtə'beɪgə] *n* (*US*) rapa svedese.
ruthless ['ruːθlɪs] *adj* spietato(a).
ruthlessness ['ruːθlɪsnɪs] *n* spietatezza.
RV *abbr* (= *revised version*) *versione riveduta della Bibbia* ♦ *n abbr* (*US*) *see* **recreational vehicle**.
rye [raɪ] *n* segale *f*.

S s

S, s [ɛs] *n* (*letter*) S, s *f or m inv*; (*US SCOL: = satisfactory*) ≈ sufficiente; **S for Sugar** ≈ S come Savona.
S *abbr* (= *saint*) S.; (= *south*) S; (*on clothes*) = *small*.
SA *abbr* = **South Africa; South America**.
Sabbath ['sæbəθ] *n* (*Jewish*) sabato; (*Christian*) domenica.
sabbatical [sə'bætɪkl] *adj*: **~ year** anno sabbatico.
sabotage ['sæbətɑːʒ] *n* sabotaggio ♦ *vt* sabotare.
saccharin(e) ['sækərɪn] *n* saccarina.
sachet ['sæʃeɪ] *n* bustina.

sack [sæk] n (*bag*) sacco ♦ vt (*dismiss*) licenziare, mandare a spasso; (*plunder*) saccheggiare; **to get the ~** essere mandato a spasso; **to give sb the ~** licenziare qn, mandare qn a spasso.

sackful ['sækful] n: **a ~ of** un sacco di.

sacking ['sækɪŋ] n tela di sacco; (*dismissal*) licenziamento.

sacrament ['sækrəmənt] n sacramento.

sacred ['seɪkrɪd] adj sacro(a).

sacred cow n (*fig: person*) intoccabile m/f; (: *institution*) caposaldo; (: *idea, belief*) dogma m.

sacrifice ['sækrɪfaɪs] n sacrificio ♦ vt sacrificare; **to make ~s (for sb)** fare (dei) sacrifici (per qn).

sacrilege ['sækrɪlɪdʒ] n sacrilegio.

sacrosanct ['sækrəusæŋkt] adj sacrosanto(a).

sad [sæd] adj triste; (*deplorable*) deplorevole.

sadden ['sædn] vt rattristare.

saddle ['sædl] n sella ♦ vt (*horse*) sellare; **to be ~d with sth** (*col*) avere qc sulle spalle.

saddlebag ['sædlbæg] n bisaccia; (*on bicycle*) borsa.

sadism ['seɪdɪzəm] n sadismo.

sadist ['seɪdɪst] n sadico/a.

sadistic [sə'dɪstɪk] adj sadico(a).

sadly ['sædlɪ] adv tristemente; (*regrettably*) sfortunatamente; **~ lacking in** penosamente privo di.

sadness ['sædnɪs] n tristezza.

sadomasochism [seɪdəu'mæsəkɪzəm] n sadomasochismo.

sae abbr (*BRIT*) = **stamped addressed envelope**; see **stamp**.

safari [sə'fɑːrɪ] n safari m inv.

safari park n zoosafari m inv.

safe [seɪf] adj sicuro(a); (*out of danger*) salvo(a), al sicuro; (*cautious*) prudente ♦ n cassaforte f; **~ from** al sicuro da; **~ and sound** sano(a) e salvo(a); **~ journey!** buon viaggio!; **(just) to be on the ~ side** per non correre rischi; **to play ~** giocare sul sicuro; **it is ~ to say that ...** si può affermare con sicurezza che ....

safe bet n: **it's a ~** è una cosa sicura.

safe-breaker ['seɪfbreɪkə*] n (*BRIT*) scassinatore m.

safe-conduct [seɪf'kɔndʌkt] n salvacondotto.

safe-cracker ['seɪfkrækə*] n = **safe-breaker**.

safe-deposit ['seɪfdɪpɔzɪt] n (*vault*) caveau m inv; (*box*) cassetta di sicurezza.

safeguard ['seɪfgɑːd] n salvaguardia ♦ vt salvaguardare.

safe haven n zona sicura or protetta.

safekeeping ['seɪf'kiːpɪŋ] n custodia.

safely ['seɪflɪ] adv sicuramente; sano(a) e salvo(a); prudentemente; **I can ~ say ...** posso tranquillamente asserire ....

safe passage n passaggio sicuro.

safe sex n sesso sicuro.

safety ['seɪftɪ] n sicurezza; **~ first!** la prudenza innanzitutto!

safety belt n cintura di sicurezza.

safety catch n sicura.

safety net n rete f di protezione.

safety pin n spilla di sicurezza.

safety valve n valvola di sicurezza.

saffron ['sæfrən] n zafferano.

sag [sæg] vi incurvarsi; afflosciarsi.

saga ['sɑːgə] n saga; (*fig*) odissea.

sage [seɪdʒ] n (*herb*) salvia; (*man*) saggio.

Sagittarius [sædʒɪ'tɛərɪəs] n Sagittario; **to be ~** essere del Sagittario.

sago ['seɪgəu] n sagù m.

Sahara [sə'hɑːrə] n: **the ~ Desert** il Deserto del Sahara.

Sahel [sæ'hɛl] n Sahel m.

said [sɛd] pt, pp of **say**.

Saigon [saɪ'gɔn] n Saigon f.

sail [seɪl] n (*on boat*) vela; (*trip*): **to go for a ~** fare un giro in barca a vela ♦ vt (*boat*) condurre, governare ♦ vi (*travel: ship*) navigare; (: *passenger*) viaggiare per mare; (*set off*) salpare; (*SPORT*) fare della vela; **they ~ed into Genoa** entrarono nel porto di Genova.

▶**sail through** vt fus (*fig*) superare senza difficoltà ♦ vi farcela senza difficoltà.

sailboat ['seɪlbəut] n (*US*) barca a vela.

sailing ['seɪlɪŋ] n (*sport*) vela; **to go ~** fare della vela.

sailing boat n barca a vela.

sailing ship n veliero.

sailor ['seɪlə*] n marinaio.

saint [seɪnt] n santo/a.

saintly ['seɪntlɪ] adj da santo(a); santo(a).

sake [seɪk] n: **for the ~ of** per, per amore di; **for pity's ~** per pietà; **for the ~ of argument** tanto per fare un esempio; **art for art's ~** l'arte per l'arte.

salad ['sæləd] n insalata; **tomato ~** insalata di pomodori.

salad bowl n insalatiera.

salad cream n (*BRIT*) (tipo di) maionese f.

salad dressing n condimento per insalata.

salad oil n olio da tavola.

salami [sə'lɑːmɪ] n salame m.

salaried ['sælərɪd] adj stipendiato(a).

salary ['sælərɪ] n stipendio.

salary scale n scala dei salari.

sale [seɪl] n vendita; (*at reduced prices*) svendita, liquidazione f; "for ~" "in vendita"; on ~ in vendita; on ~ or return da vendere o rimandare; a closing-down or (US) liquidation ~ una liquidazione; ~ and lease back n lease back m inv.

saleroom ['seɪlrum] n sala delle aste.

sales assistant n (BRIT) commesso/a.

sales clerk n (US) commesso/a.

sales conference n riunione f marketing e vendite.

sales drive n campagna di vendita, sforzo promozionale.

sales force n personale m addetto alle vendite.

salesman ['seɪlzmən] n commesso; (representative) rappresentante m.

sales manager n direttore m commerciale.

salesmanship ['seɪlzmənʃɪp] n arte f del vendere.

sales tax n (US) imposta sulle vendite.

saleswoman ['seɪlzwumən] n commessa.

salient ['seɪlɪənt] adj saliente.

saline ['seɪlaɪn] adj salino(a).

saliva [sə'laɪvə] n saliva.

sallow ['sæləu] adj giallastro(a).

sally forth, sally out ['sælɪ-] vi uscire di gran carriera.

salmon ['sæmən] n (pl inv) salmone m.

salmon trout n trota (di mare).

saloon [sə'luːn] n (US) saloon m inv, bar m inv; (BRIT AUT) berlina; (ship's lounge) salone m.

SALT [sɔːlt] n abbr (= Strategic Arms Limitation Talks/Treaty) S.A.L.T. m.

salt [sɔːlt] n sale m ♦ vt salare ♦ cpd di sale; (CULIN) salato(a); an old ~ un lupo di mare.

▶**salt away** vt ammucchiare, mettere via.

salt cellar n saliera.

salt-free ['sɔːlt'friː] adj senza sale.

saltwater ['sɔːltwɔːtə*] adj (fish etc) di mare.

salty ['sɔːltɪ] adj salato(a).

salubrious [sə'luːbrɪəs] adj salubre; (fig: district etc) raccomandabile.

salutary ['sæljutərɪ] adj salutare.

salute [sə'luːt] n saluto ♦ vt salutare.

salvage ['sælvɪdʒ] n (saving) salvataggio; (things saved) beni mpl salvati or recuperati ♦ vt salvare, mettere in salvo.

salvage vessel n scialuppa di salvataggio.

salvation [sæl'veɪʃən] n salvezza.

Salvation Army n Esercito della Salvezza.

salver ['sælvə*] n vassoio.

salvo, ~es ['sælvəu] n salva.

Samaritan [sə'mærɪtən] n: the ~s (organization) ≈ telefono amico.

same [seɪm] adj stesso(a), medesimo(a) ♦ pron: the ~ lo(la) stesso(a), gli(le) stessi(e); the ~ book as lo stesso libro di (or che); on the ~ day lo stesso giorno; at the ~ time allo stesso tempo; all or just the ~ tuttavia; to do the ~ fare la stessa cosa; to do the ~ as sb fare come qn; the ~ again (in bar etc) un altro; they're one and the ~ (person/thing) sono la stessa persona/cosa; and the ~ to you! altrettanto a lei!; ~ here! anch'io!

sample ['sɑːmpl] n campione m ♦ vt (food) assaggiare; (wine) degustare; to take a ~ prelevare un campione; free ~ campione omaggio.

sanatorium, pl **sanatoria** [sænə'tɔːrɪəm, -rɪə] n sanatorio.

sanctify ['sæŋktɪfaɪ] vt santificare.

sanctimonious [sæŋktɪ'məunɪəs] adj bigotto(a), bacchettone(a).

sanction ['sæŋkʃən] n sanzione f ♦ vt sancire, sanzionare; to impose economic ~s on or against adottare sanzioni economiche contro.

sanctity ['sæŋktɪtɪ] n santità.

sanctuary ['sæŋktjuərɪ] n (holy place) santuario; (refuge) rifugio; (for wildlife) riserva.

sand [sænd] n sabbia ♦ vt cospargere di sabbia; (also: ~ down: wood etc) cartavetrare; see also **sands**.

sandal ['sændl] n sandalo.

sandbag ['sændbæg] n sacco di sabbia.

sandblast ['sændblɑːst] vt sabbiare.

sandbox ['sændbɔks] n (US: for children) buca di sabbia.

sandcastle ['sændkɑːsl] n castello di sabbia.

sand dune n duna di sabbia.

sander ['sændə*] n levigatrice f.

sandpaper ['sændpeɪpə*] n carta vetrata.

sandpit ['sændpɪt] n (BRIT: for children) buca di sabbia.

sands [sændz] npl spiaggia.

sandstone ['sændstəun] n arenaria.

sandstorm ['sændstɔːm] n tempesta di sabbia.

sandwich ['sændwɪtʃ] n tramezzino, panino, sandwich m inv ♦ vt (also: ~ in) infilare; cheese/ham ~ sandwich al formaggio/prosciutto; to be ~ed between essere incastrato(a) fra.

sandwich board n cartello pubblicitario (portato da un uomo sandwich).

sandwich course n (BRIT) corso di formazione professionale.

sandwich man n uomo m sandwich inv.

sandy ['sændɪ] adj sabbioso(a); (colour)

color sabbia *inv*, biondo(a) rossiccio(a).
sane [seɪn] *adj* (*person*) sano(a) di mente;
(*outlook*) sensato(a).
sang [sæŋ] *pt of* sing.
sanguine ['sæŋgwɪn] *adj* ottimista.
sanitarium, *pl* **sanitaria** [sænɪ'tɛərɪəm,
-rɪə] *n* (*US*) = **sanatorium.**
sanitary ['sænɪtərɪ] *adj* (*system,
arrangements*) sanitario(a); (*clean*)
igienico(a).
sanitary towel, (*US*) **sanitary napkin** *n*
assorbente *m* (igienico).
sanitation [sænɪ'teɪʃən] *n* (*in house*) impianti
mpl sanitari; (*in town*) fognature *fpl*.
sanitation department *n* (*US*) nettezza
urbana.
sanity ['sænɪtɪ] *n* sanità mentale; (*common
sense*) buon senso.
sank [sæŋk] *pt of* sink.
San Marino [sænmə'riːnəʊ] *n* San Marino *f*.
Santa Claus [sæntə'klɔːz] *n* Babbo Natale.
Santiago [sæntɪ'aːgəʊ] *n* (*also:* ~ **de Chile**)
Santiago (del Cile) *f*.
sap [sæp] *n* (*of plants*) linfa ♦ *vt* (*strength*)
fiaccare.
sapling ['sæplɪŋ] *n* alberello.
sapphire ['sæfaɪə*] *n* zaffiro.
sarcasm ['saːkæzm] *n* sarcasmo.
sarcastic [saː'kæstɪk] *adj* sarcastico(a); **to
be** ~ fare del sarcasmo.
sarcophagus, *pl* **sarcophagi** [saː'kɔfəgəs,
-gaɪ] *n* sarcofago.
sardine [saː'diːn] *n* sardina.
Sardinia [saː'dɪnɪə] *n* Sardegna.
Sardinian [saː'dɪnɪən] *adj, n* sardo(a).
sardonic [saː'dɔnɪk] *adj* sardonico(a).
sari ['saːrɪ] *n* sari *m inv*.
sartorial [saː'tɔːrɪəl] *adj* di sartoria.
SAS *n abbr* (*BRIT MIL:* = *Special Air Service*)
*reparto dell'esercito britannico
specializzato in operazioni clandestine.*
SASE *n abbr* (*US:* = *self-addressed stamped
envelope*) *busta affrancata e con
indirizzo.*
sash [sæʃ] *n* fascia.
sash window *n* finestra a ghigliottina.
Sask. *abbr* (*Canada*) = *Saskatchewan.*
SAT *n abbr* (*US*) = *Scholastic Aptitude Test.*
sat [sæt] *pt, pp of* sit.
Sat. *abbr* (= *Saturday*) sab.
Satan ['seɪtən] *n* Satana *m*.
satanic [sə'tænɪk] *adj* satanico(a).
satchel ['sætʃl] *n* cartella.
sated ['seɪtɪd] *adj* soddisfatto(a); sazio(a).
satellite ['sætəlaɪt] *adj, n* satellite (*m*).
satellite television *n* televisione *f* via
satellite.
satiate ['seɪʃɪeɪt] *vt* saziare.

satin ['sætɪn] *n* satin *m* ♦ *adj* di *or* in satin;
with a ~ **finish** satinato(a).
satire ['sætaɪə*] *n* satira.
satirical [sə'tɪrɪkl] *adj* satirico(a).
satirist ['sætərɪst] *n* (*writer etc*)
scrittore(trice) *etc* satirico(a);
(*cartoonist*) caricaturista *m/f*.
satirize ['sætɪraɪz] *vt* satireggiare.
satisfaction [sætɪs'fækʃən] *n* soddisfazione
f; **has it been done to your** ~? ne è
rimasto soddisfatto?
satisfactory [sætɪs'fæktərɪ] *adj*
soddisfacente.
satisfied ['sætɪsfaɪd] *adj* (*customer*)
soddisfatto(a); **to be** ~ **(with sth)** essere
soddisfatto(a) (di qc).
satisfy ['sætɪsfaɪ] *vt* soddisfare; (*convince*)
convincere; **to** ~ **the requirements**
rispondere ai requisiti; **to** ~ **sb (that)**
convincere qn (che), persuadere qn
(che); **to** ~ **o.s. of sth** accertarsi di qc.
satisfying ['sætɪsfaɪŋ] *adj* soddisfacente.
satsuma [sæt'suːmə] *n* agrume di
provenienza giapponese.
saturate ['sætʃəreɪt] *vt:* **to** ~ **(with)**
saturare (di).
saturated fat ['sætʃəreɪtɪd-] *n* grassi *mpl*
saturi.
saturation [sætʃə'reɪʃən] *n* saturazione *f*.
Saturday ['sætədɪ] *n* sabato; *for phrases see
also* **Tuesday.**
sauce [sɔːs] *n* salsa; (*containing meat, fish*)
sugo.
saucepan ['sɔːspən] *n* casseruola.
saucer ['sɔːsə*] *n* piattino.
saucy ['sɔːsɪ] *adj* impertinente.
Saudi Arabia ['saʊdɪ-] *n* Arabia Saudita.
Saudi (Arabian) *adj, n* saudita (*m/f*).
sauna ['sɔːnə] *n* sauna.
saunter ['sɔːntə*] *vi* andare a zonzo,
bighellonare.
sausage ['sɔsɪdʒ] *n* salsiccia; (*salami etc*)
salame *m*.
sausage roll *n* rotolo di pasta sfoglia
ripieno di salsiccia.
sauté ['səʊteɪ] *adj* (*CULIN: potatoes*)
saltato(a); (: *onions*) soffritto(a) ♦ *vt* far
saltare; far soffriggere.
savage ['sævɪdʒ] *adj* (*cruel, fierce*)
selvaggio(a), feroce; (*primitive*)
primitivo(a) ♦ *n* selvaggio/a ♦ *vt*
attaccare selvaggiamente.
savagery ['sævɪdʒrɪ] *n* crudeltà, ferocia.
save [seɪv] *vt* (*person, belongings, COMPUT*)
salvare; (*money*) risparmiare, mettere da
parte; (*time*) risparmiare; (*food*)
conservare; (*avoid: trouble*) evitare ♦ *vi*
(*also:* ~ **up**) economizzare ♦ *n* (*SPORT*)

parata ♦ *prep* salvo, a eccezione di; **it will ~ me an hour** mi farà risparmiare un'ora; **to ~ face** salvare la faccia; **God ~ the Queen!** Dio salvi la Regina!

saving ['seɪvɪŋ] *n* risparmio ♦ *adj*: **the ~ grace of** l'unica cosa buona di; **~s** *npl* risparmi *mpl*; **to make ~s** fare economia.

savings account *n* libretto di risparmio.

savings bank *n* cassa di risparmio.

saviour, (*US*) **savior** ['seɪvjə*] *n* salvatore *m*.

savour, (*US*) **savor** ['seɪvə*] *n* sapore *m*, gusto ♦ *vt* gustare.

savoury, (*US*) **savory** ['seɪvərɪ] *adj* saporito(a); (*dish: not sweet*) salato(a).

savvy ['sævɪ] *n* (*col*) arguzia.

saw [sɔ:] *pt of* **see** ♦ *n* (*tool*) sega ♦ *vt* (*pt* **sawed**, *pp* **sawed** *or* **sawn** [sɔ:n]) segare; **to ~ sth up** fare a pezzi qc con la sega.

sawdust ['sɔ:dʌst] *n* segatura.

sawmill ['sɔ:mɪl] *n* segheria.

sawn [sɔ:n] *pp of* **saw**.

sawn-off ['sɔ:nɔf], (*US*) **sawed-off** ['sɔ:dɔf] *adj*: **~ shotgun** fucile *m* a canne mozze.

saxophone ['sæksəfəun] *n* sassofono.

say [seɪ] *n*: **to have one's ~** fare sentire il proprio parere; **to have a** *or* **some ~** avere voce in capitolo ♦ *vt* (*pt, pp* **said** [sɛd]) dire; **could you ~ that again?** potrebbe ripeterlo?; **to ~ yes/no** dire di sì/di no; **she said (that) I was to give you this** ha detto di darle questo; **my watch ~s 3 o'clock** il mio orologio fa le 3; **shall we ~ Tuesday?** facciamo martedì?; **that doesn't ~ much for him** non torna a suo credito; **when all is said and done** a conti fatti; **there is something** *or* **a lot to be said for it** ha i suoi lati positivi; **that is to ~** cioè, vale a dire; **to ~ nothing of** per non parlare di; **~ that ...** mettiamo *or* diciamo che ...; **that goes without ~ing** va da sé.

saying ['seɪŋ] *n* proverbio, detto.

SBA *n abbr* (*US*: = *Small Business Administration*) organismo ausiliario per piccole imprese.

SC *n abbr* (*US*) = **supreme court** ♦ *abbr* (*US*) = *South Carolina*.

s/c *abbr* (= *self-contained*) indipendente.

scab [skæb] *n* crosta; (*pej*) crumiro/a.

scabby ['skæbɪ] *adj* crostoso(a).

scaffold ['skæfəuld] *n* impalcatura; (*gallows*) patibolo.

scaffolding ['skæfəldɪŋ] *n* impalcatura.

scald [skɔ:ld] *n* scottatura ♦ *vt* scottare.

scalding ['skɔ:ldɪŋ] *adj* (*also*: **~ hot**) bollente.

scale [skeɪl] *n* scala; (*of fish*) squama ♦ *vt*

(*mountain*) scalare; **pay ~** scala dei salari; **~ of charges** tariffa; **on a large ~** su vasta scala; **to draw sth to ~** disegnare qc in scala; **small-~ model** modello in scala ridotta; *see also* **scales**.

▶**scale down** *vt* ridurre (proporzionalmente).

scaled-down [skeɪld'daun] *adj* su scala ridotta.

scale drawing *n* disegno in scala.

scale model *n* modello in scala.

scales [skeɪlz] *npl* bilancia.

scallion ['skæljən] *n* cipolla; (*US: shallot*) scalogna; (: *leek*) porro.

scallop ['skɔləp] *n* pettine *m*.

scalp [skælp] *n* cuoio capelluto ♦ *vt* scotennare.

scalpel ['skælpl] *n* bisturi *m inv.*

scalper ['skælpə*] *n* (*US col: of tickets*) bagarino.

scam [skæm] *n* (*col*) truffa.

scamp [skæmp] *n* (*col: child*) peste *f.*

scamper ['skæmpə*] *vi*: **to ~ away, ~ off** darsela a gambe.

scampi ['skæmpɪ] *npl* scampi *mpl.*

scan [skæn] *vt* scrutare; (*glance at quickly*) scorrere, dare un'occhiata a; (*poetry*) scandire; (*TV*) analizzare; (*RADAR*) esplorare ♦ *n* (*MED*) ecografia.

scandal ['skændl] *n* scandalo; (*gossip*) pettegolezzi *mpl.*

scandalize ['skændəlaɪz] *vt* scandalizzare.

scandalous ['skændələs] *adj* scandaloso(a).

Scandinavia [skændɪ'neɪvɪə] *n* Scandinavia.

Scandinavian [skændɪ'neɪvɪən] *adj, n* scandinavo(a).

scanner ['skænə*] *n* (*RADAR, MED*) scanner *m inv.*

scant [skænt] *adj* scarso(a).

scantily ['skæntɪlɪ] *adv*: **~ clad** *or* **dressed** succintamente vestito(a).

scanty ['skæntɪ] *adj* insufficiente; (*swimsuit*) ridotto(a).

scapegoat ['skeɪpgəut] *n* capro espiatorio.

scar [skɑ:*] *n* cicatrice *f* ♦ *vt* sfregiare.

scarce [skɛəs] *adj* scarso(a); (*copy, edition*) raro(a).

scarcely ['skɛəslɪ] *adv* appena; **~ anybody** quasi nessuno; **I can ~ believe it** faccio fatica a crederci.

scarcity ['skɛəsɪtɪ] *n* scarsità, mancanza.

scarcity value *n* valore *m* di rarità.

scare [skɛə*] *n* spavento, paura ♦ *vt* spaventare, atterrire; **to ~ sb stiff** spaventare a morte qn; **bomb ~** evacuazione *f* per sospetta presenza di un ordigno esplosivo.

▶**scare away, scare off** *vt* mettere in

fuga.

scarecrow ['skɛəkrəu] *n* spaventapasseri *m inv.*

scared [skɛəd] *adj*: **to be** ~ aver paura.

scaremonger ['skɛəmʌŋgə*] *n* allarmista *m/f.*

scarf, *pl* **scarves** [skɑːf, skɑːvz] *n* (*long*) sciarpa; (*square*) fazzoletto da testa, foulard *m inv.*

scarlet ['skɑːlɪt] *adj* scarlatto(a).

scarlet fever *n* scarlattina.

scarper ['skɑːpə*] *vi* (*BRIT col*) darsela a gambe.

SCART socket ['skɑːt-] *n* presa *f* SCART *inv.*

scarves [skɑːvz] *npl of* **scarf**.

scary ['skɛərɪ] *adj* (*col*) che fa paura.

scathing ['skeɪðɪŋ] *adj* aspro(a); **to be** ~ **about sth** essere molto critico rispetto a qc.

scatter ['skætə*] *vt* spargere; (*crowd*) disperdere ♦ *vi* disperdersi.

scatterbrained ['skætəbreɪnd] *adj* scervellato(a), sbadato(a).

scattered ['skætəd] *adj* sparso(a).

scatty ['skætɪ] *adj* (*col*) scervellato(a), sbadato(a).

scavenge ['skævɪndʒ] *vi* (*person*): **to** ~ **(for)** frugare tra i rifiuti (alla ricerca di); (*hyenas etc*) nutrirsi di carogne.

scavenger ['skævəndʒə*] *n* spazzino.

SCE *n abbr* = *Scottish Certificate of Education.*

scenario [sɪˈnɑːrɪəu] *n* (*THEAT, CINE*) copione *m*; (*fig*) situazione *f.*

scene [siːn] *n* (*THEAT, fig etc*) scena; (*of crime, accident*) scena, luogo; (*sight, view*) vista, veduta; **behind the ~s** (*also fig*) dietro le quinte; **to appear** *or* **come on the** ~ (*also fig*) entrare in scena; **the political** ~ **in Italy** il quadro politico in Italia; **to make a** ~ (*col: fuss*) fare una scenata.

scenery ['siːnərɪ] *n* (*THEAT*) scenario; (*landscape*) panorama *m.*

scenic ['siːnɪk] *adj* scenico(a); panoramico(a).

scent [sɛnt] *n* odore *m*, profumo; (*sense of smell*) olfatto, odorato; (*fig: track*) pista; **to put** *or* **throw sb off the** ~ (*fig*) far perdere le tracce a qn, sviare qn.

sceptic, (*US*) **skeptic** ['skɛptɪk] *n* scettico/a.

sceptical, (*US*) **skeptical** ['skɛptɪkl] *adj* scettico(a).

scepticism, (*US*) **skepticism** ['skɛptɪsɪzm] *n* scetticismo.

sceptre, (*US*) **scepter** ['sɛptə*] *n* scettro.

schedule ['ʃɛdjuːl, (*US*) 'skɛdjuːl] *n* programma *m*, piano; (*of trains*) orario; (*of* *prices etc*) lista, tabella ♦ *vt* fissare; **as** ~**d** come stabilito; **on** ~ in orario; **to be ahead of/behind** ~ essere in anticipo/ ritardo sul previsto; **we are working to a very tight** ~ il nostro programma di lavoro è molto intenso; **everything went according to** ~ tutto è andato secondo i piani *or* secondo il previsto.

scheduled ['ʃɛdjuːld, (*US*) 'skɛdjuːld] *adj* (*date, time*) fissato(a); (*visit, event*) programmato(a); (*train, bus, stop*) previsto(a) (sull'orario); ~ **flight** volo di linea.

schematic [skɪˈmætɪk] *adj* schematico(a).

scheme [skiːm] *n* piano, progetto; (*method*) sistema *m*; (*dishonest plan, plot*) intrigo, trama; (*arrangement*) disposizione *f*, sistemazione *f* ♦ *vt* progettare; (*plot*) ordire ♦ *vi* fare progetti; (*intrigue*) complottare; **colour** ~ combinazione *f* di colori.

scheming ['skiːmɪŋ] *adj* intrigante ♦ *n* intrighi *mpl*, macchinazioni *fpl.*

schism ['skɪzəm] *n* scisma *m.*

schizophrenia [skɪtsəˈfriːnɪə] *n* schizofrenia.

schizophrenic [skɪtsəˈfrɛnɪk] *adj, n* schizofrenico(a).

scholar ['skɔlə*] *n* erudito/a.

scholarly ['skɔləlɪ] *adj* dotto(a), erudito(a).

scholarship ['skɔləʃɪp] *n* erudizione *f*; (*grant*) borsa di studio.

school [skuːl] *n* scuola; (*in university*) scuola, facoltà *f inv* ♦ *cpd* scolare, scolastico(a) ♦ *vt* (*animal*) addestrare.

school age *n* età scolare.

schoolbook ['skuːlbuk] *n* libro scolastico.

schoolboy ['skuːlbɔɪ] *n* scolaro.

schoolchild, *pl* **-children** ['skuːltʃaɪld, -'tʃɪldrən] *n* scolaro/a.

schooldays ['skuːldeɪz] *npl* giorni *mpl* di scuola.

schoolgirl ['skuːlgɜːl] *n* scolara.

schooling ['skuːlɪŋ] *n* istruzione *f.*

school-leaver ['skuːlliːvə*] *n* (*BRIT*) ≈ neodiplomato(a).

schoolmaster ['skuːlmɑːstə*] *n* (*primary*) maestro; (*secondary*) insegnante *m.*

schoolmistress ['skuːlmɪstrɪs] *n* (*primary*) maestra; (*secondary*) insegnante *f.*

school report *n* (*BRIT*) pagella.

schoolroom ['skuːlruːm] *n* classe *f*, aula.

schoolteacher ['skuːltiːtʃə*] *n* insegnante *m/f*, docente *m/f*; (*primary*) maestro/a.

schoolyard ['skuːljɑːd] *n* (*US*) cortile *m* della scuola.

schooner ['skuːnə*] *n* (*ship*) goletta, schooner *m inv*; (*glass*) bicchiere *m* alto da sherry.

sciatica [saɪ'ætɪkə] n sciatica.
science ['saɪəns] n scienza; **the** ~**s** le scienze; (SCOL) le materie scientifiche.
science fiction n fantascienza.
scientific [saɪən'tɪfɪk] adj scientifico(a).
scientist ['saɪəntɪst] n scienziato/a.
sci-fi ['saɪfaɪ] n abbr (col) = **science fiction**.
Scilly Isles ['sɪlɪ'aɪlz] npl, **Scillies** ['sɪlɪz] npl: **the** ~ le isole Scilly.
scintillating ['sɪntɪleɪtɪŋ] adj scintillante; (wit, conversation, company) brillante.
scissors ['sɪzəz] npl forbici fpl; **a pair of** ~ un paio di forbici.
sclerosis [sklɪ'rəusɪs] n sclerosi f.
scoff [skɔf] vt (BRIT col: eat) trangugiare, ingozzare ♦ vi: **to** ~ (**at**) (mock) farsi beffe (di).
scold [skəuld] vt rimproverare.
scolding ['skəuldɪŋ] n lavata di capo, sgridata.
scone [skɔn] n focaccina da tè.
scoop [sku:p] n mestolo; (for ice cream) cucchiaio dosatore; (PRESS) colpo giornalistico, notizia (in) esclusiva.
►**scoop out** vt scavare.
►**scoop up** vt tirare su, sollevare.
scooter ['sku:tə*] n (motor cycle) motoretta, scooter m inv; (toy) monopattino.
scope [skəup] n (capacity: of plan, undertaking) portata; (: of person) capacità fpl; (opportunity) possibilità fpl; **to be within the** ~ **of** rientrare nei limiti di; **it's well within his** ~ **to ...** è perfettamente in grado di ...; **there is plenty of** ~ **for improvement** (BRIT) ci sono notevoli possibilità di miglioramento.
scorch [skɔ:tʃ] vt (clothes) strinare, bruciacchiare; (earth, grass) seccare, bruciare.
scorched earth policy [skɔ:tʃt-] n tattica della terra bruciata.
scorcher ['skɔ:tʃə*] n (col: hot day) giornata torrida.
scorching ['skɔ:tʃɪŋ] adj cocente, scottante.
score [skɔ:*] n punti mpl, punteggio; (MUS) partitura, spartito; (twenty): **a** ~ venti ♦ vt (goal, point) segnare, fare; (success) ottenere; (cut: leather, wood, card) incidere ♦ vi segnare; (FOOTBALL) fare un goal; (keep score) segnare i punti; **on that** ~ a questo riguardo; **to have an old** ~ **to settle with sb** (fig) avere un vecchio conto da saldare con qn; ~**s of people** (fig) un sacco di gente; **to** ~ **6 out of 10** prendere 6 su 10.
►**score out** vt cancellare con un segno.
scoreboard ['skɔ:bɔ:d] n tabellone m segnapunti.

scorecard ['skɔ:kɑ:d] n cartoncino segnapunti.
scoreline ['skɔ:laɪn] n (SPORT) risultato.
scorer ['skɔ:rə*] n marcatore/trice; (keeping score) segnapunti m inv.
scorn [skɔ:n] n disprezzo ♦ vt disprezzare.
scornful ['skɔ:nful] adj sprezzante.
Scorpio ['skɔ:pɪəu] n Scorpione m; **to be** ~ essere dello Scorpione.
scorpion ['skɔ:pɪən] n scorpione m.
Scot [skɔt] n scozzese m/f.
Scotch [skɔtʃ] n whisky m scozzese, scotch m.
scotch [skɔtʃ] vt (rumour etc) soffocare.
Scotch tape ® n scotch ® m.
scot-free ['skɔt'fri:] adj impunito(a); **to get off** ~ (unpunished) farla franca; (unhurt) uscire illeso(a).
Scotland ['skɔtlənd] n Scozia.
Scots [skɔts] adj scozzese.
Scotsman ['skɔtsmən] n scozzese m.
Scotswoman ['skɔtswumən] n scozzese f.
Scottish ['skɔtɪʃ] adj scozzese; **the** ~ **National Party** partito nazionalista scozzese; **the** ~ **Parliament** il Parlamento scozzese.
scoundrel ['skaundrl] n farabutto/a; (child) furfantello/a.
scour ['skauə*] vt (clean) pulire strofinando; raschiare via; ripulire; (search) battere, perlustrare.
scourer ['skauərə*] n (pad) paglietta; (powder) (detersivo) abrasivo.
scourge [skə:dʒ] n flagello.
scout [skaut] n (MIL) esploratore m; (also: **boy** ~) giovane esploratore, scout m inv.
►**scout around** vi cercare in giro.
scowl [skaul] vi accigliarsi, aggrottare le sopracciglia; **to** ~ **at** guardare torvo.
scrabble ['skræbl] vi (claw): **to** ~ (**at**) graffiare, grattare; **to** ~ **about** or **around for sth** cercare affannosamente qc ♦ n: **S**~ ® Scarabeo ®.
scraggy ['skrægɪ] adj scarno(a).
scram [skræm] vi (col) filare via.
scramble ['skræmbl] n arrampicata ♦ vi inerpicarsi; **to** ~ **out** etc uscire etc in fretta; **to** ~ **for** azzuffarsi per; **to go scrambling** (SPORT) fare il motocross.
scrambled eggs npl uova fpl strapazzate.
scrap [skræp] n pezzo, pezzetto; (fight) zuffa; (also: ~ **iron**) rottami mpl di ferro, ferraglia ♦ vt demolire; (fig) scartare; ~**s** npl (waste) scarti mpl; **to sell sth for** ~ vendere qc come ferro vecchio.
scrapbook ['skræpbuk] n album m inv di ritagli.
scrap dealer n commerciante m di

ferraglia.

scrape [skreɪp] *vt, vi* raschiare, grattare ♦ *n*: **to get into a** ~ cacciarsi in un guaio.

►**scrape through** *vi* (*succeed*) farcela per un pelo, cavarsela ♦ *vt fus* (*exam*) passare per miracolo, passare per il rotto della cuffia.

scraper ['skreɪpə*] *n* raschietto.

scrap heap *n* mucchio di rottami; **to throw sth on the** ~ (*fig*) mettere qc nel dimenticatoio.

scrap merchant *n* (*BRIT*) commerciante *m* di ferraglia.

scrap metal *n* ferraglia.

scrap paper *n* cartaccia.

scrappy ['skræpɪ] *adj* frammentario(a), sconnesso(a).

scrap yard *n* deposito di rottami; (*for cars*) cimitero delle macchine.

scratch [skrætʃ] *n* graffio ♦ *cpd*: ~ **team** squadra raccogliticcia ♦ *vt* graffiare, rigare; (*COMPUT*) cancellare ♦ *vi* grattare, graffiare; **to start from** ~ cominciare *or* partire da zero; **to be up to** ~ essere all'altezza.

scratch pad *n* (*US*) notes *m inv*, blocchetto.

scrawl [skrɔ:l] *n* scarabocchio ♦ *vi* scarabocchiare.

scrawny ['skrɔ:nɪ] *adj* scarno(a), pelle e ossa *inv*.

scream [skri:m] *n* grido, urlo ♦ *vi* urlare, gridare; **to** ~ **at sb (to do sth)** gridare a qn (di fare qc); **it was a** ~ (*fig col*) era da crepar dal ridere; **he's a** ~ (*fig col*) è una sagoma, è uno spasso.

scree [skri:] *n* ghiaione *m*.

screech [skri:tʃ] *n* strido; (*of tyres, brakes*) stridore *m* ♦ *vi* stridere.

screen [skri:n] *n* schermo; (*fig*) muro, cortina, velo ♦ *vt* schermare, fare schermo a; (*from the wind etc*) riparare; (*film*) proiettare; (*book*) adattare per lo schermo; (*candidates etc*) passare al vaglio; (*for illness*) sottoporre a controlli medici.

screen editing [-ɛdɪtɪŋ] *n* (*COMPUT*) correzione *f* e modifica su schermo.

screening ['skri:nɪŋ] *n* (*MED*) dépistage *m inv*; (*of film*) proiezione *f*; (*for security*) controlli *mpl* (di sicurezza).

screen memory *n* (*COMPUT*) memoria di schermo.

screenplay ['skri:npleɪ] *n* sceneggiatura.

screen saver *n* (*COMPUT*) screen saver *m inv*.

screen test *n* provino (cinematografico).

screw [skru:] *n* vite *f*; (*propeller*) elica ♦ *vt* avvitare; **to** ~ **sth to the wall** fissare qc al

muro con viti.

►**screw up** *vt* (*paper, material*) spiegazzare; (*col: ruin*) mandare a monte; **to** ~ **up one's face** fare una smorfia.

screwdriver ['skru:draɪvə*] *n* cacciavite *m*.

screwed-up ['skru:d'ʌp] *adj* (*col*): **she's totally** ~ è nel pallone.

screwy ['skru:ɪ] *adj* (*col*) svitato(a).

scribble ['skrɪbl] *n* scarabocchio ♦ *vt* scribacchiare ♦ *vi* scarabocchiare; **to** ~ **sth down** scribacchiare qc.

scribe [skraɪb] *n* scriba *m*.

script [skrɪpt] *n* (*CINE etc*) copione *m*; (*in exam*) elaborato *or* compito d'esame; (*writing*) scrittura.

Scripture ['skrɪptʃə*] *n* Sacre Scritture *fpl*.

scriptwriter ['skrɪptraɪtə*] *n* soggettista *m/f*.

scroll [skrəʊl] *n* rotolo di carta ♦ *vt* (*COMPUT*) scorrere.

scrotum ['skrəʊtəm] *n* scroto.

scrounge [skraʊndʒ] *vt* (*col*): **to** ~ **sth (off or from sb)** scroccare qc (a qn) ♦ *vi*: **to** ~ **on sb** vivere alle spalle di qn.

scrounger ['skraʊndʒə*] *n* scroccone/a.

scrub [skrʌb] *n* (*clean*) strofinata; (*land*) boscaglia ♦ *vt* pulire strofinando; (*reject*) annullare.

scrubbing brush ['skrʌbɪŋ-] *n* spazzolone *m*.

scruff [skrʌf] *n*: **by the** ~ **of the neck** per la collottola.

scruffy ['skrʌfɪ] *adj* sciatto(a).

scrum(mage) ['skrʌm(ɪdʒ)] *n* mischia.

scruple ['skru:pl] *n* scrupolo; **to have no** ~**s about doing sth** non avere scrupoli a fare qc.

scrupulous ['skru:pjʊləs] *adj* scrupoloso(a).

scrupulously ['skru:pjʊləslɪ] *adv* scrupolosamente; **he tries to be** ~ **fair/ honest** cerca di essere più imparziale/ onesto che può.

scrutinize ['skru:tɪnaɪz] *vt* scrutare, esaminare attentamente.

scrutiny ['skru:tɪnɪ] *n* esame *m* accurato; **under the** ~ **of sb** sotto la sorveglianza di qn.

scuba ['sku:bə] *n* autorespiratore *m*.

scuba diving *n* immersioni *fpl* subacquee.

scuff [skʌf] *vt* (*shoes*) consumare strasciticando.

scuffle ['skʌfl] *n* baruffa, tafferuglio.

scullery ['skʌlərɪ] *n* retrocucina *m or f*.

sculptor ['skʌlptə*] *n* scultore *m*.

sculpture ['skʌlptʃə*] *n* scultura.

scum [skʌm] *n* schiuma; (*pej: people*) feccia.

scupper ['skʌpə*] *vt* (*BRIT*) autoaffondare; (*fig*) far naufragare.

scurrilous ['skʌrɪləs] *adj* scurrile, volgare.
scurry ['skʌrɪ] *vi* sgambare, affrettarsi.
scurvy ['skə:vɪ] *n* scorbuto.
scuttle ['skʌtl] *n* (*NAUT*) portellino; (*also:*
coal ~) secchio del carbone ♦ *vt* (*ship*)
autoaffondare ♦ *vi* (*scamper*): **to** ~ **away,**
~ **off** darsela a gambe, scappare.
scythe [saɪð] *n* falce *f.*
SD, S. Dak. *abbr* (*US*) = *South Dakota.*
SDI *n abbr* (= *Strategic Defense Initiative*)
S.D.I. *f.*
SDLP *n abbr* (*BRIT POL*) = *Social Democratic
and Labour Party.*
SDP *n abbr* (*BRIT POL*) = *Social Democratic
Party.*
sea [si:] *n* mare *m* ♦ *cpd* marino(a), del
mare; (*ship, port*) marittimo(a), di mare;
on the ~ (*boat*) in mare; (*town*) di mare;
to go by ~ andare per mare; **by** *or* **beside
the** ~ (*holiday*) al mare; (*village*) sul mare;
to look out to ~ guardare il mare; **(out)
at** ~ al largo, heavy *or* rough ~(s) mare
grosso *or* agitato; **a** ~ **of faces** (*fig*) una
marea di gente; **to be all at** ~ (*fig*) non
sapere che pesci pigliare.
sea bed *n* fondo marino.
sea bird *n* uccello di mare.
seaboard ['si:bɔ:d] *n* costa.
sea breeze *n* brezza di mare.
seafarer ['si:fɛərə*] *n* navigante *m.*
seafaring ['si:fɛərɪŋ] *adj* (*community*)
marinaro(a); (*life*) da marinaio.
seafood ['si:fu:d] *n* frutti *mpl* di mare.
sea front *n* lungomare *m.*
seagoing ['si:gəʊɪŋ] *adj* (*ship*) d'alto
mare.
seagull ['si:gʌl] *n* gabbiano.
seal [si:l] *n* (*animal*) foca; (*stamp*) sigillo;
(*impression*) impronta del sigillo ♦ *vt*
sigillare; (*decide: sb's fate*) segnare;
(: *bargain*) concludere; ~ **of approval**
beneplacito.
▶**seal off** *vt* (*close*) sigillare; (*forbid entry to*)
bloccare l'accesso a.
sea level *n* livello del mare.
sealing wax ['si:lɪŋ-] *n* ceralacca.
sea lion *n* leone *m* marino.
sealskin ['si:lskɪn] *n* pelle *f* di foca.
seam [si:m] *n* cucitura; (*of coal*) filone *m*;
the hall was bursting at the ~**s** l'aula era
piena zeppa.
seaman ['si:mən] *n* marinaio.
seamanship ['si:mənʃɪp] *n* tecnica di
navigazione.
seamless ['si:mlɪs] *adj* senza cucitura.
seamy ['si:mɪ] *adj* malfamato(a);
squallido(a).
seance ['seɪɔns] *n* seduta spiritica.

seaplane ['si:pleɪn] *n* idrovolante *m.*
seaport ['si:pɔ:t] *n* porto di mare.
search [sə:tʃ] *n* (*for person, thing*) ricerca;
(*of drawer, pockets*) esame *m* accurato;
(*LAW: at sb's home*) perquisizione *f* ♦ *vt*
perlustrare, frugare; (*scan, examine*)
esaminare minuziosamente; (*COMPUT*)
ricercare ♦ *vi*: **to** ~ **for** ricercare; **in** ~ **of**
alla ricerca di; "~ **and replace**" (*COMPUT*)
"ricercare e sostituire".
▶**search through** *vt fus* frugare.
searcher ['sə:tʃə*] *n* chi cerca.
searching ['sə:tʃɪŋ] *adj* minuzioso(a);
penetrante; (*question*) pressante.
searchlight ['sə:tʃlaɪt] *n* proiettore *m.*
search party *n* squadra di soccorso.
search warrant *n* mandato di
perquisizione.
searing ['sɪərɪŋ] *adj* (*heat*) rovente; (*pain*)
acuto(a).
seashore ['si:ʃɔ:*] *n* spiaggia; **on the** ~
sulla riva del mare.
seasick ['si:sɪk] *adj* che soffre il mal di
mare; **to be** ~ avere il mal di mare.
seaside ['si:saɪd] *n* spiaggia; **to go to the** ~
andare al mare.
seaside resort *n* stazione *f* balneare.
season ['si:zn] *n* stagione *f* ♦ *vt* condire,
insaporire; **to be in/out of** ~ essere di/
fuori stagione; **the busy** ~ (*for shops*) il
periodo di punta; (*for hotels etc*) l'alta
stagione; **the open** ~ (*HUNTING*) la
stagione della caccia.
seasonal ['si:zənl] *adj* stagionale.
seasoned ['si:znd] *adj* (*wood*) stagionato(a);
(*fig: worker, actor, troops*) con esperienza;
a ~ **campaigner** un veterano.
seasoning ['si:znɪŋ] *n* condimento.
season ticket *n* abbonamento.
seat [si:t] *n* sedile *m*; (*in bus, train: place*)
posto; (*PARLIAMENT*) seggio; (*centre: of
government etc, of infection*) sede *f*;
(*buttocks*) didietro; (*of trousers*) fondo ♦ *vt*
far sedere; (*have room for*) avere *or*
essere fornito(a) di posti a sedere per;
are there any ~**s left?** ci sono posti?; **to
take one's** ~ prendere posto; **to be** ~**ed**
essere seduto(a); **please be** ~**ed**
accomodatevi per favore.
seat belt *n* cintura di sicurezza.
seating arrangements ['si:tɪŋ-] *npl*
sistemazione *f or* disposizione *f* dei posti.
seating capacity *n* posti *mpl* a sedere.
SEATO ['si:təʊ] *n abbr* (= *Southeast Asia
Treaty Organization*) SEATO *f.*
sea water *n* acqua di mare.
seaweed ['si:wi:d] *n* alghe *fpl.*
seaworthy ['si:wə:ðɪ] *adj* atto(a) alla

navigazione.

SEC n abbr (US: = Securities and Exchange Commission) commissione di controllo sulle operazioni in Borsa.

sec. abbr = **second**.

secateurs [sɛkə'təːz] npl forbici fpl per potare.

secede [sɪ'siːd] vi: **to ~ (from)** ritirarsi (da).

secluded [sɪ'kluːdɪd] adj isolato(a), appartato(a).

seclusion [sɪ'kluːʒən] n isolamento.

second ['sɛkənd] num secondo(a) ♦ adv (in race etc) al secondo posto; (RAIL) in seconda ♦ n (unit of time) secondo; (in series, position) secondo/a; (BRIT SCOL) laurea con punteggio discreto; (AUT: also: ~ **gear**) seconda; (COMM: imperfect) scarto ♦ vt (motion) appoggiare; [sɪ'kɔnd] (employee) distaccare; **Charles the S~** Carlo Secondo; **just a ~!** un attimo!; **~ floor** (BRIT) secondo piano; (US) primo piano; **to ask for a ~ opinion** (MED) chiedere un altro or ulteriore parere; **to have ~ thoughts (about doing sth)** avere dei ripensamenti (quanto a fare qc); **on ~ thoughts** or (US) **thought** a ripensarci, ripensandoci bene.

secondary ['sɛkəndərɪ] adj secondario(a).

secondary school n scuola secondaria; see boxed note.

SECONDARY SCHOOL

In Gran Bretagna la **secondary school** è la scuola frequentata dai ragazzi dagli 11 ai 18 anni. L'età scolare nel paese va fino ai 16 anni; vedi anche **primary school, high school**.

---

second-best [sɛkənd'bɛst] n ripiego; **as a ~** in mancanza di meglio.

second-class [sɛkənd'klɑːs] adj di seconda classe ♦ adv: **to travel ~** viaggiare in seconda (classe); **to send sth ~** spedire qc per posta ordinaria; **~ citizen** cittadino di second'ordine.

second cousin n cugino di secondo grado.

seconder ['sɛkəndə*] n sostenitore/trice.

second-guess ['sɛkənd'gɛs] vt (predict) anticipare; (after the event) giudicare col senno di poi.

second hand n (on clock) lancetta dei secondi.

second-hand [sɛkənd'hænd] adj di seconda mano, usato(a) ♦ adv (buy) di seconda mano; **to hear sth ~** venire a sapere qc da terze persone.

second-in-command ['sɛkəndɪnkə'mɑːnd] n (MIL) comandante m in seconda; (ADMIN) aggiunto.

secondly ['sɛkəndlɪ] adv in secondo luogo.

secondment [sɪ'kɔndmənt] n (BRIT) distaccamento.

second-rate [sɛkənd'reɪt] adj scadente.

Second World War n: **the ~** la seconda guerra mondiale.

secrecy ['siːkrəsɪ] n segretezza.

secret ['siːkrɪt] adj segreto(a) ♦ n segreto; **in ~** in segreto, segretamente; **to keep sth ~ (from sb)** tenere qc segreto (a qn), tenere qc nascosto (a qn); **keep it ~** che rimanga un segreto; **to make no ~ of sth** non far mistero di qc.

secret agent n agente m segreto.

secretarial [sɛkrɪ'tɛərɪəl] adj (work) da segretario/a; (college, course) di segretariato.

secretariat [sɛkrɪ'tɛərɪət] n segretariato.

secretary ['sɛkrətrɪ] n segretario/a; **S~ of State** (US POL) ≈ Ministro degli Esteri; **S~ of State (for)** (BRIT POL) ministro (di).

secretary-general ['sɛkrətrɪ'dʒɛnərl] n segretario generale.

secrete [sɪ'kriːt] vt (MED, ANAT, BIOL) secernere; (hide) nascondere.

secretion [sɪ'kriːʃən] n secrezione f.

secretive ['siːkrətɪv] adj riservato(a).

secretly ['siːkrɪtlɪ] adv in segreto, segretamente.

secret police n polizia segreta.

secret service n servizi mpl segreti.

sect [sɛkt] n setta.

sectarian [sɛk'tɛərɪən] adj settario(a).

section ['sɛkʃən] n sezione f; (of document) articolo ♦ vt sezionare, dividere in sezioni; **the business ~** (PRESS) la pagina economica.

sector ['sɛktə*] n settore m.

secular ['sɛkjulə*] adj secolare.

secure [sɪ'kjuə*] adj (free from anxiety) sicuro(a); (firmly fixed) assicurato(a), ben fermato(a); (in safe place) al sicuro ♦ vt (fix) fissare, assicurare; (get) ottenere, assicurarsi; (COMM: loan) garantire; **to make sth ~** fissare bene qc; **to ~ sth for sb** procurare qc per or a qn.

security [sɪ'kjuərɪtɪ] n sicurezza; (for loan) garanzia; **securities** npl (STOCK EXCHANGE) titoli mpl; **to increase/tighten ~** aumentare/intensificare la sorveglianza; **~ of tenure** garanzia del posto di lavoro, garanzia di titolo or di godimento.

Security Council n: **the ~** il Consiglio di Sicurezza.

security forces npl forze fpl dell'ordine.

security guard n guardia giurata.

security risk n rischio per la sicurezza.

secy. *abbr* = **secretary.**

sedan [sə'dæn] *n* (*US AUT*) berlina.

sedate [sɪ'deɪt] *adj* posato(a); calmo(a) ♦ *vt* calmare.

sedation [sɪ'deɪʃən] *n* (*MED*): **to be under ~** essere sotto l'azione di sedativi.

sedative ['sɛdɪtɪv] *n* sedativo, calmante *m*.

sedentary ['sɛdntrɪ] *adj* sedentario(a).

sediment ['sɛdɪmənt] *n* sedimento.

sedition [sɪ'dɪʃən] *n* sedizione *f*.

seduce [sɪ'djuːs] *vt* sedurre.

seduction [sɪ'dʌkʃən] *n* seduzione *f*.

seductive [sɪ'dʌktɪv] *adj* seducente.

see [siː] *vb* (*pt* **saw**, *pp* **seen** [sɔː, siːn]) *vt* vedere; (*accompany*): **to ~ sb to the door** accompagnare qn alla porta ♦ *vi* vedere; (*understand*) capire ♦ *n* sede *f* vescovile; **to ~ that** (*ensure*) badare che + *sub*, fare in modo che + *sub*; **to go and ~ sb** andare a trovare qn; **~ you soon/later/ tomorrow!** a presto/più tardi/domani!; **as far as I can ~** da quanto posso vedere; **there was nobody to be ~n** non c'era anima viva; **let me ~** (*show me*) fammi vedere; (*let me think*) vediamo (un po'); **~ for yourself** vai a vedere con i tuoi occhi; **I don't know what she ~s in him** non so che cosa ci trovi in lui.

▸**see about** *vt fus* (*deal with*) occuparsi di.

▸**see off** *vt* salutare alla partenza.

▸**see through** *vt* portare a termine ♦ *vt fus* non lasciarsi ingannare da.

▸**see to** *vt fus* occuparsi di.

seed [siːd] *n* seme *m*; (*fig*) germe *m*; (*TENNIS*) testa di serie; **to go to ~** fare seme; (*fig*) scadere.

seedless ['siːdlɪs] *adj* senza semi.

seedling ['siːdlɪŋ] *n* piantina di semenzaio.

seedy ['siːdɪ] *adj* (*shabby: person*) sciatto(a); (: *place*) cadente.

seeing ['siːɪŋ] *conj*: **~ (that)** visto che.

seek [siːk], *pt*, *pp* **sought** *vt* cercare; **to ~ advice/help from sb** chiedere consiglio/ aiuto a qn.

▸**seek out** *vt* (*person*) andare a cercare.

seem [siːm] *vi* sembrare, parere; **there ~s to be ...** sembra che ci sia ...; **it ~s (that)** ... sembra *or* pare che ... + *sub*; **what ~s to be the trouble?** cosa c'è che non va?

seemingly ['siːmɪŋlɪ] *adv* apparentemente.

seen [siːn] *pp* of **see.**

seep [siːp] *vi* filtrare, trapelare.

seer [sɪə*] *n* profeta/essa, veggente *m/f*.

seersucker ['sɪəsʌkə*] *n* cotone *m* indiano.

seesaw ['siːsɔː] *n* altalena a bilico.

seethe [siːð] *vi* ribollire; **to ~ with anger** fremere di rabbia.

see-through ['siːθruː] *adj* trasparente.

segment ['sɛgmənt] *n* segmento.

segregate ['sɛgrɪgeɪt] *vt* segregare, isolare.

segregation [sɛgrɪ'geɪʃən] *n* segregazione *f*.

Seine [seɪn] *n* Senna.

seismic ['saɪzmɪk] *adj* sismico(a).

seize [siːz] *vt* (*grasp*) afferrare; (*take possession of*) impadronirsi di; (*LAW*) sequestrare.

▸**seize up** *vi* (*TECH*) grippare.

▸**seize (up)on** *vt fus* ricorrere a.

seizure ['siːʒə*] *n* (*MED*) attacco; (*LAW*) confisca, sequestro.

seldom ['sɛldəm] *adv* raramente.

select [sɪ'lɛkt] *adj* scelto(a); (*hotel, restaurant*) chic *inv*; (*club*) esclusivo(a) ♦ *vt* scegliere, selezionare; **a ~ few** pochi eletti *mpl*.

selection [sɪ'lɛkʃən] *n* selezione *f*, scelta.

selection committee *n* comitato di selezione.

selective [sɪ'lɛktɪv] *adj* selettivo(a).

selector [sɪ'lɛktə*] *n* (*person*) selezionatore/trice; (*TECH*) selettore *m*.

self [sɛlf] *n* (*pl* **selves** [sɛlvz]): **the ~** l'io *m* ♦ *prefix* auto....

self-addressed ['sɛlfə'drɛst] *adj*: **~ envelope** busta col proprio nome e indirizzo.

self-adhesive [sɛlfəd'hiːzɪv] *adj* autoadesivo(a).

self-assertive [sɛlfə'səːtɪv] *adj* autoritario(a).

self-assurance [sɛlfə'ʃuərəns] *n* sicurezza di sé.

self-assured [sɛlfə'ʃuəd] *adj* sicuro(a) di sé.

self-catering [sɛlf'keɪtərɪŋ] *adj* (*BRIT*) in cui ci si cucina da sé; **~ apartment** appartamento (per le vacanze).

self-centred, (*US*) **self-centered** [sɛlf'sɛntəd] *adj* egocentrico(a).

self-cleaning [sɛlf'kliːnɪŋ] *adj* autopulente.

self-confessed [sɛlfkən'fɛst] *adj* (*alcoholic etc*) dichiarato(a).

self-confidence [sɛlf'kɔnfɪdəns] *n* sicurezza di sé.

self-conscious [sɛlf'kɔnʃəs] *adj* timido(a).

self-contained [sɛlfkən'teɪnd] *adj* (*BRIT: flat*) indipendente.

self-control [sɛlfkən'trəul] *n* autocontrollo.

self-defeating [sɛlfdɪ'fiːtɪŋ] *adj* futile.

self-defence, (*US*) **self-defense** [sɛlfdɪ'fɛns] *n* autodifesa; (*LAW*) legittima difesa.

self-discipline [sɛlf'dɪsɪplɪn] *n* autodisciplina.

self-employed [sɛlfɪm'plɔɪd] *adj* che lavora

in proprio.
self-esteem [sɛlfɪ'stiːm] *n* amor proprio *m*.
self-evident [sɛlf'ɛvɪdənt] *adj* evidente.
self-explanatory [sɛlfɪk'splænətərɪ] *adj*
ovvio(a).
self-governing [sɛlf'gʌvənɪŋ] *adj*
autonomo(a).
self-help ['sɛlf'hɛlp] *n* iniziativa
individuale.
self-importance [sɛlfim'pɔːtns] *n*
sufficienza.
self-indulgent [sɛlfɪn'dʌldʒənt] *adj*
indulgente verso se stesso(a).
self-inflicted [sɛlfɪn'flɪktɪd] *adj*
autoinflitto(a).
self-interest [sɛlf'ɪntrɪst] *n* interesse *m*
personale.
selfish ['sɛlfɪʃ] *adj* egoista.
selfishly ['sɛlfɪʃlɪ] *adv* egoisticamente.
selfishness ['sɛlfɪʃnɪs] *n* egoismo.
selfless ['sɛlflɪs] *adj* altruista.
selflessly ['sɛlflɪslɪ] *adv* altruisticamente.
selflessness ['sɛlflɪsnɪs] *n* altruismo.
self-made man ['sɛlfmeɪd-] *n* self-made
man *m inv*, uomo che si è fatto da sé.
self-pity [sɛlf'pɪtɪ] *n* autocommiserazione *f*.
self-portrait [sɛlf'pɔːtrɪt] *n* autoritratto.
self-possessed [sɛlfpə'zɛst] *adj*
controllato(a).
self-preservation ['sɛlfprɛzə'veɪʃən] *n*
istinto di conservazione.
self-raising [sɛlf'reɪzɪŋ], (*US*) **self-rising**
[sɛlf'raɪzɪŋ] *adj*: ~ **flour** miscela di farina e
lievito.
self-reliant [sɛlfrɪ'laɪənt] *adj* indipendente.
self-respect [sɛlfrɪs'pɛkt] *n* rispetto di sé,
amor proprio.
self-respecting [sɛlfrɪs'pɛktɪŋ] *adj* che ha
rispetto di sé.
self-righteous [sɛlf'raɪtʃəs] *adj*
soddisfatto(a) di sé.
self-rising [sɛlf'raɪzɪŋ] *adj* (*US*) = **self-
raising**.
self-sacrifice [sɛlf'sækrɪfaɪs] *n* abnegazione
f.
self-same ['sɛlfseɪm] *adj* stesso(a).
self-satisfied [sɛlf'sætɪsfaɪd] *adj*
compiaciuto(a) di sé.
self-sealing [sɛlf'siːlɪŋ] *adj* autosigillante.
self-service [sɛlf'səːvɪs] *n* autoservizio,
self-service *m*.
self-styled [sɛlf'staɪld] *adj* sedicente.
self-sufficient [sɛlfsə'fɪʃənt] *adj*
autosufficiente.
self-supporting [sɛlfsə'pɔːtɪŋ] *adj*
economicamente indipendente.
self-taught [sɛlf'tɔːt] *adj* autodidatta.
self-test ['sɛlftɛst] *n* (*COMPUT*) autoverifica.

sell, *pt, pp* **sold** [sɛl, səuld] *vt* vendere ♦ *vi*
vendersi; **to** ~ **at** *or* **for 1000 lire** essere in
vendita a 1000 lire; **to** ~ **sb an idea** (*fig*)
far accettare un'idea a qn.
▶**sell off** *vt* svendere, liquidare.
▶**sell out** *vi*: **to** ~ **out (to sb/sth)** (*COMM*)
vendere (tutto) (a qn/qc) ♦ *vt* esaurire;
the tickets are all sold out i biglietti sono
esauriti.
▶**sell up** *vi* vendere (tutto).
sell-by date ['sɛlbaɪ-] *n* scadenza.
seller ['sɛlə*] *n* venditore/trice; ~**'s market**
mercato favorevole ai venditori.
selling price ['sɛlɪŋ-] *n* prezzo di vendita.
Sellotape ® ['sɛləuteɪp] *n* (*BRIT*) nastro
adesivo, scotch ® *m*.
sellout ['sɛlaut] *n* (*betrayal*) tradimento; (*of
tickets*): **it was a** ~ registrò un tutto
esaurito.
selves [sɛlvz] *npl of* **self**.
semantic [sɪ'mæntɪk] *adj* semantico(a).
semantics [sɪ'mæntɪks] *n* semantica.
semaphore ['sɛməfɔː*] *n* segnali *mpl* con
bandiere; (*RAIL*) semaforo.
semblance ['sɛmbləns] *n* parvenza,
apparenza.
semen ['siːmən] *n* sperma *m*.
semester [sɪ'mɛstə*] *n* (*US*) semestre *m*.
semi... ['sɛmɪ] *prefix* semi... ♦ *n*: **semi**
= **semidetached (house)**.
semi-breve ['sɛmɪbriːv] *n* (*BRIT*) semibreve
f.
semicircle ['sɛmɪsəːkl] *n* semicerchio.
semicircular ['sɛmɪ'səːkjulə*] *adj*
semicircolare.
semicolon [sɛmɪ'kəulən] *n* punto e virgola.
semiconductor [sɛmɪkən'dʌktə*] *n*
semiconduttore *m*.
semiconscious [sɛmɪ'kɔnʃəs] *adj*
parzialmente cosciente.
semidetached (house) [sɛmɪdɪ'tætʃt-] *n*
(*BRIT*) casa gemella.
semifinal [sɛmɪ'faɪnl] *n* semifinale *f*.
seminar ['sɛmɪnɑː*] *n* seminario.
seminary ['sɛmɪnərɪ] *n* (*REL*: *for priests*)
seminario.
semiprecious [sɛmɪ'prɛʃəs] *adj*
semiprezioso(a).
semiquaver ['sɛmɪkweɪvə*] *n* (*BRIT*)
semicroma.
semiskilled ['sɛmɪ'skɪld] *adj*: ~ **worker**
operaio(a) non specializzato(a).
semi-skimmed ['sɛmɪ'skɪmd] *adj*
parzialmente scremato(a).
semitone ['sɛmɪtəun] *n* (*MUS*) semitono.
semolina [sɛmə'liːnə] *n* semolino.
SEN *n abbr* (*BRIT*: = *State Enrolled Nurse*)
infermiera diplomata (dopo corso

biennale).
Sen., sen. *abbr* = senator; senior.
senate ['sɛnɪt] *n* senato.
senator ['sɛnɪtə*] *n* senatore/trice.
send [sɛnd], *pt, pp* **sent** *vt* mandare; **to ~ by post** *or* (*US*) **mail** spedire per posta; **to ~ sb for sth** mandare qn a prendere qc; **to ~ word that** ... mandare a dire che ...; **she ~s (you) her love** ti saluta affettuosamente; **to ~ sb to Coventry** (*BRIT*) dare l'ostracismo a qn; **to ~ sb to sleep/into fits of laughter** far addormentare/scoppiare dal ridere qn; **to ~ sth flying** far volare via qc.
▶**send away** *vt* (*letter, goods*) spedire; (*person*) mandare via.
▶**send away for** *vt fus* richiedere per posta, farsi spedire.
▶**send back** *vt* rimandare.
▶**send for** *vt fus* mandare a chiamare, far venire; (*by post*) ordinare per posta.
▶**send in** *vt* (*report, application, resignation*) presentare.
▶**send off** *vt* (*goods*) spedire; (*BRIT SPORT: player*) espellere.
▶**send on** *vt* (*BRIT: letter*) inoltrare; (*luggage etc: in advance*) spedire in anticipo.
▶**send out** *vt* (*invitation*) diramare; (*emit: light, heat*) mandare, emanare; (*: signals*) emettere.
▶**send round** *vt* (*letter, document etc*) far circolare.
▶**send up** *vt* (*person, price*) far salire; (*BRIT: parody*) mettere in ridicolo.
sender ['sɛndə*] *n* mittente *m/f.*
send-off ['sɛndɔf] *n:* **to give sb a good ~** festeggiare la partenza di qn.
Senegal [sɛnɪ'gɔːl] *n* Senegal *m.*
Senegalese [sɛnɪgə'liːz] *adj, n* senegalese (*m/f*).
senile ['siːnaɪl] *adj* senile.
senility [sɪ'nɪlɪtɪ] *n* senilità *f.*
senior ['siːnɪə*] *adj* (*older*) più vecchio(a); (*of higher rank*) di grado più elevato ♦ *n* persona più anziana; (*in service*) persona con maggiore anzianità; **P. Jones ~ P.** Jones senior, P. Jones padre.
senior citizen *n* anziano/a.
senior high school *n* (*US*) ≈ liceo.
seniority [siːnɪ'ɔrɪtɪ] *n* anzianità; (*in rank*) superiorità.
sensation [sɛn'seɪʃən] *n* sensazione *f;* **to create a ~** fare scalpore.
sensational [sɛn'seɪʃənl] *adj* sensazionale; (*marvellous*) eccezionale.
sense [sɛns] *n* senso; (*feeling*) sensazione *f,* senso; (*meaning*) senso, significato; (*wisdom*) buonsenso ♦ *vt* sentire,

percepire; **~s** *npl* (*sanity*) ragione *f;* **it makes ~** ha senso; **there is no ~ in** (**doing**) **that** non ha senso (farlo); **~ of humour** (senso dell')umorismo; **to come to one's ~s** (*regain consciousness*) riprendere i sensi; (*become reasonable*) tornare in sé; **to take leave of one's ~s** perdere il lume *or* l'uso della ragione.
senseless ['sɛnslɪs] *adj* sciocco(a); (*unconscious*) privo(a) di sensi.
sensibilities [sɛnsɪ'bɪlɪtɪz] *npl* sensibilità *fsg.*
sensible ['sɛnsɪbl] *adj* sensato(a), ragionevole.
sensitive ['sɛnsɪtɪv] *adj:* **~ (to)** sensibile (a); **he is very ~ about it** è un tasto che è meglio non toccare con lui.
sensitivity [sɛnsɪ'tɪvɪtɪ] *n* sensibilità.
sensual ['sɛnsjuəl] *adj* sensuale.
sensuous ['sɛnsjuəs] *adj* sensuale.
sent [sɛnt] *pt, pp of* **send.**
sentence ['sɛntns] *n* (*LING*) frase *f;* (*LAW: judgement*) sentenza; (*: punishment*) condanna ♦ *vt:* **to ~ sb to death/to 5 years** condannare qn a morte/a 5 anni; **to pass ~ on sb** condannare qn.
sentiment ['sɛntɪmənt] *n* sentimento; (*opinion*) opinione *f.*
sentimental [sɛntɪ'mɛntl] *adj* sentimentale.
sentimentality [sɛntɪmɛn'tælɪtɪ] *n* sentimentalità, sentimentalismo.
sentry ['sɛntrɪ] *n* sentinella.
sentry duty *n:* **to be on ~** essere di sentinella.
Seoul [səul] *n* Seul *f.*
separable ['sɛprəbl] *adj* separabile.
separate *adj* ['sɛprɪt] separato(a) ♦ *vb* ['sɛpəreɪt] *vt* separare ♦ *vi* separarsi; **~ from** separato da; **under ~ cover** (*COMM*) in plico a parte; **to ~ into** dividere in; *see also* **separates.**
separately ['sɛprɪtlɪ] *adv* separatamente.
separates ['sɛprɪts] *npl* (*clothes*) coordinati *mpl.*
separation [sɛpə'reɪʃən] *n* separazione *f.*
Sept. *abbr* (= *September*) sett., set.
September [sɛp'tɛmbə*] *n* settembre *m; for phrases see also* **July.**
septic ['sɛptɪk] *adj* settico(a); (*wound*) infettato(a); **to go ~** infettarsi.
septicaemia, (*US*) **septicemia** [sɛptɪ'siːmɪə] *n* setticemia.
septic tank *n* fossa settica.
sequel ['siːkwl] *n* conseguenza; (*of story*) seguito.
sequence ['siːkwəns] *n* (*series*) serie *f inv;* (*order*) ordine *m;* **in ~** in ordine, di seguito; **~ of tenses** concordanza dei

tempi.
sequential [sɪ'kwɛnʃəl] *adj*: ~ **access**
(*COMPUT*) accesso sequenziale.
sequin ['siːkwɪn] *n* lustrino, paillette *f inv.*
Serb [səːb] *adj, n* = **Serbian.**
Serbia ['səːbɪə] *n* Serbia.
Serbian ['səːbɪən] *adj* serbo(a) ♦ *n* serbo/a;
(*LING*) serbo.
Serbo-Croat ['səːbəu'krəuæt] *n* (*LING*)
serbocroato.
serenade [sɛrə'neɪd] *n* serenata ♦ *vt* fare la
serenata a.
serene [sɪ'riːn] *adj* sereno(a), calmo(a).
serenity [sɪ'rɛnɪtɪ] *n* serenità, tranquillità.
sergeant ['saːdʒənt] *n* sergente *m*; (*POLICE*)
brigadiere *m.*
sergeant major *n* maresciallo.
serial ['sɪərɪəl] *n* (*PRESS*) romanzo a
puntate; (*RADIO, TV*) trasmissione *f* a
puntate ♦ *cpd* (*number*) di serie; (*COMPUT*)
seriale.
serialize ['sɪərɪəlaɪz] *vt* pubblicare a
puntate; trasmettere a puntate.
serial killer *n* serial killer *m inv.*
serial number *n* numero di serie.
series ['sɪəriːz] *n* (*pl inv*) serie *f inv*;
(*PUBLISHING*) collana.
serious ['sɪərɪəs] *adj* serio(a), grave; **are
you ~ (about it)?** parla sul serio?
seriously ['sɪərɪəslɪ] *adv* seriamente; **he's ~
rich** (*col: extremely*) ha un casino di soldi;
to take sth/sb ~ prendere qc/qn sul
serio.
seriousness ['sɪərɪəsnɪs] *n* serietà, gravità.
sermon ['səːmən] *n* sermone *m.*
serrated [sɪ'reɪtɪd] *adj* seghettato(a).
serum ['sɪərəm] *n* siero.
servant ['səːvənt] *n* domestico/a.
serve [səːv] *vt* (*employer etc*) servire,
essere a servizio di; (*purpose*) servire
a; (*customer, food, meal*) servire;
(*apprenticeship*) fare; (*prison term*)
scontare ♦ *vi* (*also TENNIS*) servire; (*soldier
etc*) prestare servizio; (*be useful*): **to ~
as/for/to do** servire da/per/per fare ♦ *n*
(*TENNIS*) servizio; **are you being ~d?** la
stanno servendo?; **to ~ on a committee/
jury** far parte di un comitato/una giuria;
it ~s him right ben gli sta, se l'è meritata;
it ~s my purpose fa al caso mio.
▶**serve out, serve up** *vt* (*food*) servire.
server ['səːvə*] *n* (*COMPUT*) server *sm inv.*
service ['səːvɪs] *n* servizio; (*AUT:
maintenance*) revisione *f*; (*REL*) funzione *f*
♦ *vt* (*car, washing machine*) revisionare;
the S~s *npl* le forze armate; **to be of ~ to
sb, to do sb a ~** essere d'aiuto a qn; **to
put one's car in for (a) ~** portare la

macchina in officina per una revisione;
dinner ~ servizio da tavola.
serviceable ['səːvɪsəbl] *adj* pratico(a), utile;
(*usable, working*) usabile.
service area *n* (*on motorway*) area di
servizio.
service charge *n* (*BRIT*) servizio.
service industries *npl* settore *m* terziario.
serviceman ['səːvɪsmən] *n* militare *m.*
service provider *n* (*COMPUT*) provider *sm
inv.*
service station *n* stazione *f* di servizio.
serviette [səːvɪ'ɛt] *n* (*BRIT*) tovagliolo.
servile ['səːvaɪl] *adj* servile.
session ['sɛʃən] *n* (*sitting*) seduta, sessione
f; (*SCOL*) anno scolastico (*or* accademico);
to be in ~ essere in seduta.
session musician *n* musicista *m/f* di studio.
set [sɛt] *n* serie *f inv*; (*RADIO, TV*)
apparecchio; (*TENNIS*) set *m inv*; (*group of
people*) mondo, ambiente *m*; (*CINE*)
scenario; (*THEAT: stage*) scene *fpl*;
(: *scenery*) scenario; (*MATH*) insieme *m*;
(*HAIRDRESSING*) messa in piega ♦ *adj*
(*fixed*) stabilito(a), determinato(a);
(*ready*) pronto(a) ♦ *vb* (*pt, pp* **set**) (*place*)
posare, mettere; (*fix*) fissare; (*assign: task,
homework*) dare, assegnare; (*adjust*)
regolare; (*decide: rules etc*) stabilire,
fissare; (*TYP*) comporre ♦ *vi* (*sun*)
tramontare; (*jam, jelly*) rapprendersi;
(*concrete*) fare presa; **to be ~ on doing**
essere deciso a fare; **to be all ~ to do sth**
essere pronto fare qc; **to be (dead) ~
against** essere completamente contrario
a; ~ **in one's ways** abitudinario; **a novel ~
in Rome** un romanzo ambientato a Roma;
to ~ to music mettere in musica; **to ~ on
fire** dare fuoco a; **to ~ free** liberare; **to ~
sth going** mettere in moto qc; **to ~ sail**
prendere il mare; **a ~ phrase** una frase
fatta; **a ~ of false teeth** una dentiera; **a ~
of dining-room furniture** una camera da
pranzo.
▶**set about** *vt fus* (*task*) intraprendere,
mettersi a; **to ~ about doing sth** mettersi
a fare qc.
▶**set aside** *vt* mettere da parte.
▶**set back** *vt* (*progress*) ritardare; **to ~
back (by)** (*in time*) mettere indietro (di); **a
house ~ back from the road** una casa a
una certa distanza dalla strada.
▶**set in** *vi* (*infection*) svilupparsi; (*compli-
cations*) intervenire; **the rain has ~ in for
the day** ormai pioverà tutto il giorno.
▶**set off** *vi* partire ♦ *vt* (*bomb*) far
scoppiare; (*cause to start*) mettere in
moto; (*show up well*) dare risalto a.

▶**set out** vi partire; (aim): **to ~ out to do** proporsi di fare ♦ vt (arrange) disporre; (state) esporre, presentare.

▶**set up** vt (organization) fondare, costituire; (record) stabilire; (monument) innalzare.

setback ['sɛtbæk] n (hitch) contrattempo, inconveniente m; (in health) ricaduta.

set menu n menù m inv fisso.

set square n squadra.

settee [sɛ'tiː] n divano, sofà m inv.

setting ['sɛtɪŋ] n ambiente m; (scenery) sfondo; (of jewel) montatura.

setting lotion n fissatore m.

settle ['sɛtl] vt (argument, matter) appianare; (problem) risolvere; (pay: bill, account) regolare, saldare; (MED: calm) calmare; (colonize: land) colonizzare ♦ vi (bird, dust etc) posarsi; (sediment) depositarsi; (also: ~ **down**) sistemarsi, stabilirsi; (become calmer) calmarsi; **to ~ to sth applicarsi a qc; to ~ for sth** accontentarsi di qc; **to ~ on sth** decidersi per qc; **that's ~d then** allora è deciso; **to ~ one's stomach** calmare il mal di stomaco.

▶**settle in** vi sistemarsi.

▶**settle up** vi: **to ~ up with sb** regolare i conti con qn.

settlement ['sɛtlmənt] n (payment) pagamento, saldo; (agreement) accordo; (colony) colonia; (village etc) villaggio, comunità f inv; **in ~ of our account** (COMM) a saldo del nostro conto.

settler ['sɛtlə*] n colonizzatore/trice.

setup ['sɛtʌp] n (arrangement) sistemazione f; (situation) situazione f.

seven ['sɛvn] num sette.

seventeen [sɛvn'tiːn] num diciassette.

seventh ['sɛvnθ] num settimo(a).

seventy ['sɛvntɪ] num settanta.

sever ['sɛvə*] vt recidere, tagliare; (relations) troncare.

several ['sɛvərl] adj, pron alcuni(e), diversi(e); ~ **of us** alcuni di noi; ~ **times** diverse volte.

severance ['sɛvərəns] n (of relations) rottura.

severance pay n indennità di licenziamento.

severe [sɪ'vɪə*] adj severo(a); (serious) serio(a), grave; (hard) duro(a); (plain) semplice, sobrio(a).

severely [sɪ'vɪəlɪ] adv (gen) severamente; (wounded, ill) gravemente.

severity [sɪ'vɛrɪtɪ] n severità; gravità; (of weather) rigore m.

sew, pt **sewed**, pp **sewn** [səu, səud, səun] vt,
vi cucire.

▶**sew up** vt ricucire; **it is all sewn up** (fig) è tutto apposto.

sewage ['suːɪdʒ] n acque fpl di scolo.

sewage works n stabilimento per la depurazione dei liquami.

sewer ['suːə*] n fogna.

sewing ['səuɪŋ] n cucito.

sewing machine n macchina da cucire.

sewn [səun] pp of **sew**.

sex [sɛks] n sesso; **to have ~ with** avere rapporti sessuali con.

sex act n atto sessuale.

sex appeal n sex appeal m inv.

sex education n educazione f sessuale.

sexism ['sɛksɪzəm] n sessismo.

sexist ['sɛksɪst] adj sessista.

sex life n vita sessuale.

sex object n oggetto sessuale; **to be treated like a ~** (woman) essere trattata da donna oggetto.

sextet [sɛks'tɛt] n sestetto.

sexual ['sɛksjuəl] adj sessuale; ~ **assault** violenza carnale; ~ **harassment** molestie fpl sessuali; ~ **intercourse** rapporti mpl sessuali.

sexy ['sɛksɪ] adj provocante, sexy inv.

Seychelles [seɪ'ʃɛlz] npl: **the ~** le Seicelle.

SF n abbr = **science fiction**.

SG n abbr (US) = **Surgeon General**.

Sgt. abbr (= sergeant) serg.

shabbiness ['ʃæbɪnɪs] n trasandatezza; squallore m; meschinità.

shabby ['ʃæbɪ] adj trasandato(a); (building) squallido(a), malandato(a); (behaviour) meschino(a).

shack [ʃæk] n baracca, capanna.

shackles ['ʃæklz] npl ferri mpl, catene fpl.

shade [ʃeɪd] n ombra; (for lamp) paralume m; (of colour) tonalità f inv; (US: window ~) veneziana; (small quantity): **a ~ of** un po' or un'ombra di ♦ vt ombreggiare, fare ombra a; ~**s** npl (US: sunglasses) occhiali mpl da sole; **in the ~** all'ombra; **a ~ smaller** un tantino più piccolo.

shadow ['ʃædəu] n ombra ♦ vt (follow) pedinare; **without** or **beyond a ~ of doubt** senz'ombra di dubbio.

shadow cabinet n (BRIT POL) governo m ombra inv.

shadowy ['ʃædəuɪ] adj ombreggiato(a), ombroso(a); (dim) vago(a), indistinto(a).

shady ['ʃeɪdɪ] adj ombroso(a); (fig: dishonest) losco(a), equivoco(a).

shaft [ʃɑːft] n (of arrow, spear) asta; (AUT, TECH) albero; (of mine) pozzo; (of lift) tromba; (of light) raggio; **ventilator ~** condotto di ventilazione.

shaggy ['ʃægɪ] *adj* ispido(a).

shake [ʃeɪk] (*pt* **shook**, *pp* **shaken** [ʃuk, 'ʃeɪkn]) *vt* scuotere; (*bottle, cocktail*) agitare ♦ *vi* tremare ♦ *n* scossa; **to ~ one's head** scuotere la testa; **to ~ hands with sb** stringere *or* dare la mano a qn.
▶**shake off** *vt* scrollare (via); (*fig*) sbarazzarsi di.
▶**shake up** *vt* scuotere.

shake-up ['ʃeɪkʌp] *n* riorganizzazione *f* drastica.

shakily ['ʃeɪkɪlɪ] *adv* (*reply*) con voce tremante; (*walk*) con passo malfermo; (*write*) con mano tremante.

shaky ['ʃeɪkɪ] *adj* (*hand, voice*) tremante; (*memory*) labile; (*knowledge*) incerto(a); (*building*) traballante.

shale [ʃeɪl] *n* roccia scistosa.

shall [ʃæl] *aux vb*: **I ~ go** andrò.

shallot [ʃə'lɔt] *n* (*BRIT*) scalogna.

shallow ['ʃæləu] *adj* poco profondo(a); (*fig*) superficiale.

sham [ʃæm] *n* finzione *f*, messinscena; (*jewellery, furniture*) imitazione *f* ♦ *adj* finto(a) ♦ *vt* fingere, simulare.

shambles ['ʃæmblz] *n* confusione *f*, baraonda, scompiglio; **the economy is (in) a complete ~** l'economia è nel caos più totale.

shambolic [ʃæm'bɔlɪk] *adj* (*col*) incasinato(a).

shame [ʃeɪm] *n* vergogna ♦ *vt* far vergognare; **it is a ~ (that/to do)** è un peccato (che + *sub*/fare); **what a ~!** che peccato!; **to put sb/sth to ~** (*fig*) far sfigurare qn/qc.

shamefaced ['ʃeɪmfeɪst] *adj* vergognoso(a).

shameful ['ʃeɪmful] *adj* vergognoso(a).

shameless ['ʃeɪmlɪs] *adj* sfrontato(a); (*immodest*) spudorato(a).

shampoo [ʃæm'pu:] *n* shampoo *m inv* ♦ *vt* fare lo shampoo a; **~ and set** shampoo e messa in piega.

shamrock ['ʃæmrɔk] *n* trifoglio (*simbolo nazionale dell'Irlanda*).

shandy ['ʃændɪ] *n* birra con gassosa.

shan't [ʃɑ:nt] = **shall not.**

shanty town ['ʃæntɪ-] *n* bidonville *f inv*.

SHAPE [ʃeɪp] *n abbr* (= *Supreme Headquarters Allied Powers, Europe*) *supremo quartier generale delle Potenze Alleate in Europa.*

shape [ʃeɪp] *n* forma ♦ *vt* (*clay, stone*) dar forma a; (*fig: ideas, character*) formare; (: *course of events*) determinare, condizionare; (*statement*) formulare; (*sb's ideas*) condizionare ♦ *vi* (*also: ~ up*: *events*) andare, mettersi; (: *person*)

cavarsela; **to take ~** prendere forma; **in the ~ of a heart** a forma di cuore; **to get o.s. into ~** rimettersi in forma; **I can't bear gardening in any ~ or form** detesto il giardinaggio d'ogni genere e specie.

-shaped [ʃeɪpt] *suffix*: **heart-~** a forma di cuore.

shapeless ['ʃeɪplɪs] *adj* senza forma, informe.

shapely ['ʃeɪplɪ] *adj* ben proporzionato(a).

share [ʃɛə*] *n* (*thing received, contribution*) parte *f*; (*COMM*) azione *f* ♦ *vt* dividere; (*have in common*) condividere, avere in comune; **to ~ out (among or between)** dividere (tra); **to ~ in** partecipare a.

share capital *n* capitale *m* azionario.

share certificate *n* certificato azionario.

shareholder ['ʃɛəhəuldə*] *n* azionista *m/f*.

share index *n* listino di Borsa.

shark [ʃɑ:k] *n* squalo, pescecane *m*.

sharp [ʃɑ:p] *adj* (*razor, knife*) affilato(a); (*point*) acuto(a), acuminato(a); (*nose, chin*) aguzzo(a); (*outline*) netto(a); (*curve, bend*) stretto(a), accentuato(a); (*cold, pain*) pungente; (*voice*) stridulo(a); (*person: quick-witted*) sveglio(a); (: *unscrupulous*) disonesto(a); (*MUS*): **C ~** do diesis ♦ *n* (*MUS*) diesis *m inv* ♦ *adv*: **at 2 o'clock ~** alle due in punto; **turn ~ left** giri tutto a sinistra; **to be ~ with sb** rimproverare qn; **look ~!** sbrigati!

sharpen ['ʃɑ:pən] *vt* affilare; (*pencil*) fare la punta a; (*fig*) aguzzare.

sharpener ['ʃɑ:pnə*] *n* (*also*: **pencil ~**) temperamatite *m inv*; (*also*: **knife ~**) affilacoltelli *m inv*.

sharp-eyed [ʃɑ:p'aɪd] *adj* dalla vista acuta.

sharpish ['ʃɑ:pɪʃ] *adv* (*BRIT col: quickly*) subito.

sharply ['ʃɑ:plɪ] *adv* (*abruptly*) bruscamente; (*clearly*) nettamente; (*harshly*) duramente, aspramente.

sharp-tempered [ʃɑ:p'tɛmpəd] *adj* irascibile.

shatter ['ʃætə*] *vt* mandare in frantumi, frantumare; (*fig: upset*) distruggere; (: *ruin*) rovinare ♦ *vi* frantumarsi, andare in pezzi.

shattered ['ʃætəd] *adj* (*grief-stricken*) sconvolto(a); (*exhausted*) a pezzi, distrutto(a).

shatterproof ['ʃætəpru:f] *adj* infrangibile.

shave [ʃeɪv] *vt* radere, rasare ♦ *vi* radersi, farsi la barba ♦ *n*: **to have a ~** farsi la barba.

shaven ['ʃeɪvn] *adj* (*head*) rasato(a), tonsurato(a).

shaver ['ʃeɪvə*] *n* (*also*: **electric ~**) rasoio

elettrico.

shaving ['ʃeɪvɪŋ] n (action) rasatura; ~s npl (of wood etc) trucioli mpl.

shaving brush n pennello da barba.

shaving cream n crema da barba.

shaving soap n sapone m da barba.

shawl [ʃɔːl] n scialle m.

she [ʃiː] pron ella, lei; **there** ~ **is** eccola; ~-**bear** orsa; ~-**elephant** elefantessa; NB: for ships, countries follow the gender of your translation.

sheaf, pl **sheaves** [ʃiːf, ʃiːvz] n covone m.

shear [ʃɪə*] vt (pt ~**ed**, pp ~**ed** or **shorn** [ʃɔːn]) (sheep) tosare.
▶**shear off** vi (break off) spezzarsi.

shears ['ʃɪəz] npl (for hedge) cesoie fpl.

sheath [ʃiːθ] n fodero, guaina; (contraceptive) preservativo.

sheathe [ʃiːð] vt rivestire, (sword) rinfoderare.

sheath knife n coltello (con fodero).

sheaves [ʃiːvz] npl of **sheaf**.

shed [ʃɛd] n capannone m ♦ vt (pt, pp **shed**) (leaves, fur etc) perdere; (tears) versare; **to** ~ **light on** (problem, mystery) far luce su.

she'd [ʃiːd] = she had; she would.

sheen [ʃiːn] n lucentezza.

sheep [ʃiːp] n (pl inv) pecora.

sheepdog ['ʃiːpdɒg] n cane m da pastore.

sheep farmer n allevatore m di pecore.

sheepish ['ʃiːpɪʃ] adj vergognoso(a), timido(a).

sheepskin ['ʃiːpskɪn] n pelle f di pecora.

sheepskin jacket n (giacca di) montone m.

sheer [ʃɪə*] adj (utter) vero(a) (e proprio(a)); (steep) a picco, perpendicolare; (transparent) trasparente ♦ adv a picco; **by** ~ **chance** per puro caso.

sheet [ʃiːt] n (on bed) lenzuolo; (of paper) foglio; (of glass) lastra; (of metal) foglio, lamina.

sheet feed n (on printer) alimentazione f di fogli.

sheet lightning n lampo diffuso.

sheet metal n lamiera.

sheet music n fogli mpl di musica.

sheik(h) [ʃeɪk] n sceicco.

shelf, pl **shelves** [ʃɛlf, ʃɛlvz] n scaffale m, mensola.

shelf life n (COMM) durata di conservazione.

shell [ʃɛl] n (on beach) conchiglia; (of egg, nut etc) guscio; (explosive) granata; (of building) scheletro, struttura ♦ vt (peas) sgranare; (MIL) bombardare, cannoneggiare.
▶**shell out** vi (col): **to** ~ **out (for)** sganciare

soldi (per).

she'll [ʃiːl] = she will; she shall.

shellfish ['ʃɛlfɪʃ] n (pl inv) (crab etc) crostaceo; (scallop etc) mollusco; (pl: as food) crostacei; molluschi.

shellsuit ['ʃɛlsuːt] n tuta di acetato.

shelter ['ʃɛltə*] n riparo, rifugio ♦ vt riparare, proteggere; (give lodging to) dare rifugio or asilo a ♦ vi ripararsi, mettersi al riparo; **to take** ~ **(from)** mettersi al riparo (da).

sheltered ['ʃɛltəd] adj (life) ritirato(a); (spot) riparato(a), protetto(a).

shelve [ʃɛlv] vt (fig) accantonare, rimandare.

shelves [ʃɛlvz] npl of **shelf**.

shelving ['ʃɛlvɪŋ] n scaffalature fpl.

shepherd ['ʃɛpəd] n pastore m ♦ vt (guide) guidare.

shepherdess ['ʃɛpədɪs] n pastora.

shepherd's pie n timballo di carne macinata e purè di patate.

sherbet ['ʃəːbət] n (BRIT: powder) polvere effervescente al gusto di frutta; (US: water ice) sorbetto.

sheriff ['ʃɛrɪf] n sceriffo.

sherry ['ʃɛrɪ] n sherry m inv.

she's [ʃiːz] = she is; she has.

Shetland ['ʃɛtlənd] n (also: **the** ~**s, the** ~ **Isles**) le (isole) Shetland.

Shetland pony n pony m inv delle Shetland.

shield [ʃiːld] n scudo ♦ vt: **to** ~ **(from)** riparare (da), proteggere (da or contro).

shift [ʃɪft] n (change) cambiamento; (of workers) turno ♦ vt spostare, muovere; (remove) rimuovere ♦ vi spostarsi, muoversi; ~ **in demand** (COMM) variazione f della domanda; **the wind has** ~**ed to the south** il vento si è girato e soffia da sud.

shift key n (on typewriter) tasto delle maiuscole.

shiftless ['ʃɪftlɪs] adj fannullone(a).

shift work n lavoro a squadre; **to do** ~ fare i turni.

shifty ['ʃɪftɪ] adj ambiguo(a); (eyes) sfuggente.

Shiite ['ʃiːaɪt] adj, n sciita (m/f).

shilling ['ʃɪlɪŋ] n (BRIT) scellino (= 12 old pence; 20 in a pound).

shilly-shally ['ʃɪlɪʃælɪ] vi tentennare, esitare.

shimmer ['ʃɪmə*] vi brillare, luccicare.

shimmering ['ʃɪmərɪŋ] adj (gen) luccicante, scintillante; (haze) tremolante; (satin etc) cangiante.

shin [ʃɪn] n tibia ♦ vi: **to** ~ **up/down a tree**

arrampicarsi in cima a/scivolare giù da un albero.

shindig ['ʃɪndɪg] *n* (*col*) festa chiassosa.

shine [ʃaɪn] *n* splendore *m*, lucentezza ♦ *vb* (*pt, pp* **shone** [ʃɔn]) *vi* (ri)splendere, brillare ♦ *vt* far brillare, far risplendere; (*torch*): **to ~ sth on** puntare qc verso.

shingle ['ʃɪŋgl] *n* (*on beach*) ciottoli *mpl*; (*on roof*) assicella di copertura.

shingles ['ʃɪŋglz] *n* (*MED*) herpes zoster *m*.

shining ['ʃaɪnɪŋ] *adj* (*surface, hair*) lucente; (*light*) brillante.

shiny ['ʃaɪnɪ] *adj* lucente, lucido(a).

ship [ʃɪp] *n* nave *f* ♦ *vt* trasportare (via mare); (*send*) spedire (via mare); (*load*) imbarcare, caricare; **on board ~** a bordo.

shipbuilder ['ʃɪpbɪldə*] *n* costruttore *m* navale.

shipbuilding ['ʃɪpbɪldɪŋ] *n* costruzione *f* navale.

ship chandler [-'tʃɑːndlə*] *n* fornitore *m* marittimo.

shipment ['ʃɪpmənt] *n* carico.

shipowner ['ʃɪpəunə*] *n* armatore *m*.

shipper ['ʃɪpə*] *n* spedizioniere *m* (marittimo).

shipping ['ʃɪpɪŋ] *n* (*ships*) naviglio; (*traffic*) navigazione *f*.

shipping agent *n* agente *m* marittimo.

shipping company *n* compagnia di navigazione.

shipping lane *n* rotta (di navigazione).

shipping line *n* = **shipping company**.

shipshape ['ʃɪpʃeɪp] *adj* in perfetto ordine.

shipwreck ['ʃɪprɛk] *n* relitto; (*event*) naufragio ♦ *vt*: **to be ~ed** naufragare, fare naufragio.

shipyard ['ʃɪpjɑːd] *n* cantiere *m* navale.

shire ['ʃaɪə*] *n* (*BRIT*) contea.

shirk [ʃəːk] *vt* sottrarsi a, evitare.

shirt [ʃəːt] *n* (*man's*) camicia; **in ~ sleeves** in maniche di camicia.

shirty ['ʃəːtɪ] *adj* (*BRIT col*) incavolato(a).

shit [ʃɪt] *excl* (*col!*) merda(*!*).

shiver ['ʃɪvə*] *n* brivido ♦ *vi* rabbrividire, tremare.

shoal [ʃəul] *n* (*of fish*) banco.

shock [ʃɔk] *n* (*impact*) urto, colpo; (*ELEC*) scossa; (*emotional*) colpo, shock *m inv*; (*MED*) shock ♦ *vt* colpire, scioccare; scandalizzare; **to give sb a ~** far venire un colpo a qn; **to be suffering from ~** essere in stato di shock; **it came as a ~ to hear that ...** è stata una grossa sorpresa sentire che ....

shock absorber *n* ammortizzatore *m*.

shocker ['ʃɔkə*] *n*: **it was a real ~** (*col*) è stata una vera bomba.

shocking ['ʃɔkɪŋ] *adj* scioccante, traumatizzante; (*scandalous*) scandaloso(a); (*very bad: weather, handwriting*) orribile; (: *results*) disastroso(a).

shockproof ['ʃɔkpruːf] *adj* antiurto *inv*.

shock therapy, shock treatment *n* (*MED*) shockterapia.

shock wave *n* onda d'urto; (*fig: usually pl*) impatto *msg*.

shod [ʃɔd] *pt, pp of* **shoe**.

shoddy ['ʃɔdɪ] *adj* scadente.

shoe [ʃuː] *n* scarpa; (*also*: **horse~**) ferro di cavallo; (*brake ~*) ganascia (del freno) ♦ *vt* (*pt, pp* **shod** [ʃɔd]) (*horse*) ferrare.

shoebrush ['ʃuːbrʌʃ] *n* spazzola per le scarpe.

shoehorn ['ʃuːhɔːn] *n* calzante *m*.

shoelace ['ʃuːleɪs] *n* stringa.

shoemaker ['ʃuːmeɪkə*] *n* calzolaio.

shoe polish *n* lucido per scarpe.

shoeshop ['ʃuːʃɔp] *n* calzoleria.

shoestring ['ʃuːstrɪŋ] *n* stringa (delle scarpe); **on a ~** (*fig: do sth*) con quattro soldi.

shoetree ['ʃuːtriː] *n* forma per scarpe.

shone [ʃɔn] *pt, pp of* **shine**.

shoo [ʃuː] *excl* sciò!, via! ♦ *vt* (*also*: **~ away**, **~ off**) cacciare (via).

shook [ʃuk] *pt of* **shake**.

shoot [ʃuːt] *n* (*on branch, seedling*) germoglio; (*shooting party*) partita di caccia; (*competition*) gara di tiro ♦ *vb* (*pt, pp* **shot** [ʃɔt]) *vt* (*game: BRIT*) cacciare, andare a caccia di; (*person*) sparare a; (*execute*) fucilare; (*film*) girare ♦ *vi* (*with gun*): **to ~ (at)** sparare (a), fare fuoco (su); (*with bow*): **to ~ (at)** tirare (su); (*FOOTBALL*) sparare, tirare (forte); **to ~ past sb** passare vicino a qn come un fulmine; **to ~ in/out** entrare/uscire come una freccia.

▶**shoot down** *vt* (*plane*) abbattere.

▶**shoot up** *vi* (*fig*) salire alle stelle.

shooting ['ʃuːtɪŋ] *n* (*shots*) sparatoria; (*murder*) uccisione *f* (a colpi d'arma da fuoco); (*HUNTING*) caccia; (*CINE*) riprese *fpl*.

shooting range *n* poligono (di tiro), tirassegno.

shooting star *n* stella cadente.

shop [ʃɔp] *n* negozio; (*workshop*) officina ♦ *vi* (*also*: **go ~ping**) fare spese; **repair ~** officina di riparazione; **to talk ~** (*fig*) parlare di lavoro.

▶**shop around** *vi* fare il giro dei negozi.

shopaholic ['ʃɔpə'hɔlɪk] *n* (*col*) maniaco/a dello shopping.

shop assistant n (BRIT) commesso/a.
shop floor n (BRIT: fig) operai mpl, maestranze fpl.
shopkeeper ['ʃɔpkiːpə*] n negoziante m/f, bottegaio/a.
shoplift ['ʃɔplɪft] vi taccheggiare.
shoplifter ['ʃɔplɪftə*] n taccheggiatore/trice.
shoplifting ['ʃɔplɪftɪŋ] n taccheggio.
shopper ['ʃɔpə*] n compratore/trice.
shopping ['ʃɔpɪŋ] n (goods) spesa, acquisti mpl.
shopping bag n borsa per la spesa.
shopping centre n centro commerciale.
shop-soiled ['ʃɔpsɔild] adj sciupato(a) a forza di stare in vetrina.
shop steward n (BRIT INDUSTRY) rappresentante m sindacale.
shop window n vetrina.
shore [ʃɔː*] n (of sea) riva, spiaggia; (of lake) riva ♦ vt: **to ~ (up)** puntellare; **on ~** a terra.
shore leave n (NAUT) franchigia.
shorn [ʃɔːn] pp of **shear**.
short [ʃɔːt] adj (not long) corto(a); (soon finished) breve; (person) basso(a); (curt) brusco(a), secco(a); (Insufficient) insufficiente ♦ n (also: **~ film**) cortometraggio; **it is ~ for** è l'abbreviazione or il diminutivo di; **a ~ time ago** poco tempo fa; **in the ~ term** nell'immediato futuro; **to be ~ of sth** essere a corto di or mancare di qc; **to run ~ of sth** rimanere senza qc; **to be in ~ supply** scarseggiare; **I'm 3 ~** me ne mancano 3; **in ~** in breve; **~ of doing a** meno che non si faccia; **everything ~ of** tutto fuorché; **to cut ~** (speech, visit) accorciare, abbreviare; (person) interrompere; **to fall ~ of** venire meno a; non soddisfare; **to stop ~** fermarsi di colpo; **to stop ~ of** non arrivare fino a; see also **shorts**.
shortage ['ʃɔːtɪdʒ] n scarsezza, carenza.
shortbread ['ʃɔːtbred] n biscotto di pasta frolla.
short-change [ʃɔːt'tʃeɪndʒ] vt: **to ~ sb** imbrogliare qn sul resto.
short-circuit [ʃɔːt'səːkɪt] n cortocircuito ♦ vt cortocircuitare ♦ vi fare cortocircuito.
shortcoming ['ʃɔːtkʌmɪŋ] n difetto.
short(crust) pastry ['ʃɔːt(krʌst)-] n (BRIT) pasta frolla.
shortcut ['ʃɔːtkʌt] n scorciatoia.
shorten ['ʃɔːtn] vt accorciare, ridurre.
shortening ['ʃɔːtnɪŋ] n grasso per pasticceria.
shortfall ['ʃɔːtfɔːl] n deficienza.

shorthand ['ʃɔːthænd] n (BRIT) stenografia; **to take sth down in ~** stenografare qc.
shorthand notebook n (BRIT) bloc-notes m inv per stenografia.
shorthand typist n (BRIT) stenodattilografo/a.
short list n (BRIT: for job) rosa dei candidati.
short-lived ['ʃɔːt'lɪvd] adj effimero(a), di breve durata.
shortly ['ʃɔːtlɪ] adv fra poco.
shortness ['ʃɔːtnɪs] n brevità; insufficienza.
shorts [ʃɔːts] npl (also: **a pair of ~**) i calzoncini.
short-sighted [ʃɔːt'saɪtɪd] adj (BRIT) miope; (fig) poco avveduto(a).
short-staffed [ʃɔːt'stɑːft] adj a corto di personale.
short story n racconto, novella.
short-tempered [ʃɔːt'tempəd] adj irascibile.
short-term ['ʃɔːttəːm] adj (effect) di or a breve durata.
short time n (INDUSTRY): **to work ~, be on ~** essere or lavorare a orario ridotto.
short wave n (RADIO) onde fpl corte.
shot [ʃɔt] pt, pp of **shoot** ♦ n sparo, colpo; (shotgun pellets) pallottole fpl; (person) tiratore m; (try) prova; (injection) iniezione f; (PHOT) foto f inv; **like a ~** come un razzo; (very readily) immediatamente; **to fire a ~ at sb/sth** sparare un colpo a qn/qc; **to have a ~ at sth/doing sth** provarci con qc/a fare qc; **a big ~** (col) un pezzo grosso, un papavero; **to get ~ of sb/sth** (col) sbarazzarsi di qn/qc.
shotgun ['ʃɔtgʌn] n fucile m da caccia.
should [ʃud] aux vb: **I ~ go now** dovrei andare ora; **he ~ be there now** dovrebbe essere arrivato ora; **I ~ go if I were you** se fossi in lei andrei; **I ~ like to** mi piacerebbe; **~ he phone...** se telefonasse....
shoulder ['ʃəuldə*] n spalla; (BRIT: of road): **hard ~** corsia d'emergenza ♦ vt (fig) addossarsi, prendere sulle proprie spalle; **to look over one's ~** guardarsi alle spalle; **to rub ~s with sb** (fig) essere a contatto con qn; **to give sb the cold ~** (fig) trattare qn con freddezza.
shoulder bag n borsa a tracolla.
shoulder blade n scapola.
shoulder strap n bretella, spallina.
shouldn't ['ʃudnt] = **should not**.
shout [ʃaut] n urlo, grido ♦ vt gridare ♦ vi urlare, gridare; **to give sb a ~** chiamare qn gridando.
▶**shout down** vt zittire gridando.

shouting ['ʃautɪŋ] *n* urli *mpl*.
shouting match *n* (*col*) vivace scambio di opinioni.
shove [ʃʌv] *vt* spingere; (*col: put*): **to ~ sth in** ficcare qc in ♦ *n* spintone *m*; **he ~d me out of the way** mi ha spinto da parte.
▶**shove off** *vi* (*NAUT*) scostarsi.
shovel ['ʃʌvl] *n* pala ♦ *vt* spalare.
show [ʃəu] *n* (*of emotion*) dimostrazione *f*, manifestazione *f*; (*semblance*) apparenza; (*exhibition*) mostra, esposizione *f*; (*THEAT, CINE*) spettacolo; (*COMM, TECH*) salone *m*, fiera ♦ *vb* (*pt* ~**ed**, *pp* **shown** [ʃəun]) *vt* far vedere, mostrare; (*courage etc*) dimostrare, dar prova di; (*exhibit*) esporre ♦ *vi* vedersi, essere visibile; **to ~ sb to his seat/to the door** accompagnare qn al suo posto/alla porta; **to ~ a profit/ loss** (*COMM*) registrare un utile/una perdita; **it just goes to ~ that ...** il che sta a dimostrare che ...; **to ask for a ~ of hands** chiedere che si voti per alzata di mano; **to be on ~** essere esposto; **it's just for ~** è solo per far scena; **who's running the ~ here?** (*col*) chi è il padrone qui?
▶**show in** *vt* far entrare.
▶**show off** *vi* (*pej*) esibirsi, mettersi in mostra ♦ *vt* (*display*) mettere in risalto; (*pej*) mettere in mostra.
▶**show out** *vt* accompagnare alla porta.
▶**show up** *vi* (*stand out*) essere ben visibile; (*col: turn up*) farsi vedere ♦ *vt* mettere in risalto; (*unmask*) smascherare.
showbiz ['ʃəubɪz] *n* (*col*) = **show business**.
show business *n* industria dello spettacolo.
showcase ['ʃəukeɪs] *n* vetrina, bacheca.
showdown ['ʃəudaun] *n* prova di forza.
shower ['ʃauə*] *n* (*also: ~ bath*) doccia; (*rain*) acquazzone *m*; (*of stones etc*) pioggia; (*US: party*) *festa* (*di fidanzamento etc*) *in cui si fanno regali alla persona festeggiata* ♦ *vi* fare la doccia ♦ *vt*: **to ~ sb with** (*gifts, abuse etc*) coprire qn di; (*missiles*) lanciare contro qn una pioggia di; **to have** *or* **take a ~** fare la doccia.
shower cap *n* cuffia da doccia.
showerproof ['ʃauəpru:f] *adj* impermeabile.
showery ['ʃauərɪ] *adj* (*weather*) con piogge intermittenti.
showground ['ʃəugraund] *n* terreno d'esposizione.
showing ['ʃəuɪŋ] *n* (*of film*) proiezione *f*.
show jumping *n* concorso ippico (di salto ad ostacoli).

showman ['ʃəumən] *n* (*at fair, circus*) impresario; (*fig*) attore *m*.
showmanship ['ʃəumənʃɪp] *n* abilità d'impresario.
shown [ʃəun] *pp of* **show**.
show-off ['ʃəuɔf] *n* (*col: person*) esibizionista *m/f*.
showpiece ['ʃəupi:s] *n* (*of exhibition*) pezzo forte; **that hospital is a ~** è un ospedale modello.
showroom ['ʃəurum] *n* sala d'esposizione.
show trial *n* processo a scopo dimostrativo (*spesso ideologico*).
showy ['ʃəuɪ] *adj* vistoso(a), appariscente.
shrank [ʃræŋk] *pt of* **shrink**.
shrapnel ['ʃræpnl] *n* shrapnel *m*.
shred [ʃred] *n* (*gen pl*) brandello; (*fig: of truth, evidence*) briciolo ♦ *vt* fare a brandelli; (*CULIN*) sminuzzare, tagliuzzare; (*documents*) distruggere, sminuzzare.
shredder ['ʃredə*] *n* (*for documents, papers*) distruttore *m* di documenti, sminuzzatrice *f*.
shrew [ʃru:] *n* (*ZOOL*) toporagno; (*fig: pej: woman*) strega.
shrewd [ʃru:d] *adj* astuto(a), scaltro(a).
shrewdness ['ʃru:dnɪs] *n* astuzia.
shriek [ʃri:k] *n* strillo ♦ *vt, vi* strillare.
shrift [ʃrɪft] *n*: **to give sb short ~** sbrigare qn.
shrill [ʃrɪl] *adj* acuto(a), stridulo(a), stridente.
shrimp [ʃrɪmp] *n* gamberetto.
shrine [ʃraɪn] *n* reliquario; (*place*) santuario.
shrink [ʃrɪŋk] *vb* (*pt* **shrank**, *pp* **shrunk** [ʃræŋk, ʃrʌŋk]) *vi* restringersi; (*fig*) ridursi ♦ *vt* (*wool*) far restringere ♦ *n* (*col: pej*) psicanalista *m/f*; **to ~ from doing sth** rifuggire dal fare qc.
shrinkage ['ʃrɪŋkɪdʒ] *n* restringimento.
shrink-wrap ['ʃrɪŋkræp] *vt* confezionare con plastica sottile.
shrivel ['ʃrɪvl] (*also: ~ up*) *vt* raggrinzare, avvizzire ♦ *vi* raggrinzirsi, avvizzire.
shroud [ʃraud] *n* lenzuolo funebre ♦ *vt*: ~**ed in mystery** avvolto(a) nel mistero.
Shrove Tuesday ['ʃrəuv-] *n* martedì *m* grasso.
shrub [ʃrʌb] *n* arbusto.
shrubbery ['ʃrʌbərɪ] *n* arbusti *mpl*.
shrug [ʃrʌg] *n* scrollata di spalle ♦ *vt, vi*: **to ~ (one's shoulders)** alzare le spalle, fare spallucce.
▶**shrug off** *vt* passare sopra a; (*cold, illness*) sbarazzarsi di.
shrunk [ʃrʌŋk] *pp of* **shrink**.

shrunken ['ʃrʌŋkən] adj rattrappito(a).
shudder ['ʃʌdə*] n brivido ♦ vi rabbrividire.
shuffle ['ʃʌfl] vt (cards) mescolare; **to ~ (one's feet)** strascicare i piedi.
shun [ʃʌn] vt sfuggire, evitare.
shunt [ʃʌnt] vt (RAIL: direct) smistare; (: divert) deviare ♦ vi: **to ~ (to and fro)** fare la spola.
shunting yard n fascio di smistamento.
shush [ʃuʃ] excl zitto(a)!
shut, pt, pp **shut** [ʃʌt] vt chiudere ♦ vi chiudersi, chiudere.
▶**shut down** vt, vi chiudere definitivamente.
▶**shut off** vt (stop: power) staccare; (: water) chiudere; (: engine) spegnere; (isolate) isolare.
▶**shut out** vt (person, noise, cold) non far entrare, (block: view) impedire, bloccare; (: memory) scacciare.
▶**shut up** vi (col: keep quiet) stare zitto(a) ♦ vt (close) chiudere; (silence) far tacere.
shutdown ['ʃʌtdaun] n chiusura.
shutter ['ʃʌtə*] n imposta; (PHOT) otturatore m.
shuttle ['ʃʌtl] n spola, navetta; (also: ~ service) servizio m navetta inv ♦ vi (subj: vehicle, person) fare la spola ♦ vt (to and fro: passengers) portare (avanti e indietro).
shuttlecock ['ʃʌtlkɔk] n volano.
shuttle diplomacy n frequenti mediazioni fpl diplomatiche.
shy [ʃaɪ] adj timido(a) ♦ vi: **to ~ away from doing sth** (fig) rifuggire dal fare qc; **to fight ~ of** tenersi alla larga da; **to be ~ of doing sth** essere restio a fare qc.
shyness ['ʃaɪnɪs] n timidezza.
Siam [saɪ'æm] n Siam m.
Siamese [saɪə'miːz] adj: **~ cat** gatto siamese; **~ twins** fratelli mpl (or sorelle fpl) siamesi.
Siberia [saɪ'bɪərɪə] n Siberia.
sibling ['sɪblɪŋ] n (formal) fratello/sorella.
Sicilian [sɪ'sɪlɪən] adj, n siciliano(a).
Sicily ['sɪsɪlɪ] n Sicilia.
sick [sɪk] adj (ill) malato(a); (vomiting): **to be ~** vomitare; (humour) macabro(a); **to feel ~** avere la nausea; **to be ~ of** (fig) averne abbastanza di; **a ~ person** un malato; **to be (off) ~** essere assente perché malato; **to fall** or **take ~** ammalarsi.
sickbag ['sɪkbæg] n sacchetto (da usarsi in caso di malessere).
sick bay n infermeria.
sick building syndrome n malattia causata da mancanza di ventilazione e luce naturale.
sicken ['sɪkn] vt nauseare ♦ vi: **to be ~ing for sth** (cold, flu etc) covare qc.
sickening ['sɪknɪŋ] adj (fig) disgustoso(a), rivoltante.
sickle ['sɪkl] n falcetto.
sick leave n congedo per malattia.
sickle-cell anaemia ['sɪklsɛl-] n anemia drepanocitica.
sickly ['sɪklɪ] adj malaticcio(a); (causing nausea) nauseante.
sickness ['sɪknɪs] n malattia; (vomiting) vomito.
sickness benefit n indennità di malattia.
sick pay n sussidio per malattia.
sickroom ['sɪkruːm] n stanza di malato.
side [saɪd] n (gen) lato; (of person, animal) fianco; (of lake) riva; (face, surface: gen) faccia; (: of paper) facciata; (fig: aspect) aspetto, lato; (team: SPORT) squadra; (: POL etc) parte f ♦ cpd (door, entrance) laterale ♦ vi: **to ~ with sb** parteggiare per qn, prendere le parti di qn; **by the ~ of** a fianco di; (road) sul ciglio di; **~ by ~** fianco a fianco; **to take ~s (with)** schierarsi (con); **the right/wrong ~** il dritto/rovescio; **from ~ to ~** da una parte all'altra; **~ of beef** quarto di bue.
sideboard ['saɪdbɔːd] n credenza.
sideboards ['saɪdbɔːdz] (BRIT), **sideburns** ['saɪdbəːnz] npl (whiskers) basette fpl.
sidecar ['saɪdkɑː*] n sidecar m inv.
side dish n contorno.
side drum n (MUS) piccolo tamburo.
side effect n (MED) effetto collaterale.
sidekick ['saɪdkɪk] n (col) compagno/a.
sidelight ['saɪdlaɪt] n (AUT) luce f di posizione.
sideline ['saɪdlaɪn] n (SPORT) linea laterale; (fig) attività secondaria.
sidelong ['saɪdlɔŋ] adj obliquo(a); **to give a ~ glance at sth** guardare qc con la coda dell'occhio.
side plate n piattino.
side road n strada secondaria.
sidesaddle ['saɪdsædl] adv all'amazzone.
side show n attrazione f.
sidestep ['saɪdstɛp] vt (question) eludere; (problem) scavalcare ♦ vi (BOXING etc) spostarsi di lato.
side street n traversa.
sidetrack ['saɪdtræk] vt (fig) distrarre.
sidewalk ['saɪdwɔːk] n (US) marciapiede m.
sideways ['saɪdweɪz] adv (move) di lato, di fianco; (look) con la coda dell'occhio.
siding ['saɪdɪŋ] n (RAIL) binario di raccordo.
sidle ['saɪdl] vi: **to ~ up (to)** avvicinarsi furtivamente (a).

SIDS *n* (= *sudden infant death syndrome*) *see* **cot death**.

siege [si:dʒ] *n* assedio; **to lay ~ to** porre l'assedio a.

siege economy *n* economia da stato d'assedio.

Sierra Leone [sɪ'erəlɪ'əun] *n* Sierra Leone *f*.

sieve [sɪv] *n* setaccio ♦ *vt* setacciare.

sift [sɪft] *vt* passare al crivello; (*fig*) vagliare ♦ *vi*: **to ~ through** esaminare minuziosamente.

sigh [saɪ] *n* sospiro ♦ *vi* sospirare.

sight [saɪt] *n* (*faculty*) vista; (*spectacle*) spettacolo; (*on gun*) mira ♦ *vt* avvistare; **in ~** in vista; **out of ~** non visibile; **at first ~** a prima vista; **to catch ~ of sth/sb** scorgere qc/qn; **to lose ~ of sb/sth** perdere di vista qn/qc; **to set one's ~s on/on doing sth** mirare a qc/a fare qc; **at ~** a vista; **I know her by ~** la conosco di vista.

sighted ['saɪtɪd] *adj* che ha il dono della vista; **partially ~** parzialmente cieco.

sightseeing ['saɪtsiːɪŋ] *n* turismo; **to go ~** visitare una località.

sightseer ['saɪtsiːə*] *n* turista *m/f*.

sign [saɪn] *n* segno; (*with hand etc*) segno, gesto; (*notice*) insegna, cartello; (*road ~*) segnale *m* ♦ *vt* firmare; **as a ~ of** in segno di; **it's a good/bad ~ of** è buon/brutto segno; **to show ~s/no ~ of doing sth** accennare/non accennare a fare qc; **plus/minus ~** segno del più/meno; **to ~ one's name** firmare, apporre la propria firma.

▶**sign away** *vt* (*rights etc*) cedere (con una firma).

▶**sign in** *vi* firmare il registro (all'arrivo).

▶**sign off** *vi* (*RADIO, TV*) chiudere le trasmissioni.

▶**sign on** *vi* (*MIL etc: enlist*) arruolarsi; (*as unemployed*) iscriversi sulla lista (dell'ufficio di collocamento); (*begin work*) prendere servizio; (*enrol*): **to ~ on for a course** iscriversi a un corso.

▶**sign out** *vi* firmare il registro (alla partenza).

▶**sign over** *vt*: **to ~ sth over to sb** cedere qc con scrittura legale a qn.

▶**sign up** (*MIL*) *vt* arruolare ♦ *vi* arruolarsi.

signal ['sɪɡnl] *n* segnale *m* ♦ *vt* (*person*) fare segno a; (*message*) comunicare per mezzo di segnali ♦ *vi*: **to ~ to sb (to do sth)** far segno a qn (di fare qc); **to ~ a left/right turn** (*AUT*) segnalare un cambiamento di direzione a sinistra/destra.

signal box *n* (*RAIL*) cabina di manovra.

signalman ['sɪɡnlmən] *n* (*RAIL*) deviatore *m*.

signatory ['sɪɡnətərɪ] *n* firmatario/a.

signature ['sɪɡnətʃə*] *n* firma.

signature tune *n* sigla musicale.

signet ring ['sɪɡnət-] *n* anello con sigillo.

significance [sɪɡ'nɪfɪkəns] *n* (*of remark*) significato; (*of event*) importanza; **that is of no ~** ciò non ha importanza.

significant [sɪɡ'nɪfɪkənt] *adj* (*improvement, amount*) notevole; (*discovery, event*) importante; (*evidence, smile*) significativo(a); **it is ~ that ...** è significativo che ....

significantly [sɪɡ'nɪfɪkəntlɪ] *adv* (*smile*) in modo eloquente; (*improve, increase*) considerevolmente, decisamente.

signify ['sɪɡnɪfaɪ] *vt* significare.

sign language *n* linguaggio dei muti.

signpost ['saɪnpəust] *n* cartello indicatore.

silage ['saɪlɪdʒ] *n* insilato.

silence ['saɪlns] *n* silenzio ♦ *vt* far tacere, ridurre al silenzio.

silencer ['saɪlənsə*] *n* (*on gun, BRIT AUT*) silenziatore *m*.

silent ['saɪlnt] *adj* silenzioso(a); (*film*) muto(a); **to keep** *or* **remain ~** tacere, stare zitto(a).

silently ['saɪlntlɪ] *adv* silenziosamente, in silenzio.

silent partner *n* (*COMM*) socio accomandante.

silhouette [sɪlu:'ɛt] *n* silhouette *f inv* ♦ *vt*: **to be ~d against** stagliarsi contro.

silicon ['sɪlɪkən] *n* silicio.

silicon chip *n* chip *m inv* al silicone.

silicone ['sɪlɪkəun] *n* silicone *m*.

silk [sɪlk] *n* seta ♦ *cpd* di seta.

silky ['sɪlkɪ] *adj* di seta, come la seta.

sill [sɪl] *n* (*window~*) davanzale *m*; (*AUT*) predellino.

silly ['sɪlɪ] *adj* stupido(a), sciocco(a); **to do something ~** fare una sciocchezza.

silo ['saɪləu] *n* silo.

silt [sɪlt] *n* limo.

silver ['sɪlvə*] *n* argento; (*money*) monete *da 5, 10, 20 o 50 pence*; (*also:* **~ware**) argenteria ♦ *cpd* d'argento.

silver foil, (*BRIT*) **silver paper** *n* carta argentata, (carta) stagnola.

silver-plated [sɪlvə'pleɪtɪd] *adj* argentato(a).

silversmith ['sɪlvəsmɪθ] *n* argentiere *m*.

silverware ['sɪlvəwɛə*] *n* argenteria, argento.

silvery ['sɪlvərɪ] *adj* (*colour*) argenteo(a); (*sound*) argentino(a).

similar ['sɪmɪlə*] *adj*: **~ (to)** simile (a).

similarity [sɪmɪ'lærɪtɪ] *n* somiglianza,

rassomiglianza.

similarly ['sɪmɪləlɪ] adv (in a similar way) allo stesso modo; (as is similar) così pure.

simile ['sɪmɪlɪ] n similitudine f.

simmer ['sɪmə*] vi cuocere a fuoco lento.

▶**simmer down** vi (fig col) calmarsi.

simper ['sɪmpə*] vi fare lo(la) smorfioso(a).

simpering ['sɪmpərɪŋ] adj lezioso(a), smorfioso(a).

simple ['sɪmpl] adj semplice; **the ~ truth** la pura verità.

simple interest n (MATH, COMM) interesse m semplice.

simple-minded [sɪmpl'maɪndɪd] adj sempliciotto(a).

simpleton ['sɪmpltən] n semplicione/a, sempliciotto/a.

simplicity [sɪm'plɪsɪtɪ] n semplicità.

simplification [sɪmplɪfɪ'keɪʃən] n semplificazione f.

simplify ['sɪmplɪfaɪ] vt semplificare.

simply ['sɪmplɪ] adv semplicemente.

simulate ['sɪmjuleɪt] vt fingere, simulare.

simulation [sɪmju'leɪʃən] n simulazione f.

simultaneous [sɪməl'teɪnɪəs] adj simultaneo(a).

simultaneously [sɪməl'teɪnɪəslɪ] adv simultaneamente, contemporaneamente.

sin [sɪn] n peccato ♦ vi peccare.

Sinai ['saɪnaɪ] n Sinai m.

since [sɪns] adv da allora ♦ prep da ♦ conj (time) da quando; (because) poiché, dato che; **~ then** da allora; **~ Monday** da lunedì; **(ever) ~ I arrived** (fin) da quando sono arrivato.

sincere [sɪn'sɪə*] adj sincero(a).

sincerely [sɪn'sɪəlɪ] adv sinceramente, **Yours ~** (at end of letter) distinti saluti.

sincerity [sɪn'sɛrɪtɪ] n sincerità.

sine [saɪn] n (MATH) seno.

sinew ['sɪnjuː] n tendine m; **~s** npl (muscles) muscoli mpl.

sinful ['sɪnful] adj peccaminoso(a).

sing, pt **sang,** pp **sung** [sɪŋ, sæŋ, sʌŋ] vt, vi cantare.

Singapore [sɪŋgə'pɔː*] n Singapore f.

singe [sɪndʒ] vt bruciacchiare.

singer ['sɪŋə*] n cantante m/f.

Singhalese [sɪŋə'liːz] adj = Sinhalese.

singing ['sɪŋɪŋ] n (of person, bird) canto; (of kettle, bullet, in ears) fischio.

single ['sɪŋgl] adj solo(a), unico(a); (unmarried: man) celibe; (: woman) nubile; (not double) semplice ♦ n (BRIT: also: ~ ticket) biglietto di (sola) andata; (record) 45 giri m inv; **not a ~ one was left** non ne è rimasto nemmeno uno; **every ~ day** tutti i santi giorni; see also **singles**.

▶**single out** vt scegliere; (distinguish) distinguere.

single bed n letto a una piazza.

single-breasted ['sɪŋglbrɛstɪd] adj a un petto.

Single European Market n: **the ~** il Mercato Unico.

single file n: **in ~** in fila indiana.

single-handed [sɪŋgl'hændɪd] adv senza aiuto, da solo(a).

single-minded [sɪŋgl'maɪndɪd] adj tenace, risoluto(a).

single parent n ragazzo padre/ragazza madre; genitore m separato; **~ family** famiglia monoparentale.

single room n camera singola.

singles ['sɪŋglz] npl (TENNIS) singolo; (US: single people) single m/fpl.

singles bar n (esp US) bar m inv per single.

single-sex school ['sɪŋgl'sɛks-] n (for boys) scuola maschile; (for girls) scuola femminile.

singly ['sɪŋglɪ] adv separatamente.

singsong ['sɪŋsɒŋ] adj (tone) cantilenante ♦ n (songs): **to have a ~** farsi una cantata.

singular ['sɪŋgjulə*] adj (LING) singolare; (unusual) strano(a), singolare ♦ n (LING) singolare m; **in the feminine ~** al femminile singolare.

singularly ['sɪŋgjuləlɪ] adv stranamente.

Sinhalese [sɪnhə'liːz] adj singalese.

sinister ['sɪnɪstə*] adj sinistro(a).

sink [sɪŋk] n lavandino, acquaio ♦ vb (pt **sank,** pp **sunk** [sæŋk, sʌŋk]) vt (ship) (fare) affondare, colare a picco; (foundations) scavare; (piles etc): **to ~ sth into** conficcare qc in ♦ vi affondare, andare a fondo; (ground etc) cedere, avvallarsi; **he sank into a chair/the mud** sprofondò in una poltrona/nel fango.

▶**sink in** vi penetrare; **it took a long time to ~ in** ci ho (or ha etc) messo molto a capirlo.

sinking ['sɪŋkɪŋ] adj: **that ~ feeling** una stretta allo stomaco.

sinking fund n (COMM) fondo d'ammortamento.

sink unit n blocco lavello.

sinner ['sɪnə*] n peccatore/trice.

Sinn Féin [ʃɪn'feɪn] n movimento separatista irlandese.

sinuous ['sɪnjuəs] adj sinuoso(a).

sinus ['saɪnəs] n (ANAT) seno.

sip [sɪp] n sorso ♦ vt sorseggiare.

siphon ['saɪfən] n sifone m ♦ vt (funds) trasferire.

▶**siphon off** vt travasare (con un sifone).

sir [sə*] n signore m; **S~ John Smith** Sir

John Smith; **yes** ~ sì, signore; **Dear S**~ (*in letter*) Egregio signor (*followed by name*); **Dear S**~**s** Spettabile ditta.
siren ['saɪərn] *n* sirena.
sirloin ['səːlɔɪn] *n* controfiletto.
sirloin steak *n* bistecca di controfiletto.
sirocco [sɪ'rɔkəu] *n* scirocco.
sisal ['saɪsəl] *n* sisal *f inv*.
sissy ['sɪsɪ] *n* (*col*) femminuccia.
sister ['sɪstə*] *n* sorella; (*nun*) suora; (*nurse*) infermiera *f* caposala *inv* ♦ *cpd*: ~ **organization** organizzazione *f* affine; ~ **ship** nave *f* gemella.
sister-in-law ['sɪstərɪnlɔː] *n* cognata.
sit, *pt, pp* **sat** [sɪt, sæt] *vi* sedere, sedersi; (*dress etc*) cadere; (*assembly*) essere in seduta ♦ *vt* (*exam*) sostenere, dare; **to** ~ **on a committee** far parte di una commissione.
▶**sit about, sit around** *vi* star seduto(a) (senza far nulla).
▶**sit back** *vi* (*in seat*) appoggiarsi allo schienale.
▶**sit down** *vi* sedersi; **to be** ~**ting down** essere seduto(a).
▶**sit in** *vi*: **to** ~ **in on a discussion** assistere ad una discussione.
▶**sit up** *vi* tirarsi su a sedere; (*not go to bed*) stare alzato(a) fino a tardi.
sitcom ['sɪtkɔm] *n abbr* (*TV*: = *situation comedy*) sceneggiato a episodi (*comico*).
sit-down ['sɪtdaun] *adj*: ~ **strike** sciopero bianco (con occupazione della fabbrica); **a** ~ **meal** un pranzo.
site [saɪt] *n* posto; (*also*: **building** ~) cantiere *m* ♦ *vt* situare.
sit-in ['sɪtɪn] *n* (*demonstration*) sit-in *m inv*.
siting ['saɪtɪŋ] *n* ubicazione *f*.
sitter ['sɪtə*] *n* (*for painter*) modello/a; (*also*: **baby** ~) babysitter *m/f inv*.
sitting ['sɪtɪŋ] *n* (*of assembly etc*) seduta; (*in canteen*) turno.
sitting member *n* (*POL*) deputato/a in carica.
sitting room *n* soggiorno.
sitting tenant *n* (*BRIT*) attuale affittuario.
situate ['sɪtjueɪt] *vt* collocare.
situated ['sɪtjueɪtɪd] *adj* situato(a).
situation [sɪtju'eɪʃən] *n* situazione *f*; "~**s vacant/wanted**" (*BRIT*) "offerte/domande di impiego".
situation comedy *n* (*THEAT*) commedia di situazione.
six [sɪks] *num* sei.
six-pack ['sɪkspæk] *n* (*esp US*) confezione *f* da sei.
sixteen [sɪks'tiːn] *num* sedici.
sixth [sɪksθ] *num* sesto(a) ♦ *n*: **the upper/**

lower ~ (*BRIT SCOL*) l'ultimo/il penultimo anno di scuola superiore.
sixty ['sɪkstɪ] *num* sessanta.
size [saɪz] *n* dimensioni *fpl*; (*of clothing*) taglia, misura; (*of shoes*) numero; (*glue*) colla; **I take** ~ **14 in a dress** ≈ porto la 44 di vestiti; **I'd like the small/large** ~ (*of soap powder etc*) vorrei la confezione piccola/grande.
▶**size up** *vt* giudicare, farsi un'idea di.
sizeable ['saɪzəbl] *adj* considerevole.
sizzle ['sɪzl] *vi* sfrigolare.
SK *abbr* (*Canada*) = Saskatchewan.
skate [skeɪt] *n* pattino; (*fish*: *pl inv*) razza ♦ *vi* pattinare.
▶**skate over, skate around** *vi* (*problem, issue*) prendere alla leggera, prendere sottogamba.
skateboard ['skeɪtbɔːd] *n* skateboard *m inv*.
skater ['skeɪtə*] *n* pattinatore/trice.
skating ['skeɪtɪŋ] *n* pattinaggio.
skating rink *n* pista di pattinaggio.
skeleton ['skɛlɪtn] *n* scheletro.
skeleton key *n* passe-partout *m inv*.
skeleton staff *n* personale *m* ridotto.
skeptic *etc* ['skɛptɪk] (*US*) = **sceptic** *etc*.
sketch [skɛtʃ] *n* (*drawing*) schizzo, abbozzo; (*THEAT etc*) scenetta comica, sketch *m inv* ♦ *vt* abbozzare, schizzare.
sketch book *n* album *m inv* per schizzi.
sketch pad *n* blocco per schizzi.
sketchy ['skɛtʃɪ] *adj* incompleto(a), lacunoso(a).
skew [skjuː] *n* (*BRIT*): **on the** ~ di traverso.
skewer ['skjuːə*] *n* spiedo.
ski [skiː] *n* sci *m inv* ♦ *vi* sciare.
ski boot *n* scarpone *m* da sci.
skid [skɪd] *n* slittamento; (*sideways slip*) sbandamento ♦ *vi* slittare; sbandare; **to go into a** ~ slittare; sbandare.
skid mark *n* segno della frenata.
skier ['skiːə*] *n* sciatore/trice.
skiing ['skiːɪŋ] *n* sci *m*.
ski instructor *n* maestro/a di sci.
ski jump *n* (*ramp*) trampolino; (*event*) salto con gli sci.
skilful, (*US*) **skillful** ['skɪlful] *adj* abile.
ski lift *n* sciovia.
skill [skɪl] *n* abilità *f inv*, capacità *f inv*; (*technique*) tecnica.
skilled [skɪld] *adj* esperto(a); (*worker*) qualificato(a), specializzato(a).
skillet ['skɪlɪt] *n* padella.
skillful *etc* ['skɪlful] (*US*) = **skilful** *etc*.
skil(l)fully ['skɪlfəlɪ] *adv* abilmente.
skim [skɪm] *vt* (*milk*) scremare; (*soup*) schiumare; (*glide over*) sfiorare ♦ *vi*: **to** ~ **through** (*fig*) scorrere, dare una scorsa a.

skimmed milk n latte m scremato.
skimp [skɪmp] vi: **to ~ on,** vt (work) fare alla carlona; (cloth etc) lesinare.
skimpy ['skɪmpɪ] adj misero(a); striminzito(a); frugale.
skin [skɪn] n pelle f; (of fruit, vegetable) buccia; (on pudding, paint) crosta ♦ vt (fruit etc) sbucciare; (animal) scuoiare, spellare; **wet** or **soaked to the ~** bagnato fino al midollo.
skin cancer n cancro alla pelle.
skin-deep [skɪn'diːp] adj superficiale.
skin diver n subacqueo.
skin diving n nuoto subacqueo.
skinflint ['skɪnflɪnt] n taccagno/a, tirchio/a.
skin graft n innesto epidermico.
skinhead ['skɪnhɛd] n skinhead m/f inv.
skinny ['skɪnɪ] adj molto magro(a).
skin test n prova di reazione cutanea.
skintight ['skɪntaɪt] adj aderente.
skip [skɪp] n saltello, balzo; (container) benna ♦ vi saltare; (with rope) saltare la corda ♦ vt (pass over) saltare; **to ~ school** (US) marinare la scuola.
ski pants npl pantaloni mpl da sci.
ski pass n ski pass m inv.
ski pole n racchetta (da sci).
skipper ['skɪpə*] n (NAUT, SPORT) capitano.
skipping rope ['skɪpɪŋ-] n (BRIT) corda per saltare.
ski resort n località f inv sciistica.
skirmish ['skɜːmɪʃ] n scaramuccia.
skirt [skɜːt] n gonna, sottana ♦ vt fiancheggiare, costeggiare.
skirting board ['skɜːtɪŋ-] n (BRIT) zoccolo.
ski run n pista (da sci).
ski suit n tuta da sci.
skit [skɪt] n parodia; scenetta satirica.
ski tow n = **ski lift**
skittle ['skɪtl] n birillo; **~s** n (game) (gioco dei) birilli mpl.
skive [skaɪv] vi (BRIT col) fare il lavativo.
skulk [skʌlk] vi muoversi furtivamente.
skull [skʌl] n cranio, teschio.
skullcap ['skʌlkæp] n (worn by Jews) zucchetto; (worn by Pope) papalina.
skunk [skʌŋk] n moffetta.
sky [skaɪ] n cielo; **to praise sb to the skies** portare alle stelle qn.
sky-blue [skaɪ'bluː] adj azzurro(a), celeste.
sky-diving ['skaɪdaɪvɪŋ] n caduta libera, paracadutismo acrobatico.
sky-high [skaɪ'haɪ] adv (throw) molto in alto ♦ adj (col) esorbitante; **prices have gone ~** (col) i prezzi sono saliti alle stelle.
skylark ['skaɪlɑːk] n allodola.
skylight ['skaɪlaɪt] n lucernario.
skyline ['skaɪlaɪn] n (horizon) orizzonte m;

(of city) profilo.
skyscraper ['skaɪskreɪpə*] n grattacielo.
slab [slæb] n lastra; (of wood) tavola; (of meat, cheese) pezzo.
slack [slæk] adj (loose) allentato(a); (slow) lento(a); (careless) negligente; (COMM: market) stagnante; (: demand) scarso(a); (period) morto(a) ♦ n (in rope etc) parte f non tesa; **business is ~** l'attività commerciale è scarsa; see also **slacks**.
slacken ['slækn] (also: ~ **off**) vi rallentare, diminuire ♦ vt allentare; (pressure) diminuire.
slacks [slæks] npl pantaloni mpl.
slag [slæg] n scorie fpl.
slag heap n ammasso di scorie.
slain [sleɪn] pp of **slay**.
slake [sleɪk] vt (one's thirst) spegnere.
slalom ['slɑːləm] n slalom m.
slam [slæm] vt (door) sbattere; (throw) scaraventare; (criticize) stroncare ♦ vi sbattere.
slammer ['slæmə*] n: **the ~** (col) la gattabuia.
slander ['slɑːndə*] n calunnia; (LAW) diffamazione f ♦ vt calunniare; diffamare.
slanderous ['slɑːndrəs] adj calunnioso(a); diffamatorio(a).
slang [slæŋ] n gergo, slang m.
slanging match ['slæŋɪŋ-] n (BRIT col) rissa verbale.
slant [slɑːnt] n pendenza, inclinazione f; (fig) angolazione f, punto di vista.
slanted ['slɑːntɪd] adj tendenzioso(a).
slanting ['slɑːntɪŋ] adj in pendenza, inclinato(a).
slap [slæp] n manata, pacca; (on face) schiaffo ♦ vt dare una manata a; schiaffeggiare ♦ adv (directly) in pieno; **it fell ~ in the middle** cadde proprio nel mezzo.
slapdash ['slæpdæʃ] adj abborracciato(a).
slaphead ['slæphɛd] n (BRIT col) imbecille m/f.
slapstick ['slæpstɪk] n (comedy) farsa grossolana.
slap-up ['slæpʌp] adj (BRIT): **a ~ meal** un pranzo (or una cena) coi fiocchi.
slash [slæʃ] vt squarciare; (face) sfregiare; (fig: prices) ridurre drasticamente, tagliare.
slat [slæt] n (of wood) stecca.
slate [sleɪt] n ardesia ♦ vt (fig: criticize) stroncare, distruggere.
slaughter ['slɔːtə*] n (of animals) macellazione f; (of people) strage f, massacro ♦ vt macellare; trucidare, massacrare.

slaughterhouse ['slɔːtəhaus] *n* macello, mattatoio.

Slav [slɑːv] *adj, n* slavo(a).

slave [sleɪv] *n* schiavo/a ♦ *vi* (*also*: ~ **away**) lavorare come uno schiavo; **to** ~ **(away) at sth/at doing sth** ammazzarsi di fatica *or* sgobbare per qc/per fare qc.

slave driver *n* (*col, pej*) schiavista *m/f*.

slave labour *n* lavoro degli schiavi; (*fig*): **we're just** ~ **here** siamo solamente sfruttati qui dentro.

slaver ['slævə*] *vi* (*dribble*) sbavare.

slavery ['sleɪvərɪ] *n* schiavitù *f*.

Slavic ['slævɪk] *adj* slavo(a).

slavish ['sleɪvɪʃ] *adj* servile; pedissequo(a).

slavishly ['sleɪvɪʃlɪ] *adv* (*copy*) pedissequamente.

Slavonic [slə'vɒnɪk] *adj* slavo(a).

slay, *pt* **slew**, *pp* **slain** [sleɪ, sluː, sleɪn] *vt* (*formal*) uccidere.

SLD *n abbr* (*BRIT*) = *Social and Liberal Democrats.*

sleazy ['sliːzɪ] *adj* trasandato(a).

sledge [slɛdʒ] *n* slitta.

sledgehammer ['slɛdʒhæmə*] *n* martello da fabbro.

sleek [sliːk] *adj* (*hair, fur*) lucido(a), lucente; (*car, boat*) slanciato(a), affusolato(a).

sleep [sliːp] *n* sonno ♦ *vi* (*pt, pp* **slept** [slɛpt]) dormire ♦ *vt*: **we can** ~ **4** abbiamo 4 posti letto, possiamo alloggiare 4 persone; **to have a good night's** ~ farsi una bella dormita; **to go to** ~ addormentarsi; **to** ~ **lightly** avere il sonno leggero; **to put to** ~ (*patient*) far addormentare; (*animal*: *euphemistic: kill*) abbattere; **to** ~ **with sb** (*euphemistic: have sex*) andare a letto con qn.

▶**sleep in** *vi* (*lie late*) alzarsi tardi; (*oversleep*) dormire fino a tardi.

sleeper ['sliːpə*] *n* (*person*) dormiente *m/f*; (*BRIT RAIL: on track*) traversina; (: *train*) treno di vagoni letto.

sleepily ['sliːpɪlɪ] *adv* con aria assonnata.

sleeping ['sliːpɪŋ] *adj* addormentato(a).

sleeping bag *n* sacco a pelo.

sleeping car *n* vagone *m* letto *inv*, carrozza *f* letto *inv*.

sleeping partner *n* (*BRIT COMM*) = **silent partner.**

sleeping pill *n* sonnifero.

sleeping sickness *n* malattia del sonno.

sleepless ['sliːplɪs] *adj* (*person*) insonne; **a** ~ **night** una notte in bianco.

sleeplessness ['sliːplɪsnɪs] *n* insonnia.

sleepwalk ['sliːpwɔːk] *vi* camminare nel sonno; (*as a habit*) essere sonnambulo(a).

sleepwalker ['sliːpwɔːkə*] *n* sonnambulo/a.

sleepy ['sliːpɪ] *adj* assonnato(a), sonnolento(a); (*fig*) addormentato(a); **to be** *or* **feel** ~ avere sonno.

sleet [sliːt] *n* nevischio.

sleeve [sliːv] *n* manica; (*of record*) copertina.

sleeveless ['sliːvlɪs] *adj* (*garment*) senza maniche.

sleigh [sleɪ] *n* slitta.

sleight [slaɪt] *n*: ~ **of hand** gioco di destrezza.

slender ['slɛndə*] *adj* snello(a), sottile; (*not enough*) scarso(a), esiguo(a).

slept [slɛpt] *pt, pp of* **sleep.**

sleuth [sluːθ] *n* (*col*) segugio.

slew [sluː] *vi* (*also*: ~ **round**) girare ♦ *pt of* **slay.**

slice [slaɪs] *n* fetta ♦ *vt* affettare, tagliare a fette; ~**d bread** pane a cassetta.

slick [slɪk] *adj* (*clever*) brillante; (*insincere*) untuoso(a), falso(a) ♦ *n* (*also*: **oil** ~) chiazza di petrolio.

slid [slɪd] *pt, pp of* **slide.**

slide [slaɪd] *n* (*in playground*) scivolo; (*PHOT*) diapositiva; (*microscope* ~) vetrino; (*BRIT*: *also*: **hair** ~) fermaglio (per capelli); (*in prices*) caduta ♦ *vb* (*pt, pp* **slid** [slɪd]) *vt* far scivolare ♦ *vi* scivolare; **to let things** ~ (*fig*) lasciare andare tutto, trascurare tutto.

slide projector *n* proiettore *m* per diapositive.

slide rule *n* regolo calcolatore.

sliding ['slaɪdɪŋ] *adj* (*door*) scorrevole; ~ **roof** (*AUT*) capotte *f inv*.

sliding scale *n* scala mobile.

slight [slaɪt] *adj* (*slim*) snello(a), sottile; (*frail*) delicato(a), fragile; (*trivial*) insignificante; (*small*) piccolo(a) ♦ *n* offesa, affronto ♦ *vt* (*offend*) offendere, fare un affronto a; **the** ~**est** il minimo (*or* la minima); **not in the** ~**est** affatto, neppure per sogno.

slightly ['slaɪtlɪ] *adv* lievemente, un po'; ~ **built** esile.

slim [slɪm] *adj* magro(a), snello(a) ♦ *vi* dimagrire, fare (*or* seguire) una dieta dimagrante.

slime [slaɪm] *n* limo, melma; viscidume *m*.

slimming ['slɪmɪŋ] *adj* (*diet, pills*) dimagrante.

slimy ['slaɪmɪ] *adj* (*also fig: person*) viscido(a); (*covered with mud*) melmoso(a).

sling [slɪŋ] *n* (*MED*) benda al collo ♦ *vt* (*pt, pp* **slung** [slʌŋ]) lanciare, tirare; **to have one's arm in a** ~ avere un braccio al collo.

slink, *pt, pp* **slunk** [slɪŋk, slʌŋk] *vi*: **to ~ away, ~ off** svignarsela.

slinky ['slɪŋkɪ] *adj* (*clothing*) aderente, attillato(a).

slip [slɪp] *n* scivolata, scivolone *m*; (*mistake*) errore *m*, sbaglio; (*underskirt*) sottoveste *f*; (*paper*) bigliettino, talloncino ♦ *vt* (*slide*) far scivolare ♦ *vi* (*slide*) scivolare; (*move smoothly*): **to ~ into/out of** scivolare in/via da; (*decline*) declinare; **to give sb the ~** sfuggire qn; **a ~ of paper** un foglietto; **a ~ of the tongue** un lapsus linguae; **to ~ sth on/off** infilarsi/togliersi qc; **to let a chance ~ by** lasciarsi scappare un'occasione; **it ~ped from her hand** le sfuggì di mano.

►**slip away** *vi* svignarsela.

►**slip in** *vt* introdurre casualmente.

►**slip out** *vi* uscire furtivamente.

slip-on ['slɪpɔn] *adj* (*gen*) comodo(a) da mettere; (*shoes*) senza allacciatura.

slipped disc ['slɪpt'] *n* spostamento della vertebre.

slipper ['slɪpə*] *n* pantofola.

slippery ['slɪpərɪ] *adj* scivoloso(a); **it's ~** si scivola.

slip road *n* (*BRIT*: *to motorway*) rampa di accesso.

slipshod ['slɪpʃɔd] *adj* sciatto(a), trasandato(a).

slip-up ['slɪpʌp] *n* granchio (*fig*).

slipway ['slɪpweɪ] *n* scalo di costruzione.

slit [slɪt] *n* fessura, fenditura; (*cut*) taglio; (*tear*) strappo ♦ *vt* (*pt, pp* **slit**) tagliare; **to ~ sb's throat** tagliare la gola a qn.

slither ['slɪðə*] *vi* scivolare, sdrucciolare.

sliver ['slɪvə*] *n* (*of glass, wood*) scheggia; (*of cheese, sausage*) fettina.

slob [slɔb] *n* (*col*) sciattone/a.

slog [slɔg] (*BRIT*) *n* faticata ♦ *vi* lavorare con accanimento, sgobbare.

slogan ['sləugən] *n* motto, slogan *m inv*.

slop [slɔp] *vi* (*also*: **~ over**) traboccare; versarsi ♦ *vt* spandere; versare ♦ *npl*: **~s** acqua sporca; sbobba.

slope [sləup] *n* pendio; (*side of mountain*) versante *m*; (*of roof*) pendenza; (*of floor*) inclinazione *f* ♦ *vi*: **to ~ down** declinare; **to ~ up** essere in salita.

sloping ['sləupɪŋ] *adj* inclinato(a).

sloppy ['slɔpɪ] *adj* (*work*) tirato(a) via; (*appearance*) sciatto(a); (*film etc*) sdolcinato(a).

slosh [slɔʃ] *vi* (*col*): **to ~ about** *or* **around** (*person*) sguazzare; (*liquid*) guazzare.

sloshed [slɔʃt] *adj* (*col*: *drunk*) sbronzo(a).

slot [slɔt] *n* fessura; (*fig*: *in timetable, RADIO, TV*) spazio ♦ *vt*: **to ~ into** introdurre in

una fessura.

sloth [sləuθ] *n* (*vice*) pigrizia, accidia; (*ZOOL*) bradipo.

slot machine *n* (*BRIT*: *vending machine*) distributore *m* automatico; (*for amusement*) slot-machine *f inv*.

slot meter *n* contatore *m* a gettoni.

slouch [slautʃ] *vi* (*when walking*) camminare dinoccolato(a); **she was ~ed in a chair** era sprofondata in una poltrona.

►**slouch about, slouch around** *vi* (*laze*) oziare.

Slovak ['sləuvæk] *adj* slovacco(a) ♦ *n* slovacco/a; (*LING*) slovacco; **the ~ Republic** la Repubblica Slovacca.

Slovakia [sləu'vækɪə] *n* Slovacchia.

Slovakian [sləu'vækɪən] *adj, n* = **Slovak**.

Slovene ['sləuviːn] *adj* sloveno(a) ♦ *n* sloveno/a; (*LING*) sloveno.

Slovenia [sləu'viːnɪə] *n* Slovenia.

Slovenian [sləu'viːnɪən] *adj, n* = **Slovene**.

slovenly ['slʌvənlɪ] *adj* sciatto(a), trasandato(a).

slow [sləu] *adj* lento(a); (*watch*): **to be ~** essere indietro ♦ *adv* lentamente ♦ *vt, vi* (*also*: **~ down, ~ up**) rallentare; "**~**" (*road sign*) "rallentare"; **at a ~ speed** a bassa velocità; **to be ~ to act/decide** essere lento ad agire/a decidere; **my watch is 20 minutes ~** il mio orologio è indietro di 20 minuti; **business is ~** (*COMM*) gli affari procedono a rilento; **to go ~** (*driver*) andare piano; (*in industrial dispute*) fare uno sciopero bianco.

slow-acting ['sləu'æktɪŋ] *adj* che agisce lentamente, ad azione lenta.

slowly ['sləulɪ] *adv* lentamente; **to drive ~** andare piano.

slow motion *n*: **in ~** al rallentatore.

slowness ['sləunɪs] *n* lentezza.

sludge [slʌdʒ] *n* fanghiglia.

slug [slʌg] *n* lumaca; (*bullet*) pallottola.

sluggish ['slʌgɪʃ] *adj* lento(a); (*business, market, sales*) stagnante, fiacco(a).

sluice [sluːs] *n* chiusa ♦ *vt*: **to ~ down** *or* **out** lavare (con abbondante acqua).

slum [slʌm] *n* catapecchia.

slumber ['slʌmbə*] *n* sonno.

slump [slʌmp] *n* crollo, caduta; (*economic*) depressione *f*, crisi *f inv* ♦ *vi* crollare; **he was ~ed over the wheel** era curvo sul volante.

slung [slʌŋ] *pt, pp of* **sling**.

slunk [slʌŋk] *pt, pp of* **slink**.

slur [slə:*] *n* pronuncia indistinta; (*stigma*) diffamazione *f*, calunnia; (*MUS*) legatura; (*smear*): **~ (on)** macchia (su) ♦ *vt* pronunciare in modo indistinto; **to cast a** ~ **on sb** calunniare qn.

slurp [slə:p] _vt, vi_ bere rumorosamente ♦ _n rumore fatto bevendo._

slurred [slə:d] _adj (pronunciation)_ inarticolato(a), disarticolato(a).

slush [slʌʃ] _n_ neve _f_ mista a fango.

slush fund _n_ fondi _mpl_ neri.

slushy ['slʌʃɪ] _adj (snow)_ che si scioglie; _(BRIT: fig)_ sdolcinato(a).

slut [slʌt] _n_ donna trasandata, sciattona.

sly [slaɪ] _adj_ furbo(a), scaltro(a); **on the** ~ di soppiatto.

SM _n abbr_ (= _sadomasochism_) sadomasochismo.

smack [smæk] _n (slap)_ pacca; _(on face)_ schiaffo ♦ _vt_ schiaffeggiare; _(child)_ picchiare ♦ _vi_: **to** ~ **of** puzzare di; **to** ~ **one's lips** fare uno schiocco con le labbra.

smacker ['smækə*] _n (col: kiss)_ bacio; (: _BRIT: pound note_) sterlina; (: _US: dollar bill_) dollaro.

small [smɔ:l] _adj_ piccolo(a); _(in height)_ basso(a); _(letter)_ minuscolo(a) ♦ _n_: **the** ~ **of the back** le reni; **to get** _or_ **grow** ~**er** _(stain, town)_ rimpicciolire; _(debt, organization, numbers)_ ridursi; **to make** ~**er** _(amount, income)_ ridurre; _(garden, object, garment)_ rimpicciolire; **in the** ~ **hours** alle ore piccole; **a** ~ **shopkeeper** un piccolo negoziante.

small ads _npl (BRIT)_ piccoli annunci _mpl._

small arms _npl_ armi _fpl_ portatili _or_ leggere.

small business _n_ piccola impresa.

small change _n_ moneta, spiccioli _mpl._

smallholder ['smɔ:lhəʊldə*] _n (BRIT)_ piccolo proprietario.

smallholding ['smɔ:lhəʊldɪŋ] _n (BRIT)_ piccola tenuta.

smallish ['smɔ:lɪʃ] _adj_ piccolino(a).

small-minded [smɔ:l'maɪndɪd] _adj_ meschino(a).

smallpox ['smɔ:lpɒks] _n_ vaiolo.

small print _n_ caratteri _mpl_ piccoli; _(on document)_ parte scritta in piccolo.

small-scale ['smɔ:lskeɪl] _adj (map, model)_ in scala ridotta; _(business, farming)_ modesto(a).

small talk _n_ chiacchiere _fpl._

small-time ['smɔ:ltaɪm] _adj (col)_ da poco; **a** ~ **thief** un ladro di polli.

small-town ['smɔ:ltaun] _adj (pej)_ provinciale, di paese.

smarmy ['smɑ:mɪ] _adj (BRIT pej)_ untuoso(a), strisciante.

smart [smɑ:t] _adj_ elegante; _(also fig: clever)_

intelligente; _(quick)_ sveglio(a) ♦ _vi_ bruciare; **the** ~ **set** il bel mondo; **to look** ~ essere elegante; **my eyes are** ~**ing** mi bruciano gli occhi.

smartcard ['smɑ:tkɑ:d] _n_ smartcard _f inv,_ carta intelligente.

smarten up ['smɑ:tn-] _vi_ farsi bello(a) ♦ _vt_ _(people)_ fare bello(a); _(things)_ abbellire.

smash [smæʃ] _n (also:_ ~**-up**) scontro, collisione _f; (sound)_ fracasso ♦ _vt_ frantumare, fracassare; _(opponent)_ annientare, schiacciare; _(hopes)_ distruggere; _(SPORT: record)_ battere ♦ _vi_ frantumarsi, andare in pezzi.

▶**smash up** _vt (car)_ sfasciare; _(room)_ distruggere.

smash-hit [smæʃ'hɪt] _n_ successone _m._

smashing ['smæʃɪŋ] _adj (col)_ favoloso(a), formidabile.

smattering ['smætərɪŋ] _n_: **a** ~ **of** un'infarinatura di.

smear [smɪə*] _n_ macchia; _(MED)_ striscio; _(insult)_ calunnia ♦ _vt_ ungere; _(fig)_ denigrare, diffamare; **his hands were** ~**ed with oil/ink** aveva le mani sporche di olio/inchiostro.

smear campaign _n_ campagna diffamatoria.

smear test _n (BRIT MED)_ Pap-test _m inv._

smell [smɛl] _n_ odore _m; (sense)_ olfatto, odorato ♦ _vb (pt, pp_ **smelt** _or_ **smelled** [smɛlt, smɛld]) _vt_ sentire (l')odore di ♦ _vi_ _(food etc)_: **to** ~ (**of**) avere odore (di); _(pej)_ puzzare, avere un cattivo odore; **it** ~**s good** ha un buon odore.

smelly ['smɛlɪ] _adj_ puzzolente.

smelt [smɛlt] _pt, pp of_ **smell** ♦ _vt (ore)_ fondere.

smile [smaɪl] _n_ sorriso ♦ _vi_ sorridere.

smiling ['smaɪlɪŋ] _adj_ sorridente.

smirk [smə:k] _n_ sorriso furbo; sorriso compiaciuto.

smith [smɪθ] _n_ fabbro.

smithy ['smɪðɪ] _n_ fucina.

smitten ['smɪtn] _adj_: ~ **with** colpito(a) da.

smock [smɒk] _n_ grembiule _m,_ camice _m._

smog [smɒg] _n_ smog _m._

smoke [sməʊk] _n_ fumo ♦ _vt, vi_ fumare; **to have a** ~ fumarsi una sigaretta; **do you** ~**?** fumi?; **to go up in** ~ _(house etc)_ bruciare, andare distrutto dalle fiamme; _(fig)_ andare in fumo.

smoked [sməʊkt] _adj (bacon, glass)_ affumicato(a).

smokeless fuel ['sməʊklɪs-] _n_ carburante _m_ che non da fumo.

smokeless zone _n (BRIT)_ zona dove sono vietati gli scarichi di fumo.

smoker ['sməukə*] *n* (*person*) fumatore/ trice; (*RAIL*) carrozza per fumatori.

smoke screen *n* cortina fumogena *or* di fumo; (*fig*) copertura.

smoke shop *n* (*US*) tabaccheria.

smoking ['sməukɪŋ] *n* fumo; "no ~" (*sign*) "vietato fumare"; **he's given up** ~ ha smesso di fumare.

smoking compartment, (*US*) **smoking car** *n* carrozza (per) fumatori.

smoky ['sməukɪ] *adj* fumoso(a); (*surface*) affumicato(a).

smolder ['sməuldə*] *vi* (*US*) = **smoulder**.

smoochy ['smu:tʃɪ] *adj* (*col*) romantico(a).

smooth [smu:ð] *adj* liscio(a); (*sauce*) omogeneo(a); (*flavour, whisky*) amabile; (*cigarette*) leggero(a); (*movement*) regolare; (*person*) mellifluo(a); (*landing, take-off, flight*) senza scosse ♦ *vt* lisciare, spianare; (*also:* ~ **out:** *difficulties*) appianare.

▶**smooth over** *vt:* **to ~ things over** (*fig*) sistemare le cose.

smoothly ['smu:ðlɪ] *adv* (*easily*) liscio; **everything went** ~ tutto andò liscio.

smother ['smʌðə*] *vt* soffocare.

smoulder, (*US*) **smolder** ['sməuldə*] *vi* covare sotto la cenere.

smudge [smʌdʒ] *n* macchia, sbavatura ♦ *vt* imbrattare, sporcare.

smug [smʌg] *adj* soddisfatto(a), compiaciuto(a).

smuggle ['smʌgl] *vt* contrabbandare; **to ~ in/out** (*goods etc*) far entrare/uscire di contrabbando.

smuggler ['smʌglə*] *n* contrabbandiere/a.

smuggling ['smʌglɪŋ] *n* contrabbando.

smut [smʌt] *n* (*grain of soot*) granello di fuliggine, (*mark*) segno nero; (*in conversation etc*) sconcezze *fpl.*

smutty ['smʌtɪ] *adj* (*fig*) osceno(a), indecente.

snack [snæk] *n* spuntino; **to have a ~** fare uno spuntino.

snack bar *n* tavola calda, snack bar *m inv.*

snag [snæg] *n* intoppo, ostacolo imprevisto.

snail [sneɪl] *n* chiocciola.

snake [sneɪk] *n* serpente *m.*

snap [snæp] *n* (*sound*) schianto, colpo secco; (*photograph*) istantanea; (*game*) rubamazzo ♦ *adj* improvviso(a) ♦ *vt* (*far*) schioccare; (*break*) spezzare di netto; (*photograph*) scattare un'istantanea di ♦ *vi* spezzarsi con un rumore secco; (*fig: person*) crollare; **to ~ at sb** rivolgersi a qn con tono brusco; (*subj: dog*) cercare di mordere qn; **to ~ open/shut** aprirsi/ chiudersi di scatto; **to ~ one's fingers at**

(*fig*) infischiarsi di; **a cold** ~ (*of weather*) un'improvvisa ondata di freddo.

▶**snap off** *vt* (*break*) schiantare.

▶**snap up** *vt* afferrare.

snap fastener *n* bottone *m* automatico.

snappy ['snæpɪ] *adj* rapido(a); **make it ~!** (*col: hurry up*) sbrigati!, svelto!

snapshot ['snæpʃɔt] *n* istantanea.

snare [snɛə*] *n* trappola.

snarl [snɑ:l] *vi* ringhiare ♦ *vt:* **to get ~ed up** (*wool, plans*) ingarbugliarsi; (*traffic*) intasarsi.

snatch [snætʃ] *n* (*fig*) furto; (*BRIT: small amount*): **~es of** frammenti *mpl* di ♦ *vt* strappare (con violenza); (*steal*) rubare ♦ *vi:* **don't ~!** non strappare le cose di mano!; **to ~ a sandwich** mangiarsi in fretta un panino; **to ~ some sleep** riuscire a dormire un po'.

▶**snatch up** *vt* raccogliere in fretta.

snazzy ['snæzɪ] *adj* (*col: clothes*) sciccoso(a).

sneak [sni:k] *vi:* **to ~ in/out** entrare/uscire di nascosto ♦ *vt:* **to ~ a look at sth** guardare di sottecchi qc.

sneakers ['sni:kəz] *npl* scarpe *fpl* da ginnastica.

sneaking ['sni:kɪŋ] *adj:* **to have a ~ feeling/ suspicion that ...** avere la vaga impressione/il vago sospetto che ....

sneaky ['sni:kɪ] *adj* falso(a), disonesto(a).

sneer [snɪə*] *vi* ghigno, sogghigno ♦ *vi* ghignare, sogghignare; **to ~ at sb/sth** farsi beffe di qn/qc.

sneeze [sni:z] *n* starnuto ♦ *vi* starnutire.

snide [snaɪd] *adj* maligno(a).

sniff [snɪf] *n* fiutata, annusata ♦ *vi* fiutare, annusare; tirare su col naso; (*in contempt*) arricciare il naso ♦ *vt* fiutare, annusare; (*glue, drug*) sniffare.

▶**sniff at** *vt fus:* **it's not to be ~ed at** non è da disprezzare.

sniffer dog ['snɪfə-] *n* cane *m* poliziotto (*per stupefacenti o esplosivi*).

snigger ['snɪgə*] *n* riso represso ♦ *vi* ridacchiare, ridere sotto i baffi.

snip [snɪp] *n* pezzetto; (*bargain*) (buon) affare *m*, occasione *f* ♦ *vt* tagliare.

sniper ['snaɪpə*] *n* franco tiratore *m*, cecchino.

snippet ['snɪpɪt] *n* frammento.

snivelling ['snɪvlɪŋ] *adj* piagnucoloso(a).

snob [snɔb] *n* snob *m/f inv.*

snobbery ['snɔbərɪ] *n* snobismo.

snobbish ['snɔbɪʃ] *adj* snob *inv.*

snog [snɔg] *vi* (*col*) pomiciare.

snooker ['snu:kə*] *n* tipo di gioco del biliardo.

snoop [snu:p] *vi:* **to ~ on sb** spiare qn; **to ~**

about curiosare.
snooper ['snuːpə*] *n* ficcanaso *m/f*.
snooty ['snuːtɪ] *adj* borioso(a), snob *inv.*
snooze [snuːz] *n* sonnellino, pisolino ♦ *vi*
fare un sonnellino.
snore [snɔː*] *vi* russare.
snoring ['snɔːrɪŋ] *n* russare *m.*
snorkel ['snɔːkl] *n* (*of swimmer*) respiratore
m a tubo.
snort [snɔːt] *n* sbuffo ♦ *vi* sbuffare ♦ *vt*
(*drugs slang*) sniffare.
snotty ['snɔtɪ] *adj* moccioso(a).
snout [snaut] *n* muso.
snow [snəu] *n* neve *f* ♦ *vi* nevicare ♦ *vt*: to be
~ed under with work essere sommerso
di lavoro.
snowball ['snəubɔːl] *n* palla di neve.
snowbound ['snəubaund] *adj* bloccato(a)
dalla neve.
snow-capped ['snəukæpt] *adj* (*mountain*)
con la cima coperta di neve; (*peak*)
coperto(a) di neve.
snowdrift ['snəudrɪft] *n* cumulo di neve
(*ammucchiato dal vento*).
snowdrop ['snəudrɔp] *n* bucaneve *m inv.*
snowfall ['snəufɔːl] *n* nevicata.
snowflake ['snəufleɪk] *n* fiocco di neve.
snowman ['snəumæn] *n* pupazzo di neve.
snowplough, (*US*) **snowplow** ['snəuplau]
n spazzaneve *m inv.*
snowshoe ['snəuʃuː] *n* racchetta da neve.
snowstorm ['snəustɔːm] *n* tormenta.
snowy ['snəuɪ] *adj* nevoso(a).
SNP *n abbr* (*BRIT POL*) = Scottish National
Party.
snub [snʌb] *vt* snobbare ♦ *n* offesa,
affronto.
snub-nosed [snʌb'nəuzd] *adj* dal naso
camuso.
snuff [snʌf] *n* tabacco da fiuto ♦ *vt* (*also:* ~
out: *candle*) spegnere.
snuff movie *n* (*col*) *film porno dove una
persona viene uccisa realmente.*
snug [snʌg] *adj* comodo(a); (*room, house*)
accogliente, comodo(a); it's a ~ fit è
attillato.
snuggle ['snʌgl] *vi*: to ~ down in bed
accovacciarsi a letto; to ~ up to sb
stringersi a qn.
snugly ['snʌglɪ] *adv* comodamente; it fits ~
(*object in pocket etc*) entra giusto giusto;
(*garment*) sta ben attillato.
SO *abbr* (*BANKING*) = standing order.

═══════════════════ *KEYWORD*

so [səu] *adv* 1 (*thus, likewise*) così; if ~ se è
così, quand'è così; I didn't do it — you did
~! non l'ho fatto io — sì che l'hai fatto!;

~ do I, ~ am I anch'io; it's 5 o'clock — ~ it
is! sono le 5 — davvero!; I hope ~ lo
spero; I think ~ penso di sì; quite ~!
esattamente!; even ~ comunque; ~ far
finora, fin qui; (*in past*) fino ad allora
2 (*in comparisons etc: to such a degree*)
così; ~ big (that) così grande (che); she's
not ~ clever as her brother lei non è
(così) intelligente come suo fratello
3: ~ much *adj* tanto(a) ♦ *adv* tanto; I've got
~ much work/money ho tanto lavoro/
tanti soldi; I love you ~ much ti amo
tanto; ~ many tanti(e)
4 (*phrases*): 10 or ~ circa 10; ~ long! (*col:
goodbye*) ciao!, ci vediamo!; ~ to speak
per così dire; ~ what? (*col*) e allora?, e
con questo?

♦ *conj* 1 (*expressing purpose*): ~ as to do in
modo *or* così da fare; we hurried ~ as not
to be late ci affrettammo per non fare
tardi; ~ (that) affinché + *sub*, perché + *sub*
2 (*expressing result*): he didn't arrive — I left
non è venuto così me ne sono andata; ~ you
see, I could have gone vedi, sarei potuto
andare; ~ that's the reason! allora è questo
il motivo!, ecco perché!

soak [səuk] *vt* inzuppare; (*clothes*) mettere
a mollo ♦ *vi* inzupparsi; (*clothes*) essere a
mollo; to be ~ed through essere fradicio.
▶**soak in** *vi* penetrare.
▶**soak up** *vt* assorbire.
soaking ['səukɪŋ] *adj* (*also:* ~ wet)
fradicio(a).
so-and-so ['səuənsəu] *n* (*somebody*) un tale;
Mr/Mrs ~ signor/signora tal dei tali.
soap [səup] *n* sapone *m.*
soapbox ['səupbɔks] *n* palco improvvisato
(*per orazioni pubbliche*).
soapflakes ['səupfleɪks] *npl* sapone *m* in
scaglie.
soap opera *n* soap opera *f inv.*
soap powder *n* detersivo.
soapsuds ['səupsʌdz] *npl* saponata.
soapy ['səupɪ] *adj* insaponato(a).
soar [sɔː*] *vi* volare in alto; (*price, morale,
spirits*) salire alle stelle.
sob [sɔb] *n* singhiozzo ♦ *vi* singhiozzare.
s.o.b. *n abbr* (*US col!:* = son of a bitch*) figlio
di puttana (*!*).
sober ['səubə*] *adj* non ubriaco(a); (*sedate*)
serio(a); (*moderate*) moderato(a); (*colour,
style*) sobrio(a).
▶**sober up** *vt* far passare la sbornia a ♦ *vi*
farsi passare la sbornia.
sobriety [səu'braɪətɪ] *n* (*not being drunk*)
sobrietà; (*seriousness, sedateness*)
sobrietà, pacatezza.

sob story n (col, pej) storia lacrimosa.
Soc. abbr (= society) Soc.
so-called ['səu'kɔːld] adj cosiddetto(a).
soccer ['sɔkə*] n calcio.
soccer pitch n campo di calcio.
soccer player n calciatore m.
sociable ['səuʃəbl] adj socievole.
social ['səuʃl] adj sociale ♦ n festa, serata.
social climber n arrampicatore/trice sociale, arrivista m/f.
social club n club m inv sociale.
Social Democrat n socialdemocratico/a.
social insurance n (US) assicurazione f sociale.
socialism ['səuʃəlɪzəm] n socialismo.
socialist ['səuʃəlɪst] adj, n socialista (m/f).
socialite ['səuʃəlaɪt] n persona in vista nel bel mondo.
socialize ['səuʃəlaɪz] vi frequentare la gente; farsi degli amici; **to ~ with** socializzare con.
social life n vita sociale.
socially ['səuʃəlɪ] adv socialmente, in società.
social science n scienze fpl sociali.
social security n previdenza sociale; **Department of S· 3·** (**DSS**) (BRIT) ≈ Istituto di Previdenza Sociale.
social services npl servizi mpl sociali.
social welfare n assistenza sociale.
social work n servizio sociale.
social worker n assistente m/f sociale.
society [sə'saɪətɪ] n società f inv; (club) società, associazione f; (also: **high ~**) alta società ♦ cpd (party, column) mondano(a).
socioeconomic ['səusɪəuiːkə'nɔmɪk] adj socio-economico(a).
sociological [səusɪə'lɔdʒɪkl] adj sociologico(a).
sociologist [səusɪ'ɔlədʒɪst] n sociologo/a.
sociology [səusɪ'ɔlədʒɪ] n sociologia.
sock [sɔk] n calzino ♦ vt (hit) dare un pugno a; **to pull one's ~s up** (fig) darsi una regolata.
socket ['sɔkɪt] n cavità f inv; (of eye) orbita; (ELEC: also: **wall ~**) presa di corrente; (: for light bulb) portalampada m inv.
sod [sɔd] n (of earth) zolla erbosa; (BRIT col!) bastardo/a (!).
▶**sod off** vi: **~ off!** (BRIT col!) levati dalle palle! (!).
soda ['səudə] n (CHEM) soda; (also: **~ water**) acqua di seltz; (US: also: **~ pop**) gassosa.
sodden ['sɔdn] adj fradicio(a).
sodium ['səudɪəm] n sodio.
sodium chloride n cloruro di sodio.
sofa ['səufə] n sofà m inv.
Sofia ['səufɪə] n Sofia.

soft [sɔft] adj (not rough) morbido(a); (not hard) soffice; (not loud) sommesso(a); (kind) gentile; (: look, smile) dolce; (not strict) indulgente; (weak) debole; (stupid) stupido(a).
soft-boiled ['sɔftbɔɪld] adj (egg) alla coque.
soft drink n analcolico.
soft drugs npl droghe fpl leggere.
soften ['sɔfn] vt ammorbidire; addolcire; attenuare ♦ vi ammorbidirsi; addolcirsi; attenuarsi.
softener ['sɔfnə*] n ammorbidente m.
soft fruit n (BRIT) ≈ frutti di bosco.
soft furnishings npl tessuti mpl d'arredo.
soft-hearted [sɔft'hɑːtɪd] adj sensibile.
softly ['sɔftlɪ] adv dolcemente; morbidamente.
softness ['sɔftnɪs] n dolcezza; morbidezza.
soft option n soluzione f (più) facile.
soft sell n persuasione f all'acquisto.
soft target n obiettivo civile (e quindi facile da colpire).
soft touch n (col): **to be a ~** lasciarsi spillare facilmente denaro.
soft toy n giocattolo di peluche.
software ['sɔftwɛə*] n software m.
software package n pacchetto di software.
soft water n acqua non calcarea.
soggy ['sɔgɪ] adj inzuppato(a).
soil [sɔɪl] n (earth) terreno, suolo ♦ vt sporcare; (fig) macchiare.
soiled [sɔɪld] adj sporco(a), sudicio(a).
sojourn ['sɔdʒɔːn] n (formal) soggiorno.
solace ['sɔlɪs] n consolazione f.
solar ['səulə*] adj solare.
solarium, pl **solaria** [sə'lɛərɪəm, -rɪə] n solarium m inv.
solar plexus [-'plɛksəs] n (ANAT) plesso solare.
solar power n energia solare.
sold [səuld] pt, pp of **sell**.
solder ['səuldə*] vt saldare ♦ n saldatura.
soldier ['səuldʒə*] n soldato, militare m ♦ vi: **to ~ on** perseverare; **toy ~** soldatino.
sold out adj (COMM) esaurito(a).
sole [səul] n (of foot) pianta (del piede); (of shoe) suola; (fish: pl inv) sogliola ♦ adj solo(a), unico(a); (exclusive) esclusivo(a).
solely ['səullɪ] adv solamente, unicamente; **I will hold you ~ responsible** la considererò il solo responsabile.
solemn ['sɔləm] adj solenne; grave; serio(a).
sole trader n (COMM) commerciante m in proprio.
solicit [sə'lɪsɪt] vt (request) richiedere, sollecitare ♦ vi (prostitute) adescare i

passanti.
solicitor [sə'lɪsɪtə*] n (*BRIT: for wills etc*) ≈
notaio; (*in court*) ≈ avvocato; *see boxed note.*

> ### SOLICITOR
>
> *Il* **solicitor** *appartiene a una delle due branche
> della professione legale britannica (vedi anche*
> **barrister***). È compito dei* **solicitor** *agire come
> consulenti in materia legale, redigere pratiche,
> preparare la documentazione legale per i
> "barrister". Contrariamente a questi ultimi, i*
> **solicitor** *non sono qualificati a rappresentare
> una parte nelle corti investite della potestà di
> decidere sui reati più gravi.*

solid ['sɔlɪd] *adj* (*not hollow*) pieno(a);
(*strong, reliable, not liquid*) solido(a); (*meal*)
sostanzioso(a); (*line*) ininterrotto(a); (*vote*)
unanime ♦ n solido; **to be on ~ ground**
essere su terraferma; (*fig*) muoversi su
terreno sicuro; **we waited 2 ~ hours**
abbiamo aspettato due ore buone.
solidarity [sɔlɪ'dærɪtɪ] n solidarietà.
solid fuel n combustibile m solido.
solidify [sə'lɪdɪfaɪ] *vi* solidificarsi ♦ *vt*
solidificare.
solidity [sə'lɪdɪtɪ] n solidità.
solid-state ['sɔlɪdsteɪt] *adj* (*ELEC*) a
transistor.
soliloquy [sə'lɪləkwɪ] n soliloquio.
solitaire [sɔlɪ'tɛə*] n (*game, gem*)
solitario.
solitary ['sɔlɪtərɪ] *adj* solitario(a).
solitary confinement n (*LAW*): **to be in ~**
essere in cella d'isolamento.
solitude ['sɔlɪtjuːd] n solitudine *f.*
solo ['səuləu] n (*MUS*) assolo.
soloist ['səuləuɪst] n solista *m/f.*
Solomon Islands ['sɔləmən-] n: **the ~** le
isole Salomone.
solstice ['sɔlstɪs] n solstizio.
soluble ['sɔljubl] *adj* solubile.
solution [sə'luːʃən] n soluzione *f.*
solve [sɔlv] *vt* risolvere.
solvency ['sɔlvənsɪ] n (*COMM*) solvenza,
solvibilità.
solvent ['sɔlvənt] *adj* (*COMM*) solvibile ♦ n
(*CHEM*) solvente *m.*
solvent abuse n abuso di colle e
solventi.
Som. *abbr* (*BRIT*) = **Somerset.**
Somali [sə'mɑːlɪ] *adj* somalo(a).
Somalia [səu'mɑːlɪə] n Somalia.
Somaliland [səu'mɑːlɪlænd] n paesi *mpl* del
corno d'Africa.
sombre, (*US*) **somber** ['sɔmbə*] *adj*
scuro(a); (*mood, person*) triste.

═══════════════════ *KEYWORD*

some [sʌm] *adj* **1** (*a certain amount or
number of*): **~ tea/water/cream** del tè/
dell'acqua/della panna; **there's ~ milk in
the fridge** c'è (del) latte nel frigo; **~
children/apples** dei bambini/delle mele;
after ~ time dopo un po'; **at ~ length** a
lungo
2 (*certain: in contrasts*) certo(a); **~ people
say that ...** alcuni dicono che ..., certa
gente dice che ...
3 (*unspecified*) un(a) certo(a), qualche; **~
woman was asking for you** una tale
chiedeva di lei; **~ day** un giorno; **~ day
next week** un giorno della prossima
settimana; **in ~ form or other** in una
forma o nell'altra
♦ *pron* **1** (*a certain number*) alcuni(e),
certi(e); **I've got ~** (*books etc*) ne ho
alcuni; **~ (of them) have been sold** alcuni
sono stati venduti
2 (*a certain amount*) un po'; **I've got ~**
(*money, milk*) ne ho un po'; **I've read ~ of
the book** ho letto parte del libro; **~ (of it)
was left** ne è rimasto un po'; **could I have
~ of that cheese?** potrei avere un po' di
quel formaggio?
♦ *adv*: **~ 10 people** circa 10 persone.

somebody ['sʌmbədɪ] *pron* qualcuno; **~ or
other** qualcuno.
someday ['sʌmdeɪ] *adv* uno di questi
giorni, un giorno o l'altro.
somehow ['sʌmhau] *adv* in un modo o
nell'altro, in qualche modo; (*for some
reason*) per qualche ragione.
someone ['sʌmwʌn] *pron* = **somebody.**
someplace ['sʌmpleɪs] *adv* (*US*) =
somewhere.
somersault ['sʌməsɔːlt] n capriola; (*in air*)
salto mortale ♦ *vi* fare una capriola (*or* un
salto mortale); (*car*) cappottare.
something ['sʌmθɪŋ] *pron* qualcosa; **~
interesting** qualcosa di interessante; **~ to
do** qualcosa da fare; **he's ~ like me** mi
assomiglia un po'; **it's ~ of a problem** è
un bel problema.
sometime ['sʌmtaɪm] *adv* (*in future*) una
volta o l'altra; (*in past*): **~ last month**
durante il mese scorso; **I'll finish it ~** lo
finirò prima o poi.
sometimes ['sʌmtaɪmz] *adv* qualche volta.
somewhat ['sʌmwɔt] *adv* piuttosto.
somewhere ['sʌmwɛə*] *adv* in *or* da
qualche parte; **~ else** da qualche altra
parte.
son [sʌn] n figlio.

sonar ['səʊnɑː*] n sonar m.
sonata [sə'nɑːtə] n sonata.
song [sɒŋ] n canzone f.
songbook ['sɒŋbʊk] n canzoniere m.
songwriter ['sɒŋraɪtə*] n compositore/trice di canzoni.
sonic ['sɒnɪk] adj (boom) sonico(a).
son-in-law ['sʌnɪnlɔː] n genero.
sonnet ['sɒnɪt] n sonetto.
sonny ['sʌnɪ] n (col) ragazzo mio.
soon [suːn] adv presto, fra poco; (early) presto; ~ afterwards poco dopo; very/quite ~ molto/abbastanza presto; as ~ as possible prima possibile; I'll do it as ~ as I can lo farò appena posso; how ~ can you be ready? fra quanto tempo sarà pronto?; see you ~! a presto!
sooner ['suːnə*] adv (time) prima; (preference): I would ~ do preferirei fare; ~ or later prima o poi; no ~ said than done detto fatto; the ~ the better prima è meglio è; no ~ had we left than ... eravamo appena partiti, quando ....
soot [sʊt] n fuliggine f.
soothe [suːð] vt calmare.
soothing ['suːðɪŋ] adj (ointment etc) calmante; (tone, words etc) rassicurante.
SOP n abbr = standard operating procedure.
sop [sɒp] n: that's only a ~ è soltanto un contentino.
sophisticated [sə'fɪstɪkeɪtɪd] adj sofisticato(a); raffinato(a); (film, mind) sottile.
sophistication [səfɪstɪ'keɪʃən] n raffinatezza; (of machine) complessità; (of argument etc) sottigliezza.
sophomore ['sɒfəmɔː*] n (US) studente/essa del secondo anno.
soporific [sɒpə'rɪfɪk] adj soporifero(a).
sopping ['sɒpɪŋ] adj (also: ~ wet) bagnato(a) fradicio(a).
soppy ['sɒpɪ] adj (pej) sentimentale.
soprano [sə'prɑːnəʊ] n (voice) soprano m; (singer) soprano m/f.
sorbet ['sɔːbeɪ] n sorbetto.
sorcerer ['sɔːsərə*] n stregone m, mago.
sordid ['sɔːdɪd] adj sordido(a).
sore [sɔː*] adj (painful) dolorante; (col: offended) offeso(a) ♦ n piaga; my eyes are ~, I have ~ eyes mi fanno male gli occhi; ~ throat mal m di gola; it's a ~ point (fig) è un punto delicato.
sorely ['sɔːlɪ] adv (tempted) fortemente.
sorrel ['sɔrəl] n acetosa.
sorrow ['sɒrəʊ] n dolore m.
sorrowful ['sɒrəʊful] adj triste.
sorry ['sɒrɪ] adj spiacente; (condition, excuse) misero(a), pietoso(a); (sight,

failure) triste; ~! scusa! (or scusi! or scusate!); (to feel ~ for sb rincrescersi per qn; I'm ~ to hear that ... mi dispiace (sentire) che ...; to be ~ about sth essere dispiaciuto or spiacente di qc.
sort [sɔːt] n specie f, genere m; (make: of coffee, car etc) tipo ♦ vt (also: ~ out: papers) classificare; ordinare; (: letters etc) smistare; (: problems) risolvere; (COMPUT) ordinare; what ~ of car? che tipo di macchina?; I shall do nothing of the ~! nemmeno per sogno!; it's ~ of awkward (col) è piuttosto difficile.
sortie ['sɔːtɪ] n sortita.
sorting office ['sɔːtɪŋ-] n ufficio m smistamento inv.
SOS n abbr (= save our souls) S.O.S. m inv.
so-so ['səʊsəʊ] adv così così.
soufflé ['suːfleɪ] n soufflé m inv.
sought [sɔːt] pt, pp of seek.
sought-after ['sɔːtɑːftə*] adj richiesto(a).
soul [səʊl] n anima, the poor ~ had nowhere to sleep il poveraccio non aveva dove dormire; I didn't see a ~ non ho visto anima viva.
soul-destroying ['səʊldɪ'strɔɪŋ] adj demoralizzante.
soulful ['səʊlful] adj pieno(a) di sentimento.
soulless ['səʊllɪs] adj senz'anima, inumano(a).
soul mate n anima gemella.
soul-searching ['səʊlsɜːtʃɪŋ] n: after much ~ dopo un profondo esame di coscienza.
sound [saʊnd] adj (healthy) sano(a); (safe, not damaged) solido(a), in buono stato; (reliable, not superficial) solido(a); (sensible) giudizioso(a), di buon senso; (valid: argument, policy, claim) valido(a) ♦ adv: ~ asleep profondamente addormentato ♦ n (noise) suono; rumore m; (GEO) stretto ♦ vt (alarm) suonare; (also: ~ out: opinions) sondare ♦ vi suonare; (fig: seem) sembrare; to be of ~ mind essere sano di mente; I don't like the ~ of it (fig: of film etc) non mi dice niente; (: of news) è preoccupante; it ~s as if ... ho l'impressione che ...; it ~s like French somiglia al francese; that ~s like them arriving mi sembra di sentirli arrivare.
▶**sound off** vi (col): to ~ off (about) (give one's opinions) fare dei grandi discorsi (su).
sound barrier n muro del suono.
soundbite ['saʊndbaɪt] n frase f incisiva.
sound effects npl effetti mpl sonori.
sound engineer n tecnico del suono.
sounding ['saʊndɪŋ] n (NAUT etc) scandagliamento.

sounding board n (MUS) cassa di risonanza; (fig): **to use sb as a ~ for one's ideas** provare le proprie idee su qn.

soundly ['saundlɪ] adv (sleep) profondamente; (beat) duramente.

soundproof ['saundpruːf] vt insonorizzare, isolare acusticamente ♦ adj insonorizzato(a), isolato(a) acusticamente.

sound system n impianto m audio inv.

soundtrack ['saundtræk] n (of film) colonna sonora.

soup [suːp] n minestra; (clear) brodo; (thick) zuppa; **in the ~** (fig) nei guai.

soup course n minestra.

soup kitchen n mensa per i poveri.

soup plate n piatto fondo.

soupspoon ['suːpspuːn] n cucchiaio da minestra.

sour ['sauə*] adj aspro(a); (fruit) acerbo(a); (milk) acido(a), fermentato(a); (fig) acido(a); **to go** or **turn ~** (milk, wine) inacidirsi; (fig: relationship, plans) guastarsi; **it's ~ grapes** (fig) è soltanto invidia.

source [sɔːs] n fonte f, sorgente f; (fig) fonte; **I have it from a reliable ~ that ...** ho saputo da fonte sicura che ....

south [sauθ] n sud m, meridione m, mezzogiorno ♦ adj del sud, sud inv, meridionale ♦ adv verso sud; **(to the) ~ of** a sud di; **the S~ of France** il sud della Francia; **to travel ~** viaggiare verso sud.

South Africa n Sudafrica m.

South African adj, n sudafricano(a).

South America n Sudamerica m, America del sud.

South American adj, n sudamericano(a).

southbound ['sauθbaund] adj (gen) diretto(a) a sud; (carriageway) sud inv.

south-east [sauθ'iːst] n sud-est m.

South-East Asia n Asia sudorientale.

southerly ['sʌðəlɪ] adj del sud.

southern ['sʌðən] adj del sud, meridionale; (wall) esposto(a) a sud; **the ~ hemisphere** l'emisfero australe.

South Pole n Polo Sud.

South Sea Islands npl: **the ~** le isole dei Mari del Sud.

South Seas npl: **the ~** i Mari del Sud.

South Vietnam n Vietnam m del Sud.

southward(s) ['sauθwəd(z)] adv verso sud.

south-west [sauθ'wɛst] n sud-ovest m.

souvenir [suːvə'nɪə*] n ricordo, souvenir m inv.

sovereign ['sɔvrɪn] adj, n sovrano(a).

sovereignty ['sɔvrəntɪ] n sovranità.

soviet ['səuvɪət] adj sovietico(a).

Soviet Union n: **the ~** l'Unione f Sovietica.

sow n [sau] scrofa ♦ vt [səu] (pt ~ed, pp sown [səun]) seminare.

soya ['sɔɪə], (US) **soy** [sɔɪ] n: **~ bean** seme m di soia; **~ sauce** salsa di soia.

sozzled ['sɔzld] adj (BRIT col) sbronzo(a).

spa [spɑː] n (resort) stazione f termale; (US: also: **health ~**) centro di cure estetiche.

space [speɪs] n spazio; (room) posto; spazio; (length of time) intervallo ♦ cpd spaziale ♦ vt (also: **~ out**) distanziare; **in a confined ~** in un luogo chiuso; **to clear a ~ for sth** fare posto per qc; **in a short ~ of time** in breve tempo; **(with)in the ~ of an hour/ three generations** nell'arco di un'ora/di tre generazioni.

space bar n (on typewriter) barra spaziatrice.

spacecraft ['speɪskrɑːft] n (pl inv) veicolo spaziale.

spaceman ['speɪsmæn] n astronauta m, cosmonauta m.

spaceship ['speɪsʃɪp] n astronave f, navicella spaziale.

space shuttle n shuttle m inv.

spacesuit ['speɪssuːt] n tuta spaziale.

spacewoman ['speɪswumən] n astronauta f, cosmonauta f.

spacing ['speɪsɪŋ] n spaziatura; **single/ double ~** (TYP etc) spaziatura singola/ doppia.

spacious ['speɪʃəs] adj spazioso(a), ampio(a).

spade [speɪd] n (tool) vanga; pala; (child's) paletta; **~s** npl (CARDS) picche fpl.

spadework ['speɪdwəːk] n (fig) duro lavoro preparatorio.

spaghetti [spə'gɛtɪ] n spaghetti mpl.

Spain [speɪn] n Spagna.

span [spæn] n (of bird, plane) apertura alare; (of arch) campata; (in time) periodo; durata ♦ vt attraversare; (fig) abbracciare.

Spaniard ['spænjəd] n spagnolo/a.

spaniel ['spænjəl] n spaniel m inv.

Spanish ['spænɪʃ] adj spagnolo(a) ♦ n (LING) spagnolo; **the ~** npl gli Spagnoli; **~ omelette** frittata di cipolle, pomodori e peperoni.

spank [spæŋk] vt sculacciare.

spanner ['spænə*] n (BRIT) chiave f inglese.

spar [spɑː*] n asta, palo ♦ vi (BOXING) allenarsi.

spare [spɛə*] adj di riserva, di scorta; (surplus) in più, d'avanzo ♦ n (part) pezzo di ricambio ♦ vt (do without) fare a meno di; (afford to give) concedere; (refrain from hurting, using) risparmiare; **to ~** (surplus) d'avanzo; **there are 2 going** ~ (BRIT) ce ne sono 2 in più; **to ~ no expense** non badare a spese; **can you ~ the time?** ha tempo?; **I've a few minutes to** ~ ho un attimino di tempo; **there is no time to** ~ non c'è tempo da perdere; **can you** ~ **(me) £10?** puoi prestarmi 10 sterline?

spare part n pezzo di ricambio.

spare room n stanza degli ospiti.

spare time n tempo libero.

spare tyre n (AUT) gomma di scorta.

spare wheel n (AUT) ruota di scorta.

sparing ['spɛərɪŋ] adj (amount) scarso(a); (use) parsimonioso(a); **to be ~ with** essere avaro(a) di.

sparingly ['spɛərɪŋlɪ] adv moderatamente.

spark [spɑːk] n scintilla.

spark(ing) plug ['spɑːk(ɪŋ)-] n candela.

sparkle ['spɑːkl] n scintillio, sfavillio ♦ vi scintillare, sfavillare; (bubble) spumeggiare, frizzare.

sparkler ['spɑːklə*] n fuoco d'artificio.

sparkling ['spɑːklɪŋ] adj scintillante, sfavillante; (wine) spumante.

sparring partner ['spɑːrɪŋ-] n sparring partner m inv; (fig) interlocutore abituale in discussioni, dibattiti, tavole rotonde ecc.

sparrow ['spærəu] n passero.

sparse [spɑːs] adj sparso(a), rado(a).

spartan ['spɑːtən] adj (fig) spartano(a).

spasm ['spæzəm] n (MED) spasmo; (fig) accesso, attacco.

spasmodic [spæz'mɔdɪk] adj spasmodico(a); (fig) intermittente.

spastic ['spæstɪk] n spastico/a.

spat [spæt] pt, pp of spit ♦ n (US) battibecco.

spate [speɪt] n (fig): ~ **of** diluvio or fiume m di; **in** ~ (river) in piena.

spatial ['speɪʃəl] adj spaziale.

spatter ['spætə*] vt, vi schizzare.

spatula ['spætjulə] n spatola.

spawn [spɔːn] vt deporre; (pej) produrre ♦ vi deporre le uova ♦ n uova fpl.

SPCA n abbr (US: = Society for the Prevention of Cruelty to Animals) ≈ E.N.P.A. m (= Ente Nazionale per la Protezione degli Animali).

SPCC n abbr (US) = Society for the Prevention of Cruelty to Children.

speak, pt **spoke**, pp **spoken** [spiːk, spəuk, 'spəukn] vt (language) parlare; (truth) dire ♦ vi parlare; **to ~ to sb/of** or **about sth** parlare a qn/di qc; ~ **up!** parli più forte!; **to** ~ **at a conference/in a debate** partecipare ad una conferenza/ad un dibattito; ~**ing!** (on telephone) sono io!; **to** ~ **one's mind** dire quello che si pensa; **he has no money to** ~ **of** non si può proprio

dire che sia ricco.

▶**speak for** vt fus: **to** ~ **for sb** parlare a nome di qn; **that picture is already spoken for** (in shop) quel quadro è già stato venduto.

speaker ['spiːkə*] n (in public) oratore/trice; (also: **loud**~) altoparlante m; (POL): **the S**~ il presidente della Camera dei Comuni (BRIT) or dei Rappresentanti (US); **are you a Welsh** ~? parla gallese?

speaking ['spiːkɪŋ] adj parlante; **Italian-**~ **people** persone che parlano italiano; **to be on** ~ **terms** parlarsi.

spear [spɪə*] n lancia.

spearhead ['spɪəhɛd] n punta di lancia; (MIL) reparto d'assalto ♦ vt (attack etc) condurre.

spearmint ['spɪəmɪnt] n (BOT etc) menta verde.

spec [spɛk] n (BRIT col): **on** ~ sperando bene; **to buy sth on** ~ comprare qc sperando di fare un affare.

special ['spɛʃl] adj speciale ♦ n (train) treno supplementare; **nothing** ~ niente di speciale; **take** ~ **care** siate particolarmente prudenti.

special agent n agente m segreto.

special correspondent n inviato speciale.

special delivery n (POST): **by** ~ per espresso.

special effects npl (CINE) effetti mpl speciali.

specialist ['spɛʃəlɪst] n specialista m/f; **a heart** ~ (MED) un cardiologo.

speciality [spɛʃɪ'ælɪtɪ], (esp US) **specialty** n specialità f inv.

specialize ['spɛʃəlaɪz] vi: **to** ~ **(in)** specializzarsi (in).

specially ['spɛʃəlɪ] adv specialmente, particolarmente.

special offer n (COMM) offerta speciale.

specialty ['spɛʃəltɪ] n (esp US) = **speciality**.

species ['spiːʃiːz] n (pl inv) specie f inv.

specific [spə'sɪfɪk] adj specifico(a); preciso(a); **to be** ~ **to** avere un legame specifico con.

specifically [spə'sɪfɪklɪ] adv (explicitly: state, warn) chiaramente, esplicitamente; (especially: design, intend) appositamente.

specification [spɛsɪfɪ'keɪʃən] n specificazione f; ~**s** npl (of car, machine) dati mpl caratteristici; (for building) dettagli mpl.

specify ['spɛsɪfaɪ] vt specificare, precisare; **unless otherwise specified** salvo indicazioni contrarie.

specimen ['spɛsɪmən] n esemplare m, modello; (MED) campione m.

specimen copy n campione m.

specimen signature n firma depositata.

speck [spɛk] n puntino, macchiolina; (*particle*) granello.

speckled ['spɛkld] adj macchiettato(a).

specs [spɛks] npl (*col*) occhiali mpl.

spectacle ['spɛktəkl] n spettacolo; see also **spectacles**.

spectacle case n (*BRIT*) fodero per gli occhiali.

spectacles ['spɛktəklz] npl (*BRIT*) occhiali mpl.

spectacular [spɛk'tækjulə*] adj spettacolare ♦ n (*CINE etc*) film m inv etc spettacolare.

spectator [spɛk'teɪtə*] n spettatore/trice.

spectator sport n sport m inv come spettacolo.

spectra ['spɛktrə] npl of **spectrum**.

spectre, (*US*) **specter** ['spɛktə*] n spettro.

spectrum, pl **spectra** ['spɛktrəm, -rə] n spettro; (*fig*) gamma.

speculate ['spɛkjuleɪt] vi speculare; (*try to guess*): **to ~ about** fare ipotesi su.

speculation [spɛkju'leɪʃən] n speculazione f; congetture fpl.

speculative ['spɛkjulətɪv] adj speculativo(a).

speculator ['spɛkjuleɪtə*] n speculatore/trice.

sped [spɛd] pt, pp of **speed**.

speech [spiːtʃ] n (*faculty*) parola; (*talk*) discorso; (*manner of speaking*) parlata; (*language*) linguaggio; (*enunciation*) elocuzione f.

speech day n (*BRIT SCOL*) giorno della premiazione.

speech impediment n difetto di pronuncia.

speechless ['spiːtʃlɪs] adj ammutolito(a), muto(a).

speech therapy n cura dei disturbi del linguaggio.

speed [spiːd] n velocità f inv; (*promptness*) prontezza; (*AUT: gear*) marcia ♦ vi (pt, pp **sped** [spɛd]): **to ~ along** procedere velocemente; **the years sped by** gli anni sono volati; (*AUT: exceed ~ limit*) andare a velocità eccessiva; **at ~** (*BRIT*) velocemente; **at full** or **top ~** a tutta velocità; **at a ~ of 70 km/h** a una velocità di 70 km l'ora; **shorthand/typing ~s** numero di parole al minuto in stenografia/dattilografia; **a five-~ gearbox** un cambio a cinque marce.

▶**speed up,** pt, pp **~ed up** vi, vt accelerare.

speedboat ['spiːdbəut] n motoscafo; fuoribordo m inv.

speedily ['spiːdɪlɪ] adv velocemente; prontamente.

speeding ['spiːdɪŋ] n (*AUT*) eccesso di velocità.

speed limit n limite m di velocità.

speedometer [spɪ'dɔmɪtə*] n tachimetro.

speed trap n (*AUT*) *tratto di strada sul quale la polizia controlla la velocità dei veicoli.*

speedway ['spiːdweɪ] n (*SPORT*) pista per motociclismo.

speedy ['spiːdɪ] adj veloce, rapido(a); (*reply*) pronto(a).

speleologist [spɛlɪ'ɔlədʒɪst] n speleologo/a.

spell [spɛl] n (*also:* **magic ~**) incantesimo; (*period of time*) (breve) periodo ♦ vt (pt, pp **spelt** or **~ed** [spɛlt, spɛld]) (*in writing*) scrivere (lettera per lettera); (*aloud*) dire lettera per lettera; (*fig*) significare; **to cast a ~ on sb** fare un incantesimo a qn; **he can't ~** fa errori di ortografia; **how do you ~ your name?** come si scrive il suo nome?; **can you ~ it for me?** me lo può dettare lettera per lettera?

spellbound ['spɛlbaund] adj incantato(a), affascinato(a).

spelling ['spɛlɪŋ] n ortografia.

spelt [spɛlt] pt, pp of **spell**.

spend, pt, pp **spent** [spɛnd, spɛnt] vt (*money*) spendere; (*time, life*) passare; **to ~ time/money/effort on sth** dedicare tempo/soldi/energie a qc.

spending ['spɛndɪŋ] n: **government ~** spesa pubblica.

spending money n denaro per le piccole spese.

spending power n potere m d'acquisto.

spendthrift ['spɛndθrɪft] n spendaccione/a.

spent [spɛnt] pt, pp of **spend** ♦ adj (*patience*) esaurito(a); (*cartridge, bullets, match*) usato(a).

sperm [spəːm] n sperma m.

sperm bank n banca dello sperma.

sperm whale n capodoglio.

spew [spjuː] vt vomitare.

sphere [sfɪə*] n sfera.

spherical ['sfɛrɪkl] adj sferico(a).

sphinx [sfɪŋks] n sfinge f.

spice [spaɪs] n spezia ♦ vt aromatizzare.

spick-and-span ['spɪkən'spæn] adj impeccabile.

spicy ['spaɪsɪ] adj piccante.

spider ['spaɪdə*] n ragno; **~'s web** ragnatela.

spiel [spiːl] n (*col*) tiritera.

spike [spaɪk] n punta; **~s** npl (*SPORT*) scarpe fpl chiodate.

spike heel n (*US*) tacco a spillo.

spiky ['spaɪkɪ] *adj* (*bush, branch*) spinoso(a); (*animal*) ricoperto(a) di aculei.

spill, *pt, pp* **spilt** *or* ~**ed** [spɪl, -t, -d] *vt* versare, rovesciare ♦ *vi* versarsi, rovesciarsi; **to** ~ **the beans** (*col*) vuotare il sacco.
►**spill out** *vi* riversarsi fuori.
►**spill over** *vi*: **to** ~ **over (into)** (*liquid*) versarsi (in); (*crowd*) riversarsi (in).

spillage ['spɪlɪdʒ] *n* (*event*) fuoriuscita; (*substance*) sostanza fuoriuscita.

spin [spɪn] *n* (*revolution of wheel*) rotazione *f*; (*AVIAT*) avvitamento; (*trip in car*) giretto ♦ *vb* (*pt, pp* **spun** [spʌn]) *vt* (*wool etc*) filare; (*wheel*) far girare; (*BRIT: clothes*) mettere nella centrifuga ♦ *vi* girare; **to ·· a yarn** raccontare una storia; **to** ~ **a coin** (*BRIT*) lanciare in aria una moneta.
►**spin out** *vt* far durare.

spina bifida ['spaɪnə'bɪfɪdə] *n* spina bifida.

spinach ['spɪnɪtʃ] *n* spinacio; (*as food*) spinaci *mpl*.

spinal ['spaɪnl] *adj* spinale.

spinal column *n* colonna vertebrale, spina dorsale.

spinal cord *n* midollo spinale.

spindly ['spɪndlɪ] *adj* lungo(a) e sottile, filiforme.

spin doctor *n* (*col*) esperto di comunicazioni responsabile dell'immagine di un partito politico.

spin-dry ['spɪn'draɪ] *vt* asciugare con la centrifuga.

spin-dryer [spɪn'draɪə*] *n* (*BRIT*) centrifuga.

spine [spaɪn] *n* spina dorsale; (*thorn*) spina.

spine-chilling ['spaɪntʃɪlɪŋ] *adj* agghiacciante.

spineless ['spaɪnlɪs] *adj* invertebrato(a), senza spina dorsale; (*fig*) smidollato(a).

spinner ['spɪnə*] *n* (*of thread*) tessitore/trice.

spinning ['spɪnɪŋ] *n* filatura.

spinning top *n* trottola.

spinning wheel *n* filatoio.

spin-off ['spɪnɔf] *n* applicazione *f* secondaria.

spinster ['spɪnstə*] *n* nubile *f*; zitella.

spiral ['spaɪərl] *n* spirale *f* ♦ *adj* a spirale ♦ *vi* (*prices*) salire vertiginosamente; **the inflationary** ~ la spirale dell'inflazione.

spiral staircase *n* scala a chiocciola.

spire ['spaɪə*] *n* guglia.

spirit ['spɪrɪt] *n* (*soul*) spirito, anima; (*ghost*) spirito, fantasma *m*; (*mood*) stato d'animo, umore *m*; (*courage*) coraggio; ~**s** *npl* (*drink*) alcolici *mpl*; **in good** ~**s** di buon umore; **in low** ~**s** triste, abbattuto(a); **community** ~, **public** ~ senso civico.

spirit duplicator *n* duplicatore *m* a spirito.

spirited ['spɪrɪtɪd] *adj* vivace, vigoroso(a); (*horse*) focoso(a).

spirit level *n* livella a bolla (d'aria).

spiritual ['spɪrɪtjuəl] *adj* spirituale ♦ *n* (*also*: **Negro** ~) spiritual *m inv*.

spiritualism ['spɪrɪtjuəlɪzəm] *n* spiritismo.

spit [spɪt] *n* (*for roasting*) spiedo; (*spittle*) sputo; (*saliva*) saliva ♦ *vi* (*pt, pp* **spat** [spæt]) sputare; (*fire, fat*) scoppiettare.

spite [spaɪt] *n* dispetto ♦ *vt* contrariare, far dispetto a; **in** ~ **of** nonostante, malgrado.

spiteful ['spaɪtful] *adj* dispettoso(a); (*tongue, remark*) maligno(a), velenoso(a).

spitroast ['spɪt'rəust] *vt* cuocere allo spiedo.

spitting ['spɪtɪŋ] *n*: "~ **prohibited**" "vietato sputare" ♦ *adj*: **to be the** ~ **image of sb** essere il ritratto vivente *or* sputato di qn.

spittle ['spɪtl] *n* saliva; sputo.

spiv [spɪv] *n* (*BRIT col*) imbroglione *m*.

splash [splæʃ] *n* spruzzo; (*sound*) tonfo; (*of colour*) schizzo ♦ *vt* spruzzare ♦ *vi* (*also*: ~ **about**) sguazzare; **to** ~ **paint on the floor** schizzare il pavimento di vernice.

splashdown ['splæʃdaun] *n* ammaraggio.

splay [spleɪ] *adj*: ~ **footed** che ha i piedi piatti.

spleen [spliːn] *n* (*ANAT*) milza.

splendid ['splendɪd] *adj* splendido(a), magnifico(a).

splendour, (*US*) **splendor** ['splendə*] *n* splendore *m*.

splice [splaɪs] *vt* (*rope*) impiombare; (*wood*) calettare.

splint [splɪnt] *n* (*MED*) stecca.

splinter ['splɪntə*] *n* scheggia ♦ *vi* scheggiarsi.

splinter group *n* gruppo dissidente.

split [splɪt] *n* spaccatura; (*fig: division, quarrel*) scissione *f* ♦ *vb* (*pt, pp* **split**) *vt* spaccare; (*party*) dividere; (*work, profits*) spartire, ripartire ♦ *vi* (*divide*) dividersi; **to do the** ~**s** fare la spaccata; **to** ~ **the difference** dividersi la differenza.
►**split up** *vi* (*couple*) separarsi, rompere; (*meeting*) sciogliersi.

split-level ['splɪtlevl] *adj* (*house*) a piani sfalsati.

split peas *npl* piselli *mpl* secchi spaccati.

split personality *n* doppia personalità.

split second *n* frazione *f* di secondo.

splitting ['splɪtɪŋ] *adj*: **a** ~ **headache** un mal di testa da impazzire.

splutter ['splʌtə*] *vi* farfugliare; sputacchiare.

spoil, *pt, pp* **spoilt** *or* ~**ed** [spɔɪl, -t, -d] *vt* (*damage*) rovinare, guastare; (*mar*) sciupare; (*child*) viziare; (*ballot paper*) rendere nullo(a), invalidare; **to be ~ing for a fight** morire dalla voglia di litigare.

spoils [spɔɪlz] *npl* bottino.

spoilsport ['spɔɪlspɔːt] *n* guastafeste *m/f inv*.

spoilt [spɔɪlt] *pt, pp of* **spoil ♦** *adj* (*child*) viziato(a); (*ballot paper*) nullo(a).

spoke [spəuk] *pt of* **speak ♦** *n* raggio.

spoken ['spəukn] *pp of* **speak**.

spokesman ['spəuksmən], **spokeswoman** [-wumən] *n* portavoce *m/f inv*.

spokesperson ['spəukspɔːsn] *n* portavoce *m/f*.

sponge [spʌndʒ] *n* spugna; (*CULIN: also: ~ cake*) pan *m* di Spagna **♦** *vt* spugnare, pulire con una spugna **♦** *vi*: **to ~ on** *or* (*US*) **off of** scroccare a.

sponge bag *n* (*BRIT*) nécessaire *m inv*.

sponge cake *n* pan *m* di Spagna.

sponger ['spʌndʒə*] *n* (*pej*) parassita *m/f*, scroccone/a.

spongy ['spʌndʒɪ] *adj* spugnoso(a).

sponsor ['spɔnsə*] *n* (*RADIO, TV, SPORT etc*) sponsor *m inv*; (*of enterprise, bill, for fund-raising*) promotore/trice **♦** *vt* sponsorizzare; patrocinare; (*POL: bill*) presentare; **I ~ed him at 3p a mile** (*in fund-raising race*) ho offerto in beneficenza 3 penny per ogni miglio che fa.

sponsorship ['spɔnsəʃɪp] *n* sponsorizzazione *f*; patrocinio.

spontaneity [spɔntə'neɪɪtɪ] *n* spontaneità.

spontaneous [spɔn'teɪnɪəs] *adj* spontaneo(a).

spoof [spuːf] *n* presa in giro, parodia.

spooky ['spuːkɪ] *adj* che fa accapponare la pelle.

spool [spuːl] *n* bobina.

spoon [spuːn] *n* cucchiaio.

spoon-feed ['spuːnfiːd] *vt* nutrire con il cucchiaio; (*fig*) imboccare.

spoonful ['spuːnful] *n* cucchiaiata.

sporadic [spə'rædɪk] *adj* sporadico(a).

sport [spɔːt] *n* sport *m inv*; (*person*) persona di spirito; (*amusement*) divertimento **♦** *vt* sfoggiare; **indoor/outdoor ~s** sport *mpl* al chiuso/all'aria aperta; **to say sth in ~** dire qc per scherzo.

sporting ['spɔːtɪŋ] *adj* sportivo(a); **to give sb a ~ chance** dare a qn una possibilità (di vincere).

sport jacket *n* (*US*) = **sports jacket**.

sports car *n* automobile *f* sportiva.

sports ground *n* campo sportivo.

sports jacket *n* giacca sportiva.

sportsman ['spɔːtsmən] *n* sportivo.

sportsmanship ['spɔːtsmənʃɪp] *n* spirito

sportivo.

sports page *n* pagina sportiva.

sportswear ['spɔːtswɛə*] *n* abiti *mpl* sportivi.

sportswoman ['spɔːtswumən] *n* sportiva.

sporty ['spɔːtɪ] *adj* sportivo(a).

spot [spɔt] *n* punto; (*mark*) macchia; (*dot: on pattern*) pallino; (*pimple*) foruncolo; (*place*) posto; (*also: ~ advertisement*) spot *m inv*; (*small amount*): **a ~ of** un po' di **♦** *vt* (*notice*) individuare, distinguere; **on the ~** sul posto; **to do sth on the ~** fare qc immediatamente *or* lì per lì; **to put sb on the ~** mettere qn in difficoltà; **to come out in ~s** coprirsi di foruncoli.

spot check *n* controllo senza preavviso.

spotless ['spɔtlɪs] *adj* immacolato(a).

spotlight ['spɔtlaɪt] *n* proiettore *m*; (*AUT*) faro ausiliario.

spot-on [spɔt'ɔn] *adj* (*BRIT*) esatto(a).

spot price *n* (*COMM*) prezzo del pronto.

spotted ['spɔtɪd] *adj* macchiato(a); a puntini, a pallini; **~ with** punteggiato(a) di.

spotty ['spɔtɪ] *adj* (*face*) foruncoloso(a).

spouse [spauz] *n* sposo/a.

spout [spaut] *n* (*of jug*) beccuccio; (*of liquid*) zampillo, getto **♦** *vi* zampillare.

sprain [spreɪn] *n* storta, distorsione *f* **♦** *vt*: **to ~ one's ankle** storcersi una caviglia.

sprang [spræŋ] *pt of* **spring**.

sprawl [sprɔːl] *vi* sdraiarsi (in modo scomposto) **♦** *n*: **urban ~** sviluppo urbanistico incontrollato; **to send sb ~ing** mandare qn a gambe all'aria.

spray [spreɪ] *n* spruzzo; (*container*) nebulizzatore *m*, spray *m inv*; (*of flowers*) mazzetto **♦** *cpd* (*deodorant*) spray *inv* **♦** *vt* spruzzare; (*crops*) irrorare.

spread [sprɛd] *n* diffusione *f*; (*distribution*) distribuzione *f*; (*PRESS, TYP: two pages*) doppia pagina; (*: across columns*) articolo a più colonne; (*CULIN*) pasta (da spalmare) **♦** *vb* (*pt, pp* **spread**) *vt* (*cloth*) stendere, distendere; (*butter etc*) spalmare; (*disease, knowledge*) propagare, diffondere **♦** *vi* stendersi, distendersi; spalmarsi; propagarsi, diffondersi; **middle-age ~** pancetta; **repayments will be ~ over 18 months** i versamenti saranno scaglionati lungo un periodo di 18 mesi.

spread-eagled ['sprɛdiːgld] *adj*: **to be** *or* **lie ~** essere disteso(a) a gambe e braccia aperte.

spreadsheet ['sprɛdʃiːt] *n* (*COMPUT*) foglio elettronico.

spree [spriː] *n*: **to go on a ~** fare baldoria.

sprig [sprɪg] *n* ramoscello.

sprightly ['spraɪtlɪ] *adj* vivace.

spring [sprɪŋ] *n* (*leap*) salto, balzo; (*bounciness*) elasticità; (*coiled metal*) molla; (*season*) primavera; (*of water*) sorgente *f* ♦ *vi* (*pt* **sprang**, *pp* **sprung** [spræŋ, sprʌŋ]) saltare, balzare ♦ *vt*: **to ~ a leak** (*pipe etc*) cominciare a perdere; **to walk with a ~ in one's step** camminare con passo elastico; **in ~, in the ~** in primavera; **to ~ from** provenire da; **to ~ into action** entrare (rapidamente) in azione; **he sprang the news on me** mi ha sorpreso con quella notizia.

►**spring up** *vi* (*problem*) presentarsi.

springboard ['sprɪŋbɔːd] *n* trampolino.

spring-clean [sprɪŋ'kliːn] *n* (*also:* **~ing**) grandi pulizie *fpl* di primavera.

spring onion *n* (*BRIT*) cipollina.

spring roll *n* involtino fritto di verdure o carne tipico della cucina cinese.

springtime ['sprɪŋtaɪm] *n* primavera.

springy ['sprɪŋɪ] *adj* elastico(a).

sprinkle ['sprɪŋkl] *vt* spruzzare; spargere; **to ~ water etc on, ~ with water etc** spruzzare dell'acqua *etc* su; **to ~ sugar etc on, ~ with sugar etc** spolverizzare di zucchero *etc*; **~d with** (*fig*) cosparso(a) di.

sprinkler ['sprɪŋklə*] *n* (*for lawn etc*) irrigatore *m*; (*for fire-fighting*) sprinkler *m inv*.

sprinkling ['sprɪŋklɪŋ] *n* (*of water*) qualche goccia; (*of salt, sugar*) pizzico.

sprint [sprɪnt] *n* scatto ♦ *vi* scattare; **the 200-metres ~** i 200 metri piani.

sprinter ['sprɪntə*] *n* velocista *m/f*.

sprite [spraɪt] *n* elfo, folletto.

spritzer ['sprɪtsə*] *n* spritz *m inv*.

sprocket ['sprɔkɪt] *n* (*on printer etc*) dente *m*, rocchetto.

sprout [spraut] *vi* germogliare.

sprouts [sprauts] *npl* (*also:* **Brussels ~**) cavolini *mpl* di Bruxelles.

spruce [spruːs] *n* abete *m* rosso ♦ *adj* lindo(a); azzimato(a).

►**spruce up** *vt* (*tidy*) mettere in ordine; (*smarten up: room etc*) abbellire; **to ~ o.s. up** farsi bello(a).

sprung [sprʌŋ] *pp of* **spring**.

spry [spraɪ] *adj* arzillo(a), sveglio(a).

SPUC *n abbr* (= *Society for the Protection of Unborn Children*) *associazione anti-abortista*.

spun [spʌn] *pt, pp of* **spin**.

spur [spəː*] *n* sperone *m*; (*fig*) sprone *m*, incentivo ♦ *vt* (*also:* **~ on**) spronare; **on the ~ of the moment** lì per lì.

spurious ['spjuərɪəs] *adj* falso(a).

spurn [spəːn] *vt* rifiutare con disprezzo, sdegnare.

spurt [spəːt] *n* getto; (*of energy*) esplosione *f* ♦ *vi* sgorgare; zampillare; **to put in or on a ~** (*runner*) fare uno scatto; (*fig: in work etc*) affrettarsi, sbrigarsi.

sputter ['spʌtə*] *vi* = **splutter**.

spy [spaɪ] *n* spia ♦ *cpd* (*film, story*) di spionaggio ♦ *vi*: **to ~ on** spiare ♦ *vt* (*see*) scorgere.

spying ['spaɪɪŋ] *n* spionaggio.

Sq. *abbr* (*in address*) = **square**.

sq. *abbr* (*MATH etc*) = **square**.

squabble ['skwɔbl] *n* battibecco ♦ *vi* bisticciarsi.

squad [skwɔd] *n* (*MIL*) plotone *m*; (*POLICE*) squadra; **flying ~** (*POLICE*) volante *f*.

squad car *n* (*BRIT POLICE*) automobile *f* della polizia.

squaddie ['skwɔdɪ] *n* (*MIL col*) burba.

squadron ['skwɔdrn] *n* (*MIL*) squadrone *m*; (*AVIAT, NAUT*) squadriglia.

squalid ['skwɔlɪd] *adj* sordido(a).

squall [skwɔːl] *n* burrasca.

squalor ['skwɔlə*] *n* squallore *m*.

squander ['skwɔndə*] *vt* dissipare.

square [skwɛə*] *n* quadrato; (*in town*) piazza; (*US: block of houses*) blocco, isolato; (*instrument*) squadra ♦ *adj* quadrato(a); (*honest*) onesto(a); (*col: ideas, person*) di vecchio stampo ♦ *vt* (*arrange*) regolare; (*MATH*) elevare al quadrato ♦ *vi* (*agree*) accordarsi; **a ~ meal** un pasto abbondante; **2 metres ~** di 2 metri per 2; **1 ~ metre** 1 metro quadrato; **we're back to ~ one** (*fig*) siamo al punto di partenza; **all ~** pari; **to get one's accounts ~** mettere in ordine i propri conti; **I'll ~ it with him** (*col*) sistemo io le cose con lui; **can you ~ it with your conscience?** (*reconcile*) puoi conciliarlo con la tua coscienza?

►**square up** *vi* (*BRIT: settle*) saldare, pagare; **to ~ up with sb** regolare i conti con qn.

square bracket *n* (*TYP*) parentesi *f inv* quadra.

squarely ['skwɛəlɪ] *adv* (*directly*) direttamente; (*honestly, fairly*) onestamente.

square root *n* radice *f* quadrata.

squash [skwɔʃ] *n* (*BRIT: drink*): **lemon/orange ~** sciroppo di limone/arancia; (*vegetable*) zucca; (*SPORT*) squash *m* ♦ *vt* schiacciare.

squat [skwɔt] *adj* tarchiato(a), tozzo(a) ♦ *vi* accovacciarsi; (*on property*) occupare abusivamente.

squatter ['skwɔtə*] *n* occupante *m/f* abusivo(a).

squawk [skwɔːk] *vi* emettere strida rauche.

squeak [skwiːk] *vi* squittire ♦ *n* (*of hinge, wheel etc*) cigolio; (*of shoes*) scricchiolio; (*of mouse etc*) squittio.

squeaky ['skwiːkɪ] *adj* (*col*) cigolante; **to be ~ clean** (*fig*) avere un'immagine pulita.

squeal [skwiːl] *vi* strillare.

squeamish ['skwiːmɪʃ] *adj* schizzinoso(a); disgustato(a).

squeeze [skwiːz] *n* pressione *f*; (*also ECON*) stretta; (*credit* ~) stretta creditizia ♦ *vt* premere; (*hand, arm*) stringere ♦ *vi*: **to ~ in** infilarsi; **to ~ past/under sth** passare vicino/sotto a qc con difficoltà; **a ~ of lemon** una spruzzata di limone.

▶**squeeze out** *vt* spremere.

squelch [skwɛltʃ] *vi* fare ciac; sguazzare.

squib [skwɪb] *n* petardo.

squid [skwɪd] *n* calamaro.

squint [skwɪnt] *vi* essere strabico(a); (*in the sunlight*) strizzare gli occhi ♦ *n*: **he has a ~** è strabico; **to ~ at sth** guardare qc di traverso; (*quickly*) dare un'occhiata a qc.

squire ['skwaɪə*] *n* (*BRIT*) proprietario terriero.

squirm [skwəːm] *vi* contorcersi.

squirrel ['skwɪrəl] *n* scoiattolo.

squirt [skwəːt] *n* schizzo ♦ *vi* schizzare; zampillare.

Sr *abbr* = **senior; sister** (*REL*).

SRC *n abbr* (*BRIT*: = *Students' Representative Council*) comitato di rappresentanza studenti.

Sri Lanka [srɪ'læŋkə] *n* Sri Lanka *m*.

SRN *n abbr* (*BRIT*: = *State Registered Nurse*) infermiera diplomata (*dopo corso triennale*).

SRO *abbr* (*US*: = *standing room only*) solo posti in piedi.

SS *abbr* = **steamship**.

SSA *n abbr* (*US*: = *Social Security Administration*) ≈ Previdenza Sociale.

SST *n abbr* (*US*) = *supersonic transport*.

ST *abbr* (*US*: = *Standard Time*) ora ufficiale.

St *abbr* = **saint; street**.

stab [stæb] *n* (*with knife etc*) pugnalata; (*col*: *try*): **to have a ~ at (doing) sth** provare a fare qc ♦ *vt* pugnalare; **to ~ sb to death** uccidere qn a coltellate.

stabbing ['stæbɪŋ] *n*: **there's been a ~** qualcuno è stato pugnalato ♦ *adj* (*pain, ache*) lancinante.

stability [stə'bɪlɪtɪ] *n* stabilità.

stabilization [steɪbəlaɪ'zeɪʃən] *n*

stabilizzazione *f*.

stabilize ['steɪbəlaɪz] *vt* stabilizzare ♦ *vi* stabilizzarsi.

stabilizer ['steɪbəlaɪzə*] *n* (*AVIAT, NAUT*) stabilizzatore *m*.

stable ['steɪbl] *n* (*for horses*) scuderia; (*for cattle*) stalla ♦ *adj* stabile; **riding ~s** maneggio.

staccato [stə'kɑːtəu] *adv* in modo staccato ♦ *adj* (*MUS*) staccato(a); (*sound*) scandito(a).

stack [stæk] *n* catasta, pila; (*col*) mucchio, sacco ♦ *vt* accatastare, ammucchiare; **there's ~s of time to finish it** (*BRIT col*) abbiamo un sacco di tempo per finirlo.

stadium ['steɪdɪəm] *n* stadio.

staff [stɑːf] *n* (*work force: gen*) personale *m*; (: *BRIT: SCOL*) personale insegnante; (: *servants*) personale di servizio; (*MIL*) stato maggiore; (*stick*) bastone *m* ♦ *vt* fornire di personale.

staffroom ['stɑːfruːm] *n* sala dei professori.

Staffs *abbr* (*BRIT*) = **Staffordshire**.

stag [stæg] *n* cervo; (*BRIT STOCK EXCHANGE*) rialzista *m/f* su nuove emissioni.

stage [steɪdʒ] *n* (*platform*) palco; (*in theatre*) palcoscenico; (*profession*): **the ~** il teatro, la scena; (*point*) fase *f*, stadio ♦ *vt* (*play*) allestire, mettere in scena; (*demonstration*) organizzare; (*fig: perform: recovery etc*) effettuare; **in ~s** per gradi; a tappe; **in the early/final ~s** negli stadi iniziali/finali; **to go through a difficult ~** attraversare un periodo difficile.

stagecoach ['steɪdʒkəutʃ] *n* diligenza.

stage door *n* ingresso degli artisti.

stage fright *n* paura del pubblico.

stagehand ['steɪdʒhænd] *n* macchinista *m*.

stage-manage ['steɪdʒmænɪdʒ] *vt* allestire le scene per; montare.

stage manager *n* direttore *m* di scena.

stagger ['stægə*] *vi* barcollare ♦ *vt* (*person*) sbalordire; (*hours, holidays*) scaglionare.

staggering ['stægərɪŋ] *adj* (*amazing*) incredibile, sbalorditivo(a).

staging post ['steɪdʒɪŋ-] *n* passaggio obbligato.

stagnant ['stægnənt] *adj* stagnante.

stagnate [stæg'neɪt] *vi* (*also fig*) stagnare.

stagnation [stæg'neɪʃən] *n* stagnazione *f*, ristagno.

stag night, stag party *n* festa di addio al celibato.

staid [steɪd] *adj* posato(a), serio(a).

stain [steɪn] *n* macchia; (*colouring*) colorante *m* ♦ *vt* macchiare; (*wood*) tingere.

stained glass window ['steɪnd-] n
vetrata.

stainless ['steɪnlɪs] adj (steel) inossidabile.

stain remover n smacchiatore m.

stair [stɛə*] n (step) gradino; ~s npl (flight of ~s) scale fpl, scala.

staircase ['stɛəkeɪs], **stairway** ['stɛəweɪ] n scale fpl, scala.

stairwell ['stɛəwɛl] n tromba delle scale.

stake [steɪk] n palo, piolo; (BETTING) puntata, scommessa ♦ vt (bet) scommettere; (risk) rischiare; (also: ~ out: area) delimitare con paletti; **to be at ~** essere in gioco; **to have a ~ in sth** avere un interesse in qc; **to ~ a claim (to sth)** rivendicare (qc).

stakeout ['steɪkaut] n sorveglianza.

stalactite ['stæləktaɪt] n stalattite f.

stalagmite ['stæləgmaɪt] n stalagmite f.

stale [steɪl] adj (bread) raffermo(a), stantio(a); (beer) svaporato(a); (smell) di chiuso.

stalemate ['steɪlmeɪt] n stallo; (fig) punto morto.

stalk [stɔːk] n gambo, stelo ♦ vt inseguire ♦ vi camminare impettito(a).

stall [stɔːl] n (BRIT: in street, market etc) bancarella; (in stable) box m inv di stalla ♦ vt (AUT) far spegnere ♦ vi (AUT) spegnersi, fermarsi; (fig) temporeggiare; ~s npl (BRIT: in cinema, theatre) platea; **newspaper/flower ~** chiosco del giornalaio/del fioraio.

stallholder ['stɔːlhəuldə*] n (BRIT) bancarellista m/f.

stallion ['stæljən] n stallone m.

stalwart ['stɔːlwət] n membro fidato.

stamen ['steɪmɛn] n stame m.

stamina ['stæmɪnə] n vigore m, resistenza.

stammer ['stæmə*] n balbuzie f ♦ vi balbettare.

stamp [stæmp] n (postage ~) francobollo; (implement) timbro; (mark, also fig) marchio, impronta; (on document) bollo; timbro ♦ vi (also: ~ one's foot) battere il piede ♦ vt battere; (letter) affrancare; (mark with a ~) timbrare; **~ed addressed envelope (sae)** busta affrancata per la risposta.

▶**stamp out** vt (fire) estinguere; (crime) eliminare; (opposition) soffocare.

stamp album n album m inv per francobolli.

stamp collecting n filatelia.

stamp duty n (BRIT) bollo.

stampede [stæm'piːd] n fuggi fuggi m inv; (of cattle) fuga precipitosa.

stamp machine n distributore m

automatico di francobolli.

stance [stæns] n posizione f.

stand [stænd] n (position) posizione f; (MIL) resistenza; (structure) supporto, sostegno; (at exhibition) stand m inv; (at market) bancarella; (booth) chiosco; (SPORT) tribuna; (also: music ~) leggìo m ♦ vb (pt, pp **stood** [stud]) vi stare in piedi; (rise) alzarsi in piedi; (be placed) trovarsi ♦ vt (place) mettere, porre; (tolerate, withstand) resistere, sopportare; **to make a ~** prendere posizione; **to take a ~ on an issue** prendere posizione su un problema; **to ~ for parliament** (BRIT) presentarsi come candidato (per il parlamento); **to ~ guard** or **watch** (MIL) essere di guardia; **it ~s to reason** è logico; **as things ~** stando così le cose; **to ~ sb a drink/meal** offrire da bere/un pranzo a qn; **I can't ~ him** non lo sopporto.

▶**stand aside** vi farsi da parte, scostarsi.

▶**stand by** vi (be ready) tenersi pronto(a) ♦ vt fus (opinion) sostenere.

▶**stand down** vi (withdraw) ritirarsi; (LAW) lasciare il banco dei testimoni.

▶**stand for** vt fus (signify) rappresentare, significare; (tolerate) sopportare, tollerare.

▶**stand in for** vt fus sostituire.

▶**stand out** vi (be prominent) spiccare.

▶**stand up** vi (rise) alzarsi in piedi.

▶**stand up for** vt fus difendere.

▶**stand up to** vt fus tener testa a, resistere a.

stand-alone ['stændələun] adj (COMPUT) stand-alone inv.

standard ['stændəd] n modello, standard m inv; (level) livello; (flag) stendardo ♦ adj (size etc) normale, standard inv; (practice) normale; (model) di serie; ~s npl (morals) principi mpl, valori mpl; **to be** or **come up to ~** rispondere ai requisiti; **below** or **not up to ~** (work) mediocre; **to apply a double ~** usare metri diversi (nel giudicare or fare etc); **~ of living** livello di vita.

standardization [stændədaɪ'zeɪʃən] n standardizzazione f.

standardize ['stændədaɪz] vt normalizzare, standardizzare.

standard lamp n (BRIT) lampada a stelo.

standard time n ora ufficiale.

stand-by ['stændbaɪ] n riserva, sostituto; **to be on ~** (gen) tenersi pronto(a); (doctor) essere di guardia; **a ~ ticket** un biglietto standby; **to fly ~** essere in lista d'attesa per un volo.

stand-by generator *n* generatore *m* d'emergenza.
stand-by passenger *n* (*AVIAT*) passeggero/a in lista d'attesa.
stand-by ticket *n* (*AVIAT*) biglietto senza garanzia.
stand-in ['stændɪn] *n* sostituto/a; (*CINE*) controfigura.
standing ['stændɪŋ] *adj* diritto(a), in piedi; (*permanent: committee*) permanente; (: *rule*) fisso(a); (: *army*) regolare; (*grievance*) continuo(a); (*duration*): **of 6 months'** ~ che dura da 6 mesi ♦ *n* rango, condizione *f*, posizione *f*; **it's a** ~ **joke** è diventato proverbiale; **he was given a** ~ **ovation** tutti si alzarono per applaudirlo; **a man of some** ~ un uomo di una certa importanza.
standing committee *n* commissione *f* permanente.
standing order *n* (*BRIT: at bank*) ordine *m* di pagamento (permanente); ~**s** *npl* (*MIL*) regolamento.
standing room *n* posto all'impiedi.
stand-off ['stændɔf] *n* (*esp US: stalemate*) situazione *f* di stallo.
standoffish [stænd'ɔfɪʃ] *adj* scostante, freddo(a).
standpat ['stændpæt] *adj* (*US*) irremovibile.
standpipe ['stændpaɪp] *n* fontanella.
standpoint ['stændpɔɪnt] *n* punto di vista.
standstill ['stændstɪl] *n*: **at a** ~ fermo(a); (*fig*) a un punto morto; **to come to a** ~ fermarsi; giungere a un punto morto.
stank [stæŋk] *pt of* stink.
stanza ['stænzə] *n* stanza (*poesia*).
staple ['steɪpl] *n* (*for papers*) graffetta; (*chief product*) prodotto principale ♦ *adj* (*food etc*) di base; (*crop, industry*) principale ♦ *vt* cucire.
stapler ['steɪplə*] *n* cucitrice *f*.
star [stɑː*] *n* stella; (*celebrity*) divo/a; (*principal actor*) vedette *f inv* ♦ *vi*: **to** ~ **(in)** essere il (*or* la) protagonista (di) ♦ *vt* (*CINE*) essere interpretato(a) da; **four-~ hotel** ≈ albergo di prima categoria; **2-~ petrol** (*BRIT*) ≈ benzina normale; **4-~ petrol** (*BRIT*) ≈ super *f*.
star attraction *n* numero principale.
starboard ['stɑːbəd] *n* dritta; **to** ~ a dritta.
starch [stɑːtʃ] *n* amido.
starched ['stɑːtʃt] *adj* (*collar*) inamidato(a).
starchy ['stɑːtʃɪ] *adj* (*food*) ricco(a) di amido.
stardom ['stɑːdəm] *n* celebrità.
stare [stɛə*] *n* sguardo fisso ♦ *vi*: **to** ~ **at** fissare.
starfish ['stɑːfɪʃ] *n* stella di mare.

stark [stɑːk] *adj* (*bleak*) desolato(a); (*simplicity, colour*) austero(a); (*reality, poverty, truth*) crudo(a) ♦ *adv*: ~ **naked** completamente nudo(a).
starkers ['stɑːkəz] *adj*: **to be** ~ (*BRIT col*) essere nudo(a) come un verme.
starlet ['stɑːlɪt] *n* (*CINE*) stellina.
starlight ['stɑːlaɪt] *n*: **by** ~ alla luce delle stelle.
starling ['stɑːlɪŋ] *n* storno.
starlit ['stɑːlɪt] *adj* stellato(a).
starry ['stɑːrɪ] *adj* stellato(a).
starry-eyed [stɑːrɪ'aɪd] *adj* (*idealistic, gullible*) ingenuo(a); (*from wonder*) meravigliato(a).
Stars and Stripes *npl*: **the** ~ la bandiera a stelle e strisce.
star sign *n* segno zodiacale.
star-studded ['stɑːstʌdɪd] *adj*: **a** ~ **cast** un cast di attori famosi.
start [stɑːt] *n* inizio; (*of race*) partenza; (*sudden movement*) sobbalzo; (*advantage*) vantaggio ♦ *vt* cominciare, iniziare; (*found: business, newspaper*) fondare, creare ♦ *vi* cominciare; (*on journey*) partire, mettersi in viaggio; (*jump*) sobbalzare; **to** ~ **doing sth** (in)cominciare a fare qc; **at the** ~ all'inizio; **for a** ~ tanto per cominciare; **to make an early** ~ partire di buon'ora; **to** ~ **(off) with ...** (*firstly*) per prima cosa ...; (*at the beginning*) all'inizio; **to** ~ **a fire** provocare un incendio.
▶**start off** *vi* cominciare; (*leave*) partire.
▶**start over** *vi* (*US*) ricominciare.
▶**start up** *vi* cominciare; (*car*) avviarsi ♦ *vt* iniziare; (*car*) avviare.
starter ['stɑːtə*] *n* (*AUT*) motorino d'avviamento; (*SPORT: official*) starter *m inv*; (: *runner, horse*) partente *m/f*; (*BRIT CULIN*) primo piatto.
starting handle ['stɑːtɪŋ-] *n* (*BRIT*) manovella d'avviamento.
starting point *n* punto di partenza.
starting price *n* prezzo *m* base *inv*.
startle ['stɑːtl] *vt* far trasalire.
startling ['stɑːtlɪŋ] *adj* sorprendente, sbalorditivo(a).
star turn *n* (*BRIT*) attrazione *f* principale.
starvation [stɑː'veɪʃən] *n* fame *f*, inedia; **to die of** ~ morire d'inedia.
starve [stɑːv] *vi* morire di fame; soffrire la fame ♦ *vt* far morire di fame, affamare; **I'm starving** muoio di fame.
stash [stæʃ] *vt*: **to** ~ **sth away** (*col*) nascondere qc.
state [steɪt] *n* stato; (*pomp*): **in** ~ in pompa ♦ *vt* dichiarare, affermare; annunciare;

to be in a ~ essere agitato(a); **the** ~ **of the art** il livello di tecnologia (or cultura etc); ~ **of emergency** stato di emergenza; ~ **of mind** stato d'animo.

state control n controllo statale.

stated ['steɪtɪd] adj fissato(a), stabilito(a).

State Department n (US) Dipartimento di Stato, ≈ Ministero degli Esteri.

state education n (BRIT) istruzione f pubblica or statale.

stateless ['steɪtlɪs] adj apolide.

stately ['steɪtlɪ] adj maestoso(a), imponente.

stately home n residenza nobiliare (d'interesse storico o artistico spesso aperta al pubblico).

statement ['steɪtmənt] n dichiarazione f; (LAW) deposizione f; (FINANCE) rendiconto; **official** ~ comunicato ufficiale; ~ **of account, bank** ~ estratto conto.

state-owned ['steɪt'əund] adj statalizzato(a).

States [steɪts] npl: **the** ~ (USA) gli Stati Uniti.

state school n scuola statale.

statesman ['steɪtsmən] n statista m.

static ['stætɪk] n (RADIO) scariche fpl ♦ adj statico(a); ~ **electricity** elettricità statica.

station ['steɪʃən] n stazione f; (rank) rango, condizione f ♦ vt collocare, disporre; **action** ~s posti mpl di combattimento; **to be** ~**ed in** (MIL) essere di stanza in.

stationary ['steɪʃənərɪ] adj fermo(a), immobile.

stationer ['steɪʃənə*] n cartolaio/a; ~**'s shop** cartoleria.

stationery ['steɪʃənərɪ] n articoli mpl di cancelleria; (writing paper) carta da lettere.

station master n (RAIL) capostazione m.

station wagon n (US) giardinetta.

statistic [stə'tɪstɪk] n statistica; see also **statistics**.

statistical [stə'tɪstɪkəl] adj statistico(a).

statistics [stə'tɪstɪks] n (science) statistica.

statue ['stætjuː] n statua.

statuesque [stætju'ɛsk] adj statuario(a).

statuette [stætju'ɛt] n statuetta.

stature ['stætʃə*] n statura.

status ['steɪtəs] n posizione f, condizione f sociale; (prestige) prestigio; (legal, marital) stato.

status quo [-'kwəu] n: **the** ~ lo statu quo.

status symbol n simbolo di prestigio.

statute ['stætjuːt] n legge f; ~**s** npl (of club etc) statuto.

statute book n codice m.

statutory ['stætjutərɪ] adj stabilito(a) dalla legge, statutario(a); ~ **meeting** (COMM) assemblea ordinaria.

staunch [stɔːntʃ] adj fidato(a), leale ♦ vt (flow) arrestare; (blood) arrestare il flusso di.

stave [steɪv] n (MUS) rigo ♦ vt: **to** ~ **off** (attack) respingere; (threat) evitare.

stay [steɪ] n (period of time) soggiorno, permanenza ♦ vi rimanere; (reside) alloggiare, stare; (spend some time) trattenersi, soggiornare; ~ **of execution** (LAW) sospensione f dell'esecuzione; **to** ~ **put** non muoversi; **to** ~ **with friends** stare presso amici; **to** ~ **the night** passare la notte.

▶**stay behind** vi restare indietro.

▶**stay in** vi (at home) stare in casa.

▶**stay on** vi restare, rimanere.

▶**stay out** vi (of house) rimanere fuori (di casa); (strikers) continuare lo sciopero.

▶**stay up** vi (at night) rimanere alzato(a).

staying power ['steɪɪŋ-] n capacità di resistenza.

STD n abbr (BRIT: = subscriber trunk dialling) teleselezione f; (= sexually transmitted disease) malattia venerea.

stead [stɛd] n (BRIT): **in sb's** ~ al posto di qn; **to stand sb in good** ~ essere utile a qn.

steadfast ['stɛdfɑːst] adj fermo(a), risoluto(a).

steadily ['stɛdɪlɪ] adv continuamente; (walk) con passo sicuro.

steady ['stɛdɪ] adj stabile, solido(a), fermo(a); (regular) costante; (boyfriend etc) fisso(a); (person) calmo(a), tranquillo(a) ♦ vt stabilizzare; calmare; **to** ~ **o.s.** ritrovare l'equilibrio.

steak [steɪk] n (meat) bistecca; (fish) trancia.

steakhouse ['steɪkhaus] n ristorante specializzato in bistecche.

steal, pt stole, pp stolen [stiːl, stəul, 'stəuln] vt rubare ♦ vi (thieve) rubare.

▶**steal away, steal off** vi svignarsela, andarsene alla chetichella.

stealth [stɛlθ] n: **by** ~ furtivamente.

stealthy ['stɛlθɪ] adj furtivo(a).

steam [stiːm] n vapore m ♦ vt trattare con vapore; (CULIN) cuocere a vapore ♦ vi fumare; (ship): **to** ~ **along** filare; **to let off** ~ (fig) sfogarsi; **under one's own** ~ (fig) da solo, con i propri mezzi; **to run out of** ~ (fig: person) non farcela più.

▶**steam up** vi (window) appannarsi; **to get** ~**ed up about sth** (fig) andare in bestia per qc.

steam engine *n* macchina a vapore; (*RAIL*) locomotiva a vapore.

steamer ['sti:mə*] *n* piroscafo, vapore *m*; (*CULIN*) pentola a vapore.

steam iron *n* ferro a vapore.

steamroller ['sti:mrəulə*] *n* rullo compressore.

steamship ['sti:mʃɪp] *n* piroscafo, vapore *m*.

steamy ['sti:mɪ] *adj* pieno(a) di vapore; (*window*) appannato(a).

steed [sti:d] *n* (*literary*) corsiero, destriero.

steel [sti:l] *n* acciaio ♦ *cpd* di acciaio.

steel band *n* banda di strumenti a percussione (*tipica dei Caribi*).

steel industry *n* industria dell'acciaio.

steel mill *n* acciaieria.

steelworks ['sti:lwə:ks] *n* acciaieria.

steely ['sti:lɪ] *adj* (*determination*) inflessibile; (*gaze*) duro(a); (*eyes*) freddo(a) come l'acciaio.

steep [sti:p] *adj* ripido(a), scosceso(a); (*price*) eccessivo(a) ♦ *vt* inzuppare; (*washing*) mettere a mollo.

steeple ['sti:pl] *n* campanile *m*.

steeplechase ['sti:pltʃeɪs] *n* corsa a ostacoli, steeplechase *m inv*.

steeplejack ['sti:pldʒæk] *n* chi ripara campanili e ciminiere.

steer [stɪə*] *n* manzo ♦ *vt* (*ship*) governare; (*car*) guidare ♦ *vi* (*NAUT: person*) governare; (: *ship*) rispondere al timone; (*car*) guidarsi; **to** ~ **clear of sb/sth** (*fig*) tenersi alla larga da qn/qc.

steering ['stɪərɪŋ] *n* (*AUT*) sterzo.

steering column *n* piantone *m* dello sterzo.

steering committee *n* comitato direttivo.

steering wheel *n* volante *m*.

stem [stɛm] *n* (*of flower, plant*) stelo; (*of tree*) fusto; (*of glass*) gambo; (*of fruit, leaf*) picciolo ♦ *vt* contenere, arginare.

▶**stem from** *vt fus* provenire da, derivare da.

stench [stɛntʃ] *n* puzzo, fetore *m*.

stencil ['stɛnsl] *n* (*of metal, cardboard*) stampino, mascherina; (*in typing*) matrice *f*.

stenographer [stɛ'nɔgrəfə*] *n* (*US*) stenografo/a.

stenography [stɛ'nɔgrəfɪ] *n* (*US*) stenografia.

step [stɛp] *n* passo; (*stair*) gradino, scalino; (*action*) mossa, azione *f* ♦ *vi*: **to** ~ **forward** fare un passo avanti; ~**s** *npl* (*BRIT*) = **stepladder**; ~ **by** ~ un passo dietro l'altro; (*fig*) poco a poco; **to be in/out of** ~ **with** (*also fig*) stare/non stare al passo con.

▶**step down** *vi* (*fig*) ritirarsi.

▶**step in** *vi* fare il proprio ingresso.

▶**step off** *vt fus* scendere da.

▶**step over** *vt fus* scavalcare.

▶**step up** *vt* aumentare; intensificare.

step aerobics *n* step *m inv*.

stepbrother ['stɛpbrʌðə*] *n* fratellastro.

stepchild ['stɛptʃaɪld] *n* figliastro/a.

stepdaughter ['stɛpdɔ:tə*] *n* figliastra.

stepfather ['stɛpfɑ:ðə*] *n* patrigno.

stepladder ['stɛplædə*] *n* scala a libretto.

stepmother ['stɛpmʌðə*] *n* matrigna.

stepping stone ['stɛpɪŋ-] *n* pietra di un guado; (*fig*) trampolino.

step Reebok ® [-'ri:bɔk] *n* step *m inv*.

stepsister ['stɛpsɪstə*] *n* sorellastra.

stepson ['stɛpsʌn] *n* figliastro.

stereo ['stɛrɪəu] *n* (*system*) sistema *m* stereofonico; (*record player*) stereo *m inv* ♦ *adj* (*also*: ~**phonic**) stereofonico(a); **in** ~ in stereofonia.

stereotype ['stɪərɪətaɪp] *n* stereotipo.

sterile ['stɛraɪl] *adj* sterile.

sterility [stɛ'rɪlɪtɪ] *n* sterilità.

sterilization [stɛrɪlaɪ'zeɪʃən] *n* sterilizzazione *f*.

sterilize ['stɛrɪlaɪz] *vt* sterilizzare.

sterling ['stə:lɪŋ] *adj* (*gold, silver*) di buona lega; (*fig*) autentico(a), genuino(a) ♦ *n* (*ECON*) (lira) sterlina; **a pound** ~ una lira sterlina.

sterling area *n* area della sterlina.

stern [stə:n] *adj* severo(a) ♦ *n* (*NAUT*) poppa.

sternum ['stə:nəm] *n* sterno.

steroid ['stɛrɔɪd] *n* steroide *m*.

stethoscope ['stɛθəskəup] *n* stetoscopio.

stevedore ['sti:vɪdɔ:*] *n* scaricatore *m* di porto.

stew [stju:] *n* stufato ♦ *vt, vi* cuocere in umido; ~**ed tea** *tè lasciato troppo in infusione*; ~**ed fruit** frutta cotta.

steward ['stju:əd] *n* (*AVIAT, NAUT, RAIL*) steward *m inv*; (*in club etc*) dispensiere *m*; (*shop* ~) rappresentante *m/f* sindacale.

stewardess ['stju:ədɛs] *n* assistente *f* di volo, hostess *f inv*.

stewardship ['stju:ədʃɪp] *n* amministrazione *f*.

stewing steak ['stju:ɪŋ-], (*US*) **stew meat** *n* carne *f* (di manzo) per stufato.

St. Ex. *abbr* = **stock exchange**.

stg *abbr* = **sterling**.

stick [stɪk] *n* bastone *m*; (*of rhubarb, celery*) gambo ♦ *vb* (*pt, pp* **stuck** [stʌk]) *vt* (*glue*) attaccare; (*thrust*): **to** ~ **sth into** conficcare *or* piantare *or* infiggere qc in; (*col*: *put*) ficcare; (: *tolerate*) sopportare

♦ vi conficcarsi; tenere; (remain) restare, rimanere; (get jammed: door, lift) bloccarsi; to ~ to (one's word, promise) mantenere; (principles) tener fede a; to get hold of the wrong end of the ~ (fig) capire male; it stuck in my mind mi è rimasto in mente.

►**stick around** vi (col) restare, fermarsi.

►**stick out, stick up** vi sporgere, spuntare ♦ vt: to ~ it out (col) tener duro.

►**stick up for** vt fus difendere.

sticker ['stɪkə*] n cartellino adesivo.

sticking plaster ['stɪkɪŋ-] n cerotto adesivo.

sticking point n (fig) punto di stallo, impasse f inv.

stickleback ['stɪklbæk] n spinarello.

stickler ['stɪklə*] n: to be a ~ for essere pignolo(a) su, tenere molto a.

stick-on ['stɪkɔn] adj (label) adesivo(a).

stick shift n (US AUT) cambio manuale.

stick-up ['stɪkʌp] n (col) rapina a mano armata.

sticky ['stɪkɪ] adj attaccaticcio(a), vischioso(a); (label) adesivo(a).

stiff [stɪf] adj rigido(a), duro(a); (muscle) legato(a), indolenzito(a); (difficult) difficile, arduo(a); (cold: manner etc) freddo(a), formale; (strong) forte; (high: price) molto alto(a); to be or feel ~ (person) essere or sentirsi indolenzito; to have a ~ neck/back avere il torcicollo/mal di schiena; to keep a ~ upper lip (BRIT fig) conservare il sangue freddo.

stiffen ['stɪfn] vt irrigidire; rinforzare ♦ vi irrigidirsi; indurirsi.

stiffness ['stɪfnɪs] n rigidità; indolenzimento; difficoltà; freddezza.

stifle ['staɪfl] vt soffocare.

stifling ['staɪflɪŋ] adj (heat) soffocante.

stigma, pl (BOT, MED) ~ta, (fig) ~s ['stɪgmə, stɪg'mɑːtə] n stigma m.

stigmata [stig'mɑːtə] npl (REL) stigmate fpl.

stile [staɪl] n cavalcasiepe m; cavalcasteccato.

stiletto [stɪ'lɛtəu] n (also: ~ heel) tacco a spillo.

still [stɪl] adj fermo(a); (quiet) silenzioso(a); (orange juice etc) non gassato(a) ♦ adv (up to this time, even) ancora; (nonetheless) tuttavia, ciò nonostante ♦ n (CINE) fotogramma m; keep ~! stai fermo!; he ~ hasn't arrived non è ancora arrivato.

stillborn ['stɪlbɔːn] adj nato(a) morto(a).

still life n natura morta.

stilt [stɪlt] n trampolo; (pile) palo.

stilted ['stɪltɪd] adj freddo(a), formale; artificiale.

stimulant ['stɪmjulənt] n stimolante m.

stimulate ['stɪmjuleɪt] vt stimolare.

stimulating ['stɪmjuleɪtɪŋ] adj stimolante.

stimulation [stɪmju'leɪʃən] n stimolazione f.

stimulus, pl **stimuli** ['stɪmjuləs, 'stɪmjulaɪ] n stimolo.

sting [stɪŋ] n puntura; (organ) pungiglione m; (col) trucco ♦ vt (pt, pp stung [stʌŋ]) pungere ♦ vi bruciare; my eyes are ~ing mi bruciano gli occhi.

stingy ['stɪndʒɪ] adj spilorcio(a), tirchio(a).

stink [stɪŋk] n fetore m, puzzo ♦ vi (pt stank, pp stunk [stæŋk, stʌŋk]) puzzare.

stinker ['stɪŋkə*] n (col) porcheria; (person) fetente m/f.

stinking ['stɪŋkɪŋ] adj (col): a ~ ... uno schifo di ..., un(a) maledetto(a) ...; ~ rich ricco(a) da far paura.

stint [stɪnt] n lavoro, compito ♦ vi: to ~ on lesinare su.

stipend ['staɪpɛnd] n stipendio, congrua.

stipendiary [staɪ'pɛndɪərɪ] adj: ~ magistrate magistrato stipendiato.

stipulate ['stɪpjuleɪt] vt stipulare.

stipulation [stɪpju'leɪʃən] n stipulazione f.

stir [stɔː*] n agitazione f, clamore m ♦ vt rimescolare; (move) smuovere, agitare ♦ vi muoversi; to give sth a ~ mescolare qc; to cause a ~ fare scalpore.

►**stir up** vt provocare, suscitare.

stir-fry ['stɔː'fraɪ] vt saltare in padella ♦ n pietanza al salto.

stirring ['stɔːrɪŋ] adj eccitante; commovente.

stirrup ['stɪrəp] n staffa.

stitch [stɪtʃ] n (SEWING) punto; (KNITTING) maglia; (MED) punto (di sutura); (pain) fitta ♦ vt cucire, attaccare; suturare.

stoat [stəut] n ermellino.

stock [stɔk] n riserva, provvista; (COMM) giacenza, stock m inv; (AGR) bestiame m; (CULIN) brodo; (FINANCE) titoli mpl, azioni fpl; (RAIL: also: rolling ~) materiale m rotabile; (descent, origin) stirpe f ♦ adj (fig: reply etc) consueto(a); solito(a), classico(a); (greeting) usuale; (COMM: goods, size) standard inv ♦ vt (have in stock) avere, vendere; well-~ed ben fornito(a); to have sth in ~ avere qc in magazzino; out of ~ esaurito(a); to take ~ (fig) fare il punto; ~s and shares valori mpl di borsa; government ~ titoli di Stato.

►**stock up** vi: to ~ up (with) fare provvista (di).

stockade [stɔ'keɪd] n palizzata.

stockbroker ['stɔkbrəukə*] n agente m di cambio.

stock control n gestione f magazzino.

stock cube n (*BRIT CULIN*) dado.
stock exchange n Borsa (valori).
stockholder ['stɔkhəuldə*] n (*FINANCE*) azionista *m/f*.
Stockholm ['stɔkhəum] n Stoccolma.
stocking ['stɔkɪŋ] n calza.
stock-in-trade ['stɔkɪn'treɪd] n (*fig*): **it's his** ~ è la sua specialità.
stockist ['stɔkɪst] n (*BRIT*) fornitore m.
stock market n (*BRIT*) Borsa, mercato finanziario.
stock phrase n cliché m inv.
stockpile ['stɔkpaɪl] n riserva ♦ vt accumulare riserve di.
stockroom ['stɔkrum] n magazzino.
stocktaking ['stɔkteɪkɪŋ] n (*BRIT COMM*) inventario.
stocky ['stɔkɪ] adj tarchiato(a), tozzo(a).
stodgy ['stɔdʒɪ] adj pesante, indigesto(a).
stoic ['stəuɪk] n stoico/a.
stoical ['stəuɪkəl] adj stoico(a).
stoke [stəuk] vt alimentare.
stoker ['stəukə*] n fochista m.
stole [stəul] pt of **steal** ♦ n stola.
stolen ['stəuln] pp of **steal**.
stolid ['stɔlɪd] adj impassibile.
stomach ['stʌmək] n stomaco; (*abdomen*) ventre m ♦ vt sopportare, digerire.
stomach ache n mal m di stomaco.
stomach pump n pompa gastrica.
stomach ulcer n ulcera allo stomaco.
stomp [stɔmp] vi: **to** ~ **in/out** etc entrare/uscire etc con passo pesante.
stone [stəun] n pietra; (*pebble*) sasso, ciottolo; (*in fruit*) nocciolo; (*MED*) calcolo; (*BRIT: weight*) = 6.348 kg.; **14 libbre** ♦ cpd di pietra ♦ vt lapidare; **within a** ~'s **throw of the station** a due passi dalla stazione.
Stone Age n: **the** ~ l'età della pietra.
stone-cold [stəun'kəuld] adj gelido(a).
stoned [stəund] adj (*col: drunk*) sbronzo(a); (*on drugs*) fuori inv.
stone-deaf [stəun'dɛf] adj sordo(a) come una campana.
stonemason ['stəunmeɪsn] n scalpellino.
stonewall [stəun'wɔːl] vi fare ostruzionismo ♦ vt ostacolare.
stonework ['stəunwəːk] n muratura.
stony ['stəunɪ] adj pietroso(a), sassoso(a).
stood [stud] pt, pp of **stand**.
stooge [stuːdʒ] n (*col*) tirapiedi *m/f* inv.
stool [stuːl] n sgabello.
stoop [stuːp] vi (*also*: **have a** ~) avere una curvatura; (*bend*) chinarsi, curvarsi; **to** ~ **to sth/doing sth** abbassarsi a qc/a fare qc.
stop [stɔp] n arresto; (*stopping place*) fermata; (*in punctuation*) punto ♦ vt

arrestare, fermare; (*break off*) interrompere; (*also*: **put a** ~ **to**) porre fine a; (*prevent*) impedire ♦ vi fermarsi; (*rain, noise etc*) cessare, finire; **to** ~ **doing sth** cessare or finire di fare qc; **to** ~ **sb (from) doing sth** impedire a qn di fare qc; **to** ~ **dead** fermarsi di colpo; ~ **it!** smettila!, basta!
►**stop by** vi passare, fare un salto.
►**stop off** vi sostare brevemente.
►**stop up** vt (*hole*) chiudere, turare.
stopcock ['stɔpkɔk] n rubinetto di arresto.
stopgap ['stɔpgæp] n (*person*) tappabuchi *m/f* inv; (*measure*) ripiego ♦ cpd (*measures, solution*) di fortuna.
stoplights ['stɔplaɪts] npl (*AUT*) stop mpl.
stopover ['stɔpəuvə*] n breve sosta; (*AVIAT*) scalo.
stoppage ['stɔpɪdʒ] n arresto, fermata; (*of pay*) trattenuta; (*strike*) interruzione f del lavoro.
stopper ['stɔpə*] n tappo.
stop press n ultimissime fpl.
stopwatch ['stɔpwɔtʃ] n cronometro.
storage ['stɔːrɪdʒ] n immagazzinamento; (*COMPUT*) memoria.
storage heater n (*BRIT*) radiatore m elettrico che accumula calore.
store [stɔː*] n provvista, riserva; (*depot*) deposito; (*BRIT: department* ~) grande magazzino; (*US: shop*) negozio ♦ vt mettere da parte; conservare; (*grain, goods*) immagazzinare; (*COMPUT*) registrare; **to set great/little** ~ **by sth** dare molta/poca importanza a qc; **who knows what is in** ~ **for us?** chissà cosa ci riserva il futuro?
►**store up** vt mettere in serbo, conservare.
storehouse ['stɔːhaus] n magazzino, deposito.
storekeeper ['stɔːkiːpə*] n (*US*) negoziante *m/f*.
storeroom ['stɔːrum] n dispensa.
storey, (*US*) **story** ['stɔːrɪ] n piano.
stork [stɔːk] n cicogna.
storm [stɔːm] n tempesta; (*also*: **thunder**~) temporale m ♦ vi (*fig*) infuriarsi ♦ vt prendere d'assalto.
storm cloud n nube f temporalesca.
storm door n controporta.
stormy ['stɔːmɪ] adj tempestoso(a), burrascoso(a).
story ['stɔːrɪ] n storia; racconto; (*PRESS*) articolo; (*US*) = **storey**.
storybook ['stɔːrɪbuk] n libro di racconti.
storyteller ['stɔːrɪtɛlə*] n narratore/trice.
stout [staut] adj solido(a), robusto(a);

(*brave*) coraggioso(a); (*fat*) corpulento(a), grasso(a) ♦ *n* birra scura.

stove [stəuv] *n* (*for cooking*) fornello; (: *small*) fornelletto; (*for heating*) stufa; **gas/electric** ~ cucina a gas/elettrica.

stow [stəu] *vt* mettere via.

stowaway ['stəuəweɪ] *n* passeggero(a) clandestino(a).

straddle ['strædl] *vt* stare a cavalcioni di.

strafe [strɑːf] *vt* mitragliare.

straggle ['strægl] *vi* crescere (*or* estendersi) disordinatamente; trascinarsi; rimanere indietro; ~**d along the coast** disseminati(e) lungo la costa.

straggler ['stræglə*] *n* sbandato/a.

straggling ['stræglɪŋ], **straggly** ['stræglɪ] *adj* (*hair*) in disordine.

straight [streɪt] *adj* (*continuous, direct*) dritto(a), (*frank*) onesto(a), franco(a); (*plain, uncomplicated*) semplice; (*THEAT: part, play*) serio(a); (*col: heterosexual*) eterosessuale ♦ *adv* **dritto**, (*drink*) liscio ♦ *n*: the ~ la linea retta; (*RAIL*) il rettilineo; (*SPORT*) la dirittura d'arrivo; **to put** *or* **get** ~ mettere in ordine, mettere ordine in; **to be (all)** ~ (*tidy*) essere a posto, essere sistemato; (*clarified*) essere chiaro; **ten** ~ **wins** dieci vittorie di fila; ~ **away**, ~ **off** (*at once*) immediatamente; ~ **off**, ~ **out** senza esitare; **I went** ~ **home** sono andato direttamente a casa.

straighten ['streɪtn] *vt* (*also*: ~ **out**) raddrizzare; **to** ~ **things out** mettere le cose a posto.

straight-faced [streɪt'feɪst] *adj* impassibile, imperturbabile ♦ *adv* con il viso serio.

straightforward [streɪt'fɔːwəd] *adj* semplice; (*frank*) onesto(a), franco(a).

strain [streɪn] *n* (*TECH*) sollecitazione *f*; (*physical*) sforzo; (*mental*) tensione *f*; (*MED*) strappo; (*streak, trace*) tendenza; elemento; (*breed*) razza; (*of virus*) tipo ♦ *vt* tendere; (*muscle*) slogare; (*ankle*) storcere; (*friendship, marriage*) mettere a dura prova; (*filter*) colare, filtrare ♦ *vi* sforzarsi; ~**s** *npl* (*MUS*) note *fpl*; **she's under a lot of** ~ è molto tesa, è sotto pressione.

strained [streɪnd] *adj* (*laugh etc*) forzato(a); (*relations*) teso(a).

strainer ['streɪnə*] *n* passino, colino.

strait [streɪt] *n* (*GEO*) stretto; **to be in dire** ~**s** (*fig*) essere nei guai.

straitjacket ['streɪtdʒækɪt] *n* camicia di forza.

strait-laced [streɪt'leɪst] *adj* puritano(a).

strand [strænd] *n* (*of thread*) filo.

strange [streɪndʒ] *adj* (*not known*)

sconosciuto(a); (*odd*) strano(a), bizzarro(a).

strangely ['streɪndʒlɪ] *adv* stranamente.

stranger ['streɪndʒə*] *n* (*unknown*) sconosciuto/a; (*from another place*) estraneo/a; **I'm a** ~ **here** non sono del posto.

strangle ['stræŋgl] *vt* strangolare.

stranglehold ['stræŋglhəuld] *n* (*fig*) stretta (mortale).

strangulation [stræŋgju'leɪʃən] *n* strangolamento.

strap [stræp] *n* cinghia; (*of slip, dress*) spallina, bretella ♦ *vt* legare con una cinghia; (*child etc*) punire (con una cinghia).

straphanging ['stræphæŋɪŋ] *n* viaggiare *m* in piedi (*su mezzi pubblici reggendosi a un sostegno*).

strapless ['stræplɪs] *adj* (*bra, dress*) senza spalline.

strapped [stræpt] *adj*: ~ **for cash** a corto di soldi; **financially** ~ finanziariamente a terra.

strapping ['stræpɪŋ] *adj* ben piantato(a).

Strasbourg ['stræzbɑːg] *n* Strasburgo *f*.

strata ['strɑːtə] *npl of* **stratum**.

stratagem ['strætɪdʒəm] *n* stratagemma *m*.

strategic [strə'tiːdʒɪk] *adj* strategico(a).

strategist ['strætɪdʒɪst] *n* stratega *m*.

strategy ['strætɪdʒɪ] *n* strategia.

stratosphere ['strætəsfɪə*] *n* stratosfera *f*.

stratum, *pl* **strata** ['strɑːtəm, 'strɑːtə] *n* strato.

straw [strɔː] *n* paglia; (*drinking* ~) cannuccia; **that's the last** ~! è la goccia che fa traboccare il vaso!

strawberry ['strɔːbərɪ] *n* fragola.

stray [streɪ] *adj* (*animal*) randagio(a) ♦ *vi* perdersi; allontanarsi, staccarsi (dal gruppo); ~ **bullet** proiettile *m* vagante.

streak [striːk] *n* striscia; (*fig: of madness etc*): **a** ~ **of** una vena di ♦ *vt* striare, screziare ♦ *vi*: **to** ~ **past** passare come un fulmine; **to have** ~**s in one's hair** avere le mèche nei capelli; **a winning/losing** ~ un periodo fortunato/sfortunato.

streaker ['striːkə*] *n* streaker *m/f inv*.

streaky ['striːkɪ] *adj* screziato(a), striato(a).

streaky bacon *n* (*BRIT*) ≈ pancetta.

stream [striːm] *n* ruscello; corrente *f*; (*of people*) fiume *m* ♦ *vt* (*SCOL*) dividere in livelli di rendimento ♦ *vi* scorrere; **to** ~ **in/out** entrare/uscire a fiotti; **against the** ~ controcorrente; **on** ~ (*new power plant etc*) in funzione, in produzione.

streamer ['striːmə*] *n* (*of paper*) stella filante.

stream feed n (*on photocopier etc*) alimentazione f continua.

streamline ['stri:mlaɪn] vt dare una linea aerodinamica a; (*fig*) razionalizzare.

streamlined ['stri:mlaɪnd] adj aerodinamico(a), affusolato(a); (*fig*) razionalizzato(a).

street [stri:t] n strada, via; **the back ~s** le strade secondarie; **to be on the ~s** (*homeless*) essere senza tetto; (*as prostitute*) battere il marciapiede.

streetcar ['stri:tkɑ:*] n (*US*) tram m inv.

street cred [-krɛd] n (*col*) credibilità presso i giovani.

street lamp n lampione m.

street lighting n illuminazione f stradale.

street map, street plan n pianta (di una città).

street market n mercato all'aperto.

streetwise ['stri:twaɪz] adj (*col*) esperto(a) dei bassifondi.

strength [strɛŋθ] n forza; (*of girder, knot etc*) resistenza, solidità; (*of chemical solution*) concentrazione f; (*of wine*) gradazione f alcolica; **on the ~ of** sulla base di, in virtù di; **below/at full ~** con gli effettivi ridotti/al completo.

strengthen ['strɛŋθən] vt rinforzare; (*muscles*) irrobustire; (*economy, currency*) consolidare.

strenuous ['strɛnjuəs] adj vigoroso(a), energico(a); (*tiring*) duro(a), pesante.

stress [strɛs] n (*force, pressure*) pressione f; (*mental strain*) tensione f; (*accent*) accento; (*emphasis*) enfasi f ♦ vt insistere su, sottolineare; **to be under ~** essere sotto tensione; **to lay great ~ on sth** dare grande importanza a qc.

stressful ['strɛsful] adj (*job*) difficile, stressante.

stretch [strɛtʃ] n (*of sand etc*) distesa; (*of time*) periodo ♦ vi stirarsi; (*extend*): **to ~ to** or **as far as** estendersi fino a; (*be enough: money, food*): **to ~ (to)** bastare (per) ♦ vt tendere, allungare; (*spread*) distendere; (*fig*) spingere (al massimo); **at a ~** ininterrottamente; **to ~ a muscle** tendere un muscolo; **to ~ one's legs** sgranchirsi le gambe.

▶**stretch out** vi allungarsi, estendersi ♦ vt (*arm etc*) allungare, tendere; (*to spread*) distendere; **to ~ out for sth** allungare la mano per prendere qc.

stretcher ['strɛtʃə*] n barella, lettiga.

stretcher-bearer ['strɛtʃəbɛərə*] n barelliere m.

stretch marks npl smagliature fpl.

strewn [stru:n] adj: **~ with** cosparso(a) di.

stricken ['strɪkən] adj provato(a); affranto(a); **~ with** colpito(a) da.

strict [strɪkt] adj (*severe*) rigido(a), severo(a); (: *order, rule*) rigoroso(a); (: *supervision*) stretto(a); (*precise*) preciso(a), stretto(a); **in ~ confidence** in assoluta confidenza.

strictly ['strɪktlɪ] adv severamente; rigorosamente; strettamente; **~ confidential** strettamente confidenziale; **~ speaking** a rigor di termini; **~ between ourselves ...** detto fra noi ....

stride [straɪd] n passo lungo ♦ vi (*pt* **strode**, *pp* **stridden** [strəʊd, 'strɪdn]) camminare a grandi passi; **to take in one's ~** (*fig*: *changes etc*) prendere con tranquillità.

strident ['straɪdnt] adj stridente.

strife [straɪf] n conflitto; litigi mpl.

strike [straɪk] n sciopero; (*of oil etc*) scoperta; (*attack*) attacco ♦ vb (*pt, pp* **struck** [strʌk]) vt colpire; (*oil etc*) scoprire, trovare; (*produce, make: coin, medal*) coniare; (: *agreement, deal*) concludere ♦ vi far sciopero, scioperare; (*attack*) attaccare; (*clock*) suonare; **to go on** or **come out on ~** mettersi in sciopero; **to ~ a match** accendere un fiammifero; **to ~ a balance** (*fig*) trovare il giusto mezzo.

▶**strike back** vi (*MIL*) fare rappresaglie; (*fig*) reagire.

▶**strike down** vt (*fig*) atterrare.

▶**strike off** vt (*from list*) cancellare; (: *doctor etc*) radiare.

▶**strike out** vt depennare.

▶**strike up** vt (*MUS*) attaccare; **to ~ up a friendship with** fare amicizia con.

strikebreaker ['straɪkbreɪkə*] n crumiro/a.

striker ['straɪkə*] n scioperante m/f; (*SPORT*) attaccante m.

striking ['straɪkɪŋ] adj impressionante.

Strimmer ® ['strɪmə*] n tagliabordi m inv.

string [strɪŋ] n spago; (*row*) fila; sequenza; catena; (*COMPUT*) stringa, sequenza; (*MUS*) corda ♦ vt (*pt, pp* **strung** [strʌŋ]): **to ~ out** disporre di fianco; **to ~ together** mettere insieme; **the ~s** npl (*MUS*) gli archi; **~ of pearls** filo di perle; **with no ~s attached** (*fig*) senza vincoli, senza obblighi; **to get a job by pulling ~s** ottenere un lavoro a forza di raccomandazioni.

string bean n fagiolino.

string(ed) instrument n (*MUS*) strumento a corda.

stringent ['strɪndʒənt] adj rigoroso(a); (*reasons, arguments*) stringente, impellente.

string quartet n quartetto d'archi.

strip [strɪp] n striscia; (SPORT): **wearing the Celtic** ~ con la divisa del Celtic ♦ vt spogliare; (also: ~ **down**: machine) smontare ♦ vi spogliarsi.
strip cartoon n fumetto.
stripe [straɪp] n striscia, riga.
striped ['straɪpt] adj a strisce or righe.
strip light n (BRIT) tubo al neon.
stripper ['strɪpə*] n spogliarellista.
strip-search ['strɪpsə:tʃ] vt: **to** ~ **sb** perquisire qn facendolo(a) spogliare ♦ n perquisizione f (facendo spogliare il perquisito).
striptease ['strɪptiːz] n spogliarello.
strive, pt **strove**, pp **striven** [straɪv, strəuv, 'strɪvn] vi: **to** ~ **to do** sforzarsi di fare.
strobe [strəub] n (also: ~ **light**) luce f stroboscopica.
strode [strəud] pt of **stride**.
stroke [strəuk] n colpo; (of piston) corsa; (MED) colpo apoplettico; (SWIMMING: style) nuoto; (caress) carezza ♦ vt accarezzare; **at a** ~ in un attimo; **on the** ~ **of 5** alle 5 in punto, allo scoccare delle 5; **a** ~ **of luck** un colpo di fortuna; **two-**~ **engine** motore a due tempi.
stroll [strəul] n giretto, passeggiatina ♦ vi andare a spasso; **to go for a** ~, **have** or **take a** ~ andare a fare un giretto or due passi.
stroller ['strəulə*] n (US) passeggino.
strong [strɒŋ] adj (gen) forte; (sturdy: table, fabric etc) solido(a); (concentrated, intense: bleach, acid) concentrato(a); (protest, letter, measures) energico(a) ♦ adv: **to be going** ~ (company) andare a gonfie vele; (person) essere attivo(a); **they are 50** ~ sono in 50; ~ **language** (swearing) linguaggio volgare.
strong-arm ['strɒŋɑːm] adj (tactics, methods) energico(a).
strongbox ['strɒŋbɒks] n cassaforte f.
stronghold ['strɒŋhəuld] n fortezza, roccaforte f.
strongly ['strɒŋlɪ] adv fortemente, con forza; solidamente; energicamente; **to feel** ~ **about sth** avere molto a cuore qc.
strongman ['strɒŋmæn] n personaggio di spicco.
strongroom ['strɒŋrum] n camera di sicurezza.
stroppy ['strɒpɪ] adj (BRIT col) scontroso(a), indisponente.
strove [strəuv] pt of **strive**.
struck [strʌk] pt, pp of **strike**.
structural ['strʌktʃərəl] adj strutturale; (CONSTR) di costruzione; di struttura.
structurally ['strʌktʃrəlɪ] adv dal punto di

vista della struttura.
structure ['strʌktʃə*] n struttura; (building) costruzione f, fabbricato.
struggle ['strʌgl] n lotta ♦ vi lottare; **to have a** ~ **to do sth** avere dei problemi per fare qc.
strum [strʌm] vt (guitar) strimpellare.
strung [strʌŋ] pt, pp of **string**.
strut [strʌt] n sostegno, supporto ♦ vi pavoneggiarsi.
strychnine ['strɪkniːn] n stricnina.
stub [stʌb] n mozzicone m; (of ticket etc) matrice f, talloncino ♦ vt: **to** ~ **one's toe (on sth)** urtare or sbattere il dito del piede (contro qc).
▶**stub out** vt: **to** ~ **out a cigarette** spegnere una sigaretta.
stubble ['stʌbl] n stoppia; (on chin) barba ispida.
stubborn ['stʌbən] adj testardo(a), ostinato(a).
stubby ['stʌbɪ] adj tozzo(a).
stucco ['stʌkəu] n stucco.
stuck [stʌk] pt, pp of **stick** ♦ adj (jammed) bloccato(a); **to get** ~ bloccarsi.
stuck-up [stʌk'ʌp] adj presuntuoso(a).
stud [stʌd] n bottoncino; borchia; (of horses) scuderia, allevamento di cavalli; (also: ~ **horse**) stallone m ♦ vt (fig): ~**ded with** tempestato(a) di.
student ['stjuːdənt] n studente/essa ♦ cpd studentesco(a); universitario(a); degli studenti; **a law/medical** ~ uno studente di legge/di medicina.
student driver n (US) conducente m/f principiante.
students' union n (BRIT: association) circolo universitario; (: building) sede f del circolo universitario.
studied ['stʌdɪd] adj studiato(a), calcolato(a).
studio ['stjuːdɪəu] n studio.
studio flat, (US) **studio apartment** n appartamento monolocale.
studious ['stjuːdɪəs] adj studioso(a); (studied) studiato(a), voluto(a).
studiously ['stjuːdɪəslɪ] adv (carefully) deliberatamente, di proposito.
study ['stʌdɪ] n studio ♦ vt studiare; esaminare ♦ vi studiare; **to make a** ~ **of sth** fare uno studio su qc; **to** ~ **for an exam** prepararsi a un esame.
stuff [stʌf] n (substance) roba; (belongings) cose fpl, roba ♦ vt imbottire; (animal: for exhibition) impagliare; (CULIN) farcire; **my nose is** ~**ed up** ho il naso chiuso; **get** ~**ed!** (col!) va' a farti fottere! (!); ~**ed toy** giocattolo di peluche.

stuffing ['stʌfɪŋ] n imbottitura; (CULIN) ripieno.

stuffy ['stʌfɪ] adj (room) mal ventilato(a), senz'aria; (ideas) antiquato(a).

stumble ['stʌmbl] vi inciampare; **to ~ across** (fig) imbattersi in.

stumbling block ['stʌmblɪŋ-] n ostacolo, scoglio.

stump [stʌmp] n ceppo; (of limb) moncone m ♦ vt: **to be ~ed for an answer** essere incapace di rispondere.

stun [stʌn] vt stordire; (amaze) sbalordire.

stung [stʌŋ] pt, pp of **sting**.

stunk [stʌŋk] pp of **stink**.

stunning ['stʌnɪŋ] adj (piece of news etc) sbalorditivo(a); (girl, dress) favoloso(a), stupendo(a).

stunt [stʌnt] n bravata; trucco pubblicitario; (AVIAT) acrobazia ♦ vt arrestare.

stunted ['stʌntɪd] adj stentato(a), rachitico(a).

stuntman ['stʌntmæn] n cascatore m.

stupefaction [stjuːpɪ'fækʃən] n stupefazione f, stupore m.

stupefy ['stjuːpɪfaɪ] vt stordire; intontire; (fig) stupire.

stupendous [stjuː'pɛndəs] adj stupendo(a), meraviglioso(a).

stupid ['stjuːpɪd] adj stupido(a).

stupidity [stjuː'pɪdɪtɪ] n stupidità.

stupidly ['stjuːpɪdlɪ] adv stupidamente.

stupor ['stjuːpə*] n torpore m.

sturdy ['stəːdɪ] adj robusto(a), vigoroso(a); solido(a).

sturgeon ['stəːdʒən] n storione m.

stutter ['stʌtə*] n balbuzie f ♦ vi balbettare.

Stuttgart ['ʃtutgart] n Stoccarda.

sty [staɪ] n (of pigs) porcile m.

stye [staɪ] n (MED) orzaiolo.

style [staɪl] n stile m; (distinction) eleganza, classe f; (hair ~) pettinatura; (of dress etc) modello, linea; **in the latest ~** all'ultima moda.

styli ['staɪlaɪ] npl of **stylus**.

stylish ['staɪlɪʃ] adj elegante.

stylist ['staɪlɪst] n: **hair ~** parrucchiere/a.

stylized ['staɪlaɪzd] adj stilizzato(a).

stylus, pl **styli** or **styluses** ['staɪləs, -laɪ] n (of record player) puntina.

Styrofoam ® ['staɪrəfəum] n (US) = **polystyrene** ♦ adj (cup) di polistirene.

suave [swɑːv] adj untuoso(a).

sub [sʌb] n abbr = **submarine**; **subscription**.

sub... [sʌb] prefix sub..., sotto....

subcommittee ['sʌbkəmɪtɪ] n sottocomitato.

subconscious [sʌb'kɔnʃəs] adj, n subcosciente (m).

subcontinent [sʌb'kɔntɪnənt] n: **the (Indian) ~** il subcontinente (indiano).

subcontract n [sʌb'kɔntrækt] subappalto ♦ vt [sʌbkən'trækt] subappaltare.

subcontractor ['sʌbkən'træktə*] n subappaltatore/trice.

subdivide [sʌbdɪ'vaɪd] vt suddividere.

subdivision ['sʌbdɪvɪʒən] n suddivisione f.

subdue [səb'djuː] vt sottomettere, soggiogare.

subdued [səb'djuːd] adj pacato(a); (light) attenuato(a); (person) poco esuberante.

sub-editor ['sʌb'ɛdɪtə*] n (BRIT) redattore(trice) aggiunto(a).

subject ['sʌbdʒɪkt] n soggetto; (citizen etc) cittadino/a; (SCOL) materia ♦ adj (liable): ~ **to** soggetto(a) a ♦ vt [səb'dʒɛkt]: **to ~ to** sottomettere a; esporre a; ~ **to confirmation in writing** a condizione di ricevere conferma scritta; **to change the ~** cambiare discorso.

subjection [səb'dʒɛkʃən] n sottomissione f, soggezione f.

subjective [səb'dʒɛktɪv] adj soggettivo(a).

subject matter n argomento; contenuto.

sub judice [sʌb'dʒuːdɪsɪ] adj (LAW) sub iudice.

subjugate ['sʌbdʒugeɪt] vt sottomettere, soggiogare.

subjunctive [səb'dʒʌŋktɪv] adj congiuntivo(a) ♦ n congiuntivo.

sublet [sʌb'lɛt] vt, vi irreg subaffittare.

sublime [sə'blaɪm] adj sublime.

subliminal [sʌb'lɪmɪnl] adj subliminale.

submachine gun ['sʌbmə'ʃiːn-] n mitra m inv.

submarine [sʌbmə'riːn] n sommergibile m.

submerge [səb'məːdʒ] vt sommergere; immergere ♦ vi immergersi.

submersion [səb'məːʃən] n sommersione f, immersione f.

submission [səb'mɪʃən] n sottomissione f; (to committee etc) richiesta, domanda.

submissive [səb'mɪsɪv] adj remissivo(a).

submit [səb'mɪt] vt sottomettere; (proposal, claim) presentare ♦ vi sottomettersi.

subnormal [sʌb'nɔːməl] adj subnormale.

subordinate [sə'bɔːdɪnət] adj, n subordinato(a).

subpoena [səb'piːnə] n (LAW) citazione f, mandato di comparizione ♦ vt (LAW) citare in giudizio.

subroutine ['sʌbruːtiːn] n (COMPUT) sottoprogramma m.

subscribe [səb'skraɪb] vi contribuire; **to ~ to** (opinion) approvare, condividere; (fund) sottoscrivere; (newspaper) abbonarsi a; essere abbonato(a) a.

subscriber [səb'skraɪbə*] n (to periodical, telephone) abbonato/a.

subscript ['sʌbskrɪpt] n deponente m.

subscription [səb'skrɪpʃən] n sottoscrizione f; abbonamento; **to take out a ~ to** abbonarsi a.

subsequent ['sʌbsɪkwənt] adj (later) successivo(a); (further) ulteriore; **~ to** in seguito a.

subsequently ['sʌbsɪkwəntlɪ] adv in seguito, successivamente.

subservient [səb'sə:vɪənt] adj: **~ (to)** remissivo(a) (a), sottomesso(a) (a).

subside [səb'saɪd] vi cedere, abbassarsi; (flood) decrescere; (wind) calmarsi.

subsidence [səb'saɪdns] n cedimento, abbassamento.

subsidiarity [səbsɪdɪ'ærɪtɪ] n (POL) principio del decentramento del potere.

subsidiary [səb'sɪdɪərɪ] adj sussidiario(a); accessorio(a); (BRIT SCOL: subject) complementare ♦ n filiale f.

subsidize ['sʌbsɪdaɪz] vt sovvenzionare.

subsidy ['sʌbsɪdɪ] n sovvenzione f.

subsist [səb'sɪst] vi: **to ~ on sth** vivere di qc.

subsistence [səb'sɪstəns] n esistenza; mezzi mpl di sostentamento.

subsistence allowance n indennità f inv di trasferta.

subsistence level n livello minimo di vita.

substance ['sʌbstəns] n sostanza; (fig) essenza; **to lack ~** (argument) essere debole.

substance abuse n abuso di sostanze tossiche.

substandard [sʌb'stændəd] adj (goods, housing) di qualità scadente.

substantial [səb'stænʃl] adj solido(a); (amount, progress etc) notevole; (meal) sostanzioso(a).

substantially [səb'stænʃəlɪ] adv sostanzialmente; **~ bigger** molto più grande.

substantiate [səb'stænʃɪeɪt] vt comprovare.

substitute ['sʌbstɪtju:t] n (person) sostituto/a; (thing) succedaneo, surrogato ♦ vt: **to ~ sth/sb for** sostituire qc/qn a.

substitute teacher n (US) supplente m/f.

substitution [sʌbstɪ'tju:ʃən] n sostituzione f.

subterfuge ['sʌbtəfju:dʒ] n sotterfugio.

subterranean [sʌbtə'reɪnɪən] adj sotterraneo(a).

subtitle ['sʌbtaɪtl] n (CINE) sottotitolo.

subtle ['sʌtl] adj sottile; (flavour, perfume) delicato(a).

subtlety ['sʌtltɪ] n sottigliezza.

subtly ['sʌtlɪ] adv sottilmente; delicatamente.

subtotal [sʌb'təutl] n somma parziale.

subtract [səb'trækt] vt sottrarre.

subtraction [səb'trækʃən] n sottrazione f.

suburb ['sʌbə:b] n sobborgo; **the ~s** la periferia.

suburban [sə'bə:bən] adj suburbano(a).

suburbia [sə'bə:bɪə] n periferia, sobborghi mpl.

subversion [səb'və:ʃən] n sovversione f.

subversive [səb'və:sɪv] adj sovversivo(a).

subway ['sʌbweɪ] n (US: underground) metropolitana; (BRIT: underpass) sottopassaggio.

subzero [sʌb'zɪərəu] adj: **~ temperatures** temperature fpl sotto zero.

succeed [sək'si:d] vi riuscire, avere successo ♦ vt succedere a; **to ~ in doing** riuscire a fare.

succeeding [sək'si:dɪŋ] adj (following) successivo(a); **~ generations** generazioni fpl future.

success [sək'sɛs] n successo.

successful [sək'sɛsful] adj (venture) coronato(a) da successo, riuscito(a); **to be ~ (in doing)** riuscire (a fare).

successfully [sək'sɛsfəlɪ] adv con successo.

succession [sək'sɛʃən] n successione f; **in ~** di seguito.

successive [sək'sɛsɪv] adj successivo(a); consecutivo(a); **on 3 ~ days** per 3 giorni consecutivi or di seguito.

successor [sək'sɛsə*] n successore m.

succinct [sək'sɪŋkt] adj succinto(a), breve.

succulent ['sʌkjulənt] adj succulento(a) ♦ n (BOT): **~s** piante fpl grasse.

succumb [sə'kʌm] vi soccombere.

such [sʌtʃ] adj (of that kind): **~ a book** un tale libro, un libro del genere; **~ books** tali libri, libri del genere; (so much): **~ courage** tanto coraggio ♦ adv: **~ a long trip** un viaggio così lungo; **~ good books** libri così buoni; **~ a lot of** talmente or così tanto(a); **making ~ a noise that** facendo un rumore tale che; **~ a long time ago** tanto tempo fa; **~ as** (like) come; **a noise ~ as to** un rumore tale da; **~ books as I have** quei pochi libri che ho; **as ~** come or in quanto tale; **I said no ~ thing** non ho detto niente del genere.

such-and-such ['sʌtʃənsʌtʃ] adj tale (after noun).

suchlike ['sʌtʃlaɪk] pron (col): **and ~** e così via.

suck [sʌk] vt succhiare; (subj: baby)

poppare; (: *pump, machine*) aspirare.
sucker ['sʌkə*] *n* (*ZOOL, TECH*) ventosa;
(*BOT*) pollone *m*; (*col*) gonzo/a, babbeo/a.
suckle ['sʌkl] *vt* allattare.
sucrose ['suːkrəuz] *n* saccarosio.
suction ['sʌkʃən] *n* succhiamento; (*TECH*)
aspirazione *f*.
suction pump *n* pompa aspirante.
Sudan [suːˈdɑːn] *n* Sudan *m*.
Sudanese [suːdəˈniːz] *adj, n* sudanese (*m/f*).
sudden ['sʌdn] *adj* improvviso(a); **all of a ~**
improvvisamente, all'improvviso.
sudden-death [sʌdnˈdɛθ] *n* (*also*: ~ **playoff**)
(*SPORT*) spareggio, bella.
suddenly ['sʌdnlɪ] *adv* bruscamente,
improvvisamente, di colpo.
suds [sʌdz] *npl* schiuma (di sapone).
sue [suː] *vt* citare in giudizio ♦ *vi*: **to ~ (for)**
intentare causa (per); **to ~ for divorce**
intentare causa di divorzio; **to ~ sb for
damages** citare qn per danni.
suede [sweɪd] *n* pelle *f* scamosciata ♦ *cpd*
scamosciato(a).
suet ['suɪt] *n* grasso di rognone.
Suez ['suːɪz] *n*: **the ~ Canal** il Canale di
Suez.
Suff. *abbr* (*BRIT*) = *Suffolk*.
suffer ['sʌfə*] *vt* soffrire, patire; (*bear*)
sopportare, tollerare; (*undergo: loss,
setback*) subire ♦ *vi* soffrire; **to ~ from**
soffrire di; **to ~ from the effects of
alcohol/a fall** risentire degli effetti
dell'alcool/di una caduta.
sufferance ['sʌfərəns] *n*: **he was only there
on ~** era più che altro sopportato lì.
sufferer ['sʌfərə*] *n* (*MED*): **~ (from)**
malato/a (di).
suffering ['sʌfərɪŋ] *n* sofferenza; (*hardship,
deprivation*) privazione *f*.
suffice [səˈfaɪs] *vi* essere sufficiente,
bastare.
sufficient [səˈfɪʃənt] *adj* sufficiente; **~
money** abbastanza soldi.
sufficiently [səˈfɪʃəntlɪ] *adv*
sufficientemente, abbastanza.
suffix ['sʌfɪks] *n* suffisso.
suffocate ['sʌfəkeɪt] *vi* (*have difficulty
breathing*) soffocare; (*die through lack of
air*) asfissiare.
suffocation [sʌfəˈkeɪʃən] *n* soffocamento;
(*MED*) asfissia.
suffrage ['sʌfrɪdʒ] *n* suffragio.
suffuse [səˈfjuːz] *vt*: **to ~ (with)** (*colour*)
tingere (di); (*light*) soffondere (di); **her
face was ~d with joy** la gioia si dipingeva
sul suo volto.
sugar ['ʃugə*] *n* zucchero ♦ *vt* zuccherare.
sugar beet *n* barbabietola da zucchero.

sugar bowl *n* zuccheriera.
sugar cane *n* canna da zucchero.
sugar-coated ['ʃugəkəutɪd] *adj* ricoperto(a)
di zucchero.
sugar lump *n* zolletta di zucchero.
sugar refinery *n* raffineria di zucchero.
sugary ['ʃugərɪ] *adj* zuccherino(a), dolce;
(*fig*) sdolcinato(a).
suggest [səˈdʒɛst] *vt* proporre, suggerire;
(*indicate*) indicare; **what do you ~ I do?**
cosa mi suggerisce di fare?
suggestion [səˈdʒɛstʃən] *n* suggerimento,
proposta.
suggestive [səˈdʒɛstɪv] *adj* suggestivo(a);
(*indecent*) spinto(a), indecente.
suicidal [suɪˈsaɪdl] *adj* suicida *inv*; (*fig*)
fatale, disastroso(a).
suicide ['suɪsaɪd] *n* (*person*) suicida *m/f*; (*act*)
suicidio; **to commit ~** suicidarsi.
suicide attempt, suicide bid *n* tentato
suicidio.
suit [suːt] *n* (*man's*) completo; (*woman's*)
completo, tailleur *m inv*; (*law~*) causa;
(*CARDS*) seme *m*, colore *m* ♦ *vt* andar bene
a *or* per; essere adatto(a) a *or* per;
(*adapt*): **to ~ sth to** adattare qc a; **to be
~ed to sth** (*suitable for*) essere adatto a
qc; **well ~ed** (*couple*) fatti l'uno per
l'altro; **to bring a ~ against sb** intentare
causa a qn; **to follow ~** (*fig*) fare
altrettanto.
suitable ['suːtəbl] *adj* adatto(a);
appropriato(a); **would tomorrow be ~?**
andrebbe bene domani?; **we found
somebody ~** abbiamo trovato la persona
adatta.
suitably ['suːtəblɪ] *adv* (*dress*) in modo
adatto; (*thank*) adeguatamente.
suitcase ['suːtkeɪs] *n* valigia.
suite [swiːt] *n* (*of rooms*) appartamento;
(*MUS*) suite *f inv*; (*furniture*): **bedroom/
dining room ~** arredo *or* mobilia per la
camera da letto/sala da pranzo; **a three-
piece ~** un salotto comprendente un
divano e due poltrone.
suitor ['suːtə*] *n* corteggiatore *m*,
spasimante *m*.
sulfate ['sʌlfeɪt] *n* (*US*) = *sulphate*.
sulfur *etc* ['sʌlfə*] (*US*) = *sulphur etc*.
sulk [sʌlk] *vi* fare il broncio.
sulky ['sʌlkɪ] *adj* imbronciato(a).
sullen ['sʌlən] *adj* scontroso(a); cupo(a).
sulphate, (*US*) **sulfate** ['sʌlfeɪt] *n* solfato;
copper ~ solfato di rame.
sulphur, (*US*) **sulfur** ['sʌlfə*] *n* zolfo.
sulphur dioxide *n* biossido di zolfo.
sulphuric, (*US*) **sulfuric** [sʌlˈfjuərɪk] *adj*: **~
acid** acido solforico.

sultan ['sʌltən] *n* sultano.
sultana [sʌl'tɑːnə] *n* (*fruit*) uva (secca) sultanina.
sultry ['sʌltrɪ] *adj* afoso(a).
sum [sʌm] *n* somma; (*SCOL etc*) addizione *f*.
▶**sum up** *vt* riassumere; (*evaluate rapidly*) valutare, giudicare ♦ *vi* riassumere.
Sumatra [suˈmɑːtrə] *n* Sumatra.
summarize ['sʌməraɪz] *vt* riassumere, riepilogare.
summary ['sʌmərɪ] *n* riassunto ♦ *adj* (*justice*) sommario(a).
summer ['sʌmə*] *n* estate *f* ♦ *cpd* d'estate, estivo(a); **in (the)** ~ d'estate.
summer camp *n* (*US*) colonia (estiva).
summerhouse ['sʌməhaus] *n* (*in garden*) padiglione *m*.
summertime ['sʌmətaɪm] *n* (*season*) estate *f*.
summer time *n* (*by clock*) ora legale (estiva).
summery ['sʌmərɪ] *adj* estivo(a).
summing-up [sʌmɪŋ'ʌp] *n* (*LAW*) ricapitolazione *f* del processo.
summit ['sʌmɪt] *n* cima, sommità; (*POL*) vertice *m*.
summit conference *n* conferenza al vertice.
summon ['sʌmən] *vt* chiamare, convocare; **to** ~ **a witness** citare un testimone.
▶**summon up** *vt* raccogliere, fare appello a.
summons *n* ordine *m* di comparizione ♦ *vt* citare; **to serve a** ~ **on sb** notificare una citazione a qn.
sumo ['suːməu] *n* (*also:* ~ **wrestling**) sumo.
sump [sʌmp] *n* (*AUT*) coppa dell'olio.
sumptuous ['sʌmptjuəs] *adj* sontuoso(a).
Sun. *abbr* (= *Sunday*) dom.
sun [sʌn] *n* sole *m*; **in the** ~ al sole; **to catch the** ~ prendere sole; **they have everything under the** ~ hanno tutto ciò che possono desiderare.
sunbathe ['sʌnbeɪð] *vi* prendere un bagno di sole.
sunbeam ['sʌnbiːm] *n* raggio di sole.
sunbed ['sʌnbɛd] *n* lettino solare.
sunblock ['sʌnblɔk] *n* crema solare a protezione totale.
sunburn ['sʌnbəːn] *n* (*tan*) abbronzatura; (*painful*) scottatura.
sunburnt ['sʌnbəːnt], **sunburned** ['sʌnbəːnd] *adj* abbronzato(a); (*painfully*) scottato(a) dal sole.
sun cream *n* crema solare.
sundae ['sʌndeɪ] *n* coppa di gelato guarnita.
Sunday ['sʌndɪ] *n* domenica; *for phrases see*

also **Tuesday.**
Sunday paper *n* giornale *m* della domenica; *see boxed note.*

SUNDAY PAPERS

I **Sunday papers** *sono i giornali che escono di domenica. Sono generalmente corredati da supplementi e riviste di argomento culturale, sportivo e di attualità ed hanno un'alta tiratura.*

Sunday school *n* ≈ scuola di catechismo.
sundial ['sʌndaɪəl] *n* meridiana.
sundown ['sʌndaun] *n* tramonto.
sundries ['sʌndrɪz] *npl* articoli diversi.
sundry ['sʌndrɪ] *adj* vari(e), diversi(e); **all and** ~ tutti quanti.
sunflower ['sʌnflauə*] *n* girasole *m*.
sung [sʌŋ] *pp of* **sing**.
sunglasses ['sʌnglɑːsɪz] *npl* occhiali *mpl* da sole.
sunk [sʌŋk] *pp of* **sink**.
sunken ['sʌŋkən] *adj* sommerso(a); (*eyes, cheeks*) infossato(a); (*bath*) incassato(a).
sunlamp ['sʌnlæmp] *n* lampada a raggi ultravioletti.
sunlight ['sʌnlaɪt] *n* (luce *f* del) sole *m*.
sunlit ['sʌnlɪt] *adj* assolato(a), soleggiato(a).
sunny ['sʌnɪ] *adj* assolato(a), soleggiato(a); (*fig*) allegro(a), felice; **it is** ~ c'è il sole.
sunrise ['sʌnraɪz] *n* levata del sole, alba.
sunroof ['sʌnruːf] *n* (*on building*) tetto a terrazzo; (*AUT*) tetto apribile.
sunscreen ['sʌnskriːn] *n* crema solare protettiva.
sunset ['sʌnsɛt] *n* tramonto.
sunshade ['sʌnʃeɪd] *n* parasole *m*.
sunshine ['sʌnʃaɪn] *n* (luce *f* del) sole *m*.
sunspot ['sʌnspɔt] *n* macchia solare.
sunstroke ['sʌnstrəuk] *n* insolazione *f*, colpo di sole.
suntan ['sʌntæn] *n* abbronzatura.
suntanned ['sʌntænd] *adj* abbronzato(a).
suntan oil *n* olio solare.
suntrap ['sʌntræp] *n* luogo molto assolato.
super ['suːpə*] *adj* (*col*) fantastico(a).
superannuation [suːpərænjuˈeɪʃən] *n* contributi *mpl* pensionistici; pensione *f*.
superb [suːˈpəːb] *adj* magnifico(a).
Super Bowl *n* (*US SPORT*) Super Bowl *m inv*.
supercilious [suːpəˈsɪlɪəs] *adj* sprezzante.
superconductor [suːpəkənˈdʌktə*] *n* superconduttore *m*.
superficial [suːpəˈfɪʃəl] *adj* superficiale.
superficially [suːpəˈfɪʃəlɪ] *adv* superficialmente.

superfluous [su'pəːfluəs] *adj* superfluo(a).

superglue ['suːpəgluː] *n* colla a presa rapida.

superhighway ['suːpəhaɪweɪ] *n* (*US*) autostrada; **the information ~** l'autostrada telematica.

superhuman [suːpə'hjuːmən] *adj* sovrumano(a).

superimpose ['suːpərɪm'pəuz] *vt* sovrapporre.

superintend [suːpərɪn'tɛnd] *vt* dirigere, sovraintendere.

superintendent [suːpərɪn'tɛndənt] *n* direttore/trice; (*POLICE*) ≈ commissario (capo).

superior [su'pɪərɪə*] *adj* superiore; (*COMM*: *goods, quality*) di prim'ordine, superiore; (*smug*: *person*) che fa il superiore ♦ *n* superiore *m/f*; **Mother S~** (*REL*) Madre *f* Superiora, Superiora.

superiority [supɪərɪ'ɔrɪtɪ] *n* superiorità.

superlative [su'pəːlətɪv] *adj* superlativo(a), supremo(a) ♦ *n* (*LING*) superlativo.

superman ['suːpəmæn] *n* superuomo.

supermarket ['suːpəmɑːkɪt] *n* supermercato.

supermodel ['suːpəmɔdl] *n* top model *m/f* *inv*.

supernatural [suːpə'nætʃərəl] *adj* soprannaturale.

supernova [suːpə'nəuvə] *n* supernova.

superpower ['suːpəpauə*] *n* (*POL*) superpotenza.

superscript ['suːpəskrɪpt] *n* esponente *m*.

supersede [suːpə'siːd] *vt* sostituire, soppiantare.

supersonic ['suːpə'sɔnɪk] *adj* supersonico(a).

superstar ['suːpəstɑː*] *adj, n* superstar (*f*) *inv*.

superstition [suːpə'stɪʃən] *n* superstizione *f*.

superstitious [suːpə'stɪʃəs] *adj* superstizioso(a).

superstore ['suːpəstɔː*] *n* (*BRIT*) grande supermercato.

supertanker ['suːpətæŋkə*] *n* superpetroliera.

supertax ['suːpətæks] *n* soprattassa.

supervise ['suːpəvaɪz] *vt* (*person etc*) sorvegliare; (*organization*) soprintendere a.

supervision [suːpə'vɪʒən] *n* sorveglianza, supervisione *f*; **under medical ~** sotto controllo medico.

supervisor ['suːpəvaɪzə*] *n* sorvegliante *m/f*, soprintendente *m/f*; (*in shop*) capocommesso/a; (*at university*) relatore/

trice.

supervisory ['suːpəvaɪzərɪ] *adj* di sorveglianza.

supine ['suːpaɪn] *adj* supino(a).

supper ['sʌpə*] *n* cena; **to have ~** cenare.

supplant [sə'plɑːnt] *vt* soppiantare.

supple ['sʌpl] *adj* flessibile; agile.

supplement *n* ['sʌplɪmənt] supplemento ♦ *vt* [sʌplɪ'mɛnt] completare, integrare.

supplementary [sʌplɪ'mɛntərɪ] *adj* supplementare.

supplementary benefit *n* (*BRIT*) forma di indennità assistenziale.

supplier [sə'plaɪə*] *n* fornitore *m*.

supply [sə'plaɪ] *vt* (*goods*): **to ~ sth (to sb)** fornire qc (a qn); (*people, organization*): **to ~ sb (with sth)** fornire a qn (qc); (*system, machine*): **to ~ sth (with sth)** alimentare qc (con qc); (*a need*) soddisfare ♦ *n* riserva, provvista; (*supplying*) approvvigionamento; (*TECH*) alimentazione *f*; **supplies** *npl* (*food*) viveri *mpl*; (*MIL*) sussistenza; **office supplies** forniture *fpl* per ufficio; **to be in short ~** scarseggiare, essere scarso(a); **the electricity/water/gas ~** l'erogazione *f* di corrente/d'acqua/di gas; **~ and demand** la domanda e l'offerta; **the car comes supplied with a radio** l'auto viene fornita completa di radio.

supply teacher *n* (*BRIT*) supplente *m/f*.

support [sə'pɔːt] *n* (*moral, financial etc*) sostegno, appoggio; (*TECH*) supporto ♦ *vt* sostenere; (*financially*) mantenere; (*uphold*) sostenere, difendere; (*SPORT*: *team*) fare il tifo per; **they stopped work in ~ (of)** hanno smesso di lavorare per solidarietà (con); **to ~ o.s.** (*financially*) mantenersi.

supporter [sə'pɔːtə*] *n* (*POL etc*) sostenitore/trice, fautore/trice; (*SPORT*) tifoso/a.

supporting [sə'pɔːtɪŋ] *adj* (*wall*) di sostegno.

supporting actor *n* attore *m* non protagonista.

supporting actress *n* attrice *f* non protagonista.

supporting role *n* ruolo non protagonista.

supportive [sə'pɔːtɪv] *adj* d'appoggio; **I have a ~ wife/family** mia moglie/la mia famiglia mi appoggia.

suppose [sə'pəuz] *vt*, *vi* supporre; immaginare; **to be ~d to do** essere tenuto(a) a fare; **always supposing (that) he comes** ammesso e non concesso che venga; **I don't ~ she'll come** non credo che venga; **he's ~d to be an expert**

dicono che sia un esperto, passa per un esperto.

supposedly [sə'pəʊzɪdlɪ] *adv* presumibilmente; (*seemingly*) apparentemente.

supposing [sə'pəʊzɪŋ] *conj* se, ammesso che + *sub*.

supposition [sʌpə'zɪʃən] *n* supposizione *f*, ipotesi *f inv*.

suppository [sə'pɒzɪtərɪ] *n* supposta, suppositorio.

suppress [sə'prɛs] *vt* reprimere; sopprimere; tenere segreto(a).

suppression [sə'prɛʃən] *n* repressione *f*; soppressione *f*.

suppressor [sə'prɛsə*] *n* (*ELEC etc*) soppressore *m*.

supremacy [su'prɛməsɪ] *n* supremazia.

supreme [su'priːm] *adj* supremo(a).

Supreme Court *n* (*US*) Corte *f* suprema; ~ **of Judicature** *corte di giudizio suprema dell'Inghilterra e del Galles*.

supremo [su'priːməu] *n* autorità *f inv* massima.

Supt. *abbr* (*POLICE*) = **superintendent**.

surcharge ['səːtʃɑːdʒ] *n* supplemento; (*extra tax*) soprattassa.

sure [ʃuə*] *adj* sicuro(a); (*definite, convinced*) sicuro(a), certo(a) ♦ *adv* (*col: US*): **that ~ is pretty, that's ~ pretty** è veramente *or* davvero carino; ~**!** (*of course*) senz'altro!, certo!; ~ **enough** infatti; **to make ~ of** assicurarsi di; **to be ~ of sth** essere sicuro di qc; **to be ~ of o.s.** essere sicuro di sé; **I'm not ~ how/ why/when** non so bene come/perché/ quando + *sub*.

sure-fire ['ʃuəfaɪə*] *adj* (*col*) infallibile.

sure-footed [ʃuə'futɪd] *adj* dal passo sicuro.

surely ['ʃuəlɪ] *adv* sicuramente; certamente; ~ **you don't mean that!** non parlerà sul serio!

surety ['ʃuərətɪ] *n* garanzia; **to go** *or* **stand ~ for sb** farsi garante per qn.

surf [səːf] *n* (*waves*) cavalloni *mpl*; (*foam*) spuma.

surface ['səːfɪs] *n* superficie *f* ♦ *vt* (*road*) asfaltare ♦ *vi* risalire alla superficie; (*fig: person*) venire a galla, farsi vivo(a); **on the ~ it seems that ...** (*fig*) superficialmente sembra che ....

surface area *n* superficie *f*.

surface mail *n* posta ordinaria.

surface-to-surface ['səːfɪstə'səːfɪs] *adj* (*MIL*) terra-terra *inv*.

surfboard ['səːfbɔːd] *n* tavola per surfing.

surfeit ['səːfɪt] *n*: **a ~ of** un eccesso di;

un'indigestione di.

surfer ['səːfə*] *n* chi pratica il surfing.

surfing ['səːfɪŋ] *n* surfing *m*.

surge [səːdʒ] *n* (*strong movement*) ondata; (*of feeling*) impeto; (*ELEC*) sovracorrente *f* ♦ *vi* (*waves*) gonfiarsi; (*ELEC: power*) aumentare improvvisamente; **to ~ forward** buttarsi avanti.

surgeon ['səːdʒən] *n* chirurgo.

Surgeon General *n* (*US*) ≈ Ministro della Sanità.

surgery ['səːdʒərɪ] *n* chirurgia; (*BRIT MED: room*) studio *or* gabinetto medico, ambulatorio; (: *session*) visita ambulatoriale; (*BRIT: of MP etc*) incontri *mpl* con gli elettori; **to undergo ~** subire un intervento chirurgico.

surgery hours *npl* (*BRIT*) orario delle visite *or* di consultazione.

surgical ['səːdʒɪkl] *adj* chirurgico(a).

surgical spirit *n* (*BRIT*) alcool denaturato.

surly ['səːlɪ] *adj* scontroso(a), burbero(a).

surmise [səː'maɪz] *vt* supporre, congetturare.

surmount [səː'maunt] *vt* sormontare.

surname ['səːneɪm] *n* cognome *m*.

surpass [səː'pɑːs] *vt* superare.

surplus ['səːpləs] *n* eccedenza; (*ECON*) surplus *m inv* ♦ *adj* eccedente, d'avanzo; **it is ~ to our requirements** eccede i nostri bisogni; ~ **stock** merce *f* in sovrappiù.

surprise [sə'praɪz] *n* sorpresa; (*astonishment*) stupore *m* ♦ *vt* sorprendere; stupire; **to take by ~** (*person*) cogliere di sorpresa; (*MIL: town, fort*) attaccare di sorpresa.

surprising [sə'praɪzɪŋ] *adj* sorprendente, stupefacente.

surprisingly [sə'praɪzɪŋlɪ] *adv* sorprendentemente; (**somewhat**) ~**, he agreed** cosa (alquanto) sorprendente, ha accettato.

surrealism [sə'rɪəlɪzəm] *n* surrealismo.

surrealist [sə'rɪəlɪst] *adj*, *n* surrealista (*m/f*).

surrender [sə'rɛndə*] *n* resa, capitolazione *f* ♦ *vi* arrendersi ♦ *vt* (*claim, right*) rinunciare a.

surrender value *n* (*COMM*) valore *m* di riscatto.

surreptitious [sʌrəp'tɪʃəs] *adj* furtivo(a).

surrogate ['sʌrəgɪt] *n* (*BRIT: substitute*) surrogato ♦ *adj* surrogato(a).

surrogate mother *n* madre *f* sostitutiva.

surround [sə'raund] *vt* circondare; (*MIL etc*) accerchiare.

surrounding [sə'raundɪŋ] *adj* circostante.

surroundings [sə'raundɪŋz] *npl* dintorni *mpl*; (*fig*) ambiente *m*.

surtax ['sɔːtæks] *n* soprattassa.
surveillance [sɔː'veɪləns] *n* sorveglianza, controllo.
survey *n* ['sɔːveɪ] (*comprehensive view: of situation, development*) quadro generale; (*study*) indagine *f*, studio; (*in housebuying etc*) perizia; (*of land*) rilevamento, rilievo topografico ♦ *vt* [sɔː'veɪ] osservare; esaminare; (*SURVEYING: building*) fare una perizia di; (: *land*) fare il rilevamento di.
surveying [sɔ'veɪɪŋ] *n* (*of land*) agrimensura.
surveyor [sɔ'veɪə*] *n* perito; (*of land*) agrimensore *m*.
survival [sɔ'vaɪvl] *n* sopravvivenza; (*relic*) reliquia, vestigio.
survival course *n* corso di sopravvivenza.
survival kit *n* equipaggiamento di prima necessità.
survive [sɔ'vaɪv] *vi* sopravvivere ♦ *vt* sopravvivere a.
survivor [sɔ'vaɪvə*] *n* superstite *m/f*, sopravvissuto/a.
susceptible [sɔ'sɛptəbl] *adj*: ~ (**to**) sensibile (a); (*disease*) predisposto(a) (a).
suspect *adj, n* ['sʌspɛkt] *adj* sospetto(a) ♦ *n* persona sospetta ♦ *vt* [sɔs'pɛkt] sospettare; (*think likely*) supporre; (*doubt*) dubitare di.
suspected [sɔs'pɛktɪd] *adj* presunto(a); **to have a** ~ **facture** avere una sospetta frattura.
suspend [sɔs'pɛnd] *vt* sospendere.
suspended animation *n*: **in a state of** ~ in stato comatoso.
suspended sentence *n* condanna con la condizionale.
suspender belt [sɔs'pɛndə*-] *n* (*BRIT*) reggicalze *m inv*.
suspenders [sɔs'pɛndəz] *npl* (*BRIT*) giarrettiere *fpl*; (*US*) bretelle *fpl*.
suspense [sɔs'pɛns] *n* apprensione *f*; (*in film etc*) suspense *m*.
suspension [sɔs'pɛnʃən] *n* (*gen, AUT*) sospensione *f*; (*of driving licence*) ritiro temporaneo.
suspension bridge *n* ponte *m* sospeso.
suspicion [sɔs'pɪʃən] *n* sospetto; **to be under** ~ essere sospettato; **arrested on** ~ **of murder** arrestato come presunto omicida.
suspicious [sɔs'pɪʃəs] *adj* (*suspecting*) sospettoso(a); (*causing suspicion*) sospetto(a); **to be** ~ **of** *or* **about sb/sth** nutrire sospetti nei riguardi di qn/qc.
suss out *vt* (*BRIT col*): **I've** ~**ed it/him out** ho capito come stanno le cose/che tipo è.
sustain [sɔs'teɪn] *vt* sostenere; sopportare;

(*suffer*) subire.
sustainable [sɔs'teɪnəbl] *adj* sostenibile.
sustained [sɔs'teɪnd] *adj* (*effort*) prolungato(a).
sustenance ['sʌstɪnəns] *n* nutrimento; mezzi *mpl* di sostentamento.
suture ['suːtʃə*] *n* sutura.
SW *abbr* (*RADIO*: = *short wave*) O.C.
swab [swɔb] *n* (*MED*) tampone *m* ♦ *vt* (*NAUT*: *also*: ~ **down**) radazzare.
swagger ['swægə*] *vi* pavoneggiarsi.
swallow ['swɔləu] *n* (*bird*) rondine *f*; (*of food*) boccone *m*; (*of drink*) sorso ♦ *vt* inghiottire; (*fig: story*) bere.
▶**swallow up** *vt* inghiottire.
swam [swæm] *pt of* **swim**.
swamp [swɔmp] *n* palude *f* ♦ *vt* sommergere.
swampy ['swɔmpɪ] *adj* palludoso(a), pantanoso(a).
swan [swɔn] *n* cigno.
swank [swæŋk] *vi* (*col*: *talk boastfully*) fare lo spaccone; (: *show off*) mettersi in mostra.
swan song *n* (*fig*) canto del cigno.
swap [swɔp] *n* scambio ♦ *vt*: **to** ~ (**for**) scambiare (con).
SWAPO ['swɑːpəu] *n abbr* = *South-West Africa People's Organization*.
swarm [swɔːm] *n* sciame *m* ♦ *vi* formicolare; (*bees*) sciamare.
swarthy ['swɔːðɪ] *adj* di carnagione scura.
swashbuckling ['swɔʃbʌklɪŋ] *adj* (*role, hero*) spericolato(a).
swastika ['swɔstɪkə] *n* croce *f* uncinata, svastica.
SWAT [swɔt] *n abbr* (*US*: = *Special Weapons and Tactics*) *reparto speciale di polizia*; **a** ~ **team** uno squadrone del reparto speciale (di polizia).
swat [swɔt] *vt* schiacciare ♦ *n* (*BRIT*: *also*: **fly** ~) ammazzamosche *m inv*.
swathe [sweɪð] *n* fascio ♦ *vt*: **to** ~ **in** (*bandages, blankets*) avvolgere in.
swatter ['swɔtə*] *n* (*also*: **fly** ~) ammazzamosche *m inv*.
sway [sweɪ] *vi* (*building*) oscillare; (*tree*) ondeggiare; (*person*) barcollare ♦ *vt* (*influence*) influenzare ♦ *n* (*rule, power*): ~ (**over**) influenza (su); **to hold** ~ **over sb** dominare qn.
Swaziland ['swɑːzɪlænd] *n* Swaziland *m*.
swear, *pt* **swore**, *pp* **sworn** [swɛə*, swɔː*, swɔːn] *vi* (*witness etc*) giurare; (*curse*) bestemmiare, imprecare ♦ *vt*: **to** ~ **an oath** prestare giuramento; **to** ~ **to sth** giurare qc.
▶**swear in** *vt* prestare giuramento a.

swearword ['swɛəwəːd] *n* parolaccia.
sweat [swɛt] *n* sudore *m*, traspirazione *f*
♦ *vi* sudare; **in a** ~ in un bagno di sudore.
sweatband ['swɛtbænd] *n* (*SPORT*) fascia
elastica (per assorbire il sudore).
sweater ['swɛtə*] *n* maglione *m*.
sweatshirt ['swɛtʃəːt] *n* maglione *m* in
cotone felpato.
sweatshop ['swɛtʃɔp] *n azienda o fabbrica
dove i dipendenti sono sfruttati.*
sweaty ['swɛtɪ] *adj* sudato(a); bagnato(a) di
sudore.
Swede [swiːd] *n* svedese *m/f*.
swede [swiːd] *n* (*BRIT*) rapa svedese.
Sweden ['swiːdn] *n* Svezia.
Swedish ['swiːdɪʃ] *adj* svedese ♦ *n* (*LING*)
svedese *m*.
sweep [swiːp] *n* spazzata; (*curve*) curva;
(*expanse*) distesa, (*range*) portata; (*also:*
chimney ~) spazzacamino ♦ *vb* (*pt, pp*
swept [swɛpt]) *vt* spazzare, scopare; (*subj:
fashion, craze*) invadere ♦ *vi* camminare
maestosamente; precipitarsi, lanciarsi;
(e)stendersi.
▶**sweep away** *vt* spazzare via, trascinare
via.
▶**sweep past** *vi* sfrecciare accanto;
passare accanto maestosamente.
▶**sweep up** *vt, vi* spazzare.
sweeper ['swiːpə*] *n* (*person*) spazzino/a;
(*machine*) spazzatrice *f*; (*FOOTBALL*)
libero.
sweeping ['swiːpɪŋ] *adj* (*gesture*) ampio(a);
(*changes, reforms*) ampio(a), radicale; **a** ~
statement un'affermazione generica.
sweepstake ['swiːpsteɪk] *n* lotteria (*spesso
abbinata alle corse dei cavalli*).
sweet [swiːt] *n* (*BRIT*) dolce *m*; (*candy*)
caramella ♦ *adj* dolce; (*fresh*) fresco(a); .
(*kind*) gentile; (*cute*) carino(a) ♦ *adv:* **to
smell/taste** ~ avere un odore/sapore
dolce; ~ **and sour** *adj* agrodolce.
sweetbread ['swiːtbrɛd] *n* animella.
sweetcorn ['swiːtkɔːn] *n* granturco dolce.
sweeten ['swiːtn] *vt* addolcire; zuccherare.
sweetener ['swiːtnə*] *n* (*CULIN*)
dolcificante *m*.
sweetheart ['swiːthɑːt] *n* innamorato/a.
sweetly ['swiːtlɪ] *adv* dolcemente.
sweetness ['swiːtnɪs] *n* sapore *m* dolce;
dolcezza.
sweet pea *n* pisello odoroso.
sweet potato *n* patata americana, patata
dolce.
sweetshop ['swiːtʃɔp] *n* (*BRIT*) ≈
pasticceria.
sweet tooth *n:* **to have a** ~ avere un
debole per i dolci.

swell [swɛl] *n* (*of sea*) mare *m* lungo ♦ *adj*
(*col: excellent*) favoloso(a) ♦ *vb* (*pt* ~**ed,** *pp*
swollen, ~**ed** ['swəulən]) *vt* gonfiare,
ingrossare; (*numbers, sales etc*)
aumentare ♦ *vi* gonfiarsi, ingrossarsi;
(*sound*) crescere; (*MED*) gonfiarsi.
swelling ['swɛlɪŋ] *n* (*MED*) tumefazione *f*,
gonfiore *m*.
sweltering ['swɛltərɪŋ] *adj* soffocante.
swept [swɛpt] *pt, pp of* **sweep.**
swerve [swəːv] *vi* deviare; (*driver*) sterzare;
(*boxer*) scartare.
swift [swɪft] *n* (*bird*) rondone *m* ♦ *adj*
rapido(a), veloce.
swiftly ['swɪftlɪ] *adv* rapidamente,
velocemente.
swiftness ['swɪftnɪs] *n* rapidità, velocità.
swig [swɪg] *n* (*col: drink*) sorsata.
swill [swɪl] *n* broda ♦ *vt* (*also:* ~ **out,** ~
down) risciacquare.
swim [swɪm] *n:* **to go for a** ~ andare a fare
una nuotata ♦ *vb* (*pt* **swam**, *pp* **swum**
[swæm, swʌm]) *vi* nuotare; (*SPORT*) fare
del nuoto; (*head, room*) girare ♦ *vt* (*river,
channel*) attraversare *or* percorrere a
nuoto; **to go** ~**ming** andare a nuotare; **to**
~ **a length** fare una vasca (a nuoto).
swimmer ['swɪmə*] *n* nuotatore/trice.
swimming ['swɪmɪŋ] *n* nuoto.
swimming baths *npl* (*BRIT*) piscina.
swimming cap *n* cuffia.
swimming costume *n* (*BRIT*) costume *m*
da bagno.
swimmingly ['swɪmɪŋlɪ] *adv:* **to go** ~
(*wonderfully*) andare a gonfie vele.
swimming pool *n* piscina.
swimming trunks *npl* costume *m* da
bagno (per uomo).
swimsuit ['swɪmsuːt] *n* costume *m* da
bagno.
swindle ['swɪndl] *n* truffa ♦ *vt* truffare.
swindler ['swɪndlə*] *n* truffatore/trice.
swine [swaɪn] *n* (*pl inv*) maiale *m*, porco;
(*col!*) porco (*!*).
swing [swɪŋ] *n* altalena; (*movement*)
oscillazione *f*; (*MUS*) ritmo; (*also:* ~
music) swing *m* ♦ *vb* (*pt, pp* **swung** [swʌŋ])
vt dondolare, far oscillare; (*also:* ~ **round**)
far girare ♦ *vi* oscillare, dondolare; (*also:*
~ **round**: *object*) roteare; (: *person*)
girarsi, voltarsi; **to be in full** ~ (*activity*)
essere in piena attività; (*party etc*) essere
nel pieno; **a** ~ **to the left** (*POL*) una svolta
a sinistra; **to get into the** ~ **of things**
entrare nel pieno delle cose; **the road** ~**s
south** la strada prende la direzione sud.
swing bridge *n* ponte *m* girevole.
swing door *n* (*BRIT*) porta battente.

swingeing ['swɪndʒɪŋ] *adj* (*BRIT: defeat*) violento(a); (: *price increase*) enorme.

swinging ['swɪŋɪŋ] *adj* (*step*) cadenzato(a), ritmico(a); (*rhythm, music*) trascinante; ~ **door** (*US*) porta battente.

swipe [swaɪp] *n* forte colpo; schiaffo ♦ *vt* (*hit*) colpire con forza; dare uno schiaffo a; (*col: steal*) sgraffignare; (*credit card etc*) far passare (nell'apposita macchinetta).

swirl [swɜːl] *n* turbine *m*, mulinello ♦ *vi* turbinare, far mulinello.

swish [swɪʃ] *adj* (*col: smart*) all'ultimo grido, alla moda ♦ *n* (*sound: of whip*) sibilo; (: *of skirts, grass*) fruscio ♦ *vi* sibilare.

Swiss [swɪs] *adj, n* (*pl inv*) svizzero(a).

Swiss French *adj* svizzero(a) francese.

Swiss German *adj* svizzero(a) tedesco(a).

switch [swɪtʃ] *n* (*for light, radio etc*) interruttore *m*; (*change*) cambiamento ♦ *vt* (*also:* ~ **round,** ~ **over**) cambiare; scambiare.
- ▶**switch off** *vt* spegnere.
- ▶**switch on** *vt* accendere; (*engine, machine*) mettere in moto, avviare; (*AUT: ignition*) inserire; (*BRIT: water supply*) aprire.

switchback ['swɪtʃbæk] *n* (*BRIT*) montagne *fpl* russe.

switchblade ['swɪtʃbleɪd] *n* (*also:* ~ **knife**) coltello a scatto.

switchboard ['swɪtʃbɔːd] *n* centralino.

switchboard operator *n* centralinista *m/f.*

Switzerland ['swɪtsələnd] *n* Svizzera.

swivel ['swɪvl] *vi* (*also:* ~ **round**) girare.

swollen ['swəulən] *pp of* **swell** ♦ *adj* (*ankle etc*) gonfio(a).

swoon [swuːn] *vi* svenire.

swoop [swuːp] *n* (*by police etc*) incursione *f*; (*of bird etc*) picchiata ♦ *vi* (*also:* ~ **down**) scendere in picchiata; (*police*): **to** ~ (**on**) fare un'incursione (in).

swop [swɔp] *n, vt* = **swap.**

sword [sɔːd] *n* spada.

swordfish ['sɔːdfɪʃ] *n* pesce *m* spada *inv.*

swore [swɔː*] *pt of* **swear.**

sworn [swɔːn] *pp of* **swear.**

swot [swɔt] *vt* sgobbare su ♦ *vi* sgobbare.

swum [swʌm] *pp of* **swim.**

swung [swʌŋ] *pt, pp of* **swing.**

sycamore ['sɪkəmɔː*] *n* sicomoro.

sycophant ['sɪkəfənt] *n* leccapiedi *m/f.*

sycophantic [sɪkə'fæntɪk] *adj* ossequioso(a), adulatore(trice).

Sydney ['sɪdnɪ] *n* Sydney *f.*

syllable ['sɪləbl] *n* sillaba.

syllabus ['sɪləbəs] *n* programma *m; on the* ~ in programma d'esame.

symbol ['sɪmbl] *n* simbolo.

symbolic(al) [sɪm'bɔlɪk(l)] *adj* simbolico(a); **to be** ~ **of sth** simboleggiare qc.

symbolism ['sɪmbəlɪzəm] *n* simbolismo.

symbolize ['sɪmbəlaɪz] *vt* simbolizzare.

symmetrical [sɪ'mɛtrɪkl] *adj* simmetrico(a).

symmetry ['sɪmɪtrɪ] *n* simmetria.

sympathetic [sɪmpə'θɛtɪk] *adj* (*showing pity*) compassionevole; (*kind*) comprensivo(a); ~ **towards** ben disposto(a) verso; **to be** ~ **to a cause** (*well-disposed*) simpatizzare per una causa.

sympathetically [sɪmpə'θɛtɪklɪ] *adv* in modo compassionevole; con comprensione.

sympathize ['sɪmpəθaɪz] *vi:* **to** ~ **with sb** compatire qn; partecipare al dolore di qn; (*understand*) capire qn.

sympathizer ['sɪmpəθaɪzə*] *n* (*POL*) simpatizzante *m/f.*

sympathy ['sɪmpəθɪ] *n* compassione *f*; **in** ~ **with** d'accordo con; (*strike*) per solidarietà con; **with our deepest** ~ con le nostre più sincere condoglianze.

symphonic [sɪm'fɔnɪk] *adj* sinfonico(a).

symphony ['sɪmfənɪ] *n* sinfonia.

symphony orchestra *n* orchestra sinfonica.

symposium [sɪm'pəuzɪəm] *n* simposio.

symptom ['sɪmptəm] *n* sintomo; indizio.

symptomatic [sɪmptə'mætɪk] *adj:* ~ (**of**) sintomatico(a) (di).

synagogue ['sɪnəgɔg] *n* sinagoga.

sync [sɪŋk] *n* (*col*): **in/out of** ~ in/fuori sincronia; (*fig: people*) **they are in** ~ sono in sintonia.

synchromesh [sɪŋkrəu'mɛʃ] *n* cambio sincronizzato.

synchronize ['sɪŋkrənaɪz] *vt* sincronizzare ♦ *vi:* **to** ~ **with** essere contemporaneo(a) a.

synchronized swimming *n* nuoto sincronizzato.

syncopated ['sɪŋkəpeɪtɪd] *adj* sincopato(a).

syndicate ['sɪndɪkɪt] *n* sindacato; (*PRESS*) agenzia di stampa.

syndrome ['sɪndrəum] *n* sindrome *f.*

synonym ['sɪnənɪm] *n* sinonimo.

synonymous [sɪ'nɔnɪməs] *adj:* ~ (**with**) sinonimo(a) (di).

synopsis, *pl* **synopses** [sɪ'nɔpsɪs, -siːz] *n* sommario, sinossi *f inv.*

syntax ['sɪntæks] *n* sintassi *f inv.*

synthesis, *pl* **syntheses** ['sɪnθəsɪs, -siːz] *n* sintesi *f inv.*

synthesizer ['sɪnθəsaɪzə*] *n* (*MUS*) sintetizzatore *m.*

synthetic [sɪn'θetɪk] *adj* sintetico(a) ♦ *n* prodotto sintetico; (*TEXTILES*) fibra sintetica.
syphilis ['sɪfɪlɪs] *n* sifilide *f.*
syphon ['saɪfən] *n, vb* = **siphon**.
Syria ['sɪrɪə] *n* Siria.
Syrian ['sɪrɪən] *adj, n* siriano(a).
syringe [sɪ'rɪndʒ] *n* siringa.
syrup ['sɪrəp] *n* sciroppo; (*also:* **golden** ~) melassa raffinata.
syrupy ['sɪrəpɪ] *adj* sciropposo(a).
system ['sɪstəm] *n* sistema *m*; (*network*) rete *f*; (*ANAT*) apparato; **it was a shock to his** ~ è stato uno shock per il suo organismo.
systematic [sɪstə'mætɪk] *adj* sistematico(a).
system disk *n* (*COMPUT*) disco del sistema.
systems analyst *n* analista *m/f* di sistemi.

T t

T, t [tiː] *n* (*letter*) T, t *m or f inv*; **T for Tommy** ≈ T come Taranto.
TA *n abbr* (*BRIT*) = **Territorial Army**.
ta [taɪ] *excl* (*BRIT col*) grazie!
tab [tæb] *n abbr* = **tabulator** ♦ *n* (*loop on coat etc*) laccetto; (*label*) etichetta; **to keep ~s on** (*fig*) tenere d'occhio.
tabby ['tæbɪ] *n* (*also:* ~ **cat**) (gatto) soriano, gatto tigrato.
tabernacle ['tæbənækl] *n* tabernacolo.
table ['teɪbl] *n* tavolo, tavola; (*chart*) tabella ♦ *vt* (*motion etc*) presentare; **to lay or set the** ~ apparecchiare *or* preparare la tavola; **to clear the** ~ sparecchiare; **league** ~ (*FOOTBALL, RUGBY*) classifica; ~ **of contents** indice *m*.
tablecloth ['teɪblklɒθ] *n* tovaglia.
table d'hôte [taːbl'dəut] *adj* (*meal*) a prezzo fisso.
table lamp *n* lampada da tavolo.
tablemat ['teɪblmæt] *n* sottopiatto.
table salt *n* sale *m* fino *or* da tavola.
tablespoon ['teɪblspuːn] *n* cucchiaio da tavola; (*also:* ~**ful**) cucchiaiata.
tablet ['tæblɪt] *n* (*MED*) compressa; (: *for sucking*) pastiglia; (*for writing*) blocco; (*of stone*) targa; ~ **of soap** (*BRIT*) saponetta.
table tennis *n* tennis *m* da tavolo, ping-pong ® *m*.

table wine *n* vino da tavola.
tabloid ['tæblɔɪd] *n* (*newspaper*) tabloid *m inv* (*giornale illustrato di formato ridotto*); **the ~s, the ~ press** i giornali popolari; *see boxed note.*

TABLOID PRESS

*Il termine **tabloid press** si riferisce ai quotidiani o ai settimanali popolari che, rispetto ai "quality papers" hanno un formato ridotto e presentano le notizie in modo più sensazionalistico e meno approfondito; vedi anche **quality press**.*

---

taboo [tə'buː] *adj, n* tabù (*m inv*).
tabulate ['tæbjuleɪt] *vt* (*data*) tabulare.
tabulator ['tæbjuleɪtə*] *n* tabulatore *m*.
tachograph ['tækəgraːf] *n* tachigrafo.
tachometer [tæ'kɒmɪtə*] *n* tachimetro.
tacit ['tæsɪt] *adj* tacito(a).
taciturn ['tæsɪtəːn] *adj* taciturno(a).
tack [tæk] *n* (*nail*) bulletta; (*stitch*) punto d'imbastitura; (*NAUT*) bordo, bordata ♦ *vt* imbullettare; imbastire ♦ *vi* bordeggiare; **to change** ~ virare di bordo; **on the wrong** ~ (*fig*) sulla strada sbagliata; **to ~ sth on to (the end of) sth** (*of letter, book*) aggiungere qc alla fine di qc.
tackle ['tækl] *n* (*equipment*) attrezzatura, equipaggiamento; (*for lifting*) paranco; (*RUGBY*) placcaggio; (*FOOTBALL*) contrasto ♦ *vt* (*difficulty*) affrontare; (*RUGBY*) placcare; (*FOOTBALL*) contrastare.
tacky ['tækɪ] *adj* colloso(a); ancora bagnato(a); (*col: shabby*) scadente.
tact [tækt] *n* tatto.
tactful ['tæktful] *adj* delicato(a), discreto(a); **to be** ~ avere tatto.
tactfully ['tæktfəlɪ] *adv* con tatto.
tactical ['tæktɪkl] *adj* tattico(a).
tactical voting *n* voto tattico.
tactician [tæk'tɪʃən] *n* tattico/a.
tactics ['tæktɪks] *n, npl* tattica.
tactless ['tæktlɪs] *adj* che manca di tatto.
tactlessly ['tæktlɪslɪ] *adv* senza tatto.
tadpole ['tædpəul] *n* girino.
taffy ['tæfɪ] *n* (*US*) caramella *f* mou *inv*.
tag [tæg] *n* etichetta; **price/name** ~ etichetta del prezzo/con il nome.
▶**tag along** *vi* seguire.
Tahiti [tə'hiːtɪ] *n* Tahiti *f.*
tail [teɪl] *n* coda; (*of shirt*) falda ♦ *vt* (*follow*) seguire, pedinare; **to turn** ~ voltare la schiena; *see also* **head**.
▶**tail away, tail off** *vi* (*in size, quality etc*) diminuire gradatamente.
tailback ['teɪlbæk] *n* (*BRIT*) ingorgo.

tail coat *n* marsina.
tail end *n* (*of train, procession etc*) coda; (*of meeting etc*) fine *f*.
tailgate ['teɪlgeɪt] *n* (*AUT*) portellone *m* posteriore.
tail light *n* (*AUT*) fanalino di coda.
tailor ['teɪlə*] *n* sarto ♦ *vt*: **to ~ sth (to)** adattare qc (alle esigenze di); **~'s (shop)** sartoria (da uomo).
tailoring ['teɪlərɪŋ] *n* (*cut*) taglio.
tailor-made ['teɪlə'meɪd] *adj* (*also fig*) fatto(a) su misura.
tailwind ['teɪlwɪnd] *n* vento di coda.
taint [teɪnt] *vt* (*meat, food*) far avariare; (*fig: reputation*) infangare.
tainted ['teɪntɪd] *adj* (*food*) guasto(a); (*water, air*) infetto(a); (*fig*) corrotto(a).
Taiwan [taɪ'wɑːn] *n* Taiwan *m*.
Tajikistan [tɑːdʒɪkɪ'stɑːn] *n* Tagikistan *m*.
take [teɪk] *vb* (*pt* **took**, *pp* **taken** [tuk, 'teɪkn]) *vt* prendere; (*gain: prize*) ottenere, vincere; (*require: effort, courage*) occorrere, volerci; (*tolerate*) accettare, sopportare; (*hold: passengers etc*) contenere; (*accompany*) accompagnare; (*bring, carry*) portare; (*conduct: meeting*) condurre; (*exam*) sostenere, presentarsi a ♦ *vi* (*dye, fire etc*) prendere; (*injection*) fare effetto; (*plant*) attecchire ♦ *n* (*CINE*) ripresa; **I ~ it that** suppongo che; **to ~ for a walk** (*child, dog*) portare a fare una passeggiata; **to ~ sb's hand** prendere qn per mano; **to ~ it upon o.s. to do sth** prendersi la responsabilità di fare qc; **to be ~n ill** avere un malore; **to be ~n with sb/sth** (*attracted*) essere tutto preso da qn/qc; **it won't ~ long** non ci vorrà molto tempo; **it ~s a lot of time/courage** occorre *or* ci vuole molto tempo/coraggio; **it will ~ at least 5 litres** contiene almeno 5 litri; **~ the first on the left** prenda la prima a sinistra; **to ~ Russian at university** fare russo all'università; **I took him for a doctor** l'ho preso per un dottore.
▶**take after** *vt fus* assomigliare a.
▶**take apart** *vt* smontare.
▶**take away** *vt* portare via; togliere; **to ~ away (from)** sottrarre (da).
▶**take back** *vt* (*return*) restituire; riportare; (*one's words*) ritirare.
▶**take down** *vt* (*building*) demolire; (*dismantle: scaffolding*) smontare; (*letter etc*) scrivere.
▶**take in** *vt* (*lodger*) prendere, ospitare; (*orphan*) accogliere; (*stray dog*) raccogliere; (*SEWING*) stringere; (*deceive*) imbrogliare, abbindolare; (*understand*)

capire; (*include*) comprendere, includere.
▶**take off** *vi* (*AVIAT*) decollare ♦ *vt* (*remove*) togliere; (*imitate*) imitare.
▶**take on** *vt* (*work*) accettare, intraprendere; (*employee*) assumere; (*opponent*) sfidare, affrontare.
▶**take out** *vt* portare fuori; (*remove*) togliere; (*licence*) prendere, ottenere; **to ~ sth out of** tirare qc fuori da; estrarre qc da; **don't ~ it out on me!** non prendertela con me!
▶**take over** *vt* (*business*) rilevare ♦ *vi*: **to ~ over from sb** prendere le consegne *or* il controllo da qn.
▶**take to** *vt fus* (*person*) prendere in simpatia; (*activity*) prendere gusto a; (*form habit of*): **to ~ to doing sth** prendere *or* cominciare a fare qc.
▶**take up** *vt* (*one's story*) riprendere; (*dress*) accorciare; (*absorb: liquids*) assorbire; (*accept: offer, challenge*) accettare; (*occupy: time, space*) occupare; (*engage in: hobby etc*) mettersi a; **to ~ up with sb** fare amicizia con qn.
takeaway ['teɪkəweɪ] *adj* (*BRIT: food*) da portar via.
take-home pay ['teɪkhəum-] *n* stipendio netto.
taken ['teɪkn] *pp of* **take**.
takeoff ['teɪkɔf] *n* (*AVIAT*) decollo.
takeout ['teɪkaut] *adj* (*US*) = **takeaway**.
takeover ['teɪkəuvə*] *n* (*COMM*) assorbimento.
takeover bid *n* offerta di assorbimento.
takings ['teɪkɪŋz] *npl* (*COMM*) incasso.
talc [tælk] *n* (*also:* **~um powder**) talco.
tale [teɪl] *n* racconto, storia; (*pej*) fandonia; **to tell ~s** fare la spia.
talent ['tælənt] *n* talento.
talented ['tæləntɪd] *adj* di talento.
talent scout *n* talent scout *m/f inv*.
talisman ['tælɪzmən] *n* talismano.
talk [tɔːk] *n* discorso; (*gossip*) chiacchiere *fpl*; (*conversation*) conversazione *f*; (*interview*) discussione *f* ♦ *vi* parlare; (*chatter*) chiacchierare; **to give a ~** tenere una conferenza; **to ~ about** parlare di; (*converse*) discorrere *or* conversare su; **to ~ sb out of/into doing** dissuadere qn da/convincere qn a fare; **to ~ shop** parlare del lavoro *or* degli affari; **~ing of films, have you seen …?** a proposito di film, ha visto …?
▶**talk over** *vt* discutere.
talkative ['tɔːkətɪv] *adj* loquace, ciarliero(a).
talking point ['tɔːkɪŋ-] *n* argomento di conversazione.

talking-to ['tɔːkɪŋtuː] n: **to give sb a good** ~ fare una bella paternale a qn.

talk show n (TV, RADIO) intervista (informale), talk show m inv.

tall [tɔːl] adj alto(a); **to be 6 feet** ~ ≈ essere alto 1 metro e 80; **how** ~ **are you?** quanto è alto?

tallboy ['tɔːlbɔɪ] n (BRIT) cassettone m alto.

tallness ['tɔːlnɪs] n altezza.

tall story n panzana, frottola.

tally ['tælɪ] n conto, conteggio ♦ vi: **to** ~ **(with)** corrispondere (a); **to keep a** ~ **of sth** tener il conto di qc.

talon ['tælən] n artiglio.

tambourine [tæmbə'riːn] n tamburello.

tame [teɪm] adj addomesticato(a); (fig: story, style) insipido(a), scialbo(a).

Tamil ['tæmɪl] adj tamil inv ♦ n tamil m/f inv; (LING) tamil m.

tamper ['tæmpə*] vi: **to** ~ **with** manomettere.

tampon ['tæmpon] n tampone m.

tan [tæn] n (also: **sun**~) abbronzatura ♦ vt abbronzare ♦ vi abbronzarsi ♦ adj (colour) marrone rossiccio inv; **to get a** ~ abbronzarsi.

tandem ['tændəm] n tandem m inv.

tandoori [tæn'duərɪ] adj nella cucina indiana, detto di carni o verdure cucinate allo spiedo in particolari forni.

tang [tæŋ] n odore m penetrante; sapore m piccante.

tangent ['tændʒənt] n (MATH) tangente f; **to go off at a** ~ (fig) partire per la tangente.

tangerine [tændʒə'riːn] n mandarino.

tangible ['tændʒəbl] adj tangibile; ~ **assets** patrimonio reale.

Tangier [tæn'dʒɪə*] n Tangeri f.

tangle ['tæŋgl] n groviglio ♦ vt aggrovigliare; **to get in(to) a** ~ finire in un groviglio.

tango ['tæŋgəu] n tango.

tank [tæŋk] n serbatoio; (for processing) vasca; (for fish) acquario; (MIL) carro armato.

tankard ['tæŋkəd] n boccale m.

tanker ['tæŋkə*] n (ship) nave f cisterna inv; (for oil) petroliera; (truck) autobotte f, autocisterna.

tanned [tænd] adj abbronzato(a).

tannin ['tænɪn] n tannino.

tanning ['tænɪŋ] n (of leather) conciatura.

tannoy ® ['tænɔɪ] n (BRIT) altoparlante m; **over the** ~ per altoparlante.

tantalizing ['tæntəlaɪzɪŋ] adj allettante.

tantamount ['tæntəmaunt] adj: ~ **to** equivalente a.

tantrum ['tæntrəm] n accesso di collera; **to**

throw a ~ fare le bizze.

Tanzania [tænzə'nɪə] n Tanzania.

Tanzanian [tænzə'nɪən] adj, n tanzaniano(a).

tap [tæp] n (on sink etc) rubinetto; (gentle blow) colpetto ♦ vt dare un colpetto a; (resources) sfruttare, utilizzare; (telephone conversation) intercettare; (telephone) mettere sotto controllo; **on** ~ (beer) alla spina; (fig: resources) a disposizione.

tap-dancing ['tæpdɑːnsɪŋ] n tip tap m.

tape [teɪp] n nastro; (also: **magnetic** ~) nastro (magnetico) ♦ vt (record) registrare (su nastro); **on** ~ (song etc) su nastro.

tape deck n piastra di registrazione.

tape measure n metro a nastro.

taper ['teɪpə*] n candelina ♦ vi assottigliarsi.

tape-record ['teɪprɪkɔːd] vt registrare (su nastro).

tape recorder n registratore m (a nastro).

tape recording n registrazione f.

tapered ['teɪpəd], **tapering** ['teɪpərɪŋ] adj affusolato(a).

tapestry ['tæpɪstrɪ] n arazzo; tappezzeria.

tape-worm ['teɪpwɜːm] n tenia, verme m solitario.

tapioca [tæpɪ'əukə] n tapioca.

tappet ['tæpɪt] n punteria.

tar [tɑː*] n catrame m; **low-/middle-**~ **cigarettes** sigarette a basso/medio contenuto di nicotina.

tarantula [tə'ræntjulə] n tarantola.

tardy ['tɑːdɪ] adj tardo(a); tardivo(a).

target ['tɑːgɪt] n bersaglio; (fig: objective) obiettivo; **to be on** ~ (project) essere nei tempi (di lavorazione).

target practice n tiro al bersaglio.

tariff ['tærɪf] n tariffa.

tarmac ['tɑːmæk] n (BRIT: on road) macadam m al catrame; (AVIAT) pista di decollo ♦ vt (BRIT) macadamizzare.

tarnish ['tɑːnɪʃ] vt offuscare, annerire; (fig) macchiare.

tarot ['tærəu] n tarocco.

tarpaulin [tɑː'pɔːlɪn] n tela incatramata.

tarragon ['tærəgən] n dragoncello.

tart [tɑːt] n (CULIN) crostata; (BRIT col: pej: woman) sgualdrina ♦ adj (flavour) aspro(a), agro(a).

▶**tart up** vt (col): **to** ~ **o.s. up** farsi bello(a); (pej) agghindarsi.

tartan ['tɑːtn] n tartan m inv.

tartar ['tɑːtə*] n (on teeth) tartaro.

tartar sauce n salsa tartara.

task [tɑːsk] n compito; **to take to** ~

rimproverare.
task force n (*MIL, POLICE*) unità operativa.
taskmaster ['tɑ:skmɑ:stə*] n: **he's a hard ~**
è un vero tiranno.
Tasmania [tæz'meɪnɪə] n Tasmania.
tassel ['tæsl] n fiocco.
taste [teɪst] n gusto; (*flavour*) sapore m,
gusto; (*fig: glimpse, idea*) idea ♦ vt gustare;
(*sample*) assaggiare ♦ vi: **to ~ of** (*fish etc*)
sapere di, avere sapore di; **what does it
~ like?** che sapore *or* gusto ha?; **it ~s like
fish** sa di pesce; **you can ~ the garlic (in
it)** (ci) si sente il sapore dell'aglio; **can I
have a ~ of this wine?** posso assaggiare
un po' di questo vino?; **to have a ~ of sth**
assaggiare qc; **to have a ~ for sth** avere
un'inclinazione per qc; **to be in bad** *or*
poor ~ essere di cattivo gusto.
taste bud n papilla gustativa.
tasteful ['teɪstful] adj di buon gusto.
tastefully ['teɪstfəlɪ] adv con gusto.
tasteless ['teɪstlɪs] adj (*food*) insipido(a);
(*remark*) di cattivo gusto.
tasty ['teɪstɪ] adj saporito(a), gustoso(a).
tattered ['tætəd] adj see **tatters**.
tatters ['tætəz] npl: **in ~** (*also:* **tattered**) a
brandelli, sbrindellato(a).
tattoo [tə'tu:] n tatuaggio; (*spectacle*)
parata militare ♦ vt tatuare.
tatty ['tætɪ] adj (*BRIT col*) malandato(a).
taught [tɔ:t] pt, pp of **teach**.
taunt [tɔ:nt] n scherno ♦ vt schernire.
Taurus ['tɔ:rəs] n Toro; **to be ~** essere del
Toro.
taut [tɔ:t] adj teso(a).
tavern ['tævən] n taverna.
tawdry ['tɔ:drɪ] adj pacchiano(a).
tawny ['tɔ:nɪ] adj fulvo(a).
tax [tæks] n imposta, tassa; (*on income*)
imposte *fpl*, tasse *fpl* ♦ vt tassare; (*fig:
strain: patience etc*) mettere alla prova;
free of ~ esentasse *inv*, esente da
imposte; **before/after ~** al lordo/netto
delle tasse.
taxable ['tæksəbl] adj imponibile.
tax allowance n detrazione *f* d'imposta.
taxation [tæk'seɪʃən] n tassazione *f*; tasse
fpl, imposte *fpl*; **system of ~** sistema *m*
fiscale.
tax avoidance n *l'evitare legalmente il
pagamento di imposte.*
tax collector n esattore *m* delle imposte.
tax disc n (*BRIT AUT*) ≈ bollo.
tax evasion n evasione *f* fiscale.
tax exemption n esenzione *f* fiscale.
tax exile n *chi ripara all'estero per
evadere le imposte.*
tax-free [tæks'fri:] adj esente da imposte.

tax haven n paradiso fiscale.
taxi ['tæksɪ] n taxi *m inv* ♦ vi (*AVIAT*) rullare.
taxidermist ['tæksɪdə:mɪst] n tassidermista
m/f.
taxi driver n tassista *m/f*.
tax inspector n (*BRIT*) ispettore *m* delle
tasse.
taxi rank, (*US*) **taxi stand** n posteggio dei
taxi.
tax payer n contribuente *m/f*.
tax rebate n rimborso fiscale.
tax relief n sgravio fiscale.
tax return n dichiarazione *f* dei redditi.
tax shelter n paradiso fiscale.
tax year n anno fiscale.
TB n abbr (= *tuberculosis*) TBC *f*.
TD n abbr (*US*) = **Treasury Department;**
(: *FOOTBALL*) = **touchdown.**
tea [ti:] n tè *m inv*; (*BRIT: snack: for children*)
merenda; **high ~** (*BRIT*) cena leggera
(*presa nel tardo pomeriggio*).
tea bag n bustina di tè.
tea break n (*BRIT*) intervallo per il tè.
teacake ['ti:keɪk] n (*BRIT*) panino dolce
all'uva.
teach, pt, pp **taught** [ti:tʃ, tɔ:t] vt: **to ~ sb
sth, ~ sth to sb** insegnare qc a qn ♦ vi
insegnare; **it taught him a lesson** (*fig*) gli
è servito da lezione.
teacher ['ti:tʃə*] n (*gen*) insegnante *m/f*; (*in
secondary school*) professore/essa; (*in
primary school*) maestro/a; **French ~**
insegnante di francese.
teacher training college n (*for primary
schools*) ≈ istituto magistrale; (*for
secondary schools*) scuola universitaria
*per l'abilitazione all'insegnamento nelle
medie superiori.*
teaching ['ti:tʃɪŋ] n insegnamento.
teaching aids npl materiali *mpl* per
l'insegnamento.
teaching hospital n (*BRIT*) clinica
universitaria.
teaching staff n (*BRIT*) insegnanti *mpl*,
personale *m* insegnante.
tea cosy n copriteiera *m inv*.
teacup ['ti:kʌp] n tazza da tè.
teak [ti:k] n teak *m*.
tea leaves npl foglie *fpl* di tè.
team [ti:m] n squadra; (*of animals*)
tiro.
▶**team up** vi: **to ~ up (with)** mettersi
insieme (a).
team games npl giochi *mpl* di squadra.
teamwork ['ti:mwə:k] n lavoro di squadra.
tea party n tè *m inv* (*ricevimento*).
teapot ['ti:pɔt] n teiera.
tear n [tɛə*] strappo; [tɪə*] lacrima ♦ vb

[tɛə*] (pt tore, pp torn [tɔ:*, tɔ:n]) vt strappare ♦ vi strapparsi; in ~s in lacrime; to burst into ~s scoppiare in lacrime; to ~ to pieces or to bits or to shreds (also fig) fare a pezzi or a brandelli.

►tear along vi (rush) correre all'impazzata.

►tear apart vt (also fig) distruggere.

►tear away vt: to ~ o.s. away (from sth) (fig) staccarsi (da qc).

►tear out vt (sheet of paper, cheque) staccare.

►tear up vt (sheet of paper etc) strappare.

tearaway ['tɛərəweɪ] n (col) monello/a.

teardrop ['tɪədrɔp] n lacrima.

tearful ['tɪəful] adj piangente, lacrimoso(a).

tear gas n gas m lacrimogeno.

tearoom ['ti:ru:m] n sala da tè.

tease [ti:z] vt canzonare; (unkindly) tormentare.

tea set n servizio da tè.

teashop ['ti:ʃɔp] n (BRIT) sala da tè.

Teasmaid ® ['ti:zmeɪd] n macchinetta per fare il tè.

teaspoon ['ti:spu:n] n cucchiaino da tè; (also: ~ful: as measurement) cucchiaino.

tea strainer n colino da tè.

teat [ti:t] n capezzolo; (of bottle) tettarella.

teatime ['ti:taɪm] n ora del tè.

tea towel n (BRIT) strofinaccio (per i piatti).

tea urn n bollitore m per il tè.

tech [tɛk] n abbr (col) = technical college; technology.

technical ['tɛknɪkl] adj tecnico(a).

technical college n ≈ istituto tecnico.

technicality [tɛknɪ'kælɪtɪ] n tecnicità; (detail) dettaglio tecnico; on a legal ~ grazie a un cavillo legale.

technically ['tɛknɪklɪ] adv dal punto di vista tecnico.

technician [tɛk'nɪʃən] n tecnico/a.

technique [tɛk'ni:k] n tecnica.

techno ['tɛknəu] n (MUS) techno f inv.

technocrat ['tɛknəkræt] n tecnocrate m/f.

technological [tɛknə'lɔdʒɪkl] adj tecnologico(a).

technologist [tɛk'nɔlədʒɪst] n tecnologo/a.

technology [tɛk'nɔlədʒɪ] n tecnologia.

teddy (bear) ['tɛdɪ-] n orsacchiotto.

tedious ['ti:dɪəs] adj noioso(a), tedioso(a).

tedium ['ti:dɪəm] n noia, tedio.

tee [ti:] n (GOLF) tee m inv.

teem [ti:m] vi abbondare, brulicare; to ~ with brulicare di; it is ~ing (with rain) piove a dirotto.

teenage ['ti:neɪdʒ] adj (fashions etc) per giovani, per adolescenti.

teenager ['ti:neɪdʒə*] n adolescente m/f.

teens [ti:nz] npl: to be in one's ~ essere adolescente.

tee-shirt ['ti:ʃə:t] n = T-shirt.

teeter ['ti:tə*] vi barcollare, vacillare.

teeth [ti:θ] npl of tooth.

teethe [ti:ð] vi mettere i denti.

teething ring ['ti:ðɪŋ-] n dentaruolo.

teething troubles npl (fig) difficoltà fpl iniziali.

teetotal ['ti:'təutl] adj astemio(a).

teetotaller, (US) teetotaler ['ti:'təutlə*] n astemio/a.

TEFL ['tɛfl] n abbr = Teaching of English as a Foreign Language.

Teflon ® ['tɛflɔn] n teflon ® m.

Tehran [tɛə'ra:n] n Tehran f.

tel. abbr (= telephone) tel.

Tel Aviv ['tɛlə'vi:v] n Tel Aviv f.

telecast ['tɛlɪka:st] vt, vi teletrasmettere.

telecommunications ['tɛlɪkəmju:nɪ'keɪʃənz] n telecomunicazioni fpl.

teleconferencing ['tɛlɪkɔnfərənsɪŋ] n teleconferenza.

telegram ['tɛlɪɡræm] n telegramma m.

telegraph ['tɛlɪɡra:f] n telegrafo.

telegraphic [tɛlɪ'ɡræfɪk] adj telegrafico(a).

telegraph pole n palo del telegrafo.

telegraph wire n filo del telegrafo.

telepathic [tɛlɪ'pæθɪk] adj telepatico(a).

telephone ['tɛlɪfəun] n telefono ♦ vt (person) telefonare a; (message) telefonare; to have a ~, (BRIT) to be on the ~ (subscriber) avere il telefono; to be on the ~ (be speaking) essere al telefono.

telephone booth, (BRIT) telephone box n cabina telefonica.

telephone call n telefonata.

telephone directory n elenco telefonico.

telephone number n numero di telefono.

telephone operator n centralinista m/f.

telephone tapping n intercettazione f telefonica.

telephonist [tə'lɛfənɪst] n (BRIT) telefonista m/f.

telephoto lens ['tɛlɪfəutəu-] n teleobiettivo.

teleprinter ['tɛlɪprɪntə*] n telescrivente f.

Teleprompter ® ['tɛlɪprɔmptə*] n (US) gobbo.

telesales ['tɛlɪseɪlz] n vendita per telefono.

telescope ['tɛlɪskəup] n telescopio ♦ vi chiudersi a telescopio; (fig: vehicles) accartocciarsi.

telescopic [tɛlɪs'kɔpɪk] adj telescopico(a); (umbrella) pieghevole.

Teletext ® ['tɛlɪtɛkst] *n* (*system*) teletext *m inv*; (*in Italy*) televideo.

telethon ['tɛlɪθən] *n* maratona televisiva.

televise ['tɛlɪvaɪz] *vt* teletrasmettere.

television ['tɛlɪvɪʒən] *n* televisione *f*; **on ~** alla televisione.

television licence *n* (*BRIT*) abbonamento alla televisione.

television programme *n* programma *m* televisivo.

television set *n* televisore *m*.

teleworking ['tɛlɪwɛːkɪŋ] *n* telelavoro.

telex ['tɛlɛks] *n* telex *m inv* ♦ *vt* trasmettere per telex ♦ *vi* mandare un telex; **to ~ sb (about sth)** informare qn via telex (di qc).

tell, *pt, pp* **told** [tɛl, təuld] *vt* dire; (*relate: story*) raccontare; (*distinguish*): **to ~ sth from** distinguere qc da ♦ *vi* (*have effect*) farsi sentire, avere effetto; **to ~ sb to do** dire a qn di fare; **to ~ sb about sth** dire a qn di qc; raccontare qc a qn; **to ~ the time** leggere l'ora; **can you ~ me the time?** può dirmi l'ora?; **(I) ~ you what ...** so io che cosa fare ...; **I couldn't ~ them apart** non riuscivo a distinguerli.
  ►**tell off** *vt* rimproverare, sgridare.
  ►**tell on** *vt fus* (*inform against*) denunciare.

teller ['tɛlə*] *n* (*in bank*) cassiere/a.

telling ['tɛlɪŋ] *adj* (*remark, detail*) rivelatore(trice).

telltale ['tɛlteɪl] *adj* (*sign*) rivelatore(trice) ♦ *n* malalingua, pettegolo/a.

telly ['tɛlɪ] *n abbr* (*BRIT col*: = *television*) tivù *f inv*.

temerity [tə'mɛrɪtɪ] *n* temerarietà.

temp [tɛmp] *abbr* (*BRIT col*: = *temporary*) *n* impiegato(a) straordinario(a) ♦ *vi* lavorare come impiegato(a) straordinario(a).

temper ['tɛmpə*] *n* (*nature*) carattere *m*; (*mood*) umore *m*; (*fit of anger*) collera ♦ *vt* (*moderate*) temperare; **to be in a ~** essere in collera; **to keep one's ~** restare calmo; **to lose one's ~** andare in collera.

temperament ['tɛmprəmənt] *n* temperamento.

temperamental [tɛmprə'mɛntl] *adj* capriccioso(a).

temperance ['tɛmpərns] *n* moderazione *f*; (*in drinking*) temperanza nel bere.

temperate ['tɛmprət] *adj* moderato(a); (*climate*) temperato(a).

temperature ['tɛmprətʃə*] *n* temperatura; **to have** *or* **run a ~** avere la febbre.

tempered ['tɛmpəd] *adj* (*steel*) temprato(a).

tempest ['tɛmpɪst] *n* tempesta.

tempestuous [tɛm'pɛstjuəs] *adj*

(*relationship, meeting*) burrascoso(a).

tempi ['tɛmpiː] *npl of* **tempo**.

template, (*US*) **templet** ['tɛmplɪt] *n* sagoma.

temple ['tɛmpl] *n* (*building*) tempio; (*ANAT*) tempia.

templet ['tɛmplɪt] *n* (*US*) = **template**.

tempo, **~s** *or* **tempi** ['tɛmpəu, 'tɛmpiː] *n* tempo; (*fig: of life etc*) ritmo.

temporal ['tɛmpərl] *adj* temporale.

temporarily ['tɛmpərərɪlɪ] *adv* temporaneamente.

temporary ['tɛmpərərɪ] *adj* temporaneo(a); (*job, worker*) avventizio(a), temporaneo(a); **~ secretary** segretaria temporanea; **~ teacher** supplente *m/f*.

temporize ['tɛmpəraɪz] *vi* temporeggiare.

tempt [tɛmpt] *vt* tentare; **to ~ sb into doing** indurre qn a fare; **to ~ed to do sth** essere tentato di fare qc.

temptation [tɛmp'teɪʃən] *n* tentazione *f*.

tempting ['tɛmptɪŋ] *adj* allettante, seducente.

ten [tɛn] *num* dieci ♦ *n* dieci; **~s of thousands** decine di migliaia.

tenable ['tɛnəbl] *adj* sostenibile.

tenacious [tə'neɪʃəs] *adj* tenace.

tenacity [tə'næsɪtɪ] *n* tenacia.

tenancy ['tɛnənsɪ] *n* affitto; condizione *f* di inquilino.

tenant ['tɛnənt] *n* inquilino/a.

tend [tɛnd] *vt* badare a, occuparsi di; (*sick etc*) prendersi cura di ♦ *vi*: **to ~ to do** tendere a fare; (*colour*): **to ~ to** tendere a.

tendency ['tɛndənsɪ] *n* tendenza.

tender ['tɛndə*] *adj* tenero(a); (*sore*) sensibile; (*fig: subject*) delicato(a) ♦ *n* (*COMM: offer*) offerta; (*money*): **legal ~** valuta (a corso legale) ♦ *vt* offrire; **to put in a ~ (for)** fare un'offerta (per); **to put work out to ~** (*BRIT*) dare lavoro in appalto; **to ~ one's resignation** presentare le proprie dimissioni.

tenderize ['tɛndəraɪz] *vt* (*CULIN*) far intenerire.

tenderly ['tɛndəlɪ] *adv* teneramente.

tenderness ['tɛndənɪs] *n* tenerezza; sensibilità.

tendon ['tɛndən] *n* tendine *m*.

tenement ['tɛnəmənt] *n* casamento.

Tenerife [tɛnə'riːf] *n* Tenerife *f*.

tenet ['tɛnət] *n* principio.

Tenn. *abbr* (*US*) = *Tennessee*.

tenner ['tɛnə*] *n* (*BRIT col*) (banconota da) dieci sterline *fpl*.

tennis ['tɛnɪs] *n* tennis *m*.

tennis ball *n* palla da tennis.

tennis court n campo da tennis.
tennis elbow n (MED) gomito del tennista.
tennis match n partita di tennis.
tennis player n tennista m/f.
tennis racket n racchetta da tennis.
tennis shoes npl scarpe fpl da tennis.
tenor ['tɛnə*] n (MUS, of speech etc) tenore m.
tenpin bowling ['tɛnpɪn-] n (BRIT) bowling m.
tense [tɛns] adj teso(a) ♦ n (LING) tempo ♦ vt (tighten: muscles) tendere.
tenseness ['tɛnsnɪs] n tensione f.
tension ['tɛnʃən] n tensione f.
tent [tɛnt] n tenda.
tentacle ['tɛntəkl] n tentacolo.
tentative ['tɛntətɪv] adj esitante, incerto(a); (conclusion) provvisorio(a).
tenterhooks ['tɛntəhuks] npl: on ~ sulle spine.
tenth [tɛnθ] num decimo(a).
tent peg n picchetto da tenda.
tent pole n palo da tenda, montante m.
tenuous ['tɛnjuəs] adj tenue.
tenure ['tɛnjuə*] n (of property) possesso; (of job) incarico; (guaranteed employment): **to have** ~ essere di ruolo.
tepid ['tɛpɪd] adj tiepido(a).
term [tə:m] n (limit) termine m; (word) vocabolo, termine; (SCOL) trimestre m; (LAW) sessione f ♦ vt chiamare, definire; ~**s** npl (conditions) condizioni fpl; (COMM) prezzi mpl, tariffe fpl; ~ **of imprisonment** periodo di prigionia; **during his** ~ **of office** durante il suo incarico; **in the short/long** ~ a breve/lunga scadenza; "**easy** ~**s**" (COMM) "facilitazioni di pagamento"; **to be on good** ~**s with** essere in buoni rapporti con; **to come to** ~ **with** (person) arrivare a un accordo con; (problem) affrontare.
terminal ['tə:mɪnl] adj finale, terminale; (disease) nella fase terminale ♦ n (ELEC, COMPUT) terminale m; (AVIAT, for oil, ore etc) terminal m inv; (BRIT: also: **coach** ~) capolinea m.
terminate ['tə:mɪneɪt] vt mettere fine a ♦ vi: **to** ~ **in** finire in or con.
termination [tə:mɪ'neɪʃən] n fine f; (of contract) rescissione f; ~ **of pregnancy** (MED) interruzione f della gravidanza.
termini ['tə:mɪnaɪ] npl of **terminus**.
terminology [tə:mɪ'nɔlədʒɪ] n terminologia.
terminus, pl **termini** ['tə:mɪnəs, 'tə:mɪnaɪ] n (for buses) capolinea m; (for trains) stazione f terminale.
termite ['tə:maɪt] n termite f.

term paper n (US UNIVERSITY) saggio scritto da consegnare a fine trimestre.
Ter(r). abbr = **terrace**.
terrace ['tɛrəs] n terrazza; (BRIT: row of houses) fila di case a schiera; **the** ~**s** npl (BRIT SPORT) le gradinate.
terraced ['tɛrɪst] adj (garden) a terrazze; (in a row: house, cottage etc) a schiera.
terrain [tɛ'reɪn] n terreno.
terrible ['tɛrɪbl] adj terribile; (weather) bruttissimo(a); (performance, report) pessimo(a).
terribly ['tɛrəblɪ] adv terribilmente; (very badly) malissimo.
terrier ['tɛrɪə*] n terrier m inv.
terrific [tə'rɪfɪk] adj incredibile, fantastico(a); (wonderful) formidabile, eccezionale.
terrify ['tɛrɪfaɪ] vt terrorizzare; **to be terrified** essere atterrito(a).
territorial [tɛrɪ'tɔ:rɪəl] adj territoriale.
territorial waters npl acque fpl territoriali.
territory ['tɛrɪtərɪ] n territorio.
terror ['tɛrə*] n terrore m.
terrorism ['tɛrərɪzəm] n terrorismo.
terrorist ['tɛrərɪst] n terrorista m/f.
terrorize ['tɛrəraɪz] vt terrorizzare.
terse [tə:s] adj (style) conciso(a); (reply) laconico(a).
tertiary ['tə:ʃərɪ] adj (gen) terziario(a); ~ **education** (BRIT) educazione f superiore post-scolastica.
Terylene ® ['tɛrəli:n] n (BRIT) terital ® m, terilene ® m.
TESL ['tɛsl] n abbr = Teaching of English as a Second Language.
TESSA ['tɛsə] n abbr (BRIT: = Tax Exempt Special Savings Account) deposito a risparmio esente da tasse.
test [tɛst] n (trial, check) prova; (: of goods in factory) controllo, collaudo; (MED) esame m; (CHEM) analisi f inv; (exam: of intelligence etc) test m inv; (: in school) compito in classe; (also: **driving** ~) esame m di guida ♦ vt provare; controllare, collaudare; esaminare; analizzare; sottoporre ad esame; **to put sth to the** ~ mettere qc alla prova; **to** ~ **sth for sth** analizzare qc alla ricerca di qc; **to** ~ **sb in history** esaminare qn in storia.
testament ['tɛstəmənt] n testamento; **the Old/New T**~ il Vecchio/Nuovo testamento.
test ban n (also: **nuclear** ~) divieto di esperimenti nucleari.
test case n (LAW, fig) caso che farà testo.
testes ['tɛsti:z] npl testicoli mpl.
test flight n volo di prova.

testicle ['tɛstɪkl] *n* testicolo.
testify ['tɛstɪfaɪ] *vi* (*LAW*) testimoniare,
deporre; **to ~ to sth** (*LAW*) testimoniare
qc; (*gen*) comprovare *or* dimostrare qc;
(*be sign of*) essere una prova di qc.
testimonial [tɛstɪ'məunɪəl] *n* (*BRIT:
reference*) benservito; (*gift*) testimonianza
di stima.
testimony ['tɛstɪmənɪ] *n* (*LAW*)
testimonianza, deposizione *f*.
testing ['tɛstɪŋ] *adj* (*difficult: time*) duro(a).
test match *n* (*CRICKET, RUGBY*) partita
internazionale.
testosterone [tɛs'tɔstərəun] *n* testosterone
m.
test paper *n* (*SCOL*) interrogazione *f*
scritta.
test pilot *n* pilota *m* collaudatore.
test tube *n* provetta.
test-tube baby ['tɛsttjuːb-] *n* bambino(a)
concepito(a) in provetta.
testy ['tɛstɪ] *adj* irritabile.
tetanus ['tɛtənəs] *n* tetano.
tetchy ['tɛtʃɪ] *adj* irritabile, irascibile.
tether ['tɛðə*] *vt* legare ♦ *n*: **at the end of
one's ~** al limite (della pazienza).
Tex. *abbr* (*US*) = *Texas*.
text [tɛkst] *n* testo.
textbook ['tɛkstbuk] *n* libro di testo.
textile ['tɛkstaɪl] *n* tessile *m*; **~s** *npl* tessuti
mpl.
textual ['tɛkstjuəl] *adj* testuale, del testo.
texture ['tɛkstʃə*] *n* tessitura; (*of skin,
paper etc*) struttura.
TGIF *abbr* (*col*) = *thank God it's Friday*.
TGWU *n abbr* (*BRIT*: = *Transport and General
Workers' Union*) *sindacato degli operai dei
trasporti e non specializzati.*
Thai [taɪ] *adj* tailandese ♦ *n* tailandese *m/f*;
(*LING*) tailandese *m*.
Thailand ['taɪlænd] *n* Tailandia.
thalidomide ® [θə'lɪdəmaɪd] *n* talidomide
® *m*.
Thames [tɛmz] *n*: **the ~** il Tamigi.
than [ðæn, ðən] *conj* che; (*with numerals,
pronouns, proper names*): **more ~ 10/me/
Maria** più di 10/me/Maria; **you know her
better ~ I do** la conosce meglio di me;
she has more apples ~ pears ha più mele
che pere; **it is better to phone ~ to write**
è meglio telefonare che scrivere; **no
sooner did he leave ~ the phone rang** non
appena uscì il telefono suonò.
thank [θæŋk] *vt* ringraziare; **~ you (very
much)** grazie (tante); **~ heavens/God!**
grazie al cielo/a Dio!; *see also* **thanks**.
thankful ['θæŋkful] *adj*: **~ (for)** riconoscente
(per); **~ for/that** (*relieved*) sollevato(a)

da/dal fatto che.
thankfully ['θæŋkfəlɪ] *adv* con
riconoscenza; con sollievo; **~ there were
few victims** grazie al cielo ci sono state
poche vittime.
thankless ['θæŋklɪs] *adj* ingrato(a).
thanks [θæŋks] *npl* ringraziamenti *mpl*,
grazie *fpl* ♦ *excl* grazie!; **~ to** *prep* grazie a.
Thanksgiving (Day) ['θæŋksgɪvɪŋ-] *n* (*US*)
giorno del ringraziamento; *see boxed note.*

THANKSGIVING

*Negli Stati Uniti il quarto giovedì di novembre
ricorre il* **Thanksgiving (Day)**, *festa nazionale
in ricordo della celebrazione con cui i Padri
Pellegrini, i puritani inglesi che fondarono la
colonia di Plymouth nel Massachusetts,
ringraziarono Dio del buon raccolto del 1621.*

═══════════════════════════ *KEYWORD*

that [ðæt](*pl* **those**) *adj* (*demonstrative*)
quel(quell', quello) *m*; quella(quell') *f*; **~
man/woman/book** quell'uomo/quella
donna/quel libro; (*not "this"*) quell'uomo/
quella donna/quel libro là; **~ one**
quello(a) là
♦ *pron* **1** (*demonstrative*) ciò; (*not "this one"*)
quello(a); **who's ~?** chi è quello là?;
what's ~? cos'è quello?; **is ~ you?** sei tu?;
I prefer this to ~ preferisco questo a
quello; **~'s what he said** questo è ciò che
ha detto; **after ~** dopo; **what happened
after ~?** che è successo dopo?; **~ is (to
say)** cioè; **at or with ~ she ... con ciò lei
...; do it like ~** fallo così
2 (*relative: direct*) che; (*: indirect*) cui; **the
book (~) I read** il libro che ho letto; **the
box (~) I put it in** la scatola in cui l'ho
messo; **the people (~) I spoke to** le
persone con cui *or* con le quali ho
parlato; **not ~ I know of** non che io
sappia
3 (*relative: of time*) in cui; **the day (~) he
came** il giorno in cui è venuto
♦ *conj* che; **he thought ~ I was ill** pensava
che io fossi malato
♦ *adv* (*demonstrative*) così; **I can't work ~
much** non posso lavorare (così) tanto; **~
high** così alto; **the wall's about ~ high
and ~ thick** il muro è alto circa così e
spesso circa così.

═══════════════════════════

thatched [θætʃt] *adj* (*roof*) di paglia; **~
cottage** cottage *m inv* col tetto di paglia.
Thatcherism ['θætʃərɪzəm] *n* thatcherismo.
thaw [θɔː] *n* disgelo ♦ *vi* (*ice*) sciogliersi;

(*food*) scongelarsi ♦ *vt* (*food*) (fare) scongelare; **it's ~ing** (*weather*) sta sgelando.

=========== KEYWORD

the [ðiː, ðə] *def art* **1** (*gen*) il(lo, l') *m*; la(l') *f*; i(gli) *mpl*; le *fpl*; **~ boy/girl/ink** il ragazzo/ la ragazza/l'inchiostro; **~ books/pencils** i libri/le matite; **~ history of ~ world** la storia del mondo; **give it to ~ postman** dallo al postino; **I haven't ~ time/money** non ho tempo/soldi; **~ rich and ~ poor** i ricchi e i poveri; **1700 lire to ~ dollar** 1700 lire per un dollaro; **paid by ~ hour** pagato a ore
2 (*in titles*): **Elizabeth ~ First** Elisabetta prima; **Peter ~ Great** Pietro il Grande
3 (*in comparisons*): **~ more he works, ~ more he earns** più lavora più guadagna; **~ sooner ~ better** prima è meglio è.

theatre, (*US*) **theater** ['θɪətə*] *n* teatro.
theatre-goer ['θɪətəgəuə*] *n* frequentatore/trice di teatri.
theatrical [θɪ'ætrɪkl] *adj* teatrale.
theft [θɛft] *n* furto.
their [ðɛə*] *adj* il(la) loro, *pl* i(le) loro.
theirs [ðɛəz] *pron* il(la) loro, *pl* i(le) loro; **it is ~** è loro; **a friend of ~** un loro amico.
them [ðɛm, ðəm] *pron* (*direct*) li(le); (*indirect*) gli, loro (*after vb*); (*stressed, after prep*: *people*) loro; (: *people, things*) essi(e); **I see ~** li vedo; **give ~ the book** dà loro *or* dagli il libro; **give me a few of ~** dammene un po' *or* qualcuno.
theme [θiːm] *n* tema *m*.
theme park *n* parco dei divertimenti a soggetto.
theme song, theme tune *n* tema musicale.
themselves [ðəm'sɛlvz] *pl pron* (*reflexive*) si; (*emphatic*) loro stessi(e); (*after prep*) se stessi(e); **between ~** tra (di) loro.
then [ðɛn] *adv* (*at that time*) allora; (*next*) poi, dopo; (*and also*) e poi ♦ *conj* (*therefore*) perciò, dunque, quindi ♦ *adj*: **the ~ president** il presidente di allora; **from ~ on** da allora in poi; **until ~** fino ad allora; **and ~ what?** e poi?, e allora?; **what do you want me to do ~?** allora cosa vuole che faccia?
theologian [θɪə'ləudʒən] *n* teologo/a.
theological [θɪə'lɔdʒɪkl] *adj* teologico(a).
theology [θɪ'ɔlədʒɪ] *n* teologia.
theorem ['θɪərəm] *n* teorema *m*.
theoretical [θɪə'rɛtɪkl] *adj* teorico(a).
theorize ['θɪəraɪz] *vi* teorizzare.
theory ['θɪərɪ] *n* teoria; **in ~** in teoria.

therapeutic(al) [θɛrə'pjuːtɪk(l)] *adj* terapeutico(a).
therapist ['θɛrəpɪst] *n* terapista *m/f*.
therapy ['θɛrəpɪ] *n* terapia.

=========== KEYWORD

there [ðɛə*] *adv* **1**: **~ is, ~ are** c'è, ci sono; **~ are 3 of them** (*people*) sono in 3; (*things*) ce ne sono 3; **~ is no-one here** non c'è nessuno qui; **~ has been an accident** c'è stato un incidente
2 (*referring to place*) là, lì; **it's ~** è là *or* lì; **up/in/down ~** lassù/là dentro/laggiù; **back ~** là dietro; **on ~** lassù; **over ~** là; **through ~** di là; **he went ~ on Friday** ci è andato venerdì; **it takes two hours to go ~ and back** ci vogliono due ore per andare e tornare; **I want that book ~** voglio quel libro là *or* lì; **~ he is!** eccolo!
3: **~, ~** (*esp to child*) su, su.

thereabouts ['ðɛərəbauts] *adv* (*place*) nei pressi, da quelle parti; (*amount*) giù di lì, all'incirca.
thereafter [ðɛər'ɑːftə*] *adv* da allora in poi.
thereby [ðɛə'baɪ] *adv* con ciò.
therefore ['ðɛəfɔː*] *adv* perciò, quindi.
there's [ðɛəz] = **there is; there has.**
thereupon [ðɛərə'pɔn] *adv* (*at that point*) a quel punto; (*formal: on that subject*) in merito.
thermal ['θəːml] *adj* (*currents, spring*) termale; (*underwear, printer*) termico(a); (*paper*) termosensibile.
thermodynamics [θəːməudaɪ'næmɪks] *n* termodinamica.
thermometer [θə'mɔmɪtə*] *n* termometro.
thermonuclear ['θəːməu'njuːklɪə*] *adj* termonucleare.
Thermos ® ['θəːməs] *n* (*also:* **~ flask**) thermos ® *m inv*.
thermostat ['θəːməstæt] *n* termostato.
thesaurus [θɪ'sɔːrəs] *n* dizionario dei sinonimi.
these [ðiːz] *pl pron, adj* questi(e).
thesis, *pl* **theses** ['θiːsɪs, 'θiːsiːz] *n* tesi *f inv*.
they [ðeɪ] *pl pron* essi(esse); (*people only*) loro; **~ say that ...** (*it is said that*) si dice che ....
they'd [ðeɪd] = **they would; they had.**
they'll [ðeɪl] = **they will; they shall.**
they're [ðɛə*] = **they are.**
they've [ðeɪv] = **they have.**
thick [θɪk] *adj* spesso(a); (*crowd*) compatto(a); (*stupid*) ottuso(a), lento(a) ♦ *n*: **in the ~ of** nel folto di; **it's 20 cm ~** ha uno spessore di 20 cm.
thicken ['θɪkən] *vi* ispessire ♦ *vt* (*sauce etc*)

ispessire, rendere più denso(a).
thicket ['θɪkɪt] *n* boscaglia.
thickly ['θɪklɪ] *adv* (*spread*) a strati spessi;
(*cut*) a fette grosse; (*populated*)
densamente.
thickness ['θɪknɪs] *n* spessore *m*.
thickset [θɪk'sɛt] *adj* tarchiato(a), tozzo(a).
thickskinned [θɪk'skɪnd] *adj* (*fig*)
insensibile.
thief, *pl* **thieves** [θi:f, θi:vz] *n* ladro/a.
thieving ['θi:vɪŋ] *n* furti *mpl*.
thigh [θaɪ] *n* coscia.
thighbone ['θaɪbəun] *n* femore *m*.
thimble ['θɪmbl] *n* ditale *m*.
thin [θɪn] *adj* sottile; (*person*) magro(a);
(*soup*) poco denso(a); (*hair, crowd*)
rado(a); (*fog*) leggero(a) ♦ *vt* (*hair*) sfoltire
♦ *vi* (*fog*) diradarsi; (*also*: ~ **out**: *crowd*)
dispersi; **to** ~ **(down)** (*sauce, paint*)
diluire; **his hair is** ~**ning** sta perdendo i
capelli.
thing [θɪŋ] *n* cosa; (*object*) oggetto;
(*contraption*) aggeggio; ~**s** *npl* (*belongings*)
cose *fpl*; **for one** ~ tanto per cominciare;
the best ~ **would be to** la cosa migliore
sarebbe di; **the** ~ **is** ... il fatto è che ...;
the main ~ **is to** ... la cosa più
importante è di ...; **first** ~ **(in the
morning)** come *or* per prima cosa (di
mattina); **last** ~ **(at night)** come *or* per
ultima cosa (di sera); **poor** ~ poveretto/a;
she's got a ~ **about mice** è terrorizzata
dai topi; **how are** ~**s?** come va?
think, *pt, pp* **thought** [θɪŋk, θɔ:t] *vi* pensare,
riflettere ♦ *vt* pensare, credere; (*imagine*)
immaginare; **to** ~ **of** pensare a; **what did
you** ~ **of them?** cosa ne ha pensato?; **to** ~
about sth/sb pensare a qc/qn; **I'll** ~ **about
it** ci penserò; **to** ~ **of doing** pensare di
fare; **I** ~ **so** penso *or* credo di sì; **to** ~ **well
of** avere una buona opinione di; **to** ~
aloud pensare ad alta voce; ~ **again!**
rifletti!, pensaci su!
▶**think out** *vt* (*plan*) elaborare; (*solution*)
trovare.
▶**think over** *vt* riflettere su; **I'd like to** ~
things over vorrei pensarci su.
▶**think through** *vt* riflettere a fondo su.
▶**think up** *vt* ideare.
thinking ['θɪŋkɪŋ] *n*: **to my (way of)** ~ a mio
parere.
think tank *n* gruppo di esperti.
thinly ['θɪnlɪ] *adv* (*cut*) a fette sottili;
(*spread*) in uno strato sottile.
thinness ['θɪnnɪs] *n* sottigliezza; magrezza.
third [θə:d] *n* terzo(a) ♦ *n* terzo/a; (*fraction*)
terzo, terza parte *f*; (*BRIT SCOL: degree*)
laurea col minimo dei voti.

third-degree burns ['θə:ddɪ'gri:-] *npl*
ustioni *fpl* di terzo grado.
thirdly ['θə:dlɪ] *adv* in terzo luogo.
third party insurance *n* (*BRIT*)
assicurazione *f* contro terzi.
third-rate [θə:d'reɪt] *adj* di qualità
scadente.
Third World *n*: **the** ~ il Terzo Mondo.
thirst [θə:st] *n* sete *f*.
thirsty ['θə:stɪ] *adj* (*person*) assetato(a), che
ha sete; **to be** ~ aver sete.
thirteen [θə:'ti:n] *num* tredici.
thirtieth ['θə:tɪɪθ] *num* trentesimo(a).
thirty ['θə:tɪ] *num* trenta.

===================================== KEYWORD

this [ðɪs] (*pl* **these**) *adj* (*demonstrative*)
questo(a); ~ **man/woman/book**
quest'uomo/questa donna/questo libro;
(*not "that"*) quest'uomo/questa donna/
questo libro qui; ~ **one** questo(a) qui; ~
time questa volta; ~ **time last year** l'anno
scorso in questo periodo; ~ **way** (*in this
direction*) da questa parte; (*in this fashion*)
così
♦ *pron* (*demonstrative*) questo(a); (*not "that
one"*) questo(a) qui; **who/what is** ~**?** chi
è/che cos'è questo?; **I prefer** ~ **to that**
preferisco questo a quello; ~ **is where I
live** io abito qui; ~ **is what he said** questo
è ciò che ha detto; **they were talking of** ~
and that stavano parlando del più e del
meno; ~ **is Mr Brown** (*in introductions,
photo*) questo è il signor Brown; (*on
telephone*) sono il signor Brown
♦ *adv* (*demonstrative*): ~ **high/long** *etc*
alto/lungo *etc* così; **it's about** ~ **high** è
alto circa così; **I didn't know things were**
~ **bad** non sapevo andasse così male.

thistle ['θɪsl] *n* cardo.
thong [θɔŋ] *n* cinghia.
thorn [θɔ:n] *n* spina.
thorny ['θɔ:nɪ] *adj* spinoso(a).
thorough ['θʌrə] *adj* (*person*) preciso(a),
accurato(a); (*search*) minuzioso(a);
(*knowledge, research*) approfondito(a),
profondo(a); (*cleaning*) a fondo.
thoroughbred ['θʌrəbrɛd] *n* (*horse*)
purosangue *m/f inv*.
thoroughfare ['θʌrəfɛə*] *n* strada
transitabile; **"no** ~**"** (*BRIT*) "divieto di
transito".
thoroughgoing ['θʌrəgəuɪŋ] *adj* (*analysis*)
approfondito(a); (*reform*) totale.
thoroughly ['θʌrəlɪ] *adv* accuratamente;
minuziosamente; in profondità; a fondo;
he ~ **agreed** fu completamente

d'accordo.

thoroughness ['θʌrənɪs] *n* precisione *f*.

those [ðəuz] *pl pron* quelli(e) ♦ *pl adj* quei(quegli) *mpl*; quelle *fpl*.

though [ðəu] *conj* benché, sebbene ♦ *adv* comunque, tuttavia; **even** ~ anche se; **it's not so easy,** ~ tuttavia non è così facile.

thought [θɔːt] *pt, pp of* **think** ♦ *n* pensiero; (*opinion*) opinione *f*; (*intention*) intenzione *f*; **after much** ~ dopo molti ripensamenti; **I've just had a** ~ mi è appena venuta un'idea; **to give sth some** ~ prendere qc in considerazione, riflettere su qc.

thoughtful ['θɔːtful] *adj* pensieroso(a), pensoso(a); ponderato(a); (*considerate*) premuroso(a).

thoughtfully ['θɔːtfəlɪ] *adv* (*pensively*) con aria pensierosa.

thoughtless ['θɔːtlɪs] *adj* sconsiderato(a); (*behaviour*) scortese.

thoughtlessly ['θɔːtlɪslɪ] *adv* sconsideratamente; scortesemente.

thought-provoking ['θɔːtprəvəukɪŋ] *adj* stimolante.

thousand ['θauzənd] *num* mille; **one** ~ mille; ~**s of** migliaia di.

thousandth ['θauzəntθ] *num* millesimo(a).

thrash [θræʃ] *vt* picchiare; bastonare; (*defeat*) battere.

▶**thrash about** *vi* dibattersi.

▶**thrash out** *vt* dibattere, sviscerare.

thrashing ['θræʃɪŋ] *n*: **to give sb a** ~ = **to thrash sb**.

thread [θrɛd] *n* filo; (*of screw*) filetto ♦ *vt* (*needle*) infilare; **to** ~ **one's way between** infilarsi tra.

threadbare ['θrɛdbɛə*] *adj* consumato(a), logoro(a).

threat [θrɛt] *n* minaccia; **to be under** ~ **of** (*closure, extinction*) rischiare di; (*exposure*) essere minacciato(a) di.

threaten ['θrɛtn] *vi* (*storm*) minacciare ♦ *vt*: **to** ~ **sb with sth/to do** minacciare qn con qc/di fare.

threatening ['θrɛtnɪŋ] *adj* minaccioso(a).

three [θriː] *num* tre.

three-dimensional [θriːdaɪ'mɛnʃənl] *adj* tridimensionale.

three-piece ['θriːpiːs]: ~ **suit** *n* completo (con gilè); ~ **suite** *n* salotto comprendente un divano e due poltrone.

three-ply [θriː'plaɪ] *adj* (*wood*) a tre strati; (*wool*) a tre fili.

three-quarters [θriː'kwɔːtəz] *npl* tre quarti *mpl*; ~ **full** pieno per tre quarti.

three-wheeler [θriː'wiːlə*] *n* (*car*) veicolo a tre ruote.

thresh [θrɛʃ] *vt* (AGR) trebbiare.

threshing machine ['θrɛʃɪŋ-] *n* trebbiatrice *f*.

threshold ['θrɛʃhəuld] *n* soglia; **to be on the** ~ **of** (*fig*) essere sulla soglia di.

threshold agreement *n* (ECON) ≈ scala mobile.

threw [θruː] *pt of* **throw**.

thrift [θrɪft] *n* parsimonia.

thrifty ['θrɪftɪ] *adj* economico(a), parsimonioso(a).

thrill [θrɪl] *n* brivido ♦ *vi* eccitarsi, tremare ♦ *vt* (*audience*) elettrizzare; **I was** ~**ed to get your letter** la tua lettera mi ha fatto veramente piacere.

thriller ['θrɪlə*] *n* film *m inv* (*or* dramma *m or* libro) del brivido.

thrilling ['θrɪlɪŋ] *adj* (*book, play etc*) pieno(a) di suspense; (*news, discovery*) entusiasmante.

thrive, *pt* **thrived, throve,** *pp* **thrived, thriven** [θraɪv, θrəuv, 'θrɪvn] *vi* crescere *or* svilupparsi bene; (*business*) prosperare; **he** ~**s on it** gli fa bene, ne gode.

thriving ['θraɪvɪŋ] *adj* (*industry etc*) fiorente.

throat [θrəut] *n* gola; **to have a sore** ~ avere (un *or* il) mal di gola.

throb [θrɔb] *n* (*of heart*) battito; (*of engine*) vibrazione *f*; (*of pain*) fitta ♦ *vi* (*heart*) palpitare; (*engine*) vibrare; (*with pain*) pulsare; **my head is** ~**bing** mi martellano le tempie.

throes [θrəuz] *npl*: **in the** ~ **of** alle prese con; in preda a; **in the** ~ **of death** in agonia.

thrombosis [θrɔm'bəusɪs] *n* trombosi *f*.

throne [θrəun] *n* trono.

throng [θrɔŋ] *n* moltitudine *f* ♦ *vt* affollare.

throttle ['θrɔtl] *n* (AUT) valvola a farfalla; (*on motorcycle*) (manopola del) gas ♦ *vt* strangolare.

through [θruː] *prep* attraverso; (*time*) per, durante; (*by means of*) per mezzo di; (*owing to*) a causa di ♦ *adj* (*ticket, train, passage*) diretto(a) ♦ *adv* attraverso; **(from) Monday** ~ **Friday** (US) da lunedì a venerdì; **I am halfway** ~ **the book** sono a metà libro; **to let sb** ~ lasciar passare qn; **to put sb** ~ **to sb** (TEL) passare qn a qn; **to be** ~ (TEL) ottenere la comunicazione; (*have finished*) avere finito; **"no** ~ **traffic"** (US) "divieto d'accesso"; **"no** ~ **road"** (BRIT) "strada senza sbocco".

throughout [θruː'aut] *prep* (*place*) dappertutto in; (*time*) per *or* durante tutto(a) ♦ *adv* dappertutto; sempre.

throughput ['θruːput] *n* (*of goods, materials*) materiale *m* in lavorazione; (COMPUT) volume *m* di dati immessi.

throve [θrəuv] pt of **thrive**.

throw [θrəu] n tiro, getto; (SPORT) lancio
♦ vt (pt **threw**, pp **thrown** [θru:, θrəun])
tirare, gettare; (SPORT) lanciare; (rider)
disarcionare; (fig) confondere; (pottery)
formare al tornio; **to ~ a party** dare una
festa; **to ~ open** (doors, windows)
spalancare; (house, gardens etc) aprire al
pubblico; (competition, race) aprire a tutti.
▶**throw about, throw around** vt (litter
etc) spargere.
▶**throw away** vt gettare or buttare via.
▶**throw off** vt sbarazzarsi di.
▶**throw out** vt buttare fuori; (reject)
respingere.
▶**throw together** vt (clothes, meal etc)
mettere insieme; (essay) buttar giù.
▶**throw up** vi vomitare.

throwaway ['θrəuəweɪ] adj da buttare.

throwback ['θrəubæk] n: **it's a ~ to** (fig) ciò
risale a.

throw-in ['θrəuɪn] n (SPORT) rimessa in
gioco.

thrown [θrəun] pp of **throw**.

thru [θru:] prep, adj, adv (US) = **through**.

thrush [θrʌʃ] n (ZOOL) tordo; (MED: esp in
children) mughetto; (: BRIT: in women)
candida.

thrust [θrʌst] n (TECH) spinta ♦ vt (pt, pp
thrust) spingere con forza; (push in)
conficcare.

thrusting ['θrʌstɪŋ] adj (troppo)
intraprendente.

thud [θʌd] n tonfo.

thug [θʌg] n delinquente m.

thumb [θʌm] n (ANAT) pollice m ♦ vt (book)
sfogliare; **to ~ a lift** fare l'autostop; **to
give sb/sth the ~s up/down** approvare/
disapprovare qn/qc.

thumb index n indice m a rubrica.

thumbnail ['θʌmneɪl] n unghia del pollice.

thumbnail sketch n descrizione f breve.

thumbtack ['θʌmtæk] n (US) puntina da
disegno.

thump [θʌmp] n colpo forte; (sound) tonfo
♦ vt battere su ♦ vi picchiare, battere.

thunder ['θʌndə*] n tuono ♦ vi tuonare;
(train etc): **to ~ past** passare con un
rombo.

thunderbolt ['θʌndəbəult] n fulmine m.

thunderclap ['θʌndəklæp] n rombo di
tuono.

thunderous ['θʌndərəs] adj fragoroso(a).

thunderstorm ['θʌndəstɔ:m] n temporale
m.

thunderstruck ['θʌndəstrʌk] adj (fig)
sbigottito(a).

thundery ['θʌndərɪ] adj temporalesco(a).

Thur(s). abbr (= Thursday) gio.

Thursday ['θɜ:zdɪ] n giovedì m inv; for
phrases see also **Tuesday**.

thus [ðʌs] adv così.

thwart [θwɔ:t] vt contrastare.

thyme [taɪm] n timo.

thyroid ['θaɪrɔɪd] n tiroide f.

tiara [tɪ'ɑ:rə] n (woman's) diadema m.

Tiber ['taɪbə*] n: **the ~** il Tevere.

Tibet [tɪ'bet] n Tibet m.

Tibetan [tɪ'betən] adj tibetano(a) ♦ n
(person) tibetano/a; (LING) tibetano.

tibia ['tɪbɪə] n tibia.

tic [tɪk] n tic m inv.

tick [tɪk] n (sound: of clock) tic tac m inv;
(mark) segno; spunta; (ZOOL) zecca; (BRIT
col): **in a ~** in un attimo; (BRIT col: credit):
to buy sth on ~ comprare qc a credito
♦ vi fare tic tac ♦ vt spuntare; **to put a ~
against sth** fare un segno di fianco a qc.
▶**tick off** vt spuntare; (person) sgridare.
▶**tick over** vi (BRIT: engine) andare al
minimo.

ticker tape ['tɪkə-] n nastro di
telescrivente; (US: in celebrations) stelle
fpl filanti.

ticket ['tɪkɪt] n biglietto; (in shop: on goods)
etichetta; (: from cash register) scontrino;
(for library) scheda; (US POL) lista dei
candidati; **to get a (parking) ~** (AUT)
prendere una multa (per sosta vietata).

ticket agency n (THEAT) agenzia di vendita
di biglietti.

ticket collector n bigliettaio.

ticket holder n persona munita di
biglietto.

ticket inspector n controllore m.

ticket office n biglietteria.

tickle ['tɪkl] n solletico ♦ vt fare il solletico
a, solleticare; (fig) stuzzicare; piacere a;
far ridere.

ticklish ['tɪklɪʃ] adj che soffre il solletico;
(which tickles: blanket, cough) che provoca
prurito.

tidal ['taɪdl] adj di marea.

tidal wave n onda anomala.

tidbit ['tɪdbɪt] n (US) = **titbit**.

tiddlywinks ['tɪdlɪwɪŋks] n gioco della
pulce.

tide [taɪd] n marea; (fig: of events) corso
♦ vt: **will £20 ~ you over till Monday?** ti
basteranno 20 sterline fino a lunedì?;
high/low ~ alta/bassa marea; **the ~ of
public opinion** l'orientamento
dell'opinione pubblica.

tidily ['taɪdɪlɪ] adv in modo ordinato; **to
arrange ~** sistemare; **to dress ~** vestirsi
per benino.

tidiness ['taɪdɪnɪs] n ordine m.

tidy ['taɪdɪ] adj (room) ordinato(a), lindo(a); (dress, work) curato(a), in ordine; (person) ordinato(a); (mind) organizzato(a) ♦ vt (also: ~ up) riordinare, mettere in ordine; **to ~ o.s. up** rassettarsi.

tie [taɪ] n (string etc) legaccio; (BRIT: also: neck~) cravatta; (fig: link) legame m; (SPORT: draw) pareggio (: match) incontro; (US RAIL) traversina ♦ vt (parcel) legare; (ribbon) annodare ♦ vi (SPORT) pareggiare; "black/white ~" "smoking/abito di rigore"; **family ~s** legami familiari; **to ~ sth in a bow** annodare qc; **to ~ a knot in sth** fare un nodo a qc.

▶**tie down** vt fissare con una corda; (fig): **to ~ sb down to** costringere qn ad accettare.

▶**tie in** vi: **to ~ in (with)** (correspond) corrispondere (a).

▶**tie on** vt (BRIT: label etc) attaccare.

▶**tie up** vt (parcel, dog) legare; (boat) ormeggiare; (arrangements) concludere; **to be ~d up** (busy) essere occupato or preso.

tie-break(er) ['taɪbreɪk(ə*)] n (TENNIS) tie-break m inv; (in quiz) spareggio.

tie-on ['taɪɔn] adj (BRIT: label) volante.

tie-pin ['taɪpɪn] n (BRIT) fermacravatta m inv.

tier [tɪə*] n fila; (of cake) strato.

Tierra del Fuego [tɪ'erədɛl'fweɪgəʊ] n Terra del Fuoco.

tie tack n (US) fermacravatta m inv.

tiff [tɪf] n battibecco.

tiger ['taɪgə*] n tigre f.

tight [taɪt] adj (rope) teso(a), tirato(a); (clothes) stretto(a); (budget, programme, bend) stretto(a); (control) severo(a), fermo(a); (col: drunk) sbronzo(a) ♦ adv (squeeze) fortemente; (shut) ermeticamente; **to be packed ~** (suitcase) essere pieno zeppo; (people) essere pigiati; **everybody hold ~!** tenetevi stretti!; see also **tights**.

tighten ['taɪtn] vt (rope) tendere; (screw) stringere; (control) rinforzare ♦ vi tendersi; stringersi.

tight-fisted [taɪt'fɪstɪd] adj avaro(a).

tight-lipped ['taɪt'lɪpt] adj: **to be ~** essere reticente; (angry) tenere le labbra serrate.

tightly ['taɪtlɪ] adv (grasp) bene, saldamente.

tightrope ['taɪtrəʊp] n corda (da acrobata).

tightrope walker n funambolo/a.

tights [taɪts] npl (BRIT) collant m inv.

tigress ['taɪgrɪs] n tigre f (femmina).

tilde ['tɪldə] n tilde f.

tile [taɪl] n (on roof) tegola; (on floor) mattonella; (on wall) piastrella ♦ vt (floor, bathroom etc) piastrellare.

tiled [taɪld] adj rivestito(a) di tegole; a mattonelle; a piastrelle.

till [tɪl] n registratore m di cassa ♦ vt (land) coltivare ♦ prep, conj = **until**.

tiller ['tɪlə*] n (NAUT) barra del timone.

tilt [tɪlt] vt inclinare, far pendere ♦ vi inclinarsi, pendere ♦ n (slope) pendio; **to wear one's hat at a ~** portare il cappello sulle ventitré; **(at) full ~** a tutta velocità.

timber ['tɪmbə*] n (material) legname m; (trees) alberi mpl da legname.

time [taɪm] n tempo; (epoch: often pl) epoca, tempo; (by clock) ora; (moment) momento; (occasion, also MATH) volta; (MUS) tempo ♦ vt (race) cronometrare; (programme) calcolare la durata di; (remark etc): **to ~ sth well/badly** scegliere il momento più/ meno opportuno per qc; **a long ~** molto tempo; **for the ~ being** per il momento; **from ~ to ~** ogni tanto; **~ after ~, ~ and again** mille volte; **in ~** (soon enough) in tempo; (after some time) col tempo; (MUS) a tempo; **at ~s** a volte; **to take one's ~** prenderla con calma; **in a week's ~** fra una settimana; **in no ~** in un attimo; **on ~** puntualmente; **to be 30 minutes behind/ ahead of ~** avere 30 minuti di ritardo/ anticipo; **by the ~ he arrived** quando è arrivato; **5 ~s 5** 5 volte 5, 5 per 5; **what ~ is it?** che ora è?, che ore sono?; **what ~ do you make it?** che ora fa?; **to have a good ~** divertirsi; **they had a hard ~ of it** è stato duro per loro; **~'s up!** è (l')ora!; **to be behind the ~s** vivere nel passato; **I've no ~ for it** (fig) non ho tempo da perdere con cose del genere; **he'll do it in his own (good) ~** (without being hurried) lo farà quando avrà (un minuto di) tempo; **he'll do it in** or (US) **on his own ~** (out of working hours) lo farà nel suo tempo libero; **the bomb was ~d to explode 5 minutes later** la bomba era stata regolata in modo da esplodere 5 minuti più tardi.

time-and-motion study ['taɪmənd 'məʊʃən-] n analisi f inv dei tempi e dei movimenti.

time bomb n bomba a orologeria.

time card n cartellino (da timbrare).

time clock n orologio m marcatempo inv.

time-consuming ['taɪmkənsjuːmɪŋ] adj che richiede molto tempo.

time difference n differenza di fuso orario.

time frame n tempi mpl.

time-honoured, (*US*) **time-honored** ['taɪmɔnəd] *adj* consacrato(a) dal tempo.

timekeeper ['taɪmkiːpə*] *n* (*SPORT*) cronometrista *m/f*.

time lag *n* intervallo, ritardo; (*in travel*) differenza di fuso orario.

timeless ['taɪmlɪs] *adj* eterno(a).

time limit *n* limite *m* di tempo.

timely ['taɪmlɪ] *adj* opportuno(a).

time off *n* tempo libero.

timer ['taɪmə*] *n* (*in kitchen*) contaminuti *m inv*; (*TECH*) timer *m inv*, temporizzatore *m*.

time-saving ['taɪmseɪvɪŋ] *adj* che fa risparmiare tempo.

time scale *n* tempi *mpl* d'esecuzione.

time-sharing ['taɪmʃɛərɪŋ] *n* (*COMPUT*) divisione *f* di tempo.

time sheet *n* = **time card**.

time signal *n* segnale *m* orario.

time switch *n* interruttore *m* a tempo.

timetable ['taɪmteɪbl] *n* orario; (*programme of events etc*) programma *m*.

time zone *n* fuso orario.

timid ['tɪmɪd] *adj* timido(a); (*easily scared*) pauroso(a).

timidity [tɪ'mɪdɪtɪ] *n* timidezza.

timing ['taɪmɪŋ] *n* sincronizzazione *f*; (*fig*) scelta del momento opportuno, tempismo; (*SPORT*) cronometraggio.

timing device *n* (*on bomb*) timer *m inv*.

timpani ['tɪmpənɪ] *npl* timpani *mpl*.

tin [tɪn] *n* stagno; (*also*: ~ **plate**) latta; (*BRIT*: *can*) barattolo (di latta), lattina, scatola; (*for baking*) teglia; **a** ~ **of paint** un barattolo di tinta *or* vernice.

tin foil *n* stagnola.

tinge [tɪndʒ] *n* sfumatura ♦ *vt*: ~**d with** tinto(a) di.

tingle ['tɪŋgl] *vi* (*cheeks, skin: from cold*) pungere, pizzicare; (: *from bad circulation*) formicolare.

tinker ['tɪŋkə*] *n* stagnino ambulante; (*gipsy*) zingaro/a.

▶**tinker with** *vt fus* armeggiare intorno a; cercare di riparare.

tinkle ['tɪŋkl] *vi* tintinnare ♦ *n* (*col*): **to give sb a** ~ dare un colpo di telefono a qn.

tin mine *n* miniera di stagno.

tinned [tɪnd] *adj* (*BRIT*: *food*) in scatola.

tinnitus [tɪ'naɪtəs] *n* (*MED*) ronzio auricolare.

tinny ['tɪnɪ] *adj* metallico(a).

tin-opener ['tɪnəupnə*] *n* (*BRIT*) apriscatole *m inv*.

tinsel ['tɪnsl] *n* decorazioni *fpl* natalizie (*argentate*).

tint [tɪnt] *n* tinta; (*for hair*) shampoo *m inv*

colorante ♦ *vt* (*hair*) fare uno shampoo colorante a.

tinted ['tɪntɪd] *adj* (*hair*) tinto(a); (*spectacles, glass*) colorato(a).

tiny ['taɪnɪ] *adj* minuscolo(a).

tip [tɪp] *n* (*end*) punta; (*protective: on umbrella etc*) puntale *m*; (*gratuity*) mancia; (*for coal*) discarica; (*for rubbish*) immondezzaio; (*advice*) suggerimento ♦ *vt* (*waiter*) dare la mancia a; (*tilt*) inclinare; (*overturn: also*: ~ **over**) capovolgere; (*empty: also*: ~ **out**) scaricare; (*predict: winner*) pronosticare; (: *horse*) dare vincente; **he ~ped out the contents of the box** ha rovesciato il contenuto della scatola.

▶**tip off** *vt* fare una soffiata a.

tip-off ['tɪpɔf] *n* (*hint*) soffiata.

tipped ['tɪpt] *adj* (*BRIT*: *cigarette*) col filtro; **steel-~** con la punta d'acciaio.

Tipp-Ex ® ['tɪpɛks] *n* (*BRIT*) liquido correttore.

tipple ['tɪpl] (*BRIT*) *vi* sbevazzare ♦ *n*: **to have a** ~ prendere un bicchierino.

tipster ['tɪpstə*] *n* (*RACING*) *chi vende informazioni sulle corse e altre manifestazioni oggetto di scommesse*.

tipsy ['tɪpsɪ] *adj* brillo(a).

tiptoe ['tɪptəu] *n*: **on** ~ in punta di piedi.

tiptop ['tɪptɔp] *adj*: **in** ~ **condition** in ottime condizioni.

tirade [taɪ'reɪd] *n* filippica.

tire ['taɪə*] *vt* stancare ♦ *vi* stancarsi ♦ *n* (*US*) = **tyre**.

▶**tire out** *vt* sfinire, spossare.

tired ['taɪəd] *adj* stanco(a); **to be/feel/look** ~ essere/sentirsi/sembrare stanco; **to be** ~ **of** essere stanco *or* stufo di.

tiredness ['taɪədnɪs] *n* stanchezza.

tireless ['taɪəlɪs] *adj* instancabile.

tiresome ['taɪəsəm] *adj* noioso(a).

tiring ['taɪərɪŋ] *adj* faticoso(a).

tissue ['tɪʃuː] *n* tessuto; (*paper handkerchief*) fazzolettino di carta.

tissue paper *n* carta velina.

tit [tɪt] *n* (*bird*) cinciallegra; (*col: breast*) tetta; **to give** ~ **for tat** rendere pan per focaccia.

titanium [tɪ'teɪnɪəm] *n* titanio.

titbit ['tɪtbɪt], (*US*) **tidbit** ['tɪdbɪt] *n* (*food*) leccornia; (*news*) notizia ghiotta.

titillate ['tɪtɪleɪt] *vt* titillare.

titivate ['tɪtɪveɪt] *vt* agghindare.

title ['taɪtl] *n* titolo; (*LAW: right*): ~ (**to**) diritto (a).

title deed *n* (*LAW*) titolo di proprietà.

title page n frontespizio.
title role n ruolo or parte f principale.
titter ['tɪtə*] vi ridere scioccamente.
tittle-tattle ['tɪtltætl] n chiacchiere fpl, pettegolezzi mpl.
titular ['tɪtjulə*] adj (in name only) nominale.
tizzy ['tɪzɪ] n (col): **to be in a** ~ essere in agitazione.
T-junction ['tiː'dʒʌŋkʃən] n incrocio a T.
TM n abbr (= transcendental meditation) M.T. f; (COMM) = **trademark**.
TN abbr (US) = Tennessee.
TNT n abbr (= trinitrotoluene) T.N.T. m.

================= KEYWORD

to [tuː, tə] prep 1 (direction) a; **to go** ~ **France/London/school** andare in Francia/a Londra/a scuola; **to go** ~ **town** andare in città; **to go** ~ **Paul's/the doctor's** andare da Paul/dal dottore; **the road** ~ **Edinburgh** la strada per Edimburgo; ~ **the left/right** a sinistra/destra
2 (as far as) (fino) a; **from here** ~ **London** da qui a Londra; **to count** ~ **10** contare fino a 10; **from 40** ~ **50 people** da 40 a 50 persone
3 (with expressions of time): **a quarter** ~ **5** le 5 meno un quarto; **it's twenty** ~ **3** sono le 3 meno venti
4 (for, of): **the key** ~ **the front door** la chiave della porta d'ingresso; **a letter** ~ **his wife** una lettera per la moglie
5 (expressing indirect object) a; **to give sth** ~ **sb** dare qc a qn; **give it** ~ **me** dammelo; **to talk** ~ **sb** parlare a qn; **it belongs** ~ **him** gli appartiene, è suo; **to be a danger** ~ **sb/sth** rappresentare un pericolo per qn/qc
6 (in relation to) a; **3 goals** ~ **2** 3 goal a 2; **30 miles** ~ **the gallon** ≈ 11 chilometri con un litro; **4 apples** ~ **the kilo** 4 mele in un chilo
7 (purpose, result): **to come** ~ **sb's aid** venire in aiuto a qn; **to sentence sb** ~ **death** condannare a morte qn; ~ **my surprise** con mia sorpresa
♦ with vb 1 (simple infinitive): ~ **go/eat** etc andare/mangiare etc
2 (following another vb): **to want/try/start** ~ **do** volere/cercare di/cominciare a fare
3 (with vb omitted): **I don't want** ~ non voglio (farlo); **you ought** ~ devi (farlo)
4 (purpose, result) per; **I did it** ~ **help you** l'ho fatto per aiutarti
5 (equivalent to relative clause): **I have**

things ~ **do** ho da fare; **the main thing is** ~ **try** la cosa più importante è provare
6 (after adjective etc): **ready** ~ **go** pronto(a) a partire; **too old/young** ~ ... troppo vecchio(a)/giovane per ...
♦ adv: **to push the door** ~ accostare la porta; **to go** ~ **and fro** andare e tornare.

toad [təud] n rospo.
toadstool ['təudstuːl] n fungo (velenoso).
toady ['təudɪ] vi adulare.
toast [təust] n (CULIN) toast m, pane m abbrustolito; (drink, speech) brindisi m inv
♦ vt (CULIN) abbrustolire; (drink to) brindare a; **a piece** or **slice of** ~ una fetta di pane abbrustolito.
toaster ['təustə*] n tostapane m inv.
toastmaster ['təustmɑːstə*] n direttore m dei brindisi.
toast rack n portatoast m inv.
tobacco [tə'bækəu] n tabacco; **pipe** ~ tabacco da pipa.
tobacconist [tə'bækənɪst] n tabaccaio/a; ~'**s (shop)** tabaccheria.
Tobago [tə'beɪɡəu] n see **Trinidad and Tobago**.
toboggan [tə'bɔɡən] n toboga m inv; (child's) slitta.
today [tə'deɪ] adv, n (also fig) oggi (m inv); **what day is it** ~? che giorno è oggi?; **what date is it** ~? quanti ne abbiamo oggi?; ~ **is the 4th of March** (oggi) è il 4 di marzo; ~'**s paper** il giornale di oggi; **a fortnight** ~ quindici giorni a oggi.
toddler ['tɔdlə*] n bambino/a che impara a camminare.
toddy ['tɔdɪ] n grog m inv.
to-do [tə'duː] n (fuss) storie fpl.
toe [təu] n dito del piede; (of shoe) punta
♦ vt: **to** ~ **the line** (fig) stare in riga, conformarsi; **big** ~ alluce m; **little** ~ mignolino.
TOEFL ['təufl] n abbr = Test(ing) of English as a Foreign Language.
toehold ['təuhəuld] n punto d'appoggio.
toenail ['təuneɪl] n unghia del piede.
toffee ['tɔfɪ] n caramella.
toffee apple n (BRIT) mela caramellata.
tofu ['təufuː] n tofu m (latte di soia non fermentato).
toga ['təuɡə] n toga.
together [tə'ɡɛðə*] adv insieme; (at same time) allo stesso tempo; ~ **with** insieme a.
togetherness [tə'ɡɛðənɪs] n solidarietà; intimità.
toggle switch ['tɔɡl-] n (COMPUT) tasto bistabile.
Togo ['təuɡəu] n Togo.

togs [tɔgz] *npl* (*col: clothes*) vestiti *mpl*.
toil [tɔɪl] *n* travaglio, fatica ♦ *vi* affannarsi; sgobbare.
toilet ['tɔɪlət] *n* (*BRIT: lavatory*) gabinetto ♦ *cpd* (*soap etc*) da toletta; **to go to the** ~ andare al gabinetto *or* al bagno.
toilet bag *n* (*BRIT*) nécessaire *m inv* da toilette.
toilet bowl *n* vaso *or* tazza del gabinetto.
toilet paper *n* carta igienica.
toiletries ['tɔɪlɪtrɪz] *npl* articoli *mpl* da toletta.
toilet roll *n* rotolo di carta igienica.
toilet water *n* acqua di colonia.
to-ing and fro-ing ['tuːɪŋən'frəʊɪŋ] *n* (*BRIT*) andirivieni *m inv*.
token ['təʊkən] *n* (*sign*) segno; (*voucher*) buono ♦ *cpd* (*fee, strike*) simbolico(a); **book/record** ~ (*BRIT*) buono-libro/-disco; **by the same** ~ (*fig*) per lo stesso motivo.
tokenism ['təʊkənɪzəm] *n* (*POL*) concessione *f* pro forma *inv*.
Tokyo ['təʊkjəʊ] *n* Tokyo *f*.
told [təʊld] *pt, pp of* **tell**.
tolerable ['tɔlərəbl] *adj* (*bearable*) tollerabile; (*fairly good*) passabile.
tolerably ['tɔlərəblɪ] *adv* (*good, comfortable*) abbastanza.
tolerance ['tɔlərns] *n* (*also TECH*) tolleranza.
tolerant ['tɔlərnt] *adj*: ~ (**of**) tollerante (nei confronti di).
tolerate ['tɔləreɪt] *vt* sopportare; (*MED, TECH*) tollerare.
toleration [tɔlə'reɪʃən] *n* tolleranza.
toll [təʊl] *n* (*tax, charge*) pedaggio ♦ *vi* (*bell*) suonare; **the accident** ~ **on the roads** il numero delle vittime della strada.
tollbridge ['təʊlbrɪdʒ] *n* ponte *m* a pedaggio.
toll call *n* (*US TEL*) (telefonata) interurbana.
toll-free ['təʊl'friː] (*US*) *adj* senza addebito, gratuito(a) ♦ *adv* gratuitamente; ~ **number** ≈ numero verde.
tomato, ~**es** [tə'mɑːtəʊ] *n* pomodoro.
tomb [tuːm] *n* tomba.
tombola [tɔm'bəʊlə] *n* tombola.
tomboy ['tɔmbɔɪ] *n* maschiaccio.
tombstone ['tuːmstəʊn] *n* pietra tombale.
tomcat ['tɔmkæt] *n* gatto.
tomorrow [tə'mɔrəʊ] *adv, n* (*also fig*) domani (*m inv*); **the day after** ~ dopodomani; **a week** ~ domani a otto; ~ **morning** domani mattina.
ton [tʌn] *n* tonnellata (*BRIT*: = *1016 kg; 20 cwt; US = 907 kg; metric = 1000 kg*); (*NAUT: also*: **register** ~) tonnellata di stazza (= *2.83 cu.m; 100 cu.ft*); ~**s of** (*col*) un

mucchio *or* sacco di.
tonal ['təʊnl] *adj* tonale.
tone [təʊn] *n* tono; (*of musical instrument*) timbro ♦ *vi* intonarsi.
►**tone down** *vt* (*colour, criticism, sound*) attenuare.
►**tone up** *vt* (*muscles*) tonificare.
tone-deaf [təʊn'dɛf] *adj* che non ha orecchio (musicale).
toner ['təʊnə*] *n* (*for photocopier*) colorante *m* organico, toner *m*.
Tonga ['tɔŋgə] *n* isole *fpl* Tonga.
tongs [tɔŋz] *npl* tenaglie *fpl*; (*for coal*) molle *fpl*; (*for hair*) arricciacapelli *m inv*.
tongue [tʌŋ] *n* lingua; ~ **in cheek** (*fig*) ironicamente.
tongue-tied ['tʌŋtaɪd] *adj* (*fig*) muto(a).
tongue-twister ['tʌŋtwɪstə*] *n* scioglilingua *m inv*.
tonic ['tɔnɪk] *n* (*MED*) ricostituente *m*; (*skin* ~) tonico; (*MUS*) nota tonica; (*also*: ~ **water**) acqua tonica.
tonight [tə'naɪt] *adv* stanotte; (*this evening*) stasera ♦ *n* questa notte; questa sera; **I'll see you** ~ ci vediamo stasera.
tonnage ['tʌnɪdʒ] *n* (*NAUT*) tonnellaggio, stazza.
tonne [tʌn] *n* (*BRIT: metric ton*) tonnellata.
tonsil ['tɔnsl] *n* tonsilla; **to have one's** ~**s out** farsi operare di tonsille.
tonsillitis [tɔnsɪ'laɪtɪs] *n* tonsillite *f*; **to have** ~ avere la tonsillite.
too [tuː] *adv* (*excessively*) troppo; (*also*) anche; **it's** ~ **sweet** è troppo dolce; **I went** ~ ci sono andato anch'io; ~ **much** *adv* troppo ♦ *adj* troppo(a); ~ **many** *adj* troppi(e); ~ **bad!** tanto peggio!; peggio così!
took [tʊk] *pt of* **take**.
tool [tuːl] *n* utensile *m*, attrezzo; (*fig: person*) strumento ♦ *vt* lavorare con un attrezzo.
tool box *n* cassetta *f* portautensili *inv*.
tool kit *n* cassetta di attrezzi.
toot [tuːt] *vi* suonare; (*with car horn*) suonare il clacson.
tooth, *pl* **teeth** [tuːθ, tiːθ] *n* (*ANAT, TECH*) dente *m*; **to clean one's teeth** lavarsi i denti; **to have a** ~ **out** *or* (*US*) **pulled** farsi togliere un dente; **by the skin of one's teeth** per il rotto della cuffia.
toothache ['tuːθeɪk] *n* mal *m* di denti; **to have** ~ avere il mal di denti.
toothpaste ['tuːθpeɪst] *n* dentifricio.
toothpick ['tuːθpɪk] *n* stuzzicadenti *m inv*.
tooth powder *n* dentifricio in polvere.
top [tɔp] *n* (*of mountain, page, ladder*) cima; (*of box, cupboard, table*) sopra *m inv*, parte *f*

superiore; (*lid: of box, jar*) coperchio; (: *of bottle*) tappo; (*toy*) trottola; (*DRESS: blouse etc*) camicia (*or* maglietta *etc*); (*of pyjamas*) giacca ♦ *adj* più alto(a); (*in rank*) primo(a); (*best*) migliore ♦ *vt* (*exceed*) superare; (*be first in*) essere in testa a; **on ~ of** sopra, in cima a; (*in addition to*) oltre a; **from ~ to toe** (*BRIT*) dalla testa ai piedi; **at the ~ of the stairs/page/street** in cima alle scale/alla pagina/alla strada; **the ~ of the milk** (*BRIT*) la panna; **at ~ speed** a tutta velocità; **at the ~ of one's voice** (*fig*) a squarciagola; **over the ~** (*col: behaviour etc*) eccessivo(a); **to go over the ~** esagerare.

▶**top up,** (*US*) **top off** *vt* riempire.
topaz ['təupæz] *n* topazio.
top-class ['tɔp'klɑːs] *adj* di prim'ordine.
topcoat ['tɔpkəut] *n* soprabito.
topflight ['tɔpflaɪt] *adj* di primaria importanza.
top floor *n* ultimo piano.
top hat *n* cilindro.
top-heavy [tɔp'hɛvɪ] *adj* (*object*) con la parte superiore troppo pesante.
topic ['tɔpɪk] *n* argomento.
topical ['tɔpɪkəl] *adj* d'attualità.
topless ['tɔplɪs] *adj* (*bather etc*) col seno scoperto; **~ swimsuit** topless *m inv*.
top-level ['tɔplɛvl] *adj* (*talks*) ad alto livello.
topmost ['tɔpməust] *adj* il(la) più alto(a).
top-notch ['tɔp'nɔtʃ] *adj* (*col: player, performer*) di razza; (: *school, car*) eccellente.
topography [tə'pɔgrəfɪ] *n* topografia.
topping ['tɔpɪŋ] *n* (*CULIN*) guarnizione *f*.
topple ['tɔpl] *vt* rovesciare, far cadere ♦ *vi* cadere; traballare.
top-ranking ['tɔp'ræŋkɪŋ] *adj* di massimo grado.
top-secret ['tɔp'siːkrɪt] *adj* segretissimo(a).
top-security ['tɔpsɪ'kjuərɪtɪ] *adj* (*BRIT*) di massima sicurezza.
topsy-turvy ['tɔpsɪ'təːvɪ] *adj, adv* sottosopra (*inv*).
top-up ['tɔpʌp] *n*: **would you like a ~?** vuole che le riempia il bicchiere (*or* la tazza *etc*)?
top-up loan *n* (*BRIT*) prestito integrativo.
torch [tɔːtʃ] *n* torcia; (*BRIT: electric*) lampadina tascabile.
tore [tɔː*] *pt of* **tear**.
torment *n* ['tɔːmɛnt] tormento ♦ *vt* [tɔː'mɛnt] tormentare; (*fig: annoy*) infastidire.
torn [tɔːn] *pp of* **tear** ♦ *adj*: **~ between** (*fig*) combattuto(a) tra.
tornado, **~es** [tɔː'neɪdəu] *n* tornado.

torpedo, **~es** [tɔː'piːdəu] *n* siluro.
torpedo boat *n* motosilurante *f*.
torpor ['tɔːpə*] *n* torpore *m*.
torrent ['tɔrnt] *n* torrente *m*.
torrential [tə'rɛnʃl] *adj* torrenziale.
torrid ['tɔrɪd] *adj* torrido(a); (*fig*) denso(a) di passione.
torso ['tɔːsəu] *n* torso.
tortoise ['tɔːtəs] *n* tartaruga.
tortoiseshell ['tɔːtəʃɛl] *adj* di tartaruga.
tortuous ['tɔːtjuəs] *adj* tortuoso(a).
torture ['tɔːtʃə*] *n* tortura ♦ *vt* torturare.
torturer ['tɔːtʃərə*] *n* torturatore/trice.
Tory ['tɔːrɪ] *adj* tory *inv*, conservatore(trice) ♦ *n* tory *m/f inv*, conservatore/trice.
toss [tɔs] *vt* gettare, lanciare; (*BRIT: pancake*) far saltare; (*head*) scuotere ♦ *n* (*movement: of head etc*) movimento brusco; (*of coin*) lancio; **to win/lose the ~** vincere/perdere a testa o croce; (*SPORT*) vincere/perdere il sorteggio; **to ~ a coin** fare a testa o croce; **to ~ up for sth** fare a testa o croce per qc; **to ~ and turn** (*in bed*) girarsi e rigirarsi.
tot [tɔt] *n* (*BRIT: drink*) bicchierino; (*child*) bimbo/a.
▶**tot up** *vt* (*BRIT: figures*) sommare.
total ['təutl] *adj* totale ♦ *n* totale *m* ♦ *vt* (*add up*) sommare; (*amount to*) ammontare a; **in ~** in tutto.
totalitarian [təutælɪ'tɛərɪən] *adj* totalitario(a).
totality [təu'tælɪtɪ] *n* totalità.
totally ['təutəlɪ] *adv* completamente.
tote bag ['təut-] *n* sporta.
totem pole ['təutəm-] *n* totem *m inv*.
totter ['tɔtə*] *vi* barcollare; (*object, government*) vacillare.
touch [tʌtʃ] *n* tocco; (*sense*) tatto; (*contact*) contatto; (*FOOTBALL*) fuori gioco *m* ♦ *vt* toccare; **a ~ of** (*fig*) un tocco di; un pizzico di; **to get in ~ with** mettersi in contatto con; **to lose ~** (*friends*) perdersi di vista; **I'll be in ~** mi farò sentire; **to be out of ~ with events** essere tagliato fuori; **the personal ~** una nota personale; **to put the finishing ~es to sth** dare gli ultimi ritocchi a qc.
▶**touch on** *vt fus* (*topic*) sfiorare, accennare a.
▶**touch up** *vt* (*improve*) ritoccare.
touch-and-go ['tʌtʃən'gəu] *adj* incerto(a); **it was ~ with the sick man** il malato era tra la vita e la morte.
touchdown ['tʌtʃdaun] *n* atterraggio; (*on sea*) ammaraggio; (*US FOOTBALL*) meta.
touched [tʌtʃt] *adj* commosso(a); (*col*)

tocco(a), toccato(a).
touching ['tʌtʃɪŋ] *adj* commovente.
touchline ['tʌtʃlaɪn] *n* (*SPORT*) linea
laterale.
touch-sensitive ['tʌtʃ'sɛnsɪtɪv] *adj*
sensibile al tatto.
touch-type ['tʌtʃtaɪp] *vi* dattilografare
(senza guardare i tasti).
touchy ['tʌtʃɪ] *adj* (*person*) suscettibile.
tough [tʌf] *adj* duro(a); (*resistant*)
resistente; (*meat*) duro(a), tiglioso(a);
(*journey*) faticoso(a), duro(a); (*person:
rough*) violento(a), brutale ♦ *n* (*gangster
etc*) delinquente *m/f*; ~ **luck!** che sfortuna!
toughen ['tʌfn] *vt* indurire, rendere più
resistente.
toughness ['tʌfnɪs] *n* durezza; resistenza.
toupee ['tu:peɪ] *n* parrucchino.
tour [tuə*] *n* viaggio; (*also*: **package** ~)
viaggio organizzato; (*of town, museum*)
visita; (*by artist*) tournée *f inv* ♦ *vt* visitare;
to go on a ~ **of** (*region, country*) fare il
giro di; (*museum, castle*) visitare; **to go on**
~ andare in tournée.
tour guide *n* accompagnatore/trice
turistico(a).
touring ['tuərɪŋ] *n* turismo.
tourism ['tuərɪzəm] *n* turismo.
tourist ['tuərɪst] *n* turista *m/f* ♦ *adv* (*travel*)
in classe turistica ♦ *cpd* turistico(a); **the** ~
trade il turismo.
tourist class *n* (*AVIAT*) classe *f* turistica.
tourist office *n* pro loco *f inv*.
tournament ['tuənəmənt] *n* torneo.
tourniquet ['tuənɪkeɪ] *n* (*MED*) laccio
emostatico, pinza emostatica.
tour operator *n* (*BRIT*) operatore *m*
turistico.
tousled ['tauzld] *adj* (*hair*) arruffato(a).
tout [taut] *vi*: **to** ~ **for** procacciare,
raccogliere; cercare clienti per ♦ *n* (*BRIT:
also*: **ticket** ~) bagarino; **to** ~ **sth (around)**
(*BRIT*) cercare di (ri)vendere qc.
tow [təu] *vt* rimorchiare ♦ *n* rimorchio; **"on**
~**"**, (*US*) **"in** ~**"** (*AUT*) "veicolo rimor-
chiato"; **to give sb a** ~ rimorchiare qn.
toward(s) [tə'wɔːd(z)] *prep* verso; (*of
attitude*) nei confronti di; (*of purpose*) per;
~ **noon/the end of the year** verso
mezzogiorno/la fine dell'anno; **to feel
friendly** ~ **sb** provare un sentimento
d'amicizia per qn.
towel ['tauəl] *n* asciugamano; (*also*: **tea** ~)
strofinaccio; **to throw in the** ~ (*fig*)
gettare la spugna.
towelling ['tauəlɪŋ] *n* (*fabric*) spugna.
towel rail, (*US*) **towel rack** *n*
portasciugamano.

tower ['tauə*] *n* torre *f* ♦ *vi* (*building,
mountain*) innalzarsi; **to** ~ **above** or **over
sb/sth** sovrastare qn/qc.
tower block *n* (*BRIT*) palazzone *m*.
towering ['tauərɪŋ] *adj* altissimo(a),
imponente.
towline ['təulaɪn] *n* (cavo da) rimorchio.
town [taun] *n* città *f inv*; **to go to** ~ andare
in città; (*fig*) mettercela tutta; **in (the)** ~
in città; **to be out of** ~ essere fuori città.
town centre *n* centro (città).
town clerk *n* segretario comunale.
town council *n* consiglio comunale.
town crier [-'kraɪə*] *n* (*BRIT*) banditore/
trice.
town hall *n* ≈ municipio.
townie ['taunɪ] *n* (*BRIT col*) uno/a di città.
town plan *n* pianta della città.
town planner *n* urbanista *m/f*.
town planning *n* urbanistica.
township ['taunʃɪp] *n* township *f inv*.
townspeople ['taunzpiːpl] *npl* cittadinanza,
cittadini *mpl*.
towpath ['təupɑːθ] *n* alzaia.
towrope ['təurəup] *n* (cavo da) rimorchio.
tow truck *n* (*US*) carro *m* attrezzi *inv*.
toxic ['tɔksɪk] *adj* tossico(a).
toxin ['tɔksɪn] *n* tossina.
toy [tɔɪ] *n* giocattolo.
▶**toy with** *vt fus* giocare con; (*idea*)
accarezzare, trastullarsi con.
toyshop ['tɔɪʃɔp] *n* negozio di giocattoli.
trace [treɪs] *n* traccia ♦ *vt* (*draw*) tracciare;
(*follow*) seguire; (*locate*) rintracciare;
without ~ (*disappear*) senza lasciare
traccia; **there was no** ~ **of it** non ne
restava traccia.
trace element *n* oligoelemento.
trachea [trə'kɪə] *n* (*ANAT*) trachea.
tracing paper ['treɪsɪŋ-] *n* carta da ricalco.
track [træk] *n* (*mark: of person, animal*)
traccia; (*on tape, SPORT; path: gen*) pista;
(: *of bullet etc*) traiettoria; (: *of suspect,
animal*) pista, tracce *fpl*; (*RAIL*) binario,
rotaie *fpl*; (*COMPUT*) traccia, pista ♦ *vt*
seguire le tracce di; **to keep** ~ **of** seguire;
to be on the right ~ (*fig*) essere sulla
buona strada.
▶**track down** *vt* (*prey*) scovare; snidare;
(*sth lost*) rintracciare.
tracker dog ['trækə-] *n* (*BRIT*) cane *m*
poliziotto *inv*.
track events *npl* (*SPORT*) prove *fpl* su pista.
tracking station ['trækɪŋ-] *n* (*SPACE*)
osservatorio spaziale.
track meet *n* (*US*) meeting *m inv* di atletica.
track record *n*: **to have a good** ~ (*fig*)
avere un buon curriculum.

tracksuit ['træksuːt] n tuta sportiva.

tract [trækt] n (GEO) tratto, estensione f; (pamphlet) opuscolo, libretto; **respiratory** ~ (ANAT) apparato respiratorio.

traction ['trækʃən] n trazione f.

tractor ['træktə*] n trattore m.

trade [treɪd] n commercio; (skill, job) mestiere m; (industry) industria, settore m ♦ vi commerciare; **to** ~ **with/in** commerciare con/in; **foreign** ~ commercio estero; **Department of T~ and Industry (DTI)** (BRIT) ≈ Ministero del Commercio.

▶**trade in** vt (old car etc) dare come pagamento parziale.

trade barrier n barriera commerciale.

trade deficit n bilancio commerciale in deficit.

Trade Descriptions Act n (BRIT) legge f a tutela del consumatore.

trade discount n sconto sul listino.

trade fair n fiera campionaria.

trade-in ['treɪdɪn] n: **to take as a** ~ accettare in permuta.

trade-in price n prezzo di permuta.

trademark ['treɪdmɑːk] n marchio di fabbrica.

trade mission n missione f commerciale.

trade name n marca, nome m depositato.

trade-off ['treɪdɔf] n compromesso, accomodamento.

trader ['treɪdə*] n commerciante m/f.

trade secret n segreto di fabbricazione.

tradesman ['treɪdzmən] n fornitore m; (shopkeeper) negoziante m.

trade union n sindacato.

trade unionist [-'juːnjənɪst] n sindacalista m/f.

trade wind n aliseo.

trading ['treɪdɪŋ] n commercio.

trading estate n (BRIT) zona industriale.

trading stamp n bollo premio.

tradition [trə'dɪʃən] n tradizione f; ~**s** npl tradizioni, usanze fpl.

traditional [trə'dɪʃənl] adj tradizionale.

traffic ['træfɪk] n traffico ♦ vi: **to** ~ **in** (pej: liquor, drugs) trafficare in.

traffic calming [-'kɑːmɪŋ] n uso di accorgimenti per rallentare il traffico in zone abitate.

traffic circle n (US) isola rotatoria.

traffic island n salvagente m, isola f spartitraffico inv.

traffic jam n ingorgo (del traffico).

trafficker ['træfɪkə*] n trafficante m/f.

traffic lights npl semaforo.

traffic offence n (BRIT) infrazione f al codice stradale.

traffic sign n cartello stradale.

traffic violation n (US) = **traffic offence**.

traffic warden n addetto/a al controllo del traffico e del parcheggio.

tragedy ['trædʒədɪ] n tragedia.

tragic ['trædʒɪk] adj tragico(a).

trail [treɪl] n (tracks) tracce fpl, pista; (path) sentiero; (of smoke etc) scia ♦ vt trascinare, strascicare; (follow) seguire ♦ vi essere al traino; (dress etc) strusciare; (plant) arrampicarsi; strisciare; **to be on sb's** ~ essere sulle orme di qn.

▶**trail away, trail off** vi (sound) affievolirsi; (interest, voice) spegnersi a poco a poco.

▶**trail behind** vi essere al traino.

trailer ['treɪlə*] n (AUT) rimorchio; (US) roulotte f inv; (CINE) prossimamente m inv.

trailer truck n (US) autoarticolato.

train [treɪn] n treno; (of dress) coda, strascico; (BRIT: series): ~ **of events** serie f di avvenimenti a catena ♦ vt (apprentice, doctor etc) formare; (sportsman) allenare; (dog) addestrare; (memory) esercitare; (point: gun etc): **to** ~ **sth on** puntare qc contro ♦ vi formarsi; allenarsi; (learn a skill) fare pratica, fare tirocinio; **to go by** ~ andare in or col treno; **one's** ~ **of thought** il filo dei propri pensieri; **to** ~ **sb to do sth** preparare qn a fare qc.

train attendant n (US) addetto/a ai vagoni letto.

trained [treɪnd] adj qualificato(a); allenato(a); addestrato(a).

trainee [treɪ'niː] n allievo/a; (in trade) apprendista m/f; **he's a** ~ **teacher** sta facendo tirocinio come insegnante.

trainer ['treɪnə*] n (SPORT) allenatore/trice; (of dogs etc) addestratore/trice; ~**s** npl (shoes) scarpe fpl da ginnastica.

training ['treɪnɪŋ] n formazione f; allenamento; addestramento; **in** ~ (SPORT) in allenamento; (fit) in forma.

training college n istituto professionale.

training course n corso di formazione professionale.

traipse [treɪps] vi: **to** ~ **in/out** etc entrare/uscire etc trascinandosi.

trait [treɪt] n tratto.

traitor ['treɪtə*] n traditore/trice.

trajectory [trə'dʒɛktərɪ] n traiettoria.

tram [træm] n (BRIT: also: ~**car**) tram m inv.

tramline ['træmlaɪn] n linea tranviaria.

tramp [træmp] n (person) vagabondo/a; (col: pej: woman) sgualdrina ♦ vi camminare con passo pesante ♦ vt (walk through: town, streets) percorrere a piedi.

trample ['træmpl] vt: **to** ~ (**underfoot**)

calpestare.

trampoline ['træmpəli:n] *n* trampolino.

trance [trɑ:ns] *n* trance *f inv*; (*MED*) catalessi *f inv*; **to go into a ~** cadere in trance.

tranquil ['træŋkwɪl] *adj* tranquillo(a).

tranquillity, (*US*) **tranquility** [træŋ'kwɪlɪtɪ] *n* tranquillità.

tranquillizer, (*US*) **tranquilizer** ['træŋkwɪlaɪzə*] *n* (*MED*) tranquillante *m*.

transact [træn'zækt] *vt* (*business*) trattare.

transaction [træn'zækʃən] *n* transazione *f*; **~s** *npl* (*minutes*) atti *mpl*; **cash ~** operazione *f* in contanti.

transatlantic ['trænzət'læntɪk] *adj* transatlantico(a).

transcend [træn'sɛnd] *vt* trascendere; (*excel over*) superare.

transcendental [trænsɛn'dɛntl] *adj*: **~ meditation** meditazione *f* trascendentale.

transcribe [træn'skraɪb] *vt* trascrivere.

transcript ['trænskrɪpt] *n* trascrizione *f*.

transcription [træn'skrɪpʃən] *n* trascrizione *f*.

transept ['trænsɛpt] *n* transetto.

transfer *n* ['trænsfə*] (*gen, also SPORT*) trasferimento; (*POL: of power*) passaggio; (*picture, design*) decalcomania; (: *stick-on*) autoadesivo ♦ *vt* [træns'fə:*] trasferire; passare; decalcare; **by bank ~** tramite trasferimento bancario; **to ~ the charges** (*BRIT TEL*) telefonare con addebito al ricevente.

transferable [træns'fə:rəbl] *adj* trasferibile; **not ~** non cedibile, personale.

transfix [træns'fɪks] *vt* trafiggere; (*fig*): **~ed with fear** paralizzato dalla paura.

transform [træns'fɔ:m] *vt* trasformare.

transformation [trænsfə'meɪʃən] *n* trasformazione *f*.

transformer [træns'fɔ:mə*] *n* (*ELEC*) trasformatore *m*.

transfusion [træns'fju:ʒən] *n* trasfusione *f*.

transgress [træns'grɛs] *vt* (*go beyond*) infrangere; (*violate*) trasgredire, infrangere.

tranship [træn'ʃɪp] *vt* trasbordare.

transient ['trænzɪənt] *adj* transitorio(a), fugace.

transistor [træn'zɪstə*] *n* (*ELEC*) transistor *m inv*; (*also*: **~ radio**) radio *f inv* a transistor.

transit ['trænzɪt] *n*: **in ~** in transito.

transit camp *n* campo (di raccolta) profughi.

transition [træn'zɪʃən] *n* passaggio, transizione *f*.

transitional [træn'zɪʃənl] *adj* di transizione.

transitive ['trænzɪtɪv] *adj* (*LING*) transitivo(a).

transit lounge *n* (*AVIAT*) sala di transito.

transitory ['trænzɪtərɪ] *adj* transitorio(a).

translate [trænz'leɪt] *vt* tradurre; **to ~ (from/into)** tradurre (da/in).

translation [trænz'leɪʃən] *n* traduzione *f*; (*SCOL: as opposed to prose*) versione *f*.

translator [trænz'leɪtə*] *n* traduttore/trice.

translucent [trænz'lu:snt] *adj* traslucido(a).

transmission [trænz'mɪʃən] *n* trasmissione *f*.

transmit [trænz'mɪt] *vt* trasmettere.

transmitter [trænz'mɪtə*] *n* trasmettitore *m*.

transparency [træns'pɛərnsɪ] *n* (*PHOT*) diapositiva.

transparent [træns'pærnt] *adj* trasparente.

transpire [træns'paɪə*] *vi* (*happen*) succedere; **it finally ~d that ...** alla fine si è venuto a sapere che ....

transplant *vt* [træns'plɑ:nt] trapiantare ♦ *n* ['trænsplɑ:nt] trapianto; **to have a heart ~** subire un trapianto cardiaco.

transport *n* ['trænspɔ:t] trasporto ♦ *vt* [træns'pɔ:t] trasportare; **public ~** mezzi *mpl* pubblici; **Department of T~** (*BRIT*) Ministero dei Trasporti.

transportation ['trænspɔ:'teɪʃən] *n* (*mezzo di*) trasporto; (*of prisoners*) deportazione *f*; **Department of T~** (*US*) Ministero dei Trasporti.

transport café *n* (*BRIT*) trattoria per camionisti.

transpose [træns'pəuz] *vt* trasporre.

transsexual [trænz'sɛksjuəl] *adj, n* transessuale (*m/f*).

transverse ['trænzvə:s] *adj* trasversale.

transvestite [trænz'vɛstaɪt] *n* travestito/a.

trap [træp] *n* (*snare, trick*) trappola; (*carriage*) calesse *m* ♦ *vt* prendere in trappola, intrappolare; (*immobilize*) bloccare; (*jam*) chiudere, schiacciare; **to set** *or* **lay a ~ (for sb)** tendere una trappola (a qn); **to ~ one's finger in the door** chiudersi il dito nella porta; **shut your ~!** (*col*) chiudi quella boccaccia!

trap door *n* botola.

trapeze [trə'pi:z] *n* trapezio.

trapper ['træpə*] *n* cacciatore *m* di animali da pelliccia.

trappings ['træpɪŋz] *npl* ornamenti *mpl*; indoratura, sfarzo.

trash [træʃ] *n* (*pej: goods*) ciarpame *m*; (: *nonsense*) sciocchezze *fpl*; (*US: rubbish*) rifiuti *mpl*, spazzatura.

trash can *n* (*US*) secchio della spazzatura.

trashy ['træʃɪ] *adj* (*col*) scadente.

trauma ['trɔ:mə] *n* trauma *m*.

traumatic [trɔːˈmætɪk] *adj* (*PSYCH*, *fig*) traumatico(a), traumatizzante.

travel [ˈtrævl] *n* viaggio; viaggi *mpl* ♦ *vi* viaggiare; (*move*) andare, spostarsi ♦ *vt* (*distance*) percorrere; **this wine doesn't ~ well** questo vino non resiste agli spostamenti.

travel agency *n* agenzia (di) viaggi.

travel agent *n* agente *m* di viaggio.

travel brochure *n* dépliant *m* di viaggi.

traveller, (*US*) **traveler** [ˈtrævlə*] *n* viaggiatore/trice; (*COMM*) commesso viaggiatore.

traveller's cheque, (*US*) **traveler's check** *n* assegno turistico.

travelling, (*US*) **traveling** [ˈtrævlɪŋ] *n* viaggi *mpl* ♦ *adj* (*circus*, *exhibition*) itinerante ♦ *cpd* (*bag*, *clock*) da viaggio; (*expenses*) di viaggio.

travel(l)ing salesman *n* commesso viaggiatore.

travelogue [ˈtrævəlɔg] *n* (*book*, *film*) diario *or* documentario di viaggio; (*talk*) conferenza sui viaggi.

travel sickness *n* mal *m* d'auto (*or* di mare *or* d'aria).

traverse [ˈtrævəs] *vt* traversare, attraversare.

travesty [ˈtrævəstɪ] *n* parodia.

trawler [ˈtrɔːlə*] *n* peschereccio (a strascico).

tray [treɪ] *n* (*for carrying*) vassoio; (*on desk*) vaschetta.

treacherous [ˈtrɛtʃərəs] *adj* traditore(trice); **road conditions today are ~** oggi il fondo stradale è pericoloso.

treachery [ˈtrɛtʃərɪ] *n* tradimento.

treacle [ˈtriːkl] *n* melassa.

tread [trɛd] *n* passo; (*sound*) rumore *m* di passi; (*of tyre*) battistrada *m inv* ♦ *vi* (*pt* trod, *pp* **trodden** [trɔd, ˈtrɔdn]) camminare.

▶**tread on** *vt fus* calpestare.

treadle [ˈtrɛdl] *n* pedale *m*.

treas. *abbr* = **treasurer**.

treason [ˈtriːzn] *n* tradimento.

treasure [ˈtrɛʒə*] *n* tesoro ♦ *vt* (*value*) tenere in gran conto, apprezzare molto; (*store*) custodire gelosamente.

treasure hunt *n* caccia al tesoro.

treasurer [ˈtrɛʒərə*] *n* tesoriere/a.

treasury [ˈtrɛʒərɪ] *n* tesoreria; (*POL*): **the T~**, (*US*) **the T~ Department** ≈ il Ministero del Tesoro.

treasury bill *n* buono del tesoro.

treat [triːt] *n* regalo ♦ *vt* trattare; (*MED*) curare; (*consider*) considerare; **it was a ~** mi (*or* ci *etc*) ha fatto veramente piacere; **to ~ sb to sth** offrire qc a qn; **to ~ sth as**

a joke considerare qc uno scherzo.

treatise [ˈtriːtɪz] *n* trattato.

treatment [ˈtriːtmənt] *n* trattamento; **to have ~ for sth** (*MED*) farsi curare qc.

treaty [ˈtriːtɪ] *n* patto, trattato.

treble [ˈtrɛbl] *adj* triplo(a), triplice ♦ *n* (*MUS*) soprano *m/f* ♦ *vt* triplicare ♦ *vi* triplicarsi.

treble clef *n* chiave *f* di violino.

tree [triː] *n* albero.

tree-lined [ˈtriːlaɪnd] *adj* fiancheggiato(a) da alberi.

treetop [ˈtriːtɔp] *n* cima di un albero.

tree trunk *n* tronco d'albero.

trek [trɛk] *n* (*hike*) spedizione *f*; (*tiring walk*) camminata sfiancante ♦ *vi* (*as holiday*) fare dell'escursionismo.

trellis [ˈtrɛlɪs] *n* graticcio, pergola.

tremble [ˈtrɛmbl] *vi* tremare; (*machine*) vibrare.

trembling [ˈtrɛmblɪŋ] *n* tremito ♦ *adj* tremante.

tremendous [trɪˈmɛndəs] *adj* (*enormous*) enorme; (*excellent*) meraviglioso(a), formidabile.

tremendously [trɪˈmɛndəslɪ] *adv* incredibilmente; **he enjoyed it ~** gli è piaciuto da morire.

tremor [ˈtrɛmə*] *n* tremore *m*, tremito; (*also*: **earth ~**) scossa sismica.

trench [trɛntʃ] *n* trincea.

trench coat *n* trench *m inv*.

trench warfare *n* guerra di trincea.

trend [trɛnd] *n* (*tendency*) tendenza; (*of events*) corso; (*fashion*) moda; **~ towards/ away from** tendenza a/ad allontanarsi da; **to set the ~** essere all'avanguardia; **to set a ~** lanciare una moda.

trendy [ˈtrɛndɪ] *adj* (*idea*) di moda; (*clothes*) all'ultima moda.

trepidation [trɛpɪˈdeɪʃn] *n* trepidazione *f*, agitazione *f*.

trespass [ˈtrɛspəs] *vi*: **to ~ on** entrare abusivamente in; (*fig*) abusare di; **"no ~ing"** "proprietà privata", "vietato l'accesso".

trespasser [ˈtrɛspəsə*] *n* trasgressore *m*; **"~s will be prosecuted"** "i trasgressori saranno puniti secondo i termini di legge".

trestle [ˈtrɛsl] *n* cavalletto.

trestle table *n* tavola su cavalletti.

trial [ˈtraɪəl] *n* (*LAW*) processo; (*test: of machine etc*) collaudo; (*hardship*) prova, difficoltà *f inv*; (*worry*) cruccio; **~s** *npl* (*ATHLETICS*) prove *fpl* di qualificazione; **horse ~s** concorso ippico; **to be on ~** essere sotto processo; **~ by jury** processo penale con giuria; **to be sent for ~** essere

rinviato a giudizio; **to bring sb to** ~ **(for a crime)** portare qn in giudizio (per un reato); **by** ~ **and error** a tentoni.
trial balance *n* (*COMM*) bilancio di verifica.
trial basis *n*: **on a** ~ in prova.
trial run *n* periodo di prova.
triangle ['traɪæŋgl] *n* (*MATH, MUS*) triangolo.
triangular [traɪ'æŋgjʊlə*] *adj* triangolare.
triathlon [traɪ'æθlən] *n* triathlon *m inv*.
tribal ['traɪbəl] *adj* tribale.
tribe [traɪb] *n* tribù *f inv*.
tribesman ['traɪbzmən] *n* membro della tribù.
tribulation [trɪbjuˈleɪʃən] *n* tribolazione *f*.
tribunal [traɪ'bjuːnl] *n* tribunale *m*.
tributary ['trɪbjuːtərɪ] *n* (*river*) tributario, affluente *m*.
tribute ['trɪbjuːt] *n* tributo, omaggio; **to pay** ~ **to** rendere omaggio a.
trice [traɪs] *n*: **in a** ~ in un attimo.
trick [trɪk] *n* trucco; (*clever act*) stratagemma *m*; (*joke*) tiro; (*CARDS*) presa ♦ *vt* imbrogliare, ingannare; **to play a** ~ **on sb** giocare un tiro a qn; **it's a** ~ **of the light** è un effetto ottico; **that should do the** ~ (*col*) vedrai che funziona; **to** ~ **sb into doing sth** convincere qn a fare qc con l'inganno; **to** ~ **sb out of sth** fregare qc a qn.
trickery ['trɪkərɪ] *n* inganno.
trickle ['trɪkl] *n* (*of water etc*) rivolo; gocciolio ♦ *vi* gocciolare; **to** ~ **in/out** (*people*) entrare/uscire alla spicciolata.
trick question *n* domanda *f* trabocchetto *inv*.
trickster ['trɪkstə*] *n* imbroglione/a.
tricky ['trɪkɪ] *adj* difficile, delicato(a).
tricycle ['traɪsɪkl] *n* triciclo.
trifle ['traɪfl] *n* sciocchezza; (*BRIT CULIN*) ≈ zuppa inglese ♦ *adv*: **a** ~ **long** un po' lungo ♦ *vi*: **to** ~ **with** prendere alla leggera.
trifling ['traɪflɪŋ] *adj* insignificante.
trigger ['trɪgə*] *n* (*of gun*) grilletto.
▶**trigger off** *vt* dare l'avvio a.
trigonometry [trɪgə'nɔmətrɪ] *n* trigonometria.
trilby ['trɪlbɪ] *n* (*BRIT: also:* ~ **hat**) cappello floscio di feltro.
trill [trɪl] *n* (*of bird, MUS*) trillo.
trilogy ['trɪlədʒɪ] *n* trilogia.
trim [trɪm] *adj* ordinato(a); (*house, garden*) ben tenuto(a); (*figure*) snello(a) ♦ *n* (*haircut etc*) spuntata, regolata; (*embellishment*) finiture *fpl*; (*on car*) guarnizioni *fpl* ♦ *vt* spuntare; (*decorate*): **to** ~ **(with)** decorare (con); (*NAUT: a sail*) orientare; **to keep in (good)** ~

mantenersi in forma.
trimmings ['trɪmɪŋz] *npl* decorazioni *fpl*; (*extras: gen CULIN*) guarnizione *f*.
Trinidad and Tobago ['trɪnɪdæd-] *n* Trinidad e Tobago *m*.
Trinity ['trɪnɪtɪ] *n*: **the** ~ la Trinità.
trinket ['trɪŋkɪt] *n* gingillo; (*piece of jewellery*) ciondolo.
trio ['triːəʊ] *n* trio.
trip [trɪp] *n* viaggio; (*excursion*) gita, escursione *f*; (*stumble*) passo falso ♦ *vi* inciampare; (*go lightly*) camminare con passo leggero; **on a** ~ in viaggio.
▶**trip up** *vi* inciampare ♦ *vt* fare lo sgambetto a.
tripartite [traɪ'pɑːtaɪt] *adj* (*agreement*) tripartito(a); (*talks*) a tre.
tripe [traɪp] *n* (*CULIN*) trippa; (*pej: rubbish*) sciocchezze *fpl*, fesserie *fpl*.
triple ['trɪpl] *adj* triplo(a) ♦ *adv*: ~ **the distance/the speed** tre volte più lontano/più veloce.
triple jump *n* triplo salto.
triplets ['trɪplɪts] *npl* bambini(e) trigemini(e).
triplicate ['trɪplɪkət] *n*: **in** ~ in triplice copia.
tripod ['traɪpɔd] *n* treppiede *m*.
Tripoli ['trɪpəlɪ] *n* Tripoli *f*.
tripper ['trɪpə*] *n* (*BRIT*) gitante *m/f*.
tripwire ['trɪpwaɪə*] *n* filo in tensione che fa scattare una trappola, allarme etc.
trite [traɪt] *adj* banale, trito(a).
triumph ['traɪʌmf] *n* trionfo ♦ *vi*: **to** ~ **(over)** trionfare (su).
triumphal [traɪ'ʌmfl] *adj* trionfale.
triumphant [traɪ'ʌmfənt] *adj* trionfante.
trivia ['trɪvɪə] *npl* banalità *fpl*.
trivial ['trɪvɪəl] *adj* (*matter*) futile; (*excuse, comment*) banale; (*amount*) irrisorio(a); (*mistake*) di poco conto.
triviality [trɪvɪ'ælɪtɪ] *n* frivolezza; (*trivial detail*) futilità.
trivialize ['trɪvɪəlaɪz] *vt* sminuire.
trod [trɔd] *pt of* **tread**.
trodden ['trɔdn] *pp of* **tread**.
trolley ['trɔlɪ] *n* carrello; (*in hospital*) lettiga.
trolley bus *n* filobus *m inv*.
trollop ['trɔləp] *n* prostituta.
trombone [trɔm'bəʊn] *n* trombone *m*.
troop [truːp] *n* gruppo; (*MIL*) squadrone *m*; ~**s** *npl* (*MIL*) truppe *fpl*; ~**ing the colour** (*BRIT: ceremony*) sfilata della bandiera.
▶**troop in** *vi* entrare a frotte.
▶**troop out** *vi* uscire a frotte.
troop carrier *n* (*plane*) aereo per il trasporto (di) truppe; (*NAUT: also:*

troopship) nave *f* per il trasporto (di) truppe.

trooper ['tru:pə*] *n* (*MIL*) soldato di cavalleria; (*US*: *policeman*) poliziotto (della polizia di stato).

troopship ['tru:pʃɪp] *n* nave *f* per il trasporto (di) truppe.

trophy ['trəufi] *n* trofeo.

tropic ['trɔpɪk] *n* tropico; **in the ~s** ai tropici; **T~ of Cancer/Capricorn** tropico del Cancro/Capricorno.

tropical ['trɔpɪkəl] *adj* tropicale.

trot [trɔt] *n* trotto ♦ *vi* trottare; **on the ~** (*BRIT fig*) di fila, uno(a) dopo l'altro(a).

►**trot out** *vt* (*excuse*, *reason*) tirar fuori; (*names*, *facts*) recitare di fila.

trouble ['trʌbl] *n* (*problems*) difficoltà *fpl*; problemi *mpl*; (*worry*) preoccupazione *f*; (*bother*, *effort*) sforzo; (*with sth mechanical*) noie *fpl*; (*POL*) conflitti *mpl*, disordine *m*; (*MED*): **stomach** *etc* ~ disturbi *mpl* gastrici *etc* ♦ *vt* disturbare; (*worry*) preoccupare ♦ *vi*: **to** ~ **to do** disturbarsi a fare; ~**s** *npl* (*POL etc*) disordini *mpl*; **to be in** ~ avere dei problemi; (*for doing wrong*) essere nei guai; **to go to the** ~ **of doing** darsi la pena di fare; **it's no ~!** di niente!; **what's the** ~? cosa c'è che non va?; **the** ~ **is ... c'è che ...**, il guaio è che ...; **to have** ~ **doing sth** avere delle difficoltà a fare qc; **please don't** ~ **yourself** non si disturbi.

troubled ['trʌbld] *adj* (*person*) preoccupato(a), inquieto(a); (*epoch*, *life*) agitato(a), difficile.

trouble-free ['trʌblfriː] *adj* senza problemi.

troublemaker ['trʌblmeɪkə*] *n* elemento disturbatore, agitatore/trice.

troubleshooter ['trʌblʃuːtə*] *n* (*in conflict*) conciliatore *m*.

troublesome ['trʌblsəm] *adj* fastidioso(a), seccante.

trouble spot *n* zona calda.

troubling ['trʌblɪŋ] *adj* (*thought*) preoccupante; **these are** ~ **times** questi sono tempi difficili.

trough [trɔf] *n* (*also*: **drinking** ~) abbeveratoio; (*also*: **feeding** ~) trogolo, mangiatoia; (*channel*) canale *m*; ~ **of low pressure** (*METEOROLOGY*) depressione *f*.

trounce [trauns] *vt* (*defeat*) sgominare.

troupe [truːp] *n* troupe *f inv*.

trouser press *n* stirapantaloni *m inv*.

trousers ['trauzəz] *npl* pantaloni *mpl*, calzoni *mpl*; **short** ~ (*BRIT*) calzoncini *mpl*.

trouser suit *n* (*BRIT*) completo *m or* tailleur *m inv* pantalone *inv*.

trousseau, *pl* ~**x** *or* ~**s** ['truːsəu, -z] *n* corredo da sposa.

trout [traut] *n* (*pl inv*) trota.

trowel ['trauəl] *n* cazzuola.

truant ['truənt] *n*: **to play** ~ (*BRIT*) marinare la scuola.

truce [truːs] *n* tregua.

truck [trʌk] *n* autocarro, camion *m inv*; (*RAIL*) carro merci aperto; (*for luggage*) carrello *m* portabagagli *inv*.

truck driver, (*US*) **trucker** ['trʌkə*] *n* camionista *m/f*.

truck farm *n* (*US*) orto industriale.

trucking ['trʌkɪŋ] *n* (*esp US*) autotrasporto.

trucking company *n* (*esp US*) impresa di trasporti.

truculent ['trʌkjulənt] *adj* aggressivo(a), brutale.

trudge [trʌdʒ] *vi* trascinarsi pesantemente.

true [truː] *adj* vero(a); (*accurate*) accurato(a), esatto(a); (*genuine*) reale; (*faithful*) fedele; (*wall*, *beam*) a piombo; (*wheel*) centrato(a); **to come** ~ avverarsi; **to life** verosimile.

truffle ['trʌfl] *n* tartufo.

truly ['truːlɪ] *adv* veramente; (*truthfully*) sinceramente; (*faithfully*) fedelmente; **yours** ~ (*in letter-writing*) distinti saluti.

trump [trʌmp] *n* (*CARDS*) atout *m inv*; **to turn up** ~**s** (*fig*) fare miracoli.

trump card *n* atout *m inv*; (*fig*) asso nella manica.

trumped-up [trʌmpt'ʌp] *adj* inventato(a).

trumpet ['trʌmpɪt] *n* tromba.

truncated [trʌŋ'keɪtɪd] *adj* tronco(a).

truncheon ['trʌntʃən] *n* sfollagente *m inv*.

trundle ['trʌndl] *vt*, *vi*: **to** ~ **along** rotolare rumorosamente.

trunk [trʌŋk] *n* (*of tree*, *person*) tronco; (*of elephant*) proboscide *f*; (*case*) baule *m*; (*US AUT*) bagagliaio.

trunk call *n* (*BRIT TEL*) (telefonata) interurbana.

trunk road *n* (*BRIT*) strada principale.

trunks [trʌŋks] *npl* (*also*: **swimming** ~) calzoncini *mpl* da bagno.

truss [trʌs] *n* (*MED*) cinto erniario ♦ *vt*: **to** ~ (**up**) (*CULIN*) legare.

trust [trʌst] *n* fiducia; (*LAW*) amministrazione *f* fiduciaria; (*COMM*) trust *m inv* ♦ *vt* (*have confidence in*) fidarsi di; (*rely on*) contare su; (*entrust*): **to** ~ **sth to sb** affidare qc a qn; (*hope*): **to** ~ (**that**) sperare (che); **you'll have to take it on** ~ deve credermi sulla parola; **in** ~ (*LAW*) in amministrazione fiduciaria.

trust company *n* trust *m inv*.

trusted ['trʌstɪd] *adj* fidato(a).

trustee [trʌs'tiː] *n* (*LAW*) amministratore(trice) fiduciario(a); (*of*

school etc) amministratore/trice.
trustful ['trʌstful] *adj* fiducioso(a).
trust fund *n* fondo fiduciario.
trusting ['trʌstɪŋ] *adj* = **trustful**.
trustworthy ['trʌstwəːðɪ] *adj* fidato(a), degno(a) di fiducia.
trusty ['trʌstɪ] *adj* fidato(a).
truth, ~s [truːθ, truːðz] *n* verità *f inv*.
truthful ['truːθful] *adj* (*person*) sincero(a); (*description*) veritiero(a), esatto(a).
truthfully ['truːθəlɪ] *adv* sinceramente.
truthfulness ['truːθəlnɪs] *n* veracità.
try [traɪ] *n* prova, tentativo; (*RUGBY*) meta ◆ *vt* (*LAW*) giudicare; (*test*: *sth new*) provare; (*strain*: *patience, person*) mettere alla prova ◆ *vi* provare; **to** ~ **to do** provare a fare; (*seek*) cercare di fare; **to give sth a** ~ provare qc; **to** ~ **one's (very) best** *or* **one's (very) hardest** mettercela tutta.
►**try on** *vt* (*clothes*) provare, mettere alla prova; **to** ~ **it on** (*fig*) cercare di farla.
►**try out** *vt* provare, mettere alla prova.
trying ['traɪɪŋ] *adj* (*day, experience*) logorante, pesante; (*child*) difficile, insopportabile.
tsar [zaː*] *n* zar *m inv*.
T-shirt ['tiːʃəːt] *n* maglietta.
T-square ['tiːskwɛə*] *n* riga a T.
TT *adj abbr* (*BRIT col*) = **teetotal** ◆ *abbr* (*US*) = *Trust Territory*.
tub [tʌb] *n* tinozza; mastello; (*bath*) bagno.
tuba ['tjuːbə] *n* tuba.
tubby ['tʌbɪ] *adj* grassoccio(a).
tube [tjuːb] *n* tubo; (*BRIT*: *underground*) metropolitana; (*for tyre*) camera d'aria; (*col*: *television*): **the** ~ la tele.
tubeless ['tjuːblɪs] *adj* (*tyre*) senza camera d'aria.
tuber ['tjuːbə*] *n* (*BOT*) tubero.
tuberculosis (TB) [tjubəːkjuˈləusɪs] *n* tubercolosi *f*.
tube station *n* (*BRIT*) stazione *f* del metrò.
tubing ['tjuːbɪŋ] *n* tubazione *f*; **a piece of** ~ un tubo.
tubular ['tjuːbjulə*] *adj* tubolare.
TUC *n abbr* (*BRIT*: = *Trades Union Congress*) confederazione *f* dei sindacati britannici.
tuck [tʌk] *n* (*SEWING*) piega ◆ *vt* (*put*) mettere.
►**tuck away** *vt* riporre.
►**tuck in** *vt* mettere dentro; (*child*) rimboccare ◆ *vi* (*eat*) mangiare di buon appetito; abbuffarsi.
►**tuck up** *vt* (*child*) rimboccare.
tuck shop *n* negozio di pasticceria (*in una scuola*).
Tue(s). *abbr* (= *Tuesday*) mar.
Tuesday ['tjuːzdɪ] *n* martedì *m inv*; (**the**

date) **today is** ~ **23rd March** oggi è martedì 23 marzo; **on** ~ martedì; **on** ~**s** di martedì; **every** ~ tutti i martedì; **every other** ~ ogni due martedì; **last/next** ~ martedì scorso/prossimo; ~ **next** martedì prossimo; **the following** ~ (*in past*) il martedì successivo; (*in future*) il martedì dopo; **a week/fortnight on** ~, ~ **week/ fortnight** martedì fra una settimana/ quindici giorni; **the** ~ **before last** martedì di due settimane fa; **the** ~ **after next** non questo martedì ma il prossimo; ~ **morning/lunchtime/afternoon/evening** martedì mattina/all'ora di pranzo/ pomeriggio/sera; ~ **night** martedì sera; (*overnight*) martedì notte; ~**'s newspaper** il giornale di martedì.
tuft [tʌft] *n* ciuffo.
tug [tʌg] *n* (*ship*) rimorchiatore *m* ◆ *vt* tirare con forza.
tug-of-love [tʌgəvˈlʌv] *n* contesa per la custodia dei figli; ~ **children** bambini *mpl* coinvolti nella contesa per la custodia.
tug-of-war [tʌgəvˈwɔː*] *n* tiro alla fune.
tuition [tjuːˈɪʃən] *n* (*BRIT*: *lessons*) lezioni *fpl*; (*US*: *fees*) tasse *fpl* scolastiche (*or* universitarie).
tulip ['tjuːlɪp] *n* tulipano.
tumble ['tʌmbl] *n* (*fall*) capitombolo ◆ *vi* capitombolare, ruzzolare; (*somersault*) fare capriole ◆ *vt* far cadere; **to** ~ **to sth** (*col*) realizzare qc.
tumbledown ['tʌmbldaun] *n* cadente, diroccato(a).
tumble dryer *n* (*BRIT*) asciugatrice *f*.
tumbler ['tʌmblə*] *n* bicchiere *m* (senza stelo).
tummy ['tʌmɪ] *n* (*col*) pancia.
tumour, (*US*) **tumor** ['tjuːmə*] *n* tumore *m*.
tumult ['tjuːmʌlt] *n* tumulto.
tumultuous [tjuːˈmʌltjuəs] *adj* tumultuoso(a).
tuna ['tjuːnə] *n* (*pl inv*) (*also*: ~ **fish**) tonno.
tune [tjuːn] *n* (*melody*) melodia, aria ◆ *vt* (*MUS*) accordare; (*RADIO, TV, AUT*) regolare, mettere a punto; **to be in/out of** ~ (*instrument*) essere accordato(a)/ scordato(a); (*singer*) essere intonato(a)/ stonato(a); **to the** ~ **of** (*fig*: *amount*) per la modesta somma di; **in** ~ **with** (*fig*) in accordo con.
►**tune in** *vi* (*RADIO, TV*): **to** ~ **in (to)** sintonizzarsi (su).
►**tune up** *vi* (*musician*) accordare lo strumento.
tuneful ['tjuːnful] *adj* melodioso(a).
tuner ['tjuːnə*] *n* (*radio set*) sintonizzatore *m*; **piano** ~ accordatore/trice di

pianoforte.
tuner amplifier n amplificatore m di sintonia.
tungsten ['tʌŋstn] n tungsteno.
tunic ['tjuːnɪk] n tunica.
tuning ['tjuːnɪŋ] n messa a punto.
tuning fork n diapason m inv.
Tunis ['tjuːnɪs] n Tunisi f.
Tunisia [tjuːˈnɪzɪə] n Tunisia.
Tunisian [tjuːˈnɪzɪən] adj, n tunisino(a).
tunnel ['tʌnl] n galleria ♦ vi scavare una galleria.
tunnel vision n (MED) riduzione f del campo visivo; (fig) visuale f ristretta.
tunny ['tʌnɪ] n tonno.
turban ['təːbən] n turbante m.
turbid ['təːbɪd] adj torbido(a).
turbine ['təːbaɪn] n turbina.
turbo ['təːbəʊ] n turbo m inv.
turbojet ['təːbəʊˈdʒɛt] n turboreattore m.
turboprop ['təːbəʊˈprɔp] n turboelica m inv.
turbot ['təːbət] n (pl inv) rombo gigante.
turbulence ['təːbjuləns] n turbolenza.
turbulent ['təːbjulənt] adj turbolento(a); (sea) agitato(a).
tureen [təˈriːn] n zuppiera.
turf [təːf] n terreno erboso; (clod) zolla ♦ vt coprire di zolle erbose; **the T~** l'ippodromo.
▶**turf out** vt (col) buttar fuori.
turf accountant n (BRIT) allibratore m.
turgid ['təːdʒɪd] adj (speech) ampolloso(a), pomposo(a).
Turin [tjuəˈrɪn] n Torino f.
Turk [təːk] n turco/a.
Turkey ['təːkɪ] n Turchia.
turkey ['təːkɪ] n tacchino.
Turkish ['təːkɪʃ] adj turco(a) ♦ n (LING) turco.
Turkish bath n bagno turco.
Turkish delight n gelatine ricoperte di zucchero a velo.
turmeric ['təːmərɪk] n curcuma.
turmoil ['təːmɔɪl] n confusione f, tumulto.
turn [təːn] n giro; (in road) curva; (tendency: of mind, events) tendenza; (performance) numero; (MED) crisi f inv, attacco ♦ vt girare, voltare; (milk) far andare a male; (shape: wood, metal) tornire; (change): **to ~ sth into** trasformare qc in ♦ vi girare; (person: look back) girarsi, voltarsi; (reverse direction) girarsi indietro; (change) cambiare; (become) diventare; **to ~ into** trasformarsi in; **a good ~** un buon servizio; **a bad ~** un brutto tiro; **it gave me quite a ~** mi ha fatto prendere un bello spavento; **"no left ~"** (AUT) "divieto di svolta a sinistra"; **it's your ~**

tocca a lei; **in ~** a sua volta; a turno; **to take ~s (at sth)** fare (qc) a turno; **at the ~ of the year/century** alla fine dell'anno/del secolo; **to take a ~ for the worse** (situation, events) volgere al peggio; (patient, health) peggiorare; **to ~ left/right** girare a sinistra/destra.
▶**turn about** vi girarsi indietro.
▶**turn away** vi girarsi (dall'altra parte) ♦ vt (reject: person) mandar via; (: business) rifiutare.
▶**turn back** vi ritornare, tornare indietro.
▶**turn down** vt (refuse) rifiutare; (reduce) abbassare; (fold) ripiegare.
▶**turn in** vi (col: go to bed) andare a letto ♦ vt (fold) voltare in dentro.
▶**turn off** vi (from road) girare, voltare ♦ vt (light, radio, engine etc) spegnere.
▶**turn on** vt (light, radio etc) accendere; (engine) avviare.
▶**turn out** vt (light, gas) chiudere, spegnere; (produce: goods) produrre; (: novel, good pupils) creare ♦ vi (appear, attend: troops, doctor etc) presentarsi; **to ~ out to be ...** rivelarsi ..., risultare ....
▶**turn over** vi (person) girarsi; (car oto) capovolgersi ♦ vt girare.
▶**turn round** vi girare; (person) girarsi.
▶**turn up** vi (person) arrivare, presentarsi; (lost object) saltar fuori ♦ vt (collar, sound, gas etc) alzare.
turnabout ['təːnəbaut], **turnaround** ['təːnəraund] n (fig) dietrofront m inv.
turncoat ['təːnkaut] n voltagabbana m/f inv.
turned-up ['təːndʌp] adj (nose) all'insù.
turning ['təːnɪŋ] n (in road) curva; (side road) strada laterale; **the first ~ on the right** la prima a destra.
turning circle n (BRIT) diametro di sterzata.
turning point n (fig) svolta decisiva.
turning radius n (US) = **turning circle**.
turnip ['təːnɪp] n rapa.
turnout ['təːnaut] n presenza, affluenza.
turnover ['təːnəʊvə*] n (COMM: amount of money) giro di affari; (: of goods) smercio; (CULIN): **apple** etc ~ sfogliatella alle mele etc; **there is a rapid ~ in staff** c'è un ricambio molto rapido di personale.
turnpike ['təːnpaik] n (US) autostrada a pedaggio.
turnstile ['təːnstail] n tornella.
turntable ['təːnteibl] n (on record player) piatto.
turn-up ['təːnʌp] n (BRIT: on trousers) risvolto.
turpentine ['təːpəntain] n (also: **turps**)

acqua ragia.

turquoise [təːˈkwɔɪz] *n* (*stone*) turchese *m* ♦ *adj* color turchese; di turchese.

turret [ˈtʌrɪt] *n* torretta.

turtle [ˈtəːtl] *n* testuggine *f*.

turtleneck (sweater) [ˈtəːtlnɛk-] *n* maglione *m* con il collo alto.

Tuscan [ˈtʌskən] *adj, n* toscano(a).

Tuscany [ˈtʌskənɪ] *n* Toscana.

tusk [tʌsk] *n* zanna.

tussle [ˈtʌsl] *n* baruffa, mischia.

tutor [ˈtjuːtə*] *n* (*in college*) docente *m/f* (*responsabile di un gruppo di studenti*); (*private teacher*) precettore *m*.

tutorial [tjuːˈtɔːrɪəl] *n* (*SCOL*) lezione *f* con discussione (*a un gruppo limitato*).

tuxedo [tʌkˈsiːdəu] *n* (*US*) smoking *m inv*.

TV [tiːˈviː] *n abbr* (= *television*) tivù *f inv*.

TV dinner *n* pasto surgelato pronto in due minuti.

twaddle [ˈtwɔdl] *n* scemenze *fpl*.

twang [twæŋ] *n* (*of instrument*) suono vibrante; (*of voice*) accento nasale ♦ *vi* vibrare ♦ *vt* (*guitar*) pizzicare le corde di.

tweak [twiːk] *vt* (*nose*) pizzicare; (*ear, hair*) tirare.

tweed [twiːd] *n* tweed *m inv*.

tweezers [ˈtwiːzəz] *npl* pinzette *fpl*.

twelfth [twɛlfθ] *num* dodicesimo(a).

Twelfth Night *n* la notte dell'Epifania.

twelve [twɛlv] *num* dodici; **at** ~ alle dodici, a mezzogiorno; (*midnight*) a mezzanotte.

twentieth [ˈtwɛntɪɪθ] *num* ventesimo(a).

twenty [ˈtwɛntɪ] *num* venti.

twerp [twəːp] *n* (*col*) idiota *m/f*.

twice [twaɪs] *adv* due volte; ~ **as much** due volte tanto; ~ **a week** due volte alla settimana; **she is** ~ **your age** ha il doppio dei suoi anni.

twiddle [ˈtwɪdl] *vt, vi*: **to** ~ (**with**) **sth** giocherellare con qc; **to** ~ **one's thumbs** (*fig*) girarsi i pollici.

twig [twɪɡ] *n* ramoscello ♦ *vt, vi* (*col*) capire.

twilight [ˈtwaɪlaɪt] *n* (*evening*) crepuscolo; (*morning*) alba; **in the** ~ nella penombra.

twill [twɪl] *n* spigato.

twin [twɪn] *adj, n* gemello(a).

twin(-bedded) room [ˈtwɪn(ˈbɛdɪd)-] *n* stanza con letti gemelli.

twin beds *npl* letti *mpl* gemelli.

twin-carburettor [ˈtwɪnkaːbjuˈrɛtə*] *adj* a doppio carburatore.

twine [twaɪn] *n* spago, cordicella ♦ *vi* (*plant*) attorcigliarsi; (*road*) serpeggiare.

twin-engined [ˈtwɪnˈɛndʒɪnd] *adj* a due motori; ~ **aircraft** bimotore *m*.

twinge [twɪndʒ] *n* (*of pain*) fitta; **a** ~ **of conscience/regret** un rimorso/rimpianto.

twinkle [ˈtwɪŋkl] *n* scintillio ♦ *vi* scintillare; (*eyes*) brillare.

twin town *n* città *f inv* gemella.

twirl [twəːl] *n* piroetta ♦ *vt* far roteare ♦ *vi* roteare.

twist [twɪst] *n* torsione *f*; (*in wire, flex*) storta; (*in story*) colpo di scena; (*bend*) svolta, piega ♦ *vt* attorcigliare; (*weave*) intrecciare; (*roll around*) arrotolare; (*fig*) deformare ♦ *vi* attorcigliarsi; arrotolarsi; (*road*) serpeggiare; **to** ~ **one's ankle/wrist** (*MED*) slogarsi la caviglia/il polso.

twisted [ˈtwɪstɪd] *adj* (*wire, rope*) attorcigliato(a); (*ankle, wrist*) slogato(a); (*fig: logic, mind*) contorto(a).

twit [twɪt] *n* (*col*) minchione/a.

twitch [twɪtʃ] *n* tiratina; (*nervous*) tic *m inv* ♦ *vi* contrarsi; avere un tic.

two [tuː] *num* due; ~ **by** ~, **in** ~**s** a due a due; **to put** ~ **and** ~ **together** (*fig*) trarre le conclusioni.

two-bit [tuːˈbɪt] *adj* (*esp US: col, pej*) da quattro soldi.

two-door [tuːˈdɔː*] *adj* (*AUT*) a due porte.

two-faced [ˈtuːˈfeɪst] *adj* (*pej: person*) falso(a).

twofold [ˈtuːfəuld] *adv*: **to increase** ~ aumentare del doppio ♦ *adj* (*increase*) doppio(a); (*reply*) in due punti.

two-piece [ˈtuːˈpiːs] *n* (*also*: ~ **suit**) due pezzi *m inv*; (*also*: ~ **swimsuit**) (costume *m* da bagno a) due pezzi *m inv*.

two-seater [ˈtuːˈsiːtə*] *n* (*plane*) biposto; (*car*) macchina a due posti.

twosome [ˈtuːsəm] *n* (*people*) coppia.

two-stroke [ˈtuːstrəuk] *n* (*engine*) due tempi *m inv* ♦ *adj* a due tempi.

two-tone [ˈtuːtəun] *adj* (*colour*) bicolore.

two-way [ˈtuːweɪ] *adj* (*traffic*) a due sensi; ~ **radio** radio *f inv* ricetrasmittente.

TX *abbr* (*US*) = *Texas*.

tycoon [taɪˈkuːn] *n*: (**business**) ~ magnate *m*.

type [taɪp] *n* (*category*) genere *m*; (*model*) modello; (*example*) tipo; (*TYP*) tipo, carattere *m* ♦ *vt* (*letter etc*) battere (a macchina), dattilografare; **what** ~ **do you want?** che tipo vuole?; **in bold/italic** ~ in grassetto/corsivo.

type-cast [ˈtaɪpkaːst] *adj* (*actor*) a ruolo fisso.

typeface [ˈtaɪpfeɪs] *n* carattere *m* tipografico.

typescript [ˈtaɪpskrɪpt] *n* dattiloscritto.

typeset [ˈtaɪpsɛt] *vt* comporre.

typesetter [ˈtaɪpsɛtə*] *n* compositore *m*.

typewriter ['taɪpraɪtə*] n macchina da scrivere.
typewritten ['taɪprɪtn] adj dattiloscritto(a), battuto(a) a macchina.
typhoid ['taɪfɔɪd] n tifoidea.
typhoon [taɪ'fuːn] n tifone m.
typhus ['taɪfəs] n tifo.
typical ['tɪpɪkl] adj tipico(a).
typify ['tɪpɪfaɪ] vt essere tipico(a) di.
typing ['taɪpɪŋ] n dattilografia.
typing error n errore m di battitura.
typing pool n ufficio m dattilografia inv.
typist ['taɪpɪst] n dattilografo/a.
typo ['taɪpəu] n abbr (col: = typographical error) refuso.
typography [taɪ'pɔgrəfɪ] n tipografia.
tyranny ['tɪrənɪ] n tirannia.
tyrant ['taɪərnt] n tiranno.
tyre, (US) **tire** ['taɪə*] n pneumatico, gomma.
tyre pressure n pressione f (delle gomme).
Tyrol [tɪ'rəul] n Tirolo.
Tyrolean [tɪrə'liːən], **Tyrolese** [tɪrə'liːz] adj, n tirolese (m/f).
Tyrrhenian Sea [tɪ'riːmiən-] n: **the** ~ il mar Tirreno.

U u

U, u [juː] n (letter) U, u m or f inv; **U for Uncle** ≈ U come Udine.
U n abbr (BRIT CINE: = universal) per tutti.
UAW n abbr (US: = United Automobile Workers) sindacato degli operai automobilistici.
UB40 n abbr (BRIT: = unemployment benefit form 40) modulo per la richiesta del sussidio di disoccupazione.
U-bend ['juːbɛnd] n (in pipe) sifone m.
ubiquitous [juː'bɪkwɪtəs] adj onnipresente.
UCAS ['juːkæs] n abbr (BRIT) = Universities and Colleges Admissions Service.
UDA n abbr (BRIT: = Ulster Defence Association) organizzazione paramilitare protestante.
UDC n abbr (BRIT) = Urban District Council.
udder ['ʌdə*] n mammella.
UDI abbr (BRIT POL) = unilateral declaration of independence.
UDR n abbr (BRIT: = Ulster Defence Regiment) reggimento dell'esercito britannico in Irlanda del Nord.

UEFA [juː'eɪfə] n abbr (= Union of European Football Associations) U.E.F.A. f.
UFO ['juːfəu] n abbr (= unidentified flying object) UFO m inv.
Uganda [juː'gændə] n Uganda.
Ugandan [juː'gændən] adj, n ugandese (m/f).
UGC n abbr (BRIT: = University Grants Committee) organo che autorizza sovvenzioni alle università.
ugh [əːh] excl puah!
ugliness ['ʌglɪnɪs] n bruttezza.
ugly ['ʌglɪ] adj brutto(a).
UHF abbr = ultra-high frequency.
UHT adj abbr (= ultra-heat treated): ~ **milk** n latte m UHT.
UK n abbr see **United Kingdom**.
Ukraine [juː'kreɪn] n Ucraina.
Ukrainian [juː'kreɪnɪən] adj ucraino(a) ♦ n (person) ucraino/a; (LING) ucraino.
ulcer ['ʌlsə*] n ulcera; **mouth** ~ afta.
Ulster ['ʌlstə*] n Ulster m.
ulterior [ʌl'tɪərɪə*] adj ulteriore; ~ **motive** secondo fine m.
ultimata [ʌltɪ'meɪtə] npl of **ultimatum**.
ultimate ['ʌltɪmɪt] adj ultimo(a), finale; (authority) massimo(a), supremo(a) ♦ n: **the** ~ **in luxury** il non plus ultra del lusso.
ultimately ['ʌltɪmɪtlɪ] adv alla fine; in definitiva, in fin dei conti.
ultimatum, pl ~**s** or **ultimata** [ʌltɪ'meɪtəm, -tə] n ultimatum m inv.
ultrasonic [ʌltrə'sɔnɪk] adj ultrasonico(a).
ultrasound [ʌltrə'saund] n (MED) ecografia.
ultraviolet ['ʌltrə'vaɪəlɪt] adj ultravioletto(a).
umbilical [ʌm'bɪlɪkl] adj: ~ **cord** cordone m ombelicale.
umbrage ['ʌmbrɪdʒ] n: **to take** ~ offendersi, impermalirsi.
umbrella [ʌm'brɛlə] n ombrello; **under the** ~ **of** (fig) sotto l'egida di.
umlaut ['umlaut] n Umlaut m inv.
umpire ['ʌmpaɪə*] n arbitro.
umpteen [ʌmp'tiːn] adj non so quanti(e); **for the** ~**th time** per l'ennesima volta.
UMW n abbr (= United Mineworkers of America) unione dei minatori d'America.
UN n abbr see **United Nations**.
unabashed [ʌnə'bæʃt] adj imperturbato(a).
unabated [ʌnə'beɪtɪd] adj non diminuito(a).
unable [ʌn'eɪbl] adj: **to be** ~ **to** non potere, essere nell'impossibilità di; (not to know how to) essere incapace di, non sapere.
unabridged [ʌnə'brɪdʒd] adj integrale.
unacceptable [ʌnək'sɛptəbl] adj (proposal, behaviour) inaccettabile; (price)

impossibile.

unaccompanied [ʌnə'kʌmpənɪd] *adj* (*child, lady*) non accompagnato(a); (*singing, song*) senza accompagnamento.

unaccountably [ʌnə'kauntəblɪ] *adv* inesplicabilmente.

unaccounted [ʌnə'kauntɪd] *adj*: **two passengers are ~ for** due passeggeri mancano all'appello.

unaccustomed [ʌnə'kʌstəmd] *adj* insolito(a); **to be ~ to sth** non essere abituato(a) a qc.

unacquainted [ʌnə'kweɪntɪd] *adj*: **to be ~ with** (*facts*) ignorare, non essere al corrente di.

unadulterated [ʌnə'dʌltəreɪtɪd] *adj* (*gen*) puro(a); (*wine*) non sofisticato(a).

unaffected [ʌnə'fektɪd] *adj* (*person, behaviour*) naturale, spontaneo(a); (*emotionally*): **to be ~ by** non essere toccato(a) da.

unafraid [ʌnə'freɪd] *adj*: **to be ~** non aver paura.

unaided [ʌn'eɪdɪd] *adv* senza aiuto.

unanimity [juːnə'nɪmɪtɪ] *n* unanimità.

unanimous [juː'nænɪməs] *adj* unanime.

unanimously [juː'nænɪməslɪ] *adv* all'unanimità.

unanswered [ʌn'ɑːnsəd] *adj* (*question, letter*) senza risposta; (*criticism*) non confutato(a).

unappetizing [ʌn'æpɪtaɪzɪŋ] *adj* poco appetitoso(a).

unappreciative [ʌnə'priːʃɪətɪv] *adj* che non apprezza.

unarmed [ʌn'ɑːmd] *adj* (*person*) disarmato(a); (*combat*) senz'armi.

unashamed [ʌnə'ʃeɪmd] *adj* sfacciato(a); senza vergogna.

unassisted [ʌnə'sɪstɪd] *adj, adv* senza nessun aiuto.

unassuming [ʌnə'sjuːmɪŋ] *adj* modesto(a), senza pretese.

unattached [ʌnə'tætʃt] *adj* senza legami, libero(a).

unattended [ʌnə'tendɪd] *adj* (*car, child, luggage*) incustodito(a).

unattractive [ʌnə'træktɪv] *adj* privo(a) di attrattiva, poco attraente.

unauthorized [ʌn'ɔːθəraɪzd] *adj* non autorizzato(a).

unavailable [ʌnə'veɪləbl] *adj* (*article, room, book*) non disponibile; (*person*) impegnato(a).

unavoidable [ʌnə'vɔɪdəbl] *adj* inevitabile.

unavoidably [ʌnə'vɔɪdəblɪ] *adv* (*detained*) per cause di forza maggiore.

unaware [ʌnə'wɛə*] *adj*: **to be ~ of** non

sapere, ignorare.

unawares [ʌnə'wɛəz] *adv* di sorpresa, alla sprovvista.

unbalanced [ʌn'bælənst] *adj* squilibrato(a).

unbearable [ʌn'bɛərəbl] *adj* insopportabile.

unbeatable [ʌn'biːtəbl] *adj* imbattibile.

unbeaten [ʌn'biːtn] *adj* (*team, army*) imbattuto(a); (*record*) insuperato(a).

unbecoming [ʌnbɪ'kʌmɪŋ] *adj* (*unseemly: language, behaviour*) sconveniente; (*unflattering: garment*) che non dona.

unbeknown(st) [ʌnbɪ'nəun(st)] *adv*: **~ to** all'insaputa di.

unbelief [ʌnbɪ'liːf] *n* incredulità.

unbelievable [ʌnbɪ'liːvəbl] *adj* incredibile.

unbelievingly [ʌnbɪ'liːvɪŋlɪ] *adv* con aria incredula.

unbend [ʌn'bend] *vb* (*irreg*) *vi* distendersi ♦ *vt* (*wire*) raddrizzare.

unbending [ʌn'bendɪŋ] *adj* (*fig*) inflessibile, rigido(a).

unbias(s)ed [ʌn'baɪəst] *adj* obiettivo(a), imparziale.

unblemished [ʌn'blemɪʃt] *adj* senza macchia.

unblock [ʌn'blɔk] *vt* (*pipe, road*) sbloccare.

unborn [ʌn'bɔːn] *adj* non ancora nato(a).

unbounded [ʌn'baundɪd] *adj* sconfinato(a), senza limite.

unbreakable [ʌn'breɪkəbl] *adj* infrangibile.

unbridled [ʌn'braɪdld] *adj* sbrigliato(a).

unbroken [ʌn'brəukən] *adj* (*intact*) intero(a); (*continuous*) continuo(a); (*record*) insuperato(a).

unbuckle [ʌn'bʌkl] *vt* slacciare.

unburden [ʌn'bəːdn] *vt*: **to ~ o.s.** sfogarsi.

unbutton [ʌn'bʌtn] *vt* sbottonare.

uncalled-for [ʌn'kɔːldfɔː*] *adj* (*remark*) fuori luogo *inv*; (*action*) ingiustificato(a).

uncanny [ʌn'kænɪ] *adj* misterioso(a), strano(a).

unceasing [ʌn'siːsɪŋ] *adj* incessante.

unceremonious [ʌnserɪ'məunɪəs] *adj* (*abrupt, rude*) senza tante cerimonie.

uncertain [ʌn'səːtn] *adj* incerto(a); **it's ~ whether ...** non è sicuro se ...; **in no ~ terms** chiaro e tondo, senza mezzi termini.

uncertainty [ʌn'səːtntɪ] *n* incertezza.

unchallenged [ʌn'tʃælɪndʒd] *adj* incontestato(a); **to go ~** non venire contestato, non trovare opposizione.

unchanged [ʌn'tʃeɪndʒd] *adj* immutato(a).

uncharitable [ʌn'tʃærɪtəbl] *adj* duro(a), severo(a).

uncharted [ʌn'tʃɑːtɪd] *adj* inesplorato(a).

unchecked [ʌn'tʃekt] *adj* incontrollato(a).

uncivilized [ʌn'sɪvɪlaɪzd] *adj* (*gen*)

selvaggio(a); (fig) incivile, barbaro(a).
uncle ['ʌŋkl] n zio.
unclear [ʌn'klɪə*] adj non chiaro(a); **I'm still ~ about what I'm supposed to do** non ho ancora ben capito cosa dovrei fare.
uncoil [ʌn'kɔɪl] vt srotolare ♦ vi srotolarsi, svolgersi.
uncomfortable [ʌn'kʌmfətəbl] adj scomodo(a); (uneasy) a disagio, agitato(a); (situation) sgradevole.
uncomfortably [ʌn'kʌmfətəblɪ] adv scomodamente; (uneasily: say) con voce inquieta; (: think) con inquietudine.
uncommitted [ʌnkə'mɪtɪd] adj (attitude, country) neutrale.
uncommon [ʌn'kɔmən] adj raro(a), insolito(a), non comune.
uncommunicative [ʌnkə'mjuːnɪkətɪv] adj poco comunicativo(a), chiuso(a).
uncomplicated [ʌn'kɔmplɪkeɪtɪd] adj semplice, poco complicato(a).
uncompromising [ʌn'kɔmprəmaɪzɪŋ] adj intransigente, inflessibile.
unconcerned [ʌnkən'səːnd] adj (unworried) tranquillo(a); **to be ~ about** non darsi pensiero di, non preoccuparsi di or per.
unconditional [ʌn'kən'dɪʃənl] adj incondizionato(a), senza condizioni.
uncongenial [ʌnkən'dʒiːnɪəl] adj (work, surroundings) poco piacevole.
unconnected [ʌnkə'nɛktɪd] adj (unrelated) senza connessione, senza rapporto; **to be ~ with** essere estraneo(a) a.
unconscious [ʌn'kɔnʃəs] adj privo(a) di sensi, svenuto(a); (unaware) inconsapevole, inconscio(a) ♦ n: **the ~** l'inconscio; **to knock sb ~** far perdere i sensi a qn con un pugno.
unconsciously [ʌn'kɔnʃəslɪ] adv inconsciamente.
unconstitutional [ʌnkɔnstɪ'tjuːʃənl] adj incostituzionale.
uncontested [ʌnkən'tɛstɪd] adj (champion) incontestato(a); (POL: seat) non disputato(a).
uncontrollable [ʌnkən'trəuləbl] adj incontrollabile, indisciplinato(a).
uncontrolled [ʌnkən'trəuld] adj (child, dog, emotion) sfrenato(a); (inflation, price rises) che sfugge al controllo.
unconventional [ʌnkən'vɛnʃənl] adj poco convenzionale.
unconvinced [ʌnkən'vɪnst] adj: **to be** or **remain ~** non essere convinto(a).
unconvincing [ʌnkən'vɪnsɪŋ] adj non convincente, poco persuasivo(a).
uncork [ʌn'kɔːk] vt stappare.
uncorroborated [ʌnkə'rɔbəreɪtɪd] adj non

convalidato(a).
uncouth [ʌn'kuːθ] adj maleducato(a), grossolano(a).
uncover [ʌn'kʌvə*] vt scoprire.
unctuous ['ʌŋktjuəs] adj untuoso(a).
undamaged [ʌn'dæmɪdʒd] adj (goods) in buono stato; (fig: reputation) intatto(a).
undaunted [ʌn'dɔːntɪd] adj intrepido(a).
undecided [ʌndɪ'saɪdɪd] adj indeciso(a).
undelivered [ʌndɪ'lɪvəd] adj non recapitato(a); **if ~ return to sender** in caso di mancato recapito rispedire al mittente.
undeniable [ʌndɪ'naɪəbl] adj innegabile, indiscutibile.
under ['ʌndə*] prep sotto; (less than) meno di; al disotto di; (according to) secondo, in conformità a ♦ adv (al) disotto; **from ~ sth** da sotto a or dal disotto di qc; **~ there** là sotto; **in ~ 2 hours** in meno di 2 ore; **~ anaesthetic** sotto anestesia; **~ discussion** in discussione; **~ repair** in riparazione; **~ the circumstances** date le circostanze.
under... ['ʌndə*] prefix sotto..., sub....
under-age [ʌndər'eɪdʒ] adj minorenne.
underarm ['ʌndərɑːm] n ascella ♦ adj ascellare ♦ adv da sotto in su.
undercapitalized [ʌndə'kæpɪtəlaɪzd] adj carente di capitali.
undercarriage ['ʌndəkærɪdʒ] n (BRIT AVIAT) carrello (d'atterraggio).
undercharge [ʌndə'tʃɑːdʒ] vt far pagare di meno a.
underclass ['ʌndəklɑːs] n sottoproletariato.
underclothes ['ʌndəkləuðz] npl biancheria (intima).
undercover ['ʌndəkʌvə*] adj segreto(a), clandestino(a).
undercurrent ['ʌndəkʌrənt] n corrente f sottomarina.
undercut [ʌndə'kʌt] vt irreg vendere a prezzo minore di.
underdeveloped ['ʌndədɪ'vɛləpt] adj sottosviluppato(a).
underdog ['ʌndədɔg] n oppresso/a.
underdone [ʌndə'dʌn] adj (CULIN) poco cotto(a).
under-employment [ʌndərɪm'plɔɪmənt] n sottoccupazione f.
underestimate [ʌndər'ɛstɪmeɪt] vt sottovalutare.
underexposed [ʌndərɪks'pəuzd] adj (PHOT) sottoesposto(a).
underfed [ʌndə'fɛd] adj denutrito(a).
underfoot [ʌndə'fut] adv sotto i piedi.
under-funded ['ʌndə'fʌndɪd] adj insufficientemente sovvenzionato(a).
undergo [ʌndə'gəu] vt irreg subire;

(*treatment*) sottoporsi a; **the car is ~ing repairs** la macchina è in riparazione.

undergraduate [ʌndə'grædjuɪt] *n* studente(essa) universitario(a) ♦ *cpd*: ~ **courses** corsi *mpl* di laurea.

underground ['ʌndəgraund] *n* metropolitana; (*POL*) movimento clandestino ♦ *adj* sotterraneo(a); (*fig*) clandestino(a); (*ART*, *CINE*) underground *inv* ♦ *adv* sottoterra; clandestinamente.

undergrowth ['ʌndəgrəuθ] *n* sottobosco.

underhand(ed) [ʌndə'hænd(ɪd)] *adj* (*fig*) furtivo(a), subdolo(a).

underinsured [ʌndərɪn'ʃuəd] *adj* non sufficientemente assicurato(a).

underlie [ʌndə'laɪ] *vt irreg* essere alla base di; **the underlying cause** il motivo di fondo.

underline [ʌndə'laɪn] *vt* sottolineare.

underling ['ʌndəlɪŋ] *n* (*pej*) subalterno/a, tirapiedi *m/f inv*.

undermanning [ʌndə'mænɪŋ] *n* carenza di personale.

undermentioned [ʌndə'menʃənd] *adj* (riportato(a)) qui sotto *or* qui di seguito.

undermine [ʌndə'maɪn] *vt* minare.

underneath [ʌndə'niːθ] *adv* sotto, disotto ♦ *prep* sotto, al di sotto di.

undernourished [ʌndə'nʌrɪʃt] *adj* denutrito(a).

underpaid [ʌndə'peɪd] *adj* mal pagato(a).

underpants ['ʌndəpænts] *npl* (*BRIT*) mutande *fpl*, slip *m inv*.

underpass ['ʌndəpɑːs] *n* (*BRIT*) sottopassaggio.

underpin [ʌndə'pɪn] *vt* puntellare; (*argument*, *case*) corroborare.

underplay [ʌndə'pleɪ] *vt* minimizzare.

underpopulated [ʌndə'pɔpjuleɪtɪd] *adj* scarsamente popolato(a), sottopopolato(a).

underprice [ʌndə'praɪs] *vt* vendere a un prezzo inferiore al dovuto.

underprivileged [ʌndə'prɪvɪlɪdʒd] *adj* svantaggiato(a).

underrate [ʌndə'reɪt] *vt* sottovalutare.

underscore [ʌndə'skɔː*] *vt* sottolineare.

underseal ['ʌndəsiːl] *vt* rendere stagno il fondo di.

undersecretary [ʌndə'sekrətrɪ] *n* sottosegretario.

undersell ['ʌndə'sel] *vt irreg* (*competitors*) vendere a prezzi più bassi di.

undershirt ['ʌndəʃəːt] *n* (*US*) maglietta.

undershorts ['ʌndəʃɔːts] *npl* (*US*) mutande *fpl*, slip *m inv*.

underside ['ʌndəsaɪd] *n* disotto.

undersigned ['ʌndəsaɪnd] *adj*, *n*

sottoscritto(a).

underskirt ['ʌndəskəːt] *n* sottoveste *f*.

understaffed [ʌndə'stɑːft] *adj* a corto di personale.

understand [ʌndə'stænd] *vb* (*irreg*: *like* **stand**) *vt*, *vi* capire, comprendere; **I ~ that ...** sento che ...; credo di capire che ...; **to make o.s. understood** farsi capire.

understandable [ʌndə'stændəbl] *adj* comprensibile.

understanding [ʌndə'stændɪŋ] *adj* comprensivo(a) ♦ *n* comprensione *f*; (*agreement*) accordo; **on the ~ that ...** a patto che *or* a condizione che ...; **to come to an ~ with sb** giungere ad un accordo con qn.

understate [ʌndə'steɪt] *vt* minimizzare, sminuire.

understatement [ʌndə'steɪtmənt] *n*: **that's an ~!** a dire poco!

understood [ʌndə'stud] *pt*, *pp of* **understand** ♦ *adj* inteso(a); (*implied*) sottinteso(a).

understudy ['ʌndəstʌdɪ] *n* sostituto/a, attore/trice supplente.

undertake [ʌndə'teɪk] *vt irreg* intraprendere; **to ~ to do sth** impegnarsi a fare qc.

undertaker ['ʌndəteɪkə*] *n* impresario di pompe funebri.

undertaking [ʌndə'teɪkɪŋ] *n* impresa; (*promise*) promessa.

undertone ['ʌndətəun] *n* (*low voice*) tono sommesso; (*of criticism etc*) vena, sottofondo; **in an ~** sottovoce.

undervalue [ʌndə'væljuː] *vt* svalutare, sottovalutare.

underwater [ʌndə'wɔːtə*] *adv* sott'acqua ♦ *adj* subacqueo(a).

underwear ['ʌndəwɛə*] *n* biancheria (intima).

underweight [ʌndə'weɪt] *adj* al di sotto del giusto peso; (*person*) sottopeso *inv*.

underworld ['ʌndəwəːld] *n* (*of crime*) malavita.

underwrite ['ʌndəraɪt] *vt* (*FINANCE*) sottoscrivere; (*INSURANCE*) assicurare.

underwriter ['ʌndəraɪtə*] *n* sottoscrittore/ trice; assicuratore/trice.

undeserving [ʌndɪ'zəːvɪŋ] *adj*: **to be ~ of** non meritare, non essere degno di.

undesirable [ʌndɪ'zaɪərəbl] *adj* indesiderabile, sgradito(a).

undeveloped [ʌndɪ'veləpt] *adj* (*land*, *resources*) non sfruttato(a).

undies ['ʌndɪz] *npl* (*col*) robina, biancheria intima da donna.

undiluted [ʌndaɪ'luːtɪd] *adj* non diluito(a).

undiplomatic [ʌndɪplə'mætɪk] *adj* poco

diplomatico(a).
undischarged ['ʌndɪs'tʃɑːdʒd] adj: ~
bankrupt fallito non riabilitato.
undisciplined [ʌn'dɪsɪplɪnd] adj
indisciplinato(a).
undisguised [ʌndɪs'gaɪzd] adj (dislike,
amusement etc) palese.
undisputed [ʌndɪs'pjuːtɪd] adj
indiscusso(a).
undistinguished [ʌndɪs'tɪŋgwɪʃt] adj
mediocre, qualunque.
undisturbed [ʌndɪs'təːbd] adj tranquillo(a);
to leave sth ~ lasciare qc così com'è.
undivided [ʌndɪ'vaɪdɪd] adj: **I want your** ~
attention esigo tutta la sua attenzione.
undo [ʌn'duː] vt irreg disfare.
undoing [ʌn'duːɪŋ] n rovina, perdita.
undone [ʌn'dʌn] pp of **undo; to come** ~
slacciarsi.
undoubted [ʌn'dautɪd] adj sicuro(a),
certo(a).
undoubtedly [ʌn'dautɪdlɪ] aav senza alcun
dubbio.
undress [ʌn'drɛs] vi spogliarsi.
undrinkable [ʌn'drɪŋkəbl] adj (unpalatable)
imbevibile; (poisonous) non potabile.
undue [ʌn'djuː] adj eccessivo(a).
undulating ['ʌndjuleɪtɪŋ] adj ondeggiante;
ondulato(a).
unduly [ʌn'djuːlɪ] adv eccessivamente.
undying [ʌn'daɪɪŋ] adj imperituro(a).
unearned [ʌn'əːnd] adj (praise, respect)
immeritato(a); ~ **income** rendita.
unearth [ʌn'əːθ] vt dissotterrare; (fig)
scoprire.
unearthly [ʌn'əːθlɪ] adj soprannaturale;
(hour) impossibile.
uneasy [ʌn'iːzɪ] adj a disagio; (worried)
preoccupato(a); **to feel** ~ **about doing sth**
non sentirsela di fare qc.
uneconomic(al) ['ʌniːkə'nɔmɪk(l)] adj non
economico(a), antieconomico(a).
uneducated [ʌn'ɛdjukeɪtɪd] adj senza
istruzione, incolto(a).
unemployed [ʌnɪm'plɔɪd] adj
disoccupato(a) ♦ npl: **the** ~ i disoccupati.
unemployment [ʌnɪm'plɔɪmənt] n
disoccupazione f.
unemployment benefit, (US)
unemployment compensation n
sussidio di disoccupazione.
unending [ʌn'ɛndɪŋ] adj senza fine.
unenviable [ʌn'ɛnvɪəbl] adj poco
invidiabile.
unequal [ʌn'iːkwəl] adj (length, objects)
disuguale; (amounts) diverso(a); (division
of labour) ineguale.
unequalled, (US) **unequaled** [ʌn'iːkwəld]

adj senza pari, insuperato(a).
unequivocal [ʌnɪ'kwɪvəkəl] adj (answer)
inequivocabile; (person) esplicito(a),
chiaro(a).
unerring [ʌn'əːrɪŋ] adj infallibile.
UNESCO [juː'nɛskəu] n abbr (= United
Nations Educational, Scientific and Cultural
Organization) U.N.E.S.C.O. f.
unethical [ʌn'ɛθɪkəl] adj (methods) poco
ortodosso(a), non moralmente
accettabile; (doctor's behaviour)
contrario(a) all'etica professionale.
uneven [ʌn'iːvn] adj ineguale; (ground)
disuguale, accidentato(a); (heartbeat)
irregolare.
uneventful [ʌnɪ'vɛntful] adj senza
sorprese, tranquillo(a).
unexceptional [ʌnɪk'sɛpʃənl] adj che non
ha niente d'eccezionale.
unexciting [ʌnɪk'saɪtɪŋ] adj (news) poco
emozionante; (film, evening) poco
interessante.
unexpected [ʌnɪk'spɛktɪd] adj inatteso(a),
imprevisto(a).
unexpectedly [ʌnɪk'spɛktɪdlɪ] adv
inaspettatamente.
unexplained [ʌnɪk'spleɪnd] adj
inspiegato(a).
unexploded [ʌnɪk'spləudɪd] adj
inesploso(a).
unfailing [ʌn'feɪlɪŋ] adj (supply, energy)
inesauribile; (remedy) infallibile.
unfair [ʌn'fɛə*] adj: ~ **(to)** ingiusto(a) (nei
confronti di); **it's** ~ **that** ... non è giusto
che ... + sub.
unfair dismissal n licenziamento
ingiustificato.
unfairly [ʌn'fɛəlɪ] adv ingiustamente.
unfaithful [ʌn'feɪθful] adj infedele.
unfamiliar [ʌnfə'mɪlɪə*] adj sconosciuto(a),
strano(a); **to be** ~ **with sth** non essere
pratico di qc, non avere familiarità con
qc.
unfashionable [ʌn'fæʃnəbl] adj (clothes)
fuori moda inv; (district) non alla moda.
unfasten [ʌn'fɑːsn] vt slacciare; sciogliere.
unfathomable [ʌn'fæðəməbl] adj
insondabile.
unfavourable, (US) **unfavorable**
[ʌn'feɪvərəbl] adj sfavorevole.
unfavo(u)rably [ʌn'feɪvərəblɪ] adv: **to look**
~ **upon** vedere di malocchio.
unfeeling [ʌn'fiːlɪŋ] adj insensibile,
duro(a).
unfinished [ʌn'fɪnɪʃt] adj incompiuto(a).
unfit [ʌn'fɪt] adj inadatto(a); (ill) non in
forma; (incompetent): ~ **(for)**
incompetente (in); (: work, MIL) inabile

(a); ~ **for habitation** inabitabile.
unflagging [ʌn'flægɪŋ] adj instancabile.
unflappable [ʌn'flæpəbl] adj calmo(a),
composto(a).
unflattering [ʌn'flætərɪŋ] adj (dress,
hairstyle) che non dona.
unflinching [ʌn'flɪntʃɪŋ] adj che non
indietreggia, risoluto(a).
unfold [ʌn'fəuld] vt spiegare; (fig) rivelare
♦ vi (view) distendersi; (story) svelarsi.
unforeseeable ['ʌnfɔː'siːəbl] adj
imprevedibile.
unforeseen [ʌnfɔː'siːn] adj imprevisto(a).
unforgettable [ʌnfə'gɛtəbl] adj
indimenticabile.
unforgivable [ʌnfə'gɪvəbl] adj
imperdonabile.
unformatted [ʌn'fɔːmætɪd] adj (disk, text)
non formattato(a).
unfortunate [ʌn'fɔːtʃnɪt] adj sfortunato(a);
(event, remark) infelice.
unfortunately [ʌn'fɔːtʃnɪtlɪ] adv
sfortunatamente, purtroppo.
unfounded [ʌn'faundɪd] adj infondato(a).
unfriendly [ʌn'frɛndlɪ] adj poco
amichevole, freddo(a).
unfulfilled [ʌnful'fɪld] adj (ambition) non
realizzato(a); (prophecy) che non si è
avverato(a); (desire) insoddisfatto(a);
(promise) non mantenuto(a); (terms of
contract) non rispettato(a); (person)
frustrato(a).
unfurl [ʌn'fəːl] vt spiegare.
unfurnished [ʌn'fəːnɪʃt] adj non
ammobiliato(a).
ungainly [ʌn'geɪnlɪ] adj goffo(a),
impacciato(a).
ungodly [ʌn'gɔdlɪ] adj empio(a); **at an** ~
hour a un'ora impossibile.
ungrateful [ʌn'greɪtful] adj ingrato(a).
unguarded [ʌn'gɑːdɪd] adj: **in an** ~ **moment**
in un momento di distrazione.
unhappily [ʌn'hæpɪlɪ] adv (unfortunately)
purtroppo, sfortunatamente.
unhappiness [ʌn'hæpɪnɪs] n infelicità.
unhappy [ʌn'hæpɪ] adj infelice; ~ **with**
(arrangements etc) insoddisfatto(a) di.
unharmed [ʌn'hɑːmd] adj incolume,
sano(a) e salvo(a).
UNHCR n abbr (= United Nations High
Commission for Refugees) Alto
Commissariato delle Nazioni Unite per
Rifugiati.
unhealthy [ʌn'hɛlθɪ] adj (gen) malsano(a);
(person) malaticcio(a).
unheard-of [ʌn'həːdɔv] adj inaudito(a),
senza precedenti.
unhelpful [ʌn'hɛlpful] adj poco disponibile.

unhesitating [ʌn'hɛzɪteɪtɪŋ] adj (loyalty)
che non vacilla; (reply, offer) pronto(a),
immediato(a).
unholy [ʌn'həulɪ] adj: **an** ~ **alliance**
un'alleanza nefasta; **he returned at an** ~
hour è tornato ad un'ora indecente.
unhook [ʌn'huk] vt sganciare; sfibbiare.
unhurt [ʌn'həːt] adj incolume, sano(a) e
salvo(a).
unhygienic [ʌnhaɪ'dʒiːnɪk] adj non
igienico(a).
UNICEF ['juːnɪsɛf] n abbr (= United Nations
International Children's Emergency Fund)
U.N.I.C.E.F. m.
unicorn ['juːnɪkɔːn] n unicorno.
unidentified [ʌnaɪ'dɛntɪfaɪd] adj non
identificato(a).
uniform ['juːnɪfɔːm] n uniforme f, divisa
♦ adj uniforme.
uniformity [juːnɪ'fɔːmɪtɪ] n uniformità.
unify ['juːnɪfaɪ] vt unificare.
unilateral [juːnɪ'lætərəl] adj unilaterale.
unimaginable [ʌnɪ'mædʒɪnəbl] adj
inimmaginabile, inconcepibile.
unimaginative [ʌnɪ'mædʒɪnətɪv] adj
privo(a) di fantasia, a corto di idee.
unimpaired [ʌnɪm'pɛəd] adj intatto(a), non
danneggiato(a).
unimportant [ʌnɪm'pɔːtənt] adj senza
importanza, di scarsa importanza.
unimpressed [ʌnɪm'prɛst] adj niente
affatto impressionato(a).
uninhabited [ʌnɪn'hæbɪtɪd] adj
disabitato(a).
uninhibited [ʌnɪn'hɪbɪtɪd] adj senza
inibizioni; senza ritegno.
uninjured [ʌn'ɪndʒəd] adj incolume.
uninspiring [ʌnɪn'spaɪərɪŋ] adj banale.
unintelligent [ʌnɪn'tɛlɪdʒənt] adj poco
intelligente.
unintentional [ʌnɪn'tɛnʃənəl] adj
involontario(a).
unintentionally [ʌnɪn'tɛnʃnəlɪ] adv senza
volerlo, involontariamente.
uninvited [ʌnɪn'vaɪtɪd] adj non invitato(a).
uninviting [ʌnɪn'vaɪtɪŋ] adj (place, food) non
invitante, poco invitante; (offer) poco
allettante.
union ['juːnjən] n unione f; (also: **trade** ~)
sindacato ♦ cpd sindacale; **the U**~ (US) gli
stati dell'Unione.
unionize ['juːnjənaɪz] vt sindacalizzare,
organizzare in sindacato.
Union Jack n bandiera nazionale
britannica.
**Union of Soviet Socialist Republics
(USSR)** n Unione f delle Repubbliche
Socialiste Sovietiche (U.R.S.S.).

union shop n stabilimento in cui tutti gli operai sono tenuti ad aderire ad un sindacato.

unique [ju:'ni:k] adj unico(a).

unisex ['ju:niseks] adj unisex inv.

Unison ['ju:nisn] n (trade union) sindacato generale dei funzionari.

unison ['ju:nisn] n: **in** ~ all'unisono.

unit ['ju:nit] n unità f inv; (section: of furniture etc) elemento; (team, squad) reparto, squadra; **production** ~ reparto m produzione inv; **sink** ~ blocco m lavello inv.

unit cost n costo unitario.

unite [ju:'nait] vt unire ♦ vi unirsi.

united [ju:'naitid] adj unito(a); (efforts) congiunto(a).

United Arab Emirates npl Emirati mpl Arabi Uniti.

United Kingdom (UK) n Regno Unito.

United Nations (Organization) (UN, UNO) n (Organizzazione f delle) Nazioni Unite (O.N.U.).

United States (of America) (US, USA) n Stati mpl Uniti (d'America) (USA).

unit price n prezzo unitario.

unit trust n (BRIT COMM) fondo d'investimento.

unity ['ju:niti] n unità.

Univ. abbr = **university**.

universal [ju:ni'və:sl] adj universale.

universe ['ju:nivə:s] n universo.

university [ju:ni'və:siti] n università f inv ♦ cpd (student, professor, education) universitario(a); (year) accademico(a).

university degree n laurea.

unjust [ʌn'dʒʌst] adj ingiusto(a).

unjustifiable ['ʌndʒʌsti'faiəbl] adj ingiustificabile.

unjustified [ʌn'dʒʌstifaid] adj ingiustificato(a); (TYP) non allineato(a).

unkempt [ʌn'kempt] adj trasandato(a); spettinato(a).

unkind [ʌn'kaind] adj poco gentile, villano(a).

unkindly [ʌn'kaindli] adv (speak) in modo sgarbato; (treat) male.

unknown [ʌn'nəun] adj sconosciuto(a); ~ **to me ...** a mia insaputa ...; ~ **quantity** (MATH, fig) incognita.

unladen [ʌn'leidn] adj (ship, weight) a vuoto.

unlawful [ʌn'lɔ:ful] adj illecito(a), illegale.

unleaded ['ʌn'ledid] adj senza piombo; ~ **petrol** benzina verde or senza piombo.

unleash [ʌn'li:ʃ] vt sguinzagliare; (fig) scatenare.

unleavened [ʌn'levnd] adj non lievitato(a), azzimo(a).

unless [ʌn'les] conj a meno che (non) + sub; ~ **otherwise stated** salvo indicazione contraria; ~ **I am mistaken** se non mi sbaglio.

unlicensed [ʌn'laisənst] adj (BRIT) senza licenza per la vendita di alcolici.

unlike [ʌn'laik] adj diverso(a) ♦ prep a differenza di, contrariamente a.

unlikelihood [ʌn'laiklihud] adj improbabilità.

unlikely [ʌn'laikli] adj improbabile; (explanation) inverosimile.

unlimited [ʌn'limitid] adj illimitato(a).

unlisted [ʌn'listid] adj (US TEL): **to be** ~ non essere sull'elenco; (STOCK EXCHANGE) non quotato(a).

unlit [ʌn'lit] adj (room) senza luce; (road) non illuminato(a).

unload [ʌn'ləud] vt scaricare.

unlock [ʌn'lɔk] vt aprire.

unlucky [ʌn'lʌki] adj sfortunato(a); (object, number) che porta sfortuna, di malaugurio; **to be** ~ (person) essere sfortunato, non avere fortuna.

unmanageable [ʌn'mænidʒəbl] adj (tool, vehicle) poco maneggevole; (situation) impossibile.

unmanned [ʌn'mænd] adj (spacecraft) senza equipaggio.

unmannerly [ʌn'mænəli] adj maleducato(a).

unmarked [ʌn'mɑ:kt] adj (unstained) pulito(a), senza macchie; ~ **police car** civetta della polizia.

unmarried [ʌn'mærid] adj non sposato(a); (man only) scapolo, celibe; (woman only) nubile.

unmarried mother n ragazza f madre inv.

unmask [ʌn'mɑ:sk] vt smascherare.

unmatched [ʌn'mætʃt] adj senza uguali.

unmentionable [ʌn'menʃnəbl] adj (vice, topic) innominabile; (word) irripetibile.

unmerciful [ʌn'mə:siful] adj spietato(a).

unmistakable [ʌnmis'teikəbl] adj indubbio(a); facilmente riconoscibile.

unmitigated [ʌn'mitigeitid] adj (disaster etc) totale, assoluto(a).

unnamed [ʌn'neimd] adj (nameless) senza nome; (anonymous) anonimo(a).

unnatural [ʌn'nætʃrəl] adj innaturale; contro natura.

unnecessary [ʌn'nesəsəri] adj inutile, superfluo(a).

unnerve [ʌn'nə:v] vt (subj: accident) sgomentare; (: hostile attitude) bloccare; (: long wait, interview) snervare.

unnoticed [ʌn'nəutist] adj: **to go** or **pass** ~ passare inosservato(a).

UNO ['juːnəu] *n abbr see* **United Nations Organization**.

unobservant [ʌnəb'zɔːvənt] *adj*: **to be ~** non avere spirito di osservazione.

unobtainable [ʌnəb'teɪnəbl] *adj (TEL)* non ottenibile.

unobtrusive [ʌnəb'truːsɪv] *adj* discreto(a).

unoccupied [ʌn'ɔkjupaɪd] *adj (house)* vuoto(a); *(seat, MIL: zone)* libero(a), non occupato(a).

unofficial [ʌnə'fɪʃl] *adj* non ufficiale; *(strike)* non dichiarato(a) dal sindacato.

unopened [ʌn'əupənd] *adj (letter)* non aperto(a); *(present)* ancora incartato(a).

unopposed [ʌnə'pəuzd] *adj* senza incontrare opposizione.

unorthodox [ʌn'ɔːθədɔks] *adj* non ortodosso(a).

unpack [ʌn'pæk] *vi* disfare la valigia *(or le valigie)*.

unpaid [ʌn'peɪd] *adj (holiday)* non pagato(a); *(work)* non retribuito(a); *(bill, debt)* da pagare.

unpalatable [ʌn'pælətəbl] *adj (food)* immangiabile; *(drink)* imbevibile; *(truth)* sgradevole.

unparalleled [ʌn'pærəlɛld] *adj* incomparabile, impareggiabile.

unpatriotic ['ʌnpætrɪ'ɔtɪk] *adj (person)* poco patriottico(a); *(speech, attitude)* antipatriottico(a).

unplanned [ʌn'plænd] *adj (visit)* imprevisto(a); *(baby)* non previsto(a).

unpleasant [ʌn'plɛznt] *adj* spiacevole; *(person, remark)* antipatico(a); *(day, experience)* brutto(a).

unplug [ʌn'plʌg] *vt* staccare.

unpolluted [ʌnpə'luːtɪd] *adj* non inquinato(a).

unpopular [ʌn'pɔpjulə*] *adj* impopolare; **to make o.s. ~ (with)** rendersi antipatico (a); *(subj: politician etc)* alienarsi le simpatie (di).

unprecedented [ʌn'prɛsɪdəntɪd] *adj* senza precedenti.

unpredictable [ʌnprɪ'dɪktəbl] *adj* imprevedibile.

unprejudiced [ʌn'prɛdʒudɪst] *adj (not biased)* obiettivo(a), imparziale; *(having no prejudices)* senza pregiudizi.

unprepared [ʌnprɪ'pɛəd] *adj (person)* impreparato(a); *(speech)* improvvisato(a).

unprepossessing [ʌnpriːpə'zɛsɪŋ] *adj* insulso(a).

unpretentious [ʌnprɪ'tɛnʃəs] *adj* senza pretese.

unprincipled [ʌn'prɪnsɪpld] *adj* senza scrupoli.

unproductive [ʌnprə'dʌktɪv] *adj* improduttivo(a); *(discussion)* sterile.

unprofessional ['ʌnprə'fɛʃənl] *adj*: **~ conduct** scorrettezza professionale.

unprofitable [ʌn'prɔfɪtəbl] *adj (financially)* non redditizio(a); *(job, deal)* poco lucrativo(a).

UNPROFOR ['ʌnprəfɔː*] *n abbr (= United Nations Protection Force)* reparto di protezione dell'ONU.

unprotected ['ʌnprə'tɛktɪd] *adj (sex)* non protetto(a).

unprovoked [ʌnprə'vəukt] *adj* non provocato(a).

unpunished [ʌn'pʌnɪʃt] *adj*: **to go ~** restare impunito(a).

unqualified [ʌn'kwɔlɪfaɪd] *adj (worker)* non qualificato(a); *(in professions)* non abilitato(a); *(success)* assoluto(a), senza riserve.

unquestionably [ʌn'kwɛstʃənəblɪ] *adv* indiscutibilmente.

unquestioning [ʌn'kwɛstʃənɪŋ] *adj (obedience, acceptance)* cieco(a).

unravel [ʌn'rævl] *vt* dipanare, districare.

unreal [ʌn'rɪəl] *adj* irreale.

unrealistic [ʌnrɪə'lɪstɪk] *adj (idea)* illusorio(a); *(estimate)* non realistico(a).

unreasonable [ʌn'riːznəbl] *adj* irragionevole; **to make ~ demands on sb** voler troppo da qn.

unrecognizable [ʌn'rɛkəgnaɪzəbl] *adj* irriconoscibile.

unrecognized [ʌn'rɛkəgnaɪzd] *adj (talent, genius)* misconosciuto(a); *(POL: regime)* non ufficialmente riconosciuto(a).

unrecorded [ʌnrɪ'kɔːdɪd] *adj* non documentato(a), non registrato(a).

unrefined [ʌnrɪ'faɪnd] *adj (sugar, petroleum)* greggio(a); *(person)* rozzo(a).

unrehearsed [ʌnrɪ'həːst] *adj (THEAT etc)* improvvisato(a); *(spontaneous)* imprevisto(a).

unrelated [ʌnrɪ'leɪtɪd] *adj*: **~ (to)** senza rapporto (con); *(by family)* non imparentato(a) (con).

unrelenting [ʌnrɪ'lɛntɪŋ] *adj* implacabile; accanito(a).

unreliable [ʌnrɪ'laɪəbl] *adj (person, machine)* che non dà affidamento; *(news, source of information)* inattendibile.

unrelieved [ʌnrɪ'liːvd] *adj (monotony)* uniforme.

unremitting [ʌnrɪ'mɪtɪŋ] *adj* incessante, infaticabile.

unrepeatable [ʌnrɪ'piːtəbl] *adj (offer)* unico(a).

unrepentant [ʌnrɪ'pɛntənt] *adj* impenitente.
unrepresentative [ʌnrɛprɪ'zɛntətɪv] *adj* atipico(a), poco rappresentativo(a).
unreserved [ʌnrɪ'zəːvd] *adj* (*seat*) non prenotato(a), non riservato(a); (*approval, admiration*) senza riserve.
unresponsive [ʌnrɪs'pɔnsɪv] *adj* che non reagisce.
unrest [ʌn'rɛst] *n* agitazione *f*.
unrestricted [ʌnrɪ'strɪktɪd] *adj* (*power, time*) illimitato(a); (*access*) libero(a).
unrewarded [ʌnrɪ'wɔːdɪd] *adj* non ricompensato(a).
unripe [ʌn'raɪp] *adj* acerbo(a).
unrivalled, (*US*) **unrivaled** [ʌn'raɪvəld] *adj* senza pari.
unroll [ʌn'rəul] *vt* srotolare.
unruffled [ʌn'rʌfld] *adj* (*person*) calmo(a) e tranquillo(a), imperturbato(a); (*hair*) a posto.
unruly [ʌn'ruːlɪ] *adj* indisciplinato(a).
unsafe [ʌn'seɪf] *adj* pericoloso(a), rischioso(a); ~ **to drink** non potabile; ~ **to eat** non commestibile.
unsaid [ʌn'sɛd] *adj*: **to leave sth** ~ passare qc sotto silenzio.
unsaleable, (*US*) **unsalable** [ʌn'seɪləbl] *adj* invendibile.
unsatisfactory ['ʌnsætɪs'fæktərɪ] *adj* che lascia a desiderare, insufficiente.
unsavoury, (*US*) **unsavory** [ʌn'seɪvərɪ] *adj* (*fig: person*) losco(a); (: *reputation, subject*) disgustoso(a), ripugnante.
unscathed [ʌn'skeɪðd] *adj* incolume.
unscientific ['ʌnsaɪən'tɪfɪk] *adj* poco scientifico(a).
unscrew [ʌn'skruː] *vt* svitare.
unscrupulous [ʌn'skruːpjuləs] *adj* senza scrupoli.
unseat [ʌn'siːt] *vt* (*rider*) disarcionare; (*fig: an official*) spodestare.
unsecured [ʌnsɪ'kjuəd] *adj*: ~ **creditor** creditore *m* chirografario.
unseeded [ʌn'siːdɪd] *adj* (*SPORT*) che non è una testa di serie.
unseemly [ʌn'siːmlɪ] *adj* sconveniente.
unseen [ʌn'siːn] *adj* (*person*) inosservato(a); (*danger*) nascosto(a).
unselfish [ʌn'sɛlfɪʃ] *adj* (*person*) altruista; (*act*) disinteressato(a).
unsettled [ʌn'sɛtld] *adj* (*person, future*) incerto(a); (*question*) non risolto(a); (*weather, market*) instabile; **to feel** ~ sentirsi disorientato(a).
unsettling [ʌn'sɛtlɪŋ] *adj* inquietante.
unshak(e)able [ʌn'ʃeɪkəbl] *adj* irremovibile.

unshaven [ʌn'ʃeɪvn] *adj* non rasato(a).
unsightly [ʌn'saɪtlɪ] *adj* brutto(a), sgradevole a vedersi.
unskilled [ʌn'skɪld] *adj*: ~ **worker** manovale *m*.
unsociable [ʌn'səuʃəbl] *adj* (*person*) poco socievole; (*behaviour*) antipatico(a).
unsocial [ʌn'səuʃəl] *adj*: ~ **hours** orario sconveniente.
unsold [ʌn'səuld] *adj* invenduto(a).
unsolicited [ʌnsə'lɪsɪtɪd] *adj* non richiesto(a).
unsophisticated [ʌnsə'fɪstɪkeɪtɪd] *adj* semplice, naturale.
unsound [ʌn'saund] *adj* (*health*) debole, cagionevole; (*in construction: floor, foundations*) debole, malsicuro(a); (*policy, advice*) poco sensato(a); (*judgment, investment*) poco sicuro(a).
unspeakable [ʌn'spiːkəbl] *adj* (*bad*) abominevole.
unspoken [ʌn'spəukən] *adj* (*words*) non detto(a); (*agreement, approval*) tacito(a).
unsteady [ʌn'stɛdɪ] *adj* instabile, malsicuro(a).
unstinting [ʌn'stɪntɪŋ] *adj* (*support*) incondizionato(a); (*generosity*) illimitato(a); (*praise*) senza riserve.
unstuck [ʌn'stʌk] *adj*: **to come** ~ scollarsi; (*fig*) fare fiasco.
unsubstantiated [ʌnsəb'stænʃɪeɪtɪd] *adj* (*rumour, accusation*) infondato(a).
unsuccessful [ʌnsək'sɛsful] *adj* (*writer, proposal*) che non ha successo; (*marriage, attempt*) mal riuscito(a), fallito(a); **to be** ~ (*in attempting sth*) non riuscire; non avere successo; (*application*) non essere considerato(a).
unsuccessfully [ʌnsək'sɛsfəlɪ] *adv* senza successo.
unsuitable [ʌn'suːtəbl] *adj* inadatto(a); (*moment*) inopportuno(a).
unsuited [ʌn'suːtɪd] *adj*: **to be** ~ **for** *or* **to** non essere fatto(a) per.
unsung ['ʌn'sʌŋ] *adj*: **an** ~ **hero** un eroe misconosciuto.
unsupported [ʌnsə'pɔːtɪd] *adj* (*claim*) senza fondamento; (*theory*) non dimostrato(a).
unsure [ʌn'ʃuə*] *adj*: ~ **(of** *or* **about)** incerto(a) (su); **to be** ~ **of o.s.** essere insicuro(a).
unsuspecting [ʌnsə'spɛktɪŋ] *adj* che non sospetta niente.
unsweetened [ʌn'swiːtnd] *adj* senza zucchero.
unswerving [ʌn'swəːvɪŋ] *adj* fermo(a).
unsympathetic ['ʌnsɪmpə'θɛtɪk] *adj* (*attitude*) poco incoraggiante; (*person*)

antipatico(a); ~ **(to)** non solidale (verso).
untangle [ʌn'tæŋgl] vt sbrogliare.
untapped [ʌn'tæpt] adj (resources) non sfruttato(a).
untaxed [ʌn'tækst] adj (goods) esente da imposte; (income) non imponibile.
unthinkable [ʌn'θɪŋkəbl] adj impensabile, inconcepibile.
unthinkingly ['ʌn'θɪŋkɪŋlɪ] adv senza pensare.
untidy [ʌn'taɪdɪ] adj (room) in disordine; (appearance, work) trascurato(a); (person, writing) disordinato(a).
untie [ʌn'taɪ] vt (knot, parcel) disfare; (prisoner, dog) slegare.
until [ʌn'tɪl] prep fino a; (after negative) prima di ♦ conj finché, fino a quando; (in past, after negative) prima che + sub, prima di + infinitive; ~ **now** finora; ~ **then** fino ad allora; **from morning** ~ **night** dalla mattina alla sera.
untimely [ʌn'taɪmlɪ] adj intempestivo(a), inopportuno(a); (death) prematuro(a).
untold [ʌn'təʊld] adj incalcolabile; indescrivibile.
untouched [ʌn'tʌtʃt] adj (not used etc) non toccato(a), intatto(a); (safe: person) incolume; (unaffected): ~ **by** insensibile a.
untoward [ʌntə'wɔːd] adj sfortunato(a), sconveniente.
untrained ['ʌn'treɪnd] adj (worker) privo(a) di formazione professionale; (troops) privo(a) di addestramento; **to the** ~ **eye** ad un occhio inesperto.
untrammelled [ʌn'træmld] adj illimitato(a).
untranslatable [ʌntrænz'leɪtəbl] adj intraducibile.
untrue [ʌn'truː] adj (statement) falso(a), non vero(a).
untrustworthy [ʌn'trʌstwəːðɪ] adj di cui non ci si può fidare.
unusable [ʌn'juːzəbl] adj inservibile, inutilizzabile.
unused [ʌn'juːzd] adj (new) nuovo(a); (not made use of) non usato(a), non utilizzato(a); **to be** ~ **to sth/to doing sth** non essere abituato(a) a qc/a fare qc.
unusual [ʌn'juːʒuəl] adj insolito(a), eccezionale, raro(a).
unusually [ʌn'juːʒuəlɪ] adv insolitamente.
unveil [ʌn'veɪl] vt scoprire, svelare.
unwanted [ʌn'wɒntɪd] adj non desiderato(a).
unwarranted [ʌn'wɒrəntɪd] adj ingiustificato(a).
unwary [ʌn'wɛərɪ] adj incauto(a).
unwavering [ʌn'weɪvərɪŋ] adj fermo(a),

incrollabile.
unwelcome [ʌn'wɛlkəm] adj (gen) non gradito(a); **to feel** ~ sentire che la propria presenza non è gradita.
unwell [ʌn'wɛl] adj indisposto(a); **to feel** ~ non sentirsi bene.
unwieldy [ʌn'wiːldɪ] adj poco maneggevole.
unwilling [ʌn'wɪlɪŋ] adj: **to be** ~ **to do** non voler fare.
unwillingly [ʌn'wɪlɪŋlɪ] adv malvolentieri.
unwind [ʌn'waɪnd] vb (irreg) vt svolgere, srotolare ♦ vi (relax) rilassarsi.
unwise [ʌn'waɪz] adj (decision, act) avventato(a).
unwitting [ʌn'wɪtɪŋ] adj involontario(a).
unworkable [ʌn'wəːkəbl] adj (plan etc) inattuabile.
unworthy [ʌn'wəːðɪ] adj indegno(a); **to be** ~ **of sth/to do sth** non essere degno di qc/di fare qc.
unwrap [ʌn'ræp] vt disfare; (present) aprire.
unwritten [ʌn'rɪtn] adj (agreement) tacito(a).
unzip [ʌn'zɪp] vt aprire (la chiusura lampo di).

═════════════════════ **KEYWORD**

up [ʌp] prep su; **he went** ~ **the stairs/the hill** è salito su per le scale/sulla collina; **the cat was** ~ **a tree** il gatto era su un albero; **they live further** ~ **the street** vivono un po' più su nella stessa strada
♦ adv **1** (upwards, higher) su, in alto; ~ **in the sky/the mountains** su nel cielo/in montagna; ~ **there** lassù; ~ **above** su in alto; ~ **with Leeds United!** viva il Leeds United!
2: **to be** ~ (out of bed) essere alzato(a); (prices, level) essere salito(a); (building) essere terminato(a); (tent) essere piantato(a); (curtains, shutters, wallpaper) essere su; "**this side** ~" "alto"; **to be** ~ **(by)** (in price, value) essere salito(a) or aumentato(a) (di); **when the year was** ~ (finished) finito l'anno; **time's** ~ il tempo è scaduto; **he's well** ~ **in** or **on politics** (BRIT) è molto informato di or sulla politica
3: ~ **to** (as far as) fino a; ~ **to now** finora
4: **to be** ~ **to** (depending on): **it's** ~ **to you** sta a lei, dipende da lei; (equal to): **he's not** ~ **to it** (job, task etc) non ne è all'altezza; (col: be doing): **what is he** ~ **to?** cosa sta combinando?; **what's** ~? (col: wrong) che c'è?; **what's** ~ **with him?** che ha?, che gli prende?
♦ n: ~**s and downs** alti e bassi mpl

♦ vi (col): she ~ped and left improvvisamente se ne andò.

up-and-coming ['ʌpənd'kʌmɪŋ] adj pieno(a) di promesse, promettente.

upbeat ['ʌpbiːt] n (MUS) tempo in levare; (in economy, prosperity) incremento ♦ adj (col) ottimistico(a).

upbraid [ʌp'breɪd] vt rimproverare.

upbringing['ʌpbrɪŋɪŋ] n educazione f.

upcoming ['ʌpkʌmɪŋ] adj imminente, prossimo(a).

update [ʌp'deɪt] vt aggiornare.

upend [ʌp'ɛnd] vt rovesciare.

upfront [ʌp'frʌnt] adj (col) franco(a), aperto(a) ♦ adv (pay) subito.

upgrade [ʌp'greɪd] vt promuovere; (job) rivalutare; (COMPUT) far passare a potenza superiore.

upheaval [ʌp'hiːvl] n sconvolgimento; tumulto.

uphill [ʌp'hɪl] adj in salita; (fig: task) difficile ♦ adv: to go ~ andare in salita, salire.

uphold [ʌp'həuld] vt irreg approvare; sostenere.

upholstery [ʌp'həulstərɪ] n tappezzeria.

upkeep ['ʌpkiːp] n manutenzione f.

up-market [ʌp'maːkɪt] adj (product) che si rivolge ad una fascia di mercato superiore.

upon [ə'pɔn] prep su.

upper ['ʌpə*] adj superiore ♦ n (of shoe) tomaia; the ~ class ≈ l'alta borghesia.

upper case n maiuscolo.

upper-class [ʌpə'klɑːs] adj dell'alta borghesia; (district) signorile; (accent) aristocratico(a); (attitude) snob inv.

uppercut ['ʌpəkʌt] n uppercut m inv, montante m.

upper hand n: to have the ~ avere il coltello dalla parte del manico.

Upper House n: the ~ (in Britain) la Camera Alta, la Camera dei Lords; (in US etc) il Senato.

uppermost ['ʌpəməust] adj il(la) più alto(a); predominante; it was ~ in my mind è stata la mia prima preoccupazione.

Upper Volta [-'vɔltə] n Alto Volta m.

upright ['ʌpraɪt] adj diritto(a); verticale; (fig) diritto(a), onesto(a) ♦ n montante m.

uprising ['ʌpraɪzɪŋ] n insurrezione f, rivolta.

uproar ['ʌprɔː*] n tumulto, clamore m.

uproarious [ʌp'rɔːrɪəs] adj clamoroso(a); (hilarious) esilarante; ~ laughter risata sonora.

uproot [ʌp'ruːt] vt sradicare.

upset n ['ʌpsɛt] turbamento ♦ vt [ʌp'sɛt] (irreg: like set) (glass etc) rovesciare; (plan, stomach) scombussolare; (person: offend) contrariare; (: grieve) addolorare; sconvolgere ♦ adj [ʌp'sɛt] contrariato(a); addolorato(a); (stomach) scombussolato(a), disturbato(a); to have a stomach ~ (BRIT) avere lo stomaco in disordine or scombussolato; to get ~ contrariarsi; addolorarsi.

upset price n (US, Scottish) prezzo di riserva.

upsetting [ʌp'sɛtɪŋ] adj (saddening) sconvolgente; (offending) offensivo(a); (annoying) fastidioso(a).

upshot ['ʌpʃɔt] n risultato; the ~ of it all was that ... la conclusione è stata che ....

upside down ['ʌpsaɪd-] adv sottosopra; to turn ~ capovolgere; (fig) mettere sottosopra.

upstage ['ʌp'steɪdʒ] vt: to ~ sb rubare la scena a qn.

upstairs [ʌp'stɛəz] adv, adj di sopra, al piano superiore ♦ n piano di sopra.

upstart ['ʌpstɑːt] n parvenu m inv.

upstream [ʌp'striːm] adv a monte.

upsurge ['ʌpsəːdʒ] n (of enthusiasm etc) ondata.

uptake ['ʌpteɪk] n: he is quick/slow on the ~ è pronto/lento di comprendonio.

uptight [ʌp'taɪt] adj (col) teso(a).

up-to-date ['ʌptə'deɪt] adj moderno(a); aggiornato(a).

upturn ['ʌptəːn] n (in luck) svolta favorevole; (in value of currency) rialzo.

upturned ['ʌptəːnd] adj (nose) all'insù.

upward ['ʌpwəd] adj ascendente; verso l'alto.

upwardly-mobile ['ʌpwədlɪ'məubaɪl] n: to be ~ salire nella scala sociale.

upward(s) ['ʌpwəd(z)] adv in su, verso l'alto.

URA n abbr (US: = Urban Renewal Administration) amministrazione per il rinnovamento urbano.

Ural Mountains ['juərəl-] npl: the ~ (also: the Urals) gli Urali, i Monti Urali.

uranium [juə'reɪnɪəm] n uranio.

Uranus [juə'reɪnəs] n (planet) Urano.

urban ['əːbən] adj urbano(a).

urbane [əː'beɪn] adj civile, urbano(a), educato(a).

urbanization [əːbənaɪ'zeɪʃən] n urbanizzazione f.

urchin ['əːtʃɪn] n monello; sea ~ riccio di mare.

Urdu ['uəduː] n urdu m inv.

urge [əːdʒ] n impulso, stimolo ♦ vt (caution

etc) raccomandare vivamente; **to ~ sb to do** esortare qn a fare, spingere qn a fare; raccomandare a qn di fare.
▶**urge on** *vt* spronare.
urgency ['ɔːdʒənsɪ] *n* urgenza; (*of tone*) insistenza.
urgent ['ɔːdʒənt] *adj* urgente; (*earnest, persistent: plea*) pressante; (: *tone*) insistente, incalzante.
urgently ['ɔːdʒəntlɪ] *adv* d'urgenza, urgentemente; con insistenza.
urinal ['juərɪnl] *n* (*BRIT: building*) vespasiano; (: *vessel*) orinale *m*, pappagallo.
urinate ['juərɪneɪt] *vi* orinare.
urine ['juərɪn] *n* orina.
urn [ɔːn] *n* urna; (*also:* **tea ~**) bollitore *m* per il tè.
Uruguay ['juərəgwaɪ] *n* Uruguay *m*.
Uruguayan [juərə'gwaɪən] *adj*, *n* uruguaiano(a).
US *n abbr see* **United States**.
us [ʌs] *pron* ci; (*stressed, after prep*) noi.
USA *n abbr* (*GEO*) *see* **United States (of America)**; (*MIL*) = *United States Army*.
usable ['juːzəbl] *adj* utilizzabile, usabile.
USAF *n abbr* = *United States Air Force*.
usage ['juːzɪdʒ] *n* uso.
USCG *n abbr* = *United States Coast Guard*.
USDA *n abbr* = *United States Department of Agriculture*.
USDAW ['ʌzdɔː] *n abbr* (*BRIT:* = *Union of Shop, Distributive and Allied Workers*) *sindacato dei dipendenti di negozi, reti di distribuzione e simili.*
USDI *n abbr* = *United States Department of the Interior*.
use *n* [juːs] uso; impiego, utilizzazione *f* ♦ *vt* [juːz] usare, utilizzare, servirsi di; **she ~d to do it** lo faceva (una volta), era solita farlo; **in ~** in uso; **out of ~** fuori uso; **to be of ~** essere utile, servire; **to make ~ of sth** far uso di qc, utilizzare qc; **ready for ~** pronto per l'uso; **it's no ~** non serve, è inutile; **to have the ~ of** poter usare; **what's this ~d for?** a che serve?; **to be ~d to** avere l'abitudine di; **to get ~d to** abituarsi a, fare l'abitudine a.
▶**use up** *vt* finire; (*supplies*) dare fondo a; (*left-overs*) utilizzare.
used [juːzd] *adj* (*car*) d'occasione.
useful ['juːsful] *adj* utile; **to come in ~** fare comodo, tornare utile.
usefulness ['juːsfəlnɪs] *n* utilità.
useless ['juːslɪs] *adj* inutile; (*unusable: object*) inservibile.
user ['juːzə*] *n* utente *m/f*; (*of petrol, gas etc*) consumatore/trice.

user-friendly ['juːzə'frɛndlɪ] *adj* orientato(a) all'utente.
USES *n abbr* = *United States Employment Service*.
usher ['ʌʃə*] *n* usciere *m*; (*in cinema*) maschera ♦ *vt:* **to ~ sb in** far entrare qn.
usherette [ʌʃə'rɛt] *n* (*in cinema*) maschera.
USIA *n abbr* = *United States Information Agency*.
USM *n abbr* = *United States Mint; United States Mail*.
USN *n abbr* = *United States Navy*.
USPHS *n abbr* = *United States Public Health Service*.
USPO *n abbr* = *United States Post Office*.
USS *abbr* = *United States Ship* (*or Steamer*).
USSR *n abbr see* **Union of Soviet Socialist Republics**.
usu. *abbr* = **usually**.
usual ['juːʒuəl] *adj* solito(a); **as ~** come al solito, come d'abitudine.
usually ['juːʒuəlɪ] *adv* di solito.
usurer ['juːʒərə*] *adj* usuraio/a.
usurp [juː'zəːp] *vt* usurpare.
UT *abbr* (*US*) = *Utah*.
utensil [juː'tɛnsl] *n* utensile *m*.
uterus ['juːtərəs] *n* utero.
utilitarian [juːtɪlɪ'tɛərɪən] *adj* utilitario(a).
utility [juː'tɪlɪtɪ] *n* utilità; (*also:* **public ~**) servizio pubblico.
utility room *n locale adibito alla stiratura dei panni etc*.
utilization [juːtɪlaɪ'zeɪʃən] *n* utilizzazione *f*.
utilize ['juːtɪlaɪz] *vt* utilizzare; sfruttare.
utmost ['ʌtməust] *adj* estremo(a) ♦ *n:* **to do one's ~** fare il possibile *or* di tutto; **of the ~ importance** della massima importanza; **it is of the ~ importance that ...** è estremamente importante che ... + *sub*.
utter ['ʌtə*] *adj* assoluto(a), totale ♦ *vt* pronunciare, proferire; emettere.
utterance ['ʌtərəns] *n* espressione *f*; parole *fpl*.
utterly ['ʌtəlɪ] *adv* completamente, del tutto.
U-turn ['juː'təːn] *n* inversione *f* a U; (*fig*) voltafaccia *m inv*.
Uzbekistan [ʌzbɛkɪ'stɑːn] *n* Uzbekistan.

V v

V, v [vi:] n (letter) V, v m or f inv; **V for Victor** ≈ V come Venezia.
v abbr (= verse; = vide: see) v.; (= volt) V.; (= versus) contro.
VA, Va. abbr (US) = Virginia.
vac [væk] n abbr (BRIT col) = **vacation**.
vacancy ['veɪkənsɪ] n (job) posto libero; (room) stanza libera; "no vacancies" "completo"; **have you any vacancies?** (office) avete bisogno di personale?; (hotel) avete una stanza?
vacant ['veɪkənt] adj (job, seat etc) libero(a); (expression) assente.
vacant lot n terreno non occupato; (for sale) terreno in vendita.
vacate [və'keɪt] vt lasciare libero(a).
vacation [və'keɪʃən] n (esp US) vacanze fpl; **to take a ~** prendere una vacanza, prendere le ferie; **on ~** in vacanza, in ferie.
vacation course n corso estivo.
vaccinate ['væksɪneɪt] vt vaccinare.
vaccination [væksɪ'neɪʃən] n vaccinazione f.
vaccine ['væksiːn] n vaccino.
vacuum ['vækjuːm] n vuoto.
vacuum bottle n (US) = **vacuum flask**.
vacuum cleaner n aspirapolvere m inv.
vacuum flask n (BRIT) thermos ® m inv.
vacuum-packed ['vækjuːm'pækt] adj confezionato(a) sottovuoto.
vagabond ['vægəbɔnd] n vagabondo/a.
vagary ['veɪgərɪ] n capriccio.
vagina [və'dʒaɪnə] n vagina.
vagrancy ['veɪgrənsɪ] n vagabondaggio.
vagrant ['veɪgrənt] n vagabondo/a.
vague [veɪg] adj vago(a); (blurred: photo, memory) sfocato(a); **I haven't the ~st idea** non ho la minima or più pallida idea.
vaguely ['veɪglɪ] adv vagamente.
vain [veɪn] adj (useless) inutile, vano(a); (conceited) vanitoso(a); **in ~** inutilmente, invano.
valance ['væləns] n volant m inv, balza.
valedictory [vælɪ'dɪktərɪ] adj di commiato.
valentine ['væləntaɪn] n (also: ~ card) cartolina or biglietto di San Valentino.
valet ['vælɪt] n cameriere m personale.

valet parking n parcheggio effettuato da un dipendente (dell'albergo etc).
valet service n (for clothes) servizio di lavanderia; (for car) servizio completo di lavaggio.
valiant ['vælɪənt] adj valoroso(a), coraggioso(a).
valid ['vælɪd] adj valido(a), valevole; (excuse) valido(a).
validate ['vælɪdeɪt] vt (contract, document) convalidare; (argument, claim) comprovare.
validity [və'lɪdɪtɪ] n validità.
valise [və'liːz] n borsa da viaggio.
valley ['vælɪ] n valle f.
valour, (US) **valor** ['vælə*] n valore m.
valuable ['væljuəbl] adj (jewel) di (grande) valore; (time) prezioso(a); **~s** npl oggetti mpl di valore.
valuation [vælju'eɪʃən] n valutazione f, stima.
value ['væljuː] n valore m ♦ vt (fix price) valutare, dare un prezzo a; (cherish) apprezzare, tenere a; **to be of great ~ to sb** avere molta importanza per qn; **to lose (in) ~** (currency) svalutarsi; (property) perdere (di) valore; **to gain (in) ~** (currency) guadagnare; (property) aumentare di valore; **you get good ~ (for money) in that shop** si compra bene in quel negozio.
value added tax (VAT) n (BRIT) imposta sul valore aggiunto (I.V.A.).
valued ['væljuːd] adj (appreciated) stimato(a), apprezzato(a).
valuer ['væljuə*] n stimatore/trice.
valve [vælv] n valvola.
vampire ['væmpaɪə*] n vampiro.
van [væn] n (AUT) furgone m; (BRIT RAIL) vagone m.
V and A n abbr (BRIT) = Victoria and Albert Museum.
vandal ['vændl] n vandalo/a.
vandalism ['vændəlɪzəm] n vandalismo.
vandalize ['vændəlaɪz] vt vandalizzare.
vanguard ['vænguːd] n avanguardia.
vanilla [və'nɪlə] n vaniglia ♦ cpd (ice cream) alla vaniglia.
vanish ['vænɪʃ] vi svanire, scomparire.
vanity ['vænɪtɪ] n vanità.
vanity case n valigetta per cosmetici.
vantage ['vaːntɪdʒ] n: **~ point** posizione f or punto di osservazione; (fig) posizione vantaggiosa.
vaporize ['veɪpəraɪz] vt vaporizzare ♦ vi vaporizzarsi.
vapour, (US) **vapor** ['veɪpə*] n vapore m.
variable ['vɛərɪəbl] adj variabile; (mood)

mutevole ♦ *n* fattore *m* variabile, variabile *f.*

variance ['vɛərɪəns] *n*: **to be at ~ (with)** essere in disaccordo (con); (*facts*) essere in contraddizione (con).

variant ['vɛərɪənt] *n* variante *f.*

variation [vɛərɪ'eɪʃən] *n* variazione *f*; (*in opinion*) cambiamento.

varicose ['værɪkəus] *adj*: ~ **veins** varici *fpl.*

varied ['vɛərɪd] *adj* vario(a), diverso(a).

variety [və'raɪətɪ] *n* varietà *f inv*; (*quantity*): **a wide ~ of ...** una vasta gamma di ...; **for a ~ of reasons** per una serie di motivi.

variety show *n* spettacolo di varietà.

various ['vɛərɪəs] *adj* vario(a), diverso(a); (*several*) parecchi(e), molti(e); **at ~ times** in momenti diversi; (*several*) diverse volte.

varnish ['vɑːnɪʃ] *n* vernice *f*; (*for nails*) smalto ♦ *vt* verniciare; **to ~ one's nails** mettersi lo smalto sulle unghie.

vary ['vɛərɪ] *vt, vi* variare, mutare; **to ~ (with *or* according to)** variare (con *or* a seconda di).

varying ['vɛərɪɪŋ] *adj* variabile.

vase [vɑːz] *n* vaso.

vasectomy [væ'sɛktəmɪ] *n* vasectomia.

Vaseline ® ['væsɪliːn] *n* vaselina.

vast [vɑːst] *adj* vasto(a); (*amount, success*) enorme.

vastly ['vɑːstlɪ] *adv* enormemente.

vastness ['vɑːstnɪs] *n* vastità.

VAT [væt] *n abbr* (*BRIT*) *see* **value added tax.**

vat [væt] *n* tino.

Vatican ['vætɪkən] *n*: **the ~** il Vaticano.

vatman ['vætmæn] *n* (*BRIT col*): **the ~ ≈** l'ispettore *m* dell'IVA; (*Inland Revenue*) (il) fisco.

vault [vɔːlt] *n* (*of roof*) volta; (*tomb*) tomba; (*in bank*) camera blindata; (*jump*) salto ♦ *vt* (*also*: ~ **over**) saltare (d'un balzo).

vaunted ['vɔːntɪd] *adj*: **much-~** tanto celebrato(a).

VC *n abbr* (*BRIT*: = *Victoria Cross*) medaglia al coraggio; = **vice-chairman.**

VCR *n abbr see* **video cassette recorder.**

VD *n abbr see* **venereal disease.**

VDU *n abbr see* **visual display unit.**

veal [viːl] *n* vitello.

veer [vɪə*] *vi* girare; virare.

veg. [vɛdʒ] *n abbr* (*BRIT col*: = *vegetable(s)*) ≈ contorno.

vegan ['viːgən] *n* (*BRIT*) vegetaliano/a.

vegeburger, veggieburger ['vɛdʒɪbəːgə*] *n* hamburger *m inv* vegetariano.

vegetable ['vɛdʒtəbl] *n* verdura, ortaggio ♦ *adj* vegetale.

vegetable garden *n* orto.

vegetarian [vɛdʒɪ'tɛərɪən] *adj, n* vegetariano(a).

vegetate ['vɛdʒɪteɪt] *vi* vegetare.

vegetation [vɛdʒɪ'teɪʃən] *n* vegetazione *f.*

vegetative ['vɛdʒɪtətɪv] *adj* (*also BOT*) vegetativo(a).

vehemence ['viːɪməns] *n* veemenza, violenza.

vehement ['viːɪmənt] *adj* veemente, violento(a); profondo(a).

vehicle ['viːɪkl] *n* veicolo; (*fig*) mezzo.

vehicular [vɪ'hɪkjulə*] *adj*: **"no ~ traffic"** "chiuso al traffico di veicoli".

veil [veɪl] *n* velo ♦ *vt* velare; **under a ~ of secrecy** (*fig*) protetto da una cortina di segretezza.

veiled [veɪld] *adj* (*also fig*) velato(a).

vein [veɪn] *n* vena; (*on leaf*) nervatura; (*fig: mood*) vena, umore *m.*

Velcro ® ['vɛlkrəu] *n* velcro ® *m inv.*

vellum ['vɛləm] *n* (*writing paper*) carta patinata.

velocity [vɪ'lɒsɪtɪ] *n* velocità *f inv.*

velour [və'luə*] *n* velours *m inv.*

velvet ['vɛlvɪt] *n* velluto.

vending machine ['vɛndɪŋ-] *n* distributore *m* automatico.

vendor ['vɛndə*] *n* venditore/trice; **street ~** venditore ambulante.

veneer [və'nɪə*] *n* impiallacciatura; (*fig*) vernice *f.*

venerable ['vɛnərəbl] *adj* venerabile.

venereal disease (VD) [vɪ'nɪərɪəl-] *n* malattia venerea.

Venetian [vɪ'niːʃən] *adj, n* veneziano(a).

Venetian blind *n* (tenda alla) veneziana.

Venezuela [vɛnɪ'zweɪlə] *n* Venezuela *m.*

Venezuelan [vɛnɪ'zweɪlən] *adj, n* venezuelano(a).

vengeance ['vɛndʒəns] *n* vendetta; **with a ~** (*fig*) davvero; furiosamente.

vengeful ['vɛndʒful] *adj* vendicativo(a).

Venice ['vɛnɪs] *n* Venezia.

venison ['vɛnɪsn] *n* carne *f* di cervo.

venom ['vɛnəm] *n* veleno.

venomous ['vɛnəməs] *adj* velenoso(a).

vent [vɛnt] *n* foro, apertura; (*in dress, jacket*) spacco ♦ *vt* (*fig: one's feelings*) sfogare, dare sfogo a.

ventilate ['vɛntɪleɪt] *vt* (*room*) dare aria a, arieggiare.

ventilation [vɛntɪ'leɪʃən] *n* ventilazione *f.*

ventilation shaft *n* condotto di aerazione.

ventilator ['vɛntɪleɪtə*] *n* ventilatore *m.*

ventriloquist [vɛn'trɪləkwɪst] *n* ventriloquo/a.

venture ['vɛntʃə*] *n* impresa (rischiosa) ♦ *vt* rischiare, azzardare ♦ *vi* arrischiarsi, azzardarsi; **a business** ~ un'iniziativa commerciale; **to** ~ **to do sth** azzardarsi a fare qc.

venture capital n capitale m di rischio.

venue ['vɛnjuː] n luogo di incontro; (SPORT) luogo (designato) per l'incontro.

Venus ['viːnəs] n (planet) Venere m.

veracity [vəˈræsɪtɪ] n veridicità.

veranda(h) [vəˈrændə] n veranda.

verb [vəːb] n verbo.

verbal ['vəːbəl] adj verbale; (translation) letterale.

verbally ['vəːbəlɪ] adv a voce.

verbatim [vəːˈbeɪtɪm] adv, adj parola per parola.

verbose [vəːˈbəʊs] adj verboso(a).

verdict ['vəːdɪkt] n verdetto; (opinion) giudizio, parere m; ~ **of guilty/not guilty** verdetto di colpevolezza/non colpevolezza.

verge [vəːdʒ] n bordo, orlo; **"soft ~s"** (BRIT) "banchina cedevole"; **on the** ~ **of doing** sul punto di fare.
▶**verge on** vt fus rasentare.

verger ['vəːdʒə*] n (REL) sagrestano.

verification [vɛrɪfɪˈkeɪʃən] n verifica.

verify ['vɛrɪfaɪ] vt verificare; (prove the truth of) confermare.

veritable ['vɛrɪtəbl] adj vero(a).

vermin ['vəːmɪn] npl animali mpl nocivi; (insects) insetti mpl parassiti.

vermouth ['vəːməθ] n vermut m inv.

vernacular [vəˈnækjʊlə*] n vernacolo.

versatile ['vəːsətaɪl] adj (person) versatile; (machine, tool etc) (che si presta a) molti usi.

verse [vəːs] n (of poem) verso; (stanza) stanza, strofa; (in bible) versetto; (no pl: poetry) versi mpl; **in** ~ in versi.

versed [vəːst] adj: **(well-)**~ **in** versato(a) in.

version ['vəːʃən] n versione f.

versus ['vəːsəs] prep contro.

vertebra, pl ~**e** ['vəːtɪbrə, -briː] n vertebra.

vertebrate ['vəːtɪbrɪt] n vertebrato.

vertebrae ['vəːtɪbriː] npl of **vertebra**.

vertical ['vəːtɪkl] adj, n verticale (m).

vertically ['vəːtɪklɪ] adv verticalmente.

vertigo ['vəːtɪgəʊ] n vertigine f; **to suffer from** ~ soffrire di vertigini.

verve [vəːv] n brio; entusiasmo.

very ['vɛrɪ] adv molto ♦ adj: **the** ~ **book which** proprio il libro che; ~ **much** moltissimo; ~ **well** molto bene; ~ **little** molto poco; **the** ~ **end** proprio alla fine; **the** ~ **last** proprio l'ultimo; **at the** ~ **least** almeno; **the** ~ **thought (of it) alarms me** il solo pensiero mi spaventa, sono spaventato solo al pensiero.

vespers ['vɛspəz] npl vespro.

vessel ['vɛsl] n (ANAT) vaso; (NAUT) nave f; (container) recipiente m.

vest [vɛst] n (BRIT) maglia; (: sleeveless) canottiera; (US: waistcoat) gilè m inv ♦ vt: **to** ~ **sb with sth, to** ~ **sth in sb** conferire qc a qn.

vested interest n: **to have a** ~ **in doing** avere tutto l'interesse a fare; ~**s** npl (COMM) diritti mpl acquisiti.

vestibule ['vɛstɪbjuːl] n vestibolo.

vestige ['vɛstɪdʒ] n vestigio.

vestment ['vɛstmənt] n (REL) paramento liturgico.

vestry ['vɛstrɪ] n sagrestia.

Vesuvius [vɪˈsuːvɪəs] n Vesuvio.

vet [vɛt] n abbr (= veterinary surgeon) veterinario ♦ vt esaminare minuziosamente; (text) rivedere; **to** ~ **sb for a job** raccogliere delle informazioni dettagliate su qn prima di offrirgli un posto.

veteran ['vɛtərn] n veterano; (also: war ~) reduce m ♦ adj: **she's a** ~ **campaigner for** ... lotta da sempre per ....

veteran car n auto f inv d'epoca (anteriore al 1919).

veterinarian [vɛtrɪˈnɛərɪən] n (US) = **veterinary surgeon**.

veterinary ['vɛtrɪnərɪ] adj veterinario(a).

veterinary surgeon n (BRIT) veterinario.

veto ['viːtəʊ] n (pl ~**es**) veto ♦ vt opporre il veto a; **to put a** ~ **on** opporre il veto a.

vetting ['vɛtɪŋ] n: **positive** ~ indagine per accertare l'idoneità di un aspirante ad una carica ufficiale.

vex [vɛks] vt irritare, contrariare.

vexed [vɛkst] adj (question) controverso(a), dibattuto(a).

VFD n abbr (US) = voluntary fire department.

VG abbr (BRIT: SCOL etc: = very good) ottimo.

VHF abbr (= very high frequency) VHF.

VI abbr (US) = Virgin Islands.

via ['vaɪə] prep (by way of) via; (by means of) tramite.

viability [vaɪəˈbɪlɪtɪ] n attuabilità.

viable ['vaɪəbl] adj attuabile; vitale.

viaduct ['vaɪədʌkt] n viadotto.

vial ['vaɪəl] n fiala.

vibes [vaɪbz] npl (col): **I got good/bad** ~ ho trovato simpatica/antipatica l'atmosfera.

vibrant ['vaɪbrənt] adj (sound) vibrante; (colour) vivace, vivo(a).

vibraphone ['vaɪbrəfəʊn] n vibrafono.

vibrate [vaɪˈbreɪt] vi: **to** ~ **(with)** vibrare (di); (resound) risonare (di).

vibration [vaɪˈbreɪʃən] n vibrazione f.

vibrator [vaɪˈbreɪtə*] n vibratore m.

vicar ['vɪkə*] *n* pastore *m*.

vicarage ['vɪkərɪdʒ] *n* presbiterio.

vicarious [vɪ'kɛərɪəs] *adj* sofferto(a) al posto di un altro; **to get ~ pleasure out of sth** trarre piacere indirettamente da qc.

vice [vaɪs] *n (evil)* vizio; *(TECH)* morsa.

vice- [vaɪs] *prefix* vice ....

vice-chairman [vaɪs'tʃɛəmən] *n* vicepresidente *m*.

vice-chancellor [vaɪs'tʃɑ:nsələ*] *n (BRIT SCOL)* rettore *m (per elezione)*.

vice-president [vaɪs'prɛzɪdənt] *n* vicepresidente *m*.

viceroy ['vaɪsrɔɪ] *n* viceré *m inv*.

vice squad *n* (squadra del) buon costume *f*.

vice versa ['vaɪsɪ'vɔ:sə] *adv* viceversa.

vicinity [vɪ'sɪnɪtɪ] *n* vicinanze *fpl*.

vicious ['vɪʃəs] *adj (remark)* maligno(a), cattivo(a); *(blow)* violento(a); **a ~ circle** un circolo vizioso.

viciousness ['vɪʃəsnɪs] *n* malignità, cattiveria; ferocia.

vicissitudes [vɪ'sɪsɪtjuːdz] *npl* vicissitudini *fpl*.

victim ['vɪktɪm] *n* vittima; **to be the ~ of** essere vittima di.

victimization [vɪktɪmaɪ'zeɪʃən] *n* persecuzione *f*; rappresaglie *fpl*.

victimize ['vɪktɪmaɪz] *vt* perseguitare; compiere delle rappresaglie contro.

victor ['vɪktə*] *n* vincitore *m*.

Victorian [vɪk'tɔːrɪən] *adj* vittoriano(a).

victorious [vɪk'tɔːrɪəs] *adj* vittorioso(a).

victory ['vɪktərɪ] *n* vittoria; **to win a ~ over sb** riportare una vittoria su qn.

video ['vɪdɪəʊ] *cpd* video... ♦ *n (~ film)* video *m inv*; *(also: ~ cassette)* videocassetta; *(also: ~ cassette recorder)* videoregistratore *m*.

video camera *n* videocamera.

video cassette *n* videocassetta.

video (cassette) recorder *n* videoregistratore *m*.

videodisc ['vɪdɪəʊdɪsk] *n* disco ottico.

video game *n* videogioco.

video nasty *n video estremamente violento o porno*.

videophone ['vɪdɪəʊfəʊn] *n* videotelefono.

video recording *n* registrazione *f* su video.

video tape *n* videotape *m inv*.

vie [vaɪ] *vi*: **to ~ with** competere con, rivaleggiare con.

Vienna [vɪ'ɛnə] *n* Vienna.

Vietnam, Viet Nam [vjɛt'næm] *n* Vietnam *m*.

Vietnamese [vjɛtnə'miːz] *adj* vietnamita

♦ *n* vietnamita *m/f*; *(LING)* vietnamita *m*.

view [vjuː] *n* vista, veduta; *(opinion)* opinione *f* ♦ *vt (situation)* considerare; *(house)* visitare; **on ~** *(in museum etc)* esposto(a); **to be in** *or* **within ~ (of sth)** essere in vista (di qc); **in full ~ of sb** sotto gli occhi di qn; **an overall ~ of the situation** una visione globale della situazione; **in my ~** a mio avviso, secondo me; **in ~ of the fact that** considerato che; **to take** *or* **hold the ~ that ...** essere dell'opinione che ...; **with a ~ to doing sth** con l'intenzione di fare qc.

viewdata ['vjuːdeɪtə] *n (BRIT) sistema di televideo*.

viewer ['vjuːə*] *n (viewfinder)* mirino; *(small projector)* visore *m*; *(TV)* telespettatore/trice.

viewfinder ['vjuːfaɪndə*] *n* mirino.

viewpoint ['vjuːpɔɪnt] *n* punto di vista.

vigil ['vɪdʒɪl] *n* veglia; **to keep ~** vegliare.

vigilance ['vɪdʒɪləns] *n* vigilanza.

vigilant ['vɪdʒɪlənt] *adj* vigile.

vigilante [vɪdʒɪ'læntɪ] *n cittadino che si fa giustizia da solo*.

vigorous ['vɪgərəs] *adj* vigoroso(a).

vigour, *(US)* **vigor** [vɪgə*] *n* vigore *m*.

vile [vaɪl] *adj (action)* vile; *(smell)* disgustoso(a), nauseante; *(temper)* pessimo(a).

vilify ['vɪlɪfaɪ] *vt* diffamare.

villa ['vɪlə] *n* villa.

village ['vɪlɪdʒ] *n* villaggio.

villager ['vɪlɪdʒə*] *n* abitante *m/f* di villaggio.

villain ['vɪlən] *n (scoundrel)* canaglia; *(criminal)* criminale *m*; *(in novel etc)* cattivo.

VIN *n abbr (US)* = *vehicle identification number*.

vinaigrette [vɪneɪ'grɛt] *n* vinaigrette *f inv*.

vindicate ['vɪndɪkeɪt] *vt* comprovare; giustificare.

vindication [vɪndɪ'keɪʃən] *n*: **in ~ of** per giustificare; a discolpa di.

vindictive [vɪn'dɪktɪv] *adj* vendicativo(a).

vine [vaɪn] *n* vite *f*; *(climbing plant)* rampicante *m*.

vinegar ['vɪnɪgə*] *n* aceto.

vine grower *n* viticoltore *m*.

vine-growing ['vaɪngrəʊɪŋ] *adj* viticolo(a)

♦ *n* viticoltura.

vineyard ['vɪnjɑːd] *n* vigna, vigneto.

vintage ['vɪntɪdʒ] *n (year)* annata, produzione *f*; **the 1970 ~** il vino del 1970.

vintage car *n* auto *f inv* d'epoca.

vintage wine *n* vino d'annata.

vinyl ['vaɪnl] *n* vinile *m*.

viola [vɪ'əulə] *n* viola.

violate ['vaɪəleɪt] *vt* violare.

violation [vaɪə'leɪʃən] *n* violazione *f*; **in ~ of sth** violando qc.

violence ['vaɪələns] *n* violenza; (POL etc) incidenti *mpl* violenti.

violent [vaɪələnt] *adj* violento(a); **a ~ dislike of sb/sth** una violenta avversione per qn/qc.

violently ['vaɪələntlɪ] *adv* violentemente; (ill, angry) terribilmente.

violet ['vaɪələt] *adj* (colour) viola inv, violetto(a) ♦ *n* (plant) violetta.

violin [vaɪə'lɪn] *n* violino.

violinist [vaɪə'lɪnɪst] *n* violinista *m/f*.

VIP *n abbr* (= very important person) V.I.P. *m/f* inv.

viper ['vaɪpə*] *n* vipera.

viral ['vaɪərəl] *adj* virale.

virgin ['və:dʒɪn] *n* vergine *f* ♦ *adj* vergine inv; **she is a ~** lei è vergine; **the Blessed V~** la Beatissima Vergine.

virginity [və:'dʒɪnɪtɪ] *n* verginità.

Virgo ['və:gəu] *n* (sign) Vergine *f*; **to be ~** essere della Vergine.

virile ['vɪraɪl] *adj* virile.

virility [vɪ'rɪlɪtɪ] *n* virilità.

virtual ['və:tjuəl] *adj* effettivo(a), vero(a); (COMPUT, PHYSICS) virtuale; (in effect): **it's a ~ impossibility** è praticamente impossibile; **the ~ leader** il capo all'atto pratico.

virtually ['və:tjuəlɪ] *adv* (almost) praticamente; **it is ~ impossible** è praticamente impossibile.

virtual reality *n* realtà *f* inv virtuale.

virtue ['və:tju:] *n* virtù *f* inv; (advantage) pregio, vantaggio; **by ~ of** grazie a.

virtuosity [və:tju'ɔsɪtɪ] *n* virtuosismo.

virtuoso [və:tju'əuzəu] *n* virtuoso.

virtuous ['və:tjuəs] *adj* virtuoso(a).

virulent ['vɪrulənt] *adj* virulento(a).

virus ['vaɪərəs] *n* virus *m* inv.

visa ['vi:zə] *n* visto.

vis-à-vis [vi:zə'vi:] *prep* rispetto a, nei riguardi di.

viscount ['vaɪkaunt] *n* visconte *m*.

viscous ['vɪskəs] *adj* viscoso(a).

vise [vaɪs] *n* (US TECH) = **vice**.

visibility [vɪzɪ'bɪlɪtɪ] *n* visibilità.

visible ['vɪzəbl] *adj* visibile; **~ exports/ imports** esportazioni *fpl*/importazioni *fpl* visibili.

visibly ['vɪzəblɪ] *adv* visibilmente.

vision ['vɪʒən] *n* (sight) vista; (foresight, in dream) visione *f*.

visionary ['vɪʒənərɪ] *n* visionario/a.

visit ['vɪzɪt] *n* visita; (stay) soggiorno ♦ *vt*

(person) andare a trovare; (place) visitare; **to pay a ~ to** (person) fare una visita a; (place) andare a visitare; **on a private/official ~** in visita privata/ ufficiale.

visiting ['vɪzɪtɪŋ] *adj* (speaker, professor, team) ospite.

visiting card *n* biglietto da visita.

visiting hours *npl* orario delle visite.

visitor ['vɪzɪtə*] *n* visitatore/trice; (guest) ospite *m/f*.

visitors' book *n* libro d'oro; (in hotel) registro.

visor ['vaɪzə*] *n* visiera.

VISTA ['vɪstə] *n abbr* (= Volunteers in Service to America) volontariato in zone depresse degli Stati Uniti.

vista ['vɪstə] *n* vista, prospettiva.

visual ['vɪzjuəl] *adj* visivo(a); visuale; ottico(a).

visual aid *n* sussidio visivo.

visual arts *npl* arti *fpl* figurative.

visual display unit (VDU) *n* unità *f* inv di visualizzazione.

visualize ['vɪzjuəlaɪz] *vt* immaginare, figurarsi; (foresee) prevedere.

visually ['vɪzjuəlɪ] *adv*: **~ appealing** piacevole a vedersi; **~ handicapped** con una menomazione della vista.

vital ['vaɪtl] *adj* vitale; **of ~ importance (to sb/sth)** di vitale importanza (per qn/qc).

vitality [vaɪ'tælɪtɪ] *n* vitalità.

vitally ['vaɪtəlɪ] *adv* estremamente.

vital statistics *npl* (of population) statistica demografica; (col: woman's) misure *fpl*.

vitamin ['vɪtəmɪn] *n* vitamina.

vitiate ['vɪʃɪeɪt] *vt* viziare.

vitreous ['vɪtrɪəs] *adj* (rock) vetroso(a); (china, enamel) vetrificato(a).

vitriolic [vɪtrɪ'ɔlɪk] *adj* (fig) caustico(a).

viva ['vaɪvə] *n* (also: ~ **voce**) (esame *m*) orale.

vivacious [vɪ'veɪʃəs] *adj* vivace.

vivacity [vɪ'væsɪtɪ] *n* vivacità.

vivid ['vɪvɪd] *adj* vivido(a).

vividly ['vɪvɪdlɪ] *adv* (describe) vividamente; (remember) con precisione.

vivisection [vɪvɪ'sɛkʃən] *n* vivisezione *f*.

vixen ['vɪksn] *n* volpe *f* femmina; (pej: woman) bisbetica.

viz *abbr* (= vide licet: namely) cioè.

VLF *abbr* (= very low frequency) bassissima frequenza.

V-neck ['vi:nɛk] *n* maglione *m* con lo scollo a V.

VOA *n abbr* (= Voice of America) voce *f* dell'America (alla radio).

vocabulary [vəu'kæbjulərɪ] *n* vocabolario.

vocal ['vəukl] *adj* (*MUS*) vocale;
(*communication*) verbale; (*noisy*)
rumoroso(a).

vocal cords *npl* corde *fpl* vocali.

vocalist ['vəukəlıst] *n* cantante *m/f* (*in un gruppo*).

vocation [vəu'keıʃən] *n* vocazione *f*.

vocational [vəu'keıʃənl] *adj* professionale;
~ **guidance** orientamento professionale;
~ **training** formazione *f* professionale.

vociferous [və'sıfərəs] *adj* rumoroso(a).

vodka ['vɔdkə] *n* vodka *f inv.*

vogue [vəug] *n* moda; (*popularity*)
popolarità, voga; **to be in ~, be the ~**
essere di moda.

voice [vɔıs] *n* voce *f* ♦ *vt* (*opinion*)
esprimere; **in a loud/soft ~** a voce alta/
bassa; **to give ~ to** esprimere.

voice mail *n* servizio di segreteria
telefonica.

voice-over ['vɔısəuvə*] *n* voce *f* fuori
campo *inv.*

void [vɔıd] *n* vuoto ♦ *adj:* ~ **of** privo(a) di.

voile [vɔıl] *n* voile *m.*

vol. *abbr* (= *volume*) vol.

volatile ['vɔlətaıl] *adj* volatile; (*fig*) volubile.

volcanic [vɔl'kænık] *adj* vulcanico(a).

volcano, ~es [vɔl'keınəu] *n* vulcano.

volition [və'lıʃən] *n:* **of one's own ~** di
propria volontà.

volley ['vɔlı] *n* (*of gunfire*) salva; (*of stones
etc*) raffica, gragnola; (*TENNIS etc*) volata.

volleyball ['vɔlıbɔ:l] *n* pallavolo *f.*

volt [vəult] *n* volt *m inv.*

voltage ['vəultıdʒ] *n* tensione *f*, voltaggio;
high/low ~ alta/bassa tensione.

voluble ['vɔljubl] *adj* loquace, ciarliero(a).

volume ['vɔlju:m] *n* volume *m*; (*of tank*)
capacità *f inv*; ~ **one/two** (*of book*) volume
primo/secondo; **his expression spoke ~s**
la sua espressione lasciava capire tutto.

volume control *n* (*RADIO, TV*) regolatore *m*
or manopola del volume.

voluminous [və'lu:mınəs] *adj*
voluminoso(a); (*notes etc*) abbondante.

voluntarily ['vɔləntrılı] *adv*
volontariamente; gratuitamente.

voluntary ['vɔləntərı] *adj* volontario(a);
(*unpaid*) gratuito(a), non retribuito(a).

voluntary liquidation *n* (*COMM*)
liquidazione *f* volontaria.

volunteer [vɔlən'tıə*] *n* volontario/a ♦ *vi*
(*MIL*) arruolarsi volontario; **to ~ to do**
offrire (volontariamente) di fare.

voluptuous [və'lʌptjuəs] *adj* voluttuoso(a).

vomit ['vɔmıt] *n* vomito ♦ *vt, vi* vomitare.

voracious [və'reıʃəs] *adj* (*appetite*)
smisurato(a); (*reader*) avido(a).

vote [vəut] *n* voto, suffragio; (*cast*) voto;
(*franchise*) diritto di voto ♦ *vi* votare ♦ *vt*
(*gen*) votare; (*sum of money etc*) votare a
favore di; **to ~ to do sth** votare a favore
di fare qc; **he was ~d secretary** è stato
eletto segretario; **to put sth to the ~, to
take a ~ on sth** mettere qc ai voti; ~ **for/
against** voto a favore/contrario; **to pass a
~ of confidence/no confidence** dare il
voto di fiducia/sfiducia; ~ **of thanks**
discorso di ringraziamento.

voter ['vəutə*] *n* elettore/trice.

voting ['vəutıŋ] *n* scrutinio.

voting paper *n* (*BRIT*) scheda elettorale.

voting right *n* diritto di voto.

vouch [vautʃ]: **to ~ for** *vt fus* farsi garante
di.

voucher ['vautʃə*] *n* (*for meal, petrol*)
buono; (*receipt*) ricevuta; **travel ~**
voucher *m inv*, tagliando.

vow [vau] *n* voto, promessa solenne ♦ *vi*
giurare; **to take** *or* **make a ~ to do sth**
fare voto di fare qc.

vowel ['vauəl] *n* vocale *f.*

voyage ['vɔııdʒ] *n* viaggio per mare,
traversata.

voyeur [vwɑ:'jə:*] *n* guardone/a.

VP *n abbr* (= *vice-president*) V.P.

vs *abbr* (= *versus*) contro.

VSO *n abbr* (*BRIT*: = *Voluntary Service
Overseas*) servizio volontario in paesi
sottosviluppati.

VT, Vt. *abbr* (*US*) = *Vermont*.

vulgar ['vʌlgə*] *adj* volgare.

vulgarity [vʌl'gærıtı] *n* volgarità.

vulnerability [vʌlnərə'bılıtı] *n*
vulnerabilità.

vulnerable ['vʌlnərəbl] *adj* vulnerabile.

vulture ['vʌltʃə*] *n* avvoltoio.

W w

W, w ['dʌblju:] *n* (*letter*) W, w *m or f inv*; **W
for William** ≈ W come Washington.

W *abbr* (= *west*) O; (*ELEC:* = *watt*) w.

WA *abbr* (*US*) = *Washington*.

wad [wɔd] *n* (*of cotton wool, paper*) tampone
m; (*of banknotes etc*) fascio.

wadding ['wɔdıŋ] *n* imbottitura.

waddle ['wɔdl] *vi* camminare come una
papera.

wade [weɪd] vi: **to ~ through** camminare a stento in ♦ vt guadare.

wafer ['weɪfə*] n (CULIN) cialda; (REL) ostia; (COMPUT) wafer m inv.

wafer-thin ['weɪfə'θɪn] adj molto sottile.

waffle ['wɔfl] n (CULIN) cialda; (col) ciance fpl; riempitivo ♦ vi cianciare; parlare a vuoto.

waffle iron n stampo per cialde.

waft [wɔft] vt portare ♦ vi diffondersi.

wag [wæg] vt agitare, muovere ♦ vi agitarsi; **the dog ~ged its tail** il cane scodinzolò.

wage [weɪdʒ] n (also: ~s) salario, paga ♦ vt: **to ~ war** fare la guerra; **a day's ~s** un giorno di paga.

wage claim n rivendicazione f salariale.

wage differential n differenza di salario.

wage earner n salariato/a.

wage freeze n blocco dei salari.

wage packet n (BRIT) busta f paga inv.

wager ['weɪdʒə*] n scommessa.

waggle ['wægl] vt dimenare, agitare ♦ vi dimenarsi, agitarsi.

wag(g)on ['wægən] n (horse-drawn) carro; (truck) furgone m; (BRIT RAIL) vagone m (merci).

wail [weɪl] n gemito; (of siren) urlo ♦ vi gemere; urlare.

waist [weɪst] n vita, cintola.

waistcoat ['weɪskəut] n panciotto, gilè m inv.

waistline ['weɪstlaɪn] n (giro di) vita.

wait [weɪt] n attesa ♦ vi aspettare, attendere; **to ~ for** aspettare; **to keep sb ~ing** far aspettare qn; **~ a moment!** (aspetti) un momento!; **"repairs while you ~"** "riparazioni lampo"; **I can't ~ to ...** (fig) non vedo l'ora di ...; **to lie in ~ for** stare in agguato a.

▶**wait behind** vi rimanere (ad aspettare).

▶**wait on** vt fus servire.

▶**wait up** vi restare alzato(a) (ad aspettare); **don't ~ up for me** non rimanere alzato per me.

waiter ['weɪtə*] n cameriere m.

waiting ['weɪtɪŋ] n: **"no ~"** (BRIT AUT) "divieto di sosta".

waiting list n lista d'attesa.

waiting room n sala d'aspetto or d'attesa.

waitress ['weɪtrɪs] n cameriera.

waive [weɪv] vt rinunciare a, abbandonare.

waiver ['weɪvə*] n rinuncia.

wake [weɪk] vb (pt **woke**, ~**d**, pp **woken**, ~**d** [wəuk, 'wəukn]) vt (also: ~ **up**) svegliare ♦ vi (also: ~ **up**) svegliarsi ♦ n (for dead person) veglia funebre; (NAUT) scia; **to ~ up to sth** (fig) rendersi conto di qc; **in the ~ of** sulla scia di; **to follow in sb's ~** (fig) seguire le tracce di qn.

waken ['weɪkn] vt, vi = **wake**.

Wales [weɪlz] n Galles m.

walk [wɔːk] n passeggiata; (short) giretto; (gait) passo, andatura; (path) sentiero; (in park etc) sentiero, vialetto ♦ vi camminare; (for pleasure, exercise) passeggiare ♦ vt (distance) fare or percorrere a piedi; (dog) accompagnare, portare a passeggiare; **10 minutes' ~ from** 10 minuti di cammino or a piedi da; **to go for a ~** andare a fare quattro passi; andare a fare una passeggiata; **from all ~s of life** di tutte le condizioni sociali; **~ in one's sleep** essere sonnambulo(a); **I'll ~ you home** ti accompagno a casa.

▶**walk out** vi (go out) uscire; (as protest) uscire (in segno di protesta); (strike) scendere in sciopero; **to ~ out on sb** piantare in asso qn.

walkabout ['wɔːkəbaut] n: **to go (on a) ~** avere incontri informali col pubblico (durante una visita ufficiale).

walker ['wɔːkə*] n (person) camminatore/ trice.

walkie-talkie ['wɔːkɪ'tɔːkɪ] n walkie-talkie m inv.

walking ['wɔːkɪŋ] n camminare m; **it's within ~ distance** ci si arriva a piedi.

walking holiday n vacanza fatta di lunghe camminate.

walking shoes npl scarpe fpl da passeggio.

walking stick n bastone m da passeggio.

Walkman ® ['wɔːkmən] n walkman ® m inv.

walk-on ['wɔːkɔn] adj (THEAT: part) da comparsa.

walkout ['wɔːkaut] n (of workers) sciopero senza preavviso or a sorpresa.

walkover ['wɔːkəuvə*] n (col) vittoria facile, gioco da ragazzi.

walkway ['wɔːkweɪ] n passaggio pedonale.

wall [wɔːl] n muro; (internal, of tunnel, cave) parete f; **to go to the ~** (fig: firm etc) fallire.

▶**wall in** vt (garden etc) circondare con un muro.

wall cupboard n pensile m.

walled [wɔːld] adj (city) fortificato(a).

wallet ['wɔlɪt] n portafoglio.

wallflower ['wɔːlflauə*] n violacciocca; **to be a ~** (fig) fare da tappezzeria.

wall hanging n tappezzeria.

wallop ['wɔləp] vt (col) pestare.

wallow ['wɔləu] vi sguazzare, rotolarsi; **to ~ in one's grief** crogiolarsi nel proprio dolore.

wallpaper ['wɔːlpeɪpə*] n carta da parati.

wall-to-wall ['wɔːltə'wɔːl] *adj*: ~ **carpeting** moquette *f*.

walnut ['wɔːlnʌt] *n* noce *f*; (*tree*) noce *m*.

walrus, *pl* ~ *or* ~**es** ['wɔːlrəs] *n* tricheco.

waltz [wɔːlts] *n* valzer *m inv* ♦ *vi* ballare il valzer.

wan [wɔn] *adj* pallido(a), smorto(a); triste.

wand [wɔnd] *n* (*also*: **magic** ~) bacchetta (magica).

wander ['wɔndə*] *vi* (*person*) girare senza meta, girovagare; (*thoughts*) vagare; (*river*) serpeggiare.

wanderer ['wɔndərə*] *n* vagabondo/a.

wandering ['wɔndrɪŋ] *adj* (*tribe*) nomade; (*minstrel, actor*) girovago(a); (*path, river*) tortuoso(a); (*glance, mind*) distratto(a).

wane [weɪn] *vi* (*moon*) calare; (*reputation*) declinare.

wangle ['wæŋgl] (*BRIT col*) *vt* procurare (con l'astuzia) ♦ *n* astuzia.

wanker ['wæŋkə*] *n* (*col!*) segaiolo (*!*); (*as insult*) coglione (*!*) *m*.

want [wɔnt] *vt* volere; (*need*) aver bisogno di; (*lack*) mancare di ♦ *n* (*poverty*) miseria, povertà; ~**s** *npl* (*needs*) bisogni *mpl*; **for** ~ **of** per mancanza di; **to** ~ **to do** volere fare; **to** ~ **sb to do** volere che qn faccia; **you're** ~**ed on the phone** la vogliono al telefono; **"cook** ~**ed"** "cercasi cuoco".

want ads *npl* (*US*) piccoli annunci *mpl*.

wanting ['wɔntɪŋ] *adj*: **to be** ~ **(in)** mancare (di); **to be found** ~ non risultare all'altezza.

wanton ['wɔntn] *adj* sfrenato(a); senza motivo.

war [wɔː*] *n* guerra; **to go to** ~ entrare in guerra.

warble ['wɔːbl] *n* (*of bird*) trillo ♦ *vi* trillare.

war cry *n* grido di guerra.

ward [wɔːd] *n* (*in hospital: room*) corsia; (: *section*) reparto; (*POL*) circoscrizione *f*; (*LAW: child*) pupillo/a.

▶**ward off** *vt* parare, schivare.

warden ['wɔːdn] *n* (*of institution*) direttore/trice; (*of park, game reserve*) guardiano/a; (*BRIT: also*: **traffic** ~) addetto/a al controllo del traffico e del parcheggio.

warder ['wɔːdə*] *n* (*BRIT*) guardia carceraria.

wardrobe ['wɔːdrəub] *n* (*cupboard*) guardaroba *m inv*, armadio; (*clothes*) guardaroba; (*THEAT*) costumi *mpl*.

warehouse ['wɛəhaus] *n* magazzino.

wares [wɛəz] *npl* merci *fpl*.

warfare ['wɔːfɛə*] *n* guerra.

war game *n* war game *m inv*.

warhead ['wɔːhɛd] *n* (*MIL*) testata, ogiva.

warily ['wɛərɪlɪ] *adv* cautamente, con prudenza.

warlike ['wɔːlaɪk] *adj* guerriero(a).

warm [wɔːm] *adj* caldo(a); (*welcome, applause*) caloroso(a); (*person, greeting*) cordiale; (*heart*) d'oro; (*supporter*) convinto(a); **it's** ~ fa caldo; **I'm** ~ ho caldo; **to keep sth** ~ tenere qc al caldo; **with my** ~**est thanks** con i miei più sentiti ringraziamenti.

▶**warm up** *vi* scaldarsi, riscaldarsi; (*athlete, discussion*) riscaldarsi ♦ *vt* scaldare, riscaldare; (*engine*) far scaldare.

warm-blooded ['wɔːm'blʌdɪd] *adj* a sangue caldo.

war memorial *n* monumento ai caduti.

warm-hearted [wɔːm'hɑːtɪd] *adj* affettuoso(a).

warmly ['wɔːmlɪ] *adv* caldamente; calorosamente; vivamente.

warmonger ['wɔːmʌŋgə*] *n* guerrafondaio.

warmongering ['wɔːmʌŋgrɪŋ] *n* bellicismo.

warmth [wɔːmθ] *n* calore *m*.

warm-up ['wɔːmʌp] *n* (*SPORT*) riscaldamento.

warn [wɔːn] *vt* avvertire, avvisare; **to** ~ **sb not to do sth** *or* **against doing sth** avvertire qn di non fare qc.

warning ['wɔːnɪŋ] *n* avvertimento; (*notice*) avviso; **without (any)** ~ senza preavviso; **gale** ~ avviso di burrasca.

warning light *n* spia luminosa.

warning triangle *n* (*AUT*) triangolo.

warp [wɔːp] *n* (*TEXTILES*) ordito ♦ *vi* deformarsi ♦ *vt* deformare; (*fig*) corrompere.

warpath ['wɔːpɑːθ] *n*: **to be on the** ~ (*fig*) essere sul sentiero di guerra.

warped [wɔːpt] *adj* (*wood*) curvo(a); (*fig: character, sense of humour etc*) contorto(a).

warrant ['wɔrnt] *n* (*LAW: to arrest*) mandato di cattura; (: *to search*) mandato di perquisizione ♦ *vt* (*justify, merit*) giustificare.

warrant officer (WO) *n* sottufficiale *m*.

warranty ['wɔrəntɪ] *n* garanzia; **under** ~ (*COMM*) in garanzia.

warren ['wɔrən] *n* (*of rabbits*) tana.

warring ['wɔrɪŋ] *adj* (*interests etc*) opposto(a), in lotta; (*nations*) in guerra.

warrior ['wɔrɪə*] *n* guerriero/a.

Warsaw ['wɔːsɔː] *n* Varsavia.

warship ['wɔːʃɪp] *n* nave *f* da guerra.

wart [wɔːt] *n* verruca.

wartime ['wɔːtaɪm] *n*: **in** ~ in tempo di guerra.

wary ['wɛərɪ] *adj* prudente; **to be** ~ **about**

or **of doing sth** andare cauto nel fare qc.
was [wɔz] *pt of* **be.**
wash [wɔʃ] *vt* lavare; (*sweep, carry: sea etc*)
portare, trascinare ♦ *vi* lavarsi ♦ *n:* **to give**
sth a ~ lavare qc, dare una lavata a qc;
to have a ~ lavarsi; **he was ~ed**
overboard fu trascinato in mare (dalle
onde).
▸**wash away** *vt* (*stain*) togliere lavando;
(*subj: river etc*) trascinare via.
▸**wash down** *vt* lavare.
▸**wash off** *vi* andare via con il lavaggio.
▸**wash up** *vi* lavare i piatti; (*US: have a*
wash) lavarsi.
Wash. *abbr* (*US*) = Washington.
washable ['wɔʃəbl] *adj* lavabile.
washbasin ['wɔʃbeɪsn] *n* lavabo.
washcloth ['wɔʃklɔθ] *n* (*US*) pezzuola (per
lavarsi).
washer ['wɔʃə*] *n* (*TECH*) rondella.
washing ['wɔʃɪŋ] *n* (*BRIT: linen etc*) bucato;
dirty ~ biancheria da lavare.
washing line *n* (*BRIT*) corda del bucato.
washing machine *n* lavatrice f.
washing powder *n* (*BRIT*) detersivo (in
polvere).
Washington ['wɔʃɪŋtən] *n* Washington f.
washing-up [wɔʃɪŋ'ʌp] *n* (*dishes*) piatti *mpl*
sporchi; **to do the** ~ lavare i piatti,
rigovernare.
washing-up liquid *n* (*BRIT*) detersivo
liquido (per stoviglie).
wash-out ['wɔʃaut] *n* (*col*) disastro.
washroom ['wɔʃrum] *n* gabinetto.
wasn't ['wɔznt] = **was not.**
Wasp, WASP [wɔsp] *n abbr* (*US:* = *White*
Anglo-Saxon Protestant) W.A.S.P. *m*
(*protestante bianco anglosassone*).
wasp [wɔsp] *n* vespa.
waspish ['wɔspɪʃ] *adj* litigioso(a).
wastage ['weɪstɪdʒ] *n* spreco; (*in*
manufacturing) scarti *mpl*.
waste [weɪst] *n* spreco; (*of time*) perdita;
(*rubbish*) rifiuti *mpl* ♦ *adj* (*material*) di
scarto; (*food*) avanzato(a); (*energy, heat*)
sprecato(a); (*land, ground: in city*)
abbandonato(a); (: *in country*) incolto(a)
♦ *vt* sprecare; (*time, opportunity*) perdere;
~**s** *npl* distesa desolata; **it's a** ~ **of money**
sono soldi sprecati; **to go to** ~ andare
sprecato; **to lay** ~ devastare.
▸**waste away** *vi* deperire.
wastebasket ['weɪstbɑːskɪt] *n* =
wastepaper basket.
waste disposal (unit) *n* (*BRIT*) eliminatore
m di rifiuti.
wasteful ['weɪstful] *adj* sprecone(a);
(*process*) dispendioso(a).

waste ground *n* (*BRIT*) terreno incolto *or*
abbandonato.
wasteland ['weɪstlænd] *n* terra desolata.
wastepaper basket ['weɪstpeɪpə-] *n*
cestino per la carta straccia.
waste pipe *n* tubo di scarico.
waste products *npl* (*INDUSTRY*) materiali
mpl di scarto.
waster ['weɪstə*] *n* (*col*) buono/a a nulla.
watch [wɔtʃ] *n* (*wrist~*) orologio; (*act of*
watching) sorveglianza; (*guard: MIL, NAUT*)
guardia; (*NAUT: spell of duty*) quarto ♦ *vt*
(*look at*) osservare; (: *match, programme*)
guardare; (*spy on, guard*) sorvegliare,
tenere d'occhio; (*be careful of*) fare
attenzione a ♦ *vi* osservare, guardare;
(*keep guard*) fare *or* montare la guardia;
to keep a close ~ **on sb/sth** tener bene
d'occhio qn/qc; ~ **how you drive/what**
you're doing attento a come guidi/quel
che fai.
▸**watch out** *vi* fare attenzione.
watchband ['wɔtʃbænd] *n* (*US*) cinturino
da orologio.
watchdog ['wɔtʃdɔg] *n* cane *m* da guardia;
(*fig*) sorvegliante *m/f*.
watchful ['wɔtʃful] *adj* attento(a), vigile.
watchmaker ['wɔtʃmeɪkə*] *n* orologiaio/a.
watchman ['wɔtʃmən] *n* guardiano; (*also:*
night ~) guardiano notturno.
watch stem *n* (*US*) corona di carica.
watch strap *n* cinturino da orologio.
watchword ['wɔtʃwəːd] *n* parola d'ordine.
water [wɔːtə*] *n* acqua ♦ *vt* (*plant*)
annaffiare ♦ *vi* (*eyes*) piangere; **in British**
~**s** nelle acque territoriali britanniche;
I'd like a drink of ~ vorrei un bicchier
d'acqua; **to pass** ~ orinare; **to make sb's**
mouth ~ far venire l'acquolina in bocca
a qn.
▸**water down** *vt* (*milk*) diluire; (*fig: story*)
edulcorare.
water closet *n* (*BRIT*) W.C. *m inv*, gabinetto.
watercolour, (*US*) **watercolor**
['wɔːtəkʌlə*] *n* (*picture*) acquerello; ~**s** *npl*
colori *mpl* per acquerelli.
water-cooled ['wɔːtəkuːld] *adj*
raffreddato(a) ad acqua.
watercress ['wɔːtəkres] *n* crescione *m*.
waterfall ['wɔːtəfɔːl] *n* cascata.
waterfront ['wɔːtəfrʌnt] *n* (*seafront*)
lungomare *m*; (*at docks*) banchina.
water heater *n* scaldabagno.
water hole *n* pozza d'acqua.
water ice *n* (*BRIT*) sorbetto.
watering can ['wɔːtərɪŋ-] *n* annaffiatoio.
water level *n* livello dell'acqua; (*of flood*)
livello delle acque.

water lily *n* ninfea.
waterline ['wɔ:təlaɪn] *n* (*NAUT*) linea di galleggiamento.
waterlogged ['wɔ:tələgd] *adj* saturo(a) d'acqua; imbevuto(a) d'acqua; (*football pitch etc*) allagato(a).
watermark ['wɔ:təmɑ:k] *n* (*on paper*) filigrana.
watermelon ['wɔ:təmɛlən] *n* anguria, cocomero.
water polo *n* pallanuoto *f*.
waterproof ['wɔ:təpru:f] *adj* impermeabile.
water-repellent ['wɔ:tərɪ'pɛlənt] *adj* idrorepellente.
watershed ['wɔ:təʃɛd] *n* (*GEO, fig*) spartiacque *m*.
water-skiing ['wɔ:təski:ɪŋ] *n* sci *m* acquatico.
water softener *n* addolcitore *m*; (*substance*) anti-calcare *m*.
water tank *n* serbatoio d'acqua.
watertight ['wɔ:tətaɪt] *adj* stagno(a).
water vapour *n* vapore *m* acqueo.
waterway ['wɔ:təweɪ] *n* corso d'acqua navigabile.
waterworks ['wɔ:təwə:ks] *npl* impianto idrico.
watery ['wɔ:tərɪ] *adj* (*colour*) slavato(a); (*coffee*) acquoso(a).
watt [wɔt] *n* watt *m inv*.
wattage ['wɔtɪdʒ] *n* wattaggio.
wattle ['wɔtl] *n* graticcio.
wave [weɪv] *n* onda; (*of hand*) gesto, segno; (*in hair*) ondulazione *f*; (*fig: of enthusiasm, strikes etc*) ondata ♦ *vi* fare un cenno con la mano; (*flag*) sventolare ♦ *vt* (*handkerchief*) sventolare ♦ (*stick*) brandire; (*hair*) ondulare; **short/medium/long** ~ (*RADIO*) onde corte/medie/lunghe; **the new** ~ (*CINE, MUS*) la new wave; **to** ~ **sb goodbye, to** ~ **goodbye to sb** fare un cenno d'addio a qn; **he** ~**d us over to his table** ci invitò con un cenno al suo tavolo.
▶**wave aside, wave away** *vt* (*person*): **to** ~ **sb aside** fare cenno a qn di spostarsi; (*fig: suggestion, objection*) respingere, rifiutare; (: *doubts*) scacciare.
waveband ['weɪvbænd] *n* gamma di lunghezze d'onda.
wavelength ['weɪvlɛŋθ] *n* lunghezza d'onda.
waver ['weɪvə*] *vi* vacillare; (*voice*) tremolare.
wavy ['weɪvɪ] *adj* ondulato(a); ondeggiante.
wax [wæks] *n* cera ♦ *vt* dare la cera a; (*car*) lucidare ♦ *vi* (*moon*) crescere.
waxworks ['wækswə:ks] *npl* cere *fpl*; museo delle cere.

way [weɪ] *n* via, strada; (*path, access*) passaggio; (*distance*) distanza; (*direction*) parte *f*, direzione *f*; (*manner*) modo, stile *m*; (*habit*) abitudine *f*; (*condition*) condizione *f*; **which** ~? — **this** ~ da che parte *or* in quale direzione? — da questa parte *or* per di qua; **to crawl one's** ~ **to** ... raggiungere ... strisciando; **he lied his** ~ **out of it** se l'è cavata mentendo; **to lose one's** ~ perdere la strada; **on the** ~ (*en route*) per strada; (*expected*) in arrivo; **you pass it on your** ~ **home** ci passi davanti andando a casa; **to be on one's** ~ essere in cammino *or* sulla strada; **to be in the** ~ bloccare il passaggio; (*fig*) essere tra i piedi *or* d'impiccio; **to keep out of sb's** ~ evitare qn; **it's a long** ~ **away** è molto lontano da qui; **the village is rather out of the** ~ il villaggio è abbastanza fuori mano; **to go out of one's** ~ **to do** (*fig*) mettercela tutta *or* fare di tutto per fare; **to be under** ~ (*work, project*) essere in corso; **to make** ~ (**for sb/sth**) far strada (a qn/qc); (*fig*) lasciare il posto *or* far largo (a qn/qc); **to get one's own** ~ fare come si vuole; **put it the right** ~ **up** (*BRIT*) mettilo in piedi dalla parte giusta; **to be the wrong** ~ **round** essere al contrario; **he's in a bad** ~ è ridotto male; **in a** ~ in un certo senso; **in some** ~**s** sotto certi aspetti; **in the** ~ **of** come; **by** ~ **of** (*through*) attraverso; (*as a sort of*) come; "~ **in**" "entrata", "ingresso"; "~ **out**" "uscita"; **the** ~ **back** la via del ritorno; **this** ~ **and that** di qua e di là; "**give** ~" (*BRIT AUT*) "dare la precedenza"; **no** ~! (*col*) assolutamente no!
waybill ['weɪbɪl] *n* (*COMM*) bolla di accompagnamento.
waylay [weɪ'leɪ] *vt irreg* tendere un agguato a; attendere al passaggio; (*fig*): **I got waylaid** ho avuto un contrattempo.
wayside ['weɪsaɪd] *n* bordo della strada; **to fall by the** ~ (*fig*) perdersi lungo la strada.
way station *n* (*US RAIL*) stazione *f* secondaria; (*fig*) tappa.
wayward ['weɪwəd] *adj* capriccioso(a); testardo(a).
WC *n abbr* (*BRIT*: = *water closet*) W.C. *m inv*, gabinetto.
WCC *n abbr* (= *World Council of Churches*) Consiglio Ecumenico delle Chiese.
we [wi:] *pl pron* noi; **here** ~ **are** eccoci.
weak [wi:k] *adj* debole; (*health*) precario(a); (*beam etc*) fragile; (*tea, coffee*) leggero(a); **to grow** ~(**er**) indebolirsi.

weaken ['wiːkən] *vi* indebolirsi ♦ *vt* indebolire.

weak-kneed ['wiːk'niːd] *adj* (*fig*) debole, codardo(a).

weakling ['wiːklɪŋ] *n* smidollato/a; debole *m/f*.

weakly ['wiːklɪ] *adj* deboluccio(a), gracile ♦ *adv* debolmente.

weakness ['wiːknɪs] *n* debolezza; (*fault*) punto debole, difetto.

wealth [wɛlθ] *n* (*money, resources*) ricchezza, richezze *fpl*; (*of details*) abbondanza, profusione *f*.

wealthy ['wɛlθɪ] *adj* ricco(a).

wean [wiːn] *vt* svezzare.

weapon ['wɛpən] *n* arma.

wear [wɛə*] *n* (*use*) uso; (*deterioration through use*) logorio, usura; (*clothing*): **sports/baby** ~ abbigliamento sportivo/ per neonati ♦ *vb* (*pt* **wore**, *pp* **worn** |wɔː*, wɔːn]) *vt* (*clothes*) portare; mettersi; (*look, smile, beard etc*) avere; (*damage: through use*) consumare ♦ *vi* (*last*) durare; (*rub etc through*) consumarsi; ~ **and tear** usura, consumo; **town/evening** ~ abiti *mpl* or tenuta da città/sera; **to** ~ **a hole in sth** bucare qc a furia di usarlo.

► **wear away** *vt* consumare; erodere ♦ *vi* consumarsi; essere eroso(a).

► **wear down** *vt* consumare; (*strength*) esaurire.

► **wear off** *vi* sparire lentamente.

► **wear on** *vi* passare.

► **wear out** *vt* consumare; (*person, strength*) esaurire.

wearable ['wɛərəbl] *adj* indossabile.

wearily ['wɪərɪlɪ] *adv* stancamente.

weariness ['wɪərɪnɪs] *n* stanchezza.

wearisome ['wɪərɪsəm] *adj* (*tiring*) estenuante; (*boring*) noioso(a).

weary ['wɪərɪ] *adj* stanco(a); (*tiring*) faticoso(a) ♦ *vt* stancare ♦ *vi*: **to** ~ **of** stancarsi di.

weasel ['wiːzl] *n* (*ZOOL*) donnola.

weather ['wɛðə*] *n* tempo ♦ *vt* (*wood*) stagionare; (*storm, crisis*) superare; **what's the** ~ **like?** che tempo fa?; **under the** ~ (*fig: ill*) poco bene.

weather-beaten ['wɛðəbiːtn] *adj* (*person*) segnato(a) dalle intemperie; (*building*) logorato(a) dalle intemperie.

weather forecast *n* previsioni *fpl* del tempo, bollettino meteorologico.

weatherman ['wɛðəmæn] *n* meteorologo.

weatherproof ['wɛðəpruːf] *adj* (*garment*) impermeabile.

weather report *n* bollettino meteorologico.

weather vane *n* = **weather cock**.

weave, *pt* **wove,** *pp* **woven** [wiːv, wəuv, 'wəuvn] *vt* (*cloth*) tessere; (*basket*) intrecciare ♦ *vi* (*fig: pt, pp* ~**d**: *move in and out*) zigzagare.

weaver ['wiːvə*] *n* tessitore/trice.

weaving ['wiːvɪŋ] *n* tessitura.

web [wɛb] *n* (*of spider*) ragnatela; (*on foot*) palma; (*fabric, also fig*) tessuto; **the (World Wide) W**~ la Rete.

webbed [wɛbd] *adj* (*foot*) palmato(a).

webbing ['wɛbɪŋ] *n* (*on chair*) cinghie *fpl*.

website ['wɛbsaɪt] *n* (*COMPUT*) site.

wed [wɛd] *vt* (*pt, pp* **wedded**) sposare ♦ *n*: **the newly-**~**s** gli sposi novelli.

Wed. *abbr* (= *Wednesday*) mer.

we'd [wiːd] = **we had; we would**.

wedded ['wɛdɪd] *pt, pp of* **wed**.

wedding ['wɛdɪŋ] *n* matrimonio; **silver/ golden** ~ nozze *fpl* d'argento/d'oro.

wedding anniversary *n* anniversario di matrimonio.

wedding day *n* giorno delle nozze *or* del matrimonio.

wedding dress *n* abito nuziale.

wedding present *n* regalo di nozze.

wedding ring *n* fede *f*.

wedge [wɛdʒ] *n* (*of wood etc*) cuneo; (*under door etc*) zeppa; (*of cake*) spicchio, fetta ♦ *vt* mettere una zeppa sotto (*or* in); **to** ~ **a door open** tenere aperta una porta con un fermo.

wedge-heeled shoes ['wɛdʒhiːld-] *npl* scarpe *fpl* con tacco a zeppa.

wedlock ['wɛdlɔk] *n* vincolo matrimoniale.

Wednesday ['wɛdnzdɪ] *n* mercoledì *m inv*; *for phrases see also* **Tuesday.**

wee [wiː] *adj* (*Scottish*) piccolo(a).

weed [wiːd] *n* erbaccia ♦ *vt* diserbare.

► **weed out** *vt* fare lo spoglio di.

weed-killer ['wiːdkɪlə*] *n* diserbante *m*.

weedy ['wiːdɪ] *adj* (*man*) allampanato.

week [wiːk] *n* settimana; **once/twice a** ~ una volta/due volte alla settimana; **in 2** ~**s' time** fra 2 settimane, fra 15 giorni; **Tuesday** ~**, a** ~ **on Tuesday** martedì a otto.

weekday ['wiːkdeɪ] *n* giorno feriale; (*COMM*) giornata lavorativa; **on** ~**s** durante la settimana.

weekend [wiːk'ɛnd] *n* fine settimana *m or f inv*, weekend *m inv*.

weekly ['wiːklɪ] *adv* ogni settimana, settimanalmente ♦ *adj, n* settimanale (*m*).

weep, *pt, pp* **wept** [wiːp, wɛpt] *vi* (*person*) piangere; (*MED: wound etc*) essudare.

weeping willow ['wiːpɪŋ-] *n* salice *m* piangente.

weepy ['wi:pɪ] n (col) film m inv or storia strappalacrime.
weigh [weɪ] vt, vi pesare; **to ~ anchor** salpare or levare l'ancora; **to ~ the pros and cons** valutare i pro e i contro.
▸**weigh down** vt (branch) piegare; (fig: with worry) opprimere, caricare.
▸**weigh out** vt (goods) pesare.
▸**weigh up** vt valutare.
weighbridge ['weɪbrɪdʒ] n bascula.
weighing machine ['weɪɪŋ-] n pesa.
weight [weɪt] n peso; **sold by ~** venduto(a) a peso; **~s and measures** pesi e misure; **to put on/lose ~** ingrassare/dimagrire.
weighting ['weɪtɪŋ] n: **~ allowance** indennità f inv speciale (per carovita etc).
weightlessness ['weɪtlɪsnɪs] n mancanza di peso.
weightlifter ['weɪtlɪftə*] n pesista m.
weight training n: **to do ~** allenarsi con i pesi.
weighty ['weɪtɪ] adj pesante; (fig) importante, grave.
weir [wɪə*] n diga.
weird [wɪəd] adj strano(a), bizzarro(a); (eerie) soprannaturale.
weirdo ['wɪədəu] n (col) tipo/a allucinante.
welcome ['wɛlkəm] adj benvenuto(a) ♦ n accoglienza, benvenuto ♦ vt accogliere cordialmente; (also: bid ~) dare il benvenuto a; (be glad of) rallegrarsi di; **to be ~** essere il(la) benvenuto(a); **to make sb ~** accogliere bene qn; **you're ~** (after thanks) prego; **you're ~ to try** provi pure.
welcoming ['wɛlkəmɪŋ] adj accogliente.
weld [wɛld] n saldatura ♦ vt saldare.
welder ['wɛldə*] n (person) saldatore m.
welding ['wɛldɪŋ] n saldatura (autogena).
welfare ['wɛlfɛə*] n benessere m.
welfare state n stato sociale.
welfare work n assistenza sociale.
well [wɛl] n pozzo ♦ adv bene ♦ adj: **to be ~** (person) stare bene ♦ excl allora!; ma!; ebbene!; **~ done!** bravo(a)!; **get ~ soon!** guarisci presto!; **to do ~ in sth** riuscire in qc; **to be doing ~** stare bene; **to think ~ of sb** avere una buona opinione di qn; **I don't feel ~** non mi sento bene; **as ~** (in addition) anche; **X as ~ as Y** sia X che Y; **he did as ~ as he could** ha fatto come meglio poteva; **you might as ~ tell me** potresti anche dirmelo; **it would be as ~ to ask** sarebbe bene chiedere; **~, as I was saying** ... dunque, come stavo dicendo ....
▸**well up** vi (tears, emotions) sgorgare.
we'll [wi:l] = we will; we shall.
well-behaved ['wɛlbɪ'heɪvd] adj ubbidiente.
well-being ['wɛl'bi:ɪŋ] n benessere m.

well-bred ['wɛl'brɛd] adj educato(a), beneducato(a).
well-built ['wɛl'bɪlt] adj (person) ben fatto(a).
well-chosen ['wɛl'tʃəuzn] adj (remarks, words) ben scelto(a), appropriato(a).
well-developed ['wɛldɪ'vɛləpt] adj sviluppato(a).
well-disposed ['wɛldɪs'pəuzd] adj: **~ to(wards)** bendisposto(a) verso.
well-dressed ['wɛl'drɛst] adj ben vestito(a), vestito(a) bene.
well-earned ['wɛl'ə:nd] adj (rest) meritato(a).
well-groomed ['wɛl'gru:md] adj curato(a), azzimato(a).
well-heeled ['wɛl'hi:ld] adj (col: wealthy) agiato(a), facoltoso(a).
well-informed ['wɛlɪn'fɔ:md] adj ben informato(a).
Wellington ['wɛlɪŋtən] n Wellington f.
wellingtons ['wɛlɪŋtənz] npl (also: **wellington boots**) stivali mpl di gomma.
well-kept ['wɛl'kɛpt] adj (house, grounds, secret) ben tenuto(a); (hair, hands) ben curato(a).
well-known ['wɛl'nəun] adj noto(a), famoso(a).
well-mannered ['wɛl'mænəd] adj ben educato(a).
well-meaning ['wɛl'mi:nɪŋ] adj ben intenzionato(a).
well-nigh ['wɛl'naɪ] adv: **~ impossible** quasi impossibile.
well-off ['wɛl'ɔf] adj benestante, danaroso(a).
well-read ['wɛl'rɛd] adj colto(a).
well-spoken ['wɛl'spəukn] adj che parla bene.
well-stocked ['wɛl'stɔkt] adj (shop, larder) ben fornito(a).
well-timed ['wɛl'taɪmd] adj opportuno(a).
well-to-do ['wɛltə'du:] adj abbiente, benestante.
well-wisher ['wɛlwɪʃə*] n ammiratore/trice; **letters from ~s** lettere fpl di incoraggiamento.
well-woman clinic ['wɛlwumən-] n ≈ consultorio (familiare).
Welsh [wɛlʃ] adj gallese ♦ n (LING) gallese m; **the ~** npl i gallesi; **the ~ National Assembly** il Parlamento gallese.
Welshman, Welshwoman ['wɛlʃmən, -wumən] n gallese m/f.
Welsh rarebit n crostino al formaggio.
welter ['wɛltə*] n massa, mucchio.
went [wɛnt] pt of **go**.
wept [wɛpt] pt, pp of **weep**.

were [wə:*] pt of **be**.

we're [wɪə*] = **we are**.

weren't [wə:nt] = **were not**.

werewolf, pl **-wolves** ['wɪəwulf, -wulvz] n licantropo, lupo mannaro (col).

west [wɛst] n ovest m, occidente m, ponente m ♦ adj (a) ovest inv, occidentale ♦ adv verso ovest; **the W~** l'Occidente.

westbound ['wɛstbaund] adj (traffic) diretto(a) a ovest; (carriageway) ovest inv.

West Country n: **the ~** il sud-ovest dell'Inghilterra.

westerly ['wɛstəlɪ] adj (wind) occidentale, da ovest.

western ['wɛstən] adj occidentale, dell'ovest ♦ n (CINE) western m inv.

westerner ['wɛstənə*] n occidentale m/f.

westernized ['wɛstənaɪzd] adj occidentalizzato(a).

West German adj, n tedesco(a) occidentale.

West Germany n Germania Occidentale.

West Indian adj delle Indie Occidentali ♦ n abitante m/f (or originario/a) delle Indie Occidentali.

West Indies [-'ɪndɪz] npl: **the ~** le Indie Occidentali.

Westminster ['wɛstmɪnstə*] n il parlamento (britannico).

westward(s) ['wɛstwəd(z)] adv verso ovest.

wet [wɛt] adj umido(a), bagnato(a); (soaked) fradicio(a); (rainy) piovoso(a) ♦ vt: **to ~ one's pants** or **o.s.** farsi la pipì addosso; **to get ~** bagnarsi; "**~ paint**" "vernice fresca".

wet blanket n (fig) guastafeste m/f inv.

wetness ['wɛtnɪs] n umidità.

wet suit n tuta da sub.

we've [wi:v] = **we have**.

whack [wæk] vt picchiare, battere.

whacked [wækt] adj (col: tired) sfinito(a), a pezzi.

whale [weɪl] n (ZOOL) balena.

whaler ['weɪlə*] n (ship) baleniera.

whaling ['weɪlɪŋ] n caccia alla balena.

wharf, pl **wharves** [wɔːf, wɔːvz] n banchina.

================== KEYWORD

what [wɔt] adj **1** (in direct/indirect questions) che; quale; **~ size is it?** che taglia è?; **~ colour is it?** di che colore è?; **~ books do you want?** quali or che libri vuole?; **for ~ reason?** per quale motivo?

2 (in exclamations) che; **~ a mess!** che disordine!

♦ pron **1** (interrogative) che cosa, cosa, che;

~'s in there? cosa c'è lì dentro?; **~ is his address?** qual è il suo indirizzo?; **~ will it cost?** quanto costerà?; **~ are you doing?** che or (che) cosa fai?; **~ are you talking about?** di che cosa parli?; **~'s happening?** che or (che) cosa succede?; **~ is it called?** come si chiama?; **~ about me?** e io?; **~ about doing ...?** e se facessimo ...?

2 (relative) ciò che, quello che; **I saw ~ you did** ho visto quello che hai fatto; **I saw ~ was on the table** ho visto cosa c'era sul tavolo; **~ I want is a cup of tea** ciò che voglio adesso è una tazza di tè

3 (indirect use) (che) cosa; **he asked me ~ she had said** mi ha chiesto che cosa avesse detto; **tell me ~ you're thinking about** dimmi a cosa stai pensando; **I don't know ~ to do** non so cosa fare

♦ excl (disbelieving) cosa!, come!

whatever [wɔt'ɛvə*] adj: **~ book** qualunque or qualsiasi libro + sub

♦ pron: **do ~ is necessary/you want** faccia qualunque or qualsiasi cosa sia necessaria/lei voglia; **~ happens** qualunque cosa accada; **no reason ~** or **whatsoever** nessuna ragione affatto or al mondo; **~ it costs** costi quello che costi.

whatsoever [wɔtsəu'ɛvə*] adj, pron = **whatever**.

wheat [wi:t] n grano, frumento.

wheatgerm ['wi:tdʒə:m] n germe m di grano.

wheatmeal ['wi:tmi:l] n farina integrale di frumento.

wheedle ['wi:dl] vt: **to ~ sb into doing sth** convincere qn a fare qc (con lusinghe); **to ~ sth out of sb** ottenere qc da qn (con lusinghe).

wheel [wi:l] n ruota; (AUT: also: **steering ~**) volante m; (NAUT) (ruota del) timone m ♦ vt spingere ♦ vi (also: **~ round**) girare.

wheelbarrow ['wi:lbærəu] n carriola.

wheelbase ['wi:lbeɪs] n interasse m.

wheelchair ['wi:ltʃeə*] n sedia a rotelle.

wheel clamp n (AUT) morsetto m bloccaruota inv.

wheeler-dealer ['wi:lə'di:lə*] n trafficone m, maneggione m.

wheelie-bin ['wi:lɪbɪn] n (BRIT) bidone m (della spazzatura) a rotelle.

wheeling ['wi:lɪŋ] n: **~ and dealing** maneggi mpl.

wheeze [wi:z] n respiro affannoso ♦ vi ansimare.

wheezy ['wi:zɪ] adj (person) che respira con affanno; (breath) sibilante.

━━━━━━━━━━━━━━━━━ KEYWORD

when [wɛn] adv quando; ~ **did it happen?** quando è successo?
♦ conj 1 (at, during, after the time that) quando; **she was reading** ~ **I came in** quando sono entrato lei leggeva; **that was** ~ **I needed you** era allora che avevo bisogno di te
2 (on, at which): **on the day** ~ **I met him** il giorno in cui l'ho incontrato; **one day** ~ **it was raining** un giorno che pioveva
3 (whereas) quando, mentre; **you said I was wrong** ~ **in fact I was right** mi hai detto che avevo torto, quando in realtà avevo ragione.

whenever [wɛn'ɛvə*] adv quando mai ♦ conj quando; (every time that) ogni volta che; **I go** ~ **I can** ci vado ogni volta che posso.
where [wɛə*] adv, conj dove; **this is** ~ è qui che; ~ **are you from?** di dov'è?; ~ **possible** quando è possibile, se possibile.
whereabouts ['wɛərəbauts] adv dove ♦ n: **sb's** ~ luogo dove qn si trova.
whereas [wɛər'æz] conj mentre.
whereby [wɛə'baɪ] adv (formal) per cui.
whereupon [wɛərə'pɔn] adv al che.
wherever [wɛər'ɛvə*] adv dove mai ♦ conj dovunque + sub; **sit** ~ **you like** si sieda dove vuole.
wherewithal ['wɛəwɪðɔːl] n: **the** ~ **(to do sth)** i mezzi (per fare qc).
whet [wɛt] vt (appetite etc) stimolare.
whether ['wɛðə*] conj se; **I don't know** ~ **to accept or not** non so se accettare o no; **it's doubtful** ~ è poco probabile che; ~ **you go or not** che lei vada o no.
whey [weɪ] n siero.

━━━━━━━━━━━━━━━━━ KEYWORD

which [wɪtʃ] adj 1 (interrogative: direct, indirect) quale; ~ **picture do you want?** quale quadro vuole?; ~ **one?** quale?; ~ **one of you did it?** chi di voi lo ha fatto?
2: **in** ~ **case** nel qual caso; **by** ~ **time** e a quel punto
♦ pron 1 (interrogative) quale; ~ **(of these) are yours?** quali di questi sono suoi?; ~ **of you are coming?** chi di voi viene?
2 (relative) che; (: indirect) cui, il (la) quale; **the apple** ~ **you ate/** ~ **is on the table** la mela che hai mangiato/che è sul tavolo; **the chair on** ~ **you are sitting** la sedia sulla quale or su cui sei seduto; **the book of** ~ **we were speaking** il libro del quale stavamo parlando; **he said he knew,** ~ **is true** ha detto che lo sapeva, il

che è vero; **I don't mind** ~ non mi importa quale; **after** ~ dopo di che.

whichever [wɪtʃ'ɛvə*] adj: **take** ~ **book you prefer** prenda qualsiasi libro che preferisce; ~ **book you take** qualsiasi libro prenda; ~ **way you** ... in qualunque modo lei ... + sub.
whiff [wɪf] n odore m; **to catch a** ~ **of sth** sentire l'odore di qc.
while [waɪl] n momento ♦ conj mentre; (as long as) finché; (although) sebbene + sub; **for a** ~ per un po'; **in a** ~ tra poco; **all the** ~ tutto il tempo; **we'll make it worth your** ~ faremo in modo che le valga la pena.
▶**while away** vt (time) far passare.
whilst [waɪlst] conj = while.
whim [wɪm] n capriccio.
whimper ['wɪmpə*] n piagnucolio ♦ vi piagnucolare.
whimsical ['wɪmzɪkl] adj (person) capriccioso(a); (look) strano(a).
whine [waɪn] n gemito ♦ vi gemere; uggiolare; piagnucolare.
whip [wɪp] n frusta; (for riding) frustino; (POL: person) capogruppo ♦ vt frustare; (CULIN: cream etc) sbattere; (snatch) sollevare (or estrarre) bruscamente; see boxed note.
▶**whip up** vt (cream) montare, sbattere; (col: meal) improvvisare; (: stir up: support, feeling) suscitare, stimolare.

┌─────────────────────────────┐
│ **WHIP**   │
│   │
│ Nel Parlamento britannico i **whip** sono parlamentari incaricati di mantenere la disciplina tra i deputati del loro partito durante le votazioni e di verificare la loro presenza in aula. │
└─────────────────────────────┘

whiplash ['wɪplæʃ] n (MED: also: ~ **injury**) colpo di frusta.
whipped cream ['wɪpt-] n panna montata.
whipping boy ['wɪpɪŋ-] n (fig) capro espiatorio.
whip-round ['wɪpraund] n (BRIT) colletta.
whirl [wəːl] n turbine m ♦ vt (far) girare rapidamente; (far) turbinare ♦ vi turbinare; (dancers) volteggiare; (leaves, dust) sollevarsi in un vortice.
whirlpool ['wəːlpuːl] n mulinello.
whirlwind ['wəːlwɪnd] n turbine m.
whirr [wəː*] vi ronzare.
whisk [wɪsk] n (CULIN) frusta; frullino ♦ vt sbattere, frullare; **to** ~ **sb away** or **off** portar via qn a tutta velocità.
whiskers ['wɪskəz] npl (of animal) baffi mpl;

(*of man*) favoriti *mpl*.
whisky, (*Irish, US*) **whiskey** ['wɪskɪ] *n*
whisky *m inv*.
whisper ['wɪspə*] *n* bisbiglio, sussurro;
(*rumour*) voce *f* ♦ *vt, vi* bisbigliare,
sussurrare; **to ~ sth to sb** bisbigliare qc
a qn.
whispering ['wɪspərɪŋ] *n* bisbiglio.
whist [wɪst] *n* (*BRIT*) whist *m*.
whistle ['wɪsl] *n* (*sound*) fischio; (*object*)
fischietto ♦ *vi, vt* fischiare; **to ~ a tune**
fischiettare un motivetto.
whistle-stop ['wɪslstɔp] *adj*: **~ tour** (*POL,
fig*) rapido giro.
Whit [wɪt] *n* Pentecoste *f*.
white [waɪt] *adj* bianco(a); (*with fear*)
pallido(a) ♦ *n* bianco; (*person*) bianco/a;
to turn *or* **go ~** (*person*) sbiancare; (*hair*)
diventare bianco; **the ~s** (*washing*) i capi
bianchi; **tennis ~s** completo da tennis.
whitebait ['waɪtbeɪt] *n* bianchetti *mpl*.
white-collar worker ['waɪtkɔlə-] *n*
impiegato/a.
white elephant *n* (*fig*) oggetto (*or*
progetto) costoso ma inutile.
white goods *npl* (*appliances*)
elettrodomestici *mpl*; (*linens*) biancheria
per la casa.
white-hot [waɪt'hɔt] *adj* (*metal*)
incandescente.
White House *n*: **the ~** la Casa Bianca; *see
boxed note*.

WHITE HOUSE

La **White House** è la residenza ufficiale del
presidente degli Stati Uniti e ha sede a
Washington DC. Spesso il termine viene usato
per indicare l'esecutivo del governo
statunitense.

---

white lie *n* bugia pietosa.
whiteness ['waɪtnɪs] *n* bianchezza.
white noise *n* rumore *m* bianco.
white paper *n* (*POL*) libro bianco.
whitewash ['waɪtwɔʃ] *n* (*paint*) bianco di
calce ♦ *vt* imbiancare; (*fig*) coprire.
whiting ['waɪtɪŋ] *n* (*pl inv*) merlango.
Whit Monday *n* lunedì *m inv* di
Pentecoste.
Whitsun ['wɪtsn] *n* Pentecoste *f*.
whittle ['wɪtl] *vt*: **to ~ away, ~ down**
ridurre, tagliare.
whizz [wɪz] *vi* passare sfrecciando.
whizz kid *n* (*col*) prodigio.
WHO *n abbr* (= *World Health Organization*)
O.M.S. *f* (= *Organizzazione mondiale della
sanità*).

════════════════════ KEYWORD

who [huː] *pron* **1** (*interrogative*) chi; **~ is it?,
~'s there?** chi è?
2 (*relative*) che; **the man ~ spoke to me**
l'uomo che ha parlato con me; **those ~
can swim** quelli che sanno nuotare.

---

whodunit [huːˈdʌnɪt] *n* (*col*) giallo.
whoever [huːˈɛvə*] *pron*: **~ finds it**
chiunque lo trovi; **ask ~ you like** lo
chieda a chiunque vuole; **~ told you that?**
chi mai gliel'ha detto?
whole [həʊl] *adj* (*complete*) tutto(a),
completo(a); (*not broken*) intero(a),
intatto(a) ♦ *n* (*total*) totale *m*; (*sth not
broken*) tutto; **the ~ lot (of it)** tutto; **the ~
lot (of them)** tutti; **the ~ of the time** tutto
il tempo; **the ~ of the town** la città
intera; **on the ~, as a ~** nel complesso,
nell'insieme; **~ villages were destroyed**
interi paesi furono distrutti.
wholehearted [həʊlˈhɑːtɪd] *adj*
sincero(a).
wholemeal ['həʊlmiːl] *adj* (*BRIT: flour, bread*)
integrale.
whole note *n* (*US*) semibreve *f*.
wholesale ['həʊlseɪl] *n* commercio *or*
vendita all'ingrosso ♦ *adj* all'ingrosso;
(*destruction*) totale.
wholesaler ['həʊlseɪlə*] *n* grossista
m/f.
wholesome ['həʊlsəm] *adj* sano(a);
(*climate*) salubre.
wholewheat ['həʊlwiːt] *adj* = **wholemeal**.
wholly ['həʊlɪ] *adv* completamente, del
tutto.

════════════════════ KEYWORD

whom [huːm] *pron* **1** (*interrogative*) chi; **~
did you see?** chi hai visto?; **to ~ did you
give it?** a chi lo hai dato?
2 (*relative*) che, *prep* + il (la) quale; **the
man ~ I saw** l'uomo che ho visto; **the
man to ~ I spoke** l'uomo al *or* con il quale
ho parlato; **those to ~ I spoke** le persone
alle *or* con le quali ho parlato.

---

whooping cough ['huːpɪŋ-] *n* pertosse
f.
whoops [wuːps] *excl*: **~-a-daisy!** ops!
whoosh [wuːʃ] *n*: **it came out with a ~**
(*sauce etc*) è uscito di getto; (*air*) è uscito
con un sibilo.
whopper ['wɔpə*] *n* (*col: lie*) balla; (: *large
thing*) cosa enorme.
whopping ['wɔpɪŋ] *adj* (*col: big*) enorme.
whore [hɔː*] *n* (*pej*) puttana.

=================================== KEYWORD

whose [huːz] *adj* **1** (*possessive: interrogative*) di chi; ~ **book is this?**, ~ **is this book?** di chi è questo libro?; ~ **daughter are you?** di chi sei figlia?; ~ **pencil have you taken?** di chi è la matita che hai preso? **2** (*possessive: relative*): **the man** ~ **son you rescued** l'uomo il cui figlio hai salvato *or* a cui hai salvato il figlio; **the girl** ~ **sister you were speaking to** la ragazza alla cui sorella stavi parlando ♦ *pron* di chi; ~ **is this?** di chi è questo?; **I know** ~ **it is** so di chi è.

Who's Who ['huːz'huː] *n elenco di personalità.*

why [waɪ] *adv, conj* perché ♦ *excl* (*surprise*) ma guarda un po'!; (*remonstrating*) ma (via)!; (*explaining*) ebbene!; ~ **not?** perché no?; ~ **not do it now?** perché non farlo adesso?; **the reason** ~ il motivo per cui.

whyever [waɪ'ɛvə*] *adv* perché mai.

WI *n abbr* (*BRIT*: = Women's Institute) circolo femminile ♦ *abbr* (*GEO*) = **West Indies**; (*US*) = **Wisconsin**.

wick [wɪk] *n* lucignolo, stoppino.

wicked ['wɪkɪd] *adj* cattivo(a), malvagio(a); (*mischievous*) malizioso(a); (*terrible: prices, weather*) terribile.

wicker ['wɪkə*] *n* vimine *m*; (*also:* ~**work**) articoli *mpl* di vimini.

wicket ['wɪkɪt] *n* (*CRICKET*) porta; area tra le due porte.

wicket keeper *n* (*CRICKET*) portiere *m*.

wide [waɪd] *adj* largo(a); (*region, knowledge*) vasto(a); (*choice*) ampio(a) ♦ *adv*: **to open** ~ spalancare; **to shoot** ~ tirare a vuoto *or* fuori bersaglio; **it is 3 metres** ~ è largo 3 metri.

wide-angle lens ['waɪdæŋgl-] *n* grandangolare *m*.

wide-awake [waɪdə'weɪk] *adj* completamente sveglio(a).

wide-eyed [waɪd'aɪd] *adj* con gli occhi spalancati.

widely ['waɪdlɪ] *adv* (*different*) molto, completamente; (*believed*) generalmente; ~ **spaced** molto distanziati(e); **to be** ~ **read** (*author*) essere molto letto; (*reader*) essere molto colto.

widen ['waɪdn] *vt* allargare, ampliare.

wideness ['waɪdnɪs] *n* larghezza; vastità; ampiezza.

wide open *adj* spalancato(a).

wide-ranging [waɪd'reɪndʒɪŋ] *adj* (*survey, report*) vasto(a); (*interests*) svariato(a).

widespread ['waɪdsprɛd] *adj* (*belief etc*) molto *or* assai diffuso(a).

widow ['wɪdəu] *n* vedova.

widowed ['wɪdəud] *adj* (che è rimasto(a)) vedovo(a).

widower ['wɪdəuə*] *n* vedovo.

width [wɪdθ] *n* larghezza; **it's 7 metres in** ~ è largo 7 metri.

widthways ['wɪdθweɪz] *adv* trasversalmente.

wield [wiːld] *vt* (*sword*) maneggiare; (*power*) esercitare.

wife, *pl* **wives** [waɪf, waɪvz] *n* moglie *f*.

wig [wɪg] *n* parrucca.

wigging ['wɪgɪŋ] *n* (*BRIT col*) lavata di capo.

wiggle ['wɪgl] *vt* dimenare, agitare ♦ *vi* (*loose screw etc*) traballare; (*worm*) torcersi.

wiggly ['wɪglɪ] *adj* (*line*) ondulato(a), sinuoso(a).

wild [waɪld] *adj* (*animal, plant*) selvatico(a); (*countryside, appearance*) selvaggio(a); (*sea*) tempestoso(a); (*idea, life*) folle; (*col: angry*) arrabbiato(a), furibondo(a); (*enthusiastic*): **to be** ~ **about** andar pazzo(a) per ♦ *n*: **the** ~ la natura; ~**s** *npl* regione *f* selvaggia.

wild card *n* (*COMPUT*) wild card *m inv.*

wildcat ['waɪldkæt] *n* gatto(a) selvatico(a).

wildcat strike *n* ≈ sciopero selvaggio.

wilderness ['wɪldənɪs] *n* deserto.

wildfire ['waɪldfaɪə*] *n*: **to spread like** ~ propagarsi rapidamente.

wild-goose chase [waɪld'guːs-] *n* (*fig*) pista falsa.

wildlife ['waɪldlaɪf] *n* natura.

wildly ['waɪldlɪ] *adv* (*applaud*) freneticamente; (*hit, guess*) a casaccio; (*happy*) follemente.

wiles [waɪlz] *npl* astuzie *fpl.*

wilful, (*US*) **willful** ['wɪlful] *adj* (*person*) testardo(a); ostinato(a); (*action*) intenzionale; (*crime*) premeditato(a).

=================================== KEYWORD

will [wɪl] *aux vb* **1** (*forming future tense*): **I** ~ **finish it tomorrow** lo finirò domani; **I** ~ **have finished it by tomorrow** lo finirò entro domani; ~ **you do it? – yes I** ~/**no I won't** lo farai? – sì (lo farò)/no (non lo farò); **the car won't start** la macchina non parte **2** (*in conjectures, predictions*): **he** ~ *or* **he'll be there by now** dovrebbe essere arrivato a quest'ora; **that** ~ **be the postman** sarà il postino **3** (*in commands, requests, offers*): ~ **you be quiet!** vuoi stare zitto?; ~ **you sit down?**

(*politely*) prego, si accomodi; (*angrily*) vuoi metterti seduto?; ~ **you come?** vieni anche tu?; ~ **you help me?** mi aiuti?, mi puoi aiutare?; **you won't lose it,** ~ **you?** non lo perderai, vero?; ~ **you have a cup of tea?** vorrebbe una tazza di tè?; **I won't put up with it!** non lo accetterò!

♦ *vt* (*pt, pp* ~**ed**): **to** ~ **sb to do** pregare tra sé perché qn faccia; **he** ~**ed himself to go on** continuò grazie a un grande sforzo di volontà

♦ *n* **1** (*desire*) volontà; **against sb's** ~ contro la volontà *or* il volere di qn; **to do sth of one's own free** ~ fare qc di propria volontà

2 (*LAW*) testamento; **to make a/one's** ~ fare testamento.

willful ['wɪlful] *adj* (*US*) = **wilful**.

willing ['wɪlɪŋ] *adj* volonteroso(a) ♦ *n*: **to show** ~ dare prova di buona volontà; ~ **to do** disposto(a) a fare.

willingly ['wɪlɪŋlɪ] *adv* volentieri.

willingness ['wɪlɪŋnɪs] *n* buona volontà.

will-o'-the-wisp [wɪləðə'wɪsp] *n* (*also fig*) fuoco fatuo.

willow ['wɪləu] *n* salice *m*.

will power *n* forza di volontà.

willy-nilly ['wɪlɪ'nɪlɪ] *adv* volente o nolente.

wilt [wɪlt] *vi* appassire.

Wilts [wɪlts] *abbr* (*BRIT*) = **Wiltshire**.

wily ['waɪlɪ] *adj* furbo(a).

wimp [wɪmp] *n* (*col*) mezza calzetta.

win [wɪn] *n* (*in sports etc*) vittoria ♦ *vb* (*pt, pp* **won** [wʌn]) *vt* (*battle, prize*) vincere; (*money*) guadagnare; (*popularity*) conquistare; (*contract*) aggiudicarsi ♦ *vi* vincere.

▶**win over,** (*BRIT*) **win round** *vt* convincere.

wince [wɪns] *n* trasalimento, sussulto ♦ *vi* trasalire.

winch [wɪntʃ] *n* verricello, argano.

Winchester disk ['wɪntʃɪstə-] *n* (*COMPUT*) disco Winchester.

wind *n* [wɪnd] vento; (*MED*) flatulenza, ventosità ♦ *vb* [waɪnd] (*pt, pp* **wound** [waund]) *vt* attorcigliare; (*wrap*) avvolgere; (*clock, toy*) caricare; (*take breath away*: [wɪnd] far restare senza fiato ♦ *vi* (*road, river*) serpeggiare; **the** ~**(s)** (*MUS*) i fiati; **into** *or* **against the** ~ controvento; **to get** ~ **of sth** venire a sapere qc; **to break** ~ scoreggiare (*col*).

▶**wind down** *vt* (*car window*) abbassare; (*fig: production, business*) diminuire.

▶**wind up** *vt* (*clock*) caricare; (*debate*) concludere.

windbreak ['wɪndbreɪk] *n* frangivento.

windcheater ['wɪndtʃiːtə*], (*US*) **windbreaker** ['wɪndbreɪkə*] *n* giacca a vento.

winder ['waɪndə*] *n* (*BRIT: on watch*) corona di carica.

windfall ['wɪndfɔːl] *n* colpo di fortuna.

winding ['waɪndɪŋ] *adj* (*road*) serpeggiante; (*staircase*) a chiocciola.

wind instrument *n* (*MUS*) strumento a fiato.

windmill ['wɪndmɪl] *n* mulino a vento.

window ['wɪndəu] *n* (*gen, COMPUT*) finestra; (*in car, train*) finestrino; (*in shop etc*) vetrina; (*also*: ~ **pane**) vetro.

window box *n* cassetta da fiori.

window cleaner *n* (*person*) pulitore *m* di finestre.

window dressing *n* allestimento della vetrina.

window envelope *n* busta a finestra.

window frame *n* telaio di finestra.

window ledge *n* davanzale *m*.

window pane *n* vetro.

window-shopping ['wɪndəuʃɔpɪŋ] *n*: **to go** ~ andare a vedere le vetrine.

windowsill ['wɪndəusɪl] *n* davanzale *m*.

windpipe ['wɪndpaɪp] *n* trachea.

wind power *n* energia eolica.

windscreen ['wɪndskriːn], (*US*) **windshield** ['wɪndʃiːld] *n* parabrezza *m inv*.

windscreen washer *n* lavacristallo.

windscreen wiper *n* tergicristallo.

windshield ['wɪndʃiːld] *n* (*US*) = **windscreen**.

windsurfing ['wɪndsəːfɪŋ] *n* windsurf *m inv*.

windswept ['wɪndswept] *adj* spazzato(a) dal vento.

wind tunnel *n* galleria aerodinamica *or* del vento.

windy ['wɪndɪ] *adj* ventoso(a); **it's** ~ c'è vento.

wine [waɪn] *n* vino ♦ *vt*: **to** ~ **and dine sb** offrire un ottimo pranzo a qn.

wine bar *n* enoteca.

wine cellar *n* cantina.

wine glass *n* bicchiere *m* da vino.

wine list *n* lista dei vini.

wine merchant *n* commerciante *m* di vino.

wine tasting *n* degustazione *f* dei vini.

wine waiter *n* sommelier *m inv*.

wing [wɪŋ] *n* ala; (*THEAT*) quinte *fpl*.

winger ['wɪŋə*] *n* (*SPORT*) ala.

wing mirror *n* (*BRIT*) specchietto retrovisore esterno.

wing nut *n* galletto.

wingspan ['wɪŋspæn], **wingspread** ['wɪŋsprɛd] *n* apertura alare, apertura d'ali.
wink [wɪŋk] *n* occhiolino, strizzatina d'occhi ♦ *vi* ammiccare, fare l'occhiolino.
winkle ['wɪŋkl] *n* litorina.
winner ['wɪnə*] *n* vincitore/trice.
winning ['wɪnɪŋ] *adj* (*team*) vincente; (*goal*) decisivo(a); (*charming*) affascinante; *see also* **winnings**.
winning post *n* traguardo.
winnings ['wɪnɪŋz] *npl* vincite *fpl*.
winsome ['wɪnsəm] *adj* accattivante.
winter ['wɪntə*] *n* inverno; **in** ~ d'inverno, in inverno.
winter sports *npl* sport *mpl* invernali.
wintry ['wɪntrɪ] *adj* invernale.
wipe [waɪp] *n* pulita, passata ♦ *vt* pulire (strofinando); (*dishes*) asciugare; **to give sth a** ~ dare una pulita *or* una passata a qc; **to** ~ **one's nose** soffiarsi il naso.
▶**wipe off** *vt* cancellare; (*stains*) togliere strofinando.
▶**wipe out** *vt* (*debt*) pagare, liquidare; (*memory*) cancellare; (*destroy*) annientare.
▶**wipe up** *vt* asciugare.
wire ['waɪə*] *n* filo; (*ELEC*) filo elettrico; (*TEL*) telegramma *m* ♦ *vt* (*ELEC: house*) fare l'impianto elettrico di; (: *circuit*) installare; (*also:* ~ **up**) collegare, allacciare.
wire brush *n* spazzola metallica.
wire cutters [-kʌtəz] *npl* tronchese *m or f*.
wireless ['waɪəlɪs] *n* (*BRIT*) telegrafia senza fili; (*set*) (apparecchio *m*) radio *f inv*.
wire netting *n* rete *f* metallica.
wire service *n* (*US*) = **news agency**.
wire-tapping ['waɪə'tæpɪŋ] *n* intercettazione *f* telefonica.
wiring ['waɪərɪŋ] *n* (*ELEC*) impianto elettrico.
wiry ['waɪərɪ] *adj* magro(a) e nerboruto(a).
Wis(c). *abbr* (*US*) = **Wisconsin**.
wisdom ['wɪzdəm] *n* saggezza; (*of action*) prudenza.
wisdom tooth *n* dente *m* del giudizio.
wise [waɪz] *adj* saggio(a); (*advice, remark*) prudente; **I'm none the** ~**r** ne so come prima.
▶**wise up** *vi* (*col*): **to** ~ **up to** divenire più consapevole di.
... wise [waɪz] *suffix*: **time**~ per quanto riguarda il tempo, in termini di tempo.
wisecrack ['waɪzkræk] *n* battuta spiritosa.
wish [wɪʃ] *n* (*desire*) desiderio; (*specific desire*) richiesta ♦ *vt* desiderare, volere; **best** ~**es** (*on birthday etc*) i migliori

auguri; **with best** ~**es** (*in letter*) cordiali saluti, con i migliori saluti; **give her my best** ~**es** le faccia i migliori auguri da parte mia; **to** ~ **sb goodbye** dire arrivederci a qn; **he** ~**ed me well** mi augurò di riuscire; **to** ~ **to do/sb to do** desiderare *or* volere fare/che qn faccia; **to** ~ **for** desiderare; **to** ~ **sth on sb** rifilare qc a qn.
wishbone ['wɪʃbəun] *n* forcella.
wishful ['wɪʃful] *adj*: **it's** ~ **thinking** è prendere i desideri per realtà.
wishy-washy ['wɪʃɪ'wɔʃɪ] *adj* insulso(a).
wisp [wɪsp] *n* ciuffo, ciocca; (*of smoke, straw*) filo.
wistful ['wɪstful] *adj* malinconico(a); (*nostalgic*) nostalgico(a).
wit [wɪt] *n* (*gen pl*) intelligenza; presenza di spirito; (*wittiness*) spirito, arguzia; (*person*) bello spirito; **to be at one's** ~**s' end** (*fig*) non sapere più cosa fare; **to have** *or* **keep one's** ~**s about one** avere presenza di spirito; **to** ~ *adv* cioè.
witch [wɪtʃ] *n* strega.
witchcraft ['wɪtʃkrɑːft] *n* stregoneria.
witch doctor *n* stregone *m*.
witch-hunt ['wɪtʃhʌnt] *n* (*fig*) caccia alle streghe.

══════════════ = *KEYWORD*

with [wɪð, wɪθ] *prep* **1** (*in the company of*) con; **I was** ~ **him** ero con lui; **we stayed** ~ **friends** siamo stati da amici; **I'll be** ~ **you in a minute** vengo subito
2 (*descriptive*) con; **a room** ~ **a view** una camera con vista (sul mare *or* sulle montagne *etc*); **the man** ~ **the grey hat/blue eyes** l'uomo con il cappello grigio/gli occhi blu
3 (*indicating manner, means, cause*): ~ **tears in her eyes** con le lacrime agli occhi; **red** ~ **anger** rosso(a) dalla rabbia; **to shake** ~ **fear** tremare di paura; **covered** ~ **snow** coperto(a) di neve
4: **I'm** ~ **you** (*I understand*) la seguo; **I'm not really** ~ **it today** (*col*) oggi sono un po' fuori.

withdraw [wɪθ'drɔː] *vb* (*irreg*) *vt* ritirare; (*money from bank*) ritirare, prelevare ♦ *vi* ritirarsi; **to** ~ **into o.s.** chiudersi in se stesso.
withdrawal [wɪθ'drɔːəl] *n* ritiro; prelievo; (*of army*) ritirata; (*MED*) stato di privazione.
withdrawal symptoms *npl* crisi *f* di astinenza.
withdrawn [wɪθ'drɔːn] *pp of* **withdraw** ♦ *adj*

distaccato(a).

wither ['wɪðə*] vi appassire.

withered ['wɪðəd] adj appassito(a); (limb) atrofizzato(a).

withhold [wɪθ'həuld] vt irreg (money) trattenere; (permission): **to ~ (from)** rifiutare (a); (information): **to ~ (from)** nascondere (a).

within [wɪð'ɪn] prep all'interno di; (in time, distances) entro ♦ adv all'interno, dentro; **~ sight of** in vista di; **~ a mile of** entro un miglio da; **~ the week** prima della fine della settimana; **~ an hour from now** da qui a un'ora; **to be ~ the law** restare nei limiti della legge.

without [wɪð'aut] prep senza; **to go** or **do ~** sth fare a meno di qc; **~ anybody knowing** senza che nessuno lo sappia.

withstand [wɪθ'stænd] vt irreg resistere a.

witness ['wɪtnɪs] n (person) testimone m/f ♦ vt (event) essere testimone di; (document) attestare l'autenticità di ♦ vi: **to ~ to sth/having seen sth** testimoniare qc/di aver visto qc; **to bear ~ to sth** testimoniare qc; **~ for the prosecution/ defence** testimone a carico/discarico.

witness box, (US) **witness stand** n banco dei testimoni.

witticism ['wɪtɪsɪzəm] n spiritosaggine f.

witty ['wɪtɪ] adj spiritoso(a).

wives [waɪvz] npl of **wife**.

wizard ['wɪzəd] n mago.

wizened ['wɪznd] adj raggrinzito(a).

wk abbr = **week**.

Wm. abbr = **William**.

WO n abbr see **warrant officer**.

wobble ['wɔbl] vi tremare; (chair) traballare.

wobbly ['wɔblɪ] adj (hand, voice) tremante; (table, chair) traballante; (object about to fall) che oscilla pericolosamente.

woe [wəu] n dolore m; disgrazia.

woeful ['wəuful] adj (sad) triste; (deplorable) deplorevole.

wok [wɔk] n wok m inv (padella concava usata nella cucina cinese).

woke [wəuk] pt of **wake**.

woken ['wəukn] pp of **wake**.

wolf, pl **wolves** [wulf, wulvz] n lupo.

woman, pl **women** ['wumən, 'wɪmɪn] n donna ♦ cpd: **~ doctor** n dottoressa; **~ friend** n amica; **~ teacher** n insegnante f; **women's page** n (PRESS) rubrica femminile.

womanize ['wumənaɪz] vi essere un donnaiolo.

womanly ['wumənlɪ] adj femminile.

womb [wu:m] n (ANAT) utero.

women ['wɪmɪn] npl of **woman**.

Women's (Liberation) Movement n (also: **Women's Lib**) Movimento per la Liberazione della Donna.

won [wʌn] pt, pp of **win**.

wonder ['wʌndə*] n meraviglia ♦ vi: **to ~ whether** domandarsi se; **to ~ at** essere sorpreso(a) di; meravigliarsi di; **to ~ about** domandarsi di; pensare a; **it's no ~ that** c'è poco or non c'è da meravigliarsi che + sub.

wonderful ['wʌndəful] adj meraviglioso(a).

wonderfully ['wʌndəfəlɪ] adv (+ adjective) meravigliosamente; (+ verb) a meraviglia.

wonky ['wɔŋkɪ] adj (BRIT col) traballante.

wont [wəunt] n: **as is his/her ~** com'è solito/a fare.

won't [wəunt] = **will not**.

woo [wu:] vt (woman) fare la corte a.

wood [wud] n legno; (timber) legname m; (forest) bosco ♦ cpd di bosco, silvestre.

wood carving n scultura in legno, intaglio.

wooded ['wudɪd] adj boschivo(a); boscoso(a).

wooden ['wudn] adj di legno; (fig) rigido(a); inespressivo(a).

woodland ['wudlənd] n zona boscosa.

woodpecker ['wudpekə*] n picchio.

wood pigeon n colombaccio, palomba.

woodwind ['wudwɪnd] npl (MUS): **the ~** i legni.

woodwork ['wudwə:k] n parti fpl in legno; (craft, subject) falegnameria.

woodworm ['wudwə:m] n tarlo del legno.

woof [wuf] n (of dog) bau bau m ♦ vi abbaiare; **~, ~!** bau bau!

wool [wul] n lana; **to pull the ~ over sb's eyes** (fig) fargliela a qn.

woollen, (US) **woolen** ['wulən] adj di lana ♦ n: **~s** indumenti mpl di lana.

woolly, (US) **wooly** ['wulɪ] adj lanoso(a); (fig: ideas) confuso(a).

woozy ['wu:zɪ] adj (col) stordito(a).

word [wə:d] n parola; (news) notizie fpl ♦ vt esprimere, formulare; **~ for ~** parola per parola, testualmente; **what's the ~ for "pen" in Italian?** come si dice "pen" in italiano?; **to put sth into ~s** esprimere qc a parole; **in other ~s** in altre parole; **to have a ~ with sb** scambiare due parole con qn; **to have ~s with sb** (quarrel with) avere un diverbio con qn; **to break/keep one's ~** non mantenere/mantenere la propria parola; **I'll take your ~ for it** la crederò sulla parola; **to send ~ of** avvisare di; **to leave ~ (with** or **for sb) that ...** lasciare detto (a qn) che ....

wording ['wɔːdɪŋ] *n* formulazione *f*.
word of mouth *n* passaparola *m*; **I learned it by** *or* **through** ~ lo so per sentito dire.
word-perfect ['wɔːd'pəfɪkt] *adj* (*speech etc*) imparato(a) a memoria.
word processing *n* word processing *m*, elaborazione *f* testi.
word processor *n* word processor *m inv*.
wordwrap ['wɔːdræp] *n* (*COMPUT*) ritorno carrello automatico.
wordy ['wɔːdɪ] *adj* verboso(a), prolisso(a).
wore [wɔː*] *pt of* **wear**.
work [wɔːk] *n* lavoro; (*ART, LITERATURE*) opera ♦ *vi* lavorare; (*mechanism, plan etc*) funzionare; (*medicine*) essere efficace ♦ *vt* (*clay, wood etc*) lavorare; (*mine etc*) sfruttare; (*machine*) far funzionare; **to be at** ~ **(on sth)** lavorare (a qc); **to set to** ~, **to start** ~ mettersi all'opera; **to go to** ~ andare al lavoro; **to be out of** ~ essere disoccupato(a); **to** ~ **one's way through a book** riuscire a leggersi tutto un libro; **to** ~ **one's way through college** lavorare per pagarsi gli studi; **to** ~ **hard** lavorare sodo; **to** ~ **loose** allentarsi; *see also* **works**.
▶**work on** *vt fus* lavorare a; (*principle*) basarsi su; **he's** ~**ing on the car** sta facendo dei lavori alla macchina.
▶**work out** *vi* (*plans etc*) riuscire, andare bene; (*SPORT*) allenarsi ♦ *vt* (*problem*) risolvere; (*plan*) elaborare; **it** ~**s out at £100** fa 100 sterline.
workable ['wɔːkəbl] *adj* (*solution*) realizzabile.
workaholic [wɔːkə'hɔlɪk] *n* stacanovista *m/f*.
workbench ['wɔːkbɛntʃ] *n* banco (da lavoro).
worked up *adj*: **to get** ~ andare su tutte le furie; eccitarsi.
worker ['wɔːkə*] *n* lavoratore/trice; (*esp AGR, INDUSTRY*) operaio/a; **office** ~ impiegato/a.
work force *n* forza lavoro.
work-in ['wɔːkɪn] *n* (*BRIT*) sciopero alla rovescia.
working ['wɔːkɪŋ] *adj* (*day*) feriale; (*tools, conditions*) di lavoro; (*clothes*) da lavoro; (*wife*) che lavora; (*partner*) attivo(a); **in** ~ **order** funzionante; ~ **knowledge** conoscenza pratica.
working capital *n* (*COMM*) capitale *m* d'esercizio.
working class *n* classe *f* operaia *or* lavoratrice ♦ *adj*: **working-class** operaio(a).
working man *n* lavoratore *m*.
working party *n* (*BRIT*) commissione *f*.

working week *n* settimana lavorativa.
work-in-progress ['wɔːkɪn'prəugrɛs] *n* (*products*) lavoro in corso; (*value*) valore *m* del manufatto in lavorazione.
workload ['wɔːkləud] *n* carico di lavoro.
workman ['wɔːkmən] *n* operaio.
workmanship ['wɔːkmənʃɪp] *n* (*of worker*) abilità; (*of thing*) fattura.
workmate ['wɔːkmeɪt] *n* collega *m/f*.
workout ['wɔːkaut] *n* (*SPORT*) allenamento.
work permit *n* permesso di lavoro.
works [wɔːks] *n* (*BRIT*: *factory*) fabbrica ♦ *npl* (*of clock, machine*) meccanismo; **road** ~ opere stradali.
works council *n* consiglio aziendale.
work sheet *n* (*COMPUT*) foglio col programma di lavoro.
workshop ['wɔːkʃɔp] *n* officina.
work station *n* stazione *f* di lavoro.
work study *n* studio di organizzazione del lavoro.
worktop ['wɔːktɔp] *n* piano di lavoro.
work-to-rule ['wɔːktə'ruːl] *n* (*BRIT*) sciopero bianco.
world [wɔːld] *n* mondo ♦ *cpd* (*tour*) del mondo; (*record, power, war*) mondiale; **all over the** ~ in tutto il mondo; **to think the** ~ **of sb** pensare un gran bene di qn; **out of this** ~ (*fig*) formidabile; **what in the** ~ **is he doing?** che cavolo sta facendo?; **to do sb a** ~ **of good** fare un gran bene a qn; **W**~ **War One/Two** la prima/seconda guerra mondiale.
world champion *n* campione/essa mondiale.
World Cup *n* (*FOOTBALL*) Coppa del Mondo.
world-famous [wɔːld'feɪməs] *adj* di fama mondiale.
worldly ['wɔːldlɪ] *adj* di questo mondo.
world music *n* musica etnica.
World Series *n*: **the** ~ (*US BASEBALL*) la finalissima di baseball.
world-wide ['wɔːld'waɪd] *adj* universale.
worm [wɔːm] *n* verme *m*.
worn [wɔːn] *pp of* **wear** ♦ *adj* usato(a).
worn-out ['wɔːnaut] *adj* (*object*) consumato(a), logoro(a); (*person*) sfinito(a).
worried ['wʌrɪd] *adj* preoccupato(a); **to be** ~ **about sth** essere preoccupato per qc.
worrier ['wʌrɪə*] *n* ansioso/a.
worrisome ['wʌrɪsəm] *adj* preoccupante.
worry ['wʌrɪ] *n* preoccupazione *f* ♦ *vt* preoccupare ♦ *vi* preoccuparsi; **to** ~ **about** *or* **over sth/sb** preoccuparsi di qc/ per qn.
worrying ['wʌrɪɪŋ] *adj* preoccupante.

worse [wə:s] *adj* peggiore ♦ *adv*, *n* peggio; **a change for the ~** un peggioramento; **to get ~, to grow ~** peggiorare; **he is none the ~ for it** non ha avuto brutte conseguenze; **so much the ~ for you!** tanto peggio per te!

worsen ['wə:sn] *vt*, *vi* peggiorare.

worse off *adj* in condizioni (economiche) peggiori; (*fig*): **you'll be ~ this way** così sarà peggio per lei; **he is now ~ than before** ora è in condizioni peggiori di prima.

worship ['wə:ʃɪp] *n* culto ♦ *vt* (*God*) adorare, venerare; (*person*) adorare; **Your W~** (*to mayor*) signor sindaco; (*to judge*) signor giudice.

worshipper ['wə:ʃɪpə*] *n* adoratore/trice; (*in church*) fedele *m/f*, devoto/a.

worst [wə:st] *adj* il(la) peggiore ♦ *adv*, *n* peggio; **at ~** al peggio, per male che vada; **to come off ~** avere la peggio; **if the ~ comes to the ~** nel peggiore dei casi.

worst-case ['wə:st'keɪs] *adj*: **the ~ scenario** la peggiore delle ipotesi.

worsted ['wustɪd] *n*: (**wool**) **~** lana pettinata.

worth [wə:θ] *n* valore *m* ♦ *adj*: **to be ~** valere; **how much is it ~?** quanto vale?; **it's ~ it** ne vale la pena; **it's not ~ the trouble** non ne vale la pena; **50 pence ~ of apples** 50 pence di mele.

worthless ['wə:θlɪs] *adj* di nessun valore.

worthwhile ['wə:θ'waɪl] *adj* (*activity*) utile; (*cause*) lodevole; **a ~ book** un libro che vale la pena leggere.

worthy ['wə:ðɪ] *adj* (*person*) degno(a); (*motive*) lodevole; **~ of** degno di.

━━━━━━━━━━━━━━━━━━ KEYWORD

would [wud] *aux vb* **1** (*conditional tense*): **if you asked him he ~ do it** se glielo chiedesse lo farebbe; **if you had asked him he ~ have done it** se glielo avesse chiesto lo avrebbe fatto
2 (*in offers, invitations, requests*): **~ you like a biscuit?** vorrebbe *or* vuole un biscotto?; **~ you ask him to come in?** lo faccia entrare, per cortesia; **~ you open the window please?** apra la finestra, per favore
3 (*in indirect speech*): **I said I ~ do it** ho detto che l'avrei fatto
4 (*emphatic*): **it WOULD have to snow today!** doveva proprio nevicare oggi!
5 (*insistence*): **she ~n't do it** non ha voluto farlo
6 (*conjecture*): **it ~ have been midnight** sarà stata mezzanotte; **it ~ seem so** sembrerebbe proprio di sì
7 (*indicating habit*): **he ~ go there on Mondays** andava lì ogni lunedì.

would-be ['wudbi:] *adj* (*pej*) sedicente.

wound *vb* [waund] *pt*, *pp of* **wind** ♦ *n*, *vt* [wu:nd] *n* ferita ♦ *vt* ferire; **~ed in the leg** ferito(a) alla gamba.

wove [wəuv] *pt of* **weave**.

WP *abbr* (*BRIT col*: = weather permitting) tempo permettendo ♦ *n abbr* = **word processing; word processor**.

WPC *n abbr* (*BRIT*: = woman police constable) donna poliziotto.

wpm *abbr* (= words per minute) p.p.m.

WRAC *n abbr* (*BRIT*: = Women's Royal Army Corps*) ausiliarie dell'esercito.

WRAF *n abbr* (*BRIT*: = Women's Royal Air Force*) ausiliarie dell'aeronautica militare.

wrangle ['ræŋgl] *n* litigio ♦ *vi* litigare.

wrap [ræp] *n* (*stole*) scialle *m*; (*cape*) mantellina ♦ *vt* (*also:* **~ up**) avvolgere; (*parcel*) incartare; **under ~s** segreto.

wrapper ['ræpə*] *n* (*of book*) copertina; (*on chocolate*) carta.

wrapping paper ['ræpɪŋ-] *n* carta da pacchi; (*for gift*) carta da regali.

wrath [rɔθ] *n* collera, ira.

wreak [ri:k] *vt* (*destruction*) portare, causare; **to ~ vengeance on** vendicarsi su; **to ~ havoc on** portare scompiglio in.

wreath, ~s [ri:θ, ri:ðz] *n* corona.

wreck [rɛk] *n* (*sea disaster*) naufragio; (*ship*) relitto; (*pej: person*) rottame *m* ♦ *vt* demolire; (*ship*) far naufragare; (*fig*) rovinare.

wreckage ['rɛkɪdʒ] *n* rottami *mpl*; (*of building*) macerie *fpl*; (*of ship*) relitti *mpl*.

wrecker ['rɛkə*] *n* (*US: breakdown van*) carro *m* attrezzi *inv*.

WREN [rɛn] *n abbr* (*BRIT*) membro del WRNS.

wren [rɛn] *n* (*ZOOL*) scricciolo.

wrench [rɛntʃ] *n* (*TECH*) chiave *f*; (*tug*) torsione *f* brusca; (*fig*) strazio ♦ *vt* strappare; storcere; **to ~ sth from** strappare qc a *or* da.

wrest [rɛst] *vt*: **to ~ sth from sb** strappare qc a qn.

wrestle ['rɛsl] *vi*: **to ~ (with sb)** lottare (con qn); **to ~ with** (*fig*) combattere *or* lottare contro.

wrestler ['rɛslə*] *n* lottatore/trice.

wrestling ['rɛslɪŋ] *n* lotta; (*also:* **all-in ~**: *BRIT*) catch *m*, lotta libera.

wrestling match *n* incontro di lotta (*or*

lotta libera).

wretch [retʃ] *n* disgraziato/a, sciagurato/a; **little** ~! (*often humorous*) birbante!

wretched ['retʃɪd] *adj* disgraziato(a); (*col*: *weather, holiday*) orrendo(a), orribile; (: *child, dog*) pestifero(a).

wriggle ['rɪgl] *n* contorsione *f* ♦ *vi* dimenarsi; (*snake, worm*) serpeggiare, muoversi serpeggiando.

wring *pt, pp* **wrung** [rɪŋ, rʌŋ] *vt* torcere; (*wet clothes*) strizzare; (*fig*): **to ~ sth out of** strappare qc a.

wringer ['rɪŋə*] *n* strizzatoio (manuale).

wringing ['rɪŋɪŋ] *adj* (*also*: ~ **wet**) bagnato(a) fradicio(a).

wrinkle ['rɪŋkl] *n* (*on skin*) ruga; (*on paper etc*) grinza ♦ *vt* corrugare; raggrinzire ♦ *vi* corrugarsi; raggrinzirsi.

wrinkled ['rɪŋkld], **wrinkly** ['rɪŋklɪ] *adj* (*fabric, paper*) stropicciato(a); (*surface*) corrugato(a), increspato(a); (*skin*) rugoso(a).

wrist [rɪst] *n* polso.

wristband ['rɪstbænd] *n* (*of shirt*) polsino; (*of watch*) cinturino.

wrist watch *n* orologio da polso.

writ [rɪt] *n* ordine *m*; mandato; **to issue a ~ against sb, serve a ~ on sb** notificare un mandato di comparizione a qn.

write, *pt* **wrote**, *pp* **written** [raɪt, rəut, 'rɪtn] *vt, vi* scrivere; **to ~ sb a letter** scrivere una lettera a qn.

▶**write away** *vi*: **to ~ away for** (*information*) richiedere per posta; (*goods*) ordinare per posta.

▶**write down** *vt* annotare; (*put in writing*) mettere per iscritto.

▶**write off** *vt* (*debt*) cancellare; (*depreciate*) deprezzare; (*smash up: car*) distruggere.

▶**write out** *vt* scrivere; (*copy*) ricopiare.

▶**write up** *vt* redigere.

write-off ['raɪtɔf] *n* perdita completa; **the car is a ~** la macchina va bene per il demolitore.

write-protect ['raɪtprə'tɛkt] *vt* (*COMPUT*) proteggere contro scrittura.

writer ['raɪtə*] *n* autore/trice, scrittore/trice.

write-up ['raɪtʌp] *n* (*review*) recensione *f*.

writhe [raɪð] *vi* contorcersi.

writing ['raɪtɪŋ] *n* scrittura; (*of author*) scritto, opera; **in ~** per iscritto; **in my own ~** scritto di mio pugno.

writing desk *n* scrivania, scrittoio.

writing paper *n* carta da scrivere.

written ['rɪtn] *pp of* **write**.

WRNS *n abbr* (*BRIT*: = *Women's Royal Naval Service*) ausiliarie della marina militare.

wrong [rɔŋ] *adj* sbagliato(a); (*not suitable*) inadatto(a); (*wicked*) cattivo(a); (*unfair*) ingiusto(a) ♦ *adv* in modo sbagliato, erroneamente ♦ *n* (*evil*) male *m*; (*injustice*) torto ♦ *vt* fare torto a; **to be ~** (*answer*) essere sbagliato; (*in doing, saying*) avere torto; **you are ~ to do it** ha torto a farlo; **you are ~ about that, you've got it ~** si sbaglia; **to be in the ~** avere torto; **what's ~?** cosa c'è che non va?; **there's nothing ~** va tutto bene; **what's ~ with the car?** cos'ha la macchina che non va?; **to go ~** (*person*) sbagliarsi; (*plan*) fallire, non riuscire; (*machine*) guastarsi; **it's ~ to steal, stealing is ~** è male rubare.

wrongdoer ['rɔŋduːə*] *n* malfattore/trice.

wrong-foot [rɔŋ'fut] *vt* (*SPORT; also fig*) prendere in contropiede.

wrongful ['rɔŋful] *adj* illegittimo(a); ingiusto(a); **~ dismissal** licenziamento ingiustificato.

wrongly ['rɔŋlɪ] *adv* (*accuse, dismiss*) a torto; (*answer, do, count*) erroneamente; (*treat*) ingiustamente.

wrong number *n*: **you have the ~** (*TEL*) ha sbagliato numero.

wrong side *n* (*of cloth*) rovescio.

wrote [rəut] *pt of* **write**.

wrought [rɔːt] *adj*: **~ iron** ferro battuto.

wrung [rʌŋ] *pt, pp of* **wring**.

WRVS *n abbr* (*BRIT*) = *Women's Royal Voluntary Service*.

wry [raɪ] *adj* storto(a).

wt. *abbr* = **weight**.

WV, W. Va. *abbr* (*US*) = *West Virginia*.

WWW *n abbr* (= *World Wide Web*): **the ~** la Rete.

WY, Wyo. *abbr* (*US*) = *Wyoming*.

WYSIWYG ['wɪzɪwɪg] *abbr* (*COMPUT*) = *what you see is what you get*.

X x

X, x [ɛks] *n* (*letter*) X, x *f or m inv*; (*BRIT CINE*: *old*) ≈ film vietato ai minori di 18 anni; **X for Xmas** ≈ X come Xeres.

Xerox ® ['zɪərɔks] *n* (*also*: ~ **machine**) fotocopiatrice *f*; (*photocopy*) fotocopia ♦ *vt* fotocopiare.

XL *abbr* = *extra large*.

Xmas ['ɛksməs] *n abbr* = **Christmas**.

X-rated ['ɛks'reɪtɪd] *adj* (*US: film*) ≈ vietato ai minori di 18 anni.
X-ray ['ɛks'reɪ] *n* raggio X; (*photograph*) radiografia ♦ *vt* radiografare; **to have an** ~ farsi fare una radiografia.
xylophone ['zaɪləfəun] *n* xilofono.

Y y

Y, y [waɪ] *n* (*letter*) Y, y *f or m inv*; **Y for Yellow,** (*US*) **Y for Yoke** ≈ Y come Yacht.
yacht [jɔt] *n* panfilo, yacht *m inv*.
yachting ['jɔtɪŋ] *n* yachting *m*, sport *m* della vela.
yachtsman ['jɔtsmən] *n* yachtsman *m inv*.
yam [jæm] *n* igname *m*; (*sweet potato*) patata dolce.
Yank [jæŋk], **Yankee** ['jæŋkɪ] *n* (*pej*) yankee *m/f inv*, nordamericano/a.
yank [jæŋk] *n* strattone *m* ♦ *vt* tirare, dare uno strattone a.
yap [jæp] *vi* (*dog*) guaire.
yard [jɑːd] *n* (*of house etc*) cortile *m*; (*US: garden*) giardino; (*measure*) iarda (= *914 mm; 3 feet*); **builder's** ~ deposito di materiale da costruzione.
yardstick ['jɑːdstɪk] *n* (*fig*) misura, criterio.
yarn [jɑːn] *n* filato; (*tale*) lunga storia.
yawn [jɔːn] *n* sbadiglio ♦ *vi* sbadigliare.
yawning ['jɔːnɪŋ] *adj* (*gap*) spalancato(a).
yd. *abbr* = **yard.**
yeah [jɛə] *adv* (*col*) sì.
year [jɪə*] *n* (*gen, SCOL*) anno; (*referring to harvest, wine etc*) annata; **every** ~ ogni anno, tutti gli anni; **this** ~ quest'anno; ~ **in,** ~ **out** anno dopo anno; **she's three** ~**s old** ha tre anni; **a** *or* **per** ~ all'anno.
yearbook ['jɪəbuk] *n* annuario.
yearly ['jɪəlɪ] *adj* annuale ♦ *adv* annualmente; **twice-**~ semestrale.
yearn [jɔːn] *vi*: **to** ~ **for sth/to do** desiderare ardentemente qc/di fare.
yearning ['jɔːnɪŋ] *n* desiderio intenso.
yeast [jiːst] *n* lievito.
yell [jɛl] *n* urlo ♦ *vi* urlare.
yellow ['jɛləu] *adj* giallo(a).
yellow fever *n* febbre *f* gialla.
yellowish ['jɛləuɪʃ] *adj* giallastro(a), giallognolo(a).
Yellow Pages ® *npl* pagine *fpl* gialle.
Yellow Sea *n*: **the** ~ il mar Giallo.

yelp [jɛlp] *n* guaito, uggiolio ♦ *vi* guaire, uggiolare.
Yemen ['jɛmən] *n* Yemen *m*.
yen [jɛn] *n* (*currency*) yen *m inv*; (*craving*): ~ **for/to do** gran voglia di/di fare.
yeoman ['jəumən] *n*: **Y**~ **of the Guard** guardiano della Torre di Londra.
yes [jɛs] *adv, n* sì (*m inv*); **to say** ~ **(to)** dire di sì (a), acconsentire (a).
yesterday ['jɛstədɪ] *adv, n* ieri (*m inv*); ~ **morning/evening** ieri mattina/sera; **the day before** ~ l'altro ieri; **all day** ~ ieri tutto il giorno.
yet [jɛt] *adv* ancora; già ♦ *conj* ma, tuttavia; **it is not finished** ~ non è ancora finito; **the best** ~ il migliore finora; **as** ~ finora; ~ **again** di nuovo; **must you go just** ~? deve andarsene di già?, **a few days** ~ ancora qualche giorno.
yew [juː] *n* tasso (*albero*).
Y-fronts ® ['waɪfrʌnts] *npl* (*BRIT*) slip *m inv* da uomo.
YHA *n abbr* (*BRIT*: = *Youth Hostels Association*) Y.H.A. *f.*
Yiddish ['jɪdɪʃ] *n* yiddish *m*.
yield [jiːld] *n* resa, (*of crops etc*) raccolto ♦ *vt* produrre, rendere; (*surrender*) cedere ♦ *vi* cedere; (*US AUT*) dare la precedenza; **a** ~ **of 5%** un profitto *or* un interesse del 5%.
YMCA *n abbr* (= *Young Men's Christian Association*) Y.M.C.A. *m.*
yob(bo) ['jɔb(əu)] *n* (*BRIT col*) bullo.
yodel ['jəudl] *vi* cantare lo jodel *or* alla tirolese.
yoga ['jəugə] *n* yoga *m.*
yog(h)ourt, yog(h)urt ['jəugət] *n* iogurt *m inv.*
yoke [jəuk] *n* giogo ♦ *vt* (*also*: ~ **together**: *oxen*) aggiogare.
yolk [jəuk] *n* tuorlo, rosso d'uovo.
yonder ['jɔndə*] *adv* là.
yonks [jɔŋks] *npl*: **for** ~ (*col*) da una vita.
Yorks [jɔːks] *abbr* (*BRIT*) = *Yorkshire.*

═══════════════════════════ *KEYWORD*

you [juː] *pron* **1** (*subject*) tu; (*: polite form*) lei; (*: pl*) voi; (*: very formal*) loro; ~ **Italians enjoy your food** a voi italiani piace mangiare bene; ~ **and I will go** andiamo io e te (*or* lei ed io); **if I was** *or* **were** ~ se fossi in te (*or* lei *etc*)
2 (*object: direct*) ti; la; vi; loro (*after vb*); (*: indirect*) ti; le; vi; loro (*after vb*); **I know** ~ ti (*or* la *or* vi) conosco; **I'll see** ~ **tomorrow** ci vediamo domani; **I gave it to** ~ te l'ho dato; gliel'ho dato; ve l'ho dato; l'ho dato loro

3 (*stressed, after prep, in comparisons*) te; lei; voi; loro; **I told YOU to do it** ho detto a TE (*or a* LEI *etc*) di farlo; **she's younger than** ~ è più giovane di te (*or lei etc*) **4** (*impers: one*) si; **fresh air does** ~ **good** l'aria fresca fa bene; ~ **never know** non si sa mai.

you'd [ju:d] = **you had; you would.**
you'll [ju:l] = **you will; you shall.**
young [jʌŋ] *adj* giovane ♦ *npl* (*of animal*) piccoli *mpl*; (*people*): **the** ~ i giovani, la gioventù; **a** ~ **man** un giovanotto; **a** ~ **lady** una signorina; **a** ~ **woman** una giovane donna; **the** ~**er generation** la nuova generazione; **my** ~**er brother** il mio fratello minore.
youngish ['jʌŋɪʃ] *adj* abbastanza giovane.
youngster ['jʌŋstə*] *n* giovanotto/a; (*child*) bambino/a.
your [jɔ:*] *adj* il(la) tuo(a), *pl* i(le) tuoi(tue); (*polite form*) il(la) suo(a), *pl* i(le) suoi(sue); (*pl*) il(la) vostro(a), *pl* i(le) vostri(e); (: *very formal*) il(la) loro, *pl* i(le) loro.
you're [juə*] = **you are.**
yours [jɔ:z] *pron* il(la) tuo(a), *pl* i(le) tuoi(tue); (*polite form*) il(la) suo(a), *pl* i(le) suoi(sue); (*pl*) il(la) vostro(a), *pl* i(le) vostri(e); (: *very formal*) il(la) loro, *pl* i(le) loro; ~ **sincerely/faithfully** (*in letter*) cordiali/distinti saluti; **a friend of** ~ un tuo (*or* suo *etc*) amico; **is it** ~? è tuo (*or* suo *etc*)?
yourself [jɔ:'sɛlf] *pron* (*reflexive*) ti; (: *polite form*) si; (*after prep*) te; se; (*emphatic*) tu stesso(a); lei stesso(a); **you** ~ **told me** me l'hai detto proprio tu, tu stesso me l'hai detto.
yourselves [jɔ:'sɛlvz] *pl pron* (*reflexive*) vi; (: *polite form*) si; (*after prep*) voi; loro; (*emphatic*) voi stessi(e); loro stessi(e).
youth [ju:θ] *n* gioventù *f*; (*young man: pl* ~**s** [ju:ðz]) giovane *m*, ragazzo *m*; **in my** ~ da giovane, quando ero giovane.
youth club *n* centro giovanile.
youthful ['ju:θful] *adj* giovane; da giovane; giovanile.
youthfulness ['ju:θfəlnɪs] *n* giovinezza.
youth hostel *n* ostello della gioventù.
youth movement *n* movimento giovanile.
you've [ju:v] = **you have.**
yowl [jaul] *n* (*of dog, person*) urlo; (*of cat*) miagolio ♦ *vi* urlare; miagolare.
yr *abbr* = **year.**
YT *abbr* (*Canada*) = **Yukon Territory.**
Yugoslav ['ju:gəusla:v] *adj, n* jugoslavo(a).
Yugoslavia [ju:gəu'sla:vɪə] *n* Jugoslavia.
Yugoslavian [ju:gəu'sla:vɪən] *adj, n*

jugoslavo(a).
Yule log [ju:l-] *n* ceppo nel caminetto a Natale.
yuppie ['jʌpɪ] *adj, n* (*col*) yuppie (*m/f*) inv.
YWCA *n abbr* (= *Young Women's Christian Association*) Y.W.C.A. *m.*

Z z

Z, z [zɛd, (*US*) zi:] *n* (*letter*) Z, z *f or m* inv; **Z for Zebra** ≈ Z come Zara.
Zaire [za:'ɪə*] *n* Zaire *m.*
Zambia ['zæmbɪə] *n* Zambia *m.*
Zambian ['zæmbɪən] *adj, n* zambiano(a).
zany ['zeɪnɪ] *adj* un po' pazzo(a).
zap [zæp] *vt* (*COMPUT*) cancellare.
zeal [zi:l] *n* zelo; entusiasmo.
zealot ['zɛlət] *n* zelota *m/f.*
zealous ['zɛləs] *adj* zelante; premuroso(a).
zebra ['zi:brə] *n* zebra.
zebra crossing *n* (*BRIT*) (passaggio pedonale a) strisce *fpl*, zebre *fpl.*
zenith ['zɛnɪθ] *n* zenit *m* inv; (*fig*) culmine *m.*
zero ['zɪərəu] *n* zero; **5° below** ~ 5° sotto zero.
zero hour *n* l'ora zero.
zero option *n* (*POL*) opzione *f* zero.
zero-rated ['zɪərəu'reɪtɪd] *adj* (*BRIT*) ad aliquota zero.
zest [zɛst] *n* gusto; (*CULIN*) buccia.
zigzag ['zɪgzæg] *n* zigzag *m* inv ♦ *vi* zigzagare.
Zimbabwe [zɪm'ba:bwɪ] *n* Zimbabwe *m.*
Zimbabwean [zɪm'ba:bwɪən] *adj* dello Zimbabwe.
Zimmer ® ['zɪmə*] *n* (*also*: ~ **frame**) deambulatore *m.*
zinc [zɪŋk] *n* zinco.
Zionism ['zaɪənɪzəm] *n* sionismo.
Zionist ['zaɪənɪst] *adj* sionistico(a) ♦ *n* sionista *m/f.*
zip [zɪp] *n* (*also*: ~ **fastener,** (*US*) ~**per**) chiusura *f or* cerniera *f* lampo inv; (*energy*) energia, forza ♦ *vt* (*also*: ~ **up**) chiudere con una cerniera lampo.
zip code *n* (*US*) codice *m* di avviamento postale.
zither ['zɪðə*] *n* cetra.
zodiac ['zəudɪæk] *n* zodiaco.
zombie ['zɔmbɪ] *n* (*fig*): **like a** ~ come un morto che cammina.

zone [zəun] *n* zona.
zoo [zuː] *n* zoo *m inv*.
zoological [zuə'lɔdʒɪkl] *adj* zoologico(a).
zoologist [zuː'ɔlədʒɪst] *n* zoologo/a.
zoology [zuː'ɔlədʒɪ] *n* zoologia.
zoom [zuːm] *vi*: **to ~ past** sfrecciare; **to ~ in**

(on sb/sth) (*PHOT, CINE*) zumare (su qn/qc).
zoom lens *n* zoom *m inv*, obiettivo a
  focale variabile.
zucchini [zuː'kiːnɪ] *n* (*pl inv*) (*US*) zucchina.
Zulu ['zuːluː] *adj*, *n* zulù (*m/f*) *inv*.
Zürich ['zjuərɪk] *n* Zurigo *f*.

ITALIAN IN ACTION

INGLESE ATTIVO

Contributors/Collaboratori

Loredana Riu   Daphne Day   Gabriella Bacchelli

Coordination/Coordinamento

Isobel Gordon

INTRODUZIONE

Il supplemento INGLESE ATTIVO vi aiuterà ad esprimervi in modo semplice e corretto, usando espressioni tipiche della lingua realmente parlata.

La sezione LOCUZIONI DI BASE contiene centinaia di frasi seguite dalla traduzione degli elementi chiave, utilizzabili nella costruzione di moltissime altre frasi.

Nella sezione sulla corrispondenza troverete diversi modelli di lettere in inglese, sia personali che commerciali, le formule più comuni usate per iniziare e concludere una lettera, indicazioni su dove e come scrivere indirizzo e mittente sulla busta e così via. Troverete anche un esempio di curriculum vitae, una domanda di assunzione e utili consigli su come adattare questi modelli alle vostre particolari esigenze.

C'è inoltre una sezione a parte sull'invio di fax e di messaggi di posta elettronica e sui diversi tipi di conversazioni telefoniche.

Siamo sicuri che, assieme al dizionario, il supplemento INGLESE ATTIVO, sarà uno strumento prezioso per aiutarvi a scrivere e a comunicare in inglese nel modo più corretto, naturale e adatto ad ogni situazione.

INDICE

INTRODUCTION

The aim of ITALIAN IN ACTION is to help you express yourself simply but correctly in fluent, natural Italian.

The SENTENCE BUILDER section provides hundreds of phrases in which the key elements have been translated, providing an invaluable point of reference when you then construct your own sentences.

The section on correspondence provides practical models of personal and business letters, job applications and CVs, together with examples of standard opening and closing formulae and information on how to address an envelope. This section also offers guidance notes to help the user adapt these models to his/her needs.

A separate section covers fax and e-mail correspondence as well as all the expressions you might need to make different types of phone calls.

We hope you will find ITALIAN IN ACTION both relevant and useful and that, used in conjunction with the dictionary, it will improve your understanding and enjoyment of Italian.

CONTENTS

❏ *Gusti e preferenze*

Per dire ciò che ci piace

I like cakes.	*Mi piacciono ...*
I like things to be in their proper place.	*Mi piace che ...*
I really liked the film.	*... mi è piaciuto molto.*
I love going to clubs.	*Adoro ...*
What I like best about Matthew are his eyes.	*Quello che mi piace di più ...*
What I enjoy most is an evening with friends.	*La cosa che mi piace di più è ...*
I very much enjoyed the trip to the vineyards.	*... mi è piaciuta molto.*
I've never tasted **anything better than** this chicken.	*... niente di meglio di ...*
I've got a weakness for chocolate cakes.	*Ho un debole per ...*
You can't beat a good cup of tea.	*Non c'è niente come ...*
There's nothing quite like a nice hot bath!	*Non c'è niente di meglio di ...*
My favourite dish is risotto.	*Il mio ... preferito ...*
Reading is **one of my favourite** pastimes.	*... uno dei miei ... preferiti.*
I don't mind being alone.	*Non mi dispiace ...*

Per dire ciò che non ci piace

I don't like fish.	*Non mi piace ...*
I don't like him **at all**.	*... non mi piace per niente.*
I'm not very keen on speaking in public.	*Non mi piace molto ...*
I'm not particularly keen on the idea.	*Non è che ... mi faccia impazzire.*
I hate chemistry.	*Odio ...*
I loathe sport.	*Detesto ...*
I can't stand being lied to.	*Non sopporto ...*
If there's one thing I hate it's ironing.	*Se c'è una cosa che odio è ...*

Per esprimere una preferenza

I prefer pop **to** classical music.	*Preferisco ... alla ...*
I would rather live in Rome.	*Preferirei ...*
I'd rather starve **than** ask him a favour.	*Preferirei ... piuttosto che ...*

Per esprimere indifferenza

It's all the same to me.	*Per me fa lo stesso.*
I have no particular preference.	*Non ho preferenze.*
As you like.	*Come vuoi.*
It doesn't matter in the least.	*Non ha nessuna importanza.*
I don't mind.	*È indifferente.*

Rivolgendosi ad altri

Do you like chocolate?	*Ti piace ...*
Do you like cooking?	*Ti piace ...*
Which do you like better: football or cricket?	*Cosa preferisci ...*
Which would you rather have: the red one or the black one?	*Quale preferisci ...*
Do you prefer living in the town or in the country?	*Preferisci ...*
What do you like best on television?	*Cosa ti piace di più ...*

❏ *Opinioni*

Per chiedere l'opinione di qualcuno

What do you think about it?	*Cosa ne pensa?*
What do you think about divorce?	*Cosa pensa del ...*
What do you think of his behaviour?	*Come ti sembra ...*
I'd like to know what you think of his work.	*Vorrei sapere cosa pensi del ...*
I would like to know your views on this.	*Mi piacerebbe sapere il suo parere o la sua opinione su ...*
What is your opinion on the team's chances of success?	*Qual è la sua opinione sulle ...*
Could you give me your opinion on this proposal?	*Potrebbe dirmi cosa pensa di ...*
In your opinion, are men and women equal?	*A suo parere o avviso ...*
In your opinion, is this the best solution?	*Secondo lei ...*

Per esprimere un'opinione

You are right.	*Hai ragione.*
He is wrong.	*Ha torto.*
He was wrong to resign.	*Ha sbagliato a ...*
I think it ought to be possible.	*Penso che ...*
I think it's a bit premature.	*Credo che sia ...*
I think it's quite natural.	*Mi sembra che sia ...*
Personally, I think that it's a waste of money.	*Personalmente, ritengo che sia ...*
I have the impression that her parents don't understand her.	*Ho l'impressione che ...*
I'm sure he is completely sincere.	*Sono sicuro che ...*
I'm convinced that there are other possibilities.	*Sono convinto che ...*
In my opinion, he hasn't changed.	*A mio parere o avviso ...*
In my view, he's their best player.	*Secondo me ...*

Per rispondere senza dare un'opinione

It depends.	*Dipende.*
It all depends on what you mean by patriotism.	*Dipende da cosa intendi per ...*
I'd rather not express an opinion.	*Preferisco non pronunciarmi.*
Actually, I've never thought about it.	*A dire il vero, non ci ho mai pensato.*

❏ *Approvazione e accordo*

I think it's an excellent idea.	*Mi sembra una magnifica idea.*
What a good idea!	*Ottima idea!*
I was very impressed by his speech.	*Ho apprezzato moltissimo ...*
It's a very good thing.	*È un'ottima cosa.*
I think you're right to be wary.	*Secondo me hai ragione a ...*
Newspapers are right to publish these stories.	*... fanno bene a ...*

You were **right to** leave your bags in left-luggage.	Hai fatto bene a ...
Third World countries **rightly believe that** most pollution comes from developed countries.	... ritengono giustamente che ...
You're quite **justified in** complaining.	Non hai torto a ...
I share this view.	Condivido l'opinione.
I fully share your concern.	Condivido pienamente la sua ...
We support the creation of jobs.	Siamo favorevoli alla ...
We are in favour of a united Europe.	Siamo a favore dell' ...
It is true that mistakes were made.	È vero che ...
I agree with you.	Sono d'accordo con lei.
I entirely agree with you.	Sono assolutamente d'accordo con lei.

❏ *Disapprovazione e dissenso*

I think he was wrong to borrow so much money.	Trovo che abbia sbagliato a ...
It's a pity that you didn't tell me.	È un peccato che ...
It is regrettable that they allowed this to happen.	C'è da rammaricarsi che ...
I dislike the idea **intensely.**	... non mi piace per niente.
I can't stand lies.	Non sopporto ...
We are against hunting.	Siamo contro ...
We do not condone violence.	Crediamo che ... sia ingiustificabile o non abbia scusanti.
I am opposed to compulsory screening.	Sono contrario al ...
I don't share this point of view.	Non condivido questo punto di vista.
I am disappointed by his attitude.	Sono deluso del ...
I am deeply disappointed.	Sono profondamente deluso.
You shouldn't have said that.	Non avresti dovuto ...
What gives him the right to act like this?	Che diritto ha di ...
I disagree.	Non sono d'accordo.
We don't agree with them.	Non siamo d'accordo con ...
I totally disagree with what he said.	Non sono affatto d'accordo con ...

It is not true to say that the disaster was inevitable.　　*Non è vero che ...*
You are wrong!　　*Ti sbagli!*

❏ *Scuse*

Per chiedere scusa

Sorry.　　*Scusa.*
Oh, sorry! I've got the wrong number.　　*Oh, scusi!*
Sorry to bother you.　　*Scusi se la disturbo.*
I'm sorry I woke you.　　*Scusa se ...*
I'm terribly sorry about the misunderstanding.　　*Sono terribilmente spiacente per ...*
I do apologize.　　*La prego di scusarmi.*
We hope our readers **will** excuse this oversight.　　*Preghiamo ... di ...*

... ammettendo responsabilità

It's my fault; I should have left earlier.　　*È colpa mia, sarei dovuto ...*
I shouldn't have laughed at her.　　*Non avrei dovuto ...*
We were wrong not to check this information.　　*Abbiamo sbagliato a non ...*
I take full responsibility for what I did.　　*Mi assumo la piena responsabilità delle ...*
If only I had done my homework!　　*Se solo avessi ...*

... declinando responsabilità

It's not my fault.　　*Non è colpa mia.*
It isn't my fault if we're late.　　*Non è colpa mia se ...*
I didn't do it on purpose.　　*Non l'ho fatto apposta.*
I had no option.　　*Non ho potuto fare altrimenti.*

But I thought that it was okay to park here.　　*Pensavo che ...*
I thought I was doing the right thing in warning him.　　*Credevo di fare bene ad ...*

Per esprimere rammarico

I'm sorry, but it's impossible.	*Mi dispiace, ma ...*
I'm afraid we're fully booked.	*Purtroppo ...*
Unfortunately we are unable to meet your request.	*Purtroppo non siamo in grado di ...*

❏ *Spiegazioni*

Cause

I didn't buy anything **because** I had no money.	*... perché ...*
I arrived late **because of** the traffic.	*... a causa del ...*
Since you insist, I'll come again tomorrow.	*Visto o dato che ...*
As I lived near the library, I used it a lot.	*Siccome ...*
I got through it **thanks to** the support of my friends.	*... grazie all'...*
Given the present situation, finding a job will be difficult.	*Vista o Data ...*
Given that there is an economic crisis, it is difficult to find work.	*Dato che ...*
Considering how many problems we had, we did well.	*Considerando ...*
It was a broken axle **that caused** the derailment.	*È stata ... che ha causato ...*
He resigned **for** health **reasons.**	*... per motivi di ...*
The theatre is closing, **due to** lack of funds.	*... per ...*
The project was abandoned **owing to** legal problems.	*... a causa di ...*
Many cancers **are linked to** smoking.	*... sono legati al ...*
The problem is that people are afraid of computers.	*Il problema è che ...*
The drop in sales **is the result of** high interest rates.	*... è il risultato dei ...*
The quarrel **resulted from** a misunderstanding.	*... ha avuto origine da ...*

Per spiegare le conseguenze di una situazione

I have to leave tonight; **so** I can't come with you.	*... quindi ...*
Distribution has been improved **so that** readers now get their newspaper earlier.	*... cosicché ...*
This cider is fermented for a very short time and is **consequently** low in alcohol.	*... di conseguenza ...*

Our lack of consultation **has resulted in** a duplication of effort.	... ha avuto come conseguenza ...
That's why they are easy to remember.	Ecco perché ...

❏ *Paragoni*

Gambling **can be compared to** a drug.	Si può paragonare ... a ...
The gas has a smell **that can be compared to** rotten eggs.	... paragonabile a ...
The shape of Italy **is often compared to** a boot.	... è spesso paragonata a ...
The noise **was comparable to** that of a large motorbike.	... era paragonabile a ...
Africa is still underpopulated **compared with** Asia.	Paragonata all'...
In the UK, the rate of inflation increased slightly **compared to** the previous year.	... rispetto all'...
What is so special about a holiday in Florida **as compared to** one in Spain?	... a paragone di ...
This story **is like** a fairy tale.	... sembra ...
He loved this countryside, which **reminded him of** Ireland.	... gli ricordava ...
Frightening levels of unemployment, **reminiscent of those** of the 30s.	... che ricordano ...
The snowboard **is the equivalent** on snow **of** the skateboard.	... è l'equivalente dello ...
This sum **corresponds to** six months' salary.	... corrisponde a ...
A 'bap'? **It's the same thing as** a bread roll.	È esattamente come ...
It comes to the same thing in terms of calories.	... è perfettamente equivalente.
This record **is no better and no worse than** the others.	... non è né meglio né peggio degli ...

Sottolineando le differenze ...

No catastrophe **can compare with** Chernobyl.	... non ha uguali.
Modern factories **cannot be compared with** those our grandparents worked in.	... non si possono paragonare con ...
The actions of this group **are in no way comparable to** those of terrorists.	... non hanno niente in comune con ...
The newspaper reports **differ** on this point.	... si differenziano ...

The history of the United States **in no way resembles** our own.	*... non assomiglia affatto alla ...*
There are worse things than losing a European cup final.	*C'è di peggio che ...*
This film **is less** interesting **than** his first one.	*... è meno ... del ...*
Women's life expectancy is 81 years, **while** men's is 72.	*... mentre ...*
While the consumption of wine and beer is decreasing, the consumption of bottled water is increasing.	*Mentre ...*

❏ *Richieste e offerte*

Richieste

I'd like another beer.	*Vorrei*
I'd like to know the times of trains to Edinburgh.	*Vorrei ...*
Could you give us a hand?	*Potresti ...*
Can you tell Eleanor the good news?	*Puoi ...*
Could you please show me the way out?	*Potrebbe per cortesia ...*
Could I ask you for a few minutes of your time?	*Può concedermi ...*
Be an angel, pop to the baker's for me.	*Sii gentile ...*
If you wouldn't mind waiting for a moment.	*Se non le dispiace ...*
Would you mind opening the window?	*Le spiacerebbe ...*
Would you be very kind and save my seat for me?	*Potrebbe farmi la cortesia di ...*
I would be grateful if you could reply as soon as possible.	*Le sarei grato se ...*

Offerte

I can come and pick you up **if** you like.	*Posso ... se ...*
I could go with you.	*Potrei ...*
Do you fancy a bit of Stilton?	*Ti va ...*
How about a pear tart?	*Che ne dici di ...*
Would you like to see my photos?	*Vi piacerebbe ...*

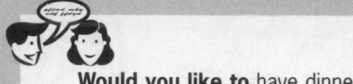

Would you like to have dinner with me one evening?   *Ti andrebbe di ...*

Do you want me to go and get your car?   *Vuoi che ...*

❏ *Consigli e suggerimenti*

Per chiedere un consiglio

What would you do, if you were me?   *Cosa faresti, al posto mio?*

Would you accept, **if you were me?**   *Se fossi in me ...*

What's your opinion on this?   *Cosa ne pensi?*

What, in your opinion, should be done to reduce pollution?   *Cosa bisognerebbe fare, secondo voi, per ...*

What would you advise?   *Cosa consigli?*

What would you advise me to do?   *Cosa mi consigli di fare?*

Which would you recommend, Majorca or Ibiza?   *Quale ci consiglia ...*

If we were to sponsor a player, **who would you recommend?**   *... chi raccomanderesti?*

What strategy **do you suggest?**   *Che ... proponi?*

How would you deal with unemployment?   *Come affrontereste ...*

Per dare un suggerimento

If I were you, I'd be a bit wary.   *Se fossi in te ...*

If I were you I wouldn't say anything.   *Al posto tuo ...*

Take my advice, buy your tickets in advance.   *Se posso darle un consiglio ...*

A word of advice: read the instructions.   *Un consiglio ...*

A useful tip: always have some pasta in your cupboard.   *Un consiglio ...*

As you like languages, **you ought to** train as a translator.   *... dovresti ...*

You should see a specialist.   *Dovresti ...*

You would do well to see a solicitor.   *Faresti bene a ...*

You would do better to spend the money on a new car.   *Faresti meglio a ...*

You could perhaps ask someone to go with you.	Forse potresti ...
You could try being a little more understanding.	Potresti ...
Perhaps you should speak to a plumber about it.	Forse dovresti ...
Perhaps we ought to try a different approach.	Forse dovremmo ...
Why don't you phone him?	Perché non ...
How about renting a video?	E se ...
How about 3 March at 10.30am?	lo proporrei ...
It might be better to give her money rather than jewellery.	Forse sarebbe meglio ...
It would be better to wait a bit.	Sarebbe meglio ...

Avvertimenti

I warn you, I intend to get my own back.	Ti avverto ...
I'd better warn you that he knows you did it.	Ti avverto che ...
Don't forget to keep a copy of your income tax return.	Ricordati di ...
Remember: appearances can be deceptive.	Non fidarti: l'apparenza inganna.
Beware of buying tickets from touts.	Diffidate dei ...
Whatever you do, don't leave your camera in the car.	Soprattutto, non ... mai ...
If you don't book early you risk being disappointed.	... rischi di ...

❏ Intenzioni e desideri

Per chiedere a qualcuno cosa intenda fare

What are you going to do?	Cosa pensi di fare?
What will you do if you fail your exams?	Cosa farai se ...
What are you going to do when you get back? Do you have anything planned?	Cosa conti di fare ... Hai dei progetti?
Can we expect you next Sunday?	Vi aspettiamo ...
Are you planning to spend all of the holiday here?	Conti di ...
Are you planning on staying long?	Conti di ...

What are you planning to do with your collection?	*Cosa conti di fare della ...*
What are you thinking of doing?	*Cosa pensi di fare?*
Do you intend to go into teaching?	*Hai intenzione di ...*
Are you thinking of making another film in Europe?	*Conta di ...*

Per esprimere le proprie intenzioni

I was planning to go to New York on 8 July.	*Pensavo di ...*
She plans to go to India for a year.	*Prevede di ...*
There are plans to build a new stadium.	*È prevista ...*
The bank **intends to** close a hundred branches.	*... ha intenzione di ...*
I am thinking of giving up politics.	*Sto pensando di ...*
I have decided to get a divorce.	*Ho deciso di ...*
I have made up my mind to stop smoking.	*Ho deciso di ...*
We never had any intention of talking to the press.	*Non è mai stata nostra intenzione ...*
That's settled, we'll go to Florida in May.	*È deciso ...*
For me, living abroad **is out of the question.**	*... è fuori discussione.*

Desideri

I'd like to be able to play as well as him.	*Vorrei ...*
I'd like to go hang-gliding.	*Mi piacerebbe ...*
I would like my photos to be published.	*Vorrei che ...*
I would like to have had a brother.	*Mi sarebbe piaciuto avere ...*
I want to act in films.	*Voglio ...*
Ian **wanted at all costs** to prevent his boss finding out.	*... voleva a tutti i costi ...*
We wish to preserve our independence.	*È nostro desiderio ...*
I hope to have children.	*Spero di ...*
We hope that children will watch this programme with their parents.	*Ci auguriamo che ...*
Do you dream of winning the lottery?	*Sogni di ...*
I dream of having a big house.	*Il mio sogno sarebbe di ...*

❏ *Obbligo*

I must find somewhere to live.	*Devo ...*
We really must see each other more often!	*Dobbiamo assolutamente ...*
If you're going to Poland, **you must** learn Polish.	*... devi ...*
He made his secretary answer all his calls.	*... esigeva che ...*
My mother **makes me** eat spinach.	*... mi costringe a ...*
The hijackers **demanded that** the plane fly to New York.	*... hanno preteso che ...*
A serious illness **forced me to** cancel my holiday.	*... mi ha costretto a ...*
He was obliged to borrow more and more money.	*Ha dovuto ...*
Mary **had no choice but to** invite him.	*... non poteva fare altro che ...*
The only thing you can do is say no.	*Non puoi fare altro che ...*
Many mothers **have to** work; **they have no other option.**	*... devono ... non hanno scelta.*
She had the baby adopted because **she had no other option.**	*... non poteva fare altrimenti.*
School **is compulsory** until the age of sixteen.	*... è obbligatoria ...*
It is essential to know some history, if we are to understand the situation.	*È indispensabile ...*

❏ *Permesso*

Per chiedere il permesso

Can I use the phone?	*Posso ...*
Can I ask you something?	*Posso ...*
Is it okay if I come now, or is it too early?	*Va bene se ...*
Do you mind if I smoke?	*Le dà fastidio se ...*
Do you mind if I open the window?	*Le spiace se ...*
Would you mind if I had a look in your briefcase, madam?	*Permette che ...*
Could I have permission to leave early?	*Posso ...*

Per concedere il permesso

Do as you please.	*Fate come volete.*
Go ahead!	*Faccia pure!*
No, of course I don't mind.	*No, non ci sono problemi.*
I have nothing against it.	*Non ho niente in contrario.*
Pupils **are allowed to** wear what they like.	*... possono ...*

Per negare il permesso

I forbid you to go out!	*Ti proibisco di ...*
It's forbidden.	*È vietato.*
Smoking in the toilet **is forbidden.**	*È vietato ...*
Child labour is **strictly forbidden by** a UN convention.	*... assolutamente proibito da ...*
No entry.	*Vietato l'ingresso.*
No parking.	*Sosta vietata.*
It's not allowed.	*Non è permesso.*
You are not allowed to swim in the lake.	*È vietato ...*
We weren't allowed to eat or drink while on duty.	*Non potevamo ...*
That's out of the question.	*È fuori discussione.*

❏ Certezza, probabilità e possibilità

Certezza

Undoubtedly, there will be problems.	*... senz'altro ...*
There is no doubt that the country's image has suffered.	*Non c'è alcun dubbio che ...*
It's bound to cause trouble.	*Sicuramente ...*
Clearly the company is in difficulties.	*È evidente che ...*
A foreign tourist is **quite obviously** a rare sight here.	*... ovviamente ...*
It is undeniable that she was partly to blame.	*È innegabile che ...*
I am sure you will like my brother.	*Sono sicuro che ...*
I am sure that I will win.	*Sono sicuro di ...*
I'm sure that I won't get bored working with him.	*Sono sicuro che ...*

| I am **certain that** we are on the right track. | *Sono sicuro che ...* |
| I am **convinced that** there are other solutions. | *Sono convinto che ...* |

Probabilità

The price of petrol will **probably** rise.	*È probabile che ...*
Inflation will **very probably** exceed 10%.	*Molto probabilmente ...*
It is highly probable that they will abandon the project.	*È molto probabile che ...*
The trend **is likely** to continue.	*È probabile che ...*
80% of skin problems **undoubtedly** have psychological origins.	*... senza dubbio ...*
They were **no doubt** right.	*... senza dubbio ...*
The construction work **should** start in April.	*... dovrebbero ...*
He must have forgotten to open the windows.	*Deve avere ...*

Possibilità

It's **possible.**	*È possibile.*
It is possible that they got your name from the electoral register.	*È possibile che ...*
It is not impossible that he has gone to Manchester.	*Non è da escludersi che ...*
That might be more expensive.	*Potrebbe essere ...*
He may have misunderstood.	*Potrebbe avere ...*
This virus **may** be extremely infectious.	*... potrebbe ...*
It may be that it will take time to achieve peace.	*Potrebbe darsi che ...*
In a few months everything **could** change.	*... potrebbe ...*
Perhaps I am mistaken.	*Puo darsi che ...*

❏ Dubbio, improbabilità e impossibilità

Dubbio

I'm not sure it's useful.	*Non sono sicuro che sia ...*
I'm not sure I'll manage.	*Non sono sicuro di ...*
I'm not sure that it's a good idea.	*Non sono sicuro che ...*

We **cannot be sure that** the problem will be solved.	*Non sappiamo con certezza se ...*
I very much doubt he'll adapt to not working.	*Dubito fortemente che ...*
Is it wise? **I doubt it.**	*Ne dubito.*
He began **to have doubts about** his doctor's competence.	*... dubitare della ...*
I wonder if we've made much progress in this area.	*Mi domando se ...*
There is no guarantee that a vaccine can be developed.	*Non è sicuro che ...*
Nobody knows exactly what happened.	*Non si sa esattamente ...*

Improbabilità

He **probably won't** change his mind.	*Probabilmente non ...*
It is unlikely that there'll be any tickets left.	*È poco probabile che ...*
I'd be surprised if they had your size.	*Mi sorprenderebbe se ...*
They are not likely to get the Nobel prize for Economics!	*È improbabile che ...*
There is not much chance the growth rate will exceed 1.5%.	*Ci sono poche probabilità che ...*
There's no danger we'll get bored.	*Non c'è pericolo di ...*
It would be amazing if everything went according to plan.	*Sarebbe sorprendente che ...*

Impossibilità

It's impossible.	*È impossibile.*
It is not possible for the government to introduce this bill before the recess.	*Non è possibile per ...*
This information **cannot be** wrong.	*È impossibile che ...*
There is no chance of their helping us.	*Non c'è alcuna possibilità che ...*

❏ *Saluti*

Hello!	*Ciao!* o *Salve!*
Hi!	*Ciao!*
Good morning!	*Buongiorno!*

Good afternoon!	Buonasera!
Good evening!	Buonasera!
How's it going?	Come va?
How's things?	Come vanno le cose?
How's life?	Come va la vita?
How are you?	Come sta?

Come rispondere

Very well, and you?	Molto bene grazie, e lei?
Fine, thanks.	Bene, grazie.
So-so.	Così così.
Could be worse.	Potrebbe andare peggio.

Per fare le presentazioni

This is Charles.	Questo è ...
Let me introduce you to my girlfriend.	Le presento ...
I'd like you to meet my husband.	Ti voglio far conoscere ...
I don't believe you know one another.	Non credo che vi conosciate.

Cosa dire durante le presentazioni

Pleased to meet you.	Piacere.
How do you do?	Molto piacere.
Hi, I'm Jane.	Ciao, sono ...

Accomiatarsi

Bye!	Ciao!
Goodbye!	Arrivederci!
Good night!	Buonanotte!
See you!	Ci vediamo!
See you later!	A più tardi!

See you soon!	*A presto!*
See you tomorrow!	*A domani!*
See you next week!	*Alla settimana prossima!*
See you Thursday!	*A giovedì!*

Auguri

Happy Birthday!	*Buon compleanno!*
Many happy returns!	*Cento di questi giorni!*
Happy Christmas!	*Buon Natale!*
Happy New Year!	*Buon Anno!*
Happy Anniversary!	*Buon anniversario!*
Congratulations!	*Congratulazioni!* o *Complimenti!*
Welcome!	*Benvenuti!*
Good luck!	*Buona fortuna!*
Safe journey!	*Buon viaggio!*
Get well soon!	*Guarisci presto!*
Take care!	*Stammi bene!*
Have fun!	*Divertiti!*
Cheers!	*Cin cin!* o *Salute!*
Enjoy your meal!	*Buon appetito!*

❑ *Corrispondenza*

Come intestare una lettera in Gran Bretagna

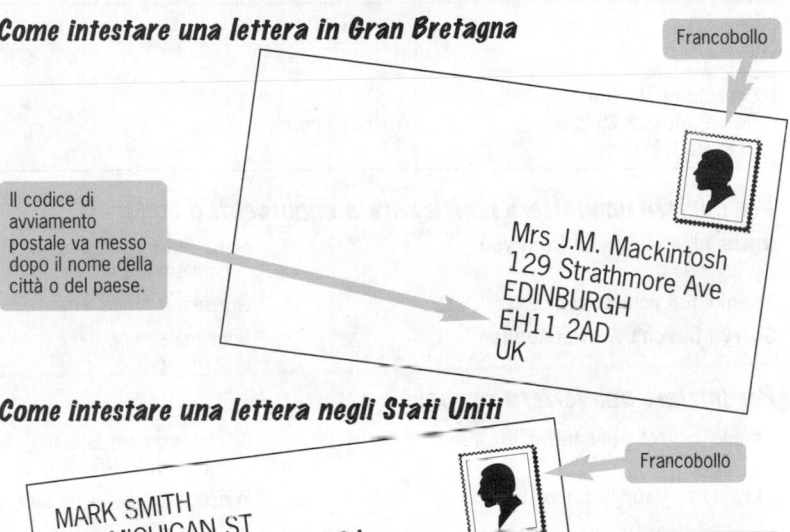

Francobollo

Il codice di avviamento postale va messo dopo il nome della città o del paese.

Mrs J.M. Mackintosh
129 Strathmore Ave
EDINBURGH
EH11 2AD
UK

Come intestare una lettera negli Stati Uniti

Francobollo

MARK SMITH
968 MICHIGAN ST
SEATTLE WA   98060-1024
USA

Il codice di avviamento postale (**zip code**) va messo dopo il nome della città e l'abbreviazione dello stato.

Abbreviazioni usate comunemente negli indirizzi

Ave = avenue	Dr = drive	Pl = place	Sq = square
Cres = crescent	Gdns = gardens	Rd = road	St = street

Formule di apertura e chiusura standard

Per scrivere a conoscenti o amici

Dear Mr and Mrs Roberts	Yours *(abbastanza formale)*
Dear Kate and Jeremy	With best wishes
Dear Aunt Jane and Uncle Alan	Love from
Dear Granny	Lots of love from *(informale)*

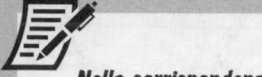

Nella corrispondenza formale

Dear Sirs Dear Sir Dear Madam Dear Sir or Madam Dear Professor Meldrum Dear Ms Gilmour	Yours faithfully Yours sincerely

Per iniziare una lettera indirizzata a conoscenti o amici

It was lovely to hear from you.

Mi ha fatto molto piacere ricevere tue notizie.

Thanks for your letter ...

Grazie per la tua lettera ...

Sorry I haven't written sooner.

Scusami se non ti ho scritto prima.

Per iniziare una lettera formale

Thank you for your letter of ...

La ringrazio per la Sua lettera del ...

In reply to your letter of ...

In risposta alla Sua lettera del ...

With reference to ...

In riferimento a ...

We are writing to you to ...

Le scriviamo per ...

We are pleased to inform you ...

Siamo lieti di comunicarle ...

We regret to inform you ...

Siamo spiacenti di comunicarle ...

Per concludere una lettera indirizzata a conoscenti o amici

Write soon.

Scrivimi presto.

Give my regards to ...

Salutami ...

... sends his/her best wishes.

Saluti da ...

Give my love to ...

Dà un bacio da parte mia a ...

Per chiudere una lettera formale

I look forward to hearing from you.

Resto in attesa di una Sua cortese risposta.

Thanking you in advance for your help.

RingraziandoLa anticipatamente del Suo aiuto.

If you require any further information please do not hesitate to contact me.

Resto a Sua disposizione per eventuali ulteriori informazioni.

❏ *Lettera di ringraziamento*

Indirizzo del mittente.

18 Slateford Ave
Leeds
LS24 3PR

25th May 2000

Data.

Dear Gran and Grandpa,

Thank you both very much for the CDs which you sent me for my birthday. They are two of my favourite groups and I'll really enjoy listening to them.

There's not much news here. I seem to be spending most of my time studying for my exams which start in two weeks. I'm hoping to pass all of them but I'm not looking forward to the Maths exam as that's my worst subject.

Mum says that you're off to Crete on holiday next week, so I hope that you have a great time and come back with a good tan.

Per le alternative, vedi pag.21.

Tony sends his love.

With love from

❏ *Prenotazione alberghiera*

109 Bellview Road
Cumbernauld
CA7 4TX

14th June 2000 ←

Data.

Mrs Elaine Crawford ←
Manager
Poppywell Cottage
Westleigh
Devon
DV3 8SP

Nome e indirizzo del destinatario della lettera.

Dear Mrs Crawford,

My sister stayed with you last year and has highly recommended your guest house.

I would like to reserve a family room for one week from 18th to 24th August of this year. I would be obliged if you would let me know how much this would be for two adults and two children, and whether you have a room available on those dates.

Questa formula va usata quando si conosce il nome della persona a cui si scrive.

I hope to hear from you soon.

Yours sincerely, ←

Andrew Naismith

❏ *Lettera di reclamo*

Per le
alternative,
vedi
pag.22.

85 Rush Lane
Triptown
Lancs
LC4 2DT

20th February 2000

Woodpecker Restaurant
145 Main Street
Triptown
Lancs
LC4 3EF

Dear Sir/Madam

I was to have dined in your restaurant last Thursday by way of celebrating my wedding anniversary with my wife and young son but am writing to let you know of our great dissatisfaction.

I had reserved a corner table for two with a view of the lake. However, when we arrived we had to wait for more than 20 minutes for a table and even then, not in the area which I had chosen. There was no highchair for my son as was promised and your staff made no effort whatsoever to accommodate our needs. In fact, they were downright discourteous. Naturally we went elsewhere, and not only have you lost any future custom from me, but I will be sure to advise my friends and colleagues against your establishment.

Yours faithfully

T. Greengage

Questa formula va usata
quando non si conosce il nome
della persona a cui si scrive.

❏ *Curriculum Vitae*

CURRICULUM VITAE

Name: Rosalind A. Williamson

Address: 11 North Street, Barnton NE6 2BT

Telephone: 01294 476230

E-mail: rosalindw@metalcomp.co.uk

Date of Birth: 18/4/1973

Nationality: British

Marital Status: Single

CAREER

2/97 to date: Sales and Marketing Executive, Metal Company plc, Barnton

11/95-1/97: Marketing Assistant, Metal Company plc

QUALIFICATIONS

1991-1995: University of Newby
BA (Hons) Italian with French – 2:1

1984-1991: Barnton Comprehensive School
A-levels: English Literature (D), French (B), Italian (A)
GCSEs: Art, Chemistry, English Language, English Literature, French, German, Italian, Maths

OTHER SKILLS

Computer literate (Word for Windows, Excel, QuarkXPress), good keyboarding skills, full, clean driving licence.

INTERESTS

Travel (have travelled extensively throughout Europe and North America), riding and sailing.

REFEREES

Ms Alice Bluegown
Sales and Marketing Manager
Metal Company plc
Barnton
NE4 3KL

Dr I.O. Sono
Department of Italian
University of Newby
Newby
S13 2RR

❏ *Ricerca di lavoro*

11 North Street
Barnton
NE6 2BT

18 August 2000

The Personnel Director
Clifton Manufacturing Ltd
Firebrick House
Clifton
MK45 6RB

Dear Sir or Madam

Questa formula va utilizzata se non si conosce il sesso della persona a cui si sta scrivendo. Se invece si conosce il nome della persona a cui si sta scrivendo, per esempio:
Mrs Lynn Kerr
Personnel Director
Clifton Manufacturing Ltd ecc.
la lettera va iniziata con la seguente formula:
Dear Mrs Kerr

With reference to your advertisement in the Guardian of 15 August, I wish to apply for the position of Marketing Manager in your company.

I am currently employed as a Sales and Marketing Executive for the Metal Company in Barnton where my main role is maintaining and developing links with our customers within the UK and producing material for marketing purposes.

I am interested in this position as it offers an opportunity to apply my sales and marketing skills in a new and challenging direction. I enclose my Curriculum Vitae for your consideration. Please do not hesitate to contact me if you require any further details.

Yours faithfully

Questa formula va usata quando non si conosce il nome della persona a cui si scrive.

Rosalind Williamson

Enc.

= **enclosures.** Da aggiungere se si allegano alla lettera ulteriori informazioni, p. es. un curriculum vitae.

❏ *Convocazione ad un colloquio di lavoro*

> Le aziende spesso inseriscono un numero di riferimento nella corrispondenza per facilitarne l'archiviazione.

CLIFTON MANUFACTURING LTD.

Firebrick House • Clifton MK45 6RB
Tel: (01367) 345 900 • Fax: (01367) 345 901
E-mail: personnel@cliftman.co.uk

Ref: RW/LK

27 August 2000

Ms Rosalind Williamson
11 North Street
Barnton
NE6 2BT

Dear Ms Williamson

Following your recent application for the position of Marketing Manager, I would like to invite you to attend an interview at the above office on Friday 3 September at 11am.

The interview will be conducted by the Sales and Marketing Director and myself and should last approximately one hour.

If this date does not suit please notify Jane Simpson on extension 3287 to arrange an alternative date.

We look forward to meeting you.

Yours sincerely

> Questa formula va usata se la lettera comincia con **Dear Ms Williamson** ecc.

Lynn Kerr

Lynn Kerr (Mrs)
Personnel Director

❏ *Fax*

Brown & Sons

Northport Enterprise Park
Birmingham B45 6JH
Tel: 0121 346 3287
Fax: 0121 346 3288
E-mail: orders@brownandsons.co.uk

FAX

To: Emma Scott, Westcott Hotel

Date: 6 November 2000

From: Malcolm Marshall

No. of pages to follow: 1

Re your order of 23 October for 100 tablecloths (Catalogue number 435789), I regret to inform you that these items are currently out of stock.

The next delivery will be in approximately four weeks' time. However, if this delay is unacceptable to you, please can you let me know so that I can cancel the order.

I am sorry for any inconvenience this may cause.

Regards

Malcolm Marshall

IF THERE ARE ANY PROBLEMS WITH THIS MESSAGE, PLEASE CONTACT
CLAIRE NEWPORT ON 0121 346 3287

❏ *Posta elettronica*

Mandare un messaggio

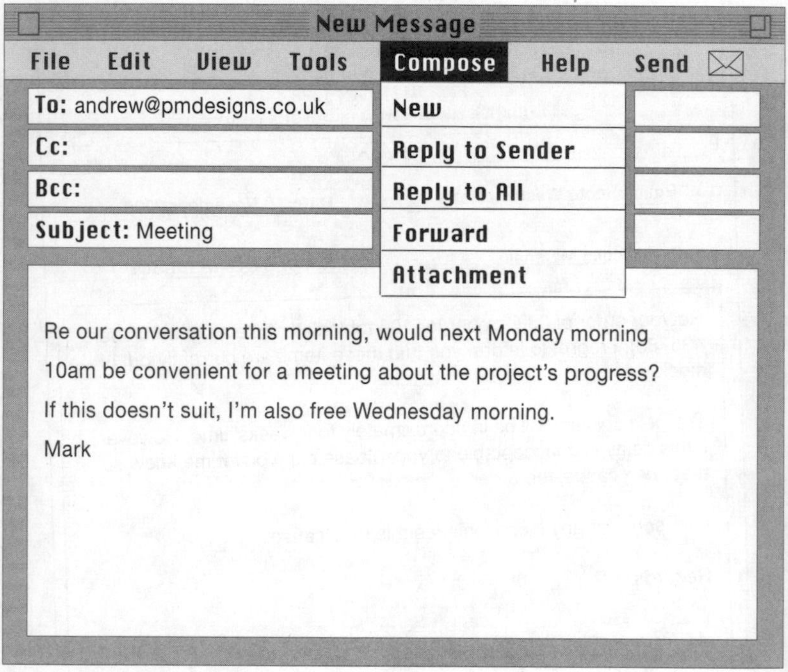

New Message						
File	**Edit**	**View**	**Tools**	**Compose**	**Help**	**Send** ✉

To: andrew@pmdesigns.co.uk

Cc:

Bcc:

Subject: Meeting

New

Reply to Sender

Reply to All

Forward

Attachment

Re our conversation this morning, would next Monday morning
10am be convenient for a meeting about the project's progress?
If this doesn't suit, I'm also free Wednesday morning.
Mark

New Message	Componi messaggio
File	File
Edit	Modifica
View	Visualizza
Tools	Strumenti
Compose	Componi
Help	Help
Send	Invia
New	Componi messaggio
Reply to Sender	Rispondi all'autore

❑ *Posta elettronica*

Ricevere un messaggio

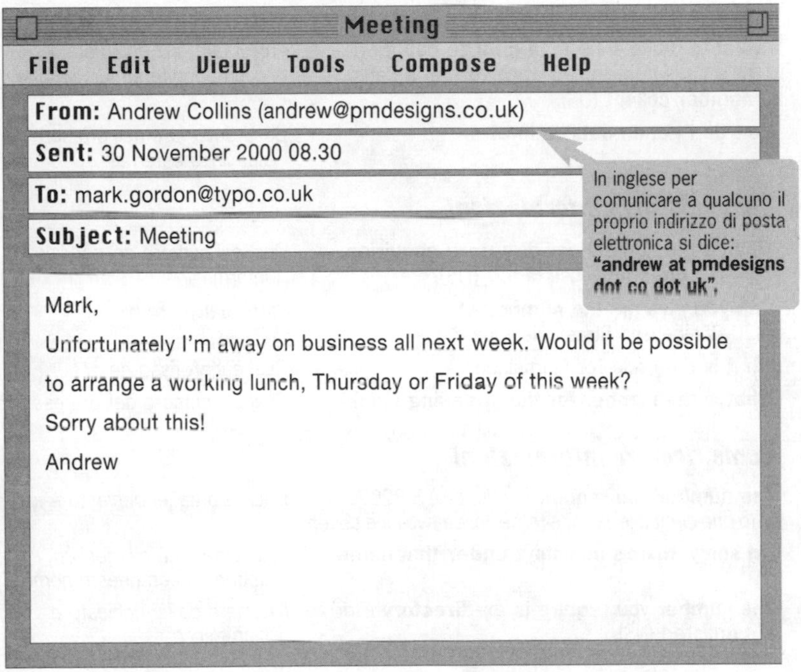

Meeting					
File	**Edit**	**View**	**Tools**	**Compose**	**Help**

From: Andrew Collins (andrew@pmdesigns.co.uk)

Sent: 30 November 2000 08.30

To: mark.gordon@typo.co.uk

Subject: Meeting

> In inglese per comunicare a qualcuno il proprio indirizzo di posta elettronica si dice: **"andrew at pmdesigns dot co dot uk"**,

Mark,

Unfortunately I'm away on business all next week. Would it be possible to arrange a working lunch, Thursday or Friday of this week?

Sorry about this!

Andrew

Reply to All	Rispondi a tutti
Forward	Inoltra
Attachment	Inserisci file
To	A
Cc (carbon copy)	Cc
Bcc (blind carbon copy)	Ccn
Subject	Oggetto
From	Da
Sent	Data

❏ *Telefono*

Diversi tipi di telefonate

Local/national call.

Comunicazione urbana/interurbana.

I want to make an international call.

Vorrei chiamare all'estero.

I want to make a reverse-charge call *(Brit)* to a Paris number o I want to call a Paris number collect *(US)*.

Vorrei fare una chiamata a ... con addebito al destinatario.

How do I get an outside line?

Cosa devo fare per ottenere una linea esterna?

Come chiedere informazioni

What is the number for directory enquiries *(Brit)* o directory assistance *(US)*?

Qual è il numero del servizio informazioni?

Can you give me the number of Europost, 20 Cumberland Street, Newquay?

Vorrei il numero di ...

What is the code for Martinique?

Qual è il prefisso del ...

What is the number for the speaking clock?

Qual è il numero dell'ora esatta?

Come ricevere informazioni

The number you require is 0181-613 3297.
(*o-one-eight-one six-one-three three-two-nine-seven*)

Il numero da lei richiesto è ...

I'm sorry, there's no listing under that name.

Spiacente, non c'è nessun abbonato con questo nome.

The number you require is ex-directory *(Brit)* o unlisted *(US)*.

Il numero da lei richiesto è fuori elenco.

Quando l'abbonato risponde

Could I speak to Mr Sanderson, please?

Vorrei o Potrei parlare con ...

Could you put me through to Dr Evans, please?

Può passarmi ...

Can I have extension 6578, please?

Può passarmi l'interno ...

I'll call back in half an hour.

Richiamo tra ...

Would you ask him to ring me when he gets back?

Può chiedergli di richiamarmi appena rientra?

Risponde il centralino

Who shall I say is calling?

Chi parla?

I'm putting you through.

Glielo passo.

I have a call from Tokyo for Mrs Thomson.	C'è una chiamata da ... per ...
I've got Miss Martin on the line.	Ho in linea ...
Dr Roberts is on another line. Do you want to wait?	... è occupato sull'altra linea, attende?
Please hold.	Attenda, prego.
There's no reply.	Non risponde.
Would you like to leave a message?	Desidera lasciare un messaggio?

Messaggi registrati

The number you have dialled has not been recognized. Please hang up.	Il numero selezionato è inesistente. Si prega di riattaccare.
The number you have dialled has been changed to 0171-789 0044.	L'abbonato ha cambiato numero. Il nuovo numero è ...
All the lines are busy right now. Please try again later.	A causa dell'ingente traffico, non ci è possibile dar seguito alla sua chiamata. La preghiamo di richiamare più tardi.
Hello, you have reached Sunspot Insurance. Please wait, your call will be answered shortly.	Buongiorno, siete in linea con ... Vi preghiamo di attendere: un operatore risponderà appena possibile.
Hello, you are through to Emma and Matthew Hargreaves. Please leave a message after the tone and we'll get back to you. Thanks.	Buongiorno, risponde la segreteria telefonica di ... Lasciate un messaggio dopo il bip, sarete richiamati al più presto.

Per rispondere al telefono

Hello, it's Anne speaking.	Pronto, sono ...
Speaking.	Sono io.
Who's speaking?	Chi parla?

In caso di difficoltà

I can't get through.	Non riesco a prendere la linea.
Their phone is out of order.	Il loro telefono è guasto.
We have been cut off.	È caduta la linea.
I must have dialled the wrong number.	Credo di aver sbagliato numero.
We've got a crossed line.	C'è un'interferenza sulla linea.
This is a very bad line.	La linea è molto disturbata.

❏ Likes, dislikes and preferences

Saying what you like

Mi piacciono i dolci.	*I like ...*
Mi piace che le cose siano al loro posto.	*I like ...*
Il film **mi è piaciuto.**	*I liked ...*
La visita ai vigneti **mi è piaciuta molto.**	*I very much enjoyed ...*
Adoro andare in discoteca.	*I love ...*
La cosa che mi piace di più è passare una serata con amici.	*What I like most is ...*
Il mio piatto **preferito** è il risotto.	*My favourite ...*
Leggere è **uno dei miei** passatempi **preferiti.**	*... one of my favourite ...*
Ho un debole per i dolci al cioccolato.	*I've got a weakness for ...*
Vado matto per la musica jazz.	*I'm crazy about ...*
Non c'è niente di meglio di un bel bagno caldo!	*There's nothing better than ...*
Non mi dispiace stare da solo.	*I don't mind ...*

Saying what you dislike

Non mi piace il pesce.	*I don't like ...*
Non mi piace molto parlare in pubblico.	*I'm not very keen on ...*
La birra **non mi piace per niente.**	*I don't like ... at all.*
Il suo comportamento **non mi piace per niente.**	*I don't like ... at all.*
Odio la chimica.	*I hate ...*
Detesto lo sport.	*I loathe ...*
Non sopporto che mi si dicano bugie.	*I can't stand ...*
Se c'è una cosa che odio è aspettare sotto la pioggia.	*What I hate most is ...*
Non è che l'idea **mi faccia impazzire.**	*I'm not madly keen on ...*

Saying what you prefer

Preferisco il rock **alla** musica classica.	*I prefer ... to ...*
Preferirei vivere a Parigi.	*I would rather ...*
Preferirei morire di fame **piuttosto che** chiedergli un favore.	*I'd rather ... than ...*
Mi piacerebbe di più lavorare a casa.	*I'd rather ...*

Expressing indifference

Per me fa lo stesso.	It's all the same to me.
Non ho preferenze.	I have no particular preference.
Coe vuole or **preferisce.**	As you like.
Non ha nessuna importanza.	It doesn't matter in the least.
È indifferente.	I don't mind.
Fai come credi, **per me è uguale.**	... it's all the same to me.

Asking what someone likes

Ti piacciono le patate fritte?	Do you like ...
Ti piace cucinare?	Do you like ...
Le piace vivere in città?	Do you like ...
Cosa preferisci: il mare o la montagna?	Which do you like better ...
Quale preferisci: il rosso o il nero?	Which do you prefer ...
Preferisci vivere in città o in campagna?	Do you prefer ...
Cosa ti piace di più in un uomo?	What do you like best ...

❏ *Opinions*

Asking for opinions

Cosa pensa del divorzio?	What do you think about ...
Cosa ne pensa?	What do you think about it?
Potrebbe dirmi la sua opinione su questo programma?	Could you tell me your opinion of ...
Vorrei sapere cosa pensi del suo lavoro.	I'd like to know what you think of ...
Qual è la sua opinione sulle probabilità di successo?	What is your opinion on ...
Mi piacerebbe sentire il suo parere su questo problema.	I'd like to hear your views on ...
Come ti sembra il suo modo di fare?	What do you think of ...
A suo parere, c'è parità tra uomini e donne?	In your opinion ...
A suo avviso, lui c'entra?	In your view ...
Secondo te, bisognerebbe ripensarci?	In your opinion ...

Expressing opinions

Hai ragione.	*You are right.*
Ha torto.	*He is wrong.*
Ha sbagliato a dimettersi.	*He was wrong to ...*
Sono sicuro che sia in buonafede.	*I'm sure he's ...*
Sono convinto che esistano altre soluzioni.	*I'm convinced that ...*
Sono convinto che sia la soluzione migliore.	*I'm sure that it's ...*
Penso che sarà possibile.	*I think ...*
Penso che tu sbagli.	*I think ...*
Credo che sia un po' prematuro.	*I think it's ...*
Credo che sia in ritardo.	*I think he's ...*
Mi sembra che sia normale.	*I think it's ...*
A mio parere, non è cambiato.	*In my opinion ...*
A mio avviso, è il caso di intervenire.	*In my opinion ...*
Per me, ha sbagliato.	*In my view ...*
Secondo me, è stato un grave errore.	*In my view ...*
Personalmente, ritengo che sia denaro sprecato.	*Personally, I think that it's ...*
Ho l'impressione che i suoi non la capiscano.	*I have the impression that ...*

Being noncommittal

Non ho un'opinione precisa al riguardo.	*I have no particular opinion on this.*
A dire il vero, non ci ho mai pensato.	*Actually, I have never thought about it.*
Dipende da cosa intendi per patriottismo.	*It all depends what you mean by ...*
Dipende.	*It depends.*
Preferisco non pronunciarmi.	*I'd rather not express an opinion.*

❏ *Approval and agreement*

Mi sembra una magnifica idea.	*I think it's an excellent idea.*
Ottima idea!	*What a good idea!*

Hai fatto bene a lasciare le valigie al deposito bagagli.	*You were right to ...*
Ho apprezzato moltissimo il suo articolo sul razzismo.	*I was very impressed by ...*
I giornali **fanno bene a** pubblicare queste notizie.	*... are right to ...*
Secondo me lei **ha ragione a** diffidarne.	*I think you're right to ...*
È un'ottima cosa.	*It's a very good thing.*
Non hai torto a lamentarti.	*You're quite justified in ...*
Condivido la sua opinione.	*I share your view.*
Condivido pienamente la sua apprensione.	*I fully share your ...*
Siamo favorevoli alla creazione di posti di lavoro.	*We are in favour of ...*
Siamo a favore dell'Europa unita.	*We are in favour of ...*
Ritengono giustamente che l'inquinamento provenga dalla fabbrica.	*They rightly believe that ...*
Sono d'accordo con lei.	*I agree with you.*
Sono pienamente d'accordo con te.	*I entirely agree with you.*
È vero che ci sono meno matrimoni oggi.	*It is true that ...*

❏ *Disapproval and disagreement*

Non sono d'accordo.	*I disagree.*
Non siamo d'accordo con loro.	*We don't agree with ...*
Non sono affatto d'accordo con quello che ha detto.	*I totally disagree with ...*
Non è vero che il risultato era inevitabile.	*It is not true to say that ...*
Ti sbagli!	*You are wrong!*
Non condivido il punto di vista degli euroscettici.	*I don't share the ... point of view.*
Siamo contro la caccia.	*We are against ...*
L'idea **non mi piace per niente.**	*I dislike ... intensely.*
Non sopporto le bugie.	*I can't stand ...*
La violenza **è ingiustificabile.**	*... cannot be justified.*
Sono contrario al test obbligatorio per l'AIDS.	*I am opposed to ...*
Trovo che abbia sbagliato a chiedere un prestito così grosso.	*I think he was wrong to ...*
Non avresti dovuto parlargli così.	*You shouldn't have ...*
Sono deluso del suo atteggiamento.	*I am disappointed by ...*

Sono profondamente deluso.	I am deeply disappointed.
È un peccato che costi così caro.	It's a pity that ...
È deplorevole che non siano in grado di trovare una soluzione.	It is highly regrettable that ...
Non possiamo permettere che la situazione peggiori.	We must not allow ...
Che diritto ha di agire così?	What gives him the right to ...

❏ *Apologies*

How to say sorry

Scusi.	Sorry.
Oh, scusi! Devo aver sbagliato piano.	Oh, sorry!
Scusi se la disturbo.	Sorry to bother you.
Scusa se ti ho svegliato.	I am sorry I ...
Mi dispiace per tutto quello che è successo.	I am sorry about ...
La prego di scusarmi.	I do apologize.
Preghiamo i lettori di scusare questa omissione.	We hope our readers will ...

Admitting responsibility

È colpa mia, sarei dovuto partire prima.	It's my fault, I should have ...
Non avrei dovuto ridere di lei.	I shouldn't have ...
Abbiamo sbagliato a non verificare questa informazione.	We were wrong not to ...
Mi assumo la piena responsabilità delle mie azioni.	I take full responsibility for ...
Purtroppo abbiamo commesso un errore nel conteggio.	We unfortunately made a mistake ...

Disclaiming responsibility

Non è colpa mia.	It's not my fault.
Non è colpa mia se siamo in ritardo.	It isn't my fault if ...
Non l'ho fatto apposta.	I didn't do it on purpose.
Non ho potuto fare altrimenti.	I had no option.

Mi era sembrato di capire che si potesse parcheggiare qui.	*I thought that ...*
Credevo di far bene a dirglielo.	*I thought I was doing the right thing in ...*

Apologizing for being unable to do something

Mi dispiace, ma è impossibile.	*I'm sorry, but ...*
Non posso fare altrimenti.	*I have no other option.*
Sono spiacente, ma purtroppo siamo al completo.	*I'm sorry, but unfortunately ...*
Siamo desolati di non poter soddisfare la sua richiesta.	*We are very sorry we ...*

❏ *Explanations*

Oauses

Sono arrivato in ritardo **a causa del** traffico.	*... because of ...*
Il programma è stato abbandonato **a causa di** problemi legali	*.... owing to ...*
Ha detto che è qui **per via del** fratello.	*... because of ...*
Sono riuscito a cavarmela **grazie all'**aiuto dei miei amici.	*... thanks to ...*
Non ho comprato niente **perché** non ho soldi.	*... because ...*
Visto *or* **dato che** insisti, tornerò domani.	*Since ...*
Siccome abitavo vicino alla biblioteca ci andavo spesso.	*As ...*
Vista la situazione attuale, non si può sperare in un miglioramento immediato.	*Given ...*
Dato che c'è una crisi economica, è difficile trovare lavoro.	*Given that ...*
Dati i problemi che abbiamo avuto, non ce la siamo cavata male.	*Considering ...*
È stata la rottura di un asse **che ha causato** il deragliamento.	*It was ... that caused ...*
Si è dimesso **per motivi di** salute.	*... for ... reasons.*
Il teatro chiude **per** mancanza di fondi.	*... due to ...*
Molte forme di tumore **sono legate al** fumo.	*... are linked to ...*
Il problema è che la gente è intimorita dai computer.	*The problem is that ...*
Il calo delle vendite **è il risultato dei** tassi d'interesse alti.	*... is the result of ...*

Consequences

Devo partire stasera, **quindi** non potrò venire con te.	... so ...
I contadini ora possono coltivare più terra, **col risultato che** la produzione di riso è aumentata.	... with the result that ...
La distribuzione è stata migliorata, **e dunque** i lettori riceveranno prima il loro giornale.	... and so ...
Il nuovo sidro viene fermentato molto poco e **di conseguenza** ha un basso contenuto alcolico.	... consequently ...
La mancanza di fondi **ha portato ad** un rallentamento del progetto.	... has resulted in ...
Sono tutti uguali **e perciò** è facile confondersi.	... and so ...

❏ Comparisons

Questo trattamento costa poco **se lo si paragona ad** altri.	... if one compares it to ...
Si può paragonare il gioco d'azzardo **a** una droga.	... can be compared to ...
Il gas di scarico ha un odore **simile a** quello delle uova marce.	... similar to ...
Il Vittoriale di d'Annunzio **è spesso paragonato a** una nave.	... is often compared to ...
Il rumore **era paragonabile a** quello di una grossa moto.	... was comparable to ...
L'Africa è ancora un continente sottopopolato **paragonato all'**Asia.	... compared with ...
L'Irlanda, **a paragone dell'**Islanda, ha un clima tropicale.	Compared to ...
In Francia, gli investimenti pubblicitari sono aumentati leggermente **rispetto all'**anno precedente.	... compared to ...
Questa storia **sembra** una favola.	... is like ...
Amava questa campagna che **gli ricordava** l'Irlanda.	... reminded him of ...
Livelli di disoccupazione **che ricordano** quelli degli anni '30.	... reminiscent of ...
La televisione **è l'equivalente** moderno **dei** circhi romani.	... is the ... equivalent of ...
Questa cifra **corrisponde a** sei mesi di stipendio.	... amounts to ...
'La schiacciata'? **È la stessa cosa che** la focaccia.	It's the same thing as ...
In termini di calorie **è equivalente.**	It comes to the same thing ...

| Questo disco **non è né migliore né peggiore dell'**ultimo. | *... is no better and no worse than ...* |

Stressing differences

Nessuna catastrofe **può essere paragonata a** quella di Černobyl.	*No ... can compare with ...*
Le fabbriche moderne **non si possono paragonare a** quelle in cui lavoravano i nostri nonni.	*... cannot be compared with ...*
Le azioni di questo gruppo **non hanno niente in comune con** le attività terroristiche.	*... are in no way comparable to ...*
I due personaggi **si differenziano** anche nei loro rapporti con le donne.	*... differ ...*
La storia degli Stati Uniti **non assomiglia affatto alla** nostra.	*... in no way resembles ...*
C'è di peggio che perdere la finale di coppa Europa.	*There are worse things than ...*
Questo film **è meno** interessante **del** suo film d'esordio.	*... is less ... than ...*
Questo programma **è più** interessante **rispetto a** quello che ho visto ieri.	*... is more ... than ...*
La durata media della vita delle donne è di 81 anni, **mentre** quella degli uomini è di 72.	*... while ...*

❏ *Requests and offers*

Requests

Vorrei un'altra birra.	*I'd like ...*
Vorrei sapere gli orari dei treni per Padova.	*I'd like to ...*
Potrebbe darci una mano?	*Could you ...*
Può dare lei la buona notizia a Cinzia?	*Can you ...*
Sii gentile, fai un salto in panetteria.	*Be an angel ...*
Se non le dispiace attendere un attimo ...	*If you wouldn't mind ...*
Sarebbe così gentile da darci la ricetta?	*Would you be so kind as to ...*
Potrebbe farmi la cortesia di tenermi il posto?	*Would you be very kind and ...*

Potrebbe per cortesia indicarmi l'uscita? *Could you please ...*

Può concedermi qualche minuto? *Could you spare me ...*

Le spiacerebbe aprire la finestra? *Would you mind ...*

Gradirei che mi comunicaste la decisione entro venerdì. *I would be grateful if ...*

Le sarei grato se provvedesse affinché questo non si ripeta più. *I would be grateful if ...*

Offers

Posso passare a prenderti, **se** vuoi. *I can ... if ...*

Potrei accompagnarti io. *I could ...*

Ti va un po' di gelato? *Do you fancy ...*

Vi piacerebbe vedere le mie foto? *Would you like to ...*

Che ne diresti di una crostata alle pere? *Do you fancy ...*

Vuoi che vada a prendere la macchina? *Do you want me to ...*

Le andrebbe di venire a cena con me una di queste sere? *Would you like to ...*

❑ *Advice and suggestions*

Asking for advice or suggestions

Cosa faresti, al posto mio? *What would you do, if you were me?*

È una questione complicata. **Tu cosa ne pensi?** *What's your opinion?*

Quale ci consiglia, Majorca o Ibiza? *Which would you recommend ...*

Cosa mi consiglia? *What would you advise?*

Cosa mi consiglia di fare? *What would you advise me to do?*

Se volessimo sponsorizzare un corridore, **chi raccomanderebbe?** *... who would you recommend?*

Che strategia **proponi?** *What ... do you suggest?*

Cosa bisognerebbe fare, secondo voi, per ridurre l'inquinamento? *What, in your opinion, should be done to ...*

Come affrontereste la disoccupazione? *How would you deal with ...*

Offering advice or suggestions

Se posso darle un consiglio, tenga le negative.	*If I may give you a bit of advice ...*
Un consiglio: leggete le istruzioni.	*A word of advice ...*
Se fossi in lei non mi fiderei.	*If I were you ...*
Al posto tuo non ne farei parola.	*If I were you ...*
Perché non gli telefoni?	*Why don't you ...*
Lei dovrebbe andare da uno specialista.	*You should ...*
Forse dovresti parlarne con un idraulico.	*Perhaps you should ...*
Farebbe bene a consultare un avvocato.	*You would do well to ...*
Faresti meglio a spendere quei soldi per comprare una macchina nuova.	*You would do better to ...*
Forse potrebbe chiedere a qualcuno di tradurglielo.	*You could perhaps ...*
Potresti essere un po' più comprensivo.	*You could ...*
Dato che hai senso del ritmo **dovresti** imparare a ballare.	*... you ought to ...*
Forse dovremmo tentare un approccio diverso.	*Perhaps we ought to ...*
E se noleggiassimo un video?	*How about ...*
Io proporrei il 3 marzo alle 10 e 30.	*How about ...*
Sarebbe bello rivedersi a Parigi.	*It would be nice to ...*
Forse sarebbe meglio regalarle dei soldi anziché dei gioielli.	*It might be better to ...*
Sarebbe meglio attendere i risultati del referendum.	*It would be better to ...*

Warnings

Soprattutto, non lasciare **mai** la macchina fotografica in auto.	*Whatever you do, don't ...*
Diffidate dei bagarini.	*Beware of ...*
Non fidarti: l'apparenza inganna.	*Remember: appearances can be deceptive.*
Se non prenoti per tempo **rischi** di non trovare posto.	*... you risk ...*
Ti avverto, mi vendicherò.	*I warn you ...*
Si ricordi di tenere una copia della dichiarazione dei redditi.	*Don't forget to ...*

❏ *Intentions and desires*

Asking what someone intends to do

Che progetti avete?	*What are your plans?*
Cosa conti di fare quando torni? **Hai dei progetti?**	*What are you going to do ... Do you have anything planned?*
Cosa conta di fare della sua collezione?	*What are you planning to do with ...*
Conta di restare molto tempo?	*Are you planning on ...*
Conta di girare un altro film in Europa?	*Are you thinking of ...*
Come pensi di fare?	*What are you thinking of doing?*
Cosa pensi di fare dopo la laurea?	*What are you thinking of doing ...*
Cosa farai se non passi agli esami?	*What will you do if ...*
Vi aspettiamo domenica prossima, d'accordo?	*We'll expect you ...*
Hai intenzione di seguire questa carriera?	*Do you intend to ...*

Talking about intentions

Pensavo di andare ad Ajaccio l'8 luglio.	*I was planning to ...*
Contiamo di vendere oltre centomila dischi.	*We reckon to ...*
Sto pensando di ritirarmi dalla politica.	*I am thinking of ...*
Prevede di trascorrere un anno in India.	*She plans to ...*
È prevista la costruzione di un nuovo stadio.	*There are plans to ...*
Ho deciso di divorziare.	*I have decided to ...*
È deciso, andiamo in Florida.	*That's settled ...*
È mia intenzione dirglielo prima possibile.	*I intend to ...*
La banca **ha intenzione di** chiudere oltre un centinaio di succursali.	*... intends to ...*
Non è mai stata nostra intenzione parlare male della stampa.	*We never had any intention of ...*
Per me vivere all'estero **è fuori discussione**.	*... is out of the question.*

Wishes

Voglio fare del cinema.	I want to ...
Vorrei suonare come Louis Armstrong.	I'd like to ...
Vorrei che le mie foto venissero pubblicate.	I would like ...
Mi piacerebbe fare qualche sport.	I'd like to ...
Mi sarebbe piaciuto avere un fratello.	I would have liked to ...
Spero di potermi sposare e avere dei bambini.	I hope to ...
Ci auguriamo che i bambini guardino questo programma con igenitori.	We hope that ...
Carlos **voleva a tutti i costi** impedire al capo di scoprirlo.	... wanted at all costs to ...
Sogni di vincere alla lotteria?	Do you dream of ...
Il mio sogno è quello di avere una casa grande.	I dream of ...
È nostro desiderio mantenere buoni rapporti.	We wish to ...

❑ Obligation

Devo trovare un alloggio.	I must ...
Dobbiamo assolutamente rivederci prima del 23!	We really must ...
Se vieni in Polonia **devi** imparare il polacco.	... you must ...
La scuola **è obbligatoria** come il servizio militare.	... is compulsory ...
Esigeva che la sua guardia del corpo dormisse nel corridoio.	He made ...
Mia madre **mi costringe a** mangiare spinaci.	... makes me ...
I dirottatori **hanno chiesto che** l'aereo ripartisse alla volta di New York.	... demanded that ...
Un attacco d'asma **mi ha costretto a** interrompere il viaggio.	... forced me to ...
Ha dovuto chiedere in prestito sempre più soldi.	... was obliged to ...
Non puoi fare altro che rifiutare.	You have no choice but to ...
Ha dato il bambino in adozione perché **non poteva fare altrimenti.**	... she had no other option.
Molte madri **sono obbligate a** lavorare, **non hanno scelta.**	... have to ...; they have no other option.
È indispensabile conoscere un po' la storia per comprendere la situazione.	It is essential to ...

❏ *Permission*

Asking for permission

Posso usare il telefono?	*Could I ...*
Posso chiederle qualcosa?	*Can I ...*
Va bene se vengo ora, o è troppo presto?	*Is it alright if ...*
Le spiace se apro la finestra?	*Do you mind if ...*
Le dà fastidio se fumo?	*Do you mind if ...*
Permette che guardi nella sua valigetta, signora?	*Would you mind if ...*
Posso avere il permesso di andare via prima?	*May I have permission to ...*

Giving permission

Fate come volete.	*Do as you please.*
Vai pure!	*Of course you can go!*
Non ho niente in contrario.	*I have nothing against it.*
Alle 8 **mi hanno detto che potevo** andarmene.	*... they told me I could ...*
I ragazzi **possono** uscire due volte alla settimana.	*... are allowed to ...*
Ti permetto di andarci se mi prometti di telefonare quando arrivi.	*I'll let you ...*

Saying something is not allowed

Ti proibisco di uscire!	*I forbid you to ...*
È proibito.	*It's forbidden.*
È vietato fumare nella toilette.	*... is forbidden.*
Vietato l'ingresso.	*No entry.*
Sosta vietata.	*No parking.*
Divieto di sosta.	*No parking.*
Non è permesso.	*It's not allowed.*
Proibisce ai bambini **di** vedere i nonni.	*She forbids ... to ...*
Il lavoro infantile **è formalmente proibito da** una convenzione dell'ONU.	*... is strictly forbidden by ...*
Non potevamo né mangiare né bere, in servizio.	*We weren't allowed to ...*
È fuori discussione.	*That's out of the question.*
Non se ne parla nemmeno.	*It's out of the question.*

❏ *Certainty, probability and possibility*

Certainty

Ci saranno **senz'altro** dei problemi.	*Undoubtedly ...*
È evidente che l'azienda è in difficoltà.	*Clearly ...*
È innegabile che fosse in parte colpa sua.	*It is undeniable that ...*
Non c'è alcun dubbio che l'immagine del paese ne abbia risentito.	*There is no doubt that ...*
Vedere un turista è **ovviamente** una cosa rarissima.	*... quite obviously ...*
Sono sicuro che mio fratello ti piacerà.	*I am sure that ...*
Sono sicuro che siamo sulla pista giusta.	*I am certain that ...*
Sono sicuro di vincere.	*I am sure that I ...*
Ho la certezza di non annoiarmi, lavorando con lui.	*I am sure that ...*
Sono convinto che esistano altre soluzioni.	*I am convinced that ...*

Probability

L'80% dei problemi dermatologici è **senza dubbio** di origine psicologica.	*... undoubtedly ...*
È probabile che il costo della benzina aumenti.	*... probably ...*
Bisogna **probabilmente** rivedere i dati.	*... probably ...*
L'inflazione supererà **molto probabilmente** il 100%.	*... very probably ...*
Deve avere dimenticato di aprire la finestra.	*He must have ...*
I lavori di costruzione **dovrebbero** iniziare ad aprile.	*... should ...*
Potrebbe darsi che stiano osservando le nostre reazioni.	*It is quite possible that ...*

Possibility

È possibile.	*It is possible.*
È possibile che l'America sia stata scoperta dai cinesi.	*It is possible that ...*
Potrebbe essere più costoso.	*That might be ...*
Tra qualche mese **potrebbe** cambiare tutto.	*... could ...*
Questo virus **potrebbe** essere estremamente contagioso.	*... may ...*
Non è da escludersi che sia andato a Parigi.	*It is not impossible that ...*

Può darsi che ci voglia del tempo per concludere la pace. *It may be that ...*
Magari sbaglio.   *Perhaps ...*

❑ *Doubt, improbability and impossibility*

Doubt

Non sono sicuro che sia utile.   *I'm not sure it's ...*
Non sono sicuro di aver ragione.   *I'm not sure ...*
Non sono certo che sia una buona idea.   *I'm not sure that it's ...*
Mi domando se abbiamo fatto molti progressi in   *I wonder if ...*
  questo campo.
È saggio? **Ne dubito.**   *I doubt it.*
Cominciò a **dubitare della** competenza del proprio   *... have doubts about ...*
  medico.
Dubito fortemente che possa adattarsi alla situazione.   *I very much doubt ...*
Non è sicuro che riesca ad arrivare in tempo.   *There is no certainty
                                                                   that ...*
Non sappiamo con certezza se è stato lui.   *We don't know for sure
                                                                   that ...*
Non si sa esattamente cosa sia successo.   *Nobody knows exactly ...*

Improbability

Probabilmente non cambierà idea.   *... probably won't ...*
È poco probabile che siano rimasti dei biglietti.   *It is unlikely that ...*
Mi sorprenderebbe se avessero il tuo numero.   *I'd be surprised if ...*
Non rischiamo di annoiarci.   *There's no danger of ...*
Ci sono poche probabilità che il tasso di crescita   *It is unlikely that ...*
  superi l'1,5%.
Sarebbe da stupirsi se tutto andasse liscio.   *It would be amazing if ...*

Impossibility

È impossibile.   *It's impossible.*
Non è possibile per l'80% dei giovani continuare gli   *It is not possible for ...*
  studi superiori.

È impossibile che quest'informazione sia falsa.	*... cannot be ...*
Non c'è alcuna possibilità che ci aiutino.	*There is no chance of ...*

❑ *Greetings*

Ciao!	*Hello! or Hi!*
Salve! *(more formal)*	*Hello!*
Come sta?	*How are you?*
Come va?	*How's it going?*
Come vanno le cose?	*How's things?*
Come va la vita?	*How's life?*
Buongiorno!	*Good morning!*
Buonasera!	*Good afternoon! or Good evening!*

What to say in reply

Molto bene grazie, e lei?	*Fine thanks, and you?*
Benone!	*Great!*
Così così.	*So-so.*
Non c'è male.	*Not so bad.*

Introductions

Questo è Charles.	*This is ...*
Le presento la mia ragazza.	*May I introduce ...*
Le voglio far conoscere mio marito.	*I'd like you to meet ...*

Replying to an introduction

Piacere.	*Pleased to meet you.*
Molto lieto.	*How do you do*

Leavetaking

Arrivederci!	*Goodbye!*
Buonanotte!	*Good night!*

Ciao!	*Bye!*
Ci vediamo!	*See you!*
A più tardi!	*See you later!*
A presto!	*See you soon!*
A domani!	*See you tomorrow!*
Alla settimana prossima!	*See you next week!*
A giovedì!	*See you Thursday!*

Best wishes

Buon compleanno!	*Happy Birthday!*
Cento di questi giorni!	*Many happy returns!*
Buon anniversario!	*Happy Anniversary!*
Buon Natale!	*Merry Christmas!*
Buon Anno!	*Happy New Year!*
Congratulazioni!	*Congratulations!*
Buon viaggio!	*Safe journey!*
Buon appetito!	*Enjoy your meal!*
Buona fortuna!	*Good luck!*
Divertiti!	*Have fun!*
Cin cin!	*Cheers!*
Buon riposo!	*Sleep well!*
Benvenuti!	*Welcome!*
Guarisci presto!	*Get well soon!*
Stammi bene!	*Take care!*

❏ *Correspondence*

How to address an envelope

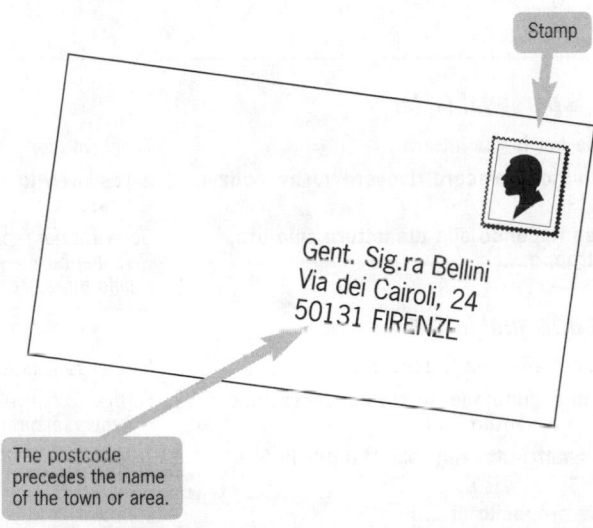

Stamp

Gent. Sig.ra Bellini
Via dei Cairoli, 24
50131 FIRENZE

The postcode
precedes the name
of the town or area.

Common abbreviations used in addresses

Egr. = Egregio	P.zza = Piazza	Spett. = Spettabile
Gent. – Gentile	Sig. = Signor	V. = Via
P.le = Piazzale	Sig.ra = Signora	V.le = Viale

Standard opening and closing formulae

In personal correspondence

Caro Signor Bianchi	Cari saluti *(quite informal)*
Cara Giovanna	A presto
Carissimo Pietro	Ti abbraccio affettuosamente
Cari Anna e Marco	Un abbraccio
Cara zia Bruna	Baci *(very informal)*

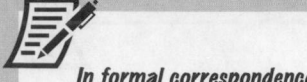

In formal correspondence

Egregio Sig. Millo Egr. Dott. Marsi Gent. Sig.ra Coretti Gent. Dott. Milesi Spett. Ditta	Distinti saluti Cordiali saluti

Starting a personal letter

Ti ringrazio per la tua lettera.	*Thank you for your letter.*
Mi ha fatto molto piacere ricevere vostre notizie.	*It was lovely to have your news.*
Scusami se rispondo alla tua lettera solo ora, ma purtroppo ...	*Sorry for not replying sooner but unfortunately ...*

Starting a formal letter

In riferimento alla Sua lettera del ...	*Further to your letter of ...*
Le scrivo in seguito alla nostra conversazione telefonica avvenuta il ...	*Further to our telephone conversation of ...*
Desidero innanzitutto ringraziarLa per la Sua lettera.	*Thank you very much for your letter.*
Le scrivo a proposito di ...	*I am writing to you about ...*
Abbiamo il piacere d'informarLa che ...	*We are pleased to inform you that ...*
... ci dispiace doverLa informare che ...	*... we regret to inform you that ...*

Ending a personal letter

Tanti saluti anche a ...	*Best wishes to ...*
Dà un bacione da parte mia anche a ...	*Give my love to ...*
Mi raccomando, scrivimi presto!	*Write soon!*
Non vedo l'ora di avere vostre notizie.	*I look forward to hearing from you.*

Ending a formal letter

RingraziandoLa anticipatamente, Le porgo i miei più cordiali saluti.	*Thanking you in advance. Yours sincerely ...*
In attesa di una Vostra gentile risposta, invio distinti saluti.	*I look forward to hearing from you. Yours sincerely ...*

❏ *Thank you letter*

Livorno, 7 gennaio 2000

Date.

Cari Simona e Gianluca,

grazie ancora per la stupenda festa di Capodanno. È stato un piacere immenso rivedere tanti vecchi amici che avevamo un po' perso di vista.

Non vediamo l'ora di incontrarvi di nuovo per fare una chiacchierata e per mostrarvi le foto che Stefano ha scattato durante la festa. Che ne dite di venire da noi a prendere un aperitivo e vedere le foto? Vi telefoneremo la settimana prossima per accordarci sulla data.

Una caro abbraccio

For alternatives see p51.

Annamaria e Stefano

❏ *Hotel booking*

Massimo Lupini
Via G. Murat, 12
00190 Roma

Roma, 3 maggio 2000

Name and address of sender.

Date.

Name and address of letter's recipient.

Spett. Direzione
Hotel Roma
Piazza Garibaldi, 4
38100 Trento

Spett. Direzione,

in seguito alla nostra conversazione telefonica del 28 aprile, vi scrivo per prenotare una camera singola per le notti del 16, 17 e 18 c.m. presso il vostro albergo. Arriverò a Trento mercoledì 16 verso le 23 e ripartirò sabato 19 in tarda mattinata.

Vi sarei grato se poteste confermarmi le tariffe e la prenotazione via fax al numero 06-6389836.

In attesa di un vostro gentile riscontro, invio cordiali saluti.

Massimo Lupini

❏ *Letter of complaint*

Sig. e Sig.ra Colli
Via Ibsen, 3
10100 Torino

Torino, 2 gennaio 2000

Hotel da Vinci
Via Cavour, 2
56100 Pisa

Spett. Direzione,

mio marito ed io abbiamo trascorso la notte del
22 dicembre presso il vostro albergo, avendo
regolarmente prenotato una camera per quella data.
Vi scriviamo per esprimere il nostro disappunto per
il servizio riservatoci.

Avevamo chiesto espressamente una camera
silenziosa ed invece ci è stata assegnata una camera
che dava sulla strada con la conseguenza che il
rumore del traffico ci ha tenuti svegli tutta la notte.
Come se ciò non bastasse, la mattina dopo è stato
impossibile avere la colazione prima della nostra
partenza alle 6 e 30.

La sosta presso di voi, che doveva permetterci di
riposare nel corso di un lungo viaggio, non ha fatto
che stancarci ancora di più.

Non solo non faremo mai più uso del vostro albergo,
ma lo sconsiglieremo vivamente ai nostri amici.

Distinti saluti

H. Colli

For
alternatives
see p52.

❏ *Curriculum Vitae*

CURRICULUM VITAE

If you have British or American qualifications you should give them, followed by a brief description in Italian.

Nome e cognome	Michela Grini
Indirizzo	Piazza Annali 23, Varese
Telefono	0332 45 67 89
Data di nascita	7 novembre 1971
Nazionalità	italiana

Titoli di studio

Diploma di ragioneria conseguito presso l'Istituto Fermi di Varese nel 1989

Diploma di dattilografia conseguito presso l'Istituto Manzoni di Varese.

Lingue

Ottima conoscenza della lingua inglese parlata e scritta

Buona conoscenza della lingua francese parlata e scritta

Esperienze Professionali

1995 a oggi

Asole Costruzioni S.p.A. di Varese, con mansioni di segretaria personale dell'Amministratore unico

1993 - 1995

Presti S.p.A. di Varese, con mansioni di segretaria personale dell'Amministratore

1990 - 1992

Impresa Lanic di Varese, con mansioni di segretaria dattilografa

Varie

Conoscenza dei principali programmi di videoscrittura e di gestione ufficio
Patente di guida

❏ *Job application*

Michela Grini
Piazza Annali, 23
21100 Varese

Varese, 20 ottobre 2000

INFOCOMP Sistemi Informatici
Ufficio Assunzioni
Via del Fiore, 9
25100 Brescia

Spett. INFOCOMP,

ho letto con molto interesse il Vostro annuncio
pubblicato su "La Gazzetta di Brescia" di oggi
e vorrei propormi per l'incarico di segretaria
bilingue. Come risulta dalla copia del
curriculum che allego, ho maturato una vasta
esperienza come segretaria, ho un'ottima
conoscenza delle lingue e possiedo buone
conoscenze informatiche.

Resto in attesa di una Vostra cortese risposta
e colgo l'occasione per inviarVi i miei più
cordiali saluti.

For alternatives see p52.

Michela Grini

❏ *Invitation to interview*

It is becoming very common to include an e-mail address in correspondence.

INFOCOMP Sistemi Informatici
Via del Fiore, 9 • 25100 BRESCIA
Tel.: 030-4829847 • e-mail: infocomp@com.it

Sig.ra Michela Grini
Piazza Annali, 23
21100 VARESE

Brescia, 29 ottobre 2000

Rif: am6

This is used to aid filing of correspondence.

Gent. Sig.ra Grini,

in risposta alla Sua recente candidatura al posto di segretaria bilingue, sono lieto di invitarLa ad un colloquio con il nostro direttore generale, Dott. Carlo Robini, lunedì 7 novembre alle ore 10 presso i nostri uffici di Brescia.

Qualora fosse impossibilitata a presentarsi al colloquio in tale data, La prego di contattare la nostra segretaria, Sig.ra Maria Ponzi (tel. 030-4829850), per concordare un altro appuntamento.

Cordiali saluti

Giancarlo Marchesini

Dott. Giancarlo Marchesini
Capo Ufficio Personale

The forms of address **Dott.** and **Dott.ssa** precede the names of all graduates.

❏ *Fax*

Studio legale Dott. Bini

Via Ghiberti, 25
33105 FIRENZE
Tel: 055–3453821
Fax: 055–3453822

FAX

Per: Sig. Carlo Salesi

Da: Maria Nelli

Oggetto: richiesta listini

Data: 19 novembre, 2000

Pagine: 1, inclusa questa

Gent. Sig. Salesi,

dovendo acquistare urgentemente 2 stampanti laser per il nostro studio,
Le scrivo per avere qualche informazione sulle stampanti fornite dalla
Sua ditta. Avremmo bisogno di un modello adatto alla stampa della
modulistica per le dichiarazioni dei redditi che possa servire anche per
le normali operazioni d'ufficio (invio lettere, ecc.).

Le sarei estremamente grata se potesse inviarmi al più presto via fax un
elenco completo delle stampanti attualmente disponibili specificando le
caratteristiche tecniche di ciascun esemplare e il prezzo.

Distinti saluti

Maria Nelli

PER PROBLEMI DI RICEZIONE DEL FAX CONTATTARE IL NUMERO
055–3453821

❏ E-mail

Sending messages

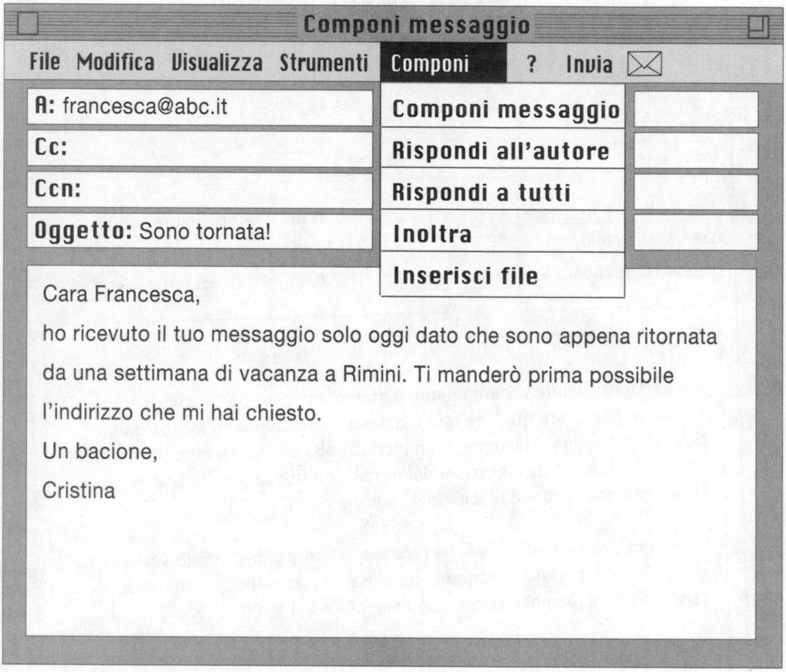

Componi messaggio			

File Modifica Uisualizza Strumenti **Componi** ? Inuia ✉

A: francesca@abc.it	**Componi messaggio**
Cc:	**Rispondi all'autore**
Ccn:	**Rispondi a tutti**
Oggetto: Sono tornata!	**Inoltra**
	Inserisci file

Cara Francesca,

ho ricevuto il tuo messaggio solo oggi dato che sono appena ritornata
da una settimana di vacanza a Rimini. Ti manderò prima possibile
l'indirizzo che mi hai chiesto.

Un bacione,

Cristina

File	File
Modifica	Edit
Visualizza	View
Strumenti	Tools
Componi	Compose
Invia	Send
Componi messaggio	New
Rispondi all'autore	Reply to sender
Rispondi a tutti	Reply to all

❑ E-mail

Receiving messages

Re: Sono tornata!					
File	Modifica	Visualizza	Strumenti	Componi	?

Da: Francesca Maggi (francesca@abc.it)

Data: 28 giugno, 2000

A: cristina_benelli@abc.it

Oggetto: Re: Sono tornata!

> In Italian, when telling someone your e-mail address you say: **"francesca chiocciolina abo punto It"**.

Cara Cristina,

adesso capisco dov'eri finita per tutto questo tempo! Ti sei divertita a Rimini? Scrivimi presto e raccontami tutto.

Ciao,

Francesca

PS. Non preoccuparti per quell'indirizzo: l'ho già trovato.

Inoltra	Forward
Inserisci file	Attachment
A	To
Cc (copia carbone)	Cc
Ccn (copia carbone nascosta)	Bcc
Oggetto	Subject
Da	From
Data	Sent

❏ *Telephone*

Different types of call

Chiamata urbana/interurbana/internazionale. — *Local/national/international call.*

Vorrei fare una telefonata internazionale. — *I want to make an international call.*

Vorrei fare una telefonata a carico del destinatario — *I want to make a reverse-charge call (Brit) or I want to call collect (US).*

Asking for information

Vorrei il numero della ditta Decapex di Vercelli. — *I'd like the number of ...*
Qual è il prefisso di Livorno? — *What is the code for ...*
Posso telefonare in Colombia direttamente? — *Can I dial direct to ...*
Qual è il prefisso per telefonare in Francia? — *What is the code for calling ...*

Receiving information

Il numero da lei richiesto è: 0432 37 49 95. — *The number you require is ...*
(zero quattro tre due tre sette quattro nove nove cinque)

Mi dispiace, ma non c'è nessun abbonato con questo nome. — *I'm sorry, but there's no listing under that name.*

Mi dispiace, il numero da lei richiesto è fuori elenco. — *... the number you have asked for is ex-directory (Brit) or unlisted (US).*

When your number answers

Vorrei parlare con il signor Matta, per favore. — *Could I speak to ...*
Mia può passare l'interno 516, per cortesia? — *Could I have extension ...*
Richiamerò più tardi. — *I'll try again later.*
Potrei lasciare un messaggio? — *Can I leave a message?*
Potrebbe chiedergli di chiamarmi quando rientra? — *Would you ask him to call me when he gets back?*

The switchboard operator speaks

Pronto, Hotel Rex, desidera? — *Hello ... can I help you?*
Chi parla, per cortesia? — *Who's calling ...*
Glielo passo subito. — *I'm putting you through now.*
C'è una telefonata in linea da Tokyo per la signora Marelli. — *I have a call from ... for ...*

C'è la signorina Martini **in linea.** ..... *is on the line.*

Non risponde nessuno. *There's no reply.*

Attenda in linea, prego or **Rimanga in linea,** *Hold the line ...*
per favore.

Vuole lasciare un messaggio? *Would you like to leave a*
messsage?

Recorded messages

Telecom Italia: **informazione gratuita. Il numero** *You have not been charged*
da lei selezionato è inesistente. *for this call. The number*
you have dialled has not
been recognised

Telecom Italia: **servizio gratuito. L'utente da lei** *You have not been charged*
chiamato ha cambiato numero. Attenda in *for this call. This number*
linea senza riagganciare poiché stiamo *has been changed. Please*
inoltrando automaticamente la sua chiamata *hold while we transfer your*
al nuovo numero 040–45 63 02. Per le *call. The new number is ...*
prossime comunicazioni la preghiamo di
utilizzare la nuova numerazione. Grazie.

Benvenuti al servizio assistenza della ditta *Welcome to ... customer*
Se.Ge.Co. *services.*

Tutte le linee sono momentaneamente occupate. *All the lines are busy right*
La preghiamo di attendere. La sua chiamata *now. Please hold the line*
sarà inoltrata prima possibile. *and we will deal with your*
call as soon as possible.

Risponde la segreteria telefonica della famiglia *You have reached ... Please*
Boni. **Lasciate un messaggio dopo il segnale** *leave a message after the*
acustico. Grazie. *tone.*

Answering the telephone

Pronto, sono Anna. *Hello, this is ...*

Sì, sono io. *Speaking.*

Chi parla? *Who's calling?*

When in trouble

Non riesco a prendere la linea. *I can't get through.*

L'apparecchio è fuori servizio. *The phone is out of order.*

È caduta la linea. *We've been cut off.*

Ho sbagliato numero. *I must have dialled the wrong*
number.

C'è un'interferenza sulla linea. *We've got a crossed line.*

La linea è molto disturbata. *This is a very bad line.*